SELECTED ENVIRONMENTAL LAW STATUTES

1996–97 EDUCATIONAL EDITION

WEST PUBLISHING CO.
ST. PAUL, MINN., 1996

610 Opperman Drive
P.O. Box 64526
St. Paul, MN 55164–0526
1–800–328–9352

ISBN 0–314–09977–8
ISSN 1076–6936

TEXT IS PRINTED ON 10% POST CONSUMER RECYCLED PAPER

PUBLISHER'S EXPLANATION

The study and practice of environmental law is almost wholly shaded by federal legislation, the most pervasive of which is compiled in this pamphlet of Selected Environmental Law Statutes.

These Acts of Congress are amended through February 15, 1996.

The statutes contained in this pamphlet bear not only the title and section classifications of the United States Code, but also their Congressional Act and section designations. The popular names of the corresponding Acts and related acronyms are identified in the Margin Index on the back cover.

Appendices contain, in excerpted form, other legislative and regulatory provisions that are the frequent companions of environmental law study.

To reach all of the judicial constructions, historical notes and additional annotative material pertaining to any given statutory provision, the reader should review that provision in the United States Code Annotated or consult the other special research aids noted in this pamphlet following each section. The latter include references to the decisions of the Supreme Court of the United States; citations to United States Code Annotated provisions; the Code of Federal Regulations; the Key Number Digest System; Corpus Juris Secundum; West's Federal Forms; Federal Jury Practice and Instructions; West's Federal Practice Manual; Federal Practice and Procedure; and Administrative Law and Practice. WESTLAW supplements the United States Code Annotated electronically and provides many useful materials for additional research. (See the WESTLAW guide following this explanation.)

THE PUBLISHER

July, 1996

*

WESTLAW® ELECTRONIC RESEARCH GUIDE

Coordinating Legal Research with WESTLAW

The *Selected Environmental Law Statutes* pamphlet is an essential aid to legal research. WESTLAW provides a vast, online library of over 7000 collections of documents and services that can supplement research begun in this publication, encompassing:

- Federal and state primary law (statutes, regulations, rules, and case law), including West's editorial enhancements, such as headnotes, Key Number classifications, annotations
- Secondary law resources (texts and treatises published by West Publishing Company and by other publishers, as well as law reviews)
- Legal news
- Directories of attorneys and experts
- Court records and filings
- Citators

Specialized topical subsets of these resources have been created for more than thirty areas of practice.

In addition to legal information, there are general news and reference databases and a broad array of specialized materials frequently useful in connection with legal matters, covering accounting, business, environment, ethics, finance, medicine, social and physical sciences.

This guide will focus on a few aspects of WESTLAW use to supplement research begun in this publication, and will direct you to additional sources of assistance.

Databases

A database is a collection of documents with some features in common. It may contain statutes, court decisions, administrative materials, commentaries, news or other information. Each database has a unique identifier, used in many WESTLAW commands to select a database of interest. For example, the database containing cases decided by the United States Courts of Appeal has the identifier CTA; the cases of a specific state are contained in a database having identifier XX-CS, where XX is the state's postal code.

The WESTLAW Directory is a comprehensive list of databases with information about each database, including the types of documents each contains. The first page of a standard or customized WESTLAW Directory is displayed upon signing on to WESTLAW, except when prior, saved research is resumed. To access the WESTLAW Directory at any time, enter DB.

A special subdirectory, accessible from the main WESTLAW Directory, lists databases applicable to Environmental Law research. For your convenience, such a list is also included at the end of this Guide.

For information as to currentness and search tips regarding any WESTLAW database, enter the SCOPE command SC followed by the database identifier (e.g., SC CTA). It is not necessary to include the identifier to obtain scope information about the currently selected database.

WESTLAW Highlights

Use of this publication may be supplemented through the WESTLAW Bulletins (WLB and WSB-XX) and various Topical Highlights, including Environmental Law Highlights (WTH-ENV). Highlights databases contain summaries of significant judicial, legislative and administrative developments and are updated daily; they are searchable both from an automatic list of recent documents and using general WESTLAW search methods for documents accumulated over time. The full text of any judicial decision may be retrieved by entering FIND.

Consult the WESTLAW Directory (enter DB) for a complete, current listing of other highlights databases.

Retrieving a Specific Case

The FIND command can be used to quickly retrieve a case whose citation is known. For example:

FI 15 F.3d 1100

Updating Case Law Research

There are a variety of citator services on WESTLAW for use in updating research.

Insta-Cite® may be used to verify citations, find parallel citations, ascertain the history of a case, and see whether it remains valid law. References are also provided to secondary sources, such as Corpus Juris Secundum®, that cite the case. To view the Insta-Cite history of a displayed case, simply enter the command IC. To view the Insta-Cite history of a selected case, enter a command in this form:

IC 992 F.2d 401

Shepard's® Citations provides a comprehensive list of cases and publications that have cited a particular case, with explanatory analysis to indicate how the citing cases have treated the case, e.g., "followed," "explained." To view the Shepard's Citations about a displayed case, enter the command SH. Add a case citation, if necessary, as in the prior Insta-Cite example.

For the latest citing references, not yet incorporated in Shepard's Citations, use Shepard's PreView® (SP command) and QuickCite™ (QC command), in the same way.

To see a complete list of publications covered by any of the citator services, enter its service abbreviation (IC, SH, SP or QC) followed by PUBS. To ascertain the scope of coverage for any of the services, enter the SCOPE command (SC) followed by the appropriate service abbreviation. For the complete list of commands available in a citator service, enter its service abbreviation (IC, SH, SP or QC) followed by CMDS.

Retrieving Statutes, Court Rules and Regulations

The United States Code and United States Code - Annotated are searchable databases on WESTLAW (identifiers USC and USCA, respectively), as are federal court rules (US-RULES) and regulations (CFR).

Annotated and/or unannotated versions of state statutes (XX-ST and XX-ST-ANN, respectively) and state court rules (XX-RULES) are also searchable on WESTLAW, as are the administrative codes of many states (XX-ADC).

In addition, the FIND command may be used to retrieve specific provisions by citation, obviating the need for database selection or search. To FIND a desired document, enter FI, followed by the citation of the desired document, using the full name of the publication, or one of the abbreviated styles recognized by WESTLAW.

If WESTLAW does not recognize the style you enter, you may enter one of the following, using US or any other state code in place of XX:

FI XX-ST	Displays templates for compiled statutes
FI XX-LEGIS	Displays templates for legislation
FI XX-RULES	Displays templates for rules
FI XX-ORDERS	Displays templates for court orders

Alternatively, entering FI followed by the publication's full name or an accepted abbreviation will normally display templates, useful jump possibilities, or helpful information necessary to complete the FIND process. For example:

FI USCA	Displays templates for United States Code - Annotated
FI FRAP	Displays templates for Federal Rules of Appellate Procedure
FI FRCP	Displays templates for Federal Rules of Civil Procedure
FI FRCRP	Displays templates for Federal Rules of Criminal Procedure
FI FRE	Displays templates for Federal Rules of Evidence
FI CFR	Displays templates for Code of Federal Regulations
FI FR	Displays templates for Federal Register

To view the complete list of FINDable documents and associated prescribed forms, enter FI PUBS.

Updating Research in re Statutes, Rules and Regulations

When viewing a statute, rule or regulation on WESTLAW after a search or FIND command, it is easy to update your research. A message will appear if relevant amendments, repeals or other new material are available through the UPDATE feature. Entering the UPDATE command will display such material.

Documents used to update federal statutes, rules, and regulations are searchable in the United States Public Laws (US-PL), Federal Orders (US-ORDERS) and Federal Register (FR) databases, respectively. For many states, similar material is contained in Legislative Service (XX-LEGIS), Court Orders (XX-ORDERS) and Administrative Register (XX-ADR) databases. Consult the WESTLAW Directory for availability in a specific state.

When documents citing a statute, rule or regulation are of interest, Shepard's Citations on WESTLAW may be of assistance. That service covers federal constitutional provisions, statutes and administrative provisions, and corresponding materials from many states. The command SH PUBS displays a directory of publications which may be Shepardized on WESTLAW. Consult the WESTLAW manual for more information about citator services.

Using WESTLAW as a Citator

For research beyond the coverage of any citator service, go directly to the databases (cases, for example) containing citing documents and use standard WESTLAW search techniques to retrieve documents citing specific constitutional provisions, statutes, standard jury instructions or other authorities.

Fortunately, the specific portion of a citation is often reasonably distinctive, such as 22:636.1, 301.65, 401(k), 12-21-5, 12052. When it is, a search on that specific portion alone may retrieve applicable documents without any substantial number of inapplicable ones (unless the number happens to be coincidentally popular in another context).

Similarly, if the citation involves more than one number, such as 42 U.S.C.A. § 1201, a search containing both numbers (e.g., 42 +5 1201) is likely to produce mostly desired information, even though the component numbers are common.

If necessary, the search may be limited in several ways:

A. Switch from a general database to one containing mostly cases within the subject area of the cite being researched;

B. Use a connector (&, /S, /P, etc.) to narrow the search to documents including terms which are highly likely to accompany the correct citation in the context of the issue being researched;

C. Include other citation information in the query. Because of the variety of citation formats used in documents, this option should be used primarily where other options prove insufficient. Below are illustrative queries for any database containing federal cases:

("Environmental Response" C.E.R.C.L.A. Superfund /5 104)
(42 /5 9604)

will retrieve cases citing 42 U.S.C.A. Section 9604;

U.S.C.A.Const! Const.! Constitution /7 4 +2 1

will retrieve cases citing the United States Constitution Article IV, § 1; and

Fed.R.Civ! F.R.Civ! F.R.C.P! R.Civ! Civil Civ.! /7 16

will retrieve cases citing Federal Civil Procedure Rule 16.

Alternative Retrieval Methods

WIN® (WESTLAW Is Natural™) allows you to frame your issue in plain English to retrieve documents:

Is a successor corporation liable for prior pollution ("hazardous waste")?

Alternatively, retrieval may be focused by use of the Terms and Connectors method:

DI(CORPORAT! /P SUCCESSOR /P POLLUT! ("HAZARDOUS WASTE"))

In databases with Key Numbers, either of the above examples will identify Corporations ⚷445.1 as a Key Number collecting headnotes relevant to this issue if there are pertinent cases.

Since the Key Numbers are affixed to points of law by trained specialists based on conceptual understanding of the case, relevant cases that were not retrieved by either of the language-dependent methods will often be found at a Key Number.

Similarly, citations in retrieved documents (to cases, statutes, rules, etc.) may suggest additional, fruitful research using other WESTLAW databases (e.g., annotated statutes, rules) or services (e.g., citator services).

Key Number Search

Frequently, case law research rapidly converges on a few topics, headings and Key Numbers within West's Key Number System that are likely to contain relevant cases. These may be discovered from known, relevant reported cases from any jurisdiction; Library References in West publications; browsing in a digest; or browsing the Key Number System on WESTLAW using the JUMP feature or the KEY command.

Once discovered, topics, subheadings or Key Numbers are useful as search terms (in databases containing reported cases) alone or with other search terms, to focus the search within a narrow range of potentially relevant material.

For example, to retrieve cases with at least one headnote classified to Corporations 🔑445.1, sign on to a caselaw database and enter

101k445.1 [use with other search terms, if desired]

The topic name (Corporations) is replaced by its numerical equivalent (101) and the 🔑 by the letter k. A list of topics and their numerical equivalents is in the WESTLAW Reference Manual and is displayed in WESTLAW when the KEY command is entered.

Other topics of special interest are listed below.

Agriculture (23)
Electricity (145)
Fish (176)
Game (187)
Health and Environment (199)
Mines and Minerals (260)
Navigable Waters (270)
Nuisance (279)
Waters and Water Courses (405)
Zoning and Planning (414)

Using JUMP

WESTLAW's JUMP feature allows you to move from one document to another or from one part of a document to another, then easily return to your original place, without losing your original result. Opportunities to move in this manner are marked in the text with a JUMP symbol (▶). Whenever you see the JUMP symbol, you may move to the place designated by the adjacent reference by using the Tab, arrow keys or mouse click to position the cursor on the JUMP symbol, then pressing Enter or clicking again with the mouse.

Within the text of a court opinion, JUMP arrows are adjacent to case cites and federal statute cites, and adjacent to parenthesized numbers marking discussions corresponding to headnotes.

On a screen containing the text of a headnote, the JUMP arrows allow movement to the corresponding discussion in the text of the opinion,

▶ (3)

and allow browsing West's Key Number System beginning at various heading levels:

▶ 101 CORPORATIONS
▶ 101XI Corporate Powers and Liabilities
▶ 101XI(C) Property and Conveyances
▶ 101k441 Conveyances by Corporations
▶ 101k445.1 k. Assumption of transferor's liabilities.

To return from a JUMP, enter GB (except for JUMPs between a headnote and the corresponding discussion in opinion, for which there is a matching number in parenthesis in both headnote and opinion). Returns from successive JUMPs (e.g., from case to cited case to case cited by cited case) without intervening returns may be accomplished by repeated entry of GB or by using the MAP command.

General Information

The information provided above illustrates some of the ways WESTLAW can complement research using this publication. However, this brief overview illustrates only some of the power of WESTLAW. The full range of WESTLAW search techniques is available to support your research.

Please consult the WESTLAW Reference Manual for additional information or assistance or call West's Reference Attorneys at 1-800-REF-ATTY (1-800-733-2889).

For information about subscribing to WESTLAW, please call 1-800-328-0109.

Environmental Law Databases

Federal Case Law, Statutes, Regulations and Administrative Materials

Federal Cases (FENV-CS)

Cases from the U.S. Supreme Court, courts of appeals, district courts, bankruptcy courts, Claims Court, and related federal and territorial courts.

U.S. Supreme Court Cases (FENV-SCT)

Cases from the U.S. Supreme Court.

U.S. Courts of Appeals Cases (FENV-CTA)

Cases from the U.S. courts of appeals.

U.S. District Courts Cases (FENV-DCT)

Cases from the U.S. district courts.

United States Code Annotated® (FENV-USCA)

Documents from the United States Code Annotated, including court rules and appendixes.

Federal Register (FENV-FR)

Documents from the Federal Register.

Code of Federal Regulations (FENV-CFR)

Documents from the Code of Federal Regulations.

Congressional Record (CR)

Documents from the Congressional Record.

United States Public Laws (US-PL)

Enrolled bills passed by both houses of the current session of the U.S. Congress.

Billcast (BC)

Summaries of congressional bills and predictions of a bill's chance of passing each stage of the legislative process.

Bills—All States & Congress—Summaries & Full Text Combined (BILLS)

Summary bill tracking materials (summaries of bills and status information) for all states and Congress, as well as the full text of bills from several states.

Bill Tracking—Federal—Summaries & Status (US-BILLTRK)

Summaries and status information concerning pending and recently passed federal bills.

Environmental Data Resources—Consent Decrees—Superfund (EDR-CONSENT)

EPA and United States District Court Consent Decrees that determine liability for Superfund site cleanup.

Chemical Regulations Reporter (FENV-CHEM)

Documents report on and analyze legislative, judicial and administrative activities that affect chemical manufacturers and users, including right-to-know regulations and biotechnology controls, with summaries of current developments, digests of court and administrative agency decisions, and the full text of proposed and final rules, notices, and other materials, and emphasizing actions by the Environmental Protection Agency to enforce the Toxic Substance Control Act and the Federal Insecticide, Fungicide and Rodenticide Act.

E.P.A. Decisions (FENV-EPA)

Orders and decisions released by the Environmental Protection Agency (EPA).

E.P.A. Federal Insecticide, Fungicide and Rodenticide Act Decisions (FENV-FIFRA)

Orders and decisions released by the EPA concerning Federal Insecticide, Fungicide and Rodenticide Act issues.

E.P.A. Resource Conservation and Recovery Act Decisions (FENV-RCRA)

Orders and decisions released by the EPA concerning Resource Conservation and Recovery Act issues.

E.P.A. Toxic Substances Control Act Decisions (FENV-TSCA)

Orders and decisions released by the EPA concerning Toxic Substances Control Act issues.

E.P.A. General Counsel Memoranda (FENV-GCM)

Memoranda prepared by the EPA's General Counsel stating official interpretations of the environmental statutes and regulations administered by the EPA.

Environmental Law—News Releases (FENV-NR)

Releases and announcements of regulatory action and other current matters by the E.P.A., the U.S. Department of the Interior (D.O.I.) and the U.S. Justice Department's Environment and Natural Resources Division.

Ocean Resources and Wildlife Reporter (FENV-ORW)

Adjudicative decisions, orders, opinion letters and other materials released by the National Oceanic and Atmospheric Administration (NOAA) of the U.S. Department of Commerce and U.S. Fish and Wildlife Service (FWS) of the U.S. Department of the Interior.

OSHA Inspection and Enforcement Reports (OSHA-INSPCT)

The most current OSHA inspection repoorts available through OSHA-DATA.

State Case Law, Statutes and Regulations

Multistate Cases (MENV-CS)

Cases from all 50 states and the District of Columbia.

Individual State Cases (XXENV-CS)

Cases from a specific state. (XX represents the postal abbreviation for the state.)

Multistate Administrative Decisions (MENV-ADMIN)

Administrative decisions released by state agencies pertaining to environmental issues.

Individual State Environmental Law Decisions (XXENV-ADMIN)

Administrative decisions from more than 20 states, including Alabama, California, Florida, Georgia, Illinois, Iowa, Kansas, Kentucky, Louisiana, Maryland, Massachusetts, Michigan, Minnesota, Nebraska, New Jersey, New York, Ohio, Oregon, Pennsylvania, Rhode Island, Tennessee, Vermont, Washington and Wisconsin.

Regulation Tracking—All States (ST-REGTRK)

Summaries and status information concerning pending and recently adopted regulations from all 50 states.

Regulation Tracking—Individual States (XX-REGTRK)

Summaries and status information concerning pending and recently passed regulations from a specific state. (XX represents the state's postal abbreviation.)

Superfund Amendments and Reauthorization Act of 1986 Legislative History (SARA-LH)

Comprehensive legislative history of the Superfund Amendments and Reauthorization Act of 1986 (SARA), P.L. 99-499.

Specialized Databases

West's Legal Directory—Environmental (WLD-ENV)

Profiles of law firms, branch offices, and biographical records of attorneys that practice environmental law.

Aquatic Sciences and Fisheries Abstracts—DIALOG® (ASFA)

Citations to 5,000 primary journals, monographs, conference proceedings and technical reports about science, technology and management of marine and freshwater environments.

BNA Chemical Regulation Daily (BNA-CRD)

Documents prepared daily by The Bureau of National Affairs, Inc. that report on and analyze legislative, judicial and administrative activities affecting the regulation of chemicals and toxic substances.

BNA's Environmental Law Database (BNA-ENV)

Documents from the BNA-CHEM and BNA-ER databases.

BNA Headlines (BNA-BHL)

A single document listing headlines of reports available in current issues of BNA daily databases.

BNA International Environment Daily (BNA-IED)

Documents prepared daily by The Bureau of National Affairs, Inc. that report on and analyze legislative, judicial and administrative activities affecting the environment worldwide.

BNA National Environment Daily (BNA-NED)

Documents prepared daily by The Bureau of National Affairs, Inc. that report on and analyze legislative, judicial and administrative activities affecting pollution control and environmental protection.

BNA State Environment Daily (BNA-SED)

Documents prepared daily by The Bureau of National Affairs, Inc. that report on and analyze legislative, judicial and administrative activities, including environmental information from the state courts, legislatures, and regulatory agencies, and coverage of the effect of federal legislation on local jurisdictions or industries.

BNA Toxics Law Daily (BNA-TLD)

Documents prepared daily by The Bureau of National Affairs, Inc. that report on and analyze legislative, judicial and administrative activities affecting radioactive and toxic waste management.

Chapman and Hall Chemical Database—DIALOG® (C&HCHEM)

Complete text of two major chemical dictionaries from Chapman & Hall Ltd., Dictionary of Organic Compounds (5th edition) and Dictionary of Organometallic Compounds.

Chemical Regulation Reporter (BNA-CHEM)

Articles from the Chemical Regulation Reporter, a Bureau of National Affairs, Inc. (BNA) weekly publication that reports on and analyzes legislative, judicial and administrative activities affecting chemical manufacturers and users.

Chemical Safety Newsbase—1981 to Present—DIALOG® (CHEMSAFETY)

Information on the hazardous and possibly hazardous effects of chemicals and processes encountered by workers in industry and laboratories.

Energyline®—DIALOG® (ENERGYLINE)

The online version of Energy Information Abstracts; also includes 8,000 energy and environment-related records dating back to 1971 from The Energy Index.

Environment Reporter (BNA-ER)

Articles from the Environment Reporter, a Bureau of National Affairs, Inc. (BNA) weekly publication that reports on and analyzes legislative, judicial and administrative activities affecting pollution control and environmental management.

Environmental Compliance & Litigation Strategy - Leader Pubs. (ENVTCLST)

Environmental Compliance and Litigation Strategy provides updates on environmental legislation. Topics include property rights, sick building syndrome, and other environmental hazards. Regular features include Case Notes, Regulatory Update, and News in Brief.

Environmental Liability Reports - Dow Jones (ENVLIABR)

The database consists of articles from Environmental Liability Report, a newsletter published weekly.

Environmental News - Dow Jones (ENVNEWS)

This database contains articles covering news about the Environments. Topics include pollution control, waste management, the Environmental Protection Agency, and the Interior Department.

Environmental Problems & Remediation - Dow Jones (ENVPBRM)

The database consists of articles from Environmental Problems & Remediation, a newsletter, published monthly.

Environmental Radiation Technology - Dow Jones (ENVRMT)

The database consits of articles from Environmental Remediation Technology, a newsletter, published bi-weekly.

Environmental Bibliography—DIALOG® (ENV-BIB)

Covers the fields of general human ecology, atmospheric studies, energy, land resources, water resources, and nutrition and health.

Environmental Data Resources—Civil Enforcement Docket (EDR-DOCKET)

Documents identifying defendants that are listed on the EPA's system for tracking civil judicial cases filed by the Department of Justice on behalf of the EPA.

Environmental Data Resources—Combined Materials (EDR-COMB)

Database contains all currently available Environmental Data Resources (EDR) materials and combines EDR-CA, EDR-ROD, EDR-NPLSETS, EDR-DOCKET, EDR-CERCLIS, EDR-TRIS, EDR-TSCA.

Environmental Data Resources—Compliance Records (EDR-COMPLY)

Documents from EDR-DOCKET and EDR-RCRIS.

Environmental Data Resources—Comprehensive Environmental Response, Compensation and Liability System—CERCLIS (EDR-CERCLIS)

Information on over 36,000 sites identified by the EPA as abandoned, inactive or uncontrolled hazardous waste sites.

Environmental Data Resources—Emergency Response Notification System (EDR-ERNS)

Information on approximately 50,000 sites where a spill of a hazardous material occurred.

Environmental Data Resources—Facility Index System (EDR-FINDS)

Index information on over 400,000 sites tracked by the EPA. Records contain facility information and reference to other EPA information systems, including CERCLIS, RCRIS, DOCKET, TRIS, TSCA, FURS, FRDS, SIA, CICIS and PADS.

Environmental Data Resources—National Priorities List [NPL] and Potentially Responsible Parties [PRP] (EDR-NPLPRP)

Information on sites that have been identified for priority cleanup under the Superfund program and parties that the EPA has identified as being potentially responsible for site cleanup.

Environmental Data Resources—National Priorities List [NPL] and Superfund Enforcement Tracking System [PRP] (EDR-NPLSETS)

Documents indicating sites that have been identified for priority cleanup under the Superfund program, and the parties that the EPA has identified as being potentially responsible for site cleanup.

Environmental Data Resources—Radius Map™ Reports (EDR-MAP)

Ordering information for EDR Radius Map™ Reports which provide geographic presentations of toxic sites on or near target properties in the United States.

Environmental Data Resources—Resource Conservation and Recovery Information System (EDR-RCRIS)

Information on over 400,000 sites where hazardous waste is generated, transported, stored, treated or disposed. Hazardous waste compliance and enforcement information is available for over 4,000 sites.

Environmental Data Resources—Site Liability Records (EDR-SITE)

Documents from EDR-CERCLIS, EDR-TRIS, EDR-TSCA and EDR-NPLSETS. Documents are records for a single physical site.

Environmental Data Resources—Consent Agreements (EDR-CA)

EPA and U.S. District Court Consent Agreements that determine liability for Superfund site cleanup.

Environmental Data Resources—Superfund Materials (EDR-SFUND)

Documents from EDR-CA, EDR-ROD and EDR-NPLSETS. Documents are records for a single physical site.

Environmental Data Resources—Superfund Records of Decision (EDR-ROD)

EPA decisions that direct the cleanup effort at a Superfund site.

Environmental Data Resources—Toxic Substance Control Act (EDR-TSCA)

Records of toxic chemical importing and manufacturing sites.

Environmental Law Reporter—Complete (ELR)

Documents from the Environmental Law Reporter, excluding full-text statutes and indexes, which is published by the Environmental Law Institute.

Environmental Law Reporter—Administrative Materials (ELR-ADMIN)

Administrative materials from the Environmental Law Reporter, including (1) Policy Guidance documents; (2) a Federal Regulations outline; (3) a list of Federal Executive Orders that relate to environmental laws; and (4) Special Collections of EPA Administrative Law Judge decisions.

Environmental Law Reporter—Bibliography (ELR-BIB)

Major subject matter headings from the Environmental Law Reporter, law review bibliography with a list of the environmental law-related articles from law reviews and other legal journals.

Environmental Law Reporter—Litigation (ELR-LIT)

Federal cases and selected state cases, from the Environmental Law Reporter, including ELR Digests summarizing the cases.

Environmental Law Reporter—News & Analysis (ELR-NEWS)

Dialogues, comments, articles, recent developments, summaries and key late developments covering activities of the U.S. Congress, state legislatures, federal and state courts, the Environmental Protection Agency, and other federal and state agencies.

Environmental Law Reporter—Pending Litigation (ELR-PEND)

Summaries of pleadings and other documents filed in cases before federal and state courts and administrative agencies since 1970, including the names and addresses of counsel and a list of those summarized documents available in full text from the Environmental Law Institute.

Environmental Law Reporter—Statutes and International Agreements (ELR-STIA)

Summaries of the approximately 60 most significant federal environmental law statutes and the full text of international agreements, treaties and conventions.

Environmental Law Reporter—Superfund (ELR-SF)

Documents relating to Superfund, the Comprehensive Environmental Response, Compensation and Liability Act of 1980 (CERCLA) and the Superfund Amendments and Reauthorization Act of 1986 (SARA).

Environmental Law Reporter—Update (ELR-UPDATE)

Current information on cases, legislation and other congressional activity, as well as summaries of recent administrative actions with a list of settlements.

Environmental Organization Computer Readable Directory (ENV-DIR)

Listings of public and private organizations, including legislative committees, that deal with environmental concerns.

Geoarchive—DIALOG® (GEOARCHIVE)

Documents covering all types of information sources in geoscience.

Geobasef—DIALOG® (GEOBASE)

Covers the worldwide literature on geography, geology, ecology and their related disciplines.

GEOREF, Database of the American Geological Institute—DIALOG® (GEOREF)

Covers worldwide technical literature on geology and geophysics.

Gower Federal Service—Interior Board of Land Appeals Decisions (GFS)

Documents released by the Interior Board of Land Appeals (IBLA).

Life Sciences Collection—DIALOG® (LIFE-SCI)

Abstracts and bibliographic citations from recent worldwide research literature in major areas of biology, medicine, biochemistry, ecology and microbiology, and in some aspects of agriculture and veterinary science.

Meteorological and Geoastrophysical Abstracts—DIALOG® (METEOR-ABS)

Current citations in English for the most important meteorological and geoastrophysical research published in worldwide literature sources.

Occupational Safety & Health—NIOSH®—DIALOG® (OSH)

Citations to more than 400 journal titles as well as over 70,000 monographs and technical reports. OSH covers all aspects of occupational safety and health, and includes such topics as hazardous agents, unsafe workplace environment and toxicology.

Oceanic Abstracts 1964 to Present—DIALOG® (OCEAN-ABS)

Articles indexing technical literature published worldwide on marine-related subjects.

Pollution Abstracts—DIALOG® (POLLUTION)

References to environmentally related literature on pollution, its sources and its control.

Registry of Toxic Effects of Chemical Substances—DIALOG® (RTECS)

Basic toxicity information for over 100,000 chemical substances.

State Environmental Records (EDR-STATE)

All currently available materials of state environmental records from the 50 states and the District of Columbia.

Toxline®—DIALOG® (TOXLINE)

Documents that cover the adverse effects of chemicals, drugs and physical agents on living systems.

TRIS—DIALOG® (TRIS)

The Transportation Research Information Service (TRIS) provides research information on air, highway, rail and maritime transport; mass transit; and other transportation modes. Subjects included are regulations and legislation, energy, environmental and maintenance technology, and operations, traffic control and communications.

TSCA Chemical Substances Inventory—DIALOG® (CHEMSUBS)

A non-bibliographic dictionary listing of chemical substances derived from the Initial Inventory of the Toxic Substances Control Act Chemical Substances Inventory. Presence on the list does not mean the substance is "in use"—rather the substance is manufactured or transported in the United States in sufficient quantities to require the chemical to be part of the inventory. The database can be used to determine whether a non-confidential substance has been registered with the EPA.

WESTLAW Topical Highlights—Environmental Law (WTH-ENV)

Summaries of recent federal and state judicial, legislative and administrative developments affecting environmental law.

Water Resources Abstracts—DIALOG® (WR-ABS)

Abstracts of water-related topics in the life, physical and social sciences, as well as the engineering and legal aspects of the conservation, control, use and management of water.

Texts and Periodicals

API Energy Business News Index—DIALOG® (APIBIZ)

Corresponds to the print publication Petroleum/Energy Business News Index. Provides cover-to-cover indexing of 25 primary publications and selected coverage of some 200 additional technical journals related to the petroleum and energy industries.

Clean Air Act 1990 Amendments Law and Practice (JW-CLEANAIR)

The full, substantive text of the treatise Clean Air Act 1990 Amendments Law and Practice and any current cumulative supplements, by Professor John-Mark Stensvaag of the University of Iowa College of Law.

Environmental Law (ENVLAW)

The full text of the treatise Environmental Law by William H. Rodgers, Jr.

Environmental Law (ENTL)

Articles, notes or other materials published in Environmental Law. Full coverage begins with volume 12 (1981).

Environmental Law—Law Reviews, Texts and Bar Journals (ENV-TP)

Documents from law reviews, texts, CLE course materials, bar journals and legal practice-oriented periodicals.

Hazardous Waste Law and Practice (JW-HAZWASTE)

The full, substantive text of the treatise Hazardous Waste Law and Practice and its current cumulative supplements, by Professor John-Mark Stensvaag of the University of Iowa College of Law.

Superfund Law and Procedure (SUPERFUND)

The full text of the treatise Superfund Law and Procedure by Allan J. Topol and Rebecca Snow.

Sustainable Environmental Law (ELI-SENVL)

The full text of the Environmental Law Institute treatise Sustainable Environmental law by Celia Campbell-Mohn, Barry Breen, and J. William Futrell.

TABLE OF CONTENTS

Page

PUBLISHER'S EXPLANATION ---- III
WESTLAW® ELECTRONIC RESEARCH GUIDE ---- V

TITLE 7. AGRICULTURE

Act

Federal Insecticide, Fungicide, and Rodenticide Act ---- 1

TITLE 15. COMMERCE AND TRADE

Toxic Substances Control Act ---- 52

TITLE 16. CONSERVATION

Multiple-Use Sustained-Yield Act of 1960 ---- 126
Coastal Zone Management Act of 1972 ---- 128
Endangered Species Act of 1973 ---- 155
Forest and Rangeland Renewable Resources Planning Act of 1974 ---- 190
Forest and Rangeland Renewable Resources Research Act of 1978 ---- 190
Renewable Resources Extension Act of 1978 ---- 190
Wood Residue Utilization Act of 1980 ---- 190

TITLE 30. MINERAL LANDS AND MINING

Surface Mining Control and Reclamation ---- 221

TITLE 33. NAVIGATION AND NAVIGABLE WATERS

Water Pollution Prevention and Control ---- 309
Ocean Dumping ---- 480
Oil Pollution Act of 1990 ---- 504

TITLE 42. THE PUBLIC HEALTH AND WELFARE

Safety of Public Water Systems ---- 541
National Environmental Policy ---- 589
Solid Waste Disposal ---- 608
Air Pollution Prevention and Control ---- 717
Comprehensive Environmental Response, Compensation and Liability ---- 1010
Emergency Planning and Community Right-To-Know ---- 1103
Pollution Prevention Act of 1990 ---- 1127

TITLE 43. PUBLIC LANDS

Federal Land Policy and Management ---- 1133

APPENDICES

App.		Page
A.	Occupational Safety and Health Act	1181
B.	Code of Federal Regulations, Title 40—Protection of Environment	1209
C.	Administrative Procedure Act	1271
D.	Equal Access to Justice Act	1297

TITLE 7—AGRICULTURE

ENVIRONMENTAL PESTICIDE CONTROL

FEDERAL INSECTICIDE, FUNGICIDE, AND RODENTICIDE ACT [FIFRA § ______]

(7 U.S.C.A. §§ 136 to 136y.)

CHAPTER 6—INSECTICIDES AND ENVIRONMENTAL PESTICIDE CONTROL

SUBCHAPTER II—ENVIRONMENTAL PESTICIDE CONTROL

Sec.

136. Definitions.
- (a) Active ingredient.
- (b) Administrator.
- (c) Adulterated.
- (d) Animal.
- (e) Certified applicator, etc.
- (f) Defoliant.
- (g) Desiccant.
- (h) Device.
- (i) District court.
- (j) Environment.
- (k) Fungus.
- (*l*) Imminent hazard.
- (m) Inert ingredient.
- (n) Ingredient statement.
- (*o*) Insect.
- (p) Label and labeling.
- (q) Misbranded.
- (r) Nematode.
- (s) Person.
- (t) Pest.
- (u) Pesticide.
- (v) Plant regulator.
- (w) Producer and produce.
- (x) Protect health and the environment.
- (y) Registrant.
- (z) Registration.
- (aa) State.
- (bb) Unreasonable adverse effects on the environment.
- (cc) Weed.
- (dd) Establishment.
- (ee) To use any registered pesticide in a manner inconsistent with its labeling.
- (ff) Outstanding data requirement.
- (gg) To distribute or sell.

136a. Registration of pesticides.
- (a) Requirement of registration.
- (b) Exemptions.
- (c) Procedure for registration.
- (d) Classification of pesticides.
- (e) Products with same formulation and claims.
- (f) Miscellaneous.

136a–1. Reregistration of registered pesticides.
- (a) General rule.
- (b) Reregistration phases.
- (c) Phase one.
- (d) Phase two.
- (e) Phase three.
- (f) Phase four.
- (g) Phase five.
- (h) Compensation of data submitter.
- (i) Fees.
- (j) Exemption of certain registrants.
- (k) Reregistration and expedited processing fund.
- (*l*) Judicial review.

136b. Transferred.

136c. Experimental use permits.
- (a) Issuance.
- (b) Temporary tolerance level.
- (c) Use under permit.
- (d) Studies.
- (e) Revocation.
- (f) State issuance of permits.
- (g) Exemption for agricultural research agencies.

136d. Administrative review; suspension.
- (a) Cancellation after five years.
- (b) Cancellation and change in classification.
- (c) Suspension.
- (d) Public hearings and scientific review.
- (e) Conditional registration.
- (f) General provisions.
- (g) Notice for stored pesticides with canceled or suspended registrations.
- (h) Judicial review.

136e. Registration of establishments.
- (a) Requirement.
- (b) Registration.
- (c) Information required.
- (d) Confidential records and information.

136f. Books and records.
- (a) Requirements.
- (b) Inspection.

Sec.
136g. Inspection of establishments, etc.
(a) In general.
(b) Warrants.
(c) Enforcement.
136h. Protection of trade secrets and other information.
(a) In general.
(b) Disclosure.
(c) Disputes.
(d) Limitations.
(e) Disclosure to contractors.
(f) Penalty for disclosure by Federal employees.
(g) Disclosure to foreign and multinational pesticide producers.
136i. Use of restricted use pesticides; applicators.
(a) Certification procedure.
(b) State plans.
(c) Instruction in integrated pest management techniques.
(d) In general.
(e) Separate standards.
136i–1. Pesticide recordkeeping.
(a) Requirements.
(b) Access.
(c) Health care personnel.
(d) Penalty.
(e) Federal or State provisions.
(f) Surveys and reports.
(g) Regulations.
136j. Unlawful acts.
(a) In general.
(b) Exemptions.
136k. Stop sale, use, removal, and seizure.
(a) Stop sale, etc., orders.
(b) Seizure.
(c) Disposition after condemnation.
(d) Court costs, etc.
136*l*. Penalties.
(a) Civil penalties.
(b) Criminal penalties.
136m. Indemnities.
(a) Requirement.
(b) Amount of payment.
136n. Administrative procedure; judicial review.
(a) District court review.
(b) Review by court of appeals.
(c) Jurisdiction of district courts.
(d) Notice of judgments.
136*o*. Imports and exports.
(a) Pesticides and devices intended for export.
(b) Cancellation notices furnished to foreign governments.
(c) Importation of pesticides and devices.
(d) Cooperation in international efforts.
(e) Regulations.

Sec.
136p. Exemption of Federal and State agencies.
136q. Storage, disposal, transportation, and recall.
(a) Storage, disposal, and transportation.
(b) Recalls.
(c) Storage costs.
(d) Administration of storage, disposal, transportation, and recall programs.
(e) Container design.
(f) Pesticide residue removal.
(g) Pesticide container study.
(h) Relationship to Solid Waste Disposal Act.
136r. Research and monitoring.
(a) Research.
(b) National monitoring plan.
(c) Monitoring.
136s. Solicitation of comments; notice of public hearings.
(a) Secretary of Agriculture.
(b) Views.
(c) Notice.
136t. Delegation and cooperation.
(a) Delegation.
(b) Cooperation.
136u. State cooperation, aid, and training.
(a) Cooperative agreements.
(b) Contracts for training.
(c) Information and education.
136v. Authority of States.
(a) In general.
(b) Uniformity.
(c) Additional uses.
136w. Authority of Administrator.
(a) In general.
(b) Exemption of pesticides.
(c) Other authority.
(d) Scientific advisory panel.
(e) Peer review.
136w–1. State primary enforcement responsibility.
(a) In general.
(b) Special rules.
(c) Administrator.
136w–2. Failure by the State to assure enforcement of State pesticide use regulations.
(a) Referral.
(b) Notice.
(c) Construction.
136w–3. Identification of pests; cooperation with Department of Agriculture's program.
(a) In general.
(b) Control availability.
(c) Integrated Pest Management.
136w–4. Annual report.
136x. Severability.
136y. Authorization of appropriations.

Related Provisions

See, also, Toxic Substances Control, 15 U.S.C.A. § 2601 et seq., post.

WEST'S FEDERAL FORMS

Enforcement and review of decisions and orders of administrative agencies, see § 851 et seq.
Jurisdiction and venue in district courts, see § 1003 et seq.

CODE OF FEDERAL REGULATIONS

Arbitration of pesticide data disputes, see 29 CFR 1440.1.
Assistance for continuing environmental programs, etc., see 40 CFR 35.001 et seq.
Special classes of merchandise, see 19 CFR 12.110 et seq.

LAW REVIEW COMMENTARIES

Confidential business information versus the public's right to disclosure—Biotechnology renews the challenge. Stanley H. Abramson, 34 U.Kansas L.Rev. 681 (1986).

Criminal sanctions under federal and state environmental statutes. Richard H. Allan, 14 Ecology L.Q. 117 (1987).

Toxic tort litigation and the causation element: Is there any hope of reconciliation? Ora Fred Harris, Jr., 40 Southwestern (Tex.) L.J. 909 (1986).

WESTLAW ELECTRONIC RESEARCH

See WESTLAW guide following the Explanation pages of this pamphlet.

SUBCHAPTER II—ENVIRONMENTAL PESTICIDE CONTROL

§ 136. Definitions [FIFRA § 2]

For purposes of this subchapter—

(a) Active ingredient.—The term "active ingredient" means—

(1) in the case of a pesticide other than a plant regulator, defoliant, or desiccant, an ingredient which will prevent, destroy, repel, or mitigate any pest;

(2) in the case of a plant regulator, an ingredient which, through physiological action, will accelerate or retard the rate of growth or rate of maturation or otherwise alter the behavior of ornamental or crop plants or the product thereof;

(3) in the case of a defoliant, an ingredient which will cause the leaves or foliage to drop from a plant; and

(4) in the case of a desiccant, an ingredient which will artificially accelerate the drying of plant tissue.

(b) Administrator.—The term "Administrator" means the Administrator of the Environmental Protection Agency.

(c) Adulterated.—The term "adulterated" applies to any pesticide if—

(1) its strength or purity falls below the professed standard of quality as expressed on its labeling under which it is sold;

(2) any substance has been substituted wholly or in part for the pesticide; or

(3) any valuable constituent of the pesticide has been wholly or in part abstracted.

(d) Animal.—The term "animal" means all vertebrate and invertebrate species, including but not limited to man and other mammals, birds, fish, and shellfish.

(e) Certified applicator, etc.—

(1) Certified applicator.—The term "certified applicator" means any individual who is certified under section 136i of this title as authorized to use or supervise the use of any pesticide which is classified for restricted use. Any applicator who holds or applies registered pesticides, or uses dilutions of registered pesticides consistent with subsection (ee) of this section, only to provide a service of controlling pests without delivering any unapplied pesticide to any person so served is not deemed to be a seller or distributor of pesticides under this subchapter.

(2) Private applicator.—The term "private applicator" means a certified applicator who uses or supervises the use of any pesticide which is classified for restricted use for purposes of producing any agricultural commodity on property owned or rented by the applicator or the applicator's employer or (if applied without compensation other than trading of personal services between producers of agricultural commodities) on the property of another person.

(3) Commercial applicator.—The term "commercial applicator" means an applicator (whether or not the applicator is a private applicator with respect to some uses) who uses or supervises the use of any pesticide which is classified for restricted use for any purpose or on any property other than as provided by paragraph (2).

(4) Under the direct supervision of a certified applicator.—Unless otherwise prescribed by its labeling, a pesticide shall be considered to be applied under the direct supervision of a certified applicator if it is applied by a competent person acting under the instructions and control of a certified applicator who is available if and when needed, even though such certified applicator is not physically present at the time and place the pesticide is applied.

(f) Defoliant.—The term "defoliant" means any substance or mixture of substances intended for causing the leaves or foliage to drop from a plant, with or without causing abscission.

(g) Desiccant.—The term "desiccant" means any substance or mixture of substances intended for artificially accelerating the drying of plant tissue.

(h) Device.—The term "device" means any instrument or contrivance (other than a firearm) which is intended for trapping, destroying, repelling, or mitigating any pest or any other form of plant or animal life (other than man and other than bacteria, virus, or other microorganism on or in living man or other living animals); but not including equipment used for the application of pesticides when sold separately therefrom.

(i) District court.—The term "district court" means a United States district court, the District

Court of Guam, the District Court of the Virgin Islands, and the highest court of American Samoa.

(j) Environment.—The term "environment" includes water, air, land, and all plants and man and other animals living therein, and the interrelationships which exist among these.

(k) Fungus.—The term "fungus" means any non-chlorophyll-bearing thallophyte (that is, any non-chlorophyll-bearing plant of a lower order than mosses and liverworts), as for example, rust, smut, mildew, mold, yeast, and bacteria, except those on or in living man or other animals and those on or in processed food, beverages, or pharmaceuticals.

(*l*) Imminent hazard.—The term "imminent hazard" means a situation which exists when the continued use of a pesticide during the time required for cancellation proceeding would be likely to result in unreasonable adverse effects on the environment or will involve unreasonable hazard to the survival of a species declared endangered or threatened by the Secretary pursuant to the Endangered Species Act of 1973.

(m) Inert ingredient.—The term "inert ingredient" means an ingredient which is not active.

(n) Ingredient statement.—The term "ingredient statement" means a statement which contains—

(1) the name and percentage of each active ingredient, and the total percentage of all inert ingredients, in the pesticide; and

(2) if the pesticide contains arsenic in any form, a statement of the percentages of total and water soluble arsenic, calculated as elementary arsenic.

(*o*) Insect.—The term "insect" means any of the numerous small invertebrate animals generally having the body more or less obviously segmented, for the most part belonging to the class insecta, comprising six-legged, usually winged forms, as for example, beetles, bugs, bees, flies, and to other allied classes of arthropods whose members are wingless and usually have more than six legs, as for example, spiders, mites, ticks, centipedes, and wood lice.

(p) Label and labeling.—

(1) Label.—The term "label" means the written, printed, or graphic matter on, or attached to, the pesticide or device or any of its containers or wrappers.

(2) Labeling.—The term "labeling" means all labels and all other written, printed, or graphic matter—

(A) accompanying the pesticide or device at any time; or

(B) to which reference is made on the label or in literature accompanying the pesticide or device, except to current official publications of the Environmental Protection Agency, the United States Departments of Agriculture and Interior, the Department of Health and Human Services, State experiment stations, State agricultural colleges, and other similar Federal or State institutions or agencies authorized by law to conduct research in the field of pesticides.

(q) Misbranded.—

(1) A pesticide is misbranded if—

(A) its labeling bears any statement, design, or graphic representation relative thereto or to its ingredients which is false or misleading in any particular;

(B) it is contained in a package or other container or wrapping which does not conform to the standards established by the Administrator pursuant to section 136w(c)(3) of this title;

(C) it is an imitation of, or is offered for sale under the name of, another pesticide;

(D) its label does not bear the registration number assigned under section 136e of this title to each establishment in which it was produced;

(E) any word, statement, or other information required by or under authority of this subchapter to appear on the label or labeling is not prominently placed thereon with such conspicuousness (as compared with other words, statements, designs, or graphic matter in the labeling) and in such terms as to render it likely to be read and understood by the ordinary individual under customary conditions of purchase and use;

(F) the labeling accompanying it does not contain directions for use which are necessary for effecting the purpose for which the product is intended and if complied with, together with any requirements imposed under section 136a(d) of this title, are adequate to protect health and the environment;

(G) the label does not contain a warning or caution statement which may be necessary and if complied with, together with any requirements imposed under section 136a(d) of this title, is adequate to protect health and the environment; or

(H) in the case of a pesticide not registered in accordance with section 136a of this title and intended for export, the label does not contain, in words prominently placed thereon with such conspicuousness (as compared with other words, statements, designs, or graphic matter in the labeling) as to render it likely to be noted by the ordinary individual under customary conditions of purchase and use, the following: "Not Registered for Use in the United States of America".

(2) A pesticide is misbranded if—

(A) the label does not bear an ingredient statement on that part of the immediate container (and on the outside container or wrapper of the retail package, if there be one, through which the ingredient statement on the immediate container cannot be clearly read) which is presented or displayed under customary conditions or purchase, except that a pesticide is not misbranded under this subparagraph if—

(i) The size or form of the immediate container, or the outside container or wrapper of the retail package, makes it impracticable to place the ingredient statement on the part which is presented or displayed under customary conditions of purchase; and

(ii) the ingredient statement appears prominently on another part of the immediate container, or outside container or wrapper, permitted by the Administrator;

(B) the labeling does not contain a statement of the use classification under which the product is registered;

(C) there is not affixed to its container, and to the outside container or wrapper of the retail package, if there be one, through which the required information on the immediate container cannot be clearly read, a label bearing—

(i) the name and address of the producer, registrant, or person for whom produced;

(ii) the name, brand, or trademark under which the pesticide is sold;

(iii) the net weight or measure of the content, except that the Administrator may permit reasonable variations; and

(iv) when required by regulation of the Administrator to effectuate the purposes of this subchapter, the registration number assigned to the pesticide under this subchapter, and the use classification; and

(D) the pesticide contains any substance or substances in quantities highly toxic to man, unless the label shall bear, in addition to any other matter required by this subchapter—

(i) the skull and crossbones;

(ii) the word "poison" prominently in red on a background of distinctly contrasting color; and

(iii) a statement of a practical treatment (first aid or otherwise) in case of poisoning by the pesticide.

(r) Nematode.—The term "nematode" means invertebrate animals of the phylum nemathelminthes and class nematoda, that is, unsegmented round worms with elongated, fusiform, or saclike bodies covered with cuticle, and inhabiting soil, water, plants, or plant parts; may also be called nemas or eelworms.

(s) Person.—The term "person" means any individual, partnership, association, corporation, or any organized group of persons whether incorporated or not.

(t) Pest.—The term "pest" means (1) any insect, rodent, nematode, fungus, weed, or (2) any other form of terrestrial or aquatic plant or animal life or virus, bacteria, or other micro-organism (except viruses, bacteria, or other micro-organisms on or in living man or other living animals) which the Administrator declares to be a pest under section 136w(c)(1) of this title.

(u) Pesticide.—The term "pesticide" means (1) any substance or mixture of substances intended for preventing, destroying, repelling, or mitigating any pest, and (2) any substance or mixture of substances intended for use as a plant regulator, defoliant, or desiccant, except that the term "pesticide" shall not include any article that is a "new animal drug" within the meaning of section 321(w) of Title 21, that has been determined by the Secretary of Health and Human Services not to be a new animal drug by a regulation establishing conditions of use for the article, or that is an animal feed within the meaning of section 321(x) of Title 21 bearing or containing a new animal drug.

(v) Plant regulator.—The term "plant regulator" means any substance or mixture of substances intended, through physiological action, for accelerating or retarding the rate of growth or rate of maturation, or for otherwise altering the behavior of plants or the produce thereof, but shall not include substances to the extent that they are intended as plant nutrients, trace elements, nutritional chemicals, plant inoculants, and soil amendments. Also, the term "plant regulator" shall not be required to include any of such of those nutrient mixtures or soil amendments as are commonly known as vitamin-hormone horticultural products, intended for improvement, maintenance, survival, health, and propagation of plants, and as are not for pest destruction and are nontoxic, nonpoisonous in the undiluted packaged concentration.

(w) Producer and produce.—The term "producer" means the person who manufactures, prepares, compounds, propagates, or processes any pesticide or device or active ingredient used in producing a pesticide. The term "produce" means to manufacture, prepare, compound, propagate, or process any pesticide or device or active ingredient used in producing a pesticide. The dilution by individuals of formulated pesticides for their own use and according to the directions on registered labels shall not of itself result in such individuals being included in the definition of "producer" for the purposes of this subchapter.

(x) Protect health and the environment.—The terms "protect health and the environment" and "protection of health and the environment" mean protection against any unreasonable adverse effects on the environment.

(y) Registrant.—The term "registrant" means a person who has registered any pesticide pursuant to the provisions of this subchapter.

(z) Registration.—The term "registration" includes reregistration.

(aa) State.—The term "State" means a State, the District of Columbia, the Commonwealth of Puerto Rico, the Virgin Islands, Guam, the Trust Territory of the Pacific Islands, and American Samoa.

(bb) Unreasonable adverse effects on the environment.—The term "unreasonable adverse effects on the environment" means any unreasonable risk to man or the environment, taking into account the economic, social, and environmental costs and benefits of the use of any pesticide.

(cc) Weed.—The term "weed" means any plant which grows where not wanted.

(dd) Establishment.—The term "establishment" means any place where a pesticide or device or active ingredient used in producing a pesticide is produced, or held, for distribution or sale.

(ee) To use any registered pesticide in a manner inconsistent with its labeling.—The term "to use any registered pesticide in a manner inconsistent with its labeling" means to use any registered pesticide in a manner not permitted by the labeling, except that the term shall not include (1) applying a pesticide at any dosage, concentration, or frequency less than that specified on the labeling unless the labeling specifically prohibits deviation from the specified dosage, concentration, or frequency, (2) applying a pesticide against any target pest not specified on the labeling if the application is to the crop, animal, or site specified on the labeling, unless the Administrator has required that the labeling specifically state that the pesticide may be used only for the pests specified on the labeling after the Administrator has determined that the use of the pesticide against other pests would cause an unreasonable adverse effect on the environment, (3) employing any method of application not prohibited by the labeling unless the labeling specifically states that the product may be applied only by the methods specified on the labeling, (4) mixing a pesticide or pesticides with a fertilizer when such mixture is not prohibited by the labeling, (5) any use of a pesticide in conformance with section 136c, 136p, or 136v of this title, or (6) any use of a pesticide in a manner that the Administrator determines to be consistent with the purposes of this subchapter. After March 31, 1979, the term shall not include the use of a pesticide for agricultural or forestry purposes at a dilution less than label dosage unless before or after that date the Administrator issues a regulation or advisory opinion consistent with the study provided for in section 27(b) of the Federal Pesticide Act of 1978, which regulation or advisory opinion specifically requires the use of definite amounts of dilution.

(ff) Outstanding data requirement.—

(1) In general. The term "outstanding data requirement" means a requirement for any study, information, or data that is necessary to make a determination under section 136a(c)(5) of this title and which study, information, or data—

(A) has not been submitted to the Administrator; or

(B) if submitted to the Administrator, the Administrator has determined must be resubmitted because it is not valid, complete, or adequate to make a determination under section 136a(c)(5) of this title and the regulations and guidelines issued under such section.

(2) Factors. In making a determination under paragraph (1)(B) respecting a study, the Administrator shall examine, at a minimum, relevant protocols, documentation of the conduct and analysis of the study, and the results of the study to determine whether the study and the results of the study fulfill the data requirement for which the study was submitted to the Administrator.

(gg) To distribute or sell.—The term "to distribute or sell" means to distribute, sell, offer for sale, hold for distribution, hold for sale, hold for shipment, ship, deliver for shipment, release for shipment, or receive and (having so received) deliver or offer to deliver. The term does not include the holding or application of registered pesticides or use dilutions thereof by any applicator who provides a service of controlling pests without delivering any unapplied pesticide to any person so served.

(June 25, 1947, ch. 125, § 2, as added Oct. 21, 1972, Pub.L. 92–516, § 2, 86 Stat. 975, and amended Dec. 28, 1973, Pub.L. 93–205, § 13(f), 87 Stat. 903; Nov. 28, 1975, Pub.L. 94–140, § 9, 89 Stat. 754; Sept. 30, 1978, Pub.L. 95–396, § 1, 92 Stat. 819; Oct. 17, 1979, Pub.L. 96–88, Title V, § 509(b), 93 Stat. 695; Oct. 25, 1988, Pub.L. 100–532, Title I, § 101, Title VI, § 601(a), Title VIII, § 801(a), 102 Stat. 2655, 2677, 2679; Dec. 13, 1991, Pub.L. 102–237, Title X, § 1006(a)(1), (2), (b)(3)(A), (B), 105 Stat. 1894, 1895.)

References in Text

The Endangered Species Act of 1973, referred to in subsec. (*l*), is Pub.L. 93–205, Dec. 28, 1973, 87 Stat. 884, as amended, which is classified principally to chapter 35 (§ 1531 et seq.) of Title 16, Conservation.

Section 27(b) of Federal Pesticide Act of 1978, referred to in subsec. (ee), is section 27(b) of Pub.L. 95–396, Sept. 30, 1978, 92 Stat. 841, which required the Administrator of the Environmental Protection Agency to report to the Senate Committee on Agriculture, Nutrition, and Forestry and to the House Committee on Agriculture not later than 9 months after Sept. 30, 1978, in respect to fee collection from pesticide registrants, not later than 6 months after Sept. 30, 1978 in respect to pesticide uses, and not later than 9 months after Sept. 30, 1978 in respect to problems of minor uses of pesticides not specifically permitted by labeling.

Effective Date of 1991 Amendment

Amendments by Pub.L. 102–237 effective Dec. 13, 1991, see section 1101(a) of Pub.L. 102–237, set out as a note under section 1421 of this title.

Effective Date of 1988 Amendment

Section 901 of Pub.L. 100–532 provided that: "Except as otherwise provided in this Act, the amendments made by this Act [see Short Title of 1988 Amendment note set out under this section] shall take effect on the expiration of 60 days after the date of enactment of this Act [October 25, 1988]."

Effective Date

Section 4 of Pub.L. 92–516, Oct. 21, 1972, 86 Stat. 998, as amended Pub.L. 94–140, § 4, Nov. 28, 1975, 89 Stat. 752; Pub.L. 95–396, § 28, Sept. 30, 1978, 92 Stat. 842, provided that:

"**(a)** Except as otherwise provided in the Federal Insecticide, Fungicide, and Rodenticide Act [this subchapter], as amended by this Act and as otherwise provided by this section, the amendments made by this Act [see Short Title note set out under this section] shall take effect at the close of the date of the enactment of this Act [Oct. 21, 1972], provided if regulations are necessary for the implementation of any provision that becomes effective on the date of enactment, such regulations shall be promulgated and shall become effective within 90 days from the date of enactment of this Act.

"**(b)** The provisions of the Federal Insecticide, Fungicide, and Rodenticide Act [this subchapter] and the regulations thereunder as such existed prior to the enactment of this Act shall remain in effect until superseded by the amendments made by this Act and regulations thereunder.

"**(c)(1)** Two years after the enactment of this Act the Administrator shall have promulgated regulations providing for the registration and classification of pesticides under the provisions of this Act and thereafter shall register all new applications under such provisions.

"**(2)** Any requirements that a pesticide be registered for use only by a certified applicator shall not be effective until five years from the date of enactment of this Act.

"**(3)** A period of five years from date of enactment shall be provided for certification of applicators.

"**(A)** One year after the enactment of this Act the Administrator shall have prescribed the standards for the certification of applicators.

"**(B)** Each State desiring to certify applicators shall submit a State plan to the Administrator for the purpose provided by section 4(b).

"**(C)** As promptly as possible but in no event more than one year after submission of a State plan, the Administrator shall approve the State plan or disapprove it and indicate the reasons for disapproval. Consideration of plans resubmitted by States shall be expedited.

"**(4)** One year after the enactment of this Act the Administrator shall have promulgated and shall make effective regulations relating to the registration of establishments, permits for experimental use, and the keeping of books and records under the provisions of this Act.

"**(d)** No person shall be subject to any criminal or civil penalty imposed by the Federal Insecticide, Fungicide, and Rodenticide Act, as amended by this Act, for any act (or failure to act) occurring before the expiration of 60 days after the Administrator has published effective regulations in the Federal Register and taken such other action as may be necessary to permit compliance with the provisions under which the penalty is to be imposed.

"**(e)** For purposes of determining any criminal or civil penalty or liability to any third person in respect of any act or omission occurring before the expiration of the periods referred to in this section, the Federal Insecticide, Fungicide, and Rodenticide Act shall be treated as continuing in effect as if this Act had not been enacted."

Short Title of 1988 Amendment

Section 1(a) of Pub.L. 100–532 provided that: "This Act [enacting section 136a–1 of this title, amending sections 136, 136a, 136b, 136c, 136d, 136f, 136g, 136h, 136i, 136j, 136k, 136*l*, 136m, 136n, 136*o*, 136p, 136q, 136s, 136v, 136w, 136w–1, 136w–2, and 136y of this title, and enacting provisions set out as notes under sections 136, 136m, and 136y of this title] may be cited as the 'Federal Insecticide, Fungicide, and Rodenticide Act Amendments of 1988'."

Short Title

Section 1(a) of Act June 25, 1947, c. 125, as added Oct. 21, 1972, Pub.L. 92–516, § 2, 86 Stat. 973, provided that: "This Act [enacting this subchapter] may be cited as the 'Federal Insecticide, Fungicide, and Rodenticide Act'."

CODE OF FEDERAL REGULATIONS

Arbitration of pesticide data disputes, see 29 CFR 1440.1.

Debarment and suspension under EPA assistance programs, see 40 CFR 32.100 et seq.

Tolerances and exemptions for pesticide chemicals in or on raw agricultural commodities, see 40 CFR 180.1 et seq.

LAW REVIEW COMMENTARIES

Application of handicap discrimination laws to AIDS patients. 22 U.S.F.L.Rev. 317 (1988).

Chemical trespass? Overview of statutory and regulatory efforts to control pesticide drift. Sarah E. Redfield, 73 Ky.L.J. 855 (1984–85).

Confidential business information versus the public's right to disclosure—Biotechnology renews the challenge. Stanley H. Abramson, 34 U.Kansas L.Rev. 681 (1986).

Criminal sanctions under federal and state environmental statutes. Richard H. Allan, 14 Ecology L.Q. 117 (1987).

Environmental claims in bankruptcy: Policy conflicts, procedural pitfalls and problematic precedent. Thomas G. Gruenert, 32 S.Tex. L.Rev. 399 (1991).

Erosion of mens rea in environmental criminal prosecution. Ruth Ann Weidel, John R. Mayo and F. Michael Zachara, 21 Seton Hall L.Rev. 1125 (1991).

Federal regulation of agricultural biotechnologies. Thomas O. McGarity, 20 U.Mich.J.L.Ref. 1089 (1987).

Hazardous wastes in New Jersey: An overview. Anne F. Morris, 38 Rutgers L.Rev. 623 (1986).

Limiting lender liability under CERCLA by administrative rule. Frona M. Powell, 75 Marq.L.Rev. 139 (1991).

Long-range planning in environmental and health regulatory agencies. Richard N.L. Andrews, 20 Ecology L.Q. 515 (1993).

Prosecution of corporations and corporate officers for environmental crimes: Limiting one's exposure for environmental criminal liability. Kenneth A. Hodson, Sarah N. McGiffert and Marianne T. Bayardi, 34 Ariz.L.Rev. 553 (1992).

Remedies for hazardous or toxic substance-related personal injuries: A discussion of the usefulness of regulatory standards. Donald W. Stever, 25 Houston L.Rev. 801 (1988).

Toxic tort litigation and the causation element: Is there any hope of reconciliation? Ora Fred Harris, Jr., 40 Southwestern (Tex.) L.J. 909 (1986).

LIBRARY REFERENCES

Agriculture ⇐9.11(1).
Health and Environment ⇐25.5(1).
C.J.S. Agriculture §§ 95, 96, 100.

C.J.S. Health and Environment § 61 et seq.

WESTLAW ELECTRONIC RESEARCH

Agricultural cases: 23k (add key number)

United States Supreme Court

Appellate review, pesticide manufacturer's action challenging constitutionality of binding arbitration provisions of 1978 amendments of Act, see Thomas v. Union Carbide Agr. Products Co., 1985, 105 S.Ct. 3325, 473 U.S. 568, 87 L.Ed.2d 409.

§ 136a. Registration of pesticides [FIFRA § 3]

(a) Requirement of registration.—Except as provided by this subchapter, no person in any State may distribute or sell to any person any pesticide that is not registered under this subchapter. To the extent necessary to prevent unreasonable adverse effects on the environment, the Administrator may by regulation limit the distribution, sale, or use in any State of any pesticide that is not registered under this subchapter and that is not the subject of an experimental use permit under section 136c of this title or an emergency exemption under section 136p of this title.

(b) Exemptions.—A pesticide which is not registered with the Administrator may be transferred if—

(1) the transfer is from one registered establishment to another registered establishment operated by the same producer solely for packaging at the second establishment or for use as a constituent part of another pesticide produced at the second establishment; or

(2) the transfer is pursuant to and in accordance with the requirements of an experimental use permit.

(c) Procedure for registration.—

(1) Statement required.—Each applicant for registration of a pesticide shall file with the Administrator a statement which includes—

(A) the name and address of the applicant and of any other person whose name will appear on the labeling;

(B) the name of the pesticide;

(C) a complete copy of the labeling of the pesticide, a statement of all claims to be made for it, and any directions for its use;

(D) the complete formula of the pesticide;

(E) a request that the pesticide be classified for general use or for restricted use, or for both; and

(F) except as otherwise provided in paragraph (2)(D), if requested by the Administrator, a full description of the tests made and the results thereof upon which the claims are based, or alternatively a citation to data that appear in the public literature or that previously had been submitted to the Administrator and that the Administrator may consider in accordance with the following provisions:

(i) With respect to pesticides containing active ingredients that are initially registered under this subchapter after September 30, 1978, data submitted to support the application for the original registration of the pesticide, or an application for an amendment adding any new use to the registration and that pertains solely to such new use, shall not, without the written permission of the original data submitter, be considered by the Administrator to support an application by another person during a period of ten years following the date the Administrator first registers the pesticide, except that such permission shall not be required in the case of defensive data.

(ii) Except as otherwise provided in clause (i), with respect to data submitted after December 31, 1969, by an applicant or registrant to support an application for registration, experimental use permit, or amendment adding a new use to an existing registration, to support or maintain in effect an existing registration, or for reregistration, the Administrator may, without the permission of the original data submitter, consider any such item of data in support of an application by any other person (hereinafter in this subparagraph referred to as the "applicant") within the fifteen-year period following the date the data were originally submitted only if the applicant has made an offer to compensate the original data submitter and submitted such offer to the Administrator accompanied by evidence of delivery to the original data submitter of the offer. The terms and amount of compensation may be fixed by agreement between the original data submitter and the applicant, or, failing such agreement, binding arbitration under this subparagraph. If, at the end of ninety days after the date of delivery to the original data submitter of the offer to compensate, the original data submitter and the applicant have neither agreed on the amount and terms of compensation nor on a procedure for reaching an agreement on the amount and terms of compensation, either person may initiate binding arbitration proceedings by requesting the Federal Mediation and Conciliation Service to appoint an arbitrator from the roster of arbitrators maintained by such Service. The procedure and rules of the

Service shall be applicable to the selection of such arbitrator and to such arbitration proceedings, and the findings and determination of the arbitrator shall be final and conclusive, and no official or court of the United States shall have power or jurisdiction to review any such findings and determination, except for fraud, misrepresentation, or other misconduct by one of the parties to the arbitration or the arbitrator where there is a verified complaint with supporting affidavits attesting to specific instances of such fraud, misrepresentation, or other misconduct. The parties to the arbitration shall share equally in the payment of the fee and expenses of the arbitrator. If the Administrator determines that an original data submitter has failed to participate in a procedure for reaching an agreement or in an arbitration proceeding as required by this subparagraph, or failed to comply with the terms of an agreement or arbitration decision concerning compensation under this subparagraph, the original data submitter shall forfeit the right to compensation for the use of the data in support of the application. Notwithstanding any other provision of this subchapter, if the Administrator determines that an applicant has failed to participate in a procedure for reaching an agreement or in an arbitration proceeding as required by this subparagraph, or failed to comply with the terms of an agreement or arbitration decision concerning compensation under this subparagraph, the Administrator shall deny the application or cancel the registration of the pesticide in support of which the data were used without further hearing. Before the Administrator takes action under either of the preceding two sentences, the Administrator shall furnish to the affected person, by certified mail, notice of intent to take action and allow fifteen days from the date of delivery of the notice for the affected person to respond. If a registration is denied or canceled under this subparagraph, the Administrator may make such order as the Administrator deems appropriate concerning the continued sale and use of existing stocks of such pesticide. Registration action by the Administrator shall not be delayed pending the fixing of compensation.

(iii) After expiration of any period of exclusive use and any period for which compensation is required for the use of an item of data under clauses (i) and (ii), the Administrator may consider such item of data in support of an application by any other applicant without the permission of the original data submitter and without an offer having been received to compensate the original data submitter for the use of such item of data.

(2) Data in support of registration.—

(A) The Administrator shall publish guidelines specifying the kinds of information which will be required to support the registration of a pesticide and shall revise such guidelines from time to time. If thereafter the Administrator requires any additional kind of information under subparagraph (B) of this paragraph, the Administrator shall permit sufficient time for applicants to obtain such additional information. The Administrator, in establishing standards for data requirements for the registration of pesticides with respect to minor uses, shall make such standards commensurate with the anticipated extent of use, pattern of use, and the level and degree of potential exposure of man and the environment to the pesticide. The Administrator shall not require a person to submit, in relation to a registration or reregistration of a pesticide for minor agricultural use under this subchapter, any field residue data from a geographic area where the pesticide will not be registered for such use. In the development of these standards, the Administrator shall consider the economic factors of potential national volume of use, extent of distribution, and the impact of the cost of meeting the requirements on the incentives for any potential registrant to undertake the development of the required data. Except as provided by section 136h of this title, within 30 days after the Administrator registers a pesticide under this subchapter the Administrator shall make available to the public the data called for in the registration statement together with such other scientific information as the Administrator deems relevant to the Administrator's decision.

(B)(i) If the Administrator determines that additional data are required to maintain in effect an existing registration of a pesticide, the Administrator shall notify all existing registrants of the pesticide to which the determination relates and provide a list of such registrants to any interested person.

(ii) Each registrant of such pesticide shall provide evidence within ninety days after receipt of notification that it is taking appropriate steps to secure the additional data that are required. Two or more registrants may agree to develop jointly, or to share in the cost of developing, such data if they agree and advise the Administrator of their intent within ninety days after notification.

Any registrant who agrees to share in the cost of producing the data shall be entitled to examine and rely upon such data in support of maintenance of such registration. The Administrator shall issue a notice of intent to suspend the registration of a pesticide in accordance with the procedures prescribed by clause (iv) if a registrant fails to comply with this clause.

(iii) If, at the end of sixty days after advising the Administrator of their agreement to develop jointly, or share in the cost of developing, data, the registrants have not further agreed on the terms of the data development arrangement or on a procedure for reaching such agreement, any of such registrants may initiate binding arbitration proceedings by requesting the Federal Mediation and Conciliation Service to appoint an arbitrator from the roster of arbitrators maintained by such Service. The procedure and rules of the Service shall be applicable to the selection of such arbitrator and to such arbitration proceedings, and the findings and determination of the arbitrator shall be final and conclusive, and no official or court of the United States shall have power or jurisdiction to review any such finding and determination, except for fraud, misrepresentation, or other misconduct by one of the parties to the arbitration or the arbitrator where there is a verified complaint with supporting affidavits attesting to specific instances of such fraud, misrepresentation, or other misconduct. All parties to the arbitration shall share equally in the payment of the fee and expenses of the arbitrator. The Administrator shall issue a notice of intent to suspend the registration of a pesticide in accordance with the procedures prescribed by clause (iv) if a registrant fails to comply with this clause.

(iv) Notwithstanding any other provision of this subchapter, if the Administrator determines that a registrant, within the time required by the Administrator, has failed to take appropriate steps to secure the data required under this subparagraph, to participate in a procedure for reaching agreement concerning a joint data development arrangement under this subparagraph or in an arbitration proceeding as required by this subparagraph, or to comply with the terms of an agreement or arbitration decision concerning a joint data development arrangement under this subparagraph, the Administrator may issue a notice of intent to suspend such registrant's registration of the pesticide for which additional data is required. The Administrator may include in the notice of intent to suspend such provisions as the Administrator deems appropriate concerning the continued sale and use of existing stocks of such pesticide. Any suspension proposed under this subparagraph shall become final and effective at the end of thirty days from receipt by the registrant of the notice of intent to suspend, unless during that time a request for hearing is made by a person adversely affected by the notice or the registrant has satisfied the Administrator that the registrant has complied fully with the requirements that served as a basis for the notice of intent to suspend. If a hearing is requested, a hearing shall be conducted under section 136d(d) of this title. The only matters for resolution at that hearing shall be whether the registrant has failed to take the action that served as the basis for the notice of intent to suspend the registration of the pesticide for which additional data is required, and whether the Administrator's determination with respect to the disposition of existing stocks is consistent with this subchapter. If a hearing is held, a decision after completion of such hearing shall be final. Notwithstanding any other provision of this subchapter, a hearing shall be held and a determination made within seventy-five days after receipt of a request for such hearing. Any registration suspended under this subparagraph shall be reinstated by the Administrator if the Administrator determines that the registrant has complied fully with the requirements that served as a basis for the suspension of the registration.

(v) Any data submitted under this subparagraph shall be subject to the provisions of paragraph (1)(D). Whenever such data are submitted jointly by two or more registrants, an agent shall be agreed on at the time of the joint submission to handle any subsequent data compensation matters for the joint submitters of such data.

(C) Within nine months after September 30, 1978, the Administrator shall, by regulation, prescribe simplified procedures for the registration of pesticides, which shall include the provisions of subparagraph (D) of this paragraph.

(D) Exemption. No applicant for registration of a pesticide who proposes to purchase a registered pesticide from another producer in order to formulate such purchased pesticide into the pesticide that is the subject of the application shall be required to—

(i) submit or cite data pertaining to such purchased product; or

(ii) offer to pay reasonable compensation otherwise required by paragraph (1)(D) of this subsection for the use of any such data.

(3) Time for acting with respect to application.—

(A) The Administrator shall review the data after receipt of the application and shall, as expeditiously as possible, either register the pesticide in accordance with paragraph (5), or notify the applicant of the Administrator's determination that it does not comply with the provisions of the subchapter in accordance with paragraph (6).

(B)(i) The Administrator shall, as expeditiously as possible, review and act on any application received by the Administrator that—

(I) proposes the initial or amended registration of an end-use pesticide that, if registered as proposed, would be identical or substantially similar in composition and labeling to a currently-registered pesticide identified in the application, or that would differ in composition and labeling from such currently-registered pesticide only in ways that would not significantly increase the risk of unreasonable adverse effects on the environment; or

(II) proposes an amendment to the registration of a registered pesticide that does not require scientific review of data.

(ii) In expediting the review of an application for an action described in clause (i), the Administrator shall—

(I) within 45 days after receiving the application, notify the registrant whether or not the application is complete and, if the application is found to be incomplete, reject the application;

(II) within 90 days after receiving a complete application, notify the registrant if the application has been granted or denied; and

(III) if the application is denied, notify the registrant in writing of the specific reasons for the denial of the application.

(4) Notice of application.—The Administrator shall publish in the Federal Register, promptly after receipt of the statement and other data required pursuant to paragraphs (1) and (2), a notice of each application for registration of any pesticide if it contains any new active ingredient or if it would entail a changed use pattern. The notice shall provide for a period of 30 days in which any Federal agency or any other interested person may comment.

(5) Approval of registration.—The Administrator shall register a pesticide if the Administrator determines that, when considered with any restrictions imposed under subsection (d) of this section—

(A) its composition is such as to warrant the proposed claims for it;

(B) its labeling and other material required to be submitted comply with the requirements of this subchapter;

(C) it will perform its intended function without unreasonable adverse effects on the environment; and

(D) when used in accordance with widespread and commonly recognized practice it will not generally cause unreasonable adverse effects on the environment.

The Administrator shall not make any lack of essentiality a criterion for denying registration of any pesticide. Where two pesticides meet the requirements of this paragraph, one should not be registered in preference to the other. In considering an application for the registration of a pesticide, the Administrator may waive data requirements pertaining to efficacy, in which event the Administrator may register the pesticide without determining that the pesticide's composition is such as to warrant proposed claims of efficacy. If a pesticide is found to be efficacious by any State under section 136v(c) of this title, a presumption is established that the Administrator shall waive data requirements pertaining to efficacy for use of the pesticide in such State.

(6) Denial of registration.—If the Administrator determines that the requirements of paragraph (5) for registration are not satisfied, the Administrator shall notify the applicant for registration of the Administrator's determination and of the Administrator's reasons (including the factual basis) therefor, and that, unless the applicant corrects the conditions and notifies the Administrator thereof during the 30-day period beginning with the day after the date on which the applicant receives the notice, the Administrator may refuse to register the pesticide. Whenever the Administrator refuses to register a pesticide, the Administrator shall notify the applicant of the Administrator's decision and of the Administrator's reasons (including the factual basis) therefor. The Administrator shall promptly publish in the Federal Register notice of such denial of registration and the reasons therefor. Upon such notification, the applicant for registration or other interested person with the concurrence of the applicant shall have the same remedies as provided for in section 136d of this title.

(7) Registration under special circumstances.—Notwithstanding the provisions of paragraph (5)—

(A) The Administrator may conditionally register or amend the registration of a pesticide if the Administrator determines that (i) the pesticide and proposed use are identical or substantially similar to any currently registered pesticide and use thereof, or differ only in ways that would not significantly increase the risk of unreasonable adverse effects on the environment, and (ii) approving the registration or amendment in the manner proposed by the applicant would not significantly increase the risk of any unreasonable adverse effect on the environment. An applicant seeking conditional registration or amended registration under this subparagraph shall submit such data as would be required to obtain registration of a similar pesticide under paragraph (5). If the applicant is unable to submit an item of data because it has not yet been generated, the Administrator may register or amend the registration of the pesticide under such conditions as will require the submission of such data not later than the time such data are required to be submitted with respect to similar pesticides already registered under this subchapter.

(B) The Administrator may conditionally amend the registration of a pesticide to permit additional uses of such pesticide notwithstanding that data concerning the pesticide may be insufficient to support an unconditional amendment, if the Administrator determines that (i) the applicant has submitted satisfactory data pertaining to the proposed additional use, and (ii) amending the registration in the manner proposed by the applicant would not significantly increase the risk of any unreasonable adverse effect on the environment. Notwithstanding the foregoing provisions of this subparagraph, no registration of a pesticide may be amended to permit an additional use of such pesticide if the Administrator has issued a notice stating that such pesticide, or any ingredient thereof, meets or exceeds risk criteria associated in whole or in part with human dietary exposure enumerated in regulations issued under this subchapter, and during the pendency of any risk-benefit evaluation initiated by such notice, if (I) the additional use of such pesticide involves a major food or feed crop, or (II) the additional use of such pesticide involves a minor food or feed crop and the Administrator determines, with the concurrence of the Secretary of Agriculture, there is available an effective alternative pesticide that does not meet or exceed such risk criteria. An applicant seeking amended registration under this subparagraph shall submit such data as would be required to obtain registration of a similar pesticide under paragraph (5). If the applicant is unable to submit an item of data (other than data pertaining to the proposed additional use) because it has not yet been generated, the Administrator may amend the registration under such conditions as will require the submission of such data not later than the time such data are required to be submitted with respect to similar pesticides already registered under this subchapter.

(C) The Administrator may conditionally register a pesticide containing an active ingredient not contained in any currently registered pesticide for a period reasonably sufficient for the generation and submission of required data (which are lacking because a period reasonably sufficient for generation of the data has not elapsed since the Administrator first imposed the data requirement) on the condition that by the end of such period the Administrator receives such data and the data do not meet or exceed risk criteria enumerated in regulations issued under this subchapter, and on such other conditions as the Administrator may prescribe. A conditional registration under this subparagraph shall be granted only if the Administrator determines that use of the pesticide during such period will not cause any unreasonable adverse effect on the environment, and that use of the pesticide is in the public interest.

(8) Interim administrative review.—Notwithstanding any other provision of this subchapter, the Administrator may not initiate a public interim administrative review process to develop a risk-benefit evaluation of the ingredients of a pesticide or any of its uses prior to initiating a formal action to cancel, suspend, or deny registration of such pesticide, required under this subchapter, unless such interim administrative process is based on a validated test or other significant evidence raising prudent concerns of unreasonable adverse risk to man or to the environment. Notice of the definition of the terms "validated test" and "other significant evidence" as used herein shall be published by the Administrator in the Federal Register.

(d) Classification of pesticides.—

(1) Classification for general use, restricted use, or both.—

(A) As a part of the registration of a pesticide the Administrator shall classify it as being for general use or for restricted use. If the Administrator determines that some of the uses for which the pesticide is registered should be for general use and that other uses for which it is registered should be for restricted use, the Administrator shall classify it for both general use and restricted use. Pesticide uses may be classified by regulation on the initial classification, and registered pesticides may be classified prior to reregistration. If some of the uses of the pesticide are classified for general use, and other uses are classified for restricted use, the directions relating to its general uses shall be clearly separated and distinguished from those directions relating to its restricted uses. The Administrator may require that its packaging and labeling for restricted uses shall be clearly distinguishable from its packaging and labeling for general uses.

(B) If the Administrator determines that the pesticide, when applied in accordance with its directions for use, warnings and cautions and for the uses for which it is registered, or for one or more of such uses, or in accordance with a widespread and commonly recognized practice, will not generally cause unreasonable adverse effects on the environment, the Administrator will classify the pesticide, or the particular use or uses of the pesticide to which the determination applies, for general use.

(C) If the Administrator determines that the pesticide, when applied in accordance with its directions for use, warnings and cautions and for the uses for which it is registered, or for one or more of such uses, or in accordance with a widespread and commonly recognized practice, may generally cause, without additional regulatory restrictions, unreasonable adverse effects on the environment, including injury to the applicator, the Administrator shall classify the pesticide, or the particular use or uses to which the determination applies, for restricted use:

(i) If the Administrator classifies a pesticide, or one or more uses of such pesticide, for restricted use because of a determination that the acute dermal or inhalation toxicity of the pesticide presents a hazard to the applicator or other persons, the pesticide shall be applied for any use to which the restricted classification applies only by or under the direct supervision of a certified applicator.

(ii) If the Administrator classifies a pesticide, or one or more uses of such pesticide, for restricted use because of a determination that its use without additional regulatory restriction may cause unreasonable adverse effects on the environment, the pesticide shall be applied for any use to which the determination applies only by or under the direct supervision of a certified applicator, or subject to such other restrictions as the Administrator may provide by regulation. Any such regulation shall be reviewable in the appropriate court of appeals upon petition of a person adversely affected filed within 60 days of the publication of the regulation in final form.

(2) Change in classification.—If the Administrator determines that a change in the classification of any use of a pesticide from general use to restricted use is necessary to prevent unreasonable adverse effects on the environment, the Administrator shall notify the registrant of such pesticide of such determination at least forty-five days before making the change and shall publish the proposed change in the Federal Register. The registrant, or other interested person with the concurrence of the registrant, may seek relief from such determination under section 136d(b) of this title.

(3) Change in classification from restricted use to general use.—The registrant of any pesticide with one or more uses classified for restricted use may petition the Administrator to change any such classification from restricted to general use. Such petition shall set out the basis for the registrant's position that restricted use classification is unnecessary because classification of the pesticide for general use would not cause unreasonable adverse effects on the environment. The Administrator, within sixty days after receiving such petition, shall notify the registrant whether the petition has been granted or denied. Any denial shall contain an explanation therefor and any such denial shall be subject to judicial review under section 136n of this title.

(e) Products with same formulation and claims.—Products which have the same formulation, are manufactured by the same person, the labeling of which contains the same claims, and the labels of which bear a designation identifying the product as the same pesticide may be registered as a single pesticide; and additional names and labels shall be added to the registration by supplemental statements.

(f) Miscellaneous.—

(1) Effect of change of labeling or formulation.—If the labeling or formulation for a pesticide is changed, the registration shall be amended to reflect such change if the Administrator determines that the change will not violate any provision of this subchapter.

(2) Registration not a defense.—In no event shall registration of an article be construed as a defense for the commission of any offense under this subchapter. As long as no cancellation proceedings are in effect registration of a pesticide shall be prima facie evidence that the pesticide, its labeling and packaging comply with the registration provisions of the subchapter.

(3) Authority to consult other federal agencies.—In connection with consideration of any registration or application for registration under this section, the Administrator may consult with any other Federal agency.

(June 25, 1947, c. 125, § 3, as added Oct. 21, 1972, Pub.L. 92–516, § 2, 86 Stat. 979, and amended Nov. 28, 1975, Pub.L. 94–140, § 12, 89 Stat. 755; Sept. 30, 1978, Pub.L. 95–396, §§ 2(a), 3–8, 92 Stat. 820, 824–827; Oct. 25, 1988, Pub.L. 100–532, Title I, §§ 102(b), 103, Title VI, § 601(b)(1), Title VIII, § 801(b), 102 Stat. 2667, 2677, 2680; Nov. 28, 1990, Pub.L. 101–624, Title XIV, § 1492, 104 Stat. 3628; Dec. 13, 1991, Pub.L. 102–237, Title X, § 1006(a)(3), (b)(1), (2), (c), 105 Stat. 1894–1896.)

Codification

Section 1006(c) of Pub.L. 102–237 provided that the phrase sought to be struck out of subsec. (c)(2)(D) of this section by section 102(v)(2)(A) of Pub.L. 100–532 is to be deemed to be "an end–use product", rather than "an end use product", as such phrase appeared in section 102(b)(2)(A) of Pub.L. 100–532.

Effective Date of 1991 Amendment

Amendments by Pub.L. 102–237 effective Dec. 13, 1991, see section 1101(a) of Pub.L. 102–237, set out as a note under section 1421 of this title.

Severability of Provisions

If any provision of Pub.L. 101–624 or the application thereof to any person or circumstance is held invalid, such invalidity not to affect other provisions or applications of Pub.L. 101–624 which can be given effect without regard to the invalid provision or application, see section 2519 of Pub.L. 101–624, set out as a note under section 1421 of this title.

Biological Pesticide Handling Study

Section 1498 of Pub.L. 101–624, provided that:

"**(a) Study.**—Not later than September 30, 1992, the National Academy of Sciences shall conduct a study of the biological control programs and registration procedures utilized by the Food and Drug Administration, the Animal and Plant Health Inspection Service, and the Environmental Protection Agency.

"**(b) Development of procedures.**—Not later than 1 year after the completion of the study under subsection (a), the agencies and offices described in such subsection shall develop and implement a common process for reviewing and approving biological control applications that are submitted to such agencies and offices that shall be based on the study conducted under such subsection and the recommendation of the National Academy of Sciences, and other public comment."

CODE OF FEDERAL REGULATIONS

Arbitration of pesticide data disputes, see 29 CFR 1440.1.
Debarment and suspension under EPA assistance programs, see 40 CFR 32.100 et seq.
Registration—
 Data requirements, see 40 CFR 158.20 et seq.
 Packaging requirements, see 40 CFR 157.20 et seq.
 Reregistration and classification, see 40 CFR 162.1 et seq.
 Standards for, see 40 CFR 155.23 et seq.

Registration—Cont'd

LAW REVIEW COMMENTARIES

Cipollone decision: Providing guidelines for federal preemption of product liability claims. Marc Z. Edell and Harriet Dinegar Milks, 150 N.J.Law. 37 (Mag.) (JAN. 1993).

Compensating manufacturers submitting health and safety data to support product registrations after Ruckelshaus v. Monsanto. 61 Ind.L.J. 189 (1985–1986).

LIBRARY REFERENCES

Agriculture ⚿9.
C.J.S. Agriculture § 83 et seq.

WESTLAW ELECTRONIC RESEARCH

Agricultural cases: 23k (add key number)

United States Supreme Court

Holding in *Northern Pipeline* case that Congress may not vest in non-Article III court the power to adjudicate a traditional contract action arising under State law without litigants' consent was not controlling in pesticide manufacturer's action challenging constitutionality of binding arbitration provision of 1978 amendments to FIFRA, see Thomas v. Union Carbide Agr. Products Co., 1985, 105 S.Ct. 3325, 473 U.S. 568, 87 L.Ed.2d 409.

§ 136a–1. Reregistration of registered pesticides [FIFRA § 4]

(a) General rule.—The Administrator shall reregister, in accordance with this section, each registered pesticide containing any active ingredient contained in any pesticide first registered before November 1, 1984, except for any pesticide as to which the Administrator has determined, after November 1, 1984, and before the effective date of this section, that—

(1) there are no outstanding data requirements; and

(2) the requirements of section 136a(c)(5) of this title have been satisfied.

(b) Reregistration phases.—Reregistrations of pesticides under this section shall be carried out in the following phases:

(1) The first phase shall include the listing under subsection (c) of this section of the active ingredients of the pesticides that will be reregistered.

(2) The second phase shall include the submission to the Administrator under subsection (d) of this section of notices by registrants respecting their intention to seek reregistration, identification by registrants of missing and inadequate data for such pesticides, and commitments by registrants to replace such missing or inadequate data within the applicable time period.

(3) The third phase shall include submission to the Administrator by registrants of the information required under subsection (e) of this section.

(4) The fourth phase shall include an independent, initial review by the Administrator under sub-

section (f) of this section of submissions under phases two and three, identification of outstanding data requirements, and the issuance, as necessary, of requests for additional data.

(5) The fifth phase shall include the review by the Administrator under subsection (g) of this section of data submitted for reregistration and appropriate regulatory action by the Administrator.

(c) Phase one.—

(1) Priority for reregistration.—For purposes of the reregistration of the pesticides described in subsection (a) of this section, the Administrator shall list the active ingredients of pesticides and shall give priority to, among others, active ingredients (other than active ingredients for which registration standards have been issued before the effective date of this section) that—

(A) are in use on or in food or feed and may result in postharvest residues;

(B) may result in residues of potential toxicological concern in potable ground water, edible fish, or shellfish;

(C) have been determined by the Administrator before the effective date of this section to have significant outstanding data requirements; or

(D) are used on crops, including in greenhouses and nurseries, where worker exposure is most likely to occur.

(2) Reregistration lists.—For purposes of reregistration under this section, the Administrator shall by order—

(A) not later than 70 days after the effective date of this section, list pesticide active ingredients for which registration standards have been issued before such effective date;

(B) not later than 4 months after such effective date, list the first 150 pesticide active ingredients, as determined under paragraph (1);

(C) not later than 7 months after such effective date, list the second 150 pesticide active ingredients, as determined under paragraph (1); and

(D) not later than 10 months after such effective date, list the remainder of the pesticide active ingredients, as determined under paragraph (1).

Each list shall be published in the Federal Register.

(3) Judicial review.—The content of a list issued by the Administrator under paragraph (2) shall not be subject to judicial review.

(4) Notice to registrants.—On the publication of a list of pesticide active ingredients under paragraph (2), the Administrator shall send by certified mail to the registrants of the pesticides containing such active ingredients a notice of the time by which the registrants are to notify the Administrator under subsection (d) of this section whether the registrants intend to seek or not to seek reregistration of such pesticides.

(d) Phase two.—

(1) In general.—The registrant of a pesticide that contains an active ingredient listed under subparagraph (B), (C), or (D) of subsection (c)(2) of this section shall submit to the Administrator, within the time period prescribed by paragraph (4), the notice described in paragraph (2) and any information, commitment, or offer described in paragraph (3).

(2) Notice of intent to seek or not to seek reregistration.—

(A) The registrant of a pesticide containing an active ingredient listed under subparagraph (B), (C), or (D) of subsection (c)(2) of this section shall notify the Administrator by certified mail whether the registrant intends to seek or does not intend to seek reregistration of the pesticide.

(B) If a registrant submits a notice under subparagraph (A) of an intention not to seek reregistration of a pesticide, the Administrator shall publish a notice in the Federal Register stating that such a notice has been submitted.

(3) Missing or inadequate data.—Each registrant of a pesticide that contains an active ingredient listed under subparagraph (B), (C), or (D) of subsection (c)(2) of this section and for which the registrant submitted a notice under paragraph (2) of an intention to seek reregistration of such pesticide shall submit to the Administrator—

(A) in accordance with regulations issued by the Administrator under section 136a of this title, an identification of—

(i) all data that are required by regulation to support the registration of the pesticide with respect to such active ingredient;

(ii) data that were submitted by the registrant previously in support of the registration of the pesticide that are inadequate to meet such regulations; and

(iii) data identified under clause (i) that have not been submitted to the Administrator; and

(B) either—

(i) a commitment to replace the data identified under subparagraph (A)(ii) and submit the data identified under subparagraph (A)(iii) within the applicable time period prescribed by paragraph (4)(B); or

(ii) an offer to share in the cost to be incurred by a person who has made a commitment under clause (i) to replace or submit the data and an offer to submit to arbitration as described by section 136a(c)(2)(B) of this title with regard to such cost sharing.

For purposes of a submission by a registrant under subparagraph (A)(ii), data are inadequate if the data are derived from a study with respect to which the registrant is unable to make the certification prescribed by subsection (e)(1)(G) of this section that the registrant possesses or has access to the raw data used in or generated by such study. For purposes of a submission by a registrant under such subparagraph, data shall be considered to be inadequate if the data are derived from a study submitted before January 1, 1970, unless it is demonstrated to the satisfaction of the Administrator that such data should be considered to support the registration of the pesticide that is to be reregistered.

(4) Time periods.—

(A) A submission under paragraph (2) or (3) shall be made—

(i) in the case of a pesticide containing an active ingredient listed under subsection (c)(2)(B) of this section, not later than 3 months after the date of publication of the listing of such active ingredient;

(ii) in the case of a pesticide containing an active ingredient listed under subsection (c)(2)(C) of this section, not later than 3 months after the date of publication of the listing of such active ingredient; and

(iii) in the case of a pesticide containing an active ingredient listed under subsection (c)(2)(D) of this section, not later than 3 months after the date of publication of the listing of such active ingredient.

On application, the Administrator may extend a time period prescribed by this subparagraph if the Administrator determines that factors beyond the control of the registrant prevent the registrant from complying with such period.

(B) A registrant shall submit data in accordance with a commitment entered into under paragraph (3)(B) within a reasonable period of time, as determined by the Administrator, but not more than 48 months after the date the registrant submitted the commitment. The Administrator, on application of a registrant, may extend the period prescribed by the preceding sentence by no more than 2 years if extraordinary circumstances beyond the control of the registrant prevent the registrant from submitting data within such prescribed period.

(5) Cancellation and removal.—

(A) If the registrant of a pesticide does not submit a notice under paragraph (2) or (3) within the time prescribed by paragraph (4)(A), the Administrator shall issue a notice of intent to cancel the registration of such registrant for such pesticide and shall publish the notice in the Federal Register and allow 60 days for the submission of comments on the notice. On expiration of such 60 days, the Administrator, by order and without a hearing, may cancel the registration or take such other action, including extension of applicable time periods, as may be necessary to enable reregistration of such pesticide by another person.

(B)(i) If—

(I) no registrant of a pesticide containing an active ingredient listed under subsection (c)(2) of this section notifies the Administrator under paragraph (2) that the registrant intends to seek reregistration of any pesticide containing that active ingredient;

(II) no such registrant complies with paragraph (3)(A); or

(III) no such registrant makes a commitment under paragraph (3)(B) to replace or submit all data described in clauses (ii) and (iii) of paragraph (3)(A);

the Administrator shall publish in the Federal Register a notice of intent to remove the active ingredient from the list established under subsection (c)(2) of this section and a notice of intent to cancel the registrations of all pesticides containing such active ingredient and shall provide 60 days for comment on such notice.

(ii) After the 60-day period has expired, the Administrator, by order, may cancel any such registration without hearing, except that the Administrator shall not cancel a registration under this subparagraph if—

(I) during the comment period a person acquires the rights of the registrant in that registration;

(II) during the comment period that person furnishes a notice of intent to reregister the pesticide in accordance with paragraph (2); and

(III) not later than 120 days after the publication of the notice under this subparagraph, that person has complied with paragraph (3) and the fee prescribed by subsection (i)(1) of this section has been paid.

(6) Suspensions and penalties.—The Administrator shall issue a notice of intent to suspend the registration of a pesticide in accordance with the procedures prescribed by section 136a(c)(2)(B)(iv) of this title if the Administrator determines that (A) progress is insufficient to ensure the submission of the data required for such pesticide under a commitment made under paragraph (3)(B) within the time period prescribed by paragraph (4)(B) or (B) the registrant has not submitted such data to the Administrator within such time period.

(e) Phase three.—

(1) Information about studies.—Each registrant of a pesticide that contains an active ingredient listed under subparagraph (B), (C), or (D) of subsection (c)(2) of this section who has submitted a notice under subsection (d)(2) of this section of an intent to seek the reregistration of such pesticide shall submit, in accordance with the guidelines issued under paragraph (4), to the Administrator—

(A) a summary of each study concerning the active ingredient previously submitted by the registrant in support of the registration of a pesticide containing such active ingredient and considered by the registrant to be adequate to meet the requirements of section 136a of this title and the regulations issued under such section;

(B) a summary of each study concerning the active ingredient previously submitted by the registrant in support of the registration of a pesticide containing such active ingredient that may not comply with the requirements of section 136a of this title and the regulations issued under such section but which the registrant asserts should be deemed to comply with such requirements and regulations;

(C) a reformat of the data from each study summarized under subparagraph (A) or (B) by the registrant concerning chronic dosing, onncogenicity, reproductive effects, mutagenicity, neurotoxicity, teratogenicity, or residue chemistry of the active ingredient that were submitted to the Administrator before January 1, 1982;

(D) where data described in subparagraph (C) are not required for the active ingredient by regulations issued under section 136a of this title, a reformat of acute and subchronic dosing data submitted by the registrant to the Administrator before January 1, 1982, that the registrant considers to be adequate to meet the requirements of section 136a of this title and the regulations issued under such section;

(E) an identification of data that are required to be submitted to the Administrator under section 136d(a)(2) of this title indicating an adverse effect of the pesticide;

(F) an identification of any other information available that in the view of the registrant supports the registration;

(G) a certification that the registrant or the Administrator possesses or has access to the raw data used in or generated by the studies that the registrant summarized under subparagraph (A) or (B);

(H) either—

(i) a commitment to submit data to fill each outstanding data requirement identified by the registrant; or

(ii) an offer to share in the cost of developing such data to be incurred by a person who has made a commitment under clause (i) to submit such data, and an offer to submit to arbitration as described by section 136a(c)(2)(B) of this title with regard to such cost sharing; and

(I) evidence of compliance with section 136a(c)(1)(D)(ii) of this title and regulations issued thereunder with regard to previously submitted data as if the registrant were now seeking the original registration of the pesticide.

A registrant who submits a certification under subparagraph (G) that is false shall be considered to have violated this subchapter and shall be subject to the penalties prescribed by section 136*l* of this title.

(2) Time periods.—

(A) The information required by paragraph (1) shall be submitted to the Administrator—

(i) in the case of a pesticide containing an active ingredient listed under subsection (c)(2)(B) of this section, not later than 12 months after the date of publication of the listing of such active ingredient;

(ii) in the case of a pesticide containing an active ingredient listed under subsection (c)(2)(C) of this section, not later than 12 months after the date of publication of the listing of such active ingredient; and

(iii) in the case of a pesticide containing an active ingredient listed under subsection (c)(2)(D) of this section, not later than 12 months after the date of publication of the listing of such active ingredient.

(B) A registrant shall submit data in accordance with a commitment entered into under paragraph (1)(H) within a reasonable period of time, as determined by the Administrator, but not more than 48 months after the date the registrant submitted the commitment under such paragraph. The Administrator, on application of a registrant, may extend the period prescribed by the preceding sentence by no more than 2 years if extraordinary circumstances beyond the control of the registrant prevent the registrant from submitting data within such prescribed period.

(3) Cancellation.—

(A) If the registrant of a pesticide fails to submit the information required by paragraph (1) within the time prescribed by paragraph (2), the Administrator, by order and without hearing, shall cancel the registration of such pesticide.

(B)(i) If the registrant of a pesticide submits the information required by paragraph (1) within the time prescribed by paragraph (2) and such information does not conform to the guidelines for submissions established by the Administrator, the Administrator shall determine whether the registrant made a good faith attempt to conform its submission to such guidelines.

(ii) If the Administrator determines that the registrant made a good faith attempt to conform its submission to such guidelines, the Administrator shall provide the registrant a reasonable period of time to make any necessary changes or corrections.

(iii)(I) If the Administrator determines that the registrant did not make a good faith attempt to conform its submission to such guidelines, the Administrator may issue a notice of intent to cancel the registration. Such a notice shall be sent to the registrant by certified mail.

(II) The registration shall be canceled without a hearing or further notice at the end of 30 days after receipt by the registrant of the notice unless during that time a request for a hearing is made by the registrant.

(III) If a hearing is requested, a hearing shall be conducted under section 136d(d) of this title, except that the only matter for resolution at the hearing shall be whether the registrant made a good faith attempt to conform its submission to such guidelines. The hearing shall be held and a determination made within 75 days after receipt of a request for hearing.

(4) Guidelines.—

(A) Not later than 1 year after the effective date of this section, the Administrator, by order, shall issue guidelines to be followed by registrants in—

(i) summarizing studies;

(ii) reformatting studies;

(iii) identifying adverse information; and

(iv) identifying studies that have been submitted previously that may not meet the requirements of section 136a of this title or regulations issued under such section, under paragraph (1).

(B) Guidelines issued under subparagraph (A) shall not be subject to judicial review.

(5) Monitoring.—The Administrator shall monitor the progress of registrants in acquiring and submitting the data required under paragraph (1).

(f) Phase four.—

(1) Independent review and identification of outstanding data requirements.—

(A) The Administrator shall review the submissions of all registrants of pesticides containing a particular active ingredient under subsections (d)(3) and (e)(1) of this section to determine if such submissions identified all the data that are missing or inadequate for such active ingredient. To assist the review of the Administrator under this subparagraph, the Administrator may require a registrant seeking reregistration to submit complete copies of studies summarized under subsection (e)(1) of this section.

(B) The Administrator shall independently identify and publish in the Federal Register the outstanding data requirements for each active ingredient that is listed under subparagraph (B), (C), or (D) of subsection (c)(2) of this section and that is contained in a pesticide to be reregistered under this section. The Administrator, at the same time, shall issue a notice under section 136a(c)(2)(B) of this title for the submission of the additional data that are required to meet such requirements.

(2) Time periods.—

(A) The Administrator shall take the action required by paragraph (1)—

(i) in the case of a pesticide containing an active ingredient listed under subsection (c)(2)(B) of this section, not later than 18 months after the date of the listing of such active ingredient;

(ii) in the case of a pesticide containing an active ingredient listed under subsection (c)(2)(C) of this section, not later than 24 months after the date of the listing of such active ingredient; and

(iii) in the case of a pesticide containing an active ingredient listed under subsection (c)(2)(D) of this section, not later than 33 months after the date of the listing of such active ingredient.

(B) If the Administrator issues a notice to a registrant under paragraph (1)(B) for the submission of additional data, the registrant shall submit such data within a reasonable period of time, as determined by the Administrator, but not to exceed 48 months after the issuance of such notice. The Administrator, on application of a registrant, may extend the period prescribed by the preceding sentence by no more than 2 years if extraordinary circumstances beyond the control of the registrant prevent the registrant from submitting data within such prescribed period.

(3) Suspensions and penalties.—The Administrator shall issue a notice of intent to suspend the registration of a pesticide in accordance with the procedures prescribed by section 136a(c)(2)(B)(iv) of this title if the Administrator determines that (A) tests necessary to fill an outstanding data requirement for such pesticide have not been initiated within 1 year after the issuance of a notice under paragraph (1)(B), or (B) progress is insufficient to ensure submission of the data referred to in clause (A) within the time period prescribed by paragraph (2)(B) or the required data have not been submitted to the Administrator within such time period.

(g) Phase five.—

(1) Data review.—The Administrator shall conduct a thorough examination of all data submitted under this section concerning an active ingredient listed under subsection (c)(2) of this section and of all other available data found by the Administrator to be relevant.

(2) Reregistration and other actions.—

(A) Within 1 year after the submission of all data concerning an active ingredient of a pesticide under subsection (f) of this section, the Administrator shall determine whether pesticides containing such active ingredient are eligible for reregistration. For extraordinary circumstances, the Administrator may extend such period for not more than 1 additional year.

(B) Before reregistering a pesticide, the Administrator shall obtain any needed product-specific data regarding the pesticide by use of section 136a(c)(2)(B) of this title and shall review such data within 90 days after its submission. The Administrator shall require that data under this subparagraph be submitted to the Administrator not later than 8 months after a determination of eligibility under subparagraph (A) has been made for each active ingredient of the pesticide, unless the Administrator determines that a longer period is required for the generation of the data.

(C) After conducting the review required by paragraph (1) for each active ingredient of a pesticide and the review required by subparagraph (B) of this paragraph, the Administrator shall determine whether to reregister a pesticide by determining whether such pesticide meets the requirements of section 136a(c)(5) of this title. If the Administrator determines that a pesticide is eligible to be reregistered, the Administrator shall reregister such pesticide within 6 months after the submission of the data concerning such pesticide under subparagraph (B).

(D) If after conducting a review under paragraph (1) or subparagraph (B) of this paragraph the Administrator determines that a pesticide should not be reregistered, the Administrator shall take appropriate regulatory action.

(h) Compensation of data submitter.—If data that are submitted by a registrant under subsection (d), (e), (f), or (g) of this section are used to support the application of another person under section 136a of this title, the registrant who submitted such data shall be entitled to compensation for the use of such data as prescribed by section 136a(c)(1)(D) of this title. In determining the amount of such compensation, the fees paid by the registrant under this section shall be taken into account.

(i) Fees.—

(1) Initial fee for food or feed use pesticide active ingredients.—The registrants of pesticides that contain an active ingredient that is listed under subparagraph (B), (C), or (D) of subsection (c)(2) of this section and that is an active ingredient of any pesticide registered for a major food or feed use shall collectively pay a fee of $50,000 on submission of information under paragraphs (2) and (3) of subsection (d) of this section for such ingredient.

(2) Final fee for food or feed use pesticide active ingredients.—

(A) The registrants of pesticides that contain an active ingredient that is listed under subparagraph (B), (C), or (D) of subsection (c)(2) of this section and that is an active ingredient of any pesticide registered for a major food or feed use shall collectively pay a fee of $100,000—

(i) on submission of information for such ingredient under subsection (e)(1) of this section if data are reformatted under subsection (e)(1)(C) of this section; or

(ii) on submission of data for such ingredient under subsection (e)(2)(B) of this section if data are not reformatted under subsection (e)(1)(C) of this section.

(B) The registrants of pesticides that contain an active ingredient that is listed under subsection (c)(2)(A) of this section and that is an active ingredient of any pesticide registered for a major food or feed use shall collectively pay a fee of $150,000 at such time as the Administrator shall prescribe.

(3) Fees for other pesticide active ingredients.—

(A) The registrants of pesticides that contain an active ingredient that is listed under subparagraph (B), (C), or (D) of subsection (c)(2) of this section and that is not an active ingredient of any pesticide registered for a major food or feed use shall collectively pay fees in amounts determined by the Administrator. Such fees may not be less than one-half of, nor greater than, the fees required by paragraphs (1) and (2). A registrant shall pay such fees at the times corresponding to the times fees prescribed by paragraphs (1) and (2) are to be paid.

(B) The registrants of pesticides that contain an active ingredient that is listed under subsection (c)(2)(A) of this section and that is not an active ingredient of any pesticide that is registered for a major food or feed use shall collectively pay a fee of not more than $100,000 and not less than $50,000 at such time as the Administrator shall prescribe.

(4) Reduction or waiver of fees for minor use and other pesticides.—

(A) An active ingredient that is contained only in pesticides that are registered solely for agricultural or nonagricultural minor uses, or a pesticide the value or volume of use of which is small, shall be exempt from the fees prescribed by paragraph (3).

(B) An antimicrobial active ingredient, the production level of which does not exceed 1,000,000 pounds per year, shall be exempt from the fees prescribed by paragraph (3). For purposes of this subparagraph, the term "antimicrobial active ingredient" means any active ingredient that is contained only in pesticides that are not registered for any food or feed use and that are—

(i) sanitizers intended to reduce the number of living bacteria or viable virus particles on inanimate surface or in water or air;

(ii) bacteriostats intended to inhibit the growth of bacteria in the presence of moisture;

(iii) disinfectants intended to destroy or irreversibly inactivate bacteria, fungi, or viruses on surfaces or inanimate objects;

(iv) sterilizers intended to destroy viruses and all living bacteria, fungi, and their spores on inanimate surfaces; or

(v) fungicides or fungistats.

(C)(i) Notwithstanding any other provision of this subsection, in the case of a small business registrant of a pesticide, the registrant shall pay a fee for the reregistration of each active ingredient of the pesticide that does not exceed an amount determined in accordance with this subparagraph.

(ii) If during the 3–year period prior to reregistration the average annual gross revenue of the registrant from pesticides containing such active ingredient is—

(I) less than $5,000,000, the registrant shall pay 0.5 percent of such revenue;

(II) $5,000,000 or more but less than $10,000,000, the registrant shall pay 1 percent of such revenue; or

(III) $10,000,000 or more, the registrant shall pay 1.5 percent of such revenue, but not more than $150,000.

(iii) For the purpose of this subparagraph, a small business registrant is a corporation, partnership, or unincorporated business that—

(I) has 150 or fewer employees; and

(II) during the 3–year period prior to reregistration, had an average annual gross revenue from chemicals that did not exceed $40,000,000.

(5) Maintenance fee.—

(A) Subject to other provisions of this paragraph, each registrant of a pesticide shall pay an annual fee by January 15 of each year of—

(i) $650 for the first registration; and

(ii) $1,300 for each additional registration, except that no fee shall be charged for more than 200 registrations held by any registrant.

(B) In the case of a pesticide that is registered for a minor agricultural use, the Administrator may reduce or waive the payment of the fee imposed under this paragraph if the Administrator determines that the fee would significantly reduce the availability of the pesticide for the use.

(C) The amount of each fee prescribed under subparagraph (A) shall be adjusted by the Administrator to a level that will result in the collection under this paragraph of, to the extent practicable, an aggregate amount of $14,000,000 each fiscal year.

(D) The maximum annual fee payable under this paragraph by—

(i) a registrant holding not more than 50 pesticide registrations shall be $55,000; and

(ii) a registrant holding over 50 registrations shall be $95,000.

(E)(i) For a small business, the maximum annual fee payable under this paragraph by—

(I) a registrant holding not more than 50 pesticide registrations shall be $38,500; and

(II) a registrant holding over 50 pesticide registrations shall be $66,500.

(ii) For purposes of clause (i), the term "small business" means a corporation, partnership, or unincorporated business that—

(I) has 150 or fewer employees; and

(II) during the 3–year period prior to the most recent maintenance fee billing cycle, had an average annual gross revenue from chemicals that did not exceed $40,000,000.

(F) If any fee prescribed by this paragraph with respect to the registration of a pesticide is not paid by a registrant by the time prescribed, the Administrator, by order and without hearing, may cancel the registration.

(G) The authority provided under this paragraph shall terminate on September 30, 1997.

(6) Other fees.—During the period beginning on October 25, 1988, and ending on September 30, 1997, the Administrator may not levy any other fees for the registration of a pesticide under this subchapter except as provided in paragraphs (1) through (5).

(7) Apportionment.—

(A) If two or more registrants are required to pay any fee prescribed by paragraph (1), (2), or (3) with respect to a particular active ingredient, the fees for such active ingredient shall be apportioned among such registrants on the basis of the market share in United States sales of the active ingredient for the 3 calendar years preceding the date of payment of such fee, except that—

(i) small business registrants that produce the active ingredient shall pay fees in accordance with paragraph (4)(C); and

(ii) registrants who have no market share but who choose to reregister a pesticide containing such active ingredient shall pay the lesser of—

(I) 15 percent of the reregistration fee; or

(II) a proportionate amount of such fee based on the lowest percentage market share held by any registrant active in the marketplace.

In no event shall registrants who have no market share but who choose to reregister a pesticide containing such active ingredient collectively pay more than 25 percent of the total active ingredient reregistration fee.

(B) The Administrator, by order, may require any registrant to submit such reports as the Administrator determines to be necessary to allow the Administrator to determine and apportion fees under this subsection or to determine the registrant's eligibility for a reduction or waiver of a fee.

(C) If any such report is not submitted by a registrant after receiving notice of such report requirement, or if any fee prescribed by this subsection (other than paragraph (5)) for an active ingredient is not paid by a registrant to the Administrator by the time prescribed under this subsection, the Administrator, by order and without hearing, may cancel each registration held by such registrant of a pesticide containing the active ingredient with respect to which the fee is imposed. The Administrator shall reapportion the fee among the remaining registrants and notify the registrants that the registrants are required to pay to the Administrator any unpaid balance of the fee within 30 days after receipt of such notice.

(j) Exemption of certain registrants.—The requirements of subsections (d), (e), (f), and (i) (other than subsection (i)(5)) of this section regarding data concerning an active ingredient and fees for review of such data shall not apply to any person who is the registrant of a pesticide to the extent that, under section 136a(c)(2)(D) of this title the person would not be required to submit or cite such data to obtain an initial registration of such pesticide.

(k) Reregistration and expedited processing fund.—

(1) Establishment.—There shall be established in the Treasury of the United States a reregistration and expedited processing fund.

(2) Source and use.—All fees collected by the Administrator under subsection (i) of this section shall be deposited into the fund and shall be available to the Administrator, without fiscal year limitation, to carry out reregistration and expedited processing of similar applications.

(3) Expedited processing of similar applications.—

(A) The Administrator shall use for each of the fiscal years 1992, 1993, and 1994, 1/7th of the maintenance fees collected, up to $2 million each year to obtain sufficient personnel and resources to assure the expedited processing and review of any application that—

(i) proposes the initial or amended registration of an end-use pesticide that, if registered as proposed, would be identical or substantially similar in composition and labeling to a currently-registered pesticide identified in the application, or that would differ in composition and labeling from any such currently-registered pesticide only in ways that would not significantly increase the risk of unreasonable adverse effects on the environment; or

(ii) proposes an amendment to the registration of a registered pesticide that does not require scientific review of data.

(B) Any amounts made available under subparagraph (A) shall be used to obtain sufficient personnel and resources to carry out the activities described in such subparagraph that are in addition to the personnel and resources available to carry out such activities on October 25, 1988.

(4) Unused funds.—Money in the fund not currently needed to carry out this section shall be—

(A) maintained on hand or on deposit;

(B) invested in obligations of the United States or guaranteed thereby; or

(C) invested in obligations, participations, or other instruments that are lawful investments for fiduciary, trust, or public funds.

(5) Accounting.—The Administrator shall—

(A) provide an annual accounting of the fees collected and disbursed from the fund; and

(B) take all steps necessary to ensure that expenditures from such fund are used only to carry out this section.

***(l)* Judicial review.**—Any failure of the Administrator to take any action required by this section shall be subject to judicial review under the procedures prescribed by section 136n(b) of this title.

(June 25, 1947, c. 125, § 4, formerly § 3A, as added Oct. 25, 1988, Pub.L. 100-532, Title I, § 102(a), 102 Stat. 2655, and renumbered Oct. 25, 1988, Pub.L. 100-532, Title VIII, § 801(q)(2)(A), 102 Stat. 2683; amended Nov. 28, 1990, Pub.L. 101-624, Title XIV, § 1493, 104 Stat. 3628; Dec. 13, 1991 Pub.L. 102-237, Title X, § 1006(a)(4), (e), (f), 105 Stat. 1895-1897.)

References in Text

For effective date of this section, referred to in subsec. (c), see section 901 of Pub.L. 100-532, set out as a note under section 136 of this title.

Effective Date of 1991 Amendment

Amendments by Pub.L. 102-237 effective Dec. 13, 1991, see section 1101(a) of Pub.L. 102-237, set out as a note under section 1421 of this title.

Effective Date

Section effective 60 days after October 25, 1988, see section 901 of Pub.L. 100-532, set out as a note under section 136 of this title.

Prior Provisions

A prior section 4 of the Federal Insecticide, Fungicide, and Rodenticide Act was transferred by Pub.L. 100-532, Title VIII, § 801(q)(1)(A), (B), Oct. 25, 1988, 102 Stat. 2683, as follows:

1. Subsections (a), (b), and (c) were transferred to section 136i of this title and are set out as subsections (a), (b), and (c) thereof.

2. The section heading was deleted.

Severability of Provisions

If any provision of Pub.L. 101-624 or the application thereof to any person or circumstance is held invalid, such invalidity not to affect other provisions or applications of Pub.L. 101-624 which can be given effect without regard to the invalid provision or application, see section 2519 of Pub.L. 101-624, set out as a note under section 1421 of this title.

§ 136b. Transferred [FIFRA former § 4]

Codification

Section, June 25, 1947, c. 125, § 4, as added Oct. 21, 1972, Pub.L. 92-516, § 2, 86 Stat. 983, and amended Nov. 28, 1975, Pub.L. 94-140, §§ 5, 11, 89 Stat. 753, 754; Sept. 30, 1978, Pub.L. 95-396, § 9, 92 Stat. 827; Pub.L. 100-532, Title VIII, § 801(c), (q)(1)(B), Oct. 25, 1988, 102 Stat. 2681, 2683, which related to use of restricted use pesticides and certification of applicators, was transferred to section 136i(a) to (c) of this title by Pub.L. 100-532, Title VIII, § 801(q)(1)(A), Oct. 25, 1988, 102 Stat. 2683.

§ 136c. Experimental use permits [FIFRA § 5]

(a) Issuance.—Any person may apply to the Administrator for an experimental use permit for a pesticide. The Administrator shall review the application. After completion of the review, but not later than one hundred and twenty days after receipt of the application and all required supporting data, the Administrator shall either issue the permit or notify the applicant of the Administrator's determination not to issue the permit and the reasons therefor. The applicant may correct the application or request a waiver of the conditions for such permit within thirty days of receipt by the applicant of such notification. The Administrator may issue an experimental use permit only if the Administrator determines that the applicant needs such permit in order to accumulate information necessary to register a pesticide under section 136a of this title. An application for an experimental use permit may be filed at any time.

(b) Temporary tolerance level.—If the Administrator determines that the use of a pesticide may reasonably be expected to result in any residue on or in food or feed, the Administrator may establish a temporary tolerance level for the residue of the pesticide before issuing the experimental use permit.

(c) Use under permit.—Use of a pesticide under an experimental use permit shall be under the supervision of the Administrator, and shall be subject to such terms and conditions and be for such period of time as the Administrator may prescribe in the permit.

(d) Studies.—When any experimental use permit is issued for a pesticide containing any chemical or combination of chemicals which has not been included in any previously registered pesticide, the Administrator may specify that studies be conducted to detect whether the use of the pesticide under the permit may cause unreasonable adverse effects on the environment. All results of such studies shall be reported to the Administrator before such pesticide may be registered under section 136a of this title.

(e) Revocation.—The Administrator may revoke any experimental use permit, at any time, if the Administrator finds that its terms or conditions are being violated, or that its terms and conditions are inadequate to avoid unreasonable adverse effects on the environment.

(f) State issuance of permits.—Notwithstanding the foregoing provisions of this section, the Administrator shall, under such terms and conditions as the Administrator may by regulations prescribe, authorize any State to issue an experimental use permit for a pesticide. All provisions of section 136i of this title relating to State plans shall apply with equal force to a State plan for the issuance of experimental use permits under this section.

(g) Exemption for agricultural research agencies.—Notwithstanding the foregoing provisions of this section, the Administrator may issue an experimental use permit for a pesticide to any public or private agricultural research agency or educational institution which applies for such permit. Each permit shall not exceed more than a one-year period or such other specific time as the Administrator may prescribe. Such permit shall be issued under such terms and conditions restricting the use of the pesticide as the Administrator may require. Such pesticide may be used only by such research agency or educational institution for purposes of experimentation.

(June 25, 1947, c. 125, § 5, as added Oct. 21, 1972, Pub.L. 92–516, § 2, 86 Stat. 983, and amended Nov. 28, 1975, Pub.L. 94–140, § 10, 89 Stat. 754; Sept. 30, 1978, Pub.L. 95–396, § 10, 92 Stat. 828; Oct. 25, 1988, Pub.L. 100–532, Title VIII, § 801(d), (q)(1)(D), 102 Stat. 2681, 2683; Dec. 13, 1991, Pub.L. 102–237, Title X, § 1006(b)(1), 105 Stat. 1895.)

Effective Date of 1991 Amendment

Amendment by section 1006(b)(1) of Pub.L. 102–237 effective Dec. 13, 1991, see section 1101(a) of Pub.L. 102–237, set out as a note under section 1421 of this title.

CODE OF FEDERAL REGULATIONS

Policies and procedures, see 40 CFR 172.1 et seq.
Debarment and suspension under EPA assistance programs, see 40 CFR 32.100 et seq.

LIBRARY REFERENCES

Agriculture ⚷9.
C.J.S. Agriculture § 83 et seq.

WESTLAW ELECTRONIC RESEARCH

Agricultural cases: 23k (add key number)

§ 136d. Administrative review; suspension [FIFRA § 6]

(a) Cancellation after five years.—

(1) Procedure.—The Administrator shall cancel the registration of any pesticide at the end of the five-year period which begins on the date of its registration (or at the end of any five year period thereafter) unless the registrant, or other interested person with the concurrence of the registrant, before the end of such period, requests in accordance with regulations prescribed by the Administrator that the registration be continued in effect. The Administrator may permit the continued sale and use of existing stocks of a pesticide whose registration is canceled under this subsection or subsection (b) of this section to such extent, under such conditions, and for such uses as the Administrator may specify if the Administrator determines that such sale or use is not inconsistent with the purposes of this subchapter and will not have unreasonable adverse effects on the environment. The Administrator shall publish in the Federal Register, at least 30 days prior to the expiration of such five-year period, notice that the registration will be canceled if the registrant or other interested person with the concurrence of the registrant does not request that the registration be continued in effect.

(2) Information.—If at any time after the registration of a pesticide the registrant has additional factual information regarding unreasonable adverse effects on the environment of the pesticide, the registrant shall submit such information to the Administrator.

(b) Cancellation and change in classification.—If it appears to the Administrator that a pesticide or its labeling or other material required to be submitted does not comply with the provisions of this subchapter or, when used in accordance with widespread and commonly recognized practice, generally causes unreasonable adverse effects on the environment, the Administrator may issue a notice of the Administrator's intent either—

(1) to cancel its registration or to change its classification together with the reasons (including the factual basis) for the Administrator's action, or

(2) to hold a hearing to determine whether or not its registration should be canceled or its classification changed.

Such notice shall be sent to the registrant and made public. In determining whether to issue any such notice, the Administrator shall include among those factors to be taken into account the impact of the action proposed in such notice on production and prices of agricultural commodities, retail food prices, and otherwise on the agricultural economy. At least 60 days prior to sending such notice to the registrant or making public such notice, whichever occurs first, the Administrator shall provide the Secretary of Agriculture with a copy of such notice and an analysis of such impact on the agricultural economy. If the Secretary comments in writing to the Administrator regarding the notice and analysis within 30 days after receiving them, the Administrator shall publish in the Federal Register (with the notice) the comments of the Secretary and the response of the Administrator with regard to the Secretary's comments. If the Secretary does not comment in writing to the Administrator regarding the notice and analysis within 30 days after receiving them, the Administrator may notify the registrant and make public the notice at any time after such 30-day period notwithstanding the foregoing 60-day time requirement. The time requirements imposed by the preceding 3 sentences may be waived or modified to the extent agreed upon by the Administrator and the Secretary. Notwithstanding any other provision of this subsection and section 136w(d) of this title, in the event that the Administrator determines that suspension of a pesticide registration is necessary to prevent an imminent hazard to human health, then upon such a finding the Administrator may waive the requirement of notice to and consultation with the Secretary of Agriculture pursuant to this subsection and of submission to the Scientific Advisory Panel pursuant to section 136w(d) of this title and proceed in accordance with subsection (c) of this section. The proposed action shall become final and effective at the end of 30 days from receipt by the registrant, or publication, of a notice issued under paragraph (1), whichever occurs later, unless within that time either (i) the registrant makes the necessary corrections, if possible, or (ii) a request for a hearing is made by a person adversely affected by the notice. In the event a hearing is held pursuant to such a request or to the Administrator's determination under paragraph (2), a decision pertaining to registration or classification issued after completion of such hearing shall be final. In taking any final action under this subsection, the Administrator shall consider restricting a pesticide's use or uses as an alternative to cancellation and shall fully explain the reasons for these restrictions, and shall include among those factors to be taken into account the impact of such final action on production and prices of agricultural commodities, retail food prices, and otherwise on the agricultural economy, and the Administrator shall publish in the Federal Register an analysis of such impact.

(c) Suspension.—

(1) Order.—If the Administrator determines that action is necessary to prevent an imminent hazard during the time required for cancellation or change in classification proceedings, the Administrator may, by order, suspend the registration of the pesticide immediately. No order of suspension may be issued unless the Administrator has issued or at the same time issues notice of the Administrator's intention to cancel the registration or change the classification of the pesticide. Except as provided in paragraph (3), the Administrator shall notify the registrant prior to issuing any suspension order. Such notice shall include findings pertaining to the question of "imminent hazard". The registrant shall then have an opportunity, in accordance with the provisions of paragraph (2), for an expedited hearing before the Administrator on the question of whether an imminent hazard exists.

(2) Expedite hearing.—If no request for a hearing is submitted to the Administrator within five days of the registrant's receipt of the notification provided for by paragraph (1), the suspension order may be issued and shall take effect and shall not be reviewable by a court. If a hearing is requested, it shall commence within five days of the receipt of the request for such hearing unless the registrant and the Administrator agree that it shall commence at a later time. The hearing shall be held in accordance with the provisions of subchapter II of chapter 5 of Title 5, except that the presiding officer need not be a certified administrative law judge. The presiding officer shall have ten days from the conclusion of the presentation of evidence to submit recommended findings and conclusions to the Administrator, who shall then have seven days to render a final order on the issue of suspension.

(3) Emergency order.—Whenever the Administrator determines that an emergency exists that does not permit the Administrator to hold a hearing before suspending, the Administrator may issue a suspension order in advance of notification to the registrant. In that case, paragraph (2) shall apply except that (A) the order of suspension shall be in effect pending the expeditious completion of the remedies provided by that paragraph and the issuance of a final order on suspension, and (B) no party other than the registrant and the Administrator shall participate except that any person adversely affected may file briefs within the time allotted by the Administrator's rules. Any person so filing briefs shall be considered a party to such proceeding for the purposes of section 136n(b) of this title.

(4) Judicial review.—A final order on the question of suspension following a hearing shall be reviewable in accordance with section 136n of this title, notwithstanding the fact that any related cancellation proceedings have not been completed. Any order of suspension entered prior to a hearing before the Administrator shall be subject to immediate review in an action by the registrant or other interested person with the concurrence of the registrant in an appropriate district court, solely to determine whether the order of suspension was arbitrary, capricious or an abuse of discretion, or whether the order was issued in accordance with the procedures established by law. The effect of any order of the court will be only to stay the effectiveness of the suspension order, pending the Administrator's final decision with respect to cancellation or change in classification. This action may be maintained simultaneously with any administrative review proceeding under this section. The commencement of proceedings under this paragraph shall not operate as a stay of order, unless ordered by the court.

(d) Public hearings and scientific review.—In the event a hearing is requested pursuant to subsection (b) of this section or determined upon by the Administrator pursuant to subsection (b) of this section, such hearing shall be held after due notice for the purpose of receiving evidence relevant and material to the issues raised by the objections filed by the applicant or other interested parties, or to the issues stated by the Administrator, if the hearing is called by the Administrator rather than by the filing of objections. Upon a showing of relevance and reasonable scope of evidence sought by any party to a public hearing, the Hearing Examiner shall issue a subpena to compel testimony or production of documents from any person. The Hearing Examiner shall be guided by the principles of the Federal Rules of Civil Procedure in making any order for the protection of the witness or the content of documents produced and shall order the payment of reasonable fees and expenses as a condition to requiring testimony of the witness. On contest, the subpena may be enforced by an appropriate United States district court in accordance with the principles stated herein. Upon the request of any party to a public hearing and when in the Hearing Examiner's judgment it is necessary or desirable, the Hearing Examiner shall at any time before the hearing record is closed refer to a Committee of the National Academy of Sciences the relevant questions of scientific fact involved in the public hearing. No member of any committee of the National Academy of Sciences established to carry out the functions of this section shall have a financial or other conflict of interest with respect to any matter considered by such committee. The Committee of the National Academy of Sciences shall report in writing to the Hearing Examiner within 60 days after such referral on these questions of scientific fact. The report shall be made public and shall be considered as part of the hearing record. The Administrator shall enter into appropriate arrangements with the National Academy of Sciences to assure an objective and competent scientific review of the questions presented to Committees of the Academy and to provide such other scientific advisory services as may be required by the Administrator for carrying out the purposes of this subchapter. As soon as practicable after completion of the hearing (including the report of the Academy) but not later than 90 days thereafter, the Administrator shall evaluate the data and reports before the Administrator and issue an order either revoking the Administrator's notice of intention issued pursuant to this section, or shall issue an order either canceling the registration, changing the classification, denying the registration, or requiring modification of the labeling or packaging of the article. Such order shall be based only on substantial evidence of record of such hearing and shall set forth detailed findings of fact upon which the order is based.

(e) Conditional registration.—

(1) The Administrator shall issue a notice of intent to cancel a registration issued under section 136a(c)(7) of this title if (A) the Administrator, at any time during the period provided for satisfaction of any condition imposed, determines that the registrant has failed to initiate and pursue appropriate action toward fulfilling any condition imposed, or (B) at the end of the period provided for satisfaction of any condition imposed, that condition has not been met. The Administrator may permit the continued sale and use of existing stocks of a pesticide whose conditional registration has been canceled under this subsection to such extent, under such conditions, and for such uses as the Administrator may specify if the Administrator determines that such sale or use is not inconsistent with the purposes of this subchapter and will not have unreasonable adverse effects on the environment.

(2) A cancellation proposed under this subsection shall become final and effective at the end of thirty days from receipt by the registrant of the notice of intent to cancel unless during that time a request for hearing is made by a person adversely affected by the notice. If a hearing is requested, a hearing shall be conducted under subsection (d) of this section. The only matters for resolution at that hearing shall be whether the registrant has initiated and pursued appropriate action to comply with the condition or conditions within the time provided or whether the condition or conditions have been satisfied within the time provided, and whether the Administrator's determination with respect to the disposition of existing stocks is consistent with this subchapter. A decision after completion of such hearing shall be final. Notwithstanding any other provision of this section, a hearing shall be held and a determination made within seventy-five days after receipt of a request for such hearing.

(f) General provisions.—

(1) Voluntary cancellation.—

(A) A registrant may, at any time, request that a pesticide registration of the registrant be canceled or amended to terminate one or more pesticide uses.

(B) Before acting on a request under subparagraph (A), the Administrator shall publish in the Federal Register a notice of the receipt of the request and provide for a 30–day period in which the public may comment.

(C) In the case of a pesticide that is registered for a minor agricultural use, if the Administrator determines that the cancellation or termination of uses would adversely affect the availability of the pesticide for use, the Administrator—

(i) shall publish in the Federal Register a notice of the receipt of the request and make reasonable efforts to inform persons who so use the pesticide of the request; and

(ii) may not approve or reject the request until the termination of the 90–day period beginning on the date of publication of the notice in the Federal Register, except that the Administrator may waive the 90–day period upon the request of the registrant or if the Administrator determines that the continued use of the pesticide would pose an unreasonable adverse effect on the environment.

(D) Subject to paragraph (3)(B), after complying with this paragraph, the Administrator may approve or deny the request.

(2) Publication of notice.—A notice of denial of registration, intent to cancel, suspension, or intent to suspend issued under this subchapter or a notice issued under subsection (c)(4) or (d)(5)(A) of section 136a–1 of this title shall be published in the Federal Register and shall be sent by certified mail, return receipt requested, to the registrant's or applicant's address of record on file with the Administrator. If the mailed notice is returned to the Administrator as undeliverable at that address, if delivery is refused, or if the Administrator otherwise is unable to accomplish delivery of the notice to the registrant or applicant after making reasonable efforts to do so, the notice shall be deemed to have been received by the registrant or applicant on the date the notice was published in the Federal Register.

(3) Transfer of registration of pesticides registered for minor agricultural uses.—In the case of a pesticide that is registered for a minor agricultural use:

(A) During the 90–day period referred to in paragraph (1)(C)(ii), the registrant of the pesticide may notify the Administrator of an agreement between the registrant and a person or persons (including persons who so use the pesticide) to transfer the registration of the pesticide, in lieu of canceling or amending the registration to terminate the use.

(B) An application for transfer of registration, in conformance with any regulations the Administrator may adopt with respect to the transfer of the pesticide registrations, must be submitted to the Administrator within 30 days of the date of notification provided pursuant to subparagraph (A). If such an application is submitted, the Administrator shall approve the transfer and shall not approve the request for voluntary cancellation or amendment to terminate use unless the Administrator determines that the continued use of the pesticide would cause an unreasonable adverse effect on the environment.

(C) If the Administrator approves the transfer and the registrant transfers the registration of the pesticide, the Administrator shall not cancel or amend the registration to delete the use or rescind the transfer of the registration, during the 180–day period beginning on the date of the approval of the transfer unless the Administrator determines that the continued use of the pesticide would cause an unreasonable adverse effect on the environment.

(D) The new registrant of the pesticide shall assume the outstanding data and other requirements for the pesticide that are pending at the time of the transfer.

(g) Notice for stored pesticides with canceled or suspended registrations.—

(1) **In general.**—Any producer or exporter of pesticides, registrant of a pesticide, applicant for registration of a pesticide, applicant for or holder of an experimental use permit, commercial applicator, or any person who distributes or sells any pesticide, who possesses any pesticide which has had its registration canceled or suspended under this section shall notify the Administrator and appropriate State and local officials of—

(A) such possession,

(B) the quantity of such pesticide such person possesses, and

(C) the place at which such pesticide is stored.

(2) **Copies.**—The Administrator shall transmit a copy of each notice submitted under this subsection to the regional office of the Environmental Protection Agency which has jurisdiction over the place of pesticide storage identified in the notice.

(h) **Judicial review.**—Final orders of the Administrator under this section shall be subject to judicial review pursuant to section 136n of this title.

(June 25, 1947, c. 125, § 6, as added Oct. 21, 1972, Pub.L. 92–516, § 2, 86 Stat. 984, and amended Nov. 28, 1975, Pub.L. 94–140, § 1, 89 Stat. 751; Mar. 27, 1978, Pub.L. 95–251, § 2(a)(2), 92 Stat. 183; Sept. 30, 1978, Pub.L. 95–396, §§ 11, 12, 92 Stat. 828; Nov. 8, 1984, Pub.L. 98–620, Title IV, § 402(4)(A), 98 Stat. 3357; Oct. 25, 1988, Pub.L. 100–532, Title II, § 201, Title IV, § 404, Title VIII, § 801(e), (q)(2)(B), 102 Stat. 2668, 2674, 2681, 2683; Nov. 28, 1990, Pub.L. 101–624, Title XIV, § 1494, 104 Stat. 3628; Dec. 13, 1991, Pub.L. 102–237, Title X, § 1006(a)(5), (b)(1), (2), (3)(C)–(E), 105 Stat. 1895, 1896.)

Effective Date of 1991 Amendment

Amendments by Pub.L. 102–237 effective Dec. 13, 1991, see section 1101(a) of Pub.L. 102–237, set out as a note under section 1421 of this title.

Severability of Provisions

If any provision of Pub.L. 101–624 or the application thereof to any person or circumstance is held invalid, such invalidity not to affect other provisions or applications of Pub.L. 101–624 which can be given effect without regard to the invalid provision or application, see section 2519 of Pub.L. 101–624, set out as a note under section 1421 of this title.

CODE OF FEDERAL REGULATIONS

Debarment and suspension under EPA assistance programs, see 40 CFR 32.100 et seq.
Registration, reregistration, and classification, see 40 CFR 162.1 et seq.
Rules of practice, see 40 CFR 164.1 et seq.

LIBRARY REFERENCES

Agriculture ⚷9.
Health and Environment ⚷25.15(1).
C.J.S. Agriculture § 83 et seq.
C.J.S. Health and Environment § 82 et seq.

WESTLAW ELECTRONIC RESEARCH

Agricultural cases: 23k (add key number)

§ 136e. Registration of establishments [FIFRA § 7]

(a) **Requirement.**—No person shall produce any pesticide subject to this subchapter or active ingredient used in producing a pesticide subject to this subchapter in any State unless the establishment in which it is produced is registered with the Administrator. The application for registration of any establishment shall include the name and address of the establishment and of the producer who operates such establishment.

(b) **Registration.**—Whenever the Administrator receives an application under subsection (a) of this section, the Administrator shall register the establishment and assign it an establishment number.

(c) **Information required.**—

(1) Any producer operating an establishment registered under this section shall inform the Administrator within 30 days after it is registered of the types and amounts of pesticides and, if applicable, active ingredients used in producing pesticides—

(A) which the producer is currently producing;

(B) which the producer has produced during the past year; and

(C) which the producer has sold or distributed during the past year.

The information required by this paragraph shall be kept current and submitted to the Administrator annually as required under such regulations as the Administrator may prescribe.

(2) Any such producer shall, upon the request of the Administrator for the purpose of issuing a stop sale order pursuant to section 136k of this title, inform the Administrator of the name and address of any recipient of any pesticide produced in any registered establishment which the producer operates.

(d) **Confidential records and information.**—Any information submitted to the Administrator pursuant to subsection (c) of this section other than the names of the pesticides or active ingredients used in producing pesticides produced, sold, or distributed at an establishment shall be considered confidential and shall be subject to the provisions of section 136h of this title.

(June 25, 1947, c. 125, § 7, as added Oct. 21, 1972, Pub.L. 92–516, § 2, 86 Stat. 987, and amended Sept. 30, 1978, Pub.L. 95–396, § 13, 92 Stat. 829; Dec. 13, 1991, Pub.L. 102–237, Title X, § 1006(b)(1), (3)(F), (G), 105 Stat. 1895, 1896.)

Effective Date of 1991 Amendment

Amendments by Pub.L. 102–237 effective Dec. 13, 1991, see section 1101(a) of Pub.L. 102–237, set out as a note under section 1421 of this title.

CODE OF FEDERAL REGULATIONS

Debarment and suspension under EPA assistance programs, see 40 CFR 32.100 et seq.
Procedures and reporting, requirements, see 40 CFR 167.1 et seq.

LIBRARY REFERENCES

Agriculture ⇨9.
C.J.S. Agriculture § 83 et seq.

WESTLAW ELECTRONIC RESEARCH

Agricultural cases: 23k (add key number)

§ 136f. Books and records [FIFRA § 8]

(a) Requirements.—The Administrator may prescribe regulations requiring producers, registrants, and applicants for registration to maintain such records with respect to their operations and the pesticides and devices produced as the Administrator determines are necessary for the effective enforcement of this subchapter and to make the records available for inspection and copying in the same manner as provided in subsection (b) of this section. No records required under this subsection shall extend to financial data, sales data other than shipment data, pricing data, personnel data, and research data (other than data relating to registered pesticides or to a pesticide for which an application for registration has been filed).

(b) Inspection.—For the purposes of enforcing the provisions of this subchapter, any producer, distributor, carrier, dealer, or any other person who sells or offers for sale, delivers or offers for delivery any pesticide or device subject to this subchapter, shall, upon request of any officer or employee of the Environmental Protection Agency or of any State or political subdivision, duly designated by the Administrator, furnish or permit such person at all reasonable times to have access to, and to copy: (1) all records showing the delivery, movement, or holding of such pesticide or device, including the quantity, the date of shipment and receipt, and the name of the consignor and consignee; or (2) in the event of the inability of any person to produce records containing such information, all other records and information relating to such delivery, movement, or holding of the pesticide or device. Any inspection with respect to any records and information referred to in this subsection shall not extend to financial data, sales data other than shipment data, pricing data, personnel data; and research data (other than data relating to registered pesticides or to a pesticide for which an application for registration has been filed). Before undertaking an inspection under this subsection, the officer or employee must present to the owner, operator, or agent in charge of the establishment or other place where pesticides or devices are held for distribution or sale, appropriate credentials and a written statement as to the reason for the inspection, including a statement as to whether a violation of the law is suspected. If no violation is suspected, an alternate and sufficient reason shall be given in writing. Each such inspection shall be commenced and completed with reasonable promptness.

(June 25, 1947, c. 125, § 8, as added Oct. 21, 1972, Pub.L. 92–516, § 2, 86 Stat. 987, and amended Sept. 30, 1978, Pub.L. 95–396, § 14, 92 Stat. 829; Oct. 25, 1988, Pub.L. 100–532, Title III, § 301, 102 Stat. 2668; Dec. 13, 1991, Pub.L. 102–237, Title X, § 1006(b)(1), 105 Stat. 1895.)

Effective Date of 1991 Amendment

Amendment by section 1006(b)(1) of Pub.L. 102–237 effective Dec. 13, 1991, see section 1101(a) of Pub.L. 102–237, set out as a note under section 1421 of this title.

CODE OF FEDERAL REGULATIONS

Debarment and suspension under EPA assistance programs, see 40 CFR 32.100 et seq.
Maintenance, etc., requirements, see 40 CFR 169.1 et seq.

LIBRARY REFERENCES

Agriculture ⇨9.
C.J.S. Agriculture § 83 et seq.

WESTLAW ELECTRONIC RESEARCH

Agricultural cases: 23k (add key number)

§ 136g. Inspection of establishments, etc. [FIFRA § 9]

(a) In general. (1) For purposes of enforcing the provisions of this subchapter, officers or employees of the Environmental Protection Agency or of any State duly designated by the Administrator are authorized to enter at reasonable times (A) any establishment or other place where pesticides or devices are held for distribution or sale for the purpose of inspecting and obtaining samples of any pesticides or devices, packaged, labeled, and released for shipment, and samples of any containers or labeling for such pesticides or devices, or (B) any place where there is being held any pesticide the registration of which has been suspended or canceled for the purpose of determining compliance with section 136q of this title.

(2) Before undertaking such inspection, the officers or employees must present to the owner, operator, or agent in charge of the establishment or other place where pesticides or devices are held for distribution or sale, appropriate credentials and a written statement as to the reason for the inspection, including a statement as to whether a violation of the law is suspected. If no violation is suspected, an alternate and sufficient reason shall be given in writing. Each such inspection shall be commenced and completed with reasonable promptness. If the officer or employee obtains any samples, prior to leaving the premises, the officer or employee shall give to the owner, operator, or agent in

charge a receipt describing the samples obtained and, if requested, a portion of each such sample equal in volume or weight to the portion retained. If an analysis is made of such samples, a copy of the results of such analysis shall be furnished promptly to the owner, operator, or agent in charge.

(b) Warrants.—For purposes of enforcing the provisions of this subchapter and upon a showing to an officer or court of competent jurisdiction that there is reason to believe that the provisions of this subchapter have been violated, officers or employees duly designated by the Administrator are empowered to obtain and to execute warrants authorizing—

(1) entry, inspection, and copying of records for purposes of this section or section 136f of this title;

(2) inspection and reproduction of all records showing the quantity, date of shipment, and the name of consignor and consignee of any pesticide or device found in the establishment which is adulterated, misbranded, not registered (in the case of a pesticide) or otherwise in violation of this subchapter and in the event of the inability of any person to produce records containing such information, all other records and information relating to such delivery, movement, or holding of the pesticide or device; and

(3) the seizure of any pesticide or device which is in violation of this subchapter.

(c) Enforcement.—

(1) Certification of facts to Attorney General.—The examination of pesticides or devices shall be made in the Environmental Protection Agency or elsewhere as the Administrator may designate for the purpose of determining from such examinations whether they comply with the requirements of this subchapter. If it shall appear from any such examination that they fail to comply with the requirements of this subchapter, the Administrator shall cause notice to be given to the person against whom criminal or civil proceedings are contemplated. Any person so notified shall be given an opportunity to present the person's views, either orally or in writing, with regard to such contemplated proceedings, and if in the opinion of the Administrator it appears that the provisions of this subchapter have been violated by such person, then the Administrator shall certify the facts to the Attorney General, with a copy of the results of the analysis or the examination of such pesticide for the institution of a criminal proceeding pursuant to section 136*l*(b) of this title or a civil proceeding under section 136*l*(a) of this title, when the Administrator determines that such action will be sufficient to effectuate the purposes of this subchapter.

(2) Notice not required.—The notice of contemplated proceedings and opportunity to present views set forth in this subsection are not prerequisites to the institution of any proceeding by the Attorney General.

(3) Warning notices.—Nothing in this subchapter shall be construed as requiring the Administrator to institute proceedings for prosecution of minor violations of this subchapter whenever the Administrator believes that the public interest will be adequately served by a suitable written notice of warning.

(June 25, 1947, c. 125, § 9, as added Oct. 21, 1972, Pub.L. 92–516, § 2, 86 Stat. 1988, and amended Oct. 25, 1988, Pub.L. 100–532, Title III, § 302, 102 Stat. 2669; Dec. 13, 1991, Pub.L. 102–237, Title X, § 1006(b)(1), (3)(H), (I), 105 Stat. 1895, 1896.)

Effective Date of 1991 Amendment

Amendments by Pub.L. 102–237 effective Dec. 13, 1991, see section 1101(a) of Pub.L. 102–237, set out as a note under section 1421 of this title.

CODE OF FEDERAL REGULATIONS

Debarment and suspension under EPA assistance programs, see 40 CFR 32.100 et seq.

LIBRARY REFERENCES

Agriculture ⚷9.
C.J.S. Agriculture § 83 et seq.

WESTLAW ELECTRONIC RESEARCH

Agricultural cases: 23k (add key number)

§ 136h. Protection of trade secrets and other information [FIFRA § 10]

(a) In general.—In submitting data required by this subchapter, the applicant may (1) clearly mark any portions thereof which in the applicant's opinion are trade secrets or commercial or financial information and (2) submit such market material separately from other material required to be submitted under this subchapter.

(b) Disclosure.—Notwithstanding any other provision of this subchapter and subject to the limitations in subsections (d) and (e) of this section, the Administrator shall not make public information which in the Administrator's judgment contains or relates to trade secrets or commercial or financial information obtained from a person and privileged or confidential, except that, when necessary to carry out the provisions of this subchapter, information relating to formulas of products acquired by authorization of this subchapter may be revealed to any Federal agency consulted and may be revealed at a public hearing or in findings of fact issued by the Administrator.

(c) Disputes.—If the Administrator proposes to release for inspection information which the applicant or registrant believes to be protected from disclosure under subsection (b) of this section, the Administrator shall notify the applicant or registrant, in writing, by certified mail. The Administrator shall not thereafter make available for inspection such data until thirty days after receipt of the notice by the applicant or registrant. During this period, the applicant or registrant may institute an action in an appropriate district court for a declaratory judgment as to whether such information is subject to protection under subsection (b) of this section.

(d) Limitations.—

(1) All information concerning the objectives, methodology, results, or significance of any test or experiment performed on or with a registered or previously registered pesticide or its separate ingredients, impurities, or degradation products, and any information concerning the effects of such pesticide on any organism or the behavior of such pesticide in the environment, including, but not limited to, data on safety to fish and wildlife, humans and other mammals, plants, animals, and soil, and studies on persistence, translocation and fate in the environment, and metabolism, shall be available for disclosure to the public. The use of such data for any registration purpose shall be governed by section 136a of this title. This paragraph does not authorize the disclosure of any information that—

(A) discloses manufacturing or quality control processes,

(B) discloses the details of any methods for testing, detecting, or measuring the quantity of any deliberately added inert ingredient of a pesticide, or

(C) discloses the identity or percentage quantity of any deliberately added inert ingredient of a pesticide,

unless the Administrator has first determined that disclosure is necessary to protect against an unreasonable risk of injury to health or the environment.

(2) Information concerning production, distribution, sale, or inventories of a pesticide that is otherwise entitled to confidential treatment under subsection (b) of this section may be publicly disclosed in connection with a public proceeding to determine whether a pesticide, or any ingredient of a pesticide, causes unreasonable adverse effects on health or the environment, if the Administrator determines that such disclosure is necessary in the public interest.

(3) If the Administrator proposes to disclose information described in clause (A), (B), or (C) of paragraph (1) or in paragraph (2) of this subsection, the Administrator shall notify by certified mail the submitter of such information of the intent to release such information. The Administrator may not release such information, without the submitter's consent, until thirty days after the submitter has been furnished such notice. Where the Administrator finds that disclosure of information described in clause (A), (B), or (C) of paragraph (1) of this subsection is necessary to avoid or lessen an imminent and substantial risk of injury to the public health, the Administrator may set such shorter period of notice (but not less than ten days) and such method of notice as the Administrator finds appropriate. During such period the data submitter may institute an action in an appropriate district court to enjoin or limit the proposed disclosure. The court may enjoin disclosure, or limit the disclosure or the parties to whom disclosure shall be made, to the extent that—

(A) in the case of information described in clause (A), (B), or (C) of paragraph (1) of this subsection, the proposed disclosure is not required to protect against an unreasonable risk of injury to health or the environment; or

(B) in the case of information described in paragraph (2) of this subsection, the public interest in availability of the information in the public proceeding does not outweigh the interests in preserving the confidentiality of the information.

(e) Disclosure to contractors.—Information otherwise protected from disclosure to the public under subsection (b) of this section may be disclosed to contractors with the United States and employees of such contractors if, in the opinion of the Administrator, such disclosure is necessary for the satisfactory performance by the contractor of a contract with the United States for the performance of work in connection with this subchapter and under such conditions as the Administrator may specify. The Administrator shall require as a condition to the disclosure of information under this subsection that the person receiving it take such security precautions respecting the information as the Administrator shall by regulation prescribe.

(f) Penalty for disclosure by Federal employees.—**(1)** Any officer or employee of the United States or former officer or employee of the United States who, by virtue of such employment or official position, has obtained possession of, or has access to, material the disclosure of which is prohibited by subsection (b) of this section, and who, knowing that disclosure of such material is prohibited by such subsection, willfully discloses the material in any manner to any person not entitled to receive it, shall be fined not more than

$10,000 or imprisoned for not more than one year, or both. Section 1905 of title 18 shall not apply with respect to the publishing, divulging, disclosure, or making known of, or making available, information reported or otherwise obtained under this subchapter. Nothing in this subchapter shall preempt any civil remedy under State or Federal law for wrongful disclosure of trade secrets.

(2) For the purposes of this section, any contractor with the United States who is furnished information as authorized by subsection (e) of this section, or any employee of any such contractor, shall be considered to be an employee of the United States.

(g) Disclosure to foreign and multinational pesticide producers.—(1) The Administrator shall not knowingly disclose information submitted by an applicant or registrant under this subchapter to any employee or agent of any business or other entity engaged in the production, sale, or distribution of pesticides in countries other than the United States or in addition to the United States or to any other person who intends to deliver such data to such foreign or multinational business or entity unless the applicant or registrant has consented to such disclosure. The Administrator shall require an affirmation from any person who intends to inspect data that such person does not seek access to the data for purposes of delivering it or offering it for sale to any such business or entity or its agents or employees and will not purposefully deliver or negligently cause the data to be delivered to such business or entity or its agents or employees. Notwithstanding any other provision of this subsection, the Administrator may disclose information to any person in connection with a public proceeding under law or regulation, subject to restrictions on the availability of information contained elsewhere in this subchapter, which information is relevant to a determination by the Administrator with respect to whether a pesticide, or any ingredient of a pesticide, causes unreasonable adverse effects on health or the environment.

(2) The Administrator shall maintain records of the names of persons to whom data are disclosed under this subsection and the persons or organizations they represent and shall inform the applicant or registrant of the names and affiliations of such persons.

(3) Section 1001 of Title 18 shall apply to any affirmation made under paragraph (1) of this subsection.

(June 25, 1947, c. 125, § 10, as added Oct. 21, 1972, Pub.L. 92–516, § 2, 86 Stat. 989, and amended Sept. 30, 1978, Pub.L. 95–396, § 15, 92 Stat. 829; Nov. 8, 1984, Pub.L. 98–620, Title IV, § 402(4)(B), 98 Stat. 3357; Nov. 8, 1984, Pub.L. 98–620, Title IV, § 402(4)(B), 98 Stat. 3357; Oct. 25, 1988, Pub.L. 100–532, Title VIII, § 801(f), 102 Stat. 2682; Dec. 13, 1991, Pub.L. 102–237, Title X, § 1006(b)(1), (2), (3)(J), 105 Stat. 1895, 1896.)

Effective Date of 1991 Amendment

Amendments by Pub.L. 102–237 effective Dec. 13, 1991, see section 1101(a) of Pub.L. 102–237, set out as a note under section 1421 of this title.

CODE OF FEDERAL REGULATIONS

Availability of information, see 40 CFR 2.100 et seq.
Debarment and suspension under EPA assistance programs, see 40 CFR 32.100 et seq.

LIBRARY REFERENCES

Agriculture ⚷9.
Trade Regulations ⚷861.
C.J.S. Agriculture § 83 et seq.
C.J.S. Trade-Marks, Trade-Names, and Unfair Competition § 237.

WESTLAW ELECTRONIC RESEARCH

Agricultural cases: 23k (add key number)

§ 136i. Use of restricted use pesticides; applicators [FIFRA § 11]

(a) Certification procedure.—

(1) Federal certification.—In any State for which a State plan for applicator certification has not been approved by the Administrator, the Administrator, in consultation with the Governor of such State, shall conduct a program for the certification of applicators of pesticides. Such program shall conform to the requirements imposed upon the States under the provisions of subsection (a)(2) of this section and shall not require private applicators to take any examination to establish competency in the use of pesticides. Prior to the implementation of the program, the Administrator shall publish in the Federal Register for review and comment a summary of the Federal plan for applicator certification and shall make generally available within the State copies of the plan. The Administrator shall hold public hearings at one or more locations within the State if so requested by the Governor of such State during the thirty days following publication of the Federal Register notice inviting comment on the Federal plan. The hearings shall be held within thirty days following receipt of the request from the Governor. In any State in which the Administrator conducts a certification program, the Administrator may require any person engaging in the commercial application, sale, offering for sale, holding for sale, or distribution of any pesticide one or more uses of which have been classified for restricted use to maintain such records and submit such reports concerning the commercial application, sale, or distribution of such pesticide as the Administrator may by regulation prescribe. Subject to paragraph (2), the Administrator shall prescribe standards for the certification of applicators of pesticides. Such standards shall provide that to be certified, an individual must be determined to be competent with respect to the use and handling of pesticides, or to the use and handling of the pesticide or class of pesticides covered by such individual's certification. The certification standard for a private applicator shall, under a State plan submitted for approval, be deemed fulfilled by the applicator completing a certification form. The Administrator shall further assure that such form contains adequate information and affirmations to carry out the intent of this subchapter, and may include in the form an affirmation that the private applicator has completed a training program approved by the Administrator so long as the program does not require the private applicator to take, pursuant to a requirement prescribed by the Administrator, any examination to establish competency in the use of the pesticide. The Administrator may require any pesticide dealer participating in a certification program to be licensed under a State licensing program approved by the Administrator.

(2) State certification.—If any State, at any time, desires to certify applicators of pesticides, the Governor of such State shall submit a State plan for such purpose. The Administrator shall approve the plan submitted by any State, or any modification thereof, if such plan in the Administrator's judgment—

(A) designates a State agency as the agency responsible for administering the plan throughout the State;

(B) contains satisfactory assurances that such agency has or will have the legal authority and qualified personnel necessary to carry out the plan;

(C) gives satisfactory assurances that the State will devote adequate funds to the administration of the plan;

(D) provides that the State agency will make such reports to the Administrator in such form and containing such information as the Administrator may from time to time require; and

(E) contains satisfactory assurances that State standards for the certification of applicators of pesticides conform with those standards prescribed by the Administrator under paragraph (1).

Any State certification program under this section shall be maintained in accordance with the State plan approved under this section.

(b) State plans.—If the Administrator rejects a plan submitted under subsection (a)(2) of this section, the Administrator shall afford the State submitting the plan due notice and opportunity for hearing before so doing. If the Administrator approves a plan submitted under subsection (a)(2) of this section, then such State shall certify applicators of pesticides with respect to such State. Whenever the Administrator determines that a State is not administering the certification program in accordance with the plan approved under this section, the Administrator shall so notify the State and provide for a hearing at the request of the State, and, if appropriate corrective action is not taken within a reasonable time, not to exceed ninety days, the Administrator shall withdraw approval of such plan.

(c) Instruction in integrated pest management techniques.—Standards prescribed by the Administrator for the certification of applicators of pesticides under subsection (a) of this section, and State plans submitted to the Administrator under subsection (a) of this section, shall include provisions for making instructional materials concerning integrated pest management techniques available to individuals at their request in accordance with the provisions of section 136u(c) of this title, but such plans may not require that any individual receive instruction concerning such techniques or be shown to be competent with respect to the use of such techniques. The Administrator and States implementing such plans shall provide that all interested individuals are notified of the availability of such instructional materials.

(d) In general.—No regulations prescribed by the Administrator for carrying out the provisions of this subchapter shall require any private applicator to maintain any records or file any reports or other documents.

(e) Separate standards.—When establishing or approving standards for licensing or certification, the Administrator shall establish separate standards for commercial and private applicators.

(June 25, 1947, c. 125, § 11, formerly §§ 4 and 11, as added Oct. 21, 1972, Pub.L. 92–516, § 2, 86 Stat. 983, 989, and amended Nov. 28, 1975, Pub.L. 94–140, §§ 5, 11, 89 Stat. 753, 754; Sept. 30, 1978, Pub.L. 95–396, § 9, 92 Stat. 827; renumbered and amended Oct. 25, 1988, Pub.L. 100–532, Title VIII, § 801(c), (q)(1)(A)–(C), 102 Stat. 2681, 2683; Dec. 13, 1991, Pub.L. 102–237, Title X, § 1006(a)(6), (b)(1), (2), (3)(K), 105 Stat. 1895, 1896.)

Effective Date of 1991 Amendment

Amendments by Pub.L. 102–237 effective Dec. 13, 1991, see section 1101(a) of Pub.L. 102–237, set out as a note under section 1421 of this title.

CODE OF FEDERAL REGULATIONS

Debarment and suspension under EPA assistance programs, see 40 CFR 32.100 et seq.

LIBRARY REFERENCES

Agriculture ⚷9.
C.J.S. Agriculture § 83 et seq.

WESTLAW ELECTRONIC RESEARCH

Agricultural cases: 23k (add key number)

§ 136i–1. Pesticide recordkeeping

(a) Requirements.—(1) The Secretary of Agriculture, in consultation with the Administrator of the Environmental Protection Agency, shall require certified applicators of restricted use pesticides (of the type described under section 136a(d)(1)(C) of this title) to maintain records comparable to records maintained by commercial applicators of pesticides in each State. If there is no State requirement for the maintenance of records, such applicator shall maintain records that contain the product name, amount, approximate date of application, and location of application of each such pesticide used for a 2-year period after such use.

(2) Within 30 days of a pesticide application, a commercial certified applicator shall provide a copy of records maintained under paragraph (1) to the person for whom such application was provided.

(b) Access.—Records maintained under subsection (a) of this section shall be made available to any Federal or State agency that deals with pesticide use or any health or environmental issue related to the use of pesticides, on the request of such agency. Each such Federal agency shall conduct surveys and record the data from individual applicators to facilitate statistical analysis for environmental and agronomic purposes, but in no case may a government agency release data, including the location from which the data was derived, that would directly or indirectly reveal the identity of individual producers. In the case of Federal agencies, such access to records maintained under subsection (a) of this section shall be through the Secretary of Agriculture, or the Secretary's designee. State agency requests for access to records maintained under subsection (a) of this section shall be through the lead State agency so designated by the State.

(c) Health care personnel.—When a health professional determines that pesticide information maintained under this section is necessary to provide medical treatment or first aid to an individual who may have been exposed to pesticides for which the information is maintained, upon request persons required to maintain records under subsection (a) of this section shall promptly provide record and available label information to that health professional. In the case of an emergency, such record information shall be provided immediately.

(d) Penalty.—The Secretary of Agriculture shall be responsible for the enforcement of subsections (a), (b), and (c) of this section. A violation of such subsection shall—

(1) in the case of the first offense, be subject to a fine of not more than $500; and

(2) in the case of subsequent offenses, be subject to a fine of not less than $1,000 for each violation, except that the penalty shall be less than $1,000 if the Secretary determines that the person made a good faith effort to comply with such subsection.

(e) Federal or State provisions.—The requirements of this section shall not affect provisions of other Federal or State laws.

(f) Surveys and reports.—The Secretary of Agriculture and the Administrator of the Environmental Protection Agency, shall survey the records maintained under subsection (a) of this section to develop and maintain a data base that is sufficient to enable the Secretary and the Administrator to publish annual comprehensive reports concerning agricultural and nonagricultural pesticide use. The Secretary and Administrator shall enter into a memorandum of understanding to define their respective responsibilities under this subsection in order to avoid duplication of effort. Such reports shall be transmitted to Congress not later than April 1 of each year.

(g) Regulations.—The Secretary of Agriculture and the Administrator of the Environmental Protection Agency shall promulgate regulations on their respective areas of responsibility implementing this section within 180 days after November 28, 1990.

(Nov. 28, 1990, Pub.L. 101–624, Title XIV, § 1491, 104 Stat. 3627; Dec. 13, 1991, Pub.L. 102–237, Title X, § 1006(d), 105 Stat. 1896.)

Codification

Section was enacted as part of the Food, Agriculture, Conservation and Trade Act of 1990, and not as part of the Federal Insecticide, Fungicide, and Rodenticide Act, which comprises this subchapter.

Effective Date of 1991 Amendment

Amendment by Pub.L. 102–237 effective Dec. 13, 1991, see section 1101(a) of Pub.L. 102–237, set out as a note under section 1421 of this title.

Severability of Provisions

If any provision of Pub.L. 101–624 or the application thereof to any person or circumstance is held invalid, such invalidity not to affect other provisions or applications of Pub.L. 101–624 which can be given effect without regard to the invalid provision or application, see section 2519 of Pub.L. 101–624, set out as a note under section 1421 of this title.

LAW REVIEW COMMENTARIES

Survey of federal and state environmental crime legislation. Edward F. Novak and Charles W. Steese, 34 Ariz.L.Rev. 571 (1992).

§ 136j. Unlawful acts [FIFRA § 12]

(a) In general.—

(1) Except as provided by subsection (b) of this section, it shall be unlawful for any person in any State to distribute or sell to any person—

(A) any pesticide that is not registered under section 136a of this title or whose registration has been canceled or suspended, except to the extent that distribution or sale otherwise has been authorized by the Administrator under this subchapter;

(B) any registered pesticide if any claims made for it as a part of its distribution or sale substantially differ from any claims made for it as a part of the statement required in connection with its registration under section 136a of this title;

(C) any registered pesticide the composition of which differs at the time of its distribution or sale from its composition as described in the statement required in connection with its registration under section 136a of this title;

(D) any pesticide which has not been colored or discolored pursuant to the provisions of section 136w(c)(5) of this title;

(E) any pesticide which is adulterated or misbranded; or

(F) any device which is misbranded.

(2) It shall be unlawful for any person—

(A) to detach, alter, deface, or destroy, in whole or in part, any labeling required under this subchapter;

(B) to refuse to—

(i) prepare, maintain, or submit any records required by or under section 136c, 136e, 136f, 136i, or 136q of this title;

(ii) submit any reports required by or under section 136c, 136d, 136e, 136f, 136i, or 136q of this title; or

(iii) allow any entry, inspection, copying of records, or sampling authorized by this subchapter;

(C) to give a guaranty or undertaking provided for in subsection (b) of this section which is false in any particular, except that a person who receives and relies upon a guaranty authorized under subsection (b) of this section may give a guaranty to the same effect, which guaranty shall contain, in addition to the person's own name and address, the name and address of the person residing in the United States from whom the person received the guaranty or undertaking;

(D) to use for the person's own advantage or to reveal, other than to the Administrator, or officials or employees of the Environmental Protection Agency or other Federal executive agencies, or to the courts, or to physicians, pharmacists, and other qualified persons, needing such information for the performance of their duties, in accordance with such directions as the Administrator may prescribe, any information acquired by authority of this subchapter which is confidential under this subchapter;

(E) who is a registrant, wholesaler, dealer, retailer, or other distributor to advertise a product registered under this subchapter for restricted use without giving the classification of the product assigned to it under section 136a of this title;

(F) to distribute or sell, or to make available for use, or to use, any registered pesticide classified for restricted use for some or all purposes other than in accordance with section 136a(d) of this title and any regulations thereunder, except that it shall not be unlawful to sell, under regulations issued by the Administrator, a restricted use pesticide to a person who is not a certified applicator for application by a certified applicator;

(G) to use any registered pesticide in a manner inconsistent with its labeling;

(H) to use any pesticide which is under an experimental use permit contrary to the provisions of such permit;

(I) to violate any order issued under section 136k of this title;

(J) to violate any suspension order issued under section 136a(c)(2)(B), 136a–1, or 136d of this title;

(K) to violate any cancellation order issued under this subchapter or to fail to submit a notice in accordance with section 136d(g) of this title;

(L) who is a producer to violate any of the provisions of section 136e of this title;

(M) to knowingly falsify all or part of any application for registration, application for experimental use permit, any information submitted to the Administrator pursuant to section 136e of this title, any records required to be maintained pursuant to this subchapter, any report filed under this subchapter, or any information marked as confidential and submitted to the Administrator under any provision of this subchapter;

(N) who is a registrant, wholesaler, dealer, retailer, or other distributor to fail to file reports required by this subchapter;

(O) to add any substance to, or take any substance from, any pesticide in a manner that may defeat the purpose of this subchapter;

(P) to use any pesticide in tests on human beings unless such human beings (i) are fully informed of the nature and purposes of the test and of any physical and mental health consequences which are reasonably foreseeable therefrom, and (ii) freely volunteer to participate in the test;

(Q) to falsify all or part of any information relating to the testing of any pesticide (or any ingredient, metabolite, or degradation product thereof), including the nature of any protocol, procedure, substance, organism, or equipment used, observation made, or conclusion or opinion formed, submitted to the Administrator, or that the person knows will be furnished to the Administrator or will become a part of any records required to be maintained by this subchapter;

(R) to submit to the Administrator data known to be false in support of a registration; or

(S) to violate any regulation issued under section 136a(a) or 136q of this title.

(b) Exemptions.—The penalties provided for a violation of paragraph (1) of subsection (a) of this section shall not apply to—

(1) any person who establishes a guaranty signed by, and containing the name and address of, the registrant or person residing in the United States from whom the person purchased or received in good faith the pesticide in the same unbroken package, to the effect that the pesticide was lawfully registered at the time of sale and delivery to the person, and that it complies with the other requirements of this subchapter, and in such case the guarantor shall be subject to the penalties which would otherwise attach to the person holding the guaranty under the provisions of this subchapter;

(2) any carrier while lawfully shipping, transporting, or delivering for shipment any pesticide or device, if such carrier upon request of any officer or employee duly designated by the Administrator shall permit such officer or employee to copy all of its records concerning such pesticide or device;

(3) any public official while engaged in the performance of the official duties of the public official;

(4) any person using or possessing any pesticide as provided by an experimental use permit in effect with respect to such pesticide and such use or possession; or

(5) any person who ships a substance or mixture of substances being put through tests in which the purpose is only to determine its value for pesticide purposes or to determine its toxicity or other properties and from which the user does not expect to receive any benefit in pest control from its use.

(June 25, 1947, c. 125, § 12, as added Oct. 21, 1972, Pub.L. 92–516, § 2, 86 Stat. 989, and amended Sept. 30, 1978, Pub.L. 95–396, § 16, 92 Stat. 832; Oct. 25, 1988, Pub.L. 100–532, Title VI, §§ 601(b)(2), 603, Title VIII, § 801(g), (q)(2)(B), 102 Stat. 2677, 2678, 2682, 2683; Dec. 13, 1991, Pub.L. 102–237, Title X, § 1006(a)(7), (b)(3)(L)–(O), 105 Stat. 1895, 1896.)

Effective Date of 1991 Amendment

Amendments by Pub.L. 102–237 effective Dec. 13, 1991, see section 1101(a) of Pub.L. 102–237, set out as a note under section 1421 of this title.

CODE OF FEDERAL REGULATIONS

Arbitration of pesticide data disputes, see 29 CFR 1440.1.
Availability of information, see 40 CFR 2.100 et seq.
Debarment and suspension under EPA, assistance programs, see 40 CFR 32.100 et seq.

LIBRARY REFERENCES

Agriculture ⚷9, 16.
C.J.S. Agriculture §§ 30 et seq., 83 et seq.

WESTLAW ELECTRONIC RESEARCH

Agricultural cases: 23k (add key number)

§ 136k. Stop sale, use, removal, and seizure [FIFRA § 13]

(a) Stop sale, etc., orders.—Whenever any pesticide or device is found by the Administrator in any State and there is reason to believe on the basis of inspection or tests that such pesticide or device is in violation of any of the provisions of this subchapter, or that such pesticide or device has been or is intended to be distributed or sold in violation of any such provisions, or when the registration of the pesticide has been canceled by a final order or has been suspended, the Administrator may issue a written or printed "stop sale, use, or removal" order to any person who owns, controls, or has custody of such pesticide or device, and after receipt of such order no person shall sell, use, or remove the pesticide or device described in the order except in accordance with the provisions of the order.

(b) Seizure.—Any pesticide or device that is being transported or, having been transported, remains unsold or in original unbroken packages, or that is sold or offered for sale in any State, or that is imported from a foreign country, shall be liable to be proceeded against in any district court in the district where it is found and seized for confiscation by a process in rem for condemnation if—

(1) in the case of a pesticide—

(A) it is adulterated or misbranded;

(B) it is not registered pursuant to the provisions of section 136a of this title;

(C) its labeling fails to bear the information required by this subchapter;

(D) it is not colored or discolored and such coloring or discoloring is required under this subchapter; or

(E) any of the claims made for it or any of the directions for its use differ in substance from the representations made in connection with its registration;

(2) in the case of a device, it is misbranded; or

(3) in the case of a pesticide or device, when used in accordance with the requirements imposed under this subchapter and as directed by the labeling, it nevertheless causes unreasonable adverse effects on the environment.

In the case of a plant regulator, defoliant, or desiccant, used in accordance with the label claims and recommendations, physical or physiological effects on plants or parts thereof shall not be deemed to be injury, when such effects are the purpose for which the plant regulator, defoliant, or desiccant was applied.

(c) Disposition after condemnation.—If the pesticide or device is condemned it shall, after entry of the decree, be disposed of by destruction or sale as the court may direct and the proceeds, if sold, less the court costs, shall be paid into the Treasury of the United States, but the pesticide or device shall not be sold contrary to the provisions of this subchapter or the laws of the jurisdiction in which it is sold. On payment of the costs of the condemnation proceedings and the execution and delivery of a good and sufficient bond conditioned that the pesticide or device shall not be sold or otherwise disposed of contrary to the provisions of the subchapter or the laws of any jurisdiction in which sold, the court may direct that such pesticide or device be delivered to the owner thereof. The proceedings of such condemnation cases shall conform, as near as may be to the proceedings in admiralty, except that either party may demand trial by jury of any issue of fact joined in any case, and all such proceedings shall be at the suit of and in the name of the United States.

(d) Court costs, etc.—When a decree of condemnation is entered against the pesticide or device, court costs and fees, storage, and other proper expenses shall be awarded against the person, if any, intervening as claimant of the pesticide or device.

(June 25, 1947, c. 125, § 13, as added Oct. 21, 1972, Pub.L. 92–516, § 2, 86 Stat. 991, and amended Oct. 25, 1988, Pub.L. 100–532, Title VIII, § 801(h), 102 Stat. 2682.)

CODE OF FEDERAL REGULATIONS

Debarment and suspension under EPA assistance programs, see 40 CFR 32.100 et seq.

WEST FEDERAL FORMS

Forfeiture proceedings, matters pertaining to, see § 5851 et seq.

LIBRARY REFERENCES

Agriculture ⚿9.
C.J.S. Agriculture § 83 et seq.

WESTLAW ELECTRONIC RESEARCH

Agricultural cases: 23k (add key number)

§ 136*l*. Penalties [FIFRA § 14]

(a) Civil penalties.—

(1) In general.—Any registrant, commercial applicator, wholesaler, dealer, retailer, or other distributor who violates any provision of this subchapter may be assessed a civil penalty by the Administrator of not more than $5,000 for each offense.

(2) Private applicator.—Any private applicator or other person not included in paragraph (1) who violates any provision of this subchapter subsequent to receiving a written warning from the Administrator or following a citation for a prior violation, may be assessed a civil penalty by the Administrator of not more than $1,000 for each offense, except that any applicator not included under paragraph (1) of this subsection who holds or applies registered pesticides, or uses dilutions of registered pesticides, only to provide a service of controlling pests without delivering any unapplied pesticide to any person so served, and who violates any provision of this subchapter may be assessed a civil penalty by the Administrator of not more than $500 for the first offense nor more than $1,000 for each subsequent offense.

(3) Hearing.—No civil penalty shall be assessed unless the person charged shall have been given notice and opportunity for a hearing on such charge in the county, parish, or incorporated city of the residence of the person charged.

(4) Determination of penalty.—In determining the amount of the penalty, the Administrator shall consider the appropriateness of such penalty to the size of the business of the person charged, the effect on the person's ability to continue in business, and the gravity of the violation. Whenever the Administrator finds that the violation occurred despite the exercise of due care or did not cause significant harm to health or the environment, the Administrator may issue a warning in lieu of assessing a penalty.

(5) References to Attorney General.—In case of inability to collect such civil penalty or failure of any person to pay all, or such portion of such civil penalty as the Administrator may determine, the Administrator shall refer the matter to the Attorney General, who shall recover such amount by action in the appropriate United States district court.

(b) Criminal penalties.—

(1) In general.—

(A) Any registrant, applicant for a registration, or producer who knowingly violates any provision of this subchapter shall be fined not more than $50,000 or imprisoned for not more than 1 year, or both.

(B) Any commercial applicator of a restricted use pesticide, or any other person not described in subparagraph (A) who distributes or sells pesticides or devices, who knowingly violates any provision of this subchapter shall be fined not more than $25,000 or imprisoned for not more than 1 year, or both.

(2) Private applicator.—Any private applicator or other person not included in paragraph (1) who knowingly violates any provision of this subchapter shall be guilty of a misdemeanor and shall on conviction be fined not more than $1,000, or imprisoned for not more than 30 days, or both.

(3) Disclosure of information.—Any person, who, with intent to defraud, uses or reveals information relative to formulas of products acquired under the authority of section 136a of this title, shall be fined not more than $10,000, or imprisoned for not more than three years, or both.

(4) Acts of officers, agents, etc.—When construing and enforcing the provisions of this subchapter, the act, omission, or failure of any officer, agent, or other person acting for or employed by any person shall in every case be also deemed to be the act, omission, or failure of such person as well as that of the person employed.

(June 25, 1947, c. 125, § 14, as added Oct. 21, 1972, Pub.L. 92–516, § 2, 86 Stat. 992, and amended Sept. 30, 1978, Pub.L. 95–396, § 17, 92 Stat. 832; Oct. 25, 1988, Pub.L. 100–532, Title VI, § 604, 102 Stat. 2678; Dec. 13, 1991, Pub.L. 102–237, Title X, § 1006(a)(8), 105 Stat. 1895.)

Effective Date of 1991 Amendment

Amendments by section 1006(a)(8) of Pub.L. 102–237 effective Dec. 13, 1991, see section 1101(a) of Pub.L. 102–237, set out as a note under section 1421 of this title.

CODE OF FEDERAL REGULATIONS

Debarment and suspension under EPA assistance programs, see 40 CFR 32.100 et seq.

LIBRARY REFERENCES

Agriculture ⚷9, 16.
C.J.S. Agriculture §§ 30 et seq., 83 et seq.

WESTLAW ELECTRONIC RESEARCH

Agricultural cases: 23k (add key number)

§ 136m. Indemnities [FIFRA § 15]

(a) General indemnification.—

(1) In general.—Except as otherwise provided in this section, if—

(A) the Administrator notifies a registrant under section 136d(c)(1) of this title that the Administrator intends to suspend a registration or that an emergency order of suspension of a registration under section 136d(c)(3) of this title has been issued;

(B) the registration in question is suspended under section 136d(c) of this title, and thereafter is canceled under section 136d(b), 136d(d), or 136d(f) of this title; and

(C) any person who owned any quantity of the pesticide immediately before the notice to the registrant under subparagraph (A) suffered losses by reason of suspension or cancellation of the registration;

the Administrator shall make an indemnity payment to the person.

(2) Exception.—Paragraph (1) shall not apply if the Administrator finds that the person—

(A) had knowledge of facts that, in themselves, would have shown that the pesticide did not meet the requirements of section 136a(c)(5) of this title for registration; and

(B) continued thereafter to produce the pesticide without giving timely notice of such facts to the Administrator.

(3) Report.—If the Administrator takes an action under paragraph (1) that requires the payment of indemnification, the Administrator shall report to the Committee on Agriculture of the House of Representatives, the Committee on Agriculture, Nutrition, and Forestry of the Senate, and the Committees on Appropriations of the House of Representatives and the Senate on—

(A) the action taken that requires the payment of indemnification;

(B) the reasons for taking the action;

(C) the estimated cost of the payment; and

(D) a request for the appropriation of funds for the payment.

(4) Appropriation.—The Administrator may not make a payment of indemnification under paragraph (1) unless a specific line item appropriation of funds has been made in advance for the payment.

(b) Indemnification of end users, dealers, and distributors.—

(1) End users.—If—

(A) the Administrator notifies a registrant under section 136d(c)(1) of this title that the Administrator intends to suspend a registration or that an emergency order of suspension of a registration under section 136d(c)(3) of this title, has been issued;

(B) the registration in question is suspended under section 136d(c) of this title, and thereafter is canceled under section 136d(b), 136d(d), or 136d(f) of this title; and

(C) any person who, immediately before the notice to the registrant under subparagraph (A), owned any quantity of the pesticide for purposes of applying or using the pesticide as an end user, rather than for purposes of distributing or selling it or further processing it for distribution or sale, suffered a loss by reason of the suspension or cancellation of the pesticide;

the person shall be entitled to an indemnity payment under this subsection for such quantity of the pesticide.

(2) Dealers and distributors.—

(A) Any registrant, wholesaler, dealer, or other distributor (hereinafter in this paragraph referred to as a "seller") of a registered pesticide who distributes or sells the pesticide directly to any person not described as an end user in paragraph (1)(C) shall, with respect to any quantity of the pesticide that such person cannot use or resell as a result of the suspension or cancellation of the pesticide, reimburse such person for the cost of first acquiring the pesticide from the seller (other than the cost of transportation, if any), unless the seller provided to the person at the time of distribution or sale a notice, in writing, that the pesticide is not subject to reimbursement by the seller.

(B) If—

(i) the Administrator notifies a registrant under section 136d(c)(1) of this title that the Administrator intends to suspend a registration or that an emergency order of suspension of a registration under section 136d(c)(3) of this title has been issued;

(ii) the registration in question is suspended under section 136d(c) of this title, and thereafter is canceled under section 136d(b), 136d(d), or 136d(f) of this title;

(iii) any person who, immediately before the notice to the registrant under clause (i)—

(I) had not been notified in writing by the seller, as provided under subparagraph (A), that any quantity of the pesticide owned by such person is not subject to reimbursement by the seller in the event of suspension or cancellation of the pesticide; and

(II) owned any quantity of the pesticide for purposes of—

(aa) distributing or selling it; or

(bb) further processing it for distribution or sale directly to an end user;

suffered a loss by reason of the suspension or cancellation of the pesticide; and

(iv) the Administrator determines on the basis of a claim of loss submitted to the Administrator by the person, that the seller—

(I) did not provide the notice specified in subparagraph (A) to such person; and

(II) is and will continue to be unable to provide reimbursement to such person, as provided under subparagraph (A), for the loss referred to in clause (iii), as a result of the insolvency or bankruptcy of the seller and the seller's resulting inability to provide such reimbursement;

the person shall be entitled to an indemnity payment under this subsection for such quantity of the pesticide.

(C) If an indemnity payment is made by the United States under this paragraph, the United States shall be subrogated to any right that would otherwise be held under this paragraph by a seller who is unable to make a reimbursement in accordance with this paragraph with regard to reimbursements that otherwise would have been made by the seller.

(3) Source.—Any payment required to be made under paragraph (1) or (2) shall be made from the appropriation provided under section 1304 of Title 31.

(4) Administrative settlement.—An administrative settlement of a claim for such indemnity may be made in accordance with the third paragraph of section 2414 of Title 28 and shall be regarded as if it were made under that section for purposes of section 1304 of Title 31.

(c) Amount of payment.—

(1) In general.—The amount of an indemnity payment under subsection (a) or (b) of this section to any person shall be determined on the basis of the cost of the pesticide owned by the person (other than the cost of transportation, if any) immediately before the issuance of the notice to the registrant referred to in subsection (a)(1)(A), (b)(1)(A), or (b)(2)(B)(i) of this section, except that in no event shall an indemnity payment to any person exceed the fair market value of the pesticide owned by the person immediately before the issuance of the notice.

(2) Special rule.—Notwithstanding any other provision of this subchapter, the Administrator may provide a reasonable time for use or other disposal of the pesticide. In determining the quantity of any pesticide for which indemnity shall be paid under this section, proper adjustment shall be made for any pesticide used or otherwise disposed of by the owner.

(June 25, 1947, c. 125, § 15, as added Oct. 21, 1972, Pub.L. 92–516, § 2, 86 Stat. 993, and amended Oct. 25, 1988, Pub.L. 100–532, Title V, § 501(a), 102 Stat. 2674.)

Effective Date of 1988 Amendment

Section 501(a) of Pub.L. 100–532 provided in part that the amendment of this section by Pub.L. 100–532 (which completely revised this section) was effective 180 days after October 25, 1988.

Interim Payments

Section 501(b) of Pub.L. 100–532 provided that:

"**(b) Interim payments**

"**(1) Source.**—Any obligation of the Administrator to pay an indemnity arising under section 15 [this section], as it existed prior to the effective date of the amendment made by this section, shall be made from the appropriation provided under section 1304 of title 31, United States Code [section 1304 of Title 31, Money and Finance].

"**(2) Administrative settlement.**—An administrative settlement of a claim for such indemnity may be made in accordance with the third paragraph of section 2414 of title 28, United States Code [section 2414 of Title 28, Judiciary and Judicial Procedure], and shall be regarded as if it were made under that section for purposes of section 1304 of title 31, United States Code [section 1304 of Title 31]."

CODE OF FEDERAL REGULATIONS

Debarment and suspension under EPA assistance programs, see 40 CFR 32.100 et seq.

LIBRARY REFERENCES

Agriculture ⚷9.
C.J.S. Agriculture § 83 et seq.

WESTLAW ELECTRONIC RESEARCH

Agricultural cases: 23k (add key number)

§ 136n. Administrative procedure; judicial review [FIFRA § 16]

(a) District court review.—Except as is otherwise provided in this subchapter, the refusal of the Administrator to cancel or suspend a registration or to change a classification not following a hearing and other final actions of the Administrator not committed to the discretion of the Administrator by law are judicially reviewable by the district courts of the United States.

(b) Review by court of appeals.—In the case of actual controversy as to the validity of any order issued by the Administrator following a public hearing, any person who will be adversely affected by such order and who had been a party to the proceedings may obtain judicial review by filing in the United States court of appeals for the circuit wherein such person resides or has a place of business, within 60 days after the entry of such order, a petition praying that the order be set aside in whole or in part. A copy of the petition shall be forthwith transmitted by the clerk of the court to the Administrator or any officer designated by the Administrator for that purpose, and thereupon the Administrator shall file in the court the record of the proceedings on which the Administrator based the Administrator's order, as provided in section 2112 of Title 28. Upon the filing of such petition the court shall have exclusive jurisdiction to affirm or set aside the order complained of in whole or in part. The court shall consider all evidence of record. The order of the Administrator shall be sustained if it is supported by substantial evidence when considered on the record as a whole. The judgment of the court affirming or setting aside, in whole or in part, any order under this section shall be final, subject to review by the Supreme Court of the United States upon certiorari or certification as provided in section 1254 of Title 28. The commencement of proceedings under this section shall not, unless specifically ordered by the court to the contrary, operate as a stay of an order.

(c) Jurisdiction of district courts.—The district courts of the United States are vested with jurisdiction specifically to enforce, and to prevent and restrain violations of, this subchapter.

(d) Notice of judgments.—The Administrator shall, by publication in such manner as the Administrator may prescribe, give notice of all judgments entered in actions instituted under the authority of this subchapter.

(June 25, 1947, c. 125, § 16, as added Oct. 21, 1972, Pub.L. 92–516, § 2, 86 Stat. 994, and amended Nov. 8, 1984, Pub.L. 98–620, Title IV, § 402(4)(C), 98 Stat. 3357; Oct. 25, 1988, Pub.L. 100–532, Title VIII, § 801(i), 102 Stat. 2682; Dec. 13, 1991, Pub.L. 102–237, Title X, § 1006(b)(1), (2), (3)(P), 105 Stat. 1895, 1896.)

Effective Date of 1991 Amendment

Amendments by Pub.L. 102–237 effective Dec. 13, 1991, see section 1101(a) of Pub.L. 102–237, set out as a note under section 1421 of this title.

Federal Practice and Procedure

Review of administrative decisions in courts of appeals, see Wright, Miller, Cooper & Gressman: Jurisdiction § 3941.

CODE OF FEDERAL REGULATIONS

Debarment and suspension under EPA assistance programs, see 40 CFR 32.100 et seq.

LIBRARY REFERENCES

Agriculture ⚷9.
Health and Environment ⚷25.15(1).
C.J.S. Agriculture § 83 et seq.
C.J.S. Health and Environment § 82 et seq.

WESTLAW ELECTRONIC RESEARCH

Agricultural cases: 23k (add key number)

§ 136*o*. Imports and exports [FIFRA § 17]

(a) Pesticides and devices intended for export.—Notwithstanding any other provision of this subchapter, no pesticide or device or active ingredient used in producing a pesticide intended solely for export to any foreign country shall be deemed in violation of this subchapter—

(1) when prepared or packed according to the specifications or directions of the foreign purchaser, except that producers of such pesticides and devices and active ingredients used in producing pesticides shall be subject to sections 136(p), (q)(1)(A), (C), (D), (E), (G), and (H), 136(q)(2)(A), (B), (C)(i) and (iii), and (D), 136e, and 136f of this title; and

(2) in the case of any pesticide other than a pesticide registered under section 136a or sold under section 136d(a)(1) of this title, if, prior to export, the foreign purchaser has signed a statement acknowledging that the purchaser understands that such pesticide is not registered for use in the United States and cannot be sold in the United States under this subchapter.

A copy of that statement shall be transmitted to an appropriate official of the government of the importing country.

(b) Cancellation notices furnished to foreign governments.—Whenever a registration, or a cancellation or suspension of the registration of a pesticide becomes effective, or ceases to be effective, the Administrator shall transmit through the State Department notification thereof to the governments of other countries and to appropriate international agencies. Such notification shall, upon request, include all information related to the cancellation or suspension of the registration of the pesticide and information concerning other pesticides that are registered under section 136a of this title and that could be used in lieu of such pesticide.

(c) Importation of pesticides and devices.—The Secretary of the Treasury shall notify the Administrator of the arrival of pesticides and devices and shall deliver to the Administrator, upon the Administrator's request, samples of pesticides or devices which are being imported into the United States, giving notice to the owner or consignee, who may appear before the Administrator and have the right to introduce testimony. If it appears from the examination of a sample that it is adulterated, or misbranded or otherwise violated the provisions set forth in this subchapter, or is otherwise injurious to health or the environment, the pesticide or device may be refused admission, and the Secretary of the Treasury shall refuse delivery to the consignee and shall cause the destruction of any pesticide or device refused delivery which shall not be exported by the consignee within 90 days from the date of notice of such refusal under such regulations as the Secretary of the Treasury may prescribe. The Secretary of the Treasury may deliver to the consignee such pesticide or device pending examination and decision in the matter on execution of bond for the amount of the full invoice value of such pesticide or device, together with the duty thereon, and on refusal to return such pesticide or device for any cause to the custody of the Secretary of the Treasury, when demanded, for the purpose of excluding them from the country, or for any other purpose, said consignee shall forfeit the full amount of said bond. All charges for storage, cartage, and labor on pesticides or devices which are refused admission or delivery shall be paid by the owner or consignee, and in default of such payment shall constitute a lien against any future importation made by such owner or consignee.

(d) Cooperation in international efforts.—The Administrator shall, in cooperation with the Department of State and any other appropriate Federal agency, participate and cooperate in any international efforts to develop improved pesticide research and regulations.

(e) Regulations.—The Secretary of the Treasury, in consultation with the Administrator, shall prescribe regulations for the enforcement of subsection (c) of this section.

(June 25, 1947, c. 125, § 17, as added Oct. 21, 1972, Pub.L. 92–516, § 2, 86 Stat. 995, and amended Sept. 30, 1978, Pub.L. 95–396, § 18(a), 92 Stat. 833; Oct. 25, 1988, Pub.L. 100–532, Title VIII, § 801(j), 102 Stat. 2682; Dec. 13, 1991, Pub.L. 102–237, Title X, § 1006(a)(9), (b)(2), 105 Stat. 1895.)

Effective Date of 1991 Amendment

Amendments by Pub.L. 102–237 effective Dec. 13, 1991, see section 1101(a) of Pub.L. 102–237, set out as a note under section 1421 of this title.

CODE OF FEDERAL REGULATIONS

Debarment and suspension under EPA assistance programs, see 40 CFR 32.100 et seq.
Special classes of merchandise, see 19 CFR 12.110 to 12.117.

LIBRARY REFERENCES

Agriculture ⚷9.
C.J.S. Agriculture § 83 et seq.

WESTLAW ELECTRONIC RESEARCH

Agricultural cases: 23k (add key number)

§ 136p. Exemption of Federal and State agencies [FIFRA § 18]

The Administrator may, at the Administrator's discretion, exempt any Federal or State agency from any provision of this subchapter if the Administrator determines that emergency conditions exist which require such exemption. The Administrator, in determining whether or not such emergency conditions exist, shall consult with the Secretary of Agriculture and the Governor of any State concerned if they request such determination.

(June 25, 1947, c. 125, § 18, as added Oct. 21, 1972, Pub.L. 92–516, § 2, 86 Stat. 995, and amended Nov. 28, 1975, Pub.L. 94–140, § 8, 89 Stat. 754; Oct. 25, 1988, Pub.L. 100–532, Title VIII, § 801(k), 102 Stat. 2682; Dec. 13, 1991, Pub.L. 102–237, Title X, § 1006(b)(1), (2), 105 Stat. 1895.)

Effective Date of 1991 Amendment

Amendments by Pub.L. 102–237 effective Dec. 13, 1991, see section 1101(a) of Pub.L. 102–237, set out as a note under section 1421 of this title.

CODE OF FEDERAL REGULATIONS

Debarment and suspension under EPA assistance programs, see 40 CFR 32.100 et seq.
Policies and procedures, see 40 CFR 166.1 et seq.

LIBRARY REFERENCES

Agriculture ⚷9.
C.J.S. Agriculture § 83 et seq.

WESTLAW ELECTRONIC RESEARCH

Agricultural cases: 23k (add key number)

§ 136q. Storage, disposal, transportation, and recall [FIFRA § 19]

(a) Storage, disposal, and transportation.—

(1) Data requirements and registration of pesticides.—The Administrator may require under section 136a or 136d of this title that—

(A) the registrant or applicant for registration of a pesticide submit or cite data or information regarding methods for the safe storage and disposal of excess quantities of the pesticide to support the registration or continued registration of a pesticide;

(B) the labeling of a pesticide contain requirements and procedures for the transportation, storage, and disposal of the pesticide, any container of the pesticide, any rinsate containing the pesticide, or any other material used to contain or collect excess or spilled quantities of the pesticide; and

(C) the registrant of a pesticide provide evidence of sufficient financial and other resources to carry out a recall plan under subsection (b) of this section, and provide for the disposition of the pesticide, in the event of suspension and cancellation of the pesticide.

(2) Pesticides.—The Administrator may by regulation, or as part of an order issued under section 136d of this title or an amendment to such an order—

(A) issue requirements and procedures to be followed by any person who stores or transports a pesticide the registration of which has been suspended or canceled;

(B) issue requirements and procedures to be followed by any person who disposes of stocks of a pesticide the registration of which has been suspended; and

(C) issue requirements and procedures for the disposal of any pesticide the registration of which has been canceled.

(3) Containers, rinsates, and other materials.—The Administrator may by regulation, or as part of an order issued under section 136d of this title or an amendment to such an order—

(A) issue requirements and procedures to be followed by any person who stores or transports any container of a pesticide the registration of which has been suspended or canceled, any rinsate containing the pesticide, or any other material used to contain or collect excess or spilled quantities of the pesticide;

(B) issue requirements and procedures to be followed by any person who disposes of stocks of any container of a pesticide the registration of which has been suspended, any rinsate containing the pesticide, or any other material used to contain or collect excess or spilled quantities of the pesticide; and

(C) issue requirements and procedures for the disposal of any container of a pesticide the registration of which has been canceled, any rinsate containing the pesticide, or any other material used to contain or collect excess or spilled quantities of the pesticide.

(b) Recalls.—

(1) In general.—If the registration of a pesticide has been suspended and canceled under section 136d of this title, and if the Administrator finds that recall of the pesticide is necessary to protect health or the environment, the Administrator shall order a recall of the pesticide in accordance with this subsection.

(2) Voluntary recall.—If, after determining under paragraph (1) that a recall is necessary, the Administrator finds that voluntary recall by the registrant and others in the chain of distribution may be as safe and effective as a mandatory recall, the Administrator shall request the registrant of the pesticide to submit, within 60 days of the request, a plan for the voluntary recall of the pesticide. If such a plan is requested and submitted, the Administrator shall approve the plan and order the registrant to conduct the recall in accordance with the plan unless the Administrator determines, after an informal hearing, that the plan is inadequate to protect health or the environment.

(3) Mandatory recall.—If, after determining under paragraph (1) that a recall is necessary, the Administrator does not request the submission of a plan under paragraph (2) or finds such a plan to be inadequate, the Administrator shall issue a regulation that prescribes a plan for the recall of the pesticide. A regulation issued under this paragraph may apply to any person who is or was a registrant, distributor, or seller of the pesticide, or any successor in interest to such a person.

(4) Recall procedure.—A regulation issued under this subsection may require any person that is subject to the regulation to—

(A) arrange to make available one or more storage facilities to receive and store the pesticide to which the recall program applies, and inform the Administrator of the location of each such facility;

(B) accept and store at such a facility those existing stocks of such pesticide that are tendered by any other person who obtained the pesticide directly or indirectly from the person that is subject to such regulation;

(C) on the request of a person making such a tender, provide for proper transportation of the pesticide to a storage facility; and

(D) take such reasonable steps as the regulation may prescribe to inform persons who may be holders of the pesticide of the terms of the recall regulation and how those persons may tender the pesticide and arrange for transportation of the pesticide to a storage facility.

(5) Contents of recall plan.—A recall plan established under this subsection shall include—

(A) the level in the distribution chain to which the recall is to extend, and a schedule for recall; and

(B) the means to be used to verify the effectiveness of the recall.

(6) Requirements or procedures.—No requirement or procedure imposed in accordance with paragraph (2) of subsection (a) may require the recall of existing stocks of the pesticide except as provided by this subsection.

(c) Storage costs.—

(1) Submission of plan.—A registrant who wishes to become eligible for reimbursement of storage costs incurred as a result of a recall prescribed under subsection (b) of this section for a pesticide whose registration has been suspended and canceled shall, as soon as practicable after the suspension of the registration of the pesticide, submit to the Administrator a plan for the storage and disposal of the pesticide that meets criteria established by the Administrator by regulation.

(2) Reimbursement.—Within a reasonable period of time after such storage costs are incurred and paid by the registrant, the Administrator shall reimburse the registrant, on request, for—

(A) none of the costs incurred by the registrant before the date of submission of the plan referred to in paragraph (1) to the Administrator;

(B) 100 percent of the costs incurred by the registrant after the date of submission of the plan to the Administrator or the date of cancellation of the registration of the pesticide, whichever is later, but before the approval of the plan by the Administrator;

(C) 50 percent of the costs incurred by the registrant during the 1-year period beginning on the date of the approval of the plan by the Administrator or the date of cancellation of the registration of the pesticide, whichever is later;

(D) none of the costs incurred by the registrant during the 3-year period beginning on the 366th day following approval of the plan by the Administrator or the date of cancellation of the registration of the pesticide, whichever is later; and

(E) 25 percent of the costs incurred by the registrant during the period beginning on the first day of the 5th year following the date of the approval of the plan by the Administrator or the date of cancellation of the registration of the pesticide, whichever is later, and ending on the date that a disposal permit for the pesticide is issued by a State or an alternative plan for disposal of the pesticide in accordance with applicable law has been developed.

(d) Administration of storage, disposal, transportation, and recall programs.—

(1) Voluntary agreements.—Nothing in this section shall be construed as preventing or making unlawful any agreement between a seller and a buyer of any pesticide or other substance regarding the ultimate allocation of the costs of storage, transportation, or disposal of a pesticide.

(2) Rule and regulation review.—Section 136w(a)(4) of this title shall not apply to any regulation issued under subsection (a)(2) or (b) of this section.

(3) Limitations.—No registrant shall be responsible under this section for a pesticide the registration of which is held by another person. No distributor or seller shall be responsible under this section for a pesticide that the distributor or seller did not hold or sell.

(4) Seizure and penalties.—If the Administrator finds that a person who is subject to a regulation or order under subsection (a)(2) or (b) of this section has failed substantially to comply with that regulation or order, the Administrator may take action under section 136k or 136*l* of this title or obtain injunctive relief under section 136n(c) of this title against such person or any successor in interest of any such person.

(e) Container design.—

(1) Procedures.—

(A) Not later than 3 years after the effective date of this subsection, the Administrator shall, in consultation with the heads of other interested Federal agencies, promulgate regulations for the design of pesticide containers that will promote the safe storage and disposal of pesticides.

(B) The regulations shall ensure, to the fullest extent practicable, that the containers—

(i) accommodate procedures used for the removal of pesticides from the containers and the rinsing of the containers;

(ii) facilitate the safe use of the containers, including elimination of splash and leakage of pesticides from the containers;

(iii) facilitate the safe disposal of the containers; and

(iv) facilitate the safe refill and reuse of the containers.

(2) Compliance.—The Administrator shall require compliance with the regulations referred to in paragraph (1) not later than 5 years after the effective date of this subsection.

(f) Pesticide residue removal.—

(1) Procedures.—

(A) Not later than 3 years after the effective date of this subsection, the Administrator shall, in consultation with the heads of other interested Federal agencies, promulgate regulations prescribing procedures and standards for the removal of pesticides from containers prior to disposal.

(B) The regulations may—

(i) specify, for each major type of pesticide container, procedures and standards providing for, at a minimum, triple rinsing or the equivalent degree of pesticide removal;

(ii) specify procedures that can be implemented promptly and easily in various circumstances and conditions;

(iii) provide for reuse, whenever practicable, or disposal of rinse water and residue; and

(iv) be coordinated with requirements for the rinsing of containers imposed under the Solid Waste Disposal Act (42 U.S.C. 6901 et seq.).

(C) The Administrator may, at the discretion of the Administrator, exempt products intended solely for household use from the requirements of this subsection.

(2) Compliance.—Effective beginning 5 years after the effective date of this subsection, a State may not exercise primary enforcement responsibility under section 136w–1 of this title, or certify an applicator under section 136i of this title, unless the Administrator determines that the State is carrying out an adequate program to ensure compliance with this subsection.

(3) Solid Waste Disposal Act.—Nothing in this subsection shall affect the authorities or requirements concerning pesticide containers under the Solid Waste Disposal Act (42 U.S.C. 6901).

(g) Pesticide container study.—

(1) Study.—

(A) The Administrator shall conduct a study of options to encourage or require—

(i) the return, refill, and reuse of pesticide containers;

(ii) the development and use of pesticide formulations that facilitate the removal of pesticide residues from containers; and

(iii) the use of bulk storage facilities to reduce the number of pesticide containers requiring disposal.

(B) In conducting the study, the Administrator shall—

(i) consult with the heads of other interested Federal agencies, State agencies, industry groups, and environmental organizations; and

(ii) assess the feasibility, costs, and environmental benefits of encouraging or requiring various measures or actions.

(2) Report.—Not later than 2 years after the effective date of this subsection, the Administrator shall submit to Congress a report describing the results of the study required under paragraph (1).

(h) Relationship to Solid Waste Disposal Act.—Nothing in this section shall diminish the authorities or requirements of the Solid Waste Disposal Act (42 U.S.C. 6901 et seq.).

(June 25, 1947, c. 125, § 19, as added Oct. 21, 1972, Pub.L. 92–516, § 2, 86 Stat. 995, and amended Sept. 30, 1978, Pub.L. 95–396, § 19, 92 Stat. 833; Oct. 25, 1988, Pub.L. 100–532, Title IV, §§ 401–403, Title VIII, § 801(q)(1)(D), 102 Stat. 2669–2672, 2683.)

References in Text

For effective date of this subsection, referred to in text, see section 901 of Pub.L. 100–532, set out as a note under section 136 of this title.

The Solid Waste Disposal Act, referred to in text, is Title II of Pub.L. 89–272, Oct. 20, 1965, 79 Stat. 997, as amended generally by Pub.L. 94–580, § 2, Oct. 21, 1976, 90 Stat. 2795, which is classified generally to chapter 82 (section 6901 et seq.) of Title 42. For complete classification of this Act to the Code, see Short Title note set out under section 6901 of Title 42 and Tables volume.

CODE OF FEDERAL REGULATIONS

Debarment and suspension under EPA assistance programs, see 40 CFR 32.100 et seq.
Procedures applicable, see 40 CFR 165.1 et seq.
Registration, reregistration, and classification, see 40 CFR 162.1 et seq.

LIBRARY REFERENCES

Agriculture ⚷9.
C.J.S. Agriculture § 83 et seq.

WESTLAW ELECTRONIC RESEARCH

Agricultural cases: 23k (add key number)

§ 136r. Research and monitoring [FIFRA § 20]

(a) Research.—The Administrator shall undertake research including research by grant or contract with other Federal agencies, universities, or others as may be necessary to carry out the purposes of this subchapter, and the Administrator shall conduct research into integrated pest management in coordination with the Secretary of Agriculture. The Administrator shall also take care to ensure that such research does not duplicate research being undertaken by any other Federal agency.

(b) National monitoring plan.—The Administrator shall formulate and periodically revise, in cooperation with other Federal, State, or local agencies, a national plan for monitoring pesticides.

(c) Monitoring.—The Administrator shall undertake such monitoring activities, including, but not limited to monitoring in air, soil, water, man, plants, and animals, as may be necessary for the implementation of this subchapter and of the national pesticide monitoring plan. The Administrator shall establish procedures for the monitoring of man and animals and their environment for incidential[1] pesticide exposure, including, but not limited to, the quantification of incidental human and environmental pesticide pollution and the secular trends thereof, and identification of the sources of contamination and their relationship to human and environmental effects. Such activities shall be carried out in cooperation with other Federal, State, and local agencies.

(June 25, 1947, c. 125, § 20, as added Oct. 21, 1972, Pub.L. 92–516, § 2, 86 Stat. 996, and amended Sept. 30, 1978, Pub.L. 95–396, § 20, 92 Stat. 834; Dec. 13, 1991, Pub.L. 102–237, Title X, § 1006(a)(10), (b)(1), 105 Stat. 1895.)

[1] So in original. Probably should be "incidental".

Effective Date of 1991 Amendment

Amendments by section 1006(a)(10), (b)(1) of Pub.L. 102–237 effective Dec. 13, 1991, see section 1101(a) of Pub.L. 102–237, set out as a note under section 1421 of this title.

CODE OF FEDERAL REGULATIONS

Debarment and suspension under EPA assistance programs, see 40 CFR 32.100 et seq.
Granting policies and procedures, see 40 CFR 30.100 et seq.
Subagreements, see 40 CFR 33.001 et seq.

LIBRARY REFERENCES

Agriculture ⚷9.
Health and Environment ⚷25.5(9).
C.J.S. Agriculture § 83 et seq.
C.J.S. Health and Environment § 65 et seq.

WESTLAW ELECTRONIC RESEARCH

Agricultural cases: 23k (add key number)

§ 136s. Solicitation of comments; notice of public hearings [FIFRA § 21]

(a) Secretary of Agriculture.—The Administrator, before publishing regulations under this subchapter, shall solicit the views of the Secretary of Agriculture in accordance with the procedure described in section 136w(a) of this title.

(b) Views.—In addition to any other authority relating to public hearings and solicitation of views, in connection with the suspension or cancellation of a pesticide registration or any other actions authorized under this subchapter, the Administrator may, at the Administrator's discretion, solicit the views of all interested persons, either orally or in writing, and seek such advice from scientists, farmers, farm organizations, and other qualified persons as the Administrator deems proper.

(c) Notice.—In connection with all public hearings under this subchapter the Administrator shall publish timely notice of such hearings in the Federal Register.

(June 25, 1947, c. 125, § 21, as added Oct. 21, 1972, Pub.L. 92–516, § 2, 86 Stat. 996, and amended Nov. 28, 1975, Pub.L. 94–140, § 2(b), 89 Stat. 752; Oct. 25, 1988, Pub.L. 100–532, Title VIII, § 801(*l*), 102 Stat. 2682; Dec. 13, 1991, Pub.L. 102–237, Title X, § 1006(b)(1), (2), 105 Stat. 1895.)

Effective Date of 1991 Amendment

Amendments by Pub.L. 102–237 effective Dec. 13, 1991, see section 1101(a) of Pub.L. 102–237, set out as a note under section 1421 of this title.

CODE OF FEDERAL REGULATIONS

Debarment and suspension under EPA assistance programs, see 40 CFR 32.100 et seq.
Registration, reregistration and classification, see 40 CFR 162.1 et seq.

LIBRARY REFERENCES

Agriculture ⚷9.
C.J.S. Agriculture § 83 et seq.

WESTLAW ELECTRONIC RESEARCH

Agricultural cases: 23k (add key number)

§ 136t. Delegation and cooperation [FIFRA § 22]

(a) Delegation.—All authority vested in the Administrator by virtue of the provisions of this subchapter may with like force and effect be executed by such employees of the Environmental Protection Agency as the Administrator may designate for the purpose.

(b) Cooperation.—The Administrator shall cooperate with Department of Agriculture, any other Federal agency, and any appropriate agency of any State or any political subdivision thereof, in carrying out the provisions of this subchapter, and in securing uniformity of regulations.

(June 25, 1947, c. 125, § 22, as added Oct. 21, 1972, Pub.L. 92–516, § 2, 86 Stat. 996.)

CODE OF FEDERAL REGULATIONS

Debarment and suspension under EPA assistance programs, see 40 CFR 32.100 et seq.

LIBRARY REFERENCES

Agriculture ⚷9.
Health and Environment ⚷25.5(9).
C.J.S. Agriculture § 83 et seq.
C.J.S. Health and Environment § 65 et seq.

WESTLAW ELECTRONIC RESEARCH

Agricultural cases: 23k (add key number)

§ 136u. State cooperation, aid, and training [FIFRA § 23]

(a) Cooperative agreements.—The Administrator may enter into cooperative agreements with States and Indian tribes—

(1) to delegate to any State or Indian tribe the authority to cooperate in the enforcement of this subchapter through the use of its personnel or facilities, to train personnel of the State or Indian tribe to cooperate in the enforcement of this subchapter, and to assist States and Indian tribes in implementing cooperative enforcement programs through grants-in-aid; and

(2) to assist States in developing and administering State programs, and Indian tribes that enter into cooperative agreements, to train and certify applicators consistent with the standards the Administrator prescribes.

Effective with the fiscal year beginning October 1, 1978, there are authorized to be appropriated annually such funds as may be necessary for the Administrator to provide through cooperative agreements an amount equal to 50 percent of the anticipated cost to each State or Indian tribe, as agreed to under such cooperative agreements, of conducting training and certification programs during such fiscal year. If funds sufficient to pay 50 percent of the costs for any year are not appropriated, the share of each State and Indian tribe shall be reduced in a like proportion in allocating available funds.

(b) Contracts for training.—In addition, the Administrator may enter into contracts with Federal, State, or Indian tribal agencies for the purpose of encouraging the training of certified applicators.

(c) Information and education.—The Administrator shall, in cooperation with the Secretary of Agriculture, use the services of the cooperative State extension services to inform and educate pesticide users about accepted uses and other regulations made under this subchapter.

(June 25, 1947, c. 125, § 23, as added Oct. 21, 1972, Pub.L. 92–516, § 2, 86 Stat. 996, and amended Sept. 30, 1978, Pub.L. 95–396, § 21, 92 Stat. 834.)

CODE OF FEDERAL REGULATIONS

Assistance for continuing environmental programs, etc., see 40 CFR 35.001 et seq.
Grant policies and procedures, see 40 CFR 30.100 et seq.
Subagreements, see 40 CFR 33.001 et seq.
Training grants, etc., see 40 CFR 45.100 et seq.

LIBRARY REFERENCES

Agriculture ⚷9.
C.J.S. Agriculture § 83 et seq.

WESTLAW ELECTRONIC RESEARCH

Agricultural cases: 23k (add key number)

§ 136v. Authority of States [FIFRA § 24]

(a) In general.—A State may regulate the sale or use of any federally registered pesticide or device in the State, but only if and to the extent the regulation does not permit any sale or use prohibited by this subchapter.

(b) Uniformity.—Such State shall not impose or continue in effect any requirements for labeling or packaging in addition to or different from those required under this subchapter.

(c) Additional uses.—

(1) A State may provide registration for additional uses of federally registered pesticides formulated for distribution and use within that State to meet special local needs in accord with the purposes of this subchapter and if registration for such use has not previously been denied, disapproved, or canceled by the Administrator. Such registration shall be deemed registration under section 136a of this title for all purposes of this subchapter, but shall

authorize distribution and use only within such State.

(2) A registration issued by a State under this subsection shall not be effective for more than ninety days if disapproved by the Administrator within that period. Prior to disapproval, the Administrator shall, except as provided in paragraph (3) of this subsection, advise the State of the Administrator's intention to disapprove and the reasons therefor, and provide the State time to respond. The Administrator shall not prohibit or disapprove a registration issued by a State under this subsection (A) on the basis of lack of essentiality of a pesticide or (B) except as provided in paragraph (3) of this subsection, if its composition and use patterns are similar to those of a federally registered pesticide.

(3) In no instance may a State issue a registration for a food or feed use unless there exists a tolerance or exemption under the Federal Food, Drug, and Cosmetic Act [21 U.S.C.A. § 301 et seq.] that permits the residues of the pesticides on the food or feed. If the Administrator determines that a registration issued by a State is inconsistent with the Federal Food, Drug, and Cosmetic Act, or the use of, a pesticide under a registration issued by a State constitutes an imminent hazard, the Administrator may immediately disapprove the registration.

(4) If the Administrator finds, in accordance with standards set forth in regulations issued under section 136w of this title, that a State is not capable of exercising adequate controls to assure that State registration under this section will be in accord with the purposes of this subchapter or has failed to exercise adequate controls, the Administrator may suspend the authority of the State to register pesticides until such time as the Administrator is satisfied that the State can and will exercise adequate controls. Prior to any such suspension, the Administrator shall advise the State of the Administrator's intention to suspend and the reasons therefor and provide the State time to respond.

(June 25, 1947, c. 125, § 24, as added Oct. 21, 1972, Pub.L. 92–516, § 2, 86 Stat. 997, and amended Sept. 30, 1978, Pub.L. 95–396, § 22, 92 Stat. 835; Oct. 25, 1988, Pub.L. 100–532, Title VIII, § 801(m), 102 Stat. 2682.)

CODE OF FEDERAL REGULATIONS

Availability of information, see 40 CFR 2.100 et seq.
Debarment and suspension under EPA assistance programs, see 40 CFR 32.100 et seq.
State issuance of experimental use permits, see 40 CFR 170.20 et seq.

LIBRARY REFERENCES

Agriculture ⚷9.
C.J.S. Agriculture § 83 et seq.

WESTLAW ELECTRONIC RESEARCH

Agricultural cases: 23k (add key number)

United States Supreme Court

This chapter providing no clear or manifest indication that Congress sought to supplant local authority over pesticide regulation impliedly, although amendments turned chapter into comprehensive regulatory statute, and substantial portions of field were still left vacant, including issue of local government permit scheme for actual use of pesticides, see Wisconsin Public Intervenor v. Mortier, 1991, 111 S.Ct. 2476.

§ 136w. Authority of Administrator [FIFRA § 25]

(a) In general.—

(1) Regulations.—The Administrator is authorized, in accordance with the procedure described in paragraph (2), to prescribe regulations to carry out the provisions of this subchapter. Such regulations shall take into account the difference in concept and usage between various classes of pesticides and differences in environmental risk and the appropriate data for evaluating such risk between agricultural and nonagricultural pesticides.

(2) Procedure.—

(A) Proposed regulations.—At least 60 days prior to signing any proposed regulation for publication in the Federal Register, the Administrator shall provide the Secretary of Agriculture with a copy of such regulation. If the Secretary comments in writing to the Administrator regarding any such regulation within 30 days after receiving it, the Administrator shall publish in the Federal Register (with the proposed regulation) the comments of the Secretary and the response of the Administrator with regard to the Secretary's comments. If the Secretary does not comment in writing to the Administrator regarding the regulation within 30 days after receiving it, the Administrator may sign such regulation for publication in the Federal Register any time after such 30-day period notwithstanding the foregoing 60-day time requirement.

(B) Final regulations.—At least 30 days prior to signing any regulation in final form for publication in the Federal Register, the Administrator shall provide the Secretary of Agriculture with a copy of such regulation. If the Secretary comments in writing to the Administrator regarding any such final regulation within 15 days after receiving it, the Administrator shall publish in the Federal Register (with the final regulation) the comments of the Secretary, if requested by the Secretary, and the response of the Administrator concerning the Secretary's comments. If the Secretary does not comment in writing to the Administrator regarding the regulation within 15 days after receiving it, the Administrator may sign such regulation for publication in the Federal Register at any time after such 15-day period notwithstanding the foregoing 30-day time requirement. In taking any final action under this subsection, the Administrator shall include among those factors to be taken into account the effect of the regulation on production and prices of agricultural commodities, retail food prices, and otherwise on the agricultural economy, and the Administrator shall publish in the Federal Register an analysis of such effect.

(C) Time requirements.—The time requirements imposed by subparagraphs (A) and (B) may be waived or modified to the extent agreed upon by the Administrator and the Secretary.

(D) Publication in the Federal Register.—The Administrator shall, simultaneously with any notification to the Secretary of Agriculture under this paragraph prior to the issuance of any proposed or final regulation, publish such notification in the Federal Register.

(3) Congressional committees.—At such time as the Administrator is required under paragraph (2) of this subsection to provide the Secretary of Agriculture with a copy of proposed regulations and a copy of the final form of regulations, the Administrator shall also furnish a copy of such regulations to the Committee on Agriculture of the House of Representatives and the Committee on Agriculture, Nutrition, and Forestry of the Senate.

(4) Congressional review of regulations.—Simultaneously with the promulgation of any rule or regulation under this subchapter, the Administrator shall transmit a copy thereof to the Secretary of the Senate and the Clerk of the House of Representatives. The rule or regulation shall not become effective until the passage of 60 calendar days after the rule or regulation is so transmitted.

(b) Exemption of pesticides.—The Administrator may exempt from the requirements of this subchapter by regulation any pesticide which the Administrator determines either (1) to be adequately regulated by another Federal agency, or (2) to be of a character which is unnecessary to be subject to this subchapter in order to carry out the purposes of this subchapter.

(c) Other authority.—The Administrator, after notice and opportunity for hearing, is authorized—

(1) to declare a pest any form of plant or animal life (other than man and other than bacteria, virus, and other micro-organisms on or in living man or other living animals) which is injurious to health or the environment;

(2) to determine any pesticide which contains any substance or substances in quantities highly toxic to man;

(3) to establish standards (which shall be consistent with those established under the authority of the Poison Prevention Packaging Act (Public Law 91–601) [15 U.S.C.A. § 1471 et seq.]) with respect to the package, container, or wrapping in which a pesticide or device is enclosed for use or consumption, in order to protect children and adults from serious injury or illness resulting from accidental ingestion or contact with pesticides or devices regulated by this subchapter as well as to accomplish the other purposes of this subchapter;

(4) to specify those classes of devices which shall be subject to any provision of section 136(q)(1) or section 136e of this title upon the Administrator's determination that application of such provision is necessary to effectuate the purposes of this subchapter;

(5) to prescribe regulations requiring any pesticide to be colored or discolored if the Administrator determines that such requirement is feasible and is necessary for the protection of health and the environment; and

(6) to determine and establish suitable names to be used in the ingredient statement.

(d) Scientific advisory panel.—The Administrator shall submit to an advisory panel for comment as to the impact on health and the environment of the action proposed in notices of intent issued under section 136d(b) of this title and of the proposed and final form of regulations issued under subsection (a) of this section within the same time periods as provided for the comments of the Secretary of Agriculture under such section 136d(b) and subsection (a) of this section. The time requirements for notices of intent and proposed and final forms of regulation may not be modified or waived unless in addition to meeting the requirements of section 136d(b) of this title or subsection (a) of this section, as applicable, the advisory panel has failed to comment on the proposed action within the prescribed time period or has agreed to the modification or waiver. The Administrator shall also solicit from the advisory panel comments, evaluations, and recommendations for operating guidelines to improve the effectiveness and quality of scientific analyses made by personnel of the Environmental Protection Agency that lead to decisions by the Administrator in carrying out the provisions of this subchapter. The comments, evaluations, and recommendations of the advisory panel submitted under this subsection and the response of the Administrator shall be published in the Federal Register in the same manner as provided for publication of the comments of the Secretary of Agriculture under such sections. The chairman of the advisory panel, after consultation with the Administrator, may create temporary subpanels on specific projects to assist the full advisory panel in expediting and preparing its evaluations, comments, and recommendations. The subpanels may be composed of scientists other than members of the advisory panel, as deemed necessary for the purpose of evaluating scientific studies relied upon by the Administrator with respect to proposed action. Such additional scientists shall be selected by the advisory panel. The panel referred to in this subsection shall consist of 7 members appointed by the Administrator from a list of 12 nominees, 6 nominated by the National Institutes of Health and 6 by the National Science Foundation utilizing a system of staggered terms of appointment. Members of the panel shall be selected on the basis of their professional qualifications to assess the effects of the impact of pesticides on health and the environment. To the extent feasible to insure multidisciplinary representation, the panel membership shall include representation for the disciplines of toxicology, pathology, environmental biology, and related sciences. If a vacancy occurs on the panel due to expiration of a term, resignation, or any other reason, each replacement shall be selected by the Administrator from a group of 4 nominees, 2 submitted by each of the nominating entities named in this subsection. The Administrator may extend the term of a panel member until the new member is appointed to fill the vacancy. If a vacancy occurs due to resignation, or reason other than expiration of a term, the Administrator shall appoint a member to serve during the unexpired term utilizing the nomination process set forth in this subsection. Should the list of nominees provided under this subsection be unsatisfactory, the Administrator may request an additional set of nominees from the nominating entities. The Administrator may require such information from the nominees to the advisory panel as the Administrator deems necessary, and the Administrator shall publish in the Federal Register the name, address, and professional affiliations of each nominee. Each member of the panel shall receive per diem compensation at a rate not in excess of that fixed for GS–18 of the General Schedule as may be determined by the Administrator, except that any such member who holds another office or position under the Federal Government the compensation for which exceeds such rate may elect to receive compensation at the rate provided for such other office or position in lieu of the compensation provided by this subsection. In order to assure the objectivity of the advisory panel, the Administrator shall promulgate regulations regarding conflicts of interest with respect to the members of the panel. The advisory panel established under this subsection shall be permanent. In performing the functions assigned by this subchapter, the panel shall consult and coordinate its activities with the Science Advisory Board established under the Environmental Research, Development, and Demonstration Authorization Act of 1978 [42 U.S.C.A. § 4365]. Whenever the Administrator exercises authority under section 136d(c) of this title to immediately suspend the registration of any pesticide to prevent an imminent hazard, the Administrator shall promptly submit to the advisory panel for comment, as to the impact on health and the environment, the action taken to suspend the registration of such pesticide.

(e) Peer review.—The Administrator shall, by written procedures, provide for peer review with respect to the design, protocols, and conduct of major scientific studies conducted under this subchapter by the Environmental Protection Agency or by any other Federal agency, any State or political subdivision thereof, or any institution or individual under grant, contract, or cooperative agreement from or with the Environmental Protection Agency. In such procedures, the Administrator shall also provide for peer review, using the advisory panel established under subsection (d) of this section or appropriate experts appointed by the Administrator from a current list of nominees maintained by such panel, with respect to the results of any such scientific studies relied upon by the Administrator with respect to actions the Administrator may take relating to the change in classification, suspension, or cancellation of a pesticide. Whenever the Administrator determines that circumstances do not permit the peer review of the results of any such scientific study prior to the Administrator's exercising authority under section 136d(c) of this title to immediately suspend the registration of any pesticide to prevent an imminent hazard, the Administrator shall promptly thereafter provide for the conduct of peer review as provided in this sentence. The evaluations and relevant documentation constituting the peer review that relate to the proposed scientific studies and the results of the completed scientific studies shall be included in the submission for comment forwarded by the Administrator to the advisory panel as provided in subsection (d) of this section. As used in this subsection, the term "peer review" shall mean an independent evaluation by scientific experts, either within or outside the Environmental Protection Agency, in the appropriate disciplines.

(June 25, 1947, c. 125, § 25, as added Oct. 21, 1972, Pub.L. 92–516, § 2, 86 Stat. 997, and amended Nov. 28, 1975, Pub.L. 94–140, §§ 2(a), 6, 7, 89 Stat. 751, 753; S.Res. 4, Feb. 4, 1977; Sept. 30, 1978, Pub.L. 95–396, § 23, 92 Stat. 836; Dec. 17, 1980, Pub.L. 96–539, §§ 1, 2(a), 4, 94 Stat. 3194, 3195; Dec. 2, 1983, Pub.L. 98–201, § 1, 97 Stat. 1379; Nov. 8, 1984, Pub.L. 98–620, Title IV, § 402(4)(D), 98 Stat. 3357; June 27, 1988, Pub.L. 100–352, § 6(i), 102 Stat. 664; Oct. 25, 1988, Pub.L. 100–532, Title VI, §§ 602, 605, Title VIII, § 801(n), 102 Stat. 2678, 2679, 2683; Dec. 13, 1991, Pub.L. 102–237, Title X, § 1006(b)(1), (2), 105 Stat. 1895.)

References in Text

The Environmental Research, Development, and Demonstration Authorization Act of 1978, referred to in subsec. (d), is Pub.L. 95–155, Nov. 8, 1977, 91 Stat. 1257, as amended. Provisions of the Act establishing the Science Advisory Board are classified to section 4365 of Title 42, The Public Health and Welfare. For complete classification of this Act to the Code, see Tables volume.

Effective Date of 1991 Amendment

Amendments by Pub.L. 102–237 effective Dec. 13, 1991, see section 1101(a) of Pub.L. 102–237, set out as a note under section 1421 of this title.

Transfer of Functions

Any reference in any provision of law enacted before Jan. 4, 1995, to a function, duty, or authority of the Clerk of the House of Representatives treated as referring, with respect to that function, duty, or authority, to the officer of the House of Representatives exercising that function, duty, or authority, as determined by the Committee on House Oversight of the House of Representatives, see section 2(1) of Pub.L. 104–14, set out as a note preceding section 21 of Title 2, The Congress.

CODE OF FEDERAL REGULATIONS

Acceptance of certain pesticides and disposal and storage of pesticides and containers, see 40 CFR 165.1 et seq.
Books and records of production and distribution, see 40 CFR 169.1 et seq.
Certification of applicators, see 40 CFR 171.1 et seq.
Debarment and suspension under EPA assistance programs, see 40 CFR 32.100 et seq.
Enforcement, see 40 CFR 162.1 et seq.
Exemption of Federal and State agencies under emergency conditions, see 40 CFR 166.1 et seq.
Experimental use permits, see 40 CFR 172.1 et seq.
Policies and procedures for State and local assistance, see 40 CFR 35.001 et seq.
Procurement of supplies, services, and construction under assistance agreements of Environmental Protection Agency, see 40 CFR 33.001 et seq.
Registration of pesticide-producing establishments, submission of reports, and labeling, see 40 CFR 167.1.
Rescission of State primary enforcement responsibility for pesticide use violations, see 40 CFR 173.1 et seq.
Worker protection standards, see 40 CFR 170.1 et seq.

LIBRARY REFERENCES

Agriculture ⇔9.
Health and Environment ⇔25.5(9).
C.J.S. Agriculture § 83 et seq.
C.J.S. Health and Environment § 65 et seq.

WESTLAW ELECTRONIC RESEARCH

Agricultural cases: 23k (add key number)

§ 136w–1. State primary enforcement responsibility [FIFRA § 26]

(a) In general.—For the purposes of this subchapter, a State shall have primary enforcement responsibility for pesticide use violations during any period for which the Administrator determines that such State—

(1) has adopted adequate pesticide use laws and regulations, except that the Administrator may not require a State to have pesticide use laws that are more stringent than this subchapter;

(2) has adopted and is implementing adequate procedures for the enforcement of such State laws and regulations; and

(3) will keep such records and make such reports showing compliance with paragraphs (1) and (2) of this subsection as the Administrator may require by regulation.

(b) Special rules.—Notwithstanding the provisions of subsection (a) of this section, any State that enters into a cooperative agreement with the Administrator under section 136u of this title for the enforcement of pesticide use restrictions shall have the primary enforcement responsibility for pesticide use violations. Any State that has a plan approved by the Administrator in accordance with the requirements of section 136i of this title that the Administrator determines meets the criteria set out in subsection (a) of this section shall have the primary enforcement responsibility for pesticide use violations. The Administrator shall make such determinations with respect to State plans under section 136i of this title in effect on September 30, 1978, not later than six months after that date.

(c) Administrator.—The Administrator shall have primary enforcement responsibility for those States that do not have primary enforcement responsibility under this subchapter. Notwithstanding the provisions of section 136(e)(1) of this title, during any period when the Administrator has such enforcement responsibility, section 136f(b) of this title shall apply to the books and records of commercial applicators and to any applicator who holds or applies pesticides, or uses dilutions of pesticides, only to provide a service of controlling pests without delivering any unapplied pesticide to any person so served, and section 136g(a) of this title shall apply to the establishment or other place where pesticides or devices are held for application by such persons with respect to pesticides or devices held for such application.

(June 25, 1947, c. 125, § 26, as added Sept. 30, 1978, Pub.L. 95–396, § 24(2), 92 Stat. 836, and amended Oct. 25, 1988, Pub.L. 100–532, Title VIII, § 801(*o*), (q)(1)(D), 102 Stat. 2683; Dec. 13, 1991, Pub.L. 102–237, Title X, § 1006(a)(11), 105 Stat. 1895.)

Effective Date of 1991 Amendment

Amendment by section 1006(a)(11) of Pub.L. 102–237 effective Dec. 13, 1991, see section 1101(a) of Pub.L. 102–237, set out as a note under section 1421 of this title.

LIBRARY REFERENCES

Agriculture ⇔9.
C.J.S. Agriculture § 83 et seq.

WESTLAW ELECTRONIC RESEARCH

Agricultural cases: 23k (add key number)

§ 136w-2. Failure by the State to assure enforcement of State pesticide use regulations [FIFRA § 27]

(a) Referral.—Upon receipt of any complaint or other information alleging or indicating a significant violation of the pesticide use provisions of this subchapter, the Administrator shall refer the matter to the appropriate State officials for their investigation of the matter consistent with the requirements of this subchapter. If, within thirty days, the State has not commenced appropriate enforcement action, the Administrator may act upon the complaint or information to the extent authorized under this subchapter.

(b) Notice.—Whenever the Administrator determines that a State having primary enforcement responsibility for pesticide use violations is not carrying out (or cannot carry out due to the lack of adequate legal authority) such responsibility, the Administrator shall notify the State. Such notice shall specify those aspects of the administration of the State program that are determined to be inadequate. The State shall have ninety days after receipt of the notice to correct any deficiencies. If after that time the Administrator determines that the State program remains inadequate, the Administrator may rescind, in whole or in part, the State's primary enforcement responsibility for pesticide use violations.

(c) Construction.—Neither section 136w-1 of this title nor this section shall limit the authority of the Administrator to enforce this subchapter, where the Administrator determines that emergency conditions exist that require immediate action on the part of the Administrator and the State authority is unwilling or unable adequately to respond to the emergency.

(June 25, 1947, c. 125, § 27, as added Sept. 30, 1978, Pub.L. 95-396, § 24(2), 92 Stat. 837, and amended Oct. 25, 1988, Pub.L. 100-532, Title VIII, § 801(p), 102 Stat. 2683.)

CODE OF FEDERAL REGULATIONS

Rescission of State primary enforcement responsibility for pesticide use violations, see 40 CFR 173.1 et seq.

LIBRARY REFERENCES

Agriculture ⇐9.
C.J.S. Agriculture § 83 et seq.

WESTLAW ELECTRONIC RESEARCH

Agricultural cases: 23k (add key number)

§ 136w-3. Identification of pests; cooperation with Department of Agriculture's program [FIFRA § 28]

(a) In general.—The Administrator, in coordination with the Secretary of Agriculture, shall identify those pests that must be brought under control. The Administrator shall also coordinate and cooperate with the Secretary of Agriculture's research and implementation programs to develop and improve the safe use and effectiveness of chemical, biological, and alternative methods to combat and control pests that reduce the quality and economical production and distribution of agricultural products to domestic and foreign consumers.

(b) Pest control availability.—

(1) In general.—The Administrator, in cooperation with the Secretary of Agriculture, shall identify—

(A) available methods of pest control by crop or animal;

(B) minor pest control problems, both in minor crops and minor or localized problems in major crops; and

(C) factors limiting the availability of specific pest control methods, such as resistance to control methods and regulatory actions limiting the availability of control methods.

(2) Report.—The Secretary of Agriculture shall, not later than 180 days after November 28, 1990, and annually thereafter, prepare a report and send the report to the Administrator. The report shall—

(A) contain the information described in paragraph (1) and the information required by section 5882 of this title;

(B) identify the crucial pest control needs where a shortage of control methods is indicated by the information described in paragraph (1); and

(C) describe in detail research and extension efforts designed to address the needs identified in subparagraph (B).

(c) Integrated pest management.—The Administrator, in cooperation with the Secretary of Agriculture, shall develop approaches to the control of pests based on integrated pest management that respond to the needs of producers, with a special emphasis on minor pests.

(June 25, 1947, c. 125, § 28, as added Sept. 30, 1978, Pub.L. 95-396, § 24(2), 92 Stat. 838, and amended Nov. 28, 1990, Pub.L. 101-624, Title XIV, § 1495, 104 Stat. 3629.)

Severability of Provisions

If any provision of Pub.L. 101-624 or the application thereof to any person or circumstance is held invalid, such invalidity not to affect other provisions or applications of Pub.L. 101-624 which can be given effect without regard to the invalid provision or application, see section 2519 of Pub.L. 101-624, set out as a note under section 1421 of this title.

LIBRARY REFERENCES

Agriculture ⇐9.

C.J.S. Agriculture § 83 et seq.

WESTLAW ELECTRONIC RESEARCH

Agricultural cases: 23k (add key number)

§ 136w–4. Annual report [FIFRA § 29]

The Administrator shall submit an annual report to Congress before February 16 of each year and the first report shall be due February 15, 1979. The report shall include the total number of applications for conditional registration under sections 136a(c)(7)(B) and 136a(c)(7)(C) of this title that were filed during the immediately preceding fiscal year, and, with respect to those applications approved, the Administrator shall report the Administrator's findings in each case, the conditions imposed and any modification of such conditions in each case, and the quantities produced of such pesticides.

(June 25, 1947, c. 125, § 29, as added Sept. 30, 1978, Pub.L. 95–396, § 24(2), 92 Stat. 838.)

WESTLAW ELECTRONIC RESEARCH

Agricultural cases: 23k (add key number)

§ 136x. Severability [FIFRA § 30]

If any provision of this subchapter or the application thereof to any person or circumstance is held invalid, the invalidity shall not affect other provisions or applications of this subchapter which can be given effect without regard to the invalid provision or application, and to this end the provisions of this subchapter are severable.

(June 25, 1947, c. 125, § 30, formerly § 26, as added Oct. 21, 1972, Pub.L. 92–516, § 2, 86 Stat. 998, and renumbered Sept. 30, 1978, Pub.L. 95–396, § 24(1), 92 Stat. 836.)

LIBRARY REFERENCES

Statutes ⇐64(2).

C.J.S. Statutes § 96 et seq.

WESTLAW ELECTRONIC RESEARCH

Agricultural cases: 23k (add key number)

§ 136y. Authorization of appropriations [FIFRA § 31]

There is authorized to be appropriated to carry out this subchapter (other than section 136u(a) of this title)—

(1) $83,000,000 for fiscal year 1989, of which not more than $13,735,500 shall be available for research under this subchapter;

(2) $95,000,000 for fiscal year 1990, of which not more than $14,343,600 shall be available for research under this subchapter; and

(3) $95,000,000 for fiscal year 1991, of which not more than $14,978,200 shall be available for research under this subchapter.

(June 25, 1947, c. 125, § 31, formerly § 27, as added Oct. 21, 1972, Pub.L. 92–516, § 2, 86 Stat. 998, amended July 2, 1975, Pub.L. 94–51, 89 Stat. 257; Oct. 10, 1975, Pub.L. 94–109, 89 Stat. 571; Nov. 28, 1975, Pub.L. 94–140, § 3, 89 Stat. 752, and renumbered and amended Sept. 30, 1978, Pub.L. 95–396, §§ 24(1), 25, 92 Stat. 836, 838; Dec. 17, 1980, Pub.L. 96–539, § 3, 94 Stat. 3195; Dec. 2, 1983, Pub.L. 98–201, § 2, 97 Stat. 1380; Dec. 23, 1985, Pub.L. 99–198, Title XVII, § 1768, 99 Stat. 1656; Oct. 25, 1988, Pub.L. 100–532, Title VII, § 701, 102 Stat. 2679.)

Effective Date of 1988 Amendment

Section 701 of Pub.L. 100–532 provided in part that amendment by Pub.L. 100–532 was effective Oct. 1, 1988.

LIBRARY REFERENCES

United States ⇐85.
C.J.S. United States § 123.

WESTLAW ELECTRONIC RESEARCH

Agricultural cases: 23k (add key number)

TITLE 15—COMMERCE AND TRADE

TOXIC SUBSTANCES CONTROL

TOXIC SUBSTANCES CONTROL ACT [TSCA § ______]

(15 U.S.C.A. §§ 2601 to 2692)

CHAPTER 53—TOXIC SUBSTANCES CONTROL

SUBCHAPTER I—CONTROL OF TOXIC SUBSTANCES

Sec.
2601. Findings, policy, and intent.
(a) Findings.
(b) Policy.
(c) Intent of Congress.
2602. Definitions.
2603. Testing of chemical substances and mixtures.
(a) Testing requirements.
(b) Testing requirement rule.
(c) Exemption.
(d) Notice.
(e) Priority list.
(f) Required actions.
(g) Petition for standards for the development of test data.
2604. Manufacturing and processing notices.
(a) In general.
(b) Submission of test data.
(c) Extension of notice period.
(d) Content of notice; publications in the Federal Register.
(e) Regulation pending development of information.
(f) Protection against unreasonable risks.
(g) Statement of reasons for not taking action.
(h) Exemptions.
(i) Definitions.
2605. Regulation of hazardous chemical substances and mixtures.
(a) Scope of regulation.
(b) Quality control.
(c) Promulgation of subsection (a) rules.
(d) Effective date.
(e) Polychlorinated biphenyls.
2606. Imminent hazards.
(a) Action authorized and required.
(b) Relief authorized.
(c) Venue and consolidation.
(d) Action under section 2605 of this title.
(e) Representation.
(f) Definition.
2607. Reporting and retention of information.
(a) Reports.
(b) Inventory.
(c) Records.
(d) Health and safety studies.

Sec.
2607. Reporting and retention of information.
(e) Notice to Administrator of substantial risks.
(f) Definitions.
2608. Relationship to other Federal laws.
(a) Laws not administered by the Administrator.
(b) Laws administered by the Administrator.
(c) Occupational safety and health.
(d) Coordination.
2609. Research, development, collection, dissemination, and utilization of data.
(a) Authority.
(b) Data systems.
(c) Screening techniques.
(d) Monitoring.
(e) Basic research.
(f) Training.
(g) Exchange of research and development results.
2610. Inspections and subpoenas.
(a) In general.
(b) Scope.
(c) Subpoenas.
2611. Exports.
(a) In general.
(b) Notice.
2612. Entry into customs territory of the United States.
(a) In general.
(b) Rules.
2613. Disclosure of data.
(a) In general.
(b) Data from health and safety studies.
(c) Designation and release of confidential data.
(d) Criminal penalty for wrongful disclosure.
(e) Access by Congress.
2614. Prohibited acts.
2615. Penalties.
(a) Civil.
(b) Criminal.
2616. Specific enforcement and seizure.
(a) Specific enforcement.
(b) Seizure.
2617. Preemption.
(a) Effect on State law.
(b) Exemption.
2618. Judicial review.
(a) In general.
(b) Additional submissions and presentations; modifications.
(c) Standard of review.
(d) Fees and costs.

Sec.
2618. Judicial review.
(e) Other remedies.
2619. Citizens' civil actions.
(a) In general.
(b) Limitation.
(c) General.
(d) Consolidation.
2620. Citizens' petitions.
(a) In general.
(b) Procedures.
2621. National defense waiver.
2622. Employee protection.
(a) In general.
(b) Remedy.
(c) Review.
(d) Enforcement.
(e) Exclusion.
2623. Employment effects.
(a) In general.
(b) Investigations.
2624. Studies.
(a) Indemnification study.
(b) Classification, storage, and retrieval study.
2625. Administration.
(a) Cooperation of Federal agencies.
(b) Fees.
(c) Action with respect to categories.
(d) Assistance office.
(e) Financial disclosures.
(f) Statement of basis and purpose.
(g) Assistant Administrator.
2626. Development and evaluation of test methods.
(a) In general.
(b) Approval by Secretary.
(c) Repealed.
2627. State programs.
(a) In general.
(b) Approval by Administrator.
(c) Annual reports.
(d) Authorization.
2628. Authorization of appropriations.
2629. Annual report.

SUBCHAPTER II–ASBESTOS HAZARD EMERGENCY RESPONSE

2641. Congressional findings and declaration of purpose.
(a) Findings.
(b) Purpose.
2642. Definitions.
2643. EPA regulations.
(a) In general.
(b) Inspection.
(c) Circumstances requiring response actions.
(d) Response actions.
(e) Implementation.
(f) Operations and maintenance.
(g) Periodic surveillance.
(h) Transportation and disposal.
(i) Management plans.
(j) Changes in regulations.
(k) Changes in guidance document.
(*l*) Treatment of Department of Defense schools.
(m) Waiver.
2644. Requirements if EPA fails to promulgate regulations.
(a) In general.
Sec.
2644. Requirements if EPA fails to promulgate regulations.
(b) Inspection.
(c) Operation and maintenance.
(d) Management plan.
(e) Building occupant protection.
(f) Transportation and disposal.
2645. Submission to State Governor.
(a) Submission.
(b) Governor requirements.
(c) Management plan review.
(d) Deferral of submission.
(e) Status reports.
2646. Contractor and laboratory accreditation.
(a) Contractor accreditation.
(b) Accreditation by State.
(c) Accreditation by Administrator-approved course.
(d) Laboratory accreditation.
(e) Financial assistance contingent on use of accredited persons.
(f) List of EPA–approved courses.
2647. Enforcement.
(a) Penalties.
(b) Relationship to subchapter I of this chapter.
(c) Enforcement considerations.
(d) Citizen complaints.
(e) Citizen petitions.
(f) Citizen civil actions with respect to EPA regulations.
(f) Failure to obtain accreditation; penalty.
2648. Emergency authority.
(a) Emergency action.
(b) Injunctive relief.
2649. State and Federal law.
(a) No preemption.
(b) Cost and damage awards.
(c) State may establish more requirements.
(d) No Federal cause of action.
(e) Intent of Congress.
2650. Asbestos contractors and local educational agencies.
(a) Study.
(b) State action.
2651. Public protection.
(a) Public protection.
(b) Labor Department review.
2652. Asbestos Ombudsman.
(a) Appointment.
(b) Duties.
2653. EPA Study of asbestos-containing material in public buildings.
2654. Transitional rules.
2655. Worker protection.
(a) Prohibition on certain activities.
(b) Employee training and equipment.
(c) Definition of emergency repair.
2656. Training grants.
(a) Grants.
(b) Authorization.

SUBCHAPTER III—INDOOR RADON ABATEMENT

2661. National goal.
2662. Definitions.
2663. EPA Citizen's Guide.
(a) Publication.
(b) Information included.
2664. Model construction standards and techniques.

Sec.
2665. Technical assistance to States for radon programs.
(a) Required activities.
(b) Discretionary assistance.
(c) Information provided to professional organizations.
(d) Proficiency rating program and training seminar.
(e) Authorization.
(f) Redesignated (e).
2666. Grant assistance to States for radon programs.
(a) In general.
(b) Application.
(c) Eligible activities.
(d) Preference to certain States.
(e) Priority activities and projects.
(f) Federal share.
(g) Assistance to local governments.
(h) Information.
(i) Limitations.
(j) Authorization.
2667. Radon in schools.
(a) Authority.
(b) Authorization.
2668. Regional radon training centers.
(a) Funding programs.
(b) Purpose of the centers.
(c) Applications.
(d) Selection criteria.
(e) Termination of funding.
(f) Authorization.
2669. Study of radon in Federal buildings.
(a) Study requirements.
(b) High-risk Federal buildings.
(c) Study designs.
(d) Information on risks and testing.
(e) Study deadline.
(f) Report to Congress.
2670. Regulations.
2671. Additional authorizations.

SUBCHAPTER IV—LEAD EXPOSURE REDUCTION
2681. Definitions.

Sec.
2682. Lead-based paint activities training and certification.
(a) Regulations.
(b) Lead-based paint activities.
(c) Renovation and remodeling.
2683. Identification of dangerous levels of lead.
2684. Authorized State programs.
(a) Approval.
(b) Approval of disapproval.
(c) Withdrawal of authorization.
(d) Model State program.
(e) Other State requirements.
(f) State and local certification.
(g) Grants to States.
(h) Enforcement by Administrator.
2685. Lead abatement and measurement.
(a) Program to promote lead exposure abatement.
(b) Standards for environmental sampling laboratories.
(c) Exposure studies.
(d) Public education.
(e) Technical assistance.
(f) Products for lead-based paint activities.
2686. Lead hazard information pamphlet.
(a) Lead hazard information pamphlet.
(b) Renovation of target housing.
2687. Regulations.
2688. Control of lead-based paint hazards at Federal facilities.
2689. Prohibited acts.
2690. Relationship to other Federal law.
2691. General provisions relating to administrative proceedings.
(a) Applicability.
(b) Rulemaking docket.
(c) Inspection and copying.
(d) Explanation.
(e) Judicial review.
(f) Effective date.
2692. Authorization of appropriations.

Related Provisions

See, also, Environmental Pesticide Control, 7 U.S.C.A. § 136 et seq., ante.

West's Federal Forms

Claim to article arrested, see § 11227.
Judgment of condemnation, forfeiture and destruction, see § 4543.
Jurisdiction and venue in district courts, see § 1003 et seq.
Service of process, see § 1201 et seq.
Subpoenas, see § 3981 et seq.

CODE OF FEDERAL REGULATIONS

Asbestos, see 40 CFR 763.100.
Asbestos—
Recordkeeping, see 40 CFR 763.114.
Chemical imports and exports, see 40 CFR 707.60 et seq.
Premanufacture notification, exemptions, see 40 CFR 723.175.
Rulemaking procedures, see 40 CFR 750.1 et seq.

WESTLAW ELECTRONIC RESEARCH

See WESTLAW guide following the Explanation pages of this pamphlet.

SUBCHAPTER I—CONTROL OF TOXIC SUBSTANCES

§ 2601. Findings, policy, and intent [TSCA § 2]

(a) Findings

The Congress finds that—

(1) human beings and the environment are being exposed each year to a large number of chemical substances and mixtures;

(2) among the many chemical substances and mixtures which are constantly being developed and produced, there are some whose manufacture, processing, distribution in commerce, use, or disposal may present an unreasonable risk of injury to health or the environment; and

(3) the effective regulation of interstate commerce in such chemical substances and mixtures also necessitates the regulation of intrastate commerce in such chemical substances and mixtures.

(b) Policy

It is the policy of the United States that—

(1) adequate data should be developed with respect to the effect of chemical substances and mixtures on health and the environment and that the development of such data should be the responsibility of those who manufacture and those who process such chemical substances and mixtures;

(2) adequate authority should exist to regulate chemical substances and mixtures which present an unreasonable risk of injury to health or the environment, and to take action with respect to chemical substances and mixtures which are imminent hazards; and

(3) authority over chemical substances and mixtures should be exercised in such a manner as not to impede unduly or create unnecessary economic barriers to technological innovation while fulfilling the primary purpose of this chapter to assure that such innovation and commerce in such chemical substances and mixtures do not present an unreasonable risk of injury to health or the environment.

(c) Intent of Congress

It is the intent of Congress that the Administrator shall carry out this chapter in a reasonable and prudent manner, and that the Administrator shall consider the environmental, economic, and social impact of any action the Administrator takes or proposes to take under this chapter.

(Oct. 11, 1976, Pub.L. 94–469, Title I, § 2, 90 Stat. 2003, redesignated Title I, Oct. 22, 1986, Pub.L. 99–519, § 3(c)(1), 100 Stat. 2989.)

Effective Date

Section 31 of Pub.L. 94–469, Oct. 11, 1976, 90 Stat. 2051, provided that: "Except as provided in section 4(f) [section 2603(f) of this title], this Act [enacting this subchapter] shall take effect on January 1, 1977."

Short Title of 1992 Amendments

Pub.L. 102–550, Title X, § 1021(c), Oct. 28, 1992, 106 Stat. 3924, provided that: "This subtitle [enacting subchapter IV of this chapter and amending sections 2606, 2610, 2612, 2615, 2616, 2618, and 2619 of this title] may be cited as the 'Lead–Based Paint Exposure Reduction Act'."

Short Title

Section 1 of Pub.L. 94–469, Oct. 11, 1976, 90 Stat. 2003, provided that: "This Act [enacting this chapter] may be cited as the 'Toxic Substances Control Act'."

West's Federal Practice Manual

Pesticides and toxic substances, see § 4385.10.

CODE OF FEDERAL REGULATIONS

Policies and procedures for the awarding of grants, see 40 CFR 30.100 et seq.

LAW REVIEW COMMENTARIES

Compensating manufacturers submitting health and safety data to support product registrations after Ruckelshaus v. Monsanto. 61 Ind.L.J. 189 (1985–1986).

Criminal sanctions under federal and state environmental statutes. Richard H. Allan, 14 Ecology L.Q. 117 (1987).

Economizing on the sins of our past: Cleaning up our hazardous wastes. Barbara Ann White, 25 Houston L.Rev. 899 (1988).

Environmental auditing: What your client doesn't know hurts the most. William L. Earl, 60 Fla.Bar J. 47 (1986).

Environmental claims in bankruptcy: Policy conflicts, procedural pitfalls and problematic precedent. Thomas G. Gruenert, 32 S.Tex. L.Rev. 399 (1991).

Environmental Law/Annual survey of significant developments. Thomas J. Elliott, 58 Pa.B.A.Q. 107 (1987).

Hazardous wastes in New Jersey: An overview. Anne F. Morris, 38 Rutgers L.Rev. 623 (1986).

Interstate waste: A key issue in resolving the national hazardous waste capacity crisis. B.J. Wynne, III and Terri Hamby, 32 S.Tex. L.Rev. 601 (1991).

Life and times of a CERCLA claim in bankruptcy: An examination of hazardous waste liability in bankruptcy proceedings. 67 St. John's L.Rev. 55 (1993).

Limiting lender liability under CERCLA by administrative rule. Frona M. Powell, 75 Marq.L.Rev. 139 (1991).

Long-range planning in environmental and health regulatory agencies. Richard N.L. Andrews, 20 Ecology L.Q. 515 (1993).

"More good than harm": A first principle for environmental agencies and reviewing courts. Edward W. Warren and Gary E. Marchant, 20 Ecology L.Q. 379 (1993).

Prosecution of corporations and corporate officers for environmental crimes: Limiting one's exposure for environmental criminal liability. Kenneth A. Hodson, Sarah N. McGiffert and Marianne T. Bayardi, 34 Ariz.L.Rev. 553 (1992).

Responding to a government environmental investigation: Shaping the defense. Francis J. Burke, Jr., Karen A. Potts, Leigh Lani Brown, Robin L. De Respino and Michael R. Hall, 34 Ariz.L.Rev. 509 (1992).

Secured creditor exemption under CERCLA. Robert J. Vincze, 62 J.Kan.B.A. 18 (1993).

Toward resolution of insurance coverage questions in toxic tort litigation. Janine Bauer and Arnold Lakind, 38 Rutgers L.Rev. 677 (1986).

Toxic tort litigation and the causation element: Is there any hope of reconciliation? Ora Fred Harris, Jr., 40 Southwestern (Tex.) L.J. 909 (1986).

LIBRARY REFERENCES

Health and Environment ⟹25.5(3).
C.J.S. Health and Environment § 91 et seq.

§ 2602. Definitions [TSCA § 3]

As used in this chapter:

(1) the [1] term "Administrator" means the Administrator of the Environmental Protection Agency.

(2)(A) Except as provided in subparagraph (B), the term "chemical substance" means any organic or inorganic substance of a particular molecular identity, including—

(i) any combination of such substances occurring in whole or in part as a result of a chemical reaction or occurring in nature and

(ii) any element or uncombined radical.

(B) Such term does not include—

(i) any mixture,

(ii) any pesticide (as defined in the Federal Insecticide, Fungicide, and Rodenticide Act [7 U.S.C.A. § 136 et seq.]) when manufactured, processed, or distributed in commerce for use as a pesticide,

(iii) tobacco or any tobacco product,

(iv) any source material, special nuclear material, or byproduct material (as such terms are defined in the Atomic Energy Act of 1954 [42 U.S.C.A. § 2011 et seq.] and regulations issued under such Act),

(v) any article the sale of which is subject to the tax imposed by section 4181 of the Internal Revenue Code of 1986 [26 U.S.C.A. § 4181] (determined without regard to any exemptions from such tax provided by section 4182 or 4221 or any other provision of such Code), and

(vi) any food, food additive, drug, cosmetic, or device (as such terms are defined in section 201 of the Federal Food, Drug, and Cosmetic Act [21 U.S.C.A. § 321]) when manufactured, processed, or distributed in commerce for use as a food, food additive, drug, cosmetic, or device.

The term "food" as used in clause (vi) of this subparagraph includes poultry and poultry products (as defined in sections 4(e) and 4(f) of the Poultry Products Inspection Act [21 U.S.C.A. § 453(e) and (f)]), meat and meat food products (as defined in section 1(j) of the Federal Meat Inspection Act [21 U.S.C.A. § 601(j)]), and eggs and egg products (as defined in section 4 of the Egg Products Inspection Act [21 U.S.C.A. § 1033]).

(3) The term "commerce" means trade, traffic, transportation, or other commerce (A) between a place in a State and any place outside of such State, or (B) which affects trade, traffic, transportation, or commerce described in clause (A).

(4) The terms "distribute in commerce" and "distribution in commerce" when used to describe an action taken with respect to a chemical substance or mixture or article containing a substance or mixture mean to sell, or the sale of, the substance, mixture, or article in commerce; to introduce or deliver for introduction into commerce, or the introduction or delivery for introduction into commerce of, the substance, mixture, or article; or to hold, or the holding of, the substance, mixture, or article after its introduction into commerce.

(5) The term "environment" includes water, air, and land and the interrelationship which exists among and between water, air, and land and all living things.

(6) The term "health and safety study" means any study of any effect of a chemical substance or mixture on health or the environment or on both, including underlying data and epidemiological studies, studies of occupational exposure to a chemical substance or mixture, toxicological, clinical, and ecological studies of a chemical substance or mixture, and any test performed pursuant to this chapter.

(7) The term "manufacture" means to import into the customs territory of the United States (as defined in general note 2 of the Harmonized Tariff Schedule of the United States), produce, or manufacture.

(8) The term "mixture" means any combination of two or more chemical substances if the combination does not occur in nature and is not, in whole or in part, the result of a chemical reaction; except that such term does include any combination which occurs, in whole or in part, as a result of a chemical reaction if none of the chemical substances comprising the combination is a new chemical substance and if the combination could have been manufactured for commercial purposes without a chemical reaction at the time the chemical substances comprising the combination were combined.

(9) The term "new chemical substance" means any chemical substance which is not included in the chemical substance list compiled and published under section 2607(b) of this title.

(10) The term "process" means the preparation of a chemical substance or mixture, after its manufacture, for distribution in commerce—

(A) in the same form or physical state as, or in a different form or physical state from, that in which it was received by the person so preparing such substance or mixture, or

(B) as part of an article containing the chemical substance or mixture.

(11) The term "processor" means any person who processes a chemical substance or mixture.

(12) The term "standards for the development of test data" means a prescription of—

(A) the—

(i) health and environmental effects, and

(ii) information relating to toxicity, persistence, and other characteristics which affect health and the environment, for which test data for a chemical substance or mixture are to be developed and any analysis that is to be performed on such data, and

(B) to the extent necessary to assure that data respecting such effects and characteristics are reliable and adequate—

(i) the manner in which such data are to be developed,

(ii) the specification of any test protocol or methodology to be employed in the development of such data, and

(iii) such other requirements as are necessary to provide such assurance.

(13) The term "State" means any State of the United States, the District of Columbia, the Commonwealth of Puerto Rico, the Virgin Islands, Guam, the Canal Zone, American Samoa, the Northern Mariana Islands, or any other territory or possession of the United States.

(14) The term "United States", when used in the geographic sense, means all of the States.

(Oct. 11, 1976, Pub.L. 94–469, Title I, § 3, 90 Stat. 2004; Oct. 22, 1986, Pub.L. 99–514, § 2, 100 Stat. 2095; redesignated Title I, Oct. 22, 1986, Pub.L. 99–519, § 3(c)(1), 100 Stat. 2989, and amended Pub.L. 100–418, Title I, § 1214(e)(1), Aug. 23, 1988, 102 Stat. 1156.)

[1] So in original.

LAW REVIEW COMMENTARIES

Federal regulation of agricultural biotechnologies. Thomas O. McGarity, 20 U.Mich.J.L.Ref. 1089 (1987).

LIBRARY REFERENCES

Health and Environment ⚷25.5(9).
C.J.S. Health and Environment § 65 et seq.

§ 2603. Testing of chemical substances and mixtures [TSCA § 4]

(a) Testing requirements

If the Administrator finds that—

(1)(A)(i) the manufacture, distribution in commerce, processing, use, or disposal of a chemical substance or mixture, or that any combination of such activities, may present an unreasonable risk of injury to health or the environment,

(ii) there are insufficient data and experience upon which the effects of such manufacture, distribution in commerce, processing, use, or disposal of such substance or mixture or of any combination of such activities on health or the environment can reasonably be determined or predicted, and

(iii) testing of such substance or mixture with respect to such effects is necessary to develop such data; or

(B)(i) a chemical substance or mixture is or will be produced in substantial quantities, and (I) it enters or may reasonably be anticipated to enter the environment in substantial quantities or (II) there is or may be significant or substantial human exposure to such substance or mixture,

(ii) there are insufficient data and experience upon which the effects of the manufacture, distribution in commerce, processing, use, or disposal of such substance or mixture or of any combination of such activities on health or the environment can reasonably be determined or predicted, and

(iii) testing of such substance or mixture with respect to such effects is necessary to develop such data; and

(2) in the case of a mixture, the effects which the mixture's manufacture, distribution in commerce, processing, use, or disposal or any combination of such activities may have on health or the environment may not be reasonably and more efficiently determined or predicted by testing the chemical substances which comprise the mixture;

the Administrator shall by rule require that testing be conducted on such substance or mixture to develop data with respect to the health and environmental effects for which there is an insufficiency of data and experience and which are relevant to a determination that the manufacture, distribution in commerce, processing, use, or disposal of such substance or mixture, or that any combination of such activities, does or does not present an unreasonable risk of injury to health or the environment.

(b) Testing requirement rule

(1) A rule under subsection (a) of this section shall include—

(A) identification of the chemical substance or mixture for which testing is required under the rule,

(B) standards for the development of test data for such substance or mixture, and

(C) with respect to chemical substances which are not new chemical substances and to mixtures, a specification of the period (which period may not be of unreasonable duration) within which the persons required to conduct the testing shall submit to the Administrator data developed in accordance with the standards referred to in subparagraph (B).

In determining the standards and period to be included, pursuant to subparagraphs (B) and (C), in a rule under subsection (a) of this section, the Administrator's considerations shall include the relative costs of the various test protocols and methodologies which may be required under the rule and the reasonably foreseeable availability of the facilities and personnel needed to perform the testing required under the rule. Any such rule may require the submission to the Administrator of preliminary data during the period prescribed under subparagraph (C).

(2)(A) The health and environmental effects for which standards for the development of test data may be prescribed include carcinogenesis, mutagenesis, teratogenesis, behavioral disorders, cumulative or synergistic effects, and any other effect which may present an unreasonable risk of injury to health or the environment. The characteristics of chemical substances and mixtures for which such standards may be prescribed include persistence, acute toxicity, subacute toxicity, chronic toxicity, and any other characteristic which may present such a risk. The methodologies that may be prescribed in such standards include epidemiologic studies, serial or hierarchical tests, in vitro tests, and whole animal tests, except that before prescribing epidemiologic studies of employees, the Administrator shall consult with the Director of the National Institute for Occupational Safety and Health.

(B) From time to time, but not less than once each 12 months, the Administrator shall review the adequacy of the standards for development of data prescribed in rules under subsection (a) of this section and shall, if necessary, institute proceedings to make appropriate revisions of such standards.

(3)(A) A rule under subsection (a) of this section respecting a chemical substance or mixture shall require the persons described in subparagraph (B) to conduct tests and submit data to the Administrator on such substance or mixture, except that the Administrator may permit two or more of such persons to designate one such person or a qualified third party to conduct such tests and submit such data on behalf of the persons making the designation.

(B) The following persons shall be required to conduct tests and submit data on a chemical substance or mixture subject to a rule under subsection (a) of this section:

(i) Each person who manufactures or intends to manufacture such substance or mixture if the Administrator makes a finding described in subsection (a)(1)(A)(ii) or (a)(1)(B)(ii) of this section with respect to the manufacture of such substance or mixture.

(ii) Each person who processes or intends to process such substance or mixture if the Administrator makes a finding described in subsection (a)(1)(A)(ii) or (a)(1)(B)(ii) of this section with respect to the processing of such substance or mixture.

(iii) Each person who manufactures or processes or intends to manufacture or process such substance or mixture if the Administrator makes a finding described in subsection (a)(1)(A)(ii) or (a)(1)(B)(ii) of this section with respect to the distribution in commerce, use, or disposal of such substance or mixture.

(4) Any rule under subsection (a) of this section requiring the testing of and submission of data for a particular chemical substance or mixture shall expire at the end of the reimbursement period (as defined in subsection (c)(3)(B) of this section) which is applicable to test data for such substance or mixture unless the Administrator repeals the rule before such date; and a rule under subsection (a) of this section requiring the testing of and submission of data for a category of chemical substances or mixtures shall expire with respect to a chemical substance or mixture included in the category at the end of the reimbursement period (as so defined) which is applicable to test data for such substance or mixture unless the Administrator before such date repeals the application of the rule to such substance or mixture or repeals the rule.

(5) Rules issued under subsection (a) of this section (and any substantive amendment thereto or repeal thereof) shall be promulgated pursuant to section 553 of Title 5 except that (A) the Administrator shall give interested persons an opportunity for the oral presentation of data, views, or arguments, in addition to an opportunity to make written submissions; (B) a transcript shall be made of any oral presentation; and (C) the Administrator shall make and publish with the rule the findings described in paragraph (1)(A) or (1)(B) of subsection (a) of this section and, in the case of a rule respecting a mixture, the finding described in paragraph (2) of such subsection.

(c) Exemption

(1) Any person required by a rule under subsection (a) of this section to conduct tests and submit data on a chemical substance or mixture may apply to the Administrator (in such form and manner as the Administrator shall prescribe) for an exemption from such requirement.

(2) If, upon receipt of an application under paragraph (1), the Administrator determines that—

(A) the chemical substance or mixture with respect to which such application was submitted is equivalent to a chemical substance or mixture for which data has been submitted to the Administrator in accordance with a rule under subsection (a) of this section or for which data is being developed pursuant to such a rule, and

(B) submission of data by the applicant on such substance or mixture would be duplicative of data which has been submitted to the Administrator in accordance with such rule or which is being developed pursuant to such rule,

the Administrator shall exempt, in accordance with paragraph (3) or (4), the applicant from conducting tests and submitting data on such substance or mixture under the rule with respect to which such application was submitted.

(3)(A) If the exemption under paragraph (2) of any person from the requirement to conduct tests and submit test data on a chemical substance or mixture is granted on the basis of the existence of previously submitted test data and if such exemption is granted during the reimbursement period for such test data (as prescribed by subparagraph (B)), then (unless such person and the persons referred to in clauses (i) and (ii) agree on the amount and method of reimbursement) the Administrator shall order the person granted the exemption to provide fair and equitable reimbursement (in an amount determined under rules of the Administrator)—

(i) to the person who previously submitted such test data, for a portion of the costs incurred by such person in complying with the requirement to submit such data, and

(ii) to any other person who has been required under this subparagraph to contribute with respect to such costs, for a portion of the amount such person was required to contribute.

In promulgating rules for the determination of fair and equitable reimbursement to the persons described in clauses (i) and (ii) for costs incurred with respect to a chemical substance or mixture, the Administrator shall, after consultation with the Attorney General and the Federal Trade Commission, consider all relevant factors, including the effect on the competitive position of the person required to provide reimbursement in relation to the person to be reimbursed and the share of the market for such substance or mixture of the person required to provide reimbursement in relation to the share of such market of the persons to be reimbursed. An order under this subparagraph shall, for purposes of judicial review, be considered final agency action.

(B) For purposes of subparagraph (A), the reimbursement period for any test data for a chemical substance or mixture is a period—

(i) beginning on the date such data is submitted in accordance with a rule promulgated under subsection (a) of this section, and

(ii) ending—

(I) five years after the date referred to in clause (i), or

(II) at the expiration of a period which begins on the date referred to in clause (i) and which is equal to the period which the Administrator determines was necessary to develop such data,

whichever is later.

(4)(A) If the exemption under paragraph (2) of any person from the requirement to conduct tests and submit test data on a chemical substance or mixture is granted on the basis of the fact that test data is being developed by one or more persons pursuant to a rule promulgated under subsection (a) of this section, then (unless such person and the persons referred to in clauses (i) and (ii) agree on the amount and method of reimbursement) the Administrator shall order the person granted the exemption to provide fair and equitable reimbursement (in an amount determined under rules of the Administrator)—

(i) to each such person who is developing such test data, for a portion of the costs incurred by each such person in complying with such rule, and

(ii) to any other person who has been required under this subparagraph to contribute with respect to the costs of complying with such rule, for a portion of the amount such person was required to contribute.

In promulgating rules for the determination of fair and equitable reimbursement to the persons described in clauses (i) and (ii) for costs incurred with respect to a chemical substance or mixture, the Administrator shall, after consultation with the Attorney General and the Federal Trade Commission, consider the factors described in the second sentence of paragraph (3)(A). An order under this subparagraph shall, for purposes of judicial review, be considered final agency action.

(B) If any exemption is granted under paragraph (2) on the basis of the fact that one or more persons are developing test data pursuant to a rule promulgated under subsection (a) of this section and if after such exemption is granted the Administrator determines that no such person has complied with such rule, the Administrator shall (i) after providing written notice to the person who holds such exemption and an opportunity for a hearing, by order terminate such exemption, and (ii) notify in writing such person of the requirements of the rule with respect to which such exemption was granted.

(d) Notice

Upon the receipt of any test data pursuant to a rule under subsection (a) of this section, the Administrator shall publish a notice of the receipt of such data in the Federal Register within 15 days of its receipt. Subject to section 2613 of this title, each such notice shall (1) identify the chemical substance or mixture for which data have been received; (2) list the uses or intended uses of such substance or mixture and the information required by the applicable standards for the development of test data; and (3) describe the nature of the test data developed. Except as otherwise provided in section 2613 of this title, such data shall be made available by the Administrator for examination by any person.

(e) Priority list

(1)(A) There is established a committee to make recommendations to the Administrator respecting the chemical substances and mixtures to which the Administrator should give priority consideration for the promulgation of a rule under subsection (a) of this section. In making such a recommendation with respect to any chemical substance or mixture, the committee shall consider all relevant factors, including—

(i) the quantities in which the substance or mixture is or will be manufactured,

(ii) the quantities in which the substance or mixture enters or will enter the environment,

(iii) the number of individuals who are or will be exposed to the substance or mixture in their places of employment and the duration of such exposure,

(iv) the extent to which human beings are or will be exposed to the substance or mixture,

(v) the extent to which the substance or mixture is closely related to a chemical substance or mixture which is known to present an unreasonable risk of injury to health or the environment,

(vi) the existence of data concerning the effects of the substance or mixture on health or the environment,

(vii) the extent to which testing of the substance or mixture may result in the development of data upon which the effects of the substance or mixture on health or the environment can reasonably be determined or predicted, and

(viii) the reasonably foreseeable availability of facilities and personnel for performing testing on the substance or mixture.

The recommendations of the committee shall be in the form of a list of chemical substances and mixtures which shall be set forth, either by individual substance or mixture or by groups of substances or mixtures, in the order in which the committee determines the Administrator should take action under subsection (a) of this section with respect to the substances and mixtures. In establishing such list, the committee shall give priority attention to those chemical substances and mixtures which are known to cause or contribute to or which are suspected of causing or contributing to cancer, gene mutations, or birth defects. The committee shall designate chemical substances and mixtures on the list with respect to which the committee determines the Administrator should, within 12 months of the date on which such substances and mixtures are first designated, initiate a proceeding under subsection (a) of this section. The total number of chemical substances and mixtures on the list which are designated under the preceding sentence may not, at any time, exceed 50.

(B) As soon as practicable but not later than nine months after January 1, 1977, the committee shall publish in the Federal Register and transmit to the Administrator the list and designations required by subparagraph (A) together with the reasons for the committee's inclusion of each chemical substance or mixture on the list. At least every six months after the date of the transmission to the Administrator of the list pursuant to the preceeding[1] sentence, the committee shall make such revisions in the list as it determines to be necessary and shall transmit them to the Administrator together with the committee's reasons for the revisions. Upon receipt of any such revision, the Administrator shall publish in the Federal Register the list with such revision, the reasons for such revision, and the designations made under subparagraph (A). The Administrator shall provide reasonable opportunity to any interested person to file with the Administrator written comments on the committee's list, any revision of such list by the committee, and designations made by the committee, and shall make such comments available to the public. Within the 12-month period beginning on the date of the first inclusion on the list of a chemical substance or mixture designated by the committee under subparagraph (A) the Administrator shall with respect to such chemical substance or mixture either initiate a rulemaking proceeding under subsection (a) of this section or if such a proceeding is not initiated within such period, publish in the Federal Register the Administrator's reason for not initiating such a proceeding.

(2)(A) The committee established by paragraph (1)(A) shall consist of eight members as follows:

(i) One member appointed by the Administrator from the Environmental Protection Agency.

(ii) One member appointed by the Secretary of Labor from officers or employees of the Department of Labor engaged in the Secretary's activities under the Occupational Safety and Health Act of 1970 [29 U.S.C.A. § 651 et seq.].

(iii) One member appointed by the Chairman of the Council on Environmental Quality from the Council or its officers or employees.

(iv) One member appointed by the Director of the National Institute for Occupational Safety and Health from officers or employees of the Institute.

(v) One member appointed by the Director of the National Institute of Environmental Health Sciences from officers or employees of the Institute.

(vi) One member appointed by the Director of the National Cancer Institute from officers or employees of the Institute.

(vii) One member appointed by the Director of the National Science Foundation from officers or employees of the Foundation.

(viii) One member appointed by the Secretary of Commerce from officers or employees of the Department of Commerce.

(B)(i) An appointed member may designate an individual to serve on the committee on the member's behalf. Such a designation may be made only with the approval of the applicable appointing authority and only if the individual is from the entity from which the member was appointed.

(ii) No individual may serve as a member of the committee for more than four years in the aggregate. If any member of the committee leaves the entity from which the member was appointed, such member may not continue as a member of the committee, and the member's position shall be considered to be vacant. A vacancy in the committee shall be filled in the same manner in which the original appointment was made.

(iii) Initial appointments to the committee shall be made not later than the 60th day after January 1, 1977. Not later than the 90th day after such date the members of the committee shall hold a meeting for the selection of a chairperson from among their number.

(C)(i) No member of the committee, or designee of such member, shall accept employment or compensation from any person subject to any requirement of this chapter or of any rule promulgated or order issued thereunder, for a period of at least 12 months after termination of service on the committee.

(ii) No person, while serving as a member of the committee, or designee of such member, may own any stocks or bonds, or have any pecuniary interest, of substantial value in any person engaged in the manufacture, processing, or distribution in commerce of any chemical substance or mixture subject to any requirement of this chapter or of any rule promulgated or order issued thereunder.

(iii) The Administrator, acting through attorneys of the Environmental Protection Agency, or the Attorney General may bring an action in the appropriate district court of the United States to restrain any violation of this subparagraph.

(D) The Administrator shall provide the committee such administrative support services as may be necessary to enable the committee to carry out its function under this subsection.

(f) Required actions

Upon the receipt of—

(1) any test data required to be submitted under this chapter, or

(2) any other information available to the Administrator,

which indicates to the Administrator that there may be a reasonable basis to conclude that a chemical substance or mixture presents or will present a significant risk of serious or widespread harm to human beings from cancer, gene mutations, or birth defects, the Administrator shall, within the 180-day period beginning on the date of the receipt of such data or information, initiate appropriate action under section 2604, 2605, or 2606 of this title to prevent or reduce to a sufficient extent such risk or publish in the Federal Register a finding that such risk is not unreasonable. For good cause shown the Administrator may extend such period for an additional period of not more than 90 days. The Administrator shall publish in the Federal Register notice of any such extension and the reasons therefor. A finding by the Administrator that a risk is not unreasonable shall be considered agency action for purposes of judicial review under chapter 7 of Title 5. This subsection shall not take effect until two years after January 1, 1977.

(g) Petition for standards for the development of test data

A person intending to manufacture or process a chemical substance for which notice is required under section 2604(a) of this title and who is not required under a rule under subsection (a) of this section to conduct tests and submit data on such substance may petition the Administrator to prescribe standards for the development of test data for such substance. The Administrator shall by order either grant or deny any such petition within 60 days of its receipt. If the petition is granted, the Administrator shall prescribe such standards for such substance within 75 days of the date the petition is granted. If the petition is denied, the Administrator shall publish, subject to section 2613 of this title, in the Federal Register the reasons for such denial.

(Oct. 11, 1976, Pub.L. 94–469, Title I, § 4, 90 Stat. 2006, redesignated Title I, Oct. 22, 1986, Pub.L. 99–519, § 3(c)(1), 100 Stat. 2989.)

[1] So in original. Probably should be "preceding".

West's Federal Practice Manual

Pesticides and toxic substances, see § 4385.10.

CODE OF FEDERAL REGULATIONS

Guidelines—
Chemical fate testing, see 40 CFR 796.1050 et seq.
Environmental effects testing, see 40 CFR 797.1050 et seq.
Good laboratory practice standards, see 40 CFR 792.1 et seq.
Health effects testing, see 40 CFR 798.1100 et seq.
Identification of specific chemical substance and mixture testing requirements, see 40 CFR 799.1 et seq.
Reimbursement for testing data costs, see 40 CFR 791.1 et seq.
Testing consent agreements and rules, see 40 CFR 790.1 et seq.

LAW REVIEW COMMENTARIES

Federal regulation of agricultural biotechnologies. Thomas O. McGarity, 20 U.Mich.J.L.Ref. 1089 (1987).

Responding to a government environmental investigation: Shaping the defense. Francis J. Burke, Jr., Karen A. Potts, Leigh Lani Brown, Robin L. De Respino and Michael R. Hall, 34 Ariz.L.Rev. 509 (1992).

LIBRARY REFERENCES

Health and Environment ⟹25.5(3).
C.J.S. Health and Environment § 91 et seq.

§ 2604. Manufacturing and processing notices [TSCA § 5]

(a) In general

(1) Except as provided in subsection (h) of this section, no person may—

(A) manufacture a new chemical substance on or after the 30th day after the date on which the Administrator first publishes the list required by section 2607(b) of this title, or

(B) manufacture or process any chemical substance for a use which the Administrator has determined, in accordance with paragraph (2), is a significant new use,

unless such person submits to the Administrator, at least 90 days before such manufacture or processing, a notice, in accordance with subsection (d) of this section, of such person's intention to manufacture or process such substance and such person complies with any applicable requirement of subsection (b) of this section.

(2) A determination by the Administrator that a use of a chemical substance is a significant new use with respect to which notification is required under paragraph (1) shall be made by a rule promulgated after a consideration of all relevant factors, including—

(A) the projected volume of manufacturing and processing of a chemical substance,

(B) the extent to which a use changes the type or form of exposure of human beings or the environment to a chemical substance,

(C) the extent to which a use increases the magnitude and duration of exposure of human beings or the environment to a chemical substance, and

(D) the reasonably anticipated manner and methods of manufacturing, processing, distribution in commerce, and disposal of a chemical substance.

(b) Submission of test data

(1)(A) If (i) a person is required by subsection (a)(1) of this section to submit a notice to the Administrator before beginning the manufacture or processing of a chemical substance, and (ii) such person is required to submit test data for such substance pursuant to a rule promulgated under section 2603 of this title before the submission of such notice, such person shall submit to the Administrator such data in accordance with such rule at the time notice is submitted in accordance with subsection (a)(1) of this section.

(B) If—

(i) a person is required by subsection (a)(1) of this section to submit a notice to the Administrator, and

(ii) such person has been granted an exemption under section 2603(c) of this title from the requirements of a rule promulgated under section 2603 of this title before the submission of such notice,

such person may not, before the expiration of the 90 day period which begins on the date of the submission in accordance with such rule of the test data the submission or development of which was the basis for the exemption, manufacture such substance if such person is subject to subsection (a)(1)(A) of this section or manufacture or process such substance for a significant new use if the person is subject to subsection (a)(1)(B) of this section.

(2)(A) If a person—

(i) is required by subsection (a)(1) of this section to submit a notice to the Administrator before beginning the manufacture or processing of a chemical substance listed under paragraph (4), and

(ii) is not required by a rule promulgated under section 2603 of this title before the submission of such notice to submit test data for such substance,

such person shall submit to the Administrator data prescribed by subparagraph (B) at the time notice is submitted in accordance with subsection (a)(1) of this section.

(B) Data submitted pursuant to subparagraph (A) shall be data which the person submitting the data believes show that—

(i) in the case of a substance with respect to which notice is required under subsection (a)(1)(A) of this section, the manufacture, processing, distribution in commerce, use, and disposal of the chemical substance or any combination of such activities will not present an unreasonable risk of injury to health or the environment, or

(ii) in the case of a chemical substance with respect to which notice is required under subsection (a)(1)(B) of this section, the intended significant new use of the chemical substance will not present an unreasonable risk of injury to health or the environment.

(3) Data submitted under paragraph (1) or (2) shall be made available, subject to section 2613 of this title, for examination by interested persons.

(4)(A)(i) The Administrator may, by rule, compile and keep current a list of chemical substances with respect to which the Administrator finds that the manufacture, processing, distribution in commerce, use, or disposal, or any combination of such activities, presents or may present an unreasonable risk of injury to health or the environment.

(ii) In making a finding under clause (i) that the manufacture, processing, distribution in commerce, use, or disposal of a chemical substance or any combination of such activities presents or may present an unreasonable risk of injury to health or the environment, the Administrator shall consider all relevant factors, including—

(I) the effects of the chemical substance on health and the magnitude of human exposure to such substance; and

(II) the effects of the chemical substance on the environment and the magnitude of environmental exposure to such substance.

(B) The Administrator shall, in prescribing a rule under subparagraph (A) which lists any chemical substance, identify those uses, if any, which the Administrator determines, by rule under subsection (a)(2) of this section, would constitute a significant new use of such substance.

(C) Any rule under subparagraph (A), and any substantive amendment or repeal of such a rule, shall be promulgated pursuant to the procedures specified in section 553 of title 5, except that (i) the Administrator shall give interested persons an opportunity for the oral presentation of data, views, or arguments, in addition to an opportunity to make written submissions, (ii) a transcript shall be kept of any oral presentation, and (iii) the Administrator shall make and publish with the rule the finding described in subparagraph (A).

(c) Extension of notice period

The Administrator may for good cause extend for additional periods (not to exceed in the aggregate 90 days) the period, prescribed by subsection (a) or (b) of this section before which the manufacturing or processing of a chemical substance subject to such subsection may begin. Subject to section 2613 of this title, such an extension and the reasons therefor shall be published in the Federal Register and shall constitute a final agency action subject to judicial review.

(d) Content of notice; publications in the Federal Register

(1) The notice required by subsection (a) of this section shall include—

(A) insofar as known to the person submitting the notice or insofar as reasonably ascertainable, the information described in subparagraphs (A), (B), (C), (D), (F), and (G) of section 2607(a)(2) of this title, and

(B) in such form and manner as the Administrator may prescribe, any test data in the possession or control of the person giving such notice which are related to the effect of any manufacture, processing, distribution in commerce, use, or disposal of such substance or any article containing such substance, or of any combination of such activities, on health or the environment, and

(C) a description of any other data concerning the environmental and health effects of such substance, insofar as known to the person making the notice or insofar as reasonably ascertainable.

Such a notice shall be made available, subject to section 2613 of this title, for examination by interested persons.

(2) Subject to section 2613 of this title, not later than five days (excluding Saturdays, Sundays and legal holidays) after the date of the receipt of a notice under subsection (a) of this section or of data under subsection (b) of this section, the Administrator shall publish in the Federal Register a notice which—

(A) identifies the chemical substance for which notice or data has been received;

(B) lists the uses or intended uses of such substance; and

(C) in the case of the receipt of data under subsection (b) of this section, describes the nature of the tests performed on such substance and any data which was developed pursuant to subsection (b) of this section or a rule under section 2603 of this title.

A notice under this paragraph respecting a chemical substance shall identify the chemical substance by generic class unless the Administrator determines that more specific identification is required in the public interest.

(3) At the beginning of each month the Administrator shall publish a list in the Federal Register of (A) each chemical substance for which notice has been received under subsection (a) of this section and for which the notification period prescribed by subsection (a), (b), or (c) of this section has not expired, and (B) each chemical substance for which such notification period has expired since the last publication in the Federal Register of such list.

(e) Regulation pending development of information

(1)(A) If the Administrator determines that—

(i) the information available to the Administrator is insufficient to permit a reasoned evaluation of the health and environmental effects of a chemical substance with respect to which notice is required by subsection (a) of this section; and

(ii)(I) in the absence of sufficient information to permit the Administrator to make such an evaluation, the manufacture, processing, distribution in commerce, use, or disposal of such substance, or any combination of such activities, may present an unreasonable risk of injury to health or the environment, or

(II) such substance is or will be produced in substantial quantities, and such substance either enters or may reasonably be anticipated to enter the environment in substantial quantities or there is or may be significant or substantial human exposure to the substance,

the Administrator may issue a proposed order, to take effect on the expiration of the notification period applicable to the manufacturing or processing of such substance under subsection (a), (b), or (c) of this section, to prohibit or limit the manufacture, processing, distribution in commerce, use, or disposal of such substance or to prohibit or limit any combination of such activities.

(B) A proposed order may not be issued under subparagraph (A) respecting a chemical substance (i) later than 45 days before the expiration of the notification period applicable to the manufacture or processing of such substance under subsection (a), (b), or (c) of this section, and (ii) unless the Administrator has, on or before the issuance of the proposed order, notified, in writing, each manufacturer or processor, as the case may be, of such substance of the determination which underlies such order.

(C) If a manufacturer or processor of a chemical substance to be subject to a proposed order issued under subparagraph (A) files with the Administrator (within the 30-day period beginning on the date such manufacturer or processor received the notice required by subparagraph (B)(ii)) objections specifying with particularity the provisions of the order deemed objectionable and stating the grounds therefor, the proposed order shall not take effect.

(2)(A)(i) Except as provided in clause (ii), if with respect to a chemical substance with respect to which notice is required by subsection (a) of this section, the Administrator makes the determination described in paragraph (1)(A) and if—

(I) the Administrator does not issue a proposed order under paragraph (1) respecting such substance, or

(II) the Administrator issues such an order respecting such substance but such order does not take effect because objections were filed under paragraph (1)(C) with respect to it,

the Administrator, through attorneys of the Environmental Protection Agency, shall apply to the United States District Court for the District of Columbia or the United States district court for the judicial district in which the manufacturer or processor, as the case may be, of such substance is found, resides, or transacts business for an injunction to prohibit or limit the manufacture, processing, distribution in commerce, use, or disposal of such substance (or to prohibit or limit any combination of such activities).

(ii) If the Administrator issues a proposed order under paragraph (1)(A) respecting a chemical substance but such order does not take effect because objections have been filed under paragraph (1)(C) with respect to it, the Administrator is not required to apply for an injunction under clause (i) respecting such substance if the Administrator determines, on the basis of such objections, that the determinations under paragraph (1)(A) may not be made.

(B) A district court of the United States which receives an application under subparagraph (A)(i) for an injunction respecting a chemical substance shall issue such injunction if the court finds that—

(i) the information available to the Administrator is insufficient to permit a reasoned evaluation of the health and environmental effects of a chemical substance with respect to which notice is required by subsection (a) of this section; and

(ii)(I) in the absence of sufficient information to permit the Administrator to make such an evaluation, the manufacture, processing, distribution in commerce, use, or disposal of such substance, or any combination of such activities, may present an unreasonable risk of injury to health or the environment, or

(II) such substance is or will be produced in substantial quantities, and such substance either enters or may reasonably be anticipated to enter the environment in substantial quantities or there is or may be significant or substantial human exposure to the substance.

(C) Pending the completion of a proceeding for the issuance of an injunction under subparagraph (B) respecting a chemical substance, the court may, upon application of the Administrator made through attorneys of the Environmental Protection Agency, issue a temporary restraining order or a preliminary injunction to prohibit the manufacture, processing, distribution in commerce, use, or disposal of such a substance (or any combination of such activities) if the court finds that the notification period applicable under subsection (a), (b), or (c) of this section to the manufacturing or processing of such substance may expire before such proceeding can be completed.

(D) After the submission to the Administrator of test data sufficient to evaluate the health and environmental effects of a chemical substance subject to an injunction issued under subparagraph (B) and the evaluation of such data by the Administrator, the district court of the United States which issued such injunction shall, upon petition, dissolve the injunction unless the Administrator has initiated a proceeding for the issuance of a rule under section 2605(a) of this title respecting the substance. If such a proceeding has been initiated, such court shall continue the injunction in effect until the effective date of the rule promulgated in such proceeding or, if such proceeding is terminated without the promulgation of a rule, upon the termination of the proceeding, whichever occurs first.

(f) Protection against unreasonable risks

(1) If the Administrator finds that there is a reasonable basis to conclude that the manufacture, processing, distribution in commerce, use, or disposal of a chemical substance with respect to which notice is required by subsection (a) of this section, or that any combination of such activities, presents or will present an unreasonable risk of injury to health or environment before a rule promulgated under section 2605 of this title can protect against such risk, the Administrator shall, before the expiration of the notification period applicable under subsection (a), (b), or (c) of this section to the manufacturing or processing of such substance, take the action authorized by paragraph (2) or (3) to the extent necessary to protect against such risk.

(2) The Administrator may issue a proposed rule under section 2605(a) of this title to apply to a chemical substance with respect to which a finding was made under paragraph (1)—

(A) a requirement limiting the amount of such substance which may be manufactured, processed, or distributed in commerce,

(B) a requirement described in paragraph (2), (3), (4), (5), (6), or (7) of section 2605(a) of this title, or

(C) any combination of the requirements referred to in subparagraph (B).

Such a proposed rule shall be effective upon its publication in the Federal Register. Section 2605(d)(2)(B) of this title shall apply with respect to such rule.

(3)(A) The Administrator may—

(i) issue a proposed order to prohibit the manufacture, processing, or distribution in commerce of a substance with respect to which a finding was made under paragraph (1), or

(ii) apply, through attorneys of the Environmental Protection Agency, to the United States District Court for the District of Columbia or the United States district court for the judicial district in which the manufacturer, or processor, as the case may be, of such substance, is found, resides, or transacts business for an injunction to prohibit the manufacture, processing, or distribution in commerce of such substance.

A proposed order issued under clause (i) respecting a chemical substance shall take effect on the expiration of the notification period applicable under subsection (a), (b), or (c) of this section to the manufacture or processing of such substance.

(B) If the district court of the United States to which an application has been made under subparagraph (A)(ii) finds that there is a reasonable basis to conclude that the manufacture, processing, distribution in commerce, use, or disposal of the chemical substance with respect to which such application was made, or that any combination of such activities, presents or will present an unreasonable risk of injury to health or the environment before a rule promulgated under section 2605 of this title can protect against such risk, the court shall issue an injunction to prohibit the manufacture, processing, or distribution in commerce of such substance or to prohibit any combination of such activities.

(C) The provisions of subparagraphs (B) and (C) of subsection (e)(1) of this section shall apply with respect to an order issued under clause (i) of subparagraph (A); and the provisions of subparagraph (C) of subsection (e)(2) of this section shall apply with respect to an injunction issued under subparagraph (B).

(D) If the Administrator issues an order pursuant to subparagraph (A)(i) respecting a chemical substance and objections are filed in accordance with subsection (e)(1)(C) of this section, the Administrator shall seek an injunction under subparagraph (A)(ii) respecting such substance unless the Administrator determines, on the basis of such objections, that such substance does not or will not present an unreasonable risk of injury to health or the environment.

(g) Statement of reasons for not taking action

If the Administrator has not initiated any action under this section or section 2605 or 2606 of this title to prohibit or limit the manufacture, processing, distribution in commerce, use, or disposal of a chemical substance, with respect to which notification or data is required by subsection (a)(1)(B) or (b) of this section, before the expiration of the notification period applicable to the manufacturing or processing of such substance, the Administrator shall publish a statement of the Administrator's reasons for not initiating such action. Such a statement shall be published in the Federal Register before the expiration of such period. Publication of such statement in accordance with the preceding sentence is not a prerequisite to the manufacturing or processing of the substance with respect to which the statement is to be published.

(h) Exemptions

(1) The Administrator may, upon application, exempt any person from any requirement of subsection (a) or (b) of this section to permit such person to manufacture or process a chemical substance for test marketing purposes—

(A) upon a showing by such person satisfactory to the Administrator that the manufacture, processing, distribution in commerce, use, and disposal of such substance, and that any combination of such activities, for such purposes will not present any unreasonable risk of injury to health or the environment, and

(B) under such restrictions as the Administrator considers appropriate.

(2)(A) The Administrator may, upon application, exempt any person from the requirement of subsection (b)(2) of this section to submit data for a chemical substance. If, upon receipt of an application under the preceding sentence, the Administrator determines that—

(i) the chemical substance with respect to which such application was submitted is equivalent to a chemical substance for which data has been submitted to the Administrator as required by subsection (b)(2) of this section, and

(ii) submission of data by the applicant on such substance would be duplicative of data which has been submitted to the Administrator in accordance with such subsection,

the Administrator shall exempt the applicant from the requirement to submit such data on such substance. No exemption which is granted under this subparagraph with respect to the submission of data for a chemical substance may take effect before the beginning of the reimbursement period applicable to such data.

(B) If the Administrator exempts any person, under subparagraph (A), from submitting data required under subsection (b)(2) of this section for a chemical substance because of the existence of previously submitted data and if such exemption is granted during the reimbursement period for such data, then (unless such person and the persons referred to in clauses (i) and (ii) agree on the amount and method of reimbursement) the Administrator shall order the person granted the exemption to provide fair and equitable reimbursement (in an amount determined under rules of the Administrator)—

(i) to the person who previously submitted the data on which the exemption was based, for a portion of the costs incurred by such person in complying with the requirement under subsection (b)(2) of this section to submit such data, and

(ii) to any other person who has been required under this subparagraph to contribute with respect to such costs, for a portion of the amount such person was required to contribute.

In promulgating rules for the determination of fair and equitable reimbursement to the persons described in clauses (i) and (ii) for costs incurred with respect to a chemical substance, the Administrator shall, after consultation with the Attorney General and the Federal Trade Commission, consider all relevant factors, including the effect on the competitive position of the person required to provide reimbursement in relation to the persons to be reimbursed and the share of the market for such substance of the person required to provide reimbursement in relation to the share of such market of the persons to be reimbursed. For purposes of judicial review, an order under this subparagraph shall be considered final agency action.

(C) For purposes of this paragraph, the reimbursement period for any previously submitted data for a chemical substance is a period—

(i) beginning on the date of the termination of the prohibition, imposed under this section, on the manufacture or processing of such substance by the person who submitted such data to the Administrator, and

(ii) ending—

(I) five years after the date referred to in clause (i), or

(II) at the expiration of a period which begins on the date referred to in clause (i) and is equal to the period which the Administrator determines was necessary to develop such data,

whichever is later.

(3) The requirements of subsections (a) and (b) of this section do not apply with respect to the manufacturing or processing of any chemical substance which is manufactured or processed, or proposed to be manufactured or processed, only in small quantities (as defined by the Administrator by rule) solely for purposes of—

(A) scientific experimentation or analysis, or

(B) chemical research on, or analysis of such substance or another substance, including such research or analysis for the development of a product,

if all persons engaged in such experimentation, research, or analysis for a manufacturer or processor are notified (in such form and manner as the Administrator may prescribe) of any risk to health which the manufacturer, processor, or the Administrator has reason to believe may be associated with such chemical substance.

(4) The Administrator may, upon application and by rule, exempt the manufacturer of any new chemical substance from all or part of the requirements of this section if the Administrator determines that the manufacture, processing, distribution in commerce, use, or disposal of such chemical substance, or that any combination of such activities, will not present an unreasonable risk of injury to health or the environment. A rule promulgated under this paragraph (and any substantive amendment to, or repeal of, such a rule) shall be promulgated in accordance with paragraphs (2) and (3) of section 2605(c) of this title.

(5) The Administrator may, upon application, make the requirements of subsections (a) and (b) of this section inapplicable with respect to the manufacturing or processing of any chemical substance (A) which exists temporarily as a result of a chemical reaction in the manufacturing or processing of a mixture or another chemical substance, and (B) to which there is no, and will not be, human or environmental exposure.

(6) Immediately upon receipt of an application under paragraph (1) or (5) the Administrator shall publish in the Federal Register notice of the receipt of such application. The Administrator shall give interested persons an opportunity to comment upon any such application and shall, within 45 days of its receipt, either approve or deny the application. The Administrator shall publish in the Federal Register notice of the approval or denial of such an application.

(i) Definitions

For purposes of this section, the terms "manufacture" and "process" mean manufacturing or processing for commercial purposes.

(Oct. 11, 1976, Pub.L. 94–469, Title I, § 5, 90 Stat. 2012, redesignated Title I, Oct. 22, 1986, Pub.L. 99–519, § 3(c)(1), 100 Stat. 2989.)

West's Federal Practice Manual

Pesticides and toxic substances, see § 4385.10.

CODE OF FEDERAL REGULATIONS

Metalworking fluids, use requirements for certain chemical substances, see 40 CFR 747.115, 747.195, 747.200.
Premanufacture notification exemptions, see 40 CFR 723.175.
Significant new uses for specific chemical substances, see 40 CFR 721.109 et seq.

LIBRARY REFERENCES

Health and Environment ⚷25.5(3).
C.J.S. Health and Environment § 91 et seq.

§ 2605. Regulation of hazardous chemical substances and mixtures [TSCA § 6]

(a) Scope of regulation

If the Administrator finds that there is a reasonable basis to conclude that the manufacture, processing, distribution in commerce, use, or disposal of a chemical substance or mixture, or that any combination of such activities, presents or will present an unreasonable risk of injury to health or the environment, the Administrator shall by rule apply one or more of the following requirements to such substance or mixture to the extent necessary to protect adequately against such risk using the least burdensome requirements:

(1) A requirement (A) prohibiting the manufacturing, processing, or distribution in commerce of such substance or mixture, or (B) limiting the amount of such substance or mixture which may be manufactured, processed, or distributed in commerce.

(2) A requirement—

(A) prohibiting the manufacture, processing, or distribution in commerce of such substance or mixture for (i) a particular use or (ii) a particular use in a concentration in excess of a level specified by the Administrator in the rule imposing the requirement, or

(B) limiting the amount of such substance or mixture which may be manufactured, processed, or distributed in commerce for (i) a particular use or (ii) a particular use in a concentration in excess of a level specified by the Administrator in the rule imposing the requirement.

(3) A requirement that such substance or mixture or any article containing such substance or mixture be marked with or accompanied by clear and adequate warnings and instructions with respect to its use, distribution in commerce, or disposal or with respect to any combination of such activities. The form and content of such warnings and instructions shall be prescribed by the Administrator.

(4) A requirement that manufacturers and processors of such substance or mixture make and retain records of the processes used to manufacture or process such substance or mixture and monitor or conduct tests which are reasonable and necessary to assure compliance with the requirements of any rule applicable under this subsection.

(5) A requirement prohibiting or otherwise regulating any manner or method of commercial use of such substance or mixture.

(6)(A) A requirement prohibiting or otherwise regulating any manner or method of disposal of such substance or mixture, or of any article containing such substance or mixture, by its manufacturer or processor or by any other person who uses, or disposes of, it for commercial purposes.

(B) A requirement under subparagraph (A) may not require any person to take any action which would be in violation of any law or requirement of, or in effect for, a State or political subdivision, and shall require each person subject to it to notify each State and political subdivision in which a required disposal may occur of such disposal.

(7) A requirement directing manufacturers or processors of such substance or mixture (A) to give notice of such unreasonable risk of injury to distributors in commerce of such substance or mixture and, to the extent reasonably ascertainable, to other persons in possession of such substance or mixture or exposed to such substance or mixture, (B) to give public notice of such risk of injury, and (C) to replace or repurchase such substance or mixture as elected by the person to which the requirement is directed.

Any requirement (or combination of requirements) imposed under this subsection may be limited in application to specified geographic areas.

(b) Quality control

If the Administrator has a reasonable basis to conclude that a particular manufacturer or processor is manufacturing or processing a chemical substance or mixture in a manner which unintentionally causes the chemical substance or mixture to present or which will cause it to present an unreasonable risk of injury to health or the environment—

(1) the Administrator may by order require such manufacturer or processor to submit a description of the relevant quality control procedures followed in the manufacturing or processing of such chemical substance or mixture; and

(2) if the Administrator determines—

(A) that such quality control procedures are inadequate to prevent the chemical substance or mixture from presenting such risk of injury, the Administrator may order the manufacturer or processor to revise such quality control procedures to the extent necessary to remedy such inadequacy; or

(B) that the use of such quality control procedures has resulted in the distribution in commerce of chemical substances or mixtures which present an unreasonable risk of injury to health or the environment, the Administrator may order the manufacturer or processor to (i) give notice of such risk to processors or distributors in commerce of any such substance or mixture, or to both, and, to the extent reasonably ascertainable, to any other person in possession of or exposed to any such substance, (ii) to give public notice of such risk, and (iii) to provide such replacement or repurchase of any such substance or mixture as is necessary to adequately protect health or the environment.

A determination under subparagraph (A) or (B) of paragraph (2) shall be made on the record after opportunity for hearing in accordance with section 554 of Title 5. Any manufacturer or processor subject to a requirement to replace or repurchase a chemical substance or mixture may elect either to replace or repurchase the substance or mixture and shall take either such action in the manner prescribed by the Administrator.

(c) Promulgation of subsection (a) rules

(1) In promulgating any rule under subsection (a) of this section with respect to a chemical substance or mixture, the Administrator shall consider and publish a statement with respect to—

(A) the effects of such substance or mixture on health and the magnitude of the exposure of human beings to such substance or mixture,

(B) the effects of such substance or mixture on the environment and the magnitude of the exposure of the environment to such substance or mixture,

(C) the benefits of such substance or mixture for various uses and the availability of substitutes for such uses, and

(D) the reasonably ascertainable economic consequences of the rule, after consideration of the effect on the national economy, small business, technological innovation, the environment, and public health.

If the Administrator determines that a risk of injury to health or the environment could be eliminated or reduced to a sufficient extent by actions taken under another Federal law (or laws) administered in whole or in part by the Administrator, the Administrator may not promulgate a rule under subsection (a) of this section to protect against such risk of injury unless the Administrator finds, in the Administrator's discretion, that it is in the public interest to protect against such risk under this chapter. In making such a finding the Administrator shall consider (i) all relevant aspects of the risk, as determined by the Administrator in the Administrator's discretion, (ii) a comparison of the estimated costs of complying with actions taken under this chapter and under such law (or laws), and (iii) the relative efficiency of actions under this chapter and under such law (or laws) to protect against such risk of injury.

(2) When prescribing a rule under subsection (a) of this section the Administrator shall proceed in accordance with section 553 of Title 5 (without regard to any reference in such section to sections 556 and 557 of such title), and shall also (A) publish a notice of proposed rulemaking stating with particularity the reason for the proposed rule; (B) allow interested persons to submit written data, views, and arguments, and make all such submissions publicly available; (C) provide an opportunity for an informal hearing in accordance with paragraph (3); (D) promulgate, if appropriate, a final rule based on the matter in the rulemaking record (as defined in section 2618(a) of this title), and (E) make and publish with the rule the finding described in subsection (a) of this section.

(3) Informal hearings required by paragraph (2)(C) shall be conducted by the Administrator in accordance with the following requirements:

(A) Subject to subparagraph (B), an interested person is entitled—

(i) to present such person's position orally or by documentary submissions (or both), and

(ii) if the Administrator determines that there are disputed issues of material fact it is necessary to resolve, to present such rebuttal submissions and to conduct (or have conducted under subparagraph (B)(ii)) such cross-examination of persons as the Administrator determines (I) to be appropriate, and (II) to be required for a full and true disclosure with respect to such issues.

(B) The Administrator may prescribe such rules and make such rulings concerning procedures in such hearings to avoid unnecessary costs or delay. Such rules or rulings may include (i) the imposition of reasonable time limits on each interested person's oral presentations, and (ii) requirements that any cross-examination to which a person may be entitled under subparagraph (A) be conducted by the Administrator on behalf of that person in such manner as the Administrator determines (I) to be appropriate, and (II) to be required for a full and true disclosure with respect to disputed issues of material fact.

(C)(i) Except as provided in clause (ii), if a group of persons each of whom under subparagraphs (A) and (B) would be entitled to conduct (or have conducted) cross-examination and who are determined by the Administrator to have the same or similar interests in the proceeding cannot agree upon a single representative of such interests for purposes of cross-examination, the Administrator may make rules and rulings (I) limiting the representation of such interest for such purposes, and (II) governing the manner in which such cross-examination shall be limited.

(ii) When any person who is a member of a group with respect to which the Administrator has made a determination under clause (i) is unable to agree upon group representation with the other members of the group, then such person shall not be denied under the authority of clause (i) the opportunity to conduct (or have conducted) cross-examination as to issues affecting the person's particular interests if (I) the person satisfies the Administrator that the person has made a reasonable and good faith effort to reach agreement upon group representation with the other members of the group and (II) the Administrator determines that there are substantial and relevant issues which are not adequately presented by the group representative.

(D) A verbatim transcript shall be taken of any oral presentation made, and cross-examination conducted in any informal hearing under this subsection. Such transcript shall be available to the public.

(4)(A) The Administrator may, pursuant to rules prescribed by the Administrator, provide compensation for reasonable attorneys' fees, expert witness fees, and other costs of participating in a rulemaking proceeding for the promulgation of a rule under subsection (a) of this section to any person—

(i) who represents an interest which would substantially contribute to a fair determination of the issues to be resolved in the proceeding, and

(ii) if—

(I) the economic interest of such person is small in comparison to the costs of effective participation in the proceeding by such person, or

(II) such person demonstrates to the satisfaction of the Administrator that such person does not have sufficient resources adequately to participate in the proceeding without compensation under this subparagraph.

In determining for purposes of clause (i) if an interest will substantially contribute to a fair determination of the issues to be resolved in a proceeding, the Administrator shall take into account the number and complexity of such issues and the extent to which representation of such interest will contribute to widespread public participation in the proceeding and representation of a fair balance of interests for the resolution of such issues.

(B) In determining whether compensation should be provided to a person under subparagraph (A) and the amount of such compensation, the Administrator shall take into account the financial burden which will be incurred by such person in participating in the rulemaking proceeding. The Administrator shall take such action as may be necessary to ensure that the aggregate amount of compensation paid under this paragraph in any fiscal year to all persons who, in rulemaking proceedings in which they receive compensation, are persons who either—

(i) would be regulated by the proposed rule, or

(ii) represent persons who would be so regulated,

may not exceed 25 per centum of the aggregate amount paid as compensation under this paragraph to all persons in such fiscal year.

(5) Paragraph (1), (2), (3), and (4) of this subsection apply to the promulgation of a rule repealing, or making a substantive amendment to, a rule promulgated under subsection (a) of this section.

(d) Effective date

(1) The Administrator shall specify in any rule under subsection (a) of this section the date on which it shall take effect, which date shall be as soon as feasible.

(2)(A) The Administrator may declare a proposed rule under subsection (a) of this section to be effective upon its publication in the Federal Register and until the effective date of final action taken, in accordance with subparagraph (B), respecting such rule if—

(i) the Administrator determines that—

(I) the manufacture, processing, distribution in commerce, use, or disposal of the chemical substance or mixture subject to such proposed rule or any combination of such activities is likely to result in an unreasonable risk of serious or widespread injury to health or the environment before such effective date; and

(II) making such proposed rule so effective is necessary to protect the public interest; and

(ii) in the case of a proposed rule to prohibit the manufacture, processing, or distribution of a chemical substance or mixture because of the risk determined under clause (i)(I), a court has in an action under section 2606 of this title granted relief with respect to such risk associated with such substance or mixture.

Such a proposed rule which is made so effective shall not, for purposes of judicial review, be considered final agency action.

(B) If the Administrator makes a proposed rule effective upon its publication in the Federal Register, the Administrator shall, as expeditiously as possible, give interested persons prompt notice of such action, provide reasonable opportunity, in accordance with paragraphs (2) and (3) of subsection (c) of this section, for a hearing on such rule, and either promulgate such rule (as proposed or with modifications) or revoke it; and if such a hearing is requested, the Administrator shall commence the hearing within five days from the date such request is made unless the Administrator and the person making the request agree upon a later date for the hearing to begin, and after the hearing is concluded the Administrator shall, within ten days of the conclusion of the hearing, either promulgate such rule (as proposed or with modifications) or revoke it.

(e) Polychlorinated biphenyls

(1) Within six months after January 1, 1977, the Administrator shall promulgate rules to—

(A) prescribe methods for the disposal of polychlorinated biphenyls, and

(B) require polychlorinated biphenyls to be marked with clear and adequate warnings, and instructions with respect to their processing, distribution in commerce, use, or disposal or with respect to any combination of such activities.

Requirements prescribed by rules under this paragraph shall be consistent with the requirements of paragraphs (2) and (3).

(2)(A) Except as provided under subparagraph (B), effective one year after January 1, 1977, no person may manufacture, process, or distribute in commerce or use any polychlorinated biphenyl in any manner other than in a totally enclosed manner.

(B) The Administrator may by rule authorize the manufacture, processing, distribution in commerce or use (or any combination of such activities) of any polychlorinated biphenyl in a manner other than in a totally enclosed manner if the Administrator finds that such manufacture, processing, distribution in commerce, or use (or combination of such activities) will not present an unreasonable risk of injury to health or the environment.

(C) For the purposes of this paragraph, the term "totally enclosed manner" means any manner which will ensure that any exposure of human beings or the environment to a polychlorinated biphenyl will be insignificant as determined by the Administrator by rule.

(3)(A) Except as provided in subparagraphs (B) and (C)—

(i) no person may manufacture any polychlorinated biphenyl after two years after January 1, 1977, and

(ii) no person may process or distribute in commerce any polychlorinated biphenyl after two and one-half years after such date.

(B) Any person may petition the Administrator for an exemption from the requirements of subparagraph (A), and the Administrator may grant by rule such an exemption if the Administrator finds that—

(i) an unreasonable risk of injury to health or environment would not result, and

(ii) good faith efforts have been made to develop a chemical substance which does not present an unreasonable risk of injury to health or the environment and which may be substituted for such polychlorinated biphenyl.

An exemption granted under this subparagraph shall be subject to such terms and conditions as the Administrator may prescribe and shall be in effect for such period (but not more than one year from the date it is granted) as the Administrator may prescribe.

(C) Subparagraph (A) shall not apply to the distribution in commerce of any polychlorinated biphenyl if such polychlorinated biphenyl was sold for purposes other than resale before two and one half years after October 11, 1976.

(4) Any rule under paragraph (1), (2)(B), or (3)(B) shall be promulgated in accordance with paragraphs (2), (3), and (4) of subsection (c) of this section.

(5) This subsection does not limit the authority of the Administrator, under any other provision of this chapter or any other Federal law, to take action respecting any polychlorinated biphenyl.

(Oct. 11, 1976, Pub.L. 94–469, Title I, § 6, 90 Stat. 2020, redesignated Title I, Oct. 22, 1986, Pub.L. 99–519, § 3(c)(1), 100 Stat. 2989.)

West's Federal Practice Manual

Pertinent federal legislation, see § 1475.7.
Pesticides and toxic substances, see § 4385.10.

CODE OF FEDERAL REGULATIONS

Asbestos, see 40 CFR 763.100.
Fully halogenated chlorofluoroalkanes, see 40 CFR 762.1 et seq.
Manufacturing, processing, distribution in commerce, and use prohibitions respecting polychlorinated biphenyls, see 40 CFR 761.1 et seq.
Rulemaking procedures, see 40 CFR 750.1 et seq.
Storage and disposal of waste material, see 40 CFR 775.180 et seq.

LAW REVIEW COMMENTARIES

Affirmative judicial case management: A viable solution to the toxic product litigation crisis. 38 Maine L.Rev. 339 (1986).

Federal preemption of state impediments to siting of PCB disposal facilities. William L. Andreen, 63 NC L.Rev. 811 (1985).

Federal regulation of agricultural biotechnologies. Thomas O. McGarity, 20 U.Mich.J.L.Ref. 1089 (1987).

"More good than harm": A first principle for environmental agencies and reviewing courts. Edward W. Warren and Gary E. Marchant, 20 Ecology L.Q. 379 (1993).

LIBRARY REFERENCES

Health and Environment ⟹25.5(3).
C.J.S. Health and Environment § 91 et seq.

§ 2606. Imminent hazards [TSCA § 7]

(a) Actions authorized and required

(1) The Administrator may commence a civil action in an appropriate district court of the United States—

(A) for seizure of an imminently hazardous chemical substance or mixture or any article containing such a substance or mixture,

(B) for relief (as authorized by subsection (b) of this section) against any person who manufactures, processes, distributes in commerce, or uses, or disposes of, an imminently hazardous chemical substance or mixture or any article containing such a substance or mixture, or

(C) for both such seizure and relief.

A civil action may be commenced under this paragraph notwithstanding the existence of a rule under section 2603, 2604, 2605 of this title, or subchapter IV of this chapter or an order under section 2604 of this title or subchapter IV of this chapter, and notwithstanding the pendency of any administrative or judicial proceeding under any provision of this chapter.

(2) If the Administrator has not made a rule under section 2605(a) of this title immediately effective (as authorized by section 2605(d)(2)(A)(i) of this title) with respect to an imminently hazardous chemical substance or mixture, the Administrator shall commence in a district court of the United States with respect to such substance or mixture or article containing such substance or mixture a civil action described in subparagraph (A), (B), or (C) of paragraph (1).

(b) Relief authorized

(1) The district court of the United States in which an action under subsection (a) of this section is brought shall have jurisdiction to grant such temporary or permanent relief as may be necessary to protect health or the environment from the unreasonable risk associated with the chemical substance, mixture, or article involved in such action.

(2) In the case of an action under subsection (a) of this section brought against a person who manufactures, processes, or distributes in commerce a chemical substance or mixture or an article containing a chemical substance or mixture, the relief authorized by paragraph (1) may include the issuance of a mandatory order requiring (A) in the case of purchasers of such substance, mixture, or article known to the defendant, notification to such purchasers of the risk associated with it; (B) public notice of such risk; (C) recall; (D) the replacement or repurchase of such substance, mixture, or article; or (E) any combination of the actions described in the preceding clauses.

(3) In the case of an action under subsection (a) of this section against a chemical substance, mixture, or article, such substance, mixture, or article may be proceeded against by process of libel for its seizure and condemnation. Proceedings in such an action shall conform as nearly as possible to proceedings in rem in admiralty.

(c) Venue and consolidation

(1)(A) An action under subsection (a) of this section against a person who manufactures, processes, or distributes a chemical substance or mixture or an article containing a chemical substance or mixture may be brought in the United States District Court for the District of Columbia, or for any judicial district in which any of the defendants is found, resides, or transacts business; and process in such an action may be served on a defendant in any other district in which such defendant resides or may be found. An action under subsection (a) of this section against a chemical substance, mixture, or article may be brought in any United States district court within the jurisdiction of which the substance, mixture, or article is found.

(B) In determining the judicial district in which an action may be brought under subsection (a) of this section in instances in which such action may be brought in more than one judicial district, the Administrator shall take into account the convenience of the parties.

(C) Subpeonas[1] requiring attendance of witnesses in an action brought under subsection (a) of this section may be served in any judicial district.

(2) Whenever proceedings under subsection (a) of this section involving identical chemical substances, mixtures, or articles are pending in courts in two or more judicial districts, they shall be consolidated for trial by order of any such court upon application reasonably made by any party in interest, upon notice to all parties in interest.

(d) Action under section 2605 of this title

Where appropriate, concurrently with the filing of an action under subsection (a) of this section or as soon thereafter as may be practicable, the Administrator shall initiate a proceeding for the promulgation of a rule under section 2605(a) of this title.

(e) Representation

Notwithstanding any other provision of law, in any action under subsection (a) of this section, the Administrator may direct attorneys of the Environmental Protection Agency to appear and represent the Administrator in such an action.

(f) Definition

For the purposes of subsection (a) of this section, the term "imminently hazardous chemical substance or mixture" means a chemical substance or mixture which presents an imminent and unreasonable risk of serious or widespread injury to health or the environment. Such a risk to health or the environment shall be considered imminent if it is shown that the manufacture, processing, distribution in commerce, use, or disposal of the chemical substance or mixture, or that any combination of such activities, is likely to result in such injury to health or the environment before a final rule under section 2605 of this title can protect against such risk.

(Oct. 11, 1976, Pub.L. 94–469, Title I, § 7, 90 Stat. 2026, redesignated Title I, Oct. 22, 1986, Pub.L. 99–519, § 3(c)(1), 100 Stat. 2989; Oct. 28, 1992, Pub.L. 102–550, Title X, § 1021(b)(1), 106 Stat. 3923.)

[1] So in original.

Effective Date of 1992 Amendments

Amendment by Pub.L. 102–550 effective Oct. 28, 1992, see section 2 of Pub.L. 102–550, set out as a note under section 5301 of Title 42, The Public Health and Welfare.

West's Federal Forms

Complaint,
Forfeiture, see § 5851 et seq.

LAW REVIEW COMMENTARIES

Interstate waste: A key issue in resolving the national hazardous waste capacity crisis. B.J. Wynne, III and Terri Hamby, 32 S.Tex. L.Rev. 601 (1991).

The once and future EPA lender regulations: Limiting lender liability for the cleanup of hazardous wastes. Jeffrey M. Gaba, 47 Consumer Fin.L.Q.Rep. 355 (1993).

LIBRARY REFERENCES

Health and Environment ⚷25.5(3).
C.J.S. Health and Environment § 91 et seq.

§ 2607. Reporting and retention of information [TSCA § 8]

(a) Reports

(1) The Administrator shall promulgate rules under which—

(A) each person (other than a small manufacturer or processor) who manufactures or processes or proposes to manufacture or process a chemical substance (other than a chemical substance described in subparagraph (B)(ii)) shall maintain such records, and shall submit to the Administrator such reports, as the Administrator may reasonably require, and

(B) each person (other than a small manufacturer or processor) who manufactures or processes or proposes to manufacture or process—

(i) a mixture, or

(ii) a chemical substance in small quantities (as defined by the Administrator by rule) solely for purposes of scientific experimentation or analysis or chemical research on, or analysis of, such substance or another substance, including any such research or analysis for the development of a product,

shall maintain records and submit to the Administrator reports but only to the extent the Administrator determines the maintenance of records or submission of reports, or both, is necessary for the effective enforcement of this chapter.

The Administrator may not require in a rule promulgated under this paragraph the maintenance of records or the submission of reports with respect to changes in the proportions of the components of a mixture unless the Administrator finds that the maintenance of such records or the submission of such reports, or both, is necessary for the effective enforcement of this chapter. For purposes of the compilation of the list of chemical substances required under subsection (b) of this section, the Administrator shall promulgate rules pursuant to this subsection not later than 180 days after January 1, 1977.

(2) The Administrator may require under paragraph (1) maintenance of records and reporting with respect to the following insofar as known to the person making the report or insofar as reasonably ascertainable:

(A) The common or trade name, the chemical identity, and the molecular structure of each chemical substance or mixture for which such a report is required.

(B) The categories or proposed categories of use of each such substance or mixture.

(C) The total amount of each such substance and mixture manufactured or processed, reasonable estimates of the total amount to be manufactured or processed, the amount manufactured or processed for each of its categories of use, and reasonable estimates of the amount to be manufactured or processed for each of its categories of use or proposed categories of use.

(D) A description of the byproducts resulting from the manufacture, processing, use, or disposal of each such substance or mixture.

(E) All existing data concerning the environmental and health effects of such substance or mixture.

(F) The number of individuals exposed, and reasonable estimates of the number who will be exposed, to such substance or mixture in their places of employment and the duration of such exposure.

(G) In the initial report under paragraph (1) on such substance or mixture, the manner or method of its disposal, and in any subsequent report on such substance or mixture, any change in such manner or method.

To the extent feasible, the Administrator shall not require under paragraph (1), any reporting which is unnecessary or duplicative.

(3)(A)(i) The Administrator may by rule require a small manufacturer or processor of a chemical substance to submit to the Administrator such information respecting the chemical substance as the Administrator may require for publication of the first list of chemical substances required by subsection (b) of this section.

(ii) The Administrator may by rule require a small manufacturer or processor of a chemical substance or mixture—

(I) subject to a rule proposed or promulgated under section 2603, 2604(b)(4), or 2605 of this title, or an order in effect under section 2604(e) of this title, or

(II) with respect to which relief has been granted pursuant to a civil action brought under section 2604 or 2606 of this title,

to maintain such records on such substance or mixture, and to submit to the Administrator such reports on such substance or mixture, as the Administrator may reasonably require. A rule under this clause requiring reporting may require reporting with respect to the matters referred to in paragraph (2).

(B) The Administrator, after consultation with the Administrator of the Small Business Administration, shall by rule prescribe standards for determining the manufacturers and processors which qualify as small manufacturers and processors for purposes of this paragraph and paragraph (1).

(b) Inventory

(1) The Administrator shall compile, keep current, and publish a list of each chemical substance which is manufactured or processed in the United States. Such list shall at least include each chemical substance which any person reports, under section 2604 of this title or subsection (a) of this section, is manufactured or processed in the United States. Such list may not include any chemical substance which was not manufactured or processed in the United States within three years before the effective date of the rules promulgated pursuant to the last sentence of subsection (a)(1) of this section. In the case of a chemical substance for which a notice is submitted in accordance with section 2604 of this title, such chemical substance shall be included in such list as of the earliest date (as determined by the Administrator) on which such substance was manufactured or processed in the United States. The Administrator shall first publish such a list not later than 315 days after January 1, 1977. The Administrator shall not include in such list any chemical substance which is manufactured or processed only in small quantities (as defined by the Administrator by rule) solely for purposes of scientific experimentation or analysis or chemical research on, or analysis of, such substance or another substance, including such research or analysis for the development of a product.

(2) To the extent consistent with the purposes of this chapter, the Administrator may, in lieu of listing, pursuant to paragraph (1), a chemical substance individually, list a category of chemical substances in which such substance is included.

(c) Records

Any person who manufactures, processes, or distributes in commerce any chemical substance or mixture shall maintain records of significant adverse reactions to health or the environment, as determined by the Administrator by rule, alleged to have been caused by the substance or mixture. Records of such adverse reactions to the health of employees shall be retained for a period of 30 years from the date such reactions were first reported to or known by the person maintaining such records. Any other record of such adverse reactions shall be retained for a period of five years from the date the information contained in the record was first reported to or known by the person maintaining the record. Records required to be maintained under this subsection shall include records of consumer allegations of personal injury or harm to health, reports of occupational disease or injury, and reports or complaints of injury to the environment submitted to the manufacturer, processor, or distributor in commerce from any source. Upon request of any duly designated representative of the Administrator, each person who is required to maintain records under this subsection shall permit the inspection of such records and shall submit copies of such records.

(d) Health and safety studies

The Administrator shall promulgate rules under which the Administrator shall require any person who manufactures, processes, or distributes in commerce or who proposes to manufacture, process, or distribute in commerce any chemical substance or mixture (or with respect to paragraph (2), any person who has possession of a study) to submit to the Administrator—

(1) lists of health and safety studies (A) conducted or initiated by or for such person with respect to such substance or mixture at any time, (B) known to such person, or (C) reasonably ascertainable by such person, except that the Administrator may exclude certain types or categories of studies from the requirements of this subsection if the Administrator finds that submission of lists of such studies are unnecessary to carry out the purposes of this chapter; and

(2) copies of any study contained on a list submitted pursuant to paragraph (1) or otherwise known by such person.

(e) Notice to Administrator of substantial risks

Any person who manufactures, processes, or distributes in commerce a chemical substance or mixture and who obtains information which reasonably supports the conclusion that such substance or mixture presents a substantial risk of injury to health or the environment shall immediately inform the Administrator of such information unless such person has actual knowledge that the Administrator has been adequately informed of such information.

(f) Definitions

For purposes of this section, the terms "manufacture" and "process" mean manufacture or process for commercial purposes.

(Oct. 11, 1976, Pub.L. 94–469, Title I, § 8, 90 Stat. 2027, redesignated Title I, Oct. 22, 1986, Pub.L. 99–519, § 3(c)(1), 100 Stat. 2989.)

CODE OF FEDERAL REGULATIONS

Data reporting requirements for certain chemical substances and mixtures, see 40 CFR 716.1 et seq.
Health and safety data reporting, see 40 CFR 716.1 et seq., 717.1 et seq.
Inventory reporting regulations, see 40 CFR 710.1 et seq.
Reporting and recordkeeping requirements for specific chemicals, see 40 CFR 704.1 et seq., 761.180 et seq.
Significant adverse reactions to health or environment caused by chemicals, recordkeeping, see 40 CFR 717.1 et seq.

LAW REVIEW COMMENTARIES

Federal regulation of agricultural biotechnologies. Thomas O. McGarity, 20 U.Mich.J.L.Ref. 1089 (1987).

LIBRARY REFERENCES

Health and Environment ⚷25.5(9).
C.J.S. Health and Environment § 65 et seq.

§ 2608. Relationship to other Federal laws [TSCA § 9]

(a) Laws not administered by the Administrator

(1) If the Administrator has reasonable basis to conclude that the manufacture, processing, distribution in commerce, use, or disposal of a chemical substance or mixture, or that any combination of such activities, presents or will present an unreasonable risk of injury to health or the environment and determines, in the Administrator's discretion, that such risk may be prevented or reduced to a sufficient extent by action taken under a Federal law not administered by the Administrator, the Administrator shall submit to the agency which administers such law a report which describes such risk and includes in such description a specification of the activity or combination of activities which the Administrator has reason to believe so presents such risk. Such report shall also request such agency—

(A)(i) to determine if the risk described in such report may be prevented or reduced to a sufficient extent by action taken under such law, and

(ii) if the agency determines that such risk may be so prevented or reduced, to issue an order declaring whether or not the activity or combination of activities specified in the description of such risk presents such risk; and

(B) to respond to the Administrator with respect to the matters described in subparagraph (A).

Any report of the Administrator shall include a detailed statement of the information on which it is based and shall be published in the Federal Register. The agency receiving a request under such a report shall make the requested determination, issue the requested order, and make the requested response within such time as the Administrator specifies in the request, but such time specified may not be less than 90 days from the date the request was made. The response of an agency shall be accompanied by a detailed statement of the findings and conclusions of the agency and shall be published in the Federal Register.

(2) If the Administrator makes a report under paragraph (1) with respect to a chemical substance or mixture and the agency to which such report was made either—

(A) issues an order declaring that the activity or combination of activities specified in the description of the risk described in the report does not present the risk described in the report, or

(B) initiates, within 90 days of the publication in the Federal Register of the response of the agency under paragraph (1), action under the law (or laws) administered by such agency to protect against such risk associated with such activity or combination of activities,

the Administrator may not take any action under section 2605 or 2606 of this title with respect to such risk.

(3) If the Administrator has initiated action under section 2605 or 2606 of this title with respect to a risk associated with a chemical substance or mixture which was the subject of a report made to an agency under paragraph (1), such agency shall before taking action under the law (or laws) administered by it to protect against such risk consult with the Administrator for the purpose of avoiding duplication of Federal action against such risk.

(b) Laws administered by the Administrator

The Administrator shall coordinate actions taken under this chapter with actions taken under other Federal laws administered in whole or in part by the Administrator. If the Administrator determines that a risk to health or the environment associated with a chemical substance or mixture could be eliminated or reduced to a sufficient extent by actions taken under the authorities contained in such other Federal laws, the Administrator shall use such authorities to protect against such risk unless the Administrator determines, in the Administrator's discretion, that it is in the public interest to protect against such risk by actions taken under this chapter. This subsection shall not be construed to relieve the Administrator of any requirement imposed on the Administrator by such other Federal laws.

(c) Occupational safety and health

In exercising any authority under this chapter, the Administrator shall not, for purposes of section 653(b)(1) of Title 29, be deemed to be exercising statutory authority to prescribe or enforce standards or regulations affecting occupational safety and health.

(d) Coordination

In administering this chapter, the Administrator shall consult and coordinate with the Secretary of Health and Human Services and the heads of any other appropriate Federal executive department or agency, any relevant independent regulatory agency, and any other appropriate instrumentality of the Federal Government for the purpose of achieving the maximum enforcement of this chapter while imposing the least burdens of duplicative requirements on those subject to the chapter and for other purposes. The Administrator shall, in the report required by section 2629 of this title, report annually to the Congress on actions taken to coordinate with such other Federal departments, agencies, or instrumentalities, and on actions taken to coordinate the authority under this chapter with the authority granted under other Acts referred to in subsection (b) of this section.

(Oct. 11, 1976, Pub.L. 94–469, Title I, § 9, 90 Stat. 2030; Oct. 17, 1979, Pub.L. 96–88, Title V, § 509(b), 93 Stat. 695; redesignated Title I, Oct. 22, 1986, Pub.L. 99–519, § 3(c)(1), 100 Stat. 2989.)

CODE OF FEDERAL REGULATIONS

Asbestos recordkeeping, see 40 CFR 763.114.
Ineligibility after violations, see 40 CFR 32.100.
Procurement under assistance programs, see 40 CFR 33.001.

LIBRARY REFERENCES

Health and Environment ⚖25.5(2).
C.J.S. Health and Environment § 61 et seq.

§ 2609. Research, development, collection, dissemination, and utilization of data [TSCA § 10]

(a) Authority

The Administrator shall, in consultation and cooperation with the Secretary of Health and Human Services and with other heads of appropriate departments and agencies, conduct such research, development, and monitoring as is necessary to carry out the purposes of this chapter. The Administrator may enter into contracts and may make grants for research, development, and monitoring under this subsection. Contracts may be entered into under this subsection without regard to section 3324(a) and (b) of Title 31 and section 5 of Title 41.

(b) Data systems

(1) The Administrator shall establish, administer, and be responsible for the continuing activities of an interagency committee which shall design, establish, and coordinate an efficient and effective system, within the Environmental Protection Agency, for the collection, dissemination to other Federal departments and agencies, and use of data submitted to the Administrator under this chapter.

(2)(A) The Administrator shall, in consultation and cooperation with the Secretary of Health and Human Services and other heads of appropriate departments and agencies design, establish, and coordinate an efficient and effective system for the retrieval of toxicological and other scientific data which could be useful to the Administrator in carrying out the purposes of this chapter. Systematized retrieval shall be developed for use by all Federal and other departments and agencies with responsibilities in the area of regulation or study of chemical substances and mixtures and their effect on health or the environment.

(B) The Administrator, in consultation and cooperation with the Secretary of Health and Human Services, may make grants and enter into contracts for the development of a data retrieval system described in subparagraph (A). Contracts may be entered into under this subparagraph without regard to section 3324(a) and (b) of Title 31 and section 5 of Title 41.

(c) Screening techniques

The Administrator shall coordinate, with the Assistant Secretary for Health of the Department of Health and Human Services, research undertaken by the Administrator and directed toward the development of rapid, reliable, and economical screening techniques for carcinogenic, mutagenic, teratogenic, and ecological effects of chemical substances and mixtures.

(d) Monitoring

The Administrator shall, in consultation and cooperation with the Secretary of Health and Human Services, establish and be responsible for research aimed at the development, in cooperation with local, State, and Federal agencies, of monitoring techniques and instruments which may be used in the detection of toxic chemical substances and mixtures and which are reliable, economical, and capable of being implemented under a wide variety of conditions.

(e) Basic research

The Administrator shall, in consultation and cooperation with the Secretary of Health and Human Services, establish research programs to develop the fundamental scientific basis of the screening and monitoring techniques described in subsections (c) and (d) of this section, the bounds of the reliability of such techniques, and the opportunities for their improvement.

(f) Training

The Administrator shall establish and promote programs and workshops to train or facilitate the training of Federal laboratory and technical personnel in existing or newly developed screening and monitoring techniques.

(g) Exchange of research and development results

The Administrator shall, in consultation with the Secretary of Health and Human Services and other heads of appropriate departments and agencies, establish and coordinate a system for exchange among Federal, State, and local authorities of research and development results respecting toxic chemical substances and mixtures, including a system to facilitate and promote the development of standard data format and analysis and consistent testing procedures.

(Oct. 11, 1976, Pub.L. 94–469, Title I, § 10, 90 Stat. 2031; Oct. 17, 1979, Pub.L. 96–88, Title V, § 509(b), 93 Stat. 695; Sept. 3, 1982, Pub.L. 97–258, § 4(b), 96 Stat. 1067; redesignated Title I, Oct. 22, 1986, Pub.L. 99–519, § 3(c)(1), 100 Stat. 2989.)

LIBRARY REFERENCES

Health and Environment ⚷25.5(9).
C.J.S. Health and Environment § 65 et seq.

§ 2610. Inspections and subpoenas [TSCA § 11]

(a) In general

For purposes of administering this chapter, the Administrator, and any duly designated representative of the Administrator, may inspect any establishment, facility, or other premises in which chemical substances, mixtures, or products subject to subchapter IV of this chapter are manufactured, processed, stored, or held before or after their distribution in commerce and any conveyance being used to transport chemical substances, mixtures, such products or such articles in connection with distribution in commerce. Such an inspection may only be made upon the presentation of appropriate credentials and of a written notice to the owner, operator, or agent in charge of the premises or conveyance to be inspected. A separate notice shall be given for each such inspection, but a notice shall not be required for each entry made during the period covered by the inspection. Each such inspection shall be commenced and completed with reasonable promptness and shall be conducted at reasonable times, within reasonable limits, and in a reasonable manner.

(b) Scope

(1) Except as provided in paragraph (2), an inspection conducted under subsection (a) of this section shall extend to all things within the premises or conveyance inspected (including records, files, papers, processes, controls, and facilities) bearing on whether the requirements of this chapter applicable to the chemical substances, mixtures, or products subject to subchapter IV of this chapter within such premises or conveyance have been complied with.

(2) No inspection under subsection (a) of this section shall extend to—

(A) financial data,

(B) sales data (other than shipment data),

(C) pricing data,

(D) personnel data, or

(E) research data (other than data required by this chapter or under a rule promulgated thereunder),

unless the nature and extent of such data are described with reasonable specificity in the written notice required by subsection (a) of this section for such inspection.

(c) Subpoenas

In carrying out this chapter, the Administrator may by subpoena require the attendance and testimony of witnesses and the production of reports, papers, documents, answers to questions, and other information that the Administrator deems necessary. Witnesses shall be paid the same fees and mileage that are paid witnesses in the courts of the United States. In the event of contumacy, failure, or refusal of any person to obey any such subpoena, any district court of the United States in which venue is proper shall have jurisdiction to order any such person to comply with such subpoena. Any failure to obey such an order of the court is punishable by the court as a contempt thereof.

(Oct. 11, 1976, Pub.L. 94–469, Title I, § 11, 90 Stat. 2032, redesignated Title I, Oct. 22, 1986, Pub.L. 99–519, § 3(c)(1), 100 Stat. 2989; Oct. 28, 1992, Pub.L. 102–550, Title X, § 1021(b)(2), (3), 106 Stat. 3923.)

Effective Date of 1992 Amendments

Amendment by Pub.L. 102–550 effective Oct. 28, 1992, see section 2 of Pub.L. 102–550, set out as a note under section 5301 of Title 42, The Public Health and Welfare.

West's Federal Forms

Administrative subpoenas, enforcement of, see § 5901 et seq.

LIBRARY REFERENCES

Health and Environment ⚷25.5(9).
C.J.S. Health and Environment § 65 et seq.

§ 2611. Exports [TSCA § 12]

(a) In general

(1) Except as provided in paragraph (2) and subsection (b) of this section, this chapter (other than section 2607 of this title) shall not apply to any chemical substance, mixture, or to an article containing a chemical substance or mixture, if—

(A) it can be shown that such substance, mixture, or article is being manufactured, processed, or distributed in commerce for export from the United States, unless such substance, mixture, or article was, in fact, manufactured, processed, or distributed in commerce, for use in the United States, and

(B) such substance, mixture, or article (when distributed in commerce), or any container in which it is enclosed (when so distributed), bears a stamp or label stating that such substance, mixture, or article is intended for export.

(2) Paragraph (1) shall not apply to any chemical substance, mixture, or article if the Administrator finds that the substance, mixture, or article will present an unreasonable risk of injury to health within the United States or to the environment of the United States. The Administrator may require, under section 2603 of this title, testing of any chemical substance or mixture exempted from this chapter by paragraph (1) for the purpose of determining whether or not such substance or mixture presents an unreasonable risk of injury to health within the United States or to the environment of the United States.

(b) Notice

(1) If any person exports or intends to export to a foreign country a chemical substance or mixture for which the submission of data is required under section 2603 or 2604(b) of this title, such person shall notify the Administrator of such exportation or intent to export and the Administrator shall furnish to the government of such country notice of the availability of the data submitted to the Administrator under such section for such substance or mixture.

(2) If any person exports or intends to export to a foreign country a chemical substance or mixture for which an order has been issued under section 2604 of this title or a rule has been proposed or promulgated under section 2604 or 2605 of this title, or with respect to which an action is pending, or relief has been granted under section 2604 or 2606 of this title, such person shall notify the Administrator of such exportation or intent to export and the Administrator shall furnish to the government of such country notice of such rule, order, action, or relief.

(Oct. 11, 1976, Pub.L. 94–469, Title I, § 12, 90 Stat. 2033, redesignated Title I, Oct. 22, 1986, Pub.L. 99–519, § 3(c)(1), 100 Stat. 2989.)

CODE OF FEDERAL REGULATIONS

Chemical imports and exports, see 40 CFR 707.60 et seq.

LIBRARY REFERENCES

Health and Environment ⚷25.5(3).
C.J.S. Health and Environment § 91 et seq.

§ 2612. Entry into customs territory of the United States [TSCA § 13]

(a) In general

(1) The Secretary of the Treasury shall refuse entry into the customs territory of the United States (as defined in general note 2 of the Harmonized Tariff Schedule of the United States) of any chemical substance, mixture, or article containing a chemical substance or mixture offered for such entry if—

(A) it fails to comply with any rule in effect under this chapter, or

(B) it is offered for entry in violation of section 2604 of this title, 2605 of this title, or subchapter IV of this chapter, a rule or order under section 2604 of this title, 2605 of this title, or subchapter IV of this chapter, or an order issued in a civil action brought under section 2604 of this title, 2606 of this title, or subchapter IV of this chapter.

(2) If a chemical substance, mixture, or article is refused entry under paragraph (1), the Secretary of the Treasury shall notify the consignee of such entry refusal, shall not release it to the consignee, and shall cause its disposal or storage (under such rules as the Secretary of the Treasury may prescribe) if it has not been exported by the consignee within 90 days from the date of receipt of notice of such refusal, except that the Secretary of the Treasury may, pending a review by the Administrator of the entry refusal, release to the consignee such substance, mixture, or article on execution of bond for the amount of the full invoice of such substance, mixture, or article (as such value is set forth in the customs entry), together with the duty thereon. On failure to return such substance, mixture, or article for any cause to the custody of the Secretary of the Treasury when demanded, such consignee shall be liable to the United States for liquidated damages equal to the full amount of such bond. All charges for storage, cartage, and labor on and for disposal of substances, mixtures, or articles which are refused entry or release under this section shall be paid by the owner or consignee, and in default of such payment shall constitute a lien against any future entry made by such owner or consignee.

(b) Rules

The Secretary of the Treasury, after consultation with the Administrator, shall issue rules for the administration of subsection (a) of this section.

(Oct. 11, 1976, Pub.L. 94–469, Title I, § 13, 90 Stat. 2034, redesignated Title I, Oct. 22, 1986, Pub.L. 99–519, § 3(c)(1), 100 Stat. 2989, and amended Aug. 23, 1988, Pub.L. 100–418, Title I, § 1214(e)(2), 102 Stat. 1156; Oct. 28, 1992, Pub.L. 102–550, Title X, § 1021(b)(4), 106 Stat. 3923.)

Effective Date of 1992 Amendments

Amendment by Pub.L. 102–550 effective Oct. 28, 1992, see section 2 of Pub.L. 102–550, set out as a note under section 5301 of Title 42, The Public Health and Welfare.

CODE OF FEDERAL REGULATIONS

United States Customs Service, chemical substances, see 19 CFR 12.118 et seq.

LIBRARY REFERENCES

Customs Duties ⇐63.
C.J.S. Customs Duties § 92 et seq.

§ 2613. Disclosure of data [TSCA § 14]

(a) In general

Except as provided by subsection (b) of this section, any information reported to, or otherwise obtained by, the Administrator (or any representative of the Administrator) under this chapter, which is exempt from disclosure pursuant to subsection (a) of section 552 of Title 5 by reason of subsection (b)(4) of such section, shall, notwithstanding the provisions of any other section of this chapter, not be disclosed by the Administrator or by any officer or employee of the United States, except that such information—

(1) shall be disclosed to any officer or employee of the United States—

(A) in connection with the official duties of such officer or employee under any law for the protection of health or the environment, or

(B) for specific law enforcement purposes;

(2) shall be disclosed to contractors with the United States and employees of such contractors if in the opinion of the Administrator such disclosure is necessary for the satisfactory performance by the contractor of a contract with the United States entered into on or after October 11, 1976, for the performance of work in connection with this chapter and under such conditions as the Administrator may specify;

(3) shall be disclosed if the Administrator determines it necessary to protect health or the environment against an unreasonable risk of injury to health or the environment; or

(4) may be disclosed when relevant in any proceeding under this chapter, except that disclosure in such a proceeding shall be made in such manner as to preserve confidentiality to the extent practicable without impairing the proceeding.

In any proceeding under section 552(a) of Title 5 to obtain information the disclosure of which has been denied because of the provisions of this subsection, the Administrator may not rely on section 552(b)(3) of such title to sustain the Administrator's action.

(b) Data from health and safety studies

(1) Subsection (a) of this section does not prohibit the disclosure of—

(A) any health and safety study which is submitted under this chapter with respect to—

(i) any chemical substance or mixture which, on the date on which such study is to be disclosed has been offered for commercial distribution, or

(ii) any chemical substance or mixture for which testing is required under section 2603 of this title or for which notification is required under section 2604 of this title, and

(B) any data reported to, or otherwise obtained by, the Administrator from a health and safety study which relates to a chemical substance or mixture described in clause (i) or (ii) of subparagraph (A).

This paragraph does not authorize the release of any data which discloses processes used in the manufacturing or processing of a chemical substance or mixture or, in the case of a mixture, the release of data disclosing the portion of the mixture comprised by any of the chemical substances in the mixture.

(2) If a request is made to the Administrator under subsection (a) of section 552 of Title 5 for information which is described in the first sentence of paragraph (1) and which is not information described in the second sentence of such paragraph, the Administrator may not deny such request on the basis of subsection (b)(4) of such section.

(c) Designation and release of confidential data

(1) In submitting data under this chapter, a manufacturer, processor, or distributor in commerce may (A) designate the data which such person believes is entitled to confidential treatment under subsection (a) of this section, and (B) submit such designated data separately from other data submitted under this chapter. A designation under this paragraph shall be made in writing and in such manner as the Administrator may prescribe.

(2)(A) Except as provided by subparagraph (B), if the Administrator proposes to release for inspection data which has been designated under paragraph (1)(A), the Administrator shall notify, in writing and by certified mail, the manufacturer, processor, or distributor in commerce who submitted such data of the intent to release such data. If the release of such data is to be made pursuant to a request made under section 552(a) of Title 5, such notice shall be given immediately upon approval of such request by the Administrator. The Administrator may not release such data until the expiration of 30 days after the manufacturer, processor, or distributor in commerce submitting such data has received the notice required by this subparagraph.

(B)(i) Subparagraph (A) shall not apply to the release of information under paragraph (1), (2), (3), or (4) of subsection (a) of this section, except that the Administrator may not release data under paragraph (3) of subsection (a) of this section unless the Administrator has notified each manufacturer, processor, and distributor in commerce who submitted such data of such release. Such notice shall be made in writing by certified mail at least 15 days before the release of such data, except that if the Administrator determines that the release of such data is necessary to protect against an imminent, unreasonable risk of injury to health or the environment, such notice may be made by such means as the Administrator determines will provide notice at least 24 hours before such release is made.

(ii) Subparagraph (A) shall not apply to the release of information described in subsection (b)(1) of this section other than information described in the second sentence of such subsection.

(d) Criminal penalty for wrongful disclosure

(1) Any officer or employee of the United States or former officer or employee of the United States, who by virtue of such employment or official position has obtained possession of, or has access to, material the disclosure of which is prohibited by subsection (a) of this section, and who knowing that disclosure of such material is prohibited by such subsection, willfully discloses the material in any manner to any person not entitled to receive it, shall be guilty of a misdemeanor and fined not more than $5,000 or imprisoned for not more than one year, or both. Section 1905 of Title 18 does not apply with respect to the publishing, divulging, disclosure, or making known of, or making available, information reported or otherwise obtained under this chapter.

(2) For the purposes of paragraph (1), any contractor with the United States who is furnished information as authorized by subsection (a)(2) of this section, and any employee of any such contractor, shall be considered to be an employee of the United States.

(e) Access by Congress

Notwithstanding any limitation contained in this section or any other provision of law, all information reported to or otherwise obtained by the Administrator (or any representative of the Administrator) under this chapter shall be made available, upon written request of any duly authorized committee of the Congress, to such committee.

(Oct. 11, 1976, Pub.L. 94–469, Title I, § 14, 90 Stat. 2034, redesignated Title I, Oct. 22, 1986, Pub.L. 99–519, § 3(c)(1), 100 Stat. 2989.)

CODE OF FEDERAL REGULATIONS

Confidentiality of business information, see 40 CFR 2.306.

LAW REVIEW COMMENTARIES

Trade secret misappropriation: A review and analysis of Massachusetts Law. Laurence H. Reece, III, 71 Mass.L.Rev. 171 (1986).

LIBRARY REFERENCES

Records ⚷54.
C.J.S. Records § 60 et seq.

§ 2614. Prohibited acts [TSCA § 15]

It shall be unlawful for any person to—

(1) fail or refuse to comply with (A) any rule promulgated or order issued under section 2603 of this title, (B) any requirement prescribed by section 2604 or 2605 of this title, (C) any rule promulgated or order issued under section 2604 or 2605 of this title, or (D) any requirement of subchapter II of this chapter or any rule promulgated or order issued under subchapter II of this chapter;

(2) use for commercial purposes a chemical substance or mixture which such person knew or had reason to know was manufactured, processed, or distributed in commerce in violation of section 2604 or 2605 of this title, a rule or order under section 2604 or 2605 of this title, or an order issued in action brought under section 2604 or 2606 of this title;

(3) fail or refuse to (A) establish or maintain records, (B) submit reports, notices, or other information, or (C) permit access to or copying of records, as required by this chapter or a rule thereunder; or

(4) fail or refuse to permit entry or inspection as required by section 2610 of this title.

(Oct. 11, 1976, Pub.L. 94–469, Title I, § 15, 90 Stat. 2036, redesignated Title I and amended Oct. 22, 1986, Pub.L. 99–519, §§ 3(b)(1), (c)(1), 100 Stat. 2988, 2989.)

LAW REVIEW COMMENTARIES

Survey of federal and state environmental crime legislation. Edward F. Novak and Charles W. Steese, 34 Ariz.L.Rev. 571 (1992).

LIBRARY REFERENCES

Health and Environment ⟹37.
C.J.S. Health and Environment § 48 et seq.

§ 2615. Penalties [TSCA § 16]

(a) Civil

(1) Any person who violates a provision of section 2614 or 2689 of this title shall be liable to the United States for a civil penalty in an amount not to exceed $25,000 for each such violation. Each day such a violation continues shall, for purposes of this subsection, constitute a separate violation of section 2614 or 2689 of this title.

(2)(A) A civil penalty for a violation of section 2614 or 2689 of this title shall be assessed by the Administrator by an order made on the record after opportunity (provided in accordance with this subparagraph) for a hearing in accordance with section 554 of Title 5. Before issuing such an order, the Administrator shall give written notice to the person to be assessed a civil penalty under such order of the Administrator's proposal to issue such order and provide such person an opportunity to request, within 15 days of the date the notice is received by such person, such a hearing on the order.

(B) In determining the amount of a civil penalty, the Administrator shall take into account the nature, circumstances, extent, and gravity of the violation or violations and, with respect to the violator, ability to pay, effect on ability to continue to do business, any history of prior such violations, the degree of culpability, and such other matters as justice may require.

(C) The Administrator may compromise, modify, or remit, with or without conditions, any civil penalty which may be imposed under this subsection. The amount of such penalty, when finally determined, or the amount agreed upon in compromise, may be deducted from any sums owing by the United States to the person charged.

(3) Any person who requested in accordance with paragraph (2)(A) a hearing respecting the assessment of a civil penalty and who is aggrieved by an order assessing a civil penalty may file a petition for judicial review of such order with the United States Court of Appeals for the District of Columbia Circuit or for any other circuit in which such person resides or transacts business. Such a petition may only be filed within the 30-day period beginning on the date the order making such assessment was issued.

(4) If any person fails to pay an assessment of a civil penalty—

(A) after the order making the assessment has become a final order and if such person does not file a petition for judicial review of the order in accordance with paragraph (3), or

(B) after a court in an action brought under paragraph (3) has entered a final judgment in favor of the Administrator,

the Attorney General shall recover the amount assessed (plus interest at currently prevailing rates from the date of the expiration of the 30-day period referred to in paragraph (3) or the date of such final judgment, as the case may be) in an action brought in any appropriate district court of the United States. In such an action, the validity, amount, and appropriateness of such penalty shall not be subject to review.

(b) Criminal

Any person who knowingly or willfully violates any provision of section 2614 or 2689 of this title, shall, in addition to or in lieu of any civil penalty which may be imposed under subsection (a) of this section for such violation, be subject, upon conviction, to a fine of not more than $25,000 for each day of violation, or to imprisonment for not more than one year, or both.

(Oct. 11, 1976, Pub.L. 94–469, Title I, § 16, 90 Stat. 2037, redesignated Title I, Oct. 22, 1986, Pub.L. 99–519, § 3(c)(1), 100 Stat. 2989; Oct. 28, 1992, Pub.L. 102–550, Title X, § 1021(b)(5), 106 Stat. 3923.)

Effective Date of 1992 Amendments

Amendment by Pub.L. 102–550 effective Oct. 28, 1992, see section 2 of Pub.L. 102–550, set out as a note under section 5301 of Title 42, The Public Health and Welfare.

CODE OF FEDERAL REGULATIONS

Rules of practice, see 40 CFR 22.01 et seq.

LAW REVIEW COMMENTARIES

Hazardous Waste: A threat to the lender's environment. Marcy Sharon Cohen, 19 UCC L.J. 99 (1986).

Prosecution of corporations and corporate officers for environmental crimes: Limiting one's exposure for environmental criminal liability. Kenneth A. Hodson, Sarah N. McGiffert and Marianne T. Bayardi, 34 Ariz.L.Rev. 553 (1992).

Responding to a government environmental investigation: Shaping the defense. Francis J. Burke, Jr., Karen A. Potts, Leigh Lani Brown, Robin L. De Respino and Michael R. Hall, 34 Ariz.L.Rev. 509 (1992).

Responsible corporate officer: Designated felon or legal fiction? Brenda S. Hustis and John Y. Gotanda, 25 Loy.U.Chi.L.J. 169 (1994).

Survey of federal and state environmental crime legislation. Edward F. Novak and Charles W. Steese, 34 Ariz.L.Rev. 571 (1992).

LIBRARY REFERENCES

Health and Environment ⚖25.5(10), 38.
C.J.S. Health and Environment §§ 49, 103 et seq.

§ 2616. Specific enforcement and seizure [TSCA § 17]

(a) Specific enforcement

(1) The district courts of the United States shall have jurisdiction over civil actions to—

(A) restrain any violation of section 2614 or 2689 of this title,

(B) restrain any person from taking any action prohibited by section 2604 of this title, 2605 of this title, or subchapter IV of this chapter, or by a rule or order under section 2604 of this title, 2605 of this title, or subchapter IV of this chapter,

(C) compel the taking of any action required by or under this chapter, or

(D) direct any manufacturer or processor of a chemical substance, mixture, or product subject to subchapter IV of this subchapter manufactured or processed in violation of section 2604 of this title, 2605 of this title, or subchapter IV of this chapter, or a rule or order under section 2604 of this title, 2605 of this title, or subchapter IV of this chapter, and distributed in commerce, (i) to give notice of such fact to distributors in commerce of such substance, mixture, or product and, to the extent reasonably ascertainable, to other persons in possession of such substance, mixture, or product or exposed to such substance, mixture, or product, (ii) to give public notice of such risk of injury, and (iii) to either replace or repurchase such substance, mixture, or product, whichever the person to which the requirement is directed elects.

(2) A civil action described in paragraph (1) may be brought—

(A) in the case of a civil action described in subparagraph (A) of such paragraph, in the United States district court for the judicial district wherein any act, omission, or transaction constituting a violation of section 2614 of this title occurred or wherein the defendant is found or transacts business, or

(B) in the case of any other civil action described in such paragraph, in the United States district court for the judicial district wherein the defendant is found or transacts business.

In any such civil action process may be served on a defendant in any judicial district in which a defendant resides or may be found. Subpoenas requiring attendance of witnesses in any such action may be served in any judicial district.

(b) Seizure

Any chemical substance, mixture, or product subject to subchapter IV of this chapter which was manufactured, processed, or distributed in commerce in violation of this chapter or any rule promulgated or order issued under this chapter or any article containing such a substance or mixture shall be liable to be proceeded against, by process of libel, for the seizure and condemnation of such substance, mixture, product, or article, in any district court of the United States within the jurisdiction of which such substance, mixture, product, or article is found. Such proceedings shall conform as nearly as possible to proceedings in rem in admiralty.

(Oct. 11, 1976, Pub.L. 94–469, Title I, § 17, 90 Stat. 2037, redesignated Title I, Oct. 22, 1986, Pub.L. 99–519, § 3(c)(1), 100 Stat. 2989; Oct. 28, 1992, Pub.L. 102–550, Title X, § 1021(b)(6), (7), 106 Stat. 3923.)

Codification

Section 1021(b)(6) of Pub.L. 102–550, which directed that subsec. (a) of this section be amended "as follows:" and which provided for subsec. heading and for par. (1) of such subsec., but which failed to account for par. (2) of such subsec., was executed by substituting subsec. heading and par. (1) for existing subsec. heading and par. (1), and by retaining existing par. (2).

Effective Date of 1992 Amendments

Amendment by Pub.L. 102–550 effective Oct. 28, 1992, see section 2 of Pub.L. 102–550, set out as a note under section 5301 of Title 42, The Public Health and Welfare.

LIBRARY REFERENCES

Health and Environment ⚖25.5(10).
C.J.S. Health and Environment § 103 et seq.

§ 2617. Preemption [TSCA § 18]

(a) Effect on State law

(1) Except as provided in paragraph (2), nothing in this chapter shall affect the authority of any State or political subdivision of a State to establish or continue in effect regulation of any chemical substance, mixture, or article containing a chemical substance or mixture.

(2) Except as provided in subsection (b) of this section—

(A) if the Administrator requires by a rule promulgated under section 2603 of this title the testing of a chemical substance or mixture, no State or political subdivision may, after the effective date of such rule, establish or continue in effect a requirement for the testing of such substance or mixture for purposes similar to those for which testing is required under such rule; and

(B) if the Administrator prescribes a rule or order under section 2604 or 2605 of this title (other than a rule imposing a requirement described in subsection (a)(6) of section 2605 of this title) which is applicable to a chemical substance or mixture, and which is designed to protect against a risk of injury to health or the environment associated with such substance or mixture, no State or political subdivision of a State may, after the effective date of such requirement, establish or continue in effect, any requirement which is applicable to such substance or mixture, or an article containing such substance or mixture, and which is designed to protect against such risk unless such requirement (i) is identical to the requirement prescribed by the Administrator, (ii) is adopted under the authority of the Clean Air Act [42 U.S.C.A. § 7401 et seq.] or any other Federal law, or (iii) prohibits the use of such substance or mixture in such State or political subdivision (other than its use in the manufacture or processing of other substances or mixtures).

(b) Exemption

Upon application of a State or political subdivision of a State the Administrator may by rule exempt from subsection (a)(2) of this section, under such conditions as may be prescribed in such rule, a requirement of such State or political subdivision designed to protect against a risk of injury to health or the environment associated with a chemical substance, mixture, or article containing a chemical substance or mixture if—

(1) compliance with the requirement would not cause the manufacturing, processing, distribution in commerce, or use of the substance, mixture, or article to be in violation of the applicable requirement under this chapter described in subsection (a)(2) of this section, and

(2) the State or political subdivision requirement (A) provides a significantly higher degree of protection from such risk than the requirement under this chapter described in subsection (a)(2) of this section and (B) does not, through difficulties in marketing, distribution, or other factors, unduly burden interstate commerce.

(Oct. 11, 1976, Pub.L. 94–469, Title I, § 18, 90 Stat. 2038, redesignated Title I, Oct. 22, 1986, Pub.L. 99–519, § 3(c)(1), 100 Stat. 2989.)

West's Federal Practice Manual

Pesticides and toxic substances, see § 4385.10.

LIBRARY REFERENCES

States ⚷4.10.
C.J.S. States § 24.

§ 2618. Judicial review [TSCA § 19]

(a) In general

(1)(A) Not later than 60 days after the date of the promulgation of a rule under section 2603(a), 2604(a)(2), 2604(b)(4), 2605(a), 2605(e), or 2607 or under subchapter II or IV of this chapter, any person may file a petition for judicial review of such rule with the United States Court of Appeals for the District of Columbia Circuit or for the circuit in which such person resides or in which such person's principal place of business is located. Courts of appeals of the United States shall have exclusive jurisdiction of any action to obtain judicial review (other than in an enforcement proceeding) of such a rule if any district court of the United States would have had jurisdiction of such action but for this subparagraph.

(B) Courts of appeals of the United States shall have exclusive jurisdiction of any action to obtain judicial review (other than in an enforcement proceeding) of an order issued under subparagraph (A) or (B) of section 2605(b)(1) of this title if any district court of the United States would have had jurisdiction of such action but for this subparagraph.

(2) Copies of any petition filed under paragraph (1)(A) shall be transmitted forthwith to the Administrator and to the Attorney General by the clerk of the court with which such petition was filed. The provisions of section 2112 of Title 28 shall apply to the filing of the rulemaking record of proceedings on which the Administrator based the rule being reviewed under this section and to the transfer of proceedings between United States courts of appeals.

(3) For purposes of this section, the term "rulemaking record" means—

(A) the rule being reviewed under this section;

(B) in the case of a rule under section 2603(a) of this title, the finding required by such section, in the case of a rule under section 2604(b)(4) of this title, the finding required by such section, in the case of a rule under section 2605(a) of this title the finding required by section 2604(f) or 2605(a) of this title, as the case may be, in the case of a rule under section 2605(a) of this title, the statement required by section 2605(c)(1) of this title, and in the case of a rule under section 2605(e) of this title, the findings required by paragraph (2)(B) or (3)(B) of such section, as the case may be and in the case of a rule under subchapter IV of this chapter, the finding required for the issuance of such a rule;

(C) any transcript required to be made of oral presentations made in proceedings for the promulgation of such rule;

(D) any written submission of interested parties respecting the promulgation of such rule; and

(E) any other information which the Administrator considers to be relevant to such rule and which the Administrator identified, on or before the date of the promulgation of such rule, in a notice published in the Federal Register.

(b) Additional submissions and presentations; modifications

If in an action under this section to review a rule the petitioner or the Administrator applies to the court for leave to make additional oral submissions or written presentations respecting such rule and shows to the satisfaction of the court that such submissions and presentations would be material and that there were reasonable grounds for the submissions and failure to make such submissions and presentations in the proceeding before the Administrator, the court may order the Administrator to provide additional opportunity to make such submissions and presentations. The Administrator may modify or set aside the rule being reviewed or make a new rule by reason of the additional submissions and presentations and shall file such modified or new rule with the return of such submissions and presentations. The court shall thereafter review such new or modified rule.

(c) Standard of review

(1)(A) Upon the filing of a petition under subsection (a)(1) of this section for judicial review of a rule, the court shall have jurisdiction (i) to grant appropriate relief, including interim relief, as provided in chapter 7 of Title 5, and (ii) except as otherwise provided in subparagraph (B), to review such rule in accordance with chapter 7 of Title 5.

(B) Section 706 of Title 5 shall apply to review of a rule under this section, except that—

(i) in the case of review of a rule under section 2603(a), 2604(b)(4), 2605(a), or 2605(e) of this title, the standard for review prescribed by paragraph (2)(E) of such section 706 shall not apply and the court shall hold unlawful and set aside such rule if the court finds that the rule is not supported by substantial evidence in the rulemaking record (as defined in subsection (a)(3) of this section) taken as a whole;

(ii) in the case of review of a rule under section 2605(a) of this title, the court shall hold unlawful and set aside such rule if it finds that—

(I) a determination by the Administrator under section 2605(c)(3) of this title that the petitioner seeking review of such rule is not entitled to conduct (or have conducted) cross-examination or to present rebuttal submissions, or

(II) a rule of, or ruling by, the Administrator under section 2605(c)(3) of this title limiting such petitioner's cross-examination or oral presentations,

has precluded disclosure of disputed material facts which was necessary to a fair determination by the Administrator of the rulemaking proceeding taken as a whole; and section 706(2)(D) shall not apply with respect to a determination, rule, or ruling referred to in subclause (I) or (II); and

(iii) the court may not review the contents and adequacy of—

(I) any statement required to be made pursuant to section 2605(c)(1) of this title, or

(II) any statement of basis and purpose required by section 553(c) of Title 5, to be incorporated in the rule

except as part of a review of the rulemaking record taken as a whole.

The term "evidence" as used in clause (i) means any matter in the rulemaking record.

(C) A determination, rule, or ruling of the Administrator described in subparagraph (B)(ii) may be reviewed only in an action under this section and only in accordance with such subparagraph.

(2) The judgment of the court affirming or setting aside, in whole or in part, any rule reviewed in accordance with this section shall be final, subject to review by the Supreme Court of the United States upon certiorari or certification, as provided in section 1254 of Title 28.

(d) Fees and costs

The decision of the court in an action commenced under subsection (a) of this section, or of the Supreme Court of the United States on review of such a decision, may include an award of costs of suit and reasonable fees for attorneys and expert witnesses if the court determines that such an award is appropriate.

(e) Other remedies

The remedies as provided in this section shall be in addition to and not in lieu of any other remedies provided by law.

(Oct. 11, 1976, Pub.L. 94–469, Title I, § 19, 90 Stat. 2039, redesignated Title I and amended Oct. 22, 1986, Pub.L. 99–519, § 3(b)(2), (c)(1), 100 Stat. 2989; Oct. 28, 1992, Pub.L. 102–550, Title X, § 1021(b)(8), 106 Stat. 3923.)

Effective Date of 1992 Amendments

Amendment by Pub.L. 102–550 effective Oct. 28, 1992, see section 2 of Pub.L. 102–550, set out as a note under section 5301 of Title 42, The Public Health and Welfare.

ADMINISTRATIVE LAW

Venue, see Koch § 8.52.

LAW REVIEW COMMENTARIES

Interstate waste: A key issue in resolving the national hazardous waste capacity crisis. B.J. Wynne, III and Terri Hamby, 32 S.Tex. L.Rev. 601 (1991).

"More good than harm": A first principle for environmental agencies and reviewing courts. Edward W. Warren and Gary E. Marchant, 20 Ecology L.Q. 379 (1993).

LIBRARY REFERENCES

Health and Environment ⚯25.15(6).
C.J.S. Health and Environment § 85 et seq.

§ 2619. Citizens' civil actions [TSCA § 20]

(a) In general

Except as provided in subsection (b) of this section, any person may commence a civil action—

(1) against any person (including (A) the United States, and (B) any other governmental instrumentality or agency to the extent permitted by the eleventh amendment to the Constitution) who is alleged to be in violation of this chapter or any rule promulgated under section 2603, 2604, or 2605 of this title, or subchapter II or IV of this chapter, or order issued under section 2604 of this title or subchapter II or IV of this chapter to restrain such violation, or

(2) against the Administrator to compel the Administrator to perform any act or duty under this chapter which is not discretionary.

Any civil action under paragraph (1) shall be brought in the United States district court for the district in which the alleged violation occurred or in which the defendant resides or in which the defendant's principal place of business is located. Any action brought under paragraph (2) shall be brought in the United States District Court for the District of Columbia, or the United States district court for the judicial district in which the plaintiff is domiciled. The district courts of the United States shall have jurisdiction over suits brought under this section, without regard to the amount in controversy or the citizenship of the parties. In any civil action under this subsection process may be served on a defendant in any judicial district in which the defendant resides or may be found and subpoenas for witnesses may be served in any judicial district.

(b) Limitation

No civil action may be commenced—

(1) under subsection (a)(1) of this section to restrain a violation of this chapter or rule or order under this chapter—

(A) before the expiration of 60 days after the plaintiff has given notice of such violation (i) to the Administrator, and (ii) to the person who is alleged to have committed such violation, or

(B) if the Administrator has commenced and is diligently prosecuting a proceeding for the issuance of an order under section 2615(a)(2) of this title to require compliance with this chapter or with such rule or order or if the Attorney General has commenced and is diligently prosecuting a civil action in a court of the United States to require compliance with this chapter or with such rule or order, but if such proceeding or civil action is commenced after the giving of notice, any person giving such notice may intervene as a matter of right in such proceeding or action; or

(2) under subsection (a)(2) of this section before the expiration of 60 days after the plaintiff has given notice to the Administrator of the alleged failure of the Administrator to perform an act or duty which is the basis for such action or, in the case of an action under such subsection for the failure of the Administrator to file an action under section 2606 of this title, before the expiration of ten days after such notification.

Notice under this subsection shall be given in such manner as the Administrator shall prescribe by rule.

(c) General

(1) In any action under this section, the Administrator, if not a party, may intervene as a matter of right.

(2) The court, in issuing any final order in any action brought pursuant to subsection (a) of this section, may award costs of suit and reasonable fees for attorneys and expert witnesses if the court determines that such an award is appropriate. Any court, in issuing its decision in an action brought to review such an order, may award costs of suit and reasonable fees for attorneys if the court determines that such an award is appropriate.

(3) Nothing in this section shall restrict any right which any person (or class of persons) may have under any statute or common law to seek enforcement of this chapter or any rule or order under this chapter or to seek any other relief.

(d) Consolidation

When two or more civil actions brought under subsection (a) of this section involving the same defendant and the same issues or violations are pending in two or more judicial districts, such pending actions, upon application of such defendants to such actions which is made to a court in which any such action is brought, may, if such court in its discretion so decides, be consolidated for trial by order (issued after giving all parties reasonable notice and opportunity to be heard) of such court and tried in—

(1) any district which is selected by such defendant and in which one of such actions is pending.

(2) a district which is agreed upon by stipulation between all the parties to such actions and in which one of such actions is pending, or

(3) a district which is selected by the court and in which one of such actions is pending.

The court issuing such an order shall give prompt notification of the order to the other courts in which the civil actions consolidated under the order are pending.

(Oct. 11, 1976, Pub.L. 94–469, Title I, § 20, 90 Stat. 2041, redesignated Title I and amended Oct. 22, 1986, Pub.L. 99–519, § 3(b)(3), (c)(1), 100 Stat. 2989; Oct. 28, 1992, Pub.L. 102–550, Title X, § 1021(b)(9), 106 Stat. 3923.)

Effective Date of 1992 Amendments

Amendment by Pub.L. 102–550 effective Oct. 28, 1992, see section 2 of Pub.L. 102–550, set out as a note under section 5301 of Title 42, The Public Health and Welfare.

CODE OF FEDERAL REGULATIONS

Notice of intent to sue, see 40 CFR 702.60.

LAW REVIEW COMMENTARIES

Warrior and the Druid—the DOD and environmental law. Michael Donnelly and James G. Van Ness, 33 Fed.Bar News 37 (1986).

LIBRARY REFERENCES

United States ⚷124.
C.J.S. United States § 175.

§ 2620. Citizens' petitions [TSCA § 21]

(a) In general

Any person may petition the Administrator to initiate a proceeding for the issuance, amendment, or repeal of a rule under section 2603, 2605, or 2607 of this title or an order under section 2604(e) or 2605(b)(2) of this title.

(b) Procedures

(1) Such petition shall be filed in the principal office of the Administrator and shall set forth the facts which it is claimed establish that it is necessary to issue, amend, or repeal a rule under section 2603, 2605, or 2607 of this title or an order under section 2604(e), 2605(b)(1)(A), or 2605(b)(1)(B) of this title.

(2) The Administrator may hold a public hearing or may conduct such investigation or proceeding as the Administrator deems appropriate in order to determine whether or not such petition should be granted.

(3) Within 90 days after filing of a petition described in paragraph (1), the Administrator shall either grant or deny the petition. If the Administrator grants such petition, the Administrator shall promptly commence an appropriate proceeding in accordance with section 2603, 2604, 2605, or 2607 of this title. If the Administrator denies such petition, the Administrator shall publish in the Federal Register the Administrator's reasons for such denial.

(4)(A) If the Administrator denies a petition filed under this section (or if the Administrator fails to grant or deny such petition within the 90-day period) the petitioner may commence a civil action in a district court of the United States to compel the Administrator to initiate a rulemaking proceeding as requested in the petition. Any such action shall be filed within 60 days after the Administrator's denial of the petition or, if the Administrator fails to grant or deny the petition within 90 days after filing the petition, within 60 days after the expiration of the 90-day period.

(B) In an action under subparagraph (A) respecting a petition to initiate a proceeding to issue a rule under section 2603, 2605, or 2607 of this title or an order under section 2604(e) or 2605(b)(2) of this title, the petitioner shall be provided an opportunity to have such petition considered by the court in a de novo proceeding. If the petitioner demonstrates to the satisfaction of the court by a preponderance of the evidence that—

(i) in the case of a petition to initiate a proceeding for the issuance of a rule under section 2603 of this title or an order under section 2604(e) of this title—

(I) information available to the Administrator is insufficient to permit a reasoned evaluation of the health and environmental effects of the chemical substance to be subject to such rule or order; and

(II) in the absence of such information, the substance may present an unreasonable risk to health or the environment, or the substance is or will be produced in substantial quantities and it enters or may reasonably be anticipated to enter the environment in substantial quantities or there is or may be significant or substantial human exposure to it; or

(ii) in the case of a petition to initiate a proceeding for the issuance of a rule under section 2605 or 2607 of this title or an order under section 2605(b)(2) of this title, there is a reasonable basis to conclude that the issuance of such a rule or order is necessary to protect health or the environment against an unreasonable risk of injury to health or the environment.[1]

the court shall order the Administrator to initiate the action requested by the petitioner. If the court finds that the extent of the risk to health or the environment alleged by the petitioner is less than the extent of risks to health or the environment with respect to which the Administrator is taking action under this chapter and there are insufficient resources available to the Administrator to take the action requested by the petitioner, the court may permit the Administrator to defer initiating the action requested by the petitioner until such time as the court prescribes.

(C) The court in issuing any final order in any action brought pursuant to subparagraph (A) may award costs of suit and reasonable fees for attorneys and expert witnesses if the court determines that such an award is appropriate. Any court, in issuing its decision in an action brought to review such an order, may award costs of suit and reasonable fees for attorneys if the court determines that such an award is appropriate.

(5) The remedies under this section shall be in addition to, and not in lieu of, other remedies provided by law.

(Oct. 11, 1976, Pub.L. 94–469, Title I, § 21, 90 Stat. 2042, redesignated Title I, Oct. 22, 1986, Pub.L. 99–519, § 3(c)(1), 100 Stat. 2989.)

1 So in original. The period should probably be a semicolon.

LIBRARY REFERENCES

United States ⟹140.
C.J.S. United States § 198 et seq.

§ 2621. National defense waiver [TSCA § 22]

The Administrator shall waive compliance with any provision of this chapter upon a request and determination by the President that the requested waiver is necessary in the interest of national defense. The Administrator shall maintain a written record of the basis upon which such waiver was granted and make such record available for in camera examination when relevant in a judicial proceeding under this chapter. Upon the issuance of such a waiver, the Administrator shall publish in the Federal Register a notice that the waiver was granted for national defense purposes, unless, upon the request of the President, the Administrator determines to omit such publication because the publication itself would be contrary to the interests of national defense, in which event the Administrator shall submit notice thereof to the Armed Services Committees of the Senate and the House of Representatives.

(Oct. 11, 1976, Pub.L. 94–469, Title I, § 22, 90 Stat. 2044, redesignated Title I, Oct. 22, 1986, Pub.L. 99–519, § 3(c)(1), 100 Stat. 2989.)

Change of Name

Any reference in any provision of law enacted before Jan. 4, 1995, to the Committee on Armed Services of the House of Representatives treated as referring to the Committee on National Security of the House of Representatives, see section 1(a)(1) of Pub.L. 104–14, set out as a note preceding section 21 of Title 2, The Congress.

LIBRARY REFERENCES

War and National Emergency ⟹38.
C.J.S. War and National Defense § 46.

§ 2622. Employee protection [TSCA § 23]

(a) In general

No employer may discharge any employee or otherwise discriminate against any employee with respect to the employee's compensation, terms, conditions, or privileges of employment because the employee (or any person acting pursuant to a request of the employee) has—

(1) commenced, caused to be commenced, or is about to commence or cause to be commenced a proceeding under this chapter;

(2) testified or is about to testify in any such proceeding; or

(3) assisted or participated or is about to assist or participate in any manner in such a proceeding or in any other action to carry out the purposes of this chapter.

(b) Remedy

(1) Any employee who believes that the employee has been discharged or otherwise discriminated against by any person in violation of subsection (a) of this section may, within 30 days after such alleged violation occurs, file (or have any person file on the employee's behalf) a complaint with the Secretary of Labor (hereinafter in this section referred to as the "Secretary") alleging such discharge or discrimination. Upon receipt of such a complaint, the Secretary shall notify the person named in the complaint of the filing of the complaint.

(2)(A) Upon receipt of a complaint filed under paragraph (1), the Secretary shall conduct an investigation of the violation alleged in the complaint. Within 30 days of the receipt of such complaint, the Secretary shall complete such investigation and shall notify in writing the complainant (and any person acting on behalf of the complainant) and the person alleged to have committed such violation of the results of the investigation conducted pursuant to this paragraph. Within ninety days of the receipt of such complaint the Secretary shall, unless the proceeding on the complaint is terminated by the Secretary on the basis of a settlement entered into by the Secretary and the person alleged to have committed such violation, issue an order either providing the relief prescribed by subparagraph (B) or denying the complaint. An order of the Secretary shall be made on the record after notice and opportunity for agency hearing. The Secretary may not enter into a settlement terminating a proceeding on a complaint without the participation and consent of the complainant.

(B) If in response to a complaint filed under paragraph (1) the Secretary determines that a violation of subsection (a) of this section has occurred, the Secretary shall order (i) the person who committed such violation to take affirmative action to abate the violation, (ii) such person to reinstate the complainant to the complainant's former position together with the compensation (including back pay), terms, conditions, and privileges of the complainant's employment, (iii) compensatory damages, and (iv) where appropriate, exemplary damages. If such an order issued, the Secretary, at the request of the complainant, shall assess against the person against whom the order is issued a sum equal to the aggregate amount of all costs and expenses (including attorney's fees) reasonably incurred, as determined by the Secretary, by the complainant for, or in connection with, the bringing of the complaint upon which the order was issued.

(c) Review

(1) Any employee or employer adversely affected or aggrieved by an order issued under subsection (b) of this section may obtain review of the order in the United States Court of Appeals for the circuit in which the violation, with respect to which the order was issued, allegedly occurred. The petition for review must be filed within sixty days from the issuance of the Secretary's order. Review shall conform to chapter 7 of Title 5.

(2) An order of the Secretary, with respect to which review could have been obtained under paragraph (1), shall not be subject to judicial review in any criminal or other civil proceeding.

(d) Enforcement

Whenever a person has failed to comply with an order issued under subsection (b)(2) of this section, the Secretary shall file a civil action in the United States district court for the district in which the violation was found to occur to enforce such order. In actions brought under this subsection, the district courts shall have jurisdiction to grant all appropriate relief, including injunctive relief and compensatory and exemplary damages.

(e) Exclusion

Subsection (a) of this section shall not apply with respect to any employee who, acting without direction from the employee's employer (or any agent of the employer), deliberately causes a violation of any requirement of this chapter.

(Oct. 11, 1976, Pub.L. 94–469, Title I, § 23, 90 Stat. 2044; Nov. 8, 1984, Pub.L. 98–620, Title IV, § 402(19), 98 Stat. 3358; redesignated Title I, Oct. 22, 1986, Pub.L. 99–519, § 3(c)(1), 100 Stat. 2989.)

West's Federal Practice Manual

Pertinent federal legislation, see § 1475.7.

CODE OF FEDERAL REGULATIONS

Procedures for the handling of discrimination complaints, see 29 CFR 24.1 et seq.

LIBRARY REFERENCES

Labor Relations ⚷9.5.
C.J.S. Labor Relations § 2.

§ 2623. Employment effects [TSCA § 24]

(a) In general

The Administrator shall evaluate on a continuing basis the potential effects on employment (including reductions in employment or loss of employment from threatened plant closures) of—

(1) the issuance of a rule or order under section 2603, 2604, or 2605 of this title, or

(2) a requirement of section 2604 or 2605 of this title.

(b) Investigations

(1) Any employee (or any representative of an employee) may request the Administrator to make an investigation of—

(A) a discharge or layoff or threatened discharge or layoff of the employee, or

(B) adverse or threatened adverse effects on the employee's employment,

allegedly resulting from a rule or order under section 2603, 2604, or 2605 of this title or a requirement of section 2604 or 2605 of this title. Any such request shall be made in writing, shall set forth with reasonable particularity the grounds for the request, and shall be signed by the employee, or representative of such employee, making the request.

(2)(A) Upon receipt of a request made in accordance with paragraph (1) the Administrator shall (i) conduct the investigation requested, and (ii) if requested by any interested person, hold public hearings on any matter involved in the investigation unless the Administrator, by order issued within 45 days of the date such hearings are requested, denies the request for the hearings because the Administrator determines there are no reasonable grounds for holding such hearings. If the Administrator makes such a determination, the Administrator shall notify in writing the person requesting the hearing of the determination and the reasons therefor and shall publish the determination and the reasons therefor in the Federal Register.

(B) If public hearings are to be held on any matter involved in an investigation conducted under this subsection—

(i) at least five days' notice shall be provided the person making the request for the investigation and any person identified in such request,

(ii) such hearings shall be held in accordance with section 2605(c)(3) of this title, and

(iii) each employee who made or for whom was made a request for such hearings and the employer of such employee shall be required to present information respecting the applicable matter referred to in paragraph (1)(A) or (1)(B) together with the basis for such information.

(3) Upon completion of an investigation under paragraph (2), the Administrator shall make findings of fact, shall make such recommendations as the Administrator deems appropriate, and shall make available to the public such findings and recommendations.

(4) This section shall not be construed to require the Administrator to amend or repeal any rule or order in effect under this chapter.

(Oct. 11, 1976, Pub.L. 94–469, Title I, § 24, 90 Stat. 2045, redesignated Title I, Oct. 22, 1986, Pub.L. 99–519, § 3(c)(1), 100 Stat. 2989.)

§ 2624. Studies [TSCA § 25]

(a) Indemnification study

The Administrator shall conduct a study of all Federal laws administered by the Administrator for the purpose of determining whether and under what conditions, if any, indemnification should be accorded any person as a result of any action taken by the Administrator under any such law. The study shall—

(1) include an estimate of the probable cost of any indemnification programs which may be recommended;

(2) include an examination of all viable means of financing the cost of any recommended indemnification; and

(3) be completed and submitted to Congress within two years from the effective date of enactment of this chapter.

The General Accounting Office shall review the adequacy of the study submitted to Congress pursuant to paragraph (3) and shall report the results of its review to the Congress within six months of the date such study is submitted to Congress.

(b) Classification, storage, and retrieval study

The Council on Environmental Quality, in consultation with the Administrator, the Secretary of Health and Human Services, the Secretary of Commerce, and the heads of other appropriate Federal departments or agencies, shall coordinate a study of the feasibility of establishing (1) a standard classification system for chemical substances and related substances, and (2) a standard means for storing and for obtaining rapid access to information respecting such substances. A report on such study shall be completed and submitted to Congress not later than 18 months after the effective date of enactment of this chapter.

(Oct. 11, 1976, Pub.L. 94–469, Title I, § 25, 90 Stat. 2046; Oct. 17, 1979, Pub.L. 96–88, Title V, § 509(b), 93 Stat. 695; redesignated Title I, Oct. 22, 1986, Pub.L. 99–519, § 3(c)(1), 100 Stat. 2989.)

§ 2625. Administration [TSCA § 26]

(a) Cooperation of Federal agencies

Upon request by the Administrator, each Federal department and agency is authorized—

(1) to make its services, personnel, and facilities available (with or without reimbursement) to the Administrator to assist the Administrator in the administration of this chapter; and

(2) to furnish to the Administrator such information, data, estimates, and statistics, and to allow the Administrator access to all information in its possession as the Administrator may reasonably determine to be necessary for the administration of this chapter.

(b) Fees

(1) The Administrator may, by rule, require the payment of a reasonable fee from any person required to submit data under section 2603 or 2604 of this title to defray the cost of administering this chapter. Such rules shall not provide for any fee in excess of $2,500 or, in the case of a small business concern, any fee in excess of $100. In setting a fee under this paragraph, the Administrator shall take into account the ability to pay of the person required to submit the data and the cost to the Administrator of reviewing such data. Such rules may provide for sharing such a fee in any case in which the expenses of testing are shared under section 2603 or 2604 of this title.

(2) The Administrator, after consultation with the Administrator of the Small Business Administration, shall by rule prescribe standards for determining the persons which qualify as small business concerns for purposes of paragraph (1).

(c) Action with respect to categories

(1) Any action authorized or required to be taken by the Administrator under any provision of this chapter with respect to a chemical substance or mixture may be taken by the Administrator in accordance with that provision with respect to a category of chemical substances or mixtures. Whenever the Administrator takes action under a provision of this chapter with respect to a category of chemical substances or mixtures, any reference in this chapter to a chemical substance or mixture (insofar as it relates to such action) shall be deemed to be a reference to each chemical substance or mixture in such category.

(2) For purposes of paragraph (1):

(A) The term "category of chemical substances" means a group of chemical substances the members of which are similar in molecular structure, in physical, chemical, or biological properties, in use, or in mode of entrance into the human body or into the environment, or the members of which are in some other way suitable for classification as such for purposes of this chapter, except that such term does not mean a group of chemical substances which are grouped together solely on the basis of their being new chemical substances.

(B) The term "category of mixtures" means a group of mixtures the members of which are similar in molecular structure, in physical, chemical, or biological properties, in use, or in the mode of entrance into the human body or into the environment, or the members of which are in some other way suitable for classification as such for purposes of this chapter.

(d) Assistance office

The Administrator shall establish in the Environmental Protection Agency an identifiable office to provide technical and other nonfinancial assistance to manufacturers and processors of chemical substances and mixtures respecting the requirements of this chapter applicable to such manufacturers and processors, the policy of the Agency respecting the application of such requirements to such manufacturers and processors, and the means and methods by which such manufacturers and processors may comply with such requirements.

(e) Financial disclosures

(1) Except as provided under paragraph (3), each officer or employee of the Environmental Protection Agency and the Department of Health and Human Services who—

(A) performs any function or duty under this chapter, and

(B) has any known financial interest (i) in any person subject to this chapter or any rule or order in effect under this chapter, or (ii) in any person who applies for or receives any grant or contract under this chapter,

shall, on February 1, 1978, and on February 1 of each year thereafter, file with the Administrator or the Secretary of Health and Human Services (hereinafter in this subsection referred to as the "Secretary"), as appropriate, a written statement concerning all such interests held by such officer or employee during the preceding calendar year. Such statement shall be made available to the public.

(2) The Administrator and the Secretary shall—

(A) act within 90 days of January 1, 1977—

(i) to define the term "known financial interests" for purposes of paragraph (1), and

(ii) to establish the methods by which the requirement to file written statements specified in paragraph (1) will be monitored and enforced, including appropriate provisions for review by the Administrator and the Secretary of such statements; and

(B) report to the Congress on June 1, 1978, and on June 1 of each year thereafter with respect to such statements and the actions taken in regard thereto during the preceding calendar year.

(3) The Administrator may by rule identify specific positions with the Environmental Protection Agency, and the Secretary may by rule identify specific positions with the Department of Health and Human Services, which are of a nonregulatory or nonpolicymaking nature, and the Administrator and the Secretary may by rule provide that officers or employees occupying such positions shall be exempt from the requirements of paragraph (1).

(4) This subsection does not supersede any requirement of chapter 11 of Title 18.

(5) Any officer or employee who is subject to, and knowingly violates, this subsection or any rule issued thereunder, shall be fined not more than $2,500 or imprisoned not more than one year, or both.

(f) Statement of basis and purpose

Any final order issued under this chapter shall be accompanied by a statement of its basis and purpose. The contents and adequacy of any such statement shall not be subject to judicial review in any respect.

(g) Assistant Administrator

(1) The President, by and with the advice and consent of the Senate, shall appoint an Assistant Administrator for Toxic Substances of the Environmental Protection Agency. Such Assistant Adminis-

trator shall be qualified individual who is, by reason of background and experience, especially qualified to direct a program concerning the effects of chemicals on human health and the environment. Such Assistant Administrator shall be responsible for (A) the collection of data, (B) the preparation of studies, (C) the making of recommendations to the Administrator for regulatory and other actions to carry out the purposes and to facilitate the administration of this chapter, and (D) such other functions as the Administrator may assign or delegate.

(2) The Assistant Administrator to be appointed under paragraph (1) shall be in addition to the Assistant Administrators of the Environmental Protection Agency authorized by section 1(d) of Reorganization Plan No. 3 of 1970.

(Oct. 11, 1976, Pub.L. 94–469, Title I, § 26, 90 Stat. 2046; Oct. 17, 1979, Pub.L. 96–88, Title V, § 509(b), 93 Stat. 695; Sept. 13, 1982, Pub.L. 97–258, § 4(b), 96 Stat. 1067; redesignated Title I, Oct. 22, 1986, Pub.L. 99–519, § 3(c)(1), 100 Stat. 2989.)

CODE OF FEDERAL REGULATIONS

Requirements for reporting financial interests, see 40 CFR 3.300 to 3.305.

LIBRARY REFERENCES

Health and Environment ⚷25.5(9).
C.J.S. Health and Environment § 65 et seq.

§ 2626. Development and evaluation of test methods [TSCA § 27]

(a) In general

The Secretary of Health and Human Services, in consultation with the Administrator and acting through the Assistant Secretary for Health, may conduct, and make grants to public and nonprofit private entities and enter into contracts with public and private entities for, projects for the development and evaluation of inexpensive and efficient methods (1) for determining and evaluating the health and environmental effects of chemical substances and mixtures, and their toxicity, persistence, and other characteristics which affect health and the environment, and (2) which may be used for the development of test data to meet the requirements of rules promulgated under section 2603 of this title. The Administrator shall consider such methods in prescribing under section 2603 of this title standards for the development of test data.

(b) Approval by Secretary

No grant may be made or contract entered into under subsection (a) of this section unless an application therefor has been submitted to and approved by the Secretary. Such an application shall be submitted in such form and manner and contain such information as the Secretary may require. The Secretary may apply such conditions to grants and contracts under subsection (a) of this section as the Secretary determines are necessary to carry out the purposes of such subsection. Contracts may be entered into under such subsection without regard to section 3324(a) and (b) of Title 31 and section 5 of Title 41.

(c) Repealed. Pub.L. 104–66, Title I, § 1061(a), Dec. 21, 1995, 109 Stat. 719

(Oct. 11, 1976, Pub.L. 94–469, Title I, § 27, 90 Stat. 2049; Oct. 17, 1979, Pub.L. 96–88, Title V, § 509(b), 93 Stat. 695; Sept. 13, 1982, Pub.L. 97–258, § 4(b), 96 Stat. 1067; redesignated Title I, Oct. 22, 1986, Pub.L. 99–519, § 3(c)(1), 100 Stat. 2989; Dec. 21, 1995, Pub.L. 104–66, Title I, § 1061(a), 109 Stat. 719.)

§ 2627. State programs [TSCA § 28]

(a) In general

For the purpose of complementing (but not reducing) the authority of, or actions taken by, the Administrator under this chapter, the Administrator may make grants to States for the establishment and operation of programs to prevent or eliminate unreasonable risks within the States to health or the environment which are associated with a chemical substance or mixture and with respect to which the Administrator is unable or is not likely to take action under this chapter for their prevention or elimination. The amount of a grant under this subsection shall be determined by the Administrator, except that no grant for any State program may exceed 75 per centum of the establishment and operation costs (as determined by the Administrator) of such program during the period for which the grant is made.

(b) Approval by Administrator

(1) No grant may be made under subsection (a) of this section unless an application therefor is submitted to and approved by the Administrator. Such an application shall be submitted in such form and manner as the Administrator may require and shall—

(A) set forth the need of the applicant for a grant under subsection (a) of this section,

(B) identify the agency or agencies of the State which shall establish or operate, or both, the program for which the application is submitted,

(C) describe the actions proposed to be taken under such program,

(D) contain or be supported by assurances satisfactory to the Administrator that such program shall, to the extent feasible, be integrated with other programs of the applicant for environmental and public health protection,

(E) provide for the making of such reports and evaluations as the Administrator may require, and

(F) contain such other information as the Administrator may prescribe.

(2) The Administrator may approve an application submitted in accordance with paragraph (1) only if the applicant has established to the satisfaction of the Administrator a priority need, as determined under rules of the Administrator, for the grant for which the application has been submitted. Such rules shall take into consideration the seriousness of the health effects in a State which are associated with chemical substances or mixtures, including cancer, birth defects, and gene mutations, the extent of the exposure in a State of human beings and the environment to chemical substances and mixtures, and the extent to which chemical substances and mixtures are manufactured, processed, used, and disposed of in a State.

(c) Annual reports

Not later than six months after the end of each of the fiscal years 1979, 1980, and 1981, the Administrator shall submit to the Congress a report respecting the programs assisted by grants under subsection (a) of this section in the preceding fiscal year and the extent to which the Administrator has disseminated information respecting such programs.

(d) Authorization

For the purpose of making grants under subsection (a) of this section, there are authorized to be appropriated $1,500,000 for each of the fiscal years 1982 and 1983. Sums appropriated under this subsection shall remain available until expended.

(Oct. 11, 1976, Pub.L. 94–469, Title I, § 28, 90 Stat. 2049; Dec. 29, 1981, Pub.L. 97–129, § 1(a), 95 Stat. 1686; redesignated Title I, Oct. 22, 1986, Pub.L. 99–519, § 3(c)(1), 100 Stat. 2989.)

§ 2628. Authorization of appropriations [TSCA § 29]

There are authorized to be appropriated to the Administrator for purposes of carrying out this chapter (other than sections 2626 and 2627 of this title and subsections (a) and (c) through (g) of section 2609 of this title) $58,646,000 for the fiscal year 1982 and $62,000,000 for the fiscal year 1983. No part of the funds appropriated under this section may be used to construct any research laboratories.

(Oct. 11, 1976, Pub.L. 94–469, Title I, § 29, 90 Stat. 2050; Dec. 29, 1981, Pub.L. 97–129, § 1(b), 95 Stat. 1686; redesignated Title I, Oct. 22, 1986, Pub.L. 99–519, § 3(c)(1), 100 Stat. 2989.)

§ 2629. Annual report [TSCA § 30]

The Administrator shall prepare and submit to the President and the Congress on or before January 1, 1978, and on or before January 1 of each succeeding year a comprehensive report on the administration of this chapter during the preceding fiscal year. Such reports shall include—

(1) a list of the testing required under section 2603 of this title during the year for which the report is made and an estimate of the costs incurred during such year by the persons required to perform such tests;

(2) the number of notices received during such year under section 2604 of this title, the number of such notices received during such year under such section for chemical substances subject to a section 2603 rule, and a summary of any action taken during such year under section 2604(g) of this title;

(3) a list of rules issued during such year under section 2605 of this title;

(4) a list, with a brief statement of the issues, of completed or pending judicial actions under this chapter and administrative actions under section 2615 of this title during such year;

(5) a summary of major problems encountered in the administration of this chapter; and

(6) such recommendations for additional legislation as the Administrator deems necessary to carry out the purposes of this chapter.

(Oct. 11, 1976, Pub.L. 94–469, Title I, § 30, 90 Stat. 2050, redesignated Title I, Oct. 22, 1986, Pub.L. 99–519, § 3(c)(1), 100 Stat. 2989.)

SUBCHAPTER II—ASBESTOS HAZARD EMERGENCY RESPONSE

§ 2641. Congressional findings and purpose [TSCA § 201]

(a) Findings

The Congress finds the following:

(1) The Environmental Protection Agency's rule on local educational agency inspection for, and notification of, the presence of friable asbestos-containing material in school buildings includes neither standards for the proper identification of asbestos-containing material and appropriate response actions with respect to friable asbestos-containing material, nor a requirement that response actions with respect to friable asbestos-containing material be carried out in a safe and complete manner once actions are found to be necessary. As a result of the lack of regulatory guidance from the Environmental Protection Agency, some schools have not

undertaken response action while many others have undertaken expensive projects without knowing if their action is necessary, adequate, or safe. Thus, the danger of exposure to asbestos continues to exist in schools, and some exposure actually may have increased due to the lack of Federal standards and improper response action.

(2) There is no uniform program for accrediting persons involved in asbestos identification and abatement, nor are local educational agencies required to use accredited contractors for asbestos work.

(3) The guidance provided by the Environmental Protection Agency in its "Guidance for Controlling Asbestos–Containing Material in Buildings" is insufficient in detail to ensure adequate responses. Such guidance is intended to be used only until the regulations required by this subchapter become effective.

(4) Because there are no Federal standards whatsoever regulating daily exposure to asbestos in other public and commercial buildings, persons in addition to those comprising the Nation's school population may be exposed daily to asbestos.

(b) Purpose

The purpose of this subchapter is—

(1) to provide for the establishment of Federal regulations which require inspection for asbestos-containing material and implementation of appropriate response actions with respect to asbestos-containing material in the Nation's schools in a safe and complete manner;

(2) to mandate safe and complete periodic reinspection of school buildings following response actions, where appropriate; and

(3) to require the Administrator to conduct a study to find out the extent of the danger to human health posed by asbestos in public and commercial buildings and the means to respond to any such danger.

(Pub.L. 94–469, Title II, § 201, as added Pub.L. 99–519, § 2, Oct. 22, 1986, 100 Stat. 2970.)

Short Title

Section 1 of Pub.L. 99–519, Oct. 22, 1986, 100 Stat. 2970 [which added title II (this subchapter) to the Toxic Substances Control Act and also enacted section 4022 of Title 20, Education, amended sections 2614, 2618, and 2619 of this title and sections 4014 and 4021 of Title 20, and enacted provisions set out as notes under sections 4014 and 4022 of Title 20] provided that Pub.L. 99–519 may be cited as the "Asbestos Hazard Emergency Response Act of 1986."

LAW REVIEW COMMENTARIES

Environmental Law/Annual survey of significant developments. Thomas J. Elliott, 58 Pa.B.A.Q. 107 (1987).

LIBRARY REFERENCES

Health and Environment ⚿25.5(1).
Schools ⚿73.
Health and Environment §§ 61 et seq., 91 et seq., 106 to 133 et seq.
Schools and School Districts §§ 252, 262.

§ 2642. Definitions [TSCA § 202]

For purposes of this subchapter—

(1) Accredited asbestos contractor

The term "accredited asbestos contractor" means a person accredited pursuant to the provisions of section 2646 of this title.

(2) Administrator

The term "Administrator" means the Administrator of the Environmental Protection Agency.

(3) Asbestos

The term "asbestos" means asbestiform varieties of—

(A) chrysotile (serpentine),
(B) crocidolite (riebeckite),
(C) amosite (cummingtonite-grunerite),
(D) anthophyllite,
(E) tremolite, or
(F) actinolite.

(4) Asbestos-containing material

The term "asbestos-containing material" means any material which contains more than 1 percent asbestos by weight.

(5) EPA guidance document

The term "Guidance for Controlling Asbestos–Containing Material in Buildings", means the Environmental Protection Agency document with such title as in effect on March 31, 1986.

(6) Friable asbestos-containing material

The term "friable asbestos-containing material" means any asbestos-containing material applied on ceilings, walls, structural members, piping, duct work, or any other part of a building which when dry may be crumbled, pulverized, or reduced to powder by hand pressure. The term includes non-friable asbestos-containing material after such previously non-friable material becomes damaged to the extent that when dry it may be crumbled, pulverized, or reduced to powder by hand pressure.

(7) Local educational agency

The term "local educational agency" means—

(A) any local educational agency as defined in section 8801 of Title 20,

(B) the owner of any private, nonprofit elementary or secondary school building, and

(C) the governing authority of any school operated under the defense dependents' education system provided for under the Defense Dependents' Education Act of 1978 (20 U.S.C. 921 et seq.).

(8) Most current guidance document

The term "most current guidance document" means the Environmental Protection Agency's "Guidance for Controlling Asbestos–Containing Material in Buildings" as modified by the Environmental Protection Agency after March 31, 1986.

(9) Non-profit elementary or secondary school

The term "non-profit elementary or secondary school" means any elementary or secondary school (as defined in section 8801 of Title 20) owned and operated by one or more nonprofit corporations or associations no part of the net earnings of which inures, or may lawfully inure, to the benefit of any private shareholder or individual.

(10) Public and commercial building

The term "public and commercial building" means any building which is not a school building, except that the term does not include any residential apartment building of fewer than 10 units.

(11) Response action

The term "response action" means methods that protect human health and the environment from asbestos-containing material. Such methods include methods described in chapters 3 and 5 of the Environmental Protection Agency's "Guidance for Controlling Asbestos–Containing Materials in Buildings".

(12) School

The term "school" means any elementary or secondary school as defined in section 8801 of Title 20.

(13) School building

The term "school building" means—

(A) any structure suitable for use as a classroom, including a school facility such as a laboratory, library, school eating facility, or facility used for the preparation of food,

(B) any gymnasium or other facility which is specially designed for athletic or recreational activities for an academic course in physical education,

(C) any other facility used for the instruction of students or for the administration of educational or research programs, and

(D) any maintenance, storage, or utility facility, including any hallway, essential to the operation of any facility described in subparagraphs (A), (B), or (C).

(14) State

The term "State" means a State, the District of Columbia, the Commonwealth of Puerto Rico, Guam, American Samoa, the Northern Marianas, the Trust Territory of the Pacific Islands, and the Virgin Islands.

(Pub.L. 94–469, Title II, § 202, as added Pub.L. 99–519, § 2, Oct. 22, 1986, 100 Stat. 2971, and amended Pub.L. 103–382, Title III, § 391(c)(1)–(3), Oct. 20, 1994, 108 Stat. 4022.)

LIBRARY REFERENCES

Health and Environment ⚖25.5(1).
C.J.S. Health and Environment §§ 61 et seq., 91 et seq., 106 to 133 et seq.

§ 2643. EPA regulations [TSCA § 203]

(a) In general

Within 360 days after October 22, 1986, the Administrator shall promulgate regulations as described in subsections (b) through (i) of this section. With respect to regulations described in subsections (b), (c), (d), (e), (f), (g), and (i) of this section, the Administrator shall issue an advanced notice of proposed rulemaking within 60 days after October 22, 1986, and shall propose regulations within 180 days after October 22, 1986. Any regulation promulgated under this section must protect human health and the environment.

(b) Inspection

The Administrator shall promulgate regulations which prescribe procedures, including the use of personnel accredited under section 2646(b) or (c) of this title and laboratories accredited under section 2646(d) of this title, for determining whether asbestos-containing material is present in a school building under the authority of a local educational agency. The regulations shall provide for the exclusion of any school building, or portion of a school building, if (1) an inspection of such school building (or portion) was completed before the effective date of the regulations, and (2) the inspection meets the procedures and other requirements of the regulations under this subchapter or of the "Guidance for Controlling Asbestos–Containing Materials in Buildings" (unless the Administrator determines that an inspection in accordance with the guidance document is inadequate). The regulations shall require inspection of any school building (or portion of a school building) that is not excluded by the preceding sentence.

(c) Circumstances requiring response actions

(1) The Administrator shall promulgate regulations which define the appropriate response action in a

school building under the authority of a local educational agency in at least the following circumstances:

(A) Damage

Circumstances in which friable asbestos-containing material or its covering is damaged, deteriorated, or delaminated.

(B) Significant damage

Circumstances in which friable asbestos-containing material or its covering is significantly damaged, deteriorated, or delaminated.

(C) Potential damage

Circumstances in which—

(i) friable asbestos-containing material is in an area regularly used by building occupants, including maintenance personnel, in the course of their normal activities, and

(ii) there is a reasonable likelihood that the material or its covering will become damaged, deteriorated, or delaminated.

(D) Potential significant damage

Circumstances in which—

(i) friable asbestos-containing material is in an area regularly used by building occupants, including maintenance personnel, in the course of their normal activities, and

(ii) there is a reasonable likelihood that the material or its covering will become significantly damaged, deteriorated, or delaminated.

(2) In promulgating such regulations, the Administrator shall consider and assess the value of various technologies intended to improve the decisionmaking process regarding response actions and the quality of any work that is deemed necessary, including air monitoring and chemical encapsulants.

(d) Response actions

(1) In general

The Administrator shall promulgate regulations describing a response action in a school building under the authority of a local educational agency, using the least burdensome methods which protect human health and the environment. In determining the least burdensome methods, the Administrator shall take into account local circumstances, including occupancy and use patterns within the school building and short- and long-term costs.

(2) Response action for damaged asbestos

In the case of a response action for the circumstances described in subsection (c)(1)(A) of this section, methods for responding shall include methods identified in chapters 3 and 5 of the "Guidance for Controlling Asbestos-Containing Material in Buildings".

(3) Response action for significantly damaged asbestos

In the case of a response action for the circumstances described in subsection (c)(1)(B) of this section, methods for responding shall include methods identified in chapter 5 of the "Guidance for Controlling Asbestos–Containing Material in Buildings".

(4) Response action for potentially damaged asbestos

In the case of a response action for the circumstances described in subsection (c)(1)(C) of this section, methods for responding shall include methods identified in chapters 3 and 5 of the "Guidance for Controlling Asbestos–Containing Material in Buildings", unless preventive measures will eliminate the reasonable likelihood that the asbestos-containing material will become damaged, deteriorated, or delaminated.

(5) Response action for potentially significantly damaged asbestos

In the case of a response action for the circumstances described in subsection (c)(1)(D) of this section, methods for responding shall include methods identified in chapter 5 of the "Guidance for Controlling Asbestos–Containing Material in Buildings", unless preventive measures will eliminate the reasonable likelihood that the asbestos-containing material will become significantly damaged, deteriorated, or delaminated.

(6) Preventive measures defined

For purposes of this section, the term "preventive measures" means actions which eliminate the reasonable likelihood of asbestos-containing material becoming damaged, deteriorated, or delaminated, or significantly damaged [1] deteriorated, or delaminated (as the case may be) or which protect human health and the environment.

(7) The Administrator shall, not later than 30 days after enactment of this paragraph, publish and distribute to all local education agencies and State Governors information or an advisory to—

(A) facilitate public understanding of the comparative risks associated with in-place management of asbestos-containing building materials and removals;

(B) promote the least burdensome response actions necessary to protect human health, safety, and the environment; and

(C) describe the circumstances in which asbestos removal is necessary to protect human health.

Such information or advisory shall be based on the best available scientific evidence and shall be revised, republished, and redistributed as appropriate, to reflect new scientific findings.

(e) Implementation

The Administrator shall promulgate regulations requiring the implementation of response actions in school buildings under the authority of a local educational agency and, where appropriate, for the determination of when a response action is completed. Such regulations shall include standards for the education and protection of both workers and building occupants for the following phases of activity:

(1) Inspection.

(2) Response Action.[2]

(3) Post-response action, including any periodic reinspection of asbestos-containing material and long-term surveillance activity.

(f) Operations and maintenance

The Administrator shall promulgate regulations to require implementation of an operations and maintenance and repair program as described in chapter 3 of the "Guidance for Controlling Asbestos–Containing Materials in Buildings" for all friable asbestos-containing material in a school building under the authority of a local educational agency.

(g) Periodic surveillance

The Administrator shall promulgate regulations to require the following:

(1) An identification of the location of friable and non-friable asbestos in a school building under the authority of a local educational agency.

(2) Provisions for surveillance and periodic reinspection of such friable and non-friable asbestos.

(3) Provisions for education of school employees, including school service and maintenance personnel, about the location of and safety procedures with respect to such friable and non-friable asbestos.

(h) Transportation and disposal

The Administrator shall promulgate regulations which prescribe standards for transportation and disposal of asbestos-containing waste material to protect human health and the environment. Such regulations shall include such provisions related to the manner in which transportation vehicles are loaded and unloaded as will assure the physical integrity of containers of asbestos-containing waste material.

(i) Management plans

(1) In general

The Administrator shall promulgate regulations which require each local educational agency to develop an asbestos management plan for school buildings under its authority, to begin implementation of such plan within 990 days after October 22, 1986, and to complete implementation of such plan in a timely fashion. The regulations shall require that each plan include the following elements, wherever relevant to the school building:

(A) An inspection statement describing inspection and response action activities carried out before October 22, 1986.

(B) A description of the results of the inspection conducted pursuant to regulations under subsection (b) of this section, including a description of the specific areas inspected.

(C) A detailed description of measures to be taken to respond to any friable asbestos-containing material pursuant to the regulations promulgated under subsections (c), (d), and (e) of this section, including the location or locations at which a response action will be taken, the method or methods of response action to be used, and a schedule for beginning and completing response actions.

(D) A detailed description of any asbestos-containing material which remains in the school building once response actions are undertaken pursuant to the regulations promulgated under subsections (c), (d), and (e) of this section.

(E) A plan for periodic reinspection and long-term surveillance activities developed pursuant to regulations promulgated under subsection (g) of this section, and a plan for operations and maintenance activities developed pursuant to regulations promulgated under subsection (f) of this section.

(F) With respect to the person or persons who inspected for asbestos-containing material and who will design or carry out response actions with respect to the friable asbestos-containing material, one of the following statements:

(i) If the State has adopted a contractor accreditation plan under section 2646(b) of this title, a statement that the person (or persons) is accredited under such plan.

(ii) A statement that the local educational agency used (or will use) persons who have been accredited by another State which has adopted a contractor accreditation plan under section 2646(b) of this title or is accredited pursuant to an Administrator-approved course under section 2646(c) of this title.

(G) A list of the laboratories that analyzed any bulk samples of asbestos-containing material found in the school building or air samples taken to detect asbestos in the school building and a statement that each laboratory has been accredited pursuant to the accreditation program under section 2646(d) of this title.

(H) With respect to each consultant who contributed to the management plan, the name of the consultant and one of the following statements:

(i) If the State has adopted a contractor accreditation plan under section 2646(b) of this title, a statement that the consultant is accredited under such plan.

(ii) A statement that the contractor is accredited by another State which has adopted a contractor accreditation plan under section 2646(b) of this title or is accredited pursuant to an Administrator-approved course under section 2646(c) of this title.

(I) An evaluation of resources needed to successfully complete response actions and carry out reinspection, surveillance, and operation and maintenance activities.

(2) Statement by contractor

A local educational agency may require each management plan to contain a statement signed by an accredited asbestos contractor that such contractor has prepared or assisted in the preparation of such plan, or has reviewed such plan, and that such plan is in compliance with the applicable regulations and standards promulgated or adopted pursuant to this section and other applicable provisions of law. Such a statement may not be signed by a contractor who, in addition to preparing or assisting in preparing the management plan, also implements (or will implement) the management plan.

(3) Warning labels

(A) The regulations shall require that each local educational agency which has inspected for and discovered any asbestos-containing material with respect to a school building shall attach a warning label to any asbestos-containing material still in routine maintenance areas (such as boiler rooms) of the school building, including—

(i) friable asbestos-containing material which was responded to by a means other than removal, and

(ii) asbestos-containing material for which no response action was carried out.

(B) The warning label shall read, in print which is readily visible because of large size or bright color, as follows: **"CAUTION: ASBESTOS. HAZARDOUS. DO NOT DISTURB WITHOUT PROPER TRAINING AND EQUIPMENT."**

(4) Plan may be submitted in stages

A local educational agency may submit a management plan in stages, with each submission of the agency covering only a portion of the school buildings under the agency's authority, if the agency determines that such action would expedite the identification and abatement of hazardous asbestos-containing material in the school buildings under the authority of the agency.

(5) Public availability

A copy of the management plan developed under the regulations shall be available in the administrative offices of the local educational agency for inspection by the public, including teachers, other school personnel, and parents. The local educational agency shall notify parent, teacher, and employee organizations of the availability of such plan.

(6) Submission to State Governor

Each plan developed under this subsection shall be submitted to the State Governor under section 2645 of this title.

(j) Changes in regulations

Changes may be made in the regulations promulgated under this section only by rule in accordance with section 553 of Title 5. Any such change must protect human health and the environment.

(k) Changes in guidance document

Any change made in the "Guidance for Controlling Asbestos-Containing Material in Buildings" shall be made only by rule in accordance with section 553 of Title 5, unless a regulation described in this section dealing with the same subject matter is in effect. Any such change must protect human health and the environment.

(*l*) Treatment of Department of Defense schools

(1) Secretary to act in lieu of governor

In the administration of this subchapter, any function, duty, or other responsibility imposed on a Governor of a State shall be carried out by the Secretary of Defense with respect to any school operated under the defense dependents' education system provided for under the Defense Dependents' Education Act of 1978 (20 U.S.C. 921 et seq.).

(2) Regulations

The Secretary of Defense, in cooperation with the Administrator, shall, to the extent feasible and consistent with the national security, take such action as may be necessary to provide for the identification, inspection, and management (including abatement) of asbestos in any building used by the Department of Defense as an overseas school for dependents of members of the Armed Forces. Such identification, inspection, and management (including abatement) shall, subject to the preceding sentence, be carried out in a manner comparable to the manner in which a local educational agency is required to carry out such activities with respect to a school building under this subchapter.

(m) Waiver

The Administrator, upon request by a Governor and after notice and comment and opportunity for a public hearing in the affected State, may waive some or all of the requirements of this section and section 2644 of this title with respect to such State if it has established and is implementing a program of asbestos inspection and management that contains requirements that are at least as stringent as the requirements of this section and section 2644 of this title.

(Pub.L. 94–469, Title II, § 203, as added Pub.L. 99–519, § 2, Oct. 22, 1986, 100 Stat. 2972, and amended Pub.L. 101–637, § 13, Nov. 28, 1990, 104 Stat. 4593.)

1 So in original. Probably should be followed by a comma.

2 So in original. Probably should not be capitalized.

References in Text

Enactment of this paragraph, referred to in subsec. (d)(7), probably means the date of enactment of Pub.L. 101–637, Nov. 28, 1990, 104 Stat. 4589, which was approved Nov. 28, 1990.

CODE OF FEDERAL REGULATIONS

Asbestos, reporting commercial and industrial uses of, materials found in schools, abatement projects, etc., see 40 CFR 763.60 et seq.

LAW REVIEW COMMENTARIES

Asbestos abatement (the insurance crisis): A solution is still up in the ambient air. Note, 38 Syracuse L.Rev. 1349 (1987).

LIBRARY REFERENCES

Health and Environment ⚷25.5(1).

C.J.S. Health and Environment §§ 61 et seq., 91 et seq., 106 to 133 et seq.

§ 2644. Requirements if EPA fails to promulgate regulations [TSCA § 204]

(a) In general

(1) Failure to promulgate

If the Administrator fails to promulgate within the prescribed period—

(A) regulations described in section 2643(b) of this title (relating to inspection);

(B) regulations described in section 2643(c), (d), (e), (f), (g), and (i) of this title (relating to responding to asbestos); or

(C) regulations described in section 2643(h) of this title (relating to transportation and disposal);

each local educational agency shall carry out the requirements described in this section in subsection (b); subsections (c), (d), and (e); or subsection (f); respectively, in accordance with the Environmental Protection Agency's most current guidance document.

(2) Stay by court

If the Administrator has promulgated regulations described in paragraph (1)(A), (B), or (C) within the prescribed period, but the effective date of such regulations has been stayed by a court for a period of more than 30 days, a local educational agency shall carry out the pertinent requirements described in this subsection in accordance with the Environmental Protection Agency's most current guidance document.

(3) Effective period

The requirements of this section shall be in effect until such time as the Administrator promulgates the pertinent regulations or until the stay is lifted (as the case may be).

(b) Inspection

(1) Except as provided in paragraph (2), the local educational agency, within 540 days after October 22, 1986, shall conduct an inspection for asbestos-containing material, using personnel accredited under section 2646(b) or (c) of this title and laboratories accredited under section 2646(d) of this title, in each school building under its authority.

(2) The local educational agency may exclude from the inspection requirement in paragraph (1) any school building, or portion of a school building, if (A) an inspection of such school building (or portion) was completed before the date on which this section goes into effect, and (B) the inspection meets the inspection requirements of this section.

(c) Operation and maintenance

The local educational agency shall, within 720 days after October 22, 1986, develop and begin implementation of an operation and maintenance plan with respect to friable asbestos-containing material in a school building under its authority. Such plan shall provide for the education of school service and maintenance personnel about safety procedures with respect to asbestos-containing material, including friable asbestos-containing material.

(d) Management plan

(1) In general

The local educational agency shall—

(A) develop a management plan for responding to asbestos-containing material in each school building under its authority and submit such plan to the Governor under section 2645 of this title within 810 days after October 22, 1986,

(B) begin implementation of such plan within 990 days after October 22, 1986, and

(C) complete implementation of such plan in a timely fashion.

(2) Plan requirements

The management plan shall—

(A) include the elements listed in section 2643(i)(1) of this title including an inspection statement as described in paragraph (3) of this section,[1]

(B) provide for the attachment of warning labels as described in section 2643(i)(3) of this title,

(C) be prepared in accordance with the most current guidance document,

(D) meet the standard described in paragraph (4) for actions described in that paragraph, and

(E) be submitted to the State Governor under section 2645 of this title.

(3) Inspection statement

The local educational agency shall complete an inspection statement, covering activities carried out before October 22, 1986, which meets the following requirements:

(A) The statement shall include the following information:

(i) The dates of inspection.

(ii) The name, address, and qualifications of each inspector.

(iii) A description of the specific areas inspected.

(iv) A list of the laboratories that analyzed any bulk samples of asbestos-containing material or air samples of asbestos found in any school building and a statement describing the qualifications of each laboratory.

(v) The results of the inspection.

(B) The statement shall state whether any actions were taken with respect to any asbestos-containing material found to be present, including a specific reference to whether any actions were taken in the boiler room of the building. If any such action was taken, the following items of information shall be included in the statement:

(i) The location or locations at which the action was taken.

(ii) A description of the method of action.

(iii) The qualifications of the persons who conducted the action.

(4) Standard

The ambient interior concentration of asbestos after the completion of actions described in the most current guidance document, other than the type of action described in sections 2643(f) of this title and subsection (c) of this section, shall not exceed the ambient exterior concentration, discounting any contribution from any local stationary source. Either a scanning electron microscope or a transmission electron microscope shall be used to determine the ambient interior concentration. In the absence of reliable measurements, the ambient exterior concentration shall be deemed to be—

(A) less than 0.003 fibers per cubic centimeter if a scanning electron microscope is used, and

(B) less than 0.005 fibers per cubic centimeter if a transmission electron microscope is used.

(5) Public availability

A copy of the management plan shall be available in the administrative offices of the local educational agency for inspection by the public, including teachers, other school personnel, and parents. The local educational agency shall notify parent, teacher, and employee organizations of the availability of such plan.

(e) Building occupant protection

The local educational agency shall provide for the protection of building occupants during each phase of activity described in this section.

(f) Transportation and disposal

The local educational agency shall provide for the transportation and disposal of asbestos in accordance with the most recent version of the Environmental Protection Agency's "Asbestos Waste Management Guidance" (or any successor to such document).

(Pub.L. 94–469, Title II, § 204, as added Pub.L. 99–519, § 2, Oct. 22, 1986, 100 Stat. 2977.)

[1] So in original. Probably should be "subsection".

CODE OF FEDERAL REGULATIONS

Asbestos, reporting commercial and industrial uses of, materials found in schools, abatement projects, etc., see 40 CFR 763.60 et seq.

LIBRARY REFERENCES

Health and Environment ⚷25.5(1).
C.J.S. Health and Environment §§ 61 et seq., 91 et seq., 106 to 133 et seq.

§ 2645. Submission to State Governor [TSCA § 205]

(a) Submission

Within 720 days after October 22, 1986 (or within 810 days if there are no regulations under section 2643(i) of this title) a local educational agency shall submit a management plan developed pursuant to regulations promulgated under section 2643(i) of this title (or under section 2644(d) of this title if there are no regulations) to the Governor of the State in which the local educational agency is located.

(b) Governor requirements

Within 360 days after October 22, 1986, the Governor of each State—

(1) shall notify local educational agencies in the State of where to submit their management plans under this section, and

(2) may establish administrative procedures for reviewing management plans submitted under this section.

If the Governor establishes procedures under paragraph (2), the Governor shall designate to carry out the reviews those State officials who are responsible for implementing environmental protection or other public health programs, or with authority over asbestos programs, in the State.

(c) Management plan review

(1) Review of plan

The Governor may disapprove a management plan within 90 days after the date of receipt of the plan if the plan—

(A) does not conform with the regulations under section 2643(i) of this title (or with section 2644(d) of this title if there are no regulations),

(B) does not assure that contractors who are accredited pursuant to this subchapter will be used to carry out the plan, or

(C) does not contain a response action schedule which is reasonable and timely, taking into account circumstances relevant to the speed at which the friable asbestos-containing material in the school buildings under the local educational agency's authority should be responded to, including human exposure to the asbestos while the friable asbestos-containing material remains in the school building, and the ability of the local educational agency to continue to provide educational services to the community.

(2) Revision of plan

If the State Governor disapproves a plan, the State Governor shall explain in writing to the local educational agency the reasons why the plan was disapproved and the changes that need to be made in the plan. Within 30 days after the date on which notice is received of disapproval of its plan, the local educational agency shall revise the plan to conform with the State Governor's suggested changes. The Governor may extend the 30-day period for not more than 90 days.

(d) Deferral of submission

(1) Request for deferral

A local educational agency may request a deferral, to May 9, 1989, of the deadline under subsection (a) of this section. Upon approval of such a request, the deadline under subsection (a) of this section is deferred until May 9, 1989, for the local educational agency which submitted the request. Such a request may cover one or more schools under the authority of the agency and shall include a list of all the schools covered by the request. A local educational agency shall file any such request with the State Governor by October 12, 1988, and shall include with the request either of the following statements:

(A) A statement—

(i) that the State in which the agency is located has requested from the Administrator, before June 1, 1988, a waiver under section 2643(m) of this title; and

(ii) that gives assurance that the local educational agency has carried out the notification and, in the case of a public school, public meeting required by paragraph (2).

(B) A statement, the accuracy of which is sworn to by a responsible official of the agency (by notarization or other means of certification), that includes the following with respect to each school for which a deferral is sought in the request:

(i) A statement that, in spite of the fact that the local educational agency has made a good faith effort to meet the deadline for submission of a management plan under subsection (a) of this section, the agency will not be able to meet the deadline. The statement shall include a brief explanation of the reasons why the deadline cannot be met.

(ii) A statement giving assurance that the local educational agency has made available for inspection by the public, at each school for which a deferral is sought in the request, at least one of the following documents:

(I) A solicitation by the local educational agency to contract with an accredited asbestos contractor for inspection or management plan development.

(II) A letter attesting to the enrollment of school district personnel in an Environmental Protection Agency-accredited training course for inspection and management plan development.

(III) Documentation showing that an analysis of suspected asbestos-containing material from the school is pending at an accredited laboratory.

(IV) Documentation showing that an inspection or management plan has been completed in at least one other school under the local educational agency's authority.

(iii) A statement giving assurance that the local educational agency has carried out the notification and, in the case of a public school, public meeting required by paragraph (2).

(iv) A proposed schedule outlining all significant activities leading up to submission of a management plan by May 9, 1989, including inspection of the school (if not completed at the time of the request) with a deadline of no later than December 22, 1988, for entering into a signed contract with an accredited asbestos contractor for inspection (unless such inspections are to be performed by school personnel), laboratory analysis of material from the school suspected of containing asbestos, and development of the management plan.

(2) Notification and public meeting

Before filing a deferral request under paragraph (1), a local educational agency shall notify affected parent, teacher, and employee organizations of its intent to file such a request. In the case of a deferral request for a public school, the local educational agency shall discuss the request at a public meeting of the school board with jurisdiction over the school, and affected parent, teacher, and employee organizations shall be notified in advance of the time and place of such meeting.

(3) Response by Governor

(A) Not later than 30 days after the date on which a Governor receives a deferral request under paragraph (1) from a local educational agency, the Governor shall respond to the local educational agency in writing by acknowledging whether the request is complete or incomplete. If the request is incomplete, the Governor shall identify in the response the items that are missing from the request.

(B) A local educational agency may correct any deficiencies in an incomplete deferral request and refile the request with the Governor. In any case in which the local educational agency decides to refile the request, the agency shall refile the request, and the Governor shall respond to such refiled request in the manner described in subparagraph (A), no later than 15 days after the local educational agency has received a response from the Governor under subparagraph (A).

(C) Approval of a deferral request under this subsection occurs only upon the receipt by a local educational agency of a written acknowledgment from the Governor that the agency's deferral request is complete.

(4) Submission and review of plan

A local educational agency whose deferral request is approved shall submit a management plan to the Governor not later than May 9, 1989. Such management plan shall include a copy of the deferral request and the statement accompanying such request. Such management plan shall be reviewed in accordance with subsection (c) of this section, except that the Governor may extend the 30–day period for revision of the plan under subsection (c)(2) of this section for only an additional 30 days (for a total of 60 days).

(5) Implementation of plan

The approval of a deferral request from a local educational agency shall not be considered to be a waiver or exemption from the requirement under section 2643(i) of this title for the local educational agency to begin implementation of its management plan by July 9, 1989.

(6) EPA notice

(A) Not later than 15 days after July 18, 1988, the Administrator shall publish in the Federal Register the following:

(i) A notice describing the opportunity to file a request for deferral under this subsection.

(ii) A list of the State offices (including officials (if available) in each State as designated under subsection (b) of this section) with which deferral requests should be filed.

(B) As soon as practicable, but in no event later than 30 days, after July 18, 1988, the Administrator shall mail a notice describing the opportunity to file a request for deferral under this subsection to each local educational agency and to each State office in the list published under subparagraph (A).

(e) Status reports

(1) Not later than December 31, 1988, the Governor of each State shall submit to the Administrator a written statement on the status of management plan submissions and deferral requests by local educational agencies in the State. The statement shall be made available to local educational agencies in the State and shall contain the following:

(A) A list containing each local educational agency that submitted a management plan by October 12, 1988.

(B) A list containing each local educational agency whose deferral request was approved.

(C) A list containing each local educational agency that failed to submit a management plan by October 12, 1988, and whose deferral request was disapproved.

(D) A list containing each local educational agency that failed to submit a management plan by October 12, 1988, and did not submit a deferral request.

(2) Not later than December 31, 1989, the Governor of each State shall submit to the Administrator an updated version of the written statement submitted under paragraph (1). The statement shall be made available to local educational agencies in the State and shall contain the following:

(A) A list containing each local educational agency whose management plan was submitted and not disapproved as of October 9, 1989.

(B) A list containing each local educational agency whose management plan was submitted and disapproved, and which remains disapproved, as of October 9, 1989.

(C) A list containing each local educational agency that submitted a management plan after May 9, 1989, and before October 10, 1989.

(D) A list containing each local educational agency that failed to submit a management plan as of October 9, 1989.

(Pub.L. 94–469, Title II, § 205, as added Pub.L. 99–519, § 2, Oct. 22, 1986, 100 Stat. 2979, and amended Pub.L. 100–368, §§ 1(a), 2, July 18, 1988, 102 Stat. 829, 831.)

LIBRARY REFERENCES

Health and Environment ⚷25.5(1).
C.J.S. Health and Environment §§ 61 et seq., 91 et seq., 106 to 133 et seq.

§ 2646. Contractor and laboratory accreditation [TSCA § 206]

(a) Contractor accreditation

A person may not—

(1) inspect for asbestos-containing material in a school building under the authority of a local educational agency or in a public or commercial building,

(2) prepare a management plan for such a school, or

(3) design or conduct response actions, other than the type of action described in sections 2643(f) and 2644(c) of this title, with respect to friable asbestos-containing material in such a school or in a public or commercial building,

unless such person is accredited by a State under subsection (b) of this section or is accredited pursuant to an Administrator-approved course under subsection (c) of this section.

(b) Accreditation by State

(1) Model plan

(A) Persons to be accredited

Within 180 days after October 22, 1986, the Administrator, in consultation with affected organizations, shall develop a model contractor accreditation plan for States to give accreditation to persons in the following categories:

(i) Persons who inspect for asbestos-containing material in school buildings under the authority of a local educational agency or in public or commercial buildings.

(ii) Persons who prepare management plans for such schools.

(iii) Persons who design or carry out response actions, other than the type of action described in sections 2643(f) and 2644(c) of this title, with respect to friable asbestos-containing material in such schools or in public or commercial buildings.

(B) Plan requirements

The plan shall include a requirement that any person in a category listed in paragraph (1) achieve a passing grade on an examination and participate in continuing education to stay informed about current asbestos inspection and response action technology. The examination shall demonstrate the knowledge of the person in areas that the Administrator prescribes as necessary and appropriate in each of the categories. Such examinations may include requirements for knowledge in the following areas:

(i) Recognition of asbestos-containing material and its physical characteristics.

(ii) Health hazards of asbestos and the relationship between asbestos exposure and disease.

(iii) Assessing the risk of asbestos exposure through a knowledge of percentage weight of asbestos-containing material, viability, age, deterioration, location and accessibility of materials, and advantages and disadvantages of dry and wet response action methods.

(iv) Respirators and their use, care, selection, degree of protection afforded, fitting, testing, and maintenance and cleaning procedures.

(v) Appropriate work practices and control methods, including the use of high efficiency particle absolute vacuums, the use of amended water, and principles of negative air pressure equipment use and procedures.

(vi) Preparing a work area for response action work, including isolating work areas to prevent bystander or public exposure to asbestos, decontamination procedures, and procedures for dismantling work areas after completion of work.

(vii) Establishing emergency procedures to respond to sudden releases.

(viii) Air monitoring requirements and procedures.

(ix) Medical surveillance program requirements.

(x) Proper asbestos waste transportation and disposal procedures.

(xi) Housekeeping and personal hygiene practices, including the necessity of showers, and procedures to prevent asbestos exposure to an employee's family.

(2) State adoption of plan

Each State shall adopt a contractor accreditation plan at least as stringent as the model plan developed by the Administrator under paragraph (1), within 180 days after the commencement of the first regular session of the legislature of such State which is convened following the date on which the Administrator completes development of the model plan. In the case of a school operated under the defense dependents' education system provided for under the Defense Dependents' Education Act of 1978 (20 U.S.C. 921 et seq.), the Secretary of Defense shall adopt a contractor accreditation plan at least as stringent as that model.

(c) Accreditation by Administrator-approved course

(1) Course approval

Within 180 days after October 22, 1986, the Administrator shall ensure that any Environmental Protection Agency-approved asbestos training course is consistent with the model plan (including testing requirements) developed under subsection (b) of this section. A contractor may be accredited by taking and passing such a course.

(2) Treatment of persons with previous EPA asbestos training

A person who—

(A) completed an Environmental Protection Agency-approved asbestos training course before October 22, 1986, and

(B) passed (or passes) an asbestos test either before or after October 22, 1986,

may be accredited under paragraph (1) if the Administrator determines that the course and test are equivalent to the requirements of the model plan developed under subsection (b) of this section. If the Administrator so determines, the person shall be considered accredited for the purposes of this subchapter until a date that is one year after the date on which the State in which such person is employed establishes an accreditation program pursuant to subsection (b) of this section.

(3) Lists of courses

The Administrator, in consultation with affected organizations, shall publish (and revise as necessary)—

(A) a list of asbestos courses and tests in effect before October 22, 1986, which qualify for equivalency treatment under paragraph (2), and

(B) a list of asbestos courses and tests which the Administrator determines under paragraph (1) are consistent with the model plan and which will qualify a contractor for accreditation under such paragraph.

(d) Laboratory accreditation

(1) The Administrator shall provide for the development of an accreditation program for laboratories by the National Bureau of Standards in accordance with paragraph (2). The Administrator shall transfer such funds as are necessary to the National Institute of Standards and Technology to carry out such program.

(2) The National Institute of Standards and Technology, upon request by the Administrator, shall, in consultation with affected organizations—

(A) within 360 days after October 22, 1986, develop an accreditation program for laboratories which conduct qualitative and semi-quantitative analyses of bulk samples of asbestos-containing material, and

(B) within 720 days after October 22, 1986, develop an accreditation program for laboratories which conduct analyses of air samples of asbestos from school buildings under the authority of a local educational agency.

(3) A laboratory which plans to carry out any such analysis shall comply with the requirements of the accreditation program.

(e) Financial assistance contingent on use of accredited persons

(1) A school which is an applicant for financial assistance under section 505 of the Asbestos School Hazard Abatement Act of 1984 [20 U.S.C.A. § 4014] is not eligible for such assistance unless the school, in carrying out the requirements of this subchapter—

(A) uses a person (or persons)—

(i) who is accredited by a State which has adopted an accreditation plan based on the model plan developed under subsection (b) of this section, or

(ii) who is accredited pursuant to an Administrator-approved course under subsection (c) of this section, and

(B) uses a laboratory (or laboratories) which is accredited under the program developed under subsection (d) of this section.

(2) This subsection shall apply to any financial assistance provided under the Asbestos School Hazard Abatement Act of 1984 [20 U.S.C.A. § 4011 et seq.] for activities performed after the following dates:

(A) In the case of activities performed by persons, after the date which is one year after October 22, 1986.

(B) In the case of activities performed by laboratories, after the date which is 180 days after the date on which a laboratory accreditation program is completed under subsection (d) of this section.

(f) List of EPA-approved courses

Not later than August 31, 1988, and every three months thereafter until August 31, 1991, the Administrator shall publish in the Federal Register a list of all Environmental Protection Agency-approved asbestos training courses for persons to achieve accreditation in each category described in subsection (b)(1)(A) of this section and for laboratories to achieve accreditation. The Administrator may continue publishing such a list after August 31, 1991, at such times as the Administrator considers it useful. The list shall include the name and address of each approved trainer and, to the extent available, a list of all the geographic sites where training courses will take place. The Administrator shall provide a copy of the list to each State official on the list published by the Administrator under section 2645(d)(6) of this title and to each regional office of the Environmental Protection Agency.

(Pub.L. 94–469, Title II, § 206, as added Pub.L. 99–519, § 2, Oct. 22, 1986, 100 Stat. 2980, and amended Pub.L. 100–368, § 3, July 18, 1988, 102 Stat. 832; Pub.L. 100–418, Title V, § 5115(c), Aug. 23, 1988, 102 Stat. 1433; Pub.L. 101–637, § 15(a)(1), (2), Nov. 28, 1990, 104 Stat. 4596.)

Change of Name

"National Institute of Standards and Technology" was substituted for "National Bureau of Standards" in subsec. (d)(1), (2) on authority of Pub.L. 100–418, Title V, § 5115(c), Aug. 23, 1988, 102 Stat. 1433, which directed that any reference to the National Bureau of Standards be deemed to refer to the National Institute of Standards and Technology.

Effective Date of 1990 Amendment

Section 15(c) of Pub.L. 101–637 provided that: "This section [amending subsecs. (a)(1), (3) and (b)(1)(A)(i), (iii) of this section and section 2647(g) of this title and enacting provisions set out as notes under this section] shall take effect upon the expiration of the 12-month period following the date of the enactment of this Act [November 28, 1990]. The Administrator may extend the effective date for a period not to exceed one year if the Administrator determines that accredited asbestos contractors are needed to perform school-site abatement required under the Asbestos Hazard Emergency Response Act (15 U.S.C. 2641) [probably means section 2 of Pub.L. 99–519, Oct. 22, 1986, 100 Stat. 2970, which is generally classified to section 2641 et seq. of this title, for distribution of this Act to the Code, see Short Title note set out under section 2601 of this title and Tables] and such an extension is necessary to ensure effective implementation of section 203 of the Toxic Substances Control Act [section 2643 of this title]."

LIBRARY REFERENCES

Health and Environment ⚷25.5(1).

C.J.S. Health and Environment §§ 61 et seq., 91 et seq., 106 to 133 et seq.

§ 2647. Enforcement [TSCA § 207]

(a) Penalties

Any local educational agency—

(1) which fails to conduct an inspection pursuant to regulations under section 2643(b) of this title or under section 2644(b) of this title,

(2) which knowingly submits false information to the Governor regarding any inspection pursuant to regulations under section 2643(i) of this title or knowingly includes false information in any inspection statement under section 2644(d)(3) of this title,

(3) which fails to develop a management plan pursuant to regulations under section 2643(i) of this title or under section 2644(d) of this title,

(4) which carries out any activity prohibited by section 2655 of this title, or

(5) which knowingly submits false information to the Governor regarding a deferral request under section 2645(d) of this title.[1]

is liable for a civil penalty of not more than $5,000 for each day during which the violation continues. Any civil penalty under this subsection shall be assessed and collected in the same manner, and subject to the same provisions, as in the case of civil penalties assessed and collected under section 2615 of this title. For purposes of this subsection, a "violation" means a failure to comply with respect to a single school building. The court shall order that any civil penalty collected under this subsection be used by the local educational agency for purposes of complying with this subchapter. Any portion of a civil penalty remaining unspent after compliance by a local educational agency is completed shall be deposited into the Asbestos Trust Fund established by section 4022 of Title 20.

(b) Relationship to subchapter I of this chapter

A local educational agency is not liable for any civil penalty under subchapter I of this chapter for failing or refusing to comply with any rule promulgated or order issued under this subchapter.

(c) Enforcement considerations

(1) In determining the amount of a civil penalty to be assessed under subsection (a) of this section against a local educational agency, the Administrator shall consider—

(A) the significance of the violation;

(B) the culpability of the violator, including any history of previous violations under this chapter;

(C) the ability of the violator to pay the penalty; and

(D) the ability of the violator to continue to provide educational services to the community.

(2) Any action ordered by a court in fashioning relief under section 2619 of this title shall be consistent with regulations promulgated under section 2643 of this title (or with the requirements of section 2644 of this title if there are no regulations).

(d) Citizen complaints

Any person may file a complaint with the Administrator or with the Governor of the State in which the school building is located with respect to asbestos-containing material in a school building. If the Administrator or Governor receives a complaint under this subsection containing allegations which provide a reasonable basis to believe that a violation of this chapter has occurred, the Administrator or Governor shall investigate and respond (including taking enforcement action where appropriate) to the complaint within a reasonable period of time.

(e) Citizen petitions

(1) Any person may petition the Administrator to initiate a proceeding for the issuance, amendment, or repeal of a regulation or order under this subchapter.

(2) Such petition shall be filed in the principal office of the Administrator and shall set forth the facts which it is claimed establish that it is necessary to issue, amend, or repeal a regulation or order under this subchapter.

(3) The Administrator may hold a public hearing or may conduct such investigation or proceeding as the Administrator deems appropriate in order to determine whether or not such petition should be granted.

(4) Within 90 days after filing of a petition described in paragraph (1), the Administrator shall either grant or deny the petition. If the Administrator grants such petition, the Administrator shall promptly commence an appropriate proceeding in accordance with this subchapter. If the Administrator denies such petition, the Administrator shall publish in the Federal Register the Administrator's reasons for such denial. The granting or denial of a petition under this subsection shall not affect any deadline or other requirement of this subchapter.

(f) Citizen civil actions with respect to EPA regulations

(1) Any person may commence a civil action without prior notice against the Administrator to compel the Administrator to meet the deadlines in section 2643 of this title for issuing advanced notices of proposed rulemaking, proposing regulations, and promulgating regulations. Any such action shall be brought in the district court of the United States for the District of Columbia.

(2) In any action brought under paragraph (1) in which the court finds the Administrator to be in violation of any deadline in section 2643 of this title, the court shall set forth a schedule for promulgating the regulations required by section 2643 of this title and shall order the Administrator to comply with such schedule. The court may extend any deadline (which has not already occurred) in section 2644(b), 2644(c), or 2644(d) of this title for a period of not more than 6 months, if the court-ordered schedule will result in final promulgation of the pertinent regulations within the extended period. Such deadline extensions may not be granted by the court beginning 720 days after October 22, 1986.

(3) Section 2619 of this title shall apply to civil actions described in this subsection, except to the extent inconsistent with this subsection.

(g) Failure to obtain accreditation; penalty

Any contractor who—

(1) inspects for asbestos-containing material in a school, public or commercial building;

(2) designs or conducts response actions with respect to friable asbestos-containing material in a school, public or commercial building; or

(3) employs individuals to conduct response actions with respect to friable asbestos-containing material in a school, public or commercial building;

and who fails to obtain the accreditation under section 2646 of this title, or in the case of employees to require or provide for the accreditation required, is liable for a civil penalty of not more than $5,000 for each day during which the violation continues, unless such contractor is a direct employee of the Federal Government.

(Pub.L. 94–469, Title II, § 207, as added Pub.L. 99–519, § 2, Oct. 22, 1986, 100 Stat. 2983, and amended Pub.L. 100–368, § 5, July 18, 1988, 102 Stat. 833; Pub.L. 101–647, § 15(a)(4), Nov. 28, 1990, 104 Stat. 4596.)

1 So in original. A comma was probably intended.

Effective Date of 1990 Amendment

Amendment of subsec. (g) by Pub.L. 101–637, effective upon the expiration of the 12-month period following the date of enactment of Pub.L. 101–637, Nov. 28, 1990, 104 Stat. 4589, which was approved Nov. 28, 1990, and subject to extension, see section 15(c) of Pub.L. 101–637, set out as a note under section 2646 of this title.

LIBRARY REFERENCES

Health and Environment ⇔38.
C.J.S. Health and Environment §§ 49, 50, 134 to 139, 151 to 156.

§ 2648. Emergency authority [TSCA § 208]

(a) Emergency action

(1) Authority

Whenever—

(A) the presence of airborne asbestos or the condition of friable asbestos-containing material in a school building governed by a local educational agency poses an imminent and substantial endangerment to human health or the environment, and

(B) the local educational agency is not taking sufficient action (as determined by the Administrator or the Governor) to respond to the airborne asbestos or friable asbestos-containing material,

the Administrator or the Governor of a State is authorized to act to protect human health or the environment.

(2) Limitations on Governor's action

The Governor of a State shall notify the Administrator within a reasonable period of time before the Governor plans to take an emergency action under this subsection. After such notification, if the Administrator takes an emergency action with respect to the same hazard, the Governor may not carry out (or continue to carry out, if the action has been started) the emergency action.

(3) Notification

The following notification shall be provided before an emergency action is taken under this subsection:

(A) In the case of a Governor taking the action, the Governor shall notify the local educational agency concerned.

(B) In the case of the Administrator taking the action, the Administrator shall notify both the local educational agency concerned and the Governor of the State in which such agency is located.

(4) Cost recovery

The Administrator or the Governor of a State may seek reimbursement for all costs of an emergency action taken under this subsection in the United States District Court for the District of Columbia or for the district in which the emergency action occurred. In any action seeking reimbursement from a local educational agency, the action shall be brought in the United States District Court for the district in which the local educational agency is located.

(b) Injunctive relief

Upon receipt of evidence that the presence of airborne asbestos or the condition of friable asbestos-containing material in a school building governed by a local educational agency poses an imminent and substantial endangerment to human health or the environment—

(1) the Administrator may request the Attorney General to bring suit, or

(2) the Governor of a State may bring suit,

to secure such relief as may be necessary to respond to the hazard. The district court of the United States in the district in which the response will be carried out shall have jurisdiction to grant such relief, including injunctive relief.

(Pub.L. 94–469, Title II, § 208, as added Pub.L. 99–519, § 2, Oct. 22, 1986, 100 Stat. 2985.)

LIBRARY REFERENCES

Health and Environment ⇔25.5(1).
C.J.S. Health and Environment §§ 61 et seq., 91 et seq., 106 to 133 et seq.

§ 2649. State and Federal law [TSCA § 209]

(a) No preemption

Nothing in this subchapter shall be construed, interpreted, or applied to preempt, displace, or supplant any other State or Federal law, whether statutory or common.

(b) Cost and damage awards

Nothing in this subchapter or any standard, regulation, or requirement promulgated pursuant to this subchapter shall be construed or interpreted to preclude any court from awarding costs and damages associated with the abatement, including the removal, of asbestos-containing material, or a portion of such costs, at any time prior to the actual date on which such material is removed.

(c) State may establish more requirements

Nothing in this subchapter shall be construed or interpreted as preempting a State from establishing any additional liability or more stringent requirements with respect to asbestos in school buildings within such State.

(d) No Federal cause of action

Nothing in this subchapter creates a cause of action or in any other way increases or diminishes the liability of any person under any other law.

(e) Intent of Congress

It is not the intent of Congress that this subchapter or rules, regulations, or orders issued pursuant to this subchapter be interpreted as influencing, in either the plaintiff's or defendant's favor, the disposition of any civil action for damages relating to asbestos. This subsection does not affect the authority of any court to make a determination in an adjudicatory proceeding under applicable State law with respect to the admission into evidence or any other use of this subchapter or rules, regulations, or orders issued pursuant to this subchapter.

(Pub.L. 94–469, Title II, § 209, as added Pub.L. 99–519, § 2, Oct. 22, 1986, 100 Stat. 2986.)

LIBRARY REFERENCES

States ⚷18.31.
C.J.S. States § 24.

§ 2650. Asbestos contractors and local educational agencies [TSCA § 210]

(a) Study

(1) General requirement

The Administrator shall conduct a study on the availability of liability insurance and other forms of assurance against financial loss which are available to local educational agencies and asbestos contractors with respect to actions required under this subchapter. Such study shall examine the following:

(A) The extent to which liability insurance and other forms of assurance against financial loss are available to local educational agencies and asbestos contractors.

(B) The extent to which the cost of insurance or other forms of assurance against financial loss has increased and the extent to which coverage has become less complete.

(C) The extent to which any limitation in the availability of insurance or other forms of assurance against financial loss is the result of factors other than standards of liability in applicable law.

(D) The extent to which the existence of the regulations required by subsections (c) and (d) of section 2643 of this title and the accreditation of contractors under section 2646 of this title has affected the availability or cost of insurance or other forms of assurance against financial loss.

(E) The extent to which any limitation on the availability of insurance or other forms of assurance against financial loss is inhibiting inspections for asbestos-containing material or the development or implementation of management plans under this subchapter.

(F) Identification of any other impediments to the timely completion of inspections or the development and implementation of management plans under this subchapter.

(2) Interim report

Not later than April 1, 1988, the Administrator shall submit to the Congress an interim report on the progress of the study required by this subsection, along with preliminary findings based on information collected to that date.

(3) Final report

Not later than October 1, 1990, the Administrator shall submit to the Congress a final report on the study required by this subsection, including final findings based on the information collected.

(b) State action

On the basis of the interim report or the final report of the study required by subsection (a) of this section, a State may enact or amend State law to establish or modify a standard of liability for local educational agencies or asbestos contractors with respect to actions required under this subchapter.

(Pub.L. 94–469, Title II, § 210, as added Pub.L. 99–519, § 2, Oct. 22, 1986, 100 Stat. 2986.)

LIBRARY REFERENCES

Schools ⚷78.
C.J.S. Schools and School Districts § 270 et seq.

§ 2651. Public protection [TSCA § 211]

(a) Public protection

No State or local educational agency may discriminate against a person in any way, including firing a person who is an employee, because the person provided information relating to a potential violation of this subchapter to any other person, including a State or the Federal Government.

(b) Labor Department review

Any public or private employee or representative of employees who believes he or she has been fired or otherwise discriminated against in violation of subsection (a) of this section may within 90 days after the alleged violation occurs apply to the Secretary of Labor for a review of the firing or alleged discrimination. The review shall be conducted in accordance with section 660(c) of Title 29.

(Pub.L. 94–469, Title II, § 211, as added Pub.L. 99–519, § 2, Oct. 22, 1986, 100 Stat. 2987.)

LIBRARY REFERENCES

Schools ⚷141(2).
C.J.S. Schools and School Districts § 201 et seq.

§ 2652. Asbestos Ombudsman [TSCA § 212]

(a) Appointment

The Administrator shall appoint an Asbestos Ombudsman, who shall carry out the duties described in subsection (b) of this section.

(b) Duties

The duties of the Asbestos Ombudsman are—

(1) to receive complaints, grievances, and requests for information submitted by any person with respect to any aspect of this subchapter,

(2) to render assistance with respect to the complaints, grievances, and requests received, and

(3) to make such recommendations to the Administrator as the Ombudsman considers appropriate.

(Pub.L. 94–469, Title II, § 212, as added Pub.L. 99–519, § 2, Oct. 22, 1986, 100 Stat. 2987.)

CODE OF FEDERAL REGULATIONS

Asbestos, reporting commercial and industrial uses of, materials found in schools, abatement projects, etc., see 40 CFR 763.60 et seq.

LIBRARY REFERENCES

Health and Environment ⚷25.5(9).
C.J.S. Health and Environment §§ 65, 66, 103, 107, 140 et seq.

§ 2653. EPA study of asbestos-containing material in public buildings [TSCA § 213]

Within 360 days after October 22, 1986, the Administrator shall conduct and submit to the Congress the results of a study which shall—

(1) assess the extent to which asbestos-containing materials are present in public and commercial buildings;

(2) assess the condition of asbestos-containing material in commercial buildings and the likelihood that persons occupying such buildings, including service and maintenance personnel, are, or may be, exposed to asbestos fibers;

(3) consider and report on whether public and commercial buildings should be subject to the same inspection and response action requirements that apply to school buildings;

(4) assess whether existing Federal regulations adequately protect the general public, particularly abatement personnel, from exposure to asbestos during renovation and demolition of such buildings; and

(5) include recommendations that explicitly address whether there is a need to establish standards for, and regulate asbestos exposure in, public and commercial buildings.

(Pub.L. 94–469, Title II, § 213, as added Pub.L. 99–519, § 2, Oct. 22, 1986, 100 Stat. 2987.)

LIBRARY REFERENCES

Health and Environment ⚷25.5(1).
C.J.S. Health and Environment §§ 61 et seq., 91 et seq., 106 to 133 et seq.

§ 2654. Transitional rules [TSCA § 214]

Any regulation of the Environmental Protection Agency under subchapter I of this chapter which is inconsistent with this subchapter shall not be in effect after October 22, 1986. Any advanced notice of proposed rulemaking, any proposed rule, and any regulation of the Environmental Protection Agency in effect before October 22, 1986, which is consistent with the regulations required under section 2643 of this title shall remain in effect and may be used to meet the requirements of section 2643 of this title, except that any such regulation shall be enforced under this chapter.

(Pub.L. 94–469, Title II, § 214, as added Pub.L. 99–519, § 2, Oct. 22, 1986, 100 Stat. 2988.)

LIBRARY REFERENCES

Health and Environment ⚷25.5(1).
C.J.S. Health and Environment §§ 61 et seq., 91 et seq., 106 to 133 et seq.

§ 2655. Worker protection [TSCA § 215]

(a) Prohibition on certain activities

Until the local educational agency with authority over a school has submitted a management plan (for the school) which the State Governor has not disapproved as of the end of the period for review and revision of the plan under section 2645 of this title, the local educational agency may not do either of the following in the school:

(1) Perform, or direct an employee to perform, renovations or removal of building materials, except emergency repairs, in the school, unless—

(A) the school is carrying out work under a grant awarded under section 4014 of Title 20; or

(B) an inspection that complies with the requirements of regulations promulgated under section 2643 of this title has been carried out in the school and the agency complies with the following sections of title 40 of the Code of Federal Regulations:

(i) Paragraphs (g), (h), and (i) of section 763.90 (response actions).

(ii) Appendix D to subpart E of part 763 (transport and disposal of asbestos waste).

(2) Perform, or direct an employee to perform, operations and maintenance activities in the school, unless the agency complies with the following sections of title 40 of the Code of Federal Regulations:

(A) Section 763.91 (operations and maintenance), including appendix B to subpart E of part 763.

(B) Paragraph (a)(2) of section 763.92 (training and periodic surveillance).

(b) Employee training and equipment

Any school employee who is directed to conduct emergency repairs involving any building material containing asbestos or suspected of containing asbestos, or to conduct operations and maintenance activities, in a school—

(1) shall be provided the proper training to safely conduct such work in order to prevent potential exposure to asbestos; and

(2) shall be provided the proper equipment and allowed to follow work practices that are necessary to safely conduct such work in order to prevent potential exposure to asbestos.

(c) Definition of emergency repair

For purposes of this section, the term "emergency repair" means a repair in a school building that was not planned and was in response to a sudden, unexpected event that threatens either—

(1) the health or safety of building occupants; or

(2) the structural integrity of the building.

(Pub.L. 94–469, Title II, § 215, as added Pub.L. 100–368, § 4(a), July 18, 1988, 102 Stat. 832.)

Effective Date

Section 4(c) of Pub.L. 100–368 provided that: "Section 215 of the Toxic Substances Control Act, as added by subsection (a), [this section] shall take effect on October 12, 1988."

§ 2656. Training grants [TSCA § 216]

(a) Grants

The Administrator is authorized to award grants under this section to nonprofit organizations that demonstrate experience in implementing and operating health and safety asbestos training and education programs for workers who are or will be engaged in asbestos-related activities (including State and local governments, colleges and universities, joint labor-management trust funds, and nonprofit government employee organizations) to establish and, or, operate asbestos training programs on a not-for-profit basis. Applications for grants under this subsection shall be submitted in such form and manner, and contain such information, as the Administrator prescribes.

(b) Authorization

Of such sums as are authorized to be appropriated pursuant to section 4021(a) of Title 20 for the fiscal years 1991, 1992, 1993, 1994, and 1995, not more than $5,000,000 are authorized to be appropriated to carry out this section in each such fiscal year.

(Pub.L. 94–469, Title II, § 216, as added Pub.L. 101–637, § 16(a)(1), Nov. 28, 1990, 104 Stat. 4597.)

Effective Date

Section 16(b) of Pub.L. 101–637 provided that: "Section 216 of the Toxic Substances Control Act [this section], as added by subsection (a), shall take effect on the date of the enactment of this Act [Nov. 28, 1990]."

SUBCHAPTER III—INDOOR RADON ABATEMENT

§ 2661. National goal [TSCA § 301]

The national long-term goal of the United States with respect to radon levels in buildings is that the air within buildings in the United States should be as free of radon as the ambient air outside of buildings.

(Pub.L. 94–469, Title III, § 301, as added Pub.L. 100–551, § 1(a), Oct. 28, 1988, 102 Stat. 2755.)

LIBRARY REFERENCES

Health and Environment ⚷25.6, 32.
C.J.S. Health and Environment §§ 28 to 36, 52, 91 to 105, 125 to 154.

WESTLAW ELECTRONIC RESEARCH

Health and Environment cases: 199k (add key number).

§ 2662. Definitions [TSCA § 302]

For purposes of this subchapter:

(1) The term "local educational agency" means—

(A) any local educational agency as defined in section 8801 of Title 20;

(B) the owner of any nonprofit elementary or secondary school building; and

(C) the governing authority of any school operated pursuant to section 241 of Title 20, as in effect before enactment of the Improving America's Schools Act of 1994, or successor authority, relating to impact aid for children who reside on Federal property.

(2) The term "nonprofit elementary or secondary school" has the meaning given such term by section 2642(8) of this title,[1]

(3) The term "radon" means the radioactive gaseous element and its short-lived decay products produced by the disintegration of the element radium occurring in air, water, soil, or other media.

(4) The term "school building" has the meaning given such term by section 2642(13) of this title.

(Pub.L. 94–469, Title III, § 302, as added Pub.L. 100–551, § 1(a), Oct. 28, 1988, 102 Stat. 2755, and amended Pub.L. 103–382, Title III, §§ 391(c)(4), 392(b)(2), Oct. 20, 1994, 108 Stat. 4022, 4026.)

[1] So in original. Probably should be "2642(9)".

References in Text

Section 198 of the Elementary and Secondary Education Act of 1965, referred to in par. (1)(A), was section 198 of Pub.L. 89–10 classified to section 2854 of Title 20, Education prior to the enactment of Pub.L. 100–297, which generally amended and reorganized Pub.L. 89–10. The term "local educational agency" defined in section 2854 of Title 20 and referred to in parenthetical reference of par. (1)(A) as "(20 U.S.C. 3381)" is now defined in section 2891 of Title 20.

§ 2663. EPA Citizen's Guide [TSCA § 303]

(a) Publication

In order to make continuous progress toward the long-term goal established in section 2661 of this title, the Administrator of the Environmental Protection Agency shall, not later than June 1, 1989, publish and make available to the public an updated version of its document titled "A Citizen's Guide to Radon". The Administrator shall revise and republish the guide as necessary thereafter.

(b) Information included

(1) Action levels

The updated citizen's guide published as provided in subsection (a) of this section shall include a description of a series of action levels indicating the health risk associated with different level of radon exposure.

(2) Other information

The updated citizen's guide shall also include information with respect to each of the following:

(A) The increased health risk associated with the exposure of potentially sensitive populations to different levels of radon.

(B) The increased health risk associated with the exposure to radon of persons engaged in potentially risk-increasing behavior.

(C) The cost and technological feasibility of reducing radon concentrations within existing and new buildings.

(D) The relationship between short-term and long-term testing techniques and the relationship between (i) measurements based on both such techniques, and (ii) the actions levels set forth as provided in paragraph (1).

(E) Outdoor radon levels around the country.

(Pub.L. 94–469, Title III, § 303, as added Pub.L. 100–551, § 1(a), Oct. 28, 1988, 102 Stat. 2755.)

LIBRARY REFERENCES

Health and Environment ⚖25.5, 32.
C.J.S. Health and Environment §§ 28 to 36, 52 to 153.

§ 2664. Model construction standards and techniques [TSCA § 304]

The Administrator of the Environmental Protection Agency shall develop model construction standards and techniques for controlling radon levels within new buildings. To the maximum extent possible, these standards and techniques should be developed with the assistance of organizations involved in establishing national building construction standards and techniques. The Administrator shall make a draft of the document containing the model standards and techniques available for public review and comment. The model standards and techniques shall provide for geographic differences in construction types and materials, geology, weather, and other variables that may affect radon levels in new buildings. The Administrator shall make final model standards and techniques available to the public by June 1, 1990. The Administrator shall work to ensure that organizations responsible for developing national model building codes, and authorities which regulate building construction within States or political subdivisions within States, adopt the Agency's model standards and techniques.

(Pub.L. 94–469, Title III, § 304, as added Pub.L. 100–551, § 1(a), Oct. 28, 1988, 102 Stat. 2756.)

§ 2665. Technical assistance to States for radon programs [TSCA § 305]

(a) Required activities

The Administrator (or another Federal department or agency designated by the Administrator) shall develop and implement activities designed to assist State radon programs. These activities may include, but are not limited to, the following:

(1) Establishment of a clearinghouse of radon related information, including mitigation studies, public information materials, surveys of radon levels, and other relevant information.

(2) Operation of a voluntary proficiency program for rating the effectiveness of radon measurement devices and methods, the effectiveness of randon

mitigation devices and methods, and the effectiveness of private firms and individuals offering radon-related architecture, design, engineering, measurement, and mitigation services. The proficiency program under this subparagraph shall be in operation within one year after October 28, 1988.

(3) Design and implementation of training seminars for State and local officials and private and professional firms dealing with radon and addressing topics such as monitoring, analysis, mitigation, health effects, public information, and program design.

(4) Publication of public information materials concerning radon health risks and methods of radon mitigation.

(5) Operation of cooperative projects between the Environmental Protection Agency's Radon Action Program and the State's radon program. Such projects shall include the Home Evaluation Program, in which the Environmental Protection Agency evaluates homes and States demonstrate mitigation methods in these homes. To the maximum extent practicable, consistent with the objectives of the evaluation and demonstration, homes of low-income persons should be selected for evaluation and demonstration.

(6) Demonstration of radon mitigation methods in various types of structures and in various geographic settings and publication of findings. In the case of demonstration of such methods in homes, the Administrator should select homes of low-income persons, to the maximum extent practicable and consistent with the objectives of the demonstration.

(7) Establishment of a national data base with data organized by State concerning the location and amounts of radon.

(8) Development and demonstration of methods of radon measurement and mitigation that take into account unique characteristics, if any, of nonresidential buildings housing child care facilities.

(b) Discretionary assistance

Upon request of a State, the Administrator (or another Federal department or agency designated by the Administrator) may provide technical assistance to such State in development or implementation of programs addressing radon. Such assistance may include, but is not limited to, the following:

(1) Design and implementation of surveys of the location and occurrence of radon within a State.

(2) Design and implementation of public information and education programs.

(3) Design and implementation of State programs to control radon in existing or new structures.

(4) Assessment of mitigation alternatives in unusual or unconventional structures.

(5) Design and implementation of methods for radon measurement and mitigation for nonresidential buildings housing child care facilities.

(c) Information provided to professional organizations

The Administrator, or another Federal department or agency designated by the Administrator, shall provide appropriate information concerning technology and methods of radon assessment and mitigation to professional organizations representing private firms involved in building design, engineering, and construction.

(d) Proficiency rating program and training seminar

(1) Authorization

There is authorized to be appropriated not more than $1,500,000 for the purposes of initially establishing the proficiency rating program under subsection (a)(2) of this section and the training seminars under subsection (a)(3) of this section.

(2) Charge imposed

To cover the operating costs of such proficiency rating program and training seminars, the Administrator shall impose on persons applying for a proficiency rating and on private and professional firms participating in training seminars such charges as may be necessary to defray the costs of the program or seminars. No such charge may be imposed on any State or local government.

(3) Special account

Funds derived from the charges imposed under paragraph (2) of this subsection shall be deposited in a special account in the Treasury. Amounts in the special account are authorized to be appropriated only for purposes of administering such proficiency rating program or training seminars or for reimbursement of funds appropriated to the Administrator to initially establish such program or seminars.

(4) Reimbursement of General Fund

During the first three years of the program and seminars, the Administrator shall make every effort, consistent with the goals and successful operation of the program and seminars, to set charges imposed under paragraph (2) of this subsection so that an amount in excess of operation costs is collected. Such excess amount shall be used to reimburse the General Fund of the Treasury for the full amount appropriated to initially establish the program and seminars.

(5) Research

The Administrator shall, in conjunction with other Federal agencies, conduct research to develop, test, and evaluate radon and radon progeny measurement methods and protocols. The purpose of such research shall be to assess the ability of those methods and protocols to accurately assess exposure to radon progeny. Such research shall include—

(A) conducting comparisons among radon and radon progeny measurement techniques;

(B) developing measurement protocols for different building types under varying operating conditions; and

(C) comparing the exposures estimated by stationary monitors and protocols to those measured by personal monitors, and issue guidance documents that—

(i) provide information on the results of research conducted under this paragraph; and

(ii) describe model State radon measurement and mitigation programs.

(6) Mandatory proficiency testing program study

(A) The Administrator shall conduct a study to determine the feasibility of establishing a mandatory proficiency testing program that would require that—

(i) any product offered for sale, or device used in connection with a service offered to the public, for the measurement of radon meets minimum performance criteria; and

(ii) any operator of a device, or person employing a technique, used in connection with a service offered to the public for the measurement of radon meets a minimum level of proficiency.

(B) The study shall also address procedures for—

(i) ordering the recall of any product sold for the measurement of radon which does not meet minimum performance criteria;

(ii) ordering the discontinuance of any service offered to the public for the measurement of radon which does not meet minimum performance criteria; and

(iii) establishing adequate quality assurance requirements for each company offering radon measurement services to the public to follow.

The study shall identify enforcement mechanisms necessary to the success of the program. The Administrator shall report the findings of the study with recommendations to Congress by March 1, 1991.

(7) User fee

In addition to any charge imposed pursuant to paragraph (2), the Administrator shall collect user fees from persons seeking certification under the radon proficiency program in an amount equal to $1,500,000 to cover the Environmental Protection Agency's cost of conducting research pursuant to paragraph (5) for each of the fiscal years 1991, 1992, 1993, 1994, and 1995. Such funds shall be deposited in the account established pursuant to paragraph (3).

(e) Authorization

(1) There is authorized to be appropriated for the purposes of carrying out sections 2663, 2664 of this title, and this section an amount not to exceed $3,000,000 for each of fiscal years 1989, 1990, and 1991.

(2) No amount appropriated under this subsection may be used by the Environmental Protection Agency to administer the grant program under section 2666 of this title.

(3) No amount appropriated under this subsection may be used to cover the costs of the proficiency rating program under subsection (a)(2) of this section.

(f) Redesignated (e)

(Pub.L. 94–469, Title III, § 305, as added Pub.L. 100–551, § 1(a), Oct. 28, 1988, 102 Stat. 2756, and amended Pub.L. 101–508, Title X, § 10202, Nov. 5, 1990, 104 Stat. 1388–393; Pub.L. 104–66, Title II, § 2021(*l*), Dec. 21, 1995, 109 Stat. 728.)

References in Text

Section 403(c) of the Superfund Amendments and Authorization Act of 1986, referred to in subsec. (d) is Pub.L. 99–499, § 403(c), Oct. 17, 1986, 100 Stat. 1758, which is set out as a note under section 7401 of Title 42, Public Health and Welfare.

LIBRARY REFERENCES

Health and Environment ⚷25.5(2) to (4), 32.
C.J.S. Health and Environment §§ 28 to 36, 52, 61 et seq., 91 to 133.

§ 2666. Grant assistance to States for radon programs [TSCA § 306]

(a) In general

For each fiscal year, upon application of the Governor of a State, the Administrator may make a grant, subject to such terms and conditions as the Administrator considers appropriate, under this section to the State for the purpose of assisting the State in the development and implementation of programs for the assessment and mitigation of radon.

(b) Application

An application for a grant under this section in any fiscal year shall contain such information as the Administrator shall require, including each of the following:

(1) A description of the seriousness and extent of radon exposure in the State.

(2) An identification of the State agency which has the primary responsibility for radon programs and which will receive the grant, a description of the roles and responsibilities of the lead State agency and any other State agencies involved in radon programs, and description of the roles and responsibilities of any municipal, district, or areawide organization involved in radon programs.

(3) A description of the activities and programs related to radon which the State proposes in such year.

(4) A budget specifying Federal and State funding of each element of activity of the grant application.

(5) A 3-year plan which outlines long range program goals and objectives, tasks necessary to achieve them, and resource requirements for the entire 3-year period, including anticipated State funding levels and desired Federal funding levels. This clause shall apply only for the initial year in which a grant application is made.

(c) Eligible activities

Activities eligible for grant assistance under this section are the following:

(1) Survey of radon levels, including special surveys of geographic areas or classes of buildings (such as, among others, public buildings, school buildings, high-risk residential construction types).

(2) Development of public information and educational materials concerning radon assessment, mitigation, and control programs.

(3) Implementation of programs to control radon in existing and new structures.

(4) Purchase by the State of radon measurement equipment or devices.

(5) Purchase and maintenance of analytical equipment connected to radon measurement and analysis, including costs of calibration of such equipment.

(6) Payment of costs of Environmental Protection Agency-approved training programs related to radon for permanent State or local employees.

(7) Payment of general overhead and program administration costs.

(8) Development of a data storage and management system for information concerning radon occurrence, levels, and programs.

(9) Payment of costs of demonstration of radon mitigation methods and technologies as approved by the Administrator, including State participation in the Environmental Protection Agency Home Evaluation Program.

(10) A toll-free radon hotline to provide information and technical assistance.

(d) Preference to certain States

Beginning in fiscal year 1991, the Administrator shall give a preference for grant assistance under this section to States that have made reasonable efforts to ensure the adoption, by the authorities which regulate building construction within that State or political subdivisions within States, of the model construction standards and techniques for new buildings developed under section 2664 of this title.

(e) Priority activities and projects

The Administrator shall support eligible activities contained in State applications with the full amount of available funds. In the event that State applications for funds exceed the total funds available in a fiscal year, the Administrator shall give priority to activities or projects proposed by States based on each of the following criteria:

(1) The seriousness and extent of the radon contamination problem to be addressed.

(2) The potential for the activity or project to bring about reduction in radon levels.

(3) The potential for development of innovative radon assessment techniques, mitigation measures as approved by the Administrator, or program management approaches which may be of use to other States.

(4) Any other uniform criteria that the Administrator deems necessary to promote the goals of the grant program and that the Administrator provides to State before the application process.

(f) Federal share

The Federal share of the cost of radon program activities implemented with Federal assistance under this section in any fiscal year shall not exceed 75 percent of the costs incurred by the State in implementing such program in the first year of a grant to such State, 60 percent in the second year, and 50 percent in the third year. Federal assistance shall be made on the condition that the non-Federal share is provided from non-Federal funds.

(g) Assistance to local governments

States may, at the Governor's discretion, use funds from grants under this section to assist local governments in implementation of activities eligible for assistance under paragraphs (2), (3), and (6) of subsection (c) of this section.

(h) Information

(1) The Administrator may request such information, data, and reports developed by the State as he considers necessary to make the determination of continuing eligibility under this section.

(2) Any State receiving funds under this section shall provide to the Administrator all radon-related information generated in its activities, including the results of radon surveys, mitigation demonstration projects, and risk communication studies.

(3) Any State receiving funds under this section shall maintain, and make available to the public, a list of firms and individuals within the State that have received a passing rating under the Environmental Protection Agency proficiency rating program referred to in section 2665(a)(2) of this title. The list shall also include the address and phone number of such firms and individuals, together with the proficiency rating received by each. The Administrator shall make such list available to the public at appropriate locations in each State which does not receive funds under this section unless the State assumes such responsibility.

(i) Limitations

(1) No grant may be made under this section in any fiscal year to a State which in the preceding fiscal year received a grant under this section unless the Administrator determines that such State satisfactorily implemented the activities funded by the grant in such preceding fiscal year.

(2) The costs of implementing paragraphs (4) and (9) of subsection (c) of this section shall not in the aggregate exceed 50 percent of the amount of any grant awarded under this section to a State in a fiscal year. In implementing such paragraphs, a State should make every effort, consistent with the goals and successful operation of the State radon program to give a preference to low-income persons.

(3) The costs of general overhead and program administration under subsection (c)(7) of this section shall not exceed 25 percent of the amount of any grant awarded under this section to a State in a fiscal year.

(4) A State may use funds received under this section for financial assistance to persons only to the extent such assistance is related to demonstration projects or the purchase and analysis of radon measurement devices.

(j) Authorization

(1) There is authorized to be appropriated for grant assistance under this section an amount not to exceed $10,000,000 for each of fiscal years 1989, 1990, and 1991.

(2) There is authorized to be appropriated for the purpose of administering the grant program under this section such sums as may be necessary for each of such fiscal years.

(3) Notwithstanding any other provision of this section, not more than 10 percent of the amount appropriated to carry out this section may be used to make grants to any one State.

(4) Funds not obligated to States in the fiscal year for which funds are appropriated under this section shall remain available for obligation during the next fiscal year.

(5) No amount appropriated under this subsection may be used to cover the costs of the proficiency rating program under section 2665(a)(2) of this title.

(Pub.L. 94–469, Title III, § 306, as added Pub.L. 100–551, § 1(a), Oct. 28, 1988, 102 Stat. 2758.)

§ 2667. Radon in schools [TSCA § 307]

(a) Study of radon in schools

(1) Authority

The Administrator shall conduct a study for the purpose of determining the extent of radon contamination in the Nation's school buildings.

(2) List of high probability areas

In carrying out such study, the Administrator shall identify and compile a list of areas within the United States which the Administrator determines have a high probability of including schools which have elevated levels of radon.

(3) Basis of list

In compiling such list, the Administrator shall make such determinations on the basis of, among other things, each of the following:

(A) Geological data.

(B) Data on high radon levels in homes and other structures nearby any such school.

(C) Physical characteristics of the school buildings.

(4) Survey

In conducting such study the Administrator shall design a survey which when completed allows Congress to characterize the extent of radon contamination in schools in each State. The survey shall include testing from a representative sample of schools in each high-risk area identified in paragraph (1) and shall include additional testing, to the extent resources are available for such testing. The survey also shall include any reliable testing data supplied by States, schools, or other parties.

(5) Assistance

(A) The Administrator shall make available to the appropriate agency of each State, as designated by the Governor of such State, a list of high risk areas within each State, including a delineation of such areas and any other data available to the Administrator for schools in that State. To assist such agencies, the Administrator also shall provide guidance and data detailing the risks associated with high radon levels, technical guidance and related information concerning testing for radon within schools, and methods of reducing radon levels.

(B) In addition to the assistance authorized by subparagraph (A), the Administrator is authorized to make available to the appropriate agency of each State as designated by the Governor of such State, devices suitable for use by such agencies in conducting tests for radon within the schools under the jurisdiction of any such State agency. The Administrator is authorized to make available to such agencies the use of laboratories of the Environmental Protection Agency, or to recommend laboratories, to evaluate any such devices for the presence of radon levels.

(6) Diagnostic and remedial efforts

The Administrator is authorized to select, from high-risk areas identified in paragraph (2), school buildings for purposes of enabling the Administrator to undertake diagnostic and remedial efforts to reduce the levels of radon in such school buildings. Such diagnostic and remedial efforts shall be carried out with a view to developing technology and expertise for the purpose of making such technology and expertise available to any local educational agency and the several States.

(7) Status report

On or before October 1, 1989, the Administrator shall submit to the Congress a status report with respect to action taken by the Administrator in conducting the study required by this section, including the results of the Administrator's diagnostic and remedial work. On or before October 1, 1989, the Administrator shall submit a final report setting forth the results of the study conducted pursuant to this section, including the results of the Administrator's diagnostic and remedial work, and the recommendations of the Administrator.

(b) Authorization

For the purpose of carrying out the provisions of paragraph (6) of subsection (a) of this section, there are authorized to be appropriated such sums, not to exceed $500,000, as may be necessary. For the purpose of carrying out the provisions of this section other than such paragraph (6), there are authorized to be appropriated such sums, not to exceed $1,000,000, as may be necessary.

(Pub.L. 94–469, Title III, § 307, as added Pub.L. 100–551, § 1(a), Oct. 28, 1988, 102 Stat. 2761.)

§ 2668. Regional radon training centers [TSCA § 308]

(a) Funding program

Upon application of colleges, universities, institutions of higher learning, or consortia of such institutions, the Administrator may make a grant or cooperative agreement, subject to such terms and conditions as the Administrator considers appropriate, under this section to the applicant for the purpose of establishing and operating a regional radon training center.

(b) Purpose of the centers

The purpose of a regional radon training center is to develop information and provide training to Federal and State officials, professional and private firms, and the public regarding the health risks posed by radon and demonstrated methods of radon measurement and mitigation.

(c) Applications

Any colleges, universities, institutions of higher learning or consortia of such institutions may submit an application for funding under this section. Such applications shall be submitted to the Administrator in such form and containing such information as the Administrator may require.

(d) Selection criteria

The Administrator shall support at least 3 eligible applications with the full amount of available funds. The Administrator shall select recipients of funding under this section to ensure that funds are equitably allocated among regions of the United States, and on the basis of each of the following criteria:

(1) The extent to which the applicant's program will promote the purpose described in subsection (b) of this section.

(2) The demonstrated expertise of the applicant regarding radon measurement and mitigation methods and other radon-related issues.

(3) The demonstrated expertise of the applicant in radon training and in activities relating to information development and dissemination.

(4) The seriousness of the radon problem in the region.

(5) The geographical coverage of the proposed center.

(6) Any other uniform criteria that the Administrator deems necessary to promote the purpose described in subsection (b) of this section and that the Administrator provides to potential applicants prior to the application process.

(e) Termination of funding

No funding may be given under this section in any fiscal year to an applicant which in the preceding fiscal year received funding under this section unless the Administrator determines that the recipient satisfactorily implemented the activities that were funded in the preceding year.

(f) Authorization

There is authorized to be appropriated to carry out the program under this section not to exceed $1,000,000 for each of fiscal years 1989, 1990, and 1991.

(Pub.L. 94–469, Title III, § 308, as added Pub.L. 100–551, § 1(a), Oct. 28, 1988, 102 Stat. 2762.)

§ 2669. Study of radon in Federal buildings [TSCA § 309]

(a) Study requirement

The head of each Federal department or agency that owns a Federal building shall conduct a study for the purpose of determining the extent of radon contamination in such buildings. Such study shall include, in the case of a Federal building using a nonpublic water source (such as a well or other groundwater), radon contamination of the water.

(b) High-risk Federal buildings

(1) The Administrator shall identify and compile a list of areas within the United States which the Administrator, in consultation with Federal departments and agencies, determines have a high probability of including Federal buildings which have elevated levels of radon.

(2) In compiling such list, the Administrator shall make such determinations on the basis of, among other things, the following:

(A) Geological data.

(B) Data on high radon levels in homes and other structures near any such Federal building.

(C) Physical characteristics of the Federal buildings.

(c) Study designs

Studies required under subsection (a) of this section shall be based on design criteria specified by the Administrator. The head of each Federal department or agency conducting such a study shall submit, not later than July 1, 1989, a study design to the Administrator for approval. The study design shall follow the most recent Environmental Protection Agency guidance documents, including "A Citizen's Guide to Radon"; the "Interim Protocol for Screening and Follow Up: Radon and Radon Decay Products Measurements"; the "Interim Indoor Radon & Radon Decay Product Measurement Protocol"; and any other recent guidance documents. The study design shall include testing data from a representative sample of Federal buildings in each high-risk area identified in subsection (b) of this section. The study design also shall include additional testing data to the extent resources are available, including any reliable data supplied by Federal agencies, States, or other parties.

(d) Information on risks and testing

(1) The Administrator shall provide to the departments or agencies conducting studies under subsection (a) of this section the following:

(A) Guidance and data detailing the risks associated with high radon levels.

(B) Technical guidance and related information concerning testing for radon within Federal buildings and water supplies.

(C) Technical guidance and related information concerning methods for reducing radon levels.

(2) In addition to the assistance required by paragraph (1), the Administrator is authorized to make available, on a cost reimbursable basis, to the departments or agencies conducting studies under subsection (a) of this section devices suitable for use by such departments or agencies in conducting tests for radon within Federal buildings. For the purpose of assisting such departments or agencies in evaluating any such devices for the presence of radon levels, the Administrator is authorized to recommend laboratories or to make available to such departments or agencies, on a cost reimbursable basis, the use of laboratories of the Environmental Protection Agency.

(e) Study deadline

Not later than June 1, 1990, the head of each Federal department or agency conducting a study under subsection (a) of this section shall complete the study and provide the study to the Administrator.

(f) Report to Congress

Not later than October 1, 1990, the Administrator shall submit a report to the Congress describing the results of the studies conducted pursuant to subsection (a) of this section.

(Pub.L. 94–469, Title III, § 309, as added Pub.L. 100–551, § 1(a), Oct. 28, 1988, 102 Stat. 2763.)

§ 2670. Regulations [TSCA § 310]

The Administrator is authorized to issue such regulations as may be necessary to carry out the provisions of this subchapter.

(Pub.L. 94–469, Title III, § 310, as added Pub.L. 100–551, § 1(a), Oct. 28, 1988, 102 Stat. 2764.)

§ 2671. Additional authorizations [TSCA § 311]

Amounts authorized to be appropriated in this subchapter for purposes of carrying out the provisions of this subchapter are in addition to amounts authorized to be appropriated under other provisions of law for radon-related activities.

(Pub.L. 94–469, Title III, § 311, as added Pub.L. 100–551, § 1(a), Oct. 28, 1988, 102 Stat. 2764.)

SUBCHAPTER IV—LEAD EXPOSURE REDUCTION

§ 2681. Definitions [TSCA § 401]

For the purposes of this subchapter:

(1) Abatement

The term "abatement" means any set of measures designed to permanently eliminate lead-based paint hazards in accordance with standards established by the Administrator under this subchapter. Such term includes—

(A) the removal of lead-based paint and lead-contaminated dust, the permanent containment or encapsulation of lead-based paint, the replacement of lead-painted surfaces or fixtures, and the removal or covering of lead-contaminated soil; and

(B) all preparation, cleanup, disposal, and postabatement clearance testing activities associated with such measures.

(2) Accessible surface

The term, "accessible surface" means an interior or exterior surface painted with lead-based paint that is accessible for a young child to mouth or chew.

(3) Deteriorated paint

The term "deteriorated paint" means any interior or exterior paint that is peeling, chipping, chalking or cracking or any paint located on an interior or exterior surface or fixture that is damaged or deteriorated.

(4) Evaluation

The term "evaluation" means risk assessment, inspection, or risk assessment and inspection.

(5) Friction surface

The term "friction surface" means an interior or exterior surface that is subject to abrasion or friction, including certain window, floor, and stair surfaces.

(6) Impact surface

The term "impact surface" means an interior or exterior surface that is subject to damage by repeated impacts, for example, certain parts of door frames.

(7) Inspection

The term "inspection" means (A) a surface-by-surface investigation to determine the presence of lead-based paint, as provided in section 4822(c) of Title 42, and (B) the provision of a report explaining the results of the investigation.

(8) Interim controls

The term "interim controls" means a set of measures designed to reduce temporarily human exposure or likely exposure to lead-based paint hazards, including specialized cleaning, repairs, maintenance, painting, temporary containment, ongoing monitoring of lead-based paint hazards or potential hazards, and the establishment and operation of management and resident education programs.

(9) Lead-based paint

The term "lead-based paint" means paint or other surface coatings that contain lead in excess of 1.0 milligrams per centimeter squared or 0.5 percent by weight or (A) in the case of paint or other surface coatings on target housing, such lower level as may be established by the Secretary of Housing and Urban Development, as defined in section 4822(c) of Title 42, or (B) in the case of any other paint or surface coatings, such other level as may be established by the Administrator.

(10) Lead-based paint hazard

The term "lead-based paint hazard" means any condition that causes exposure to lead from lead-contaminated dust, lead-contaminated soil, lead-contaminated paint that is deteriorated or present in accessible surfaces, friction surfaces, or impact surfaces that would result in adverse human health effects as established by the Administrator under this subchapter.

(11) Lead-contaminated dust

The term "lead-contaminated dust" means surface dust in residential dwellings that contains an area or mass concentration of lead in excess of levels determined by the Administrator under this subchapter to pose a threat of adverse health effects in pregnant women or young children.

(12) Lead-contaminated soil

The term "lead-contaminated soil" means bare soil on residential real property that contains lead at or in excess of the levels determined to be hazardous to human health by the Administrator under this subchapter.

(13) Reduction

The term "reduction" means measures designed to reduce or eliminate human exposure to lead-based paint hazards through methods including interim controls and abatement.

(14) Residential dwelling

The term "residential dwelling" means—

(A) a single-family dwelling, including attached structures such as porches and stoops; or

(B) a single-family dwelling unit in a structure that contains more than 1 separate residential dwelling unit, and in which each such unit is used or occupied, or intended to be used or occupied, in whole or in part, as the home or residence of 1 or more persons.

(15) Residential real property

The term "residential real property" means real property on which there is situated 1 or more residential dwellings used or occupied, or intended to be used or occupied, in whole or in part, as the home or residence of 1 or more persons.

(16) Risk assessment

The term "risk assessment" means an on-site investigation to determine and report the existence, nature, severity and location of lead-based paint hazards in residential dwellings, including—

(A) information gathering regarding the age and history of the housing and occupancy by children under age 6;

(B) visual inspection;

(C) limited wipe sampling or other environmental sampling techniques;

(D) other activity as may be appropriate; and

(E) provision of a report explaining the results of the investigation.

(17) Target housing

The term "target housing" means any housing constructed prior to 1978, except housing for the elderly or persons with disabilities (unless any child who is less than 6 years of age resides or is expected to reside in such housing for the elderly or persons with disabilities) or any 0-bedroom dwelling. In the case of jurisdictions which banned the sale or use of lead-based paint prior to 1978, the Secretary of Housing and Urban Development, at the Secretary's discretion, may designate an earlier date.

(Pub.L. 94–469, Title IV, § 401, as added Pub.L. 102–550, Title X, § 1021(a), Oct. 28, 1992, 106 Stat. 3912.)

Effective Date

Section effective Oct. 28, 1992, see section 2 of Pub.L. 102–550, set out as a note under section 5301 of Title 42, The Public Health and Welfare.

LIBRARY REFERENCES

Health and Environment ⚷25.5(3).
C.J.S. Health and Environment §§ 95 et seq., 106 et seq., 129 et seq.

§ 2682. Lead-based paint activities training and certification [TSCA § 402]

(a) Regulations

(1) In general

Not later than 18 months after October 28, 1992, the Administrator shall, in consultation with the Secretary of Labor, the Secretary of Housing and Urban Development, and the Secretary of Health and Human Services (acting through the Director of the National Institute for Occupational Safety and Health), promulgate final regulations governing lead-based paint activities to ensure that individuals engaged in such activities are properly trained; that training programs are accredited; and that contractors engaged in such activities are certified. Such regulations shall contain standards for performing lead-based paint activities, taking into account reliability, effectiveness, and safety. Such regulations shall require that all risk assessment, inspection, and abatement activities performed in target housing shall be performed by certified contractors, as such term is defined in section 4851b of Title 42. The provisions of this section shall supersede the provisions set forth under the heading "Lead Abatement Training and Certification" and under the heading "Training Grants" in title III of the Act entitled "An Act making appropriations for the Departments of Veterans Affairs and Housing and Urban Development, and for sundry independent agencies, commissions, corporations, and offices for the fiscal year ending September 30, 1992, and for other purposes", Public Law 102–139, and upon the enactment of this section the provisions set forth in such public law under such headings shall cease to have any force and effect.

(2) Accreditation of training programs

Final regulations promulgated under paragraph (1) shall contain specific requirements for the accreditation of lead-based paint activities training programs for workers, supervisors, inspectors and planners, and other individuals involved in lead-based paint activities, including but not limited to, each of the following:

(A) Minimum requirements for the accreditation of training providers.

(B) Minimum training curriculum requirements.

(C) Minimum training hour requirements.

(D) Minimum hands-on training requirements.

(E) Minimum trainee competency and proficiency requirements.

(F) Minimum requirements for training program quality control.

(3) Accreditation and certification fees

The Administrator (or the State in the case of an authorized State program) shall impose a fee on—

(A) persons operating training programs accredited under this subchapter; and

(B) lead-based paint activities contractors certified in accordance with paragraph (1).

The fees shall be established at such level as is necessary to cover the costs of administering and enforcing the standards and regulations under this section which are applicable to such programs and contractors. The fee shall not be imposed on any State, local government, or nonprofit training program. The Administrator (or the State in the case of an authorized State program) may waive the fee for lead-based paint activities contractors under subparagraph (A) for the purpose of training their own employees.

(b) Lead-based paint activities

For purposes of this subchapter, the term "lead-based paint activities" means—

(1) in the case of target housing, risk assessment, inspection, and abatement; and

(2) in the case of any public building constructed before 1978, commercial building, bridge, or other structure or superstructure, identification of lead-based paint and materials containing lead-based paint, deleading, removal of lead from bridges, and demolition.

For purposes of paragraph (2), the term "deleading" means activities conducted by a person who offers to eliminate lead-based paint or lead-based paint hazards or to plan such activities.

(c) Renovation and remodeling

(1) Guidelines

In order to reduce the risk of exposure to lead in connection with renovation and remodeling of target housing, public buildings constructed before 1978, and commercial buildings, the Administrator shall, within 18 months after October 28, 1992, promulgate guidelines for the conduct of such renovation and remodeling activities which may create a risk of exposure to dangerous levels of lead. The Administrator shall disseminate such guidelines to persons engaged in such renovation and remodeling through hardware and paint stores, employee organizations, trade groups, State and local agencies, and through other appropriate means.

(2) Study of certification

The Administrator shall conduct a study of the extent to which persons engaged in various types of renovation and remodeling activities in target housing, public buildings constructed before 1978, and commercial buildings are exposed to lead in the conduct of such activities or disturb lead and create a lead-based paint hazard on a regular or occasional basis. The Administrator shall complete such study and publish the results thereof within 30 months after October 28, 1992.

(3) Certification determination

Within 4 years after October 28, 1992, the Administrator shall revise the regulations under subsection (a) of this section to apply the regulations to renovation or remodeling activities in target housing, public buildings constructed before 1978, and commercial buildings that create lead-based paint hazards. In determining which contractors are engaged in such activities, the Administrator shall utilize the results of the study under paragraph (2) and consult with the representatives of labor organizations, lead-based paint activities contractors, persons engaged in remodeling and renovation, experts in lead health effects, and others. If the Administrator determines that any category of contractors engaged in renovation or remodeling does not require certification, the Administrator shall publish an explanation of the basis for that determination.

(Pub.L. 94–469, Title IV, § 402, as added Pub.L. 102–550, Title X, § 1021(a), Oct. 28, 1992, 106 Stat. 3914.)

References in Text

Reference in subsec. (a)(1) to provisions set forth under certain specified headings in Pub.L. 102–139 is a reference to provisions set out as a note under section 4822 of Title 42, The Public Health and Welfare, relating to lead-based paint abatement training and certification requirements and training grants.

Effective Date

Section effective Oct. 28, 1992, see section 2 of Pub.L. 102–550, set out as a note under section 5301 of Title 42, The Public Health and Welfare.

§ 2683. Identification of dangerous levels of lead [TSCA § 403]

Within 18 months after October 28, 1992, the Administrator shall promulgate regulations which shall identify, for purposes of this subchapter, and the Residential Lead–Based Paint Hazard Reduction Act of 1992 [42 U.S.C.A. § 4851 et seq.], lead-based paint hazards, lead-contaminated dust, and lead-contaminated soil.

(Pub.L. 94–469, Title IV, § 403, as added Pub.L. 102–550, Title X, § 1021(a), Oct. 28, 1992, 106 Stat. 3916.)

References in Text

The Residential Lead-Based Paint Hazard Reduction Act of 1992, referred to in text, is Pub.L. 102–550, Title X, § 1001 et seq., Oct. 28, 1992, 106 Stat. 3897, which is classified generally to chapter 63A (section 4851 et seq.) of Title 42, The Public Health and Welfare. For complete classification of that Act to the Code see Short Title note under section 4851 of Title 42 and Tables.

Effective Date

Section effective Oct. 28, 1992, see section 2 of Pub.L. 102–550, set out as a note under section 5301 of Title 42, The Public Health and Welfare.

§ 2684. Authorized State programs [TSCA § 404]

(a) Approval

Any State which seeks to administer and enforce the standards, regulations, or other requirements established under section 2682 or 2686 of this title, or both, may, after notice and opportunity for public hearing, develop and submit to the Administrator an application, in such form as the Administrator shall require, for authorization of such a State program. Any such State may also certify to the Administrator at the time of submitting such program that the State program meets the requirements of paragraphs (1) and (2) of subsection (b) of this section. Upon submission of such certification, the State program shall be deemed to be authorized under this section, and shall apply in such State in lieu of the corresponding Federal program under section 2682 or 2686 of this title, or both, as the case may be, until such time as the Administrator disapproves the program or withdraws the authorization.

(b) Approval or disapproval

Within 180 days following submission of an application under subsection (a) of this section, the Administrator shall approve or disapprove the application. The Administrator may approve the application only if, after notice and after opportunity for public hearing, the Administrator finds that—

(1) the State program is at least as protective of human health and the environment as the Federal program under section 2682 or 2686 of this title or both, as the case may be, and

(2) such State program provides adequate enforcement.

Upon authorization of a State program under this section, it shall be unlawful for any person to violate or fail or refuse to comply with any requirement of such program.

(c) Withdrawal of authorization

If a State is not administering and enforcing a program authorized under this section in compliance with standards, regulations, and other requirements of this subchapter, the Administrator shall so notify the State and, if corrective action is not completed within a reasonable time, not to exceed 180 days, the Administrator shall withdraw authorization of such program and establish a Federal program pursuant to this subchapter.

(d) Model State program

Within 18 months after October 28, 1992, the Administrator shall promulgate a model State program which may be adopted by any State which seeks to administer and enforce a State program under this title. Such model program shall, to the extent practicable, encourage States to utilize existing State and local certification and accreditation programs and procedures. Such program shall encourage reciprocity among the States with respect to the certification under section 2682 of this title.

(e) Other State requirements

Nothing in this subchapter shall be construed to prohibit any State or political subdivision thereof from imposing any requirements which are more stringent than those imposed by this subchapter.

(f) State and local certification

The regulations under this subchapter shall, to the extent appropriate, encourage States to seek program authorization and to use existing State and local certification and accreditation procedures, except that a State or local government shall not require more than 1 certification under this section for any lead-based paint activities contractor to carry out lead-based paint activities in the State or political subdivision thereof.

(g) Grants to States

The Administrator is authorized to make grants to States to develop and carry out authorized State programs under this section. The grants shall be subject to such terms and conditions as the Administrator may establish to further the purposes of this subchapter.

(h) Enforcement by Administrator

If a State does not have a State program authorized under this section and in effect by the date which is 2 years after promulgation of the regulations under section 2682 or 2686 of this title, the Administrator shall, by such date, establish a Federal program for section 2682 or 2686 of this title (as the case may be) for such State and administer and enforce such program in such State.

(Pub.L. 94–469, Title IV, § 404, as added Pub.L. 102–550, Title X, § 1021(a), Oct. 28, 1992, 106 Stat. 3916.)

Effective Date

Section effective Oct. 28, 1992, see section 2 of Pub.L. 102–550, set out as a note under section 5301 of Title 42, The Public Health and Welfare.

§ 2685. Lead abatement and measurement [TSCA § 405]

(a) Program to promote lead exposure abatement

The Administrator, in cooperation with other appropriate Federal departments and agencies, shall conduct a comprehensive program to promote safe, effective, and affordable monitoring, detection, and abatement of lead-based paint and other lead exposure hazards.

(b) Standards for environmental sampling laboratories

(1) The Administrator shall establish protocols, criteria, and minimum performance standards for laboratory analysis of lead in paint films, soil, and dust. Within 2 years after October 28, 1992, the Administrator, in consultation with the Secretary of Health and Human Services, shall establish a program to certify laboratories as qualified to test substances for lead content unless the Administrator determines, by the date specified in this paragraph, that effective voluntary accreditation programs are in place and operating on a nationwide basis at the time of such determination. To be certified under such program, a laboratory shall, at a minimum, demonstrate an ability to test substances accurately for lead content.

(2) Not later than 24 months after October 28, 1992, and annually thereafter, the Administrator shall publish and make available to the public a list of certified or accredited environmental sampling laboratories.

(3) If the Administrator determines under paragraph (1) that effective voluntary accreditation programs are in place for environmental sampling laboratories, the Administrator shall review the performance and effectiveness of such programs within 3 years after such determination. If, upon such review, the Administrator determines that the voluntary accreditation programs are not effective in assuring the quality and consistency of laboratory analyses, the Administrator shall, not more than 12 months thereafter, establish a certification program that meets the requirements of paragraph (1).

(c) Exposure studies

(1) The Secretary of Health and Human Services (hereafter in this subsection referred to as the "Secretary"), acting through the Director of the Centers for Disease Control (CDC), and the Director of the National Institute of Environmental Health Sciences, shall jointly conduct a study of the sources of lead exposure in children who have elevated blood lead levels (or other indicators of elevated lead body burden), as defined by the Director of the Centers for Disease Control.

(2) The Secretary, in consultation with the Director of the National Institute for Occupational Safety and Health, shall conduct a comprehensive study of means to reduce hazardous occupational lead abatement exposures. This study shall include, at a minimum, each of the following—

(A) Surveillance and intervention capability in the States to identify and prevent hazardous exposures to lead abatement workers.

(B) Demonstration of lead abatement control methods and devices and work practices to identify and prevent hazardous lead exposures in the workplace.

(C) Evaluation, in consultation with the National Institute of Environmental Health Sciences, of health effects of low and high levels of occupational lead exposures on reproductive, neurological, renal, and cardiovascular health.

(D) Identification of high risk occupational settings to which prevention activities and resources should be targeted.

(E) A study assessing the potential exposures and risks from lead to janitorial and custodial workers.

(3) The studies described in paragraphs (1) and (2) shall, as appropriate, examine the relative contributions to elevated lead body burden from each of the following:

(A) Drinking water.

(B) Food.

(C) Lead-based paint and dust from lead-based paint.

(D) Exterior sources such as ambient air and lead in soil.

(E) Occupational exposures, and other exposures that the Secretary determines to be appropriate.

(4) Not later than 30 months after October 28, 1992, the Secretary shall submit a report to the Congress concerning the studies described in paragraphs (1) and (2).

(d) Public education

(1) The Administrator, in conjunction with the Secretary of Health and Human Services, acting through the Director of the Agency for Toxic Substances and Disease Registry, and in conjunction with the Secretary of Housing and Urban Development, shall sponsor public education and outreach activities to increase public awareness of—

(A) the scope and severity of lead poisoning from household sources;

(B) potential exposure to sources of lead in schools and childhood day care centers;

(C) the implications of exposures for men and women, particularly those of childbearing age;

(D) the need for careful, quality, abatement and management actions;

(E) the need for universal screening of children;

(F) other components of a lead poisoning prevention program;

(G) the health consequences of lead exposure resulting from lead-based paint hazards;

(H) risk assessment and inspection methods for lead-based paint hazards; and

(I) measures to reduce the risk of lead exposure from lead-based paint.

(2) The activities described in paragraph (1) shall be designed to provide educational services and information to—

(A) health professionals;

(B) the general public, with emphasis on parents of young children;

(C) homeowners, landlords, and tenants;

(D) consumers of home improvement products;

(E) the residential real estate industry; and

(F) the home renovation industry.

(3) In implementing the activities described in paragraph (1), the Administrator shall assure coordination with the President's Commission on Environmental Quality's education and awareness campaign on lead poisoning.

(4) The Administrator, in consultation with the Chairman of the Consumer Product Safety Commission, shall develop information to be distributed by retailers of home improvement products to provide consumers with practical information related to the hazards of renovation and remodeling where lead-based paint may be present.

(e) Technical assistance

(1) Clearinghouse

Not later than 6 months after October 28, 1992, the Administrator shall establish, in consultation with the Secretary of Housing and Urban Development and the Director of the Centers for Disease Control, a National Clearinghouse on Childhood Lead Poisoning (hereinafter in this section referred to as "Clearinghouse"). The Clearinghouse shall—

(A) collect, evaluate, and disseminate current information on the assessment and reduction of lead-based paint hazards, adverse health effects, sources of exposure, detection and risk assessment methods, environmental hazards abatement, and clean-up standards;

(B) maintain a rapid-alert system to inform certified lead-based paint activities contractors of significant developments in research related to lead-based paint hazards; and

(C) perform any other duty that the Administrator determines necessary to achieve the purposes of this chapter.

(2) Hotline

Not later than 6 months after October 28, 1992, the Administrator, in cooperation with other Federal agencies and with State and local governments, shall establish a single lead-based paint hazard hotline to provide the public with answers to questions about lead poisoning prevention and referrals to the Clearinghouse for technical information.

(f) Products for lead-based paint activities

Not later than 30 months after October 28, 1992, the President shall, after notice and opportunity for comment, establish by rule appropriate criteria, testing protocols, and performance characteristics as are necessary to ensure, to the greatest extent possible and consistent with the purposes and policy of this subchapter, that lead-based paint hazard evaluation and reduction products introduced into commerce after a period specified in the rule are effective for the intended use described by the manufacturer. The rule shall identify the types or classes of products that are subject to such rule. The President, in implementation of the rule, shall, to the maximum extent possible, utilize independent testing laboratories, as appropriate, and consult with such entities and others in developing the rules. The President may delegate the authorities under this subsection to the Environmental

Protection Agency or the Secretary of Commerce or such other appropriate agency.

(Pub.L. 94–469, Title IV, § 405, as added Pub.L. 102–550, Title X, § 1021(a), Oct. 28, 1992, 106 Stat. 3917.)

Effective Date

Section effective Oct. 28, 1992, see section 2 of Pub.L. 102–550, set out as a note under section 5301 of Title 42, The Public Health and Welfare.

§ 2686. Lead hazard information pamphlet [TSCA § 406]

(a) Lead hazard information pamphlet

Not later than 2 years after October 28, 1992, after notice and opportunity for comment, the Administrator of the Environmental Protection Agency, in consultation with the Secretary of Housing and Urban Development and with the Secretary of Health and Human Services, shall publish, and from time to time revise, a lead hazard information pamphlet to be used in connection with this subchapter and section 4852d of Title 42. The pamphlet shall—

(1) contain information regarding the health risks associated with exposure to lead;

(2) provide information on the presence of lead-based paint hazards in federally assisted, federally owned, and target housing;

(3) describe the risks of lead exposure for children under 6 years of age, pregnant women, women of childbearing age, persons involved in home renovation, and others residing in a dwelling with lead-based paint hazards;

(4) describe the risks of renovation in a dwelling which lead-based paint hazards;

(5) provide information on approved methods for evaluating and reducing lead-based paint hazards and their effectiveness in identifying, reducing, eliminating, or preventing exposure to lead-based paint hazards;

(6) advise persons how to obtain a list of contractors certified pursuant to this title in lead-based paint hazard evaluation and reduction in the area in which the pamphlet is to be used;

(7) state that a risk assessment or inspection for lead-based paint is recommended prior to the purchase, lease, or renovation of target housing;

(8) state that certain State and local laws impose additional requirements related to lead-based paint in housing and provide a listing of Federal, State, and local agencies in each State, including address and telephone number, that can provide information about applicable laws and available governmental and private assistance and financing; and

(9) provide such other information about environmental hazards associated with residential real property as the Administrator deems appropriate.

(b) Renovation of target housing

Within 2 years after October 28, 1992, the Administrator shall promulgate regulations under this subsection to require each person who performs for compensation a renovation of target housing to provide a lead hazard information pamphlet to the owner and occupant of such housing prior to commencing the renovation.

(Pub.L. 94–469, Title IV, § 406, as added Pub.L. 102–550, Title X, § 1021(a), Oct. 28, 1992, 106 Stat. 3920.)

Effective Date

Section effective Oct. 28, 1992, see section 2 of Pub.L. 102–550, set out as a note under section 5301 of Title 42, The Public Health and Welfare.

§ 2687. Regulations [TSCA § 407]

The regulations of the Administrator under this subchapter shall include such recordkeeping and reporting requirements as may be necessary to insure the effective implementation of this subchapter. The regulations may be amended from time to time as necessary.

(Pub.L. 94–469, Title IV, § 407, as added Pub.L. 102–550, Title X, § 1021(a), Oct. 28, 1992, 106 Stat. 3921.)

Effective Date

Section effective Oct. 28, 1992, see section 2 of Pub.L. 102–550, set out as a note under section 5301 of Title 42, The Public Health and Welfare.

§ 2688. Control of lead-based paint hazards at Federal facilities [TSCA § 408]

Each department, agency, and instrumentality of executive, legislative, and judicial branches of the Federal Government (1) having jurisdiction over any property or facility, or (2) engaged in any activity resulting, or which may result, in a lead-based paint hazard, and each officer, agent, or employee thereof, shall be subject to, and comply with, all Federal, State, interstate, and local requirements, both substantive and procedural (including any requirement for certification, licensing, recordkeeping, or reporting or any provisions for injunctive relief and such sanctions as may be imposed by a court to enforce such relief) respecting lead-based paint, lead-based paint activities, and lead-based paint hazards in the same manner, and to the same extent as any nongovernmental entity is subject to such requirements, including the payment of reasonable service charges. The Federal, State, interstate, and local substantive and procedural requirements referred to in this subsection include, but are not limited to, all administrative orders and all civil and administrative penalties and fines regardless of whether such penalties or fines are punitive or coercive in nature, or whether imposed for isolated, intermittent or continuing violations. The United States hereby expressly waives any immunity otherwise applicable to the United States with respect to any such substantive or procedural requirement (including, but not limited to, any injunctive relief, administrative order, or civil or administrative penalty or fine referred to in the preceding sentence, or reasonable service charge). The reasonable service charges referred to in this section include, but are not limited to, fees or charges assessed for certification and licensing, as well as any other nondiscriminatory charges that are assessed in connection with a Federal, State, interstate, or local lead-based paint, lead-based paint activities, or lead-based paint hazard activities program. No agent, employee, or officer of the United States shall be personally liable for any civil penalty under any Federal, State, interstate, or local law relating to lead-based paint, lead-based paint activities, or lead-based paint hazards with respect to any act or omission within the scope of his official duties.

(Pub.L. 94–469, Title IV, § 408, as added Pub.L. 102–550, Title X, § 1021(a), Oct. 28, 1992, 106 Stat. 3921.)

Effective Date

Section effective Oct. 28, 1992, see section 2 of Pub.L. 102–550, set out as a note under section 5301 of Title 42, The Public Health and Welfare.

§ 2689. Prohibited acts [TSCA § 409]

It shall be unlawful for any person to fail or refuse to comply with a provision of this subchapter or with any rule or order issued under this subchapter.

(Pub.L. 94–469, Title IV, § 409, as added Pub.L. 102–550, Title X, § 1021(a), Oct. 28, 1992, 106 Stat. 3921.)

Effective Date

Section effective Oct. 28, 1992, see section 2 of Pub.L. 102–550, set out as a note under section 5301 of Title 42, The Public Health and Welfare.

§ 2690. Relationship to other Federal law [TSCA § 410]

Nothing in this subchapter shall affect the authority of other appropriate Federal agencies to establish or enforce any requirements which are at least as stringent as those established pursuant to this subchapter.

(Pub.L. 94–469, Title IV, § 410, as added Pub.L. 102–550, Title X, § 1021(a), Oct. 28, 1992, 106 Stat. 3921.)

Effective Date

Section effective Oct. 28, 1992, see section 2 of Pub.L. 102–550, set out as a note under section 5301 of Title 42, The Public Health and Welfare.

§ 2691. General provisions relating to administrative proceedings [TSCA § 411]

(a) Applicability

This section applies to the promulgation or revision of any regulation issued under this subchapter.

(b) Rulemaking docket

Not later than the date of proposal of any action to which this section applies, the Administrator shall establish a rulemaking docket for such action (hereinafter in this subsection referred to as a "rule"). Whenever a rule applies only within a particular State, a second (identical) docket shall be established in the appropriate regional office of the Environmental Protection Agency.

(c) Inspection and copying

(1) The rulemaking docket required under subsection (b) of this section shall be open for inspection by the public at reasonable times specified in the notice of proposed rulemaking. Any person may copy documents contained in the docket. The Administrator shall provide copying facilities which may be used at the expense of the person seeking copies, but the Administrator may waive or reduce such expenses in such instances as the public interest requires. Any person may request copies by mail if the person pays the expenses, including personnel costs to do the copying.

(2)(A) Promptly upon receipt by the agency, all written comments and documentary information on the proposed rule received from any person for inclusion in the docket during the comment period shall be placed in the docket. The transcript of public hearings, if any, on the proposed rule shall also be included in the docket promptly upon receipt from the person who transcribed such hearings. All documents which become available after the proposed rule has been published and which the Administrator determines are of central relevance to the rulemaking shall be placed in the docket as soon as possible after their availability.

(B) The drafts of proposed rules submitted by the Administrator to the Office of Management and Budget for any interagency review process prior to proposal of any such rule, all documents accompanying such drafts, and all written comments thereon by other agencies and all written responses to such written comments by the Administrator shall be placed in the docket no later than the date of proposal of the rule. The drafts of the final rule submitted for such review process prior to promulgation and all such written comments thereon, all documents accompanying such drafts, and written responses thereto shall be placed in the docket no later than the date of promulgation.

(d) Explanation

(1) The promulgated rule shall be accompanied by an explanation of the reasons for any major changes in the promulgated rule from the proposed rule.

(2) The promulgated rule shall also be accompanied by a response to each of the significant comments, criticisms, and new data submitted in written or oral presentations during the comment period.

(3) The promulgated rule may not be based (in part or whole) on any information or data which has not been placed in the docket as of the date of such promulgation.

(e) Judicial review

The material referred to in subsection (c)(2)(B) of this section shall not be included in the record for judicial review.

(f) Effective date

The requirements of this section shall take effect with respect to any rule the proposal of which occurs after 90 days after October 28, 1992.

(Pub.L. 94–469, Title IV, § 411, as added Pub.L. 102–550, Title X, § 1021(a), Oct. 28, 1992, 106 Stat. 3922.)

Effective Date

Section effective Oct. 28, 1992, see section 2 of Pub.L. 102–550, set out as a note under section 5301 of Title 42, The Public Health and Welfare.

§ 2692. Authorization of appropriations [TSCA § 412]

There are authorized to be appropriated to carry out the purposes of this subchapter such sums as may be necessary.

(Pub.L. 94–469, Title IV, § 412, as added Pub.L. 102–550, Title X, § 1021(a), Oct. 28, 1992, 106 Stat. 3923.)

Effective Date

Section effective Oct. 28, 1992, see section 2 of Pub.L. 102–550, set out as a note under section 5301 of Title 42, The Public Health and Welfare.

TITLE 16—CONSERVATION

RENEWABLE SURFACE RESOURCES OF NATIONAL FORESTS

MULTIPLE–USE SUSTAINED–YIELD ACT OF 1960 [MUSYA § ___]

(16 U.S.C.A. §§ 528 to 531)

CHAPTER 2—NATIONAL FORESTS

Sec.

528. Development and administration of renewable surface resources for multiple use and sustained yield of products and services; Congressional declaration of policy and purpose.
529. Authorization of development and administration; consideration to relative values of resources; areas of wilderness.
530. Cooperation for purposes of development and administration with State and local governmental agencies and others.
531. Definitions.

§ 528. Development and administration of renewable surface resources for multiple use and sustained yield of products and services; Congressional declaration of policy and purpose [MUSYA § 1]

It is the policy of the Congress that the national forests are established and shall be administered for outdoor recreation, range, timber, watershed, and wildlife and fish purposes. The purposes of sections 528 to 531 of this title are declared to be supplemental to, but not in derogation of, the purposes for which the national forests were established as set forth in section 475 of this title. Nothing herein shall be construed as affecting the jurisdiction or responsibilities of the several States with respect to wildlife and fish on the national forests. Nothing herein shall be construed so as to affect the use or administration of the mineral resources of national forest lands or to affect the use or administration of Federal lands not within national forests.

(Pub.L. 86–517, § 1, June 12, 1960, 74 Stat. 215.)

Short Title

Section 5 of Pub.L. 86–517, as added Pub.L. 94–588, § 19, Oct. 22, 1976, 90 Stat. 2962, provided that: "This Act [enacting sections 528 to 531 of this title] may be cited as the 'Multiple–Use Sustained–Yield Act of 1960'."

CROSS REFERENCES

Forest and Rangeland renewable resources program—
Coordination of purposes and administration with sections 528 to 531 of this title, see sections 1600, 1602, 1604, and 1607 of this title.
Promulgation of regulations under principles of sections 528 to 531 of this title, see section 1604 of this title.
Surface coal mining operations, prohibition on national forest lands unless in compliance with sections 528 to 531 of this title, see section 1272 of Title 30, Mineral Lands and Mining.
Wilderness Act, noninterference with purposes for which national forests established under sections 528 to 531 of this title, see section 1133 of this title.
Wildlife, fish, and game conservation and rehabilitation programs not to limit Secretary's authority under sections 528 to 531 of this title, see section 670h of this title.

WEST'S FEDERAL PRACTICE MANUAL

Conservation of fish and wildlife, see § 4389.55.
Federal land policy and management, see § 4389.25 et seq.

CODE OF FEDERAL REGULATIONS

Administration of forest development transportation system, see 36 CFR 212.1 et seq.
Wilderness—primitive areas, see 36 CFR 293.1 et seq.
"Woodsy Owl" symbol, use of, see 36 CFR 272.1 et seq.

LAW REVIEW COMMENTARIES

A market approach to water resource allocation—a system unique to the West or a blueprint for future water allocation in the East? Robert C. Kerr, 1 Cooley L.Rev. 337 (1983).

§ 529. Authorization of development and administration; consideration to relative values of resources; areas of wilderness [MUSYA § 2]

The Secretary of Agriculture is authorized and directed to develop and administer the renewable surface resources of the national forests for multiple use and sustained yield of the several products and services obtained therefrom. In the administration of the national forests due consideration shall be given to the relative values of the various resources in particular areas. The establishment and maintenance of areas of wilderness are consistent with the purposes and provisions of sections 528 to 531 of this title.

(Pub.L. 86–517, § 2, June 12, 1960, 74 Stat. 215.)

CODE OF FEDERAL REGULATIONS

Administration of forest development transportation system, see 36 CFR 212.1 et seq.
Wilderness—primitive areas, see 36 CFR 293.1 et seq.
"Woodsy Owl" symbol, use of, see 36 CFR 272.1 et seq.

LIBRARY REFERENCES

Woods and Forests ⚷7.
C.J.S. Woods and Forests § 13.

§ 530. Cooperation for purposes of development and administration with State and local governmental agencies and others [MUSYA § 3]

In the effectuation of sections 528 to 531 of this title the Secretary of Agriculture is authorized to cooperate with interested State and local governmental agencies and others in the development and management of the national forests.

(Pub.L. 86–517, § 3, June 12, 1960, 74 Stat. 215.)

CODE OF FEDERAL REGULATIONS

Administration of forest development transportation system, see 36 CFR 212.1 et seq.
Wilderness—primitive areas, see 36 CFR 293.1 et seq.
"Woodsy Owl" symbol, use of, see 36 CFR 272.1 et seq.

LIBRARY REFERENCES

States ⚷4.19.
C.J.S. States §§ 1, 7.

§ 531. Definitions [MUSYA § 4]

As used in sections 528 to 531 of this title the following terms shall have the following meanings:

(a) "Multiple use" means: The management of all the various renewable surface resources of the national forests so that they are utilized in the combination that will best meet the needs of the American people; making the most judicious use of the land for some or all of these resources or related services over areas large enough to provide sufficient latitude for periodic adjustments in use to conform to changing needs and conditions; that some land will be used for less than all of the resources; and harmonious and coordinated management of the various resources, each with the other, without impairment of the productivity of the land, with consideration being given to the relative values of the various resources, and not necessarily the combination of uses that will give the greatest dollar return or the greatest unit output.

(b) "Sustained yield of the several products and services" means the achievement and maintenance in perpetuity of a high-level annual or regular periodic output of the various renewable resources of the national forests without impairment of the productivity of the land.

(Pub.L. 86–517, § 4, June 12, 1960, 74 Stat. 215.)

CODE OF FEDERAL REGULATIONS

Administration of forest development transportation system, see 36 CFR 212.1 et seq.
Wilderness—primitive areas, see 36 CFR 293.1 et seq.
"Woodsy Owl" symbol, use of, see 36 CFR 272.1 et seq.

COASTAL ZONE MANAGEMENT

COASTAL ZONE MANAGEMENT ACT OF 1972 [CZMA § ___]

(16 U.S.C.A. §§ 1451 to 1464)

CHAPTER 33—COASTAL ZONE MANAGEMENT

Sec.

1451. Congressional findings.
1452. Congressional declaration of policy.
1453. Definitions.
1454. Management program development grants.
  (a) Authorization.
  (b) Program requirements.
  (c) Limits on grants.
  (d) Grants for completion of development and implementation of management programs; limits and eligibility requirements.
  (e) Allocation of grants.
  (f) Reversion of unobligated grants.
  (g) Grants to other political subdivisions.
  (h) Submission of program for review and approval.
  (i) Expiration date of grant authority.
1455. Administrative grants.
  (a) Authorization; matching funds.
  (b) Grants to coastal States; requirements.
  (c) Allocation of grants to coastal States.
  (d) Mandatory adoption of State management program for coastal zone.
  (e) Amendment or modification of State management program for coastal zone.
1455a. Coastal resource improvement program.
  (a) Definitions.
  (b) Resource management improvement grants.
  (c) Uses, terms and conditions of grants.
  (d) State matching contributions; ratio; maximum amount of grants.
  (e) Allocation of grants to local governments and other agencies.
  (f) Other technical and financial assistance.
1455b. Protecting coastal waters.
  (a) In general.
  (b) Program contents.
  (c) Program submission, approval, and implementation.
  (d) Technical assistance.
  (e) Inland coastal zone boundaries.
  (f) Financial assistance.
  (g) Guidance for coastal nonpoint source pollution control.
  (h) Authorizations of appropriations.
  (i) Definitions.
1456. Coordination and cooperation.
  (a) Federal agencies.
  (b) Adequate consideration of views of Federal agencies.
  (c) Consistency of Federal activities with State management programs; Presidential exemption; certification.

Sec.

1456. Coordination and cooperation.
  (d) Applications of local governments for Federal assistance; relationship of activities with the enforceable policies of an approved coastal State's management program.
  (e) Construction with other laws.
  (f) Construction with existing requirements of water and air pollution programs.
  (g) Concurrence with programs which affect inland areas.
  (h) Mediation of disagreements.
  (i) Application fee for appeals.
1456a. Coastal Zone Management Fund.
  (a) Administration and coordination by Secretary; financial assistance; audit; rules and regulations.
  (b) Grants; calculations; purposes and priority of proceeds; supervision by Secretary.
  (c) Grants; study and planning; consequences affecting coastal zone relating to new or expanded energy facilities; limits on grants.
  (d) Loans; coastal energy activity requiring new or improved public facilities or services; guarantees; relief from inability to meet obligations.
  (e) Rules and regulations; financial assistance, formula, and procedures; criteria for review; criteria and procedures for repayment; loan requirements, terms, and conditions; interest rates.
  (f) Guarantees; terms and conditions; full faith and credit; fees; interest; payments; defaults; enforcement by Attorney General; insufficient funds.
  (g) Eligibility requirements; apportionment of assistance.
  (h) Coastal Energy Impact Fund; establishment.
  (i) Land use or water use decisions; intercession of Secretary prohibited.
  (j) Report to Congress; evaluations.
  (k) Basis of Secretary's administration of financial assistance.
  (*l*) Definitions.
1456b. Coastal zone enhancement.
  (a) Coastal zone enhancement objective defined.
  (b) Limits on grants.
  (c) Evaluation of State proposals by Secretary.
  (d) Promulgation of regulations by Secretary.
  (e) No State contribution required.
  (f) Funding.
  (g) Eligibility; suspension of State for noncompliance.
1456c. Technical assistance.
1457. Public hearings.

Sec.
1458. Review of performance.
(a) Evaluation of adherence with terms of grants.
(b) Public comments; notice of public meetings; reports.
(c) Suspension of financial assistance for noncompliance; notification of Governor by Secretary; length of suspension.
(d) Withdrawal of approval of program; withdrawal of financial assistance.
(e) Notice and hearing.
(f) Repealed.
1459. Records and audit.
(a) Maintenance of records by recipients of grants or financial assistance.
(b) Access by Secretary and Comptroller General to records, books, etc., of recipients of grants or financial assistance for audit and examination.
1460. Walter B. Jones excellence in coastal zone management awards.
(a) Establishment.
(b) Annual selection of recipients.
(c) Solicitation of nominations from coastal states; consultation with experts.
(d) Solicitation of nominations from coastal States and the National Sea Grant College Program.
(e) Funding; types of awards.
1461. National Estuarine Research Reserve System.
(a) Establishment of System.
(b) Designation of National Estuarine Reserves.
(c) Estuarine Research Guidelines.

Sec.
1461. National Estuarine Research Reserve System.
(d) Promotion and coordination of Estuarine research.
(e) Financial assistance.
(f) Evaluation of System performance.
(g) Report.
1462. Coastal zone management reports.
(a) Biennial reports.
(b) Recommendations for legislation.
(c) Review of other federal programs; report to Congress.
1463. Rules and regulations.
1463a. Omitted.
1463b. National Coastal Resources Research and Development Institute.
(a) Establishment by Secretary; administration.
(b) Purposes of Institute.
(c) Determination of Institute policies.
(d) Establishment of Advisory Council; functions and composition.
(e) Administration of Institute.
(f) Evaluation of Institute by Secretary.
(g) Report to Secretary.
(h) Access to Institute books, records and documents.
(i) Statute of Institute employees.
(j) Authorization of appropriations.
1464. Authorization of appropriations.
(a) Sums appropriated to Secretary.
(b) Sums appropriated to Fund.
(c) Limitations.
(d) Reversion to Secretary of unobligated State funds; availability of funds.

Related Provisions

See, also, Federal Land Policy and Management, 43 U.S.C.A. § 1701 et seq., post and Outer Continental Shelf Resource Management, 43 U.S.C.A. § 1801 et seq., post.

CROSS REFERENCES

Adjacent coastal state with approved management program under this chapter, issuance of license for—
Deepwater port, see sections 1503 and 1508 of Title 33, Navigation and Navigable Waters.
Ocean thermal energy conversion facility, see sections 9111 and 9115 of Title 42, The Public Health and Welfare.
Coastal Barrier Resources System—
Availability of federal expenditures or financial assistance for projects under this chapter, see section 3505 of this title.
Report to Congress to contain conservation recommendations based on management plans approved under this chapter, see section 3509 of this title.
Construction of this chapter with Outer Continental Shelf Lands Act, see section 1866 of Title 43, Public Lands.
Development and production pursuant to oil and gas lease in outer Continental Shelf, other than Gulf of Mexico, effect of management program under this chapter on approval, see section 1351 of Title 43.
State recreational boating safety and facilities improvement program—
Approval if consultation with state officials responsible for program under this chapter, see section 13102 of Title 46, Shipping.
Guidelines and standards for to include environmental standards consistent with this chapter, see section 13101 of Title 46.

CODE OF FEDERAL REGULATIONS

Coastal energy impact program, see 15 CFR 931.1 et seq.
Federal consistency with approved coastal management programs, see 15 CFR 930.1 et seq.
Program development and approval, see 15 CFR 923.1 et seq.
Program development grants, see 15 CFR 926.1 et seq.

WESTLAW ELECTRONIC RESEARCH

See WESTLAW guide following the Explanation pages of this pamphlet.

§ 1451. Congressional findings [CZMA § 302]

The Congress finds that—

(a) There is a national interest in the effective management, beneficial use, protection, and development of the coastal zone.

(b) The coastal zone is rich in a variety of natural, commercial, recreational, ecological, industrial, and esthetic resources of immediate and potential value to the present and future well-being of the Nation.

(c) The increasing and competing demands upon the lands and waters of our coastal zone occasioned by population growth and economic development, including requirements for industry, commerce, residential development, recreation, extraction of mineral resources and fossil fuels, transportation and navigation, waste disposal, and harvesting of fish, shellfish, and other living marine resources, have resulted in the loss of living marine resources, wildlife, nutrient-rich areas, permanent and adverse changes to ecological systems, decreasing open space for public use, and shoreline erosion.

(d) The habitat areas of the coastal zone, and the fish, shellfish, other living marine resources, and wildlife therein, are ecologically fragile and consequently extremely vulnerable to destruction by man's alterations.

(e) Important ecological, cultural, historic, and esthetic values in the coastal zone which are essential to the well-being of all citizens are being irretrievably damaged or lost.

(f) New and expanding demands for food, energy, minerals, defense needs, recreation, waste disposal, transportation, and industrial activities in the Great Lakes, territorial sea, exclusive economic zone, and Outer Continental Shelf are placing stress on these areas and are creating the need for resolution of serious conflicts among important and competing uses and values in coastal and ocean waters; [1]

(g) Special natural and scenic characteristics are being damaged by ill-planned development that threatens these values.

(h) In light of competing demands and the urgent need to protect and to give high priority to natural systems in the coastal zone, present state and local institutional arrangements for planning and regulating land and water uses in such areas are inadequate.

(i) The key to more effective protection and use of the land and water resources of the coastal zone is to encourage the states to exercise their full authority over the lands and waters in the coastal zone by assisting the states, in cooperation with Federal and local governments and other vitally affected interests, in developing land and water use programs for the coastal zone, including unified policies, criteria, standards, methods, and processes for dealing with land and water use decisions of more than local significance.

(j) The national objective of attaining a greater degree of energy self-sufficiency would be advanced by providing Federal financial assistance to meet state and local needs resulting from new or expanded energy activity in or affecting the coastal zone.

(k) Land uses in the coastal zone, and the uses of adjacent lands which drain into the coastal zone, may significantly affect the quality of coastal waters and habitats, and efforts to control coastal water pollution from land use activities must be improved.

(*l*) Because global warming may result in a substantial sea level rise with serious adverse effects in the coastal zone, coastal states must anticipate and plan for such an occurrence.

(m) Because of their proximity to and reliance upon the ocean and its resources, the coastal states have substantial and significant interests in the protection, management, and development of the resources of the exclusive economic zone that can only be served by the active participation of coastal states in all Federal programs affecting such resources and, wherever appropriate, by the development of state ocean resource plans as part of their federally approved coastal zone management programs.

(Pub.L. 89–454, Title III, § 302, as added Oct. 27, 1972, Pub.L. 92–583, 86 Stat. 1280, and amended July 26, 1976, Pub.L. 94–370, § 2, 90 Stat. 1013; Oct. 17, 1980, Pub.L. 96–464, § 2, 94 Stat. 2060; Nov. 5, 1990, Pub.L. 101–508, Title VI, § 6203(a), 104 Stat. 1388–300)

[1] So in original. Probably should be a period.

Short Title of 1990 Amendment

Section 6201 of Pub.L. 101–508 provided that: "This subtitle [enacting sections 1455b, 1456c and 1460 of this title, amending this section and sections 1452, 1453, 1454, 1455, 1455a, 1456, 1456a, 1456b, 1458, 1461 and 1464 of this title, and enacting provisions set out as notes under this section and section 1455 of this title] may be cited as the 'Coastal Zone Act Reauthorization Amendments of 1990'."

Short Title

Section 301 of Pub.L. 89–454, Title III, as added Pub.L. 92–583, Oct. 27, 1972, 86 Stat. 1280, provided that: "This title [enacting this chapter] may be cited as the 'Coastal Zone Management Act of 1972'."

CODE OF FEDERAL REGULATIONS

Approval of state programs, requirements, see 15 CFR 923.3 et seq.

LAW REVIEW COMMENTARIES

American and British offshore oil development. Uisdean R. Vass. 21 Tulsa L.J. 23 (1985).

Environmental claims in bankruptcy: Policy conflicts, procedural pitfalls and problematic precedent. Thomas G. Gruenert, 32 S.Tex. L.Rev. 399 (1991).

Staring down the barrel of *Nollan:* Can the Coastal Commission dodge the bullet? Note, 9 Whittier L.Rev. 579 (1987).

Library References

Health and Environment ⚷25.5(4).
Zoning and Planning ⚷1 et seq.
C.J.S. Health and Environment § 91 et seq.
C.J.S. Zoning and Land Planning § 2 et seq.

§ 1452. Congressional declaration of policy [CZMA § 303]

The Congress finds and declares that it is the national policy—

(1) to preserve, protect, develop, and where possible, to restore or enhance, the resources of the

Nation's coastal zone for this and succeeding generations;

(2) to encourage and assist the states to exercise effectively their responsibilities in the coastal zone through the development and implementation of management programs to achieve wise use of the land and water resources of the coastal zone, giving full consideration to ecological, cultural, historic, and esthetic values as well as the needs for compatible economic development, which programs should at least provide for—

(A) the protection of natural resources, including wetlands, floodplains, estuaries, beaches, dunes, barrier islands, coral reefs, and fish and wildlife and their habitat, within the coastal zone,

(B) the management of coastal development to minimize the loss of life and property caused by improper development in flood-prone, storm surge, geological hazard, and erosion-prone areas and in areas likely to be affected by or vulnerable to sea level rise, land subsidence, and saltwater intrusion, and by the destruction of natural protective features such as beaches, dunes, wetlands, and barrier islands.[1]

(C) the management of coastal development to improve, safeguard, and restore the quality of coastal waters, and to protect natural resources and existing uses of those waters,

(D) priority consideration being given to coastal-dependent uses and orderly processes for siting major facilities related to national defense, energy, fisheries development, recreation, ports and transportation, and the location, to the maximum extent practicable, of new commercial and industrial developments in or adjacent to areas where such development already exists,

(E) public access to the coasts for recreation purposes,

(F) assistance in the redevelopment of deteriorating urban waterfronts and ports, and sensitive preservation and restoration of historic, cultural, and esthetic coastal features,

(G) the coordination and simplification of procedures in order to ensure expedited governmental decisionmaking for the management of coastal resources,

(H) continued consultation and coordination with, and the giving of adequate consideration to the views of, affected Federal agencies,

(I) the giving of timely and effective notification of, and opportunities for public and local government participation in, coastal management decisionmaking,

(J) assistance to support comprehensive planning, conservation, and management for living marine resources, including planning for the siting of pollution control and aquaculture facilities within the coastal zone, and improved coordination between State and Federal coastal zone management agencies and State and wildlife agencies, and

(K) the study and development, in any case in which the Secretary considers it to be appropriate, of plans for addressing the adverse effects upon the coastal zone of land subsidence and of sea level rise; and

(3) to encourage the preparation of special area management plans which provide for increased specificity in protecting significant natural resources, reasonable coastal-dependent economic growth, improved protection of life and property in hazardous areas, including those areas likely to be affected by land subsidence, sea level rise, or fluctuating water levels of the Great Lakes, and improved predictability in governmental decisionmaking;

(4) to encourage the participation and cooperation of the public, state and local governments, and interstate and other regional agencies, as well as of the Federal agencies having programs affecting the coastal zone, in carrying out the purposes of this chapter;

(5) to encourage coordination and cooperation with and among the appropriate Federal, State, and local agencies, and international organizations where appropriate, in collection, analysis, synthesis, and dissemination of coastal management information, research results, and technical assistance, to support State and Federal regulation of land use practices affecting the coastal and ocean resources of the United States; and

(6) to respond to changing circumstances affecting the coastal environment and coastal resource management by encouraging States to consider such issues as ocean uses potentially affecting the coastal zone.

(Pub.L. 89–454, Title III, § 303, as added Oct. 27, 1972, Pub.L. 92–583, 86 Stat. 1281, as amended Oct. 17, 1980, Pub.L. 96–464, § 3, 94 Stat. 2060; Nov. 5, 1990, Pub.L. 101–508, Title VI, § 6203(b), 104 Stat. 1388–301; Pub.L. 102–587, Title II, § 2205(b)(2), Nov. 4, 1992, 106 Stat. 5050.)

[1] So in original. The period probably should be a comma.

Codification

Section 2205(b)(2) of Pub.L. 102–587 amended section 6203(b)(1) of Pub.L. 101–508 to correct the language to be substituted for by such section 6203(b)(1), which amendment required no change in text.

Amendment of par. (2) by section 6203(b)(1) of Pub.L. 101–508 was executed as the probable intent of Congress by substituting new language for existing phrase "as well as to needs for" notwithstanding directory language reciting that the language to be stricken read "as well as the needs for".

CODE OF FEDERAL REGULATIONS

Coastal zone management regulations, purpose, see 15 CFR 923.1 et seq.
Floodplain, wetlands review, see 10 CFR 1022.1 et seq.
Improving coastal zone management, see 15 CFR 923.101 et seq.

CROSS REFERENCES

Administrative grants, see section 1455 of this title.
Coastal resource improvement program, "eligible coastal state" as meaning coastal state making satisfactory progress in activities designed to result in significant improvement in achieving coastal management objectives, see section 1455a of this title.
Eligibility to receive financial assistance under coastal energy impact program, see section 1456a of this title.
Review of performance of coastal states with respect to coastal management, see section 1458 of this title.

§ 1453. Definitions [CZMA § 304]

For purposes of this chapter—

(1) The term "coastal zone" means the coastal waters (including the lands therein and thereunder) and the adjacent shorelands (including the waters therein and thereunder), strongly influenced by each other and in proximity to the shorelines of the several coastal states, and includes islands, transitional and intertidal areas, salt marshes, wetlands, and beaches. The zone extends, in Great Lakes waters, to the international boundary between the United States and Canada and, in other areas, seaward to the outer limit of State title and ownership under the Submerged Lands Act (43 U.S.C. 1301 et seq.), the Act of March 2, 1917, (48 U.S.C. 749), the Covenant to Establish a Commonwealth of the Northern Mariana Islands in Political Union with the United States of America, as approved by the Act of March 24, 1976 (48 U.S.C. 1681 note), or section 1 of the Act of November 20, 1963 (48 U.S.C. 1705), as applicable. The zone extends inland from the shorelines only to the extent necessary to control shorelands, the uses of which have a direct and significant impact on the coastal waters, and to control those geographical areas which are likely to be affected by or vulnerable to sea level rise. Excluded from the coastal zone are lands the use of which is by law subject solely to the discretion of or which is held in trust by the Federal Government, its officers, or agents.

(2) The term "coastal resource of national significance" means any coastal wetland, beach, dune, barrier island, reef, estuary, or fish and wildlife habitat, if any such area is determined by a coastal state to be of substantial biological or natural storm protective value.

(3) The term "coastal waters" means (A) in the Great Lakes area, the waters within the territorial jurisdiction of the United States consisting of the Great Lakes, their connecting waters, harbors, roadsteads, and estuary-type areas such as bays, shallows, and marshes and (B) in other areas, those waters, adjacent to the shorelines, which contain a measurable quantity or percentage of sea water, including, but not limited to, sounds, bays, lagoons, bayous, ponds, and estuaries.

(4) The term "coastal state" means a state of the United States in, or bordering on, the Atlantic, Pacific, or Arctic Ocean, the Gulf of Mexico, Long Island Sound, or one or more of the Great Lakes. For the purposes of this chapter, the term also includes Puerto Rico, the Virgin Islands, Guam, the Commonwealth of the Northern Mariana Islands, and the Trust Territories of the Pacific Islands, and American Samoa.

(5) The term "coastal energy activity" means any of the following activities if, and to the extent that (A) the conduct, support, or facilitation of such activity requires and involves the siting, construction, expansion, or operation of any equipment or facility; and (B) any technical requirement exists which, in the determination of the Secretary, necessitates that the siting, construction, expansion, or operation of such equipment or facility be carried out in, or in close proximity to, the coastal zone of any coastal state;

(i) Any Outer Continental Shelf energy activity.

(ii) Any transportation, conversion, treatment, transfer, or storage of liquified natural gas.

(iii) Any transportation, transfer, or storage of oil, natural gas, or coal (including, but not limited to, by means of any deepwater port, as defined in section 1502(10) of Title 33).

For purposes of this paragraph, the siting, construction, expansion, or operation of any equipment or facility shall be "in close proximity to" the coastal zone of any coastal state if such siting, construction, expansion, or operation has, or is likely to have, a significant effect on such coastal zone.

(6) The term "energy facilities" means any equipment or facility which is or will be used primarily—

(A) in the exploration for, or the development, production, conversion, storage, transfer, processing, or transportation of, any energy resource; or

(B) for the manufacture, production, or assembly of equipment, machinery, products, or devices which are involved in any activity described in subparagraph (A).

The term includes, but is not limited to (i) electric generating plants; (ii) petroleum refineries and associated facilities; (iii) gasification plants; (iv) facilities used for the transportation, conversion, treatment, transfer, or storage of liquified natural gas;

(v) uranium enrichment or nuclear fuel processing facilities; (vi) oil and gas facilities, including platforms, assembly plants, storage depots, tank farms, crew and supply bases, and refining complexes; (vii) facilities including deepwater ports, for the transfer of petroleum; (viii) pipelines and transmission facilities; and (ix) terminals which are associated with any of the foregoing.

(6a) The term "enforceable policy" means State policies which are legally binding through constitutional provisions, laws, regulations, land use plans, ordinances, or judicial or administrative decisions, by which a State exerts control over private and public land and water uses and natural resources in the coastal zone.

(7) The term "estuary" means that part of a river or stream or other body of water having unimpaired connection with the open sea, where the sea water is measurably diluted with fresh water derived from land drainage. The term includes estuary-type areas of the Great Lakes.

(8) The term "estuarine sanctuary" means a research area which may include any part or all of an estuary and any island, transitional area, and upland in, adjoining, or adjacent to such estuary, and which constitutes to the extent feasible a natural unit, set aside to provide scientists and students the opportunity to examine over a period of time the ecological relationships within the area.

(9) The term "Fund" means the Coastal Zone Management Fund established under section 1456a(b) of this title.

(10) The term "land use" means activities which are conducted in, or on the shorelands within, the coastal zone, subject to the requirements outlined in section 1456(g) of this title.

(11) The term "local government" means any political subdivision of, or any special entity created by, any coastal state which (in whole or part) is located in, or has authority over, such state's coastal zone and which (A) has authority to levy taxes, or to establish and collect user fees, or (B) provides any public facility or public service which is financed in whole or part by taxes or user fees. The term includes, but is not limited to, any school district, fire district, transportation authority, and any other special purpose district or authority.

(12) The term "management program" includes, but is not limited to, a comprehensive statement in words, maps, illustrations, or other media of communication, prepared and adopted by the state in accordance with the provisions of this chapter, setting forth objectives, policies, and standards to guide public and private uses of lands and waters in the coastal zone.

(13) The term "Outer Continental Shelf energy activity" means any exploration for, or any development or production of, oil or natural gas from the Outer Continental Shelf (as defined in section 1331(a) of Title 43) or the siting, construction, expansion, or operation of any new or expanded energy facilities directly required by such exploration, development, or production.

(14) The term "person" means any individual; any corporation, partnership, association, or other entity organized or existing under the laws of any state; the Federal Government; any state, regional, or local government; or any entity of any such Federal, state, regional, or local government.

(15) The term "public facilities and public services" means facilities or services which are financed, in whole or in part, by any state or political subdivision thereof, including, but not limited to, highways and secondary roads, parking, mass transit, docks, navigation aids, fire and police protection, water supply, waste collection and treatment (including drainage), schools and education, and hospitals and health care. Such term may also include any other facility or service so financed which the Secretary finds will support increased population.

(16) The term "Secretary" means the Secretary of Commerce.

(17) The term "special area management plan" means a comprehensive plan providing for natural resource protection and reasonable coastal-dependent economic growth containing a detailed and comprehensive statement of policies; standards and criteria to guide public and private uses of lands and waters; and mechanisms for timely implementation in specific geographic areas within the coastal zone.

(18) The term "water use" means a use, activity, or project conducted in or on waters within the coastal zone.

(Pub.L. 89–454, Title III, § 304, as added Oct. 27, 1972, Pub.L. 92–583, 86 Stat. 1281, and amended July 26, 1976, Pub.L. 94–370, § 3, 90 Stat. 1013; Oct. 17, 1980, Pub.L. 96–464, § 4, 94 Stat. 2061; Nov. 5, 1990, Pub.L. 101–508, Title VI, § 6204, 104 Stat. 1388–302; Nov. 4, 1992, Pub.L. 102–587, Title II, § 2205(b)(3)–(7), 106 Stat. 5050, 5051.)

Codification

Amendment of par. (1) by section 6204(a) of Pub.L. 101–508 was executed to the second sentence of par. (1), notwithstanding directory language reciting that it be executed to the third sentence, as the probable intent of Congress.

References in Text

The Submerged Lands Act, referred to in par. (1), is Act May 22, 1953, c. 65, 67 Stat. 29, as amended, which is classified generally to subchapters I and II (sections 1301 et seq., 1311 et seq.) of chapter 29 of Title 43, Public Lands. For complete classification of this Act to the Code, see Short Title note set out under section 1301 of Title 43 and Tables.

The Act of March 2, 1917, referred to in par. (1), is Act Mar. 2, 1917, c. 145, 39 Stat. 961, as amended, known as the Puerto Rican Federal Relations Act and also popularly known as the Jones Act, which is classified principally to chapter 4 (section 731 et seq.) of Title 48, Territories and Insular Possessions. Section 8 of this Act is classified to section 749 of Title 48. For complete classification of this Act to the Code, see Short Title note set out under section 731 of Title 48 and Tables.

The Act of March 24, 1976, referred to in par. (1), is Pub.L. 94–241, Mar. 24, 1976, 90 Stat. 263, as amended, which is classified as a note entitled "Covenant to Establish Commonwealth of Northern Mariana Islands in Political Union with the United States of America" under section 1681 of Title 48, Territories and Insular Possessions.

Section 1 of the Act of November 20, 1963, referred to in par. (1), is section 1 of Pub.L. 88–183, Nov. 20, 1963, 77 Stat. 338, which was formerly classified to section 1701 of Title 48, Possessions and Insular Territories. Such section, which related to the authority of the Secretary of the Interior to transfer tidelands, submerged lands, and filled lands to the governments of Guam, Virgin Islands and American Samoa, was repealed by Pub.L. 93–435, § 5, Oct. 5, 1974, 88 Stat. 1212. Similar provisions were enacted by section 1 of Pub.L. 93–435, Oct. 5, 1974, 88 Stat. 1210, as amended, and are classified to section 1705 of Title 48.

CODE OF FEDERAL REGULATIONS

Terms defined, see 15 CFR 921.2 et seq., 923.2 et seq.

CROSS REFERENCES

Marine environment defined as coastal zone for purposes of—
National sea grant college program, see section 1122 of Title 33, Navigation and Navigable Waters.
Ocean pollution research and development and monitoring, see section 1702 of Title 33.

§ 1454. Management program development grants [CZMA § 305]

(a) In fiscal years 1991, 1992, and 1993, the Secretary may make a grant annually to any coastal state without an approved program if the coastal state demonstrates to the satisfaction of the Secretary that the grant will be used to develop a management program consistent with the requirements set forth in section 1455 of this title. The amount of any such grant shall not exceed $200,000 in any fiscal year, and shall require State matching funds according to a 4–to–1 ratio of Federal–to–State contributions. After an initial grant is made to a coastal state pursuant to this subsection, no subsequent grant shall be made to that coastal state pursuant to this subsection unless the Secretary finds that the coastal state is satisfactorily developing its management program. No coastal state is eligible to receive more than two grants pursuant to this subsection.

(b) Any coastal state which has completed the development of its management program shall submit such program to the Secretary for review and approval pursuant to section 1455 of this title.

(Pub.L. 89–454, Title III, § 305, as added Oct. 27, 1972, Pub.L. 92–583, 86 Stat. 1282, and amended Jan. 2, 1975, Pub.L. 93–612, § 1(1), 88 Stat. 1974; July 26, 1976, Pub.L. 94–370, § 4, 90 Stat. 1015; Nov. 5, 1990, Pub.L. 101–508, Title VI, § 6205, 104 Stat. 1388–302; Nov. 4, 1992, Pub.L. 102–587, Title II, § 2205(b)(1)(A), 106 Stat. 5050.)

CROSS REFERENCES

Administrative grants depended on meeting program requirements, see section 1455 of this title.
Coastal zone for purposes of jurisdiction over subsoil and seabed of outer Continental Shelf defined as boundaries of coastal zone identified under this section, see section 1331 of Title 43, Public Lands.
Congressional consent for two or more coastal States to enter into agreements or compacts for developing and administering coordinated coastal zone planning, policies, and programs pursuant to this section and section 1455 of this title, see section 1456b of this title.
Eligibility for financial assistance under coastal energy impact program depended on receipt of grant under subsecs. (c) and (d) of this section, see section 1456a of this title.
Regulations for management of outer Continental Shelf leasing program to consider management program developed under this section, see section 1344 of Title 43, Public Lands.
Resource management improvement grants for redevelopment of deteriorating and underutilized urban waterfronts and ports and for access to public beaches and other public coastal areas, see section 1455a of this title.

CODE OF FEDERAL REGULATIONS

Applications for program development grants, see 15 CFR 923.90 et seq.
Outer Continental Shelf—
Geological and geophysical explorations of, see 30 CFR 251.0 et seq.
Oil and gas and sulphur operations in, see 30 CFR 250.0 et seq.
Program development and approval, see 15 CFR 923.1 et seq.
Program development grants, allocation of funds to states, see 15 CFR 926.1 et seq.
Uses subject to management, see 15 CFR 923.11 et seq.

LIBRARY REFERENCES

United States ⟹82(1).
C.J.S. United States § 122.

§ 1455. Administrative grants [CZMA § 306]

(a) Authorization; matching funds

The Secretary may make grants to any coastal state for the purpose of administering that state's management program, if the state matches any such grant according to the following ratios of Federal–to–State contributions for the applicable fiscal year:

(1) For those States for which programs were approved prior to enactment of the Coastal Zone Act Reauthorization Amendments of 1990, 1 to 1 for any fiscal year.

(2) For programs approved after enactment of the Coastal Zone Act Reauthorization Amendments of 1990, 4 to 1 for the first fiscal year, 2.3 to 1 for

the second fiscal year, 1.5 to 1 for the third fiscal year, and 1 to 1 for each fiscal year thereafter.

(b) Grants to coastal States; requirements

The Secretary may make a grant to a coastal state under subsection (a) of this section only if the Secretary finds that the management program of the coastal state meets all applicable requirements of this chapter and has been approved in accordance with subsection (d) of this section.

(c) Allocation of grants to coastal States

Grants under this section shall be allocated to coastal states with approved programs based on rules and regulations promulgated by the Secretary which shall take into account the extent and nature of the shoreline and area covered by the program, population of the area, and other relevant factors. The Secretary shall establish, after consulting with the coastal states, maximum and minimum grants for any fiscal year to promote equity between coastal states and effective coastal management.

(d) Mandatory adoption of State management program for coastal zone

Before approving a management program submitted by a coastal state, the Secretary shall find the following:

(1) The State has developed and adopted a management program for its coastal zone in accordance with rules and regulations promulgated by the Secretary, after notice, and with the opportunity of full participation by relevant Federal agencies, State agencies, local governments, regional organizations, port authorities, and other interested parties and individuals, public and private, which is adequate to carry out the purposes of this chapter and is consistent with the policy declared in section 1452 of this title.

(2) The management program includes each of the following required program elements:

(A) An identification of the boundaries of the coastal zone subject to the management program.

(B) A definition of what shall constitute permissible land uses and water uses within the coastal zone which have a direct and significant impact on the coastal waters.

(C) An inventory and designation of areas of particular concern within the coastal zone.

(D) An identification of the means by which the State proposes to exert control over the land uses and water uses referred to in subparagraph (B), including a list of relevant State constitutional provisions, laws, regulations, and judicial decisions.

(E) Broad guidelines on priorities of uses in particular areas, including specifically those uses of lowest priority.

(F) A description of the organizational structure proposed to implement such management program, including the responsibilities and interrelationships of local, areawide, State, regional, and interstate agencies in the management process.

(G) A definition of the term 'beach' and a planning process for the protection of, and access to, public beaches and other public coastal areas of environmental, recreational, historical, esthetic, ecological, or cultural value.

(H) A planning process for energy facilities likely to be located in, or which may significantly affect, the coastal zone, including a process for anticipating the management of the impacts resulting from such facilities.

(I) A planning process for assessing the effects of, and studying and evaluating ways to control, or lessen the impact of, shoreline erosion, and to restore areas adversely affected by such erosion.

(3) The State has—

(A) coordinated its program with local, areawide, and interstate plans applicable to areas within the coastal zone—

(i) existing on January 1 of the year in which the State's management program is submitted to the Secretary; and

(ii) which have been developed by a local government, an areawide agency, a regional agency, or an interstate agency; and

(B) established an effective mechanism for continuing consultation and coordination between the management agency designated pursuant to paragraph (6) and with local governments, interstate agencies, regional agencies, and areawide agencies within the coastal zone to assure the full participation of those local governments and agencies in carrying out the purposes of this chapter; except that the Secretary shall not find any mechanism to be effective for purposes of this subparagraph unless it requires that—

(i) the management agency, before implementing any management program decision which would conflict with any local zoning ordinance, decision, or other action, shall send a notice of the management program decision to any local government whose zoning authority is affected;

(ii) within the 30-day period commencing on the date of receipt of that notice, the local government may submit to the management agency written comments on the management program decision, and any recommendation for alternatives; and

(iii) the management agency, if any comments are submitted to it within the 30–day period by any local government—

(I) shall consider the comments;

(II) may, in its discretion, hold a public hearing on the comments; and

(III) may not take any action within the 30–day period to implement the management program decision.

(4) The State has held public hearings in the development of the management program.

(5) The management program and any changes thereto have been reviewed and approved by the Governor of the State.

(6) The Governor of the State has designated a single State agency to receive and administer grants for implementing the management program.

(7) The State is organized to implement the management program.

(8) The management program provides for adequate consideration of the national interest involved in planning for, and managing the coastal zone, including the siting of facilities such as energy facilities which are of greater than local significance. In the case of energy facilities, the Secretary shall find that the State has given consideration to any applicable national or interstate energy plan or program.

(9) The management program includes procedures whereby specific areas may be designated for the purpose of preserving or restoring them for their conservation, recreational, ecological, historical, or esthetic values.

(10) The State, acting through its chosen agency or agencies (including local governments, areawide agencies, regional agencies, or interstate agencies) has authority for the management of the coastal zone in accordance with the management program. Such authority shall include power—

(A) to administer land use and water use regulations to control development to ensure compliance with the management program, and to resolve conflicts among competing uses; and

(B) to acquire fee simple and less than fee simple interests in land, waters, and other property through condemnation or other means when necessary to achieve conformance with the management program.

(11) The management program provides for any one or a combination of the following general techniques for control of land uses and water uses within the coastal zone:

(A) State establishment of criteria and standards for local implementation, subject to administrative review and enforcement.

(B) Direct State land and water use planning and regulation.

(C) State administrative review for consistency with the management program of all development plans, projects, or land and water use regulations, including exceptions and variances thereto, proposed by any State or local authority or private developer, with power to approve or disapprove after public notice and an opportunity for hearings.

(12) The management program contains a method of assuring that local land use and water use regulations within the coastal zone do not unreasonably restrict or exclude land uses and water uses of regional benefit.

(13) The management program provides for—

(A) the inventory and designation of areas that contain one or more coastal resources of national significance; and

(B) specific and enforceable standards to protect such resources.

(14) The management program provides for public participation in permitting processes, consistency determinations, and other similar decisions.

(15) The management program provides a mechanism to ensure that all State agencies will adhere to the program.

(16) The management program contains enforceable policies and mechanisms to implement the applicable requirements of the Coastal Nonpoint Pollution Control Program of the State required by section 1455b of this title.

(e) Amendment or modification of State management program for coastal zone

A coastal state may amend or modify a management program which it has submitted and which has been approved by the Secretary under this section, subject to the following conditions:

(1) The State shall promptly notify the Secretary of any proposed amendment, modification, or other program change and submit it for the Secretary's approval. The Secretary may suspend all or part of any grant made under this section pending State submission of the proposed amendments, modification, or other program change.

(2) Within 30 days after the date the Secretary receives any proposed amendment, the Secretary shall notify the State whether the Secretary approves or disapproves the amendment, or whether the Secretary finds it is necessary to extend the review of the proposed amendment for a period not to exceed 120 days after the date the Secretary received the proposed amendment. The Secretary may extend this period only as necessary to meet the requirements of the National Environmental Policy Act of 1969 (42 U.S.C. 4321 et seq.). If the Secretary does not notify the coastal state that the Secretary approves or disapproves the amendment within that period, then the amendment shall be conclusively presumed as approved.

(3)(A) Except as provided in subparagraph (B), a coastal state may not implement any amendment, modification, or other change as part of its approved management program unless the amendment, modification, or other change is approved by the Secretary under this subsection.

(B) The Secretary, after determining on a preliminary basis, that an amendment, modification, or other change which has been submitted for approval under this subsection is likely to meet the program approval standards in this section, may permit the State to expend funds awarded under this section to begin implementing the proposed amendment, modification, or change. This preliminary approval shall not extend for more than 6 months and may not be renewed. A proposed amendment, modification, or change which has been given preliminary approval and is not finally approved under this paragraph shall not be considered an enforceable policy for purposes of section 1456 of this title.

(Pub.L. 89–454, Title III, § 306, as added Oct. 27, 1972, Pub.L. 92–583, 86 Stat. 1283, and amended Jan. 2, 1975, Pub.L. 93–612, § 1(2), 88 Stat. 1974; July 26, 1976, Pub.L. 94–370, § 5, 90 Stat. 1017; Oct. 17, 1980, Pub.L. 96–464, § 5(a), 94 Stat. 2062; April 7, 1986, Pub.L. 99–272, Title VI, § 6043(b)(1), (c), 100 Stat. 124, 125; Nov. 5, 1990, Pub.L. 101–508, Title VI, § 6206(a), 104 Stat. 1388–303; Nov. 4, 1992, Pub.L. 102–587, Title II, § 2205(b)(1)(A), (B), (8), 106 Stat. 5050, 5051.)

References in Text

The enactment of the Coastal Zone Act Reauthorization Amendments of 1990, referred to in subsec. (a)(1), (2), is probably a reference to the date of enactment of Pub.L. 101–508, Title VI, Subtitle C (section 6201 et seq.), Nov. 5, 1990, 104 Stat. 1388–303, which was approved Nov. 5, 1990.

The National Environmental Policy Act of 1969, referred to in subsec. (e)(2), is Pub.L. 91–190, Jan. 1, 1970, 83 Stat. 852, as amended, which is classified generally to chapter 55 (section 4321 et seq.) of Title 42, The Public Health and Welfare. For complete classification of this Act to the Code, see Short Title note set out under section 4321 of Title 42 and Tables.

Additional Program Requirements

Section 6206(b) of Pub.L. 101–508 provided that:

"Each State which submits a management program for approval under section 306 of the Coastal Zone Management Act of 1972, as amended by this subtitle [this section, as amended by section 6206(a), Pub.L. 101–508] (including a State which submitted a program before the date of enactment of this Act [Nov. 5, 1990]), shall demonstrate to the Secretary—

"(1) that the program complies with section 306(d)(14) and (15) of that Act [subsec. (d)(14) and (15) of this section] by not later than 3 years after the date of the enactment of this Act [Nov. 5, 1990]; and

"(2) that the program complies with section 306(d)(16) of that Act [subsec. (d)(16) of this section] by not later than 30 months after the date of publication of final guidance under section 6217(g) of this Act [section 1455b at this title]."

CROSS REFERENCES

Authorization of appropriations, see section 1464 of this title.
Boundary of Coastal Barrier Resources System—
Copy of filed map provided to state coastal zone management agency, see section 3503 of this title.
Modification by state coastal zone management agency, see section 3503 of this title.
Coastal resource improvement program, "eligible coastal state" as meaning a coastal state that has a management program approved under this section, see section 1455a of this title.
Congressional consent for two or more coastal States to enter into agreements or compacts for developing and administering coordinated coastal zone planning, policies, and programs pursuant to this section and section 1454 of this title, see section 1456b of this title.
Eligibility for financial assistance under coastal energy impact program depended on whether management program has been approved under this section, see section 1456a of this title.
Management program development grants before state qualifies for grant under this section, see section 1454 of this title.
Management program under this section not to be approved unless views of Federal agencies principally affected by such program adequately considered, see section 1456 of this title.
Necessity of state concurrence with consistency certification for licensing of—
Geological and geophysical exploratory plans in coastal zone of outer Continental Shelf, see section 1340 of Title 43, Public Lands.
Oil and gas production and development in coastal zone of outer Continental Shelf other than Gulf of Mexico, see section 1351 of Title 43.
Regulations for management of outer Continental Shelf leasing program to consider management program developed under this section, see section 1344 of Title 43.
Withdrawal of approval of management program for failure to adhere to terms of grant or cooperative agreement funded under this section, see section 1458 of this title.

CODE OF FEDERAL REGULATIONS

Allocation, see 15 CFR 923.92 et seq.
Approved management programs, amendment of, see 15 CFR 923.80 et seq.
Development and production plan, see 30 CFR 250.34–2 et seq.
Federal-state consultation, see 15 CFR 923.51 et seq.
Improving coastal zone management, see 15 CFR 923.101 et seq.
Plan coordination, see 15 CFR 923.56 et seq.
State review of actions, land and water uses, management program, see 15 CFR 923.44 et seq.

LAW REVIEW COMMENTARIES

Governmentally created erosion on the seashore: The Fifth Amendment washed away. Leslie M. MacRae, 89 Dick.L.Rev. 101 (1984).

LIBRARY REFERENCES

United States ⚯82(1).
C.J.S. United States § 122.

§ 1455a. Coastal resource improvement program [CZMA § 306A]

(a) Definitions

For purposes of this section—

(1) The term "eligible coastal state" means a coastal state that for any fiscal year for which a grant is applied for under this section—

(A) has a management program approved under section 1455 of this title; and

(B) in the judgment of the Secretary, is making satisfactory progress in activities designed to result in significant improvement in achieving the coastal management objectives specified in section 1452(2)(A) through (K) of this title.

(2) The term "urban waterfront and port" means any developed area that is densely populated and is being used for, or has been used for, urban residential recreational, commercial, shipping or industrial purposes.

(b) Resource management improvement grants

The Secretary may make grants to any eligible coastal state to assist that state in meeting one or more of the following objectives:

(1) The preservation or restoration of specific areas of the state that (A) are designated under the management program procedures required by section 1455(d)(9) of this title because of their conservation recreational, ecological, or esthetic values, or (B) contain one or more coastal resources of national significance, or for the purpose of restoring and enhancing shellfish production by the purchase and distribution of clutch material on publicly owned reef tracts.

(2) The redevelopment of deteriorating and underutilized urban waterfronts and ports that are designated in the state's management program pursuant to section 1455(d)(2)(C) of this title as areas of particular concern.

(3) The provision of access to public beaches and other public coastal areas and to coastal waters in accordance with the planning process required under section 1455(d)(2)(G) of this title.

(c) Uses, terms and conditions of grants

(1) Each grant made by the Secretary under this section shall be subject to such terms and conditions as may be appropriate to ensure that the grant is used for purposes consistent with this section.

(2) Grants made under this section may be used for—

(A) the acquisition of fee simple and other interests in land;

(B) low-cost construction projects determined by the Secretary to be consistent with the purposes of this section, including but not limited to, paths, walkways, fences, parks, and the rehabilitation of historic buildings and structures; except that not more than 50 per centum of any grant made under this section may be used for such construction projects;

(C) in the case of grants made for objectives described in subsection (b)(2) of this section—

(i) the rehabilitation or acquisition of piers to provide increased public use, including compatible commercial activity,

(ii) the establishment of shoreline stabilization measures including the installation or rehabilitation of bulkheads for the purpose of public safety or increasing public access and use, and

(iii) the removal or replacement of pilings where such action will provide increased recreational use of urban waterfront areas,

but activities provided for under this paragraph shall not be treated as construction projects subject to the limitations in paragraph (B);

(D) engineering designs, specifications, and other appropriate reports; and

(E) educational, interpretive, and management costs and such other related costs as the Secretary determines to be consistent with the purposes of this section.

(d) State matching contributions; ratio; maximum amount of grants

(1) The Secretary may make grants to any coastal state for the purpose of carrying out the project or purpose for which such grants are awarded, if the state matches any such grant according to the following ratios of Federal to state contributions for the applicable fiscal year: 4 to 1 for fiscal year 1986; 2.3 to 1 for fiscal year 1987; 1.5 to 1 for fiscal year 1988; and 1 to 1 for each fiscal year after fiscal year 1988.

(2) Grants provided under this section may be used to pay a coastal state's share of costs required under any other Federal program that is consistent with the purposes of this section.

(3) The total amount of grants made under this section to any eligible coastal state for any fiscal year may not exceed an amount equal to 10 per centum of the total amount appropriated to carry out this section for such fiscal year.

(e) Allocation of grants to local governments and other agencies

With the approval of the Secretary, an eligible coastal state may allocate to a local government, an areawide agency designated under section 3334 of Title 42, a regional agency, or an interstate agency, a portion of any grant made under this section for the purpose of carrying out this section; except that such an allocation shall not relieve that state of the responsibility for ensuring that any funds so allocated are applied in furtherance of the state's approved management program.

(f) Other technical and financial assistance

In addition to providing grants under this section, the Secretary shall assist eligible coastal states and their local governments in identifying and obtaining other sources of available Federal technical and financial assistance regarding the objectives of this section.

(Pub.L. 89–454, Title III, § 306A, as added Oct. 17, 1980, Pub.L. 96–464, § 6, 94 Stat. 2062, as amended April 7, 1986, Pub.L. 99–272, Title VI, § 6043(b)(2), 100 Stat. 124; Nov. 5, 1990, Pub.L. 101–508, Title VI, §§ 6207, 6216(a), 104 Stat. 1388–307, 1388–314; Nov. 4, 1992, Pub.L. 102–587, Title II, § 2205(b)(9)–(12), 106 Stat. 5051.)

Codification

Section 6216a of Pub.L. 101–508 directed the amendment of section 306a(b)(1) of the Coastal Zone Management Act of 1972. There is no such section of such Act. Section 306A(b)(1) of such Act is classified to subsec. (b)(1) of this section, and such amendment was executed to such subsec. as the probable intent of Congress.

CROSS REFERENCES

Authorization of appropriations, see section 1464 of this title.

Exclusions from cost of administering management program, see section 1455 of this title.

CODE OF FEDERAL REGULATIONS

Floodplain, wetlands review, see 10 CFR 1022.1 et seq.

LIBRARY REFERENCES

Health and Environment ⚡25.5(4).

C.J.S. Health and Environment § 91 et seq.

§ 1455b. Protecting coastal waters

(a) In general

(1) Program development

Not later than 30 months after the date of the publication of final guidance under subsection (g) of this section, each State for which a management program has been approved pursuant to section 306 of the Coastal Zone Management Act of 1972 [16 U.S.C.A. § 1455] shall prepare and submit to the Secretary and the Administrator a Coastal Nonpoint Pollution Control Program for approval pursuant to this section. The purpose of the program shall be to develop and implement management measures for nonpoint source pollution to restore and protect coastal waters, working in close conjunction with other State and local authorities.

(2) Program coordination

A State program under this section shall be coordinated closely with State and local water quality plans and programs developed pursuant to sections 1288, 1313, 1329, and 1330 of Title 33 and with State plans developed pursuant to the Coastal Zone Management Act of 1972 [this chapter], as amended by this Act [Pub.L. 101–508, Title VI, Subtitle C]. The program shall serve as an update and expansion of the State nonpoint source management program developed under section 1329 at Title 33, as the program under that section relates to land and water uses affecting coastal waters.

(b) Program contents

Each State program under this section shall provide for the implementation, at a minimum, of management measures in conformity with the guidance published under subsection (g) of this section, to protect coastal waters generally, and shall also contain the following:

(1) Identifying land uses

The identification of, and a continuing process for identifying, land uses which, individually or cumulatively, may cause or contribute significantly to a degradation of—

(A) those coastal waters where there is a failure to attain or maintain applicable water quality standards or protect designated uses, as determined by the State pursuant to its water quality planning processes; or

(B) those coastal waters that are threatened by reasonably foreseeable increases in pollution loadings from new or expanding sources.

(2) Identifying critical coastal areas

The identification of, and a continuing process for identifying, critical coastal areas adjacent to coastal waters referred to in paragraph (1)(A) and (B), within which any new land uses or substantial expansion of existing land uses shall be subject to management measures in addition to those provided for in subsection (g) of this section.

(3) Management measures

The implementation and continuing revision from time to time of additional management measures applicable to the land uses and areas identified pursuant to paragraphs (1) and (2) that are necessary to achieve and maintain applicable water quality standards under section 1313 of Title 33 and protect designated uses.

(4) Technical assistance

The provision of technical and other assistance to local governments and the public for implementing the measures referred to in paragraph (3), which may include assistance in developing ordinances and regulations, technical guidance, and modeling to predict and assess the effectiveness of such measures, training, financial incentives, demonstration projects, and other innovations to protect coastal water quality and designated uses.

(5) Public participation

Opportunities for public participation in all aspects of the program, including the use of public notices and opportunities for comment, nomination procedures, public hearings, technical and financial assistance, public education, and other means.

(6) Administrative coordination

The establishment of mechanisms to improve coordination among State agencies and between State and local officials responsible for land use programs and permitting, water quality permitting and enforcement, habitat protection, and public health and safety, through the use of joint project review, memoranda of agreement, or other mechanisms.

(7) State coastal zone boundary modification

A proposal to modify the boundaries of the State coastal zone as the coastal management agency of the State determines is necessary to implement the recommendations made pursuant to subsection (e) of this section. If the coastal management agency does not have the authority to modify such boundaries, the program shall include recommendations for such modifications to the appropriate State authority.

(c) Program submission, approval, and implementation

(1) Review and approval

Within 6 months after the date of submission by a State of a program pursuant to this section, the Secretary and the Administrator shall jointly review the program. The program shall be approved if—

(A) the Secretary determines that the portions of the program under the authority of the Secretary meet the requirements of this section and the Administrator concurs with that determination; and

(B) the Administrator determines that the portions of the program under the authority of the Administrator meet the requirements of this section and the Secretary concurs with that determination.

(2) Implementation of approved program

If the program of a State is approved in accordance with paragraph (1), the State shall implement the program, including the management measures included in the program pursuant to subsection (b) of this section, through—

(A) changes to the State plan for control of nonpoint source pollution approved under section 1329 of Title 33; and

(B) changes to the State coastal zone management program developed under section 306 of the Coastal Zone Management Act of 1972 [16 U.S.C.A. § 1455], as amended by this Act.

(3) Withholding coastal management assistance

If the Secretary finds that a coastal State has failed to submit an approvable program as required by this section, the Secretary shall withhold for each fiscal year until such a program is submitted a portion of grants otherwise available to the State for the fiscal year under section 306 of the Coastal Zone Management Act of 1972 [16 U.S.C.A. § 1455], as follows:

(A) 10 percent for fiscal year 1996.

(B) 15 percent for fiscal year 1997.

(C) 20 percent for fiscal year 1998.

(D) 30 percent for fiscal year 1999 and each fiscal year thereafter.

The Secretary shall make amounts withheld under this paragraph available to coastal States having programs approved under this section.

(4) Withholding water pollution control assistance

If the Administrator finds that a coastal State has failed to submit an approvable program as required by this section, the Administrator shall withhold from grants available to the State under section 1329 of Title 33, for each fiscal year until such a program is submitted, an amount equal to a percentage of the grants awarded to the State for the preceding fiscal year under that section, as follows:

(A) For fiscal year 1996, 10 percent of the amount awarded for fiscal year 1995.

(B) For fiscal year 1997, 15 percent of the amount awarded for fiscal year 1996.

(C) For fiscal year 1998, 20 percent of the amount awarded for fiscal year 1997.

(D) For fiscal year 1999 and each fiscal year thereafter, 30 percent of the amount awarded for fiscal year 1998 or other preceding fiscal year.

The Administrator shall make amounts withheld under this paragraph available to States having programs approved pursuant to this subsection.

(d) Technical assistance

The Secretary and the Administrator shall provide technical assistance to coastal States and local governments in developing and implementing programs under this section. Such assistance shall include—

(1) methods for assessing water quality impacts associated with coastal land uses;

(2) methods for assessing the cumulative water quality effects of coastal development;

(3) maintaining and from time to time revising an inventory of model ordinances, and providing other assistance to coastal States and local governments in identifying, developing, and implementing pollution control measures; and

(4) methods to predict and assess the effects of coastal land use management measures on coastal water quality and designated uses.

(e) Inland coastal zone boundaries

(1) Review

The Secretary, in consultation with the Administrator of the Environmental Protection Agency, shall, within 18 months after November 5, 1990, review the inland coastal zone boundary of each coastal State program which has been approved or is proposed for approval under section 306 of the Coastal Zone Management Act of 1972 [16 U.S.C.A. § 1455], and evaluate whether the State's coastal zone boundary extends inland to the extent necessary to control the land and water uses that have a significant impact on coastal waters of the State.

(2) Recommendation

If the Secretary, in consultation with the Administrator, finds that modifications to the inland boundaries of a State's coastal zone are necessary for that State to more effectively manage land and water uses to protect coastal waters, the Secretary, in consultation with the Administrator, shall recommend appropriate modifications in writing to the affected State.

(f) Financial assistance

(1) In general

Upon request of a State having a program approved under section 306 of the Coastal Zone Management Act of 1972 [16 U.S.C.A. § 1455], the Secretary, in consultation with the Administrator, may provide grants to the State for use for developing a State program under this section.

(2) Amount

The total amount of grants to a State under this subsection shall not exceed 50 percent of the total cost to the State of developing a program under this section.

(3) State share

The State share of the cost of an activity carried out with a grant under this subsection shall be paid from amounts from non-Federal sources.

(4) Allocation

Amounts available for grants under this subsection shall be allocated among States in accordance with regulations issued pursuant to section 306(c) of the Coastal Zone Management Act of 1972 [16 U.S.C.A. § 1455(c)], except that the Secretary may use not more than 25 percent of amounts available for such grants to assist States which the Secretary, in consultation with the Administrator, determines are making exemplary progress in preparing a State program under this section or have extreme needs with respect to coastal water quality.

(g) Guidance for coastal nonpoint source pollution control

(1) In general

The Administrator, in consultation with the Secretary and the Director of the United States Fish and Wildlife Service and other Federal agencies, shall publish (and periodically revise thereafter) guidance for specifying management measures for sources of nonpoint pollution in coastal waters.

(2) Content

Guidance under this subsection shall include, at a minimum—

(A) a description of a range of methods, measures, or practices, including structural and nonstructural controls and operation and maintenance procedures, that constitute each measure;

(B) a description of the categories and subcategories of activities and locations for which each measure may be suitable;

(C) an identification of the individual pollutants or categories or classes of pollutants that may be controlled by the measures and the water quality effects of the measures;

(D) quantitative estimates of the pollution reduction effects and costs of the measures;

(E) a description of the factors which should be taken into account in adapting the measures to specific sites or locations; and

(F) any necessary monitoring techniques to accompany the measures to assess over time the success of the measures in reducing pollution loads and improving water quality.

(3) Publication

The Administrator, in consultation with the Secretary, shall publish—

(A) proposed guidance pursuant to this subsection not later than 6 months after November 5, 1990; and

(B) final guidance pursuant to this subsection not later than 18 months after such date.

(4) Notice and comment

The Administrator shall provide to coastal States and other interested persons an opportunity to provide written comments on proposed guidance under this subsection.

(5) Management measures

For purposes of this subsection, the term "management measures" means economically achievable measures for the control of the addition of pollutants from existing and new categories and classes of nonpoint sources of pollution, which reflect the greatest degree of pollutant reduction achievable through the application of the best available nonpoint pollution control practices, technologies, processes, siting criteria, operating methods, or other alternatives.

(h) Authorizations of appropriations

(1) Administrator

There is authorized to be appropriated to the Administrator for use for carrying out this section not more than $1,000,000 for each of fiscal years 1992, 1993, and 1994.

(2) Secretary

(A) Of amounts appropriated to the Secretary for a fiscal year under section 318(a)(4) of the Coastal Zone Management Act of 1972 [16 U.S.C.A. § 1464(a)(4)], as amended by this Act [Pub.L. 101–508, Title VI, Subtitle C], not more than $1,000,000 shall be available for use by the Secretary for carrying out this section for that fiscal year, other than for providing in the form of grants under subsection (f) of this section.

(B) There is authorized to be appropriated to the Secretary for use for providing in the form of grants under subsection (f) of this section not more than—

(i) $6,000,000 for fiscal year 1992;

(ii) $12,000,000 for fiscal year 1993;

(iii) $12,000,000 for fiscal year 1994; and

(iv) $12,000,000 for fiscal year 1995.

(i) Definitions

In this section—

(1) the term "Administrator" means the Administrator of the Environmental Protection Agency;

(2) the term "coastal state" has the meaning given the term "coastal State" under section 304 of the Coastal Zone Management Act of 1972 (16 U.S.C. 1453) [16 U.S.C.A. § 1453];

(3) each of the terms "coastal waters" and "coastal zone" has the meaning that term has in the Coastal Zone Management Act of 1972 [this chapter];

(4) the term "coastal management agency" means a State agency designated pursuant to section 306(d)(6) of the Coastal Zone Management Act of 1972 [16 U.S.C.A. § 1455(d)(6)];

(5) the term "land use" includes a use of waters adjacent to coastal waters; and

(6) the term "Secretary" means the Secretary of Commerce.

(Pub.L. 101–508, Title VI, § 6217, Nov. 5, 1990, 104 Stat. 1388–314; Pub.L. 102–587, Title II, § 2205(b)(1)(A), (B), (24), Nov. 4, 1992, 106 Stat. 5050, 5052.)

References in Text

The Coastal Zone Management Act of 1972, referred to in subsecs. (a)(2) and (i)(3), is Pub.L. 89–454, Title III (section 301 et seq.), as added Pub.L. 92–583, Oct. 27, 1972, 86 Stat. 1280, as amended, which is classified generally to this chapter.

As amended by this Act, referred to in subsecs. (a)(2), (c)(2)(B) and (h)(2), is a reference to the amendment of the Coastal Zone Management Act of 1972 by Pub.L. 101–508, Title VI, Subtitle C (section 6201 et seq.), Nov. 5, 1990, 104 Stat. 1388–299, known as the Coastal Zone Act Reauthorization Amendments of 1990, which is classified generally to this chapter.

For complete classification of these Acts to the Code, see Short Title and Short Title of Amendment notes set out under section 1451 of this title and Tables.

Codification

Section was enacted as part of the Coastal Zone Act Reauthorization Amendments of 1990, and not as part of the Coastal Zone Management Act of 1972, which comprises this chapter.

WEST'S FEDERAL PRACTICE MANUAL

Preservation of coastal waters, see § 4389.50.

Code Of Federal Regulations

Floodplain, wetlands review, see 10 CFR 1022.1 et seq.

§ 1456. Coordination and cooperation [CZMA § 307]

(a) Federal agencies

In carrying out his functions and responsibilities under this chapter, the Secretary shall consult with, cooperate with, and, to the maximum extent practicable, coordinate his activities with other interested Federal agencies.

(b) Adequate consideration of views of Federal agencies

The Secretary shall not approve the management program submitted by a state pursuant to section 1455 of this title unless the views of Federal agencies principally affected by such program have been adequately considered.

(c) Consistency of Federal activities with State management programs; Presidential exemption; certification

(1)(A) Each Federal agency activity within or outside the coastal zone that affects any land or water use or natural resource of the coastal zone shall be carried out in a manner which is consistent to the maximum extent practicable with the enforceable policies of approved State management programs. A Federal agency activity shall be subject to this paragraph unless it is subject to paragraph (2) or (3).

(B) After any final judgment, decree, or order of any Federal court that is appealable under section 1291 or 1292 of Title 28, or under any other applicable provision of Federal law, that a specific Federal agency activity is not in compliance with subparagraph (A), and certification by the Secretary that mediation under subsection (h) of this section is not likely to result in such compliance, the President may, upon written request from the Secretary, exempt from compliance those elements of the Federal agency activity that are found by the Federal court to be inconsistent with an approved State program, if the President determines that the activity is in the paramount interest of the United States. No such exemption shall be granted on the basis of a lack of appropriations unless the President has specifically requested such appropriations as part of the budgetary process, and the Congress has failed to make available the requested appropriations.

(C) Each Federal agency carrying out an activity subject to paragraph (1) shall provide a consistency determination to the relevant State agency designated under section 1455(d)(6) of this title at the earliest practicable time, but in no case later than 90 days before final approval of the Federal activity unless both the Federal agency and the State agency agree to a different schedule.

(2) Any Federal agency which shall undertake any development project in the coastal zone of a state shall insure that the project is, to the maximum extent practicable, consistent with the enforceable policies of approved state management programs.

(3)(A) After final approval by the Secretary of a state's management program, any applicant for a required Federal license or permit to conduct an activity, in or outside of the coastal zone, affecting any land or water use or natural resource of the coastal zone of that state shall provide in the application to the licensing or permitting agency a certification that the proposed activity complies with the enforceable policies of the state's approved program and that such activity will be conducted in a manner consistent with the program. At the same time, the applicant shall furnish to the state or its designated agency a copy of the certification, with all necessary information and data. Each coastal state shall establish procedures for public notice in the case of all such certifications and, to the extent it deems appropriate, procedures for public hearings in connection therewith. At the earliest practicable time, the state or its designated agency shall notify the Federal agency concerned that the state concurs with or objects to the applicant's certification. If the state or its designated agency fails to furnish the required notification within six months after receipt of its copy of the applicant's certification, the state's concurrence with the certification shall be conclusively presumed. No license or permit shall be granted by the Federal agency until the state or its designated agency has concurred with the applicant's certification or until, by the state's failure to act, the concurrence is conclusively presumed, unless the Secretary, on his own initiative or upon appeal by the applicant, finds, after providing a reasonable opportunity for detailed comments from the Federal agency involved and from the state, that the activity is consistent with the objectives of this chapter or is otherwise necessary in the interest of national security.

(B) After the management program of any coastal state has been approved by the Secretary under section 1455 of this title, any person who submits to the Secretary of the Interior any plan for the exploration or development of, or production from, any area which has been leased under the Outer Continental Shelf Lands Act (43 U.S.C. 1331 et seq.) and regulations under such Act shall, with respect to any exploration, development, or production described in such plan and affecting any land or water use or natural resource of the coastal zone of such state, attach to such plan a certification that each activity which is described in detail in such plan complies with the enforceable policies of such state's approved management program and will be carried out in a manner consistent with such program. No Federal official or agency shall grant such person any license or permit for any activity described in detail in such plan until such state or its designated agency receives a copy of such certification and plan, together with any other necessary data and information, and until—

(i) such state or its designated agency, in accordance with the procedures required to be established by such state pursuant to subparagraph (A), concurs with such person's certification and notifies the Secretary and the Secretary of the Interior of such concurrence;

(ii) concurrence by such state with such certification is conclusively presumed as provided for in subparagraph (A), except if such state fails to concur with or object to such certification within three months after receipt of its copy of such certification and supporting information, such state shall provide the Secretary, the appropriate federal agency, and such person with a written statement describing the status of review and the basis for further delay in issuing a final decision, and if such statement is not so provided, concurrence by such state with such certification shall be conclusively presumed; or

(iii) the Secretary finds, pursuant to subparagraph (A), that each activity which is described in detail in such plan is consistent with the objectives of this chapter or is otherwise necessary in the interest of national security.

If a state concurs or is conclusively presumed to concur, or if the Secretary makes such a finding, the provisions of subparagraph (A) are not applicable with respect to such person, such state, and any Federal license or permit which is required to conduct any activity affecting land uses or water uses in the coastal zone of such state which is described in detail in the plan to which such concurrence or finding applies. If such state objects to such certification and if the Secretary fails to make a finding under clause (iii) with respect to such certification, or if such person fails substantially to comply with such plan as submitted, such person shall submit an amendment to such plan, or a new plan, to the Secretary of the Interior. With respect to any amendment or new plan submitted to the Secretary of the Interior pursuant to the preceding sentence, the applicable time period for purposes of concurrence by conclusive presumption under subparagraph (A) is 3 months.

(d) Applications of local governments for Federal assistance; relationship of activities with the enforceable policies of an approved coastal State's management program

State and local governments submitting applications for Federal assistance under other Federal programs, in or outside of the coastal zone, affecting any land or water use of[1] natural resource of the coastal zone shall indicate the views of the appropriate state or local agency as to the relationship of such activities to the approved management program for the coastal zone. Such applications shall be submitted and coordinated in accordance with the provisions of section 6506 of Title 31. Federal agencies shall not approve proposed projects that are inconsistent with the enforceable policies of a coastal state's management program, except upon a finding by the Secretary that such project is consistent with the purposes of this chapter or necessary in the interest of national security.

(e) Construction with other laws

Nothing in this chapter shall be construed—

(1) to diminish either Federal or state jurisdiction, responsibility, or rights in the field of planning, development, or control of water resources, submerged lands, or navigable waters; nor to displace, supersede, limit, or modify any interstate compact or the jurisdiction or responsibility of any legally established joint or common agency of two or more states or of two or more states and the Federal Government; nor to limit the authority of Congress to authorize and fund projects;

(2) as superseding, modifying, or repealing existing laws applicable to the various Federal agencies; nor to affect the jurisdiction, powers, or prerogatives of the International Joint Commission, United States and Canada, the Permanent Engineering Board, and the United States operating entity or entities established pursuant to the Columbia River Basin Treaty, signed at Washington, January 17, 1961, or the International Boundary and Water Commission, United States and Mexico.

(f) Construction with existing requirements of water and air pollution programs

Notwithstanding any other provision of this chapter, nothing in this chapter shall in any way affect any requirement (1) established by the Federal Water Pollution Control Act, as amended [33 U.S.C.A. § 1251 et seq.], or the Clean Air Act, as amended [42 U.S.C.A. § 7401 et seq.], or (2) established by the Federal Government or by any state or local government pursuant to such Acts. Such requirements shall be incorporated in any program developed pursuant to this chapter and shall be the water pollution control and air pollution control requirements applicable to such program.

(g) Concurrence with programs which affect inland areas

When any state's coastal zone management program, submitted for approval or proposed for modification pursuant to section 1455 of this title, includes requirements as to shorelands which also would be subject to any Federally supported national land use program which may be hereafter enacted, the Secretary, prior to approving such program, shall obtain the concurrence of the Secretary of the Interior, or such other Federal official as may be designated to administer the national land use program, with respect to that portion of the coastal zone management program affecting such inland areas.

(h) Mediation of disagreements

In case of serious disagreement between any Federal agency and a coastal state—

(1) in the development or the initial implementation of a management program under section 1454 of this title; or

(2) in the administration of a management program approved under section 1455 of this title;

the Secretary, with the cooperation of the Executive Office of the President, shall seek to mediate the differences involved in such disagreement. The process of such mediation shall, with respect to any disagreement described in paragraph (2), include public hearings which shall be conducted in the local area concerned.

(i) Application fee for appeals

(1) With respect to appeals under subsections (c)(3) and (d) of this section which are submitted after November 5, 1990, the Secretary shall collect an application fee of not less than $200 for minor appeals and not less than $500 for major appeals, unless the Secretary, upon consideration of an applicant's request for a fee waiver, determines that the applicant is unable to pay the fee.

(2)(A) The Secretary shall collect such other fees as are necessary to recover the full costs of administering and processing such appeals under subsection (c) of this section.

(B) If the Secretary waives the application fee under paragraph (1) for an applicant, the Secretary shall waive all other fees under this subsection for the applicant.

(3) Fees collected under this subsection shall be deposited into the Coastal Zone Management Fund established under section 1456a of this title.

(Pub.L. 89–454, Title III, § 307, as added Oct. 27, 1972, Pub.L. 92–583, 86 Stat. 1285, and amended July 26, 1976, Pub.L. 94–370, § 6, 90 Stat. 1018; Sept. 18, 1978, Pub.L. 95–372, Title V, § 504, 92 Stat. 693; Nov. 5, 1990, Pub.L. 101–508, Title VI, § 6208, 104 Stat. 1388–307; Nov. 4, 1992, Pub.L. 102–587, Title II, § 2205(b)(13), (14), 106 Stat. 5051.)

1 So in original. Probably should be "or".

CROSS REFERENCES

Coastal zone management reports, see section 1462 of this title.

Management program for which grants are made under section 1454(d) of this title not considered approved program for purposes of this section, see section 1454 of this title.

Necessity of state concurrence with consistency certification for licensing of—

Geological and geophysical exploratory plans in coastal zone of outer Continental Shelf, see section 1340 of Title 43, Public Lands.

Oil and gas production and development in coastal zone of outer Continental Shelf, other than Gulf of Mexico, see section 1351 of Title 43.

Water quality standards or criteria included within term "water use", see section 1453 of this title.

WEST'S FEDERAL PRACTICE MANUAL

Federal wetlands regulatory legislation, see § 6237.

CODE OF FEDERAL REGULATIONS

Air and water pollution control requirements, see 15 CFR 923.45 et seq.

Federal consistency with approved coastal management programs, see 15 CFR 930.1 et seq.

Federal-state consultation, see 15 CFR 923.51 et seq.

Necessity of state concurrence with consistency certification for licensing of—Cont'd

LAW REVIEW COMMENTARIES

Groundwater pollution I: The problem and the law. Robert L. Glicksman and George Cameron Coggins, 35 U.Kan.L.Rev. 75 (1986).

United States Supreme Court

State regulation or control not preempted, except in cases of actual conflict between federal and state law, see California Coastal Com'n v. Granite Rock Co., Cal.1987, 107 S.Ct. 1419, 480 U.S. 572, 94 L.Ed.2d 577.

Consistency determination, phrase "directly affecting" in subsec. (c), see Secretary of the Interior v. California, 1984, 104 S.Ct. 656, 78 L.Ed.2d 496.

Injunction, sale of Pacific tracts for oil and gas leasing, stay pending determination of whether sale was activity "directly affecting" coastal zone, Clark v. California, 1983, 104 S.Ct. 540, 78 L.Ed.2d 376, motion denied 164 S.Ct. 968, 79 L.Ed.2d 207.

§ 1456a. Coastal Zone Management Fund [CZMA § 308]

(a)(1) The obligations of any coastal state or unit of general purpose local government to repay loans made pursuant to this section as in effect before November 5, 1990, and any repayment schedule established pursuant to this chapter as in effect before November 5, 1990, are not altered by any provision of this chapter. Such loans shall be repaid under authority of this subsection and the Secretary may issue regulations governing such repayment. If the Secretary finds that any coastal state or unit of local government is unable to meet its obligations pursuant to this subsection because the actual increases in employment and related population resulting from coastal energy activity and the facilities associated with such activity do not provide adequate revenues to enable such State or unit to meet such obligations in accordance with the appropriate repayment schedule, the Secretary shall, after review of the information submitted by such State or unit, take any of the following actions:

(A) Modify the terms and conditions of such loan.

(B) Refinance the loan.

(C) Recommend to the Congress that legislation be enacted to forgive the loan.

(2) Loan repayments made pursuant to this subsection shall be retained by the Secretary as offsetting collections, and shall be deposited into the Coastal Zone Management Fund established under subsection (b) of this section.

(b)(1) The Secretary shall establish and maintain a fund, to be known as the "Coastal Zone Management Fund", which shall consist of amounts retained and deposited into the Fund under subsection (a) of this section and fees deposited into the Fund under section 1456(i)(3) of this title.

(2) Subject to amounts provided in appropriation Acts, amounts in the Fund shall be available to the Secretary for use for the following:

(A) Expenses incident to the administration of this chapter, in an amount not to exceed—

(i) $5,000,000 for fiscal year 1991;

(ii) $5,225,000 for fiscal year 1992;

(iii) $5,460,125 for fiscal year 1993;

(iv) $5,705,830 for fiscal year 1994; and

(v) $5,962,593 for fiscal year 1995.

(B) After use under subparagraph (A)—

(i) projects to address management issues which are regional in scope, including interstate projects;

(ii) demonstration projects which have high potential for improving coastal zone management, especially at the local level;

(iii) emergency grants to State coastal zone management agencies to address unforeseen or disaster-related circumstances;

(iv) appropriate awards recognizing excellence in coastal zone management as provided in section 1460 of this title;

(v) program development grants as authorized by section 1454 of this title; and

(vi) to provide financial support to coastal states for use for investigating and applying the public trust doctrine to implement State management programs approved under section 1455 of this title.

(3) On December 1 of each year, the Secretary shall transmit to the Congress an annual report on the Fund, including the balance of the Fund and an itemization of all deposits into and disbursements from the Fund in the preceding fiscal year.

(Pub.L. 89–454, Title III, § 308, as added July 26, 1976, Pub.L. 94–370, § 7, 90 Stat. 1019, and amended Sept. 18, 1978, Pub.L. 95–372, Title V, §§ 501, 503(a)–(d), 92 Stat. 690, 692, 693; Oct. 17, 1980, Pub.L. 96–464, § 7, 94 Stat. 2064; April 7, 1986, Pub.L. 99–272, Title VI, § 6047, 100 Stat. 128; Nov. 5, 1990, Pub.L. 101–508, Title VI, § 6209, 104 Stat. 1388–308; Nov. 4, 1992, Pub.L. 102–587, Title II, § 2205(b)(1)(A), (B), (15)–(18), 106 Stat. 5050, 5052.)

CROSS REFERENCES

Access to books and records of recipients of grants or financial assistance for audit and examination, see section 1459 of this title.

Authorization of appropriations, see section 1464 of this title.

Coastal zone management reports, see section 1462 of this title.

Criteria established under subsec. (g)(1) of this section used to determine eligibility for interstate grants, see section 1456b of this title.

"Fund" as used in this chapter as meaning the Coastal Energy Impact Fund, see section 1453 of this title.

CODE OF FEDERAL REGULATIONS

Coastal energy impact program, see 15 CFR 931.1 et seq.

LIBRARY REFERENCES

Health and Environment ⚷25.5(4).
C.J.S. Health and Environment § 91 et seq.

§ 1456b. Coastal zone enhancement grants [CZMA § 309]

(a) Coastal zone enhancement objective defined

For purposes of this section, the term "coastal zone enhancement objective" means any of the following objectives:

(1) Protection, restoration, or enhancement of the existing coastal wetlands base, or creation of new coastal wetlands.

(2) Preventing or significantly reducing threats to life and destruction of property by eliminating development and redevelopment in high-hazard areas, managing development in other hazard areas, and anticipating and managing the effects of potential sea level rise and Great Lakes level rise.

(3) Attaining increased opportunities for public access, taking into account current and future public access needs, to coastal areas of recreational, historical, aesthetic, ecological, or cultural value.

(4) Reducing marine debris entering the Nation's coastal and ocean environment by managing uses and activities that contribute to the entry of such debris.

(5) Development and adoption of procedures to assess, consider, and control cumulative and secondary impacts of coastal growth and development, including the collective effect on various individual uses or activities on coastal resources, such as coastal wetlands and fishery resources.

(6) Preparing and implementing special area management plans for important coastal areas.

(7) Planning for the use of ocean resources.

(8) Adoption of procedures and enforceable policies to help facilitate the siting of energy facilities and Government facilities and energy-related activities and Government activities which may be of greater than local significance.

(b) Limits on grants

Subject to the limitations and goals established in this section, the Secretary may make grants to coastal states to provide funding for development and submission for Federal approval of program changes that support attainment of one or more coastal zone enhancement objectives.

(c) Evaluation of State proposals by Secretary

The Secretary shall evaluate and rank State proposals for funding under this section, and make funding awards based on those proposals, taking into account the criteria established by the Secretary under subsection (d) of this section. The Secretary shall ensure that funding decisions under this section take into consideration the fiscal and technical needs of proposing States and the overall merit of each proposal in terms of benefits to the public.

(d) Promulgation of regulations by Secretary

Within 12 months following November 5, 1990, and consistent with the notice and participation requirements established in section 1463 of this title the Secretary shall promulgate regulations concerning coastal zone enhancement grants that establish—

(1) specific and detailed criteria that must be addressed by a coastal state (including the State's priority needs for improvement as identified by the Secretary after careful consultation with the State) as part of the State's development and implementation of coastal zone enhancement objectives;

(2) administrative or procedural rules or requirements as necessary to facilitate the development and implementation of such objectives by coastal states; and

(3) other funding award criteria as are necessary or appropriate to ensure that evaluations of proposals, and decisions to award funding, under this section are based on objective standards applied fairly and equitably to those proposals.

(e) No State contribution required

A State shall not be required to contribute any portion of the cost of any proposal for which funding is awarded under this section.

(f) Funding

Beginning in fiscal year 1991, not less than 10 percent and not more than 20 percent of the amounts appropriated to implement sections 1455 and 1455a of this title shall be retained by the Secretary for use in implementing this section, up to a maximum of $10,000,000 annually.

(g) Eligibility; suspension of State for noncompliance

If the Secretary finds that the State is not undertaking the actions committed to under the terms of the grant, the Secretary shall suspend the State's eligibility for further funding under this section for at least one year.

(Pub.L. 89–454, Title III, § 309, as added July 26, 1976, Pub.L. 94–370, § 8, 90 Stat. 1028, and amended Oct. 17, 1980, Pub.L. 96–464, § 8, 94 Stat. 2064; Nov. 5, 1990, Pub.L. 101–508, Title VI, § 6210, 104 Stat. 1388–309; Nov. 4, 1992, Pub.L. 102–587, Title II, § 2205(b)(1)(B), 106 Stat. 5050.)

Codification

Section 6210 of Pub.L. 101–508 directed the amendment of section 309 of the Coastal Zone Management Act of 1972 (16 U.S.C. 1452b). Section 309 of such Act is this section, and such amendment was executed to this section as the probable intent of Congress.

CROSS REFERENCES

Authorization of appropriations, see section 1464 of this title.

WEST'S FEDERAL PRACTICE MANUAL

Preservation of coastal waters, see § 4389.50.

§ 1456c. Technical Assistance [CZMA § 310]

(a) The Secretary shall conduct a program of technical assistance and management-oriented research necessary to support the development and implementation of State coastal management program amendments under section 1456b of this title, and appropriate to the furtherance of international cooperative efforts and technical assistance in coastal zone management. Each department, agency, and instrumentality of the executive branch of the Federal Government may assist the Secretary, on a reimbursable basis or otherwise, in carrying out the purposes of this section, including the furnishing of information to the extent permitted by law, the transfer of personnel with their consent and without prejudice to their position and rating, and the performance of any research, study, and technical assistance which does not interfere with the performance of the primary duties of such department, agency, or instrumentality. The Secretary may enter into contracts or other arrangements with any qualified person for the purposes of carrying out this subsection.

(b)(1) The Secretary shall provide for the coordination of technical assistance, studies, and research activities under this section with any other such activities that are conducted by or subject to the authority of the Secretary.

(2) The Secretary shall make the results of research and studies conducted pursuant to this section available to coastal states in the form of technical assistance publications, workshops, or other means appropriate.

(3) The Secretary shall consult with coastal states on a regular basis regarding the development and implementation of the program established by this section.

(Pub.L. 89–454, Title III, § 310, as added Nov. 5, 1990, Pub.L. 101–508, Title VI, § 6211, 104 Stat. 1388–311.)

Prior Provisions

A prior section 1456c, Pub.L. 89–454, Title III, § 310, as added Pub.L. 94–370, § 9, July 26, 1976, 90 Stat. 1029, which related to research and technical assistance for coastal zone management, was repealed by Pub.L. 99–272, Title VI, § 6045(1), Apr. 7, 1986, 100 Stat. 127.

§ 1457. Public hearings [CZMA § 311]

All public hearings required under this chapter must be announced at least thirty days prior to the hearing date. At the time of the announcement, all agency materials pertinent to the hearings, including documents, studies, and other data, must be made available to the public for review and study. As similar materials are subsequently developed, they shall be made available to the public as they become available to the agency.

(Pub.L. 89–454, Title III, § 311, formerly § 308, as added Oct. 27, 1972, Pub.L. 92–583, 86 Stat. 1287, and renumbered July 26, 1976, Pub.L. 94–370, § 7, 90 Stat. 1019.)

CODE OF FEDERAL REGULATIONS

Public hearings, see 15 CFR 923.58 et seq.

LIBRARY REFERENCES

Health and Environment ⟹25.5(9).
C.J.S. Health and Environment § 65 et seq.

§ 1458. Review of performance [CZMA § 312]

(a) Evaluation of adherence with terms of grants

The Secretary shall conduct a continuing review of the performance of coastal states with respect to coastal management. Each review shall include a written evaluation with an assessment and detailed findings concerning the extent to which the state has implemented and enforced the program approved by the Secretary, addressed the coastal management needs identified in section 1452(2)(A) through (K) of this title, and adhered to the terms of any grant, loan, or cooperative agreement funded under this chapter.

(b) Public comments; notice of public meetings; reports

In evaluating a coastal state's performance, the Secretary shall conduct the evaluation in an open and public manner, and provide full opportunity for public participation, including holding public meetings in the State being evaluated and providing opportunities for the submission of written and oral comments by the public. The Secretary shall provide the public with at least 45 days' notice of such public meetings by placing a notice in the Federal Register, by publication of timely notices in newspapers of general circulation within the State being evaluated, and by communications with persons and organizations known to be interested in the evaluation. Each evaluation shall be prepared in report form and shall include written responses to the written comments received during the evaluation process. The final report of the evaluation shall be completed within 120 days after the last public meeting held in the State being evaluated. Copies of the evaluation shall be immediately provided to all persons and organizations participating in the evaluation process.

(c) Suspension of financial assistance for noncompliance; notification of Governor by Secretary; length of suspension

(1) The Secretary may suspend payment of any portion of financial assistance extended to any coastal state under this chapter, and may withdraw any unexpended portion of such assistance, if the Secretary determines that the coastal state is failing to adhere to (A) the management program or a State plan developed to manage a national estuarine reserve established under section 1461 of this title, or a portion of the program or plan approved by the Secretary, or (B) the terms of any grant or cooperative agreement funded under this chapter.

(2) Financial assistance may not be suspended under paragraph (1) unless the Secretary provides the Governor of the coastal state with—

(A) written specifications and a schedule for the actions that should be taken by the State in order that such suspension of financial assistance may be withdrawn; and

(B) written specifications stating how those funds from the suspended financial assistance shall be expended by the coastal state to take the actions referred to in subparagraph (A).

(3) The suspension of financial assistance may not last for less than 6 months or more than 36 months after the date of suspension.

(d) Withdrawal of approval of program; withdrawal of financial assistance

The Secretary shall withdraw approval of the management program of any coastal state and shall withdraw financial assistance available to that State under this chapter as well as any unexpended portion of such assistance, if the Secretary determines that the coastal state has failed to take the actions referred to in subsection (c)(2)(A) of this section.

(e) Notice and hearing

Management program approval and financial assistance may not be withdrawn under subsection (d) of this section, unless the Secretary gives the coastal state notice of the proposed withdrawal and an opportunity for a public hearing on the proposed action. Upon the withdrawal of management program approval under this subsection (d) of this section, the Secretary shall provide the coastal state with written specifications of the actions that should be taken, or not engaged in, by the state in order that such withdrawal may be canceled by the Secretary.

(f) Repealed. Pub.L. 101–508, Title VI, § 6212(d), Nov. 5, 1990, 104 Stat. 1388—311.

(Pub.L. 89–454, Title III, § 312, formerly § 309, as added Oct. 27, 1972, Pub.L. 92–583, 86 Stat. 1287, renumbered and amended July 26, 1976, Pub.L. 94–370, §§ 7, 10, 90 Stat. 1019, 1029; Oct. 17, 1980, Pub.L. 96–464, § 9(a), 94 Stat. 2065; April 7, 1986, Pub.L. 99–272, Title VI, § 6043(a), 100 Stat. 124; Nov. 5, 1990, Pub.L. 101–508, Title VI, §§ 6212, 6216(b), 104 Stat. 1388–311, 1388–314; Nov. 4, 1992, Pub.L. 102–587, Title II, § 2205(b)(1)(A), (C), 106 Stat. 5050.)

CROSS REFERENCES

Coastal zone management reports, see section 1462 of this title.

CODE OF FEDERAL REGULATIONS

Approved management programs, termination of, see 15 CFR 923.80 et seq.

LIBRARY REFERENCES

Health and Environment ⟹25.15.
C.J.S. Health and Environment § 82 et seq.

§ 1459. Records and audit [CZMA § 313]

(a) Maintenance of records by recipients of grants or financial assistance

Each recipient of a grant under this chapter or of financial assistance under section 1456a of this title, as in effect before November 5, 1990, shall keep such records as the Secretary shall prescribe, including records which fully disclose the amount and disposition of the funds received under the grant and of the proceeds of such assistance, the total cost of the project or undertaking supplied by other sources, and such other records as will facilitate an effective audit.

(b) Access by Secretary and Comptroller General to records, books, etc., of recipients of grants or financial assistance for audit and examination

The Secretary and the Comptroller General of the United States, or any of their duly authorized representatives, shall—

(1) after any grant is made under this chapter or any financial assistance is provided under section 1456a of this title, as in effect before November 5, 1990; and

(2) until the expiration of 3 years after—

(A) completion of the project, program, or other undertaking for which such grant was made or used, or

(B) repayment of the loan or guaranteed indebtedness for which such financial assistance was provided,

have access for purposes of audit and examination to any record, book, document, and paper which belongs to or is used or controlled by, any recipient of the grant funds or any person who entered into any transaction relating to such financial assistance and which is pertinent for purposes of determining if the grant funds or the proceeds of such financial assistance are being, or were, used in accordance with the provisions of this chapter.

(Pub.L. 89–454, Title III, § 313, formerly § 310, as added Oct. 27, 1972, Pub.L. 92–583, 86 Stat. 1287, renumbered and amended July 26, 1976, Pub.L. 94–370, §§ 7, 11, 90 Stat. 1019, 1030; Nov. 4, 1992, Pub.L. 102–587, Title II, § 2205(b)(19), 106 Stat. 5052.)

Codification

Another section 313 of Pub.L. 89–454, Title III, as added Pub.L. 101–508, Title VI, § 6213, Nov. 5, 1990, 104 Stat. 1388—312, is classified to section 1460 of this title, set out post.

CROSS REFERENCES

Financial assistance under coastal energy impact program subject to audit, see section 1456a of this title.

§ 1460. Walter B. Jones excellence in coastal zone management awards [CZMA § 314]

(a) Establishment

The Secretary shall, using sums in the Coastal Zone Management Fund established under section 1456a of this title and other amounts available to carry out this chapter (other than amounts appropriated to carry out sections 1454, 1455, 1455a, 1456, 1456c, and 1461 of this title), implement a program to promote excellence in coastal zone management by identifying and acknowledging outstanding accomplishments in the field.

(b) Annual selection of recipients

The Secretary shall select annually—

(1) one individual, other than an employee or officer of the Federal Government, whose contribution to the field of coastal zone management has been the most significant;

(2) 5 local governments which have made the most progress in developing and implementing the coastal zone management principles embodied in this chapter; and

(3) up to 10 graduate students whose academic study promises to contribute materially to development of new or improved approaches to coastal zone management.

(c) Solicitation of nominations from coastal states; consultation with experts

In making selections under subsection (b)(2) of this section the Secretary shall solicit nominations from the coastal states, and shall consult with experts in local government planning and land use.

(d) Solicitation of nominations from coastal states and the National Sea Grant College Program

In making selections under subsection (b)(3) of this section the Secretary shall solicit nominations from coastal states and the National Sea Grant College Program.

(e) Funding; types of awards

Using sums in the Coastal Zone Management Fund established under section 1456a of this title and other amounts available to carry out this chapter (other than amounts appropriated to carry out sections 1454, 1455, 1455a, 1456, 1456c, and 1461 of this title), the Secretary shall establish and execute appropriate awards, to be known as the "Walter B. Jones Awards," including—

(1) cash awards in an amount not to exceed $5,000 each;

(2) research grants; and

(3) public ceremonies to acknowledge such awards.

(Pub.L. 89–454, Title III, § 314, formerly § 313, as added Nov. 5, 1990, Pub.L. 101–508, Title VI, § 6213, 104 Stat. 1388–312, renumbered § 314 and amended Nov. 4, 1992, Pub.L. 102–587, Title II, § 2205(b)(20), 106 Stat. 5052.)

Codification

Another section 313 of Pub.L. 89–454, Title III, formerly 310, as added Pub.L. 92–583, Oct. 27, 1972, 86 Stat. 1287, renumbered and amended Pub.L. 94–370, §§ 7, 11, July 26, 1976, 90 Stat. 1019, 1030, is classified to section 1459 of this title, set out ante.

Prior Provisions

A prior section 1460, Pub.L. 89–454, Title III, § 314, formerly § 311, as added Pub.L. 92–583, Oct. 27, 1972, 86 Stat. 1287, and renumbered Pub.L. 94–370, § 7, July 26, 1976, 90 Stat. 1019, which related to the establishment of the Coastal Zone Management Advisory Committee, was repealed by Pub.L. 99–272, Title VI, § 6045(2), Apr. 7, 1986, 100 Stat. 127.

§ 1461. National Estuarine Research Reserve System [CZMA § 315]

(a) Establishment of System

There is established the National Estuarine Research Reserve System (hereinafter referred to in this section as the "System") that consists of—

(1) each estuarine sanctuary designated under this section as in effect before April 7, 1986; and

(2) each estuarine area designated as a national estuarine reserve under subsection (b) of this section.

Each estuarine sanctuary referred to in paragraph (1) is hereby designated as a national estuarine reserve.

(b) Designation of National Estuarine Reserves

After April 7, 1986, the Secretary may designate an estuarine area as a national estuarine reserve if—

(1) the Governor of the coastal state in which the area is located nominates the area for that designation; and

(2) the Secretary finds that—

(A) the area is a representative estuarine ecosystem that is suitable for long-term research and contributes to the biogeographical and typological balance of the System;

(B) the law of the coastal state provides long-term protection for reserve resources to ensure a stable environment for research;

(C) designation of the area as a reserve will serve to enhance public awareness and understanding of estuarine areas, and provide suitable opportunities for public education and interpretation; and

(D) the coastal state in which the area is located has complied with the requirements of any regulations issued by the Secretary to implement this section.

(c) Estuarine Research Guidelines

The Secretary shall develop guidelines for the conduct of research within the System that shall include—

(1) a mechanism for identifying, and establishing priorities among, the coastal management issues that should be addressed through coordinated research within the System;

(2) the establishment of common research principles and objectives to guide the development of research programs within the System;

(3) the identification of uniform research methodologies which will ensure comparability of data, the broadest application of research results, and the maximum use of the System for research purposes;

(4) the establishment of performance standards upon which the effectiveness of the research efforts and the value of reserves within the System in addressing the coastal management issues identified in paragraph (1) may be measured; and

(5) the consideration of additional sources of funds for estuarine research than the funds authorized under this chapter, and strategies for encouraging the use of such funds within the System, with particular emphasis on mechanisms established under subsection (d) of this section.

In developing the guidelines under this section, the Secretary shall consult with prominent members of the estuarine research community.

(d) Promotion and coordination of Estuarine research

The Secretary shall take such action as is necessary to promote and coordinate the use of the System for research purposes including—

(1) requiring that the National Oceanic and Atmospheric Administration, in conducting or supporting estuarine research, give priority consideration to research that uses the System; and

(2) consulting with other Federal and State agencies to promote use of one or more reserves within the System by such agencies when conducting estuarine research.

(e) Financial assistance

(1) The Secretary may, in accordance with such rules and regulations as the Secretary shall promulgate, make grants—

(A) to a coastal state—

(i) for purposes of acquiring such lands and waters, and any property interests therein, as are necessary to ensure the appropriate long-term management of an area as a national estuarine reserve,

(ii) for purposes of operating or managing a national estuarine reserve and constructing appropriate reserve facilities, or

(iii) for purposes of conducting educational or interpretive activities; and

(B) to any coastal state or public or private person for purposes of supporting research and monitoring within a national estuarine reserve that are consistent with the research guidelines developed under subsection (c) of this section.

(2) Financial assistance provided under paragraph (1) shall be subject to such terms and conditions as the Secretary considers necessary or appropriate to protect the interests of the United States, including requiring coastal states to execute suitable title documents setting forth the property interest or interests of the United States in any lands and waters acquired in whole or part with such financial assistance.

(3)(A) The amount of the financial assistance provided under paragraph (1)(A)(i) with respect to the acquisition of lands and waters, or interests therein, for any one national estuarine reserve may not exceed an amount equal to 50 percent of the costs of the lands, waters, and interests therein or $5,000,000, whichever amount is less.

(B) The amount of the financial assistance provided under paragraph (1)(A)(ii) and (iii) and paragraph (1)(B) may not exceed 70 percent of the costs incurred to achieve the purposes described in those paragraphs with respect to a reserve; except that the amount of the financial assistance provided under paragraph (1)(A)(iii) may be up to 100 percent of any costs for activities that benefit the entire System.

(f) Evaluation of System performance

(1) The Secretary shall periodically evaluate the operation and management of each national estuarine reserve, including education and interpretive activities, and the research being conducted within the reserve.

(2) If evaluation under paragraph (1) reveals that the operation and management of the reserve is deficient, or that the research being conducted within the reserve is not consistent with the research guidelines developed under subsection (c) of this section, the Secretary may suspend the eligibility of that reserve for financial assistance under subsection (e) of this section until the deficiency or inconsistency is remedied.

(3) The Secretary may withdraw the designation of an estuarine area as a national estuarine reserve if evaluation under paragraph (1) reveals that—

(A) the basis for any one or more of the findings made under subsection (b)(2) of this section regarding that area no longer exists; or

(B) a substantial portion of the research conducted within the area, over a period of years, has not been consistent with the research guidelines developed under subsection (c) of this section.

(g) Report

The Secretary shall include in the report required under section 1462 of this title information regarding—

(1) new designations of national estuarine reserves;

(2) any expansion of existing national estuarine reserves;

(3) the status of the research program being conducted within the System; and

(4) a summary of the evaluations made under subsection (f) of this section.

(Pub.L. 89–454, Title III, § 315, formerly § 312, as added Oct. 27, 1972, Pub.L. 92–583, 86 Stat. 1288, renumbered and amended July 26, 1976, Pub.L. 94–370, §§ 7, 12, 90 Stat. 1019, 1030; Oct. 17, 1980, Pub.L. 96–464, § 11, 94 Stat. 2067; April 7, 1986, Pub.L. 99–272, Title VI, § 6044, 100 Stat. 125; Nov. 5, 1990, Pub.L. 101–508, Title VI, § 6214, 104 Stat. 1388–313; Nov. 4, 1992, Pub.L. 102–587, Title II, § 2205(b)(1)(A), (B), (21), (22), 106 Stat. 5050, 5052.)

CODE OF FEDERAL REGULATIONS

Designation of National Estuarine Sanctuaries, see 15 CFR 921.30 et seq.
National estuarine sanctuary program regulations, see 15 CFR 921.1 et seq.
Potential research projects, see 15 CFR 921.41 et seq.
Program evaluation, see 15 CFR 921.34 et seq.

§ 1462. Coastal zone management reports [CZMA § 316]

(a) Biennial reports

The Secretary shall consult with the Congress on a regular basis concerning the administration of this chapter and shall prepare and submit to the President for transmittal to the Congress a report summarizing the administration of this chapter during each period of two consecutive fiscal years. Each report, which shall be transmitted to the Congress not later than April 1 of the year following the close of the biennial period to which it pertains, shall include, but not be restricted to (1) an identification of the state programs approved pursuant to this chapter during the preceding Federal fiscal year and a description of those programs; (2) a listing of the states participating in the provisions of this chapter and a description of the status of each state's programs and its accomplishments during the preceding Federal fiscal year; (3) an itemization of the allocation of funds to the various coastal states and a break-down of the major projects and areas on which these funds were expended; (4) an identification of any state programs which have been reviewed and disapproved, and a statement of the reasons for such action; (5) a summary of evaluation findings prepared in accordance with subsection (a) of section 1458 of this title, and a description of any sanctions imposed under subsections (c) and (d) of section 1458 of this title; (6) a listing of all activities and projects which, pursuant to the provisions of subsection (c) or subsection (d) of section 1456 of this title, are not consistent with an applicable approved state management program; (7) a summary of the regulations issued by the Secretary or in effect during the preceding Federal fiscal year; (8) a summary of a coordinated national strategy and program for the Nation's coastal zone including identification and discussion of Federal, regional, state, and local responsibilities and functions therein; (9) a summary of outstanding problems arising in the administration of this chapter in order of priority; (10) a description of the economic, environmental, and social consequences of energy activity affecting the coastal zone and an evaluation of the effectiveness of financial assistance under section 1456a of this title in dealing with such consequences; (11) a description and evaluation of applicable interstate and regional planning and coordination mechanisms developed by the coastal states; (12) a summary and evaluation of the research, studies, and training conducted in support of coastal zone management; and (13) such other information as may be appropriate.

(b) Recommendations for legislation

The report required by subsection (a) of this section shall contain such recommendations for additional legislation as the Secretary deems necessary to achieve the objectives of this chapter and enhance its effective operation.

(c) Review of other federal programs; report to Congress

(1) The Secretary shall conduct a systematic review of Federal programs, other than this chapter, that affect coastal resources for purposes of identifying conflicts between the objectives and administration of such programs and the purposes and policies of this chapter. Not later than 1 year after October 17, 1980, the Secretary shall notify each Federal agency having appropriate jurisdiction of any conflict between its program and the purposes and policies of this chapter identified as a result of such review.

(2) The Secretary shall promptly submit a report to the Congress consisting of the information required under paragraph (1) of this subsection. Such report shall include recommendations for changes necessary to resolve existing conflicts among Federal laws and programs that affect the uses of coastal resources.

(Pub.L. 89–454, Title III, § 316, formerly § 313, as added Oct. 27, 1972, Pub.L. 92–583, 86 Stat. 1288, renumbered and amended July 26, 1976, Pub.L. 94–370, §§ 7, 13, 90 Stat. 1019, 1030; Oct. 17, 1980, Pub.L. 96–464, § 10, 94 Stat. 2066; Nov. 4, 1992, Pub.L. 102–587, Title II, § 2205(b)(23), 106 Stat. 5052.)

§ 1463. Rules and regulations [CZMA § 317]

The Secretary shall develop and promulgate, pursuant to section 553 of title 5, after notice and opportunity for full participation by relevant Federal agencies, state agencies, local governments, regional organizations, port authorities, and other interested parties, both public and private, such rules and regulations as may be necessary to carry out the provisions of this chapter.

(Pub.L. 89–454, Title III, § 317, formerly § 314, as added Oct. 27, 1972, Pub.L. 92–583, 86 Stat. 1288, and renumbered July 26, 1976, Pub.L. 94–370, § 7, 90 Stat. 1019.)

§ 1463a. Omitted

§ 1463b. National Coastal Resources Research and Development Institute

(a) Establishment by Secretary; administration

The Secretary of Commerce shall provide for the establishment of a National Coastal Resources Research and Development Institute (hereinafter in this section referred to as the "Institute") to be administered by the Oregon State Marine Science Center.

(b) Purposes of Institute

The Institute shall conduct research and carry out educational and demonstration projects designed to promote the efficient and responsible development of ocean and coastal resources, including arctic resources. Such projects shall be based on biological, geological, genetic, economic and other scientific research applicable to the purposes of this section and shall include studies on the economic diversification and environmental protection of the Nation's coastal areas.

(c) Determination of Institute policies

(1) The policies of the Institute shall be determined by a Board of Governors composed of—

(A) two representatives appointed by the Governor of Oregon;

(B) one representative appointed by the Governor of Alaska;

(C) one representative appointed by the Governor of Washington;

(D) one representative appointed by the Governor of California; and

(E) one representative appointed by the Governor of Hawaii.

(2) Such policies shall include the selection, on a nationally competitive basis, of the research, projects, and studies to be supported by the Institute in accordance with the purposes of this section.

(d) Establishment of Advisory Council; functions and composition

(1) The Board of Governors shall establish an Advisory Council composed of specialists in ocean and coastal resources from the academic community.

(2) To the maximum extent practicable, the Advisory Council shall be composed of such specialists from every coastal region of the Nation.

(3) The Advisory Council shall provide such advice to the Board of Governors as such Board shall request, including recommendations regarding the support of research, projects, and studies in accordance with the purposes of this section.

(e) Administration of Institute

The Institute shall be administered by a Director who shall be appointed by the Chancellor of the Oregon Board of Higher Education in consultation with the Board of Governors.

(f) Evaluation of Institute by Secretary

The Secretary of Commerce shall conduct an ongoing evaluation of the activities of the Institute to ensure that funds received by the Institute under this section are used in a manner consistent with the provisions of this section.

(g) Report to Secretary

The Institute shall report to the Secretary of Commerce on its activities within 2 years after July 17, 1984.

(h) Access to Institute books, records and documents

The Comptroller General of the United States, and any of his duly authorized representatives, shall have access, for the purpose of audit and examination, to any books, documents, papers and records of the Institute that are pertinent to the funds received under this section.

(i) Status of Institute employees

Employees of the Institute shall not, by reason of such employment, be considered to be employees of the Federal Government for any purpose.

(j) Authorization of appropriations

For the purposes of this section, there are authorized to be appropriated in each fiscal year $5,000,000, commencing with fiscal year 1985.

(July 17, 1984, Pub.L. 98–364, title II, § 201, 98 Stat. 443.)

Codification

This section was not enacted as part of the Coastal Zone Management Act of 1972, which comprises this chapter.

§ 1464. Authorization of appropriations [CZMA § 318]

(a) Sums appropriated to Secretary

There are authorized to be appropriated to the Secretary—

(1) such sums, not to exceed $750,000 for each of the fiscal years occurring during the period beginning October 1, 1990, and ending September 30, 1993, as may be necessary for grants under section 1454 of this title, to remain available until expended;

(2) such sums, not to exceed $42,000,000 for the fiscal year ending September 30, 1991, $48,890,000 for the fiscal year ending September 30, 1992, $58,870,000 for the fiscal year ending September 30, 1993, $67,930,000 for the fiscal year ending September 30, 1994, and $90,090,000 for the fiscal year ending September 30, 1995, as may be necessary for grants under sections 1455, 1455A, and 1456b of this title, to remain available until expended;

(3) such sums, not to exceed $6,000,000 for the fiscal year ending September 30, 1991, $6,270,000 for the fiscal year ending September 30, 1992, $6,552,000 for the fiscal year ending September 30, 1993, $6,847,000 for the fiscal year ending September 30, 1994, and $7,155,000 for the fiscal year ending September 30, 1995, as may be necessary for grants under section 1461 of this title, to remain available until expended; and

(4) such sums, not to exceed $10,000,000 for each of the fiscal years occurring during the period beginning October 1, 1990, and ending September 30, 1995, as may be necessary for activities under section 1456c of this title and for administrative expenses incident to the administration of this chapter; except that expenditures for such administrative expenses shall not exceed $5,000,000 in any such fiscal year.

(b) Sums appropriated to Fund

There are authorized to be appropriated until October 1, 1986, to the Fund, such sums, not to exceed $800,000,000, for the purposes of carrying out the provisions of section 1456a of this title, other than subsection (b), of which not to exceed $150,000,000 shall be for purposes of subsections (c)(1), (c)(2) and (c)(3) of such section.

(c) Limitations

Federal funds received from other sources shall not be used to pay a coastal state's share of costs under section 1455 or 1456b of this title.

(d) Reversion to Secretary of unobligated State funds; availability of funds

The amount of any grant, or portion of a grant, made to a State under any section of this chapter which is not obligated by such State during the fiscal year, or during the second fiscal year after the fiscal year, for which it was first authorized to be obligated by such State shall revert to the Secretary. The Secretary shall add such reverted amount to those funds available for grants under the section for such reverted amount was originally made available.

(Pub.L. 89–454, Title III, § 318, formerly § 315, as added Oct. 27, 1972, Pub.L. 92–583, 86 Stat. 1289, amended Jan. 2, 1975, Pub.L. 93–612, § 1(3), 88 Stat. 1974, renumbered and amended July 26, 1976, Pub.L. 94–370, §§ 7, 14, 90 Stat. 1019, 1031; Sept. 18, 1978, Pub.L. 95–372, Title V, §§ 502, 503(e), (f), 92 Stat. 692, 693; Oct. 17, 1980, Pub.L. 96–464, § 13, 94 Stat. 2070; April 7, 1986, Pub.L. 99–272, Title VI, § 6046, 100 Stat. 127; Nov. 7, 1986, Pub.L. 99–626, § 7, 100 Stat. 3506; Nov. 5, 1990, Pub.L. 101–508, Title VI, § 6215, 104 Stat. 1388–313.)

ENDANGERED SPECIES

ENDANGERED SPECIES ACT OF 1973 [ESA § ___]

(16 U.S.C.A. §§ 1531 to 1544)

CHAPTER 35—ENDANGERED SPECIES

Sec.

1531. Congressional findings and declaration of purposes and policy.
   (a) Findings.
   (b) Purposes.
   (c) Policy.
1532. Definitions.
1533. Determination of endangered species and threatened species.
   (a) Generally.
   (b) Basis for determinations.
   (c) Lists.
   (d) Protective regulations.
   (e) Similarity of appearance cases.
   (f) Recovery plans.
   (g) Monitoring.
   (h) Agency guidelines; publication in Federal Register; scope; proposals and amendments; notice and opportunity for comments.
   (i) Submission to State agency of justification for regulations inconsistent with State agency's comments or petition.
1534. Land acquisition.
   (a) Implementation of conservation program; authorization of Secretary and Secretary of Agriculture.
   (b) Availability of funds for acquisition of lands, waters, etc.
1535. Cooperation with States.
   (a) Generally.
   (b) Management agreements.
   (c) Cooperative agreements.
   (d) Allocation of funds.
   (e) Review of State programs.
   (f) Conflicts between Federal and State laws.
   (g) Transition.
   (h) Regulations.
   (i) Appropriations.
1536. Interagency cooperation.
   (a) Federal agency actions and consultations.
   (b) Opinion of Secretary.
   (c) Biological assessment.
   (d) Limitation on commitment of resources.
   (e) Endangered Species Committee.
   (f) Promulgation of regulations; form and contents of exemption application.
   (g) Application for exemption; report to Committee.
   (h) Grant of exemption.
   (i) Review by Secretary of State; violation of international treaty or other international obligation of United States.
   (j) Exemption for national security reasons.
   (k) Exemption decision not considered major Federal action; environmental impact statement.

Sec.

1536. Interagency cooperation.
   (*l*) Committee order granting exemption; cost of mitigation and enhancement measures; report by applicant to Council on Environmental Quality.
   (m) Notice requirement for citizen suits not applicable.
   (n) Judicial review.
   (*o*) Exemption as providing exception on taking of endangered species.
   (p) Exemptions in Presidentially declared disaster areas.
1537. International cooperation.
   (a) Financial assistance.
   (b) Encouragement of foreign programs.
   (c) Personnel.
   (d) Investigations.
1537a. Convention implementation.
   (a) Management Authority and Scientific Authority.
   (b) Management Authority functions.
   (c) Scientific Authority functions; determinations.
   (d) Reservations by the United States under Convention.
   (e) Wildlife preservation in Western Hemisphere.
1538. Prohibited acts.
   (a) Generally.
   (b) Species held in captivity or controlled environment.
   (c) Violation of Convention.
   (d) Imports and exports.
   (e) Reports.
   (f) Designation of ports.
   (g) Violations.
1539. Exceptions.
   (a) Permits.
   (b) Hardship exemptions.
   (c) Notice and review.
   (d) Permit and exemption policy.
   (e) Alaska natives.
   (f) Pre–Act endangered species parts exemption; application and certification; regulation; validity of sales contract; separability of provisions; renewal of exemption; expiration of renewal certification.
   (g) Burden of proof.
   (h) Certain antique articles; importation; port designation; application for return of articles.
   (i) Noncommercial transshipments.
   (j) Experimental populations.
1540. Penalties and enforcement.
   (a) Civil penalties.
   (b) Criminal violations.
   (c) District court jurisdiction.
   (d) Rewards and certain incidental expenses.
   (e) Enforcement.

Sec.
1540. Penalties and enforcement.
(f) Regulations.
(g) Citizen suits.
(h) Coordination with other laws.
1541. Endangered plants.
1542. Authorization of appropriations.
(a) In general.
(b) Exemption from chapter.
(c) Convention implementation.
1543. Construction with Marine Mammal Protection Act of 1972.
1544. Annual cost analysis by the Fish and Wildlife Service.

CROSS REFERENCES

Conservation of Antarctic fauna and flora—
Assessment of penalty not to preclude assessment of penalty under this chapter, see section 2407 of this title.
Conviction of offense not to preclude conviction of offense under this chapter, see section 2408 of this title.
Permit applications with respect to native mammal, bird or plant endangered or threatened submitted to appropriate Secretary, see section 2404 of this title.
Construction of this chapter with subsistence management and use provisions of Alaska National Interest Lands Conservation Act, see section 3125 of this title.
Depletion or depleted for purposes of marine mammal protection defined as case in which species or population stock listed as endangered or threatened, see section 1362 of this title.
Imminent hazard for purposes of pesticide control defined as continued use of pesticide likely to result in hazard to survival of species declared endangered or threatened, see section 136 of Title 7, Agriculture.
Licensing procedures for small hydroelectric power projects not to exempt project from requirements of this chapter, see section 2705 of this title.
Nongame fish and wildlife for purposes of fish and wildlife conservation defined as vertebrate animals not endangered or threatened, see section 2902 of this title.

§ 1531. Congressional findings and declaration of purposes and policy [ESA § 2]

(a) Findings

The Congress finds and declares that—

(1) various species of fish, wildlife, and plants in the United States have been rendered extinct as a consequence of economic growth and development untempered by adequate concern and conservation;

(2) other species of fish, wildlife, and plants have been so depleted in numbers that they are in danger of or threatened with extinction;

(3) these species of fish, wildlife, and plants are of esthetic, ecological, educational, historical, recreational, and scientific value to the Nation and its people;

(4) the United States has pledged itself as a sovereign state in the international community to conserve to the extent practicable the various species of fish or wildlife and plants facing extinction, pursuant to—

(A) migratory bird treaties with Canada and Mexico;

(B) the Migratory and Endangered Bird Treaty with Japan;

(C) the Convention on Nature Protection and Wildlife Preservation in the Western Hemisphere;

(D) the International Convention for the Northwest Atlantic Fisheries;

(E) the International Convention for the High Seas Fisheries of the North Pacific Ocean;

(F) the Convention on International Trade in Endangered Species of Wild Fauna and Flora; and

(G) other international agreements; and

(5) encouraging the States and other interested parties, through Federal financial assistance and a system of incentives, to develop and maintain conservation programs which meet national and international standards is a key to meeting the Nation's international commitments and to better safeguarding, for the benefit of all citizens, the Nation's heritage in fish, wildlife, and plants.

(b) Purposes

The purposes of this chapter are to provide a means whereby the ecosystems upon which endangered species and threatened species depend may be conserved, to provide a program for the conservation of such endangered species and threatened species, and to take such steps as may be appropriate to achieve the purposes of the treaties and conventions set forth in subsection (a) of this section.

(c) Policy

(1) It is further declared to be the policy of Congress that all Federal departments and agencies shall seek to conserve endangered species and threatened species and shall utilize their authorities in furtherance of the purposes of this chapter.

(2) It is further declared to be the policy of Congress that Federal agencies shall cooperate with State and local agencies to resolve water resource issues in concert with conservation of endangered species.

(Pub.L. 93–205, § 2, Dec. 28, 1973, 87 Stat. 884; Pub.L. 96–159, § 1, Dec. 28, 1979, 93 Stat. 1225; Pub.L. 97–304, § 9(a), Oct. 13, 1982, 96 Stat. 1426; Pub.L. 100–478, Title I, § 1013(a), Oct. 7, 1988, 102 Stat. 2315.)

Short Title

Section 1 of Pub.L. 93–205 provided: "That this Act [enacting this chapter, amending sections 460k–1, 460*l*–9, 668dd, 715i, 715s, 1362, 1371, 1372 and 1402 of this title and section 136 of title 7, Agriculture, repealing sections 668aa to 668cc–6 of this title, and enacting provisions set out as notes under this section] may be cited as the 'Endangered Species Act of 1973'."

Relationship of Other Act to Endangered Species Act of 1973

Pub.L. 102–251, Title III, § 305, Mar. 9, 1992, 106 Stat. 66, provided that: "The special areas defined in section 3(24) of the Magnuson Fishery Conservation and Management Act (16 U.S.C. 1802(24)) [section 1802(24) of this title] shall be considered places that are subject to the jurisdiction of the United States for the purposes of the Endangered Species Act of 1973 (16 U.S.C. 1531 et seq.) [this chapter]."

[Section 305 of Pub.L. 102–251 effective on the date on which the Agreement between the United States and the Union of Soviet Socialist Republics on the Maritime Boundary, signed June 1, 1990, enters into force for the United States, with authority to prescribe implementing regulations effective Mar. 9, 1992, but with no such regulation to be effective until the date on which the Agreement enters into force for the United States, see section 308 of Pub.L. 102–251, set out as a note under section 773 of this title.]

CODE OF FEDERAL REGULATIONS

Endangered and threatened wildlife and plants, see 50 CFR 17.1 et seq.

CROSS REFERENCES

Granting of permits and exemptions for taking endangered species to be conditioned on finding that such grant will be consistent with the purposes and policy set forth in this section, see section 1539 of this title.

West's Federal Forms

Complaint, see § 1713 and comment thereunder.

LAW REVIEW COMMENTARIES

American and British offshore oil development. Uisdean R. Vass. 21 Tulsa L.J. 23 (1985).

Conservation obligations under the Endangered Species Act: A case study of the Yellowstone grizzly bear. Comment, 64 U.Colo. L.Rev. 607 (1993).

Effectiveness of judicial review under the 1979 Amendment to the Endangered Species Act. 7 J. Energy L. & Pol'y 145 (1986).

Environmental claims in bankruptcy: Policy conflicts, procedural pitfalls and problematic precedent. Thomas G. Gruenert, 32 S.Tex. L.Rev. 399 (1991).

Grazing management on the public lands: Opening the process to public participation. Joseph M. Feller, 26 Land and Water L.Rev. 571 (1991).

Is the "Endangered Species Act" endangered? David P. Berschauer, 21 Sw.U.L.Rev. 991 (1992).

Protecting national park system buffer zones: Existing, proposed, and suggested authority. John W. Hiscock. 7 J.Energy L. & Pol'y 35 (1986).

Public interest and intimidation suits: A new approach. Joseph J. Brecher, 28 Santa Clara L.Rev. 105 (1988).

Regulated taking of threatened species under the Endangered Species Act. Note, 39 Hast.L.J. 399 (1988).

Sierra Club v. Clark: The government cries wolf. Keith J. Halleland. 1985, 11 Wm.Mitchell L.Rev. 969.

LIBRARY REFERENCES

Fish ⇐8, 10, 12, 14.
Game ⇐3½, 5, 7 to 10.
Health and Environment ⇐25.5.
States ⇐4.19.
United States ⇐55, 85.
C.J.S. Fish §§ 26, 28 et seq., 36, 38 et seq.
C.J.S. Game §§ 7, 10 et seq., 16 to 18.
C.J.S. Health and Environment §§ 61 to 66, 69, 71 to 73, 78 to 80, 82 to 86, 88 to 90, 94, 104, 110, 115 to 126, 128, 129, 132, 133, 135, 137 to 140, 142, 144 to 153.
C.J.S. States § 28.
C.J.S. United States §§ 71, 73, 123.

United States Supreme Court

Protection of endangered species, under this chapter, to be accorded the highest priority, see Tennessee Valley Authority v. Hill, Tenn.1978, 98 S.Ct. 2279, 437 U.S. 153, 57 L.Ed.2d 117.

§ 1532. Definitions [ESA § 3]

For the purposes of this chapter—

(1) The term "alternative courses of action" means all alternatives and thus is not limited to original project objectives and agency jurisdiction.

(2) The term "commercial activity" means all activities of industry and trade, including, but not limited to, the buying or selling of commodities and activities conducted for the purpose of facilitating such buying and selling: *Provided, however,* That it does not include exhibition of commodities by museums or similar cultural or historical organizations.

(3) The terms "conserve", "conserving", and "conservation" mean to use and the use of all methods and procedures which are necessary to bring any endangered species or threatened species to the point at which the measures provided pursuant to this chapter are no longer necessary. Such methods and procedures include, but are not limited to, all activities associated with scientific resources management such as research, census, law enforcement, habitat acquisition and maintenance, propagation, live trapping, and transplantation, and, in the extraordinary case where population pressures within a given ecosystem cannot be otherwise relieved, may include regulated taking.

(4) The term "Convention" means the Convention on International Trade in Endangered Species of Wild Fauna and Flora, signed on March 3, 1973, and the appendices thereto.

(5)(A) The term "critical habitat" for a threatened or endangered species means—

(i) the specific areas within the geographical area occupied by the species, at the time it is listed in accordance with the provisions of section 1533 of this title, on which are found those physical or biological features (I) essential to the conservation of the species and (II) which may require special management considerations or protection; and

(ii) specific areas outside the geographical area occupied by the species at the time it is listed in accordance with the provisions of section 1533 of this title, upon a determination by the Secretary that such areas are essential for the conservation of the species.

(B) Critical habitat may be established for those species now listed as threatened or endangered species for which no critical habitat has heretofore been established as set forth in subparagraph (A) of this paragraph.

(C) Except in those circumstances determined by the Secretary, critical habitat shall not include the entire geographical area which can be occupied by the threatened or endangered species.

(6) The term "endangered species" means any species which is in danger of extinction throughout all or a significant portion of its range other than a species of the Class Insecta determined by the Secretary to constitute a pest whose protection under the provisions of this chapter would present an overwhelming and overriding risk to man.

(7) The term "Federal agency" means any department, agency, or instrumentality of the United States.

(8) The term "fish or wildlife" means any member of the animal kingdom, including without limitation any mammal, fish, bird (including any migratory, nonmigratory, or endangered bird for which protection is also afforded by treaty or other international agreement), amphibian, reptile, mollusk, crustacean, arthropod or other invertebrate, and includes any part, product, egg, or offspring thereof, or the dead body or parts thereof.

(9) The term "foreign commerce" includes, among other things, any transaction—

(A) between persons within one foreign country;

(B) between persons in two or more foreign countries;

(C) between a person within the United States and a person in a foreign country; or

(D) between persons within the United States, where the fish and wildlife in question are moving in any country or countries outside the United States.

(10) The term "import" means to land on, bring into, or introduce into, or attempt to land on, bring into, or introduce into, any place subject to the jurisdiction of the United States, whether or not such landing, bringing, or introduction constitutes an importation within the meaning of the customs laws of the United States.

(11) Repealed. Pub.L. 97–304, § 4(b), Oct. 13, 1982, 96 Stat. 1420.

(12) The term "permit or license applicant" means, when used with respect to an action of a Federal agency for which exemption is sought under section 1536 of this title, any person whose application to such agency for a permit or license has been denied primarily because of the application of section 1536(a) of this title to such agency action.

(13) The term "person" means an individual, corporation, partnership, trust, association, or any other private entity; or any officer, employee, agent, department, or instrumentality of the Federal Government, of any State, municipality, or political subdivision of a State, or of any foreign government; any State, municipality, or political subdivision of a State; or any other entity subject to the jurisdiction of the United States.

(14) The term "plant" means any member of the plant kingdom, including seeds, roots and other parts thereof.

(15) The term "Secretary" means, except as otherwise herein provided, the Secretary of the Interior or the Secretary of Commerce as program responsibilities are vested pursuant to the provisions of Reorganization Plan Numbered 4 of 1970; except that with respect to the enforcement of the provisions of this chapter and the Convention which pertain to the importation or exportation of terrestrial plants, the term also means the Secretary of Agriculture.

(16) The term "species" includes any subspecies of fish or wildlife or plants, and any distinct population segment of any species of vertebrate fish or wildlife which interbreeds when mature.

(17) The term "State" means any of the several States, the District of Columbia, the Commonwealth of Puerto Rico, American Samoa, the Virgin Islands, Guam, and the Trust Territory of the Pacific Islands.

(18) The term "State agency" means any State agency, department, board, commission, or other governmental entity which is responsible for the management and conservation of fish, plant, or wildlife resources within a State.

(19) The term "take" means to harass, harm, pursue, hunt, shoot, wound, kill, trap, capture, or collect, or to attempt to engage in any such conduct.

(20) The term "threatened species" means any species which is likely to become an endangered species within the foreseeable future throughout all or a significant portion of its range.

(21) The term "United States", when used in a geographical context, includes all States.

(Pub.L. 93–205, § 3, Dec. 28, 1973, 87 Stat. 885; Pub.L. 94–359, § 5, July 12, 1976, 90 Stat. 913; Pub.L. 95–632, § 2, Nov. 10, 1978, 92 Stat. 3751; Pub.L. 96–159, § 2, Dec. 28, 1979, 93 Stat. 1225; Pub.L. 97–304, § 4(b), Oct. 13, 1982, 96 Stat. 1420; Pub.L. 100–478, Title I, § 1001, Oct. 7, 1988, 102 Stat. 2306.)

CROSS REFERENCES

Judicial review of any decision of Endangered Species Committee by any "person" as defined in this section, see section 1536 of this title.

CODE OF FEDERAL REGULATIONS

Endangered species regulations concerning terrestrial plants, see 7 CFR 355.1 et seq.

LAW REVIEW COMMENTARIES

Conservation obligations under the Endangered Species Act: A case study of the Yellowstone grizzly bear. Comment, 64 U.Colo. L.Rev. 607 (1993).

§ 1533. Determination of endangered species and threatened species [ESA § 4]

(a) Generally

(1) The Secretary shall by regulation promulgated in accordance with subsection (b) of this section determine whether any species is an endangered species or a threatened species because of any of the following factors:

(A) the present or threatened destruction, modification, or curtailment of its habitat or range;

(B) overutilization for commercial, recreational, scientific, or educational purposes;

(C) disease or predation;

(D) the inadequacy of existing regulatory mechanisms; or

(E) other natural or manmade factors affecting its continued existence.

(2) With respect to any species over which program responsibilities have been vested in the Secretary of Commerce pursuant to Reorganization Plan Numbered 4 of 1970—

(A) in any case in which the Secretary of Commerce determines that such species should—

(i) be listed as an endangered species or a threatened species, or

(ii) be changed in status from a threatened species to an endangered species,

he shall so inform the Secretary of the Interior, who shall list such species in accordance with this section;

(B) in any case in which the Secretary of Commerce determines that such species should—

(i) be removed from any list published pursuant to subsection (c) of this section, or

(ii) be changed in status from an endangered species to a threatened species,

he shall recommend such action to the Secretary of the Interior, and the Secretary of the Interior, if he concurs in the recommendation, shall implement such action; and

(C) the Secretary of the Interior may not list or remove from any list any such species, and may not change the status of any such species which are listed, without a prior favorable determination made pursuant to this section by the Secretary of Commerce.

(3) The Secretary, by regulation promulgated in accordance with subsection (b) of this section and to the maximum extent prudent and determinable—

(A) shall, concurrently with making a determination under paragraph (1) that a species is an endangered species or a threatened species, designate any habitat of such species which is then considered to be critical habitat; and

(B) may, from time-to-time thereafter as appropriate, revise such designation.

(b) Basis for determinations

(1)(A) The Secretary shall make determinations required by subsection (a)(1) of this section solely on the basis of the best scientific and commercial data available to him after conducting a review of the status of the species and after taking into account those efforts, if any, being made by any State or foreign nation, or any political subdivision of a State or foreign nation, to protect such species, whether by predator control, protection of habitat and food supply, or other conservation practices, within any area under its jurisdiction, or on the high seas.

(B) In carrying out this section, the Secretary shall give consideration to species which have been—

(i) designated as requiring protection from unrestricted commerce by any foreign nation, or pursuant to any international agreement; or

(ii) identified as in danger of extinction, or likely to become so within the foreseeable future, by any State agency or by any agency of a foreign nation that is responsible for the conservation of fish or wildlife or plants.

(2) The Secretary shall designate critical habitat, and make revisions thereto, under subsection (a)(3) of this section on the basis of the best scientific data available and after taking into consideration the economic impact, and any other relevant impact, of specifying any particular area as critical habitat. The Secretary may exclude any area from critical habitat if he determines that the benefits of such exclusion outweigh the benefits of specifying such area as part of the critical habitat, unless he determines, based on the best scientific and commercial data available, that the failure to designate such area as critical habitat will result in the extinction of the species concerned.

(3)(A) To the maximum extent practicable, within 90 days after receiving the petition of an interested person under section 553(e) of Title 5 to add a species to, or to remove a species from, either of the lists published under subsection (c) of this section, the Secretary shall make a finding as to whether the petition presents substantial scientific or commercial information indicating that the petitioned action may be warranted. If such a petition is found to present such information, the Secretary shall promptly commence a review of the status of the species concerned. The Secretary shall promptly publish each finding made under this subparagraph in the Federal Register.

(B) Within 12 months after receiving a petition that is found under subparagraph (A) to present substantial information indicating that the petitioned action may be warranted, the Secretary shall make one of the following findings:

(i) The petitioned action is not warranted, in which case the Secretary shall promptly publish such finding in the Federal Register.

(ii) The petitioned action is warranted, in which case the Secretary shall promptly publish in the Federal Register a general notice and the complete text of a proposed regulation to implement such action in accordance with paragraph (5).

(iii) The petitioned action is warranted, but that—

(I) the immediate proposal and timely promulgation of a final regulation implementing the petitioned action in accordance with paragraphs (5) and (6) is precluded by pending proposals to determine whether any species is an endangered species or a threatened species, and

(II) expeditious progress is being made to add qualified species to either of the lists published under subsection (c) of this section and to remove from such lists species for which the protections of this chapter are no longer necessary,

in which case the Secretary shall promptly publish such finding in the Federal Register, together with a description and evaluation of the reasons and data on which the finding is based.

(C)(i) A petition with respect to which a finding is made under subparagraph (B)(iii) shall be treated as a petition that is resubmitted to the Secretary under subparagraph (A) on the date of such finding and that presents substantial scientific or commercial information that the petitioned action may be warranted.

(ii) Any negative finding described in subparagraph (A) and any finding described in subparagraph (B)(i) or (iii) shall be subject to judicial review.

(iii) The Secretary shall implement a system to monitor effectively the status of all species with respect to which a finding is made under subparagraph (B)(iii) and shall make prompt use of the authority under paragraph 7 to prevent a significant risk to the well being of any such species.

(D)(i) To the maximum extent practicable, within 90 days after receiving the petition of an interested person under section 553(e) of Title 5, to revise a critical habitat designation, the Secretary shall make a finding as to whether the petition presents substantial scientific information indicating that the revision may be warranted. The Secretary shall promptly publish such finding in the Federal Register.

(ii) Within 12 months after receiving a petition that is found under clause (i) to present substantial information indicating that the requested revision may be warranted, the Secretary shall determine how he intends to proceed with the requested revision, and shall promptly publish notice of such intention in the Federal Register.

(4) Except as provided in paragraphs (5) and (6) of this subsection, the provisions of section 553 of Title 5 (relating to rulemaking procedures), shall apply to any regulation promulgated to carry out the purposes of this chapter.

(5) With respect to any regulation proposed by the Secretary to implement a determination, designation, or revision referred to in subsection (a)(1) or (3) of this section, the Secretary shall—

(A) not less than 90 days before the effective date of the regulation—

(i) publish a general notice and the complete text of the proposed regulation in the Federal Register, and

(ii) give actual notice of the proposed regulation (including the complete text of the regulation) to the State agency in each State in which the species is believed to occur, and to each county or equivalent jurisdiction in which the species is believed to occur, and invite the comment of such agency, and each such jurisdiction, thereon;

(B) insofar as practical, and in cooperation with the Secretary of State, give notice of the proposed regulation to each foreign nation in which the species is believed to occur or whose citizens harvest the species on the high seas, and invite the comment of such nation thereon;

(C) give notice of the proposed regulation to such professional scientific organizations as he deems appropriate;

(D) publish a summary of the proposed regulation in a newspaper of general circulation in each area of the United States in which the species is believed to occur; and

(E) promptly hold one public hearing on the proposed regulation if any person files a request for such a hearing within 45 days after the date of publication of general notice.

(6)(A) Within the one-year period beginning on the date on which general notice is published in accordance with paragraph (5)(A)(i) regarding a proposed regulation, the Secretary shall publish in the Federal Register—

(i) if a determination as to whether a species is an endangered species or a threatened species, or a revision of critical habitat, is involved, either—

(I) a final regulation to implement such determination,

(II) a final regulation to implement such revision or a finding that such revision should not be made,

(III) notice that such one-year period is being extended under subparagraph (B)(i), or

(IV) notice that the proposed regulation is being withdrawn under subparagraph (B)(ii), together with the finding on which such withdrawal is based; or

(ii) subject to subparagraph (C), if a designation of critical habitat is involved, either—

(I) a final regulation to implement such designation, or

(II) notice that such one-year period is being extended under such subparagraph.

(B)(i) If the Secretary finds with respect to a proposed regulation referred to in subparagraph (A)(i) that there is substantial disagreement regarding the sufficiency or accuracy of the available data relevant to the determination or revision concerned, the Secretary may extend the one-year period specified in subparagraph (A) for not more than six months for purposes of soliciting additional data.

(ii) If a proposed regulation referred to in subparagraph (A)(i) is not promulgated as a final regulation within such one-year period (or longer period if extension under clause (i) applies) because the Secretary finds that there is not sufficient evidence to justify the action proposed by the regulation, the Secretary shall immediately withdraw the regulation. The finding on which a withdrawal is based shall be subject to judicial review. The Secretary may not propose a regulation that has previously been withdrawn under this clause unless he determines that sufficient new information is available to warrant such proposal.

(iii) If the one-year period specified in subparagraph (A) is extended under clause (i) with respect to a proposed regulation, then before the close of such extended period the Secretary shall publish in the Federal Register either a final regulation to implement the determination or revision concerned, a finding that the revision should not be made, or a notice of withdrawal of the regulation under clause (ii), together with the finding on which the withdrawal is based.

(C) A final regulation designating critical habitat of an endangered species or a threatened species shall be published concurrently with the final regulation implementing the determination that such species is endangered or threatened, unless the Secretary deems that—

(i) it is essential to the conservation of such species that the regulation implementing such determination be promptly published; or

(ii) critical habitat of such species is not then determinable, in which case the Secretary, with respect to the proposed regulation to designate such habitat, may extend the one-year period specified in subparagraph (A) by not more than one additional year, but not later than the close of such additional year the Secretary must publish a final regulation, based on such data as may be available at that time, designating, to the maximum extent prudent, such habitat.

(7) Neither paragraph (4), (5), or (6) of this subsection nor section 553 of Title 5 shall apply to any regulation issued by the Secretary in regard to any emergency posing a significant risk to the well-being of any species of fish or wildlife or plants, but only if—

(A) at the time of publication of the regulation in the Federal Register the Secretary publishes therein detailed reasons why such regulation is necessary; and

(B) in the case such regulation applies to resident species of fish or wildlife, or plants, the Secretary gives actual notice of such regulation to the State agency in each State in which such species is believed to occur.

Such regulation shall, at the discretion of the Secretary, take effect immediately upon the publication of the regulation in the Federal Register. Any regulation promulgated under the authority of this paragraph shall cease to have force and effect at the close of the 240-day period following the date of publication unless, during such 240-day period, the rulemaking procedures which would apply to such regulation without regard to this paragraph are complied with. If at any time after issuing an emergency regulation the Secretary determines, on the basis of the best appropriate data available to him, that substantial evidence does not exist to warrant such regulation, he shall withdraw it.

(8) The publication in the Federal Register of any proposed or final regulation which is necessary or appropriate to carry out the purposes of this chapter shall include a summary by the Secretary of the data on which such regulation is based and shall show the relationship of such data to such regulation; and if such regulation designates or revises critical habitat, such summary shall, to the maximum extent practicable, also include a brief description and evaluation of those activities (whether public or private) which, in the opinion of the Secretary, if undertaken may adversely modify such habitat, or may be affected by such designation.

(c) Lists

(1) The Secretary of the Interior shall publish in the Federal Register a list of all species determined by him or the Secretary of Commerce to be endangered species and a list of all species determined by him or the Secretary of Commerce to be threatened species. Each list shall refer to the species contained therein by scientific and common name or names, if any, specify with respect to each such species over what portion of its range it is endangered or threatened, and specify any critical habitat within such range. The Secretary shall from time to time revise each list published under the authority of this subsection to reflect recent determinations, designations, and revisions made in accordance with subsections (a) and (b) of this section.

(2) The Secretary shall—

(A) conduct, at least once every five years, a review of all species included in a list which is published pursuant to paragraph (1) and which is in effect at the time of such review; and

(B) determine on the basis of such review whether any such species should—

(i) be removed from such list;

(ii) be changed in status from an endangered species to a threatened species; or

(iii) be changed in status from a threatened species to an endangered species.

Each determination under subparagraph (B) shall be made in accordance with the provisions of subsections (a) and (b) of this section.

(d) Protective regulations

Whenever any species is listed as a threatened species pursuant to subsection (c) of this section, the Secretary shall issue such regulations as he deems necessary and advisable to provide for the conservation of such species. The Secretary may by regulation prohibit with respect to any threatened species any act prohibited under section 1538(a)(1) of this title, in the case of fish or wildlife, or section 1538(a)(2) of this title, in the case of plants, with respect to endangered species; except that with respect to the taking of resident species of fish or wildlife, such regulations shall apply in any State which has entered into a cooperative agreement pursuant to section 1535(c) of this title only to the extent that such regulations have also been adopted by such State.

(e) Similarity of appearance cases

The Secretary may, by regulation of commerce or taking, and to the extent he deems advisable, treat any species as an endangered species or threatened species even though it is not listed pursuant to this section if he finds that—

(A) such species so closely resembles in appearance, at the point in question, a species which has been listed pursuant to such section that enforcement personnel would have substantial difficulty in attempting to differentiate between the listed and unlisted species;

(B) the effect of this substantial difficulty is an additional threat to an endangered or threatened species; and

(C) such treatment of an unlisted species will substantially facilitate the enforcement and further the policy of this chapter.

(f) Recovery plans

(1) The Secretary shall develop and implement plans (hereinafter in this subsection referred to as "recovery plans") for the conservation and survival of endangered species and threatened species listed pursuant to this section, unless he finds that such a plan will not promote the conservation of the species. The Secretary, in developing and implementing recovery plans, shall, to the maximum extent practicable—

(A) give priority to those endangered species or threatened species, without regard to taxonomic classification, that are most likely to benefit from such plans, particularly those species that are, or may be, in conflict with construction or other development projects or other forms of economic activity;

(B) incorporate in each plan—

(i) a description of such site-specific management actions as may be necessary to achieve the plan's goal for the conservation and survival of the species;

(ii) objective, measurable criteria which, when met, would result in a determination, in accordance with the provisions of this section, that the species be removed from the list; and

(iii) estimates of the time required and the cost to carry out those measures needed to achieve the plan's goal and to achieve intermediate steps toward that goal.

(2) The Secretary, in developing and implementing recovery plans, may procure the services of appropriate public and private agencies and institutions, and other qualified persons. Recovery teams appointed pursuant to this subsection shall not be subject to the Federal Advisory Committee Act.

(3) The Secretary shall report every two years to the Committee on Environment and Public Works of the Senate and the Committee on Merchant Marine and Fisheries of the House of Representatives on the status of efforts to develop and implement recovery plans for all species listed pursuant to this section and on the status of all species for which such plans have been developed.

(4) The Secretary shall, prior to final approval of a new or revised recovery plan, provide public notice and an opportunity for public review and comment on such plan. The Secretary shall consider all information presented during the public comment period prior to approval of the plan.

(5) Each Federal agency shall, prior to implementation of a new or revised recovery plan, consider all information presented during the public comment period under paragraph (4).

(g) Monitoring

(1) The Secretary shall implement a system in cooperation with the States to monitor effectively for not less than five years the status of all species which have recovered to the point at which the measures provided pursuant to this chapter are no longer necessary and which, in accordance with the provisions of this section, have been removed from either of the lists published under subsection (c) of this section.

(2) The Secretary shall make prompt use of the authority under paragraph 7 of subsection (b) of this section to prevent a significant risk to the well being of any such recovered species.

(h) Agency guidelines; publication in Federal Register; scope; proposals and amendments: notice and opportunity for comments

The Secretary shall establish, and publish in the Federal Register, agency guidelines to insure that the purposes of this section are achieved efficiently and effectively. Such guidelines shall include, but are not limited to—

(1) procedures for recording the receipt and the disposition of petitions submitted under subsection (b)(3) of this section;

(2) criteria for making the findings required under such subsection with respect to petitions;

(3) a ranking system to assist in the identification of species that should receive priority review under subsection (a)(1) of this section; and

(4) a system for developing and implementing, on a priority basis, recovery plans under subsection (f) of this section.

The Secretary shall provide to the public notice of, and opportunity to submit written comments on, any guideline (including any amendment thereto) proposed to be established under this subsection.

(i) Submission to State agency of justification for regulations inconsistent with State agency's comments or petition

If, in the case of any regulation proposed by the Secretary under the authority of this section, a State agency to which notice thereof was given in accordance with subsection (b)(5)(A)(ii) of this section files comments disagreeing with all or part of the proposed regulation, and the Secretary issues a final regulation which is in conflict with such comments, or if the Secretary fails to adopt a regulation pursuant to an action petitioned by a State agency under subsection (b)(3) of this section, the Secretary shall submit to the State agency a written justification for his failure to adopt regulations consistent with the agency's comments or petition.

(Pub.L. 93–205, § 4, Dec. 28, 1973, 87 Stat. 886; Pub.L. 94–359, § 1, July 12, 1976, 90 Stat. 911; Pub.L. 95–632, §§ 11, 13, Nov. 10, 1978, 92 Stat. 3764, 3766; Pub.L. 96–159, § 3, Dec. 28, 1979, 93 Stat. 1225; Pub.L. 97–304, § 2(a), Oct. 13, 1982, 96 Stat. 1411; Pub.L. 100–478, Title I, §§ 1002–1004, Oct. 7, 1988, 102 Stat. 2306.)

References in Text

The Federal Advisory Committee Act, referred to in text, is set out in Appendix 2 to Title 5, Government Organization and Employees.

Abolition of House Committee on Merchant Marine and Fisheries

Committee on Merchant Marine and Fisheries of House of Representatives abolished and any reference in any provision of law enacted before Jan. 4, 1995, to the Committee on Merchant Marine and Fisheries of the House of Representatives treated as referring to the Committee on Agriculture of the House of Representatives, in the case of a provision of law relating to inspection of seafood or seafood products, the Committee on National Security of the House of Representatives, in the case of a provision of law relating to interoceanic canals, the Merchant Marine Academy and State Maritime Academies, or national security aspects of merchant marine, the Committee on Resources of the House of Representatives, in the case of a provision of law relating to fisheries, wildlife, international fishing agreements marine affairs (including coastal zone management) except for measures relating to oil and other pollution of navigable waters, or oceanography, the Committee on Science of the House of Representatives, in the case of a provision of law relating to marine research, and the Committee on Transportation and Infrastructure of the House of Representatives, in the case of a provision of law relating to a matter other than a matter described above, see section 1(b)(3) of Pub.L. 104–14, set out as a note preceding section 21 of Title 2, The Congress.

CROSS REFERENCES

Acquisition of areas of land suitable for conservation of endangered and threatened species in conservation recreational areas, see section 460k–1 of this title.

Areas of lands or waters acquired through migratory bird conservation provisions administered in accordance with treaty obligations to protect endangered and threatened species, see section 715i of this title.

Citizen suits to compel Secretary to apply protective regulation or against Secretary to perform nondiscretionary act or duty under this section, see section 1540.

Conservation program with respect to National Forest System to include fish, wildlife, and plants listed as endangered or threatened species pursuant to this section, see section 1534 of this title.

Cooperative agreements by state agencies for implementation of public land conservation and rehabilitation programs to provide adequate protection for endangered and threatened species, see section 670h of this title.

Cooperative agreements with States not to affect protective regulations issued under this section, see section 1535 of this title.

Duty of Marine Mammal Commission to recommend revisions of endangered and threatened species list, see section 1402 of this title.

Federal agencies to utilize their authorities in furtherance of purposes of this chapter by carrying out program for conservation of endangered or threatened species listed pursuant to this section, see section 1536 of this title.

International cooperation and encouragement of foreign programs for conservation of endangered or threatened species listed pursuant to this section, see section 1537 of this title.

Listing of endangered or threatened species in accordance with this section as determinative of "critical habitat", see section 1532 of this title.

National Wildlife Refuge System to include lands acquired or reserved for protection of endangered and threatened species, see section 715s of this title.

Prohibited acts, see section 1538 of this title.

Regulations on hunting and fishing of endangered and threatened species on lands not within National Wildlife Refuge System, see section 668dd of this title.

WEST'S FEDERAL FORMS

Complaint to enjoin violations, see § 1713.

CODE OF FEDERAL REGULATIONS

Coal mining exploration plans, see 43 CFR 3482.1 et seq.

Compliance with National Environmental Policy Act, see 7 CFR 650.1 et seq.

General provisions, see 50 CFR 217.1 et seq.

Identification of—

Endangered and threatened wildlife and plants, United States Fish and Wildlife Service, see 50 CFR 17.1 et seq.

Threatened fish and wildlife, National Marine Fisheries Service, see 60 CFR 227.1 et seq.

Listing endangered and threatened species and designating critical habitat, see 50 CFR 424.01 et seq.

LAW REVIEW COMMENTARIES

Conservation obligations under the Endangered Species Act: A case study of the Yellowstone grizzly bear. Comment, 64 U.Colo. L.Rev. 607 (1993).

Endangered Species Act and its implementation by the U.S. Department of Interior and Commerce. Oliver A. Houck, 64 U.Colo. L.Rev. 277 (1993).

§ 1534. Land acquisition [ESA § 5]

(a) Implementation of conservation program; authorization of Secretary and Secretary of Agriculture

The Secretary, and the Secretary of Agriculture with respect to the National Forest System, shall establish and implement a program to conserve fish, wildlife, and plants, including those which are listed as endangered species or threatened species pursuant to section 1533 of this title. To carry out such a program, the appropriate Secretary—

(1) shall utilize the land acquisition and other authority under the Fish and Wildlife Act of 1956, as amended [16 U.S.C.A. § 742a et seq.], the Fish and Wildlife Coordination Act, as amended [16 U.S.C.A. § 661 et seq.], and the Migratory Bird Conservation Act [16 U.S.C.A. § 715 et seq.], as appropriate; and

(2) is authorized to acquire by purchase, donation, or otherwise, lands, waters, or interest therein, and such authority shall be in addition to any other land acquisition authority vested in him.

(b) Availability of funds for acquisition of lands, waters, etc.

Funds made available pursuant to the Land and Water Conservation Fund Act of 1965, as amended [16 U.S.C.A. § 460*l*–4 et seq.], may be used for the purpose of acquiring lands, waters, or interests therein under subsection (a) of this section.

(Pub.L. 93–205, § 5, Dec. 28, 1973, 87 Stat. 889; Pub.L. 95–632, § 12, Nov. 10, 1978, 92 Stat. 3766.)

References in Text

The Fish and Wildlife Act of 1956, as amended, referred to in subsec. (a)(1), is Act Aug. 8, 1956, c. 1036, 70 Stat. 119, as amended, which is classified generally to sections 742a et seq. of this title. For complete classification of this Act to the Code, see Short Title note set out under section 742a of this title and Tables volume.

The Fish and Wildlife Coordination Act, as amended, referred to in subsec. (a)(1), is Act Mar. 10, 1934, c. 55, 48 Stat. 401, as amended, which is classified generally to sections 661 to 666c of this title. For complete classification of this Act to the Code, see Short Title note set out under section 661 of this title and Tables volume.

The Migratory Bird Conservation Act, referred to in subsec. (a)(1), is Act Feb. 18, 1929, c. 257, 45 Stat. 1222, as amended, which is classified generally to subchapter III (section 715 et seq.) of chapter 7 of this title. For complete classification of this Act to the Code, see section 715 of this title and Tables volume.

The Land and Water Conservation Fund Act of 1965, as amended, referred to in subsec. (b), is Pub.L. 88–578, Sept. 3, 1964, 78 Stat. 897, as amended, which is classified to section 460*l*–4 et seq. of this title. For complete classification of this Act to the Code, see Short Title note set out under section 460*l*–4 of this title and Tables volume.

CROSS REFERENCES

Land and water conservation fund, acquisition for National Wildlife Refuge System of land or water for endangered and threatened species, see section 460*l*–9 of this title.

Snake River Birds of Prey National Conservation Area, land exchanges, see 16 USCA § 460iii–4.

§ 1535. Cooperation with States [ESA § 6]

(a) Generally

In carrying out the program authorized by this chapter, the Secretary shall cooperate to the maximum extent practicable with the States. Such cooperation shall include consultation with the States concerned before acquiring any land or water, or interest therein, for the purpose of conserving any endangered species or threatened species.

(b) Management agreements

The Secretary may enter into agreements with any State for the administration and management of any area established for the conservation of endangered species or threatened species. Any revenues derived from the administration of such areas under these agreements shall be subject to the provisions of section 715s of this title.

(c) Cooperative agreements

(1) In furtherance of the purposes of this chapter, the Secretary is authorized to enter into a cooperative agreement in accordance with this section with any State which establishes and maintains an adequate and active program for the conservation of endangered species and threatened species. Within one hundred and twenty days after the Secretary receives a certified copy of such a proposed State program, he shall make a determination whether such program is in accordance with this chapter. Unless he determines, pursuant to this paragraph, that the State program is not in accordance with this chapter, he shall enter into a cooperative agreement with the State for the purpose of assisting in implementation of the State program. In order for a State program to be deemed an adequate and active program for the conservation of endangered species and threatened species, the Secretary must find, and annually thereafter reconfirm such finding, that under the State program—

(A) authority resides in the State agency to conserve resident species of fish or wildlife determined by the State agency or the Secretary to be endangered or threatened;

(B) the State agency has established acceptable conservation programs, consistent with the purposes and policies of this chapter, for all resident species of fish or wildlife in the State which are deemed by the Secretary to be endangered or threatened, and has furnished a copy of such plan and program together with all pertinent details, information, and data requested to the Secretary;

(C) the State agency is authorized to conduct investigations to determine the status and requirements for survival of resident species of fish and wildlife;

(D) the State agency is authorized to establish programs, including the acquisition of land or aquatic habitat or interests therein, for the conservation of resident endangered or threatened species of fish or wildlife; and

(E) provision is made for public participation in designating resident species of fish or wildlife as endangered or threatened; or

that under the State program—

(i) the requirements set forth in subparagraphs (C), (D), and (E) of this paragraph are complied with, and

(ii) plans are included under which immediate attention will be given to those resident species of fish and wildlife which are determined by the Secretary or the State agency to be endangered or threatened and which the Secretary and the State agency agree are most urgently in need of conservation programs; except that a cooperative agreement entered into with a State whose program is deemed adequate and active pursuant to clause (i) and this clause shall not affect the applicability of prohibitions set forth in or authorized pursuant to section 1533(d) of this title or section 1538(a)(1) of this title with respect to the taking of any resident endangered or threatened species.

(2) In furtherance of the purposes of this chapter, the Secretary is authorized to enter into a cooperative agreement in accordance with this section with any State which establishes and maintains an adequate and active program for the conservation of endangered species and threatened species of plants. Within one hundred and twenty days after the Secretary receives a certified copy of such a proposed State program, he shall make a determination whether such program is in accordance with this chapter. Unless he determines, pursuant to this paragraph, that the State program is not in accordance with this chapter, he shall enter into a cooperative agreement with the State for the purpose of assisting in implementation of the State program. In order for a State program to be deemed an adequate and active program for the conservation of endangered species of plants and threatened species of plants, the Secretary must find, and annually thereafter reconfirm such finding, that under the State program—

(A) authority resides in the State agency to conserve resident species of plants determined by the State agency or the Secretary to be endangered or threatened;

(B) the State agency has established acceptable conservation programs, consistent with the purposes and policies of this chapter, for all resident species of plants in the State which are deemed by the Secretary to be endangered or threatened, and has furnished a copy of such plan and program together with all pertinent details, information, and data requested to the Secretary;

(C) the State agency is authorized to conduct investigations to determine the status and requirements for survival of resident species of plants; and

(D) provision is made for public participation in designating resident species of plants as endangered or threatened; or

that under the State program—

(i) the requirements set forth in subparagraphs (C) and (D) of this paragraph are complied with, and

(ii) plans are included under which immediate attention will be given to those resident species of plants which are determined by the Secretary or the State agency to be endangered or threatened and which the Secretary and the State agency agree are most urgently in need of conservation programs; except that a cooperative agreement entered into with a State whose program is deemed adequate and active pursuant to clause (i) and this clause shall not affect the applicability of prohibitions set forth in or authorized pursuant to section 1533(d) or section 1538(a)(1) of this title with respect to the taking of any resident endangered or threatened species.

(d) Allocation of funds

(1) The Secretary is authorized to provide financial assistance to any State, through its respective State agency, which has entered into a cooperative agreement pursuant to subsection (c) of this section to assist in development of programs for the conservation of endangered and threatened species or to assist in monitoring the status of candidate species pursuant to subparagraph (C) of section 1533(b)(3) of this title and recovered species pursuant to section 1533(g) of this title. The Secretary shall allocate each annual appropriation made in accordance with the provisions of subsection (i) of this section to such States based on consideration of—

(A) the international commitments of the United States to protect endangered species or threatened species;

(B) the readiness of a State to proceed with a conservation program consistent with the objectives and purposes of this chapter;

(C) the number of endangered species and threatened species within a State;

(D) the potential for restoring endangered species and threatened species within a State;

(E) the relative urgency to initiate a program to restore and protect an endangered species or threatened species in terms of survival of the species;

(F) the importance of monitoring the status of candidate species within a State to prevent a significant risk to the well being of any such species; and

(G) the importance of monitoring the status of recovered species within a State to assure that such species do not return to the point at which the measures provided pursuant to this chapter are again necessary.

So much of the annual appropriation made in accordance with provisions of subsection (i) of this section allocated for obligation to any State for any fiscal year as remains unobligated at the close thereof is authorized to be made available to that State until the close of the succeeding fiscal year. Any amount allocated to any State which is unobligated at the end of the period during which it is available for expenditure is authorized to be made available for expenditure by the Secretary in conducting programs under this section.

(2) Such cooperative agreements shall provide for (A) the actions to be taken by the Secretary and the States; (B) the benefits that are expected to be derived in connection with the conservation of endangered or threatened species; (C) the estimated cost of these actions; and (D) the share of such costs to be borne by the Federal Government and by the States; except that—

(i) the Federal share of such program costs shall not exceed 75 percent of the estimated program cost stated in the agreement; and

(ii) the Federal share may be increased to 90 percent whenever two or more States having a common interest in one or more endangered or threatened species, the conservation of which may be enhanced by cooperation of such States, enter jointly into an agreement with the Secretary.

The Secretary may, in his discretion, and under such rules and regulations as he may prescribe, advance funds to the State for financing the United States pro rata share agreed upon in the cooperative agreement. For the purposes of this section, the non-Federal share may, in the discretion of the Secretary, be in the form of money or real property, the value of which will be determined by the Secretary, whose decision shall be final.

(e) Review of State programs

Any action taken by the Secretary under this section shall be subject to his periodic review at no greater than annual intervals.

(f) Conflicts between Federal and State laws

Any State law or regulation which applies with respect to the importation or exportation of, or interstate or foreign commerce in, endangered species or threatened species is void to the extent that it may effectively (1) permit what is prohibited by this chapter or by any regulation which implements this chapter, or (2) prohibit what is authorized pursuant to an exemption or permit provided for in this chapter or in any regulation which implements this chapter. This chapter shall not otherwise be construed to void any State law or regulation which is intended to conserve migratory, resident, or introduced fish or wildlife, or to permit or prohibit sale of such fish or wildlife. Any State law or regulation respecting the taking of an endangered species or threatened species may be more restrictive than the exemptions or permits provided for in this chapter or in any regulation which implements this chapter but not less restrictive than the prohibitions so defined.

(g) Transition

(1) For purposes of this subsection, the term "establishment period" means, with respect to any State, the period beginning on December 28, 1973 and ending on whichever of the following dates first occurs: (A) the date of the close of the 120-day period following the adjournment of the first regular session of the legislature of such State which commences after December 28, 1973, or (B) the date of the close of the 15-month period following December 28, 1973.

(2) The prohibitions set forth in or authorized pursuant to sections 1533(d) and 1538(a)(1)(B) of this title shall not apply with respect to the taking of any resident endangered species or threatened species (other than species listed in Appendix I to the Convention or otherwise specifically covered by any other treaty or Federal law) within any State—

(A) which is then a party to a cooperative agreement with the Secretary pursuant to subsection (c) of this section (except to the extent that the taking of any such species is contrary to the law of such State); or

(B) except for any time within the establishment period when—

(i) the Secretary applies such prohibition to such species at the request of the State, or

(ii) the Secretary applies such prohibition after he finds, and publishes his finding, that an emergency exists posing a significant risk to the well-being of such species and that the prohibition must be applied to protect such species. The Secretary's finding and publication may be made without regard to the public hearing or comment provisions of section 553 of Title 5 or any other provision of this chapter; but such prohibition shall expire 90 days after the date of its imposition unless the Secretary further extends such prohibition by publishing notice and a statement of justification of such extension.

(h) Regulations

The Secretary is authorized to promulgate such regulations as may be appropriate to carry out the provisions of this section relating to financial assistance to States.

(i) Appropriations

(1) To carry out the provisions of this section for fiscal years after September 30, 1988, there shall be deposited into a special fund known as the cooperative endangered species conservation fund, to be administered by the Secretary, an amount equal to 5 percent of the combined amounts covered each fiscal year into the Federal aid to wildlife restoration fund under section 669b of this title, and paid, transferred, or otherwise credited each fiscal year to the Sport Fishing Restoration Account established under 1016 of the Act of July 18, 1984.

(2) Amounts deposited into the special fund are authorized to be appropriated annually and allocated in accordance with subsection (d) of this section.

(Pub.L. 93–205, § 6, Dec. 28, 1973, 87 Stat. 889; Pub.L. 95–212, Dec. 19, 1977, 91 Stat. 1493; Pub.L. 95–632, § 10, Nov. 10, 1978, 92 Stat. 3762; Pub.L. 96–246, May 23, 1980, 94 Stat. 348; Pub.L. 97–304, §§ 3, 8(b), Oct. 13, 1982, 96 Stat. 1416, 1426; Pub.L. 100–478, Title I, § 1005, Oct. 7, 1988, 102 Stat. 2307.)

References in Text

Section 1016 of the Act of July 18, 1984, referred to in subsec. (i), probably means Pub.L. 98–369, Div. A, Title X, § 1016, July 18, 1984, 98 Stat. 1019, which enacted section 9504 of Title 26, Internal Revenue Code, amended section 9503 of Title 26, repealed section 13107 of Title 46, Shipping, and enacted provisions set out as a note under section 9504 of Title 26.

CROSS REFERENCES

Authorization of appropriations, see section 1542 of this title.
Citizen suit to compel Secretary to apply prohibitions with respect to taking of any resident endangered or threatened species within any State, see section 1540 of this title.
Exception to prohibited acts, see section 1538 of this title.
Regulations on hunting and fishing of endangered and threatened species on lands not within National Wildlife Refuge System, see section 668dd of this title.
Resident species of fish or wildlife, protective regulations applicable in any State which has entered into cooperative agreement only to extent such regulations have also been adopted by such State, see section 1533 of this title.

WEST'S FEDERAL FORMS

Complaint to enjoin violations, see § 1713.

CODE OF FEDERAL REGULATIONS

Cooperation with states in conservation efforts, see 50 CFR 81.1 et seq., 225.1 et seq.

LAW REVIEW COMMENTARIES

Georges bank—Common ground or continued battleground? Donna R. Christie, 23 San Diego L.Rev. 491 (1986).

The Fishery Conversation and Management Act: The states' role in domestic and international fishery management. Leslie M. MacRae, 88 Dick.L.Rev. 306 (1984).

LIBRARY REFERENCES

States ⚡4.19.
C.J.S. States §§ 1, 7.

United States Supreme Court

State imposed environmental regulation of mining operations on national forest lands, see California Coastal Commission v. Granite Rock Company, Cal.1987, 107 S.Ct. 1419.

§ 1536. Interagency cooperation [ESA § 7]

(a) Federal agency actions and consultations

(1) The Secretary shall review other programs administered by him and utilize such programs in furtherance of the purposes of this chapter. All other Federal agencies shall, in consultation with and with the assistance of the Secretary, utilize their authorities in furtherance of the purposes of this chapter by carrying out programs for the conservation of endangered species and threatened species listed pursuant to section 1533 of this title.

(2) Each Federal agency shall, in consultation with and with the assistance of the Secretary, insure that any action authorized, funded, or carried out by such agency (hereinafter in this section referred to as an "agency action") is not likely to jeopardize the continued existence of any endangered species or threatened species or result in the destruction or adverse modification of habitat of such species which is determined by the Secretary, after consultation as appropriate with affected States, to be critical, unless such agency has been granted an exemption for such action by the Committee pursuant to subsection (h) of this section. In fulfilling the requirements of this paragraph each agency shall use the best scientific and commercial data available.

(3) Subject to such guidelines as the Secretary may establish, a Federal agency shall consult with the Secretary on any prospective agency action at the request of, and in cooperation with, the prospective permit or license applicant if the applicant has reason to believe that an endangered species or a threatened species may be present in the area affected by his project and that implementation of such action will likely affect such species.

(4) Each Federal agency shall confer with the Secretary on any agency action which is likely to jeopardize the continued existence of any species proposed to be listed under section 1533 of this title or result in the destruction or adverse modification of critical habitat proposed to be designated for such species. This paragraph does not require a limitation on the commitment of resources as described in subsection (d) of this section.

(b) Opinion of Secretary

(1)(A) Consultation under subsection (a)(2) of this section with respect to any agency action shall be concluded within the 90-day period beginning on the date on which initiated or, subject to subparagraph (B), within such other period of time as is mutually agreeable to the Secretary and the Federal agency.

(B) In the case of an agency action involving a permit or license applicant, the Secretary and the Federal agency may not mutually agree to conclude consultation within a period exceeding 90 days unless the Secretary, before the close of the 90th day referred to in subparagraph (A)—

(i) if the consultation period proposed to be agreed to will end before the 150th day after the date on which consultation was initiated, submits to the applicant a written statement setting forth—

(I) the reasons why a longer period is required,

(II) the information that is required to complete the consultation, and

(III) the estimated date on which consultation will be completed; or

(ii) if the consultation period proposed to be agreed to will end 150 or more days after the date on which consultation was initiated, obtains the consent of the applicant to such period.

The Secretary and the Federal agency may mutually agree to extend a consultation period established under the preceding sentence if the Secretary, before the close of such period, obtains the consent of the applicant to the extension.

(2) Consultation under subsection (a)(3) of this section shall be concluded within such period as is agreeable to the Secretary, the Federal agency, and the applicant concerned.

(3)(A) Promptly after conclusion of consultation under paragraph (2) or (3) of subsection (a) of this section, the Secretary shall provide to the Federal agency and the applicant, if any, a written statement setting forth the Secretary's opinion, and a summary of the information on which the opinion is based, detailing how the agency action affects the species or its critical habitat. If jeopardy or adverse modification is found, the Secretary shall suggest those reasonable and prudent alternatives which he believes would not violate subsection (a)(2) of this section and can be taken by the Federal agency or applicant in implementing the agency action.

(B) Consultation under subsection (a)(3) of this section, and an opinion issued by the Secretary incident to such consultation, regarding an agency action shall be treated respectively as a consultation under subsection (a)(2) of this section, and as an opinion issued after consultation under such subsection, regarding that action if the Secretary reviews the action before it is commenced by the Federal agency and finds, and notifies such agency, that no significant changes have been made with respect to the action and that no significant change has occurred regarding the information used during the initial consultation.

(4) If after consultation under subsection (a)(2) of this section, the Secretary concludes that—

(A) the agency action will not violate such subsection, or offers reasonable and prudent alternatives which the Secretary believes would not violate such subsection;

(B) the taking of an endangered species or a threatened species incidental to the agency action will not violate such subsection; and

(C) if an endangered species or threatened species of a marine mammal is involved, the taking is authorized pursuant to section 1371(a)(5) of this title;

the Secretary shall provide the Federal agency and the applicant concerned, if any, with a written statement that—

(i) specifies the impact of such incidental taking on the species,

(ii) specifies those reasonable and prudent measures that the Secretary considers necessary or appropriate to minimize such impact,

(iii) in the case of marine mammals, specifies those measures that are necessary to comply with section 1371(a)(5) of this title with regard to such taking, and

(iv) sets forth the terms and conditions (including, but not limited to, reporting requirements) that must be complied with by the Federal agency or applicant (if any), or both, to implement the measures specified under clauses (ii) and (iii).

(c) Biological assessment

(1) To facilitate compliance with the requirements of subsection (a)(2) of this section, each Federal agency shall, with respect to any agency action of such agency for which no contract for construction has been entered into and for which no construction has begun on November 10, 1978, request of the Secretary information whether any species which is listed or proposed to be listed may be present in the area of such proposed action. If the Secretary advises, based on the best scientific and commercial data available, that such species may be present, such agency shall conduct a biological assessment for the purpose of identifying any endangered species or threatened species which is likely to be affected by such action. Such assessment shall be completed within 180 days after the date on which initiated (or within such other period as is mutually agreed to by the Secretary and such agency, except that if a permit or license applicant is involved, the 180-day period may not be extended unless such agency provides the applicant, before the close of such period, with a written statement setting forth the estimated length of the proposed extension and the reasons therefor) and, before any contract for construction is entered into and before construction is begun with respect to such action. Such assessment may be undertaken as part of a Federal agency's compliance with the requirements of section 102 of the National Environmental Policy Act of 1969 (42 U.S.C. 4332).

(2) Any person who may wish to apply for an exemption under subsection (g) of this section for that action may conduct a biological assessment to identify any endangered species or threatened species which is likely to be affected by such action. Any such biological assessment must, however, be conducted in cooperation with the Secretary and under the supervision of the appropriate Federal agency.

(d) Limitation on commitment of resources

After initiation of consultation required under subsection (a)(2) of this section, the Federal agency and the permit or license applicant shall not make any irreversible or irretrievable commitment of resources with respect to the agency action which has the effect of foreclosing the formulation or implementation of any reasonable and prudent alternative measures which would not violate subsection (a)(2) of this section.

(e) Endangered Species Committee

(1) There is established a committee to be known as the Endangered Species Committee (hereinafter in this section referred to as the "Committee").

(2) The Committee shall review any application submitted to it pursuant to this section and determine in accordance with subsection (h) of this section whether or not to grant an exemption from the requirements of subsection (a)(2) of this section for the action set forth in such application.

(3) The Committee shall be composed of seven members as follows:

(A) The Secretary of Agriculture.

(B) The Secretary of the Army.

(C) The Chairman of the Council of Economic Advisors.

(D) The Administrator of the Environmental Protection Agency.

(E) The Secretary of the Interior.

(F) The Administrator of the National Oceanic and Atmospheric Administration.

(G) The President, after consideration of any recommendations received pursuant to subsection (g)(2)(B) of this section shall appoint one individual from each affected State, as determined by the Secretary, to be a member of the Committee for the consideration of the application for exemption for an agency action with respect to which such recommendations are made, not later than 30 days after an application is submitted pursuant to this section.

(4)(A) Members of the Committee shall receive no additional pay on account of their service on the Committee.

(B) While away from their homes or regular places of business in the performance of services for the Committee, members of the Committee shall be allowed travel expenses, including per diem in lieu of subsistence, in the same manner as persons employed intermittently in the Government service are allowed expenses under section 5703 of Title 5.

(5)(A) Five members of the Committee or their representatives shall constitute a quorum for the transaction of any function of the Committee, except that, in no case shall any representative be considered in determining the existence of a quorum for the transaction of any function of the Committee if that function involves a vote by the Committee on any matter before the Committee.

(B) The Secretary of the Interior shall be the Chairman of the Committee.

(C) The Committee shall meet at the call of the Chairman or five of its members.

(D) All meetings and records of the Committee shall be open to the public.

(6) Upon request of the Committee, the head of any Federal agency is authorized to detail, on a nonreimbursable basis, any of the personnel of such agency to the Committee to assist it in carrying out its duties under this section.

(7)(A) The Committee may for the purpose of carrying out its duties under this section hold such hearings, sit and act at such times and places, take such testimony, and receive such evidence, as the Committee deems advisable.

(B) When so authorized by the Committee, any member or agent of the Committee may take any action which the Committee is authorized to take by this paragraph.

(C) Subject to the Privacy Act [5 U.S.C.A. § 552a], the Committee may secure directly from any Federal agency information necessary to enable it to carry out its duties under this section. Upon request of the Chairman of the Committee, the head of such Federal agency shall furnish such information to the Committee.

(D) The Committee may use the United States mails in the same manner and upon the same conditions as a Federal agency.

(E) The Administrator of General Services shall provide to the Committee on a reimbursable basis such administrative support services as the Committee may request.

(8) In carrying out its duties under this section, the Committee may promulgate and amend such rules, regulations, and procedures, and issue and amend such orders as it deems necessary.

(9) For the purpose of obtaining information necessary for the consideration of an application for an exemption under this section the Committee may issue subpenas for the attendance and testimony of witnesses and the production of relevant papers, books, and documents.

(10) In no case shall any representative, including a representative of a member designated pursuant to paragraph (3)(G) of this subsection, be eligible to cast a vote on behalf of any member.

(f) Promulgation of regulations; form and contents of exemption application

Not later than 90 days after November 10, 1978, the Secretary shall promulgate regulations which set forth the form and manner in which applications for exemption shall be submitted to the Secretary and the information to be contained in such applications. Such regulations shall require that information submitted in an application by the head of any Federal agency with respect to any agency action include, but not be limited to—

(1) a description of the consultation process carried out pursuant to subsection (a)(2) of this section between the head of the Federal agency and the Secretary; and

(2) a statement describing why such action cannot be altered or modified to conform with the requirements of subsection (a)(2) of this section.

(g) Application for exemption; report to Committee

(1) A Federal agency, the Governor of the State in which an agency action will occur, if any, or a permit or license applicant may apply to the Secretary for an exemption for an agency action of such agency if, after consultation under subsection (a)(2) of this section, the Secretary's opinion under subsection (b) of this section indicates that the agency action would violate subsection (a)(2) of this section. An application for an exemption shall be considered initially by the Secretary in the manner provided for in this subsection, and shall be considered by the Committee for a final determination under subsection (h) of this section after a report is made pursuant to paragraph (5). The applicant for an exemption shall be referred to as the "exemption applicant" in this section.

(2)(A) An exemption applicant shall submit a written application to the Secretary, in a form prescribed under subsection (f) of this section, not later than 90 days after the completion of the consultation process; except that, in the case of any agency action involving a permit or license applicant, such application shall be submitted not later than 90 days after the date on which the Federal agency concerned takes final agency action with respect to the issuance of the permit or license. For purposes of the preceding sentence, the term "final agency action" means (i) a disposition by an agency with respect to the issuance of a permit or license that is subject to administrative review, whether or not such disposition is subject to judicial review; or (ii) if administrative review is sought with respect to such disposition, the decision resulting after such review. Such application shall set forth the reasons why the exemption applicant considers that the agency action meets the requirements for an exemption under this subsection.

(B) Upon receipt of an application for exemption for an agency action under paragraph (1), the Secretary shall promptly (i) notify the Governor of each affected State, if any, as determined by the Secretary, and request the Governors so notified to recommend individuals to be appointed to the Endangered Species Committee for consideration of such application; and (ii) publish notice of receipt of the application in the Federal Register, including a summary of the information contained in the application and a description of the agency action with respect to which the application for exemption has been filed.

(3) The Secretary shall within 20 days after the receipt of an application for exemption, or within such other period of time as is mutually agreeable to the exemption applicant and the Secretary—

(A) determine that the Federal agency concerned and the exemption applicant have—

(i) carried out the consultation responsibilities described in subsection (a) of this section in good faith and made a reasonable and responsible effort to develop and fairly consider modifications or reasonable and prudent alternatives to the proposed agency action which would not violate subsection (a)(2) of this section;

(ii) conducted any biological assessment required by subsection (c) of this section; and

(iii) to the extent determinable within the time provided herein, refrained from making any irreversible or irretrievable commitment of resources prohibited by subsection (d) of this section; or

(B) deny the application for exemption because the Federal agency concerned or the exemption applicant have not met the requirements set forth in subparagraph (A)(i), (ii), and (iii).

The denial of an application under subparagraph (B) shall be considered final agency action for purposes of chapter 7 of Title 5.

(4) If the Secretary determines that the Federal agency concerned and the exemption applicant have met the requirements set forth in paragraph (3)(A)(i), (ii), and (iii) he shall, in consultation with the Members of the Committee, hold a hearing on the application for exemption in accordance with sections 554, 555, and 556 (other than subsection (b)(1) and (2) thereof) of Title 5 and prepare the report to be submitted pursuant to paragraph (5).

(5) Within 140 days after making the determinations under paragraph (3) or within such other period of time as is mutually agreeable to the exemption applicant and the Secretary, the Secretary shall submit to the Committee a report discussing—

(A) the availability of reasonable and prudent alternatives to the agency action, and the nature and extent of the benefits of the agency action and of alternative courses of action consistent with conserving the species or the critical habitat;

(B) a summary of the evidence concerning whether or not the agency action is in the public interest and is of national or regional significance;

(C) appropriate reasonable mitigation and enhancement measures which should be considered by the Committee; and

(D) whether the Federal agency concerned and the exemption applicant refrained from making any irreversible or irretrievable commitment of resources prohibited by subsection (d) of this section.

(6) To the extent practicable within the time required for action under subsection (g) of this section, and except to the extent inconsistent with the requirements of this section, the consideration of any application for an exemption under this section and the conduct of any hearing under this subsection shall be in accordance with sections 554, 555, and 556 (other than subsection (b)(3) of section 556) of Title 5.

(7) Upon request of the Secretary, the head of any Federal agency is authorized to detail, on a nonreimbursable basis, any of the personnel of such agency to the Secretary to assist him in carrying out his duties under this section.

(8) All meetings and records resulting from activities pursuant to this subsection shall be open to the public.

(h) Grant of exemption

(1) The Committee shall make a final determination whether or not to grant an exemption within 30 days after receiving the report of the Secretary pursuant to subsection (g)(5) of this section. The Committee shall grant an exemption from the requirements of subsection (a)(2) of this section for an agency action if, by a vote of not less than five of its members voting in person—

(A) it determines on the record, based on the report of the Secretary, the record of the hearing held under subsection (g)(4) of this section and on such other testimony or evidence as it may receive, that—

(i) there are no reasonable and prudent alternatives to the agency action;

(ii) the benefits of such action clearly outweigh the benefits of alternative courses of action consistent with conserving the species or its critical habitat, and such action is in the public interest;

(iii) the action is of regional or national significance; and

(iv) neither the Federal agency concerned nor the exemption applicant made any irreversible or irretrievable commitment of resources prohibited by subsection (d) of this section; and

(B) it establishes such reasonable mitigation and enhancement measures, including, but not limited to, live propagation, transplantation, and habitat acquisition and improvement, as are necessary and appropriate to minimize the adverse effects of the agency action upon the endangered species, threatened species, or critical habitat concerned.

Any final determination by the Committee under this subsection shall be considered final agency action for purposes of chapter 7 of Title 5.

(2)(A) Except as provided in subparagraph (B), an exemption for an agency action granted under paragraph (1) shall constitute a permanent exemption with respect to all endangered or threatened species for the purposes of completing such agency action—

(i) regardless whether the species was identified in the biological assessment; and

(ii) only if a biological assessment has been conducted under subsection (c) of this section with respect to such agency action.

(B) An exemption shall be permanent under subparagraph (A) unless—

(i) the Secretary finds, based on the best scientific and commercial data available, that such exemption would result in the extinction of a species that was not the subject of consultation under subsection (a)(2) of this section or was not identified in any biological assessment conducted under subsection (c) of this section, and

(ii) the Committee determines within 60 days after the date of the Secretary's finding that the exemption should not be permanent.

If the Secretary makes a finding described in clause (i), the Committee shall meet with respect to the matter within 30 days after the date of the finding.

(i) Review by Secretary of State; violation of international treaty or other international obligation of United States

Notwithstanding any other provision of this chapter, the Committee shall be prohibited from considering for exemption any application made to it, if the Secretary of State, after a review of the proposed agency action and its potential implications, and after hearing, certifies, in writing, to the Committee within 60 days of any application made under this section that the granting of any such exemption and the carrying out of such action would be in violation of an international treaty obligation or other international obligation of the United States. The Secretary of State shall, at the time of such certification, publish a copy thereof in the Federal Register.

(j) Exemption for national security reasons

Notwithstanding any other provision of this chapter, the Committee shall grant an exemption for any agency action if the Secretary of Defense finds that such exemption is necessary for reasons of national security.

(k) Exemption decision not considered major Federal action; environmental impact statement

An exemption decision by the Committee under this section shall not be a major Federal action for purposes of the National Environmental Policy Act of 1969 [42 U.S.C.A. § 4321 et seq.]: *Provided*, That an environmental impact statement which discusses the impacts upon endangered species or threatened species or their critical habitats shall have been previously prepared with respect to any agency action exempted by such order.

(*l*) Committee order granting exemption; cost of mitigation and enhancement measures; report by applicant to Council on Environmental Quality

(1) If the Committee determines under subsection (h) of this section that an exemption should be granted with respect to any agency action, the Committee shall issue an order granting the exemption and specifying the mitigation and enhancement measures established pursuant to subsection (h) of this section which shall be carried out and paid for by the exemption applicant in implementing the agency action. All necessary mitigation and enhancement measures shall be authorized prior to the implementing of the agency action and funded concurrently with all other project features.

(2) The applicant receiving such exemption shall include the costs of such mitigation and enhancement measures within the overall costs of continuing the proposed action. Notwithstanding the preceding sentence the costs of such measures shall not be treated as project costs for the purpose of computing benefit-cost or other ratios for the proposed action. Any applicant may request the Secretary to carry out such mitigation and enhancement measures. The costs incurred by the Secretary in carrying out any such measures shall be paid by the applicant receiving the exemption. No later than one year after the granting of an exemption, the exemption applicant shall submit to the Council on Environmental Quality a report describing its compliance with the mitigation and enhancement measures prescribed by this section. Such a report shall be submitted annually until all such mitigation and enhancement measures have been completed. Notice of the public availability of such reports shall be published in the Federal Register by the Council on Environmental Quality.

(m) Notice requirement for citizen suits not applicable

The 60-day notice requirement of section 1540(g) of this title shall not apply with respect to review of any final determination of the Committee under subsection (h) of this section granting an exemption from the requirements of subsection (a)(2) of this section.

(n) Judicial review

Any person, as defined by section 1532(13) of this title, may obtain judicial review, under chapter 7 of Title 5, of any decision of the Endangered Species Committee under subsection (h) of this section in the United States Court of Appeals for (1) any circuit wherein the agency action concerned will be, or is being, carried out, or (2) in any case in which the agency action will be, or is being, carried out outside of any circuit, the District of Columbia, by filing in such court within 90 days after the date of issuance of the decision, a written petition for review. A copy of such petition shall be transmitted by the clerk of the court to the Committee and the Committee shall file in the court the record in the proceeding, as provided in section 2112, of Title 28. Attorneys designated by the Endangered Species Committee may appear for, and represent the Committee in any action for review under this subsection.

(*o*) Exemption as providing exception on taking of endangered species

Notwithstanding sections 1533(d) and 1538(a)(1)(B) and (C) of this title, sections 1371 and 1372 of this title, or any regulation promulgated to implement any such section—

(1) any action for which an exemption is granted under subsection (h) of this section shall not be considered to be a taking of any endangered species or threatened species with respect to any activity which is necessary to carry out such action; and

(2) any taking that is in compliance with the terms and conditions specified in a written statement provided under subsection (b)(4)(iv) of this section shall not be considered to be a prohibited taking of the species concerned.

(p) Exemptions in Presidentially declared disaster areas

In any area which has been declared by the President to be a major disaster area under the Disaster Relief and Emergency Assistance Act [42 U.S.C.A. § 5121 et seq.], the President is authorized to make the determinations required by subsections (g) and (h) of this section for any project for the repair or replacement of a public facility substantially as it existed prior to the disaster under section 405 or 406 of the Disaster Relief and Emergency Assistance Act [42 U.S.C.A. §§ 5171 or 5172], and which the President determines (1) is necessary to prevent the recurrence of such a natural disaster and to reduce the potential loss of human life, and (2) to involve an emergency situation which does not allow the ordinary procedures of this section to be followed. Notwithstanding any other provision of this section, the Committee shall accept the determinations of the President under this subsection.

(Pub.L. 93–205, § 7, Dec. 28, 1973, 87 Stat. 892; Pub.L. 95–632, § 3, Nov. 10, 1978, 92 Stat. 3752; Pub.L. 96–159, § 4, Dec. 28, 1979, 93 Stat. 1226; Pub.L. 97–304, §§ 4(a), 8(b), Oct. 13, 1982, 96 Stat. 1417, 1426; Pub.L. 99–659, Title IV, § 411(b), (c), Nov. 14, 1986, 100 Stat. 3742; Pub.L. 100–707, Title I, § 109(g), Nov. 23, 1988, 102 Stat. 4709.)

References in Text

The Privacy Act, referred to in subsec. (e)(7)(C), is Pub.L. 93–579, Dec. 31, 1974, 88 Stat. 1896, as amended, which enacted section 552a of Title 5, Government Organization and Employees, and provisions set out as notes under section 552a of Title 5. For complete classification of this Act to the Code, see Short Title note set out under section 552a of Title 5 and Tables volume.

The National Environmental Policy Act of 1969, referred to in subsec. (k), is Pub.L. 91–190, Jan. 1, 1970, 83 Stat. 852, as amended, which is classified generally to chapter 55 (section 4321 et seq.) of Title 42, The Public Health and Welfare. Section 102 of the National Environmental Policy Act of 1969, referred to in subsec. (c)(1), is classified to section 4332 of Title 42. For complete classification of this Act to the Code, see Short Title note set out under section 4321 of Title 42 and Tables Volume.

The Disaster Relief and Emergency Assistance Act (redesignated "The Robert T. Stafford Disaster Relief and Emergency Assistance Act" by Pub.L. 93–288, § 1, as amended by 100–707, § 102(a)), referred to in subsec. (p), is Pub.L. 93–288, May 22, 1974, 88 Stat. 143, as amended, which is classified principally to chapter 68 (section 5121 et seq.) of Title 42, The Public Health and Welfare. Sections 405 and 406 of the Disaster and Emergency Assistance Act are classified to sections 5171 and 5172 of Title 42. For complete classification of this Act to the Code, see Short Title note set out under section 5121 of Title 42 and Tables volume.

WEST'S FEDERAL FORMS

Complaint to enjoin violations, see § 1713.

CROSS REFERENCES

Authorization of appropriations, see section 1542 of this title.
Experimental populations, exception, see section 1539 of this title.
"Permit or license applicant" defined when used with respect to an action of a Federal agency for which an exemption is sought under this section, see section 1532 of this title.

West's Federal Forms

Enforcement and review of decisions and orders of administrative agencies, see § 851 et seq.

CODE OF FEDERAL REGULATIONS

Critical habitats, see 50 CFR 17.94 et seq.

LAW REVIEW COMMENTARIES

Conservation obligations under the Endangered Species Act: A case study of the Yellowstone grizzly bear. Comment, 64 U.Colo. L.Rev. 607 (1993).

Effectiveness of judicial review under the 1979 Amendment to the Endangered Species Act. 7 J.Energy L. & Pol'y 145 (1986).

Endangered Species Act and its implementation by the U.S. Department of Interior and Commerce. Oliver A. Houck, 64 U.Colo. L.Rev. 277 (1993).

Protecting Public Values in the Platte River. Eric Pearson and J. David Aiken 20 Creighton L.Rev. 361 (1986–1987).

Warrior and the Druid—the DOD and environmental law. Michael Donnelly and James G. Van Ness, 33 Fed.Bar News 37 (1986).

§ 1537. International cooperation [ESA § 8]

(a) Financial assistance

As a demonstration of the commitment of the United States to the worldwide protection of endangered species and threatened species, the President may, subject to the provisions of section 1306 of Title 31, use foreign currencies accruing to the United States Government under the Agricultural Trade Development and Assistance Act of 1954 [7 U.S.C.A. § 1691 et seq.] or any other law to provide to any foreign country (with its consent) assistance in the development and management of programs in that country which the Secretary determines to be necessary or useful for the conservation of any endangered species or threatened species listed by the Secretary pursuant to section 1533 of this title. The President shall provide assistance (which includes, but is not limited to, the acquisition, by lease or otherwise, of lands, waters, or interests therein) to foreign countries under this section under such terms and conditions as he deems appropriate. Whenever foreign currencies are available for the provision of assistance under this section, such currencies shall be used in preference to funds appropriated under the authority of section 1542 of this title.

(b) Encouragement of foreign programs

In order to carry out further the provisions of this chapter, the Secretary, through the Secretary of State, shall encourage—

(1) foreign countries to provide for the conservation of fish or wildlife and plants including endangered species and threatened species listed pursuant to section 1533 of this title;

(2) the entering into of bilateral or multilateral agreements with foreign countries to provide for such conservation; and

(3) foreign persons who directly or indirectly take fish or wildlife or plants in foreign countries or on the high seas for importation into the United States for commercial or other purposes to develop and carry out with such assistance as he may provide, conservation practices designed to enhance such fish or wildlife or plants and their habitat.

(c) Personnel

After consultation with the Secretary of State, the Secretary may—

(1) assign or otherwise make available any officer or employee of his department for the purpose of cooperating with foreign countries and international organizations in developing personnel resources and programs which promote the conservation of fish or wildlife or plants; and

(2) conduct or provide financial assistance for the educational training of foreign personnel, in this country or abroad, in fish, wildlife, or plant management, research and law enforcement and to render professional assistance abroad in such matters.

(d) Investigations

After consultation with the Secretary of State and the Secretary of the Treasury, as appropriate, the Secretary may conduct or cause to be conducted such law enforcement investigations and research abroad as he deems necessary to carry out the purposes of this chapter.

(Pub.L. 93–205, § 8, Dec. 28, 1973, 87 Stat. 892; Pub.L. 96–159, § 5, Dec. 28, 1979, 93 Stat. 1228.)

References in Text

The Agricultural Trade Development and Assistance Act of 1954, referred to in subsec. (a), is Act July 10, 1954, c. 469, 68 Stat. 454, as amended, which is classified generally to chapter 41 (section 1691 et seq.) of Title 7, Agriculture. For complete classification of this Act to the Code, see Short Title note set out under section 1691 of Title 7 and Tables volume.

Codification

In subsec. (a), "section 1306 of Title 31" was substituted for "section 1415 of the Supplemental Appropriation Act, 1953 (31 U.S.C. 724)" on authority of Pub.L. 97–258, § 4(b), Sept. 13, 1982, 96 Stat. 1067, the first section of which enacted Title 31, Money and Finance.

Conservation of Sea Turtles; Importation of Shrimp

Pub.L. 101–162, Title VI, § 609, Nov. 21, 1989, 103 Stat. 1037, provided that:

"**(a)** The Secretary of State, in consultation with the Secretary of Commerce, shall, with respect to those species of sea turtles the conservation of which is the subject of regulations promulgated by the Secretary of Commerce on June 29, 1987—

"**(1)** initiate negotiations as soon as possible for the development of bilateral or multilateral agreements with other nations for the protection and conservation of such species of sea turtles;

"**(2)** initiate negotiations as soon as possible with all foreign governments which are engaged in, or which have persons or companies engaged in, commercial fishing operations which, as determined by the Secretary of Commerce, may affect adversely such species of sea turtles, for the purpose of entering into bilateral and multilateral treaties with such countries to protect such species of sea turtles;

"**(3)** encourage such other agreements to promote the purposes of this section with other nations for the protection of specific ocean and land regions which are of special significance to the health and stability of such species of sea turtles;

"**(4)** initiate the amendment of any existing international treaty for the protection and conservation of such species of sea turtles to which the United States is a party in order to make such treaty consistent with the purposes and policies of this section; and

"**(5)** provide to the Congress by not later than one year after the date of enactment of this section [Nov. 21, 1989]

"**(A)** a list of each nation which conducts commercial shrimp fishing operations within the geographic range of distribution of such sea turtles;

"**(B)** a list of each nation which conducts commercial shrimp fishing operations which may affect adversely such species of sea turtles; and

"**(C)** a full report on—

"**(i)** the results of his efforts under this section; and

"**(ii)** the status of measures taken by each nation listed pursuant to paragraph (A) or (B) to protect and conserve such sea turtles.

"**(b)(1) In general.**—The importation of shrimp or products from shrimp which have been harvested with commercial fishing technology which may affect adversely such species of sea turtles shall be prohibited not later than May 1, 1991, except as provided in paragraph (2).

"**(2) Certification procedure.**—The ban on importation of shrimp or products from shrimp pursuant to paragraph (1) shall not apply if the President shall determine and certify to the Congress not later than May 1, 1991, and annually thereafter that—

"**(A)** the government of the harvesting nation has provided documentary evidence of the adoption of a regulatory program governing the incidental taking of such sea turtles in the course of such harvesting that is comparable to that of the United States; and

"**(B)** the average rate of that incidental taking by the vessels of the harvesting nation is comparable to the average rate of incidental taking of sea turtles by United States vessels in the course of such harvesting; or

"**(C)** the particular fishing environment of the harvesting nation does not pose a threat of the incidental taking of such sea turtles in the course of such harvesting."

WEST'S FEDERAL FORMS

Complaint to enjoin violations, see § 1713.

§ 1537a. Convention implementation [ESA § 8A]

(a) Management Authority and Scientific Authority

The Secretary of the Interior (hereinafter in this section referred to as the "Secretary") is designated as the Management Authority and the Scientific Authority for purposes of the Convention and the respective functions of each such Authority shall be carried out through the United States Fish and Wildlife Service.

(b) Management Authority functions

The Secretary shall do all things necessary and appropriate to carry out the functions of the Management Authority under the Convention.

(c) Scientific Authority functions; determinations

(1) The Secretary shall do all things necessary and appropriate to carry out the functions of the Scientific Authority under the Convention.

(2) The Secretary shall base the determinations and advice given by him under Article IV of the Convention with respect to wildlife upon the best available biological information derived from professionally accepted wildlife management practices; but is not required to make, or require any State to make, estimates of population size in making such determinations or giving such advice.

(d) Reservations by the United States under Convention

If the United States votes against including any species in Appendix I or II of the Convention and does not enter a reservation pursuant to paragraph (3) of Article XV of the Convention with respect to that species, the Secretary of State, before the 90th day after the last day on which such a reservation could be entered, shall submit to the Committee on Merchant Marine and Fisheries of the House of Representatives, and to the Committee on the Environment and Public Works of the Senate, a written report setting forth the reasons why such a reservation was not entered.

(e) Wildlife Preservation in Western Hemisphere

(1) The Secretary of the Interior (hereinafter in this subsection referred to as the "Secretary"), in cooperation with the Secretary of State, shall act on behalf of, and represent, the United States in all regards as required by the Convention on Nature Protection and Wildlife Preservation in the Western Hemisphere (56 Stat. 1354, T.S. 982, hereinafter in this subsection referred to as the "Western Convention"). In the discharge of these responsibilities, the Secretary and the Secretary of State shall consult with the Secretary of Agriculture, the Secretary of Commerce, and the heads of other agencies with respect to matters relating to or affecting their areas of responsibility.

(2) The Secretary and the Secretary of State shall, in cooperation with the contracting parties to the Western Convention and, to the extent feasible and appropriate, with the participation of State agencies, take such steps as are necessary to implement the Western Convention. Such steps shall include, but not be limited to—

(A) cooperation with contracting parties and international organizations for the purpose of developing personnel resources and programs that will facilitate implementation of the Western Convention;

(B) identification of those species of birds that migrate between the United States and other contracting parties, and the habitats upon which those species depend, and the implementation of cooperative measures to ensure that such species will not become endangered or threatened; and

(C) identification of measures that are necessary and appropriate to implement those provisions of the Western Convention which address the protection of wild plants.

(3) No later than September 30, 1985, the Secretary and the Secretary of State shall submit a report to Congress describing those steps taken in accordance with the requirements of this subsection and identifying the principal remaining actions yet necessary for comprehensive and effective implementation of the Western Convention.

(4) The provisions of this subsection shall not be construed as affecting the authority, jurisdiction, or responsibility of the several States to manage, control, or regulate resident fish or wildlife under State law or regulations.

(Pub.L. 93–205, § 8A, as added Pub.L. 96–159, § 6(a)(1), Dec. 28, 1979, 93 Stat. 1228, and amended Pub.L. 97–304, § 5, Oct. 13, 1982, 96 Stat. 1421.)

Abolition of House Committee on Merchant Marine and Fisheries

Committee on Merchant Marine and Fisheries of House of Representatives abolished and any reference in any provision of law enacted before Jan. 4, 1995, to the Committee on Merchant Marine and Fisheries of the House of Representatives treated as referring to the Committee on Agriculture of the House of Representatives, in the case of a provision of law relating to inspection of seafood or seafood products, the Committee on National Security of the House of Representatives, in the case of a provision of law relating to interoceanic canals, the Merchant Marine Academy and State Maritime Academies, or national security aspects of merchant marine, the Committee on Resources of the House of Representatives, in the case of a provision of law relating to fisheries, wildlife, international fishing agreements marine affairs (including coastal zone management) except for measures relating to oil and other pollution of navigable waters, or oceanography, the Committee on Science of the House of Representatives, in the case of a provision of law relating to marine research, and the Committee on Transportation and Infrastructure of the House of Representatives, in the case of a provision of law relating to a matter other than a matter described above, see section 1(b)(3) of Pub.L. 104–14, set out as a note preceding section 21 of Title 2, The Congress.

CROSS REFERENCES

Authorization of appropriations, see section 1542 of this title.

WEST'S FEDERAL FORMS

Complaint to enjoin violations, see § 1713.

CODE OF FEDERAL REGULATIONS

Endangered species convention, see 50 CFR 23.1 et seq.

§ 1538. Prohibited acts [ESA § 9]

(a) Generally

(1) Except as provided in sections 1535(g)(2) and 1539 of this title, with respect to any endangered species of fish or wildlife listed pursuant to section 1533 of this title it is unlawful for any person subject to the jurisdiction of the United States to—

(A) import any such species into, or export any such species from the United States;

(B) take any such species within the United States or the territorial sea of the United States;

(C) take any such species upon the high seas;

(D) possess, sell, deliver, carry, transport, or ship, by any means whatsoever, any such species taken in violation of subparagraphs (B) and (C);

(E) deliver, receive, carry, transport, or ship in interstate or foreign commerce, by any means whatsoever and in the course of a commercial activity, any such species;

(F) sell or offer for sale in interstate or foreign commerce any such species; or

(G) violate any regulation pertaining to such species or to any threatened species of fish or wildlife listed pursuant to section 1533 of this title and promulgated by the Secretary pursuant to authority provided by this chapter.

(2) Except as provided in sections 1535(g)(2) and 1539 of this title, with respect to any endangered

species of plants listed pursuant to section 1533 of this title, it is unlawful for any person subject to the jurisdiction of the United States to—

(A) import any such species into, or export any such species from, the United States;

(B) remove and reduce to possession any such species from areas under Federal jurisdiction; maliciously damage or destroy any such species on any such area; or remove, cut, dig up, or damage or destroy any such species on any other area in knowing violation of any law or regulation of any State or in the course of any violation of a State criminal trespass law;

(C) deliver, receive, carry, transport, or ship in interstate or foreign commerce, by any means whatsoever and in the course of a commercial activity, any such species;

(D) sell or offer for sale in interstate or foreign commerce any such species; or

(E) violate any regulation pertaining to such species or to any threatened species of plants listed pursuant to section 1533 of this title and promulgated by the Secretary pursuant to authority provided by this chapter.

(b) Species held in captivity or controlled environment

(1) The provisions of subsections (a)(1)(A) and (a)(1)(G) of this section shall not apply to any fish or wildlife which was held in captivity or in a controlled environment on (A) December 28, 1973, or (B) the date of the publication in the Federal Register of a final regulation adding such fish or wildlife species to any list published pursuant to subsection (c) of section 1533 of this title: *Provided,* That such holding and any subsequent holding or use of the fish or wildlife was not in the course of a commercial activity. With respect to any act prohibited by subsections (a)(1)(A) and (a)(1)(G) of this section which occurs after a period of 180 days from (i) December 28, 1973, or (ii) the date of publication in the Federal Register of a final regulation adding such fish or wildlife species to any list published pursuant to subsection (c) of section 1533 of this title, there shall be a rebuttable presumption that the fish or wildlife involved in such act is not entitled to the exemption contained in this subsection.

(2)(A) The provisions of subsection (a)(1) of this section shall not apply to—

(i) any raptor legally held in captivity or in a controlled environment on November 10, 1978; or

(ii) any progeny of any raptor described in clause (i);

until such time as any such raptor or progeny is intentionally returned to a wild state.

(B) Any person holding any raptor or progeny described in subparagraph (A) must be able to demonstrate that the raptor or progeny does, in fact, qualify under the provisions of this paragraph, and shall maintain and submit to the Secretary, on request, such inventories, documentation, and records as the Secretary may by regulation require as being reasonably appropriate to carry out the purposes of this paragraph. Such requirements shall not unnecessarily duplicate the requirements of other rules and regulations promulgated by the Secretary.

(c) Violation of Convention

(1) It is unlawful for any person subject to the jurisdiction of the United States to engage in any trade in any specimens contrary to the provisions of the Convention, or to possess any specimens traded contrary to the provisions of the Convention, including the definitions of terms in Article I thereof.

(2) Any importation into the United States of fish or wildlife shall, if—

(A) such fish or wildlife is not an endangered species listed pursuant to section 1533 of this title but is listed in Appendix II to the Convention,

(B) the taking and exportation of such fish or wildlife is not contrary to the provisions of the Convention and all other applicable requirements of the Convention have been satisfied,

(C) the applicable requirements of subsections (d), (e), and (f) of this section have been satisfied, and

(D) such importation is not made in the course of a commercial activity,

be presumed to be an importation not in violation of any provision of this chapter or any regulation issued pursuant to this chapter.

(d) Imports and exports

(1) In general.—It is unlawful for any person, without first having obtained permission from the Secretary, to engage in business—

(A) as an importer or exporter of fish or wildlife (other than shellfish and fishery products which (i) are not listed pursuant to section 1533 of this title as endangered species or threatened species, and (ii) are imported for purposes of human or animal consumption or taken in waters under the jurisdiction of the United States or on the high seas for recreational purposes) or plants; or

(B) as an importer or exporter of any amount of raw or worked African elephant ivory.

(2) **Requirements.**—Any person required to obtain permission under paragraph (1) of this subsection shall—

(A) keep such records as will fully and correctly disclose each importation or exportation of fish, wildlife, plants, or African elephant ivory made by him and the subsequent disposition made by him with respect to such fish, wildlife, plants, or ivory;

(B) at all reasonable times upon notice by a duly authorized representative of the Secretary, afford such representative access to his place of business, an opportunity to examine his inventory of imported fish, wildlife, plants, or African elephant ivory and the records required to be kept under subparagraph (A) of this paragraph, and to copy such records; and

(C) file such reports as the Secretary may require.

(3) **Regulations.**—The Secretary shall prescribe such regulations as are necessary and appropriate to carry out the purposes of this subsection.

(4) **Restriction on consideration of value or amount of African elephant ivory imported or exported.**—In granting permission under this subsection for importation or exportation of African elephant ivory, the Secretary shall not vary the requirements for obtaining such permission on the basis of the value or amount of ivory imported or exported under such permission.

(e) Reports

It is unlawful for any person importing or exporting fish or wildlife (other than shellfish and fishery products which (1) are not listed pursuant to section 1533 of this title as endangered or threatened species, and (2) are imported for purposes of human or animal consumption or taken in waters under the jurisdiction of the United States or on the high seas for recreational purposes) or plants to fail to file any declaration or report as the Secretary deems necessary to facilitate enforcement of this chapter or to meet the obligations of the Convention.

(f) Designation of ports

(1) It is unlawful for any person subject to the jurisdiction of the United States to import into or export from the United States any fish or wildlife (other than shellfish and fishery products which (A) are not listed pursuant to section 1533 of this title as endangered species or threatened species, and (B) are imported for purposes of human or animal consumption or taken in waters under the jurisdiction of the United States or on the high seas for recreational purposes) or plants, except at a port or ports designated by the Secretary of the Interior. For the purpose of facilitating enforcement of this chapter and reducing the costs thereof, the Secretary of the Interior, with approval of the Secretary of the Treasury and after notice and opportunity for public hearing, may, by regulation, designate ports and change such designations. The Secretary of the Interior, under such terms and conditions as he may prescribe, may permit the importation or exportation at nondesignated ports in the interest of the health or safety of the fish or wildlife or plants, or for other reasons if, in his discretion, he deems it appropriate and consistent with the purpose of this subsection.

(2) Any port designated by the Secretary of the Interior under the authority of section 668cc–4(d) of this title, shall, if such designation is in effect on December 27, 1973, be deemed to be a port designated by the Secretary under paragraph (1) of this subsection until such time as the Secretary otherwise provides.

(g) Violations

It is unlawful for any person subject to the jurisdiction of the United States to attempt to commit, solicit another to commit, or cause to be committed, any offense defined in this section.

(Pub.L. 93–205, § 9, Dec. 28, 1973, 87 Stat. 893; Pub.L. 95–632, § 4, Nov. 10, 1978, 92 Stat. 3760; Pub.L. 97–304, § 9(b), Oct. 13, 1982, 96 Stat. 1426; Pub.L. 100–478, Title I, § 1006, Title II, § 2301, Oct. 7, 1988, 102 Stat. 2308, 2321; Pub.L. 100–653, Title IX, § 905, Nov. 14, 1988, 102 Stat. 3835.)

References in Text

Section 668cc–4(d) of this title, referred to in subsec. (f)(2), was repealed by Pub.L. 93–205, § 14, Dec. 28, 1973, 87 Stat. 903.

Human Activities Within Proximity of Whales

Pub.L. 103–238, § 17, Apr. 30, 1994, 108 Stat. 559, provided that:

"**(a) Lawful approaches.**—In waters of the United States surrounding the State of Hawaii, it is lawful for a person subject to the jurisdiction of the United States to approach, by any means other than an aircraft, no closer than 100 years to a humpback whale, regardless of whether the approach is made in waters designated under section 222.31 of title 50, Code of Federal Regulations, as cow/calf waters.

"**(b) Termination of legal effect of certain regulations.**—Subsection (b) of section 222.31 of title 50, Code of Federal Regulations, shall cease to be in force and effect."

Cross References

Exemption as providing exception on taking of endangered species, see section 1536 of this title.
Issuance of protective regulations, see section 1533 of this title.
Penalties and enforcement, see section 1540 of this title.
Permits and hardship exemptions, see section 1539 of this title.
Taking of resident endangered or threatened species, cooperative agreements with States, see section 1535 of this title.

WEST'S FEDERAL FORMS

Complaint to enjoin violations, see § 1713.

CODE OF FEDERAL REGULATIONS

Importation of wild animals, birds, fish, insects, etc., see 19 CFR 12.26 et seq.
Off-road vehicles on public lands, see 43 CFR 8340.0–1 et seq.
Plants, see 50 CFR 17.61 et seq., 17.71 et seq.
Wildlife, see 50 CFR 17.21 et seq., 17.31 et seq.

LAW REVIEW COMMENTARIES

Endangered Species Act and its implementation by the U.S. Department of Interior and Commerce. Oliver A. Houck, 64 U.Colo. L.Rev. 277 (1993).

Warrior and the Druid—the DOD and environmental law. Michael Donnelly and James G. Van Ness, 33 Fed.Bar News 37 (1986).

Library References

Customs Duties ⚷22.
Fish ⚷13.
Game ⚷7.
United States ⚷41.
C.J.S. Customs Duties § 30.
C.J.S. Fish § 28 et seq.
C.J.S. Game §§ 1, 5.
C.J.S. United States § 41.

WESTLAW ELECTRONIC RESEARCH

United States: 393k (add key number)

§ 1539. Exceptions [ESA § 10]

(a) Permits

(1) The Secretary may permit, under such terms and conditions as he shall prescribe—

(A) any act otherwise prohibited by section 1538 of this title for scientific purposes or to enhance the propagation or survival of the affected species, including, but not limited to, acts necessary for the establishment and maintenance of experimental populations pursuant to subsection (j) of this section; or

(B) any taking otherwise prohibited by section 1538(a)(1)(B) of this title if such taking is incidental to, and not the purpose of, the carrying out of an otherwise lawful activity.

(2)(A) No permit may be issued by the Secretary authorizing any taking referred to in paragraph (1)(B) unless the applicant therefor submits to the Secretary a conservation plan that specifies—

(i) the impact which will likely result from such taking;

(ii) what steps the applicant will take to minimize and mitigate such impacts, and the funding that will be available to implement such steps;

(iii) what alternative actions to such taking the applicant considered and the reasons why such alternatives are not being utilized; and

(iv) such other measures that the Secretary may require as being necessary or appropriate for purposes of the plan.

(B) If the Secretary finds, after opportunity for public comment, with respect to a permit application and the related conservation plan that—

(i) the taking will be incidental;

(ii) the applicant will, to the maximum extent practicable, minimize and mitigate the impacts of such taking;

(iii) the applicant will ensure that adequate funding for the plan will be provided;

(iv) the taking will not appreciably reduce the likelihood of the survival and recovery of the species in the wild; and

(v) the measures, if any, required under subparagraph (A)(iv) will be met;

and he has received such other assurances as he may require that the plan will be implemented, the Secretary shall issue the permit. The permit shall contain such terms and conditions as the Secretary deems necessary or appropriate to carry out the purposes of this paragraph, including, but not limited to, such reporting requirements as the Secretary deems necessary for determining whether such terms and conditions are being complied with.

(C) The Secretary shall revoke a permit issued under this paragraph if he finds that the permittee is not complying with the terms and conditions of the permit.

(b) Hardship exemptions

(1) If any person enters into a contract with respect to a species of fish or wildlife or plant before the date of the publication in the Federal Register of notice of consideration of that species as an endangered species and the subsequent listing of that species as an endangered species pursuant to section 1533 of this title will cause undue economic hardship to such person under the contract, the Secretary, in order to minimize such hardship, may exempt such person from the application of section 1538(a) of this title to the extent the Secretary deems appropriate if such person applies to him for such exemption and includes with such application such information as the Secretary may require to prove such hardship; except that (A) no such exemption shall be for a duration of more than one year from the date of publication in the Federal Register of notice of consideration of the species concerned, or shall apply to a quantity of fish or wildlife or plants in excess of that specified by the Secretary; (B) the one-year period for those species of fish or wildlife listed by the Secretary as endangered prior to December 28, 1973 shall expire in accordance with the terms of section 668cc–3 of this title; and (C) no such exemption may be granted for the importation or exportation of a specimen listed in

Appendix I of the Convention which is to be used in a commercial activity.

(2) As used in this subsection, the term "undue economic hardship" shall include, but not be limited to:

(A) substantial economic loss resulting from inability caused by this chapter to perform contracts with respect to species of fish and wildlife entered into prior to the date of publication in the Federal Register of a notice of consideration of such species as an endangered species;

(B) substantial economic loss to persons who, for the year prior to the notice of consideration of such species as an endangered species, derived a substantial portion of their income from the lawful taking of any listed species, which taking would be made unlawful under this chapter; or

(C) curtailment of subsistence taking made unlawful under this chapter by persons (i) not reasonably able to secure other sources of subsistence; and (ii) dependent to a substantial extent upon hunting and fishing for subsistence; and (iii) who must engage in such curtailed taking for subsistence purposes.

(3) The Secretary may make further requirements for a showing of undue economic hardship as he deems fit. Exceptions granted under this section may be limited by the Secretary in his discretion as to time, area, or other factor of applicability.

(c) Notice and review

The Secretary shall publish notice in the Federal Register of each application for an exemption or permit which is made under this section. Each notice shall invite the submission from interested parties, within thirty days after the date of the notice, of written data, views, or arguments with respect to the application; except that such thirty-day period may be waived by the Secretary in an emergency situation where the health or life of an endangered animal is threatened and no reasonable alternative is available to the applicant, but notice of any such waiver shall be published by the Secretary in the Federal Register within ten days following the issuance of the exemption or permit. Information received by the Secretary as a part of any application shall be available to the public as a matter of public record at every stage of the proceeding.

(d) Permit and exemption policy

The Secretary may grant exceptions under subsections (a)(1)(A) and (b) of this section only if he finds and publishes his finding in the Federal Register that (1) such exceptions were applied for in good faith, (2) if granted and exercised will not operate to the disadvantage of such endangered species, and (3) will be consistent with the purposes and policy set forth in section 1531 of this title.

(e) Alaska natives

(1) Except as provided in paragraph (4) of this subsection the provisions of this chapter shall not apply with respect to the taking of any endangered species or threatened species, or the importation of any such species taken pursuant to this section, by—

(A) any Indian, Aleut, or Eskimo who is an Alaskan Native who resides in Alaska; or

(B) any non-native permanent resident of an Alaskan native village;

if such taking is primarily for subsistence purposes. Non-edible byproducts of species taken pursuant to this section may be sold in interstate commerce when made into authentic native articles of handicrafts and clothing; except that the provisions of this subsection shall not apply to any non-native resident of an Alaskan native village found by the Secretary to be not primarily dependent upon the taking of fish and wildlife for consumption or for the creation and sale of authentic native articles of handicrafts and clothing.

(2) Any taking under this subsection may not be accomplished in a wasteful manner.

(3) As used in this subsection—

(i) The term "subsistence" includes selling any edible portion of fish or wildlife in native villages and towns in Alaska for native consumption within native villages or towns; and

(ii) The term "authentic native articles of handicrafts and clothing" means items composed wholly or in some significant respect of natural materials, and which are produced, decorated, or fashioned in the exercise of traditional native handicrafts without the use of pantographs, multiple carvers, or other mass copying devices. Traditional native handicrafts include, but are not limited to, weaving, carving, stitching, sewing, lacing, beading, drawing, and painting.

(4) Notwithstanding the provisions of paragraph (1) of this subsection, whenever the Secretary determines that any species of fish or wildlife which is subject to taking under the provisions of this subsection is an endangered species or threatened species, and that such taking materially and negatively affects the threatened or endangered species, he may prescribe regulations upon the taking of such species by any such Indian, Aleut, Eskimo, or non-Native Alaskan resident of an Alaskan native village. Such regulations may be established with reference to species,

geographical description of the area included, the season for taking, or any other factors related to the reason for establishing such regulations and consistent with the policy of this chapter. Such regulations shall be prescribed after a notice and hearings in the affected judicial districts of Alaska and as otherwise required by section 1373 of this title, and shall be removed as soon as the Secretary determines that the need for their impositions has disappeared.

(f) Pre-Act endangered species parts exemption; application and certification; regulation; validity of sales contract; separability of provisions; renewal of exemption; expiration of renewal certification

(1) As used in this subsection—

(A) The term "pre-Act endangered species part" means—

(i) any sperm whale oil, including derivatives thereof, which was lawfully held within the United States on December 28, 1973, in the course of a commercial activity; or

(ii) any finished scrimshaw product, if such product or the raw material for such product was lawfully held within the United States on December 28, 1973, in the course of a commercial activity.

(B) The term "scrimshaw product" means any art form which involves the substantial etching or engraving of designs upon, or the substantial carving of figures, patterns, or designs from, any bone or tooth of any marine mammal of the order Cetacea. For purposes of this subsection, polishing or the adding of minor superficial markings does not constitute substantial etching, engraving, or carving.

(2) The Secretary, pursuant to the provisions of this subsection, may exempt, if such exemption is not in violation of the Convention, any pre-Act endangered species part from one or more of the following prohibitions:

(A) The prohibition on exportation from the United States set forth in section 1538(a)(1)(A) of this title.

(B) Any prohibition set forth in section 1538(a)(1)(E) or (F) of this title.

(3) Any person seeking an exemption described in paragraph (2) of this subsection shall make application therefor to the Secretary in such form and manner as he shall prescribe, but no such application may be considered by the Secretary unless the application—

(A) is received by the Secretary before the close of the one-year period beginning on the date on which regulations promulgated by the Secretary to carry out this subsection first take effect;

(B) contains a complete and detailed inventory of all pre-Act endangered species parts for which the applicant seeks exemption;

(C) is accompanied by such documentation as the Secretary may require to prove that any endangered species part or product claimed by the applicant to be a pre-Act endangered species part is in fact such a part; and

(D) contains such other information as the Secretary deems necessary and appropriate to carry out the purposes of this subsection.

(4) If the Secretary approves any application for exemption made under this subsection, he shall issue to the applicant a certificate of exemption which shall specify—

(A) any prohibition in section 1538(a) of this title which is exempted;

(B) the pre-Act endangered species parts to which the exemption applies;

(C) the period of time during which the exemption is in effect, but no exemption made under this subsection shall have force and effect after the close of the three-year period beginning on the date of issuance of the certificate unless such exemption is renewed under paragraph (8); and

(D) any term or condition prescribed pursuant to paragraph (5)(A) or (B), or both, which the Secretary deems necessary or appropriate.

(5) The Secretary shall prescribe such regulations as he deems necessary and appropriate to carry out the purposes of this subsection. Such regulations may set forth—

(A) terms and conditions which may be imposed on applicants for exemptions under this subsection (including, but not limited to, requirements that applicants register inventories, keep complete sales records, permit duly authorized agents of the Secretary to inspect such inventories and records, and periodically file appropriate reports with the Secretary); and

(B) terms and conditions which may be imposed on any subsequent purchaser of any pre-Act endangered species part covered by an exemption granted under this subsection;

to insure that any such part so exempted is adequately accounted for and not disposed of contrary to the provisions of this chapter. No regulation prescribed by the Secretary to carry out the purposes of this subsection shall be subject to section 1533(f)(2)(A)(i) of this title.

(6)(A) Any contract for the sale of pre-Act endangered species parts which is entered into by the Administrator of General Services prior to the effective date of this subsection and pursuant to the notice published in the Federal Register on January 9, 1973, shall not be rendered invalid by virtue of the fact that fulfillment of such contract may be prohibited under section 1538(a)(1)(F) of this title.

(B) In the event that this paragraph is held invalid, the validity of the remainder of this chapter, including the remainder of this subsection, shall not be affected.

(7) Nothing in this subsection shall be construed to—

(A) exonerate any person from any act committed in violation of paragraphs (1)(A), (1)(E), or (1)(F) of section 1538(a) of this title prior to July 12, 1976; or

(B) immunize any person from prosecution for any such act.

(8)(A)(i) [1] Any valid certificate of exemption which was renewed after October 13, 1982, and was in effect on March 31, 1988, shall be deemed to be renewed for a six-month period beginning on October 7, 1988. Any person holding such a certificate may apply to the Secretary for one additional renewal of such certificate for a period not to exceed 5 years beginning on October 7, 1988.

(B) If the Secretary approves any application for renewal of an exemption under this paragraph, he shall issue to the applicant a certificate of renewal of such exemption which shall provide that all terms, conditions, prohibitions, and other regulations made applicable by the previous certificate shall remain in effect during the period of the renewal.

(C) No exemption or renewal of such exemption made under this subsection shall have force and effect after the expiration date of the certificate of renewal of such exemption issued under this paragraph.

(D) No person may, after January 31, 1984, sell or offer for sale in interstate or foreign commerce, any pre-Act finished scrimshaw product unless such person holds a valid certificate of exemption issued by the Secretary under this subsection, and unless such product or the raw material for such product was held by such person on October 13, 1982.

(9) Repealed. Pub.L. 100–478, Title I, § 1011(d), Oct. 7, 1988, 102 Stat. 2314.

(g) Burden of proof

In connection with any action alleging a violation of section 1538 of this title, any person claiming the benefit of any exemption or permit under this chapter shall have the burden of proving that the exemption or permit is applicable, has been granted, and was valid and in force at the time of the alleged violation.

(h) Certain antique articles; importation; port designation; application for return of articles

(1) Sections 1533(d) and 1538(a) and (c) of this title do not apply to any article which—

(A) is not less than 100 years of age;

(B) is composed in whole or in part of any endangered species or threatened species listed under section 1533 of this title;

(C) has not been repaired or modified with any part of any such species on or after December 28, 1973; and

(D) is entered at a port designated under paragraph (3).

(2) Any person who wishes to import an article under the exception provided by this subsection shall submit to the customs officer concerned at the time of entry of the article such documentation as the Secretary of the Treasury, after consultation with the Secretary of the Interior, shall by regulation require as being necessary to establish that the article meets the requirements set forth in paragraph (1)(A), (B), and (C).

(3) The Secretary of the Treasury, after consultation with the Secretary of the Interior, shall designate one port within each customs region at which articles described in paragraph (1)(A), (B), and (C) must be entered into the customs territory of the United States.

(4) Any person who imported, after December 27, 1973, and on or before November 10, 1978, any article described in paragraph (1) which—

(A) was not repaired or modified after the date of importation with any part of any endangered species or threatened species listed under section 1533 of this title;

(B) was forfeited to the United States before November 10, 1978, or is subject to forfeiture to the United States on such date of enactment, pursuant to the assessment of a civil penalty under section 1540 of this title; and

(C) is in the custody of the United States on November 10, 1978;

may, before the close of the one-year period beginning on November 10, 1978, make application to the Secretary for return of the article. Application shall be made in such form and manner, and contain such documentation, as the Secretary prescribes. If on the basis of any such application which is timely filed, the Secretary is satisfied that the requirements of this paragraph are met with respect to the article concerned, the Secretary shall return the article to the applicant and the importation of such article shall, on and after the date of return, be deemed to be a lawful importation under this chapter.

(i) Noncommercial transshipments

Any importation into the United States of fish or wildlife shall, if—

(1) such fish or wildlife was lawfully taken and exported from the country of origin and country of reexport, if any;

(2) such fish or wildlife is in transit or transshipment through any place subject to the jurisdiction of the United States en route to a country where such fish or wildlife may be lawfully imported and received;

(3) the exporter or owner of such fish or wildlife gave explicit instructions not to ship such fish or wildlife through any place subject to the jurisdiction of the United States, or did all that could have reasonably been done to prevent transshipment, and the circumstances leading to the transshipment were beyond the exporter's or owner's control;

(4) the applicable requirements of the Convention have been satisfied; and

(5) such importation is not made in the course of a commercial activity,

be an importation not in violation of any provision of this chapter or any regulation issued pursuant to this chapter while such fish or wildlife remains in the control of the United States Customs Service.

(j) Experimental populations

(1) For purposes of this subsection, the term "experimental population" means any population (including any offspring arising solely therefrom) authorized by the Secretary for release under paragraph (2), but only when, and at such times as, the population is wholly separate geographically from nonexperimental populations of the same species.

(2)(A) The Secretary may authorize the release (and the related transportation) of any population (including eggs, propagules, or individuals) of an endangered species or a threatened species outside the current range of such species if the Secretary determines that such release will further the conservation of such species.

(B) Before authorizing the release of any population under subparagraph (A), the Secretary shall by regulation identify the population and determine, on the basis of the best available information, whether or not such population is essential to the continued existence of an endangered species or a threatened species.

(C) For the purposes of this chapter, each member of an experimental population shall be treated as a threatened species; except that—

(i) solely for purposes of section 1536 of this title (other than subsection (a)(1) thereof), an experimental population determined under subparagraph (B) to be not essential to the continued existence of a species shall be treated, except when it occurs in an area within the National Wildlife Refuge System or the National Park System, as a species proposed to be listed under section 1533 of this title; and

(ii) critical habitat shall not be designated under this chapter for any experimental population determined under subparagraph (B) to be not essential to the continued existence of a species.

(3) The Secretary, with respect to populations of endangered species or threatened species that the Secretary authorized, before October 13, 1982, for release in geographical areas separate from the other populations of such species, shall determine by regulation which of such populations are an experimental population for the purposes of this subsection and whether or not each is essential to the continued existence of an endangered species or a threatened species.

(Pub.L. 93–205, § 10, Dec. 28, 1973, 87 Stat. 896; Pub.L. 94–359, §§ 2, 3, July 12, 1976, 90 Stat. 911, 912; Pub.L. 95–632, § 5, Nov. 10, 1978, 92 Stat. 3760; Pub.L. 96–159, § 7, Dec. 28, 1979, 93 Stat. 1230; Pub.L. 97–304, § 6(1) to (3), (4)(A)(5), (6), Oct. 13, 1982, 96 Stat. 1422–1424; Pub.L. 100–478, Title I, §§ 1011, 1013(b), (c), Oct. 7, 1988, 102 Stat. 2314, 2315.)

[1] So in original. No. cl. (ii) has been enacted.

References in Text

Section 668cc–3 of this title, referred to in subsec. (b), was repealed by Pub.L. 93–205, § 14, Dec. 28, 1973, 87 Stat. 903.

Pre-Act, referred to in subsec. (f), means the period prior to the effective date of the Endangered Species Act of 1973, Dec. 28, 1973.

Subsec. (f) of section 1533 of this title, referred to in subsec. (f)(5), which related to promulgation of regulations by the Secretary was struck out, and subsec. (g) of section 1533 of this title was redesignated as subsec. (f), by Pub.L. 97–304, § (2)(a)(4)(B), (C), Oct. 13, 1982, 96 Stat. 1415. For provisions related to promulgation of regulations, see subsecs. (b) and (h) of section 1533 of this title.

Effective date of this subsection, referred to in subsec. (f)(6)(A), probably means the date of enactment of subsec. (f) by section 2 of Pub.L. 94–359, July 12, 1976.

Scrimshaw Exemptions

Pub.L. 103–238, § 18, Apr. 30, 1994, 108 Stat. 559, provided that: "Notwithstanding any other provision of law, any valid certificate of exemption renewed by the Secretary (or deemed to be renewed) under section 10(f)(8) of the Endangered Species Act of 1973 (16 U.S.C. 1539(f)(8) [subsec. (f)(8) of this section]) for any person holding such a certificate with respect to the possession of pre-Act finished scrimshaw products or raw material for such products shall remain valid for a period not to exceed 5 years beginning on the date of enactment of this Act [Apr. 30, 1994]."

CROSS REFERENCES

Provisions of this section as exception to prohibited acts, see section 1538 of this title.

WEST'S FEDERAL FORMS

Complaint to enjoin violations, see § 1713.

CODE OF FEDERAL REGULATIONS

Exemptions—
 Application procedure, see 50 CFR 451.01 et seq.
 Consideration of application by Secretary, see 50 CFR 452.01 et seq.
 General provisions, see 50 CFR 450.01 et seq.
 Pre-Act endangered species, see 50 CFR 222.1 et seq.
 Review of application by Endangered Species Committee, see 50 CFR 453.01 et seq.
General permit procedures—
 National Marine Fisheries Service, see 50 CFR 220.1 et seq.
 United States Fish and Wildlife Service, see 50 CFR 13.1 et seq.
Plants, see 50 CFR 17.62 et seq., 17.72 et seq.
Subsistence uses by Alaska natives, see 36 CFR 13.40 et seq.
Surface coal mining and reclamation operations, see 30 CFR 773.1 et seq.
Wildlife, see 50 CFR 17.22 et seq., 17.32 et seq.

LAW REVIEW COMMENTARIES

Endangered Species Act and its implementation by the U.S. Department of Interior and Commerce. Oliver A. Houck, 64 U.Colo. L.Rev. 277 (1993).

LIBRARY REFERENCES

Food ⇨8.
Game ⇨3½.
C.J.S. Food § 18.
C.J.S. Game § 7.

WESTLAW ELECTRONIC RESEARCH

Food cases: 178k (add key number)
Game cases: 187k (add key number)

§ 1540. Penalties and enforcement [ESA § 11]

(a) Civil penalties

(1) Any person who knowingly violates, and any person engaged in business as an importer or exporter of fish, wildlife, or plants who violates, any provision of this chapter, or any provision of any permit or certificate issued hereunder, or of any regulation issued in order to implement subsection (a)(1)(A), (B), (C), (D), (E), or (F), (a)(2)(A), (B), (C), or (D), (c), (d) (other than regulation relating to recordkeeping or filing of reports), (f) or (g) of section 1538 of this title, may be assessed a civil penalty by the Secretary of not more than $25,000 for each violation. Any person who knowingly violates, and any person engaged in business as an importer or exporter of fish, wildlife, or plants who violates, any provision of any other regulation issued under this chapter may be assessed a civil penalty by the Secretary of not more than $12,000 for each such violation. Any person who otherwise violates any provision of this chapter, or any regulation, permit, or certificate issued hereunder, may be assessed a civil penalty by the Secretary of not more than $500 for each such violation. No penalty may be assessed under this subsection unless such person is given notice and opportunity for a hearing with respect to such violation. Each violation shall be a separate offense. Any such civil penalty may be remitted or mitigated by the Secretary. Upon any failure to pay a penalty assessed under this subsection, the Secretary may request the Attorney General to institute a civil action in a district court of the United States for any district in which such person is found, resides, or transacts business to collect the penalty and such court shall have jurisdiction to hear and decide any such action. The court shall hear such action on the record made before the Secretary and shall sustain his action if it is supported by substantial evidence on the record considered as a whole.

(2) Hearings held during proceedings for the assessment of civil penalties authorized by paragraph (1) of this subsection shall be conducted in accordance with section 554 of Title 5. The Secretary may issue subpenas for the attendance and testimony of witnesses and the production of relevant papers, books, and documents, and administer oaths. Witnesses summoned shall be paid the same fees and mileage that are paid to witnesses in the courts of the United States. In case of contumacy or refusal to obey a subpena served upon any person pursuant to this paragraph, the district court of the United States for any district in which such person is found or resides or transacts business, upon application by the United States and after notice to such person, shall have jurisdiction to issue an order requiring such person to appear and give testimony before the Secretary or to appear and produce documents before the Secretary, or both, and any failure to obey such order of the court may be punished by such court as a contempt thereof.

(3) Notwithstanding any other provision of this chapter, no civil penalty shall be imposed if it can be shown by a preponderance of the evidence that the defendant committed an act based on a good faith belief that he was acting to protect himself or herself, a member of his or her family, or any other individual from bodily harm, from any endangered or threatened species.

(b) Criminal violations

(1) Any person who knowingly violates any provision of this chapter, of any permit or certificate issued hereunder, or of any regulation issued in order to implement subsection (a)(1)(A), (B), (C), (D), (E), or (F); (a)(2)(A), (B), (C), or (D), (c), (d) (other than a regulation relating to recordkeeping, or filing of reports), (f), or (g) of section 1538 of this title shall, upon conviction, be fined not more than $50,000 or imprisoned for not more than one year, or both. Any person who knowingly violates any provision of any other regulation issued under this chapter shall, upon conviction, be fined not more than $25,000 or imprisoned for not more than six months, or both.

(2) The head of any Federal agency which has issued a lease, license, permit, or other agreement authorizing a person to import or export fish, wildlife, or plants, or to operate a quarantine station for imported wildlife, or authorizing the use of Federal lands, including grazing of domestic livestock, to any person who is convicted of a criminal violation of this chapter or any regulation, permit, or certificate issued hereunder may immediately modify, suspend, or revoke each lease, license, permit or other agreement. The Secretary shall also suspend for a period of up to one year, or cancel, any Federal hunting or fishing permits or stamps issued to any person who is convicted of a criminal violation of any provision of this chapter or any regulation, permit, or certificate issued hereunder. The United States shall not be liable for the payments of any compensation, reimbursement, or damages in connection with the modification, suspension, or revocation of any leases, licenses, permits, stamps, or other agreements pursuant to this section.

(3) Notwithstanding any other provision of this chapter, it shall be a defense to prosecution under this subsection if the defendant committed the offense based on a good faith belief that he was acting to protect himself or herself, a member of his or her family, or any other individual, from bodily harm from any endangered or threatened species.

(c) District court jurisdiction

The several district courts of the United States, including the courts enumerated in section 460 of Title 28, shall have jurisdiction over any actions arising under this chapter. For the purpose of this chapter, American Samoa shall be included within the judicial district of the District Court of the United States for the District of Hawaii.

(d) Rewards and certain incidental expenses

The Secretary or the Secretary of the Treasury shall pay, from sums received as penalties, fines, or forfeitures of property for any violation of this chapter or any regulation issued hereunder (1) a reward to any person who furnishes information which leads to an arrest, a criminal conviction, civil penalty assessment, or forfeiture of property for any violation of this chapter or any regulation issued hereunder, and (2) the reasonable and necessary costs incurred by any person in providing temporary care for any fish, wildlife, or plant pending the disposition of any civil or criminal proceeding alleging a violation of this chapter with respect to that fish, wildlife, or plant. The amount of the reward, if any, is to be designated by the Secretary or the Secretary of the Treasury, as appropriate. Any officer or employee of the United States or any State or local government who furnishes information or renders service in the performance of his official duties is ineligible for payment under this subsection. Whenever the balance of sums received under this section and section 3375(d) of this title, as penalties or fines, or from forfeitures of property, exceed $500,000, the Secretary of the Treasury shall deposit an amount equal to such excess balance in the cooperative endangered species conservation fund established under section 1535(i) of this title.

(e) Enforcement

(1) The provisions of this chapter and any regulations or permits issued pursuant thereto shall be enforced by the Secretary, the Secretary of the Treasury, or the Secretary of the Department in which the Coast Guard is operating, or all such Secretaries. Each such Secretary may utilize by agreement, with or without reimbursement, the personnel, services, and facilities of any other Federal agency or any State agency for purposes of enforcing this chapter.

(2) The judges of the district courts of the United States and the United States magistrate judges may, within their respective jurisdictions, upon proper oath or affirmation showing probable cause, issue such warrants or other process as may be required for enforcement of this chapter and any regulation issued thereunder.

(3) Any person authorized by the Secretary, the Secretary of the Treasury, or the Secretary of the Department in which the Coast Guard is operating, to enforce this chapter may detain for inspection and inspect any package, crate, or other container, including its contents, and all accompanying documents, upon importation or exportation. Such person may make arrests without a warrant for any violation of this chapter if he has reasonable grounds to believe that the person to be arrested is committing the violation in his presence or view, and may execute and serve any arrest warrant, search warrant, or other warrant or civil or criminal process issued by any officer or court of competent jurisdiction for enforcement of this chapter. Such person so authorized may search and seize, with or without a warrant, as authorized by law. Any fish, wildlife, property, or item so seized shall be held by any person authorized by the Secretary, the Secretary of the Treasury, or the Secretary of the Department in which the Coast Guard is

operating pending disposition of civil or criminal proceedings, or the institution of an action in rem for forfeiture of such fish, wildlife, property, or item pursuant to paragraph (4) of this subsection; except that the Secretary may, in lieu of holding such fish, wildlife, property, or item, permit the owner or consignee to post a bond or other surety satisfactory to the Secretary, but upon forfeiture of any such property to the United States, or the abandonment or waiver of any claim to any such property, it shall be disposed of (other than by sale to the general public) by the Secretary in such a manner, consistent with the purposes of this chapter, as the Secretary shall by regulation prescribe.

(4)(A) All fish or wildlife or plants taken, possessed, sold, purchased, offered for sale or purchase, transported, delivered, received, carried, shipped, exported, or imported contrary to the provisions of this chapter, any regulation made pursuant thereto, or any permit or certificate issued hereunder shall be subject to forfeiture to the United States.

(B) All guns, traps, nets, and other equipment, vessels, vehicles, aircraft, and other means of transportation used to aid the taking, possessing, selling, purchasing, offering for sale or purchase, transporting, delivering, receiving, carrying, shipping, exporting, or importing of any fish or wildlife or plants in violation of this chapter, any regulation made pursuant thereto, or any permit or certificate issued thereunder shall be subject to forfeiture to the United States upon conviction of a criminal violation pursuant to subsection (b)(1) of this section.

(5) All provisions of law relating to the seizure, forfeiture, and condemnation of a vessel for violation of the customs laws, the disposition of such vessel or the proceeds from the sale thereof, and the remission or mitigation of such forfeiture, shall apply to the seizures and forfeitures incurred, or alleged to have been incurred, under the provisions of this chapter, insofar as such provisions of law are applicable and not inconsistent with the provisions of this chapter; except that all powers, rights, and duties conferred or imposed by the customs laws upon any officer or employee of the Treasury Department shall, for the purposes of this chapter, be exercised or performed by the Secretary or by such persons as he may designate.

(6) The Attorney General of the United States may seek to enjoin any person who is alleged to be in violation of any provision of this chapter or regulation issued under authority thereof.

(f) Regulations

The Secretary, the Secretary of the Treasury, and the Secretary of the Department in which the Coast Guard is operating, are authorized to promulgate such regulations as may be appropriate to enforce this chapter, and charge reasonable fees for expenses to the Government connected with permits or certificates authorized by this chapter including processing applications and reasonable inspections, and with the transfer, board, handling, or storage of fish or wildlife or plants and evidentiary items seized and forfeited under this chapter. All such fees collected pursuant to this subsection shall be deposited in the Treasury to the credit of the appropriation which is current and chargeable for the cost of furnishing the services. Appropriated funds may be expended pending reimbursement from parties in interest.

(g) Citizen suits

(1) Except as provided in paragraph (2) of this subsection any person may commence a civil suit on his own behalf—

(A) to enjoin any person, including the United States and any other governmental instrumentality or agency (to the extent permitted by the eleventh amendment to the Constitution), who is alleged to be in violation of any provision of this chapter or regulation issued under the authority thereof; or

(B) to compel the Secretary to apply, pursuant to section 1535(g)(2)(B)(ii) of this title, the prohibitions set forth in or authorized pursuant to section 1533(d) or 1538(a)(1)(B) of this title with respect to the taking of any resident endangered species or threatened species within any State; or

(C) against the Secretary where there is alleged a failure of the Secretary to perform any act or duty under section 1533 of this title which is not discretionary with the Secretary.

The district courts shall have jurisdiction, without regard to the amount in controversy or the citizenship of the parties, to enforce any such provision or regulation, or to order the Secretary to perform such act or duty, as the case may be. In any civil suit commenced under subparagraph (B) the district court shall compel the Secretary to apply the prohibition sought if the court finds that the allegation that an emergency exists is supported by substantial evidence.

(2)(A) No action may be commenced under subparagraph (1)(A) of this section—

(i) prior to sixty days after written notice of the violation has been given to the Secretary, and to any alleged violator of any such provision or regulation;

(ii) if the Secretary has commenced action to impose a penalty pursuant to subsection (a) of this section; or

(iii) if the United States has commenced and is diligently prosecuting a criminal action in a court of the United States or a State to redress a violation of any such provision or regulation.

(B) No action may be commenced under subparagraph (1)(B) of this section—

(i) prior to sixty days after written notice has been given to the Secretary setting forth the reasons why an emergency is thought to exist with respect to an endangered species or a threatened species in the State concerned; or

(ii) if the Secretary has commenced and is diligently prosecuting action under section 1535(g)(2)(B)(ii) of this title to determine whether any such emergency exists.

(C) No action may be commenced under subparagraph (1)(C) of this section prior to sixty days after written notice has been given to the Secretary; except that such action may be brought immediately after such notification in the case of an action under this section respecting an emergency posing a significant risk to the well-being of any species of fish or wildlife or plants.

(3)(A) Any suit under this subsection may be brought in the judicial district in which the violation occurs.

(B) In any such suit under this subsection in which the United States is not a party, the Attorney General, at the request of the Secretary, may intervene on behalf of the United States as a matter of right.

(4) The court, in issuing any final order in any suit brought pursuant to paragraph (1) of this subsection, may award costs of litigation (including reasonable attorney and expert witness fees) to any party, whenever the court determines such award is appropriate.

(5) The injunctive relief provided by this subsection shall not restrict any right which any person (or class of persons) may have under any statute or common law to seek enforcement of any standard or limitation or to seek any other relief (including relief against the Secretary or a State agency).

(h) Coordination with other laws

The Secretary of Agriculture and the Secretary shall provide for appropriate coordination of the administration of this chapter with the administration of the animal quarantine laws (21 U.S.C. 101–105, 111–135b, and 612–614) and section 306 of the Tariff Act of 1930 (19 U.S.C. 1306). Nothing in this chapter or any amendment made by this Act shall be construed as superseding or limiting in any manner the functions of the Secretary of Agriculture under any other law relating to prohibited or restricted importations or possession of animals and other articles and no proceeding or determination under this chapter shall preclude any proceeding or be considered determinative of any issue of fact or law in any proceeding under any Act administered by the Secretary of Agriculture. Nothing in this chapter shall be construed as superseding or limiting in any manner the functions and responsibilities of the Secretary of the Treasury under the Tariff Act of 1930 [19 U.S.C.A. § 1202 et seq.], including, without limitation, section 527 of that Act (19 U.S.C. 1527), relating to the importation of wildlife taken, killed, possessed, or exported to the United States in violation of the laws or regulations of a foreign country.

(Pub.L. 93–205, § 11, Dec. 28, 1973, 87 Stat. 897; Pub.L. 94–359, § 4, July 12, 1976, 90 Stat. 913; Pub.L. 95–632, §§ 6–8, Nov. 10, 1978, 92 Stat. 3761, 3762; Pub.L. 97–79, § 9(e), Nov. 16, 1981, 95 Stat. 1079; Pub.L. 97–304, §§ 7, 9(c), Oct. 13, 1982, 96 Stat. 1425, 1427; Pub.L. 98–327, § 4, June 25, 1984, 98 Stat. 271; Pub.L. 100–478, Title I, § 1007, Oct. 7, 1988, 102 Stat. 2309; Pub.L. 101–650, Title III, § 321, Dec. 1, 1990, 104 Stat. 5117.)

References in Text

The customs laws, referred to in subsec. (e)(5), are classified generally to Title 19, Customs Duties.

The amendments "made by this Act", referred to in subsec. (h), refer to the amendments made by Pub.L. 93–205, which amended sections 460k–1, 460*l*–9, 668dd, 715i, 715s, 1362, 1371, 1372 and 1402 of this title and section 136 of Title 7, Agriculture, and repealed sections 668aa to 668cc–6 of this title.

The Tariff Act of 1930, referred to in subsec. (h), is Act June 17, 1930, c. 497, 46 Stat. 590, as amended, which is classified generally to chapter 4 (section 1202 et seq.) of Title 19, Customs Duties. For complete classification of this Act to the Code, see section 1654 of Title 19 and Tables volume.

Change of Name

United States magistrate appointed under section 631 of Title 28, Judiciary and Judicial Procedure, to be known as United States magistrate judge after Dec. 1, 1990, with any reference to United States magistrate or magistrate in Title 28, in any other Federal statute, etc., deemed a reference to United States magistrate judge appointed under section 631 of Title 28, see section 321 of Pub.L. 101–650, set out as a note under section 631 of Title 28.

CROSS REFERENCES

Application for return of antique articles subject to forfeiture pursuant to assessment of civil penalty under this section, see section 1539 of this title.

Notice requirement for citizen suits not applicable with respect to review of final determination of Endangered Species Committee granting exemption from consultations for Federal agencies, see section 1536 of this title.

Federal Practice and Procedure

Expansion of standing by Congress, see Wright, Miller & Cooper: Jurisdiction 2d § 3531.13.

West's Federal Practice Manual

Attorney fees, see § 7683.25.

West's Federal Forms

Administrative subpenas, enforcement of, see § 5901 et seq.
Complaint to enjoin actions in violation of this chapter, see § 1713 and Comment thereunder.
Contempt proceedings, see § 5651 et seq.
Exceptions to pretrial order on behalf of plaintiffs, see § 2811.5 and Comment thereunder.
Initial appearance before magistrate, see § 7041 et seq.
Intervention, matters pertaining to, see § 3111 et seq.
Jurisdiction and venue in district courts, matters pertaining to, see § 1003 et seq.
Magistrate's arrest warrants, see § 7031 et seq.
Preliminary injunctions, matters pertaining to, see § 5271 et seq.
Pretrial order—injunctive relief, see § 2806.10 and Comment thereunder.
Production of documents, motions and orders pertaining to, see § 3551 et seq.
Sentence and fine, see § 7531 et seq.
Taxation of costs, see § 4612 et seq.

CODE OF FEDERAL REGULATIONS

Civil procedures—
National Oceanic and Atmospheric Administration, see 15 CFR 904.100 et seq.
United States Fish and Wildlife Service, see 50 CFR 11.1 et seq.
Endangered species regulations concerning terrestrial plants, see 7 CFR 355.1 et seq.
Establishment of ports for importation, exportation, and reexportation of plants, see 50 CFR 24.1 et seq.
General permit procedures, see 50 CFR 13.1 et seq.
Importation, exportation, and transportation of wildlife, see 50 CFR 14.1 et seq.
Rules of practice governing proceedings under certain acts, see 7 CFR 380.1 et seq.
Seizure, forfeiture, and disposal procedures—
Animal and Plant Health Inspection Service, see 7 CFR 356.1 et seq.
National Marine Fisheries Service, see 50 CFR 219.1 et seq.
United States Fish and Wildlife Service, see 50 CFR 12.1 et seq.

LAW REVIEW COMMENTARIES

Reducing attorneys' fees for partial success: A comment on Hensley and Blum. Dan B. Dobbs, Wis.L.Rev. 835 (1986).

The market test for attorney fee awards: Is the hourly rate test mandatory? Dan B. Dobbs, 28 Ariz.L.Rev. 1 (1986).

Warrior and the Druid—the DOD and environmental law. Michael Donnelly and James G. Van Ness, 33 Fed.Bar News 37 (1986).

LIBRARY REFERENCES

Fish ⚡14.
Game ⚡8.
C.J.S. Fish § 38 et seq.
C.J.S. Game § 16.

§ 1541. Endangered plants [ESA § 12]

The Secretary of the Smithsonian Institution, in conjunction with other affected agencies, is authorized and directed to review (1) species of plants which are now or may become endangered or threatened and (2) methods of adequately conserving such species, and to report to Congress, within one year after December 28, 1973, the results of such review including recommendations for new legislation or the amendment of existing legislation.

(Pub.L. 93–205, § 12, Dec. 28, 1973, 87 Stat. 901.)

LIBRARY REFERENCES

Health and Environment ⚡25.5.
C.J.S. Health and Environment §§ 61 to 66, 69, 71 to 73, 78 to 80, 82 to 86, 88 to 90, 94, 104, 110, 115 to 126, 128, 129, 132, 133, 135, 137 to 140, 142, 144 to 153.

§ 1542. Authorization of appropriations [ESA § 15]

(a) In general

Except as provided in subsections (b), (c), and (d) of this section, there are authorized to be appropriated—

(1) not to exceed $35,000,000 for fiscal year 1988, $36,500,000 for fiscal year 1989, $38,000,000 for fiscal year 1990, $39,500,000 for fiscal year 1991, and $41,500,000 for fiscal year 1992 to enable the Department of the Interior to carry out such functions and responsibilities as it may have been given under this chapter;

(2) not to exceed $5,750,000 for fiscal year 1988, $6,250,000 for each of fiscal years 1989 and 1990, and $6,750,000 for each of fiscal years 1991 and 1992 to enable the Department of Commerce to carry out such functions and responsibilities as it may have been given under this chapter; and

(3) not to exceed $2,200,000 for fiscal year 1988, $2,400,000 for each of fiscal years 1989 and 1990, and $2,600,000 for each of fiscal years 1991 and 1992, to enable the Department of Agriculture to carry out its functions and responsibilities with respect to the enforcement of this chapter and the Convention which pertain to the importation or exportation of plants.

(b) Exemptions from chapter

There are authorized to be appropriated to the Secretary to assist him and the Endangered Species Committee in carrying out their functions under sections 1536(e), (g), and (h) of this title not to exceed $600,000 for each of fiscal years 1988, 1989, 1990, 1991, and 1992.

(c) Convention implementation

There are authorized to be appropriated to the Department of the Interior for purposes of carrying out section 1537a(e) of this title not to exceed $400,000 for each of fiscal years 1988, 1989, and 1990, and $500,000 for each of fiscal years 1991 and 1992, and such sums shall remain available until expended.

(Pub.L. 93–205, § 15, Dec. 28, 1973, 87 Stat. 903; Pub.L. 94–325, June 30, 1976, 90 Stat. 724; Pub.L. 95–632, § 9, Nov. 10, 1978, 92 Stat. 3762; Pub.L. 96–159, § 8, Dec. 28, 1979, 93 Stat. 1230; Pub.L. 97–304, § 8(a), Oct. 13, 1982, 96 Stat. 1425; Pub.L. 100–478, Title I, § 1009, Oct. 7, 1988, 102 Stat. 2312.)

CROSS REFERENCES

International cooperation, use of foreign currencies when available in preference to funds appropriated under this section, see section 1537 of this title.

§ 1543. Construction with Marine Mammal Protection Act of 1972 [ESA § 17]

Except as otherwise provided in this chapter, no provision of this chapter shall take precedence over any more restrictive conflicting provision of the Marine Mammal Protection Act of 1972 [16 U.S.C.A. § 1361 et seq.].

(Pub.L. 93–205, § 17, Dec. 28, 1973, 87 Stat. 903.)

References in Text

The Marine Mammal Protection Act of 1972, referred to in text, is Pub.L. 92–522, Oct. 21, 1972, 86 Stat. 1027, as amended, which is classified generally to chapter 31 (section 1361 et seq.) of this title. For complete classification of this Act to the Code, see Short Title note set out under section 1361 of this title and Tables volume.

§ 1544. Annual cost analysis by the Fish and Wildlife Service [ESA § 18]

On or before January 15, 1990, and each January 15 thereafter, the Secretary of the Interior, acting through the Fish and Wildlife Service, shall submit to the Congress an annual report covering the preceding fiscal year which shall contain—

(1) an accounting on a species by species basis of all reasonably identifiable Federal expenditures made primarily for the conservation of endangered or threatened species pursuant to this chapter; and

(2) an accounting on a species by species basis of all reasonably identifiable expenditures made primarily for the conservation of endangered or threatened species pursuant to this chapter by States receiving grants under section 1535 of this title.

(Pub.L. 93–205, § 18, as added Pub.L. 100–478, Title I, § 1012, Oct. 7, 1988, 102 Stat. 2314.)

LIBRARY REFERENCES

United States ⇐41.
C.J.S. United States § 41.

WESTLAW ELECTRONIC RESEARCH

United States cases: 393k(add key number)

FOREST AND RANGELAND RESOURCES

FOREST AND RANGELAND RENEWABLE RESOURCES PLANNING ACT OF 1974 [FRRRPA § ___]

(16 U.S.C.A. §§ 1600 to 1614)

FOREST AND RANGELAND RENEWABLE RESOURCES RESEARCH ACT OF 1978 [FRRRRA § ___]

(16 U.S.C.A. §§ 1641 to 1647)

RENEWABLE RESOURCES EXTENSION ACT OF 1978 [RREA § ___]

(16 U.S.C.A. §§ 1671 to 1676)

WOOD RESIDUE UTILIZATION ACT OF 1980 [WRUA § ___]

(16 U.S.C.A. §§ 1681 to 1687)

CHAPTER 36—FOREST AND RANGELAND RENEWABLE RESOURCES PLANNING

SUBCHAPTER I—PLANNING

Sec.
1600. Congressional findings.
1601. Renewable Resource Assessment.
(a) Preparation by Secretary of Agriculture; time of preparation, updating and contents.
(b) Contents of Assessments.
(c) Public involvement; consultation with governmental departments and agencies.
(d) Congressional policy of multiple use sustained yield management; examination and certification of lands; estimate of appropriations necessary for reforestation and other treatment; budget requirements; authorization of appropriations.
(e) Report on herbicides and pesticides.
1602. Renewable Resource Program; preparation by Secretary of Agriculture and transmittal to President; purpose and development of program; time of preparation, updating and contents.
1603. National Forest System resource inventories; development, maintenance, and updating by Secretary of Agriculture as part of Assessment.
1604. National Forest System land and resource management plans.
(a) Development, maintenance, and revision by Secretary of Agriculture as part of Program; coordination.

Sec.
1604. National Forest System land and resource management plans.
(b) Criteria.
(c) Incorporation of standards and guidelines by Secretary; time of completion; progress reports; existing management plans.
(d) Public participation in management plans; availability of plans; public meetings.
(e) Required assurances.
(f) Required provisions.
(g) Promulgation of regulations for development and revision of plans; environmental considerations; resource management guidelines; guidelines for land management plans.
(h) Scientific committee to aid in promulgation of regulations; termination; revision committees; clerical and technical assistance; compensation of committee members.
(i) Consistency of resource plans, permits, contracts, and other instruments with land management plans; revision.
(j) Effective date of land management plans and revisions.
(k) Development of land management plans.
(*l*) Program evaluation; process for estimating long-term costs and benefits; summary of data included in annual report.
(m) Establishment of standards to ensure culmination of mean annual increment of growth; silvicultural practices; salvage harvesting; exceptions.
1605. Protection, use and management of renewable resources on non-Federal lands; utilization of As-

Sec.

sessment, surveys and Program by Secretary of Agriculture to assist States, etc.

1606. Budget requests by President for Forest Service activities.
(a) Transmittal to Speaker of House and President of Senate of Assessment, Program and Statement of Policy used in framing requests; time for transmittal; implementation by President of programs established under Statement of Policy unless Statement subsequently disapproved by Congress; time for disapproval.
(b) Contents of requests to show extent of compliance of projected programs and policies with policies approved by Congress; requests not conforming to approved policies; expenditure of appropriations.
(c) Annual evaluation report to Congress of Program components; time of submission; status of major research programs; application of findings; status, etc., of cooperative forestry assistance programs and activities.
(d) Required contents of annual evaluation report.
(e) Additional required contents of annual evaluation report.
(f) Form of annual evaluation report.

1606a. Reforestation Trust Fund.
(a) Establishment; source of funds.
(b) Transfer of certain tariff receipts to Trust Fund; fiscal year limitation; quarterly transfers; adjustment of estimates.
(c) Report to Congress; printing as House and Senate document; investments; sale and redemption of obligations; credits for Trust Fund.
(d) Obligations from Trust Fund.

1607. National Forest System renewable resources; development and administration by Secretary of Agriculture in accordance with multiple use and sustained yield concepts for products and services; target year for operational posture of resources; budget requests.

1608. National Forest Transportation System.
(a) Congressional declaration of policy; time for development; method of financing; financing of forest development roads.
(b) Construction of temporary roadways in connection with timber contracts, and other permits or leases.
(c) Standards of roadway construction.

1609. National Forest System.
(a) Congressional declaration of constituent elements and purposes; lands etc., included within; return of lands to public domain.
(b) Location of Forest Service offices.

1610. Implementation of provisions by Secretary of Agriculture; utilization of information and data of other organizations; avoidance of duplication of planning, etc.; "renewable resources" defined.

1611. Timber.
(a) Limitations on removal; variations in allowable sale quantity; public participation.
(b) Salvage harvesting.

1612. Public participation.
(a) Adequate notice and opportunity to comment.
(b) Advisory boards.

1613. Promulgation of regulations.

1614. Severability of provisions.

Sec.

SUBCHAPTER II—RESEARCH

1641. Congressional statement of findings; application of provisions with planning provisions.

1642. Investigations, experiments, tests, and other activities.
(a) Authorization; scope and purposes of activities.
(b) Development of periodic Renewable Resources Assessment through survey and analysis of conditions.
(c) Program of research and study relative to health and productivity of domestic forest ecosystems; advisory committee; reports.
(d) Other studies and activities.

1643. Implementation of provisions.
(a) Establishment and maintenance of research facilities; acquisition, expenditures, etc., for property.
(b) Acceptance, holding, and administration of gifts, donations, and bequests; use and investment of gifts, proceeds, etc.; funding requirements.
(c) Cooperation with Federal, State, and other governmental agencies, public and private agencies, etc.; funding requirements for contributions from cooperators.

1644. Competitive grants; scope and purposes; prerequisites.

1645. General provisions.
(a) Availability of funds to cooperators and grantees.
(b) Coordination of cooperative aid and grants with other aid and grant authorities.
(c) Dissemination of knowledge and technology developed from research activities; cooperation with specified entities.
(d) Additional implementative authorities.
(e) Construction of statutory provisions.
(f) Definitions.

1646. Authorization of appropriations.

1647. Other Federal programs.
(a) Repeal of statutory authorities relating to investigation, experiments, and tests in reforestation and forest products.
(b) Force and effect of cooperative and other agreements under repealed statutory authorities relating to investigation, etc., in reforestation and forest products.
(c) Issuance of rules and regulations for implementation of provisions and coordination with agricultural research, extension, and teaching provisions.
(d) Availability of funds appropriated under repealed statutory authorities relating to investigation, etc., in reforestation and forest products.

1648. Recycling research.
(a) Findings.
(b) Recycling research program.
(c) Authorization of appropriations.

1649. Forestry Student Grant Program.
(a) Establishment.
(b) Student grants.
(c) Eligibility.
(d) Authorization of appropriations.

SUBCHAPTER III—EXTENSION PROGRAMS

1671. Congressional statement of findings.

Sec.
1672. General program authorization.
(a) Types of programs; preconditions and cooperation with State program directors, etc.
(b) "Eligible colleges and universities" defined.
(c) Use of appropriate educational methods required; scope of methods.
1673. State programs.
(a) Development by State program director, etc., of comprehensive and coordinated program by mutual agreement; consultations; review procedure.
(b) Encouragement by State director, etc., of cooperation between county and State extension staffs and appropriate Federal and State agencies and organizations.
(c) Administration and coordination of program by State director; exception.
(d) Appointment and use of advisory committees by State director, etc.; composition of advisory committees.
(e) "State" defined.
1674. Renewable Resources Extension Program plan.
(a) Preparation and submission to Congress; purposes; contents.
(b) Considerations governing preparation.
(c) Annual report to Congress.
(d) Review of activities and evaluation of progress.
1674a. Expanded programs.
(a) In general.
(b) Activities.
1675. Authorization of appropriations; criteria for eligibility of States for funds.
1676. Issuance of rules and regulations for implementation of provisions and coordination with agricultural, research, extension, and teaching provisions.

SUBCHAPTER IV—WOOD RESIDUE UTILIZATION
1681. Congressional statement of purpose.
1682. Pilot projects and demonstrations.
(a) Establishment, implementation.
(b) Scope; residue removal credits.
1683. Pilot projects; requirements; residue removal credits as compensation; implementation guidelines.
1684. Annual reports.
1685. Regulations.
1686. Definitions.
1687. Authorization of appropriations.

SUBCHAPTER I—PLANNING

§ 1600. Congressional findings [FRRRPA § 2]

The Congress finds that—

(1) the management of the Nation's renewable resources is highly complex and the uses, demand for, and supply of the various resources are subject to change over time;

(2) the public interest is served by the Forest Service, Department of Agriculture, in cooperation with other agencies, assessing the Nation's renewable resources, and developing and preparing a national renewable resource program, which is periodically reviewed and updated;

(3) to serve the national interest, the renewable resource program must be based on a comprehensive assessment of present and anticipated uses, demand for, and supply of renewable resources from the Nation's public and private forests and rangelands, through analysis of environmental and economic impacts, coordination of multiple use and sustained yield opportunities as provided in the Multiple-Use Sustained-Yield Act of 1960 (74 Stat. 215; 16 U.S.C. 528–531), and public participation in the development of the program;

(4) the new knowledge derived from coordinated public and private research programs will promote a sound technical and ecological base for effective management, use, and protection of the Nation's renewable resources;

(5) inasmuch as the majority of the Nation's forests and rangeland is under private, State, and local governmental management and the Nation's major capacity to produce goods and services is based on these nonfederally managed renewable resources, the Federal Government should be a catalyst to encourage and assist these owners in the efficient long-term use and improvement of these lands and their renewable resources consistent with the principles of sustained yield and multiple use;

(6) the Forest Service, by virtue of its statutory authority for management of the National Forest System, research and cooperative programs, and its role as an agency in the Department of Agriculture, has both a responsibility and an opportunity to be a leader in assuring that the Nation maintains a natural resource conservation posture that will meet the requirements of our people in perpetuity; and

(7) recycled timber product materials are as much a part of our renewable forest resources as are the trees from which they originally came, and in order to extend our timber and timber fiber resources and reduce pressures for timber production from Federal lands, the Forest Service should expand its research in the use of recycled and waste timber product materials, develop techniques for the substitution of these secondary materials for primary materials, and promote and encourage the use of recycled timber product materials.

(Pub.L. 93–378, § 2, as added Pub.L. 94–588, § 2, Oct. 22, 1976, 90 Stat. 2949.)

References in Text

The Multiple-Use Sustained-Yield Act of 1960, referred to in par. (3), is Pub.L. 86–517, June 12, 1960, 74 Stat. 215, which is classified to sections 528 to 531 of this title.

Short Title

Section 1 of Pub.L. 93–378, Aug. 17, 1974, 88 Stat. 476, provided: "That this Act [which enacted this subchapter] may be cited as the 'Forest and Rangeland Renewable Resources Planning Act of 1974'."

CROSS REFERENCES

Clarification of lands outside boundaries of conservation areas, see section 1635 of Title 43, Public Lands.

Cooperative forestry assistance policies and directives to complement provisions of subchapter, see section 2101 of this title.

LAW REVIEW COMMENTARIES

Comment, the National Forest Management Act of 1976: A critical look at two trees in the NFMA forest. 22 Land & Water L.Rev. 413 (1987).

Federal management of forests and marine fisheries. Richard P. Gale, 25 Natural Resources J. 275 (1985).

LIBRARY REFERENCES

Logs and Logging ⚷21.
Public Lands ⚷1 to 21.
United States ⚷85.
Woods and Forests ⚷1 et seq.
C.J.S. Logs and Logging § 29.
C.J.S. Public Lands §§ 3 to 25.
C.J.S. United States § 123.
C.J.S. Woods and Forests §§ 1, 2.

§ 1601. Renewable Resource Assessment [FRRRPA § 3(a)]

(a) Preparation by Secretary of Agriculture; time of preparation, updating and contents

In recognition of the vital importance of America's renewable resources of the forest, range, and other associated lands to the Nation's social and economic well-being, and of the necessity for a long term perspective in planning and undertaking related national renewable resource programs administered by the Forest Service, the Secretary of Agriculture shall prepare a Renewable Resource Assessment (hereinafter called the "Assessment"). The Assessment shall be prepared not later than December 31, 1975, and shall be updated during 1979 and each tenth year thereafter, and shall include but not be limited to—

(1) an analysis of present and anticipated uses, demand for, and supply of the renewable resources, with consideration of the international resource situation, and an emphasis of pertinent supply and demand and price relationship trends;

(2) an inventory, based on information developed by the Forest Service and other Federal agencies, of present and potential renewable resources, and an evaluation of opportunities for improving their yield of tangible and intangible goods and services, together with estimates of investment costs and direct and indirect returns to the Federal Government;

(3) a description of Forest Service programs and responsibilities in research, cooperative programs and management of the National Forest System, their interrelationships, and the relationship of these programs and responsibilities to public and private activities;

(4) a discussion of important policy considerations, laws, regulations, and other factors expected to influence and affect significantly the use, ownership, and management of forest, range, and other associated lands; and

(5) an analysis of the potential effects of global climate change on the condition of renewable resources on the forests and rangelands of the United States; and

(6) an analysis of the rural and urban forestry opportunities to mitigate the buildup of atmospheric carbon dioxide and reduce the risk of global climate change,[1]

(b) Contents of Assessments

The Secretary shall report in the 1979 and subsequent Assessments on:

(1) the additional fiber potential in the National Forest System including, but not restricted to, forest mortality, growth, salvage potential, potential increased forest products sales, economic constraints, alternate markets, contract considerations, and other multiple use considerations;

(2) the potential for increased utilization of forest and wood product wastes in the National Forest System and on other lands, and of urban wood wastes and wood product recycling, including recommendations to the Congress for actions which would lead to increased utilization of material now being wasted both in the forests and in manufactured products; and

(3) the milling and other wood fiber product fabrication facilities and their location in the United States, noting the public and private forested areas that supply such facilities, assessing the degree of utilization into product form of harvested trees by such facilities, and setting forth the technology appropriate to the facilities to improve utilization either individually or in aggregate units of harvested trees and to reduce wasted wood fibers. The Secretary shall set forth a program to encourage the adoption by these facilities of these technologies for improving wood fiber utilization.

(c) Public involvement; consultation with governmental departments and agencies

In developing the reports required under subsection (b) of this section, the Secretary shall provide opportunity for public involvement and shall consult with other interested governmental departments and agencies.

(d) Congressional policy of multiple use sustained yield management; examination and certification of lands; estimate of appropriations necessary for reforestation and other treatment; budget requirements; authorization of appropriations

(1) It is the policy of the Congress that all forested lands in the National Forest System shall be maintained in appropriate forest cover with species of trees, degree of stocking, rate of growth, and conditions of stand designed to secure the maximum benefits of multiple use sustained yield management in accordance with land management plans. Accordingly, the Secretary is directed to identify and report to the Congress annually at the time of submission of the President's budget together with the annual report provided for under section 1606(c) of this title, beginning with submission of the President's budget for fiscal year 1978, the amount and location by forests and States and by productivity class, where practicable, of all lands in the National Forest System where objectives of land management plans indicate the need to reforest areas that have been cut-over or otherwise denuded or deforested, and all lands with stands of trees that are not growing at their best potential rate of growth. All national forest lands treated from year to year shall be examined after the first and third growing seasons and certified by the Secretary in the report provided for under this subsection as to stocking rate, growth rate in relation to potential and other pertinent measures. Any lands not certified as satisfactory shall be returned to the backlog and scheduled for prompt treatment. The level and types of treatment shall be those which secure the most effective mix of multiple use benefits.

(2) Notwithstanding the provisions of section 1607 of this title, the Secretary shall annually for eight years following October 22, 1976, transmit to the Congress in the manner provided in this subsection an estimate of the sums necessary to be appropriated, in addition to the funds available from other sources, to replant and otherwise treat an acreage equal to the acreage to be cut over that year, plus a sufficient portion of the backlog of lands found to be in need of treatment to eliminate the backlog within the eight-year period. After such eight-year period, the Secretary shall transmit annually to the Congress an estimate of the sums necessary to replant and otherwise treat all lands being cut over and maintain planned timber production on all other forested lands in the National Forest System so as to prevent the development of a backlog of needed work larger than the needed work at the beginning of the fiscal year. The Secretary's estimate of sums necessary, in addition to the sums available under other authorities, for accomplishment of the reforestation and other treatment of National Forest System lands under this section shall be provided annually for inclusion in the President's budget and shall also be transmitted to the Speaker of the House and the President of the Senate together with the annual report provided for under section 1606(c) of this title at the time of submission of the President's budget to the Congress beginning with the budget for fiscal year 1978. The sums estimated as necessary for reforestation and other treatment shall include moneys needed to secure seed, grow seedlings, prepare sites, plant trees, thin, remove deleterious growth and underbrush, build fence to exclude livestock and adverse wildlife from regeneration areas and otherwise establish and improve growing forests to secure planned production of trees and other multiple use values.

(3) Effective for the fiscal year beginning October 1, 1977, and each fiscal year thereafter, there is hereby authorized to be appropriated for the purpose of reforesting and treating lands in the National Forest System $200,000,000 annually to meet requirements of this subsection (d). All sums appropriated for the purposes of this subsection shall be available until expended.

(e) Report on herbicides and pesticides

The Secretary shall submit an annual report to the Congress on the amounts, types, and uses of herbicides and pesticides used in the National Forest System, including the beneficial or adverse effects of such uses.

(Pub.L. 93–378, § 3(a) [formerly § 2(a)], (c)–(e), Aug. 17, 1974, 88 Stat. 476, renumbered and amended Pub.L. 94–588, §§ 2, 3, 4, Oct. 22, 1976, 90 Stat. 2949, 2950; amended Pub.L. 101–624, Title XXIV, § 2408(a), Nov. 28, 1990, 104 Stat. 4061.)

[1] So in original. Probably should be a period.

Codification

Section is constituted as follows:

Subsec. (a) consists of section 3(a), formerly 2(a), of Pub.L. 93–378, as renumbered by section 2 of Pub.L. 94–588. Section 3(b), formerly section 2(b), of Pub.L. 93–378 amended section 581h of this title.

Subsec. (b) consists of section 3(c) of Pub.L. 93–378, as added by section 3 of Pub.L. 94–588.

Subsec. (c) consists of section 3(d) of Pub.L. 93–378, as added by section 3 of Pub.L. 94–588.

Subsec. (d) consists of section 3(d) of Pub.L. 93–378, as added by section 4 of Pub.L. 94–588.

Subsec. (e) consists of section 3(e) of Pub.L. 93–378, as added by section 4 of Pub.L. 94–588.

Presidential Commission on State and Private Forests

Section 1245 of Pub.L. 101–624, as amended Pub.L. 102–237, Title X, § 1018(b), Dec. 13, 1991, 105 Stat. 1905, provided that:

"**(a) Establishment.**—The President shall establish a Commission on State and Private Forests (hereafter in this section referred to as the 'Commission') which shall assess the status of the State and private forest lands of the United States, the problems affecting these lands, and the potential contribution of these lands to the renewable natural resource needs of the United States associated with their improved management and protection.

"(b) **Composition.**—The Commission shall be composed of 25 members to be appointed by the President, including Federal, State, and local officials, timber industry representatives, nonindustrial private forest landowners, conservationists, and community leaders. No more than five members shall be appointed from any one State. Not fewer than 20 members shall be appointed by the President from nominations submitted by the following Members of Congress:

"(1) The chairman of the Committee on Agriculture of the House of Representatives.

"(2) The ranking minority member of the Committee on Agriculture of the House of Representatives.

"(3) The chairman of the Committee on Agriculture, Nutrition, and Forestry of the Senate.

"(4) The ranking minority member of the Committee on Agriculture, Nutrition, and Forestry of the Senate.

"(c) **Vacancy.**—A vacancy on the Commission shall be filled by appointment by the President in the manner provided in subsection (b).

"(d) **Chairperson.**—The Commission shall elect a chairperson from among the members of the Commission by a majority vote.

"(e) **Meetings.**—The Commission shall meet at the call of the chairperson or a majority of the members of the Commission.

"(f) **Duties.**—

"(1) **Study.**—The Commission shall conduct a study that shall include—

"(A) an assessment using existing inventories of the current status of the State and private forest lands of the United States, including—

"(i) ownership status and past and future trends;

"(ii) the production of timber and nontimber resources from such lands; and

"(iii) landowner attitudes toward the protection and management of these lands;

"(B) a review of the problems affecting the State and private forest lands of the United States, including—

"(i) resource losses to insects, disease, fire, and damaging weather;

"(ii) inadequate reforestation;

"(iii) fragmentation and conversion of the forest land base; and

"(iv) management options;

"(C) constraints on, and opportunities for, providing multiresource outputs from forest lands;

"(D) administrative and legislative recommendations for addressing the problems and capitalizing on the potential of these lands for contributing to the renewable natural resource needs of the United States.

"(2) **Findings and recommendations.**—On the basis of its study, the Commission shall make findings and develop recommendations for consideration by the President with respect to the future demands placed on State and private forests in meeting both commodity and noncommodity needs of the United States in anticipation of impending changes in the management of the national forests, especially with regard to timber harvest. This assessment should focus on the role of State and private forest lands and help to identify means of improving their contribution to meeting the timber and nontimber needs of the United States.

"(3) **Report.**—The Commission shall submit to the President, not later than December 1, 1992, a report containing its findings and recommendations. The President shall submit the report to the Committee on Agriculture of the House of Representatives and the Committee on Agriculture, Nutrition, and Forestry of the Senate, and the report is authorized to be printed as a House Document.

"(g) **Operations in general.**—

"(1) **Agency cooperation.**—The heads of executive agencies, the General Accounting Office, the Office of Technology Assessment, and the Congressional Budget Office shall cooperate with the Commission.

"(2) **Compensation.**—Members of the Commission shall serve without compensation for work on the Commission. While away from their homes or regular places of business in the performance of duties of the Commission, members of the Commission shall be allowed travel expenses, including per diem in lieu of subsistence, as authorized by law for persons serving intermittently in the Government service under section 5703 of title 5 of the United States Code [section 5703 of Title 5, Government Organization and Employees].

"(3) **Director.**—To the extent there are sufficient funds available to the Commission and subject to such rules as may be adopted by the Commission, the Commission, without regard to the provisions of title 5 of the United States Code governing appointments in the competitive service and without regard to the provisions of chapter 51 and subchapter III of chapter 53 of such title [section 5101 et seq. and 5331 et seq. of Title 5, respectively] relating to the classification and General Schedule pay rates, may—

"(A) appoint and fix the compensation of a director; and

"(B) appoint and fix the compensation of such additional personnel as the Commission determines necessary to assist it to carry out its duties and functions.

"(4) **Staff and services.**—On the request of the Commission, the heads of executive agencies, the Comptroller General, and the Director of the Office of Technology Assessment may furnish the Commission with such office, personnel or support services as the head of the agency, or office, and the chairperson of the Commission agree are necessary to assist the Commission to carry out its duties and functions. The Commission shall not be required to pay, or reimburse, any agency for office, personnel or support services provided by this subsection.

"(5) **Exemptions.**—

"(A) **FACA.**—The Commission shall be exempt from sections 7(d), 10(e), 10(f), and 14 of the Federal Advisory Committee Act (5 U.S.C. App. 2, 1 et seq.) [sections 7(d), 10(e), 10(f), and 14 of Appendix 2 of Title 5].

"(B) **Title 5.**—The Commission shall be exempt from the requirements of sections 4301 through 4305 of title 5 of the United States Code [sections 4301 through 4305 of Title 5].

"(h) **Authorization of appropriations and spending authority.**—

"(1) **Authorization of appropriations.**—There is authorized to be appropriated such sums as are necessary to implement this section.

"(2) **Spending authority.**—Any spending authority (as defined in section 401 of the Congressional Budget Act of 1974 [section 651 of Title 2, The Congress]) provided in this title [Title XII of Pub.L. 101–624, Nov. 28, 1990, 104 Stat. 3521, for distribution of which see Tables] shall be effective for any fiscal year only to such extent or in such amounts as are provided in appropriation Acts.

"(i) **Termination.**—The Presidential Commission on State and Private Forests shall cease to exist 90 days following the submission of its report to the President."

CROSS REFERENCES

Annual evaluation report to Congress of Program components, see section 1606 of this title.

Budget requests for National Forest System renewable resources, see section 1607.

Development of periodic Renewable Resource Assessment through survey and analysis of conditions, see section 1642.

Eligibility of States for appropriated funds, see section 1675 of this title.

Expenditure of Trust amounts for reforestation, see section 1606a of this title.

Renewable Resources Extension Program, preparation, see section 1674 of this title.

Responsibilities of Secretary and Department of Agriculture for coordination of agricultural research, etc., with periodic renewable resource assessment, see section 3121 of Title 7, Agriculture.

§ 1602. Renewable Resource Program; preparation by Secretary of Agriculture and transmittal to President; purpose and development of program; time of preparation, updating and contents [FRRRPA § 4]

In order to provide for periodic review of programs for management and administration of the National Forest System, for research, for cooperative State and private Forest Service programs, and for conduct of other Forest Service activities in relation to the findings of the Assessment, the Secretary of Agriculture, utilizing information available to the Forest Service and other agencies within the Department of Agriculture, including data prepared pursuant to section 1010a of Title 7, shall prepare and transmit to the President a recommended Renewable Resource Program (hereinafter called the "Program"). The Program transmitted to the President may include alternatives, and shall provide in appropriate detail for protection, management, and development of the National Forest System, including forest development roads and trails; for cooperative Forest Service programs; and for research. The Programs shall be developed in accordance with principles set forth in the Multiple–Use Sustained–Yield Act of June 12, 1960 (74 Stat. 215; 16 U.S.C. 528–531), and the National Environmental Policy Act of 1969 (83 Stat. 852) [42 U.S.C.A. § 4321 et seq.]. The Program shall be prepared not later than December 31, 1975, to cover the four-year period beginning October 1, 1976, and at least each of the four fiscal decades next following such period, and shall be updated no later than during the first half of the fiscal year ending September 30, 1980, and the first half of each fifth fiscal year thereafter to cover at least each of the four fiscal decades beginning next after such updating. The Program shall include, but not be limited to—

(1) an inventory of specific needs and opportunities for both public and private program investments. The inventory shall differentiate between activities which are of a capital nature and those which are of an operational nature;

(2) specific identification of Program outputs, results anticipated, and benefits associated with investments in such a manner that the anticipated costs can be directly compared with the total related benefits and direct and indirect returns to the Federal Government;

(3) a discussion of priorities for accomplishment of inventoried Program opportunities, with specified costs, outputs, results, and benefits;

(4) a detailed study of personnel requirements as needed to implement and monitor existing and ongoing programs; and

(5) Program recommendations which—

(A) evaluate objectives for the major Forest Service programs in order that multiple-use and sustained-yield relationships among and within the renewable resources can be determined;

(B) explain the opportunities for owners of forests and rangeland to participate in programs to improve and enhance the condition of the land and the renewable resource products therefrom;

(C) recognize the fundamental need to protect and, where appropriate, improve the quality of soil, water, and air resources;

(D) state national goals that recognize the interrelationships between and interdependence within the renewable resources;

(E) evaluate the impact of the export and import of raw logs upon domestic timber supplies and prices; and

(F) account for the effects of global climate change on forest and rangeland conditions, including potential effects on the geographic ranges of species, and on forest and rangeland products.

(Pub.L. 93–378, § 4, formerly § 3, Aug. 17, 1974, 88 Stat. 477, renumbered and amended Pub.L. 94–588, §§ 2, 5, Oct. 22, 1976, 90 Stat. 2949, 2951; amended Pub.L. 101–624, Title XXIV, 2408(b), Nov. 28, 1990, 104 Stat. 4061.)

References in Text

The Multiple–Use Sustained–Yield Act of 1960, referred to in text, is Pub.L. 86–517, June 12, 1960, 74 Stat. 215, as amended, which is classified to sections 528 to 531 of this title.

The National Environmental Policy Act of 1969, referred to in text, is Pub.L. 91–190, Jan. 1, 1970, 83 Stat. 852, as amended, which is classified generally to chapter 55 (section 4321 et seq.) of Title 42, the Public Health and Welfare.

CROSS REFERENCES

Annual report by Secretary of Agriculture in aiding Congressional oversight activities, see section 1606 of this title.

Budget requests for forest service activities, transmittal to Congress of Program, see section 1606 of this title.

Development, etc., of land and resources management plans for units of National Forest System, see section 1604 of this title.

Responsibility of Department of Agriculture for coordination of all agricultural research with periodic renewable resources assessment and program, see section 3121 of Title 7, Agriculture.

§ 1603. National Forest System resource inventories; development, maintenance, and updating by Secretary of Agriculture as part of Assessment [FRRRPA § 5]

As a part of the Assessment, the Secretary of Agriculture shall develop and maintain on a continuing basis a comprehensive and appropriately detailed inventory of all National Forest System lands and renewable resources. This inventory shall be kept current so as to reflect changes in conditions and identify new and emerging resources and values.

(Pub.L. 93–378, § 5, formerly § 4, Aug. 17, 1974, 88 Stat. 477, renumbered Pub.L. 94–588, § 2, Oct. 22, 1976, 90 Stat. 2949.)

§ 1604. National Forest System land and resource management plans [FRRRPA § 6]

(a) Development, maintenance, and revision by Secretary of Agriculture as part of Program; coordination

As a part of the Program provided for by section 1602 of this title, the Secretary of Agriculture shall develop, maintain, and, as appropriate, revise land and resource management plans for units of the National Forest System, coordinated with the land and resource management planning processes of State and local governments and other Federal agencies.

(b) Criteria

In the development and maintenance of land management plans for use on units of the National Forest System, the Secretary shall use a systematic interdisciplinary approach to achieve integrated consideration of physical, biological, economic, and other sciences.

(c) Incorporation of standards and guidelines by Secretary; time of completion; progress reports; existing management plans

The Secretary shall begin to incorporate the standards and guidelines required by this section in plans for units of the National Forest System as soon as practicable after October 22, 1976 and shall attempt to complete such incorporation for all such units by no later than September 30, 1985. The Secretary shall report to the Congress on the progress of such incorporation in the annual report required by section 1606(c) of this title. Until such time as a unit of the National Forest System is managed under plans developed in accordance with this subchapter, the management of such unit may continue under existing land and resource management plans.

(d) Public participation in management plans; availability of plans; public meetings

The Secretary shall provide for public participation in the development, review, and revision of land management plans including, but not limited to, making the plans or revisions available to the public at convenient locations in the vicinity of the affected unit for a period of at least three months before final adoption, during which period the Secretary shall publicize and hold public meetings or comparable processes at locations that foster public participation in the review of such plans or revisions.

(e) Required assurances

In developing, maintaining, and revising plans for units of the National Forest System pursuant to this section, the Secretary shall assure that such plans—

(1) provide for multiple use and sustained yield of the products and services obtained therefrom in accordance with the Multiple–Use Sustained–Yield Act of 1960 [16 U.S.C.A. §§ 528–531], and, in particular, include coordination of outdoor recreation, range, timber, watershed, wildlife and fish, and wilderness; and

(2) determine forest management systems, harvesting levels, and procedures in the light of all of the uses set forth in subsection (c)(1) of this section, the definition of the terms "multiple use" and "sustained yield" as provided in the Multiple–Use Sustained–Yield Act of 1960, and the availability of lands and their suitability for resource management.

(f) Required provisions

Plans developed in accordance with this section shall—

(1) form one integrated plan for each unit of the National Forest System, incorporating in one document or one set of documents, available to the public at convenient locations, all of the features required by this section;

(2) be embodied in appropriate written material, including maps and other descriptive documents, reflecting proposed and possible actions, including the planned timber sale program and the proportion of probable methods of timber harvest within the unit necessary to fulfill the plan;

(3) be prepared by an interdisciplinary team. Each team shall prepare its plan based on inventories of the applicable resources of the forest;

(4) be amended in any manner whatsoever after final adoption after public notice, and, if such amendment would result in a significant change in such plan, in accordance with the provisions of subsections (e) and (f) of this section and public involvement comparable to that required by subsection (d) of this section; and

(5) be revised (A) from time to time when the Secretary finds conditions in a unit have significantly changed, but at least every fifteen years, and (B) in accordance with the provisions of subsections (e) and (f) of this section and public involvement comparable to that required by subsection (d) of this section.

(g) Promulgation of regulations for development and revision of plans; environmental considerations; resource management guidelines; guidelines for land management plans

As soon as practicable, but not later than two years after October 22, 1976, the Secretary shall in accordance with the procedures set forth in section 553 of Title 5 promulgate regulations, under the principles of the Multiple-Use Sustained-Yield Act of 1960 [16 U.S.C.A. §§ 528-531], that set out the process for the development and revision of the land management plans, and the guidelines and standards prescribed by this subsection. The regulations shall include, but not be limited to—

(1) specifying procedures to insure that land management plans are prepared in accordance with the National Environmental Policy Act of 1969 [42 U.S.C.A. § 4321 et seq.], including, but not limited to, direction on when and for what plans an environmental impact statement required under section 102(2)(C) of that Act [42 U.S.C.A. § 4332(2)(C)] shall be prepared;

(2) specifying guidelines which—

(A) require the identification of the suitability of lands for resource management;

(B) provide for obtaining inventory data on the various renewable resources, and soil and water, including pertinent maps, graphic material, and explanatory aids; and

(C) provide for methods to identify special conditions or situations involving hazards to the various resources and their relationship to alternative activities;

(3) specifying guidelines for land management plans developed to achieve the goals of the Program which—

(A) insure consideration of the economic and environmental aspects of various systems of renewable resource management, including the related systems of silviculture and protection of forest resources, to provide for outdoor recreation (including wilderness), range, timber, watershed, wildlife, and fish;

(B) provide for diversity of plant and animal communities based on the suitability and capability of the specific land area in order to meet overall multiple-use objectives, and within the multiple-use objectives of a land management plan adopted pursuant to this section, provide, where appropriate, to the degree practicable, for steps to be taken to preserve the diversity of tree species similar to that existing in the region controlled by the plan;

(C) insure research on and (based on continuous monitoring and assessment in the field) evaluation of the effects of each management system to the end that it will not produce substantial and permanent impairment of the productivity of the land;

(D) permit increases in harvest levels based on intensified management practices, such as reforestation, thinning, and tree improvement if (i) such practices justify increasing the harvests in accordance with the Multiple-Use Sustained-Yield Act of 1960, and (ii) such harvest levels are decreased at the end of each planning period if such practices cannot be successfully implemented or funds are not received to permit such practices to continue substantially as planned;

(E) insure that timber will be harvested from National Forest System lands only where—

(i) soil, slope, or other watershed conditions will not be irreversibly damaged;

(ii) there is assurance that such lands can be adequately restocked within five years after harvest;

(iii) protection is provided for streams, streambanks, shorelines, lakes, wetlands, and other bodies of water from detrimental changes in water temperatures, blockages of water courses, and deposits of sediment, where harvests are likely to seriously and adversely affect water conditions or fish habitat; and

(iv) the harvesting system to be used is not selected primarily because it will give the greatest dollar return or the greatest unit output of timber; and

(F) insure that clearcutting, seed tree cutting, shelterwood cutting, and other cuts designed to regenerate an even-aged stand of timber will be used as a cutting method on National Forest System lands only where—

(i) for clearcutting, it is determined to be the optimum method, and for other such cuts it is determined to be appropriate, to meet the objectives and requirements of the relevant land management plan;

(ii) the interdisciplinary review as determined by the Secretary has been completed and the potential environmental, biological, esthetic, engineering, and economic impacts on each advertised sale area have been assessed, as well as the consistency of the sale with the multiple use of the general area;

(iii) cut blocks, patches, or strips are shaped and blended to the extent practicable with the natural terrain;

(iv) there are established according to geographic areas, forest types, or other suitable classifications the maximum size limits for areas to be cut in one harvest operation, including provision to exceed the established limits after appropriate public notice and review by the responsible Forest Service officer one level above the Forest Service officer who normally would approve the harvest proposal: *Provided*, That such limits shall not apply to the size of areas harvested as a result of natural catastrophic conditions such as fire, insect and disease attack, or windstorm; and

(v) such cuts are carried out in a manner consistent with the protection of soil, watershed, fish, wildlife, recreation, and esthetic resources, and the regeneration of the timber resource.

(h) Scientific committee to aid in promulgation of regulations; termination; revision committees; clerical and technical assistance; compensation of committee members

(1) In carrying out the purposes of subsection (g) of this section, the Secretary of Agriculture shall appoint a committee of scientists who are not officers or employees of the Forest Service. The committee shall provide scientific and technical advice and counsel on proposed guidelines and procedures to assure that an effective interdisciplinary approach is proposed and adopted. The committee shall terminate upon promulgation of the regulations, but the Secretary may, from time to time, appoint similar committees when considering revisions of the regulations. The views of the committees shall be included in the public information supplied when the regulations are proposed for adoption.

(2) Clerical and technical assistance, as may be necessary to discharge the duties of the committee, shall be provided from the personnel of the Department of Agriculture.

(3) While attending meetings of the committee, the members shall be entitled to receive compensation at a rate of $100 per diem, including traveltime, and while away from their homes or regular places of business they may be allowed travel expenses, including per diem in lieu of subsistence, as authorized by section 5703 of Title 5 for persons in the Government service employed intermittently.

(i) Consistency of resource plans, permits, contracts, and other instruments with land management plans; revision

Resource plans and permits, contracts, and other instruments for the use and occupancy of National Forest System lands shall be consistent with the land management plans. Those resource plans and permits, contracts, and other such instruments currently in existence shall be revised as soon as practicable to be made consistent with such plans. When land management plans are revised, resource plans and permits, contracts, and other instruments, when necessary, shall be revised as soon as practicable. Any revision in present or future permits, contracts, and other instruments made pursuant to this section shall be subject to valid existing rights.

(j) Effective date of land management plans and revisions

Land management plans and revisions shall become effective thirty days after completion of public participation and publication of notification by the Secretary as required under subsection (d) of this section.

(k) Development of land management plans

In developing land management plans pursuant to this subchapter, the Secretary shall identify lands within the management area which are not suited for timber production, considering physical, economic, and other pertinent factors to the extent feasible, as determined by the Secretary, and shall assure that, except for salvage sales or sales necessitated to protect other multiple-use values, no timber harvesting shall occur on such lands for a period of 10 years. Lands once identified as unsuitable for timber production shall continue to be treated for reforestation purposes, particularly with regard to the protection of other multiple-use values. The Secretary shall review his decision to classify these lands as not suited for timber production at least every 10 years and shall return these lands to timber production whenever he determines that conditions have changed so that they have become suitable for timber production.

(*l*) Program evaluation; process for estimating long-term costs and benefits; summary of data included in annual report

The Secretary shall—

(1) formulate and implement, as soon as practicable, a process for estimating long-terms[1] costs and benefits to support the program evaluation requirements of this subchapter. This process shall include requirements to provide information on a representative sample basis of estimated expenditures associated with the reforestation, timber stand improvement, and sale of timber from the National Forest System, and shall provide a comparison of these expenditures to the return to the Government resulting from the sale of timber; and

(2) include a summary of data and findings resulting from these estimates as a part of the annual

report required pursuant to section 1606(c) of this title, including an identification on a representative sample basis of those advertised timber sales made below the estimated expenditures for such timber as determined by the above cost process; and

(m) Establishment of standards to ensure culmination of mean annual increment of growth; silvicultural practices; salvage harvesting; exceptions

The Secretary shall establish—

(1) standards to insure that, prior to harvest, stands of trees throughout the National Forest System shall generally have reached the culmination of mean annual increment of growth (calculated on the basis of cubic measurement or other methods of calculation at the discretion of the Secretary): *Provided*, That these standards shall not preclude the use of sound silvicultural practices, such as thinning or other stand improvement measures: *Provided further*, That these standards shall not preclude the Secretary from salvage or sanitation harvesting of timber stands which are substantially damaged by fire, windthrow or other catastrophe, or which are in imminent danger from insect or disease attack; and

(2) exceptions to these standards for the harvest of particular species of trees in management units after consideration has been given to the multiple uses of the forest including, but not limited to, recreation, wildlife habitat, and range and after completion of public participation processes utilizing the procedures of subsection (d) of this section.

(Pub.L. 93–378, § 6, formerly § 5, Aug. 17, 1974, 88 Stat. 477, renumbered and amended Pub.L. 94–588, §§ 2, 6, 12(a), Oct. 22, 1976, 90 Stat. 2949, 2952, 2958.)

[1] So in original. Probably should be "long-term".

References in Text

The Multiple–Use Sustained–Yield Act of 1960, referred to in subsecs. (e) and (g), is Pub.L. 86–517, June 12, 1960, 74 Stat. 215, as amended, which is classified to sections 528 to 531 of this title.

The National Environmental Policy Act of 1969, referred to in subsec. (g)(1), is Pub.L. 91–190, Jan. 1, 1970, 83 Stat. 852, as amended, which is classified generally to chapter 55 (section 4321 et seq.) of Title 42, the Public Health and Welfare.

Forest Land and Resource Management Plans of Forest Service and Bureau of Land Management

Pub.L. 101–121, Title III, § 312, Oct. 23, 1989, 103 Stat. 743, provided that: "The Forest Service and Bureau of Land Management are to continue to complete as expeditiously as possible development of their respective Forest Land and Resource Management Plans to meet all applicable statutory requirements. Notwithstanding the date in section 6(c) of the NFMA (16 U.S.C. 1600)[subsec. (c) of this section], the Forest Service, and the Bureau of Land Management under separate authority, may continue the management of lands within their jurisdiction under existing land and resource management plans pending the completion of new plans. Nothing shall limit judicial review of particular activities on these lands: *Provided, however*, That there shall be no challenges to any existing plan on the sole basis that the plan in its entirety is outdated, or in the case of the Bureau of Land Management, solely on the basis that the plan does not incorporate information available subsequent to the completion of the existing plan: *Provided further*, That any and all particular activities to be carried out under existing plans may nevertheless be challenged."

Similar provisions were contained in the following prior Appropriations Acts:

Pub.L. 100–446, Title III, § 314, Sept. 27, 1988, 102 Stat. 1825.

Pub.L. 100–202, § 101(g)[Title III, § 314], Dec. 22, 1987, 101 Stat. 1329–254.

Pub.L. 99–591, Title I, § 101(h)[Title II, § 201], Oct. 30, 1986, 100 Stat. 3341–268.

Pub.L. 99–500, Title I, § 101(h)[Title II, § 201], Oct. 18, 1986, 100 Stat. 1783–268.

CROSS REFERENCES

Applicability of provisions of National Forest timber utilization program notwithstanding this section, see section 539d of this title.

Comprehensive management plan consistent with requirements of this section, see section 542d of this title.

Forest Service leases and permits, see section 8855 of Title 42, Public Health and Welfare.

Grazing leases and permits, see section 1752 of Title 43, Public Lands.

Oregon Cascades Recreation Area, development of management direction for Area in accordance with this section, see section 460*oo*(g) of this title.

Spring Mountain National Recreation Area, management plan, applicability to this section, see 16 USCA § 460hh–4.

WEST'S FEDERAL PRACTICE MANUAL

Conservation of fish and wildlife, see § 4389.55.

Federal land policy and management, see § 4389.25 et seq.

CODE OF FEDERAL REGULATIONS

Planning, applicability, and procedures, see 36 CFR 219.1 et seq.

LAW REVIEW COMMENTARIES

Federal lands and local communities. Eric T. Freyfogle, 27 Ariz. L.Rev. 653 (1985).

Section 6(k) of the National Forest Management Act: The bottom line on below-cost timber sales? Comment, 1987 Utah L.Rev. 373 (No. 2).

Taking account of the ecosystem on the public domain: Law and ecology in the greater Yellowstone region. Robert B. Keiter, 60 U.Colo.L.Rev. 923 (1989).

§ 1605. Protection, use and management of renewable resources on non-Federal lands; utilization of Assessment, surveys and Program by Secretary of Agriculture to assist States, etc. [FRRRPA § 7]

The Secretary of Agriculture may utilize the Assessment, resource surveys, and Program prepared pursuant to this subchapter to assist States and other organizations in proposing the planning for the protection, use, and management of renewable resources on non-Federal land.

(Pub.L. 93–378, § 7, formerly § 6, Aug. 17, 1974, 88 Stat. 478, renumbered Pub.L. 94–588, § 2, Oct. 22, 1976, 90 Stat. 2949.)

§ 1606. Budget requests by President for Forest Service activities [FRRRPA § 8]

(a) Transmittal to Speaker of House and President of Senate of Assessment, Program and Statement of Policy used in framing requests; time for transmittal; implementation by President of programs established under Statement of Policy unless Statement subsequently disapproved by Congress; time for disapproval

On the date Congress first convenes in 1976 and thereafter following each updating of the Assessment and the Program, the President shall transmit to the Speaker of the House of Representatives and the President of the Senate, when Congress convenes, the Assessment as set forth in section 1601 of this title and the Program as set forth in section 1602 of this title, together with a detailed Statement of Policy intended to be used in framing budget requests by that Administration for Forest Service activities for the five- or ten-year program period beginning during the term of such Congress for such further action deemed appropriate by the Congress. Following the transmission of such Assessment, Program, and Statement of Policy, the President shall, subject to other actions of the Congress, carry out programs already established by law in accordance with such Statement of Policy or any subsequent amendment or modification thereof approved by the Congress, unless, before the end of the first period of ninety calendar days of continuous session of Congress after the date on which the President of the Senate and the Speaker of the House are recipients of the transmission of such Assessment, Program, and Statement of Policy, either House adopts a resolution reported by the appropriate committee of jurisdiction disapproving the Statement of Policy. For the purpose of this subsection, the continuity of a session shall be deemed to be broken only by an adjournment sine die, and the days on which either House is not in session because of an adjournment of more than three days to a day certain shall be excluded in the computation of the ninety-day period. Notwithstanding any other provision of this subchapter, Congress may revise or modify the Statement of Policy transmitted by the President, and the revised or modified Statement of Policy shall be used in framing budget requests.

(b) Contents of requests to show extent of compliance of projected programs and policies with policies approved by Congress; requests not conforming to approved policies; expenditure of appropriations

Commencing with the fiscal budget for the year ending September 30, 1977, requests presented by the President to the Congress governing Forest Service activities shall express in qualitative and quantitative terms the extent to which the programs and policies projected under the budget meet the policies approved by the Congress in accordance with subsection (a) of this section. In any case in which such budget so presented recommends a course which fails to meet the policies so established, the President shall specifically set forth the reason or reasons for requesting the Congress to approve the lesser programs or policies presented. Amounts appropriated to carry out the policies approved in accordance with subsection (a) of this section shall be expended in accordance with the Congressional Budget and Impoundment Control Act of 1974.

(c) Annual evaluation report to Congress of Program components; time of submission; status of major research programs; application of findings; status, etc., of cooperative forestry assistance programs and activities

For the purpose of providing information that will aid Congress in its oversight responsibilities and improve the accountability of agency expenditures and activities, the Secretary of Agriculture shall prepare an annual report which evaluates the component elements of the Program required to be prepared by section 1602 of this title which shall be furnished to the Congress at the time of submission of the annual fiscal budget commencing with the third fiscal year after August 17, 1974. With regard to the research component of the program, the report shall include, but not be limited to, a description of the status of major research programs, significant findings, and how these findings will be applied in National Forest System management and in cooperative State and private Forest Service programs. With regard to the cooperative forestry assistance part of the Program, the report shall include, but not be limited to, a description of the status, accomplishments, needs, and work backlogs for the programs and activities conducted under the Cooperative Forestry Assistance Act of 1978 [16 U.S.C.A. § 2101 et seq.].

(d) Required contents of annual evaluation report

These annual evaluation reports shall set forth progress in implementing the Program required to be prepared by section 1602 of this title, together with accomplishments of the Program as they relate to the objectives of the Assessment. Objectives should be set forth in qualitative and quantitative terms and accomplishments should be reported accordingly. The report shall contain appropriate measurements of pertinent costs and benefits. The evaluation shall assess the balance between economic factors and environmental quality factors. Program benefits shall include, but not be limited to, environmental quality factors such as esthetics, public access, wildlife habitat, recreational and wilderness use, and economic factors such as the excess of cost savings over the value of foregone benefits and the rate of return on renewable resources.

(e) Additional required contents of annual evaluation report

The reports shall indicate plans for implementing corrective action and recommendations for new legislation where warranted.

(f) Form of annual evaluation report

The reports shall be structured for Congress in concise summary form with necessary detailed data in appendices.

(Pub.L. 93–378, § 11, formerly § 7, Aug. 17, 1974, 88 Stat. 478, renumbered § 8 and amended Pub.L. 94–588, §§ 2, 7, 12(b), Oct. 22, 1976, 90 Stat. 2949, 2956, 2958; Pub.L. 95–313, § 12, July 1, 1978, 92 Stat. 374; renumbered § 11 Pub.L. 101–624, Title XII, § 1215(1), Nov. 28, 1990, 104 Stat. 3525.)

References in Text

Congressional Budget and Impoundment Control Act of 1974, referred to in subsec. (b), is Pub.L. 93–344, July 12, 1974, 88 Stat. 297, as amended. For complete classification of this Act to the Code, see Short Title note set out under section 621 of Title 2, The Congress, and Tables volume.

The Cooperative Forestry Assistance Act of 1978, referred to in subsec. (c), is Pub.L. 95–313, July 1, 1978, 92 Stat. 365, which is classified principally to chapter 41 (section 2101 et seq.) of this title. For complete classification of this Act to the Code, see Short Title note set out under section 2101 of this title and Tables volume.

Statement of Policy

Pub.L. 96–514, Title III, § 310, Dec. 12, 1980, 94 Stat. 2984, provided that:

"The Statement of Policy transmitted by the President to the Speaker of the House of Representatives and the President of the Senate on June 19, 1980, as required under section 8 of the Forest and Rangeland Renewable Resources Planning Act of 1974 [this section], is revised and modified to read as follows:

"STATEMENT OF POLICY

"BASIC PRINCIPLES

"It is the policy of the United States—

"(1) forests and rangeland, in all ownerships, should be managed to maximize their net social and economic contributions to the Nation's well being, in an environmentally sound manner.

"(2) the Nation's forested land, except such public land that is determined by law or policy to be maintained in its existing or natural state, should be managed at levels that realize its capabilities to satisfy the Nation's need for food, fiber, energy, water, soil stability, wildlife and fish, recreation, and esthetic values.

"(3) the productivity of suitable forested land, in all ownerships, should be maintained and enhanced to minimize the inflationary impacts of wood product prices on the domestic economy and permit a net export of forest products by the year 2030.

"(4) in order to achieve this goal, it is recognized that in the major timber growing regions most of the commercial timber lands will have to be brought to and maintained, where possible, at 90 percent of their potential level of growth, consistent with the provisions of the National Forest Management Act of 1976 on Federal lands, so that all resources are utilized in the combination that will best meet the needs of the American people.

"(5) forest and rangeland protection programs should be improved to more adequately protect forest and rangeland resources from fire, erosion, insects, disease, and the introduction or spread of noxious weeds, insects, and animals.

"(6) the Federal agencies carrying out the policies contained in this Statement will cooperate and coordinate their efforts to accomplish the goals contained in this Statement and will consult, coordinate, and cooperate with the planning efforts of the States.

"(7) in carrying out the Assessment and the Program under the Forest and Rangeland Renewable Resources Planning Act of 1974 [this subchapter] and the Appraisal and the Program under the Soil and Water Resources Conservation Act of 1977 [section 2001 et seq. of this title], the Secretary of Agriculture shall assure that resource and economic information and evaluation data will be continually improved so that the best possible information is always available for use by Federal agencies and the public.

"RANGE LAND DATA BASE AND ITS IMPROVEMENT

"The data on and understanding of the cover and condition of range lands is less refined than the data on and understanding of commercial forest land. Range lands have significant value in the production of water and protection of watersheds; the production of fish and wildlife food and habitat; recreation; and the production of livestock forage. An adequate data base on the cover and condition of range lands should be developed by the year 1990. Currently, cattle production from these lands is annually estimated at 213 million animal unit months of livestock forage. These lands should be maintained and enhanced, including their water and other resource values, so that they can annually provide 310 million animal units months of forage by the year 2030, along with other benefits.

"GENERAL ACCEPTANCE OF HIGH BOUND PROGRAM

"Congress generally accepts the 'high-bound' program described on pages 7 through 18 of the 1980 Report to Congress on the Nation's Renewable Resources prepared by the Secretary of Agriculture. However, Congress finds that the 'high-bound' program may not be sufficient to accomplish the goals contained in this statement, particularly in the areas of range and watershed resources, State and private forest cooperation and timber management.

"STATE AND PRIVATE LANDS

"States and owners of private forest and rangelands will be encouraged, consistent with their individual objectives, to manage their land in support of this Statement of Policy. The State and private forestry and range programs of the Forest Service will be essential to the furtherance of this Statement of Policy.

"FUNDING THE GOALS

"In order to accomplish the policy goals contained in this statement by the year 2030, the Federal Government should adequately fund programs of research (including cooperative research), extension, cooperative forestry assistance and protection, and improved management of the forest and rangelands. The Secretary of Agriculture shall continue his efforts to evaluate the cost-effectiveness of the renewable resource programs."

CROSS REFERENCES

Report at time of annual report under this section of amount and location of lands required to be reforested, see section 1601 of this title.

Report in annual report of progress of incorporation of standards and guidelines in plans for units of National Forest System, see section 1604 of this title.

Submission of annual reports with reports required by this section, see section 1684 of this title.

CODE OF FEDERAL REGULATIONS

Conservation and environmental programs, see 7 CFR 701.1 et seq.

§ 1606a. Reforestation Trust Fund

(a) Establishment; source of funds

There is established in the Treasury of the United States a trust fund, to be known as the Reforestation Trust Fund (hereinafter in this section referred to as the "Trust Fund"), consisting of such amounts as are transferred to the Trust Fund under subsection (b)(1) of this section and any interest earned on investment of amounts in the Trust Fund under subsection (c)(2) of this section.

(b) Transfer of certain tariff receipts to Trust Fund; fiscal year limitation; quarterly transfers; adjustment of estimates

(1) Subject to the limitation in paragraph (2), the Secretary of the Treasury shall transfer to the Trust Fund an amount equal to the sum of the tariffs received in the Treasury after January 1, 1989, under headings 4401 through 4412 and subheadings 4418.50.00, 4418.90.20, 4420.10.00, 4420.90.80, 4421.90.10 through 4421.90.20, and 4421.90.70 of chapter 44, subheadings 6808.00.00 and 6809.11.00 of chapter 68 and subheading 9614.10.00 of chapter 96 of the Harmonized Tariff Schedule of the United States.

(2) The Secretary shall not transfer more than $30,000,000 to the Trust Fund for any fiscal year.

(3) The amounts required to be transferred to the Trust Fund under paragraph (1) shall be transferred at least quarterly from the general fund of the Treasury to the Trust Fund on the basis of estimates made by the Secretary of the Treasury. Proper adjustment shall be made in the amounts subsequently transferred to the extent prior estimates were in excess of or less than the amounts required to be transferred.

(c) Report to Congress; printing as House and Senate document; investments; sale and redemption of obligations; credits for Trust Fund

(1) It shall be the duty of the Secretary of the Treasury to hold the Trust Fund, and (after consultation with the Secretary of Agriculture) to report to the Congress each year on the financial condition and the results of the operations of the Trust Fund during the preceding fiscal year and on its expected condition and operations during the next fiscal year. Such report shall be printed as both a House and Senate document of the session of the Congress to which the report is made.

(2)(A) It shall be the duty of the Secretary of the Treasury to invest such portion of the Trust Fund as is not, in his judgment, required to meet current withdrawals. Such investments may be made only in interest-bearing obligations of the United States or in obligations guaranteed as to both principal and interest by the United States. For such purpose, such obligations may be acquired (i) on original issue at the issue price, or (ii) by purchase of outstanding obligations at the market price. The purposes for which obligations of the United States may be issued under chapter 31 of Title 31 are hereby extended to authorize the issuance at par of special obligations exclusively to the Trust Fund. Such special obligations shall bear interest at a rate equal to the average rate of interest, computed as to the end of the calendar month next preceding the date of such issue, borne by all marketable interest-bearing obligations of the United States then forming a part of the Public Debt; except that where such average rate is not a multiple of one-eighth of 1 percent, the rate of interest of such special obligations shall be the multiple of one-eighth of 1 percent next lower than such average rate. Such special obligations shall be issued only if the Secretary of the Treasury determines that the purchase of other interest-bearing obligations of the United States, or of obligations guaranteed as to both principal and interest by the United States on original issue or at the market price, is not in the public interest.

(B) Any obligation acquired by the Trust Fund (except special obligations issued exclusively to the Trust Fund) may be sold by the Secretary of the Treasury at the market price, and such special obligations may be redeemed at par plus accrued interest.

(C) The interest on, and the proceeds from the sale or redemption of, any obligations held in the Trust Fund shall be credited to and form a part of the Trust Fund.

(d) Obligations from Trust Fund

The Secretary of Agriculture is hereafter authorized to obligate such sums as are available in the Trust Fund (including any amounts not obligated in previous fiscal years) for—

(1) reforestation and timber stand improvement as specified in section (3)(d) of the Forest and Rangeland Renewable Resources Planning Act of 1974 (16 U.S.C. 1601(d)); and

(2) properly allocable administrative costs of the Federal Government for the activities specified above.

(Pub.L. 96–451, Title III, § 303, Oct. 14, 1980, 94 Stat. 1991; Pub.L. 97–424, Title IV, § 422, Jan. 6, 1983, 96 Stat. 2164; Pub.L. 99–190, § 101(d) [Title II, § 201], Dec. 19, 1985, 99 Stat. 1245; Pub.L. 100–418, Title I, § 1214(r), Aug. 23, 1988, 102 Stat. 1160.)

Codification

Section was not enacted as part of the Forest and Rangeland Renewable Resources Planning Act of 1974, which comprises this subchapter.

In subsec. (c)(2)(A), "chapter 31 of Title 31" was substituted for "the Second Liberty Bond Act, as amended" on authority of Pub.L. 97–258, § 4(b), Sept. 13, 1982, 96 Stat. 1067, the first section of which enacted Title 31, Money and Finance.

§ 1607. National Forest System renewable resources; development and administration by Secretary of Agriculture in accordance with multiple use and sustained yield concepts for products and services; target year for operational posture of resources; budget requests [FRRRPA § 9]

The Secretary of Agriculture shall take such action as will assure that the development and administration of the renewable resources of the National Forest System are in full accord with the concepts for multiple use and sustained yield of products and services as set forth in the Multiple-Use Sustained-Yield Act of 1960 [16 U.S.C.A. §§ 528–531]. To further these concepts, the Congress hereby sets the year 2000 as the target year when the renewable resources of the National Forest System shall be in an operating posture whereby all backlogs of needed treatment for their restoration shall be reduced to a current basis and the major portion of planned intensive multiple-use sustained-yield management procedures shall be installed and operating on an environmentally-sound basis. The annual budget shall contain requests for funds for an orderly program to eliminate such backlogs: *Provided*, That when the Secretary finds that (1) the backlog of areas that will benefit by such treatment has been eliminated, (2) the cost of treating the remainder of such area exceeds the economic and environmental benefits to be secured from their treatment, or (3) the total supplies of the renewable resources of the United States are adequate to meet the future needs of the American people, the budget request for these elements of restoration may be adjusted accordingly.

(Pub.L. 93–378, § 9, formerly § 8, Aug. 17, 1974, 88 Stat. 479, renumbered Pub.L. 94–588, § 2, Oct. 22, 1976, 90 Stat. 2949.)

References in Text

The Multiple-Use Sustained-Yield Act of 1960, referred to in text, is Pub.L. 86–517, June 12, 1960, 74 Stat. 215, as amended, which is classified to sections 528 to 531 of this title.

§ 1608. National Forest Transportation System [FRRRPA § 10]

(a) Congressional declaration of policy; time for development; method of financing; financing of forest development roads

The Congress declares that the installation of a proper system of transportation to service the National Forest System, as is provided for in sections 532 to 538 of this title, shall be carried forward in time to meet anticipated needs on an economical and environmentally sound basis, and the method chosen for financing the construction and maintenance of the transportation system should be such as to enhance local, regional, and national benefits: *Provided*, That limitations on the level of obligations for construction of forest roads by timber purchasers shall be established in annual appropriation Acts.

(b) Construction of temporary roadways in connection with timber contracts, and other permits or leases

Unless the necessity for a permanent road is set forth in the forest development road system plan, any road constructed on land of the National Forest System in connection with a timber contract or other permit or lease shall be designed with the goal of reestablishing vegetative cover on the roadway and areas where the vegetative cover has been disturbed by the construction of the road, within ten years after the termination of the contract, permit, or lease either through artificial or natural means. Such action shall be taken unless it is later determined that the road is needed for use as a part of the National Forest Transportation System.

(c) Standards of roadway construction

Roads constructed on National Forest System lands shall be designed to standards appropriate for the intended uses, considering safety, cost of transportation, and impacts on land and resources.

(Pub.L. 93–378, § 10, formerly § 9, Aug. 17, 1974, 88 Stat. 479, renumbered and amended Pub.L. 94–588, §§ 2, 8, Oct. 22, 1976, 90 Stat. 2949, 2956; Pub.L. 97–100, Title II, § 201, Dec. 23, 1981, 95 Stat. 1405.)

CODE OF FEDERAL REGULATIONS

Forest highways, see 23 CFR 660.101 et seq.

§ 1609. National Forest System [FRRRPA § 11]

(a) Congressional declaration of constituent elements and purposes; lands etc., included within; return of lands to public domain

Congress declares that the National Forest System consists of units of federally owned forest, range, and related lands throughout the United States and its territories, united into a nationally significant system dedicated to the long-term benefit for present and future generations, and that it is the purpose of this section to include all such areas into one integral system. The "National Forest System" shall include all national forest lands reserved or withdrawn from the public domain of the United States, all national forest lands acquired through purchase, exchange, donation, or other means, the national grasslands and land utilization projects administered under title III of the Bankhead-Jones Farm Tenant Act [7 U.S.C.A. § 1010 et seq.], and other lands, waters, or interests therein which are administered by the Forest Service or are designated for administration through the Forest Service as a part of the system. Notwithstanding the provisions of section 473 of this title, no land now or hereafter reserved or withdrawn from the public domain as national forests pursuant to section 471 of this title, or any act supplementary to and amendatory thereof, shall be returned to the public domain except by an act of Congress.

(b) Location of Forest Service offices

The on-the-ground field offices, field supervisory offices, and regional offices of the Forest Service shall be so situated as to provide the optimum level of convenient, useful services to the public, giving priority to the maintenance and location of facilities in rural areas and towns near the national forest and Forest Service program locations in accordance with the standards in section 3122(b) of Title 42.

(Pub.L. 93–378, § 11, formerly § 10, Aug. 17, 1974, 88 Stat. 480, renumbered and amended Pub.L. 94–588, §§ 2, 9, Oct. 22, 1976, 90 Stat. 2949, 2957.)

References in Text

The Bankhead-Jones Farm Tenant Act, referred to in subsec. (a), is Act July 22, 1937, c. 517, 50 Stat. 522, as amended. Title III of the Bankhead-Jones Farm Tenant Act is classified generally to subchapter III (section 1010 et seq.) of chapter 33 of Title 7, Agriculture.

Section 471 of this title, referred to in subsec. (a), was repealed by Pub.L. 94–579, Title VII, § 704(a), Oct. 21, 1976, 90 Stat. 2792.

Land Conveyances Involving Joliet Army Ammunition Plant, Illinois

Pub.L. 104–106, Title XXIX, Feb. 10, 1996, 110 Stat. 594, provided for the conversion of the Joliet Army Ammunition Plant to the Midewin National Tallgrass Prairie, Illinois, and the conveyance of certain real property at the Arsenal for a national cemetery, a Will County, Illinois, landfill, and industrial parks to replace all or a part of lost economic activity, with provisions prohibiting construction of title to restrict or lessen the degree of cleanup required to be carried out under environmental laws, and provisions authorizing retention of real property used for environmental cleanup by the Secretary of the Army until the transfer occurs.

LAW REVIEW COMMENTARIES

National forest lands, defined as in this section for purposes of, Spring Mountain National Recreation Area, see 16 USCA § 460hhh.

§ 1610. Implementation of provisions by Secretary of Agriculture; utilization of information and data of other organizations; avoidance of duplication of planning, etc.; "renewable resources" defined [FRRRPA § 12]

In carrying out this subchapter, the Secretary of Agriculture shall utilize information and data available from other Federal, State, and private organizations and shall avoid duplication and overlap of resource assessment and program planning efforts of other Federal agencies. The term "renewable resources" shall be construed to involve those matters within the scope of responsibilities and authorities of the Forest Service on August 17, 1974, and on the date of enactment of any legislation amendatory or supplementary to this subchapter.

(Pub.L. 93–378, § 12, formerly § 11, Aug. 17, 1974, 88 Stat. 480, renumbered and amended Pub.L. 94–588, §§ 2, 10, Oct. 22, 1976, 90 Stat. 2949, 2957.)

§ 1611. Timber [FRRRPA § 13]

(a) Limitations on removal; variations in allowable sale quantity; public participation

The Secretary of Agriculture shall limit the sale of timber from each national forest to a quantity equal to or less than a quantity which can be removed from such forest annually in perpetuity on a sustained-yield basis: *Provided,* That, in order to meet overall multiple-use objectives, the Secretary may establish an allowable sale quantity for any decade which departs from the projected long-term average sale quantity that would otherwise be established: *Provided further,* That any such planned departure must be consistent with the multiple-use management objectives of the land management plan. Plans for variations in the allowable sale quantity must be made with public participation as required by section 1604(d) of this title. In addition, within any decade, the Secretary may sell a quantity in excess of the annual allowable sale quantity established pursuant to this section in the case of any national forest so long as the average sale quantities of timber from such national forest over the decade covered by the plan do not exceed such quantity limitation. In those cases where a forest has less than two hundred thousand acres of commercial forest land, the Secretary may use two or more forests for purposes of determining the sustained yield.

(b) Salvage harvesting

Nothing in subsection (a) of this section shall prohibit the Secretary from salvage or sanitation harvesting of timber stands which are substantially damaged by fire, windthrow, or other catastrophe, or which are in imminent danger from insect or disease attack. The Secretary may either substitute such timber for timber that would otherwise be sold under the plan or, if not feasible, sell such timber over and above the plan volume.

(Pub.L. 93–378, § 13, as added Pub.L. 94–588, § 11, Oct. 22, 1976, 90 Stat. 2957.)

Emergency Salvage Timber Sale Program

Pub.L. 104–19, Title II, § 2001, July 27, 1995, 109 Stat. 240, provided that:

"**(a) Definitions.**—For purposes of this section:

"(1) The term 'appropriate committees of Congress' means the Committee on Resources, the Committee on Agriculture, and the

Committee on Appropriations of the House of Representatives and the Committee on Energy and Natural Resources, the Committee on Agriculture, Nutrition, and Forestry, and the Committee on Appropriations of the Senate.

"(2) The term 'emergency period' means the period beginning on the date of the enactment of this section [July 27, 1995] and ending on September 30, 1997.

"(3) The term 'salvage timber sale' means a timber sale for which an important reason for entry includes the removal of disease- or insect-infested trees, dead, damaged, or down trees, or trees affected by fire or imminently susceptible to fire or insect attack. Such term also includes the removal of associated trees or trees lacking the characteristics of a healthy and viable ecosystem for the purpose of ecosystem improvement or rehabilitation, except that any such sale must include an identifiable salvage component of trees described in the first sentence.

"(4) The term 'Secretary concerned' means—

"(A) the Secretary of Agriculture, with respect to lands within the National Forest System; and

"(B) the Secretary of the Interior, with respect to Federal lands under the jurisdiction of the Bureau of Land Management.

"(b) **Completion of salvage timber sales.**—

"(1) **Salvage timber sales.**—Using the expedited procedures provided in subsection (c), the Secretary concerned shall prepare, advertise, offer, and award contracts during the emergency period for salvage timber sales from Federal lands described in subsection (a)(4). During the emergency period, the Secretary concerned is to achieve, to the maximum extent feasible, a salvage timber sale volume level above the programmed level to reduce the backlogged volume of salvage timber. The preparation, advertisement, offering, and awarding of such contracts shall be performed utilizing subsection (c) and notwithstanding any other provision of law, including a law under the authority of which any judicial order may be outstanding on or after the date of the enactment of this Act [July 27, 1995].

"(2) **Use of salvage sale funds.**—To conduct salvage timber sales under this subsection, the Secretary concerned may use salvage sale funds otherwise available to the Secretary concerned.

"(3) **Sales in preparation.**—Any salvage timber sale in preparation on the date of the enactment of this Act [July 27, 1995] shall be subject to the provisions of this section.

"(c) **Expedited procedures for emergency salvage timber sales.**—

"(1) **Sale documentation.**—

"(A) **Preparation.**—For each salvage timber sale conducted under subsection (b), the Secretary concerned shall prepare a document that combines an environmental assessment under section 102(2) of the National Environmental Policy Act of 1969 (42 U.S.C. 4332(2)) [section 4332(2) of Title 42, The Public Health and Welfare] (including regulations implementing such section) and a biological evaluation under section 7(a)(2) of the Endangered Species Act of 1973 (16 U.S.C. 1536(a)(2)) [section 1536(a)(2) of this title] and other applicable Federal law and implementing regulations. A document embodying decisions relating to salvage timber sales proposed under authority of this section shall, at the sole discretion of the Secretary concerned and to the extent the Secretary concerned considers appropriate and feasible, consider the environmental effects of the salvage timber sale and the effect, if any, on threatened or endangered species, and to the extent the Secretary concerned, at his sole discretion, considers appropriate and feasible, be consistent with any standards and guidelines from the management plans applicable to the National Forest or Bureau of Land Management District on which the salvage timber sale occurs.

"(B) **Use of existing materials.**—In lieu of preparing a new document under this paragraph, the Secretary concerned may use a document prepared pursuant to the National Environmental Policy Act of 1969 (42 U.S.C. 4321 et seq.) [section 4321 et seq. of Title 42] before the date of the enactment of this Act [July 27, 1995], a biological evaluation written before such date, or information collected for such a document or evaluation if the document, evaluation, or information applies to the Federal lands covered by the proposed sale.

"(C) **Scope and content.**—The scope and content of the documentation and information prepared, considered, and relied on under this paragraph is at the sole discretion of the Secretary concerned.

"(2) **Reporting requirements.**—Not later than August 30, 1995, the Secretary concerned shall submit a report to the appropriate committees of Congress on the implementation of this section. The report shall be updated and resubmitted to the appropriate committees of Congress every six months thereafter until the completion of all salvage timber sales conducted under subsection (b). Each report shall contain the following:

"(A) The volume of salvage timber sales sold and harvested, as of the date of the report, for each National Forest and each district of the Bureau of Land Management.

"(B) The available salvage volume contained in each National Forest and each district of the Bureau of Land Management.

"(C) A plan and schedule for an enhanced salvage timber sale program for fiscal years 1995, 1996, and 1997 using the authority provided by this section for salvage timber sales.

"(D) A description of any needed resources and personnel, including personnel reassignments, required to conduct an enhanced salvage timber sale program through fiscal year 1997.

"(E) A statement of the intentions of the Secretary concerned with respect to the salvage timber sale volume levels specified in the joint explanatory statement of managers accompanying the conference report on H.R. 1158, House Report 104–124.

"(3) **Advancement of sales authorized.**—The Secretary concerned may begin salvage timber sales under subsection (b) intended for a subsequent fiscal year before the start of such fiscal year if the Secretary concerned determines that performance of such salvage timber sales will not interfere with salvage timber sales intended for a preceding fiscal year.

"(4) **Decisions.**—The Secretary concerned shall design and select the specific salvage timber sales to be offered under subsection (b) on the basis of the analysis contained in the document or documents prepared pursuant to paragraph (1) to achieve, to the maximum extent feasible, a salvage timber sale volume level above the program level.

"(5) **Sale preparation.**—

"(A) **Use of available authorities.**—The Secretary concerned shall make use of all available authority, including the employment of private contractors and the use of expedited fire contracting procedures, to prepare and advertise salvage timber sales under subsection (b).

"(B) **Exemptions.**—The preparation, solicitation, and award of salvage timber sales under subsection (b) shall be exempt from—

"(i) the requirements of the Competition in Contracting Act (41 U.S.C. 253 et seq.) [probably means the Competition in Contracting Act of 1984, Pub.L. 98–369, Div. B, Title VIII, July 18, 1984, 98 Stat. 1175, for classifications to which see Short Title note under section 251 of Title 41, Public Contracts, and Tables] and the implementing regulations in the Federal Acquisition Regulation issued pursuant to section 25(c) of the Office of Federal Procurement Policy Act (41 U.S.C. 421(c)) [section 421(c) of Title 41] and any departmental acquisition regulations; and

"(ii) the notice and publication requirements in section 18 of such Act (41 U.S.C. 416) [section 416 of Title 41] and 8(e) of the Small Business Act (15 U.S.C. 637(e)) [section 637(e) of Title 15, Commerce and Trade] and the implementing regulations in the Federal Acquisition Regulations and any departmental acquisition regulations.

"(C) **Incentive payment recipients; report.**—The provisions of section 3(d)(1) of the Federal Workforce Restructuring Act of 1994 (Public Law 103–226; 5 U.S.C. 5597 note) [set out as a note under section 5597 of Title 5, Government Organization and Employees] shall not apply to any former employee of the Secretary concerned who received a voluntary separation incentive payment authorized by such Act [Pub.L. 103–226, Mar. 30, 1994, 108 Stat. 111, for classifications to which see Short Title note under section 2101 of Title 5 and Tables] and accepts employment pursuant to this paragraph. The Director of the Office of Personnel Management and the Secretary concerned shall provide a summary report to the appropriate committees of Congress, the Committee on Government Reform and Oversight of the House of Representatives, and the Committee on Governmental Affairs of the Senate regarding the number of incentive payment recipients who were rehired, their terms of reemployment, their job classifications, and an explanation, in the judgment of the agencies involved of how such reemployment without repayment of the incentive payments received is consistent with the original waiver provisions of such Act. This report shall not be conducted in a manner that would delay the rehiring of any former employees under this paragraph, or affect the normal confidentiality of Federal employees.

"(6) **Cost considerations.**—Salvage timber sales undertaken pursuant to this section shall not be precluded because the costs of such activities are likely to exceed the revenues derived from such activities.

"(7) **Effect of salvage sales.**—The Secretary concerned shall not substitute salvage timber sales conducted under subsection (b) for planned non-salvage timber sales.

"(8) **Reforestation of salvage timber sale parcels.**—The Secretary concerned shall plan and implement reforestation of each parcel of land harvested under a salvage timber sale conducted under subsection (b) as expeditiously as possible after completion of the harvest on the parcel, but in no case later than any applicable restocking period required by law or regulation.

"(9) **Effect on judicial decisions.**—The Secretary concerned may conduct salvage timber sales under subsection (b) notwithstanding any decision, restraining order, or injunction issued by a United States court before the date of the enactment of this section [July 27, 1995].

"(d) **Direction to complete timber sales on lands covered by option 9.**—Notwithstanding any other law (including a law under the authority of which any judicial order may be outstanding on or after the date of enactment of this Act [July 27, 1995]), the Secretary concerned shall expeditiously prepare, offer, and award timber sale contracts on Federal lands described in the 'Record of Decision for Amendments to Forest Service and Bureau of Land Management Planning Documents Within the Range of the Northern Spotted Owl', signed by the Secretary of the Interior and the Secretary of Agriculture on April 13, 1994. The Secretary concerned may conduct timber sales under this subsection notwithstanding any decision, restraining order, or injunction issued by a United States court before the date of the enactment of this section. The issuance of any regulation pursuant to section 4(d) of the Endangered Species Act of 1973 (16 U.S.C. 1533(d)) [section 1533(d) of this title] to ease or reduce restrictions on non-Federal lands within the range of the northern spotted owl shall be deemed to satisfy the requirements of section 102(2)(C) of the National Environmental Policy Act of 1969 (42 U.S.C. 4332(2)(C)) [section 4332(2)(C) of Title 42], given the analysis included in the Final Supplemental Impact Statement on the Management of the Habitat for Late Successional and Old Growth Forest Related Species Within the Range of the Northern Spotted Owl, prepared by the Secretary of Agriculture and the Secretary of the Interior in 1994, which is, or may be, incorporated by reference in the administrative record of any such regulation. The issuance of any such regulation pursuant to section 4(d) of the Endangered Species Act of 1973 (16 U.S.C. 1533(d)) shall not require the preparation of an environmental impact statement under section 102(2)(C) of the National Environmental Policy Act of 1969 (42 U.S.C. 4332(2)(C)).

"(e) **Administrative review.**—Salvage timber sales conducted under subsection (b), timber sales conducted under subsection (d), and any decision of the Secretary concerned in connection with such sales, shall not be subject to administrative review.

"(f) **Judicial review.**—

"(1) **Place and time of filing.**—A salvage timber sale to be conducted under subsection (b), and a timber sale to be conducted under subsection (d), shall be subject to judicial review only in the United States district court for the district in which the affected Federal lands are located. Any challenge to such sale must be filed in such district court within 15 days after the date of initial advertisement of the challenged sale. The Secretary concerned may not agree to, and a court may not grant, a waiver of the requirements of this paragraph.

"(2) **Effect of filing on agency action.**—For 45 days after the date of the filing of a challenge to a salvage timber sale to be conducted under subsection (b) or a timber sale to be conducted under subsection (d), the Secretary concerned shall take no action to award the challenged sale.

"(3) **Prohibition on restraining orders, preliminary injunctions, and relief pending review.**—No restraining order, preliminary injunction, or injunction pending appeal shall be issued by any court of the United States with respect to any decision to prepare, advertise, offer, award, or operate a salvage timber sale pursuant to subsection (b) or any decision to prepare, advertise, offer, award, or operate a timber sale pursuant to subsection (d). Section 705 of title 5, United States Code, shall not apply to any challenge to such a sale.

"(4) **Standard of review.**—The courts shall have authority to enjoin permanently, order modification of, or void an individual salvage timber sale if it is determined by a review of the record that the decision to prepare, advertise, offer, award, or operate such sale was arbitrary and capricious or otherwise not in accordance with applicable law (other than those laws specified in subsection (i)).

"(5) **Time for decision.**—Civil actions filed under this subsection shall be assigned for hearing at the earliest possible date. The court shall render its final decision relative to any challenge within 45 days from the date such challenge is brought, unless the court determines that a longer period of time is required to satisfy the requirement of the United States Constitution. In order to reach a decision within 45 days, the district court may assign all or part of any such case or cases to one or more Special Masters, for prompt review and recommendations to the court.

"(6) **Procedures.**—Notwithstanding any other provision of law, the court may set rules governing the procedures of any proceeding brought under this subsection which set page limits on briefs and time limits on filing briefs and motions and other actions which are shorter than the limits specified in the Federal rules of civil or appellate procedure.

"(7) **Appeal.**—Any appeal from the final decision of a district court in an action brought pursuant to this subsection shall be filed not later than 30 days after the date of decision.

"(g) **Exclusion of certain Federal lands.**—

"(1) **Exclusion.**—The Secretary concerned may not select, authorize, or undertake any salvage timber sale under subsection (b) with respect to lands described in paragraph (2).

"(2) **Description of excluded lands.**—The lands referred to in paragraph (1) are as follows:

"(A) Any area on Federal lands included in the National Wilderness Preservation System.

"(B) Any roadless area on Federal lands designated by Congress for wilderness study in Colorado or Montana.

"(C) Any roadless area on Federal lands recommended by the Forest Service or Bureau of Land Management for wilderness designation in its most recent land management plan in effect as of the date of the enactment of this Act [July 27, 1995].

"(D) Any area on Federal lands on which timber harvesting for any purpose is prohibited by statute.

"(h) **Rulemaking.**—The Secretary concerned is not required to issue formal rules under section 553 of title 5, United States Code, to implement this section or carry out the authorities provided by this section.

"(i) **Effect on other laws.**—The documents and procedures required by this section for the preparation, advertisement, offering, awarding, and operation of any salvage timber sale subject to subsection (b) and any timber sale under subsection (d) shall be deemed to satisfy the requirements of the following applicable Federal laws (and regulations implementing such laws):

"(1) The Forest and Rangeland Renewable Resources Planning Act of 1974 (16 U.S.C. 1600 et seq.) [section 1600 et seq. of this title].

"(2) The Federal Land Policy and Management Act of 1976 (43 U.S.C. 1701 et seq.) [section 1701 et seq. of Title 43, Public Lands].

"(3) The National Environmental Policy Act of 1969 (42 U.S.C. 4321 et seq.) [section 4321 et seq. of Title 42].

"(4) The Endangered Species Act of 1973 (16 U.S.C. 1531 et seq.) [section 1531 et seq. of this title].

"(5) The National Forest Management Act of 1976 (16 U.S.C. 472a et seq.) [Pub.L. 94–588, Oct. 22, 1976, 90 Stat. 2949, for classifications to which see Short Title note under section 1600 of this Title and Tables].

"(6) The Multiple-Use Sustained-Yield Act of 1960 (16 U.S.C. 528 et seq.) [section 528 et seq. of this title].

"(7) Any compact, executive agreement, convention, treaty, and international agreement, and implementing legislation related thereto.

"(8) All other applicable Federal environmental and natural resource laws.

"**(j) Expiration date.**—The authority provided by subsections (b) and (d) shall expire on December 31, 1996. The terms and conditions of this section shall continue in effect with respect to salvage timber sale contracts offered under subsection (b) and timber sale contracts offered under subsection (d) until the completion of performance of the contracts.

"**(k) Award and release of previously offered and unawarded timber sale contracts.**—

"**(1) Award and release required.**—Notwithstanding any other provision of law, within 45 days after the date of the enactment of this Act [July 27, 1995], the Secretary concerned shall act to award, release, and permit to be completed in fiscal years 1995 and 1996, with no change in originally advertised terms, volumes, and bid prices, all timber sale contracts offered or awarded before that date in any unit of the National Forest System or district of the Bureau of Land Management subject to section 318 of Public Law 101–121 (103 Stat. 745) [not classified to the Code]. The return of the bid bond of the high bidder shall not alter the responsibility of the Secretary concerned to comply with this paragraph.

"**(2) Threatened or endangered bird species.**—No sale unit shall be released or completed under this subsection if any threatened or endangered bird species is known to be nesting within the acreage that is the subject of the sale unit.

"**(3) Alternative offer in case of delay.**—If for any reason a sale cannot be released and completed under the terms of this subsection within 45 days after the date of the enactment of this Act [July 27, 1995], the Secretary concerned shall provide the purchaser an equal volume of timber, of like kind and value, which shall be subject to the terms of the original contract and shall not count against current allowable sale quantities.

"**(*l*) Effect on plans, policies, and activities.**—Compliance with this section shall not require or permit any administrative action, including revisions, amendment, consultation, supplementation, or other action, in or for any land management plan, standard, guideline, policy, regional guide, or multiforest plan because of implementation or impacts, site-specific or cumulative, of activities authorized or required by this section, except that any such administrative action with respect to salvage timber sales is permitted to the extent necessary, at the sole discretion of the Secretary concerned, to meet the salvage timber sale goal specified in subsection (b)(1) of this section or to reflect the effects of the salvage program. The Secretary concerned shall not rely on salvage timber sales as the basis for administrative action limiting other multiple use activities nor be required to offer a particular salvage timber sale. No project decision shall be required to be halted or delayed by such documents or guidance, implementation, or impacts."

§ 1612. Public participation [FRRRPA § 14]

(a) Adequate notice and opportunity to comment

In exercising his authorities under this subchapter and other laws applicable to the Forest Service, the Secretary, by regulation, shall establish procedures, including public hearings where appropriate, to give the Federal, State, and local governments and the public adequate notice and an opportunity to comment upon the formulation of standards, criteria, and guidelines applicable to Forest Service programs.

(b) Advisory boards

In providing for public participation in the planning for and management of the National Forest System, the Secretary, pursuant to the Federal Advisory Committee Act (86 Stat. 770) and other applicable law, shall establish and consult such advisory boards as he deems necessary to secure full information and advice on the execution of his responsibilities. The membership of such boards shall be representative of a cross section of groups interested in the planning for and management of the National Forest System and the various types of use and enjoyment of the lands thereof.

(Pub.L. 93–378, § 14, as added Pub.L. 94–588, § 11, Oct. 22, 1976, 90 Stat. 2958.)

References in Text

The Federal Advisory Committee Act, referred to in text, is Pub.L. 92–463, Oct. 6, 1972, 86 Stat. 770, which is set out in Appendix 2 to Title 5, Government Organization and Employees.

Forest Service Decision Making and Appeals Reform

Pub.L. 102–381, Title III, § 322, Oct. 5, 1992, 106 Stat. 1419, provided that:

"**(a) In general.**—In accordance with this section, the Secretary of Agriculture, acting through the Chief of the Forest Service, shall establish a notice and comment process for proposed actions of the Forest Service concerning projects and activities implementing land and resource management plans developed under the Forest and Rangeland Renewable Resources Planning Act of 1974 (16 U.S.C. 1601 et seq.) and shall modify the procedure for appeals of decisions concerning such projects.

"**(b) Notice and comment.**—

"**(1) Notice.**—Prior to proposing an action referred to in subsection (a), the Secretary shall give notice of the proposed action, and the availability of the action for public comment by—

"**(A)** promptly mailing notice about the proposed action to any person who has requested it in writing, and to persons who are known to have participated in the decisionmaking process; and,

"**(B)(i)** in the case of an action taken by the Chief of the Forest Service, publishing notice of action in the Federal Register; or

"**(ii)** in the case of any other action referred to in subsection (a), publishing notice of the action in a newspaper of general circulation that has previously been identified in the Federal Register as the newspaper in which notice under this paragraph may be published.

"**(2) Comment.**—The Secretary shall accept comments on the proposed action within 30 days after publication of the notice in accordance with paragraph (1).

"**(c) Right to appeal.**—Not later than 45 days after the date of issuance of a decision of the Forest Service concerning actions referred to in subsection (a), a person who was involved in the public comment process under subsection (b) through submission of written or oral comments or by otherwise notifying the Forest Service of their interest in the proposed action may file an appeal.

"**(d) Disposition of an appeal.**—

"**(1) Informal disposition.**—

"**(A) In general.**—Subject to subparagraph (B), a designated employee of the Forest Service shall offer to meet with each individual who files an appeal in accordance with subsection (c) and attempt to dispose of the appeal.

"**(B) Time and location of the meeting.**—Each meeting in accordance with subparagraph (A) shall take place—

"**(i)** not later than 15 days after the closing date for filing an appeal; and "(ii) at a location designated by the Chief of the Forest Service that is in the vicinity of the lands affected by the decision.

"(2) **Formal review.**—If the appeal is not disposed of in accordance with paragraph (1), an appeals review officer designated by the Chief of the Forest Service shall review the appeal and recommend in writing, to the official responsible for deciding the appeal, the appropriate disposition of the appeal. The official responsible for deciding the appeal shall then decide the appeal. The appeals review officer shall be a line officer at least at the level of the agency official who made the initial decision on the project or activity that is under appeal, who has not participated in the initial decision and will not be responsible for implementation of the initial decision after the appeal is decided.

"(3) **Time for disposition.**—Disposition of appeals under this subsection shall be completed not later than 30 days after the closing date for filing of an appeal, provided that the Forest Service may extend the closing date by an additional 15 days.

"(4) If the Secretary fails to decide the appeal within the 45–day period, the decision on which the appeal is based shall be deemed to be a final agency action for the purpose of chapter 7 of title 5, United States Code [5 U.S.C.A. § 701 et seq.].

"(e) **Stay.**—Unless the Chief of the Forest Service determines that an emergency situation exists with respect to a decision of the Forest Service, implementation of the decision shall be stayed during the period beginning on the date of the decision—

"(1) for 45 days, if an appeal is not filed, or

"(2) for an additional 15 days after the date of the disposition of an appeal under this section, if the agency action is deemed final under subsection (d)(4)."

CODE OF FEDERAL REGULATIONS

Procedures for public involvement, see 36 CFR 216.1 et seq.

§ 1613. Promulgation of regulations [FRRRPA § 15]

The Secretary of Agriculture shall prescribe such regulations as he determines necessary and desirable to carry out the provisions of this subchapter.

(Pub.L. 93–378, § 15, as added Pub.L. 94–588, § 11, Oct. 22, 1976, 90 Stat. 2958.)

CODE OF FEDERAL REGULATIONS

Planning, applicability and procedures, see 36 CFR 219.1 et seq.

§ 1614. Severability of provisions [FRRRPA § 16]

If any provision of this subchapter or the application thereof to any person or circumstances is held invalid, the validity of the remainder of this subchapter and of the application of such provision to other persons and circumstances shall not be affected thereby.

(Pub.L. 93–378, § 16, as added Pub.L. 94–588, § 11, Oct. 22, 1976, 90 Stat. 2958.)

SUBCHAPTER II—RESEARCH

§ 1641. Congressional statement of findings; application of provisions with planning provisions [FRRRRA § 2]

(a) Findings

(1) Congress finds that scientific discoveries and technological advances must be made and applied to support the protection, management, and utilization of the Nation's renewable resources. It is the purpose of this subchapter to authorize the Secretary of Agriculture (hereinafter in this subchapter referred to as the "Secretary") to implement a comprehensive program of forest and rangeland renewable resources research and dissemination of the findings of such research.

(2) Congress further finds that the forest and rangeland renewable resources of the world are threatened by deforestation due to conversion to agriculture of lands better suited to other uses, overgrazing, over-harvesting, and other causes that pose a direct adverse threat to people, the global environment, and the world economy.

(b) Application of provisions with planning provisions

This subchapter shall be deemed to complement the policies and direction set forth in the Forest and Rangeland Renewable Resources Planning Act of 1974 [16 U.S.C.A. § 1600 et seq.]

(c) Purpose

It is the purpose of this subchapter to authorize the Secretary to expand research activities to encompass international forestry and natural resource issues on a global scale.

(Pub.L. 95–307, § 2, June 30, 1978, 92 Stat. 353; Pub.L. 101–513, Title VI, § 611(a)(1), formerly § 607(a)(1), Nov. 5, 1990, 104 Stat. 2072, renumbered § 611(a)(1), Pub.L. 102–574, § 2(a)(1), Oct. 29, 1992, 106 Stat. 4593.)

References in Text

The Forest and Rangeland Renewable Resources Planning Act of 1974, referred to in text, is Pub.L. 93–378, Aug. 17, 1974, 88 Stat. 476, as amended, which is classified generally to subchapter I (section 1600 et seq.) of this chapter.

Effective Date

Section 9 of Pub.L. 95–307 which provided that Pub.L. 95–307 (enacting this subchapter, repealing sections 581 to 581i of this title, and enacting provisions set out as a note under section 1600 of this title) is effective Oct. 1, 1978, was amended generally by Pub.L. 101–624 and is classified to section 1648 of this title.

Short Title

Section 1 of Pub.L. 95–307, June 30, 1978, 92 Stat. 353, provided: "That this Act [enacting this subchapter] may be cited as the 'Forest and Rangeland Renewable Resources Research Act of 1978'."

§ 1642. Investigations, experiments, tests, and other activities [FRRRRA § 3]

(a) Authorization; scope and purposes of activities

The Secretary is authorized to conduct, support, and cooperate in investigations, experiments, tests, and other activities the Secretary deems necessary to obtain, analyze, develop, demonstrate, and disseminate scientific information about protecting, managing, and utilizing forest and rangeland renewable resources in rural, suburban, and urban areas. The activities conducted, supported, or cooperated in by the Secretary under this subchapter shall include, but not be limited to, the five major areas of renewable resource research identified in paragraphs (1) through (5) of this subsection.

(1) Renewable resource management research shall include, as appropriate, research activities related to managing, reproducing, planting, and growing vegetation on forests and rangelands for timber, forage, water, fish and wildlife, esthetics, recreation, wilderness, energy production, activities related to energy conservation, and other purposes, including activities for encouraging improved reforestation of forest lands from which timber has been harvested; determining the role of forest and rangeland management in the productive use of forests and rangelands, in diversified agriculture, and in mining, transportation, and other industries; and developing alternatives for the management of forests and rangelands that will make possible the most effective use of their multiple products and services.

(2) Renewable resource environmental research shall include, as appropriate, research activities related to understanding and managing surface and subsurface water flow, preventing and controlling erosion, and restoring damaged or disturbed soils on forest and rangeland watersheds; maintaining and improving wildlife and fish habitats; managing vegetation to reduce air and water pollution, provide amenities, and for other purposes; and understanding, predicting, and modifying weather, climatic, and other environmental conditions that affect the protection and management of forests and rangelands.

(3) Renewable resource protection research shall include, as appropriate, research activities related to protecting vegetation and other forest and rangeland resources, including threatened and endangered flora and fauna, as well as wood and wood products in storage or use, from fires, insects, diseases, noxious plants, animals, air pollutants, and other agents through biological, chemical, and mechanical control methods and systems; and protecting people, natural resources, and property from fires in rural areas.

(4) Renewable resource utilization research shall include, as appropriate, research activities related to harvesting, transporting, processing, marketing, distributing, and utilizing wood and other materials derived from forest and rangeland renewable resources; recycling and fully utilizing wood fiber; producing and conserving energy; and testing forest products, including necessary fieldwork associated therewith.

(5) Renewable resource assessment research shall include, as appropriate, research activities related to developing and applying scientific knowledge and technology in support of the survey and analysis of forest and rangeland renewable resources described in subsection (b) of this section.

(b) Development of periodic Renewable Resource Assessment through survey and analysis of conditions

(1) To ensure the availability of adequate data and scientific information for development of the periodic Renewable Resource Assessment provided for in section 1601 of this title, the Secretary of Agriculture shall make and keep current a comprehensive survey and analysis of the present and prospective conditions of and requirements for renewable resources of the forests and rangelands of the United States and of the supplies of such renewable resources, including a determination of the present and potential productivity of the land, and of such other facts as may be necessary and useful in the determination of ways and means needed to balance the demand for and supply of these renewable resources, benefits, and uses in meeting the needs of the people of the United States. The Secretary shall conduct the survey and analysis under such plans as the Secretary may determine to be fair and equitable, and cooperate with appropriate officials of each State and, either through them or directly, with private or other entities.

(2) In implementing this subsection, the Secretary is authorized to develop and implement improved methods of survey and analysis of forest inventory information, for which purposes there are hereby authorized to be appropriated annually $10,000,000.

(c) Program of research and study relative to health and productivity of domestic forest ecosystems; advisory committee; reports

(1) The Secretary, acting through the United States Forest Service, shall establish not later than 180 days after October 24, 1988, a 10-year program (hereinafter in this subsection referred to as the "Program") to—

(A) increase the frequency of forest inventories in matters that relate to atmospheric pollution and conduct such surveys as are necessary to monitor long-term trends in the health and productivity of domestic forest ecosystems;

(B) determine the scope of the decline in the health and productivity of domestic forest ecosystems;

(C) accelerate and expand existing research efforts (including basic forest ecosystem research) to evaluate the effects of atmospheric pollutants on forest ecosystems and their role in the decline in domestic forest health and productivity;

(D) study the relationship between atmospheric pollution and other climatological, chemical, physical, and biological factors that may affect the health and productivity of domestic forest ecosystems;

(E) develop recommendations for solving or mitigating problems related to the effects of atmospheric pollution on the health and productivity of domestic forest ecosystems;

(F) foster cooperation among Federal, State, and private researchers and encourage the exchange of scientific information on the effects of atmospheric pollutants on forest ecosystems among the United States, Canada, European nations, and other nations;

(G) support the long-term funding of research programs and related efforts to determine the causes of declines in the health and productivity of domestic forest ecosystems and the effects of atmospheric pollutants on the health and productivity of domestic forest ecosystems; and

(H) enlarge the Eastern Hardwood Cooperative by devoting additional resources to field analysis of the response of hardwood species to atmospheric pollution, and other factors that may affect the health and productivity of these ecosystems.

(2) The Secretary shall establish a committee to advise the Secretary in developing and carrying out the Program, which shall be composed of scientists with training and experience in various disciplines, including atmospheric, ecological, and biological sciences. Such scientists shall be selected from among individuals who are actively performing research for Federal or State agencies or for private industries, institutions, or organizations.

(3) The Secretary shall coordinate the Program with existing research efforts of Federal and State agencies and private industries, institutions, or organizations.

(4) The Secretary shall submit to the President and to Congress the following reports:

(A) Not less than 30 days before establishing the Program, the Secretary shall submit an initial program report—

(i) discussing existing information about declining health and productivity of forest ecosystems on public and private lands in North America and Europe;

(ii) outlining the findings and status of all current research and monitoring efforts in North America and Europe on the causes and effects of atmospheric pollution on the health and productivity of forest ecosystems;

(iii) describing the Program; and

(iv) estimating the cost of implementing the Program for each fiscal year of its duration.

(B) Not later than January 15, 1990, and January 15 of each year thereafter, during which the Program is in operation following the year in which the initial program report is submitted, the Secretary shall submit an annual report—

(i) updating information about declining health and productivity of forest ecosystems on public and private lands in North America and Europe;

(ii) updating the findings and status of all current research and monitoring efforts in North America and Europe on the causes and effects of atmospheric pollution on the health and productivity of forest ecosystems, including efforts conducted under the Program;

(iii) recommending additional research and monitoring efforts to be undertaken under the Program to determine the effects of atmospheric pollution on the health and productivity of domestic forest ecosystems; and

(iv) recommending methods for solving or mitigating problems stemming from the effects of atmospheric pollution on the health and productivity of domestic forest ecosystems.

(C) Not later than 10 years after the date on which the initial program report is submitted, the Secretary shall submit a final report—

(i) reviewing existing information about declining health and productivity of forest ecosystems on public and private lands in North America and Europe;

(ii) reviewing the nature and findings of all research and monitoring efforts conducted under the Program and any other relevant research and monitoring efforts related to the effects of atmospheric pollution on forest ecosystem; and

(iii) making final recommendations for solving or mitigating problems stemming from the effects of atmospheric pollution on the health and productivity of domestic forest ecosystems.

(d) Other studies and activities

The Secretary is authorized to conduct, support, and cooperate in studies and other activities the Secretary deems necessary to—

(1) evaluate renewable resource management problems associated with urban-forest interface;

(2) assess effects of changes in Federal revenue codes on private forest management and investment; and

(3) develop improved delivery systems for information and technical assistance provided to private landowners.

(Pub.L. 95–307, § 3, June 30, 1978, 92 Stat. 353; Pub.L. 96–294, Title II, § 254, June 30, 1980, 94 Stat. 707; Pub.L. 100–521, § 3, Oct. 24, 1988, 102 Stat. 2601; Pub.L. 101–624, Title XII, § 1241(a), Nov. 28, 1990, 104 Stat. 3544.)

Short Title of 1988 Amendment

Section 1 of Pub.L. 100–521, Oct. 4, 1988, 102 Stat. 2601, provided that: "This Act [which added subsec. (c) of this section and enacted provisions set out as notes under this section] may be cited as the 'Forest Ecosystems and Atmospheric Pollution Research Act of 1988'."

Southern Forest Regeneration Program

Section 1242 of Pub.L. 101–624 provided that:

"(a) **Establishment.**—The Secretary of Agriculture shall make a grant to a State for the establishment, within such State, of a center, to be known as the 'Southern Forest Regeneration Center' (hereafter referred to in this section as the 'Center'), to study forest regeneration problems and forest productivity in the southern region of the United States.

"(b) **Duties of Center.**—The Center shall study forest regeneration problems and forest productivity in the southern region of the United States, including—

"(1) nursery management concerns that will lead to improved seedling quality;

"(2) forest management practices that account for environmental stresses; and

"(3) the development of low-cost forest regeneration methods that provide options for wood products, species diversity, wildlife habitat, and production of clean air and water.

"(c) **Establishment of other programs.**—The Secretary of Agriculture may establish other programs in other regions of the United States, or a comprehensive National program, to carry out the purposes of this section as the Secretary determines appropriate.

"(d) **Authorization of appropriations.**—There are authorized to be appropriated such sums as may be necessary to carry out this section."

Semiarid Agroforestry Research Center

Section 1243 of Pub.L. 101–624 provided that:

"(a) **Semiarid Agroforestry Research, Development, and Demonstration Center.**—The Secretary of Agriculture shall establish at the Forestry Sciences Laboratory of the United States Forest Service, in Lincoln, Nebraska, a Semiarid Agroforestry Research, Development, and Demonstration Center (hereafter referred to in this section as the 'Center') and appoint a Director to manage and coordinate the program established at the Center under subsection (b).

"(b) **Program.**—The Secretary shall establish a program at the Center and seek the participation of Federal or State governmental entities, land-grant colleges or universities, State agricultural experiment stations, State and private foresters, the National Arbor Day Foundation, and other nonprofit foundations in such program to conduct or assist research, investigations, studies, and surveys to—

"(1) develop sustainable agroforestry systems on semiarid lands that minimize topsoil loss and water contamination and stabilize or enhance crop productivity;

"(2) adapt, demonstrate, document, and model the effectiveness of agroforestry systems under different farming systems and soil or climate conditions;

"(3) develop dual use agroforestry systems compatible with paragraphs (1) and (2) which would provide high-value forestry products for commercial sale from semiarid land;

"(4) develop and improve the drought and pest resistance characteristics of trees for conservation forestry and agroforestry applications in semiarid regions, including the introduction and breeding of trees suited for the Great Plains region of the United States;

"(5) develop technology transfer programs that increase farmer and public acceptance of sustainable agroforestry systems;

"(6) develop improved windbreak and shelterbelt technologies for drought preparedness, soil and water conservation, environmental quality, and biological diversity on semiarid lands;

"(7) develop technical and economic concepts for sustainable agroforestry on semiarid lands, including the conduct of economic analyses of the costs and benefits of agroforestry systems and the development of models to predict the economic benefits under soil or climate conditions;

"(8) provide international leadership in the development and exchange of agroforestry practices on semiarid lands worldwide;

"(9) support research on the effects of agroforestry systems on semiarid lands in mitigating nonpoint source water pollution;

"(10) support research on the design, establishment, and maintenance of tree and shrub plantings to regulate the deposition of snow along roadways; and

"(11) conduct sociological, demographic, and economic studies as needed to develop strategies for increasing the use of forestry conservation and agroforestry practices.

"(c) **Information collection and dissemination.**—The Secretary shall establish at the Center a program, to be known as the National Clearinghouse on Agroforestry Conservation and Promotion to—

"(1) collect, analyze, and disseminate information on agroforestry conservation technologies and practices; and

"(2) promote the use of such information by landowners and those organizations associated with forestry and tree promotion.

"(d) **Authorization of appropriations.**—There are authorized to be appropriated $5,000,000 annually to carry out this section."

Forest Ecosystems and Atmospheric Pollution Research; Congressional Statement of Findings

Section 2 of Pub.L. 100–521 provided that:

"Congress finds that—

"(1) the health and productivity of forests in certain regions of the United States are declining;

"(2) there is a special concern about the decline of certain hardwood species, particularly sugar maples and oaks, in the eastern United States and the effects of atmospheric pollutants on the health and productivity of these forests;

"(3) declines in the productivity of certain commercially important Southern pine species have been measured;

"(4) existing research indicates that atmospheric pollution, including ozone, acidic deposition, and heavy metals, may contribute to this decline;

"(5) there is an urgent need to expand and better coordinate existing Federal, State, and private research, including research by private industry, to determine the cause of changes in the health and productivity of domestic forest ecosystems and to monitor and evaluate the effects of atmospheric pollutants on such ecosystems; and

"(6) such research and monitoring should not impede efforts to control atmospheric pollutants."

§ 1643. Implementation of provisions [FRRRRA § 4(a)–(c)]

(a) Establishment and maintenance of research facilities; acquisition, expenditures, etc., for property

In implementing this subchapter, the Secretary is authorized to establish and maintain a system of experiment stations, research laboratories, experimental areas, and other forest and rangeland research facilities. The Secretary is authorized, with donated or appropriated funds, to acquire by lease, donation, purchase, exchange, or otherwise, land or interests in land within the United States needed to implement this subchapter, to make necessary expenditures to examine, appraise, and survey such property, and to do all things incident to perfecting title thereto in the United States.

(b) Acceptance, holding, and administration of gifts, donations, and bequests; use and investment of gifts, proceeds, etc.; funding requirements

In implementing this subchapter, the Secretary is authorized to accept, hold, and administer gifts, donations, and bequests of money, real property, or personal property from any source not otherwise prohibited by law and to use such gifts, donations, and bequests to (1) establish or operate any forest and rangeland research facility within the United States, or (2) perform any forest and rangeland renewable resource research activity authorized by this subchapter. Such gifts, donations, and bequests, or the proceeds thereof, and money appropriated for these purposes shall be deposited in the Treasury in a special fund. At the request of the Secretary, the Secretary of the Treasury may invest or reinvest any money in the fund that in the opinion of the Secretary is not needed for current operations. Such investments shall be in public debt securities with maturities suitable for the needs of the fund and bearing interest at prevailing market rates. There are hereby authorized to be expended from such fund such amounts as may be specified in annual appropriation Acts, which shall remain available until expended.

(c) Cooperation with international, Federal, State, and other governmental agencies, public and private agencies, etc.; funding requirements for contributions from cooperators

In implementing this subchapter, the Secretary may cooperate with international, Federal, State, and other governmental agencies, with public or private agencies, institutions, universities, and organizations, and with businesses and individuals in the United States and in other countries. The Secretary may receive money and other contributions from cooperators under such conditions as the Secretary may prescribe. Any money contributions received under this subsection shall be credited to the applicable appropriation or fund to be used for the same purposes and shall remain available until expended as the Secretary may direct for use in conducting research activities authorized by this subchapter and in making refunds to contributors.

(Pub.L. 95–307, § 4(a)–(c), June 30, 1978, 92 Stat. 354; Pub.L. 101–513, Title VI, § 611(a)(2), formerly § 607(a)(2), Nov. 5, 1990, 104 Stat. 2072, renumbered § 611(a)(2), Pub.L. 102–574, § 2(a)(1), Oct. 29, 1992, 106 Stat. 4593.)

§ 1644. Competitive grants; scope and purposes; prerequisites [FRRRRA § 5]

In addition to any grants made under other laws, the Secretary is authorized to make competitive grants that will further research activities authorized by this subchapter to Federal, State, and other governmental agencies, public or private agencies, institutions, universities, and organizations, and businesses and individuals in the United States. In making these grants, the Secretary shall emphasize basic and applied research activities that are important to achieving the purposes of this subchapter, and shall obtain, through review by qualified scientists and other methods, participation in research activities by scientists throughout the United States who have expertise in matters related to forest and rangeland renewable resources. Grants under this section shall be made at the discretion of the Secretary under whatever conditions the Secretary may prescribe, after publicly soliciting research proposals, allowing sufficient time for submission of the proposals, and considering qualitative, quantitative, financial, administrative, and other factors that the Secretary deems important in judging, comparing, and accepting the proposals. The Secretary may reject any or all proposals received under this section if the Secretary determines that it is in the public interest to do so.

(Pub.L. 95–307, § 5, June 30, 1978, 92 Stat. 355.)

CODE OF FEDERAL REGULATIONS

Competitive research grants program, see 7 CFR 3201.1 et seq.

§ 1645. General provisions [FRRRRA § 6]

(a) Availability of funds to cooperators and grantees

The Secretary may make funds available to cooperators and grantees under this subchapter without regard to the provisions of section 3324(a) and (b) of Title 31, which prohibits advances of public money.

(b) Coordination of cooperative aid and grants with other aid and grant authorities

To avoid duplication, the Secretary shall coordinate cooperative aid and grants under this subchapter with cooperative aid and grants the Secretary makes under any other authority.

(c) Dissemination of knowledge and technology developed from research activities; cooperation with specified entities

The Secretary shall use the authorities and means available to the Secretary to disseminate the knowledge and technology developed from research activities conducted under or supported by this subchapter. In meeting this responsibility, the Secretary shall cooperate, as the Secretary deems appropriate, with the entities identified in subsection (d)(3) of this section and with others.

(d) Additional implementative authorities

In implementing this subchapter, the Secretary, as the Secretary deems appropriate and practical, shall—

(1) use, and encourage cooperators and grantees to use, the best available scientific skills from a variety of disciplines within and outside the fields of agriculture and forestry;

(2) seek, and encourage cooperators and grantees to seek, a proper mixture of short-term and long-term research and a proper mixture of basic and applied research;

(3) avoid unnecessary duplication and coordinate activities under this section among agencies of the Department of Agriculture and with other affected Federal departments and agencies, State agricultural experiment stations, State extension services, State foresters or equivalent State officials, forestry schools, and private research organizations; and

(4) encourage the development, employment, retention, and exchange of qualified scientists and other specialists through postgraduate, postdoctoral, and other training, national and international exchange of scientists, and other incentives and programs to improve the quality of forest and rangeland renewable resources research.

(e) Construction of statutory provisions

This subchapter shall be construed as supplementing all other laws relating to the Department of Agriculture and shall not be construed as limiting or repealing any existing law or authority of the Secretary except as specifically cited in this subchapter.

(f) Definitions

For the purposes of this subchapter, the terms "United States" and "State" shall include each of the several States, the District of Columbia, the Commonwealth of Puerto Rico, the Virgin Islands of the United States, the Commonwealth of the Northern Mariana Islands, the Trust Territory of the Pacific Islands, and the territories and possessions of the United States.

(Pub.L. 95–307, § 6, June 30, 1978, 92 Stat. 355.)

Codification

In subsec. (a), "section 3324(a) and (b) of Title 31" was substituted for "section 3648 of the Revised Statutes (31 U.S.C. 529)" on authority of Pub.L. 97–258, § 4(b), Sept. 13, 1982, 96 Stat. 1067, the first section of which enacted Title 31, Money and Finance.

§ 1646. Authorization of appropriations [FRRRRA § 7]

There are hereby authorized to be appropriated annually such sums as may be needed to implement this subchapter. Funds appropriated under this subchapter shall remain available until expended.

(Pub.L. 95–307, § 7, June 30, 1978, 92 Stat. 356.)

§ 1647. Other Federal programs [FRRRRA § 8]

(a) Repeal of statutory authorities relating to investigation, experiments, and tests in reforestation and forest products

The Act of May 22, 1928, known as the McSweeney-McNary Act (45 Stat. 699–702, as amended; 16 U.S.C. 581, 581a, 581b–581i), is hereby repealed.

(b) Force and effect of cooperative and other agreements under repealed statutory authorities relating to investigation, etc., in reforestation and forest products

Contracts and cooperative and other agreements under the McSweeney-McNary Act shall remain in effect until revoked or amended by their own terms or under other provisions of law.

(c) Issuance of rules and regulations for implementation of provisions and coordination with agricultural research, extension, and teaching provisions

The Secretary is authorized to issue such rules and regulations as the Secretary deems necessary to implement the provisions of this subchapter and to coordinate this subchapter with title XIV of the Food and Agriculture Act of 1977 [7 U.S.C.A. § 3101 et seq.].

(d) Availability of funds appropriated under repealed statutory authorities relating to investigation, etc., in reforestation and forest products

Funds appropriated under the authority of the McSweeney-McNary Act shall be available for expenditure for the programs authorized under this subchapter.

(Pub.L. 95–307, § 8, June 30, 1978, 92 Stat. 356.)

References in Text

The Food and Agriculture Act of 1977, referred to in subsec. (c), is Pub.L. 95–113, Sept. 29, 1977, 91 Stat. 913, as amended. Title XIV of the Food and Agriculture Act of 1977, known as the "National Agricultural Research, Extension, and Teaching Policy Act of 1977", is classified principally to chapter 64 (section 3101 et seq.) of Title 7, Agriculture.

§ 1648. Recycling research [FRRRRA § 9]

(a) Findings

Congress finds that—

(1) the United States is amassing vast amounts of solid wastes, which is presenting an increasing problem for municipalities in locating suitable disposal sites;

(2) a large proportion of these wastes consists of paper and other wood wastes;

(3) less than one-third of these paper and wood wastes are recycled;

(4) additional recycling would result in reduced solid waste landfill disposal and would contribute to a reduced rate of removal of standing timber from forest lands; and

(5) additional research is needed to develop technological advances to address barriers to increased recycling of paper and wood wastes and utilization of products consisting of recycled materials.

(b) Recycling research program

The Secretary is authorized to conduct, support, and cooperate in an expanded wood fiber recycling research program, including the acquisition of necessary equipment. The Secretary shall seek to ensure that the program includes the cooperation and support of private industry and that program goals include the application of such research to industry and consumer needs.

(c) Authorization of appropriations

In addition to any other funds made available to implement section 1642 of this title, for the 5-year period beginning on October 1, 1990, there are authorized to be appropriated annually $10,000,000 to implement this section.

(Pub.L. 95–307, § 9, as added Pub.L. 101–624, Title XII, § 1241(b), Nov. 28, 1990, 104 Stat. 3544.)

Prior Provisions

A prior section 9 of Pub.L. 95–307, June 30, 1978, 92 Stat. 357, which provided the effective date for Pub.L. 95–307, was set out as a note under section 1641 of this title prior to general amendment by Pub.L. 101–624.

§ 1649. Forestry Student Grant Program [FRRRRA § 10]

(a) Establishment

The Secretary shall establish a program, to be known as the "Forestry Student Grant Program" (hereafter referred to in this section as the "Program"), to provide assistance to expand the professional education of forestry, natural resources, and environmental scientists.

(b) Student grants

Under the Program the Secretary shall provide assistance for the establishment of a competitive grant fellowship program to assist graduate, and undergraduate minority and female, students attending institutions having programs in forestry and natural resources.

(c) Eligibility

The Secretary shall ensure that students concentrating in the following studies shall be eligible for assistance under subsection (b) of this section:

(1) Forestry.

(2) Biology and forest organisms.

(3) Ecosystem function and management.

(4) Human-forest interaction.

(5) International trade, competition, and cooperation.%

(6) Wood as a raw material.

(7) Economics and policy.

(d) Authorization of appropriations

There are authorized to be appropriated such sums as may be necessary to carry out this section.

(Pub.L. 95–307, § 10, as added Pub.L. 101–624, Title XII, § 1252, Nov. 28, 1990, 104 Stat. 3553.)

SUBCHAPTER III—EXTENSION PROGRAMS

§ 1671. Congressional statement of findings [RREA § 2]

Congress finds that—

(1) the extension program of the Department of Agriculture and the extension activities of each State provide useful and productive educational programs for private forest and range landowners and processors and consumptive and nonconsumptive users of forest and rangeland renewable resources, and these educational programs complement research and assistance programs conducted by the Department of Agriculture;

(2) to meet national goals, it is essential that all forest and rangeland renewable resources (hereinafter in this subchapter referred to as "renewable resources"), including fish and wildlife, forage, outdoor recreation opportunities, timber, and water, be fully considered in designing educational programs for landowners, processors, and users;

(3) more efficient utilization and marketing of renewable resources extend available supplies of such resources, provide products to consumers at prices less than they would otherwise be, and promote reasonable returns on the investments of landowners, processors, and users;

(4) trees and forests in urban areas improve the esthetic quality, reduce noise, filter impurities from the air and add oxygen to it, save energy by moderating temperature extremes, control wind and water erosion, and provide habitat for wildlife; and

(5) trees and shrubs used as shelterbelts protect farm lands from wind and water erosion, promote moisture accumulation in the soil, and provide habitat for wildlife.

(Pub.L. 95–306, § 2, June 30, 1978, 92 Stat. 349.)

Effective and Termination Dates

Section 8 of Pub.L. 95–306, as amended Pub.L. 100–231, § 2(2), Jan. 5, 1988, 101 Stat. 1565, provided that: "The provisions of this Act [enacting this subchapter and provisions set out as a note under section 1600 of this title] shall be effective for the period beginning October 1, 1978, and ending September 30, 2000."

Short Title

Section 1 of Pub.L. 95–306, June 30, 1978, 92 Stat. 349, provided: "That this Act [enacting this subchapter] may be cited as the 'Renewable Resources Extension Act of 1978'."

§ 1672. General program authorization [RREA § 3]

(a) Types of programs; preconditions and cooperation with State program directors, etc.

The Secretary of Agriculture (hereinafter in this subchapter referred to as the "Secretary"), under conditions the Secretary may prescribe and in cooperation with the State directors of cooperative extension service programs and eligible colleges and universities, shall—

(1) provide educational programs that enable individuals to recognize, analyze, and resolve problems dealing with renewable resources, including forest- and range-based outdoor recreation opportunities, trees and forests in urban areas, and trees and shrubs in shelterbelts;

(2) use educational programs to disseminate the results of research on renewable resources;

(3) conduct educational programs that transfer the best available technology to those involved in the management and protection of forests and rangelands and the processing and use of their associated renewable resources;

(4) develop and implement educational programs that give special attention to the educational needs of small, private nonindustrial forest landowners;

(5) develop and implement educational programs in range and fish and wildlife management;

(6) assist in providing continuing education programs for professionally trained individuals in fish and wildlife, forest, range, and watershed management and related fields;

(7) help forest and range landowners in securing technical and financial assistance to bring appropriate expertise to bear on their problems;

(8) help identify areas of needed research regarding renewable resources;

(9) in cooperation with State foresters or equivalent State officials, promote public understanding of the energy conservation, economic, social, environmental, and psychological values of trees and open space in urban and community area environments and expand knowledge of the ecological relationships and benefits of trees and related resources in urban and community environments; and

(10) conduct a comprehensive natural resource and environmental education program for landowners and managers, public officials, and the public, with particular emphasis on youth.

(b) "Eligible colleges and universities" defined

As used in this subchapter, the term "eligible colleges and universities" means colleges and universities eligible to be supported and maintained, in whole or in part, with funds made available under the provisions of the Act of July 2, 1862 (12 Stat. 503–505, as amended; 7 U.S.C. 301–305, 307, 308), and the Act of August 30, 1890 (26 Stat. 417–419, as amended; 7 U.S.C. 321–326, 328), including Tuskegee Institute, and colleges and universities eligible for assistance under the Act of October 10, 1962 (76 Stat. 806–807, as amended; 16 U.S.C. 582a, 582a–1–582a–7).

(c) Use of appropriate educational methods required; scope of methods

In implementing this section, all appropriate educational methods may be used, including, but not limited to, meetings, short courses, workshops, tours, demonstrations, publications, news releases, and radio and television programs.

(Pub.L. 95–306, § 3, June 30, 1978, 92 Stat. 349; Pub.L. 101–624, Title XII, §§ 1219(b)(1), 1251(b), Nov. 28, 1990, 104 Stat. 3538, 3552; Pub.L. 102–237, Title X, § 1018(2), Dec. 13, 1991, 105 Stat. 1905.)

References in Text

The Act of July 2, 1862 (12 Stat. 503–505, as amended; 7 U.S.C. 301–305, 307, 308), referred to in subsec. (b), is Act July 2, 1862, c. 130, 12 Stat. 503, as amended, popularly known as the Morrill Act and also as the First Morrill Act, which is classified generally to subchapter I (section 301 et seq.) of chapter 13 of Title 7, Agriculture.

The Act of August 30, 1890 (26 Stat. 417–419, as amended; 7 U.S.C. 321–326, 328), referred to in subsec. (b), is Act Aug. 30, 1890, c. 841, 26 Stat. 417, as amended, popularly known as the Agricultural College Act of 1890 and also as the Second Morrill Act, which is classified generally to subchapter II (section 321 et seq.) of chapter 13 of Title 7.

The Act of October 10, 1962 (76 Stat. 806–807, as amended), referred to in subsec. (b), is Pub.L. 87–788, Oct. 10, 1962, 76 Stat. 806, as amended, known as the McIntire-Stennis Act of 1962, which is classified generally to subchapter III (section 582a et seq.) of chapter 3 of this title.

Effective Date of 1991 Amendment

Amendments by Pub.L. 102–237 effective Dec. 13, 1991, see section 1101(a) of Pub.L. 102–237, set out as a note under section 1421 of Title 7, Agriculture.

§ 1673. State programs [RREA § 4]

(a) Development by State program director, etc., of comprehensive and coordinated program by mutual agreement; consultations; review procedure

The State director of cooperative extension programs (hereinafter in this subchapter referred to as the "State director") and the administrative heads of extension for eligible colleges and universities in each State shall jointly develop, by mutual agreement, a single comprehensive and coordinated renewable resources extension program in which the role of each eligible college and university is well-defined. In meeting this responsibility, the State director and the administrative heads of extension for eligible colleges and universities shall consult and seek agreement with the administrative technical representatives and the forestry representatives provided for by the Secretary in implementation of the Act of October 10, 1962 (76 Stat. 806–807, as amended; 16 U.S.C. 582a, 582a–1–582a–7), in the State. Each State's renewable resources extension program shall be submitted to the Secretary annually. The National Agricultural Research and Extension Users Advisory Board established under section 3123 of Title 7 shall review and make recommendations to the Secretary pertaining to programs conducted under this subchapter.

(b) Encouragement by State director, etc., of cooperation between county and State extension staffs and appropriate Federal and State agencies and organizations

The State director and the administrative heads of extension for eligible colleges and universities in each State shall encourage close cooperation between extension staffs at the county and State levels, and State and Federal research organizations dealing with renewable resources, State and Federal agencies that manage forests and rangelands and their associated renewable resources, State and Federal agencies that have responsibilities associated with the processing or use of renewable resources, and other agencies or organizations the State director and administrative heads of extension deem appropriate.

(c) Administration and coordination of program by State director; exception

Each State renewable resources extension program shall be administered and coordinated by the State director, except that, in States having colleges eligible to receive funds under the Act of August 30, 1890 (26 Stat. 417–419, as amended; 7 U.S.C. 321–326, 328), including Tuskegee Institute, the State renewable resources extension program shall be administered by the State director and the administrative head or heads of extension for the college or colleges eligible to receive such funds.

(d) Appointment and use of advisory committees by State director, etc.; composition of advisory committees

In meeting the provisions of this section, each State director and administrative heads of extension for eligible colleges and universities shall appoint and use one or more advisory committees comprised of forest and range landowners, professionally trained individuals in fish and wildlife, forest, range, and watershed management, and related fields, as appropriate, and other suitable persons.

(e) "State" defined

For the purposes of this subchapter, the term "State" means any one of the fifty States, the Commonwealth of Puerto Rico, Guam, the District of Columbia, and the Virgin Islands of the United States.

(Pub.L. 95–306, § 4, June 30, 1978, 92 Stat. 350.)

References in Text

The Act of October 10, 1962 (76 Stat. 806–807, as amended), referred to in subsec. (a), is Pub.L. 87–788, Oct. 10, 1962, 76 Stat. 806, as amended, known as the McIntire-Stennis Act of 1962, which is classified generally to subchapter III (section 582a et seq.) of chapter 3 of this title.

The Act of August 30, 1890 (26 Stat. 417–419, as amended; 7 U.S.C. 321–326, 328), referred to in subsec. (c), is Act Aug. 30, 1890, c. 841, 26 Stat. 417, as amended, popularly known as the Agricultural College Act of 1890 and also as the Second Morrill Act, which is classified generally to subchapter II (section 321 et seq.) of chapter 13 of Title 7, Agriculture.

§ 1674. Renewable Resources Extension Program plan [RREA § 5]

(a) Preparation and submission to Congressional committees; purposes; contents

The Secretary shall prepare a five-year plan for implementing this subchapter, which is to be called the "Renewable Resources Extension Program" and shall submit such plan to the Committee on Agriculture of the House of Representatives and the Committee on Agriculture, Nutrition, and Forestry of the Senate no later than the last day of the first half of the fiscal year ending September 30, 1980, and the last day of the first half of each fifth fiscal year thereafter. The Renewable Resources Extension Program shall provide national emphasis and direction as well as guidance to State directors and administrative heads of extension for eligible colleges and universities in the development of their respective State renewable resources extension programs, which are to be appropriate in terms of the conditions, needs, and opportunities in each State. The Renewable Resources Extension Program shall contain, but not be limited to, brief outlines of general extension programs for fish and wildlife management (for both game and nongame species), range management, timber management (including brief outlines of general extension programs for timber utilization, timber harvesting, timber marketing, wood utilization, and wood products marketing), and watershed management (giving special attention to water quality protection), as well as brief outlines of general extension programs for recognition and enhancement of forest- and range-based outdoor recreation opportunities, for urban and community forestry activities, and for planting and management of trees and shrubs in shelterbelts, and give special attention to water quality protection and natural resource and environmental education for landowners and managers, public officials, and the public.

(b) Considerations governing preparation

In preparing the Renewable Resources Extension Program, the Secretary shall take into account the respective capabilities of private forests and rangelands for yielding renewable resources and the relative needs for such resources identified in the periodic Renewable Resource Assessment provided for in section 1601 of this title and the periodic appraisal of land and water resources provided for in section 2004 of this title.

(c) Annual report to Congress

To provide information that will aid Congress in its oversight responsibilities and to provide accountability in implementing this subchapter, the Secretary shall prepare an annual report, which shall be furnished to Congress at the time of submission of each annual fiscal budget, beginning with the annual fiscal budget for the fiscal year ending September 30, 1981. The annual report shall set forth accomplishments of the Renewable Resources Extension Program, its strengths and weaknesses, recommendations for improvement, and costs of program administration, each with respect to the preceding fiscal year.

(d) Review of activities and evaluation of progress

To assist Congress and the public in evaluating the Renewable Resources Extension Program, the program shall include a review of activities undertaken in response to the preceding five-year plan and an evaluation of the progress made toward accomplishing the goals and objectives set forth in such preceding plan. Such review and evaluation shall be displayed in the program, for the Nation as a whole, and for each State.

(Pub.L. 95–306, § 5, June 30, 1978, 92 Stat. 351; Pub.L. 100–231, § 3, Jan. 5, 1988, 101 Stat. 1565; Pub.L. 101–624, Title XII, §§ 1219(b)(2), 1251(c), Nov. 28, 1990, 104 Stat. 3539, 3553.)

§ 1674a. Expanded programs [RREA § 5A]

(a) In general

The Secretary, acting through the Extension Service and the State cooperative extension services, and in consultation with State foresters or equivalent State officials, school boards, and universities, shall expand forestry and natural resources education programs conducted under this subchapter for private forest owners and managers, public officials, youth, and the general public, and shall include guidelines for the transfer of technology.

(b) Activities

(1) In general

In expanding the programs conducted under this subchapter, the Secretary shall ensure that activities are undertaken to promote policies and practices that enhance the health, vitality, productivity, economic value, and environmental attributes of the forest lands of the United States.

(2) Types

The activities referred to in paragraph (1) shall include—

(A) demonstrating and teaching landowners and forest managers the concepts of multiple-use and sustainable natural resource management;

(B) conducting comprehensive environmental education programs that assist citizens to participate in environmentally positive activities such as tree planting, recycling, erosion prevention, and waste management; and

(C) educational programs and materials that will improve the capacity of schools, local governments and resource agencies to deliver forestry and natural resources information to young people, environmentally concerned citizens, and action groups.

(Pub.L. 95–306, § 5A, as added Pub.L. 101–624, Title XII, § 1251(a), Nov. 28, 1990, 104 Stat. 3552.)

§ 1675. Authorization of appropriations; criteria for eligibility of States for funds [RREA § 6]

There are authorized to be appropriated to implement this subchapter $15,000,000 for the fiscal year ending September 30, 1988, and $15,000,000 for each of the next twelve fiscal years. Generally, States shall be eligible for funds appropriated under this subchapter according to the respective capabilities of their private forests and rangelands for yielding renewable resources and relative needs for such resources identified in the periodic Renewable Resource Assessment provided for in section 1601 of this title and the periodic appraisal of land and water resources provided for in section 2004 of this title.

(Pub.L. 95–306, § 6, June 30, 1978, 92 Stat. 352; Pub.L. 100–231, § 2(1), Jan. 5, 1988, 101 Stat. 1565.)

§ 1676. Issuance of rules and regulations for implementation of provisions and coordination with agricultural, research, extension, and teaching provisions [RREA § 7]

The Secretary is authorized to issue such rules and regulations as the Secretary deems necessary to implement the provisions of this subchapter and to coordinate this subchapter with title XIV of the Food and Agriculture Act of 1977 [7 U.S.C.A. § 3101 et seq.].
(Pub.L. 95–306, § 7, June 30, 1978, 92 Stat. 352.)

References in Text

The Food and Agriculture Act of 1977, referred to in text, is Pub.L. 95–113, Sept. 29, 1977, 91 Stat. 913, as amended. Title XIV of the Food and Agriculture Act of 1977, known as the "National Agricultural Research, Extension, and Teaching Policy Act of 1977", is classified principally to chapter 64 (section 3101 et seq.) of Title 7, Agriculture.

SUBCHAPTER IV—WOOD RESIDUE UTILIZATION

§ 1681. Congressional statement of purpose [WRUA § 2]

The purpose of this subchapter is to develop, demonstrate, and make available information on feasible methods that have potential for commercial application to increase and improve utilization, in residential, commercial, and industrial or powerplant applications, of wood residues resulting from timber harvesting and forest protection and management activities occurring on public and private forest lands, and from the manufacture of forest products, including woodpulp.
(Pub.L. 96–554, § 2, Dec. 19, 1980, 94 Stat. 3257.)

Short Title

Section 1 of Pub.L. 96–554, Dec. 19, 1980, 94 Stat. 3257, provided: "That this Act [enacting this subchapter] may be cited as the 'Wood Residue Utilization Act of 1980'."

§ 1682. Pilot projects and demonstrations [WRUA § 3]

(a) Establishment, implementation

The Secretary may establish pilot projects and demonstrations to carry out the purposes of this subchapter. The pilot projects and demonstrations established under this section (1) may be operated by the Secretary; or (2) may be carried out through contracts or agreements with owners of private forest lands or other persons, or in conjunction with projects, contracts, or agreements entered into under any other authority which the Secretary may possess: *Provided,* That nothing contained in this subchapter shall abrogate or modify provisions of existing contracts or agreements, including contracts or agreements for the sale of national forest timber, except to the extent such changes are mutually agreed to by the parties to such contracts or agreements.

(b) Scope; residue removal credits

Pilot projects and demonstrations carried out under this section may include, but are not limited to (1) establishment and operation of utilization demonstration areas; (2) establishment and operation of fuel wood concentration and distribution centers; and (3) construction of access roads needed to facilitate wood residue utilization: *Provided,* That residue removal credits may be utilized by the Secretary only as provided in section 1683 of this title.
(Pub.L. 96–554, § 3, Dec. 19, 1980, 94 Stat. 3257.)

CROSS REFERENCES

Authorization of appropriations for pilot projects and demonstrations, see section 1687 of this title.

§ 1683. Projects; requirements; residue removal credits as compensation; implementation guidelines [WRUA § 4]

The Secretary may carry out pilot wood residue utilization projects under which purchasers of National Forest System timber under contracts awarded prior to October 1, 1986, may, except as otherwise provided in this section, be required to remove wood residues not purchased by them to points of prospective use in return for compensation in the form of "residue removal credits." Such projects may be carried out where the Secretary identifies situations in which pilot wood residue utilization projects on the National Forest System can provide important information on various methods and approaches to increasing the utilization, in residential, commercial, and industrial or powerplant applications, of wood residues and where such information cannot reasonably be obtained unless the pilot projects are done in conjunction with normal National Forest timber sale activities. The residue removal credits shall be applied against the amount payable for the timber purchased and shall represent the anticipated cost of removal of wood residues. The following guidelines shall apply to projects carried out under this section:

(1) Except in cases where wood residue removal is determined to be necessary for fire prevention, site preparation for regeneration, wildlife habitat improvement, or other land management purposes, the Secretary may not provide for removal of wood residues in instances where the anticipated cost of removal would exceed the anticipated value.

(2) The residue removal credits authorized by this section shall not exceed the amount payable by

the purchaser for timber after the application of all other designated charges and credits.

(3) The Secretary may sell the wood residues removed to points of prospective use for not less than their appraised value.

(4) Pilot projects, demonstrations, and other programs established pursuant to this subchapter shall be carried out in a manner which does not result in an adverse effect on the furnishing of timber, free of charge, under any other provision of law.

(5) Wood residues shall be collected from a site so as to avoid soil depletion or erosion giving full consideration to the protection of wildlife habitat.

(6) For the purposes of section 500 of this title, (A) any residue removal credit applied under this section shall be considered as "money received" or "moneys received", respectively, and (B) the "money received" or "moneys received", respectively, from the sales of wood residues removed to points of prospective use shall be the proceeds of the sales less the sum of any residue removal credit applied with respect to such residues plus any costs incurred by the Forest Service in processing and storing such residues.

(Pub.L. 96–554, § 4, Dec. 19, 1980, 94 Stat. 3257.)

CROSS REFERENCES

Authorization of appropriations, see section 1687 of this title.
Residue removal credits, see section 1682.

§ 1684. Annual reports [WRUA § 5]

The Secretary shall make annual reports to the Congress on the programs authorized by this subchapter. These reports shall be submitted with the reports required under section 1606(c) of this title.

(Pub.L. 96–554, § 5, Dec. 19, 1980, 94 Stat. 3258.)

§ 1685. Regulations [WRUA § 6]

The Secretary shall issue such regulations as the Secretary deems necessary to implement the provisions of this subchapter.

(Pub.L. 96–554, § 6, Dec. 19, 1980, 94 Stat. 3258.)

§ 1686. Definitions [WRUA § 7]

For purposes of this subchapter, the term:

(1) "Anticipated cost of removal" means the projected cost of removal of wood residues from timber sales areas to points of prospective use, as determined by the Secretary at the time of advertisement of the timber sales contract in accordance with appropriate appraisal and sale procedures.

(2) "Anticipated value" means the projected value of wood residues as fuel or other merchantable wood products, as determined by the Secretary at the time of advertisement of the timber sales contract in accordance with appropriate appraisal and sale procedures.

(3) "Points of prospective use" means the locations where the wood residues are sold or otherwise put to use, as determined by the Secretary in accordance with appropriate appraisal and sale procedures.

(4) "Person" means an individual, partnership, joint-stock company, corporation, association, trust, estate, or any other legal entity, or any agency of Federal or State government or of a political subdivision of a State.

(5) "Secretary" means the Secretary of Agriculture.

(6) "Wood residues" includes, but is not limited to, logging slash, down timber material, woody plants, and standing live or dead trees which do not meet utilization standards because of size, species, merchantable volume, or economic selection criteria and which, in the case of live trees, are surplus to growing stock needs.

(Pub.L. 96–554, § 7, Dec. 19, 1980, 94 Stat. 3258.)

§ 1687. Authorization of appropriations [WRUA § 8]

There is hereby authorized to be appropriated not to exceed $25,000,000 for each of the fiscal years 1982, 1983, 1984, 1985, and 1986 to carry out the pilot projects and demonstrations authorized by section 1682 of this title, the residue removal credits authorized by section 1683 of this title, and the other provisions of this subchapter: *Provided,* That not to exceed $2,500,000 of such amount may be appropriated for administrative expenses to carry out this subchapter for the period beginning October 1, 1981, and ending September 30, 1986. Such sums shall be in addition to those provided under other provisions of law and shall remain available until expended.

(Pub.L. 96–554, § 8, Dec. 19, 1980, 94 Stat. 3259.)

TITLE 30—MINERAL LANDS AND MINING

SURFACE MINING CONTROL AND RECLAMATION

SURFACE MINING CONTROL AND RECLAMATION ACT OF 1977 [SMCRA § ___]

(30 U.S.C.A. §§ 1201, 1202, 1211, 1221 to 1230a, 1231 to 1243, 1251 to 1279, 1281, 1291 to 1309, 1311 to 1316, 1321 to 1328)

MINING AND MINERAL RESOURCES RESEARCH INSTITUTE ACT OF 1984 [MMRRIA § ___]

(30 U.S.C.A. §§ 1221 to 1230)

CHAPTER 25—SURFACE MINING CONTROL AND RECLAMATION

SUBCHAPTER I—STATEMENT OF FINDINGS AND POLICY

Sec.
1201. Congressional findings.
1202. Statement of purpose.

SUBCHAPTER II—OFFICE OF SURFACE MINING RECLAMATION AND ENFORCEMENT

1211. Office of Surface Mining Reclamation and Enforcement.
- (a) Establishment.
- (b) Appointment, compensation, duties, etc., of Director; employees.
- (c) Duties of Secretary.
- (d) Restriction on use of Federal coal mine health and safety inspectors.
- (e) Repealed.
- (f) Conflict of interest; penalties; rules and regulations; report to Congress.
- (g) Petition for issuance, amendment, or repeal of rule; filing; hearing or investigation; notice of denial.

SUBCHAPTER III—STATE MINING AND MINERAL RESOURCES RESEARCH INSTITUTES

1221. Authorization of State allotments to institutes.
1222. Research funds to institutes.
- (a) Authorization of appropriations.
- (b) Application for funds; contents.
- (c) Research facilities; selection of institutes; designation of funds for scholarships and fellowships.
- (d) Requirements for receipt of funds.

Sec.
1222. Research funds to institutes.
- (e) Restriction on application of funds.

1223. Funding criteria.
1224. Duties of Secretary.
- (a) Consulting with other agencies; prescribing rules and regulations; furnishing advice and assistance; coordinating research.
- (b) Annual ascertainment of compliance.
- (c) Annual report to Congress.

1225. Effect on colleges and universities.
1226. Research.
- (a) Coordination with existing programs; availability of information to public.
- (b) Effect on Federal agencies.
- (c) Availability of results to public.
- (d) Authorization of appropriation.

1227. Center for cataloging.
1228. Interagency cooperation.
1229. Committee on Mining and Mineral Resources Research.
- (a) Appointment; composition.
- (b) Consultation and recommendations.
- (c) Compensation, travel, subsistence and related expenses.
- (d) Chairmanship of Committee.
- (e) National plan for research.
- (f) Application of Federal Advisory Committee Act.

1230. Eligibility criteria.
1230a. Strategic Resources Generic Mineral Technology.
- (a) Establishment.
- (b) Functions.
- (c) Criteria.
- (d) Authorization of appropriations.

SUBCHAPTER IV—ABANDONED MINE RECLAMATIONS

1231. Abandoned Mine Reclamation Fund.
- (a) Establishment; administration; State funds.

Sec.
1231. Abandoned Mine Reclamation Fund.
(b) Sources of deposits to fund.
(c) Use of moneys.
(d) Moneys available upon appropriation; no fiscal year limitation.
(e) Interest.
1232. Reclamation fee.
(a) Payment; rate.
(b) Due date.
(c) Submission of statement.
(d) Penalty.
(e) Civil action to recover fee.
(f) Cooperation from other agencies.
(g) Allocation of funds.
(h) Transfer of funds to Combined Fund.
1233. Objectives of fund.
(a) Priorities.
(b) Utilities and other facilities.
(c) Inventory.
1234. Eligible lands and water.
1235. State reclamation of program.
(a) Promulgation of regulations.
(b) Submission of State Reclamation Plan and annual projects.
(c) Restriction.
(d) Approval of State program; withdrawal.
(e) Contents of State Reclamation Plan.
(f) Annual application for support; contents.
(g) Costs.
(h) Grant of funds.
(i) Program monitorship.
(j) Annual report to Secretary.
(k) Eligible lands of Indian tribes.
(*l*) State liability.
1236. Reclamation of rural lands.
(a) Agreements with landowners for conservation treatment.
(b) Conservation and development plans.
(c) Agreement to effect plan.
(d) Financial and other assistance; determination by Secretary.
(e) Termination of agreements.
(f) Preservation and surrender of history and allotments.
(g) Rules and regulations.
(h) Utilization of Soil Conservation Service.
1237. Acquisition and reclamation of land adversely affected by past coal mining practices.
(a) Findings of fact; notice; right of entry.
(b) Studies or exploratory work.
(c) Requirements for acquisition of affected land.
(d) Title to affected land; value.
(e) State participation; grants.
(f) Rules and regulations.
(g) Public sale; notice and hearing.
(h) Construction or rehabilitation of housing for disabled, displaced, or dislocated persons; grants.
1238. Liens.
(a) Filing of statement and appraisal.
(b) Petition.
(c) Recordation.
1239. Filling voids and sealing tunnels.
(a) Congressional declaration of hazardous conditions.
(b) Limitation on funds.

Sec.
1239. Filling voids and sealing tunnels.
(c) Expenditures in States or Indian reservation.
(d) Disposal of mine wastes.
(e) Land acquisition.
1240. Emergency powers.
1240a. Certification.
(a) Certification of completion of coal reclamation.
(b) Eligible lands, waters, and facilities.
(c) Priorities.
(d) Specific sites and areas not eligible.
(e) Utilities and other facilities.
(f) Need for activities or construction of specified public facilities.
(g) Application of other provisions.
1241. Annual report to Congress.
1242. Powers of Secretary or State.
(a) Engage in work, promulgate rules and regulations, etc., to implement and administer this subchapter.
(b) Engage in cooperative projects.
(c) Request for action to restrain interference with regard to this subchapter.
(d) Construct and operate plants for control and treatment of water pollution resulting from mine drainage.
(e) Transfer funds.
1243. Interagency cooperation.

SUBCHAPTER V—CONTROL OF THE ENVIRONMENTAL IMPACTS OF SURFACE COAL MINING

1251. Environmental protection standards.
1251a. Abandoned coal refuse sites.
1252. Initial regulatory procedures.
(a) State regulation.
(b) Interim standards.
(c) Full compliance with environmental protection performance standards.
(d) Permit application.
(e) Federal enforcement program.
(f) Interim period.
1253. State programs.
(a) Regulation of surface coal mining and reclamation operations; submittal to Secretary; time limit; demonstration of effectiveness.
(b) Approval of program.
(c) Notice of disapproval.
(d) Inability of State to take action.
1254. Federal programs.
(a) Promulgation and implementation by Secretary for State.
(b) Federal enforcement of State program.
(c) Notice and hearing.
(d) Review of permits.
(e) Submission of State program after implementation of Federal program.
(f) Validity of Federal program permits under superseding State program.
(g) Preemption of State statutes or regulations.
(h) Coordination of issuance and review of Federal program permits with any other Federal or State permit process.
1255. State laws.

Sec.
1256. Permits.
(a) Persons engaged in surface coal mining within State; time limit; exception.
(b) Term.
(c) Termination.
(d) Renewal.
1257. Application requirements.
(a) Fee.
(b) Submittal; contents.
(c) Assistance to small coal operators.
(d) Reclamation plan.
(e) Public inspection.
(f) Insurance certificate.
(g) Blasting plan.
(h) Reimbursement of costs.
1258. Reclamation plan requirements.
1259. Performance bonds.
(a) Filing with regulatory authority; scope; number and amount.
(b) Liability period; execution.
(c) Bond of applicant without separate surety; alternate system.
(d) Deposit of cash or securities.
(e) Adjustments.
1260. Permit approval or denial.
(a) Basis for decision; notification of applicant and local government officials; burden of proof.
(b) Requirements for approval.
(c) Schedule of violations.
(d) Prime farmland mining permit.
(e) Modification of prohibition.
1261. Revision of permits.
(a) Application and revised reclamation plan; requirements; extensions to area covered.
(b) Transfer, assignment, or sale of rights under permit.
(c) Review of outstanding permits.
1262. Coal exploration permits.
(a) Regulations; contents.
(b) Confidential information.
(c) Penalties.
(d) Limitation on removal of coal.
(e) Law governing exploration of Federal lands.
1263. Public notice and public hearings.
(a) Submittal of advertisement to regulatory authority; notification of local governmental bodies.
(b) Objections to permit applications; informal conference; record.
(c) Prior Federal coal lease hearing as evidence.
1264. Decisions of regulatory authority and appeals.
(a) Issuance of findings within 60 days after informal conference.
(b) Decision without informal conference; notification within a reasonable time.
(c) Request for rehearing on reasons for final determination; time; issuance of decision.
(d) Temporary relief.
(e) Power of regulatory authority with respect to rehearing.
(f) Right to appeal in accordance with section 1276 of this title.
1265. Environmental protection performance standards.
(a) Permit requirement.
(b) General standards.

Sec.
1265. Environmental protection performance standards.
(c) Procedures; exception to original contour restoration requirements.
(d) Steep-slope surface coal mining standards.
(e) Variances to original contour restoration requirements.
(f) Standards and criteria for coal mine waste piles.
1266. Surface effects of underground coal mining operations.
(a) Rules and regulations.
(b) Permit requirements.
(c) Suspension of underground coal mining operations in urbanized areas.
(d) Applicability of this subchapter to surface operations and surface impacts incident to underground coal mining operations.
1267. Inspections and monitoring.
(a) Inspections of surface coal mining and reclamation operations.
(b) Records and reports; monitoring systems; evaluation of results.
(c) Inspection intervals.
(d) Maintenance of sign.
(e) Violations.
(f) Availability of information to public.
(g) Conflict of interest; penalty; publication of regulations; report to Congress.
(h) Review; procedures for inspections.
1268. Penalties.
(a) Civil penalties for violations of permit conditions and provisions of this subchapter.
(b) Hearing.
(c) Notice of violation; action required of violator; waiver of legal rights.
(d) Civil action to recover civil penalties.
(e) Willful violations.
(f) Corporate violations.
(g) False statements, representations, or certifications.
(h) Failure to correct violation.
(i) Effect on additional enforcement right or procedure available under State law.
1269. Release of performance bonds or deposits.
(a) Filing of request; submittal of copy of advertisement; notification by letter of intent to seek release.
(b) Inspection and evaluation; notification of decision.
(c) Requirements for release.
(d) Notice of disapproval.
(e) Notice to municipality.
(f) Objections to release; hearing.
(g) Informal conference.
(h) Power of regulatory authority with respect to informal conference.
1270. Citizens suits.
(a) Civil action to compel compliance with this chapter.
(b) Limitation on bringing of action.
(c) Venue; intervention.
(d) Costs; filing of bonds.
(e) Effect on other enforcement methods.
(f) Action for damages.
1271. Enforcement.
(a) Notice of violation; Federal inspection; waiver of notification period; cessation order; affir-

Sec.
1271. Enforcement.
mative obligation on operator; suspension or revocation of permits; contents of notices and orders.
(b) Inadequate State enforcement; notice and hearing.
(c) Civil action for relief.
(d) Sanctions; effect on additional enforcement rights under State law.
1272. Designating areas unsuitable for surface coal mining.
(a) Establishment of State planning process; standards; State process requirements; integration with present and future land use planning and regulation processes; savings provisions.
(b) Review of Federal lands.
(c) Petition; intervention; decision.
(d) Statement.
(e) Prohibition on certain Federal public and private surface coal mining operations.
1273. Federal lands.
(a) Promulgation and implementation of Federal lands program.
(b) Incorporation of requirements into any lease, permit, or contract issued by Secretary which may involve surface coal mining and reclamation operations.
(c) State cooperative agreements.
(d) Development of program to assure no unreasonable denial to any class of coal purchasers.
1274. Public agencies, public utilities, and public corporations.
1275. Review by Secretary.
(a) Application for review of order or notice; investigation; hearing; notice.
(b) Findings of fact; issuance of decision.
(c) Temporary relief; issuance of order or decision granting or denying relief.
(d) Notice and hearing with respect to section 1271 order to show cause.
(e) Costs.
1276. Judicial review.
(a) Review by United States District Court; venue; filing of petition; time.
(b) Evidence; conclusiveness of findings; orders.
(c) Temporary relief; prerequisites.
(d) Stay of action, order, or decision of Secretary.
(e) Action of State regulatory authority.
1277. Special bituminous coal mines.
(a) Issuance of separate regulations; criteria.
(b) New bituminous coal surface mines.
(c) Scope of alternative regulations.
1278. Surface mining operations not subject to this chapter.
1279. Anthracite coal mines.

SUBCHAPTER VI—DESIGNATION OF LANDS UNSUITABLE FOR NONCOAL MINING

1281. Designation procedures.
(a) Review of Federal land areas for unsuitability for noncoal mining.
(b) Criteria considered in determining designations.
(c) Petition for exclusion; contents; hearing; temporary land withdrawal.

Sec.
1281. Designation procedures.
(d) Limitation on designations; rights preservation; regulations.
(e) Statement.
(f) Area withdrawal.
(g) Right to appeal.

SUBCHAPTER VII—ADMINISTRATIVE AND MISCELLANEOUS PROVISIONS

1291. Definitions.
1292. Other Federal laws.
(a) Construction of chapter as superseding, amending, modifying, or repealing certain laws.
(b) Effect on authority of Secretary or heads of other Federal agencies.
(c) Cooperation.
(d) Major Federal action.
1293. Employee protection.
(a) Retaliatory practices prohibited.
(b) Review by Secretary; investigation; notice; hearing; findings of fact; judicial review.
(c) Costs.
1294. Penalty.
1295. Grants to States.
(a) Assisting any State in development, administration, and enforcement of State programs under this chapter.
(b) Assisting any State in development, administration, and enforcement of its State programs.
(c) Increases in annual grants.
1296. Annual report to President and Congress.
1297. Separability of provisions.
1298. Alaskan surface coal mine study.
(a) Contract with National Academy of Sciences-National Academy of Engineering.
(b) Report to President and Congress.
(c) Draft of legislation.
(d) Modification of applicability of environmental protection provisions of this chapter to surface coal mining operations in Alaska; publication in Federal Register; hearing.
(e) Interim regulations.
(f) Authorization of appropriations.
1299. Study of reclamation standards for surface mining of other minerals.
(a) Contract with National Academy of Sciences-National Academy of Engineering; requirements.
(b) Submittal of study with legislative recommendation to President and Congress.
(c) Authorization of appropriations.
1300. Indian lands.
(a) Study of regulation of surface mining; consultation with tribe; proposed legislation.
(b) Submittal of study to Congress.
(c) Compliance with interim environmental protection standards of this chapter.
(d) Compliance with permanent environmental protection standards of this chapter.
(e) Inclusion and enforcement of terms and conditions of leases.
(f) Approval of changes in terms and conditions of leases.
(g) Participation of tribes.
(h) Jurisdictional status.

Sec.
1300. Indian lands.
(i) Grants.
1301. Environmental practices.
1302. Authorization of appropriations.
1303. Coordination of regulatory and inspection activities.
1304. Surface owner protection.
(a) Applicability.
(b) Lease of coal deposits governed by section 201 of this title.
(c) Consent to lease by surface owner.
(d) Preferences.
(e) "Surface owner" defined.
(f) Exception.
(g) Effect on property rights of United States or any other landowner.
1305. Federal lessee protection.
1306. Effect on rights of owner of coal in Alaska to conduct surface mining operations.
1307. Water rights and replacement.
1308. Advance appropriations.
1309. Certification and training of blasters.
1309a. Subsidence.
(a) Requirements.
(b) Regulations.
1309b. Research.

SUBCHAPTER VIII—UNIVERSITY COAL RESEARCH LABORATORIES

1311. Establishment of university coal research laboratories.
(a) Designation by Secretary of Energy.
(b) Criteria.
(c) Location of coal laboratories.
(d) Period for submission of applications for designation; contents.
(e) Time limit.

Sec.
1312. Financial assistance.
1313. Limitation on payments.
1314. Payments; Federal share of operating expenses.
1315. Advisory Council on Coal Research.
(a) Establishment; members.
(b) Furnishing advice to Secretary of Energy.
(c) Annual report to President; transmittal to Congress.
(d) Compensation and travel expenses.
(e) Alternate members.
1316. Authorization of appropriations.

SUBCHAPTER IX—ENERGY RESOURCE GRADUATE FELLOWSHIPS

1321. Fellowship awards.
(a) Graduate study and research in areas of applied science and engineering relating to production, conservation, and utilization of fuels and energy.
(b) Term.
(c) Replacement awards.
1322. Fellowship recipients.
1323. Distribution of fellowships.
1324. Stipends and allowances.
1325. Limitation on fellowships.
1326. Fellowship conditions.
1327. Authorization of appropriations.
1328. Research, development projects, etc., relating to alternative coal mining technologies.
(a) Authority of Secretary of the Interior to conduct, promote, etc.
(b) Contracts and grants.
(c) Authorization of appropriations.
(d) Publication in Federal Register; report to Congress.
(e) Availability of information to public.

Related Provisions

See, also, Solid Waste Disposal, 42 U.S.C.A. § 6901 et seq., post; and Uranium Mill Tailings Radiation Control, 42 U.S.C.A. § 7901 et seq., post.

CROSS REFERENCES

Integration of hazardous waste regulations with regulations promulgated under this chapter, see section 6905 of Title 42, The Public Health and Welfare.

Surface coal mining and reclamation permits issued under this chapter as hazardous waste permits, see section 6925 of Title 42.

West's Federal Forms

Depositions, see § 3271 et seq.

Jurisdiction and venue in district courts, see § 1003 et seq.

Preliminary injunctions and temporary restraining orders, see § 5271 et seq.

Production of documents, motions and orders pertaining to, see § 3551 et seq.

Sentence and fine, see § 7531 et seq.

Subpoenas, see § 3981 et seq.

West's Federal Practice Manual

Minerals on federal lands, see § 5301 et seq.

CODE OF FEDERAL REGULATIONS

Abandoned mine reclamation funds, see 30 CFR 872.1 et seq.

Civil penalties, see 30 CFR 723.1 et seq.

Federal enforcement, see 30 CFR 843.1 et seq.

Federal inspections and monitoring, see 30 CFR 842.1 et seq.

Grants for program development, administration and enforcement, see 30 CFR 735.1 et seq.

Indian reclamation programs, see 30 CFR 888.1 et seq.

Permit requirements for special categories of mining, see 30 CFR 785.1 et seq.

Reclamation requirements, generally, see 30 CFR 874.1 et seq.

Rural abandoned mine program, see 7 CFR 632.1 et seq.

Secretary of interior, powers and duties, generally, see 30 CFR 700.1 et seq.

State programs for conduct of surface mine operations, see 30 CFR Chap. VII, Subchap. T.

LAW REVIEW COMMENTARIES

Groundwater pollution I: The problem and the law. Robert L. Glicksman and George Cameron Coggins, 35 U.Kan.L.Rev. 75 (1986).

Pennsylvania's implementation of the Surface Mining Control and Reclamation Act: An assessment of how "cooperative federalism" can make state regulatory programs more effective. John C. Dernbach, 19 U.Mich.J.L.Ref. 903 (1986).

WESTLAW ELECTRONIC RESEARCH

See WESTLAW guide following the Explanation pages of this pamphlet.

SUBCHAPTER I—STATEMENT OF FINDINGS AND POLICY

§ 1201. Congressional findings [SMCRA § 101]

The Congress finds and declares that—

(a) extraction of coal and other minerals from the earth can be accomplished by various methods of mining, including surface mining;

(b) coal mining operations presently contribute significantly to the Nation's energy requirements; surface coal mining constitutes one method of extraction of the resource; the overwhelming percentage of the Nation's coal reserves can only be extracted by underground mining methods, and it is, therefore, essential to the national interest to insure the existence of an expanding and economically healthy underground coal mining industry;

(c) many surface mining operations result in disturbances of surface areas that burden and adversely affect commerce and the public welfare by destroying or diminishing the utility of land for commercial, industrial, residential, recreational, agricultural, and forestry purposes, by causing erosion and landslides, by contributing to floods, by polluting the water, by destroying fish and wildlife habitats, by impairing natural beauty, by damaging the property of citizens, by creating hazards dangerous to life and property by degrading the quality of life in local communities, and by counteracting governmental programs and efforts to conserve soil, water, and other natural resources;

(d) the expansion of coal mining to meet the Nation's energy needs makes even more urgent the establishment of appropriate standards to minimize damage to the environment and to productivity of the soil and to protect the health and safety of the public.[1]

(e) surface mining and reclamation technology are now developed so that effective and reasonable regulation of surface coal mining operations by the States and by the Federal Government in accordance with the requirements of this chapter is an appropriate and necessary means to minimize so far as practicable the adverse social, economic, and environmental effects of such mining operations;

(f) because of the diversity in terrain, climate, biologic, chemical, and other physical conditions in areas subject to mining operations, the primary governmental responsibility for developing, authorizing, issuing, and enforcing regulations for surface mining and reclamation operations subject to this chapter should rest with the States;

(g) surface mining and reclamation standards are essential in order to insure that competition in interstate commerce among sellers of coal produced in different States will not be used to undermine the ability of the several States to improve and maintain adequate standards on coal mining operations within their borders;

(h) there are a substantial number of acres of land throughout major regions of the United States disturbed by surface and underground coal on which little or no reclamation was conducted, and the impacts from these unreclaimed lands impose social and economic costs on residents in nearby and adjoining areas as well as continuing to impair environmental quality;

(i) while there is a need to regulate surface mining operations for minerals other than coal, more data and analyses are needed to serve as a basis for effective and reasonable regulation of such operations;

(j) surface and underground coal mining operations affect interstate commerce, contribute to the economic well-being, security, and general welfare of the Nation and should be conducted in an environmentally sound manner; and

(k) the cooperative effort established by this chapter is necessary to prevent or mitigate adverse environmental effects of present and future surface coal mining operations.

(Aug. 3, 1977, Pub.L. 95–87, Title I, § 101, 91 Stat. 447.)

[1] So in original. The period probably should be a semicolon.

Short Title of 1990 Amendment

Pub.L. 101–508, Title VI, Subtitle A, Nov. 5, 1990, 104 Stat. 1388–289, provided that: "This subtitle [enacting section 1240a of this title, amending sections 1231, 1232, 1233, 1234, 1235, 1236, 1237, 1239, 1257 and 1302 of this title, and enacting provisions set out as a note under section 1231 of this title] may be cited as the 'Abandoned Mine Reclamation Act of 1990'."

Pub.L. 101–498, Nov. 2, 1990, 104 Stat. 1207, provided that: "This Act [enacting section 1230a of this title] may be cited as the 'Strategic and Critical Minerals Act of 1990'."

Short Title

Section 1 of Pub.L. 95–87, Aug. 3, 1977, 91 Stat. 447, provided: "That this Act [enacting this chapter] may be cited as the 'Surface Mining Control and Reclamation Act of 1977'."

Section 11 of Pub.L. 98–409, as added Pub.L. 100–483, § 12, Oct. 12, 1988, 102 Stat. 2341, provided that: "This Act [classified to subchapter III of this chapter] may be cited as the 'Mining and Mineral Resources Research Institute Act of 1984'."

West's Federal Practice Manual

Federal statutes after 1935, see § 1475.7.
Minerals on federal lands, see § 5301 et seq.

CODE OF FEDERAL REGULATIONS

Abandoned mine reclamation fund—fee collection and coal production reporting, see 30 CFR 870.1 et seq.
Appalachia—
Mine fire control, see 30 CFR 880.1 et seq.
Subsidence and stripmine rehabilitation, see 30 CFR 881.1 et seq.

Areas unsuitable for coal mining, criteria for designation, see 30 CFR 762.1 et seq.
Blasters-training, examination and certification, see 30 CFR Chap. VII, Subchap. M.
Bonding and insurance requirements, see 30 CFR Chap. VII, Subchap. J.
Bureau of Indian Affairs, coal mining exploration and reclamation of lands, see 25 CFR 216.1 et seq.
Coal management, see 43 CFR Chap. II, Subchap. C, Group 3400.
Coal operation permits and exploration systems, see 30 CFR Chap. VII, Subchap. G.
Employees, protection, see 30 CFR Chap. VII, Subchap. P.
Federal inspection and monitoring, see 30 CFR 842.1 et seq.
Federal lands program, see 30 CFR Chap. VII, Subchap. D.
General regulatory provisions, restrictions and exemptions, see 30 CFR Chap. VII, Subchap. A.
Grants—
  Mining and mineral research institutes and projects, see 30 CFR Chap. VII, Subchap. S.
  Program development, administration and enforcement, see 30 CFR 735.1 et seq.
  State reclamation, see 30 CFR 886.1 et seq.
Indian lands program, see 30 CFR Chap. VII, Subchap. E.
Initial program regulations, see 30 CFR Chap. VII, Subchap. B.
Performance standards, permanent programs, see 30 CFR Chap. VII, Subchap. K.
Procedures under Surface Mining Control and Reclamation Act of 1977, see 30 CFR 301.1 et seq.
Records and files, maintenance, see 30 CFR 212.50 et seq.
Secretary of Interior, hearings and appeals procedure, see 43 CFR 4.1 et seq.
Small operator assistance, see 30 CFR Chap. VII, Subchap. H.
State inspection and enforcement, see 30 CFR 840.1 et seq.
State program submissions—
  Approval or disapproval, procedures and criteria, see 30 CFR 732.1 et seq.
  Scope and content requirements, see 30 CFR 731.1 et seq.
State programs for conduct of surface mine operations, see 30 CFR Chap. VII, Subchap. T.

LAW REVIEW COMMENTARIES

A proposal for extension of the Occupational Safety and Health Act to indian-owned businesses on reservations. 18 U.Mich.J.L.Ref. 473 (1985).

Environmental claims in bankruptcy: Policy conflicts, procedural pitfalls and problematic precedent. Thomas G. Gruenert, 32 S.Tex. L.Rev. 399 (1991).

First decade of the implementation of the Surface Mining Control and Reclamation Act of 1977 in Oklahoma. Theodore M. Vestal, 23 Tulsa L.J. 593 (1988).

Illinois coal mine subsidence law updated. Robert E. Beck, So.Ill. L.J. 379 (1985).

LIBRARY REFERENCES

Mines and Minerals ⚷92.6.
C.J.S. Mines and Minerals § 239.

§ 1202. Statement of purpose [SMCRA § 102]

It is the purpose of this chapter to—

(a) establish a nationwide program to protect society and the environment from the adverse effects of surface coal mining operations;

(b) assure that the rights of surface landowners and other persons with a legal interest in the land or appurtenances thereto are fully protected from such operations;

(c) assure that surface mining operations are not conducted where reclamation as required by this chapter is not feasible;

(d) assure that surface coal mining operations are so conducted as to protect the environment;

(e) assure that adequate procedures are undertaken to reclaim surface areas as contemporaneously as possible with the surface coal mining operations;

(f) assure that the coal supply essential to the Nation's energy requirements, and to its economic and social well-being is provided and strike a balance between protection of the environment and agricultural productivity and the Nation's need for coal as an essential source of energy;

(g) assist the States in developing and implementing a program to achieve the purposes of this chapter;

(h) promote the reclamation of mined areas left without adequate reclamation prior to August 3, 1977, and which continue, in their unreclaimed condition, to substantially degrade the quality of the environment, prevent or damage the beneficial use of land or water resources, or endanger the health or safety of the public;

(i) assure that appropriate procedures are provided for the public participation in the development, revision, and enforcement of regulations, standards, reclamation plans, or programs established by the Secretary or any State under this chapter;

(j) provide a means for development of the data and analyses necessary to establish effective and reasonable regulation of surface mining operations for other minerals;

(k) encourage the full utilization of coal resources through the development and application of underground extraction technologies;

(*l*) stimulate, sponsor, provide for and/or supplement present programs for the conduct of research investigations, experiments, and demonstrations, in the exploration, extraction, processing, development, and production of minerals and the training of mineral engineers and scientists in the field of mining, minerals resources, and technology, and the establishment of an appropriate research and training center in various States; and

(m) wherever necessary, exercise the full reach of Federal constitutional powers to insure the protection of the public interest through effective control of surface coal mining operations.

(Aug. 3, 1977, Pub.L. 95–87, Title I, § 102, 91 Stat. 448.)

CODE OF FEDERAL REGULATIONS

Areas unsuitable for mining, see 30 CFR Chap. VII, Subchap. F.
General performance standards—
Surface mining, see 30 CFR 715.10 et seq.
Underground mining, see 30 CFR 717.10 et seq.
General regulatory provisions, restrictions and exemptions, see 30 CFR Chap. VII, Subchap. A.
Inspection and enforcement procedure, see 30 CFR Chap. VII, Subchap. L.
Performance standards, permanent program, general provisions, see 30 CFR 810.1 et seq.
Permit requirements for special categories of mining, see 30 CFR 785.1 et seq.
Special permanent program performance standards—
Anthracite mines in Pennsylvania, see 30 CFR 820.1 et seq.
In situ processing, see 30 CFR 828.1 et seq.
Mountaintop removal, see 30 CFR 824.1 et seq.
State programs for conduct of surface mine operations, see 30 CFR Chap. VII, Subchap. T.

SUBCHAPTER II—OFFICE OF SURFACE MINING RECLAMATION AND ENFORCEMENT

CROSS REFERENCES

Office defined, see section 1291 of this title.

§ 1211. Office of Surface Mining Reclamation and Enforcement [SMCRA § 201]

(a) Establishment

There is established in the Department of the Interior, the Office of Surface Mining Reclamation and Enforcement (hereinafter referred to as the "Office").

(b) Appointment, compensation, duties, etc., of Director; employees

The Office shall have a Director who shall be appointed by the President, by and with the advice and consent of the Senate, and shall be compensated at the rate provided for level V of the Executive Schedule under section 5315 [1] of Title 5, and such other employees as may be required. Pursuant to section 5108 of Title 5, and after consultation with the Secretary, the Director of the Office of Personnel Management shall determine the necessary number of positions in general schedule employees in grade 16, 17, and 18 to perform functions of this subchapter and shall allocate such positions to the Secretary. The Director shall have the responsibilities provided under subsection (c) of this section and those duties and responsibilities relating to the functions of the Office which the Secretary may assign, consistent with this chapter. Employees of the Office shall be recruited on the basis of their professional competence and capacity to administer the provisions of this chapter. The Office may use, on a reimbursable basis when appropriate, employees of the Department and other Federal agencies to administer the provisions of this chapter, providing that no legal authority, program, or function in any Federal agency which has as its purpose promoting the development or use of coal or other mineral resources or regulating the health and safety of miners under provisions of the Federal Coal Mine Health and Safety Act of 1969 (83 Stat. 742) [30 U.S.C.A. § 801 et seq.], shall be transferred to the Office.

(c) Duties of Secretary

The Secretary, acting through the Office, shall—

(1) administer the programs for controlling surface coal mining operations which are required by this chapter; review and approve or disapprove State programs for controlling surface coal mining operations and reclaiming abandoned mined lands; make those investigations and inspections necessary to insure compliance with this chapter; conduct hearings, administer oaths, issue subpenas, and compel the attendance of witnesses and production of written or printed material as provided for in this chapter; issue cease-and-desist orders; review and vacate or modify or approve orders and decisions; and order the suspension, revocation, or withholding of any permit for failure to comply with any of the provisions of this chapter or any rules and regulations adopted pursuant thereto;

(2) publish and promulgate such rules and regulations as may be necessary to carry out the purposes and provisions of this chapter;

(3) administer the State grant-in-aid program for the development of State programs for surface and mining and reclamation operations provided for in subchapter V of this chapter;

(4) administer the program for the purchase and reclamation of abandoned and unreclaimed mined areas pursuant to subchapter IV of this chapter;

(5) administer the surface mining and reclamation research and demonstration project authority provided for in this chapter;

(6) consult with other agencies of the Federal Government having expertise in the control and reclamation of surface mining operations and assist States, local governments, and other eligible agencies in the coordination of such programs;

(7) maintain a continuing study of surface mining and reclamation operations in the United States;

(8) develop and maintain an Information and Data Center on Surface Coal Mining, Reclamation, and Surface Impacts of Underground Mining, which will make such data available to the public and the Federal, regional, State, and local agencies conducting or concerned with land use planning and agencies concerned with surface and underground mining and reclamation operations;

(9) assist the States in the development of State programs for surface coal mining and reclamation operations which meet the requirements of this chapter, and at the same time, reflect local requirements and local environmental and agricultural conditions;

(10) assist the States in developing objective scientific criteria and appropriate procedures and institutions for determining those areas of a State to be designated unsuitable for all or certain types of surface coal mining pursuant to section 1272 of this title;

(11) monitor all Federal and State research programs dealing with coal extraction and use and recommend to Congress the research and demonstration projects and necessary changes in public policy which are designated to (A) improve feasibility of underground coal mining, and (B) improve surface mining and reclamation techniques directed at eliminating adverse environmental and social impacts;

(12) cooperate with other Federal agencies and State regulatory authorities to minimize duplication of inspections, enforcement, and administration of this chapter; and

(13) perform such other duties as may be provided by law and relate to the purposes of this chapter.

(d) Restriction on use of Federal coal mine health and safety inspectors

The Director shall not use either permanently or temporarily any person charged with responsibility of inspecting coal mines under the Federal Coal Mine Health and Safety Act of 1969 [30 U.S.C.A. § 801 et seq.], unless he finds and publishes such finding in the Federal Register, that such activities would not interfere with such inspections under the 1969 Act.

(e) Repealed. Pub.L. 96–511, § 4(b), Dec. 11, 1980, 94 Stat. 2826

(f) Conflict of interest; penalties; rules and regulations; report to Congress

No employee of the Office or any other Federal employee performing any function or duty under this chapter shall have a direct or indirect financial interest in underground or surface coal mining operations. Whoever knowingly violates the provisions of the above sentence shall, upon conviction, be punished by a fine of not more than $2,500, or by imprisonment for not more than one year, or both. The Director shall (1) within sixty days after August 3, 1977, publish regulations, in accordance with section 553 of Title 5, to establish the methods by which the provisions of this subsection will be monitored and enforced, including appropriate provisions for the filing by such employees and the review of statements and supplements thereto concerning their financial interests which may be affected by this subsection, and (2) report to the Congress as part of the annual report (section 1296 of this title) on the actions taken and not taken during the preceding calendar year under this subsection.

(g) Petition for issuance, amendment, or repeal of rule; filing; hearing or investigation; notice of denial

(1) After the Secretary has adopted the regulations required by section 1251 of this title, any person may petition the Director to initiate a proceeding for the issuance, amendment, or repeal of a rule under this chapter.

(2) Such petitions shall be filed in the principal office of the Director and shall set forth the facts which it is claimed established that it is necessary to issue, amend, or repeal a rule under this chapter.

(3) The Director may hold a public hearing or may conduct such investigation or proceeding as the Director deems appropriate in order to determine whether or not such petition should be granted.

(4) Within ninety days after filing of a petition described in paragraph (1), the Director shall either grant or deny the petition. If the Director grants such petition, the Director shall promptly commence an appropriate proceeding in accordance with the provisions of this chapter. If the Director denies such petition, the Director shall so notify the petitioner in writing setting forth the reasons for such denial.

(Aug. 3, 1977, Pub.L. 95–87, Title II, § 201, 91 Stat. 449; March 7, 1978, Pub.L. 95–240, Title I, § 100, 92 Stat. 109; 1978 Reorg. Plan No. 2, § 102, eff. Jan. 1, 1979, 43 F.R. 36037, 92 Stat. 3783; Dec. 11, 1980, Pub.L. 96–511, § 4(b), 94 Stat. 2826.)

1 So in original. Probably should be "section 5316".

Travel and Per Diem Expenses of State and Tribal Personnel Attending Sponsored Training

Pub.L. 103–332, Title I, Sept. 30, 1994, 108 Stat. 2510, provided in part: "That notwithstanding any other provision of law, appropriations for the Office of Surface Mining Reclamation and Enforcement may provide for the travel and per diem expenses of State and tribal personnel attending Office of Surface Mining Reclamation and Enforcement sponsored training."

Similar provisions were contained in the following appropriations Acts:

Pub.L. 103–138, Title I, Nov. 11, 1993, 107 Stat. 1389.
Pub.L. 102–381, Title I, Oct. 5, 1992, 106 Stat. 1387.
Pub.L. 102–154, Title I, Nov. 13, 1991, 105 Stat. 1002.
Pub.L. 101–512, Title I, Nov. 5, 1990, 104 Stat. 1927.
Pub.L. 101–121, Title I, Oct. 23, 1989, 103 Stat. 712.
Pub.L. 101–446, Title I, Sept. 27, 1988, 102 Stat. 1793.

CROSS REFERENCES

Conflict of interests of employees of State regulatory authorities, see section 1267 of this title.

West's Federal Forms

Administrative subpenas, enforcement of, see § 5901 et seq.

CODE OF FEDERAL REGULATIONS

Abandoned mine land reclamation, see 30 CFR Chap. VII, Subchap. R.
Areas unsuitable for mining, see 30 CFR Chap. VII, Subchap. F.
Employees, responsibility and conduct, see 43 CFR 20.735–1 et seq.
General performance standards—
Surface mining, see 30 CFR 715.10 et seq.
Underground mining, see 30 CFR 717.10 et seq.
General regulatory provisions, restrictions and exemptions, see 30 CFR Chap. VII, Subchap. A.
Grants for program development, administration and enforcement, see 30 CFR 735.1 et seq.
Inspection and enforcement procedure, see 30 CFR Chap. VII, Subchap. L.
Performance standards, permanent program, general provisions, see 30 CFR 810.1 et seq.
Permit requirements for special categories of mining, see 30 CFR 785.1 et seq.
Program regulations—
Civil penalties, see 30 CFR 723.1 et seq.
Enforcement procedures, see 30 CFR 722.1 et seq.
Restriction on financial interests of—
Federal employees, see 30 CFR 706.1 et seq.
State employees, see 30 CFR 705.1 et seq.
Special permanent program performance standards—
Anthracite mines in Pennsylvania, see 30 CFR 820.1 et seq.
In situ processing, see 30 CFR 828.1 et seq.
Mountaintop removal, see 30 CFR 824.1 et seq.
State programs for conduct of surface mine operations, see 30 CFR Chap. VII, Subchap. T.

LIBRARY REFERENCES

Mines and Minerals ⚷92.6.
C.J.S. Mines and Minerals § 239.

United States Supreme Court

Goals of this section, pollution control, preserving productive capacity of lands, etc., see Hodel v. Indiana, 1981, 101 S.Ct. 2376, 452 U.S. 314, 69 L.Ed.2d 40, concurring opinion 101 S.Ct. 2389, 452 U.S. 264, 69 L.Ed.2d 1.

SUBCHAPTER III—STATE MINING AND MINERAL RESOURCES RESEARCH INSTITUTES

Short Title

For authority to cite Pub.L. 98–409, Aug. 29, 1984, 98 Stat. 1536, which enacted this subchapter, as the Mining and Mineral Resources Research Institute Act of 1984, see section 11 of Pub.L. 98–409, set out as a note under section 1201 of this title.

CROSS REFERENCES

Authorization of appropriations to carry out the provisions of this subchapter, see section 1457a of Title 43, Public Lands.

§ 1221. Authorization of State allotments to institutes [MMRRIA § 1]

(a)(1) There are authorized to be appropriated to the Secretary of the Interior (hereafter in this subchapter referred to as the "Secretary") funds adequate to provide for each participating State $400,000 for each of the fiscal years ending September 30, 1990, through September 30, 1994, to assist the States in carrying on the work of a competent and qualified mining and mineral resources research institute or center (hereafter in this subchapter referred to as the "institute") at one public college or university in the State which meets the eligibility criteria established in section 1230 of this title.

(2)(A) Funds appropriated under this section shall be made available for grants to be matched on a basis of no less than 2 non-Federal dollars for each Federal dollar.

(B) If there is more than one such eligible college or university in a State, funds appropriated under this subchapter shall, in the absence of a designation to the contrary by act of the legislature of the State, be granted to one such college or university designated by the Governor of the State.

(C) Where a State does not have a public college or university eligible under section 1230 of this title, the Committee on Mining and Mineral Resources Research established in section 1229 of this title (hereafter in this subchapter referred to as the "Committee") may allocate the State's allotment to one private college or university which it determines to be eligible under such section.

(b) It shall be the duty of each institute to plan and conduct, or arrange for a component or components of the college or university with which it is affiliated to conduct research, investigations, demonstrations, and experiments of either, or both, a basic or practical nature in relation to mining and mineral resources, and to provide for the training of mineral engineers and scientists through such research, investigations, demonstrations, and experiments. The subject of such research, investigation, demonstration, experiment, and training may include exploration; extraction; processing; development; production of fuel and nonfuel mineral resources; mining and mineral technology; supply and demand for minerals; conservation and best use of available supplies of minerals; the economic, legal, social, engineering, recreational, biological, geographic, ecological, and other aspects of mining, mineral resources, and mineral reclamation. Such research, investigation, demonstration, experiment and training shall consider the interrelationship with the natural environment, the varying conditions and needs of the respective States, and mining and mineral resources research projects being conducted by agencies of the Federal and State governments and other institutes.

(Pub.L. 98–409, § 1, Aug. 29, 1984, 98 Stat. 1536; Pub.L. 100–483, §§ 2–4, Oct. 12, 1988, 102 Stat. 2339.)

Codification

Section was not enacted as part of the Surface Mining Control and Reclamation Act of 1977 which comprises this chapter.

CROSS REFERENCES

Funding criteria for institutes under this section, see section 1223 of this title.

CODE OF FEDERAL REGULATIONS

Grants for mining and mineral research institutes and projects, see 30 CFR Chap. VII, Subchap. S.

LIBRARY REFERENCES

Mines and Minerals ⚖92.9.
C.J.S. Mines and Minerals § 229 et seq.

§ 1222. Research funds to institutes [MMRRIA § 2]

(a) Authorization of appropriations

There is authorized to be appropriated to the Secretary not more than $15,000,000 for each of the fiscal years ending September 30, 1990, through September 30, 1994, which shall remain available until expended. Such funds when appropriated shall be made available to an institute or to institutes participating in a generic mineral technology center to meet the necessary expenses for purposes of—

(1) specific mineral research and demonstration projects of broad application, which could not otherwise be undertaken, including the expenses of planning and coordinating regional mining and mineral resources research projects by two or more institutes; and

(2) research into any aspects of mining and mineral resources problems related to the mission of the Department of the Interior, which are deemed by the Committee to be desirable and are not otherwise being studied.

(b) Application for funds; contents

Each application for funds under subsection (a) of this section shall state, among other things, the nature of the project to be undertaken; the period during which it will be pursued; the qualifications of the personnel who will direct and conduct it; the estimated costs; the importance of the project to the Nation, region, or State concerned; its relation to other known research projects theretofore pursued or being pursued; the extent to which the proposed project will provide opportunity for the training of mining and mineral engineers and scientists; and the extent of participation by nongovernmental sources in the project.

(c) Research facilities; selection of institutes; designation of funds for scholarships and fellowships

The Committee shall review all such funding applications and recommend to the Secretary the use of the institutes, insofar as practicable, to perform special research. Recommendations shall be made without regard to the race, religion, or sex of the personnel who will conduct and direct the research, and on the basis of the facilities available in relation to the particular needs of the research project; special geographic, geologic, or climatic conditions within the immediate vicinity of the institute; any other special requirements of the research project; and the extent to which such project will provide an opportunity for training individuals as mineral engineers and scientists. The Committee shall recommend to the Secretary the designation and utilization of such portions of the funds authorized to be appropriated by this section as it deems appropriate for the purpose of providing scholarships, graduate fellowships, and postdoctoral fellowships.

(d) Requirements for receipt of funds

No funds shall be made available under subsection (a) of this section except for a project approved by the Secretary and all funds shall be made available upon the basis of merit of the project, the need for the knowledge which it is expected to produce when completed, and the opportunity it provides for the training of individuals as mineral engineers and scientists.

(e) Restriction on application of funds

No funds made available under this section shall be applied to the acquisition by purchase or lease of any land or interests therein, or the rental, purchase, construction, preservation, or repair of any building.

(Pub.L. 98–409, § 2, Aug. 29, 1984, 98 Stat. 1537; Pub.L. 100–483, § 5, Oct. 12, 1988, 102 Stat. 2339.)

Codification

Section was not enacted as part of the Surface Mining Control and Reclamation Act of 1977 which comprises this chapter.

CROSS REFERENCES

Funding criteria for institutes under this section, see section 1223 of this title.

LIBRARY REFERENCES

United States ⚖82(2).
C.J.S. United States § 122.

§ 1223. Funding criteria [MMRRIA § 3]

(a) Funds available to institutes under sections 1221 and 1222 of this title shall be paid at such times and in such amounts during each fiscal year as determined by the Secretary, and upon vouchers approved by him. Each institute shall—

(1) set forth its plan to provide for the training of individuals as mineral engineers and scientists under a curriculum appropriate to the field of mineral resources and mineral engineering and related fields;

(2) set forth policies and procedures which assure that Federal funds made available under this subchapter for any fiscal year will suoplement and, to the extent practicable, increase the level of funds that would, in the absence of such Federal funds, be made available for purposes of this subchapter, and in no case supplant such funds; and

(3) have an officer appointed by its governing authority who shall receive and account for all funds paid under the provisions of this subchapter and shall make an annual report to the Secretary on or before the first day of September of each year, on work accomplished and the status of projects underway, together with a detailed statement of the amounts received under any provisions of this subchapter during the preceding fiscal year, and of its disbursements on schedules prescribed by the Secretary.

If any of the funds received by the authorized receiving officer of any institute under the provisions of this subchapter shall by any action or contingency be found by the Secretary to have been improperly diminished, lost, or misapplied, such funds shall be replaced by the State concerned and until so replaced no subsequent appropriation shall be allotted or paid to any institute of such State.

(b) The institutes are authorized and encouraged to plan and conduct programs under this subchapter in cooperation with each other and with such other agencies and individuals as may contribute to the solution of the mining and mineral resources problems involved. Moneys appropriated pursuant to this subchapter shall be available for paying the necessary expenses of planning, coordinating, and conducting such cooperative research.

(Pub.L. 98–409, § 3, Aug. 29, 1984, 98 Stat. 1538.)

Codification

Section was not enacted as part of the Surface Mining Control and Reclamation Act of 1977 which comprises this chapter.

CROSS REFERENCES

Duty of Secretary to ascertain compliance with this section, see section 1224 of this title.

§ 1224. Duties of Secretary [MMRRIA § 4]

(a) Consulting with other agencies; prescribing rules and regulations; furnishing advice and assistance; coordinating research

The Secretary, acting through the Director of the United States Bureau of Mines, shall administer this subchapter and, after full consultation with other interested Federal agencies, shall prescribe such rules and regulations as may be necessary to carry out its provisions. The Secretary shall furnish such advice and assistance as will best promote the purposes of this subchapter, shall participate in coordinating research initiated under this subchapter by the institutes, shall indicate to them such lines of inquiry that seem most important, and shall encourage and assist in the establishment and maintenance of cooperation by and between the institutes and between them and other research organizations, the United States Department of the Interior, and other Federal establishments.

(b) Annual ascertainment of compliance

On or before the first day of July in each year beginning after August 29, 1984, the Secretary shall ascertain whether the requirements of section 1223(a) of this title have been met as to each institute and State.

(c) Annual report to Congress

The Secretary shall make an annual report to the Congress of the receipts, expenditures, and work of the institutes in all States under the provisions of this subchapter. The Secretary's report shall indicate whether any portion of an appropriation available for allotment to any State has been withheld and, if so, the reason therefor.

(Pub.L. 98–409, § 4, Aug. 29, 1984, 98 Stat. 1538; Pub.L. 100–483, § 6, Oct. 12, 1988, 102 Stat. 2340; Pub.L. 102–285, § 10(b), May 18, 1992, 106 Stat. 172.)

Codification

Section was not enacted as part of the Surface Mining Control and Reclamation Act of 1977 which comprises this chapter.

Change of Name

Pub.L. 102–285, § 10(b), May 18, 1992, 106 Stat. 172, provided that, on and after May 18, 1992, the Bureau of Mines is redesignated and shall thereafter be known as the United States Bureau of Mines. See note under section 1 of Title 30, Mineral Lands and Mining.

CODE OF FEDERAL REGULATIONS

Secretary of Interior, general scope of authority and responsibility, see 30 CFR 700.1 et seq.

§ 1225. Effect on colleges and universities [MMRRIA § 5]

Nothing in this subchapter shall be construed to impair or modify the legal relationship existing between any of the colleges or universities under whose direction an institute is established and the government of the State in which it is located, and nothing in this subchapter shall in any way be construed to authorize Federal control or direction of education at any college or university.

(Pub.L. 98–409, § 5, Aug. 29, 1984, 98 Stat. 1539.)

Codification

Section was not enacted as part of the Surface Mining Control and Reclamation Act of 1977 which comprises this chapter.

§ 1226. Research [MMRRIA § 6]

(a) Coordination with existing programs; availability of information to public

The Secretary shall obtain the continuing advice and cooperation of all agencies of the Federal Government concerned with mining and mineral resources, of State and local governments, and of private institutions and individuals to assure that the programs authorized by this subchapter will supplement and not be redundant with respect to established mining and minerals research programs, and to stimulate research in otherwise neglected areas, and to contribute to a comprehensive nationwide program of mining and minerals research, with due regard for the protection and conservation of the environment. The Secretary shall make generally available information and reports on projects completed, in progress, or planned under the provisions of this subchapter, in addition to any direct publication of information by the institutes themselves.

(b) Effect on Federal agencies

Nothing in this subchapter is intended to give or shall be construed as giving the Secretary any authority over mining and mineral resources research conducted by any agency of the Federal Government, or as repealing or diminishing existing authorities or responsibilities of any agency of the Federal Government to plan and conduct, contract for, or assist in research in its area of responsibility and concern with regard to mining and mineral resources.

(c) Availability of results to public

No research, demonstration, or experiment shall be carried out under this subchapter by an institute financed by grants under this subchapter, unless all uses, products, processes, patents, and other developments resulting therefrom, with such exception or limitation, if any, as the Secretary may find necessary in the public interest, are made available promptly to the general public. Patentable inventions shall be governed by the provisions of Public Law 96–517. Nothing contained in this section shall deprive the owner of any background patent relating to any such activities of any rights which that owner may have under that patent.

(d) Authorization of appropriation

(1) There is authorized to be appropriated to the Secretary $450,000 for each of the fiscal years ending September 30, 1990, through September 30, 1994, to administer this subchapter. No funds may be withheld by the Secretary for administrative expenses from those authorized to be appropriated by sections 1221 and 1222 of this title.

(2) There are authorized to be appropriated to the Secretary such sums as are necessary for the printing and publishing of the results of activities carried out by institutes and generic mineral technology centers under this subchapter, but such appropriations shall not exceed $550,000 in any single fiscal year.

(Pub.L. 98–409, § 6, Aug. 29, 1984, 98 Stat. 1539; Pub.L. 100–483, § 7, Oct. 12, 1988, 102 Stat. 2340.)

Codification

Section was not enacted as part of the Surface Mining Control and Reclamation Act of 1977 which comprises this chapter.

CROSS REFERENCES

Research, development projects, etc., relating to alternative coal mining technologies, availability of information to public, see section 1328 of this title.

§ 1227. Center for cataloging [MMRRIA § 7]

The Secretary shall establish a center for cataloging current and projected scientific research in all fields of mining and mineral resources. Each Federal agency doing mining and mineral resources research shall cooperate by providing the cataloging center with information on work underway or scheduled by it. The cataloging center shall classify and maintain for public use a catalog of mining and mineral resources research and investigation projects in progress or scheduled by all Federal agencies and by such non-Federal agencies of government, colleges, universities, private institutions, firms, and individuals as may make such information available.

(Pub.L. 98–409, § 7, Aug. 29, 1984, 98 Stat. 1540.)

Codification

Section was not enacted as part of the Surface Mining Control and Reclamation Act of 1977 which comprises this chapter.

§ 1228. Interagency cooperation [MMRRIA § 8]

The President shall, by such means as he deems appropriate, clarify agency responsibility for Federal mining and mineral resources research and provide for interagency coordination of such research, including the research authorized by this subchapter. Such coordination shall include—

(1) continuing review of the adequacy of the Government-wide program in mining and mineral resources research;

(2) identification and elimination of duplication and overlap between agency programs;

(3) identification of technical needs in various mining and mineral resources research categories;

(4) recommendations with respect to allocation of technical effort among Federal agencies;

(5) review of technical manpower needs, and findings concerning management policies to improve the quality of the Government-wide research effort; and

(6) actions to facilitate interagency communication at management levels.

(Pub.L. 98–409, § 8, Aug. 29, 1984, 98 Stat. 1540.)

Codification

Section was not enacted as part of the Surface Mining Control and Reclamation Act of 1977 which comprises this chapter.

§ 1229. Committee on Mining and Mineral Resources Research [MMRRIA § 9]

(a) Appointment; composition

The Secretary shall appoint a Committee on Mining and Mineral Resources Research composed of—

(1) the Assistant Secretary of the Interior responsible for minerals and mining research, or his delegate;

(2) the Director, United States Bureau of Mines, or his delegate;

(3) the Director, United States Geological Survey, or his delegate;

(4) the Director of the National Science Foundation, or his delegate;

(5) the President, National Academy of Sciences, or his delegate;

(6) the President, National Academy of Engineering, or his delegate; and

(7) not more than 7 other persons who are knowledgeable in the fields of mining and mineral resources research, including two university administrators involved in the conduct of programs authorized by this subchapter, 3 representatives from the mining industry, a working miner, and a representative from the conservation community. In making these six appointments, the Secretary shall consult with interested groups.

(b) Consultation and recommendations

The Committee shall consult with, and make recommendations to, the Secretary on all matters relating to mining and mineral resources research and the determinations that are required to be made under this subchapter. The Secretary shall consult with, and consider recommendations of, such Committee in such matters.

(c) Compensation, travel, subsistence and related expenses

Committee members, other than officers or employees of Federal, State, or local governments, shall be, for each day (including traveltime) during which they are performing Committee business, paid at a rate fixed by the Secretary but not [1] excess of the daily equivalent of the maximum rate of pay for grade GS–18 of the General Schedule under section 5332 of Title 5, and shall be fully reimbursed for travel, subsistence, and related expenses.

(d) Chairmanship of Committee

The Committee shall be jointly chaired by the Assistant Secretary of the Interior responsible for minerals and mining and a person to be elected by the Committee from among the members referred to in paragraphs (5), (6), and (7) of subsection (a) of this section.

(e) National plan for research

The Committee shall develop a national plan for research in mining and mineral resources, considering ongoing efforts in the universities, the Federal Government, and the private sector, and shall formulate and recommend a program to implement the plan utilizing resources provided for under this subchapter. The Committee shall submit such plan to the Secretary, the President, and the Congress on or before March 1, 1986, and shall submit an annual update of such plan by January 15 of each calendar year.

(f) Application of Federal Advisory Committee Act

Section 10 of the Federal Advisory Committee Act (5 U.S.C. App.) shall not apply to the Committee.

(Pub.L. 98–409, § 9, Aug. 29, 1984, 98 Stat. 1540; Pub.L. 100–483, §§ 8, 9, Oct. 12, 1988, 102 Stat. 2340; Pub.L. 102–285, § 10(b), May 18, 1992, 106 Stat. 172.)

[1] So in original. Probably should be followed by "in".

Codification

Section was not enacted as part of the Surface Mining Control and Reclamation Act of 1977 which comprises this chapter.

Change of Name

Pub.L. 102–285, § 10(b), May 18, 1992, 106 Stat. 172, provided that, on and after May 18, 1992, the Bureau of Mines is redesignated and shall thereafter be known as the United States Bureau of Mines. See note under section 1 of Title 30, Mineral Lands and Mining.

Reports to Congressional Committees

Section 11 of Pub.L. 100–483 provided that:

"(a) **Report on Programs.**—The Committee on Mining and Mineral Resources Research established under section 9 of the Mining and Mineral Resources Research Institute Act of 1984 (30 U.S.C. 1229) [this section] shall submit a report by January 15, 1992, to the Committee on Interior and Insular Affairs of the United States House of Representatives and the Committee on Energy and Natural Resources of the United States Senate on the programs established under that Act [this subchapter]. Such report may be submitted in conjunction with the annual plan update required by section 9(e) of such Act (30 U.S.C. 1229(e) [subsec. (e) of this section] and shall include, but not necessarily be limited to, each of the following:

"(1) A review of the activities of the institutes and generic mineral technology centers established under the Mining and Mineral Resources Research Institute Act of 1984 [this subchapter].

"(2) A review of each institute's eligibility pursuant to section 10 of the Mining and Mineral Resources Research Institute Act of 1984 (30 U.S.C. 1230) [section 1230 of this title].

"(3) A review of each generic mineral technology center's eligibility. In conducting such review the committee shall consider the following criteria:

"(A) Relevance and effectiveness of the research conducted.

"(B) Need for further research in the generic area.

"(4) Recommendations on establishing a mechanism by which new generic mineral technology centers can be established and existing centers can be phased-out or consolidated upon the completion of their mission.

"(b) **Report on Proposal for Center.**—The committee shall submit a proposal to establish a Generic Mineral Technology Center on Strategic and Critical Minerals to the Committee on Interior and Insular Affairs of the United States House of Representatives and the Committee on Energy and Natural Resources of the United States Senate by January 15, 1990."

CROSS REFERENCES

Allocation, by Committee, of State allotment for institute to private college or university, see section 1221 of this title.

§ 1230. Eligibility criteria [MMRRIA § 10]

(a) The Committee shall determine the eligibility of a college or university to participate as a mining and mineral resources research institute under this subchapter using criteria which include—

(1) the presence of a substantial program of graduate instruction and research in mining or mineral extraction or closely related fields which has a demonstrated history of achievement;

(2) evidence of institutional commitment for the purposes of this subchapter;

(3) evidence that such institution has or can obtain significant industrial cooperation in activities within the scope of this subchapter; and

(4) the presence of an engineering program in mining or minerals extraction that is accredited by the Accreditation Board for Engineering and Technology, or evidence of equivalent institutional capability as determined by the Committee.

(b)(1) Notwithstanding the provisions of subsection (a) of this section, those colleges or universities which, on October 12, 1988, have a mining or mineral resources research institute program which has been found to be eligible pursuant to this subchapter shall continue to be eligible subject to review at least once during the period authorized by the Mining and Mineral Resources Research Institute Amendments of 1988, under the provisions of subsection (a) of this section. The results of such review shall be submitted by January 15, 1992, pursuant to section 11(a)(2) of the Mining and Mineral Resources Research Institute Amendments of 1988.

(2) Generic mineral technology centers established by the Secretary under this subchapter are to be composed of institutes eligible pursuant to subsection (a) of this section. Existing generic mineral technology centers shall continue to be eligible under this subchapter subject to at least one review prior to January 15, 1992, pursuant to section 11(a)(3) of the Mining and Mineral Resources Research Institute Amendments of 1988.

(Pub.L. 98–409, § 10, Aug. 29, 1984, 98 Stat. 1541; Pub.L. 100–483, § 10, Oct. 12, 1988, 102 Stat. 2340.)

References in Text

The Mining and Mineral Resources Research Institute Amendments of 1988, referred to in subsec. (b)(1), is Pub.L. 100–483, Oct. 12, 1988, 102 Stat. 2341, which amended this subchapter. Section 11(a)(2), (3) of such Amendments of 1988, referred to in subsec. (b)(1), (2), is set out as a note under section 1229 of this title.

Codification

Section was not enacted as part of the Surface Mining Control and Reclamation Act of 1977 which comprises this chapter.

CROSS REFERENCES

Allocation, by Committee, of State allotment for institute to private college or university in absence of public college or university eligible under this section, see section 1221 of this title.

§ 1230a. Strategic Resources Generic Mineral Technology Center [MMRRIA § 12]

(a) Establishment

The Secretary of Interior is authorized and directed to establish a Strategic Resources Mineral Technology Center (hereinafter referred to as the "center") for the purpose of improving existing, and developing new, technologies that will decrease the dependence of the United States on supplies of strategic and critical minerals.

(b) Functions

The center shall—

(1) provide for studies and technology development in the areas of mineral extraction and refining processes, product substitution and conservation of mineral resources through recycling and advanced processing and fabrication methods;

(2) identify new deposits of strategic and critical mineral resources; and

(3) facilitate the transfer of information, studies, and technologies developed by the center to the private sector.

(c) Criteria

The Secretary shall establish the center referred to in subsection (a) of this section at a university that—

(1) does not currently host a generic mineral technology center;

(2) has established advanced degree programs in geology and geological engineering, and metallurgical and mining engineering;

(3) has expertise in materials and advanced processing research; and

(4) is located west of the 100th meridian.

(d) Authorization of appropriations

There is authorized to be appropriated such sums as may be necessary to carry out this section.

(Pub.L. 98–409, § 12, as added Pub.L. 101–498, § 2, Nov. 2, 1990, 104 Stat. 1207.)

SUBCHAPTER IV—ABANDONED MINE RECLAMATIONS

CROSS REFERENCES

Administration of this subchapter, duty of Secretary, see section 1211 of this title.

State programs for regulation of surface coal mining and reclamation operations, see section 1253 of this title.

§ 1231. Abandoned Mine Reclamation Fund [SMCRA § 401]

(a) Establishment; administration; State funds

There is created on the books of the Treasury of the United States a trust fund to be known as the Abandoned Mine Reclamation Fund (hereinafter referred to as the "fund") which shall be administered by the Secretary of the Interior. State abandoned mine reclamation funds (State funds) generated by grants from this subchapter shall be established by each State pursuant to an approved State program.

(b) Sources of deposits to fund

The fund shall consist of amounts deposited in the fund, from time to time derived from—

(1) the reclamation fees levied under section 1232 of this title;

(2) any user charge imposed on or for land reclaimed pursuant to this subchapter after expenditures for maintenance have been deducted;

(3) donations by persons, corporations, associations, and foundations for the purposes of this subchapter;

(4) recovered moneys as provided for in this subchapter; and

(5) interest credited to the fund under subsection (e) of this section.

(c) Use of moneys

Moneys in the fund may be used for the following purposes:

(1) reclamation and restoration of land and water resources adversely affected by past coal mining, including but not limited to reclamation and restoration of abandoned surface mine areas, abandoned coal processing areas, and abandoned coal refuse disposal areas; sealing and filling abandoned deep mine entries and voids; planting of land adversely affected by past coal mining to prevent erosion and sedimentation; prevention, abatement, treatment, and control of water pollution created by coal mine drainage including restoration of stream beds, and construction and operation of water treatment plants; prevention, abatement, and control of burning coal refuse disposal areas and burning coal in situ; prevention, abatement, and control of coal mine subsidence; and establishment of self-sustaining, individual State administered programs to insure private property against damages caused by land subsidence resulting from underground coal mining in those States which have reclamation plans approved in accordance with section 1253 of this title: *Provided*, That funds used for this purpose shall not exceed $3,000,000 of the funds made available to any State under section 1232(g)(1) of this title;

(2) for transfer on an annual basis to the Secretary of Agriculture for use under section 1236 of this title;

(3) acquisition and filling of voids and sealing of tunnels, shafts, and entryways under section 1239 of this title;

(4) acquisition of land as provided for in this subchapter;

(5) enforcement and collection of the reclamation fee provided for in section 1232 of this title;

(6) studies by the Department of the Interior to such extent or in such amounts as are provided in appropriation Acts with public and private organizations to provide information, advice, and technical assistance, including research and demonstration projects conducted in accordance with section 3501 of the Omnibus Budget Reconciliation Act of 1986, conducted for the purposes of this subchapter;

(7) restoration, reclamation, abatement, control, or prevention of adverse effects of coal mining which constitutes an emergency as provided for in this subchapter;

(8) grants to the States to accomplish the purposes of this subchapter;

(9) administrative expenses of the United States and each State to accomplish the purposes of this subchapter;

(10) for use under section 1240a of this title;

(11) for the purpose of section 1257(c) of this title, except that not more than $10,000,000 shall annually be available for such purpose;

(12) for the purpose described in section 1232(h) of this title; and

(13) all other necessary expenses to accomplish the purposes of this subchapter.

(d) Moneys available upon appropriation; no fiscal year limitation

Moneys from the fund shall be available for the purposes of this subchapter, only when appropriated therefor, and such appropriations shall be made without fiscal year limitations.

(e) Interest

The Secretary of the Interior shall notify the Secretary of the Treasury as to what portion of the fund is not, in his judgment, required to meet current withdrawals. The Secretary of the Treasury shall invest such portion of the fund in public debt securities with maturities suitable for the needs of such fund and bearing interest at rates determined by the Secretary of the Treasury, taking into consideration current market yields on outstanding marketable obligations of the United States of comparable maturities. The income on such investments shall be credited to, and form a part of, the fund.

(Aug. 3, 1977, Pub.L. 95–87, Title IV, § 401, 91 Stat. 456; Oct. 12, 1984, Pub.L. 98–473, Title I, § 101(c), 98 Stat. 1837, 1875; Pub.L. 101–508, Title VI, § 6002, Nov. 5, 1990, 104 Stat. 1388–289; Oct. 24, 1992, Pub.L. 102–486, Title XIX, § 19143(b)(3)(A), Title XXV, § 2504(c)(1), 106 Stat. 3056, 3105.)

References in Text

Section 3501 of the Omnibus Budget Reconciliation Act of 1986, referred to in subsec. (c)(6), is section 3501 of Pub.L. 99–509, Title III, Oct. 21, 1986, 100 Stat. 1891.

Effective Date of 1990 Amendment

Section 6014 of Pub.L. 101–508 provided that: "The amendments made by this subtitle [enacting section 1240a of this title, amending this section and sections 1232 to 1237, 1239, 1257 and 1302 of this title, and enacting provisions set out as notes under this section] shall take effect at the beginning of the first fiscal year immediately following the fiscal year in which this subtitle is enacted [Pub.L. 101–508 was approved on Nov. 5, 1990; the next fiscal year began on Oct. 1, 1991]."

Savings Provisions

Section 6013 of Pub.L. 101–508 provided that: "Nothing in this subtitle [Subtitle A (section 6001 et seq.) of Pub.L. 101–508, Title VI, Nov. 5, 1990, 104 Stat. 1388–289, for distribution of which, see Short Title of 1990 Amendment note set out under section 1201 of title and Tables] shall be construed to affect the certifications made by the State of Wyoming, the State of Montana, and the State of Louisiana to the Secretary of the Interior prior to the date of enactment of this subtitle [Nov. 5, 1990] that such State has completed the reclamation of eligible abandoned coal mine lands."

CROSS REFERENCES

Authorization of appropriation of funds reserved by this section for test borings and core samplings in connection with applications for surface coal mining and reclamation permits, see section 1302 of this title.

Fund defined, see section 1291 of this title.

Reclamation of rural lands, availability of funds, see section 1236 of this title.

CODE OF FEDERAL REGULATIONS

Abandoned mine reclamation funds, see 30 CFR 872.1 et seq.

State reclamation grants, see 30 CFR 886.1 et seq.

LAW REVIEW COMMENTARIES

Illinois coal mine subsidence law updated. Robert E. Beck, So.Ill. L.J. 379 (1985).

LIBRARY REFERENCES

Mines and Minerals ⇐92.6, 92.9.

C.J.S. Mines and Minerals §§ 229 et seq., 239.

§ 1232. Reclamation fee [SMCRA § 402]

(a) Payment; rate

All operators of coal mining operations subject to the provisions of this chapter shall pay to the Secretary of the Interior, for deposit in the fund, a reclamation fee of 35 cents per ton of coal produced by surface coal mining and 15 cents per ton of coal produced by underground mining or 10 per centum of the value of the coal at the mine, as determined by the Secretary, whichever is less, except that the reclamation fee for lignite coal shall be at a rate of 2 per centum of the value of the coal at the mine, or 10 cents per ton, whichever is less.

(b) Due date

Such fee shall be paid no later than thirty days after the end of each calendar quarter beginning with the first calendar quarter occurring after August 3, 1977, and ending September 30, 2004, after which time the fee shall be established at a rate to continue to provide for the deposit referred to in subsection (h) of this section.

(c) Submission of statement

Together with such reclamation fee, all operators of coal mine operations shall submit a statement of the amount of coal produced during the calendar quarter, the method of coal removal and the type of coal, the accuracy of which shall be sworn to by the operator and notarized. Such statement shall include an identification of the permittee of the surface coal mining operation, any operator in addition to the permittee, the owner of the coal, the preparation plant, tipple, or loading point for the coal and the person purchasing the coal from the operator. The report shall also specify the number of the permit required under section 1256 of this title and the mine safety and health identification number. Each quarterly report shall contain a notification of any changes in the information required by this subsection since the date of the preceding quarterly report. The information contained in the quarterly reports under this subsection shall be maintained by the Secretary in a computerized database.

(d) Penalty

(1) Any person, corporate officer, agent or director, on behalf of a coal mine operator, who knowingly makes any false statement, representation or certification, or knowingly fails to make any statement, representation or certification required in this section shall, upon conviction, be punished by a fine of not more than $10,000, or by imprisonment for not more than one year, or both.

(2) The Secretary shall conduct such audits of coal production and the payment of fees under this subchapter as may be necessary to ensure full compliance with the provisions of this subchapter. For purposes of performing such audits the Secretary (or any duly designated officer, employee, or representative of the Secretary) shall, at all reasonable times, upon request, have access to, and may copy, all books, papers, and other documents of any person subject to the provisions of this subchapter. The Secretary may at any time conduct audits of any surface coal mining and reclamation operation, including without limitation, tipples and preparation plants, as may be necessary in the judgment of the Secretary to ensure full and complete payment of the fees under this subchapter.

(e) Civil action to recover fee

Any portion of the reclamation fee not properly or promptly paid pursuant to this section shall be recoverable, with statutory interest, from coal mine operators, in any court of competent jurisdiction in any action at law to compel payment of debts.

(f) Cooperation from other agencies

All Federal and State agencies shall fully cooperate with the Secretary of the Interior in the enforcement of this section. Whenever the Secretary believes that any person has not paid the full amount of the fee payable under subsection (a) of this section the Secretary shall notify the Federal agency responsible for ensuring compliance with the provisions of section 4121 of Title 26.

(g) Allocation of Funds

(1) Except as provided in subsection (h) of this section, moneys deposited into the fund shall be allocated by the Secretary to accomplish the purposes of this subchapter as follows:

(A) 50 percent of the reclamation fees collected annually in any State (other than fees collected with respect to Indian lands) shall be allocated annually by the Secretary to the State, subject to such State having each of the following:

(i) An approved abandoned mine reclamation program pursuant to section 1235 of this title.

(ii) Lands and waters which are eligible pursuant to section 1234 of this title (in the case of a State not certified under section 1240a(a) of this title) or pursuant to section 1240a(b) of this title (in the case of a State certified under section 1240a(a) of this title).

(B) 50 percent of the reclamation fees collected annually with respect to Indian lands shall be allocated annually by the Secretary to the Indian tribe having jurisdiction over such lands, subject to such tribe having each of the following:

(i) An approved abandoned mine reclamation program pursuant to section 1235 of this title.

(ii) Lands and waters which are eligible pursuant to section 1234 of this title (in the case of an Indian tribe not certified under section 1240a(a) of this title) or pursuant to section 1240a(b) of this title (in the case of a tribe certified under section 1240a(a) of this title).

(C) The funds allocated by the Secretary under this paragraph to States and Indian tribes shall only be used for annual reclamation project construction and program administration grants.

(D) To the extent not expended within 3 years after the date of any grant award under this paragraph, such grant shall be available for expenditure by the Secretary in any area under paragraph (2), (3), (4), or (5).

(2) 20 percent of the amounts available in the fund in any fiscal year which are not allocated under paragraph (1) in that fiscal year (including that interest accruing as provided in section 1231(e) of this title and including funds available for reallocation pursuant to paragraph (1)(D)), shall be allocated to the Secretary only for the purpose of making the annual transfer to the Secretary of Agriculture under section 1231(c)(2) of this title.

(3) Amounts available in the fund which are not allocated to States and Indian tribes under paragraph (1) or allocated under paragraphs (2) and (5) are authorized to be expended by the Secretary for any of the following:

(A) For the purpose of section 1257(c) of this title, either directly or through grants to the States, subject to the limitation contained in section 1231(c)(11) of this title.

(B) For the purpose of section 1240 of this title (relating to emergencies).

(C) For the purpose of meeting the objectives of the fund set forth in section 1233(a) of this title for eligible lands and waters pursuant to section 1234 of this title in States and on Indian lands where the State or Indian tribe does not have an approved abandoned mine reclamation program pursuant to section 1235 of this title.

(D) For the administration of this subchapter by the Secretary.

(4)(A) Amounts available in the fund which are not allocated under paragraphs (1), (2), and (5) or expended under paragraph (3) in any fiscal year are authorized to be expended by the Secretary under this paragraph for the reclamation or drainage abatement of lands and waters within unreclaimed sites which are mined for coal or which were affected by such mining, wastebanks, coal processing or other coal mining processes and left in an inadequate reclamation status.

(B) Funds made available under this paragraph may be used for reclamation or drainage abatement at a site referred to in subparagraph (A) if the Secretary makes either of the following findings:

(i) A finding that the surface coal mining operation occurred during the period beginning on August 4, 1977, and ending on or before the date on which the Secretary approved a State program pursuant to section 1253 of this title for a State in which the site is located, and that any funds for reclamation or abatement which are available pursuant to a bond or other form of financial guarantee or from any other source are not sufficient to provide for adequate reclamation or abatement at the site.

(ii) A finding that the surface coal mining operation occurred during the period beginning on August 4, 1977, and ending on or before November 5, 1990, and that the surety of such mining operator became insolvent during such period, and as of November 5, 1990, funds immediately available from proceedings relating to such insolvency, or from any financial guarantee or other source are not sufficient to provide for adequate reclamation or abatement at the site.

(C) In determining which sites to reclaim pursuant to this paragraph, the Secretary shall follow the priorities stated in paragraphs (1) and (2) of section 1233(a) of this title. The Secretary shall ensure that priority is given to those sites which are in the immediate vicinity of a residential area or which have an adverse economic impact upon a local community.

(D) Amounts collected from the assessment of civil penalties under section 1268 of this title are authorized to be appropriated to carry out this paragraph.

(E) Any State may expend grants made available under paragraphs (1) and (5) for reclamation and abatement of any site referred to in subparagraph (A) if the State, with the concurrence of the Secretary, makes either of the findings referred to in clause (i) or (ii) of subparagraph (B) and if the State determines that the reclamation priority of the site is the same or more urgent than the reclamation priority for eligible lands and waters pursuant to section 1234 of this title under the priorities stated in paragraphs (1) and (2) of section 1233(a) of this title.

(F) For the purposes of the certification referred to in section 1240a(a) of this title, sites referred to in subparagraph (A) of this paragraph shall be considered as having the same priorities as those stated in section 1233(a) of this title for eligible lands and waters pursuant to section 1234 of this title. All sites referred to in subparagraph (A) of this paragraph within any State shall be reclaimed prior to such State making the certification referred to in section 1240a(a) of this title.

(5) The Secretary shall allocate 40 percent of the amount in the fund after making the allocation referred to in paragraph (1) for making additional annual grants to States and Indian tribes which are not certified under section 1240a(a) of this title to supplement grants received by such States and Indian tribes pursuant to paragraph (1)(C) until the priorities stated in paragraphs (1) and (2) of section 1233(a) of this title have been achieved by such State or Indian tribe. The allocation of such funds for the purpose of making such expenditures shall be through a formula based on the amount of coal historically produced in the State or from the Indian lands concerned prior to August 3, 1977. Funds allocated or expended by the Secretary under paragraph (2), (3), or (4) of this subsection for any State or Indian tribe shall not be deducted against any allocation of funds to the State or Indian tribe under paragraph (1) or under this paragraph.

(6) Any State may receive and retain, without regard to the 3–year limitation referred to in paragraph (1)(D), up to 10 percent of the total of the grants made annually to such State under paragraphs (1) and (5) if such amounts are deposited into either—

(A) a special trust fund established under State law pursuant to which such amounts (together with all interest earned on such amounts) are expended by the State solely to achieve the priorities stated in section 1233(a) of this title after September 30, 1995, or

(B) an acid mine drainage abatement and treatment fund established under State law as provided in paragraph (7).

(7)(A) Any State may establish under State law an acid mine drainage abatement and treatment fund from which amounts (together with all interest earned on such amounts) are expended by the State to implement, in consultation with the Soil Conservation Service, acid mine drainage abatement and treatment plans approved by the Secretary. Such plans shall provide for the comprehensive abatement of the causes and treatment of the effects of acid mine drainage within qualified hydrologic units affected by coal mining practices.

(B) The plan shall include, but shall not be limited to, each of the following:

(i) An identification of the qualified hydrologic unit.

(ii) The extent to which acid mine drainage is affecting the water quality and biological resources within the hydrologic unit.

(iii) An identification of the sources of acid mine drainage within the hydrologic unit.

(iv) An identification of individual projects and the measures proposed to be undertaken to abate and treat the causes or effects of acid mine drainage within the hydrologic unit.

(v) The cost of undertaking the proposed abatement and treatment measures.

(vi) An identification of existing and proposed sources of funding for such measures.

(vii) An analysis of the cost-effectiveness and environmental benefits of abatement and treatment measures.

(C) The Secretary may approve any plan under this paragraph only after determining that such plan meets the requirements of this paragraph. In conducting an analysis of the items referred to in clauses (iv), (v), and (vii) the Director of the Office of Surface Mining shall obtain the comments of the Director of the United States Bureau of Mines. In approving plans under this paragraph, the Secretary shall give a priority to those plans which will be implemented in coordination with measures undertaken by the Secretary of Agriculture under section 1236 of this title.

(D) For purposes of this paragraph, the term "qualified hydrologic unit" means a hydrologic unit—

(i) in which the water quality has been significantly affected by acid mine drainage from coal mining practices in a manner which adversely impacts biological resources; and

(ii) which contains lands and waters which are—

(I) eligible pursuant to section 1234 of this title and include any of the priorities stated in paragraph (1), (2), or (3) of section 1233(a) of this title and

(II) proposed to be the subject of the expenditures by the State (from amounts available from the forfeiture of bonds required under section 1259 of this title or from other State sources) to mitigate acid mine drainage.

(8) Of the funds available for expenditure under this subsection in any fiscal year, the Secretary shall allocate annually not less than $2,000,000 for expenditure in each State, and for each Indian tribe, having an approved abandoned mine reclamation program pursuant to section 1235 of this title and eligible lands and waters pursuant to section 1234 of this title so long as an allocation of funds to such State or such tribe is necessary to achieve the priorities stated in paragraphs (1) and (2) of section 1233(a) of this title.

(h) Transfer of funds to Combined Fund

(1) In the case of any fiscal year beginning on or after October 1, 1995, with respect to which fees are required to be paid under this section, the Secretary shall, as of the beginning of such fiscal year and before any allocation under subsection (g) of this section, make the transfer provided in paragraph (2).

(2) The Secretary shall transfer from the fund to the United Mine Workers of America Combined Benefit Fund established under section 9702 of Title 26 for any fiscal year an amount equal to the sum of—

(A) the amount of the interest which the Secretary estimates will be earned and paid to the Fund during the fiscal year, plus

(B) the amount by which the amount described in subparagraph (A) is less than $70,000,000.

(3)(A) The aggregate amount which may be transferred under paragraph (2) for any fiscal year shall not exceed the amount of expenditures which the trustees of the Combined Fund estimate will be debited against the unassigned beneficiaries premium account under section 9704(e) of Title 26 for the fiscal year of the Combined Fund in which the transfer is made.

(B) The aggregate amount which may be transferred under paragraph (2)(B) for all fiscal years shall not exceed an amount equivalent to all interest earned and paid to the fund after September 30, 1992, and before October 1, 1995.

(4) If, for any fiscal year, the amount transferred is more or less than the amount required to be transferred, the Secretary shall appropriately adjust the amount transferred for the next fiscal year.

(Aug. 3, 1977, Pub.L. 95–87, Title IV, § 402, 91 Stat. 457; May 7, 1987, Pub.L. 100–34, Title I, § 101, 101 Stat. 300; Pub.L. 101–508, Title VI, §§ 6003, 6004, Nov. 5, 1990, 104 Stat. 1388–290, 1388–291; May 18, 1992, Pub.L. 102–285, § 10(b), 106 Stat. 172; Oct. 24, 1992, Pub.L. 102–486, Title XIX, § 19143(b)(1), (2), (3)(B), Title XXV, § 2515, 106 Stat. 3056, 3113.)

Change of Name

Pub.L. 102–285, § 10(b), May 18, 1992, 106 Stat. 172, provided that, on and after May 18, 1992, the Bureau of Mines is redesignated and shall thereafter be known as the United States Bureau of Mines. See note under section 1 of Title 30, Mineral Lands and Mining.

Effective Date of 1990 Amendment

Amendment by Pub.L. 101–508 effective Oct. 1, 1991, see section 6014 of Pub.L. 101–508, set out as a note under section 1231 of this title.

Savings Provisions

Nothing in Subtitle A (section 6001 et seq.) of Title VI of Pub.L. 101–508, construed to affect the certifications made by the States of Wyoming, Montana, and Louisiana to the Secretary of the Interior prior to Nov. 5, 1990, that each such State has completed the reclamation of eligible abandoned coal mine lands, see section 6013 of Pub.L. 101–508, set out as a note under section 1231 of this title.

CROSS REFERENCES

Grant of reclamation fee moneys to State reclamation programs, see section 1235 of this title.

Limitation on funds available for filling voids and sealing tunnels, see section 1239 of this title.

Limitation on use of funds allocated pursuant to this section, see section 1231 of this title.

CODE OF FEDERAL REGULATIONS

Abandoned mine reclamation funds, see 30 CFR 872.1 et seq.

Fee collection and coal production reporting, see 30 CFR 870.1 et seq.

State reclamation—

Grants, see 30 CFR 886.1 et seq.

Plans, see 30 CFR 884.1 et seq.

LAW REVIEW COMMENTARIES

Illinois coal mine subsidence law updated. Robert E. Beck, So.Ill. L.J. 379 (1985).

§ 1233. Objectives of fund [SMCRA § 403]

(a) Priorities

Expenditure of moneys from the fund on lands and water eligible pursuant to section 1234 of this title for the purposes of this subchapter, except as provided for under section 1240a of this title, shall reflect the following priorities in the order stated:

(1) the protection of public health, safety, general welfare, and property from extreme danger of adverse effects of coal mining practices;

(2) the protection of public health, safety, and general welfare from adverse effects of coal mining practices;

(3) the restoration of land and water resources and the environment previously degraded by adverse effects of coal mining practices including measures for the conservation and development of soil, water (excluding channelization), woodland, fish and wildlife, recreation resources, and agricultural productivity.[1]

(4) the protection, repair, replacement, construction, or enhancement of public facilities such as utilities, roads, recreation, and conservation facilities adversely affected by coal mining practices;

(5) the development of publicly owned land adversely affected by coal mining practices including land acquired as provided in this subchapter for recreation and historic purposes, conservation, and reclamation purposes and open space benefits.

(b) Utilities and other facilities

(1) Any State or Indian tribe not certified under section 1240a(a) of this title may expend up to 30 percent of the funds allocated to such State or Indian tribe in any year through the grants made available under paragraphs (1) and (5) of section 1232(g) of this title for the purpose of protecting, repairing, replacing, constructing, or enhancing facilities relating to water supply, including water distribution facilities and treatment plants, to replace water supplies adversely affected by coal mining practices.

(2) If the adverse effect on water supplies referred to in this subsection occurred both prior to and after August 3, 1977, or as the case may be, the dates (and under the criteria) set forth under section 1232(g)(4)(B) of this title, section 1234 of this title shall not be construed to prohibit a State or Indian tribe referred to in paragraph (1) from using funds referred to in such paragraph for the purposes of this subsection if the State or Indian tribe determines that such adverse effects occurred predominantly prior to August 3, 1977, or as the case may be, the dates (and under the criteria) set forth under section 1232(g)(4)(B) of this title.

(c) Inventory

For the purposes of assisting in the planning and evaluation of reclamation projects pursuant to section 1235 of this title, and assisting in making the certification referred to in section 1240a(a) of this title, the Secretary shall maintain an inventory of eligible lands and waters pursuant to section 1234 of this title which meet the priorities stated in paragraphs (1) and (2) of subsection (a) of this section. Under standardized procedures established by the Secretary, States and Indian tribes with approved abandoned mine reclamation programs pursuant to section 1235 of this title may offer amendments to update the inventory as it applies to eligible lands and waters under the jurisdiction of such States or tribes. The Secretary shall provide such States and tribes with the financial and technical assistance necessary for the purpose of making inventory amendments. The Secretary shall compile and maintain an inventory for States and Indian lands in the case when a State or Indian tribe does not have an approved abandoned mine reclamation program pursuant to section 1235 of this title. On a regular basis, but not less than annually, the projects completed under this subchapter shall be so noted on the inventory under standardized procedures established by the Secretary.

(Aug. 3, 1977, Pub.L. 95–87, Title IV, § 403, 91 Stat. 458; Pub.L. 101–508, Title VI, § 6005, Nov. 5, 1990, 104 Stat. 1388–294; Oct. 24, 1992, Pub.L. 102–486, Title XXV, § 2504(c)(2), (e), 106 Stat. 3105, 3106.)

[1] So in original. The period probably should be a semicolon.

Effective Date of 1990 Amendment

Amendment by Pub.L. 101–508 effective Oct. 1, 1991, see section 6014 of Pub.L. 101–508, set out as a note under section 1231 of this title.

Savings Provisions

Nothing in Subtitle A (section 6001 et seq.) of Title VI of Pub.L. 101–508, construed to affect the certifications made by the States of Wyoming, Montana, and Louisiana to the Secretary of the Interior prior to Nov. 5, 1990, that each such State has completed the reclamation of eligible abandoned coal mine lands, see section 6013 of Pub.L. 101–508, set out as a note under section 1231 of this title.

CROSS REFERENCES

Allocation of reclamation fees if objectives set out in this section are met, see section 1232 of this title.

CODE OF FEDERAL REGULATIONS

Reclamation requirements, general provisions, see 30 CFR 874.1 et seq.
State reclamation plans, see 30 CFR 884.1 et seq.

§ 1234. Eligible lands and water [SMCRA § 404]

Lands and water eligible for reclamation or drainage abatement expenditures under this subchapter are those which were mined for coal or which were affected by such mining, wastebanks, coal processing, or other coal mining processes, except as provided for under section 1240a of this title, and abandoned or left in an inadequate reclamation status prior to August 3, 1977, and for which there is no continuing reclamation responsibility under State or other Federal laws. For other provisions relating to lands and waters eligible for such expenditures, see section 1232(g)(4) of this title, section 1233(b)(1) of this title and section 1239 of this title. Surface coal mining operations on lands eligible for remining shall not affect the eligibility of such lands for reclamation and restoration under this subchapter after the release of the bond or deposit for any such operation as provided under section 1269 of this title. In the event the bond or deposit for a surface coal mining operation on lands eligible for remining is forfeited, funds available under this subchapter may be used if the amount of such bond or deposit is not sufficient to provide for adequate reclamation or abatement, except that if conditions warrant the Secretary shall immediately exercise his authority under section 1240 of this title.

(Aug. 3, 1977, Pub.L. 95–87, Title IV, § 404, 91 Stat. 459; Pub.L. 101–508, Title VI, § 6006, Nov. 5, 1990, 104 Stat. 1388–295; Oct. 24, 1992, Pub.L. 102–486, Title XXV, § 2503(d), 106 Stat. 3103.)

Effective Date of 1990 Amendment

Amendment by Pub.L. 101–508 effective Oct. 1, 1991, see section 6014 of Pub.L. 101–508, set out as a note under section 1231 of this title.

Savings Provisions

Nothing in Subtitle A (section 6001 et seq.) of Title VI of Pub.L. 101–508, construed to affect the certifications made by the States of Wyoming, Montana, and Louisiana to the Secretary of the Interior prior to Nov. 5, 1990, that each such State has completed the reclamation of eligible abandoned coal mine lands, see section 6013 of Pub.L. 101–508, set out as a note under section 1231 of this title.

CROSS REFERENCES

Filling of voids and sealing tunnels, disregard of provisions of this section, see section 1239 of this title.
Indian tribes with eligible lands, treatment as States under this subchapter, see section 1235 of this title.
Objectives for expenditures on eligible lands and water, see section 1233 of this title.

CODE OF FEDERAL REGULATIONS

Reclamation requirements, general provisions, see 30 CFR 874.1 et seq.
State reclamation plans, see 30 CFR 884.1 et seq.

§ 1235. State reclamation program [SMCRA § 405]

(a) Promulgation of regulations

Not later than the end of the one hundred and eighty-day period immediately following August 3, 1977, the Secretary shall promulgate and publish in the Federal Register regulations covering implementation of an abandoned mine reclamation program incorporating the provisions of this subchapter and establishing procedures and requirements for preparation submission, and approval of State programs consisting of the plan and annual submissions of projects.

(b) Submission of State Reclamation Plan and annual projects

Each State having within its borders coal mined lands eligible for reclamation under this subchapter, may submit to the Secretary a State Reclamation Plan and annual projects to carry out the purposes of this subchapter.

(c) Restriction

The Secretary shall not approve, fund, or continue to fund a State abandoned mine reclamation program unless that State has an approved State regulatory program pursuant to section 1253 of this title.

(d) Approval of State program; withdrawal

If the Secretary determines that a State has developed and submitted a program for reclamation of abandoned mines and has the ability and necessary State legislation to implement the provisions of this subchapter, sections 1232 and 1240 of this title excepted, the Secretary shall approve such State program and shall grant to the State exclusive responsibility and authority to implement the provisions of the approved program: *Provided*, That the Secretary shall withdraw such approval and authorization if he determines upon the basis of information provided under this section that the State program is not in compliance with the procedures, guidelines, and requirements established under subsection (a) of this section.

(e) Contents of State Reclamation Plan

Each State Reclamation Plan shall generally identify the areas to be reclaimed, the purposes for which the reclamation is proposed, the relationship of the lands to be reclaimed and the proposed reclamation to surrounding areas, the specific criteria for ranking and identifying projects to be funded, and the legal authority and programmatic capability to perform such work in conformance with the provisions of this subchapter.

(f) Annual application for support; contents

On an annual basis, each State having an approved State Reclamation Plan may submit to the Secretary an application for the support of the State program and implementation of specific reclamation projects. Such annual requests shall include such information as may be requested by the Secretary including:

(1) a general description of each proposed project;

(2) a priority evaluation of each proposed project;

(3) a statement of the estimated benefits in such terms as: number of acres restored, miles of stream improved, acres of surface lands protected from subsidence, population protected from subsidence, air pollution, hazards of mine and coal refuse disposal area fires;

(4) an estimate of the cost for each proposed project;

(5) in the case of proposed research and demonstration projects, a description of the specific techniques to be evaluated or objective to be attained;

(6) an identification of lands or interest therein to be acquired and the estimated cost; and

(7) in each year after the first in which a plan is filed under this subchapter, an inventory of each project funded under the previous year's grant: which inventory shall include details of financial expenditures on such project together with a brief description of each such project, including project locations, landowner's name, acreage, type of reclamation performed.

(g) Costs

The costs for each proposed project under this section shall include: actual construction costs, actual operation and maintenance costs of permanent facilities, planning and engineering costs, construction inspection costs, and other necessary administrative expenses.

(h) Grant of funds

Upon approval of State Reclamation Plan by the Secretary and of the surface mine regulatory program pursuant to section 1253 of this title, the Secretary shall grant, on an annual basis, funds to be expended in such State pursuant to section 1232(g) of this title and which are necessary to implement the State reclamation program as approved by the Secretary.

(i) Program monitorship

The Secretary, through his designated agents, will monitor the progress and quality of the program. The States shall not be required at the start of any project to submit complete copies of plans and specifications.

(j) Annual report to Secretary

The Secretary shall require annual and other reports as may be necessary to be submitted by each State administering the approved State reclamation program with funds provided under this subchapter. Such reports shall include that information which the Secretary deems necessary to fulfill his responsibilities under this subchapter.

(k) Eligible lands of Indian tribes

Indian tribes having within their jurisdiction eligible lands pursuant to section 1234 of this title or from which coal is produced, shall be considered as a "State" for the purposes of this subchapter except[1] for purposes of subsection (c) of this section with respect to the Navajo, Hopi and Crow Indian Tribes.

(*l*) State liability

No State shall be liable under any provision of Federal law for any costs or damages as a result of action taken or omitted in the course of carrying out a State abandoned mine reclamation plan approved under this section. This subsection shall not preclude liability for costs or damages as a result of gross negligence or intentional misconduct by the State. For purposes of the preceding sentence, reckless, willful, or wanton misconduct shall constitute gross negligence.

(Aug. 3, 1977, Pub.L. 95–87, Title IV, § 405, 91 Stat. 459; July 11, 1987, Pub.L. 100–71, Title I, 101 Stat. 416; Pub.L. 101–508, Title VI, §§ 6007, 6012(d)(1), (2), Nov. 5, 1990, 104 Stat. 1388–295, 1388–298.)

1 So in original. Probably should be ", except".

Effective Date of 1990 Amendment

Amendment by Pub.L. 101–508 effective Oct. 1, 1991, see section 6014 of Pub.L. 101–508, set out as a note under section 1231 of this title.

Savings Provisions

Nothing in Subtitle A (section 6001 et seq.) of Title VI of Pub.L. 101–508, construed to affect the certifications made by the States of Wyoming, Montana, and Louisiana to the Secretary of the Interior prior to Nov. 5, 1990, that each such State has completed the reclamation of eligible abandoned coal mine lands, see section 6013 of Pub.L. 101–508, set out as a note under section 1231 of this title.

CROSS REFERENCES

Expenditure of excess reclamation fees by additional grants to State reclamation programs, see section 1232 of this title.

CODE OF FEDERAL REGULATIONS

Indian reclamation programs, see 30 CFR 888.1 et seq.
Secretary of Interior, general scope of authority and responsibility, see 30 CFR 700.1 et seq.
State programs for conduct of surface mine operations, see 30 CFR Chap. VII, Subchap. T.
State reclamation—
Grants, see 30 CFR 886.1 et seq.
Plans, see 30 CFR 884.1 et seq.

§ 1236. Reclamation of rural lands [SMCRA § 406]

(a) Agreements with landowners for conservation treatment

In order to provide for the control and prevention of erosion and sediment damages from unreclaimed mined lands, and to promote the conservation and development of soil and water resources of unreclaimed mined lands and lands affected by mining, the Secretary of Agriculture is authorized to enter into agreements of not more than ten years with landowners (including owners of water rights), residents, and tenants, and individually or collectively, determined by him to have control for the period of the agreement of lands in question therein, providing for land stabilization, erosion, and sediment control, and reclamation through conservation treatment, including measures for the conservation and development of soil, water (excluding stream channelization), woodland, wildlife, and recreation resources, and agricultural productivity of such lands. Such agreements shall be made by the Secretary with the owners, including owners of water rights, residents, or tenants (collectively or individually) of the lands in question.

(b) Conservation and development plans

The landowner, including the owner of water rights, resident, or tenant shall furnish to the Secretary of Agriculture a conservation and development plan setting forth the proposed land uses and conservation treatment which shall be mutually agreed by the Secretary of Agriculture and the landowner, including owner of water rights, resident, or tenant to be needed on the lands for which the plan was prepared. In those instances where it is determined that the water rights or water supply of a tenant, landowner, including owner of water rights, resident, or tenant have been adversely affected by a surface or underground coal mine operation which has removed or disturbed a stratum so as to significantly affect the hydrologic balance, such plan may include proposed measures to enhance water quality or quantity by means of joint action with other affected landowners, including owner of water rights, residents, or tenants in consultation with appropriate State and Federal agencies.

(c) Agreement to effect plan

Such plan shall be incorporated in an agreement under which the landowner, including owner of water rights, resident, or tenant shall agree with the Secretary of Agriculture to effect the land uses and conservation treatment provided for in such plan on the lands described in the agreement in accordance with the terms and conditions thereof.

(d) Financial and other assistance; determination by Secretary

In return for such agreement by the landowner, including owner of water rights, resident, or tenant, the Secretary of Agriculture is authorized to furnish financial and other assistance to such landowner, including owner of water rights, resident, or tenant, in such amounts and subject to such conditions as the Secretary of Agriculture determines are appropriate in the public interest for carrying out the land use and conservation treatment set forth in the agreement. Grants made under this section, depending on the income-producing potential of the land after reclaiming, shall provide up to 80 per centum of the cost of carrying out such land uses and conservation treatment on not more than one hundred and twenty acres of land occupied by such owner, including water rights owners, resident, or tenant, or on not more than one hundred and twenty acres of land which has been purchased jointly by such landowners, including water rights owners, residents, or tenants, under an agreement for the enhancement of water quality or quantity or on land which has been acquired by an appropriate State or local agency for the purpose of implementing such agreement; except the Secretary may reduce the matching cost share where he determines that (1) the main benefits to be derived from the project are related to improving offsite water quality, offsite esthetic values, or other offsite benefits, and (2) the matching share requirement would place a burden on the landowner which would probably prevent him from participating in the program: *Provided, however*, That the Secretary of Agriculture may allow for land use and conservation treatment on such lands occupied by any such owner in excess of such one hundred and twenty acre limitation up to three hundred and twenty acres, but in such event the amount of the grant to such landowner to carry out such reclamation on such lands shall be reduced proportionately. Notwithstanding any other provision of this section with regard to acreage limitations, the Secretary of Agriculture may carry out reclamation treatment projects to control erosion and improve water quality on all lands within a hydrologic unit, consisting of not more than 25,000 acres, if the Secretary determines that treatment of such lands as a hydrologic unit will achieve greater reduction in the adverse effects of past surface mining practices than would be achieved if reclamation was done on individual parcels of land.

(e) Termination of agreements

The Secretary of Agriculture may terminate any agreement with a landowner including water rights owners, operator, or occupier by mutual agreement if the Secretary of Agriculture determines that such termination would be in the public interest, and may agree to such modification of agreements previously entered into hereunder as he deems desirable to carry out the purposes of this section or to facilitate the practical administration of the program authorized herein.

(f) Preservation and surrender of history and allotments

Notwithstanding any other provision of law, the Secretary of Agriculture, to the extent he deems it desirable to carry out the purposes of this section, may provide in any agreement hereinunder for (1) preservation for a period not to exceed the period covered by the agreement and an equal period thereafter of the cropland, crop acreage, and allotment history applicable to land covered by the agreement for the purpose of any Federal program under which such history is used as a basis for an allotment or other limitation on the production of such crop; or (2) surrender of any such history and allotments.

(g) Rules and regulations

The Secretary of Agriculture shall be authorized to issue such rules and regulations as he determines are necessary to carry out the provisions of this section.

(h) Utilization of Soil Conservation Service

In carrying out the provisions of this section, the Secretary of Agriculture shall utilize the services of the Soil Conservation Service.

(i) Repealed. Pub.L. 101–508, Title VI, § 6012(c), Nov. 5, 1990, 104 Stat. 1388–298.

(Aug. 3, 1977, Pub.L. 95–87, Title IV, § 406, 91 Stat. 460; Dec. 22, 1981, Pub.L. 97–98, Title XV, § 1551, 95 Stat. 1344; Pub.L. 101–508, Title VI, §§ 6008, 6012(c), (d)(3), Nov. 5, 1990, 104 Stat. 1388–295, 1388–298.)

Effective Date of 1990 Amendment

Amendment by Pub.L. 101–508 effective Oct. 1, 1991, see section 6014 of Pub.L. 101–508, set out as a note under section 1231 of this title.

Savings Provisions

Nothing in Subtitle A (section 6001 et seq.) of Title VI of Pub.L. 101–508, construed to affect the certifications made by the States of Wyoming, Montana, and Louisiana to the Secretary of the Interior prior to Nov. 5, 1990, that each such State has completed the reclamation of eligible abandoned coal mine lands, see section 6013 of Pub.L. 101–508, set out as a note under section 1231 of this title.

CROSS REFERENCES

Abandoned Mine Reclamation Fund moneys, use for purposes of this section, see section 1231 of this title.

Payments received under this section, exclusion from gross income, see section 126 of Title 26, Internal Revenue Code.

CODE OF FEDERAL REGULATIONS

Rural abandoned mine program, see 7 CFR 632.1 et seq.

§ 1237. Acquisition and reclamation of land adversely affected by past coal mining practices [SMCRA § 407]

(a) Findings of fact; notice; right of entry

If the Secretary or the State pursuant to an approved State program, makes a finding of fact that—

(1) land or water resources have been adversely affected by past coal mining practices; and

(2) the adverse effects are at a stage where, in the public interest, action to restore, reclaim, abate, control, or prevent should be taken; and

(3) the owners of the land or water resources where entry must be made to restore, reclaim, abate, control, or prevent the adverse effects of past coal mining practices are not known, or readily available; or

(4) the owners will not give permission for the United States, the States, political subdivisions, their agents, employees, or contractors to enter upon such property to restore, reclaim, abate, control, or prevent the adverse effects of past coal mining practices;

then, upon giving notice by mail to the owners if known or if not known by posting notice upon the premises and advertising once in a newspaper of general circulation in the municipality in which the land lies, the Secretary, his agents, employees, or contractors, or the State pursuant to an approved State program, shall have the right to enter upon the property adversely affected by past coal mining practices and any other property to have access to such property to do all things necessary or expedient to restore, reclaim, abate, control, or prevent the adverse effects. Such entry shall be construed as an exercise of the police power for the protection of public health, safety, and general welfare and shall not be construed as an act of condemnation of property nor of trespass thereon. The moneys expended for such work and the benefits accruing to any such premises so entered upon shall be chargeable against such land and shall mitigate or offset any claim in or any action brought by any owner of any interest in such premises for any alleged damages by virtue of such entry: *Provided, however,* That this provision is not intended to create new rights of action or eliminate existing immunities.

(b) Studies or exploratory work

The Secretary, his agents, employees, or contractors or the State pursuant to an approved State program, shall have the right to enter upon any property for the purpose of conducting studies or exploratory work to determine the existence of adverse effects of past coal mining practices and to determine the feasibility of restoration, reclamation, abatement, control, or prevention of such adverse effects. Such entry shall be construed as an exercise of the police power for the protection of public health, safety, and general welfare and shall not be construed as an act of condemnation of property nor trespass thereon.

(c) Requirements for acquisition of affected land

The Secretary or the State pursuant to an approved State program, may acquire any land, by purchase, donation, or condemnation, which is adversely affected by past coal mining practices if the Secretary determines that acquisition of such land is necessary to successful reclamation and that—

(1) the acquired land, after restoration, reclamation, abatement, control, or prevention of the adverse effects of past coal mining practices, will serve recreation and historic purposes, conservation and reclamation purposes or provide open space benefits; and

(2) permanent facilities such as a treatment plant or a relocated stream channel will be constructed on the land for the restoration, reclamation, abatement, control, or prevention of the adverse effects of past coal mining practices; or

(3) acquisition of coal refuse disposal sites and all coal refuse thereon will serve the purposes of this subchapter or that public ownership is desirable to meet emergency situations and prevent recurrences of the adverse effects of past coal mining practices.

(d) Title to affected land; value

Title to all lands acquired pursuant to this section shall be in the name of the United States or, if acquired by a State pursuant to an approved program, title shall be in the name of the State. The price paid for land acquired under this section shall reflect the market value of the land as adversely affected by past coal mining practices.

(e) State participation; grants

States are encouraged as part of their approved State programs, to reclaim abandoned and unreclaimed mined lands within their boundaries and, if necessary, to acquire or to transfer such lands to the Secretary or the appropriate State regulatory authority under appropriate Federal regulations. The Secretary is authorized to make grants on a matching basis to States in such amounts as he deems appropriate for the purpose of carrying out the provisions of this subchapter but in no event shall any grant exceed 90 per centum of the cost of acquisition of the lands for which the grant is made. When a State has made any such land available to the Federal Government under this subchapter, such State shall have a preference right to purchase such lands after reclamation at fair market value less the State portion of the original acquisition price. Notwithstanding the provisions of paragraph (1) of subsection (c) of this section, reclaimed land may be sold to the State or local government in which it is located at a price less than fair market value, which in no case shall be less than the cost to the United States of the purchase and reclamation of the land, as negotiated by the Secretary, to be used for a valid public purpose. If any land sold to a State or local government under this paragraph is not used for a valid public purpose as specified by the Secretary in the terms of the sales agreement then all right, title, and interest in such land shall revert to the United States. Money received from such sale shall be deposited in the fund.

(f) Rules and regulations

The Secretary, in formulating regulations for making grants to the States to acquire land pursuant to this section, shall specify that acquired land meet the criteria provided for in subsections (c) and (d) of this section. The Secretary may provide by regulation that money derived from the lease, rental, or user charges of such acquired land and facilities thereon will be deposited in the fund.

(g) Public sale; notice and hearing

(1) Where land acquired pursuant to this section is deemed to be suitable for industrial, commercial, residential, or recreational development, the Secretary may sell or authorize the States to sell such land by

public sale under a system of competitive bidding, at not less than fair market value and under such other regulations promulgated to insure that such lands are put to proper use consistent with local and State land use plans, if any, as determined by the Secretary.

(2) The Secretary or the State pursuant to an approved State program, when requested after appropriate public notice shall hold a public hearing, with the appropriate notice, in the county or counties or the appropriate subdivisions of the State in which lands acquired pursuant to this section are located. The hearings shall be held at a time which shall afford local citizens and governments the maximum opportunity to participate in the decision concerning the use or disposition of the lands after restoration, reclamation, abatement, control, or prevention of the adverse effects of past coal mining practices.

(h) Construction or rehabilitation of housing for disabled, displaced, or dislocated persons; grants

In addition to the authority to acquire land under subsection (d) of this section the Secretary is authorized to use money in the fund to acquire land by purchase, donation, or condemnation, and to reclaim and transfer acquired land to any State or to a political subdivision thereof, or to any person, firm, association, or corporation, if he determines that such is an integral and necessary element of an economically feasible plan for the project to construct or rehabilitate housing for persons disabled as the result of employment in the mines or work incidental thereto, persons displaced by acquisition of land pursuant to this section, or persons dislocated as the result of adverse effects of coal mining practices which constitute an emergency as provided in section 1240 of this title or persons dislocated as the result of natural disasters or catastrophic failures from any cause. Such activities shall be accomplished under such terms and conditions as the Secretary shall require, which may include transfers of land with or without monetary consideration: *Provided*, That to the extent that the consideration is below the fair market value of the land transferred, no portion of the difference between the fair market value and the consideration shall accrue as a profit to such persons, firm, association, or corporation. No part of the funds provided under this subchapter may be used to pay the actual construction costs of housing. The Secretary may carry out the purposes of this subsection directly or he may make grants and commitments for grants, and may advance money under such terms and conditions as he may require to any State, or any department, agency, or instrumentality of a State, or any public body or nonprofit organization designated by a State.

(Aug. 3, 1977, Pub.L. 95–87, Title IV, §,407, 91 Stat. 462; Pub.L. 101–508, Title VI, § 6012(d)(4)–(7), Nov. 5, 1990, 104 Stat. 1388–298.)

Effective Date of 1990 Amendment

Amendment by Pub.L. 101–508 effective Oct. 1, 1991, see section 6014 of Pub.L. 101–508, set out as a note under section 1231 of this title.

Savings Provisions

Nothing in Subtitle A (section 6001 et seq.) of Title VI of Pub.L. 101–508, construed to affect the certifications made by the States of Wyoming, Montana, and Louisiana to the Secretary of the Interior prior to Nov. 5, 1990, that each such State has completed the reclamation of eligible abandoned coal mine lands, see section 6013 of Pub.L. 101–508, set out as a note under section 1231 of this title.

CODE OF FEDERAL REGULATIONS

Abandoned mine land reclamation, see 30 CFR Chap. VII, Subchap. R.

Secretary of Interior, general scope of authority and responsibility, see 30 CFR 700.1 et seq.

§ 1238. Liens [SMCRA § 408]

(a) Filing of statement and appraisal

Within six months after the completion of projects to restore, reclaim, abate, control, or prevent adverse effects of past coal mining practices on privately owned land, the Secretary or the State, pursuant to an approved State program, shall itemize the moneys so expended and may file a statement thereof in the office of the county in which the land lies which has the responsibility under local law for the recording of judgments against land, together with a notarized appraisal by an independent appraiser of the value of the land before the restoration, reclamation, abatement, control, or prevention of adverse effects of past coal mining practices if the moneys so expended shall result in a significant increase in property value. Such statement shall constitute a lien upon the said land. The lien shall not exceed the amount determined by the appraisal to be the increase in the market value of the land as a result of the restoration, reclamation, abatement, control, or prevention of the adverse effects of past coal mining practices. No lien shall be filed against the property of any person, in accordance with this subsection, who owned the surface prior to May 2, 1977, and who neither consented to nor participated in nor exercised control over the mining operation which necessitated the reclamation performed hereunder.

(b) Petition

The landowner may proceed as provided by local law to petition within sixty days of the filing of the lien, to determine the increase in the market value of the land as a result of the restoration, reclamation, abatement, control, or prevention of the adverse effects of past coal mining practices. The amount reported to be the increase in value of the premises shall constitute the amount of the lien and shall be recorded with the statement herein provided. Any party aggrieved by the decision may appeal as provided by local law.

(c) Recordation

The lien provided in this section shall be entered in the county office in which the land lies and which has responsibility under local law for the recording of judgments against land. Such statement shall constitute a lien upon the said land as of the date of the expenditure of the moneys and shall have priority as a lien second only to the lien of real estate taxes imposed upon said land.

(Aug. 3, 1977, Pub.L. 95–87, Title IV, § 408, 91 Stat. 465.)

CODE OF FEDERAL REGULATIONS

Reclamation on private land, see 30 CFR 882.1 et seq.

§ 1239. Filling voids and sealing tunnels [SMCRA § 409]

(a) Congressional declaration of hazardous conditions

The Congress declares that voids, and open and abandoned tunnels, shafts, and entryways resulting from any previous mining operation, constitute a hazard to the public health or safety and that surface impacts of any underground or surface mining operation may degrade the environment. The Secretary, at the request of the Governor of any State, or the governing body of an Indian tribe, is authorized to fill such voids, seal such abandoned tunnels, shafts, and entryways, and reclaim surface impacts of underground or surface mines which the Secretary determines could endanger life and property, constitute a hazard to the public health and safety, or degrade the environment. State regulatory authorities are authorized to carry out such work pursuant to an approved abandoned mine reclamation program.

(b) Limitation on funds

Funds available for use in carrying out the purpose of this section shall be limited to those funds which must be allocated to the respective States or Indian tribes under the provisions of paragraphs (1) and (5) of section 1232(g) of this title.

(c) Expenditures in States or Indian reservations

(1) The Secretary may make expenditures and carry out the purposes of this section in such States where requests are made by the Governor or governing body of an Indian tribe for those reclamation projects which meet the priorities stated in section 1233(a)(1) of this title, except that for the purposes of this section the reference to coal in section 1233(a)(1) of this title shall not apply.

(2) The provisions of section 1234 of this title shall apply to this section, with the exception that such mined lands need not have been mined for coal.

(3) The Secretary shall not make any expenditures for the purposes of this section in those States which have made the certification referred to in section 1240a(a) of this title.

(d) Disposal of mine wastes

In those instances where mine waste piles are being reworked for conservation purposes, the incremental costs of disposing of the wastes from such operations by filling voids and sealing tunnels may be eligible for funding providing that the disposal of these wastes meets the purposes of this section.

(e) Land acquisition

The Secretary may acquire by purchase, donation, easement, or otherwise such interest in land as he determines necessary to carry out the provisions of this section.

(Aug. 3, 1977, Pub.L. 95–87, Title IV, § 409, 91 Stat. 465; Pub.L. 101–508, Title VI, § 6009, Nov. 5, 1990, 104 Stat. 1388–296.)

Effective Date of 1990 Amendment

Amendment by Pub.L. 101–508 effective Oct. 1, 1991, see section 6014 of Pub.L. 101–508, set out as a note under section 1231 of this title.

Savings Provisions

Nothing in Subtitle A (section 6001 et seq.) of Title VI of Pub.L. 101–508, construed to affect the certifications made by the States of Wyoming, Montana, and Louisiana to the Secretary of the Interior prior to Nov. 5, 1990, that each such State has completed the reclamation of eligible abandoned coal mine lands, see section 6013 of Pub.L. 101–508, set out as a note under section 1231 of this title.

CROSS REFERENCES

Abandoned Mine Reclamation Fund moneys, use for purposes of this section, see section 1231 of this title.

Allocation of reclamation fees if objectives set out in this section are met, see section 1232 of this title.

CODE OF FEDERAL REGULATIONS

Abandoned mine land reclamation, see 30 CFR Chap. VII, Subchap. R.

§ 1240. Emergency powers [SMCRA § 410]

(a) The Secretary is authorized to expend moneys from the fund for the emergency restoration, reclamation, abatement, control, or prevention of adverse effects of coal mining practices, on eligible lands, if the Secretary makes a finding of fact that—

(1) an emergency exists constituting a danger to the public health, safety, or general welfare; and

(2) no other person or agency will act expeditiously to restore, reclaim, abate, control, or prevent the adverse effects of coal mining practices.

(b) The Secretary, his agents, employees, and contractors shall have the right to enter upon any land where the emergency exists and any other land to have access to the land where the emergency exists to restore, reclaim, abate, control, or prevent the adverse effects of coal mining practices and to do all things necessary or expedient to protect the public health, safety, or general welfare. Such entry shall be construed as an exercise of the police power and shall not be construed as an act of condemnation of property nor of trespass thereof. The moneys expended for such work and the benefits accruing to any such premises so entered upon shall be chargeable against such land and shall mitigate or offset any claim in or any action brought by any owner of any interest in such premises for any alleged damages by virtue of such entry: *Provided, however,* That this provision is not intended to create new rights of action or eliminate existing immunities.

(Aug. 3, 1977, Pub.L. 95–87, Title IV, § 410, 91 Stat. 466.)

CROSS REFERENCES

Construction of housing for persons dislocated by an emergency as provided in this section, see section 1237 of this title.

State reclamation program, exception from implementation of this section, see section 1235 of this title.

CODE OF FEDERAL REGULATIONS

Reclamation on private land, see 30 CFR 882.1 et seq.

Rights of entry, see 30 CFR 877.1 et seq.

§ 1240a. Certification [SMCRA § 411]

(a) Certification of completion of coal reclamation

The Governor of a State, or the head of a governing body of an Indian tribe, with an approved abandoned mine reclamation program under section 1235 of this title may certify to the Secretary that all of the priorities stated in section 1233(a) of this title for eligible lands and waters pursuant to section 1234 of this title have been achieved. The Secretary, after notice in the Federal Register and opportunity for public comment, shall concur with such certification if the Secretary determines that such certification is correct.

(b) Eligible lands, waters, and facilities

If the Secretary has concurred in a State or tribal certification under subsection (a) of this section, for purposes of determining the eligibility of lands and waters for annual grants under section 1232(g)(1) of this title, section 1234 of this title shall not apply, and eligible lands, waters, and facilities shall be those—

(1) which were mined or processed for minerals or which were affected by such mining or processing, and abandoned or left in an inadequate reclamation status prior to August 3, 1977; and

(2) for which there is no continuing reclamation responsibility under State or other Federal laws.

In determining the eligibility under this subsection of Federal lands, waters, and facilities under the jurisdiction of the Forest Service or Bureau of Land Management, in lieu of the August 3, 1977, date referred to in paragraph (1) the applicable date[1] shall be August 28, 1974, and November 26, 1980, respectively.

(c) Priorities

Expenditures of moneys for lands, waters, and facilities referred to in subsection (b) of this section shall reflect the following objectives and priorities in the order stated (in lieu of the priorities set forth in section 1233 of this title):

(1) The protection of public health, safety, general welfare, and property from extreme danger of adverse effects of mineral mining and processing practices.

(2) The protection of public health, safety, and general welfare from adverse effects of mineral mining and processing practices.

(3) The restoration of land and water resources and the environment previously degraded by the adverse effects of mineral mining and processing practices.

(d) Specific sites and areas not eligible

Sites and areas designated for remedial action pursuant to the Uranium Mill Tailings Radiation Control Act of 1978 (42 U.S.C. 7901 and following) or which have been listed for remedial action pursuant to the Comprehensive Environmental Response Compensation and Liability Act of 1980 (42 U.S.C. 9601 and following) shall not be eligible for expenditures from the Fund under this section.

(e) Utilities and other facilities

Reclamation projects involving the protection, repair, replacement, construction, or enhancement of utilities, such as those relating to water supply, roads, and such other facilities serving the public adversely affected by mineral mining and processing practices, and the construction of public facilities in communities impacted by coal or other mineral mining and processing practices, shall be deemed part of the objectives set forth, and undertaken as they relate to the priorities stated in subsection (c) of this section.

(f) Need for activities or construction of specified public facilities

Notwithstanding subsection (e) of this section, where the Secretary has concurred in the certification referenced in subsection (a) of this section and where the Governor of a State or the head of a governing body of an Indian tribe determines there is a need for activities or construction of specific public facilities related to the coal or minerals industry in States impacted by coal or minerals development and the Secretary concurs in such need, then the State or Indian tribe, as the case may be, may use annual grants made available under section 1232(g)(1) of this title to carry out such activities or construction.

(g) Application of other provisions

The provisions of sections 1237 and 1238 of this title shall apply to subsections (a) through (e) of this section, except that for purposes of this section the references to coal in sections 1237 and 1238 of this title shall not apply.

(Pub.L. 95–87, Title IV, § 411, as added Nov. 5, 1990, Pub.L. 101–508, Title VI, § 6010, 104 Stat. 1388–296.)

[1] So in original. Probably should be "dates".

References in Text

The Uranium Mill Tailings Radiation Control Act of 1978, referred to in subsec. (d), is Pub.L. 95–604, Nov. 8, 1978, 92 Stat. 3021, as amended, which is classified principally to chapter 88 (section 7901 et seq.) of Title 42, The Public Health and Welfare. For complete classification of this Act to the Code, see Short Title note set out under section 7901 of Title 42 and Tables.

The Comprehensive Environmental Response Compensation and Liability Act of 1980, referred to in subsec. (d), is Pub.L. 96–510, Dec. 11, 1980, 94 Stat. 2767, as amended, which is classified principally to chapter 103 (sections 9601 et seq.) of Title 42, The Public Health and Welfare. For complete classification of this Act to the Code, see Short Title note set out under section 9601 of Title 42 and Tables.

Codification

Another section 411 of Pub.L. 95–87 is classified to section 1241 of this title. Such section is redesignated section 412 of Pub.L. 95–87, eff. Oct. 1, 1991, pursuant to sections 6010(1) and 6014 of Pub.L. 101–508. Such section remains classified to section 1241 of this title after such redesignation on Oct. 1, 1991.

Effective Date

Section effective Oct. 1, 1991, see section 6014 of Pub.L. 101–508, set out as a note under section 1231 of this title.

Savings Provisions

Nothing in Subtitle A (section 6001 et seq.) of Title VI of Pub.L. 101–508, construed to affect the certifications made by the States of Wyoming, Montana, and Louisiana to the Secretary of the Interior prior to Nov. 5, 1990, that each such State has completed the reclamation of eligible abandoned coal mine lands, see section 6013 of Pub.L. 101–508, set out as a note under section 1231 of this title.

§ 1241. Annual report to Congress [SMCRA § 411]

Not later than January 1, 1978, and annually thereafter, the Secretary or the State pursuant to an approved State program, shall report to the Congress on operations under the fund together with his recommendations as to future uses of the fund.

(Pub.L. 95–87, Title IV, § 412, formerly § 411, Aug. 3, 1977, 91 Stat. 466, renumbered Pub.L. 101–508, Title VI, § 6010(1), Nov. 5, 1990, 104 Stat. 1388–296.)

§ 1242. Powers of Secretary or State [SMCRA § 412]

(a) Engage in work, promulgate rules and regulations, etc., to implement and administer this subchapter

The Secretary or the State pursuant to an approved State program, shall have the power and authority, if not granted it otherwise, to engage in any work and to do all things necessary or expedient, including promulgation of rules and regulations, to implement and administer the provisions of this subchapter.

(b) Engage in cooperative projects

The Secretary or the State pursuant to an approved State program, shall have the power and authority to engage in cooperative projects under this subchapter with any other agency of the United States of America, any State and their governmental agencies.

(c) Request for action to restrain interference with regard to this subchapter

The Secretary or the State pursuant to an approved State program, may request the Attorney General, who is hereby authorized to initiate, in addition to any other remedies provided for in this subchapter, in any court of competent jurisdiction, an action in equity for an injunction to restrain any interference with the exercise of the right to enter or to conduct any work provided in this subchapter.

(d) Construct and operate plants for control and treatment of water pollution resulting from mine drainage

The Secretary or the State pursuant to an approved State program, shall have the power and authority to construct and operate a plant or plants for the control and treatment of water pollution resulting from mine drainage. The extent of this control and treatment may be dependent upon the ultimate use of the water: *Provided*, That the above provisions of this paragraph shall not be deemed in any way to repeal or supersede any portion of the Federal Water Pollution Control Act (33 U.S.C.A. 1151, et seq. as amended) [33 U.S.C.A. § 1251 et seq.] and no control or treatment under this subsection shall in any way be less than that required under the Federal Water Pollution Control Act. The construction of a plant or plants may include major interceptors and other facilities appurtenant to the plant.

(e) Transfer funds

The Secretary may transfer funds to other appropriate Federal agencies, in order to carry out the reclamation activities authorized by this subchapter.

(Pub.L. 95–87, Title IV, § 413, formerly § 412, Aug. 3, 1977, 91 Stat. 466, renumbered Pub.L. 101–508, Title VI, § 6010(1), Nov. 5, 1990, 104 Stat. 1388–296.)

CODE OF FEDERAL REGULATIONS

Abandoned mine land reclamation, see 30 CFR Chap. VII, Subchap. R.

Secretary of Interior, general scope of authority and responsibility, see 30 CFR 700.1 et seq.

§ 1243. Interagency cooperation [SMCRA § 413]

All departments, boards, commissioners, and agencies of the United States of America shall cooperate with the Secretary by providing technical expertise, personnel, equipment, materials, and supplies to implement and administer the provisions of this subchapter.

(Pub.L. 95–87, Title IV, § 414, formerly § 413, Aug. 3, 1977, 91 Stat. 467, renumbered Pub.L. 101–508, Title VI, § 6010(1), Nov. 5, 1990, 104 Stat. 1388–296.)

SUBCHAPTER V—CONTROL OF THE ENVIRONMENTAL IMPACTS OF SURFACE COAL MINING

CROSS REFERENCES

Deduction of mining and solid waste reclamation and closing costs incurred pursuant to provisions of this subchapter, see section 468 of Title 26, Internal Revenue Code.

Duty of Secretary to administer State grant-in-aid program provided in this subchapter, see section 1211 of this title.

National environmental policy, see section 4321 et seq. of Title 42, The Public Health and Welfare.

§ 1251. Environmental protection standards [SMCRA § 501]

(a) Not later than the end of the ninety-day period immediately following August 3, 1977, the Secretary shall promulgate and publish in the Federal Register regulations covering an interim regulatory procedure for surface coal mining and reclamation operations setting mining and reclamation performance standards based on and incorporating the provisions set out in section 1252(c) of this title. The issuance of the interim regulations shall be deemed not to be a major Federal action within the meaning of section 4332(2)(c) of Title 42. Such regulations, which shall be concise and written in plain, understandable language shall not be promulgated and published by the Secretary until he has—

(A) published proposed regulations in the Federal Register and afforded interested persons and State and local governments a period of not less than thirty days after such publication to submit written comments thereon;

(B) obtained the written concurrence of the Administrator of the Environmental Protection Agency with respect to those regulations promulgated under this section which relate to air or water quality standards promulgated under the authority of the Federal Water Pollution Control Act, as amended (33 U.S.C.A. 1151–1175) [33 U.S.C.A. § 1251 et seq.]; and the Clean Air Act, as amended (42 U.S.C.A. 1857 et seq.) [42 U.S.C.A. § 7401 et seq.]; and

(C) held at least one public hearing on the proposed regulations.

The date, time, and place of any hearing held on the proposed regulations shall be set out in the publication of the proposed regulations. The Secretary shall consider all comments and relevant data presented at such hearing before final promulgation and publication of the regulations.

(b) Not later than one year after August 3, 1977, the Secretary shall promulgate and publish in the Federal Register regulations covering a permanent regulatory procedure for surface coal mining and reclamation operations performance standards based on and conforming to the provisions of this subchapter and establishing procedures and requirements for preparation, submission, and approval of State programs; and development and implementation of Federal programs under the subchapter. The Secretary shall promulgate these regulations, which shall be concise and written in plain, understandable language in accordance with the procedures in subsection (a) of this section.

(Aug. 3, 1977, Pub.L. 95–87, Title V, § 501, 91 Stat. 467.)

CROSS REFERENCES

Adoption of regulations under this section as major action for purposes of National Environmental Policy Act of 1969, see section 1292 of this title.

Environmental protection performance standards, see section 1265 of this title.

Judicial review of standards promulgated pursuant to this section, see section 1276 of this title.

Interim regulations for certain Alaskan coal mines, see section 1298 of this title.

Proceedings for issuance, amendment or repeal of rule following adoption of regulations required by this section, see section 1211 of this title.

Review of permits under previously approved State programs, time limit regulations for conformity to Federal program, see section 1254 of this title.

Surface effects of underground coal mining operations, rules and regulations, see section 1266 of this title.

West's Federal Practice Manual

Minerals on federal lands, see § 5301 et seq.

CODE OF FEDERAL REGULATIONS

Areas unsuitable for mining, see 30 CFR Chap. VII, Subchap. F.
Computation of time for purposes of rules and regulations, see 30 CFR 700.15.
General performance standards—
Surface mining, see 30 CFR 715.10 et seq.
Underground mining, see 30 CFR 717.10 et seq.
Government financed highway or construction, exemption for coal extraction, see 30 CFR 707.1 et seq.
Inspection and enforcement procedure, see 30 CFR Chap. VII, Subchap. L.
Non-Federal and non-Indian lands, permanent regulatory programs, see 30 CFR Chap. VII, Subchap. C.
Permanent program performance standards—
General provisions, see 30 CFR 810.1 et seq.
Surface mining, see 30 CFR 816.1 et seq.
Underground mining, see 30 CFR 817.1 et seq.
Permanent regulatory program, see 30 CFR 701.1 et seq.
Permit requirements for special categories of mining, see 30 CFR 785.1 et seq.
Program regulations—
Civil penalties, see 30 CFR 723.1 et seq.
Enforcement procedures, see 30 CFR 722.1 et seq.
Secretary of Interior, general scope of authority and responsibility, see 30 CFR 700.1 et seq.
Special permanent program performance standards—
Anthracite mines in Pennsylvania, see 30 CFR 820.1 et seq.
In situ processing, see 30 CFR 828.1 et seq.
Mountaintop removal, see 30 CFR 824.1 et seq.

LAW REVIEW COMMENTARIES

Pennsylvania surface mining legislation: A regulatory mire. Comment (1986) 47 U.Pitt.L.Rev. 517.

LIBRARY REFERENCES

Mines and Minerals ⚖92.6, 92.9.
C.J.S. Mines and Minerals §§ 229 et seq., 239.

§ 1251a. Abandoned coal refuse sites

(1) Notwithstanding any other provision of the Surface Mining Control and Reclamation Act of 1977 [30 U.S.C.A. § 1201 et seq.] to the contrary, the Secretary of the Interior shall, within one year after the enactment of this Act, publish proposed regulations in the Federal Register, and after opportunity for public comment publish final regulations, establishing environmental protection performance and reclamation standards, and separate permit systems applicable to operations for the on-site reprocessing of abandoned coal refuse and operations for the removal of abandoned coal refuse on lands that would otherwise be eligible for expenditure under section 404 and section 402(g)(4) of the Surface Mining Control and Reclamation Act of 1977 [30 U.S.C.A. §§ 1234 and 1232(g)(4)].

(2) The standards and permit systems referred to in paragraph (1) shall distinguish between those operations which reprocess abandoned coal refuse on-site, and those operations which completely remove abandoned coal refuse from a site for the direct use of such coal refuse, or for the reprocessing of such coal refuse, at another location. Such standards and permit systems shall be premised on the distinct differences between operations for the on-site reprocessing, and operations for the removal, of abandoned coal refuse and other types of surface coal mining operations.

(3) The Secretary of the Interior may devise a different standard than any of those set forth in section 515 and section 516 of the Surface Mining Control and Reclamation Act of 1977 [30 U.S.C.A. §§ 1265 and 1266], and devise a separate permit system, if he determines, on a standard-by-standard basis, that a different standard may facilitate the on-site reprocessing, or the removal, of abandoned coal refuse in a manner that would provide the same level of environmental protection as under section 515 and section 516 [30 U.S.C.A. §§ 1265 and 1266].

(4) Not later than 30 days prior to the publication of the proposed regulations referred to in this subsection, the Secretary shall submit a report to the Committee on Interior and Insular Affairs of the United States House of Representatives, and the Committee on Energy and Natural Resources of the United States Senate containing a detailed description of any environmental protection performance and reclamation standards, and separate permit systems, devised pursuant to this subsection.

(Pub.L. 102–486, Title XXV, § 2503(e), Oct. 24, 1992, 106 Stat. 3103.)

References in Text

Enactment of this act, referred to in paragraph (1), probably means the date of enactment of Pub.L. 102–486, 106 Stat. 2776, which was approved Oct. 24, 1992.

The Surface Mining Control and Reclamation Act of 1977, referred to in paragraphs (1) and (3), is Pub.L. 95–87, Aug. 3, 1977, 91 Stat. 445, as amended, which is classified generally to this chapter. For complete classification of this Act to the Code, see Short Title note set out under section 1201 of this title and Tables.

Codification

Section was not enacted as part of the Surface Mining Control and Reclamation Act of 1977 which comprises this chapter.

Change of Name

Any reference in any provision of law enacted before Jan. 4, 1995, to the Committee on Natural Resources of the House of Representatives treated as referring to the Committee on Resources of the House of Representatives, see section 1(a)(8) of Pub.L. 104–14, set out as a note preceding section 21 of Title 2, The Congress.

Committee on Interior and Insular Affairs of the House of Representatives changed to Committee on Natural Resources of the House of Representatives on Jan. 5, 1993, by House Resolution No. 5, One Hundred Third Congress.

§ 1252. Initial regulatory procedures [SMCRA § 502]

(a) State regulation

No person shall open or develop any new or previously mined or abandoned site for surface coal mining operations on lands on which such operations are regulated by a State unless such person has obtained a permit from the State's regulatory authority.

(b) Interim standards

All surface coal mining operations on lands on which such operations are regulated by a State which commence operations pursuant to a permit issued on or after six months from August 3, 1977, shall comply, and such permits shall contain terms requiring compliance with, the provisions set out in subsection (c) of this section. Prior to final disapproval of a State program or prior to promulgation of a Federal program or a Federal lands program pursuant to this chapter, a State may issue such permits.

(c) Full compliance with environmental protection performance standards

On and after nine months from August 3, 1977, all surface coal mining operations on lands on which such operations are regulated by a State shall comply with the provisions of subsections (b)(2), (b)(3), (b)(5), (b)(10), (b)(13), (b)(15), (b)(19), and (d) of section 1265 of this title or, where a surface coal mining operation will remove an entire coal seam or seams running through the upper fraction of a mountain, ridge, or hill by removing all of the overburden and creating a level plateau or a gently rolling contour with no highwalls remaining, such operation shall comply with the requirements of section 1265(c)(4) and (5) of this title without regard to the requirements of section 1265(b)(3) or (d)(2) and (3) of this title, with respect to lands from which overburden and the coal seam being mined have not been removed: *Provided, however,* That surface coal mining operations in operation pursuant to a permit issued by a State before August 3, 1977, issued to a person as defined in section 1291(19) of this title in existence prior to May 2, 1977 and operated by a person whose total annual production of coal from surface and underground coal mining operations does not exceed one hundred thousand tons shall not be subject to the provisions of this subsection except with reference to the provision of section 1265(d)(1) of this title until January 1, 1979.

(d) Permit application

Not later than two months following the approval of a State program pursuant to section 1253 of this title or the implementation of a Federal program pursuant to section 1254 of this title, regardless of litigation contesting that approval or implementation, all operators of surface coal mines in expectation of operating such mines after the expiration of eight months from the approval of a State program or the implementation of a Federal program, shall file an application for a permit with the regulatory authority. Such application shall cover those lands to be mined after the expiration of eight months from the approval of a State program or the implementation of a Federal program. The regulatory authority shall process such applications and grant or deny a permit within eight months after the date of approval of the State program or the implementation of the Federal program, unless specially enjoined by a court of competent jurisdiction, but in no case later than forty-two months from August 3, 1977.

(e) Federal enforcement program

Within six months after August 3, 1977, the Secretary shall implement a Federal enforcement program which shall remain in effect in each State as surface coal mining operations are required to comply with the provisions of this chapter, until the State program has been approved pursuant to this chapter or until a Federal program has been implemented pursuant to this chapter. The enforcement program shall—

(1) include inspections of surface coal mine sites which may be made (but at least one inspection for every site every six months), without advance notice to the mine operator and for the purpose of ascertaining compliance with the standards of subsections (b) and (c) above. The Secretary shall order any necessary enforcement action to be implemented pursuant to the Federal enforcement provision of this subchapter to correct violations identified at the inspections;

(2) provide that upon receipt of inspection reports indicating that any surface coal mining operation has been found in violation of subsections (b) and (c) above, during not less than two consecutive State inspections or upon receipt by the Secretary of information which would give rise to reasonable belief that such standards are being violated by any surface coal mining operation, the Secretary shall order the immediate inspection of such operation by Federal inspectors and the necessary enforcement actions, if any, to be implemented pursuant to the Federal enforcement provisions of this subchapter. When the Federal inspection results from information provided to the Secretary by any person, the Secretary shall notify such person when the Federal inspection is proposed to be carried out and such person shall be allowed to accompany the inspector during the inspection;

(3) provide that the State regulatory agency file with the Secretary and with a designated Federal office centrally located in the county or area in which the inspected surface coal mine is located copies of inspection reports made;

(4) provide that moneys authorized by section 1302 of this title shall be available to the Secretary prior to the approval of a State program pursuant to this chapter to reimburse the State for conducting those inspections in which the standards of this

chapter are enforced and for the administration of this section.[1]

(5) for purposes of this section, the term "Federal inspector" means personnel of the Office of Surface Mining Reclamation and Enforcement and such additional personnel of the United States Geological Survey, Bureau of Land Management, or of the Mining Enforcement and Safety Administration so designated by the Secretary, or such other personnel of the Forest Service, Soil Conservation Service, or the Agricultural Stabilization and Conservation Service as arranged by appropriate agreement with the Secretary on a reimbursable or other basis;[2]

(f) Interim period

Following the final disapproval of a State program, and prior to promulgation of a Federal program or a Federal lands program pursuant to this chapter, including judicial review of such a program, existing surface coal mining operations may continue surface mining operations pursuant to the provisions of this section. During such period no new permits shall be issued by the State whose program has been disapproved. Permits which lapse during such period may continue in full force and effect until promulgation of a Federal program or a Federal lands program.

(Aug. 3, 1977, Pub.L. 95–87, Title V, § 502, 91 Stat. 468.)

[1] So in original. The period probably should be a semicolon.

[2] So in original. The semicolon probably should be a period.

CROSS REFERENCES

Application for permit under Federal or State program by holders of permits issued by State regulatory authority pursuant to this section, see section 1256 of this title.
Authorization of appropriations for implementation of this section, see section 1302 of this title.
Enforcement, see section 1271 of this title.
Interim regulations incorporating provisions of this section, see section 1251 of this title.
Penalties for violations of Federal enforcement pursuant to this section, see section 1268 of this title.
State cooperative agreements for regulation of Federal lands, compliance with this section, see section 1273 of this title.
State regulation of surface coal mining and reclamation operations during injunction, see section 1253 of this title.

CODE OF FEDERAL REGULATIONS

Initial program regulations, see 30 CFR 710.1 et seq.
Permanent program performance standards—
Surface mining, see 30 CFR 816.1 et seq.
Underground mining, see 30 CFR 817.1 et seq.
Reimbursements to States pursuant to this section, see 30 CFR 725.1 et seq.

§ 1253. State programs [SMCRA § 503]

(a) Regulation of surface coal mining and reclamation operations; submittal to Secretary; time limit; demonstration of effectiveness

Each State in which there are or may be conducted surface coal mining operations on non-Federal lands, and which wishes to assume exclusive jurisdiction over the regulation of surface coal mining and reclamation operations, except as provided in sections 1271 and 1273 of this title and subchapter IV of this chapter, shall submit to the Secretary, by the end of the eighteen-month period beginning on August 3, 1977, a State program which demonstrates that such State has the capability of carrying out the provisions of this chapter and meeting its purposes through—

(1) a State law which provides for the regulation of surface coal mining and reclamation operations in accordance with the requirements of this chapter;

(2) a State law which provides sanctions for violations of State laws, regulations, or conditions of permits concerning surface coal mining and reclamation operations, which sanctions shall meet the minimum requirements of this chapter, including civil and criminal actions, forfeiture of bonds, suspensions, revocations, and withholding of permits, and the issuance of cease-and-desist orders by the State regulatory authority or its inspectors;

(3) a State regulatory authority with sufficient administrative and technical personnel, and sufficient funding to enable the State to regulate surface coal mining and reclamation operations in accordance with the requirements of this chapter;

(4) a State law which provides for the effective implementations, maintenance, and enforcement of a permit system, meeting the requirements of this subchapter for the regulations of surface coal mining and reclamation operations for coal on lands within the State;

(5) establishment of a process for the designation of areas as unsuitable for surface coal mining in accordance with section 1272 of this title provided that the designation of Federal lands unsuitable for mining shall be performed exclusively by the Secretary after consultation with the State; and [1]

(6) establishment for the purposes of avoiding duplication, of a process for coordinating the review and issuance of permits for surface coal mining and reclamation operations with any other Federal or State permit process applicable to the proposed operations; and

(7) rules and regulations consistent with regulations issued by the Secretary pursuant to this chapter.

(b) Approval of program

The Secretary shall not approve any State program submitted under this section until he has—

(1) solicited and publicly disclosed the views of the Administrator of the Environmental Protection Agency, the Secretary of Agriculture, and the heads of other Federal agencies concerned with or having

special expertise pertinent to the proposed State program;

(2) obtained the written concurrence of the Administrator of the Environmental Protection Agency with respect to those aspects of a State program which relate to air or water quality standards promulgated under the authority of the Federal Water Pollution Control Act, as amended (33 U.S.C.A. 1151–1175) [33 U.S.C.A. § 1251 et seq.], and the Clean Air Act, as amended (42 U.S.C.A. 1857 et seq.) [42 U.S.C.A. § 7401 et seq.];

(3) held at least one public hearing on the State program within the State; and

(4) found that the State has the legal authority and qualified personnel necessary for the enforcement of the environmental protection standards.

The Secretary shall approve or disapprove a State program, in whole or in part, within six full calendar months after the date such State program was submitted to him.

(c) Notice of disapproval

If the Secretary disapproves any proposed State program in whole or in part, he shall notify the State in writing of his decision and set forth in detail the reasons therefor. The State shall have sixty days in which to resubmit a revised State program or portion thereof. The Secretary shall approve or disapprove the resubmitted State program or portion thereof within sixty days from the date of resubmission.

(d) Inability of State to take action

For the purposes of this section and section 1254 of this title, the inability of a State to take any action the purpose of which is to prepare, submit or enforce a State program, or any portion thereof, because the action is enjoined by the issuance of an injunction by any court of competent jurisdiction shall not result in a loss of eligibility for financial assistance under subchapters IV and VII of this chapter or in the imposition of a Federal program. Regulation of the surface coal mining and reclamation operations covered or to be covered by the State program subject to the injunction shall be conducted by the State pursuant to section 1252 of this title, until such time as the injunction terminates or for one year, whichever is shorter, at which time the requirements of this section and section 1254 of this title shall again be fully applicable.

(Aug. 3, 1977, Pub.L. 95–87, Title V, § 503, 91 Stat. 470.)

[1] So in original.

CROSS REFERENCES

Approval of State program as major action for purposes of National Environmental Policy Act of 1969, see section 1292 of this title.
Designation of areas unsuitable for surface coal mining, see section 1272 of this title.
Enforcement of program, see section 1271 of this title.
Federal programs in absence of State programs, see section 1254 of this title.
Insurance of private property against land subsidence in States having programs approved in accordance with this section, see section 1231 of this title.
Penalties for violation of State programs, conditions for program approval, see section 1268 of this title.
Permits—
Generally, see section 1256 of this title.
Applications, see section 1252 of this title.
State program defined, see section 1291 of this title.
State reclamation program, see section 1235 of this title.
State regulations for certification and training of blasters, see section 1309 of this title.

CODE OF FEDERAL REGULATIONS

Areas unsuitable for mining, see 30 CFR Chap. VII, Subchap. F.
Inspection and enforcement procedure—
Federal, see 30 CFR 843.1 et seq.
State, see 30 CFR 840.1 et seq.
Non-federal and non-Indian land, permanent regulatory programs, see 30 CFR Chap. VII, Subchap. C.
Performance standards, permanent programs, general provisions, see 30 CFR 810.1 et seq.
Permit requirements for special categories of mining, see 30 CFR 785.1 et seq.
Special permanent program performance standards—
Anthracite mines in Pennsylvania, see 30 CFR 820.1 et seq.
In situ processing, see 30 CFR 828.1 et seq.
Mountaintop removal, see 30 CFR 824.1 et seq.
State programs for conduct of surface mine operations, see 30 CFR Chap. VII, Subchap. T.

§ 1254. Federal programs [SMCRA § 504]

(a) Promulgation and implementation by Secretary for State

The Secretary shall prepare and, subject to the provisions of this section, promulgate and implement a Federal program for a State no later than thirty-four months after August 3, 1977, if such State—

(1) fails to submit a State program covering surface coal mining and reclamation operations by the end of the eighteen-month period beginning on August 3, 1977;

(2) fails to resubmit an acceptable State program within sixty days of disapproval of a proposed State program: *Provided*, That the Secretary shall not implement a Federal program prior to the expiration of the initial period allowed for submission of a State program as provided for in clause (1) of this subsection; or

(3) fails to implement, enforce, or maintain its approved State program as provided for in this chapter.

If State compliance with clause (1) of this subsection requires an act of the State legislature, the Secretary may extend the period of submission of a State program up to an additional six months. Promulgation and implementation of a Federal program vests the Secretary with exclusive jurisdiction for the regulation and control of surface coal mining and reclamation operations taking place on lands within any State not in compliance with this chapter. After promulgation and implementation of a Federal program the Secretary shall be the regulatory authority. If a Federal program is implemented for a State, section 1272(a), (c), and (d) of this title shall not apply for a period of one year following the date of such implementation. In promulgating and implementing a Federal program for a particular State the Secretary shall take into consideration the nature of that State's terrain, climate, biological, chemical, and other relevant physical conditions.

(b) Federal enforcement of State program

In the event that a State has a State program for surface coal mining, and is not enforcing any part of such program, the Secretary may provide for the Federal enforcement, under the provisions of section 1271 of this title, of that part of the State program not being enforced by such State.

(c) Notice and hearing

Prior to promulgation and implementation of any proposed Federal program, the Secretary shall give adequate public notice and hold a public hearing in the affected State.

(d) Review of permits

Permits issued pursuant to a previously approved State program shall be valid but reviewable under a Federal program. Immediately following promulgation of a Federal program, the Secretary shall undertake to review such permits to determine that the requirements of this chapter are not violated. If the Secretary determines any permit to have been granted contrary to the requirements of this chapter, he shall so advise the permittee and provide him an opportunity for hearing and a reasonable opportunity for submission of a new application and reasonable time, within a time limit prescribed in regulations promulgated pursuant to section 1251(b) of this title, to conform ongoing surface mining and reclamation operations to the requirements of the Federal program.

(e) Submission of State program after implementation of Federal program

A State which has failed to obtain the approval of a State program prior to implementation of a Federal program may submit a State program at any time after such implementation. Upon the submission of such a program, the Secretary shall follow the procedures set forth in section 1253(b) of this title and shall approve or disapprove the State program within six months after its submittal. Approval of a State program shall be based on the determination that the State has the capability of carrying out the provisions of this chapter and meeting its purposes through the criteria set forth in section 1253(a)(1) through (6) of this title. Until a State program is approved as provided under this section, the Federal program shall remain in effect and all actions taken by the Secretary pursuant to such Federal program, including the terms and conditions of any permit issued thereunder shall remain in effect.

(f) Validity of Federal program permits under superseding State program

Permits issued pursuant to the Federal program shall be valid under any superseding State program: *Provided*, That the Federal permittee shall have the right to apply for a State permit to supersede his Federal permit. The State regulatory authority may review such permits to determine that the requirements of this chapter and the approved State program are not violated. Should the State program contain additional requirements not contained in the Federal program, the permittee will be provided opportunity for hearing and a reasonable time, within a time limit prescribed in regulations promulgated pursuant to section 1251 of this title, to conform ongoing surface mining and reclamation operations to the additional State requirements.

(g) Preemption of State statutes or regulations

Whenever a Federal program is promulgated for a State pursuant to this chapter, any statutes or regulations of such State which are in effect to regulate surface mining and reclamation operations subject to this chapter shall, insofar as they interfere with the achievement of the purposes and the requirements of this chapter and the Federal program, be preempted and superseded by the Federal program. The Secretary shall set forth any State law or regulation which is preempted and superseded by the Federal program.

(h) Coordination of issuance and review of Federal program permits with any other Federal or State permit process

Any Federal program shall include a process for coordinating the review and issuance of permits for surface mining and reclamation operations with any other Federal or State permit process applicable to the proposed operation.

(Aug. 3, 1977, Pub.L. 95–87, Title V, § 504, 91 Stat. 471.)

CROSS REFERENCES

Designation of areas unsuitable for surface coal mining, see section 1272 of this title.
Enforcement of program, see section 1271 of this title.
Federal program defined, see section 1291 of this title.
Federal regulations for certification and training of blasters, see section 1309 of this title.
Inability of State to act on State program due to injunction, effect on applicability of this section, see section 1253 of this title.

Permits—
Generally, see section 1256 of this title.
Applications, see section 1252 of this title.
Promulgation of Federal program as major action for purposes of National Environmental Policy Act of 1969, see section 1292 of this title.

West's Federal Practice Manual

Minerals on federal lands, see § 5301 et seq.

CODE OF FEDERAL REGULATIONS

Areas unsuitable for mining, see 30 CFR Chap. VII, Subchap. F.
Inspection and enforcement procedure—
Federal enforcement, see 30 CFR 843.1 et seq.
Federal inspections and monitoring, see 30 CFR 842.1 et seq.
Non-federal and non-Indian lands, permanent regulatory programs, see 30 CFR Chap. VII, Subchap. C.
Performance standards—
General provisions, see 30 CFR 810.1 et seq.
Surface mining, see 30 CFR 816.1 et seq.
Underground mining, see 30 CFR 817.1 et seq.
Permit requirements for special categories of mining, see 30 CFR 785.1 et seq.
Special permanent program performance standards—
Anthracite mines in Pennsylvania, see 30 CFR 820.1 et seq.
In situ processing, see 30 CFR 828.1 et seq.
Mountaintop removal, see 30 CFR 824.1 et seq.
State programs for conduct of surface mine operations, see 30 CFR Chap. VII, Subchap. T.

§ 1255. State laws [SMCRA § 505]

(a) No State law or regulation in effect on August 3, 1977, or which may become effective thereafter, shall be superseded by any provision of this chapter or any regulation issued pursuant thereto, except insofar as such State law or regulation is inconsistent with the provisions of this chapter.

(b) Any provision of any State law or regulation in effect upon August 3, 1977, or which may become effective thereafter, which provides for more stringent land use and environmental controls and regulations of surface coal mining and reclamation operation than do the provisions of this chapter or any regulation issued pursuant thereto shall not be construed to be inconsistent with this chapter. The Secretary shall set forth any State law or regulation which is construed to be inconsistent with this chapter. Any provision of any State law or regulation in effect on August 3, 1977, or which may become effective thereafter, which provides for the control and regulation of surface mining and reclamation operations for which no provision is contained in this chapter shall not be construed to be inconsistent with this chapter.

(Aug. 3, 1977, Pub.L. 95–87, Title V, § 505, 91 Stat. 473.)

CODE OF FEDERAL REGULATIONS

Performance standards, permanent program, general provisions, see 30 CFR 810.1 et seq.
State programs for conduct of surface mine operations, see 30 CFR Chap. VII, Subchap. T.

§ 1256. Permits [SMCRA § 506]

(a) Persons engaged in surface coal mining within State; time limit; exception

No later than eight months from the date on which a State program is approved by the Secretary, pursuant to section 1253 of this title, or no later than eight months from the date on which the Secretary has promulgated a Federal program for a State not having a State program pursuant to section 1254 of this title, no person shall engage in or carry out on lands within a State any surface coal mining operations unless such person has first obtained a permit issued by such State pursuant to an approved State program or by the Secretary pursuant to a Federal program; except a person conducting surface coal mining operations under a permit from the State regulatory authority, issued in accordance with the provisions of section 1252 of this title, may conduct such operations beyond such period if an application for a permit has been filed in accordance with the provisions of this chapter, but the initial administrative decision has not been rendered.

(b) Term

All permits issued pursuant to the requirements of this chapter shall be issued for a term not to exceed five years: *Provided*, That if the applicant demonstrates that a specified longer term is reasonably needed to allow the applicant to obtain necessary financing for equipment and the opening of the operation and if the application is full and complete for such specified longer term, the regulatory authority may grant a permit for such longer term. A successor in interest to a permittee who applies for a new permit within thirty days of succeeding to such interest and who is able to obtain the bond coverage of the original permittee may continue surface coal mining and reclamation operations according to the approved mining and reclamation plan of the original permittee until such successor's application is granted or denied.

(c) Termination

A permit shall terminate if the permittee has not commenced the surface coal mining operations covered by such permit within three years of the issuance of the permit: *Provided*, That the regulatory authority may grant reasonable extensions of time upon a showing that such extensions are necessary by reason of litigation precluding such commencement or threatening substantial economic loss to the permittee, or by reason of conditions beyond the control and without the fault or negligence of the permittee: *Provided further*, That in the case of a coal lease issued under the Federal Mineral Leasing Act, as amended [30 U.S.C.A. § 181 et seq.], extensions of time may not extend beyond the period allowed for diligent development in accordance with section 7 of that Act [30 U.S.C.A. § 207]: *Provided further*, That with respect to coal to be mined for use in a synthetic fuel facility or specific major electric generating facility, the permittee shall be deemed to have commenced surface mining operations at such time as the construction of the synthetic fuel or generating facility is initiated.

(d) Renewal

(1) Any valid permit issued pursuant to this chapter shall carry with it the right of successive renewal upon expiration with respect to areas within the boundaries of the existing permit. The holders of the permit may apply for renewal and such renewal shall be issued (provided that on application for renewal the burden shall be on the opponents of renewal), subsequent to fulfillment of the public notice requirements of sections 1263 and 1264 of this title unless it is established that and written findings by the regulatory authority are made that—

(A) the terms and conditions of the existing permit are not being satisfactorily met;

(B) the present surface coal mining and reclamation operation is not in compliance with the environmental protection standards of this chapter and the approved State plan or Federal program pursuant to this chapter; or

(C) the renewal requested substantially jeopardizes the operator's continuing responsibility on existing permit areas;

(D) the operator has not provided evidence that the performance bond in effect for said operation will continue in full force and effect for any renewal requested in such application as well as any additional bond the regulatory authority might require pursuant to section 1259 of this title; or

(E) any additional revised or updated information required by the regulatory authority has not been provided. Prior to the approval of any renewal of permit the regulatory authority shall provide notice to the appropriate public authorities.

(2) If an application for renewal of a valid permit includes a proposal to extend the mining operation beyond the boundaries authorized in the existing permit, the portion of the application for renewal of a valid permit which addresses any new land areas shall be subject to the full standards applicable to new applications under this chapter: *Provided, however*, That if the surface coal mining operations authorized by a permit issued pursuant to this chapter were not subject to the standards contained in section 1260(b)(5)(A) and (B) of this title by reason of complying with the proviso of section 1260(b)(5) of this title, then the portion of the application for renewal of the permit which addresses any new land areas previously identified in the reclamation plan submitted pursuant to section 1258 of this title shall not be subject to the standards contained in section 1260(b)(5)(A) and (B) of this title.

(3) Any permit renewal shall be for a term not to exceed the period of the original permit established by this chapter. Application for permit renewal shall be made at least one hundred and twenty days prior to the expiration of the valid permit.

(Aug. 3, 1977, Pub.L. 95–87, Title V, § 506, 91 Stat. 473.)

CODE OF FEDERAL REGULATIONS

Approval or denial of State programs, see 30 CFR 732.1 et seq.
Permit requirements for special categories of mining, see 30 CFR 785.1 et seq.
Secretary of Interior, hearings and appeals procedure, see 43 CFR 4.1 et seq.
Special program performance standards, mountaintop removal, see 30 CFR 824.1 et seq.

§ 1257. Application requirements [SMCRA § 507]

(a) Fee

Each application for a surface coal mining and reclamation permit pursuant to an approved State program or a Federal program under the provisions of this chapter shall be accompanied by a fee as determined by the regulatory authority. Such fee may be less than but shall not exceed the actual or anticipated cost of reviewing, administering, and enforcing such permit issued pursuant to a State or Federal program. The regulatory authority may develop procedures so as to enable the cost of the fee to be paid over the term of the permit.

(b) Submittal; contents

The permit application shall be submitted in a manner satisfactory to the regulatory authority and shall contain, among other things—

(1) the names and addresses of (A) the permit applicant; (B) every legal owner of record of the property (surface and mineral), to be mined; (C) the holders of record of any leasehold interest in the property; (D) any purchaser of record of the property under a real estate contract; and (E) the operator if he is a person different from the applicant; and (F) if any of these are business entities other than a single proprietor, the names and addresses of the principals, officers, and resident agent;

(2) the names and addresses of the owners of record of all surface and subsurface areas adjacent to any part of the permit area;

(3) a statement of any current or previous surface coal mining permits in the United States held by the applicant and the permit identification and each pending application;

(4) if the applicant is a partnership, corporation, association, or other business entity, the following where applicable: the names and addresses of every officer, partner, director, or person performing a function similar to a director, of the applicant, together with the name and address of any person owning, of record 10 per centum or more of any class of voting stock of the applicant and a list of all names under which the applicant, partner, or principal shareholder previously operated a surface mining operation within the United States within the five-year period preceding the date of submission of the application;

(5) a statement of whether the applicant, any subsidiary, affiliate, or persons controlled by or under common control with the applicant, has ever held a Federal or State mining permit which in the five-year period prior to the date of submission of the application has been suspended or revoked or has had a mining bond or similar security deposited in lieu of bond forfeited and, if so, a brief explanation of the facts involved;

(6) a copy of the applicant's advertisement to be published in a newspaper of general circulation in the locality of the proposed site at least once a week for four successive weeks, and which includes the ownership, a description of the exact location and boundaries of the proposed site sufficient so that the proposed operation is readily locatable by local residents, and the location of where the application is available for public inspection;

(7) a description of the type and method of coal mining operation that exists or is proposed, the engineering techniques proposed or used, and the equipment used or proposed to be used;

(8) the anticipated or actual starting and termination dates of each phase of the mining operation and number of acres of land to be affected;

(9) the applicant shall file with the regulatory authority on an accurate map or plan, to an appropriate scale, clearly showing the land to be affected as of the date of the application, the area of land within the permit area upon which the applicant has the legal right to enter and commence surface mining operations and shall provide to the regulatory authority a statement of those documents upon which the applicant bases his legal right to enter and commence surface mining operations on the area affected, and whether that right is the subject of pending court litigation: *Provided*, That nothing in this chapter shall be construed as vesting in the regulatory authority the jurisdiction to adjudicate property title disputes.[1]

(10) the name of the watershed and location of the surface stream or tributary into which surface and pit drainage will be discharged;

(11) a determination of the probable hydrologic consequences of the mining and reclamation operations, both on and off the mine site, with respect to the hydrologic regime, quantity and quality of water in surface and ground water systems including the dissolved and suspended solids under seasonal flow conditions and the collection of sufficient data for the mine site and surrounding areas so that an assessment can be made by the regulatory authority of the probable cumulative impacts of all anticipated mining in the area upon the hydrology of the area and particularly upon water availability: *Provided, however*, That this determination shall not be required until such time as hydrologic information on the general area prior to mining is made available from an appropriate Federal or State agency: *Provided further*, That the permit shall not be approved until such information is available and is incorporated into the application;

(12) when requested by the regulatory authority, the climatological factors that are peculiar to the locality of the land to be affected, including the average seasonal precipitation, the average direction and velocity of prevailing winds, and the seasonal temperature ranges;

(13) accurate maps to an appropriate scale clearly showing (A) the land to be affected as of the date of application and (B) all types of information set forth on topographical maps of the United States Geological Survey of a scale of 1:24,000 or 1:25,000 or larger, including all manmade features and significant known archeological sites existing on the date of application. Such a map or plan shall among other things specified by the regulatory authority show all boundaries of the land to be affected, the boundary lines and names of present owners of record of all surface areas abutting the permit area, and the location of all buildings within one thousand feet of the permit area;

(14) cross-section maps or plans of the land to be affected including the actual area to be mined, prepared by or under the direction of and certified by a qualified registered professional engineer, or professional geologist with assistance from experts in related fields such as land surveying and landscape architecture, showing pertinent elevation and location of test borings or core samplings and depicting the following information: the nature and

depth of the various strata of overburden; the location of subsurface water, if encountered, and its quality; the nature and thickness of any coal or rider seam above the coal seam to be mined; the nature of the stratum immediately beneath the coal seam to be mined; all mineral crop lines and the strike and dip of the coal to be mined, within the area of land to be affected; existing or previous surface mining limits; the location and extent of known workings of any underground mines, including mine openings to the surface; the location of aquifers; the estimated elevation of the water table; the location of spoil, waste, or refuse areas and topsoil preservation areas; the location of all impoundments for waste or erosion control; any settling or water treatment facility; constructed or natural drainways and the location of any discharges to any surface body of water on the area of land to be affected or adjacent thereto; and profiles at appropriate cross sections of the anticipated final surface configuration that will be achieved pursuant to the operator's proposed reclamation plan;

(15) a statement of the result of test borings or core samplings from the permit area, including logs of the drill holes; the thickness of the coal seam found, an analysis of the chemical properties of such coal; the sulfur content of any coal seam; chemical analysis of potentially acid or toxic forming sections of the overburden; and chemical analysis of the stratum lying immediately underneath the coal to be mined except that the provisions of this paragraph (15) may be waived by the regulatory authority with respect to the specific application by a written determination that such requirements are unnecessary;

(16) for those lands in the permit application which a reconnaissance inspection suggests may be prime farm lands, a soil survey shall be made or obtained according to standards established by the Secretary of Agriculture in order to confirm the exact location of such prime farm lands, if any; and

(17) information pertaining to coal seams, test borings, core samplings, or soil samples as required by this section shall be made available to any person with an interest which is or may be adversely affected: *Provided*, That information which pertains only to the analysis of the chemical and physical properties of the coal (excepting information regarding such mineral or elemental content which is potentially toxic in the environment) shall be kept confidential and not made a matter of public record.

(c) Assistance to small coal operators

(1) If the regulatory authority finds that the probable total annual production at all locations of a coal surface mining operator will not exceed 300,000 tons, the cost of the following activities, which shall be performed by a qualified public or private laboratory or such other public or private qualified entity designated by the regulatory authority, shall be assumed by the regulatory authority upon the written request of the operator in connection with a permit application:

(A) The determination of probable hydrologic consequences required by subsection (b)(11) of this section, including the engineering analyses and designs necessary for the determination.

(B) The development of cross-section maps and plans required by subsection (b)(14) of this section.

(C) The geologic drilling and statement of results of test borings and core samplings required by subsection (b)(15) of this section.

(D) The collection of archaeological information required by subsection (b)(13) of this section and any other archaeological and historical information required by the regulatory authority, and the preparation of plans necessitated thereby.

(E) Pre-blast surveys required by section 1265(b)(15)(E) of this title.

(F) The collection of site-specific resource information and production of protection and enhancement plans for fish and wildlife habitats and other environmental values required by the regulatory authority under this chapter.

(2) The Secretary shall provide or assume the cost of training coal operators that meet the qualifications stated in paragraph (1) concerning the preparation of permit applications and compliance with the regulatory program, and shall ensure that qualified coal operators are aware of the assistance available under this subsection.

(d) Reclamation plan

Each applicant for a permit shall be required to submit to the regulatory authority as part of the permit application a reclamation plan which shall meet the requirements of this chapter.

(e) Public inspection

Each applicant for a surface coal mining and reclamation permit shall file a copy of his application for public inspection with the recorder at the courthouse of the county or an appropriate public office approved by the regulatory authority where the mining is proposed to occur, except for that information pertaining to the coal seam itself.

(f) Insurance certificate

Each applicant for a permit shall be required to submit to the regulatory authority as part of the permit application a certificate issued by an insurance company authorized to do business in the United States certifying that the applicant has a public liability insurance policy in force for the surface mining and reclamation operations for which such permit is sought, or evidence that the applicant has satisfied other State or Federal self-insurance requirements. Such policy shall provide for personal injury and property damage protection in an amount adequate to compensate any persons damaged as a result of surface coal mining and reclamation operations including use of explosives and entitled to compensation under the applicable provisions of State law. Such policy shall be maintained in full force and effect during the terms of the permit or any renewal, including the length of all reclamation operations.

(g) Blasting plan

Each applicant for a surface coal mining and reclamation permit shall submit to the regulatory authority as part of the permit application a blasting plan which shall outline the procedures and standards by which the operator will meet the provisions of section 1265(b)(15) of this title.

(h) Reimbursement of costs

A coal operator that has received assistance pursuant to subsection (c)(1) or (2) of this section shall reimburse the regulatory authority for the cost of the services rendered if the program administrator finds that the operator's actual and attributed annual production of coal for all locations exceeds 300,000 tons during the 12 months immediately following the date on which the operator is issued the surface coal mining and reclamation permit.

(Aug. 3, 1977, Pub.L. 95–87, Title V, § 507, 91 Stat. 474; Pub.L. 101–508, Title VI, § 6011, Nov. 5, 1990, 104 Stat. 1388–297; Oct. 24, 1992, Pub.L. 102–486, Title XXV, § 2513, 106 Stat. 3112.)

[1] So in original. The period probably should be a semicolon.

References in Text

This chapter, referred to in subsecs. (a), (b)(9), (c)(1)(F), and (d), was in the original "this Act", meaning Pub.L. 95–87, Aug. 3, 1977, 91 Stat. 445, as amended, which enacted this chapter and amended section 1114 of Title 18, Crimes and Criminal Procedure. For complete classification of this Act to the Code, see Short Title note set out under section 1201 of this title and Tables.

Effective Date of 1990 Amendment

Amendment by Pub.L. 101–508 effective Oct. 1, 1991, see section 6014 of Pub.L. 101–508, set out as a note under section 1231 of this title.

Savings Provisions

Nothing in Subtitle A (section 6001 et seq.) of Title VI of Pub.L. 101–508, construed to affect the certifications made by the States of Wyoming, Montana, and Louisiana to the Secretary of the Interior prior to Nov. 5, 1990, that each such State has completed the reclamation of eligible abandoned coal mine lands, see section 6013 of Pub.L. 101–508, set out as a note under section 1231 of this title.

CROSS REFERENCES

Approval or denial of permit, see section 1260 of this title.
Authorization of appropriations for implementation of this section, see section 1302 of this title.
Environmental protection performance standards, permit requirement, see section 1265 of this title.
Reclamation plan requirements, see section 1258 of this title.
Soil surveys made pursuant to this section, use in requirements for release of performance bonds or deposits, see section 1269 of this title.
Surface coal mining operations on Indian lands, compliance with requirements as stringent as those of this section, see section 1300 of this title.
Use of reclamation fees for test borings and core samplings taken pursuant to this section, see section 1231 of this title.

CODE OF FEDERAL REGULATIONS

Approval or denial of State programs, see 30 CFR 732.1 et seq.
Federal inspections and monitoring, see 30 CFR 842.1 et seq.
Performance standards—
Surface mining, see 30 CFR 816.1 et seq.
Underground mining, see 30 CFR 817.1 et seq.
Permit requirements for special categories of mining, see 30 CFR 785.1 et seq.
Surface mining permit applications, see 30 CFR 779.1 et seq.

LAW REVIEW COMMENTARIES

Encouraging safety through insurance-based incentives: financial responsibility for hazardous wastes. Jeffrey Kehne, 96 Yale L.J. 403 (1986).

§ 1258. Reclamation plan requirements [SMCRA § 508]

(a) Each reclamation plan submitted as part of a permit application pursuant to any approved State program or a Federal program under the provisions of this chapter shall include, in the degree of detail necessary to demonstrate that reclamation required by the State or Federal program can be accomplished, a statement of:

(1) the identification of the lands subject to surface coal mining operations over the estimated life of those operations and the size, sequence, and timing of the subareas for which it is anticipated that individual permits for mining will be sought;

(2) the condition of the land to be covered by the permit prior to any mining including:

(A) the uses existing at the time of the application, and if the land has a history of previous mining, the uses which preceded any mining; and

(B) the capability of the land prior to any mining to support a variety of uses giving consideration to soil and foundation characteristics, topography, and vegetative cover, and, if applicable, a soil survey prepared pursuant to section 1257(b)(16) of this title; and

(C) the productivity of the land prior to mining, including appropriate classification as prime farm lands, as well as the average yield of food, fiber, forage, or wood products from such lands obtained under high levels of management;

(3) the use which is proposed to be made of the land following reclamation, including a discussion of the utility and capacity of the reclaimed land to support a variety of alternative uses and the relationship of such use to existing land use policies and plans, and the comments of any owner of the surface, State and local governments or agencies thereof which would have to initiate, implement, approve or authorize the proposed use of the land following reclamation;

(4) a detailed description of how the proposed postmining land use is to be achieved and the necessary support activities which may be needed to achieve the proposed land use;

(5) the engineering techniques proposed to be used in mining and reclamation and a description of the major equipment; a plan for the control of surface water drainage and of water accumulation; a plan, where appropriate, for backfilling, soil stabilization, and compacting, grading, and appropriate revegetation; a plan for soil reconstruction, replacement, and stabilization, pursuant to the performance standards in section 1265(b)(7)(A), (B), (C), and (D) of this title, for those food, forage, and forest lands identified in section 1265(b)(7) of this title; an estimate of the cost per acre of the reclamation, including a statement as to how the permittee plans to comply with each of the requirements set out in section 1265 of this title;

(6) the consideration which has been given to maximize the utilization and conservation of the solid fuel resource being recovered so that reaffecting the land in the future can be minimized;

(7) a detailed estimated timetable for the accomplishment of each major step in the reclamation plan;

(8) the consideration which has been given to making the surface mining and reclamation operations consistent with surface owner plans, and applicable State and local land use plans and programs;

(9) the steps to be taken to comply with applicable air and water quality laws and regulations and any applicable health and safety standards;

(10) the consideration which has been given to developing the reclamation plan in a manner consistent with local physical environmental, and climatological conditions;

(11) all lands, interests in lands, or options on such interests held by the applicant or pending bids on interests in lands by the applicant, which lands are contiguous to the area to be covered by the permit;

(12) the results of test boring which the applicant has made at the area to be covered by the permit, or other equivalent information and data in a form satisfactory to the regulatory authority, including the location of subsurface water, and an analysis of the chemical properties including acid forming properties of the mineral and overburden: *Provided*, That information which pertains only to the analysis of the chemical and physical properties of the coal (excepting information regarding such mineral or elemental contents which is potentially toxic in the environment) shall be kept confidential and not made a matter of public record;

(13) a detailed description of the measures to be taken during the mining and reclamation process to assure the protection of:

(A) the quality of surface and ground water systems, both on- and off-site, from adverse effects of the mining and reclamation process;

(B) the rights of present users to such water; and

(C) the quantity of surface and ground water systems, both on- and off-site, from adverse effects of the mining and reclamation process or to provide alternative sources of water where such protection of quantity cannot be assured;

(14) such other requirements as the regulatory authority shall prescribe by regulations.

(b) Any information required by this section which is not on public file pursuant to State law shall be held in confidence by the regulatory authority.

(Aug. 3, 1977, Pub.L. 95–87, Title V, § 508, 91 Stat. 478.)

CROSS REFERENCES

Permits, see section 1256 of this title.
Reclamation plan defined, see section 1291 of this title.
Surface coal mining operations on Indian lands, compliance with requirements as stringent as those of this section, see section 1300 of this title.

CODE OF FEDERAL REGULATIONS

Approval or denial of State programs, see 30 CFR 732.1 et seq.
Performance standards—
Surface mining, see 30 CFR 816.1 et seq.
Underground mining, see 30 CFR 817.1 et seq.
Permit requirements for special categories of mining, see 30 CFR 785.1 et seq.
Special program performance standards, mountaintop removal, see 30 CFR 824.1 et seq.

§ 1259. Performance bonds [SMCRA § 509]

(a) Filing with regulatory authority; scope; number and amount

After a surface coal mining and reclamation permit application has been approved but before such a permit is issued, the applicant shall file with the regulatory authority, on a form prescribed and furnished by the regulatory authority, a bond for performance payable, as appropriate, to the United States or to the

State, and conditional upon faithful performance of all the requirements of this chapter and the permit. The bond shall cover that area of land within the permit area upon which the operator will initiate and conduct surface coal mining and reclamation operations within the initial term of the permit. As succeeding increments of surface coal mining and reclamation operations are to be initiated and conducted within the permit area, the permittee shall file with the regulatory authority an additional bond or bonds to cover such increments in accordance with this section. The amount of the bond required for each bonded area shall depend upon the reclamation requirements of the approved permit; shall reflect the probable difficulty of reclamation giving consideration to such factors as topography, geology of the site, hydrology, and revegetation potential, and shall be determined by the regulatory authority. The amount of the bond shall be sufficient to assure the completion of the reclamation plan if the work had to be performed by the regulatory authority in the event of forfeiture and in no case shall the bond for the entire area under one permit be less than $10,000.

(b) Liability period; execution

Liability under the bond shall be for the duration of the surface coal mining and reclamation operation and for a period coincident with operator's responsibility for revegetation requirements in section 1265 of this title. The bond shall be executed by the operator and a corporate surety licensed to do business in the State where such operation is located, except that the operator may elect to deposit cash, negotiable bonds of the United States Government or such State, or negotiable certificates of deposit of any bank organized or transacting business in the United States. The cash deposit or market value of such securities shall be equal to or greater than the amount of the bond required for the bonded area.

(c) Bond of applicant without separate surety; alternate system

The regulatory authority may accept the bond of the applicant itself without separate surety when the applicant demonstrates to the satisfaction of the regulatory authority the existence of a suitable agent to receive service of process and a history of financial solvency and continuous operation sufficient for authorization to self-insure or bond such amount or in lieu of the establishment of a bonding program, as set forth in this section, the Secretary may approve as part of a State or Federal program an alternative system that will achieve the objectives and purposes of the bonding program pursuant to this section.

(d) Deposit of cash or securities

Cash or securities so deposited shall be deposited upon the same terms as the terms upon which surety bonds may be deposited. Such securities shall be security for the repayment of such negotiable certificate of deposit.

(e) Adjustments

The amount of the bond or deposit required and the terms of each acceptance of the applicant's bond shall be adjusted by the regulatory authority from time to time as affected land acreages are increased or decreased or where the cost of future reclamation changes.

(Aug. 3, 1977, Pub.L. 95–87, Title V, § 509, 91 Stat. 479.)

CROSS REFERENCES

Applicability of this section to anthracite coal mines, see section 1279 of this title.
Bond to secure payment of damages to surface estate held by Federal permittees or lessees, see section 1305 of this title.
Continuation of performance bonds on renewal of permits, see section 1256 of this title.
Environmental protection performance standards, see section 1265 of this title.
Permit area defined, see section 1291 of this title.
Surface coal mining operations on Indian lands, compliance with requirements as stringent as those of this section, see section 1300 of this title.

CODE OF FEDERAL REGULATIONS

Approval or denial of State programs, see 30 CFR 732.1 et seq.
Permit requirements for special categories of mining, see 30 CFR 785.1 et seq.

§ 1260. Permit approval or denial [SMCRA § 510]

(a) Basis for decision; notification of applicant and local government officials; burden of proof

Upon the basis of a complete mining application and reclamation plan or a revision or renewal thereof, as required by this chapter and pursuant to an approved State program or Federal program under the provisions of this chapter, including public notification and an opportunity for a public hearing as required by section 1263 of this title, the regulatory authority shall grant, require modification of, or deny the application for a permit in a reasonable time set by the regulatory authority and notify the applicant in writing. The applicant for a permit, or revision of a permit, shall have the burden of establishing that his application is in compliance with all the requirements of the applicable State or Federal program. Within ten days after the granting of a permit, the regulatory authority shall notify the local governmental officials in the local political subdivision in which the area of land to be affected is located that a permit has been issued and shall describe the location of the land.

(b) Requirements for approval

No permit or revision application shall be approved unless the application affirmatively demonstrates and the regulatory authority finds in writing on the basis of the information set forth in the application or from information otherwise available which will be documented in the approval, and made available to the applicant, that—

(1) the permit application is accurate and complete and that all the requirements of this chapter and the State or Federal program have been complied with;

(2) the applicant has demonstrated that reclamation as required by this chapter and the State or Federal program can be accomplished under the reclamation plan contained in the permit application;

(3) the assessment of the probable cumulative impact of all anticipated mining in the area on the hydrologic balance specified in section 1257(b) of this title has been made by the regulatory authority and the proposed operation thereof has been designed to prevent material damage to hydrologic balance outside permit area;

(4) the area proposed to be mined is not included within an area designated unsuitable for surface coal mining pursuant to section 1272 of this title or is not within an area under study for such designation in an administrative proceeding commenced pursuant to section 1272(a)(4)(D) or section 1272(c) of this title (unless in such an area as to which an administrative proceeding has commenced pursuant to section 1272(a)(4)(D) of this title, the operator making the permit application demonstrates that, prior to January 1, 1977, he has made substantial legal and financial commitments in relation to the operation for which he is applying for a permit);

(5) the proposed surface coal mining operation, if located west of the one hundredth meridian west longitude, would—

(A) not interrupt, discontinue, or preclude farming on alluvial valley floors that are irrigated or naturally subirrigated, but, excluding undeveloped range lands which are not significant to farming on said alluvial valley floors and those lands as to which the regulatory authority finds that if the farming that will be interrupted, discontinued, or precluded is of such small acreage as to be of negligible impact on the farm's agricultural production, or

(B) not materially damage the quantity or quality of water in surface or underground water systems that supply these valley floors in (A) of subsection (b)(5) of this section:

Provided, That this paragraph (5) shall not affect those surface coal mining operations which in the year preceding August 3, 1977, (I) produced coal in commercial quantities, and were located within or adjacent to alluvial valley floors or (II) had obtained specific permit approval by the State regulatory authority to conduct surface coal mining operations within said alluvial valley floors.

With respect to such surface mining operations which would have been within the purview of the foregoing proviso but for the fact that no coal was so produced in commercial quantities and no such specific permit approval was so received, the Secretary, if he determines that substantial financial and legal commitments were made by an operator prior to January 1, 1977, in connection with any such operation, is authorized, in accordance with such regulations as the Secretary may prescribe, to enter into an agreement with that operator pursuant to which the Secretary may, notwithstanding any other provision of law, lease other Federal coal deposits to such operator in exchange for the relinquishment by such operator of his Federal lease covering coal deposits involving such mining operations, or pursuant to section 1716 of Title 43, convey to the fee holder of any such coal deposits involving such mining operations the fee title to other available Federal coal deposits in exchange for the fee title to such deposits so involving such mining operations. It is the policy of the Congress that the Secretary shall develop and carry out a coal exchange program to acquire private fee coal precluded from being mined by the restrictions of this paragraph (5) in exchange for Federal coal which is not so precluded. Such exchanges shall be made under section 1716 of Title 43;

(6) in cases where the private mineral estate has been severed from the private surface estate, the applicant has submitted to the regulatory authority—

(A) the written consent of the surface owner to the extraction of coal by surface mining methods; or

(B) a conveyance that expressly grants or reserves the right to extract the coal by surface mining methods; or

(C) if the conveyance does not expressly grant the right to extract coal by surface mining methods, the surface-subsurface legal relationship shall be determined in accordance with State law: *Provided*, That nothing in this chapter shall be construed to authorize the regulatory authority to adjudicate property rights disputes.

(c) Schedule of violations

The applicant shall file with his permit application a schedule listing any and all notices of violations of this chapter and any law, rule, or regulation of the United States, or of any department or agency in the United States pertaining to air or water environmental protection incurred by the applicant in connection with any surface coal mining operation during the three-year period prior to the date of application. The schedule shall also indicate the final resolution of any such notice of violation. Where the schedule or other information available to the regulatory authority indicates that any surface coal mining operation owned or controlled by the applicant is currently in violation of this chapter or such other laws referred to [1] this subsection, the permit shall not be issued until the applicant submits proof that such violation has been corrected or is in the process of being corrected to the satisfaction of the regulatory authority, department, or agency which has jurisdiction over such violation and no permit shall be issued to an applicant after a finding by the regulatory authority, after opportunity for hearing, that the applicant, or the operator specified in the application, controls or has controlled mining operations with a demonstrated pattern of willful violations of this chapter of such nature and duration with such resulting irreparable damage to the environment as to indicate an intent not to comply with the provisions of this chapter.

(d) Prime farmland mining permit

(1) In addition to finding the application in compliance with subsection (b) of this section, if the area proposed to be mined contains prime farmland pursuant to section 1257(b)(16) of this title, the regulatory authority shall, after consultation with the Secretary of Agriculture, and pursuant to regulations issued hereunder by the Secretary of [2] Interior with the concurrence of the Secretary of Agriculture, grant a permit to mine on prime farmland if the regulatory authority finds in writing that the operator has the technological capability to restore such mined area, within a reasonable time, to equivalent or higher levels of yield as non-mined prime farmland in the surrounding area under equivalent levels of management and can meet the soil reconstruction standards in section 1265(b)(7) of this title. Except for compliance with subsection (b) of this section, the requirements of this paragraph (1) shall apply to all permits issued after August 3, 1977.

(2) Nothing in this subsection shall apply to any permit issued prior to August 3, 1977, or to any revisions or renewals thereof, or to any existing surface mining operations for which a permit was issued prior to August 3, 1977.

(e) Modification of prohibition

After October 24, 1992, the prohibition of subsection (c) of this section shall not apply to a permit application due to any violation resulting from an unanticipated event or condition at a surface coal mining operation on lands eligible for remining under a permit held by the person making such application. As used in this subsection, the term "violation" has the same meaning as such term has under subsection (c) of this section. The authority of this subsection and section 1265(b)(20)(B) of this title shall terminate on September 30, 2004.

(Aug. 3, 1977, Pub.L. 95–87, Title V, § 510, 91 Stat. 480; Oct. 24, 1992, Pub.L. 102–486, Title XXV, § 2503(a), 106 Stat. 3102.)

[1] So in original. Probably should be followed by "in".

[2] So in original. Probably should be "of the".

CROSS REFERENCES

Permits generally, see section 1256 of this title.
Public notice and public hearings for permits, see section 1263 of this title.
Surface coal mining operations on Indian lands, compliance with requirements as stringent as those of this section, see section 1300 of this title.

CODE OF FEDERAL REGULATIONS

Approval or denial of State programs, see 30 CFR 732.1 et seq.
Areas unsuitable for mining, see 30 CFR Chap. VII, Subchap. F.
Federal enforcement, see 30 CFR 843.1 et seq.
Information collection, see 30 CFR 716.10.
Permit requirements for special categories of mining, see 30 CFR 785.1 et seq.
Prime farmland performance standards, initial program regulations—
Generally, see 30 CFR 716.7.
Secretary of Interior, hearings and appeals procedure, see 43 CFR 4.1 et seq.
Special program performance standards—
In situ processing, see 30 CFR 828.1 et seq.
Mountaintop removal, see 30 CFR 824.1 et seq.

United States Supreme Court

Prime farmlands provision of this section, validity, see Hodel v. Indiana, 1981, 101 S.Ct. 2376, 452 U.S. 314, 69 L.Ed.2d 40, concurring opinion 101 S.Ct. 2389, 452 U.S. 264, 69 L.Ed.2d 1.

§ 1261. Revision of permits [SMCRA § 511]

(a) Application and revised reclamation plan; requirements; extensions to area covered

(1) During the term of the permit the permittee may submit an application for a revision of the permit, together with a revised reclamation plan, to the regulatory authority.

(2) An application for a revision of a permit shall not be approved unless the regulatory authority finds that reclamation as required by this chapter and the State or Federal program can be accomplished under the revised reclamation plan. The revision shall be approved or disapproved within a period of time established by the State or Federal program. The

regulatory authority shall establish guidelines for a determination of the scale or extent of a revision request for which all permit application information requirements and procedures, including notice and hearings, shall apply: *Provided,* That any revisions which propose significant alterations in the reclamation plan shall, at a minimum, be subject to notice and hearing requirements.

(3) Any extensions to the area covered by the permit except incidental boundary revisions must be made by application for another permit.

(b) Transfer, assignment, or sale of rights under permit

No transfer, assignment, or sale of the rights granted under any permit issued pursuant to this chapter shall be made without the written approval of the regulatory authority.

(c) Review of outstanding permits

The regulatory authority shall within a time limit prescribed in regulations promulgated by the regulatory authority, review outstanding permits and may require reasonable revision or modification of the permit provisions during the term of such permit: *Provided,* That such revision or modification shall be based upon a written finding and subject to notice and hearing requirements established by the State or Federal program.

(Aug. 3, 1977, Pub.L. 95–87, Title V, § 511, 91 Stat. 483.)

CROSS REFERENCES

Deduction for expenses incurred for reclamation or closing activities conducted under reclamation plan submitted pursuant to this section, see section 468 of Title 26, Internal Revenue Code.

Public notice and public hearings for permits, see section 1263 of this title.

Reclamation plan requirements, see section 1258 of this title.

CODE OF FEDERAL REGULATIONS

Approval or denial of State programs, see 30 CFR 732.1 et seq.

Permit requirements for special categories of mining, see 30 CFR 785.1 et seq.

Secretary of Interior, hearings and appeals procedure, see 43 CFR 4.1 et seq.

§ 1262. Coal exploration permits [SMCRA § 512]

(a) Regulations; contents

Each State or Federal program shall include a requirement that coal exploration operations which substantially disturb the natural land surface be conducted in accordance with exploration regulations issued by the regulatory authority. Such regulations shall include, at a minimum (1) the requirement that prior to conducting any exploration under this section, any person must file with the regulatory authority notice of intention to explore and such notice shall include a description of the exploration area and the period of supposed exploration and (2) provisions for reclamation in accordance with the performance standards in section 1265 of this title of all lands disturbed in exploration, including excavations, roads, drill holes, and the removal of necessary facilities and equipment.

(b) Confidential information

Information submitted to the regulatory authority pursuant to this subsection as confidential concerning trade secrets or privileged commercial or financial information which relates to the competitive rights of the person or entity intended to explore the described area shall not be available for public examination.

(c) Penalties

Any person who conducts any coal exploration activities which substantially disturb the natural land surface in violation of this section or regulations issued pursuant thereto shall be subject to the provisions of section 1268 of this title.

(d) Limitation on removal of coal

No operator shall remove more than two hundred and fifty tons of coal pursuant to an exploration permit without the specific written approval of the regulatory authority.

(e) Law governing exploration of Federal lands

Coal exploration on Federal lands shall be governed by section 4 of the Federal Coal Leasing Amendments Act of 1975 (90 Stat. 1085).

(Aug. 3, 1977, Pub.L. 95–87, Title V, § 512, 91 Stat. 483.)

CROSS REFERENCES

Surface coal mining operations defined to exclude coal explorations, see section 1291 of this title.

CODE OF FEDERAL REGULATIONS

Approval or denial of State programs, see 30 CFR 732.1 et seq.

Areas unsuitable for mining, see 30 CFR Chap. VII, Subchap. F.

Inspection and enforcement procedure, see 30 CFR Chap. VII, Subchap. L.

Performance standards, permanent program, general provisions, see 30 CFR 810.1 et seq.

Secretary of Interior, general scope of authority and responsibility, see 30 CFR 700.1 et seq.

§ 1263. Public notice and public hearings [SMCRA § 513]

(a) Submittal of advertisement to regulatory authority; notification of local governmental bodies

At the time of submission of an application for a surface coal mining and reclamation permit, or revision of an existing permit, pursuant to the provisions of this chapter or an approved State program, the applicant shall submit to the regulatory authority a copy of his advertisement of the ownership, precise location, and boundaries of the land to be affected. At the time of submission such advertisement shall be placed by the applicant in a local newspaper of general circulation in the locality of the proposed surface mine at least once a week for four consecutive weeks. The regulatory authority shall notify various local governmental bodies, planning agencies, and sewage and water treatment authorities, of[1] water companies in the locality in which the proposed surface mining will take place, notifying them of the operator's intention to surface mine a particularly described tract of land and indicating the application's permit number and where a copy of the proposed mining and reclamation plan may be inspected. These local bodies, agencies, authorities, or companies may submit written comments within a reasonable period established by the regulatory authority on the mining applications with respect to the effect of the proposed operation on the environment which are within their area of responsibility. Such comments shall immediately be transmitted to the applicant by the regulatory authority and shall be made available to the public at the same locations as are the mining applications.

(b) Objections to permit applications; informal conference; record

Any person having an interest which is or may be adversely affected or the officer or head of any Federal, State, or local governmental agency or authority shall have the right to file written objections to the proposed initial or revised application for a permit for surface coal mining and reclamation operation with the regulatory authority within thirty days after the last publication of the above notice. Such objections shall immediately be transmitted to the applicant by the regulatory authority and shall be made available to the public. If written objections are filed and an informal conference requested, the regulatory authority shall then hold an informal conference in the locality of the proposed mining, if requested within a reasonable time of the receipt of such objections or request. The date, time and location of such informal conference shall be advertised by the regulatory authority in a newspaper of general circulation in the locality at least two weeks prior to the scheduled conference date. The regulatory authority may arrange with the applicant upon request by any party to the administrative proceeding access to the proposed mining area for the purpose of gathering information relevant to the proceeding. An electronic or stenographic record shall be made of the conference proceeding, unless waived by all parties. Such record shall be maintained and shall be accessible to the parties until final release of the applicant's performance bond. In the event all parties requesting the informal conference stipulate agreement prior to the requested informal conference and withdraw their request, such informal conference need not be held.

(c) Prior Federal coal lease hearing as evidence

Where the lands included in an application for a permit are the subject of a Federal coal lease in connection with which hearings were held and determinations were made under section 201(a)(3)(A), (B) and (C) of this title, such hearings shall be deemed as to the matters covered to satisfy the requirements of this section and section 1264 of this title and such determinations shall be deemed to be a part of the record and conclusive for purposes of sections 1260, 1264 of this title and this section.

(Aug. 3, 1977, Pub.L. 95–87, Title V, § 513, 91 Stat. 484.)

[1] So in original. Probably should be "or".

CROSS REFERENCES

Decisions of regulatory authority and appeals, see section 1264 of this title.
Permits—
Generally, see section 1256 of this title.
Approval or denial, see section 1260 of this title.
Release of performance bonds or deposits, see section 1269 of this title.

CODE OF FEDERAL REGULATIONS

Approval or denial of State programs, see 30 CFR 732.1 et seq.
Permit requirements for special categories of mining, see 30 CFR 785.1 et seq.

§ 1264. Decisions of regulatory authority and appeals [SMCRA § 514]

(a) Issuance of findings within 60 days after informal conference

If an informal conference has been held pursuant to section 1263(b) of this title, the regulatory authority shall issue and furnish the applicant for a permit and persons who are parties to the administrative proceedings with the written finding of the regulatory authority, granting or denying the permit in whole or in part and stating the reasons therefor, within the sixty days of said hearings.

(b) Decision without informal conference; notification within a reasonable time

If there has been no informal conference held pursuant to section 1263(b) of this title, the regulatory authority shall notify the applicant for a permit within a reasonable time as determined by the regulatory authority and set forth in regulations, taking into account the time needed for proper investigation of the site, the complexity of the permit application, and whether or not written objection to the application has been filed, whether the application has been approved or disapproved in whole or in part.

(c) Request for rehearing on reasons for final determination; time; issuance of decision

If the application is approved, the permit shall be issued. If the application is disapproved, specific reasons therefor must be set forth in the notification. Within thirty days after the applicant is notified of the final decision of the regulatory authority on the permit application, the applicant or any person with an interest which is or may be adversely affected may request a hearing on the reasons for the final determination. The regulatory authority shall hold a hearing within thirty days of such request and provide notification to all interested parties at the time that the applicant is so notified. If the Secretary is the regulatory authority the hearing shall be of record and governed by section 554 of Title 5. Where the regulatory authority is the State, such hearing shall be of record, adjudicatory in nature and no person who presided at a conference under section 1263(b) of this title shall either preside at the hearing or participate in this decision thereon or in any administrative appeal therefrom. Within thirty days after the hearing the regulatory authority shall issue and furnish the applicant, and all persons who participated in the hearing, with the written decision of the regulatory authority granting or denying the permit in whole or in part and stating the reasons therefor.

(d) Temporary relief

Where a hearing is requested pursuant to subsection (c) of this section, the Secretary, where the Secretary is the regulatory authority, or the State hearing authority may, under such conditions as it may prescribe, grant such temporary relief as it deems appropriate pending final determination of the proceedings if—

(1) all parties to the proceedings have been notified and given an opportunity to be heard on a request for temporary relief;

(2) the person requesting such relief shows that there is a substantial likelihood that he will prevail on the merits of the final determination of the proceeding; and

(3) such relief will not adversely affect the public health or safety or cause significant imminent environmental harm to land, air, or water resources.

(e) Power of regulatory authority with respect to rehearing

For the purpose of such hearing, the regulatory authority may administer oaths, subpoena witnesses, or written or printed materials, compel attendance of the witness, or production of the materials, and take evidence including but not limited to site inspections of the land to be affected and other surface coal mining operations carried on by the applicant in the general vicinity of the proposed operation. A verbatim record of each public hearing required by this chapter shall be made, and a transcript made available on the motion of any party or by order of the regulatory authority.

(f) Right to appeal in accordance with section 1276 of this title

Any applicant or any person with an interest which is or may be adversely affected who has participated in the administrative proceedings as an objector, and who is aggrieved by the decision of the regulatory authority, or if the regulatory authority fails to act within the time limits specified in this chapter shall have the right to appeal in accordance with section 1276 of this title.

(Aug. 3, 1977, Pub.L. 95–87, Title V, § 514, 91 Stat. 485.)

CROSS REFERENCES

Permits generally, see section 1256 of this title.
Prior Federal coal lease hearing as evidence, see section 1263 of this title.

CODE OF FEDERAL REGULATIONS

Approval or denial of State programs, see 30 CFR 732.1 et seq.
Permit requirements for special categories of mining, see 30 CFR 785.1 et seq.
Secretary of Interior, hearings and appeals procedure, see 43 CFR 4.1 et seq.

§ 1265. Environmental protection performance standards [SMCRA § 515]

(a) Permit requirement

Any permit issued under any approved State or Federal program pursuant to this chapter to conduct surface coal mining operations shall require that such surface coal mining operations will meet all applicable performance standards of this chapter, and such other requirements as the regulatory authority shall promulgate.

(b) General standards

General performance standards shall be applicable to all surface coal mining and reclamation operations and shall require the operation as a minimum to—

(1) conduct surface coal mining operations so as to maximize the utilization and conservation of the solid fuel resource being recovered so that reaffecting the land in the future through surface coal mining can be minimized;

(2) restore the land affected to a condition capable of supporting the uses which it was capable of supporting prior to any mining, or higher or better uses of which there is reasonable likelihood, so long as such use or uses do not present any actual or probable hazard to public health or safety or pose

any actual or probable threat of water diminution or pollution, and the permit applicants' declared proposed land use following reclamation is not deemed to be impractical or unreasonable, inconsistent with applicable land use policies and plans, involves unreasonable delay in implementation, or is violative of Federal, State, or local law;

(3) except as provided in subsection (c) of this section with respect to all surface coal mining operations backfill, compact (where advisable to insure stability or to prevent leaching of toxic materials), and grade in order to restore the approximate original contour of the land with all highwalls, spoil piles, and depressions eliminated (unless small depressions are needed in order to retain moisture to assist revegetation or as otherwise authorized pursuant to this chapter): *Provided, however*, That in surface coal mining which is carried out at the same location over a substantial period of time where the operation transects the coal deposit, and the thickness of the coal deposits relative to the volume of the overburden is large and where the operator demonstrates that the overburden and other spoil and waste materials at a particular point in the permit area or otherwise available from the entire permit area is insufficient, giving due consideration to volumetric expansion, to restore the approximate original contour, the operator, at a minimum, shall backfill, grade, and compact (where advisable) using all available overburden and other spoil and waste materials to attain the lowest practicable grade but not more than the angle of repose, to provide adequate drainage and to cover all acid-forming and other toxic materials, in order to achieve an ecologically sound land use compatible with the surrounding region: *And provided further*, That in surface coal mining where the volume of overburden is large relative to the thickness of the coal deposit and where the operator demonstrates that due to volumetric expansion the amount of overburden and other spoil and waste materials removed in the course of the mining operation is more than sufficient to restore the approximate original contour, the operator shall after restoring the approximate contour, backfill, grade, and compact (where advisable) the excess overburden and other spoil and waste materials to attain the lowest grade but not more than the angle of repose, and to cover all acid-forming and other toxic materials, in order to achieve an ecologically sound land use compatible with the surrounding region and that such overburden or spoil shall be shaped and graded in such a way as to prevent slides, erosion, and water pollution and is revegetated in accordance with the requirements of this chapter;

(4) stabilize and protect all surface areas including spoil piles affected by the surface coal mining and reclamation operation to effectively control erosion and attendant air and water pollution;

(5) remove the topsoil from the land in a separate layer, replace it on the backfill area, or if not utilized immediately, segregate it in a separate pile from other spoil and when the topsoil is not replaced on a backfill area within a time short enough to avoid deterioration of the topsoil, maintain a successful cover by quick growing plant or other means thereafter so that the topsoil is preserved from wind and water erosion, remains free of any contamination by other acid or toxic material, and is in a usable condition for sustaining vegetation when restored during reclamation, except if topsoil is of insufficient quantity or of poor quality for sustaining vegetation, or if other strata can be shown to be more suitable for vegetation requirements, then the operator shall remove, segregate, and preserve in a like manner such other strata which is best able to support vegetation;

(6) restore the topsoil or the best available subsoil which is best able to support vegetation;

(7) for all prime farm lands as identified in section 1257(b)(16) of this title to be mined and reclaimed, specifications for soil removal, storage, replacement, and reconstruction shall be established by the Secretary of Agriculture, and the operator shall, as a minimum, be required to—

(A) segregate the A horizon of the natural soil, except where it can be shown that other available soil materials will create a final soil having a greater productive capacity; and if not utilized immediately, stockpile this material separately from other spoil, and provide needed protection from wind and water erosion or contamination by other acid or toxic material;

(B) segregate the B horizon of the natural soil, or underlying C horizons or other strata, or a combination of such horizons or other strata that are shown to be both texturally and chemically suitable for plant growth and that can be shown to be equally or more favorable for plant growth than the B horizon, in sufficient quantities to create in the regraded final soil a root zone of comparable depth and quality to that which existed in the natural soil; and if not utilized immediately, stockpile this material separately from other spoil, and provide needed protection from wind and water erosion or contamination by other acid or toxic material;

(C) replace and regrade the root zone material described in (B) above with proper compaction and uniform depth over the regraded spoil material; and

(D) redistribute and grade in a uniform manner the surface soil horizon described in subparagraph (A);

(8) create, if authorized in the approved mining and reclamation plan and permit, permanent impoundments of water on mining sites as part of reclamation activities only when it is adequately demonstrated that—

(A) the size of the impoundment is adequate for its intended purposes;

(B) the impoundment dam construction will be so designed as to achieve necessary stability with an adequate margin of safety compatible with that of structures constructed under Public Law 83–566 (16 U.S.C. 1006);

(C) the quality of impounded water will be suitable on a permanent basis for its intended use and that discharges from the impoundment will not degrade the water quality below water quality standards established pursuant to applicable Federal and State law in the receiving stream;

(D) the level of water will be reasonably stable;

(E) final grading will provide adequate safety and access for proposed water users; and

(F) such water impoundments will not result in the diminution of the quality or quantity of water utilized by adjacent or surrounding landowners for agricultural, industrial[1] recreational, or domestic uses;

(9) conducting[2] any augering operation associated with surface mining in a manner to maximize recoverability of mineral reserves remaining after the operation and reclamation are complete; and seal all auger holes with an impervious and noncombustible material in order to prevent drainage except where the regulatory authority determines that the resulting impoundment of water in such auger holes may create a hazard to the environment or the public health or safety: *Provided*, That the permitting authority may prohibit augering if necessary to maximize the utilization, recoverability or conservation of the solid fuel resources or to protect against adverse water quality impacts;

(10) minimize the disturbances to the prevailing hydrologic balance at the mine-site and in associated offsite areas and to the quality and quantity of water in surface and ground water systems both during and after surface coal mining operations and during reclamation by—

(A) avoiding acid or other toxic mine drainage by such measures as, but not limited to—

(i) preventing or removing water from contact with toxic producing deposits;

(ii) treating drainage to reduce toxic content which adversely affects downstream water upon being released to water courses;

(iii) casing, sealing, or otherwise managing boreholes, shafts, and wells and keep[3] acid or other toxic drainage from entering ground and surface waters;

(B)(i) conducting surface coal mining operations so as to prevent, to the extent possible using the best technology currently available, additional contributions of suspended solids to streamflow, or runoff outside the permit area, but in no event shall contributions be in excess of requirements set by applicable State or Federal law;

(ii) constructing any siltation structures pursuant to subparagraph (B)(i) of this subsection prior to commencement of surface coal mining operations, such structures to be certified by a qualified registered engineer or a qualified registered professional land surveyor in any State which authorizes land surveyors to prepare and certify such maps or plans to be constructed as designed and as approved in the reclamation plan;

(C) cleaning out and removing temporary or large settling ponds or other siltation structures from drainways after disturbed areas are revegetated and stabilized; and depositing the silt and debris at a site and in a manner approved by the regulatory authority;

(D) restoring recharge capacity of the mined area to approximate premining conditions;

(E) avoiding channel deepening or enlargement in operations requiring the discharge of water from mines;

(F) preserving throughout the mining and reclamation process the essential hydrologic functions of alluvial valley floors in the arid and semiarid areas of the country; and

(G) such other actions as the regulatory authority may prescribe;

(11) with respect to surface disposal of mine wastes, tailings, coal processing wastes, and other wastes in areas other than the mine working or excavations, stabilize all waste piles in designated areas through construction in compacted layers including the use of incombustible and impervious materials if necessary and assure the final contour of the waste pile will be compatible with natural surroundings and that the site can and will be stabilized and revegetated according to the provisions of this chapter;

(12) refrain from surface coal mining within five hundred feet from active and abandoned underground mines in order to prevent breakthroughs and to protect health or safety of miners: *Provided*, That the regulatory authority shall permit an operator to mine near, through or partially through an abandoned underground mine or closer to an active underground mine if (A) the nature, timing, and sequencing of the approximate coincidence of specific surface mine activities with specific underground mine activities are jointly approved by the regulatory authorities concerned with surface mine regulation and the health and safety of underground miners, and (B) such operations will result in improved resource recovery, abatement of water pollution, or elimination of hazards to the health and safety of the public;

(13) design, locate, construct, operate, maintain, enlarge, modify, and remove or abandon, in accordance with the standards and criteria developed pursuant to subsection (f) of this section, all existing and new coal mine waste piles consisting of mine wastes, tailings, coal processing wastes, or other liquid and solid wastes, and used either temporarily or permanently as dams or embankments;

(14) insure that all debris, acid-forming materials, toxic materials, or materials constituting a fire hazard are treated or buried and compacted or otherwise disposed of in a manner designed to prevent contamination of ground or surface waters and that contingency plans are developed to prevent sustained combustion;

(15) insure that explosives are used only in accordance with existing State and Federal law and the regulations promulgated by the regulatory authority, which shall include provisions to—

(A) provide adequate advance written notice to local governments and residents who might be affected by the use of such explosives by publication of the planned blasting schedule in a newspaper of general circulation in the locality and by mailing a copy of the proposed blasting schedule to every resident living within one-half mile of the proposed blasting site and by providing daily notice to resident/occupiers in such areas prior to any blasting;

(B) maintain for a period of at least three years and make available for public inspection upon request a log detailing the location of the blasts, the pattern and depth of the drill holes, the amount of explosives used per hole, and the order and length of delay in the blasts;

(C) limit the type of explosives and detonating equipment, the size, the timing and frequency of blasts based upon the physical conditions of the site so as to prevent (i) injury to persons, (ii) damage to public and private property outside the permit area, (iii) adverse impacts on any underground mine, and (iv) change in the course, channel, or availability of ground or surface water outside the permit area;

(D) require that all blasting operations be conducted by trained and competent persons as certified by the regulatory authority;

(E) provide that upon the request of a resident or owner of a man-made dwelling or structure within one-half mile of any portion of the permitted area the applicant or permittee shall conduct a pre-blasting survey of such structures and submit the survey to the regulatory authority and a copy to the resident or owner making the request. The area of the survey shall be decided by the regulatory authority and shall include such provisions as the Secretary shall promulgate.

(16) insure that all reclamation efforts proceed in an environmentally sound manner and as contemporaneously as practicable with the surface coal mining operations: *Provided, however*, That where the applicant proposes to combine surface mining operations with underground mining operations to assure maximum practical recovery of the mineral resources, the regulatory authority may grant a variance for specific areas within the reclamation plan from the requirement that reclamation efforts proceed as contemporaneously as practicable to permit underground mining operations prior to reclamation:

(A) if the regulatory authority finds in writing that:

(i) the applicant has presented, as part of the permit application, specific, feasible plans for the proposed underground mining operations;

(ii) the proposed underground mining operations are necessary or desirable to assure maximum practical recovery of the mineral resource and will avoid multiple disturbance of the surface;

(iii) the applicant has satisfactorily demonstrated that the plan for the underground mining operations conforms to requirements for underground mining in the jurisdiction and that permits necessary for the underground mining operations have been issued by the appropriate authority;

(iv) the areas proposed for the variance have been shown by the applicant to be necessary for the implementing of the proposed underground mining operations;

(v) no substantial adverse environmental damage, either on-site or off-site, will result from the delay in completion of reclamation as required by this chapter;

(vi) provisions for the off-site storage of spoil will comply with paragraph (22);

(B) if the Secretary has promulgated specific regulations to govern the granting of such variances in accordance with the provisions of this subsection and section 1251 of this title, and has imposed such additional requirements as he deems necessary;

(C) if variances granted under the provisions of this subsection are to be reviewed by the regulatory authority not more than three years from the date of issuance of the permit; and

(D) if liability under the bond filed by the applicant with the regulatory authority pursuant to section 1259(b) of this title shall be for the duration of the underground mining operations and until the requirements of this subsection and section 1269 of this title have been fully complied with.[4]

(17) insure that the construction, maintenance, and postmining conditions of access roads into and across the site of operations will control or prevent erosion and siltation, pollution of water, damage to fish or wildlife or their habitat, or public or private property;

(18) refrain from the construction of roads or other access ways up a stream bed or drainage channel or in such proximity to such channel so as to seriously alter the normal flow of water;

(19) establish on the regraded areas, and all other lands affected, a diverse, effective, and permanent vegetative cover of the same seasonal variety native to the area of land to be affected and capable of self-regeneration and plant succession at least equal in extent of cover to the natural vegetation of the area; except, that introduced species may be used in the revegetation process where desirable and necessary to achieve the approved postmining land use plan;

(20)(A) assume the responsibility for successful revegetation, as required by paragraph (19) above, for a period of five full years after the last year of augmented seeding, fertilizing, irrigation, or other work in order to assure compliance with paragraph (19) above, except in those areas or regions of the country where the annual average precipitation is twenty-six inches or less, then the operator's assumption of responsibility and liability will extend for a period of ten full years after the last year of augmented seeding, fertilizing, irrigation, or other work: *Provided,* That when the regulatory authority approves a long-term intensive agricultural postmining land use, the applicable five- or ten-year period of responsibility for revegetation shall commence at the date of initial planting for such long-term intensive agricultural postmining land used: *Provided further,* That when the regulatory authority issues a written finding approving a long-term, intensive, agricultural postmining land use as part of the mining and reclamation plan, the authority may grant exception to the provisions of paragraph (19) above;

(B) on lands eligible for remining assume the responsibility for successful revegetation for a period of two full years after the last year of augmented seeding, fertilizing, irrigation, or other work in order to assure compliance with the applicable standards, except in those areas or regions of the country where the annual average precipitation is twenty-six inches or less, then the operator's assumption of responsibility and liability will be extended for a period of five full years after the last year of augmented seeding, fertilizing, irrigation, or other work in order to assure compliance with the applicable standards.

(21) protect offsite areas from slides or damage occurring during the surface coal mining and reclamation operations, and not deposit spoil material or locate any part of the operations or waste accumulations outside the permit area;

(22) place all excess spoil material resulting from coal surface mining and reclamation activities in such a manner that—

(A) spoil is transported and placed in a controlled manner in position for concurrent compaction and in such a way to assure mass stability and to prevent mass movement;

(B) the areas of disposal are within the bonded permit areas and all organic matter shall be removed immediately prior to spoil placement;

(C) appropriate surface and internal drainage systems and diversion ditches are used so as to prevent spoil erosion and movement;

(D) the disposal area does not contain springs, natural water courses or wet weather seeps unless lateral drains are constructed from the wet areas to the main underdrains in such a manner that filtration of the water into the spoil pile will be prevented;

(E) if placed on a slope, the spoil is placed upon the most moderate slope among those upon which, in the judgment of the regulatory authority, the spoil could be placed in compliance with all the requirements of this chapter, and shall be placed, where possible, upon, or above, a natural terrace, bench, or berm, if such placement provides additional stability and prevents mass movement;

(F) where the toe of the spoil rests on a downslope, a rock toe buttress, of sufficient size to prevent mass movement, is constructed;

(G) the final configuration is compatible with the natural drainage pattern and surroundings and suitable for intended uses;

(H) design of the spoil disposal area is certified by a qualified registered professional engineer in conformance with professional standards; and

(I) all other provisions of this chapter are met.[5]

(23) meet such other criteria as are necessary to achieve reclamation in accordance with the purposes of this chapter, taking into consideration the physical, climatological, and other characteristics of the site; and [6]

(24) to the extent possible using the best technology currently available, minimize disturbances and adverse impacts of the operation on fish, wildlife, and related environmental values, and achieve enhancement of such resources where practicable;

(25) provide for an undisturbed natural barrier beginning at the elevation of the lowest coal seam to be mined and extending from the outslope for such distance as the regulatory authority shall determine shall be retained in place as a barrier to slides and erosion.

(c) Procedures; exception to original contour restoration requirements

(1) Each State program may and each Federal program shall include procedures pursuant to which the regulatory authority may permit surface mining operations for the purposes set forth in paragraph (3) of this subsection.

(2) Where an applicant meets the requirements of paragraphs (3) and (4) of this subsection a permit without regard to the requirement to restore to approximate original contour set forth in subsection (b)(3) or (d)(2) and (3) of this section may be granted for the surface mining of coal where the mining operation will remove an entire coal seam or seams running through the upper fraction of a mountain, ridge, or hill (except as provided in subsection (c)(4)(A) hereof) by removing all of the overburden and creating a level plateau or a gently rolling contour with no highwalls remaining, and capable of supporting postmining uses in accord with the requirements of this subsection.

(3) In cases where an industrial, commercial, agricultural, residential or public facility (including recreational facilities) use is proposed or [7] the postmining use of the affected land, the regulatory authority may grant a permit for a surface mining operation of the nature described in subsection (c)(2) of this section where—

(A) after consultation with the appropriate land use planning agencies, if any, the proposed postmining land use is deemed to constitute an equal or better economic or public use of the affected land, as compared with premining use;

(B) the applicant presents specific plans for the proposed postmining land use and appropriate assurances that such use will be—

(i) compatible with adjacent land uses;

(ii) obtainable according to data regarding expected need and market;

(iii) assured of investment in necessary public facilities;

(iv) supported by commitments from public agencies where appropriate;

(v) practicable with respect to private financial capability for completion of the proposed use;

(vi) planned pursuant to a schedule attached to the reclamation plan so as to integrate the mining operation and reclamation with the postmining land use; and

(vii) designed by a registered engineer in conformance with professional standards established to assure the stability, drainage, and configuration necessary for the intended use of the site;

(C) the proposed use would be consistent with adjacent land uses, and existing State and local land use plans and programs;

(D) the regulatory authority provides the governing body of the unit of general-purpose government in which the land is located and any State or Federal agency which the regulatory agency, in its discretion, determines to have an interest in the proposed use, an opportunity of not more than sixty days to review and comment on the proposed use;

(E) all other requirements of this chapter will be met.

(4) In granting any permit pursuant to this subsection the regulatory authority shall require that—

(A) the toe of the lowest coal seam and the overburden associated with it are retained in place as a barrier to slides and erosion;

(B) the reclaimed area is stable;

(C) the resulting plateau or rolling contour drains inward from the outslopes except at specified points;

(D) no damage will be done to natural watercourses;

(E) spoil will be placed on the mountaintop bench as is necessary to achieve the planned postmining land use: *Provided*, That all excess spoil material not retained on the mountaintop shall be placed in accordance with the provisions of subsection (b)(22) of this section;

(F) insure stability of the spoil retained on the mountaintop and meet the other requirements of this chapter;[8]

(5) The regulatory authority shall promulgate specific regulations to govern the granting of permits in accord with the provisions of this subsection, and may impose such additional requirements as he deems to be necessary.

(6) All permits granted under the provisions of this subsection shall be reviewed not more than three years from the date of issuance of the permit, unless the applicant affirmatively demonstrates that the proposed development is proceeding in accordance with the terms of the approved schedule and reclamation plan.

(d) Steep-slope surface coal mining standards

The following performance standards shall be applicable to steep-slope surface coal mining and shall be in addition to those general performance standards required by this section: *Provided, however*, That the provisions of this subsection (d) shall not apply to those situations in which an operator is mining on flat or gently rolling terrain, on which an occasional steep slope is encountered through which the mining operation is to proceed, leaving a plain or predominantly flat area or where an operator is in compliance with provisions of subsection (c) hereof:

(1) Insure that when performing surface coal mining on steep slopes, no debris, abandoned or disabled equipment, spoil material, or waste mineral matter be placed on the downslope below the bench or mining cut: *Provided*, That spoil material in excess of that required for the reconstruction of the approximate original contour under the provisions of subsection (b)(3) or (d)(2) of this section shall be permanently stored pursuant to subsection (b)(22) of this section.

(2) Complete backfilling with spoil material shall be required to cover completely the highwall and return the site to the appropriate original contour, which material will maintain stability following mining and reclamation.

(3) The operator may not disturb land above the top of the highwall unless the regulatory authority finds that such disturbance will facilitate compliance with the environmental protection standards of this section: *Provided, however*, That the land disturbed above the highwall shall be limited to that amount necessary to facilitate said compliance.

(4) For the purposes of this subsection (d), the term "steep slope" is any slope above twenty degrees or such lesser slope as may be defined by the regulatory authority after consideration of soil, climate, and other characteristics of a region or State.

(e) Variances to original contour restoration requirements

(1) Each State program may and each Federal program shall include procedures pursuant to which the regulatory authority may permit variances for the purposes set forth in paragraph (3) of this subsection, provided that the watershed control of the area is improved; and further provided complete backfilling with spoil material shall be required to cover completely the highwall which material will maintain stability following mining and reclamation.

(2) Where an applicant meets the requirements of paragraphs (3) and (4) of this subsection a variance from the requirement to restore to approximate original contour set forth in subsection (d)(2) of this section may be granted for the surface mining of coal where the owner of the surface knowingly requests in writing, as a part of the permit application that such a variance be granted so as to render the land, after reclamation, suitable for an industrial, commercial, residential, or public use (including recreational facilities) in accord with the further provisions of (3) and (4) of this subsection.

(3)(A) After consultation with the appropriate land use planning agencies, if any, the potential use of the affected land is deemed to constitute an equal or better economic or public use;

(B) is designed and certified by a qualified registered professional engineer in conformance with professional standards established to assure the stability, drainage, and configuration necessary for the intended use of the site; and

(C) after approval of the appropriate state environmental agencies, the watershed of the affected land is deemed to be improved.

(4) In granting a variance pursuant to this subsection the regulatory authority shall require that only such amount of spoil will be placed off the mine bench as is necessary to achieve the planned postmining land use, insure stability of the spoil retained on the bench, meet all other requirements of this chapter, and all spoil placement off the mine bench must comply with subsection (b)(22) of this section.

(5) The regulatory authority shall promulgate specific regulations to govern the granting of variances in accord with the provisions of this subsection, and may impose such additional requirements as he deems to be necessary.

(6) All exceptions granted under the provisions of this subsection shall be reviewed not more than three years from the date of issuance of the permit, unless the permittee affirmatively demonstrates that the proposed development is proceeding in accordance with the terms of the reclamation plan.

(f) Standards and criteria for coal mine waste piles

The Secretary, with the written concurrence of the Chief of Engineers, shall establish within one hundred and thirty-five days from August 3, 1977, standards and criteria regulating the design, location, construction, operation, maintenance, enlargement, modification, removal, and abandonment of new and existing coal mine waste piles referred to in subsection (b)(13) of this section and section 1266(b)(5) of this title. Such standards and criteria shall conform to the standards and criteria used by the Chief of Engineers to insure that flood control structures are safe and effectively perform their intended function. In addition to engineering and other technical specifications the standards and criteria developed pursuant to this subsection must include provisions for: review and approval of plans and specifications prior to construction, enlargement, modification, removal, or abandonment; performance of periodic inspections during construction; issuance of certificates of approval upon completion of construction; performance of periodic safety inspections; and issuance of notices for required remedial or maintenance work.

(Aug. 3, 1977, Pub.L. 95–87, Title V, § 515, 91 Stat. 486; Oct. 18, 1986, Pub.L. 99–500, Title I, § 101(h), [Title I, § 123], 100 Stat. 3341–267; Oct. 30, 1986, Pub.L. 99–591, Title I, § 101(h), [Title I, § 123], 100 Stat. 3341–267; Oct. 24, 1992, Pub.L. 102–486, Title XXV, § 2503(b), 106 Stat. 3102.)

1 So in original. Probably should be followed by a comma.

2 So in original. Probably should be "conduct".

3 So in original. Probably should be "keeping".

4 So in original. The period probably should be a semicolon.

5 So in original. The period probably should be a semicolon.

6 So in original. The word "and" probably should appear at end of par. (24).

7 So in original. Probably should be "for".

8 So in original. The semicolon probably should be a period.

CROSS REFERENCES

Alternative regulations for anthracite coal mines in lieu of this section, see section 1279 of this title.
Approximate original contour defined, see section 1291 of this title.
Blasting plan part of permit application, outline of compliance with provisions of this section, see section 1257 of this title.
Compliance with provisions of this section by State-regulated surface coal mining operations, see section 1252 of this title.
Departure, on experimental basis, from standards promulgated under this section, see section 1301 of this title.
Judicial review of standards promulgated pursuant to this section, see section 1276 of this title.
Performance bonds—
Generally, see section 1259 of this title.
Release upon revegetation of land in accordance with approved reclamation plan, see section 1269 of this title.
Prime farmland mining permits, ability of applicants to meet soil reconstruction standards of this section, see section 1260 of this title.
Reclamation in accordance with this section of lands subjected to coal exploration, see section 1262 of this title.
Reclamation plan requirements, see section 1258 of this title.
Surface coal mining operations on Indian lands, compliance with requirements as stringent as those of this section, see section 1300 of this title.
Underground coal mining permits, operation in accordance with standards of this section, see section 1266 of this title.

CODE OF FEDERAL REGULATIONS

Approval or denial of State programs, see 30 CFR 732.1 et seq.
General performance standards, initial program regulations—
Surface mining, see 30 CFR 715.10 et seq.
Underground mining, see 30 CFR 717.10 et seq.
Permanent program performance standards—
General provisions, see 30 CFR 810.1 et seq.
Surface mining, see 30 CFR 816.1 et seq.
Underground mining, see 30 CFR 817.1 et seq.
Permit requirements for special categories of mining, see 30 CFR 785.1 et seq.
Secretary of Interior, general scope of authority and responsibility, see 30 CFR 700.1 et seq.
Special performance standards, initial program regulations—see 30 CFR 716.1 et seq.
Special permanent program performance standards—
In situ processing, see 30 CFR 828.1 et seq.
Mountaintop removal, see 30 CFR 824.1 et seq.

LAW REVIEW COMMENTARIES

Illinois coal mine subsidence law updated. Robert E. Beck, So.Ill. L.J. 379 (1985).

United States Supreme Court

Steep-slope mining standards provisions of this section, constitutionality, see Hodel v. Virginia Surface Min. & Reclamation Ass'n Inc., 1981, 101 S.Ct. 2352, 452 U.S. 264, 69 L.Ed.2d 1, concurring opinion 101 S.Ct. 2389, 452 U.S. 264, 69 L.Ed.2d 1.

§ 1266. Surface effects of underground coal mining operations [SMCRA § 516]

(a) Rules and regulations

The Secretary shall promulgate rules and regulations directed toward the surface effects of underground coal mining operations, embodying the following requirements and in accordance with the procedures established under section 1251 of this title: *Provided, however,* That in adopting any rules and regulations the Secretary shall consider the distinct difference between surface coal mining and underground coal mining. Such rules and regulations shall not conflict with nor supersede any provision of the Federal Coal Mine Health and Safety Act of 1969 [30 U.S.C.A. § 801 et seq.] nor any regulation issued pursuant thereto, and shall not be promulgated until the Secretary has obtained the written concurrence of the head of the department which administers such Act.

(b) Permit requirements

Each permit issued under any approved State or Federal program pursuant to this chapter and relating to underground coal mining shall require the operator to—

(1) adopt measures consistent with known technology in order to prevent subsidence causing material damage to the extent technologically and economically feasible, maximize mine stability, and maintain the value and reasonably foreseeable use of such surface lands, except in those instances where the mining technology used requires planned subsidence in a predictable and controlled manner: *Provided*, That nothing in this subsection shall be construed to prohibit the standard method of room and pillar mining;

(2) seal all portals, entryways, drifts, shafts, or other openings between the surface and underground mine working when no longer needed for the conduct of the mining operations;

(3) fill or seal exploratory holes no longer necessary for mining, maximizing to the extent technologically and economically feasible return of mine and processing waste, tailings, and any other waste incident to the mining operation, to the mine workings or excavations;

(4) with respect to surface disposal of mine wastes, tailings, coal processing wastes, and other wastes in areas other than the mine workings or excavations, stabilize all waste piles created by the permittee from current operations through construction in compacted layers including the use of incombustible and impervious materials if necessary and assure that the leachate will not degrade below water quality standards established pursuant to applicable Federal and State law surface or ground waters and that the final contour of the waste accumulation will be compatible with natural surroundings and that the site is stabilized and revegetated according to the provisions of this section;

(5) design, locate, construct, operate, maintain, enlarge, modify, and remove, or abandon, in accordance with the standards and criteria developed pursuant to section 1265(f) of this title, all existing and new coal mine waste piles consisting of mine wastes, tailings, coal processing wastes, or other liquid and solid wastes and used either temporarily or permanently as dams or embankments;

(6) establish on regraded areas and all other lands affected, a diverse and permanent vegetative cover capable of self-regeneration and plant succession and at least equal in extent of cover to the natural vegetation of the area;

(7) protect offsite areas from damages which may result from such mining operations;

(8) eliminate fire hazards and otherwise eliminate conditions which constitute a hazard to health and safety of the public;

(9) minimize the disturbances of the prevailing hydrologic balance at the minesite and in associated offsite areas and to the quantity of water in surface ground water systems both during and after coal mining operations and during reclamation by—

(A) avoiding acid or other toxic mine drainage by such measures as, but not limited to—

(i) preventing or removing water from contact with toxic producing deposits;

(ii) treating drainage to reduce toxic content which adversely affects downstream water upon being released to water courses;

(iii) casing, sealing, or otherwise managing boreholes, shafts, and wells to keep acid or other toxic drainage from entering ground and surface waters; and

(B) conducting surface coal mining operations so as to prevent, to the extent possible using the best technology currently available, additional contributions of suspended solids to streamflow or runoff outside the permit area (but in no event shall such contributions be in excess of requirements set by applicable State or Federal law), and avoiding channel deepening or enlargement in operations requiring the discharge of water from mines;

(10) with respect to other surface impacts not specified in this subsection including the construction of new roads or the improvement or use of existing roads to gain access to the site of such activities and for haulage, repair areas, storage areas, processing areas, shipping areas, and other areas upon which are sited structures, facilities, or other property or materials on the surface, resulting from or incident to such activities, operate in accordance with the standards established under section 1265 of this title for such effects which result from surface coal mining operations: *Provided*, That the Secretary shall make such modifications in the requirements imposed by this paragraph as are necessary to accommodate the distinct difference between surface and underground coal mining;

(11) to the extent possible using the best technology currently available, minimize disturbances and adverse impacts of the operation on fish, wildlife, and related environmental values, and achieve enhancement of such resources where practicable;

(12) locate openings for all new drift mines working acid-producing or iron-producing coal seams in such a manner as to prevent a gravity discharge of water from the mine.

(c) Suspension of underground coal mining operations in urbanized areas

In order to protect the stability of the land, the regulatory authority shall suspend underground coal mining under urbanized areas, cities, towns, and communities and adjacent to industrial or commercial buildings, major impoundments, or permanent streams if he finds imminent danger to inhabitants of the urbanized areas, cities, towns, and communities.

(d) Applicability of this subchapter to surface operations and surface impacts incident to underground coal mining operations

The provisions of this subchapter relating to State and Federal programs, permits, bonds, inspections and enforcement, public review, and administrative and judicial review shall be applicable to surface operations and surface impacts incident to an underground coal mine with such modifications to the permit application requirements, permit approval or denial procedures, and bond requirements as are necessary to accommodate the distinct difference between surface and underground coal mining. The Secretary shall promulgate such modifications in accordance with the rulemaking procedure established in section 1251 of this title.

(Aug. 3, 1977, Pub.L. 95–87, Title V, § 516, 91 Stat. 495.)

CROSS REFERENCES

Alternative regulations for anthracite coal mines in lieu of this section, see section 1279 of this title.
Coal exploration permits, see section 1262 of this title.
Definitions, see section 1291 of this title.
Departure, on experimental basis, from standards promulgated under this section, see section 1301 of this title.
Environmental protection performance standards, see section 1265 of this title.
Judicial review of standards promulgated pursuant to this section, see section 1276 of this title.
Surface coal mining operations on Indian lands, compliance with requirements as stringent as those of this section, see section 1300 of this title.

CODE OF FEDERAL REGULATIONS

Approval or denial of State programs, see 30 CFR 732.1 et seq.
General performance standards—
Surface mining, see 30 CFR 715.10 et seq.
Underground mining, see 30 CFR 717.10 et seq.
Permanent program performance standards—
General provisions, see 30 CFR 810.1 et seq.
Surface mining, see 30 CFR 816.1 et seq.
Underground mining, see 30 CFR 817.1 et seq.
Permit requirements for special categories of mining, see 30 CFR 785.1 et seq.
Secretary of Interior, general scope of authority and responsibility, see 30 CFR 700.1 et seq.
Special program performance standards, in situ processing, see 30 CFR 828.1 et seq.

§ 1267. Inspections and monitoring [SMCRA § 517]

(a) Inspections of surface coal mining and reclamation operations

The Secretary shall cause to be made such inspections of any surface coal mining and reclamation operations as are necessary to evaluate the administration of approved State programs, or to develop or enforce any Federal program, and for such purposes authorized representatives of the Secretary shall have a right of entry to, upon, or through any surface coal mining and reclamation operations.

(b) Records and reports; monitoring systems; evaluation of results

For the purpose of developing or assisting in the development, administration, and enforcement of any approved State or Federal program under this chapter or in the administration and enforcement of any permit under this chapter, or of determining whether any person is in violation of any requirement of any such State or Federal program or any other requirement of this chapter—

(1) the regulatory authority shall require any permittee to (A) establish and maintain appropriate records, (B) make monthly reports to the regulatory authority, (C) install, use, and maintain any necessary monitoring equipment or methods, (D) evaluate results in accordance with such methods, at such locations, intervals, and in such manner as a regulatory authority shall prescribe, and (E) provide such other information relative to surface coal mining and reclamation operations as the regulatory authority deems reasonable and necessary;

(2) for those surface coal mining and reclamation operations which remove or disturb strata that serve as aquifers which significantly insure the hydrologic balance of water use either on or off the mining site, the regulatory authority shall specify those—

(A) monitoring sites to record the quantity and quality of surface drainage above and below the minesite as well as in the potential zone of influence;

(B) monitoring sites to record level, amount, and samples of ground water and aquifers potentially affected by the mining and also directly below the lowermost (deepest) coal seam to be mined;

(C) records of well logs and borehole data to be maintained; and

(D) monitoring sites to record precipitation.

The monitoring data collection and analysis required by this section shall be conducted according to standards and procedures set forth by the regulatory authority in order to assure their reliability and validity; and

(3) the authorized representatives of the regulatory authority, without advance notice and upon presentation of appropriate credentials (A) shall have the right of entry to, upon, or through any surface coal mining and reclamation operations or any premises in which any records required to be maintained under paragraph (1) of this subsection are located; and (B) may at reasonable times, and without delay, have access to and copy any records, inspect any monitoring equipment or method of operation required under this chapter.

(c) Inspection intervals

The inspections by the regulatory authority shall (1) occur on an irregular basis averaging not less than one partial inspection per month and one complete inspection per calendar quarter for the surface coal mining and reclamation operation covered by each permit; (2) occur without prior notice to the permittee or his agents or employees except for necessary onsite meetings with the permittee; and (3) include the filing of inspection reports adequate to enforce the requirements of and to carry out the terms and purposes of this chapter.

(d) Maintenance of sign

Each permittee shall conspicuously maintain at the entrances to the surface coal mining and reclamation operations a clearly visible sign which sets forth the name, business address, and phone number of the permittee and the permit number of the surface coal mining and reclamation operations.

(e) Violations

Each inspector, upon detection of each violation of any requirement of any State or Federal program or of this chapter, shall forthwith inform the operator in writing, and shall report in writing any such violation to the regulatory authority.

(f) Availability of information to public

Copies of any records, reports, inspection materials, or information obtained under this subchapter by the regulatory authority shall be made immediately available to the public at central and sufficient locations in the county, multicounty, and State area of mining so that they are conveniently available to residents in the areas of mining.

(g) Conflict of interest; penalty; publication of regulations; report to Congress

No employee of the State regulatory authority performing any function or duty under this chapter shall have a direct or indirect financial interest in any underground or surface coal mining operation. Whoever knowingly violates the provisions of this subsection shall, upon conviction, be punished by a fine of not more than $2,500, or by imprisonment of not more than one year, or by both. The Secretary shall (1) within sixty days after August 3, 1977, publish in the Federal Register, in accordance with section 553 of Title 5, regulations to establish methods by which the provisions of this subsection will be monitored and enforced by the Secretary and such State regulatory authority, including appropriate provisions for the filing by such employees and the review of statements and supplements thereto concerning any financial interest which may be affected by this subsection, and (2) report to the Congress as part of the Annual Report (section 1296 of this title) on actions taken and not taken during the preceding year under this subsection.

(h) Review; procedures for inspections

(1) Any person who is or may be adversely affected by a surface mining operation may notify the Secretary or any representative of the Secretary responsible for conducting the inspection, in writing, of any violation of this chapter which he has reason to believe exists at the surface mining site. The Secretary shall, by regulation, establish procedures for informal review of any refusal by a representative of the Secretary to issue a citation with respect to any such alleged violation. The Secretary shall furnish such persons requesting the review a written statement of the reasons for the Secretary's final disposition of the case.

(2) The Secretary shall also, by regulation, establish procedures to insure that adequate and complete inspections are made. Any such person may notify the Secretary of any failure to make such inspections, after which the Secretary shall determine whether adequate and complete inspections have been made. The Secretary shall furnish such persons a written statement of the reasons for the Secretary's determination that adequate and complete inspections have or have not been conducted.

(Aug. 3, 1977, Pub.L. 95–87, Title V, § 517, 91 Stat. 498.)

CROSS REFERENCES

Conflict of interests of employees of Office or of other Federal employees, see section 1211 of this title.

Surface coal mining operations on Indian lands, compliance with requirements as stringent as those of this section, see section 1300 of this title.

CODE OF FEDERAL REGULATIONS

Approval or denial of State programs, see 30 CFR 732.1 et seq.
Areas unsuitable for mining, petition for designation or termination of previous designation, see 30 CFR 769.1 et seq.
Inspection and enforcement procedure, see 30 CFR Chap. VII, Subchap. L.
Maintenance, substituted federal enforcement or approval withdrawal of state programs, see 30 CFR 733.1 et seq.
Performance standards, permanent program, general provisions, see 30 CFR 810.1 et seq.
Permit requirements for special categories of mining, see 30 CFR 785.1 et seq.
Restriction on financial interests of—
Federal employees, see 30 CFR 706.1 et seq.
State employees, see 30 CFR 705.1 et seq.
Secretary of Interior, general scope of authority and responsibility, see 30 CFR 700.1 et seq.
Special program performance standards—
In situ processing, see 30 CFR 828.1 et seq.
Mountaintop removal, see 30 CFR 824.1 et seq.

§ 1268. Penalties [SMCRA § 518]

(a) Civil penalties for violations of permit conditions and provisions of this subchapter

In the enforcement of a Federal program or Federal lands program, or during Federal enforcement pursuant to section 1252 of this title or during Federal enforcement of a State program pursuant to section 1271 of this title, any permittee who violates any permit condition or who violates any other provision of this subchapter, may be assessed a civil penalty by the Secretary, except that if such violation leads to the issuance of a cessation order under section 1271 of this title, the civil penalty shall be assessed. Such penalty shall not exceed $5,000 for each violation. Each day of continuing violation may be deemed a separate violation for purposes of penalty assessments. In determining the amount of the penalty, consideration shall be given to the permittee's history of previous violations at the particular surface coal mining operation; the seriousness of the violation, including any irreparable harm to the environment and any hazard to the health or safety of the public; whether the permittee was negligent; and the demonstrated good faith of the permittee charged in attempting to achieve rapid compliance after notification of the violation.

(b) Hearing

A civil penalty shall be assessed by the Secretary only after the person charged with a violation described under subsection (a) of this section has been given an opportunity for a public hearing. Where such a public hearing has been held, the Secretary shall make findings of fact, and he shall issue a written decision as to the occurrence of the violation and the amount of the penalty which is warranted, incorporating, when appropriate, an order therein requiring that the penalty be paid. When appropriate, the Secretary shall consolidate such hearings with other proceedings under section 1271 of this title. Any hearing under this section shall be of record and shall be subject to section 554 of Title 5. Where the person charged with such a violation fails to avail himself of the opportunity for a public hearing, a civil penalty shall be assessed by the Secretary after the Secretary has determined that a violation did occur, and the amount of the penalty which is warranted, and has issued an order requiring that the penalty be paid.

(c) Notice of violation; action required of violator; waiver of legal rights

Upon the issuance of a notice or order charging that a violation of this chapter has occurred, the Secretary shall inform the operator within thirty days of the proposed amount of said penalty. The person charged with the penalty shall then have thirty days to pay the proposed penalty in full or, if the person wishes to contest either the amount of the penalty or the fact of the violation, forward the proposed amount to the Secretary for placement in an escrow account. If through administrative or judicial review of the proposed penalty, it is determined that no violation occurred, or that the amount of the penalty should be reduced, the Secretary shall within thirty days remit the appropriate amount to the person, with interest at the rate of 6 percent, or at the prevailing Department of the Treasury rate, whichever is greater. Failure to forward the money to the Secretary within thirty days shall result in a waiver of all legal rights to contest the violation or the amount of the penalty.

(d) Civil action to recover civil penalties

Civil penalties owed under this chapter, may be recovered in a civil action brought by the Attorney General at the request of the Secretary in any appropriate district court of the United States.

(e) Willful violations

Any person who willfully and knowingly violates a condition of a permit issued pursuant to a Federal program, a Federal lands program or Federal enforcement pursuant to section 1252 of this title or during Federal enforcement of a State program pursuant to section 1271 of this title or fails or refuses to comply with any order issued under section 1271 or section 1276 of this title, or any order incorporated in a final decision issued by the Secretary under this chapter, except an order incorporated in a decision issued under subsection (b) of this section or section 1294 of this title, shall, upon conviction, be punished by a fine of not more than $10,000, or by imprisonment for not more than one year or both.

(f) Corporate violations

Whenever a corporate permittee violates a condition of a permit issued pursuant to a Federal program, a Federal lands program or Federal enforcement pursuant to section 1252 of this title or Federal enforcement of a State program pursuant to section 1271 of this title or fails or refuses to comply with any order issued under section 1271 of this title, or any order incorporated in a final decision issued by the Secretary under this chapter except an order incorporated in a decision issued under subsection (b) of this section or section 1293 of this title, any director, officer, or agent of such corporation who willfully and knowingly authorized, ordered, or carried out such violation, failure, or refusal shall be subject to the same civil penalties, fines, and imprisonment that may be imposed upon a person under subsections (a) and (e) of this section.

(g) False statements, representations, or certifications

Whoever knowingly makes any false statement, representation, or certification, or knowingly fails to make any statement, representation, or certification in any application, record, report, plant, or other document filed or required to be maintained pursuant to a Federal program or a Federal lands program or any order of decision issued by the Secretary under this chapter, shall, upon conviction, be punished by a fine of not more than $10,000, or by imprisonment for not more than one year or both.

(h) Failure to correct violation

Any operator who fails to correct a violation for which a citation has been issued under section 1271(a) of this title within the period permitted for its correction (which period shall not end until the entry of a final order by the Secretary, in the case of any review proceedings under section 1275 of this title initiated by the operator wherein the Secretary orders, after an expedited hearing, the suspension of the abatement requirements of the citation after determining that the operator will suffer irreparable loss or damage from the application of those requirements, or until the entry of an order of the court, in the case of any review proceedings under section 1276 of this title initiated by the operator wherein the court orders the suspension of the abatement requirements of the citation), shall be assessed a civil penalty of not less than $750 for each day during which such failure or violation continues.

(i) Effect on additional enforcement right or procedure available under State law

As a condition of approval of any State program submitted pursuant to section 1253 of this title, the civil and criminal penalty provisions thereof shall, at a minimum, incorporate penalties no less stringent than those set forth in this section, and shall contain the same or similar procedural requirements relating thereto. Nothing herein shall be construed so as to eliminate any additional enforcement right or procedures which are available under State law to a State regulatory authority but which are not specifically enumerated herein.

(Aug. 3, 1977, Pub.L. 95–87, Title V, § 518, 91 Stat. 499.)

CROSS REFERENCES

Coal exploration permits, penalties for violations, see section 1262 of this title.

Judicial review of penalty determinations by Secretary, see section 1276 of this title.

CODE OF FEDERAL REGULATIONS

Approval or denial of State programs, see 30 CFR 732.1 et seq.

Civil penalties, see 30 CFR 723.1 et seq.

Inspection and enforcement procedure, see 30 CFR Chap. VII, Subchap. L.

Secretary of Interior, hearings and appeals procedure, see 43 CFR 4.1 et seq.

United States Supreme Court

Civil penalties provision of this section, due process challenge, see Hodel v. Virginia Surface Min. & Reclamation Ass'n, Inc., 1981, 101 S.Ct. 2352, 452 U.S. 264, 69 L.Ed.2d 1, concurring opinion 101 S.Ct. 2389, 452 U.S. 264, 69 L.Ed.2d 1.

§ 1269. Release of performance bonds or deposits [SMCRA § 519]

(a) Filing of request; submittal of copy of advertisement; notification by letter of intent to seek release

The permittee may file a request with the regulatory authority for the release of all or part of a performance bond or deposit. Within thirty days after any application for bond or deposit release has been filed with the regulatory authority, the operator shall submit a copy of an advertisement placed at least once a week for four successive weeks in a newspaper of general circulation in the locality of the surface coal mining operation. Such advertisement shall be considered part of any bond release application and shall contain a notification of the precise location of the land affected, the number of acres, the permit and the date approved, the amount of the bond filed and the portion sought to be released, and the type and appropriate dates of reclamation work performed, and a description of the results achieved as they relate to the operator's approved reclamation plan. In addition, as part of any bond release application, the applicant shall submit copies of letters which he has sent to adjoining property owners, local governmental bodies, planning agencies, and sewage and water treatment authorities, or water companies in the locality in which the surface coal mining and reclamation activities took place, notifying them of his intention to seek release from the bond.

(b) Inspection and evaluation; notification of decision

Upon receipt of the notification and request, the regulatory authority shall within thirty days conduct an inspection and evaluation of the reclamation work involved. Such evaluation shall consider, among other things, the degree of difficulty to complete any remaining reclamation, whether pollution of surface and subsurface water is occurring, the probability of continuance of future occurrence of such pollution, and the estimated cost of abating such pollution. The regulatory authority shall notify the permittee in writing of its decision to release or not to release all or part of the performance bond or deposit within sixty days from the filing of the request, if no public hearing is held pursuant to subsection (f) of this section, and if there has been a public hearing held pursuant to subsection (f) of this section, within thirty days thereafter.

(c) Requirements for release

The regulatory authority may release in whole or in part said bond or deposit if the authority is satisfied the reclamation covered by the bond or deposit or portion thereof has been accomplished as required by this chapter according to the following schedule:

(1) When the operator completes the backfilling, regrading, and drainage control of a bonded area in accordance with his approved reclamation plan, the release of 60 per centum of the bond or collateral for the applicable permit area.

(2) After revegetation has been established on the regraded mined lands in accordance with the approved reclamation plan. When determining the amount of bond to be released after successful revegetation has been established, the regulatory authority shall retain that amount of bond for the revegetated area which would be sufficient for a third party to cover the cost of reestablishing revegetation and for the period specified for operator responsibility in section 1265 of this title of reestablishing revegetation. No part of the bond or deposit shall be released under this paragraph so long as the lands to which the release would be applicable are contributing suspended solids to streamflow or runoff outside the permit area in excess of the requirements set by section 1265(b)(10) of this title or until soil productivity for prime farm lands has returned to equivalent levels of yield as nonmined land of the same soil type in the surrounding area under equivalent management practices as determined from the soil survey performed pursuant to section 1257(b)(16) of this title. Where a silt dam is to be retained as a permanent impoundment pursuant to section 1265(b)(8) of this title, the portion of bond may be released under this paragraph so long as provisions for sound future maintenance by the operator or the landowner have been made with the regulatory authority.

(3) When the operator has completed successfully all surface coal mining and reclamation activities, the release of the remaining portion of the bond, but not before the expiration of the period specified for operator responsibility in section 1265 of this title: *Provided, however,* That no bond shall be fully released until all reclamation requirements of this chapter are fully met.

(d) Notice of disapproval

If the regulatory authority disapproves the application for release of the bond or portion thereof, the authority shall notify the permittee, in writing, stating the reasons for disapproval and recommending corrective actions necessary to secure said release and allowing opportunity for a public hearing.

(e) Notice to municipality

When any application for total or partial bond release is filed with the regulatory authority, the regulatory authority shall notify the municipality in which a surface coal mining operation is located by certified mail at least thirty days prior to the release of all or a portion of the bond.

(f) Objections to release; hearing

Any person with a valid legal interest which might be adversely affected by release of the bond or the responsible officer or head of any Federal, State, or local governmental agency which has jurisdiction by law or special expertise with respect to any environmental, social, or economic impact involved in the operation, or is authorized to develop and enforce environmental standards with respect to such operations shall have the right to file written objections to the proposed release from bond to the regulatory authority within thirty days after the last publication of the above notice. If written objections are filed, and a hearing requested, the regulatory authority shall inform all the interested parties, of the time and place of the hearing, and hold a public hearing in the locality of the surface coal mining operation proposed for bond release within thirty days of the request for such hearing. The date, time, and location of such public hearings shall be advertised by the regulatory authority in a newspaper of general circulation in the locality for two consecutive weeks, and shall hold a public hearing in the locality of the surface coal mining operation proposed for bond release or at the

State capital at the option of the objector, within thirty days of the request for such hearing.

(g) Informal conference

Without prejudice to the rights of the objectors, the applicant, or the responsibilities of the regulatory authority pursuant to this section, the regulatory authority may establish an informal conference as provided in section 1263 of this title to resolve such written objections.

(h) Power of regulatory authority with respect to informal conference

For the purpose of such hearing the regulatory authority shall have the authority and is hereby empowered to administer oaths, subpena witnesses, or written or printed materials, compel the attendance of witnesses, or production of the materials, and take evidence including but not limited to inspections of the land affected and other surface coal mining operations carried on by the applicant in the general vicinity. A verbatim record of each public hearing required by this chapter shall be made, and a transcript made available on the motion of any party or by order of the regulatory authority.

(Aug. 3, 1977, Pub.L. 95–87, Title V, § 519, 91 Stat. 501.)

CROSS REFERENCES

Applicability of this section to anthracite coal mines, see section 1279 of this title.
Environmental protection performance standards, see section 1265 of this title.
Surface coal mining operations on Indian lands, compliance with requirements as stringent as those of this section, see section 1300 of this title.

CODE OF FEDERAL REGULATIONS

Approval or denial of State programs, see 30 CFR 732.1 et seq.
Permit requirements for special categories of mining, see 30 CFR 785.1 et seq.

§ 1270. Citizens suits [SMCRA § 520]

(a) Civil action to compel compliance with this chapter

Except as provided in subsection (b) of this section, any person having an interest which is or may be adversely affected may commence a civil action on his own behalf to compel compliance with this chapter—

(1) against the United States or any other governmental instrumentality or agency to the extent permitted by the eleventh amendment to the Constitution which is alleged to be in violation of the provisions of this chapter or of any rule, regulation, order or permit issued pursuant thereto, or against any other person who is alleged to be in violation of any rule, regulation, order or permit issued pursuant to this subchapter; or

(2) against the Secretary or the appropriate State regulatory authority to the extent permitted by the eleventh amendment to the Constitution where there is alleged a failure of the Secretary or the appropriate State regulatory authority to perform any act or duty under this chapter which is not discretionary with the Secretary or with the appropriate State regulatory authority.

The district courts shall have jurisdiction, without regard to the amount in controversy or the citizenship of the parties.

(b) Limitation on bringing of action

No action may be commenced—

(1) under subsection (a)(1) of this section—

(A) prior to sixty days after the plaintiff has given notice in writing of the violation (i) to the Secretary, (ii) to the State in which the violation occurs, and (iii) to any alleged violator; or

(B) if the Secretary or the State has commenced and is diligently prosecuting a civil action in a court of the United States or a State to require compliance with the provisions of this chapter, or any rule, regulation, order, or permit issued pursuant to this chapter, but in any such action in a court of the United States any person may intervene as a matter of right; or

(2) under subsection (a)(2) of this section prior to sixty days after the plaintiff has given notice in writing of such action to the Secretary, in such manner as the Secretary shall by regulation prescribe, or to the appropriate State regulatory authority, except that such action may be brought immediately after such notification in the case where the violation or order complained of constitutes an imminent threat to the health or safety of the plaintiff or would immediately affect a legal interest of the plaintiff.

(c) Venue; intervention

(1) Any action respecting a violation of this chapter or the regulations thereunder may be brought only in the judicial district in which the surface coal mining operation complained of is located.

(2) In such action under this section, the Secretary, or the State regulatory authority, if not a party, may intervene as a matter of right.

(d) Costs; filing of bonds

The court, in issuing any final order in any action brought pursuant to subsection (a) of this section, may award costs of litigation (including attorney and expert witness fees) to any party, whenever the court determines such award is appropriate. The court may, if a temporary restraining order or preliminary injunction is sought require the filing of a bond or equivalent security in accordance with the Federal Rules of Civil Procedure.

(e) Effect on other enforcement methods

Nothing in this section shall restrict any right which any person (or class of persons) may have under any statute or common law to seek enforcement of any of the provisions of this chapter and the regulations thereunder, or to seek any other relief (including relief against the Secretary or the appropriate State regulatory authority).

(f) Action for damages

Any person who is injured in his person or property through the violation by any operator of any rule, regulation, order, or permit issued pursuant to this chapter may bring an action for damages (including reasonable attorney and expert witness fees) only in the judicial district in which the surface coal mining operation complained of is located. Nothing in this subsection shall affect the rights established by or limits imposed under State Workmen's Compensation laws.

(Aug. 3, 1977, Pub.L. 95–87, Title V, § 520, 91 Stat. 503.)

CROSS REFERENCES

Judicial review of State regulatory authority action, effect on rights under this section, see section 1276 of this title.

West's Federal Practice Manual

Intervention of right, see § 8838 et seq.

CODE OF FEDERAL REGULATIONS

Notice of citizen suits, see 30 CFR 700.13.

§ 1271. Enforcement [SMCRA § 521]

(a) Notice of violation; Federal inspection; waiver of notification period; cessation order; affirmative obligation on operator; suspension or revocation of permits; contents of notices and orders

(1) Whenever, on the basis of any information available to him, including receipt of information from any person, the Secretary has reason to believe that any person is in violation of any requirement of this chapter or any permit condition required by this chapter, the Secretary shall notify the State regulatory authority, if one exists, in the State in which such violation exists. If no such State authority exists or the State regulatory authority fails within ten days after notification to take appropriate action to cause said violation to be corrected or to show good cause for such failure and transmit notification of its action to the Secretary, the Secretary shall immediately order Federal inspection of the surface coal mining operation at which the alleged violation is occurring unless the information available to the Secretary is a result of a previous Federal inspection of such surface coal mining operation. The ten-day notification period shall be waived when the person informing the Secretary provides adequate proof that an imminent danger of significant environmental harm exists and that the State has failed to take appropriate action. When the Federal inspection results from information provided to the Secretary by any person, the Secretary shall notify such person when the Federal inspection is proposed to be carried out and such person shall be allowed to accompany the inspector during the inspection.

(2) When, on the basis of any Federal inspection, the Secretary or his authorized representative determines that any condition or practices exist, or that any permittee is in violation of any requirement of this chapter or any permit condition required by this chapter, which condition, practice, or violation also creates an imminent danger to the health or safety of the public, or is causing, or can reasonably be expected to cause significant, imminent environmental harm to land, air, or water resources, the Secretary or his authorized representative shall immediately order a cessation of surface coal mining and reclamation operations or the portion thereof relevant to the condition, practice, or violation. Such cessation order shall remain in effect until the Secretary or his authorized representative determines that the condition, practice, or violation has been abated, or until modified, vacated, or terminated by the Secretary or his authorized representative pursuant to paragraph (5) of this subsection. Where the Secretary finds that the ordered cessation of surface coal mining and reclamation operations, or any portion thereof, will not completely abate the imminent danger to health or safety of the public or the significant imminent environmental harm to land, air, or water resources, the Secretary shall, in addition to the cessation order, impose affirmative obligations on the operator requiring him to take whatever steps the Secretary deems necessary to abate the imminent danger or the significant environmental harm.

(3) When, on the basis of a Federal inspection which is carried out during the enforcement of a Federal program or a Federal lands program, Federal inspection pursuant to section 1252, or section 1254(b) of this title, or during Federal enforcement of a State program in accordance with subsection (b) of this section, the Secretary or his authorized representative determines that any permittee is in violation of any requirement of this chapter or any permit condition required by this chapter; but such violation does not create an imminent danger to the health or safety of the public, or cannot be reasonably expected to cause significant, imminent environmental harm to land, air,

or water resources, the Secretary or authorized representative shall issue a notice to the permittee or his agent fixing a reasonable time but not more than ninety days for the abatement of the violation and providing opportunity for public hearing.

If, upon expiration of the period of time as originally fixed or subsequently extended, for good cause shown and upon the written finding of the Secretary or his authorized representative, the Secretary or his authorized representative finds that the violation has not been abated, he shall immediately order a cessation of surface coal mining and reclamation operations or the portion thereof relevant to the violation. Such cessation order shall remain in effect until the Secretary or his authorized representative determines that the violation has been abated, or until modified, vacated, or terminated by the Secretary or his authorized representative pursuant to paragraph (5) of this subsection. In the order of cessation issued by the Secretary under this subsection, the Secretary shall determine the steps necessary to abate the violation in the most expeditious manner possible, and shall include the necessary measures in the order.

(4) When, on the basis of a Federal inspection which is carried out during the enforcement of a Federal program or a Federal lands program, Federal inspection pursuant to section 1252 or section 1254 of this title or during Federal enforcement of a State program in accordance with subsection (b) of this section, the Secretary or his authorized representative determines that a pattern of violations of any requirements of this chapter or any permit conditions required by this chapter exists or has existed, and if the Secretary or his authorized representative also find that such violations are caused by the unwarranted failure of the permittee to comply with any requirements of this chapter or any permit conditions, or that such violations are willfully caused by the permittee, the Secretary or his authorized representative shall forthwith issue an order to the permittee to show cause as to why the permit should not be suspended or revoked and shall provide opportunity for a public hearing. If a hearing is requested the Secretary shall inform all interested parties of the time and place of the hearing. Upon the permittee's failure to show cause as to why the permit should not be suspended or revoked, the Secretary or his authorized representative shall forthwith suspend or revoke the permit.

(5) Notices and orders issued pursuant to this section shall set forth with reasonable specificity the nature of the violation and the remedial action required, the period of time established for abatement, and a reasonable description of the portion of the surface coal mining and reclamation operation to which the notice or order applies. Each notice or order issued under this section shall be given promptly to the permittee or his agent by the Secretary or his authorized representative who issues such notice or order, and all such notices and orders shall be in writing and shall be signed by such authorized representatives. Any notice or order issued pursuant to this section may be modified, vacated, or terminated by the Secretary or his authorized representative. A copy of any such order or notice shall be sent to the State regulatory authority in the State in which the violation occurs: *Provided*, That any notice or order issued pursuant to this section which requires cessation of mining by the operator shall expire within thirty days of actual notice to the operator unless a public hearing is held at the site or within such reasonable proximity to the site that any viewings of the site can be conducted during the course of public hearing.

(b) Inadequate State enforcement; notice and hearing

Whenever on the basis of information available to him, the Secretary has reason to believe that violations of all or any part of an approved State program result from a failure of the State to enforce such State program or any part thereof effectively, he shall after public notice and notice to the State, hold a hearing thereon in the State within thirty days of such notice. If as a result of said hearing the Secretary finds that there are violations and such violations result from a failure of the State to enforce all or any part of the State program effectively, and if he further finds that the State has not adequately demonstrated its capability and intent to enforce such State program, he shall give public notice of such finding. During the period beginning with such public notice and ending when such State satisfies the Secretary that it will enforce this chapter, the Secretary shall enforce, in the manner provided by this chapter, any permit condition required under this chapter, shall issue new or revised permits in accordance with requirements of this chapter, and may issue such notices and orders as are necessary for compliance therewith: *Provided*, That in the case of a State permittee who has met his obligations under such permit and who did not willfully secure the issuance of such permit through fraud or collusion, the Secretary shall give the permittee a reasonable time to conform ongoing surface mining and reclamation to the requirements of this chapter before suspending or revoking the State permit.

(c) Civil action for relief

The Secretary may request the Attorney General to institute a civil action for relief, including a permanent or temporary injunction, restraining order, or any other appropriate order in the district court of the United States for the district in which the surface coal mining and reclamation operation is located or in which the permittee thereof has his principal office, whenever such permittee or his agent (A) violates or fails or refuses to comply with any order or decision issued by the Secretary under this chapter, or (B) interferes with, hinders, or delays the Secretary or his authorized representatives in carrying out the provisions of this chapter, or (C) refuses to admit such authorized representative to the mine, or (D) refuses to permit inspection of the mine by such authorized representative, or (E) refuses to furnish any information or report requested by the Secretary in furtherance of the provisions of this chapter, or (F) refuses to permit access to, and copying of, such records as the Secretary determines necessary in carrying out the provisions of this chapter. Such court shall have jurisdiction to provide such relief as may be appropriate. Temporary restraining orders shall be issued in accordance with rule 65 of the Federal Rules of Civil Procedure, as amended. Any relief granted by the court to enforce an order under clause (A) of this section shall continue in effect until the completion or final termination of all proceedings for review of such order under this subchapter, unless, prior thereto, the district court granting such relief sets it aside or modifies it.

(d) Sanctions; effect on additional enforcement rights under State law

As a condition of approval of any State program submitted pursuant to section 1253 of this title, the enforcement provisions thereof shall, at a minimum, incorporate sanctions no less stringent than those set forth in this section, and shall contain the same or similar procedural requirements relating thereto. Nothing herein shall be construed so as to eliminate any additional enforcement rights or procedures which are available under State law to a State regulatory authority but which are not specifically enumerated herein.

(Aug. 3, 1977, Pub.L. 95–87, Title V, § 521, 91 Stat. 504.)

CROSS REFERENCES

Federal enforcement of State programs pursuant to this section, see section 1254 of this title.

Imminent danger to the health and safety of the public defined, see section 1291 of this title.

Penalties for violations, see section 1268 of this title.

Retaliatory practices against employees aiding in enforcement of this chapter, see section 1293 of this title.

Review by Secretary of notices or orders issued under this section, see section 1275 of this title.

State programs for regulation of surface coal mining and reclamation operations, see section 1253 of this title.

Temporary judicial relief from orders issued under certain provisions of this section, see section 1276 of this title.

CODE OF FEDERAL REGULATIONS

Inspection and enforcement procedure, see 30 CFR Chap. VII, Subchap. L.

Non-federal and non-Indian lands, permanent regulatory programs, see 30 CFR Chap. VII, Subchap. C.

Secretary of Interior, hearings and appeals procedure, see 43 CFR 4.1 et seq.

United States Supreme Court

Cessation order on basis of federal inspection, due process challenge to this section, see Hodel v. Virginia Surface Min. & Reclamation Ass'n, Inc., 1981, 101 S.Ct. 2352, 452 U.S. 264, 69 L.Ed.2d 1, concurring opinion 101 S.Ct. 2389, 452 U.S. 264, 69 L.Ed.2d 1.

§ 1272. Designating areas unsuitable for surface coal mining [SMCRA § 522]

(a) Establishment of State planning process; standards; State process requirements; integration with present and future land use planning and regulation processes; savings provisions

(1) To be eligible to assume primary regulatory authority pursuant to section 1253 of this title, each State shall establish a planning process enabling objective decisions based upon competent and scientifically sound data and information as to which, if any, land areas of a State are unsuitable for all or certain types of surface coal mining operations pursuant to the standards set forth in paragraphs (2) and (3) of this subsection but such designation shall not prevent the mineral exploration pursuant to the chapter of any area so designated.

(2) Upon petition pursuant to subsection (c) of this section, the State regulatory authority shall designate an area as unsuitable for all or certain types of surface coal mining operations if the State regulatory authority determines that reclamation pursuant to the requirements of this chapter is not technologically and economically feasible.

(3) Upon petition pursuant to subsection (c) of this section, a surface area may be designated unsuitable for certain types of surface coal mining operations if such operations will—

(A) be incompatible with existing State or local land use plans or programs; or

(B) affect fragile or historic lands in which such operations could result in significant damage to important historic, cultural, scientific, and esthetic values and natural systems; or

(C) affect renewable resource lands in whic[illegible] such operations could result in a substantial loss [illegible] reduction of long-range productivity of water sup[illegible] or of food or fiber products, and such land[illegible] include aquifers and aquifer recharge area[illegible]

(D) affect natural hazard lands in whic[illegible] operations could substantially endanger [illegible] property, such lands to include areas subject to frequent flooding and areas of unstable geology.

(4) To comply with this section, a State must demonstrate it has developed or is developing a process which includes—

(A) a State agency responsible for surface coal mining lands review;

(B) a data base and an inventory system which will permit proper evaluation of the capacity of different land areas of the State to support and permit reclamation of surface coal mining operations;

(C) a method or methods for implementing land use planning decisions concerning surface coal mining operations; and

(D) proper notice, opportunities for public participation, including a public hearing prior to making any designation or redesignation, pursuant to this section.

(5) Determinations of the unsuitability of land for surface coal mining, as provided for in this section, shall be integrated as closely as possible with present and future land use planning and regulation processes at the Federal, State, and local levels.

(6) The requirements of this section shall not apply to lands on which surface coal mining operations are being conducted on August 3, 1977, or under a permit issued pursuant to this chapter, or where substantial legal and financial commitments in such operation were in existence prior to January 4, 1977.

(b) Review of Federal lands

The Secretary shall conduct a review of the Federal lands to determine, pursuant to the standards set forth in paragraphs (2) and (3) of subsection (a) of this section, whether there are areas on Federal lands which are unsuitable for all or certain types of surface coal mining operations: *Provided, however*, That the Secretary may permit surface coal mining on Federal lands prior to the completion of this review. When the Secretary determines an area on Federal lands to be unsuitable for all or certain types of surface coal mining operations, he shall withdraw such area or [illegible]ondition any mineral leasing or mineral entries in a [illegible]nner so as to limit surface coal mining operations [illegible]h area. Where a Federal program has been [illegible]ted in a State pursuant to section 1254 of [illegible]e Secretary shall implement a process for [illegible] areas unsuitable for surface coal mining [illegible] lands within such State and such [illegible]porate the standards and proce- [illegible] Prior to designating Federal [illegible]h mining, the Secretary shall [illegible]riate State and local agencies.

(c) Petition; intervention; decision

Any person having an interest which is or may be adversely affected shall have the right to petition the regulatory authority to have an area designated as unsuitable for surface coal mining operations, or to have such a designation terminated. Such a petition shall contain allegations of facts with supporting evidence which would tend to establish the allegations. Within ten months after receipt of the petition the regulatory authority shall hold a public hearing in the locality of the affected area, after appropriate notice and publication of the date, time, and location of such hearing. After a person having an interest which is or may be adversely affected has filed a petition and before the hearing, as required by this subsection, any person may intervene by filing allegations of facts with supporting evidence which would tend to establish the allegations. Within sixty days after such hearing, the regulatory authority shall issue and furnish to the petitioner and any other party to the hearing, a written decision regarding the petition, and the reasons therefore.[1] In the event that all the petitioners stipulate agreement prior to the requested hearing, and withdraw their request, such hearing need not be held.

(d) Statement

Prior to designating any land areas as unsuitable for surface coal mining operations, the regulatory authority shall prepare a detailed statement on (i) the potential coal resources of the area, (ii) the demand for coal resources, and (iii) the impact of such designation on the environment, the economy, and the supply of coal.

(e) Prohibition on certain Federal public and private surface coal mining operations

After August 3, 1977, and subject to valid existing rights no surface coal mining operations except those which exist on August 3, 1977, shall be permitted—

(1) on any lands within the boundaries of units of the National Park System, the National Wildlife Refuge Systems, the National System of Trails, the National Wilderness Preservation System, the Wild and Scenic Rivers System, including study rivers designated under section 1276(a) of Title 16 and National Recreation Areas designated by Act of Congress;

(2) on any Federal lands within the boundaries of any national forest: *Provided, however*, That surface coal mining operations may be permitted on such lands if the Secretary finds that there are no significant recreational, timber, economic, or other values which may be incompatible with such surface mining operations and—

(A) surface operations and impacts are incident to an underground coal mine; or

(B) where the Secretary of Agriculture determines, with respect to lands which do not have significant forest cover within those national forests west of the 100th meridian, that surface mining is in compliance with the Multiple-Use Sustained-Yield Act of 1960 [16 U.S.C.A. §§ 528–531], the Federal Coal Leasing Amendments Act of 1975, the National Forest Management Act of 1976, and the provisions of this chapter: *And provided further*, That no surface coal mining operations may be permitted within the boundaries of the Custer National Forest;

(3) which will adversely affect any publicly owned park or places included in the National Register of Historic Sites unless approved jointly by the regulatory authority and the Federal, State, or local agency with jurisdiction over the park or the historic site;

(4) within one hundred feet of the outside right-of-way line of any public road, except where mine access roads or haulage roads join such right-of-way line and except that the regulatory authority may permit such roads to be relocated or the area affected to lie within one hundred feet of such road, if after public notice and opportunity for public hearing in the locality a written finding is made that the interests of the public and the landowners affected thereby will be protected; or

(5) within three hundred feet from any occupied dwelling, unless waived by the owner thereof, nor within three hundred feet of any public building, school, church, community, or institutional building, public park, or within one hundred feet of a cemetery.

(Aug. 3, 1977, Pub.L. 95–87, Title V, § 522, 91 Stat. 507.)

1 So in original. Probably should be "therefor".

CROSS REFERENCES

Designation of lands unsuitable for noncoal mining, see section 1281 of this title.
Duties of Secretary under this section in connection with Federal lands program, see section 1273 of this title.
Duty of Secretary to assist States in developing criteria and procedures for determining areas unsuitable for surface coal mining, see section 1211 of this title.
Federal programs implemented for States, applicability of certain provisions of this section, see section 1254 of this title.
Permit approval or denial, suitability of area for surface coal mining, see section 1260 of this title.
State program provisions for designation of areas unsuitable for coal mining, see section 1253 of this title.

West's Federal Practice Manual

Permissive intervention, see § 8843 et seq.

CODE OF FEDERAL REGULATIONS

Approval or denial of State programs, see 30 CFR 732.1 et seq.
Areas unsuitable for mining, see 30 CFR Chap. VII, Subchap. F.
Environment, see 43 CFR 3461.0–3 et seq.
Federal program for a State, see 30 CFR 736.1 et seq.
Secretary of Interior, hearings and appeals procedure, see 43 CFR 4.1 et seq.

§ 1273. Federal lands [SMCRA § 523]

(a) Promulgation and implementation of Federal lands program

No later than one year after August 3, 1977, the Secretary shall promulgate and implement a Federal lands program which shall be applicable to all surface coal mining and reclamation operations taking place pursuant to any Federal law on any Federal lands: *Provided*, That except as provided in section 1300 of this title the provisions of this chapter shall not be applicable to Indian lands. The Federal lands program shall, at a minimum, incorporate all of the requirements of this chapter and shall take into consideration the diverse physical, climatological, and other unique characteristics of the Federal lands in question. Where Federal lands in a State with an approved State program are involved, the Federal lands program shall, at a minimum, include the requirements of the approved State program: *Provided*, That the Secretary shall retain his duties under sections 201(a), (2)(B)[1] and 201(a)(3) of this title, and shall continue to be responsible for designation of Federal lands as unsuitable for mining in accordance with section 1272(b) of this title.

(b) Incorporation of requirements into any lease, permit, or contract issued by Secretary which may involve surface coal mining and reclamation operations

The requirements of this chapter and the Federal lands program or an approved State program for State regulation of surface coal mining on Federal lands under subsection (c) of this section, whichever is applicable, shall be incorporated by reference or otherwise in any Federal mineral lease, permit, or contract issued by the Secretary which may involve surface coal mining and reclamation operations. Incorporation of such requirements shall not, however, limit in any way the authority of the Secretary to subsequently issue new regulations, revise the Federal lands program to deal with changing conditions or changed technology, and to require any surface mining and reclamation operations to conform with the requirements of this chapter and the regulations issued pursuant to this chapter.

(c) State cooperative agreements

Any State with an approved State program [illegible] elect to enter into a cooperative agreement wit[illegible] Secretary to provide for State regulation of s[illegible] coal mining and reclamation operations on [illegible] lands within the State, provided the Secretar[illegible] mines in writing that such State has the necessary personnel and funding to fully implement such a cooperative agreement in accordance with the provision of this chapter. States with cooperative agreements existing on August 3, 1977, may elect to continue regulation on Federal lands within the State, prior to approval by the Secretary of their State program, or imposition of a Federal program, provided that such existing cooperative agreement is modified to fully comply with the initial regulatory procedures set forth in section 1252 of this title. Nothing in this subsection shall be construed as authorizing the Secretary to delegate to the States his duty to approve mining plans on Federal lands, to designate certain Federal lands as unsuitable for surface coal mining pursuant to section 1272 of this title, or to regulate other activities taking place on Federal lands.

(d) Development of program to assure no unreasonable denial to any class of coal purchasers

The Secretary shall develop a program to assure that with respect to the granting of permits, leases, or contracts for coal owned by the United States, that no class of purchasers of the mined coal shall be unreasonably denied purchase thereof.

(Aug. 3, 1977, Pub.L. 95–87, Title V, § 523, 91 Stat. 510.)

1 So in original. Probably should be "201(a)(2)(B)".

CROSS REFERENCES

Authorization of appropriations for implementation of this section, see section 1302 of this title.
Federal lands program defined, see section 1291 of this title.
Grants to States, increase for State regulation of Federal lands, see section 1295 of this title.
Implementation of Federal lands program as not constituting major action for purposes of National Environmental Policy Act, see section 1292 of this title.
Judicial review of standards promulgated pursuant to this section, see section 1276 of this title.
State programs, exclusive jurisdiction of surface coal mining and reclamation operations except as provided in this section, see section 1253 of this title.

CODE OF FEDERAL REGULATIONS

Areas unsuitable for mining, petition for designation or termination of previous designation, see 30 CFR 769.1 et seq.
General performance standards—
Surface mining, see 30 CFR 715.10 et seq.
Underground mining, see 30 CFR 717.10 et seq.
Inspection and enforcement procedure, see 30 CFR Chap. VII, Subchap. L.
...tary of Interior, general scope of authority and responsibility, ...e 30 CFR 700.1 et seq.
...rams for conduct of surface mine operations, see 30 CFR ... VII, Subchap. T.

...blic agencies, public utilities, ...d public corporations [SMCRA ...]

... instrumentality of Federal, ...nt, including any publicly ... owned corporation of Federal, State, or local government, which proposes to engage in surface coal mining operations which are subject to the requirements of this chapter shall comply with the provisions of this subchapter.

(Aug. 3, 1977, Pub.L. 95–87, Title V, § 524, 91 Stat. 511.)

§ 1275. Review by Secretary [SMCRA § 525]

(a) Application for review of order or notice; investigation; hearing; notice

(1) A permittee issued a notice or order by the Secretary pursuant to the provisions of paragraphs (2) and (3) of subsection (a) of section 1271 of this title, or pursuant to a Federal program or the Federal lands program or any person having an interest which is or may be adversely affected by such notice or order or by any modification, vacation, or termination of such notice or order, may apply to the Secretary for review of the notice or order within thirty days of receipt thereof or within thirty days of its modification, vacation, or termination. Upon receipt of such application, the Secretary shall cause such investigation to be made as he deems appropriate. Such investigation shall provide an opportunity for a public hearing, at the request of the applicant or the person having an interest which is or may be adversely affected, to enable the applicant or such person to present information relating to the issuance and continuance of such notice or order or the modification, vacation, or termination thereof. The filing of an application for review under this subsection shall not operate as a stay of any order or notice.

(2) The permittee and other interested persons shall be given written notice of the time and place of the hearing at least five days prior thereto. Any such hearing shall be of record and shall be subject to section 554 of Title 5.

(b) Findings of fact; issuance of decision

Upon receiving the report of such investigation, the Secretary shall make findings of fact, and shall issue a written decision, incorporating therein an order vacating, affirming, modifying, or terminating the notice or order, or the modification, vacation, or termination of such notice or order complained of and incorporate his findings therein. Where the application for review concerns an order for cessation of surface coal mining and reclamation operations issued pursuant to the provisions of paragraph (2) or (3) of subsection (a) of section 1271 of this title, the Secretary shall issue the written decision within thirty days of the receipt of the application for review, unless temporary relief has been granted by the Secretary pursuant to subsection

(c) of this section or by the court pursuant to subsection (c) of section 1276 of this title.

(c) Temporary relief; issuance of order or decision granting or denying relief

Pending completion of the investigation and hearing required by this section, the applicant may file with the Secretary a written request that the Secretary grant temporary relief from any notice or order issued under section 1271 of this title, a Federal program or the Federal lands program together with a detailed statement giving reasons for granting such relief. The Secretary shall issue an order or decision granting or denying such relief expeditiously: *Provided*, That where the applicant requests relief from an order for cessation of coal mining and reclamation operations issued pursuant to paragraph (2) or (3) of subsection (a) of section 1271 of this title, the order or decision on such a request shall be issued within five days of its receipt. The Secretary may grant such relief, under such conditions as he may prescribe, if—

(1) a hearing has been held in the locality of the permit area on the request for temporary relief in which all parties were given an opportunity to be heard;

(2) the applicant shows that there is substantial likelihood that the findings of the Secretary will be favorable to him; and

(3) such relief will not adversely affect the health or safety of the public or cause significant, imminent environmental harm to land, air, or water resources.

(d) Notice and hearing with respect to section 1271 order to show cause

Following the issuance of an order to show cause as to why a permit should not be suspended or revoked pursuant to section 1271 of this title, the Secretary shall hold a public hearing after giving written notice of the time, place, and date thereof. Any such hearing shall be of record and shall be subject to section 554 of Title 5. Within sixty days following the public hearing, the Secretary shall issue and furnish to the permittee and all other parties to the hearing a written decision, and the reasons therefor, concerning suspension or revocation of the permit. If the Secretary revokes the permit, the permittee shall immediately cease surface coal mining operations on the permit area and shall complete reclamation within a period specified by the Secretary, or the Secretary shall declare as forfeited the performance bonds for the operation.

(e) Costs

Whenever an order is issued under this section, or as a result of any administrative proceeding under this chapter, at the request of any person, a sum equal to the aggregate amount of all costs and expenses (including attorney fees) as determined by the Secretary to have been reasonably incurred by such person for or in connection with his participation in such proceedings, including any judicial review of agency actions, may be assessed against either party as the court, resulting from judicial review or the Secretary, resulting from administrative proceedings, deems proper.

(Aug. 3, 1977, Pub.L. 95–87, Title V, § 525, 91 Stat. 511.)

CROSS REFERENCES

Penalties for violations, see section 1268 of this title.

Temporary judicial relief from orders or decisions issued pursuant to this section, see section 1276 of this title.

CODE OF FEDERAL REGULATIONS

Civil penalties, see 30 CFR 841.1 et seq.

Federal enforcement, see 30 CFR 843.1 et seq.

Secretary of Interior, hearings and appeals procedure, see 43 CFR 4.1 et seq.

§ 1276. Judicial review [SMCRA § 526]

(a) Review by United States District Court; venue; filing of petition; time

(1) Any action of the Secretary to approve or disapprove a State program or to prepare or promulgate a Federal program pursuant to this chapter shall be subject to judicial review by the United States District Court for the District which includes the capital of the State whose program is at issue. Any action by the Secretary promulgating national rules or regulations including standards pursuant to sections 1251, 1265, 1266, and 1273 of this title shall be subject to judicial review in the United States District Court for the District of Columbia Circuit. Any other action constituting rulemaking by the Secretary shall be subject to judicial review only by the United States District Court for the District in which the surface coal mining operation is located. Any action subject to judicial review under this subsection shall be affirmed unless the court concludes that such action is arbitrary, capricious, or otherwise inconsistent with law. A petition for review of any action subject to judicial review under this subsection shall be filed in the appropriate Court within sixty days from the date of such action, or after such date if the petition is based solely on grounds arising after the sixtieth day. Any such petition may be made by any person who participated in the administrative proceedings and who is aggrieved by the action of the Secretary.

(2) Any order or decision issued by the Secret[illegible] in a civil penalty proceeding or any other procee[illegible] required to be conducted pursuant to section [illegible] Title 5 shall be subject to judicial review on or [illegible] 30 days from the date of such order or de[illegible] accordance with subsection (b) of this secti[illegible]

United States District Court for the District in which the surface coal mining operation is located. In the case of a proceeding to review an order or decision issued by the Secretary under the penalty section of this chapter, the court shall have jurisdiction to enter an order requiring payment of any civil penalty assessment enforced by its judgment. This availability of review established in this subsection shall not be construed to limit the operations of rights established in section 1270 of this title.

(b) Evidence; conclusiveness of findings; orders

The courts shall hear such petition or complaint solely on the record made before the Secretary. Except as provided in subsection (a) of this section, the findings of the Secretary if supported by substantial evidence on the record considered as a whole, shall be conclusive. The court may affirm, vacate, or modify any order or decision or may remand the proceedings to the Secretary for such further action as it may direct.

(c) Temporary relief; prerequisites

In the case of a proceeding to review any order or decision issued by the Secretary under this chapter, including an order or decision issued pursuant to subsection (c) or (d) of section 1275 of this title pertaining to any order issued under paragraph (2), (3), or (4) of subsection (a) of section 1271 of this title for cessation of coal mining and reclamation operations, the court may, under such conditions as it may prescribe, grant such temporary relief as it deems appropriate pending final determination of the proceedings if—

(1) all parties to the proceedings have been notified and given an opportunity to be heard on a request for temporary relief;

(2) the person requesting such relief shows that there is a substantial likelihood that he will prevail on the merits of the final determination of the proceeding; and

(3) such relief will not adversely affect the public health or safety or cause significant imminent environmental harm to land, air, or water resources.

Stay of action, order, or decision of Secretary

commencement of a proceeding under this sec- not, unless specifically ordered by the court, stay of the action, order, or decision of

egulatory authority

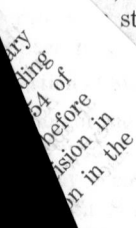

egulatory authority pursuant to m shall be subject to judicial etent jurisdiction in accor- out the availability of such review shall not be construed to limit the operation of the rights established in section 1270 of this title except as provided therein.

(Aug. 3, 1977, Pub.L. 95–87, Title V, § 526, 91 Stat. 512.)

CROSS REFERENCES

Decisions of regulatory authority, right to appeal in accordance with this section, see section 1264 of this title.
Penalties for violations, see section 1268 of this title.
Review by Secretary, see section 1275 of this title.

§ 1277. Special bituminous coal mines [SMCRA § 527]

(a) Issuance of separate regulations; criteria

The regulatory authority is authorized to issue separate regulations for those special bituminous coal surface mines located west of the 100th meridian west longitude which meet the following criteria:

(1) the excavation of the specific mine pit takes place on the same relatively limited site for an extended period of time;

(2) the excavation of the specific mine pit follows a coal seam having an inclination of fifteen degrees or more from the horizontal, and continues in the same area proceeding downward with lateral expansion of the pit necessary to maintain stability or as necessary to accommodate the orderly expansion of the total mining operation;

(3) the excavation of the specific mine pit involves the mining of more than one coal seam and mining has been initiated on the deepest coal seam contemplated to be mined in the current operation;

(4) the amount of material removed is large in proportion to the surface area disturbed;

(5) there is no practicable alternative method of mining the coal involved;

(6) there is no practicable method to reclaim the land in the manner required by this chapter; and

(7) the specific mine pit has been actually producing coal since January 1, 1972, in such manner as to meet the criteria set forth in this section, and, because of past duration of mining, is substantially committed to a mode of operation which warrants exceptions to some provisions of this subchapter.

(b) New bituminous coal surface mines

Such separate regulations shall also contain a distinct part to cover and pertain to new bituminous coal surface mines which may be developed after August 3, 1977, on lands immediately adjacent to lands upon which are located special bituminous mines existing on January 1, 1972. Such new mines shall meet the criteria of subsection (a) of this section except for paragraphs (3) and (7), and all requirements of State law, notwithstanding in whole or part the regulations issued pursuant to subsection (c) of this section. In the event of an amendment or revision to the State's regulatory program, regulations, or decisions made thereunder governing such mines, the Secretary shall issue such additional regulations as necessary to meet the purposes of this chapter.

(c) Scope of alternative regulations

Such alternative regulations may pertain only to the standards governing onsite handling of spoils, elimination of depressions capable of collecting water, creation of impoundments, and regrading to the approximate original contour and shall specify that remaining highwalls are stable. All other performance standards in this subchapter shall apply to such mines.

(Aug. 3, 1977, Pub.L. 95–87, Title V, § 527, 91 Stat. 513.)

CROSS REFERENCES

Approximate original contour defined, see section 1291 of this title.

CODE OF FEDERAL REGULATIONS

Permit requirements for special categories of mining, see 30 CFR 785.1 et seq.
Secretary of Interior, general scope of authority and responsibility, see 30 CFR 700.1 et seq.
Special bituminous coal mine performance standards, initial program regulations, see 30 CFR 716.4.
Special permanent program performance standards for special bituminous coal mines in Wyoming, see 30 CFR 825.1 et seq.

§ 1278. Surface mining operations not subject to this chapter [SMCRA § 528]

The provisions of this chapter shall not apply to any of the following activities:

(1) the extraction of coal by a landowner for his own noncommercial use from land owned or leased by him; and

(2) the extraction of coal as an incidental part of Federal, State or local government-financed highway or other construction under regulations established by the regulatory authority.

(Aug. 3, 1977, Pub.L. 95–87, Title V, § 528, 91 Stat. 514; May 7, 1987, Pub.L. 100–34, Title II, § 201(a), 101 Stat. 300.)

CROSS REFERENCES

Deduction of expenses incurred for mining reclamation or closing activities in accordance with reclamation plan submitted pursuant to this section, see section 468 of Title 26, Internal Revenue Code.
Surface coal mining operations defined, see section 1291 of this title.

CODE OF FEDERAL REGULATIONS

Government financed highway or construction, exemption for coal extraction, see 30 CFR 707.1 et seq.
Secretary of Interior, general scope of authority and responsibility, see 30 CFR 700.1 et seq.

§ 1279. Anthracite coal mines [SMCRA § 529]

(a) The Secretary is authorized to and shall issue separate regulations according to time schedules established in this chapter for anthracite coal surface mines, if such mines are regulated by environmental protection standards of the State in which they are located. Such alternative regulations shall adopt, in each instance, the environmental protection provisions of the State regulatory program in existence on August 3, 1977, in lieu of sections 1265 and 1266 of this title. Provisions of sections 1259 and 1269 of this title are applicable except for specified bond limits and period of revegetation responsibility. All other provisions of this chapter apply and the regulation issued by the Secretary of Interior for each State anthracite regulatory program shall so reflect: *Provided, however*, That upon amendment of a State's regulatory program for anthracite mining or regulations thereunder in force in lieu of the above-cited sections of this chapter, the Secretary shall issue such additional regulations as necessary to meet the purposes of this chapter.

(b) The Secretary of Interior shall report to Congress biennially, commencing on December 31, 1977, as to the effectiveness of such State anthracite regulatory programs operating in conjunction with this chapter with respect to protecting the environment and such reports shall include those recommendations the Secretary deems necessary for program changes in order to better meet the environmental protection objectives of this chapter.

(Aug. 3, 1977, Pub.L. 95–87, Title V, § 529, 91 Stat. 514.)

CODE OF FEDERAL REGULATIONS

Anthracite coal mine standards, initial program regulations, see 30 CFR 716.5.
Permit requirements for special categories of mining, see 30 CFR 785.1 et seq.
Secretary of Interior, general scope of authority and responsibility, see 30 CFR 700.1 et seq.
Special program performance standards, anthracite mines in Pennsylvania, see 30 CFR 820.1 et seq.

SUBCHAPTER VI—DESIGNATION OF LANDS UNSUITABLE FOR NONCOAL MINING

§ 1281. Designation procedures [SMCRA § 601]

(a) Review of Federal land areas for unsuitability for noncoal mining

With respect to Federal lands within any State, the Secretary of Interior may, and if so requested by the Governor of such State shall, review any area within such lands to assess whether it may be unsuitable for mining operations for minerals or materials other than coal, pursuant to the criteria and procedures of this section.

(b) Criteria considered in determining designations

An area of Federal land may be designated under this section as unsuitable for mining operations if (1) such area consists of Federal land of a predominantly urban or suburban character, used primarily for residential or related purposes, the mineral estate of which remains in the public domain, or (2) such area consists of Federal land where mining operations would have an adverse impact on lands used primarily for residential or related purposes.

(c) Petition for exclusion; contents; hearing; temporary land withdrawal

Any person having an interest which is or may be adversely affected shall have the right to petition the Secretary to seek exclusion of an area from mining operations pursuant to this section or the redesignation of an area or part thereof as suitable for such operations. Such petition shall contain allegations of fact with supporting evidence which would tend to substantiate the allegations. The petitioner shall be granted a hearing within a reasonable time and finding with reasons therefor upon the matter of their petition. In any instance where a Governor requests the Secretary to review an area, or where the Secretary finds the national interest so requires, the Secretary may temporarily withdraw the area to be reviewed from mineral entry or leasing pending such review: *Provided, however*, That such temporary withdrawal be ended as promptly as practicable and in no event shall exceed two years.

(d) Limitation on designations; rights preservation; regulations

In no event is a land area to be designated unsuitable for mining operations under this section on which mining operations are being conducted prior to the holding of a hearing on such petition in accordance with subsection (c) of this section. Valid existing rights shall be preserved and not affected by such designation. Designation of an area as unsuitable for mining operations under this section shall not prevent subsequent mineral exploration of such area, except that such exploration shall require the prior written consent of the holder of the surface estate, which consent shall be filed with the Secretary. The Secretary may promulgate, with respect to any designated area, regulations to minimize any adverse effects of such exploration.

(e) Statement

Prior to any designation pursuant to this section, the Secretary shall prepare a detailed statement on (i) the potential mineral resources of the area, (ii) the demand for such mineral resources, and (iii) the impact of such designation or the absence of such designation on the environment, economy, and the supply of such mineral resources.

(f) Area withdrawal

When the Secretary designates an area of Federal lands as unsuitable for all or certain types of mining operations for minerals and materials other than coal pursuant to this section he may withdraw such area from mineral entry or leasing, or condition such entry or leasing so as to limit such mining operations in accordance with his determination, if the Secretary also determines, based on his analysis pursuant to subsection (e) of this section, that the benefits resulting from such designation would be greater than the benefits to the regional or national economy which could result from mineral development of such area.

(g) Right to appeal

Any party with a valid legal interest who has appeared in the proceedings in connection with the Secretary's determination pursuant to this section and who is aggrieved by the Secretary's decision (or by his failure to act within a reasonable time) shall have the right of appeal for review by the United States district court for the district in which the pertinent area is located.

(Aug. 3, 1977, Pub.L. 95–87, Title VI, § 601, 91 Stat. 515.)

CROSS REFERENCES

Designation of areas unsuitable for surface coal mining, see section 1272 of this title.

LIBRARY REFERENCES

Mines and Minerals ⚷92.6, 92.9.
C.J.S. Mines and Minerals §§ 229 et seq., 239.

SUBCHAPTER VII—ADMINISTRATIVE AND MISCELLANEOUS PROVISIONS

CROSS REFERENCES

Inability of State to take action concerning State program, effect on eligibility for financial assistance under this subchapter, see section 1253 of this title.

§ 1291. Definitions [SMCRA § 701]

For the purposes of this chapter—

(1) "alluvial valley floors" means the unconsolidated stream laid deposits holding streams where water availability is sufficient for subirrigation or flood irrigation agricultural activities but does not include upland areas which are generally overlain by a thin veneer of colluvial deposits composed chiefly of debris from sheet erosion, deposits by unconcentrated runoff or slope wash, together with

talus, other mass movement accumulation and windblown deposits;

(2) "approximate original contour" means that surface configuration achieved by backfilling and grading of the mined area so that the reclaimed area, including any terracing or access roads, closely resembles the general surface configuration of the land prior to mining and blends into and complements the drainage pattern of the surrounding terrain, with all highwalls and spoil piles eliminated; water impoundments may be permitted where the regulatory authority determines that they are in compliance with section 1265(b)(8) of this title;

(3) "commerce" means trade, traffic, commerce, transportation, transmission, or communication among the several States, or between a State and any other place outside thereof, or between points in the same State which directly or indirectly affect interstate commerce;

(4) "Federal lands" means any land, including mineral interests, owned by the United States without regard to how the United States acquired ownership of the land and without regard to the agency having responsibility for management thereof, except Indian lands: *Provided*, That for the purposes of this chapter lands or mineral interests east of the one hundredth meridian west longitude owned by the United States and entrusted to or managed by the Tennessee Valley Authority shall not be subject to sections 1304 (Surface Owner Protection) and 1305 (Federal Lessee Protection) of this title.[1]

(5) "Federal lands program" means a program established by the Secretary pursuant to section 1273 of this title to regulate surface coal mining and reclamation operations on Federal lands;

(6) "Federal program" means a program established by the Secretary pursuant to section 1254 of this title to regulate surface coal mining and reclamation operations on lands within a State in accordance with the requirements of this chapter;

(7) "fund" means the Abandoned Mine Reclamation Fund established pursuant to section 1231 of this title;

(8) "imminent danger to the health and safety of the public" means the existence of any condition or practice, or any violation of a permit or other requirement of this chapter in a surface coal mining and reclamation operation, which condition, practice, or violation could reasonably be expected to cause substantial physical harm to persons outside the permit area before such condition, practice, or violation can be abated. A reasonable expectation of death or serious injury before abatement exists if a rational person, subjected to the same conditions or practices giving rise to the peril, would not expose himself or herself to the danger during the time necessary for abatement;

(9) "Indian lands" means all lands, including mineral interests, within the exterior boundaries of any Federal Indian reservation, notwithstanding the issuance of any patent, and including rights-of-way, and all lands including mineral interests held in trust for or supervised by an Indian tribe;

(10) "Indian tribe" means any Indian tribe, band, group, or community having a governing body recognized by the Secretary;

(11) "lands within any State" or "lands within such State" means all lands within a State other than Federal lands and Indian lands;

(12) "Office" means the Office of Surface Mining Reclamation and Enforcement established pursuant to subchapter II of this chapter;

(13) "operator" means any person, partnership, or corporation engaged in coal mining who removes or intends to remove more than two hundred and fifty tons of coal from the earth by coal mining within twelve consecutive calendar months in any one location;

(14) "other minerals" means clay, stone, sand, gravel, metalliferous and nonmetalliferous ores, and any other solid material or substances of commercial value excavated in solid form from natural deposits on or in the earth, exclusive of coal and those minerals which occur naturally in liquid or gaseous form;

(15) "permit" means a permit to conduct surface coal mining and reclamation operations issued by the State regulatory authority pursuant to a State program or by the Secretary pursuant to a Federal program;

(16) "permit applicant" or "applicant" means a person applying for a permit;

(17) "permit area" means the area of land indicated on the approved map submitted by the operator with his application, which area of land shall be covered by the operator's bond as required by section 1259 of this title and shall be readily identifiable by appropriate markers on the site;

(18) "permittee" means a person holding a permit;

(19) "person" means an individual, partnership, association, society, joint stock company, firm, company, corporation, or other business organization;

(20) the term "prime farmland" shall have the same meaning as that previously prescribed by the Secretary of Agriculture on the basis of such factors as moisture availability, temperature regime, chemical balance, permeability, surface layer composition,

susceptibility to flooding, and erosion characteristics, and which historically have been used for intensive agricultural purposes, and as published in the Federal Register.[1]

(21) "reclamation plan" means a plan submitted by an applicant for a permit under a State program or Federal program which sets forth a plan for reclamation of the proposed surface coal mining operations pursuant to section 1258 of this title;

(22) "regulatory authority" means the State regulatory authority where the State is administering this chapter under an approved State program or the Secretary where the Secretary is administering this chapter under a Federal program;

(23) "Secretary" means the Secretary of the Interior, except where otherwise described;

(24) "State" means a State of the United States, the District of Columbia, the Commonwealth of Puerto Rico, the Virgin Islands, American Samoa, and Guam;

(25) "State program" means a program established by a State pursuant to section 1253 of this title to regulate surface coal mining and reclamation operations, on lands within such State in accord with the requirements of this chapter and regulations issued by the Secretary pursuant to this chapter;

(26) "State regulatory authority" means the department or agency in each State which has primary responsibility at the State level for administering this chapter;

(27) "surface coal mining and reclamation operations" means surface mining operations and all activities necessary and incident to the reclamation of such operations after August 3, 1977;

(28) "surface coal mining operations" means—

(A) activities conducted on the surface of lands in connection with a surface coal mine or subject to the requirements of section 1266 of this title surface operations and surface impacts incident to an underground coal mine, the products of which enter commerce or the operations of which directly or indirectly affect interstate commerce. Such activities include excavation for the purpose of obtaining coal including such common methods as contour, strip, auger, mountaintop removal, box cut, open pit, and area mining, the uses of explosives and blasting, and in situ distillation or retorting, leaching or other chemical or physical processing, and the cleaning, concentrating, or other processing or preparation, loading of coal for interstate commerce at or near the mine site: *Provided, however*, That such activities do not include the extraction of coal incidental to the extraction of other minerals where coal does not exceed 16⅔ per centum of the tonnage of minerals removed for purposes of commercial use or sale or coal explorations subject to section 1262 of this title; and

(B) the areas upon which such activities occur or where such activities disturb the natural land surface. Such areas shall also include any adjacent land the use of which is incidental to any such activities, all lands affected by the construction of new roads or the improvement or use of existing roads to gain access to the site of such activities and for haulage, and excavations, workings, impoundments, dams, ventilation shafts, entryways, refuse banks, dumps, stockpiles, overburden piles, spoil banks, culm banks, tailings, holes or depressions, repair areas, storage areas, processing areas, shipping areas and other areas upon which are sited structures, facilities, or other property or materials on the surface, resulting from or incident to such activities; and

(29) "unwarranted failure to comply" means the failure of a permittee to prevent the occurrence of any violation of his permit or any requirement of this chapter due to indifference, lack of diligence, or lack of reasonable care, or the failure to abate any violation of such permit or the chapter due to indifference, lack of diligence, or lack of reasonable care;

(30) "lignite coal" means consolidated lignitic coal having less than 8,300 British thermal units per pound, moist and mineral matter free;

(31) the term "coal laboratory", as used in subchapter VIII of this chapter, means a university coal research laboratory established and operated pursuant to a designation made under section 1311 of this title;

(32) the term "institution of higher education" as used in subchapters VIII and IX of this chapter, means any such institution as defined by section 1141(a) of Title 20;

(33) the term "unanticipated event or condition" as used in section 1260(e) of this title means an event or condition encountered in a remining operation that was not contemplated by the applicable surface coal mining and reclamation permit; and

(34) the term "lands eligible for remining" means those lands that would otherwise be eligible for expenditures under section 1234 or under section 1232(g)(4) of this title.

(Aug. 3, 1977, Pub.L. 95–87, Title VII, § 701, 91 Stat. 516; Oct. 24, 1992, Pub.L. 102–486, Title XXV, § 2503(c), 106 Stat. 3103.)

1 So in original. The period probably should be a semicolon.

CROSS REFERENCES

Certain persons as defined by this section subject to environmental performance standards for surface coal mining operations, see section 1252 of this title.
Surface mining operations not subject to this chapter, see section 1278 of this title.

CODE OF FEDERAL REGULATIONS

Definitions—
Generally, see 30 CFR 700.5.
Initial regulatory program, see 30 CFR 710.5.
Permanent regulatory program, see 30 CFR 701.5.
Federal enforcement, see 30 CFR 843.1 et seq.
General performance standards—
Surface mining, see 30 CFR 715.10 et seq.
Underground mining, see 30 CFR 717.10 et seq.
Permanent regulatory program, see 30 CFR 701.1 et seq.
Permit requirements for special categories of mining, see 30 CFR 785.1 et seq.
Secretary of Interior, general scope of authority and responsibility, see 30 CFR 700.1 et seq.
Special program performance standards—
In situ processing, see 30 CFR 828.1 et seq.
Mountaintop removal, see 30 CFR 824.1 et seq.

LIBRARY REFERENCES

Mines and Minerals ⚷92.6, 92.9.
C.J.S. Mines and Minerals §§ 229 et seq., 239.

§ 1292. Other Federal laws [SMCRA § 702]

(a) Construction of chapter as superseding, amending, modifying, or repealing certain laws

Nothing in this chapter shall be construed as superseding, amending, modifying, or repealing the Mining and Minerals Policy Act of 1970 (30 U.S.C. 21a), the National Environmental Policy Act of 1969 (42 U.S.C. 4321–47), or any of the following Acts or with any rule or regulation promulgated thereunder, including, but not limited to—

(1) The Federal Metal and Nonmetallic Mine Safety Act (30 U.S.C. 721–740).

(2) The Federal Coal Mine Health and Safety Act of 1969 (83 Stat. 742) [30 U.S.C.A. § 801 et seq.].

(3) The Federal Water Pollution Control Act (79 Stat. 903), as amended (33 U.S.C. 1151–1175) [33 U.S.C.A. § 1251 et seq.], the State laws enacted pursuant thereto, or other Federal laws relating to preservation of water quality.

(4) The Clean Air Act, as amended (42 U.S.C. 1857 et seq.) [42 U.S.C.A. § 7401 et seq.].

(5) The Solid Waste Disposal Act (42 U.S.C. 3251–3259) [42 U.S.C.A. § 6901 et seq.].

(6) The Refuse Act of 1899 (33 U.S.C. 407).

(7) The Fish and Wildlife Coordination Act of 1934 (16 U.S.C. 661–666c).

(8) The Mineral Leasing Act of 1920, as amended (30 U.S.C. 181 et seq.).

(b) Effect on authority of Secretary or heads of other Federal agencies

Nothing in this chapter shall affect in any way the authority of the Secretary or the heads of other Federal agencies under other provisions of law to include in any lease, license, permit, contract, or other instrument such conditions as may be appropriate to regulate surface coal mining and reclamation operations on land under their jurisdiction.

(c) Cooperation

To the greatest extent practicable each Federal agency shall cooperate with the Secretary and the States in carrying out the provisions of this chapter.

(d) Major Federal action

Approval of the State programs, pursuant to section 1253(b) of this title, promulgation of Federal programs, pursuant to section 1254 of this title, and implementation of the Federal lands programs, pursuant to section 1273 of this title, shall not constitute a major action within the meaning of section 102(2)(C) of the National Environmental Policy Act of 1969 (42 U.S.C. 4332). Adoption of regulations under section 1251(b) of this title shall constitute a major action within the meaning of section 102(2)(C) of the National Environmental Policy Act of 1969 (42 U.S.C. 4332).

(Aug. 3, 1977, Pub.L. 95–87, Title VII, § 702, 91 Stat. 519.)

CODE OF FEDERAL REGULATIONS

Permanent regulatory program, see 30 CFR 701.1 et seq.

§ 1293. Employee protection [SMCRA § 703]

(a) Retaliatory practices prohibited

No person shall discharge, or in any other way discriminate against, or cause to be fired or discriminated against, any employee or any authorized representative of employees by reason of the fact that such employee or representative has filed, instituted, or caused to be filed or instituted any proceeding under this chapter, or has testified or is about to testify in any proceeding resulting from the administration or enforcement of the provisions of this chapter.

(b) Review by Secretary; investigation; notice; hearing; findings of fact; judicial review

Any employee or a representative of employees who believes that he has been fired or otherwise discriminated against by any person in violation of subsection (a) of this section may, within thirty days after such alleged violation occurs, apply to the Secretary for a review of such firing or alleged discrimination. A copy of the application shall be sent to the person or operator who will be the respondent. Upon receipt of such application, the Secretary shall cause such investigation to be made as he deems appropriate. Such investigation shall provide an opportunity for a public hearing at the request of any party to such review to enable the parties to present information relating to the alleged violation. The parties shall be given written notice of the time and place of the hearing at least five days prior to the hearing. Any such hearing shall be of record and shall be subject to section 554 of Title 5. Upon receiving the report of such investigation the Secretary shall make findings of fact. If he finds that a violation did occur, he shall issue a decision incorporating therein his findings and an order requiring the party committing the violation to take such affirmative action to abate the violation as the Secretary deems appropriate, including, but not limited to, the rehiring or reinstatement of the employee or representative of employees to his former position with compensation. If he finds that there was no violation, he will issue a finding. Orders issued by the Secretary under this subsection shall be subject to judicial review in the same manner as orders and decisions of the Secretary are subject to judicial review under this chapter.

(c) Costs

Whenever an order is issued under this section to abate any violation, at the request of the applicant a sum equal to the aggregate amount of all costs and expenses (including attorneys' fees) to have been reasonably incurred by the applicant for, or in connection with, the institution and prosecution of such proceedings, shall be assessed against the persons committing the violation.

(Aug. 3, 1977, Pub.L. 95–87, Title VII, § 703, 91 Stat. 520.)

CROSS REFERENCES

Corporate violations, penalties, see section 1268 of this title.
Enforcement of this chapter, see section 1271 of this title.

CODE OF FEDERAL REGULATIONS

Secretary of Interior, hearings and appeals procedure, see 43 CFR 4.1 et seq.

§ 1294. Penalty [SMCRA § 704]

Any person who shall, except as permitted by law, willfully resist, prevent, impede, or interfere with the Secretary or any of his agents in the performance of duties pursuant to this chapter shall be punished by a fine of not more than $5,000 or by imprisonment for not more than one year, or both.

(Aug. 3, 1977, Pub.L. 95–87, Title VII, § 704, 91 Stat. 520.)

CROSS REFERENCES

Penalty for wilful violations of this section, see section 1268 of this title.

§ 1295. Grants to States [SMCRA § 705]

(a) Assisting any State in development, administration, and enforcement of State programs under this chapter

The Secretary is authorized to make annual grants to any State for the purpose of assisting such State in developing, administering, and enforcing State programs under this chapter. Except as provided in subsection (c) of this section, such grants shall not exceed 80 per centum of the total costs incurred during the first year, 60 per centum of total costs incurred during the second year, and 50 per centum of the total costs incurred during each year thereafter.

(b) Assisting any State in development, administration, and enforcement of its State programs

The Secretary is authorized to cooperate with and provide assistance to any State for the purpose of assisting it in the development, administration, and enforcement of its State programs. Such cooperation and assistance shall include—

(1) technical assistance and training including provision of necessary curricular and instruction materials, in the development, administration, and enforcement of the State programs; and

(2) assistance in preparing and maintaining a continuing inventory of information on surface coal mining and reclamation operations for each State for the purposes of evaluating the effectiveness of the State programs. Such assistance shall include all Federal departments and agencies making available data relevant to surface coal mining and reclamation operations and to the development, administration, and enforcement of State programs concerning such operations.

(c) Increases in annual grants

If, in accordance with section 1273(d) of this title, a State elects to regulate surface coal mining and reclamation operations on Federal lands, the Secretary may increase the amount of the annual grants under subsection (a) of this section by an amount which he determines is approximately equal to the amount the Federal Government would have expended for such regulation if the State had not made such election.

(Aug. 3, 1977, Pub.L. 95–87, Title VII, § 705, 91 Stat. 520.)

CROSS REFERENCES

Authorization of appropriations for implementation of this section, see section 1302 of this title.

CODE OF FEDERAL REGULATIONS

Grants for program development, administration and enforcement, see 30 CFR 735.1 et seq.
Permanent regulatory program, see 30 CFR 701.1 et seq.

§ 1296. Annual report to President and Congress [SMCRA § 706]

The Secretary shall submit annually to the President and the Congress a report concerning activities conducted by him, the Federal Government, and the States pursuant to this chapter. Among other matters, the Secretary shall include in such report recommendations for additional administrative or legislative action as he deems necessary and desirable to accomplish the purposes of this chapter.

(Aug. 3, 1977, Pub.L. 95–87, Title VII, § 706, 91 Stat. 521.)

CROSS REFERENCES

Report to Congress concerning conflicts of interest of employees performing functions or duties under this chapter—
Federal employees, see section 1211 of this title.
State employees, see section 1267 of this title.

§ 1297. Separability of provisions [SMCRA § 707]

If any provision of this chapter or the applicability thereof to any person or circumstances is held invalid, the remainder of this chapter and the application of such provision to other persons or circumstances shall not be affected thereby.

(Aug. 3, 1977, Pub.L. 95–87, Title VII, § 707, 91 Stat. 521.)

§ 1298. Alaskan surface coal mine study [SMCRA § 708]

(a) Contract with National Academy of Sciences–National Academy of Engineering

The Secretary is directed to contract to such extent or in such amounts as are provided in advance in appropriation Acts with the National Academy of Sciences–National Academy of Engineering for an in-depth study of surface coal mining conditions in the State of Alaska in order to determine which, if any, of the provisions of this chapter should be modified with respect to surface coal mining operations in Alaska.

(b) Report to President and Congress

The Secretary shall report on the findings of the study to the President and Congress no later than two years after August 3, 1977.

(c) Draft of legislation

The Secretary shall include in his report a draft of legislation to implement any changes recommended to this chapter.

(d) Modification of applicability of environmental protection provisions of this chapter to surface coal mining operations in Alaska; publication in Federal Register; hearing

Until one year after the Secretary has made this report to the President and Congress, or three years after August 3, 1977, whichever comes first, the Secretary is authorized to modify the applicability of any environmental protection provision of this chapter, or any regulation issued pursuant thereto, to any surface coal mining operation in Alaska from which coal has been mined during the year preceding August 3, 1977, if he determines that it is necessary to insure the continued operation of such surface coal mining operation. The Secretary may exercise this authority only after he has (1) published notice of proposed modification in the Federal Register and in a newspaper of general circulation in the area of Alaska in which the affected surface coal mining operation is located, and (2) held a public hearing on the proposed modification in Alaska.

(e) Interim regulations

In order to allow new mines in Alaska to continue orderly development, the Secretary is authorized to issue interim regulations pursuant to section 1251(b) of this title including those modifications to the environmental standards as required based on the special physical, hydrological and climatic conditions in Alaska but with the purpose of protecting the environment to an extent equivalent to those standards for the other coal regions.

(f) Authorization of appropriations

There is authorized to be appropriated for the purpose of this section $250,000: *Provided,* That no new budget authority is authorized to be appropriated for fiscal year 1977.

(Aug. 3, 1977, Pub.L. 95–87, Title VII, § 708, 91 Stat. 521.)

CODE OF FEDERAL REGULATIONS

Coal mines in Alaska, performance standards, initial program regulations, see 30 CFR 716.6.
Permanent regulatory program, see 30 CFR 701.1 et seq.
Secretary of Interior, general scope of authority and responsibility, see 30 CFR 700.1 et seq.

§ 1299. Study of reclamation standards for surface mining of other minerals [SMCRA § 709]

(a) Contract with National Academy of Sciences–National Academy of Engineering; requirements

The Chairman of the Council on Environmental Quality is directed to contract to such extent or in such amounts as are provided in appropriation Acts with the National Academy of Sciences–National Academy of Engineering, other Government agencies or private groups as appropriate, for an in-depth study of current and developing technology for surface and open pit mining and reclamation for minerals other than coal designed to assist in the establishment of effective and reasonable regulation of surface and open pit mining and reclamation for minerals other than coal. The study shall—

(1) assess the degree to which the requirements of this chapter can be met by such technology and the costs involved;

(2) identify areas where the requirements of this chapter cannot be met by current and developing technology;

(3) in those instances describe requirements most comparable to those of this chapter which could be met, the costs involved, and the differences in reclamation results between these requirements and those of this chapter; and

(4) discuss alternative regulatory mechanisms designed to insure the achievement of the most beneficial postmining land use for areas affected by surface and open pit mining.

(b) Submittal of study with legislative recommendation to President and Congress

The study together with specific legislative recommendations shall be submitted to the President and the Congress no later than eighteen months after August 3, 1977: *Provided*, That, with respect to surface or open pit mining for sand and gravel the study shall be submitted no later than twelve months after August 3, 1977: *Provided further*, That with respect to mining for oil shale and tar sands that a preliminary report shall be submitted no later than twelve months after August 3, 1977.

(c) Authorization of appropriations

There are hereby authorized to be appropriated for the purpose of this section $500,000: *Provided*, That no new budget authority is authorized to be appropriated for fiscal year 1977.

(Aug. 3, 1977, Pub.L. 95–87, Title VII, § 709, 91 Stat. 522.)

§ 1300. Indian lands [SMCRA § 710]

(a) Study of regulation of surface mining; consultation with tribe; proposed legislation

The Secretary is directed to study the question of the regulation of surface mining on Indian lands which will achieve the purpose of this chapter and recognize the special jurisdictional status of these lands. In carrying out this study the Secretary shall consult with Indian tribes. The study report shall include proposed legislation designed to allow Indian tribes to elect to assume full regulatory authority over the administration and enforcement of regulation of surface mining of coal on Indian lands.

(b) Submittal of study to Congress

The study report required by subsection (a) of this section together with drafts of proposed legislation and the view of each Indian tribe which would be affected shall be submitted to the Congress as soon as possible but not later than January 1, 1978.

(c) Compliance with interim environmental protection standards of this chapter

On and after one hundred and thirty-five days from August 3, 1977, all surface coal mining operations on Indian lands shall comply with requirements at least as stringent as those imposed by subsections (b)(2), (b)(3), (b)(5), (b)(10), (b)(13), (b)(19), and (d) of section 1265 of this title and the Secretary shall incorporate the requirements of such provisions in all existing and new leases issued for coal on Indian lands.

(d) Compliance with permanent environmental protection standards of this chapter

On and after thirty months from August 3, 1977, all surface coal mining operations on Indian lands shall comply with requirements at least as stringent as those imposed by sections 1257, 1258, 1259, 1260, 1265, 1266, 1267, and 1269 of this title and the Secretary shall incorporate the requirements of such provisions in all existing and new leases issued for coal on Indian lands.

(e) Inclusion and enforcement of terms and conditions of leases

With respect to leases issued after August 3, 1977, the Secretary shall include and enforce terms and conditions in addition to those required by subsections (c) and (d) of this section as may be requested by the Indian tribe in such leases.

(f) Approval of changes in terms and conditions of leases

Any change required by subsection (c) or (d) of this section in the terms and conditions of any coal lease on Indian lands existing on August 3, 1977, shall require the approval of the Secretary.

(g) Participation of tribes

The Secretary shall provide for adequate participation by the various Indian tribes affected in the study authorized in this section and not more than $700,000 of the funds authorized in section 1302(a) of this title shall be reserved for this purpose.

(h) Jurisdictional status

The Secretary shall analyze and make recommendations regarding the jurisdictional status of Indian Lands [1] outside the exterior boundaries of Indian reservations: *Provided*, That nothing in this chapter shall change the existing jurisdictional status of Indian Lands [1].

(i) Grants

The Secretary shall make grants to the Navajo, Hopi, Northern Cheyenne, and Crow tribes to assist such tribes in developing regulations and programs for regulating surface coal mining and reclamation operations on Indian lands, except that nothing in this subsection may be construed as providing such tribes with the authorities set forth under section 1253 of this title. Grants made under this subsection shall be used to establish an office of surface mining regulation for each such tribe. Each such office shall—

(1) develop tribal regulations and program policies with respect to surface mining;

(2) assist the Office of Surface Mining Reclamation and Enforcement established by section 1211 of this title in the inspection and enforcement of surface mining activities on Indian lands, including, but not limited to, permitting, mine plan review, and bond release; and

(3) sponsor employment training and education in the area of mining and mineral resources.

(Aug. 3, 1977, Pub.L. 95–87, Title VII, § 710, 91 Stat. 523; Oct. 24, 1992, Pub.L. 102–486, Title XXV, § 2514, 106 Stat. 3112.)

1 So in original. Probably should be "lands".

CROSS REFERENCES

Applicability of this chapter to Indian lands, see section 1273 of this title.

Authorization of appropriations for implementation of this section, see section 1302 of this title.

CODE OF FEDERAL REGULATIONS

Indian reclamation program, see 30 CFR 888.1 et seq.

§ 1301. Environmental practices [SMCRA § 711]

In order to encourage advances in mining and reclamation practices or to allow post-mining land use for industrial, commercial, residential, or public use (including recreational facilities), the regulatory authority with approval by the Secretary may authorize departures in individual cases on an experimental basis from the environmental protection performance standards promulgated under sections 1265 and 1266 of this title. Such departures may be authorized if (i) the experimental practices are potentially more or at least as environmentally protective, during and after mining operations, as those required by promulgated standards; (ii) the mining operations approved for particular land-use or other purposes are not larger or more numerous than necessary to determine the effectiveness and economic feasibility of the experimental practices; and (iii) the experimental practices do not reduce the protection afforded public health and safety below that provided by promulgated standards.

(Aug. 3, 1977, Pub.L. 95–87, Title VII, § 711, 91 Stat. 523.)

CODE OF FEDERAL REGULATIONS

Permanent regulatory program, see 30 CFR 701.1 et seq.

Permit requirements for special categories of mining, see 30 CFR 785.1 et seq.

§ 1302. Authorization of appropriations [SMCRA § 712]

There is authorized to be appropriated to the Secretary for the purposes of this chapter the following sums; and all such funds appropriated shall remain available until expended:

(a) For the implementation and funding of sections 1252, 1273, and 1300 of this title, there are authorized to be appropriated to the Secretary of the Interior the sum of $10,000,000 for the fiscal year ending September 30, 1978, $25,000,000 for each of the two succeeding fiscal years, and in such fiscal years such additional amounts as may be necessary for increases in salary, pay, retirement, other employee benefits authorized by law, and other nondiscretionary costs.

(b) For the implementation and funding of section 1257(c) of this title, see the provisions of section 1231(c)(11) of this title.

(c) For the implementation and funding of section 1295 of this title and for the administrative and other purposes of this chapter, except as otherwise provided for in this chapter, authorization is provided for the sum of $20,000,000 for the fiscal year ending September 30, 1978, and $30,000,000 for each of the two succeeding fiscal years and such funds that are required thereafter.

(d) In order that the implementation of the requirements of this chapter may be initiated in a timely and orderly manner, the Secretary is authorized, subject to the approval of the appropriation Committees of the House and of the Senate, to utilize not to exceed $2,000,000 of the appropriations otherwise available to him for the fiscal year ending September 30, 1977, for the administration and other purposes of this chapter.

(Aug. 3, 1977, Pub.L. 95–87, Title VII, § 712, 91 Stat. 524; Aug. 11, 1978, Pub.L. 95–343, § 1, 92 Stat. 473; Pub.L. 101–508, Title VI, § 6012(b), Nov. 5, 1990, 104 Stat. 1388–298.)

Effective Date of 1990 Amendment

Amendment by Pub.L. 101–508 effective Oct. 1, 1991, see section 6014 of Pub.L. 101–508, set out as a note under section 1231 of this title.

Savings Provisions

Nothing in Subtitle A (section 6001 et seq.) of Title VI of Pub.L. 101–508, construed to affect the certifications made by the States of Wyoming, Montana, and Louisiana to the Secretary of the Interior prior to Nov. 5, 1990, that each such State has completed the reclamation of eligible abandoned coal mine lands, see section 6013 of Pub.L. 101–508, set out as a note under section 1231 of this title.

CROSS REFERENCES

Abandoned Mine Reclamation Fund, sources of deposit, see section 1231 of this title.
Advance appropriations for payments under this chapter, see section 1308 of this title.
Initial Federal enforcement program, reimbursement of States for enforcement from moneys authorized by this section, see section 1252 of this title.
Limitation of funding concerning Indian lands, see section 1300 of this title.

§ 1303. Coordination of regulatory and inspection activities [SMCRA § 713]

(a) The President shall, to the extent appropriate, and in keeping with the particular enforcement requirements of each Act referred to herein, insure the coordination of regulatory and inspection activities among the departments, agencies, and instrumentalities to which such activities are assigned by this chapter, by the Clean Air Act [42 U.S.C.A. § 7401 et seq.], by the Water Pollution Control Act [33 U.S.C.A. § 1251 et seq.], by the Department of Energy Organization Act [42 U.S.C.A. § 7107 et seq.], and by existing or subsequently enacted Federal mine safety and health laws, except that no such coordination shall be required with respect to mine safety and health inspections, advance notice of which is or may be prohibited by existing or subsequently enacted Federal mine safety and health laws.

(b) The President may execute the coordination required by this section by means of an Executive order, or by any other mechanism he determines to be appropriate.

(Aug. 3, 1977, Pub.L. 95–87, Title VII, § 713, 91 Stat. 524.)

CODE OF FEDERAL REGULATIONS

Permanent regulatory program, see 30 CFR 701.1 et seq.

§ 1304. Surface owner protection [SMCRA § 714]

(a) Applicability

The provisions of this section shall apply where coal owned by the United States under land the surface rights to which are owned by a surface owner as defined in this section is to be mined by methods other than underground mining techniques.

(b) Lease of coal deposits governed by section 201 of this title

Any coal deposits subject to this section shall be offered for lease pursuant to section 201(a) of this title.

(c) Consent to lease by surface owner

The Secretary shall not enter into any lease of Federal coal deposits until the surface owner has given written consent to enter and commence surface mining operations and the Secretary has obtained evidence of such consent. Valid written consent given by any surface owner prior to August 3, 1977, shall be deemed sufficient for the purposes of complying with this section.

(d) Preferences

In order to minimize disturbance to surface owners from surface coal mining of Federal coal deposits and to assist in the preparation of comprehensive land-use plans required by section 201(a) of this title, the Secretary shall consult with any surface owner whose land is proposed to be included in a leasing tract and shall ask the surface owner to state his preference for or against the offering of the deposit under his land for lease. The Secretary shall, in his discretion but to the maximum extent practicable, refrain from leasing coal deposits for development by methods other than underground mining techniques in those areas where a significant number of surface owners have stated a preference against the offering of the deposits for lease.

(e) "Surface owner" defined

For the purpose of this section the term "surface owner" means the natural person or persons (or corporation, the majority stock of which is held by a person or persons who meet the other requirements of this section) who—

(1) hold legal or equitable title to the land surface;

(2) have their principal place of residence on the land; or personally conduct farming or ranching operations upon a farm or ranch unit to be affected by surface coal mining operations; or receive directly a significant portion of their income, if any, from such farming or ranching operations; and

(3) have met the conditions of paragraphs (1) and (2) for a period of at least three years prior to the granting of the consent.

In computing the three-year period the Secretary may include periods during which title was owned by a relative of such person by blood or marriage during which period such relative would have met the requirements of this subsection.

(f) Exception

This section shall not apply to Indian lands.

(g) Effect on property rights of United States or any other landowner

Nothing in this section shall be construed as increasing or diminishing any property rights by the United States or by any other landowner.

(Aug. 3, 1977, Pub.L. 95–87, Title VII, § 714, 91 Stat. 524.)

CROSS REFERENCES

Exemption of Tennessee Valley Authority lands from provisions of this section, see section 1291 of this title.
Indian lands, see section 1304 of this title.

CODE OF FEDERAL REGULATIONS

Permanent regulatory program, see 30 CFR 701.1 et seq.

§ 1305. Federal lessee protection [SMCRA § 715]

In those instances where the coal proposed to be mined by surface coal mining operations is owned by the Federal Government and the surface is subject to a lease or a permit issued by the Federal Government, the application for a permit shall include either:

(1) the written consent of the permittee or lessee of the surface lands involved to enter and commence surface coal mining operations on such land, or in lieu thereof;

(2) evidence of the execution of a bond or undertaking to the United States or the State, whichever is applicable, for the use and benefit of the permittee or lessee of the surface lands involved to secure payment of any damages to the surface estate which the operations will cause to the crops, or to the tangible improvements of the permittee or lessee of the surface lands as may be determined by the parties involved, or as determined and fixed in an action brought against the operator or upon the bond in a court of competent jurisdiction. This bond is in addition to the performance bond required for reclamation under this chapter.

(Aug. 3, 1977, Pub.L. 95–87, Title VII, § 715, 91 Stat. 525.)

CROSS REFERENCES

Exemption of Tennessee Valley Authority lands from provisions of this section, see section 1291 of this title.
Performance bonds, see section 1259 of this title.

CODE OF FEDERAL REGULATIONS

Permanent regulatory program, see 30 CFR 701.1 et seq.

§ 1306. Effect on rights of owner of coal in Alaska to conduct surface mining operations [SMCRA § 716]

Nothing in this chapter shall be construed as increasing or diminishing the rights of any owner of coal in Alaska to conduct or authorize surface coal mining operations for coal which has been or is hereafter conveyed out of Federal ownership to the State of Alaska or pursuant to the Alaska Native Claims Settlement Act [43 U.S.C.A. § 1601 et seq.]: *Provided*, That such surface coal mining operations meet the requirements of this chapter.

(Aug. 3, 1977, Pub.L. 95–87, Title VII, § 716, 91 Stat. 526.)

CODE OF FEDERAL REGULATIONS

Permanent regulatory program, see 30 CFR 701.1 et seq.

§ 1307. Water rights and replacement [SMCRA § 717]

(a) Nothing in this chapter shall be construed as affecting in any way the right of any person to enforce or protect, under applicable law, his interest in water resources affected by a surface coal mining operation.

(b) The operator of a surface coal mine shall replace the water supply of an owner of interest in real property who obtains all or part of his supply of water for domestic, agricultural, industrial, or other legitimate use from an underground or surface source where such supply has been affected by contamination, diminution, or interruption proximately resulting from such surface coal mine operation.

(Aug. 3, 1977, Pub.L. 95–87, Title VII, § 717, 91 Stat. 526.)

CODE OF FEDERAL REGULATIONS

Permanent regulatory program, see 30 CFR 701.1 et seq.

§ 1308. Advance appropriations [SMCRA § 718]

Notwithstanding any other provision of this chapter, no authority to make payments under this chapter shall be effective except to such extent or in such amounts as are provided in advance in appropriation Acts.

(Aug. 3, 1977, Pub.L. 95–87, Title VII, § 718, 91 Stat. 526.)

CROSS REFERENCES

Authorization of appropriations, see section 1302 of this title.

§ 1309. Certification and training of blasters [SMCRA § 719]

In accordance with this chapter, the Secretary of the Interior (or the approved State regulatory authority as provided for in section 1253 of this title) shall promulgate regulations requiring the training, examination, and certification of persons engaging in or directly responsible for blasting or use of explosives in surface coal mining operations.

(Aug. 3, 1977, Pub.L. 95–87, Title VII, § 719, 91 Stat. 526.)

CODE OF FEDERAL REGULATIONS

Permanent regulatory program, see 30 CFR 701.1 et seq.
Secretary of Interior, general scope of authority and responsibility, see 30 CFR 700.1 et seq.

§ 1309a. Subsidence [SMCRA § 720]

(a) Requirements

Underground coal mining operations conducted after October 24, 1992, shall comply with each of the following requirements:

(1) Promptly repair, or compensate for, material damage resulting from subsidence caused to any occupied residential dwelling and structures related thereto, or non-commercial building due to underground coal mining operations. Repair of damage shall include rehabilitation, restoration, or replacement of the damaged occupied residential dwelling and structures related thereto, or non-commercial building. Compensation shall be provided to the owner of the damaged occupied residential dwelling and structures related thereto or non-commercial building and shall be in the full amount of the diminution in value resulting from the subsidence. Compensation may be accomplished by the purchase, prior to mining, of a noncancellable premium-prepaid insurance policy.

(2) Promptly replace any drinking, domestic, or residential water supply from a well or spring in existence prior to the application for a surface coal mining and reclamation permit, which has been affected by contamination, diminution, or interruption resulting from underground coal mining operations.

Nothing in this section shall be construed to prohibit or interrupt underground coal mining operations.

(b) Regulations

Within one year after October 24, 1992, the Secretary shall, after providing notice and opportunity for public comment, promulgate final regulations to implement subsection (a) of this section.

(Pub.L. 95–87, Title VII, § 720, as added Pub.L. 102–486, Title XXV, § 2504(a)(1), Oct. 24, 1992, 106 Stat. 3104.)

Review of Existing Requirements and Report to Congress

Section 2504(a)(2) of Pub.L. 102–486 provided that:

"(A) The Secretary of the Interior shall review existing requirements related to underground coal mine subsidence and natural gas and petroleum pipeline safety. Such review shall consider the following with respect to subsidence: notification; mitigation; coordination; requirements of the Natural Gas Pipeline Safety Act and the Hazardous Liquid Pipeline Safety Act [section 1671 et seq. and section 2001 et seq. of Appendix to Title 49, Transportation]; and the status of Federal, State and local laws, as well as common law, with respect to prevention or mitigation of damage from subsidence.

"(B) The review shall also include a survey of the status of Federal, State, and local laws, as well as common law, with respect to the responsibilities of the relevant parties for costs resulting from damage due to subsidence or from mitigation efforts undertaken to prevent damage from subsidence.

"(C) In conducting the review, the Secretary of the Interior shall consult with the Secretary of Transportation, the Attorney General of the United States, appropriate officials of relevant States, and owners and representatives of natural gas and petroleum pipeline companies and coal companies.

"(D) The Secretary of the Interior shall submit a report detailing the results of the review to the Committee on Energy and Natural Resources of the United States Senate and the Committee on Interior and Insular Affairs of the United States House of Representatives within 18 months of enactment of this Act [Oct. 24, 1992]. Where appropriate, the Secretary of the Interior shall commence a rulemaking to address any deficiencies in existing law determined in the review under subparagraph (A) regarding notification, coordination and mitigation."

§ 1309b. Research [SMCRA § 721]

The Office of Surface Mining Reclamation and Enforcement is authorized to conduct studies, research and demonstration projects relating to the implementation of, and compliance with, subchapter V of this chapter, and provide technical assistance to states for that purpose. Prior to approving any such studies, research or demonstration projects the Director, Office of Surface Mining Reclamation and Enforcement, shall first consult with the Director, Bureau of Mines, and obtain a determination from such Director that the Bureau of Mines is not already conducting like or similar studies, research or demonstration projects. Studies, research and demonstration projects for the purposes of subchapter IV of this chapter shall only be conducted in accordance with section 1231(c)(6) of this title.

(Pub.L. 95–87, Title VII, § 721, as added Pub.L. 102–486, Title XXV, § 2504(c)(3), Oct. 24, 1992, 106 Stat. 3105.)

SUBCHAPTER VIII—UNIVERSITY COAL RESEARCH LABORATORIES

CROSS REFERENCES

Coal laboratory defined, see section 1291 of this title.

§ 1311. Establishment of university coal research laboratories [SMCRA § 801]

(a) Designation by Secretary of Energy

The Secretary of Energy, after consultation with the National Academy of Engineering, shall designate thirteen institutions of higher education at which university coal research laboratories will be established and operated. Ten such designations shall be made as provided in subsection (e) of this section and the remaining three shall be made in fiscal year 1980.

(b) Criteria

In making designations under this section, the Secretary of Energy shall consider the following criteria:

(1) Those ten institutions of higher education designated as provided in subsection (e) of this section shall be located in a State with abundant coal reserves.

(2) The institution of higher education shall have experience in coal research, expertise in several areas of coal research, and potential or currently active, outstanding programs in coal research.

(3) The institution of higher education has the capacity to establish and operate the coal laboratories to be assisted under this subchapter.

(c) Location of coal laboratories

Not more than one coal laboratory established pursuant to this subchapter shall be located in a single State and at least one coal laboratory shall be established within each of the major coal provinces recognized by the United States Bureau of Mines, including Alaska.

(d) Period for submission of applications for designation; contents

The Secretary of Energy shall establish a period, not in excess of ninety days after August 3, 1977, for the submission of applications for designation under this section. Any institution of higher education desiring to be designated under this subchapter shall submit an application to the Secretary of Energy in such form, at such time, and containing or accompanied by such information as the Secretary of Energy may reasonably require. Each application shall—

(1) describe the facilities to be established for coal energy resources and conversion research and research on related environmental problems including facilities for interdisciplinary academic research projects by the combined efforts of specialists such as mining engineers, mineral engineers, geochemists, mineralogists, mineral economists, fuel scientists, combustion engineers, mineral preparation engineers, coal petrographers, geologists, chemical engineers, civil engineers, mechanical engineers, and ecologists;

(2) set forth a program for the establishment of a test laboratory for coal characterization which, in addition, may be used as a site for the exchange of coal research activities by representatives of private industry engaged in coal research and characterization;

(3) set forth a program for providing research and development activities for students engaged in advanced study in any discipline which is related to the development of adequate energy supplies in the United States. The research laboratory shall be associated with an ongoing educational and research program on extraction and utilization of coal.

(e) Time limit

The Secretary of Energy shall designate the ten institutions of higher education under this section not later than ninety days after the date on which such applications are to be submitted.

(Aug. 3, 1977, Pub.L. 95–87, Title VIII, § 801, 91 Stat. 526; Nov. 9, 1978, Pub.L. 95–617, Title VI, § 604(a), (c), 92 Stat. 3166, 3167; May 18, 1992, Pub.L. 102–285, § 10(b), 106 Stat. 172.)

Change of Name

Pub.L. 102–285, § 10(b), May 18, 1992, 106 Stat. 172, provided that, on and after May 18, 1992, the Bureau of Mines is redesignated and shall thereafter be known as the United States Bureau of Mines. See note under section 1 of Title 30, Mineral Lands and Mining.

CROSS REFERENCES

Authorization of appropriations for coal laboratories, see section 1316 of this title.
Coal laboratory defined, see section 1291 of this title.
Financial assistance for coal laboratories, see section 1312 of this title.

LIBRARY REFERENCES

Mines and Minerals ⇐92.6, 92.9.
C.J.S. Mines and Minerals §§ 229 et seq., 239.

§ 1312. Financial assistance [SMCRA § 802]

(a) The Secretary of Energy is authorized to make grants to any institution of higher education designated under section 1311 of this title to pay the Federal share of the cost of establishing (including the construction of such facilities as may be necessary) and maintaining a coal laboratory.

(b) Each institution of higher education designated pursuant to section 1311 of this title shall submit an application to the Secretary of Energy. Each such application shall—

(1) set forth the program to be conducted at the coal laboratory which includes the purposes set forth in section 1311(d) of this title;

(2) provide assurances that the university will pay from non-Federal sources the remaining costs of carrying out the program set forth;

(3) provide such fiscal control and fund accounting procedures as may be necessary to assure the proper disbursement of and accounting for Federal funds received under this subchapter;

(4) provide for making an annual report which shall include a description of the activities conducted at the coal laboratory and an evaluation of the success of such activities, and such other necessary reports in such form and containing such information as the Secretary of Energy may require, and for keeping such records and affording such access thereto as may be necessary to assure the correctness and verification of such reports; and

(5) set forth such policies and procedures as will insure that Federal funds made available under this section for any fiscal year will be so used as to

supplement and, to the extent practical, increase the level of funds that would, in the absence of such Federal funds, be made available for the purposes of the activities described in subsections (d)(1), (2), and (3) of section 1311 of this title, and in no case supplant such funds.

(Aug. 3, 1977, Pub.L. 95–87, Title VIII, § 802, 91 Stat. 527; Nov. 9, 1978, Pub.L. 95–617, Title VI, § 604(c), 92 Stat. 3167.)

§ 1313. Limitation on payments [SMCRA § 803]

(a) No institutions of higher education may receive more than $4,000,000 for the construction of its coal research laboratory, including initially installed fixed equipment, nor may it receive more than $1,500,000 for initially installed movable equipment, nor may it receive more than $500,000 for new program startup expenses.

(b) No institution of higher education may receive more than $1,500,000 per year from the Federal Government for operating expenses.

(Aug. 3, 1977, Pub.L. 95–87, Title VIII, § 803, 91 Stat. 528.)

§ 1314. Payments; Federal share of operating expenses [SMCRA § 804]

(a) From the amounts appropriated pursuant to section 1316 of this title, the Secretary of Energy shall pay to each institution of higher education having an application approved under this subchapter an amount equal to the Federal share of the cost of carrying out that application. Such payments may be in installments, by way of reimbursement, or by way of advance with necessary adjustments on account of underpayments or overpayments.

(b) The Federal share of operating expenses for any fiscal year shall not exceed 50 per centum of the cost of the operation of a coal research laboratory.

(Aug. 3, 1977, Pub.L. 95–87, Title VIII, § 804, 91 Stat. 528; Nov. 9, 1978, Pub.L. 95–617, Title VI, § 604(c), 92 Stat. 3167.)

§ 1315. Advisory Council on Coal Research [SMCRA § 805]

(a) Establishment; members

There is established an Advisory Council on Coal Research which shall be composed of—

(1) the Secretary of Energy, who shall be Chairman;

(2) the Director of the United States Bureau of Mines of the Department of the Interior;

(3) the President of the National Academy of Sciences;

(4) the President of the National Academy of Engineering;

(5) the Director of the United States Geological Survey; and

(6) six members appointed by the Secretary of Energy from among individuals who, by virtue of experience or training, are knowledgeable in the field of coal research and mining, and who are representatives of institutions of higher education, industrial users of coal and coal-derived fuels, the coal industry, mine workers, nonindustrial consumer groups, and institutions concerned with the preservation of the environment.

(b) Furnishing advice to Secretary of Energy

The Advisory Council shall advise the Secretary of Energy with respect to the general administration of this subchapter, and furnish such additional advice as he may request.

(c) Annual report to President; transmittal to Congress

The Advisory Council shall make an annual report of its findings and recommendations (including recommendations for changes in the provisions of this subchapter) to the President not later than December 31 of each calendar year. The President shall transmit each such report to the Congress.

(d) Compensation and travel expenses

(1) Members of the Council who are not regular officers or employees of the United States Government shall, while serving on business of the Council, be entitled to receive compensation at rates fixed by the Secretary of Energy but not exceeding the daily rate prescribed for GS–18 of the General Schedule under section 5332 of Title 5 and while so serving away from their homes or regular places of business, they may be allowed travel expenses, including per diem in lieu of subsistence, as authorized by section 5703 of Title 5 for persons in the Government service employed intermittently.

(2) Members of the Council who are officers or employees of the Government shall be reimbursed for travel, subsistence, and other necessary expenses incurred by them in carrying out their duties on the Council.

(e) Alternate members

Whenever a member of the Council appointed under clauses (1) through (5) is unable to attend a meeting, that member shall appoint an appropriate alternate to represent him for that meeting.

(Aug. 3, 1977, Pub.L. 95–87, Title VIII, § 805, 91 Stat. 528; Nov. 9, 1978, Pub.L. 95–617, Title VI, § 604(c), 92 Stat. 3167; May 18, 1992, Pub.L. 102–285, § 10(b), 106 Stat. 172.)

Change of Name

Pub.L. 102–285, § 10(b), May 18, 1992, 106 Stat. 172, provided that, on and after May 18, 1992, the Bureau of Mines is redesignated and shall thereafter be known as the United States Bureau of Mines. See note under section 1 of Title 30, Mineral Lands and Mining.

§ 1316. Authorization of appropriations [SMCRA § 806]

(a) For the ten institutions referred to in the last sentence of section 1311(a) of this title, there are authorized to be appropriated not to exceed $30,000,000 for the fiscal year ending September 30, 1979 (including the cost of construction, equipment, and startup expenses), and not to exceed $7,500,000 for the fiscal year 1980 and for each fiscal year thereafter through the fiscal year ending before October 1, 1984, to carry out the provisions of this subchapter.

(b) For the three remaining institutions referred to in the last sentence of section 1311(a) of this title, there are authorized to be appropriated not to exceed $6,500,000 for the fiscal year 1980 (including the cost of construction, equipment, and startup expenses), and not to exceed $2,000,000 for each fiscal year after fiscal year 1980 ending before October 1, 1984, to carry out the provisions of this subchapter.

(Aug. 3, 1977, Pub.L. 95–87, Title VIII, § 806, 91 Stat. 529; Nov. 9, 1978, Pub.L. 95–617, Title VI, § 604(b), 92 Stat. 3166.)

CROSS REFERENCES

Payment of Federal share of operating expenses from amounts appropriated pursuant to this section, see section 1314 of this title.

SUBCHAPTER IX—ENERGY RESOURCE GRADUATE FELLOWSHIPS

CROSS REFERENCES

Institution of higher education defined, see section 1291 of this title.

§ 1321. Fellowship awards [SMCRA § 901]

(a) Graduate study and research in areas of applied science and engineering relating to production, conservation, and utilization of fuels and energy

The Secretary of Energy is authorized to award under the provisions of this subchapter not to exceed one thousand fellowships for the fiscal year ending September 30, 1979, and each of the five succeeding fiscal years. Fellowships shall be awarded under the provisions of this subchapter for graduate study and research in those areas of applied science and engineering that are related to the production, conservation, and utilization of fuels and energy. Fellowships shall be awarded to students in programs leading to master's degrees. Such fellowships may be awarded for graduate study and research at any institution of higher education, library, archive, or any other research center approved by the Secretary of Energy after consultation with the Secretary of Education.

(b) Term

Such fellowships shall be awarded for such periods as the Secretary of Energy may determine, but not to exceed two years.

(c) Replacement awards

In addition to the number of fellowships authorized to be awarded by subsection (a) of this section, the Secretary of Energy is authorized to award fellowships equal to the number previously awarded during any fiscal year under this subchapter but vacated prior to the end of the period for which they were awarded; except that each fellowship awarded under this subsection shall be for such period of graduate work or research, not in excess of the remainder of the period for which the fellowship which it replaces was awarded as the Secretary of Energy may determine.

(Aug. 3, 1977, Pub.L. 95–87, Title IX, § 901, 91 Stat. 529; Aug. 4, 1977, Pub.L. 95–91, Title III, § 301(a), Title VII, §§ 703, 707, 91 Stat. 577, 606, 607; Oct. 17, 1979, Pub.L. 96–88, Title III, § 301(a)(1), Title V, § 507, 93 Stat. 677, 692.)

LIBRARY REFERENCES

Colleges and Universities ⚷9.25(1).
C.J.S. Colleges and Universities § 28.

§ 1322. Fellowship recipients [SMCRA § 902]

Recipients of fellowships under this subchapter shall be—

(a) persons who have been accepted by an institution of higher education for graduate study leading to an advanced degree or for a professional degree, and

(b) persons who plan a career in the field of energy resources, production, or utilization.

(Aug. 3, 1977, Pub.L. 95–87, Title IX, § 902, 91 Stat. 530.)

§ 1323. Distribution of fellowships [SMCRA § 903]

In awarding fellowships under the provisions of this subchapter, the Secretary of Energy shall endeavor to provide equitable distribution of such fellowships throughout the Nation, except that the Secretary of Energy shall give special attention to institutions of higher education, libraries, archives, or other research centers which have a demonstrated capacity to offer courses of study or research in the field of energy resources and conservation and conversion and related disciplines. In carrying out his responsibilities under this section, the Secretary of Energy shall take into consideration the projected need for highly trained engineers and scientists in the field of energy sources.

(Aug. 3, 1977, Pub.L. 95–87, Title IX, § 903, 91 Stat. 530; Aug. 4, 1977, Pub.L. 95–91, Title III, § 301(a), Title VII, §§ 703, 707, 91 Stat. 577, 606, 607.)

§ 1324. Stipends and allowances [SMCRA § 904]

(a) Each person awarded a fellowship under this subchapter shall receive a stipend of not more than $10,000 for each academic year of study. An additional amount of $500 for each such calendar year of study shall be paid to such person on account of each of his dependents.

(b) In addition to the amount paid to such person pursuant to subsection (a) of this section there shall be paid to the institution of higher education at which each such person is pursuing his course of study, 100 per centum of the amount paid to such person less the amount paid on account of such person's dependents, to such person less any amount charged such person for tuition.

(Aug. 3, 1977, Pub.L. 95–87, Title IX, § 904, 91 Stat. 530.)

CROSS REFERENCES

Conditions for receipt of stipends and allowances, see section 1326 of this title.

§ 1325. Limitation on fellowships [SMCRA § 905]

No fellowship shall be awarded under this subchapter for study at a school or department of divinity. For the purpose of this section, the term "school or department of divinity" means an institution or department or branch of an institution, whose program is specifically for the education of students to prepare them to become ministers of religion or to enter upon some other religious vocation or to prepare them to teach theological subjects.

(Aug. 3, 1977, Pub.L. 95–87, Title IX, § 905, 91 Stat. 530.)

§ 1326. Fellowship conditions [SMCRA § 906]

(a) A person awarded a fellowship under the provisions of this subchapter shall continue to receive the payments provided in section 1324(a) of this title only during such periods as the Secretary of Energy finds that he is maintaining satisfactory proficiency in, and devoting essentially full time to, study or research in the field in which such fellowship was awarded, in an institution of higher education, and is not engaging in gainful employment other than part-time employment in teaching, research, or similar activities, approved by the Secretary of Energy.

(b) The Secretary of Energy shall require reports containing such information in such forms and to be filed at such times as he determines necessary from each person awarded a fellowship under the provisions of this subchapter. Such reports shall be accompanied by a certificate from an appropriate official at the institution of higher education, library, archive, or other research center approved by the Secretary of Energy, stating that such person is making satisfactory progress in, and is devoting essentially full time to the research for which the fellowship was awarded.

(Aug. 3, 1977, Pub.L. 95–87, Title IX, § 906, 91 Stat. 530; Aug. 4, 1977, Pub.L. 95–91, Title III, § 301(a), Title VII, §§ 703, 707, 91 Stat. 577, 606, 607.)

§ 1327. Authorization of appropriations [SMCRA § 907]

There are authorized to be appropriated $11,000,000 for the fiscal year ending September 30, 1979, and for each of the five succeeding fiscal years. For payments for the initial awarding of fellowships awarded under this subchapter, there are authorized to be appropriated for the fiscal year ending September 30, 1979, and for each of the five succeeding fiscal years, such sums as may be necessary in order that fellowships already awarded might be completed.

(Aug. 3, 1977, Pub.L. 95–87, Title IX, § 907, 91 Stat. 531.)

§ 1328. Research, development projects, etc., relating to alternative coal mining technologies [SMCRA § 908]

(a) Authority of Secretary of the Interior to conduct, promote, etc.

The Secretary of the Interior is authorized to conduct and promote the coordination and acceleration of, research, studies, surveys, experiments, demonstration projects, and training relating to—

(1) the development and application of coal mining technologies which provide alternatives to surface disturbance and which maximize the recovery of available coal resources, including the improvement of present underground mining methods, methods for the return of underground mining wastes to the mine void, methods for the underground mining of thick coal seams and very deep seams; and

(2) safety and health in the application of such technologies, methods, and means.

(b) Contracts and grants

In conducting the activities authorized by this section, the Secretary of the Interior may enter into contracts with and make grants to qualified institutions, agencies, organizations, and persons.

(c) Authorization of appropriations

There are authorized to be appropriated to the Secretary of the Interior, to carry out the purposes of this section, $35,000,000 for each fiscal year beginning with the fiscal year 1979, and for each year thereafter for the next four years.

(d) Publication in Federal Register; report to Congress

At least sixty days before any funds are obligated for any research studies, surveys, experiments or demonstration projects to be conducted or financed under this chapter in any fiscal year, the Secretary of the Interior in consultation with the heads of other Federal agencies having the authority to conduct or finance such projects, shall determine and publish such determinations in the Federal Register that such projects are not being conducted or financed by any other Federal agency. On December 31 of each calendar year, the Secretary shall report to the Congress on the research studies, surveys, experiments or demonstration projects, conducted or financed under this chapter, including, but not limited to, a statement of the nature and purpose of each project, the Federal cost thereof, the identity and affiliation of the persons engaged in such projects, the expected completion date of the projects and the relationship of the projects to other such projects of a similar nature.

(e) Availability of information to public

Subject to the patent provisions of section 306(d) of this Act, all information and data resulting from any research studies, surveys, experiments, or demonstration projects conducted or financed under this chapter shall be promptly made available to the public.

(Aug. 3, 1977, Pub.L. 95–87, Title IX, § 908, 91 Stat. 531; Aug. 4, 1977, Pub.L. 95–91, Title III, § 301(a), Title VII, §§ 703, 707, 91 Stat. 577, 606, 607; Sept. 10, 1982, Pub.L. 97–257, Title I, § 100, 96 Stat. 841.)

References in Text

Section 306(d) of this Act, referred to in subsec. (e), was classified to section 1226(d) of this title and was omitted from the Code pursuant to the replacement of subchapter III (section 1221 et seq.) of this chapter by Pub.L. 98–409. See section 1226(c) of this title.

*

TITLE 33—NAVIGATION AND NAVIGABLE WATERS

WATER POLLUTION PREVENTION AND CONTROL

FEDERAL WATER POLLUTION CONTROL ACT [FWPCA § ___]

(33 U.S.C.A. §§ 1251 to 1387)

CHAPTER 26—WATER POLLUTION PREVENTION AND CONTROL

SUBCHAPTER I—RESEARCH AND RELATED PROGRAMS

Sec.

1251. Congressional declaration of goals and policy.
  (a) Restoration and maintenance of chemical, physical and biological integrity of Nation's waters; national goals for achievement of objective.
  (b) Congressional recognition, preservation, and protection of primary responsibilities and rights of States.
  (c) Congressional policy toward Presidential activities with foreign countries.
  (d) Administrator of Environmental Protection Agency to administer chapter.
  (e) Public participation in development, revision, and enforcement of any regulation, etc.
  (f) Procedures utilized for implementing chapter.
  (g) Authority of States over water.

1252. Comprehensive programs for water pollution control.
  (a) Preparation and development.
  (b) Planning for reservoirs; storage for regulation of streamflow.
  (c) Basins; grants to State agencies.
  (d) Repealed.

1252a. Reservoir projects, water storage; modification; storage for other than for water quality, opinion of Federal agency, committee resolutions of approval; provisions inapplicable to projects with certain prescribed water quality benefits in relation to total project benefits.

1253. Interstate cooperation and uniform laws.

1254. Research, investigations, training, and information.
  (a) Establishment of national programs; cooperation; investigations; water quality surveillance system; reports.
  (b) Authorized activities of Administrator.
  (c) Research and studies on harmful effects of pollutants; cooperation with Secretary of Health and Human Services.
  (d) Sewage treatment; identification and measurement of effects of pollutants; augmented streamflow.
  (e) Field laboratory and research facilities.
  (f) Great Lakes water quality research.
  (g) Treatment works pilot training programs; employment needs forecasting; training projects and grants; research fellowships; technical training; report to the President and transmittal to Congress.
  (h) Lake pollution.
  (i) Oil pollution control studies.
  (j) Solid waste disposal equipment for vessels.
  (k) Land acquisition.
  (*l*) Collection and dissemination of scientific knowledge on effects and control of pesticides in water.
  (m) Waste oil disposal study.
  (n) Comprehensive studies of effects of pollution on estuaries and estuarine zones; reports.
  (*o*) Methods of reducing total flow of sewage and unnecessary water consumption; reports.
  (p) Agricultural pollution.
  (q) Sewage in rural areas; national clearinghouse for alternative treatment information; clearinghouse on small flows.
  (r) Research grants to colleges and universities.
  (s) River Study Centers.
  (t) Thermal discharges.
  (u) Authorization of appropriations.

1254a. Research on effects of pollutants.

1255. Grants for research and development.
  (a) Demonstration projects covering storm waters, advanced waste treatment and water purification methods, and joint treatment systems for municipal and industrial wastes.
  (b) Demonstration projects for advanced treatment and environmental enhancement techniques to control pollution in river basins.
  (c) Research and demonstration projects for prevention of water pollution by industry.
  (d) Accelerated and priority development of waste management and waste treatment methods and identification and measurement methods.
  (e) Research and demonstration projects covering agricultural pollution and pollution from sewage in rural areas; dissemination of information.
  (f) Limitations.
  (g) Maximum grants.
  (h) Authorization of appropriations.
  (i) Assistance for research and demonstration projects.
  (j) Assistance for recycle, reuse, and land treatment projects.

Sec.
1256. Grants for pollution control programs.
(a) Authorization of appropriations for State and interstate programs.
(b) Allotments.
(c) Maximum annual payments.
(d) Limitations.
(e) Grants prohibited to States not establishing water quality monitoring procedures or adequate emergency and contingency plans.
(f) Conditions.
(g) Reallotment of unpaid allotments.
1257. Mine water pollution control demonstrations.
(a) Comprehensive approaches to elimination or control of mine water pollution.
(b) Consistency of projects with objectives of Appalachian Regional Development Act of 1965.
(c) Watershed selection.
(d) Conditions upon Federal participation.
(e) Authorization of appropriations.
1257a. State demonstration programs for cleanup of abandoned mines for use as waste disposal sites; authorization of appropriations.
1258. Pollution control in the Great Lakes.
(a) Demonstration projects.
(b) Conditions of Federal participation.
(c) Authorization of appropriations.
(d) Lake Erie demonstration program.
(e) Authorization of appropriations for Lake Erie demonstration program.
1259. Training grants and contracts.
1260. Applications; allocation.
1261. Scholarships.
1262. Definitions and authorizations.
1263. Alaska village demonstration projects.
(a) Central community facilities for safe water; elimination or control of pollution.
(b) Utilization of personnel and facilities of Department of Health and Human Services.
(c) Omitted.
(d) Authorization of appropriations.
(e) Study to develop comprehensive program for achieving sanitation services; report to Congress.
(f) Technical, financial, and management assistance.
(g) Definitions.
1264. Omitted.
1265. In-place toxic pollutants.
1266. Hudson River reclamation demonstration project.
1267. Chesapeake Bay.
1268. Great Lakes.
(a) Findings, purpose, and definitions.
(b) Great Lakes National Program Office.
(c) Great Lakes management.
(d) Great Lakes research.
(e) Research and management coordination.
(f) Interagency Cooperation.
(g) Relationship to existing Federal and State laws and international treaties.
(h) Authorizations of Great Lakes appropriations.
1269. Long Island Sound.
(a) Continuation of Management Conference; establishment of office.
(b) Administration and staffing of office.
(c) Duties of the office.
(d) Grants.
(e) Authorizations.

Sec.
1270. Lake Champlain Management Conference.
(a) Establishment.
(b) Membership.
(c) Technical advisory committee.
(d) Research program.
(e) Pollution prevention, control, and restoration plan.
(f) Grant assistance.
(g) Definition.
1271. Sediment survey and monitoring.
(a) Survey.
(b) Monitoring.

SUBCHAPTER II—GRANTS FOR CONSTRUCTION OF TREATMENT WORKS

1281. Congressional declaration of purpose.
(a) Development and implementation of waste treatment management plans and practices.
(b) Application of technology: confined disposal of pollutants; consideration of advanced techniques.
(c) Waste treatment management area and scope.
(d) Waste treatment management construction of revenue producing facilities.
(e) Waste treatment management integration of facilities.
(f) Waste treatment management "open space" and recreational considerations.
(g) Grants to construct publicly owned treatment works.
(h) Grants to construct privately owned treatment works.
(i) Waste treatment management methods, processes, and techniques to reduce energy requirements.
(j) Grants for treatment works utilizing processes and techniques of guidelines under section 1314(d)(3) of this title.
(k) Limitation on use of grants for publicly owned treatment works.
(*l*) Grants for facility plans, or plans, specifications, and estimates for proposed project for construction of treatment works; limitations, allotments, advances, etc.
(m) Grants for State of California projects.
(n) Water quality problems; funds, scope, etc.
(*o*) Capital financing plan.
(p) Time limit on resolving certain disputes.
1281a. Total treatment system funding.
1281b. Availability of Farmers Home Administration funds for non-Federal share.
1282. Federal share.
(a) Amount of grants for treatment works.
(b) Amount of grants for construction of treatment works not commenced prior to July 1, 1971.
(c) Availability of sums allotted to Puerto Rico.
1283. Plans, specifications, estimates, and payments.
(a) Submission; contractual nature of approval by Administrator; agreement on eligible costs; single grant.
(b) Periodic payments.
(c) Final payments.
(d) Projects eligible.

Sec.
1283. Plans, specifications, estimates, and payments.
(e) Technical and legal assistance in administration and enforcement of contracts; intervention in civil actions.
(f) Design/build projects.
1284. Limitations and conditions.
(a) Determinations by Administrator.
(b) Additional determinations; issuance of guidelines; approval by Administrator; system of charges.
(c) Applicability of reserve capacity restrictions to primary, secondary, or advanced waste treatment facilities or related interceptors.
(d) Engineering requirements; certification by owner and operator; contractual assurances, etc.
1285. Allotment of grant funds.
(a) Funds for fiscal years during period June 30, 1972, and September 30, 1977; determination of amount.
(b) Availability and use of funds allotted for fiscal years during period June 30, 1972, and September 30, 1977; reallotment.
(c) Funds for fiscal years during period October 1, 1977, and September 30, 1981; funds for fiscal years 1982 to 1990; determination of amount.
(d) Availability and use of funds; reallotment.
(e) Minimum allotment; additional appropriations; ratio of amount available.
(f) Omitted.
(g) Reservation of funds; State management assistance.
(h) Alternate systems for small communities.
(i) Set-aside for innovative and alternative projects.
(j) Water quality management plan; reservation of funds for nonpoint source management.
(k) New York City Convention Center.
(*l*) Marine estuary reservation.
(m) Discretionary deposits into State water pollution control revolving funds.
1286. Reimbursement and advanced construction.
(a) Publicly owned treatment works construction initiated after June 30, 1966, but before July 1, 1973; reimbursement formula.
(b) Publicly owned treatment works construction initiated between June 30, 1956, and June 30, 1966; reimbursement formula.
(c) Application for reimbursement.
(d) Allocation of funds.
(e) Authorization of appropriations.
(f) Additional funds.
1287. Authorization of appropriations.
1288. Areawide waste treatment management.
(a) Identification and designation of areas having substantial water quality control problems.
(b) Planning process.
(c) Regional operating agencies.
(d) Conformity of works with area plan.
(e) Permits not to conflict with approved plans.
(f) Grants.
(g) Technical assistance by Administrator.
(h) Technical assistance by Secretary of the Army.
(i) State best management practices program.
(j) Agricultural cost sharing.
1289. Basin planning.
(a) Preparation of Level B plans.
(b) Reporting requirements.

Sec.
1289. Basin planning.
(c) Authorization of appropriations.
1290. Annual survey.
1291. Sewage collection systems.
(a) Existing and new systems.
(b) Use of population density as test.
(c) Pollutant discharges from separate storm sewer systems.
1292. Definitions.
1293. Loan guarantees.
(a) State or local obligations issued exclusively to Federal Financing Bank for publicly owned treatment works; determination of eligibility of project by Administrator.
(b) Conditions for issuance.
(c) Fees for application investigation and issuance of commitment guarantee.
(d) Commitment for repayment.
1293a. Contained spoil disposal facilities.
(a) Construction, operation, and maintenance; period; conditions; requirements.
(b) Time for establishment; consideration of area needs; requirements.
(c) Written agreement requirement; terms of agreement.
(d) Waiver of construction costs contribution from non-Federal interests; findings of participation in waste treatment facilities for general geographical area and compliance with water quality standards; waiver of payments in event of written agreement before occurrence of findings.
(e) Federal payment of costs for disposal of dredged spoil from project.
(f) Title to lands, easements, and rights-of-way; retention by non-Federal interests; conveyance of facilities; agreement of transferee.
(g) Federal licenses or permits; charges; remission of charge.
(h) Provisions applicable to Great Lakes and their connecting channels.
(i) Research, study, and experimentation program relating to dredged spoil extended to navigable waters, etc.; cooperative program; scope of program; utilization of facilities and personnel of Federal agency.
(j) Period for depositing dredged materials.
(k) Study and monitoring program.
1294. Public information and education on recycling and reuse of wastewater, use of land treatment, and reduction of wastewater volume.
1295. Requirements for American materials.
1296. Determination of priority of projects.
1297. Guidelines for cost-effectiveness analysis.
1298. Cost effectiveness.
(a) Congressional statement of policy.
(b) Determination by Administrator as prerequisite to approval of grant.
(c) Value engineering review.
(d) Projects affected.
1299. State certification of projects.

SUBCHAPTER III—STANDARDS AND ENFORCEMENT

1311. Effluent limitations.
(a) Illegality of pollutant discharges except in compliance with law.

Sec.
1311. Effluent limitations.
(b) Timetable for achievement of objectives.
(c) Modification of timetable.
(d) Review and revision of effluent limitations.
(e) All point discharge source application of effluent limitations.
(f) Illegality of discharge of radiological, chemical, or biological warfare agents, high-level radioactive waste, or medical waste.
(g) Modifications for certain nonconventional pollutants.
(h) Modification of secondary treatment requirements.
(i) Municipal time extensions.
(j) Modification procedures.
(k) Innovative technology.
(*l*) Toxic pollutants.
(m) Modification of effluent limitation requirements for point sources.
(n) Fundamentally different factors.
(*o*) Application fees.
(p) Modified permit for coal remining operations.
1312. Water quality related effluent limitations.
(a) Establishment.
(b) Modifications of effluent limitations.
(c) Delay in application of other limitations.
1313. Water quality standards and implementation plans.
(a) Existing water quality standards.
(b) Proposed regulations.
(c) Review; revised standards; publication.
(d) Identification of areas with insufficient controls; maximum daily load; certain effluent limitations revision.
(e) Continuing planning process.
(f) Earlier compliance.
(g) Heat standards.
(h) Thermal water quality standards.
1313a. Revised water quality standards.
1314. Information and guidelines.
(a) Criteria development and publication.
(b) Effluent limitation guidelines.
(c) Pollution discharge elimination procedures.
(d) Secondary treatment information; alternative waste treatment management techniques; innovative and alternative wastewater treatment processes; facilities deemed equivalent of secondary treatment.
(e) Best management practices for industry.
(f) Identification and evaluation of nonpoint sources of pollution; processes, procedures, and methods to control pollution.
(g) Guidelines for pretreatment of pollutants.
(h) Test procedures guidelines.
(i) Guidelines for monitoring, reporting, enforcement, funding, personnel, and manpower.
(j) Lake restoration guidance manual.
(k) Agreements with Secretaries of Agriculture, Army, and Interior to provide maximum utilization of programs to achieve and maintain water quality; transfer of funds; authorization of appropriations.
(*l*) Individual control strategies for toxic pollutants.
(m) Schedule for review of Guidelines.
1315. State reports on water quality; transmittal to Congress.

Sec.
1316. National standards of performance.
(a) Definitions.
(b) Categories of sources; Federal standards of performance for new sources.
(c) State enforcement of standards of performance.
(d) Protection from more stringent standards.
(e) Illegality of operation of new sources in violation of applicable standards of performance.
1317. Toxic and pretreatment effluent standards.
(a) Toxic pollutant list; revision; hearing; promulgation of standards; effective date; consultation.
(b) Pretreatment standards; hearing; promulgation; compliance period; revision; application to State and local laws.
(c) New sources of pollutants into publicly owned treatment works.
(d) Operation in violation of standards unlawful.
(e) Compliance date extension for innovative pretreatment systems.
1318. Records and reports; inspections.
(a) Maintenance; monitoring equipment; entry; access to information.
(b) Availability to public; trade secrets exception; penalty for disclosure of confidential information.
(c) Application of State law.
(d) Access by Congress.
1319. Enforcement.
(a) State enforcement; compliance orders.
(b) Civil actions.
(c) Criminal penalties.
(d) Civil penalties; factors considered determining amount.
(e) State liability for judgments and expenses.
(f) Wrongful introduction of pollutants into treatment works.
(g) Administrative penalties.
1320. International pollution abatement.
(a) Hearing; participation by foreign nations.
(b) Functions and responsibilities of Administrator not affected.
(c) Hearing board; composition; findings of fact; recommendations; implementation of board's decision.
(d) Report by alleged polluter.
(e) Compensation of board members.
(f) Enforcement proceedings.
1321. Oil and hazardous substance liability.
(a) Definitions.
(b) Congressional declaration of policy against discharges of oil or hazardous substances; designation of hazardous substances; study of higher standard of care incentives and report to Congress; liability; penalties; civil actions: penalty limitations, separate offenses, jurisdiction, mitigation of damages and costs, recovery of removal costs and alternative remedies.
(c) Removal of discharged oil or hazardous substances; National Contingency Plan.
(d) Marine disaster discharges.
(e) Judicial relief.
(f) Liability for actual costs of removal.
(g) Third party liability.
(h) Rights against third parties who caused or contributed to discharge.

Sec.
1321. Oil and hazardous substance liability.
(i) Recovery of removal costs.
(j) Regulations; penalty.
(k) Authorization of appropriations; supplemental appropriations.
(*l*) Administration.
(m) Boarding and inspection of vessels; arrest; execution of warrants or other process.
(n) Jurisdiction.
(*o*) Obligation for damages unaffected; local authority not preempted; existing Federal authority not modified or affected.
(p) Financial responsibility.
(q) Establishment of maximum limit of liability with respect to onshore or offshore facilities.
(r) Liability limitations not to limit liability under other legislation.
1322. Marine sanitation devices.
(a) Definitions.
(b) Federal standards of performance.
(c) Initial standards; effective dates; revision; waiver.
(d) Vessels owned and operated by United States.
(e) Pre-promulgation consultation.
(f) Regulation by States or political subdivisions thereof; complete prohibition upon discharge of sewage.
(g) Sales limited to certified devices; certification of test device; recordkeeping; reports.
(h) Sale and resale of properly equipped vessels; operability of certified marine sanitation devices.
(i) Jurisdiction to restrain violations; contempts.
(j) Penalties.
(k) Enforcement authority.
(*l*) Boarding and inspection of vessels; execution of warrants and other process.
(m) Enforcement in United States possessions.
(n) Uniform national discharge standards for vessels of the Armed Forces.
1323. Federal facilities pollution control.
1324. Clean lakes.
(a) Establishment and scope of program.
(b) Financial assistance to States.
(c) Maximum amount of grant; authorization of appropriations.
(d) Demonstration program.
1325. National Study Commission.
(a) Establishment.
(b) Membership; chairman.
(c) Contract authority.
(d) Cooperation of departments, agencies, and instrumentalities of executive branch.
(e) Report to Congress.
(f) Compensation and allowances.
(g) Appointment of personnel.
(h) Authorization of appropriation.
1326. Thermal discharges.
(a) Effluent limitations that will assure protection and propagation of balanced, indigenous population of shellfish, fish, and wildlife.
(b) Cooling water intake structures.
(c) Period of protection from more stringent effluent limitations following discharge point source modification commenced after October 18, 1972.

Sec.
1327. Omitted.
1328. Aquaculture.
(a) Authority to permit discharge of specific pollutants.
(b) Procedures and guidelines.
(c) State administration.
1329. Nonpoint source management programs.
(a) State assessment reports.
(b) State management programs.
(c) Administrative provisions.
(d) Approval or disapproval of reports and management programs.
(e) Local management programs; technical assistance.
(f) Technical assistance for states.
(g) Interstate management conference.
(h) Grant program.
(i) Grants for protecting groundwater quality.
(j) Authorization of appropriations.
(k) Consistency of other programs and projects with management programs.
(*l*) Collection of information.
(m) Reports of Administrator.
(n) Set aside for administrative personnel.
1330. National estuary program.
(a) Management conference.
(b) Purposes of conference.
(c) Members of conference.
(d) Utilization of existing data.
(e) Period of conference.
(f) Approval and implementation of plans.
(g) Grants.
(h) Grant reporting.
(i) Authorization of appropriations.
(j) Research.
(k) Definitions.

SUBCHAPTER IV—PERMITS AND LICENSES

1341. Certification.
(a) Compliance with applicable requirements; application; procedures; license suspension.
(b) Compliance with other provisions of law setting applicable water quality requirements.
(c) Authority of Secretary of the Army to permit use of spoil disposal areas by Federal licensees or permittees.
(d) Limitations and monitoring requirements of certification.
1342. National pollutant discharge elimination system.
(a) Permits for discharge of pollutants.
(b) State permit programs.
(c) Suspension of Federal program upon submission of State program; withdrawal of approval of State program; return of State program to Administrator.
(d) Notification of Administrator.
(e) Waiver of notification requirement.
(f) Point source categories.
(g) Other regulations for safe transportation, handling, carriage, storage, and stowage of pollutants.
(h) Violation of permit conditions; restriction or prohibition upon introduction of pollutant by source not previously utilizing treatment works.

Sec.
1342. National pollutant discharge elimination system.
(i) Federal enforcement not limited.
(j) Public information.
(k) Compliance with permits.
(*l*) Limitation on permit requirement.
(m) Additional pretreatment of conventional pollutants not required.
(n) Partial permit program.
(*o*) Anti-Backsliding.
(p) Municipal and industrial stormwater discharges.
1343. Ocean discharge criteria.
(a) Issuance of permits.
(b) Waiver.
(c) Guidelines for determining degradation of waters.
1344. Permits for dredged or fill material.
(a) Discharge into navigable waters at specified disposal sites.
(b) Specification for disposal sites.
(c) Denial or restriction of use of defined areas as disposal sites.
(d) "Secretary" defined.
(e) General permits on State, regional, or nationwide basis.
(f) Non-prohibited discharge of dredged or fill material.
(g) State administration.
(h) Determination of State's authority to issue permits under State program; approval; notification; transfers to State program.
(i) Withdrawal of approval.
(j) Copies of applications for State permits and proposed general permits to be transmitted to Administrator.
(k) Waiver.
(*l*) Categories of discharges not subject to requirements.
(m) Comments on permit applications or proposed general permits by Secretary of Interior acting through Director of United States Fish and Wildlife Service.
(n) Enforcement authority not limited.
(*o*) Public availability of permits and permit applications.
(p) Compliance.
(q) Minimization of duplication, needless paperwork, and delays in issuance; agreements.
(r) Federal projects specifically authorized by Congress.
(s) Violation of permits.
(t) Navigable waters within State jurisdiction.
1345. Disposal or use of sewage sludge.
(a) Permit.
(b) Issuance of permit; regulations.
(c) State permit program.
(d) Regulations.
(e) Manner of sludge disposal.
(f) Implementation of regulations.
(g) Studies and projects.

SUBCHAPTER V—GENERAL PROVISIONS

1361. Administration.
(a) Authority of Administrator to prescribe regulations.
(b) Utilization of other agency officers and employees.

Sec.
1361. Administration.
(c) Recordkeeping.
(d) Audit.
(e) Awards for outstanding technological achievement or innovative processes, methods, or devices in waste treatment and pollution abatement programs.
(f) Detail of Environmental Protection Agency personnel to State water pollution control agencies.
1362. Definitions.
1363. Water Pollution Control Advisory Board.
(a) Establishment; composition; terms of office.
(b) Functions.
(c) Clerical and technical assistance.
1364. Emergency powers.
(a) Emergency powers.
(b) Repealed.
1365. Citizen suits.
(a) Authorization; jurisdiction.
(b) Notice.
(c) Venue; intervention by Administrator; United States interests protected.
(d) Litigation costs.
(e) Statutory or common law rights not restricted.
(f) Effluent standard or limitation.
(g) Citizen.
(h) Civil action by State Governors.
1366. Appearance.
1367. Employee protection.
(a) Discrimination against persons filing, instituting, or testifying in proceedings under this chapter prohibited.
(b) Application for review; investigation; hearing; review.
(c) Costs and expenses.
(d) Deliberate violations by employee acting without direction from his employer or his agent.
(e) Investigations of employment reductions.
1368. Federal procurement.
(a) Contracts with violators prohibited.
(b) Notification of agencies.
(c) Omitted.
(d) Exemptions.
(e) Annual report to Congress.
1369. Administrative procedure and judicial review.
(a) Subpenas.
(b) Review of Administrator's action; selection of court; fees.
(c) Additional evidence.
1370. State authority.
1371. Authority under other laws and regulations.
(a) Impairment of authority or functions of officials and agencies; treaty provisions.
(b) Discharges of pollutants into navigable waters.
(c) Action of Administrator deemed major Federal action; construction of National Environmental Policy Act of 1969.
(d) Consideration of international water pollution control agreements.
1372. Labor standards.
1373. Public health agency coordination.
1374. Effluent Standards and Water Quality Information Advisory Committee.
(a) Establishment; membership; term.
(b) Action on proposed regulations.

Sec.
1374. Effluent Standards and Water Quality Information Advisory Committee.
(c) Secretary; legal counsel; compensation.
(d) Quorum; special panel.
(e) Rules.
1375. Reports to Congress.
(a) Implementation of chapter objectives; status and progress of programs.
(b) Detailed estimates and comprehensive study on costs; State estimates, survey form.
(c) Status of combined sewer overflows in municipal treatment works operations.
(d) Legislative recommendations on program requiring coordination between water supply and wastewater control plans as condition for construction grants; public hearing.
(e) State revolving fund report.
1376. Authorization of appropriations.
1377. Indian tribes.
(a) Policy.
(b) Assessment of sewage treatment needs; report.
(c) Reservation of funds.
(d) Cooperative agreements.
(e) Treatment as States.
(f) Grants for nonpoint source programs.
(g) Alaska native organizations.
(h) Definitions.

SUBCHAPTER VI—STATE WATER POLLUTION CONTROL REVOLVING FUNDS

1381. Grants to States for establishment of revolving funds.
(a) General authority.

Sec.
1381. Grants to States for establishment of revolving funds.
(b) Schedule of grant payments.
1382. Capitalization grant agreements.
(a) General rule.
(b) Specific requirements.
1383. Water pollution control revolving loan funds.
(a) Requirements for obligation of grant funds.
(b) Administration.
(c) Projects eligible for assistance.
(d) Types of assistance.
(e) Limitation to prevent double benefits.
(f) Consistency with planning requirements.
(g) Priority list requirement.
(h) Eligibility of non-federal share of construction grant projects.
1384. Allotment of funds.
(a) Formula.
(b) Reservation of funds for planning.
(c) Allotment period.
1385. Corrective action.
(a) Notification of noncompliance.
(b) Withholding of payments.
(c) Reallotment of withheld payments.
1386. Audits, reports, and fiscal controls; intended use plan.
(a) Fiscal control and auditing procedures.
(b) Annual federal audits.
(c) Intended use plan.
(d) Annual report.
(e) Annual federal oversight review.
(f) Applicability of subchapter II provisions.
1387. Authorization of appropriations.

Related Provisions

See, also, Safety of Public Water Systems, 42 U.S.C.A. § 300f et seq., post; Water Resources Research, 42 U.S.C.A. § 10301 et seq., post.

CROSS REFERENCES

Amortization of pollution control facilities, see section 169 of Title 26, Internal Revenue Code.

Appalachian regional development, grants for construction of sewage treatment works, see section 212 of the Appendix to Title 40, Public Buildings, Property, and Works.

Atomic energy, authority of Administrator under this chapter, see section 2022 of Title 42, The Public Health and Welfare.

Coal leases, provisions requiring compliance with this chapter, see section 201 of Title 30, Mineral Lands and Mining.

Colorado River Basin Project—
Applicability of this chapter, see section 1577 of Title 43, Public Lands.
Salinity control, see sections 1595 and 1597 of Title 43.

Conditions for issuance of license for ownership, etc., of deepwater port, see section 1503 of this title.

Construction of the Surface Mining Control and Reclamation Act of 1977 as not superseding, etc., this chapter, see section 1292 of Title 30, Mineral Lands and Mining.

Coordination of regulatory and inspection activities, see section 1303 of Title 30.

Deepwater port considered as "new source" for purposes of this chapter, see section 1502 of this title.

Definition of "dumping" for purposes of ocean dumping, see section 1402 of this title.

Demonstrations of energy-related pollution control technologies, see section 4363a of Title 42, The Public Health and Welfare.

Discharge of pollutants from vessels engaged in recovery or exploration of deep sea minerals subject to this chapter, see section 1419 of Title 30, Mineral Lands and Mining.

Establishment of contained spoil disposal facilities pursuant to requirements of this chapter, see section 1293a of this title.

Mine drainage, construction and operation of plants for control and treatment of water pollution, see section 1242 of Title 30, Mineral Lands and Mining.

Noise emission standards, consideration of standards under this chapter, see section 4905 of Title 42, The Public Health and Welfare.

Notification to National Response Center of any release of hazardous substance from vessel, see section 9603 of Title 42.

Pinelands National Reserve, plan for implementation of provisions of this chapter, see section 471i of Title 16, Conservation.

Power plant fuel use, applicable environmental requirements, see section 8302 of Title 42, The Public Health and Welfare.

Reclamation and irrigation projects, applicability of this chapter, see section 421h of Title 43, Public Lands.

Requirements of this chapter to be incorporated into requirements for coastal zone management, see section 1456 of Title 16, Conservation.

Rural communities assistance for solid waste disposal, see section 6949 of Title 42, The Public Health and Welfare.

Science Advisory Board, availability of proposed environmental criteria documents, standards, limitations or regulations, see section 4365 of Title 42.

Solid waste disposal—
Construction with this chapter, see section 6905 of Title 42.
Creation of greater amounts of waste by virtue of this chapter, see section 6901 of Title 42.

Solid waste management information and guidelines, see section 6907 of Title 42.

Supplements to Federal grant-in-aid programs for Appalachian regional development, see section 214 of the Appendix to Title 40, Public Buildings, Property, and Works.
Surface coal mining, regulations setting mining and reclamation performance standards, see section 1251 of Title 30, Mineral Lands and Mining.
Urban mass transportation, compliance with requirements of this chapter, see section 1604 of Title 49, Transportation.
Water research and development, cooperation with Federal agencies, State and local governments, etc., see section 10303 of Title 42, The Public Health and Welfare.

West's Federal Forms

Complaints in admiralty charging oil pollution, see §§ 11097, 11098, 11098.5.
Contempt proceedings, see § 5651 et seq.
Judgment for oil spill cleanup costs, penalty, see § 11755 and Comment thereunder.
Jurisdiction and venue in district courts, see 1003 et seq.
Preliminary injunctions and temporary restraining orders, see § 5271 et seq.
Production of documents, motions and orders, see § 3551 et seq.
Taxation of costs, see § 4612 et seq.

West's Federal Practice Manual

Concurrent Claims Court jurisdiction, see § 1834.

CODE OF FEDERAL REGULATIONS

Administration of federal contracts, grants or loans, see 40 CFR 15.1 et seq.
Civil penalties for violation of oil pollution prevention regulations, see 40 CFR 114.1 et seq.
Effluent guidelines and standards, see 40 CFR 401.10 et seq.
General regulatory policies, see 33 CFR 320.1 et seq.
Guidelines establishing test procedures for analysis of pollutants, see 40 CFR 136.1 et seq.
Oil pollution regulations, see 33 CFR Chap. I, Subchap. O.
Pollution removal damage claims, see 33 CFR 25.101 et seq.
Public participation in programs, see 40 CFR 25.1 et seq.
Research and demonstration grants, see 40 CFR 40.100 et seq.
Rural clean water program, see 7 CFR 634.1 et seq.
State and local assistance, see 40 CFR 35.001 et seq.
Water quality planning and management, see 40 CFR 130.0 et seq.

LAW REVIEW COMMENTARIES

Hazardous Waste: A threat to the lender's environment. Marcy Sharon Cohen, 19 UCC L.J. 99 (1986).

United States Supreme Court

Interstate water pollution, preemption of state nuisance law, see International Paper Co. v. Harmel Ouellette et al., 1987, 107 S.Ct. 805, 93 L.Ed.2d 883.

WESTLAW ELECTRONIC RESEARCH

See WESTLAW guide following the Explanation pages of this pamphlet.

SUBCHAPTER I—RESEARCH AND RELATED PROGRAMS

§ 1251. Congressional declaration of goals and policy [FWPCA § 101]

(a) Restoration and maintenance of chemical, physical and biological integrity of Nation's waters; national goals for achievement of objective

The objective of this chapter is to restore and maintain the chemical, physical, and biological integrity of the Nation's waters. In order to achieve this objective it is hereby declared that, consistent with the provisions of this chapter—

(1) it is the national goal that the discharge of pollutants into the navigable waters be eliminated by 1985;

(2) it is the national goal that wherever attainable, an interim goal of water quality which provides for the protection and propagation of fish, shellfish, and wildlife and provides for recreation in and on the water be achieved by July 1, 1983;

(3) it is the national policy that the discharge of toxic pollutants in toxic amounts be prohibited;

(4) it is the national policy that Federal financial assistance be provided to construct publicly owned waste treatment works;

(5) it is the national policy that areawide waste treatment management planning processes be developed and implemented to assure adequate control of sources of pollutants in each State;

(6) it is the national policy that a major research and demonstration effort be made to develop technology necessary to eliminate the discharge of pollutants into the navigable waters, waters of the contiguous zone, and the oceans; and

(7) it is the national policy that programs for the control of nonpoint sources of pollution be developed and implemented in an expeditious manner so as to enable the goals of this chapter to be met through the control of both point and nonpoint sources of pollution.

(b) Congressional recognition, preservation, and protection of primary responsibilities and rights of States

It is the policy of the Congress to recognize, preserve, and protect the primary responsibilities and rights of States to prevent, reduce, and eliminate pollution, to plan the development and use (including restoration, preservation, and enhancement) of land and water resources, and to consult with the Administrator in the exercise of his authority under this chapter. It is the policy of Congress that the States manage the construction grant program under this chapter and implement the permit programs under sections 1342 and 1344 of this title. It is further the policy of the Congress to support and aid research relating to the prevention, reduction, and elimination of pollution and to provide Federal technical services and financial aid to State and interstate agencies and municipalities in connection with the prevention, reduction, and elimination of pollution.

(c) Congressional policy toward Presidential activities with foreign countries

It is further the policy of Congress that the President, acting through the Secretary of State and such national and international organizations as he determines appropriate, shall take such action as may be necessary to insure that to the fullest extent possible all foreign countries shall take meaningful action for the prevention, reduction, and elimination of pollution in their waters and in international waters and for the achievement of goals regarding the elimination of discharge of pollutants and the improvement of water quality to at least the same extent as the United States does under its laws.

(d) Administrator of Environmental Protection Agency to administer chapter

Except as otherwise expressly provided in this chapter, the Administrator of the Environmental Protection Agency (hereinafter in this chapter called "Administrator") shall administer this chapter.

(e) Public participation in development, revision, and enforcement of any regulation, etc.

Public participation in the development, revision, and enforcement of any regulation, standard, effluent limitation, plan, or program established by the Administrator or any State under this chapter shall be provided for, encouraged, and assisted by the Administrator and the States. The Administrator, in cooperation with the States, shall develop and publish regulations specifying minimum guidelines for public participation in such processes.

(f) Procedures utilized for implementing chapter

It is the national policy that to the maximum extent possible the procedures utilized for implementing this chapter shall encourage the drastic minimization of paperwork and interagency decision procedures, and the best use of available manpower and funds, so as to prevent needless duplication and unnecessary delays at all levels of government.

(g) Authority of States over water

It is the policy of Congress that the authority of each State to allocate quantities of water within its jurisdiction shall not be superseded, abrogated or otherwise impaired by this chapter. It is the further policy of Congress that nothing in this chapter shall be construed to supersede or abrogate rights to quantities of water which have been established by any State. Federal agencies shall co-operate with State and local agencies to develop comprehensive solutions to prevent, reduce and eliminate pollution in concert with programs for managing water resources.

(June 30, 1948, c. 758, Title I, § 101, Oct. 18, 1972, as added Pub.L. 92–500, § 2, 86 Stat. 816, and amended Dec. 27, 1977, Pub.L. 95–217, §§ 5(a), 26(b), 91 Stat. 1567, 1575; Feb. 4, 1987, Pub.L. 100–4, Title III, § 316(b), 101 Stat. 60.)

Short Title of 1994 Amendments

Pub.L. 103–431, § 1, Oct. 31, 1994, 108 Stat. 4396, provided that: "This Act [amending section 1311 of this title] may be cited as the 'Ocean Pollution Reduction Act'."

Short Title of 1990 Amendments

Pub.L. 101–596, § 1, Nov. 16, 1990, 104 Stat. 3000, provided that: "This Act [enacting sections 1269 and 1270 and amending sections 1268 and 1324 of this title, and enacting note provisions under this section and section 1270 of this title] may be cited as the 'Great Lakes Critical Programs Act of 1990'."

Pub.L. 101–596, Title II, § 201, Nov. 16, 1990, 104 Stat. 3004, provided that: "This part [enacting section 1269 and amending section 1416 of this title] may be cited as the 'Long Island Sound Improvement Act of 1990'."

Pub.L. 101–596, Title III, § 301, Nov. 16, 1990, 104 Stat. 3006, provided that: "This title [enacting section 1270 and amending section 1324(d)(2) of this title and enacting note provision under section 1270 of this title] may be cited as the 'Lake Champlain Special Designation Act of 1990'."

Short Title

Section 519, formerly 518, of Act June 30, 1948, c. 758, Title V, as added Oct. 18, 1972, Pub.L. 92–500, § 2, 86 Stat. 896, amended Dec. 27, 1977, Pub.L. 95–217, § 2, 91 Stat. 1566, and renumbered Feb. 4, 1987, Pub.L. 100–4, Title V, § 506, 101 Stats. 76, provided that: "This Act [enacting this chapter] may be cited as the 'Federal Water Pollution Control Act' (commonly referred to as the Clean Water Act)."

Savings Provisions

Section 4 of Pub.L. 92–500, Oct. 18, 1972, 86 Stat. 896, provided that:

"(a) No suit, action, or other proceeding lawfully commenced by or against the Administrator or any other officer or employee of the United States in his official capacity or in relation to the discharge of his official duties under the Federal Water Pollution Control Act as in effect immediately prior to the date of enactment of this Act [Oct. 18, 1972] shall abate by reason of the taking effect of the amendment made by section 2 of this Act [which enacted this chapter]. The court may, on its own motion or that of any party made at any time within twelve months after such taking effect, allow the same to be maintained by or against the Administrator or such officer or employee.

"(b) All rules, regulations, orders, determinations, contracts, certifications, authorizations, delegations, or other actions duly issued, made, or taken by or pursuant to the Federal Water Pollution Control Act as in effect immediately prior to the date of enactment of this Act [Oct. 18, 1972], and pertaining to any functions, powers, requirements, and duties under the Federal Water Pollution Control Act as in effect immediately prior to the date of enactment of this Act [Oct. 18, 1972] shall continue in full force and effect after the date of enactment of this Act [Oct. 18, 1972] until modified or rescinded in accordance with the Federal Water Pollution Control Act as amended by this Act [this chapter].

"(c) The Federal Water Pollution Control Act as in effect immediately prior to the date of enactment of this Act [Oct. 18, 1972] shall remain applicable to all grants made from funds authorized for the fiscal year ending June 30, 1972, and prior fiscal years, including any increases in the monetary amount of any such grant which may be paid from authorizations for fiscal years beginning after June 30, 1972, except as specifically otherwise provided in section 202 of the Federal Water Pollution Control Act as amended by this Act [section 1282 of this title] and in subsection (c) of section 3 of this Act."

Separability of Provisions

Section 512 of Act June 30, 1948, c. 758, Title V, as added Oct. 18, 1972, Pub.L. 92–500, § 2, 86 Stat. 894, provided that: "If any provision of this Act [this chapter], or the application of any provision of this Act [this chapter] to any person or circumstance, is held invalid, the application of such provision to other persons or circumstances, and the remainder of this Act [this chapter], shall not be affected thereby."

National Shellfish Indicator Program

Pub.L. 102-567, Title III, § 308, Oct. 29, 1992, 106 Stat. 4286, provided that:

"(a) Establishment of a research program.—The Secretary of Commerce, in cooperation with the Secretary of Health and Human Services and the Administrator of the Environmental Protection Agency, shall establish and administer a 5-year national shellfish research program (hereafter in this section referred to as the 'Program') for the purpose of improving existing classification systems for shellfish growing waters using the latest technological advancements in microbiology and epidemiological methods. Within 12 months after the date of enactment of this Act [Oct. 29, 1992], the Secretary of Commerce, in cooperation with the advisory committee established under subsection (b) and the Consortium, shall develop a comprehensive 5-year plan for the Program which shall at a minimum provide for—

"(1) an environmental assessment of commercial shellfish growing areas in the United States, including an evaluation of the relationships between indicators of fecal contamination and human enteric pathogens;

"(2) the evaluation of such relationships with respect to potential health hazards associated with human consumption of shellfish;

"(3) a comparison of the current microbiological methods used for evaluating indicator bacteria and human enteric pathogens in shellfish and shellfish growing waters with new technological methods designed for this purpose;

"(4) the evaluation of current and projected systems for human sewage treatment in eliminating viruses and other human enteric pathogens which accumulate in shellfish;

"(5) the design of epidemiological studies to relate microbiological data, sanitary survey data, and human shellfish consumption date to actual hazards to health associated with such consumption; and

"(6) recommendations for revising Federal shellfish standards and improving the capabilities of Federal and State agencies to effectively manage shellfish and ensure the safety of shellfish intended for human consumption.

"(b) Advisory committee.—(1) For the purpose of providing oversight of the Program on a continuing basis, an advisory committee (hereafter in this section referred to as the 'Committee') shall be established under a memorandum of understanding between the Interstate Shellfish Sanitation Conference and the National Marine Fisheries Service.

"(2) The Committee shall—

"(A) identify priorities for achieving the purpose of the Program;

"(B) review and recommend approval or disapproval of Program work plans and plans of operation;

"(C) review and comment on all subcontracts and grants to be awarded under the Program;

"(D) receive and review progress reports from the Consortium and program subcontractors and grantees; and

"(E) provide such other advice on the Program as is appropriate.

"(3) The Committee shall consist of at least ten members and shall include—

"(A) three members representing agencies having authority under State law to regulate the shellfish industry, of whom one shall represent each of the Atlantic, Pacific, and Gulf of Mexico shellfish growing regions;

"(B) three members representing persons engaged in the shellfish industry in the Atlantic, Pacific, and Gulf of Mexico shellfish growing regions (who shall be appointed from among at least six recommendations by the industry members of the Interstate Shellfish sanitation Conference Executive Board), of whom one shall represent the shellfish industry in each region;

"(C) three members, of whom one shall represent each of the following Federal agencies; the National Oceanic and Atmospheric Administration, the Environmental Protection Agency, and the Food and Drug Administration; and

"(D) one member representing the Shellfish Institute of North America.

"(4) The Chairman of the Committee shall be selected from among the Committee members described in paragraph (3)(A).

"(5) The Committee shall establish and maintain a subcommittee of scientific experts to provide advice, assistance, and information relevant to research funded under the Program, except that no individual who is awarded, or whose application is being considered for, a grant or subcontract under the Program may serve on such subcommittee. The membership of the subcommittee shall, to the extent practicable, be regionally balanced with experts who have scientific knowledge concerning each of the Atlantic, Pacific, and Gulf of Mexico shellfish growing regions. Scientists from the National Academy of Sciences and appropriate Federal agencies (including the National Oceanic and Atmospheric Administration, Food and Drug Administration, Centers for Disease Control, National Institutes of Health, Environmental Protection Agency, and National Science Foundation) shall be considered for membership on the subcommittee.

"(6) Members of the Committee and its scientific subcommittee established under this subsection shall not be paid for serving on the Committee or subcommittee, but shall receive travel expenses as authorized by section 5703 of title 5, United states Code [section 5703 of Title 5, Government Organization and Employees].

"(c) Contract with consortium.—Within 30 days after the date of enactment of this Act [Oct. 29, 1992], the Secretary of Commerce shall seek to enter into a cooperative agreement or contract with the Consortium under which the Consortium will—

"(1) be the academic administrative organization and fiscal agent for the Program;

"(2) award and administer such grants and subcontracts as are approved by the Committee under subsection (b);

"(3) develop and implement a scientific peer review process for evaluating grant and subcontractor applications prior to review by the Committee;

"(4) in cooperation with the Secretary of Commerce and the Committee, procure the services of a scientific project director;

"(5) develop and submit budgets, progress reports, work plans, and plans of operation for the Program to the Secretary of Commerce and the Committee; and

"(6) make available to the Committee such staff, information, and assistance as the Committee may reasonably require to carry out its activities.

"(d) Reporting requirements.—Within 3 months after the date of enactment of this Act [Oct. 29, 1992] and within each of the next three consecutive 3-month intervals, the Secretary of Commerce shall provide Congress with written assessments of Federal efforts to implement this section. In addition, the Secretary of Commerce shall submit an annual report to Congress on the Program, including a description of the research funded under the Program and the results of such research.

"(e) Authorization of appropriations.—(1) Of the sums authorized under section 4(a) of the National Oceanic and Atmospheric Administration Marine Fisheries Program Authorization act (Public Law 98-210; 97 Stat. 1409) [section 4(a) of Pub.L. 98-210, Dec. 6, 1983, 97 Stat. 1409, which is not classified to the Code], there are authorized to be appropriated to the Secretary of Commerce $5,200,000 for each of the fiscal years 1993 through 1997 for carrying out the Program. Of the amounts appropriated pursuant to this authorization, not more than 5 percent of such appropriation may be used for administrative purposes by the National Oceanic and Atmospheric Administration. The remaining 95 percent of such appropriation shall be used to meet the administrative and scientific objectives of the Program.

"(2) The Interstate Shellfish Sanitation Conference shall not administer appropriations authorized under this section, but may be reimbursed from such appropriations for its expenses in arranging for travel, meetings, workshops, or conferences necessary to carry out the Program.

"(f) Definitions.—As used in this section, the term—

"(1) 'Consortium' means the Louisiana Universities Marine Consortium; and

"(2) 'shellfish' means any species of oyster, clam, or mussel that is harvested for human consumption."

International Trade Study

Section 6 of Pub.L. 92-500, Oct. 18, 1972, 86 Stat. 896, provided that:

"**(a)** The Secretary of Commerce, in cooperation with other interested Federal agencies and with representatives of industry and the public, shall undertake immediately an investigation of study to determine—

"**(1)** the extent to which pollution abatement and control programs will be imposed on, or voluntarily undertaken by, United States manufacturers in the near future and the probable short- and long-range effects of the costs of such programs (computed to the greatest extent practicable on an industry-by-industry basis) on (A) the production costs of such domestic manufacturers, and (B) the market prices of the goods produced by them:

"**(2)** the probable extent to which pollution abatement and control programs will be implemented in foreign industrial nations in the near future and the extent to which the production costs (computed to the greatest extent practicable on an industry-by-industry basis) of foreign manufacturers will be affected by the costs of such programs;

"**(3)** the probable competitive advantage which any article manufactured in a foreign nation will likely have in relation to a comparable article made in the United States if that foreign nation—

"**(A)** does not require its manufacturers to implement pollution abatement and control programs.

"**(B)** requires a lesser degree of pollution abatement and control in its programs, or

"**(C)** in any way reimburses or otherwise subsidizes its manufacturers for the costs of such program;

"**(4)** alternative means by which any competitive advantage accruing to the products of any foreign nation as a result of any factor described in paragraph (3) may be (A) accurately and quickly determined, and (B) equalized, for example, by the imposition of a surcharge or duty, on a foreign product in an amount necessary to compensate for such advantage; and

"**(5)** the impact, if any, which the imposition of a compensating tariff of other equalizing measure may have in encouraging foreign nations to implement pollution and abatement control programs.

"**(b)** The Secretary shall make an initial report to the President and Congress within six months after the date of enactment of this section [Oct. 18, 1972] of the results of the study and investigation carried out pursuant to this section and shall make additional reports thereafter at such times as he deems appropriate taking into account the development of relevant data, but not less than once every twelve months."

International Agreements

Section 7 of Pub.L. 92–500, Oct. 18, 1972, 86 Stat. 896, provided that: "The President shall undertake to enter into international agreement to apply uniform standards of performance for the control of the discharge and emission of pollutants from new sources, uniform controls over the discharge and emission of toxic pollutants, and uniform controls over the discharge of pollutants into the ocean. For this purpose the President shall negotiate multilateral treaties, conventions, resolutions, or other agreements, and formulate, present, or support proposals at the United Nations and other appropriate international forums."

Sex Discrimination

Section 13 of Pub.L. 92–500, Oct. 18, 1972, 86 Stat. 903, provided that: "No person in the United States shall on the ground of sex be excluded from participation in, be denied the benefits of, or be subjected to discrimination under any program or activity receiving Federal assistance under this Act [see Short Title note above] the Federal Water Pollution Control Act [this chapter], or the Environmental Financing Act. This section shall be enforced through agency provisions and rules similar to those already established, with respect to racial and other discrimination, under title VI of the Civil Rights Act of 1964 [section 2000d et seq. of Title 42, The Public Health and Welfare]. However, this remedy is not exclusive and will not prejudice or cut off any other legal remedies available to a discriminatee."

CROSS REFERENCES

Modification of secondary treatment requirements, see section 1311 of this title.

Report to Congress to include recommendations concerning policy to reduce pollution, see section 1252 of this title.

CODE OF FEDERAL REGULATIONS

Procedures for decisionmaking, see 40 CFR 124.1 et seq.
Procurement under assistance agreements, see 40 CFR 33.001 et seq.
Public participation in programs, see 40 CFR 25.1 et seq.

LAW REVIEW COMMENTARIES

American and British offshore oil development. Uisdean R. Vass. 21 Tulsa L.J. 23 (1985).

Beyond words of exhortation: The congressional prescription for vigorous federal enforcement of the Clean Water Act. William L. Andreen, 55 Geo.Wash.L.Rev. 202 (1987).

Citizen suits under the Clean Water Act. 38 Rutgers L.Rev. 813 (1986).

Confidential business information versus the public's right to disclosure—Biotechnology renews the challenge. Stanley H. Abramson, 34 U.Kansas L.Rev. 681 (1986).

Congressional ambiguity allows EPA's safety valve to remain open. 35 Catholic U.L.Rev. 595 (1986).

Crude legislation: Liability and compensation under the Oil Pollution Act of 1990. 23 Rutgers L.J. 597 (1992).

Damming agricultural drainage: The effect of wetland preservation and federal regulation on agricultural drainage in Minnesota. Mark J. Hanson, 13 Wm.Mitchell L.Rev. 135 (1987).

Economizing on the sins of our past: Cleaning up our hazardous wastes. Barbara Ann White, 25 Houston L.Rev. 899 (1988).

Environmental auditing: What your client doesn't know hurts the most. William L. Earl, 60 Fla.Bar J. 47 (1986).

Environmental element in Florida condemnation proceedings. Marcus A. Castillo, 61 Fla.B.J. 60 (May 1987).

Environmental Law/Annual survey of significant developments. Thomas J. Elliott, 58 Pa.B.A.Q. 107 (1987).

Erosion of mens rea in environmental criminal prosecution. Ruth Ann Weidel, John R. Mayo and F. Michael Zachara, 21 Seton Hall L.Rev. 1125 (1991).

Federal preemption and private legal remedies for pollution. Robert L. Glicksman (1985), 134 U.Pa.L.Rev. 121.

Federal regulation of environmental releases of genetically manipulated microorganisms. Edward L. Korwek and Peter L. de la Cruz (1985) 11 Rutgers Computer & Tech.Law J. 301.

Florida's assumption of federal dredge-and-fill jurisdiction. Martin R. Dix and Scott Denson, 67 Fla.B.J. 56 (April 1993).

Fundamentally different factor variances under the Clean Water Act: Should they be applicable to toxic pollutants? (1983–84) 29 Vill.L.Rev. 771.

Grazing management on the public lands: Opening the process to public participation. Joseph M. Feller, 26 Land and Water L.Rev. 571 (1991).

Hazardous wastes in New Jersey: An overview. Anne F. Morris, 38 Rutgers L.Rev. 623 (1986).

How well can states enforce their environmental laws when the polluter is the United States Government? 18 Rutgers L.J. 123 (1986).

Interstate waste: A key issue in resolving the national hazardous waste capacity crisis. B.J. Wynne, III and Terri Hamby, 32 S.Tex. L.Rev. 601 (1991).

Limiting lender liability under CERCLA by administrative rule. Frona M. Powell, 75 Marq.L.Rev. 139 (1991).

New Jersey clean up your "act": Some reflections on the Spill Compensation and Control Act. Francis E.P. McCarter, 38 Rutgers L.Rev. 637 (1986).

No longer just a cost of doing business: Criminal liability of corporate officials for violations of the Clean Water Act and Resource Conservation and Recovery Act. G. Nelson Smith, III, 53 La.L.Rev. 119 (1992).

North American commission on the environment. Stephen L. Kass and Michael B. Gerrard, 209 N.Y.L.J. 3 (May 28, 1993).

Oil and gas exemptions under RCRA and CERCLA: Are they still "safe harbors" eleven years later? Michael M. Gibson and David P. Young, 32 S.Tex.L.Rev. 361 (1991).

Oil Pollution Act of 1990: Opening a new era in federal and Texas regulation of oil spill prevention, containment and cleanup, and liability. J.B. Ruhl and Michael J. Jewell, 32 S.Tex.L.Rev. 475 (1991).

Private enforcement of the Clean Air Act and the Clean Water Act. 35 Am.U.L.Rev. 127 (1985).

Property owner liability for environmental contamination in California. Michael B. Hingerty, 22 U.S.F.L.Rev. 31 (1987).

Regulation of batture pollution and ecology. Stan Millan, 33 Loyola (La.) L.Rev. 921 (1988).

Resolving conflicts between bankruptcy law and the state police power. Ellen E. Sward, 1987 Wis.L.Rev. 403 (1987).

The federal consistency doctrine: Coastal zone management and "new federalism". Tim Eichenberg and Jack Archer, 14 Ecology L.Q. 9 (1987).

The Federal Water Pollution Control Act's antidegradation policy and its application to groundwater. 20 U.S.F.L.Rev. 633 (1986).

Toward a national groundwater act: Current contamination and future courses of action. Thomas D. Marks, 61 Fla.B.J. 10 (April 1987).

Toward resolution of insurance coverage questions in toxic tort litigation. Janine Bauer and Arnold Lakind, 38 Rutgers L.Rev. 677 (1986).

Toxic tort litigation and the causation element: Is there any hope of reconciliation? Ora Fred Harris, Jr., 40 Southwestern (Tex.) L.J. 909 (1986).

LIBRARY REFERENCES

Health and Environment ⟹25.7(3).
C.J.S. Health and Environment § 106.

United States Supreme Court

Interstate pollution, discharge of sewage into Lake Michigan, this chapter displacing federal common law of nuisance, see City of Milwaukee v. Illinois and Michigan, 1981, 101 S.Ct. 1784, 451 U.S. 304, 68 L.Ed.2d 114.

Preemption of federal common law of nuisance in area of water pollution, see Middlesex County Sewerage Authority v. National Sea Clammers Ass'n, 1981, 101 S.Ct. 2615, 453 U.S. 1, 69 L.Ed.2d 435.

Public nuisance in interstate or navigable waters, application of federal common law not inconsistent with this chapter, see Illinois v. City of Milwaukee, 1972, 92 S.Ct. 1385, 406 U.S. 91, 31 L.Ed.2d 712.

§ 1252. Comprehensive programs for water pollution control [FWPCA § 102]

(a) Preparation and development

The Administrator shall, after careful investigation, and in cooperation with other Federal agencies, State water pollution control agencies, interstate agencies, and the municipalities and industries involved, prepare or develop comprehensive programs for preventing, reducing, or eliminating the pollution of the navigable waters and ground waters and improving the sanitary condition of surface and underground waters. In the development of such comprehensive programs due regard shall be given to the improvements which are necessary to conserve such waters for the protection and propagation of fish and aquatic life and wildlife, recreational purposes, and the withdrawal of such waters for public water supply, agricultural, industrial, and other purposes. For the purpose of this section, the Administrator is authorized to make joint investigations with any such agencies of the condition of any waters in any State or States, and of the discharges of any sewage, industrial wastes, or substance which may adversely affect such waters.

(b) Planning for reservoirs; storage for regulation of streamflow

(1) In the survey or planning of any reservoir by the Corps of Engineers, Bureau of Reclamation, or other Federal agency, consideration shall be given to inclusion of storage for regulation of streamflow, except that any such storage and water releases shall not be provided as a substitute for adequate treatment or other methods of controlling waste at the source.

(2) The need for and the value of storage for regulation of streamflow (other than for water quality) including but not limited to navigation, salt water intrusion, recreation, esthetics, and fish and wildlife, shall be determined by the Corps of Engineers, Bureau of Reclamation, or other Federal agencies.

(3) The need for, the value of, and the impact of, storage for water quality control shall be determined by the Administrator, and his views on these matters shall be set forth in any report or presentation to Congress proposing authorization or construction of any reservoir including such storage.

(4) The value of such storage shall be taken into account in determining the economic value of the entire project of which it is a part, and costs shall be allocated to the purpose of regulation of streamflow in a manner which will insure that all project purposes, share equitably in the benefit of multiple-purpose construction.

(5) Costs of regulation of streamflow features incorporated in any Federal reservoir or other impoundment under the provisions of this chapter shall be determined and the beneficiaries identified and if the benefits are widespread or national in scope, the costs of such features shall be nonreimbursable.

(6) No license granted by the Federal Energy Regulatory Commission for a hydroelectric power project shall include storage for regulation of streamflow for the purpose of water quality control unless the Administrator shall recommend its inclusion and such reservoir storage capacity shall not exceed such proportion of the total storage required for the water quality control plan as the drainage area of such reservoir bears to the drainage area of the river basin or basins involved in such water quality control plan.

(c) Basins; grants to State agencies

(1) The Administrator shall, at the request of the Governor of a State, or a majority of the Governors

when more than one State is involved, make a grant to pay not to exceed 50 per centum of the administrative expenses of a planning agency for a period not to exceed three years, which period shall begin after October 18, 1972, if such agency provides for adequate representation of appropriate State, interstate, local, or (when appropriate) international interests in the basin or portion thereof involved and is capable of developing an effective, comprehensive water quality control plan for a basin or portion thereof.

(2) Each planning agency receiving a grant under this subsection shall develop a comprehensive pollution control plan for the basin or portion thereof which—

(A) is consistent with any applicable water quality standards effluent and other limitations, and thermal discharge regulations established pursuant to current law within the basin;

(B) recommends such treatment works as will provide the most effective and economical means of collection, storage, treatment, and elimination of pollutants and recommends means to encourage both municipal and industrial use of such works;

(C) recommends maintenance and improvement of water quality within the basin or portion thereof and recommends methods of adequately financing those facilities as may be necessary to implement the plan; and

(D) as appropriate, is developed in cooperation with, and is consistent with any comprehensive plan prepared by the Water Resources Council, any areawide waste management plans developed pursuant to section 1288 of this title, and any State plan developed pursuant to section 1313(e) of this title.

(3) For the purposes of this subsection the term "basin" includes, but is not limited to, rivers and their tributaries, streams, coastal waters, sounds, estuaries, bays, lakes, and portions thereof as well as the lands drained thereby.

(d) Repealed. Pub.L. 104–66, Title II, § 2021(a), Dec. 21, 1995, 109 Stat. 726

(June 30, 1948, c. 758, Title I, § 102, as added Oct. 18, 1972, Pub.L. 92–500, § 2, 86 Stat. 817, and amended Aug. 4, 1977, Pub.L. 95–91, Title IV, § 402(a)(i)(A), 91 Stat. 583; Dec. 27, 1977, Pub.L. 95–217, § 5(b), 91 Stat. 1567; Dec. 21, 1995, Pub.L. 104–66, Title II, § 2021(a), 109 Stat. 726.)

Environmental Dredging

Pub.L. 101–640, Title III, § 312, Nov. 28, 1990, 104 Stat. 4639, provided that:

"**(a) Operation and maintenance of navigation projects.**—Whenever necessary to meet the requirements of the Federal Water Pollution Control Act [33 U.S.C.A. § 1251 et seq.], the Secretary, in consultation with the Administrator of the Environmental Protection Agency, may remove, as part of operation and maintenance of a navigation project, contaminated sediments outside the boundaries of and adjacent to the navigation channel.

"**(b) Nonproject specific.**—

"**(1) In general.**—The Secretary may remove contaminated sediments from the navigable waters of the United States for the purpose of environmental enhancement and water quality improvement if such removal is requested by a non-Federal sponsor and the sponsor agrees to pay 50 percent of the cost of such removal.

"**(2) Maximum amount.**—The Secretary may not expend more than $10,000,000 in a fiscal year to carry out this subsection.

"**(c) Joint plan requirement.**—The Secretary may only remove contaminated sediments under subsection (b) in accordance with a joint plan developed by the Secretary and interested Federal, State, and local government officials. Such plan must include an opportunity for public comment, a description of the work to be undertaken, the method to be used for dredged material disposal, the roles and responsibilities of the Secretary and non-Federal sponsors, and identification of sources of funding.

"**(d) Disposal costs.**—Costs of disposal of contaminated sediments removed under this section shall be a non-Federal responsibility.

"**(e) Limitation on statutory construction.**—Nothing in this section shall be construed to affect the rights and responsibilities of any person under the Comprehensive Environmental Response, Compensation, and Liability Act of 1980 [42 U.S.C.A. § 9601 et seq.].

"**(f) Termination date.**—This section shall not be effective after the last day of the 5-year period beginning on the date of the enactment of this Act [Nov. 28, 1990]; except that the Secretary may complete any project commenced under this section on or before such last day."

CROSS REFERENCES

Modification of project for regulation of streamflow, see section 1252a of this title.

Report to Congress, progress and problems associated with developing comprehensive plans under this section, see section 1375 of this title.

CODE OF FEDERAL REGULATIONS

Administration of federal contracts, grants, or loans, see 40 CFR 15.1 et seq.

LAW REVIEW COMMENTARIES

Grazing management on the public lands: Opening the process to public participation. Joseph M. Feller, 26 Land and Water L.Rev. 571 (1991).

Resurgence of presidential budgetmaking initiative: A proposal to reform the Impoundment Control Act of 1974. 63 Texas L.Rev. 693 (1984).

Toward a national groundwater act: Current contamination and future courses of action. Thomas D. Marks, 61 Fla.B.J. 10 (April 1987).

Library References

Health and Environment ⚷25.7(3).
C.J.S. Health and Environment § 106.

§ 1252a. Reservoir projects, water storage; modification; storage for other than for water quality, opinion of Federal agency, committee resolutions of approval; provisions inapplicable to projects with certain prescribed water quality benefits in relation to total project benefits [FWPCA § 102A]

In the case of any reservoir project authorized for construction by the Corps of Engineers, Bureau of

Reclamation, or other Federal agency when the Administrator of the Environmental Protection Agency determines pursuant to section 1252(b) of this title that any storage in such project for regulation of streamflow for water quality is not needed, or is needed in a different amount, such project may be modified accordingly by the head of the appropriate agency, and any storage no longer required for water quality may be utilized for other authorized purposes of the project when, in the opinion of the head of such agency, such use is justified. Any such modification of a project where the benefits attributable to water quality are 15 per centum or more but not greater than 25 per centum of the total project benefits shall take effect only upon the adoption of resolutions approving such modification by the appropriate committees of the Senate and House of Representatives. The provisions of the section shall not apply to any project where the benefits attributable to water quality exceed 25 per centum of the total project benefits.

(March 7, 1974, Pub.L. 93–251, Title I, § 65, 88 Stat. 30.)

Codification

Section was not enacted as part of the Federal Water Pollution Control Act which comprises this chapter.

Library References

Health and Environment ⚷25.7(3).
Waters and Water Courses ⚷243.
C.J.S. Health and Environment § 106.
C.J.S. Waters § 350.

§ 1253. Interstate cooperation and uniform laws [FWPCA § 103]

(a) The Administrator shall encourage cooperative activities by the States for the prevention, reduction, and elimination of pollution, encourage the enactment of improved and, so far as practicable, uniform State laws relating to the prevention, reduction, and elimination of pollution; and encourage compacts between States for the prevention and control of pollution.

(b) The consent of the Congress is hereby given to two or more States to negotiate and enter into agreements or compacts, not in conflict with any law or treaty of the United States, for (1) cooperative effort and mutual assistance for the prevention and control of pollution and the enforcement of their respective laws relating thereto, and (2) the establishment of such agencies, joint or otherwise, as they may deem desirable for making effective such agreements and compacts. No such agreement or compact shall be binding or obligatory upon any State a party thereto unless and until it has been approved by the Congress.

(June 30, 1948, c. 758, Title I, § 103, as added Oct. 18, 1972, Pub.L. 92–500, § 2, 86 Stat. 818.)

Library References

States ⚷6.
C.J.S. States § 31 et seq.

§ 1254. Research, investigations, training, and information [FWPCA § 104]

(a) Establishment of national programs; cooperation; investigations; water quality surveillance system; reports

The Administrator shall establish national programs for the prevention, reduction, and elimination of pollution and as part of such programs shall—

(1) in cooperation with other Federal, State, and local agencies, conduct and promote the coordination and acceleration of, research, investigations, experiments, training, demonstrations, surveys, and studies relating to the causes, effects, extent, prevention, reduction, and elimination of pollution;

(2) encourage, cooperate with, and render technical services to pollution control agencies and other appropriate public or private agencies, institutions, and organizations, and individuals, including the general public, in the conduct of activities referred to in paragraph (1) of this subsection;

(3) conduct, in cooperation with State water pollution control agencies and other interested agencies, organizations and persons, public investigations concerning the pollution of any navigable waters, and report on the results of such investigations;

(4) establish advisory committees composed of recognized experts in various aspects of pollution and representatives of the public to assist in the examination and evaluation of research progress and proposals and to avoid duplication of research;

(5) in cooperation with the States, and their political subdivisions, and other Federal agencies establish, equip, and maintain a water quality surveillance system for the purpose of monitoring the quality of the navigable waters and ground waters and the contiguous zone and the oceans and the Administrator shall, to the extent practicable, conduct such surveillance by utilizing the resources of the National Aeronautics and Space Administration, the National Oceanic and Atmospheric Administration, the United States Geological Survey, and the Coast Guard, and shall report on such quality in the report required under subsection (a) of section 1375 of this title; and

(6) initiate and promote the coordination and acceleration of research designed to develop the most effective practicable tools and techniques for measuring the social and economic costs and benefits of activities which are subject to regulation under this chapter; and shall transmit a report on the results of such research to the Congress not later than January 1, 1974.

(b) Authorized activities of Administrator

In carrying out the provisions of subsection (a) of this section the Administrator is authorized to—

(1) collect and make available, through publications and other appropriate means, the results of and other information, including appropriate recommendations by him in connection therewith, pertaining to such research and other activities referred to in paragraph (1) of subsection (a) of this section;

(2) cooperate with other Federal departments and agencies, State water pollution control agencies, interstate agencies, other public and private agencies, institutions, organizations, industries involved, and individuals, in the preparation and conduct of such research and other activities referred to in paragraph (1) of subsection (a) of this section;

(3) make grants to State water pollution control agencies, interstate agencies, other public or nonprofit private agencies, institutions, organizations, and individuals, for purposes stated in paragraph (1) of subsection (a) of this section;

(4) contract with public or private agencies, institutions, organizations, and individuals, without regard to section 3324(a) and (b) of title 31 and section 5 of title 41, referred to in paragraph (1) of subsection (a) of this section;

(5) establish and maintain research fellowships at public or nonprofit private educational institutions or research organizations;

(6) collect and disseminate, in cooperation with other Federal departments and agencies, and with other public or private agencies, institutions, and organizations having related responsibilities, basic data on chemical, physical, and biological effects of varying water quality and other information pertaining to pollution and the prevention, reduction, and elimination thereof; and

(7) develop effective and practical processes, methods, and prototype devices for the prevention, reduction, and elimination of pollution.

(c) Research and studies on harmful effects of pollutants; cooperation with Secretary of Health and Human Services

In carrying out the provisions of subsection (a) of this section the Administrator shall conduct research on, and survey the results of other scientific studies on, the harmful effects on the health or welfare of persons caused by pollutants. In order to avoid duplication of effort, the Administrator shall, to the extent practicable, conduct such research in cooperation with and through the facilities of the Secretary of Health and Human Services.

(d) Sewage treatment; identification and measurement of effects of pollutants; augmented streamflow

In carrying out the provisions of this section the Administrator shall develop and demonstrate under varied conditions (including conducting such basic and applied research, studies, and experiments as may be necessary):

(1) Practicable means of treating municipal sewage, and other waterborne wastes to implement the requirements of section 1281 of this title;

(2) Improved methods and procedures to identify and measure the effects of pollutants, including those pollutants created by new technological developments; and

(3) Methods and procedures for evaluating the effects on water quality of augmented streamflows to control pollution not susceptible to other means of prevention, reduction, or elimination.

(e) Field laboratory and research facilities

The Administrator shall establish, equip, and maintain field laboratory and research facilities, including, but not limited to, one to be located in the northeastern area of the United States, one in the Middle Atlantic area, one in the southeastern area, one in the midwestern area, one in the southwestern area, one in the Pacific Northwest, and one in the State of Alaska, for the conduct of research, investigations, experiments, field demonstrations and studies, and training relating to the prevention, reduction and elimination of pollution. Insofar as practicable, each such facility shall be located near institutions of higher learning in which graduate training in such research might be carried out. In conjunction with the development of criteria under section 1343 of this title, the Administrator shall construct the facilities authorized for the National Marine Water Quality Laboratory established under this subsection.

(f) Great Lakes water quality research

The Administrator shall conduct research and technical development work, and make studies, with respect to the quality of the waters of the Great Lakes, including an analysis of the present and projected future water quality of the Great Lakes under varying conditions of waste treatment and disposal, an evaluation of the water quality needs of those to be served by such waters, an evaluation of municipal, industrial, and vessel waste treatment and disposal practices with respect to such waters, and a study of alternate means of solving pollution problems (including additional waste treatment measures) with respect to such waters.

(g) Treatment works pilot training programs; employment needs forecasting; training projects and grants; research fellowships; technical training; report to the President and transmittal to Congress

(1) For the purpose of providing an adequate supply of trained personnel to operate and maintain existing and future treatment works and related activities, and for the purpose of enhancing substantially the proficiency of those engaged in such activities, the Administrator shall finance pilot programs, in cooperation with State and interstate agencies, municipalities, educational institutions, and other organizations and individuals, of manpower development and training and retraining of persons in, on entering into, the field of operation and maintenance of treatment works and related activities. Such program and any funds expended for such a program shall supplement, not supplant, other manpower and training programs and funds available for the purposes of this paragraph. The Administrator is authorized, under such terms and conditions as he deems appropriate, to enter into agreements with one or more States, acting jointly or severally, or with other public or private agencies or institutions for the development and implementation of such a program.

(2) The Administrator is authorized to enter into agreements with public and private agencies and institutions, and individuals to develop and maintain an effective system for forecasting the supply of, and demand for, various professional and other occupational categories needed for the prevention, reduction, and elimination of pollution in each region, State, or area of the United States and, from time to time, to publish the results of such forecasts.

(3) In furtherance of the purposes of this chapter, the Administrator is authorized to—

(A) make grants to public or private agencies and institutions and to individuals for training projects, and provide for the conduct of training by contract with public or private agencies and institutions and with individuals without regard to section 3324(a) and (b) of title 31 and section 5 of title 41;

(B) establish and maintain research fellowships in the Environmental Protection Agency with such stipends and allowances, including traveling and subsistence expenses, as he may deem necessary to procure the assistance of the most promising research fellows; and

(C) provide, in addition to the program established under paragraph (1) of this subsection, training in technical matters relating to the causes, prevention, reduction, and elimination of pollution for personnel of public agencies and other persons with suitable qualifications.

(4) The Administrator shall submit, through the President, a report to the Congress not later than December 31, 1973, summarizing the actions taken under this subsection and the effectiveness of such actions, and setting forth the number of persons trained, the occupational categories for which training was provided, the effectiveness of other Federal, State, and local training programs in this field, together with estimates of future needs, recommendations on improving training programs, and such other information and recommendations, including legislative recommendations, as he deems appropriate.

(h) Lake pollution

The Administrator is authorized to enter into contracts with, or make grants to, public or private agencies and organizations and individuals for (A) the purpose of developing and demonstrating new or improved methods for the prevention, removal, reduction, and elimination of pollution in lakes, including the undesirable effects of nutrients and vegetation, and (B) the construction of publicly owned research facilities for such purpose.

(i) Oil pollution control studies

The Administrator, in cooperation with the Secretary of the Department in which the Coast Guard is operating, shall—

(1) engage in such research, studies, experiments, and demonstrations as he deems appropriate, relative to the removal of oil from any waters and to the prevention, control, and elimination of oil and hazardous substances pollution;

(2) publish from time to time the results of such activities; and

(3) from time to time, develop and publish in the Federal Register specifications and other technical information on the various chemical compounds used in the control of oil and hazardous substances spills.

In carrying out this subsection, the Administrator may enter into contracts with, or make grants to, public or private agencies and organizations and individuals.

(j) Solid waste disposal equipment for vessels

The Secretary of the department in which the Coast Guard is operating shall engage in such research, studies, experiments, and demonstrations as he deems appropriate relative to equipment which is to be installed on board a vessel and is designed to receive, retain, treat, or discharge human body wastes and the wastes from toilets and other receptacles intended to receive or retain body wastes with particular emphasis on equipment to be installed on small recreational vessels. The Secretary of the department in which the Coast Guard is operating shall report to Congress the results of such research, studies, experiments, and demonstrations prior to the effective date of any regulations established under section 1322 of this title. In carrying out this subsection the Secretary of the department in which the Coast Guard is operating may enter into contracts with, or make grants to, public or private organizations and individuals.

(k) Land acquisition

In carrying out the provisions of this section relating to the conduct by the Administrator of demonstration projects and the development of field laboratories and research facilities, the Administrator may acquire land and interests therein by purchase, with appropriated or donated funds, by donation, or by exchange for acquired or public lands under his jurisdiction which he classifies as suitable for disposition. The values of the properties so exchanged either shall be approximately equal, or if they are not approximately equal, the values shall be equalized by the payment of cash to the grantor or to the Administrator as the circumstances require.

(*l*) Collection and dissemination of scientific knowledge on effects and control of pesticides in water

(1) The Administrator shall, after consultation with appropriate local, State, and Federal agencies, public and private organizations, and interested individuals, as soon as practicable but not later than January 1, 1973, develop and issue to the States for the purpose of carrying out this chapter the latest scientific knowledge available in indicating the kind and extent of effects on health and welfare which may be expected from the presence of pesticides in the water in varying quantities. He shall revise and add to such information whenever necessary to reflect developing scientific knowledge.

(2) The President shall, in consultation with appropriate local, State, and Federal agencies, public and private organizations, and interested individuals, conduct studies and investigations of methods to control the release of pesticides into the environment which study shall include examination of the persistency of pesticides in the water environment and alternatives thereto. The President shall submit reports, from time to time, on such investigations to Congress together with his recommendations for any necessary legislation.

(m) Waste oil disposal study

(1) The Administrator shall, in an effort to prevent degradation of the environment from the disposal of waste oil, conduct a study of (A) the generation of used engine, machine, cooling, and similar waste oil, including quantities generated, the nature and quality of such oil, present collecting methods and disposal practices, and alternate uses of such oil; (B) the long-term, chronic biological effects of the disposal of such waste oil; and (C) the potential market for such oils, including the economic and legal factors relating to the sale of products made from such oils, the level of subsidy, if any, needed to encourage the purchase by public and private nonprofit agencies of products from such oil, and the practicability of Federal procurement, on a priority basis, of products made from such oil. In conducting such study, the Administrator shall consult with affected industries and other persons.

(2) The Administrator shall report the preliminary results of such study to Congress within six months after October 18, 1972, and shall submit a final report to Congress within 18 months after such date.

(n) Comprehensive studies of effects of pollution on estuaries and estuarine zones; reports

(1) The Administrator shall, in cooperation with the Secretary of the Army, the Secretary of Agriculture, the Water Resources Council, and with other appropriate Federal, State, interstate, or local public bodies and private organizations, institutions, and individuals, conduct and promote, and encourage contributions to, continuing comprehensive studies of the effects of pollution, including sedimentation, in the estuaries and estuarine zones of the United States on fish and wildlife, on sport and commercial fishing, on recreation, on water supply and water power, and on other beneficial purposes. Such studies shall also consider the effect of demographic trends, the exploitation of mineral resources and fossil fuels, land and industrial development, navigation, flood and erosion control, and other uses of estuaries and estuarine zones upon the pollution of the waters therein.

(2) In conducting such studies, the Administrator shall assemble, coordinate, and organize all existing pertinent information on the Nation's estuaries and estuarine zones; carry out a program of investigations and surveys to supplement existing information in representative estuaries and estuarine zones; and identify the problems and areas where further research and study are required.

(3) The Administrator shall submit to Congress, from time to time, reports of the studies authorized by this subsection but at least one such report during any six-year period. Copies of each such report shall be made available to all interested parties, public and private.

(4) For the purpose of this subsection, the term "estuarine zones" means an environmental system consisting of an estuary and those transitional areas

which are consistently influenced or affected by water from an estuary such as, but not limited to, salt marshes, coastal and intertidal areas, bays, harbors, lagoons, inshore waters, and channels, and the term "estuary" means all or part of the mouth of a river or stream or other body of water having unimpaired natural connection with open sea and within which the sea water is measurably diluted with fresh water derived from land drainage.

(*o*) Methods of reducing total flow of sewage and unnecessary water consumption; reports

(1) The Administrator shall conduct research and investigations on devices, systems, incentives, pricing policy, and other methods of reducing the total flow of sewage, including, but not limited to, unnecessary water consumption in order to reduce the requirements for, and the costs of, sewage and waste treatment services. Such research and investigations shall be directed to develop devices, systems, policies, and methods capable of achieving the maximum reduction of unnecessary water consumption.

(2) The Administrator shall report the preliminary results of such studies and investigations to the Congress within one year after October 18, 1972, and annually thereafter in the report required under subsection (a) of section 1375 of this title. Such report shall include recommendations for any legislation that may be required to provide for the adoption and use of devices, systems, policies, or other methods of reducing water consumption and reducing the total flow of sewage. Such report shall include an estimate of the benefits to be derived from adoption and use of such devices, systems, policies, or other methods and also shall reflect estimates of any increase in private, public, or other cost that would be occasioned thereby.

(p) Agricultural pollution

In carrying out the provisions of subsection (a) of this section the Administrator shall, in cooperation with the Secretary of Agriculture, other Federal agencies, and the States, carry out a comprehensive study and research program to determine new and improved methods and the better application of existing methods of preventing, reducing, and eliminating pollution from agriculture, including the legal, economic, and other implications of the use of such methods.

(q) Sewage in rural areas; national clearinghouse for alternative treatment information; clearinghouse on small flows

(1) The Administrator shall conduct a comprehensive program of research and investigation and pilot project implementation into new and improved methods of preventing, reducing, storing, collecting, treating, or otherwise eliminating pollution from sewage in rural and other areas where collection of sewage in conventional, communitywide sewage collection systems is impractical, uneconomical, or otherwise infeasible, or where soil conditions or other factors preclude the use of septic tank and drainage field systems.

(2) The Administrator shall conduct a comprehensive program of research and investigation and pilot project implementation into new and improved methods for the collection and treatment of sewage and other liquid wastes combined with the treatment and disposal of solid wastes.

(3) The Administrator shall establish, either within the Environmental Protection Agency, or through contract with an appropriate public or private non-profit organization, a national clearinghouse which shall (A) receive reports and information resulting from research, demonstrations, and other projects funded under this chapter related to paragraph (1) of this subsection and to subsection (e)(2) of section 1255 of this title; (B) coordinate and disseminate such reports and information for use by Federal and State agencies, municipalities, institutions, and persons in developing new and improved methods pursuant to this subsection; and (C) provide for the collection and dissemination of reports and information relevant to this subsection from other Federal and State agencies, institutions, universities, and persons.

(4) Small flows clearinghouse.—

Notwithstanding section 1285(d) of this title, from amounts that are set aside for a fiscal year under section 1285(i) of this title and are not obligated by the end of the 24-month period of availability for such amounts under section 1285(d) of this title, the Administrator shall make available $1,000,000 or such unobligated amount, whichever is less, to support a national clearinghouse within the Environmental Protection Agency to collect and disseminate information on small flows of sewage and innovative or alternative wastewater treatment processes and techniques, consistent with paragraph (3). This paragraph shall apply with respect to amounts set aside under section 1285(i) of this title for which the 24-month period of availability referred to in the preceding sentence ends on or after September 30, 1986.

(r) Research grants to colleges and universities

The Administrator is authorized to make grants to colleges and universities to conduct basic research into the structure and function of freshwater aquatic ecosystems, and to improve understanding of the ecological characteristics necessary to the maintenance of the chemical, physical, and biological integrity of freshwater aquatic ecosystems.

(s) River Study Centers

The Administrator is authorized to make grants to one or more institutions of higher education (regionally located and to be designated as "River Study Centers") for the purpose of conducting and reporting on interdisciplinary studies on the nature of river systems, including hydrology, biology, ecology, economics, the relationship between river uses and land uses, and the effects of development within river basins on river systems and on the value of water resources and water related activities. No such grant in any fiscal year shall exceed $1,000,000.

(t) Thermal discharges

The Administrator shall, in cooperation with State and Federal agencies and public and private organizations, conduct continuing comprehensive studies of the effects and methods of control of thermal discharges. In evaluating alternative methods of control the studies shall consider (1) such data as are available on the latest available technology, economic feasibility including cost-effectiveness analysis, and (2) the total impact on the environment, considering not only water quality but also air quality, land use, and effective utilization and conservation of freshwater and other natural resources. Such studies shall consider methods of minimizing adverse effects and maximizing beneficial effects of thermal discharges. The results of these studies shall be reported by the Administrator as soon as practicable, but not later than 270 days after October 18, 1972, and shall be made available to the public and the States, and considered as they become available by the Administrator in carrying out section 1326 of this title and by the States in proposing thermal water quality standards.

(u) Authorization of appropriations

There is authorized to be appropriated (1) not to exceed $100,000,000 per fiscal year for the fiscal year ending June 30, 1973, the fiscal year ending June 30, 1974, and the fiscal year ending June 30, 1975, not to exceed $14,039,000 for the fiscal year ending September 30, 1980, not to exceed $20,697,000 for the fiscal year ending September 30, 1981, not to exceed $22,770,000 for the fiscal year ending September 30, 1982, such sums as may be necessary for fiscal years 1983 through 1985, and not to exceed $22,770,000 per fiscal year for each of the fiscal years 1986 through 1990, for carrying out the provisions of this section, other than subsections (g)(1) and (2), (p), (r), and (t) of this section, except that such authorizations are not for any research, development, or demonstration activity pursuant to such provisions; (2) not to exceed $7,500,000 for fiscal years 1973, 1974, and 1975, $2,000,000 for fiscal year 1977, $3,000,000 for fiscal year 1978, $3,000,000 for fiscal year 1979, $3,000,000 for fiscal year 1980, $3,000,000 for fiscal year 1981, $3,000,000 for fiscal year 1982, such sums as may be necessary for fiscal years 1983 through 1985, and $3,000,000 per fiscal year for each of the fiscal years 1986 through 1990, for carrying out the provisions of subsection (g)(1) of this section; (3) not to exceed $2,500,000 for fiscal years 1973, 1974, and 1975, $1,000,000 for fiscal year 1977, $1,500,000 for fiscal year 1978, $1,500,000 for fiscal year 1979, $1,500,000 for fiscal year 1980, $1,500,000 for fiscal year 1981, $1,500,000 for fiscal year 1982, such sums as may be necessary for fiscal years 1983 through 1985, and $1,500,000 per fiscal year for each of the fiscal years 1986 through 1990, for carrying out the provisions of subsection (g)(2) of this section; (4) not to exceed $10,000,000 for each of the fiscal years ending June 30, 1973, June 30, 1974, and June 30, 1975, for carrying out the provisions of subsection (p) of this section; (5) not to exceed $15,000,000 per fiscal year for the fiscal years ending June 30, 1973, June 30, 1974, and June 30, 1975, for carrying out the provisions of subsection (r) of this section; and (6) not to exceed $10,000,000 per fiscal year for the fiscal years ending June 30, 1973, June 30, 1974, and June 30, 1975, for carrying out the provisions of subsection (t) of this section.

(June 30, 1948, c. 758, Title I, § 104, as added Oct. 18, 1972, Pub.L. 92–500, § 2, 86 Stat. 819, and amended Dec. 28, 1973, Pub.L. 93–207, § 1(1), 87 Stat. 906; Jan. 2, 1975, Pub.L. 93–592, § 1, 88 Stat. 1924; Dec. 27, 1977, Pub.L. 95–217, §§ 4(a), (b), 6, 7, 91 Stat. 1566, 1567; Nov. 2, 1978, Pub.L. 95–576, § 1(a), 92 Stat. 2467; Oct. 17, 1979, Pub.L. 96–88, title V, § 509(b), 93 Stat. 695; Oct. 21, 1980, Pub.L. 96–483, § 1(a), 94 Stat. 2360; Feb. 4, 1987, Pub.L. 100–4, Title I, §§ 101(a), 102, 101 Stat. 8, 9; Nov. 13, 1991, Pub.L. 102–154, Title I, 105 Stat. 1000; May 18, 1992, Pub.L. 102–285, § 10(a), 106 Stat. 171.)

Change of Name

Pub.L. 102–285, § 10(a), May 18, 1992, 106 Stat. 171, redesignated the Geological Survey and provided that on and after May 18, 1992, it shall be known as the United States Geological Survey. An earlier statute [Pub.L. 102–154, Title I, Nov. 13, 1991, 105 Stat. 1000] had provided for the identical change of name effective on and after Nov. 13, 1991. See note under section 31 of Title 43, Public Lands.

CROSS REFERENCES

Authorization of appropriations to carry out this chapter other than this section, see section 1376 of this title.

Coordination of programs under this section with study for achieving sanitation services in Alaskan villages, see section 1263 of this title.

Dissemination of information obtained under this section, see section 1255 of this title.

Federal standards for marine sanitation devices, see section 1322 of this title.

Grants to municipalities to assist in operation and maintenance of projects which received grants under this section, see section 1255 of this title.

CODE OF FEDERAL REGULATIONS

Fellowships, see 40 CFR 46.100 et seq.

Research and demonstration grants, see 40 CFR 40.100 et seq.
Training assistance, see 40 CFR 45.100 et seq.

LAW REVIEW COMMENTARIES

From elephants to mice: The development of EBMUD's program to control small source wastewater discharges. Raoul Stewardson, 20 Ecology L.Q. 441 (1993).

Library References

Health and Environment ⟹25.7(3).
C.J.S. Health and Environment § 106.

§ 1254a. Research on effects of pollutants

In carrying out the provisions of section 1254(a) of this title, the Administrator shall conduct research on the harmful effects on the health and welfare of persons caused by pollutants in water, in conjunction with the United States Fish and Wildlife Service, the National Oceanic and Atmospheric Administration, and other Federal, State, and interstate agencies carrying on such research. Such research shall include, and shall place special emphasis on, the effect that bioaccumulation of these pollutants in aquatic species has upon reducing the value of aquatic commercial and sport industries. Such research shall further study methods to reduce and remove these pollutants from the relevant affected aquatic species so as to restore and enhance these valuable resources.

(Pub.L. 100–4, Title I, § 105, Feb. 4, 1987, 101 Stat. 15.)

Codification

Section was enacted as part of the Water Quality Act of 1987, and not as part of the Federal Water Pollution Control Act, which comprises this chapter.

LIBRARY REFERENCES

Navigable Waters ⟹35.
C.J.S. Health and Environment § 106 et seq.
C.J.S. Navigable Waters § 11.

§ 1255. Grants for research and development [FWPCA § 105]

(a) Demonstration projects covering storm waters, advanced waste treatment and water purification methods, and joint treatment systems for municipal and industrial wastes

The Administrator is authorized to conduct in the Environmental Protection Agency, and to make grants to any State, municipality, or intermunicipal or interstate agency for the purpose of assisting in the development of—

(1) any project which will demonstrate a new or improved method of preventing, reducing, and eliminating the discharge into any waters of pollutants from sewers which carry storm water or both storm water and pollutants; or

(2) any project which will demonstrate advanced waste treatment and water purification methods (including the temporary use of new or improved chemical additives which provide substantial immediate improvements to existing treatment processes), or new or improved methods of joint treatment systems for municipal and industrial wastes;

and to include in such grants such amounts as are necessary for the purpose of reports, plans, and specifications in connection therewith.

(b) Demonstration projects for advanced treatment and environmental enhancement techniques to control pollution in river basins

The Administrator is authorized to make grants to any State or States or interstate agency to demonstrate, in river basins or portions thereof, advanced treatment and environmental enhancement techniques to control pollution from all sources, within such basins or portions thereof, including nonpoint sources, together with in stream[1] water quality improvement techniques.

(c) Research and demonstration projects for prevention of water pollution by industry

In order to carry out the purposes of section 1311 of this title, the Administrator is authorized to (1) conduct in the Environmental Protection Agency, (2) make grants to persons, and (3) enter into contracts with persons, for research and demonstration projects for prevention of pollution of any waters by industry including, but not limited to, the prevention, reduction, and elimination of the discharge of pollutants. No grant shall be made for any project under this subsection unless the Administrator determines that such project will develop or demonstrate a new or improved method of treating industrial wastes or otherwise prevent pollution by industry, which method shall have industrywide application.

(d) Accelerated and priority development of waste management and waste treatment methods and identification and measurement methods

In carrying out the provisions of this section, the Administrator shall conduct, on a priority basis, an accelerated effort to develop, refine, and achieve practical application of:

(1) waste management methods applicable to point and nonpoint sources of pollutants to eliminate the discharge of pollutants, including, but not limited to, elimination of runoff of pollutants and the effects of pollutants from inplace or accumulated sources;

(2) advanced waste treatment methods applicable to point and nonpoint sources, including inplace or accumulated sources of pollutants, and methods for

reclaiming and recycling water and confining pollutants so they will not migrate to cause water or other environmental pollution; and

(3) improved methods and procedures to identify and measure the effects of pollutants on the chemical, physical, and biological integrity of water, including those pollutants created by new technological developments.

(e) Research and demonstration projects covering agricultural pollution and pollution from sewage in rural areas; dissemination of information

(1) The Administrator is authorized to (A) make, in consultation with the Secretary of Agriculture, grants to persons for research and demonstration projects with respect to new and improved methods of preventing, reducing, and eliminating pollution from agriculture, and (B) disseminate, in cooperation with the Secretary of Agriculture, such information obtained under this subsection, section 1254(p) of this title, and section 1314 of this title as will encourage and enable the adoption of such methods in the agricultural industry.

(2) The Administrator is authorized, (A) in consultation with other interested Federal agencies, to make grants for demonstration projects with respect to new and improved methods of preventing, reducing, storing, collecting, treating, or otherwise eliminating pollution from sewage in rural and other areas where collection of sewage in conventional, community-wide sewage collection systems is impractical, uneconomical, or otherwise infeasible, or where soil conditions or other factors preclude the use of septic tank and drainage field systems, and (B) in cooperation with other interested Federal and State agencies, to disseminate such information obtained under this subsection as will encourage and enable the adoption of new and improved methods developed pursuant to this subsection.

(f) Limitations

Federal grants under subsection (a) of this section shall be subject to the following limitations:

(1) No grant shall be made for any project unless such project shall have been approved by the appropriate State water pollution control agency or agencies and by the Administrator;

(2) No grant shall be made for any project in an amount exceeding 75 per centum of cost thereof as determined by the Administrator; and

(3) No grant shall be made for any project unless the Administrator determines that such project will serve as a useful demonstration for the purpose set forth in clause (1) or (2) of subsection (a) of this section.

(g) Maximum grants

Federal grants under subsections (c) and (d) of this section shall not exceed 75 per centum of the cost of the project.

(h) Authorization of appropriations

For the purpose of this section there is authorized to be appropriated $75,000,000 per fiscal year for the fiscal year ending June 30, 1973, the fiscal year ending June 30, 1974, and the fiscal year ending June 30, 1975, and from such appropriations at least 10 per centum of the funds actually appropriated in each fiscal year shall be available only for the purposes of subsection (e) of this section.

(i) Assistance for research and demonstration projects

The Administrator is authorized to make grants to a municipality to assist in the costs of operating and maintaining a project which received a grant under this section, section 1254 of this title, or section 1263 of this title prior to December 27, 1977, so as to reduce the operation and maintenance costs borne by the recipients of services from such project to costs comparable to those for projects assisted under subchapter II of this chapter.

(j) Assistance for recycle, reuse, and land treatment projects

The Administrator is authorized to make a grant to any grantee who received an increased grant pursuant to section 1282(a)(2) of this title. Such grant may pay up to 100 per centum of the costs of technical evaluation of the operation of the treatment works, costs of training of persons (other than employees of the grantee), and costs of disseminating technical information on the operation of the treatment works.

(June 30, 1948, c. 758, Title I, § 105, as added Oct. 18, 1972, Pub.L. 92–500, § 2, 86 Stat. 825, and amended Jan. 2, 1975, Pub.L. 93–592, § 2, 88 Stat. 1925; Dec. 27, 1977, Pub.L. 95–217, §§ 8, 9, 91 Stat. 1568.)

[1] So in original.

CROSS REFERENCES

Alaska village demonstration projects, study to develop comprehensive program for achieving sanitation services to be coordinated with projects covering pollution from sewage in rural areas, see section 1263 of this title.

Authorization of appropriations to carry out the provisions of this chapter other than this section, see section 1376 of this title.

National clearinghouse to receive reports and information on projects covering pollution from sewage in rural areas, see section 1254 of this title.

CODE OF FEDERAL REGULATIONS

Administration of federal contracts, grants, or loans, see 40 CFR 15.1 et seq.

Debarment and suspension under Environmental Protection Agency assistance programs, see 40 CFR 32.100 et seq.

General regulation by Environmental Protection Agency of assistance programs, see 40 CFR 30.100 et seq.

Research and demonstration grants, see 40 CFR 40.100 et seq.

Library References

Health and Environment ⚬25.7(3).
C.J.S. Health and Environment § 106.

§ 1256. Grants for pollution control programs [FWPCA § 106]

(a) Authorization of appropriations for State and interstate programs

There are hereby authorized to be appropriated the following sums, to remain available until expended, to carry out the purposes of this section—

(1) $60,000,000 for the fiscal year ending June 30, 1973; and

(2) $75,000,000 for the fiscal year ending June 30, 1974, and the fiscal year ending June 30, 1975, $100,000,000 per fiscal year for the fiscal years 1977, 1978, 1979, and 1980, $75,000,000 per fiscal year for the fiscal years 1981 and 1982, such sums as may be necessary for fiscal years 1983 through 1985, and $75,000,000 per fiscal year for each of the fiscal years 1986 through 1990;

for grants to States and to interstate agencies to assist them in administering programs for the prevention, reduction, and elimination of pollution, including enforcement directly or through appropriate State law enforcement officers or agencies.

(b) Allotments

From the sums appropriated in any fiscal year, the Administrator shall make allotments to the several States and interstate agencies in accordance with regulations promulgated by him on the basis of the extent of the pollution problem in the respective States.

(c) Maximum annual payments

The Administrator is authorized to pay to each State and interstate agency each fiscal year either—

(1) the allotment of such State or agency for such fiscal year under subsection (b) of this section, or

(2) the reasonable costs as determined by the Administrator of developing and carrying out a pollution program by such State or agency during such fiscal year,

which ever amount is the lesser.

(d) Limitations

No grant shall be made under this section to any State or interstate agency for any fiscal year when the expenditure of non-Federal funds by such State or interstate agency during such fiscal year for the recurrent expenses of carrying out its pollution control program are less than the expenditure by such State or interstate agency of non-Federal funds for such recurrent program expenses during the fiscal year ending June 30, 1971.

(e) Grants prohibited to states not establishing water quality monitoring procedures or adequate emergency and contingency plans

Beginning in fiscal year 1974 the Administrator shall not make any grant under this section to any State which has not provided or is not carrying out as a part of its program—

(1) the establishment and operation of appropriate devices, methods, systems, and procedures necessary to monitor, and to compile and analyze data on (including classification according to eutrophic condition), the quality of navigable waters and to the extent practicable, ground waters including biological monitoring; and provision for annually updating such data and including it in the report required under section 1315 of this title;

(2) authority comparable to that in section 1364 of this title and adequate contingency plans to implement such authority.

(f) Conditions

Grants shall be made under this section on condition that—

(1) Such State (or interstate agency) files with the Administrator within one hundred and twenty days after October 18, 1972:

(A) a summary report of the current status of the State pollution control program, including the criteria used by the State in determining priority of treatment works; and

(B) such additional information, data, and reports as the Administrator may require.

(2) No federally assumed enforcement as defined in section 1319(a)(2) of this title is in effect with respect to such State or interstate agency.

(3) Such State (or interstate agency) submits within one hundred and twenty days after October 18, 1972, and before October 1 of each year thereafter for the Administrator's approval of its program for the prevention, reduction, and elimination of pollution in accordance with purposes and provisions of this chapter in such form and content as the Administrator may prescribe.

(g) Reallotment of unpaid allotments

Any sums allotted under subsection (b) of this section in any fiscal year which are not paid shall be reallotted by the Administrator in accordance with regulations promulgated by him.

(June 30, 1948, c. 758, Title I, § 106, as added Oct. 18, 1972, Pub.L. 92–500, § 2, 86 Stat. 827, and amended Jan. 2, 1975, Pub.L. 93–592, § 3, 88 Stat. 1925; April 21, 1976, Pub.L. 94–273, § 3(20), 90 Stat. 377; Dec. 27, 1977, Pub.L. 95–217, § 4(c), 91 Stat. 1566; Oct. 21, 1980, Pub.L. 96–483, § 1(b), 94 Stat. 2360; Feb. 4, 1987, Pub.L. 100–4, Title I, § 101(b), 101 Stat. 9.)

CODE OF FEDERAL REGULATIONS

Administration of federal contracts, grants, or loans, see 40 CFR 15.1 et seq.
State and local assistance, see 40 CFR 35.001 et seq.
Water quality planning and management, see 40 CFR 130.0 et seq.

LAW REVIEW COMMENTARIES

Long-range planning in environmental and health regulatory agencies. Richard N.L. Andrews, 20 Ecology L.Q. 515 (1993).

Library References

Health and Environment ⚷25.7(3).
C.J.S. Health and Environment § 106.

§ 1257. Mine water pollution control demonstrations [FWPCA § 107]

(a) Comprehensive approaches to elimination or control of mine water pollution

The Administrator in cooperation with the Appalachian Regional Commission and other Federal agencies is authorized to conduct, to make grants for, or to contract for, projects to demonstrate comprehensive approaches to the elimination or control of acid or other mine water pollution resulting from active or abandoned mining operations and other environmental pollution affecting water quality within all or part of a watershed or river basin, including siltation from surface mining. Such projects shall demonstrate the engineering and economic feasibility and practicality of various abatement techniques which will contribute substantially to effective and practical methods of acid or other mine water pollution elimination or control, and other pollution affecting water quality, including techniques that demonstrate the engineering and economic feasibility and practicality of using sewage sludge materials and other municipal wastes to diminish or prevent pollution affecting water quality from acid, sedimentation, or other pollutants and in such projects to restore affected lands to usefulness for forestry, agriculture, recreation, or other beneficial purposes.

(b) Consistency of projects with objectives of Appalachian Regional Development Act of 1965

Prior to undertaking any demonstration project under this section in the Appalachian region (as defined in section 403 of the Appalachian Regional Development Act of 1965, as amended [40 App. U.S.C.A. § 403]), the Appalachian Regional Commission shall determine that such demonstration project is consistent with the objectives of the Appalachian Regional Development Act of 1965, as amended [40 App. U.S.C.A. § 1 et seq.].

(c) Watershed selection

The Administrator, in selecting watersheds for the purposes of this section, shall be satisfied that the project area will not be affected adversely by the influx of acid or other mine water pollution from nearby sources.

(d) Conditions upon Federal participation

Federal participation in such projects shall be subject to the conditions—

(1) that the State shall acquire any land or interests therein necessary for such project; and

(2) that the State shall provide legal and practical protection to the project area to insure against any activities which will cause future acid or other mine water pollution.

(e) Authorization of appropriations

There is authorized to be appropriated $30,000,000 to carry out the provisions of this section, which sum shall be available until expended.

(June 30, 1948, c. 758, Title I, § 107, as added Oct. 18, 1972, Pub.L. 92–500, § 2, 86 Stat. 828.)

CROSS REFERENCES

Authorization of appropriations to carry out the provisions of this chapter other than this section, see section 1376 of this title.

CODE OF FEDERAL REGULATIONS

Research and demonstration grants, see 40 CFR 40.100 et seq.

Library References

Health and Environment ⚷25.7(9).
C.J.S. Health and Environment § 108 et seq.

§ 1257a. State demonstration programs for cleanup of abandoned mines for use as waste disposal sites; authorization of appropriations

The Administrator of the Environmental Protection Agency is authorized to make grants to States to undertake a demonstration program for the cleanup of State-owned abandoned mines which can be used as hazardous waste disposal sites. The State shall pay 10 per centum of project costs. At a minimum, the Administrator shall undertake projects under such program in the States of Ohio, Illinois, and West Virginia. There are authorized to be appropriated $10,000,000 per fiscal year for each of the fiscal years ending September 30, 1982, September 30, 1983, and September 30, 1984, to carry out this section. Such projects shall be undertaken in accordance with all applicable laws and regulations.

(Oct. 21, 1980, Pub.L. 96–483, § 12, 94 Stat. 2363.)

Codification

Section was not enacted as part of the Federal Water Pollution Control Act, which comprises this chapter.

Library References

Health and Environment ⇐25.7(9).
C.J.S. Health and Environment § 108 et seq.

§ 1258. Pollution control in the Great Lakes [FWPCA § 108]

(a) Demonstration projects

The Administrator, in cooperation with other Federal departments, agencies, and instrumentalities is authorized to enter into agreements with any State, political subdivision, interstate agency, or other public agency, or combination thereof, to carry out one or more projects to demonstrate new methods and techniques and to develop preliminary plans for the elimination or control of pollution, within all or any part of the watersheds of the Great Lakes. Such projects shall demonstrate the engineering and economic feasibility and practicality of removal of pollutants and prevention of any polluting matter from entering into the Great Lakes in the future and other reduction and remedial techniques which will contribute substantially to effective and practical methods of pollution prevention, reduction, or elimination.

(b) Conditions of Federal participation

Federal participation in such projects shall be subject to the condition that the State, political subdivision, interstate agency, or other public agency, or combination thereof, shall pay not less than 25 per centum of the actual project costs, which payment may be in any form, including, but not limited to, land or interests therein that is needed for the project, and personal property or services the value of which shall be determined by the Administrator.

(c) Authorization of appropriations

There is authorized to be appropriated $20,000,000 to carry out the provisions of subsections (a) and (b) of this section, which sum shall be available until expended.

(d) Lake Erie demonstration program

(1) In recognition of the serious conditions which exist in Lake Erie, the Secretary of the Army, acting through the Chief of Engineers, is directed to design and develop a demonstration waste water management program for the rehabilitation and environmental repair of Lake Erie. Prior to the initiation of detailed engineering and design, the program, along with the specific recommendations of the Chief of Engineers, and recommendations for its financing, shall be submitted to the Congress for statutory approval. This authority is in addition to, and not in lieu of, other waste water studies aimed at eliminating pollution emanating from select sources around Lake Erie.

(2) This program is to be developed in cooperation with the Environmental Protection Agency, other interested departments, agencies, and instrumentalities of the Federal Government, and the States and their political subdivisions. This program shall set forth alternative systems for managing waste water on a regional basis and shall provide local and State governments with a range of choice as to the type of system to be used for the treatment of waste water. These alternative systems shall include both advanced waste treatment technology and land disposal systems including aerated treatment-spray irrigation technology and will also include provisions for the disposal of solid wastes, including sludge. Such program should include measures to control point sources of pollution, area sources of pollution, including acid-mine drainage, urban runoff and rural runoff, and in place sources of pollution, including bottom loads, sludge banks, and polluted harbor dredgings.

(e) Authorization of appropriations for Lake Erie demonstration program

There is authorized to be appropriated $5,000,000 to carry out the provisions of subsection (d) of this section, which sum shall be available until expended.

(June 30, 1948, c. 758, Title I, § 108, as added Oct. 18, 1972, Pub.L. 92–500, § 2, 86 Stat. 828.)

Cross References

Authorization of appropriations to carry out the provisions of this chapter other than this section, see section 1376 of this title.

CODE OF FEDERAL REGULATIONS

Research and demonstration grants, see 40 CFR 40.100 et seq.

Library References

Health and Environment ⇐25.7(4).
C.J.S. Health and Environment § 108 et seq.

§ 1259. Training grants and contracts [FWPCA § 109]

(a) The Administrator is authorized to make grants to or contracts with institutions of higher education, or combinations of such institutions, to assist them in planning, developing, strengthening, improving, or carrying out programs or projects for the preparation of undergraduate students to enter an occupation which involves the design, operation, and maintenance of treatment works, and other facilities whose purpose is water quality control. Such grants or contracts may include payment of all or part of the cost of programs or projects such as—

(A) planning for the development or expansion of programs or projects for training persons in the operation and maintenance of treatment works;

(B) training and retraining of faculty members;

(C) conduct of short-term or regular session institutes for study by persons engaged in, or preparing to engage in, the preparation of students preparing to enter an occupation involving the operation and maintenance of treatment works;

(D) carrying out innovative and experimental programs of cooperative education involving alternate periods of full-time or part-time academic study at the institution and periods of full-time or part-time employment involving the operation and maintenance of treatment works; and

(E) research into, and development of, methods of training students or faculty, including the preparation of teaching materials and the planning of curriculum.

(b)(1) The Administrator may pay 100 per centum of any additional cost of construction of treatment works required for a facility to train and upgrade waste treatment works operation and maintenance personnel and for the costs of other State treatment works operator training programs, including mobile training units, classroom rental, specialized instructors, and instructional material.

(2) The Administrator shall make no more than one grant for such additional construction in any State (to serve a group of States, where, in his judgment, efficient training programs require multi-State programs), and shall make such grant after consultation with and approval by the State or States on the basis of (A) the suitability of such facility for training operation and maintenance personnel for treatment works throughout such State or States; and (B) a commitment by the State agency or agencies to carry out at such facility a program of training approved by the Administrator. In any case where a grant is made to serve two or more States, the Administrator is authorized to make an additional grant for a supplemental facility in each such State.

(3) The Administrator may make such grant out of the sums allocated to a State under section 1285 of this title, except that in no event shall the Federal cost of any such training facilities exceed $500,000.

(4) The Administrator may exempt a grant under this section from any requirement under section 1284(a)(3) of this title. Any grantee who received a grant under this section prior to enactment of the Clean Water Act of 1977 shall be eligible to have its grant increased by funds made available under such Act.

(June 30, 1948, c. 758, Title I, § 109, as added Oct. 18, 1972, Pub.L. 92–500, § 2, 86 Stat. 829, and amended Dec. 27, 1977, Pub.L. 95–217, § 10, 91 Stat. 1568.)

Cross References

Annual reports by Administrator of his activities under sections 1259 to 1261 of this title, including recommendations for revisions, see sections 1262 and 1375 of this title.
Application for grants, see section 1260 of this title.
Authorization of appropriations, see section 1262 of this title.
Definition of "institution of higher education" and "academic year", see section 1262 of this title.
Equitable distribution of grants throughout the United States, see section 1260 of this title.

CODE OF FEDERAL REGULATIONS

Training assistance, see 40 CFR 45.100 et seq.

Library References

Health and Environment ⚷25.7(21), (22).
C.J.S. Health and Environment § 106 et seq.

§ 1260. Applications; allocation [FWPCA § 110]

(1) A grant or contract authorized by section 1259 of this title may be made only upon application to the Administrator at such time or times and containing such information as he may prescribe, except that no such application shall be approved unless it—

(A) sets forth programs, activities, research, or development for which a grant is authorized under section 1259 of this title and describes the relation to any program set forth by the applicant in an application, if any, submitted pursuant to section 1261 of this title;

(B) provides such fiscal control and fund accounting procedures as may be necessary to assure proper disbursement of and accounting for Federal funds paid to the applicant under this section; and

(C) provides for making such reports, in such form and containing such information, as the Administrator may require to carry out his functions under this section, and for keeping such records and for affording such access thereto as the Administrator may find necessary to assure the correctness and verification of such reports.

(2) The Administrator shall allocate grants or contracts under section 1259 of this title in such manner as will most nearly provide an equitable distribution of the grants or contracts throughout the United States among institutions of higher education which show promise of being able to use funds effectively for the purpose of this section.

(3)(A) Payments under this section may be used in accordance with regulations of the Administrator, and subject to the terms and conditions set forth in an application approved under paragraph (1), to pay part of the compensation of students employed in connection with the operation and maintenance of treatment works, other than as an employee in connection with the operation and maintenance of treatment works or as an employee in any branch of the Government of the United States, as part of a program for which a grant has been approved pursuant to this section.

(B) Departments and agencies of the United States are encouraged, to the extent consistent with efficient administration, to enter into arrangements with institutions of higher education for the full-time, part-time, or temporary employment, whether in the competitive or excepted service, of students enrolled in programs set forth in applications approved under paragraph (1).

(June 30, 1948, c. 758, Title I, § 110, as added Oct. 18, 1972, Pub.L. 92–500, § 2, 86 Stat. 830.)

Cross References

Annual reports by Administrator of his activities under sections 1259 to 1261 of this title, including recommendations for revisions, see sections 1262 and 1375 of this title.

Approval of programs of institutions of higher education for purposes of scholarships, see section 1261 of this title.

Definition of "institution of higher education" and "academic year", see section 1262 of this title.

§ 1261. Scholarships [FWPCA § 111]

(1) The Administrator is authorized to award scholarships in accordance with the provisions of this section for undergraduate study by persons who plan to enter an occupation involving the operation and maintenance of treatment works. Such scholarships shall be awarded for such periods as the Administrator may determine but not to exceed four academic years.

(2) The Administrator shall allocate scholarships under this section among institutions of higher education with programs approved under the provisions of this section for the use of individuals accepted into such programs in such manner and according to such plan as will insofar as practicable—

(A) provide an equitable distribution of such scholarships throughout the United States; and

(B) attract recent graduates of secondary schools to enter an occupation involving the operation and maintenance of treatment works.

(3) The Administrator shall approve a program of any institution of higher education for the purposes of this section only upon application by the institution and only upon his finding—

(A) that such program has a principal objective the education and training of persons in the operation and maintenance of treatment works;

(B) that such program is in effect and of high quality, or can be readily put into effect and may reasonably be expected to be of high quality;

(C) that the application describes the relation of such program to any program, activity, research, or development set forth by the applicant in an application, if any, submitted pursuant to section 1260 of this title; and

(D) that the application contains satisfactory assurances that (i) the institution will recommend to the Administrator for the award of scholarships under this section, for study in such program, only persons who have demonstrated to the satisfaction of the institution a serious intent, upon completing the program, to enter an occupation involving the operation and maintenance of treatment works, and (ii) the institution will make reasonable continuing efforts to encourage recipients of scholarships under this section, enrolled in such program, to enter occupations involving the operation and maintenance of treatment works upon completing the program.

(4)(A) The Administrator shall pay to persons awarded scholarships under this section such stipends (including such allowances for subsistence and other expenses for such persons and their dependents) as he may determine to be consistent with prevailing practices under comparable supported programs.

(B) The Administrator shall (in addition to the stipends paid to persons under paragraph (1)) pay to the institution of higher education at which such person is pursuing his course of study such amount as he may determine to be consistent with prevailing practices under comparable federally supported programs.

(5) A person awarded a scholarship under the provisions of this section shall continue to receive the payments provided in this section only during such periods as the Administrator finds that he is maintaining satisfactory proficiency and devoting full time to study or research in the field in which such scholarship was awarded in an institution of higher education, and is not engaging in gainful employment other than employment approved by the Administrator by or pursuant to regulation.

(6) The Administrator shall by regulation provide that any person awarded a scholarship under this section shall agree in writing to enter and remain in an occupation involving the design, operation, or maintenance of treatment works for such period after completion of his course of studies as the Administrator determines appropriate.

(June 30, 1948, c. 758, Title I, § 111, as added Oct. 18, 1972, Pub.L. 92–500, § 2, 86 Stat. 831.)

Cross References

Annual reports by Administrator of his activities under sections 1259 to 1261 of this title, including recommendations for revisions, see sections 1262 and 1375 of this title.
Application for grants or contracts, see section 1260 of this title.
Definition of "institution of higher education" and "academic year", see section 1262 of this title.

CODE OF FEDERAL REGULATIONS

Training assistance, see 40 CFR 45.100 et seq.

Library References

Colleges and Universities ⇐9.
C.J.S. Colleges and Universities § 29 et seq.

§ 1262. Definitions and authorizations [FWPCA § 112]

(a) As used in sections 1259 through 1262 of this title—

(1) The term "institution of higher education" means an educational institution described in the first sentence of section 1141 of title 20 (other than an institution of any agency of the United States) which is accredited by a nationally recognized accrediting agency or association approved by the Administrator for this purpose. For purposes of this subsection, the Administrator shall publish a list of nationally recognized accrediting agencies or associations which he determines to be reliable authority as to the quality of training offered.

(2) The term "academic year" means an academic year or its equivalent, as determined by the Administrator.

(b) The Administrator shall annually report his activities under sections 1259 through 1262 of this title, including recommendations for needed revisions in the provisions thereof.

(c) There are authorized to be appropriated $25,000,000 per fiscal year for the fiscal years ending June 30, 1973, June 30, 1974, and June 30, 1975, $6,000,000 for the fiscal year ending September 30, 1977, $7,000,000 for the fiscal year ending September 30, 1978, $7,000,000 for the fiscal year ending September 30, 1979, $7,000,000 for the fiscal year ending September 30, 1980, $7,000,000 for the fiscal year ending September 30, 1981, $7,000,000 for the fiscal year ending September 30, 1982, such sums as may be necessary for fiscal years 1983 through 1985, and $7,000,000 per fiscal year for each of the fiscal years 1986 through 1990, to carry out sections 1259 through 1262 of this title.

(June 30, 1948, c. 758, Title I, § 112, as added Oct. 18, 1972, Pub.L. 92–500, § 2, 86 Stat. 832, and amended Jan. 2, 1975, Pub.L. 93–592, § 4, 88 Stat. 1925; Dec. 27, 1977, Pub.L. 95–217, § 4(d), 91 Stat. 1566; Oct. 21, 1980, Pub.L. 96–483, § 1(c), 94 Stat. 2360; Feb. 4, 1987, Pub.L. 100–4, Title I, § 101(c), 101 Stat. 9.)

Cross References

Authorization of appropriations to carry out the provisions of this chapter other than this section, see section 1376 of this title.

§ 1263. Alaska village demonstration projects [FWPCA § 113]

(a) Central community facilities for safe water; elimination or control of pollution

The Administrator is authorized to enter into agreements with the State of Alaska to carry out one or more projects to demonstrate methods to provide for central community facilities for safe water and eliminate or control of pollution in those native villages of Alaska without such facilities. Such project shall include provisions for community safe water supply systems, toilets, bathing and laundry facilities, sewage disposal facilities, and other similar facilities, and educational and informational facilities and programs relating to health and hygiene. Such demonstration projects shall be for the further purpose of developing preliminary plans for providing such safe water and such elimination or control of pollution for all native villages in such State.

(b) Utilization of personnel and facilities of Department of Health and Human Services

In carrying out this section the Administrator shall cooperate with the Secretary of Health and Human Services for the purpose of utilizing such of the personnel and facilities of that Department as may be appropriate.

(c) Omitted

(d) Authorization of appropriations

There is authorized to be appropriated not to exceed $2,000,000 to carry out this section. In addition, there is authorized to be appropriated to carry out this section not to exceed $200,000 for the fiscal year ending September 30, 1978, and $220,000 for the fiscal year ending September 30, 1979.

(e) Study to develop comprehensive program for achieving sanitation services; report to Congress

The Administrator is authorized to coordinate with the Secretary of the Department of Health and Human Services, the Secretary of the Department of Housing and Urban Development, the Secretary of the Department of the Interior, the Secretary of the Department of Agriculture, and the heads of any other departments or agencies he may deem appropriate to conduct a joint study with representatives of the State of Alaska and the appropriate Native organizations (as defined in Public Law 92–203) to develop a comprehensive program for achieving adequate sanitation services in Alaska villages. This study shall be coordinated with the programs and projects authorized by sections 1254(q) and 1255(e)(2) of this title. The Administrator shall submit a report of the results of the study, together with appropriate supporting data and such recommendations as he deems desirable, to the Committee on Environment and Public Works of the Senate and to the Committee on Public Works and Transportation of the House of Representatives not later than December 31, 1979. The Administrator shall also submit recommended administrative actions, procedures, and any proposed legislation necessary to implement the recommendations of the study no later than June 30, 1980.

(f) Technical, financial, and management assistance

The Administrator is authorized to provide technical, financial and management assistance for operation and maintenance of the demonstration projects constructed under this section, until such time as the recommendations of subsection (e) of this section are implemented.

(g) Definitions

For the purpose of this section, the term "village" shall mean an incorporated or unincorporated community with a population of ten to six hundred people living within a two-mile radius. The term "sanitation services" shall mean water supply, sewage disposal, solid waste disposal and other services necessary to maintain generally accepted standards of personal hygiene and public health.

(June 30, 1948, c. 758, Title I, § 113, as added Oct. 18, 1972, Pub.L. 92–500, § 2, 86 Stat. 832, and amended Dec. 27, 1977, Pub.L. 95–217, § 11, 91 Stat. 1568; Oct. 17, 1979, Pub.L. 96–88, title V, § 509(b), 93 Stat. 695.)

Change of Name

Any reference in any provision of law enacted before Jan. 4, 1995, to the Committee on Public Works and Transportation of the House of Representatives treated as referring to the Committee on Transportation and Infrastructure of the House of Representatives, see section 1(a)(9) of Pub.L. 104–14, set out as a note preceding section 21 of Title 2, The Congress.

Cross References

Authorization of appropriations to carry out the provisions of this chapter other than this section, see section 1376 of this title.
Grants to municipalities to assist in costs of operating and maintaining projects which received grants under this section, see section 1255 of this title.

CODE OF FEDERAL REGULATIONS

Research and demonstration projects, see 40 CFR 40.100 et seq.

Library References

Health and Environment ⚷25.7(21).
C.J.S. Health and Environment § 106 et seq.

§ 1264. Omitted

§ 1265. In-place toxic pollutants [FWPCA § 115]

The Administrator is directed to identify the location of in-place pollutants with emphasis on toxic pollutants in harbors and navigable waterways and is authorized, acting through the Secretary of the Army, to make contracts for the removal and appropriate disposal of such materials from critical port and harbor areas. There is authorized to be appropriated $15,000,000 to carry out the provisions of this section, which sum shall be available until expended.

(June 30, 1948, c. 758, Title I, § 115, as added Oct. 18, 1972, Pub.L. 92–500, § 2, 86 Stat. 833.)

Cross References

Authorization of appropriations to carry out the provisions of this chapter other than this section, see section 1376 of this title.
Hudson River reclamation demonstration project, funds available, see section 1266 of this title.

Library References

Health and Environment ⚷25.7(20), (22).
C.J.S. Health and Environment §§ 106 et seq., 113 et seq.

§ 1266. Hudson River reclamation demonstration project [FWPCA § 116]

(a) The Administrator is authorized to enter into contracts and other agreements with the State of New York to carry out a project to demonstrate methods for the selective removal of polychlorinated biphenyls contaminating bottom sediments of the Hudson River, treating such sediments as required, burying such sediments in secure landfills, and installing monitoring systems for such landfills. Such demonstration project shall be for the purpose of determining the feasibility of indefinite storage in secure landfills of toxic substances and of ascertaining the improvement of the rate of recovery of a toxic contaminated national waterway. No pollutants removed pursuant to this paragraph shall be placed in any landfill unless the Administrator first determines that disposal of the pollutants in such landfill would provide a higher standard of protection of the public health, safety, and welfare than disposal of such pollutants by any other method including, but not limited to, incineration or a chemical destruction process.

(b) The Administrator is authorized to make grants to the State of New York to carry out this section from funds allotted to such State under section 1285(a) of this title, except that the amount of any such grant shall be equal to 75 per centum of the cost of the project and such grant shall be made on condition that non-Federal sources provide the remainder of the cost of such project. The authority of this section shall be available until September 30, 1983. Funds allotted to the State of New York under section 1285(a) of this title shall be available under this subsection only to the extent that funds are not available, as determined by the Administrator, to the State of New York for the work authorized by this section under section 1265 or 1321 of this title or a comprehensive hazardous substance response and clean up fund. Any funds used under the authority of this subsection shall be deducted from any estimate of the needs of the State of New York prepared under section 1375(b) of this title. The Administrator may not obligate or expend more than $20,000,000 to carry out this section.

(June 30, 1948, c. 758, Title I, § 116, as added Oct. 21, 1980, Pub.L. 96–483, § 10, 94 Stat. 2363.)

Library References

Health and Environment ⇐25.7(21).
C.J.S. Health and Environment § 106 et seq.

§ 1267. Chesapeake Bay [FWPCA § 117]

(a) Office

The Administrator shall continue the Chesapeake Bay Program and shall establish and maintain in the Environmental Protection Agency an office, division, or branch of Chesapeake Bay Programs to—

(1) collect and make available, through publications and other appropriate means, information pertaining to the environmental quality of the Chesapeake Bay (hereinafter in this subsection referred to as the "Bay");

(2) coordinate Federal and State efforts to improve the water quality of the Bay;

(3) determine the impact of sediment deposition in the Bay and identify the sources, rates, routes, and distribution patterns of such sediment deposition; and

(4) determine the impact of natural and man-induced environmental changes on the living resources of the Bay and the relationships among such changes, with particular emphasis placed on the impact of pollutant loadings of nutrients, chlorine, acid precipitation, dissolved oxygen, and toxic pollutants, including organic chemicals and heavy metals, and with special attention given to the impact of such changes on striped bass.

(b) Interstate development plan grants

(1) Authority

The Administrator shall, at the request of the Governor of a State affected by the interstate management plan developed pursuant to the Chesapeake Bay Program (hereinafter in this section referred to as the "plan"), make a grant for the purpose of implementing the management mechanisms contained in the plan if such State has, within 1 year after February 4, 1987, approved and committed to implement all or substantially all aspects of the plan. Such grants shall be made subject to such terms and conditions as the Administrator considers appropriate.

(2) Submission of proposal

A State or combination of States may elect to avail itself of the benefits of this subsection by submitting to the Administrator a comprehensive proposal to implement management mechanisms contained in the plan which shall include (A) a description of proposed abatement actions which the State or combination of States commits to take within a specified time period to reduce pollution in the Bay and to meet applicable water quality standards, and (B) the estimated cost of the abatement actions proposed to be taken during the next fiscal year. If the Administrator finds that such proposal is consistent with the national policies set forth in section 1251(a) of this title and will contribute to the achievement of the national goals set forth in such section, the Administrator shall approve such proposal and shall finance the costs of implementing segments of such proposal.

(3) Federal share

Grants under this subsection shall not exceed 50 percent of the costs of implementing the management mechanisms contained in the plan in any fiscal year and shall be made on condition that non-Federal sources provide the remainder of the cost of implementing the management mechanisms contained in the plan during such fiscal year.

(4) Administrative costs

Administrative costs in the form of salaries, overhead, or indirect costs for services provided and charged against programs or projects supported by funds made available under this subsection shall not exceed in any one fiscal year 10 percent of the annual Federal grant made to a State under this subsection.

(c) Reports

Any State or combination of States that receives a grant under subsection (b) of this section shall, within 18 months after the date of receipt of such grant and biennially thereafter, report to the Administrator on the progress made in implementing the interstate management plan developed pursuant to the Chesapeake Bay Program. The Administrator shall transmit each such report along with the comments of the Administrator on such report to Congress.

(d) Authorization of appropriations

There are hereby authorized to be appropriated the following sums, to remain available until expended, to carry out the purposes of this section:

(1) $3,000,000 per fiscal year for each of the fiscal years 1987, 1988, 1989, and 1990, to carry out subsection (a) of this section; and

(2) $10,000,000 per fiscal year for each of the fiscal years 1987, 1988, 1989, and 1990, for grants to States under subsection (b) of this section.

(June 30, 1948, c. 758, Title I, § 117, as added Feb. 4, 1987, Pub.L. 100–4, Title I, § 103, 101 Stat. 10.)

LIBRARY REFERENCES

Navigable Waters ⟹35.
C.J.S. Health and Environment § 106 et seq.
C.J.S. Navigable Waters § 11.

§ 1268. Great Lakes [FWPCA § 118]

(a) Findings, purpose, and definitions

(1) Findings

The Congress finds that—

(A) the Great Lakes are a valuable national resource, continuously serving the people of the United States and other nations as an important source of food, fresh water, recreation, beauty, and enjoyment;

(B) the United States should seek to attain the goals embodied in the Great Lakes Water Quality Agreement of 1978, as amended by the Water Quality Agreement of 1987 and any other agreements and amendments, with particular emphasis on goals related to toxic pollutants; and

(C) the Environmental Protection Agency should take the lead in the effort to meet those goals, working with other Federal agencies and State and local authorities.

(2) Purpose

It is the purpose of this section to achieve the goals embodied in the Great Lakes Water Quality Agreement of 1978, as amended by the Water Quality Agreement of 1987 and any other agreements and amendments, through improved organization and definition of mission on the part of the Agency, funding of State grants for pollution control in the Great Lakes area, and improved accountability for implementation of such agreement.

(3) Definitions

For purposes of this section, the term—

(A) "Agency" means the Environmental Protection Agency;

(B) "Great Lakes" means Lake Ontario, Lake Erie, Lake Huron (including Lake St. Clair), Lake Michigan, and Lake Superior, and the connecting channels (Saint Mary's River, Saint Clair River, Detroit River, Niagara River, and Saint Lawrence River to the Canadian Border);

(C) "Great Lakes System" means all the streams, rivers, lakes, and other bodies of water within the drainage basin of the Great Lakes;

(D) "Program Office" means the Great Lakes National Program Office established by this section;

(E) "Research Office" means the Great Lakes Research Office established by subsection (d) of this section;

(F) "area of concern" means a geographic area located within the Great Lakes, in which beneficial uses are impaired and which has been officially designated as such under Annex 2 of the Great Lakes Water Quality Agreement;

(G) "Great Lakes States" means the States of Illinois, Indiana, Michigan, Minnesota, New York, Ohio, Pennsylvania, and Wisconsin;

(H) "Great Lakes Water Quality Agreement" means the bilateral agreement, between the United States and Canada which was signed in 1978 and amended by the Protocol of 1987;

(I) "Lakewide Management Plan" means a written document which embodies a systematic and comprehensive ecosystem approach to restoring and protecting the beneficial uses of the open waters of each of the Great Lakes, in accordance with article VI and Annex 2 of the Great Lakes Water Quality Agreement; and

(J) "Remedial Action Plan" means a written document which embodies a systematic and comprehensive ecosystem approach to restoring and protecting the beneficial uses of areas of concern, in accordance with article VI and Annex 2 of the Great Lakes Water Quality Agreement.

(b) Great Lakes National Program Office

The Great Lakes National Program Office (previously established by the Administrator) is hereby established within the Agency. The Program Office shall be headed by a Director who, by reason of management experience and technical expertise relating to the Great Lakes, is highly qualified to direct the development of programs and plans on a variety of Great Lakes issues. The Great Lakes National Program Office shall be located in a Great Lakes State.

(c) Great Lakes management

(1) Functions

The Program Office shall—

(A) in cooperation with appropriate Federal, State, tribal, and international agencies, and in accordance with section 1251(e) of this title, develop and implement specific action plans to carry out the responsibilities of the United States under the Great Lakes Water Quality Agreement of 1978, as amended by the Water Quality Agreement of 1987 and any other agreements and amendments,; [1]

(B) establish a Great Lakes system-wide surveillance network to monitor the water quality of the Great Lakes, with specific emphasis on the monitoring of toxic pollutants;

(C) serve as the liaison with, and provide information to, the Canadian members of the International Joint Commission and the Canadian counterpart to the Agency;

(D) coordinate actions of the Agency (including actions by headquarters and regional offices thereof) aimed at improving Great Lakes water quality; and

(E) coordinate actions of the Agency with the actions of other Federal agencies and State and local authorities, so as to ensure the input of those agencies and authorities in developing water quality strategies and obtain the support of those agencies and authorities in achieving the objectives of such agreement.

(2) Great Lakes water quality guidance

(A) By June 30, 1991, the Administrator, after consultation with the Program Office, shall publish in the Federal Register for public notice and comment proposed water quality guidance for the Great Lakes System. Such guidance shall conform with the objectives and provisions of the Great Lakes Water Quality Agreement, shall be no less restrictive than the provisions of this chapter and national water quality criteria and guidance, shall specify numerical limits on pollutants in ambient Great Lakes waters to protect human health, aquatic life, and wildlife, and shall provide guidance to the Great Lakes States on minimum water quality standards, antidegradation policies, and implementation procedures for the Great Lakes System.

(B) By June 30, 1992, the Administrator, in consultation with the Program Office, shall publish in the Federal Register, pursuant to this section and the Administrator's authority under this chapter, final water quality guidance for the Great Lakes System.

(C) Within two years after such Great Lakes guidance is published, the Great Lakes States shall adopt water quality standards, antidegradation policies, and implementation procedures for waters within the Great Lakes System which are consistent with such guidance. If a Great Lakes State fails to adopt such standards, policies, and procedures, the Administrator shall promulgate them not later than the end of such two-year period. When reviewing any Great Lakes State's water quality plan, the agency shall consider the extent to which the State has complied with the Great Lakes guidance issued pursuant to this section.

(3) Remedial action plans

(A) For each area of concern for which the United States has agreed to draft a Remedial Action Plan, the Program Office shall ensure that the Great Lakes State in which such area of concern is located—

(i) submits a Remedial Action Plan to the Program Office by June 30, 1991;

(ii) submits such Remedial Action Plan to the International Joint Commission by January 1, 1992; and

(iii) includes such Remedial Action Plans within the State's water quality plan by January 1, 1993.

(B) For each area of concern for which Canada has agreed to draft a Remedial Action Plan, the Program Office shall, pursuant to subparagraph (c)(1)(C) of this section, work with Canada to assure the submission of such Remedial Action Plans to the International Joint Commission by June 30, 1991, and to finalize such Remedial Action Plans by January 1, 1993.

(C) For any area of concern designated as such subsequent to November 16, 1990, the Program Office shall (i) if the United States has agreed to draft the Remedial Action Plan, ensure that the Great Lakes State in which such area of concern is located submits such Plan to the Program Office within two years of the area's designation, submits it to the International Joint Commission no later than six months after submitting it to the Program Office, and includes such Plan in the State's water quality plan no later than one year after submitting it to the Commission; and (ii) if Canada has agreed to draft the Remedial Action Plan, work with Canada, pursuant to subparagraph (c)(1)(C) of this section, to ensure the submission of such Plan to the International Joint Commission within two years of the area's designation and the finalization of such Plan no later than eighteen months after submitting it to such Commission.

(D) The Program Office shall compile formal comments on individual Remedial Action Plans made by the International Joint Commission pursuant to section 4(d) of Annex 2 of the Great Lakes Water Quality Agreement and, upon request by a member of the public, shall make such comments available for inspection and copying. The Program Office shall also make available, upon request, formal comments made by the Environmental Protection Agency on individual Remedial Action Plans.

(4) Lakewide Management Plans

The Administrator, in consultation with the Program Office shall—

(A) by January 1, 1992, publish in the Federal Register a proposed Lakewide Management Plan for Lake Michigan and solicit public comments;

(B) by January 1, 1993, submit a proposed Lakewide Management Plan for Lake Michigan to the International Joint Commission for review; and

(C) by January 1, 1994, publish in the Federal Register a final Lakewide Management Plan for Lake Michigan and begin implementation.

Nothing in this subparagraph shall preclude the simultaneous development of Lakewide Management Plans for the other Great Lakes.

(5) Spills of oil and hazardous materials

The Program Office, in consultation with the Coast Guard, shall identify areas within the Great Lakes which are likely to experience numerous or voluminous spills of oil or other hazardous materials from land based facilities, vessels, or other sources and, in consultation with the Great Lakes States, shall identify weaknesses in Federal and State programs and systems to prevent and respond to such spills. This information shall be included on at least a biennial basis in the report required by this section.

(6) 5-year plan and program

The Program Office shall develop, in consultation with the States, a five-year plan and program for reducing the amount of nutrients introduced into the Great Lakes. Such program shall incorporate any management program for reducing nutrient runoff from nonpoint sources established under section 1329 of this title and shall include a program for monitoring nutrient runoff into, and ambient levels in, the Great Lakes.

(7) 5-year study and demonstration projects

(A) The Program Office shall carry out a five-year study and demonstration projects relating to the control and removal of toxic pollutants in the Great Lakes, with emphasis on the removal of toxic pollutants from bottom sediments. In selecting locations for conducting demonstration projects under this paragraph, priority consideration shall be given to projects at the following locations: Saginaw Bay, Michigan; Sheboygan Harbor, Wisconsin; Grand Calumet River, Indiana; Ashtabula River, Ohio; and Buffalo River, New York.

(B) The Program Office shall—

(i) by December 31, 1990, complete chemical, physical, and biological assessments of the contaminated sediments at the locations selected for the study and demonstration projects;

(ii) by December 31, 1990, announce the technologies that will be demonstrated at each location and the numerical standard of protection intended to be achieved at each location;

(iii) by December 31, 1992, complete full or pilot scale demonstration projects on site at each location of promising technologies to remedy contaminated sediments; and

(iv) by December 31, 1993, issue a final report to Congress on its findings.

(C) The Administrator, after providing for public review and comment, shall publish information concerning the public health and environmental consequences of contaminants in Great Lakes sediment. Information published pursuant to this subparagraph shall include specific numerical limits to protect health, aquatic life, and wildlife from the bioaccumulation of toxins. The Administrator shall, at a minimum, publish information pursuant to this subparagraph within 2 years of November 16, 1990.

(8) Administrator's responsibility

The Administrator shall ensure that the Program Office enters into agreements with the various organizational elements of the Agency involved in Great Lakes activities and the appropriate State agencies specifically delineating—

(A) the duties and responsibilities of each such element in the Agency with respect to the Great Lakes;

(B) the time periods for carrying out such duties and responsibilities; and

(C) the resources to be committed to such duties and responsibilities.

(9) Budget item

The Administrator shall, in the Agency's annual budget submission to Congress, include a funding request for the Program Office as a separate budget line item.

(10) Comprehensive report

Within 90 days after the end of each fiscal year, the Administrator shall submit to Congress a comprehensive report which—

(A) describes the achievements in the preceding fiscal year in implementing the Great Lakes Water Quality Agreement of 1978, as amended by the Water Quality Agreement of 1987 and any other agreements and amendments, and shows by categories (including judicial enforcement, research, State cooperative efforts, and general administration) the amounts expended on Great Lakes water quality initiatives in such preceding fiscal year;

(B) describes the progress made in such preceding fiscal year in implementing the system of surveillance of the water quality in the Great Lakes System, including the monitoring of groundwater and sediment, with particular reference to toxic pollutants;

(C) describes the long-term prospects for improving the condition of the Great Lakes; and

(D) provides a comprehensive assessment of the planned efforts to be pursued in the succeeding fiscal year for implementing the Great Lakes Water Quality Agreement of 1978, as amended by the Water Quality Agreement of 1987 and any other agreements and amendments,,[1] which assessment shall—

(i) show by categories (including judicial enforcement, research, State cooperative efforts, and general administration) the amount anticipated to be expended on Great Lakes water quality initiatives in the fiscal year to which the assessment relates; and

(ii) include a report of current programs administered by other Federal agencies which make available resources to the Great Lakes water quality management efforts.

(11) Confined disposal facilities

(A) The Administrator, in consultation with the Assistant Secretary of the Army for Civil Works, shall develop and implement, within one year of November 16, 1990, management plans for every Great Lakes confined disposal facility.

(B) The plan shall provide for monitoring of such facilities, including—

(i) water quality at the site and in the area of the site;

(ii) sediment quality at the site and in the area of the site;

(iii) the diversity, productivity, and stability of aquatic organisms at the site and in the area of the site; and

(iv) such other conditions as the Administrator deems appropriate.

(C) The plan shall identify the anticipated use and management of the site over the following twenty-year period including the expected termination of dumping at the site, the anticipated need for site management, including pollution control, following the termination of the use of the site.

(D) The plan shall identify a schedule for review and revision of the plan which shall not be less frequent than five years after adoption of the plan and every five years thereafter.

(d) Great Lakes research

(1) Establishment of Research Office

There is established within the National Oceanic and Atmospheric Administration the Great Lakes Research Office.

(2) Identification of issues

The Research Office shall identify issues relating to the Great Lakes resources on which research is needed. The Research Office shall submit a report to Congress on such issues before the end of each fiscal year which shall identify any changes in the Great Lakes system[2] with respect to such issues.

(3) Inventory

The Research Office shall identify and inventory Federal, State, university, and tribal environmental research programs (and, to the extent feasible, those of private organizations and other nations) relating to the Great Lakes system,[2] and shall update that inventory every four years.

(4) Research exchange

The Research Office shall establish a Great Lakes research exchange for the purpose of facilitating the rapid identification, acquisition, retrieval, dissemination, and use of information concerning research projects which are ongoing or completed and which affect the Great Lakes System.

(5) Research program

The Research Office shall develop, in cooperation with the Coordination Office, a comprehensive environmental research program and data base for the Great Lakes system.[2] The data base shall include, but not be limited to, data relating to water quality, fisheries, and biota.

(6) Monitoring

The Research Office shall conduct, through the Great Lakes Environmental Research Laboratory, the National Sea Grant College program, other Federal laboratories, and the private sector, appropriate research and monitoring activities which address priority issues and current needs relating to the Great Lakes.

(7) Location

The Research Office shall be located in a Great Lakes State.

(e) Research and management coordination

(1) Joint plan

Before October 1 of each year, the Program Office and the Research Office shall prepare a joint research plan for the fiscal year which begins in the following calendar year.

(2) Contents of plan

Each plan prepared under paragraph (1) shall—

(A) identify all proposed research dedicated to activities conducted under the Great Lakes Water Quality Agreement of 1978, as amended by the Water Quality Agreement of 1987 and any other agreements and amendments,; [1]

(B) include the Agency's assessment of priorities for research needed to fulfill the terms of such Agreement; and

(C) identify all proposed research that may be used to develop a comprehensive environmental data base for the Great Lakes System and establish priorities for development of such data base.

(3) Health research report

(A) Not later than September 30, 1994, the Program Office, in consultation with the Research Office, the Agency for Toxic Substances and Disease Registry, and Great Lakes States shall submit to the Congress a report assessing the adverse effects of water pollutants in the Great Lakes System on the health of persons in Great Lakes States and the health of fish, shellfish, and wildlife in the Great Lakes System. In conducting research in support of this report, the Administrator may, where appropriate, provide for research to be conducted under cooperative agreements with Great Lakes States.

(B) There is authorized to be appropriated to the Administrator to carry out this section not to exceed $3,000,000 for each of fiscal years 1992, 1993, and 1994.

(f) Interagency cooperation

The head of each department, agency, or other instrumentality of the Federal Government which is engaged in, is concerned with, or has authority over programs relating to research, monitoring, and planning to maintain, enhance, preserve, or rehabilitate the environmental quality and natural resources of the Great Lakes, including the Chief of Engineers of the Army, the Chief of the Soil Conservation Service, the Commandant of the Coast Guard, the Director of the Fish and Wildlife Service, and the Administrator of the National Oceanic and Atmospheric Administration, shall submit an annual report to the Administrator with respect to the activities of that agency or office affecting compliance with the Great Lakes Water Quality Agreement of 1978, as amended by the Water Quality Agreement of 1987 and any other agreements and amendments,.[1]

(g) Relationship to existing Federal and State laws and international treaties

Nothing in this section shall be construed to affect the jurisdiction, powers, or prerogatives of any department, agency, or officer of the Federal Government or of any State government, or of any tribe, nor any powers, jurisdiction, or prerogatives of any international body created by treaty with authority relating to the Great Lakes.

(h) Authorizations of Great Lakes appropriations

There are authorized to be appropriated to the Administrator to carry out this section not to exceed $11,000,000 per fiscal year for the fiscal years 1987, 1988, 1989, and 1990, and $25,000,000 for fiscal year 1991. Of the amounts appropriated each fiscal year—

(1) 40 percent shall be used by the Great Lakes National Program Office on demonstration projects on the feasibility of controlling and removing toxic pollutants;

(2) 7 percent shall be used by the Great Lakes National Program Office for the program of nutrient monitoring; and

(3) 30 percent or $3,300,000, whichever is the lesser, shall be transferred to the National Oceanic and Atmospheric Administration for use by the Great Lakes Research Office.

(June 30, 1948, c. 758, Title I, § 118, as added Feb. 4, 1987, Pub.L. 100–4, Title I, § 104, 101 Stat. 11 and amended Nov. 18, 1988, Pub.L. 100–688, Title I, § 1008, 102 Stat. 4151; Nov. 16, 1990, Pub.L. 101–596, Title I, §§ 101–106, 104 Stat. 3000–3004.)

[1] So in original.

[2] So in original. Probably should be capitalized.

Great Lakes Remedial Action Plans

Pub.L. 101–640, Title IV, § 401, Nov. 28, 1990, 104 Stat. 4644, provided that:

"(a) Assistance.—The Secretary is authorized to provide technical, planning, and engineering assistance to States and local governments in the development and implementation of remedial action plans for areas of concern in the Great Lakes identified under the Great Lakes

Water Quality Agreement of 1978. Non-Federal interests shall contribute 50 percent of the costs of such assistance.

"**(b) Maximum amount.**—The Secretary may not expend more than $3,000,000 in a fiscal year to carry out this section."

LIBRARY REFERENCES

Navigable Waters ⇔35.
C.J.S. Health and Environment § 106 et seq.
C.J.S. Navigable Waters § 11.

§ 1269. Long Island Sound [FWPCA § 119]

(a) Continuation of Management Conference; establishment of Office

The Administrator shall continue the Management Conference of the Long Island Sound Study (hereinafter referred to as the "Conference") as established pursuant to section 1270 of this title, and shall establish an office (hereinafter referred to as the "Office") to be located on or near Long Island Sound.

(b) Administration and staffing of Office

The Office shall be headed by a Director, who shall be detailed by the Administrator, following consultation with the Administrators of EPA regions I and II, from among the employees of the Agency who are in civil service. The Administrator shall delegate to the Director such authority and detail such additional staff as may be necessary to carry out the duties of the Director under this section.

(c) Duties of the Office

The Office shall assist the Management Conference of the Long Island Sound Study in carrying out its goals. Specifically, the Office shall—

(1) assist and support the implementation of the Comprehensive Conservation and Management Plan for Long Island Sound developed pursuant to section 1270 of this title;

(2) conduct or commission studies deemed necessary for strengthened implementation of the Comprehensive Conservation and Management Plan including, but not limited to—

(A) population growth and the adequacy of wastewater treatment facilities,

(B) the use of biological methods for nutrient removal in sewage treatment plants,

(C) contaminated sediments, and dredging activities,

(D) nonpoint source pollution abatement and land use activities in the Long Island Sound watershed,

(E) wetland protection and restoration,

(F) atmospheric deposition of acidic and other pollutants into Long Island Sound,

(G) water quality requirements to sustain fish, shellfish, and wildlife populations, and the use of indicator species to assess environmental quality,

(H) State water quality programs, for their adequacy pursuant to implementation of the Comprehensive Conservation and Management Plan, and

(I) options for long-term financing of wastewater treatment projects and water pollution control programs.

(3) coordinate the grant, research and planning programs authorized under this section;

(4) coordinate activities and implementation responsibilities with other Federal agencies which have jurisdiction over Long Island Sound and with national and regional marine monitoring and research programs established pursuant to the Marine Protection, Research, and Sanctuaries Act;

(5) provide administrative and technical support to the conference;

(6) collect and make available to the public publications, and other forms of information the conference determines to be appropriate, relating to the environmental quality of Long Island Sound;

(7) not more than two years after the date of the issuance of the final Comprehensive Conservation and Management Plan for Long Island Sound under section 1270 of this title, and biennially thereafter, issue a report to the Congress which—

(A) summarizes the progress made by the States in implementing the Comprehensive Conservation and Management Plan;

(B) summarizes any modifications to the Comprehensive Conservation and Management Plan in the twelve-month period immediately preceding such report; and

(C) incorporates specific recommendations concerning the implementation of the Comprehensive Conservation and Management Plan; and

(8) convene conferences and meetings for legislators from State governments and political subdivisions thereof for the purpose of making recommendations for coordinating legislative efforts to facilitate the environmental restoration of Long Island Sound and the implementation of the Comprehensive Conservation and Management Plan.

(d) Grants

(1) The Administrator is authorized to make grants for projects and studies which will help implement the Long Island Sound Comprehensive Conservation and Management Plan. Special emphasis shall be given to implementation, research and planning, enforcement, and citizen involvement and education.

(2) State, interstate, and regional water pollution control agencies, and other public or nonprofit private agencies, institutions, and organizations held to be eligible for grants pursuant to this subsection.

(3) Citizen involvement and citizen education grants under this subsection shall not exceed 95 per centum of the costs of such work. All other grants under this subsection shall not exceed 50 per centum of the research, studies, or work. All grants shall be made on the condition that the non-Federal share of such costs are provided from non-Federal sources.

(e) Authorizations

(1) There is authorized to be appropriated to the Administrator for the implementation of this section, other than subsection (d) of this section, such sums as may be necessary for each of the fiscal years 1991 through 1996.

(2) There is authorized to be appropriated to the Administrator for the implementation of subsection (d) of this section not to exceed $3,000,000 for each of the fiscal years 1991 through 1996.

(June 30, 1948, c. 758, Title I, § 119, as added Nov. 16, 1990, Pub.L. 101-596, Title II, § 202, 104 Stat. 3004.)

References in Text

The Marine Protection, Research, and Sanctuaries Act, referred to in subsec. (c)(4), is Pub.L. 92-532, Oct. 23, 1972, 86 Stat. 1052, as amended, which is classified principally to chapter 27 (§ 1401 et seq.) of this title. For complete classification of this Act to the Code, see Short Title note set out under section 1401 of this title and Tables.

§ 1270. Lake Champlain Management Conference [FWPCA § 120]

(a) Establishment

There is established a Lake Champlain Management Conference to develop a comprehensive pollution prevention, control, and restoration plan for Lake Champlain. The Administrator shall convene the management conference within ninety days of November 16, 1990.

(b) Membership

The Members of the Management Conference shall be comprised of—

(1) the Governors of the States of Vermont and New York;

(2) each interested Federal agency, not to exceed a total of five members;

(3) the Vermont and New York Chairpersons of the Vermont, New York, Quebec Citizens Advisory Committee for the Environmental Management of Lake Champlain;

(4) four representatives of the State legislature of Vermont;

(5) four representatives of the State legislature of New York;

(6) six persons representing local governments having jurisdiction over any land or water within the Lake Champlain basin, as determined appropriate by the Governors; and

(7) eight persons representing affected industries, nongovernmental organizations, public and private educational institutions, and the general public, as determined appropriate by the trigovernmental Citizens Advisory Committee for the Environmental Management of Lake Champlain, but not to be current members of the Citizens Advisory Committee.

(c) Technical Advisory Committee

(1) The Management Conference shall, not later than one hundred and twenty days after November 16, 1990, appoint a Technical Advisory Committee.

(2) Such Technical Advisory Committee shall consist of officials of: appropriate departments and agencies of the Federal Government; the State governments of New York and Vermont; and governments of political subdivisions of such States; and public and private research institutions.

(d) Research program

(1) The Management Conference shall establish a multi-disciplinary environmental research program for Lake Champlain. Such research program shall be planned and conducted jointly with the Lake Champlain Research Consortium.

(e) Pollution prevention, control, and restoration plan

(1) Not later than three years after November 16, 1990, the Management Conference shall publish a pollution prevention, control, and restoration plan (hereafter in this section referred to as the "Plan") for Lake Champlain.

(2) The Plan developed pursuant to this section shall—

(A) identify corrective actions and compliance schedules addressing point and nonpoint sources of pollution necessary to restore and maintain the chemical, physical, and biological integrity of water quality, a balanced, indigenous population of shellfish, fish and wildlife, recreational, and economic activities in and on the lake;

(B) incorporate environmental management concepts and programs established in State and Federal plans and programs in effect at the time of the development of such plan;

(C) clarify the duties of Federal and State agencies in pollution prevention and control activities, and to the extent allowable by law, suggest a timetable for adoption by the appropriate Federal and State agencies to accomplish such duties within a reasonable period of time;

(D) describe the methods and schedules for funding of programs, activities, and projects identified in the Plan, including the use of Federal funds and other sources of funds; and

(E) include a strategy for pollution prevention and control that includes the promotion of pollution prevention and management practices to reduce the amount of pollution generated in the Lake Champlain basin.

(3) The Administrator, in cooperation with the Management Conference, shall provide for public review and comment on the draft Plan. At a minimum, the Management Conference shall conduct one public meeting to hear comments on the draft plan in the State of New York and one such meeting in the State of Vermont.

(4) Not less than one hundred and twenty days after the publication of the Plan required pursuant to this section, the Administrator shall approve such plan if the plan meets the requirements of this section and the Governors of the States of New York and Vermont concur.

(5) Upon approval of the plan, such plan shall be deemed to be an approved management program for the purposes of section 1329(h) of this title and such plan shall be deemed to be an approved comprehensive conservation and management plan pursuant to section 1330 of this title.

(f) Grant assistance

(1) The Administrator may, in consultation with the Management Conference, make grants to State, interstate, and regional water pollution control agencies, and public or nonprofit agencies, institutions, and organizations.

(2) Grants under this subsection shall be made for assisting research, surveys, studies, and modeling and technical and supporting work necessary for the development of the Plan and for retaining expert consultants in support of litigation undertaken by the State of New York and the State of Vermont to compel cleanup or obtain cleanup damage costs from persons responsible for pollution of Lake Champlain.

(3) The amount of grants to any person under this subsection for a fiscal year shall not exceed 75 per centum of the costs of such research, survey, study and work and shall be made available on the condition that non-Federal share of such costs are provided from non-Federal sources.

(4) The Administrator may establish such requirements for the administration of grants as he determines to be appropriate.

(g) Definition

For the purposes of this section, the term "Lake Champlain drainage basin" means all or part of Clinton, Franklin, Warren, Essex, and Washington counties in the State of New York and all or part of Franklin, Grand Isle, Chittenden, Addison, Rutland, Lamoille, Orange, Washington, Orleans, and Caledonia counties in Vermont, that contain all of the streams, rivers, lakes, and other bodies of water, including wetlands, that drain into Lake Champlain.

(h) Statutory interpretation

Nothing in this section shall be construed so as to affect the jurisdiction or powers of—

(1) any department or agency of the Federal Government or any State government; or

(2) any international organization or entity related to Lake Champlain created by treaty or memorandum to which the United States is a signatory.

(i) Authorization

There are authorized to be appropriated to the Environmental Protection Agency to carry out this section $2,000,000 for each of fiscal years 1991, 1992, 1993, 1994, and 1995.

(June 30, 1948, c. 758, Title I, § 120, as added Nov. 16, 1990, Pub.L. 101-596, Title III, § 303, 104 Stat. 3006.)

Federal Program Coordination

Section 304 of Pub.L. 101-596 provided that:

[Federal Program Coordination]

"(a) **Designation of Lake Champlain as a Special Project Area Under the Agricultural Conservation Program.**—

"(1) **In general.**—Notwithstanding any other provision of law, the Lake Champlain basin, as defined under section 120(h) of the Federal Water Pollution Control Act [section 1270(h) of this title], shall be designated by the Secretary of Agriculture as a special project area under the Agricultural Conservation Program established under section 8(b) of the Soil Conservation and Domestic Allotment Act (16 U.S.C. 590h(b)) [section 590h(b) of title 16, conservation].

"(2) **Technical assistance reimbursement.**—To carry out the purposes of this subsection, the technical assistance reimbursement from the Agricultural Stabilization and Conservation Service authorized under the Soil Conservation and Domestic Allotment Act [16 U.S.C.A. § 590a et seq.], shall be increased from 5 per centum to 10 per centum.

"(3) **Comprehensive agricultural monitoring.**—The Secretary, in consultation with the Management Conference and appropriate State and Federal agencies, shall develop a comprehensive agricultural monitoring and evaluation network for all major drainages within the Lake Champlain basin.

"(4) **Allocation of funds.**—In allocating funds under this subsection, the Secretary of Agriculture shall consult with the Management Conference established under section 120 of the Federal Water Pollution Control Act [section 1270 of this title] and to the extent allowable by law, allocate funds to those agricultural enterprises located at sites that the Management Conference determines to be priority sites, on the basis of a concern for ensuring implementation of nonpoint source pollution controls throughout the Lake Champlain basin.

"(b) **Cooperation of the United States Geological Survey of the Department of the Interior.**—For the purpose of enhancing and expanding basic data collection and monitoring in operation in the Lake Champlain basin, as defined under section 120 of the Federal Water Pollution Control Act [section 1270 of this title], the Secretary of the Interior, acting through the heads of water resources divisions of the New York and New England districts of the United States Geological Survey, shall—

"(1) in cooperation with appropriate universities and private research institutions, and the appropriate officials of the appropriate departments and agencies of the States of New York and Vermont, develop an integrated geographic information system of the Lake Champlain basin;

"(2) convert all partial recording sites in the Lake Champlain basin to continuous monitoring stations with full gauging capabilities and status; and

"(3) establish such additional continuous monitoring station sites in the Lake Champlain basin as are necessary to carry out basic data collection and monitoring, as defined by the Secretary of the Interior, including groundwater mapping, and water quality and sediment data collection.

"(c) **Cooperation of the United States Fish and Wildlife Service of the Department of the Interior.**—

"(1) **Resource conservation program.**—The Secretary of the Interior, acting through the United States Fish and Wildlife Service, in cooperation with the Lake Champlain Fish and Wildlife Management Cooperative and the Management Conference established pursuant to this subsection shall—

"(A) establish and implement a fisheries resources restoration, development and conservation program, including dedicating a level of hatchery production within the Lake Champlain basin at or above the level that existed immediately preceding the date of enactment of this Act [November 16, 1990]; and

"(B) conduct a wildlife species and habitat assessment survey in the Lake Champlain basin, including—

"(i) a survey of Federal threatened and endangered species, listed or proposed for listing under the Endangered Species Act of 1973 (16 U.S.C. 1531 et seq.), New York State and State of Vermont threatened and endangered species and other species of special concern, migratory nongame species of management concern, and national resources plan species;

"(ii) a survey of wildlife habitats such as islands, wetlands, and riparian areas; and

"(iii) a survey of migratory bird populations breeding, migrating and wintering within the Lake Champlain basin.

"(2) To accomplish the purposes of paragraph (1), the Director of the United States Fish and Wildlife Service is authorized to carry out activities related to—

"(A) controlling sea lampreys and other nonindigenous aquatic animal nuisances;

"(B) improving the health of fishery resources;

"(C) conducting investigations about and assessing the status of fishery resources, and disseminating that information to all interested parties; and

"(D) conducting and periodically updating a survey of the fishery resources and their habitats and food chains in the Lake Champlain basin.

"(d) **Authorizations.**—(1) There is authorized to be appropriated to the Department of Agriculture $2,000,000 for each of fiscal years 1991, 1992, 1993, 1994, and 1995 to carry out subsection (a) of this section.

"(2) There is authorized to be appropriated to the Department of Interior $1,000,000 for each of fiscal years 1991, 1992, 1993, 1994, and 1995 to carry out subsections (b) and (c) of this section."

SUBCHAPTER II—GRANTS FOR CONSTRUCTION OF TREATMENT WORKS

CROSS REFERENCES

Consideration of international water pollution control agreements in development of the ranking in order of priority of needs for construction of treatment works, see section 1371 of this title.

Grants to municipalities to reduce operation and maintenance costs to costs comparable to those for projects assisted under this subchapter, see section 1255 of this title.

Priority to applications from public bodies situated in areas affected by major disasters, see section 5153 of Title 42, The Public Health and Welfare.

Prohibition on making of grants until review and revision of water quality standards, see section 1313a of this title.

§ 1271. Sediment survey and monitoring [NCSAMA § 503]

(a) Survey

(1) In general

The Administrator, in consultation with the Administrator of the National Oceanic and Atmospheric Administration and the Secretary, shall conduct a comprehensive national survey of data regarding aquatic sediment quality in the United States. The Administrator shall compile all existing information on the quantity, chemical and physical composition, and geographic location of pollutants in aquatic sediment, including the probable source of such pollutants and identification of those sediments which are contaminated pursuant to section 501(b)(4).

(2) Report

Not later than 24 months after October 31, 1992, the Administrator shall report to the Congress the findings, conclusions, and recommendations of such survey, including recommendations for actions necessary to prevent contamination of aquatic sediments and to control sources of contamination.

(b) Monitoring

(1) In general

The Administrator, in consultation with the Administrator of the National Oceanic and Atmospheric Administration and the Secretary, shall conduct a comprehensive and continuing program to assess aquatic sediment quality. The program conducted pursuant to this subsection shall, at a minimum—

(A) identify the location of pollutants in aquatic sediment;

(B) identify the extent of pollutants in sediment and those sediments which are contaminated pursuant to section 501(b)(4);

(C) establish methods and protocols for monitoring the physical, chemical, and biological effects of pollutants in aquatic sediment and of contaminated sediment;

(D) develop a system for the management, storage, and dissemination of data concerning aquatic sediment quality;

(E) provide an assessment of aquatic sediment quality trends over time;

(F) identify locations where pollutants in sediment may pose a threat to the quality of drinking water supplies, fisheries resources, and marine habitats; and

(G) establish a clearing house for information on technology, methods, and practices available for the remediation, decontamination, and control of sediment contamination.

(2) Report

The Administrator shall submit to Congress a report on the findings of the monitoring under paragraph (1) on the date that is 2 years after the date specified in subsection (a)(2) of this section and biennially thereafter.

(Pub.L. 102–580, Title V, § 503, Oct. 31, 1992, 106 Stat. 4865.)

References in Text

Section 501(b)(4), referred to in subsecs. (a)(1) and (b)(1)(B), is section 501(b)(4) of Pub.L. 102–580, Title V, Oct. 31, 1992, 106 Stat. 4864, which is classified in a note entitled "Definitions" and set out under this section.

Codification

Section was enacted as part of the Water Resources Development Act of 1992 and the National Contaminated Sediment Assessment and Management Act, and not as part of the Federal Water Pollution Control Act, which comprises this chapter.

Short Title

Section 501(a) of Pub.L. 102–580 provided that: "This title [Pub.L. 102–580, Title V, Oct. 31, 1992, 106 Stat. 4864, which enacted this section, amended sections 1412, 1413, 1414, 1415, 1416, 1420 and 1421 of this title, and enacted provisions set out as notes under section 1271 of this title; for distribution of Pub.L. 102–580 to the Code, see Short Title note set out under section 2201 of this title and Tables] may be cited as the 'National Contaminated Sediment Assessment and Management Act'."

Authorization of Appropriations

Section 509(b)of Pub.L. 102–580 provided that: "There is authorized to be appropriated to the Administrator to carry out sections 502 [set out as a note under this section] and 503 [this section] such sums as may be necessary."

Availability of Contaminated Sediments Information

Section 327 of Pub.L. 102–580 provided that:

"(a) **Study.**—The Secretary shall—

"(1) conduct a national study on information that is currently available on contaminated sediments of the surface waters of the United States; and

"(2) compile information obtained in such study for the purpose of identifying the location and nature of contaminated sediments in the Nation.

"(b) **Report.**—Not later than 1 year after the date of the enactment of this Act [Oct. 31, 1992], the Secretary shall transmit to the Committee on Public Works and Transportation of the House of Representatives and the Committee on Environment and Public Works of the Senate a report on the results of the study conducted under subsection (a), including recommendations for the collection of additional date on the contaminated sediments and including the compilation of information referred to in subsection (a)."

[Any reference in any provision of law enacted before Jan. 4, 1995, to the Committee on Public Works and Transportation of the House of Representatives treated as referring to the Committee on Transportation and Infrastructure of the House of Representatives, see section 1(a)(9) of Pub.L. 104–14, set out as a note preceding section 21 of Title 2, The Congress.]

Definitions

Section 501(b) of Pub.L. 102–580 provided that:

"(b) **Definitions.**—For the purposes of sections 502 [set out as a note under this section] and 503 of this title [this section]—

"(1) the term 'aquatic sediment' means sediment underlying the navigable water of the United States;

"(2) the term 'navigable waters' has the same meaning as in section 502(7) of the Federal Water Pollution Control Act (33 U.S.C. 1362(7) [section 1362(7) of this title]);

"(3) the term 'pollutant' has the same meaning as in section 502(6) of the Federal Water Pollution Control act (33 U.S.C. 1362(6) [section 1362(6) of this title]); except that such term does not include dredge spoil, rock, sand, or cellar dirt;

"(4) the term 'contaminated sediment' means aquatic sediment which—

"(A) contains chemical substances in excess of appropriate geochemical, toxicological or sediment quality criteria or measures; or

"(B) is otherwise considered by the Administrator to pose a threat to human health or the environment; and

"(5) the term 'Administrator' means the Administrator of the Environmental Protection Agency."

National Contaminated Sediment Task Force

Section 502 of Pub.L. 102–580 provided that:

"**Sec. 502. National contaminated sediment task force.**

"(a) **Establishment.**—There is established a National Contaminated Sediment Task Force (hereinafter referred to in this section as the 'Task Force'). The Task Force shall—

"(1) advise the Administrator and the Secretary in the implementation of this title [Pub.L. 102–580, Title V, Oct. 31, 1992, 106 Stat. 4864, which enacted this section, amended sections 1412, 1413, 1414, 1415, 1416, 1420 and 1421 of this title, and enacted provisions set out as notes under section 1271 of this title; for distribution of Pub.L. 102–580 to the Code, see Short Title note set out under section 2201 of this title and Tables];

"(2) review and comment on reports concerning aquatic sediment quality and the extent and seriousness of aquatic sediment contamination throughout the Nation;

"(3) review and comment on programs for the research and development of aquatic sediment restoration methods, practices, and technologies;

"(4) review and comment on the selection of pollutants for development of aquatic sediment criteria and the schedule for the development of such criteria;

"(5) advise appropriate officials in the development of guidelines for restoration of contaminated sediment;

"(6) make recommendations to appropriate officials concerning practices and measures—

"(A) to prevent the contamination of aquatic sediments; and

"(B) to control sources of sediment contamination; and

"(7) review and assess the means and methods for locating and constructing permanent, cost-effective long-term disposal sites for the disposal of dredged material that is not suitable for ocean dumping (as determined under the Marine Protection, Research, and Sanctuaries Act of 1972 (33 U.S.C. 1401 et seq.) [Section 1401 et seq. of this title]).

"(b) Membership.—

"(1) **In general.**—The membership of the Task Force shall include 1 representative of each of the following:

"(A) The Administrator.

"(B) The Secretary.

"(C) The National Oceanic and Atmospheric Administration.

"(D) The United States Fish and Wildlife Service.

"(E) The Geological Survey.

"(F) The Department of Agriculture.

"(2) **Additional members of the Task Force shall be jointly selected by the Administrator and the Secretary, and shall include—**

"(A) not more than 3 representatives of States;

"(B) not more than 3 representatives of ports, agriculture, and manufacturing; and

"(C) not more than 3 representatives of public interest organizations with a demonstrated interest in aquatic sediment contamination.

"(3) **Cochairmen.**—The Administrator and the Secretary shall serve as cochairmen of the Task Force.

"(4) **Clerical and Technical assistance.**—Such clerical and technical assistance as may be necessary to discharge the duties of the Task Force shall be provided by the personnel of the Environmental Protection agency and the Army Corps of Engineers.

"(5) **Compensation for additional members.**—The additional members of the Task Force selected under paragraph (2) shall, while attending meetings or conferences of the Task Force, be compensated at a rate to be fixed by the cochairmen, but not to exceed the daily equivalent of the base rate of pay in effect for grade GS–15 of the General Schedule under section 5332 of title 5, United States Code [section 5332 of Title 5, Government Organization and Employees], for each day (including travel time) during which they are engaged in the actual performance of duties vested in the Task Force. While away from their homes or regular places of business in the performance of services for the Task Force, such members shall be allowed travel expenses, including per diem in lieu of subsistence, in the same manner as persons employed intermittently in the Government service are allowed expenses under section 5703(b) of title 5, United States Code [section 5703(b) of Title 5].

"(c) **Report.**—Within 2 years after the date of the enactment of this Act [Oct. 31, 1992], the Task Force shall submit to Congress a report stating the findings and recommendations of the Task Force."

§ 1281. Congressional declaration of purpose [FWPCA § 201]

(a) Development and implementation of waste treatment management plans and practices

It is the purpose of this subchapter to require and to assist the development and implementation of waste treatment management plans and practices which will achieve the goals of this chapter.

(b) Application of technology: confined disposal of pollutants; consideration of advanced techniques

Waste treatment management plans and practices shall provide for the application of the best practicable waste treatment technology before any discharge into receiving waters, including reclaiming and recycling of water, and confined disposal of pollutants so they will not migrate to cause water or other environmental pollution and shall provide for consideration of advanced waste treatment techniques.

(c) Waste treatment management area and scope

To the extent practicable, waste treatment management shall be on an areawide basis and provide control or treatment of all point and nonpoint sources of pollution, including in place or accumulated pollution sources.

(d) Waste treatment management construction of revenue producing facilities

The Administrator shall encourage waste treatment management which results in the construction of revenue producing facilities providing for—

(1) the recycling of potential sewage pollutants through the production of agriculture, silviculture, or aquaculture products, or any combination thereof;

(2) the confined and contained disposal of pollutants not recycled;

(3) the reclamation of wastewater; and

(4) the ultimate disposal of sludge in a manner that will not result in environmental hazards.

(e) Waste treatment management integration of facilities

The Administrator shall encourage waste treatment management which results in integrating facilities for sewage treatment and recycling with facilities to treat, dispose of, or utilize other industrial and municipal wastes, including but not limited to solid waste and waste heat and thermal discharges. Such integrated facilities shall be designed and operated to produce revenues in excess of capital and operation and maintenance costs and such revenues shall be used by the designated regional management agency to aid in financing other environmental improvement programs.

(f) Waste treatment management "open space" and recreational considerations

The Administrator shall encourage waste treatment management which combines "open space" and recreational considerations with such management.

(g) Grants to construct publicly owned treatment works

(1) The Administrator is authorized to make grants to any State, municipality, or intermunicipal or interstate agency for the construction of publicly owned treatment works. On and after October 1, 1984, grants under this subchapter shall be made only for projects for secondary treatment or more stringent treatment, or any cost effective alternative thereto, new interceptors and appurtenances, and infiltration-in-flow correction. Notwithstanding the preceding sentences, the Administrator may make grants on and after October 1, 1984, for (A) any project within the definition set forth in section 1292(2) of this title, other than for a project referred to in the preceding sentence, and (B) any purpose for which a grant may be made under sections[1] 1329(h) and (i) of this title (including any innovative and alternative approaches for the control of nonpoint sources of pollution), except that not more than 20 per centum (as determined by the Governor of the State) of the amount allotted to a State under section 1285 of this title for any fiscal year shall be obligated in such State under authority of this sentence.

(2) The Administrator shall not make grants from funds authorized for any fiscal year beginning after

June 30, 1974, to any State, municipality, or intermunicipal or interstate agency for the erection, building, acquisition, alteration, remodeling, improvement, or extension of treatment works unless the grant applicant has satisfactorily demonstrated to the Administrator that—

(A) alternative waste management techniques have been studied and evaluated and the works proposed for grant assistance will provide for the application of the best practicable waste treatment technology over the life of the works consistent with the purposes of this subchapter; and

(B) as appropriate, the works proposed for grant assistance will take into account and allow to the extent practicable the application of technology at a later date which will provide for the reclaiming or recycling of water or otherwise eliminate the discharge of pollutants.

(3) The Administrator shall not approve any grant after July 1, 1973, for treatment works under this section unless the applicant shows to the satisfaction of the Administrator that each sewer collection system discharging into such treatment works is not subject to excessive infiltration.

(4) The Administrator is authorized to make grants to applicants for treatment works grants under this section for such sewer system evaluation studies as may be necessary to carry out the requirements of paragraph (3) of this subsection. Such grants shall be made in accordance with rules and regulations promulgated by the Administrator. Initial rules and regulations shall be promulgated under this paragraph not later than 120 days after October 18, 1972.

(5) The Administrator shall not make grants from funds authorized for any fiscal year beginning after September 30, 1978, to any State, municipality, or intermunicipal or interstate agency for the erection, building, acquisition, alteration, remodeling, improvement, or extension of treatment works unless the grant applicant has satisfactorily demonstrated to the Administrator that innovative and alternative wastewater treatment processes and techniques which provide for the reclaiming and reuse of water, otherwise eliminate the discharge of pollutants, and utilize recycling techniques, land treatment, new or improved methods of waste treatment management for municipal and industrial waste (discharged into municipal systems) and the confined disposal of pollutants, so that pollutants will not migrate to cause water or other environmental pollution, have been fully studied and evaluated by the applicant taking into account subsection (d) of this section and taking into account and allowing to the extent practicable the more efficient use of energy and resources.

(6) The Administrator shall not make grants from funds authorized for any fiscal year beginning after September 30, 1978, to any State, municipality, or intermunicipal or interstate agency for the erection, building, acquisition, alteration, remodeling, improvement, or extension of treatment works unless the grant applicant has satisfactorily demonstrated to the Administrator that the applicant has analyzed the potential recreation and open space opportunities in the planning of the proposed treatment works.

(h) Grants to construct privately owned treatment works

A grant may be made under this section to construct a privately owned treatment works serving one or more principal residences or small commercial establishments constructed prior to, and inhabited on, December 27, 1977, where the Administrator finds that—

(1) a public body otherwise eligible for a grant under subsection (g) of this section has applied on behalf of a number of such units and certified that public ownership of such works is not feasible;

(2) such public body has entered into an agreement with the Administrator which guarantees that such treatment works will be properly operated and maintained and will comply with all other requirements of section 1284 of this title and includes a system of charges to assure that each recipient of waste treatment services under such a grant will pay its proportionate share of the cost of operation and maintenance (including replacement); and

(3) the total cost and environmental impact of providing waste treatment services to such residences or commercial establishments will be less than the cost of providing a system of collection and central treatment of such wastes.

(i) Waste treatment management methods, processes, and techniques to reduce energy requirements

The Administrator shall encourage waste treatment management methods, processes, and techniques which will reduce total energy requirements.

(j) Grants for treatment works utilizing processes and techniques of guidelines under section 1314(d)(3) of this title

The Administrator is authorized to make a grant for any treatment works utilizing processes and techniques meeting the guidelines promulgated under section 1314(d)(3) of this title, if the Administrator determines it is in the public interest and if in the cost effectiveness study made of the construction grant application for the purpose of evaluating alternative treatment works, the life cycle cost of the treatment works for which the grant is to be made does not exceed the life cycle cost of the most cost effective alternative by more than 15 per centum.

(k) Limitation on use of grants for publicly owned treatment works

No grant made after November 15, 1981, for a publicly owned treatment works, other than for facility planning and the preparation of construction plans and specifications, shall be used to treat, store, or convey the flow of any industrial user into such treatment works in excess of a flow per day equivalent to fifty thousand gallons per day of sanitary waste. This subsection shall not apply to any project proposed by a grantee which is carrying out an approved project to prepare construction plans and specifications for a facility to treat wastewater, which received its grant approval before May 15, 1980. This subsection shall not be in effect after November 15, 1981.

(*l*) Grants for facility plans, or plans, specifications, and estimates for proposed project for construction of treatment works; limitations, allotments, advances, etc.

(1) After December 29, 1981, Federal grants shall not be made for the purpose of providing assistance solely for facility plans, or plans, specifications, and estimates for any proposed project for the construction of treatment works. In the event that the proposed project receives a grant under this section for construction, the Administrator shall make an allowance in such grant for non-Federal funds expended during the facility planning and advanced engineering and design phase at the prevailing Federal share under section 1282(a) of this title, based on the percentage of total project costs which the Administrator determines is the general experience for such projects.

(2)(A) Each State shall use a portion of the funds allotted to such State each fiscal year, but not to exceed 10 per centum of such funds, to advance to potential grant applicants under this subchapter the costs of facility planning or the preparation of plans, specifications, and estimates.

(B) Such an advance shall be limited to the allowance for such costs which the Administrator establishes under paragraph (1) of this subsection, and shall be provided only to a potential grant applicant which is a small community and which in the judgment of the State would otherwise be unable to prepare a request for a grant for construction costs under this section.

(C) In the event a grant for construction costs is made under this section for a project for which an advance has been made under this paragraph, the Administrator shall reduce the amount of such grant by the allowance established under paragraph (1) of this subsection. In the event no such grant is made, the State is authorized to seek repayment of such advance on such terms and conditions as it may determine.

(m) Grants for State of California projects

(1) Notwithstanding any other provisions of this subchapter, the Administrator is authorized to make a grant from any funds otherwise allotted to the State of California under section 1285 of this title to the project (and in the amount) specified in Order WQG 81–1 of the California State Water Resources Control Board.

(2) Notwithstanding any other provision of this chapter, the Administrator shall make a grant from any funds otherwise allotted to the State of California to the city of Eureka, California, in connection with project numbered C–06–2772, for the purchase of one hundred and thirty-nine acres of property as environmental mitigation for siting of the proposed treatment plant.

(3) Notwithstanding any other provision of this chapter, the Administrator shall make a grant from any funds otherwise allotted to the State of California to the city of San Diego, California, in connection with that city's aquaculture sewage process (total resources recovery system) as an innovative and alternative waste treatment process.

(n) Water quality problems; funds, scope, etc.

(1) On and after October 1, 1984, upon the request of the Governor of an affected State, the Administrator is authorized to use funds available to such State under section 1285 of this title to address water quality problems due to the impacts of discharges from combined storm water and sanitary sewer overflows, which are not otherwise eligible under this subsection, where correction of such discharges is a major priority for such State.

(2) Beginning fiscal year 1983, the Administrator shall have available $200,000,000 per fiscal year in addition to those funds authorized in section 1287 of this title to be utilized to address water quality problems of marine bays and estuaries subject to lower levels of water quality due to the impacts of discharges from combined storm water and sanitary sewer overflows from adjacent urban complexes, not otherwise eligible under this subsection. Such sums may be used as deemed appropriate by the Administrator as provided in paragraphs (1) and (2) of this subsection, upon the request of and demonstration of water quality benefits by the Governor of an affected State.

(o) Capital financing plan

The Administrator shall encourage and assist applicants for grant assistance under this subchapter to develop and file with the Administrator a capital financing plan which, at a minimum—

(1) projects the future requirements for waste treatment services within the applicant's jurisdiction for a period of no less than ten years;

(2) projects the nature, extent, timing, and costs of future expansion and reconstruction of treatment works which will be necessary to satisfy the applicant's projected future requirements for waste treatment services; and

(3) sets forth with specificity the manner in which the applicant intends to finance such future expansion and reconstruction.

(p) Time limit on resolving certain disputes

In any case in which a dispute arises with respect to the awarding of a contract for construction of treatment works by a grantee of funds under this subchapter and a party to such dispute files an appeal with the Administrator under this subchapter for resolution of such dispute, the Administrator shall make a final decision on such appeal within 90 days of the filing of such appeal.

(June 30, 1948, c. 758, Title II, § 201, as added Oct. 18, 1972, Pub.L. 92–500, § 2, 86 Stat. 833, and amended Dec. 27, 1977, Pub.L. 95–217, §§ 12–16, 91 Stat. 1569, 1570; Oct. 21, 1980, Pub.L. 96–483, §§ 2(d), 3, 94 Stat. 2361; Dec. 29, 1981, Pub.L. 97–117, §§ 2(a), 3(a), 4–6, 10(c), 95 Stat. 1623–1626; Feb. 4, 1987, Pub.L. 100–4, Title II, § 201, Title III, § 316(c), 101 Stat. 15, 60.)

1 So in original. Probably should be "section".

CROSS REFERENCES

Action of Administrator deemed major Federal action for purposes of environmental policy, see section 1371 of this title.
Allotment of additional funds, see section 1286 of this title.
Amount of grants for treatment works, see section 1282 of this title.
Areawide waste treatment management planning process consistent with this section, see section 1288 of this title.
Cost-effectiveness, Congressional statement of policy, see section 1298 of this title.
Definition of "treatment works", see section 1292 of this title.
Grants for sewage collection systems, see section 1291 of this title.
Grants to designated regional operating agencies, see section 1288 of this title.
Grants to State for reasonable costs of administration of any aspects of this section, see section 1285 of this title.
Guidelines for cost-effectiveness analysis, see section 1297 of this title.
Matters determinable prior to approval of grant under this section, see section 1284 of this title.
Plans, specifications, and estimates for project for construction of treatment works plant, see section 1283 of this title.
Promulgation of guidelines for identifying innovative and alternative wastewater treatment processes referred to in this section, see section 1314 of this title.
Publication of information on alternative waste treatment management techniques available to implement this section, see section 1314 of this title.
Report of estimated costs to Congress, see section 1375 of this title.
Terms and conditions for extension of timetable for achievement of objectives, see section 1311 of this title.
Treatment of amount of grant under this section in excess of costs of construction of treatment works as grant of the Federal share of cost of construction of a sewage collection system, see section 1281a of this title.

Library References

Health and Environment ⇐25.7(21).
C.J.S. Health and Environment § 106 et seq.

§ 1281a. Total treatment system funding

Notwithstanding any other provision of law, in any case where the Administrator of the Environmental Protection Agency finds that the total of all grants made under section 1281 of this title for the same treatment works exceeds the actual construction costs for such treatment works (as defined in this chapter) such excess amount shall be a grant of the Federal share (as defined in this chapter) of the cost of construction of a sewage collection system if—

(1) such sewage collection system was constructed as part of the same total treatment system as the treatment works for which such grants under section 1281 of this title were approved, and

(2) an application for assistance for the construction of such sewage collection system was filed in accordance with section 3102 of Title 42 before all such grants under section 1281 of this title were made and such grant under section 3102 of Title 42 could not be approved due to lack of funding under such section 3102 of Title 42.

The total of all grants for sewage collection systems made under this section shall not exceed $2,800,000.

(Dec. 27, 1977, Pub.L. 95–217, § 78, 91 Stat. 1611.)

Codification

Section was enacted as part of the Clean Water Act of 1977, Pub.L. 95–217, and not as part of the Federal Water Pollution Control Act, June 30, 1948, c. 758, as added Oct. 18, 1972, Pub.L. 92–500, 86 Stat. 816, which comprises this chapter.

Library References

Health and Environment ⇐25.7(21).
C.J.S. Health and Environment § 106 et seq.

§ 1281b. Availability of Farmers Home Administration funds for non-Federal share

Notwithstanding any other provision of law, Federal assistance made available by the Farmers Home Administration to any political subdivision of a State may be used to provide the non-Federal share of the cost of any construction project carried out under section 1281 of this title.

(Pub.L. 100–4, Title II, § 202(f), Feb. 4, 1987, 101 Stat. 16.)

Codification

Section was enacted as part of the Water Quality Act of 1987, and not as part of the Federal Water Pollution Control Act, which comprises this chapter.

LIBRARY REFERENCES

Navigable Waters ⟹35.
C.J.S. Health and Environment § 106 et seq.
C.J.S. Navigable Waters § 11.

§ 1282. Federal share [FWPCA § 202]

(a) Amount of grants for treatment works

(1) The amount of any grant for treatment works made under this chapter from funds authorized for any fiscal year beginning after June 30, 1971, and ending before October 1, 1984, shall be 75 per centum of the cost of construction thereof (as approved by the Administrator), and for any fiscal year beginning on or after October 1, 1984, shall be 55 per centum of the cost of construction thereof (as approved by the Administrator), unless modified to a lower percentage rate uniform throughout a State by the Governor of that State with the concurrence of the Administrator. Within ninety days after October 21, 1980, the Administrator shall issue guidelines for concurrence in any such modification, which shall provide for the consideration of the unobligated balance of sums allocated to the State under section 1285 of this title, the need for assistance under this subchapter in such State, and the availability of State grant assistance to replace the Federal share reduced by such modification. The payment of any such reduced Federal share shall not constitute an obligation on the part of the United States or a claim on the part of any State or grantee to reimbursement for the portion of the Federal share reduced in any such State. Any grant (other than for reimbursement) made prior to October 18, 1972, from any funds authorized for any fiscal year beginning after June 30, 1971, shall, upon the request of the applicant, be increased to the applicable percentage under this section. Notwithstanding the first sentence of this paragraph, in any case where a primary, secondary, or advanced waste treatment facility or its related interceptors or a project for infiltration-in-flow correction has received a grant for erection, building, acquisition, alteration, remodeling, improvement, extension, or correction before October 1, 1984, all segments and phases of such facility, interceptors, and project for infiltration-in-flow correction shall be eligible for grants at 75 per centum of the cost of construction thereof for any grant made pursuant to a State obligation which obligation occurred before October 1, 1990. Notwithstanding the first sentence of this paragraph, in the case of a project for which an application for a grant under this subchapter has been made to the Administrator before October 1, 1984, and which project is under judicial injunction on such date prohibiting its construction, such project shall be eligible for grants at 75 percent of the cost of construction thereof. Notwithstanding the first sentence of this paragraph, in the case of the Wyoming Valley Sanitary Authority project mandated by judicial order under a proceeding begun prior to October 1, 1984, and a project for wastewater treatment for Altoona, Pennsylvania, such projects shall be eligible for grants at 75 percent of the cost of construction thereof.

(2) The amount of any grant made after September 30, 1978, and before October 1, 1981, for any eligible treatment works or significant portion thereof utilizing innovative or alternative wastewater treatment processes and techniques referred to in section 1281(g)(5) of this title shall be 85 per centum of the cost of construction thereof, unless modified by the Governor of the State with the concurrence of the Administrator to a percentage rate no less than 15 per centum greater than the modified uniform percentage rate in which the Administrator has concurred pursuant to paragraph (1) of this subsection. The amount of any grant made after September 30, 1981, for any eligible treatment works or unit processes and techniques thereof utilizing innovative or alternative wastewater treatment processes and techniques referred to in section 1281(g)(5) of this title shall be a percentage of the cost of construction thereof equal to 20 per centum greater than the percentage in effect under paragraph (1) of this subsection for such works or unit processes and techniques, but in no event greater that 85 per centum of the cost of construction thereof. No grant shall be made under this paragraph for construction of a treatment works in any State unless the proportion of the State contribution to the non-Federal share of construction costs for all treatment works in such State receiving a grant under this paragraph is the same as or greater than the proportion of the State contribution (if any) to the non-Federal share of construction costs for all treatment works receiving grants in such State under paragraph (1) of this subsection.

(3) In addition to any grant made pursuant to paragraph (2) of this subsection, the Administrator is authorized to make a grant to fund all of the costs of the modification or replacement of any facilities constructed with a grant made pursuant to paragraph (2) if the Administrator finds that such facilities have not met design performance specifications unless such failure is attributable to negligence on the part of any person and if such failure has significantly increased capital or operating and maintenance expenditures. In addition, the Administrator is authorized to make a

grant to fund all of the costs of the modification or replacement of biodisc equipment (rotating biological contractors) in any publicly owned treatment works if the Administrator finds that such equipment has failed to meet design performance specifications, unless such failure is attributable to negligence on the part of any person, and if such failure has significantly increased capital or operating and maintenance expenditures.

(4) For the purposes of this section, the term "eligible treatment works" means those treatment works in each State which meet the requirements of section 1281(g)(5) of this title and which can be fully funded from funds available for such purpose in such State.

(b) Amount of grants for construction of treatment works not commenced prior to July 1, 1971

The amount of the grant for any project approved by the Administrator after January 1, 1971, and before July 1, 1971, for the construction of treatment works, the actual erection, building or acquisition of which was not commenced prior to July 1, 1971, shall, upon the request of the applicant, be increased to the applicable percentage under subsection (a) of this section for grants for treatment works from funds for fiscal years beginning after June 30, 1971, with respect to the cost of such actual erection, building, or acquisition. Such increased amount shall be paid from any funds allocated to the State in which the treatment works is located without regard to the fiscal year for which such funds were authorized. Such increased amount shall be paid for such project only if—

(1) a sewage collection system that is a part of the same total waste treatment system as the treatment works for which such grant was approved is under construction or is to be constructed for use in conjunction with such treatment works, and if the cost of such sewage collection system exceeds the cost of such treatment works, and

(2) the State water pollution control agency or other appropriate State authority certifies that the quantity of available ground water will be insufficient, inadequate, or unsuitable for public use, including the ecological preservation and recreational use of surface water bodies, unless effluents from publicly-owned treatment works after adequate treatment are returned to the ground water consistent with acceptable technological standards.

(c) Availability of sums allotted to Puerto Rico

Notwithstanding any other provision of law, sums allotted to the Commonwealth of Puerto Rico under section 1285 of this title for fiscal year 1981 shall remain available for obligation for the fiscal year for which authorized and for the period of the next succeeding twenty-four months. Such sums and any unobligated funds available to Puerto Rico from allotments for fiscal years ending prior to October 1, 1981, shall be available for obligation by the Administrator of the Environmental Protection Agency only to fund the following systems: Aguadilla, Arecibo, Mayaguez, Carolina, and Camuy Hatillo. These funds may be used by the Commonwealth of Puerto Rico to fund the non-Federal share of the costs of such projects. To the extent that these funds are used to pay the non-Federal share, the Commonwealth of Puerto Rico shall repay to the Environmental Protection Agency such amounts on terms and conditions developed and approved by the Administrator in consultation with the Governor of the Commonwealth of Puerto Rico. Agreement on such terms and conditions, including the payment of interest to be determined by the Secretary of the Treasury, shall be reached prior to the use of these funds for the Commonwealth's non-Federal share. No Federal funds awarded under this provision shall be used to replace local governments funds previously expended on these projects.

(June 30, 1948, c. 758, Title II, § 202, as added Oct. 18, 1972, Pub.L. 92–500, § 2, 86 Stat. 834, and amended Dec. 27, 1977, Pub.L. 95–217, § 17, 91 Stat. 1571; Oct. 21, 1980, Pub.L. 96–483, § 9, 94 Stat. 2362; Dec. 29, 1981, Pub.L. 97–117, §§ 7, 8(a), (b), 95 Stat. 1625; Oct. 19, 1982, Pub.L. 97–357, Title V, § 501, 96 Stat. 1712; Feb. 4, 1987, Pub.L. 100–4, Title II, § 202(a)–(d), 101 Stat. 15, 16.)

CROSS REFERENCES

Allowance in construction grants for non-Federal funds expended during facility planning, etc., stage, see section 1281 of this title.

Grants to grantees who received an increased grant under this section, see section 1255 of this title.

Increase in Federal share for construction of treatment works utilizing innovative processes pursuant to this section, see section 1285 of this title.

Library References

Health and Environment ⚷25.7(21).
C.J.S. Health and Environment § 106 et seq.

§ 1283. Plans, specifications, estimates, and payments [FWPCA § 203]

(a) Submission; contractual nature of approval by Administrator; agreement on eligible costs; single grant

(1) Each applicant for a grant shall submit to the Administrator for his approval, plans, specifications, and estimates for each proposed project for the construction of treatment works for which a grant is applied for under section 1281(g)(1) of this title from funds allotted to the State under section 1285 of this title and which otherwise meets the requirements of

this chapter. The Administrator shall act upon such plans, specifications, and estimates as soon as practicable after the same have been submitted, and his approval of any such plans, specifications, and estimates shall be deemed a contractual obligation of the United States for the payment of its proportional contribution to such project.

(2) Agreement on eligible costs

(A) Limitation on modifications

Before taking final action on any plans, specifications, and estimates submitted under this subsection after the 60th day following February 4, 1987, the Administrator shall enter into a written agreement with the applicant which establishes and specifies which items of the proposed project are eligible for Federal payments under this section. The Administrator may not later modify such eligibility determinations unless they are found to have been made in violation of applicable Federal statutes and regulations.

(B) Limitation on effect

Eligibility determinations under this paragraph shall not preclude the Administrator from auditing a project pursuant to section 1361 of this title, or other authority, or from withholding or recovering Federal funds for costs which are found to be unreasonable, unsupported by adequate documentation, or otherwise unallowable under applicable Federal cost principles, or which are incurred on a project which fails to meet the design specifications or effluent limitations contained in the grant agreement and permit pursuant to section 1342 of this title for such project.

(3) In the case of a treatment works that has an estimated total cost of $8,000,000 or less (as determined by the Administrator), and the population of the applicant municipality is twenty-five thousand or less (according to the most recent United States census), upon completion of an approved facility plan, a single grant may be awarded for the combined Federal share of the cost of preparing construction plans and specifications, and the building and erection of the treatment works.

(b) Periodic payments

The Administrator shall, from time to time as the work progresses, make payments to the recipient of a grant for costs of construction incurred on a project. These payments shall at no time exceed the Federal share of the cost of construction incurred to the date of the voucher covering such payment plus the Federal share of the value of the materials which have been stockpiled in the vicinity of such construction in conformity to plans and specifications for the project.

(c) Final payments

After completion of a project and approval of the final voucher by the Administrator, he shall pay out of the appropriate sums the unpaid balance of the Federal share payable on account of such project.

(d) Projects eligible

Nothing in this chapter shall be construed to require, or to authorize the Administrator to require, that grants under this chapter for construction of treatment works be made only for projects which are operable units usable for sewage collection, transportation, storage, waste treatment, or for similar purposes without additional construction.

(e) Technical and legal assistance in administration and enforcement of contracts; intervention in civil actions

At the request of a grantee under this subchapter, the Administrator is authorized to provide technical and legal assistance in the administration and enforcement of any contract in connection with treatment works assisted under this subchapter, and to intervene in any civil action involving the enforcement of such a contract.

(f) Design/build projects

(1) Agreement

Consistent with State law, an applicant who proposes to construct waste water treatment works may enter into an agreement with the Administrator under this subsection providing for the preparation of construction plans and specifications and the erection of such treatment works, in lieu of proceeding under the other provisions of this section.

(2) Limitation on projects

Agreements under this subsection shall be limited to projects under an approved facility plan which projects are—

(A) treatment works that have an estimated total cost of $8,000,000 or less; and

(B) any of the following types of waste water treatment systems: aerated lagoons, trickling filters, stabilization ponds, land application systems, sand filters, and subsurface disposal systems.

(3) Required terms

An agreement entered into under this subsection shall—

(A) set forth an amount agreed to as the maximum Federal contribution to the project, based upon a competitively bid document of basic design data and applicable standard construction specifications and a determination of the federally eligible costs of the project at the applicable Federal share under section 1282 of this title;

(B) set forth dates for the start and completion of construction of the treatment works by the applicant and a schedule of payments of the Federal contribution to the project;

(C) contain assurances by the applicant that (i) engineering and management assistance will be provided to manage the project; (ii) the proposed treatment works will be an operable unit and will meet all the requirements of this subchapter; and (iii) not later than 1 year after the date specified as the date of completion of construction of the treatment works, the treatment works will be operating so as to meet the requirements of any applicable permit for such treatment works under section 1342 of this title;

(D) require the applicant to obtain a bond from the contractor in an amount determined necessary by the Administrator to protect the Federal interest in the project; and

(E) contain such other terms and conditions as are necessary to assure compliance with this subchapter (except as provided in paragraph (4) of this subsection).

(4) Limitation on application

Subsections (a), (b), and (c) of this section shall not apply to grants made pursuant to this subsection.

(5) Reservation to assure compliance

The Administrator shall reserve a portion of the grant to assure contract compliance until final project approval as defined by the Administrator. If the amount agreed to under paragraph (3)(A) exceeds the cost of designing and constructing the treatment works, the Administrator shall reallot the amount of the excess to the State in which such treatment works are located for the fiscal year in which such audit is completed.

(6) Limitation on obligations

The Administrator shall not obligate more than 20 percent of the amount allotted to a State for a fiscal year under section 1285 of this title for grants pursuant to this subsection.

(7) Allowance

The Administrator shall determine an allowance for facilities planning for projects constructed under this subsection in accordance with section 1281(*l*) of this title.

(8) Limitation on Federal contributions

In no event shall the Federal contribution for the cost of preparing construction plans and specifications and the building and erection of treatment works pursuant to this subsection exceed the amount agreed upon under paragraph (3).

(9) Recovery action

In any case in which the recipient of a grant made pursuant to this subsection does not comply with the terms of the agreement entered into under paragraph (3), the Administrator is authorized to take such action as may be necessary to recover the amount of the Federal contribution to the project.

(10) Prevention of double benefits

A recipient of a grant made pursuant to this subsection shall not be eligible for any other grants under this subchapter for the same project.

(June 30, 1948, c. 758, Title II, § 203, as added Oct. 18, 1972, Pub.L. 92–500, § 2, 86 Stat. 835, and amended Jan. 2, 1974, Pub.L. 93–243, § 2, 87 Stat. 1069; Dec. 27, 1977, Pub.L. 95–217, §§ 18, 19, 91 Stat. 1571, 1572; Oct. 21, 1980, Pub.L. 96–483, § 6, 94 Stat. 2362; Dec. 29, 1981, Pub.L. 97–117, § 9, 95 Stat. 1626; Feb. 4, 1987, Pub.L. 100–4, Title II, §§ 203, 204, 101 Stat. 16, 17.)

CROSS REFERENCES

Certification by State for priority of grant for construction of treatment works, see section 1284 of this title.

Sums obligated under this section to be credited to State to which last allotted, see section 1285 of this title.

Timetable for achievement of effluent limitations for publicly owned treatment works approved under this section, see section 1311 of this title.

Library References

Health and Environment ⚷25.7(21).
C.J.S. Health and Environment § 106 et seq.

§ 1284. Limitations and conditions [FWPCA § 204]

(a) Determinations by Administrator

Before approving grants for any project for any treatment works under section 1281(g)(1) of this title the Administrator shall determine—

(1) that any required areawide waste treatment management plan under section 1288 of this title (A) is being implemented for such area and the proposed treatment works are included in such plan, or (B) is being developed for such area and reasonable progress is being made toward its implementation and the proposed treatment works will be included in such plan;

(2) that (A) the State in which the project is to be located (i) is implementing any required plan under section 1313(e) of this title and the proposed treatment works are in conformity with such plan, or (ii) is developing such a plan and the proposed treatment works will be in conformity with such plan, and (B) such State is in compliance with section 1315(b) of this title;

(3) that such works have been certified by the appropriate State water pollution control agency as entitled to priority over such other works in the State in accordance with any applicable State plan under section 1313(e) of this title, except that any priority list developed pursuant to section 1313(e)(3)(H) of this title may be modified by such State in accordance with regulations promulgated by the Administrator to give higher priority for grants for the Federal share of the cost of preparing construction drawings and specifications for any treatment works utilizing processes and techniques meeting the guidelines promulgated under section 1314(d)(3) of this title and for grants for the combined Federal share of the cost of preparing construction drawings and specifications and the building and erection of any treatment works meeting the requirements of the next to the last sentence of section 1283(a) of this title which utilizes processes and techniques meeting the guidelines promulgated under section 1314(d)(3) of this title;.[1]

(4) that the applicant proposing to construct such works agrees to pay the non-Federal costs of such works and has made adequate provisions satisfactory to the Administrator for assuring proper and efficient operation, including the employment of trained management and operations personnel, and the maintenance of such works in accordance with a plan of operation approved by the State water pollution control agency or, as appropriate, the interstate agency, after construction thereof;

(5) that the size and capacity of such works relate directly to the needs to be served by such works, including sufficient reserve capacity. The amount of reserve capacity provided shall be approved by the Administrator on the basis of a comparison of the cost of constructing such reserves as a part of the works to be funded and the anticipated cost of providing expanded capacity at a date when such capacity will be required, after taking into account, in accordance with regulations promulgated by the Administrator, efforts to reduce total flow of sewage and unnecessary water consumption. The amount of reserve capacity eligible for a grant under this subchapter shall be determined by the Administrator taking into account the projected population and associated commercial and industrial establishments within the jurisdiction of the applicant to be served by such treatment works as identified in an approved facilities plan, an areawide plan under section 1288 of this title, or an applicable municipal master plan of development. For the purpose of this paragraph, section 1288 of this title, and any such plan, projected population shall be determined on the basis of the latest information available from the United States Department of Commerce or from the States as the Administrator, by regulation, determines appropriate. Beginning October 1, 1984, no grant shall be made under this subchapter to construct that portion of any treatment works providing reserve capacity in excess of existing needs (including existing needs of residential, commercial, industrial, and other users) on the date of approval of a grant for the erection, building, acquisition, alteration, remodeling, improvement, or extension of a project for secondary treatment or more stringent treatment or new interceptors and appurtenances, except that in no event shall reserve capacity of a facility and its related interceptors to which this subsection applies be in excess of existing needs on October 1, 1990. In any case in which an applicant proposes to provide reserve capacity greater than that eligible for Federal financial assistance under this subchapter, the incremental costs of the additional reserve capacity shall be paid by the applicant;

(6) that no specification for bids in connection with such works shall be written in such a manner as to contain proprietary, exclusionary, or discriminatory requirements other than those based upon performance, unless such requirements are necessary to test or demonstrate a specific thing or to provide for necessary interchangeability of parts and equipment. When in the judgment of the grantee, it is impractical or uneconomical to make a clear and accurate description of the technical requirements, a "brand name or equal" description may be used as a means to define the performance or other salient requirements of a procurement, and in doing so the grantee need not establish the existence of any source other than the brand or source so named.

(b) Additional determinations; issuance of guidelines; approval by Administrator; system of charges

(1) Notwithstanding any other provision of this subchapter, the Administrator shall not approve any grant for any treatment works under section 1281(g)(1) of this title after March 1, 1973, unless he shall first have determined that the applicant (A) has adopted or will adopt a system of charges to assure that each recipient of waste treatment services within the applicant's jurisdiction, as determined by the Administrator, will pay its proportionate share (except as otherwise provided in this paragraph) of the costs of operation and maintenance (including replacement) of any waste treatment services provided by the applicant; and (B) has legal, institutional, managerial, and financial capability to insure adequate construction, operation, and maintenance of treatment works

throughout the applicant's jurisdiction, as determined by the Administrator. In any case where an applicant which, as of December 27, 1977, uses a system of dedicated ad valorem taxes and the Administrator determines that the applicant has a system of charges which results in the distribution of operation and maintenance costs for treatment works within the applicant's jurisdiction, to each user class, in proportion to the contribution to the total cost of operation and maintenance of such works by each user class (taking into account total waste water loading of such works, the constituent elements of the wastes, and other appropriate factors), and such applicant is otherwise in compliance with clause (A) of this paragraph with respect to each industrial user, then such dedicated ad valorem tax system shall be deemed to be the user charge system meeting the requirements of clause (A) of this paragraph for the residential user class and such small non-residential user classes as defined by the Administrator. In defining small non-residential users, the Administrator shall consider the volume of wastes discharged into the treatment works by such users and the constituent elements of such wastes as well as such other factors as he deems appropriate. A system of user charges which imposes a lower charge for low-income residential users (as defined by the Administrator) shall be deemed to be a user charge system meeting the requirements of clause (A) of this paragraph if the Administrator determines that such system was adopted after public notice and hearing.

(2) The Administrator shall, within one hundred and eighty days after October 18, 1972, and after consultation with appropriate State, interstate, municipal, and intermunicipal agencies, issue guidelines applicable to payment of waste treatment costs by industrial and nonindustrial recipients of waste treatment services which shall establish (A) classes of users of such services, including categories of industrial users; (B) criteria against which to determine the adequacy of charges imposed on classes and categories of users reflecting all factors that influence the cost of waste treatment, including strength, volume, and delivery flow rate characteristics of waste; and (C) model systems and rates of user charges typical of various treatment works serving municipal-industrial communities.

(3) Approval by the Administrator of a grant to an interstate agency established by interstate compact for any treatment works shall satisfy any other requirement that such works be authorized by Act of Congress.

(4) A system of charges which meets the requirement of clause (A) of paragraph (1) of this subsection may be based on something other than metering the sewage or water supply flow of residential recipients of waste treatment services, including ad valorem taxes. If the system of charges is based on something other than metering the Administrator shall require (A) the applicant to establish a system by which the necessary funds will be available for the proper operation and maintenance of the treatment works; and (B) the applicant to establish a procedure under which the residential user will be notified as to that portion of his total payment which will be allocated to the cost of the waste treatment services.

(c) Applicability of reserve capacity restrictions to primary, secondary, or advanced waste treatment facilities or related interceptors

The next to the last sentence of paragraph (5) of subsection (a) of this section shall not apply in any case where a primary, secondary, or advanced waste treatment facility or its related interceptors has received a grant for erection, building, acquisition, alteration, remodeling, improvement, or extension before October 1, 1984, and all segments and phases of such facility and interceptors shall be funded based on a 20-year reserve capacity in the case of such facility and a 20-year reserve capacity in the case of such interceptors, except that, if a grant for such interceptors has been approved prior to December 29, 1981, such interceptors shall be funded based on the approved reserve capacity not to exceed 40 years.

(d) Engineering requirements; certification by owner and operator; contractual assurances, etc.

(1) A grant for the construction of treatment works under this subchapter shall provide that the engineer or engineering firm supervising construction or providing architect engineering services during construction shall continue its relationship to the grant applicant for a period of one year after the completion of construction and initial operation of such treatment works. During such period such engineer or engineering firm shall supervise operation of the treatment works, train operating personnel, and prepare curricula and training material for operating personnel. Costs associated with the implementation of this paragraph shall be eligible for Federal assistance in accordance with this subchapter.

(2) On the date one year after the completion of construction and initial operation of such treatment works, the owner and operator of such treatment works shall certify to the Administrator whether or not such treatment works meet the design specifications and effluent limitations contained in the grant agreement and permit pursuant to section 1342 of this title for such works. If the owner and operator of such treatment works cannot certify that such treat-

ment works meet such design specifications and effluent limitations, any failure to meet such design specifications and effluent limitations shall be corrected in a timely manner, to allow such affirmative certification, at other than Federal expense.

(3) Nothing in this section shall be construed to prohibit a grantee under this subchapter from requiring more assurances, guarantees, or indemnity or other contractual requirements from any party to a contract pertaining to a project assisted under this subchapter, than those provided under this subsection.

(June 30, 1948, c. 758, Title II, § 204, as added Oct. 18, 1972, Pub.L. 92–500, § 2, 86 Stat. 835, and amended Dec. 27, 1977, Pub.L. 95–217, §§ 20–24, 91 Stat. 1572, 1573; Oct. 21, 1980, Pub.L. 96–483, § 2(a), (b), 94 Stat. 2360, 2361; Dec. 29, 1981, Pub.L. 97–117, §§ 10(a), (b), 11, 12, 95 Stat. 1626, 1627; Feb. 4, 1987, Pub.L. 100–4, Title II, § 205(a)–(c), 101 Stat. 18.)

1 So in original. The par. ends with both a period and semicolon.

CROSS REFERENCES

Exemption of training grants from requirements of this section, see section 1259 of this title.

Grants for construction of privately owned treatment works, see section 1281 of this title.

Grants to any State from amount reserved to such State for the reasonable costs of administration, see section 1285 of this title.

State permit programs, compliance with this section, see section 1342 of this title.

CODE OF FEDERAL REGULATIONS

General pretreatment regulations for existing and new sources of pollution, see 40 CFR 403.1 et seq.

Library References

Health and Environment ⟹25.7(21).
C.J.S. Health and Environment § 106 et seq.

§ 1285. Allotment of grant funds [FWPCA § 205]

(a) Funds for fiscal years during period June 30, 1972, and September 30, 1977; determination of amount

Sums authorized to be appropriated pursuant to section 1287 of this title for each fiscal year beginning after June 30, 1972, and before September 30, 1977, shall be allotted by the Administrator not later than the January 1st immediately preceding the beginning of the fiscal year for which authorized, except that the allotment for fiscal year 1973 shall be made not later than 30 days after October 18, 1972. Such sums shall be allotted among the States by the Administrator in accordance with regulations promulgated by him, in the ratio that the estimated cost of constructing all needed publicly owned treatment works in each State bears to the estimated cost of construction of all needed publicly owned treatment works in all of the States. For the fiscal years ending June 30, 1973, and June 30, 1974, such ratio shall be determined on the basis of table III of House Public Works Committee Print No. 92–50. For the fiscal year ending June 30, 1975, such ratio shall be determined one-half on the basis of table I of House Public Works Committee Print Numbered 93–28 and one-half on the basis of table II of such print, except that no State shall receive an allotment less than that which it received for the fiscal year ending June 30, 1972, as set forth in table III of such print. Allotments for fiscal years which begin after the fiscal year ending June 30, 1975, shall be made only in accordance with a revised cost estimate made and submitted to Congress in accordance with section 1375(b) of this title and only after such revised cost estimate shall have been approved by law specifically enacted after October 18, 1972.

(b) Availability and use of funds allotted for fiscal years during period June 30, 1972, and September 30, 1977; reallotment

(1) Any sums allotted to a State under subsection (a) of this section shall be available for obligation under section 1283 of this title on and after the date of such allotment. Such sums shall continue available for obligation in such State for a period of one year after the close of the fiscal year for which such sums are authorized. Any amounts so allotted which are not obligated by the end of such one-year period shall be immediately reallotted by the Administrator, in accordance with regulations promulgated by him, generally on the basis of the ratio used in making the last allotment of sums under this section. Such reallotted sums shall be added to the last allotments made to the States. Any sum made available to a State by reallotment under this subsection shall be in addition to any funds otherwise allotted to such State for grants under this subchapter during any fiscal year.

(2) Any sums which have been obligated under section 1283 of this title and which are released by the payment of the final voucher for the project shall be immediately credited to the State to which such sums were last allotted. Such released sums shall be added to the amounts last allotted to such State and shall be immediately available for obligation in the same manner and to the same extent as such last allotment.

(c) Funds for fiscal years during period October 1, 1977, and September 30, 1981; funds for fiscal years 1982 to 1990; determination of amount

(1) Sums authorized to be appropriate pursuant to section 1287 of this title for the fiscal years during the period beginning October 1, 1977, and ending September 30, 1981, shall be allotted for each such year by the Administrator not later than the tenth day which begins after December 27, 1977. Notwithstanding any other provision of law, sums authorized for the fiscal years ending September 30, 1978, September 30, 1979, September 30, 1980, and September 30, 1981,

shall be allotted in accordance with table 3 of Committee Print Numbered 95–30 of the Committee on Public Works and Transportation of the House of Representatives.

(2) Sums authorized to be appropriated pursuant to section 1287 of this title for the fiscal years 1982, 1983, 1984, and 1985 shall be allotted for each such year by the Administrator not later than the tenth day which begins after December 29, 1981. Notwithstanding any other provision of law, sums authorized for the fiscal year ending September 30, 1982, shall be allotted in accordance with table 3 of Committee Print Numbered 95–30 of the Committee on Public Works and Transportation of the House of Representatives. Sums authorized for the fiscal years ending September 30, 1983, September 30, 1984, September 30, 1985, and September 30, 1986, shall be allotted in accordance with the following table:

States:	
Alabama	.011398
Alaska	.006101
Arizona	.006885
Arkansas	.006668
California	.072901
Colorado	.008154
Connecticut	.012487
Delaware	.004965
District of Columbia	.004965
Florida	.034407
Georgia	.017234
Hawaii	.007895
Idaho	.004965
Illinois	.046101
Indiana	.024566
Iowa	.013796
Kansas	.009201
Kentucky	.012973
Louisiana	.011205
Maine	.007788
Maryland	.024653
Massachusetts	.034608
Michigan	.043829
Minnesota	.018735
Mississippi	.009184
Missouri	.028257
Montana	.004965
Nebraska	.005214
Nevada	.004965
New Hampshire	.010186
New Jersey	.041654
New Mexico	.004965
New York	.113097
North Carolina	.018396
North Dakota	.004965
Ohio	.057383
Oklahoma	.008235
Oregon	.011515
Pennsylvania	.040377
Rhode Island	.006750
South Carolina	.010442
South Dakota	.004965
Tennessee	.014807
Texas	.038726
Utah	.005371
Vermont	.004965
Virginia	.020861
Washington	.017726
West Virginia	.015890
Wisconsin	.027557
Wyoming	.004965
Samoa	.000915
Guam	.000662
Northern Marianas	.000425
Puerto Rico	.013295
Pacific Trust Territories	.001305
Virgin Islands	.000531
United States totals	.999996

(3) Fiscal years 1987–1990

Sums authorized to be appropriated pursuant to section 1287 of this title for the fiscal years 1987, 1988, 1989, and 1990 shall be allotted for each such year by the Administrator not later than the 10th day which begins after February 4, 1987. Sums authorized for such fiscal years shall be allotted in accordance with the following table:

States:	
Alabama	.011309
Alaska	.006053
Arizona	.006831
Arkansas	.006616
California	.072333
Colorado	.008090
Connecticut	.012390
Delaware	.004965
District of Columbia	.004965
Florida	.034139
Georgia	.017100
Hawaii	.007833
Idaho	.004965
Illinois	.045741
Indiana	.024374
Iowa	.013688
Kansas	.009129
Kentucky	.012872
Louisiana	.011118
Maine	.007829
Maryland	.024461
Massachusetts	.034338
Michigan	.043487
Minnesota	.018589
Mississippi	.009112
Missouri	.028037
Montana	.004965

States:	
Nebraska	.005173
Nevada	.004965
New Hampshire	.010107
New Jersey	.041329
New Mexico	.004965
New York	.111632
North Carolina	.018253
North Dakota	.004965
Ohio	.056936
Oklahoma	.008171
Oregon	.011425
Pennsylvania	.040062
Rhode Island	.006791
South Carolina	.010361
South Dakota	.004965
Tennessee	.014692
Texas	.046226
Utah	.005329
Vermont	.004965
Virginia	.020698
Washington	.017588
West Virginia	.015766
Wisconsin	.027342
Wyoming	.004965
American Samoa	.000908
Guam	.000657
Northern Marianas	.000422
Puerto Rico	.013191
Pacific Trust Territories	.001295
Virgin Islands	.000527

(d) Availability and use of funds; reallotment

Sums allotted to the States for a fiscal year shall remain available for obligation for the fiscal year for which authorized and for the period of the next succeeding twelve months. The amount of any allotment not obligated by the end of such twenty-four-month period shall be immediately reallotted by the Administrator on the basis of the same ratio as applicable to sums allotted for the then current fiscal year, except that none of the funds reallotted by the Administrator for fiscal year 1978 and for fiscal years thereafter shall be allotted to any State which failed to obligate any of the funds being reallotted. Any sum made available to a State by reallotment under this subsection shall be in addition to any funds otherwise allotted to such State for grants under this subchapter during any fiscal year.

(e) Minimum allotment; additional appropriations; ratio of amount available

For the fiscal years 1978, 1979, 1980, 1981, 1982, 1983, 1984, 1985, 1986, 1987, 1988, 1989, and 1990, no State shall receive less than one-half of 1 per centum of the total allotment under subsection (c) of this section, except that in the case of Guam, Virgin Islands, American Samoa, and the Trust Territories not more than thirty-three one-hundredths of 1 per centum in the aggregate shall be allotted to all four of these jurisdictions. For the purpose of carrying out this subsection there are authorized to be appropriated, subject to such amounts as are provided in appropriation Acts, not to exceed $75,000,000 for each of fiscal years 1978, 1979, 1980, 1981, 1982, 1983, 1984, 1985, 1986, 1987, 1988, 1989, and 1990. If for any fiscal year the amount appropriated under authority of this subsection is less than the amount necessary to carry out this subsection, the amount each State receives under this subsection for such year shall bear the same ratio to the amount such State would have received under this subsection in such year if the amount necessary to carry it out had been appropriated as the amount appropriated for such year bears to the amount necessary to carry out this subsection for such year.

(f) Omitted

(g) Reservation of funds; State management assistance

(1) The Administrator is authorized to reserve each fiscal year not to exceed 2 per centum of the amount authorized under section 1287 of this title for purposes of the allotment made to each State under this section on or after October 1, 1977, except in the case of any fiscal year beginning on or after October 1, 1981, and ending before October 1, 1994, in which case the percentage authorized to be reserved shall not exceed 4 per centum.[1] or $400,000 whichever amount is the greater. Sums so reserved shall be available for making grants to such State under paragraph (2) of this subsection for the same period as sums are available from such allotment under subsection (d) of this section, and any such grant shall be available for obligation only during such period. Any grant made from sums reserved under this subsection which has not been obligated by the end of the period for which available shall be added to the amount last allotted to such State under this section and shall be immediately available for obligation in the same manner and to the same extent as such last allotment. Sums authorized to be reserved by this paragraph shall be in addition to and not in lieu of any other funds which may be authorized to carry out this subsection.

(2) The Administrator is authorized to grant to any State from amounts reserved to such State under this subsection, the reasonable costs of administering any aspects of sections 1281, 1283, 1284, and 1292 of this title the responsibility for administration of which the Administrator has delegated to such State. The Administrator may increase such grant to take into account the reasonable costs of administering an approved program under section 1342 or 1344 of this

title, administering a state-wide waste treatment management planning program under section 1288(b)(4) of this title, and managing waste treatment construction grants for small communities.

(h) Alternate systems for small communities

The Administrator shall set aside from funds authorized for each fiscal year beginning on or after October 1, 1978, a total (as determined by the Governor of the State) of not less than 4 percent nor more than 7½ percent of the sums allotted to any State with a rural population of 25 per centum or more of the total population of such State, as determined by the Bureau of the Census. The Administrator may set aside no more than 7½ percent of the sums allotted to any other State for which the Governor requests such action. Such sums shall be available only for alternatives to conventional sewage treatment works for municipalities having a population of three thousand five hundred or less, or for the highly dispersed sections of larger municipalities, as defined by the Administrator.

(i) Set-aside for innovative and alternative projects

Not less than ½ of 1 percent of funds allotted to a State for each of the fiscal years ending September 30, 1979, through September 30, 1990, under subsection (c) of this section shall be expended only for increasing the Federal share of grants for construction of treatment works utilizing innovative processes and techniques pursuant to section 1282(a)(2) of this title. Including the expenditures authorized by the preceding sentence, a total of 2 percent of the funds allotted to a State for each of the fiscal years ending September 30, 1979, and September 30, 1980, and 3 percent of the funds allotted to a State for the fiscal year ending September 30, 1981, under subsection (c) of this section shall be expended only for increasing grants for construction of treatment works pursuant to section 1282(a)(2) of this title. Including the expenditures authorized by the first sentence of this subsection, a total (as determined by the Governor of the State) of not less than 4 percent nor more than 7½ percent of the funds allotted to such State under subsection (c) of this section for each of the fiscal years ending September 30, 1982, through September 30, 1990, shall be expended only for increasing the Federal share of grants for construction of treatment works pursuant to section 1282(a)(2) of this title.

(j) Water quality management plan; reservation of funds for nonpoint source management

(1) The Administrator shall reserve each fiscal year not to exceed 1 per centum of the sums allotted and available for obligation to each State under this section for each fiscal year beginning on or after October 1, 1981, or $100,000, whichever amount is the greater.

(2) Such sums shall be used by the Administrator to make grants to the States to carry out water quality management planning, including, but not limited to—

(A) identifying most cost effective and locally acceptable facility and non-point measures to meet and maintain water quality standards;

(B) developing an implementation plan to obtain State and local financial and regulatory commitments to implement measures developed under subparagraph (A);

(C) determining the nature, extent, and causes of water quality problems in various areas of the State and interstate region, and reporting on these annually; and

(D) determining those publicly owned treatment works which should be constructed with assistance under this subchapter, in which areas and in what sequence, taking into account the relative degree of effluent reduction attained, the relative contributions to water quality of other point or nonpoint sources, and the consideration of alternatives to such construction, and implementing section 1313(e) of this title.

(3) In carrying out planning with grants made under paragraph (2) of this subsection, a State shall develop jointly with local, regional, and interstate entities, a plan for carrying out the program and give funding priority to such entities and designated or undesignated public comprehensive planning organizations to carry out the purposes of this subsection. In giving such priority, the State shall allocate at least 40 percent of the amount granted to such State for a fiscal year under paragraph (2) of this subsection to regional public comprehensive planning organizations in such State and appropriate interstate organizations for the development and implementation of the plan described in this paragraph. In any fiscal year for which the Governor, in consultation with such organizations and with the approval of the Administrator, determines that allocation of at least 40 percent of such amount to such organizations will not result in significant participation by such organizations in water quality management planning and not significantly assist in development and implementation of the plan described in this paragraph and achieving the goals of this chapter, the allocation to such organization may be less than 40 percent of such amount.

(4) All activities undertaken under this subsection shall be in coordination with other related provisions of this chapter.

(5) Nonpoint source reservation.—

In addition to the sums reserved under paragraph (1), the Administrator shall reserve each fiscal year for each State 1 percent of the sums allotted and available for obligation to such State under this section for each fiscal year beginning on or after October 1, 1986, or $100,000, whichever is greater, for the purpose of carrying out section 1329 of this title. Sums so reserved in a State in any fiscal year for which such State does not request the use of such sums, to the extent such sums exceed $100,000, may be used by such State for other purposes under this subchapter.

(k) New York City Convention Center

The Administrator shall allot to the State of New York from sums authorized to be appropriated for the fiscal year ending September 30, 1982, an amount necessary to pay the entire cost of conveying sewage from the Convention Center of the city of New York to the Newtown sewage treatment plant, Brooklyn-Queens area, New York. The amount allotted under this subsection shall be in addition to and not in lieu of any other amounts authorized to be allotted to such State under this chapter.

(*l*) Marine estuary reservation

(1) Reservation of funds

(A) General rule

Prior to making allotments among the States under subsection (c) of this section, the Administrator shall reserve funds from sums appropriated pursuant to section 1287 of this title for each fiscal year beginning after September 30, 1986.

(B) Fiscal years 1987 and 1988

For each of fiscal years 1987 and 1988 the reservation shall be 1 percent of the sums appropriated pursuant to section 1287 of this title for such fiscal year.

(C) Fiscal years 1989 and 1990

For each of fiscal years 1989 and 1990 the reservation shall be 1½ percent of the funds appropriated pursuant to section 1287 of this title for such fiscal year.

(2) Use of funds

Of the sums reserved under this subsection, two-thirds shall be available to address water quality problems of marine bays and estuaries subject to lower levels of water quality due to the impacts of discharges from combined storm water and sanitary sewer overflows from adjacent urban complexes, and one-third shall be available for the implementation of section 1330 of this title, relating to the national estuary program.

(3) Period of availability

Sums reserved under this subsection shall be subject to the period of availability for obligation established by subsection (d) of this section.

(4) Treatment of certain body of water

For purposes of this section and section 1281(n) of this title, Newark Bay, New Jersey, and the portion of the Passaic River up to Little Falls, in the vicinity of Beatties Dam, shall be treated as a marine bay and estuary.

(m) Discretionary deposits into State water pollution control revolving funds

(1) From construction grant allotments

In addition to any amounts deposited in a water pollution control revolving fund established by a State under subchapter VI of this chapter, upon request of the Governor of such State, the Administrator shall make available to the State for deposit, as capitalization grants, in such fund in any fiscal year beginning after September 30, 1986, such portion of the amounts allotted to such State under this section for such fiscal year as the Governor considers appropriate; except that (A) in fiscal year 1987, such deposit may not exceed 50 percent of the amounts allotted to such State under this section for such fiscal year, and (B) in fiscal year 1988, such deposit may not exceed 75 percent of the amounts allotted to such State under this section for this fiscal year.

(2) Notice requirement

The Governor of a State may make a request under paragraph (1) for a deposit into the water pollution control revolving fund of such State—

(A) in fiscal year 1987 only if no later than 90 days after February 4, 1987, and

(B) in each fiscal year thereafter only if 90 days before the first day of such fiscal year,

the State provides notice of its intent to make such deposit.

(3) Exception

Sums reserved under section 1285(j) of this title shall not be available for obligation under this subsection.

(June 30, 1948, c. 758, Title II, § 205, as added Oct. 18, 1972, Pub.L. 92–500, § 2, 86 Stat. 837, and amended Jan. 2, 1974, Pub.L. 93–243, § 1, 87 Stat. 1069; Dec. 27, 1977, Pub.L. 95–217, §§ 25, 26(a), 27, 28, 91 Stat. 1574, 1575; Oct. 21, 1980, Pub.L. 96–483, § 11, 94 Stat. 2363; Dec. 29, 1981, Pub.L. 97–117, §§ 8(c), 13–16, 95 Stat. 1625, 1627–1629; Feb. 4, 1987, Pub.L. 100–4, Title II, §§ 206(a)–(c), 207–210, 212(b), Title III, § 316(d), 101 Stat. 19–21, 27, 60.)

[1] So in original. Probably should be a comma.

Change of Name

Any reference in any provision of law enacted before Jan. 4, 1995, to the Committee on Public Works and Transportation of the House of Representatives treated as referring to the Committee on Transportation and Infrastructure of the House of Representatives, see section 1(a)(9) of Pub.L. 104–14, set out as a note preceding section 21 of Title 2, The Congress.

CROSS REFERENCES

Amount of grants for treatment works, see section 1282 of this title.
Availability of sums allotted to Puerto Rico, see section 1282 of this title.
Hudson River reclamation project, grants from funds allotted to State of New York under this section, see section 1266 of this title.
Submission of plans, specifications, etc., for proposed project for construction of treatment works, see section 1283 of this title.
Training grants from sums allocated to a State under this section, see section 1259 of this title.
Water quality problems, use of funds available under this section, see section 1281 of this title.

CODE OF FEDERAL REGULATIONS

Administration of federal contracts, grants or loans, see 40 CFR 15.1 et seq.
State and local assistance, see 40 CFR 35.001 et seq.
Water quality planning and management, see 40 CFR 130.0 et seq.

Library References

Health and Environment ⟹25.7(21).
C.J.S. Health and Environment § 106 et seq.

United States Supreme Court

Construction of word "sums" with phrase "all sums" within provisions of this section, see Train v. City of New York, 1975, 95 S.Ct. 839, 420 U.S. 35, 43 L.Ed.2d 1.

§ 1286. Reimbursement and advanced construction [FWPCA § 206]

(a) Publicly owned treatment works construction initiated after June 30, 1966, but before July 1, 1973; reimbursement formula

Any publicly owned treatment works in a State on which construction was initiated after June 30, 1966, but before July 1, 1973, which was approved by the appropriate State water pollution control agency and which the Administrator finds meets the requirements of section 1158 of this title in effect at the time of the initiation of construction shall be reimbursed a total amount equal to the difference between the amount of Federal financial assistance, if any, received under such section 1158 of this title for such project and 50 per centum of the cost of such project, or 55 per centum of the project cost where the Administrator also determines that such treatment works was constructed in conformity with a comprehensive metropolitan treatment plan as described in section 1158(f) of this title as in effect immediately prior to October 18, 1972. Nothing in this subsection shall result in any such works receiving Federal grants from all sources in excess of 80 per centum of the cost of such project.

(b) Publicly owned treatment works construction initiated between June 30, 1956, and June 30, 1966; reimbursement formula

Any publicly owned treatment works constructed with or eligible for Federal financial assistance under this Act in a State between June 30, 1956, and June 30, 1966, which was approved by the State water pollution control agency and which the Administrator finds meets the requirements of section 1158 of this title prior to October 18, 1972 but which was constructed without assistance under such section 1158 of this title or which received such assistance in an amount less than 30 per centum of the cost of such project shall qualify for payments and reimbursement of State or local funds used for such project from sums allocated to such State under this section in an amount which shall not exceed the difference between the amount of such assistance, if any, received for such project and 30 per centum of the cost of such project.

(c) Application for reimbursement

No publicly owned treatment works shall receive any payment or reimbursement under subsection (a) or (b) of this section unless an application for such assistance is filed with the Administrator within the one year period which begins on October 18, 1972. Any application filed within such one year period may be revised from time to time, as may be necessary.

(d) Allocation of funds

The Administrator shall allocate to each qualified project under subsection (a) of this section each fiscal year for which funds are appropriated under subsection (e) of this section an amount which bears the same ratio to the unpaid balance of the reimbursement due such project as the total of such funds for such year bears to the total unpaid balance of reimbursement due all such approved projects on the date of enactment of such appropriation. The Administrator shall allocate to each qualified project under subsection (b) of this section each fiscal year for which funds are appropriated under subsection (e) of this section an amount which bears the same ratio to the unpaid balance of the reimbursement due such project as the total of such funds for such year bears to the total unpaid balance of reimbursement due all such approved projects on the date of enactment of such appropriation.

(e) Authorization of appropriations

There is authorized to be appropriated to carry out subsection (a) of this section not to exceed $2,600,000,000 and, to carry out subsection (b) of this section, not to exceed $750,000,000. The authorizations contained in this subsection shall be the sole source of funds for reimbursements authorized by this section.

(f) Additional funds

(1) In any case where a substantial portion of the funds allotted to a State for the current fiscal year under this subchapter have been obligated under section 1281(g) of this title, or will be so obligated in a timely manner (as determined by the Administrator), and there is construction of any treatment works project without the aid of Federal funds and in accordance with all procedures and all requirements applicable to treatment works projects, except those procedures and requirements which limit construction of projects to those constructed with the aid of previously allotted Federal funds, the Administrator, upon his approval of an application made under this subsection therefor, is authorized to pay the Federal share of the cost of construction of such project when additional funds are allotted to the State under this subchapter if prior to the construction of the project the Administrator approves plans, specifications, and estimates therefor in the same manner as other treatment works projects. The Administrator may not approve an application under this subsection unless an authorization is in effect for the first fiscal year in the period for which the application requests payment and such requested payment for that fiscal year does not exceed the State's expected allotment from such authorization. The Administrator shall not be required to make such requested payment for any fiscal year—

(A) to the extent that such payment would exceed such State's allotment of the amount appropriated for such fiscal year; and

(B) unless such payment is for a project which, on the basis of an approved funding priority list of such State, is eligible to receive such payment based on the allotment and appropriation for such fiscal year.

To the extent that sufficient funds are not appropriated to pay the full Federal share with respect to a project for which obligations under the provisions of this subsection have been made, the Administrator shall reduce the Federal share to such amount less than 75 per centum as such appropriations do provide.

(2) In determining the allotment for any fiscal year under this subchapter, any treatment works project constructed in accordance with this section and without the aid of Federal funds shall not be considered completed until an application under the provisions of this subsection with respect to such project has been approved by the Administrator, or the availability of funds from which this project is eligible for reimbursement has expired, whichever first occurs.

(June 30, 1948, c. 758, Title II, § 206, as added Oct. 18, 1972, Pub.L. 92–500, § 2, 86 Stat. 836, and amended Dec. 28, 1973, Pub.L. 93–207, § 1(2), 87 Stat. 906; Dec. 27, 1977, Pub.L. 95–217, § 29(a), 91 Stat. 1576; Oct. 21, 1980, Pub.L. 96–483, § 5, 94 Stat. 2361.)

CROSS REFERENCES

Authorization of appropriations to carry out this chapter other than this section, see section 1376 of this title.
Authorization of appropriations to carry out this subchapter other than subsec. (e) of this section, see section 1287 of this title.
Loan guarantees, see section 1293 of this title.

Library References

Health and Environment ⇨25.7(21).
C.J.S. Health and Environment § 106 et seq.

§ 1287. Authorization of appropriations [FWPCA § 207]

There is authorized to be appropriated to carry out this subchapter, other than sections 1286(e), 1288 and 1289 of this title, for the fiscal year ending June 30, 1973, not to exceed $5,000,000,000, for the fiscal year ending June 30, 1974, not to exceed $6,000,000,000, and for the fiscal year ending June 30, 1975, not to exceed $7,000,000,000, and subject to such amounts as are provided in appropriation Acts, for the fiscal year ending September 30, 1977, $1,000,000,000 for the fiscal year ending September 30, 1978, $4,500,000,000 and for the fiscal years ending September 30, 1979, September 30, 1980, not to exceed $5,000,000,000; for the fiscal year ending September 30, 1981, not to exceed $2,548,837,000; and for the fiscal years ending September 30, 1982, September 30, 1983, September 30, 1984, and September 30, 1985, not to exceed $2,400,000,000 per fiscal year; and for each of the fiscal years ending September 30, 1986, September 30, 1987, and September 30, 1988, not to exceed $2,400,000,000; and for each of the fiscal years ending September 30, 1989, and September 30, 1990, not to exceed $1,200,000,000.

(June 30, 1948, c. 758, Title II, § 207, as added Oct. 18, 1972, Pub.L. 92–500, § 2, 86 Stat. 839, and amended Dec. 28, 1973, Pub.L. 93–207, § 1(3), 87 Stat. 906; Dec. 27, 1977, Pub.L. 95–217, § 30, 91 Stat. 1576; Aug. 13, 1981, Pub.L. 97–35, Title XVIII, § 1801(a), 95 Stat. 764; Dec. 29, 1981, Pub.L. 97–117, § 17, 95 Stat. 1630; Feb. 4, 1987, Pub.L. 100–4, Title II, § 211, 101 Stat. 21.)

CROSS REFERENCES

Authorization of appropriations to carry out this chapter other than this section, see section 1376 of this title.
Time for allotment of sums authorized to be appropriated pursuant to this section for fiscal years during period beginning Oct. 1, 1977, and ending Sept. 30, 1981, see section 1285 of this title.
Water quality problems, funds available, see section 1281 of this title.

Library References

Health and Environment ⚷25.7(21).
C.J.S. Health and Environment § 106 et seq.

§ 1288. Areawide waste treatment management [FWPCA § 208]

(a) Identification and designation of areas having substantial water quality control problems

For the purpose of encouraging and facilitating the development and implementation of areawide waste treatment management plans—

(1) The Administrator, within ninety days after October 18, 1972, and after consultation with appropriate Federal, State, and local authorities, shall by regulation publish guidelines for the identification of those areas which, as a result of urban-industrial concentrations or other factors, have substantial water quality control problems.

(2) The Governor of each State, within sixty days after publication of the guidelines issued pursuant to paragraph (1) of this subsection, shall identify each area within the State which, as a result of urban-industrial concentrations or other factors, has substantial water quality control problems. Not later than one hundred and twenty days following such identification and after consultation with appropriate elected and other officials of local governments having jurisdiction in such areas, the Governor shall designate (A) the boundaries of each such area, and (B) a single representative organization, including elected officials from local governments or their designees, capable of developing effective areawide waste treatment management plans for such area. The Governor may in the same manner at any later time identify any additional area (or modify an existing area) for which he determines areawide waste treatment management to be appropriate, designate the boundaries of such area, and designate an organization capable of developing effective areawide waste treatment management plans for such area.

(3) With respect to any area which, pursuant to the guidelines published under paragraph (1) of this subsection, is located in two or more States, the Governors of the respective States shall consult and cooperate in carrying out the provisions of paragraph (2), with a view toward designating the boundaries of the interstate area having common water quality control problems and for which areawide waste treatment management plans would be most effective, and toward designating, within one hundred and eighty days after publication of guidelines issued pursuant to paragraph (1) of this subsection, of a single representative organization capable of developing effective areawide waste treatment management plans for such area.

(4) If a Governor does not act, either by designating or determining not to make a designation under paragraph (2) of this subsection, within the time required by such paragraph, or if, in the case of an interstate area, the Governors of the States involved do not designate a planning organization within the time required by paragraph (3) of this subsection, the chief elected officials of local governments within an area may by agreement designate (A) the boundaries for such an area, and (B) a single representative organization including elected officials from such local governments, or their designees, capable of developing an areawide waste treatment management plan for such area.

(5) Existing regional agencies may be designated under paragraphs (2), (3), and (4) of this subsection.

(6) The State shall act as a planning agency for all portions of such State which are not designated under paragraphs (2), (3), or (4) of this subsection.

(7) Designations under this subsection shall be subject to the approval of the Administrator.

(b) Planning process

(1)(A) Not later than one year after the date of designation of any organization under subsection (a) of this section such organization shall have in operation a continuing areawide waste treatment management planning process consistent with section 1281 of this title. Plans prepared in accordance with this process shall contain alternatives for waste treatment management, and be applicable to all wastes generated within the area involved. The initial plan prepared in accordance with such process shall be certified by the Governor and submitted to the Administrator not later than two years after the planning process is in operation.

(B) For any agency designated after 1975 under subsection (a) of this section and for all portions of a State for which the State is required to act as the planning agency in accordance with subsection (a)(6) of this section, the initial plan prepared in accordance with such process shall be certified by the Governor and submitted to the Administrator not later than three years after the receipt of the initial grant award authorized under subsection (f) of this section.

(2) Any plan prepared under such process shall include, but not be limited to—

(A) the identification of treatment works necessary to meet the anticipated municipal and industrial waste treatment needs of the area over a twenty-year period, annually updated (including an analysis of alternative waste treatment systems), including any requirements for the acquisition of land for treatment purposes; the necessary waste water collection and urban storm water runoff systems; and a program to provide the necessary financial arrangements for the development of such treatment works, and an identification of open space and recreation opportunities that can be expected to result from improved water quality, including consideration of potential use of lands associated with treatment works and increased access to water-based recreation;

(B) the establishment of construction priorities for such treatment works and time schedules for the initiation and completion of all treatment works;

(C) the establishment of a regulatory program to—

(i) implement the waste treatment management requirements of section 1281(c) of this title,

(ii) regulate the location, modification, and construction of any facilities within such area which may result in any discharge in such area, and

(iii) assure that any industrial or commercial wastes discharged into any treatment works in such area meet applicable pretreatment requirements;

(D) the identification of those agencies necessary to construct, operate, and maintain all facilities required by the plan and otherwise to carry out the plan;

(E) the identification of the measures necessary to carry out the plan (including financing), the period of time necessary to carry out the plan, the costs of carrying out the plan within such time, and the economic, social, and environmental impact of carrying out the plan within such time;

(F) a process to (i) identify, if appropriate, agriculturally and silviculturally related nonpoint sources of pollution, including return flows from irrigated agriculture, and their cumulative effects, runoff from manure disposal areas, and from land used for livestock and crop production, and (ii) set forth procedures and methods (including land use requirements) to control to the extent feasible such sources;

(G) a process to (i) identify, if appropriate, mine-related sources of pollution including new, current, and abandoned surface and underground mine runoff, and (ii) set forth procedures and methods (including land use requirements) to control to the extent feasible such sources;

(H) a process to (i) identify construction activity related sources of pollution, and (ii) set forth procedures and methods (including land use requirements) to control to the extent feasible such sources;

(I) a process to (i) identify, if appropriate, salt water intrusion into rivers, lakes, and estuaries resulting from reduction of fresh water flow from any cause, including irrigation, obstruction, ground water extraction, and diversion, and (ii) set forth procedures and methods to control such intrusion to the extent feasible where such procedures and methods are otherwise a part of the waste treatment management plan;

(J) a process to control the disposition of all residual waste generated in such area which could affect water quality; and

(K) a process to control the disposal of pollutants on land or in subsurface excavations within such area to protect ground and surface water quality.

(3) Areawide waste treatment management plans shall be certified annually by the Governor or his designee (or Governors or their designees, where more than one State is involved) as being consistent with applicable basin plans and such areawide waste treatment management plans shall be submitted to the Administrator for his approval.

(4)(A) Whenever the Governor of any State determines (and notifies the Administrator) that consistency with a statewide regulatory program under section 1313 of this title so requires, the requirements of clauses (F) through (K) of paragraph (2) of this subsection shall be developed and submitted by the Governor to the Administrator for approval for application to a class or category of activity throughout such State.

(B) Any program submitted under subparagraph (A) of this paragraph which, in whole or in part, is to control the discharge or other placement of dredged or fill material into the navigable waters shall include the following:

(i) A consultation process which includes the State agency with primary jurisdiction over fish and wildlife resources.

(ii) A process to identify and manage the discharge or other placement of dredged or fill material which adversely affects navigable waters, which shall complement and be coordinated with a State program under section 1344 of this title conducted pursuant to this chapter.

(iii) A process to assure that any activity conducted pursuant to a best management practice will comply with the guidelines established under section 1344(b)(1) of this title, and sections 1317 and 1343 of this title.

(iv) A process to assure that any activity conducted pursuant to a best management practice can be terminated or modified for cause including, but not limited to, the following:

(I) violation of any condition of the best management practice;

(II) change in any activity that requires either a temporary or permanent reduction or elimination of the discharge pursuant to the best management practice.

(v) A process to assure continued coordination with Federal and Federal-State water-related planning and reviewing processes, including the National Wetlands Inventory.

(C) If the Governor of a State obtains approval from the Administrator of a statewide regulatory program which meets the requirements of subparagraph (B) of this paragraph and if such State is administering a permit program under section 1344 of this title, no person shall be required to obtain an individual permit pursuant to such section, or to comply with a general permit issued pursuant to such section, with respect to any appropriate activity within such State for which a best management practice has been approved by the Administrator under the program approved by the Administrator pursuant to this paragraph.

(D)(i) Whenever the Administrator determines after public hearing that a State is not administering a program approved under this section in accordance with the requirements of this section, the Administrator shall so notify the State, and if appropriate corrective action is not taken within a reasonable time, not to exceed ninety days, the Administrator shall withdraw approval of such program. The Administrator shall not withdraw approval of any such program unless he shall first have notified the State, and made public, in writing, the reasons for such withdrawal.

(ii) In the case of a State with a program submitted and approved under this paragraph, the Administrator shall withdraw approval of such program under this subparagraph only for a substantial failure of the State to administer its program in accordance with the requirements of this paragraph.

(c) Regional operating agencies

(1) The Governor of each State, in consultation with the planning agency designated under subsection (a) of this section, at the time a plan is submitted to the Administrator, shall designate one or more waste treatment management agencies (which may be an existing or newly created local, regional, or State agency or political subdivision) for each area designated under subsection (a) of this section and submit such designations to the Administrator.

(2) The Administrator shall accept any such designation, unless, within 120 days of such designation, he finds that the designated management agency (or agencies) does not have adequate authority—

(A) to carry out appropriate portions of an areawide waste treatment management plan developed under subsection (b) of this section;

(B) to manage effectively waste treatment works and related facilities serving such area in conformance with any plan required by subsection (b) of this section;

(C) directly or by contract, to design and construct new works, and to operate and maintain new and existing works as required by any plan developed pursuant to subsection (b) of this section;

(D) to accept and utilize grants, or other funds from any source, for waste treatment management purposes;

(E) to raise revenues, including the assessment of waste treatment charges;

(F) to incur short- and long-term indebtedness;

(G) to assure in implementation of an areawide waste treatment management plan that each participating community pays its proportionate share of treatment costs;

(H) to refuse to receive any wastes from any municipality or subdivision thereof, which does not comply with any provisions of an approved plan under this section applicable to such area; and

(I) to accept for treatment industrial wastes.

(d) Conformity of works with area plan

After a waste treatment management agency having the authority required by subsection (c) of this section has been designated under such subsection for an area and a plan for such area has been approved under subsection (b) of this section, the Administrator shall not make any grant for construction of a publicly owned treatment works under section 1281(g)(1) of this title within such area except to such designated agency and for works in conformity with such plan.

(e) Permits not to conflict with approved plans

No permit under section 1342 of this title shall be issued for any point source which is in conflict with a plan approved pursuant to subsection (b) of this section.

(f) Grants

(1) The Administrator shall make grants to any agency designated under subsection (a) of this section for payment of the reasonable costs of developing and operating a continuing areawide waste treatment management planning process under subsection (b) of this section.

(2) For the two-year period beginning on the date the first grant is made under paragraph (1) of this subsection to an agency, if such first grant is made before October 1, 1977, the amount of each such grant to such agency shall be 100 per centum of the costs of developing and operating a continuing areawide waste treatment management planning process under subsection (b) of this section, and thereafter the amount granted to such agency shall not exceed 75 per centum of such costs in each succeeding one-year period. In the case of any other grant made to an agency under such paragraph (1) of this subsection, the amount of such grant shall not exceed 75 per centum of the costs of developing and operating a continuing areawide waste treatment management planning process in any year.

(3) Each applicant for a grant under this subsection shall submit to the Administrator for his approval each proposal for which a grant is applied for under this subsection. The Administrator shall act upon such proposal as soon as practicable after it has been submitted, and his approval of that proposal shall be deemed a contractual obligation of the United States for the payment of its contribution to such proposal, subject to such amounts as are provided in appropriation Acts. There is authorized to be appropriated to carry out this subsection not to exceed $50,000,000 for the fiscal year ending June 30, 1973, not to exceed $100,000,000 for the fiscal year ending June 30, 1974, not to exceed $150,000,000 per fiscal year for the fiscal years ending June 30, 1975, September 30, 1977, September 30, 1978, September 30, 1979, and September 30, 1980, not to exceed $100,000,000 per fiscal year for the fiscal years ending September 30, 1981, and September 30, 1982, and such sums as may be necessary for fiscal years 1983 through 1990.

(g) Technical assistance by Administrator

The Administrator is authorized, upon request of the Governor or the designated planning agency, and without reimbursement, to consult with, and provide technical assistance to, any agency designated under subsection (a) of this section in the development of areawide waste treatment management plans under subsection (b) of this section.

(h) Technical assistance by Secretary of the Army

(1) The Secretary of the Army, acting through the Chief of Engineers, in cooperation with the Administrator is authorized and directed, upon request of the Governor or the designated planning organization, to consult with, and provide technical assistance to, any agency designed [1] under subsection (a) of this section in developing and operating a continuing areawide waste treatment management planning process under subsection (b) of this section.

(2) There is authorized to be appropriated to the Secretary of the Army, to carry out this subsection, not to exceed $50,000,000 per fiscal year for the fiscal years ending June 30, 1973, and June 30, 1974.

(i) State best management practices program

(1) The Secretary of the Interior, acting through the Director of the United States Fish and Wildlife Service, shall, upon request of the Governor of a State, and without reimbursement, provide technical assistance to such State in developing a statewide program for submission to the Administrator under subsection (b)(4)(B) of this section and in implementing such program after its approval.

(2) There is authorized to be appropriated to the Secretary of the Interior $6,000,000 to complete the National Wetlands Inventory of the United States, by December 31, 1981, and to provide information from such Inventory to States as it becomes available to assist such States in the development and operation of programs under this chapter.

(j) Agricultural cost sharing

(1) The Secretary of Agriculture, with the concurrence of the Administrator, and acting through the Soil Conservation Service and such other agencies of the Department of Agriculture as the Secretary may designate, is authorized and directed to establish and administer a program to enter into contracts, subject to such amounts as are provided in advance by appropriation acts, of not less than five years nor more than ten years with owners and operators having control of rural land for the purpose of installing and maintaining measures incorporating best management practices to control nonpoint source pollution for improved water quality in those States or areas for which the Administrator has approved a plan under subsection (b) of this section where the practices to which the contracts apply are certified by the management agency designated under subsection (c)(1) of this section to be consistent with such plans and will result in improved water quality. Such contracts may be entered into during the period ending not later than September 31, 1988. Under such contracts the land owner or operator shall agree—

(i) to effectuate a plan approved by a soil conservation district, where one exists, under this section for his farm, ranch, or other land substantially in accordance with the schedule outlined therein unless any requirement thereof is waived or modified by the Secretary;

(ii) to forfeit all rights to further payments or grants under the contract and refund to the United States all payments and grants received thereunder, with interest, upon his violation of the contract at any stage during the time he has control of the land if the Secretary, after considering the recommendations of the soil conservation district, where one exists, and the Administrator, determines that such violation is of such a nature as to warrant termination of the contract, or to make refunds or accept such payment adjustments as the Secretary may deem appropriate if he determines that the violation by the owner or operator does not warrant termination of the contract;

(iii) upon transfer of his right and interest in the farm, ranch, or other land during the contract period to forfeit all rights to further payments or grants under the contract and refund to the United States all payments or grants received thereunder, with interest, unless the transferee of any such land agrees with the Secretary to assume all obligations of the contract;

(iv) not to adopt any practice specified by the Secretary on the advice of the Administrator in the contract as a practice which would tend to defeat the purposes of the contract;

(v) to such additional provisions as the Secretary determines are desirable and includes in the contract to effectuate the purposes of the program or to facilitate the practical administration of the program.

(2) In return for such agreement by the landowner or operator the Secretary shall agree to provide technical assistance and share the cost of carrying out those conservation practices and measures set forth in the contract for which he determines that cost sharing is appropriate and in the public interest and which are approved for cost sharing by the agency designated to implement the plan developed under subsection (b) of this section. The portion of such cost (including labor) to be shared shall be that part which the Secretary determines is necessary and appropriate to effectuate the installation of the water quality management practices and measures under the contract, but not to exceed 50 per centum of the total cost of the measures set forth in the contract; except the Secretary may increase the matching cost share where he determines that (1) the main benefits to be derived from the measures are related to improving offsite water quality, and (2) the matching share requirement would place a burden on the landowner which would probably prevent him from participating in the program.

(3) The Secretary may terminate any contract with a landowner or operator by mutual agreement with the owner or operator if the Secretary determines that such termination would be in the public interest, and may agree to such modification of contracts previously entered into as he may determine to be desirable to carry out the purposes of the program or facilitate the practical administration thereof or to accomplish equitable treatment with respect to other conservation, land use, or water quality programs.

(4) In providing assistance under this subsection the Secretary will give priority to those areas and sources that have the most significant effect upon water quality. Additional investigations or plans may be made, where necessary, to supplement approved water quality management plans, in order to determine priorities.

(5) The Secretary shall, where practicable, enter into agreements with soil conservation districts, State soil and water conservation agencies, or State water quality agencies to administer all or part of the program established in this subsection under regulations developed by the Secretary. Such agreements shall provide for the submission of such reports as the Secretary deems necessary, and for payment by the United States of such portion of the costs incurred in the administration of the program as the Secretary may deem appropriate.

(6) The contracts under this subsection shall be entered into only in areas where the management agency designated under subsection (c)(1) of this section assures an adequate level of participation by owners and operators having control of rural land in such areas. Within such areas the local soil conservation district, where one exists, together with the Secretary of Agriculture, will determine the priority of assistance among individual land owners and operators to assure that the most critical water quality problems are addressed.

(7) The Secretary, in consultation with the Administrator and subject to section 1314(k) of this title, shall, not later than September 30, 1978, promulgate regulations for carrying out this subsection and for support and cooperation with other Federal and non-Federal agencies for implementation of this subsection.

(8) This program shall not be used to authorize or finance projects that would otherwise be eligible for assistance under the terms of Public Law 83–566 [16 U.S.C.A. § 1001 et seq.].

(9) There are hereby authorized to be appropriated to the Secretary of Agriculture $200,000,000 for fiscal year 1979, $400,000,000 for fiscal year 1980, $100,000,000 for fiscal year 1981, $100,000,000 for fiscal year 1982, and such sums as may be necessary for fiscal years 1983 through 1990, to carry out this subsection. The program authorized under this subsection shall be in addition to, and not in substitution of, other programs in such area authorized by this or any other public law.

(June 30, 1948, c. 758, Title II, § 208, as added Oct. 18, 1972, Pub.L. 92–500, § 2, 86 Stat. 839, and amended Dec. 27, 1977, Pub.L. 95–217, §§ 4(e), 31, 32, 33(a), 34, 35, 91 Stat. 1566, 1576–1579; Oct. 21, 1980, Pub.L. 96–483, § 1(d), (e), 94 Stat. 2360; Feb. 4, 1987, Pub.L. 100–4, Title I, § 101(d), (e), 101 Stat. 9.)

1 So in original probably should read "designated".

CROSS REFERENCES

Authorization of appropriations to carry out this chapter, other than subsec. (f) and (h), see section 1376 of this title.
Authorization of appropriations to carry out this subchapter other than this section, see section 1287 of this title.
Basin planning, see section 1289 of this title.
Continuing planning processes incorporating all elements of any areawide waste management plan under this section, see section 1313 of this title.
Designation of agency designated under this section for purposes of developing solid waste disposal plans, see section 6946 of Title 42. The Public Health and Welfare.
Exclusion from gross income of portion of payments received under this section, see section 126 of Title 26, Internal Revenue Code.
Grants to State agencies for development of pollution control plan for basin in conjunction with any areawide waste management plan developed pursuant to this section, see section 1252 of this title.
Grants to States for reasonable costs of administration of an approved program, see section 1285 of this title.
Identification and evaluation of nonpoint sources of pollution, see section 1314 of this title.
Limitations and conditions of grants, see section 1284 of this title.
"Municipality" defined for purposes of this chapter, see section 1362 of this title.
Non-prohibited discharge of dredged or fill material resulting from any activity with respect to which a State has an approved program under this section, see section 1344 of this title.
Reports to Congress on progress of plans developed under this section, see section 1375 of this title.

CODE OF FEDERAL REGULATIONS

General pretreatment regulations for existing and new sources of pollution, see 40 CFR 403.1 et seq.
Rural clean water program, see 7 CFR 634.1 et seq.
State and local assistance, see 40 CFR 35.001 et seq.
Water quality planning and management, see 40 CFR 130.0 et seq.

§ 1289. Basin planning [FWPCA § 209]

(a) Preparation of Level B plans

The President, acting through the Water Resources Council, shall, as soon as practicable, prepare a Level B plan under the Water Resources Planning Act [42 U.S.C.A. § 1962 et seq.] for all basins in the United States. All such plans shall be completed not later than January 1, 1980, except that priority in the preparation of such plans shall be given to those basins and portions thereof which are within those areas designated under paragraphs (2), (3), and (4) of subsection (a) of section 1288 of this title.

(b) Reporting requirements

The President, acting through the Water Resources Council, shall report annually to Congress on progress being made in carrying out this section. The first such report shall be submitted not later than January 31, 1973.

(c) Authorization of appropriations

There is authorized to be appropriated to carry out this section not to exceed $200,000,000.

(June 30, 1948, c. 758, Title II, § 209, as added Oct. 18, 1972, Pub.L. 92–500, § 2, 86 Stat. 843.)

CROSS REFERENCES

Authorization of appropriations to carry out this chapter other than this section, see section 1376 of this title.
Authorization of appropriations to carry out this subchapter other than this section, see section 1287 of this title.
Continuing planning processes resulting in plans for all navigable waters incorporating plans under this section, see section 1313 of this title.
Reports to Congress on progress of plans developed under this section, see section 1375 of this title.

LIBRARY REFERENCES

Health and Environment ⚷25.5(1).
C.J.S. Health and Environment § 61 et seq.

§ 1290. Annual survey [FWPCA § 210]

The Administrator shall annually make a survey to determine the efficiency of the operation and maintenance of treatment works constructed with grants made under this chapter, as compared to the efficiency planned at the time the grant was made. The results of such annual survey shall be included in the report required under section 1375(a) of this title.

(June 30, 1948, c. 758, Title II, § 210, as added Oct. 18, 1972, Pub.L. 92–500, § 2, 86 Stat. 843.)

CROSS REFERENCES

Reports to Congress containing a summary of the results of the survey taken under this section, see section 1375 of this title.

§ 1291. Sewage collection systems [FWPCA § 211]

(a) Existing and new systems

No grant shall be made for a sewage collection system under this subchapter unless such grant (1) is for replacement or major rehabilitation of an existing collection system and is necessary to the total integrity and performance of the waste treatment works servicing such community, or (2) is for a new collection system in an existing community with sufficient existing or planned capacity adequately to treat such collected sewage and is consistent with section 1281 of this title.

(b) Use of population density as test

If the Administrator uses population density as a test for determining the eligibility of a collector sewer for assistance it shall be only for the purpose of evaluating alternatives and determining the needs for such system in relation to ground or surface water quality impact.

(c) Pollutant discharges from separate storm sewer systems

No grant shall be made under this subchapter from funds authorized for any fiscal year during the period beginning October 1, 1977, and ending September 30, 1990, for treatment works for control of pollutant discharges from separate storm sewer systems.

(June 30, 1948, c. 758, Title II, § 211, as added Oct. 18, 1972, Pub.L. 92–500, § 2, 86 Stat. 843, and amended Dec. 27, 1977, Pub.L. 95–217, § 36, 91 Stat. 1581; Dec. 29, 1981, Pub.L. 97–117, § 2(b), 95 Stat. 1623; Feb. 4, 1987, Pub.L. 100–4, Title II, § 206(d), 101 Stat. 20.)

LIBRARY REFERENCES

Health and Environment ⚷25.7(21).
C.J.S. Health and Environment § 106 et seq.

§ 1292. Definitions [FWPCA § 212]

As used in this subchapter—

(1) The term "construction" means any one or more of the following: preliminary planning to determine the feasibility of treatment works, engineering, architectural, legal, fiscal, or economic investigations or studies, surveys, designs, plans, working drawings, specifications, procedures, field testing of innovative or alternative waste water treatment processes and techniques meeting guidelines promulgated under section 1314(d)(3) of this title, or other necessary actions, erection, building, acquisition, alteration, remodeling, improvement, or extension of treatment works, or the inspection or supervision of any of the foregoing items.

(2)(A) The term "treatment works" means any devices and systems used in the storage, treatment, recycling, and reclamation of municipal sewage or industrial wastes of a liquid nature to implement section 1281 of this title, or necessary to recycle or reuse water at the most economical cost over the estimated life of the works, including intercepting sewers, outfall sewers, sewage collection systems, pumping, power, and other equipment, and their appurtenances; extensions, improvements, remodeling, additions, and alterations thereof; elements essential to provide a reliable recycled supply such as standby treatment units and clear well facilities; and any works, including site acquisition of the land that will be an integral part of the treatment process (including land used for the storage of treated wastewater in land treatment systems prior to land application) or is used for ultimate disposal of residues resulting from such treatment.

(B) In addition to the definition contained in subparagraph (A) of this paragraph, "treatment works" means any other method or system for preventing, abating, reducing, storing, treating, separating, or disposing of municipal waste, including storm water runoff, or industrial waste, including waste in combined storm water and sanitary sewer systems. Any application for construction grants which includes wholly or in part such methods or systems shall, in accordance with guidelines published by the Administrator pursuant to subparagraph (C) of this paragraph, contain adequate data and analysis demonstrating such proposal to be, over the life of such works, the most cost efficient alternative to comply with sections 1311 or 1312 of this title, or the requirements of section 1281 of this title.

(C) For the purposes of subparagraph (B) of this paragraph, the Administrator shall, within one hundred and eighty days after October 18, 1972, publish and thereafter revise no less often than annually, guidelines for the evaluation of methods, including cost-effective analysis, described in subparagraph (B) of this paragraph.

(3) The term "replacement" as used in this subchapter means those expenditures for obtaining and installing equipment, accessories, or appurtenances during the useful life of the treatment works necessary to maintain the capacity and performance for which such works are designed and constructed.

(June 30, 1948, c. 758, Title II, § 212, as added Oct. 18, 1972, Pub.L. 92–500, § 2, 86 Stat. 844, and amended Dec. 27, 1977, Pub.L. 95–217, § 37, 91 Stat. 1581; Dec. 29, 1981, Pub.L. 97–117, § 8(d), 95 Stat. 1626.)

CROSS REFERENCES

Estimate of costs of treatment works as defined in this section, see section 1375 of this title.
Grants for projects within definition set forth in this section, see section 1281 of this title.
Grants to States for reasonable cost of administering this section, see section 1285 of this title.
Permits for disposal or use of sewage sludge, see section 1345 of this title.
Pretreatment standards for prevention of discharge of pollutant through treatment works as defined in this section, see section 1317 of this title.
Violation of permit conditions, see section 1342 of this title.

§ 1293. Loan guarantees [FWPCA § 213]

(a) State or local obligations issued exclusively to Federal Financing Bank for publicly owned treatment works; determination of eligibility of project by Administrator

Subject to the conditions of this section and to such terms and conditions as the Administrator determines to be necessary to carry out the purposes of this subchapter, the Administrator is authorized to guarantee, and to make commitments to guarantee, the principal and interest (including interest accruing between the date of default and the date of the payment in full of the guarantee) of any loan, obligation, or participation therein of any State, municipality, or intermunicipal or interstate agency issued directly and exclusively to the Federal Financing Bank to finance that part of the cost of any grant-eligible project for the construction of publicly owned treatment works not paid for with Federal financial assistance under this subchapter (other than this section), which project the Administrator has determined to be eligible for such financial assistance under this subchapter, including, but not limited to, projects eligible for reimbursement under section 1286 of this title.

(b) Conditions for issuance

No guarantee, or commitment to make a guarantee, may be made pursuant to this section—

(1) unless the Administrator certifies that the issuing body is unable to obtain on reasonable terms sufficient credit to finance its actual needs without such guarantee; and

(2) unless the Administrator determines that there is a reasonable assurance of repayment of the loan, obligation, or participation therein.

A determination of whether financing is available at reasonable rates shall be made by the Secretary of the Treasury with relationship to the current average yield on outstanding marketable obligations of municipalities of comparable maturity.

(c) Fees for application investigation and issuance of commitment guarantee

The Administrator is authorized to charge reasonable fees for the investigation of an application for a guarantee and for the issuance of a commitment to make a guarantee.

(d) Commitment for repayment

The Administrator, in determining whether there is a reasonable assurance of repayment, may require a commitment which would apply to such repayment. Such commitment may include, but not be limited to, any funds received by such grantee from the amounts appropriated under section 1286 of this title.

(June 30, 1948, c. 758, Title II, § 213, as added Oct. 19, 1976, Pub.L. 94–558, 90 Stat. 2639, and amended Oct. 21, 1980, Pub.L. 96–483, § 2(e), 94 Stat. 2361.)

CODE OF FEDERAL REGULATIONS

Administration of federal contracts, grants, or loans, see 40 CFR 15.1 et seq.

Loan guarantees for construction of treatment works, see 40 CFR 39.100 et seq.

LIBRARY REFERENCES

Health and Environment ⚷25.7(21).

C.J.S. Health and Environment § 106 et seq.

§ 1293a. Contained spoil disposal facilities

(a) Construction, operation, and maintenance; period; conditions; requirements

The Secretary of the Army, acting through the Chief of Engineers, is authorized to construct, operate, and maintain, subject to the provisions of subsection (c) of this section, contained spoil disposal facilities of sufficient capacity for a period not to exceed ten years, to meet the requirements of this section. Before establishing each such facility, the Secretary of the Army shall obtain the concurrence of appropriate local governments and shall consider the views and recommendations of the Administrator of the Environmental Protection Agency and shall comply with requirements of section 1171 of this title, and of the National Environmental Policy Act of 1969 [42 U.S.C.A. § 4321 et seq.]. Section 401 of this title shall not apply to any facility authorized by this section.

(b) Time for establishment; consideration of area needs; requirements

The Secretary of the Army, acting through the Chief of Engineers, shall establish the contained spoil disposal facilities authorized in subsection (a) of this section at the earliest practicable date, taking into consideration the views and recommendations of the Administrator of the Environmental Protection Agency as to those areas which, in the Administrator's judgment, are most urgently in need of such facilities and pursuant to the requirements of the National Environmental Policy Act of 1969 [42 U.S.C.A. § 4321 et seq.] and the Federal Water Pollution Control Act [33 U.S.C.A. § 1251 et seq.].

(c) Written agreement requirement; terms of agreement

Prior to construction of any such facility, the appropriate State or States, interstate agency, municipality, or other appropriate political subdivision of the State shall agree in writing to (1) furnish all lands, easements, and rights-of-way necessary for the construction, operation, and maintenance of the facility; (2) contribute to the United States 25 per centum of the construction costs, such amount to be payable either in cash prior to construction, in installments during construction, or in installments, with interest at a rate to be determined by the Secretary of the Treasury, as of the beginning of the fiscal year in which construction is initiated, on the basis of the computed average interest rate payable by the Treasury upon its outstanding marketable public obligations, which are neither due or callable for redemption for fifteen years from date of issue; (3) hold and save the United States free from damages due to construction, operation, and maintenance of the facility; and (4) except as provided in subsection (f) of this section, maintain the facility after completion of its use for disposal purposes in a manner satisfactory to the Secretary of the Army.

(d) Waiver of construction costs contribution from non-Federal interests; findings of participation in waste treatment facilities for general geographical area and compliance with water quality standards; waiver of payments in event of written agreement before occurrence of findings

The requirement for appropriate non-Federal interest or interests to furnish an agreement to contribute 25 per centum of the construction costs as set forth in subsection (c) of this section shall be waived by the Secretary of the Army upon a finding by the Administrator of the Environmental Protection Agency that for the area to which such construction applies, the State or States involved, interstate agency, municipality, and other appropriate political subdivision of the State and industrial concerns are participating in and in compliance with an approved plan for the general geographical area of the dredging activity for construction, modification, expansion, or rehabilitation of waste treatment facilities and the Administrator has found that applicable water quality standards are not being violated. In the event such findings occur after the appropriate non-Federal interest or interests have entered into the agreement required by subsection (c) of this section, any payments due after the date of such findings as part of the required local contribution of 25 per centum of the construction costs shall be waived by the Secretary of the Army.

(e) Federal payment of costs for disposal of dredged spoil from project

Notwithstanding any other provision of law, all costs of disposal of dredged spoil from the project for the Great Lakes connecting channels, Michigan, shall be borne by the United States.

(f) Title to lands; easements, and rights-of-way; retention by non-Federal interests; conveyance of facilities; agreement of transferee

The participating non-Federal interest or interests shall retain title to all lands, easements, and rights-of-way furnished by it pursuant to subsection (c) of this section. A spoil disposal facility owned by a non-Federal interest or interests may be conveyed to another party only after completion of the facility's use for disposal purposes and after the transferee agrees in writing to use or maintain the facility in a manner which the Secretary of the Army determines to be satisfactory.

(g) Federal licenses or permits; charges; remission of charge

Any spoil disposal facilities constructed under the provisions of this section shall be made available to Federal licensees or permittees upon payment of an appropriate charge for such use. Twenty-five per centum of such charge shall be remitted to the participating non-Federal interest or interests except for those excused from contributing to the construction costs under subsections (d) and (e) of this section.

(h) Provisions applicable to Great Lakes and their connecting channels

This section, other than subsection (i), shall be applicable only to the Great Lakes and their connecting channels.

(i) Research, study, and experimentation program relating to dredged spoil extended to navigable waters, etc.; cooperative program; scope of program; utilization of facilities and personnel of Federal agency

The Chief of Engineers, under the direction of the Secretary of the Army, is hereby authorized to extend to all navigable waters, connecting channels, tributary streams, other waters of the United States and waters contiguous to the United States, a comprehensive program of research, study, and experimentation relating to dredged spoil. This program shall be carried out in cooperation with other Federal and State agencies, and shall include, but not be limited to, investigations on the characteristics of dredged spoil, and alternative methods of its disposal. To the extent that such study shall include the effects of such dredge spoil on water quality, the facilities and personnel of the Environmental Protection Agency shall be utilized.

(j) Period for depositing dredged materials

The Secretary of the Army, acting through the Chief of Engineers, is authorized to continue to deposit dredged materials into a contained spoil disposal facility constructed under this section until the Secretary determines that such facility is no longer needed for such purpose or that such facility is completely full.

(k) Study and monitoring program

(1) Study

The Secretary of the Army, acting through the Chief of Engineers, shall conduct a study of the materials disposed of in contained spoil disposal facilities constructed under this section for the purpose of determining whether or not toxic pollutants are present in such facilities and for the purpose of determining the concentration levels of each of such pollutants in such facilities.

(2) Report

Not later than 1 year after November 17, 1988, the Secretary shall transmit to Congress a report on the results of the study conducted under paragraph (1).

(3) Inspection and monitoring program

The Secretary shall conduct a program to inspect and monitor contained spoil disposal facilities constructed under this section for the purpose of determining whether or not toxic pollutants are leaking from such facilities.

(4) Toxic pollutant defined

For purposes of this subsection, the term "toxic pollutant" means those toxic pollutants referred to in sections 1311(b)(2)(C) and 1311(b)(2)(D) of this title and such other pollutants as the Secretary, in consultation with the Administrator of the Environmental Protection Agency, determines are appropriate based on their effects on human health and the environment.

(Dec. 31, 1970, Pub.L. 91–611, Title I, § 123, 84 Stat. 1823, March 7, 1974, Pub.L. 93–251, Title I, § 23, 88 Stat. 20; Pub.L. 100–676, § 24, Nov. 17, 1988, 102 Stat. 4027.)

Codification

Section was not enacted as part of the Federal Water Pollution Control Act, which comprises this chapter.

LIBRARY REFERENCES

Health and Environment ⚖25.7(21).
C.J.S. Health and Environment § 106 et seq.

§ 1294. Public information and education on recycling and reuse of wastewater, use of land treatment, and reduction of wastewater volume [FWPCA § 214]

The Administrator shall develop and operate within one year of December 27, 1977, a continuing program of public information and education on recycling and reuse of wastewater (including sludge), the use of land treatment, and methods for the reduction of wastewater volume.

(June 30, 1948, c. 758, Title II, § 214, as added Dec. 27, 1977, Pub.L. 95–217, § 38, 91 Stat. 1581.)

LAW REVIEW COMMENTARIES

From elephants to mice: The development of EBMUD's program to control small source wastewater discharges. Raoul Stewardson, 20 Ecology L.Q. 441 (1993).

§ 1295. Requirements for American materials [FWPCA § 215]

Notwithstanding any other provision of law, no grant for which application is made after February 1, 1978, shall be made under this subchapter for any treatment works unless only such unmanufactured articles, materials, and supplies as have been mined or produced in the United States, and only such manufactured articles, materials, and supplies as have been manufactured in the United States, substantially all from articles, materials, or supplies mined, produced, or manufactured, as the case may be, in the United States will be used in such treatment works. This section shall not apply in any case where the Administrator determines, based upon those factors the Administrator deems relevant, including the available resources of the agency, it to be inconsistent with the public interest (including multilateral government procurement agreements) or the cost to be unreasonable, or if articles, materials, or supplies of the class or kind to be used or the articles, materials, or supplies from which they are manufactured are not mined, produced, or manufactured, as the case may be, in the United States in sufficient and reasonably available commercial quantities and of a satisfactory quality.

(June 30, 1948, c. 758, Title II, § 215, as added Dec. 27, 1977, Pub.L. 95–217, § 39, 91 Stat. 1581.)

§ 1296. Determination of priority of projects [FWPCA § 216]

Notwithstanding any other provision of this chapter, the determination of the priority to be given each category of projects for construction of publicly owned treatment works within each State shall be made solely by that State, except that if the Administrator, after a public hearing, determines that a specific project will not result in compliance with the enforceable requirements of this chapter, such project shall be removed from the State's priority list and such State shall submit a revised priority list. These categories shall include, but not be limited to (A) secondary treatment, (B) more stringent treatment, (C) infiltration-in-flow correction, (D) major sewer system rehabilitation, (E) new collector sewers and appurtenances, (F) new interceptors and appurtenances, and (G) correction of combined sewer overflows. Not less than 25 per centum of funds allocated to a State in any fiscal year under this subchapter for construction of publicly owned treatment works in such State shall be obligated for those types of projects referred to in clauses (D), (E), (F), and (G) of this section, if such projects are on such State's priority list for that year and are otherwise eligible for funding in that fiscal year. It is the policy of Congress that projects for wastewater treatment and management undertaken with Federal financial assistance under this chapter by any State, municipality, or intermunicipal or interstate agency shall be projects which, in the estimation of the State, are designed to achieve optimum water quality management, consistent with the public health and water quality goals and requirements of this chapter.

(June 30, 1948, c. 758, Title II, § 216, as added Dec. 27, 1977, Pub.L. 95–217, § 40, 91 Stat. 1582, and amended Dec. 29, 1981, Pub.L. 97–117, § 18, 95 Stat. 1630.)

§ 1297. Guidelines for cost-effectiveness analysis [FWPCA § 217]

Any guidelines for cost-effectiveness analysis published by the Administrator under this subchapter shall provide for the identification and selection of cost effective alternatives to comply with the objectives and goals of this chapter and sections 1281(b), 1281(d), 1281(g)(2)(A), and 1311(b)(2)(B) of this title.

(June 30, 1948, c. 758, Title II, § 217, as added Dec. 27, 1977, Pub.L. 95–217, § 41, 91 Stat. 1582.)

§ 1298. Cost effectiveness [FWPCA § 218]

(a) Congressional statement of policy

It is the policy of Congress that a project for waste treatment and management undertaken with Federal financial assistance under this chapter by any State, municipality, or intermunicipal or interstate agency shall be considered as an overall waste treatment system for waste treatment and management, and shall be that system which constitutes the most economical and cost-effective combination of devices and systems used in the storage, treatment, recycling, and reclamation of municipal sewage or industrial wastes of a liquid nature to implement section 1281 of this title, or necessary to recycle or reuse water at the most economical cost over the estimated life of the works, including intercepting sewers, outfall sewers, sewage collection systems, pumping power, and other equipment, and their appurtenances; extension, improvements, remodeling, additions, and alterations thereof; elements essential to provide a reliable recycled supply such as standby treatment units and clear well facilities; and any works, including site acquisition of the land that will be an integral part of the treatment process (including land use for the storage of treated wastewater in land treatment systems prior to land application) or which is used for ultimate disposal of residues resulting from such treatment; water efficiency measures and devices; and any other method or system for preventing, abating, reducing, storing, treating, separating, or disposing of municipal waste, including storm water runoff, or industrial waste, including waste in combined storm water and sanitary sewer systems; to meet the requirements of this chapter.

(b) Determination by Administrator as prerequisite to approval of grant

In accordance with the policy set forth in subsection (a) of this section, before the Administrator approves any grant to any State, municipality, or intermunicipal or interstate agency for the erection, building, acquisition, alteration, remodeling, improvement, or extension of any treatment works the Administrator shall determine that the facilities plan of which such treatment works are a part constitutes the most economical and cost-effective combination of treatment works over the life of the project to meet the requirements of this chapter, including, but not limited to, consideration of construction costs, operation, maintenance, and replacement costs.

(c) Value engineering review

In furtherance of the policy set forth in subsection (a) of this section, the Administrator shall require value engineering review in connection with any treatment works, prior to approval of any grant for the erection, building, acquisition, alteration, remodeling, improvement, or extension of such treatment works, in any case in which the cost of such erection, building, acquisition, alteration, remodeling, improvement, or extension is projected to be in excess of $10,000,000. For purposes of this subsection, the term "value engineering review" means a specialized cost control technique which uses a systematic and creative approach to identify and to focus on unnecessarily high cost in a project in order to arrive at a cost saving without sacrificing the reliability or efficiency of the project.

(d) Projects affected

This section applies to projects for waste treatment and management for which no treatment works including a facilities plan for such project have received Federal financial assistance for the preparation of construction plans and specifications under this chapter before December 29, 1981.

(June 30, 1948, c. 758, Title II, § 218, as added Dec. 29, 1981, Pub.L. 97–117, § 19, 95 Stat. 1630.)

LIBRARY REFERENCES

Health and Environment ⟹25.7(1).
C.J.S. Health and Environment § 106 et seq.

§ 1299. State certification of projects [FWPCA § 219]

Whenever the Governor of a State which has been delegated sufficient authority to administer the construction grant program under this subchapter in that State certifies to the Administrator that a grant application meets applicable requirements of Federal and State law for assistance under this subchapter, the

Administrator shall approve or disapprove such application within 45 days of the date of receipt of such application. If the Administrator does not approve or disapprove such application within 45 days of receipt, the application shall be deemed approved. If the Administrator disapproves such application the Administrator shall state in writing the reasons for such disapproval. Any grant approved or deemed approved under this section shall be subject to amounts provided in appropriation Acts.

(June 30, 1948, c. 758, Title II, § 219, as added Dec. 29, 1981, Pub.L. 97–117, § 20, 95 Stat. 1630.)

LIBRARY REFERENCES

Health and Environment ⚷25.7(10).
C.J.S. Health and Environment § 106 et seq.

SUBCHAPTER III—STANDARDS AND ENFORCEMENT

§ 1311. Effluent limitations [FWPCA § 301]

(a) Illegality of pollutant discharges except in compliance with law

Except as in compliance with this section and sections 1312, 1316, 1317, 1328, 1342, and 1344 of this title, the discharge of any pollutant by any person shall be unlawful.

(b) Timetable for achievement of objectives

In order to carry out the objective of this chapter there shall be achieved—

(1)(A) not later than July 1, 1977, effluent limitations for point sources, other than publicly owned treatment works, (i) which shall require the application of the best practicable control technology currently available as defined by the Administrator pursuant to section 1314(b) of this title, or (ii) in the case of a discharge into a publicly owned treatment works which meets the requirements of subparagraph (B) of this paragraph, which shall require compliance with any applicable pretreatment requirements and any requirements under section 1317 of this title; and

(B) for publicly owned treatment works in existence on July 1, 1977, or approved pursuant to section 1283 of this title prior to June 30, 1974 (for which construction must be completed within four years of approval), effluent limitations based upon secondary treatment as defined by the Administrator pursuant to section 1314(d)(1) of this title; or,

(C) not later than July 1, 1977, any more stringent limitation, including those necessary to meet water quality standards, treatment standards, or schedules of compliance, established pursuant to any State law or regulations (under authority preserved by section 1370 of this title) or any other Federal law or regulation, or required to implement any applicable water quality standard established pursuant to this chapter.

(2)(A) for pollutants identified in subparagraphs (C), (D), and (F) of this paragraph, effluent limitations for categories and classes of point sources, other than publicly owned treatment works, which (i) shall require application of the best available technology economically achievable for such category or class, which will result in reasonable further progress toward the national goal of eliminating the discharge of all pollutants, as determined in accordance with regulations issued by the Administrator pursuant to section 1314(b)(2) of this title, which such effluent limitations shall require the elimination of discharges of all pollutants if the Administrator finds, on the basis of information available to him (including information developed pursuant to section 1325 of this title), that such elimination is technologically and economically achievable for a category or class of point sources as determined in accordance with regulations issued by the Administrator pursuant to section 1314(b)(2) of this title, or (ii) in the case of the introduction of a pollutant into a publicly owned treatment works which meets the requirements of subparagraph (B) of this paragraph, shall require compliance with any applicable pretreatment requirements and any other requirement under section 1317 of this title;

(B) Repealed. Pub.L. 97–117, § 21(b), Dec. 29, 1981, 95 Stat. 1632.

(C) with respect to all toxic pollutants referred to in table 1 of Committee Print Numbered 95–30 of the Committee on Public Works and Transportation of the House of Representatives compliance with effluent limitations in accordance with subparagraph (A) of this paragraph as expeditiously as practicable but in no case later than three years after the date such limitations are promulgated under section 1314(b) of this title, and in no case later than March 31, 1989;

(D) for all toxic pollutants listed under paragraph (1) of subsection (a) of section 1317 of this title which are not referred to in subparagraph (C) of this paragraph compliance with effluent limitations in accordance with subparagraph (A) of this paragraph as expeditiously as practicable, but in no case later than three years after the date such limitations are promulgated under section 1314(b) of this title, and in no case later than March 31, 1989;

(E) as expeditiously as practicable but in no case later than three years after the date such limitations are promulgated under section 1314(b) of this title, and in no case later than March 31, 1989, compliance with effluent limitations for categories and classes of point sources, other than publicly owned treatment works, which in the case of pollutants identified pursuant to section 1314(a)(4) of this title shall require application of the best conventional pollutant control technology as determined in accordance with regulations issued by the Administrator pursuant to section 1314(b)(4) of this title; and

(F) for all pollutants (other than those subject to subparagraphs (C), (D), or (E) of this paragraph) compliance with effluent limitations in accordance with subparagraph (A) of this paragraph as expeditiously as practicable but in no case later than 3 years after the date such limitations are established, and in no case later than March 31, 1989.

(3)(A) for effluent limitations under paragraph (1)(A)(i) of this subsection promulgated after January 1, 1982, and requiring a level of control substantially greater or based on fundamentally different control technology than under permits for an industrial category issued before such date, compliance as expeditiously as practicable but in no case later than three years after the date such limitations are promulgated under section 1314(b) of this title, and in no case later than March 31, 1989; and

(B) for any effluent limitation in accordance with paragraph (1)(A)(i), (2)(A)(i), or (2)(E) of this subsection established only on the basis of section 1342(a)(1) of this title in a permit issued after February 4, 1987, compliance as expeditiously as practicable but in no case later than three years after the date such limitations are established, and in no case later than March 31, 1989.

(c) Modification of timetable

The Administrator may modify the requirements of subsection (b)(2)(A) of this section with respect to any point source for which a permit application is filed after July 1, 1977, upon a showing by the owner or operator of such point source satisfactory to the Administrator that such modified requirements (1) will represent the maximum use of technology within the economic capability of the owner or operator; and (2) will result in reasonable further progress toward the elimination of the discharge of pollutants.

(d) Review and revision of effluent limitations

Any effluent limitation required by paragraph (2) of subsection (b) of this section shall be reviewed at least every five years and, if appropriate, revised pursuant to the procedure established under such paragraph.

(e) All point discharge source application of effluent limitations

Effluent limitations established pursuant to this section or section 1312 of this title shall be applied to all point sources of discharge of pollutants in accordance with the provisions of this chapter.

(f) Illegality of discharge of radiological, chemical, or biological warfare agents, high-level radioactive waste, or medical waste

Notwithstanding any other provisions of this chapter it shall be unlawful to discharge any radiological, chemical, or biological warfare agent, any high-level radioactive waste, or any medical waste into the navigable waters.

(g) Modifications for certain nonconventional pollutants

(1) General authority

The Administrator, with the concurrence of the State, may modify the requirements of subsection (b)(2)(A) of this section with respect to the discharge from any point source of ammonia, chlorine, color, iron, and total phenols (4AAP) (when determined by the Administrator to be a pollutant covered by subsection (b)(2)(F) of this section) and any other pollutant which the Administrator lists under paragraph (4) of this subsection.

(2) Requirements for granting modifications

A modification under this subsection shall be granted only upon a showing by the owner or operator of a point source satisfactory to the Administrator that—

(A) such modified requirements will result at a minimum in compliance with the requirements of subsection (b)(1)(A) or (C) of this section, whichever is applicable;

(B) such modified requirements will not result in any additional requirements on any other point or nonpoint source; and

(C) such modification will not interfere with the attainment or maintenance of that water quality which shall assure protection of public water supplies, and the protection and propagation of a balanced population of shellfish, fish, and wildlife, and allow recreational activities, in and on the water and such modification will not result in the discharge of pollutants in quantities which may reasonably be anticipated to pose an unacceptable risk to human health or the environment because of bioaccumulation, persistency in the environment, acute toxicity, chronic toxicity (including carcinogenicity, mutagenicity or teratogenicity), or synergistic propensities.

(3) Limitation on authority to apply for subsection (c) modification

If an owner or operator of a point source applies for a modification under this subsection with respect to the discharge of any pollutant, such owner or operator shall be eligible to apply for modification under subsection (c) of this section with respect to such pollutant only during the same time period as he is eligible to apply for a modification under this subsection.

(4) Procedures for listing additional pollutants

(A) General authority

Upon petition of any person, the Administrator may add any pollutant to the list of pollutants for which modification under this section is authorized (except for pollutants identified pursuant to section 1314(a)(4) of this title, toxic pollutants subject to section 1317(a) of this title, and the thermal component of discharges) in accordance with the provisions of this paragraph.

(B) Requirements for listing

(i) Sufficient information

The person petitioning for listing of an additional pollutant under this subsection shall submit to the Administrator sufficient information to make the determinations required by this subparagraph.

(ii) Toxic criteria determination

The Administrator shall determine whether or not the pollutant meets the criteria for listing as a toxic pollutant under section 1317(a) of this title.

(iii) Listing as toxic pollutant

If the Administrator determines that the pollutant meets the criteria for listing as a toxic pollutant under section 1317(a) of this title, the Administrator shall list the pollutant as a toxic pollutant under section 1317(a) of this title.

(iv) Nonconventional criteria determination

If the Administrator determines that the pollutant does not meet the criteria for listing as a toxic pollutant under such section and determines that adequate test methods and sufficient data are available to make the determinations required by paragraph (2) of this subsection with respect to the pollutant, the Administrator shall add the pollutant to the list of pollutants specified in paragraph (1) of this subsection for which modifications are authorized under this subsection.

(C) Requirements for filing of petitions

A petition for listing of a pollutant under this paragraph—

(i) must be filed not later than 270 days after the date of promulgation of an applicable effluent guideline under section 1314 of this title;

(ii) may be filed before promulgation of such guideline; and

(iii) may be filed with an application for a modification under paragraph (1) with respect to the discharge of such pollutant.

(D) Deadline for approval of petition

A decision to add a pollutant to the list of pollutants for which modifications under this subsection are authorized must be made within 270 days after the date of promulgation of an applicable effluent guideline under section 1314 of this title.

(E) Burden of proof

The burden of proof for making the determinations under subparagraph (B) shall be on the petitioner.

(5) Removal of pollutants

The Administrator may remove any pollutant from the list of pollutants for which modifications are authorized under this subsection if the Administrator determines that adequate test methods and sufficient data are no longer available for determining whether or not modifications may be granted with respect to such pollutant under paragraph (2) of this subsection.

(h) Modification of secondary treatment requirements

The Administrator, with the concurrence of the State, may issue a permit under section 1342 of this title which modifies the requirements of subsection (b)(1)(B) of this section with respect to the discharge of any pollutant from a publicly owned treatment works into marine waters, if the applicant demonstrates to the satisfaction of the Administrator that—

(1) there is an applicable water quality standard specific to the pollutant for which the modification is requested, which has been identified under section 1314(a)(6) of this title;

(2) the discharge of pollutants in accordance with such modified requirements will not interfere, alone or in combination with pollutants from other sources, with the attainment or maintenance of that water quality which assures protection of public water supplies and the protection and propagation of a balanced, indigenous population of shellfish,

fish, and wildlife, and allows recreational activities, in and on the water;

(3) the applicant has established a system for monitoring the impact of such discharge on a representative sample of aquatic biota, to the extent practicable, and the scope of such monitoring is limited to include only those scientific investigations which are necessary to study the effects of the proposed discharge;

(4) such modified requirements will not result in any additional requirements on any other point or nonpoint source;

(5) all applicable pretreatment requirements for sources introducing waste into such treatment works will be enforced;

(6) in the case of any treatment works serving a population of 50,000 or more, with respect to any toxic pollutant introduced into such works by an industrial discharger for which pollutant there is no applicable pretreatment requirement in effect, sources introducing waste into such works are in compliance with all applicable pretreatment requirements, the applicant will enforce such requirements, and the applicant has in effect a pretreatment program which, in combination with the treatment of discharges from such works, removes the same amount of such pollutant as would be removed if such works were to apply secondary treatment to discharges and if such works had no pretreatment program with respect to such pollutant;

(7) to the extent practicable, the applicant has established a schedule of activities designed to eliminate the entrance of toxic pollutants from nonindustrial sources into such treatment works;

(8) there will be no new or substantially increased discharges from the point source of the pollutant to which the modification applies above that volume of discharge specified in the permit;

(9) the applicant at the time such modification becomes effective will be discharging effluent which has received at least primary or equivalent treatment and which meets the criteria established under section 1314(a)(1) of this title after initial mixing in the waters surrounding or adjacent to the point at which such effluent is discharged.

For the purposes of this subsection the phrase "the discharge of any pollutant into marine waters" refers to a discharge into deep waters of the territorial sea or the waters of the contiguous zone, or into saline estuarine waters where there is strong tidal movement and other hydrological and geological characteristics which the Administrator determines necessary to allow compliance with paragraph (2) of this subsection, and section 1251(a)(2) of this title. For the purposes of paragraph (9), "primary or equivalent treatment" means treatment by screening, sedimentation, and skimming adequate to remove at least 30 percent of the biological oxygen demanding material and of the suspended solids in the treatment works influent, and disinfection, where appropriate. A municipality which applies secondary treatment shall be eligible to receive a permit pursuant to this subsection which modifies the requirements of subsection (b)(1)(B) of this section with respect to the discharge of any pollutant from any treatment works owned by such municipality into marine waters. No permit issued under this subsection shall authorize the discharge of sewage sludge into marine waters. In order for a permit to be issued under this subsection for the discharge of a pollutant into marine waters, such marine waters must exhibit characteristics assuring that water providing dilution does not contain significant amounts of previously discharged effluent from such treatment works. No permit issued under this subsection shall authorize the discharge of any pollutant into saline estuarine waters which at the time of application do not support a balanced indigenous population of shellfish, fish and wildlife, or allow recreation in and on the waters or which exhibit ambient water quality below applicable water quality standards adopted for the protection of public water supplies, shellfish, fish and wildlife or recreational activities or such other standards necessary to assure support and protection of such uses. The prohibition contained in the preceding sentence shall apply without regard to the presence or absence of a causal relationship between such characteristics and the applicant's current or proposed discharge. Notwithstanding any other provisions of this subsection, no permit may be issued under this subsection for discharge of a pollutant into the New York Bight Apex consisting of the ocean waters of the Atlantic Ocean westward of 73 degrees 30 minutes west longitude and northward of 40 degrees 10 minutes north latitude.

(i) Municipal time extensions

(1) Where construction is required in order for a planned or existing publicly owned treatment works to achieve limitations under subsection (b)(1)(B) or (b)(1)(C) of this section, but (A) construction cannot be completed within the time required in such subsection, or (B) the United States has failed to make financial assistance under this chapter available in time to achieve such limitations by the time specified in such subsection, the owner or operator of such treatment works may request the Administrator (or if appropriate the State) to issue a permit pursuant to section 1342 of this title or to modify a permit issued pursuant to that section to extend such time for compliance.

Any such request shall be filed with the Administrator (or if appropriate the State) within 180 days after February 4, 1987. The Administrator (or if appropriate the State) may grant such request and issue or modify such a permit, which shall contain a schedule of compliance for the publicly owned treatment works based on the earliest date by which such financial assistance will be available from the United States and construction can be completed, but in no event later than July 1, 1988, and shall contain such other terms and conditions, including those necessary to carry out subsections (b) through (g) of section 1281 of this title, section 1317 of this title, and such interim effluent limitations applicable to that treatment works as the Administrator determines are necessary to carry out the provisions of this chapter.

(2)(A) Where a point source (other than a publicly owned treatment works) will not achieve the requirements of subsections (b)(1)(A) and (b)(1)(C) of this section and—

(i) if a permit issued prior to July 1, 1977, to such point source is based upon a discharge into a publicly owned treatment works; or

(ii) if such point source (other than a publicly owned treatment works) had before July 1, 1977, a contract (enforceable against such point source) to discharge into a publicly owned treatment works; or

(iii) if either an application made before July 1, 1977, for a construction grant under this chapter for a publicly owned treatment works, or engineering or architectural plans or working drawings made before July 1, 1977, for a publicly owned treatment works, show that such point source was to discharge into such publicly owned treatment works,

and such publicly owned treatment works is presently unable to accept such discharge without construction, and in the case of a discharge to an existing publicly owned treatment works, such treatment works has an extension pursuant to paragraph (1) of this subsection, the owner or operator of such point source may request the Administrator (or if appropriate the State) to issue or modify such a permit pursuant to such section 1342 of this title to extend such time for compliance. Any such request shall be filed with the Administrator (or if appropriate the State) within 180 days after December 27, 1977, or the filing of a request by the appropriate publicly owned treatment works under paragraph (1) of this subsection, whichever is later. If the Administrator (or if appropriate the State) finds that the owner or operator of such point source has acted in good faith, he may grant such request and issue or modify such a permit, which shall contain a schedule of compliance for the point source to achieve the requirements of subsections (b)(1)(A) and (C) of this section and shall contain such other terms and conditions, including pretreatment and interim effluent limitations and water conservation requirements applicable to that point source, as the Administrator determines are necessary to carry out the provisions of this chapter.

(B) No time modification granted by the Administrator (or if appropriate the State) pursuant to paragraph (2)(A) of this subsection shall extend beyond the earliest date practicable for compliance or beyond the date of any extension granted to the appropriate publicly owned treatment works pursuant to paragraph (1) of this subsection, but in no event shall it extend beyond July 1, 1988; and no such time modification shall be granted unless (i) the publicly owned treatment works will be in operation and available to the point source before July 1, 1988, and will meet the requirements of subsections (b)(1)(B) and (C) of this section after receiving the discharge from that point source; and (ii) the point source and the publicly owned treatment works have entered into an enforceable contract requiring the point source to discharge into the publicly owned treatment works, the owner or operator of such point source to pay the costs required under section 1284 of this title, and the publicly owned treatment works to accept the discharge from the point source; and (iii) the permit for such point source requires that point source to meet all requirements under section 1317(a) and (b) of this title during the period of such time modification.

(j) Modification procedures

(1) Any application filed under this section for a modification of the provisions of—

(A) subsection (b)(1)(B) of this section under subsection (h) of this section shall be filed not later that [1] the 365th day which begins after December 29, 1981, except that a publicly owned treatment works which prior to December 31, 1982, had a contractual arrangement to use a portion of the capacity of an ocean outfall operated by another publicly owned treatment works which has applied for or received modification under subsection (h) of this section, may apply for a modification of subsection (h) of this section in its own right not later than 30 days after February 4, 1987, and except as provided in paragraph (5);

(B) subsection (b)(2)(A) of this section as it applies to pollutants identified in subsection (b)(2)(F) of this section shall be filed not later than 270 days after the date of promulgation of an applicable effluent guideline under section 1314 of this title or not later than 270 days after December 27, 1977, whichever is later.

(2) Subject to paragraph (3) of this section, any application for a modification filed under subsection (g) of this section shall not operate to stay any requirement under this chapter, unless in the judgment of the Administrator such a stay or the modification sought will not result in the discharge of pollutants in quantities which may reasonably be anticipated to pose an unacceptable risk to human health or the environment because of bioaccumulation, persistency in the environment, acute toxicity, chronic toxicity (including carcinogenicity, mutagenicity, or teratogenicity), or synergistic propensities, and that there is a substantial likelihood that the applicant will succeed on the merits of such application. In the case of an application filed under subsection (g) of this section, the Administrator may condition any stay granted under this paragraph on requiring the filing of a bond or other appropriate security to assure timely compliance with the requirements from which a modification is sought.

(3) Compliance requirements under subsection (g)

(A) Effect of filing

An application for a modification under subsection (g) of this section and a petition for listing of a pollutant as a pollutant for which modifications are authorized under such subsection shall not stay the requirement that the person seeking such modification or listing comply with effluent limitations under this chapter for all pollutants not the subject of such application or petition.

(B) Effect of disapproval

Disapproval of an application for a modification under subsection (g) of this section shall not stay the requirement that the person seeking such modification comply with all applicable effluent limitations under this chapter.

(4) Deadline for subsection (g) decision

An application for a modification with respect to a pollutant filed under subsection (g) of this section must be approved or disapproved not later than 365 days after the date of such filing; except that in any case in which a petition for listing such pollutant as a pollutant for which modifications are authorized under such subsection is approved, such application must be approved or disapproved not later than 365 days after the date of approval of such petition.

(5) Extension of application deadline

(A) In general

In the 180–day period beginning on October 31, 1994, the city of San Diego, California, may apply for a modification pursuant to subsection (h) of this section of the requirements of subsection (b)(1)(B) of this section with respect to biological oxygen demand and total suspended solids in the effluent discharged into marine waters.

(B) Application

An application under this paragraph shall include a commitment by the applicant to implement a waste water reclamation program that, at a minimum, will—

(i) achieve a system capacity of 45,000,000 gallons of reclaimed waste water per day by January 1, 2010; and

(ii) result in a reduction in the quantity of suspended solids discharged by the applicant into the marine environment during the period of the modification.

(C) Additional conditions

The Administrator may not grant a modification pursuant to an application submitted under this paragraph unless the Administrator determines that such modification will result in removal of not less than 58 percent of the biological oxygen demand (on an annual average) and not less than 80 percent of total suspended solids (on a monthly average) in the discharge to which the application applies.

(D) Preliminary decision deadline

The Administrator shall announce a preliminary decision on an application submitted under this paragraph not later than 1 year after the date the application is submitted.

(k) Innovative technology

In the case of any facility subject to a permit under section 1342 of this title which proposes to comply with the requirements of subsection (b)(2)(A) or (b)(2)(E) of this section by replacing existing production capacity with an innovative production process which will result in an effluent reduction significantly greater than that required by the limitation otherwise applicable to such facility and moves toward the national goal of eliminating the discharge of all pollutants, or with the installation of an innovative control technique that has a substantial likelihood for enabling the facility to comply with the applicable effluent limitation by achieving a significantly greater effluent reduction than that required by the applicable effluent limitation and moves toward the national goal of eliminating the discharge of all pollutants, or by achieving the required reduction with an innovative system that has the potential for significantly lower costs than the systems which have been determined by the Administrator to be economically achievable, the Administrator (or the State with an approved program under section 1342 of this title, in consultation with the

Administrator) may establish a date for compliance under subsection (b)(2)(A) or (b)(2)(E) of this section no later than two years after the date for compliance with such effluent limitation which would otherwise be applicable under such subsection, if it is also determined that such innovative system has the potential for industrywide application.

(*l*) Toxic pollutants

Other than as provided in subsection (n) of this section, the Administrator may not modify any requirement of this section as it applies to any specific pollutant which is on the toxic pollutant list under section 1317(a)(1) of this title.

(m) Modification of effluent limitation requirements for point sources

(1) The Administrator, with the concurrence of the State, may issue a permit under section 1342 of this title which modifies the requirements of subsections (b)(1)(A) and (b)(2)(E) of this section, and of section 1343 of this title, with respect to effluent limitations to the extent such limitations relate to biochemical oxygen demand and pH from discharges by an industrial discharger in such State into deep waters of the territorial seas, if the applicant demonstrates and the Administrator finds that—

(A) the facility for which modification is sought is covered at the time of the enactment of this subsection by National Pollutant Discharge Elimination System permit number CA0005894 or CA0005282;

(B) the energy and environmental costs of meeting such requirements of subsections (b)(1)(A) and (b)(2)(E) of this section and section 1343 of this title exceed by an unreasonable amount the benefits to be obtained, including the objectives of this chapter;

(C) the applicant has established a system for monitoring the impact of such discharges on a representative sample of aquatic biota;

(D) such modified requirements will not result in any additional requirements on any other point or nonpoint source;

(E) there will be no new or substantially increased discharges from the point source of the pollutant to which the modification applies above that volume of discharge specified in the permit;

(F) the discharge is into waters where there is strong tidal movement and other hydrological and geological characteristics which are necessary to allow compliance with this subsection and section 1251(a)(2) of this title;

(G) the applicant accepts as a condition to the permit a contractual obligation to use funds in the amount required (but not less than $250,000 per year for ten years) for research and development of water pollution control technology, including but not limited to closed cycle technology;

(H) the facts and circumstances present a unique situation which, if relief is granted, will not establish a precedent or the relaxation of the requirements of this chapter applicable to similarly situated discharges; and

(I) no owner or operator of a facility comparable to that of the applicant situated in the United States has demonstrated that it would be put at a competitive disadvantage to the applicant (or the parent company or any subsidiary thereof) as a result of the issuance of a permit under this subsection.

(2) The effluent limitations established under a permit issued under paragraph (1) shall be sufficient to implement the applicable State water quality standards, to assure the protection of public water supplies and protection and propagation of a balanced, indigenous population of shellfish, fish, fauna, wildlife, and other aquatic organisms, and to allow recreational activities in and on the water. In setting such limitations, the Administrator shall take into account any seasonal variations and the need for an adequate margin of safety, considering the lack of essential knowledge concerning the relationship between effluent limitations and water quality and the lack of essential knowledge of the effects of discharges on beneficial uses of the receiving waters.

(3) A permit under this subsection may be issued for a period not to exceed five years, and such a permit may be renewed for one additional period not to exceed five years upon a demonstration by the applicant and a finding by the Administrator at the time of application for any such renewal that the provisions of this subsection are met.

(4) The Administrator may terminate a permit issued under this subsection if the Administrator determines that there has been a decline in ambient water quality of the receiving waters during the period of the permit even if a direct cause and effect relationship cannot be shown: *Provided,* That if the effluent from a source with a permit issued under this subsection is contributing to a decline in ambient water quality of the receiving waters, the Administrator shall terminate such permit.

(n) Fundamentally different factors

(1) General rule

The Administrator, with the concurrence of the State, may establish an alternative requirement under subsection (b)(2) of this section or section 1317(b) of this title for a facility that modifies the requirements of national effluent limitation guidelines or categorical pretreatment standards that would otherwise be applicable to such facility, if the owner or operator of such facility demonstrates to the satisfaction of the Administrator that—

(A) the facility is fundamentally different with respect to the factors (other than cost) specified in section 1314(b) or 1314(g) of this title and considered by the Administrator in establishing such national effluent limitation guidelines or categorical pretreatment standards;

(B) the application—

(i) is based solely on information and supporting data submitted to the Administrator during the rulemaking for establishment of the applicable national effluent limitation guidelines or categorical pretreatment standard specifically raising the factors that are fundamentally different for such facility; or

(ii) is based on information and supporting data referred to in clause (i) and information and supporting data the applicant did not have a reasonable opportunity to submit during such rulemaking;

(C) the alternative requirement is no less stringent than justified by the fundamental difference; and

(D) the alternative requirement will not result in a non-water quality environmental impact which is markedly more adverse than the impact considered by the Administrator in establishing such national effluent limitation guideline or categorical pretreatment standard.

(2) Time limit for applications

An application for an alternative requirement which modifies the requirements of an effluent limitation or pretreatment standard under this subsection must be submitted to the Administrator within 180 days after the date on which such limitation or standard is established or revised, as the case may be.

(3) Time limit for decision

The Administrator shall approve or deny by final agency action an application submitted under this subsection within 180 days after the date such application is filed with the Administrator.

(4) Submission of information

The Administrator may allow an applicant under this subsection to submit information and supporting data until the earlier of the date the application is approved or denied or the last day that the Administrator has to approve or deny such application.

(5) Treatment of pending applications

For the purposes of this subsection, an application for an alternative requirement based on fundamentally different factors which is pending on February 4, 1987, shall be treated as having been submitted to the Administrator on the 180th day following February 4, 1987. The applicant may amend the application to take into account the provisions of this subsection.

(6) Effect of submission of application

An application for an alternative requirement under this subsection shall not stay the applicant's obligation to comply with the effluent limitation guideline or categorical pretreatment standard which is the subject of the application.

(7) Effect of denial

If an application for an alternative requirement which modifies the requirements of an effluent limitation or pretreatment standard under this subsection is denied by the Administrator, the applicant must comply with such limitation or standard as established or revised, as the case may be.

(8) Reports

By January 1, 1997, and January 1 of every odd-numbered year thereafter, the Administrator shall submit to the Committee on Environment and Public Works of the Senate and the Committee on Transportation and Infrastructure of the House of Representatives a report on the status of applications for alternative requirements which modify the requirements of effluent limitations under this section or section 1314 of this title or any national categorical pretreatment standard under section 1317(b) of this title filed before, on, or after February 4, 1987.

(*o*) Application fees

The Administrator shall prescribe and collect from each applicant fees reflecting the reasonable administrative costs incurred in reviewing and processing applications for modifications submitted to the Administrator pursuant to subsections (c), (g), (i), (k), (m), and (n) of this section, section 1314(d)(4) of this title, and section 1326(a) of this title. All amounts collected by the Administrator under this subsection shall be deposited into a special fund of the Treasury entitled "Water Permits and Related Services" which shall thereafter be available for appropriation to carry out activities of the Environmental Protection Agency for which such fees were collected.

(p) Modified permit for coal remining operations

(1) In general

Subject to paragraphs (2) through (4) of this subsection, the Administrator, or the State in any case which the State has an approved permit program under section 1342(b) of this title, may issue a permit under section 1342 of this title which modifies the requirements of subsection (b)(2)(A) of this section with respect to the pH level of any pre-existing discharge, and with respect to pre-existing discharges of iron and manganese from the remined area of any coal remining operation or with respect to the pH level or level of iron or manganese in any pre-existing discharge affected by the remining operation. Such modified requirements shall apply the best available technology economically achievable on a case-by-case basis, using best professional judgment, to set specific numerical effluent limitations in each permit.

(2) Limitations

The Administrator or the State may only issue a permit pursuant to paragraph (1) if the applicant demonstrates to the satisfaction of the Administrator or the State, as the case may be, that the coal remining operation will result in the potential for improved water quality from the remining operation but in no event shall such a permit allow the pH level of any discharge, and in no event shall such a permit allow the discharges of iron and manganese, to exceed the levels being discharged from the remined area before the coal remining operation begins. No discharge from, or affected by, the remining operation shall exceed State water quality standards established under section 1313 of this title.

(3) Definitions

For purposes of this subsection—

(A) Coal remining operation

The term "coal remining operation" means a coal mining operation which begins after February 4, 1987, at a site on which coal mining was conducted before August 3, 1977.

(B) Remined area

The term "remined area" means only that area of any coal remining operation on which coal mining was conducted before August 3, 1977.

(C) Pre-existing discharge

The term "pre-existing discharge" means any discharge at the time of permit application under this subsection.

(4) Applicability of strip mining laws

Nothing in this subsection shall affect the application of the Surface Mining Control and Reclamation Act of 1977 [30 U.S.C.A. § 1201 et seq.] to any coal remining operation, including the application of such Act to suspended solids.

(June 30, 1948, c. 758, Title III, § 301, as added Oct. 18, 1972, Pub.L. 92–500, § 2, 86 Stat. 844, and amended Dec. 27, 1977, Pub.L. 95–217, §§ 42–47, 53(c), 91 Stat. 1582–1586, 1590; Dec. 29, 1981, Pub.L. 97–117, §§ 21, 22(a)–(d), 95 Stat. 1631, 1632; Jan. 8, 1983, Pub.L. 97–440, 96 Stat. 2289; Feb. 4, 1987, Pub.L. 100–4, Title III, §§ 301(a)–(e), 302(a)–(d), 303(a), (b)(1), (c)–(f), 304(a), 305, 306(a), (b), 307, 101 Stat. 29–37; Nov. 18, 1988, Pub.L. 100–688, Title III, § 3202(b), 102 Stat. 4154; Oct. 31 1994, Pub.L. 103–431, § 2, 108 Stat. 4396; Dec. 21, 1995, Pub.L. 104–66, Title II, § 2021(b), 109 Stat. 727.)

1 So in original. Probably should be "than".

References in Text

The effective date of the Surface Mining Control and Reclamation Act of 1977, referred to in subsec. (p)(3)(A) and (B), probably means the date of enactment of Pub.L. 95–87, which was approved Aug. 3, 1977.

The Surface Mining Control and Reclamation Act of 1977, referred to in subsec. (p)(4), is Pub.L. 95–87, Aug. 3, 1977, 91 Stat. 445, as amended, which is classified generally to chapter 25 (section 1201 et seq.) of Title 30, Mineral Lands and Mining.

Change of Name

Any reference in any provision of law enacted before Jan. 4, 1995, to the Committee on Public Works and Transportation of the House of Representatives treated as referring to the Committee on Transportation and Infrastructure of the House of Representatives, see section 1(a)(9) of Pub.L. 104–14, set out as a note preceding section 21 of Title 2, The Congress.

CROSS REFERENCES

Criminal penalties for violation of this section, see section 1319 of this title.
Definition of "effluent standard or limitation" for purposes of citizen suits, see section 1365 of this title.
Definition of "treatment works", see section 1292 of this title.
Development and publication of information on factors necessary for protection of public water supplies, see section 1314 of this title.
Employee protection, deliberate violations by employee acting without direction from employer, see section 1367 of this title.
Guidelines for cost-effectiveness analysis, see section 1297 of this title.
Identification of areas with insufficient effluent limitations, see section 1313 of this title.
National Study Commission, establishment, see section 1325 of this title.
Permits for discharge of pollutants, see section 1342 of this title.
Permits for dredged or fill material, see section 1344 of this title.
Research and demonstration projects to carry out the purposes of this section, see section 1255 of this title.
Review of Administrator's actions, see section 1369 of this title.
State certification of applicants for federal license, see section 1341 of this title.
Thermal discharges, effluent limitations for protection and propagation of shellfish, etc., see section 1326 of this title.
Toxic and pretreatment effluent standards, see section 1317 of this title.
Water quality related effluent limitations, see section 1312 of this title.

CODE OF FEDERAL REGULATIONS

Criteria and standards for the National Pollutant Discharge Elimination System, see 40 CFR 125.1 et seq.

Effluent guidelines and standards, see 40 CFR Chap. I, Subchap. N.
Guidelines establishing test procedures for analysis of pollutants, see 40 CFR 136.1 et seq.
Secondary treatment regulation, see 40 CFR 133.100 et seq.

LAW REVIEW COMMENTARIES

Congressional ambiguity allows EPA's safety valve to remain open. 35 Catholic U.L.Rev. 595 (1986).

Erosion of mens rea in environmental criminal prosecution. Ruth Ann Weidel, John R. Mayo and F. Michael Zachara, 21 Seton Hall L.Rev. 1125 (1991).

Encouraging safety through insurance-based incentives: financial responsibility for hazardous wastes. Jeffrey Kehne, 96 Yale L.J. 403 (1986).

From elephants to mice: The development of EBMUD's program to control small source wastewater discharges. Raoul Stewardson, 20 Ecology L.Q. 441 (1993).

Fundamentally different factor variances under the Clean Water Act: Should they be applicable to toxic pollutants? (1983–84) 29 Vill.L.Rev. 771.

Long-range planning in environmental and health regulatory agencies. Richard N.L. Andrews, 20 Ecology L.Q. 515 (1993).

"More good than harm": A first principle for environmental agencies and reviewing courts. Edward W. Warren and Gary E. Marchant, 20 Ecology L.Q. 379 (1993).

Responsible corporate officer: Designated felon or legal fiction? Brenda S. Hustis and John Y. Gotanda, 25 Loy.U.Chi.L.J. 169 (1994).

Toxic tort litigation and the causation element: Is there any hope of reconciliation? Ora Fred Harris, Jr., 40 Southwestern (Tex.) L.J. 909 (1986).

LIBRARY REFERENCES

Health and Environment ⚷25.7(10).
C.J.S. Health and Environment § 106 et seq.

United States Supreme Court

Court's authority to impose more stringent effluent limitations under federal common law than those imposed by federal agency, City of Milwaukee v. Illinois and Michigan, 1981, 101 S.Ct. 1784, 451 U.S. 304, 68 L.Ed.2d 114, certiorari denied 105 S.Ct. 979, 980, 83 L.Ed.2d 981.

Issuance of fundamentally different factor variances with respect to toxic pollutants, see Chemical Mfrs. Ass'n v. National Resources Defense Council, Inc., 1985, 105 S.Ct. 1102, 470 U.S. 116, 84 L.Ed.2d 90.

Regulations setting effluent limitations, existing point sources, allowance for individual variations, see E.I. du Pont de Nemours & Co. v. Train, 1977, 97 S.Ct. 965, 430 U.S. 112, 51 L.Ed.2d 204.

§ 1312. Water quality related effluent limitations [FWPCA § 302]

(a) Establishment

Whenever, in the judgment of the Administrator or as identified under section 1314(*l*) of this title, discharges of pollutants from a point source or group of point sources, with the application of effluent limitations required under section 1311(b)(2) of this title, would interfere with the attainment or maintenance of that water quality in a specific portion of the navigable waters which shall assure protection of public health, public water supplies, agricultural and industrial uses, and the protection and propagation of a balanced population of shellfish, fish and wildlife, and allow recreational activities in and on the water, effluent limitations (including alternative effluent control strategies) for such point source or sources shall be established which can reasonably be expected to contribute to the attainment or maintenance of such water quality.

(b) Modifications of effluent limitations

(1) Notice and hearing

Prior to establishment of any effluent limitation pursuant to subsection (a) of this section, the Administrator shall publish such proposed limitation and within 90 days of such publication hold a public hearing.

(2) Permits

(A) No reasonable relationship

The Administrator, with the concurrence of the State, may issue a permit which modifies the effluent limitations required by subsection (a) of this section for pollutants other than toxic pollutants if the applicant demonstrates at such hearing that (whether or not technology or other alternative control strategies are available) there is no reasonable relationship between the economic and social costs and the benefits to be obtained (including attainment of the objective of this chapter) from achieving such limitation.

(B) Reasonable progress

The Administrator, with the concurrence of the State, may issue a permit which modifies the effluent limitations required by subsection (a) of this section for toxic pollutants for a single period not to exceed 5 years if the applicant demonstrates to the satisfaction of the Administrator that such modified requirements (i) will represent the maximum degree of control within the economic capability of the owner and operator of the source, and (ii) will result in reasonable further progress beyond the requirements of section 1311(b)(2) of this title toward the requirements of subsection (a) of this section.

(c) Delay in application of other limitations

The establishment of effluent limitations under this section shall not operate to delay the application of any effluent limitation established under section 1311 of this title.

(June 30, 1948, c. 758, Title III, § 302, as added Oct. 18, 1972, Pub.L. 92–500, § 2, 86 Stat. 846, and amended Feb. 4, 1987, Pub.L. 100–4, Title III, § 308(e), 101 Stat. 39.)

CROSS REFERENCES

Alternate methods for preventing, etc., municipal waste as within definition of "treatment works," see section 1292 of this title.
Approval of continuing planning process, see section 1313 of this title.
Best management practices for industry, see section 1314 of this title.

Certification from State of compliance with provisions of this section, see section 1341 of this title.
Discharge of pollutants as unlawful except as when in compliance with this section, see section 1311 of this title.
Effluent standards for purposes of citizen suits, see section 1365 of this title.
Enforcement of provisions of this section, see section 1319 of this title.
Permits for discharge of pollutants, see section 1342 of this title.
Review of Administrator's actions, see section 1369 of this title.
Violations by employees acting without direction from employer, see section 1367 of this title.

ADMINISTRATIVE LAW

Cost/benefit requirements, see Koch § 4.35.

LIBRARY REFERENCES

Health and Environment ⚖25.7(10).
C.J.S. Health and Environment § 106 et seq.

§ 1313. Water quality standards and implementation plans [FWPCA § 303]

(a) Existing water quality standards

(1) In order to carry out the purpose of this chapter, any water quality standard applicable to interstate waters which was adopted by any State and submitted to, and approved by, or is a waiting approval by, the Administrator pursuant to this Act as in effect immediately prior to October 18, 1972, shall remain in effect unless the Administrator determined that such standard is not consistent with the applicable requirements of this Act as in effect immediately prior to October 18, 1972. If the Administrator makes such a determination he shall, within three months after October 18, 1972, notify the State and specify the changes needed to meet such requirements. If such changes are not adopted by the State within ninety days after the date of such notification, the Administrator shall promulgate such changes in accordance with subsection (b) of this section.

(2) Any State which, before October 18, 1972, has adopted, pursuant to its own law, water quality standards applicable to intrastate waters shall submit such standards to the Administrator within thirty days after October 18, 1972. Each such standard shall remain in effect, in the same manner and to the same extent as any other water quality standard established under this chapter unless the Administrator determines that such standard is inconsistent with the applicable requirements of this Act as in effect immediately prior to October 18, 1972. If the Administrator makes such a determination he shall not later than the one hundred and twentieth day after the date of submission of such standards, notify the State and specify the changes needed to meet such requirements. If such changes are not adopted by the State within ninety days after such notification, the Administrator shall promulgate such changes in accordance with subsection (b) of this section.

(3)(A) Any State which prior to October 18, 1972, has not adopted pursuant to its own laws water quality standards applicable to intrastate waters shall, not later than one hundred and eighty days after October 18, 1972, adopt and submit such standards to the Administrator.

(B) If the Administrator determines that any such standards are consistent with the applicable requirements of this Act as in effect immediately prior to October 18, 1972, he shall approve such standards.

(C) If the Administrator determines that any such standards are not consistent with the applicable requirements of this Act as in effect immediately prior to October 18, 1972, he shall, not later than the ninetieth day after the date of submission of such standards, notify the State and specify the changes to meet such requirements. If such changes are not adopted by the State within ninety days after the date of notification, the Administrator shall promulgate such standards pursuant to subsection (b) of this section.

(b) Proposed regulations

(1) The Administrator shall promptly prepare and publish proposed regulations setting forth water quality standards for a State in accordance with the applicable requirements of this Act as in effect immediately prior to October 18, 1972, if—

(A) the State fails to submit water quality standards within the times prescribed in subsection (a) of this section.

(B) a water quality standard submitted by such State under subsection (a) of this section is determined by the Administrator not to be consistent with the applicable requirements of subsection (a) of this section.

(2) The Administrator shall promulgate any water quality standard published in a proposed regulation not later than one hundred and ninety days after the date he publishes any such proposed standard, unless prior to such promulgation, such State has adopted a water quality standard which the Administrator determines to be in accordance with subsection (a) of this section.

(c) Review; revised standards; publication

(1) The Governor of a State or the State water pollution control agency of such State shall from time to time (but at least once each three year period beginning with October 18, 1972) hold public hearings for the purpose of reviewing applicable water quality standards and, as appropriate, modifying and adopting

standards. Results of such review shall be made available to the Administrator.

(2)(A) Whenever the State revises or adopts a new standard, such revised or new standard shall be submitted to the Administrator. Such revised or new water quality standard shall consist of the designated uses of the navigable waters involved and the water quality criteria for such waters based upon such uses. Such standards shall be such as to protect the public health or welfare, enhance the quality of water and serve the purposes of this chapter. Such standards shall be established taking into consideration their use and value for public water supplies, propagation of fish and wildlife, recreational purposes, and agricultural, industrial, and other purposes, and also taking into consideration their use and value for navigation.

(B) Whenever a State reviews water quality standards pursuant to paragraph (1) of this subsection, or revises or adopts new standards pursuant to this paragraph, such State shall adopt criteria for all toxic pollutants listed pursuant to section 1317(a)(1) of this title for which criteria have been published under section 1314(a) of this title, the discharge or presence of which in the affected waters could reasonably be expected to interfere with those designated uses adopted by the State, as necessary to support such designated uses. Such criteria shall be specific numerical criteria for such toxic pollutants. Where such numerical criteria are not available, whenever a State reviews water quality standards pursuant to paragraph (1), or revises or adopts new standards pursuant to this paragraph, such State shall adopt criteria based on biological monitoring or assessment methods consistent with information published pursuant to section 1314(a)(8) of this title. Nothing in this section shall be construed to limit or delay the use of effluent limitations or other permit conditions based on or involving biological monitoring or assessment methods or previously adopted numerical criteria.

(3) If the Administrator, within sixty days after the date of submission of the revised or new standard, determines that such standard meets the requirements of this chapter, such standard shall thereafter be the water quality standard for the applicable waters of that State. If the Administrator determines that any such revised or new standard is not consistent with the applicable requirements of this chapter, he shall not later than the ninetieth day after the date of submission of such standard notify the State and specify the changes to meet such requirements. If such changes are not adopted by the State within ninety days after the date of notification, the Administrator shall promulgate such standard pursuant to paragraph (4) of this subsection.

(4) The Administrator shall promptly prepare and publish proposed regulations setting forth a revised or new water quality standard for the navigable waters involved—

(A) if a revised or new water quality standard submitted by such State under paragraph (3) of this subsection for such waters is determined by the Administrator not to be consistent with the applicable requirements of this chapter, or

(B) in any case where the Administrator determines that a revised or new standard is necessary to meet the requirements of this chapter.

The Administrator shall promulgate any revised or new standard under this paragraph not later than ninety days after he publishes such proposed standards, unless prior to such promulgation, such State has adopted a revised or new water quality standard which the Administrator determines to be in accordance with this chapter.

(d) Identification of areas with insufficient controls; maximum daily load; certain effluent limitations revision

(1)(A) Each State shall identify those waters within its boundaries for which the effluent limitations required by section 1311(b)(1)(A) and section 1311(b)(1)(B) of this title are not stringent enough to implement any water quality standard applicable to such waters. The State shall establish a priority ranking for such waters, taking into account the severity of the pollution and the uses to be made of such waters.

(B) Each State shall identify those waters or parts thereof within its boundaries for which controls on thermal discharges under section 1311 of this title are not stringent enough to assure protection and propagation of a balanced indigenous population of shellfish, fish, and wildlife.

(C) Each State shall establish for the waters identified in paragraph (1)(A) of this subsection, and in accordance with the priority ranking, the total maximum daily load, for those pollutants which the Administrator identifies under section 1314(a)(2) of this title as suitable for such calculation. Such load shall be established at a level necessary to implement the applicable water quality standards with seasonal variations and a margin of safety which takes into account any lack of knowledge concerning the relationship between effluent limitations and water quality.

(D) Each State shall estimate for the waters identified in paragraph (1)(B) of this subsection the total maximum daily thermal load required to assure protection and propagation of a balanced, indigenous population of shellfish, fish, and wildlife. Such estimates shall take into account the normal water temperatures, flow rates, seasonal variations, existing sources of heat input, and the dissipative capacity of the identified waters or parts thereof. Such estimates shall include a calculation of the maximum heat input that can be made into each such part and shall include a margin of safety which takes into account any lack of knowledge concerning the development of thermal water quality criteria for such protection and propagation in the identified waters or parts thereof.

(2) Each State shall submit to the Administrator from time to time, with the first such submission not later than one hundred and eighty days after the date of publication of the first identification of pollutants under section 1314(a)(2)(D) of this title, for his approval the waters identified and the loads established under paragraphs (1)(A), (1)(B), (1)(C), and (1)(D) of this subsection. The Administrator shall either approve or disapprove such identification and load not later than thirty days after the date of submission. If the Administrator approves such identification and load, such State shall incorporate them into its current plan under subsection (e) of this section. If the Administrator disapproves such identification and load, he shall not later than thirty days after the date of such disapproval identify such waters in such State and establish such loads for such waters as he determines necessary to implement the water quality standards applicable to such waters and upon such identification and establishment the State shall incorporate them into its current plan under subsection (e) of this section.

(3) For the specific purpose of developing information, each State shall identify all waters within its boundaries which it has not identified under paragraph (1)(A) and (1)(B) of this subsection and estimate for such waters the total maximum daily load with seasonal variations and margins of safety, for those pollutants which the Administrator identifies under section 1314(a)(2) of this title as suitable for such calculation and for thermal discharges, at a level that would assure protection and propagation of a balanced indigenous population of fish, shellfish, and wildlife.

(4) Limitations on revision of certain effluent limitations

(A) Standard not attained

For waters identified under paragraph (1)(A) where the applicable water quality standard has not yet been attained, any effluent limitation based on a total maximum daily load or other waste load allocation established under this section may be revised only if (i) the cumulative effect of all such revised effluent limitations based on such total maximum daily load or waste load allocation will assure the attainment of such water quality standard, or (ii) the designated use which is not being attained is removed in accordance with regulations established under this section.

(B) Standard attained

For waters identified under paragraph (1)(A) where the quality of such waters equals or exceeds levels necessary to protect the designated use for such waters or otherwise required by applicable water quality standards, any effluent limitation based on a total maximum daily load or other waste load allocation established under this section, or any water quality standard established under this section, or any other permitting standard may be revised only if such revision is subject to and consistent with the antidegradation policy established under this section.

(e) Continuing planning process

(1) Each State shall have a continuing planning process approved under paragraph (2) of this subsection which is consistent with this chapter.

(2) Each State shall submit not later than 120 days after October 18, 1972, to the Administrator for his approval a proposed continuing planning process which is consistent with this chapter. Not later than thirty days after the date of submission of such a process the Administrator shall either approve or disapprove such process. The Administrator shall from time to time review each State's approved planning process for the purpose of insuring that such planning process is at all times consistent with this chapter. The Administrator shall not approve any State permit program under subchapter IV of this chapter for any State which does not have an approved continuing planning process under this section.

(3) The Administrator shall approve any continuing planning process submitted to him under this section which will result in plans for all navigable waters within such State, which include, but are not limited to, the following:

(A) effluent limitations and schedules of compliance at least as stringent as those required by section 1311(b)(1), section 1311(b)(2), section 1316, and section 1317 of this title, and at least as stringent as any requirements contained in any applicable water quality standard in effect under authority of this section;

(B) the incorporation of all elements of any applicable area-wide waste management plans under section 1288 of this title, and applicable basin plans under section 1289 of this title;

(C) total maximum daily load for pollutants in accordance with subsection (d) of this section;

(D) procedures for revision;

(E) adequate authority for intergovernmental cooperation;

(F) adequate implementation, including schedules of compliance, for revised or new water quality standards, under subsection (c) of this section;

(G) controls over the disposition of all residual waste from any water treatment processing;

(H) an inventory and ranking, in order of priority, of needs for construction of waste treatment works required to meet the applicable requirements of sections 1311 and 1312 of this title.

(f) Earlier compliance

Nothing in this section shall be construed to affect any effluent limitation, or schedule of compliance required by any State to be implemented prior to the dates set forth in sections 1311(b)(1) and 1311(b)(2) of this title nor to preclude any State from requiring compliance with any effluent limitation or schedule of compliance at dates earlier than such dates.

(g) Heat standards

Water quality standards relating to heat shall be consistent with the requirements of section 1326 of this title.

(h) Thermal water quality standards

For the purposes of this chapter the term "water quality standards" includes thermal water quality standards.

(June 30, 1948, c. 758, Title III, § 303, as added Oct. 18, 1972, Pub.L. 92–500, § 2, 86 Stat. 846, and amended Feb. 4, 1987, Pub.L. 100–4, Title III, § 308(d), Title IV, § 404(b), 101 Stat. 39, 68.)

CROSS REFERENCES

Approval of grants for treatment works, certification for priority, see section 1284 of this title.

License or permit to conduct activities resulting in discharge into navigable waters, certification by State of compliance with this section, see section 1341 of this title.

Period of protection from more stringent effluent limitations following discharge point source modification, see section 1326 of this title.

Planning process, consistency with State wide regulatory program, see section 1288 of this title.

Pollution control plans for basins, development in cooperation with State plan developed pursuant to this section, see section 1252 of this title.

Publication of information on and the identification of pollutants suitable for maximum daily load measurement correlated with the achievement of water quality objectives, see section 1314 of this title.

Reports to Congress on progress and problems associated with plans under this section, see section 1375 of this title.

Time for completion of review, revision, and adoption or promulgation of revised or new water quality standards, see section 1313a of this title.

Water quality management plan, see section 1285 of this title.

CODE OF FEDERAL REGULATIONS

Water quality planning and management, see 40 CFR 130.0 et seq.
Water quality standards, see 40 CFR 131.1 et seq.

LAW REVIEW COMMENTARIES

Federal regulation of environmental releases of genetically manipulated microorganisms. Edward L. Korwek and Peter L. de la Cruz (1985) 11 Rutgers Computer & Tech.Law J. 301.

From elephants to mice: The development of EBMUD's program to control small source wastewater discharges. Raoul Stewardson, 20 Ecology L.Q. 441 (1993).

Grazing management on the public lands: Opening the process to public participation. Joseph M. Feller, 26 Land and Water L.Rev. 571 (1991).

"More good than harm": A first principle for environmental agencies and reviewing courts. Edward W. Warren and Gary E. Marchant, 20 Ecology L.Q. 379 (1993).

Resolving conflicts between bankruptcy law and the state police power. Ellen E. Sward, 1987 Wis.L.Rev. 403 (1987).

Toward a national groundwater act: Current contamination and future courses of action. Thomas D. Marks, 61 Fla.B.J. 10 (April 1987).

United States Supreme Court

Clean Water Act provision requiring state to institute comprehensive standards establishing water quality goals for intrastate waters, consisting of designated uses of navigable waters involved and water quality criteria for those waters based on those uses, requires that a project for which water quality certification is required be consistent with both designated use and water quality criteria, see PUD No. 1 of Jefferson County v. Washington Dept. of Ecology, 1994, 114 S.Ct. 1900, 128 L.Ed.2d 716.

Limitation on permit authority, discharged materials to meet applicable standards, see U.S. v. Pennsylvania Indus. Chemical Corp., 1973, 93 S.Ct. 1804, 411 U.S. 655, 36 L.Ed.2d 567.

Preemption of state requirements on sewage discharge, initial federal standards, see Lake Carriers' Ass'n v. MacMullan, 1972, 92 S.Ct. 1749, 406 U.S. 498, 32 L.Ed. 257.

LIBRARY REFERENCES

Health and Environment ⇐25.7(10).
C.J.S. Health and Environment § 106 et seq.

§ 1313a. Revised water quality standards

The review, revision, and adoption or promulgation of revised or new water quality standards pursuant to section 303(c) of the Federal Water Pollution Control Act [33 U.S.C.A. § 1313(c)] shall be completed by the date three years after December 29, 1981. No grant shall be made under title II of the Federal Water Pollution Control Act [33 U.S.C.A. § 1281 et seq.] after such date until water quality standards are reviewed and revised pursuant to section 303(c), [33 U.S.C.A. § 1313(c)] except where the State has in good faith submitted such revised water quality standards and the Administrator has not acted to approve or disapprove such submission within one hundred and twenty days of receipt.

(Dec. 29, 1981, Pub.L. 97–117, § 24, 95 Stat. 1632.)

Codification

Section was enacted as part of the Municipal Wastewater Treatment Construction Grant Amendments of 1981, and not as part of the Federal Water Pollution Control Act, which comprises this chapter.

LIBRARY REFERENCES

Health and Environment ⚖25.7(10).
C.J.S. Health and Environment § 106 et seq.

§ 1314. Information and guidelines [FWPCA § 304]

(a) Criteria development and publication

(1) The Administrator, after consultation with appropriate Federal and State agencies and other interested persons, shall develop and publish, within one year after October 18, 1972 (and from time to time thereafter revise) criteria for water quality accurately reflecting the latest scientific knowledge (A) on the kind and extent of all identifiable effects on health and welfare including, but not limited to, plankton, fish, shellfish, wildlife, plant life, shorelines, beaches, esthetics, and recreation which may be expected from the presence of pollutants in any body of water, including ground water; (B) on the concentration and dispersal of pollutants, or their byproducts, through biological, physical, and chemical processes; and (C) on the effects of pollutants on biological community diversity, productivity, and stability, including information on the factors affecting rates of eutrophication and rates of organic and inorganic sedimentation for varying types of receiving waters.

(2) The Administrator, after consultation with appropriate Federal and State agencies and other interested persons, shall develop and publish, within one year after October 18, 1972 (and from time to time thereafter revise) information (A) on the factors necessary to restore and maintain the chemical, physical, and biological integrity of all navigable waters, ground waters, waters of the contiguous zone, and the oceans; (B) on the factors necessary for the protection and propagation of shellfish, fish, and wildlife for classes and categories of receiving waters and to allow recreational activities in and on the water; and (C) on the measurement and classification of water quality; and (D) for the purpose of section 1313 of this title, on and the identification of pollutants suitable for maximum daily load measurement correlated with the achievement of water quality objectives.

(3) Such criteria and information and revisions thereof shall be issued to the States and shall be published in the Federal Register and otherwise made available to the public.

(4) The Administrator shall, within 90 days after December 27, 1977, and from time to time thereafter, publish and revise as appropriate information identifying conventional pollutants, including but not limited to, pollutants classified as biological oxygen demanding, suspended solids, fecal coliform, and pH. The thermal component of any discharge shall not be identified as a conventional pollutant under this paragraph.

(5)(A) The Administrator, to the extent practicable before consideration of any request under section 1311(g) of this title and within six months after December 27, 1977, shall develop and publish information on the factors necessary for the protection of public water supplies, and the protection and propagation of a balanced population of shellfish, fish and wildlife, and to allow recreational activities, in and on the water.

(B) The Administrator, to the extent practicable before consideration of any application under section 1311(h) of this title and within six months after December 27, 1977, shall develop and publish information on the factors necessary for the protection of public water supplies, and the protection and propagation of a balanced indigenous population of shellfish, fish and wildlife, and to allow recreational activities, in and on the water.

(6) The Administrator shall, within three months after December 27, 1977, and annually thereafter, for purposes of section 1311(h) of this title publish and revise as appropriate information identifying each water quality standard in effect under this chapter or State law, the specific pollutants associated with such water quality standard, and the particular waters to which such water quality standard applies.

(7) Guidance to states

The Administrator, after consultation with appropriate State agencies and on the basis of criteria and information published under paragraphs (1) and (2) of this subsection, shall develop and publish, within 9 months after February 4, 1987, guidance to the States on performing the identification required by subsection (*l*)(1) of this section.

(8) Information on water quality criteria

The Administrator, after consultation with appropriate State agencies and within 2 years after February 4, 1987, shall develop and publish information on methods for establishing and measuring water quality criteria for toxic pollutants on other bases than pollutant-by-pollutant criteria, including biological monitoring and assessment methods.

(b) Effluent limitation guidelines

For the purpose of adopting or revising effluent limitations under this chapter the Administrator shall, after consultation with appropriate Federal and State agencies and other interested persons, publish within one year of October 18, 1972, regulations, providing guidelines for effluent limitations, and, at least annually thereafter, revise, if appropriate, such regulations. Such regulations shall—

(1)(A) identify, in terms of amounts of constituents and chemical, physical, and biological characteristics of pollutants, the degree of effluent reduction attainable through the application of the best practicable control technology currently available for classes and categories of point sources (other than publicly owned treatment works); and

(B) specify factors to be taken into account in determining the control measures and practices to be applicable to point sources (other than publicly owned treatment works) within such categories or classes. Factors relating to the assessment of best practicable control technology currently available to comply with subsection (b)(1) of section 1311 of this title shall include consideration of the total cost of application of technology in relation to the effluent reduction benefits to be achieved from such application, and shall also take into account the age of equipment and facilities involved, the process employed, the engineering aspects of the application of various types of control techniques, process changes, non-water quality environmental impact (including energy requirements), and such other factors as the Administrator deems appropriate;

(2)(A) identify, in terms of amounts of constituents and chemical, physical, and biological characteristics of pollutants, the degree of effluent reduction attainable through the application of the best control measures and practices achievable including treatment techniques, process and procedure innovations, operating methods, and other alternatives for classes and categories of point sources (other than publicly owned treatment works); and

(B) specify factors to be taken into account in determining the best measures and practices available to comply with subsection (b)(2) of section 1311 of this title to be applicable to any point source (other than publicly owned treatment works) within such categories or classes. Factors relating to the assessment of best available technology shall take into account the age of equipment and facilities involved, the process employed, the engineering aspects of the application of various types of control techniques, process changes, the cost of achieving such effluent reduction, non-water quality environmental impact (including energy requirements), and such other factors as the Administrator deems appropriate;

(3) identify control measures and practices available to eliminate the discharge of pollutants from categories and classes of point sources, taking into account the cost of achieving such elimination of the discharge of pollutants; and

(4)(A) identify, in terms of amounts of constituents and chemical, physical, and biological characteristics of pollutants, the degree of effluent reduction attainable through the application of the best conventional pollutant control technology (including measures and practices) for classes and categories of point sources (other than publicly owned treatment works); and

(B) specify factors to be taken into account in determining the best conventional pollutant control technology measures and practices to comply with section 1311(b)(2)(E) of this title to be applicable to any point source (other than publicly owned treatment works) within such categories or classes. Factors relating to the assessment of best conventional pollutant control technology (including measures and practices) shall include consideration of the reasonableness of the relationship between the costs of attaining a reduction in effluents and the effluent reduction benefits derived, and the comparison of the cost and level of reduction of such pollutants from the discharge from publicly owned treatment works to the cost and level of reduction of such pollutants from a class or category of industrial sources, and shall take into account the age of equipment and facilities involved, the process employed, the engineering aspects of the application of various types of control techniques, process changes, non-water quality environmental impact (including energy requirements), and such other factors as the Administrator deems appropriate.

(c) Pollution discharge elimination procedures

The Administrator, after consultation, with appropriate Federal and State agencies and other interested persons, shall issue to the States and appropriate water pollution control agencies within 270 days after October 18, 1972 (and from time to time thereafter) information on the processes, procedures, or operating methods which result in the elimination or reduction of the discharge of pollutants to implement standards of performance under section 1316 of this title. Such information shall include technical and other data, including costs, as are available on alternative methods of elimination or reduction of the discharge of pollutants. Such information, and revisions thereof, shall be published in the Federal Register and otherwise shall be made available to the public.

(d) Secondary treatment information; alternative waste treatment management techniques; innovative and alternative wastewater treatment processes; facilities deemed equivalent of secondary treatment

(1) The Administrator, after consultation with appropriate Federal and State agencies and other interested persons, shall publish within sixty days after October 18, 1972 (and from time to time thereafter) information, in terms of amounts of constituents and chemical, physical, and biological characteristics of pollutants, on the degree of effluent reduction attainable through the application of secondary treatment.

(2) The Administrator, after consultation with appropriate Federal and State agencies and other interested persons, shall publish within nine months after October 18, 1972 (and from time to time thereafter) information on alternative waste treatment management techniques and systems available to implement section 1281 of this title.

(3) The Administrator, after consultation with appropriate Federal and State agencies and other interested persons, shall promulgate within one hundred and eighty days after December 27, 1977, guidelines for identifying and evaluating innovative and alternative wastewater treatment processes and techniques referred to in section 1281(g)(5) of this title.

(4) For the purposes of this subsection, such biological treatment facilities as oxidation ponds, lagoons, and ditches and trickling filters shall be deemed the equivalent of secondary treatment. The Administrator shall provide guidance under paragraph (1) of this subsection on design criteria for such facilities, taking into account pollutant removal efficiencies and, consistent with the objectives of this chapter, assuring that water quality will not be adversely affected by deeming such facilities as the equivalent of secondary treatment.

(e) Best management practices for industry

The Administrator, after consultation with appropriate Federal and State agencies and other interested persons, may publish regulations, supplemental to any effluent limitations specified under subsections (b) and (c) of this section for a class or category of point sources, for any specific pollutant which the Administrator is charged with a duty to regulate as a toxic or hazardous pollutant under section 1317(a)(1) or 1321 of this title, to control plant site runoff, spillage or leaks, sludge or waste disposal, and drainage from raw material storage which the Administrator determines are associated with or ancillary to the industrial manufacturing or treatment process within such class or category of point sources and may contribute significant amounts of such pollutants to navigable waters. Any applicable controls established under this subsection shall be included as a requirement for the purposes of section 1311, 1312, 1316, 1317, or 1343 of this title, as the case may be, in any permit issued to a point source pursuant to section 1342 of this title.

(f) Identification and evaluation of nonpoint sources of pollution; processes, procedures, and methods to control pollution

The Administrator, after consultation with appropriate Federal and State agencies and other interested persons, shall issue to appropriate Federal agencies, the States, water pollution control agencies, and agencies designated under section 1288 of this title, within one year after October 18, 1972 (and from time to time thereafter) information including (1) guidelines for identifying and evaluating the nature and extent of nonpoint sources of pollutants, and (2) processes, procedures, and methods to control pollution resulting from—

(A) agricultural and silvicultural activities, including runoff from fields and crop and forest lands;

(B) mining activities, including runoff and siltation from new, currently operating, and abandoned surface and underground mines;

(C) all construction activity, including runoff from the facilities resulting from such construction;

(D) the disposal of pollutants in wells or in subsurface excavations;

(E) salt water intrusion resulting from reductions of fresh water flow from any cause, including extraction of ground water, irrigation, obstruction, and diversion; and

(F) changes in the movement, flow, or circulation of any navigable waters or ground waters, including changes caused by the construction of dams, levees, channels, causeways, or flow diversion facilities.

Such information and revisions thereof shall be published in the Federal Register and otherwise made available to the public.

(g) Guidelines for pretreatment of pollutants

(1) For the purpose of assisting States in carrying out programs under section 1342 of this title, the Administrator shall publish, within one hundred and twenty days after October 18, 1972, and review at least annually thereafter and, if appropriate, revise guidelines for pretreatment of pollutants which he determines are not susceptible to treatment by publicly owned treatment works. Guidelines under this subsection shall be established to control and prevent the discharge into the navigable waters, the contiguous zone, or the ocean (either directly or through publicly owned treatment works) of any pollutant which interferes with, passes through, or otherwise is incompatible with such works.

(2) When publishing guidelines under this subsection, the Administrator shall designate the category or categories of treatment works to which the guidelines shall apply.

(h) Test procedures guidelines

The Administrator shall, within one hundred and eighty days from October 18, 1972, promulgate guidelines establishing test procedures for the analysis of pollutants that shall include the factors which must be provided in any certification pursuant to section 1341 of this title or permit application pursuant to section 1342 of this title.

(i) Guidelines for monitoring, reporting, enforcement, funding, personnel, and manpower

The Administrator shall (1) within sixty days after October 18, 1972, promulgate guidelines for the purpose of establishing uniform application forms and other minimum requirements for the acquisition of information from owners and operators of point-sources of discharge subject to any State program under section 1342 of this title, and (2) within sixty days from October 18, 1972, promulgate guidelines establishing the minimum procedural and other elements of any State program under section 1342 of this title, which shall include:

(A) monitoring requirements;

(B) reporting requirements (including procedures to make information available to the public);

(C) enforcement provisions; and

(D) funding, personnel qualifications, and manpower requirements (including a requirement that no board or body which approves permit applications or portions thereof shall include, as a member, any person who receives, or has during the previous two years received, a significant portion of his income directly or indirectly from permit holders or applicants for a permit).

(j) Lake restoration guidance manual

The Administrator shall, within 1 year after February 4, 1987, and biennially thereafter, publish and disseminate a lake restoration guidance manual describing methods, procedures, and processes to guide State and local efforts to improve, restore, and enhance water quality in the Nation's publicly owned lakes.

(k) Agreements with Secretaries of Agriculture, Army, and Interior to provide maximum utilization of programs to achieve and maintain water quality; transfer of funds; authorization of appropriations

(1) The Administrator shall enter into agreements with the Secretary of Agriculture, the Secretary of the Army, and the Secretary of the Interior, and the heads of such other departments, agencies, and instrumentalities of the United States as the Administrator determines, to provide for the maximum utilization of other Federal laws and programs for the purpose of achieving and maintaining water quality through appropriate implementation of plans approved under section 1288 of this title and nonpoint source pollution management programs approved under section 1329 of this title.

(2) The Administrator is authorized to transfer to the Secretary of Agriculture, the Secretary of the Army, and the Secretary of the Interior and the heads of such other departments, agencies, and instrumentalities of the United States as the Administrator determines, any funds appropriated under paragraph (3) of this subsection to supplement funds otherwise appropriated to programs authorized pursuant to any agreement under paragraph (1).

(3) There is authorized to be appropriated to carry out the provisions of this subsection, $100,000,000 per fiscal year for the fiscal years 1979 through 1983 and such sums as may be necessary for fiscal years 1984 through 1990.

(*l*) Individual control strategies for toxic pollutants

(1) State list of navigable waters and development of strategies

Not later than 2 years after February 4, 1987, each State shall submit to the Administrator for review, approval, and implementation under this subsection—

(A) a list of those waters within the State which after the application of effluent limitations required under section 1311(b)(2) of this title cannot reasonably be anticipated to attain or maintain (i) water quality standards for such waters reviewed, revised, or adopted in accordance with section 1313(c)(2)(B) of this title, due to toxic pollutants, or (ii) that water quality which shall assure protection of public health, public water supplies, agricultural and industrial uses, and the protection and propagation of a balanced population of shellfish, fish and wildlife, and allow recreational activities in and on the water;

(B) a list of all navigable waters in such State for which the State does not expect the applicable standard under section 1313 of this title will be achieved after the requirements of sections 1311(b), 1316, and 1317(b) of this title are met, due entirely or substantially to discharges from point sources of any toxic pollutants listed pursuant to section 1317(a) of this title;

(C) for each segment of the navigable waters included on such lists, a determination of the specific point sources discharging any such toxic pollutant which is believed to be preventing or impairing such water quality and the amount of each such toxic pollutant discharged by each such source; and

(D) for each such segment, an individual control strategy which the State determines will produce a reduction in the discharge of toxic pollutants from point sources identified by the State under this paragraph through the establishment of effluent limitations under section 1342 of this title and water quality standards under section 1313(c)(2)(B) of this title, which reduction is sufficient, in combination with existing controls on point and nonpoint sources of pollution, to achieve the applicable water quality standard as soon as possible, but not later than 3 years after the date of the establishment of such strategy.

(2) Approval or disapproval

Not later than 120 days after the last day of the 2-year period referred to in paragraph (1), the Administrator shall approve or disapprove the control strategies submitted under paragraph (1) by any State.

(3) Administrator's action

If a State fails to submit control strategies in accordance with paragraph (1) or the Administrator does not approve the control strategies submitted by such State in accordance with paragraph (1), then, not later than 1 year after the last day of the period referred to in paragraph (2), the Administrator, in cooperation with such State and after notice and opportunity for public comment, shall implement the requirements of paragraph (1) in such State. In the implementation of such requirements, the Administrator shall, at a minimum, consider for listing under this subsection any navigable waters for which any person submits a petition to the Administrator for listing not later than 120 days after such last day.

(m) Schedule for review of guidelines

(1) Publication

Within 12 months after February 4, 1987, and biennially thereafter, the Administrator shall publish in the Federal Register a plan which shall—

(A) establish a schedule for the annual review and revision of promulgated effluent guidelines, in accordance with subsection (b) of this section;

(B) identify categories of sources discharging toxic or nonconventional pollutants for which guidelines under subsection (b)(2) of this section and section 1316 of this title have not previously been published; and

(C) establish a schedule for promulgation of effluent guidelines for categories identified in subparagraph (B), under which promulgation of such guidelines shall be no later than 4 years after February 4, 1987, for categories identified in the first published plan or 3 years after the publication of the plan for categories identified in later published plans.

(2) Public review

The Administrator shall provide for public review and comment on the plan prior to final publication.

(June 30, 1948, c. 758, Title III, § 304, as added Oct. 18, 1972, Pub.L. 92–500, § 2, 86 Stat. 850, and amended Dec. 27, 1977, Pub.L. 95–217, §§ 48–51, 62(b), 91 Stat. 1587, 1588, 1598; Dec. 29, 1981, Pub.L. 97–117, § 23, 95 Stat. 1632; Feb. 4, 1987, Pub.L. 100–4, Title I, § 101(f), Title III, §§ 308(a), (c), (f), 315(c), 316(e), 101 Stat. 9, 38–40, 52, 61.)

CROSS REFERENCES

Authorization of appropriations to carry out this chapter other than this section, see section 1376 of this title.
Definition of "construction" as including field testing of innovative techniques meeting guidelines promulgated under this section, see section 1292 of this title.
Dissemination of information gained under this section, see section 1255 of this title.
Establishment of total maximum daily load for pollutants identified under this section, see section 1313 of this title.
Grants for treatment works utilizing guidelines under this section, see section 1281 of this title.
Higher priority for grants for cost of preparing construction drawings for treatment works utilizing processes meeting guidelines promulgated under this section, see section 1284 of this title.
Permits for discharge of pollutants, see section 1342 of this title.
Program of cooperation for utilizing wastewater control systems utilizing innovative treatment processes for which guidelines have been promulgated under this section, see section 1323 of this title.
Regulations for carrying out agricultural cost sharing, subject to this section, see section 1288 of this title.
Standards for commercial vessels on the Great Lakes requiring at minimum the equivalent of secondary treatment as defined under this section, see section 1322 of this title.
State reports on water quality, see section 1315 of this title.
Subpoena for obtaining information under this section, see section 1369 of this title.
Timetable for achievement of effluent limitations, see section 1311 of this title.
Toxic and pretreatment effluent standards, see section 1317 of this title.
Waiver of requirements for transmittal of State permit applications to Administrator, see section 1344 of this title.

CODE OF FEDERAL REGULATIONS

Criteria and standards for the National Pollutant Discharge Elimination System, see 40 CFR 125.1 et seq.
Effluent guidelines and standards, see 40 CFR Chap. I, Subchap. N.
Guidelines establishing test procedures for analysis of pollutants, see 40 CFR 136.1 et seq.
Secondary treatment regulation, see 40 CFR 133.100 et seq.

LAW REVIEW COMMENTARIES

From elephants to mice: The development of EBMUD's program to control small source wastewater discharges. Raoul Stewardson, 20 Ecology L.Q. 441 (1993).

Long-range planning in environmental and health regulatory agencies. Richard N.L. Andrews, 20 Ecology L.Q. 515 (1993).

Toward a national groundwater act: Current contamination and future courses of action. Thomas D. Marks, 61 Fla.B.J. 10 (April 1987).

United States Supreme Court

Guidelines under this section, use in regulations establishing existing point source effluent limitations, see E.I. du Pont de Nemours & Co. v. Train, 1977, 97 S.Ct. 965, 430 U.S. 112, 51 L.Ed.2d 204.

LIBRARY REFERENCES

Health and Environment ⟹25.7(10).
C.J.S. Health and Environment § 106 et seq.

§ 1315. State reports on water quality; transmittal to Congress [FWPCA § 305]

(a) Omitted.

(b)(1) Each State shall prepare and submit to the Administrator by April 1, 1975, and shall bring up to date by April 1, 1976, and biennially thereafter, a report which shall include—

(A) a description of the water quality of all navigable waters in such State during the preceding year, with appropriate supplemental descriptions as shall be required to take into account seasonal, tidal, and other variations, correlated with the quality of water required by the objective of this chapter (as identified by the Administrator pursuant to criteria published under section 1314(a) of this title) and the water quality described in subparagraph (B) of this paragraph;

(B) an analysis of the extent to which all navigable waters of such State provide for the protection and propagation of a balanced population of shellfish, fish, and wildlife, and allow recreational activities in and on the water;

(C) an analysis of the extent to which the elimination of the discharge of pollutants and a level of water quality which provides for the protection and propagation of a balanced population of shellfish, fish, and wildlife and allows recreational activities in and on the water, have been or will be achieved by the requirements of this chapter, together with recommendations as to additional action necessary to achieve such objectives and for what waters such additional action is necessary;

(D) an estimate of (i) the environmental impact, (ii) the economic and social costs necessary to achieve the objective of this chapter in such State, (iii) the economic and social benefits of such achievement, and (iv) an estimate of the date of such achievement; and

(E) a description of the nature and extent of nonpoint sources of pollutants, and recommendations as to the programs which must be undertaken to control each category of such sources, including an estimate of the costs of implementing such programs.

(2) The Administrator shall transmit such State reports, together with an analysis thereof, to Congress on or before October 1, 1975, and October 1, 1976, and biennially thereafter.

(June 30, 1948, c. 758, Title III, § 305, as added Oct. 18, 1972, Pub.L. 92–500, § 2, 86 Stat. 853, and amended Dec. 27, 1977, Pub.L. 95–217, § 52, 91 Stat. 1589.)

CROSS REFERENCES

Grants prohibited to States not complying with requirements of this section, see section 1256 of this title.
Records required to be kept for carrying out the requirements of this section, see section 1318 of this title.
Subpoenas for obtaining information under this section, see section 1369 of this title.

CODE OF FEDERAL REGULATIONS

Water quality planning and management, see 40 CFR 130.0 et seq.

§ 1316. National standards of performance [FWPCA § 306]

(a) Definitions

For purposes of this section:

(1) The term "standard of performance" means a standard for the control of the discharge of pollutants which reflect the greatest degree of effluent reduction which the Administrator determines to be achievable through application of the best available demonstrated control technology, processes, operating methods, or other alternatives, including, where practicable, a standard permitting no discharge of pollutants.

(2) The term "new source" means any source, the construction of which is commenced after the publication of proposed regulations prescribing a standard of performance under this section which will be applicable to such source, if such standard is thereafter promulgated in accordance with this section.

(3) The term "source" means any building, structure, facility, or installation from which there is or may be the discharge of pollutants.

(4) The term "owner or operator" means any person who owns, leases, operates, controls, or supervises a source.

(5) The term "construction" means any placement, assembly, or installation of facilities or equipment (including contractual obligations to purchase such facilities or equipment) at the premises where such equipment will be used, including preparation work at such premises.

(b) Categories of sources; Federal standards of performance for new sources

(1)(A) The Administrator shall, within ninety days after October 18, 1972, publish (and from time to time thereafter shall revise) a list of categories of sources, which shall, at the minimum, include:

pulp and paper mills;
paperboard, builders paper and board mills;
meat product and rendering processing;
dairy product processing;
grain mills;
canned and preserved fruits and vegetables processing;
canned and preserved seafood processing;
sugar processing;
textile mills;
cement manufacturing;
feedlots;
electroplating;
organic chemicals manufacturing;
inorganic chemicals manufacturing;
plastic and synthetic materials manufacturing;
soap and detergent manufacturing;
fertilizer manufacturing;
petroleum refining;
iron and steel manufacturing;
nonferrous metals manufacturing;
phosphate manufacturing;
steam electric powerplants;
ferroalloy manufacturing;
leather tanning and finishing;
glass and asbestos manufacturing;
rubber processing; and
timber products processing.

(B) As soon as practicable, but in no case more than one year, after a category of sources is included in a list under subparagraph (A) of this paragraph, the Administrator shall propose and publish regulations establishing Federal standards of performance for new sources within such category. The Administrator shall afford interested persons an opportunity for written comment on such proposed regulations. After considering such comments, he shall promulgate, within one hundred and twenty days after publication of such proposed regulations, such standards with such adjustments as he deems appropriate. The Administrator shall, from time to time, as technology and alternatives change, revise such standards following the procedure required by this subsection for promulgation of such standards. Standards of performance, or revisions thereof, shall become effective upon promulgation. In establishing or revising Federal standards of performance for new sources under this section, the Administrator shall take into consideration the cost of achieving such effluent reduction, and any non-water quality, environmental impact and energy requirements.

(2) The Administrator may distinguish among classes, types, and sizes within categories of new sources for the purpose of establishing such standards and shall consider the type of process employed (including whether batch or continuous).

(3) The provisions of this section shall apply to any new source owned or operated by the United States.

(c) State enforcement of standards of performance

Each State may develop and submit to the Administrator a procedure under State law for applying and enforcing standards of performance for new sources located in such State. If the Administrator finds that the procedure and the law of any State require the application and enforcement of standards of performance to at least the same extent as required by this section, such State is authorized to apply and enforce such standards of performance (except with respect to new sources owned or operated by the United States).

(d) Protection from more stringent standards

Notwithstanding any other provision of this chapter, any point source the construction of which is commenced after October 18, 1972, and which is so constructed as to meet all applicable standards of performance shall not be subject to any more stringent standard of performance during a ten-year period beginning on the date of completion of such construction or during the period of depreciation or amortization of such facility for the purposes of section 167 or 169 (or both) of title 26 whichever period ends first.

(e) Illegality of operation of new sources in violation of applicable standards of performance

After the effective date of standards of performance promulgated under this section, it shall be unlawful for any owner or operator of any new source to operate such source in violation of any standard of performance applicable to such source.

(June 30, 1948, c. 758, Title III, § 306, as added Oct. 18, 1972, Pub.L. 92–500, § 2, 86 Stat. 854.)

CROSS REFERENCES

Applicant for Federal license or permit, certification of compliance with provisions of this section, see section 1341 of this title.

Approval of continuing planning processes resulting in plans including effluent limitations and schedules of compliance as stringent as those required by this section, see section 1313 of this title.

Employee protection, employees in deliberate violation of this section, see section 1367 of this title.

Enforcement of conditions of this section, see section 1319 of this title.

Federal facilities, exemptions from requirements of this chapter other than this section, see section 1323 of this title.

Illegality of pollutant discharges except in compliance with this section, see section 1311 of this title.

Information on the processes and procedures resulting in reduction or elimination of pollutants to implement standards of performance under this section, see section 1314 of this title.
Judicial review of administrator's action in promulgating standards under this section, see section 1369 of this title.
Notice of citizen actions, see section 1365 of this title.
Notice of intent to propose standard of performance for new source required by this section, see section 1374 of this title.
Permit for discharge of any pollutant by new source as defined under this section deemed major Federal action, see section 1371 of this title.
Permits for discharge of pollutants meeting requirements of this section, see section 1342 of this title.
State permit program, see section 1342 of this title.
Thermal discharges, protection and propagation of fish and wildlife, see section 1326 of this title.

CODE OF FEDERAL REGULATIONS

Effluent guidelines and standards, see 40 CFR Chap. I, Subchap. N.

LAW REVIEW COMMENTARIES

Warrior and the Druid—the DOD and environmental law. Michael Donnelly and James G. Van Ness, 33 Fed.Bar News 37 (1986).

LIBRARY REFERENCES

Health and Environment ⚷25.7(10).
C.J.S. Health and Environment § 106 et seq.

§ 1317. Toxic and pretreatment effluent standards [FWPCA § 307]

(a) Toxic pollutant list; revision; hearing; promulgation of standards; effective date; consultation

(1) On and after December 27, 1977, the list of toxic pollutants or combination of pollutants subject to this chapter shall consist of those toxic pollutants listed in table 1 of Committee Print Numbered 95–30 of the Committee on Public Works and Transportation of the House of Representatives, and the Administrator shall publish, not later than the thirtieth day after December 27, 1977, that list. From time to time thereafter, the Administrator may revise such list and the Administrator is authorized to add to or remove from such list any pollutant. The Administrator in publishing any revised list, including the addition or removal of any pollutant from such list, shall take into account toxicity of the pollutant, its persistence, degradability, the usual or potential presence of the affected organisms in any waters, the importance of the affected organisms, and the nature and extent of the effect of the toxic pollutant on such organisms. A determination of the Administrator under this paragraph shall be final except that if, on judicial review, such determination was based on arbitrary and capricious action of the Administrator, the Administrator shall make a redetermination.

(2) Each toxic pollutant listed in accordance with paragraph (1) of this subsection shall be subject to effluent limitations resulting from the application of the best available technology economically achievable for the applicable category or class of point sources established in accordance with sections 1311(b)(2)(A) and 1314(b)(2) of this title. The Administrator, in his discretion, may publish in the Federal Register a proposed effluent standard (which may include a prohibition) establishing requirements for a toxic pollutant which, if an effluent limitation is applicable to a class or category of point sources, shall be applicable to such category or class only if such standard imposes more stringent requirements. Such published effluent standard (or prohibition) shall take into account the toxicity of the pollutant, its persistence, degradability, the usual or potential presence of the affected organisms in any waters, the importance of the affected organisms and the nature and extent of the effect of the toxic pollutant on such organisms, and the extent to which effective control is being or may be achieved under other regulatory authority. The Administrator shall allow a period of not less than sixty days following publication of any such proposed effluent standard (or prohibition) for written comment by interested persons on such proposed standard. In addition, if within thirty days of publication of any such proposed effluent standard (or prohibition) any interested person so requests, the Administrator shall hold a public hearing in connection therewith. Such a public hearing shall provide an opportunity for oral and written presentations, such cross-examination as the Administrator determines is appropriate on disputed issues of material fact, and the transcription of a verbatim record which shall be available to the public. After consideration of such comments and any information and material presented at any public hearing held on such proposed standard or prohibition, the Administrator shall promulgate such standard (or prohibition) with such modification as the Administrator finds are justified. Such promulgation by the Administrator shall be made within two hundred and seventy days after publication of proposed standard (or prohibition). Such standard (or prohibition) shall be final except that if, on judicial review, such standard was not based on substantial evidence, the Administrator shall promulgate a revised standard. Effluent limitations shall be established in accordance with sections 1311(b)(2)(A) and 1314(b)(2) of this title for every toxic pollutant referred to in table 1 of Committee Print Numbered 95–30 of the Committee on Public Works and Transportation of the House of Representatives as soon as practicable after December 27, 1977, but no later than July 1, 1980. Such effluent limitations or effluent standards (or prohibitions) shall be established for every other toxic pollutant listed under paragraph (1) of this subsection as soon as practicable after it is so listed.

(3) Each such effluent standard (or prohibition) shall be reviewed and, if appropriate, revised at least every three years.

(4) Any effluent standard promulgated under this section shall be at that level which the Administrator determines provides an ample margin of safety.

(5) When proposing or promulgating any effluent standard (or prohibition) under this section, the Administrator shall designate the category or categories of sources to which the effluent standard (or prohibition) shall apply. Any disposal of dredged material may be included in such a category of sources after consultation with the Secretary of the Army.

(6) Any effluent standard (or prohibition) established pursuant to this section shall take effect on such date or dates as specified in the order promulgating such standard, but in no case, more than one year from the date of such promulgation. If the Administrator determines that compliance within one year from the date of promulgation is technologically infeasible for a category of sources, the Administrator may establish the effective date of the effluent standard (or prohibition) for such category at the earliest date upon which compliance can be feasibly attained by sources within such category, but in no event more than three years after the date of such promulgation.

(7) Prior to publishing any regulations pursuant to this section the Administrator shall, to the maximum extent practicable within the time provided, consult with appropriate advisory committees, States, independent experts, and Federal departments and agencies.

(b) Pretreatment standards; hearing; promulgation; compliance period; revision; application to State and local laws

(1) The Administrator shall, within one hundred and eighty days after October 18, 1972, and from time to time thereafter, publish proposed regulations establishing pretreatment standards for introduction of pollutants into treatment works (as defined in section 1292 of this title) which are publicly owned for those pollutants which are determined not to be susceptible to treatment by such treatment works or which would interfere with the operation of such treatment works. Not later than ninety days after such publication, and after opportunity for public hearing, the Administrator shall promulgate such pretreatment standards. Pretreatment standards under this subsection shall specify a time for compliance not to exceed three years from the date of promulgation and shall be established to prevent the discharge of any pollutant through treatment works (as defined in section 1292 of this title) which are publicly owned, which pollutant interferes with, passes through, or otherwise is incompatible with such works. If, in the case of any toxic pollutant under subsection (a) of this section introduced by a source into a publicly owned treatment works, the treatment by such works removes all or any part of such toxic pollutant and the discharge from such works does not violate that effluent limitation or standard which would be applicable to such toxic pollutant if it were discharged by such source other than through a publicly owned treatment works, and does not prevent sludge use or disposal by such works in accordance with section 1345 of this title, then the pretreatment requirements for the sources actually discharging such toxic pollutant into such publicly owned treatment works may be revised by the owner or operator of such works to reflect the removal of such toxic pollutant by such works.

(2) The Administrator shall, from time to time, as control technology, processes, operating methods, or other alternatives change, revise such standards following the procedure established by this subsection for promulgation of such standards.

(3) When proposing or promulgating any pretreatment standard under this section, the Administrator shall designate the category or categories of sources to which such standard shall apply.

(4) Nothing in this subsection shall affect any pretreatment requirement established by any State or local law not in conflict with any pretreatment standard established under this subsection.

(c) New sources of pollutants into publicly owned treatment works

In order to insure that any source introducing pollutants into a publicly owned treatment works, which source would be a new source subject to section 1316 of this title if it were to discharge pollutants, will not cause a violation of the effluent limitations established for any such treatment works, the Administrator shall promulgate pretreatment standards for the category of such sources simultaneously with the promulgation of standards of performance under section 1316 of this title for the equivalent category of new sources. Such pretreatment standards shall prevent the discharge of any pollutant into such treatment works, which pollutant may interfere with, pass through, or otherwise be incompatible with such works.

(d) Operation in violation of standards unlawful

After the effective date of any effluent standard or prohibition or pretreatment standard promulgated under this section, it shall be unlawful for any owner or operator of any source to operate any source in violation of any such effluent standard or prohibition or pretreatment standard.

(e) Compliance date extension for innovative pretreatment systems

In the case of any existing facility that proposes to comply with the pretreatment standards of subsection (b) of this section by applying an innovative system that meets the requirements of section 1311(k) of this title, the owner or operator of the publicly owned treatment works receiving the treated effluent from such facility may extend the date for compliance with the applicable pretreatment standard established under this section for a period not to exceed 2 years—

(1) if the Administrator determines that the innovative system has the potential for industrywide application, and

(2) if the Administrator (or the State in consultation with the Administrator, in any case in which the State has a pretreatment program approved by the Administrator)—

(A) determines that the proposed extension will not cause the publicly owned treatment works to be in violation of its permit under section 1342 of this title or of section 1345 of this title or to contribute to such a violation, and

(B) concurs with the proposed extension.

(June 30, 1948, c. 758, Title III, § 307, as added Oct. 18, 1972, Pub.L. 92–500, § 2, 86 Stat. 856, and amended Dec. 27, 1977, Pub.L. 95–217, §§ 53(a), (b), 54(a), 91 Stat. 1589–1591; Feb. 4, 1987, Pub.L. 100–4, Title III, § 309(a), 101 Stat. 41.)

Change of Name

Any reference in any provision of law enacted before Jan. 4, 1995, to the Committee on Public Works and Transportation of the House of Representatives treated as referring to the Committee on Transportation and Infrastructure of the House of Representatives, see section 1(a)(9) of Pub.L. 104–14, set out as a note preceding section 21 of Title 2, The Congress.

CROSS REFERENCES

Application for Federal license or permit, certificate of compliance with this section, see section 1341 of this title.
Approval of continuing planning process which includes effluent limitations as stringent as those in this section, see section 1313 of this title.
Areawide waste treatment management, see section 1288 of this title.
Best management practices for industry, see section 1314 of this title.
Definition of "hazardous substance" for purposes of liability and compensation for hazardous substances releases, see section 9601 of Title 42, The Public Health and Welfare.
Employee protection, deliberate violations by employee, see section 1367 of this title.
Enforcement of provisions of this chapter, see section 1319 of this title.
Federal facilities pollution control, exemption from provisions of this chapter other than this section, see section 1323 of this title.
Illegality of pollutant discharges except when in compliance with this section, see section 1311 of this title.
Judicial review of Administrator's actions, see section 1369 of this title.
Non-prohibited discharge of dredged or fill material, see section 1344 of this title.
Notice of action brought with respect to violation of this section, see section 1365 of this title.
Notice of action on proposed toxic effluent standard required by this section, see section 1374 of this title.
Permits for discharge of pollutants, see section 1342 of this title.
State permit programs, see section 1342 of this title.

CODE OF FEDERAL REGULATIONS

Effluent guidelines and standards, see 40 CFR Chap. I, Subchap. N.
Guidelines establishing test procedures for analysis of pollutants, see 40 CFR 136.1 et seq.
Public hearings on effluent standards for toxic pollutants, see 40 CFR 104.1 et seq.
Toxic pollutant effluent standards, see 40 CFR 129.1 et seq.

ADMINISTRATIVE LAW

Separation of functions in rulemaking procedures, see Koch § 4.72.

LAW REVIEW COMMENTARIES

Congressional ambiguity allows EPA's safety valve to remain open. 35 Catholic U.L.Rev. 595 (1986).

Economizing on the sins of our past: Cleaning up our hazardous wastes. Barbara Ann White, 25 Houston L.Rev. 899 (1988).

From elephants to mice: The development of EBMUD's program to control small source wastewater discharges. Raoul Stewardson, 20 Ecology L.Q. 441 (1993).

Long-range planning in environmental and health regulatory agencies. Richard N.L. Andrews, 20 Ecology L.Q. 515 (1993).

The once and future EPA lender regulations: Limiting lender liability for the cleanup of hazardous wastes. Jeffrey M. Gaba, 47 Consumer Fin.L.Q.Rep. 355 (1993).

LIBRARY REFERENCES

Health and Environment ⚷25.7(12).
C.J.S. Health and Environment § 107 et seq.

§ 1318. Records and reports; inspections [FWPCA § 308]

(a) Maintenance; monitoring equipment; entry; access to information

Whenever required to carry out the objective of this chapter, including but not limited to (1) developing or assisting in the development of any effluent limitation, or other limitation, prohibition, or effluent standard, pretreatment standard, or standard of performance under this chapter; (2) determining whether any person is in violation of any such effluent limitation, or other limitation, prohibition or effluent standard, pretreatment standard, or standard of performance; (3) any requirement established under this section; or (4) carrying out sections 1315, 1321, 1342, 1344 (relating to State permit programs), 1345, and 1364 of this title—

(A) the Administrator shall require the owner or operator of any point source to (i) establish and maintain such records, (ii) make such reports, (iii) install, use, and maintain such monitoring equipment or methods (including where appropriate, biological monitoring methods), (iv) sample such effluents (in accordance with such methods, at such locations, at such intervals, and in such manner as the Administrator shall prescribe), and (v) provide such other information as he may reasonably require; and

(B) the Administrator or his authorized representative (including an authorized contractor acting as a representative of the Administrator), upon presentation of his credentials—

(i) shall have a right of entry to, upon, or through any premises in which an effluent source is located or in which any records required to be maintained under clause (A) of this subsection are located, and

(ii) may at reasonable times have access to and copy any records, inspect any monitoring equipment or method required under clause (A), and sample any effluents which the owner or operator of such source is required to sample under such clause.

(b) Availability to public; trade secrets exception; penalty for disclosure of confidential information

Any records, reports, or information obtained under this section (1) shall, in the case of effluent data, be related to any applicable effluent limitations, toxic, pretreatment, or new source performance standards, and (2) shall be available to the public, except that upon a showing satisfactory to the Administrator by any person that records, reports, or information, or particular part thereof (other than effluent data), to which the Administrator has access under this section, if made public would divulge methods or processes entitled to protection as trade secrets of such person, the Administrator shall consider such record, report, or information, or particular portion thereof confidential in accordance with the purposes of section 1905 of Title 18. Any authorized representative of the Administrator (including an authorized contractor acting as a representative of the Administrator) who knowingly or willfully publishes, divulges, discloses, or makes known in any manner or to any extent not authorized by law any information which is required to be considered confidential under this subsection shall be fined not more than $1,000 or imprisoned not more than 1 year, or both. Nothing in this subsection shall prohibit the Administrator or an authorized representative of the Administrator (including any authorized contractor acting as a representative of the Administrator) from disclosing records, reports, or information to other officers, employees, or authorized representatives of the United States concerned with carrying out this chapter or when relevant in any proceeding under this chapter.

(c) Application of State law

Each State may develop and submit to the Administrator procedures under State law for inspection, monitoring, and entry with respect to point sources located in such State. If the Administrator finds that the procedures and the law of any State relating to inspection, monitoring, and entry are applicable to at least the same extent as those required by this section, such State is authorized to apply and enforce its procedures for inspection, monitoring, and entry with respect to point sources located in such State (except with respect to point sources owned or operated by the United States).

(d) Access by Congress

Notwithstanding any limitation contained in this section or any other provision of law, all information reported to or otherwise obtained by the Administrator (or any representative of the Administrator) under this chapter shall be made available, upon written request of any duly authorized committee of Congress, to such committee.

(June 30, 1948, ch. 758, title III, § 308, as added Oct. 18, 1972, Pub.L. 92–500, § 2, 86 Stat. 858, and amended Dec. 27, 1977, Pub.L. 95–217, § 67(c)(1), 91 Stat. 1606; Feb. 4, 1987, Pub.L. 100–4, Title III, § 310, Title IV, § 406(d)(1), 101 Stat. 41, 73.)

CROSS REFERENCES

Enforcement action for violation of any condition which implements this section, see section 1319 of this title.

Guidelines for use of imminent hazard, enforcement, and emergency response authorities, see section 9606 of Title 42, The Public Health and Welfare.

Non-prohibited discharge of dredged or fill material, see section 1344 of this title.

Permits for discharge of pollutants, see section 1342 of this title.

CODE OF FEDERAL REGULATIONS

Electrical and electronic components point source category, see 40 CFR 469.10 et seq.

General pretreatment regulations for existing and new sources of pollution, see 40 CFR 403.1 et seq.

Iron and steel manufacturing point source category, see 40 CFR 420.01 et seq.

Metal finishing point source category, see 40 CFR 433.10 et seq.

Plastics molding and forming point source category, see 40 CFR 463.1 et seq.

Public information, see 40 CFR 2.100 et seq.

Secondary treatment regulation, see 40 CFR 133.100 et seq.

Toxic pollutant effluent standards, see 40 CFR 129.1 et seq.

LAW REVIEW COMMENTARIES

From elephants to mice: The development of EBMUD's program to control small source wastewater discharges. Raoul Stewardson, 20 Ecology L.Q. 441 (1993).

Warrior and the Druid—the DOD and environmental law. Michael Donnelly and James G. Van Ness, 33 Fed.Bar News 37 (1986).

LIBRARY REFERENCES

Health and Environment ⚷25.7(18).

C.J.S. Health and Environment § 113 et seq.

§ 1319. Enforcement [FWPCA § 309]

(a) State enforcement; compliance orders

(1) Whenever, on the basis of any information available to him, the Administrator finds that any person is in violation of any condition or limitation which implements section 1311, 1312, 1316, 1317, 1318, 1328, or 1345 of this title in a permit issued by a State under an approved permit program under section 1342 or 1344 of this title he shall proceed under his authority in paragraph (3) of this subsection or he shall notify the person in alleged violation and such State of such finding. If beyond the thirtieth day after the Administrator's notification the State has not commenced appropriate enforcement action, the Administrator shall issue an order requiring such person to comply with such condition or limitation or shall bring a civil action in accordance with subsection (b) of this section.

(2) Whenever, on the basis of information available to him, the Administrator finds that violations of permit conditions or limitations as set forth in paragraph (1) of this subsection are so widespread that such violations appear to result from a failure of the State to enforce such permit conditions or limitations effectively, he shall so notify the State. If the Administrator finds such failure extends beyond the thirtieth day after such notice, he shall give public notice of such finding. During the period beginning with such public notice and ending when such State satisfies the Administrator that it will enforce such conditions and limitations (hereafter referred to in this section as the period of "federally assumed enforcement"), except where an extension has been granted under paragraph (5)(B) of this subsection, the Administrator shall enforce any permit condition or limitation with respect to any person—

(A) by issuing an order to comply with such condition or limitation, or

(B) by bringing a civil action under subsection (b) of this section.

(3) Whenever on the basis of any information available to him the Administrator finds that any person is in violation of section 1311, 1312, 1316, 1317, 1318, 1328, or 1345 of this title, or is in violation of any permit condition or limitation implementing any of such sections in a permit issued under section 1342 of this title by him or by a State or in a permit issued under section 1344 of this title by a State, he shall issue an order requiring such person to comply with such section or requirement, or he shall bring a civil action in accordance with subsection (b) of this section.

(4) A copy of any order issued under this subsection shall be sent immediately by the Administrator to the State in which the violation occurs and other affected States. In any case in which an order under this subsection (or notice to a violator under paragraph (1) of this subsection) is issued to a corporation, a copy of such order (or notice) shall be served on any appropriate corporate officers. An order issued under this subsection relating to a violation of section 1318 of this title shall not take effect until the person to whom it is issued has had an opportunity to confer with the Administrator concerning the alleged violation.

(5)(A) Any order issued under this subsection shall be by personal service, shall state with reasonable specificity the nature of the violation, and shall specify a time for compliance not to exceed thirty days in the case of a violation of an interim compliance schedule or operation and maintenance requirement and not to exceed a time the Administrator determines to be reasonable in the case of a violation of a final deadline, taking into account the seriousness of the violation and any good faith efforts to comply with applicable requirements.

(B) The Administrator may, if he determines (i) that any person who is a violator of, or any person who is otherwise not in compliance with, the time requirements under this chapter or in any permit issued under this chapter, has acted in good faith, and has made a commitment (in the form of contracts or other securities) of necessary resources to achieve compliance by the earliest possible date after July 1, 1977, but not later than April 1, 1979; (ii) that any extension under this provision will not result in the imposition of any additional controls on any other point or nonpoint source; (iii) that an application for a permit under section 1342 of this title was filed for such person prior to December 31, 1974; and (iv) that the facilities necessary for compliance with such requirements are under construction, grant an extension of the date referred to in section 1311(b)(1)(A) of this title to a date which will achieve compliance at the earliest time possible but not later than April 1, 1979.

(6) Whenever, on the basis of information available to him, the Administrator finds (A) that any person is in violation of section 1311(b)(1)(A) or (C) of this title, (B) that such person cannot meet the requirements for a time extension under section 1311(i)(2) of this title, and (C) that the most expeditious and appropriate means of compliance with this chapter by such person is to discharge into a publicly owned treatment works, then, upon request of such person, the Administrator may issue an order requiring such person to comply with this chapter at the earliest date practicable, but not later than July 1, 1983, by discharging into a publicly owned treatment works if such works concur with such order. Such order shall include a schedule of compliance.

(b) Civil actions

The Administrator is authorized to commence a civil action for appropriate relief, including a permanent or temporary injunction, for any violation for which he is authorized to issue a compliance order under subsection (a) of this section. Any action under this subsection may be brought in the district court of the United States for the district in which the defendant is located or resides or is doing business, and such court shall have jurisdiction to restrain such violation and to require compliance. Notice of the commencement of such action shall be given immediately to the appropriate State.

(c) Criminal penalties

(1) Negligent violations

Any person who—

(A) negligently violates section 1311, 1312, 1316, 1317, 1318, 1321(b)(3), 1328, or 1345 of this title, or any permit condition or limitation implementing any of such sections in a permit issued under section 1342 of this title by the Administrator or by a State, or any requirement imposed in a pretreatment program approved under section 1342(a)(3) or 1342(b)(8) of this title or in a permit issued under section 1344 of this title by the Secretary of the Army or by a State; or

(B) negligently introduces into a sewer system or into a publicly owned treatment works any pollutant or hazardous substance which such person knew or reasonably should have known could cause personal injury or property damage or, other than in compliance with all applicable Federal, State, or local requirements or permits, which causes such treatment works to violate any effluent limitation or condition in any permit issued to the treatment works under section 1342 of this title by the Administrator or a State;

shall be punished by a fine of not less than $2,500 nor more than $25,000 per day of violation, or by imprisonment for not more than 1 year, or by both. If a conviction of a person is for a violation committed after a first conviction of such person under this paragraph, punishment shall be by a fine of not more than $50,000 per day of violation, or by imprisonment of not more than 2 years, or by both.

(2) Knowing violations

Any person who—

(A) knowingly violates section 1311, 1312, 1316, 1317, 1318, 1321(b)(3), 1328, or 1345 of this title, or any permit condition or limitation implementing any of such sections in a permit issued under section 1342 of this title by the Administrator or by a State, or any requirement imposed in a pretreatment program approved under section 1342(a)(3) or 1342(b)(8) of this title or in a permit issued under section 1344 of this title by the Secretary of the Army or by a State; or

(B) knowingly introduces into a sewer system or into a publicly owned treatment works any pollutant or hazardous substance which such person knew or reasonably should have known could cause personal injury or property damage or, other than in compliance with all applicable Federal, State, or local requirements or permits, which causes such treatment works to violate any effluent limitation or condition in a permit issued to the treatment works under section 1342 of this title by the Administrator or a State;

shall be punished by a fine of not less than $5,000 nor more than $50,000 per day of violation, or by imprisonment for not more than 3 years, or by both. If a conviction of a person is for a violation committed after a first conviction of such person under this paragraph, punishment shall be by a fine of not more than $100,000 per day of violation, or by imprisonment of not more than 6 years, or by both.

(3) Knowing endangerment

(A) General rule

Any person who knowingly violates section 1311, 1312, 1313, 1316, 1317, 1318, 1328, or 1345 of this title, or any permit condition or limitation implementing any of such sections in a permit issued under section 1342 of this title by the Administrator or by a State, or in a permit issued under section 1344 of this title by the Secretary of the Army or by a State, and who knows at that time that he thereby places another person in imminent danger of death or serious bodily injury, shall, upon conviction, be subject to a fine of not more than $250,000 or imprisonment of not more than 15 years, or both. A person which is an organization shall, upon conviction of violating this subparagraph, be subject to a fine of not more than $1,000,000. If a conviction of a person is for a violation committed after a first conviction of such person under this paragraph, the maximum punishment shall be doubled with respect to both fine and imprisonment.

(B) Additional provisions

For the purpose of subparagraph (A) of this paragraph—

(i) in determining whether a defendant who is an individual knew that his conduct placed another person in imminent danger of death or serious bodily injury—

(I) the person is responsible only for actual awareness or actual belief that he possessed; and

(II) knowledge possessed by a person other than the defendant but not by the defendant himself may not be attributed to the defendant;

except that in proving the defendant's possession of actual knowledge, circumstantial evidence may be used, including evidence that the defendant took affirmative steps to shield himself from relevant information;

(ii) it is an affirmative defense to prosecution that the conduct charged was consented to by the person endangered and that the danger and conduct charged were reasonably foreseeable hazards of—

(I) an occupation, a business, or a profession; or

(II) medical treatment or medical or scientific experimentation conducted by professionally approved methods and such other person had been made aware of the risks involved prior to giving consent;

and such defense may be established under this subparagraph by a preponderance of the evidence;

(iii) the term "organization" means a legal entity, other than a government, established or organized for any purpose, and such term includes a corporation, company, association, firm, partnership, joint stock company, foundation, institution, trust, society, union, or any other association of persons; and

(iv) the term "serious bodily injury" means bodily injury which involves a substantial risk of death, unconsciousness, extreme physical pain, protracted and obvious disfigurement, or protracted loss or impairment of the function of a bodily member, organ, or mental faculty.

(4) False statements

Any person who knowingly makes any false material statement, representation, or certification in any application, record, report, plan, or other document filed or required to be maintained under this chapter or who knowingly falsifies, tampers with, or renders inaccurate any monitoring device or method required to be maintained under this chapter, shall upon conviction, be punished by a fine of not more than $10,000, or by imprisonment for not more than 2 years, or by both. If a conviction of a person is for a violation committed after a first conviction of such person under this paragraph, punishment shall be by a fine of not more than $20,000 per day of violation, or by imprisonment of not more than 4 years, or by both.

(5) Treatment of single operational upset

For purposes of this subsection, a single operational upset which leads to simultaneous violations of more than one pollutant parameter shall be treated as a single violation.

(6) Responsible corporate officer as "person"

For the purpose of this subsection, the term "person" means, in addition to the definition contained in section 1362(5) of this title, any responsible corporate officer.

(7) Hazardous substance defined

For the purpose of this subsection, the term "hazardous substance" means (A) any substance designated pursuant to section 1321(b)(2)(A) of this title, (B) any element, compound, mixture, solution, or substance designated pursuant to section 9602 of Title 42, (C) any hazardous waste having the characteristics identified under or listed pursuant to section 3001 of the Solid Waste Disposal Act [42 U.S.C.A. § 6921] (but not including any waste the regulation of which under the Solid Waste Disposal Act [42 U.S.C.A. § 6901 et seq.] has been suspended by Act of Congress), (D) any toxic pollutant listed under section 1317(a) of this title, and (E) any imminently hazardous chemical substance or mixture with respect to which the Administrator has taken action pursuant to section 2606 of Title 15.

(d) Civil penalties; factors considered in determining amount

Any person who violates section 1311, 1312, 1316, 1317, 1318, 1328, or 1345 of this title, or any permit condition or limitation implementing any of such sections in a permit issued under section 1342 of this title by the Administrator, or by a State, or in a permit issued under section 1344 of this title by a State,,[1] or any requirement imposed in a pretreatment program approved under section 1342(a)(3) or 1342(b)(8) of this title, and any person who violates any order issued by the Administrator under subsection (a) of this section, shall be subject to a civil penalty not to exceed $25,000 per day for each violation. In determining the amount of a civil penalty the court shall consider the seriousness of the violation or violations, the economic benefit (if any) resulting from the violation, any history of such violations, any good-faith efforts to comply with the applicable requirements, the economic impact of the penalty on the violator, and such other matters as justice may require. For purposes of this subsection, a single operational upset which leads to simultaneous violations of more than one pollutant parameter shall be treated as a single violation.

(e) State liability for judgments and expenses

Whenever a municipality is a party to a civil action brought by the United States under this section, the State in which such municipality is located shall be joined as a party. Such State shall be liable for payment of any judgment, or any expenses incurred as a result of complying with any judgment, entered against the municipality in such action to the extent that the laws of that State prevent the municipality from raising revenues needed to comply with such judgment.

(f) Wrongful introduction of pollutants into treatments works

Whenever, on the basis of any information available to him, the Administrator finds that an owner or operator of any source is introducing a pollutant into a treatment works in violation of subsection (d) of section 1317 of this title, the Administrator may notify the owner or operator of such treatment works and the State of such violation. If the owner or operator of the treatment works does not commence appropriate enforcement action within 30 days of the date of such notification, the Administrator may commence a civil action for appropriate relief, including but not limited to, a permanent or temporary injunction, against the owner or operator of such treatment works. In any such civil action the Administrator shall join the owner or operator of such source as a party to the action. Such action shall be brought in the district court of the United States in the district in which the treatment works is located. Such court shall have jurisdiction to restrain such violation and to require the owner or operator of the treatment works and the owner or operator of the source to take such action as may be necessary to come into compliance with this chapter. Notice of commencement of any such action shall be given to the State. Nothing in this subsection shall be construed to limit or prohibit any other authority the Administrator may have under this chapter.

(g) Administrative penalties

(1) Violations

Whenever on the basis of any information available—

(A) the Administrator finds that any person has violated section 1311, 1312, 1316, 1317, 1318, 1328, or 1345 of this title, or has violated any permit condition or limitation implementing any of such sections in a permit issued under section 1342 of this title by the Administrator or by a State, or in a permit issued under section 1344 of this title by a State, or

(B) the Secretary of the Army (hereinafter in this subsection referred to as the "Secretary") finds that any person has violated any permit condition or limitation in a permit issued under section 1344 of this title by the Secretary,

the Administrator or Secretary, as the case may be, may, after consultation with the State in which the violation occurs, assess a class I civil penalty or a class II civil penalty under this subsection.

(2) Classes of penalties

(A) Class I

The amount of a class I civil penalty under paragraph (1) may not exceed $10,000 per violation, except that the maximum amount of any class I civil penalty under this subparagraph shall not exceed $25,000. Before issuing an order assessing a civil penalty under this subparagraph, the Administrator or the Secretary, as the case may be, shall give to the person to be assessed such penalty written notice of the Administrator's or Secretary's proposal to issue such order and the opportunity to request, within 30 days of the date the notice is received by such person, a hearing on the proposed order. Such hearing shall not be subject to section 554 or 556 of Title 5, but shall provide a reasonable opportunity to be heard and to present evidence.

(B) Class II

The amount of a class II civil penalty under paragraph (1) may not exceed $10,000 per day for each day during which the violation continues; except that the maximum amount of any class II civil penalty under this subparagraph shall not exceed $125,000. Except as otherwise provided in this subsection, a class II civil penalty shall be assessed and collected in the same manner, and subject to the same provisions, as in the case of civil penalties assessed and collected after notice and opportunity for a hearing on the record in accordance with section 554 of Title 5. The Administrator and the Secretary may issue rules for discovery procedures for hearings under this subparagraph.

(3) Determining amount

In determining the amount of any penalty assessed under this subsection, the Administrator or the Secretary, as the case may be, shall take into account the nature, circumstances, extent and gravity of the violation, or violations, and, with respect to the violator, ability to pay, any prior history of such violations, the degree of culpability, economic benefit or savings (if any) resulting from the violation, and such other matters as justice may require. For purposes of this subsection, a single operational upset which leads to simultaneous violations of more than one pollutant parameter shall be treated as a single violation.

(4) Rights of interested persons

(A) Public notice

Before issuing an order assessing a civil penalty under this subsection the Administrator or Secretary, as the case may be, shall provide public notice of and reasonable opportunity to comment on the proposed issuance of such order.

(B) Presentation of evidence

Any person who comments on a proposed assessment of a penalty under this subsection shall be given notice of any hearing held under this subsection and of the order assessing such penalty. In any hearing held under this subsection, such person shall have a reasonable opportunity to be heard and to present evidence.

(C) Rights of interested persons to a hearing

If no hearing is held under paragraph (2) before issuance of an order assessing a penalty under this subsection, any person who commented on the proposed assessment may petition, within 30 days after the issuance of such order, the Administrator or Secretary, as the case may be, to set aside such order and to provide a hearing on the penalty. If the evidence presented by the petitioner in support of the petition is material and was not considered in the issuance of the order, the Administrator or Secretary shall immediately set aside such order and provide a hearing in accordance with paragraph (2)(A) in the case of a class I civil penalty and paragraph (2)(B) in the case of a class II civil penalty. If the Administrator or Secretary denies a hearing under this subparagraph, the Administrator or Secretary shall provide to the petitioner, and publish in the Federal Register, notice of and the reasons for such denial.

(5) Finality of order

An order issued under this subsection shall become final 30 days after its issuance unless a petition for judicial review is filed under paragraph (8) or a hearing is requested under paragraph (4)(C). If such a hearing is denied, such order shall become final 30 days after such denial.

(6) Effect of order

(A) Limitation on actions under other sections

Action taken by the Administrator or the Secretary, as the case may be, under this subsection shall not affect or limit the Administrator's or Secretary's authority to enforce any provision of this chapter; except that any violation—

(i) with respect to which the Administrator or the Secretary has commenced and is diligently prosecuting an action under this subsection,

(ii) with respect to which a State has commenced and is diligently prosecuting an action under a State law comparable to this subsection, or

(iii) for which the Administrator, the Secretary, or the State has issued a final order not subject to further judicial review and the violator has paid a penalty assessed under this subsection, or such comparable State law, as the case may be,

shall not be the subject of a civil penalty action under subsection (d) of this section or section 1321(b) of this title or section 1365 of this title.

(B) Applicability of limitation with respect to citizen suits

The limitations contained in subparagraph (A) on civil penalty actions under section 1365 of this title shall not apply with respect to any violation for which—

(i) a civil action under section 1365(a)(1) of this title has been filed prior to commencement of an action under this subsection, or

(ii) notice of an alleged violation of section 1365(a)(1) of this title has been given in accordance with section 1365(b)(1)(A) of this title prior to commencement of an action under this subsection and an action under section 1365(a)(1) of this title with respect to such alleged violation is filed before the 120th day after the date on which such notice is given.

(7) Effect of action on compliance

No action by the Administrator or the Secretary under this subsection shall affect any person's obligation to comply with any section of this chapter or with the terms and conditions of any permit issued pursuant to section 1342 or 1344 of this title.

(8) Judicial review

Any person against whom a civil penalty is assessed under this subsection or who commented on the proposed assessment of such penalty in accordance with paragraph (4) may obtain review of such assessment—

(A) in the case of assessment of a class I civil penalty, in the United States District Court for the District of Columbia or in the district in which the violation is alleged to have occurred, or

(B) in the case of assessment of a class II civil penalty, in United States Court of Appeals for the District of Columbia Circuit or for any other circuit in which such person resides or transacts business,

by filing a notice of appeal in such court within the 30-day period beginning on the date the civil penalty order is issued and by simultaneously sending a copy of such notice by certified mail to the Administrator or the Secretary, as the case may be, and the Attorney General. The Administrator or the Secretary shall promptly file in such court a certified copy of the record on which the order was issued. Such court shall not set aside or remand such order unless there is not substantial evidence in the record, taken as a whole, to support the finding of a violation or unless the Administrator's or Secretary's assessment of the penalty constitutes an abuse of discretion and shall not impose additional civil penalties for the same violation unless the Administrator's or Secretary's assessment of the penalty constitutes an abuse of discretion.

(9) Collection

If any person fails to pay an assessment of a civil penalty—

(A) after the order making the assessment has become final, or

(B) after a court in an action brought under paragraph (8) has entered a final judgment in favor of the Administrator or the Secretary, as the case may be,

the Administrator or the Secretary shall request the Attorney General to bring a civil action in an appropriate district court to recover the amount assessed (plus interest at currently prevailing rates from the date of the final order or the date of the final judgment, as the case may be). In such an action, the validity, amount, and appropriateness of such penalty shall not be subject to review. Any person who fails to pay on a timely basis the amount of an assessment of a civil penalty as described in the first sentence of this paragraph shall be required to pay, in addition to such amount and interest, attorneys fees and costs for collection proceedings and a quarterly nonpayment penalty for each quarter during which such failure to pay persists. Such nonpayment penalty shall be in an amount equal to 20 percent of the aggregate amount of such person's penalties and nonpayment penalties which are unpaid as of the beginning of such quarter.

(10) Subpoenas

The Administrator or Secretary, as the case may be, may issue subpoenas for the attendance and testimony of witnesses and the production of relevant papers, books, or documents in connection with hearings under this subsection. In case of contumacy or refusal to obey a subpoena issued pursuant to this paragraph and served upon any person, the district court of the United States for any district in which such person is found, resides, or transacts business, upon application by the United States and after notice to such person, shall have jurisdiction to issue an order requiring such person to appear and give testimony before the administrative law judge or to appear and produce documents before the administrative law judge, or both, and any failure to obey such order of the court may be punished by such court as a contempt thereof.

(11) Protection of existing procedures

Nothing in this subsection shall change the procedures existing on the day before February 4, 1987, under other subsections of this section for issuance and enforcement of orders by the Administrator.

(June 30, 1948, c. 758, Title III, § 309, as added Oct. 18, 1972, Pub.L. 92–500, § 2, 86 Stat. 859, and amended Dec. 27, 1977, Pub.L. 95–217, §§ 54(b), 55, 56, 67(c)(2), 91 Stat. 1591, 1592, 1606; Feb. 4, 1987, Pub.L. 100–4, Title III, §§ 312, 313(a)(1), (b)(1), (c), 314(a), 101 Stat. 42, 45, 46; Aug. 18, 1990, Pub.L. 101–380, Title IV, § 4301(c), 104 Stat. 537.)

[1] So in original.

CROSS REFERENCES

Condition of grant to State that no federally assumed enforcement as defined in this section is in effect, see section 1256 of this title.

Costs of response incurred by Federal Government in connection with discharge recoverable in action brought under this section, see section 9607 of Title 42, The Public Health and Welfare.

Guidelines for use of imminent hazard, enforcement, and emergency response authorities, see section 9606 of Title 42.

Jurisdiction of district courts to apply civil penalties under this section, see section 1365 of this title.

Liability of owner or operator for costs of removal incurred in connection with a discharge of oil or hazardous substance, see section 1321 of this title.

National pollutant discharge elimination system, authority of Administrator to take action under this section, see section 1342 of this title.

Permits for dredged or fill material, authority of Administrator to take action under this section, see section 1344 of this title.

Prohibition of Federal procurement contracts with persons convicted under this section, see section 1368 of this title.

West's Federal Forms

Indictment, false statements in reports filed with Environmental Protection Agency, see § 7135.5.

Federal Jury Practice and Instructions

Elements of offense, discharging pollutant into natural waterway, see Devitt and Blackmar § 64.02 Notes.

CODE OF FEDERAL REGULATIONS

General pretreatment regulations for existing and new sources of pollution, see 40 CFR 403:1 et seq.

LAW REVIEW COMMENTARIES

Citizen-suit provisions under the Federal Water Pollution Control Act: Are remedies available for past violations? Comment, 19 Conn. L.Rev. 589 (1987).

Considerations of the scienter requirement and the responsible corporate officer doctrine for knowing violations of environmental statutes. Kevin L. Colbert, 33 S.Tex.L.Rev. 699 (1992).

Criminal sanctions under federal and state environmental statutes. Richard H. Allan, 14 Ecology L.Q. 117 (1987).

Erosion of mens rea in environmental criminal prosecution. Ruth Ann Weidel, John R. Mayo and F. Michael Zachara, 21 Seton Hall L.Rev. 1125 (1991).

From elephants to mice: The development of EBMUD's program to control small source wastewater discharges. Raoul Stewardson, 20 Ecology L.Q. 441 (1993).

Listing and debarment: The Stealth bombers. Edward L. Grimsley, 5 S.C.Law. 22 (Nov.–Dec. 1993).

Prosecution of corporations and corporate officers for environmental crimes: Limiting one's exposure for environmental criminal liability. Kenneth A. Hodson, Sarah N. McGiffert and Marianne T. Bayardi, 34 Ariz.L.Rev. 553 (1992).

Responding to a government environmental investigation: Shaping the defense. Francis J. Burke, Jr., Karen A. Potts, Leigh Lani Brown, Robin L. De Respino and Michael R. Hall, 34 Ariz.L.Rev. 509 (1992).

Responsible corporate officer: Designated felon or legal fiction? Brenda S. Hustis and John Y. Gotanda, 25 Loy.U.Chi.L.J. 169 (1994).

Survey of federal and state environmental crime legislation. Edward F. Novak and Charles W. Steese, 34 Ariz.L.Rev. 571 (1992).

Warrior and the Druid—the DOD and environmental law. Michael Donnelly and James G. Van Ness, 33 Fed.Bar News 37 (1986).

LIBRARY REFERENCES

Health and Environment ⇔25.7(17).
C.J.S. Health and Environment § 113 et seq.

§ 1320. International pollution abatement [FWPCA § 310]

(a) Hearing; participation by foreign nations

Whenever the Administrator, upon receipts of reports, surveys, or studies from any duly constituted international agency, has reason to believe that pollution is occurring which endangers the health or welfare of persons in a foreign country, and the Secretary of State requests him to abate such pollution, he shall give formal notification thereof to the State water pollution control agency of the State or States in which such discharge or discharges originate and to the appropriate interstate agency, if any. He shall also promptly call such a hearing, if he believes that such pollution is occurring in sufficient quantity to warrant such action, and if such foreign country has given the United States essentially the same rights with respect to the prevention and control of pollution occurring in that country as is given that country by this subsection. The Administrator, through the Secretary of State, shall invite the foreign country which may be adversely affected by the pollution to attend and participate in the hearing, and the representative of such country shall, for the purpose of the hearing and any further proceeding resulting from such hearing, have all the rights of a State water pollution control agency. Nothing in this subsection shall be construed to modify, amend, repeal, or otherwise affect the provisions of the 1909 Boundary Waters Treaty between Canada and the United States or the Water Utilization Treaty of 1944 between Mexico and the United States (59 Stat. 1219), relative to the control and abatement of pollution in waters covered by those treaties.

(b) Functions and responsibilities of Administrator not affected

The calling of a hearing under this section shall not be construed by the courts, the Administrator, or any person as limiting, modifying, or otherwise affecting the functions and responsibilities of the Administrator under this section to establish and enforce water quality requirements under this chapter.

(c) Hearing board; composition; findings of fact; recommendations; implementation of board's decision

The Administrator shall publish in the Federal Register a notice of a public hearing before a hearing board of five or more persons appointed by the Administrator. A majority of the members of the board and the chairman who shall be designated by the Administrator shall not be officers or employees of Federal, State, or local governments. On the basis of the evidence presented at such hearing, the board shall within sixty days after completion of the hearing make findings of fact as to whether or not such pollution is occurring and shall thereupon by decision, incorporating its findings therein, make such recommendations to abate the pollution as may be appropriate and shall transmit such decision and the record of the hearings to the Administrator. All such decisions shall be public. Upon receipt of such decision, the Administrator shall promptly implement the board's decision in accordance with the provisions of this chapter.

(d) Report by alleged polluter

In connection with any hearing called under this subsection, the board is authorized to require any person whose alleged activities result in discharges causing or contributing to pollution to file with it in such forms as it may prescribe, a report based on existing data, furnishing such information as may reasonably be required as to the character, kind, and quantity of such discharges and the use of facilities or other means to prevent or reduce such discharges by the person filing such a report. Such report shall be made under oath or otherwise, as the board may prescribe, and shall be filed with the board within such reasonable period as it may prescribe, unless additional time is granted by it. Upon a showing satisfactory to the board by the person filing such report that such report or portion thereof (other than effluent data), to which the Administrator has access under this section, if made public would divulge trade secrets or secret processes of such person, the board shall consider such report or portion thereof confidential for the purposes of section 1905 of title 18. If any person required to file any report under this paragraph shall fail to do so within the time fixed by the board for filing the same, and such failure shall continue for thirty days after notice of such default, such person shall forfeit to the United States the sum of $1,000 for each and every day of the continuance of such failure, which forfeiture shall be payable into the Treasury of the United States, and shall be recoverable in a civil suit in the name of the United States in the district court of the United States where such person has his principal office or in any district in which he does business. The Administrator may upon application therefor remit or mitigate any forfeiture provided for under this subsection.

(e) Compensation of board members

Board members, other than officers or employees of Federal, State, or local governments, shall be for each day (including travel-time) during which they are performing board business, entitled to receive compensation at a rate fixed by the Administrator but not in excess of the maximum rate of pay for grade GS–18, as provided in the General Schedule under section 5332 of title 5, and shall, notwithstanding the limitations of sections 5703 and 5704 of title 5, be fully reimbursed for travel, subsistence and related expenses.

(f) Enforcement proceedings

When any such recommendation adopted by the Administrator involves the institution of enforcement proceedings against any person to obtain the abatement of pollution subject to such recommendation, the Administrator shall institute such proceedings if he believes that the evidence warrants such proceedings. The district court of the United States shall consider and determine de novo all relevant issues, but shall receive in evidence the record of the proceedings before the conference or hearing board. The court shall have jurisdiction to enter such judgment and orders enforcing such judgment as it deems appropriate or to remand such proceedings to the Administrator for such further action as it may direct.

(June 30, 1948, c. 758, Title III, § 310, as added Oct. 18, 1972, Pub.L. 92–500, § 2, 86 Stat. 860.)

LIBRARY REFERENCES

International Law ⚬=10.
C.J.S. International Law § 12.

§ 1321. Oil and hazardous substance liability [FWPCA § 311]

(a) Definitions

For the purpose of this section, the term—

(1) "oil" means oil of any kind or in any form, including, but not limited to, petroleum, fuel oil, sludge, oil refuse, and oil mixed with wastes other than dredged spoil;

(2) "discharge" includes, but is not limited to, any spilling, leaking, pumping, pouring, emitting, emptying or dumping, but excludes (A) discharges in compliance with a permit under section 1342 of this title, (B) discharges resulting from circumstances identified and reviewed and made a part of the public record with respect to a permit issued or modified under section 1342 of this title, and subject to a condition in such permit, and (C) continuous or anticipated intermittent discharges from a point source, identified in a permit or permit application under section 1342 of this title, which are caused by events occurring within the scope of relevant operating or treatment systems;

(3) "vessel" means every description of watercraft or other artificial contrivance used, or capable of being used, as a means of transportation on water other than a public vessel;

(4) "public vessel" means a vessel owned or bareboat-chartered and operated by the United States, or by a State or political subdivision thereof, or by a foreign nation, except when such vessel is engaged in commerce;

(5) "United States" means the States, the District of Columbia, the Commonwealth of Puerto Rico, the Commonwealth of the Northern Mariana Islands, Guam, American Samoa, the Virgin Islands, and the Trust Territory of the Pacific Islands;

(6) "owner or operator" means (A) in the case of a vessel, any person owning, operating, or chartering by demise, such vessel, and (B) in the case of an onshore facility, and an offshore facility, any person owning or operating such onshore facility or offshore facility, and (C) in the case of any abandoned offshore facility, the person who owned or operated such facility immediately prior to such abandonment;

(7) "person" includes an individual, firm, corporation, association, and a partnership.

(8) "remove" or "removal" refers to containment and removal of the oil or hazardous substances from

the water and shorelines or the taking of such other actions as may be necessary to minimize or mitigate damage to the public health or welfare, including, but not limited to, fish, shellfish, wildlife, and public and private property, shorelines, and beaches;

(9) "contiguous zone" means the entire zone established or to be established by the United States under article 24 of the Convention on the Territorial Sea and the Contiguous Zone;

(10) "onshore facility" means any facility (including, but not limited to, motor vehicles and rolling stock) of any kind located in, on, or under, any land within the United States other than submerged land;

(11) "offshore facility" means any facility of any kind located in, on, or under, any of the navigable waters of the United States, and any facility of any kind which is subject to the jurisdiction of the United States and is located in, on, or under any other waters, other than a vessel or a public vessel;

(12) "act of God" means an act occasioned by an unanticipated grave natural disaster;

(13) "barrel" means 42 United States gallons at 60 degrees Fahrenheit;

(14) "hazardous substance" means any substance designated pursuant to subsection (b)(2) of this section;

(15) "inland oil barge" means a non-self-propelled vessel carrying oil in bulk as cargo and certificated to operate only in the inland waters of the United States, while operating in such waters;

(16) "inland waters of the United States" means those waters of the United States lying inside the baseline from which the territorial sea is measured and those waters outside such baseline which are a part of the Gulf Intracoastal Waterway;

(17) "otherwise subject to the jurisdiction of the United States" means subject to the jurisdiction of the United States by virtue of United States citizenship, United States vessel documentation or numbering, or as provided for by international agreement to which the United States is a party;

(18) "Area Committee" means an Area Committee established under subsection (j) of this section;

(19) "Area Contingency Plan" means an Area Contingency Plan prepared under subsection (j) of this section;

(20) "Coast Guard District Response Group" means a Coast Guard District Response Group established under subsection (j) of this section;

(21) "Federal On–Scene Coordinator" means a Federal On–Scene Coordinator designated in the National Contingency Plan;

(22) "National Contingency Plan" means the National Contingency Plan prepared and published under subsection (d) of this section;

(23) "National Response Unit" means the National Response Unit established under subsection (j) of this section; and

(24) "worst case discharge" means—

(A) in the case of a vessel, a discharge in adverse weather conditions of its entire cargo; and

(B) in the case of an offshore facility or onshore facility, the largest foreseeable discharge in adverse weather conditions.

(b) Congressional declaration of policy against discharges of oil or hazardous substances; designation of hazardous substances; study of higher standard of care incentives and report to Congress; liability; penalties; civil actions: penalty limitations, separate offenses, jurisdiction, mitigation of damages and costs, recovery of removal costs; alternative remedies and withholding clearance of vessels

(1) The Congress hereby declares that it is the policy of the United States that there should be no discharges of oil or hazardous substances into or upon the navigable waters of the United States, adjoining shorelines, or into or upon the waters of the contiguous zone, or in connection with activities under the Outer Continental Shelf Lands Act [43 U.S.C.A. § 1331 et seq.] or the Deepwater Port Act of 1974 [33 U.S.C.A. § 1501 et seq.], or which may affect natural resources belonging to, appertaining to, or under the exclusive management authority of the United States (including resources under the Magnuson Fishery Conservation and Management Act [16 U.S.C.A. § 1801 et seq.]).

(2)(A) The Administrator shall develop, promulgate, and revise as may be appropriate, regulations designating as hazardous substances, other than oil as defined in this section, such elements and compounds which, when discharged in any quantity into or upon the navigable waters of the United States or adjoining shorelines or the waters of the contiguous zone or in connection with activities under the Outer Continental Shelf Lands Act [43 U.S.C.A. § 1331 et seq.] or the Deepwater Port Act of 1974 [33 U.S.C.A. § 1501 et seq.], or which may affect natural resources belonging to, appertaining to, or under the exclusive management authority of the United States (including resources under the Magnuson Fishery Conservation and Management Act [16 U.S.C.A. § 1801 et seq.]), present an imminent and substantial danger to the public health or welfare, including, but not limited to, fish, shellfish, wildlife, shorelines, and beaches.

(B) The Administrator shall within 18 months after November 2, 1978, conduct a study and report to the Congress on methods, mechanisms, and procedures to create incentives to achieve a higher standard of care in all aspects of the management and movement of hazardous substances on the part of owners, operators, or persons in charge of onshore facilities, offshore facilities, or vessels. The Administrator shall include in such study (1) limits of liability, (2) liability for third party damages, (3) penalties and fees, (4) spill prevention plans, (5) current practices in the insurance and banking industries, and (6) whether the penalty enacted in subclause (bb) of clause (iii) of subparagraph (B) of subsection (b)(2) of section 311 of Public Law 92–500 should be enacted.

(3) The discharge of oil or hazardous substances (i) into or upon the navigable waters of the United States, adjoining shorelines, or into or upon the waters of the contiguous zone, or (ii) in connection with activities under the Outer Continental Shelf Lands Act [43 U.S.C.A. § 1331 et seq.] or the Deepwater Port Act of 1974 [33 U.S.C.A. § 1501 et seq.], or which may affect natural resources belonging to, appertaining to, or under the exclusive management authority of the United States (including resources under the Magnuson Fishery Conservation and Management Act [16 U.S.C.A. § 1801 et seq.]), in such quantities as may be harmful as determined by the President under paragraph (4) of this subsection, is prohibited, except (A) in the case of such discharges into the waters of the contiguous zone or which may affect natural resources belonging to, appertaining to, or under the exclusive management authority of the United States (including resources under the Magnuson Fishery Conservation and Management Act), where permitted under the Protocol of 1978 Relating to the International Convention for the Prevention of Pollution from Ships, 1973, and (B) where permitted in quantities and at times and locations or under such circumstances or conditions as the President may, by regulation, determine not to be harmful. Any regulations issued under this subsection shall be consistent with maritime safety and with marine and navigation laws and regulations and applicable water quality standards.

(4) The President shall by regulation determine for the purposes of this section those quantities of oil and any hazardous substances the discharge of which may be harmful to the public health or welfare or the environment of the United States, including but not limited to fish, shellfish, wildlife, and public and private property, shorelines, and beaches.

(5) Any person in charge of a vessel or of an onshore facility or an offshore facility shall, as soon as he has knowledge of any discharge of oil or a hazardous substance from such vessel or facility in violation of paragraph (3) of this subsection, immediately notify the appropriate agency of the United States Government of such discharge. The Federal agency shall immediately notify the appropriate State agency of any State which is, or may reasonably be expected to be, affected by the discharge of oil or a hazardous substance. Any such person (A) in charge of a vessel from which oil or a hazardous substance is discharged in violation of paragraph (3) (i) of this subsection, or (B) in charge of a vessel from which oil or a hazardous substance is discharged in violation of paragraph (3)(ii) of this subsection and who is otherwise subject to the jurisdiction of the United States at the time of the discharge, or (C) in charge of an onshore facility or an offshore facility, who fails to notify immediately such agency of such discharge shall, upon conviction, be fined in accordance with Title 18, or imprisoned for not more than 5 years, or both. Notification received pursuant to this paragraph shall not be used against any such natural person in any criminal case, except a prosecution for perjury or for giving a false statement.

(6) Administrative penalties

(A) Violations

Any owner, operator, or person in charge of any vessel, onshore facility, or offshore facility—

(i) from which oil or a hazardous substance is discharged in violation of paragraph (3), or

(ii) who fails or refuses to comply with any regulation issued under subsection (j) of this section to which that owner, operator, or person in charge is subject,

may be assessed a class I or class II civil penalty by the Secretary of the department in which the Coast Guard is operating or the Administrator.

(B) Classes of penalties

(i) Class I

The amount of a class I civil penalty under subparagraph (A) may not exceed $10,000 per violation, except that the maximum amount of any class I civil penalty under this subparagraph shall not exceed $25,000. Before assessing a civil penalty under this clause, the Administrator or Secretary, as the case may be, shall give to the person to be assessed such penalty written notice of the Administrator's or Secretary's proposal to assess the penalty and the opportunity to request, within 30 days of the date the notice is received by such person, a hearing on the proposed penalty. Such hearing shall not be subject to section 554 or 556 of Title 5, but shall provide a reasonable opportunity to be heard and to present evidence.

(ii) Class II

The amount of a class II civil penalty under subparagraph (A) may not exceed $10,000 per day for each day during which the violation continues; except that the maximum amount of any class II civil penalty under this subparagraph shall not exceed $125,000. Except as otherwise provided in this subsection, a class II civil penalty shall be assessed and collected in the same manner, and subject to the same provisions, as in the case of civil penalties assessed and collected after notice and opportunity for a hearing on the record in accordance with section 554 of Title 5. The Administrator and Secretary may issue rules for discovery procedures for hearings under this paragraph.

(C) Rights of interested persons

(i) Public notice

Before issuing an order assessing a class II civil penalty under this paragraph the Administrator or Secretary, as the case may be, shall provide public notice of and reasonable opportunity to comment on the proposed issuance of such order.

(ii) Presentation of evidence

Any person who comments on a proposed assessment of a class II civil penalty under this paragraph shall be given notice of any hearing held under this paragraph and of the order assessing such penalty. In any hearing held under this paragraph, such person shall have a reasonable opportunity to be heard and to present evidence.

(iii) Rights of interested persons to a hearing

If no hearing is held under subparagraph (B) before issuance of an order assessing a class II civil penalty under this paragraph, any person who commented on the proposed assessment may petition, within 30 days after the issuance of such order, the Administrator or Secretary, as the case may be, to set aside such order and to provide a hearing on the penalty. If the evidence presented by the petitioner in support of the petition is material and was not considered in the issuance of the order, the Administrator or Secretary shall immediately set aside such order and provide a hearing in accordance with subparagraph (B)(ii). If the Administrator or Secretary denies a hearing under this clause, the Administrator or Secretary shall provide to the petitioner, and publish in the Federal Register, notice of and the reasons for such denial.

(D) Finality of order

An order assessing a class II civil penalty under this paragraph shall become final 30 days after its issuance unless a petition for judicial review is filed under subparagraph (G) or a hearing is requested under subparagraph (C)(iii). If such a hearing is denied, such order shall become final 30 days after such denial.

(E) Effect of order

Action taken by the Administrator or Secretary, as the case may be, under this paragraph shall not affect or limit the Administrator's or Secretary's authority to enforce any provision of this chapter; except that any violation—

(i) with respect to which the Administrator or Secretary has commenced and is diligently prosecuting an action to assess a class II civil penalty under this paragraph, or

(ii) for which the Administrator or Secretary has issued a final order assessing a class II civil penalty not subject to further judicial review and the violator has paid a penalty assessed under this paragraph,

shall not be the subject of a civil penalty action under section 1319(d), 1319(g), or 1365 of this title or under paragraph (7).

(F) Effect of action on compliance

No action by the Administrator or Secretary under this paragraph shall affect any person's obligation to comply with any section of this chapter.

(G) Judicial review

Any person against whom a civil penalty is assessed under this paragraph or who commented on the proposed assessment of such penalty in accordance with subparagraph (C) may obtain review of such assessment—

(i) in the case of assessment of a class I civil penalty, in the United States District Court for the District of Columbia or in the district in which the violation is alleged to have occurred, or

(ii) in the case of assessment of a class II civil penalty, in United States Court of Appeals for the District of Columbia Circuit or for any other circuit in which such person resides or transacts business,

by filing a notice of appeal in such court within the 30–day period beginning on the date the civil penalty order is issued and by simultaneously sending a copy of such notice by certified mail to the Administrator or Secretary, as the case may be, and the Attorney General. The Administrator or Secretary shall promptly file in such court a certified copy of the record on which the order was issued. Such court shall not set aside or remand such order unless there is not substantial evidence in the record, taken as a whole, to support the finding of a violation or unless the Administrator's or Secretary's assessment of the penalty constitutes an abuse of discretion and shall not impose additional civil penalties for the same violation unless the Administrator's or Secretary's assessment of the penalty constitutes an abuse of discretion.

(H) Collection

If any person fails to pay an assessment of a civil penalty—

(i) after the assessment has become final, or

(ii) after a court in an action brought under subparagraph (G) has entered a final judgment in favor of the Administrator or Secretary, as the case may be,

the Administrator or Secretary shall request the Attorney General to bring a civil action in an appropriate district court to recover the amount assessed (plus interest at currently prevailing rates from the date of the final order or the date of the final judgment, as the case may be). In such an action, the validity, amount, and appropriateness of such penalty shall not be subject to review. Any person who fails to pay on a timely basis the amount of an assessment of a civil penalty as described in the first sentence of this subparagraph shall be required to pay, in addition to such amount and interest, attorneys fees and costs for collection proceedings and a quarterly nonpayment penalty for each quarter during which such failure to pay persists. Such nonpayment penalty shall be in an amount equal to 20 percent of the aggregate amount of such person's penalties and nonpayment penalties which are unpaid as of the beginning of such quarter.

(I) Subpoenas

The Administrator or Secretary, as the case may be, may issue subpoenas for the attendance and testimony of witnesses and the production of relevant papers, books, or documents in connection with hearings under this paragraph. In case of contumacy or refusal to obey a subpoena issued pursuant to this subparagraph and served upon any person, the district court of the United States for any district in which such person is found, resides, or transacts business, upon application by the United States and after notice to such person, shall have jurisdiction to issue an order requiring such person to appear and give testimony before the administrative law judge or to appear and produce documents before the administrative law judge, or both, and any failure to obey such order of the court may be punished by such court as a contempt thereof.

(7) Civil penalty action

(A) Discharge, generally

Any person who is the owner, operator, or person in charge of any vessel, onshore facility, or offshore facility from which oil or a hazardous substance is discharged in violation of paragraph (3), shall be subject to a civil penalty in an amount up to $25,000 per day of violation or an amount up to $1,000 per barrel of oil or unit of reportable quantity of hazardous substances discharged.

(B) Failure to remove or comply

Any person described in subparagraph (A) who, without sufficient cause—

(i) fails to properly carry out removal of the discharge under an order of the President pursuant to subsection (c) of this section; or

(ii) fails to comply with an order pursuant to subsection (e)(1)(B) of this section;

shall be subject to a civil penalty in an amount up to $25,000 per day of violation or an amount up to 3 times the costs incurred by the Oil Spill Liability Trust Fund as a result of such failure.

(C) Failure to comply with regulation

Any person who fails or refuses to comply with any regulation issued under subsection (j) of this section shall be subject to a civil penalty in an amount up to $25,000 per day of violation.

(D) Gross negligence

In any case in which a violation of paragraph (3) was the result of gross negligence or willful misconduct of a person described in subparagraph (A), the person shall be subject to a civil penalty of not less than $100,000, and not more than $3,000 per barrel of oil or unit of reportable quantity of hazardous substance discharged.

(E) Jurisdiction

An action to impose a civil penalty under this paragraph may be brought in the district court of the United States for the district in which the defendant is located, resides, or is doing business, and such court shall have jurisdiction to assess such penalty.

(F) Limitation

A person is not liable for a civil penalty under this paragraph for a discharge if the person has been assessed a civil penalty under paragraph (6) for the discharge.

(8) Determination of amount

In determining the amount of a civil penalty under paragraphs (6) and (7), the Administrator, Secretary, or the court, as the case may be, shall consider the seriousness of the violation or violations, the economic benefit to the violator, if any, resulting from the violation, the degree of culpability involved, any other penalty for the same incident, any history of prior violations, the nature, extent, and degree of success of any efforts of the violator to minimize or mitigate the effects of the discharge, the economic impact of the penalty on the violator, and any other matters as justice may require.

(9) Mitigation of damage

In addition to establishing a penalty for the discharge of oil or a hazardous substance, the Administrator or the Secretary of the department in which the Coast Guard is operating may act to mitigate the damage to the public health or welfare caused by such discharge. The cost of such mitigation shall be deemed a cost incurred under subsection (c) of this section for the removal of such substance by the United States Government.

(10) Recovery of removal costs

Any costs of removal incurred in connection with a discharge excluded by subsection (a)(2)(C) of this section shall be recoverable from the owner or operator of the source of the discharge in an action brought under section 1319(b) of this title.

(11) Limitation

Civil penalties shall not be assessed under both this section and section 1319 of this title for the same discharge.

(12) Withholding clearance

If any owner, operator, or person in charge of a vessel is liable for a civil penalty under this subsection, or if reasonable cause exists to believe that the owner, operator, or person in charge may be subject to a civil penalty under this subsection, the Secretary of the Treasury, upon the request of the Secretary of the department in which the Coast Guard is operating or the Administrator, shall with respect to such vessel refuse or revoke—

(A) the clearance required by section 91 of the Appendix to Title 46;

(B) a permit to proceed under section 313 of the Appendix to Title 46; and

(C) a permit to depart required under section 1443 of Title 19;

as applicable. Clearance or a permit refused or revoked under this paragraph may be granted upon the filing of a bond or other surety satisfactory to the Secretary of the department in which the Coast Guard is operating or the Administrator.

(c) Federal removal authority

(1) General removal requirement

(A) The President shall, in accordance with the National Contingency Plan and any appropriate Area Contingency Plan, ensure effective and immediate removal of a discharge, and mitigation or prevention of a substantial threat of a discharge, of oil or a hazardous substance—

(i) into or on the navigable waters;

(ii) on the adjoining shorelines to the navigable waters;

(iii) into or on the waters of the exclusive economic zone; or

(iv) that may affect natural resources belonging to, appertaining to, or under the exclusive management authority of the United States.

(B) In carrying out this paragraph, the President may—

(i) remove or arrange for the removal of a discharge, and mitigate or prevent a substantial threat of a discharge, at any time;

(ii) direct or monitor all Federal, State, and private actions to remove a discharge; and

(iii) remove and, if necessary, destroy a vessel discharging, or threatening to discharge, by whatever means are available.

(2) Discharge posing substantial threat to public health or welfare

(A) If a discharge, or a substantial threat of a discharge, of oil or a hazardous substance from a vessel, offshore facility, or onshore facility is of such a size or character as to be a substantial threat to the public health or welfare of the United States (including but not limited to fish, shellfish, wildlife, other natural resources, and the public and private beaches and shorelines of the United States), the President shall direct all Federal, State, and private actions to remove the discharge or to mitigate or prevent the threat of the discharge.

(B) In carrying out this paragraph, the President may, without regard to any other provision of law governing contracting procedures or employment of personnel by the Federal Government—

(i) remove or arrange for the removal of the discharge, or mitigate or prevent the substantial threat of the discharge; and

(ii) remove and, if necessary, destroy a vessel discharging, or threatening to discharge, by whatever means are available.

(3) Actions in accordance with National Contingency Plan

(A) Each Federal agency, State, owner or operator, or other person participating in efforts under this subsection shall act in accordance with the National Contingency Plan or as directed by the President.

(B) An owner or operator participating in efforts under this subsection shall act in accordance with the National Contingency Plan and the applicable response plan required under subsection (j) of this section, or as directed by the President.

(4) Exemption from liability

(A) A person is not liable for removal costs or damages which result from actions taken or omitted to be taken in the course of rendering care, assistance, or advice consistent with the National Contingency Plan or as otherwise directed by the President.

(B) Subparagraph (A) does not apply—

(i) to a responsible party;

(ii) to a response under the Comprehensive Environmental Response, Compensation, and Liability Act of 1980 (42 U.S.C. 9601 et seq.);

(iii) with respect to personal injury or wrongful death; or

(iv) if the person is grossly negligent or engages in willful misconduct.

(C) A responsible party is liable for any removal costs and damages that another person is relieved of under subparagraph (A).

(5) Obligation and liability of owner or operator not affected

Nothing in this subsection affects—

(A) the obligation of an owner or operator to respond immediately to a discharge, or the threat of a discharge, of oil; or

(B) the liability of a responsible party under the Oil Pollution Act of 1990 [33 U.S.C.A. § 2701 et seq.].

(6) Responsible party defined

For purposes of this subsection, the term "responsible party" has the meaning given that term under section 1001 of the Oil Pollution Act of 1990 [33 U.S.C.A. § 2701].

(d) National Contingency Plan

(1) Preparation by President

The President shall prepare and publish a National Contingency Plan for removal of oil and hazardous substances pursuant to this section.

(2) Contents

The National Contingency Plan shall provide for efficient, coordinated, and effective action to minimize damage from oil and hazardous substance discharges, including containment, dispersal, and removal of oil and hazardous substances, and shall include, but not be limited to, the following:

(A) Assignment of duties and responsibilities among Federal departments and agencies in coordination with State and local agencies and port authorities including, but not limited to, water pollution control and conservation and trusteeship of natural resources (including conservation of fish and wildlife).

(B) Identification, procurement, maintenance, and storage of equipment and supplies.

(C) Establishment or designation of Coast Guard strike teams, consisting of—

(i) personnel who shall be trained, prepared, and available to provide necessary services to carry out the National Contingency Plan;

(ii) adequate oil and hazardous substance pollution control equipment and material; and

(iii) a detailed oil and hazardous substance pollution and prevention plan, including measures to protect fisheries and wildlife.

(D) A system of surveillance and notice designed to safeguard against as well as ensure earliest possible notice of discharges of oil and hazardous substances and imminent threats of such discharges to the appropriate State and Federal agencies.

(E) Establishment of a national center to provide coordination and direction for operations in carrying out the Plan.

(F) Procedures and techniques to be employed in identifying, containing, dispersing, and removing oil and hazardous substances.

(G) A schedule, prepared in cooperation with the States, identifying—

(i) dispersants, other chemicals, and other spill mitigating devices and substances, if any, that may be used in carrying out the Plan,

(ii) the waters in which such dispersants, other chemicals, and other spill mitigating devices and substances may be used, and

(iii) the quantities of such dispersant, other chemicals, or other spill mitigating device or substance which can be used safely in such waters,

which schedule shall provide in the case of any dispersant, chemical, spill mitigating device or substance, or waters not specifically identified in such schedule that the President, or his delegate, may, on a case-by-case basis, identify the dispersants, other chemicals, and other spill mitigating devices and substances which may be used, the waters in which they may be used, and the quantities which can be used safely in such waters.

(H) A system whereby the State or States affected by a discharge of oil or hazardous substance may act where necessary to remove such discharge and such State or States may be reimbursed in accordance with the Oil Pollution Act of 1990 [33 U.S.C.A. § 2701 et seq.], in the case of any discharge of oil from a vessel or facility, for the reasonable costs incurred for that removal, from the Oil Spill Liability Trust Fund.

(I) Establishment of criteria and procedures to ensure immediate and effective Federal identification of, and response to, a discharge, or the threat of a discharge, that results in a substantial threat to the public health or welfare of the United States, as required under subsection (c)(2) of this section.

(J) Establishment of procedures and standards for removing a worst case discharge of oil, and for mitigating or preventing a substantial threat of such a discharge.

(K) Designation of the Federal official who shall be the Federal On-Scene Coordinator for each area for which an Area Contingency Plan is required to be prepared under subsection (j) of this section;

(L) Establishment of procedures for the coordination of activities of—

(i) Coast Guard strike teams established under subparagraph (C);

(ii) Federal On-Scene Coordinators designated under subparagraph (K);

(iii) District Response Groups established under subsection (j) of this section; and

(iv) Area Committees established under subsection (j) of this section.

(M) A fish and wildlife response plan, developed in consultation with the United States Fish and Wildlife Service, the National Oceanic and Atmospheric Administration, and other interested parties (including State fish and wildlife conservation officials), for the immediate and effective protection, rescue, and rehabilitation of, and the minimization of risk of damage to, fish and wildlife resources and their habitat that are harmed or that may be jeopardized by a discharge.

(3) Revisions and amendments

The President may, from time to time, as the President deems advisable, revise or otherwise amend the National Contingency Plan.

(4) Actions in accordance with National Contingency Plan

After publication of the National Contingency Plan, the removal of oil and hazardous substances and actions to minimize damage from oil and hazardous substance discharges shall, to the greatest extent possible, be in accordance with the National Contingency Plan.

(e) Civil enforcement

(1) Orders protecting public health

In addition to any action taken by a State or local government, when the President determines that there may be an imminent and substantial threat to the public health or welfare of the United States, including fish, shellfish, and wildlife, public and private property, shorelines, beaches, habitat, and other living and nonliving natural resources under the jurisdiction or control of the United States, because of an actual or threatened discharge of oil or a hazardous substance from a vessel or facility in violation of subsection (b) of this section, the President may—

(A) require the Attorney General to secure any relief from any person, including the owner or operator of the vessel or facility, as may be necessary to abate such endangerment; or

(B) after notice to the affected State, take any other action under this section, including issuing administrative orders, that may be necessary to protect the public health and welfare.

(2) Jurisdiction of district courts

The district courts of the United States shall have jurisdiction to grant any relief under this subsection that the public interest and the equities of the case may require.

(f) Liability for actual costs of removal

(1) Except where an owner or operator can prove that a discharge was caused solely by (A) an act of God, (B) an act of war, (C) negligence on the part of

the United States Government, or (D) an act or omission of a third party without regard to whether any such act or omission was or was not negligent, or any combination of the foregoing clauses, such owner or operator of any vessel from which oil or a hazardous substance is discharged in violation of subsection (b)(3) of this section shall, notwithstanding any other provision of law, be liable to the United States Government for the actual costs incurred under subsection (c) of this section for the removal of such oil or substance by the United States Government in an amount not to exceed, in the case of an inland oil barge $125 per gross ton of such barge, or $125,000, whichever is greater, and in the case of any other vessel, $150 per gross ton of such vessel (or, for a vessel carrying oil or hazardous substances as cargo, $250,000), whichever is greater, except that where the United States can show that such discharge was the result of willful negligence or willful misconduct within the privity and knowledge of the owner, such owner or operator shall be liable to the United States Government for the full amount of such costs. Such costs shall constitute a maritime lien on such vessel which may be recovered in an action in rem in the district court of the United States for any district within which any vessel may be found. The United States may also bring an action against the owner or operator of such vessel in any court of competent jurisdiction to recover such costs.

(2) Except where an owner or operator of an onshore facility can prove that a discharge was caused solely by (A) an act of God, (B) an act of war, (C) negligence on the part of the United States Government, or (D) an act or omission of a third party without regard to whether any such act or omission was or was not negligent, or any combination of the foregoing clauses, such owner or operator of any such facility from which oil or a hazardous substance is discharged in violation of subsection (b)(3) of this section shall be liable to the United States Government for the actual costs incurred under subsection (c) of this section for the removal of such oil or substance by the United States Government in an amount not to exceed $50,000,000, except that where the United States can show that such discharge was the result of willful negligence or willful misconduct within the privity and knowledge of the owner, such owner or operator shall be liable to the United States Government for the full amount of such costs. The United States may bring an action against the owner or operator of such facility in any court of competent jurisdiction to recover such costs. The Administrator is authorized, by regulation, after consultation with the Secretary of Commerce and the Small Business Administration, to establish reasonable and equitable classifications of those onshore facilities having a total fixed storage capacity of 1,000 barrels or less which he determines because of size, type, and location do not present a substantial risk of the discharge of oil or a hazardous substance in violation of subsection (b)(3) of this section, and apply with respect to such classifications differing limits of liability which may be less than the amount contained in this paragraph.

(3) Except where an owner or operator of an offshore facility can prove that a discharge was caused solely by (A) an act of God, (B) an act of war, (C) negligence on the part of the United States Government, or (D) an act or omission of a third party without regard to whether any such act or omission was or was not negligent, or any combination of the foregoing clauses, such owner or operator of any such facility from which oil or a hazardous substance is discharged in violation of subsection (b)(3) of this section shall, notwithstanding any other provision of law, be liable to the United States Government for the actual costs incurred under subsection (c) of this section for the removal of such oil or substance by the United States Government in an amount not to exceed $50,000,000, except that where the United States can show that such discharge was the result of willful negligence or willful misconduct within the privity and knowledge of the owner, such owner or operator shall be liable to the United States Government for the full amount of such costs. The United States may bring an action against the owner or operator of such a facility in any court of competent jurisdiction to recover such costs.

(4) The costs of removal of oil or a hazardous substance for which the owner or operator of a vessel or onshore or offshore facility is liable under subsection (f) of this section shall include any costs or expenses incurred by the Federal Government or any State government in the restoration or replacement of natural resources damaged or destroyed as a result of a discharge of oil or a hazardous substance in violation of subsection (b) of this section.

(5) The President, or the authorized representative of any State, shall act on behalf of the public as trustee of the natural resources to recover for the costs of replacing or restoring such resources. Sums recovered shall be used to restore, rehabilitate, or acquire the equivalent of such natural resources by the appropriate agencies of the Federal Government, or the State government.

(g) Third party liability

Where the owner or operator of a vessel (other than an inland oil barge) carrying oil or hazardous substances as cargo or an onshore or offshore facility which handles or stores oil or hazardous substances in bulk, from which oil or a hazardous substance is discharged in violation of subsection (b) of this section, alleges that such discharge was caused solely by an act or omission of a third party, such owner or operator shall pay to the United States Government the actual costs incurred under subsection (c) of this section for removal of such oil or substance and shall be entitled by subrogation to all rights of the United States Government to recover such costs from such third party under this subsection. In any case where an owner or operator of a vessel, of an onshore facility, or of an offshore facility, from which oil or a hazardous substance is discharged in violation of subsection (b)(3) of this section, proves that such discharge of oil or hazardous substance was caused solely by an act or omission of a third party, or was caused solely by such an act or omission in combination with an act of God, an act of war, or negligence on the part of the United States Government, such third party shall, notwithstanding any other provision of law, be liable to the United States Government for the actual costs incurred under subsection (c) of this section for removal of such oil or substance by the United States Government, except where such third party can prove that such discharge was caused solely by (A) an act of God, (B) an act of war, (C) negligence on the part of the United States Government, or (D) an act or omission of another party without regard to whether such act or omission was or was not negligent, or any combination of the foregoing clauses. If such third party was the owner or operator of a vessel which caused the discharge of oil or a hazardous substance in violation of subsection (b)(3) of this section, the liability of such third party under this subsection shall not exceed, in the case of an inland oil barge $125 per gross ton of such barge, or $125,000, whichever is greater, and in the case of any other vessel, $150 per gross ton of such vessel (or, for a vessel carrying oil or hazardous substances as cargo, $250,000), whichever is greater. In any other case the liability of such third party shall not exceed the limitation which would have been applicable to the owner or operator of the vessel or the onshore or offshore facility from which the discharge actually occurred if such owner or operator were liable. If the United States can show that the discharge of oil or a hazardous substance in violation of subsection (b)(3) of this section was the result of willful negligence or willful misconduct within the privity and knowledge of such third party, such third party shall be liable to the United States Government for the full amount of such removal costs. The United States may bring an action against the third party in any court of competent jurisdiction to recover such removal costs.

(h) Rights against third parties who caused or contributed to discharge

The liabilities established by this section shall in no way affect any rights which (1) the owner or operator of a vessel or of an onshore facility or an offshore facility may have against any third party whose acts may in any way have caused or contributed to such discharge, or (2) The [1] United States Government may have against any third party whose actions may in any way have caused or contributed to the discharge of oil or hazardous substance.

(i) Recovery of removal costs

In any case where an owner or operator of a vessel or an onshore facility or an offshore facility from which oil or a hazardous substance is discharged in violation of subsection (b)(3) of this section acts to remove such oil or substance in accordance with regulations promulgated pursuant to this section, such owner or operator shall be entitled to recover the reasonable costs incurred in such removal upon establishing, in a suit which may be brought against the United States Government in the United States Court of Federal Claims, that such discharge was caused solely by (A) an act of God, (B) an act of war, (C) negligence on the part of the United States Government, or (D) an act or omission of a third party without regard to whether such act or omission was or was not negligent, or of any combination of the foregoing causes.

(j) National response system

(1) In general

Consistent with the National Contingency Plan required by subsection (c)(2) of this section, as soon as practicable after October 18, 1972, and from time to time thereafter, the President shall issue regulations consistent with maritime safety and with marine and navigation laws (A) establishing methods and procedures for removal of discharged oil and hazardous substances, (B) establishing criteria for the development and implementation of local and regional oil and hazardous substance removal contingency plans, (C) establishing procedures, methods, and equipment and other requirements for equipment to prevent discharges of oil and hazardous substances from vessels and from onshore facilities and offshore facilities, and to contain such discharges, and (D) governing the inspection of vessels carrying cargoes of oil and hazardous substances and the inspection of such cargoes in order to reduce the likelihood of discharges of oil from vessels in violation of this section.

(2) **National response unit**

The Secretary of the department in which the Coast Guard is operating shall establish a National Response Unit at Elizabeth City, North Carolina. The Secretary, acting through the National Response Unit—

(A) shall compile and maintain a comprehensive computer list of spill removal resources, personnel, and equipment that is available worldwide and within the areas designated by the President pursuant to paragraph (4), which shall be available to Federal and State agencies and the public;

(B) shall provide technical assistance, equipment, and other resources requested by a Federal On-Scene Coordinator;

(C) shall coordinate use of private and public personnel and equipment to remove a worst case discharge, and to mitigate or prevent a substantial threat of such a discharge, from a vessel, offshore facility, or onshore facility operating in or near an area designated by the President pursuant to paragraph (4);

(D) may provide technical assistance in the preparation of Area Contingency Plans required under paragraph (4);

(E) shall administer Coast Guard strike teams established under the National Contingency Plan;

(F) shall maintain on file all Area Contingency Plans approved by the President under this subsection; and

(G) shall review each of those plans that affects its responsibilities under this subsection.

(3) **Coast guard district response groups**

(A) The Secretary of the department in which the Coast Guard is operating shall establish in each Coast Guard district a Coast Guard District Response Group.

(B) Each Coast Guard District Response Group shall consist of—

(i) the Coast Guard personnel and equipment, including firefighting equipment, of each port within the district;

(ii) additional prepositioned equipment; and

(iii) a district response advisory staff.

(C) Coast Guard district response groups—

(i) shall provide technical assistance, equipment, and other resources when required by a Federal On-Scene Coordinator;

(ii) shall maintain all Coast Guard response equipment within its district;

(iii) may provide technical assistance in the preparation of Area Contingency Plans required under paragraph (4); and

(iv) shall review each of those plans that affect its area of geographic responsibility.

(4) **Area committees and area contingency plans**

(A) There is established for each area designated by the President an Area Committee comprised of members appointed by the President from qualified personnel of Federal, State, and local agencies.

(B) Each Area Committee, under the direction of the Federal On-Scene Coordinator for its area, shall—

(i) prepare for its area the Area Contingency Plan required under subparagraph (C);

(ii) work with State and local officials to enhance the contingency planning of those officials and to assure preplanning of joint response efforts, including appropriate procedures for mechanical recovery, dispersal, shoreline cleanup, protection of sensitive environmental areas, and protection, rescue, and rehabilitation of fisheries and wildlife; and

(iii) work with State and local officials to expedite decisions for the use of dispersants and other mitigating substances and devices.

(C) Each Area Committee shall prepare and submit to the President for approval an Area Contingency Plan for its area. The Area Contingency Plan shall—

(i) when implemented in conjunction with the National Contingency Plan, be adequate to remove a worst case discharge, and to mitigate or prevent a substantial threat of such a discharge, from a vessel, offshore facility, or onshore facility operating in or near the area;

(ii) describe the area covered by the plan, including the areas of special economic or environmental importance that might be damaged by a discharge;

(iii) describe in detail the responsibilities of an owner or operator and of Federal, State, and local agencies in removing a discharge, and in mitigating or preventing a substantial threat of a discharge;

(iv) list the equipment (including firefighting equipment), dispersants or other mitigating substances and devices, and personnel available to an owner or operator and Federal, State, and local agencies, to ensure an effective and immediate removal of a discharge, and to ensure mitigation or prevention of a substantial threat of a discharge;

(v) describe the procedures to be followed for obtaining an expedited decision regarding the use of dispersants;

(vi) describe in detail how the plan is integrated into other Area Contingency Plans and vessel, offshore facility, and onshore facility response plans approved under this subsection, and into operating procedures of the National Response Unit;

(vii) include any other information the President requires; and

(viii) be updated periodically by the Area Committee.

(D) The President shall—

(i) review and approve Area Contingency Plans under this paragraph; and

(ii) periodically review Area Contingency Plans so approved.

(5) Tank vessel and facility response plans

(A) The President shall issue regulations which require an owner or operator of a tank vessel or facility described in subparagraph (B) to prepare and submit to the President a plan for responding, to the maximum extent practicable, to a worst case discharge, and to a substantial threat of such a discharge, of oil or a hazardous substance.

(B) The tank vessels and facilities referred to in subparagraph (A) are the following:

(i) A tank vessel, as defined under section 2101 of Title 46.

(ii) An offshore facility.

(iii) An onshore facility that, because of its location, could reasonably be expected to cause substantial harm to the environment by discharging into or on the navigable waters, adjoining shorelines, or the exclusive economic zone.

(C) A response plan required under this paragraph shall—

(i) be consistent with the requirements of the National Contingency Plan and Area Contingency Plans;

(ii) identify the qualified individual having full authority to implement removal actions, and require immediate communications between that individual and the appropriate Federal official and the persons providing personnel and equipment pursuant to clause (iii);

(iii) identify, and ensure by contract or other means approved by the President the availability of, private personnel and equipment necessary to remove to the maximum extent practicable a worst case discharge (including a discharge resulting from fire or explosion), and to mitigate or prevent a substantial threat of such a discharge;

(iv) describe the training, equipment testing, periodic unannounced drills, and response actions of persons on the vessel or at the facility, to be carried out under the plan to ensure the safety of the vessel or facility and to mitigate or prevent the discharge, or the substantial threat of a discharge;

(v) be updated periodically; and

(vi) be resubmitted for approval of each significant change.

(D) With respect to any response plan submitted under this paragraph for an onshore facility that, because of its location, could reasonably be expected to cause significant and substantial harm to the environment by discharging into or on the navigable waters or adjoining shorelines or the exclusive economic zone, and with respect to each response plan submitted under this paragraph for a tank vessel or offshore facility, the President shall—

(i) promptly review such response plan;

(ii) require amendments to any plan that does not meet the requirements of this paragraph;

(iii) approve any plan that meets the requirements of this paragraph; and

(iv) review each plan periodically thereafter.

(E) A tank vessel, offshore facility, or onshore facility required to prepare a response plan under this subsection may not handle, store, or transport oil unless—

(i) in the case of a tank vessel, offshore facility, or onshore facility for which a response plan is reviewed by the President under subparagraph (D), the plan has been approved by the President; and

(ii) the vessel or facility is operating in compliance with the plan.

(F) Notwithstanding subparagraph (E), the President may authorize a tank vessel, offshore facility, or onshore facility to operate without a response plan approved under this paragraph, until not later than 2 years after the date of the submission to the President of a plan for the tank vessel or facility, if the owner or operator certifies that the owner or operator has ensured by contract or other means approved by the President the availability of private personnel and equipment necessary to respond, to the maximum extent practicable, to a worst case discharge or a substantial threat of such a discharge.

(G) The owner or operator of a tank vessel, offshore facility, or onshore facility may not claim as a defense to liability under title I of the Oil Pollution Act of 1990 [section 2701 et seq. of this title] that the owner or operator was acting in accordance with an approved response plan.

(H) The Secretary shall maintain, in the Vessel Identification System established under chapter 125 of Title 46, the dates of approval and review of a response plan under this paragraph for each tank vessel that is a vessel of the United States.

(6) Equipment requirements and inspection

Not later than 2 years after August 18, 1990, the President shall require—

(A) periodic inspection of containment booms, skimmers, vessels, and other major equipment used to remove discharges; and

(B) vessels operating on navigable waters and carrying oil or a hazardous substance in bulk as cargo to carry appropriate removal equipment that employs the best technology economically feasible and that is compatible with the safe operation of the vessel.

(7) Area drills

The President shall periodically conduct drills of removal capability, without prior notice, in areas for which Area Contingency Plans are required under this subsection and under relevant tank vessel and facility response plans. The drills may include participation by Federal, State, and local agencies, the owners and operators of vessels and facilities in the area, and private industry. The President may publish annual reports on these drills, including assessments of the effectiveness of the plans and a list of amendments made to improve plans.

(8) United States Government not liable

The United States Government is not liable for any damages arising from its actions or omissions relating to any response plan required by this section.

(k) Repealed. Pub.L. 101–380, Title I, § 2002(b)(2), Aug. 18, 1990, 104 Stat. 507

(*l*) Administration

The President is authorized to delegate the administration of this section to the heads of those Federal departments, agencies, and instrumentalities which he determines to be appropriate. Each such department, agency, and instrumentality, in order to avoid duplication of effort, shall, whenever appropriate, utilize the personnel, services, and facilities of other Federal departments, agencies, and instrumentalities.

(m) Administrative provisions

(1) For vessels

Anyone authorized by the President to enforce the provisions of this section with respect to any vessel may, except as to public vessels—

(A) board and inspect any vessel upon the navigable waters of the United States or the waters of the contiguous zone,

(B) with or without a warrant, arrest any person who in the presence or view of the authorized person violates the provisions of this section or any regulation issued thereunder, and

(C) execute any warrant or other process issued by an officer or court of competent jurisdiction.

(2) For facilities

(A) Recordkeeping

Whenever required to carry out the purposes of this section, the Administrator or the Secretary of the Department in which the Coast Guard is operating shall require the owner or operator of a facility to which this section applies to establish and maintain such records, make such reports, install, use, and maintain such monitoring equipment and methods, and provide such other information as the Administrator or Secretary, as the case may be, may require to carry out the objectives of this section.

(B) Entry and inspection

Whenever required to carry out the purposes of this section, the Administrator or the Secretary of the Department in which the Coast Guard is operating or an authorized representative of the Administrator or Secretary, upon presentation of appropriate credentials, may—

(i) enter and inspect any facility to which this section applies, including any facility at which any records are required to be maintained under subparagraph (A); and

(ii) at reasonable times, have access to and copy any records, take samples, and inspect any monitoring equipment or methods required under subparagraph (A).

(C) Arrests and execution of warrants

Anyone authorized by the Administrator or the Secretary of the department in which the Coast Guard is operating to enforce the provisions of this section with respect to any facility may—

(i) with or without a warrant, arrest any person who violates the provisions of this section or any regulation issued thereunder in the presence or view of the person so authorized; and

(ii) execute any warrant or process issued by an officer or court of competent jurisdiction.

(D) Public access

Any records, reports, or information obtained under this paragraph shall be subject to the same public access and disclosure requirements which are applicable to records, reports, and information obtained pursuant to section 1318 of this title.

(n) Jurisdiction

The several district courts of the United States are invested with jurisdiction for any actions, other than actions pursuant to subsection (i)(1) of this section, arising under this section. In the case of Guam and the Trust Territory of the Pacific Islands, such actions may be brought in the district court of Guam, and in the case of the Virgin Islands such actions may be brought in the district court of the Virgin Islands. In the case of American Samoa and the Trust Territory of the Pacific Islands, such actions may be brought in the District Court of the United States for the District of Hawaii and such court shall have jurisdiction of such actions. In the case of the Canal Zone, such actions may be brought in the United States District Court for the District of the Canal Zone.

(*o*) Obligation for damages unaffected; local authority not preempted; existing Federal authority not modified or affected

(1) Nothing in this section shall affect or modify in any way the obligations of any owner or operator of any vessel, or of any owner or operator of any onshore facility or offshore facility to any person or agency under any provision of law for damages to any publicly owned or privately owned property resulting from a discharge of any oil or hazardous substance or from the removal of any such oil or hazardous substance.

(2) Nothing in this section shall be construed as preempting any State or political subdivision thereof from imposing any requirement or liability with respect to the discharge of oil or hazardous substance into any waters within such State.

(3) Nothing in this section shall be construed as affecting or modifying any other existing authority of any Federal department, agency, or instrumentality, relative to onshore or offshore facilities under this chapter or any other provision of law, or to affect any State or local law not in conflict with this section.

(p) Repealed. Pub.L. 101–380, Title II, § 2002(b)(4), Aug. 18, 1990, 104 Stat. 507

(q) Establishment of maximum limit of liability with respect to onshore or offshore facilities

The President is authorized to establish, with respect to any class or category of onshore or offshore facilities, a maximum limit of liability under subsections (f)(2) and (3) of this section of less than $50,000,000, but not less than $8,000,000.

(r) Liability limitations not to limit liability under other legislation

Nothing in this section shall be construed to impose, or authorize the imposition of, any limitation on liability under the Outer Continental Shelf Lands Act [43 U.S.C. 1331 et seq.] or the Deepwater Port Act of 1974 [33 U.S.C. 1501 et seq.].

(s) Oil Spill Liability Trust Fund

The Oil Spill Liability Trust Fund established under section 9509 of Title 26 shall be available to carry out subsections (b), (c), (d), (j), and (*l*) of this section as those subsections apply to discharges, and substantial threats of discharges, of oil. Any amounts received by the United States under this section shall be deposited in the Oil Spill Liability Trust Fund.

(June 30, 1948, c. 758, Title III, § 311, as added Oct. 18, 1972, Pub.L. 92–500, § 2, 86 Stat. 862, and amended Dec. 28, 1973, Pub.L. 93–207, § 1(4), 87 Stat. 906; Dec. 27, 1977, Pub.L. 95–217, §§ 57, 58(a)–(g), (i), (k)–(m), 91 Stat. 1593–1596; Nov. 2, 1978, Pub.L. 95–576, § 1(b), 92 Stat. 2467; Oct. 21, 1980, Pub.L. 96–478, § 13(b), 94 Stat. 2303; Oct. 21, 1980, Pub.L. 96–483, § 8, 94 Stat. 2362; Dec. 22, 1980, Pub.L. 96–561, Title II, § 238(b), 94 Stat. 3300; April 2, 1982, Pub.L. 97–164, Title I, § 161(5), 96 Stat. 49; Feb. 4, 1987, Pub.L. 100–4, Title V, § 502(b), 101 Stat. 75; Aug. 18, 1990, Pub.L. 101–380, Title II, § 2002(b), Title IV, §§ 4201(a), (b), (b)[(c)], 4202(a), (c), 4204, 4301(a), (b), 4305, 4306, 104 Stat. 507, 523, 525, 527, 532, 533, 540, 541; Oct. 6, 1992, Pub.L. 102–388, Title III, § 349, 106 Stat. 1554; Oct. 29, 1992, Pub.L. 102–572, Title IX, § 902(b)(1), 106 Stat. 4516.)

[1] So in original.

References in Text

The Comprehensive Environmental Response, Compensation, and Liability Act of 1980, referred to in subsec. (c)(4)(B)(ii), is Pub.L. 96–510, Dec. 11, 1980, 94 Stat. 2767, as amended, which is principally classified to chapter 103 (section 9601 et seq.) of Title 42, The Public Health and Welfare. For complete classification of this Act to the Code, see Short Title note set out under section 9601 of Title 42 and Tables.

The Oil Pollution Act of 1990, referred to in subsecs. (c)(5)(B), (c)(6), (d)(2)(H) and (j)(5)(H), is Pub.L. 101–380, Aug. 18, 1990, 104 Stat. 484, which is principally classified to chapter 40 (section 2701 et seq.) of this title. Section 1001 of the Act is classified to section 2701 of this title. For complete classification of this Act to the Code, see Short Title note set out under section 2701 of this title and Tables.

Codification

"Not later than 2 years after August 18, 1990", appearing in subsec. (j)(6), was, in the original, "not later than 2 years after the date of enactment of this section", and was editorially translated according to the probable intent of Congress in enacting subsec. (j)(6) by Pub.L. 101–380, 104 Stat. 484, which was approved Aug. 18, 1990.

Change of Name

References to United States Claims Court deemed to refer to United States Court of Federal Claims and references to Claims Court deemed to refer to Court of Federal Claims, see section 902(b) of Pub.L. 102–572, set out as a note under section 171 of Title 28, Judiciary and Judicial Procedure.

Effective Date of 1992 Amendments

Amendment by Title IX of Pub.L. 102–572 effective Oct. 29, 1992, see section 911 of Pub.L. 102–572, set out as a note under section 171 of Title 28, Judiciary and Judicial Procedure.

Oil Spill Liability Under Oil Pollution Act of 1990

Section 2002(a) of Pub.L. 101–380 provided that: "Subsections (f), (g), (h), and (i) of section 311 of the Federal Water Pollution Control Act (33 U.S.C. 1321) [subsecs. (f), (g), (h), and (i) of this section] shall not apply with respect to any incident for which liability is established under section 1002 of this Act [section 2702 of this title]."

Transfer to Oil Spill Liability Trust Fund of Moneys Remaining in Revolving Fund Upon Its Repeal

Section 2002(b)(2) of Pub.L. 101–380 provided that: "Subsection (k) [of this section] is repealed. Any amounts remaining in the revolving fund established under that subsection shall be deposited in the [Oil Spill Liability Trust] Fund. The [Oil Spill Liability Trust] Fund shall assume all liability incurred by the revolving fund established under that subsection."

Revision of National Contingency Plan

Section 4201(c) of Pub.L. 101–380 provided that: "Not later than one year after the date of the enactment of this Act [Aug. 18, 1990], the President shall revise and republish the National Contingency Plan prepared under section 311(c)(2) of the Federal Water Pollution Control Act [subsec. (c)(2) of this section] (as in effect immediately before the date of the enactment of this Act [Aug. 18, 1990]) to implement the amendments made by this section [amending subsecs. (a), (c), and (d) of this section] and section 4202 [amending subsecs. (j) and (*o*) of this section]."

Implementation of National Planning and Response System

Section 4202(b) of Pub.L. 101–380 provided that:

"**(1) Area committees and contingency plans.—(A)** Not later than 6 months after the date of the enactment of this Act [Aug. 18, 1990], the President shall designate the areas for which Area Committees are established under section 311(j)(4) of the Federal Water Pollution Control Act [subsec. (j)(4) of this section], as amended by this Act. In designating such areas, the President shall ensure that all navigable waters, adjoining shorelines, and waters of the exclusive economic zone are subject to an Area Contingency Plan under that section.

"**(B)** Not later than 18 months after the date of the enactment of this Act [Aug. 18, 1990], each Area Committee established under that section [subsec. (j)(4) of this section] shall submit to the President the Area Contingency Plan required under that section.

"**(C)** Not later than 24 months after the date of the enactment of this Act [Aug. 18, 1990], the President shall—

"**(i)** promptly review each plan;

"**(ii)** require amendments to any plan that does not meet the requirements of section 311(j)(4) of the Federal Water Pollution Control Act [subsec. (j)(4) of this section]; and

"**(iii)** approve each plan that meets the requirements of that section.

"**(2) National response unit.**—Not later than one year after the date of the enactment of this Act [Aug. 18, 1990], the Secretary of the department in which the Coast Guard is operating shall establish a National Response Unit in accordance with section 311(j)(2) of the Federal Water Pollution Control Act, as amended by this Act [subsec. (j)(2) of this section].

"**(3) Coast guard district response groups.**—Not later than 1 year after the date of the enactment of this Act [Aug. 18, 1990], the Secretary of the department in which the Coast Guard is operating shall establish Coast Guard District Response Groups in accordance with section 311(j)(3) of the Federal Water Pollution Control Act, as amended by this Act [subsec. (j)(3) of this section].

"**(4) Tank vessel and facility response plans; transition provision; effective date of prohibition.—(A)** Not later than 24 months after the date of the enactment of this Act [Aug. 18, 1990], the President shall issue regulations for tank vessel and facility response plans under section 311(j)(5) of the Federal Water Pollution Control Act, as amended by this Act [subsec. (j)(5) of this section].

"**(B)** During the period beginning 30 months after the date of the enactment of this paragraph [Aug. 18, 1990], and ending 36 months after that date of enactment, a tank vessel or facility for which a response plan is required to be prepared under section 311(j)(5) of the Federal Water Pollution Control Act [subsec. (j)(5) of this section], as amended by this Act, may not handle, store, or transport oil unless the owner or operator thereof has submitted such a plan to the President.

"**(C)** Subparagraph (E) of section 311(j)(5) of the Federal Water Pollution Control Act [subsec. (j)(5) of this section], as amended by this Act, shall take effect 36 months after the date of the enactment of this Act [Aug. 18, 1990]."

Deposit of Certain Penalties Into Oil Spill Liability Trust Fund

Penalties paid pursuant to this section and sections 1319(c) and 1501 et seq., respectively, of this title, deposited in the Oil Spill Liability Trust Fund created under section 9509 of Title 26, Internal Revenue Code, see section 4304 of Pub.L. 101–380, set out as a note under section 9509 of Title 26.

CROSS REFERENCES

Authorization of appropriations to carry out this chapter with certain exceptions, see section 1376 of this title.

Coordination of guidelines for use of imminent hazard, enforcement, and emergency response authorities with powers under this section, see section 9606 of Title 42, The Public Health and Welfare.

Definition of "hazardous substance" for purposes of comprehensive environmental response, compensation, and liability provisions, see section 9601 of Title 42.

Definition of "removal costs" for purposes of offshore oil spill pollution fund, see section 1811 of Title 43, Public Lands.

Demonstration of financial responsibility in accordance with this section, see section 1653 of Title 43.

Designation of hazardous substance under this section as constituting hazardous material in relation to vessels and seamen, see section 2101 of Title 46, Shipping.

Effective date of regulations issued pursuant to this section, see section 9652 of Title 42, The Public Health and Welfare.

Establishment and maintenance of records to carry out this section, see section 1318 of this title.

Establishment of reportable released quantities of hazardous substances, see section 9602 of Title 42, The Public Health and Welfare.

Federal oil pollution preventive measures on the high seas, availability of revolving fund monies, see section 1486 of this title.

Hazardous Substance Superfund, payment of claims incurred as result of carrying out national contingency plan established under this section, see section 9611 of Title 42, The Public Health and Welfare.

Hudson River reclamation demonstration project, see section 1266 of this title.

Oil within meaning of this section as included in definition of "material", see section 1402 of this title.

Prohibition of discharge of oil from any offshore facility or vessel, see section 1821 of Title 43, Public Lands.

Regulations respecting assessment of damages to natural resources, see section 9651 of Title 42, The Public Health and Welfare.

Regulations supplemental to effluent limitations for specific hazardous pollutants, see section 1314 of this title.

Removal of oil in accordance with National Contingency Plan established pursuant to this section, see section 1517 of this title.

Revision of National Contingency Plan, see section 9605 of Title 42, The Public Health and Welfare.

Transfer of unobligated funds under this section, see section 9654 of Title 42.

Federal Practice and Procedure

Exceptions to sovereign immunity, see Wright, Miller & Cooper: Jurisdiction 2d § 3656 et seq.

Federal Jury Practice and Instructions

Liability of corporation, see Devitt and Blackmar § 64.08.

West's Federal Forms

Complaint for cleanup expense, see § 11098.5 and Comment thereunder.
Complaints in admiralty charging oil pollution, see §§ 11097, 11098.
Judgment for oil spill cleanup costs, penalty, see § 11755 and Comment thereunder.

West's Federal Practice Manual

Concurrent Claims Court jurisdiction, see § 1834.

CODE OF FEDERAL REGULATIONS

Civil penalties for violation of oil pollution prevention regulations, see 40 CFR 114.1 et seq.
Designation of substances, reportable quantities, and notification requirements for release of substances, see 40 CFR 302.1 et seq.
Financial responsibility for oil pollution—Alaska pipeline, see 33 CFR 131.1 et seq.
Financial responsibility for water pollution, see 33 CFR 130.1 et seq.
Hazardous substances—
 Designation, see 40 CFR 116.1 et seq.
 Determination of reportable quantities, see 40 CFR 117.1 et seq.
Inspection and certification, see 46 CFR 71.01 et seq., 91.01 et seq., 189.01 et seq.
Liability limits for small onshore storage facilities, see 40 CFR 113.1 et seq.
Limitations on discharge of oil, see 40 CFR 110.1 et seq., 112.1 et seq.
Oil pollution regulations, see 33 CFR Chap. I, Subchap. O.
Pollution contingency plan, see 40 CFR 300.1 et seq.
Pollution of coastal and navigable waters, reports by United States Customs Service officers, see 19 CFR 4.0 et seq.
Pollution removal damage claims, see 33 CFR 25.101 et seq.
Trans-Alaska pipeline liability fund, see 43 CFR 29.1 et seq.

LAW REVIEW COMMENTARIES

Encouraging safety through insurance-based incentives: financial responsibility for hazardous wastes. Jeffrey Kehne, 96 Yale L.J. 403 (1986).
Groundwater contamination claims in Connecticut. Dean M. Cordiano and Lynn Anne Glover, 60 Conn.B.J. 167 (1986).
Liability of parent corporations for hazardous waste cleanup and damages. 99 Harvard L.Rev. 986 (1986).
New Jersey clean up your "act": Some reflections on the Spill Compensation and Control Act. Francis E.P. McCarter, 38 Rutgers L.Rev. 637 (1986).
Oil Pollution Act of 1990: Opening a new era in federal and Texas regulation of oil spill prevention, containment and cleanup, and liability. J.B. Ruhl and Michael J. Jewell, 32 S.Tex.L.Rev. 475 (1991).
Regulation of batture pollution and ecology. Stan Millan, 33 Loyola (La.) L.Rev. 921 (1988).
Responding to a government environmental investigation: Shaping the defense. Francis J. Burke, Jr., Karen A. Potts, Leigh Lani Brown, Robin L. De Respino and Michael R. Hall, 34 Ariz. L.Rev. 509 (1992).
Survey of federal and state environmental crime legislation. Edward F. Novak and Charles W. Steese, 34 Ariz.L.Rev. 571 (1992).
The once and future EPA lender regulations: Limiting lender liability for the cleanup of hazardous wastes. Jeffrey M. Gaba, 47 Consumer Fin.L.Q.Rep. 355 (1993).

United States Supreme Court

Hearing in which civil penalty imposed not "quasi-criminal" so as to implicate constitutional protection against compulsory self-incrimination as regards use of statutory reporting requirements, see U.S. v. Ward, 1980, 100 S.Ct. 2636, 448 U.S. 242, 65 L.Ed.2d 742, rehearing denied 101 S.Ct. 37, 448 U.S. 916, 65 L.Ed.2d 1179.

State regulation or control, oil spills, waiver of preemption, Askew v. American Waterways Operators Inc., 1973, 93 S.Ct. 1590, 411 U.S. 325, 36 L.Ed.2d 280.

§ 1322. Marine sanitation devices [FWPCA § 312]

(a) Definitions

For the purpose of this section, the term—

(1) "new vessel" includes every description of watercraft or other artificial contrivance used, or capable of being used, as a means of transportation on the navigable waters, the construction of which is initiated after promulgation of standards and regulations under this section;

(2) "existing vessel" includes every description of watercraft or other artificial contrivance used, or capable of being used, as a means of transportation on the navigable waters, the construction of which is initiated before promulgation of standards and regulations under this section;

(3) "public vessel" means a vessel owned or bareboat chartered and operated by the United States, by a State or political subdivision thereof, or by a foreign nation, except when such vessel is engaged in commerce;

(4) "United States" includes the States, the District of Columbia, the Commonwealth of Puerto Rico, the Virgin Islands, Guam, American Samoa, the Canal Zone, and the Trust Territory of the Pacific Islands;

(5) "marine sanitation device" includes any equipment for installation on board a vessel which is designed to receive, retain, treat, or discharge sewage, and any process to treat such sewage;

(6) "sewage" means human body wastes and the wastes from toilets and other receptacles intended to receive or retain body wastes except that, with respect to commercial vessels on the Great Lakes, such term shall include graywater;

(7) "manufacturer" means any person engaged in the manufacturing, assembling, or importation of marine sanitation devices or of vessels subject to standards and regulations promulgated under this section;

(8) "person" means an individual, partnership, firm, corporation, association, or agency of the United States, but does not include an individual on board a public vessel;

(9) "discharge" includes, but is not limited to, any spilling, leaking, pumping, pouring, emitting, emptying or dumping;

(10) "commercial vessels" means those vessels used in the business of transporting property for compensation or hire, or in transporting property in the business of the owner, lessee, or operator of the vessel;

(11) "graywater" means galley, bath, and shower water;

(12) "discharge incidental to the normal operation of a vessel"—

(A) means a discharge, including—

(i) graywater, bilge water, cooling water, weather deck runoff, ballast water, oil water separator effluent, and any other pollutant discharge from the operation of a marine propulsion system, shipboard maneuvering system, crew habitability system, or installed major equipment, such as an aircraft carrier elevator or a catapult, or from a protective, preservative, or absorptive application to the hull of the vessel; and

(ii) a discharge in connection with the testing, maintenance, and repair of a system described in clause (i) whenever the vessel is waterborne; and

(B) does not include—

(i) a discharge of rubbish, trash, garbage, or other such material discharged overboard;

(ii) an air emission resulting from the operation of a vessel propulsion system, motor driven equipment, or incinerator; or

(iii) a discharge that is not covered by part 122.3 of title 40, Code of Federal Regulations (as in effect on February 10, 1996);

(13) "marine pollution control device" means any equipment or management practice, for installation or use on board a vessel of the Armed Forces, that is—

(A) designed to receive, retain, treat, control, or discharge a discharge incidental to the normal operation of a vessel; and

(B) determined by the Administrator and the Secretary of Defense to be the most effective equipment or management practice to reduce the environmental impacts of the discharge consistent with the considerations set forth in subsection (n)(2)(B) of this section; and

(14) "vessel of the Armed Forces" means—

(A) any vessel owned or operated by the Department of Defense, other than a time or voyage chartered vessel; and

(B) any vessel owned or operated by the Department of Transportation that is designated by the Secretary of the department in which the Coast Guard is operating as a vessel equivalent to a vessel described in subparagraph (A).

(b) Federal standards of performance

(1) As soon as possible, after October 18, 1972, and subject to the provisions of section 1254(j) of this title, the Administrator, after consultation with the Secretary of the department in which the Coast Guard is operating, after giving appropriate consideration to the economic costs involved, and within the limits of available technology, shall promulgate Federal standards of performance for marine sanitation devices (hereafter in this section referred to as "standards") which shall be designed to prevent the discharge of untreated or inadequately treated sewage into or upon the navigable waters from new vessels and existing vessels, except vessels not equipped with installed toilet facilities. Such standards and standards established under subsection (c)(1)(B) of this section shall be consistent with maritime safety and the marine and navigation laws and regulations and shall be coordinated with the regulations issued under this subsection by the Secretary of the department in which the Coast Guard is operating. The Secretary of the department in which the Coast Guard is operating shall promulgate regulations, which are consistent with standards promulgated under this subsection and subsection (c) of this section and with maritime safety and the marine and navigation laws and regulations governing the design, construction, installation, and operation of any marine sanitation device on board such vessels.

(2) Any existing vessel equipped with a marine sanitation device on the date of promulgation of initial standards and regulations under this section, which device is in compliance with such initial standards and regulations, shall be deemed in compliance with this section until such time as the device is replaced or is found not to be in compliance with such initial standards and regulations.

(c) Initial standards; effective dates; revision; waiver

(1)(A) Initial standards and regulations under this section shall become effective for new vessels two years after promulgation; and for existing vessels five years after promulgation. Revisions of standards and regulations shall be effective upon promulgation, unless another effective date is specified, except that no revision shall take effect before the effective date of the standard or regulation being revised.

(B) The Administrator shall, with respect to commercial vessels on the Great Lakes, establish standards which require at a minimum the equivalent of secondary treatment as defined under section 1314(d) of this title. Such standards and regulations shall take effect for existing vessels after such time as the Administrator determines to be reasonable for the upgrading of marine sanitation devices to attain such standard.

(2) The Secretary of the department in which the Coast Guard is operating with regard to his regulatory authority established by this section, after consultation with the Administrator, may distinguish among classes, type, and sizes of vessels as well as between new and existing vessels, and may waive applicability of standards and regulations as necessary or appropriate for such classes, types, and sizes of vessels (including existing vessels equipped with marine sanitation devices on the date of promulgation of the initial standards required by this section), and, upon application, for individual vessels.

(d) Vessels owned and operated by the United States

The provisions of this section and the standards and regulations promulgated hereunder apply to vessels owned and operated by the United States unless the Secretary of Defense finds that compliance would not be in the interest of national security. With respect to vessels owned and operated by the Department of Defense, regulations under the last sentence of subsection (b)(1) of this section and certifications under subsection (g)(2) of this section shall be promulgated and issued by the Secretary of Defense.

(e) Pre-promulgation consultation

Before the standards and regulations under this section are promulgated, the Administrator and the Secretary of the department in which the Coast Guard is operating shall consult with the Secretary of State; the Secretary of Health and Human Services; the Secretary of Defense; the Secretary of the Treasury; the Secretary of Commerce; other interested Federal agencies; and the States and industries interested; and otherwise comply with the requirements of section 553 of title 5.

(f) Regulation by States or political subdivisions thereof; complete prohibition upon discharge of sewage

(1)(A) Except as provided in subparagraph (B), after the effective date of the initial standards and regulations promulgated under this section, no State or political subdivision thereof shall adopt or enforce any statute or regulation of such State or political subdivision with respect to the design, manufacture, or installation or use of any marine sanitation device on any vessel subject to the provisions of this section.

(B) A State may adopt and enforce a statute or regulation with respect to the design, manufacture, or installation or use of any marine sanitation device on a houseboat, if such statute or regulation is more stringent than the standards and regulations promulgated under this section. For purposes of this paragraph, the term "houseboat" means a vessel which, for a period of time determined by the State in which the vessel is located, is used primarily as a residence and is not used primarily as a means of transportation.

(2) If, after promulgation of the initial standards and regulations and prior to their effective date, a vessel is equipped with a marine sanitation device in compliance with such standards and regulations and the installation and operation of such device is in accordance with such standards and regulations, such standards and regulations shall, for the purposes of paragraph (1) of this subsection, become effective with respect to such vessel on the date of such compliance.

(3) After the effective date of the initial standards and regulations promulgated under this section, if any State determines that the protection and enhancement of the quality of some or all of the waters within such State require greater environmental protection, such State may completely prohibit the discharge from all vessels of any sewage, whether treated or not, into such waters, except that no such prohibition shall apply until the Administrator determines that adequate facilities for the safe and sanitary removal and treatment of sewage from all vessels are reasonably available for such water to which such prohibition would apply. Upon application of the State, the Administrator shall make such determination within 90 days of the date of such application.

(4)(A) If the Administrator determines upon application by a State that the protection and enhancement of the quality of specified waters within such State requires such a prohibition, he shall by regulation completely prohibit the discharge from a vessel of any sewage (whether treated or not) into such waters.

(B) Upon application by a State, the Administrator shall, by regulation, establish a drinking water intake zone in any waters within such State and prohibit the discharge of sewage from vessels within that zone.

(g) Sales limited to certified devices; certification of test device; recordkeeping; reports

(1) No manufacturer of a marine sanitation device shall sell, offer for sale, or introduce or deliver for introduction in interstate commerce, or import into the United States for sale or resale any marine sanitation device manufactured after the effective date of the standards and regulations promulgated under this section unless such device is in all material respects substantially the same as a test device certified under this subsection.

(2) Upon application of the manufacturer, the Secretary of the department in which the Coast Guard is operating shall so certify a marine sanitation device if he determines, in accordance with the provisions of this paragraph, that it meets the appropriate standards and regulations promulgated under this section. The Secretary of the department in which the Coast Guard is operating shall test or require such testing of the device in accordance with procedures set forth by the Administrator as to standards of performance and for such other purposes as may be appropriate. If the Secretary of the department in which the Coast Guard is operating determines that the device is satisfactory from the standpoint of safety and any other requirements of maritime law or regulation, and after consideration of the design, installation, operation, material, or other appropriate factors, he shall certify the device. Any device manufactured by such manufacturer which is in all material respects substantially the same as the certified test device shall be deemed to be in conformity with the appropriate standards and regulations established under this section.

(3) Every manufacturer shall establish and maintain such records, make such reports, and provide such information as the Administrator or the Secretary of the department in which the Coast Guard is operating may reasonably require to enable him to determine whether such manufacturer has acted or is acting in compliance with this section and regulations issued thereunder and shall, upon request of an officer or employee duly designated by the Administrator or the Secretary of the department in which the Coast Guard is operating, permit such officer or employee at reasonable times to have access to and copy such records. All information reported to or otherwise obtained by the Administrator or the Secretary of the Department in which the Coast Guard is operating or their representatives pursuant to this subsection which contains or relates to a trade secret or other matter referred to in section 1905 of title 18 shall be considered confidential for the purpose of that section, except that such information may be disclosed to other officers or employees concerned with carrying out this section. This paragraph shall not apply in the case of the construction of a vessel by an individual for his own use.

(h) Sale and resale of properly equipped vessels; operability of certified marine sanitation devices

After the effective date of standards and regulations promulgated under this section, it shall be unlawful—

(1) for the manufacturer of any vessel subject to such standards and regulations to manufacture for sale, to sell or offer for sale, or to distribute for sale or resale any such vessel unless it is equipped with a marine sanitation device which is in all material respects substantially the same as the appropriate test device certified pursuant to this section;

(2) for any person, prior to the sale or delivery of a vessel subject to such standards and regulations to the ultimate purchaser, wrongfully to remove or render inoperative any certified marine sanitation device or element of design of such device installed in such vessel;

(3) for any person to fail or refuse to permit access to or copying of records or to fail to make reports or provide information required under this section; and

(4) for a vessel subject to such standards and regulations to operate on the navigable waters of the United States, if such vessel is not equipped with an operable marine sanitation device certified pursuant to this section.

(i) Jurisdiction to restrain violations; contempts

The district courts of the United States shall have jurisdictions to restrain violations of subsection (g)(1) of this section and subsections (h)(1) through (3) of this section. Actions to restrain such violations shall be brought by, and in, the name of the United States. In case of contumacy or refusal to obey a subpena served upon any person under this subsection, the district court of the United States for any district in which such person is found or resides or transacts business, upon application by the United States and after notice to such person, shall have jurisdiction to issue an order requiring such person to appear and give testimony or to appear and produce documents, and any failure to obey such order of the court may be punished by such court as a contempt thereof.

(j) Penalties

Any person who violates subsection (g)(1) of this section, clause (1) or (2) of subsection (h) of this section, or subsection (n)(8) of this section, shall be liable to a civil penalty of not more than $5,000 for each violation. Any person who violates clause (4) of subsection (h) of this section or any regulation issued pursuant to this section shall be liable to a civil penalty of not more than $2,000 for each violation. Each violation shall be a separate offense. The Secretary of the department in which the Coast Guard is operating may assess and compromise any such penalty. No penalty shall be assessed until the person charged shall have been given notice and an opportunity for a hearing on such charge. In determining the amount of the penalty, or the amount agreed upon in compromise, the gravity of the violation, and the demonstrated good faith of the person charged in attempting to achieve rapid compliance, after notification of a violation, shall be considered by said Secretary.

(k) Enforcement authority

The provisions of this section shall be enforced by the Secretary of the department in which the Coast

Guard is operating and he may utilize by agreement, with or without reimbursement, law enforcement officers or other personnel and facilities of the Administrator, other Federal agencies, or the States to carry out the provisions of this section. The provisions of this section may also be enforced by a State.

(*l*) Boarding and inspection of vessels; execution of warrants and other process

Anyone authorized by the Secretary of the department in which the Coast Guard is operating to enforce the provisions of this section may, except as to public vessels, (1) board and inspect any vessel upon the navigable waters of the United States and (2) execute any warrant or other process issued by an officer or court of competent jurisdiction.

(m) Enforcement in United States possessions

In the case of Guam and the Trust Territory of the Pacific Islands, actions arising under this section may be brought in the district court of Guam, and in the case of the Virgin Islands such actions may be brought in the district court of the Virgin Islands. In the case of American Samoa and the Trust Territory of the Pacific Islands, such actions may be brought in the District Court of the United States for the District of Hawaii and such court shall have jurisdiction of such actions. In the case of the Canal Zone, such actions may be brought in the District Court for the District of the Canal Zone.

(n) Uniform national discharge standards for vessels of the Armed Forces.—

(1) Applicability

This subsection shall apply to vessels of the Armed Forces and discharges, other than sewage, incidental to the normal operation of a vessel of the Armed Forces, unless the Secretary of Defense finds that compliance with this subsection would not be in the national security interests of the United States.

(2) Determination of discharges required to be controlled by marine pollution control devices

(A) In general

The Administrator and the Secretary of Defense, after consultation with the Secretary of the department in which the Coast Guard is operating, the Secretary of Commerce, and interested States, shall jointly determine the discharges incidental to the normal operation of a vessel of the Armed Forces for which it is reasonable and practicable to require use of a marine pollution control device to mitigate adverse impacts on the marine environment. Notwithstanding subsection (a)(1) of section 553 of Title 5, the Administrator and the Secretary of Defense shall promulgate the determinations in accordance with such section. The Secretary of Defense shall require the use of a marine pollution control device on board a vessel of the Armed Forces in any case in which it is determined that the use of such a device is reasonable and practicable.

(B) Considerations

In making a determination under subparagraph (A), the Administrator and the Secretary of Defense shall take into consideration—

(i) the nature of the discharge;

(ii) the environmental effects of the discharge;

(iii) the practicability of using the marine pollution control device;

(iv) the effect that installation or use of the marine pollution control device would have on the operation or operational capability of the vessel;

(v) applicable United States law;

(vi) applicable international standards; and

(vii) the economic costs of the installation and use of the marine pollution control device.

(3) Performance standards for marine pollution control devices

(A) In general

For each discharge for which a marine pollution control device is determined to be required under paragraph (2), the Administrator and the Secretary of Defense, in consultation with the Secretary of the department in which the Coast Guard is operating, the Secretary of State, the Secretary of Commerce, other interested Federal agencies, and interested States, shall jointly promulgate Federal standards of performance for each marine pollution control device required with respect to the discharge. Notwithstanding subsection (a)(1) of section 553 of Title 5, the Administrator and the Secretary of Defense shall promulgate the standards in accordance with such section.

(B) Considerations

In promulgating standards under this paragraph, the Administrator and the Secretary of Defense shall take into consideration the matters set forth in paragraph (2)(B).

(C) Classes, types, and sizes of vessels

The standards promulgated under this paragraph may—

(i) distinguish among classes, types, and sizes of vessels;

(ii) distinguish between new and existing vessels; and

(ii) provide for a waiver of the applicability of the standards as necessary or appropriate to a particular class, type, age, or size of vessel.

(4) Regulations for use of marine pollution control devices

The Secretary of Defense, after consultation with the Administrator and the Secretary of the department in which the Coast Guard is operating, shall promulgate such regulations governing the design, construction, installation, and use of marine pollution control devices on board vessels of the Armed Forces as are necessary to achieve the standards promulgated under paragraph (3).

(5) Deadlines; effective date

(A) Determinations

The Administrator and the Secretary of Defense shall—

(i) make the initial determinations under paragraph (2) not later than 2 years after February 10, 1996; and

(ii) every 5 years—

(I) review the determinations; and

(II) if necessary, revise the determinations based on significant new information.

(B) Standards

The Administrator and the Secretary of Defense shall—

(i) promulgate standards of performance for a marine pollution control device under paragraph (3) not later than 2 years after the date of a determination under paragraph (2) that the marine pollution control device is required; and

(ii) every 5 years—

(I) review the standards; and

(II) if necessary, revise the standards, consistent with paragraph (3)(B) and based on significant new information.

(C) Regulations

The Secretary of Defense shall promulgate regulations with respect to a marine pollution control device under paragraph (4) as soon as practicable after the Administrator and the Secretary of Defense promulgate standards with respect to the device under paragraph (3), but not later than 1 year after the Administrator and the Secretary of Defense promulgate the standards. The regulations promulgated by the Secretary of Defense under paragraph (4) shall become effective upon promulgation unless another effective date is specified in the regulations.

(D) Petition for review

The Governor of any State may submit a petition requesting that the Secretary of Defense and the Administrator review a determination under paragraph (2) or a standard under paragraph (3), if there is significant new information, not considered previously, that could reasonably result in a change to the particular determination or standard after consideration of the matters set forth in paragraph (2)(B). The petition shall be accompanied by the scientific and technical information on which the petition is based. The Administrator and the Secretary of Defense shall grant or deny the petition not later than 2 years after the date of receipt of the petition.

(6) Effect on other laws

(A) Prohibition on regulation by States or political subdivisions of States

Beginning on the effective date of—

(i) a determination under paragraph (2) that it is not reasonable and practicable to require use of a marine pollution control device regarding a particular discharge incidental to the normal operation of a vessel of the Armed Forces; or

(ii) regulations promulgated by the Secretary of Defense under paragraph (4);

except as provided in paragraph (7), neither a State nor a political subdivision of a State may adopt or enforce any statute or regulation of the State or political subdivision with respect to the discharge or the design, construction, installation, or use of any marine pollution control device required to control discharges from a vessel of the Armed Forces.

(B) Federal laws

This subsection shall not affect the application of section 1321 of this title to discharges incidental to the normal operation of a vessel.

(7) Establishment of State no-discharge zones

(A) State prohibition

(i) In general

After the effective date of—

(I) a determination under paragraph (2) that it is not reasonable and practicable to require use of a marine pollution control device regarding a particular discharge incidental to the normal operation of a vessel of the Armed Forces; or

(II) regulations promulgated by the Secretary of Defense under paragraph (4);

if a State determines that the protection and enhancement of the quality of some or all of the waters within the State require greater environmental protection, the State may prohibit 1 or more discharges incidental to the normal operation of a vessel, whether treated or not treated, into the waters. No prohibition shall apply until the Administrator makes the determinations described in subclauses (II) and (III) of subparagraph (B)(i).

(ii) Documentation

To the extent that a prohibition under this paragraph would apply to vessels of the Armed Forces and not to other types of vessels, the State shall document the technical or environmental basis for the distinction.

(B) Prohibition by the Administrator

(i) In general

Upon application of a State, the Administrator shall by regulation prohibit the discharge from a vessel of 1 or more discharges incidental to the normal operation of a vessel, whether treated or not treated, into the waters covered by the application if the Administrator determines that—

(I) the protection and enhancement of the quality of the specified waters within the State require a prohibition of the discharge into the waters;

(II) adequate facilities for the safe and sanitary removal of the discharge incidental to the normal operation of a vessel are reasonably available for the waters to which the prohibition would apply; and

(III) the prohibition will not have the effect of discriminating against a vessel of the Armed Forces by reason of the ownership or operation by the Federal Government, or the military function, of the vessel.

(ii) Approval or disapproval

The Administrator shall approve or disapprove an application submitted under clause (i) not later than 90 days after the date on which the application is submitted to the Administrator. Notwithstanding clause (i)(II), the Administrator shall not disapprove an application for the sole reason that there are not adequate facilities to remove any discharge incidental to the normal operation of a vessel from vessels of the Armed Forces.

(C) Applicability to foreign flagged vessels

A prohibition under this paragraph—

(i) shall not impose any design, construction, manning, or equipment standard on a foreign flagged vessel engaged in innocent passage unless the prohibition implements a generally accepted international rule or standard; and

(ii) that relates to the prevention, reduction, and control of pollution shall not apply to a foreign flagged vessel engaged in transit passage unless the prohibition implements an applicable international regulation regarding the discharge of oil, oily waste, or any other noxious substance into the waters.

(8) Prohibition relating to vessels of the Armed Forces

After the effective date of the regulations promulgated by the Secretary of Defense under paragraph (4), it shall be unlawful for any vessel of the Armed Forces subject to the regulations to—

(A) operate in the navigable waters of the united States or the waters of the contiguous zone, if the vessel is not equipped with any required marine pollution control device meeting standards established under this subsection; or

(B) discharge overboard any discharge incidental to the normal operation of a vessel in waters with respect to which a prohibition on the discharge has been established under paragraph (7).

(9) Enforcement

This subsection shall be enforceable, as provided in subsections (j) and (k) of this section, against any agency of the United States responsible for vessels of the Armed Forces notwithstanding any immunity asserted by the agency.

(June 30, 1948, c. 758, Title III, § 312, as added Oct. 18, 1972, Pub.L. 92–500, § 2, 86 Stat. 871, and amended Dec. 27, 1977, Pub.L. 95–217, § 59, 91 Stat. 1596; Oct. 17, 1979, Pub.L. 96–88, Title V, § 509(b), 93 Stat. 695; Feb. 4, 1987, Pub.L. 100–4, Title III, § 311, 101 Stat. 42; Feb. 10, 1996, Pub.L. 104–106, Title III, § 325(b) to (c)(2), 110 Stat. 254.)

Discharges from Vessels of the Armed Forces

Section 325(a) of Pub.L. 104–106 provided that: "The purposes of this section [amending this section and section 1362 of this title and enacting provisions set out as notes under this section] are to—

"(1) enhance the operational flexibility of vessels of the Armed Forces domestically and internationally;

"(2) stimulate the development of innovative vessel pollution control technology; and

"(3) advance the development by the United States Navy of environmentally sound ships."

Cooperation in Standards Development

Section 325(d) of Pub.L. 104–106 provided that: "The Administrator of the Environmental Protection Agency and the Secretary of Defense may, by mutual agreement, with or without reimbursement, provide for the use of information, reports, personnel, or other resources of the Environmental Protection Agency or the Department of Defense to carry out section 312(n) of the Federal Water Pollution Control Act (as added by subsection (b) [subsec. (n) of this section]), including the use of the resources—

"(1) to determine—

"(A) the nature and environmental effect of discharges incidental to the normal operation of a vessel of the Armed Forces;

"(B) the practicability of using marine pollution control devices on vessels of the Armed Forces; and

"(C) the effect that installation or use of marine pollution control devices on vessels of the Armed Forces would have on the operation or operational capability of the vessels; and

"(2) to establish performance standards for marine pollution control devices on vessels of the Armed Forces."

Construction, Renovation, Operation, and Maintenance of Pumpout Stations and Waste Reception Facilities

Pub.L. 102–587, Title V, Subtitle F, § 5601 et seq., Nov. 4, 1992, 106 Stat. 5086, provided that:

"Sec. 5601. Short title.

"This subtitle [subtitle F, §§ 5601 to 5608, of Title V of Pub.L. 102–587, amending sections 777c and 777g of Title 16, Conservation and enacting this note] may be cited as the 'Clean Vessel Act of 1992'.

"Sec. 5602. Findings; purpose.

"(a) **Findings.**—The Congress finds the following:

"(1) The discharge of untreated sewage by vessels is prohibited under Federal law in all areas within the navigable waters of the United States.

"(2) The discharge of treated sewage by vessels is prohibited under either Federal or State law in many of the United States bodies of water where recreational boaters operate.

"(3) There is currently an inadequate number of pumpout stations for type III marine sanitation devices where recreational vessels normally operate.

"(4) Sewage discharged by recreational vessels because of an inadequate number of pumpout stations is a substantial contributor to localized degradation of water quality in the United States.

"(b) **Purpose.**—The purpose of this subtitle is to provide funds to States for the construction, renovation, operation, and maintenance of pumpout stations and waste reception facilities.

"Sec. 5603. Determination and plan regarding State marine sanitation device pumpout station needs.

"(a) **Survey.**—Within 3 months after the notification under section 5605(b), each coastal State shall conduct a survey to determine—

"(1) the number and location of all operational pumpout stations and waste reception facilities at public and private marinas, mooring areas, docks, and other boating access facilities within the coastal zone of the State; and

"(2) the number of recreational vessels in the coastal waters of the State with type III marine sanitation devices or portable toilets, and the areas of those coastal waters where those vessels congregate.

"(b) **Plan.**—Within 6 months after the notification under section 5605(b), and based on the survey conducted under subsection (a), each coastal State shall—

"(1) develop and submit to the Secretary of the Interior a plan for any construction or renovation of pumpout stations and waste reception facilities that are necessary to ensure that, based on the guidance issued under section 5605(a), there are pumpout stations and waste reception facilities in the State that are adequate and reasonably available to meet the needs of recreational vessels using the coastal waters of the State; and

"(2) submit to the Secretary of the Interior with that plan a list of all stations and facilities in the coastal zone of the State which are operational on the date of submittal.

"(c) **Plan approval.**—

"(1) **In general.**—Not later than 60 days after a plan is submitted by a State under subsection (b), the Secretary of the Interior shall approve or disapprove the plan, based on—

"(A) the adequacy of the survey conducted by the State under subsection (a); and

"(B) the ability of the plan, based on the guidance issued under section 5605(a), to meet the construction and renovation needs of the recreational vessels identified in the survey.

"(2) **Notification of State; modification.**—The Secretary of the Interior shall promptly notify the affected Governor of the approval or disapproval of a plan. If a plan is disapproved, the Secretary of the Interior shall recommend necessary modifications and return the plan to the affected Governor.

"(3) **Resubmittal.**—Not later than 60 days after receiving a plan returned by the Secretary of the Interior, the Governor shall make the appropriate changes and resubmit the plan.

"(d) **Indication of stations and facilities on NOAA charts.**—

"(1) **In general.**—The Under Secretary of Commerce for Oceans and Atmosphere shall indicate, on charts published by the National Oceanic and Atmospheric Administration for the use of operators of recreational vessels, the locations of pumpout stations and waste reception facilities.

"(2) **Notification of NOAA.**—

"(A) **Lists of stations and facilities.**—The Secretary of the Interior shall transmit to the Under Secretary of Commerce for Oceans and Atmosphere each list of operational stations and facilities submitted by a State under subsection (b)(2), by not later than 30 days after the date of receipt of that list.

"(B) **Completion of project.**—The Director of the United States Fish and Wildlife Service shall notify the Under Secretary of the location of each station or facility at which a construction or renovation project is completed by a State with amounts made available under the Act of August 9, 1950 (16 U.S.C. 777a et seq.), as amended by this subtitle [section 777 et seq. of Title 16, Conservation], by not later than 30 days after the date of notification by a State of the completion of the project.

"Sec. 5604. Funding.

"(a) [Omitted. Subsec. (a) amended section 777c of Title 16, Conservation]

"(b) [Omitted. Subsec. (b) amended section 777g of Title 16, Conservation]

"(c) **Grant program.**—

"(1) **Matching grants.**—The Secretary of the Interior may obligate an amount not to exceed the amount made available under section 4(b)(2) of the Act of August 9, 1950 (16 U.S.C. 777c(b)(2), as amended by this Act) [section 777c(b)(2) of Title 16], to make grants to—

"(A) coastal States to pay not more than 75 percent of the cost to a coastal State of—

"(i) conducting a survey under section 5603(a);

"(ii) developing and submitting a plan and accompanying list under section 5603(b);

"(iii) constructing and renovating pumpout stations and waste reception facilities; and

"(iv) conducting a program to educate recreational boaters about the problem of human body waste discharges from vessels and inform them of the location of pumpout stations and waste reception facilities.

"(B) inland States, which can demonstrate to the Secretary of the Interior that there are an inadequate number of pumpout stations and waste reception facilities to meet the needs of recreational vessels in the waters of that State, to pay 75 percent of the cost to that State of—

"(i) constructing and renovating pumpout stations and waste reception facilities in the inland State; and

"(ii) conducting a program to educate recreational boaters about the problem of human body waste discharges from vessels and inform them of the location of pumpout stations and waste reception facilities.

"(2) **Priority.**—In awarding grants under this subsection, the Secretary of the Interior shall give priority consideration to grant applications that—

"(A) in coastal States, propose constructing and renovating pumpout stations and waste reception facilities in accordance with a coastal State's plan approved under section 5603(c);

"(B) provide for public/private partnership efforts to develop and operate pumpout stations and waste receptions facilities; and

"(C) propose innovative ways to increase the availability and use of pumpout stations and waste reception facilities.

"(d) **Disclaimer.**—Nothing in this subtitle shall be interpreted to preclude a State from carrying out the provisions of this subtitle with funds other than those described in this section.

"**Sec. 5605. Guidance and notification.**

"(a) **Issuance of guidance.**—Not later than 3 months after the date of the enactment of this subtitle [Nov. 4, 1992], the Secretary of the Interior shall, after consulting with the Administrator of the Environmental Protection Agency, the Under Secretary of Commerce for Oceans and Atmosphere, and the Commandant of the Coast Guard, issue for public comment pumpout station and waste reception facility guidance. The Secretary of the Interior shall finalize the guidance not later than 6 months after the date of enactment of this subtitle [Nov. 4, 1992]. The guidance shall include—

"(1) guidance regarding the types of pumpout stations and waste reception facilities that may be appropriate for construction, renovation, operation, or maintenance with amounts available under the Act of August 9, 1950 (16 U.S.C. 777a et seq.) [section 777 et seq. of Title 16], as amended by this subtitle, and appropriate location of the stations and facilities within a marina or boatyard;

"(2) guidance defining what constitutes adequate and reasonably available pumpout stations and waste reception facilities in boating areas;

"(3) guidance on appropriate methods for disposal of vessel sewage from pumpout stations and waste reception facilities;

"(4) guidance on appropriate connector fittings to facilitate the sanitary and expeditious discharge of sewage from vessels;

"(5) guidance on the waters most likely to be affected by the discharge of sewage from vessels; and

"(6) other information that is considered necessary to promote the establishment of pumpout facilities to reduce sewage discharges from vessels and to protect United States waters.

"(b) **Notification.**—Not later than one month after the guidance issued under subsection (a) is finalized, the Secretary of the Interior shall provide notification in writing to the fish and wildlife, water pollution control, and coastal zone management authorities of each State, of—

"(1) the availability of amounts under the Act of August 9, 1950 (16 U.S.C. 777a et seq.) [section 777 et seq. of Title 16] to implement the Clean Vessel Act of 1992 [subtitle F of Title V of Pub.L. 102–587 amending sections 777c and 777g of Title 16 and enacting this note]; and

"(2) the guidance developed under subsection (a).

"**Sec. 5606. Effect on State funding eligibility.**

"This subtitle shall not be construed or applied to jeopardize any funds available to a coastal State under the Act of August 9, 1950 (16 U.S.C. 777a et seq.) [section 777 et seq. of Title 16], if the coastal State is, in good faith, pursuing a survey and plan designed to meet the purposes of this subtitle.

"**Sec. 5607. Applicability.**

"The requirements of section 5603 shall not apply to a coastal State if within six months after the date of enactment of this subtitle [Nov. 4, 1992] the Secretary of the Interior certifies that—

"(1) the State has developed and is implementing a plan that will ensure that there will be pumpout stations and waste reception facilities adequate to meet the needs of recreational vessels in the coastal waters of the State; or

"(2) existing pumpout stations and waste reception facilities in the coastal waters of the State are adequate to meet those needs.

"**Sec. 5608. Definitions.**

"For the purposes of this subtitle the term:

"(1) 'coastal State'—

"(A) means a State of the United States in, or bordering on the Atlantic, Pacific, or Arctic Ocean; and Gulf of Mexico; Long Island Sound; or one or more of the Great Lakes;

"(B) includes Puerto Rico, the Virgin Islands, Guam, the Commonwealth of the Northern Mariana Islands, and American Samoa; and

"(C) does not include a State for which the ratio of the number of recreational vessels in the State numbered under chapter 123 of title 46, United States Code [section 12301 et seq. of Title 46, Shipping], to number of miles of shoreline (as that term is defined in section 926.2(d) of title 15, Code of Federal Regulations, as in effect on January 1, 1991), is less than one.

"(2) 'coastal waters' means—

"(A) in the Great Lakes area, the waters within the territorial jurisdiction of the United States consisting of the Great Lakes, their connecting waters, harbors, roadsteads, and estuary-type areas such as bays, shallows, and marches; and

"(B) in other areas, those waters, adjacent to the shorelines, which contain a measurable percentage of sea water, including sounds, bay, lagoons, bayous, ponds, and estuaries.

"(3) 'coastal zone' has the same meaning that term has in section 304(1) of the Coastal Zone Management Act of 1972 (16 U.S.C. 1453(1)) [section 1453(1) of Title 16];

"(4) 'inland State' means a State which is not a coastal state;

"(5) 'type III marine sanitation device' means any equipment for installation on board a vessel which is specifically designed to receive, retain, and discharge human body wastes;

"(6) 'pumpout station' means a facility that pumps or receive human body wastes out of type III marine sanitation devices installed on board vessels;

"(7) 'recreation vessel' means a vessel—

"(A) manufactured for operation, or operated, primarily for pleasure; or

"(B) leased, rented, or chartered to another for the latter's

"(8) 'waste reception facility' means a facility specifically designed to receive wastes from portable toilets carried on vessels, and does not include lavatories."

CROSS REFERENCES

Definition of "material" for purposes of ocean dumping as not including sewage from vessels within the meaning of this section, see section 1402 of this title.

Definition of "pollutant" as not including sewage from vessels within the meaning of this section, see section 1362 of this title.

Solid waste disposal equipment for vessels, see section 1254 of this title.

LAW REVIEW COMMENTARIES

Oklahoma v. EPA Does the Clean Water Act provide an effective remedy to downstream states or is there still room left for federal common law. Maria V. Maurrasse, 45 U.Miami L.Rev. 1037 (1991).

CODE OF FEDERAL REGULATIONS

Standards for marine sanitation devices, see 33 CFR 159.1 et seq., 40 CFR 140.1 et seq.

LIBRARY REFERENCES

Health and Environment ⟹25.7(1).

C.J.S. Health and Environment §§ 106, 125.

§ 1323. Federal facilities pollution control [FWPCA § 313]

(a) Each department, agency, or instrumentality of the executive, legislative, and judicial branches of the Federal Government (1) having jurisdiction over any property or facility, or (2) engaged in any activity resulting, or which may result, in the discharge or runoff of pollutants, and each officer, agent, or employee thereof in the performance of his official duties, shall be subject to, and comply with, all Federal, State, interstate, and local requirements, administrative authority, and process and sanctions respecting the control and abatement of water pollution in the same manner, and to the same extent as any nongovernmental entity including the payment of reasonable service charges. The preceding sentence shall apply (A) to any requirement whether substantive or procedural (including any recordkeeping or reporting requirement, any requirement respecting permits and any other requirement, whatsoever), (B) to the exercise of any Federal, State, or local administrative authority, and (C) to any process and sanction, whether enforced in Federal, State, or local courts or in any other manner. This subsection shall apply notwithstanding any immunity of such agencies, officers, agents, or employees under any law or rule of law. Nothing in this section shall be construed to prevent any department, agency, or instrumentality of the Federal Government, or any officer, agent, or employee thereof in the performance of his official duties, from removing to the appropriate Federal district court any proceeding to which the department, agency, or instrumentality or officer, agent, or employee thereof is subject pursuant to this section, and any such proceeding may be removed in accordance with section 1441 et seq. of title 28. No officer, agent, or employee of the United States shall be personally liable for any civil penalty arising from the performance of his official duties, for which he is not otherwise liable, and the United States shall be liable only for those civil penalties arising under Federal law or imposed by a State or local court to enforce an order or the process of such court. The President may exempt any effluent source of any department, agency, or instrumentality in the executive branch from compliance with any such a requirement if he determines it to be in the paramount interest of the United States to do so; except that no exemption may be granted from the requirements of section 1316 or 1317 of this title. No such exemptions shall be granted due to lack of appropriation unless the President shall have specifically requested such appropriation as a part of the budgetary process and the Congress shall have failed to make available such requested appropriation. Any exemption shall be for a period not in excess of one year, but additional exemptions may be granted for periods of not to exceed one year upon the President's making a new determination. The President shall report each January to the Congress all exemptions from the requirements of this section granted during the preceding calendar year, together with his reason for granting such exemption. In addition to any such exemption of a particular effluent source, the President may, if he determines it to be in the paramount interest of the United States to do so, issue regulations exempting from compliance with the requirements of this section any weaponry, equipment, aircraft, vessels, vehicles, or other classes or categories of property, and access to such property, which are owned or operated by the Armed Forces of the United States (including the Coast Guard) or by the National Guard of any State and which are uniquely military in nature. The President shall reconsider the need for such regulations at three-year intervals.

(b)(1) The Administrator shall coordinate with the head of each department, agency, or instrumentality of the Federal Government having jurisdiction over any property or facility utilizing federally owned wastewater facilities to develop a program of cooperation for utilizing wastewater control systems utilizing those innovative treatment processes and techniques for which guidelines have been promulgated under section 1314(d)(3) of this title. Such program shall include an inventory of property and facilities which could utilize such processes and techniques.

(2) Construction shall not be initiated for facilities for treatment of wastewater at any Federal property or facility after September 30, 1979, if alternative methods for wastewater treatment at such property or facility utilizing innovative treatment processes and techniques, including but not limited to methods utilizing recycle and reuse techniques and land treatment are not utilized, unless the life cycle cost of the alternative treatment works exceeds the life cycle cost of the most cost effective alternative by more than 15 per centum. The Administrator may waive the application of this paragraph in any case where the Administrator determines it to be in the public interest, or that compliance with this paragraph would interfere with the orderly compliance with conditions of a permit issued pursuant to section 1342 of this title.

(June 30, 1948, c. 758, Title III, § 313, as added Oct. 18, 1972, Pub.L. 92–500, § 2, 86 Stat. 875, and amended Dec. 27, 1977, Pub.L. 95–217, §§ 60, 61(a), 91 Stat. 1597, 1598.)

CROSS REFERENCES

Citizen suits to enforce effluent standards, see section 1365 of this title.

LAW REVIEW COMMENTARIES

Hazardous Waste Law for the federal employee after the Federal Facility Compliance Act of 1992. Stephen J. Darmody, 40 Fed. B.News & J. 650 (Nov./Dec. 1993).

How well can states enforce their environmental laws when the polluter is the United States Government? 18 Rutgers L.J. 123 (1986).

Warrior and the Druid—the DOD and environmental law. Michael Donnelly and James G. Van Ness, 33 Fed.Bar News 37 (1986).

LIBRARY REFERENCES

Health and Environment ⚖25.7(3).
C.J.S. Health and Environment § 106.

United States Supreme Court

Phrase "arising under" federal law, as used in Clean Water Act to exclude cases in which plaintiff relies on state law, and even when state's exercise of power of particular circumstances is expressly permitted, suggested only uncertain waiver and was not the required clear waiver necessary to waive sovereign immunity, for purposes of determining whether national government could be subjected to punitive fines, see United States Department of Energy v. Ohio, 1992, 112 S.Ct. 1627, 118 L.Ed.2d 255.

Federal installations, compliance with state requirements, necessity of state permit from state with federally approved program, see Environmental Protection Agency v. California, ex rel. State Water Resources Control Bd., 1976, 96 S.Ct. 2022, 426 U.S. 200, 48 L.Ed.2d 578.

§ 1324. Clean lakes [FWPCA § 314]

(a) Establishment and scope of program

(1) State program requirements

Each State on a biennial basis shall prepare and submit to the Administrator for his approval—

(A) an identification and classification according to eutrophic condition of all publicly owned lakes in such State;

(B) a description of procedures, processes, and methods (including land use requirements), to control sources of pollution of such lakes;

(C) a description of methods and procedures, in conjunction with appropriate Federal agencies, to restore the quality of such lakes;

(D) methods and procedures to mitigate the harmful effects of high acidity, including innovative methods of neutralizing and restoring buffering capacity of lakes and methods of removing from lakes toxic metals and other toxic substances mobilized by high acidity;

(E) a list and description of those publicly owned lakes in such State for which uses are known to be impaired, including those lakes which are known not to meet applicable water quality standards or which require implementation of control programs to maintain compliance with applicable standards and those lakes in which water quality has deteriorated as a result of high acidity that may reasonably be due to acid deposition; and

(F) an assessment of the status and trends of water quality in lakes in such State, including but not limited to, the nature and extent of pollution loading from point and nonpoint sources and the extent to which the use of lakes is impaired as a result of such pollution, particularly with respect to toxic pollution.

(2) Submission as part of 1315(b)(1) report

The information required under paragraph (1) shall be included in the report required under section 1315(b)(1) of this title, beginning with the report required under such section by April 1, 1988.

(3) Report of Administrator

Not later than 180 days after receipt from the States of the biennial information required under paragraph (1), the Administrator shall submit to the Committee on Public Works and Transportation of the House of Representatives and the Committee on Environment and Public Works of the Senate a report on the status of water quality in lakes in the United States, including the effectiveness of the methods and procedures described in paragraph (1)(D).

(4) Eligibility requirement

Beginning after April 1, 1988, a State must have submitted the information required under paragraph (1) in order to receive grant assistance under this section.

(b) Financial assistance to States

The Administrator shall provide financial assistance to States in order to carry out methods and procedures approved by him under subsection (a) of this section. The Administrator shall provide financial assistance to States to prepare the identification and classification surveys required in subsection (a)(1) of this section.

(c) Maximum amount of grant; authorization of appropriations

(1) The amount granted to any State for any fiscal year under subsection (b) of this section shall not exceed 70 per centum of the funds expended by such State in such year for carrying out approved methods and procedures under subsection (a) of this section.

(2) There is authorized to be appropriated $50,000,000 for the fiscal year ending June 30, 1973; $100,000,000 for the fiscal year 1974; $150,000,000 for the fiscal year 1975, $50,000,000 for fiscal year 1977, $60,000,000 for fiscal year 1978, $60,000,000 for fiscal year 1979, $60,000,000 for fiscal year 1980, $30,000,000 for fiscal year 1981, $30,000,000 for fiscal year 1982, such sums as may be necessary for fiscal years 1983 through 1985, and $30,000,000 per fiscal year for each of the fiscal years 1986 through 1990 for grants to States under subsection (b) of this section which such sums shall remain available until expended. The Administrator shall provide for an equitable distribution of such sums to the States with approved methods and procedures under subsection (a) of this section.

(d) Demonstration program

(1) General requirements

The Administrator is authorized and directed to establish and conduct at locations throughout the Nation a lake water quality demonstration program. The program shall, at a minimum—

(A) develop cost effective technologies for the control of pollutants to preserve or enhance lake water quality while optimizing multiple lakes uses;

(B) control nonpoint sources of pollution which are contributing to the degradation of water quality in lakes;

(C) evaluate the feasibility of implementing regional consolidated pollution control strategies;

(D) demonstrate environmentally preferred techniques for the removal and disposal of contaminated lake sediments;

(E) develop improved methods for the removal of silt, stumps, aquatic growth, and other obstructions which impair the quality of lakes;

(F) construct and evaluate silt traps and other devices or equipment to prevent or abate the deposit of sediment in lakes; and

(G) demonstrate the costs and benefits of utilizing dredged material from lakes in the reclamation of despoiled land.

(2) Geographical requirements

Demonstration projects authorized by this subsection shall be undertaken to reflect a variety of geographical and environmental conditions. As a priority, the Administrator shall undertake demonstration projects at Lake Champlain, New York and Vermont; Lake Houston, Texas; Beaver Lake, Arkansas; Greenwood Lake and Belcher Creek, New Jersey; Deal Lake, New Jersey; Alcyon Lake, New Jersey; Gorton's Pond, Rhode Island; Lake Washington, Rhode Island; Lake Bomoseen, Vermont; Sauk Lake, Minnesota; and Lake Worth, Texas.

(3) Reports

By January 1, 1997, and January 1 of every odd-numbered year thereafter, the Administrator shall report to the Committee on Transportation and Infrastructure of the House of Representatives and the Committee on Environment and Public Works of the Senate on work undertaken pursuant to this subsection. Upon completion of the program authorized by this subsection, the Administrator shall submit to such committees a final report on the results of such program, along with recommendations for further measures to improve the water quality of the Nation's lakes.

(4) Authorization of appropriations

(A) In general

There is authorized to be appropriated to carry out this subsection not to exceed $40,000,000 for fiscal years beginning after September 30, 1986, to remain available until expended.

(B) Special authorizations

(i) Amount

There is authorized to be appropriated to carry out subsection (b) of this section with respect to subsection (a)(1)(D) of this section not to exceed $15,000,000 for fiscal years beginning after September 30, 1986, to remain available until expended.

(ii) Distribution of funds

The Administrator shall provide for an equitable distribution of sums appropriated pursuant to this subparagraph among States carrying out approved methods and procedures. Such distribution shall be based on the relative needs of each such State for the mitigation of the harmful effects on lakes and other surface waters of high acidity that may reasonably be due to acid deposition or acid mine drainage.

(iii) Grants as additional assistance

The amount of any grant to a State under this subparagraph shall be in addition to, and not in lieu of, any other Federal financial assistance.

(June 30, 1948, c. 758, Title III, § 314, as added Oct. 18, 1972, Pub.L. 92–500, § 2, 86 Stat. 875, and amended Dec. 27, 1977, Pub.L. 95–217, §§ 4(f), 62(a), 91 Stat. 1567, 1598; Oct. 21, 1980, Pub.L. 96–483, § 1(f), 94 Stat. 2360; Feb. 4, 1987, Pub.L. 100–4, Title I, § 101(g), Title III, § 315(a), (b), (d), 101 Stat. 9, 49, 50, 52; Nov. 16, 1990, Pub.L. 101–596, Title III, § 302, 104 Stat. 3006; Dec. 21, 1995, Pub.L. 104–66, Title II, § 2021(c), 109 Stat. 727.)

Change of Name

Any reference in any provision of law enacted before Jan. 4, 1995, to the Committee on Public Works and Transportation of the House of Representatives treated as referring to the Committee on Transportation and Infrastructure of the House of Representatives, see section 1(a)(9) of Pub.L. 104–14, set out as a note preceding section 21 of Title 2, The Congress.

CROSS REFERENCES

Authorization of appropriations to carry out this chapter other than this section, see section 1376 of this title.

LIBRARY REFERENCES

Health and Environment ⚯25.7(4).
C.J.S. Health and Environment § 108 et seq.

§ 1325. National Study Commission [FWPCA § 315]

(a) Establishment

There is established a National Study Commission, which shall make a full and complete investigation and study of all of the technological aspects of achieving, and all aspects of the total economic, social, and environmental effects of achieving or not achieving, the effluent limitations and goals set forth for 1983 in section 1311(b)(2) of this title.

(b) Membership; chairman

Such Commission shall be composed of fifteen members, including five members of the Senate, who are members of the Environment and Public Works committee, appointed by the President of the Senate, five members of the House, who are members of the Public Works and Transportation committee, appointed by the Speaker of the House, and five members of the public appointed by the President. The Chairman of such Commission shall be elected from among its members.

(c) Contract authority

In the conduct of such study, the Commission is authorized to contract with the National Academy of Sciences and the National Academy of Engineering (acting through the National Research Council), the National Institute of Ecology, Brookings Institution, and other nongovernmental entities, for the investigation of matters within their competence.

(d) Cooperation of departments, agencies, and instrumentalities of executive branch

The heads of the departments, agencies and instrumentalities of the executive branch of the Federal Government shall cooperate with the Commission in carrying out the requirements of this section, and shall furnish to the Commission such information as the Commission deems necessary to carry out this section.

(e) Report to Congress

A report shall be submitted to the Congress of the results of such investigation and study, together with recommendations, not later than three years after October 18, 1972.

(f) Compensation and allowances

The members of the Commission who are not officers or employees of the United States, while attending conferences or meetings of the Commission or while otherwise serving at the request of the Chairman shall be entitled to receive compensation at a rate not in excess of the maximum rate of pay for Grade GS–18, as provided in the General Schedule under section 5332 of title 5, including traveltime and while away from their homes or regular places of business they may be allowed travel expenses, including per diem in lieu of subsistence as authorized by law for persons in the Government service employed intermittently.

(g) Appointment of personnel

In addition to authority to appoint personnel subject to the provisions of title 5 governing appointments in the competitive service, and to pay such personnel in accordance with the provisions of chapter 51 and subchapter III of chapter 53 of such title relating to classification and General Schedule pay rates, the Commission shall have authority to enter into contracts with private or public organizations who shall furnish the Commission with such administrative and technical personnel as may be necessary to carry out the purpose of this section. Personnel furnished by such organizations under this subsection are not, and shall not be considered to be, Federal employees for any purposes, but in the performance of their duties shall be guided by the standards which apply to employees of the legislative branches under rules 41 and 43 of the Senate and House of Representatives, respectively.

(h) Authorization of appropriation

There is authorized to be appropriated, for use in carrying out this section, not to exceed $17,250,000.

(June 30, 1948, c. 758, Title III, § 315, as added Oct. 18, 1972, Pub.L. 92–500, § 2, 86 Stat. 875, and amended Dec. 28, 1973, Pub.L. 93–207, § 1(5), 87 Stat. 906; Jan. 2, 1975, Pub.L. 93–592, § 5, 88 Stat. 1925; March 23, 1976, Pub.L. 94–238, 90 Stat. 250; H.Res. 988, Oct. 8, 1974; S.Res. 4, Feb. 4, 1977.)

Change of Name

Any reference in any provision of law enacted before Jan. 4, 1995, to the Committee on Public Works and Transportation of the House of Representatives treated as referring to the Committee on Transportation and Infrastructure of the House of Representatives, see section 1(a)(9) of Pub.L. 104–14, set out as a note preceding section 21 of Title 2, The Congress.

CROSS REFERENCES

Authorization of appropriations to carry out this chapter other than this section, see section 1376 of this title.

Timetable for achievement of objectives, see section 1311 of this title.

§ 1326. Thermal discharges [FWPCA § 316]

(a) Effluent limitations that will assure protection and propagation of balanced, indigenous population of shellfish, fish, and wildlife

With respect to any point source otherwise subject to the provisions of section 1311 of this title or section 1316 of this title, whenever the owner or operator of any such source, after opportunity for public hearing, can demonstrate to the satisfaction of the Administrator (or, if appropriate, the State) that any effluent limitation proposed for the control of the thermal component of any discharge from such source will require effluent limitations more stringent than necessary to assure the projection [1] and propagation of a balanced, indigenous population of shellfish, fish, and wildlife in and on the body of water into which the discharge is to be made, the Administrator (or, if appropriate, the State) may impose an effluent limitation under such sections for such plant, with respect to the thermal component of such discharge (taking into account the interaction of such thermal component with other pollutants), that will assure the protection and propagation of a balanced, indigenous population of shellfish, fish, and wildlife in and on that body of water.

(b) Cooling water intake structures

Any standard established pursuant to section 1311 of this title or section 1316 of this title and applicable to a point source shall require that the location, design, construction, and capacity of cooling water intake structures reflect the best technology available for minimizing adverse environmental impact.

(c) Period of protection from more stringent effluent limitations following discharge point source modification commenced after October 18, 1972

Notwithstanding any other provision of this chapter, any point source of a discharge having a thermal component, the modification of which point source is commenced after October 18, 1972, and which, as modified, meets effluent limitations established under section 1311 of this title or, if more stringent, effluent limitations established under section 1313 of this title and which effluent limitations will assure protection and propagation of a balanced, indigenous population of shellfish, fish, and wildlife in or on the water into which the discharge is made, shall not be subject to any more stringent effluent limitation with respect to the thermal component of its discharge during a ten year period beginning on the date of completion of such modification or during the period of depreciation or amortization of such facility for the purpose of section 167 or 169 (or both) of title 26, whichever period ends first.

(June 30, 1948, c. 758, Title III, § 316, as added Oct. 18, 1972, Pub.L. 92–500, § 2, 86 Stat. 876.)

[1] So in original. Probably should be "protection".

CROSS REFERENCES

Water quality standards relating to heat to be consistent with requirements of this section, see section 1313 of this title.

CODE OF FEDERAL REGULATIONS

Effluent guidelines and standards, see 40 CFR 401.10 et seq.

LIBRARY REFERENCES

Health and Environment ⟹25.7(12).
C.J.S. Health and Environment § 107 et seq.

§ 1327. Omitted

§ 1328. Aquaculture [FWPCA § 318]

(a) Authority to permit discharge of specific pollutants

The Administrator is authorized, after public hearings, to permit the discharge of a specific pollutant or pollutants under controlled conditions associated with an approved aquaculture project under Federal or State supervision pursuant to section 1342 of this title.

(b) Procedures and guidelines

The Administrator shall by regulation establish any procedures and guidelines which the Administrator deems necessary to carry out this section. Such regulations shall require the application to such discharge of each criterion, factor, procedure, and requirement applicable to a permit issued under section 1342 of this title, as the Administrator determines necessary to carry out the objective of this chapter.

(c) State administration

Each State desiring to administer its own permit program within its jurisdiction for discharge of a specific pollutant or pollutants under controlled conditions associated with an approved aquaculture project may do so if upon submission of such program the Administrator determines such program is adequate to carry out the objective of this chapter.

(June 30, 1948, c. 758, Title III, § 318, as added Oct. 18, 1972, Pub.L. 92–500, § 2, 86 Stat. 877, and amended Dec. 27, 1977, Pub.L. 95–217, § 63, 91 Stat. 1599.)

CROSS REFERENCES

Enforcement of provisions of this section, see section 1319 of this title.
Illegality of pollutant discharges except as in compliance with this section, see section 1311 of this title.
Permit for discharge of pollutants except as provided in this section, see section 1342 of this title.

CODE OF FEDERAL REGULATIONS

Environmental Protection Agency administered permit programs: the National Pollutant Discharge Elimination System, see 40 CFR 122.1 et seq.
State program requirements, see 40 CFR 123.1 et seq.

§ 1329. Nonpoint source management programs [FWPCA § 319]

(a) State assessment reports

(1) Contents

The Governor of each State shall, after notice and opportunity for public comment, prepare and submit to the Administrator for approval, a report which—

(A) identifies those navigable waters within the State which, without additional action to control nonpoint sources of pollution, cannot reasonably be expected to attain or maintain applicable water quality standards or the goals and requirements of this chapter;

(B) identifies those categories and subcategories of nonpoint sources or, where appropriate, particular nonpoint sources which add significant pollution to each portion of the navigable waters identified under subparagraph (A) in amounts which contribute to such portion not meeting such water quality standards or such goals and requirements;

(C) describes the process, including intergovernmental coordination and public participation, for identifying best management practices and measures to control each category and subcategory of nonpoint sources and, where appropriate, particular nonpoint sources identified under subparagraph (B) and to reduce, to the maximum extent practicable, the level of pollution resulting from such category, subcategory, or source; and

(D) identifies and describes State and local programs for controlling pollution added from nonpoint sources to, and improving the quality of, each such portion of the navigable waters, including but not limited to those programs which are receiving Federal assistance under subsections (h) and (i) of this section.

(2) Information used in preparation

In developing the report required by this section, the State (A) may rely upon information developed pursuant to sections 1288, 1313(e), 1314(f), 1315(b), and 1324 of this title, and other information as appropriate, and (B) may utilize appropriate elements of the waste treatment management plans developed pursuant to sections 1288(b) and 1313 of this title, to the extent such elements are consistent with and fulfill the requirements of this section.

(b) State management programs

(1) In general

The Governor of each State, for that State or in combination with adjacent States, shall, after notice and opportunity for public comment, prepare and submit to the Administrator for approval a management program which such State proposes to implement in the first four fiscal years beginning after the date of submission of such management program for controlling pollution added from nonpoint sources to the navigable waters within the State and improving the quality of such waters.

(2) Specific contents

Each management program proposed for implementation under this subsection shall include each of the following:

(A) An identification of the best management practices and measures which will be undertaken to reduce pollutant loadings resulting from each category, subcategory, or particular nonpoint source designated under paragraph (1)(B), taking into account the impact of the practice on ground water quality.

(B) An identification of programs (including, as appropriate, nonregulatory or regulatory programs for enforcement, technical assistance, financial assistance, education, training, technology transfer, and demonstration projects) to achieve implementation of the best management practices by the categories, subcategories, and particular nonpoint sources designated under subparagraph (A).

(C) A schedule containing annual milestones for (i) utilization of the program implementation methods identified in subparagraph (B), and (ii) implementation of the best management practices identified in subparagraph (A) by the categories, subcategories, or particular nonpoint sources designated under paragraph (1)(B). Such schedule shall provide for utilization of the best management practices at the earliest practicable date.

(D) A certification of the attorney general of the State or States (or the chief attorney of any State water pollution control agency which has independent legal counsel) that the laws of the State or States, as the case may be, provide adequate authority to implement such management program or, if there is not such adequate authority, a list of such additional authorities as will be necessary to implement such management program. A schedule and commitment by the State or States to seek such additional authorities as expeditiously as practicable.

(E) Sources of Federal and other assistance and funding (other than assistance provided under subsections (h) and (i) of this section) which will be available in each of such fiscal years for supporting implementation of such practices and measures and the purposes for which such assistance will be used in each of such fiscal years.

(F) An identification of Federal financial assistance programs and Federal development projects for which the State will review individual assistance applications or development projects for their effect on water quality pursuant to the procedures set forth in Executive Order 12372 as in effect on September 17, 1983, to determine whether such assistance applications or development projects would be consistent with the program prepared under this subsection; for the purposes of this subparagraph, identification shall not be limited to the assistance programs or development projects subject to Executive Order 12372 but may include any programs listed in the most recent Catalog of Federal Domestic Assistance which may have an effect on the purposes and objectives of the State's nonpoint source pollution management program.

(3) Utilization of local and private experts

In developing and implementing a management program under this subsection, a State shall, to the maximum extent practicable, involve local public and private agencies and organizations which have expertise in control of nonpoint sources of pollution.

(4) Development on watershed basis

A State shall, to the maximum extent practicable, develop and implement a management program under this subsection on a watershed-by-watershed basis within such State.

(c) Administrative provisions

(1) Cooperation requirement

Any report required by subsection (a) of this section and any management program and report required by subsection (b) of this section shall be developed in cooperation with local, substate regional, and interstate entities which are actively planning for the implementation of nonpoint source pollution controls and have either been certified by the Administrator in accordance with section 1288 of this title, have worked jointly with the State on water quality management planning under section 1285(j) of this title, or have been designated by the State legislative body or Governor as water quality management planning agencies for their geographic areas.

(2) Time period for submission of reports and management programs

Each report and management program shall be submitted to the Administrator during the 18–month period beginning on February 4, 1987.

(d) Approval or disapproval of reports and management programs

(1) Deadline

Subject to paragraph (2), not later than 180 days after the date of submission to the Administrator of any report or management program under this section (other than subsections (h), (i), and (k) of this section), the Administrator shall either approve or disapprove such report or management program, as the case may be. The Administrator may approve a portion of a management program under this subsection. If the Administrator does not disapprove a report, management program, or portion of a management program in such 180–day period, such report, management program, or portion shall be deemed approved for purposes of this section.

(2) Procedure for disapproval

If, after notice and opportunity for public comment and consultation with appropriate Federal and State agencies and other interested persons, the Administrator determines that—

(A) the proposed management program or any portion thereof does not meet the requirements of subsection (b)(2) of this section or is not likely to satisfy, in whole or in part, the goals and requirements of this chapter;

(B) adequate authority does not exist, or adequate resources are not available, to implement such program or portion;

(C) the schedule for implementing such program or portion is not sufficiently expeditious; or

(D) the practices and measures proposed in such program or portion are not adequate to reduce the level of pollution in navigable waters in the State resulting from nonpoint sources and to improve the quality of navigable waters in the State;

the Administrator shall within 6 months of the receipt of the proposed program notify the State of any revisions or modifications necessary to obtain approval. The State shall thereupon have an additional 3 months to submit its revised management program and the Administrator shall approve or disapprove such revised program within three months of receipt.

(3) Failure of State to submit report

If a Governor of a State does not submit the report required by subsection (a) of this section within the period specified by subsection (c)(2) of this section, the Administrator shall, within 30 months after February 4, 1987, prepare a report for such State which makes the identifications required by paragraphs (1)(A) and (1)(B) of subsection (a) of this section. Upon completion of the requirement of the preceding sentence and after notice and opportunity for comment, the Administrator shall report to Congress on his actions pursuant to this section.

(e) Local management programs; technical assistance

If a State fails to submit a management program under subsection (b) of this section or the Administrator does not approve such a management program, a local public agency or organization which has expertise in, and authority to, control water pollution resulting from nonpoint sources in any area of such State which the Administrator determines is of sufficient geographic size may, with approval of such State, request the Administrator to provide, and the Administrator shall provide, technical assistance to such agency or organization in developing for such area a management program which is described in subsection (b) of this section and can be approved pursuant to subsection (d) of this section. After development of such management program, such agency or organization shall submit such management program to the Administrator for approval. If the Administrator approves such management program, such agency or organization shall be eligible to receive financial assistance under subsection (h) of this section for implementation of such management program as if such agency or organization were a State for which a report submitted under subsection (a) of this section and a management program submitted under subsection (b) of this section were approved under this section. Such financial assistance shall be subject to the same terms and conditions as assistance provided to a State under subsection (h) of this section.

(f) Technical assistance for States

Upon request of a State, the Administrator may provide technical assistance to such State in developing a management program approved under subsection (b) of this section for those portions of the navigable waters requested by such State.

(g) Interstate management conference

(1) Convening of conference; notification; purpose

If any portion of the navigable waters in any State which is implementing a management program approved under this section is not meeting applicable water quality standards or the goals and requirements of this chapter as a result, in whole or in part, of pollution from nonpoint sources in another State, such State may petition the Administrator to convene, and the Administrator shall convene, a management conference of all States which contribute significant pollution resulting from nonpoint sources to such portion. If, on the basis of information available, the Administrator determines that a State is not meeting applicable water quality standards or the goals and requirements of this chapter as a result, in whole or in part, of significant pollution from nonpoint sources in another State, the Administrator shall notify such States. The Administrator may convene a management conference under this paragraph not later than 180 days after giving such notification, whether or not the State which is not meeting such standards requests such conference. The purpose of such conference shall be to develop an agreement among such States to reduce the level of pollution in such portion resulting from nonpoint sources and to improve the water quality of such portion. Nothing in such agreement shall supersede or abrogate rights to quantities of water which have been established by interstate water compacts, Supreme Court decrees, or State water laws. This subsection shall not apply to any pollution which is subject to the Colorado River Basin Salinity Control Act [43 U.S.C.A. § 1571 et seq.]. The requirement that the Administrator convene a management conference shall not be subject to the provisions of section 1365 of this title.

(2) State management program requirement

To the extent that the States reach agreement through such conference, the management programs of the States which are parties to such agreements and which contribute significant pollution to the navigable waters or portions thereof not meeting applicable water quality standards or goals and requirements of this chapter will be revised to reflect such agreement. Such management programs shall be consistent with Federal and State law.

(h) Grant program

(1) Grants for implementation of management programs

Upon application of a State for which a report submitted under subsection (a) of this section and a management program submitted under subsection (b) of this section is approved under this section, the Administrator shall make grants, subject to such terms and conditions as the Administrator considers appropriate, under this subsection to such State for the purpose of assisting the State in implementing such management program. Funds reserved pursuant to section 1285(j)(5) of this title may be used to develop and implement such management program.

(2) Applications

An application for a grant under this subsection in any fiscal year shall be in such form and shall contain such other information as the Administrator may require, including an identification and description of the best management practices and measures which the State proposes to assist, encourage, or require in such year with the Federal assistance to be provided under the grant.

(3) Federal share

The Federal share of the cost of each management program implemented with Federal assistance under this subsection in any fiscal year shall not exceed 60 percent of the cost incurred by the State in implementing such management program and shall be made on condition that the non-Federal share is provided from non-Federal sources.

(4) Limitation on grant amounts

Notwithstanding any other provision of this subsection, not more than 15 percent of the amount appropriated to carry out this subsection may be used to make grants to any one State, including any grants to any local public agency or organization with authority to control pollution from nonpoint sources in any area of such State.

(5) Priority for effective mechanisms

For each fiscal year beginning after September 30, 1987, the Administrator may give priority in making grants under this subsection, and shall give consideration in determining the Federal share of any such grant, to States which have implemented or are proposing to implement management programs which will—

(A) control particularly difficult or serious nonpoint source pollution problems, including, but not limited to, problems resulting from mining activities;

(B) implement innovative methods or practices for controlling nonpoint sources of pollution, including regulatory programs where the Administrator deems appropriate;

(C) control interstate nonpoint source pollution problems; or

(D) carry out ground water quality protection activities which the Administrator determines are part of a comprehensive nonpoint source pollution control program, including research, planning, ground water assessments, demonstration programs, enforcement, technical assistance, education, and training to protect ground water quality from nonpoint sources of pollution.

(6) Availability for obligation

The funds granted to each State pursuant to this subsection in a fiscal year shall remain available for obligation by such State for the fiscal year for which appropriated. The amount of any such funds not obligated by the end of such fiscal year shall be available to the Administrator for granting to other States under this subsection in the next fiscal year.

(7) Limitation on use of funds

States may use funds from grants made pursuant to this section for financial assistance to persons only to the extent that such assistance is related to the costs of demonstration projects.

(8) Satisfactory progress

No grant may be made under this subsection in any fiscal year to a State which in the preceding fiscal year received a grant under this subsection unless the Administrator determines that such State made satisfactory progress in such preceding fiscal year in meeting the schedule specified by such State under subsection (b)(2) of this section.

(9) Maintenance of effort

No grant may be made to a State under this subsection in any fiscal year unless such State enters into such agreements with the Administrator as the Administrator may require to ensure that such State will maintain its aggregate expenditures from all other sources for programs for controlling pollution added to the navigable waters in such State from nonpoint sources and improving the quality of such waters at or above the average level of such expenditures in its two fiscal years preceding February 4, 1987.

(10) Request for information

The Administrator may request such information, data, and reports as he considers necessary to make the determination of continuing eligibility for grants under this section.

(11) Reporting and other requirements

Each State shall report to the Administrator on an annual basis concerning (A) its progress in meeting the schedule of milestones submitted pursuant to subsection (b)(2)(C) of this section, and (B) to the extent that appropriate information is available, reductions in nonpoint source pollutant loading and improvements in water quality for those navigable waters or watersheds within the State which were identified pursuant to subsection (a)(1)(A) of this section resulting from implementation of the management program.

(12) Limitation on administrative costs

For purposes of this subsection, administrative costs in the form of salaries, overhead, or indirect costs for services provided and charged against activities and programs carried out with a grant under this subsection shall not exceed in any fiscal year 10 percent of the amount of the grant in such year, except that costs of implementing enforcement and regulatory activities, education, training, technical assistance, demonstration projects, and technology transfer programs shall not be subject to this limitation.

(i) Grants for protecting groundwater quality

(1) Eligible applicants and activities

Upon application of a State for which a report submitted under subsection (a) of this section and a plan submitted under subsection (b) of this section is approved under this section, the Administrator shall make grants under this subsection to such State for the purpose of assisting such State in carrying out groundwater quality protection activities which the Administrator determines will advance the State toward implementation of a comprehensive nonpoint source pollution control program. Such activities shall include, but not be limited to, research, planning, groundwater assessments, demonstration programs, enforcement, technical assistance, education and training to protect the quality of groundwater and to prevent contamination of groundwater from nonpoint sources of pollution.

(2) Applications

An application for a grant under this subsection shall be in such form and shall contain such information as the Administrator may require.

(3) Federal share; maximum amount

The Federal share of the cost of assisting a State in carrying out groundwater protection activities in any fiscal year under this subsection shall be 50 percent of the costs incurred by the State in carrying out such activities, except that the maximum amount of Federal assistance which any State may receive under this subsection in any fiscal year shall not exceed $150,000.

(4) Report

The Administrator shall include in each report transmitted under subsection (m) of this section a report on the activities and programs implemented under this subsection during the preceding fiscal year.

(j) Authorization of appropriations

There is authorized to be appropriated to carry out subsections (h) and (i) of this section not to exceed $70,000,000 for fiscal year 1988, $100,000,000 per fiscal year for each of fiscal years 1989 and 1990, and $130,000,000 for fiscal year 1991; except that for each of such fiscal years not to exceed $7,500,000 may be made available to carry out subsection (i) of this section. Sums appropriated pursuant to this subsection shall remain available until expended.

(k) Consistency of other programs and projects with management programs

The Administrator shall transmit to the Office of Management and Budget and the appropriate Federal departments and agencies a list of those assistance programs and development projects identified by each State under subsection (b)(2)(F) of this section for which individual assistance applications and projects will be reviewed pursuant to the procedures set forth in Executive Order 12372 as in effect on September 17, 1983. Beginning not later than sixty days after receiving notification by the Administrator, each Federal department and agency shall modify existing regulations to allow States to review individual development projects and assistance applications under the identified Federal assistance programs and shall accommodate, according to the requirements and definitions of Executive Order 12372, as in effect on September 17, 1983, the concerns of the State regarding the consistency of such applications or projects with the State nonpoint source pollution management program.

(*l*) Collection of information

The Administrator shall collect and make available, through publications and other appropriate means, information pertaining to management practices and implementation methods, including, but not limited to, (1) information concerning the costs and relative efficiencies of best management practices for reducing nonpoint source pollution; and (2) available data concerning the relationship between water quality and implementation of various management practices to control nonpoint sources of pollution.

(m) Reports of Administrator

(1) Annual reports

Not later than January 1, 1988, and each January 1 thereafter, the Administrator shall transmit to the Committee on Public Works and Transportation of the House of Representatives and the Committee on Environment and Public Works of the Senate, a report for the preceding fiscal year on the activities and programs implemented under this section and the progress made in reducing pollution in the navigable waters resulting from nonpoint sources and improving the quality of such waters.

(2) Final report

Not later than January 1, 1990, the Administrator shall transmit to Congress a final report on the activities carried out under this section. Such report, at a minimum, shall—

(A) describe the management programs being implemented by the States by types and amount of affected navigable waters, categories and subcategories of nonpoint sources, and types of best management practices being implemented;

(B) describe the experiences of the States in adhering to schedules and implementing best management practices;

(C) describe the amount and purpose of grants awarded pursuant to subsections (h) and (i) of this section;

(D) identify, to the extent that information is available, the progress made in reducing pollutant loads and improving water quality in the navigable waters;

(E) indicate what further actions need to be taken to attain and maintain in those navigable waters (i) applicable water quality standards, and (ii) the goals and requirements of this chapter;

(F) include recommendations of the Administrator concerning future programs (including enforcement programs) for controlling pollution from nonpoint sources; and

(G) identify the activities and programs of departments, agencies, and instrumentalities of the United States which are inconsistent with the management programs submitted by the States and recommend modifications so that such activities and programs are consistent with and assist the States in implementation of such management programs.

(n) Set aside for administrative personnel

Not less than 5 percent of the funds appropriated pursuant to subsection (j) of this section for any fiscal year shall be available to the Administrator to maintain personnel levels at the Environmental Protection Agency at levels which are adequate to carry out this section in such year.

(June 30, 1948, c. 758, Title III, § 319, as added Feb. 4, 1987, Pub.L. 100–4, Title III, § 316(a), 101 Stat. 52.)

Change of Name

Any reference in any provision of law enacted before Jan. 4, 1995, to the Committee on Public Works and Transportation of the House of Representatives treated as referring to the Committee on Transportation and Infrastructure of the House of Representatives, see section 1(a)(9) of Pub.L. 104–14, set out as a note preceding section 21 of Title 2, The Congress.

LIBRARY REFERENCES

Navigable Waters ⚷35.
C.J.S. Health and Environment § 106 et seq.
C.J.S. Navigable Waters § 11.

§ 1330. National estuary program [FWPCA § 320]

(a) Management conference

(1) Nomination of estuaries

The Governor of any State may nominate to the Administrator an estuary lying in whole or in part within the State as an estuary of national significance and request a management conference to develop a comprehensive management plan for the estuary. The nomination shall document the need for the conference, the likelihood of success, and information relating to the factors in paragraph (2).

(2) Convening of conference

(A) In general

In any case where the Administrator determines, on his own initiative or upon nomination of a State under paragraph (1), that the attainment or maintenance of that water quality in an estuary which assures protection of public water supplies and the protection and propagation of a balanced, indigenous population of shellfish, fish, and wildlife, and allows recreational activities, in and on the water, requires the control of point and nonpoint sources of pollution to supplement existing controls of pollution in more than one State, the Administrator shall select such estuary and convene a management conference.

(B) Priority consideration

The Administrator shall give priority consideration under this section to Long Island Sound, New York and Connecticut; Narragansett Bay, Rhode Island; Buzzards Bay, Massachusetts; Massachusetts Bay, Massachusetts (including Cape Cod Bay and Boston Harbor); Puget Sound, Washington; New York-New Jersey Harbor, New York and New Jersey; Delaware Bay, Delaware and New Jersey; Delaware Inland Bays, Delaware; Albemarle Sound, North Carolina; Sarasota Bay, Florida; San Francisco Bay, California; Santa Monica Bay, California; Galveston Bay, Texas; Barataria-Terrebonne Bay estuary complex, Louisiana; Indian River Lagoon, Florida; and Peconic Bay, New York.

(3) Boundary dispute exception

In any case in which a boundary between two States passes through an estuary and such boundary is disputed and is the subject of an action in any court, the Administrator shall not convene a management conference with respect to such estuary before a final adjudication has been made of such dispute.

(b) Purposes of conference

The purposes of any management conference convened with respect to an estuary under this subsection shall be to—

(1) assess trends in water quality, natural resources, and uses of the estuary;

(2) collect, characterize, and assess data on toxics, nutrients, and natural resources within the estuarine zone to identify the causes of environmental problems;

(3) develop the relationship between the inplace loads and point and nonpoint loadings of pollutants to the estuarine zone and the potential uses of the zone, water quality, and natural resources;

(4) develop a comprehensive conservation and management plan that recommends priority corrective actions and compliance schedules addressing point and nonpoint sources of pollution to restore and maintain the chemical, physical, and biological integrity of the estuary, including restoration and maintenance of water quality, a balanced indigenous population of shellfish, fish and wildlife, and recreational activities in the estuary, and assure that the designated uses of the estuary are protected;

(5) develop plans for the coordinated implementation of the plan by the States as well as Federal and local agencies participating in the conference;

(6) monitor the effectiveness of actions taken pursuant to the plan; and

(7) review all Federal financial assistance programs and Federal development projects in accordance with the requirements of Executive Order 12372, as in effect on September 17, 1983, to determine whether such assistance program or project would be consistent with and further the purposes and objectives of the plan prepared under this section.

For purposes of paragraph (7), such programs and projects shall not be limited to the assistance programs and development projects subject to Executive Order 12372, but may include any programs listed in the most recent Catalog of Federal Domestic Assistance which may have an effect on the purposes and objectives of the plan developed under this section.

(c) Members of conference

The members of a management conference convened under this section shall include, at a minimum, the Administrator and representatives of—

(1) each State and foreign nation located in whole or in part in the estuarine zone of the estuary for which the conference is convened;

(2) international, interstate, or regional agencies or entities having jurisdiction over all or a significant part of the estuary;

(3) each interested Federal agency, as determined appropriate by the Administrator;

(4) local governments having jurisdiction over any land or water within the estuarine zone, as determined appropriate by the Administrator; and

(5) affected industries, public and private educational institutions, and the general public, as determined appropriate by the Administrator.

(d) Utilization of existing data

In developing a conservation and management plan under this section, the management conference shall survey and utilize existing reports, data, and studies relating to the estuary that have been developed by or made available to Federal, interstate, State, and local agencies.

(e) Period of conference

A management conference convened under this section shall be convened for a period not to exceed 5 years. Such conference may be extended by the Administrator, and if terminated after the initial period, may be reconvened by the Administrator at any time thereafter, as may be necessary to meet the requirements of this section.

(f) Approval and implementation of plans

(1) Approval

Not later than 120 days after the completion of a conservation and management plan and after providing for public review and comment, the Administrator shall approve such plan if the plan meets the requirements of this section and the affected Governor or Governors concur.

(2) Implementation

Upon approval of a conservation and management plan under this section, such plan shall be implemented. Funds authorized to be appropriated under subchapters II and VI of this chapter and section 1329 of this title may be used in accordance with the applicable requirements of this chapter to assist States with the implementation of such plan.

(g) Grants

(1) Recipients

The Administrator is authorized to make grants to State, interstate, and regional water pollution control agencies and entities, State coastal zone management agencies, interstate agencies, other public or nonprofit private agencies, institutions, organizations, and individuals.

(2) Purposes

Grants under this subsection shall be made to pay for assisting research, surveys, studies, and modeling and other technical work necessary for the development of a conservation and management plan under this section.

(3) Federal share

The amount of grants to any person (including a State, interstate, or regional agency or entity) under this subsection for a fiscal year shall not exceed 75 percent of the costs of such research, survey, studies, and work and shall be made on condition that the non-Federal share of such costs are provided from non-Federal sources.

(h) Grant reporting

Any person (including a State, interstate, or regional agency or entity) that receives a grant under subsection (g) of this section shall report to the Administrator not later than 18 months after receipt of such grant and biennially thereafter on the progress being made under this section.

(i) Authorization of appropriations

There are authorized to be appropriated to the Administrator not to exceed $12,000,000 per fiscal year for each of fiscal years 1987, 1988, 1989, 1990, and 1991 for—

(1) expenses related to the administration of management conferences under this section, not to exceed 10 percent of the amount appropriated under this subsection;

(2) making grants under subsection (g) of this section; and

(3) monitoring the implementation of a conservation and management plan by the management conference or by the Administrator, in any case in which the conference has been terminated.

The Administrator shall provide up to $5,000,000 per fiscal year of the sums authorized to be appropriated under this subsection to the Administrator of the National Oceanic and Atmospheric Administration to carry out subsection (j) of this section.

(j) Research

(1) Programs

In order to determine the need to convene a management conference under this section or at the request of such a management conference, the Administrator shall coordinate and implement, through the National Marine Pollution Program Office and the National Marine Fisheries Service of the National Oceanic and Atmospheric Administration, as appropriate, for one or more estuarine zones—

(A) a long-term program of trend assessment monitoring measuring variations in pollutant concentrations, marine ecology, and other physical or biological environmental parameters which may affect estuarine zones, to provide the Administrator the capacity to determine the potential and actual effects of alternative management strategies and measures;

(B) a program of ecosystem assessment assisting in the development of (i) baseline studies which determine the state of estuarine zones and the effects of natural and anthropogenic changes, and (ii) predictive models capable of translating information on specific discharges or general pollutant loadings within estuarine zones into a set of probable effects on such zones;

(C) a comprehensive water quality sampling program for the continuous monitoring of nutrients, chlorine, acid precipitation dissolved oxygen, and potentially toxic pollutants (including organic chemicals and metals) in estuarine zones, after consultation with interested State, local, interstate, or international agencies and review and analysis of all environmental sampling data presently collected from estuarine zones; and

(D) a program of research to identify the movements of nutrients, sediments and pollutants through estuarine zones and the impact of nutrients, sediments, and pollutants on water quality, the ecosystem, and designated or potential uses of the estuarine zones.

(2) Reports

The Administrator, in cooperation with the Administrator of the National Oceanic and Atmospheric Administration, shall submit to the Congress no less often than biennially a comprehensive report on the activities authorized under this subsection including—

(A) a listing of priority monitoring and research needs;

(B) an assessment of the state and health of the Nation's estuarine zones, to the extent evaluated under this subsection;

(C) a discussion of pollution problems and trends in pollutant concentrations with a direct or indirect effect on water quality, the ecosystem, and designated or potential uses of each estuarine zone, to the extent evaluated under this subsection; and

(D) an evaluation of pollution abatement activities and management measures so far implemented to determine the degree of improvement toward the objectives expressed in subsection (b)(4) of this section.

(k) Definitions

For purposes of this section, the terms "estuary" and "estuarine zone" have the meanings such terms have in section 1254(n)(4) of this title, except that the term "estuarine zone" shall also include associated aquatic ecosystems and those portions of tributaries draining into the estuary up to the historic height of migration of anadromous fish or the historic head of tidal influence, whichever is higher.

(June 30, 1948, c. 758, Title III, § 320, as added Feb. 4, 1987, Pub.L. 100–4, Title III, § 317(b), 101 Stat. 61, and amended Dec. 22, 1987, § 101(f) [Title II], Pub.L. 100–202, 101 Stat. 1329–197; Nov. 14, 1988, Pub.L. 100–653, Title X, § 1004, 102 Stat. 3836; Nov. 18, 1988, Pub.L. 100–688, Title II, § 2001, 102 Stat. 4152.)

SUBCHAPTER IV—PERMITS AND LICENSES

CROSS REFERENCES

Continuing planning process, approval of State permit program, see section 1313 of this title.

§ 1341. Certification [FWPCA § 401]

(a) Compliance with applicable requirements; application; procedures; license suspension

(1) Any applicant for a Federal license or permit to conduct any activity including, but not limited to, the construction or operation of facilities, which may result in any discharge into the navigable waters, shall provide the licensing or permitting agency a certification from the State in which the discharge originates or will originate, or, if appropriate, from the interstate water pollution control agency having jurisdiction over the navigable waters at the point where the discharge originates or will originate, that any such discharge will comply with the applicable provisions of sections 1311, 1312, 1313, 1316, and 1317 of this title. In the case of any such activity for which there is not an applicable effluent limitation or other limitation under sections 1311(b) and 1312 of this title, and there is not an applicable standard under sections 1316 and 1317 of this title, the State shall so certify, except that any such certification shall not be deemed to satisfy section 1371(c) of this title. Such State or interstate agency shall establish procedures for public notice in the case of all applications for certification by it and, to the extent it deems appropriate, procedures for public hearings in connection with specific applications. In any case where a State or interstate agency has no authority to give such a certification, such certification shall be from the Administrator. If the State, interstate agency, or Administrator, as the case may be, fails or refuses to act on a request for certification, within a reasonable period of time (which shall not exceed one year) after receipt of such request, the certification requirements of this subsection shall be waived with respect to such Federal application. No license or permit shall be granted until the certification required by this section has been obtained or has been waived as provided in the preceding sentence. No license or permit shall be granted if certification has been denied by the State, interstate agency, or the Administrator, as the case may be.

(2) Upon receipt of such application and certification the licensing or permitting agency shall immediately notify the Administrator of such application and certification. Whenever such a discharge may affect, as determined by the Administrator, the quality of the waters of any other State, the Administrator within thirty days of the date of notice of application for such Federal license or permit shall so notify such other State, the licensing or permitting agency, and the applicant. If, within sixty days after receipt of such notification, such other State determines that such discharge will affect the quality of its waters so as to violate any water quality requirements in such State, and within such sixty-day period notifies the Administrator and the licensing or permitting agency in writing of its objection to the issuance of such license or permit and requests a public hearing on such objection, the licensing or permitting agency shall hold such a hearing. The Administrator shall at such hearing submit his evaluation and recommendations with respect to any such objection to the licensing or permitting agency. Such agency, based upon the recommendations of such State, the Administrator, and upon any additional evidence, if any, presented to the agency at the hearing, shall condition such license or permit in such manner as may be necessary to insure compliance with applicable water quality requirements. If the imposition of conditions cannot insure such compliance such agency shall not issue such license or permit.

(3) The certification obtained pursuant to paragraph (1) of this subsection with respect to the construction of any facility shall fulfill the requirements of this subsection with respect to certification in connection with any other Federal license or permit required for the operation of such facility unless, after notice to the certifying State, agency, or Administrator, as the case may be, which shall be given by the Federal agency to whom application is made for such operating license or permit, the State, or if appropriate, the interstate agency or the Administrator, notifies such agency within sixty days after receipt of such notice that there is no longer reasonable assurance that there will be compliance with the applicable provisions of sections 1311, 1312, 1313, 1316, and 1317 of this title because of changes since the construction license or permit certification was issued in (A) the construction or operation of the facility, (B) the characteristics of the waters into which such discharge is made, (C) the water quality criteria applicable to such waters or (D) applicable effluent limitations or other requirements. This paragraph shall be inapplicable in any case where the applicant for such operating license or permit has failed to provide the certifying State, or, if appropriate, the interstate agency or the Administrator, with notice of any proposed changes in the construction or operation of the facility with respect to which a construction license or permit has been granted, which changes may result in violation of section 1311, 1312, 1313, 1316, or 1317 of this title.

(4) Prior to the initial operation of any federally licensed or permitted facility or activity which may

result in any discharge into the navigable waters and with respect to which a certification has been obtained pursuant to paragraph (1) of this subsection, which facility or activity is not subject to a Federal operating license or permit, the licensee or permittee shall provide an opportunity for such certifying State, or, if appropriate, the interstate agency or the Administrator to review the manner in which the facility or activity shall be operated or conducted for the purposes of assuring that applicable effluent limitations or other limitations or other applicable water quality requirements will not be violated. Upon notification by the certifying State, or if appropriate, the interstate agency or the Administrator that the operation of any such federally licensed or permitted facility or activity will violate applicable effluent limitations or other limitations or other water quality requirements such Federal agency may, after public hearing, suspend such license or permit. If such license or permit is suspended, it shall remain suspended until notification is received from the certifying State, agency, or Administrator, as the case may be, that there is reasonable assurance that such facility or activity will not violate the applicable provisions of section 1311, 1312, 1313, 1316, or 1317 of this title.

(5) Any Federal license or permit with respect to which a certification has been obtained under paragraph (1) of this subsection may be suspended or revoked by the Federal agency issuing such license or permit upon the entering of a judgment under this chapter that such facility or activity has been operated in violation of the applicable provisions of section 1311, 1312, 1313, 1316, or 1317 of this title.

(6) Except with respect to a permit issued under section 1342 of this title, in any case where actual construction of a facility has been lawfully commenced prior to April 3, 1970, no certification shall be required under this subsection for a license or permit issued after April 3, 1970, to operate such facility, except that any such license or permit issued without certification shall terminate April 3, 1973, unless prior to such termination date the person having such license or permit submits to the Federal agency which issued such license or permit a certification and otherwise meets the requirements of this section.

[(7) Redesignated (6)].

(b) Compliance with other provisions of law setting applicable water quality requirements

Nothing in this section shall be construed to limit the authority of any department or agency pursuant to any other provision of law to require compliance with any applicable water quality requirements. The Administrator shall, upon the request of any Federal department or agency, or State or interstate agency, or applicant, provide, for the purpose of this section, any relevant information on applicable effluent limitations, or other limitations, standards, regulations, or requirements, or water quality criteria, and shall, when requested by any such department or agency or State or interstate agency, or applicant, comment on any methods to comply with such limitations, standards, regulations, requirements, or criteria.

(c) Authority of Secretary of the Army to permit use of spoil disposal areas by Federal licensees or permittees

In order to implement the provisions of this section, the Secretary of the Army, acting through the Chief of Engineers, is authorized, if he deems it to be in the public interest, to permit the use of spoil disposal areas under his jurisdiction by Federal licensees or permittees, and to make an appropriate charge for such use. Moneys received from such licensees or permittees shall be deposited in the Treasury as miscellaneous receipts.

(d) Limitations and monitoring requirements of certification

Any certification provided under this section shall set forth any effluent limitations and other limitations, and monitoring requirements necessary to assure that any applicant for a Federal license or permit will comply with any applicable effluent limitations and other limitations, under section 1311 or 1312 of this title, standard of performance under section 1316 of this title, or prohibition, effluent standard, or pretreatment standard under section 1317 of this title, and with any other appropriate requirement of State law set forth in such certification, and shall become a condition on any Federal license or permit subject to the provisions of this section.

(June 30, 1948, c. 758, Title IV, § 401, as added Oct. 18, 1972, Pub.L. 92–500, § 2, 86 Stat. 877, and amended Dec. 27, 1977, Pub.L. 95–217, §§ 61(b), 64, 91 Stat. 1598, 1599.)

CROSS REFERENCES

Citizen suits for violation of effluent standards, see section 1365 of this title.

Licensing authority of any Federal agency under environmental policy provisions, see section 1371 of this title.

Test procedures for analysis of pollutants to include factors to be provided in any certification pursuant to this section, see section 1314 of this title.

United States Supreme Court

State could impose minimum flow condition as condition for water quality certification for hydroelectric project under Clean Water Act provision allowing states to condition certification upon any limitations necessary to ensure compliance with state water quality standards or any other "appropriate requirement of State law", see PUD No. 1 of Jefferson County v. Washington Dept. of Ecology, 1994, 114 S.Ct. 1900, 128 L.Ed.2d 716.

LIBRARY REFERENCES

Health and Environment ⇔25.7(13).
C.J.S. Health and Environment § 107 et seq.

§ 1342. National pollutant discharge elimination system [FWPCA § 402]

(a) Permits for discharge of pollutants

(1) Except as provided in sections 1328 and 1344 of this title, the Administrator may, after opportunity for public hearing, issue a permit for the discharge of any pollutant, or combination of pollutants, notwithstanding section 1311(a) of this title, upon condition that such discharge will meet either (A) all applicable requirements under sections 1311, 1312, 1316, 1317, 1318, and 1343 of this title, or (B) prior to the taking of necessary implementing actions relating to all such requirements, such conditions as the Administrator determines are necessary to carry out the provisions of this chapter.

(2) The Administrator shall prescribe conditions for such permits to assure compliance with the requirements of paragraph (1) of this subsection, including conditions on data and information collection, reporting, and such other requirements as he deems appropriate.

(3) The permit program of the Administrator under paragraph (1) of this subsection, and permits issued thereunder, shall be subject to the same terms, conditions, and requirements as apply to a State permit program and permits issued thereunder under subsection (b) of this section.

(4) All permits for discharges into the navigable waters issued pursuant to section 407 of this title shall be deemed to be permits issued under this subchapter, and permits issued under this subchapter shall be deemed to be permits issued under section 407 of this title, and shall continue in force and effect for their term unless revoked, modified, or suspended in accordance with the provisions of this chapter.

(5) No permit for a discharge into the navigable waters shall be issued under section 407 of this title after October 18, 1972. Each application for a permit under section 407 of this title, pending on October 18, 1972, shall be deemed to be an application for a permit under this section. The Administrator shall authorize a State, which he determines has the capability of administering a permit program which will carry out the objectives of this chapter to issue permits for discharges into the navigable waters within the jurisdiction of such State. The Administrator may exercise the authority granted him by the preceding sentence only during the period which begins on October 18, 1972, and ends either on the ninetieth day after the date of the first promulgation of guidelines required by section 1314(i)(2) of this title, or the date of approval by the Administrator of a permit program for such State under subsection (b) of this section, whichever date first occurs, and no such authorization to a State shall extend beyond the last day of such period. Each such permit shall be subject to such conditions as the Administrator determines are necessary to carry out the provisions of this chapter. No such permit shall issue if the Administrator objects to such issuance.

(b) State permit programs

At any time after the promulgation of the guidelines required by subsection (i)(2) of section 1314 of this title, the Governor of each State desiring to administer its own permit program for discharges into navigable waters within its jurisdiction may submit to the Administrator a full and complete description of the program it proposes to establish and administer under State law or under an interstate compact. In addition, such State shall submit a statement from the attorney general (or the attorney for those State water pollution control agencies which have independent legal counsel), or from the chief legal officer in the case of an interstate agency, that the laws of such State, or the interstate compact, as the case may be, provide adequate authority to carry out the described program. The Administrator shall approve each submitted program unless he determines that adequate authority does not exist:

(1) To issue permits which—

(A) apply, and insure compliance with, any applicable requirements of sections 1311, 1312, 1316, 1317, and 1343 of this title;

(B) are for fixed terms not exceeding five years; and

(C) can be terminated or modified for cause including, but not limited to, the following:

(i) violation of any condition of the permit;

(ii) obtaining a permit by misrepresentation, or failure to disclose fully all relevant facts;

(iii) change in any condition that requires either a temporary or permanent reduction or elimination of the permitted discharge;

(D) control the disposal of pollutants into wells;

(2)(A) To issue permits which apply, and insure compliance with, all applicable requirements of section 1318 of this title; or

(B) To inspect, monitor, enter, and require reports to at least the same extent as required in section 1318 of this title;

(3) To insure that the public, and any other State the waters of which may be affected, receive notice of each application for a permit and to provide an opportunity for public hearing before a ruling on each such application;

(4) To insure that the Administrator receives notice of each application (including a copy thereof) for a permit;

(5) To insure that any State (other than the permitting State), whose waters may be affected by the issuance of a permit may submit written recommendations to the permitting State (and the Administrator) with respect to any permit application and, if any part of such written recommendations are not accepted by the permitting State, that the permitting State will notify such affected State (and the Administrator) in writing of its failure to so accept such recommendations together with its reasons for so doing;

(6) To insure that no permit will be issued if, in the judgment of the Secretary of the Army acting through the Chief of Engineers, after consultation with the Secretary of the department in which the Coast Guard is operating, anchorage and navigation of any of the navigable waters would be substantially impaired thereby;

(7) To abate violations of the permit or the permit program, including civil and criminal penalties and other ways and means of enforcement;

(8) To insure that any permit for a discharge from a publicly owned treatment works includes conditions to require the identification in terms of character and volume of pollutants of any significant source introducing pollutants subject to pretreatment standards under section 1317(b) of this title into such works and a program to assure compliance with such pretreatment standards by each such source, in addition to adequate notice to the permitting agency of (A) new introductions into such works of pollutants from any source which would be a new source as defined in section 1316 of this title if such source were discharging pollutants, (B) new introductions of pollutants into such works from a source which would be subject to section 1311 of this title if it were discharging such pollutants, or (C) a substantial change in volume or character of pollutants being introduced into such works by a source introducing pollutants into such works at the time of issuance of the permit. Such notice shall include information on the quality and quantity of effluent to be introduced into such treatment works and any anticipated impact of such change in the quantity or quality of effluent to be discharged from such publicly owned treatment works; and

(9) To insure that any industrial user of any publicly owned treatment works will comply with sections 1284(b), 1317, and 1318 of this title.

(c) Suspension of Federal program upon submission of State program; withdrawal of approval of State program; return of State program to Administrator

(1) Not later than ninety days after the date on which a State has submitted a program (or revision thereof) pursuant to subsection (b) of this section, the Administrator shall suspend the issuance of permits under subsection (a) of this section as to those discharges subject to such program unless he determines that the State permit program does not meet the requirements of subsection (b) of this section or does not conform to the guidelines issued under section 1314(i)(2) of this title. If the Administrator so determines, he shall notify the State of any revisions or modifications necessary to conform to such requirements or guidelines.

(2) Any State permit program under this section shall at all times be in accordance with this section and guidelines promulgated pursuant to section 1314(i)(2) of this title.

(3) Whenever the Administrator determines after public hearing that a State is not administering a program approved under this section in accordance with requirements of this section, he shall so notify the State and, if appropriate corrective action is not taken within a reasonable time, not to exceed ninety days, the Administrator shall withdraw approval of such program. The Administrator shall not withdraw approval of any such program unless he shall first have notified the State, and made public, in writing, the reasons for such withdrawal.

(4) Limitations on partial permit program returns and withdrawals.

A State may return to the Administrator administration, and the Administrator may withdraw under paragraph (3) of this subsection approval, of—

(A) a State partial permit program approved under subsection (n)(3) of this section only if the entire permit program being administered by the State department or agency at the time is returned or withdrawn; and

(B) a State partial permit program approved under subsection (n)(4) of this section only if an entire phased component of the permit program being administered by the State at the time is returned or withdrawn.

(d) Notification of Administrator

(1) Each State shall transmit to the Administrator a copy of each permit application received by such State

and provide notice to the Administrator of every action related to the consideration of such permit application, including each permit proposed to be issued by such State.

(2) No permit shall issue (A) if the Administrator within ninety days of the date of his notification under subsection (b)(5) of this section objects in writing to the issuance of such permit, or (B) if the Administrator within ninety days of the date of transmittal of the proposed permit by the State objects in writing to the issuance of such permit as being outside the guidelines and requirements of this chapter. Whenever the Administrator objects to the issuance of a permit under this paragraph such written objection shall contain a statement of the reasons for such objection and the effluent limitations and conditions which such permit would include if it were issued by the Administrator.

(3) The Administrator may, as to any permit application, waive paragraph (2) of this subsection.

(4) In any case where, after December 27, 1977, the Administrator, pursuant to paragraph (2) of this subsection, objects to the issuance of a permit, on request of the State, a public hearing shall be held by the Administrator on such objection. If the State does not resubmit such permit revised to meet such objection within 30 days after completion of the hearing, or, if no hearing is requested within 90 days after the date of such objection, the Administrator may issue the permit pursuant to subsection (a) of this section for such source in accordance with the guidelines and requirements of this chapter.

(e) Waiver of notification requirement

In accordance with guidelines promulgated pursuant to subsection (i)(2) of section 1314 of this title, the Administrator is authorized to waive the requirements of subsection (d) of this section at the time he approves a program pursuant to subsection (b) of this section for any category (including any class, type, or size within such category) of point sources within the State submitting such program.

(f) Point source categories

The Administrator shall promulgate regulations establishing categories of point sources which he determines shall not be subject to the requirements of subsection (d) of this section in any State with a program approved pursuant to subsection (b) of this section. The Administrator may distinguish among classes, types, and sizes within any category of point sources.

(g) Other regulations for safe transportation, handling, carriage, storage, and stowage of pollutants

Any permit issued under this section for the discharge of pollutants into the navigable waters from a vessel or other floating craft shall be subject to any applicable regulations promulgated by the Secretary of the department in which the Coast Guard is operating, establishing specifications for safe transportation, handling, carriage, storage, and stowage of pollutants.

(h) Violation of permit conditions; restriction or prohibition upon introduction of pollutant by source not previously utilizing treatment works

In the event any condition of a permit for discharges from a treatment works (as defined in section 1292 of this title) which is publicly owned is violated, a State with a program approved under subsection (b) of this section or the Administrator, where no State program is approved or where the Administrator determines pursuant to section 1319(a) of this title that a State with an approved program has not commenced appropriate enforcement action with respect to such permit, may proceed in a court of competent jurisdiction to restrict or prohibit the introduction of any pollutant into such treatment works by a source not utilizing such treatment works prior to the finding that such condition was violated.

(i) Federal enforcement not limited

Nothing in this section shall be construed to limit the authority of the Administrator to take action pursuant to section 1319 of this title.

(j) Public information

A copy of each permit application and each permit issued under this section shall be available to the public. Such permit application or permit, or portion thereof, shall further be available on request for the purpose of reproduction.

(k) Compliance with permits

Compliance with a permit issued pursuant to this section shall be deemed compliance, for purposes of sections 1319 and 1365 of this title, with sections 1311, 1312, 1316, 1317, and 1343 of this title, except any standard imposed under section 1317 of this title for a toxic pollutant injurious to human health. Until December 31, 1974, in any case where a permit for discharge has been applied for pursuant to this section, but final administrative disposition of such application has not been made, such discharge shall not be a violation of (1) section 1311, 1316, or 1342 of this title, or (2) section 407 of this title, unless the Administrator or other plaintiff proves that final administrative disposition of such application has not been made because of the failure of the applicant to furnish information reasonably required or requested in order to process the application. For the 180-day period beginning on October 18, 1972, in the case of any point source discharging any pollutant or combination of pollutants immediately prior to such date which source is not subject to section 407 of this title, the discharge by such source shall not be a violation of this chapter if such a source applies for a permit for discharge pursuant to this section within such 180-day period.

(*l*) Limitation on permit requirement

(1) Agricultural return flows

The Administrator shall not require a permit under this section for discharges composed entirely of return flows from irrigated agriculture, nor shall the Administrator directly or indirectly, require any State to require such a permit.

(2) Stormwater runoff from oil, gas, and mining operations

The Administrator shall not require a permit under this section, nor shall the Administrator directly or indirectly require any State to require a permit, for discharges of stormwater runoff from mining operations or oil and gas exploration, production, processing, or treatment operations or transmission facilities, composed entirely of flows which are from conveyances or systems of conveyances (including but not limited to pipes, conduits, ditches, and channels) used for collecting and conveying precipitation runoff and which are not contaminated by contact with, or do not come into contact with, any overburden, raw material, intermediate products, finished product, byproduct, or waste products located on the site of such operations.

(m) Additional pretreatment of conventional pollutants not required

To the extent a treatment works (as defined in section 1292 of this title) which is publicly owned is not meeting the requirements of a permit issued under this section for such treatment works as a result of inadequate design or operation of such treatment works, the Administrator, in issuing a permit under this section, shall not require pretreatment by a person introducing conventional pollutants identified pursuant to section 1314(a)(4) of this title into such treatment works other than pretreatment required to assure compliance with pretreatment standards under subsection (b)(8) of this section and section 1317(b)(1) of this title. Nothing in this subsection shall affect the Administrator's authority under sections 1317 and 1319 of this title, affect State and local authority under sections 1317(b)(4) and 1370 of this title, relieve such treatment works of its obligations to meet requirements established under this chapter, or otherwise preclude such works from pursuing whatever feasible options are available to meet its responsibility to comply with its permit under this section.

(n) Partial permit program

(1) State submission

The Governor of a State may submit under subsection (b) of this section a permit program for a portion of the discharges into the navigable waters in such State.

(2) Minimum coverage

A partial permit program under this subsection shall cover, at a minimum, administration of a major category of the discharges into the navigable waters of the State or a major component of the permit program required by subsection (b) of this section.

(3) Approval of major category partial permit programs

The Administrator may approve a partial permit program covering administration of a major category of discharges under this subsection if—

(A) such program represents a complete permit program and covers all of the discharges under the jurisdiction of a department or agency of the State; and

(B) the Administrator determines that the partial program represents a significant and identifiable part of the State program required by subsection (b) of this section.

(4) Approval of major component partial permit programs

The Administrator may approve under this subsection a partial and phased permit program covering administration of a major component (including discharge categories) of a State permit program required by subsection (b) of this section if—

(A) the Administrator determines that the partial program represents a significant and identifiable part of the State program required by subsection (b) of this section; and

(B) the State submits, and the Administrator approves, a plan for the State to assume administration by phases of the remainder of the State program required by subsection (b) of this section by a specified date not more than 5 years after submission of the partial program under this subsection and agrees to make all reasonable efforts to assume such administration by such date.

(o) Anti-backsliding

(1) General prohibition

In the case of effluent limitations established on the basis of subsection (a)(1)(B) of this section, a permit may not be renewed, reissued, or modified on the basis of effluent guidelines promulgated under section 1314(b) of this title subsequent to the original issuance of such permit, to contain effluent limitations which are less stringent than the comparable effluent limitations in the previous permit. In the case of effluent limitations established on the basis of section 1311(b)(1)(C) or section 1313(d) or (e) of this title, a permit may not be renewed, reissued, or modified to contain effluent limitations which are less stringent than the comparable effluent limitations in the previous permit except in compliance with section 1313(d)(4) of this title.

(2) Exceptions

A permit with respect to which paragraph (1) applies may be renewed, reissued, or modified to contain a less stringent effluent limitation applicable to a pollutant if—

(A) material and substantial alterations or additions to the permitted facility occurred after permit issuance which justify the application of a less stringent effluent limitation;

(B)(i) information is available which was not available at the time of permit issuance (other than revised regulations, guidance, or test methods) and which would have justified the application of a less stringent effluent limitation at the time of permit issuance; or

(ii) the Administrator determines that technical mistakes or mistaken interpretations of law were made in issuing the permit under subsection (a)(1)(B) of this section;

(C) a less stringent effluent limitation is necessary because of events over which the permittee has no control and for which there is no reasonably available remedy;

(D) the permittee has received a permit modification under section 1311(c), 1311(g), 1311(h), 1311(i), 1311(k), 1311(n), or 1326(a) of this title; or

(E) the permittee has installed the treatment facilities required to meet the effluent limitations in the previous permit and has properly operated and maintained the facilities but has nevertheless been unable to achieve the previous effluent limitations, in which case the limitations in the reviewed, reissued, or modified permit may reflect the level of pollutant control actually achieved (but shall not be less stringent than required by effluent guidelines in effect at the time of permit renewal, reissuance, or modification).

Subparagraph (B) shall not apply to any revised waste load allocations or any alternative grounds for translating water quality standards into effluent limitations, except where the cumulative effect of such revised allocations results in a decrease in the amount of pollutants discharged into the concerned waters, and such revised allocations are not the result of a discharger eliminating or substantially reducing its discharge of pollutants due to complying with the requirements of this chapter or for reasons otherwise unrelated to water quality.

(3) Limitations

In no event may a permit with respect to which paragraph (1) applies be renewed, reissued, or modified to contain an effluent limitation which is less stringent than required by effluent guidelines in effect at the time the permit is renewed, reissued, or modified. In no event may such a permit to discharge into waters be renewed, reissued, or modified to contain a less stringent effluent limitation if the implementation of such limitation would result in a violation of a water quality standard under section 1313 of this title applicable to such waters.

(p) Municipal and industrial stormwater discharges

(1) General rule

Prior to October 1, 1994, the Administrator or the State (in the case of a permit program approved under section 1342 of this title) shall not require a permit under this section for discharges composed entirely of stormwater.

(2) Exceptions

Paragraph (1) shall not apply with respect to the following stormwater discharges:

(A) A discharge with respect to which a permit has been issued under this section before February 4, 1987.

(B) A discharge associated with industrial activity.

(C) A discharge from a municipal separate storm sewer system serving a population of 250,000 or more.

(D) A discharge from a municipal separate storm sewer system serving a population of 100,000 or more but less than 250,000.

(E) A discharge for which the Administrator or the State, as the case may be, determines that the stormwater discharge contributes to a violation of a water quality standard or is a significant contributor of pollutants to waters of the United States.

(3) Permit requirements

(A) Industrial discharges

Permits for discharges associated with industrial activity shall meet all applicable provisions of this section and section 1311 of this title.

(B) Municipal discharge

Permits for discharges from municipal storm sewers—

(i) may be issued on a system- or jurisdiction-wide basis;

(ii) shall include a requirement to effectively prohibit non-stormwater discharges into the storm sewers; and

(iii) shall require controls to reduce the discharge of pollutants to the maximum extent practicable, including management practices, control techniques and system, design and engineering methods, and such other provisions as the Administrator or the State determines appropriate for the control of such pollutants.

(4) Permit application requirements

(A) Industrial and large municipal discharges

Not later than 2 years after February 4, 1987, the Administrator shall establish regulations setting forth the permit application requirements for stormwater discharges described in paragraphs (2)(B) and (2)(C). Applications for permits for such discharges shall be filed no later than 3 years after February 4, 1987. Not later than 4 years after February 4, 1987, the Administrator or the State, as the case may be, shall issue or deny each such permit. Any such permit shall provide for compliance as expeditiously as practicable, but in no event later than 3 years after the date of issuance of such permit.

(B) Other municipal discharges

Not later than 4 years after February 4, 1987, the Administrator shall establish regulations setting forth the permit application requirements for stormwater discharges described in paragraph (2)(D). Applications for permits for such discharges shall be filed no later than 5 years after February 4, 1987. Not later than 6 years after February 4, 1987, the Administrator or the State, as the case may be, shall issue or deny each such permit. Any such permit shall provide for compliance as expeditiously as practicable, but in no event later than 3 years after the date of issuance of such permit.

(5) Studies

The Administrator, in consultation with the States, shall conduct a study for the purposes of—

(A) identifying those stormwater discharges or classes of stormwater discharges for which permits are not required pursuant to paragraphs (1) and (2) of this subsection;

(B) determining, to the maximum extent practicable, the nature and extent of pollutants in such discharges; and

(C) establishing procedures and methods to control stormwater discharges to the extent necessary to mitigate impacts on water quality.

Not later than October 1, 1988, the Administrator shall submit to Congress a report on the results of the study described in subparagraphs (A) and (B). Not later than October 1, 1989, the Administrator shall submit to Congress a report on the results of the study described in subparagraph (C).

(6) Regulations

Not later than October 1, 1993, the Administrator, in consultation with State and local officials, shall issue regulations (based on the results of the studies conducted under paragraph (5)) which designate stormwater discharges, other than those discharges described in paragraph (2), to be regulated to protect water quality and shall establish a comprehensive program to regulate such designated sources. The program shall, at a minimum, (A) establish priorities, (B) establish requirements for State stormwater management programs, and (C) establish expeditious deadlines. The program may include performance standards, guidelines, guidance, and management practices and treatment requirements, as appropriate.

(June 30, 1948, c. 758, Title IV, § 402, as added Oct. 18, 1972, Pub.L. 92–500, § 2, 86 Stat. 880, and amended Dec. 27, 1977, Pub.L. 95–217, §§ 33(c), 50, 54(c)(1), 65, 66, 91 Stat. 1577, 1588, 1591, 1599, 1600; Feb. 4, 1987, Pub.L. 100–4, Title IV, §§ 401 to 404(a), (c), formerly (d), 405, 101 Stat. 65 to 67, 69; Oct. 31, 1992, Pub.L. 102–580, Title III, § 364, 106 Stat. 4862; Dec. 21, 1995, Pub.L. 104–66, Title II, § 2021(e)(2), 109 Stat. 727.)

Stormwater Permit Requirements

Pub.L. 102–240, Title I, § 1068, Dec. 18, 1991, 105 Stat. 2007, provided that:

"**(a) General rule.**—Notwithstanding the requirements of sections 402(p)(2)(B), (C), and (D) of the Federal Water Pollution Control Act [subsec. (p)(2)(B), (C), and (D) of this section], permit application deadlines for stormwater discharges associated with industrial activities from facilities that are owned or operated by a municipality shall be established by the Administrator of the Environmental Protection Agency (hereinafter in this section referred to as the 'Administrator') pursuant to the requirements of this section.

"**(b) Permit applications.**—

"**(1) Individual applications.**—The Administrator shall require individual permit applications for discharges described in subsection (a) on or before October 1, 1992; except that any municipality that has participated in a timely part I group application for an industrial activity discharging stormwater that is denied such participation in a group application or for which a group application is denied shall not be required to submit an individual application until the 180th day following the date on which the denial is made.

"(2) **Group applications.**—With respect to group applications for permits for discharges described in subsection (a), the Administrator shall require—

"(A) part I applications on or before September 30, 1991, except that any municipality with a population of less than 250,000 shall not be required to submit a part I application before May 18, 1992; and

"(B) part II applications on or before October 1, 1992, except that any municipality with a population of less than 250,000 shall not be required to submit a part II application before May 17, 1993.

"(c) **Municipalities with less than 100,000 population.**—The Administrator shall not require any municipality with a population of less than 100,000 to apply for or obtain a permit for any stormwater discharge associated with an industrial activity other than an airport, powerplant, or uncontrolled sanitary landfill owned or operated by such municipality before October 1, 1992, unless such permit is required by section 402(p)(2)(A) or (E) of the Federal Water Pollution Control Act [subsec. (p)(2)(A) or (E) of this section].

"(d) **Uncontrolled sanitary landfill defined.**—For the purposes of this section, the term 'uncontrolled sanitary landfill' means a landfill or open dump, whether in operation or closed, that does not meet the requirements for run-on and run-off controls established pursuant to subtitle D of the Solid Waste Disposal Act [section 6941 et seq. of Title 42, The Public Health and Welfare].

"(e) **Limitation on statutory construction.**—Nothing in this section shall be construed to affect any application or permit requirement, including any deadline, to apply for or obtain a permit for stormwater discharges subject to section 402(p)(2)(A) or (E) of the Federal Water Pollution Control Act [subsec. (p)(2)(A) or (E) of this section].

"(f) **Regulations.**—The Administrator shall issue final regulations with respect to general permits for stormwater discharges associated with industrial activity on or before February 1, 1992."

CROSS REFERENCES

Aquaculture discharges of specific pollutants under controlled conditions, see section 1328 of this title.
Certification by owner of treatment works of compliance with permit specifications, see section 1284 of this title.
Citizen suits for violation of permit, see section 1365 of this title.
Control of specific pollutants as requirement for permit under this section, see section 1314 of this title.
Discharge of dredged or fill material not prohibited by this section, see section 1344 of this title.
Enforcement for violations of permits, see section 1319 of this title.
Establishment and maintenance of records, see section 1318 of this title.
Exclusion of discharge in compliance with permit from definition of "discharge", see section 1321 of this title.
Federal facilities pollution control, waiver of conditions, see section 1323 of this title.
Federally permitted release as meaning discharges in compliance with a permit under this section, see section 9601 of Title 42, The Public Health and Welfare.
Grants for reasonable costs of administering an approved program under this section, see section 1285 of this title.
Illegality of pollutant discharges except in compliance with this section, see section 1311 of this title.
Issuance of permits after promulgation of guidelines for determination of degradation of waters of territorial seas, see section 1343 of this title.
Necessity of permit for construction of facility lawfully commenced on certain date, see section 1341 of this title.
Permit for disposal or use of sewage sludge, see section 1345 of this title.
Permit under this section deemed major Federal action, see section 1371 of this title.
Permit under this section not to conflict with a plan approved pursuant to section 1288 of this title, see section 1288 of this title.
Public health agency coordination, see section 1373 of this title.
Review of Administrator's action in issuing or denying permit, see section 1369 of this title.
Solid or dissolved material in domestic sewage or solid or dissolved materials or industrial discharges which are point sources subject to permits under this section excluded from definition of "solid waste", see section 6903 of Title 42.
State implementation of permit programs under this section, see section 1251 of this title.

CODE OF FEDERAL REGULATIONS

Criteria and standards for National Pollutant Discharge Elimination System, see 40 CFR 125.1 et seq.
Environmental Protection Agency administered permit programs: the National Pollutant Discharge Elimination System, see 40 CFR 122.1 et seq.
General pretreatment regulations for existing and new sources of pollution, see 40 CFR 403.1 et seq.
State program requirements, see 40 CFR 123.1 et seq.

LAW REVIEW COMMENTARIES

Environmental Law/Annual survey of significant developments. Thomas J. Elliott, 58 Pa.B.A.Q. 107 (1987).

From elephants to mice: The development of EBMUD's program to control small source wastewater discharges. Raoul Stewardson, 20 Ecology L.Q. 441 (1993).

New Jersey clean up your "act": Some reflections on the Spill Compensation and Control Act. Francis E.P. McCarter, 38 Rutgers L.Rev. 637 (1986).

Oklahoma v. EPA Does the Clean Water Act provide an effective remedy to downstream states or is there still room left for federal common law. Maria V. Maurrasse, 45 U.Miami L.Rev. 1037 (1991).

Regulation of batture pollution and ecology. Stan Millan, 33 Loyola (La.) L.Rev. 921 (1988).

Toward a national groundwater act: Current contamination and future courses of action. Thomas D. Marks, 61 Fla.B.J. 10 (April 1987).

LIBRARY REFERENCES

Health and Environment ⚷25.7(13).
C.J.S. Health and Environment § 107 et seq.

United States Supreme Court

Federal permits, necessity for public hearings, see Costle v. Pacific Legal Foundation, 1980, 100 S.Ct. 1095, 445 U.S. 198, 63 L.Ed.2d 329.

§ 1343. Ocean discharge criteria [FWPCA § 403]

(a) Issuance of permits

No permit under section 1342 of this title for a discharge into the territorial sea, the waters of the contiguous zone, or the oceans shall be issued, after promulgation of guidelines established under subsection (c) of this section, except in compliance with such guidelines. Prior to the promulgation of such guidelines, a permit may be issued under such section 1342 of this title if the Administrator determines it to be in the public interest.

(b) Waiver

The requirements of subsection (d) of section 1342 of this title may not be waived in the case of permits for discharges into the territorial sea.

(c) Guidelines for determining degradation of waters

(1) The Administrator shall, within one hundred and eighty days after October 18, 1972 (and from time to time thereafter), promulgate guidelines for determining the degradation of the waters of the territorial seas, the contiguous zone, and the oceans, which shall include:

(A) the effect of disposal of pollutants on human health or welfare, including but not limited to plankton, fish, shellfish, wildlife, shorelines, and beaches;

(B) the effect of disposal of pollutants on marine life including the transfer, concentration, and dispersal of pollutants or their byproducts through biological, physical, and chemical processes; changes in marine ecosystem diversity, productivity, and stability; and species and community population changes;

(C) the effect of disposal, of pollutants on esthetic, recreation, and economic values;

(D) the persistence and permanence of the effects of disposal of pollutants;

(E) the effect of the disposal of varying rates, of particular volumes and concentrations of pollutants;

(F) other possible locations and methods of disposal or recycling of pollutants including land-based alternatives; and

(G) the effect on alternate uses of the oceans, such as mineral exploitation and scientific study.

(2) In any event where insufficient information exists on any proposed discharge to make a reasonable judgment on any of the guidelines established pursuant to this subsection no permit shall be issued under section 1342 of this title.

(June 30, 1948, c. 758, Title IV, § 403, as added Oct. 18, 1972, Pub.L. 92–500, § 2, 86 Stat. 883.)

CROSS REFERENCES

Best management practices for industry, see section 1314 of this title.
Determination of State's authority to issue permits for dredged or fill material, see section 1344 of this title.
Field laboratory and research facilities, see section 1254 of this title.
Modification of effluent limitation requirements for point sources, see section 1311 of this title.
Permits for discharge of pollutants, see section 1342 of this title.
Planning process to assure compliance with this section, see section 1288 of this title.

§ 1344. Permits for dredged or fill material [FWPCA § 404]

(a) Discharge into navigable waters at specified disposal sites

The Secretary may issue permits, after notice and opportunity for public hearings for the discharge of dredged or fill material into the navigable waters at specified disposal sites. Not later than the fifteenth day after the date an applicant submits all the information required to complete an application for a permit under this subsection, the Secretary shall publish the notice required by this subsection.

(b) Specification for disposal sites

Subject to subsection (c) of this section, each such disposal site shall be specified for each such permit by the Secretary (1) through the application of guidelines developed by the Administrator, in conjunction with the Secretary, which guidelines shall be based upon criteria comparable to the criteria applicable to the territorial seas, the contiguous zone, and the ocean under section 1343(c) of this title, and (2) in any case where such guidelines under clause (1) alone would prohibit the specification of a site, through the application additionally of the economic impact of the site on navigation and anchorage.

(c) Denial or restriction of use of defined areas as disposal sites

The Administrator is authorized to prohibit the specification (including the withdrawal of specification) of any defined area as a disposal site, and he is authorized to deny or restrict the use of any defined area for specification (including the withdrawal of specification) as a disposal site, whenever he determines, after notice and opportunity for public hearings, that the discharge of such materials into such area will have an unacceptable adverse effect on municipal water supplies, shellfish beds and fishery areas (including spawning and breeding areas), wildlife, or recreational areas. Before making such determination, the Administrator shall consult with the Secretary. The Administrator shall set forth in writing and make public his findings and his reasons for making any determination under this subsection.

(d) "Secretary" defined

The term "Secretary" as used in this section means the Secretary of the Army, acting through the Chief of Engineers.

(e) General permits on State, regional, or nationwide basis

(1) In carrying out his functions relating to the discharge of dredged or fill material under this section, the Secretary may, after notice and opportunity for public hearing, issue general permits on a State, regional, or nationwide basis for any category of activities involving discharges of dredged or fill material if the Secretary determines that the activities in such category are similar in nature, will cause only minimal adverse environmental effects when performed separately, and will have only minimal cumulative adverse

effect on the environment. Any general permit issued under this subsection shall (A) be based on the guidelines described in subsection (b)(1) of this section, and (B) set forth the requirements and standards which shall apply to any activity authorized by such general permit.

(2) No general permit issued under this subsection shall be for a period of more than five years after the date of its issuance and such general permit may be revoked or modified by the Secretary if, after opportunity for public hearing, the Secretary determines that the activities authorized by such general permit have an adverse impact on the environment or such activities are more appropriately authorized by individual permits.

(f) Non-prohibited discharge of dredged or fill material

(1) Except as provided in paragraph (2) of this subsection, the discharge of dredged or fill material—

(A) from normal farming, silviculture, and ranching activities such as plowing, seeding, cultivating, minor drainage, harvesting for the production of food, fiber, and forest products, or upland soil and water conservation practices;

(B) for the purpose of maintenance, including emergency reconstruction of recently damaged parts, of currently serviceable structures such as dikes, dams, levees, groins, riprap, breakwaters, causeways, and bridge abutments or approaches, and transportation structures;

(C) for the purpose of construction or maintenance of farm or stock ponds or irrigation ditches, or the maintenance of drainage ditches;

(D) for the purpose of construction of temporary sedimentation basins on a construction site which does not include placement of fill material into the navigable waters;

(E) for the purpose of construction or maintenance of farm roads or forest roads, or temporary roads for moving mining equipment, where such roads are constructed and maintained, in accordance with best management practices, to assure that flow and circulation patterns and chemical and biological characteristics of the navigable waters are not impaired, that the reach of the navigable waters is not reduced, and that any adverse effect on the aquatic environment will be otherwise minimized;

(F) resulting from any activity with respect to which a State has an approved program under section 1288(b)(4) of this title which meets the requirements of subparagraphs (B) and (C) of such section,

is not prohibited by or otherwise subject to regulation under this section or section 1311(a) or 1342 of this title (except for effluent standards or prohibitions under section 1317 of this title).

(2) Any discharge of dredged or fill material into the navigable waters incidental to any activity having as its purpose bringing an area of the navigable waters into a use to which it was not previously subject, where the flow or circulation of navigable waters may be impaired or the reach of such waters be reduced, shall be required to have a permit under this section.

(g) State administration

(1) The Governor of any State desiring to administer its own individual and general permit program for the discharge of dredged or fill material into the navigable waters (other than those waters which are presently used, or are susceptible to use in their natural condition or by reasonable improvement as a means to transport interstate or foreign commerce shoreward to their ordinary high water mark, including all waters which are subject to the ebb and flow of the tide shoreward to their mean high water mark, or mean higher high water mark on the west coast, including wetlands adjacent thereto) within its jurisdiction may submit to the Administrator a full and complete description of the program it proposes to establish and administer under State law or under an interstate compact. In addition, such State shall submit a statement from the attorney general (or the attorney for those State agencies which have independent legal counsel), or from the chief legal officer in the case of an interstate agency, that the laws of such State, or the interstate compact, as the case may be, provide adequate authority to carry out the described program.

(2) Not later than the tenth day after the date of the receipt of the program and statement submitted by any State under paragraph (1) of this subsection, the Administrator shall provide copies of such program and statement to the Secretary and the Secretary of the Interior, acting through the Director of the United States Fish and Wildlife Service.

(3) Not later than the ninetieth day after the date of the receipt by the Administrator of the program and statement submitted by any State, under paragraph (1) of this subsection, the Secretary and the Secretary of the Interior, acting through the Director of the United States Fish and Wildlife Service, shall submit any comments with respect to such program and statement to the Administrator in writing.

(h) Determination of State's authority to issue permits under State program; approval; notification; transfers to State program

(1) Not later than the one-hundred-twentieth day after the date of the receipt by the Administrator of a program and statement submitted by any State under paragraph (1) of this subsection, the Administrator shall determine, taking into account any comments submitted by the Secretary and the Secretary of the Interior, acting through the Director of the United States Fish and Wildlife Service, pursuant to subsection (g) of this section, whether such State has the following authority with respect to the issuance of permits pursuant to such program:

(A) To issue permits which—

(i) apply, and assure compliance with, any applicable requirements of this section, including, but not limited to, the guidelines established under subsection (b)(1) of this section, and sections 1317 and 1343 of this title;

(ii) are for fixed terms not exceeding five years; and

(iii) can be terminated or modified for cause including, but not limited to, the following:

(I) violation of any condition of the permit;

(II) obtaining a permit by misrepresentation, or failure to disclose fully all relevant facts;

(III) change in any condition that requires either a temporary or permanent reduction or elimination of the permitted discharge.

(B) To issue permits which apply, and assure compliance with, all applicable requirements of section 1318 of this title, or to inspect, monitor, enter, and require reports to at least the same extent as required in section 1318 of this title.

(C) To assure that the public, and any other State the waters of which may be affected, receive notice of each application for a permit and to provide an opportunity for public hearing before a ruling on each such application.

(D) To assure that the Administrator receives notice of each application (including a copy thereof) for a permit.

(E) To assure that any State (other than the permitting State), whose waters may be affected by the issuance of a permit may submit written recommendations to the permitting State (and the Administrator) with respect to any permit application and, if any part of such written recommendations are not accepted by the permitting State, that the permitting State will notify such affected State (and the Administrator) in writing of its failure to so accept such recommendations together with its reasons for so doing.

(F) To assure that no permit will be issued if, in the judgment of the Secretary, after consultation with the Secretary of the department in which the Coast Guard is operating, anchorage and navigation of any of the navigable waters would be substantially impaired thereby.

(G) To abate violations of the permit or the permit program, including civil and criminal penalties and other ways and means of enforcement.

(H) To assure continued coordination with Federal and Federal-State water-related planning and review processes.

(2) If, with respect to a State program submitted under subsection (g)(1) of this section, the Administrator determines that such State—

(A) has the authority set forth in paragraph (1) of this subsection, the Administrator shall approve the program and so notify (i) such State and (ii) the Secretary, who upon subsequent notification from such State that it is administering such program, shall suspend the issuance of permits under subsections (a) and (e) of this section for activities with respect to which a permit may be issued pursuant to such State program; or

(B) does not have the authority set forth in paragraph (1) of this subsection, the Administrator shall so notify such State, which notification shall also describe the revisions or modifications necessary so that such State may resubmit such program for a determination by the Administrator under this subsection.

(3) If the Administrator fails to make a determination with respect to any program submitted by a State under subsection (g)(1) of this section within one-hundred-twenty days after the date of the receipt of such program, such program shall be deemed approved pursuant to paragraph (2)(A) of this subsection and the Administrator shall so notify such State and the Secretary who, upon subsequent notification from such State that it is administering such program, shall suspend the issuance of permits under subsection (a) and (e) of this section for activities with respect to which a permit may be issued by such State.

(4) After the Secretary receives notification from the Administrator under paragraph (2) or (3) of this subsection that a State permit program has been approved, the Secretary shall transfer any applications for permits pending before the Secretary for activities with respect to which a permit may be issued pursuant to such State program to such State for appropriate action.

(5) Upon notification from a State with a permit program approved under this subsection that such State intends to administer and enforce the terms and conditions of a general permit issued by the Secretary under subsection (e) of this section with respect to activities in such State to which such general permit applies, the Secretary shall suspend the administration and enforcement of such general permit with respect to such activities.

(i) Withdrawal of approval

Whenever the Administrator determines after public hearing that a State is not administering a program approved under subsection (h)(2)(A) of this section, in accordance with this section, including, but not limited to, the guidelines established under subsection (b)(1) of this section, the Administrator shall so notify the State, and, if appropriate corrective action is not taken within a reasonable time, not to exceed ninety days after the date of the receipt of such notification, the Administrator shall (1) withdraw approval of such program until the Administrator determines such corrective action has been taken, and (2) notify the Secretary that the Secretary shall resume the program for the issuance of permits under subsections (a) and (e) of this section for activities with respect to which the State was issuing permits and that such authority of the Secretary shall continue in effect until such time as the Administrator makes the determination described in clause (1) of this subsection and such State again has an approved program.

(j) Copies of applications for State permits and proposed general permits to be transmitted to Administrator

Each State which is administering a permit program pursuant to this section shall transmit to the Administrator (1) a copy of each permit application received by such State and provide notice to the Administrator of every action related to the consideration of such permit application, including each permit proposed to be issued by such State, and (2) a copy of each proposed general permit which such State intends to issue. Not later than the tenth day after the date of the receipt of such permit application or such proposed general permit, the Administrator shall provide copies of such permit application or such proposed general permit to the Secretary and the Secretary of the Interior, acting through the Director of the United States Fish and Wildlife Service. If the Administrator intends to provide written comments to such State with respect to such permit application or such proposed general permit, he shall so notify such State not later than the thirtieth day after the date of the receipt of such application or such proposed general permit and provide such written comments to such State, after consideration of any comments made in writing with respect to such application or such proposed general permit by the Secretary and the Secretary of the Interior, acting through the Director of the United States Fish and Wildlife Service, not later than the ninetieth day after the date of such receipt. If such State is so notified by the Administrator, it shall not issue the proposed permit until after the receipt of such comments from the Administrator, or after such ninetieth day, whichever first occurs. Such State shall not issue such proposed permit after such ninetieth day if it has received such written comments in which the Administrator objects (A) to the issuance of such proposed permit and such proposed permit is one that has been submitted to the Administrator pursuant to subsection (h)(1)(E) of this section, or (B) to the issuance of such proposed permit as being outside the requirements of this section, including, but not limited to, the guidelines developed under subsection (b)(1) of this section unless it modifies such proposed permit in accordance with such comments. Whenever the Administrator objects to the issuance of a permit under the preceding sentence such written objection shall contain a statement of the reasons for such objection and the conditions which such permit would include if it were issued by the Administrator. In any case where the Administrator objects to the issuance of a permit, on request of the State, a public hearing shall be held by the Administrator on such objection. If the State does not resubmit such permit revised to meet such objection within 30 days after completion of the hearing or, if no hearing is requested within 90 days after the date of such objection, the Secretary may issue the permit pursuant to subsection (a) or (e) of this section, as the case may be, for such source in accordance with the guidelines and requirements of this chapter.

(k) Waiver

In accordance with guidelines promulgated pursuant to subsection (i)(2) of section 1314 of this title, the Administrator is authorized to waive the requirements of subsection (j) of this section at the time of the approval of a program pursuant to subsection (h)(2)(A) of this section for any category (including any class, type, or size within such category) of discharge within the State submitting such program.

(*l*) Categories of discharges not subject to requirements

The Administrator shall promulgate regulations establishing categories of discharges which he determines shall not be subject to the requirements of subsection (j) of this section in any State with a program approved pursuant to subsection (h)(2)(A) of this section. The Administrator may distinguish among classes, types, and sizes within any category of discharges.

(m) Comments on permit applications or proposed general permits by Secretary of the Interior acting through Director of United States Fish and Wildlife Service

Not later than the ninetieth day after the date on which the Secretary notifies the Secretary of the

Interior, acting through the Director of the United States Fish and Wildlife Service that (1) an application for a permit under subsection (a) of this section has been received by the Secretary, or (2) the Secretary proposes to issue a general permit under subsection (e) of this section, the Secretary of the Interior, acting through the Director of the United States Fish and Wildlife Service, shall submit any comments with respect to such application or such proposed general permit in writing to the Secretary.

(n) Enforcement authority not limited

Nothing in this section shall be construed to limit the authority of the Administrator to take action pursuant to section 1319 of this title.

(*o*) Public availability of permits and permit applications

A copy of each permit application and each permit issued under this section shall be available to the public. Such permit application or portion thereof, shall further be available on request for the purpose of reproduction.

(p) Compliance

Compliance with a permit issued pursuant to this section, including any activity carried out pursuant to a general permit issued under this section, shall be deemed compliance, for purposes of sections 1319 and 1365 of this title, with sections 1311, 1317, and 1343 of this title.

(q) Minimization of duplication, needless paperwork, and delays in issuance; agreements

Not later than the one-hundred-eightieth day after December 27, 1977, the Secretary shall enter into agreements with the Administrator, the Secretaries of the Departments of Agriculture, Commerce, Interior, and Transportation, and the heads of other appropriate Federal agencies to minimize, to the maximum extent practicable, duplication, needless paperwork, and delays in the issuance of permits under this section. Such agreements shall be developed to assure that, to the maximum extent practicable, a decision with respect to an application for a permit under subsection (a) of this section will be made not later than the ninetieth day after the date the notice for such application is published under subsection (a) of this section.

(r) Federal projects specifically authorized by Congress

The discharge of dredged or fill material as part of the construction of a Federal project specifically authorized by Congress, whether prior to or on or after December 27, 1977, is not prohibited by or otherwise subject to regulation under this section, or a State program approved under this section, or section 1311(a) or 1342 of this title (except for effluent standards or prohibitions under section 1317 of this title), if information on the effects of such discharge, including consideration of the guidelines developed under subsection (b)(1) of this section, is included in an environmental impact statement for such project pursuant to the National Environmental Policy Act of 1969 [42 U.S.C.A. § 4321 et seq.] and such environmental impact statement has been submitted to Congress before the actual discharge of dredged or fill material in connection with the construction of such project and prior to either authorization of such project or an appropriation of funds for such construction.

(s) Violation of permits

(1) Whenever on the basis of any information available to him the Secretary finds that any person is in violation of any condition or limitation set forth in a permit issued by the Secretary under this section, the Secretary shall issue an order requiring such person to comply with such condition or limitation, or the Secretary shall bring a civil action in accordance with paragraph (3) of this subsection.

(2) A copy of any order issued under this subsection shall be sent immediately by the Secretary to the State in which the violation occurs and other affected States. Any order issued under this subsection shall be by personal service and shall state with reasonable specificity the nature of the violation, specify a time for compliance, not to exceed thirty days, which the Secretary determines is reasonable, taking into account the seriousness of the violation and any good faith efforts to comply with applicable requirements. In any case in which an order under this subsection is issued to a corporation, a copy of such order shall be served on any appropriate corporate officers.

(3) The Secretary is authorized to commence a civil action for appropriate relief, including a permanent or temporary injunction for any violation for which he is authorized to issue a compliance order under paragraph (1) of this subsection. Any action under this paragraph may be brought in the district court of the United States for the district in which the defendant is located or resides or is doing business, and such court shall have jurisdiction to restrain such violation and to require compliance. Notice of the commencement of such acton[1] shall be given immediately to the appropriate State.

(4) Any person who violates any condition or limitation in a permit issued by the Secretary under this section, and any person who violates any order issued by the Secretary under paragraph (1) of this subsection, shall be subject to a civil penalty not to exceed $25,000 per day for each violation. In determining the amount of a civil penalty the court shall consider the seriousness of the violation or violations, the economic benefit (if any) resulting from the violation, any history of such violations, any good-faith efforts to comply with the applicable requirements, the economic impact of the penalty on the violator, and such other matters as justice may require.

(t) Navigable waters within State jurisdiction

Nothing in this section shall preclude or deny the right of any State or interstate agency to control the discharge of dredged or fill material in any portion of the navigable waters within the jurisdiction of such State, including any activity of any Federal agency, and each such agency shall comply with such State or interstate requirements both substantive and procedural to control the discharge of dredged or fill material to the same extent that any person is subject to such requirements. This section shall not be construed as affecting or impairing the authority of the Secretary to maintain navigation.

(June 30, 1948, c. 758, Title IV, § 404, as added Oct. 18, 1972, Pub.L. 92–500, § 2, 86 Stat. 884, and amended Dec. 27, 1977, Pub.L. 95–217, § 67(a), (b), 91 Stat. 1600; Feb. 4, 1987, Pub.L. 100–4, Title III, § 313(d), 101 Stat. 45.)

[1] So in original. Probably should read "action".

CROSS REFERENCES

Areawide waste treatment management, compliance with guidelines established under this section, see section 1288 of this title.
Definition of "federally permitted release", see section 9601 of Title 42, The Public Health and Welfare.
Enforcement of permit provisions, see section 1319 of this title.
Grant to State for reasonable cost of administering an approved program under this section, see section 1285 of this title.
Illegality of pollutant discharges except as in compliance with this section, see section 1311 of this title.
Permits for discharge of pollutants, see section 1342 of this title.
Records and reports, see section 1318 of this title.
State management of permit program, see section 1254 of this title.

CODE OF FEDERAL REGULATIONS

Enforcement, supervision and inspection, see 33 CFR 326.1 et seq.
General regulatory policies, see 33 CFR 320.1 et seq.
Nationwide permits, see 33 CFR 330.1 et seq.
Permits for discharges of dredged or fill material into waters of the United States, see 33 CFR 323.1 et seq.
Procedures applicable to dredged and fill material, see 40 CFR 230.1 et seq., 231.1 et seq.
Processing of Department of the Army permits, see 33 CFR 325.1 et seq.
Public hearings, see 33 CFR 327.1 et seq.
State program transfer regulations, see 40 CFR 233.1 et seq.

LAW REVIEW COMMENTARIES

Comprehensive Wetlands Conservation and Management Act of 1991: A restructuring of section 404 that affords inadequate protection for clerical wetlands. Dennis Collins Swords, 53 La.L.Rev. 163 (1992).

Damming agricultural drainage: The effect of wetland preservation and federal regulation on agricultural drainage in Minnesota. Mark J. Hanson, 13 Wm.Mitchell L.Rev. 135 (1987).

Florida's assumption of federal dredge-and-fill jurisdiction. Martin R. Dix and Scott Denson, 67 Fla.B.J. 56 (April 1993).

Navigating through the Wetlands Act. Marsha Wolf and Lewis Goldshore, 120 N.J.L.J. 645 (1987).

Regulation of batture pollution and ecology. Stan Millan, 33 Loyola (La.) L.Rev. 921 (1988).

Section 404(f) of the Clean Water Act: Trench warfare over maintenance of agricultural drainage ditches. Benjamin H. Grumbles, 17 Wm.Mitchell L.Rev. 1021 (1991).

Section 404 of the Clean Water Act—permits for placement of solid fill—judicial review. Peter L. Koff, Laurie Burt and Catherine L. Farrell, 29 Ann.Surv.Mass.L. 354 (1982).

The Clean Water Act—More Section 404: The Supreme Court gets its feet wet. 65 Boston U.L.Rev. 995 (1985).

Wetlands and agricultural: Environmental regulation and the limits of private property. Gerald Torres, 34 U.Kan.L.Rev. 539 (1986).

LIBRARY REFERENCES

Health and Environment ⚷25.7(13).
C.J.S. Health and Environment § 107 et seq.

§ 1345. Disposal or use of sewage sludge [FWPCA § 405]

(a) Permit

Notwithstanding any other provision of this chapter or of any other law, in any case where the disposal of sewage sludge resulting from the operation of a treatment works as defined in section 1292 of this title (including the removal of in-place sewage sludge from one location and its deposit at another location) would result in any pollutant from such sewage sludge entering the navigable waters, such disposal is prohibited except in accordance with a permit issued by the Administrator under section 1342 of this title.

(b) Issuance of permit; regulations

The Administrator shall issue regulations governing the issuance of permits for the disposal of sewage sludge subject to subsection (a) of this section and section 1342 of this title. Such regulations shall require the application to such disposal of each criterion, factor, procedure, and requirement applicable to a permit issued under section 1342 of this title.

(c) State permit program

Each State desiring to administer its own permit program for disposal of sewage sludge subject to subsection (a) of this section within its jurisdiction may do so in accordance with section 1342 of this title.

(d) Regulations

(1) Regulations

The Administrator, after consultation with appropriate Federal and State agencies and other interested persons, shall develop and publish, within one year after December 27, 1977, and from time to time thereafter, regulations providing guidelines for the disposal of sludge and the utilization of sludge for various purposes. Such regulations shall—

(A) identify uses for sludge, including disposal;

(B) specify factors to be taken into account in determining the measures and practices applicable to each such use or disposal (including publication of information on costs);

(C) identify concentrations of pollutants which interfere with each such use or disposal.

The Administrator is authorized to revise any regulation issued under this subsection.

(2) Identification and regulation of toxic pollutants

(A) On basis of available information

(i) Proposed regulations

Not later than November 30, 1986,[1] the Administrator shall identify those toxic pollutants which, on the basis of available information on their toxicity, persistence, concentration, mobility, or potential for exposure, may be present in sewage sludge in concentrations which may adversely affect public health or the environment, and propose regulations specifying acceptable management practices for sewage sludge containing each such toxic pollutant and establishing numerical limitations for each such pollutant for each use identified under paragraph (1)(A).

(ii) Final regulations

Not later than August 31, 1987, and after opportunity for public hearing, the Administrator shall promulgate the regulations required by subparagraph (A)(i).

(B) Others

(i) Proposed regulations

Not later than July 31, 1987, the Administrator shall identify those toxic pollutants not identified under subparagraph (A)(i) which may be present in sewage sludge in concentrations which may adversely affect public health or the environment, and propose regulations specifying acceptable management practices for sewage sludge containing each such toxic pollutant and establishing numerical limitations for each pollutant for each such use identified under paragraph (1)(A).

(ii) Final regulations

Not later than June 15, 1988, the Administrator shall promulgate the regulations required by subparagraph (B)(i).

(C) Review

From time to time, but not less often than every 2 years, the Administrator shall review the regulations promulgated under this paragraph for the purpose of identifying additional toxic pollutants and promulgating regulations for such pollutants consistent with the requirements of this paragraph.

(D) Minimum standards; compliance date

The management practices and numerical criteria established under subparagraphs (A), (B), and (C) shall be adequate to protect public health and the environment from any reasonably anticipated adverse effects of each pollutant. Such regulations shall require compliance as expeditiously as practicable but in no case later than 12 months after their publication, unless such regulations require the construction of new pollution control facilities, in which case the regulations shall require compliance as expeditiously as practicable but in no case later than two years from the date of their publication.

(3) Alternative standards

For purposes of this subsection, if, in the judgment of the Administrator, it is not feasible to prescribe or enforce a numerical limitation for a pollutant identified under paragraph (2), the Administrator may instead promulgate a design, equipment, management practice, or operational standard, or combination thereof, which in the Administrator's judgment is adequate to protect public health and the environment from any reasonably anticipated adverse effects of such pollutant. In the event the Administrator promulgates a design or equipment standard under this subsection, the Administrator shall include as part of such standard such requirements as will assure the proper operation and maintenance of any such element of design or equipment.

(4) Conditions on permits

Prior to the promulgation of the regulations required by paragraph (2), the Administrator shall impose conditions in permits issued to publicly owned treatment works under section 1342 of this title or take such other measures as the Administrator deems appropriate to protect public health and the environment from any adverse effects which may occur from toxic pollutants in sewage sludge.

(5) Limitation on statutory construction

Nothing in this section is intended to waive more stringent requirements established by this chapter or any other law.

(e) Manner of sludge disposal

The determination of the manner of disposal or use of sludge is a local determination, except that it shall be unlawful for any person to dispose of sludge from a publicly owned treatment works or any other treatment works treating domestic sewage for any use for which regulations have been established pursuant to subsection (d) of this section, except in accordance with such regulations.

(f) Implementation of regulations

(1) Through section 1342 permits

Any permit issued under section 1342 of this title to a publicly owned treatment works or any other treatment works treating domestic sewage shall include requirements for the use and disposal of sludge that implement the regulations established pursuant to subsection (d) of this section, unless such requirements have been included in a permit issued under the appropriate provisions of subtitle C of the Solid Waste Disposal Act [42 U.S.C.A. § 6921 et seq.], part C of the Safe Drinking Water Act [42 U.S.C.A. § 300h et seq.], the Marine Protection, Research, and Sanctuaries Act of 1972 [33 U.S.C.A. § 1401 et seq.], or the Clean Air Act [42 U.S.C.A. § 7401 et seq.], or under State permit programs approved by the Administrator, where the Administrator determines that such programs assure compliance with any applicable requirements of this section. Not later than December 15, 1986,[2] the Administrator shall promulgate procedures for approval of State programs pursuant to this paragraph.

(2) Through other permits

In the case of a treatment works described in paragraph (1) that is not subject to section 1342 of this title and to which none of the other above listed permit programs nor approved State permit authority apply, the Administrator may issue a permit to such treatment works solely to impose requirements for the use and disposal of sludge that implement the regulations established pursuant to subsection (d) of this section. The Administrator shall include in the permit appropriate requirements to assure compliance with the regulations established pursuant to subsection (d) of this section. The Administrator shall establish procedures for issuing permits pursuant to this paragraph.

(g) Studies and projects

(1) Grant program; information gathering

The Administrator is authorized to conduct or initiate scientific studies, demonstration projects, and public information and education projects which are designed to promote the safe and beneficial management or use of sewage sludge for such purposes as aiding the restoration of abandoned mine sites, conditioning soil for parks and recreation areas, agricultural and horticultural uses, and other beneficial purposes. For the purposes of carrying out this subsection, the Administrator may make grants to State water pollution control agencies, other public or nonprofit agencies, institutions, organizations, and individuals. In cooperation with other Federal departments and agencies, other public and private agencies, institutions, and organizations, the Administrator is authorized to collect and disseminate information pertaining to the safe and beneficial use of sewage sludge.

(2) Authorization of appropriations

For the purposes of carrying out the scientific studies, demonstration projects, and public information and education projects authorized in this section, there is authorized to be appropriated for fiscal years beginning after September 30, 1986, not to exceed $5,000,000.

(June 30, 1948, c. 758, Title IV, § 405, as added Oct. 18, 1972, Pub.L. 92–500, § 2, 86 Stat. 884, and amended Dec. 27, 1977, Pub.L. 95–217, §§ 54(d), 68, 91 Stat. 1591, 1606; Feb. 4, 1987, Pub.L. 100–4, Title IV, § 406(a), (b), (c), (f), 101 Stat. 71, 72, 74.)

1 So in original. Subsec. (d)(2) was enacted by Pub.L. 100–4, which was approved Feb. 4, 1987.

2 So in original. Subsec. (f) was enacted by Pub.L. 100–4, which was approved Feb. 4, 1987.

CROSS REFERENCES

Enforcement provisions, see section 1319 of this title.
Pretreatment standards, see section 1317 of this title.

CODE OF FEDERAL REGULATIONS

Classification of solid waste disposal facilities and practices, see 40 CFR 257.1 et seq.
Environmental Protection Agency administered permit programs: the National Pollutant Discharge Elimination System, see 40 CFR 122.1 et seq.
General pretreatment regulations for existing and new sources of pollution, see 40 CFR 403.1 et seq.
State program requirements, see 40 CFR 123.1 et seq.

LAW REVIEW COMMENTARIES

Regulation of batture pollution and ecology. Stan Millan, 33 Loyola (La.) L.Rev. 921 (1988).

LIBRARY REFERENCES

Health and Environment ⟹25.7(13).
C.J.S. Health and Environment § 107 et seq.

SUBCHAPTER V—GENERAL PROVISIONS

§ 1361. Administration [FWPCA § 501]

(a) Authority of Administrator to prescribe regulations

The Administrator is authorized to prescribe such regulations as are necessary to carry out his functions under this chapter.

(b) Utilization of other agency officers and employees

The Administrator, with the consent of the head of any other agency of the United States, may utilize such officers and employees of such agency as may be found necessary to assist in carrying out the purposes of this chapter.

(c) Recordkeeping

Each recipient of financial assistance under this chapter shall keep such records as the Administrator shall prescribe, including records which fully disclose the amount and disposition by such recipient of the proceeds of such assistance, the total cost of the project or undertaking in connection with which such assistance is given or used, and the amount of that portion of the cost of the project or undertaking supplied by other sources, and such other records as will facilitate effective audit.

(d) Audit

The Administrator and the Comptroller General of the United States, or any of their duly authorized representatives, shall have access, for the purpose of audit and examination, to any books, documents, papers, and records of the recipients that are pertinent to the grants received under this chapter. For the purpose of carrying out audits and examinations with respect to recipients of Federal assistance under this chapter, the Administrator is authorized to enter into noncompetitive procurement contracts with independent State audit organizations, consistent with chapter 75 of Title 31. Such contracts may only be entered into to the extent and in such amounts as may be provided in advance in appropriation Acts.

(e) Awards for outstanding technological achievement or innovative processes, methods, or devices in waste treatment and pollution abatement programs

(1) It is the purpose of this subsection to authorize a program which will provide official recognition by the United States Government to those industrial organizations and political subdivisions of States which during the preceding year demonstrated an outstanding technological achievement or an innovative process, method, or device in their waste treatment and pollution abatement programs. The Administrator shall, in consultation with the appropriate State water pollution control agencies, establish regulations under which such recognition may be applied for and granted, except that no applicant shall be eligible for an award under this subsection if such applicant is not in total compliance with all applicable water quality requirements under this chapter, or otherwise does not have a satisfactory record with respect to environmental quality.

(2) The Administrator shall award a certificate or plaque of suitable design to each industrial organization or political subdivision which qualifies for such recognition under regulations established under this subsection.

(3) The President of the United States, the Governor of the appropriate State, the Speaker of the House of Representatives, and the President pro tempore of the Senate shall be notified of the award by the Administrator and the awarding of such recognition shall be published in the Federal Register.

(f) Detail of Environmental Protection Agency personnel to State water pollution control agencies

Upon the request of a State water pollution control agency, personnel of the Environmental Protection Agency may be detailed to such agency for the purpose of carrying out the provisions of this chapter.

(June 30, 1948, c. 758, Title V, § 501, as added Oct. 18, 1972, Pub.L. 92–500, § 2, 86 Stat. 885, and amended Feb. 4, 1987, Pub.L. 100–4, Title V, § 501, 101 Stat. 75.)

CODE OF FEDERAL REGULATIONS

Civil penalties for violation of oil pollution prevention regulations, see 40 CFR 114.1 et seq.
Criteria and standards for the National Pollutant Discharge Elimination System, see 40 CFR 125.1 et seq.
Designation of substances, reportable quantities, and notification requirements for release of substances, see 40 CFR 302.1 et seq.
Effluent guidelines and standards, see 40 CFR Chap. I, Subch. N.
Guidelines establishing test procedures for analysis of pollutants, see 40 CFR 136.1 et seq.
Guidelines for specification of disposal sites for dredged or fill material, see 40 CFR 230.1 et seq.
Judicial review under Environmental Protection Agency administered statutes, see 40 CFR 23.1 et seq.
Oil pollution prevention, see 40 CFR 112.1 et seq.
Public information, see 40 CFR 2.100 et seq.
Secondary treatment regulation, see 40 CFR 133.100 et seq.
State and local assistance, see 40 CFR 35.001 et seq.
Toxic pollutant effluent standards, see 40 CFR 129.1 et seq.

LAW REVIEW COMMENTARIES

From elephants to mice: The development of EBMUD's program to control small source wastewater discharges. Raoul Stewardson, 20 Ecology L.Q. 441 (1993).

LIBRARY REFERENCES

Health and Environment ⟹25.7(3).
C.J.S. Health and Environment § 106.

§ 1362. Definitions [FWPCA § 502]

Except as otherwise specifically provided, when used in this chapter:

(1) The term "State water pollution control agency" means the State agency designated by the Governor having responsibility for enforcing State laws relating to the abatement of pollution.

(2) The term "interstate agency" means an agency of two or more States established by or pursuant to an agreement or compact approved by the Congress, or any other agency of two or more States, having substantial powers or duties pertaining to the control of

pollution as determined and approved by the Administrator.

(3) The term "State" means a State, the District of Columbia, the Commonwealth of Puerto Rico, the Virgin Islands, Guam, American Samoa, the Commonwealth of the Northern Mariana Islands, and the Trust Territory of the Pacific Islands.

(4) The term "municipality" means a city, town, borough, county, parish, district, association, or other public body created by or pursuant to State law and having jurisdiction over disposal of sewage, industrial wastes, or other wastes, or an Indian tribe or an authorized Indian tribal organization, or a designated and approved management agency under section 1288 of this title.

(5) The term "person" means an individual, corporation, partnership, association, State, municipality, commission, or political subdivision of a State, or any interstate body.

(6) The term "pollutant" means dredged spoil, solid waste, incinerator residue, sewage, garbage, sewage sludge, munitions, chemical wastes, biological materials, radioactive materials, heat, wrecked or discarded equipment, rock, sand, cellar dirt and industrial, municipal, and agricultural waste discharged into water. This term does not mean (A) "sewage from vessels or a discharge incidental to the normal operation of a vessel of the Armed Forces" within the meaning of section 1322 of this title; or (B) water, gas, or other material which is injected into a well to facilitate production of oil or gas, or water derived in association with oil or gas production and disposed of in a well, if the well used either to facilitate production or for disposal purposes is approved by authority of the State in which the well is located, and if such State determines that such injection or disposal will not result in the degradation of ground or surface water resources.

(7) The term "navigable waters" means the waters of the United States, including the territorial seas.

(8) The term "territorial seas" means the belt of the seas measured from the line of ordinary low water along that portion of the coast which is in direct contact with the open sea and the line marking the seaward limit of inland waters, and extending seaward a distance of three miles.

(9) The term "contiguous zone" means the entire zone established or to be established by the United States under article 24 of the Convention of the Territorial Sea and the Contiguous Zone.

(10) The term "ocean" means any portion of the high seas beyond the contiguous zone.

(11) The term "effluent limitation" means any restriction established by a State or the Administrator on quantities, rates, and concentrations of chemical, physical, biological, and other constituents which are discharged from point sources into navigable waters, the waters of the contiguous zone, or the ocean, including schedules of compliance.

(12) The term "discharge of a pollutant" and the term "discharge of pollutants" each means (A) any addition of any pollutant to navigable waters from any point source, (B) any addition of any pollutant to the waters of the contiguous zone or the ocean from any point source other than a vessel or other floating craft.

(13) The term "toxic pollutant" means those pollutants, or combinations of pollutants, including disease-causing agents, which after discharge and upon exposure, ingestion, inhalation or assimilation into any organism, either directly from the environment or indirectly by ingestion through food chains, will, on the basis of information available to the Administrator, cause death, disease, behavioral abnormalities, cancer, genetic mutations, physiological malfunctions (including malfunctions in reproduction) or physical deformations, in such organisms or their offspring.

(14) The term "point source" means any discernible, confined and discrete conveyance, including but not limited to any pipe, ditch, channel, tunnel, conduit, well, discrete fissure, container, rolling stock, concentrated animal feeding operation, or vessel or other floating craft, from which pollutants are or may be discharged. This term does not include agricultural stormwater discharges and return flows from irrigated agriculture.

(15) The term "biological monitoring" shall mean the determination of the effects on aquatic life, including accumulation of pollutants in tissue, in receiving waters due to the discharge of pollutants (A) by techniques and procedures, including sampling of organisms representative of appropriate levels of the food chain appropriate to the volume and the physical, chemical, and biological characteristics of the effluent, and (B) at appropriate frequencies and locations.

(16) The term "discharge" when used without qualification includes a discharge of a pollutant, and a discharge of pollutants.

(17) The term "schedule of compliance" means a schedule of remedial measures including an enforceable sequence of actions or operations leading to compliance with an effluent limitation, other limitation, prohibition, or standard.

(18) The term "industrial user" means those industries identified in the Standard Industrial Classification Manual, Bureau of the Budget, 1967, as amended and supplemented, under the category of "Division D—Manufacturing" and such other classes of significant waste producers as, by regulation, the Administrator deems appropriate.

(19) The term "pollution" means the man-made or man-induced alteration of the chemical, physical, biological, and radiological integrity of water.

(20) The term "medical waste" means isolation wastes; infectious agents; human blood and blood products; pathological wastes; sharps; body parts; contaminated bedding; surgical wastes and potentially contaminated laboratory wastes; dialysis wastes; and such additional medical items as the Administrator shall prescribe by regulation.

(June 30, 1948, c. 758, Title V, § 502, as added Oct. 18, 1972, Pub.L. 92–500, § 2, 86 Stat. 886, and amended Dec. 27, 1977, Pub.L. 95–217, § 33(b), 91 Stat. 1577; Feb. 4, 1987, Pub.L. 100–4, Title V, §§ 502(a), 503, 101 Stat. 75; Nov. 18, 1988, Pub.L. 100–688, Title III, § 3202(a), 102 Stat. 4154; Feb. 10, 1996, Pub.L. 104–106, Title III, § 325(c)(3), 110 Stat. 259.)

CROSS REFERENCES

Definition of "person" for purposes of—
  Criminal penalties, see section 1319 of this title.
  Violation of permits, see section 1344 of this title.
Definition of "territorial sea" and "contiguous zone" see section 9601 of Title 42, The Public Health and Welfare.
Ocean thermal energy conversion facility or plantship not deemed vessel for purposes of this section, see section 9117 of Title 42.
State certifying authority, amortization of pollution control facilities, see section 169 of Title 26, Internal Revenue Code.
Vessel or other floating craft engaged in commercial recovery or exploration as vessel under this section, see section 1419 of Title 30, Mineral Lands and Mining.

LAW REVIEW COMMENTARIES

Damming agricultural drainage: The effect of wetland preservation and federal regulation on agricultural drainage in Minnesota. Mark J. Hanson, 13 Wm.Mitchell L.Rev. 135 (1987).

Erosion of mens rea in environmental criminal prosecution. Ruth Ann Weidel, John R. Mayo and F. Michael Zachara, 21 Seton Hall L.Rev. 1125 (1991).

Federal regulation of environmental releases of genetically manipulated microorganisms. Edward L. Korwek and Peter L. de la Cruz (1985) 11 Rutgers Computer & Tech.Law J. 301.

Listing and debarment: The Stealth bombers. Edward L. Grimsley, 5 S.C.Law. 22 (Nov.–Dec. 1993).

§ 1363. Water Pollution Control Advisory Board [FWPCA § 503]

(a) Establishment; composition; terms of office

(1) There is hereby established in the Environmental Protection Agency a Water Pollution Control Advisory Board, composed of the Administrator or his designee, who shall be Chairman, and nine members appointed by the President, none of whom shall be Federal officers or employees. The appointed members, having due regard for the purposes of this chapter, shall be selected from among representatives of various State, interstate, and local governmental agencies, of public or private interests contributing to, affected by, or concerned with pollution, and of other public and private agencies, organizations, or groups demonstrating an active interest in the field of pollution prevention and control, as well as other individuals who are expert in this field.

(2)(A) Each member appointed by the President shall hold office for a term of three years, except that (i) any member appointed to fill a vacancy occurring prior to the expiration of the term for which his predecessor was appointed shall be appointed for the remainder of such term, and (ii) the terms of office of the members first taking office after June 30, 1956, shall expire as follows: three at the end of one year after such date, three at the end of two years after such date, and three at the end of three years after such date, as designated by the President at the time of appointment, and (iii) the term of any member under the preceding provisions shall be extended until the date on which his successor's appointment is effective. None of the members appointed by the President shall be eligible for reappointment within one year after the end of his preceding term.

(B) The members of the Board who are not officers or employees of the United States, while attending conferences or meetings of the Board or while serving at the request of the Administrator, shall be entitled to receive compensation at a rate to be fixed by the Administrator, but not exceeding $100 per diem, including travel-time, and while away from their homes or regular places of business they may be allowed travel expenses, including per diem in lieu of subsistence, as authorized by law for persons in the Government service employed intermittently.

(b) Functions

The Board shall advise, consult with, and make recommendations to the Administrator on matters of policy relating to the activities and functions of the Administrator under this chapter.

(c) Clerical and technical assistance

Such clerical and technical assistance as may be necessary to discharge the duties of the Board shall be provided from the personnel of the Environmental Protection Agency.

(June 30, 1948, c. 758, Title V, § 503, as added Oct. 18, 1972, Pub.L. 92–500, § 2, 86 Stat. 887.)

LIBRARY REFERENCES

Health and Environment ⚷25.7(3).
C.J.S. Health and Environment § 106.

§ 1364. Emergency powers [FWPCA § 504]

(a) Emergency powers

Notwithstanding any other provision of this chapter, the Administrator upon receipt of evidence that a pollution source or combination of sources is presenting an imminent and substantial endangerment to the health of persons or to the welfare of persons where such endangerment is to the livelihood of such persons, such as inability to market shellfish, may bring suit on behalf of the United States in the appropriate district court to immediately restrain any person causing or contributing to the alleged pollution to stop the discharge of pollutants causing or contributing to such pollution or to take such other action as may be necessary.

(b) Repealed. Pub.L. 96–510, title III, § 304(a), Dec. 11, 1980, 94 Stat. 2809

(June 30, 1948, c. 758, Title V, § 504, as added Oct. 18, 1972, Pub.L. 92–500, § 2, 86 Stat. 888, and amended Dec. 27, 1977, Pub.L. 95–217, § 69, 91 Stat. 1607; Dec. 11, 1980, Pub.L. 96–510, Title III, § 304(a), 94 Stat. 2809.)

CROSS REFERENCES

Guidelines for using imminent hazard, enforcement, and emergency response authorities, see section 9606 of Title 42, The Public Health and Welfare.

Prohibition of grants to states not providing as part of their program authority comparable to that in this section, see section 1256 of this title.

Records and reports, see section 1318 of this title.

Transfer of funds appropriated under this section, see section 9654 of Title 42, The Public Health and Welfare.

LAW REVIEW COMMENTARIES

Groundwater contamination claims in Connecticut. Dean M. Cordiano and Lynn Anne Glover, 60 Conn.B.J. 167 (1986).

§ 1365. Citizen suits [FWPCA § 505]

(a) Authorization; jurisdiction

Except as provided in subsection (b) of this section and section 1319(g)(6) of this title, any citizen may commence a civil action on his own behalf—

(1) against any person (including (i) the United States, and (ii) any other governmental instrumentality or agency to the extent permitted by the eleventh amendment to the Constitution) who is alleged to be in violation of (A) an effluent standard or limitation under this chapter or (B) an order issued by the Administrator or a State with respect to such a standard or limitation, or

(2) against the Administrator where there is alleged a failure of the Administrator to perform any act or duty under this chapter which is not discretionary with the Administrator.

The district courts shall have jurisdiction, without regard to the amount in controversy or the citizenship of the parties, to enforce such an effluent standard or limitation, or such an order, or to order the Administrator to perform such act or duty, as the case may be, and to apply any appropriate civil penalties under section 1319(d) of this title.

(b) Notice

No action may be commenced—

(1) under subsection (a)(1) of this section—

(A) prior to sixty days after the plaintiff has given notice of the alleged violation (i) to the Administrator, (ii) to the State in which the alleged violation occurs, and (iii) to any alleged violator of the standard, limitation, or order, or

(B) if the Administrator or State has commenced and is diligently prosecuting a civil or criminal action in a court of the United States, or a State to require compliance with the standard, limitation, or order, but in any such action in a court of the United States any citizen may intervene as a matter of right.

(2) under subsection (a)(2) of this section prior to sixty days after the plaintiff has given notice of such action to the Administrator,

except that such action may be brought immediately after such notification in the case of an action under this section respecting a violation of sections 1316 and 1317(a) of this title. Notice under this subsection shall be given in such manner as the Administrator shall prescribe by regulation.

(c) Venue; intervention by Administrator; United States interests protected

(1) Any action respecting a violation by a discharge source of an effluent standard or limitation or an order respecting such standard or limitation may be brought under this section only in the judicial district in which such source is located.

(2) In such action under this section, the Administrator, if not a party, may intervene as a matter of right.

(3) Protection of interests of United States

Whenever any action is brought under this section in a court of the United States, the plaintiff shall serve a copy of the complaint on the Attorney General and the Administrator. No consent judgment shall be entered in an action in which the United States is not a party prior to 45 days following the receipt of a copy of the proposed consent judgment by the Attorney General and the Administrator.

(d) Litigation costs

The court, in issuing any final order in any action brought pursuant to this section, may award costs of litigation (including reasonable attorney and expert witness fees) to any prevailing or substantially prevailing party, whenever the court determines such award is appropriate. The court may, if a temporary restraining order or preliminary injunction is sought, require the filing of a bond or equivalent security in accordance with the Federal Rules of Civil Procedure.

(e) Statutory or common law rights not restricted

Nothing in this section shall restrict any right which any person (or class of persons) may have under any statute or common law to seek enforcement of any effluent standard or limitation or to seek any other relief (including relief against the Administrator or a State agency).

(f) Effluent standard or limitation

For purposes of this section, the term "effluent standard or limitation under this chapter" means (1) effective July 1, 1973, an unlawful act under subsection (a) of section 1311 of this title; (2) an effluent limitation or other limitation under section 1311 or 1312 of this title; (3) standard of performance under section 1316 of this title; (4) prohibition, effluent standard or pretreatment standards under section 1317 of this title; (5) certification under section 1341 of this title; (6) a permit or condition thereof issued under section 1342 of this title, which is in effect under this chapter (including a requirement applicable by reason of section 1323 of this title); or (7) a regulation under section 1345(d) of this title,.[1]

(g) Citizen

For the purposes of this section the term "citizen" means a person or persons having an interest which is or may be adversely affected.

(h) Civil action by State Governors

A Governor of a State may commence a civil action under subsection (a) of this section, without regard to the limitations of subsection (b) of this section, against the Administrator where there is alleged a failure of the Administrator to enforce an effluent standard or limitation under this chapter the violation of which is occurring in another State and is causing an adverse effect on the public health or welfare in his State, or is causing a violation of any water quality requirement in his State.

(June 30, 1948, c. 758, Title V, § 505, as added Oct. 18, 1972, Pub.L. 92–500, § 2, 86 Stat. 888, and amended Feb. 4, 1987, Pub.L. 100–4, Title III, § 314(c), Title IV, § 406(d)(2), Title V, §§ 504, 505(c), 101 Stat. 49, 73, 75, 76.)

[1] So in original.

CROSS REFERENCES

Compliance with permit as compliance, for purposes of this section, with other provisions of this chapter, see sections 1342 and 1344 of this title.

West's Federal Practice Manual

Attorney's fees, see § 7683.27.
Intervention as of right, see § 8839.

CODE OF FEDERAL REGULATIONS

Notice prior to suit, see 40 CFR 135.1 et seq.

LAW REVIEW COMMENTARIES

Citizen-suit provisions under the Federal Water Pollution Control Act: Are remedies available for past violations? Comment, 19 Conn. L.Rev. 589 (1987).

Citizen suits under the Clean Water Act. 38 Rutgers L.Rev. 813 (1986).

Environmental Law/Annual survey of significant developments. Thomas J. Elliott, 58 Pa.B.A.Q. 107 (1987).

From elephants to mice: The development of EBMUD's program to control small source wastewater discharges. Raoul Stewardson, 20 Ecology L.Q. 441 (1993).

Interpreting the citizen suit provision of the Clean Water Act. Note, 37 Case W.Res.L.Rev. 515 (1986–87).

Note, citizen suits and civil penalties under the Clean Water Act. 85 Mich.L.Rev. 1656 (1987).

Note, effective assistance of counsel: *Strickland* and the Illinois Death Penalty Statute. U.Ill.L.Rev. 131 (1987).

Oklahoma v. EPA Does the Clean Water Act provide an effective remedy to downstream states or is there still room left for federal common law. Maria V. Maurrasse, 45 U.Miami L.Rev. 1037 (1991).

Preemption of state common law remedies by federal environmental statutes: *International Paper Co. v. Ouellette*. Randolph L. Hill, 14 Ecology L.Q. 541 (1987).

Warrior and the Druid—the DOD and environmental law. Michael Donnelly and James G. Van Ness, 33 Fed.Bar News 37 (1986).

United States Supreme Court

Inclusion in citizen suit sections of both Clean Water Act (CWA) and Resource Conservation and Recovery Act (RCRA) of United States as "person" went only to clauses subjecting government to suit, and broader waiver could not be inferred; authorization of district courts to impose punitive fines under Acts' civil penalties sections excluded United States from among "persons" who may be fined, see United States Department of Energy v. Ohio, 1992, 112 S.Ct. 1627, 118 L.Ed.2d 255.

Law governing, action by state in federal court alleging public nuisance by water pollution, see Illinois v. City of Milwaukee, 1972, 92 S.Ct. 1385, 406 U.S. 91, 31 L.Ed.2d 712.

§ 1366. Appearance [FWPCA § 506]

The Administrator shall request the Attorney General to appear and represent the United States in any civil or criminal action instituted under this chapter to which the Administrator is a party. Unless the Attorney General notifies the Administrator within a reasonable time, that he will appear in a civil action, attorneys who are officers or employees of the Environmental Protection Agency shall appear and represent the United States in such action.

(June 30, 1948, c. 758, Title V, § 506, as added Oct. 18, 1972, Pub.L. 92–500, § 2, 86 Stat. 889.)

LIBRARY REFERENCES

Attorney General ⚷6.
C.J.S. Attorney General § 7 et seq.

§ 1367. Employee protection [FWPCA § 507]

(a) Discrimination against persons filing, instituting, or testifying in proceedings under this chapter prohibited

No person shall fire, or in any other way discriminate against, or cause to be fired or discriminated against, any employee or any authorized representative of employees by reason of the fact that such employee or representative has filed, instituted, or caused to be filed or instituted any proceeding under this chapter, or has testified or is about to testify in any proceeding resulting from the administration or enforcement of the provisions of this chapter.

(b) Application for review; investigation; hearing; review

Any employee or a representative of employees who believes that he has been fired or otherwise discriminated against by any person in violation of subsection (a) of this section may, within thirty days after such alleged violation occurs, apply to the Secretary of Labor for a review of such firing or alleged discrimination. A copy of the application shall be sent to such person who shall be the respondent. Upon receipt of such application, the Secretary of Labor shall cause such investigation to be made as he deems appropriate. Such investigation shall provide an opportunity for a public hearing at the request of any party to such review to enable the parties to present information relating to such alleged violation. The parties shall be given written notice of the time and place of the hearing at least five days prior to the hearing. Any such hearing shall be of record and shall be subject to section 554 of Title 5. Upon receiving the report of such investigation, the Secretary of Labor shall make findings of fact. If he finds that such violation did occur, he shall issue a decision, incorporating an order therein and his findings, requiring the party committing such violation to take such affirmative action to abate the violation as the Secretary of Labor deems appropriate, including, but not limited to, the rehiring or reinstatement of the employee or representative of employees to his former position with compensation. If he finds that there was no such violation, he shall issue an order denying the application. Such order issued by the Secretary of Labor under this subparagraph shall be subject to judicial review in the same manner as orders and decisions of the Administrator are subject to judicial review under this chapter.

(c) Costs and expenses

Whenever an order is issued under this section to abate such violation, at the request of the applicant, a sum equal to the aggregate amount of all costs and expenses (including the attorney's fees), as determined by the Secretary of Labor, to have been reasonably incurred by the applicant for, or in connection with, the institution and prosecution of such proceedings, shall be assessed against the person committing such violation.

(d) Deliberate violations by employee acting without direction from his employer or his agent

This section shall have no application to any employee who, acting without direction from his employer (or his agent) deliberately violates any prohibition of effluent limitation or other limitation under section 1311 or 1312 of this title, standards of performance under section 1316 of this title, effluent standard, prohibition or pretreatment standard under section 1317 of this title, or any other prohibition or limitation established under this chapter.

(e) Investigations of employment reductions

The Administrator shall conduct continuing evaluations of potential loss or shifts of employment which may result from the issuance of any effluent limitation or order under this chapter, including, where appropriate, investigating threatened plant closures or reductions in employment allegedly resulting from such limitation or order. Any employee who is discharged or laid-off, threatened with discharge or lay-off, or otherwise discriminated against by any person because of the alleged results of any effluent limitation or order issued under this chapter, or any representative of such employee, may request the Administrator to conduct a full investigation of the matter. The Administrator shall thereupon investigate the matter and, at the request of any party, shall hold public hearings on not less than five days notice, and shall at such hearings require the parties, including the employer involved, to present information relating to the actual or potential effect of such limitation or order on employment and on any alleged discharge, lay-off, or other discrimination and the detailed reasons or justification therefor. Any such hearing shall be of record and shall be subject to section 554 of Title 5. Upon receiving the report of such investigation, the Administrator shall make findings of fact as to the effect of such effluent limitation or order on employment and on the alleged discharge, lay-off, or discrimination and shall make such recommendations as he deems appropriate. Such report, findings, and recommendations shall be available to the public. Nothing in this subsection shall be construed to require or authorize the Administrator to modify or withdraw any effluent limitation or order issued under this chapter.

(June 30, 1948, c. 758, Title V, § 507, as added Oct. 18, 1972, Pub.L. 92–500, § 2, 86 Stat. 890.)

CROSS REFERENCES

Subpoena for carrying out this section, see section 1369 of this title.

CODE OF FEDERAL REGULATIONS

Complaint procedures, see 29 CFR 24.1 et seq.
Employee protection hearings, see 40 CFR 108.1 et seq.

LIBRARY REFERENCES

Labor Relations ⟹372.
C.J.S. Labor Relations § 356 et seq.

§ 1368. Federal procurement [FWPCA § 508]

(a) Contracts with violators prohibited

No Federal agency may enter into any contract with any person, who has been convicted of any offense under section 1319(c) of this title, for the procurement of goods, materials, and services if such contract is to be performed at any facility at which the violation which gave rise to such conviction occurred, and if such facility is owned, leased, or supervised by such person. The prohibition in the preceding sentence shall continue until the Administrator certifies that the condition giving rise to such conviction has been corrected.

(b) Notification of agencies

The Administrator shall establish procedures to provide all Federal agencies with the notification necessary for the purposes of subsection (a) of this section.

(c) Omitted

(d) Exemptions

The President may exempt any contract, loan, or grant from all or part of the provisions of this section where he determines such exemption is necessary in the paramount interest of the United States and he shall notify the Congress of such exemption.

(e) Annual report to Congress

The President shall annually report to the Congress on measures taken in compliance with the purpose and intent of this section, including, but not limited to, the progress and problems associated with such compliance.

(f) Contractor certification or contract clause in acquisition of commercial items

(1) No certification by a contractor, and no contract clause, may be required in the case of a contract for the acquisition of commercial items in order to implement a prohibition or requirement of this section or a prohibition or requirement issued in the implementation of this section.

(2) In paragraph (1), the term "commercial item" has the meaning given such term in section 403(12) of Title 41.

(June 30, 1948, c. 758, Title V, § 508, as added Oct. 18, 1972, Pub.L. 92–500, § 2, 86 Stat. 891, and amended Oct. 13, 1994, Pub.L. 103–355, Title VIII, § 8301(a), 108 Stat. 3396.)

CODE OF FEDERAL REGULATIONS

Procurement under assistance agreements, see 40 CFR 33.001 et seq.

LAW REVIEW COMMENTARIES

Listing and debarment: The Stealth bombers. Edward L. Grimsley, 5 S.C.Law. 22 (Nov.–Dec. 1993).

LIBRARY REFERENCES

Health and Environment ⟹25.7(22).
C.J.S. Health and Environment § 106 et seq.

§ 1369. Administrative procedure and judicial review [FWPCA § 509]

(a) Subpenas

(1) For purposes of obtaining information under section 1315 of this title, or carrying out section 1367(e) of this title, the Administrator may issue subpenas for the attendance and testimony of witnesses and the production of relevant papers, books, and documents, and he may administer oaths. Except for effluent data, upon a showing satisfactory to the Administrator that such papers, books, documents, or information or particular part thereof, if made public, would divulge trade secrets or secret processes, the Administrator shall consider such record, report, or information or particular portion thereof confidential in accordance with the purposes of section 1905 of title 18, except that such paper, book, document, or information may be disclosed to other officers, employees, or authorized representatives of the United States concerned with carrying out this chapter, or when relevant in any proceeding under this chapter. Witnesses summoned shall be paid the same fees and mileage that are paid witnesses in the courts of the United States. In case of contumacy or refusal to obey a subpena served upon any person under this subsection, the district court of the United States for any district in which such person is found or resides or transacts business, upon application by the United States and after notice to such person, shall have jurisdiction to issue an order requiring such person to appear and give testimony before the Administrator, to appear and produce papers, books, and documents before the Administrator, or both, and any failure to

obey such order of the court may be punished by such court as a contempt thereof.

(2) The district courts of the United States are authorized, upon application by the Administrator, to issue subpenas for attendance and testimony of witnesses and the production of relevant papers, books, and documents, for purposes of obtaining information under sections 1314(b) and (c) of this title. Any papers, books, documents, or other information or part thereof, obtained by reason of such a subpena shall be subject to the same requirements as are provided in paragraph (1) of this subsection.

(b) Review of Administrator's action; selection of court; fees

(1) Review of the Administrator's action (A) in promulgating any standard of performance under section 1316 of this title, (B) in making any determination pursuant to section 1316(b)(1)(C) of this title, (C) in promulgating any effluent standard, prohibition, or pretreatment standard under section 1317 of this title, (D) in making any determination as to a State permit program submitted under section 1342(b) of this title, (E) in approving or promulgating any effluent limitation or other limitation under section 1311, 1312, 1316, or 1345 of this title, (F) in issuing or denying any permit under section 1342 of this title, and (G) in promulgating any individual control strategy under section 1314(*l*) of this title, may be had by any interested person in the Circuit Court of Appeals of the United States for the Federal judicial district in which such person resides or transacts business which is directly affected by such action upon application by such person. Any such application shall be made within 120 days from the date of such determination, approval, promulgation, issuance or denial, or after such date only if such application is based solely on grounds which arose after such 120th day.

(2) Action of the Administrator with respect to which review could have been obtained under paragraph (1) of this subsection shall not be subject to judicial review in any civil or criminal proceeding for enforcement.

(3) Award of fees

In any judicial proceeding under this subsection, the court may award costs of litigation (including reasonable attorney and expert witness fees) to any prevailing or substantially prevailing party whenever it determines that such award is appropriate.

(c) Additional evidence

In any judicial proceeding brought under subsection (b) of this section in which review is sought of a determination under this chapter required to be made on the record after notice and opportunity for hearing, if any party applies to the court for leave to adduce additional evidence, and shows to the satisfaction of the court that such additional evidence is material and that there were reasonable grounds for the failure to adduce such evidence in the proceeding before the Administrator, the court may order such additional evidence (and evidence in rebuttal thereof) to be taken before the Administrator, in such manner and upon such terms and conditions as the court may deem proper. The Administrator may modify his findings as to the facts, or make new findings, by reason of the additional evidence so taken and he shall file such modified or new findings, and his recommendation, if any, for the modification or setting aside of his original determination, with the return of such additional evidence.

(June 30, 1948, c. 758, Title V, § 509, as added Oct. 18, 1972, Pub.L. 92–500, § 2, 86 Stat. 891, and amended Dec. 28, 1973, Pub.L. 93–207, § 1(6), 87 Stat. 906; Feb. 4, 1987, Pub.L. 100–4, Title III, § 308(b), Title IV, § 406(d)(3), Title V, § 505(a), (b), 101 Stat. 39, 73, 75; Jan. 8, 1988, Pub.L. 100–236, § 2, 101 Stat. 1732.)

CODE OF FEDERAL REGULATIONS

Judicial review under Environmental Protection Agency administered statutes, see 40 CFR 23.1 et seq.
Public information, see 40 CFR 2.100 et seq.

West's Federal Forms

Administrative subpoenas, enforcement of, see § 5901 et seq.

United States Supreme Court

Jurisdiction, court of appeals review of federal administrator's objection to state permit, see Crown Simpson Pulp Co. v. Costle, 1980, 100 S.Ct. 1093, 445 U.S. 193, 63 L.Ed.2d 312.

§ 1370. State authority [FWPCA § 510]

Except as expressly provided in this chapter, nothing in this chapter shall (1) preclude or deny the right of any State or political subdivision thereof or interstate agency to adopt or enforce (A) any standard or limitation respecting discharges of pollutants, or (B) any requirement respecting control or abatement of pollution; except that if an effluent limitation, or other limitation, effluent standard, prohibition, pretreatment standard, or standard of performance is in effect under this chapter, such State or political subdivision or interstate agency may not adopt or enforce any effluent limitation, or other limitation, effluent standard, prohibition, pretreatment standard, or standard of performance which is less stringent than the effluent limitation, or other limitation, effluent standard, prohibition, pretreatment standard, or standard of performance under this chapter; or (2) be construed as impairing or in any manner affecting any right or jurisdiction of the States with respect to the waters (including boundary waters) of such States.

(June 30, 1948, c. 758, Title V, § 510, as added Oct. 18, 1972, Pub.L. 92–500, § 2, 86 Stat. 893.)

CROSS REFERENCES

Timetable for achievement of effluent limitations, see section 1311 of this title.

LAW REVIEW COMMENTARIES

New Jersey clean up your "act": Some reflections on the Spill Compensation and Control Act. Francis E.P. McCarter, 38 Rutgers L.Rev. 637 (1986).

LIBRARY REFERENCES

Health and Environment ⚷25.7(10).
C.J.S. Health and Environment § 106 et seq.

§ 1371. Authority under other laws and regulations [FWPCA § 511]

(a) Impairment of authority or functions of officials and agencies; treaty provisions

This chapter shall not be construed as (1) limiting the authority or functions of any officer or agency of the United States under any other law or regulation not inconsistent with this chapter; (2) affecting or impairing the authority of the Secretary of the Army (A) to maintain navigation or (B) under the Act of March 3, 1899, (30 Stat. 1112); except that any permit issued under section 1344 of this title shall be conclusive as to the effect on water quality of any discharge resulting from any activity subject to section 403 of this title, or (3) affecting or impairing the provisions of any treaty of the United States.

(b) Discharges of pollutants into navigable waters

Discharges of pollutants into the navigable waters subject to the Rivers and Harbors Act of 1910 (36 Stat. 593; 33 U.S.C. 421) and the Supervisory Harbors Act of 1888 (25 Stat. 209; 33 U.S.C. 441–451b) shall be regulated pursuant to this chapter, and not subject to such Act of 1910 and the Act of 1888 except as to effect on navigation and anchorage.

(c) Action of the Administrator deemed major Federal action; construction of the National Environmental Policy Act of 1969

(1) Except for the provision of Federal financial assistance for the purpose of assisting the construction of publicly owned treatment works as authorized by section 1281 of this title, and the issuance of a permit under section 1342 of this title for the discharge of any pollutant by a new source as defined in section 1316 of this title, no action of the Administrator taken pursuant to this chapter shall be deemed a major Federal action significantly affecting the quality of the human environment within the meaning of the National Environmental Policy Act of 1969 (83 Stat. 852) [42 U.S.C.A. § 4321 et seq.]; and

(2) Nothing in the National Environmental Policy Act of 1969 (83 Stat. 852) shall be deemed to—

(A) authorize any Federal agency authorized to license or permit the conduct of any activity which may result in the discharge of a pollutant into the navigable waters to review any effluent limitation or other requirement established pursuant to this chapter or the adequacy of any certification under section 1341 of this title; or

(B) authorize any such agency to impose, as a condition precedent to the issuance of any license or permit, any effluent limitation other than any such limitation established pursuant to this chapter.

(d) Consideration of international water pollution control agreements

Notwithstanding this chapter or any other provision of law, the Administrator (1) shall not require any State to consider in the development of the ranking in order of priority of needs for the construction of treatment works (as defined in subchapter II of this chapter), any water pollution control agreement which may have been entered into between the United States and any other nation, and (2) shall not consider any such agreement in the approval of any such priority ranking.

(June 30, 1948, c. 758, Title V, § 511, as added Oct. 18, 1972, Pub.L. 92–500, § 2, 86 Stat. 893, and amended Jan. 2, 1974, Pub.L. 93–243, § 3, 87 Stat. 1069.)

CROSS REFERENCES

Permits and licenses, compliance with requirements, see section 1341 of this title.

LIBRARY REFERENCES

Health and Environment ⚷25.7(3).
C.J.S. Health and Environment § 106.

§ 1372. Labor standards [FWPCA § 513]

The Administrator shall take such action as may be necessary to insure that all laborers and mechanics employed by contractors or subcontractors on treatment works for which grants are made under this chapter shall be paid wages at rates not less than those prevailing for the same type of work on similar construction in the immediate locality, as determined by the Secretary of Labor, in accordance with the Davis-Bacon Act (46 Stat. 1494; 40 U.S.C., sec. 276a through 276a–5). The Secretary of Labor shall have, with respect to the labor standards specified in this subsection,[1] the authority and functions set forth in

Reorganization Plan Numbered 14 of 1950 (15 F.R. 3176) and section 276c of Title 40.

(June 30, 1948, c. 758, Title V, § 513, as added Oct. 18, 1972, Pub.L. 92–500, § 2, 86 Stat. 894.)

[1] So in original. Probably should be "section".

CODE OF FEDERAL REGULATIONS

Labor standards provisions applicable to contracts covering federally financed and assisted construction, see 29 CFR 5.1 et seq.
Procedures for predetermination of wage rates, see 29 CFR 1.1 et seq.

LIBRARY REFERENCES

Labor Relations ⚬=1128.
C.J.S. Labor Relations § 1038.

§ 1373. Public health agency coordination [FWPCA § 514]

The permitting agency under section 1342 of this title shall assist the applicant for a permit under such section in coordinating the requirements of this chapter with those of the appropriate public health agencies.

(June 30, 1948, c. 758, Title V, § 514, as added Oct. 18, 1972, Pub.L. 92–500, § 2, 86 Stat. 894.)

§ 1374. Effluent Standards and Water Quality Information Advisory Committee [FWPCA § 515]

(a) Establishment; membership; term

(1) There is established on [1] Effluent Standards and Water Quality Information Advisory Committee, which shall be composed of a Chairman and eight members who shall be appointed by the Administrator within sixty days after October 18, 1972.

(2) All members of the Committee shall be selected from the scientific community, qualified by education, training, and experience to provide, assess, and evaluate scientific and technical information on effluent standards and limitations.

(3) Members of the Committee shall serve for a term of four years, and may be reappointed.

(b) Action on proposed regulations

(1) No later than one hundred and eighty days prior to the date on which the Administrator is required to publish any proposed regulations required by section 1314(b) of this title, any proposed standard of performance for new sources required by section 1316 of this title, or any proposed toxic effluent standard required by section 1317 of this title, he shall transmit to the Committee a notice of intent to propose such regulations. The Chairman of the Committee within ten days after receipt of such notice may publish a notice of a public hearing by the Committee, to be held within thirty days.

(2) No later than one hundred and twenty days after receipt of such notice, the Committee shall transmit to the Administrator such scientific and technical information as is in its possession, including that presented at any public hearing, related to the subject matter contained in such notice.

(3) Information so transmitted to the Administrator shall constitute a part of the administrative record and comments on any proposed regulations or standards as information to be considered with other comments and information in making any final determinations.

(4) In preparing information for transmittal, the Committee shall avail itself of the technical and scientific services of any Federal agency, including the United States Geological Survey and any national environmental laboratories which may be established.

(c) Secretary; legal counsel; compensation

(1) The Committee shall appoint and prescribe the duties of a Secretary, and such legal counsel as it deems necessary. The Committee shall appoint such other employees as it deems necessary to exercise and fulfill its powers and responsibilities. The compensation of all employees appointed by the Committee shall be fixed in accordance with chapter 51 and subchapter III of chapter 53 of Title 5.

(2) Members of the Committee shall be entitled to receive compensation at a rate to be fixed by the President but not in excess of the maximum rate of pay for grade GS–18, as provided in the General Schedule under section 5332 of Title 5.

(d) Quorum; special panel

Five members of the Committee shall constitute a quorum, and official actions of the Committee shall be taken only on the affirmative vote of at least five members. A special panel composed of one or more members upon order of the Committee shall conduct any hearing authorized by this section and submit the transcript of such hearing to the entire Committee for its action thereon.

(e) Rules

The Committee is authorized to make such rules as are necessary for the orderly transaction of its business.

(June 30, 1948, c. 758, Title V, § 515, as added Oct. 18, 1972, Pub.L. 92–500, § 2, 86 Stat. 894.)

[1] So in original. Probably should be "an".

LIBRARY REFERENCES

United States ⚬=29.
C.J.S. United States § 34 et seq.

§ 1375. Reports to Congress [FWPCA § 516]

(a) Implementation of chapter objectives; status and progress of programs

Within ninety days following the convening of each session of Congress, the Administrator shall submit to the Congress a report, in addition to any other report required by this chapter, on measures taken toward implementing the objective of this chapter, including, but not limited to, (1) the progress and problems associated with developing comprehensive plans under section 1252 of this title, areawide plans under section 1288 of this title, basin plans under section 1289 of this title, and plans under section 1313(e) of this title; (2) a summary of actions taken and results achieved in the field of water pollution control research, experiments, studies, and related matters by the Administrator and other Federal agencies and by other persons and agencies under Federal grants or contracts; (3) the progress and problems associated with the development of effluent limitations and recommended control techniques; (4) the status of State programs, including a detailed summary of the progress obtained as compared to that planned under State program plans for development and enforcement of water quality requirements; (5) the identification and status of enforcement actions pending or completed under this chapter during the preceding year; (6) the status of State, interstate, and local pollution control programs established pursuant to, and assisted by, this chapter; (7) a summary of the results of the survey required to be taken under section 1290 of this title; (8) his activities including recommendations under sections 1259 through 1261 of this title; and (9) all reports and recommendations made by the Water Pollution Control Advisory Board.

(b) Detailed estimates and comprehensive study on costs; State estimates, survey form

(1) The Administrator, in cooperation with the States, including water pollution control agencies and other water pollution control planning agencies, shall make (A) a detailed estimate of the cost of carrying out the provisions of this chapter; (B) a detailed estimate, biennially revised, of the cost of construction of all needed publicly owned treatment works in all of the States and of the cost of construction of all needed publicly owned treatment works in each of the States; (C) a comprehensive study of the economic impact on affected units of government of the cost of installation of treatment facilities; and (D) a comprehensive analysis of the national requirements for and the cost of treating municipal, industrial, and other effluent to attain the water quality objectives as established by this chapter or applicable State law. The Administrator shall submit such detailed estimate and such comprehensive study of such cost to the Congress no later than February 10 of each odd-numbered year. Whenever the Administrator, pursuant to this subsection, requests and receives an estimate of cost from a State, he shall furnish copies of such estimate together with such detailed estimate to Congress.

(2) Notwithstanding the second sentence of paragraph (1) of this subsection, the Administrator shall make a preliminary detailed estimate called for by subparagraph (B) of such paragraph and shall submit such preliminary detailed estimate to the Congress no later than September 3, 1974. The Administrator shall require each State to prepare an estimate of cost for such State, and shall utilize the survey form EPA–1, O.M.B. No. 158–R0017, prepared for the 1973 detailed estimate, except that such estimate shall include all costs of compliance with section 1281(g)(2)(A) of this title and water quality standards established pursuant to section 1313 of this title, and all costs of treatment works as defined in section 1292(2) of this title, including all eligible costs of constructing sewage collection systems and correcting excessive infiltration or inflow and all eligible costs of correcting combined storm and sanitary sewer problems and treating storm water flows. The survey form shall be distributed by the Administrator to each State no later than January 31, 1974.

(c) Status of combined sewer overflows in municipal treatment works operations

The Administrator shall submit to the Congress by October 1, 1978, a report on the status of combined sewer overflows in municipal treatment works operations. The report shall include (1) the status of any projects funded under this chapter to address combined sewer overflows (2) a listing by State of combined sewer overflow needs identified in the 1977 State priority listings, (3) an estimate for each applicable municipality of the number of years necessary, assuming an annual authorization and appropriation for the construction grants program of $5,000,000,000, to correct combined sewer overflow problems, (4) an analysis using representative municipalities faced with major combined sewer overflow needs, of the annual discharges of pollutants from overflows in comparison to treated effluent discharges, (5) an analysis of the technological alternatives available to municipalities to correct major combined sewer overflow problems, and (6) any recommendations of the Administrator for legislation to address the problem of combined sewer overflows, including whether a separate authorization and grant program should be established by the Congress to address combined sewer overflows.

(d) Legislative recommendations on program requiring coordination between water supply and wastewater control plans as condition for construction grants; public hearing

The Administrator, in cooperation with the States, including water pollution control agencies, and other water pollution control planning agencies, and water supply and water resources agencies of the States and the United States shall submit to Congress, within two years of December 27, 1977, a report with recommendations for legislation on a program to require coordination between water supply and wastewater control plans as a condition to grants for construction of treatment works under this chapter. No such report shall be submitted except after opportunity for public hearings on such proposed report.

(e) State revolving fund report

(1) In general

Not later than February 10, 1990, the Administrator shall submit to Congress a report on the financial status and operations of water pollution control revolving funds established by the States under subchapter VI of this chapter. The Administrator shall prepare such report in cooperation with the States, including water pollution control agencies and other water pollution control planning and financing agencies.

(2) Contents

The report under this subsection shall also include the following:

(A) an inventory of the facilities that are in significant noncompliance with the enforceable requirements of this chapter;

(B) an estimate of the cost of construction necessary to bring such facilities into compliance with such requirements;

(C) an assessment of the availability of sources of funds for financing such needed construction, including an estimate of the amount of funds available for providing assistance for such construction through September 30, 1999, from the water pollution control revolving funds established by the States under subchapter VI of this chapter;

(D) an assessment of the operations, loan portfolio, and loan conditions of such revolving funds;

(E) an assessment of the effect on user charges of the assistance provided by such revolving funds compared to the assistance provided with funds appropriated pursuant to section 1287 of this title; and

(F) an assessment of the efficiency of the operation and maintenance of treatment works constructed with assistance provided by such revolving funds compared to the efficiency of the operation and maintenance of treatment works constructed with assistance provided under section 1281 of this title.

(June 30, 1948, c. 758, Title V, § 516, as added Oct. 18, 1972, Pub.L. 92–500, § 2, 86 Stat. 895, and amended Jan. 2, 1974, Pub.L. 93–243, § 4, 87 Stat. 1069; Dec. 27, 1977, Pub.L. 95–217, §§ 70–72, 91 Stat. 1608, 1609; Feb. 4, 1987, Pub.L. 100–4, Title II, § 212(c), 101 Stat. 27; Dec. 21, 1995, Pub.L. 104–66, Title II, § 2021(d), 109 Stat. 727.)

Studies and Reports

Pub.L. 100–4, Title III, § 308(g), Feb. 4, 1987, 101 Stat. 40, directed the Administrator to conduct a water quality improvement study and report the results of such study to specified Congressional committees not later than 2 years after Feb. 4, 1987.

Pub.L. 100–4, Title III, § 314(b), Feb. 4, 1987, 101 Stat. 49, directed that the Secretary of the Army and the Administrator each prepare a report on enforcement mechanisms and submit the reports to Congress not later than Dec. 1, 1988.

Pub.L. 100–4, Title IV, § 404(c), Feb. 4, 1987, 101 Stat. 69, which directed the Administrator to study the extent to which States have adopted water quality standards in accordance with section 1313a of this title and the extent to which modifications of permits issued under section 1342(a)(1)(B) of this title for the purpose of reflecting revisions of water quality standards be encouraged and to submit a report on such study to Congress not later than 2 years after Feb. 4, 1987, was repealed by Pub.L. 104–66, Title II, § 2021(e)(1), Dec. 21, 1995, 109 Stat. 727.

Pub.L. 100–4, Title V, § 516, Feb. 4, 1987, 101 Stat. 86, directed the Administrator to conduct a study of de minimis discharges and report the results of such study to specified Congressional committees not later than 1 year after Feb. 4, 1987.

Pub.L. 100–4, Title V, § 517, Feb. 4, 1987, 100 Stat. 86, directed the Administrator to conduct a study of effectiveness of innovative and alternative processes and techniques and report the results of such study to specified Congressional committees not later than 1 year after Feb. 4, 1987.

Pub.L. 100–4, Title V, § 518, Feb. 4, 1987, 101 Stat. 86, directed the Administrator to conduct a study of testing procedures and report the results of such study to specified Congressional committees not later than 1 year after Feb. 4, 1987.

Pub.L. 100–4, Title V, § 519, Feb. 4, 1987, 100 Stat. 87, directed the Administrator to conduct a study of pretreatment of toxic pollutants and report the results of such study to specified Congressional committees not later than 4 years after Feb. 4, 1987.

Pub.L. 100–4, Title V, § 520, Feb. 4, 1987, 101 Stat. 87, directed the Administrator, in conjunction with State and local agencies, to conduct studies of water pollution problems in aquifers and report the result of such studies to Congress not later than 2 years after Feb. 4, 1987.

Pub.L. 100–4, Title V, § 522, Feb. 4, 1987, 101 Stat. 88, directed the Administrator to conduct a study on sulfide corrosion and report the results of such study to specified Congressional committees not later than 1 year after Feb. 4, 1987.

Pub.L. 100–4, Title V, § 523, Feb. 4, 1987, 101 Stat. 89, directed the Administrator to conduct a study of rainfall induced infiltration into sewer systems and report the results of such study to Congress not later than 1 year after Feb. 4, 1987.

Pub.L. 100–4, Title V, § 524, Feb. 4, 1987, 101 Stat. 89, directed the Administrator to conduct a study of dam water quality and report the results of such study to Congress not later than Dec. 31, 1987.

Pub.L. 100–4, Title V, § 525, Feb. 4, 1987, 101 Stat. 89, directed the Administrator to conduct a study of pollution in Lake Pend Oreille, Idaho, and the Clark Fork River and its tributaries, Idaho, Montana, and Washington, and to report to Congress the findings and recommendations.

CROSS REFERENCES

Allotment of grant funds for construction of treatment works, see section 1285 of this title.

Annual survey of efficiency of treatment works constructed with grants made under this chapter, see section 1290 of this title.
Deduction of funds for Hudson River reclamation demonstration project from estimates prepared pursuant to this section, see section 1266 of this title.
Report on quality of navigable waters, ground water, etc., see section 1254 of this title.

§ 1376. Authorization of appropriations [FWPCA § 517]

There are authorized to be appropriated to carry out this chapter, other than sections 1254, 1255, 1256(a), 1257, 1258, 1262, 1263, 1264, 1265, 1286, 1287, 1288(f) and (h), 1289, 1314, 1321(c), (d), (i), (*l*), and (k), 1324, 1325, and 1327 of this title, $250,000,000 for the fiscal year ending June 30, 1973, $300,000,000 for the fiscal year ending June 30, 1974, $350,000,000 for the fiscal year ending June 30, 1975, $100,000,000 for the fiscal year ending September 30, 1977, $150,000,000 for the fiscal year ending September 30, 1978, $150,000,000 for the fiscal year ending September 30, 1979, $150,000,000 for the fiscal year ending September 30, 1980, $150,000,000 for the fiscal year ending September 30, 1981, $161,000,000 for the fiscal year ending September 30, 1982, such sums as may be necessary for fiscal years 1983 through 1985, and $135,000,000 per fiscal year for each of the fiscal years 1986 through 1990.

(June 30, 1948, c. 758, Title V, § 517, as added Oct. 18, 1972, Pub.L. 92–500, § 2, 86 Stat. 896, and amended Dec. 27, 1977, Pub.L. 95–217, § 4(g), 91 Stat. 1567; Oct. 21, 1980, Pub.L. 96–483, § 1(g), 94 Stat. 2360; Feb. 4, 1987, Pub.L. 100–4, Title I, § 101(h), 101 Stat. 9.)

§ 1377. Indian tribes [FWPCA § 518]

(a) Policy

Nothing in this section shall be construed to affect the application of section 1251(g) of this title, and all of the provisions of this section shall be carried out in accordance with the provisions of such section 1251(g) of this title. Indian tribes shall be treated as States for purposes of such section 1251(g) of this title.

(b) Assessment of sewage treatment needs; report

The Administrator, in cooperation with the Director of the Indian Health Service, shall assess the need for sewage treatment works to serve Indian tribes, the degree to which such needs will be met through funds allotted to States under section 1285 of this title and priority lists under section 1296 of this title, and any obstacles which prevent such needs from being met. Not later than one year after February 4, 1987, the Administrator shall submit a report to Congress on the assessment under this subsection, along with recommendations specifying (1) how the Administrator intends to provide assistance to Indian tribes to develop waste treatment management plans and to construct treatment works under this chapter, and (2) methods by which the participation in and administration of programs under this chapter by Indian tribes can be maximized.

(c) Reservation of funds

The Administrator shall reserve each fiscal year beginning after September 30, 1986, before allotments to the States under section 1285(e) of this title, one-half of one percent of the sums appropriated under section 1287 of this title. Sums reserved under this subsection shall be available only for grants for the development of waste treatment management plans and for the construction of sewage treatment works to serve Indian tribes, as defined in subsection (h) of this section and former Indian reservations in Oklahoma (as determined by the Secretary of the Interior) and Alaska Native Villages as defined in Public Law 92–203 [43 U.S.C.A. § 1601 et seq.].

(d) Cooperative agreements

In order to ensure the consistent implementation of the requirements of this chapter, an Indian tribe and the State or States in which the lands of such tribe are located may enter into a cooperative agreement, subject to the review and approval of the Administrator, to jointly plan and administer the requirements of this chapter.

(e) Treatment as States

The Administrator is authorized to treat an Indian tribe as a State for purposes of subchapter II of this chapter and sections 1254, 1256, 1313, 1315, 1318, 1319, 1324, 1329, 1341, 1342, and 1344 of this title to the degree necessary to carry out the objectives of this section, but only if—

(1) the Indian tribe has a governing body carrying out substantial governmental duties and powers;

(2) the functions to be exercised by the Indian tribe pertain to the management and protection of water resources which are held by an Indian tribe, held by the United States in trust for Indians, held by a member of an Indian tribe if such property interest is subject to a trust restriction on alienation, or otherwise within the borders of an Indian reservation; and

(3) the Indian tribe is reasonably expected to be capable, in the Administrator's judgment, of carrying out the functions to be exercised in a manner consistent with the terms and purposes of this chapter and of all applicable regulations.

Such treatment as a State may include the direct provision of funds reserved under subsection (c) of this section to the governing bodies of Indian tribes, and the determination of priorities by Indian tribes, where not determined by the Administrator in cooperation with the Director of the Indian Health Service. The Administrator, in cooperation with the Director of the Indian Health Service, is authorized to make grants under subchapter II of this chapter in an amount not to exceed 100 percent of the cost of a project. Not later than 18 months after February 4, 1987, the Administrator shall, in consultation with Indian tribes, promulgate final regulations which specify how Indian tribes shall be treated as States for purposes of this chapter. The Administrator shall, in promulgating such regulations, consult affected States sharing common water bodies and provide a mechanism for the resolution of any unreasonable consequences that may arise as a result of differing water quality standards that may be set by States and Indian tribes located on common bodies of water. Such mechanism shall provide for explicit consideration of relevant factors including, but not limited to, the effects of differing water quality permit requirements on upstream and downstream dischargers, economic impacts, and present and historical uses and quality of the waters subject to such standards. Such mechanism should provide for the avoidance of such unreasonable consequences in a manner consistent with the objective of this chapter.

(f) Grants for nonpoint source programs

The Administrator shall make grants to an Indian tribe under section 1329 of this title as though such tribe was a State. Not more than one-third of one percent of the amount appropriated for any fiscal year under section 1329 of this title may be used to make grants under this subsection. In addition to the requirements of section 1329 of this title, an Indian tribe shall be required to meet the requirements of paragraphs (1), (2), and (3) of subsection (d) of this section in order to receive such a grant.

(g) Alaska Native organizations

No provision of this chapter shall be construed to—

(1) grant, enlarge, or diminish, or in any way affect the scope of the governmental authority, if any, of any Alaska Native organization, including any federally-recognized tribe, traditional Alaska Native council, or Native council organized pursuant to the Act of June 18, 1934 (48 Stat. 987), over lands or persons in Alaska;

(2) create or validate any assertion by such organization or any form of governmental authority over lands or persons in Alaska; or

(3) in any way affect any assertion that Indian country, as defined in section 1151 of Title 18, exists or does not exist in Alaska.

(h) Definitions

For purposes of this section, the term—

(1) "Federal Indian reservation" means all land within the limits of any Indian reservation under the jurisdiction of the United States Government, notwithstanding the issuance of any patent, and including rights-of-way running through the reservation; and

(2) "Indian tribe" means any Indian tribe, band, group, or community recognized by the Secretary of the Interior and exercising governmental authority over a Federal Indian reservation.

(June 30, 1948, c. 758, Title V, § 518, as added Feb. 4, 1987, Pub.L. 100–4, Title V, § 506, 101 Stat. 76, and amended Nov. 1, 1988, Pub.L. 100–581, Title II, § 207, 102 Stat. 2940.)

References in Text

Pub.L. 92–203, referred to in subsec. (c), is Pub.L. 92–203, Dec. 18, 1971, 85 Stat. 688, as amended, popularly known as the "Alaska Native Claims Settlement Act", which is classified generally to chapter 33 (section 1601 et seq.) of Title 43, Public Lands. "Alaska Native Villages", also so referred, are defined in section 1602(c) of Title 43, defining "Native village".

SUBCHAPTER VI—STATE WATER POLLUTION CONTROL REVOLVING FUNDS

§ 1381. Grants to States for establishment of revolving funds [FWPCA § 601]

(a) General authority

Subject to the provisions of this subchapter, the Administrator shall make capitalization grants to each State for the purpose of establishing a water pollution control revolving fund for providing assistance (1) for construction of treatment works (as defined in section 1292 of this title) which are publicly owned, (2) for implementing a management program under section 1329 of this title, and (3) for developing and implementing a conservation and management plan under section 1330 of this title.

(b) Schedule of grant payments

The Administrator and each State shall jointly establish a schedule of payments under which the Administrator will pay to the State the amount of each grant to be made to the State under this subchapter. Such schedule shall be based on the State's intended use plan under section 1386(c) of this title, except that—

(1) such payments shall be made in quarterly installments, and

(2) such payments shall be made as expeditiously as possible, but in no event later than the earlier of—

(A) 8 quarters after the date such funds were obligated by the State, or

(B) 12 quarters after the date such funds were allotted to the State.

(June 30, 1948, c. 758, Title VI, § 601, as added Feb. 4, 1987, Pub.L. 100–4, Title II, § 212(a), 101 Stat. 22.)

LIBRARY REFERENCES

Navigable Waters ⇨35.
States ⇨127.
United States ⇨82(2).
C.J.S. Health and Environment § 106 et seq.
C.J.S. Navigable Waters § 11.
C.J.S. States § 228.
C.J.S. United States § 122.

§ 1382. Capitalization grant agreements [FWPCA § 602]

(a) General rule

To receive a capitalization grant with funds made available under this subchapter and section 1285(m) of this title, a State shall enter into an agreement with the Administrator which shall include but not be limited to the specifications set forth in subsection (b) of this section.

(b) Specific requirements

The Administrator shall enter into an agreement under this section with a State only after the State has established to the satisfaction of the Administrator that—

(1) the State will accept grant payments with funds to be made available under this subchapter and section 1285(m) of this title in accordance with a payment schedule established jointly by the Administrator under section 1381(b) of this title and will deposit all such payments in the water pollution control revolving fund established by the State in accordance with this subchapter;

(2) the State will deposit in the fund from State moneys an amount equal to at least 20 percent of the total amount of all capitalization grants which will be made to the State with funds to be made available under this subchapter and section 1285(m) of this title on or before the date on which each quarterly grant payment will be made to the State under this subchapter;

(3) the State will enter into binding commitments to provide assistance in accordance with the requirements of this subchapter in an amount equal to 120 percent of the amount of each such grant payment within 1 year after the receipt of such grant payment;

(4) all funds in the fund will be expended in an expeditious and timely manner;

(5) all funds in the fund as a result of capitalization grants under this subchapter and section 1285(m) of this title will first be used to assure maintenance of progress, as determined by the Governor of the State, toward compliance with enforceable deadlines, goals, and requirements of this chapter, including the municipal compliance deadline;

(6) treatment works eligible under section 1383(c)(1) of this title which will be constructed in whole or in part before fiscal year 1995 with funds directly made available by capitalization grants under this subchapter and section 1285(m) of this title will meet the requirements of, or otherwise be treated (as determined by the Governor of the State) under sections 1281(b), 1281(g)(1), 1281(g)(2), 1281(g)(3), 1281(g)(5), 1281(g)(6), 1281(n)(1), 1281(*o*), 1284(a)(1), 1284(a)(2), 1284(b)(1), 1284(d)(2), 1291, 1298, 1371(c)(1), and 1372 of this title in the same manner as treatment works constructed with assistance under subchapter II of this chapter;

(7) in addition to complying with the requirements of this subchapter, the State will commit or expend each quarterly grant payment which it will receive under this subchapter in accordance with laws and procedures applicable to the commitment or expenditure of revenues of the State;

(8) in carrying out the requirements of section 1386 of this title, the State will use accounting, audit, and fiscal procedures conforming to generally accepted government accounting standards;

(9) the State will require as a condition of making a loan or providing other assistance, as described in section 1383(d) of this title, from the fund that the recipient of such assistance will maintain project accounts in accordance with generally accepted government accounting standards; and

(10) the State will make annual reports to the Administrator on the actual use of funds in accordance with section 1386(d) of this title.

(June 30, 1948, c. 758, Title VI, § 602, as added Feb. 4, 1987, Pub.L. 100–4, Title II, § 212(a), 101 Stat. 22.)

LIBRARY REFERENCES

United States ⇨82(2).
C.J.S. United States § 122.

§ 1383. Water pollution control revolving loan funds [FWPCA § 603]

(a) Requirements for obligation of grant funds

Before a State may receive a capitalization grant with funds made available under this subchapter and section 1285(m) of this title, the State shall first establish a water pollution control revolving fund which complies with the requirements of this section.

(b) Administration

Each State water pollution control revolving fund shall be administered by an instrumentality of the State with such powers and limitations as may be required to operate such fund in accordance with the requirements and objectives of this chapter.

(c) Projects eligible for assistance

The amounts of funds available to each State water pollution control revolving fund shall be used only for providing financial assistance (1) to any municipality, intermunicipal, interstate, or State agency for construction of publicly owned treatment works (as defined in section 1292 of this title), (2) for the implementation of a management program established under section 1329 of this title, and (3) for development and implementation of a conservation and management plan under section 1330 of this title. The fund shall be established, maintained, and credited with repayments, and the fund balance shall be available in perpetuity for providing such financial assistance.

(d) Types of assistance

Except as otherwise limited by State law, a water pollution control revolving fund of a State under this section may be used only—

(1) to make loans, on the condition that—

(A) such loans are made at or below market interest rates, including interest free loans, at terms not to exceed 20 years;

(B) annual principal and interest payments will commence not later than 1 year after completion of any project and all loans will be fully amortized not later than 20 years after project completion;

(C) the recipient of a loan will establish a dedicated source of revenue for repayment of loans; and

(D) the fund will be credited with all payments of principal and interest on all loans;

(2) to buy or refinance the debt obligation of municipalities and intermunicipal and interstate agencies within the State at or below market rates, where such debt obligations were incurred after March 7, 1985;

(3) to guarantee, or purchase insurance for, local obligations where such action would improve credit market access or reduce interest rates;

(4) as a source of revenue or security for the payment of principal and interest on revenue or general obligation bonds issued by the State if the proceeds of the sale of such bonds will be deposited in the fund;

(5) to provide loan guarantees for similar revolving funds established by municipalities or intermunicipal agencies;

(6) to earn interest on fund accounts; and

(7) for the reasonable costs of administering the fund and conducting activities under this subchapter, except that such amounts shall not exceed 4 percent of all grant awards to such fund under this subchapter.

(e) Limitation to prevent double benefits

If a State makes, from its water pollution revolving fund, a loan which will finance the cost of facility planning and the preparation of plans, specifications, and estimates for construction of publicly owned treatment works, the State shall ensure that if the recipient of such loan receives a grant under section 1281(g) of this title for construction of such treatment works and an allowance under section 1281(*l*)(1) of this title for non-Federal funds expended for such planning and preparation, such recipient will promptly repay such loan to the extent of such allowance.

(f) Consistency with planning requirements

A State may provide financial assistance from its water pollution control revolving fund only with respect to a project which is consistent with plans, if any, developed under sections 1285(j), 1288, 1313(e), 1329, and 1330 of this title.

(g) Priority list requirement

The State may provide financial assistance from its water pollution control revolving fund only with respect to a project for construction of a treatment works described in subsection (c)(1) of this section if such project is on the State's priority list under section 1296 of this title. Such assistance may be provided regardless of the rank of such project on such list.

(h) Eligibility of non-Federal share of construction grant projects

A State water pollution control revolving fund may provide assistance (other than under subsection (d)(1) of this section) to a municipality or intermunicipal or interstate agency with respect to the non-Federal share of the costs of a treatment works project for which such municipality or agency is receiving assistance from the Administrator under any other authority only if such assistance is necessary to allow such project to proceed.

(June 30, 1948, c. 758, Title VI, § 603, as added Feb. 4, 1987, Pub.L. 100–4, Title II, § 212(a), 101 Stat. 23.)

LIBRARY REFERENCES

Health and Environment ⚖25.7(21).
States ⚖127.
C.J.S. Health and Environment § 106 et seq.
C.J.S. States § 228.

§ 1384. Allotment of funds [FWPCA § 604]

(a) Formula

Sums authorized to be appropriated to carry out this section for each of fiscal years 1989 and 1990 shall be allotted by the Administrator in accordance with section 1285(c) of this title.

(b) Reservation of funds for planning

Each State shall reserve each fiscal year 1 percent of the sums allotted to such State under this section for such fiscal year, or $100,000, whichever amount is greater, to carry out planning under sections 1285(j) and 1313(e) of this title.

(c) Allotment period

(1) Period of availability for grant award

Sums allotted to a State under this section for a fiscal year shall be available for obligation by the State during the fiscal year for which sums are authorized and during the following fiscal year.

(2) Reallotment of unobligated funds

The amount of any allotment not obligated by the State by the last day of the 2-year period of availability established by paragraph (1) shall be immediately reallotted by the Administrator on the basis of the same ratio as is applicable to sums allotted under subchapter II of this chapter for the second fiscal year of such 2-year period. None of the funds reallotted by the Administrator shall be reallotted to any State which has not obligated all sums allotted to such State in the first fiscal year of such 2-year period.

(June 30, 1948, c. 758, Title VI, § 604, as added Feb. 4, 1987, Pub.L. 100–4, Title II, § 212(a), 101 Stat. 25.)

§ 1385. Corrective action [FWPCA § 605]

(a) Notification of noncompliance

If the Administrator determines that a State has not complied with its agreement with the Administrator under section 1382 of this title or any other requirement of this subchapter, the Administrator shall notify the State of such noncompliance and the necessary corrective action.

(b) Withholding of payments

If a State does not take corrective action within 60 days after the date a State receives notification of such action under subsection (a) of this section, the Administrator shall withhold additional payments to the State until the Administrator is satisfied that the State has taken the necessary corrective action.

(c) Reallotment of withheld payments

If the Administrator is not satisfied that adequate corrective actions have been taken by the State within 12 months after the State is notified of such actions under subsection (a) of this section, the payments withheld from the State by the Administrator under subsection (b) of this section shall be made available for reallotment in accordance with the most recent formula for allotment of funds under this subchapter.

(June 30, 1948, c. 758, Title VI, § 605, as added Feb. 4, 1987, Pub.L. 100–4, Title II, § 212(a), 101 Stat. 25.)

§ 1386. Audits, reports, and fiscal controls; intended use plan [FWPCA § 606]

(a) Fiscal control and auditing procedures

Each State electing to establish a water pollution control revolving fund under this subchapter shall establish fiscal controls and accounting procedures sufficient to assure proper accounting during appropriate accounting periods for—

(1) payments received by the fund;

(2) disbursements made by the fund; and

(3) fund balances at the beginning and end of the accounting period.

(b) Annual federal audits

The Administrator shall, at least on an annual basis, conduct or require each State to have independently conducted reviews and audits as may be deemed necessary or appropriate by the Administrator to carry out the objectives of this section. Audits of the use of funds deposited in the water pollution revolving fund established by such State shall be conducted in accordance with the auditing procedures of the General Accounting Office, including chapter 75 of Title 31.

(c) Intended use plan

After providing for public comment and review, each State shall annually prepare a plan identifying the intended uses of the amounts available to its water pollution control revolving fund. Such intended use plan shall include, but not be limited to—

(1) a list of those projects for construction of publicly owned treatment works on the State's priority list developed pursuant to section 1296 of this title and a list of activities eligible for assistance under sections 1329 and 1330 of this title;

(2) a description of the short- and long-term goals and objectives of its water pollution control revolving fund;

(3) information on the activities to be supported, including a description of project categories, discharge requirements under subchapters III and IV of this chapter, terms of financial assistance, and communities served;

(4) assurances and specific proposals for meeting the requirements of paragraphs (3), (4), (5), and (6) of section 1382(b) of this title; and

(5) the criteria and method established for the distribution of funds.

(d) Annual report

Beginning the first fiscal year after the receipt of payments under this subchapter, the State shall provide an annual report to the Administrator describing how the State has met the goals and objectives for the previous fiscal year as identified in the plan prepared for the previous fiscal year pursuant to subsection (c) of this section, including identification of loan recipients, loan amounts, and loan terms and similar details on other forms of financial assistance provided from the water pollution control revolving fund.

(e) Annual federal oversight review

The Administrator shall conduct an annual oversight review of each State plan prepared under subsection (c) of this section, each State report prepared under subsection (d) of this section, and other such materials as are considered necessary and appropriate in carrying out the purposes of this subchapter. After reasonable notice by the Administrator to the State or the recipient of a loan from a water pollution control revolving fund, the State or loan recipient shall make available to the Administrator such records as the Administrator reasonably requires to review and determine compliance with this subchapter.

(f) Applicability of subchapter II provisions

Except to the extent provided in this subchapter, the provisions of subchapter II of this chapter shall not apply to grants under this subchapter.

(June 30, 1948, c. 758, Title VI, § 606, as added Feb. 4, 1987, Pub.L. 100–4, Title II, § 212(a), 101 Stat. 25.)

§ 1387. Authorization of appropriations [FWPCA § 607]

There is authorized to be appropriated to carry out the purposes of this subchapter the following sums:

(1) $1,200,000,000 per fiscal year for each of fiscal years 1989 and 1990;

(2) $2,400,000,000 for fiscal year 1991;

(3) $1,800,000,000 for fiscal year 1992;

(4) $1,200,000,000 for fiscal year 1993; and

(5) $600,000,000 for fiscal year 1994.

(June 30, 1948, c. 758, Title VI, § 607, as added Feb. 4, 1987, Pub.L. 100–4, Title II, § 212(a), 101 Stat. 26.)

OCEAN DUMPING

MARINE PROTECTION, RESEARCH, AND SANCTUARIES ACT OF 1972 [MPRSA § ___]

(33 U.S.C.A. §§ 1401 to 1445)

CHAPTER 27—OCEAN DUMPING

Sec.
1401. Congressional finding, policy, and declaration of purpose.
- (a) Dangers of unregulated dumping.
- (b) Policy of regulation and prevention or limitation.
- (c) Regulation of dumping and transportation for dumping purposes.

1402. Definitions.

SUBCHAPTER I—REGULATION

1411. Prohibited acts.
1412. Dumping permit program.
- (a) Environmental Protection Agency permits.
- (b) Permit categories.
- (c) Sites and times for dumping.
- (d) Fish wastes.
- (e) Foreign State permits; acceptance.

1412a. Dumping of sewage sludge and industrial waste.
- (a) Emergency permits for dumping of industrial waste; issuance, etc.
- (b) "Industrial waste" defined.

1413. Dumping permit program for dredged material.
- (a) Issuance by Secretary of the Army.
- (b) Independent determination of need for dumping, other methods of disposal, and appropriate locations; alternative sites.
- (c) Concurrence by the Administrator.
- (d) Waiver of requirements.
- (e) Federal projects involving dredged material.

1414. Permit conditions.
- (a) Designated and included conditions.
- (b) Permit processing fees; reporting requirements.
- (c) General permits.
- (d) Review.
- (e) Information for review and evaluation of applications.
- (f) Public information.
- (g) Display of issued permits.
- (h) Low-level radioactive waste; research purposes.
- (i) Radioactive Material Disposal Impact Assessment; Congressional approval.

1414a. Special provisions regarding certain dumping sites.
- (a) New York Bight Apex.
- (b) Restriction on Use of the 106-Mile Site.

1414b. Ocean dumping of sewage sludge and industrial waste.
- (a) Termination of dumping.
- (b) Special dumping fees.

Sec.
1414b. Ocean dumping of sewage sludge and industrial waste.
- (c) Compliance agreements and enforcement agreements.
- (d) Penalties.
- (e) Trust account.
- (f) Use of fees and penalties.
- (g) Enforcement.
- (h) State progress reports.
- (i) EPA progress reports.
- (j) Environmental monitoring.
- (k) Definitions.

1414c. Prohibition on disposal of sewage sludge at landfills on Staten Island.
- (a) In general.
- (b) Exclusion from penalties.
- (c) Definition.

1415. Penalties.
- (a) Assessment of civil penalty by Administrator; remission or mitigation; court action for appropriate relief.
- (b) Criminal penalties.
- (c) Separate offenses.
- (d) Injunctive relief.
- (e) Liability of vessels in rem.
- (f) Revocation and suspension of permits.
- (g) Civil suits by private persons.
- (h) Emergencies.
- (i) Seizure and forfeiture.

1416. Relationship to other laws.
- (a) Voiding of preexisting licenses.
- (b) Actions under authority of Rivers and Harbors Act.
- (c) Impairment of navigation.
- (d) State programs.
- (e) Existing conservation programs not affected.
- (f) Dumping of dredged material in Long Island Sound from any Federal, etc., project.
- (g) Savings clause.

1417. Enforcement.
- (a) Utilization of other departments, agencies, and instrumentalities.
- (b) Delegation of review and evaluation authority.
- (c) Surveillance and other enforcement activity.

1418. Regulations.
1419. International cooperation.
1420. Authorization of appropriations.
1421. Annual report to Congress.

SUBCHAPTER II—RESEARCH

1441. Monitoring and research program.

Sec.
1442. Research program respecting possible long-range effects of pollution, overfishing, and man-induced changes of ocean ecosystems.
(a) Secretary of Commerce.
(b) Action with other nations.
(c) Cooperation of other departments, agencies, and independent instrumentalities.

Sec.
(d) Utilization of personnel, services, and facilities; inter-agency agreements.
1443. Cooperation with public authorities, agencies, and institutions, private agencies and institutions, and individuals; regional management plans for waste disposal; report on sewage disposal in New York metropolitan area.
1444. Annual reports.
1445. Authorization of appropriations.

Related Provisions

See, also, Water Pollution Prevention and Control, 33 U.S.C.A. § 1251 et seq., ante; Ocean Pollution Research, 33 U.S.C.A. § 1701 et seq., post; Prevention of Pollution from Ships, 33 U.S.C.A. § 1901 et seq., post; and Water Resources Research, 42 U.S.C.A. § 10301 et seq., post.

CROSS REFERENCES

Application of solid waste disposal provisions, see section 6905 of Title 42, The Public Health and Welfare.
Deepwater port license, conditions for issuance, see section 1503 of this title.
Nuclear waste, ocean disposal of, see section 10104 of Title 42, The Public Health and Welfare.

West's Federal Forms

Jurisdiction and venue in district courts, matters pertaining to, see § 1003 et seq.
Preliminary injunctions and temporary restraining orders, see § 5271 et seq.
Sentence and fine, see § 7531 et seq.

CODE OF FEDERAL REGULATIONS

Enforcement, supervision, and inspection, see 33 CFR 326.1 et seq.
General regulatory policies, see 33 CFR 320.1 et seq.
Nationwide permits, see 33 CFR 330.1 et seq.
Ocean dumping, see 40 CFR Chap. I, Subchap. H.
Permits for discharges of dredged or fill material into water of the United States, see 33 CFR 323.1 et seq.
Processing of army department permits, see 33 CFR 325.1 et seq.
Public hearings, see 33 CFR 327.1 et seq.
Public information, see 40 CFR 2.100 et seq.

WESTLAW ELECTRONIC RESEARCH

See WESTLAW guide following the Explanation pages of this pamphlet.

§ 1401. Congressional finding, policy, and declaration of purpose [MPRSA § 2]

(a) Dangers of unregulated dumping

Unregulated dumping of material into ocean waters endangers human health, welfare, and amenities, and the marine environment, ecological systems, and economic potentialities.

(b) Policy of regulation and prevention or limitation

The Congress declares that it is the policy of the United States to regulate the dumping of all types of materials into ocean waters and to prevent or strictly limit the dumping into ocean waters of any material which would adversely affect human health, welfare, or amenities, or the marine environment, ecological systems, or economic potentialities.

(c) Regulation of dumping and transportation for dumping purposes

It is the purpose of this chapter to regulate (1) the transportation by any person of material from the United States and, in the case of United States vessels, aircraft, or agencies, the Transportation of material from a location outside the United States, when in either case the transportation is for the purpose of dumping the material into ocean waters, and (2) the dumping of material transported by any person from a location outside the United States, if the dumping occurs in the territorial sea or the contiguous zone of the United States.

(Oct. 23, 1972, Pub.L. 92–532, § 2, 86 Stat. 1052; March 22, 1974, Pub.L. 93–254, § 1(1), 88 Stat. 50.)

Short Title

Section 1 of Pub.L. 92–532, Oct. 23, 1972, 86 Stat. 1052, provided: "That this Act [enacting this chapter and sections 1431 to 1434 of Title 16, Conservation] may be cited as the 'Marine Protection, Research, and Sanctuaries Act of 1972'."

LAW REVIEW COMMENTARIES

Ghosts of fishing nets past: A proposal for regulating derelict synthetic fishing nets. Comment, 63 Wash.L.Rev. 677 (1988).

§ 1402. Definitions [MPRSA § 3]

For the purposes of this chapter the term—

(a) "Administrator" means the Administrator of the Environmental Protection Agency.

(b) "Ocean waters" means those waters of the open seas lying seaward of the base line from which the territorial sea is measured, as provided for in the Convention on the Territorial Sea and the Contiguous Zone (15 UST 1606; TIAS 5639).

(c) "Material" means matter of any kind or description, including, but not limited to, dredged material, solid waste, incinerator residue, garbage, sewage, sewage sludge, munitions, radiological, chemical, and biological warfare agents, radioactive materials, chemicals, biological and laboratory waste, wreck or discarded equipment, rock, sand, excavation debris, and industrial, municipal, agricultural, and other waste; but such term does not mean sewage from vessels within the meaning of section 1322 of this title. Oil within the meaning of section 1321 of this title shall be included only to the extent that such oil is taken on board a vessel or aircraft for the purpose of dumping.

(d) "United States" includes the several States, the District of Columbia, the Commonwealth of Puerto Rico, the Canal Zone, the territories and possessions of the United States, and the Trust Territory of the Pacific Islands.

(e) "Person" means any private person or entity, or any officer, employee, agent, department, agency, or instrumentality of the Federal Government, of any State or local unit of government, or of any foreign government.

(f) "Dumping" means a disposition of material: *Provided*, That it does not mean a disposition of any effluent from any outfall structure to the extent that such disposition is regulated under the provisions of the Federal Water Pollution Control Act, as amended [33 U.S.C.A. § 1251 et seq.], under the provisions of section 407 of this title, or under the provisions of the Atomic Energy Act of 1954, as amended [42 U.S.C.A. § 2011 et seq.], nor does it mean a routine discharge of effluent incidental to the propulsion of, or operation of motor-driven equipment on, vessels: *Provided, further*, That it does not mean the construction of any fixed structure or artificial island nor the intentional placement of any device in ocean waters or on or in the submerged land beneath such waters, for a purpose other than disposal, when such construction or such placement is otherwise regulated by Federal or State law or occurs pursuant to an authorized Federal or State program: *And Provided further*, That it does not include the deposit of oyster shells, or other materials when such deposit is made for the purpose of developing, maintaining, or harvesting fisheries resources and is otherwise regulated by Federal or State law or occurs pursuant to an authorized Federal or State program.

(g) "District court of the United States" includes the District Court of Guam, the District Court of the Virgin Islands, the District Court of Puerto Rico, the District Court of the Canal Zone, and in the case of American Samoa and the Trust Territory of the Pacific Islands, the District Court of the United States for the District of Hawaii, which court shall have jurisdiction over actions arising therein.

(h) "Secretary" means the Secretary of the Army.

(i) "Dredged material" means any material excavated or dredged from the navigable waters of the United States.

(j) "High-level radioactive waste" means the aqueous waste resulting from the operation of the first cycle solvent extraction system, or equivalent and the concentrated waste from subsequent extraction cycles, or equivalent, in a facility for reprocessing irradiated reactor fuels, or irradiated fuel from nuclear power reactors.

(k) "Medical waste" means isolation wastes; infectious agents; human blood and blood products; pathological wastes; sharps; body parts; contaminated bedding; surgical wastes and potentially contaminated laboratory wastes; dialysis wastes; and such additional medical items as the Administrator shall prescribe by regulation.

(*l*) "Transport" or "transportation" refers to the carriage and related handling of any material by a vessel, or by any other vehicle, including aircraft.

(m) "Convention" means the Convention on the Prevention of Marine Pollution by Dumping of Wastes and Other Matter.

(Oct. 23, 1972, Pub.L. 92–532, § 3, 86 Stat. 1052; March 22, 1974, Pub.L. 93–254, § 1(2), 88 Stat. 50; Nov. 18, 1988, Pub.L. 100–688, Title III, § 3201(a), 102 Stat. 4153.)

SUBCHAPTER I—REGULATION

CROSS REFERENCES

Criminal penalties for improper disposition of hazardous waste, federal enforcement of, see section 6928 of Title 42, The Public Health and Welfare.

Dumping of sewage sludge and industrial waste, see section 1412a of this title.

Generators of hazardous waste, standards applicable, see section 6922 of Title 42, The Public Health and Welfare.

Transporters of hazardous waste, standards applicable, see section 6923 of Title 42.

§ 1411. Prohibited acts [MPRSA § 101]

(a) Except as may be authorized by a permit issued pursuant to section 1412 or section 1413 of this title, and subject to regulations issued pursuant to section 1418 of this title,

(1) no person shall transport from the United States, and

(2) in the case of a vessel or aircraft registered in the United States or flying the United States flag or in the case of a United States department, agency, or instrumentality, no person shall transport from any location

any material for the purpose of dumping it into ocean waters.

(b) Except as may be authorized by a permit issued pursuant to section 1412 of this title, and subject to

regulations issued pursuant to section 1418 of this title, no person shall dump any material transported from a location outside the United States (1) into the territorial sea of the United States, or (2) into a zone contiguous to the territorial sea of the United States, extending to a line twelve nautical miles seaward from the base line from which the breadth of the territorial sea is measured, to the extent that it may affect the territorial sea or the territory of the United States.
(Oct. 23, 1972, Pub.L. 92–532, Title I, § 101, 86 Stat. 1053; March 22, 1974, Pub.L. 93–254, § 1(3), 88 Stat. 51.)

Effective Date

Section 110(a) of Title I of Pub.L. 92–532, Oct. 23, 1972, 86 Stat. 1060, provided that: "This title [this subchapter] shall take effect six months after the date of the enactment of this Act [Oct. 23, 1972]."

Savings Provisions

Section 110(b) of Title I of Pub.L. 92–532, Oct. 23, 1972, 86 Stat. 1060, provided that: "No legal action begun, or right of action accrued, prior to the effective date of this title [see Effective Date note under this section] shall be affected by any provision of this title [this subchapter]."

CROSS REFERENCES

Alternative disposal methods, duty of Administrator to develop, see section 1443 of this title.
Dumping of sewage sludge and industrial waste, see section 1412a of this title.
Environmental Protection Agency permits, see 1412 of this title.

LAW REVIEW COMMENTARIES

Prosecution of corporations and corporate officers for environmental crimes: Limiting one's exposure for environmental criminal liability. Kenneth A. Hodson, Sarah N. McGiffert and Marianne T. Bayardi, 34 Ariz.L.Rev. 553 (1992).

Library References

Health and Environment ⟹25.7(3).
C.J.S. Health and Environment § 106.

§ 1412. Dumping permit program [MPRSA § 102]

(a) Environmental Protection Agency permits

Except in relation to dredged material, as provided for in section 1413 of this title, and in relation to radiological, chemical, and biological warfare agents, high-level radioactive waste, and medical waste, for which no permit may be issued, the Administrator may issue permits, after notice and opportunity for public hearings, for the transportation from the United States or, in the case of an agency or instrumentality of the United States, or in the case of a vessel or aircraft registered in the United States or flying the United States flag, for the transportation from a location outside the United States, of material for the purpose of dumping it into ocean waters, or for the dumping of material into the waters described in section 1411(b) of this title, where the Administrator determines that such dumping will not unreasonably degrade or endanger human health, welfare, or amenities, or the marine environment, ecological systems, or economic potentialities. The Administrator shall establish and apply criteria for reviewing and evaluating such permit applications, and, in establishing or revising such criteria, shall consider, but not be limited in his consideration to, the following:

(A) The need for the proposed dumping.

(B) The effect of such dumping on human health and welfare, including economic, esthetic, and recreational values.

(C) The effect of such dumping on fisheries resources, plankton, fish, shellfish, wildlife, shore lines and beaches.

(D) The effect of such dumping on marine ecosystems, particularly with respect to—

(i) the transfer, concentration, and dispersion of such material and its byproducts through biological, physical, and chemical processes.

(ii) potential changes in marine ecosystem diversity, productivity, and stability, and

(iii) species and community population dynamics.

(E) The persistence and permanence of the effects of the dumping.

(F) The effect of dumping particular volumes and concentrations of such materials.

(G) Appropriate locations and methods of disposal or recycling, including land-based alternatives and the probable impact of requiring use of such alternate locations or methods upon considerations affecting the public interest.

(H) The effect on alternate uses of oceans, such as scientific study, fishing, and other living resource exploitation, and nonliving resource exploitation.

(I) In designating recommended sites, the Administrator shall utilize wherever feasible locations beyond the edge of the Continental Shelf.

In establishing or revising such criteria, the Administrator shall consult with Federal, State, and local officials, and interested members of the general public, as may appear appropriate to the Administrator. With respect to such criteria as may affect the civil works program of the Department of the Army, the Administrator shall also consult with the Secretary. In reviewing applications for permits, the Administrator shall make such provision for consultation with interested Federal and State agencies as he deems useful or necessary. No permit shall be issued for a dumping of material which will violate applicable water quality standards. To the extent that he may do so without relaxing the requirements of this subchapter, the Administrator, in establishing or revising such criteria, shall apply the standards and criteria binding upon the United States under the Convention, including its Annexes.

(b) Permit categories

The Administrator may establish and issue various categories of permits, including the general permits described in section 1414(c) of this title.

(c) Designation of sites

(1) In general

The Administrator shall, in a manner consistent with the criteria established pursuant to subsection (a) of this section, designate sites or time periods for dumping. The Administrator shall designate sites or time periods for dumping that will mitigate adverse impact on the environment to the greatest extent practicable.

(2) Prohibitions regarding site or time period

In any case where the Administrator determines that, with respect to certain materials, it is necessary to prohibit dumping at a site or during a time period, the Administrator shall prohibit the dumping of such materials in such site or during such time period. This prohibition shall apply to any dumping at the site or during such time period. This prohibition shall apply to any dumping at the site or during the time period, including any dumping under section 1413(e) of this title.

(3) Dredged material disposal sites

In the case of dredged material disposal sites, the Administrator, in conjunction with the Secretary, shall develop a site management plan for each site designated pursuant to this section. In developing such plans, the Administrator and the Secretary shall provide opportunity for public comment. Such plans shall include, but not be limited to—

(A) a baseline assessment of conditions at the site;

(B) a program for monitoring the site;

(C) special management conditions or practices to be implemented at each site that are necessary for protection of the environment;

(D) consideration of the quantity of the material to be disposed of at the site, and the presence, nature, and bioavailability of the contaminants in the material;

(E) consideration of the anticipated use of the site over the long term, including the anticipated closure date for the site, if applicable, and any need for management of the site after the closure f the site; and

a schedule for review and revision of the ich shall not be reviewed and revised less frequently than 10 years after adoption of the plan, and every 10 years thereafter).

(4) General site management plan requirement; prohibitions

After January 1, 1995, no site shall receive a final designation unless a management plan has been developed pursuant to this section. Beginning on January 1, 1997, no permit for dumping pursuant to this chapter or authorization for dumping under section 1413(e) of this title shall be issued for a site unless such site has received a final designation pursuant to this subsection or an alternative site has been selected pursuant to section 1413(b) of this title.

(5) Management plans for previously designated sites

The Administrator shall develop a site management plan for any site designated prior to January 1, 1995, as expeditiously as practicable, but not later than January 1, 1997, giving priority consideration to management plans for designated sites that are considered to have the greatest impact on the environment.

(d) Fish wastes

No permit is required under this subchapter for the transportation for dumping or the dumping of fish wastes, except when deposited in harbors or other protected or enclosed coastal waters, or where the Administrator finds that such deposits could endanger health, the environment, or ecological systems in a specific location. Where the Administrator makes such a finding, such material may be deposited only as authorized by a permit issued by the Administrator under this section.

(e) Foreign State permits; acceptance

In the case of transportation of material, by an agency or instrumentality of the United States or by a vessel or aircraft registered in the United States or flying the United States flag, from a location in a foreign State Party to the Convention, a permit issued pursuant to the authority of that foreign State Party, in accordance with Convention requirements, and which otherwise could have been issued pursuant to subsection (a) of this section, shall be accepted, for the purposes of this subchapter, as if it were issued by the Administrator under the authority of this section: *Provided*, That in the case of an agency or instrumentality of the United States, no application shall be made for a permit to be issued pursuant to the authority of a foreign State Party to the Convention unless the Administrator concurs in the filing of such application.

(Oct. 23, 1972, Pub.L. 92–532, Title I, § 102, 86 Stat. 1054; March 22, 1974, Pub.L. 93–254, § 1(4), 88 Stat. 51; Dec. 22, 1980, Pub.L. 96–572, § 3, 94 Stat. 3345; Nov. 18, 1988, Pub.L. 100–688, Title III, § 3201(b), 102 Stat. 4153; Oct. 31, 1992, Pub.L. 102–580, Title V, § 506(a), 106 Stat. 4868.)

CROSS REFERENCES

Appropriate locations for dumping dredged material, see section 1413 of this title.
Dumping of dredged material in Long Island Sound from any Federal, etc., project, see section 1416 of this title.
"Federally permitted release" defined, see section 9601 of Title 42, The Public Health and Welfare.
General permits, conditions for, see section 1414 of this title.
Prohibited acts, see section 1411 of this title.
Revocation and suspension of permits, see section 1415 of this title.

CODE OF FEDERAL REGULATIONS

Ocean dumping, see 40 CFR Chap. I, Subchap. H.

LAW REVIEW COMMENTARIES

Ghosts of fishing nets past: A proposal for regulating derelict synthetic fishing nets. Comment, 63 Wash.L.Rev. 677 (1988).

Library References

Health and Environment ⇐25.7(13).
C.J.S. Health and Environment § 107 et seq.

§ 1412a. Dumping of sewage sludge and industrial waste

(a) Emergency permits for dumping of industrial waste; issuance, etc.

Notwithstanding section 104B of the Marine Protection, Research, and Sanctuaries Act of 1972 [42 U.S.C.A. § 1414b], after December 31, 1981, the Administrator may issue emergency permits under Title I of such Act [33 U.S.C.A. § 1411 et seq.] for the dumping of industrial waste into ocean waters, or into waters described in such section 101(b) [33 U.S.C.A. § 1411(b)], if the Administrator determines that there has been demonstrated to exist an emergency, requiring the dumping of such waste, which poses an unacceptable risk relating to human health and admits of no other feasible solution. As used herein, "emergency" refers to situations requiring action with a marked degree of urgency.

(b) "Industrial wastes" defined

For purposes of this section, the term "industrial waste" means any solid, semisolid, or liquid waste generated by a manufacturing or processing plant.

(Nov. 4, 1977, Pub.L. 95–153, § 4, 91 Stat. 1255; Dec. 22, 1980, Pub.L. 96–572, § 2, 94 Stat. 3344; Nov. 18, 1988, Pub.L. 100–688, Title I, § 1003(a), 102 Stat. 4149.)

Codification

Section was not enacted as part of the Marine Protection, Research, and Sanctuaries Act of 1972, which comprises this chapter.

CROSS REFERENCES

Cooperation with public authorities, agencies, and institutions, private agencies and institutions, and individuals, see section 1443 of this title.

LIBRARY REFERENCES

Health and Environment ⇐25.7(13), (19).
C.J.S. Health and Environment §§ 107 et seq., 113 et seq.

§ 1413. Dumping permit program for dredged material [MPRSA § 103]

(a) Issuance by Secretary of the Army

Subject to the provisions of subsections (b), (c), and (d) of this section, the Secretary may issue permits, after notice and opportunity for public hearings, for the transportation of dredged material for the purpose of dumping it into ocean waters, where the Secretary determines that the dumping will not unreasonably degrade or endanger human health, welfare, or amenities, or the marine environment, ecological systems, or economic potentialities.

(b) Independent determination of need for dumping, other methods of disposal, and appropriate locations; alternative sites

In making the determination required by subsection (a) of this section, the Secretary shall apply those criteria, established pursuant to section 1412(a) of this title, relating to the effects of the dumping. Based upon an evaluation of the potential effect of a permit denial on navigation, economic and industrial development, and foreign and domestic commerce of the United States, the Secretary shall make an independent determination as to the need for the dumping. The Secretary shall also make an independent determination as to other possible methods of disposal and as to appropriate locations for the dumping. In considering appropriate locations, he shall, to the maximum extent feasible, utilize the recommended sites designated by the Administrator pursuant to section 1412(c) of this title. In any case in which the use of a designated site is not feasible, the Secretary may, with the concurrence of the Administrator, select an alternative site. The criteria and factors established in section 1412(a) of this title relating to site selection shall be used in selecting the alternative site in a manner consistent with the application of such factors and criteria pursuant to section 1412(c) of this title. Disposal at or in the vicinity of an alternative site shall be limited to a period of not greater than 5 years unless the site is subsequently designated pursuant to section 1412(c) of this title; except that an alternative site may continue to be used for an additional period of time that shall not exceed 5 years if—

(1) no feasible disposal site has been designated by the Administrator;

(2) the continued use of the alternative site is necessary to maintain navigation and facilitate interstate or international commerce; and

(3) the Administrator determines that the continued use of the site does not pose an unacceptable risk to human health, aquatic resources, or the environment.

(c) Concurrence by the Administrator

(1) Notification

Prior to issuing a permit to any person under this section, the Secretary shall first notify the Administrator of the Secretary's intention to do so and provide necessary and appropriate information concerning the permit to the Administrator. Within 30 days of receiving such information, the Administrator shall review the information and request any additional information the Administrator deems necessary to evaluate the proposed permit.

(2) Concurrence by Administrator

Within 45 days after receiving from the Secretary all information the Administrator considers to be necessary to evaluate the proposed permit, the Administrator shall, in writing, concur with (either entirely or with conditions) or decline to concur with the determination of the Secretary as to compliance with the criteria, conditions, and restrictions established pursuant to sections 1412(a) and 1412(c) of this title relating to the environmental impact of the permit. The Administrator may request one 45–day extension in writing and the Secretary shall grant such request on receipt of the request.

(3) Effect of concurrence

In any case where the Administrator makes a determination to concur (with or without conditions) or to decline to concur within the time period specified in paragraph (2) the determination shall prevail. If the Administrator declines to concur in the determination of the Secretary no permit shall be issued. If the Administrator concurs with conditions the permit shall include such conditions. The Administrator shall state in writing the reasons for declining to concur or for the conditions of the concurrence.

(4) Failure to act

If no written documentation is made by the Administrator within the time period provided for in paragraph (2), the Secretary may issue the permit.

(5) Compliance with criteria and restrictions

Unless the Administrator grants a waiver pursuant to subsection (d) of this section, any permit issued by the Secretary shall require compliance with such criteria and restrictions.

(d) Waiver of requirements

If, in any case, the Secretary finds that, in the disposition of dredged material, there is no economically feasible method or site available other than a dumping site the utilization of which would result in non-compliance with the criteria established pursuant to section 1412(a) of this title relating to the effects of dumping or with the restrictions established pursuant to section 1412(c) of this title relating to critical areas, he shall so certify and request a waiver from the Administrator of the specific requirements involved. Within thirty days of the receipt of the waiver request, unless the Administrator finds that the dumping of the material will result in an unacceptably adverse impact on municipal water supplies, shell-fish beds, wildlife, fisheries (including spawning and breeding areas), or recreational areas, he shall grant the waiver.

(e) Federal projects involving dredged material

In connection with Federal projects involving dredged material, the Secretary may, in lieu of the permit procedure, issue regulations which will require the application to such projects of the same criteria, other factors to be evaluated, the same procedures, and the same requirements which apply to the issuance of permits under subsections (a), (b), (c), and (d) of this section and section 1414(a) and (d) of this title.

(Oct. 23, 1972, Pub.L. 92–532, Title I, § 103, 86 Stat. 1055; Oct. 31, 1992, Pub.L. 102–580, Title V, §§ 504, 506(b), 106 Stat. 4866, 4869.)

CROSS REFERENCES

Environmental Protection Agency permits, see section 1412 of this title.
"Federally permitted release" defined, see section 9601 of Title 42, The Public Health and Welfare.
General permits, see section 1414 of this title.
Prohibited acts, see section 1411 of this title.
Revocation and suspension of permits, see section 1415 of this title.

CODE OF FEDERAL REGULATIONS

Enforcement, supervision, and inspection, see 33 CFR 326.1 et seq.
General regulatory policies, see 33 CFR 320.1 et seq.
Nationwide permits, see 33 CFR 330.1 et seq.
Permits for discharges of dredged or fill material into waters of the United States, see 33 CFR 323.1 et seq.
Permits for ocean dumping of dredged material, see 33 CFR 324.1 et seq.
Processing of Department of the Army permits, see 33 CFR 325.1 et seq.
Public hearings, see 33 CFR 327.1 et seq.

LIBRARY REFERENCES

Health and Environment ⟹25.7(13).
C.J.S. Health and Environment § 107 et seq.

§ 1414. Permit conditions [MPRSA § 104]

(a) Designated and included conditions

Permits issued under this subchapter shall designate and include (1) the type of material authorized to be transported for dumping or to be dumped; (2) the amount of material authorized to be transported for dumping or to be dumped; (3) the location where such transport for dumping will be terminated or where such dumping will occur; (4) such requirements, limitations, or conditions as are necessary to assure consistency with any site management plan approved pursuant to section 1412(c) of this title; (5) any special provisions deemed necessary by the Administrator or the Secretary, as the case may be, after consultation with the Secretary of the Department in which the Coast Guard is operating, for the monitoring and surveillance of the transportation or dumping; and (6) such other matters as the Administrator or the Secretary, as the case may be, deems appropriate. Permits issued under this subchapter shall be issued for a period of not to exceed 7 years.

(b) Permit processing fees; reporting requirements

The Administrator or the Secretary, as the case may be, may prescribe such processing fees for permits and such reporting requirements for actions taken pursuant to permits issued by him under this subchapter as he deems appropriate.

(c) General permits

Consistent with the requirements of sections 1412 and 1413 of this title, but in lieu of a requirement for specific permits in such case, the Administrator or the Secretary, as the case may be, may issue general permits for the transportation for dumping, or dumping, or both, of specified materials or classes of materials for which he may issue permits, which he determines will have a minimal adverse environmental impact.

(d) Review

Any permit issued under this subchapter shall be reviewed periodically and, if appropriate, revised. The Administrator or the Secretary, as the case may be, may limit or deny the issuance of permits, or he may alter or revoke partially or entirely the terms of permits issued by him under this subchapter, for the transportation for dumping, or for the dumping, or both, of specified materials or classes of materials, where he finds, based upon monitoring data from the dump site and surrounding area, that such materials cannot be dumped consistently with the criteria and other factors required to be applied in evaluating the permit application. No action shall be taken under this subsection unless the affected person or permittee shall have been given notice and opportunity for a hearing on such action as proposed.

(e) Information for review and evaluation of applications

The Administrator or the Secretary, as the case may be, shall require an applicant for a permit under this subchapter to provide such information as he may consider necessary to review and evaluate such application.

(f) Public information

Information received by the Administrator or the Secretary, as the case may be, as a part of any application or in connection with any permit granted under this subchapter shall be available to the public as a matter of public record, at every stage of the proceeding. The final determination of the Administrator or the Secretary, as the case may be, shall be likewise available.

(g) Display of issued permits

A copy of any permit issued under this subchapter shall be placed in a conspicuous place in the vessel which will be used for the transportation or dumping authorized by such permit, and an additional copy shall be furnished by the issuing official to the Secretary of the department in which the Coast Guard is operating, or its designee.

(h) Low-level radioactive waste; research purposes

Notwithstanding any provision of this subchapter to the contrary, during the two-year period beginning on January 6, 1983, no permit may be issued under this subchapter that authorizes the dumping of any low-level radioactive waste unless the Administrator of the Environmental Protection Agency determines—

(1) that the proposed dumping is necessary to conduct research—

(A) on new technology related to ocean dumping, or

(B) to determine the degree to which the dumping of such substance will degrade the marine environment;

(2) that the scale of the proposed dumping is limited to the smallest amount of such material and the shortest duration of time that is necessary to fulfill the purposes of the research, such that the dumping will have minimal adverse impact upon human health, welfare, and amenities, and the marine environment, ecological systems, economic potentialities, and other legitimate uses;

(3) after consultation with the Secretary of Commerce, that the potential benefits of such research will outweigh any such adverse impact; and

(4) that the proposed dumping will be preceded by appropriate baseline monitoring studies of the

proposed dump site and its surrounding environment.

Each permit issued pursuant to this subsection shall be subject to such conditions and restrictions as the Administrator determines to be necessary to minimize possible adverse impacts of such dumping.

(i) Radioactive Material Disposal Impact Assessment; Congressional approval

(1) Two years after January 6, 1983, the Administrator may not issue a permit under this subchapter for the disposal of radioactive waste material until the applicant, in addition to complying with all other requirements of this subchapter, prepares, with respect to the site at which the disposal is proposed, a Radioactive Material Disposal Impact Assessment which shall include—

(A) a listing of all radioactive materials in each container to be disposed, the number of containers to be dumped, the structural diagrams of each container, the number of curies of each material in each container, and the exposure levels in rems at the inside and outside of each container;

(B) an analysis of the environmental impact of the proposed action, at the site at which the applicant desires to dispose of the material, upon human health and welfare and marine life;

(C) any adverse environmental effects at the site which cannot be avoided should the proposal be implemented;

(D) an analysis of the resulting environmental and economic conditions if the containers fail to contain the radioactive waste material when initially deposited at the specific site;

(E) a plan for the removal or containment of the disposed nuclear material if the container leaks or decomposes;

(F) a determination by each affected State whether the proposed action is consistent with its approved Coastal Zone Management Program;

(G) an analysis of the economic impact upon other users of marine resources;

(H) alternatives to the proposed action;

(I) comments and results of consultation with State officials and public hearings held in the coastal States that are nearest to the affected areas;

(J) a comprehensive monitoring plan to be carried out by the applicant to determine the full effect of the disposal on the marine environment, living resources, or human health, which plan shall include, but not be limited to, the monitoring of exterior container radiation samples, the taking of water and sediment samples, and fish and benthic animal samples, adjacent to the containers, and the acquisition of such other information as the Administrator may require; and

(K) such other information which the Administrator may require in order to determine the full effects of such disposal.

(2) The Administrator shall include, in any permit to which paragraph (1) applies, such terms and conditions as may be necessary to ensure that the monitoring plan required under paragraph (1)(J) is fully implemented, including the analysis by the Administrator of the samples required to be taken under the plan.

(3) The Administrator shall submit a copy of the assessment prepared under paragraph (1) with respect to any permit to the Committee on Merchant Marine and Fisheries of the House of Representatives and the Committee on Environment and Public Works of the Senate.

(4)(A) Upon a determination by the Administrator that a permit to which this subsection applies should be issued, the Administrator shall transmit such a recommendation to the House of Representatives and the Senate.

(B) No permit may be issued by the Administrator under this chapter for the disposal of radioactive materials in the ocean unless the Congress, by approval of a resolution described in paragraph (D) within 90 days of continuous session of the Congress beginning on the date after the date of receipt by the Senate and the House of Representatives of such recommendation, authorizes the Administrator to grant a permit to dispose of radioactive material under this chapter.

(C) For purposes of this subsection—

(1) continuity of session of the Congress is broken only by an adjournment sine die;

(2) the days on which either House is not in session because of an adjournment of more than three days to a day certain are excluded in the computation of the 90 day calendar period.

(D) For the purposes of this subsection, the term "resolution" means a joint resolution, the resolving clause of which is as follows: "That the House of Representatives and the Senate approve and authorize the Administrator of the Environmental Protection Agency to grant a permit to ______ under the Marine Protection, Research, and Sanctuaries Act of 1972 to dispose of radioactive materials in the ocean as recommended by the Administrator to the Congress on ______, 19—."; the first blank space therein to be filled with the appropriate applicant to dispose of nuclear material and the second blank therein to be filled with the date on which the Administrator submits the recommendation to the House of Representatives and the Senate.

(Oct. 23, 1972, Pub.L. 92–532, Title I, § 104, 86 Stat. 1056; Jan. 6, 1983, Pub.L. 97–424, Title IV, § 424(a), 96 Stat. 2165; Apr. 2, 1987, Pub.L. 100–17, § 133(c)(1), 101 Stat. 172; Oct. 31, 1992, Pub.L. 102–580, Title V, § 507, 106 Stat. 4869.)

Abolition of House Committee on Merchant Marine and Fisheries

Committee on Merchant Marine and Fisheries of House of Representatives abolished and any reference in any provision of law enacted before Jan. 4, 1995, to the Committee on Merchant Marine and Fisheries of the House of Representatives treated as referring to the Committee on Agriculture of the House of Representatives, in the case of a provision of law relating to inspection of seafood or seafood products, the Committee on National Security of the House of Representatives, in the case of a provision of law relating to interoceanic canals, the Merchant Marine Academy and State Maritime Academies, or national security aspects of merchant marine, the Committee on Resources of the House of Representatives, in the case of a provision of law relating to fisheries, wildlife, international fishing agreements marine affairs (including coastal zone management) except for measures relating to oil and other pollution of navigable waters, or oceanography, the Committee on Science of the House of Representatives, in the case of a provision of law relating to marine research, and the Committee on Transportation and Infrastructure of the House of Representatives, in the case of a provision of law relating to a matter other than a matter described above, see section 1(b)(3) of Pub.L. 104–14, set out as a note preceding section 21 of Title 2, The Congress.

CROSS REFERENCES

Permit categories, see section 1412 of this title.

CODE OF FEDERAL REGULATIONS

Contents of permits; revision, revocation, or limitation of ocean dumping permits, see 40 CFR 223.1 et seq.
Public information, see 40 CFR 2.100 et seq.

LIBRARY REFERENCES

Health and Environment ⟹25.7(13).
C.J.S. Health and Environment § 107 et seq.

§ 1414a. Special provisions regarding certain dumping sites [MPRSA § 104A]

(a) New York Bight Apex

(1) For purposes of this subsection—

(A) The term "Apex" means the New York Bight Apex consisting of the ocean waters of the Atlantic Ocean westward of 73 degrees 30 minutes west longitude and northward of 40 degrees 10 minutes north latitude.

(B) The term "Apex site" means that site within the Apex at which the dumping of municipal sludge occurred before October 1, 1983.

(C) The term "eligible authority" means any sewerage authority or other unit of State or local government that on November 2, 1983, was authorized under court order to dump municipal sludge at the Apex site.

(2) No person may apply for a permit under this subchapter in relation to the dumping of, or the transportation for purposes of dumping, municipal sludge within the Apex unless that person is an eligible authority.

(3) The Administrator may not issue, or renew, any permit under this subchapter that authorizes the dumping of, or the transportation for purposes of dumping, municipal sludge within the Apex after the earlier of—

(A) December 15, 1987; or

(B) the day determined by the Administrator to be the first day on which municipal sludge generated by eligible authorities can reasonably be dumped at a site designated under section 1412 of this title other than a site within the Apex.

(b) Restriction on use of the 106–mile site

The Administrator may not issue or renew any permit under this subchapter which authorizes any person, other than a person that is an eligible authority within the meaning of subsection (a)(1)(C) of this section, to dump, or to transport for the purposes of dumping, municipal sludge within the site designated under section 1412(c) of this title by the Administrator and known as the "106–Mile Ocean Waste Dump Site" (as described in 49 F.R. 19005).

(Pub.L. 92–532, Title I, § 104A, as added Nov. 17, 1986, Pub.L. 99–662, Title XI, § 1172(b), 100 Stat. 4259.)

Prior Provisions

An identical section 104A, which was added to Pub.L. 92–532 by Pub.L. 100–4, Title V, § 508(b), Feb. 4, 1987, 101 Stat. 79 and also classified to this section, was repealed by Pub.L. 100–688, Title I, § 1002, Nov. 18, 1988, 102 Stat. 4139.

LIBRARY REFERENCES

Navigable Waters ⟹35.
C.J.S. Health and Environment § 106 et seq.
C.J.S. Navigable Waters § 11.

§ 1414b. Ocean dumping of sewage sludge and industrial waste [MPRSA § 104B]

(a) Termination of dumping

(1) Prohibitions on dumping

Notwithstanding any other provision of law—

(A) on and after the 270th day after November 18, 1988, no person (including a person described in section 1414a(a)(1)(C) of this title) shall dump into ocean waters, or transport for the purpose of dumping into ocean waters, sewage sludge or industrial waste, unless such person—

(i) has entered into a compliance agreement or enforcement agreement which meets the requirements of subsection (c)(2) or (3) of this section, as applicable; and

(ii) has obtained a permit issued under section 1412 of this title which authorizes such transportation and dumping; and

(B) after December 31, 1991, it shall be unlawful for any person to dump into ocean waters, or to transport for the purposes of dumping into ocean waters, sewage sludge or industrial waste.

(2) Prohibition on new entrants

The Administrator shall not issue any permit under this chapter which authorizes a person to dump into ocean waters, or to transport for the purposes of dumping into ocean waters, sewage sludge or industrial waste, unless that person was authorized by a permit issued under section 1412 of this title or by a court order to dump into ocean waters, or to transport for the purpose of dumping into ocean waters, sewage sludge or industrial waste on September 1, 1988.

(b) Special dumping fees

(1) In general

Subject to paragraph (4), any person who dumps into ocean waters, or transports for the purpose of dumping into ocean waters, sewage sludge or industrial waste shall be liable for a fee equal to—

(A) $100 for each dry ton (or equivalent) of sewage sludge or industrial waste transported or dumped by the person on or after the 270th day after November 18, 1988 and before January 1, 1990;

(B) $150 for each dry ton (or equivalent) of sewage sludge or industrial waste transported or dumped by the person on or after January 1, 1990, and before January 1, 1991; and

(C) $200 for each dry ton (or equivalent) of sewage sludge or industrial waste transported or dumped by the person on or after January 1, 1991, and before January 1, 1992.

(2) Payment of fees

Of the amount of fees under paragraph (1) for which a person is liable, such person—

(A) shall pay into a trust account established by the person in accordance with subsection (e) of this section a sum equal to 85 percent of such amount;

(B) shall pay to the Administrator a sum equal to $15 per dry ton (or equivalent) of sewage sludge and industrial waste transported or dumped by such person, for use for agency activities as provided in subsection (f)(1) of this section;

(C) subject to paragraph (5), shall pay into the Clean Oceans Fund established by the State in which the person is located a sum equal to 50 percent of the balance of such amount after application of subparagraphs (A) and (B); and

(D) subject to paragraph (5), shall pay to the State in which the person is located a sum equal to the balance of such amount after application of subparagraphs (A), (B), and (C), for deposit into the water pollution control revolving fund established by the State under title VI of the Federal Water Pollution Control Act [33 U.S.C.A. § 1381 et seq.], as provided in subsection (f)(2) of this section.

(3) Schedule for payment

Fees under this subsection shall be paid on a quarterly basis.

(4) Waiver of fees

(A) The Administrator shall waive all fees under this subsection, other than the portion of fees required to be paid to the Administrator under paragraph (2)(B) for agency activities, for any person who has entered into a compliance agreement which meets the requirements of subsection (c)(2) of this section.

(B) The Administrator shall reimpose fees under this subsection for a person for whom such fees are waived under subparagraph (A) if the Administrator determines that—

(i) the person has failed to comply with the terms of a compliance agreement which the person entered into under subsection (c)(2) of this section; and

(ii) such failure is likely to result in the person not being able to terminate by December 31, 1991, dumping of sewage sludge or industrial waste into ocean waters.

(C) The Administrator may waive fees reimposed for a person under subparagraph (B) if the Administrator determines that the person has returned to compliance with a compliance agreement which the person entered into under subsection (c)(2) of this section.

(5) Payments prior to establishment of account

(A) In any case in which a State has not established a Clean Oceans Fund or a water pollution control revolving fund under title VI of the Federal Water Pollution Control Act [33 U.S.C.A. § 1381 et seq.], fees required to be paid by a person in that State under paragraph (2)(C) or (D), as applicable, shall be paid to the Administrator.

(B) Amounts paid to the Administrator pursuant to this paragraph shall be held by the Administrator in escrow until the establishment of the fund into which such amounts are required to be paid under paragraph (2), or until the last day of the 1-year period beginning on the date of such payment, whichever is earlier, and thereafter—

(i) if such fund has been established, shall be paid by the Administrator into the fund; or

(ii) if such fund has not been established, shall revert to the general fund of the Treasury.

(c) Compliance agreements and enforcement agreements

(1) In general

As a condition of issuing a permit under section 1412 of this title which authorizes a person to transport or dump sewage sludge or industrial waste, the Administrator shall require that, before the issuance of such permit, the person and the State in which the person is located enter into with the Administrator—

(A) a compliance agreement which meets the requirements of paragraph (2); or

(B) an enforcement agreement which meets the requirements of paragraph (3).

(2) Compliance agreements

An agreement shall be a compliance agreement for purposes of this section only if—

(A) it includes a plan negotiated by the person, the State in which the person is located, and the Administrator that will, in the opinion of the Administrator, if adhered to by the person in good faith, result in the phasing out and termination of ocean dumping, and transportation for the purpose of ocean dumping, of sewage sludge and industrial waste by such person by not later than December 31, 1991, through the design, construction, and full implementation of an alternative system for the management of sewage sludge and industrial waste transported or dumped by the person;

(B) it includes a schedule which—

(i) in the opinion of the Administrator, specifies reasonable dates by which the person shall complete the various activities that are necessary for the timely implementation of the alternative system referred to in subparagraph (A); and

(ii) meets the requirements of paragraph (4);

(C) it requires the person to notify in a timely manner the Administrator and the Governor of the State of any problems the person has in complying with the schedule referred to in subparagraph (B);

(D) it requires the Administrator and the Governor of the State to evaluate on an ongoing basis the compliance of the person with the schedule referred to in subparagraph (B);

(E) it requires the person to pay in accordance with this section all fees and penalties the person is liable for under this section; and

(F) it authorizes the person to use interim measures before completion of the alternative system referred to in subparagraph (A).

(3) Enforcement agreements

An agreement shall be an enforcement agreement for purposes of this section only if—

(A) it includes a plan negotiated by the person, the State in which the person is located, and the Administrator that will, in the opinion of the Administrator, if adhered to by the person in good faith, result in the phasing out and termination of ocean dumping, and transportation for the purpose of ocean dumping, of sewage sludge and industrial waste by such person through the design, construction, and full implementation of an alternative system for the management of sewage sludge and industrial waste transported or dumped by the person;

(B) it includes a schedule which—

(i) in the opinion of the Administrator, specifies reasonable dates by which the person shall complete the various activities that are necessary for the timely implementation of the alternative system referred to in subparagraph (A); and

(ii) meets the requirements of paragraph (4);

(C) it requires the person to notify in a timely manner the Administrator and the Governor of the State of any problems the person has in complying with the schedule referred to in subparagraph (B);

(D) it requires the Administrator and the Governor of the State to evaluate on an ongoing basis the compliance of the person with the schedule referred to in subparagraph (B);

(E) it requires the person to pay in accordance with this section all fees and penalties the person is liable for under this section; and

(F) it authorizes the person to use interim measures before completion of the alternative system referred to in subparagraph (A).

(4) Schedules

A schedule included in a compliance agreement pursuant to paragraph (2)(B) or an enforcement agreement pursuant to paragraph (3)(B) shall establish deadlines for—

(A) preparation of engineering designs and related specifications for the alternative system referred to in paragraph (2)(A) or paragraph (3)(A), as applicable;

(B) compliance with appropriate Federal, State, and local statutes, regulations, and ordinances;

(C) site and equipment acquisitions for such alternative system;

(D) construction and testing of such alternative system;

(E) operation of such alternative system at full capacity; and

(F) any other activities, including interim measures, that the Administrator considers necessary or appropriate.

(5) Clean oceans funds

(A) Each State that is a party to a compliance agreement or an enforcement agreement under this subsection shall establish an interest bearing account, to be known as a Clean Oceans Fund, into which a person shall pay fees and penalties in accordance with subsections (b)(2)(C) of this section and (d)(2)(C)(i) of this section, respectively.

(B) A State which establishes a Clean Oceans Fund pursuant to this paragraph shall allocate and pay from the fund each year, to each person in the State which has entered into a compliance agreement or enforcement agreement under this subsection, a portion of amounts in the fund on the last day of that year which is equal to the sum of—

(i) amounts paid by the person into the fund in that year as fees pursuant to subsection (b)(2)(C) of this section; and as penalties pursuant to subsection (d)(2)(C)(i) of this section;

(ii) amounts paid by the Administrator into the fund in that year as fees held in escrow for the person pursuant to subsection (b)(5)(B) of this section; and

(iii) interest on such amounts.

(C) Amounts allocated and paid to a person pursuant to subparagraph (B)—

(i) shall be used for the purposes described in subsection (e)(2)(B); and

(ii) may be used for matching Federal grants.

(D) A Clean Oceans Fund established by a State pursuant to this paragraph shall be subject to such accounting, reporting, and other requirements as may be established by the Administrator to assure accountability of payments into and out of the fund.

(6) Public participation

The Administrator shall provide an opportunity for public comment regarding the establishment and implementation of compliance agreements and enforcement agreements entered into pursuant to this section.

(d) Penalties

(1) In general

In lieu of any other civil penalty under this chapter, any person who has entered into a compliance agreement or enforcement agreement under subsection (c) of this section and who dumps or transports sewage sludge or industrial waste in violation of subsection (a)(1)(B) of this section shall be liable for a civil penalty, to be assessed by the Administrator, as follows:

(A) For each dry ton (or equivalent) of sewage sludge or industrial waste dumped or transported by the person in violation of this subsection in calendar year 1992, $600.

(B) For each dry ton (or equivalent) of sewage sludge or industrial waste dumped or transported by the person in violation of this subsection in any year after calendar year 1992, a sum equal to—

(i) the amount of penalty per dry ton (or equivalent) for a violation occurring in the preceding calendar year, plus

(ii) a percentage of such amount equal to 10 percent of such amount, plus an additional 1 percent of such amount for each full calendar year since December 31, 1991.

(2) Payment of penalty

Of the amount of penalties under paragraph (1) for which a person is liable, such person—

(A) shall pay into a trust account established by the person in accordance with subsection (e) of this section a sum which is a percentage of such amount equal to—

(i) 90 percent of such amount, reduced by

(ii) 5 percent of such amount for each full calendar year since December 31, 1991;

(B) shall pay to the Administrator a sum equal to $15 per dry ton (or equivalent) of sewage sludge and industrial waste transported or dumped by such person in that year, for use for agency activities as provided in subsection (f)(1) of this section;

(C) for violations in any year before calendar year 1995—

(i) subject to paragraph (4), shall pay into the Clean Oceans Fund established by the State in which the person is located a sum equal to 50 percent of the balance of such amount; and

(ii) subject to paragraph (4), shall pay to the State in which the person is located a sum equal to the portion of such amount which is not paid as provided in subparagraphs (A), (B), and (C), for deposit into the water pollution control revolving fund established by the State under title VI of the Federal Water Pollution Control Act [33 U.S.C.A. § 1381 et seq.], as provided in subsection (f)(2) of this section; and

(D) for violations in any year after calendar year 1994, shall pay to the State in which the person is located a sum equal to the balance of such amount, for use by the State for providing assistance under subsection (f)(3) of this section.

(3) Schedule for payment

Penalties under this subsection shall be paid on a quarterly basis.

(4) Payments prior to establishment of account

In any case in which a State has not established a Clean Oceans Fund or a water pollution control revolving fund under title VI of the Federal Water Pollution Control Act [33 U.S.C.A. § 1381 et seq.], penalties required to be paid by a person in that State under paragraph (2)(C)(i) or (ii), as applicable, shall be paid to the Administrator for holding and payment or reversion, as applicable, in the same manner as fees are held and paid or revert under subsection (b)(5) of this section.

(e) Trust account

(1) In general

A person who enters into a compliance agreement or an enforcement agreement under subsection (c) of this section shall establish a trust account for the payment and use of fees and penalties under this section.

(2) Trust account requirements

An account shall be a trust account for purposes of this subsection only if it meets, to the satisfaction of the Administrator, the following requirements:

(A) Amounts in the account may be used only with the concurrence of the person who establishes the account and the Administrator; except that the person may use amounts in the account for a purpose authorized by subparagraph (B) after 60 days after notification of the Administrator if the Administrator does not disapprove such use before the end of such 60-day period.

(B) Amounts in the account may be used only for projects which will identify, develop, and implement—

(i) an alternative system, and any interim measures, for the management of sewage sludge and industrial waste, including but not limited to any such system or measures utilizing resource recovery, recycling, thermal reduction, or composting techniques; or

(ii) improvements in pretreatment, treatment, and storage techniques for sewage sludge and industrial waste to facilitate the implementation of such alternative system or interim measures.

(C) Upon a finding by the Administrator that a person did not pay fees or penalties into an account as required by this section, or did not use amounts in the account in accordance with this subsection, the balance of the amounts in the account shall be paid to the State in which the person is located, for deposit into the water pollution control revolving fund established by the State under title VI of the Federal Water Pollution Control Act [33 U.S.C.A. § 1381 et seq.], as provided in subsection (f)(2) of this section.

(3) Use of unexpended amounts

Upon a determination by the Administrator that a person has terminated ocean dumping of sewage sludge or industrial waste, the balance of amounts in an account established by the person under this subsection shall be paid to the person for use—

(A) for debts incurred by the person in complying with this chapter or the Federal Water Pollution Control Act [33 U.S.C.A. § 1251 et seq.];

(B) in meeting the requirements of the Federal Water Pollution Control Act (33 U.S.C. 1251 et seq.) which apply to the person, including operations and maintenance; and

(C) for matching Federal grants.

(4) Use for matching Federal grants

Amounts in a trust account under this subsection may be used for matching Federal grants.

(f) Use of fees and penalties

(1) Agency activities

Of the total amount of fees and penalties paid to the Administrator in a fiscal year pursuant to subsections (b)(2)(B) and (d)(2)(B) of this section, respectively—

(A) not to exceed one-third of such total amount shall be used by the Administrator for—

(i) costs incurred or expected to be incurred in undertaking activities directly associated with the issuance under this chapter of permits for the transportation or dumping of sewage sludge and industrial waste, including the costs of any environmental assessment of the direct effects of dumping under the permits;

(ii) preparation of reports under subsection (i) of this section; and

(iii) such other research, studies, and projects the Administrator considers necessary for, and consistent with, the development and implementation of alternative systems for the management of sewage sludge and industrial waste;

(B) not to exceed one-third of such total amount shall be transferred to the Secretary of the department in which the Coast Guard is operating for use for—

(i) Coast Guard surveillance of transportation and dumping of sewage sludge and industrial waste subject to this chapter; and

(ii) such enforcement activities conducted by the Coast Guard with respect to such transportation and dumping as may be necessary to ensure to the maximum extent practicable complete compliance with the requirements of this chapter; and

(C) not to exceed one-third of such total amount shall be transferred to the Under Secretary of Commerce for Oceans and Atmosphere for use for—

(i) monitoring, research, and related activities consistent with the program developed pursuant to subsection (j)(1) of this section; and

(ii) preparing annual reports to the Congress pursuant to subsection (j)(4) of this section which describe the results of such monitoring, research, and activities.

(2) Deposits into State water pollution control revolving fund

(A) Amounts paid to a State pursuant to subsection (b)(2)(D), (d)(2)(C)(ii), or (e)(2)(C) of this section shall be deposited into the water pollution control revolving fund established by the State pursuant to title VI of the Federal Water Pollution Control Act [33 U.S.C.A. § 1381 et seq.].

(B) Amounts deposited into a State water pollution control revolving fund pursuant to this paragraph—

(i) shall not be used by the State to provide assistance to the person who paid such amounts for development or implementation of any alternative system;

(ii) shall not be considered to be State matching amounts under title VI of the Federal Water Pollution Control Act [33 U.S.C.A. § 1381 et seq.]; and

(iii) shall not be subject to State matching requirements under such title.

(3) Penalty payments to States after 1994

(A) Amounts paid to a State as penalties pursuant to subsection (d)(2)(D) of this section may be used by the State—

(i) for providing assistance to any person in the State—

(I)for implementing a management program under section 319 of the Federal Water Pollution Control Act [33 U.S.C.A. § 1329];

(II) for developing and implementing a conservation and management plan under section 320 of such [33 U.S.C.A. § 1330]; or

(III) for implementing technologies and management practices necessary for controlling pollutant inputs adversely affecting the New York Bight, as such inputs are identified in the New York Bight Restoration Plan prepared under section 2301 of the Marine Plastic Pollution Research and Control Act of 1987; and

(ii) for providing assistance to any person in the State who was not required to pay such penalties for construction of treatment works (as defined in section 212 of the Federal Water Pollution Control Act [33 U.S.C.A. § 1929]) which are publicly owned.

(B) Amounts paid to a State as penalties pursuant to subsection (d)(2)(D) of this section which are not used in accordance with subparagraph (A) shall be deposited into the water pollution control revolving fund established by the State under title VI of the Federal Water Pollution Control Act [33 U.S.C.A. § 1381 et seq.]. Amounts deposited into such a fund pursuant to this subparagraph—

(i) shall not be used by the State to provide assistance to the person who paid such amounts;

(ii) shall not be considered to be State matching amounts under title VI of the Federal Water Pollution Control Act [33 U.S.C.A. § 1381 et seq.]; and

(iii) shall not be subject to State matching requirements under such title.

(4) Deposits into Treasury as offsetting collections

Amounts of fees and penalties paid to the Administrator pursuant to subsection (b)(2)(B) or (d)(2)(B) of this section which are used by an agency in accordance with paragraph (1) shall be deposited into the Treasury as offsetting collections of the agency.

(g) Enforcement

(1) In general

Whenever, on the basis of any information available, the Administrator finds that a person is dumping or transporting sewage sludge or industrial waste in violation of subsection (a)(1) of this section, the Administrator shall issue an order requiring such person to terminate such dumping or transporting (as applicable) until such person—

(A) enters into a compliance agreement or an enforcement agreement under subsection (c) of this section; and

(B) obtains a permit under section 1412 of this title which authorizes such dumping or transporting.

(2) Requirements of order

Any order issued by the Administrator under this subsection—

(A) shall be delivered by personal service to the person named in the order;

(B) shall state with reasonable specificity the nature of the violation for which the order is issued; and

(C) shall require that the person named in the order, as a condition of dumping into ocean waters, or transporting for the purpose of dumping into ocean waters, sewage sludge or industrial waste—

(i) shall enter into a compliance agreement or an enforcement agreement under subsection (c) of this section; and

(ii) shall obtain a permit under section 1412 of this title which authorizes such dumping or transporting.

(3) Actions

The Administrator may request the Attorney General to commence a civil action for appropriate relief, including a temporary or permanent injunction and the imposition of civil penalties authorized by subsection (d)(1) of this section, for any violation of subsection (a)(1) of this section or of an order issued by the Administrator under this section. Such an action may be brought in the district court of the United States for the district in which the defendant is located, resides, or is doing business, and such court shall have jurisdiction to restrain such violation and require compliance with subsection (a)(1) of this section and any such order.

(h) State progress reports

(1) In general

The Governor of each State that is a party to a compliance agreement or an enforcement agreement under subsection (c) of this section shall submit to the Administrator on September 30 of 1989 and of every year thereafter until the Administrator determines that ocean dumping of sewage sludge and industrial waste by persons located in that State has terminated, a report which describes—

(A) the efforts of each person located in the State to comply with a compliance agreement or enforcement agreement entered into by the person pursuant to subsection (c) of this section, including the extent to which such person has complied with deadlines established by the schedule included in such agreement;

(B) activity of the State regarding permits for the construction and operation of each alternative system; and

(C) an accounting of amounts paid into and withdrawn from a Clean Oceans Fund established by the State.

(2) Failure to submit report

If a State fails to submit a report in accordance with this subsection, the Administrator shall withhold funds reserved for such State under section 205(g) of the Federal Water Pollution Control Act (33 U.S.C. 1285(g)). Funds withheld pursuant to this paragraph may, at the discretion of the Administrator, be restored to a State upon compliance with this subsection.

(i) EPA progress reports

(1) In general

Not later than December 31 of 1989 and of each year thereafter until the Administrator determines that ocean dumping of sewage sludge and industrial waste has terminated, the Administrator shall prepare and submit to the Congress a report on—

(A) progress being made by persons issued permits under section 1412 of this title for transportation or dumping of sewage sludge or industrial waste in developing alternative systems for managing sewage sludge and industrial waste;

(B) the efforts of each such person to comply with a compliance agreement or enforcement agreement entered into by the person pursuant to subsection (c) of this section, including the extent to which such person has complied with deadlines established by the schedule included in such agreement;

(C) progress being made by the Administrator and others in identifying and implementing alternative systems for the management of sewage sludge and industrial waste; and

(D) progress being made toward the termination of ocean dumping of sewage sludge and industrial waste.

(2) **Referral to Congressional committees**

Each report submitted to the Congress under this subsection shall be referred to each standing committee of the House of Representatives and of the Senate having jurisdiction over any part of the subject matter of the report.

(j) **Environmental monitoring**

(1) **In general**

The Administrator, in cooperation with the Under Secretary of Commerce for Oceans and Atmosphere, shall design a program for monitoring environmental conditions—

(A) at the Apex site (as that term is defined in section 1414a of this title);

(B) at the site designated by the Administrator under section 1412(c) of this title and known as the "106-Mile Ocean Waste Dump Site" (as described in 49 F.R. 19005);

(C) at the site at which industrial waste is dumped; and

(D) within the potential area of influence of the sewage sludge and industrial waste dumped at those sites.

(2) **Program requirements**

The program designed under paragraph (1) shall include, but is not limited to—

(A) sampling of an appropriate number of fish and shellfish species and other organisms to assess the effects of environmental conditions on living marine organisms in these areas; and

(B) use of satellite and other advanced technologies in conducting the program.

(3) **Monitoring activities**

The Administrator and the Under Secretary of Commerce for Oceans and Atmosphere shall each conduct monitoring activities consistent with the program designed under paragraph (1).

(4) **Reports**

(A) Not later than 1 year after November 18, 1988, the Administrator, in cooperation with the Under Secretary of Commerce for Oceans and Atmosphere, shall submit to the Congress a report describing the program designed pursuant to paragraph (1).

(B) Not later than December 31 of each year after the submission of a report under subparagraph (A), the Administrator and the Under Secretary of Commerce for Oceans and Atmosphere shall report to the Congress the results of monitoring activities conducted during the previous year under the program designed pursuant to paragraph (1).

(k) **Definitions**

For purposes of this section—

(1) the term "alternative system" means any method for the management of sewage sludge or industrial waste which does not require a permit under this chapter;

(2) the term "Clean Oceans Fund" means such a fund established by a State in accordance with subsection (c)(5) of this section;

(3) the term "excluded material" means—

(A) any dredged material discharged by the United States Army Corps of Engineers or discharged pursuant to a permit issued by the Secretary in accordance with section 1413 of this title; and

(B) any waste from a tuna cannery operation located in American Samoa or Puerto Rico discharged pursuant to a permit issued by the Administrator under section 1412 of this title;

(4) the term "industrial waste" means any solid, semisolid, or liquid waste generated by a manufacturing or processing plant, other than an excluded material;

(5) the term "interim measure" means any short-term method for the management of sewage sludge or industrial waste, which—

(A) is used before implementation of an alternative system; and

(B) does not require a permit under this chapter; and

(6) the term "sewage sludge" means any solid, semisolid, or liquid waste generated by a wastewater treatment plant, other than an excluded material.

(Pub.L. 92–532, Title I, § 104B, as added Pub.L. 100–688, Title I, § 1002, Nov. 18, 1988, 102 Stat. 4139.)

References in Text

The Federal Water Pollution Control Act, referred to in subsecs. (b)(2)(D), (5)(A), (d)(2)(C)(ii), (4), (e)(2)(C), (3)(A), (B), (f)(2)(A), (B)(ii), (iii), (3)(B) opening clause, (B)(ii), (iii), is Act June 30, 1948, c. 758, as amended generally by Pub.L. 92–500, § 2, Oct. 18, 1972, 86 Stat. 816, which is classified generally to chapter 26 (section 1251 et seq.) of this title. Title VI of that Act is classified to subchapter VI (Section 1381 et seq.) of chapter 26 of this title. For complete classification of this Act to the Code, see Short Title note set out under section 1251 of this title and Tables volume.

Section 2301 of the Marine Plastic Pollution Research and Control Act of 1987, referred to in subsec. (f)(3)(A)(i)(III), is section 2301 of Pub.L. 100–220, Title II, Dec. 29, 1987, 101 Stat. 1467, set out as a note under section 2267 of this title.

Short Title

Section 1001 of Pub.L. 100–688, Nov. 18, 1988, 102 Stat. 4139, provided that: "This title [adding this section and section 1414c of this title to the Marine Protection, Research, and Sanctuaries Act of 1972] may be cited as the 'Ocean Dumping Ban Act of 1988'."

§ 1414c. Prohibition on disposal of sewage sludge at landfills on Staten Island [MPRSA § 104C]

(a) In general

No person shall dispose of sewage sludge at any landfill located on Staten Island, New York.

(b) Exclusion from penalties

(1) In general

Subject to paragraph (2), a person who violates this section shall not be subject to any penalty under this chapter.

(2) Injunction

Paragraph (1) shall not prohibit the bringing of an action for, or the granting of, an injunction under section 1415 of this title with respect to a violation of this section.

(c) Definition

For purposes of this section, the term "sewage sludge" has the meaning such term has in section 1414b of this title.

(Pub.L. 92–532, Title I, § 104C, as added Pub.L. 100–688, Title I, § 1005, Nov. 18, 1988, 102 Stat. 4150.)

§ 1415. Penalties [MPRSA § 105]

(a) Assessment of civil penalty by Administrator; remission or mitigation; court action for appropriate relief

Any person who violates any provision of this subchapter, or of the regulations promulgated under this subchapter, or a permit issued under this subchapter shall be liable to a civil penalty of not more than $50,000 for each violation to be assessed by the Administrator. In addition, any person who violates this subchapter or any regulation issued under this subchapter by engaging in activity involving the dumping of medical waste shall be liable for a civil penalty of not more than $125,000 for each violation, to be assessed by the Administrator after written notice and an opportunity for a hearing. No penalty shall be assessed until the person charged shall have been given notice and an opportunity for a hearing of such violation. In determining the amount of the penalty, the gravity of the violation, prior violations, and the demonstrated good faith of the person charged in attempting to achieve rapid compliance after notification of a violation shall be considered by said Administrator. For good cause shown, the Administrator may remit or mitigate such penalty. Upon failure of the offending party to pay the penalty, the Administrator may request the Attorney General to commence an action in the appropriate district court of the United States for such relief as may be appropriate.

Any person who violates any provision of this subchapter, or of the regulations promulgated under this subchapter, or a permit issued under this subchapter shall be liable to a civil penalty of not more than $50,000 for each violation to be assessed by the Administrator. No penalty shall be assessed until the person charged shall have been given notice and an opportunity for a hearing of such violation. In determining the amount of the penalty, the gravity of the violation, prior violations, and the demonstrated good faith of the person charged in attempting to achieve rapid compliance after notification of a violation shall be considered by said Administrator. For good cause shown, the Administrator may remit or mitigate such penalty. Upon failure of the offending party to pay the penalty, the Administrator may request the Attorney General to commence an action in the appropriate district court of the United States for such relief as may be appropriate.

(b) Criminal penalties

In addition to any action that may be brought under subsection (a) of this section—

(1) any person who knowingly violates any provision of this subchapter, any regulation promulgated under this subchapter, or a permit issued under this subchapter, shall be fined under Title 18, or imprisoned for not more than 5 years, or both; and

(2) any person who is convicted of such a violation pursuant to paragraph (1) shall forfeit to the United States—

(A) any property constituting or derived from any proceeds that the person obtained, directly or indirectly, as a result of such violation; and

(B) any of the property of the person which was used, or intended to be used in any manner or part, to commit or to facilitate the commission of the violation.

(c) Separate offenses

For the purpose of imposing civil penalties and criminal fines under this section, each day of a continuing violation shall constitute a separate offense as shall the dumping from each of several vessels, or other sources.

(d) Injunctive relief

The Attorney General or his delegate may bring actions for equitable relief to enjoin an imminent or continuing violation of this subchapter, of regulations promulgated under this subchapter, or of permits issued under this subchapter, and the district courts of the United States shall have jurisdiction to grant such relief as the equities of the case may require.

(e) Liability of vessels in rem

A vessel, except a public vessel within the meaning of section 13 of the Federal Water Pollution Control Act, as amended, used in a violation, shall be liable in rem for any civil penalty assessed or criminal fine imposed and may be proceeded against in any district court of the United States having jurisdiction thereof; but no vessel shall be liable unless it shall appear that one or more of the owners, or bareboat charterers, was at the time of the violation a consenting party or privy to such violation.

(f) Revocation and suspension of permits

If the provisions of any permit issued under section 1412 or 1413 of this title are violated, the Administrator or the Secretary, as the case may be, may revoke the permit or may suspend the permit for a specified period of time. No permit shall be revoked or suspended unless the permittee shall have been given notice and opportunity for a hearing on such violation and proposed suspension or revocation.

(g) Civil suits by private persons

(1) Except as provided in paragraph (2) of this subsection any person may commence a civil suit on his own behalf to enjoin any person, including the United States and any other governmental instrumentality or agency (to the extent permitted by the eleventh amendment to the Constitution), who is alleged to be in violation of any prohibition, limitation, criterion, or permit established or issued by or under this subchapter. The district courts shall have jurisdiction, without regard to the amount in controversy or the citizenship of the parties, to enforce such prohibition, limitation, criterion, or permit, as the case may be.

(2) No action may be commenced—

(A) prior to sixty days after notice of the violation has been given to the Administrator or to the Secretary, and to any alleged violator of the prohibition, limitation, criterion, or permit; or

(B) if the Attorney General has commenced and is diligently prosecuting a civil action in a court of the United States to require compliance with the prohibition, limitation, criterion, or permit; or

(C) if the Administrator has commenced action to impose a penalty pursuant to subsection (a) of this section, or if the Administrator, or the Secretary, has initiated permit revocation or suspension proceedings under subsection (f) of this section; or

(D) if the United States has commenced and is diligently prosecuting a criminal action in a court of the United States or a State to redress a violation of this subchapter.

(3)(A) Any suit under this subsection may be brought in the judicial district in which the violation occurs.

(B) In any such suit under this subsection in which the United States is not a party, the Attorney General, at the request of the Administrator or Secretary, may intervene on behalf of the United States as a matter of right.

(4) The court, in issuing any final order in any suit brought pursuant to paragraph (1) of this subsection may award costs of litigation (including reasonable attorney and expert witness fees) to any party, whenever the court determines such award is appropriate.

(5) The injunctive relief provided by this subsection shall not restrict any right which any person (or class of persons) may have under any statute or common law to seek enforcement of any standard or limitation or to seek any other relief (including relief against the Administrator, the Secretary, or a State agency).

(h) Emergencies

No person shall be subject to a civil penalty or to a criminal fine or imprisonment for dumping materials from a vessel if such materials are dumped in an emergency to safeguard life at sea. Any such emergency dumping shall be reported to the Administrator under such conditions as he may prescribe.

(i) Seizure and forfeiture

(1) In general

Any vessel used to commit an act for which a penalty is imposed under subsection (b) of this section shall be subject to seizure and forfeiture to the United States under procedures established for seizure and forfeiture of conveyances under sections 853 and 911 of Title 21.

(2) Limitation on application

This subsection does not apply to an act committed substantially in accordance with a compliance agreement or enforcement agreement entered into by the Administrator under section 1414b(c) of this title.

(Oct. 23, 1972, Pub.L. 92–532, Title I, § 105, 86 Stat. 1057; Nov. 18, 1988, Pub.L. 100–688, Title III, § 3201(c), (d), 102 Stat. 4153; Oct. 31, 1992, Pub.L. 102–580, Title V, § 508, 106 Stat. 4869.)

CODE OF FEDERAL REGULATIONS

Rules of practice, see 40 CFR 22.01 et seq.

LIBRARY REFERENCES

Health and Environment ⟹25.7(23).

C.J.S. Health and Environment § 113 et seq.

§ 1416. Relationship to other laws [MPRSA § 106]

(a) Voiding of preexisting licenses

After the effective date of this subchapter, all licenses, permits, and authorizations other than those issued pursuant to this subchapter shall be void and of no legal effect, to the extent that they purport to authorize any activity regulated by this subchapter, and whether issued before or after the effective date of this subchapter.

(b) Actions under authority of Rivers and Harbors Act

The provisions of subsection (a) of this section shall not apply to actions taken before the effective date of this subchapter under the authority of the Rivers and Harbors Act of 1899 (30 Stat. 1151), as amended (33 U.S.C. 401 et seq.).

(c) Impairment of navigation

Prior to issuing any permit under this subchapter, if it appears to the Administrator that the disposition of material, other than dredged material, may adversely affect navigation in the territorial sea of the United States, or in the approaches to any harbor of the United States, or may create an artificial island on the Outer Continental Shelf, the Administrator shall consult with the Secretary and no permit shall be issued if the Secretary determines that navigation will be unreasonably impaired.

(d) State programs

(1) State rights preserved

Except as expressly provided in this subsection, nothing in this subchapter shall preclude or deny the right of any State to adopt or enforce any requirements respecting dumping of materials into ocean waters within the jurisdiction of the State.

(2) Federal projects

In the case of a Federal project, a State may not adopt or enforce a requirement that is more stringent than a requirement under this subchapter if the Administrator finds that such requirement—

(A) is not supported by relevant scientific evidence showing the requirement to be protective of human health, aquatic resources, or the environment;

(B) is arbitrary or capricious; or

(C) is not applicable or is not being applied to all projects without regard to Federal, State, or private participation and the Secretary of the Army concurs in such finding.

(3) Exemption from State requirements

The President may exempt a Federal project from any State requirement respecting dumping of materials into ocean waters if it is in the paramount interest of the United States to do so.

(4) Consideration of site of origin prohibited

Any requirement respecting dumping of materials into ocean waters applied by a State shall be applied without regard to the site of origin of the material to be dumped.

(e) Existing conservation programs not affected

Nothing in this subchapter shall be deemed to affect in any manner or to any extent any provision of the Fish and Wildlife Coordination Act as amended (16 U.S.C. 661–666c).

(f) Dumping of dredged material in Long Island Sound from any Federal, etc., project

In addition to other provisions of law and not withstanding the specific exclusion relating to dredged material in the first sentence in section 1412(a) of this title, the dumping of dredged material in Long Island Sound from any Federal project (or pursuant to Federal authorization) or from a dredging project by a non-Federal applicant exceeding 25,000 cubic yards shall comply with the requirements of this subchapter.

(g) Savings clause

Nothing in this subchapter shall restrict, affect or modify the rights of any person (1) to seek damages or enforcement of any standard or limitation under State law, including State common law, or (2) to seek damages under other Federal law, including maritime tort law, resulting from noncompliance with any requirement of this chapter or any permit under this chapter.

(Oct. 23, 1972, Pub.L. 92–532, Title I, § 106, 86 Stat. 1058; Dec. 22, 1980, Pub.L. 96–572, § 4, 94 Stat. 3345; Oct. 17, 1986, Pub.L. 99–499, Title I, § 127(d), 100 Stat. 1693; Nov. 16, 1990, Pub.L. 101–596, Title II, § 203, 104 Stat. 3006; Oct. 31, 1992, Pub.L. 102–580, Title V, § 505, 106 Stat. 4867.)

Codification

Amendment by section 203 of Pub.L. 101–596 has been executed to subsec. (f) of this section notwithstanding language directing amendment of subsec. (g) of this section, as the probable intent of Congress.

§ 1417. Enforcement [MPRSA § 107]

(a) Utilization of other departments, agencies, and instrumentalities

The Administrator or the Secretary, as the case may be, may, whenever appropriate, utilize by agreement, the personnel, services and facilities of other Federal departments, agencies, and instrumentalities, or State agencies or instrumentalities, whether on a reimbursable or a nonreimbursable basis, in carrying out his responsibilities under this subchapter.

(b) Delegation of review and evaluation authority

The Administrator or the Secretary may delegate responsibility and authority for reviewing and evaluating permit applications, including the decision as to whether a permit will be issued, to an officer of his agency, or he may delegate, by agreement, such responsibility and authority to the heads of other Federal departments or agencies, whether on a reimbursable or nonreimbursable basis.

(c) Surveillance and other enforcement activity

The Secretary of the department in which the Coast Guard is operating shall conduct surveillance and other appropriate enforcement activity to prevent unlawful transportation of material for dumping, or unlawful dumping. Such enforcement activity shall include, but not be limited to, enforcement of regulations issued by him pursuant to section 1418 of this title, relating to safe transportation, handling, carriage, storage, and stowage. The Secretary of the Department in which the Coast Guard is operating shall supply to the Administrator and to the Attorney General, as appropriate, such information of enforcement activities and such evidentiary material assembled as they may require in carrying out their duties relative to penalty assessments, criminal prosecutions, or other actions involving litigation pursuant to the provisions of this subchapter.

(Oct. 23, 1972, Pub.L. 92–532, Title I, § 107, 86 Stat. 1059.)

CODE OF FEDERAL REGULATIONS

Contents of permits; revision, revocation or limitation of ocean dumping permits, see 40 CFR 223.1 et seq.

LIBRARY REFERENCES

Health and Environment ⚟25.7(17).
C.J.S. Health and Environment § 113 et seq.

§ 1418. Regulations [MPRSA § 108]

In carrying out the responsibilities and authority conferred by this subchapter, the Administrator, the Secretary, and the Secretary of the department in which the Coast Guard is operating are authorized to issue such regulations as they may deem appropriate.

(Oct. 23, 1972, Pub.L. 92–532, Title I, § 108, 86 Stat. 1059.)

CROSS REFERENCES

Prohibited acts, see section 1411 of this title.
Surveillance and other enforcement activity, see section 1417 of this title.

CODE OF FEDERAL REGULATIONS

Ocean dumping, see 40 CFR Chap. I, Subchap. H.
Public information, see 40 CFR 2.100 et seq.

§ 1419. International cooperation [MPRSA § 109]

The Secretary of State, in consultation with the Administrator, shall seek effective international action and cooperation to insure protection of the marine environment, and may, for this purpose, formulate, present, or support specific proposals in the United Nations and other component international organizations for the development of appropriate international rules and regulations in support of the policy of this chapter.

(Oct. 23, 1972, Pub.L. 92–532, Title I, § 109, 86 Stat. 1060.)

LIBRARY REFERENCES

International Law ⚟10.
C.J.S. International Law § 12.

§ 1420. Authorization of appropriations [MPRSA § 111]

There are authorized to be appropriated, for purposes of carrying out this subchapter, not to exceed $12,000,000 for fiscal year 1993 and not to exceed $14,000,000 for each of the fiscal years 1994, 1995, 1996, and 1997, to remain available until expended.

(Oct. 23, 1972, Pub.L. 92–532, Title I, § 111, 86 Stat. 1060; Oct. 26, 1974, Pub.L. 93–472, 88 Stat. 1430; July 25, 1975, Pub.L. 94–62, § 1, 89 Stat. 303; June 30, 1976, Pub.L. 94–326, § 1, 90 Stat. 725; Nov. 4, 1977, Pub.L. 95–153, § 1, 91 Stat. 1255; Dec. 22, 1980, Pub.L. 96–572, § 1, 94 Stat. 3344; June 23, 1981, Pub.L. 97–16, 95 Stat. 100; Oct. 28, 1988, Pub.L. 100–536, 102 Stat. 2710; Oct. 31, 1992, Pub.L. 102–580, Title V, § 509(a), 106 Stat. 4870.)

LIBRARY REFERENCES

Health and Environment ⚟25.7(21).
C.J.S. Health and Environment § 106 et seq.

§ 1421. Annual report to Congress [MPRSA § 112]

The Administrator shall on or before February 1 of each year report to the Congress on the administration of this subchapter during the preceding fiscal year, including recommendations for additional legislation if deemed necessary. Such report shall include a description of the number of permits issued under this subchapter (including the number of permits issued by the Secretary with the concurrence of the Administrator), any actions taken under subsections (c) and (d) of section 1413 of this title, and for each permit, the site receiving the material, the volume and characteristics of material dumped (including the extent and nature of pollutants in such material), and the management practices implemented in connection with each disposal activity.

(Oct. 23, 1972, Pub.L. 92–532, Title I, § 112, 86 Stat. 1060; June 30, 1976, Pub.L. 94–326, § 2, 90 Stat. 725; Oct. 19, 1980, Pub.L. 96–470, Title II, § 209(f), 94 Stat. 2245; Oct. 31, 1992, Pub.L. 102–580, Title V, § 510, 106 Stat. 4870.)

SUBCHAPTER II—RESEARCH

CROSS REFERENCES

Comprehensive ocean pollution program, contents of, see section 1704 of this title.

§ 1441. Monitoring and research program [MPRSA § 201]

The Secretary of Commerce, in coordination with the Secretary of the Department in which the Coast Guard is operating and with the Administrator shall, within six months of October 23, 1972, initiate a comprehensive and continuing program of monitoring and research regarding the effects of the dumping of material into ocean waters or other coastal waters where the tide ebbs and flows or into the Great Lakes or their connecting waters.

(Oct. 23, 1972, Pub.L. 92–532, Title II, § 201, 86 Stat. 1060; April 7, 1986, Pub.L. 99–272, Title VI, § 6061, 100 Stat. 131.)

§ 1442. Research program respecting possible long-range effects of pollution, overfishing, and man-induced changes of ocean ecosystems [MPRSA § 202]

(a) Secretary of Commerce

(1) The Secretary of Commerce, in close consultation with other appropriate Federal departments, agencies, and instrumentalities shall, within six months of October 23, 1972, initiate a comprehensive and continuing program of research with respect to the possible long-range effects of pollution, overfishing, and man-induced changes of ocean ecosystems. These responsibilities shall include the scientific assessment of damages to the natural resources from spills of petroleum or petroleum products. In carrying out such research, the Secretary of Commerce shall take into account such factors as existing and proposed international policies affecting oceanic problems, economic considerations involved in both the protection and the use of the oceans, possible alternatives to existing programs, and ways in which the health of the oceans may best be preserved for the benefit of succeeding generations of mankind.

(2) The Secretary of Commerce shall ensure that the program under this section complements, when appropriate, the activities undertaken by other Federal agencies pursuant to subchapter I of this chapter and section 1443 of this title. That program shall include but not be limited to—

(A) the development and assessment of scientific techniques to define and quantify the degradation of the marine environment;

(B) the assessment of the capacity of the marine environment to receive materials without degradation;

(C) continuing monitoring programs to assess the health of the marine environment, including but not limited to the monitoring of bottom oxygen concentrations, contaminant levels in biota, sediments, and the water column, diseases in fish and shellfish, and changes in types and abundance of indicator species;

(D) the development of methodologies, techniques, and equipment for disposal of waste materials to minimize degradation of the marine environment.

(3) The Secretary of Commerce shall ensure that the comprehensive and continuing research program conducted under this subsection is consistent with the comprehensive plan for ocean pollution research and development and monitoring prepared under section 1703 of this title.

(b) Action with other nations

In carrying out his responsibilities under this section, the Secretary of Commerce, under the foreign policy guidance of the President and pursuant to international agreements and treaties made by the President with the advice and consent of the Senate, may act alone or in conjunction with any other nation or group of nations, and shall make known the results of his activities by such channels of communication as may appear appropriate.

(c) Cooperation of other departments, agencies, and independent instrumentalities

Each department, agency, and independent instrumentality of the Federal Government is authorized and directed to cooperate with the Secretary of Commerce in carrying out the purposes of this section and, to the extent permitted by law, to furnish such information as may be requested.

(d) Utilization of personnel, services, and facilities; inter-agency agreements

The Secretary of Commerce, is carrying out his responsibilities under this section, shall, to the extent feasible utilize the personnel, services, and facilities of other Federal departments, agencies, and instrumentalities (including those of the Coast Guard for monitoring purposes), and is authorized to enter into appropriate inter-agency agreements to accomplish this action.

(Oct. 23, 1972, Pub.L. 92–532, Title II, § 202, 86 Stat. 1060; July 25, 1975, Pub.L. 94–62, § 2, 89 Stat. 303; Oct. 6, 1980, Pub.L. 96–381, § 3, 94 Stat. 1524; Oct. 19, 1980, Pub.L. 96–470, Title II, § 201(f), 94 Stat. 2242; April 7, 1986, Pub.L. 99–272, Title VI, § 6062, 100 Stat. 131; Nov. 7, 1988, Pub.L. 100–627, Title I, § 101, 102 Stat. 3213.)

§ 1443. Cooperation with public authorities, agencies, and institutions, private agencies and institutions, and individuals; regional management plans for waste disposal; report on sewage disposal in New York metropolitan area [MPRSA § 203]

(a) The Administrator of the Environmental Protection Agency shall—

(1) conduct research, investigations, experiments, training, demonstrations, surveys, and studies for the purpose of—

(A) determining means of minimizing or ending, as soon as possible after October 6, 1980, the dumping into ocean waters, or waters described in section 1411(b) of this title, of material which may unreasonably degrade or endanger human health, welfare, or amenities, or the marine environment, ecological systems, or economic potentialities, and

(B) developing disposal methods as alternatives to the dumping described in subparagraph (A); and

(2) encourage, cooperate with, promote the coordination of, and render financial and other assistance to appropriate public authorities, agencies, and institutions (whether Federal, State, interstate, or local) and appropriate private agencies, institutions, and individuals in the conduct of research and other activities described in paragraph (1).

(b) Nothing in this section shall be construed to affect in any way the December 31, 1981, termination date, established in section 1412a of this title, for the ocean dumping of sewage sludge.

(c) The Administrator, in cooperation with the Secretary, the Secretary of Commerce, and other officials of appropriate Federal, State, and local agencies, shall assess the feasibility in coastal areas of regional management plans for the disposal of waste materials. Such plans should integrate where appropriate Federal, State, regional, and local waste disposal activities into a comprehensive regional disposal strategy. These plans should address, among other things—

(1) the sources, quantities, and types of materials that require and will require disposal;

(2) the environmental, economic, social, and human health factors (and the methods used to assess these factors) associated with disposal alternatives;

(3) the improvements in production processes, methods of disposal, and recycling to reduce the adverse effects associated with such disposal alternatives;

(4) the applicable laws and regulations governing waste disposal; and

(5) improvements in permitting processes to reduce administrative burdens.

(d) The Administrator, in cooperation with the Secretary of Commerce, shall submit to the Congress and the President, not later than one year after April 7, 1986, a report on sewage sludge disposal in the New York City metropolitan region. The report shall—

(1) consider the factors listed in subsection (c) of this section as they relate to landfilling, incineration, ocean dumping, or any other feasible disposal or reuse/recycling option;

(2) include an assessment of the cost of these alternatives; and

(3) recommend such regulatory or legislative changes as may be necessary to reduce the adverse impacts associated with sewage sludge disposal.

(Oct. 23, 1972, Pub.L. 92–532, Title II, § 203, 86 Stat. 1061; Oct. 6, 1980, Pub.L. 96–381, § 1, 94 Stat. 1523; April 7, 1986, Pub.L. 99–272, Title VI, § 6063, 100 Stat. 131.)

§ 1444. Annual reports [MPRSA § 204]

(a) In March of each year, the Secretary of Commerce shall report to the Congress on his activities under this subchapter during the previous fiscal year. The report shall include—

(1) the Secretary's findings made under section 1441 of this title, including an evaluation of the short-term ecological effects and the social and economic factors involved with the dumping;

(2) the results of activities undertaken pursuant to section 1442 of this title;

(3) with the concurrence of the Administrator and after consulting with officials of other appropriate Federal agencies, an identification of the short- and long-term research requirements associated with activities under subchapter I of this chapter, and a description of how Federal research under this subchapter and subchapter I of this chapter will meet those requirements; and

(4) activities of the Department of Commerce under section 665 of Title 16.

(b) In March of each year, the Administrator shall report to the Congress on his activities during the previous fiscal year under section 1443 of this title.

(c) On October 31 of each year, the Under Secretary shall report to the Congress the specific programs that the National Oceanic and Atmospheric Administration and the Environmental Protection Agency carried out pursuant to this subchapter in the previous fiscal year, specifically listing the amount of funds allocated to those specific programs in the previous fiscal year.

(Oct. 23, 1972, Pub.L. 92–532, Title II, § 204, formerly § 205, 86 Stat. 1061; as added Pub.L. 96–572, § 5, Dec. 22, 1980, 94 Stat. 3345, and renumbered and amended Pub.L. 99–272, Title VI, § 6065, April 7, 1986, 100 Stat. 132; Nov. 7, 1988, Pub.L. 100–627, Title I, § 102, 102 Stat. 3213.)

§ 1445. Authorization of appropriations [MPRSA § 205]

There are authorized to be appropriated for the first fiscal year after October 23, 1972, and for the next two fiscal years thereafter such sums as may be necessary to carry out this subchapter, but the sums appropriated for any such fiscal year may not exceed $6,000,000. There are authorized to be appropriated not to exceed $1,500,000 for the transition period (July 1 through September 30, 1976), not to exceed $5,600,000 for fiscal year 1977, not to exceed $6,500,000 for fiscal year 1978, not to exceed $11,396,000 for fiscal year 1981, not to exceed $12,000,000 for fiscal year 1982, not to exceed $10,635,000 for fiscal year 1986, not to exceed $11,114,000 for fiscal year 1987, not to exceed $13,500,000 for fiscal year 1989, and not to exceed $14,500,000 for fiscal year 1990.

(Oct. 23, 1972, Pub.L. 92–532, Title II, § 205, formerly § 204, 86 Stat. 1061; July 25, 1975, Pub.L. 94–62, § 3, 89 Stat. 303; June 30, 1976, Pub.L. 94–326, § 3, 90 Stat. 725; Nov. 4, 1977, Pub.L. 95–153, § 2, 91 Stat. 1255; Oct. 6, 1980, Pub.L. 96–381, § 2, 94 Stat. 1523, renumbered and amended Pub.L. 99–272, Title VI, § 6064, April 7, 1986, 100 Stat. 132; Nov. 7, 1988, Pub.L. 100–627, Title I, § 103, 102 Stat. 3213.)

LIBRARY REFERENCES

Health and Environment ⚟25.7(20).
C.J.S. Health and Environment § 113 et seq.

OIL POLLUTION

OIL POLLUTION ACT OF 1990 [OPA § ___]

(33 U.S.C.A. §§ 2701 to 2761)

CHAPTER 40—OIL POLLUTION

SUBCHAPTER I—OIL POLLUTION LIABILITY AND COMPENSATION

Sec.
2701. Definitions.
2702. Elements of liability.
(a) In general.
(b) Covered removal costs and damages.
(c) Excluded discharges.
(d) Liability of third parties.
2703. Defenses to liability.
(a) Complete defenses.
(b) Defenses as to particular claimants.
(c) Limitation on complete defense.
2704. Limits on liability.
(a) General rule.
(b) Division of liability for mobile offshore drilling units.
(c) Exceptions.
(d) Adjusting limits of liability.
2705. Interest.
(a) General rule.
(b) Period.
2706. Natural resources.
(a) Liability.
(b) Designation of trustees.
(c) Functions of trustees.
(d) Measure of damages.
(e) Damage assessment regulations.
(f) Use of recovered sums.
(g) Compliance.
2707. Recovery by foreign claimants.
(a) Required showing by foreign claimants.
(b) Discharges in foreign countries.
(c) Foreign claimant defined.
2708. Recovery by responsible party.
(a) In general.
(b) Extent of recovery.
2709. Contribution.
2710. Indemnification agreements.
(a) Agreements not prohibited.
(b) Liability not transferred.
(c) Relationship to other causes of action.
2711. Consultation on removal actions.
2712. Uses of the Fund.
(a) Uses generally.
(b) Defense to liability for Fund.
(c) Obligation of Fund by Federal officials.
(d) Access to Fund by State officials.
(e) Regulations.
(f) Rights of subrogation.
(g) Audits.
(h) Period of limitations for claims.
(i) Limitation on payment for same costs.

Sec.
2712. Uses of the Fund.
(j) Obligation in accordance with plan.
(k) Preference for private persons in area affected by discharge.
2713. Claims procedure.
(a) Presentation.
(b) Presentation to Fund.
(c) Election.
(d) Uncompensated damages.
(e) Procedure for claims against Fund.
2714. Designation of source and advertisement.
(a) Designation of source and notification.
(b) Advertisement by responsible party or guarantor.
(c) Advertisement by President.
2715. Subrogation.
(a) In general.
(b) Actions on behalf of Fund.
2716. Financial responsibility.
(a) Requirement.
(b) Sanctions.
(c) Offshore facilities.
(e)[1] Methods of financial responsibility.
(f) Claims against guarantor.
(g) Limitation on guarantor's liability.
(h) Continuation of regulations.
(i) Unified certificate.
2716a. Financial responsibilities; civil penalties.
(a) Administrative.
(b) Judicial.
2717. Litigation, jurisdiction, and venue.
(a) Review of regulations.
(b) Jurisdiction.
(c) State court jurisdiction.
(d) Assessment and collection of tax.
(e) Savings provision.
(f) Period of limitations.
2718. Relationship to other law.
(a) Preservation of State authorities; Solid Waste Disposal Act.
(b) Preservation of State funds.
(c) Additional requirements and liabilities; penalties.
(d) Federal employee liability.
2719. State financial responsibility.
2720. Differentiation among fats, oils, and greases.
(a) In general.
(b) Considerations.
(c) Exception.
(d) Omitted.

SUBCHAPTER II—PRINCE WILLIAM SOUND PROVISIONS

2731. Oil Spill Recovery Institute.
(a) Establishment of Institute.

Sec.
2731. Oil Spill Recovery Institute.
(b) Functions.
(c) Advisory Board.
(d) Scientific and Technical Committee.
(e) Director.
(f) Evaluation.
(g) Audit.
(h) Status of employees.
(i) Termination.
(j) Use of funds.
(k) Research.
(*l*) Definitions.
2732. Terminal and tanker oversight and monitoring.
(a) Short title and findings.
(b) Demonstration programs.
(c) Oil Terminal Facilities and Oil Tanker Operations Association.
(d) Regional Citizens' Advisory Councils.
(e) Committee for Terminal and Oil Tanker Operations and Environmental Monitoring.
(f) Committee for Oil Spill Prevention, Safety, and Emergency Response.
(g) Agency cooperation.
(h) Recommendations of the Council.
(i) Administrative actions.
(j) Location and compensation.
(k) Funding.
(*l*) Reports.
(m) Definitions.
(n) Savings clause.
(*o*) Alternative voluntary advisory group in lieu of Council.
2733. Bligh Reef light.
2734. Vessel traffic service system.
2735. Equipment and personnel requirements under tank vessel and facility response plans.
(a) In general.
(b) Definitions.
2736. Funding.
(a) Section 2731.
(b) Sections 2733 and 2734.
2737. Limitation.

SUBCHAPTER III—MISCELLANEOUS

2751. Savings provisions.
(a) Cross-references.
(b) Continuation of regulations.
(c) Rule of construction.
(d) Actions and rights.
(e) Admiralty and maritime law.
2752. Annual appropriations.
(a) Required.
(b) Exceptions.
2753. Outer Banks Protection.
(a) Short title.
(b) Findings.
(c) Prohibition of oil and gas leasing, exploration, and development.
(d) Additional environmental information.
(e) Environmental Sciences Review Panel.
(f) Authorization of appropriations.

Sec.
SUBCHAPTER IV—OIL POLLUTION RESEARCH AND DEVELOPMENT PROGRAM

2761. Oil pollution research and development program.
(a) Interagency Coordinating Committee on Oil Pollution Research.
(b) Oil pollution research and technology plan.
(c) Oil pollution research and development program.
(d) International cooperation.
(e) Biennial reports.
(f) Funding.
[1] No subsec. (d) was enacted.

SUBCHAPTER I—OIL POLLUTION LIABILITY AND COMPENSATION

§ 2701. Definitions [OPA § 1001]

For the purposes of this chapter, the term—

(1) "act of God" means an unanticipated grave natural disaster or other natural phenomenon of an exceptional, inevitable, and irresistible character the effects of which could not have been prevented or avoided by the exercise of due care or foresight;

(2) "barrel" means 42 United States gallons at 60 degrees fahrenheit;

(3) "claim" means a request, made in writing for a sum certain, for compensation for damages or removal costs resulting from an incident;

(4) "claimant" means any person or government who presents a claim for compensation under this subchapter;

(5) "damages" means damages specified in section 2702(b) of this title, and includes the cost of assessing these damages;

(6) "deepwater port" is a facility licensed under the Deepwater Port Act of 1974 (33 U.S.C. 1501–1524);

(7) "discharge" means any emission (other than natural seepage), intentional or unintentional, and includes, but is not limited to, spilling, leaking, pumping, pouring, emitting, emptying, or dumping;

(8) "exclusive economic zone" means the zone established by Presidential Proclamation Numbered 5030, dated March 10, 1983, including the ocean waters of the areas referred to as "eastern special areas" in Article 3(1) of the Agreement between the United States of America and the Union of Soviet Socialist Republics on the Maritime Boundary, signed June 1, 1990;

(9) "facility" means any structure, group of structures, equipment, or device (other than a vessel) which is used for one or more of the following purposes: exploring for, drilling for, producing, storing, handling, transferring, processing, or transporting oil. This term includes any motor vehicle, rolling stock, or pipeline used for one or more of these purposes;

(10) "foreign offshore unit" means a facility which is located, in whole or in part, in the territorial sea or on the continental shelf of a foreign country and which is or was used for one or more of the following purposes: exploring for, drilling for, producing, storing, handling, transferring, processing, or transporting oil produced from the seabed beneath the foreign country's territorial sea or from the foreign country's continental shelf;

(11) "Fund" means the Oil Spill Liability Trust Fund, established by section 9509 of Title 26;

(12) "gross ton" has the meaning given that term by the Secretary under part J of Title 46 [46 U.S.C.A. § 14101 et seq.];

(13) "guarantor" means any person, other than the responsible party, who provides evidence of financial responsibility for a responsible party under this chapter;

(14) "incident" means any occurrence or series of occurrences having the same origin, involving one or more vessels, facilities, or any combination thereof, resulting in the discharge or substantial threat of discharge of oil;

(15) "Indian tribe" means any Indian tribe, band, nation, or other organized group or community, but not including any Alaska Native regional or village corporation, which is recognized as eligible for the special programs and services provided by the United States to Indians because of their status as Indians and has governmental authority over lands belonging to or controlled by the tribe;

(16) "lessee" means a person holding a leasehold interest in an oil or gas lease on lands beneath navigable waters (as that term is defined in section 1301(a) of Title 43) or on submerged lands of the Outer Continental Shelf, granted or maintained under applicable State law or the Outer Continental Shelf Lands Act (43 U.S.C. 1331 et seq.);

(17) "liable" or "liability" shall be construed to be the standard of liability which obtains under section 1321 of this title;

(18) "mobile offshore drilling unit" means a vessel (other than a self-elevating lift vessel) capable of use as an offshore facility;

(19) "National Contingency Plan" means the National Contingency Plan prepared and published under section 1321(d) of this title, as amended by this Act, or revised under section 105 of the Comprehensive Environmental Response, Compensation, and Liability Act (42 U.S.C. 9605);

(20) "natural resources" includes land, fish, wildlife, biota, air, water, ground water, drinking water supplies, and other such resources belonging to, managed by, held in trust by, appertaining to, or otherwise controlled by the United States (including the resources of the exclusive economic zone), any State or local government or Indian tribe, or any foreign government;

(21) "navigable waters" means the waters of the United States, including the territorial sea;

(22) "offshore facility" means any facility of any kind located in, on, or under any of the navigable waters of the United States, and any facility of any kind which is subject to the jurisdiction of the United States and is located in, on, or under any other waters, other than a vessel or a public vessel;

(23) "oil" means oil of any kind or in any form, including, but not limited to, petroleum, fuel oil, sludge, oil refuse, and oil mixed with wastes other than dredged spoil, but does not include petroleum, including crude oil or any fraction thereof, which is specifically listed or designated as a hazardous substance under subparagraphs (A) through (F) of section 101(14) of the Comprehensive Environmental Response, Compensation, and Liability Act (42 U.S.C. 9601) and which is subject to the provisions of that Act [42 U.S.C.A. § 9601 et seq.];

(24) "onshore facility" means any facility (including, but not limited to, motor vehicles and rolling stock) of any kind located in, on, or under, any land within the United States other than submerged land;

(25) the term "Outer Continental Shelf facility" means an offshore facility which is located, in whole or in part, on the Outer Continental Shelf and is or was used for one or more of the following purposes: exploring for, drilling for, producing, storing, handling, transferring, processing, or transporting oil produced from the Outer Continental Shelf;

(26) "owner or operator" means (A) in the case of a vessel, any person owning, operating, or chartering by demise, the vessel, and (B) in the case of an onshore facility, and an offshore facility, any person owning or operating such onshore facility or offshore facility, and (C) in the case of any abandoned offshore facility, the person who owned or operated such facility immediately prior to such abandonment;

(27) "person" means an individual, corporation, partnership, association, State, municipality, commission, or political subdivision of a State, or any interstate body;

(28) "permittee" means a person holding an authorization, license, or permit for geological exploration issued under section 11 of the Outer Continental Shelf Lands Act (43 U.S.C. 1340) or applicable State law;

(29) "public vessel" means a vessel owned or bareboat chartered and operated by the United States, or by a State or political subdivision thereof, or by a foreign nation, except when the vessel is engaged in commerce;

(30) "remove" or "removal" means containment and removal of oil or a hazardous substance from water and shorelines or the taking of other actions as may be necessary to minimize or mitigate damage to the public health or welfare, including, but not limited to, fish, shellfish, wildlife, and public and private property, shorelines, and beaches;

(31) "removal costs" means the costs of removal that are incurred after a discharge of oil has occurred or, in any case in which there is a substantial threat of a discharge of oil, the costs to prevent, minimize, or mitigate oil pollution from such an incident;

(32) "responsible party" means the following:

(A) Vessels

In the case of a vessel, any person owning, operating, or demise chartering the vessel.

(B) Onshore facilities

In the case of an onshore facility (other than a pipeline), any person owning or operating the facility, except a Federal agency, State, municipality, commission, or political subdivision of a State, or any interstate body, that as the owner transfers possession and right to use the property to another person by lease, assignment, or permit.

(C) Offshore facilities

In the case of an offshore facility (other than a pipeline or a deepwater port licensed under the Deepwater Port Act of 1974 (33 U.S.C. 1501 et seq.)), the lessee or permittee of the area in which the facility is located or the holder of a right of use and easement granted under applicable State law or the Outer Continental Shelf Lands Act (43 U.S.C. 1301–1356) for the area in which the facility is located (if the holder is a different person than the lessee or permittee), except a Federal agency, State, municipality, commission, or political subdivision of a State, or any interstate body, that as owner transfers possession and right to use the property to another person by lease, assignment, or permit.

(D) Deepwater ports

In the case of a deepwater port licensed under the Deepwater Port Act of 1974 (33 U.S.C. 1501–1524), the licensee.

(E) Pipelines

In the case of a pipeline, any person owning or operating the pipeline.

(F) Abandonment

In the case of an abandoned vessel, onshore facility, deepwater port, pipeline, or offshore facility, the persons who would have been responsible parties immediately prior to the abandonment of the vessel or facility.

(33) "Secretary" means the Secretary of the department in which the Coast Guard is operating;

(34) "tank vessel" means a vessel that is constructed or adapted to carry, or that carries, oil or hazardous material in bulk as cargo or cargo residue, and that—

(A) is a vessel of the United States;

(B) operates on the navigable waters; or

(C) transfers oil or hazardous material in a place subject to the jurisdiction of the United States;

(35) "territorial seas" means the belt of the seas measured from the line of ordinary low water along that portion of the coast which is in direct contact with the open sea and the line marking the seaward limit of inland waters, and extending seaward a distance of 3 miles;

(36) "United States" and "State" mean the several States of the United States, the District of Columbia, the Commonwealth of Puerto Rico, Guam, American Samoa, the United States Virgin Islands, the Commonwealth of the Northern Marianas, and any other territory or possession of the United States; and

(37) "vessel" means every description of watercraft or other artificial contrivance used, or capable of being used, as a means of transportation on water, other than a public vessel.

(Pub.L. 101–380, Title I, § 1001, Aug. 18, 1990, 104 Stat. 486.)

References in Text

This chapter, referred to in text, was in the original this "Act", meaning Pub.L. 101–380 which, in addition to enacting this chapter, made conforming amendments and additional changes in other sections of this title as well as in Titles 14, 16, 23, 26, 43, 46, and 46 App. For complete classification to the Code see Short Title note under this section and Tables.

The Deepwater Port Act of 1974, referred to in pars. (6) and (32), is Pub.L. 93–627, Jan. 3, 1975, 88 Stat. 2126, as amended, which is classified generally to chapter 29 (§ 1501 et seq.) of this title. For complete classification of this Act to the Code, see Short Title note set out under section 1501 of this title and Tables.

The Outer Continental Shelf Lands Act, referred to in pars. (16), (28), and (32), is Act Aug. 7. 1953, c. 345, 67 Stat. 462, as amended, which is classified generally to subchapter III (§ 1331 et seq.) of chapter 29 of Title 43, Public Lands. For complete classification of this Act to the Code, see Short Title note set out under section 1331 of Title 43 and Tables.

Reference in par. (19) to the amendment of section 1321(d) of this title "by this Act" refers to the amendment by Pub.L. 101-380, Aug. 18, 1990, 104 Stat. 484.

The Comprehensive Environmental Response, Compensation, and Liability Act of 1980, referred to in pars. (19) and (23), is Pub.L. 96-510, Dec. 11, 1980, 94 Stat. 2767, as amended, which is classified principally to chapter 103 (§ 9601 et seq.) of Title 42, The Public Health and Welfare. For complete classification of this Act to the Code, see Short Title note set out under section 9601 of Title 42 and Tables.

Effective Date

Section 1020 of Pub.L. 101-380 provided that: "This Act [probably refers to title I of Pub.L. 101-380 which enacted this subchapter] shall apply to an incident occurring after the date of the enactment of this Act [Aug. 18, 1990]."

Short Title of 1995 Amendments

Pub.L. 104-55, § 1, Nov. 20, 1995, 109 Stat. 546, provided that: "This Act [enacting section 2720 of this title and amending sections 2704 and 2716 of this title] may be cited as the 'Edible Oil Regulatory Reform Act'."

Short Title

Section 1 of Pub.L. 101-380 provided that: "This Act [enacting this chapter and sections 1642 and 1656 of Title 43, Public Lands, section 3703a of Title 46, Shipping, and section 1274a of the Appendix to Title 46; amending sections 1223, 1228, 1232, 1236, 1319, 1321, 1481, 1486, 1503, 1514, and 1908 of this title, section 3145 of Title 16, Conservation, section 401 note of Title 23, Highways, sections 4612 and 9509 of Title 26, Internal Revenue Code, sections 1334, 1350, and 1653 of Title 43, sections 2101, 2302, 3318, 3715, 3718, 5116, 6101, 7101, 7106, 7107, 7109, 7302, 7502, 7503, 7505, 7701, 7702, 7703, 8101, 8104, 8502, 8503, 8702, 9101, 9302, 9308, and 12106 of Title 46, and section 1274 of the Appendix to Title 46; repealing section 1517 of this title and sections 1811, 1811 note, and 1812 to 1824 of Title 43; and enacting provisions set out as notes under sections 1203, 1223, and 1321 of this title, section 92 of Title 14, Coast Guard, section 9509 of Title 26, sections 1334, 1651, and 1653 of Title 43, sections 3703, 3703a, and 7106 of Title 46, and section 1295 of the Appendix to Title 46] may be cited as the 'Oil Pollution Act of 1990'."

LAW REVIEW COMMENTARIES

Crude legislation: Liability and compensation under the Oil Pollution Act of 1990. Daniel Kopec and Philip Peterson, 23 Rutgers L.J. 597 (1992).

§ 2702. Elements of liability [OPA § 1002]

(a) In general

Notwithstanding any other provision or rule of law, and subject to the provisions of this chapter, each responsible party for a vessel or a facility from which oil is discharged, or which poses the substantial threat of a discharge of oil, into or upon the navigable waters or adjoining shorelines or the exclusive economic zone is liable for the removal costs and damages specified in subsection (b) that result from such incident.

(b) Covered removal costs and damages

(1) Removal costs

The removal costs referred to in subsection (a) of this section are—

(A) all removal costs incurred by the United States, a State, or an Indian tribe under subsection (c), (d), (e), or (*l*) of section 1321 of this title, as amended by this Act, under the Intervention on the High Seas Act (33 U.S.C. 1471 et seq.), or under State law; and

(B) any removal costs incurred by any person for acts taken by the person which are consistent with the National Contingency Plan.

(2) Damages

The damages referred to in subsection (a) of this section are the following:

(A) Natural resources

Damages for injury to, destruction of, loss of, or loss of use of, natural resources, including the reasonable costs of assessing the damage, which shall be recoverable by a United States trustee, a State trustee, an Indian tribe trustee, or a foreign trustee.

(B) Real or personal property

Damages for injury to, or economic losses resulting from destruction of, real or personal property, which shall be recoverable by a claimant who owns or leases that property.

(C) Subsistence use

Damages for loss of subsistence use of natural resources, which shall be recoverable by any claimant who so uses natural resources which have been injured, destroyed, or lost, without regard to the ownership or management of the resources.

(D) Revenues

Damages equal to the net loss of taxes, royalties, rents, fees, or net profit shares due to the injury, destruction, or loss of real property, personal property, or natural resources, which shall be recoverable by the Government of the United States, a State, or a political subdivision thereof.

(E) Profits and earning capacity

Damages equal to the loss of profits or impairment of earning capacity due to the injury, destruction, or loss of real property, personal property, or natural resources, which shall be recoverable by any claimant.

(F) **Public services**

Damages for net costs of providing increased or additional public services during or after removal activities, including protection from fire, safety, or health hazards, caused by a discharge of oil, which shall be recoverable by a State, or a political subdivision of a State.

(c) Excluded discharges

This subchapter does not apply to any discharge—

(1) permitted by a permit issued under Federal, State, or local law;

(2) from a public vessel; or

(3) from an onshore facility which is subject to the Trans-Alaska Pipeline Authorization Act (43 U.S.C. 1651 et seq.).

(d) Liability of third parties

(1) In general

(A) Third party treated as responsible party

Except as provided in subparagraph (B), in any case in which a responsible party establishes that a discharge or threat of a discharge and the resulting removal costs and damages were caused solely by an act or omission of one or more third parties described in section 2703(a)(3) of this title (or solely by such an act or omission in combination with an act of God or an act of war), the third party or parties shall be treated as the responsible party or parties for purposes of determining liability under this subchapter.

(B) Subrogation of responsible party

If the responsible party alleges that the discharge or threat of a discharge was caused solely by an act or omission of a third party, the responsible party—

(i) in accordance with section 2713 of this title, shall pay removal costs and damages to any claimant; and

(ii) shall be entitled by subrogation to all rights of the United States Government and the claimant to recover removal costs or damages from the third party or the Fund paid under this subsection.

(2) Limitation applied

(A) Owner or operator of vessel or facility

If the act or omission of a third party that causes an incident occurs in connection with a vessel or facility owned or operated by the third party, the liability of the third party shall be subject to the limits provided in section 2704 of this title as applied with respect to the vessel or facility.

(B) Other cases

In any other case, the liability of a third party or parties shall not exceed the limitation which would have been applicable to the responsible party of the vessel or facility from which the discharge actually occurred if the responsible party were liable.

(Pub.L. 101-380, Title I, § 1002, Aug. 18, 1990, 104 Stat. 489.)

References in Text

This chapter, referred to in text, was in the original this "Act", meaning Pub.L. 101-380 which, in addition to enacting this chapter, made conforming amendments to other sections in this title as well as in Titles 14, 16, 23, 26, 43, 46 and 46 App. For complete classification to the Code see Short Title note under section 2701 of this title and Tables.

Reference in subsec. (b)(1)(A) to the amendment of section 1321 of this title "by this Act" refers to amendment by Pub.L. 101-380, Aug. 18, 1990, 104 Stat. 484.

The Intervention on the High Seas Act, referred to in subsec. (b)(1)(A), is Pub.L. 93-248, Feb. 5, 1974, 88 Stat. 8, as amended, which is classified generally to chapter 28 (§ 1471 et seq.) of this title. For complete classification of this Act to the Code, see Short Title note set out under section 1471 of this title and Tables.

The Trans-Alaska Pipeline Authorization Act, referred to in subsec. (c)(3), is title II of Pub.L. 93-153, Nov. 16, 1973, 87 Stat. 584, which is classified to chapter 34 (§ 1651 et seq.) of Title 43, Public Lands. For complete classification of this Act to the Code, see Short Title note set out under section 1651 of Title 43 and Tables.

Effective Date

Section applicable to incidents occurring after Aug. 18, 1990, see section 1020 of Pub.L. 101-380, set out as a note under section 2701 of this title.

§ 2703. Defenses to liability [OPA § 1003]

(a) Complete defenses

A responsible party is not liable for removal costs or damages under section 2702 of this title if the responsible party establishes, by a preponderance of the evidence, that the discharge or substantial threat of a discharge of oil and the resulting damages or removal costs were caused solely by—

(1) an act of God;

(2) an act of war;

(3) an act or omission of a third party, other than an employee or agent of the responsible party or a third party whose act or omission occurs in connection with any contractual relationship with the responsible party (except where the sole contractual arrangement arises in connection with carriage by a common carrier by rail), if the responsible party establishes, by a preponderance of the evidence, that the responsible party—

(A) exercised due care with respect to the oil concerned, taking into consideration the characteristics of the oil and in light of all relevant facts and circumstances; and

(B) took precautions against foreseeable acts or omissions of any such third party and the foreseeable consequences of those acts or omissions; or

(4) any combination of paragraphs (1), (2), and (3).

(b) Defenses as to particular claimants

A responsible party is not liable under section 2702 of this title to a claimant, to the extent that the incident is caused by the gross negligence or willful misconduct of the claimant.

(c) Limitation on complete defense

Subsection (a) of this section does not apply with respect to a responsible party who fails or refuses—

(1) to report the incident as required by law if the responsible party knows or has reason to know of the incident;

(2) to provide all reasonable cooperation and assistance requested by a responsible official in connection with removal activities; or

(3) without sufficient cause, to comply with an order issued under subsection (c) or (e) of section 1321 of this title, as amended by this Act, or the Intervention on the High Seas Act (33 U.S.C. 1471 et seq.).

(Pub.L. 101–380, Title I, § 1003, Aug. 18, 1990, 104 Stat. 491.)

References in Text

Reference in subsec. (c)(3), to the amendment of section 1321 of this title "by this Act" refers to amendment by Pub.L. 101–380, Aug. 18, 1990, 104 Stat. 484.

The Intervention on the High Seas Act, referred to in subsec. (c)(3), is Pub.L. 93–248, Feb. 5, 1974, 88 Stat. 8, as amended, which is classified generally to chapter 28 (§ 1471 et seq.) of this title. For complete classification of this Act to the Code, see Short Title note set out under section 1471 of this title and Tables.

Effective Date

Section applicable to incidents occurring after Aug. 18, 1990, see section 1020 of Pub.L. 101–380, set out as a note under section 2701 of this title.

§ 2704. Limits on liability [OPA § 1004]

(a) General rule

Except as otherwise provided in this section, the total of the liability of a responsible party under section 2702 of this title and any removal costs incurred by, or on behalf of, the responsible party, with respect to each incident shall not exceed—

(1) for a tank vessel (except a tank vessel on which the only oil carried as cargo is an animal fat or vegetable oil, as those terms are used in section 2720 of this title) the greater of—

(A) $1,200 per gross ton; or

(B)(i) in the case of a vessel greater than 3,000 gross tons, $10,000,000; or

(ii) in the case of a vessel of 3,000 gross tons or less, $2,000,000;

(2) for any other vessel, $600 per gross ton or $500,000, whichever is greater;

(3) for an offshore facility except a deepwater port, the total of all removal costs plus $75,000,000; and

(4) for any onshore facility and a deepwater port, $350,000,000.

(b) Division of liability for mobile offshore drilling units

(1) Treated first as tank vessel

For purposes of determining the responsible party and applying this chapter and except as provided in paragraph (2), a mobile offshore drilling unit which is being used as an offshore facility is deemed to be a tank vessel with respect to the discharge, or the substantial threat of a discharge, of oil on or above the surface of the water.

(2) Treated as facility for excess liability

To the extent that removal costs and damages from any incident described in paragraph (1) exceed the amount for which a responsible party is liable (as that amount may be limited under subsection (a)(1) of this section), the mobile offshore drilling unit is deemed to be an offshore facility. For purposes of applying subsection (a)(3) of this section the amount specified in that subsection shall be reduced by the amount for which the responsible party is liable under paragraph (1).

(c) Exceptions

(1) Acts of responsible party

Subsection (a) of this section does not apply if the incident was proximately caused by—

(A) gross negligence or willful misconduct of, or

(B) the violation of an applicable Federal safety, construction, or operating regulation by,

the responsible party, an agent or employee of the responsible party, or a person acting pursuant to a contractual relationship with the responsible party (except where the sole contractual arrangement arises in connection with carriage by a common carrier by rail).

(2) Failure or refusal of responsible party

Subsection (a) of this section does not apply if the responsible party fails or refuses—

(A) to report the incident as required by law and the responsible party knows or has reason to know of the incident;

(B) to provide all reasonable cooperation and assistance requested by a responsible official in connection with removal activities; or

(C) without sufficient cause, to comply with an order issued under subsection (c) or (e) of section 1321 of this title, as amended by this Act, or the Intervention on the High Seas Act (33 U.S.C. 1471 et seq.).

(3) OCS facility or vessel

Notwithstanding the limitations established under subsection (a) of this section and the defenses of section 2703 of this title, all removal costs incurred by the United States Government or any State or local official or agency in connection with a discharge or substantial threat of a discharge of oil from any Outer Continental Shelf facility or a vessel carrying oil as cargo from such a facility shall be borne by the owner or operator of such facility or vessel.

(d) Adjusting limits of liability

(1) Onshore facilities

Subject to paragraph (2), the President may establish by regulation, with respect to any class or category of onshore facility, a limit of liability under this section of less than $350,000,000, but not less than $8,000,000, taking into account size, storage capacity, oil throughput, proximity to sensitive areas, type of oil handled, history of discharges, and other factors relevant to risks posed by the class or category of facility.

(2) Deepwater ports and associated vessels

(A) Study

The Secretary shall conduct a study of the relative operational and environmental risks posed by the transportation of oil by vessel to deepwater ports (as defined in section 3 of the Deepwater Port Act of 1974 (33 U.S.C. 1502)) versus the transportation of oil by vessel to other ports. The study shall include a review and analysis of offshore lightering practices used in connection with that transportation, an analysis of the volume of oil transported by vessel using those practices, and an analysis of the frequency and volume of oil discharges which occur in connection with the use of those practices.

(B) Report

Not later than 1 year after August 18, 1990, the Secretary shall submit to the Congress a report on the results of the study conducted under subparagraph (A).

(C) Rulemaking proceeding

If the Secretary determines, based on the results of the study conducted under this subparagraph (A), that the use of deepwater ports in connection with the transportation of oil by vessel results in a lower operational or environmental risk than the use of other ports, the Secretary shall initiate, not later than the 180th day following the date of submission of the report to the Congress under subparagraph (B), a rulemaking proceeding to lower the limits of liability under this section for deepwater ports as the Secretary determines appropriate. The Secretary may establish a limit of liability of less than $350,000,000, but not less than $50,000,000, in accordance with paragraph (1).

(3) Periodic reports

The President shall, within 6 months after August 18, 1990, and from time to time thereafter, report to the Congress on the desirability of adjusting the limits of liability specified in subsection (a) of this section.

(4) Adjustment to reflect Consumer Price Index

The President shall, by regulations issued not less often than every 3 years, adjust the limits of liability specified in subsection (a) of this section to reflect significant increases in the Consumer Price Index.

(Pub.L. 101–380, Title I, § 1004, Aug. 18, 1990, 104 Stat. 491; Pub.L. 104–55, § 2(d)(1), Nov. 20, 1995, 109 Stat. 546.)

References in Text

This chapter, referred to in text, was in the original this "Act", meaning Pub.L. 101–380 which, in addition to enacting this chapter, made conforming amendments to other sections in this title as well as in Titles 14, 16, 23, 26, 43, 46, and 46 App. For complete classification to the Code see Short Title note under section 2701 of this title and Tables.

Reference in subsec. (c)(2)(C) to the amendment of section 1321 of this title "by this Act" refers to amendment by Pub.L. 101–380, Aug. 18, 1990, 104 Stat. 484.

The Intervention on the High Seas Act, referred to in subsec. (c)(2)(C), is Pub.L. 93–248, Feb. 5, 1974, 88 Stat. 8, as amended, which is classified generally to chapter 28 (§ 1471 et seq.) of this title. For complete classification of this Act to the Code, see Short Title note set out under section 1471 of this title and Tables.

The Deepwater Port Act of 1974, referred to in subsec. (d)(2)(A), is Pub.L. 93–627, Jan. 3, 1975, 88 Stat. 2126, as amended, which is classified generally to chapter 29 (§ 1501 et seq.) of this title. For complete classification of this Act to the Code, see Short Title note set out under section 1501 of this title and Tables.

Effective Date

Section applicable to incidents occurring after Aug. 18, 1990, see section 1020 of Pub.L. 101–380, set out as a note under section 2701 of this title.

LAW REVIEW COMMENTARIES

Crude legislation: Liability and compensation under the Oil Pollution Act of 1990. Daniel Kopec and Philip Peterson, 23 Rutgers L.J. 597 (1992).

§ 2705. Interest [OPA § 1005]

(a) General rule

The responsible party or the responsible party's guarantor is liable to a claimant for interest on the amount paid in satisfaction of a claim under this chapter for the period described in subsection (b) of this section.

(b) Period

(1) In general

Except as provided in paragraph (2), the period for which interest shall be paid is the period beginning on the 30th day following the date on which the claim is presented to the responsible party or guarantor and ending on the date on which the claim is paid.

(2) Exclusion of period due to offer by guarantor

If the guarantor offers to the claimant an amount equal to or greater than that finally paid in satisfaction of the claim, the period described in paragraph (1) does not include the period beginning on the date the offer is made and ending on the date the offer is accepted. If the offer is made within 60 days after the date on which the claim is presented under section 2713(a) of this title, the period described in paragraph (1) does not include any period before the offer is accepted.

(3) Exclusion of periods in interests of justice

If in any period a claimant is not paid due to reasons beyond the control of the responsible party or because it would not serve the interests of justice, no interest shall accrue under this section during that period.

(4) Calculation of interest

The interest paid under this section shall be calculated at the average of the highest rate for commercial and finance company paper of maturities of 180 days or less obtaining on each of the days included within the period for which interest must be paid to the claimant, as published in the Federal Reserve Bulletin.

(5) Interest not subject to liability limits

(A) In general

Interest (including prejudgment interest) under this paragraph is in addition to damages and removal costs for which claims may be asserted under section 2702 of this title and shall be paid without regard to any limitation of liability under section 2704 of this title.

(B) Payment by guarantor

The payment of interest under this subsection by a guarantor is subject to section 2716(g) of this title.

(Pub.L. 101–380, Title I, § 1005, Aug. 18, 1990, 104 Stat. 493.)

References in Text

This chapter, referred to in text, was in the original this "Act", meaning Pub.L. 101–380 which, in addition to enacting this chapter, made conforming amendments to other sections in this title as well as in Titles 14, 16, 23, 26, 43, 46, and 46 App. For complete classification to the Code see Short Title note under section 2701 of this title and Tables.

Effective Date

Section applicable to incidents occurring after Aug. 18, 1990, see section 1020 of Pub.L. 101–380, set out as a note under section 2701 of this title.

§ 2706. Natural resources [OPA § 1006]

(a) Liability

In the case of natural resource damages under section 2702(b)(2)(A) of this title, liability shall be—

(1) to the United States Government for natural resources belonging to, managed by, controlled by, or appertaining to the United States;

(2) to any State for natural resources belonging to, managed by, controlled by, or appertaining to such State or political subdivision thereof;

(3) to any Indian tribe for natural resources belonging to, managed by, controlled by, or appertaining to such Indian tribe; and

(4) in any case in which section 2707 of this title applies, to the government of a foreign country for natural resources belonging to, managed by, controlled by, or appertaining to such country.

(b) Designation of trustees

(1) In general

The President, or the authorized representative of any State, Indian tribe, or foreign government, shall act on behalf of the public, Indian tribe, or foreign country as trustee of natural resources to present a claim for and to recover damages to the natural resources.

(2) Federal trustees

The President shall designate the Federal officials who shall act on behalf of the public as trustees for natural resources under this chapter.

(3) State trustees

The Governor of each State shall designate State and local officials who may act on behalf of the public as trustee for natural resources under this chapter and shall notify the President of the designation.

(4) Indian tribe trustees

The governing body of any Indian tribe shall designate tribal officials who may act on behalf of the tribe or its members as trustee for natural resources under this chapter and shall notify the President of the designation.

(5) Foreign trustees

The head of any foreign government may designate the trustee who shall act on behalf of that government as trustee for natural resources under this chapter.

(c) Functions of trustees

(1) Federal trustees

The Federal officials designated under subsection (b)(2) of this section—

(A) shall assess natural resource damages under section 2702(b)(2)(A) of this title for the natural resources under their trusteeship;

(B) may, upon request of and reimbursement from a State or Indian tribe and at the Federal officials' discretion, assess damages for the natural resources under the State's or tribe's trusteeship; and

(C) shall develop and implement a plan for the restoration, rehabilitation, replacement, or acquisition of the equivalent, of the natural resources under their trusteeship.

(2) State trustees

The State and local officials designated under subsection (b)(3) of this section—

(A) shall assess natural resource damages under section 2702(b)(2)(A) of this title for the purposes of this chapter for the natural resources under their trusteeship; and

(B) shall develop and implement a plan for the restoration, rehabilitation, replacement, or acquisition of the equivalent, of the natural resources under their trusteeship.

(3) Indian tribe trustees

The tribal officials designated under subsection (b)(4) of this section—

(A) shall assess natural resource damages under section 2702(b)(2)(A) of this title for the purposes of this chapter for the natural resources under their trusteeship; and

(B) shall develop and implement a plan for the restoration, rehabilitation, replacement, or acquisition of the equivalent, of the natural resources under their trusteeship.

(4) Foreign trustees

The trustees designated under subsection (b)(5) of this section—

(A) shall assess natural resource damages under section 2702(b)(2)(A) of this title for the purposes of this chapter for the natural resources under their trusteeship; and

(B) shall develop and implement a plan for the restoration, rehabilitation, replacement, or acquisition of the equivalent, of the natural resources under their trusteeship.

(5) Notice and opportunity to be heard

Plans shall be developed and implemented under this section only after adequate public notice, opportunity for a hearing, and consideration of all public comment.

(d) Measure of damages

(1) In general

The measure of natural resource damages under section 2702(b)(2)(A) of this title is—

(A) the cost of restoring, rehabilitating, replacing, or acquiring the equivalent of, the damaged natural resources;

(B) the diminution in value of those natural resources pending restoration; plus

(C) the reasonable cost of assessing those damages.

(2) Determine costs with respect to plans

Costs shall be determined under paragraph (1) with respect to plans adopted under subsection (c) of this section.

(3) No double recovery

There shall be no double recovery under this chapter for natural resource damages, including with respect to the costs of damage assessment or restoration, rehabilitation, replacement, or acquisition for the same incident and natural resource.

(e) Damage assessment regulations

(1) Regulations

The President, acting through the Under Secretary of Commerce for Oceans and Atmosphere and in consultation with the Administrator of the Environmental Protection Agency, the Director of the United States Fish and Wildlife Service, and the heads of other affected agencies, not later than 2 years after August 18, 1990, shall promulgate regulations for the assessment of natural resource damages under section 2702(b)(2)(A) of this title resulting from a discharge of oil for the purpose of this chapter.

(2) **Rebuttable presumption**

Any determination or assessment of damages to natural resources for the purposes of this chapter made under subsection (d) of this section by a Federal, State, or Indian trustee in accordance with the regulations promulgated under paragraph (1) shall have the force and effect of a rebuttable presumption on behalf of the trustee in any administrative or judicial proceeding under this chapter.

(f) **Use of recovered sums**

Sums recovered under this chapter by a Federal, State, Indian, or foreign trustee for natural resource damages under section 2702(b)(2)(A) of this title shall be retained by the trustee in a revolving trust account, without further appropriation, for use only to reimburse or pay costs incurred by the trustee under subsection (c) of this section with respect to the damaged natural resources. Any amounts in excess of those required for these reimbursements and costs shall be deposited in the Fund.

(g) **Compliance**

Review of actions by any Federal official where there is alleged to be a failure of that official to perform a duty under this section that is not discretionary with that official may be had by any person in the district court in which the person resides or in which the alleged damage to natural resources occurred. The court may award costs of litigation (including reasonable attorney and expert witness fees) to any prevailing or substantially prevailing party. Nothing in this subsection shall restrict any right which any person may have to seek relief under any other provision of law.

(Pub.L. 101–380, Title I, § 1006, Aug. 18, 1990, 104 Stat. 494.)

References in Text

This chapter, referred to in text, was in the original this "Act", meaning Pub.L. 101–380 which, in addition to enacting this chapter, made conforming amendments to other sections in this title as well as in Titles 14, 16, 23, 26, 43, 46, and 46 App. For complete classification to the Code see Short Title note under section 2701 of this title and Tables.

Effective Date

Section applicable to incidents occurring after Aug. 18, 1990, see section 1020 of Pub.L. 101–380, set out as a note under section 2701 of this title.

NOAA Oil and Hazardous Substance Spill Cost Reimbursement

Pub.L. 102–567, Title II, § 205, Oct. 29, 1992, 106 Stat. 4282, provided that:

"(a) **Treatment of amounts received as reimbursement of expenses.**—Notwithstanding any other provision of law, amounts received by the United States as reimbursement of expenses related to oil or hazardous substance spill response activities, or natural resource damage assessment, restoration, rehabilitation, replacement, or acquisition activities, conducted (or to be conducted) by the National Oceanic and Atmospheric Administration—

"(1) shall be deposited into the Fund;

"(2) shall be available, without fiscal year limitation and without apportionment, for use in accordance with the law under which the activities are conducted; and

"(3) shall not be considered to be an augmentation of appropriations.

"(b) **Application.**—Subsection (a) shall apply to amounts described in subsection (a) that are received—

"(1) after the date of the enactment of this Act [Oct. 29, 1992]; or

"(2) with respect to the oil spill associated with the grounding of the EXXON VALDEZ.

"(c) **Definitions.**—For purposes of this section—

"(1) the term 'Fund' means the Damage Assessment and Restoration Revolving Fund of the National Oceanic and Atmospheric Administration referred to in title I of Public Law 101–515 under the heading 'National Oceanic and Atmospheric Administration' (104 Stat. 2105) [Pub.L. 101–515, Title I (part), Nov. 5, 1990, 104 Stat. 2105, which is not classified to the Code]; and

"(2) the term 'expenses' includes incremental and base salaries, ships, aircraft, and associated indirect costs, except the term does not include base salaries and benefits of National Oceanic and Atmospheric Administration Support Coordinators."

§ 2707. Recovery by foreign claimants [OPA § 1007]

(a) **Required showing by foreign claimants**

(1) **In general**

In addition to satisfying the other requirements of this chapter, to recover removal costs or damages resulting from an incident a foreign claimant shall demonstrate that—

(A) the claimant has not been otherwise compensated for the removal costs or damages; and

(B) recovery is authorized by a treaty or executive agreement between the United States and the claimant's country, or the Secretary of State, in consultation with the Attorney General and other appropriate officials, has certified that the claimant's country provides a comparable remedy for United States claimants.

(2) **Exceptions**

Paragraph (1)(B) shall not apply with respect to recovery by a resident of Canada in the case of an incident described in subsection (b)(4) of this section.

(b) **Discharges in foreign countries**

A foreign claimant may make a claim for removal costs and damages resulting from a discharge, or substantial threat of a discharge, of oil in or on the territorial sea, internal waters, or adjacent shoreline of a foreign country, only if the discharge is from—

(1) an Outer Continental Shelf facility or a deepwater port;

(2) a vessel in the navigable waters;

(3) a vessel carrying oil as cargo between 2 places in the United States; or

(4) a tanker that received the oil at the terminal of the pipeline constructed under the Trans–Alaska Pipeline Authorization Act (43 U.S.C. 1651 et seq.), for transportation to a place in the United States, and the discharge or threat occurs prior to delivery of the oil to that place.

(c) Foreign claimant defined

In this section, the term "foreign claimant" means—

(1) a person residing in a foreign country;

(2) the government of a foreign country; and

(3) an agency or political subdivision of a foreign country.

(Pub.L. 101–380, Title I, § 1007, Aug. 18, 1990, 104 Stat. 496.)

References in Text

This chapter, referred to in text, was in the original this "Act", meaning Pub.L. 101–380 which, in addition to enacting this chapter, made conforming amendments to other sections in this title as well as in Titles 14, 16, 23, 26, 43, 46, and 46 App. For complete classification to the Code see Short Title note under section 2701 of this title and Tables.

The Trans–Alaska Pipeline Authorization Act, referred to in subsec. (b)(4), is title II of Pub.L. 93–153, Nov. 16, 1973, 87 Stat. 584, which is classified to chapter 34 (§ 1651 et seq.) of Title 43, Public Lands. For complete classification of this Act to the Code, see Short Title note set out under section 1651 of Title 43 and Tables.

Effective Date

Section applicable to incidents occurring after Aug. 18, 1990, see section 1020 of Pub.L. 101–380, set out as a note under section 2701 of this title.

§ 2708. Recovery by responsible party [OPA § 1008]

(a) In general

The responsible party for a vessel or facility from which oil is discharged, or which poses the substantial threat of a discharge of oil, may assert a claim for removal costs and damages under section 2713 of this title only if the responsible party demonstrates that—

(1) the responsible party is entitled to a defense to liability under section 2703 of this title; or

(2) the responsible party is entitled to a limitation of liability under section 2704 of this title.

(b) Extent of recovery

A responsible party who is entitled to a limitation of liability may assert a claim under section 2713 of this title only to the extent that the sum of the removal costs and damages incurred by the responsible party plus the amounts paid by the responsible party, or by the guarantor on behalf of the responsible party, for claims asserted under section 2713 of this title exceeds the amount to which the total of the liability under section 2702 of this title and removal costs and damages incurred by, or on behalf of, the responsible party is limited under section 2704 of this title.

(Pub.L. 101–380, Title I, § 1008, Aug. 18, 1990, 104 Stat. 497.)

Effective Date

Section applicable to incidents occurring after Aug. 18, 1990, see section 1020 of Pub.L. 101–380, set out as a note under section 2701 of this title.

§ 2709. Contribution [OPA § 1009]

A person may bring a civil action for contribution against any other person who is liable or potentially liable under this chapter or another law. The action shall be brought in accordance with section 2717 of this title.

(Pub.L. 101–380, Title I, § 1009, Aug. 18, 1990, 104 Stat. 497.)

References in Text

This chapter, referred to in text, was in the original this "Act", meaning Pub.L. 101–380 which, in addition to enacting this chapter, made conforming amendments to other sections in this title as well as in Titles 14, 16, 23, 26, 43, 46, and 46 App. For complete classification to the Code see Short Title note under section 2701 of this title and Tables.

Effective Date

Section applicable to incidents occurring after Aug. 18, 1990, see section 1020 of Pub.L. 101–380, set out as a note under section 2701 of this title.

§ 2710. Indemnification agreements [OPA § 1010]

(a) Agreements not prohibited

Nothing in this chapter prohibits any agreement to insure, hold harmless, or indemnify a party to such agreement for any liability under this chapter.

(b) Liability not transferred

No indemnification, hold harmless, or similar agreement or conveyance shall be effective to transfer liability imposed under this chapter from a responsible party or from any person who may be liable for an incident under this chapter to any other person.

(c) Relationship to other causes of action

Nothing in this chapter including the provisions of subsection (b) of this section bars a cause of action that a responsible party subject to liability under this chapter, or a guarantor, has or would have, by reason of subrogation or otherwise, against any person.

(Pub.L. 101–380, Title I, § 1010, Aug. 18, 1990, 104 Stat. 498.)

References in Text

This chapter, referred to in text, was in the original this "Act", meaning Pub.L. 101–380 which, in addition to enacting this chapter, made conforming amendments to other sections in this title as well as in Titles 14, 16, 23, 26, 43, 46, and 46 App. For complete classification to the Code see Short Title note under section 2701 of this title and Tables.

Effective Date

Section applicable to incidents occurring after Aug. 18, 1990, see section 1020 of Pub.L. 101–380, set out as a note under section 2701 of this title.

§ 2711. Consultation on removal actions [OPA § 1011]

The President shall consult with the affected trustees designated under section 2706 of this title on the appropriate removal action to be taken in connection with any discharge of oil. For the purposes of the National Contingency Plan, removal with respect to any discharge shall be considered completed when so determined by the President in consultation with the Governor or Governors of the affected States. However, this determination shall not preclude additional removal actions under applicable State law.

(Pub.L. 101–380, Title I, § 1011, Aug. 18, 1990, 104 Stat. 498.)

Effective Date

Section applicable to incidents occurring after Aug. 18, 1990, see section 1020 of Pub.L. 101–380, set out as a note under section 2701 of this title.

§ 2712. Uses of the fund [OPA § 1012]

(a) Uses generally

The Fund shall be available to the President for—

(1) the payment of removal costs, including the costs of monitoring removal actions, determined by the President to be consistent with the National Contingency Plan—

(A) by Federal authorities; or

(B) by a Governor or designated State official under subsection (d) of this section;

(2) the payment of costs incurred by Federal, State, or Indian tribe trustees in carrying out their functions under section 2706 of this title for assessing natural resource damages and for developing and implementing plans for the restoration, rehabilitation, replacement, or acquisition of the equivalent of damaged resources determined by the President to be consistent with the National Contingency Plan;

(3) the payment of removal costs determined by the President to be consistent with the National Contingency Plan as a result of, and damages resulting from, a discharge, or a substantial threat of a discharge, of oil from a foreign offshore unit;

(4) the payment of claims in accordance with section 2713 of this title for uncompensated removal costs determined by the President to be consistent with the National Contingency Plan or uncompensated damages;

(5) the payment of Federal administrative, operational, and personnel costs and expenses reasonably necessary for and incidental to the implementation, administration, and enforcement of this chapter (including, but not limited to, sections 2704(d)(2) of this title, 2706(e) of this title, 4107 of this Act, 4110 of this Act, 4111 of this Act, 4112 of this Act, 4117 of this Act, 2703 of this title, 8103 of this Act, and subchapter IV of this chapter) and subsections (b), (c), (d), (j), and (*l*) of section 1321 of this title, as amended by this Act, with respect to prevention, removal, and enforcement related to oil discharges, provided that—

(A) not more than $25,000,000 in each fiscal year shall be available to the Secretary for operating expenses incurred by the Coast Guard;

(B) not more than $30,000,000 each year through the end of fiscal year 1992 shall be available to establish the National Response System under section 1321(j) of this title, as amended by this Act, including the purchase and prepositioning of oil spill removal equipment; and

(C) not more than $27,250,000 in each fiscal year shall be available to carry out subchapter IV of this chapter.

(b) Defense to liability for Fund

The Fund shall not be available to pay any claim for removal costs or damages to a particular claimant, to the extent that the incident, removal costs, or damages are caused by the gross negligence or willful misconduct of that claimant.

(c) Obligation of Fund by Federal officials

The President may promulgate regulations designating one or more Federal officials who may obligate money in accordance with subsection (a) of this section.

(d) Access to Fund by State officials

(1) Immediate removal

In accordance with regulations promulgated under this section, the President, upon the request of the Governor of a State or pursuant to an agreement with a State under paragraph (2), may obligate the Fund for payment in an amount not to exceed $250,000 for removal costs consistent with the National Contingency Plan required for the immediate removal of a discharge, or the mitigation or prevention of a substantial threat of a discharge, of oil.

(2) Agreements

(A) In general

The President shall enter into an agreement with the Governor of any interested State to establish procedures under which the Governor or a designated State official may receive payments from the Fund for removal costs pursuant to paragraph (1).

(B) Terms

Agreements under this paragraph—

(i) may include such terms and conditions as may be agreed upon by the President and the Governor of a State;

(ii) shall provide for political subdivisions of the State to receive payments for reasonable removal costs; and

(iii) may authorize advance payments from the Fund to facilitate removal efforts.

(e) Regulations

The President shall—

(1) not later than 6 months after August 18, 1990, publish proposed regulations detailing the manner in which the authority to obligate the Fund and to enter into agreements under this subsection shall be exercised; and

(2) not later than 3 months after the close of the comment period for such proposed regulations, promulgate final regulations for that purpose.

(f) Rights of subrogation

Payment of any claim or obligation by the Fund under this chapter shall be subject to the United States Government acquiring by subrogation all rights of the claimant or State to recover from the responsible party.

(g) Audits

The Comptroller General shall audit all payments, obligations, reimbursements, and other uses of the Fund, to assure that the Fund is being properly administered and that claims are being appropriately and expeditiously considered. The Comptroller General shall submit to the Congress an interim report one year after August 18, 1990. The Comptroller General shall thereafter audit the Fund as is appropriate. Each Federal agency shall cooperate with the Comptroller General in carrying out this subsection.

(h) Period of limitations for claims

(1) Removal costs

No claim may be presented under this subchapter for recovery of removal costs for an incident unless the claim is presented within 6 years after the date of completion of all removal actions for that incident.

(2) Damages

No claim may be presented under this section for recovery of damages unless the claim is presented within 3 years after the date on which the injury and its connection with the discharge in question were reasonably discoverable with the exercise of due care, or in the case of natural resource damages under section 2702(b)(2)(A) of this title, if later, the date of completion of the natural resources damage assessment under section 2706(e) of this title.

(3) Minors and incompetents

The time limitations contained in this subsection shall not begin to run—

(A) against a minor until the earlier of the date when such minor reaches 18 years of age or the date on which a legal representative is duly appointed for the minor, or

(B) against an incompetent person until the earlier of the date on which such incompetent's incompetency ends or the date on which a legal representative is duly appointed for the incompetent.

(i) Limitation on payment for same costs

In any case in which the President has paid an amount from the Fund for any removal costs or damages specified under subsection (a) of this section, no other claim may be paid from the Fund for the same removal costs or damages.

(j) Obligation in accordance with plan

(1) In general

Except as provided in paragraph (2), amounts may be obligated from the Fund for the restoration, rehabilitation, replacement, or acquisition of natural resources only in accordance with a plan adopted under section 2706(c) of this title.

(2) Exception

Paragraph (1) shall not apply in a situation requiring action to avoid irreversible loss of natural resources or to prevent or reduce any continuing danger to natural resources or similar need for emergency action.

(k) Preference for private persons in area affected by discharge

(1) In general

In the expenditure of Federal funds for removal of oil, including for distribution of supplies, construction, and other reasonable and appropriate activities, under a contract or agreement with a private person, preference shall be given, to the extent feasible and practicable, to private persons residing or doing business primarily in the area affected by the discharge of oil.

(2) Limitation

This subsection shall not be considered to restrict the use of Department of Defense resources.

(Pub.L. 101–380, Title I, § 1012, Aug. 18, 1990, 104 Stat. 498.)

References in Text

This chapter, referred to in text, was in the original this "Act", meaning Pub.L. 101–380 which, in addition to enacting this chapter, made conforming amendments to other sections in this title as well as in Titles 14, 16, 23, 26, 43, 46, and 46 App. For complete classification to the Code see Short Title note under section 2701 of this title and Tables.

References in subsec. (a)(5) to sections 4107, 4110, 4111, 4112, 4117, and 8103 of this Act refer to sections of Pub.L. 101–380 which sections are classified, respectively, to section 1223 and 1223 note of this title, 1651 note of Title 43, Public Lands, section 3703 notes of Title 46, Shipping, and section 1295 note of the Appendix to Title 46. Section 4112 of this Act, relating to a dredge modification study by the Secretary of the Army, was not classified to the Code.

References in subsec. (a)(5) to the amendment of section 1321 of this title "by this Act" refer to amendment by Pub.L. 101–380, Aug. 18, 1990, 104 Stat. 484.

Effective Date

Section applicable to incidents occurring after Aug. 18, 1990, see section 1020 of Pub.L. 101–380, set out as a note under section 2701 of this title.

§ 2713. Claims procedure [OPA § 1013]

(a) Presentation

Except as provided in subsection (b) of this section, all claims for removal costs or damages shall be presented first to the responsible party or guarantor of the source designated under section 2714(a) of this title.

(b) Presentation to Fund

(1) In general

Claims for removal costs or damages may be presented first to the Fund—

(A) if the President has advertised or otherwise notified claimants in accordance with section 2714(c) of this title.

(B) by a responsible party who may assert a claim under section 2708 of this title.

(C) by the Governor of a State for removal costs incurred by that State; or

(D) by a United States claimant in a case where a foreign offshore unit has discharged oil causing damage for which the Fund is liable under section 2712(a) of this title.

(2) Limitation on presenting claim

No claim of a person against the Fund may be approved or certified during the pendency of an action by the person in court to recover costs which are the subject of the claim.

(c) Election

If a claim is presented in accordance with subsection (a) and—

(1) each person to whom the claim is presented denies all liability for the claim, or

(2) the claim is not settled by any person by payment within 90 days after the date upon which (A) the claim was presented, or (B) advertising was begun pursuant to section 2714(b) of this title, whichever is later,

the claimant may elect to commence an action in court against the responsible party or guarantor or to present the claim to the Fund.

(d) Uncompensated damages

If a claim is presented in accordance with this section and full and adequate compensation is unavailable, a claim for the uncompensated damages and removal costs may be presented to the Fund.

(e) Procedure for claims against Fund

The President shall promulgate, and may from time to time amend, regulations for the presentation, filing, processing, settlement, and adjudication of claims under this chapter against the Fund.

(Pub.L. 101–380, Title I, § 1013, Aug. 18, 1990, 104 Stat. 501.)

References in Text

This chapter, referred to in text, was in the original this "Act", meaning Pub.L. 101–380 which, in addition to enacting this chapter, made conforming amendments to other sections in this title as well as in Titles 14, 16, 23, 26, 43, 46, and 46 App. For complete classification to the Code see Short Title note under section 2701 of this title and Tables.

Effective Date

Section applicable to incidents occurring after Aug. 18, 1990, see section 1020 of Pub.L. 101–380, set out as a note under section 2701 of this title.

§ 2714. Designation of source and advertisement [OPA § 1014]

(a) Designation of source and notification

When the President receives information of an incident, the President shall, where possible and appropriate, designate the source or sources of the discharge or threat. If a designated source is a vessel or a facility, the President shall immediately notify the responsible party and the guarantor, if known, of that designation.

(b) Advertisement by responsible party or guarantor

If a responsible party or guarantor fails to inform the President, within 5 days after receiving notification of a designation under subsection (a) of this section, of the party's or the guarantor's denial of the designation, such party or guarantor shall advertise the designation and the procedures by which claims may be presented, in accordance with regulations promulgated by the President. Advertisement under the preceding sentence shall begin no later than 15 days after the date of the designation made under subsection (a) of this section. If advertisement is not otherwise made in accordance with this subsection, the President shall promptly and at the expense of the responsible party or the guarantor involved, advertise the designation and the procedures by which claims may be presented to the responsible party or guarantor. Advertisement under this subsection shall continue for a period of no less than 30 days.

(c) Advertisement by President

If—

(1) the responsible party and the guarantor both deny a designation within 5 days after receiving notification of a designation under subsection (a) of this section,

(2) the source of the discharge or threat was a public vessel, or

(3) the President is unable to designate the source or sources of the discharge or threat under subsection (a) of this section,

the President shall advertise or otherwise notify potential claimants of the procedures by which claims may be presented to the Fund.

(Pub.L. 101–380, Title I, § 1014, Aug. 18, 1990, 104 Stat. 501.)

Effective Date

Section applicable to incidents occurring after Aug. 18, 1990, see section 1020 of Pub.L. 101–380, set out as a note under section 2701 of this title.

§ 2715. Subrogation [OPA § 1015]

(a) In general

Any person, including the Fund, who pays compensation pursuant to this chapter to any claimant for removal costs or damages shall be subrogated to all rights, claims, and causes of action that the claimant has under any other law.

(b) Actions on behalf of Fund

At the request of the Secretary, the Attorney General shall commence an action on behalf of the Fund to recover any compensation paid by the Fund to any claimant pursuant to this chapter, and all costs incurred by the Fund by reason of the claim, including interest (including prejudgment interest), administrative and adjudicative costs, and attorney's fees. Such an action may be commenced against any responsible party or (subject to section 2716 of this title) guarantor, or against any other person who is liable, pursuant to any law, to the compensated claimant or to the Fund, for the cost or damages for which the compensation was paid. Such an action shall be commenced against the responsible foreign government or other responsible party to recover any removal costs or damages paid from the Fund as the result of the discharge, or substantial threat of discharge, of oil from a foreign offshore unit.

(Pub.L. 101–380, Title I, § 1015, Aug. 18, 1990, 104 Stat. 502.)

References in Text

This chapter, referred to in text, was in the original this "Act", meaning Pub.L. 101–380 which, in addition to enacting this chapter, made conforming amendments to other sections in this title as well as in Titles 14, 16, 23, 26, 43, 46, and 46 App. For complete classification to the Code see Short Title note under section 2701 of this title and Tables.

Reference in subsec. (h) to the "effective date of this Act" probably refers to the date of enactment of Pub.L. 101–380 which was approved on Aug. 18, 1990.

Effective Date

Section applicable to incidents occurring after Aug. 18, 1990, see section 1020 of Pub.L. 101–380, set out as a note under section 2701 of this title.

§ 2716. Financial responsibility [OPA § 1016]

(a) Requirement

The responsible party for—

(1) any vessel over 300 gross tons (except a non-self-propelled vessel that does not carry oil as cargo or fuel) using any place subject to the jurisdiction of the United States; or

(2) any vessel using the waters of the exclusive economic zone to transship or lighter oil destined for a place subject to the jurisdiction of the United States;

shall establish and maintain, in accordance with regulations promulgated by the Secretary, evidence of financial responsibility sufficient to meet the maximum amount of liability to which the responsible party could be subjected under section 2704(a) or (d) of this title, in a case where the responsible party would be entitled to limit liability under that section. If the responsible party owns or operates more than one vessel, evidence of financial responsibility need be established only to meet the amount of the maximum liability applicable to the vessel having the greatest maximum liability.

(b) Sanctions

(1) Withholding clearance

The Secretary of the Treasury shall withhold or revoke the clearance required by section 91 of the Appendix to Title 46 of any vessel subject to this section that does not have the evidence of financial responsibility required for the vessel under this section.

(2) **Denying entry to or detaining vessels**

The Secretary may—

(A) deny entry to any vessel to any place in the United States, or to the navigable waters, or

(B) detain at the place,

any vessel that, upon request, does not produce the evidence of financial responsibility required for the vessel under this section.

(3) **Seizure of vessel**

Any vessel subject to the requirements of this section which is found in the navigable waters without the necessary evidence of financial responsibility for the vessel shall be subject to seizure by and forfeiture to the United States.

(c) **Offshore facilities**

(1) **In general**

Except as provided in paragraph (2), each responsible party with respect to an offshore facility shall establish and maintain evidence of financial responsibility of $150,000,000 to meet the amount of liability to which the responsible party could be subjected under section 2704(a) of this title in a case in which the responsible party would be entitled to limit liability under that section. In a case in which a person is the responsible party for more than one facility subject to this subsection, evidence of financial responsibility need be established only to meet the maximum liability applicable to the facility having the greatest maximum liability.

(2) **Deepwater ports**

Each responsible party with respect to a deepwater port shall establish and maintain evidence of financial responsibility sufficient to meet the maximum amount of liability to which the responsible party could be subjected under section 2704(a) of this title in a case where the responsible party would be entitled to limit liability under that section. If the Secretary exercises the authority under section 2704(d)(2) of this title to lower the limit of liability for deepwater ports, the responsible party shall establish and maintain evidence of financial responsibility sufficient to meet the maximum amount of liability so established. In a case in which a person is the responsible party for more than one deepwater port, evidence of financial responsibility need be established only to meet the maximum liability applicable to the deepwater port having the greatest maximum liability.

(e) [1] **Methods of financial responsibility**

Financial responsibility under this section may be established by any one, or by any combination, of the following methods which the Secretary (in the case of a vessel) or the President (in the case of a facility) determines to be acceptable: evidence of insurance, surety bond, guarantee, letter of credit, qualification as a self-insurer, or other evidence of financial responsibility. Any bond filed shall be issued by a bonding company authorized to do business in the United States. In promulgating requirements under this section, the Secretary or the President, as appropriate, may specify policy or other contractual terms, conditions, or defenses which are necessary, or which are unacceptable, in establishing evidence of financial responsibility to effectuate the purposes of this chapter.

(f) **Claims against guarantor**

Any claim for which liability may be established under section 2702 of this title may be asserted directly against any guarantor providing evidence of financial responsibility for a responsible party liable under that section for removal costs and damages to which the claim pertains. In defending against such a claim, the guarantor may invoke (1) all rights and defenses which would be available to the responsible party under this chapter, (2) any defense authorized under subsection (e) of this section, and (3) the defense that the incident was caused by the willful misconduct of the responsible party. The guarantor may not invoke any other defense that might be available in proceedings brought by the responsible party against the guarantor.

(g) **Limitation on guarantor's liability**

Nothing in this chapter shall impose liability with respect to an incident on any guarantor for damages or removal costs which exceed, in the aggregate, the amount of financial responsibility required under this chapter which that guarantor has provided for a responsible party.

(h) **Continuation of regulations**

Any regulation relating to financial responsibility, which has been issued pursuant to any provision of law repealed or superseded by this chapter, and which is in effect on the date immediately preceding the effective date of this Act, is deemed and shall be construed to be a regulation issued pursuant to this section. Such a regulation shall remain in full force and effect unless and until superseded by a new regulation issued under this section.

(i) **Unified certificate**

The Secretary may issue a single unified certificate of financial responsibility for purposes of this chapter and any other law.

(Pub.L. 101–380, Title I, § 1016, Aug. 18, 1990, 104 Stat. 502; Pub.L. 104–55, § 2(d)(2), Nov. 20, 1995, 109 Stat. 547.)

[1] No subsec. (d) has been enacted.

References in Text

This chapter, referred to in text, was in the original this "Act", meaning Pub.L. 101–380 which, in addition to enacting this chapter, made conforming amendments to other sections in this title as well as in Titles 14, 16, 23, 26, 43, 46, and 46 App. For complete classification to the Code see Short Title note under section 2701 of this title and Tables.

Effective Date

Section applicable to incidents occurring after Aug. 18, 1990, see section 1020 of Pub.L. 101–380, set out as a note under section 2701 of this title.

§ 2716a. Financial responsibility; civil penalties [OPA § 4303]

(a) Administrative

Any person who, after notice and an opportunity for a hearing, is found to have failed to comply with the requirements of section 2716 of this title or the regulations issued under that section, or with a denial or detention order issued under subsection (c)(2) of that section, shall be liable to the United States for a civil penalty, not to exceed $25,000 per day of violation. The amount of the civil penalty shall be assessed by the President by written notice. In determining the amount of the penalty, the President shall take into account the nature, circumstances, extent, and gravity of the violation, the degree of culpability, any history of prior violation, ability to pay, and such other matters as justice may require. The President may compromise, modify, or remit, with or without conditions, any civil penalty which is subject to imposition or which had been imposed under this paragraph. If any person fails to pay an assessed civil penalty after it has become final, the President may refer the matter to the Attorney General for collection.

(b) Judicial

In addition to, or in lieu of, assessing a penalty under subsection (a) of this section, the President may request the Attorney General to secure such relief as necessary to compel compliance with this section 2716 of this title, including a judicial order terminating operations. The district courts of the United States shall have jurisdiction to grant any relief as the public interest and the equities of the case may require.

(Pub.L. 101–380, Title IV, § 4303, Aug. 18, 1990, 104 Stat. 539.)

Codification

Section was not enacted as part of title I of Pub.L. 101–380 which comprises this subchapter.

Effective Date

Section applicable to incidents occurring after Aug. 18, 1990, as constituting the basis for violations of section 2716 of this title for which penalties are assessed under this section, see section 1020 of Pub.L. 101–380, set out as a note under section 2701 of this title.

§ 2717. Litigation, jurisdiction, and venue [OPA § 1017]

(a) Review of regulations

Review of any regulation promulgated under this chapter may be had upon application by any interested person only in the Circuit Court of Appeals of the United States for the District of Columbia. Any such application shall be made within 90 days from the date of promulgation of such regulations. Any matter with respect to which review could have been obtained under this subsection shall not be subject to judicial review in any civil or criminal proceeding for enforcement or to obtain damages or recovery of response costs.

(b) Jurisdiction

Except as provided in subsections (a) and (c) of this section, the United States district courts shall have exclusive original jurisdiction over all controversies arising under this chapter, without regard to the citizenship of the parties or the amount in controversy. Venue shall lie in any district in which the discharge or injury or damages occurred, or in which the defendant resides, may be found, has its principal office, or has appointed an agent for service of process. For the purposes of this section, the Fund shall reside in the District of Columbia.

(c) State court jurisdiction

A State trial court of competent jurisdiction over claims for removal costs or damages, as defined under this chapter, may consider claims under this chapter or State law and any final judgment of such court (when no longer subject to ordinary forms of review) shall be recognized, valid, and enforceable for all purposes of this chapter.

(d) Assessment and collection of tax

The provisions of subsections (a), (b), and (c) of this section shall not apply to any controversy or other matter resulting from the assessment or collection of any tax, or to the review of any regulation promulgated under Title 26.

(e) Savings provision

Nothing in this title shall apply to any cause of action or right of recovery arising from any incident which occurred prior to August 18, 1990. Such claims shall be adjudicated pursuant to the law applicable on the date of the incident.

(f) Period of limitations

(1) Damages

Except as provided in paragraphs (3) and (4), an action for damages under this chapter shall be barred unless the action is brought within 3 years after—

(A) the date on which the loss and the connection of the loss with the discharge in question are reasonably discoverable with the exercise of due care, or

(B) in the case of natural resource damages under section 2702(b)(2)(A) of this title, the date of completion of the natural resources damage assessment under section 2706(c) of this title.

(2) Removal costs

An action for recovery of removal costs referred to in section 2702(b)(1) of this title must be commenced within 3 years after completion of the removal action. In any such action described in this subsection, the court shall enter a declaratory judgment on liability for removal costs or damages that will be binding on any subsequent action or actions to recover further removal costs or damages. Except as otherwise provided in this paragraph, an action may be commenced under this subchapter for recovery of removal costs at any time after such costs have been incurred.

(3) Contribution

No action for contribution for any removal costs or damages may be commenced more than 3 years after—

(A) the date of judgment in any action under this chapter for recovery of such costs or damages, or

(B) the date of entry of a judicially approved settlement with respect to such costs or damages.

(4) Subrogation

No action based on rights subrogated pursuant to this chapter by reason of payment of a claim may be commenced under this chapter more than 3 years after the date of payment of such claim.

(5) Commencement

The time limitations contained herein shall not begin to run—

(A) against a minor until the earlier of the date when such minor reaches 18 years of age or the date on which a legal representative is duly appointed for such minor, or

(B) against an incompetent person until the earlier of the date on which such incompetent's incompetency ends or the date on which a legal representative is duly appointed for such incompetent.

(Pub.L. 101–380, Title I, § 1017, Aug. 18, 1990, 104 Stat. 504.)

References in Text

This chapter, referred to in text, was in the original this "Act", meaning Pub.L. 101–380 which, in addition to enacting this chapter, made conforming amendments to other sections in this title as well as in Titles 14, 16, 23, 26, 43, 46, and 46 App. For complete classification to the Code see Short Title note under section 2701 of this title and Tables.

Effective Date

Section applicable to incidents occurring after Aug. 18, 1990, see section 1020 of Pub.L. 101–380, set out as a note under section 2701 of this title.

§ 2718. Relationship to other law [OPA § 1018]

(a) Preservation of State authorities; Solid Waste Disposal Act

Nothing in this chapter or the Act of March 3, 1851 shall—

(1) affect, or be construed or interpreted as preempting, the authority of any State or political subdivision thereof from imposing any additional liability or requirements with respect to—

(A) the discharge of oil or other pollution by oil within such State; or

(B) any removal activities in connection with such a discharge; or

(2) affect, or be construed or interpreted to affect or modify in any way the obligations or liabilities of any person under the Solid Waste Disposal Act (42 U.S.C. 6901 et seq.) or State law, including common law.

(b) Preservation of State funds

Nothing in this chapter or in section 9509 of Title 26 shall in any way affect, or be construed to affect, the authority of any State—

(1) to establish, or to continue in effect, a fund any purpose of which is to pay for costs or damages arising out of, or directly resulting from, oil pollution or the substantial threat of oil pollution; or

(2) to require any person to contribute to such a fund.

(c) Additional requirements and liabilities; penalties

Nothing in this chapter, the Act of March 3, 1851 (46 U.S.C. 183 et seq.), or section 9509 of Title 26 shall in any way affect, or be construed to affect, the authority of the United States or any State or political subdivision thereof—

(1) to impose additional liability or additional requirements; or

(2) to impose, or to determine the amount of, any fine or penalty (whether criminal or civil in nature) for any violation of law;

relating to the discharge, or substantial threat of a discharge, of oil.

(d) Federal employee liability

For purposes of section 2679(b)(2)(B) of Title 28, nothing in this chapter shall be construed to authorize or create a cause of action against a Federal officer or employee in the officer's or employee's personal or individual capacity for any act or omission while acting within the scope of the officer's or employee's office or employment.

(Pub.L. 101–380, Title I, § 1018, Aug. 18, 1990, 104 Stat. 505.)

References in Text

This chapter, referred to in text, was in the original this "Act", meaning Pub.L. 101–380 which, in addition to enacting this chapter, made conforming amendments to other sections in this title as well as in Titles 14, 16, 23, 26, 43, 46, and 46 App. For complete classification to the Code see Short Title note under section 2701 of this title and Tables.

Reference in subsecs. (a) and (c) to "the Act of March 3, 1851" probably is a reference to Act March 3, 1851, c. 43, 9 Stat. 635, entitled "An Act to limit the liability of ship-owners, and for other purposes", which is now covered by section 181 et seq. of the Appendix to Title 46, Shipping.

The Solid Waste Disposal Act, referred to in subsec. (a)(2), is title II of Pub.L. 89–272, Oct. 20, 1965, 79 Stat. 997, as amended generally by Pub.L. 94–580, § 2, Oct. 21, 1976, 90 Stat. 2795, which is classified generally to chapter 82 (§ 6901 et seq.) of Title 42, The Public Health and Welfare. For complete classification of this Act to the Code, see Short Title note set out under section 6901 of Title 42 and Tables.

Effective Date

Section applicable to incidents occurring after Aug. 18, 1990, see section 1020 of Pub.L. 101–380, set out as a note under section 2701 of this title.

Report on Vessel Safety and Ability to Meet Legal Obligations

Pub.L. 102–241, § 32, Dec. 19, 1991, 105 Stat. 2222, provided that: "Not later than one year after the date of enactment of this Act [Dec. 19, 1991], the Secretary of Transportation shall report to Congress on the effect of section 1018 of the Oil Pollution Act of 1990 (Public Law 101–380; 104 Stat. 484) [this section] on the safety of vessels being used to transport oil and the capability of owners and operators to meet their legal obligations in the event of an oil spill."

LAW REVIEW COMMENTARIES

Crude legislation: Liability and compensation under the Oil Pollution Act of 1990. Daniel Kopec and Philip Peterson, 23 Rutgers L.J. 597 (1992).

§ 2719. State financial responsibility [OPA § 1019]

A State may enforce, on the navigable waters of the State, the requirements for evidence of financial responsibility under section 2716 of this title.

(Pub.L. 101–380, Title I, § 1019, Aug. 18, 1990, 104 Stat. 506.)

Effective Date

Section applicable to incidents occurring after Aug. 18, 1990, see section 1020 of Pub.L. 101–380, set out as a note under section 2701 of this title.

§ 2720. Differentiation among fats, oils, and greases

(a) In general

Except as provided in subsection (c) of this section, in issuing or enforcing any regulation or establishing any interpretation or guideline relating to the transportation, storage, discharge, release, emission, or disposal of a fat, oil, or grease under any Federal law, the head of that Federal agency shall—

(1) differentiate between and establish separate classes for—

(A) animal fats and oils and greases, and fish and marine mammal oils, within the meaning of paragraph (2) of section 61(a) of Title 13, and oils of vegetable origin, including oils from the seeds, nuts, and kernels referred to in paragraph (1)(A) of that section; and

(B) other oils and greases, including petroleum; and

(2) apply standards to different classes of fats and oils based on considerations in subsection (b) of this section.

(b) Considerations

In differentiating between the class of fats, oils, and greases described in subsection (a)(1)(A) of this section and the class of oils and greases described in subsection (a)(1)(B) of this section, the head of the Federal agency shall consider differences in the physical, chemical, biological, and other properties, and in the environmental effects, of the classes.

(c) Exception

The requirements of this Act shall not apply to the Food and Drug Administration and the Food Safety and Inspection Service.

(d) Omitted

(Pub.L. 104–55, § 2, Nov. 20, 1995, 109 Stat. 546.)

References in Text

This Act, referred to in subsec. (c), is Pub.L. 104–55, Nov. 20, 1995, 109 Stat. 546, which enacted this section, amended sections 2704 and 2716 of this title, and enacted provisions set out as a note under section 2701 of this title. For complete classification of this Act to the Code, see Short Title note set out under section 2701 of this title and Tables.

Codification

Section was enacted as part of the Edible Oil Regulatory Reform Act [Pub.L. 104–55] and not as part of the Oil Pollution Act of 1990 [Pub.L. 101–380] which enacted this chapter.

Section 2 of Pub.L. 104–55, which enacted this section, consisted in the original of subsecs. (a) to (d). Section 2(d) of Pub.L. 104–55, which has been omitted from the text of this section, amended sections 2704(a)(1) and 2716(a) of this title.

SUBCHAPTER II—PRINCE WILLIAM SOUND PROVISIONS

§ 2731. Oil Spill Recovery Institute [OPA § 5001]

(a) Establishment of Institute

The Secretary of Commerce shall provide for the establishment of a Prince William Sound Oil Spill

Recovery Institute (hereinafter in this section referred to as the "Institute") to be administered by the Secretary of Commerce through the Prince William Sound Science and Technology Institute and located in Cordova, Alaska.

(b) Functions

The Institute shall conduct research and carry out educational and demonstration projects designed to—

(1) identify and develop the best available techniques, equipment, and materials for dealing with oil spills in the arctic and subarctic marine environment; and

(2) complement Federal and State damage assessment efforts and determine, document, assess, and understand the long-range effects of the EXXON VALDEZ oil spill on the natural resources of Prince William Sound and its adjacent waters (as generally depicted on the map entitled "EXXON VALDEZ oil spill dated March 1990"), and the environment, the economy, and the lifestyle and well-being of the people who are dependent on them, except that the Institute shall not conduct studies or make recommendations on any matter which is not directly related to the EXXON VALDEZ oil spill or the effects thereof.

(c) Advisory Board

(1) In general

The policies of the Institute shall be determined by an advisory board, composed of 18 members appointed as follows:

(A) One representative appointed by each of the Commissioners of Fish and Game, Environmental Conservation, Natural Resources, and Commerce and Economic Development of the State of Alaska, all of whom shall be State employees.

(B) One representative appointed by each of—

(i) the Secretaries of Commerce, the Interior, Agriculture, Transportation, and the Navy; and

(ii) the Administrator of the Environmental Protection Agency;

all of whom shall be Federal employees.

(C) 4 representatives appointed by the Secretary of Commerce from among residents of communities in Alaska that were affected by the EXXON VALDEZ oil spill who are knowledgeable about fisheries, other local industries, the marine environment, wildlife, public health, safety, or education. At least 2 of the representatives shall be appointed from among residents of communities located in Prince William Sound. The Secretary shall appoint residents to serve terms of 2 years each, from a list of 8 qualified individuals to be submitted by the Governor of the State of Alaska based on recommendations made by the governing body of each affected community. Each affected community may submit the names of 2 qualified individuals for the Governor's consideration. No more than 5 of the 8 qualified persons recommended by the Governor shall be members of the same political party.

(D) 3 Alaska Natives who represent Native entities affected by the EXXON VALDEZ oil spill, at least one of whom represents an entity located in Prince William Sound, to serve terms of 2 years each from a list of 6 qualified individuals submitted by the Alaska Federation of Natives.

(E) One nonvoting representative of the Institute of Marine Science.

(F) One nonvoting representative appointed by the Prince William Sound Science and Technology Institute.

(2) Chairman—

The representative of the Secretary of Commerce shall serve as Chairman of the Advisory Board.

(3) Policies

Policies determined by the Advisory Board under this subsection shall include policies for the conduct and support, through contracts and grants awarded on a nationally competitive basis, of research, projects, and studies to be supported by the Institute in accordance with the purposes of this section.

(d) Scientific and Technical Committee

(1) In general

The Advisory Board shall establish a scientific and technical committee, composed of specialists in matters relating to oil spill containment and cleanup technology, arctic and subarctic marine ecology, and the living resources and socioeconomics of Prince William Sound and its adjacent waters, from the University of Alaska, the Institute of Marine Science, the Prince William Sound Science and Technology Institute, and elsewhere in the academic community.

(2) Functions

The Scientific and Technical Committee shall provide such advice to the Advisory Board as the Advisory Board shall request, including recommendations regarding the conduct and support of research, projects, and studies in accordance with the purposes of this section. The Advisory Board shall not request, and the Committee shall not provide, any advice which is not directly related to the EXXON VALDEZ oil spill or the effects thereof.

(e) Director

The Institute shall be administered by a Director appointed by the Secretary of Commerce. The Prince William Sound Science and Technology Institute, the Advisory Board, and the Scientific and Technical Committee may each submit independent recommendations for the Secretary's consideration for appointment as Director. The Director may hire such staff and incur such expenses on behalf of the Institute as are authorized by the Advisory Board.

(f) Evaluation

The Secretary of Commerce may conduct an ongoing evaluation of the activities of the Institute to ensure that funds received by the Institute are used in a manner consistent with this section.

(g) Audit

The Comptroller General of the United States, and any of his or her duly authorized representatives, shall have access, for purposes of audit and examination, to any books, documents, papers, and records of the Institute and its administering agency that are pertinent to the funds received and expended by the Institute and its administering agency.

(h) Status of employees

Employees of the Institute shall not, by reason of such employment, be considered to be employees of the Federal Government for any purpose.

(i) Termination

The Institute shall terminate 10 years after August 18, 1990.

(j) Use of funds

All funds authorized for the Institute shall be provided through the National Oceanic and Atmospheric Administration. No funds made available to carry out this section may be used to initiate litigation. No funds made available to carry out this section may be used for the acquisition of real property (including buildings) or construction of any building. No more than 20 percent of funds made available to carry out this section may be used to lease necessary facilities and to administer the Institute. None of the funds authorized by this section shall be used for any purpose other than the functions specified in subsection (b) of this section.

(k) Research

The Institute shall publish and make available to any person upon request the results of all research, educational, and demonstration projects conducted by the Institute. The Administrator shall provide a copy of all research, educational, and demonstration projects conducted by the Institute to the National Oceanic and Atmospheric Administration.

(*l*) Definitions

In this section, the term "Prince William Sound and its adjacent waters" means such sound and waters as generally depicted on the map entitled "EXXON VALDEZ oil spill dated March 1990".

(Pub.L. 101–380, Title V, § 5001, Aug. 18, 1990, 104 Stat. 542.)

§ 2732. Terminal and tanker oversight and monitoring [OPA § 5002]

(a) Short title and findings

(1) Short title

This section may be cited as the "Oil Terminal and Oil Tanker Environmental Oversight and Monitoring Act of 1990".

(2) Findings

The Congress finds that—

(A) the March 24, 1989, grounding and rupture of the fully loaded oil tanker, the EXXON VALDEZ, spilled 11 million gallons of crude oil in Prince William Sound, an environmentally sensitive area;

(B) many people believe that complacency on the part of the industry and government personnel responsible for monitoring the operation of the Valdez terminal and vessel traffic in Prince William Sound was one of the contributing factors to the EXXON VALDEZ oil spill;

(C) one way to combat this complacency is to involve local citizens in the process of preparing, adopting, and revising oil spill contingency plans;

(D) a mechanism should be established which fosters the long-term partnership of industry, government, and local communities in overseeing compliance with environmental concerns in the operation of crude oil terminals;

(E) such a mechanism presently exists at the Sullom Voe terminal in the Shetland Islands and this terminal should serve as a model for others;

(F) because of the effective partnership that has developed at Sullom Voe, Sullom Voe is considered the safest terminal in Europe;

(G) the present system of regulation and oversight of crude oil terminals in the United States has degenerated into a process of continual mistrust and confrontation.

(H) only when local citizens are involved in the process will the trust develop that is necessary to change the present system from confrontation to consensus;

(I) a pilot program patterned after Sullom Voe should be established in Alaska to further refine the concepts and relationships involved; and

(J) similar programs should eventually be established in other major crude oil terminals in the United States because the recent oil spills in Texas, Delaware, and Rhode Island indicate that the safe transportation of crude oil is a national problem.

(b) Demonstration programs

(1) Establishment

There are established 2 Oil Terminal and Oil Tanker Environmental Oversight and Monitoring Demonstration Programs (hereinafter referred to as "Programs") to be carried out in the State of Alaska.

(2) Advisory function

The function of these Programs shall be advisory only.

(3) Purpose

The Prince William Sound Program shall be responsible for environmental monitoring of the terminal facilities in Prince William Sound and the crude oil tankers operating in Prince William Sound. The Cook Inlet Program shall be responsible for environmental monitoring of the terminal facilities and crude oil tankers operating in Cook Inlet located South of the latitude at Point Possession and North of the latitude at Amatuli Island, including offshore facilities in Cook Inlet.

(4) Suits barred

No program, association, council, committee or other organization created by this section may sue any person or entity, public or private, concerning any matter arising under this section except for the performance of contracts.

(c) Oil Terminal Facilities and Oil Tanker Operations Association

(1) Establishment

There is established an Oil Terminal Facilities and Oil Tanker Operations Association (hereinafter in this section referred to as the "Association") for each of the Programs established under subsection (b) of this section.

(2) Membership

Each Association shall be comprised of 4 individuals as follows:

(A) One individual shall be designated by the owners and operators of the terminal facilities and shall represent those owners and operators.

(B) One individual shall be designated by the owners and operators of the crude oil tankers calling at the terminal facilities and shall represent those owners and operators.

(C) One individual shall be an employee of the State of Alaska, shall be designated by the Governor of the State of Alaska, and shall represent the State government.

(D) One individual shall be an employee of the Federal Government, shall be designated by the President, and shall represent the Federal Government.

(3) Responsibilities

Each Association shall be responsible for reviewing policies relating to the operation and maintenance of the oil terminal facilities and crude oil tankers which affect or may affect the environment in the vicinity of their respective terminals. Each Association shall provide a forum among the owners and operators of the terminal facilities, the owners and operators of crude oil tankers calling at those facilities, the United States, and the State of Alaska to discuss and to make recommendations concerning all permits, plans, and site-specific regulations governing the activities and actions of the terminal facilities which affect or may affect the environment in the vicinity of the terminal facilities and of crude oil tankers calling at those facilities.

(4) Designation of existing organization

The Secretary may designate an existing nonprofit organization as an Association under this subsection if the organization is organized to meet the purposes of this section and consists of at least the individuals listed in paragraph (2).

(d) Regional Citizens' Advisory Councils

(1) Membership

There is established a Regional Citizens' Advisory Council (hereinafter in this section referred to as the "Council") for each of the programs established by subsection (b) of this section.

(2) Membership

Each Council shall be composed of voting members and nonvoting members, as follows:

(A) Voting members

Voting members shall be Alaska residents and, except as provided in clause (vii) of this paragraph, shall be appointed by the Governor of the State of Alaska from a list of nominees provided by each of the following interests, with one representative appointed to represent each of the following interests, taking into consideration the need for regional balance on the Council:

(i) Local commercial fishing industry organizations, the members of which depend on the fisheries resources of the waters in the vicinity of the terminal facilities.

(ii) Aquaculture associations in the vicinity of the terminal facilities.

(iii) Alaska Native Corporations and other Alaska Native organizations the members of which reside in the vicinity of the terminal facilities.

(iv) Environmental organizations the members of which reside in the vicinity of the terminal facilities.

(v) Recreational organizations the members of which reside in or use the vicinity of the terminal facilities.

(vi) The Alaska State Chamber of Commerce, to represent the locally based tourist industry.

(vii)(I) For the Prince William Sound Terminal Facilities Council, one representative selected by each of the following municipalities: Cordova, Whittier, Seward, Valdez, Kodiak, the Kodiak Island Borough, and the Kenai Peninsula Borough.

(II) For the Cook Inlet Terminal Facilities Council, one representative selected by each of the following municipalities: Homer, Seldovia, Anchorage, Kenai, Kodiak, the Kodiak Island Borough, and the Kenai Peninsula Borough.

(B) Nonvoting members

One ex-officio, nonvoting representative shall be designated by, and represent, each of the following:

(i) The Environmental Protection Agency.

(ii) The Coast Guard.

(iii) The National Oceanic and Atmospheric Administration.

(iv) The United States Forest Service.

(v) The Bureau of Land Management.

(vi) The Alaska Department of Environmental Conservation.

(vii) The Alaska Department of Fish and Game.

(viii) The Alaska Department of Natural Resources.

(ix) The Division of Emergency Services, Alaska Department of Military and Veterans Affairs.

(3) Terms

(A) Duration of Councils

The term of the Councils shall continue throughout the life of the operation of the Trans-Alaska Pipeline System and so long as oil is transported to or from Cook Inlet.

(B) Three years

The voting members of each Council shall be appointed for a term of 3 years except as provided for in subparagraph (C).

(C) Initial appointments

The terms of the first appointments shall be as follows:

(i) For the appointments by the Governor of the State of Alaska, one-third shall serve for 3 years, one-third shall serve for 2 years, and one-third shall serve for one year.

(ii) For the representatives of municipalities required by subsection (d)(2)(A)(vii) of this section, a drawing of lots among the appointees shall determine that one-third of that group serves for 3 years, one-third serves for 2 years, and the remainder serves for 1 year.

(4) Self-governing

Each Council shall elect its own chairperson, select its own staff, and make policies with regard to its internal operating procedures. After the initial organizational meeting called by the Secretary under subsection (i) of this section, each Council shall be self-governing.

(5) Dual membership and conflicts of interest prohibited

(A) No individual selected as a member of the Council shall serve on the Association.

(B) No individual selected as a voting member of the Council shall be engaged in any activity which might conflict with such individual carrying out his functions as a member thereof.

(6) Duties

Each Council shall—

(A) provide advice and recommendations to the Association on policies, permits, and site-specific regulations relating to the operation and maintenance of terminal facilities and crude oil tankers which affect or may affect the environment in the vicinity of the terminal facilities;

(B) monitor through the committee established under subsection (e) of this section, the environmental impacts of the operation of the terminal facilities and crude oil tankers;

(C) monitor those aspects of terminal facilities' and crude oil tankers' operations and maintenance which affect or may affect the environment in the vicinity of the terminal facilities;

(D) review through the committee established under subsection (f) of this section, the adequacy of oil spill prevention and contingency plans for the terminal facilities and the adequacy of oil spill prevention and contingency plans for crude oil tankers, operating in Prince William Sound or in Cook Inlet;

(E) provide advice and recommendations to the Association on port operations, policies and practices;

(F) recommend to the Association—

(i) standards and stipulations for permits and site-specific regulations intended to minimize the impact of the terminal facilities' and crude oil tankers' operations in the vicinity of the terminal facilities;

(ii) modifications of terminal facility operations and maintenance intended to minimize the risk and mitigate the impact of terminal facilities, operations in the vicinity of the terminal facilities and to minimize the risk of oil spills;

(iii) modifications of crude oil tanker operations and maintenance in Prince William Sound and Cook Inlet intended to minimize the risk and mitigate the impact of oil spills; and

(iv) modifications to the oil spill prevention and contingency plans for terminal facilities and for crude oil tankers in Prince William Sound and Cook Inlet intended to enhance the ability to prevent and respond to an oil spill; and

(G) create additional committees of the Council as necessary to carry out the above functions, including a scientific and technical advisory committee to the Prince William Sound Council.

(7) No estoppel

No Council shall be held liable under State or Federal law for costs or damages as a result of rendering advice under this section. Nor shall any advice given by a voting member of a Council, or program representative or agent, be grounds for estopping the interests represented by the voting Council members from seeking damages or other appropriate relief.

(8) Scientific work

In carrying out its research, development and monitoring functions, each Council is authorized to conduct its own scientific research and shall review the scientific work undertaken by or on behalf of the terminal operators or crude oil tanker operators as a result of a legal requirement to undertake that work. Each Council shall also review the relevant scientific work undertaken by or on behalf of any government entity relating to the terminal facilities or crude oil tankers. To the extent possible, to avoid unnecessary duplication, each Council shall coordinate its independent scientific work with the scientific work performed by or on behalf of the terminal operators and with the scientific work performed by or on behalf of the operators of the crude oil tankers.

(e) Committee for Terminal and Oil Tanker Operations and Environmental Monitoring

(1) Monitoring Committee

Each Council shall establish standing Terminal and Oil Tanker Operations and Environmental Monitoring Committee (hereinafter in this section referred to as the "Monitoring Committee") to devise and manage a comprehensive program of monitoring the environmental impacts of the operations of terminal facilities and of crude oil tankers while operating in Prince William Sound and Cook Inlet. The membership of the Monitoring Committee shall be made up of members of the Council, citizens, and recognized scientific experts selected by the Council.

(2) Duties

In fulfilling its responsibilities, the Monitoring Committee shall—

(A) advise the Council on a monitoring strategy that will permit early detection of environmental impacts of terminal facility operations and crude oil tanker operations while in Prince William Sound and Cook Inlet;

(B) develop monitoring programs and make recommendations to the Council on the implementation of those programs;

(C) at its discretion, select and contract with universities and other scientific institutions to carry out specific monitoring projects authorized by the Council pursuant to an approved monitoring strategy;

(D) complete any other tasks assigned by the Council; and

(E) provide written reports to the Council which interpret and assess the results of all monitoring programs.

(f) Committee for Oil Spill Prevention, Safety, and Emergency Response

(1) Technical Oil Spill Committee

Each Council shall establish a standing technical committee (hereinafter referred to as "Oil Spill Committee") to review and assess measures designed to prevent oil spills and the planning and preparedness for responding to, containing, cleaning up, and mitigating impacts of oil spills. The membership of the Oil Spill Committee shall be made up of members of the Council, citizens, and recognized technical experts selected by the Council.

(2) Duties

In fulfilling its responsibilities, the Oil Spill Committee shall—

(A) periodically review the respective oil spill prevention and contingency plans for the terminal facilities and for the crude oil tankers while in Prince William Sound or Cook Inlet, in light of new technological developments and changed circumstances;

(B) monitor periodic drills and testing of the oil spill contingency plans for the terminal facilities and for crude oil tankers while in Prince William Sound and Cook Inlet;

(C) study wind and water currents and other environmental factors in the vicinity of the terminal facilities which may affect the ability to prevent, respond to, contain, and clean up an oil spill;

(D) identify highly sensitive areas which may require specific protective measures in the event of a spill in Prince William Sound or Cook Inlet;

(E) monitor developments in oil spill prevention, containment, response, and cleanup technology;

(F) periodically review port organization, operations, incidents, and the adequacy and maintenance of vessel traffic service systems designed to assure safe transit of crude oil tankers pertinent to terminal operations;

(G) periodically review the standards for tankers bound for, loading at, exiting from, or otherwise using the terminal facilities;

(H) complete any other tasks assigned by the Council; and

(I) provide written reports to the Council outlining its findings and recommendations.

(g) Agency cooperation

On and after the expiration of the 180–day period following August 18, 1990, each Federal department, agency, or other instrumentality shall, with respect to all permits, site-specific regulations, and other matters governing the activities and actions of the terminal facilities which affect or may affect the vicinity of the terminal facilities, consult with the appropriate Council prior to taking substantive action with respect to the permit, site-specific regulation, or other matter. This consultation shall be carried out with a view to enabling the appropriate Association and Council to review the permit, site-specific regulation, or other matters and make appropriate recommendations regarding operations, policy or agency actions. Prior consultation shall not be required if an authorized Federal agency representative reasonably believes that an emergency exists requiring action without delay.

(h) Recommendations of the Council

In the event that the Association does not adopt, or significantly modifies before adoption, any recommendation of the Council made pursuant to the authority granted to the Council in subsection (d) of this section, the Association shall provide to the Council, in writing, within 5 days of its decision, notice of its decision and a written statement of reasons for its rejection or significant modification of the recommendation.

(i) Administrative actions

Appointments, designations, and selections of individuals to serve as members of the Associations and Councils under this section shall be submitted to the Secretary prior to the expiration of the 120–day period following August 18, 1990. On or before the expiration of the 180–day period following August 18, 1990, the Secretary shall call an initial meeting of each Association and Council for organizational purposes.

(j) Location and compensation

(1) Location

Each Association and Council established by this section shall be located in the State of Alaska.

(2) Compensation

No member of an Association or Council shall be compensated for the member's services as a member of the Association or Council, but shall be allowed travel expenses, including per diem in lieu of subsistence, at a rate established by the Association or Council not to exceed the rates authorized for employees of agencies under sections 5702 and 5703 of Title 5. However, each Council may enter into contracts to provide compensation and expenses to members of the committees created under subsections (d), (e), and (f) of this section.

(k) Funding

(1) Requirement

Approval of the contingency plans required of owners and operators of the Cook Inlet and Prince

William Sound terminal facilities and crude oil tankers while operating in Alaskan waters in commerce with those terminal facilities shall be effective only so long as the respective Association and Council for a facility are funded pursuant to paragraph (2).

(2) Prince William Sound program

The owners or operators of terminal facilities or crude oil tankers operating in Prince William Sound shall provide, on an annual basis, an aggregate amount of not more than $2,000,000, as determined by the Secretary. Such amount—

(A) shall provide for the establishment and operation on the environmental oversight and monitoring program in Prince William Sound;

(B) shall be adjusted annually by the Anchorage Consumer Price Index; and

(C) may be adjusted periodically upon the mutual consent of the owners or operators of terminal facilities or crude oil tankers operating in Prince William Sound and the Prince William Sound terminal facilities Council.

(3) Cook Inlet program

The owners or operators of terminal facilities, offshore facilities, or crude oil tankers operating in Cook Inlet shall provide, on an annual basis, an aggregate amount of not more than $1,000,000, as determined by the Secretary. Such amount—

(A) shall provide for the establishment and operation of the environmental oversight and monitoring program in Cook Inlet;

(B) shall be adjusted annually by the Anchorage Consumer Price Index; and

(C) may be adjusted periodically upon the mutual consent of the owners or operators of terminal facilities, offshore facilities, or crude oil tankers operating in Cook Inlet and the Cook Inlet Council.

(*l*) Reports

(1) Associations and Councils

Prior to the expiration of the 36-month period following August 18, 1990, each Association and Council established by this section shall report to the President and the Congress concerning its activities under this section, together with its recommendations.

(2) GAO

Prior to the expiration of the 36-month period following August 18, 1990, the General Accounting Office shall report to the President and the Congress as to the handling of funds, including donated funds, by the entities carrying out the programs under this section, and the effectiveness of the demonstration programs carried out under this section, together with its recommendations.

(m) Definitions

As used in this section, the term—

(1) "terminal facilities" means—

(A) in the case of the Prince William Sound Program, the entire oil terminal complex located in Valdez, Alaska, consisting of approximately 1,000 acres including all buildings, docks (except docks owned by the City of Valdez if those docks are not used for loading of crude oil), pipes, piping, roads, ponds, tanks, crude oil tankers only while at the terminal dock, tanker escorts owned or operated by the operator of the terminal, vehicles, and other facilities associated with, and necessary for, assisting tanker movement of crude oil into and out of the oil terminal complex; and

(B) in the case of the Cook Inlet Program, the entire oil terminal complex including all buildings, docks, pipes, piping, roads, ponds, tanks, vessels, vehicles, crude oil tankers only while at the terminal dock, tanker escorts owned or operated by the operator of the terminal, emergency spill response vessels owned or operated by the operator of the terminal, and other facilities associated with, and necessary for, assisting tanker movement of crude oil into and out of the oil terminal complex;

(2) "crude oil tanker" means a tanker (as that term is defined under section 2101 of Title 46,

(A) in the case of the Prince William Sound Program, calling at the terminal facilities for the purpose of receiving and transporting oil to refineries, operating north of Middleston Island and bound for or exiting from Prince William Sound; and

(B) in the case of the Cook Inlet Program, calling at the terminal facilities for the purpose of receiving and transporting oil to refineries and operating in Cook Inlet and the Gulf of Alaska north of Amatuli Island, including tankers transiting to Cook Inlet from Prince William Sound;

(3) "vicinity of the terminal facilities" means that geographical area surrounding the environment of terminal facilities which is directly affected or may be directly affected by the operation of the terminal facilities; and

(4) "Secretary" means the Secretary of Transportation.

(n) Savings clause

(1) Regulatory authority

Nothing in this section shall be construed as modifying, repealing, superseding, or preempting any municipal, State or Federal law or regulation, or in any way affecting litigation arising from oil spills or the rights and responsibilities of the United States or the State of Alaska, or municipalities thereof, to preserve and protect the environment through regulation of land, air, and water uses, of safety, and of related development. The monitoring provided for by this section shall be designed to help assure compliance with applicable laws and regulations and shall only extend to activities—

(A) that would affect or have the potential to affect the vicinity of the terminal facilities and the area of crude oil tanker operations included in the Programs; and

(B) are subject to the United States or State of Alaska, or municipality thereof, law, regulation, or other legal requirement.

(2) Recommendations

This subsection is not intended to prevent the Association or Council from recommending to appropriate authorities that existing legal requirements should be modified or that new legal requirements should be adopted.

(*o*) Alternative voluntary advisory group in lieu of Council

The requirements of subsections (c) through (*l*) of this section, as such subsections apply respectively to the Prince William Sound Program and the Cook Inlet Program, are deemed to have been satisfied so long as the following conditions are met:

(1) Prince William Sound

With respect to the Prince William Sound Program, the Alyeska Pipeline Service Company or any of its owner companies enters into a contract for the duration of the operation of the Trans–Alaska Pipeline System with the Alyeska Citizens Advisory Committee in existence on the date of enactment of this section, or a successor organization, to fund that Committee or organization on an annual basis in the amount provided for by subsection (k)(2)(A) of this section, and the President annually certifies that the Committee or organization fosters the general goals and purposes of this section and is broadly representative of the communities and interests in the vicinity of the terminal facilities and Prince William Sound.

(2) Cook Inlet

With respect to the Cook Inlet Program, the terminal facilities, offshore facilities, or crude oil tanker owners and operators enter into a contract with a voluntary advisory organization to fund that organization on an annual basis and the President annually certifies that the organization fosters the general goals and purposes of this section and is broadly representative of the communities and interests in the vicinity of the terminal facilities and Cook Inlet.

(Pub.L. 101–380, Title V, § 5002, Aug. 18, 1990, 104 Stat. 544.)

Certification of President

For certification of Prince William Sound Regional Citizens Advisory Committee, see 56 F.R. 12439, Mar. 21, 1991.

§ 2733. Bligh Reef light [OPA § 5003]

The Secretary of Transportation shall within one year after August 18, 1990, install and ensure operation of an automated navigation light on or adjacent to Bligh Reef in Prince William Sound, Alaska, of sufficient power and height to provide long-range warning of the location of Bligh Reef.

(Pub.L. 101–380, Title V, § 5003, Aug. 18, 1990, 104 Stat. 553.)

§ 2734. Vessel traffic service system [OPA § 5004]

The Secretary of Transportation shall within one year after August 18, 1990—

(1) acquire, install, and operate such additional equipment (which may consist of radar, closed circuit television, satellite tracking systems, or other shipboard dependent surveillance), train and locate such personnel, and issue such final regulations as are necessary to increase the range of the existing VTS system in the Port of Valdez, Alaska, sufficiently to track the locations and movements of tank vessels carrying oil from the Trans–Alaska Pipeline when such vessels are transiting Prince William Sound, Alaska, and to sound an audible alarm when such tankers depart from designated navigation routes; and

(2) submit to the Committee on Commerce, Science, and Transportation of the Senate and the Committee on Merchant Marine and Fisheries of the House of Representatives a report on the feasibility and desirability of instituting positive control of tank vessel movements in Prince William Sound by Coast Guard personnel using the Port of Valdez,

Alaska, VTS system, as modified pursuant to paragraph (1).

(Pub.L. 101–380, Title V, § 5004, Aug. 18, 1990, 104 Stat. 553.)

Abolition of House Committee on Merchant Marine and Fisheries

Committee on Merchant Marine and Fisheries of House of Representatives abolished and any reference in any provision of law enacted before Jan. 4, 1995, to the Committee on Merchant Marine and Fisheries of the House of Representatives treated as referring to the Committee on Agriculture of the House of Representatives, in the case of a provision of law relating to inspection of seafood or seafood products, the Committee on National Security of the House of Representatives, in the case of a provision of law relating to interoceanic canals, the Merchant Marine Academy and State Maritime Academies, or national security aspects of merchant marine, the Committee on Resources of the House of Representatives, in the case of a provision of law relating to fisheries, wildlife, international fishing agreements marine affairs (including coastal zone management) except for measures relating to oil and other pollution of navigable waters, or oceanography, the Committee on Science of the House of Representatives, in the case of a provision of law relating to marine research, and the Committee on Transportation and Infrastructure of the House of Representatives, in the case of a provision of law relating to a matter other than a matter described above, see section 1(b)(3) of Pub.L. 104–14, set out as a note preceding section 21 of Title 2, The Congress.

§ 2735. Equipment and personnel requirements under tank vessel and facility response plans [OPA § 5005]

(a) In general

In addition to the requirements for response plans for vessels established by section 1321(j) of this title, as amended by this Act, a response plan for a tanker loading cargo at a facility permitted under the Trans–Alaska Pipeline Authorization Act (43 U.S.C. 1651 et seq.), and a response plan for such a facility, shall provide for—

(1) prepositioned oil spill containment and removal equipment in communities and other strategic locations within the geographic boundaries of Prince William Sound, including escort vessels with skimming capability; barges to receive recovered oil; heavy duty sea boom, pumping, transferring, and lightering equipment; and other appropriate removal equipment for the protection of the environment, including fish hatcheries;

(2) the establishment of an oil spill removal organization at appropriate locations in Prince William Sound, consisting of trained personnel in sufficient numbers to immediately remove, to the maximum extent practicable, a worst case discharge or a discharge of 200,000 barrels of oil, whichever is greater;

(3) training in oil removal techniques for local residents and individuals engaged in the cultivation or production of fish or fish products in Prince William Sound;

(4) practice exercises not less than 2 times per year which test the capacity of the equipment and personnel required under this paragraph; and

(5) periodic testing and certification of equipment required under this paragraph, as required by the Secretary.

(b) Definitions

In this section—

(1) the term "Prince William Sound" means all State and Federal waters within Prince William Sound, Alaska, including the approach to Hinchenbrook Entrance out to and encompassing Seal Rocks; and

(2) the term "worst case discharge" means—

(A) in the case of a vessel, a discharge in adverse weather conditions of its entire cargo; and

(B) in the case of a facility, the largest foreseeable discharge in adverse weather conditions.

(Pub.L. 101–380, Title V, § 5005, Aug. 18, 1990, 104 Stat. 553; Pub.L. 102–388, Title III, § 354, Oct. 6, 1992, 106 Stat. 1555.)

References in Text

Reference in subsec. (a) to the amendment of section 1321(j) of this title "by this Act" refers to the amendment by Pub.L. 101–380, Aug. 18, 1990, 104 Stat. 484.

The Trans–Alaska Pipeline Authorization Act, referred to in subsec. (a), is title II of Pub.L. 93–153, Nov. 16, 1973, 87 Stat. 584, which is classified to chapter 34 (§ 1651 et seq.) of Title 43, Public Lands. For complete classification of this Act to the Code, see Short Title note set out under section 1651 of Title 43 and Tables.

§ 2736. Funding [OPA § 5006]

(a) Section 2731

Amounts in the Fund shall be available, subject to appropriations, and shall remain available until expended, to carry out section 2731 of this title as follows:

(1) $5,000,000 shall be available for the first fiscal year beginning after August 18, 1990.

(2) $2,000,000 shall be available for each of the 9 fiscal years following the fiscal year described in paragraph (1).

(b) Sections 2733 and 2734

Amounts in the Fund shall be available, without further appropriations and without fiscal year limitation, to carry out sections 2733 and 2734 of this title in an amount not to exceed $5,000,000.

(Pub.L. 101–380, Title V, § 5006, August 18, 1990, 104 Stat. 554.)

§ 2737. Limitation [OPA § 5007]

Notwithstanding any other law, tank vessels that have spilled more than 1,000,000 gallons of oil into the marine environment after March 22, 1989, are prohibited from operating on the navigable waters of Prince William Sound, Alaska.

(Pub.L. 101–380, Title V, § 5007, August 18, 1990, 104 Stat. 554.)

SUBCHAPTER III—MISCELLANEOUS

§ 2751. Savings provisions [OPA § 6001]

(a) Cross-references

A reference to a law replaced by this chapter, including a reference in a regulation, order, or other law, is deemed to refer to the corresponding provision of this chapter.

(b) Continuation of regulations

An order, rule, or regulation in effect under a law replaced by this chapter continues in effect under the corresponding provision of this chapter until repealed, amended, or superseded.

(c) Rule of construction

An inference of legislative construction shall not be drawn by reason of the caption or catch line of a provision enacted by this chapter.

(d) Actions and rights

Nothing in this chapter shall apply to any rights and duties that matured, penalties that were incurred, and proceedings that were begun before August 18, 1990, except as provided by this section, and shall be adjudicated pursuant to the law applicable on the date prior to August 18, 1990.

(e) Admiralty and maritime law

Except as otherwise provided in this chapter, this chapter does not affect—

(1) admiralty and maritime law; or

(2) the jurisdiction of the district courts of the United States with respect to civil actions under admiralty and maritime jurisdiction, saving to suitors in all cases all other remedies to which they are otherwise entitled.

(Pub.L. 101–380, Title VI, § 6001, Aug. 18, 1990, 104 Stat. 554.)

References in Text

This chapter, referred to in text, was in the original this "Act", meaning Pub.L. 101–380 which, in addition to enacting this chapter, made conforming amendments to other sections in this title as well as in Titles 14, 16, 23, 26, 43, 46, and 46 App. For complete classification of Pub.L. 101–380 to the Code see Short Title note under section 2701 of this title and Tables.

§ 2752. Annual appropriations [OPA § 6002]

(a) Required

Except as provided in subsection (b) of this section, amounts in the Fund shall be available only as provided in annual appropriation Acts.

(b) Exceptions

Subsection (a) of this section, shall not apply to sections 2706(f), 2712(a)(4), or 2736(b) of this title, and shall not apply to an amount not to exceed $50,000,000 in any fiscal year which the President may make available from the Fund to carry out section 1321(c) of this title, as amended by this Act, and to initiate the assessment of natural resources damages required under section 2706 of this title. Sums to which this subsection applies shall remain available until expended.

(Pub.L. 101–380, Title VI, § 6002, Aug. 18, 1990, 104 Stat. 555.)

References in Text

Reference in subsec. (b) to the amendment of section 1321(c) of this title "by this Act" refers to the amendment by Pub.L. 101–380, Aug. 18, 1990, 104 Stat. 484.

§ 2753. Outer Banks Protection [OPA § 6003]

(a) Short title

This section may be cited as the "Outer Banks Protection Act".

(b) Findings

The Congress finds that—

(1) the Outer Banks of North Carolina is an area of exceptional environmental fragility and beauty;

(2) the annual economic benefits of commercial and recreational fishing activities to North Carolina, which could be adversely affected by oil or gas development offshore the State's coast, exceeds $1,000,000,000;

(3) the major industry in coastal North Carolina is tourism, which is subject to potentially significant disruption by offshore oil or gas development;

(4) the physical oceanographic characteristics of the area offshore North Carolina between Cape Hatteras and the mouth of the Chesapeake Bay are not well understood, being affected by Gulf Stream western boundary perturbations and accompanying warm filaments, warm and cold core rings which separate from the Gulf Stream, wind stress, outflow from the Chesapeake Bay, Gulf Stream meanders, and intrusions of Virginia coastal waters around and over the Diamond shoals;

(5) diverse and abundant fisheries resources occur in the western boundary area of the Gulf Stream offshore North Carolina, but little is understood of the complex ecological relationships between the life histories of those species and their physical, chemical, and biological environment;

(6) the environmental impact statements prepared for Outer Continental Shelf lease sales numbered 56 (1981) and 78 (1983) contain insufficient and outdated environmental information from which to make decisions on approval of additional oil and gas leasing, exploration, and development activities;

(7) the draft environmental report, dated November 1, 1989, and the preliminary final environmental report dated June 1, 1990, prepared pursuant to a July 14, 1989 memorandum of understanding between the State of North Carolina, the Department of the Interior, and the Mobil Oil Company, have not allayed concerns about the adequacy of the environmental information available to determine whether to proceed with additional offshore leasing, exploration, or development offshore North Carolina; and

(8) the National Research Council report entitled "The Adequacy of Environmental Information for Outer Continental Shelf Oil and Gas Decisions: Florida and California", issued in 1989, concluded that—

(A) information with respect to those States, which have received greater scrutiny than has North Carolina, is inadequate; and

(B) there are serious generic defects in the Minerals Management Service's methods of environmental analysis,

reinforcing concerns about the adequacy of the scientific and technical information which are the basis for a decision to lease additional tracts or approve an exploration plan offshore North Carolina, especially with respect to oceanographic, ecological, and socioeconomic information.

(c) Prohibition of oil and gas leasing, exploration, and development

(1) Prohibition

The Secretary of the Interior shall not—

(A) conduct a lease sale;

(B) issue any new leases;

(C) approve any exploration plan;

(D) approve any development and production plan;

(E) approve any application for permit to drill; or

(F) permit any drilling,

for oil or gas under the Outer Continental Shelf Lands Act [43 U.S.C.A. § 1331 et seq.] on any lands of the Outer Continental Shelf offshore North Carolina.

(2) Boundaries

For purposes of paragraph (1), the term "offshore North Carolina" means the area within the lateral seaward boundaries between areas offshore North Carolina and areas offshore—

(A) Virginia as provided in the joint resolution entitled "Joint resolution granting the consent of Congress to an agreement between the States of North Carolina and Virginia establishing their lateral seaward boundary" approved October 27, 1972 (86 Stat. 1298); and

(B) South Carolina as provided in the Act entitled "An Act granting the consent of Congress to the agreement between the States of North Carolina and South Carolina establishing their lateral seaward boundary" approved October 9, 1981 (95 Stat. 988).

(3) Duration of prohibition

(A) In general

The prohibition under paragraph (1) shall remain in effect until the later of—

(i) October 1, 1991; or

(ii) 45 days of continuous session of the Congress after submission of a written report to the Congress by the Secretary of the Interior, made after consideration of the findings and recommendations of the Environmental Sciences Review Panel under subsection (e) of this section

(I) certifying that the information available, including information acquired pursuant to subsection (d) of this section, is sufficient to enable the Secretary to carry out his responsibilities under the Outer Continental Shelf Lands Act [43 U.S.C.A. § 1331 et seq.] with respect to authorizing the activities described in paragraph (1); and

(II) including a detailed explanation of any differences between such certification and the findings and recommendations of the Environmental Sciences Review Panel under subsection (e) of this section, and a detailed justification of each such difference.

(B) Continuous session of Congress

In computing any 45–day period of continuous session of Congress under subparagraph (A)(ii)—

(i) continuity of session is broken only by an adjournment of the Congress sine die; and

(ii) the days on which either House of Congress is not in session because of an adjournment of more than 3 days to a day certain are excluded.

(d) Additional environmental information

The Secretary of the Interior shall undertake ecological and socioeconomic studies, additional physical oceanographic studies, including actual field work and the correlation of existing data, and other additional environmental studies, to obtain sufficient information about all significant conditions, processes, and environments which influence, or may be influenced by, oil and gas leasing, exploration, and development activities offshore North Carolina to enable the Secretary to carry out his responsibilities under the Outer Continental Shelf Lands Act [43 U.S.C.A. § 1331 et seq.] with respect to authorizing the activities described in subsection (c)(1) of this section. During the time that the Environmental Sciences Review Panel established under subsection (e) of this section is in existence, the Secretary of the Interior shall consult with such Panel in carrying out this subsection.

(e) Environmental Sciences Review Panel

(1) Establishment and membership

There shall be established an Environmental Sciences Review Panel, to consist of—

(A) 1 marine scientist selected by the Secretary of the Interior;

(B) 1 marine scientist selected by the Governor of North Carolina; and

(C) 1 person each from the disciplines of physical oceanography, ecology, and social science, to be selected jointly by the Secretary of the Interior and the Governor of North Carolina from a list of individuals nominated by the National Academy of Sciences.

(2) Functions

Not later than 6 months after August 18, 1990, the Environmental Sciences Review Panel shall—

(A) prepare and submit to the Secretary of the Interior findings and recommendations—

(i) assessing the adequacy of available physical oceanographic, ecological, and socioeconomic information in enabling the Secretary to carry out his responsibilities under the Outer Continental Shelf Lands Act [43 U.S.C.A. § 1331 et seq.] with respect to authorizing the activities described in subsection (c)(1) of this section; and

(ii) if such available information is not adequate for such purposes, indicating what additional information is required to enable the Secretary to carry out such responsibilities; and

(B) consult with the Secretary of the Interior as provided in subsection (d) of this section.

(3) Expenses

Each member of the Environmental Sciences Review Panel shall be reimbursed for actual travel expenses and shall receive per diem in lieu of subsistence for each day such member is engaged in the business of the Environmental Sciences Review Panel.

(4) Termination

The Environmental Sciences Review Panel shall be terminated after the submission of all findings and recommendations required under paragraph (2)(A).

(f) Authorization of appropriations

There are authorized to be appropriated to the Secretary of the Interior to carry out this section not to exceed $500,000 for fiscal year 1991, to remain available until expended.

(Pub.L. 101–380, Title VI, § 6003, Aug. 18, 1990, 104 Stat. 555.)

References in Text

The Outer Continental Shelf Lands Act, referred to in subsecs. (c), (d), and (e), is Act Aug. 7, 1953, c. 345, 67 Stat. 462, as amended, which is classified generally to subchapter III (§ 1331 et seq.) of chapter 29 of Title 43, Public Lands. For complete classification of this Act to the Code, see Short Title note set out under section 1331 of Title 43 and Tables.

SUBCHAPTER IV—OIL POLLUTION RESEARCH AND DEVELOPMENT PROGRAM

§ 2761. Oil pollution research and development program [OPA § 7001]

(a) Interagency Coordinating Committee on Oil Pollution Research

(1) Establishment

There is established an Interagency Coordinating Committee on Oil Pollution Research (hereinafter in this section referred to as the "Interagency Committee").

(2) Purposes

The Interagency Committee shall coordinate a comprehensive program of oil pollution research, technology development, and demonstration among the Federal agencies, in cooperation and coordination with industry, universities, research institutions, State governments, and other nations, as appropriate, and shall foster cost-effective research mechanisms, including the joint funding of research.

(3) Membership

The Interagency Committee shall include representatives from the Department of Commerce (including the National Oceanic and Atmospheric Administration and the National Institute of Standards and Technology), the Department of Energy, the Department of the Interior (including the Minerals Management Service and the United States Fish and Wildlife Service), the Department of Transportation (including the United States Coast Guard, the Maritime Administration, and the Research and Special Projects Administration), the Department of Defense (including the Army Corps of Engineers and the Navy), the Environmental Protection Agency, the National Aeronautics and Space Administration, and the United States Fire Administration in the Federal Emergency Management Agency, as well as such other Federal agencies as the President may designate.

A representative of the Department of Transportation shall serve as Chairman.

(b) Oil pollution research and technology plan

(1) Implementation plan

Within 180 days after August 18, 1990, the Interagency Committee shall submit to Congress a plan for the implementation of the oil pollution research, development, and demonstration program established pursuant to subsection (c) of this section. The research plan shall—

(A) identify agency roles and responsibilities;

(B) assess the current status of knowledge on oil pollution prevention, response, and mitigation technologies and effects of oil pollution on the environment;

(C) identify significant oil pollution research gaps including an assessment of major technological deficiencies in responses to past oil discharges;

(D) establish research priorities and goals for oil pollution technology development related to prevention, response, mitigation, and environmental effects;

(E) estimate the resources needed to conduct the oil pollution research and development program established pursuant to subsection (c) of this section, and timetables for completing research tasks; and

(F) identify, in consultation with the States, regional oil pollution research needs and priorities for a coordinated, multidisciplinary program of research at the regional level.

(2) Advice and guidance

The Chairman, through the Department of Transportation, shall contract with the National Academy of Sciences to—

(A) provide advice and guidance in the preparation and development of the research plan; and

(B) assess the adequacy of the plan as submitted, and submit a report to Congress on the conclusions of such assessment.

The National Institute of Standards and Technology shall provide the Interagency Committee with advice and guidance on issues relating to quality assurance and standards measurements relating to its activities under this section.

(c) Oil pollution research and development program

(1) Establishment

The Interagency Committee shall coordinate the establishment, by the agencies represented on the Interagency Committee, of a program for conducting oil pollution research and development, as provided in this subsection.

(2) Innovative oil pollution technology

The program established under this subsection shall provide for research, development, and demonstration of new or improved technologies which are effective in preventing or mitigating oil discharges and which protect the environment, including—

(A) development of improved designs for vessels and facilities, and improved operational practices;

(B) research, development, and demonstration of improved technologies to measure the ullage of a vessel tank, prevent discharges from tank vents, prevent discharges during lightering and bunkering operations, contain discharges on the deck of a vessel, prevent discharges through the use of vacuums in tanks, and otherwise contain discharges of oil from vessels and facilities;

(C) research, development, and demonstration of new or improved systems of mechanical, chemical, biological, and other methods (including the use of dispersants, solvents, and bioremediation) for the recovery, removal, and disposal of oil, including evaluation of the environmental effects of the use of such systems;

(D) research and training, in consultation with the National Response Team, to improve industry's and Government's ability to quickly and effectively remove an oil discharge, including the long-term use, as appropriate, of the National Spill Control School in Corpus Christi, Texas;

(E) research to improve information systems for decision-making, including the use of data from coastal mapping, baseline data, and other data related to the environmental effects of oil discharges, and cleanup technologies;

(F) development of technologies and methods to protect public health and safety from oil discharges, including the population directly exposed to an oil discharge;

(G) development of technologies, methods, and standards for protecting removal personnel, including training, adequate supervision, protective equipment, maximum exposure limits, and decontamination procedures;

(H) research and development of methods to restore and rehabilitate natural resources damaged by oil discharges;

(I) research to evaluate the relative effectiveness and environmental impacts of bioremediation technologies; and

(J) the demonstration of a satellite-based, dependent surveillance vessel traffic system in Narragansett Bay to evaluate the utility of such system in reducing the risk of oil discharges from vessel collisions and groundings in confined waters.

(3) Oil pollution technology evaluation

The program established under this subsection shall provide for oil pollution prevention and mitigation technology evaluation including—

(A) the evaluation and testing of technologies developed independently of the research and development program established under this subsection;

(B) the establishment, where appropriate, of standards and testing protocols traceable to national standards to measure the performance of oil pollution prevention or mitigation technologies; and

(C) the use, where appropriate, of controlled field testing to evaluate real-world application of oil discharge prevention or mitigation technologies.

(4) Oil pollution effects research

(A) The Committee shall establish a research program to monitor and evaluate the environmental effects of oil discharges. Such program shall include the following elements:

(i) The development of improved models and capabilities for predicting the environmental fate, transport, and effects of oil discharges.

(ii) The development of methods, including economic methods, to assess damages to natural resources resulting from oil discharges.

(iii) The identification of types of ecologically sensitive areas at particular risk to oil discharges and the preparation of scientific monitoring and evaluation plans, one for each of several types of ecological conditions, to be implemented in the event of major oil discharges in such areas.

(iv) The collection of environmental baseline data in ecologically sensitive areas at particular risk to oil discharges where such data are insufficient.

(B) The Department of Commerce in consultation with the Environmental Protection Agency shall monitor and scientifically evaluate the long-term environmental effects of oil discharges if—

(i) the amount of oil discharged exceeds 250,000 gallons;

(ii) the oil discharge has occurred on or after January 1, 1989; and

(iii) the Interagency Committee determines that a study of the long-term environmental effects of the discharge would be of significant scientific value, especially for preventing or responding to future oil discharges.

Areas for study may include the following sites where oil discharges have occurred: the New York/New Jersey Harbor area, where oil was discharged by an Exxon underwater pipeline, the T/B CIBRO SAVANNAH, and the M/V BT NAUTILUS; Narragansett Bay where oil was discharged by the WORLD PRODIGY; the Houston Ship Channel where oil was discharged by the RACHEL B; the Delaware River, where oil was discharged by the PRESIDENTE RIVERA, and Huntington Beach, California, where oil was discharged by the AMERICAN TRADER.

(C) Research conducted under this paragraph by, or through, the United States Fish and Wildlife Service shall be directed and coordinated by the National Wetland Research Center.

(5) Marine simulation research

The program established under this subsection shall include research on the greater use and application of geographic and vessel response simulation models, including the development of additional data bases and updating of existing data bases using, among others, the resources of the National Maritime Research Center. It shall include research and vessel simulations for—

(A) contingency plan evaluation and amendment;

(B) removal and strike team training;

(C) tank vessel personnel training; and

(D) those geographic areas where there is a significant likelihood of a major oil discharge.

(6) Demonstration projects

The United States Coast Guard, in conjunction with other such agencies in the Department of Transportation as the Secretary of Transportation may designate, shall conduct 3 port oil pollution minimization demonstration projects, one each with (A) the Port Authority of New York and New Jersey, (B) the Ports of Los Angeles and Long Beach, California, and (C) the Port of New Orleans, Louisiana, for the purpose of developing and demonstrating integrated port oil pollution prevention and cleanup systems which utilize the information and implement the improved practices and technologies developed from the research, development, and demonstration program established in this section. Such systems shall utilize improved technologies and management practices for reducing the risk of oil discharges, including, as appropriate, improved data access, computerized tracking of oil shipments, improved vessel tracking and navigation systems, advanced technology to monitor pipeline and tank conditions, improved oil spill response capability, improved capability to predict the flow and effects of oil discharges in both the inner and outer harbor areas for the purposes of making infrastructure decisions, and such other activities necessary to achieve the purposes of this section.

(7) Simulated environmental testing

Agencies represented on the Interagency Committee shall ensure the long-term use and operation of the Oil and Hazardous Materials Simulated Environmental Test Tank (OHMSETT) Research Center in New Jersey for oil pollution technology testing and evaluations.

(8) Regional research program

(A) Consistent with the research plan in subsection (b) of this section, the Interagency Committee shall coordinate a program of competitive grants to universities or other research institutions, or groups of universities or research institutions, for the purposes of conducting a coordinated research program related to the regional aspects of oil pollution, such as prevention, removal, mitigation, and the effects of discharged oil on regional environments. For the purposes of this paragraph, a region means a Coast Guard district as set out in part 3 of title 33, Code of Federal Regulations (1989).

(B) The Interagency Committee shall coordinate the publication by the agencies represented on the Interagency Committee of a solicitation for grants under this subsection. The application shall be in such form and contain such information as may be required in the published solicitation. The applications shall be reviewed by the Interagency Committee, which shall make recommendations to the appropriate granting agency represented on the Interagency Committee for awarding the grant. The granting agency shall award the grants recommended by the Interagency Committee unless the agency decides not to award the grant due to budgetary or other compelling considerations and publishes its reasons for such a determination in the Federal Register. No grants may be made by any agency from any funds authorized for this paragraph unless such grant award has first been recommended by the Interagency Committee.

(C) Any university or other research institution, or group of universities or research institutions, may apply for a grant for the regional research program established by this paragraph. The applicant must be located in the region, or in a State a part of which is in the region, for which the project is proposed as part of the regional research program. With respect to a group application, the entity or entities which will carry out the substantial portion of the proposed research must be located in the region, or in a State a part of which is in the region, for which the project is proposed as part of the regional research program.

(D) The Interagency Committee shall make recommendations on grants in such a manner as to ensure an appropriate balance within a region among the various aspects of oil pollution research, including prevention, removal, mitigation, and the effects of discharged oil on regional environments. In addition, the Interagency Committee shall make recommendations for grants based on the following criteria:

(i) There is available to the applicant for carrying out this paragraph demonstrated research resources.

(ii) The applicant demonstrates the capability of making a significant contribution to regional research needs.

(iii) The projects which the applicant proposes to carry out under the grant are consistent with the research plan under subsection (b)(1)(F) of this section and would further the objectives of the research and development program established in this section.

(E) Grants provided under this paragraph shall be for a period up to 3 years, subject to annual review by the granting agency, and provide not more than 80 percent of the costs of the research activities carried out in connection with the grant.

(F) No funds made available to carry out this subsection may be used for the acquisition of real property (including buildings) or construction of any building.

(G) Nothing in this paragraph is intended to alter or abridge the authority under existing law of any Federal agency to make grants, or enter into contracts or cooperative agreements, using funds other than those authorized in this chapter for the purposes of carrying out this paragraph.

(9) Funding

For each of the fiscal years 1991, 1992, 1993, 1994, and 1995, $6,000,000 of amounts in the Fund shall be available to carry out the regional research program in paragraph (8), such amounts to be available in equal amounts for the regional research program in each region; except that if the agencies represented on the Interagency Committee determine that regional research needs exist which cannot be addressed within such funding limits, such agencies may use their authority under paragraph (10) to make additional grants to meet such needs. For the purposes of this paragraph, the research program carried out by the Prince William Sound Oil Spill Recovery Institute established under section 2731 of this title, shall not be eligible to receive grants under this paragraph.

(10) Grants

In carrying out the research and development program established under this subsection, the agencies represented on the Interagency Committee may enter into contracts and cooperative agreements and make grants to universities, research institutions, and other persons. Such contracts, cooperative agreements, and grants shall address research and technology priorities set forth in the oil pollution research plan under subsection (b) of this section.

(11) Utilization of resources

In carrying out research under this section, the Department of Transportation shall continue to utilize the resources of the Research and Special Programs Administration of the Department of Transportation, to the maximum extent practicable.

(d) International Cooperation

In accordance with the research plan submitted under subsection (b) of this section, the Interagency Committee shall coordinate and cooperate with other nations and foreign research entities in conducting oil pollution research, development, and demonstration activities, including controlled field tests of oil discharges.

(e) Biennial Reports

The Chairman of the Interagency Committee shall submit to Congress every 2 years on October 30 a report on the activities carried out under this section in the preceding 2 fiscal years, and on activities proposed to be carried out under this section in the current 2 fiscal year period.

(f) Funding

Not to exceed $21,250,000 of amounts in the Fund shall be available annually to carry out this section except for subsection (c)(8) of this section. Of such sums—

(1) funds authorized to be appropriated to carry out the activities under subsection (c)(4) of this section shall not exceed $5,000,000 for fiscal year 1991 or $3,500,000 for any subsequent fiscal year; and

(2) not less than $2,250,000 shall be available for carrying out the activities in subsection (c)(6) of this section for fiscal years 1992, 1993, 1994, and 1995.

All activities authorized in this section, including subsection (c)(8) of this section, are subject to appropriations.

(Pub.L. 101–380, Title VII, § 7001, Aug. 18, 1990, 104 Stat. 559.)

References in Text

This chapter, referred to in subsec. (c)(8)(G), was in the original this "Act", meaning Pub.L. 101–380 which, in addition to enacting this chapter, made conforming amendments to other sections in this title as well as in Titles 14, 16, 23, 26, 43, 46, and 46 App. For complete classification of Pub.L. 101–380 to the Code see Short Title note under section 2701 of this title and Tables.

*

TITLE 42—THE PUBLIC HEALTH AND WELFARE

SAFETY OF PUBLIC WATER SYSTEMS

PUBLIC HEALTH SERVICE ACT (TITLE XIV) [PHSA § ___]

(42 U.S.C.A. §§ 300f to 300j-26)

CHAPTER 6A—PUBLIC HEALTH SERVICE

SUBCHAPTER XII—SAFETY OF PUBLIC WATER SYSTEMS

PART A—DEFINITIONS

Sec.
300f. Definitions.

PART B—PUBLIC WATER SYSTEMS

300g. Coverage.
300g-1. National drinking water regulations.
(a) National primary drinking water regulations; maximum contaminant level goals; simultaneous publication of regulations and goals.
(b) Standard setting schedules and deadlines; substitution of contaminants; additional contaminants; adequate safety margin in levels; "feasible" defined; technology, techniques, or other means to meet contaminant level; alternative treatment techniques; filtration and disinfection as required treatment techniques; amendment, review, effective date, and supersedure of regulations; addition of substances unrelated contamination.
(c) Secondary regulations; publication of proposed regulations; promulgation; amendments.
(d) Regulations; public hearings; administrative consultations.
(e) Science Advisory Board comments.
300g-2. State primary enforcement responsibility; regulations; notice and hearing; publication in Federal Register; applications.
300g-3. Enforcement of drinking water regulations.
(a) Notice to State and public water system; issuance of administrative order; civil action.
(b) Judicial determinations in appropriate Federal district courts; civil penalties; separate violations.
(c) Notice of owner or operator of public water system to persons served; regulations for form, manner, and frequency of notice; amendment of regulations to provide different types and frequencies of notice; penalties.

Sec.
300g-3. Enforcement of drinking water regulations.

(d) Notice of noncompliance with secondary drinking water regulations.
(e) State authority to adopt or enforce laws or regulations respecting drinking water regulations or public water systems unaffected.
(f) Notice and public hearing; availability of recommendations transmitted to State and public water system.
(g) Administrative order requiring compliance; notice and hearing; civil penalty; civil actions.
300g-4. Variances.
(a) Characteristics of raw water sources; specific treatment technique; notice to Administrator, reasons for variance; compliance, enforcement; approval or revision of schedules and revocation of variances; review of variances and schedules; publication in Federal Register, notice and results of review; notice to State; considerations respecting abuse of discretion in granting variances or failing to prescribe schedules; State corrective action; authority of Administrator in State without primary enforcement responsibility; alternative treatment techniques.
(b) Enforcement of schedule or other requirement.
(c) Applications for variances; regulations; reasonable time for acting.
(d) "Treatment technique requirement" defined.
300g-5. Exemptions.
(a) Requisite findings.
(b) Compliance schedule and implementation of control measures; notice and hearing; dates for compliance with schedule; extension of final date for compliance; compliance, enforcement; approval or revision of schedules and revocation of exemptions.
(c) Notice to Administrator; reasons for exemption.
(d) Review of exemptions and schedules; publication in Federal Register, notice and results of review; notice to State; considerations respecting abuse of discretion in

Sec.
300g–5. Exemptions.
granting exemptions or failing to prescribe schedules; State corrective action.
(e) "Treatment technique requirement" defined.
(f) Authority of Administrator in a State without primary enforcement responsibility.
(g) Applications for exemptions; regulations; reasonable time for acting.
300g–6. Prohibition on use of lead pipes, solder, or flux.
(a) In general.
(1) Prohibition.
(2) Public notice requirements.
(A) In general.
(B) Contents of notice.
(b) State enforcement.
(1) Enforcement of prohibition.
(2) Enforcement of public notice requirements.
(c) Penalties.
(d) "Lead free" defined.

PART C—PROTECTION OF UNDERGROUND SOURCES OF DRINKING WATER

300h. Regulations for State programs.
(a) Publication of proposed regulations; promulgation; amendments; public hearings; administrative consultations.
(b) Minimum requirements; restrictions.
(c) Temporary permits; notice and hearing.
(d) "Underground injection" defined; underground injection endangerment of drinking water sources.
300h–1. State primary enforcement responsibility.
(a) List of States in need of control program; amendment of list.
(b) State applications; notice to Administrator of compliance with revised or added requirements; approval or disapproval by Administrator; duration of State primary enforcement responsibility; public hearing.
(c) Program by Administrator for State without primary enforcement responsibility; restrictions.
(d) "Applicable underground injection control program" defined.
(e) Primary enforcement responsibility by Indian Tribe.
300h–2. Enforcement of program.
(a) Notice to State and violator; issuance of administrative order; civil action.
(b) Civil and criminal actions.
(c) Administrative orders.
(d) State authority to adopt or enforce laws or regulations respecting underground injection unaffected.
300h–3. Interim regulation of underground injections.
(a) Necessity for well operation permit; designation of one aquifer areas.
(b) Well operation permits; publication in Federal Register; notice and hearing; issuance or denial; conditions for issuance.
(c) Civil penalties; separate violations; penalties for willful violations; temporary restraining order or injunction.

Sec.
300h–3. Interim regulation of underground injections.
(d) "New underground injection well" defined.
(e) Areas with one aquifer; publication in Federal Register; commitments for Federal financial assistance.
300h–4. Optional demonstration by States relating to oil or natural gas.
(a) Approval of State underground injection control program; alternative showing of effectiveness of program by State.
(b) Revision or amendment of requirements of regulation; showing of effectiveness of program by State.
(c) Primary enforcement responsibility of State; voiding by Administrator under duly promulgated rule.
300h–5. Regulation of State programs.
300h–6. Sole source aquifer demonstration program.
(a) Purpose.
(b) "Critical aquifer protection area" defined.
(c) Application.
(d) Criteria.
(e) Contents of application.
(f) Comprehensive plan.
(g) Plans under section 208 of the Clean Water Act.
(h) Consultation and hearings.
(i) Approval or disapproval.
(j) Grants and reimbursement.
(k) Activities funded under other law.
(*l*) Savings provision.
(m) Authorization of appropriations.
300h–7. State programs to establish wellhead protection areas.
(a) State programs.
(b) Public participation.
(c) Disapproval.
(1) In general.
(2) Modification and resubmission.
(d) Federal assistance.
(e) "Wellhead protection area" defined.
(f) Prohibitions.
(1) Activities under other laws.
(2) Individual sources.
(g) Implementation.
(h) Federal agencies.
(i) Additional requirement.
(1) In general.
(2) "Annular injection" defined.
(3) Review.
(4) Disapproval.
(j) Coordination with other laws.
(k) Authorization of appropriations.

PART D—EMERGENCY POWERS

300i. Emergency powers.
(a) Actions authorized against imminent and substantial endangerment to health.
(b) Penalties for violations; separate offenses.
300i–1. Tampering with public water systems.
(a) Tampering.
(b) Attempt or threat.
(c) Civil penalty.
(d) "Tamper" defined.

Sec.

PART E—GENERAL PROVISIONS

300j. Assurances of availability of adequate supplies of chemicals necessary for treatment of water.
(a) Certification of need application.
(b) Application requirements; publication in Federal Register; waiver; certification, issuance or denial.
(c) Certification of need; issuance; executive orders; implementation of orders; equitable apportionment of orders; factors considered.
(d) Breach of contracts; defense.
(e) Penalties for noncompliance with orders; temporary restraining orders and preliminary or permanent injunctions.
(f) Termination date.

300j–1. Research, technical assistance, information, training of personnel.
(a) Specific powers and duties of Administrator.
(b) Other powers and duties of Administrator.
(c) Establishment of training programs and grants for training; training fees.
(d) Authorization of appropriations.
(e) Technical assistance for small systems; authorization of appropriations; amount to be utilized for public water systems owned or operated by Indian tribes.

300j–2. Grants for State programs.
(a) Public water systems supervision programs; applications for grants; allotment of sums; waiver of grant restrictions; notice of approval or disapproval of application; authorization of appropriations.
(b) Underground water source protection programs; applications for grants; allotment of sums; authorization of appropriations.
(c) Definitions.

300j–3. Special project grants and guaranteed loans.
(a) Special study and demonstration project grants.
(b) Limitations.
(c) Authorization of appropriations.
(d) Loan guarantees to public water systems; conditions; indebtedness limitation; regulations.

300j–3a. Grants to public sector agencies.
(a) Assistance for development and demonstration projects.
(b) Limitations.
(c) Authorization of appropriations.

300j–3b. Contaminant standards or treatment technique guidelines.

300j–4. Records and inspections.
(a) Persons subject to requirements; size of system and likely contaminants as considerations for monitoring; monitoring for unregulated contaminants; notification of availability of results; waiver or monitoring requirement; authorization of appropriations.
(b) Entry of establishments, facilities, or other property; inspections; conduct of certain tests; audit and examination of records; entry restrictions; prohibition against informing of a proposed entry.
(c) Penalty.

Sec.

300j–4. Records and inspections.
(d) Confidential information; trade secrets and secret processes; information disclosure; "information required under this section" defined.
(e) "Grantee" and "person" defined.
(f) Information regarding drinking water coolers.

300j–5. National Drinking Water Advisory Council.
(a) Establishment; membership; representation of interests; term of office, vacancies; reappointment.
(b) Functions.
(c) Compensation and allowances; travel expenses.
(d) Advisory committee termination provision inapplicable.

300j–6. Federal agencies.
(a) Compliance with Federal, State, and local requirements, etc.; scope of applicability of compliance requirements, etc.; liability for civil penalties.
(b) Waiver; national security; records available in judicial proceedings; publication in Federal Register; notice to Congressional Committees.
(c) Indian rights and sovereignty as unaffected.

300j–7. Judicial review.
(a) Courts of appeals; petition for review; actions respecting regulations; filing period; grounds arising after expiration of filing period; exclusiveness of remedy.
(b) District courts; petition for review; actions respecting variances or exemptions; filing period; grounds arising after expiration of filing period; exclusiveness of remedy.
(c) Judicial order for additional evidence before Administrator; modified or new findings; recommendation for modification or setting aside of original determination.

300j–8. Citizen's civil action.
(a) Persons subject to civil action; jurisdiction of enforcement proceedings.
(b) Conditions for commencement of civil action; notice.
(c) Intervention of right.
(d) Costs; attorney fees; expert witness fees; filing of bond.
(e) Availability of other relief.

300j–9. General provisions.
(a) Regulations; delegation of functions.
(b) Utilization of officers and employees of Federal agencies.
(c) Assignment of Agency personnel to State or interstate agencies.
(d) Payments of grants; adjustments; advances; reimbursement; installments; conditions; eligibility for grants; "nonprofit agency or institution" defined.
(e) Labor standards.
(f) Appearance and representation of Administrator through Attorney General or attorney appointees.
(g) Authority of Administrator under other provisions unaffected.
(h) Reports to Congressional Committees; review by Office of Management and Budget: submittal of comments to Congressional Committees.

Sec.
300j–9. General provisions.
(i) Discrimination prohibition; procedural requirements; prohibition inapplicable to undirected but deliberate violations.
300j–10. Appointment of scientific, etc., personnel by Administrator of Environmental Protection Agency for implementation of responsibilities; compensation.
300j–11. Indian Tribes.
(a) In general.
(b) EPA regulations.
(1) Specific provisions.
(2) Provisions where treatment as State inappropriate.

PART F—ADDITIONAL REQUIREMENTS TO REGULATE THE SAFETY OF DRINKING WATER

300j–21. Definitions.

Sec.
300j–22. Recall of drinking water coolers with lead-lined tanks.
300j–23. Drinking water coolers containing lead.
(a) Publication of lists.
(b) Prohibition.
(c) Criminal penalty.
(d) Civil penalty.
300j–24. Lead contamination in school drinking water.
(a) Distribution of drinking water cooler list.
(b) Guidance document and testing protocol.
(c) Dissemination to schools, etc.
(d) Remedial action program.
300j–25. Federal assistance for State programs regarding lead contamination in school drinking water.
(a) School drinking water programs.
(b) Limits.
(c) Authorization of appropriations.
300j–26. Certification of testing laboratories.

Related Provisions

See, also, Water Pollution Prevention and Control, 33 U.S.C.A. § 1251 et seq., ante; and Water Resources Research, 42 U.S.C.A. § 10301 et seq., post.

SUBCHAPTER XII—SAFETY OF PUBLIC WATER SYSTEMS

CROSS REFERENCES

Applicability of Solid Waste Disposal Act to activity or substance which is subject to this subchapter, see section 6905 of this title.

Comprehensive management plan for Pinelands National Reserve to include plan for implementation of this subchapter, see section 471i of Title 16, Conservation.

Proposed environmental criteria regulation under this subchapter, functions of Science Advisory Board respecting, see section 4365 of this title.

Responsiveness of research on wastewater treatment and treatment of water for potable use to needs in implementing this subchapter, see section 10303(b), (e) of this title.

West's Federal Forms

Intervention, see § 3111 et seq.

Jurisdiction and venue in district courts, see § 1003 et seq.

Preliminary injunctions and temporary restraining orders, see § 5271 et seq.

Taxation of costs, see § 4612 et seq.

CODE OF FEDERAL REGULATIONS

Decisionmaking procedures applicable to permit programs, see 40 CFR 124.1 et seq.

Environmental impact and related procedures, see 23 CFR 771.101 et seq.

Environmental protection agency grants, policies and procedures, see 40 CFR 30.100 et seq.

Implementation and enforcement of national primary drinking water regulations, see 40 CFR 142.1 et seq.

Primary and secondary drinking water provisions, see 40 CFR 141.1 et seq., 143.1 et seq.

Underground injection control programs, technical standards, see 40 CFR 146.1 et seq.

WESTLAW ELECTRONIC RESEARCH

See WESTLAW guide following the Explanation pages of this pamphlet.

PART A—DEFINITIONS

§ 300f. Definitions [PHSA § 1401]

For purposes of this subchapter:

(1) The term "primary drinking water regulation" means a regulation which—

(A) applies to public water systems;

(B) specifies contaminants which, in the judgment of the Administrator, may have any adverse effect on the health of persons;

(C) specifies for each such contaminant either—

(i) a maximum contaminant level, if, in the judgment of the Administrator, it is economically and technologically feasible to ascertain the level of such contaminant in water in public water systems, or

(ii) if, in the judgment of the Administrator, it is not economically or technologically feasible to so ascertain the level of such contaminant, each treatment technique known to the Administrator which leads to a reduction in the level of such contaminant sufficient to satisfy the requirements of section 300g–1 of this title; and

(D) contains criteria and procedures to assure a supply of drinking water which dependably complies with such maximum contaminant levels; including quality control and testing procedures to insure compliance with such levels and to insure proper operation and maintenance of the system, and requirements as to (i) the minimum quality of water which may be taken into the system and (ii) siting for new facilities for public water systems.

(2) The term "secondary drinking water regulation" means a regulation which applies to public water systems and which specifies the maximum contaminant levels which, in the judgment of the Administrator, are requisite to protect the public welfare. Such regulations may apply to any contaminant in drinking water (A) which may adversely affect the odor or appearance of such water and consequently may cause a substantial number of the persons served by the public water system providing such water to discontinue its use, or (B) which may otherwise adversely affect the public welfare. Such regulations may vary according to geographic and other circumstances.

(3) The term "maximum contaminant level" means the maximum permissible level of a contaminant in water which is delivered to any user of a public water system.

(4) The term "public water system" means a system for the provision to the public of piped water for human consumption, if such system has at least fifteen service connections or regularly serves at least twenty-five individuals. Such term includes (A) any collection, treatment, storage, and distribution facilities under control of the operator of such system and used primarily in connection with such system, and (B) any collection or pretreatment storage facilities not under such control which are used primarily in connection with such system.

(5) The term "supplier of water" means any person who owns or operates a public water system.

(6) The term "contaminant" means any physical, chemical, biological, or radiological substance or matter in water.

(7) The term "Administrator" means the Administrator of the Environmental Protection Agency.

(8) The term "Agency" means the Environmental Protection Agency.

(9) The term "Council" means the National Drinking Water Advisory Council established under section 300j–5 of this title.

(10) The term "municipality" means a city, town, or other public body created by or pursuant to State law, or an Indian Tribe.

(11) The term "Federal agency" means any department, agency, or instrumentality of the United States.

(12) The term "person" means an individual, corporation, company, association, partnership, State, municipality, or Federal agency (and includes officers, employees, and agents of any corporation, company, association, State, municipality, or Federal agency).

(13) The term "State" includes, in addition to the several States, only the District of Columbia, Guam, the Commonwealth of Puerto Rico, the Northern Mariana Islands, the Virgin Islands, American Samoa, and the Trust Territory of the Pacific Islands.

(14) The term "Indian Tribe" means any Indian tribe having a Federally recognized governing body carrying out substantial governmental duties and powers over any area.

(July 1, 1944, c. 373, Title XIV, § 1401, as added Dec. 16, 1974, Pub.L. 93–523, § 2(a), 88 Stat. 1661, and amended June 23, 1976, Pub.L. 94–317, Title III, § 301(b)(2), 90 Stat. 707; Oct. 12, 1976, Pub.L. 94–484, Title IX, § 905(b)(1), 90 Stat. 2325; Nov. 16, 1977, Pub.L. 95–190, § 8(b), 91 Stat. 1397; June 19, 1986, Pub.L. 99–339, Title III, § 302(b), 100 Stat. 666.)

Short Title

Section 1 of Act July 1, 1944, c. 373, 58 Stat. 682, provided that: "This Act [comprising this chapter] may be cited as the 'Public Health Service Act'."

Section 1 of Pub.L. 93–523, Dec. 16, 1974, 88 Stat. 1660, provided that: "This Act [which enacted this subchapter and section 349 of Title 21, Food and Drugs] may be cited as the 'Safe Drinking Water Act'."

Section 1 of Pub.L. 99–339, June 19, 1986, 100 Stat. 642, provided that: "This Act [which enacted sections 300g–6, 300h–5, to 300h–7, 300i–1, 300j–11, and 6939b of this title, and amended this section and sections 300g–1 et seq. of this title] may be cited as the 'Safe Drinking Water Act Amendments of 1986'."

Section 1 of Pub.L. 100–572, Oct. 31, 1988, 102 Stat. 2884, provided that: "This Act [which enacted part F of this subchapter and sections 247b–1 and 300j–4(f) of this title] may be cited as the 'Lead Contamination Control Act of 1988'."

LAW REVIEW COMMENTARIES

Long-range planning in environmental and health regulatory agencies. Richard N.L. Andrews, 20 Ecology L.Q. 515 (1993).

"More good than harm": A first principle for environmental agencies and reviewing courts. Edward W. Warren and Gary E. Marchant, 20 Ecology L.Q. 379 (1993).

Part B—Public Water Systems

LIBRARY REFERENCES

Waters and Water Courses ⚷196, 202.
C.J.S. Waters §§ 232 et seq., 280.

§ 300g. Coverage [PHSA § 1411]

Subject to sections 300g–4 and 300g–5 of this title, national primary drinking water regulations under this part shall apply to each public water system in each State; except that such regulations shall not apply to a public water system—

(1) which consists only of distribution and storage facilities (and does not have any collection and treatment facilities);

(2) which obtains all of its water from, but is not owned or operated by, a public water system to which such regulations apply;

(3) which does not sell water to any person; and

(4) which is not a carrier which conveys passengers in interstate commerce.

(July 1, 1944, c. 373, Title XIV, § 1411, as added Dec. 16, 1974, Pub.L. 93–523, § 2(a), 88 Stat. 1662.)

LAW REVIEW COMMENTARIES

Long-range planning in environmental and health regulatory agencies. Richard N.L. Andrews, 20 Ecology L.Q. 515 (1993).

LIBRARY REFERENCES

Waters and Water Courses ⚬64.
C.J.S. Waters § 43 et seq.

§ 300g–1. National drinking water regulations [PHSA § 1412]

(a) National primary drinking water regulations; maximum contaminant level goals; simultaneous publication of regulations and goals

(1) Effective on June 19, 1986, each national interim or revised primary drinking water regulation promulgated under this section before June 19, 1986, shall be deemed to be a national primary drinking water regulation under subsection (b) of this section. No such regulation shall be required to comply with the standards set forth in subsection (b)(4) of this section unless such regulation is amended to establish a different maximum contaminant level after June 19, 1986.

(2) After June 19, 1986, each recommended maximum contaminant level published before June 19, 1986, shall be treated as a maximum contaminant level goal.

(3) Whenever a national primary drinking water regulation is proposed under paragraph (1), (2), or (3) of subsection (b) of this section for any contaminant, the maximum contaminant level goal for such contaminant shall be proposed simultaneously. Whenever a national primary drinking water regulation is promulgated under paragraph (1), (2), or (3) of subsection (b) of this section for any contaminant, the maximum contaminant level goal for such contaminant shall be published simultaneously.

(4) Paragraph (3) shall not apply to any recommended maximum contaminant level published before June 19, 1986.

(b) Standard setting schedules and deadlines; substitution of contaminants; additional contaminants; adequate safety margin in levels; "feasible" defined; technology, techniques, or other means to meet contaminant level; alternative treatment techniques; filtration and disinfection as required treatment techniques; amendment, review, effective date, and supersedure of regulations; addition of substances unrelated to contamination

(1) In the case of those contaminants listed in the Advance Notice of Proposed Rulemaking published in volume 47, Federal Register, page 9352, and in volume 48, Federal Register, page 45502, the Administrator shall publish maximum contaminant level goals and promulgate national primary drinking water regulations—

(A) not later than 12 months after June 19, 1986, for not less than 9 of those listed contaminants;

(B) not later than 24 months after June 19, 1986, for not less than 40 of those listed contaminants; and

(C) not later than 36 months after June 19, 1986, for the remainder of such listed contaminants.

(2)(A) If the Administrator identifies a drinking water contaminant the regulation of which, in the judgment of the Administrator, is more likely to be protective of public health (taking into account the schedule for regulation under paragraph (1)) than a contaminant referred to in paragraph (1), the Administrator may publish a maximum contaminant level goal and promulgate a national primary drinking water regulation for such identified contaminant in lieu of regulating the contaminant referred to in such paragraph. There may be no more than 7 contaminants in paragraph (1) for which substitutions may be made. Regulation of a contaminant identified under this paragraph shall be in accordance with the schedule applicable to the contaminant for which the substitution is made.

(B) If the Administrator identifies one or more contaminants for substitution under this paragraph, the Administrator shall publish in the Federal Register not later than one year after June 19, 1986, a list of contaminants proposed for substitution, the contaminants referred to in paragraph (1) for which substitutions are to be made, and the basis for the judgment that regulation of such proposed substitute contaminants is more likely to be protective of public health (taking into account the schedule for regulation under such paragraph). Following a period of 60 days for public comment, the Administrator shall publish in the Federal Register a final list of contaminants to be substituted and contaminants referred to in paragraph (1) for which substitutions are to be made, together with responses to significant comments.

(C) Any contaminant referred to in paragraph (1) for which a substitution is made, pursuant to subparagraph (A) of this paragraph, shall be included on the priority list to be published by the Administrator not later than January 1, 1988, pursuant to paragraph (3)(A).

(D) The Administrator's decision to regulate a contaminant identified pursuant to this paragraph in lieu of a contaminant referred to in paragraph (1) shall not be subject to judicial review.

(3)(A) The Administrator shall publish maximum contaminant level goals and promulgate national primary drinking water regulations for each contaminant (other than a contaminant referred to in paragraph (1) or (2) for which a national primary drinking water regulation was promulgated) which, in the judgment of the Administrator, may have any adverse effect on the health of persons and which is known or anticipated to occur in public water systems. Not later than January 1, 1988, and at 3 year intervals thereafter, the Administrator shall publish a list of contaminants which are known or anticipated to occur in public water systems and which may require regulation under this chapter.

(B) For the purpose of establishing the list under subparagraph (A), the Administrator shall form an advisory working group including members from the National Toxicology Program and the Environmental Protection Agency's Offices of Drinking Water, Pesticides, Toxic Substances, Ground Water, Solid Waste and Emergency Response and any others the Administrator deems appropriate. The Administrator's consideration of priorities shall include, but not be limited to, substances referred to in section 9601(14) of this title, and substances registered as pesticides under the Federal Insecticide, Fungicide, and Rodenticide Act [7 U.S.C.A. § 136 et seq.].

(C) Not later than 24 months after the listing of contaminants under subparagraph (A), the Administrator shall publish proposed maximum contaminant level goals and national primary drinking water regulations for not less than 25 contaminants from the list established under subparagraph (A).

(D) Not later than 36 months after the listing of contaminants under subparagraph (A), the Administrator shall publish a maximum contaminant goal and promulgate a national primary drinking water regulation for those contaminants for which proposed maximum contaminant level goals and proposed national primary drinking water regulations were published under subparagraph (C).

(4) Each maximum contaminant level goal established under this subsection shall be set at the level at which no known or anticipated adverse effects on the health of persons occur and which allows an adequate margin of safety. Each national primary drinking water regulation for a contaminant for which a maximum contaminant level goal is established under this subsection shall specify a maximum level for such contaminant which is as close to the maximum contaminant level goal as is feasible.

(5) For the purposes of this subsection, the term "feasible" means feasible with the use of the best technology, treatment techniques and other means which the Administrator finds, after examination for efficacy under field conditions and not solely under laboratory conditions, are available (taking cost into consideration). For the purpose of paragraph (4), granular activated carbon is feasible for the control of synthetic organic chemicals, and any technology, treatment technique, or other means found to be the best available for the control of synthetic organic chemicals must be at least as effective in controlling synthetic organic chemicals as granular activated carbon.

(6) Each national primary drinking water regulation which establishes a maximum contaminant level shall list the technology, treatment techniques, and other means which the Administrator finds to be feasible for purposes of meeting such maximum contaminant level, but a regulation under this paragraph shall not require that any specified technology, treatment technique, or other means be used for purposes of meeting such maximum contaminant level.

(7)(A) The Administrator is authorized to promulgate a national primary drinking water regulation that requires the use of a treatment technique in lieu of establishing a maximum contaminant level, if the Administrator makes a finding that it is not economically or technologically feasible to ascertain the level of the contaminant. In such case, the Administrator shall identify those treatment techniques which, in the Administrator's judgment, would prevent known or anticipated adverse effects on the health of persons to the extent feasible. Such regulations shall specify each treatment technique known to the Administrator which meets the requirements of this paragraph, but the Administrator may grant a variance from any specified treatment technique in accordance with section 300g–4(a)(3) of this title.

(B) Any schedule referred to in this subsection for the promulgation of a national primary drinking water regulation for any contaminant shall apply in the same manner if the regulation requires a treatment technique in lieu of establishing a maximum contaminant level.

(C)(i) Not later than 18 months after June 19, 1986, the Administrator shall propose and promulgate national primary drinking water regulations specifying criteria under which filtration (including coagulation and sedimentation, as appropriate) is required as a treatment technique for public water systems supplied by surface water sources. In promulgating such rules, the Administrator shall consider the quality of source waters, protection afforded by watershed management, treatment practices (such as disinfection and length of water storage) and other factors relevant to protection of health.

(ii) In lieu of the provisions of section 300g–4 of this title the Administrator shall specify procedures by which the State determines which public water systems within its jurisdiction shall adopt filtration under the criteria of clause (i). The State may require the public water system to provide studies or other information to assist in this determination. The procedures shall provide notice and opportunity for public hearing on this determination. If the State determines that filtration is required, the State shall prescribe a schedule for compliance by the public water system with the filtration requirement. A schedule shall require compliance within 18 months of a determination made under clause (iii).

(iii) Within 18 months from the time that the Administrator establishes the criteria and procedures under this subparagraph, a State with primary enforcement responsibility shall adopt any necessary regulations to implement this subparagraph. Within 12 months of adoption of such regulations the State shall make determinations regarding filtration for all the public water systems within its jurisdiction supplied by surface waters.

(iv) If a State does not have primary enforcement responsibility for public water systems, the Administrator shall have the same authority to make the determination in clause (ii) in such State as the State would have under that clause. Any filtration requirement or schedule under this subparagraph shall be treated as if it were a requirement of a national primary drinking water regulation.

(8) Not later than 36 months after June 19, 1986, the Administrator shall propose and promulgate national primary drinking water regulations requiring disinfection as a treatment technique for all public water systems. The Administrator shall simultaneously promulgate a rule specifying criteria that will be used by the Administrator (or delegated State authorities) to grant variances from this requirement according to the provisions of sections 300g–4(a)(1)(B) and 300g–4(a)(3) of this title. In implementing section 300j–1(g) of this title the Administrator or the delegated State authority shall, where appropriate, give special consideration to providing technical assistance to small public water systems in complying with the regulations promulgated under this paragraph.

(9) Revised national primary drinking water regulations shall be amended whenever changes in technology, treatment techniques, and other means permit greater protection of the health of persons, but in any event such regulations shall be reviewed at least once every 3 years. Such review shall include an analysis of innovations or changes in technology, treatment techniques or other activities that have occurred over the previous 3-year period and that may provide for greater protection of the health of persons. The findings of such review shall be published in the Federal Register. If, after opportunity for public comment, the Administrator concludes that the technology, treatment techniques, or other means resulting from such innovations or changes are not feasible within the meaning of paragraph (5), an explanation of such conclusion shall be published in the Federal Register.

(10) National primary drinking water regulations promulgated under this subsection (and amendments thereto) shall take effect eighteen months after the date of their promulgation. Regulations under subsection (a) of this section shall be superseded by regulations under this subsection to the extent provided by the regulations under this subsection.

(11) No national primary drinking water regulation may require the addition of any substance for preventive health care purposes unrelated to contamination of drinking water.

(c) Secondary regulations; publication of proposed regulations; promulgation; amendments

The Administrator shall publish proposed national secondary drinking water regulations within 270 days after December 16, 1974. Within 90 days after publication of any such regulation, he shall promulgate such regulation with such modifications as he deems appropriate. Regulations under this subsection may be amended from time to time.

(d) Regulations; public hearings; administrative consultations

Regulations under this section shall be prescribed in accordance with section 553 of title 5 (relating to rulemaking), except that the Administrator shall provide opportunity for public hearing prior to promulgation of such regulations. In proposing and promulgating regulations under this section, the Administrator shall consult with the Secretary and the National Drinking Water Advisory Council.

(e) Science Advisory Board comments

The Administrator shall request comments from the Science Advisory Board (established under the Environmental Research, Development, and Demonstration Act of 1978) prior to proposal of a maximum contaminant level goal and national primary drinking water regulation. The Board shall respond, as it deems appropriate, within the time period applicable for promulgation of the national primary drinking water standard concerned. This subsection shall, under no circumstances, be used to delay final promulgation of any national primary drinking water standard.

(July 1, 1944, c. 373, Title XIV, § 1412, as added Dec. 16, 1974, Pub.L. 93-523, § 2(a), 88 Stat. 1662, and amended Nov. 16, 1977, Pub.L. 95-190, §§ 3(c), 12(a), 91 Stat. 1394, 1398; June 19, 1986, Pub.L. 99-339, Title I, § 101(a), (b), (c)(1), (d), (e), 100 Stat. 642-646.)

CROSS REFERENCES

Bottled drinking water standards, see section 349 of Title 21, Food and Drugs.

CODE OF FEDERAL REGULATIONS

Additional primary and secondary drinking water provisions, see 40 CFR 141.1 et seq., 143.1 et seq.

Environmental impact and related procedures, see 23 CFR 771.101 et seq.

LAW REVIEW COMMENTARIES

Long-range planning in environmental and health regulatory agencies. Richard N.L. Andrews, 20 Ecology L.Q. 515 (1993).

LIBRARY REFERENCES

Waters and Water Courses ⚷202.
C.J.S. Waters § 280.

§ 300g-2. State primary enforcement responsibility; regulations; notice and hearing; publication in Federal Register; applications [PHSA § 1413]

(a) For purposes of this subchapter, a State has primary enforcement responsibility for public water systems during any period for which the Administrator determines (pursuant to regulations prescribed under subsection (b) of this section) that such State—

(1) has adopted drinking water regulations which are no less stringent than the national primary drinking water regulations in effect under sections 300g-1(a) and 300g-1(b) of this title;

(2) has adopted and is implementing adequate procedures for the enforcement of such State regulations, including conducting such monitoring and making such inspections as the Administrator may require by regulation;

(3) will keep such records and make such reports with respect to its activities under paragraphs (1) and (2) as the Administrator may require by regulation;

(4) if it permits variances or exemptions, or both, from the requirements of its drinking water regulations which meet the requirements of paragraph (1), permits such variances and exemptions under conditions and in a manner which is not less stringent than the conditions under, and the manner in which variances and exemptions may be granted under sections 300g-4 and 300g-5 of this title;

(5) has adopted and can implement an adequate plan for the provision of safe drinking water under emergency circumstances.

(b)(1) The Administrator shall, by regulation (proposed within 180 days of December 16, 1974), prescribe the manner in which a State may apply to the Administrator for a determination that the requirements of paragraphs (1), (2), (3), and (4) of subsection (a) of this section are satisfied with respect to the State, the manner in which the determination is made, the period for which the determination will be effective, and the manner in which the Administrator may determine that such requirements are no longer met. Such regulations shall require that before a determination of the Administrator that such requirements are met or are no longer met with respect to a State may become effective, the Administrator shall notify such State of the determination and the reasons therefor and shall provide an opportunity for public hearing on the determination. Such regulations shall be promulgated (with such modifications as the Administrator deems appropriate) within 90 days of the publication of the proposed regulations in the Federal Register. The Administrator shall promptly notify in writing the chief executive officer of each State of the promulgation of regulations under this paragraph. Such notice shall contain a copy of the regulations and shall specify a State's authority under this subchapter when it is determined to have primary enforcement responsibility for public water systems.

(2) When an application is submitted in accordance with the Administrator's regulations under paragraph (1), the Administrator shall within 90 days of the date on which such application is submitted (A) make the determination applied for, or (B) deny the application and notify the applicant in writing of the reasons for his denial.

(July 1, 1944, c. 373, Title XIV, § 1413, as added Dec. 16, 1974, Pub.L. 93-523, § 2(a), 88 Stat. 1665, as amended June 19, 1986, Pub.L. 99-339, Title I, § 101(c)(2), 100 Stat. 646.)

CODE OF FEDERAL REGULATIONS

Implementation and enforcement of national primary drinking water regulations, see 40 CFR 142.1 et seq.

LIBRARY REFERENCES

States ⚷4.10.
C.J.S. States § 24.

§ 300g–3. Enforcement of drinking water regulations [PHSA § 1414]

(a) Notice to State and public water system; issuance of administrative order; civil action

(1)(A) Whenever the Administrator finds during a period during which a State has primary enforcement responsibility for public water systems (within the meaning of section 300g–2(a) of this title) that any public water system—

(i) for which a variance under section 300g–4 or an exemption under section 300g–5 of this title is not in effect, does not comply with any national primary drinking water regulation in effect under section 300g–1 of this title, or

(ii) for which a variance under section 300g–4 or an exemption under section 300g–5 of this title is in effect, does not comply with any schedule or other requirement imposed pursuant thereto,

he shall so notify the State and such public water system and provide such advice and technical assistance to such State and public water system as may be appropriate to bring the system into compliance with such regulation or requirement by the earliest feasible time.

(B) If, beyond the thirtieth day after the Administrator's notification under subparagraph (A), the State has not commenced appropriate enforcement action, the Administrator shall issue an order under subsection (g) of this section requiring the public water system to comply with such regulation or requirement or the Administrator shall commence a civil action under subsection (b) of this section.

(2) Whenever, on the basis of information available to him, the Administrator finds during a period during which a State does not have primary enforcement responsibility for public water systems that a public water system in such State—

(A) for which a variance under section 300g–4(a)(2) or an exemption under section 300g–5(f) of this title is not in effect, does not comply with any national primary drinking water regulation in effect under section 300g–1 of this title, or

(B) for which a variance under section 300g–4(a)(2) or an exemption under section 300g–5(f) of this title is in effect, does not comply with any schedule or other requirement imposed pursuant thereto,

the Administrator shall issue an order under subsection (g) of this section requiring the public water system to comply with such regulation or requirement or the Administrator shall commence a civil action under subsection (b) of this section.

(b) Judicial determinations in appropriate Federal district courts; civil penalties; separate violations

The Administrator may bring a civil action in the appropriate United States district court to require compliance with a national primary drinking water regulation, with an order issued under subsection (g) of this section, or with any schedule or other requirement imposed pursuant to a variance or exemption granted under section 300g–4 or 300g–5 of this title if—

(1) authorized under paragraph (1) or (2) of subsection (a) of this section, or

(2) if requested by (A) the chief executive officer of the State in which is located the public water system which is not in compliance with such regulation or requirement, or (B) the agency of such State which has jurisdiction over compliance by public water systems in the State with national primary drinking water regulations or State drinking water regulations.

The court may enter, in an action brought under this subsection, such judgment as protection of public health may require, taking into consideration the time necessary to comply and the availability of alternative water supplies; and, if the court determines that there has been a violation of the regulation or schedule or other requirement with respect to which the action was brought, the court may, taking into account the seriousness of the violation, the population at risk, and other appropriate factors, impose on the violator a civil penalty of not to exceed $25,000 for each day in which such violation occurs.

(c) Notice of owner or operator of public water system to persons served; regulations for form, manner, and frequency of notice; amendment of regulations to provide different types and frequencies of notice; penalties

Each owner or operator of a public water system shall give notice to the persons served by it—

(1) of any failure on the part of the public water system to—

(A) comply with an applicable maximum contaminant level or treatment technique requirement of, or a testing procedure prescribed by, a national primary drinking water regulation, or

(B) perform monitoring required by section 300j–4(a) of this title, and

(2) if the public water system is subject to a variance granted under section 300g–4(a)(1)(A) or 300g–4(a)(2) of this title for an inability to meet a maximum contaminant level requirement or is subject to an exemption granted under section 300g–5 of this title, of—

(A) the existence of such variance or exemption, and

(B) any failure to comply with the requirements of any schedule prescribed pursuant to the variance or exemption.

The Administrator shall by regulation prescribe the form, manner, and frequency for giving notice under this subsection. Within 15 months after June 19, 1986, the Administrator shall amend such regulations to provide for different types and frequencies of notice based on the differences between violations which are intermittent or infrequent and violations which are continuous or frequent. Such regulations shall also take into account the seriousness of any potential adverse health effects which may be involved. Notice of any violation of a maximum contaminant level or any other violation designated by the Administrator as posing a serious potential adverse health effect shall be given as soon as possible, but in no case later than 14 days after the violation. Notice of a continuous violation of a regulation other than a maximum contaminant level shall be given no less frequently than every 3 months. Notice of violations judged to be less serious shall be given no less frequently than annually. The Administrator shall specify the types of notice to be used to provide information as promptly and effectively as possible taking into account both the seriousness of any potential adverse health effects and the likelihood of reaching all affected persons. Notification of violations shall include notice by general circulation newspaper serving the area and, whenever appropriate, shall also include a press release to electronic media and individual mailings. Notice under this subsection shall provide a clear and readily understandable explanation of the violation, any potential adverse health effects, the steps that the system is taking to correct such violation, and the necessity for seeking alternative water supplies, if any, until the violation is corrected. Until such amended regulations are promulgated, the regulations in effect on June 19, 1986, shall remain in effect. The Administrator may also require the owner or operator of a public water system to give notice to the persons served by it of contaminant levels of any unregulated contaminant required to be monitored under section 300j–4(a) of this title. Any person who violates this subsection or regulations issued under this subsection shall be subject to a civil penalty of not to exceed $25,000.

(d) Notice of noncompliance with secondary drinking water regulations

Whenever, on the basis of information available to him, the Administrator finds that within a reasonable time after national secondary drinking water regulations have been promulgated, one or more public water systems in a State do not comply with such secondary regulations, and that such noncompliance appears to result from a failure of such State to take reasonable action to assure that public water systems throughout such State meet such secondary regulations, he shall so notify the State.

(e) State authority to adopt or enforce laws or regulations respecting drinking water regulations or public water systems unaffected

Nothing in this subchapter shall diminish any authority of a State or political subdivision to adopt or enforce any law or regulation respecting drinking water regulations or public water systems, but no such law or regulation shall relieve any person of any requirement otherwise applicable under this subchapter.

(f) Notice and public hearing; availability of recommendations transmitted to State and public water system

If the Administrator makes a finding of noncompliance (described in subparagraph (A) or (B) of subsection (a)(1) of this section) with respect to a public water system in a State which has primary enforcement responsibility, the Administrator may, for the purpose of assisting that State in carrying out such responsibility and upon the petition of such State or public water system or persons served by such system, hold, after appropriate notice, public hearings for the purpose of gathering information from technical or other experts, Federal, State, or other public officials, representatives of such public water system, persons served by such system, and other interested persons on—

(1) the ways in which such system can within the earliest feasible time be brought into compliance with the regulation or requirement with respect to which such finding was made, and

(2) the means for the maximum feasible protection of the public health during any period in which such system is not in compliance with a national primary drinking water regulation or requirement applicable to a variance or exemption.

On the basis of such hearings the Administrator shall issue recommendations which shall be sent to such

State and public water system and shall be made available to the public and communications media.

(g) Administrative order requiring compliance; notice and hearing; civil penalty; civil actions

(1) In any case in which the Administrator is authorized to bring a civil action under this section or under section 300j–4 of this title with respect to any regulation, schedule, or other requirement, the Administrator also may issue an order to require compliance with such regulation, schedule, or other requirement.

(2) An order issued under this subsection shall not take effect until after notice and opportunity for public hearing and, in the case of a State having primary enforcement responsibility for public water systems in that State, until after the Administrator has provided the State with an opportunity to confer with the Administrator regarding the proposed order. A copy of any order proposed to be issued under this subsection shall be sent to the appropriate State agency of the State involved if the State has primary enforcement responsibility for public water systems in that State. Any order issued under this subsection shall state with reasonable specificity the nature of the violation. In any case in which an order under this subsection is issued to a corporation, a copy of such order shall be issued to appropriate corporate officers.

(3)(A) Any person who violates, or fails or refuses to comply with, an order under this subsection shall be liable to the United States for a civil penalty of not more than $25,000 per day of violation.

(B) Whenever any civil penalty sought by the Administrator under this paragraph does not exceed a total of $5,000, the penalty shall be assessed by the Administrator after notice and opportunity for a hearing on the record in accordance with section 554 of Title 5.

(C) Whenever any civil penalty sought by the Administrator under this paragraph exceeds $5,000, the penalty shall be assessed by a civil action brought by the Administrator in the appropriate United States district court (as determined under the provisions of Title 28).

(D) If any person fails to pay an assessment of a civil penalty after it has become a final and unappealable order, or after the appropriate court of appeals has entered final judgment in favor of the Administrator, the Attorney General shall recover the amount for which such person is liable in any appropriate district court of the United States. In any such action, the validity and appropriateness of the final order imposing the civil penalty shall not be subject to review.

(July 1, 1944, c. 373, Title XIV, § 1414, as added Dec. 16, 1974, Pub.L. 93–523, § 2(a), 88 Stat. 1666, and amended Nov. 16, 1977, Pub.L. 95–190, § 12(b), 91 Stat. 1398; June 19, 1986, Pub.L. 99–339, Title I, §§ 102, 103, 100 Stat. 647, 648.)

CODE OF FEDERAL REGULATIONS

Implementation and enforcement of national primary drinking water regulations, see 40 CFR 142.1 et seq.

LIBRARY REFERENCES

States ⚿4.10.
C.J.S. States § 24.

§ 300g–4. Variances [PHSA § 1415]

(a) Characteristics of raw water sources; specific treatment technique; notice to Administrator, reasons for variance; compliance, enforcement; approval or revision of schedules and revocation of variances; review of variances and schedules; publication in Federal Register, notice and results of review; notice to State; considerations respecting abuse of discretion in granting variances or failing to prescribe schedules; State corrective action; authority of Administrator in a State without primary enforcement responsibility; alternative treatment techniques

Notwithstanding any other provision of this part, variances from national primary drinking water regulations may be granted as follows:

(1)(A) A State which has primary enforcement responsibility for public water systems may grant one or more variances from an applicable national primary drinking water regulation to one or more public water systems within its jurisdiction which, because of characteristics of the raw water sources which are reasonably available to the systems, cannot meet the requirements respecting the maximum contaminant levels of such drinking water regulation. A variance may only be issued to a system after the system's application of the best technology, treatment techniques, or other means, which the Administrator finds are available (taking costs into consideration). The Administrator shall propose and promulgate his finding of the best available technology, treatment techniques or other means available for each contaminant for purposes of this subsection at the time he proposes and promulgates a maximum contaminant level for each such contaminant. The Administrator's finding of best available technology, treatment techniques or other means for purposes of this subsection may vary depending on the number of persons served by the system or for other physical conditions related to engineering feasibility and costs of compliance with maximum contaminant levels as considered appropriate by the

Administrator. Before a State may grant a variance under this subparagraph, the State must find that the variance will not result in an unreasonable risk to health. If a State grants a public water system a variance under this subparagraph, the State shall prescribe at the time the variance is granted, a schedule for—

(i) compliance (including increments of progress) by the public water system with each contaminant level requirement with respect to which the variance was granted, and

(ii) implementation by the public water system of such additional control measures as the State may require for each contaminant, subject to such contaminant level requirement, during the period ending on the date compliance with such requirement is required.

Before a schedule prescribed by a State pursuant to this subparagraph may take effect, the State shall provide notice and opportunity for a public hearing on the schedule. A notice given pursuant to the preceding sentence may cover the prescribing of more than one such schedule and a hearing held pursuant to such notice shall include each of the schedules covered by the notice. A schedule prescribed pursuant to this subparagraph for a public water system granted a variance shall require compliance by the system with each contaminant level requirement with respect to which the variance was granted as expeditiously as practicable (as the State may reasonably determine).

(B) A State which has primary enforcement responsibility for public water systems may grant to one or more public water systems within its jurisdiction one or more variances from any provision of a national primary drinking water regulation which requires the use of a specified treatment technique with respect to a contaminant if the public water system applying for the variance demonstrates to the satisfaction of the State that such treatment technique is not necessary to protect the health of persons because of the nature of the raw water source of such system. A variance granted under this subparagraph shall be conditioned on such monitoring and other requirements as the Administrator may prescribe.

(C) Before a variance proposed to be granted by a State under subparagraph (A) or (B) may take effect, such State shall provide notice and opportunity for public hearing on the proposed variance. A notice given pursuant to the preceding sentence may cover the granting of more than one variance and a hearing held pursuant to such notice shall include each of the variances covered by the notice. The State shall promptly notify the Administrator of all variances granted by it. Such notification shall contain the reason for the variance (and in the case of a variance under subparagraph (A), the basis for the finding required by that subparagraph before the granting of the variance) and documentation of the need for the variance.

(D) Each public water system's variance granted by a State under subparagraph (A) shall be conditioned by the State upon compliance by the public water system with the schedule prescribed by the State pursuant to that subparagraph. The requirements of each schedule prescribed by a State pursuant to that subparagraph shall be enforceable by the State under its laws. Any requirement of a schedule on which a variance granted under that subparagraph is conditioned may be enforced under section 300g–3 of this title as if such requirement was part of a national primary drinking water regulation.

(E) Each schedule prescribed by a State pursuant to subparagraph (A) shall be deemed approved by the Administrator unless the variance for which it was prescribed is revoked by the Administrator under subparagraph (G) or the schedule is revised by the Administrator under such subparagraph.

(F) Not later than 18 months after the effective date of the interim national primary drinking water regulations the Administrator shall complete a comprehensive review of the variances granted under subparagraph (A) (and schedules prescribed pursuant thereto) and under subparagraph (B) by the States during the one-year period beginning on such effective date. The Administrator shall conduct such subsequent reviews of variances and schedules as he deems necessary to carry out the purposes of this subchapter, but each subsequent review shall be completed within each 3-year period following the completion of the first review under this subparagraph. Before conducting any review under this subparagraph, the Administrator shall publish notice of the proposed review in the Federal Register. Such notice shall (i) provide information respecting the location of data and other information respecting the variances to be reviewed (including data and other information concerning new scientific matters bearing on such variances), and (ii) advise of the opportunity to submit comments on the variances reviewed and on the need for continuing them. Upon completion of any such review, the Administrator shall publish in the Federal Register the results of his review together with findings responsive to comments submitted in connection with such review.

(G)(i) If the Administrator finds that a State has, in a substantial number of instances, abused its discretion in granting variances under subparagraph (A) or (B) or that in a substantial number of cases the State has failed to prescribe schedules in accordance with subparagraph (A), the Administrator shall notify the State of his findings. In determining if a State has abused its discretion in granting variances in a substantial number of instances, the Administrator shall consider the number of persons who are affected by the variances and if the requirements applicable to the granting of the variances were complied with. A notice under this clause shall—

(I) identify each public water system with respect to which the finding was made,

(II) specify the reasons for the finding, and

(III) as appropriate, propose revocations of specific variances or propose revised schedules or other requirements for specific public water systems granted variances, or both.

(ii) The Administrator shall provide reasonable notice and public hearing on the provisions of each notice given pursuant to clause (i) of this subparagraph. After a hearing on a notice pursuant to such clause, the Administrator shall (I) rescind the finding for which the notice was given and promptly notify the State of such rescission, or (II) promulgate (with such modifications as he deems appropriate) such variance revocations and revised schedules or other requirements proposed in such notice as he deems appropriate. Not later than 180 days after the date a notice is given pursuant to clause (i) of this subparagraph, the Administrator shall complete the hearing on the notice and take the action required by the preceding sentence.

(iii) If a State is notified under clause (i) of this subparagraph of a finding of the Administrator made with respect to a variance granted a public water system within that State or to a schedule or other requirement for a variance and if, before a revocation of such variance or a revision of such schedule or other requirement promulgated by the Administrator takes effect, the State takes corrective action with respect to such variance or schedule or other requirement which the Administrator determines makes his finding inapplicable to such variance or schedule or other requirement, the Administrator shall rescind the application of his finding to that variance or schedule or other requirement. No variance revocation or revised schedule or other requirement may take effect before the expiration of 90 days following the date of the notice in which the revocation or revised schedule or other requirement was proposed.

(2) If a State does not have primary enforcement responsibility for public water systems, the Administrator shall have the same authority to grant variances in such State as the State would have under paragraph (1) if it had primary enforcement responsibility.

(3) The Administrator may grant a variance from any treatment technique requirement of a national primary drinking water regulation upon a showing by any person that an alternative treatment technique not included in such requirement is at least as efficient in lowering the level of the contaminant with respect to which such requirement was prescribed. A variance under this paragraph shall be conditioned on the use of the alternative treatment technique which is the basis of the variance.

(b) Enforcement of schedule or other requirement

Any schedule or other requirement on which a variance granted under paragraph (1)(B) or (2) of subsection (a) of this section is conditioned may be enforced under section 300g–3 of this title as if such schedule or other requirement was part of a national primary drinking water regulation.

(c) Applications for variances; regulations: reasonable time for acting

If an application for a variance under subsection (a) of this section is made, the State receiving the application or the Administrator, as the case may be, shall act upon such application within a reasonable period (as determined under regulations prescribed by the Administrator) after the date of its submission.

(d) "Treatment technique requirement" defined

For purposes of this section, the term "treatment technique requirement" means a requirement in a national primary drinking water regulation which specifies for a contaminant (in accordance with section 300f(1)(C)(ii) of this title) each treatment technique known to the Administrator which leads to a reduction in the level of such contaminant sufficient to satisfy the requirements of section 300g–1(b)(3) of this title.

(July 1, 1944, c. 373, Title XIV, § 1415, as added Dec. 16, 1974, Pub.L. 93–523, § 2(a), 88 Stat. 1669, as amended June 19, 1986, Pub.L. 99–339, Title I, § 104, 100 Stat. 649.)

CODE OF FEDERAL REGULATIONS

Implementation and enforcement of national primary drinking water regulations, see 40 CFR 142.1 et seq.

LIBRARY REFERENCES

Waters and Water Courses ⇐64.
C.J.S. Waters § 43 et seq.

§ 300g–5. Exemptions [PHSA § 1416]

(a) Requisite findings

A State which has primary enforcement responsibility may exempt any public water system within the State's jurisdiction from any requirement respecting a maximum contaminant level or any treatment technique requirement, or from both, of an applicable national primary drinking water regulation upon a finding that—

(1) due to compelling factors (which may include economic factors), the public water system is unable to comply with such contaminant level or treatment technique requirement,

(2) the public water system was in operation on the effective date of such contaminant level or treatment technique requirement, or, for a system that was not in operation by that date, only if no reasonable alternative source of drinking water is available to such new system, and,

(3) the granting of the exemption will not result in an unreasonable risk to health.

(b) Compliance schedule and implementation of control measures; notice and hearing; dates for compliance with schedule; extension of final date for compliance; compliance, enforcement; approval or revision of schedules and revocation of exemptions

(1) If a State grants a public water system an exemption under subsection (a) of this section, the State shall prescribe, at the time the exemption is granted, a schedule for—

(A) compliance (including increments of progress) by the public water system with each contaminant level requirement and treatment technique requirement with respect to which the exemption was granted, and

(B) implementation by the public water system of such control measures as the State may require for each contaminant, subject to such contaminant level requirement or treatment technique requirement, during the period ending on the date compliance with such requirement is required.

Before a schedule prescribed by a State pursuant to this subsection may take effect, the State shall provide notice and opportunity for a public hearing on the schedule. A notice given pursuant to the preceding sentence may cover the prescribing of more than one such schedule and a hearing held pursuant to such notice shall include each of the schedules covered by the notice.

(2)(A) A schedule prescribed pursuant to this subsection for a public water system granted an exemption under subsection (a) of this section shall require compliance by the system with each contaminant level and treatment technique requirement with respect to which the exemption was granted as expeditiously as practicable (as the State may reasonably determine) but (except as provided in subparagraph (B))—

(i) in the case of an exemption granted with respect to a contaminant level or treatment technique requirement prescribed by the national primary drinking water regulations promulgated under section 300g–1(a) of this title, not later than 12 months after June 19, 1986; and

(ii) in the case of an exemption granted with respect to a contaminant level or treatment technique requirement prescribed by national primary drinking water regulations, other than a regulation referred to in section 300g–1(a) of this title, 12 months after the date of the issuance of the exemption.

(B) The final date for compliance provided in any schedule in the case of any exemption may be extended by the State (in the case of a State which has primary enforcement responsibility) or by the Administrator (in any other case) for a period not to exceed 3 years after the date of the issuance of the exemption if the public water system establishes that—

(i) the system cannot meet the standard without capital improvements which cannot be completed within the period of such exemption;

(ii) in the case of a system which needs financial assistance for the necessary improvements, the system has entered into an agreement to obtain such financial assistance; or

(iii) the system has entered into an enforceable agreement to become a part of a regional public water system; and

the system is taking all practicable steps to meet the standard.

(C) In the case of a system which does not serve more than 500 service connections and which needs financial assistance for the necessary improvements, an exemption granted under clause (i) or (ii) of subparagraph (B) may be renewed for one or more additional 2-year periods if the system establishes that it is taking all practicable steps to meet the requirements of subparagraph (B).

(3) Each public water system's exemption granted by a State under subsection (a) of this section shall be conditioned by the State upon compliance by the public water system with the schedule prescribed by the State pursuant to this subsection. The requirements of each schedule prescribed by a State pursuant to this subsection shall be enforceable by the State under its laws. Any requirement of a schedule on which an exemption granted under this section is conditioned may be enforced under section 300g–3 of this title as if such requirement was part of a national primary drinking water regulation.

(4) Each schedule prescribed by a State pursuant to this subsection shall be deemed approved by the Administrator unless the exemption for which it was prescribed is revoked by the Administrator under subsection (d)(2) of this section or the schedule is revised by the Administrator under such subsection.

(c) Notice to Administrator; reasons for exemption

Each State which grants an exemption under subsection (a) of this section shall promptly notify the Administrator of the granting of such exemption. Such notification shall contain the reasons for the exemption (including the basis for the finding required by subsection (a)(3) of this section before the exemption may be granted) and document the need for the exemption.

(d) Review of exemptions and schedules; publication in Federal Register, notice and results of review; notice to State; considerations respecting abuse of discretion in granting exemptions or failing to prescribe schedules; State corrective action

(1) Not later than 18 months after the effective date of the interim national primary drinking water regulations the Administrator shall complete a comprehensive review of the exemptions granted (and schedules prescribed pursuant thereto) by the States during the one-year period beginning on such effective date. The Administrator shall conduct such subsequent reviews of exemptions and schedules as he deems necessary to carry out the purposes of this subchapter, but each subsequent review shall be completed within each 3-year period following the completion of the first review under this subparagraph. Before conducting any review under this subparagraph, the Administrator shall publish notice of the proposed review in the Federal Register. Such notice shall (A) provide information respecting the location of data and other information respecting the exemptions to be reviewed (including data and other information concerning new scientific matters bearing on such exemptions), and (B) advise of the opportunity to submit comments on the exemptions reviewed and on the need for continuing them. Upon completion of any such review, the Administrator shall publish in the Federal Register the results of his review, together with findings responsive to comments submitted in connection with such review.

(2)(A) If the Administrator finds that a State has, in a substantial number of instances, abused its discretion in granting exemptions under subsection (a) of this section or failed to prescribe schedules in accordance with subsection (b) of this section, the Administrator shall notify the State of his findings. In determining if a State has abused its discretion in granting exemptions in a substantial number of instances, the Administrator shall consider the number of persons who are affected by the exemptions and if the requirements applicable to the granting of the exemptions were complied with. A notice under this subparagraph shall—

(i) identify each exempt public water system with respect to which the finding was made,

(ii) specify the reasons for the finding, and

(iii) as appropriate, propose revocations of specific exemptions or propose revised schedules for specific exempt public water systems, or both.

(B) The Administrator shall provide reasonable notice and public hearing on the provisions of each notice given pursuant to subparagraph (A). After a hearing on a notice pursuant to subparagraph (A), the Administrator shall (i) rescind the finding for which the notice was given and promptly notify the State of such rescission, or (ii) promulgate (with such modifications as he deems appropriate) such exemption revocations and revised schedules proposed in such notice as he deems appropriate. Not later than 180 days after the date a notice is given pursuant to subparagraph (A), the Administrator shall complete the hearing on the notice and take the action required by the preceding sentence.

(C) If a State is notified under subparagraph (A) of a finding of the Administrator made with respect to an exemption granted a public water system within that State or to a schedule prescribed pursuant to such an exemption and if before a revocation of such exemption or a revision of such schedule promulgated by the Administrator takes effect the State takes corrective action with respect to such exemption or schedule which the Administrator determines makes his finding inapplicable to such exemption or schedule, the Administrator shall rescind the application of his finding to that exemption or schedule. No exemption revocation or revised schedule may take effect before the expiration of 90 days following the date of the notice in which the revocation or revised schedule was proposed.

(e) "Treatment technique requirement" defined

For purposes of this section, the term "treatment technique requirement" means a requirement in a national primary drinking water regulation which specifies for a contaminant (in accordance with section 300f(1)(C)(ii) of this title) each treatment technique known to the Administrator which leads to a reduction in the level of such contaminant sufficient to satisfy the requirements of section 300g–1(b) of this title.

(f) Authority of Administrator in a State without primary enforcement responsibility

If a State does not have primary enforcement responsibility for public water systems, the Administrator shall have the same authority to exempt public water systems in such State from maximum contaminant level requirements and treatment technique requirements under the same conditions and in the same manner as the State would be authorized to grant exemptions under this section if it had primary enforcement responsibility.

(g) Applications for exemptions; regulations; reasonable time for acting

If an application for an exemption under this section is made, the State receiving the application or the Administrator, as the case may be, shall act upon such application within a reasonable period (as determined under regulations prescribed by the Administrator) after the date of its submission.

(July 1, 1944, c. 373, Title XIV, § 1416, as added Dec. 16, 1974, Pub.L. 93–523, § 2(a), 88 Stat. 1672, and amended Nov. 16, 1977, Pub.L. 95–190, § 10(a), 91 Stat. 1398; Dec. 5, 1980, Pub.L. 96–502, §§ 1, 4(b), 94 Stat. 2737, 2738; June 19, 1986, Pub.L. 99–339, Title I, §§ 101(c)(4), 105, 100 Stat. 646, 649.)

CODE OF FEDERAL REGULATIONS

Implementation and enforcement of national primary drinking water regulations, see 40 CFR 142.1 et seq.

LIBRARY REFERENCES

Waters and Water Courses ⚷202.
C.J.S. Waters § 280.

§ 300g–6. Prohibition on use of lead pipes, solder, or flux [PHSA § 1417]

(a) In general

(1) Prohibition

Any pipe, solder, or flux, which is used after June 19, 1986, in the installation or repair of—

(A) any public water system, or

(B) any plumbing in a residential or nonresidential facility providing water for human consumption which is connected to a public water system,

shall be lead free (within the meaning of subsection (d) of this section). This paragraph shall not apply to leaded joints necessary for the repair of cast iron pipes.

(2) Public notice requirements

(A) In general

Each public water system shall identify and provide notice to persons that may be affected by lead contamination of their drinking water where such contamination results from either or both of the following:

(i) The lead content in the construction materials of the public water distribution system.

(ii) Corrosivity of the water supply sufficient to cause leaching of lead.

The notice shall be provided in such manner and form as may be reasonably required by the Administrator. Notice under this paragraph shall be provided notwithstanding the absence of a violation of any national drinking water standard.

(B) Contents of notice

Notice under this paragraph shall provide a clear and readily understandable explanation of—

(i) the potential sources of lead in the drinking water,

(ii) potential adverse health effects,

(iii) reasonably available methods of mitigating known or potential lead content in drinking water,

(iv) any steps the system is taking to mitigate lead content in drinking water, and

(v) the necessity for seeking alternative water supplies, if any.

(b) State enforcement

(1) Enforcement of prohibition

The requirements of subsection (a)(1) of this section shall be enforced in all States effective 24 months after June 19, 1986. States shall enforce such requirements through State or local plumbing codes, or such other means of enforcement as the State may determine to be appropriate.

(2) Enforcement of public notice requirements

The requirements of subsection (a)(2) of this section shall apply in all States effective 24 months after June 19, 1986.

(c) Penalties

If the Administrator determines that a State is not enforcing the requirements of subsection (a) of this section as required pursuant to subsection (b) of this section, the Administrator may withhold up to 5 percent of Federal funds available to that State for State program grants under section 300j–2(a) of this title.

(d) "Lead free" defined

For purposes of this section, the term "lead free"—

(1) when used with respect to solders and flux refers to solders and flux containing not more than 0.2 percent lead, and

(2) when used with respect to pipes and pipe fittings refers to pipes and pipe fittings containing not more than 8.0 percent lead.

(July 1, 1944, c. 373, Title XIV, § 1417, as added June 19, 1986, Pub.L. 99–339, Title I, § 109(a)(1), 100 Stat. 651.)

PART C—PROTECTION OF UNDERGROUND SOURCES OF DRINKING WATER

LIBRARY REFERENCES

Waters and Water Courses ⚷196, 202.
C.J.S. Waters §§ 232 et seq., 280.

§ 300h. Regulations for State programs [PHSA § 1421]

(a) Publication of proposed regulations; promulgation; amendments; public hearings; administrative consultations

(1) The Administrator shall publish proposed regulations for State underground injection control programs within 180 days after December 16, 1974. Within 180 days after publication of such proposed regulations, he shall promulgate such regulations with such modifications as he deems appropriate. Any regulation under this subsection may be amended from time to time.

(2) Any regulation under this section shall be proposed and promulgated in accordance with section 553 of title 5 (relating to rulemaking), except that the Administrator shall provide opportunity for public hearing prior to promulgation of such regulations. In proposing and promulgating regulations under this section, the Administrator shall consult with the Secretary, the National Drinking Water Advisory Council, and other appropriate Federal entities and with interested State entities.

(b) Minimum requirements; restrictions

(1) Regulations under subsection (a) of this section for State underground injection programs shall contain minimum requirements for effective programs to prevent underground injection which endangers drinking water sources within the meaning of subsection (d)(2) of this section. Such regulations shall require that a State program, in order to be approved under section 300h–1 of this title—

(A) shall prohibit, effective on the date on which the applicable underground injection control program takes effect, any underground injection in such State which is not authorized by a permit issued by the State (except that the regulations may permit a State to authorize underground injection by rule);

(B) shall require (i) in the case of a program which provides for authorization of underground injection by permit, that the applicant for the permit to inject must satisfy the State that the underground injection will not endanger drinking water sources, and (ii) in the case of a program which provides for such an authorization by rule, that no rule may be promulgated which authorizes any underground injection which endangers drinking water sources;

(C) shall include inspection, monitoring, recordkeeping, and reporting requirements; and

(D) shall apply (i) as prescribed by section 300j–6(b) of this title, to underground injections by Federal agencies, and (ii) to underground injections by any other person whether or not occurring on property owned or leased by the United States.

(2) Regulations of the Administrator under this section for State underground injection control programs may not prescribe requirements which interfere with or impede—

(A) the underground injection of brine or other fluids which are brought to the surface in connection with oil or natural gas production or natural gas storage operations, or

(B) any underground injection for the secondary or tertiary recovery of oil or natural gas,

unless such requirements are essential to assure that underground sources of drinking water will not be endangered by such injection.

(3)(A) The regulations of the Administrator under this section shall permit or provide for consideration of varying geologic, hydrological, or historical conditions in different States and in different areas within a State.

(B)(i) In prescribing regulations under this section the Administrator shall, to the extent feasible, avoid promulgation of requirements which would unnecessarily disrupt State underground injection control programs which are in effect and being enforced in a substantial number or[1] States.

(ii) For the purpose of this subparagraph, a regulation prescribed by the Administrator under this section shall be deemed to disrupt a State underground injection control program only if it would be infeasible to comply with both such regulation and the State underground injection control program.

(iii) For the purpose of this subparagraph, a regulation prescribed by the Administrator under this section shall be deemed unnecessary only if, without such regulation, underground sources of drinking water will not be endangered by an underground injection.

(C) Nothing in this section shall be construed to alter or affect the duty to assure that underground sources of drinking water will not be endangered by any underground injection.

(c) Temporary permits; notice and hearing

(1) The Administrator may, upon application of the Governor of a State which authorizes underground injection by means of permits, authorize such State to issue (without regard to subsection (b)(1)(B)(i) of this section) temporary permits for underground injection which may be effective until the expiration of four years after December 16, 1974, if—

(A) the Administrator finds that the State has demonstrated that it is unable and could not reasonably have been able to process all permit applications within the time available;

(B) the Administrator determines the adverse effect on the environment of such temporary permits is not unwarranted;

(C) such temporary permits will be issued only with respect to injection wells in operation on the date on which such State's permit program approved under this part first takes effect and for which there was inadequate time to process its permit application; and

(D) the Administrator determines the temporary permits require the use of adequate safeguards established by rules adopted by him.

(2) The Administrator may, upon application of the Governor of a State which authorizes underground injection by means of permits, authorize such State to issue (without regard to subsection (b)(1)(B)(i) of this section), but after reasonable notice and hearing, one or more temporary permits each of which is applicable to a particular injection well and to the underground injection of a particular fluid and which may be effective until the expiration of four years after December 16, 1974, if the State finds, on the record of such hearing—

(A) that technology (or other means) to permit safe injection of the fluid in accordance with the applicable underground injection control program is not generally available (taking costs into consideration);

(B) that injection of the fluid would be less harmful to health than the use of other available means of disposing of waste or producing the desired product; and

(C) that available technology or other means have been employed (and will be employed) to reduce the volume and toxicity of the fluid and to minimize the potentially adverse effect of the injection on the public health.

(d) "Underground injection" defined; underground injection endangerment of drinking water sources

For purposes of this part:

(1) The term "underground injection" means the subsurface emplacement of fluids by well injection. Such term does not include the underground injection of natural gas for purposes of storage.

(2) Underground injection endangers drinking water sources if such injection may result in the presence in underground water which supplies or can reasonably be expected to supply any public water system of any contaminant, and if the presence of such contaminant may result in such system's not complying with any national primary drinking water regulation or may otherwise adversely affect the health of persons.

(July 1, 1944, c. 373, Title XIV, § 1421, as added Dec. 16, 1974, Pub.L. 93–523, § 2(a), 88 Stat. 1674, and amended Nov. 16, 1977, Pub.L. 95–190, § 6(b), 91 Stat. 1396; Dec. 5, 1980, Pub.L. 96–502, §§ 3, 4(c), 94 Stat. 2738; June 19, 1986, Pub.L. 99–339, Title II, § 201(a), 100 Stat. 653.)

1 So in original. Probably should read "of".

CODE OF FEDERAL REGULATIONS

Environmental Protection Agency,
  Administration of permit programs, see 40 CFR 122.1 et seq.
  Decisionmaking procedures applicable to permit programs, see 40 CFR 124.1 et seq.
Underground injection control program, see 40 CFR 144.1.
  Technical criteria and standards for, see 40 CFR 146.1 et seq.

LIBRARY REFERENCES

Waters and Water Courses ⚷64.
C.J.S. Waters § 43 et seq.

§ 300h–1. State primary enforcement responsibility [PHSA § 1422]

(a) List of States in need of control program; amendment of list

Within 180 days after December 16, 1974, the Administrator shall list in the Federal Register each State for which in his judgment a State underground injection control program may be necessary to assure that underground injection will not endanger drinking water sources. Such list may be amended from time to time.

(b) State applications; notice to Administrator of compliance with revised or added requirements; approval or disapproval by Administrator; duration of State primary enforcement responsibility; public hearing

(1)(A) Each State listed under subsection (a) of this section shall within 270 days after the date of promulgation of any regulation under section 300h of this title (or, if later, within 270 days after such State is first listed under subsection (a) of this section) submit to the Administrator an application which contains a showing satisfactory to the Administrator that the State—

(i) has adopted after reasonable notice and public hearings, and will implement, an underground injection control program which meets the requirements of regulations in effect under section 300h of this title; and

(ii) will keep such records and make such reports with respect to its activities under its underground injection control program as the Administrator may require by regulation.

The Administrator may, for good cause, extend the date for submission of an application by any State under this subparagraph for a period not to exceed an additional 270 days.

(B) Within 270 days of any amendment of a regulation under section 300h of this title revising or adding any requirement respecting State underground injection control programs, each State listed under subsection (a) of this section shall submit (in such form and manner as the Administrator may require) a notice to the Administrator containing a showing satisfactory to him that the State underground injection control program meets the revised or added requirement.

(2) Within ninety days after the State's application under paragraph (1)(A) or notice under paragraph (1)(B) and after reasonable opportunity for presentation of views, the Administrator shall by rule either approve, disapprove, or approve in part and disapprove in part, the State's underground injection control program.

(3) If the Administrator approves the State's program under paragraph (2), the State shall have primary enforcement responsibility for underground water sources until such time as the Administrator determines, by rule, that such State no longer meets the requirements of clause (i) or (ii) of paragraph (1)(A) of this subsection.

(4) Before promulgating any rule under paragraph (2) or (3) of this subsection, the Administrator shall provide opportunity for public hearing respecting such rule.

(c) Program by Administrator for State without primary enforcement responsibility; restrictions

If the Administrator disapproves a State's program (or part thereof) under subsection (b)(2) of this section, if the Administrator determines under subsection (b)(3) of this section that a State no longer meets the requirements of clause (i) or (ii) of subsection (b)(1)(A) of this section, or if a State fails to submit an application or notice before the date of expiration of the period specified in subsection (b)(1) of this section, the Administrator shall by regulation within 90 days after the date of such disapproval, determination, or expiration (as the case may be) prescribe (and may from time to time by regulation revise) a program applicable to such State meeting the requirements of section 300h(b) of this title. Such program may not include requirements which interfere with or impede—

(1) the underground injection of brine or other fluids which are brought to the surface in connection with oil or natural gas production or natural gas storage operations, or

(2) any underground injection for the secondary or tertiary recovery of oil or natural gas,

unless such requirements are essential to assure that underground sources of drinking water will not be endangered by such injection. Such program shall apply in such State to the extent that a program adopted by such State which the Administrator determines meets such requirements is not in effect. Before promulgating any regulation under this section, the Administrator shall provide opportunity for public hearing respecting such regulation.

(d) "Applicable underground injection control program" defined

For purposes of this subchapter, the term "applicable underground injection control program" with respect to a State means the program (or most recent amendment thereof) (1) which has been adopted by the State and which has been approved under subsection (b) of this section, or (2) which has been prescribed by the Administrator under subsection (c) of this section.

(e) Primary enforcement responsibility by Indian Tribe

An Indian Tribe may assume primary enforcement responsibility for underground injection control under this section consistent with such regulations as the Administrator has prescribed pursuant to this part and section 300j–11 of this title. The area over which such Indian Tribe exercises governmental jurisdiction need not have been listed under subsection (a) of this section, and such Tribe need not submit an application to assume primary enforcement responsibility within the 270-day deadline noted in subsection (b)(1)(A) of this section. Until an Indian Tribe assumes primary enforcement responsibility, the currently applicable underground injection control program shall continue to apply. If an applicable underground injection control program does not exist for an Indian Tribe, the Administrator shall prescribe such a program pursuant to subsection (c) of this section, and consistent with section 300h(b) of this title, within 270 days after June 19, 1986, unless an Indian Tribe first obtains approval to assume primary enforcement responsibility for underground injection control.

(July 1, 1944, c. 373, Title XIV, § 1422, as added Dec. 16, 1974, Pub.L. 93–523, § 2(a), 88 Stat. 1676, and amended Nov. 16, 1977, Pub.L. 95–190, § 6(a), 91 Stat. 1396; June 19, 1986, Pub.L. 99–339, Title II, § 201(a), Title III, § 302(c), 100 Stat. 653, 666.)

CODE OF FEDERAL REGULATIONS

Environmental Protection Agency,
 Administration of permit programs, see 40 CFR 122.1 et seq.
 Decisionmaking procedures applicable to permit programs, see 40 CFR 124.1 et seq.
Underground injection control programs,
 Additional requirements respecting, see 40 CFR 123.41 et seq.
 Technical criteria and standards for, see 40 CFR 146.1 et seq.

LIBRARY REFERENCES

States ⚿4.10.
C.J.S. States § 24.

§ 300h–2. Enforcement of program [PHSA § 1423]

(a) Notice to State and violator; issuance of administrative order; civil action

(1) Whenever the Administrator finds during a period during which a State has primary enforcement responsibility for underground water sources (within the meaning of section 300h–1(b)(3) of this title or section 300h–4(c) of this title) that any person who is subject to a requirement of an applicable underground injection control program in such State is violating such requirement, he shall so notify the State and the person violating such requirement. If beyond the thirtieth day after the Administrator's notification the State has not commenced appropriate enforcement action, the Administrator shall issue an order under subsection (c) of this section requiring the person to comply with such requirement or the Administrator shall commence a civil action under subsection (b) of this section.

(2) Whenever the Administrator finds during a period during which a State does not have primary enforcement responsibility for underground water sources that any person subject to any requirement of any applicable underground injection control program in such State is violating such requirement, the Administrator shall issue an order under subsection (c) of this section requiring the person to comply with such requirement or the Administrator shall commence a civil action under subsection (b) of this section.

(b) Civil and criminal actions

Civil actions referred to in paragraphs (1) and (2) of subsection (a) of this section shall be brought in the appropriate United States district court. Such court shall have jurisdiction to require compliance with any requirement of an applicable underground injection program or with an order issued under subsection (c) of this section. The court may enter such judgment as protection of public health may require. Any person who violates any requirement of an applicable underground injection control program or an order requiring compliance under subsection (c) of this section—

(1) shall be subject to a civil penalty of not more than $25,000 for each day of such violation, and

(2) if such violation is willful, such person may, in addition to or in lieu of the civil penalty authorized by paragraph (1), be imprisoned for not more than 3 years, or fined in accordance with Title 18, or both.

(c) Administrative orders

(1) In any case in which the Administrator is authorized to bring a civil action under this section with respect to any regulation or other requirement of this part other than those relating to—

(A) the underground injection of brine or other fluids which are brought to the surface in connection with oil or natural gas production, or

(B) any underground injection for the secondary or tertiary recovery of oil or natural gas,

the Administrator may also issue an order under this subsection either assessing a civil penalty of not more than $10,000 for each day of violation for any past or current violation, up to a maximum administrative penalty of $125,000, or requiring compliance with such regulation or other requirement, or both.

(2) In any case in which the Administrator is authorized to bring a civil action under this section with respect to any regulation, or other requirement of this part relating to—

(A) the underground injection of brine or other fluids which are brought to the surface in connection with oil or natural gas production, or

(B) any underground injection for the secondary or tertiary recovery of oil or natural gas,

the Administrator may also issue an order under this subsection either assessing a civil penalty of not more than $5,000 for each day of violation for any past or current violation, up to a maximum administrative penalty of $125,000, or requiring compliance with such regulation or other requirement, or both.

(3)(A) An order under this subsection shall be issued by the Administrator after opportunity (provided in accordance with this subparagraph) for a hearing. Before issuing the order, the Administrator shall give to the person to whom it is directed written notice of the Administrator's proposal to issue such order and the opportunity to request, within 30 days of the date the notice is received by such person, a hearing on the order. Such hearing shall not be subject to section 554 or 556 of Title 5 but shall provide a reasonable opportunity to be heard and to present evidence.

(B) The Administrator shall provide public notice of, and reasonable opportunity to comment on, any proposed order.

(C) Any citizen who comments on any proposed order under subparagraph (B) shall be given notice of any hearing under this subsection and of any order. In any hearing held under subparagraph (A), such citizen shall have a reasonable opportunity to be heard and to present evidence.

(D) Any order issued under this subsection shall become effective 30 days following its issuance unless an appeal is taken pursuant to paragraph (6).

(4)(A) Any order issued under this subsection shall state with reasonable specificity the nature of the violation and may specify a reasonable time for compliance.

(B) In assessing any civil penalty under this subsection, the Administrator shall take into account appropriate factors, including (i) the seriousness of the violation; (ii) the economic benefit (if any) resulting from the violation; (iii) any history of such violations; (iv) any good-faith efforts to comply with the applicable requirements; (v) the economic impact of the penalty on the violator; and (vi) such other matters as justice may require.

(5) Any violation with respect to which the Administrator has commenced and is diligently prosecuting an action, or has issued an order under this subsection assessing a penalty, shall not be subject to an action under subsection (b) of this section or section 300h-3(c) or 300j-8 of this title, except that the foregoing limitation on civil actions under section 300j-8 of this title shall not apply with respect to any violation for which—

(A) a civil action under section 300j-8(a)(1) of this title has been filed prior to commencement of an action under this subsection, or

(B) a notice of violation under section 300j-8(b)(1) of this title has been given before commencement of an action under this subsection and an action under section 300j-8(a)(1) of this title is filed before 120 days after such notice is given.

(6) Any person against whom an order is issued or who commented on a proposed order pursuant to paragraph (3) may file an appeal of such order with the United States District Court for the District of Columbia or the district in which the violation is alleged to have occurred. Such an appeal may only be filed within the 30-day period beginning on the date the order is issued. Appellant shall simultaneously send a copy of the appeal by certified mail to the Administrator and to the Attorney General. The Administrator shall promptly file in such court a certified copy of the record on which such order was imposed. The district court shall not set aside or remand such order unless there is not substantial evidence on the record, taken as a whole, to support the finding of a violation or, unless the Administrator's assessment of penalty or requirement for compliance constitutes an abuse of discretion. The district court shall not impose additional civil penalties for the same violation unless the Administrator's assessment of a penalty constitutes an abuse of discretion. Notwithstanding section 300j-7(a)(2) of this title, any order issued under paragraph (3) shall be subject to judicial review exclusively under this paragraph.

(7) If any person fails to pay an assessment of a civil penalty—

(A) after the order becomes effective under paragraph (3), or

(B) after a court, in an action brought under paragraph (6), has entered a final judgment in favor of the Administrator,

the Administrator may request the Attorney General to bring a civil action in an appropriate district court to recover the amount assessed (plus costs, attorneys' fees, and interest at currently prevailing rates from the date the order is effective or the date of such final judgment, as the case may be). In such an action, the validity, amount, and appropriateness of such penalty shall not be subject to review.

(8) The Administrator may, in connection with administrative proceedings under this subsection, issue subpoenas compelling the attendance and testimony of witnesses and subpoenas duces tecum, and may request the Attorney General to bring an action to enforce any subpoena under this section. The district courts shall have jurisdiction to enforce such subpoenas and impose sanction.

(d) State authority to adopt or enforce laws or regulations respecting underground injection unaffected

Nothing in this subchapter shall diminish any authority of a State or political subdivision to adopt or enforce any law or regulation respecting underground injection but no such law or regulation shall relieve any person of any requirement otherwise applicable under this subchapter.

(July 1, 1944, c. 373, Title XIV, § 1423, as added Dec. 16, 1974, Pub.L. 93-523, § 2(a), 88 Stat. 1677, and amended Dec. 5, 1980, Pub.L. 96-502, § 2(b), 94 Stat. 2738; June 19, 1986, Pub.L. 99-339, Title II, § 202, 100 Stat. 654.)

CODE OF FEDERAL REGULATIONS

Environmental Protection Agency,
Administration of permit programs, see 40 CFR 122.1 et seq.
Decisionmaking procedures applicable to permit programs, see 40 CFR 124.1 et seq.
Requirements, see 40 CFR 145.1.
Underground injection control programs, technical criteria and standards for, see 40 CFR 146.1 et seq.

LAW REVIEW COMMENTARIES

Survey of federal and state environmental crime legislation. Edward F. Novak and Charles W. Steese, 34 Ariz.L.Rev. 571 (1992).

§ 300h–3. Interim regulation of underground injections [PHSA § 1424]

(a) Necessity for well operation permit; designation of one aquifer areas

(1) Any person may petition the Administrator to have an area of a State (or States) designated as an area in which no new underground injection well may be operated during the period beginning on the date of the designation and ending on the date on which the applicable underground injection control program covering such area takes effect unless a permit for the operation of such well has been issued by the Administrator under subsection (b) of this section. The Administrator may so designate an area within a State if he finds that the area has one aquifer which is the sole or principal drinking water source for the area and which, if contaminated, would create a significant hazard to public health.

(2) Upon receipt of a petition under paragraph (1) of this subsection, the Administrator shall publish it in the Federal Register and shall provide an opportunity to interested persons to submit written data, views, or arguments thereon. Not later than the 30th day following the date of the publication of a petition under this paragraph in the Federal Register, the Administrator shall either make the designation for which the petition is submitted or deny the petition.

(b) Well operation permits; publication in Federal Register; notice and hearing; issuance or denial; conditions for issuance

(1) During the period beginning on the date an area is designated under subsection (a) of this section and ending on the date the applicable underground injection control program covering such area takes effect, no new underground injection well may be operated in such area unless the Administrator has issued a permit for such operation.

(2) Any person may petition the Administrator for the issuance of a permit for the operation of such a well in such an area. A petition submitted under this paragraph shall be submitted in such manner and contain such information as the Administrator may require by regulation. Upon receipt of such a petition, the Administrator shall publish it in the Federal Register. The Administrator shall give notice of any proceeding on a petition and shall provide opportunity for agency hearing. The Administrator shall act upon such petition on the record of any hearing held pursuant to the preceding sentence respecting such petition. Within 120 days of the publication in the Federal Register of a petition submitted under this paragraph, the Administrator shall either issue the permit for which the petition was submitted or shall deny its issuance.

(3) The Administrator may issue a permit for the operation of a new underground injection well in an area designated under subsection (a) of this section only if he finds that the operation of such well will not cause contamination of the aquifer of such area so as to create a significant hazard to public health. The Administrator may condition the issuance of such a permit upon the use of such control measures in connection with the operation of such well, for which the permit is to be issued, as he deems necessary to assure that the operation of the well will not contaminate the aquifer of the designated area in which the well is located so as to create a significant hazard to public health.

(c) Civil penalties; separate violations; penalties for willful violations; temporary restraining order or injunction

Any person who operates a new underground injection well in violation of subsection (b) of this section, (1) shall be subject to a civil penalty of not more than $5,000 for each day in which such violation occurs, or (2) if such violation is willful, such person may, in lieu of the civil penalty authorized by clause (1), be fined not more than $10,000 for each day in which such violation occurs. If the Administrator has reason to believe that any person is violating or will violate subsection (b) of this section, he may petition the United States district court to issue a temporary restraining order or injunction (including a mandatory injunction) to enforce such subsection.

(d) "New underground injection well" defined

For purposes of this section, the term "new underground injection well" means an underground injection well whose operation was not approved by appropriate State and Federal agencies before December 16, 1974.

(e) Areas with one aquifer; publication in Federal Register; commitments for Federal financial assistance

If the Administrator determines, on his own initiative or upon petition, that an area has an aquifer which is the sole or principal drinking water source for the area and which, if contaminated, would create a significant hazard to public health, he shall publish notice of that determination in the Federal Register. After the publication of any such notice, no commitment for Federal financial assistance (through a grant, contract, loan guarantee, or otherwise) may be entered into for any project which the Administrator determines may contaminate such aquifer through a recharge zone so as to create a significant hazard to public health, but a commitment for Federal financial assistance may, if authorized under another provision of law, be entered into to plan or design the project to assure that it will not so contaminate the aquifer.

(July 1, 1944, c. 373, Title XIV, § 1424, as added Dec. 16, 1974, Pub. L. 93–523, § 2(a), 88 Stat. 1678.)

CODE OF FEDERAL REGULATIONS

Review of projects affecting the Edwards Underground Reservoir, see 40 CFR 149.1 et seq.

LIBRARY REFERENCES

Health and Environment ⟹25.7(13).
C.J.S. Health and Environment § 107 et seq.

§ 300h–4. Optional demonstration by States relating to oil or natural gas [PHSA § 1425]

(a) Approval of State underground injection control program; alternative showing of effectiveness of program by State

For purposes of the Administrator's approval or disapproval under section 300h–1 of this title of that portion of any State underground injection control program which relates to—

(1) the underground injection of brine or other fluids which are brought to the surface in connection with oil or natural gas production or natural gas storage operations, or

(2) any underground injection for the secondary or tertiary recovery of oil or natural gas,

in lieu of the showing required under subparagraph (A) of section 300h–1(b)(1) of this title the State may demonstrate that such portion of the State program meets the requirements of subparagraphs (A) through (D) of section 300h(b)(1) of this title and represents an effective program (including adequate recordkeeping and reporting) to prevent underground injection which endangers drinking water sources.

(b) Revision or amendment of requirements of regulation; showing of effectiveness of program by State

If the Administrator revises or amends any requirement of a regulation under section 300h of this title relating to any aspect of the underground injection referred to in subsection (a) of this section, in the case of that portion of a State underground injection control program for which the demonstration referred to in subsection (a) of this section has been made, in lieu of the showing required under section 300h–1(b)(1)(B) of this title the State may demonstrate that, with respect to that aspect of such underground injection, the State program meets the requirements of subparagraphs (A) through (D) of section 300h(b)(1) of this title and represents an effective program (including adequate recordkeeping and reporting) to prevent underground injection which endangers drinking water sources.

(c) Primary enforcement responsibility of State; voiding by Administrator under duly promulgated rule

(1) Section 300h–1(b)(3) of this title shall not apply to that portion of any State underground injection control program approved by the Administrator pursuant to a demonstration under subsection (a) of this section (and under subsection (b) of this section where applicable).

(2) If pursuant to such a demonstration, the Administrator approves such portion of the State program, the State shall have primary enforcement responsibility with respect to that portion until such time as the Administrator determines, by rule, that such demonstration is no longer valid. Following such a determination, the Administrator may exercise the authority of subsection (c) of section 300h–1 of this title in the same manner as provided in such subsection with respect to a determination described in such subsection.

(3) Before promulgating any rule under paragraph (2), the Administrator shall provide opportunity for public hearing respecting such rule.

(July 1, 1944, c. 373, Title XIV, § 1425, as added Dec. 5, 1980, Pub.L. 96–502, § 2(a), 94 Stat. 2737, and amended June 19, 1986, Pub.L. 99–339, Title II, § 201(a), 100 Stat. 653.)

LIBRARY REFERENCES

Waters and Water Courses ⟹196, 202.
C.J.S. Waters §§ 232 et seq., 280.

§ 300h–5. Regulation of State programs [PHSA § 1426]

Not later than 18 months after June 19, 1986, the Administrator shall modify regulations issued under this chapter for Class I injection wells to identify monitoring methods, in addition to those in effect on November 1, 1985, including groundwater monitoring. In accordance with such regulations, the Administrator, or delegated State authority, shall determine the applicability of such monitoring methods, wherever appropriate, at locations and in such a manner as to provide the earliest possible detection of fluid migration into, or in the direction of, underground sources of drinking water from such wells, based on its assessment of the potential for fluid migration from the injection zone that may be harmful to human health or the environment. For purposes of this subsection, a class I injection well is defined in accordance with 40 CFR 146.05 as in effect on November 1, 1985.

(July 1, 1944, c. 373, Title XIV, § 1426, as added June 19, 1986, Pub.L. 99–339, Title II, § 201(b), 100 Stat. 653, and amended Dec. 21, 1995, Pub.L. 104–66, Title II, § 2021(f), 109 Stat. 727.)

§ 300h–6. Sole source aquifer demonstration program [PHSA § 1427]

(a) Purpose

The purpose of this section is to establish procedures for development, implementation, and assessment of demonstration programs designed to protect critical aquifer protection areas located within areas designated as sole or principal source aquifers under section 300h–3(e) of this title.

(b) "Critical aquifer protection area" defined

For purposes of this section, the term "critical aquifer protection area" means either of the following:

(1) All or part of an area located within an area for which an application or designation as a sole or principal source aquifer pursuant to section 300h–3(e) of this title, has been submitted and approved by the Administrator not later than 24 months after June 19, 1986, and which satisfies the criteria established by the Administrator under subsection (d) of this section.

(2) All or part of an area which is within an aquifer designated as a sole source aquifer as of June 19, 1986, and for which an areawide ground water quality protection plan has been approved under section 208 of the Clean Water Act [33 U.S.C.A. § 1288] prior to June 19, 1986.

(c) Application

Any State, municipal or local government or political subdivision thereof or any planning entity (including any interstate regional planning entity) that identifies a critical aquifer protection area over which it has authority or jurisdiction may apply to the Administrator for the selection of such area for a demonstration program under this section. Any applicant shall consult with other government or planning entities with authority or jurisdiction in such area prior to application. Applicants, other than the Governor, shall submit the application for a demonstration program jointly with the Governor.

(d) Criteria

Not later than 1 year after June 19, 1986, the Administrator shall, by rule, establish criteria for identifying critical aquifer protection areas under this section. In establishing such criteria, the Administrator shall consider each of the following:

(1) The vulnerability of the aquifer to contamination due to hydrogeologic characteristics.

(2) The number of persons or the proportion of population using the ground water as a drinking water source.

(3) The economic, social and environmental benefits that would result to the area from maintenance of ground water of high quality.

(4) The economic, social and environmental costs that would result from degradation of the quality of the ground water.

(e) Contents of application

An application submitted to the Administrator by any applicant for a demonstration program under this section shall meet each of the following requirements:

(1) The application shall propose boundaries for the critical aquifer protection area within its jurisdiction.

(2) The application shall designate or, if necessary, establish a planning entity (which shall be a public agency and which shall include representation of elected local and State governmental officials) to develop a comprehensive management plan (hereinafter in this section referred to as the "plan") for the critical protection area. Where a local government planning agency exists with adequate authority to carry out this section with respect to any proposed critical protection area, such agency shall be designated as the planning entity.

(3) The application shall establish procedures for public participation in the development of the plan, for review, approval, and adoption of the plan, and for assistance to municipalities and other public agencies with authority under State law to implement the plan.

(4) The application shall include a hydrogeologic assessment of surface and ground water resources within the critical protection area.

(5) The application shall include a comprehensive management plan for the proposed protection area.

(6) The application shall include the measures and schedule proposed for implementation of such plan.

(f) Comprehensive plan

(1) The objective of a comprehensive management plan submitted by an applicant under this section shall

be to maintain the quality of the ground water in the critical protection area in a manner reasonably expected to protect human health, the environment and ground water resources. In order to achieve such objective, the plan may be designed to maintain, to the maximum extent possible, the natural vegetative and hydrogeological conditions. Each of the following elements shall be included in such a protection plan:

(A) A map showing the detailed boundary of the critical protection area.

(B) An identification of existing and potential point and nonpoint sources of ground water degradation.

(C) An assessment of the relationship between activities on the land surface and ground water quality.

(D) Specific actions and management practices to be implemented in the critical protection area to prevent adverse impacts on ground water quality.

(E) Identification of authority adequate to implement the plan, estimates of program costs, and sources of State matching funds.

(2) Such plan may also include the following:

(A) A determination of the quality of the existing ground water recharged through the special protection area and the natural recharge capabilities of the special protection area watershed.

(B) Requirements designed to maintain existing underground drinking water quality or improve underground drinking water quality if prevailing conditions fail to meet drinking water standards, pursuant to this chapter and State law.

(C) Limits on Federal, State, and local government, financially assisted activities and projects which may contribute to degradation of such ground water or any loss of natural surface and subsurface infiltration of purification capability of the special protection watershed.

(D) A comprehensive statement of land use management including emergency contingency planning as it pertains to the maintenance of the quality of underground sources of drinking water or to the improvement of such sources if necessary to meet drinking water standards pursuant to this chapter and State law.

(E) Actions in the special protection area which would avoid adverse impacts on water quality, recharge capabilities, or both.

(F) Consideration of specific techniques, which may include clustering, transfer of development rights, and other innovative measures sufficient to achieve the objectives of this section.

(G) Consideration of the establishment of a State institution to facilitate and assist funding a development transfer credit system.

(H) A program for State and local implementation of the plan described in this subsection in a manner that will insure the continued, uniform, consistent protection of the critical protection area in accord with the purposes of this section.

(I) Pollution abatement measures, if appropriate.

(g) Plans under section 208 of the Clean Water Act

A plan approved before June 19, 1986, under section 208 of the Clean Water Act [33 U.S.C.A. § 1288] to protect a sole source aquifer designated under section 300h–3(e) of this title shall be considered a comprehensive management plan for the purposes of this section.

(h) Consultation and hearings

During the development of a comprehensive management plan under this section, the planning entity shall consult with, and consider the comments of, appropriate officials of any municipality and State or Federal agency which has jurisdiction over lands and waters within the special protection area, other concerned organizations and technical and citizen advisory committees. The planning entity shall conduct public hearings at places within the special protection area for the purpose of providing the opportunity to comment on any aspect of the plan.

(i) Approval or disapproval

Within 120 days after receipt of an application under this section, the Administrator shall approve or disapprove the application. The approval or disapproval shall be based on a determination that the critical protection area satisfies the criteria established under subsection (d) of this section and that a demonstration program for the area would provide protection for ground water quality consistent with the objectives stated in subsection (f) of this section. The Administrator shall provide to the Governor a written explanation of the reasons for the disapproval of any such application. Any petitioner may modify and resubmit any application which is not approved. Upon approval of an application, the Administrator may enter into a cooperative agreement with the applicant to establish a demonstration program under this section.

(j) Grants and reimbursement

Upon entering a cooperative agreement under subsection (i) of this section, the Administrator may provide to the applicant, on a matching basis, a grant of 50 per centum of the costs of implementing the plan established under this section. The Administrator may also reimburse the applicant of an approved plan up to 50 per centum of the costs of developing such plan, except for plans approved under section 208 of the Clean Water Act [33 U.S.C.A. § 1288]. The total amount of grants under this section for any one aquifer, designated under section 300h-3(e) of this title, shall not exceed $4,000,000 in any one fiscal year.

(k) Activities funded under other law

No funds authorized under this subsection[1] may be used to fund activities funded under other sections of this chapter or the Clean Water Act [33 U.S.C.A. § 1251 et seq.], the Solid Waste Disposal Act [42 U.S.C.A. § 6901 et seq.], the Comprehensive Environmental Response, Compensation, and Liability Act of 1980 [42 U.S.C.A. § 9601 et seq.] or other environmental laws.

(*l*) Savings provision

Nothing under this section shall be construed to amend, supersede or abrogate rights to quantities of water which have been established by interstate water compacts, Supreme Court decrees, or State water laws; or any requirement imposed or right provided under any Federal or State environmental or public health statute.

(m) Authorization of appropriations

There are authorized to be appropriated to carry out this section not more than the following amounts:

Fiscal year:	*Amount*
1987	$10,000,000
1988	15,000,000
1989	17,500,000
1990	17,500,000
1991	17,500,000

Matching grants under this section may also be used to implement or update any water quality management plan for a sole or principal source aquifer approved (before June 19, 1986) by the Administrator under section 208 of the Federal Water Pollution Control Act [33 U.S.C.A. § 1288].

(July 1, 1986, c. 373, Title XIV, § 1427, as added June 19, 1986, Pub.L. 99-339, Title II, § 203, 100 Stat. 657, and amended June 19, 1986, Pub.L. 99-339, Title III, § 301(f), 100 Stat. 664; Dec. 21, 1995, Pub.L. 104-66, Title II, § 2021(g), 109 Stat. 727.)

1 So in original. Probably should be "section".

§ 300h-7. State programs to establish wellhead protection areas [PHSA § 1428]

(a) State programs

The Governor or Governor's designee of each State shall, within 3 years of June 19, 1986, adopt and submit to the Administrator a State program to protect wellhead areas within their jurisdiction from contaminants which may have any adverse effect on the health of persons. Each State program under this section shall, at a minimum—

(1) specify the duties of State agencies, local governmental entities, and public water supply systems with respect to the development and implementation of programs required by this section;

(2) for each wellhead, determine the wellhead protection area as defined in subsection (e) of this section based on all reasonably available hydrogeologic information on ground water flow, recharge and discharge and other information the State deems necessary to adequately determine the wellhead protection area;

(3) identify within each wellhead protection area all potential anthropogenic sources of contaminants which may have any adverse effect on the health of persons;

(4) describe a program that contains, as appropriate, technical assistance, financial assistance, implementation of control measures, education, training, and demonstration projects to protect the water supply within wellhead protection areas from such contaminants;

(5) include contingency plans for the location and provision of alternate drinking water supplies for each public water system in the event of well or wellfield contamination by such contaminants; and

(6) include a requirement that consideration be given to all potential sources of such contaminants within the expected wellhead area of a new water well which serves a public water supply system.

(b) Public participation

To the maximum extent possible, each State shall establish procedures, including but not limited to the establishment of technical and citizens' advisory committees, to encourage the public to participate in developing the protection program for wellhead areas. Such procedures shall include notice and opportunity for public hearing on the State program before it is submitted to the Administrator.

(c) Disapproval

(1) In general

If, in the judgment of the Administrator, a State program (or portion thereof, including the definition of a wellhead protection area), is not adequate to protect public water systems as required by this section, the Administrator shall disapprove such program (or portion thereof). A State program developed pursuant to subsection (a) of this section shall be deemed to be adequate unless the Administrator determines, within 9 months of the receipt of a State program, that such program (or portion thereof) is inadequate for the purpose of protecting public water systems as required by this section from contaminants that may have any adverse effect on the health of persons. If the Administrator determines that a proposed State program (or any portion thereof) is inadequate, the Administrator shall submit a written statement of the reasons for such determination to the Governor of the State.

(2) Modification and resubmission

Within 6 months after receipt of the Administrator's written notice under paragraph (1) that any proposed State program (or portion thereof) is inadequate, the Governor or Governor's designee, shall modify the program based upon the recommendations of the Administrator and resubmit the modified program to the Administrator.

(d) Federal assistance

After the date 3 years after June 19, 1986, no State shall receive funds authorized to be appropriated under this section except for the purpose of implementing the program and requirements of paragraphs (4) and (6) of subsection (a) of this section.

(e) "Wellhead protection area" defined

As used in this section, the term "wellhead protection area" means the surface and subsurface area surrounding a water well or wellfield, supplying a public water system, through which contaminants are reasonably likely to move toward and reach such water well or wellfield. The extent of a wellhead protection area, within a State, necessary to provide protection from contaminants which may have any adverse effect on the health of persons is to be determined by the State in the program submitted under subsection (a) of this section. Not later than one year after June 19, 1986, the Administrator shall issue technical guidance which States may use in making such determinations. Such guidance may reflect such factors as the radius of influence around a well or wellfield, the depth of drawdown of the water table by such well or wellfield at any given point, the time or rate of travel of various contaminants in various hydrologic conditions, distance from the well or wellfield, or other factors affecting the likelihood of contaminants reaching the well or wellfield, taking into account available engineering pump tests or comparable data, field reconnaissance, topographic information, and the geology of the formation in which the well or wellfield is located.

(f) Prohibitions

(1) Activities under other laws

No funds authorized to be appropriated under this section may be used to support activities authorized by the Federal Water Pollution Control Act [33 U.S.C.A. § 1251 et seq.], the Solid Waste Disposal Act [42 U.S.C.A. § 6901 et seq.], the Comprehensive Environmental Response, Compensation, and Liability Act of 1980 [42 U.S.C.A. § 9601 et seq.], or other sections of this chapter.

(2) Individual sources

No funds authorized to be appropriated under this section may be used to bring individual sources of contamination into compliance.

(g) Implementation

Each State shall make every reasonable effort to implement the State wellhead area protection program under this section within 2 years of submitting the program to the Administrator. Each State shall submit to the Administrator a biennial status report describing the State's progress in implementing the program. Such report shall include amendments to the State program for water wells sited during the biennial period.

(h) Federal agencies

Each department, agency, and instrumentality of the executive, legislative, and judicial branches of the Federal Government having jurisdiction over any potential source of contaminants identified by a State program pursuant to the provisions of subsection (a)(3) of this section shall be subject to and comply with all requirements of the State program developed according to subsection (a)(4) of this section applicable to such potential source of contaminants, both substantive and procedural, in the same manner, and to the same extent, as any other person is subject to such requirements, including payment of reasonable charges and fees. The President may exempt any potential source under the jurisdiction of any department, agency, or instrumentality in the executive branch if the President determines it to be in the paramount interest of the United States to do so. No such exemption shall be granted due to the lack of an appropriation unless the President shall have specifically requested such appropriation as part of the budgetary process and the Congress shall have failed to make available such requested appropriations.

(i) Additional requirement

(1) In general

In addition to the provisions of subsection (a) of this section, States in which there are more than 2,500 active wells at which annular injection is used as of January 1, 1986, shall include in their State program a certification that a State program exists and is being adequately enforced that provides protection from contaminants which may have any adverse effect on the health of persons and which are associated with the annular injection or surface disposal of brines associated with oil and gas production.

(2) "Annular injection" defined

For purposes of this subsection, the term "annular injection" means the reinjection of brines associated with the production of oil or gas between the production and surface casings of a conventional oil or gas producing well.

(3) Review

The Administrator shall conduct a review of each program certified under this subsection.

(4) Disapproval

If a State fails to include the certification required by this subsection or if in the judgment of the Administrator the State program certified under this subsection is not being adequately enforced, the Administrator shall disapprove the State program submitted under subsection (a) of this section.

(j) Coordination with other laws

Nothing in this section shall authorize or require any department, agency, or other instrumentality of the Federal Government or State or local government to apportion, allocate or otherwise regulate the withdrawal or beneficial use of ground or surface waters, so as to abrogate or modify any existing rights to water established pursuant to State or Federal law, including interstate compacts.

(k) Authorization of appropriations

Unless the State program is disapproved under this section, the Administrator shall make grants to the State for not less than 50 or more than 90 percent of the costs incurred by a State (as determined by the Administrator) in developing and implementing each State program under this section. For purposes of making such grants there is authorized to be appropriated not more than the following amounts:

Fiscal year:	*Amount*
1987	$20,000,000
1988	20,000,000
1989	35,000,000
1990	35,000,000
1991	35,000,000

(July 1, 1944, c. 373, Title XIV, § 1428, as added June 19, 1986, Pub.L. 99–339, Title II, § 205, 100 Stat. 660, amended June 19, 1986, Pub.L. 99–339, Title III, § 301(e), 100 Stat. 664.)

PART D—EMERGENCY POWERS

§ 300i. Emergency powers [PHSA § 1431]

(a) Actions authorized against imminent and substantial endangerment to health

Notwithstanding any other provision of this subchapter the Administrator, upon receipt of information that a contaminant which is present in or is likely to enter a public water system or an underground source of drinking water may present an imminent and substantial endangerment to the health of persons, and that appropriate State and local authorities have not acted to protect the health of such persons, may take such actions as he may deem necessary in order to protect the health of such persons. To the extent he determines it to be practicable in light of such imminent endangerment, he shall consult with the State and local authorities in order to confirm the correctness of the information on which action proposed to be taken under this subsection is based and to ascertain the action which such authorities are or will be taking. The action which the Administrator may take may include (but shall not be limited to) (1) issuing such orders as may be necessary to protect the health of persons who are or may be users of such system (including travelers), including orders requiring the provision of alternative water supplies by persons who caused or contributed to the endangerment, and (2) commencing a civil action for appropriate relief, including a restraining order or permanent or temporary injunction.

(b) Penalties for violations; separate offenses

Any person who violates or fails or refuses to comply with any order issued by the Administrator under subsection (a)(1) of this section may, in an action brought in the appropriate United States district court to enforce such order, be subject to a civil penalty of not to exceed $5,000 for each day in which such violation occurs or failure to comply continues.

(July 1, 1944, c. 373, Title XIV, § 1431, as added Dec. 16, 1974, Pub.L. 93–523, § 2(a), 88 Stat. 1680, and amended June 19, 1986, Pub.L. 99–339, Title II, § 204, 100 Stat. 660.)

CROSS REFERENCES

Guidelines for using imminent hazard, enforcement, and emergency response authorities, see section 9606 of this title.

CODE OF FEDERAL REGULATIONS

Environmental Protection Agency,
 Administration of permit programs, see 40 CFR 122.1 et seq.
 Decisionmaking procedures applicable to permit programs, see 40 CFR 124.1 et seq.
Underground injection control programs, technical criteria and standards for, see 40 CFR 146.1 et seq.

LIBRARY REFERENCES

Health and Environment ⇔38.
C.J.S. Health and Environment § 49 et seq.

§ 300i–1. Tampering with public water systems [PHSA § 1432]

(a) Tampering

Any person who tampers with a public water system shall be imprisoned for not more than 5 years, or fined in accordance with Title 18, or both.

(b) Attempt or threat

Any person who attempts to tamper, or makes a threat to tamper, with a public drinking water system be imprisoned for not more than 3 years, or fined in accordance with Title 18, or both.

(c) Civil penalty

The Administrator may bring a civil action in the appropriate United States district court (as determined under the provisions of Title 28) against any person who tampers, attempts to tamper, or makes a threat to tamper with a public water system. The court may impose on such person a civil penalty of not more than $50,000 for such tampering or not more than $20,000 for such attempt or threat.

(d) "Tamper" defined

For purposes of this section, the term "tamper" means—

(1) to introduce a contaminant into a public water system with the intention of harming persons; or

(2) to otherwise interfere with the operation of a public water system with the intention of harming persons.

(July 1, 1944, c. 373, Title XIV, § 1432, as added June 19, 1986, Pub.L. 99–339, Title I, § 108, 100 Stat. 651.)

LAW REVIEW COMMENTARIES

Responsible corporate officer: Designated felon or legal fiction? Brenda S. Hustis and John Y. Gotanda, 25 Loy.U.Chi.L.J. 169 (1994).

PART E—GENERAL PROVISIONS

§ 300j. Assurances of availability of adequate supplies of chemicals necessary for treatment of water [PHSA § 1441]

(a) Certification of need application

If any person who uses chlorine, activated carbon, lime, ammonia, soda ash, potassium permanganate, caustic soda, or other chemical or substance for the purpose of treating water in any public water system or in any public treatment works determines that the amount of such chemical or substance necessary to effectively treat such water is not reasonably available to him or will not be so available to him when required for the effective treatment of such water, such person may apply to the Administrator for a certification (hereinafter in this section referred to as a "certification of need") that the amount of such chemical or substance which such person requires to effectively treat such water is not reasonably available to him or will not be so available when required for the effective treatment of such water.

(b) Application requirements; publication in Federal Register; waiver; certification, issuance or denial

(1) An application for a certification of need shall be in such form and submitted in such manner as the Administrator may require and shall (A) specify the persons the applicant determines are able to provide the chemical or substance with respect to which the application is submitted, (B) specify the persons from whom the applicant has sought such chemical or substance, and (C) contain such other information as the Administrator may require.

(2) Upon receipt of an application under this section, the Administrator shall (A) publish in the Federal Register a notice of the receipt of the application and a brief summary of it, (B) notify in writing each person whom the President or his delegate (after consultation with the Administrator) determines could be made subject to an order required to be issued upon the issuance of the certification of need applied for in such application, and (C) provide an opportunity for the submission of written comments on such application. The requirements of the preceding sentence of this paragraph shall not apply when the Administrator for good cause finds (and incorporates the finding with a brief statement of reasons therefor in the order issued) that waiver of such requirements is necessary in order to protect the public health.

(3) Within 30 days after—

(A) the date a notice is published under paragraph (2) in the Federal Register with respect to an application submitted under this section for the issuance of a certification of need, or

(B) the date on which such application is received if as authorized by the second sentence of such paragraph no notice is published with respect to such application,

the Administrator shall take action either to issue or deny the issuance of a certification of need.

(c) Certification of need; issuance; executive orders; implementation of orders; equitable apportionment of orders; factors considered

(1) If the Administrator finds that the amount of a chemical or substance necessary for an applicant under an application submitted under this section to effectively treat water in a public water system or in a public treatment works is not reasonably available to the applicant or will not be so available to him when required for the effective treatment of such water, the Administrator shall issue a certification of need. Not later than seven days following the issuance of such certification, the President or his delegate shall issue an order requiring the provision to such person of such amounts of such chemical or substance as the Administrator deems necessary in the certification of need issued for such person. Such order shall apply to such manufacturers, producers, processors, distributors, and repackagers of such chemical or substance as the President or his delegate deems necessary and appropriate, except that such order may not apply to any manufacturer, producer, or processor of such chemical or substance who manufactures, produces, or processes (as the case may be) such chemical or substance solely for its own use. Persons subject to an order issued under this section shall be given a reasonable opportunity to consult with the President or his delegate with respect to the implementation of the order.

(2) Orders which are to be issued under paragraph (1) to manufacturers, producers, and processors of a chemical or substance shall be equitably apportioned, as far as practicable, among all manufacturers, producers, and processors of such chemical or substance; and orders which are to be issued under paragraph (1) to distributors and repackagers of a chemical or substance shall be equitably apportioned, as far as practicable, among all distributors and repackagers of such chemical or substance. In apportioning orders issued under paragraph (1) to manufacturers, producers, processors, distributors, and repackagers of chlorine, the President or his delegate shall, in carrying out the requirements of the preceding sentence, consider—

(A) the geographical relationships and established commercial relationships between such manufacturers, producers, processors, distributors, and repackagers and the persons for whom the orders are issued;

(B) in the case of orders to be issued to producers of chlorine, the (i) amount of chlorine historically supplied by each such producer to treat water in public water systems and public treatment works, and (ii) share of each such producer of the total annual production of chlorine in the United States; and

(C) such other factors as the President or his delegate may determine are relevant to the apportionment of orders in accordance with the requirements of the preceding sentence.

(3) Subject to subsection (f) of this section, any person for whom a certification of need has been issued under this subsection may upon the expiration of the order issued under paragraph (1) upon such certification apply under this section for additional certifications.

(d) Breach of contracts; defense

There shall be available as a defense to any action brought for breach of contract in a Federal or State court arising out of delay or failure to provide, sell, or offer for sale or exchange a chemical or substance subject to an order issued pursuant to subsection (c)(1) of this section, that such delay or failure was caused solely by compliance with such order.

(e) Penalties for noncompliance with orders; temporary restraining orders and preliminary or permanent injunctions

(1) Whoever knowingly fails to comply with any order issued pursuant to subsection (c)(1) of this section shall be fined not more than $5,000 for each such failure to comply.

(2) Whoever fails to comply with any order issued pursuant to subsection (c)(1) of this section shall be subject to a civil penalty of not more than $2,500 for each such failure to comply.

(3) Whenever the Administrator or the President or his delegate has reason to believe that any person is violating or will violate any order issued pursuant to subsection (c)(1) of this section, he may petition a United States district court to issue a temporary restraining order or preliminary or permanent injunction (including a mandatory injunction) to enforce the provision of such order.

(f) Termination date

No certification of need or order issued under this section may remain in effect for more than one year.

(July 1, 1944, c. 373, Title XIV, § 1441, as added Dec. 16, 1974, Pub.L. 93–523, § 2(a), 88 Stat. 1680, and amended Nov. 16, 1977, Pub.L. 95–190, § 7, 91 Stat. 1396; Sept. 6, 1979, Pub.L. 96–63, § 3, 93 Stat. 411; June 19, 1986, Pub.L. 99–339, Title III, § 301(d), 100 Stat. 664.)

LIBRARY REFERENCES

Waters and Water Courses ⟹64.
C.J.S. Waters § 43 et seq.

§ 300j–1. Research, technical assistance, information, training of personnel [PHSA § 1442]

(a) Specific powers and duties of Administrator

(1) The Administrator may conduct research, studies, and demonstrations relating to the causes, diagnosis, treatment, control, and prevention of physical and mental diseases and other impairments of man resulting directly or indirectly from contaminants in water, or to the provision of a dependably safe supply of drinking water, including—

(A) improved methods (i) to identify and measure the existence of contaminants in drinking water (including methods which may be used by State and local health and water officials), and (ii) to identify the source of such contaminants;

(B) improved methods to identify and measure the health effects of contaminants in drinking water;

(C) new methods of treating raw water to prepare it for drinking, so as to improve the efficiency of water treatment and to remove contaminants from water;

(D) improved methods for providing a dependably safe supply of drinking water, including improvements in water purification and distribution, and methods of assessing the health related hazards of drinking water; and

(E) improved methods of protecting underground water sources of public water systems from contamination.

(2)(A) The Administrator shall, to the maximum extent feasible, provide technical assistance to the States and municipalities in the establishment and administration of public water system supervision programs (as defined in section 300j–2(c)(1) of this title).

(B) The Administrator is authorized to provide technical assistance and to make grants to States, or publicly owned water systems to assist in responding to and alleviating any emergency situation affecting public water systems (including sources of water for such systems) which the Administrator determines to present substantial danger to the public health. Grants provided under this subparagraph shall be used only to support those actions which (i) are necessary for preventing, limiting or mitigating danger to the public health in such emergency situation and (ii) would not, in the judgment of the Administrator, be taken without such emergency assistance. The Administrator may carry out the program authorized under this subparagraph as part of, and in accordance with the terms and conditions of, any other program of assistance for environmental emergencies which the Administrator is authorized to carry out under any other provision of law. No limitation on appropriations for any such other program shall apply to amounts appropriated under this subparagraph.

(3)(A) The Administrator shall conduct studies, and make periodic reports to Congress, on the costs of carrying out regulations prescribed under section 300g–1 of this title.

(B) Not later than eighteen months after November 16, 1977, the Administrator shall submit a report to Congress which identifies and analyzes—

(i) the anticipated costs of compliance with interim and revised national primary drinking water regulations and the anticipated costs to States and units of local governments in implementing such regulations;

(ii) alternative methods of (including alternative treatment techniques for) compliance with such regulations;

(iii) methods of paying the costs of compliance by public water systems with national primary drinking water regulations, including user charges, State or local taxes or subsidies, Federal grants (including planning or construction grants, or both), loans, and loan guarantees, and other methods of assisting in paying the costs of such compliance;

(iv) the advantages and disadvantages of each of the methods referred to in clauses (ii) and (iii);

(v) the sources of revenue presently available (and projected to be available) to public water systems to meet current and future expenses; and

(vi) the costs of drinking water paid by residential and industrial consumers in a sample of large, medium, and small public water systems and of individually owned wells, and the reasons for any differences in such costs.

The report required by this subparagraph shall identify and analyze the items required in clauses (i) through (v) separately with respect to public water systems serving small communities. The report required by this subparagraph shall include such recommendations as the Administrator deems appropriate.

(4) Omitted

(5) The Administrator shall carry out a study of methods of underground injection which do not result in the degradation of underground drinking water sources.

(6) The Administrator shall carry out a study of methods of preventing, detecting, and dealing with surface spills of contaminants which may degrade underground water sources for public water systems.

(7) The Administrator shall carry out a study of virus contamination of drinking water sources and means of control of such contamination.

(8) The Administrator shall carry out a study of the nature and extent of the impact on underground water which supplies or can reasonably be expected to supply public water systems of (A) abandoned injection or extraction wells; (B) intensive application of pesticides and fertilizers in underground water recharge areas; and (C) ponds, pools, lagoons, pits, or other surface disposal of contaminants in underground water recharge areas.

(9) The Administrator shall conduct a comprehensive study of public water supplies and drinking water sources to determine the nature, extent, sources of and means of control of contamination by chemicals or other substances suspected of being carcinogenic. Not later than six months after December 16, 1974, he shall transmit to the Congress the initial results of such study, together with such recommendations for further review and corrective action as he deems appropriate.

(10) The Administrator shall carry out a study of the reaction of chlorine and humic acids and the effects of the contaminants which result from such reaction on public health and on the safety of drinking water, including any carcinogenic effect.

(11) The Administrator shall carry out a study of polychlorinated biphenyl contamination of actual or potential sources of drinking water, contamination of such sources by other substances known or suspected to be harmful to public health, the effects of such contamination, and means of removing, treating, or otherwise controlling such contamination. To assist in carrying out this paragraph, the Administrator is authorized to make grants to public agencies and private nonprofit institutions.

(b) Other powers and duties of Administrator

In carrying out this subchapter, the Administrator is authorized to—

(1) collect and make available information pertaining to research, investigations, and demonstrations with respect to providing a dependably safe supply of drinking water together with appropriate recommendations in connection therewith;

(2) make available research facilities of the Agency to appropriate public authorities, institutions, and individuals engaged in studies and research relating to the purposes of this subchapter;

(3) make grants to, and enter into contracts with, any public agency, educational institution, and any other organization, in accordance with procedures prescribed by the Administrator, under which he may pay all or part of the costs (as may be determined by the Administrator) of any project or activity which is designed—

(A) to develop, expand, or carry out a program (which may combine training education and employment) for training persons for occupations involving the public health aspects of providing safe drinking water;

(B) to train inspectors and supervisory personnel to train or supervise persons in occupations involving the public health aspects of providing safe drinking water; or

(C) to develop and expand the capability of programs of States and municipalities to carry out the purposes of this subchapter (other than by carrying out State programs of public water system supervision or underground water source protection (as defined in section 300j–2(c) of this title)).

(c) Establishment of training programs and grants for training; training fees

The Administrator shall—

(1) provide training for, and make grants for training (including postgraduate training) of (A) personnel of State agencies which have primary enforcement responsibility and of agencies or units of local government to which enforcement responsibilities have been delegated by the State, and (B) personnel who manage or operate public water systems, and

(2) make grants for postgraduate training of individuals (including grants to educational institutions for traineeships) for purposes of qualifying such individuals to work as personnel referred to in paragraph (1).

Reasonable fees may be charged for training provided under paragraph (1)(B) to persons other than personnel of State or local agencies but such training shall be provided to personnel of State or local agencies without charge.

(d) Authorization of appropriations

There are authorized to be appropriated to carry out the provisions of this section other than subsection (a)(2)(B) of this section and provisions relating to research $15,000,000 for the fiscal year ending June 30, 1975; $25,000,000 for the fiscal year ending June 30, 1976; $35,000,000 for the fiscal year ending June 30, 1977; $17,000,000 for each of the fiscal years 1978 and 1979; $21,405,000 for the fiscal year ending September 30, 1980; $30,000,000 for the fiscal year ending September 30, 1981; and $35,000,000 for the fiscal year ending September 30, 1982. There are authorized to be appropriated to carry out subsection (a)(2)(B) of this section $8,000,000 for each of the fiscal years 1978 through 1982. There are authorized to be appropriated to carry out subsection (a)(2)(B) of this section not more than the following amounts:

Fiscal year:	*Amount*
1987	$7,650,000
1988	7,650,000
1989	8,050,000
1990	8,050,000
1991	8,050,000

There are authorized to be appropriated to carry out the provisions of this section (other than subsection (g) of this section, subsection (a)(2)(B) of this section, and provisions relating to research), not more than the following amounts:

Fiscal year:	*Amount*
1987	$35,600,000
1988	35,600,000
1989	38,020,000
1990	38,020,000
1991	38,020,000

(e) Technical assistance for small systems; authorization of appropriations; amount to be utilized for public water systems owned or operated by Indian tribes

The Administrator is authorized to provide technical assistance to small public water systems to enable such systems to achieve and maintain compliance with national drinking water regulations. Such assistance may include "circuit-rider" programs, training, and preliminary engineering studies. There are authorized to be appropriated to carry out this subsection $10,000,000 for each of the fiscal years 1987 through 1991. Not less than the greater of—

(1) 3 percent of the amounts appropriated under this subsection, or

(2) $280,000

shall be utilized for technical assistance to public water systems owned or operated by Indian tribes.

(July 1, 1944, c. 373, Title XIV, § 1442, as added Dec. 16, 1974, Pub.L. 93–523, § 2(a), 88 Stat. 1682, and amended Nov. 16, 1977, Pub.L. 95–190, §§ 2(a), 3(a), (b), (e)(1), 4, 9, 10(b), 13, 91 Stat. 1393–1395, 1397–1399; Sept. 6, 1979, Pub.L. 96–63, § 1, 93 Stat. 411; Dec. 5, 1980, Pub.L. 96–502, § 5, 94 Stat. 2738; June 19, 1986, Pub.L. 99–339, Title I, § 107, Title III, §§ 301(a), (g), 304(a), 100 Stat. 651, 663, 665, 667; Dec. 21, 1995, Pub.L. 104–66, Title II, § 2021(h), 109 Stat. 727.)

CODE OF FEDERAL REGULATIONS

Environmental Protection Agency grants, policies and procedures respecting, see 40 CFR 30.100 et seq.
Subagreements, see 40 CFR 33.001 et seq.

LIBRARY REFERENCES

Health and Environment ⇐20.
C.J.S. Health and Environment § 2 et seq.

§ 300j–2. Grants for State programs [PHSA § 1443]

(a) Public water systems supervision programs; applications for grants; allotment of sums; waiver of grant restrictions; notice of approval or disapproval of application; authorization of appropriations

(1) From allotments made pursuant to paragraph (4), the Administrator may make grants to States to carry out public water system supervision programs.

(2) No grant may be made under paragraph (1) unless an application therefor has been submitted to the Administrator in such form and manner as he may require. The Administrator may not approve an application of a State for its first grant under paragraph (1) unless he determines that the State—

(A) has established or will establish within one year from the date of such grant a public water system supervision program, and

(B) will, within that one year, assume primary enforcement responsibility for public water systems within the State.

No grant may be made to a State under paragraph (1) for any period beginning more than one year after the date of the State's first grant unless the State has assumed and maintains primary enforcement responsibility for public water systems within the State. The prohibitions contained in the preceding two sentences shall not apply to such grants when made to Indian Tribes.

(3) A grant under paragraph (1) shall be made to cover not more than 75 per centum of the grant recipient's costs (as determined under regulations of the Administrator) in carrying out, during the one-year period beginning on the date the grant is made, a public water system supervision program.

(4) In each fiscal year the Administrator shall, in accordance, with regulations, allot the sums appropriated for such year under paragraph (5) among the States on the basis of population, geographical area, number of public water systems, and other relevant factors. No State shall receive less than 1 per centum of the annual appropriation for grants under paragraph (1): *Provided,* That the Administrator may, by regulation, reduce such percentage in accordance with the criteria specified in this paragraph: *And provided further,* That such percentage shall not apply to grants allotted to Guam, American Samoa, or the Virgin Islands.

(5) The prohibition contained in the last sentence of paragraph (2) may be waived by the Administrator with respect to a grant to a State through fiscal year 1979 but such prohibition may only be waived if, in the judgment of the Administrator—

(A) the State is making a diligent effort to assume and maintain primary enforcement responsibility for public water systems within the State;

(B) the State has made significant progress toward assuming and maintaining such primary enforcement responsibility; and

(C) there is reason to believe the State will assume such primary enforcement responsibility by October 1, 1979.

The amount of any grant awarded for the fiscal years 1978 and 1979 pursuant to a waiver under this paragraph may not exceed 75 per centum of the allotment which the State would have received for such fiscal year if it had assumed and maintained such primary enforcement responsibility. The remaining 25 per centum of the amount allotted to such State for such fiscal year shall be retained by the Administrator, and the Administrator may award such amount to such State at such time as the State assumes such responsibility before the beginning of fiscal year 1980. At the beginning of each fiscal years[1] 1979 and 1980 the amounts retained by the Administrator for any preceding fiscal year and not awarded by the beginning of fiscal year 1979 or 1980 to the States to which such amounts were originally allotted may be removed from the original allotment and reallotted for fiscal year 1979 or 1980 (as the case may be) to States which have assumed primary enforcement responsibility by the beginning of such fiscal year.

(6) The Administrator shall notify the State of the approval or disapproval of any application for a grant under this section—

(A) within ninety days after receipt of such application, or

(B) not later than the first day of the fiscal year for which the grant application is made,

whichever is later.

(7) For purposes of making grants under paragraph (1) there are authorized to be appropriated $15,000,000 for the fiscal year ending June 30, 1976, $25,000,000 for the fiscal year ending June 30, 1977, $35,000,000 for fiscal year 1978, $45,000,000 for fiscal year 1979, $29,450,000 for the fiscal year ending September 30, 1980, $32,000,000 for the fiscal year ending September 30, 1981, and $34,000,000 for the fiscal year ending September 30, 1982. For the purposes of making grants under paragraph (1) there are authorized to be appropriated not more than the following amounts:

Fiscal year:	*Amount*
1987	$37,200,000
1988	37,200,000
1989	40,150,000
1990	40,150,000
1991	40,150,000

(b) Underground water source protection programs; applications for grants; allotment of sums; authorization of appropriations

(1) From allotments made pursuant to paragraph (4), the Administrator may make grants to States to carry out underground water source protection programs.

(2) No grant may be made under paragraph (1) unless an application therefor has been submitted to the Administrator in such form and manner as he may require. No grant may be made to any State under paragraph (1) unless the State has assumed primary enforcement responsibility within two years after the date the Administrator promulgates regulations for State underground injection control programs under section 300h of this title. The prohibition contained in the preceding sentence shall not apply to such grants when made to Indian Tribes.

(3) A grant under paragraph (1) shall be made to cover not more than 75 per centum of the grant recipient's costs (as determined under regulations of the Administrator) in carrying out, during the one-year period beginning on the date the grant is made, and underground water source protection program.

(4) In each fiscal year the Administrator shall, in accordance with regulations, allot the sums appropriated for such year under paragraph (5) among the States on the basis of population, geographical area, and other relevant factors.

(5) For purposes of making grants under paragraph (1) there are authorized to be appropriated $5,000,000 for the fiscal year ending June 30, 1976, $7,500,000 for the fiscal year ending June 30, 1977, $10,000,000 for each of the fiscal years 1978 and 1979, $7,795,000 for the fiscal year ending September 30, 1980, $18,000,000 for the fiscal year ending September 30, 1981, and $21,000,000 for the fiscal year ending September 30, 1982. For the purpose of making grants under paragraph (1) there are authorized to be appropriated not more than the following amounts:

Fiscal year:	*Amount*
1987	$19,700,000
1988	19,700,000
1989	20,850,000

Fiscal year:	*Amount*
1990	20,850,000
1991	20,850,000

(c) Definitions

For purposes of this section:

(1) The term "public water system supervision program" means a program for the adoption and enforcement of drinking water regulations (with such variances and exemptions from such regulations under conditions and in a manner which is not less stringent than the conditions under, and the manner in, which variances and exemptions may be granted under sections 300g–4 and 300g–5 of this title) which are no less stringent than the national primary drinking water regulations under section 300g–1 of this title, and for keeping records and making reports required by section 300g–2(a)(3) of this title.

(2) The term "underground water source protection program" means a program for the adoption and enforcement of a program which meets the requirements of regulations under section 300h of this title and for keeping records and making reports required by section 300h–1(b)(1)(A)(ii) of this title. Such term includes, where applicable, a program which meets the requirements of section 300h–4 of this title.

(July 1, 1944, c. 373, Title XIV, § 1443, as added Dec. 16, 1974, Pub.L. 93–523, § 2(a), 88 Stat. 1684, and amended Nov. 16, 1977, Pub.L. 95–190, §§ 2(b), (c), 5(a), 91 Stat. 1393, 1395; Sept. 6, 1979, Pub.L. 96–63, § 2, 93 Stat. 411; Dec. 5, 1980, Pub.L. 96–502, §§ 2(c), 4(d), 94 Stat. 2738; June 19, 1986, Pub.L. 99–339, Title III, §§ 301(b), (c), 302(d), 100 Stat. 664, 666.)

1 So in original. Probably should be "year".

CODE OF FEDERAL REGULATIONS

Grants,
Awarded by Environmental Protection Agency, see 40 CFR 30.100 et seq.
Programs for air and water pollution control, public water system, solid and hazardous waste management, pesticide enforcement and underground water source protection, see 40 CFR 35.200 et seq.
Subagreements, see 40 CFR 33.001 et seq.

LIBRARY REFERENCES

United States ⟹82(2).
C.J.S. United States § 122.

§ 300j–3. Special project grants and guaranteed loans [PHSA § 1444]

(a) Special study and demonstration project grants

The Administrator may make grants to any person for the purposes of—

(1) assisting in the development and demonstration (including construction) of any project which will demonstrate a new or improved method, approach, or technology, for providing a dependably safe supply of drinking water to the public; and

(2) assisting in the development and demonstration (including construction) of any project which will investigate and demonstrate health implications involved in the reclamation, recycling, and reuse of waste waters for drinking and the processes and methods for the preparation of safe and acceptable drinking water.

(b) Limitations

Grants made by the Administrator under this section shall be subject to the following limitations:

(1) Grants under this section shall not exceed 66⅔ per centum of the total cost of construction of any facility and 75 per centum of any other costs, as determined by the Administrator.

(2) Grants under this section shall not be made for any project involving the construction or modification of any facilities for any public water system in a State unless such project has been approved by the State agency charged with the responsibility for safety of drinking water (or if there is no such agency in a State, by the State health authority).

(3) Grants under this section shall not be made for any project unless the Administrator determines, after consulting the National Drinking Water Advisory Council, that such project will serve a useful purpose relating to the development and demonstration of new or improved techniques, methods, or technologies for the provision of safe water to the public for drinking.

(4) Priority for grants under this section shall be given where there are known or potential public health hazards which require advanced technology for the removal of particles which are too small to be removed by ordinary treatment technology.

(c) Authorization of appropriations

For the purposes of making grants under subsections (a) and (b) of this section there are authorized to be appropriated $7,500,000 for the fiscal year ending June 30, 1975; and $7,500,000 for the fiscal year ending June 30, 1976; and $10,000,000 for the fiscal year ending June 30, 1977.

(d) Loan guarantees to public water systems; conditions; indebtedness limitation; regulations

The Administrator during the fiscal years ending June 30, 1975, and June 30, 1976, shall carry out a program of guaranteeing loans made by private lenders to small public water systems for the purpose of enabling such systems to meet national primary drinking water regulations prescribed under section 300g–1 of this title. No such guarantee may be made with respect to a system unless (1) such system cannot reasonably obtain financial assistance necessary to comply with such regulations from any other source, and (2) the Administrator determines that any facilities constructed with a loan guaranteed under this subsection is not likely to be made obsolete by subsequent changes in primary regulations. The aggregate amount of indebtedness guaranteed with respect to any system may not exceed $50,000. The aggregate amount of indebtedness guaranteed under this subsection may not exceed $50,000,000. The Administrator shall prescribe regulations to carry out this subsection.

(July 1, 1944, c. 373, Title XIV, § 1444, as added Dec. 16, 1974, Pub.L. 93–523, § 2(a), 88 Stat. 1685, and amended June 19, 1986, Pub.L. 99–339, Title I, § 101(c)(3), 100 Stat. 646.)

CODE OF FEDERAL REGULATIONS

Environmental Protection Agency grants, policies and procedures respecting, see 40 CFR 30.100 et seq.
Subagreements, see 40 CFR 33.001 et seq.

LIBRARY REFERENCES

United States ⚷82(1).
C.J.S. United States § 122.

§ 300j–3a. Grants to public sector agencies

(a) Assistance for development and demonstration projects

The Administrator of the Environmental Protection Agency shall offer grants to public sector agencies for the purposes of—

(1) assisting in the development and demonstration (including construction) of any project which will demonstrate a new or improved method, approach, or technology for providing a dependably safe supply of drinking water to the public; and

(2) assisting in the development and demonstration (including construction) of any project which will investigate and demonstrate health and conservation implications involved in the reclamation, recycling, and reuse of wastewaters for drinking and agricultural use or the processes and methods for the preparation of safe and acceptable drinking water.

(b) Limitations

Grants made by the Administrator under this section shall be subject to the following limitations:

(1) Grants under this section shall not exceed 66⅔ per centum of the total cost of construction of any facility and 75 per centum of any other costs, as determined by the Administrator.

(2) Grants under this section shall not be made for any project involving the construction or modification of any facilities for any public water system in a State unless such project has been approved by the State agency charged with the responsibility for safety of drinking water (or if there is no such agency in a State, by the State health authority).

(3) Grants under this section shall not be made for any project unless the Administrator determines, after consultation, that such project will serve a useful purpose relating to the development and demonstration of new or improved techniques, methods, or technologies for the provision of safe water to the public for drinking.

(c) Authorization of appropriations

There are authorized to be appropriated for the purposes of this section $25,000,000 for fiscal year 1978.

(Nov. 8, 1977, Pub.L. 95–155, § 5, 91 Stat. 1258; Oct. 18, 1978, Pub.L. 95–477, § 7(a)(1), 92 Stat. 1511.)

Codification

Section was enacted as part of the Environmental Research, Development, and Demonstration Authorization Act of 1978, and not as part of the Public Health Service Act which comprises this chapter.

§ 300j–3b. Contaminant standards or treatment technique guidelines

(1) Not later than nine months after October 18, 1978, the Administrator shall promulgate guidelines establishing supplemental standards or treatment technique requirements for microbiological, viral, radiological, organic, and inorganic contaminants, which guidelines shall be conditions, as provided in paragraph (2), of any grant for a demonstration project for water reclamation, recycling, and reuse funded under section 300j–3a of this title or under section 300j–3(a)(2) of this title, where such project involves direct human consumption of treated wastewater. Such guidelines shall provide for sufficient control of each such contaminant, such that in the Administrator's judgement, no adverse effects on the health of persons may reasonably be anticipated to occur, allowing an adequate margin of safety.

(2) A grant referred to in paragraph (1) for a project which involves direct human consumption of treated wastewater may be awarded on or after the date of promulgation of guidelines under this section only if the applicant demonstrates to the satisfaction of the Administrator that the project—

(A) will comply with all national primary drinking water regulations under section 300g–1 of this title;

(B) will comply with all guidelines under this section; and

(C) will in other respects provide safe drinking water.

Any such grant awarded before the date of promulgation of such guidelines shall be conditioned on the applicant's agreement to comply to the maximum feasible extent with such guidelines as expeditiously as practicable following the date of promulgation thereof.

(3) Guidelines under this section may, in the discretion of the Administrator—

(A) be nationally and uniformly applicable to all projects funded under section 300j–3a of this title or section 300j–1(a)(2) of this title;

(B) vary for different classes or categories of such projects (as determined by the Administrator);

(C) be established and applicable on a project-by-project basis; or

(D) any combination of the above.

(4) Nothing in this section shall be construed to prohibit or delay the award of any grant referred to in paragraph (1) prior to the date of promulgation of such guidelines.

(Oct. 18, 1978, Pub.L. 95–477, § 7(b), 92 Stat. 1511.)

Codification

Section was enacted as part of the Environmental Research, Development, and Demonstration Authorization Act of 1979, and not as part of the Public Health Service Act which comprises this chapter.

§ 300j–4. Records and inspections [PHSA § 1445]

(a) Persons subject to requirements; size of system and likely contaminants as considerations for monitoring; monitoring for unregulated contaminants; notification of availability of results; waiver of monitoring requirement; authorization of appropriations

(1) Every person who is a supplier of water, who is or may be otherwise subject to a primary drinking water regulation prescribed under section 300g–1 of this title or to an applicable underground injection control program (as defined in section 300h–1(c) of this title), who is or may be subject to the permit requirement of section 300h–3 of this title, or to an order issued under section 300j of this title, or who is a grantee, shall establish and maintain such records, make such reports, conduct such monitoring, and provide such information as the Administrator may reasonably require by regulation to assist him in establishing regulations under this subchapter, in determining whether such person has acted or is acting in compliance with this subchapter in administering any program of financial assistance under this subchapter, in evaluating the health risks of unregulated contaminants, or in advising the public of such risks. In requiring a public water system to monitor under this subsection, the Administrator may take into consideration the system size and the contaminants likely to be found in the system's drinking water.

(2) Not later than 18 months after June 19, 1986, the Administrator shall promulgate regulations requiring every public water system to conduct a monitoring program for unregulated contaminants. The regulations shall require monitoring of drinking water supplied by the system and shall vary the frequency and schedule of monitoring requirements for systems based on the number of persons served by the system, the source of supply, and the contaminants likely to be found. Each system shall be required to monitor at least once every 5 years after the effective date of the Administrator's regulations unless the Administrator requires more frequent monitoring.

(3) Regulations under paragraph (2) shall list unregulated contaminants for which systems may be required to monitor, and shall include criteria by which the primary enforcement authority in each State could show cause for addition or deletion of contaminants from the designated list. The primary State enforcement authority may delete contaminants for an individual system, in accordance with these criteria, after obtaining approval of assessment of the contaminants potentially to be found in the system. The Administrator shall approve or disapprove such an assessment submitted by a State within 60 days. A State may add contaminants, in accordance with these criteria, without making an assessment, but in no event shall such additions increase Federal expenditures authorized by this section.

(4) Public water systems conducting monitoring of unregulated contaminants pursuant to this section shall provide the results of such monitoring to the primary enforcement authority.

(5) Notification of the availability of the results of the monitoring programs required under paragraph (2), and notification of the availability of the results of the monitoring program referred to in paragraph (6), shall be given to the persons served by the system and the Administrator.

(6) The Administrator may waive the monitoring requirement under paragraph (2) for a system which has conducted a monitoring program after January 1, 1983, if the Administrator determines the program to have been consistent with the regulations promulgated under this section.

(7) Any system supplying less than 150 service connections shall be treated as complying with this subsection if such system provides water samples or the opportunity for sampling according to rules established by the Administrator.

(8) There are authorized to be appropriated $30,000,000 in the fiscal year ending September 30, 1987[1] to remain available until expended to carry out the provisions of this subsection.

(b) Entry of establishments, facilities, or other property; inspections; conduct of certain tests; audit and examination of records; entry restrictions; prohibition against informing of a proposed entry

(1) Except as provided in paragraph (2), the Administrator, or representatives of the Administrator duly designated by him, upon presenting appropriate credentials and a written notice to any supplier of water or other person subject to (A) a national primary drinking water regulation prescribed under section 300g–1 of this title, (B) an applicable underground injection control program, or (C) any requirement to monitor an unregulated contaminant pursuant to subsection (a) of this section, or person in charge of any of the property of such supplier or other person referred to in clause (A), (B), or (C), is authorized to enter any establishment, facility, or other property of such supplier or other person in order to determine whether such supplier or other person has acted or is acting in compliance with this subchapter, including for this purpose, inspection, at reasonable times, of records, files, papers, processes, controls, and facilities, or in order to test any feature of a public water system, including its raw water source. The Administrator or the Comptroller General (or any representative designated by either) shall have access for the purpose of audit and examination to any records, reports, or information of a grantee which are required to be maintained under subsection (a) of this section or which are pertinent to any financial assistance under this subchapter.

(2) No entry may be made under the first sentence of paragraph (1) in an establishment, facility, or other property of a supplier of water or other person subject to a national primary drinking water regulation if the establishment, facility, or other property is located in a State which has primary enforcement responsibility for public water systems unless, before written notice of such entry is made, the Administrator (or his representative) notifies the State agency charged with responsibility for safe drinking water of the reasons for such entry. The Administrator shall, upon a showing by the State agency that such an entry will be detrimental to the administration of the State's program of primary enforcement responsibility, take such showing into consideration in determining whether to make such entry. No State agency which receives notice under this paragraph of an entry proposed to be made under paragraph (1) may use the information contained in the notice to inform the person whose property is proposed to be entered of the proposed entry; and if a State agency so uses such information, notice to the agency under this paragraph is not required until such time as the Administrator determines the agency has provided him satisfactory assurances that it will no longer so use information contained in a notice under this paragraph.

(c) Penalty

Whoever fails or refuses to comply with any requirement of subsection (a) of this section or to allow the Administrator, the Comptroller General, or representatives of either, to enter and conduct any audit or inspection authorized by subsection (b) of this section shall be subject to a civil penalty of not to exceed $25,000.

(d) Confidential information; trade secrets and secret processes; information disclosure; "information required under this section" defined

(1) Subject to paragraph (2), upon a showing satisfactory to the Administrator by any person that any information required under this section from such person, if made public, would divulge trade secrets or secret processes of such person, the Administrator shall consider such information confidential in accordance with the purposes of section 1905 of title 18. If the applicant fails to make a showing satisfactory to the Administrator, the Administrator shall give such applicant thirty days' notice before releasing the information to which the application relates (unless the public health or safety requires an earlier release of such information).

(2) Any information required under this section (A) may be disclosed to other officers, employees, or authorized representatives of the United States concerned with carrying out this subchapter or to committees of the Congress, or when relevant in any proceeding under this subchapter, and (B) shall be disclosed to the extent it deals with the level of contaminants in drinking water. For purposes of this subsection the term "information required under this section" means any papers, books, documents, or information, or any particular part thereof, reported to or otherwise obtained by the Administrator under this section.

(e) "Grantee" and "person" defined

For purposes of this section, (1) the term "grantee" means any person who applies for or receives financial assistance, by grant, contract, or loan guarantee under this subchapter, and (2) the term "person" includes a Federal agency.

(f) Information regarding drinking water coolers

The Administrator may utilize the authorities of this section for purposes of part F. Any person who manufactures, imports, sells, or distributes drinking water coolers in interstate commerce shall be treated as a supplier of water for purposes of applying the provisions of this section in the case of persons subject to part F.

(July 1, 1944, c. 373, Title XIV, § 1445, as added Dec. 16, 1974, Pub.L. 93–523, § 2(a), 88 Stat. 1686, and amended Nov. 16, 1977, Pub.L. 95–190, § 12(c), (d), 91 Stat. 1398; June 19, 1986, Pub.L. 99–339, Title I, § 106, Title III, § 301(h), 100 Stat. 650, 665; Oct. 31, 1988, Pub.L. 100–572, § 5, 102 Stat. 2884.)

[1] So in original. Probably should be followed by a comma.

CROSS REFERENCES

Guidelines for using imminent hazard, enforcement, and emergency response authorities, see section 9606 of this title.

CODE OF FEDERAL REGULATIONS

Environmental Protection Agency,
Administration of permit programs, see 40 CFR 122.1 et seq.
Decisionmaking procedures applicable to permit programs, see 40 CFR 124.1 et seq.
Implementation and enforcement of national primary drinking water regulations, see 40 CFR 142.1 et seq.
Policies and procedures governing requests for public information, see 40 CFR 2.100 et seq.
Underground injection control programs, technical criteria and standards for, see 40 CFR 146.1 et seq.

§ 300j–5. National Drinking Water Advisory Council [PHSA § 1446]

(a) Establishment; membership; representation of interests; term of office, vacancies; reappointment

There is established a National Drinking Water Advisory Council which shall consist of fifteen members appointed by the Administrator after consultation with the Secretary. Five members shall be appointed from the general public; five members shall be appointed from appropriate State and local agencies concerned with water hygiene and public water supply; and five members shall be appointed from representatives of private organizations or groups demonstrating an active interest in the field of water hygiene and public water supply. Each member of the Council shall hold office for a term of three years, except that—

(1) any member appointed to fill a vacancy occurring prior to the expiration of the term for which his predecessor was appointed shall be appointed for the remainder of such term; and

(2) the terms of the members first taking office shall expire as follows: Five shall expire three years after December 16, 1974, five shall expire two years after such date, and five shall expire one year after such date, as designated by the Administrator at the time of appointment.

The members of the Council shall be eligible for reappointment.

(b) Functions

The Council shall advise, consult with, and make recommendations to, the Administrator on matters relating to activities, functions, and policies of the Agency under this subchapter.

(c) Compensation and allowances; travel expenses

Members of the Council appointed under this section shall, while attending meetings or conferences of the Council or otherwise engaged in business of the Council, receive compensation and allowances at a rate to be fixed by the Administrator, but not exceeding the daily equivalent of the annual rate of basic pay in effect for grade GS–18 of the General Schedule for each day (including traveltime) during which they are engaged in the actual performance of duties vested in the Council. While away from their homes or regular places of business in the performance of services for the Council, members of the Council shall be allowed travel expenses, including per diem in lieu of subsistence, in the same manner as persons employed intermittently in the Government service are allowed expenses under section 5703(b) of title 5.

(d) Advisory committee termination provision inapplicable

Section 14(a) of the Federal Advisory Committee Act (relating to termination) shall not apply to the Council.

(July 1, 1944, c. 373, Title XIV, § 1446, as added Dec. 16, 1974, Pub.L. 93–523, § 2(a), 88 Stat. 1688.)

LIBRARY REFERENCES

United States ⇐29.
C.J.S. United States § 34 et seq.

§ 300j–6. Federal agencies [PHSA § 1447]

(a) Compliance with Federal, State, and local requirements, etc.; scope of applicability of compliance requirements, etc.; liability for civil penalties

Each Federal agency (1) having jurisdiction over any federally owned or maintained public water system or (2) engaged in any activity resulting, or which may result in, underground injection which endangers drinking water (within the meaning of section 300h(d)(2) of this title) shall be subject to, and comply with, all Federal, State, and local requirements, administrative authorities, and process and sanctions respecting the provision of safe drinking water and respecting any underground injection program in the same manner, and to the same extent, as any nongovernmental entity. The preceding sentence shall apply (A) to any requirement whether substantive or procedural (including any recordkeeping or reporting requirement, any requirement respecting permits, and any other requirement whatsoever), (B) to the exercise of any Federal, State, or local administrative authority, and (C) to any process or sanction, whether enforced in Federal, State, or local courts or in any other manner. This subsection shall apply, notwithstanding any immunity of such agencies, under any law or rule of law. No officer, agent, or employee of the United States shall be personally liable for any civil penalty under this subchapter with respect to any act or omission within the scope of his official duties.

(b) Waiver; national security; records available in judicial proceedings; publication in Federal Register; notice to Congressional Committees

The Administrator shall waive compliance with subsection (a) of this section upon request of the Secretary of Defense and upon a determination by the President that the requested waiver is necessary in the interest of national security. The Administrator shall maintain a written record of the basis upon which such waiver was granted and make such record available for in camera examination when relevant in a judicial proceeding under this subchapter. Upon the issuance of such a waiver, the Administrator shall publish in the Federal Register a notice that the waiver was granted for national security purposes, unless, upon the request of the Secretary of Defense, the Administrator determines to omit such publication because the publication itself would be contrary to the interests of national security, in which event the Administrator shall submit notice to the Armed Services Committee of the Senate and House of Representatives.

(c) Indian rights and sovereignty as unaffected

(1) Nothing in the Safe Drinking Water Amendments of 1977 shall be construed to alter or affect the status of American Indian lands or water rights nor to waive any sovereignty over Indian lands guaranteed by treaty or statute.

(2) For the purposes of this chapter, the term "Federal agency" shall not be construed to refer to or include any American Indian tribe, nor to the Secretary of the Interior in his capacity as trustee of Indian lands.

(July 1, 1944, c. 373, Title XIV, § 1447, as added Dec. 16, 1974, Pub.L. 93–523, § 2(a), 88 Stat. 1688, and amended Nov. 16, 1977, Pub.L. 95–190, § 8(a), (d), 91 Stat. 1396, 1397.)

CODE OF FEDERAL REGULATIONS

Underground injection control programs, technical criteria and standards for, see 40 CFR 146.1 et seq.

§ 300j–7. Judicial review [PHSA § 1448]

(a) Courts of appeals; petition for review; actions respecting regulations; filing period; grounds arising after expiration of filing period; exclusiveness of remedy

A petition for review of—

(1) actions pertaining to the establishment of national primary drinking water regulations (including maximum contaminant level goals) may be filed only in the United States Court of Appeals for the District of Columbia circuit; and

(2) any other action of the Administrator under this chapter may be filed in the circuit in which the petitioner resides or transacts business which is directly affected by the action.

Any such petition shall be filed within the 45-day period beginning on the date of the promulgation of the regulation or issuance of the order with respect to which review is sought or on the date of the determination with respect to which review is sought, and may be filed after the expiration of such 45-day period if the petition is based solely on grounds arising after the expiration of such period. Action of the Administrator with respect to which review could have been obtained under this subsection shall not be subject to judicial review in any civil or criminal proceeding for enforcement or in any civil action to enjoin enforcement.

(b) District courts; petition for review; actions respecting variances or exemptions; filing period; grounds arising after expiration of filing period; exclusiveness of remedy

The United States district courts shall have jurisdiction of actions brought to review (1) the granting of, or the refusing to grant, a variance or exemption under section 300g–4 or 300g–5 of this title or (2) the requirements of any schedule prescribed for a variance or exemption under such section or the failure to prescribe such a schedule. Such an action may only be brought upon a petition for review filed with the court within the 45-day period beginning on the date the action sought to be reviewed is taken or, in the case of a petition to review the refusal to grant a variance or exemption or the failure to prescribe a schedule, within the 45-day period beginning on the date action is required to be taken on the variance, exemption, or schedule, as the case may be. A petition for such review may be filed after the expiration of such period if the petition is based solely on grounds arising after the expiration of such period. Action with respect to which review could have been obtained under this subsection shall not be subject to judicial review in any civil or criminal proceeding for enforcement or in any civil action to enjoin enforcement.

(c) Judicial order for additional evidence before Administrator; modified or new findings; recommendation for modification or setting aside of original determination

In any judicial proceeding in which review is sought of a determination under this subchapter required to be made on the record after notice and opportunity for hearing, if any party applies to the court for leave to adduce additional evidence and shows to the satisfaction of the court that such additional evidence is material and that there were reasonable grounds for the failure to adduce such evidence in the proceeding before the Administrator, the court may order such additional evidence (and evidence in rebuttal thereof) to be taken before the Administrator, in such manner and upon such terms and conditions as the court may deem proper. The Administrator may modify his findings as to the facts, or make new findings, by reason of the additional evidence so taken, and he shall file such modified or new findings, and his recommendation, if any, for the modification or setting aside of his original determination, with the return of such additional evidence.

(July 1, 1944, c. 373, Title XIV, § 1448, as added Dec. 16, 1974, Pub.L. 93–523, § 2(a), 88 Stat. 1689, and amended June 19, 1986, Pub.L. 99–339, Title III, § 303, 100 Stat. 667.)

LAW REVIEW COMMENTARIES

Coordinating judicial review in administrative law. Harold H. Bruff, 39 UCLA L.Rev. 1193 (1992).

LIBRARY REFERENCES

Health and Environment ⚖25.15(1).
C.J.S. Health and Environment § 82 et seq.

§ 300j–8. Citizen's civil action [PHSA § 1449]

(a) Persons subject to civil action; jurisdiction of enforcement proceedings

Except as provided in subsection (b) of this section, any person may commence a civil action on his own behalf—

(1) against any person (including (A) the United States, and (B) any other governmental instrumentality or agency to the extent permitted by the eleventh amendment to the Constitution) who is alleged to be in violation of any requirement prescribed by or under this subchapter, or

(2) against the Administrator where there is alleged a failure of the Administrator to perform any act or duty under this subchapter which is not discretionary with the Administrator.

No action may be brought under paragraph (1) against a public water system for a violation of a requirement prescribed by or under this subchapter which occurred within the 27-month period beginning on the first day of the month in which this subchapter is enacted. The United States district courts shall have jurisdiction, without regard to the amount in controversy or the citizenship of the parties, to enforce in an action brought under this subsection any requirement prescribed by or under this subchapter or to order the Administrator to perform an act or duty described in paragraph (2), as the case may be.

(b) Conditions for commencement of civil action; notice

No civil action may be commenced—

(1) under subsection (a)(1) of this section respecting violation of a requirement prescribed by or under this subchapter—

(A) prior to sixty days after the plaintiff has given notice of such violation (i) to the Administrator, (ii) to any alleged violator of such requirement and (iii) to the State in which the violation occurs, or

(B) if the Administrator, the Attorney General, or the State has commenced and is diligently prosecuting a civil action in a court of the United States to require compliance with such requirement, but in any such action in a court of the United States any person may intervene as a matter of right; or

(2) under subsection (a)(2) of this section prior to sixty days after the plaintiff has given notice of such action to the Administrator.

Notice required by this subsection shall be given in such manner as the Administrator shall prescribe by regulation. No person may commence a civil action under subsection (a) of this section to require a State to prescribe a schedule under section 300g–4 or 300g–5 of this title for a variance or exemption, unless such person shows to the satisfaction of the court that the State has in a substantial number of cases failed to prescribe such schedules.

(c) Intervention of right

In any action under this section, the Administrator or the Attorney General, if not a party, may intervene as a matter of right.

(d) Costs; attorney fees; expert witness fees; filing of bond

The court, in issuing any final order in any action brought under subsection (a) of this section, may award costs of litigation (including reasonable attorney and expert witness fees) to any party whenever the court determines such an award is appropriate. The court may, if a temporary restraining order or preliminary injunction is sought, require the filing of a bond or equivalent security in accordance with the Federal Rules of Civil Procedure.

(e) Availability of other relief

Nothing in this section shall restrict any right which any person (or class of persons) may have under any statute or common law to seek enforcement of any requirement prescribed by or under this subchapter or to seek any other relief. Nothing in this section or in any other law of the United States shall be construed to prohibit, exclude, or restrict any State or local government from—

(1) bringing any action or obtaining any remedy or sanction in any State or local court, or

(2) bringing any administrative action or obtaining any administrative remedy or sanction,

against any agency of the United States under State or local law to enforce any requirement respecting the provision of safe drinking water or respecting any underground injection control program. Nothing in this section shall be construed to authorize judicial review of regulations or orders of the Administrator under this subchapter, except as provided in section 300j–7 of this title. For provisions providing for application of certain requirements to such agencies in the same manner as to nongovernmental entities, see section 300j–6 of this title.

(July 1, 1944, c. 373, Title XIV, § 1449, as added Dec. 16, 1974, Pub.L. 93–523, § 2(a), 88 Stat. 1690, and amended Nov. 16, 1977, Pub.L. 95–190, § 8(c), 91 Stat. 1397.)

§ 300j–9. General provisions [PHSA § 1450]

(a) Regulations; delegation of functions

(1) The Administrator is authorized to prescribe such regulations as are necessary or appropriate to carry out his functions under this subchapter.

(2) The Administrator may delegate any of his functions under this subchapter (other than prescribing regulations) to any officer or employee of the Agency.

(b) Utilization of officers and employees of Federal agencies

The Administrator, with the consent of the head of any other agency of the United States, may utilize such officers and employees of such agency as he deems necessary to assist him in carrying out the purposes of this subchapter.

(c) Assignment of Agency personnel to State or interstate agencies

Upon the request of a State or interstate agency, the Administrator may assign personnel of the Agency to such State or interstate agency for the purposes of carrying out the provisions of this subchapter.

(d) Payments of grants; adjustments; advances; reimbursement; installments; conditions; eligibility for grants; "nonprofit agency or institution" defined

(1) The Administrator may make payments of grants under this subchapter (after necessary adjustment on account of previously made underpayments or overpayments) in advance or by way of reimbursement, and in such installments and on such conditions as he may determine.

(2) Financial assistance may be made available in the form of grants only to individuals and nonprofit agencies or institutions. For purposes of this paragraph, the term "nonprofit agency or institution" means an agency or institution no part of the net earnings of which inure, or may lawfully inure, to the benefit of any private shareholder or individual.

(e) Labor standards

The Administrator shall take such action as may be necessary to assure compliance with provisions of the Act of March 3, 1931 (known as the Davis-Bacon Act; 40 U.S.C. 276a—276a–5). The Secretary of Labor shall have, with respect to the labor standards specified in this subsection, the authority and functions set forth in Reorganization Plan Numbered 14 of 1950 (15 F.R. 3176; 64 Stat. 1267) and section 276c of Title 40.

(f) Appearance and representation of Administrator through Attorney General or attorney appointees

The Administrator shall request the Attorney General to appear and represent him in any civil action instituted under this subchapter to which the Administrator is a party. Unless, within a reasonable time, the Attorney General notifies the Administrator that he will appear in such action, attorneys appointed by the Administrator shall appear and represent him.

(g) Authority of Administrator under other provisions unaffected

The provisions of this subchapter shall not be construed as affecting any authority of the Administrator under part G of subchapter II of this chapter.

(h) Reports to Congressional Committees; review by Office of Management and Budget: submittal of comments to Congressional Committees

Not later than April 1 of each year, the Administrator shall submit to the Committee on Commerce, Science, and Transportation of the Senate and the Committee on Energy and Commerce of the House of

Representatives a report respecting the activities of the Agency under this subchapter and containing such recommendations for legislation as he considers necessary. The report of the Administrator under this subsection which is due not later than April 1, 1975, and each subsequent report of the Administrator under this subsection shall include a statement on the actual and anticipated cost to public water systems in each State of compliance with the requirements of this subchapter. The Office of Management and Budget may review any report required by this subsection before its submission to such committees of Congress, but the Office may not revise any such report, require any revision in any such report, or delay its submission beyond the day prescribed for its submission, and may submit to such committees of Congress its comments respecting any such report.

(i) Discrimination prohibition; procedural requirements; prohibition inapplicable to undirected but deliberate violations

(1) No employer may discharge any employee or otherwise discriminate against any employee with respect to his compensation, terms, conditions, or privileges of employment because the employee (or any person acting pursuant to a request of the employee) has—

(A) commenced, caused to be commenced, or is about to commence or cause to be commenced a proceeding under this subchapter or a proceeding for the administration or enforcement of drinking water regulations or underground injection control programs of a State,

(B) testified or is about to testify in any such proceeding, or

(C) assisted or participated or is about to assist or participate in any manner in such a proceeding or in any other action to carry out the purposes of this subchapter.

(2)(A) Any employee who believes that he has been discharged or otherwise discriminated against by any person in violation of paragraph (1) may, within 30 days after such violation occurs, file (or have any person file on his behalf) a complaint with the Secretary of Labor (hereinafter in this subsection referred to as the "Secretary") alleging such discharge or discrimination. Upon receipt of such a complaint, the Secretary shall notify the person named in the complaint of the filing of the complaint.

(B)(i) Upon receipt of a complaint filed under subparagraph (A), the Secretary shall conduct an investigation of the violation alleged in the complaint. Within 30 days of the receipt of such complaint, the Secretary shall complete such investigation and shall notify in writing the complainant (and any person acting in his behalf) and the person alleged to have committed such violation of the results of the investigation conducted pursuant to this subparagraph. Within 90 days of the receipt of such complaint the Secretary shall, unless the proceeding on the complaint is terminated by the Secretary on the basis of a settlement entered into by the Secretary and the person alleged to have committed such violation, issue an order either providing the relief prescribed by clause (ii) or denying the complaint. An order of the Secretary shall be made on the record after notice and opportunity for agency hearing. The Secretary may not enter into a settlement terminating a proceeding on a complaint without the participation and consent of the complainant.

(ii) If in response to a complaint filed under subparagraph (A) the Secretary determines that a violation of paragraph (1) has occurred, the Secretary shall order (I) the person who committed such violation to take affirmative action to abate the violation, (II) such person to reinstate the complainant to his former position together with the compensation (including back pay), terms, conditions, and privileges of his employment, (III) compensatory damages, and (IV) where appropriate, exemplary damages. If such an order is issued, the Secretary, at the request of the complainant, shall assess against the person against whom the order is issued a sum equal to the aggregate amount of all costs and expenses (including attorneys' fees) reasonably incurred, as determined by the Secretary, by the complainant for, or in connection with, the bringing of the complaint upon which the order was issued.

(3)(A) Any person adversely affected or aggrieved by an order issued under paragraph (2) may obtain review of the order in the United States Court of Appeals for the circuit in which the violation, with respect to which the order was issued, allegedly occurred. The petition for review must be filed within sixty days from the issuance of the Secretary's order. Review shall conform to chapter 7 of Title 5. The commencement of proceedings under this subparagraph shall not, unless ordered by the court, operate as a stay of the Secretary's order.

(B) An order of the Secretary with respect to which review could have been obtained under subparagraph (A) shall not be subject to judicial review in any criminal or other civil proceeding.

(4) Whenever a person has failed to comply with an order issued under paragraph (2)(B), the Secretary shall file a civil action in the United States District Court for the district in which the violation was found to occur to enforce such order. In actions brought under this paragraph, the district courts shall have jurisdiction to grant all appropriate relief including, but not limited to, injunctive relief, compensatory, and exemplary damages.

(5) Any nondiscretionary duty imposed by this section is enforceable in mandamus proceeding brought under section 1361 of Title 28.

(6) Paragraph (1) shall not apply with respect to any employee who, acting without direction from his employer (or the employer's agent), deliberately causes a violation of any requirement of this subchapter.

(July 1, 1944, c. 373, Title XIV, § 1450, as added Dec. 16, 1974, Pub.L. 93–523, § 2(a), 88 Stat. 1691, and amended S.Res. 4, Feb. 4, 1977; H.Res. 549, Mar. 25, 1980; Nov. 8, 1984, Pub.L. 98–620, Title IV, § 402(38), 98 Stat. 3360; Nov. 2, 1994, Pub.L. 103–437, § 15(a)(2), 108 Stat. 4591.)

Change of Name

Any reference in any provision of law enacted before Jan. 4, 1995, to the Committee on Energy and Commerce of the House of Representatives treated as referring to the Committee on Commerce of the House of Representatives, except that any reference in any provision of law enacted before Jan. 4, 1995, to the Committee on Energy and Commerce of the House of Representatives treated as referring to the Committee on Agriculture of the House of Representatives, in the case of a provision of law relating to inspection of seafood or seafood products, the Committee on Banking and Financial Services of the House of Representatives, in the case of a provision of law relating to bank capital markets activities generally or to depository institution securities activities generally, and the Committee on Transportation and Infrastructure of the House of Representatives, in the case of a provision of law relating to railroads, railway labor, or railroad retirement and unemployment (except revenue measures related thereto), see section 1(a)(4) and (c)(1) of Pub.L. 104–14, set out as a note preceding section 21 of Title 2, The Congress.

CODE OF FEDERAL REGULATIONS

Environmental Protection Agency,
  Administration of permit programs, see 40 CFR 122.1 et seq.
  Decisionmaking procedures applicable to permit programs, see 40 CFR 124.1 et seq.
Grant policies and procedures, see 40 CFR 35.100 et seq.
Implementation and enforcement of national primary drinking water regulations, see 40 CFR 142.1 et seq.
Labor standards applicable to contracts covering federally financed and assisted construction, see 29 CFR 5.1 et seq.
Procedures for determination of prevailing wage rates for laborers and mechanics, see 29 CFR 1.1 et seq.
Procedures governing disposition of discrimination complaints, see 29 CFR 24.1 et seq.
Public participation in programs and activities, see 40 CFR 25.1 et seq.
Underground injection control programs, technical criteria and standards for, see 40 CFR 146.1 et seq.

LIBRARY REFERENCES

Health and Environment ⚖25.7(3).
Labor Relations ⚖7.
C.J.S. Health and Environment § 106.
C.J.S. Labor Relations § 2 et seq.

§ 300j–10. Appointment of scientific, etc., personnel by Administrator of Environmental Protection Agency for implementation of responsibilities; compensation

To the extent that the Administrator of the Environmental Protection Agency deems such action necessary to the discharge of his functions under title XIV of the Public Health Service Act [42 U.S.C.A. § 300f et seq.] (relating to safe drinking water) and under other provisions of law, he may appoint personnel to fill not more than thirty scientific, engineering, professional, legal, and administrative positions within the Environmental Protection Agency without regard to the civil service laws and may fix the compensation of such personnel not in excess of the maximum rate payable for GS–18 of the General Schedule under section 5332 of Title 5.

(Nov. 16, 1977, Pub.L. 95–190, § 11(b), 91 Stat. 1398.)

Codification

Section was enacted as part of the Safe Drinking Water Amendments of 1977, and not as part of the Public Health Service Act which comprises this chapter.

LIBRARY REFERENCES

Health and Environment ⚖25.5(9).
C.J.S. Health and Environment § 65 et seq.

§ 300j–11. Indian Tribes [PHSA § 1451]

(a) In general

Subject to the provisions of subsection (b) of this section, the Administrator—

(1) is authorized to treat Indian Tribes as States under this subchapter,

(2) may delegate to such Tribes primary enforcement responsibility for public water systems and for underground injection control, and

(3) may provide such Tribes grant and contract assistance to carry out functions provided by this subchapter.

(b) EPA regulations

(1) Specific provisions

The Administrator shall, within 18 months after June 19, 1986, promulgate final regulations specifying those provisions of this subchapter for which it is appropriate to treat Indian Tribes as States. Such treatment shall be authorized only if:

(A) the Indian Tribe is recognized by the Secretary of the Interior and has a governing body carrying out substantial governmental duties and powers;

(B) the functions to be exercised by the Indian Tribe are within the area of the Tribal Government's jurisdiction; and

(C) the Indian Tribe is reasonably expected to be capable, in the Administrator's judgment, of carrying out the functions to be exercised in a manner consistent with the terms and purposes of this subchapter and of all applicable regulations.

(2) Provisions where treatment as State inappropriate

For any provision of this subchapter where treatment of Indian Tribes as identical to States is inappropriate, administratively infeasible or otherwise inconsistent with the purposes of this subchapter, the Administrator may include in the regulations promulgated under this section, other means for administering such provision in a manner that will achieve the purpose of the provision. Nothing in this section shall be construed to allow Indian Tribes to assume or maintain primary enforcement responsibility for public water systems or for underground injection control in a manner less protective of the health of persons than such responsibility may be assumed or maintained by a State. An Indian tribe[1] shall not be required to exercise criminal enforcement jurisdiction for purposes of complying with the preceding sentence.

(July 1, 1944, c. 373, Title XIV, § 1451, as added June 19, 1986, Pub.L. 99–339, Title III, § 302(a), 100 Stat. 665.)

[1] So in original. Probably should be capitalized.

PART F—ADDITIONAL REQUIREMENTS TO REGULATE THE SAFETY OF DRINKING WATER

§ 300j–21. Definitions [PHSA § 1461]

As used in this part—

(1) Drinking water cooler.—The term "drinking water cooler" means any mechanical device affixed to drinking water supply plumbing which actively cools water for human consumption.

(2) Lead free.—The term "lead free" means, with respect to a drinking water cooler, that each part or component of the cooler which may come in contact with drinking water contains not more than 8 percent lead, except that no drinking water cooler which contains any solder, flux, or storage tank interior surface which may come in contact with drinking water shall be considered lead free if the solder, flux, or storage tank interior surface contains more than 0.2 percent lead. The Administrator may establish more stringent requirements for treating any part or component of a drinking water cooler as lead free for purposes of this part whenever he determines that any such part may constitute an important source of lead in drinking water.

(3) Local educational agency.—The term "local educational agency" means—

(A) any local educational agency as defined in section 8801 of Title 20,

(B) the owner of any private, nonprofit elementary or secondary school building, and

(C) the governing authority of any school operating under the defense dependent's education system provided for under the Defense Dependent's Education Act of 1978 (20 U.S.C. 921 and following).

(4) Repair.—The term "repair" means, with respect to a drinking water cooler, to take such corrective action as is necessary to ensure that water cooler is lead free.

(5) Replacement.—The term "replacement", when used with respect to a drinking water cooler, means the permanent removal of the water cooler and the installation of a lead free water cooler.

(6) School.—The term "school" means any elementary school or secondary school as defined in section 8801 of Title 20 and any kindergarten or day care facility.

(7) Lead-lined tank.—The term "lead-lined tank" means a water reservoir container in a drinking water cooler which container is constructed of lead or which has an interior surface which is not lead free.

(July 1, 1944, c. 373, Title XIV, § 1461, as added Oct. 31, 1988, Pub.L. 100–572, § 2(a), 102 Stat. 2884, and amended Oct. 20, 1994, Pub.L. 103–382, Title III, § 391(p), 108 Stat. 4024.)

References in Text

The Defense Dependents' Education Act of 1978, referred to in par. (3)(C), is Title XIV of Pub.L. 95–561, Nov. 1, 1978, 92 Stat. 2365, as amended, which is classified principally to chapter 25A (§ 921 et seq.) of Title 20, Education.

§ 300j–22. Recall of drinking water coolers with lead-lined tanks [PHSA § 1462]

For purposes of the Consumer Product Safety Act [15 U.S.C.A. § 2051 et seq.], all drinking water coolers identified by the Administrator on the list under section 300j–23 of this title as having a lead-lined tank shall be considered to be imminently hazardous consumer products within the meaning of section 12 of such Act (15 U.S.C. 2061). After notice and opportunity for comment, including a public hearing, the Consumer Product Safety Commission shall issue an order requiring the manufacturers and importers of such coolers to repair, replace, or recall and provide a refund for such coolers within 1 year after October 31,

1988. For purposes of enforcement, such order shall be treated as an order under section 15(d) of that Act (15 U.S.C. 2064(d)).

(July 1, 1944, c. 373, Title XIV, § 1462, as added Oct. 31, 1988, Pub.L. 100–572, § 2(a), 102 Stat. 2885.)

References in Text

The Consumer Product Safety Act, referred to in text, is Pub.L. 92–573, Oct. 27, 1972, 86 Stat. 1207, as amended, which is classified generally to chapter 47 (§ 2051 et seq.) of Title 15, Commerce and Trade.

§ 300j–23. Drinking water coolers containing lead [PHSA § 1463]

(a) Publication of lists

The Administrator shall, after notice and opportunity for public comment, identify each brand and model of drinking water cooler which is not lead free, including each brand and model of drinking water cooler which has a lead-lined tank. For purposes of identifying the brand and model of drinking water coolers under this subsection, the Administrator shall use the best information available to the Environmental Protection Agency. Within 100 days after October 31, 1988, the Administrator shall publish a list of each brand and model of drinking water cooler identified under this subsection. Such list shall separately identify each brand and model of cooler which has a lead-lined tank. The Administrator shall continue to gather information regarding lead in drinking water coolers and shall revise and republish the list from time to time as may be appropriate as new information or analysis becomes available regarding lead contamination in drinking water coolers.

(b) Prohibition

No person may sell in interstate commerce, or manufacture for sale in interstate commerce, any drinking water cooler listed under subsection (a) of this section or any other drinking water cooler which is not lead free, including a lead-lined drinking water cooler.

(c) Criminal penalty

Any person who knowingly violates the prohibition contained in subsection (b) of this section shall be imprisoned for not more than 5 years, or fined in accordance with Title 18, or both.

(d) Civil penalty

The Administrator may bring a civil action in the appropriate United States District Court (as determined under the provisions of Title 28) to impose a civil penalty on any person who violates subsection (b) of this section. In any such action the court may impose on such person a civil penalty of not more than $5,000 ($50,000 in the case of a second or subsequent violation).

(July 1, 1944, c. 373, Title XIV, § 1463, as added Oct. 31, 1988, Pub.L. 100–572, § 2(a), 102 Stat. 2885.)

§ 300j–24. Lead contamination in school drinking water [PHSA § 1464]

(a) Distribution of drinking water cooler list

Within 100 days after October 31, 1988, the Administrator shall distribute to the States a list of each brand and model of drinking water cooler identified and listed by the Administrator under section 300j–23(a) of this title.

(b) Guidance document and testing protocol

The Administrator shall publish a guidance document and a testing protocol to assist schools in determining the source and degree of lead contamination in school drinking water supplies and in remedying such contamination. The guidance document shall include guidelines for sample preservation. The guidance document shall also include guidance to assist States, schools, and the general public in ascertaining the levels of lead contamination in drinking water coolers and in taking appropriate action to reduce or eliminate such contamination. The guidance document shall contain a testing protocol for the identification of drinking water coolers which contribute to lead contamination in drinking water. Such document and protocol may be revised, republished and redistributed as the Administrator deems necessary. The Administrator shall distribute the guidance document and testing protocol to the States within 100 days after October 31, 1988.

(c) Dissemination to schools, etc.

Each State shall provide for the dissemination to local educational agencies, private nonprofit elementary or secondary schools and to day care centers of the guidance document and testing protocol published under subsection (b) of this section, together with the list of drinking water coolers published under section 300j–23(a) of this title.

(d) Remedial action program

(1) Testing and remedying lead contamination

Within 9 months after October 31, 1988, each State shall establish a program, consistent with this section, to assist local educational agencies in testing for, and remedying, lead contamination in drinking water from coolers and from other sources of lead contamination at schools under the jurisdiction of such agencies.

(2) Public availability

A copy of the results of any testing under paragraph (1) shall be available in the administrative offices of the local educational agency for inspection by the public, including teachers, other school personnel, and parents. The local educational agency shall notify parent, teacher, and employee organizations of the availability of such testing results.

(3) Coolers

In the case of drinking water coolers, such program shall include measures for the reduction or elimination of lead contamination from those water coolers which are not lead free and which are located in schools. Such measures shall be adequate to ensure that within 15 months after October 31, 1988, all such water coolers in schools under the jurisdiction of such agencies are repaired, replaced, permanently removed, or rendered inoperable unless the cooler is tested and found (within the limits of testing accuracy) not to contribute lead to drinking water.

(July 1, 1944, c. 373, Title XIV, § 1464, as added Oct. 31, 1988, Pub.L. 100–572, § 2(a), 102 Stat. 2886.)

§ 300j–25. Federal assistance for State programs regarding lead contamination in school drinking water [PHSA § 1465]

(a) School drinking water programs

The Administrator shall make grants to States to establish and carry out State programs under section 300j–24 of this title to assist local educational agencies in testing for, and remedying, lead contamination in drinking water from drinking water coolers and from other sources of lead contamination at schools under the jurisdiction of such agencies. Such grants may be used by States to reimburse local educational agencies for expenses incurred after October 31, 1988, for such testing and remedial action.

(b) Limits

Each grant under this section shall be used as by the State for testing water coolers in accordance with section 300j–24 of this title, for testing for lead contamination in other drinking water supplies under section 300j–24 of this title, or for remedial action under State programs under section 300j–24 of this title. Not more than 5 percent of the grant may be used for program administration.

(c) Authorization of appropriations

There are authorized to be appropriated to carry out this section not more than $30,000,000 for fiscal year 1989, $30,000,000 for fiscal year 1990, and $30,000,000 for fiscal year 1991.

(July 1, 1944, c. 373, Title XIV, § 1465, as added Oct. 31, 1988, Pub.L. 100–572, § 2(a), 102 Stat. 2887.)

§ 300j–26. Certification of testing laboratories

The Administrator of the Environmental Protection Agency shall assure that programs for the certification of testing laboratories which test drinking water supplies for lead contamination certify only those laboratories which provide reliable accurate testing. The Administrator (or the State in the case of a State to which certification authority is delegated under this subsection)[1] shall publish and make available to the public upon request the list of laboratories certified under this subsection.[1]

(Pub.L. 100–572, § 4, Oct. 31, 1988, 102 Stat. 2889.)

[1] So in original.

Codification

Section was enacted as part of the Lead Contamination Control Act of 1988 and not as part of the Public Health Service Act which comprises this chapter.

NATIONAL ENVIRONMENTAL POLICY

NATIONAL ENVIRONMENTAL POLICY ACT OF 1969 [NEPA § ___]

(42 U.S.C.A. §§ 4321 to 4370d)

CHAPTER 55—NATIONAL ENVIRONMENTAL POLICY

Sec.

4321. Congressional declaration of purpose.

SUBCHAPTER I—POLICIES AND GOALS

4331. Congressional declaration of national environmental policy.
   (a) Creation and maintenance of conditions under which man and nature can exist in productive harmony.
   (b) Continuing responsibility of Federal Government to use all practicable means to improve and coordinate Federal plans, functions, programs, and resources.
   (c) Responsibility of each person to contribute to preservation and enhancement of environment.

4332. Cooperation of agencies; reports; availability of information; recommendations; international and national coordination of efforts.

4333. Conformity of administrative procedures to national environmental policy.

4334. Other statutory obligations of agencies.

4335. Efforts supplemental to existing authorizations.

SUBCHAPTER II—COUNCIL ON ENVIRONMENTAL QUALITY

4341. Reports to Congress; recommendations for legislation.

4342. Establishment; membership; Chairman; appointments.

4343. Employment of personnel, experts and consultants.

4344. Duties and functions.

4345. Consultation with Citizens' Advisory Committee on Environmental Quality and other representatives.

4346. Tenure and compensation of members.

4346a. Travel reimbursement by private organizations and Federal, State, and local governments.

4346b. Expenditures in support of international activities.

4347. Authorization of appropriations.

SUBCHAPTER III—MISCELLANEOUS PROVISIONS

4361, 4361a. Repealed.

4361b. Implementation by Administrator of Environmental Protection Agency of recommendations of "CHESS" Investigative Report; waiver; inclusion of status of implementation requirements in annual revisions of plan for research, development, and demonstration.

4361c. Staff management.
   (a) Appointments for educational programs.
   (b) Post-doctoral research fellows.
   (c) Non-government research associates.
   (d) Women and minority groups.

4362. Interagency cooperation on prevention of environmental cancer and heart and lung disease.

4362a. Task Force on Environmental Cancer and Heart and Lung Disease; membership of Director of National Center for Health Statistics and of head of Center for Disease Control.

4363. Continuing and long-term environmental research and development.

4363a. Pollution control technologies demonstrations.

4364. Expenditure of funds for research and development related to regulatory program activities.
   (a) Coordination, etc., with research needs and priorities of program offices and Environmental Protection Agency.
   (b) Program offices subject to coverage.
   (c) Report to Congress; contents.

4365. Science Advisory Board.
   (a) Establishment; requests for advice by administrator of Environmental Protection Agency and Congressional committees.
   (b) Membership; Chairman; meetings; qualifications of members.
   (c) Proposed environmental criteria document, standard, limitation, or regulation; functions respecting in conjunction with Administrator.
   (d) Utilization of technical and scientific capabilities of Federal agencies and national environmental laboratories for determining adequacy of scientific and technical basis of proposed criteria document, etc.
   (e) Member committees and investigative panels; establishment; chairmanship.
   (f) Appointment and compensation of secretary and other personnel; compensation of members.
   (g) Consultation and coordination with Scientific Advisory Panel.

4366. Identification and coordination of research, development, and demonstration activities.
   (a) Consultation and cooperation of Administrator of Environmental Protection Agency with heads of Federal agencies; inclusion of activities in annual revisions of plan for research, etc.
   (b) Coordination of programs by Administrator.
   (c) Joint study by Council on Environmental Quality in consultation with Office of Science and

Sec.
4366. Identification and coordination of research, development, and demonstration activities.
Technology Policy for coordination of activities; report to President and Congress; report by President to Congress on implementation of joint study and report.
4366a. Development of data base of environmental research articles indexed by geographic location.
(a) Research journals.
(b) Index.
(c) Purchase of information.
(d) Revising list.
(e) Specific location of research projects.
4367. Reporting requirements of financial interests of officers and employees of Environmental Protection Agency.
(a) Covered officers and employees.
(b) Implementation of requirements by Administrator.
(c) Exemption of positions by Administrator.
(d) Violations; penalties.
4368. Grants to qualified citizens groups.
4368a. Utilization of talents of older Americans in projects of pollution prevention, abatement, and control.
(a) Technical assistance to environmental agencies.
(b) Pre-award certifications.
(c) Prior appropriations Acts.
4368b. General assistance program.
(a) Short title.
(b) Purposes.
(c) Definitions.
(d) General assistance program.
(e) No reduction in amounts.
(f) Expenditure of general assistance.
(g) Procedures.
(h) Authorization.
4369. Miscellaneous reports.
(a) Availability to Congressional committees.
(b) Transmittal of jurisdictional information.
(c) Comment by Government agencies and the public.
(d) Transmittal of research information to the Department of Energy.
4369a. Reports on environmental research and development activities of the Agency.
(a) Reports to keep Congressional committees fully and currently informed.
(b) Annual reports relating requested funds to activities to be carried out with those funds.
4370. Reimbursement for use of facilities.
(a) Authority to allow outside groups or individuals to use research and test facilities; reimbursement.
(b) Rules and regulations.
(c) Waiver of reimbursement by Administrator.
4370a. Assistant Administrators of Environmental Protection Agency; appointment; duties.
4370b. Availability of fees and charges to carry out Agency programs.
4370c. Environmental Protection Agency fees.
(a) Assessment and collection.
(b) Amount of fees and charges.
(c) Limit on fees and charges.
(d) Rule of construction.
(e) Uses of fees.

Sec.
4370d. Availability of funding for economically and socially disadvantaged individuals.

WESTLAW ELECTRONIC RESEARCH

See WESTLAW guide following the Explanation pages of this pamphlet.

§ 4321. Congressional declaration of purpose [NEPA § 2]

The purposes of this chapter are: To declare a national policy which will encourage productive and enjoyable harmony between man and his environment; to promote efforts which will prevent or eliminate damage to the environment and biosphere and stimulate the health and welfare of man; to enrich the understanding of the ecological systems and natural resources important to the Nation; and to establish a Council on Environmental Quality.

(Jan. 1, 1970, Pub.L. 91–190, § 2, 83 Stat. 852.)

Short Title

Section 1 of Pub.L. 91–190 Jan. 1, 1970, 83 Stat. 852, provided: "That this Act [enacting this chapter] may be cited as the 'National Environmental Policy Act of 1969'."

Environmental Enforcement

Pub.L. 101–593, Title II, Nov. 16, 1990, 104 Stat. 2962, provided that:

"Sec. 201. Short Title.

"This title may be cited as the 'Pollution Prosecution Act of 1990'.

"Sec. 202. EPA Office of Criminal Investigation.

"(a) The Administrator of the Environmental Protection Agency (hereinafter referred to as the 'Administrator') shall increase the number of criminal investigators assigned to the Office of Criminal Investigations by such numbers as may be necessary to assure that the number of criminal investigators assigned to the office—

"(1) for the period October 1, 1991, through September 30, 1992, is not less than 72;

"(2) for the period October 1, 1992, through September 30, 1993, is not less than 110;

"(3) for the period October 1, 1993, through September 30, 1994, is not less than 123;

"(4) for the period October 1, 1994, through September 30, 1995, is not less than 160;

"(5) beginning October 1, 1995, is not less than 200.

"(b) For fiscal year 1991 and in each of the following 4 fiscal years, the Administrator shall, during each such fiscal year, provide increasing numbers of additional support staff to the Office of Criminal Investigations.

"(c) The head of the Office of Criminal Investigations shall be a position in the competitive service as defined in 2102 of title 5 U.S.C. [section 2102 of Title 5, Government Organization and Employees] or a career reserve position as defined in 3132(A) of title 5 U.S.C. [section 3132(A) of Title 5] and the head of such office shall report directly, without intervening review or approval, to the Assistant Administrator for Enforcement.

"Sec. 203. Civil investigators.

"The Administrator, as soon as practicable following the date of the enactment of this Act [Nov. 16, 1990], but no later than September 30, 1991, shall increase by fifty the number of civil investigators assigned to assist the Office of Enforcement in developing and prosecuting civil and administrative actions and carrying out its other functions.

"Sec. 204. National Training Institute.

"The Administrator shall, as soon as practicable but no later than September 30, 1991 establish within the Office of Enforcement the National Enforcement Training Institute. It shall be the function of the Institute, among others, to train Federal, State, and local lawyers, inspectors, civil and criminal investigators, and technical experts in the enforcement of the Nation's environmental laws.

"Sec. 205. **Authorization.**

"For the purposes of carrying out the provisions of this Act [probably means this note], there is authorized to be appropriated to the Environmental Protection Agency $13,000,000 for fiscal year 1991, $18,000,000 for fiscal year 1992, $20,000,000 for fiscal year 1993, $26,000,000 for fiscal year 1994, and $33,000,000 for fiscal year 1995."

CROSS REFERENCES

Pacific Salmon Fishing, regulations of Secretary of Commerce under treaty not subject to this chapter, see section 3636 of Title 16, Conservation.

Federal Practice and Procedure

Environmental class actions, see Wright, Miller & Kane: Civil § 1782.

West's Federal Practice Manual

Federal environmental law, see § 4381 et seq.

LAW REVIEW COMMENTARIES

Businesses beware: Personal liability looms for environmental offenses. Joseph G. Maternowski, 62 Hennepin Law. (Mn.) 12 (Nov.–Dec. 1992).

Criminal enforcement of environmental regulations. Daniel J. Gibby and Daniel L. Eide, 67 Fla.B.J. 72 (May 1993).

DEC's proposed new SEQRA regulations. Stephen L. Kass and Michael B. Gerrard, 211 N.Y.L.J. 3 (March 25, 1994).

Grazing management on the public lands: Opening the process to public participation. Joseph M. Feller, 26 Land and Water L.Rev. 571 (1991).

Judicial review of the administrative record in NEPA litigation. Susannah T. French, 81 Cal.L.Rev. 929 (1993).

Long-range planning in environmental and health regulatory agencies. Richard N.L. Andrews, 20 Ecology L.Q. 515 (1993).

Parallel universes: NEPA lessons for the new property. Michael Herz, 93 Colum.L.Rev. 1668 (1993).

Regulation of batture pollution and ecology. Stan Millan, 33 Loyola (La.) L.Rev. 921 (1988).

LIBRARY REFERENCES

Health and Environment ⚷25.5.
C.J.S. Health and Environment § 61 et seq.

United States Supreme Court

Other statutes, not repealed by implication by this chapter, Aberdeen & Rockfish R. Co. v. Students Challenging Regulatory Agency Procedures, 1975, 95 S.Ct. 2336, 422 U.S. 289, 45 L.Ed.2d 191.

SUBCHAPTER I—POLICIES AND GOALS

§ 4331. Congressional declaration of national environmental policy [NEPA § 101]

(a) Creation and maintenance of conditions under which man and nature can exist in productive harmony

The Congress, recognizing the profound impact of man's activity on the interrelations of all components of the natural environment, particularly the profound influences of population growth, high-density urbanization, industrial expansion, resource exploitation, and new and expanding technological advances and recognizing further the critical importance of restoring and maintaining environmental quality to the overall welfare and development of man, declares that it is the continuing policy of the Federal Government, in cooperation with State and local governments, and other concerned public and private organizations, to use all practicable means and measures, including financial and technical assistance, in a manner calculated to foster and promote the general welfare, to create and maintain conditions under which man and nature can exist in productive harmony, and fulfill the social, economic, and other requirements of present and future generations of Americans.

(b) Continuing responsibility of Federal Government to use all practicable means to improve and coordinate Federal plans, functions, programs, and resources

In order to carry out the policy set forth in this chapter, it is the continuing responsibility of the Federal Government to use all practicable means, consistent with other essential considerations of national policy, to improve and coordinate Federal plans, functions, programs, and resources to the end that the Nation may—

(1) fulfill the responsibilities of each generation as trustee of the environment for succeeding generations;

(2) assure for all Americans safe, healthful, productive, and esthetically and culturally pleasing surroundings;

(3) attain the widest range of beneficial uses of the environment without degradation, risk to health or safety, or other undesirable and unintended consequences;

(4) preserve important historic, cultural, and natural aspects of our national heritage, and maintain, wherever possible, an environment which supports diversity and variety of individual choice;

(5) achieve a balance between population and resource use which will permit high standards of living and a wide sharing of life's amenities; and

(6) enhance the quality of renewable resources and approach the maximum attainable recycling of depletable resources.

(c) Responsibility of each person to contribute to preservation and enhancement of environment

The Congress recognizes that each person should enjoy a healthful environment and that each person has a responsibility to contribute to the preservation and enhancement of the environment.

(Jan. 1, 1970, Pub. L. 91–190, Title I, § 101, 83 Stat. 852.)

Federal Practice and Procedure

Environmental class actions, see Wright, Miller & Kane: Civil 2d § 1782.

LAW REVIEW COMMENTARIES

Long-range planning in environmental and health regulatory agencies. Richard N.L. Andrews, 20 Ecology L.Q. 515 (1993).

Parallel universes: NEPA lessons for the new property. Michael Herz, 93 Colum.L.Rev. 1668 (1993).

LIBRARY REFERENCES

Health and Environment ⚖25.5.
C.J.S. Health and Environment § 61 et seq.

United States Supreme Court

Environmental effect and environmental impact, terms defined, Metropolitan Edison Co. v. People Against Nuclear Energy, 1983, 103 S.Ct. 1556, 460 U.S. 766, 75 L.Ed.2d 534.

§ 4332. Cooperation of agencies; reports; availability of information; recommendations; international and national coordination of efforts [NEPA § 102]

The Congress authorizes and directs that, to the fullest extent possible: (1) the policies, regulations, and public laws of the United States shall be interpreted and administered in accordance with the policies set forth in this chapter, and (2) all agencies of the Federal Government shall—

(A) utilize a systematic, interdisciplinary approach which will insure the integrated use of the natural and social sciences and the environmental design arts in planning and in decisionmaking which may have an impact on man's environment;

(B) identify and develop methods and procedures, in consultation with the Council on Environmental Quality established by subchapter II of this chapter, which will insure that presently unquantified environmental amenities and values may be given appropriate consideration in decisionmaking along with economic and technical considerations;

(C) include in every recommendation or report on proposals for legislation and other major Federal actions significantly affecting the quality of the human environment, a detailed statement by the responsible official on—

(i) the environmental impact of the proposed action,

(ii) any adverse environmental effects which cannot be avoided should the proposal be implemented,

(iii) alternatives to the proposed action,

(iv) the relationship between local short-term uses of man's environment and the maintenance and enhancement of long-term productivity, and

(v) any irreversible and irretrievable commitments of resources which would be involved in the proposed action should it be implemented.

Prior to making any detailed statement, the responsible Federal official shall consult with and obtain the comments of any Federal agency which has jurisdiction by law or special expertise with respect to any environmental impact involved. Copies of such statement and the comments and views of the appropriate Federal, State, and local agencies, which are authorized to develop and enforce environmental standards, shall be made available to the President, the Council on Environmental Quality and to the public as provided by section 552 of Title 5, and shall accompany the proposal through the existing agency review processes;

(D) Any detailed statement required under subparagraph (C) after January 1, 1970, for any major Federal action funded under a program of grants to States shall not be deemed to be legally insufficient solely by reason of having been prepared by a State agency or official, if:

(i) the State agency or official has statewide jurisdiction and has the responsibility for such action,

(ii) the responsible Federal official furnishes guidance and participates in such preparation,

(iii) the responsible Federal official independently evaluates such statement prior to its approval and adoption, and

(iv) after January 1, 1976, the responsible Federal official provides early notification to, and solicits the views of, any other State or any Federal land management entity of any action or any alternative thereto which may have significant impacts upon such State or affected Federal land management entity and, if there is any disagreement on such impacts, prepares a written assessment of such impacts and views for incorporation into such detailed statement.

The procedures in this subparagraph shall not relieve the Federal official of his responsibilities for the scope, objectivity, and content of the entire statement or of any other responsibility under this chapter; and further, this subparagraph does not affect the legal sufficiency of statements prepared by State agencies with less than statewide jurisdiction.[1]

(E) study, develop, and describe appropriate alternatives to recommended courses of action in any proposal which involves unresolved conflicts concerning alternative uses of available resources;

(F) recognize the worldwide and long-range character of environmental problems and, where consistent with the foreign policy of the United States, lend appropriate support to initiatives, resolutions, and programs designed to maximize international cooperation in anticipating and preventing a decline in the quality of mankind's world environment;

(G) make available to States, counties, municipalities, institutions, and individuals, advice and information useful in restoring, maintaining, and enhancing the quality of the environment;

(H) initiate and utilize ecological information in the planning and development of resource-oriented projects; and

(I) assist the Council on Environmental Quality established by subchapter II of this chapter.

(Jan. 1, 1970, Pub.L. 91–190, Title I, § 102, 83 Stat. 853; Aug. 9, 1975, Pub.L. 94–83, 89 Stat. 424.)

[1] So in original. The period probably should be a semicolon.

Certain Commercial Space Launch Activities

Pub.L. 104–88, Title IV, § 401, Dec. 29, 1995, 109 Stat. 955, provided that: "The licensing of a launch vehicle or launch site operator (including any amendment, extension, or renewal of the license) under chapter 701 of title 49, United States Code [section 70101 et seq. of Title 49, Transportation], shall not be considered a major Federal action for purposes of section 102(C) of the National Environmental Policy Act of 1969 (42 U.S.C. 4332(C)) if—

"**(1)** the Department of the Army has issued a permit for the activity; and

"**(2)** the Army Corps of Engineers has found that the activity has no significant impact."

[Section 401 of Pub.L. 104–88 effective Jan. 1, 1996, see section 2 of Pub.L. 104–88, set out as a note under section 701 of Title 49, Transportation.]

CROSS REFERENCES

National marine sanctuaries, procedures for designation, preparation of draft environmental impact statement by Secretary of Commerce, see section 1434 of Title 16, Conservation.

Federal Practice and Procedure

Environmental class actions, see Wright, Miller & Kane: Civil 2d § 1782.

West's Federal Practice Manual

Environmentally concerned departments and agencies, see § 4381.10 et seq.
Mineral leases, see § 5301 et seq.
Relation to energy policy, see § 4342.5.
Relation to government contracts, see § 1530.

WEST'S FEDERAL PRACTICE MANUAL

Environmental common law background, see § 4382 et seq.
National environmental policy overview, see § 4383 et seq.

CODE OF FEDERAL REGULATIONS

Requirements, standards, etc.,
Agency for International Development, see 22 CFR 216.1 et seq.
Agricultural Stabilization and Conservation Service, see 7 CFR 799.1 et seq.
Bureau of Land Management, see 43 CFR 3040 et seq., 6290.0–2 et seq.
Civil Aeronautics Board, see 14 CFR 201.1 et seq., 261.1 et seq., 312.1 et seq., 399.1 et seq.
Coast Guard, see 46 CFR 12.01 et seq., 71.01–1 et seq., 91.01–1 et seq., 105.01–1 et seq., 176.01–1 et seq., 189.01–1 et seq.
Committee for Purchase from the Blind and Other Severely Handicapped, see 41 CFR 51–6.1 et seq.

Requirements, standards, etc.,Cont'd
Consumer Products Safety Commission, review, see 16 CFR 1021.1 et seq.
Council on Environmental Quality, see 40 CFR 1500.1 et seq., 1510.1 et seq.
Defense Department, see 32 CFR 214.1 et seq.
Energy Research and Development Administration, see 10 CFR 711.1 et seq.
Environmental Protection Agency, see 40 CFR Ch. 1.
Federal Aviation Administration, see 14 CFR 21.1 et seq., 36.1 et seq., 91.1 et seq.
Federal Highway Administration, see 23 CFR 420.101 et seq., 712.101 et seq., 751.1 et seq., 770.200 et seq., 771.1 et seq., 772.1 et seq.
Federal Maritime Commission, see 46 CFR 547.1 et seq.
Federal Trade Commission, see 16 CFR 1.1 et seq.
Food and Drug Administration, see 21 CFR 25.1 et seq.
Housing and Urban Development, see 24 CFR 58.1 et seq.
Interstate Commerce Commission, see 49 CFR 1108.1 et seq.
Law Enforcement Assistance Administration, see 28 CFR 19.1 et seq.
National Aeronautics and Space Administration, see 14 CFR 1204.200 et seq.
National Highway Traffic Safety Administration, see 49 CFR 520.1 et seq.
National Marine Fisheries Service, see 50 CFR 251.1 et seq.
Navy Department, see 32 CFR 775.1 et seq.
Nuclear Regulatory Commission, see 10 CFR 2.1 et seq., 51.1 et seq.
Occupational Safety and Health Administration, see 29 CFR 1999.1 et seq.
Office of Education, see 45 CFR 100a.185, 100b.185.
Soil Conservation Service, see 7 CFR 650.1 et seq.
Tennessee Valley Authority, see 18 CFR 305.1 et seq.
Urban Mass Transportation Administration, see 49 CFR 613.100 et seq.

LAW REVIEW COMMENTARIES

Comment, on shore oil and gas leasing on public lands: At what point does NEPA require the preparation of an environmental impact statement? 25 San Diego L.Rev. 161 (1988).

Environmental review of recombinant DNA experiments under NEPA: *Foundation on Economic Trends v. Heckler.* Note, 21 U.S.F.L.Rev. 501 (1987).

Grazing management on the public lands: Opening the process to public participation. Joseph M. Feller, 26 Land and Water L.Rev. 571 (1991).

Judicial review of the administrative record in NEPA litigation. Susannah T. French, 81 Cal.L.Rev. 929 (1993).

Parallel universes: NEPA lessons for the new property. Michael Herz, 93 Colum.L.Rev. 1668 (1993).

RCRA immunity from NEPA: The EPA has exceeded the scope of its authority. Comment, 24 San Diego L.Rev. 1249 (1987).

United States Supreme Court

Agency decisions, review, see Strycker's Bay Neighborhood Council, Inc. v. Karlen, N.Y., 1980, 100 S.Ct. 497, 444 U.S. 223, 62 L.Ed.2d 433.

Construction with other laws, see Weinberger v. Catholic Action of Hawaii/Peace Ed. Project, 1981, 102 S.Ct. 197, 454 U.S. 139, 70 L.Ed.2d 298.

Important ingredient of environmental impact statement is discussion of steps that could be taken to mitigate adverse environmental consequences, see Robertson v. Methow Valley Citizens Council, 1989, 109 S.Ct. 1835.

Judicial review of agency actions, duties and functions of court, see Aberdeen & Rockfish Ry. Co. v. Students Challenging Regulatory Agency Procedures, 1972, 93 S.Ct. 1, 409 U.S. 1207, 34 L.Ed.2d 21.

§ 4333. Conformity of administrative procedures to national environmental policy [NEPA § 103]

All agencies of the Federal Government shall review their present statutory authority, administrative regulations, and current policies and procedures for the purpose of determining whether there are any deficiencies or inconsistencies therein which prohibit full compliance with the purposes and provisions of this chapter and shall propose to the President not later than July 1, 1971, such measures as may be necessary to bring their authority and policies into conformity with the intent, purposes, and procedures set forth in this chapter.

(Jan. 1, 1970, Pub.L. 91–190, Title I, § 103, 83 Stat. 854.)

Federal Practice and Procedure

Environmental class actions, see Wright, Miller & Kane: Civil 2d § 1782.

§ 4334. Other statutory obligations of agencies [NEPA § 104]

Nothing in section 4332 or 4333 of this title shall in any way affect the specific statutory obligations of any Federal agency (1) to comply with criteria or standards of environmental quality, (2) to coordinate or consult with any other Federal or State agency, or (3) to act, or refrain from acting contingent upon the recommendations or certification of any other Federal or State agency.

(Jan. 1, 1970, Pub.L. 91–190, Title I, § 104, 83 Stat. 854.)

Federal Practice and Procedure

Environmental class actions, see Wright, Miller & Kane: Civil 2d § 1782.

West's Federal Practice Manual

Quotas for minority businesses, see § 16555.

CODE OF FEDERAL REGULATIONS

Department of Defense, environmental effects, see 32 CFR 214.1 et seq.

§ 4335. Efforts supplemental to existing authorizations [NEPA § 105]

The policies and goals set forth in this chapter are supplementary to those set forth in existing authorizations of Federal agencies.

(Jan. 1, 1970, Pub.L. 91–190, Title I, § 105, 83 Stat. 854.)

Federal Practice and Procedure

Environmental class actions, see Wright, Miller & Kane: Civil 2d § 1782.

SUBCHAPTER II—COUNCIL ON ENVIRONMENTAL QUALITY

§ 4341. Reports to Congress; recommendations for legislation [NEPA § 201]

The President shall transmit to the Congress annually beginning July 1, 1970, an Environmental Quality Report (hereinafter referred to as the "report") which shall set forth (1) the status and condition of the major natural, manmade, or altered environmental classes of the Nation, including, but not limited to, the air, the aquatic, including marine, estuarine, and fresh water, and the terrestrial environment, including, but not limited to, the forest, dryland, wetland, range, urban, suburban, and rural environment; (2) current and foreseeable trends in the quality, management and utilization of such environments and the effects of those trends on the social, economic, and other requirements of the Nation; (3) the adequacy of available natural resources for fulfilling human and economic requirements of the Nation in the light of expected population pressures; (4) a review of the programs and activities (including regulatory activities) of the Federal Government, the State and local governments, and nongovernmental entities or individuals, with particular reference to their effect on the environment and on the conservation, development and utilization of natural resources; and (5) a program for remedying the deficiencies of existing programs and activities, together with recommendations for legislation.

(Jan. 1, 1970, Pub.L. 91–190, Title II, § 201, 83 Stat. 854.)

Federal Practice and Procedure

Environmental class actions, see Wright, Miller & Kane: Civil 2d § 1782.

LIBRARY REFERENCES

Health and Environment ⚷1, 25.5.
C.J.S. Health and Environment §§ 4 et seq., 61 et seq.

§ 4342. Establishment; membership; Chairman; appointments [NEPA § 202]

There is created in the Executive Office of the President a Council on Environmental Quality (hereinafter referred to as the "Council"). The Council shall be composed of three members who shall be appointed by the President to serve at his pleasure, by and with the advice and consent of the Senate. The President shall designate one of the members of the Council to serve as Chairman. Each member shall be a person who, as a result of his training, experience, and attainments, is exceptionally well qualified to analyze and interpret environmental trends and information of all kinds; to appraise programs and activities of the Federal Government in the light of the policy set forth in subchapter I of this chapter; to be conscious of and responsive to the scientific, economic, social, esthetic, and cultural needs and interests of the Nation; and to formulate and recommend national policies to promote the improvement of the quality of the environment.

(Jan. 1, 1970, Pub.L. 91–190, Title II, § 202, 83 Stat. 854.)

Federal Practice and Procedure

Environmental class actions, see Wright, Miller & Kane: Civil 2d § 1782.

West's Federal Practice Manual

Council on Environmental Quality, see § 4382.5.

LAW REVIEW COMMENTARIES

Long-range planning in environmental and health regulatory agencies. Richard N.L. Andrews, 20 Ecology L.Q. 515 (1993).

§ 4343. Employment of personnel, experts and consultants [NEPA § 203]

(a) The Council may employ such officers and employees as may be necessary to carry out its functions under this chapter. In addition, the Council may employ and fix the compensation of such experts and consultants as may be necessary for the carrying out of its functions under this chapter, in accordance with section 3109 of title 5 (but without regard to the last sentence thereof).

(b) Notwithstanding section 1342 of title 31, the Council may accept and employ voluntary and uncompensated services in furtherance of the purposes of the Council.

(Jan. 1, 1970, Pub.L. 91–190, Title II, § 203, 83 Stat. 855; July 3, 1975, Pub.L. 94–52, § 2, 89 Stat. 258; as amended Sept. 13, 1982, Pub.L. 97–258, § 4(b), 96 Stat. 1067.)

Federal Practice and Procedure

Environmental class actions, see Wright, Miller & Kane: Civil 2d § 1782.

§ 4344. Duties and functions [NEPA § 204]

It shall be the duty and function of the Council—

(1) to assist and advise the President in the preparation of the Environmental Quality Report required by section 4341 of this title;

(2) to gather timely and authoritative information concerning the conditions and trends in the quality of the environment both current and prospective, to analyze and interpret such information for the purpose of determining whether such conditions and trends are interfering, or are likely to interfere, with the achievement of the policy set forth in subchapter I of this chapter, and to compile and submit to the President studies relating to such conditions and trends;

(3) to review and appraise the various programs and activities of the Federal Government in the light of the policy set forth in subchapter I of this chapter for the purpose of determining the extent to which such programs and activities are contributing to the achievement of such policy, and to make recommendations to the President with respect thereto;

(4) to develop and recommend to the President national policies to foster and promote the improvement of environmental quality to meet the conservation, social, economic, health, and other requirements and goals of the Nation;

(5) to conduct investigations, studies, surveys, research, and analyses relating to ecological systems and environmental quality;

(6) to document and define changes in the natural environment, including the plant and animal systems, and to accumulate necessary data and other information for a continuing analysis of these changes or trends and an interpretation of their underlying causes;

(7) to report at least once each year to the President on the state and condition of the environment; and

(8) to make and furnish such studies, reports thereon, and recommendations with respect to matters of policy and legislation as the President may request.

(Jan. 1, 1970, Pub.L. 91–190, Title II, § 204, 83 Stat. 855.)

Federal Practice and Procedure

Environmental class actions, see Wright, Miller & Kane: Civil 2d § 1782.

West's Federal Practice Manual

Council on Environmental Quality, see § 4382.5.

LAW REVIEW COMMENTARIES

Long-range planning in environmental and health regulatory agencies. Richard N.L. Andrews, 20 Ecology L.Q. 515 (1993).

§ 4345. Consultation with Citizens' Advisory Committee on Environmental Quality and other representatives [NEPA § 205]

In exercising its powers, functions, and duties under this chapter, the Council shall—

(1) consult with the Citizens' Advisory Committee on Environmental Quality established by Executive Order numbered 11472, dated May 29, 1969, and with such representatives of science, industry, agriculture, labor, conservation organizations, State and

local governments and other groups, as it deems advisable; and

(2) utilize, to the fullest extent possible, the services, facilities, and information (including statistical information) of public and private agencies and organizations, and individuals, in order that duplication of effort and expense may be avoided, thus assuring that the Council's activities will not unnecessarily overlap or conflict with similar activities authorized by law and performed by established agencies.

(Jan. 1, 1970, Pub.L. 91–190, Title II, § 205, 83 Stat. 855.)

Federal Practice and Procedure

Environmental class actions, see Wright, Miller & Kane: Civil 2d § 1782.

§ 4346. Tenure and compensation of members [NEPA § 206]

Members of the Council shall serve full time and the Chairman of the Council shall be compensated at the rate provided for Level II of the Executive Schedule Pay Rates (5 U.S.C. 5313). The other members of the Council shall be compensated at the rate provided for Level IV or[1] the Executive Schedule Pay Rates (5 U.S.C. 5315).

(Jan. 1, 1970, Pub.L. 91–190, Title II, § 206, 83 Stat. 856.)

[1] So in original. Probably should read "of".

§ 4346a. Travel reimbursement by private organizations and Federal, State, and local governments [NEPA § 207]

The Council may accept reimbursements from any private nonprofit organization or from any department, agency, or instrumentality of the Federal Government, any State, or local government, for the reasonable travel expenses incurred by an officer or employee of the Council in connection with his attendance at any conference, seminar, or similar meeting conducted for the benefit of the Council.

(Pub.L. 91–190, Title II, § 207, as added July 3, 1975, Pub.L. 94–52, § 3, 89 Stat. 258.)

§ 4346b. Expenditures in support of international activities [NEPA § 208]

The Council may make expenditures in support of its international activities, including expenditures for: (1) international travel; (2) activities in implementation of international agreements; and (3) the support of international exchange programs in the United States and in foreign countries.

(Pub.L. 91–190, Title II, § 208, as added July 3, 1975, Pub.L. 94–52, § 3, 89 Stat. 258.)

Federal Practice and Procedure

Environmental class actions, see Wright, Miller & Kane: Civil 2d § 1782.

§ 4347. Authorization of appropriations [NEPA § 209]

There are authorized to be appropriated to carry out the provisions of this chapter not to exceed $300,000 for fiscal year 1970, $700,000 for fiscal year 1971, and $1,000,000 for each fiscal year thereafter.

(Jan. 1, 1970, Pub.L. 91–190, Title II, § 209, formerly § 207, 83 Stat. 856, renumbered July 3, 1975, Pub.L. 94–52, § 3, 89 Stat. 258.)

SUBCHAPTER III—MISCELLANEOUS PROVISIONS

§ 4361. Repealed. Pub.L. 104–66, Title II, § 2021(k)(1), Dec. 21, 1995, 109 Stat. 728

Section, Pub.L. 94–475, § 5, Oct. 11, 1976, 90 Stat. 2071, related to a plan for research, development, and demonstration.

§ 4361a. Repealed. Pub.L. 104–66, Title II, § 2021(k)(2), Dec. 21, 1995, 109 Stat. 728

Section, Pub.L. 95–155, § 4, Nov. 8, 1977, 91 Stat. 1258, related to budget projections in annual revisions of the plan for research, development, and demonstration.

§ 4361b. Implementation by Administrator of Environmental Protection Agency of recommendations of "CHESS" Investigative Report; waiver; inclusion of status of implementation requirements in annual revisions of plan for research, development, and demonstration

The Administrator of the Environmental Protection Agency shall implement the recommendations of the report prepared for the House Committee on Science and Technology entitled "The Environmental Protection Agency Research Program with primary emphasis on the Community Health and Environmental Surveillance System (CHESS): An Investigative Report", unless for any specific recommendation he determines (1) that such recommendation has been implemented, (2) that implementation of such recommendation would not enhance the quality of the research, or (3) that implementation of such recommendation will require funding which is not available. Where such funding is not available, the Administrator shall request the required authorization or appropriation for such implementation. The Administrator shall report the status of such implementation in each annual revision of the five-year plan transmitted to the Congress under section 4361 of this title.

(Nov. 8, 1977, Pub.L. 95–155, § 10, 91 Stat. 1262.)

Codification

Section was enacted as part of the Environmental Research, Development and Demonstration Authorization Act of 1978, and not as part of the National Environmental Policy Act of 1969 which comprises this chapter.

§ 4361c. Staff management

(a) Appointments for educational programs

(1) The Administrator is authorized to select and appoint up to 75 full-time permanent staff members in the Office of Research and Development to pursue full-time educational programs for the purpose of (A) securing an advanced degree or (B) securing academic training, for the purpose of making a career change in order to better carry out the Agency's research mission.

(2) The Administrator shall select and appoint staff members for these assignments according to rules and criteria promulgated by him. The Agency may continue to pay the salary and benefits of the appointees as well as reasonable and appropriate relocation expenses and tuition.

(3) The term of each appointment shall be for up to one year, with a single renewal of up to one year in appropriate cases at the discretion of the Administrator.

(4) Staff members appointed to this program shall not count against any Agency personnel ceiling during the term of their appointment.

(b) Post-doctoral research fellows

(1) The Administrator is authorized to appoint up to 25 Post-doctoral Research Fellows in accordance with the provisions of section 213.3102(aa) of title 5 of the Code of Federal Regulations.

(2) Persons holding these appointments shall not count against any personnel ceiling of the Agency.

(c) Non-government research associates

(1) The Administrator is authorized and encouraged to utilize research associates from outside the Federal Government in conducting the research, development, and demonstration programs of the Agency.

(2) These persons shall be selected and shall serve according to rules and criteria promulgated by the Administrator.

(d) Women and minority groups

For all programs in this section, the Administrator shall place special emphasis on providing opportunities for education and training of women and minority groups.

(Oct. 18, 1978, Pub.L. 95–477, § 6, 92 Stat. 1510.)

Codification

Section was enacted as part of the Environmental Research, Development, and Demonstration Authorization Act of 1979, and not as part of the National Environmental Policy Act of 1969 which comprises this chapter.

Federal Practice and Procedure

Environmental class actions, see Wright, Miller & Kane: Civil 2d § 1782.

§ 4362. Interagency cooperation on prevention of environmental cancer and heart and lung disease

(a) Not later than three months after August 7, 1977, there shall be established a Task Force on Environmental Cancer and Heart and Lung Disease (hereinafter referred to as the "Task Force"). The Task Force shall include representatives of the Environmental Protection Agency, the National Cancer Institute, the National Heart, Lung, and Blood Institute, the National Institute of Occupational Safety and Health, and the National Institute on Environmental Health Sciences, and shall be chaired by the Administrator (or his delegate).

(b) The Task Force shall—

(1) recommend a comprehensive research program to determine and quantify the relationship between environmental pollution and human cancer and heart and lung disease;

(2) recommend comprehensive strategies to reduce or eliminate the risks of cancer or such other diseases associated with environmental pollution;

(3) recommend research and such other measures as may be appropriate to prevent or reduce the incidence of environmentally related cancer and heart and lung diseases;

(4) coordinate research by, and stimulate cooperation between, the Environmental Protection Agency, the Department of Health and Human Services, and such other agencies as may be appropriate to prevent environmentally related cancer and heart and lung diseases; and

(5) report to Congress, not later than one year after August 7, 1977, and annually thereafter, on the problems and progress in carrying out this section.

(Aug. 7, 1977, Pub.L. 95–95, Title IV, § 402, 91 Stat. 791, 793; Oct. 17, 1979, Pub.L. 96–88, Title V, § 509(b), 93 Stat. 695.)

Codification

Section was enacted as part of the Clean Air Act Amendments of 1977, and not as part of the National Environmental Policy Act of 1969 which comprises this chapter.

Federal Practice and Procedure

Environmental class actions, see Wright, Miller & Kane: Civil 2d § 1782.

§ 4362a. Task Force on Environmental Cancer and Heart and Lung Disease; membership of Director of National Center for Health Statistics and of head of Center for Disease Control

The Director of the National Center for Health Statistics and the head of the Center for Disease Control (or the successor to such entity) shall each serve as members of the Task Force on Environmental Cancer and Heart and Lung Disease established under section 4362 of this title.

(Nov. 9, 1978, Pub.L. 95–623, § 9, 92 Stat. 3455.)

Codification

Section was enacted as part of the Health Services Research, Health Statistics, and Health Care Technology Act of 1978, and not as part of the National Environmental Policy Act of 1969 which comprises this chapter.

Change of Name

The name of the Centers for Disease Control was changed to the Centers for Disease Control and Prevention without a conforming amendment to this section. See Pub.L. 102–531, Title III, § 312, Oct. 27, 1992, 106 Stat. 3504, enacting extensive conforming amendments and House Conference Report No. 102–1019, page 47 (1992 U.S.C.C. & A.N. page 3038) indicating the intent of Congress.

Federal Practice and Procedure

Environmental class actions, see Wright, Miller & Kane: Civil 2d § 1782.

§ 4363. Continuing and long-term environmental research and development

The Administrator of the Environmental Protection Agency shall establish a separately identified program of continuing, long-term environmental research and development for each activity listed in section 2(a) of this Act. Unless otherwise specified by law, at least 15 per centum of funds appropriated to the Administrator for environmental research and development for each activity listed in section 2(a) of this Act shall be obligated and expended for such long-term environmental research and development under this section.

(Dec. 22, 1980, Pub.L. 96–569, § 2(f), 94 Stat. 3337.)

References in Text

Section 2(a) of this Act, referred to in text, is section 2(a) of Pub.L. 96–569, Dec. 22, 1980, 94 Stat. 3335, which is not classified to the Code.

Codification

Section was enacted as part of the Environmental Research, Development, and Demonstration Authorization Act of 1981, and not as part of the National Environmental Policy Act of 1969 which comprises this chapter.

Federal Practice and Procedure

Environmental class actions, see Wright, Miller & Kane: Civil 2d § 1782.

§ 4363a. Pollution control technologies demonstrations

(1) The Administrator shall continue to be responsible for conducting and shall continue to conduct full-scale demonstrations of energy-related pollution control technologies as necessary in his judgment to fulfill the provisions of the Clean Air Act as amended [42 U.S.C.A. § 7401 et seq.] the Federal Water Pollution Control Act as amended [33 U.S.C.A. § 1251 et seq.] and other pertinent pollution control statutes.

(2) Energy-related environmental protection projects authorized to be administered by the Environmental Protection Agency under this Act, shall not be transferred administratively to the Department of Energy or reduced through budget amendment. No action shall be taken through administrative or budgetary means to diminish the ability of the Environmental Protection Agency to initiate such projects.

(April 7, 1980, Pub.L. 96–229, § 2(d), 94 Stat. 325, 327.)

References in Text

This Act, referred to in par. (2), is Pub.L. 96–229, Apr. 7, 1980, 94 Stat. 325, known as the Environmental Research, Development, and Demonstration Authorization Act of 1980, which enacted sections 4363, 4363a, 4369a, and 4370 of this title.

Codification

Section was enacted as part of the Environmental Research, Development, and Demonstration Authorization Act of 1980, and not as part of the National Environmental Policy Act of 1969 which comprises this chapter.

Federal Practice and Procedure

Environmental class actions, see Wright, Miller & Kane: Civil 2d § 1782.

§ 4364. Expenditure of funds for research and development related to regulatory program activities

(a) Coordination, etc., with research needs and priorities of program offices and Environmental Protection Agency

The Administrator of the Environmental Protection Agency shall assure that the expenditure of any funds appropriated pursuant to this Act or any other provision of law for environmental research and development related to regulatory program activities shall be coordinated with and reflect the research needs and priorities of the program offices, as well as the overall research needs and priorities of the Agency, including those defined in the five-year research plan.

(b) Program offices subject to coverage

For purposes of subsection (a) of this section, the appropriate program offices are—

(1) the Office of Air and Waste Management, for air quality activities;

(2) the Office of Water and Hazardous Materials, for water quality activities and water supply activities;

(3) the Office of Pesticides, for environmental effects of pesticides;

(4) the Office of Solid Waste, for solid waste activities;

(5) the Office of Toxic Substances, for toxic substance activities;

(6) the Office of Radiation Programs, for radiation activities; and

(7) the Office of Noise Abatement and Control, for noise activities.

(c) Report to Congress; contents

The Administrator shall submit to the President and the Congress a report concerning the most appropriate means of assuring, on a continuing basis, that the research efforts of the Agency reflect the needs and priorities of the regulatory program offices, while maintaining a high level of scientific quality. Such report shall be submitted on or before March 31, 1978.

(Nov. 8, 1977, Pub.L. 95–155, § 7, 91 Stat. 1259.)

References in Text

This Act, referred to in subsec. (a), is Pub.L. 95–155, Nov. 8, 1977, 91 Stat. 1257, as amended, known as the Environmental Research, Development, and Demonstration Authorization Act of 1978, which, to the extent classified to the Code, enacted sections 300j–3a, 4361a, 4361b, and 4363 to 4367 of this title.

Codification

Section was enacted as part of the Environmental Research, Development, and Demonstration Authorization Act of 1978, and not as part of the National Environmental Policy Act of 1969 which comprises this chapter.

§ 4365. Science Advisory Board

(a) Establishment; requests for advice by Administrator of Environmental Protection Agency and Congressional committees

The Administrator of the Environmental Protection Agency shall establish a Science Advisory Board which shall provide such scientific advice as may be requested by the Administrator, the Committee on Environment and Public Works of the United States Senate, or the Committee on Science, Space, and Technology, on Energy and Commerce, or on Public Works and Transportation of the House of Representatives.

(b) Membership; Chairman; meetings; qualifications of members

Such Board shall be composed of at least nine members, one of whom shall be designated Chairman, and shall meet at such times and places as may be designated by the Chairman of the Board in consultation with the Administrator. Each member of the Board shall be qualified by education, training, and experience to evaluate scientific and technical information on matters referred to the Board under this section.

(c) Proposed environmental criteria document, standard, limitation, or regulation; functions respecting in conjunction with Administrator

(1) The Administrator, at the time any proposed criteria document, standard, limitation, or regulation under the Clean Air Act [42 U.S.C.A. § 7401 et seq.], the Federal Water Pollution Control Act [33 U.S.C.A. § 1251 et seq.], the Resource Conservation and Recovery Act of 1976 [42 U.S.C.A. § 6901 et seq.], the Noise Control Act [42 U.S.C.A. § 4901 et seq.], the Toxic Substances Control Act [15 U.S.C.A. § 2601 et seq.], or the Safe Drinking Water Act [42 U.S.C.A. § 300f et seq.], or under any other authority of the Administrator, is provided to any other Federal agency for formal review and comment, shall make available to the Board such proposed criteria document, standard, limitation, or regulation, together with relevant scientific and technical information in the possession of the Environmental Protection Agency on which the proposed action is based.

(2) The Board may make available to the Administrator, within the time specified by the Administrator, its advice and comments on the adequacy of the scientific and technical basis of the proposed criteria document, standard, limitation, or regulation, together with any pertinent information in the Board's possession.

(d) Utilization of technical and scientific capabilities of Federal agencies and national environmental laboratories for determining adequacy of scientific and technical basis of proposed criteria document, etc.

In preparing such advice and comments, the Board shall avail itself of the technical and scientific capabilities of any Federal agency, including the Environmental Protection Agency and any national environmental laboratories.

(e) Member committees and investigative panels; establishment; chairmanship

The Board is authorized to constitute such member committees and investigative panels as the Administrator and the Board find necessary to carry out this section. Each such member committee or investigative panel shall be chaired by a member of the Board.

(f) Appointment and compensation of secretary and other personnel; compensation of members

(1) Upon the recommendation of the Board, the Administrator shall appoint a secretary, and such other employees as deemed necessary to exercise and

fulfill the Board's powers and responsibilities. The compensation of all employees appointed under this paragraph shall be fixed in accordance with chapter 51 and subchapter III of chapter 53 of Title 5.

(2) Members of the Board may be compensated at a rate to be fixed by the President but not in excess of the maximum rate of pay for grade GS–18, as provided in the General Schedule under section 5332 of Title 5.

(g) Consultation and coordination with Scientific Advisory Panel

In carrying out the functions assigned by this section, the Board shall consult and coordinate its activities with the Scientific Advisory Panel established by the Administrator pursuant to section 136w(d) of Title 7.

(Nov. 8, 1977, Pub.L. 95–155, § 8, 91 Stat. 1260, H.Res. 549, Mar. 25, 1980; Dec. 22, 1980, Pub.L. 96–569, § 3, 94 Stat. 3337; Nov. 2, 1994, Pub.L. 103–437, § 15(*o*), 108 Stat. 4593; Dec. 21, 1995, Pub.L. 104–66, Title II, § 2021(k)(3), 109 Stat. 728.)

Codification

Section was enacted as part of the Environmental Research, Development, and Demonstration Authorization Act of 1978, and not as part of the National Environmental Policy Act of 1969 which comprises this chapter.

Change of Name

Any reference in any provision of law enacted before Jan. 4, 1995, to the Committee on Energy and Commerce of the House of Representatives treated as referring to the Committee on Commerce of the House of Representatives, except that any reference in any provision of law enacted before Jan. 4, 1995, to the Committee on Energy and Commerce of the House of Representatives treated as referring to the Committee on Agriculture of the House of Representatives, in the case of a provision of law relating to inspection of seafood or seafood products, the Committee on Banking and Financial Services of the House of Representatives, in the case of a provision of law relating to bank capital markets activities generally or to depository institution securities activities generally, and the Committee on Transportation and Infrastructure of the House of Representatives, in the case of a provision of law relating to railroads, railway labor, or railroad retirement and unemployment (except revenue measures related thereto), see section 1(a)(4) and (c)(1) of Pub.L. 104–14, set out as a note preceding section 21 of Title 2, The Congress.

Any reference in any provision of law enacted before Jan. 4, 1995, to the Committee on Science, Space, and Technology of the House of Representatives treated as referring to the Committee on Science of the House of Representatives, see section 1(a)(10) of Pub.L. 104–14, set out as a note preceding section 21 of Title 2, The Congress.

Any reference in any provision of law enacted before Jan. 4, 1995, to the Committee on Public Works and Transportation of the House of Representatives treated as referring to the Committee on Transportation and Infrastructure of the House of Representatives, see section 1(a)(9) of Pub.L. 104–14, set out as a note preceding section 21 of Title 2, The Congress.

§ 4366. Identification and coordination of research, development, and demonstration activities

(a) Consultation and cooperation of Administrator of Environmental Protection Agency with heads of Federal agencies; inclusion of activities in annual revisions of plan for research, etc.

The Administrator of the Environmental Protection Agency, in consultation and cooperation with the heads of other Federal agencies, shall take such actions on a continuing basis as may be necessary or appropriate—

(1) to identify environmental research, development, and demonstration activities, within and outside the Federal Government, which may need to be more effectively coordinated in order to minimize unnecessary duplication of programs, projects, and research facilities;

(2) to determine the steps which might be taken under existing law, by him and by the heads of such other agencies, to accomplish or promote such coordination, and to provide for or encourage the taking of such steps; and

(3) to determine the additional legislative actions which would be needed to assure such coordination to the maximum extent possible.

The Administrator shall include in each annual revision of the five-year plan provided for by section 4361 of this title a full and complete report on the actions taken and determinations made during the preceding year under this subsection, and may submit interim reports on such actions and determinations at such other times as he deems appropriate.

(b) Coordination of programs by Administrator

The Administrator of the Environmental Protection Agency shall coordinate environmental research, development, and demonstration programs of such Agency with the heads of other Federal agencies in order to minimize unnecessary duplication of programs, projects, and research facilities.

(c) Joint study by Council on Environmental Quality in consultation with Office of Science and Technology Policy for coordination of activities; report to President and Congress; report by President to Congress on implementation of joint study and report

(1) In order to promote the coordination of environmental research and development activities, and to assure that the action taken and methods used (under subsection (a) of this section and otherwise) to bring about such coordination will be as effective as possible for that purpose, the Council on Environmental Quality in consultation with the Office of Science and Technology Policy shall promptly undertake and carry out a joint study of all aspects of the coordination of environmental research and development. The Chairman of the Council shall prepare a report on the results of such study, together with such recommendations (including legislative recommendations) as he deems appropriate, and shall submit such report to the President and the Congress not later than May 31, 1978.

(2) Not later than September 30, 1978, the President shall report to the Congress on steps he has taken to implement the recommendations included in the report under paragraph (1), including any recommendations he may have for legislation.

(Nov. 8, 1977, Pub.L. 95–155, § 9, 91 Stat. 1261.)

Codification

Section was enacted as part of the Environmental Research, Development, and Demonstration Authorization Act of 1978, and not as part of the National Environmental Policy Act of 1969 which comprises this chapter.

Federal Practice and Procedure

Environmental class actions, see Wright, Miller & Kane: Civil 2d § 1782.

LIBRARY REFERENCES

United States ⇐29, 31, 40, 41.
C.J.S. United States §§ 31, 34 et seq., 38 et seq.

§ 4366a. Development of data base of environmental research articles indexed by geographic location

(a) Research journals

Within 6 months following November 16, 1990, and from time to time thereafter, the Environmental Protection Agency shall identify not less than 35 important environmental research journals, conference proceedings or other reference sources in which scientific research or engineering studies related to air, water, or soil quality or pollution or other environmental issues are routinely published. In carrying out the requirements of this subsection, at least 50 journals or proceedings shall be reviewed.

(b) Index

(1) Within 12 months following November 16, 1990, and annually thereafter, the Environmental Protection Agency shall review the journals and other materials identified in subsection (a) of this section and compile, maintain and publish an index of the articles contained therein during the preceding calendar year by geographic location. A copy of such index shall be made available to the Service for distribution to the public, and a copy shall be submitted to the Congress not less than 30 days prior to the date on which it is made available to the Service.

(2) Beginning 12 months after November 16, 1990, the Agency shall identify not less than 20 materials identified in subsection (a) of this section which were published during the time period from 1970 to the year preceding enactment, and shall compile and publish a series of indices of articles contained therein by geographic location. The time frame which each index contains should not exceed 5 years.

(c) Purchase of information

The Environmental Protection Agency is authorized to enter into contracts or other arrangements for the acquisition of data and other information necessary for purposes of this Act.

(d) Revising list

The Environmental Protection Agency shall review the list of references developed under this section at least biennially and shall revise the list of sources as appropriate.

(e) Specific location of research projects

Unless exempted by the Administrator of the Environmental Protection Agency, all reports resulting from research projects sponsored by the Environmental Protection Agency and initiated after the expiration of the 36–month period following November 16, 1990 shall indicate the specific location to which the research pertains.

(Nov. 16, 1990, Pub.L. 101–617, § 4, 104 Stat. 3287.)

Termination of Section

Section expires 10 years after Nov. 16, 1990, pursuant to section 6 of Pub.L. 101–617, set out as a note under this section.

References in Text

This Act, referred to in subsec. (c), is Pub.L. 101–617, Nov. 16, 1990, 104 Stat. 3287, which is classified to this section. For complete classification of this Act to the Code, see Short Title note set out under this section and Tables.

Short Title; Congressional Findings; Purpose

Sections 1 to 3 of Pub.L. 101–617 provided that:

"Section 1. Short Title.

"This Act [enacting this section and provisions set out as notes under this section] may be cited as the 'Environmental Research Geographic Location Information Act'.

"Sec. 2. Findings.

"The Congress finds that—

"(1) at present, there is no reliable method of locating private or Government research on environmental issues by geographic location; and

"(2) a means of identifying environmental research conducted at specific geographic locations is needed for purposes such as detecting trends in environmental quality, assisting the public in learning about the quality and issues of their local environment, and providing a data base for identifying areas of critical environmental concern.

"Sec. 3. Purpose.

"The purpose of this Act [enacting this section and provisions set out as notes under this section] is to develop a data base of environmental research articles indexed by geographic location."

Authorization of Appropriations; Expiration of Section

Sections 5 and 6 of Pub.L. 101–617 provided that:

"Sec. 5. Authorizations.

"There are authorized to be appropriated such sums as may be necessary to carry out this Act [enacting this section and provisions set out as notes under this section].

"Sec. 6. Expiration of Act.

"This Act [enacting this section and provisions set out as notes under this section] shall expire 10 years after the date of its enactment [Nov. 16, 1990]."

§ 4367. Reporting requirements of financial interests of officers and employees of Environmental Protection Agency

(a) Covered officers and employees

Each officer or employee of the Environmental Protection Agency who—

(1) performs any function or duty under this Act; and

(2) has any known financial interest in any person who applies for or receives grants, contracts, or other forms of financial assistance under this Act,

shall, beginning on February 1, 1978, annually file with the Administrator a written statement concerning all such interests held by such officer or employee during the preceding calendar year. Such statement shall be available to the public.

(b) Implementation of requirements by Administrator

The Administrator shall—

(1) act within ninety days after November 8, 1977—

(A) to define the term "known financial interest" for purposes of subsection (a) of this section; and

(B) to establish the methods by which the requirement to file written statements specified in subsection (a) of this section will be monitored and enforced, including appropriate provision for the filing by such officers and employees of such statements and the review by the Administrator of such statements; and

(2) report to the Congress on June 1 of each calendar year with respect to such disclosures and the actions taken in regard thereto during the preceding calendar year.

(c) Exemption of positions by Administrator

In the rules prescribed under subsection (b) of this section, the Administrator may identify specific positions of a nonpolicymaking nature within the Administration and provide that officers or employees occupying such positions shall be exempt from the requirements of this section.

(d) Violations; penalties

Any officer or employee who is subject to, and knowingly violates, this section, shall be fined not more than $2,500 or imprisoned not more than one year, or both.

(Nov. 8, 1977, Pub.L. 95–155, § 12, 91 Stat. 1263.)

References in Text

This Act, referred to in subsec. (a)(1), (2), is Pub.L. 95–155, Nov. 8, 1977, 91 Stat. 1257, as amended, known as the Environmental Research, Development, and Demonstration Authorization Act of 1978, which, to the extent classified to the Code, enacted sections 300j–3a, 4361a, 4361b, and 4363 to 4367 of this title.

Codification

Section was enacted as part of the Environmental Research, Development, and Demonstration Authorization Act of 1978, and not as part of the National Environmental Policy Act of 1969 which comprises this chapter.

Federal Practice and Procedure

Environmental class actions, see Wright, Miller & Kane: Civil 2d § 1782.

§ 4368. Grants to qualified citizens groups

(1) There is authorized to be appropriated to the Environmental Protection Agency, for grants to qualified citizens groups in States and regions, $3,000,000.

(2) Grants under this section may be made for the purpose of supporting and encouraging participation by qualified citizens groups in determining how scientific, technological, and social trends and changes affect the future environment and quality of life of an area, and for setting goals and identifying measures for improvement.

(3) The term "qualified citizens group" shall mean a nonprofit organization of citizens having an area based focus, which is not single-issue oriented and which can demonstrate a prior record of interest and involvement in goal-setting and research concerned with improving the quality of life, including plans to identify, protect and enhance significant natural and cultural resources and the environment.

(4) A citizens group shall be eligible for assistance only if certified by the Governor in consultation with the State legislature as a bona fide organization entitled to receive Federal assistance to pursue the aims of this program. The group shall further demonstrate its capacity to employ usefully the funds for the purposes of this program and its broad-based representative nature.

(5) After an initial application for assistance under this section has been approved, the Administrator may make grants on an annual basis, on condition that the Governor recertify the group and that the applicant submits to the Administrator annually—

(A) an evaluation of the progress made during the previous year in meeting the objectives for which the grant was made;

(B) a description of any changes in the objectives of the activities; and

(C) a description of the proposed activities for the succeeding one year period.

(6) A grant made under this program shall not exceed 75 per centum of the estimated cost of the project or program for which the grant is made, and

no group shall receive more than $50,000 in any one year.

(7) No financial assistance provided under this section shall be used to support lobbying or litigation by any recipient group.

(Oct. 18, 1978, Pub.L. 95–477, § 3(d), 92 Stat. 1509.)

References in Text

This section, referred to in par. (5), means section 3 of Pub.L. 95–477, in its entirety, subsec. (d) of which enacted this section, subsecs. (a) and (b) of which were not classified to the Code, and subsec. (c) of which authorized funds for a study and report to be submitted by Oct. 18, 1980.

Codification

Section was enacted as part of the Environmental Research, Development, and Demonstration Authorization Act of 1979, and not as part of the National Environmental Policy Act of 1969 which comprises this chapter.

Federal Practice and Procedure

Environmental class actions, see Wright, Miller & Kane: Civil 2d § 1782.

LIBRARY REFERENCES

United States ⚖82(2).
C.J.S. United States § 122.

§ 4368a. Utilization of talents of older Americans in projects of pollution prevention, abatement, and control

(a) Technical assistance to environmental agencies

Notwithstanding any other provision of law relating to Federal grants and cooperative agreements, the Administrator of the Environmental Protection Agency is authorized to make grants to, or enter into cooperative agreements with, private nonprofit organizations designated by the Secretary of Labor under title V of the Older Americans Act of 1965 [42 U.S.C.A. § 3056 et seq.] to utilize the talents of older Americans in programs authorized by other provisions of law administered by the Administrator (and consistent with such provisions of law) in providing technical assistance to Federal, State, and local environmental agencies for projects of pollution prevention, abatement, and control. Funding for such grants or agreements may be made available from such programs or through title V of the Older Americans Act of 1965 [42 U.S.C.A. § 3056 et seq.] and title IV of the Job Training Partnership Act [29 U.S.C.A. § 1671 et seq.].

(b) Pre-award certifications

Prior to awarding any grant or agreement under subsection (a) of this section, the applicable Federal, State, or local environmental agency shall certify to the Administrator that such grants or agreements will not—

(1) result in the displacement of individuals currently employed by the environmental agency concerned (including partial displacement through reduction of nonovertime hours, wages, or employment benefits);

(2) result in the employment of any individual when any other person is in a layoff status from the same or substantially equivalent job within the jurisdiction of the environmental agency concerned; or

(3) affect existing contracts for services.

(c) Prior appropriations Acts

Grants or agreements awarded under this section shall be subject to prior appropriation Acts.

(June 12, 1984, Pub.L. 98–313, § 2, 98 Stat. 235.)

Codification

Section was not enacted as part of the National Environmental Policy Act of 1969 which comprises this chapter.

Short Title

Section 1 of Pub.L. 98–313, June 12, 1984, 98 Stat. 235, provided that: "This Act [enacting this section] may be cited as the 'Environmental Programs Assistance Act of 1984'."

§ 4368b. General assistance program

(a) Short title

This section may be cited as the "Indian Environmental General Assistance Program Act of 1992".

(b) Purposes

The purposes of this section are to—

(1) provide general assistance grants to Indian tribal governments and intertribal consortia to build capacity to administer environmental regulatory programs that may be delegated by the Environmental Protection Agency on Indian lands; and

(2) provide technical assistance from the Environmental Protection Agency to Indian tribal governments and intertribal consortia in the development of multimedia programs to address environmental issues on Indian lands.

(c) Definitions

For purposes of this section:

(1) The term "Indian tribal government" means any Indian tribe, band, nation, or other organized group or community, including any Alaska Native village or regional or village corporation (as defined in, or established pursuant to, the Alaska Native Claims Settlement Act (43 U.S.C.A. § 1601, et seq.)), which is recognized as eligible for the special services provided by the United States to Indians because of their status as Indians.

(2) The term "intertribal consortia" or "intertribal consortium" means a partnership between two

or more Indian tribal governments authorized by the governing bodies of those tribes to apply for and receive assistance pursuant to this section.

(3) The term "Administrator" means the Administrator of the Environmental Protection Agency.

(d) General assistance program

(1) The Administrator of the Environmental Protection Agency shall establish an Indian Environmental General Assistance Program that provides grants to eligible Indian tribal governments or intertribal consortia to cover the costs of planning, developing, and establishing environmental protection programs consistent with other applicable provisions of law providing for enforcement of such laws by Indian tribes on Indian lands.

(2) Each grant awarded for general assistance under this subsection for a fiscal year shall be no less than $75,000, and no single grant may be awarded to an Indian tribal government or intertribal consortium for more than 10 percent of the funds appropriated under subsection (h) of this section.

(3) The term of any general assistance award made under this subsection may exceed one year. Any awards made pursuant to this section shall remain available until expended. An Indian tribal government or intertribal consortium may receive a general assistance grant for a period of up to four years in each specific media area.

(e) No reduction in amounts

In no case shall the award of a general assistance grant to an Indian tribal government or intertribal consortium under this section result in a reduction of Environmental Protection Agency grants for environmental programs to that tribal government or consortium. Nothing in this section shall preclude an Indian tribal government or intertribal consortium from receiving individual media grants or cooperative agreements. Funds provided by the Environmental Protection Agency through the general assistance program shall be used by an Indian tribal government or intertribal consortium to supplement other funds provided by the Environmental Protection Agency through individual media grants or cooperative agreements.

(f) Expenditure of general assistance

Any general assistance under this section shall be expended for the purpose of planning, developing, and establishing the capability to implement programs administered by the Environmental Protection Agency and specified in the assistance agreement. Purposes and programs authorized under this section shall include the development and implementation of solid and hazardous waste programs for Indian lands. An Indian tribal government or intertribal consortium receiving general assistance pursuant to this section shall utilize such funds for programs and purposes to be carried out in accordance with the terms of the assistance agreement. Such programs and general assistance shall be carried out in accordance with the purposes and requirements of applicable provisions of law, including the Solid Waste Disposal Act (42 U.S.C. 6901 et seq.).

(g) Procedures

(1) Within 12 months following October 24, 1992, the Administrator shall promulgate regulations establishing procedures under which an Indian tribal government or intertribal consortium may apply for general assistance grants under this section.

(2) The Administrator shall publish regulations issued pursuant to this section in the Federal Register.

(3) The Administrator shall establish procedures for accounting, auditing, evaluating, and reviewing any programs or activities funded in whole or in part for a general assistance grant under this section.

(h) Authorization

There are authorized to be appropriated to carry out the provisions of this section, $15,000,000 for each of the fiscal years 1993, 1994, 1995, 1996, 1997, and 1998.

(i) Report to Congress

The Administrator shall transmit an annual report to the appropriate Committees of the Congress with jurisdiction over the applicable environmental laws and Indian tribes describing which Indian tribes or intertribal consortia have been granted approval by the Administrator pursuant to law to enforce certain environmental laws and the effectiveness of any such enforcement.

(Pub.L. 102–497, § 11, Oct. 24, 1992, 106 Stat. 3258; Pub.L. 103–155, Nov. 24, 1993, 107 Stat. 1523.)

References in Text

The Alaska Native Claims Settlement Act, referred to in subsec. (c)(1), is Pub.L. 92–203, Dec. 18, 1971, 85 Stat. 688, as amended, which is classified generally to chapter 33 (section 1601 et seq.) of Title 43, Public Lands. For complete classification of this Act to the Code, see Short Title note set out under section 1601 of this title and Tables.

The Solid Waste Disposal Act, referred to in subsec. (f), is Title II of Pub.L. 89–272, Oct. 20, 1965, 79 Stat. 997, as amended generally by Pub.L. 94–580, § 2, Oct. 21, 1976, 90 Stat. 2795, which is classified generally to chapter 82 (section 6901 et seq.) of this title. For complete classification of this Act to the Code, see Short Title note set out under section 6901 of this title and Tables.

Codification

Section was enacted as part of the Indian Environmental General Assistance Program Act of 1992 and not as part of the National Environmental Policy Act of 1969, which comprises this chapter.

§ 4369. Miscellaneous reports

(a) Availability to Congressional committees

All reports to or by the Administrator relevant to the Agency's program of research, development, and demonstration shall promptly be made available to the Committee on Science, Space, and Technology of the House of Representatives and the Committee on Environment and Public Works of the Senate, unless otherwise prohibited by law.

(b) Transmittal of jurisdictional information

The Administrator shall keep the Committee on Science, Space, and Technology of the House of Representatives and the Committee on Environment and Public Works of the Senate fully and currently informed with respect to matters falling within or related to the jurisdiction of the committees.

(c) Comment by Government agencies and the public

The reports provided for in section 5910 of this title shall be made available to the public for comment, and to the heads of affected agencies for comment and, in the case of recommendations for action, for response.

(d) Transmittal of research information to the Department of Energy

For the purpose of assisting the Department of Energy in planning and assigning priorities in research development and demonstration activities related to environmental control technologies, the Administrator shall actively make available to the Department all information on research activities and results of research programs of the Environmental Protection Agency.

(Oct. 18, 1978, Pub.L. 95–477, § 5, 92 Stat. 1510; Nov. 2, 1994, Pub.L. 103–437 § 15(c)(6), 108 Stat. 4592.)

Codification

Section was enacted as part of the Environmental Research, Development, and Demonstration Authorization Act of 1979, and not as part of the National Environmental Policy Act of 1969 which comprises this chapter.

Change of Name

Any reference in any provision of law enacted before Jan. 4, 1995, to the Committee on Science, Space, and Technology of the House of Representatives treated as referring to the Committee on Science of the House of Representatives, see section 1(a)(10) of Pub.L. 104–14, set out as a note preceding section 21 of Title 2, The Congress.

§ 4369a. Reports on environmental research and development activities of the Agency

(a) Reports to keep Congressional committees fully and currently informed

The Administrator shall keep the appropriate committees of the House and the Senate fully and currently informed about all aspects of the environmental research and development activities of the Environmental Protection Agency.

(b) Annual reports relating requested funds to activities to be carried out with those funds

Each year, at the time of the submission of the President's annual budget request, the Administrator shall make available to the appropriate committees of Congress sufficient copies of a report fully describing funds requested and the environmental research and development activities to be carried out with these funds.

(April 7, 1980, Pub.L. 96–229, § 4, 94 Stat. 328.)

Codification

Section was enacted as part of the Environmental Research, Development, and Demonstration Authorization Act of 1980, and not as part of the National Environmental Policy Act of 1969 which comprises this chapter.

§ 4370. Reimbursement for use of facilities

(a) Authority to allow outside groups or individuals to use research and test facilities; reimbursement

The Administrator is authorized to allow appropriate use of special Environmental Protection Agency research and test facilities by outside groups or individuals and to receive reimbursement or fees for costs incurred thereby when he finds this to be in the public interest. Such reimbursement or fees are to be used by the Agency to defray the costs of use by outside groups or individuals.

(b) Rules and regulations

The Administrator may promulgate regulations to cover such use of Agency facilities in accordance with generally accepted accounting, safety, and laboratory practices.

(c) Waiver of reimbursement by Administrator

When he finds it is in the public interest the Administrator may waive reimbursement or fees for outside use of Agency facilities by nonprofit private or public entities.

(April 7, 1980, Pub.L. 96–229, § 5, 94 Stat. 328.)

Codification

Section was enacted as part of the Environmental Research, Development, and Demonstration Authorization Act of 1980, and not as part of the National Environmental Policy Act of 1969 which comprises this chapter.

Federal Practice and Procedure

Environmental class actions, see Wright, Miller & Kane: Civil 2d 1782.

§ 4370a. Assistant Administrators of Environmental Protection Agency; appointment; duties

(a) The President, by and with the advice and consent of the Senate, may appoint three Assistant

Administrators of the Environmental Protection Agency in addition to—

(1) the five Assistant Administrators provided for in section 1(d) of Reorganization Plan Numbered 3 of 1970;

(2) the Assistant Administrator provided by section 2625(g) of Title 15; and

(3) the Assistant Administrator provided by section 6911a of this title.

(b) Each Assistant Administrator appointed under subsection (a) of this section shall perform such duties as the Administrator of the Environmental Protection Agency may prescribe.

(Aug. 23, 1983, Pub.L. 98–80, § 1, 97 Stat. 485.)

Codification

Section was not enacted as part of the National Environmental Policy Act of 1969 which comprises this chapter.

§ 4370b. Availability of fees and charges to carry out Agency programs

Notwithstanding any other provision of law, after September 30, 1990, amounts deposited in the Licensing and Other Services Fund from fees and charges assessed and collected by the Administrator for services and activities carried out pursuant to the statutes administered by the Environmental Protection Agency shall thereafter be available to carry out the Agency's activities in the programs for which the fees or charges are made.

(Pub.L. 101–144, Title III, Nov. 9, 1989, 103 Stat. 858.)

Codification

Section was enacted as part of the Departments of Veterans Affairs and Housing and Urban Development, and Independent Agencies Appropriations Act, 1990, and not as part of the National Environmental Policy Act of 1969, which comprises this chapter.

§ 4370c. Environmental Protection Agency fees

(a) Assessment and collection

The Administrator of the Environmental Protection Agency shall, by regulation, assess and collect fees and charges for services and activities carried out pursuant to laws administered by the Environmental Protection Agency.

(b) Amount of fees and charges

Fees and charges assessed pursuant to this section shall be in such amounts as may be necessary to ensure that the aggregate amount of fees and charges collected pursuant to this section, in excess of the amount of fees and charges collected under current law—

(1) in fiscal year 1991, is not less than $28,000,000; and

(2) in each of fiscal years 1992, 1993, 1994, and 1995, is not less than $38,000,000.

(c) Limitation on fees and charges

(1) The maximum aggregate amount of fees and charges in excess of the amounts being collected under current law which may be assessed and collected pursuant to this section in a fiscal year—

(A) for services and activities carried out pursuant ot[1] the Federal Water Pollution Control Act [33 U.S.C.A. § 1251 et seq.] is $10,000,000; and

(B) for services and activities in programs within the jurisdiction of the House Committee on Energy and Commerce and administered by the Environmental Protection Agency through the Administrator, shall be limited to such sums collected as of November 5, 1990, pursuant to sections 2625(b) and 2665(e)(2) of Title 15, and such sums specifically authorized by the Clean Air Act Amendments of 1990.

(2) Any remaining amounts required to be collected under this section shall be collected from services and programs administered by the Environmental Protection Agency other than those specified in subparagraphs (A) and (B) of paragraph (1).

(d) Rule of construction

Nothing in this section increases or diminishes the authority of the Administrator to promulgate regulations pursuant to the Independent Office Appropriations Act (31 U.S.C. 9701).

(e) Uses of fees

Fees and charges collected pursuant to this section shall be deposited into a special account for environmental services in the Treasury of the United States. Subject to appropriation Acts, such funds shall be available to the Environmental Protection Agency to carry out the activities for which such fees and charges are collected. Such funds shall remain available until expended.

(Nov. 5, 1990, Pub.L. 101–508, Title VI, § 6501, 104 Stat. 1388–320).

[1] So in original. Probably should be "to".

References in Text

The Federal Water Pollution Control Act, referred to in subsec. (c)(1)(A), is Act June 30, 1948, c. 758, as amended generally by Pub.L. 92–500, § 2, Oct. 18, 1972, 86 Stat. 816, which is classified generally to chapter 26 (section 1251 et seq.) of Title 33, Navigation and Navigable Waters. For complete classification of this Act to the Code, see Short Title note set out under section 1251 of Title 33 and Tables.

The Clean Air Act Amendments of 1990, referred to in subsec. (c)(1)(B), is Pub.L. 101–549, Nov. 15, 1990, 104 Stat. 2399. For complete classification of this Act to the Code, see Tables.

The Independent Office Appropriations Act (31 U.S.C. 9701), referred to in subsec. (d), is Act Aug. 31, 1951, c. 376, Title V, § 501, 65 Stat. 290, as extensively revised Pub.L. 97–258, Sept. 13, 1982, 96 Stat. 1051, which is classified to section 9701 of Title 31, Money and Finance. For complete classification of these Acts to the Code, see Tables.

Codification

Section was enacted as part of the Omnibus Budget Reconciliation Act of 1990 and not as part of the National Environmental Policy Act of 1969 which comprises this chapter.

Change of Name

Any reference in any provision of law enacted before Jan. 4, 1995, to the Committee on Energy and Commerce of the House of Representatives treated as referring to the Committee on Commerce of the House of Representatives, except that any reference in any provision of law enacted before Jan. 4, 1995, to the Committee on Energy and Commerce of the House of Representatives treated as referring to the Committee on Agriculture of the House of Representatives, in the case of a provision of law relating to inspection of seafood or seafood products, the Committee on Banking and Financial Services of the House of Representatives, in the case of a provision of law relating to bank capital markets activities generally or to depository institution securities activities generally, and the Committee on Transportation and Infrastructure of the House of Representatives, in the case of a provision of law relating to railroads, railway labor, or railroad retirement and unemployment (except revenue measures related thereto), see section 1(a)(4) and (c)(1) of Pub.L. 104–14, set out as a note preceding section 21 of Title 2, The Congress.

§ 4370d. Availability of funding for economically and socially disadvantaged individuals

The Administrator of the Environmental Protection Agency shall, hereafter, to the fullest extent possible, ensure that at least 8 per centum of Federal funding for prime and subcontracts awarded in support of authorized programs, including grants, loans, and contracts for wastewater treatment and leaking underground storage tanks grants, be made available to business concerns or other organizations owned or controlled by socially and economically disadvantaged individuals (within the meaning of section 637(a)(5) and (6) of Title 15), including historically black colleges and universities. For purposes of this section, economically and socially disadvantaged individuals shall be deemed to include women.

(Pub.L. 102–389, Title III, Oct. 6, 1992, 106 Stat. 1602.)

Codification

Section was enacted as part of the Departments of Veterans Affairs and Housing and Urban Development, and Independent Agencies Appropriations Act, 1993, and not as part of the National Environmental Policy Act of 1969, which comprises this chapter.

SOLID WASTE DISPOSAL

SOLID WASTE DISPOSAL ACT [SWDA § ___]

(42 U.S.C.A. §§ 6901 to 6992k)

CHAPTER 82—SOLID WASTE DISPOSAL

SUBCHAPTER I—GENERAL PROVISIONS

Sec.

6901. Congressional findings.
- (a) Solid waste.
- (b) Environment and health.
- (c) Materials.
- (d) Energy.

6901a. Congressional findings: used oil recycling.

6902. Objectives and national policy.
- (a) Objectives.
- (b) National policy.

6903. Definitions.

6904. Governmental cooperation.
- (a) Interstate cooperation.
- (b) Consent of Congress to compacts.

6905. Application of chapter and integration with other Acts.
- (a) Application of chapter.
- (b) Integration with other Acts.
- (c) Integration with the Surface Mining Control and Reclamation Act of 1977.

6906. Financial disclosure.
- (a) Statement.
- (b) Action by Administrator.
- (c) Exemption.
- (d) Penalty.

6907. Solid waste management information and guidelines.
- (a) Guidelines.
- (b) Notice.

6908. Small town environmental planning.
- (a) Establishment.
- (b) Small Town Environmental Planning Task Force.
- (c) Identification of environmental requirements.
- (d) Small Town Ombudsman.
- (e) Multi-media permits.
- (f) Definition.
- (g) Authorization.

SUBCHAPTER II—OFFICE OF SOLID WASTE: AUTHORITIES OF THE ADMINISTRATOR

6911. Office of Solid Waste and Interagency Coordinating Committee.
- (a) Office of Solid Waste.
- (b) Interagency Coordinating Committee.

6911a. Assistant Administrator of Environmental Protection Agency; appointment, etc.

6912. Authorities of Administrator.
- (a) Authorities.
- (b) Revision of regulations.
- (c) Criminal investigations.

Sec.

6913. Resource Recovery and Conservation Panels.

6914. Grants for discarded tire disposal.
- (a) Grants.
- (b) Authorization of appropriations.

6914a. Labeling of lubricating oil.

6914b. Degradable plastic ring carriers.

6914b–1. Regulations covering degradable plastic ring carriers.

6915. Annual report.

6916. General authorization.
- (a) General administration.
- (b) Resource Recovery and Conservation Panels.
- (c) Hazardous waste.
- (d) State and local support.
- (e) Criminal investigations.
- (f) Underground storage tanks.

6917. Office of ombudsman.
- (a) Establishment; functions.
- (b) Authority to render assistance.
- (c) Effect on procedures for grievance, appeals, or administrative matters.
- (d) Termination.

SUBCHAPTER III—HAZARDOUS WASTE MANAGEMENT

6921. Identification and listing of hazardous waste.
- (a) Criteria for identification or listing.
- (b) Identification and listing.
- (c) Petition by State Governor.
- (d) Small quantity generator waste.
- (e) Specified wastes.
- (f) Delisting procedures.
- (g) EP toxicity.
- (h) Additional characteristics.
- (i) Clarification of household waste exclusion.

6922. Standards applicable to generators of hazardous waste.
- (a) In general.
- (b) Waste minimization.

6923. Standards applicable to transporters of hazardous waste.
- (a) Standards.
- (b) Coordination with regulations of Secretary of Transportation.
- (c) Fuel from hazardous waste.

6924. Standards applicable to owners and operators of hazardous waste treatment, storage, and disposal facilities.
- (a) In general.
- (b) Salt dome formations, salt bed formations, underground mines and caves.
- (c) Liquids in landfills.
- (d) Prohibitions on land disposal of specified wastes.

Sec.
6924. Standards applicable to owners and operators of hazardous waste treatment, storage, and disposal facilities.
(e) Solvents and dioxins.
(f) Disposal into deep injection wells; specified subsection (d) wastes, solvents and dioxins.
(g) Additional land disposal prohibition determination.
(h) Variance from land disposal prohibitions.
(i) Publication of determination.
(j) Storage of hazardous waste prohibited from land disposal.
(k) Definition of land disposal.
(*l*) Ban on dust suppression.
(m) Treatment standards for waste subject to land disposal prohibition.
(n) Air emissions.
(*o*) Minimum technological requirements.
(p) Ground water monitoring.
(q) Hazardous waste used as fuel.
(r) Labeling.
(s) Recordkeeping.
(t) Financial responsibility provisions.
(u) Continuing releases at permitted facilities.
(v) Corrective action beyond facility boundary.
(w) Underground tanks.
(x) Mining and other special wastes.
(y) Munitions.
6925. Permits for treatment, storage, or disposal of hazardous waste.
(a) Permit requirements.
(b) Requirements of permit application.
(c) Permit issuance.
(d) Permit revocation.
(e) Interim status.
(f) Coal mining wastes and reclamation permits.
(g) Research, development and demonstration permits.
(h) Waste minimization.
(i) Interim status facilities receiving wastes after July 26, 1982.
(j) Interim status surface impoundments.
6926. Authorized State hazardous waste programs.
(a) Federal guidelines.
(b) Authorization of State program.
(c) Interim authorization.
(d) Effect of State permit.
(e) Withdrawal of authorization.
(f) Availability of information.
(g) Amendments made by 1984 act.
(h) State programs for used oil.
6927. Inspections.
(a) Access entry.
(b) Availability to public.
(c) Federal facility inspections.
(d) State-operated facilities.
(e) Mandatory inspections.
6928. Federal enforcement.
(a) Compliance orders.
(b) Public hearing.
(c) Violation of compliance orders.
(d) Criminal penalties.
(e) Knowing endangerment.
(f) Special rules.
(g) Civil penalty.
(h) Interim status corrective action.

Sec.
6929. Retention of State authority.
6930. Effective date.
(a) Preliminary notification.
(b) Effective date of regulation.
6931. Authorization of assistance to States.
(a) Authorization of appropriations.
(b) Allocation.
(c) Activities included.
6932. Transferred.
6933. Hazardous waste site inventory.
(a) State inventory programs.
(b) Environmental Protection Agency program.
(c) Grants.
(d) No impediment to immediate remedial action.
6934. Monitoring, analysis, and testing.
(a) Authority of Administrator.
(b) Previous owners and operators.
(c) Proposal.
(d) Monitoring, etc., carried out by Administrator.
(e) Enforcement.
6935. Restrictions on recycled oil.
(a) In general.
(b) Identification or listing of used oil as hazardous waste.
(c) Used oil which is recycled.
(d) Permits.
6936. Expansion during interim status.
(a) Waste piles.
(b) Landfills and surface impoundments.
6937. Inventory of Federal agency hazardous waste facilities.
(a) Program requirement; submission; availability; contents.
(b) Environmental Protection Agency program.
6938. Export of hazardous wastes.
(a) In general.
(b) Regulations.
(c) Notification.
(d) Procedures for requesting consent of the receiving country.
(e) Conveyance of written consent to exporter.
(f) International agreements.
(g) Reports.
(h) Other standards.
6939. Domestic sewage.
(a) Report.
(b) Revisions of regulations.
(c) Report on wastewater lagoon.
(d) Application of sections 6927 and 6930.
6939a. Exposure information and health assessments.
(a) Exposure information.
(b) Health assessments.
(c) Members of the public.
(d) Priority.
(e) Periodic reports.
(f) Definition.
(g) Cost recovery.
6939b. Interim control of hazardous waste injection.
(a) Underground source of drinking water.
(b) Actions under Comprehensive Environmental Response, Compensation and Liability Act.
(c) Enforcement.
(d) Definitions.
6939c. Mixed waste inventory reports and plan.
(a) Mixed waste inventory reports.

Sec.
6939c. Mixed waste inventory reports and plan.
(b) Plan for development of treatment capacities and technologies.
(c) Schedule and progress reports.
6939d. Public vessels.
(a) Waste generated on public vessels.
(b) Computation of storage period.
(c) Definitions.
(d) Relationship to other law.
6939e. Federally owned treatment works.
(a) In general.
(b) Prohibition.
(c) Enforcement.
(d) Definition.
(e) Savings clause.

SUBCHAPTER IV—STATE OR REGIONAL SOLID WASTE PLANS

6941. Objectives of subchapter.
6941a. Energy and materials conservation and recovery; Congressional findings.
6942. Federal guidelines for plans.
(a) Guidelines for identification of regions.
(b) Guidelines for State plans.
(c) Considerations for State plan guidelines.
6943. Requirements for approval of plans.
(a) Minimum requirements.
(b) Discretionary plan provisions relating to recycled oil.
(c) Energy and materials conservation and recovery feasibility planning and assistance.
(d) Size of waste-to-energy facilities.
6944. Criteria for sanitary landfills; sanitary landfills required for all disposal.
(a) Criteria for sanitary landfills.
(b) Disposal required to be in sanitary landfills, etc.
(c) Effective date.
6945. Upgrading of open dumps.
(a) Closing or upgrading of existing open dumps.
(b) Inventory.
(c) Control of hazardous disposal.
6946. Procedure for development and implementation of State plan.
(a) Identification of regions.
(b) Identification of State and local agencies and responsibilities.
(c) Interstate regions.
6947. Approval of State plan; Federal assistance.
(a) Plan approval.
(b) Eligibility of States for Federal financial assistance.
(c) Existing activities.
6948. Federal assistance.
(a) Authorization of Federal financial assistance.
(b) State allotment.
(c) Distribution of Federal financial assistance within the State.
(d) Technical assistance.
(e) Special communities.
(f) Assistance to States for discretionary program for recycled oil.
(g) Assistance to municipalities for energy and materials conservation and recovery planning activities.

Sec.
6949. Rural communities assistance.
(a) In general.
(b) Allotment.
(c) Limit.
(d) Authorization of appropriations.
6949a. Adequacy of certain guidelines and criteria.
(a) Study.
(b) Report.
(c) Revisions of guidelines and criteria.

SUBCHAPTER V—DUTIES OF THE SECRETARY OF COMMERCE IN RESOURCE AND RECOVERY

6951. Functions.
6952. Development of specifications for secondary materials.
6953. Development of markets for recovered materials.
6954. Technology promotion.
6955. Marketing policies, establishment; nondiscrimination requirement.
6956. Authorization of appropriations.

SUBCHAPTER VI—FEDERAL RESPONSIBILITIES

6961. Application of Federal, State, and local law to Federal facilities.
(a) In general.
(b) Administrative enforcement actions.
(c) Limitation on State use of funds collected from Federal Government.
6962. Federal procurement.
(a) Application of section.
(b) Procurement subject to other law.
(c) Requirements.
(d) Specifications.
(e) Guidelines.
(f) Procurement of services.
(g) Executive Office.
(h) Definitions.
(i) Procurement program.
(j) Preference for recycled toner cartridges.
6963. Cooperation with Environmental Protection Agency.
(a) General rule.
(b) Information relating to energy and materials conservation and recovery.
6964. Applicability of solid waste disposal guidelines to Executive agencies.
(a) Compliance.
(b) Licenses and permits.
6965. Chief Financial Officer report.

SUBCHAPTER VII—MISCELLANEOUS PROVISIONS

6971. Employee protection.
(a) General.
(b) Remedy.
(c) Costs.
(d) Exception.
(e) Employment shifts and loss.
(f) Occupational safety and health.
6972. Citizens' suits.
(a) In general.
(b) Actions prohibited.
(c) Notice.
(d) Intervention.
(e) Costs.

Sec.
6972. Citizens' suits.
(f) Other rights preserved.
(g) Transporters.
6973. Imminent hazard.
(a) Authority of Administrator.
(b) Violations.
(c) Immediate notice.
(d) Public participation in settlements.
6974. Petition for regulations; public participation.
(a) Petition.
(b) Public participation.
6975. Separability of provisions.
6976. Judicial review.
(a) Review of final regulations and certain petitions.
(b) Review of certain actions under sections 6925 and 6926 of this title.
6977. Grants or contracts for training projects.
(a) General authority.
(b) Purposes.
(c) Study.
6978. Payments.
(a) General rule.
(b) Prohibition.
6979. Labor standards.
6979a. Transferred.
6979b. Law enforcement authority.

SUBCHAPTER VIII—RESEARCH, DEVELOPMENT, DEMONSTRATION, AND INFORMATION

6981. Research, demonstrations, training and other activities.
(a) General authority.
(b) Management program.
(c) Authorities.
6982. Special studies; plans for research, development, and demonstrations.
(a) Glass and plastic.
(b) Composition of waste stream.
(c) Priorities study.
(d) Small-scale and low technology study.
(e) Front-end source separation.
(f) Mining waste.
(g) Sludge.
(h) Tires.
(i) Resource recovery facilities.
(j) Resource Conservation Committee.
(k) Airport landfills.
(*l*) Completion of research and studies.
(m) Drilling fluids, produced waters, and other wastes associated with the exploration, development, or production of crude oil or natural gas or geothermal energy.
(n) Materials generated from the combustion of coal and other fossil fuels.
(*o*) Cement kiln dust waste.
(p) Materials generated from the extraction, beneficiation, and processing of ores and minerals, including phosphate rock and overburden from uranium mining.
(q) Authorization of appropriations.
(r) Minimization of hazardous waste.
(s) Extending the useful life of sanitary landfills.

Sec.
6983. Coordination, collection, and dissemination of information.
(a) Information.
(b) Library.
(c) Model accounting system.
(d) Model codes.
(e) Information programs.
(f) Coordination.
(g) Special restriction.
6984. Full-scale demonstration facilities.
(a) Authority.
(b) Time limitation.
(c) Cost sharing.
(d) Prohibition.
6985. Special study and demonstration projects on recovery of useful energy and materials.
(a) Studies.
(b) Demonstration.
(c) Application of other sections.
6986. Grants for resource recovery systems and improved solid waste disposal facilities.
(a) Authority.
(b) Conditions.
(c) Limitations.
(d) Regulations.
(e) Additional limitations.
(f) Single State.
6987. Authorization of appropriations.

SUBCHAPTER IX—REGULATION OF UNDERGROUND STORAGE TANKS

6991. Definitions and exemptions.
6991a. Notification.
(a) Underground storage tanks.
(b) Agency designation.
(c) State inventories.
6991b. Release, detection, prevention, and correction regulations.
(a) Regulations.
(b) Distinctions in regulations.
(c) Requirements.
(d) Financial responsibility.
(e) New tank performance standards.
(f) Effective dates.
(g) Interim prohibition.
(h) EPA Response Program for Petroleum.
(1) Before regulations.
(2) After regulations.
(3) Priority of corrective actions.
(4) Corrective action orders.
(5) Allowable corrective actions.
(6) Recovery of costs.
(A) In general.
(B) Recovery.
(C) Effect on liability.
(i) No transfers of liability.
(ii) No bar to cause of action.
(D) Facility.
(7) State authorities.
(A) General.
(B) Cost share.
(8) Emergency procurement powers.
(9) Definition of owner.
(10) Definition of exposure assessment.

Sec.
6991b. Release, detection, prevention, and correction regulations.
(11) Facilities without financial responsibility.
6991c. Approval of State programs.
(a) Elements of State programs.
(b) Federal standards.
(c) Financial responsibility.
(d) EPA determination.
(e) Withdrawal of authorization.
6991d. Inspections, monitoring, testing and corrective action.
(a) Furnishing information.
(b) Confidentiality.
6991e. Federal enforcement.
(a) Compliance orders.
(b) Procedure.
(c) Contents of order.
(d) Civil penalties.
6991f. Federal facilities.
(a) Application of subchapter.
(b) Presidential exemption.
6991g. State authority.
6991h. Study of underground storage tanks.
(a) Petroleum tanks.
(b) Other tanks.
(c) Elements of studies.
(d) Farm and heating oil tanks.
(e) Reports.
(f) Reimbursement.
6991i. Authorization of appropriations.

SUBCHAPTER X—DEMONSTRATION MEDICAL WASTE TRACKING PROGRAM

6992. Scope of demonstration program for medical waste.
(a) Covered States.
(b) Opt out.
(c) Petition in.
(d) Expiration of demonstration program.
6992a. Listing of medical wastes.
(a) List.
(b) Exclusions from list.
6992b. Tracking of medical waste.
(a) Demonstration program.
(b) Small quantities.
(c) On-site incinerators.
(d) Type of medical waste and types of generators.
6992c. Inspections.
(a) Requirements for access.
(b) Procedures.
(c) Availability to public.
6992d. Enforcement.
(a) Compliance orders.
(b) Criminal penalties.
(c) Knowing endangerment.
(d) Civil penalties.
(e) Civil penalty policy.
6992e. Federal facilities.
(a) In general.
(b) Definition of person.
6992f. Relationship to State law.
(a) State inspections and enforcement.
(b) Retention of State authority.
(c) State forms.
6992g. Report to Congress.
(a) Final report.

Sec.
6992g. Report to Congress.
(b) Interim reports.
(c) Consultation.
6992h. Health impacts report.
6992i. General provisions.
(a) Consultation.
(b) Public comment.
(c) Relationship to subchapter III.
6992j. Effective date.
6992k. Authorization of appropriations.

CROSS REFERENCES

Applicable environmental requirements defined as including standards, limitations, or other requirements established by this chapter, see section 8302 of this title.

By product material managed in conformity with general requirements of this chapter, see section 2114 of this title.

Definitions of this chapter applied to chapter on Comprehensive Environmental Response, Compensation, and Liability, see section 9601 of this title.

Duty of Administrator under this chapter to make available to Science Advisory Board proposed environmental criteria document, see section 4365 of this title.

Hazardous waste and qualified hazardous waste disposal facility as defined in this chapter subject to taxation, see section 4682 of Title 26, Internal Revenue Code.

Health and environmental standards for uranium mill tailings consistent with requirements of this chapter, see section 2022 of this title.

Persons subject to penalties for not complying with transportation of hazardous wastes as defined by this chapter, see section 11901 of Title 49, Transportation.

Responsibility of Environmental Protection Agency for environmental, economic, and institutional aspects of solid waste projects and that such projects are consistent with guidelines provided in this chapter, see section 5919 of this title.

Surface Mining Control and Reclamation Act as not superseding, amending, modifying or repealing this chapter, see section 1292 of Title 30, Mineral Lands and Mining.

West's Federal Forms

Enforcement and review of administrative agency decisions and orders, see § 851 et seq.

Jurisdiction and venue in district courts, see § 1003 et seq.

Preliminary injunctions and temporary restraining orders, see § 5271 et seq.

Sentence and fine, see § 7531 et seq.

CODE OF FEDERAL REGULATIONS

Classification of solid waste disposal facilities and practices, see 40 CFR 257.1 et seq.

Federal waste permit program, see 40 CFR 270.1 et seq.

Hazardous waste management generally, see 40 CFR 260.1 et seq.

Identification and listing of hazardous waste, see 40 CFR 261.1 et seq.

Solid waste generally, see 40 CFR Chap. I, Subchap. I.

Solid waste management guidelines and procedures, see 40 CFR 244.100 et seq., 245.100 et seq., 246.100 et seq.

State and local assistance, see 40 CFR 35.001 et seq.

State program regulations, see 40 CFR 233.1 et seq.

LAW REVIEW COMMENTARIES

Encouraging safety through insurance-based incentives: financial responsibility for hazardous wastes. Jeffrey Kehne, 96 Yale L.J. 403 (1986).

Criminal sanctions under federal and state environmental statutes. Richard H. Allan, 14 Ecology L.Q. 117 (1987).

How well can states enforce their environmental laws when the polluter is the United States Government? 18 Rutgers L.J. 123 (1986).

Patterns of judicial interpretation of insurance coverage for hazardous waste site liability. Robert D. Chesler, Michael L. Rodburg and Cornelius C. Smith, Jr., 18 Rutgers L.J. 9 (1986).

Toward a national groundwater act: Current contamination and future courses of action. Thomas D. Marks, 61 Fla.B.J. 10 (April 1987).

Who should control hazardous waste on native American lands? Looking beyond Washington Department of Ecology v. EPA. Leslie Allen, 14 Ecology L.Q. 69 (1987).

The problem with RCRA—Do the financial responsibility provisions really work? 36 Am.U.L.Rev. 133 (1986).

WESTLAW ELECTRONIC RESEARCH

See WESTLAW guide following the Explanation pages of this pamphlet.

SUBCHAPTER I—GENERAL PROVISIONS

§ 6901. Congressional findings [SWDA § 1002]

(a) Solid waste

The Congress finds with respect to solid waste—

(1) that the continuing technological progress and improvement in methods of manufacture, packaging, and marketing of consumer products has resulted in an ever-mounting increase, and in a change in the characteristics, of the mass material discarded by the purchaser of such products;

(2) that the economic and population growth of our Nation, and the improvements in the standard of living enjoyed by our population, have required increased industrial production to meet our needs, and have made necessary the demolition of old buildings, the construction of new buildings, and the provision of highways and other avenues of transportation, which, together with related industrial, commercial, and agricultural operations, have resulted in a rising tide of scrap, discarded, and waste materials;

(3) that the continuing concentration of our population in expanding metropolitan and other urban areas has presented these communities with serious financial, management, intergovernmental, and technical problems in the disposal of solid wastes resulting from the industrial, commercial, domestic, and other activities carried on in such areas;

(4) that while the collection and disposal of solid wastes should continue to be primarily the function of State, regional, and local agencies, the problems of waste disposal as set forth above have become a matter national in scope and in concern and necessitate Federal action through financial and technical assistance and leadership in the development, demonstration, and application of new and improved methods and processes to reduce the amount of waste and unsalvageable materials and to provide for proper and economical solid waste disposal practices.

(b) Environment and health

The Congress finds with respect to the environment and health, that—

(1) although land is too valuable a national resource to be needlessly polluted by discarded materials, most solid waste is disposed of on land in open dumps and sanitary landfills;

(2) disposal of solid waste and hazardous waste in or on the land without careful planning and management can present a danger to human health and the environment;

(3) as a result of the Clean Air Act [42 U.S.C.A. § 7401 et seq.], the Water Pollution Control Act [33 U.S.C.A. § 1251 et seq.], and other Federal and State laws respecting public health and the environment, greater amounts of solid waste (in the form of sludge and other pollution treatment residues) have been created. Similarly, inadequate and environmentally unsound practices for the disposal or use of solid waste have created greater amounts of air and water pollution and other problems for the environment and for health;

(4) open dumping is particularly harmful to health, contaminates drinking water from underground and surface supplies, and pollutes the air and the land;

(5) the placement of inadequate controls on hazardous waste management will result in substantial risks to human health and the environment;

(6) if hazardous waste management is improperly performed in the first instance, corrective action is likely to be expensive, complex, and time consuming;

(7) certain classes of land disposal facilities are not capable of assuring long-term containment of certain hazardous wastes, and to avoid substantial risk to human health and the environment, reliance on land disposal should be minimized or eliminated, and land disposal, particularly landfill and surface impoundment, should be the least favored method for managing hazardous wastes; and

(8) alternatives to existing methods of land disposal must be developed since many of the cities in the United States will be running out of suitable solid waste disposal sites within five years unless immediate action is taken.

(c) Materials

The Congress finds with respect to materials, that—

(1) millions of tons of recoverable material which could be used are needlessly buried each year;

(2) methods are available to separate usable materials from solid waste; and

(3) the recovery and conservation of such materials can reduce the dependence of the United States on foreign resources and reduce the deficit in its balance of payments.

(d) Energy

The Congress finds with respect to energy, that—

(1) solid waste represents a potential source of solid fuel, oil, or gas that can be converted into energy;

(2) the need exists to develop alternative energy sources for public and private consumption in order to reduce our dependence on such sources as petroleum products, natural gas, nuclear and hydroelectric generation; and

(3) technology exists to produce usable energy from solid waste.

(Pub.L. 89–272, Title II, § 1002, as added Oct. 21, 1976, Pub.L. 94–580, § 2, 90 Stat. 2796, and amended Nov. 8, 1978, Pub.L. 95–609, § 7(a), 92 Stat. 3081; Nov. 8, 1984, Pub.L. 98–616, Title I, § 101(a), 98 Stat. 3224.)

Short Title of 1992 Amendments

Pub.L. 102–386, Title I, § 101, Oct. 6, 1992, 106 Stat. 1505, provided that: "This title [enacting sections 6908, 6939c, 6939d, 6939e, and 6965 of this title, amending sections 6903, 6924, 6927, and 6961 of this title, and enacting provisions set out as notes under sections 6939c and 6961 of this title] may be cited as the 'Federal Facility Compliance Act of 1992'."

Short Title

Section 1001 of Pub.L. 89–272, Title II, as added Pub.L. 94–580, § 2, Oct. 21, 1976, 90 Stat. 2795, provided in part that title II of Pub.L. 89–272 [enacting this chapter] may be cited as the "Solid Waste Disposal Act".

Section 1 of Pub.L. 94–580 provided that: "This Act [which enacted this chapter] may be cited as the 'Resource Conservation and Recovery Act of 1976'."

Section 1 of Pub.L. 100–582, Nov. 1, 1988, 102 Stat. 2950, provided that: "This Act [enacting subchapter X of this chapter and sections 6903(40) of this title and 3063 of Title 18, Crimes and Criminal Procedure] may be cited as the 'Medical Waste Tracking Act of 1988'."

CODE OF FEDERAL REGULATIONS

Grants, see 40 CFR 30.100 et seq., 40.100 et seq.
Hazardous waste treatment facilities, standards for owners of, see 40 CFR 264.1 et seq., 265.1 et seq.
Procurement under assistance agreements, see 40 CFR 33.001 et seq.

LAW REVIEW COMMENTARIES

America's lethal export: The growing trade in hazardous waste. 1991 U.Ill.L.Rev. 889.

Bankrupting CERCLA: Amending the Bankruptcy Code to allow CERCLA contingent claims for contribution. Kenneth W. Maxwell, 13 J. Energy, Nat. Resources, & Envtl.L. 431 (1993).

Cleaning up after federal and state pollution programs: Local government hazardous waste regulation. William L. Earl and George F. Gramling, 17 Stetson L.Rev. (Fla.) 639 (1988).

Crying wolf or is a wolf at the door?: Lender liability for environmental cleanup. Jeanmarie B. Tade, 32 S.Tex.L.Rev. 555 (1991).

Emerging federal law of mine waste: Administrative, judicial and legislative developments. John R. Jacus and Thomas E. Root, 26 Land and Water L.Rev. 461 (1991).

Erosion of mens rea in environmental criminal prosecution. Ruth Ann Weidel, John R. Mayo and F. Michael Zachara, 21 Seton Hall L.Rev. 1125 (1991).

From elephants to mice: The development of EBMUD's program to control small source wastewater discharges. Raoul Stewardson, 20 Ecology L.Q. 441 (1993).

Hazardous Waste Law for the federal employee after the Federal Facility Compliance Act of 1992. Stephen J. Darmody, 40 Fed. B.News & J. 650 (Nov./Dec. 1993).

Interaction of the Bankruptcy Code and environmental laws: Grit, the grind, and the grease. Robert R. Graves, 29 Willamette L.Rev. 297 (1993).

Interstate waste: A key issue in resolving the national hazardous waste capacity crisis. B.J. Wynne, III and Terri Hamby, 32 S.Tex. L.Rev. 601 (1991).

Limiting lender liability under CERCLA by administrative rule. Frona M. Powell, 75 Marq.L.Rev. 139 (1991).

Long-range planning in environmental and health regulatory agencies. Richard N.L. Andrews, 20 Ecology L.Q. 515 (1993).

No longer just a cost of doing business: Criminal liability of corporate officials for violations of the Clean Water Act and Resource Conservation and Recovery Act. G. Nelson Smith, III, 53 La.L.Rev. 119 (1992).

Oil and gas exemptions under RCRA and CERCLA: Are they still "safe harbors" eleven years later? Michael M. Gibson and David P. Young, 32 S.Tex.L.Rev. 361 (1991).

Prosecution of corporations and corporate officers for environmental crimes: Limiting one's exposure for environmental criminal liability. Kenneth A. Hodson, Sarah N. McGiffert and Marianne T. Bayardi, 34 Ariz.L.Rev. 553 (1992).

Recovering costs for cleaning up hazardous waste sites: An examination of state superlien statutes. Note, 63 Ind.L.J. 571 (1987–1988).

Resolving conflicts between bankruptcy law and the state police power. Ellen E. Sward, 1987 Wis.L.Rev. 403 (1987).

Responding to a government environmental investigation: Shaping the defense. Francis J. Burke, Jr., Karen A. Potts, Leigh Lani Brown, Robin L. De Respino and Michael R. Hall, 34 Ariz.L.Rev. 509 (1992).

Responsible corporate officer: Designated felon or legal fiction? Brenda S. Hustis and John Y. Gotanda, 25 Loy.U.Chi.L.J. 169 (1994).

Survey of federal and state environmental crime legislation. Edward F. Novak and Charles W. Steese, 34 Ariz.L.Rev. 571 (1992).

The once and future EPA lender regulations: Limiting lender liability for the cleanup of hazardous wastes. Jeffrey M. Gaba, 47 Consumer Fin.L.Q.Rep. 355 (1993).

§ 6901a. Congressional findings: used oil recycling

The Congress finds and declares that—

(1) used oil is a valuable source of increasingly scarce energy and materials;

(2) technology exists to re-refine, reprocess, reclaim, and otherwise recycle used oil;

(3) used oil constitutes a threat to public health and the environment when reused or disposed of improperly; and

that, therefore, it is in the national interest to recycle used oil in a manner which does not constitute a threat to public health and the environment and which conserves energy and materials.

(Oct. 15, 1980, Pub.L. 96–463, § 2, 94 Stat. 2055.)

Codification

Section was enacted as part of the Used Oil Recycling Act of 1980, and not as part of the Solid Waste Disposal Act which comprises this chapter.

Short Title

Pub. L. 96–463, § 1, Oct. 15, 1980, 94 Stat. 2055, provided that Pub. L. 96–463 [which enacted this section and sections 6914a and 6932 of this title] may be cited as the "Used Oil Recycling Act of 1980".

§ 6902. Objectives and national policy [SWDA § 1003]

(a) Objectives

The objectives of this chapter are to promote the protection of health and the environment and to conserve valuable material and energy resources by—

(1) providing technical and financial assistance to State and local governments and interstate agencies for the development of solid waste management plans (including resource recovery and resource conservation systems) which will promote improved solid waste management techniques (including more effective organizational arrangements), new and improved methods of collection, separation, and recovery of solid waste, and the environmentally safe disposal of nonrecoverable residues;

(2) providing training grants in occupations involving the design, operation, and maintenance of solid waste disposal systems;

(3) prohibiting future open dumping on the land and requiring the conversion of existing open dumps to facilities which do not pose a danger to the environment or to health;

(4) assuring that hazardous waste management practices are conducted in a manner which protects human health and the environment;

(5) requiring that hazardous waste be properly managed in the first instance thereby reducing the need for corrective action at a future date;

(6) minimizing the generation of hazardous waste and the land disposal of hazardous waste by encouraging process substitution, materials recovery, properly conducted recycling and reuse, and treatment;

(7) establishing a viable Federal-State partnership to carry out the purposes of this chapter and insuring that the Administrator will, in carrying out the provisions of subchapter III of this chapter give a high priority to assisting and cooperating with States in obtaining full authorization of State programs under subchapter III of this chapter;

(8) providing for the promulgation of guidelines for solid waste collection, transport, separation, recovery, and disposal practices and systems;

(9) promoting a national research and development program for improved solid waste management and resource conservation techniques, more effective organizational arrangements, and new and improved methods of collection, separation, and recovery, and recycling of solid wastes and environmentally safe disposal of nonrecoverable residues;

(10) promoting the demonstration, construction, and application of solid waste management, resource recovery, and resource conservation systems which preserve and enhance the quality of air, water, and land resources; and

(11) establishing a cooperative effort among the Federal, State, and local governments and private enterprise in order to recover valuable materials and energy from solid waste.

(b) National policy

The Congress hereby declares it to be the national policy of the United States that, wherever feasible, the generation of hazardous waste is to be reduced or eliminated as expeditiously as possible. Waste that is nevertheless generated should be treated, stored, or disposed of so as to minimize the present and future threat to human health and the environment.

(Pub.L. 89–272, Title II, § 1003, as added Oct. 21, 1976, Pub.L. 94–580, § 2, 90 Stat. 2798, and amended Nov. 8, 1984, Pub.L. 98–616, Title I, § 101(b), 98 Stat. 3224.)

§ 6903. Definitions [SWDA § 1004]

As used in this chapter:

(1) The term "Administrator" means the Administrator of the Environmental Protection Agency.

(2) The term "construction," with respect to any project of construction under this chapter, means (A) the erection or building of new structures and acquisition of lands or interests therein, or the acquisition, replacement, expansion, remodeling, alteration, modernization, or extension of existing structures, and (B) the acquisition and installation of initial equipment of, or required in connection with, new or newly acquired structures or the expanded, remodeled, altered, modernized or extended part of existing structures (including trucks and other motor vehicles, and tractors, cranes, and other machinery) necessary for the proper utilization and operation of the facility after completion of the project; and includes preliminary planning to determine the economic and engineering feasibility and the public health and safety aspects of the project, the engineering, architectural, legal, fiscal, and economic investigations and studies, and any surveys, designs, plans, working drawings, specifications, and other action necessary for the carrying out of the project, and (C) the inspection and supervision of

the process of carrying out the project to completion.

(2A) The term "demonstration" means the initial exhibition of a new technology process or practice or a significantly new combination or use of technologies, processes or practices, subsequent to the development stage, for the purpose of proving technological feasibility and cost effectiveness.

(3) The term "disposal" means the discharge, deposit, injection, dumping, spilling, leaking, or placing of any solid waste or hazardous waste into or on any land or water so that such solid waste or hazardous waste or any constituent thereof may enter the environment or be emitted into the air or discharged into any waters, including ground waters.

(4) The term "Federal agency" means any department, agency, or other instrumentality of the Federal Government, any independent agency or establishment of the Federal Government including any Government corporation, and the Government Printing Office.

(5) The term "hazardous waste" means a solid waste, or combination of solid wastes, which because of its quantity, concentration, or physical, chemical, or infectious characteristics may—

(A) cause, or significantly contribute to an increase in mortality or an increase in serious irreversible, or incapacitating reversible, illness; or

(B) pose a substantial present or potential hazard to human health or the environment when improperly treated, stored, transported, or disposed of, or otherwise managed.

(6) The term "hazardous waste generation" means the act or process of producing hazardous waste.

(7) The term "hazardous waste management" means the systematic control of the collection, source separation, storage, transportation, processing, treatment, recovery, and disposal of hazardous wastes.

(8) For purposes of Federal financial assistance (other than rural communities assistance), the term "implementation" does not include the acquisition, leasing, construction, or modification of facilities or equipment or the acquisition, leasing, or improvement of land.

(9) The term "intermunicipal agency" means an agency established by two or more municipalities with responsibility for planning or administration of solid waste.

(10) The term "interstate agency" means an agency of two or more municipalities in different States, or an agency established by two or more States, with authority to provide for the management of solid wastes and serving two or more municipalities located in different States.

(11) The term "long-term contract" means, when used in relation to solid waste supply, a contract of sufficient duration to assure the viability of a resource recovery facility (to the extent that such viability depends upon solid waste supply).

(12) The term "manifest" means the form used for identifying the quantity, composition, and the origin, routing, and destination of hazardous waste during its transportation from the point of generation to the point of disposal, treatment, or storage.

(13) The term "municipality" (A) means a city, town, borough, county, parish, district, or other public body created by or pursuant to State law, with responsibility for the planning or administration of solid waste management, or an Indian tribe or authorized tribal organization or Alaska Native village or organization, and (B) includes any rural community or unincorporated town or village or any other public entity for which an application for assistance is made by a State or political subdivision thereof.

(14) The term "open dump" means any facility or site where solid waste is disposed of which is not a sanitary landfill which meets the criteria promulgated under section 6944 of this title and which is not a facility for disposal of hazardous waste.

(15) The term "person" means an individual, trust, firm, joint stock company, corporation (including a government corporation), partnership, association, State, municipality, commission, political subdivision of a State, or any interstate body and shall include each department, agency, and instrumentality of the United States.

(16) The term "procurement item" means any device, good, substance, material, product, or other item whether real or personal property which is the subject of any purchase, barter, or other exchange made to procure such item.

(17) The term "procuring agency" means any Federal agency, or any State agency or agency of a political subdivision of a State which is using appropriated Federal funds for such procurement, or any person contracting with any such agency with respect to work performed under such contract.

(18) The term "recoverable" refers to the capability and likelihood of being recovered from solid waste for a commercial or industrial use.

(19) The term "recovered material" means waste material and byproducts which have been recovered or diverted from solid waste, but such term does not

include those materials and byproducts generated from, and commonly reused within, an original manufacturing process.

(20) The term "recovered resources" means material or energy recovered from solid waste.

(21) The term "resource conservation" means reduction of the amounts of solid waste that are generated, reduction of overall resource consumption, and utilization of recovered resources.

(22) The term "resource recovery" means the recovery of material or energy from solid waste.

(23) The term "resource recovery system" means a solid waste management system which provides for collection, separation, recycling, and recovery of solid wastes, including disposal of nonrecoverable waste residues.

(24) The term "resource recovery facility" means any facility at which solid waste is processed for the purpose of extracting, converting to energy, or otherwise separating and preparing solid waste for reuse.

(25) The term "regional authority" means the authority established or designated under section 6946 of this title.

(26) The term "sanitary landfill" means a facility for the disposal of solid waste which meets the criteria published under section 6944 of this title.

(26A) The term "sludge" means any solid, semisolid or liquid waste generated from a municipal, commercial, or industrial wastewater treatment plant, water supply treatment plant, or air pollution control facility or any other such waste having similar characteristics and effects.

(27) The term "solid waste" means any garbage, refuse, sludge from a waste treatment plant, water supply treatment plant, or air pollution control facility and other discarded material, including solid, liquid, semisolid, or contained gaseous material resulting from industrial, commercial, mining, and agricultural operations, and from community activities, but does not include solid or dissolved material in domestic sewage, or solid or dissolved materials in irrigation return flows or industrial discharges which are point sources subject to permits under section 1342 of title 33, or source, special nuclear, or byproduct material as defined by the Atomic Energy Act of 1954, as amended (68 Stat. 923) [42 U.S.C.A. § 2011 et seq.].

(28) The term "solid waste management" means the systematic administration of activities which provide for the collection, source separation, storage, transportation, transfer, processing, treatment, and disposal of solid waste.

(29) The term "solid waste management facility" includes—

(A) any resource recovery system or component thereof,

(B) any system, program, or facility for resource conservation, and

(C) any facility for the collection, source separation, storage, transportation, transfer, processing, treatment or disposal of solid wastes, including hazardous wastes, whether such facility is associated with facilities generating such wastes or otherwise.

(30) The terms "solid waste planning", "solid waste management", and "comprehensive planning" include planning or management respecting resource recovery and resource conservation.

(31) The term "State" means any of the several States, the District of Columbia, the Commonwealth of Puerto Rico, the Virgin Islands, Guam, American Samoa, and the Commonwealth of the Northern Mariana Islands.

(32) The term "State authority" means the agency established or designated under section 6947 of this title.

(33) The term "storage", when used in connection with hazardous waste, means the containment of hazardous waste, either on a temporary basis or for a period of years, in such a manner as not to constitute disposal of such hazardous waste.

(34) The term "treatment", when used in connection with hazardous waste, means any method, technique, or process, including neutralization, designed to change the physical, chemical, or biological character or composition of any hazardous waste so as to neutralize such waste or so as to render such waste nonhazardous, safer for transport, amendable for recovery, amenable for storage, or reduced in volume. Such term includes any activity or processing designed to change the physical form or chemical composition of hazardous waste so as to render it nonhazardous.

(35) The term "virgin material" means a raw material, including previously unused copper, aluminum, lead, zinc, iron, or other metal or metal ore, any undeveloped resource that is, or with new technology will become, a source of raw materials.

(36) The term "used oil" means any oil which has been—

(A) refined from crude oil,

(B) used, and

(C) as a result of such use, contaminated by physical or chemical impurities.

(37) The term "recycled oil" means any used oil which is reused, following its original use, for any purpose (including the purpose for which the oil was originally used). Such term includes oil which is re-refined, reclaimed, burned, or reprocessed.

(38) The term "lubricating oil" means the fraction of crude oil which is sold for purposes of reducing friction in any industrial or mechanical device. Such term includes re-refined oil.

(39) The term "re-refined oil" means used oil from which the physical and chemical contaminants acquired through previous use have been removed through a refining process.

(40) Except as otherwise provided in this paragraph, the term "medical waste" means any solid waste which is generated in the diagnosis, treatment, or immunization of human beings or animals, in research pertaining thereto, or in the production or testing of biologicals. Such term does not include any hazardous waste identified or listed under subchapter III of this chapter or any household waste as defined in regulations under subchapter III of this chapter.

(41) The term "mixed waste" means waste that contains both hazardous waste and source, special nuclear, or by-product material subject to the Atomic Energy Act of 1954 (42 U.S.C. 2011 et seq.).

(Pub.L. 89–272, Title II, § 1004, as added Oct. 21, 1976, Pub.L. 94–580, § 2, 90 Stat. 2798, and amended Nov. 8, 1978, Pub.L. 95–609, § 7(b), 92 Stat. 3081; Oct. 15, 1980, Pub.L. 96–463, § 3, 94 Stat. 2055; Oct. 21, 1980, Pub.L. 96–482, § 2, 94 Stat. 2334; Nov. 1, 1988, Pub.L. 100–582, § 3, 102 Stat. 2958; Pub.L. 102–386, Title I, §§ 103, 105(b), Oct. 6, 1992, 106 Stat. 1507, 1512.)

References in Text

The Atomic Energy Act of 1954, as amended, referred to in pars. (27) and (41), is Act Aug. 30, 1954, c. 1073, § 1, 68 Stat. 921, as amended, which is classified principally to chapter 23 (section 2011 et seq.) of this title. For complete classification of this Act to the Code, see Short Title note set out under section 2011 of this title and Tables.

CROSS REFERENCES

Disposal, hazardous waste, and treatment, as defined by this section as applied to hazardous substances releases, liability and compensation, see section 9601 of this title.

Solid waste as defined in this section as applied to synthetic fuel conversion facilities and municipal organic waste energy generation facilities, see section 5919 of this title.

LAW REVIEW COMMENTARIES

Contractors as unsuspecting responsible parties under Superfund. J. Randle Schick, 8 CBA Rec. 16 (Feb. 1994).

From elephants to mice: The development of EBMUD's program to control small source wastewater discharges. Raoul Stewardson, 20 Ecology L.Q. 441 (1993).

Interstate waste: A key issue in resolving the national hazardous waste capacity crisis. B.J. Wynne, III and Terri Hamby, 32 S.Tex. L.Rev. 601 (1991).

Used oil in the United States: Environmental impact, regulation, and management. Elizabeth A. Beiring, 41 Buffalo L.Rev. 157 (1993).

§ 6904. Governmental cooperation [SWDA § 1005]

(a) Interstate cooperation

The provisions of this chapter to be carried out by States may be carried out by interstate agencies and provisions applicable to States may apply to interstate regions where such agencies and regions have been established by the respective States and approved by the Administrator. In any such case, action required to be taken by the Governor of a State, respecting regional designation shall be required to be taken by the Governor of each of the respective States with respect to so much of the interstate region as is within the jurisdiction of that State.

(b) Consent of Congress to compacts

The consent of the Congress is hereby given to two or more States to negotiate and enter into agreements or compacts, not in conflict with any law or treaty of the United States, for—

(1) cooperative effort and mutual assistance for the management of solid waste or hazardous waste (or both) and the enforcement of their respective laws relating thereto, and

(2) the establishment of such agencies, joint or otherwise, as they may deem desirable for making effective such agreements or compacts.

No such agreement or compact shall be binding or obligatory upon any State a party thereto unless it is agreed upon by all parties to the agreement and until it has been approved by the Administrator and the Congress.

(Pub.L. 89–272, Title II, § 1005, as added Oct. 21, 1976, Pub.L. 94–580, § 2, 90 Stat. 2801.)

LAW REVIEW COMMENTARIES

Property owner liability for environmental contamination in California. Michael B. Hingerty, 22 U.S.F.L.Rev. 31 (1987).

§ 6905. Application of chapter and integration with other Acts [SWDA § 1006]

(a) Application of chapter

Nothing in this chapter shall be construed to apply to (or to authorize any State, interstate, or local authority to regulate) any activity or substance which is subject to the Federal Water Pollution Control Act [33 U.S.C.A. § 1251 et seq.], the Safe Drinking Water Act [42 U.S.C.A. § 300f et seq.], the Marine Protection, Research and Sanctuaries Act of 1972 [33 U.S.C.A. § 1401 et seq.], or the Atomic Energy Act of 1954 [42 U.S.C.A. § 2011 et seq.] except to the extent that such application (or regulation) is not inconsistent with the requirements of such Acts.

(b) Integration with other Acts

(1) The Administrator shall integrate all provisions of this chapter for purposes of administration and enforcement and shall avoid duplication, to the maximum extent practicable, with the appropriate provisions of the Clean Air Act [42 U.S.C.A. § 7401 et seq.], the Federal Water Pollution Control Act [33 U.S.C.A. § 1251 et seq.], the Federal Insecticide, Fungicide, and Rodenticide Act [7 U.S.C.A. § 136 et seq.], the Safe Drinking Water Act [42 U.S.C.A. § 300f et seq.], the Marine Protection, Research and Sanctuaries Act of 1972 [33 U.S.C.A. § 1401 et seq.], and such other Acts of Congress as grant regulatory authority to the Administrator. Such integration shall be effected only to the extent that it can be done in a manner consistent with the goals and policies expressed in this chapter and in the other acts referred to in this subsection.

(2)(A) As promptly as practicable after November 8, 1984, the Administrator shall submit a report describing—

(i) the current data and information available on emissions of polychlorinated dibenzo-p-dioxins from resource recovery facilities burning municipal solid waste;

(ii) any significant risks to human health posed by these emissions; and

(iii) operating practices appropriate for controlling these emissions.

(B) Based on the report under subparagraph (A) and on any future information on such emissions, the Administrator may publish advisories or guidelines regarding the control of dioxin emissions from such facilities. Nothing in this paragraph shall be construed to preempt or otherwise affect the authority of the Administrator to promulgate any regulations under the Clean Air Act [42 U.S.C.A. § 7401 et seq.] regarding emissions of polychlorinated dibenzo-p-dioxins.

(3) Notwithstanding any other provisions of law, in developing solid waste plans, it is the intention of this chapter that in determining the size of a waste-to-energy facility, adequate provisions shall be given to the present and reasonably anticipated future needs, including those needs created by thorough implementation of section 6962(h) of this title, of the recycling and resource recovery interests within the area encompassed by the solid waste plan.

(c) Integration with the Surface Mining Control and Reclamation Act of 1977

(1) No later than 90 days after October 21, 1980, the Administrator shall review any regulations applicable to the treatment, storage, or disposal of any coal mining wastes or overburden promulgated by the Secretary of the Interior under the Surface Mining and Reclamation Act of 1977 [30 U.S.C.A. § 1201 et seq.]. If the Administrator determines that any requirement of final regulations promulgated under any section of subchapter III of this chapter relating to mining wastes or overburden is not adequately addressed in such regulations promulgated by the Secretary, the Administrator shall promptly transmit such determination, together with suggested revisions and supporting documentation, to the Secretary.

(2) The Secretary of the Interior shall have exclusive responsibility for carrying out any requirement of subchapter III of this chapter with respect to coal mining wastes or overburden for which a surface coal mining and reclamation permit is issued or approved under the Surface Mining Control and Reclamation Act of 1977 [30 U.S.C.A. § 1201 et seq.]. The Secretary shall, with the concurrence of the Administrator, promulgate such regulations as may be necessary to carry out the purposes of this subsection and shall integrate such regulations with regulations promulgated under the Surface Mining Control and Reclamation Act of 1977.

(Pub.L. 89–272, Title II, § 1006, as added Oct. 21, 1976, Pub.L. 94–580, § 2, 90 Stat. 2802, and amended Oct. 21, 1980, Pub.L. 96–482, § 3, 94 Stat. 2334; Nov. 8, 1984, Pub.L. 98–616, Title I, § 102, Title V, § 501(f)(2), 98 Stat. 3225, 3276.)

CODE OF FEDERAL REGULATIONS

Definitions and requirements, see 10 CFR 122.1 et seq., 123.1 et seq.
Hazardous waste standards, see 40 CFR 260.1 et seq. to 271.1 et seq.

§ 6906. Financial disclosure [SWDA § 1007]

(a) Statement

Each officer or employee of the Administrator who—

(1) performs any function or duty under this chapter; and

(2) has any known financial interest in any person who applies for or receives financial assistance under this chapter

shall, beginning on February 1, 1977, annually file with the Administrator a written statement concerning all such interests held by such officer or employee during the preceding calendar year. Such statement shall be available to the public.

(b) Action by Administrator

The Administrator shall—

(1) act within ninety days after October 21, 1976—

(A) to define the term "known financial interest" for purposes of subsection (a) of this section; and

(B) to establish the methods by which the requirement to file written statements specified in subsection (a) of this section will be monitored and enforced, including appropriate provision for the filing by such officers and employees of such statements and the review by the Administrator of such statements; and

(2) report to the Congress on June 1, 1978, and of each succeeding calendar year with respect to such disclosures and the actions taken in regard thereto during the preceding calendar year.

(c) Exemption

In the rules prescribed under subsection (b) of this section, the Administrator may identify specific positions within the Environmental Protection Agency which are of a nonpolicy-making nature and provide that officers or employees occupying such positions shall be exempt from the requirements of this section.

(d) Penalty

Any officer or employee who is subject to, and knowingly violates, this section shall be fined not more than $2,500 or imprisoned not more than one year, or both.

(Pub.L. 89–272, Title II, § 1007, as added Oct. 21, 1976, Pub.L. 94–580, § 2, 90 Stat. 2802.)

CODE OF FEDERAL REGULATIONS

Responsibilities and conduct of EPA employees, generally, see 40 CFR 3.100 et seq.

§ 6907. Solid waste management information and guidelines [SWDA § 1008]

(a) Guidelines

Within one year of October 21, 1976, and from time to time thereafter, the Administrator shall, in cooperation with appropriate Federal, State, municipal, and intermunicipal agencies, and in consultation with other interested persons, and after public hearings, develop and publish suggested guidelines for solid waste management. Such suggested guidelines shall—

(1) provide a technical and economic description of the level of performance that can be attained by various available solid waste management practices (including operating practices) which provide for the protection of public health and the environment;

(2) not later than two years after October 21, 1976, describe levels of performance, including appropriate methods and degrees of control, that provide at a minimum for (A) protection of public health and welfare; (B) protection of the quality of ground waters and surface waters from leachates; (C) protection of the quality of surface waters from runoff through compliance with effluent limitations under the Federal Water Pollution Control Act, as amended [33 U.S.C.A. § 1251 et seq.]; (D) protection of ambient air quality through compliance with new source performance standards or requirements of air quality implementation plans under the Clean Air Act, as amended [42 U.S.C.A. § 7401 et seq.]; (E) disease and vector control; (F) safety; and (G) esthetics; and

(3) provide minimum criteria to be used by the States to define those solid waste management practices which constitute the open dumping of solid waste or hazardous waste and are to be prohibited under subchapter IV of this chapter.

Where appropriate, such suggested guidelines also shall include minimum information for use in deciding the adequate location, design, and construction of facilities associated with solid waste management practices, including the consideration of regional, geographic, demographic, and climatic factors.

(b) Notice

The Administrator shall notify the Committee on Environment and Public Works of the Senate and the Committee on Energy and Commerce of the House of Representatives a reasonable time before publishing any suggested guidelines or proposed regulations under this chapter of the content of such proposed suggested guidelines or proposed regulations under this chapter.

(Pub.L. 89–272, Title II, § 1008, as added Oct. 21, 1976, Pub.L. 94–580, § 2, 90 Stat. 2803, and amended S.Res. 4, Feb. 4, 1977; Nov. 8, 1978, Pub.L. 95–609, § 7(c), (d), 92 Stat. 3081; H.Res. 549, Mar. 25, 1980; Pub.L. 103–437, § 15(r), Nov. 2, 1994, 108 Stat. 4594.)

Change of Name

Any reference in any provision of law enacted before Jan. 4, 1995, to the Committee on Energy and Commerce of the House of Representatives treated as referring to the Committee on Commerce of the House of Representatives, except that any reference in any provision of law enacted before Jan. 4, 1995, to the Committee on Energy and Commerce of the House of Representatives treated as referring to the Committee on Agriculture of the House of Representatives, in the case of a provision of law relating to inspection of seafood or seafood products, the Committee on Banking and Financial Services of the House of Representatives, in the case of a provision of law relating to bank capital markets activities generally or to depository institution securities activities generally, and the Committee on Transportation and Infrastructure of the House of Representatives, in the case of a provision of law relating to railroads, railway labor, or railroad retirement and unemployment (except revenue measures related thereto), see section 1(a)(4) and (c)(1) of Pub.L. 104–14, set out as a note preceding section 21 of Title 2, The Congress.

CROSS REFERENCES

Responsibility of Environmental Protection Agency for environmental, economic, and institutional aspects of municipal waste reprocessing projects and that such projects are consistent with guidelines provided in this section, see section 5920 of this title.

Responsibility of Environmental Protection Agency for environmental, economic, and institutional aspects of solid waste projects and that such projects are consistent with guidelines provided in this section, see section 5919 of this title.

CODE OF FEDERAL REGULATIONS

Classification of solid waste disposal facilities and practices, criteria, see 40 CFR 257.1 et seq.

Solid waste management guidelines and procedures, see 40 CFR 244.100 et seq., 245.100 et seq., 246.100 et seq.

Solid wastes generally, see 40 CFR Chap. 1, Subchap. I.

LAW REVIEW COMMENTARIES

Property owner liability for environmental contamination in California. Michael B. Hingerty, 22 U.S.F.L.Rev. 31 (1987).

§ 6908. Small town environmental planning [FFCA § 109]

(a) Establishment

The Administrator of the Environmental Protection Agency (hereafter referred to as the "Administrator") shall establish a program to assist small communities in planning and financing environmental facilities. The program shall be known as the "Small Town Environmental Planning Program".

(b) Small Town Environmental Planning Task Force

(1) The Administrator shall establish a Small Town Environmental Planning Task Force which shall be composed of representatives of small towns from different areas of the United States, Federal and State governmental agencies, and public interest groups. The Administrator shall terminate the Task Force not later than 2 years after the establishment of the Task Force.

(2) The Task Force shall—

(A) identify regulations developed pursuant to Federal environmental laws which pose significant compliance problems for small towns;

(B) identify means to improve the working relationship between the Environmental Protection Agency (hereafter referred to as the Agency[1]) and small towns;

(C) review proposed regulations for the protection of the environmental and public health and suggest revisions that could improve the ability of small towns to comply with such regulations;

(D) identify means to promote regionalization of environmental treatment systems and infrastructure serving small towns to improve the economic condition of such systems and infrastructure; and

(E) provide such other assistance to the Administrator as the Administrator deems appropriate.

(c) Identification of environmental requirements

(1) Not later than 6 months after October 6, 1992, the Administrator shall publish a list of requirements under Federal environmental and public health statutes (and the regulations developed pursuant to such statutes) applicable to small towns. Not less than annually, the Administrator shall make such additions and deletions to and from the list as the Administrator deems appropriate.

(2) The Administrator shall, as part of the Small Town Environmental Planning Program under this section, implement a program to notify small communities of the regulations identified under paragraph (1) and of future regulations and requirements through methods that the Administrator determines to be effective to provide information to the greatest number of small communities, including any of the following:

(A) Newspapers and other periodicals.

(B) Other news media.

(C) Trade, municipal, and other associations that the Administrator determines to be appropriate.

(D) Direct mail.

(d) Small Town Ombudsman

The Administrator shall establish and staff an Office of the Small Town Ombudsman. The Office shall provide assistance to small towns in connection with the Small Town Environmental Planning Program and other business with the Agency. Each regional office shall identify a small town contact. The Small Town Ombudsman and the regional contacts also may assist larger communities, but only if first priority is given to providing assistance to small towns.

(e) Multi–media permits

(1) The Administrator shall conduct a study of establishing a multi-media permitting program for small towns. Such evaluation shall include an analysis of—

(A) environmental benefits and liabilities of a multi-media permitting program;

(B) the potential of using such a program to coordinate a small town's environmental and public health activities; and

(C) the legal barriers, if any, to the establishment of such a program.

(2) Within 3 years after October 6, 1992, the Administrator shall report to Congress on the results of

the evaluation performed in accordance with paragraph (1). Included in this report shall be a description of the activities conducted pursuant to subsections (a) through (d) of this section.

(f) Definition

For purposes of this section, the term "small town" means an incorporated or unincorporated community (as defined by the Administrator) with a population of less than 2,500 individuals.

(g) Authorization

There is authorized to be appropriated the sum of $500,000 to implement this section.

(Pub.L. 102–386, Title I, § 109, Oct. 6, 1992, 106 Stat. 1515.)

1 So in original. Probably should be " 'Agency" '.

Codification

Section was enacted as part of the Federal Facility Compliance Act of 1992 and not as part of the Solid Waste Disposal Act, which comprises this chapter.

SUBCHAPTER II—OFFICE OF SOLID WASTE; AUTHORITIES OF THE ADMINISTRATOR

§ 6911. Office of Solid Waste and Interagency Coordinating Committee [SWDA § 2001]

(a) Office of Solid Waste

The Administrator shall establish within the Environmental Protection Agency an Office of Solid Waste (hereinafter referred to as the "Office") to be headed by an Assistant Administrator of the Environmental Protection Agency. The duties and responsibilities (other than duties and responsibilities relating to research and development) of the Administrator under this chapter (as modified by applicable reorganization plans) shall be carried out through the Office.

(b) Interagency Coordinating Committee

(1) There is hereby established an Interagency Coordinating Committee on Federal Resource Conservation and Recovery Activities which shall have the responsibility for coordinating all activities dealing with resource conservation and recovery from solid waste carried out by the Environmental Protection Agency, the Department of Energy, the Department of Commerce, and all other Federal agencies which conduct such activities pursuant to this chapter or any other Act. For purposes of this subsection, the term "resource conservation and recovery activities" shall include, but not be limited to, all research, development and demonstration projects on resource conservation or energy, or material, recovery from solid waste, and all technical or financial assistance for State or local planning for, or implementation of, projects related to resource conservation or energy or material, recovery from solid waste. The Committee shall be chaired by the Administrator of the Environmental Protection Agency or such person as the Administrator may designate. Members of the Committee shall include representatives of the Department of Energy, the Department of Commerce, the Department of the Treasury, and each other Federal agency which the Administrator determines to have programs or responsibilities affecting resource conservation or recovery.

(2) The Interagency Coordinating Committee shall include oversight of the implementation of

(A) the May 1979 Memorandum of Understanding on Energy Recovery from Municipal Solid Waste between the Environmental Protection Agency and the Department of Energy;

(B) the May 30, 1978, Interagency Agreement between the Department of Commerce and the Environmental Protection Agency on the Implementation of the Resource Conservation and Recovery Act; and

(C) any subsequent agreements between these agencies or other Federal agencies which address Federal resource recovery or conservation activities.

(3) The Interagency Coordinating Committee shall submit to the Congress by March 1, 1981, and on March 1 each year thereafter, a five-year action plan for Federal resource conservation or recovery activities which shall identify means and propose programs to encourage resource conservation or material and energy recovery and increase private and municipal investment in resource conservation or recovery systems, especially those which provide for material conservation or recovery as well as energy conservation or recovery. Such plan shall describe, at a minimum, a coordinated and nonduplicatory plan for resource recovery and conservation activities for the Environmental Protection Agency, the Department of Energy, the Department of Commerce, and all other Federal agencies which conduct such activities.

(Pub.L. 89–272, Title II, § 2001, as added Oct. 21, 1976, Pub.L. 94–580, § 2, 90 Stat. 2804, and amended Oct. 21, 1980, Pub.L. 96–482, § 4(c), 94 Stat. 2335; Dec. 11, 1980, Pub.L. 96–510, Title III, § 307(a), 94 Stat. 2810.)

West's Federal Practice Manual

Solid waste disposal, see § 4385.5.

LIBRARY REFERENCES

Health and Environment ⚷1.
C.J.S. Health and Environment § 4 et seq.

§ 6911a. Assistant Administrator of Environmental Protection Agency; appointment, etc.

The Assistant Administrator of the Environmental Protection Agency appointed to head the Office of Solid Waste shall be in addition to the five Assistant Administrators of the Environmental Protection Agency provided for in section 1(d) of Reorganization Plan Numbered 3 of 1970 and the additional Assistant Administrator provided by the Toxic Substances Control Act [15 U.S.C.A. § 2601 et seq.], shall be appointed by the President by and with the advice and consent of the Senate.

(Dec. 11, 1980, Pub.L. 96–510, Title III, § 307(b), 94 Stat. 2810; Aug. 23, 1983, Pub.L. 98–80, § 2(c)(2)(B), 97 Stat. 485.)

Codification

Section was enacted as part of the Comprehensive Environmental Response, Compensation, and Liability Act of 1980, and not as part of the Solid Waste Disposal Act which comprises this chapter.

§ 6912. Authorities of Administrator [SWDA § 2002]

(a) Authorities

In carrying out this chapter, the Administrator is authorized to—

(1) prescribe, in consultation with Federal, State, and regional authorities, such regulations as are necessary to carry out his functions under this chapter;

(2) consult with or exchange information with other Federal agencies undertaking research, development, demonstration projects, studies, or investigations relating to solid waste;

(3) provide technical and financial assistance to States or regional agencies in the development and implementation of solid waste plans and hazardous waste management programs;

(4) consult with representatives of science, industry, agriculture, labor, environmental protection and consumer organizations, and other groups, as he deems advisable;

(5) utilize the information, facilities, personnel and other resources of Federal agencies, including the National Institute of Standards and Technology and the National Bureau of the Census, on a reimbursable basis, to perform research and analyses and conduct studies and investigations related to resource recovery and conservation and to otherwise carry out the Administrator's functions under this chapter; and

(6) to delegate to the Secretary of Transportation the performance of any inspection or enforcement function under this chapter relating to the transportation of hazardous waste where such delegation would avoid unnecessary duplication of activity and would carry out the objectives of this chapter and of the Hazardous Materials Transportation Act [49 U.S.C.A. § 1801 et seq.].

(b) Revision of regulations

Each regulation promulgated under this chapter shall be reviewed and, where necessary, revised not less frequently than every three years.

(c) Criminal investigations

In carrying out the provisions of this chapter, the Administrator, and duly-designated agents and employees of the Environmental Protection Agency, are authorized to initiate and conduct investigations under the criminal provisions of this chapter, and to refer the results of these investigations to the Attorney General for prosecution in appropriate cases.

(Pub.L. 89–272, Title II, § 2002, as added Oct. 21, 1976, Pub.L. 94–580, § 2, 90 Stat. 2804, and amended Oct. 21, 1980, Pub.L. 96–482, § 5, 94 Stat. 2335; Nov. 8, 1984, Pub.L. 98–616, Title IV, § 403(d)(4), 98 Stat. 3272; Pub.L. 100–418, Title V, § 5115(c), Aug. 23, 1988, 102 Stat. 1433.)

CODE OF FEDERAL REGULATIONS

Hazardous waste generally, see 40 CFR 260.1 et seq. to 271.1 et seq.
Identification of regions and agencies for solid waste management, see 40 CFR 255.1 et seq.

§ 6913. Resource Recovery and Conservation Panels [SWDA § 2003]

The Administrator shall provide teams of personnel, including Federal, State, and local employees or contractors (hereinafter referred to as "Resource Conservation and Recovery Panels") to provide Federal agencies, States and local governments upon request with technical assistance on solid waste management, resource recovery, and resource conservation. Such teams shall include technical, marketing, financial, and institutional specialists, and the services of such teams shall be provided without charge to States or local governments.

(Pub.L. 89–272, Title II, § 2003, as added Oct. 21, 1976, Pub.L. 94–580, § 2, 90 Stat. 2804, and amended Nov. 8, 1978, Pub.L. 95–609, § 7(e), 92 Stat. 3081; Oct. 21, 1980, Pub.L. 96–482, § 5, 94 Stat. 2355.)

§ 6914. Grants for discarded tire disposal [SWDA § 2004]

(a) Grants

The Administrator shall make available grants equal to 5 percent of the purchase price of tire shredders (including portable shredders attached to tire collection trucks) to those eligible applicants best meeting criteria promulgated under this section. An eligible applicant may be any private purchaser, public body, or public-private joint venture. Criteria for receiving grants shall be promulgated under this section and shall include the policy to offer any private purchaser the first option to receive a grant, the policy to develop widespread geographic distribution of tire shredding facilities, the need for such facilities within a geographic area, and the projected risk and viability of any such venture. In the case of an application under this section from a public body, the Administrator shall first make a determination that there are no private purchasers interested in making an application before approving a grant to a public body.

(b) Authorization of appropriations

There is authorized to be appropriated $750,000 for each of the fiscal years 1978 and 1979 to carry out this section.

(Pub.L. 89–272, Title II, § 2004, as added Oct. 21, 1976, Pub.L. 94–580, § 2, 90 Stat. 2805.)

LAW REVIEW COMMENTARIES

Oil Pollution Act of 1990: Opening a new era in federal and Texas regulation of oil spill prevention, containment and cleanup, and liability. J.B. Ruhl and Michael J. Jewell, 32 S.Tex.L.Rev. 475 (1991).

§ 6914a. Labeling of lubricating oil [SWDA § 2005]

For purposes of any provision of law which requires the labeling of commodities, lubricating oil shall be treated as lawfully labeled only if it bears the following statement, prominently displayed:

"DON'T POLLUTE—CONSERVE RESOURCES; RETURN USED OIL TO COLLECTION CENTERS".

(Pub.L. 89–272, Title II, § 2005, as added Oct. 15, 1980, Pub.L. 96–463, § 4(a), 94 Stat. 2056.)

§ 6914b. Degradable plastic ring carriers

As used in this section and section 6914b–1 of this title—

(1) the term "regulated item" means any plastic ring carrier device that contains at least one hole greater than 1¾ inches in diameter which is made, used, or designed for the purpose of packaging, transporting, or carrying multipackaged cans or bottles, and which is of a size, shape, design, or type capable, when discarded, of becoming entangled with fish or wildlife; and

(2) the term "naturally degradable material" means a material which, when discarded, will be reduced to environmentally benign subunits under the action of normal environmental forces, such as, among others, biological decomposition, photodegradation, or hydrolysis.

(Pub.L. 100–556, Title I, § 102, Oct. 28, 1988, 102 Stat. 2779.)

Codification

Section was not enacted as part of the Solid Waste Disposal Act which comprises this chapter.

Congressional Findings

Section 101 of Pub.L. 100–556 provided that: "The Congress finds that—

"(1) plastic ring carrier devices have been found in large quantities in the marine environment;

"(2) fish and wildlife have been known to have become entangled in plastic ring carriers;

"(3) nondegradable plastic ring carrier devices can remain intact in the marine environment for decades, posing a threat to fish and wildlife; and

"(4) 16 States have enacted laws requiring that plastic ring carrier devices be made from degradable material in order to reduce litter and to protect fish and wildlife."

§ 6914b–1. Regulations covering degradable plastic ring carriers

Not later than 24 months after October 28, 1988 (unless the Administrator of the Environmental Protection Agency determines that it is not feasible or that the byproducts of degradable regulated items present a greater threat to the environment than nondegradable regulated items), the Administrator of the Environmental Protection Agency shall require, by regulation, that any regulated item intended for use in the United States shall be made of naturally degradable material which, when discarded, decomposes within a period established by such regulation. The period within which decomposition must occur after being discarded shall be the shortest period of time consistent with the intended use of the item and the physical integrity required for such use. Such regulation shall allow a reasonable time for affected parties to come into compliance, including the use of existing inventories.

(Pub.L. 100–556, Title I, § 103, Oct. 28, 1988, 102 Stat. 2779.)

Codification

Section was not enacted as part of the Solid Waste Disposal Act which comprises this chapter.

§ 6915. Annual report [SWDA § 2006]

The Administrator shall transmit to the Congress and the President, not later than ninety days after the end of each fiscal year, a comprehensive and detailed report on all activities of the Office during the preceding fiscal year. Each such report shall include—

(1) a statement of specific and detailed objectives for the activities and programs conducted and assisted under this chapter;

(2) statements of the Administrator's conclusions as to the effectiveness of such activities and pro-

grams in meeting the stated objectives and the purposes of this chapter, measured through the end of such fiscal year;

(3) a summary of outstanding solid waste problems confronting the Administrator, in order of priority;

(4) recommendations with respect to such legislation which the Administrator deems necessary or desirable to assist in solving problems respecting solid waste;

(5) all other information required to be submitted to the Congress pursuant to any other provision of this chapter; and

(6) the Administrator's plans for activities and programs respecting solid waste during the next fiscal year.

(Pub.L. 89–272, Title II, § 2006, formerly § 2005, as added Oct. 21, 1976, Pub.L. 94–580, § 2, 90 Stat. 2805, renumbered Oct. 15, 1980, Pub.L. 96–463, § 4(a), 94 Stat. 2056, and amended Nov. 8, 1984, Pub.L. 98–616, Title V, § 502(b), 98 Stat. 3276.)

§ 6916. General authorization [SWDA § 2007]

(a) General administration

There are authorized to be appropriated to the Administrator for the purpose of carrying out the provisions of this chapter, $35,000,000 for the fiscal year ending September 30, 1977, $38,000,000 for the fiscal year ending September 30, 1978, $42,000,000 for the fiscal year ending September 30, 1979, $70,000,000 for the fiscal year ending September 30, 1980, $80,000,000 for the fiscal year ending September 30, 1981, $80,000,000 for the fiscal year ending September 30, 1982, $70,000,000 for the fiscal year ending September 30, 1985, $80,000,000 for the fiscal year ending September 30, 1986, $80,000,000 for the fiscal year ending September 30, 1987, and $80,000,000 for the fiscal year 1988.

(b) Resource Recovery and Conservation Panels

Not less than 20 percent of the amount appropriated under subsection (a) of this section, or $5,000,000 per fiscal year, whichever is less, shall be used only for purposes of Resource Recovery and Conservation Panels established under section 6913 of this title (including travel expenses incurred by such panels in carrying out their functions under this chapter).

(c) Hazardous waste

Not less than 30 percent of the amount appropriated under subsection (a) of this section shall be used only for purposes of carrying out subchapter III of this chapter (relating to hazardous waste) other than section 6931 of this title.

(d) State and local support

Not less than 25 per centum of the total amount appropriated under this chapter, up to the amount authorized in section 6948(a)(1) of this title, shall be used only for purposes of support to State, regional, local, and interstate agencies in accordance with subchapter IV of this chapter other than section 6948(a)(2) or 6949 of this title.

(e) Criminal investigations

There is authorized to be appropriated to the Administrator $3,246,000 for the fiscal year 1985, $2,408,300 for the fiscal year 1986, $2,529,000 for the fiscal year 1987, and $2,529,000 for the fiscal year 1988 to be used—

(1) for additional officers or employees of the Environmental Protection Agency authorized by the Administrator to conduct criminal investigations (to investigate, or supervise the investigation of, any activity for which a criminal penalty is provided) under this chapter; and

(2) for support costs for such additional officers or employees.

(f) Underground storage tanks

(1) There are authorized to be appropriated to the Administrator for the purpose of carrying out the provisions of subchapter IX of this chapter (relating to regulation of underground storage tanks), $10,000,000 for each of the fiscal years 1985 through 1988.

(2) There is authorized to be appropriated $25,000,000 for each of the fiscal years 1985 through 1988 to be used to make grants to the States for purposes of assisting the States in the development and implementation of approved State underground storage tank release detection, prevention, and correction programs under subchapter IX of this chapter.

(Pub.L. 89–272, Title II, § 2007, formerly § 2006, as added Oct. 21, 1976, Pub.L. 94–580, § 2, 90 Stat. 2805, renumbered Oct. 15, 1980, Pub.L. 96–463, § 4(a), 94 Stat. 2055, and amended Oct. 21, 1980, Pub.L. 96–482, §§ 6, 31(a), 94 Stat. 2336, 2352; Nov. 8, 1984, Pub.L. 98–616, § 2(a), (i), 98 Stat. 3222, 3223.)

§ 6917. Office of ombudsman [SWDA § 2008]

(a) Establishment; functions

The Administrator shall establish an Office of Ombudsman, to be directed by an Ombudsman. It shall be the function of the Office of Ombudsman to receive individual complaints, grievances, requests for information submitted by any person with respect to any program or requirement under this chapter.

(b) Authority to render assistance

The Ombudsman shall render assistance with respect to the complaints, grievances, and requests submitted to the Office of Ombudsman, and shall make appropriate recommendations to the Administrator.

(c) Effect on procedures for grievance, appeals, or administrative matters

The establishment of the Office of Ombudsman shall not affect any procedures for grievances, appeals, or administrative matters in any other provision of this chapter, any other provision of law, or any Federal regulation.

(d) Termination

The Office of the Ombudsman shall cease to exist 4 years after November 8, 1984.

(Pub.L. 89–272, Title II, § 2008, as added Nov. 8, 1984, Pub.L. 98–616, Title I, § 103(a), 98 Stat. 3225.)

SUBCHAPTER III—HAZARDOUS WASTE MANAGEMENT

CROSS REFERENCES

Liability of owners or operators of hazardous waste disposal facilities receiving permit under this subchapter or after the period of monitoring required by this subchapter, see section 9607 of this title.

Notification requirements respecting released substances, see section 9603 of this title.

Remedial actions provided by the President upon condition that State assure availability of hazardous waste disposal facility in compliance with requirements of this subchapter, see section 9604 of this title.

Remedy or remedial action not including offsite transport of hazardous substances, or the storage, treatment, destruction, or secure disposition offsite of such substances unless such action will create new capacity to manage in compliance with this subchapter, see section 9604 of this title.

Reports and studies concerning additional hazardous wastes and construction and operation of hazardous waste facilities, see section 9651 of this title.

Requirements for facilities, including those under this subchapter, to establish and maintain evidence of financial responsibility, promulgated no earlier than five years after December 11, 1980, see section 9608 of this title.

Rules for protection from hazards at inactive or depository uranium mill tailings sites consistent with standards required by this subchapter, see section 2022 of this title.

§ 6921. Identification and listing of hazardous waste [SWDA § 3001]

(a) Criteria for identification or listing

Not later than eighteen months after October 21, 1976, the Administrator shall, after notice and opportunity for public hearing, and after consultation with appropriate Federal and State agencies, develop and promulgate criteria for identifying the characteristics of hazardous waste, and for listing hazardous waste, which should be subject to the provisions of this subchapter, taking into account toxicity, persistence, and degradability in nature, potential for accumulation in tissue, and other related factors such as flammability, corrosiveness, and other hazardous characteristics. Such criteria shall be revised from time to time as may be appropriate.

(b) Identification and listing

(1) Not later than eighteen months after October 21, 1976, and after notice and opportunity for public hearing, the Administrator shall promulgate regulations identifying the characteristics of hazardous waste, and listing particular hazardous wastes (within the meaning of section 6903(5) of this title), which shall be subject to the provisions of this subchapter. Such regulations shall be based on the criteria promulgated under subsection (a) of this section and shall be revised from time to time thereafter as may be appropriate. The Administrator, in cooperation with the Agency for Toxic Substances and Disease Registry and the National Toxicology Program, shall also identify or list those hazardous wastes which shall be subject to the provisions of this subchapter solely because of the presence in such wastes of certain constituents (such as identified carcinogens, mutagens, or teratagens) at levels in excess of levels which endanger human health.

(2)(A) Notwithstanding the provisions of paragraph (1) of this subsection, drilling fluids, produced waters, and other wastes associated with the exploration, development, or production of crude oil or natural gas or geothermal energy shall be subject only to existing State or Federal regulatory programs in lieu of this subchapter until at least 24 months after October 21, 1980, and after promulgation of the regulations in accordance with subparagraphs (B) and (C) of this paragraph. It is the sense of the Congress that such State or Federal programs should include, for waste disposal sites which are to be closed, provisions requiring at least the following:

(i) The identification through surveying, platting, or other measures, together with recordation of such information on the public record, so as to assure that the location where such wastes are disposed of can be located in the future; except however, that no such surveying, platting, or other measure identifying the location of a disposal site for drilling fluids and associated wastes shall be required if the distance from the disposal site to the surveyed or platted location to the associated well is less than two hundred lineal feet; and

(ii) A chemical and physical analysis of a produced water and a composition of a drilling fluid suspected to contain a hazardous material, with such information to be acquired prior to closure and to be placed on the public record.

(B) Not later than six months after completion and submission of the study required by section 6982(m) of this title, the Administrator shall, after public hearings and opportunity for comment, determine either to promulgate regulations under this subchapter for drilling fluids, produced waters, and other wastes associated with the exploration, development, or production of crude oil or natural gas or geothermal energy or that such regulations are unwarranted. The Administrator shall publish his decision in the Federal Register accompanied by an explanation and justification of the reasons for it. In making the decision under this paragraph, the Administrator shall utilize the information developed or accumulated pursuant to the study required under section 6982(m) of this title.

(C) The Administrator shall transmit his decision, along with any regulations, if necessary, to both Houses of Congress. Such regulations shall take effect only when authorized by Act of Congress.

(3)(A) Notwithstanding the provisions of paragraph (1) of this subsection, each waste listed below shall, except as provided in subparagraph (B) of this paragraph, be subject only to regulation under other applicable provisions of Federal or State law in lieu of this subchapter until at least six months after the date of submission of the applicable study required to be conducted under subsection (f), (n), *(o)*, or (p) of section 6982 of this title and after promulgation of regulations in accordance with subparagraph (C) of this paragraph:

(i) Fly ash waste, bottom ash waste, slag waste, and flue gas emission control waste generated primarily from the combustion of coal or other fossil fuels.

(ii) Solid waste from the extraction, beneficiation, and processing of ores and minerals, including phosphate rock and overburden from the mining of uranium ore.

(iii) Cement kiln dust waste.

(B)(i) Owners and operators of disposal sites for wastes listed in subparagraph (A) may be required by the Administrator, through regulations prescribed under authority of section 6912 of this title—

(I) as to disposal sites for such wastes which are to be closed, to identify the locations of such sites through surveying, platting, or other measures, together with recordation of such information on the public record, to assure that the locations where such wastes are disposed of are known and can be located in the future, and

(II) to provide chemical and physical analysis and composition of such wastes, based on available information, to be placed on the public record.

(ii)(I) In conducting any study under subsection (f), (n), *(o)*, or (p), of section 6982 of this title, any officer, employee, or authorized representative of the Environmental Protection Agency, duly designated by the Administrator, is authorized, at reasonable times and as reasonably necessary for the purposes of such study, to enter any establishment where any waste subject to such study is generated, stored, treated, disposed of, or transported from; to inspect, take samples, and conduct monitoring and testing; and to have access to and copy records relating to such waste. Each such inspection shall be commenced and completed with reasonable promptness. If the officer, employee, or authorized representative obtains any samples prior to leaving the premises, he shall give to the owner, operator, or agent in charge a receipt describing the sample obtained and if requested a portion of each such sample equal in volume or weight to the portion retained. If any analysis is made of such samples, or monitoring and testing performed, a copy of the results shall be furnished promptly to the owner, operator, or agent in charge.

(II) Any records, reports, or information obtained from any person under subclause (I) shall be available to the public, except that upon a showing satisfactory to the Administrator by any person that records, reports, or information, or particular part thereof, to which the Administrator has access under this subparagraph if made public, would divulge information entitled to protection under section 1905 of Title 18, the Administrator shall consider such information or particular portion thereof confidential in accordance with the purposes of that section, except that such record, report, document, or information may be disclosed to other officers, employees, or authorized representatives of the United States concerned with carrying out this chapter. Any person not subject to the provisions of section 1905 of Title 18 who knowingly and willfully divulges or discloses any information entitled to protection under this subparagraph shall, upon conviction, be subject to a fine of not more than $5,000 or to imprisonment not to exceed one year, or both.

(iii) The Administrator may prescribe regulations, under the authority of this chapter, to prevent radiation exposure which presents an unreasonable risk to human health from the use in construction or land reclamation (with or without revegetation) of (I) solid waste from the extraction, beneficiation, and processing of phosphate rock or (II) overburden from the mining of uranium ore.

(iv) Whenever on the basis of any information the Administrator determines that any person is in violation of any requirement of this subparagraph, the Administrator shall give notice to the violator of his failure to comply with such requirement. If such violation extends beyond the thirtieth day after the Administrator's notification, the Administrator may issue an order requiring compliance within a specified time period or the Administrator may commence a civil action in the United States district court in the district in which the violation occurred for appropriate relief, including a temporary or permanent injunction.

(C) Not later than six months after the date of submission of the applicable study required to be conducted under subsection (f), (n), *(o)*, or (p), of section 6982 of this title, the Administrator shall, after public hearings and opportunity for comment, either determine to promulgate regulations under this subchapter for each waste listed in subparagraph (A) of this paragraph or determine that such regulations are unwarranted. The Administrator shall publish his determination, which shall be based on information developed or accumulated pursuant to such study, public hearings, and comment, in the Federal Register accompanied by an explanation and justification of the reasons for it.

(c) Petition by State Governor

At any time after the date eighteen months after October 21, 1976, the Governor of any State may petition the Administrator to identify or list a material as a hazardous waste. The Administrator shall act upon such petition within ninety days following his receipt thereof and shall notify the Governor of such action. If the Administrator denies such petition because of financial considerations, in providing such notice to the Governor he shall include a statement concerning such considerations.

(d) Small quantity generator waste

(1) By March 31, 1986, the Administrator shall promulgate standards under sections 6922, 6923, and 6924 of this title for hazardous waste generated by a generator in a total quantity of hazardous waste greater than one hundred kilograms but less than one thousand kilograms during a calendar month.

(2) The standards referred to in paragraph (1), including standards applicable to the legitimate use, reuse, recycling, and reclamation of such wastes, may vary from the standards applicable to hazardous waste generated by larger quantity generators, but such standards shall be sufficient to protect human health and the environment.

(3) Not later than two hundred and seventy days after November 8, 1984, any hazardous waste which is part of a total quantity generated by a generator generating greater than one hundred kilograms but less than one thousand kilograms during one calendar month and which is shipped off the premises on which such waste is generated shall be accompanied by a copy of the Environmental Protection Agency Uniform Hazardous Waste Manifest form signed by the generator. This form shall contain the following information:

(A) the name and address of the generator of the waste;

(B) the United States Department of Transportation description of the waste, including the proper shipping name, hazard class, and identification number (UN/NA), if applicable;

(C) the number and type of containers;

(D) the quantity of waste being transported; and

(E) the name and address of the facility designated to receive the waste.

If subparagraph (B) is not applicable, in lieu of the description referred to in such subparagraph (B), the form shall contain the Environmental Protection Agency identification number, or a generic description of the waste, or a description of the waste by hazardous waste characteristic. Additional requirements related to the manifest form shall apply only if determined necessary by the Administrator to protect human health and the environment.

(4) The Administrator's responsibility under this subchapter to protect human health and the environment may require the promulgation of standards under this subchapter for hazardous wastes which are generated by any generator who does not generate more than one hundred kilograms of hazardous waste in a calendar month.

(5) Until the effective date of standards required to be promulgated under paragraph (1), any hazardous waste identified or listed under section 6921 of this title generated by any generator during any calendar month in a total quantity greater than one hundred kilograms but less than one thousand kilograms, which is not treated, stored, or disposed of at a hazardous waste treatment, storage or disposal facility with a permit under section 6925 of this title, shall be disposed of only in a facility which is permitted, licensed, or registered by a State to manage municipal or industrial solid waste.

(6) Standards promulgated as provided in paragraph (1) shall, at a minimum require that all treatment, storage, or disposal of hazardous wastes generated by generators referred to in paragraph (1) shall

occur at a facility with interim status or a permit under this subchapter, except that onsite storage of hazardous waste generated by a generator generating a total quantity of hazardous waste greater than one hundred kilograms, but less than one thousand kilograms during a calendar month, may occur without the requirement of a permit for up to one hundred and eighty days. Such onsite storage may occur without the requirement of a permit for not more than six thousand kilograms for up to two hundred and seventy days if such generator must ship or haul such waste over two hundred miles.

(7)(A) Nothing in this subsection shall be construed to affect or impair the validity of regulations promulgated by the Secretary of Transportation pursuant to the Hazardous Materials Transportation Act [49 U.S.C.A. App. § 1801 et seq.].

(B) Nothing in this subsection shall be construed to affect, modify, or render invalid any requirements in regulations promulgated prior to January 1, 1983 applicable to any acutely hazardous waste identified or listed under section 6921 of this title which is generated by any generator during any calendar month in a total quantity less than one thousand kilograms.

(8) Effective March 31, 1986, unless the Administrator promulgates standards as provided in paragraph (1) of this subsection prior to such date, hazardous waste generated by any generator in a total quantity greater than one hundred kilograms but less than one thousand kilograms during a calendar month shall be subject to the following requirements until the standards referred to in paragraph (1) of this subsection have become effective:

(A) the notice requirements of paragraph (3) of this subsection shall apply and in addition, the information provided in the form shall include the name of the waste transporters and the name and address of the facility designated to receive the waste;

(B) except in the case of the onsite storage referred to in paragraph (6) of this subsection, the treatment, storage, or disposal of such waste shall occur at a facility with interim status or a permit under this subchapter;

(C) generators of such waste shall file manifest exception reports as required of generators producing greater amounts of hazardous waste per month except that such reports shall be filed by January 31, for any waste shipment occurring in the last half of the preceding calendar year, and by July 31, for any waste shipment occurring in the first half of the calendar year; and

(D) generators of such waste shall retain for three years a copy of the manifest signed by the designated facility that has received the waste.

Nothing in this paragraph shall be construed as a determination of the standards appropriate under paragraph (1).

(9) The last sentence of section 6930(b) of this title shall not apply to regulations promulgated under this subsection.

(e) Specified wastes

(1) Not later than 6 months after November 8, 1984, the Administrator shall, where appropriate, list under subsection (b)(1) of this section, additional wastes containing chlorinated dioxins or chlorinated-dibenzofurans. Not later than one year after November 8, 1984, the Administrator shall, where appropriate, list under subsection (b)(1) of this section wastes containing remaining halogenated dioxins and halogenated-dibenzofurans.

(2) Not later than fifteen months after November 8, 1984, the Administrator shall make a determination of whether or not to list under subsection (b)(1) of this section the following wastes: Chlorinated Aliphatics, Dioxin, Dimethyl Hydrazine, TDI (toluene diisocyanate), Carbamates, Bromacil, Linuron, Organo-bromines, solvents, refining wastes, chlorinated aromatics, dyes and pigments, inorganic chemical industry wastes, lithium batteries, coke byproducts, paint production wastes, and coal slurry pipeline effluent.

(f) Delisting procedures

(1) When evaluating a petition to exclude a waste generated at a particular facility from listing under this section, the Administrator shall consider factors (including additional constituents) other than those for which the waste was listed if the Administrator has a reasonable basis to believe that such additional factors could cause the waste to be a hazardous waste. The Administrator shall provide notice and opportunity for comment on these additional factors before granting or denying such petition.

(2)(A) To the maximum extent practicable the Administrator shall publish in the Federal Register a proposal to grant or deny a petition referred to in paragraph (1) within twelve months after receiving a complete application to exclude a waste generated at a particular facility from being regulated as a hazardous waste and shall grant or deny such a petition within twenty-four months after receiving a complete application.

(B) The temporary granting of such a petition prior to November 8, 1984, without the opportunity for public comment and the full consideration of such comments shall not continue for more than twenty-four months after November 8, 1984. If a final decision to grant or deny such a petition has not been promulgated after notice and opportunity for public comment within the time limit prescribed by the preceding sentence, any such temporary granting of such petition shall cease to be in effect.

(g) EP toxicity

Not later than twenty-eight months after November 8, 1984, the Administrator shall examine the deficiencies of the extraction procedure toxicity characteristic as a predictor of the leaching potential of wastes and make changes in the extraction procedure toxicity characteristic, including changes in the leaching media, as are necessary to insure that it accurately predicts the leaching potential of wastes which pose a threat to human health and the environment when mismanaged.

(h) Additional characteristics

Not later than two years after November 8, 1984, the Administrator shall promulgate regulations under this section identifying additional characteristics of hazardous waste, including measures or indicators of toxicity.

(i) Clarification of household waste exclusion

A resource recovery facility recovering energy from the mass burning of municipal solid waste shall not be deemed to be treating, storing, disposing of, or otherwise managing hazardous wastes for the purposes of regulation under this subchapter, if—

(1) such facility—

(A) receives and burns only—

(i) household waste (from single and multiple dwellings, hotels, motels, and other residential sources), and

(ii) solid waste from commercial or industrial sources that does not contain hazardous waste identified or listed under this section, and

(B) does not accept hazardous wastes identified or listed under this section, and

(2) the owner or operator of such facility has established contractual requirements or other appropriate notification or inspection procedures to assure that hazardous wastes are not received at or burned in such facility.

(Pub.L. 89–272, Title II, § 3001, as added Oct. 21, 1976, Pub.L. 94–580, § 2, 90 Stat. 2806, and amended Oct. 21, 1980, Pub.L. 96–482, § 7, 94 Stat. 2336; Nov. 8, 1984, Pub.L. 98–616, Title II, §§ 221(a), 222, 223(a), 98 Stat. 3248, 3251, 3252.)

Ash Management and Disposal

Pub.L. 101–549, Title III, § 306, Nov. 15, 1990, 104 Stat. 2584, provided that: "For a period of 2 years after the date of enactment of the Clean Air Act Amendments of 1990 [Nov. 15, 1990], ash from solid waste incineration units burning municipal waste shall not be regulated by the Administrator of the Environmental Protection Agency pursuant to section 3001 of the Solid Waste Disposal Act [this section]. Such reference and limitation shall not be construed to prejudice, endorse or otherwise affect any activity by the Administrator following the 2–year period from the date of enactment of the Clean Air Act Amendments of 1990."

CODE OF FEDERAL REGULATIONS

Hazardous waste, identification and listing of, see 40 CFR 261.1 et seq.
Hazardous waste management, generally, see 40 CFR 260.1 et seq.
Standards, see 40 CFR 262.10 et seq.

West's Federal Practice Manual

Solid waste disposal, see § 4385.5.

LAW REVIEW COMMENTARIES

Emerging federal law of mine waste: Administrative, judicial and legislative developments. John R. Jacus and Thomas E. Root, 26 Land and Water L.Rev. 461 (1991).

High penalties and citizen suits await small businesses unaware of EPCRA reporting requirements. Jeffrey T. Pender, 10 Corp. Counsel Rev. (Tex.) 81 (May 1991).

Oil and gas exemptions under RCRA and CERCLA: Are they still "safe harbors" eleven years later? Michael M. Gibson and David P. Young, 32 S.Tex.L.Rev. 361 (1991).

The once and future EPA lender regulations: Limiting lender liability for the cleanup of hazardous wastes. Jeffrey M. Gaba, 47 Consumer Fin.L.Q.Rep. 355 (1993).

Toxic tort litigation and the causation element: Is there any hope of reconciliation? Fred Harris, Jr., 40 Southwestern (Tex.) L.J. 909 (1986).

United States Supreme Court

Ash generated by resource recovery facility's incineration of municipal solid waste was subject to regulatory scheme governing hazardous waste set forth in Resource Conservation and Recovery Act, see City of Chicago v. Environmental Defense Fund, 1994, 114 S.Ct. 1588, 128 L.Ed.2d 302.

Additional disposal fee imposed by Alabama on hazardous waste generated outside of Alabama and disposed of at commercial facility in Alabama discriminated against interstate commerce in violation of the commerce clause, see Chemical Waste Management, Inc. v. Hunt, 1992, 112 S.Ct. 2009, 119 L.Ed.2d 121.

§ 6922. Standards applicable to generators of hazardous waste [SWDA § 3002]

(a) In general

Not later than eighteen months after October 21, 1976, and after notice and opportunity for public hearings and after consultation with appropriate Federal and State agencies, the Administrator shall promulgate regulations establishing such standards, applicable to generators of hazardous waste identified or listed under this subchapter, as may be necessary to protect human health and the environment. Such standards shall establish requirements respecting—

(1) recordkeeping practices that accurately identify the quantities of such hazardous waste generated, the constituents thereof which are significant in quantity or in potential harm to human health or the environment, and the disposition of such wastes;

(2) labeling practices for any containers used for the storage, transport, or disposal of such hazardous waste such as will identify accurately such waste;

(3) use of appropriate containers for such hazardous waste;

(4) furnishing of information on the general chemical composition of such hazardous waste to persons transporting, treating, storing, or disposing of such wastes;

(5) use of a manifest system and any other reasonable means necessary to assure that all such hazardous waste generated is designated for treatment, storage, or disposal in, and arrives at, treatment, storage, or disposal facilities (other than facilities on the premises where the waste is generated) for which a permit has been issued as provided in this subchapter, or pursuant to title I of the Marine Protection, Research, and Sanctuaries Act (86 Stat. 1052) [33 U.S.C.A. § 1411 et seq.]; and

(6) submission of reports to the Administrator (or the State agency in any case in which such agency carries out a permit program pursuant to this subchapter) at least once every two years, setting out—

(A) the quantities and nature of hazardous waste identified or listed under this subchapter that he has generated during the year;

(B) the disposition of all hazardous waste reported under subparagraph (A);

(C) the efforts undertaken during the year to reduce the volume and toxicity of waste generated; and

(D) the changes in volume and toxicity of waste actually achieved during the year in question in comparison with previous years, to the extent such information is available for years prior to November 8, 1984.

(b) Waste minimization

Effective September 1, 1985, the manifest required by subsection (a)(5) of this section shall contain a certification by the generator that—

(1) the generator of the hazardous waste has a program in place to reduce the volume or quantity and toxicity of such waste to the degree determined by the generator to be economically practicable; and

(2) the proposed method of treatment, storage, or disposal is that practicable method currently available to the generator which minimizes the present and future threat to human health and the environment.

(Pub.L. 89–272, Title II, § 3002, as added Oct. 21, 1976, Pub.L. 94–580, § 2, 90 Stat. 2806, and amended Nov. 8, 1978, Pub.L. 95–609, § 7(f), 92 Stat. 3082; Oct. 21, 1980, Pub.L. 96–482, § 8, 94 Stat. 2338; Nov. 8, 1984, Pub.L. 98–616, Title II, § 224(a), 98 Stat. 3252.)

CODE OF FEDERAL REGULATIONS

Generators of hazardous waste, standards applicable to, see 40 CFR 262.10 et seq.

Identification and listing of hazardous waste, see 40 CFR, 261.1 et seq.

West's Federal Practice Manual

Solid waste disposal, see § 4385.5.

LAW REVIEW COMMENTARIES

Encouraging safety through insurance-based incentives: financial responsibility for hazardous wastes. Jeffrey Kehne, 96 Yale L.J. 403 (1986).

From elephants to mice: The development of EBMUD's program to control small source wastewater discharges. Raoul Stewardson, 20 Ecology L.Q. 441 (1993).

Hazardous Waste Law for the federal employee after the Federal Facility Compliance Act of 1992. Stephen J. Darmody, 40 Fed. B.News & J. 650 (Nov./Dec. 1993).

How well can states enforce their environmental laws when the polluter is the United States Government? 18 Rutgers L.J. 123 (1986).

Interaction of the Bankruptcy Code and environmental laws: Grit, the grind, and the grease. Robert R. Graves, 29 Willamette L.Rev. 297 (1993).

"More good than harm": A first principle for environmental agencies and reviewing courts. Edward W. Warren and Gary E. Marchant, 20 Ecology L.Q. 379 (1993).

§ 6923. Standards applicable to transporters of hazardous waste [SWDA § 3003]

(a) Standards

Not later than eighteen months after October 21, 1976, and after opportunity for public hearings, the Administrator, after consultation with the Secretary of Transportation and the States, shall promulgate regulations establishing such standards, applicable to transporters of hazardous waste identified or listed under this subchapter, as may be necessary to protect human health and the environment. Such standards shall include but need not be limited to requirements respecting—

(1) recordkeeping concerning such hazardous waste transported, and their source and delivery points;

(2) transportation of such waste only if properly labeled;

(3) compliance with the manifest system referred to in section 6922(5) of this title; and

(4) transportation of all such hazardous waste only to the hazardous waste treatment, storage, or disposal facilities which the shipper designates on the manifest form to be a facility holding a permit issued under this subchapter, or pursuant to title I of the Marine Protection, Research, and Sanctuaries Act (86 Stat. 1052) [33 U.S.C.A. § 1411 et seq.].

(b) Coordination with regulations of Secretary of Transportation

In case of any hazardous waste identified or listed under this subchapter which is subject to the Hazardous Materials Transportation Act (88 Stat. 2156; 49 U.S.C. 1801 et seq.) [49 App. U.S.C.A. § 1801 et seq.], the regulations promulgated by the Administrator under this section shall be consistent with the requirements of such Act and the regulations thereunder. The Administrator is authorized to make recommendations to the Secretary of Transportation respecting the regulations of such hazardous waste under the Hazardous Materials Transportation Act and for addition of materials to be covered by such Act.

(c) Fuel from hazardous waste

Not later than two years after November 8, 1984, and after opportunity for public hearing, the Administrator shall promulgate regulations establishing standards, applicable to transporters of fuel produced (1) from any hazardous waste identified or listed under section 6921 of this title, or (2) from any hazardous waste identified or listed under section 6921 of this title and any other material, as may be necessary to protect human health and the environment. Such standards may include any of the requirements set forth in paragraphs (1) through (4) of subsection (a) of this section as may be appropriate.

(Pub.L. 89–272, Title II, § 3003, as added Oct. 21, 1976, Pub.L. 94–580, § 2, 90 Stat. 2807, and amended Nov. 8, 1978, Pub.L. 95–609, § 7(g), 92 Stat. 3082; Nov. 8, 1984, Pub.L. 98–616, Title II, § 204(b)(2), 98 Stat. 3238.)

CODE OF FEDERAL REGULATIONS

Transporters of hazardous waste, standards applicable to, see 40 CFR 263.10 et seq.

West's Federal Practice Manual

Solid waste disposal, see § 4385.5.

LAW REVIEW COMMENTARIES

How well can states enforce their environmental laws when the polluter is the United States Government? 18 Rutgers L.J. 123 (1986).

Interstate waste: A key issue in resolving the national hazardous waste capacity crisis. B.J. Wynne, III and Terri Hamby, 32 S.Tex. L.Rev. 601 (1991).

§ 6924. Standards applicable to owners and operators of hazardous waste treatment, storage, and disposal facilities [SWDA § 3004]

(a) In general

Not later than eighteen months after October 21, 1976, and after opportunity for public hearings and after consultation with appropriate Federal and State agencies, the Administrator shall promulgate regulations establishing such performance standards, applicable to owners and operators of facilities for the treatment, storage, or disposal of hazardous waste identified or listed under this subchapter, as may be necessary to protect human health and the environment. In establishing such standards the Administrator shall, where appropriate, distinguish in such standards between requirements appropriate for new facilities and for facilities in existence on the date of promulgation of such regulations. Such standards shall include, but need not be limited to, requirements respecting—

(1) maintaining records of all hazardous wastes identified or listed under this chapter which is treated, stored, or disposed of, as the case may be, and the manner in which such wastes were treated, stored, or disposed of;

(2) satisfactory reporting, monitoring, and inspection and compliance with the manifest system referred to in section 6922(5) of this title;

(3) treatment, storage, or disposal of all such waste received by the facility pursuant to such operating methods, techniques, and practices as may be satisfactory to the Administrator;

(4) the location, design, and construction of such hazardous waste treatment, disposal, or storage facilities;

(5) contingency plans for effective action to minimize unanticipated damage from any treatment, storage, or disposal of any such hazardous waste;

(6) the maintenance of operation of such facilities and requiring such additional qualifications as to ownership, continuity of operation, training for personnel, and financial responsibility (including financial responsibility for corrective action) as may be necessary or desirable; and

(7) compliance with the requirements of section 6925 of this title respecting permits for treatment, storage, or disposal.

No private entity shall be precluded by reason of criteria established under paragraph (6) from the ownership or operation of facilities providing hazardous waste treatment, storage, or disposal services where such entity can provide assurances of financial responsibility and continuity of operation consistent with the degree and duration of risks associated with the treatment, storage, or disposal of specified hazardous waste.

(b) Salt dome formations, salt bed formations, underground mines and caves

(1) Effective on November 8, 1984, the placement of any noncontainerized or bulk liquid hazardous waste in any salt dome formation, salt bed formation, underground mine, or cave is prohibited until such time as—

(A) the Administrator has determined, after notice and opportunity for hearings on the record in the affected areas, that such placement is protective of human health and the environment;

(B) the Administrator has promulgated performance and permitting standards for such facilities under this subchapter, and;

(C) a permit has been issued under section 6925(c) of this title for the facility concerned.

(2) Effective on November 8, 1984, the placement of any hazardous waste other than a hazardous waste referred to in paragraph (1) in a salt dome formation, salt bed formation, underground mine, or cave is prohibited until such time as a permit has been issued under section 6925(c) of this title for the facility concerned.

(3) No determination made by the Administrator under subsection (d), (e), or (g) of this section regarding any hazardous waste to which such subsection (d), (e), or (g) applies shall affect the prohibition contained in paragraph (1) or (2) of this subsection.

(4) Nothing in this subsection shall apply to the Department of Energy Waste Isolation Pilot Project in New Mexico.

(c) Liquids in landfills

(1) Effective 6 months after November 8, 1984, the placement of bulk or noncontainerized liquid hazardous waste or free liquids contained in hazardous waste (whether or not absorbents have been added) in any landfill is prohibited. Prior to such date the requirements (as in effect on April 30, 1983) promulgated under this section by the Administrator regarding liquid hazardous waste shall remain in force and effect to the extent such requirements are applicable to the placement of bulk or noncontainerized liquid hazardous waste, or free liquids contained in hazardous waste, in landfills.

(2) Not later than fifteen months after November 8, 1984, the Administrator shall promulgate final regulations which—

(A) minimize the disposal of containerized liquid hazardous waste in landfills, and

(B) minimize the presence of free liquids in containerized hazardous waste to be disposed of in landfills.

Such regulations shall also prohibit the disposal in landfills of liquids that have been absorbed in materials that biodegrade or that release liquids when compressed as might occur during routine landfill operations. Prior to the date on which such final regulations take effect, the requirements (as in effect on April 30, 1983) promulgated under this section by the Administrator shall remain in force and effect to the extent such requirements are applicable to the disposal of containerized liquid hazardous waste, or free liquids contained in hazardous waste, in landfills.

(3) Effective twelve months after November 8, 1984, the placement of any liquid which is not a hazardous waste in a landfill for which a permit is required under section 6925(c) of this title or which is operating pursuant to interim status granted under section 6925(e) of this title is prohibited unless the owner or operator of such landfill demonstrates to the Administrator, or the Administrator determines, that—

(A) the only reasonably available alternative to the placement in such landfill is placement in a landfill or unlined surface impoundment, whether or not permitted under section 6925(c) of this title or operating pursuant to interim status under section 6925(e) of this title, which contains, or may reasonably be anticipated to contain, hazardous waste; and

(B) placement in such owner or operator's landfill will not present a risk of contamination of any underground source of drinking water.

As used in subparagraph (B), the term "underground source of drinking water" has the same meaning as provided in regulations under the Safe Drinking Water Act (title XIV of the Public Health Service Act) [42 U.S.C.A. § 300f et seq.]

(4) No determination made by the Administrator under subsection (d), (e), or (g) of this section regarding any hazardous waste to which such subsection (d), (e), or (g) applies shall affect the prohibition contained in paragraph (1) of this subsection.

(d) Prohibitions on land disposal of specified wastes

(1) Effective 32 months after November 8, 1984 (except as provided in subsection (f) of this section with respect to underground injection into deep injection wells), the land disposal of the hazardous wastes referred to in paragraph (2) is prohibited unless the Administrator determines the prohibition on one or more methods of land disposal of such waste is not required in order to protect human health and the environment for as long as the waste remains hazardous, taking into account—

(A) the long-term uncertainties associated with land disposal,

(B) the goal of managing hazardous waste in an appropriate manner in the first instance, and

(C) the persistence, toxicity, mobility, and propensity to bioaccumulate of such hazardous wastes and their hazardous constituents.

For the purposes of this paragraph, a method of land disposal may not be determined to be protective of human health and the environment for a hazardous waste referred to in paragraph (2) (other than a hazardous waste which has complied with the pretreatment regulations promulgated under subsection (m) of this section), unless, upon application by an interested person, it has been demonstrated to the Administrator, to a reasonable degree of certainty, that there will be no migration of hazardous constituents from the disposal unit or injection zone for as long as the wastes remain hazardous.

(2) Paragraph (1) applies to the following hazardous wastes listed or identified under section 6921 of this title:

(A) Liquid hazardous wastes, including free liquids associated with any solid or sludge, containing free cyanides at concentrations greater than or equal to 1,000 mg/l.

(B) Liquid hazardous wastes, including free liquids associated with any solid or sludge, containing the following metals (or elements) or compounds of these metals (or elements) at concentrations greater than or equal to those specified below:

(i) arsenic and/or compounds (as As) 500 mg/l;

(ii) cadmium and/or compounds (as Cd) 100 mg/l;

(iii) chromium (VI and/or compounds (as Cr VI)) 500 mg/l;

(iv) lead and/or compounds (as Pb) 500 mg/l;

(v) mercury and/or compounds (as Hg) 20 mg/l;

(vi) nickel and/or compounds (as Ni) 134 mg/l;

(vii) selenium and/or compounds (as Se) 100 mg/l; and

(viii) thallium and/or compounds (as Th) 130 mg/l.

(C) Liquid hazardous waste having a pH less than or equal to two (2.0).

(D) Liquid hazardous wastes containing polychlorinated biphenyls at concentrations greater than or equal to 50 ppm.

(E) Hazardous wastes containing halogenated organic compounds in total concentration greater than or equal to 1,000 mg/kg.

When necessary to protect human health and the environment, the Administrator shall substitute more stringent concentration levels than the levels specified in subparagraphs (A) through (E).

(3) During the period ending forty-eight months after November 8, 1984, this subsection shall not apply to any disposal of contaminated soil or debris resulting from a response action taken under section 9604 or 9606 of this title or a corrective action required under this subchapter.

(e) Solvents and dioxins

(1) Effective twenty-four months after November 8, 1984 (except as provided in subsection (f) of this section with respect to underground injection into deep injection wells), the land disposal of the hazardous wastes referred to in paragraph (2) is prohibited unless the Administrator determines the prohibition of one or more methods of land disposal of such waste is not required in order to protect human health and the environment for as long as the waste remains hazardous, taking into account the factors referred to in subparagraphs (A) through (C) of subsection (d)(1) of this section. For the purposes of this paragraph, a method of land disposal may not be determined to be protective of human health and the environment for a hazardous waste referred to in paragraph (2) (other than a hazardous waste which has complied with the pretreatment regulations promulgated under subsection (m) of this section), unless upon application by an interested person it has been demonstrated to the Administrator, to a reasonable degree of certainty, that there will be no migration of hazardous constituents from the disposal unit or injection zone for as long as the wastes remain hazardous.

(2) The hazardous wastes to which the prohibition under paragraph (1) applies are as follows—

(A) dioxin-containing hazardous wastes numbered F020, F021, F022, and F023 (as referred to in the proposed rule published by the Administrator in the Federal Register for April 4, 1983), and

(B) those hazardous wastes numbered F001, F002, F003, F004, and F005 in regulations promulgated by the Administrator under section 3001 (40 C.F.R. 261.31 (July 1, 1983)), as those regulations are in effect on July 1, 1983.

(3) During the period ending forty-eight months after November 8, 1984, this subsection shall not apply to any disposal of contaminated soil or debris resulting from a response action taken under section

9604 or 9606 of this title or a corrective action required under this subchapter.

(f) Disposal into deep injection wells; specified subsection (d) wastes, solvents and dioxins

(1) Not later than forty-five months after November 8, 1984, the Administrator shall complete a review of the disposal of all hazardous wastes referred to in paragraph (2) of subsection (d) of this section and in paragraph (2) of subsection (e) of this section by underground injection into deep injection wells.

(2) Within forty-five months after November 8, 1984, the Administrator shall make a determination regarding the disposal by underground injection into deep injection wells of the hazardous wastes referred to in paragraph (2) of subsection (d) of this section and the hazardous wastes referred to in paragraph (2) of subsection (e) of this section. The Administrator shall promulgate final regulations prohibiting the disposal of such wastes into such wells if it may reasonably be determined that such disposal may not be protective of human health and the environment for as long as the waste remains hazardous, taking into account the factors referred to in subparagraphs (A) through (C) of subsection (d)(1) of this section. In promulgating such regulations, the Administrator shall consider each hazardous waste referred to in paragraph (2) of subsection (d) of this section or in paragraph (2) of subsection (e) of this section which is prohibited from disposal into such wells by any State.

(3) If the Administrator fails to make a determination under paragraph (2) for any hazardous waste referred to in paragraph (2) of subsection (d) of this section or in paragraph (2) of subsection (e) of this section within forty-five months after November 8, 1984, such hazardous waste shall be prohibited from disposal into any deep injection well.

(4) As used in this subsection, the term "deep injection well" means a well used for the underground injection of hazardous waste other than a well to which section 6979a(a) of this title applies.

(g) Additional land disposal prohibition determination

(1) Not later than twenty-four months after November 8, 1984, the Administrator shall submit a schedule to Congress for—

(A) reviewing all hazardous wastes listed (as of November 8, 1984) under section 6921 of this title other than those wastes which are referred to in subsection (d) or (e) of this section; and

(B) taking action under paragraph (5) of this subsection with respect to each such hazardous waste.

(2) The Administrator shall base the schedule on a ranking of such listed wastes considering their intrinsic hazard and their volume such that decisions regarding the land disposal of high volume hazardous wastes with high intrinsic hazard shall, to the maximum extent possible, be made by the date forty-five months after November 8, 1984. Decisions regarding low volume hazardous wastes with lower intrinsic hazard shall be made by the date sixty-six months after November 8, 1984.

(3) The preparation and submission of the schedule under this subsection shall not be subject to the Paperwork Reduction Act of 1980. No hearing on the record shall be required for purposes of preparation or submission of the schedule. The schedule shall not be subject to judicial review.

(4) The schedule under this subsection shall require that the Administrator shall promulgate regulations in accordance with paragraph (5) or make a determination under paragraph (5)—

(A) for at least one-third of all hazardous wastes referred to in paragraph (1) by the date forty-five months after November 8, 1984;

(B) for at least two-thirds of all such listed wastes by the date fifty-five months after November 8, 1984; and

(C) for all such listed wastes and for all hazardous wastes identified under section 6921 of this title by the date sixty-six months after November 8, 1984.

In the case of any hazardous waste identified or listed under section 6921 of this title after November 8, 1984, the Administrator shall determine whether such waste shall be prohibited from one or more methods of land disposal in accordance with paragraph (5) within six months after the date of such identification or listing.

(5) Not later than the date specified in the schedule published under this subsection, the Administrator shall promulgate final regulations prohibiting one or more methods of land disposal of the hazardous wastes listed on such schedule except for methods of land disposal which the Administrator determines will be protective of human health and the environment for as long as the waste remains hazardous, taking into account the factors referred to in subparagraphs (A) through (C) of subsection (d)(1) of this section. For the purposes of this paragraph, a method of land disposal may not be determined to be protective of human health and the environment (except with respect to a hazardous waste which has complied with the pretreatment regulations promulgated under subsection (m) of this section) unless, upon application by an interested person, it has been demonstrated to the Administrator, to a reasonable degree of certainty, that there will be no migration of hazardous constituents from the disposal unit or injection zone for as long as the wastes remain hazardous.

(6)(A) If the Administrator fails (by the date forty-five months after November 8, 1984) to promulgate regulations or make a determination under paragraph (5) for any hazardous waste which is included in the first one-third of the schedule published under this subsection, such hazardous waste may be disposed of in a landfill or surface impoundment only if—

(i) such facility is in compliance with the requirements of subsection (*o*) of this section which are applicable to new facilities (relating to minimum technological requirements); and

(ii) prior to such disposal, the generator has certified to the Administrator that such generator has investigated the availability of treatment capacity and has determined that the use of such landfill or surface impoundment is the only practical alternative to treatment currently available to the generator.

The prohibition contained in this subparagraph shall continue to apply until the Administrator promulgates regulations or makes a determination under paragraph (5) for the waste concerned.

(B) If the Administrator fails (by the date 55 months after November 8, 1984) to promulgate regulations or make a determination under paragraph (5) for any hazardous waste which is included in the first two-thirds of the schedule published under this subsection, such hazardous waste may be disposed of in a landfill or surface impoundment only if—

(i) such facilities in compliance with the requirements of subsection *(o)* of this section which are applicable to new facilities (relating to minimum technological requirements); and

(ii) prior to such disposal, the generator has certified to the Administrator that such generator has investigated the availability of treatment capacity and has determined that the use of such landfill or surface impoundment is the only practical alternative to treatment currently available to the generator.

The prohibition contained in this subparagraph shall continue to apply until the Administrator promulgates regulations or makes a determination under paragraph (5) for the waste concerned.

(C) If the Administrator fails to promulgate regulations, or make a determination under paragraph (5) for any hazardous waste referred to in paragraph (1) within 66 months after November 8, 1984, such hazardous waste shall be prohibited from land disposal.

(h) Variance from land disposal prohibitions

(1) A prohibition in regulations under subsection (d), (e), (f), or (g) of this section shall be effective immediately upon promulgation.

(2) The Administrator may establish an effective date different from the effective date which would otherwise apply under subsection (d), (e), (f), or (g) of this section with respect to a specific hazardous waste which is subject to a prohibition under subsection (d), (e), (f), or (g) of this section or under regulations under subsection (d), (e), (f), or (g) of this section. Any such other effective date shall be established on the basis of the earliest date on which adequate alternative treatment, recovery, or disposal capacity which protects human health and the environment will be available. Any such other effective date shall in no event be later than 2 years after the effective date of the prohibition which would otherwise apply under subsection (d), (e), (f), or (g) of this section.

(3) The Administrator, after notice and opportunity for comment and after consultation with appropriate State agencies in all affected States, may on a case-by-case basis grant an extension of the effective date which would otherwise apply under subsection (d), (e), (f), or (g) of this section or under paragraph (2) for up to one year, where the applicant demonstrates that there is a binding contractual commitment to construct or otherwise provide such alternative capacity but due to circumstances beyond the control of such applicant such alternative capacity cannot reasonably be made available by such effective date. Such extension shall be renewable once for no more than one additional year.

(4) Whenever another effective date (hereinafter referred to as a "variance") is established under paragraph (2), or an extension is granted under paragraph (3), with respect to any hazardous waste, during the period for which such variance or extension is in effect, such hazardous waste may be disposed of in a landfill or surface impoundment only if such facility is in compliance with the requirements of subsection *(o)* of this section.

(i) Publication of determination

If the Administrator determines that a method of land disposal will be protective of human health and the environment, he shall promptly publish in the Federal Register notice of such determination, together with an explanation of the basis for such determination.

(j) Storage of hazardous waste prohibited from land disposal

In the case of any hazardous waste which is prohibited from one or more methods of land disposal under this section (or under regulations promulgated by the Administrator under any provision of this section) the storage of such hazardous waste is prohibited unless such storage is solely for the purpose of the accumulation of such quantities of hazardous waste as are necessary to facilitate proper recovery, treatment or disposal.

(k) Definition of land disposal

For the purposes of this section, the term "land disposal", when used with respect to a specified hazardous waste, shall be deemed to include, but not be limited to, any placement of such hazardous waste in a landfill, surface impoundment, waste pile, injection well, land treatment facility, salt dome formation, salt bed formation, or underground mine or cave.

(*l*) Ban on dust suppression

The use of waste or used oil or other material, which is contaminated or mixed with dioxin or any other hazardous waste identified or listed under section 6921 of this title (other than a waste identified solely on the basis of ignitability), for dust suppression or road treatment is prohibited.

(m) Treatment standards for waste subject to land disposal prohibition

(1) Simultaneously with the promulgation of regulations under subsection (d), (e), (f), or (g) of this section prohibiting one or more methods of land disposal of a particular hazardous waste, and as appropriate thereafter, the Administrator shall, after notice and an opportunity for hearings and after consultation with appropriate Federal and State agencies, promulgate regulations specifying those levels or methods of treatment, if any, which substantially diminish the toxicity of the waste or substantially reduce the likelihood of migration of hazardous constituents from the waste so that short-term and long-term threats to human health and the environment are minimized.

(2) If such hazardous waste has been treated to the level or by a method specified in regulations promulgated under this subsection, such waste or residue thereof shall not be subject to any prohibition promulgated under subsection (d), (e), (f), or (g) of this section and may be disposed of in a land disposal facility which meets the requirements of this subchapter. Any regulation promulgated under this subsection for a particular hazardous waste shall become effective on the same date as any applicable prohibition promulgated under subsection (d), (e), (f), or (g) of this section.

(n) Air emissions

Not later than thirty months after November 8, 1984, the Administrator shall promulgate such regulations for the monitoring and control of air emissions at hazardous waste treatment, storage, and disposal facilities, including but not limited to open tanks, surface impoundments, and landfills, as may be necessary to protect human health and the environment.

(*o*) Minimum technological requirements

(1) The regulations under subsection (a) of this section shall be revised from time to time to take into account improvements in the technology of control and measurement. At a minimum, such regulations shall require, and a permit issued pursuant to section 6925(c) of this title after November 8, 1984, by the Administrator or a State shall require—

(A) for each new landfill or surface impoundment, each new landfill or surface impoundment unit at an existing facility, each replacement of an existing landfill or surface impoundment unit, and each lateral expansion of an existing landfill or surface impoundment unit, for which an application for a final determination regarding issuance of a permit under section 6925(c) of this title is received after November 8, 1984—

(i) the installation of two or more liners and a leachate collection system above (in the case of a landfill) and between such liners; and

(ii) ground water monitoring; and

(B) for each incinerator which receives a permit under section 6925(c) of this title after November 8, 1984, the attainment of the minimum destruction and removal efficiency required by regulations in effect on June 24, 1982.

The requirements of this paragraph shall apply with respect to all waste received after the issuance of the permit.

(2) Paragraph (1)(A)(i) shall not apply if the owner or operator demonstrates to the Administrator, and the Administrator finds for such landfill or surface impoundment, that alternative design and operating practices, together with location characteristics, will prevent the migration of any hazardous constituents into the ground water or surface water at least as effectively as such liners and leachate collection systems.

(3) The double-liner requirement set forth in paragraph (1)(A)(i) may be waived by the Administrator for any monofill, if—

(A) such monofill contains only hazardous wastes from foundry furnace emission controls or metal casting molding sand,

(B) such wastes do not contain constituents which would render the wastes hazardous for reasons other than the Extraction Procedure ("EP") toxicity characteristics set forth in regulations under this subchapter, and

(C) such monofill meets the same requirements as are applicable in the case of a waiver under section 6925(j)(2) or (4) of this title.

(4)(A) Not later than thirty months after November 8, 1984, the Administrator shall promulgate standards requiring that new landfill units, surface impoundment units, waste piles, underground tanks and land treatment units for the storage, treatment, or disposal of hazardous waste identified or listed under section 6921 of this title shall be required to utilize approved leak detection systems.

(B) For the purposes of subparagraph (A)—

(i) the term "approved leak detection system" means a system or technology which the Administrator determines to be capable of detecting leaks of hazardous constituents at the earliest practicable time; and

(ii) the term "new units" means units on which construction commences after the date of promulgation of regulations under this paragraph.

(5)(A) The Administrator shall promulgate regulations or issue guidance documents implementing the requirements of paragraph (1)(A) within two years after November 8, 1984.

(B) Until the effective date of such regulations or guidance documents, the requirement for the installation of two or more liners may be satisfied by the installation of a top liner designed, operated, and constructed of materials to prevent the migration of any constituent into such liner during the period such facility remains in operation (including any post-closure monitoring period), and a lower liner designed, operated and constructed to prevent the migration of any constituent through such liner during such period. For the purpose of the preceding sentence, a lower liner shall be deemed to satisfy such requirement if it is constructed of at least a 3-foot thick layer of recompacted clay or other natural material with a permeability of no more than $1X10^{-7}$ centimeter per second.

(6) Any permit under section 6925 of this title which is issued for a landfill located within the State of Alabama shall require the installation of two or more liners and a leachate collection system above and between such liners, notwithstanding any other provision of this chapter.

(7) In addition to the requirements set forth in this subsection, the regulations referred to in paragraph (1) shall specify criteria for the acceptable location of new and existing treatment, storage, or disposal facilities as necessary to protect human health and the environment. Within 18 months after November 8, 1984, the Administrator shall publish guidance criteria identifying areas of vulnerable hydrogeology.

(p) Ground water monitoring

The standards under this section concerning ground water monitoring which are applicable to surface impoundments, waste piles, land treatment units, and landfills shall apply to such a facility whether or not—

(1) the facility is located above the seasonal high water table;

(2) two liners and a leachate collection system have been installed at the facility; or

(3) the owner or operator inspects the liner (or liners) which has been installed at the facility.

This subsection shall not be construed to affect other exemptions or waivers from such standards provided in regulations in effect on November 8, 1984, or as may be provided in revisions to those regulations, to the extent consistent with this subsection. The Administrator is authorized on a case-by-case basis to exempt from ground water monitoring requirements under this section (including subsection (*o*) of this section) any engineered structure which the Administrator finds does not receive or contain liquid waste (nor waste containing free liquids), is designed and operated to exclude liquid from precipitation or other runoff, utilizes multiple leak detection systems within the outer layer of containment, and provides for continuing operation and maintenance of these leak detection systems during the operating period, closure, and the period required for post-closure monitoring and for which the Administrator concludes on the basis of such findings that there is a reasonable certainty hazardous constituents will not migrate beyond the outer layer of containment prior to the end of the period required for post-closure monitoring.

(q) Hazardous waste used as fuel

(1) Not later than two years after November 8, 1984, and after notice and opportunity for public hearing, the Administrator shall promulgate regulations establishing such—

(A) standards applicable to the owners and operators of facilities which produce a fuel—

(i) from any hazardous waste identified or listed under section 6921 of this title, or

(ii) from any hazardous waste identified or listed under section 6921 of this title and any other material;

(B) standards applicable to the owners and operators of facilities which burn, for purposes of energy recovery, any fuel produced as provided in subparagraph (A) or any fuel which otherwise contains any hazardous waste identified or listed under section 6921 of this title; and

(C) standards applicable to any person who distributes or markets any fuel which is produced as provided in subparagraph (A) or any fuel which otherwise contains any hazardous waste identified or listed under section 6921 of this title

as may be necessary to protect human health and the environment. Such standards may include any of the requirements set forth in paragraphs (1) through (7) of subsection (a) of this section as may be appropriate. Nothing in this subsection shall be construed to affect or impair the provisions of section 6921(b)(3) of this title. For purposes of this subsection, the term "hazardous waste listed under section 6921 of this title" includes any commercial chemical product which is listed under section 6921 of this title and which, in lieu of its original intended use, is (i) produced for use as (or as a component of) a fuel, (ii) distributed for use as a fuel, or (iii) burned as a fuel.

(2)(A) This subsection, subsection (r) of this section, and subsection (s) of this section shall not apply to petroleum refinery wastes containing oil which are converted into petroleum coke at the same facility at which such wastes were generated, unless the resulting coke product would exceed one or more characteristics by which a substance would be identified as a hazardous waste under section 6921 of this title.

(B) The Administrator may exempt from the requirements of this subsection, subsection (r) of this section, or subsection (s) of this section facilities which burn de minimis quantities of hazardous waste as fuel, as defined by the Administrator, if the wastes are burned at the same facility at which such wastes are generated; the waste is burned to recover useful energy, as determined by the Administrator on the basis of the design and operating characteristics of the facility and the heating value and other characteristics of the waste; and the waste is burned in a type of device determined by the Administrator to be designed and operated at a destruction and removal efficiency sufficient such that protection of human health and environment is assured.

(C)(i) After the date of November 8, 1984, and until standards are promulgated and in effect under paragraph (2) of this subsection, no fuel which contains any hazardous waste may be burned in any cement kiln which is located within the boundaries of any incorporated municipality with a population greater than five hundred thousand (based on the most recent census statistics) unless such kiln fully complies with regulations (as in effect on November 8, 1984 under this subchapter which are applicable to incinerators.

(ii) Any person who knowingly violates the prohibition contained in clause (i) shall be deemed to have violated section 6928(d)(2) of this title.

(r) Labeling

(1) Notwithstanding any other provision of law, until such time as the Administrator promulgates standards under subsection (q) of this section specifically superceding this requirement, it shall be unlawful for any person who is required to file a notification in accordance with paragraph (1) or (3) of section 6930 of this title to distribute or market any fuel which is produced from any hazardous waste identified or listed under section 6921 of this title, or any fuel which otherwise contains any hazardous waste identified or listed under section 6921 of this title if the invoice or the bill of sale fails—

(A) to bear the following statement: "WARNING: THIS FUEL CONTAINS HAZARDOUS WASTES", and

(B) to list the hazardous wastes contained therein.

Beginning ninety days after November 8, 1984, such statement shall be located in a conspicuous place on every such invoice or bill of sale and shall appear in conspicuous and legible type in contrast by typography, layouts, or color with other printed matter on the invoice or bill of sale.

(2) Unless the Administrator determines otherwise as may be necessary to protect human health and the environment, this subsection shall not apply to fuels produced from petroleum refining waste containing oil if—

(A) such materials are generated and reinserted onsite into the refining process;

(B) contaminants are removed; and

(C) such refining waste containing oil is converted along with normal process streams into pertroleum-derived [1] fuel products at a facility at which crude oil is refined into petroleum products and which is classified as a number SIC 2911 facility under the Office of Management and Budget Standard Industrial Classification Manual.

(3) Unless the Administrator determines otherwise as may be necessary to protect human health and the environment, this subsection shall not apply to fuels produced from oily materials, resulting from normal petroleum refining, production and transportation practices, if (A) contaminants are removed; and (B) such oily materials are converted along with normal process streams into petroleum-derived fuel products at a facility at which crude oil is refined into petroleum products and which is classified as a number SIC 2911 facility under the Office of Management and Budget Standard [2] Classification Manual.

(s) Recordkeeping

Not later than fifteen months after November 8, 1984, the Administrator shall promulgate regulations requiring that any person who is required to file a notification in accordance with subparagraph (1), (2), or (3), of section 6930(a) of this title shall maintain such records regarding fuel blending, distribution, or use as may be necessary to protect human health and the environment.

(t) Financial responsibility provisions

(1) Financial responsibility required by subsection (a) of this section may be established in accordance with regulations promulgated by the Administrator by any one, or any combination, of the following: insurance, guarantee, surety bond, letter of credit, or qualification as a self-insurer. In promulgating requirements under this section, the Administrator is authorized to specify policy or other contractual terms, conditions, or defenses which are necessary or are unacceptable in establishing such evidence of financial responsibility in order to effectuate the purposes of this chapter.

(2) In any case where the owner or operator is in bankruptcy, reorganization, or arrangement pursuant to the Federal Bankruptcy Code or where (with reasonable diligence) jurisdiction in any State court or any Federal Court cannot be obtained over an owner or operator likely to be solvent at the time of judgment, any claim arising from conduct for which evidence of financial responsibility must be provided under this section may be asserted directly against the guarantor providing such evidence of financial responsibility. In the case of any action pursuant to this subsection, such guarantor shall be entitled to invoke all rights and defenses which would have been available to the owner or operator if any action had been brought against the owner or operator by the claimant and which would have been available to the guarantor if an action had been brought against the guarantor by the owner or operator.

(3) The total liability of any guarantor shall be limited to the aggregate amount which the guarantor has provided as evidence of financial responsibility to the owner or operator under this chapter. Nothing in this subsection shall be construed to limit any other State or Federal statutory, contractual or common law liability of a guarantor to its owner or operator including, but not limited to, the liability of such guarantor for bad faith either in negotiating or in failing to negotiate the settlement of any claim. Nothing in this subsection shall be construed to diminish the liability of any person under section 9607 or 9611 of this title or other applicable law.

(4) For the purpose of this subsection, the term "guarantor" means any person, other than the owner or operator, who provides evidence of financial responsibility for an owner or operator under this section.

(u) Continuing releases at permitted facilities

Standards promulgated under this section shall require, and a permit issued after November 8, 1984, by the Administrator or a State shall require, corrective action for all releases of hazardous waste or constituents from any solid waste management unit at a treatment, storage, or disposal facility seeking a permit under this subchapter, regardless of the time at which waste was placed in such unit. Permits issued under section 6925 of this title shall contain schedules of compliance for such corrective action (where such corrective action cannot be completed prior to issuance of the permit) and assurances of financial responsibility for completing such corrective action.

(v) Corrective action beyond facility boundary

As promptly as practicable after November 8, 1984, the Administrator shall amend the standards under this section regarding corrective action required at facilities for the treatment, storage, or disposal, of hazardous waste listed or identified under section 6921 of this title to require that corrective action be taken beyond the facility boundary where necessary to protect human health and the environment unless the owner or operator of the facility concerned demonstrates to the satisfaction of the Administrator that, despite the owner or operator's best efforts, the owner or operator was unable to obtain the necessary permission to undertake such action. Such regulations shall take effect immediately upon promulgation, notwithstanding section 6930(b) of this title, and shall apply to—

(1) all facilities operating under permits issued under subsection (c) of this section, and

(2) all landfills, surface impoundments, and waste pile units (including any new units, replacements of existing units, or lateral expansions of existing units) which receive hazardous waste after July 26, 1982.

Pending promulgation of such regulations, the Administrator shall issue corrective action orders for facilities referred to in paragraphs (1) and (2), on a case-by-case basis, consistent with the purposes of this subsection.

(w) Underground tanks

Not later than March 1, 1985, the Administrator shall promulgate final permitting standards under this section for underground tanks that cannot be entered for inspection. Within forty-eight months after November 8, 1984, such standards shall be modified, if necessary, to cover at a minimum all requirements and standards described in section 6991b of this title.

(x) Mining and other special wastes

If (1) solid waste from the extraction, beneficiation or processing of ores and minerals, including phosphate rock and overburden from the mining of uranium, (2) fly ash waste, bottom ash waste, slag waste, and flue gas emission control waste generated primarily from the combustion of coal or other fossil fuels, or (3) cement kiln dust waste, is subject to regulation under this subchapter, the Administrator is authorized to modify the requirements of subsections (c), (d), (e), (f), (g), (*o*), and (u) of this section and section 6925(j) of this title, in the case of landfills or surface impoundments receiving such solid waste, to take into account the special characteristics of such wastes, the practical difficulties associated with implementation of such requirements, and site-specific characteristics, including but not limited to the climate, geology, hydrology and soil chemistry at the site, so long as such modified requirements assure protection of human health and the environment.

(y) Munitions

(1) Not later than 6 months after October 6, 1992, the Administrator shall propose, after consulting with the Secretary of Defense and appropriate State officials, regulations identifying when military munitions become hazardous waste for purposes of this subchapter and providing for the safe transportation and storage of such waste. Not later than 24 months after such date, and after notice and opportunity for comment, the Administrator shall promulgate such regulations. Any such regulations shall assure protection of human health and the environment.

(2) For purposes of this subsection, the term "military munitions" includes chemical and conventional munitions.

(Pub.L. 89–272, Title II, § 3004, as added Oct. 21, 1976, Pub.L. 94–580, § 2, 90 Stat. 2807, and amended Oct. 21, 1980, Pub.L. 96–482, § 9, 94 Stat. 2338; Nov. 8, 1984, Pub.L. 98–616, Title II, §§ 201(a), 202(a), 203, 204(b)(1), 205–209, 98 Stat. 3226, 3233, 3234, 3236, 3238–3240; Oct. 6, 1992, Pub.L. 102–386, Title I, § 107, 106 Stat. 1513.)

[1] So in original. Probably should be petroleum-derived.

[2] So in original. Probably should be Standard Industrial Classification.

CODE OF FEDERAL REGULATIONS

Definitions and requirements, see 40 CFR 122.1 et seq.
Owners and operations of hazardous waste facilities, standards applicable to, see 40 CFR 264.1 et seq., 265.1 et seq., 267.1 et seq.

West's Federal Practice Manual

Solid waste disposal, see § 4385.5.

LAW REVIEW COMMENTARIES

Bankrupting CERCLA: Amending the Bankruptcy Code to allow CERCLA contingent claims for contribution. Kenneth W. Maxwell, 13 J. Energy, Nat. Resources, & Envtl.L. 431 (1993).

Emerging federal law of mine waste: Administrative, judicial and legislative developments. John R. Jacus and Thomas E. Root, 26 Land and Water L.Rev. 461 (1991).

Encouraging safety through insurance-based incentives: financial responsibility for hazardous wastes. Jeffrey Kehne, 96 Yale L.J. 403 (1986).

Hazardous Waste Law for the federal employee after the Federal Facility Compliance Act of 1992. Stephen J. Darmody, 40 Fed. B.News & J. 650 (Nov./Dec. 1993).

How well can states enforce their environmental laws when the polluter is the United States Government? 18 Rutgers L.J. 123 (1986).

Interstate waste: A key issue in resolving the national hazardous waste capacity crisis. B.J. Wynne, III and Terri Hamby, 32 S.Tex. L.Rev. 601 (1991).

Long-range planning in environmental and health regulatory agencies. Richard N.L. Andrews, 20 Ecology L.Q. 515 (1993).

Note, enhancing the community's role in landfill siting in Illinois. U.Ill.L.Rev. 97 (1987).

Oil and gas exemptions under RCRA and CERCLA: Are they still "safe harbors" eleven years later? Michael M. Gibson and David P. Young, 32 S.Tex.L.Rev. 361 (1991).

Oil Pollution Act of 1990: Opening a new era in federal and Texas regulation of oil spill prevention, containment and cleanup, and liability. J.B. Ruhl and Michael J. Jewell, 32 S.Tex.L.Rev. 475 (1991).

The problem with RCRA—Do the financial responsibility provisions really work? 36 Am.U.L.Rev. 133 (1986).

The Resource Conservation and Recovery Act (RCRA) and the Georgia Solid Waste Management Act. Frances M. Hallahan, 38 Mercer L.Rev. 569 (1987).

§ 6925. Permits for treatment, storage, or disposal of hazardous waste [SWDA § 3005]

(a) Permit requirements

Not later than eighteen months after October 21, 1976, the Administrator shall promulgate regulations requiring each person owning or operating an existing facility or planning to construct a new facility for the treatment, storage, or disposal of hazardous waste identified or listed under this subchapter to have a permit issued pursuant to this section. Such regulations shall take effect on the date provided in section 6930 of this title and upon and after such date the treatment, storage, or disposal of any such hazardous waste and the construction of any new facility for the treatment, storage, or disposal of any such hazardous waste is prohibited except in accordance with such a permit. No permit shall be required under this section in order to construct a facility if such facility is constructed pursuant to an approval issued by the

Administrator under section 2605(e) of Title 15 for the incineration of polycholorinated[1] biphenyls and any person owning or operating such a facility may, at any time after operation or construction of such facility has begun, file an application for a permit pursuant to this section authorizing such facility to incinerate hazardous waste identified or listed under this subchapter.

(b) Requirements of permit application

Each application for a permit under this section shall contain such information as may be required under regulations promulgated by the Administrator, including information respecting—

(1) estimates with respect to the composition, quantities, and concentrations of any hazardous waste identified or listed under this subchapter, or combinations of any such hazardous waste and any other solid waste, proposed to be disposed of, treated, transported, or stored, and the time, frequency, or rate of which such waste is proposed to be disposed of, treated, transported, or stored; and

(2) the site at which such hazardous waste or the products of treatment of such hazardous waste will be disposed of, treated, transported to, or stored.

(c) Permit issuance

(1) Upon a determination by the Administrator (or a State, if applicable), of compliance by a facility for which a permit is applied for under this section with the requirements of this section and section 6924 of this title, the Administrator (or the State) shall issue a permit for such facilities. In the event permit applicants propose modification of their facilities, or in the event the Administrator (or the State) determines that modifications are necessary to conform to the requirements under this section and section 6924 of this title, the permit shall specify the time allowed to complete the modifications.

(2)(A)(i) Not later than the date four years after November 8, 1984, in the case of each application under this subsection for a permit for a land disposal facility which was submitted before such date, the Administrator shall issue a final permit pursuant to such application or issue a final denial of such application.

(ii) Not later than the date five years after November 8, 1984, in the case of each application for a permit under this subsection for an incinerator facility which was submitted before such date, the Administrator shall issue a final permit pursuant to such application or issue a final denial of such application.

(B) Not later than the date eight years after November 8, 1984, in the case of each application for a permit under this subsection for any facility (other than a facility referred to in subparagraph (A)) which was submitted before such date, the Administrator shall issue a final permit pursuant to such application or issue a final denial of such application.

(C) The time periods specified in this paragraph shall also apply in the case of any State which is administering an authorized hazardous waste program under section 6926 of this title. Interim status under subsection (e) of this section shall terminate for each facility referred to in subparagraph (A)(ii) or (B) on the expiration of the five- or eight-year period referred to in subparagraph (A) or (B), whichever is applicable, unless the owner or operator of the facility applies for a final determination regarding the issuance of a permit under this subsection within—

(i) two years after November 8, 1984 (in the case of a facility referred to in subparagraph (A)(ii)), or

(ii) four years after November 8, 1984 (in the case of a facility referred to in subparagraph (B)).

(3) Any permit under this section shall be for a fixed term, not to exceed 10 years in the case of any land disposal facility, storage facility, or incinerator or other treatment facility. Each permit for a land disposal facility shall be reviewed five years after date of issuance or reissuance and shall be modified as necessary to assure that the facility continues to comply with the currently applicable requirements of this section and section 6924 of this title. Nothing in this subsection shall preclude the Administrator from reviewing and modifying a permit at any time during its term. Review of any application for a permit renewal shall consider improvements in the state of control and measurement technology as well as changes in applicable regulations. Each permit issued under this section shall contain such terms and conditions as the Administrator (or the State) determines necessary to protect human health and the environment.

(d) Permit revocation

Upon a determination by the Administrator (or by a State, in the case of a State having an authorized hazardous waste program under section 6926 of this title) of noncompliance by a facility having a permit under this chapter with the requirements of this section or section 6924 of this title, the Administrator (or State, in the case of a State having an authorized hazardous waste program under section 6926 of this title) shall revoke such permit.

(e) Interim status

(1) Any person who—

(A) owns or operates a facility required to have a permit under this section which facility—

(i) was in existence on November 19, 1980, or

(ii) is in existence on the effective date of statutory or regulatory changes under this chapter that render the facility subject to the requirement to have a permit under this section,

(B) has complied with the requirements of section 6930(a) of this title, and

(C) has made an application for a permit under this section

shall be treated as having been issued such permit until such time as final administrative disposition of such application is made, unless the Administrator or other plaintiff proves that final administrative disposition of such application has not been made because of the failure of the applicant to furnish information reasonably required or requested in order to process the application. This paragraph shall not apply to any facility which has been previously denied a permit under this section or if authority to operate the facility under this section has been previously terminated.

(2) In the case of each land disposal facility which has been granted interim status under this subsection before November 8, 1984, interim status shall terminate on the date twelve months after November 8, 1984, unless the owner or operator of such facility—

(A) applies for a final determination regarding the issuance of a permit under subsection (c) of this section for such facility before the date twelve months after November 8, 1984; and

(B) certifies that such facility is in compliance with all applicable groundwater monitoring and financial responsibility requirements.

(3) In the case of each land disposal facility which is in existence on the effective date of statutory or regulatory changes under this chapter that render the facility subject to the requirement to have a permit under this section and which is granted interim status under this subsection, interim status shall terminate on the date twelve months after the date on which the facility first becomes subject to such permit requirement unless the owner or operator of such facility—

(A) applies for a final determination regarding the issuance of a permit under subsection (c) of this section for such facility before the date twelve months after the date on which the facility first becomes subject to such permit requirement; and

(B) certifies that such facility is in compliance with all applicable groundwater monitoring and financial responsibility requirements.

(f) Coal mining wastes and reclamation permits

Notwithstanding subsection (a) through (e) of this section, any surface coal mining and reclamation permit covering any coal mining wastes or overburden which has been issued or approved under the Surface Mining Control and Reclamation Act of 1977 [30 U.S.C.A. § 1201 et seq.] shall be deemed to be a permit issued pursuant to this section with respect to the treatment, storage, or disposal of such wastes or overburden. Regulations promulgated by the Administrator under this subchapter shall not be applicable to treatment, storage, or disposal of coal mining wastes and overburden which are covered by such a permit.

(g) Research, development and demonstration permits

(1) The Administrator may issue a research, development, and demonstration permit for any hazardous waste treatment facility which proposes to utilize an innovative and experimental hazardous waste treatment technology or process for which permit standards for such experimental activity have not been promulgated under this subchapter. Any such permit shall include such terms and conditions as will assure protection of human health and the environment. Such permits—

(A) shall provide for the construction of such facilities, as necessary, and for operation of the facility for not longer than one year (unless renewed as provided in paragraph (4)), and

(B) shall provide for the receipt and treatment by the facility of only those types and quantities of hazardous waste which the Administrator deems necessary for purposes of determining the efficacy and performance capabilities of the technology or process and the effects of such technology or process on human health and the environment, and

(C) shall include such requirements as the Administrator deems necessary to protect human health and the environment (including, but not limited to, requirements regarding monitoring, operation, insurance or bonding, financial responsibility, closure, and remedial action), and such requirements as the Administrator deems necessary regarding testing and providing of information to the Administrator with respect to the operation of the facility.

The Administrator may apply the criteria set forth in this paragraph in establishing the conditions of each permit without separate establishment of regulations implementing such criteria.

(2) For the purpose of expediting review and issuance of permits under this subsection, the Administrator may, consistent with the protection of human health and the environment, modify or waive permit application and permit issuance requirements established in the Administrator's general permit regulations except that there may be no modification or

waiver of regulations regarding financial responsibility (including insurance) or of procedures established under section 6974(b)(2) of this title regarding public participation.

(3) The Administrator may order an immediate termination of all operations at the facility at any time he determines that termination is necessary to protect human health and the environment.

(4) Any permit issued under this subsection may be renewed not more than three times. Each such renewal shall be for a period of not more than 1 year.

(h) Waste minimization

Effective September 1, 1985, it shall be a condition of any permit issued under this section for the treatment, storage, or disposal of hazardous waste on the premises where such waste was generated that the permittee certify, no less often than annually, that—

(1) the generator of the hazardous waste has a program in place to reduce the volume or quantity and toxicity of such waste to the degree determined by the generator to be economically practicable; and

(2) the proposed method of treatment, storage, or disposal is that practicable method currently available to the generator which minimizes the present and future threat to human health and the environment.

(i) Interim status facilities receiving wastes after July 26, 1982

The standards concerning ground water monitoring, unsaturated zone monitoring, and corrective action, which are applicable under section 6924 of this title to new landfills, surface impoundments, land treatment units, and waste-pile units required to be permitted under subsection (c) of this section shall also apply to any landfill, surface impoundment, land treatment unit, or waste-pile unit qualifying for the authorization to operate under subsection (e) of this section which receives hazardous waste after July 26, 1982.

(j) Interim status surface impoundments

(1) Except as provided in paragraph (2), (3), or (4), each surface impoundment in existence on November 8, 1984, and qualifying for the authorization to operate under subsection (e) of this section shall not receive, store, or treat hazardous waste after the date four years after November 8, 1984, unless such surface impoundment is in compliance with the requirements of section 6924(*o*)(1)(A) of this title which would apply to such impoundment if it were new.

(2) Paragraph (1) of this subsection shall not apply to any surface impoundment which (A) has at least one liner, for which there is no evidence that such liner is leaking; (B) is located more than one-quarter mile from an underground source of drinking water; and (C) is in compliance with generally applicable ground water monitoring requirements for facilities with permits under subsection (c) of this section.

(3) Paragraph (1) of this subsection shall not apply to any surface impoundment which (A) contains treated waste water during the secondary or subsequent phases of an aggressive biological treatment facility subject to a permit issued under section 1342 of Title 33 (or which holds such treated waste water after treatment and prior to discharge); (B) is in compliance with generally applicable ground water monitoring requirements for facilities with permits under subsection (c) of this section; and (C)(i) is part of a facility in compliance with section 1311(b)(2) of Title 33, or (ii) in the case of a facility for which no effluent guidelines required under section 1314(b)(2) of Title 33 are in effect and no permit under section 1342(a)(1) of Title 33 implementing section 1311(b)(2) of Title 33 has been issued, is part of a facility in compliance with a permit under section 1342 of Title 33, which is achieving significant degradation of toxic pollutants and hazardous constituents contained in the untreated waste stream and which has identified those toxic pollutants and hazardous constituents in the untreated waste stream to the appropriate permitting authority.

(4) The Administrator (or the State, in the case of a State with an authorized program), after notice and opportunity for comment, may modify the requirements of paragraph (1) for any surface impoundment if the owner or operator demonstrates that such surface impoundment is located, designed and operated so as to assure that there will be no migration of any hazardous constitutent [2] into ground water or surface water at any future time. The Administrator or the State shall take into account locational criteria established under section 6924(*o*)(7) of this title.

(5) The owner or operator of any surface impoundment potentially subject to paragraph (1) who has reason to believe that on the basis of paragraph (2), (3), or (4) such surface impoundment is not required to comply with the requirements of paragraph (1), shall apply to the Administrator (or the State, in the case of a State with an authorized program) not later than twenty-four months after November 8, 1984, for a determination of the applicability of paragraph (1) (in the case of paragraph (2) or (3)) or for a modification of the requirements of paragraph (1) (in the case of paragraph (4)), with respect to such surface impoundment. Such owner or operator shall provide, with such application, evidence pertinent to such decision, including:

(A) an application for a final determination regarding the issuance of a permit under subsection (c) of this section for such facility, if not previously submitted;

(B) evidence as to compliance with all applicable ground water monitoring requirements and the information and analysis from such monitoring;

(C) all reasonably ascertainable evidence as to whether such surface impoundment is leaking; and

(D) in the case of applications under paragraph (2) or (3), a certification by a registered professional engineer with academic training and experience in ground water hydrology that—

(i) under paragraph (2), the liner of such surface impoundment is designed, constructed, and operated in accordance with applicable requirements, such surface impoundment is more than one-quarter mile from an underground source of drinking water and there is no evidence such liner is leaking; or

(ii) under paragraph (3), based on analysis of those toxic pollutants and hazardous constituents that are likely to be present in the untreated waste stream, such impoundment satisfies the conditions of paragraph (3).

In the case of any surface impoundment for which the owner or operator fails to apply under this paragraph within the time provided by this paragraph or paragraph (6), such surface impoundment shall comply with paragraph (1) notwithstanding paragraph (2), (3), or (4). Within twelve months after receipt of such application and evidence and not later than thirty-six months after November 8, 1984, and after notice and opportunity to comment, the Administrator (or, if appropriate, the State) shall advise such owner or operator on the applicability of paragraph (1) to such surface impoundment or as to whether and how the requirements of paragraph (1) shall be modified and applied to such surface impoundment.

(6)(A) In any case in which a surface impoundment becomes subject to paragraph (1) after November 8, 1984, due to the promulgation of additional listings or characteristics for the identification of hazardous waste under section 6921 of this title, the period for compliance in paragraph (1) shall be four years after the date of such promulgation, the period for demonstrations under paragraph (4) and for submission of evidence under paragraph (5) shall be not later than twenty-four months after the date of such promulgation, and the period for the Administrator (or if appropriate, the State) to advise such owners or operators under paragraph (5) shall be not later than thirty-six months after the date of promulgation.

(B) In any case in which a surface impoundment is initially determined to be excluded from the requirements of paragraph (1) but due to a change in condition (including the existence of a leak) no longer satisfies the provisions of paragraph (2), (3), or (4) and therefore becomes subject to paragraph (1), the period for compliance in paragraph (1) shall be two years after the date of discovery of such change of condition, or in the case of a surface impoundment excluded under paragraph (3) three years after such date of discovery.

(7)(A) The Administrator shall study and report to the Congress on the number, range of size, construction, likelihood of hazardous constituents migrating into ground water, and potential threat to human health and the environment of existing surface impoundments excluded by paragraph (3) from the requirements of paragraph (1). Such report shall address the need, feasibility, and estimated costs of subjecting such existing surface impoundments to the requirements of paragraph (1).

(B) In the case of any existing surface impoundment or class of surface impoundments from which the Administrator (or the State, in the case of a State with an authorized program) determines hazardous constituents are likely to migrate into ground water, the Administrator (or if appropriate, the State) is authorized to impose such requirements as may be necessary to protect human health and the environment, including the requirements of section 6924(*o*) of this title which would apply to such impoundments if they were new.

(C) In the case of any surface impoundment excluded by paragraph (3) from the requirements of paragraph (1) which is subsequently determined to be leaking, the Administrator (or, if appropriate, the State) shall require compliance with paragraph (1), unless the Administrator (or, if appropriate, the State) determines that such compliance is not necessary to protect human health and the environment.

(8) In the case of any surface impoundment in which the liners and leak detection system have been installed pursuant to the requirements of paragraph (1) and in good faith compliance with section 6924(*o*) of this title and the Administrator's regulations and guidance documents governing liners and leak detection systems, no liner or leak detection system which is different from that which was so installed pursuant to paragraph (1) shall be required for such unit by the Administrator when issuing the first permit under this section to such facility. Nothing in this paragraph shall preclude the Administrator from requiring installation of a new liner when the Administrator has reason to believe that any liner installed pursuant to the requirements of this subsection is leaking.

(9) In the case of any surface impoundment which has been excluded by paragraph (2) on the basis of a liner meeting the definition under paragraph (12)(A)(ii), at the closure of such impoundment the Administrator shall require the owner or operator of such impoundment to remove or decontaminate all waste residues, all contaminated liner material, and contaminated soil to the extent practicable. If all contaminated soil is not removed or decontaminated, the owner or operator of such impoundment shall be required to comply with appropriate post-closure requirements, including but not limited to ground water monitoring and corrective action.

(10) Any incremental cost attributable to the requirements of this subsection or section 6924(*o*) of this title shall not be considered by the Administrator (or the State, in the case of a State with an authorized program under section 1342 of title 33)—

(A) in establishing effluent limitations and standards under section 1311, 1314, 1316, 1317, or 1342 of title 33 based on effluent limitations guidelines and standards promulgated any time before twelve months after November 8, 1984; or

(B) in establishing any other effluent limitations to carry out the provisions of section 1311, 1317, or 1342 of Title 33 on or before October 1, 1986.

(11)(A) If the Administrator allows a hazardous waste which is prohibited from one or more methods of land disposal under subsection (d), (e) or (g) of section 6924 of this title (or under regulations promulgated by the Administrator under such subsections) to be placed in a surface impoundment (which is operating pursuant to interim status) for storage or treatment, such impoundment shall meet the requirements that are applicable to new surface impoundments under section 6924(*o*)(1) of this title, unless such impoundment meets the requirements of paragraph (2) or (4).

(B) In the case of any hazardous waste which is prohibited from one or more methods of land disposal under subsection (d), (e), or (g) of section 6924 of this title (or under regulations promulgated by the Administrator under such subsection) the placement or maintenance of such hazardous waste in a surface impoundment for treatment is prohibited as of the effective date of such prohibition unless the treatment residues which are hazardous are, at a minimum, removed for subsequent management within one year of the entry of the waste into the surface impoundment.

(12)(A) For the purposes of paragraph (2)(A) of this subsection, the term "liner" means—

(i) a liner designed, constructed, installed, and operated to prevent hazardous waste from passing into the liner at any time during the active life of the facility; or

(ii) a liner designed, constructed, installed, and operated to prevent hazardous waste from migrating beyond the liner to adjacent subsurface soil, ground water, or surface water at any time during the active life of the facility.

(B) For the purposes of this subsection, the term "aggressive biological treatment facility" means a system of surface impoundments in which the initial impoundment of the secondary treatment segment of the facility utilizes intense mechanical aeration to enhance biological activity to degrade waste water pollutants and

(i) the hydraulic retention time in such initial impoundment is no longer than 5 days under normal operating conditions, on an annual average basis;

(ii) the hydraulic retention time in such initial impoundment is no longer than thirty days under normal operating conditions, on an annual average basis: *Provided,* That the sludge in such impoundment does not constitute a hazardous waste as identified by the extraction procedure toxicity characteristic in effect on November 8, 1984; or

(iii) such system utilizes activated sludge treatment in the first portion of secondary treatment.

(C) For the purposes of this subsection, the term "underground source or [3] drinking water" has the same meaning as provided in regulations under the Safe Drinking Water Act (title XIV of the Public Health Service Act) [42 U.S.C.A. § 300f et seq.].

(13) The Administrator may modify the requirements of paragraph (1) in the case of a surface impoundment for which the owner or operator, prior to October 1, 1984, has entered into, and is in compliance with, a consent order, decree, or agreement with the Administrator or a State with an authorized program mandating corrective action with respect to such surface impoundment that provides a degree of protection of human health and the environment which is at a minimum equivalent to that provided by paragraph (1).

(Pub.L. 89–272, Title II, § 3005, as added Oct. 21, 1976, Pub.L. 94–580, § 2, 90 Stat. 2808, and amended Nov. 8, 1978, Pub.L. 95–609, § 7(h), 92 Stat. 3082; Oct. 21, 1980, Pub.L. 96–482, §§ 10, 11, 94 Stat. 2338; Nov. 8, 1984, Pub.L. 98–616, Title II, §§ 211, 212, 213(a), (c), 214(a), 215, 224(b), 243(c), 98 Stat. 3240–3243, 3253, 3261.)

[1] So in original.

2 So in original. Probably should be constituent.

3 So in original. Probably should be "of".

CROSS REFERENCES

Federally permitted release defined as including releases in compliance with legally enforceable final permit issued pursuant to this section, see section 9601 of this title.

CODE OF FEDERAL REGULATIONS

Federal waste permit program, see 40 CFR 270.1 et seq.
Requirements, see 40 CFR 122.1 et seq., 123.1 et seq., 264.1 et seq., 265.1 et seq., 267.1 et seq.
Underground injection control program, see 40 CFR 144.1 et seq., 145.1 et seq.

West's Federal Practice Manual

Solid waste disposal, see § 4385.5.

LAW REVIEW COMMENTARIES

Erosion of mens rea in environmental criminal prosecution. Ruth Ann Weidel, John R. Mayo and F. Michael Zachara, 21 Seton Hall L.Rev. 1125 (1991).

From elephants to mice: The development of EBMUD's program to control small source wastewater discharges. Raoul Stewardson, 20 Ecology L.Q. 441 (1993).

Interstate waste: A key issue in resolving the national hazardous waste capacity crisis. B.J. Wynne, III and Terri Hamby, 32 S.Tex. L.Rev. 601 (1991).

The problem with RCRA—Do the financial responsibility provisions really work? 36 Am.U.L.Rev. 133 (1986).

§ 6926. Authorized State hazardous waste programs [SWDA § 3006]

(a) Federal guidelines

Not later than eighteen months after October 21, 1976, the Administrator, after consultation with State authorities, shall promulgate guidelines to assist States in the Development of State hazardous waste programs.

(b) Authorization of State program

Any State which seeks to administer and enforce a hazardous waste program pursuant to this subchapter may develop and, after notice and opportunity for public hearing, submit to the Administrator an application, in such form as he shall require, for authorization of such program. Within ninety days following submission of an application under this subsection, the Administrator shall issue a notice as to whether or not he expects such program to be authorized, and within ninety days following such notice (and after opportunity for public hearing) he shall publish his findings as to whether or not the conditions listed in items (1), (2), and (3) below have been met. Such State is authorized to carry out such program in lieu of the Federal program under this subchapter in such State and to issue and enforce permits for the storage, treatment, or disposal of hazardous waste (and to enforce permits deemed to have been issued under section 6935(d)(1) of this title) unless, within ninety days following submission of the application the Administrator notifies such State that such program may not be authorized and, within ninety days following such notice and after opportunity for public hearing, he finds that (1) such State program is not equivalent to the Federal program under this subchapter, (2) such program is not consistent with the Federal or State programs applicable in other States, or (3) such program does not provide adequate enforcement of compliance with the requirements of this subchapter. In authorizing a State program, the Administrator may base his findings on the Federal program in effect one year prior to submission of a State's application or in effect on January 26, 1983, whichever is later.

(c) Interim authorization

(1) Any State which has in existence a hazardous waste program pursuant to State law before the date ninety days after the date of promulgation of regulations under sections 6922, 6923, 6924, and 6925 of this title, may submit to the Administrator evidence of such existing program and may request a temporary authorization to carry out such program under this subchapter. The Administrator shall, if the evidence submitted shows the existing State program to be substantially equivalent to the Federal program under this subchapter, grant an interim authorization to the State to carry out such program in lieu of the Federal program pursuant to this subchapter for a period ending no later than January 31, 1986.

(2) The Administrator shall, by rule, establish a date for the expiration of interim authorization under this subsection.

(3) Pending interim or final authorization of a State program for any State which reflects the amendments made by the Hazardous and Solid Waste Amendments of 1984, the State may enter into an agreement with the Administrator under which the State may assist in the administration of the requirements and prohibitions which take effect pursuant to such Amendments.

(4) In the case of a State permit program for any State which is authorized under subsection (b) of this section or under this subsection, until such program is amended to reflect the amendments made by the Hazardous and Solid Waste Amendments of 1984 and such program amendments receive interim or final authorization, the Administrator shall have the authority in such State to issue or deny permits or those portions of permits affected by the requirements and prohibitions established by the Hazardous and Solid Waste Amendments of 1984. The Administrator shall coordinate with States the procedures for issuing such permits.

(d) Effect of State permit

Any action taken by a State under a hazardous waste program authorized under this section shall have the same force and effect as action taken by the Administrator under this subchapter.

(e) Withdrawal of authorization

Whenever the Administrator determines after public hearing that a State is not administering and enforcing a program authorized under this section in accordance with requirements of this section, he shall so notify the State and, if appropriate corrective action is not taken within a reasonable time, not to exceed ninety days, the Administrator shall withdraw authorization of such program and establish a Federal program pursuant to this subchapter. The Administrator shall not withdraw authorization of any such program unless he shall first have notified the State, and made public, in writing, the reasons for such withdrawal.

(f) Availability of information

No State program may be authorized by the Administrator under this section unless—

(1) such program provides for the public availability of information obtained by the State regarding facilities and sites for the treatment, storage, and disposal of hazardous waste; and

(2) such information is available to the public in substantially the same manner, and to the same degree, as would be the case if the Administrator was carrying out the provisions of this subchapter in such State.

(g) Amendments made by 1984 act

(1) Any requirement or prohibition which is applicable to the generation, transportation, treatment, storage, or disposal of hazardous waste and which is imposed under this subchapter pursuant to the amendments made by the Hazardous and Solid Waste Amendments of 1984 shall take effect in each State having an interim or finally authorized State program on the same date as such requirement takes effect in other States. The administrator shall carry out such requirement directly in each such State unless the State program is finally authorized (or is granted interim authorization as provided in paragraph (2)) with respect to such requirement.

(2) Any State which, before November 8, 1984, has an existing hazardous waste program which has been granted interim or final authorization under this section may submit to the Administrator evidence that such existing program contains (or has been amended to include) any requirement which is substantially equivalent to a requirement referred to in paragraph (1) and may request interim authorization to carry out that requirement under this subchapter. The Administrator shall, if the evidence submitted shows the State requirement to be substantially equivalent to the requirement referred to in paragraph (1), grant an interim authorization to the State to carry out such requirement in lieu of direct administration in the State by the Administrator of such requirement.

(h) State programs for used oil

In the case of used oil which is not listed or identified under this subtitle as a hazardous waste but which is regulated under section 6935 of this title, the provisions of this section regarding State programs shall apply in the same manner and to the same extent as such provisions apply to hazardous waste identified or listed under this subtitle.

(Pub.L. 89–272, Title II, § 3006, as added Oct. 21, 1976, Pub.L. 94–580, § 2, 90 Stat. 2809, and amended Nov. 8, 1978, Pub.L. 95–609, § 7(i), 92 Stat. 3082; Nov. 8, 1984, Pub.L. 98–616, Title II, §§ 225, 226(a), 227, 228, 241(b)(2), 98 Stat. 3254, 3255, 3260; Oct. 17, 1986, Pub.L. 99–499, Title II, § 205(j), 100 Stat. 1703.)

West's Federal Practice Manual

Solid waste disposal, see § 4385.5.

CROSS REFERENCES

Transfer of liability becomes effective after owner or operator of hazardous waste disposal facility notifies Administrator of Environmental Protection Agency and State where it has authorized program under this section, see section 9607 of this title.

CODE OF FEDERAL REGULATIONS

State program requirements, see 40 CFR 123.1 et seq.
State program requirements, see 40 CFR 123.1 et seq., 271.1 et seq.

LAW REVIEW COMMENTARIES

Hazardous Waste Law for the federal employee after the Federal Facility Compliance Act of 1992. Stephen J. Darmody, 40 Fed. B.News & J. 650 (Nov./Dec. 1993).

Interstate waste: A key issue in resolving the national hazardous waste capacity crisis. B.J. Wynne, III and Terri Hamby, 32 S.Tex. L.Rev. 601 (1991).

Long-range planning in environmental and health regulatory agencies. Richard N.L. Andrews, 20 Ecology L.Q. 515 (1993).

Regulatory jurisdiction over non-Indian hazardous waste in Indian country. Note, 72 Iowa L.Rev. 1091 (1987).

Resolving conflicts between bankruptcy law and the state police power. Ellen E. Sward, 1987 Wis.L.Rev. 403 (1987).

§ 6927. Inspections [SWDA § 3007]

(a) Access entry

For purposes of developing or assisting in the development of any regulation or enforcing the provisions of this chapter, any person who generates, stores, treats, transports, disposes of, or otherwise handles or has handled hazardous wastes shall, upon request of any officer, employee or representative of the Environmental Protection Agency, duly designated by the Administrator, or upon request of any duly designated officer, employee or representative of a State having an authorized hazardous waste program, furnish information relating to such wastes and permit such person at all reasonable times to have access to, and to copy all records relating to such wastes. For the purposes of developing or assisting in the development of any regulation or enforcing the provisions of this chapter, such officers, employees or representatives are authorized—

(1) to enter at reasonable times any establishment or other place where hazardous wastes are or have been generated, stored, treated, disposed of, or transported from;

(2) to inspect and obtain samples from any person of any such wastes and samples of any containers or labeling for such wastes.

Each such inspection shall be commenced and completed with reasonable promptness. If the officer, employee or representative obtains any samples, prior to leaving the premises, he shall give to the owner, operator, or agent in charge a receipt describing the sample obtained and if requested a portion of each such sample equal in volume or weight to the portion retained. If any analysis is made of such samples, a copy of the results of such analysis shall be furnished promptly to the owner, operator, or agent in charge.

(b) Availability to public

(1) Any records, reports, or information (including records, reports, or information obtained by representatives of the Environmental Protection Agency) obtained from any person under this section (including records, reports, or information obtained by representatives of the Environmental Protection Agency) shall be available to the public, except that upon a showing satisfactory to the Administrator (or the State, as the case may be) by any person that records, reports, or information, or particular part thereof, to which the Administrator (or the State, as the case may be) or any officer, employee or representative thereof has access under this section if made public, would divulge information entitled to protection under section 1905 of Title 18, such information or particular portion thereof shall be considered confidential in accordance with the purposes of that section, except that such record, report, document, or information may be disclosed to other officers, employees, or authorized representatives of the United States concerned with carrying out this chapter, or when relevant in any proceeding under this chapter.

(2) Any person not subject to the provisions of section 1905 of Title 18 who knowingly and willfully divulges or discloses any information entitled to protection under this subsection shall, upon conviction, be subject to a fine of not more than $5,000 or to imprisonment not to exceed one year, or both.

(3) In submitting data under this chapter, a person required to provide such data may—

(A) designate the data which such person believes is entitled to protection under this subsection, and

(B) submit such designated data separately from other data submitted under this chapter.

A designation under this paragraph shall be made in writing and in such manner as the Administrator may prescribe.

(4) Notwithstanding any limitation contained in this section or any other provision of law, all information reported to, or otherwise obtained by, the Administrator (or any representative of the Administrator) under this chapter shall be made available, upon written request of any duly authorized committee of the Congress, to such committee.

(c) Federal facility inspections

The Administrator shall undertake on an annual basis a thorough inspection of each facility for the treatment, storage, or disposal of hazardous waste which is owned or operated by a department, agency, or instrumentality of the United States to enforce its compliance with this subchapter and the regulations promulgated thereunder. Any State with an authorized hazardous waste program also may conduct an inspection of any such facility for purposes of enforcing the facility's compliance with the State hazardous waste program. The records of such inspections shall be available to the public as provided in subsection (b) of this section. The department, agency, or instrumentality owning or operating each such facility shall reimburse the Environmental Protection Agency for the costs of the inspection of the facility. With respect to the first inspection of each such facility occurring after October 6, 1992, the Administrator shall conduct a comprehensive ground water monitoring evaluation at the facility, unless such an evaluation was conducted during the 12–month period preceding October 6, 1992.

(d) State-operated facilities

The Administrator shall annually undertake a through inspection of every facility for the treatment, storage, or disposal of hazardous waste which is operated by a State or local government for which a permit is required under section 6925 of this title. The records of such inspection shall be available to the public as provided in subsection (b) of this section.

(e) Mandatory inspections

(1) The Administrator (or the State in the case of a State having an authorized hazardous waste program under this subchapter) shall commence a program to thoroughly inspect every facility for the treatment, storage, or disposal of hazardous waste for which a permit is required under section 6925 of this title no less often than every two years as to its compliance with this subchapter (and the regulations promulgated under this subchapter). Such inspections shall commence not later than twelve months after November 8, 1984. The Administrator shall, after notice and opportunity for public comment, promulgate regulations governing the minimum frequency and manner of such inspections, including the manner in which records of such inspections shall be maintained and the manner in which reports of such inspections shall be filed. The Administrator may distinguish between classes and categories of facilities commensurate with the risks posed by each class or category.

(2) Not later than six months after November 8, 1984, the Administrator shall submit to the Congress a report on the potential for inspections of hazardous waste treatment, storage, or disposal facilities by nongovernmental inspectors as a supplement to inspections conducted by officers, employees, or representatives of the Environmental Protection Agency or States having authorized hazardous waste programs or operating under a cooperative agreement with the Administrator. Such report shall be prepared in cooperation with the States, insurance companies offering environmental impairment insurance, independent companies providing inspection services, and other such groups as appropriate. Such report shall contain recommendations on provisions and requirements for a program of private inspections to supplement governmental inspections.

(Pub.L. 89–272, Title II, § 3007, as added Oct. 21, 1976, Pub.L. 94–580, § 2, 90 Stat. 2810, and amended Nov. 8, 1978, Pub.L. 95–609, § 7(j), 92 Stat. 3082; Oct. 21, 1980, Pub.L. 96–482, § 12, 94 Stat. 2339; Nov. 8, 1984, Pub.L. 98–616, Title II, §§ 229–231, Title V, § 502(a), 98 Stat. 3255, 3256, 3276; Oct. 6, 1992, Pub.L. 102–386, Title I, § 104, 106 Stat. 1507.)

CROSS REFERENCES

Guidelines for using the imminent hazard, enforcement, and emergency response authorities to include powers authorized by this section, see section 9606 of this title.

CODE OF FEDERAL REGULATIONS

Definitions, additional requirements, see 40 CFR 122.1 et seq.
Hazardous waste management generally, see 40 CFR 260.1 et seq. to 271.1 et seq.
Hazardous waste treatment facilities, standards for owners and operators, see 40 CFR 264.1 et seq., 265.1 et seq.
Public information, see 40 CFR 2.100 et seq.
State program requirements, see 40 CFR 123.1 et seq.

LAW REVIEW COMMENTARIES

Interstate waste: A key issue in resolving the national hazardous waste capacity crisis. B.J. Wynne, III and Terri Hamby, 32 S.Tex. L.Rev. 601 (1991).

§ 6928. Federal enforcement [SWDA § 3008]

(a) Compliance orders

(1) Except as provided in paragraph (2), whenever on the basis of any information the Administrator determines that any person has violated or is in violation of any requirement of this subchapter, the Administrator may issue an order assessing a civil penalty for any past or current violation, requiring compliance immediately or within a specified time period, or both, or the Administrator may commence a civil action in the United States district court in the district in which the violation occurred for appropriate relief, including a temporary or permanent injunction.

(2) In the case of a violation of any requirement of this subchapter where such violation occurs in a State which is authorized to carry out a hazardous waste program under section 6926 of this title, the Administrator shall give notice to the State in which such violation has occurred prior to issuing an order or commencing a civil action under this section.

(3) Any order issued pursuant to this subsection may include a suspension or revocation of any permit issued by the Administrator or a State under this subchapter and shall state with reasonable specificity the nature of the violation. Any penalty assessed in the order shall not exceed $25,000 per day of noncompliance for each violation of a requirement of this subchapter. In assessing such a penalty, the Administrator shall take into account the seriousness of the violation and any good faith efforts to comply with applicable requirements.

(b) Public hearing

Any order issued under this section shall become final unless, no later than thirty days after the order is served, the person or persons named therein request a public hearing. Upon such request the Administrator shall promptly conduct a public hearing. In connection with any proceeding under this section the Administrator may issue subpenas for the attendance and testimony of witnesses and the production of relevant papers, books, and documents, and may promulgate rules for discovery procedures.

(c) Violation of compliance orders

If a violator fails to take corrective action within the time specified in a compliance order, the Administrator may assess a civil penalty of not more than $25,000 for each day of continued noncompliance with the order and the Administrator may suspend or revoke any permit issued to the violator (whether issued by the Administrator or the State).

(d) Criminal penalties

Any person who—

(1) knowingly transports or causes to be transported any hazardous waste identified or listed under this subchapter to a facility which does not have a permit under this subchapter or pursuant to title I of the Marine Protection, Research, and Sanctuaries Act (86 Stat. 1052) [33 U.S.C.A. § 1411 et seq.],

(2) knowingly treats, stores, or disposes of any hazardous waste identified or listed under this subchapter—

(A) without a permit under this subchapter or pursuant to title I of the Marine Protection, Research, and Sanctuaries Act (86 Stat. 1052) [33 U.S.C.A § 1411 et seq.]; or

(B) in knowing violation of any material condition or requirement of such permit;

(C) in knowing violation of any material condition or requirement of any applicable interim status regulations or standards;

(3) knowingly omits material information or makes any false material statement or representation in any application, label, manifest, record, report, permit, or other document filed, maintained, or used for purposes of compliance with regulations promulgated by the Administrator (or by a State in the case of an authorized State program) under this subchapter;

(4) knowingly generates, stores, treats, transports, disposes of, exports, or otherwise handles any hazardous waste or any used oil not identified or listed as a hazardous waste under this subchapter (whether such activity took place before or takes place after the date of the enactment of this paragraph) and who knowingly destroys, alters, conceals, or fails to file any record, application, manifest, report, or other document required to be maintained or filed for purposes of compliance with regulations promulgated by the Administrator (or by a State in the case of an authorized State program) under this subchapter;

(5) knowingly transports without a manifest, or causes to be transported without a manifest, any hazardous waste or any used oil not identified or listed as a hazardous waste under this subchapter required by regulations promulgated under this subchapter (or by a State in the case of a State program authorized under this subchapter) to be accompanied by a manifest;

(6) knowingly exports a hazardous waste identified or listed under this subchapter (A) without the consent of the receiving country or, (B) where there exists an international agreement between the United States and the government of the receiving country establishing notice, export, and enforcement procedures for the transportation, treatment, storage, and disposal of hazardous wastes, in a manner which is not in conformance with such agreement; or

(7) knowingly stores, treats, transports, or causes to be transported, disposes of, or otherwise handles any used oil not identified or listed as a hazardous waste under this subchapter—

(A) in knowing violation of any material condition or requirement of a permit under this subchapter; or

(B) in knowing violation of any material condition or requirement of any applicable regulations or standards under this chapter;

shall, upon conviction, be subject to a fine of not more than $50,000 for each day of violation, or imprisonment not to exceed two years (five years in the case of a violation of paragraph (1) or (2)), or both. If the conviction is for a violation committed after a first conviction of such person under this paragraph, the maximum punishment under the respective paragraph shall be doubled with respect to both fine and imprisonment.

(e) Knowing endangerment

Any person who knowingly transports, treats, stores, disposes of, or exports any hazardous waste identified or listed under this subchapter or used oil not identified or listed as a hazardous waste under this subchapter in violation of paragraph (1), (2), (3), (4), (5), (6), or (7) of subsection (d) of this section who knows at that time that he thereby places another person in imminent danger of death or serious bodily injury, shall, upon conviction, be subject to a fine of not more than $250,000 or imprisonment for not more than fifteen years, or both. A defendant that is an organization shall, upon conviction of violating this subsection, be subject to a fine of not more than $1,000,000.

(f) Special rules

For the purposes of subsection (e) of this section—

(1) A person's state of mind is knowing with respect to—

(A) his conduct, if he is aware of the nature of his conduct;

(B) an existing circumstance, if he is aware or believes that the circumstance exists; or

(C) a result of his conduct, if he is aware or believes that his conduct is substantially certain to cause danger of death or serious bodily injury.

(2) In determining whether a defendant who is a natural person knew that his conduct placed another person in imminent danger of death or serious bodily injury—

(A) the person is responsible only for actual awareness or actual belief that he possessed; and

(B) knowledge possessed by a person other than the defendant but not by the defendant himself may not be attributed to the defendant;

Provided, That in proving the defendant's possession of actual knowledge, circumstantial evidence may be used, including evidence that the defendant took affirmative steps to shield himself from relevant information.

(3) It is an affirmative defense to a prosecution that the conduct charged was consented to by the person endangered and that the danger and conduct charged were reasonably foreseeable hazards of—

(A) an occupation, a business, or a profession; or

(B) medical treatment or medical or scientific experimentation conducted by professionally approved methods and such other person had been made aware of the risks involved prior to giving consent.

The defendant may establish an affirmative defense under this subsection by a preponderance of the evidence.

(4) All general defenses, affirmative defenses, and bars to prosecution that may apply with respect to other Federal criminal offenses may apply under subsection (e) of this section and shall be determined by the courts of the United States according to the principles of common law as they may be interpreted in the light of reason and experience. Concepts of justification and excuse applicable under this section may be developed in the light of reason and experience.

(5) The term "organization" means a legal entity, other than a government, established or organized for any purpose, and such term includes a corporation, company, association, firm, partnership, joint stock company, foundation, institution, trust, society, union, or any other association of persons.

(6) The term "serious bodily injury" means—

(A) bodily injury which involves a substantial risk of death;

(B) unconsciousness;

(C) extreme physical pain;

(D) protracted and obvious disfigurement; or

(E) protracted loss or impairment of the function of a bodily member, organ, or mental faculty.

(g) Civil penalty

Any person who violates any requirement of this subchapter shall be liable to the United States for a civil penalty in an amount not to exceed $25,000 for each such violation. Each day of such violation shall, for purposes of this subsection, constitute a separate violation.

(h) Interim status corrective action

(1) Whenever on the basis of any information the Administrator determines that there is or has been a release of hazardous waste into the environment from a facility authorized to operate under section 6925(e) of this title, the Administrator may issue an order requiring corrective action or such other response measure as he deems necessary to protect human health or the environment or the Administrator may commence a civil action in the United States district court in the district in which the facility is located for appropriate relief, including a temporary or permanent injunction.

(2) Any order issued under this subsection may include a suspension or revocation of authorization to operate under section 6925(e) of this title, shall state with reasonable specificity the nature of the required corrective action or other response measure, and shall specify a time for compliance. If any person named in an order fails to comply with the order, the Administrator may assess, and such person shall be liable to the United States for, a civil penalty in an amount not to exceed $25,000 for each day of noncompliance with the order.

(Pub.L. 89–272, Title II, § 3008, as added Oct. 21, 1976, Pub.L. 94–580, § 2, 90 Stat. 2811, and amended Nov. 8, 1978, Pub.L. 95–609, § 7(k), 92 Stat. 3082; Oct. 21, 1980, Pub.L. 96–482, § 13, 94 Stat. 2339; Nov. 8, 1984, Pub.L. 98–616, Title II, §§ 232, 233, 245(c), Title IV, § 403(d)(1)–(3), 98 Stat. 3256, 3257, 3264, 3272; Oct. 17, 1986, Pub.L. 99–499, Title II, § 205(i), 100 Stat. 1703.)

CROSS REFERENCES

Guidelines for using the imminent hazard, enforcement, and emergency response authorities to include powers authorized by this section, see section 9606 of this title.

CODE OF FEDERAL REGULATIONS

Debarment and suspension, see 40 CFR, 32.100 et seq.

Permits, rules concerning revocation and suspension of, see 40 CFR 22.01 et seq.

LAW REVIEW COMMENTARIES

Businesses beware: Personal liability looms for environmental offenses. Joseph G. Maternowski, 62 Hennepin Law. (Mn.) 12 (Nov.–Dec. 1992).

Considerations of the scienter requirement and the responsible corporate officer doctrine for knowing violations of environmental statutes. Kevin L. Colbert, 33 S.Tex.L.Rev. 699 (1992).

Corporate environmental crimes. Larry G. Gutterridge and Judith M. Praitis, 16 L.A.Law. 26 (Dec. 1993).

Criminal enforcement of environmental regulations. Daniel J. Gibby and Daniel L. Eide, 67 Fla.B.J. 72 (May 1993).

Criminal liability for violations of federal hazardous waste law: The "knowledge" of corporations and their executives. Christopher Harris, Patrick O. Cavanaugh and Robert L. Zisk, 23 Wake Forest L.Rev. 203 (1988).

Erosion of mens rea in environmental criminal prosecution. Ruth Ann Weidel, John R. Mayo and F. Michael Zachara, 21 Seton Hall L.Rev. 1125 (1991).

Hazardous Waste: A threat to the lender's environment. Marcy Sharon Cohen, 19 UCC L.J. 99 (1986).

Hazardous Waste Law for the federal employee after the Federal Facility Compliance Act of 1992. Stephen J. Darmody, 40 Fed. B.News & J. 650 (Nov./Dec. 1993).

How well can states enforce their environmental laws when the polluter is the United States Government? 18 Rutgers L.J. 123 (1986).

Interstate waste: A key issue in resolving the national hazardous waste capacity crisis. B.J. Wynne, III and Terri Hamby, 32 S.Tex. L.Rev. 601 (1991).

Prosecution of corporations and corporate officers for environmental crimes: Limiting one's exposure for environmental criminal liability. Kenneth A. Hodson, Sarah N. McGiffert and Marianne T. Bayardi, 34 Ariz.L.Rev. 553 (1992).

Responding to a government environmental investigation: Shaping the defense. Francis J. Burke, Jr., Karen A. Potts, Leigh Lani Brown, Robin L. De Respino and Michael R. Hall, 34 Ariz.L.Rev. 509 (1992).

Responsible corporate officer: Designated felon or legal fiction? Brenda S. Hustis and John Y. Gotanda, 25 Loy.U.Chi.L.J. 169 (1994).

Survey of federal and state environmental crime legislation. Edward F. Novak and Charles W. Steese, 34 Ariz.L.Rev. 571 (1992).

§ 6929. Retention of State authority [SWDA § 3009]

Upon the effective date of regulations under this subchapter no State or political subdivision may impose any requirements less stringent than those authorized under this subchapter respecting the same matter as governed by such regulations, except that if application of a regulation with respect to any matter under this subchapter is postponed or enjoined by the action of any court, no State or political subdivision shall be prohibited from acting with respect to the same aspect of such matter until such time as such regulation takes effect. Nothing in this chapter shall be construed to prohibit any State or political subdivision thereof from imposing any requirements, including those for site selection, which are more stringent than those imposed by such regulations. Nothing in this chapter (or in any regulation adopted under this chapter) shall be construed to prohibit any State from requiring that the State be provided with a copy of each manifest used in connection with hazardous waste which is generated within that State or transported to a treatment, storage, or disposal facility within that State.

(Pub.L. 89–272, Title II, § 3009, as added Oct. 21, 1976, Pub.L. 94–580, § 2, 90 Stat. 2812, and amended Oct. 21, 1980, Pub.L. 96–482, § 14, 94 Stat. 2342; Nov. 8, 1984, Pub.L. 98–616, Title II, § 213(b), 98 Stat. 3242.)

LAW REVIEW COMMENTARIES

Interstate waste: A key issue in resolving the national hazardous waste capacity crisis. B.J. Wynne, III and Terri Hamby, 32 S.Tex. L.Rev. 601 (1991).

Oil Pollution Act of 1990: Opening a new era in federal and Texas regulation of oil spill prevention, containment and cleanup, and liability. J.B. Ruhl and Michael J. Jewell, 32 S.Tex.L.Rev. 475 (1991).

United States Supreme Court

Preemption, validity of state control prohibiting importation of solid or liquid waste, see City of Philadelphia v. New Jersey, 1978, 98 S.Ct. 2531, 437 U.S. 617, 57 L.Ed.2d 475.

§ 6930. Effective date [SWDA § 3010]

(a) Preliminary notification

Not later than ninety days after promulgation of regulations under section 6921 of this title identifying by its characteristics or listing any substance as hazardous waste subject to this subchapter, any person generating or transporting such substance or owning or operating a facility for treatment, storage, or disposal of such substance shall file with the Administrator (or with States having authorized hazardous waste permit programs under section 6926 of this title) a notification stating the location and general description of such activity and the identified or listed hazardous wastes handled by such person. Not later than fifteen months after November 8, 1984—

(1) the owner or operator of any facility which produces a fuel (A) from any hazardous waste identified or listed under section 6921 of this title, (B) from such hazardous waste identified or listed under section 6921 of this title and any other material, (C) from used oil, or (D) from used oil and any other material;

(2) the owner or operator of any facility (other than a single- or two-family residence) which burns for purposes of energy recovery any fuel produced as provided in paragraph (1) or any fuel which otherwise contains used oil or any hazardous waste identified or listed under section 6921 of this title; and

(3) any person who distributes or markets any fuel which is produced as provided in paragraph (1) or any fuel which otherwise contains used oil or any hazardous waste identified or listed under section 6921 of this title

shall file with the Administrator (and with the State in the case of a State with an authorized hazardous waste program) a notification stating the location and general description of the facility, together with a description of the identified or listed hazardous waste involved and, in the case of a facility referred to in paragraph (1) or (2), a description of the production or energy recovery activity carried out at the facility and such other information as the Administrator deems necessary. For purposes of the preceding sentence, the term "hazardous waste listed under section 6921 of this title" also includes any commercial chemical product which is listed under section 6921 of this title and which, in lieu of its original intended use, is (i) produced for use as (or as a component of) a fuel, (ii) distributed for use as a fuel, or (iii) burned as a fuel. Notification shall not be required under the second sentence of this subsection in the case of facilities (such as residential boilers) where the Administrator determines that such notification is not necessary in order for the Administrator to obtain sufficient information respecting current practices of facilities using hazardous waste for energy recovery. Nothing in this subsection shall be construed to affect or impair the provisions of section 6921(b)(3) of this title. Nothing in this subsection shall affect regulatory determinations under section 6935 of this title. In revising any regulation under section 6921 of this title identifying additional characteristics of hazardous waste or listing any additional substance as hazardous waste subject to this subchapter, the Administrator may require any person referred to in the preceding provisions to file with the Administrator (or with States having authorized hazardous waste permit programs under section 6926 of this title) the notification described in the preceding provisions. Not more than one such notification shall be required to be filed with respect to the same substance. No identified or listed hazardous waste subject to this subchapter may be transported, treated, stored, or disposed of unless notification has been given as required under this subsection.

(b) Effective date of regulation

The regulations under this subchapter respecting requirements applicable to the generation, transportation, treatment, storage, or disposal of hazardous waste (including requirements respecting permits for such treatment, storage, or disposal) shall take effect on the date six months after the date of promulgation thereof (or six months after the date of revision in the case of any regulation which is revised after the date required for promulgation thereof). At the time a regulation is promulgated, the Administrator may provide for a shorter period prior to the effective date, or an immediate effective date for:

(1) a regulation with which the Administrator finds the regulated community does not need six months to come into compliance;

(2) a regulation which responds to an emergency situation; or

(3) other good cause found and published with the regulation.

(Pub.L. 89–272, Title II, § 3010, as added Oct. 21, 1976, Pub.L. 94–580, § 2, 90 Stat. 2812, and amended Oct. 21, 1980, Pub.L. 96–482, § 15, 94 Stat. 2342; Nov. 8, 1984, Pub.L. 98–616, Title II, §§ 204(a), 234, 98 Stat. 3235, 3258.)

§ 6931. Authorization of assistance to States [SWDA § 3011]

(a) Authorization of appropriations

There is authorized to be appropriated $25,000,000 for each of the fiscal years 1978 and 1979[1] $20,000,000 for fiscal year 1980, $35,000,000 for fiscal year 1981, $40,000,000 for the fiscal year 1982, $55,000,000 for the fiscal year 1985, $60,000,000 for the fiscal year 1986, $60,000,000 for the fiscal year 1987, and $60,000,000 for the fiscal year 1988 to be used to make grants to the States for purposes of assisting the States in the development and implementation of authorized State hazardous waste programs.

(b) Allocation

Amounts authorized to be appropriated under subsection (a) of this section shall be allocated among the States on the basis of regulations promulgated by the Administrator, after consultation with the States, which take into account, the extent to which hazardous waste is generated, transported, treated, stored, and disposed of within such State, the extent of exposure of human beings and the environment within such State to such waste, and such other factors as the Administrator deems appropriate.

(c) Activities included

State hazardous waste programs for which grants may be made under subsection (a) of this section may include (but shall not be limited to) planning for hazardous waste treatment, storage and disposal facilities, and the development and execution of programs to protect health and the environment from inactive facilities which may contain hazardous waste.

(Pub.L. 89–272, Title II, § 3011, as added Oct. 21, 1976, Pub.L. 94–580, § 2, 90 Stat. 2812, and amended Oct. 21, 1980, Pub.L. 96–482, §§ 16, 31(b), 94 Stat. 2342, 2352; Nov. 8, 1984, Pub.L. 98–616, § 2(b), 98 Stat. 3222.)

[1] So in original. A comma is probably needed.

CODE OF FEDERAL REGULATIONS

State and local assistance, see 40 CFR 35.001 et seq.

LAW REVIEW COMMENTARIES

How well can states enforce their environmental laws when the polluter is the United States Government? 18 Rutgers L.J. 123 (1986).

§ 6932. Transferred

Codification

Section 6932, Pub.L. 89–272, Title II, § 3012, as added Pub.L. 96–463, § 7(a), Oct. 15, 1980, 94 Stat. 2057, was redesignated section 3014 of Pub.L. 89–272, and is set out as section 6935 of this title.

§ 6933. Hazardous waste site inventory [SWDA § 3012]

(a) State inventory programs

Each State shall, as expeditiously as practicable, undertake a continuing program to compile, publish, and submit to the Administrator an inventory describing the location of each site within such State at which hazardous waste has at any time been stored or disposed of. Such inventory shall contain—

(1) a description of the location of the sites at which any such storage or disposal has taken place before the date on which permits are required under section 6925 of this title for such storage or disposal;

(2) such information relating to the amount, nature, and toxicity of the hazardous waste at each such site as may be practicable to obtain and as may be necessary to determine the extent of any health hazard which may be associated with such site;

(3) the name and address, or corporate headquarters of, the owner of each such site, determined as of the date of preparation of the inventory;

(4) an identification of the types or techniques of waste treatment or disposal which have been used at each such site; and

(5) information concerning the current status of the site, including information respecting whether or not hazardous waste is currently being treated or disposed of at such site (and if not, the date on which such activity ceased) and information respecting the nature of any other activity currently carried out at such site.

For purposes of assisting the States in compiling information under this section, the Administrator shall make available to each State undertaking a program under this section such information as is available to him concerning the items specified in paragraphs (1) through (5) with respect to the sites within such State, including such information as the Administrator is able to obtain from other agencies or departments of the United States and from surveys and studies carried out by any committee or subcommittee of the Congress. Any State may exercise the authority of section 6927 of this title for purposes of this section in the same manner and to the same extent as provided in such section in the case of States having an authorized hazardous waste program, and any State may by order require any person to submit such information as may be necessary to compile the data referred to in paragraphs (1) through (5).

(b) Environmental Protection Agency program

If the Administrator determines that any State program under subsection (a) of this section is not adequately providing information respecting the sites in such State referred to in subsection (a) of this section, the Administrator shall notify the State. If within ninety days following such notification, the State program has not been revised or amended in such manner as will adequately provide such information, the Administrator shall carry out the inventory program in such State. In any such case—

(1) the Administrator shall have the authorities provided with respect to State programs under subsection (a) of this section;

(2) the funds allocated under subsection (c) of this section for grants to States under this section may be used by the Administrator for carrying out such program in such State; and

(3) no further expenditure may be made for grants to such State under this section until such time as the Administrator determines that such State is carrying out, or will carry out, an inventory program which meets the requirements of this section.

(c) Grants

(1) Upon receipt of an application submitted by any State to carry out a program under this section, the Administrator may make grants to the States for purposes of carrying out such a program. Grants under this section shall be allocated among the several States by the Administrator based upon such regulations as he prescribes to carry out the purposes of this section. The Administrator may make grants to any State which has conducted an inventory program which effectively carried out the purposes of this section before October 21, 1980, to reimburse such State for all, or any portion of, the costs incurred by such State in conducting such program.

(2) There are authorized to be appropriated to carry out this section $25,000,000 for each of the fiscal years 1985 through 1988.

(d) No impediment to immediate remedial action

Nothing in this section shall be construed to provide that the Administrator or any State should, pending completion of the inventory required under this section, postpone undertaking any enforcement or remedial action with respect to any site at which hazardous waste has been treated, stored, or disposed of.

(Pub.L. 89–272, Title II, § 3012, as added Oct. 21, 1980, Pub.L. 96–482, § 17(a), 94 Stat. 2342, and amended Nov. 8, 1984, Pub.L. 98–616, § 2(c), 98 Stat. 3222.)

§ 6934. Monitoring, analysis, and testing [SWDA § 3013]

(a) Authority of Administrator

If the Administrator determines, upon receipt of any information, that—

(1) the presence of any hazardous waste at a facility or site at which hazardous waste is, or has been, stored, treated, or disposed of, or

(2) the release of any such waste from such facility or site

may present a substantial hazard to human health or the environment, he may issue an order requiring the owner or operator of such facility or site to conduct such monitoring, testing, analysis, and reporting with respect to such facility or site as the Administrator deems reasonable to ascertain the nature and extent of such hazard.

(b) Previous owners and operators

In the case of any facility or site not in operation at the time a determination is made under subsection (a) of this section with respect to the facility or site, if the Administrator finds that the owner of such facility or site could not reasonably be expected to have actual knowledge of the presence of hazardous waste at such facility or site and of its potential for release, he may issue an order requiring the most recent previous owner or operator of such facility or site who could reasonably be expected to have such actual knowledge to carry out the actions referred to in subsection (a) of this section.

(c) Proposal

An order under subsection (a) or (b) of this section shall require the person to whom such order is issued to submit to the Administrator within 30 days from the issuance of such order a proposal for carrying out the required monitoring, testing, analysis, and reporting. The Administrator may, after providing such person with an opportunity to confer with the Administrator respecting such proposal, require such person to carry out such monitoring, testing, analysis, and reporting in accordance with such proposal, and such modifications in such proposal as the Administrator deems reasonable to ascertain the nature and extent of the hazard.

(d) Monitoring, etc., carried out by Administrator

(1) If the Administrator determines that no owner or operator referred to in subsection (a) or (b) of this section is able to conduct monitoring, testing, analysis, or reporting satisfactory to the Administrator, if the Administrator deems any such action carried out by an owner or operator to be unsatisfactory, or if the Administrator cannot initially determine that there is an owner or operator referred to in subsection (a) or (b) of this section who is able to conduct such monitoring, testing, analysis, or reporting, he may—

(A) conduct monitoring, testing, or analysis (or any combination thereof) which he deems reasonable to ascertain the nature and extent of the hazard associated with the site concerned, or

(B) authorize a State or local authority or other person to carry out any such action,

and require, by order, the owner or operator referred to in subsection (a) or (b) of this section to reimburse the Administrator or other authority or person for the costs of such activity.

(2) No order may be issued under this subsection requiring reimbursement of the costs of any action carried out by the Administrator which confirms the results of an order issued under subsection (a) or (b) of this section.

(3) For purposes of carrying out this subsection, the Administrator or any authority or other person authorized under paragraph (1), may exercise the authorities set forth in section 6927 of this title.

(e) Enforcement

The Administrator may commence a civil action against any person who fails or refuses to comply with any order issued under this section. Such action shall be brought in the United States district court in which the defendant is located, resides, or is doing business. Such court shall have jurisdiction to require compliance with such order and to assess a civil penalty of not to exceed $5,000 for each day during which such failure or refusal occurs.

(Pub.L. 89–272, Title II, § 3013, as added Oct. 21, 1980, Pub.L. 96–482, § 17(a), 94 Stat. 2344.)

CROSS REFERENCES

Guidelines for using the imminent hazard, enforcement, and emergency response authorities to include powers authorized by this section, see section 9606 of this title.

§ 6935. Restrictions on recycled oil [SWDA § 3014]

(a) In general

Not later than one year after October 15, 1980, the Administrator shall promulgate regulations establishing such performance standards and other requirements as may be necessary to protect the public health and the environment from hazards associated with recycled oil. In developing such regulations, the Administrator shall conduct an analysis of the economic impact of the regulations on the oil recycling industry. The Administrator shall ensure that such regulations do not discourage the recovery or recycling of used oil, consistent with the protection of human health and the environment.

(b) Identification or listing of used oil as hazardous waste

Not later than twelve months after November 8, 1984, the Administrator shall propose whether to list or identify used automobile and truck crankcase oil as hazardous waste under section 6921 of this title. Not later than twenty-four months after November 8, 1984, the Administrator shall make a final determination whether to list or identify used automobile and truck crankcase oil and other used oil as hazardous wastes under section 6921 of this title.

(c) Used oil which is recycled

(1) With respect to generators and transporters of used oil identified or listed as a hazardous waste under section 6921 of this title, the standards promulgated under section 6921(d), 6922, and 6923 of this title shall not apply to such used oil if such used oil is recycled.

(2)(A) In the case of used oil which is exempt under paragraph (1), not later than twenty-four months after November 8, 1984, the Administrator shall promulgate such standards under this subsection regarding the generation and transportation of used oil which is recycled as may be necessary to protect human health and the environment. In promulgating such regulations with respect to generators, the Administrator shall take into account the effect of such regulations on environmentally acceptable types of used oil recycling and the effect of such regulations on small quantity generators and generators which are small businesses (as defined by the Administrator).

(B) The regulations promulgated under this subsection shall provide that no generator of used oil which is exempt under paragraph (1) from the standards promulgated under section 6921(d), 6922, and 6923 of this title shall be subject to any manifest requirement or any associated recordkeeping and reporting requirement with respect to such used oil if such generator—

(i) either—

(I) enters into an agreement or other arrangement (including an agreement or arrangement with an independent transporter or with an agent of the recycler) for delivery of such used oil to a recycling facility which has a permit under section 6925(c) of this title (or for which a valid permit is deemed to be in effect under subsection (d) of this section), or

(II) recycles such used oil at one or more facilities of the generator which has such a permit under section 6925 of this title (or for which a valid permit is deemed to have been issued under subsection (d) of this section);

(ii) such used oil is not mixed by the generator with other types of hazardous wastes; and

(iii) the generator maintains such records relating to such used oil, including records of agreements or other arrangements for delivery of such used oil to any recycling facility referred to in clause (i)(I), as the Administrator deems necessary to protect human health and the environment.

(3) The regulations under this subsection regarding the transportation of used oil which is exempt from the standards promulgated under section 6921(d), 6922, and 6923 of this title under paragraph (1) shall require the transporters of such used oil to deliver such used oil to a facility which has a valid permit under section 6925 of this title or which is deemed to have a valid permit under subsection (d) of this section. The Administrator shall also establish other standards for such transporters as may be necessary to protect human health and the environment.

(d) Permits

(1) The owner or operator of a facility which recycles used oil which is exempt under subsection (c)(1) of this section, shall be deemed to have a permit under this subsection for all such treatment or recycling (and any associated tank or container storage) if such owner and operator comply with standards promulgated by the Administrator under section 6924 of this title; except that the Administrator may require such owners and operators to obtain an individual permit under section 6925(c) of this title if he determines that an individual permit is necessary to protect human health and the environment.

(2) Notwithstanding any other provision of law, any generator who recycles used oil which is exempt under subsection (c)(1) of this section shall not be required to obtain a permit under section 6925(c) of this title with respect to such used oil until the Administrator has promulgated standards under section 6924 of this title regarding the recycling of such used oil.

(Pub.L. 89–272, Title II, § 3014, formerly § 3012, as added Oct. 15, 1980, Pub.L. 96–463, § 7(a), 94 Stat. 2057, renumbered and amended Nov. 8, 1984, Pub.L. 98–616, Title II, §§ 241(a), 242, Title V, § 502(g)(1), 98 Stat. 3258, 3260, 3277.)

§ 6936. Expansion during interim status [SWDA § 3015]

(a) Waste piles

The owner or operator of a waste pile qualifying for the authorization to operate under section 6925(e) of this title shall be subject to the same requirements for liners and leachate collection systems or equivalent protection provided in regulations promulgated by the Administrator under section 6924 of this title before October 1, 1982, or revised under section 6924(*o*) of this title (relating to minimum technological requirements), for new facilities receiving individual permits under subsection (c) of section 6925 of this title, with respect to each new unit, replacement of an existing unit, or lateral expansion of an existing unit that is within the waste management area identified in the permit application submitted under section 6925 of this title, and with respect to waste received beginning six months after November 8, 1984.

(b) Landfills and surface impoundments

(1) The owner or operator of a landfill or surface impoundment qualifying for the authorization to operate under section 6925(e) of this title shall be subject to the requirements of section 6924(*o*)of this title (relating to minimum technological requirements), with respect to each new unit, replacement of an existing unit, or lateral expansion of an existing unit that is within the waste management area identified in the permit application submitted under this section, and with respect to waste received beginning 6 months after November 8, 1984.

(2) The owner or operator of each unit referred to in paragraph (1) shall notify the Administrator (or the State, if appropriate) at least sixty days prior to receiving waste. The Administrator (or the State) shall require the filing, within six months of receipt of such notice, of an application for a final determination regarding the issuance of a permit for each facility submitting such notice.

(3) In the case of any unit in which the liner and leachate collection system has been installed pursuant to the requirements of this section and in good faith compliance with the Administrator's regulations and guidance documents governing liners and leachate collection systems, no liner or leachate collection system which is different from that which was so installed pursuant to this section shall be required for such unit by the Administrator when issuing the first permit under section 6925 of this title to such facility, except that the Administrator shall not be precluded from requiring installation of a new liner when the Administrator has reason to believe that any liner installed pursuant to the requirements of this section is leaking. The Administrator may, under section 6924 of this title, amend the requirements for liners and leachate collection systems required under this section as may be necessary to provide additional protection for human health and the environment.

(Pub.L. 89–272, Title II, § 3015, as added Nov. 8, 1984, Pub.L. 98–616, Title II, § 243(a), 98 Stat. 3260.)

§ 6937. Inventory of Federal agency hazardous waste facilities [SWDA § 3016]

(a) Program requirement; submission; availability; contents

Each Federal agency shall undertake a continuing program to compile, publish, and submit to the Administrator (and to the State in the case of sites in States having an authorized hazardous waste program) an inventory of each site which the Federal agency owns or operates or has owned or operated at which hazardous waste is stored, treated, or disposed of or has been disposed of at any time. The inventory shall be submitted every two years beginning January 31, 1986. Such inventory shall be available to the public as provided in section 6927(b) of this title. Information previously submitted by a Federal agency under section 9603 of this title or under section 6925 or 6930 of this title, or under this section need not be resubmitted except that the agency shall update any previous submission to reflect the latest available data and information. The inventory shall include each of the following:

(1) A description of the location of each site at which any such treatment, storage, or disposal has taken place before the date on which permits are required under section 6925 of this title for such storage, treatment, or disposal, and where hazardous waste has been disposed, a description of hydrogeology of the site and the location of withdrawal wells and surface water within one mile of the site.

(2) Such information relating to the amount, nature, and toxicity of the hazardous waste in each site as may be necessary to determine the extent of any health hazard which may be associated with any site.

(3) Information on the known nature and extent of environmental contamination at each site, including a description of the monitoring data obtained.

(4) Information concerning the current status of the site, including information respecting whether or not hazardous waste is currently being treated, stored, or disposed of at such site (and if not, the date on which such activity ceased) and information respecting the nature of any other activity currently carried out at such site.

(5) A list of sites at which hazardous waste has been disposed and environmental monitoring data has not been obtained, and the reasons for the lack of monitoring data at each site.

(6) A description of response actions undertaken or contemplated at contaminated sites.

(7) An identification of the types of techniques of waste treatment, storage, or disposal which have been used at each site.

(8) The name and address and responsible Federal agency for each site, determined as of the date of preparation of the inventory.

(b) Environmental Protection Agency program

If the Administrator determines that any Federal agency under subsection (a) of this section is not adequately providing information respecting the sites referred to in subsection (a) of this section, the Administrator shall notify the chief official of such agency. If within ninety days following such notification, the Federal agency has not undertaken a program to adequately provide such information, the Administrator shall carry out the inventory program for such agency.

(Pub.L. 89–272, Title II, § 3016, as added Nov. 8, 1984, Pub.L. 98–616, Title II, § 244, 98 Stat. 3261.)

§ 6938. Export of hazardous wastes [SWDA § 3017]

(a) In general

Beginning twenty-four months after November 8, 1984, no person shall export any hazardous waste identified or listed under this subchapter unless

(1)(A) such person has provided the notification required in subsection (c) of this section,

(B) the government of the receiving country has consented to accept such hazardous waste,

(C) a copy of the receiving country's written consent is attached to the manifest accompanying each waste shipment, and

(D) the shipment conforms with the terms of the consent of the government of the receiving country required pursuant to subsection (e) of this section or

(2) the United States and the government of the receiving country have entered into an agreement as provided for in subsection (f) of this section and the shipment conforms with the terms of such agreement.

(b) Regulations

Not later than twelve months after November 8, 1984, the Administrator shall promulgate the regulations necessary to implement this section. Such regulations shall become effective one hundred and eighty days after promulgation.

(c) Notification

Any person who intends to export a hazardous waste identified or listed under this subchapter beginning twelve months after November 8, 1984, shall, before such hazardous waste is scheduled to leave the United States, provide notification to the Administrator. Such notification shall contain the following information:

(1) the name and address of the exporter;

(2) the types and estimated quantities of hazardous waste to be exported;

(3) the estimated frequency or rate at which such waste is to be exported; and the period of time over which such waste is to be exported;

(4) the ports of entry;

(5) a description of the manner in which such hazardous waste will be transported to and treated, stored, or disposed in the receiving country; and

(6) the name and address of the ultimate treatment, storage or disposal facility.

(d) Procedures for requesting consent of the receiving country

Within thirty days of the Administrator's receipt of a complete notification under this section, the Secretary of State, acting on behalf of the Administrator, shall—

(1) forward a copy of the notification to the government of the receiving country;

(2) Advise the government that United States law prohibits the export of hazardous waste unless the receiving country consents to accept the hazardous waste;

(3) request the government to provide the Secretary with a written consent or objection to the terms of the notification; and

(4) forward to the government of the receiving country a description of the Federal regulations which would apply to the treatment, storage, and disposal of the hazardous waste in the United States.

(e) Conveyance of written consent to exporter

Within thirty days of receipt by the Secretary of State of the receiving country's written consent or objection (or any subsequent communication withdrawing a prior consent or objection), the Administrator shall forward such a consent, objection, or other communication to the exporter.

(f) International agreements

Where there exists an international agreement between the United States and the government of the receiving country establishing notice, export, and enforcement procedures for the transportation, treatment, storage, and disposal of hazardous wastes, only the requirements of subsections (a)(2) and (g) of this section shall apply.

(g) Reports

After November 8, 1984, any person who exports any hazardous waste identified or listed under section 6921 of this title shall file with the Administrator no later than March 1 of each year, a report summarizing the types, quantities, frequency, and ultimate destination of all such hazardous waste exported during the previous calendar year.

(h) Other standards

Nothing in this section shall preclude the Administrator from establishing other standards for the export of hazardous wastes under section 6922 or 6923 of this title.

(Pub.L. 89–272, Title II, § 3017, as added Nov. 8, 1984, Pub.L. 98–616, Title II, § 245(a), 98 Stat. 3262.)

West's Federal Practice Manual

Solid waste disposal, see § 4385.5.

§ 6939. Domestic sewage [SWDA § 3018]

(a) Report

The Administrator shall, not later than 15 months after November 8, 1984, submit a report to the Congress concerning those substances identified or listed under section 6921 of this title which are not regulated under this subchapter by reason of the exclusion for mixtures of domestic sewage and other wastes that pass through a sewer system to a publicly owned treatment works. Such report shall include the types, size and number of generators which dispose of such substances in this manner, the types and quantities disposed of in this manner, and the identification of significant generators, wastes, and waste constituents not regulated under existing Federal law or regulated in a manner sufficient to protect human health and the environment.

(b) Revisions of regulations

Within eighteen months after submitting the report specified in subsection (a) of this section, the Administrator shall revise existing regulations and promulgate such additional regulations pursuant to this subchapter (or any other authority of the Administrator, including section 1317 of Title 33) as are necessary to assure that substances identified or listed under section 6921 of this title which pass through a sewer system to a publicly owned treatment works are adequately controlled to protect human health and the environment.

(c) Report on wastewater lagoon

The Administrator shall, within thirty-six months after November 8, 1984, submit a report to Congress concerning wastewater lagoons at publicly owned treatment works and their effect on groundwater quality. Such report shall include—

(1) the number and size of such lagoons;

(2) the types and quantities of waste contained in such lagoons;

(3) the extent to which such waste has been or may be released from such lagoons and contaminate ground water; and

(4) available alternatives for preventing or controlling such releases.

The Administrator may utilize the authority of sections 6927 and 6934 of this title for the purpose of completing such report.

(d) Application of sections 6927 and 6930

The provisions of sections 6927 and 6930 of this title shall apply to solid or dissolved materials in domestic sewage to the same extent and in the same manner as such provisions apply to hazardous waste.

(Pub.L. 89–272, Title II, § 3018, as added Nov. 8, 1984, Pub.L. 98–616, Title II, § 246(a), 98 Stat. 3264.)

West's Federal Practice Manual

Solid waste disposal, see § 4385.5.

§ 6939a. Exposure information and health assessments [SWDA § 3019]

(a) Exposure information

Beginning on the date nine months after November 8, 1984, each application for a final determination regarding a permit under section 6925(c) of this title for a landfill or surface impoundment shall be accompanied by information reasonably ascertainable by the owner or operator on the potential for the public to be exposed to hazardous wastes or hazardous constituents through releases related to the unit. At a minimum, such information must address:

(1) reasonably foreseeable potential releases from both normal operations and accidents at the unit, including releases associated with transportation to or from the unit;

(2) the potential pathways of human exposure to hazardous wastes or constituents resulting from the releases described under paragraph (1); and

(3) the potential magnitude and nature of the human exposure resulting from such releases.

The owner or operator of a landfill or surface impoundment for which an application for such a final determination under section 6925(c) of this title has been submitted prior to November 8, 1984, shall submit the information required by this subsection to the Administrator (or the State, in the case of a State with an authorized program) no later than the date nine months after November 8, 1984.

(b) Health assessments

(1) The Administrator (or the State, in the case of a State with an authorized program) shall make the information required by subsection (a) of this section, together with other relevant information, available to the Agency for Toxic Substances and Disease Registry established by section 9604(i) of this title.

(2) Whenever in the judgment of the Administrator, or the State (in the case of a State with an authorized program), a landfill or a surface impoundment poses a substantial potential risk to human health, due to the existence of releases of hazardous constituents, the magnitude of contamination with hazardous constituents which may be the result of a release, or the magnitude of the population exposed to such release or contamination, the Administrator or the State (with the concurrence of the Administrator) may request the Administrator of the Agency for Toxic Substances and Disease Registry to conduct a health assessment in connection with such facility and take other appropriate action with respect to such risks as authorized by section 9604(b) and (i) of this title. If funds are provided in connection with such request the Administrator of such Agency shall conduct such health assessment.

(c) Members of the public

Any member of the public may submit evidence of releases of or exposure to hazardous constituents from such a facility, or as to the risks or health effects associated with such releases or exposure, to the Administrator of the Agency for Toxic Substances and Disease Registry, the Administrator, or the State (in the case of a State with an authorized program).

(d) Priority

In determining the order in which to conduct health assessments under this subsection, the Administrator of the Agency for Toxic Substances and Disease Registry shall give priority to those facilities or sites at which there is documented evidence of release of hazardous constituents, at which the potential risk to human health appears highest, and for which in the judgment of the Administrator of such Agency existing health assessment data is inadequate to assess the potential risk to human health as provided in subsection (f) of this section.

(e) Periodic reports

The Administrator of such Agency shall issue periodic reports which include the results of all the assessments carried out under this section. Such assessments or other activities shall be reported after appropriate peer review.

(f) Definition

For the purposes of this section, the term "health assessments" shall include preliminary assessments of the potential risk to human health posed by individual sites and facilities subject to this section, based on such factors as the nature and extent of contamination, the existence of potential for pathways of human exposure (including ground or surface water contamination, air emissions, and food chain contamination), the size and potential susceptibility of the community within the likely pathways of exposure, the comparison of expected human exposure levels to the short-term and long-term health effects associated with identified contaminants and any available recommended exposure or tolerance limits for such contaminants, and the comparison of existing morbidity and mortality data on diseases that may be associated with the observed levels of exposure. The assessment shall include an evaluation of the risks to the potentially affected population from all sources of such contaminants, including known point or nonpoint sources other than the site or facility in question. A purpose of such preliminary assessments shall be to help determine whether full-scale health or epidemiological studies and medical evaluations of exposed populations shall be undertaken.

(g) Cost recovery

In any case in which a health assessment performed under this section discloses the exposure of a population to the release of a hazardous substance, the costs of such health assessment may be recovered as a cost of response under section 9607 of this title from persons causing or contributing to such release of such hazardous substance or, in the case of multiple releases contributing to such exposure, to all such release.

(Pub.L. 89–272, Title II, § 3019, as added Nov. 8, 1984, Pub.L. 98–616, Title II, § 247(a), 98 Stat. 3265.)

§ 6939b. Interim control of hazardous waste injection [SWDA § 3020]

(a) Underground source of drinking water

No hazardous waste may be disposed of by underground injection—

(1) into a formation which contains (within one-quarter mile of the well used for such underground injection) an underground source of drinking water; or

(2) above such a formation.

The prohibitions established under this section shall take effect 6 months after November 8, 1984, except in the case of any State in which identical or more stringent prohibitions are in effect before such date under the Safe Drinking Water Act [42 U.S.C.A. § 300f et seq.].

(b) Actions under Comprehensive Environmental Response, Compensation and Liability Act

Subsection (a) of this section shall not apply to the injection of contaminated ground water into the aquifer from which it was withdrawn, if—

(1) such injection is—

(A) a response action taken under section 9604 or 9606 of this title, or

(B) part of corrective action required under this chapter[1]

intended to clean up such contamination;

(2) such contaminated ground water is treated to substantially reduce hazardous constituents prior to such injection; and

(3) such response action or corrective action will, upon completion, be sufficient to protect human health and the environment.

(c) Enforcement

In addition to enforcement under the provisions of this chapter, the prohibitions established under paragraphs (1) and (2) of subsection (a) of this section shall be enforceable under the Safe Drinking Water Act [42 U.S.C.A. § 300f et seq.] in any State—

(1) which has adopted identical or more stringent prohibitions under part C of the Safe Drinking Water Act [42 U.S.C.A. § 300h et seq.] and which has assumed primary enforcement responsibility under that Act [42 U.S.C.A. § 300f et seq.] for enforcement of such prohibitions; or

(2) in which the Administrator has adopted identical or more stringent prohibitions under the Safe Drinking Water Act [42 U.S.C.A. § 300f et seq.] and is exercising primary enforcement responsibility under that Act [42 U.S.C.A. § 300f et seq.] for enforcement of such prohibitions.

(d) Definitions

The terms "primary enforcement responsibility", "underground source of drinking water", "formation" and "well" have the same meanings as provided in regulations of the Administrator under the Safe Drinking Water Act [42 U.S.C.A. § 300f et seq.]. The term "Safe Drinking Water Act" means title XIV of the Public Health Service Act [42 U.S.C.A. § 300f et seq.].

(Pub.L. 89–272, Title II, § 3020, formerly § 7010, as added Nov. 8, 1984, Pub.L. 98–616, Title IV, § 405(a), 98 Stat. 3273, and renumbered and amended June 19, 1986, Pub.L. 99–339, Title II, § 201(c), 100 Stat. 654.)

[1] So in original. Probably should be followed by a comma.

§ 6939c. Mixed waste inventory reports and plan [SWDA § 3021]

(a) Mixed waste inventory reports

(1) Requirement

Not later than 180 days after October 6, 1992, the Secretary of Energy shall submit to the Administrator and to the Governor of each State in which the Department of Energy stores or generates mixed wastes the following reports:

(A) A report containing a national inventory of all such mixed wastes, regardless of the time they were generated, on a State–by–State basis.

(B) A report containing a national inventory of mixed waste treatment capacities and technologies.

(2) Inventory of wastes

The report required by paragraph (1)(A) shall include the following:

(A) A description of each type of mixed waste at each Department of Energy facility in each State, including, at a minimum, the name of the waste stream.

(B) The amount of each type of mixed waste currently stored at each Department of Energy facility in each State, set forth separately by mixed waste that is subject to the land disposal prohibition requirements of section 6924 of this title and mixed waste that is not subject to such prohibition requirements.

(C) An estimate of the amount of each type of mixed waste the Department expects to generate in the next 5 years at each Department of Energy facility in each State.

(D) A description of any waste minimization actions the Department has implemented at each Department of Energy facility in each State for each mixed waste stream.

(E) The EPA hazardous waste code for each type of mixed waste containing waste that has been characterized at each Department of Energy facility in each State.

(F) An inventory of each type of waste that has not been characterized by sampling and analysis at each Department of Energy facility in each State.

(G) The basis for the Department's determination of the applicable hazardous waste code for each type of mixed waste at each Department of Energy facility and a description of whether the determination is based on sampling and analysis conducted on the waste or on the basis of process knowledge.

(H) A description of the source of each type of mixed waste at each Department of Energy facility in each State.

(I) The land disposal prohibition treatment technology or technologies specified for the hazardous waste component of each type of mixed waste at each Department of Energy facility in each State.

(J) A statement of whether and how the radionuclide content of the waste alters or affects use of the technologies described in subparagraph (I).

(3) Inventory of treatment capacities and technologies

The report required by paragraph (1)(B) shall include the following:

(A) An estimate of the available treatment capacity for each waste described in the report required by paragraph (1)(A) for which treatment technologies exist.

(B) A description, including the capacity, number and location, of each treatment unit considered in calculating the estimate under subparagraph (A).

(C) A description, including the capacity, number and location, of any existing treatment unit that was not considered in calculating the estimate under subparagraph (A) but that could, alone or in conjunction with other treatment units, be used to treat any of the wastes described in the report required by paragraph (1)(A) to meet the requirements of regulations promulgated pursuant to section 6924(m) of this title.

(D) For each unit listed in subparagraph (C), a statement of the reasons why the unit was not included in calculating the estimate under subparagraph (A).

(E) A description, including the capacity, number, location, and estimated date of availability, of each treatment unit currently proposed to increase the treatment capacities estimated under subparagraph (A).

(F) For each waste described in the report required by paragraph (1)(A) for which the Department has determined no treatment technology exists, information sufficient to support such determination and a description of the technological approaches the Department anticipates will need to be developed to treat the waste.

(4) Comments and revisions

Not later than 90 days after the date of the submission of the reports by the Secretary of Energy under paragraph (1), the Administrator and each State which received the reports shall submit any comments they may have concerning the reports to the Department of Energy. The Secretary of Energy shall consider and publish the comments prior to publication of the final report.

(5) Requests for additional information

Nothing in this subsection limits or restricts the authority of States or the Administrator to request additional information from the Secretary of Energy.

(b) Plan for development of treatment capacities and technologies

(1) Plan requirement

(A)(i) For each facility at which the Department of Energy generates or stores mixed wastes, except any facility subject to a permit, agreement, or order described in clause (ii), the Secretary of Energy shall develop and submit, as provided in paragraph (2), a plan for developing treatment capacities and technologies to treat all of the facility's mixed wastes, regardless of the time they were generated, to the standards promulgated pursuant to section 6924(m) of this title.

(ii) Clause (i) shall not apply with respect to any facility subject to any permit establishing a schedule for treatment of such wastes, or any existing agreement or administrative or judicial order governing the treatment of such wastes, to which the State is a party.

(B) Each plan shall contain the following:

(i) For mixed wastes for which treatment technologies exist, a schedule for submitting all applicable permit applications, entering into contracts, initiating construction, conducting systems testing, commencing operations, and processing backlogged and currently generated mixed wastes.

(ii) For mixed wastes for which no treatment technologies exist, a schedule for identifying and developing such technologies, identifying the funding requirements for the identification and development of such technologies, submitting treatability study exemptions, and submitting research and development permit applications.

(iii) For all cases where the Department proposes radionuclide separation of mixed wastes, or materials derived from mixed wastes, it shall provide an estimate of the volume of waste generated by each case of radionuclide separation, the volume of waste that would exist or be generated without radionuclide separation, the estimated costs of waste treatment and disposal if radionuclide separation is used compared to the estimated costs if it is not used, and the assumptions underlying such waste volume and cost estimates.

(C) A plan required under this subsection may provide for centralized, regional, or on-site treatment of mixed wastes, or any combination thereof.

(2) Review and approval of plan

(A) For each facility that is located in a State (i) with authority under State law to prohibit land disposal of mixed waste until the waste has been treated and (ii) with both authority under State law to regulate the hazardous components of mixed waste and authorization from the Environmental Protection Agency under section 6926 of this title to regulate the hazardous components of mixed waste, the Secretary of Energy shall submit the plan required under paragraph (1) to the appropriate State regulatory officials for their review and approval, modification, or disapproval. In reviewing the plan, the State shall consider the need for regional treatment facilities. The State shall consult with the Administrator and any other State in which a facility affected by the plan is located and consider public comments in making its determination on the plan. The State shall approve, approve with modifications, or disapprove the plan within 6 months after receipt of the plan.

(B) For each facility located in a State that does not have the authority described in subparagraph (A), the Secretary shall submit the plan required under paragraph (1) to the Administrator of the Environmental Protection Agency for review and approval, modification, or disapproval. A copy of the plan also shall be provided by the Secretary to the State in which such facility is located. In reviewing the plan, the Administrator shall consider the need for regional treatment facilities. The Administrator shall consult with the State or States in which any facility affected by the plan is located and consider public comments in making a determination on the plan. The Administrator shall approve, approve with modifications, or disapprove the plan within 6 months after receipt of the plan.

(C) Upon the approval of a plan under this paragraph by the Administrator or a State, the Administrator shall issue an order under section 6928(a) of this title, or the State shall issue an order under appropriate State authority, requiring compliance with the approved plan.

(3) Public participation

Upon submission of a plan by the Secretary of Energy to the Administrator or a State, and before approval of the plan by the Administrator or a State, the Administrator or State shall publish a notice of the availability of the submitted plan and make such submitted plan available to the public on request.

(4) Revisions of plan

If any revisions of an approved plan are proposed by the Secretary of Energy or required by the Administrator or a State, the provisions of paragraphs (2) and (3) shall apply to the revisions in the same manner as they apply to the original plan.

(5) Waiver of plan requirement

(A) A State may waive the requirement for the Secretary of Energy to develop and submit a plan under this subsection for a facility located in the State if the State (i) enters into an agreement with the Secretary of Energy that addresses compliance at that facility with section 6924(j) of this title with respect to mixed waste, and (ii) issues an order requiring compliance with such agreement and which is in effect.

(B) Any violation of an agreement or order referred to in subparagraph (A) is subject to the waiver of sovereign immunity contained in section 6961(a) of this title.

(c) Schedule and progress reports

(1) Schedule

Not later than 6 months after October 6, 1992, the Secretary of Energy shall publish in the Federal Register a schedule for submitting the plans required under subsection (b) of this section.

(2) Progress reports

(A) Not later than the deadlines specified in subparagraph (B), the Secretary of Energy shall submit to the Committee on Environment and Public Works of the Senate and the Committee on Energy and Commerce of the House of Representatives a progress report containing the following:

(i) An identification, by facility, of the plans that have been submitted to States or the Administrator of the Environmental Protection Agency pursuant to subsection (b).

(ii) The status of State and Environmental Protection Agency review and approval of each such plan.

(iii) The number of orders requiring compliance with such plans that are in effect.

(iv) For the first 2 reports required under this paragraph, an identification of the plans required under such subsection (b) of this section that the Secretary expects to submit in the 12-month period following submission of the report.

(B) The Secretary of Energy shall submit a report under subparagraph (A) not later than 12 months after October 6, 1992, 24 months after such date, and 36 months after such date.

(Pub.L. 89–272, Title II, § 3021, as added Pub.L. 102–386, Title I, § 105(a)(1), Oct. 6, 1992, 106 Stat. 1508.)

Change of Name

Any reference in any provision of law enacted before Jan. 4, 1995, to the Committee on Energy and Commerce of the House of Representatives treated as referring to the Committee on Commerce of the House of Representatives, except that any reference in any provision of law enacted before Jan. 4, 1995, to the Committee on Energy and Commerce of the House of Representatives treated as referring to the Committee on Agriculture of the House of Representatives, in the case of a provision of law relating to inspection of seafood or seafood products, the Committee on Banking and Financial Services of the House of Representatives, in the case of a provision of law relating to bank capital markets activities generally or to depository institution securities activities generally, and the Committee on Transportation and Infrastructure of the House of Representatives, in the case of a provision of law relating to railroads, railway labor, or railroad retirement and unemployment (except revenue measures related thereto), see section 1(a)(4) and (c)(1) of Pub.L. 104–14, set out as a note preceding section 21 of Title 2, The Congress.

GAO Report

Section 105(c) of Pub.L. 102–386 provided that:

"(1) **Requirement.**—Not later than 18 months after the date of the enactment of this Act [Oct. 6, 1992], the Comptroller General shall submit to Congress a report on the Department of Energy's progress in complying with section 3021(b) of the Solid Waste Disposal Act [subsec. (b) of this section].

"(2) **Matters to be included.**—The report required under paragraph (1) shall contain, at a minimum, the following:

"(A) The Department of Energy's progress in submitting to the States or the Administrator of the Environmental Protection Agency a plan for each facility for which a plan is required under section 3021(b) of the Solid Waste Disposal Act [subsec. (b) of this section] and the status of State or Environmental Protection Agency review and approval of each such plan.

"(B) The Department of Energy's progress in entering into orders requiring compliance with any such plans that have been approved.

"(C) An evaluation of the completeness and adequacy of each such plan as of the date of submission of the report required under paragraph (1).

"(D) An identification of any recurring problems among the Department of Energy's submitted plans.

"(E) A description of treatment technologies and capacity that have been developed by the Department of Energy since the date of the enactment of this Act [Oct. 6, 1992] and a list of the wastes that are expected to be treated by such technologies and the facilities at which the wastes are generated or stored.

"(F) The progress made by the Department of Energy in characterizing its mixed waste streams at each such facility by sampling and analysis.

"(G) An identification and analysis of additional actions that the Department of Energy must take to—

"(i) complete submission of all plans required under such section 3021(b) [subsec. (b) of this section] for all such facilities;

"(ii) obtain the adoption of orders requiring compliance with all such plans; and

"(iii) develop mixed waste treatment capacity and technologies."

§ 6939d. Public vessels [SWDA § 3022]

(a) Waste generated on public vessels

Any hazardous waste generated on a public vessel shall not be subject to the storage, manifest, inspection, or recordkeeping requirements of this chapter until such waste is transferred to a shore facility, unless—

(1) the waste is stored on the public vessel for more than 90 days after the public vessel is placed in reserve or is otherwise no longer in service; or

(2) the waste is transferred to another public vessel within the territorial waters of the United States and is stored on such vessel or another public vessel for more than 90 days after the date of transfer.

(b) Computation of storage period

For purposes of subsection (a) of this section, the 90-day period begins on the earlier of—

(1) the date on which the public vessel on which the waste was generated is placed in reserve or is otherwise no longer in service; or

(2) the date on which the waste is transferred from the public vessel on which the waste was generated to another public vessel within the territorial waters of the United States;

and continues, without interruption, as long as the waste is stored on the original public vessel (if in reserve or not in service) or another public vessel.

(c) Definitions

For purposes of this section:

(1) The term "public vessel" means a vessel owned or bareboat chartered and operated by the United States, or by a foreign nation, except when the vessel is engaged in commerce.

(2) The terms "in reserve" and "in service" have the meanings applicable to those terms under section 7293 and sections 7304 through 7308 of Title 10 and regulations prescribed under those sections.

(d) Relationship to other law

Nothing in this section shall be construed as altering or otherwise affecting the provisions of section 7311 of Title 10.

(Pub.L. 89–272, Title II, § 3022, as added Pub.L. 102–386, Title I, § 106(a), Oct. 6, 1992, 106 Stat. 1513.)

§ 6939e. Federally owned treatment works [SWDA § 3023]

(a) In general

For purposes of section 6903(27) of this title, the phrase "but does not include solid or dissolved material in domestic sewage" shall apply to any solid or dissolved material introduced by a source into a federally owned treatment works if—

(1) such solid or dissolved material is subject to a pretreatment standard under section 1317 of Title 33, and the source is in compliance with such standard;

(2) for a solid or dissolved material for which a pretreatment standard has not been promulgated pursuant to section 1317 of Title 33, the Administrator has promulgated a schedule for establishing such a pretreatment standard which would be applicable to such solid or dissolved material not later than 7 years after October 6, 1992, such standard is promulgated on or before the date established in the schedule, and after the effective date of such standard the source is in compliance with such standard;

(3) such solid or dissolved material is not covered by paragraph (1) or (2) and is not prohibited from land disposal under subsections (d), (e), (f), or (g) of section 6924 of this title because such material has been treated in accordance with section 6924(m) of this title; or

(4) notwithstanding paragraphs (1), (2), or (3), such solid or dissolved material is generated by a household or person which generates less than 100 kilograms of hazardous waste per month unless such solid or dissolved material would otherwise be an acutely hazardous waste and subject to standards, regulations, or other requirements under this chapter notwithstanding the quantity generated.

(b) Prohibition

It is unlawful to introduce into a federally owned treatment works any pollutant that is a hazardous waste.

(c) Enforcement

(1) Actions taken to enforce this section shall not require closure of a treatment works if the hazardous waste is removed or decontaminated and such removal or decontamination is adequate, in the discretion of the Administrator or, in the case of an authorized State, of the State, to protect human health and the environment.

(2) Nothing in this subsection shall be construed to prevent the Administrator or an authorized State from ordering the closure of a treatment works if the Administrator or State determines such closure is necessary for protection of human health and the environment.

(3) Nothing in this subsection shall be construed to affect any other enforcement authorities available to the Administrator or a State under this subchapter.

(d) Definition

For purposes of this section, the term "federally owned treatment works" means a facility that is owned and operated by a department, agency, or instrumentality of the Federal Government treating wastewater, a majority of which is domestic sewage, prior to discharge in accordance with a permit issued under section 1342 of Title 33.

(e) Savings clause

Nothing in this section shall be construed as affecting any agreement, permit, or administrative or judicial order, or any condition or requirement contained in such an agreement, permit, or order, that is in existence on October 6, 1992, and that requires corrective action or closure at a federally owned treatment works or solid waste management unit or facility related to such a treatment works.

(Pub.L. 89–272, Title II, § 3023, as added Pub.L. 102–386, Title I, § 108(a), Oct. 6, 1992, 106 Stat. 1514.)

SUBCHAPTER IV—STATE OR REGIONAL SOLID WASTE PLANS

§ 6941. Objectives of subchapter [SWDA § 4001]

The objectives of this subchapter are to assist in developing and encouraging methods for the disposal of solid waste which are environmentally sound and which maximize the utilization of valuable resources including energy and materials which are recoverable from solid waste and to encourage resource conservation. Such objectives are to be accomplished through Federal technical and financial assistance to States or regional authorities for comprehensive planning pursuant to Federal guidelines designed to foster cooperation among Federal, State, and local governments and private industry. In developing such comprehensive plans, it is the intention of this chapter that in determining the size of the waste-to-energy facility, adequate provision shall be given to the present and reasonably anticipated future needs, including those needs created by thorough implementation of section 6962(h) of this title, of the recycling and resource recovery interest within the area encompassed by the planning process.

(Pub.L. 89–272, Title II, § 4001, as added Oct. 21, 1976, Pub.L. 94–580, § 2, 90 Stat. 2813, and amended Oct. 21, 1980, Pub.L. 96–482, § 32(b), 94 Stat. 2353; Nov. 8, 1984, Pub.L. 98–616, Title III, § 301(a), Title V, § 501(f)(1), 98 Stat. 3267, 3276.)

LAW REVIEW COMMENTARIES

Toward a national groundwater act: Current contamination and future courses of action. Thomas D. Marks, 61 Fla.B.J. 10 (April 1987).

§ 6941a. Energy and materials conservation and recovery; Congressional findings

The Congress finds that—

(1) significant savings could be realized by conserving materials in order to reduce the volume or quantity of material which ultimately becomes waste;

(2) solid waste contains valuable energy and material resources which can be recovered and used thereby conserving increasingly scarce and expensive fossil fuels and virgin materials;

(3) the recovery of energy and materials from municipal waste, and the conservation of energy and materials contributing to such waste streams, can have the effect of reducing the volume of the municipal waste stream and the burden of disposing of increasing volumes of solid waste;

(4) the technology to conserve resources exists and is commercially feasible to apply;

(5) the technology to recover energy and materials from solid waste is of demonstrated commercial feasibility; and

(6) various communities throughout the nation have different needs and different potentials for conserving resources and for utilizing techniques for the recovery of energy and materials from waste, and Federal assistance in planning and implementing such energy and materials conservation and recovery programs should be available to all such communities on an equitable basis in relation to their needs and potential.

(Oct. 21, 1980, Pub.L. 96–482, § 32(a), 94 Stat. 2353.)

Codification

Section was enacted as part of the Solid Waste Disposal Act Amendments of 1980, and not as part of the Solid Waste Disposal Act which comprises this chapter.

§ 6942. Federal guidelines for plans [SWDA § 4002]

(a) Guidelines for identification of regions

For purposes of encouraging and facilitating the development of regional planning for solid waste management, the Administrator, within one hundred and eighty days after October 21, 1976, and after consultation with appropriate Federal, State, and local authorities, shall by regulation publish guidelines for the identification of those areas which have common solid waste management problems and are appropriate units for planning regional solid waste management services. Such guidelines shall consider—

(1) the size and location of areas which should be included,

(2) the volume of solid waste which should be included, and

(3) the available means of coordinating regional planning with other related regional planning and for coordination of such regional planning into the State plan.

(b) Guidelines for State plans

Not later than eighteen months after October 21, 1976, and after notice and hearing, the Administrator shall, after consultation with appropriate Federal, State, and local authorities, promulgate regulations containing guidelines to assist in the development and implementation of State solid waste management plans (hereinafter in this chapter referred to as "State plans"). The guidelines shall contain methods for achieving the objectives specified in section 6941 of this title. Such guidelines shall be reviewed from time to time, but not less frequently than every three years, and revised as may be appropriate.

(c) Considerations for State plan guidelines

The guidelines promulgated under subsection (b) of this section shall consider—

(1) the varying regional, geologic, hydrologic, climatic, and other circumstances under which different solid waste practices are required in order to insure the reasonable protection of the quality of the ground and surface waters from leachate contamination, the reasonable protection of the quality of the surface waters from surface runoff contamination, and the reasonable protection of ambient air quality;

(2) characteristics and conditions of collection, storage, processing, and disposal operating methods, techniques and practices, and location of facilities where such operating methods, techniques, and practices are conducted, taking into account the nature of the material to be disposed;

(3) methods for closing or upgrading open dumps for purposes of eliminating potential health hazards;

(4) population density, distribution, and projected growth;

(5) geographic, geologic, climatic, and hydrologic characteristics;

(6) the type and location of transportation;

(7) the profile of industries;

(8) the constituents and generation rates of waste;

(9) the political, economic, organizational, financial, and management problems affecting comprehensive solid waste management;

(10) types of resource recovery facilities and resource conservation systems which are appropriate; and

(11) available new and additional markets for recovered material and energy and energy resources recovered from solid waste as well as methods for conserving such materials and energy.

(Pub.L. 89–272, Title II, § 4002, as added Oct. 21, 1976, Pub.L. 94–580, § 2, 90 Stat. 2813, and amended Oct. 21, 1980, Pub.L. 96–482, § 32(c), 94 Stat. 2353.)

CODE OF FEDERAL REGULATIONS

Guidelines, see 40 CFR 256.01 et seq.

§ 6943. Requirements for approval of plans [SWDA § 4003]

(a) Minimum requirements

In order to be approved under section 6947 of this title, each State plan must comply with the following minimum requirements—

(1) The plan shall identify (in accordance with section 6946(b) of this title) (A) the responsibilities of State, local, and regional authorities in the implementation of the State plan, (B) the distribution of Federal funds to the authorities responsible for development and implementation of the State plan, and (C) the means for coordinating regional planning and implementation under the State plan.

(2) The plan shall, in accordance with sections 6944(b) and 6945(a) of this title, prohibit the establishment of new open dumps within the State, and contain requirements that all solid waste (including solid waste originating in other States, but not including hazardous waste) shall be (A) utilized for resource recovery or (B) disposed of in sanitary landfills (within the meaning of section 6944(a) of this title) or otherwise disposed of in an environmentally sound manner.

(3) The plan shall provide for the closing or upgrading of all existing open dumps within the State pursuant to the requirements of section 6945 of this title.

(4) The plan shall provide for the establishment of such State regulatory powers as may be necessary to implement the plan.

(5) The plan shall provide that no State or local government within the State shall be prohibited under State or local law from negotiating and entering into long-term contracts for the supply of solid waste to resource recovery facilities, from entering into long-term contracts for the operation of such facilities, or from securing long-term markets for material and energy recovered from such facilities or for conserving materials or energy by reducing the volume of waste.

(6) The plan shall provide for such resource conservation or recovery and for the disposal of solid waste in sanitary landfills or any combination of practices so as may be necessary to use or dispose of such waste in a manner that is environmentally sound.

(b) Discretionary plan provisions relating to recycled oil

Any State plan submitted under this subchapter may include, at the option of the State, provisions to carry out each of the following:

(1) Encouragement, to the maximum extent feasible and consistent with the protection of the public health and the environment, of the use of recycled oil in all appropriate areas of State and local government.

(2) Encouragement of persons contracting with the State to use recycled oil to the maximum extent feasible, consistent with protection of the public health and the environment.

(3) Informing the public of the uses of recycled oil.

(4) Establishment and implementation of a program (including any necessary licensing of persons and including the use, where appropriate, of manifests) to assure that used oil is collected, transported, treated, stored, reused, and disposed of, in a manner which does not present a hazard to the public health or the environment.

Any plan submitted under this chapter before October 15, 1980, may be amended, at the option of the State, at any time after such date to include any provision referred to in this subsection.

(c) Energy and materials conservation and recovery feasibility planning and assistance

(1) A State which has a plan approved under this subchapter or which has submitted a plan for such approval shall be eligible for assistance under section 6948(a)(3) of this title if the Administrator determines that under such plan the State will—

(A) analyze and determine the economic and technical feasibility of facilities and programs to conserve resources which contribute to the waste stream or to recover energy and materials from municipal waste;

(B) analyze the legal, institutional, and economic impediments to the development of systems and facilities for conservation of energy or materials which contribute to the waste stream or for the recovery of energy and materials from municipal waste and make recommendations to appropriate governmental authorities for overcoming such impediments;

(C) assist municipalities within the State in developing plans, programs, and projects to conserve resources or recover energy and materials from municipal waste; and

(D) coordinate the resource conservation and recovery planning under subparagraph (C).

(2) The analysis referred to in paragraph (1)(A) shall include—

(A) the evaluation of, and establishment of priorities among, market opportunities for industrial and commercial users of all types (including public utilities and industrial parks) to utilize energy and materials recovered from municipal waste;

(B) comparisons of the relative costs of energy recovered from municipal waste in relation to the costs of energy derived from fossil fuels and other sources;

(C) studies of the transportation and storage problems and other problems associated with the development of energy and materials recovery technology, including curbside source separation;

(D) the evaluation and establishment of priorities among ways of conserving energy or materials which contribute to the waste stream;

(E) comparison of the relative total costs between conserving resources and disposing of or recovering such waste; and

(F) studies of impediments to resource conservation or recovery, including business practices, transportation requirements, or storage difficulties.

Such studies and analyses shall also include studies of other sources of solid waste from which energy and materials may be recovered or minimized.

(d) Size of waste-to-energy facilities

Notwithstanding any of the above requirements, it is the intention of this chapter and the planning process developed pursuant to this chapter that in determining the size of the waste-to-energy facility, adequate provision shall be given to the present and reasonably anticipated future needs of the recycling and resource recovery interest within the area encompassed by the planning process.

(Pub.L. 89–272, Title II, § 4003, as added Oct. 21, 1976, Pub.L. 94–580, § 2, 90 Stat. 2814, and amended Oct. 15, 1980, Pub.L. 96–463, § 5(a), (b), 94 Stat. 2056; Oct. 21, 1980, Pub.L. 96–482, §§ 18, 32(d), 94 Stat. 2345, 2353; Nov. 8, 1984, Pub.L. 98–616, Title III, § 301(b), Title V, § 502(h), 98 Stat. 3267, 3277.)

§ 6944. Criteria for sanitary landfills; sanitary landfills required for all disposal [SWDA § 4004]

(a) Criteria for sanitary landfills

Not later than one year after October 21, 1976, after consultation with the States, and after notice and public hearings, the Administrator shall promulgate regulations containing criteria for determining which facilities shall be classified as sanitary landfills and which shall be classified as open dumps within the meaning of this chapter. At a minimum, such criteria shall provide that a facility may be classified as a sanitary landfill and not an open dump only if there is no reasonable probability of adverse effects on health or the environment from disposal of solid waste at such facility. Such regulations may provide for the classification of the types of sanitary landfills.

(b) Disposal required to be in sanitary landfills, etc.

For purposes of complying with section 6943(2) of this title each State plan shall prohibit the establishment of open dumps and contain a requirement that disposal of all solid waste within the State shall be in compliance with such section 6943(2) of this title.

(c) Effective date

The prohibition contained in subsection (b) of this section shall take effect on the date six months after the date of promulgation of regulations under subsection (a) of this section.

(Pub.L. 89–272, Title II, § 4004, as added Oct. 21, 1976, Pub.L. 94–580, § 2, 90 Stat. 2815, and amended Nov. 8, 1984, Pub.L. 98–616, Title III, § 302(b), 98 Stat. 3268.)

CODE OF FEDERAL REGULATIONS

Solid waste disposal facilities and practices, criteria for classification of, see 40 CFR 257.1 et seq.

§ 6945. Upgrading of open dumps [SWDA § 4005]

(a) Closing or upgrading of existing open dumps

Upon promulgation of criteria under section 6907(a)(3) of this title, any solid waste management practice or disposal of solid waste or hazardous waste which constitutes the open dumping of solid waste or hazardous waste is prohibited, except in the case of any practice or disposal of solid waste under a timetable or schedule for compliance established under this section. The prohibition contained in the preceding sentence shall be enforceable under section 6972 of this title against persons engaged in the act of open dumping. For purposes of complying with section 6943(a)(2) and 6943(a)(3) of this title, each State plan shall contain a requirement that all existing disposal facilities or sites for solid waste in such State which are open dumps listed in the inventory under subsection (b) of this section shall comply with such measures as may be promulgated by the Administrator to eliminate health hazards and minimize potential health hazards. Each such plan shall establish, for any entity which demonstrates that it has considered other public or private alternatives for solid waste management to comply with the prohibition on open dumping and is unable to utilize such alternatives to so comply, a timetable or schedule for compliance for such practice or disposal of solid waste which specifies a schedule of remedial measures, including an enforceable sequence of actions or operations, leading to compliance with the prohibition on open dumping of solid waste within a reasonable time (not to exceed 5 years from the date of publication of criteria under section 6907(a)(3) of this title).

(b) Inventory

To assist the States in complying with section 6943(a)(3) of this title, not later than one year after promulgation of regulations under section 6944 of this title, the Administrator, with the cooperation of the Bureau of the Census shall publish an inventory of all disposal facilities or sites in the United States which are open dumps within the meaning of this chapter.

(c) Control of hazardous disposal

(1)(A) Not later than 36 months after November 8, 1984, each State shall adopt and implement a permit program or other system of prior approval and conditions to assure that each solid waste management facility within such State which may receive hazardous household waste or hazardous waste due to the provision of section 6921(d) of this title for small quantity generators (otherwise not subject to the requirement for a permit under section 6925 of this title) will comply with the applicable criteria promulgated under section 6944(a) and 6907(a)(3) of this title.

(B) Not later than eighteen months after the promulgation of revised criteria under section 6944(a) of this title (as required by section 6949a(c) of this title), each State shall adopt and implement a permit program or other system or [1] prior approval and conditions, to assure that each solid waste management facility within such State which may receive hazardous household waste or hazardous waste due to the provision of section 6921(d) of this title for small quantity generators (otherwise not subject to the requirement for a permit under section 6925 of this title) will comply with the criteria revised under section 6944(a) of this title.

(C) The Administrator shall determine whether each State has developed an adequate program under this paragraph. The Administrator may make such a determination in conjunction with approval, disapproval or partial approval of a State plan under section 6947 of this title.

(2)(A) In any State that the Administrator determines has not adopted an adequate program for such facilities under paragraph (1)(B) by the date provided in such paragraph, the Administrator may use the authorities available under sections 6927 and 6928 of this title to enforce the prohibition contained in subsection (a) of this section with respect of such facilities.

(B) For purposes of this paragraph, the term "requirement of this subchapter" in section 6928 of this title shall be deemed to include criteria promulgated by the Administrator under sections 6907(a)(3) and 6944(a) of this title, and the term "hazardous wastes" in section 6927 of this title shall be deemed to include solid waste at facilities that may handle hazardous household wastes or hazardous wastes from small quantity generators.

(Pub.L. 89–272, Title II, § 4005, as added Oct. 21, 1976, Pub.L. 94–580, § 2, 90 Stat. 2815, and amended Oct. 21, 1980, Pub.L. 96–482, § 19(a), (b), 94 Stat. 2345; Nov. 8, 1984, Pub.L. 98–616, Title III, § 302(c), Title IV, § 403(c), Title V, § 502(c), 98 Stat. 3268, 3272, 3276.)

[1] So in original. Probably should be "of".

§ 6946. Procedure for development and implementation of State plan [SWDA § 4006]

(a) Identification of regions

Within one hundred and eighty days after publication of guidelines under section 6942(a) of this title (relating to identification of regions), the Governor of each State, after consultation with local elected officials, shall promulgate regulations based on such guidelines identifying the boundaries of each area within the State which, as a result of urban concentrations, geographic conditions, markets, and other factors, is appropriate for carrying out regional solid waste management. Such regulations may be modified from time to time (identifying additional or different regions) pursuant to such guidelines.

(b) Identification of State and local agencies and responsibilities

(1) Within one hundred and eighty days after the Governor promulgates regulations under subsection (a) of this section, for purposes of facilitating the development and implementation of a State plan which will meet the minimum requirements of section 6943 of this title, the State, together with appropriate elected officials of general purpose units of local government, shall jointly (A) identify an agency to develop the State plan and identify one or more agencies to implement such plan, and (B) identify which solid waste management activities will, under such State plan, be planned for and carried out by the State and which such management activities will, under such State plan, be planned for and carried out by a regional or local authority or a combination of regional or local and State authorities. If a multi-functional regional agency authorized by State law to conduct solid waste planning and management (the members of which are appointed by the Governor) is in existence on October 21, 1976, the Governor shall identify such authority for purposes of carrying out within such region clause (A) of this paragraph. Where feasible, designation of the agency for the affected area designated under section 1288 of Title 33 shall be considered. A State agency identified under this paragraph shall be established or designated by the Governor of such State. Local or regional agencies identified under this paragraph shall be composed of individuals at least a majority of whom are elected local officials.

(2) If planning and implementation agencies are not identified and designated or established as required under paragraph (1) for any affected area, the governor shall, before the date two hundred and seventy days after promulgation of regulations under subsection (a) of this section, establish or designate a State agency to develop and implement the State plan for such area.

(c) Interstate regions

(1) In the case of any region which, pursuant to the guidelines published by the Administrator under section 6942(a) of this title (relating to identification of regions), would be located in two or more States, the Governors of the respective States, after consultation with local elected officials, shall consult, cooperate, and enter into agreements identifying the boundaries of such region pursuant to subsection (a) of this section.

(2) Within one hundred and eighty days after an interstate region is identified by agreement under paragraph (1), appropriate elected officials of general purpose units of local government within such region shall jointly establish or designate an agency to develop a plan for such region. If no such agency is established or designated within such period by such officials, the Governors of the respective States may, by agreement, establish or designate for such purpose a single representative organization including elected officials of general purpose units of local government within such region.

(3) Implementation of interstate regional solid waste management plans shall be conducted by units of local government for any portion of a region within their jurisdiction, or by multijurisdictional agencies or authorities designated in accordance with State law, including those designated by agreement by such units of local government for such purpose. If no such unit, agency, or authority is so designated, the respective Governors shall designate or establish a single interstate agency to implement such plan.

(4) For purposes of this subchapter, so much of an interstate regional plan as is carried out within a particular State shall be deemed part of the State plan for such State.

(Pub.L. 89–272, Title II, § 4006, as added Oct. 21, 1976, Pub.L. 94–580, § 2, 90 Stat. 2816, and amended Oct. 21, 1980, Pub.L. 96–482, § 19(b), 94 Stat. 2345.)

CODE OF FEDERAL REGULATIONS

Regions and agencies for solid waste management, identification of, see 40 CFR 255.1 et seq.

United States Supreme Court

State regulation or control, nonhazardous solid waste, see City of Philadelphia v. New Jersey, 1978, 98 S.Ct. 2531, 437 U.S. 617, 57 L.Ed.2d 475.

§ 6947. Approval of State plan; Federal assistance [SWDA § 4007]

(a) Plan approval

The Administrator shall, within six months after a State plan has been submitted for approval, approve or disapprove the plan. The Administrator shall approve a plan if he determines that—

(1) it meets the requirements of paragraphs (1), (2), (3), and (5) of section 6943 of this title; and

(2) it contains provision for revision of such plan, after notice and public hearing, whenever the Administrator, by regulation, determines—

(A) that revised regulations respecting minimum requirements have been promulgated under paragraphs (1), (2), (3), and (5) of section 6943 of this title with which the State plan is not in compliance;

(B) that information has become available which demonstrates the inadequacy of the plan to effectuate the purposes of this subchapter; or

(C) that such revision is otherwise necessary.

The Administrator shall review approved plans from time to time and if he determines that revision or corrections are necessary to bring such plan into compliance with the minimum requirements promulgated under section 6943 of this title (including new or revised requirements), he shall, after notice and opportunity for public hearing, withdraw his approval of such plan. Such withdrawal of approval shall cease to be effective upon the Administrator's determination that such complies with such minimum requirements.

(b) Eligibility of States for Federal financial assistance

(1) The Administrator shall approve a State application for financial assistance under this subchapter, and make grants to such State, if such State and local and regional authorities within such State have complied with the requirements of section 6946 of this title within the period required under such section and if such State has a State plan which has been approved by the Administrator under this subchapter.

(2) The Administrator shall approve a State application for financial assistance under this subchapter, and make grants to such State, for fiscal years 1978 and 1979 if the Administrator determines that the State plan continues to be eligible for approval under subsection (a) of this section and is being implemented by the State.

(3) Upon withdrawal of approval of a State plan under subsection (a) of this section, the Administrator shall withhold Federal financial and technical assistance under this subchapter (other than such technical assistance as may be necessary to assist in obtaining the reinstatement of approval) until such time as such approval is reinstated.

(c) Existing activities

Nothing in this subchapter shall be construed to prevent or affect any activities respecting solid waste planning or management which are carried out by State, regional, or local authorities unless such activities are inconsistent with a State plan approved by the Administrator under this subchapter.

(Pub.L. 89–272, Title II, § 4007, as added Oct. 21, 1976, Pub.L. 94–580, § 2, 90 Stat. 2817, and amended Nov. 8, 1978, Pub.L. 95–609, § 7(*l*), 92 Stat. 3082.)

§ 6948. Federal assistance [SWDA § 4008]

(a) Authorization of Federal financial assistance

(1) There are authorized to be appropriated $30,000,000 for fiscal year 1978, $40,000,000 for fiscal year 1979, $20,000,000 for fiscal year 1980, $15,000,000 for fiscal year 1981, $20,000,000 for the fiscal year 1982, and $10,000,000 for each of the fiscal years 1985 through 1988 for purposes of financial assistance to States and local, regional, and interstate authorities for the development and implementation of plans approved by the Administrator under this subchapter (other than the provisions of such plans referred to in section 6943(b) of this title, relating to feasibility planning for municipal waste energy and materials conservation and recovery).

(2)(A) The Administrator is authorized to provide financial assistance to States, counties, municipalities, and intermunicipal agencies and State and local public solid waste management authorities for implementation of programs to provide solid waste management, resource recovery, and resource conservation services and hazardous waste management. Such assistance shall include assistance for facility planning and feasibility studies; expert consultation; surveys and analyses of market needs; marketing of recovered resources; technology assessments; legal expenses; construction feasibility studies; source separation projects; and fiscal or economic investigations or studies; but such assistance shall not include any other element of construction, or any acquisition of land or interest in land, or any subsidy for the price of recovered resources. Agencies assisted under this subsection shall consider existing solid waste management and hazardous waste management services and facilities as well as facilities proposed for construction.

(B) An applicant for financial assistance under this paragraph must agree to comply with respect to the project or program assisted with the applicable requirements of section 6945 of this title and subchapter III of this chapter and apply applicable solid waste management practices, methods, and levels of control consistent with any guidelines published pursuant to section 6907 of this title. Assistance under this paragraph shall be available only for programs certified by the State to be consistent with any applicable State or areawide solid waste management plan or program. Applicants for technical and financial assistance under this section shall not preclude or foreclose consideration of programs for the recovery of recyclable materials through source separation or other resource recovery techniques.

(C) There are authorized to be appropriated $15,000,000 for each of the fiscal years 1978 and 1979 for purposes of this section. There are authorized to be appropriated $10,000,000 for fiscal year 1980, $10,000,000 for fiscal year 1981, $10,000,000 for fiscal year 1982, and $10,000,000 for each of the fiscal years 1985 through 1988 for purposes of this paragraph.

(D) There are authorized—

(i) to be made available $15,000,000 out of funds appropriated for fiscal year 1985, and

(ii) to be appropriated for each of the fiscal years 1986 though[1] 1988, $20,000,000

for grants to States (and where appropriate to regional, local, and interstate agencies) to implement programs requiring compliance by solid waste management facilities with the criteria promulgated under section 6944(a) of this title and section 6907(a)(3) of this title and with the provisions of section 6945 of this title. To the extent practicable, such programs shall require such compliance not later than thirty-six months after November 8, 1984.

(3)(A) There is authorized to be appropriated for the fiscal year beginning October 1, 1981, and for each fiscal year thereafter before October 1, 1986, $4,000,000 for purposes of making grants to States to carry out section 6943(b) of this title. No amount may be appropriated for such purposes for the fiscal year beginning on October 1, 1986, or for any fiscal year thereafter.

(B) Assistance provided by the Administrator under this paragraph shall be used only for the purposes specified in section 6943(b) of this title. Such assistance may not be used for purposes of land acquisition, final facility design, equipment purchase, construction, startup or operation activities.

(C) Where appropriate, any State receiving assistance under this paragraph may make all or any part of such assistance available to municipalities within the State to carry out the activities specified in section 6943(b)(1)(A) and (B) of this title.

(b) State allotment

The sums appropriated in any fiscal year under subsection (a)(1) of this section shall be allotted by the Administrator among all States, in the ratio that the population in each State bears to the population in all of the States, except that no State shall receive less than one-half of 1 per centum of the sums so allotted in any fiscal year. No State shall receive any grant under this section during any fiscal year when its expenditures of non-Federal funds for other than non-recurrent expenditures for solid waste management control programs will be less than its expenditures were for such programs during fiscal year 1975, except that such funds may be reduced by an amount equal to their proportionate share of any general reduction of State spending ordered by the Governor or legislature of such State. No State shall receive any grant for solid waste management programs unless the Administrator is satisfied that such grant will be so used as to supplement and, to the extent practicable, increase the level of State, local, regional, or other non-Federal funds that would in the absence of such grant be made available for the maintenance of such programs.

(c) Distribution of Federal financial assistance within the State

The Federal assistance allotted to the States under subsection (b) of this section shall be allocated by the State receiving such funds to State, local, regional, and interstate authorities carrying out planning and implementation of the State plan. Such allocation shall be based upon the responsibilities of the respective parties as determined pursuant to section 6946(b) of this title.

(d) Technical assistance

(1) The Administrator may provide technical assistance to State and local governments for purposes of developing and implementing State plans. Technical assistance respecting resource recovery and conservation may be provided through resource recovery and conservation panels, established in the Environmental Protection Agency under subchapter II of this chapter, to assist the State and local governments with respect to particular resource recovery and conservation projects under consideration and to evaluate their effect on the State plan.

(2) In carrying out this subsection, the Administrator may, upon request, provide technical assistance to States to assist in the removal or modification of legal, institutional, economic, and other impediments to the recycling of used oil. Such impediments may include laws, regulations, and policies, including State procurement policies, which are not favorable to the recycling of used oil.

(3) In carrying out this subsection, the Administrator is authorized to provide technical assistance to States, municipalities, regional authorities, and intermunicipal agencies upon request, to assist in the removal or modification of legal, institutional, and economic impediments which have the effect of impeding the development of systems and facilities to recover energy and materials from municipal waste or to conserve energy or materials which contribute to the waste stream. Such impediments may include—

(A) laws, regulations, and policies, including State and local procurement policies, which are not favorable to resource conservation and recovery policies, systems, and facilities;

(B) impediments to the financing of facilities to conserve or recover energy and materials from municipal waste through the exercise of State and local authority to issue revenue bonds and the use of State and local credit assistance; and

(C) impediments to institutional arrangements necessary to undertake projects for the conservation or recovery of energy and materials from municipal waste, including the creation of special districts, authorities, or corporations where necessary having the power to secure the supply of waste of a project, to conserve resources, to implement the project, and to undertake related activities.

(e) Special communities

(1) The Administrator, in cooperation with State and local officials, shall identify local governments within the United States (A) having a solid waste disposal facility (i) which is owned by the unit of local government, (ii) for which an order has been issued by the State to cease receiving solid waste for treatment, storage, or disposal, and (iii) which is subject to a State-approved end-use recreation plan, and (B) which are located over an aquifer which is the source of drinking water for any person or public water system and which has serious environmental problems resulting from the disposal of such solid waste, including possible methane migration.

(2) There is authorized to be appropriated to the Administrator $2,500,000 for the fiscal year 1980 and $1,500,000 for each of the fiscal years 1981 and 1982 to make grants to be used for containment and stabilization of solid waste located at the disposal sites referred to in paragraph (1). Not more than one community in any State shall be eligible for grants under this paragraph and not more than one project in any State shall be eligible for such grants. No unit of local government shall be eligible for grants under this paragraph with respect to any site which exceeds 65 acres in size.

(f) Assistance to States for discretionary program for recycled oil

(1) The Administrator may make grants to States, which have a State plan approved under section 6947 of this title, or which have submitted a State plan for approval under such section, if such plan includes the discretionary provisions described in section 6943(b) of this title. Grants under this subsection shall be for purposes of assisting the State in carrying out such discretionary provisions. No grant under this subsection may be used for construction or for the acquisition of land or equipment.

(2) Grants under this subsection shall be allotted among the States in the same manner as provided in the first sentence of subsection (b) of this section.

(3) No grant may be made under this subsection unless an application therefor is submitted to, and approved by, the Administrator. The application shall be in such form, be submitted in such manner, and contain such information as the Administrator may require.

(4) For purposes of making grants under this subsection, there are authorized to be appropriated $5,000,000 for fiscal year 1982, $5,000,000 for fiscal year 1983, and $5,000,000 for each of the fiscal years 1985 through 1988.

(g) Assistance to municipalities for energy and materials conservation and recovery planning activities

(1) The Administrator is authorized to make grants to municipalities, regional authorities, and intermunicipal agencies to carry out activities described in subparagraphs (A) and (B) of section 6943(b)(1) of this title. Such grants may be made only pursuant to an application submitted to the Administrator by the municipality which application has been approved by the State and determined by the State to be consistent with any State plan approved or submitted under this subchapter or any other appropriate planning carried out by the State.

(2) There is authorized to be appropriated for the fiscal year beginning October 1, 1981, and for each fiscal year thereafter before October 1, 1986, $8,000,000 for purposes of making grants to municipalities under this subsection. No amount may be appropriated for such purposes for the fiscal year beginning on October 1, 1986, or for any fiscal year thereafter.

(3) Assistance provided by the Administrator under this subsection shall be used only for the purposes specified in paragraph (1). Such assistance may not be used for purposes of land acquisition, final facility design, equipment purchase, construction, startup or operation activities.

(Pub.L. 89–272, Title II, § 4008, as added Oct. 21, 1976, Pub.L. 94–580, § 2, 90 Stat. 2818, and amended Oct. 15, 1980, Pub.L. 96–463, §§ 5(b), 6, 94 Stat. 2057; Oct. 21, 1980, Pub.L. 96–482, §§ 20, 31(c), (d), 32(e), (f), 94 Stat. 2345, 2352, 2354, 2355; Nov. 8, 1984, Pub.L. 98–616, § 2(d)–(g), (k), Title V, § 502(d), (e), 98 Stat. 3222, 3223, 3276.)

[1] So in original. Probably should be through.

LIBRARY REFERENCES

United States ⇐82(3).
C.J.S. United States § 122.

§ 6949. Rural communities assistance [SWDA § 4009]

(a) In general

The Administrator shall make grants to States to provide assistance to municipalities with a population of five thousand or less, or counties with a population of ten thousand or less or less than twenty persons per square mile and not within a metropolitan area, for solid waste management facilities (including equipment) necessary to meet the requirements of section 6945 of this title or restrictions on open burning or other requirements arising under the Clean Air Act [42 U.S.C.A. § 7401 et seq.] or the Federal Water Pollution Control Act [33 U.S.C.A. § 1251 et seq.]. Such assistance shall only be available—

(1) to any municipality or county which could not feasibly be included in a solid waste management system or facility serving an urbanized, multijurisdictional area because of its distance from such systems;

(2) where existing or planned solid waste management services or facilities are unavailable or insufficient to comply with the requirements of section 6945 of this title; and

(3) for systems which are certified by the State to be consistent with any plans or programs established under any State or areawide planning process.

(b) Allotment

The Administrator shall allot the sums appropriated to carry out this section in any fiscal year among the States in accordance with regulations promulgated by him on the basis of the average of the ratio which the population of rural areas of each State bears to the total population of rural areas of all the States, the ratio which the population of counties in each State having less than twenty persons per square mile bears to the total population of such counties in all the States, and the ratio which the population of such low-density counties in each State having 33 per centum or more of all families with incomes not in excess of 125 per centum of the poverty level bears to the total population of such counties in all the States.

(c) Limit

The amount of any grant under this section shall not exceed 75 per centum of the costs of the project. No assistance under this section shall be available for the acquisition of land or interests in land.

(d) Authorization of appropriations

There are authorized to be appropriated $25,000,000 for each of the fiscal years 1978 and 1979 to carry out this section. There are authorized to be appropriated $10,000,000 for the fiscal year 1980 and $15,000,000 for each of the fiscal years 1981 and 1982 to carry out this section.

(Pub.L. 89–272, Title II, § 4009, as added Oct. 21, 1976, Pub.L. 94–580, § 2, 90 Stat. 2819, and amended Pub.L. 96–482, § 31(e), Oct. 21, 1980, 94 Stat. 2353.)

CODE OF FEDERAL REGULATIONS

State and local assistance, see 40 CFR 35.001 et seq.

LIBRARY REFERENCES

United States ⚷82(3).
C.J.S. United States § 122.

§ 6949a. Adequacy of certain guidelines and criteria [SWDA § 4010]

(a) Study

The Administrator shall conduct a study of the extent to which the guidelines and criteria under this chapter (other than guidelines and criteria for facilities to which subchapter III of this chapter applies) which are applicable to solid waste management and disposal facilities, including, but not limited to landfills and surface impoundments, are adequate to protect human health and the environment from ground water contamination. Such study shall include a detailed assessment of the degree to which the criteria under section 6907(a) of this title and the criteria under section 6944 of this title regarding monitoring, prevention of contamination, and remedial action are adequate to protect ground water and shall also include recommendation with respect to any additional enforcement authorities which the Administrator, in consultation with the Attorney General, deems necessary for such purposes.

(b) Report

Not later than thirty-six months after November 8, 1984, the Administrator shall submit a report to the Congress setting forth the results of the study required under this section, together with any recommendations made by the Administrator on the basis of such study.

(c) Revisions of guidelines and criteria

Not later than March 31, 1988, the Administrator shall promulgate revisions of the criteria promulgated under paragraph (1) of section 6944(a) of this title and under section 6907(a)(3) of this title for facilities that may receive hazardous household wastes or hazardous wastes from small quantity generators under section 6921(d) of this title. The criteria shall be those necessary to protect human health and the environment and may take into account the practicable capability of such facilities. At a minimum such revisions for facilities potentially receiving such wastes should require ground water monitoring as necessary to detect contamination, establish criteria for the acceptable location of new or existing facilities, and provide for corrective action as appropriate.

(Pub.L. 89–272, Title II, § 4010, as added Nov. 8, 1984, Pub.L. 98–616, Title III, § 302(a)(1), 98 Stat. 3267.)

SUBCHAPTER V—DUTIES OF THE SECRETARY OF COMMERCE IN RESOURCE AND RECOVERY

§ 6951. Functions [SWDA § 5001]

The Secretary of Commerce shall encourage greater commercialization of proven resource recovery technology by providing—

(1) accurate specifications for recovered materials;

(2) stimulation of development of markets for recovered materials;

(3) promotion of proven technology; and

(4) a forum for the exchange of technical and economic data relating to resource recovery facilities.

(Pub.L. 89–272, Title II, § 5001, as added Oct. 21, 1976, Pub.L. 94–580, § 2, 90 Stat. 2820.)

§ 6952. Development of specifications for secondary materials [SWDA § 5002]

The Secretary of Commerce, acting through the National Institute of Standards and Technology, and in conjunction with national standards-setting organizations in resource recovery, shall, after public hearings, and not later than two years after September 1, 1979, publish guidelines for the development of specifications for the classification of materials recovered from waste which were destined for disposal. The specifications shall pertain to the physical and chemical properties and characteristics of such materials with regard to their use in replacing virgin materials in various industrial, commercial, and governmental uses. In establishing such guidelines the Secretary shall also, to the extent feasible, provide such information as may be necessary to assist Federal agencies with procurement of items containing recovered materials. The Secretary shall continue to cooperate with national standards-setting organizations, as may be necessary, to encourage the publication, promulgation and updating of standards for recovered materials and for the use of recovered materials in various industrial, commercial, and governmental uses.

(Pub.L. 89–272, Title II, § 5002, as added Oct. 21, 1976, Pub.L. 94–580, § 2, 90 Stat. 2820, and amended Oct. 21, 1980, Pub.L. 96–482, § 21(a), 94 Stat. 2346; Pub.L. 100–418, Title V, § 5115(c), Aug. 23, 1988, 102 Stat. 1433.)

§ 6953. Development of markets for recovered materials [SWDA § 5003]

The Secretary of Commerce shall within two years after September 1, 1979, take such actions as may be necessary to—

(1) identify the geographical location of existing or potential markets for recovered materials;

(2) identify the economic and technical barriers to the use of recovered materials; and

(3) encourage the development of new uses for recovered materials.

(Pub.L. 89–272, Title II, § 5003, as added Oct. 21, 1976, Pub.L. 94–580, § 2, 90 Stat. 2821, and amended Oct. 21, 1980, Pub.L. 96–482, § 21(b), 94 Stat. 2346.)

§ 6954. Technology promotion [SWDA § 5004]

The Secretary of Commerce is authorized to evaluate the commercial feasibility of resource recovery facilities and to publish the results of such evaluation, and to develop a data base for purposes of assisting persons in choosing such a system.

(Pub.L. 89–272, Title II, § 5004, as added Oct. 21, 1976, Pub.L. 94–580, § 2, 90 Stat. 2821.)

§ 6955. Marketing policies, establishment; nondiscrimination requirement [SWDA § 5005]

In establishing any policies which may affect the development of new markets for recovered materials and in making any determination concerning whether or not to impose monitoring or other controls on any marketing or transfer of recovered materials, the Secretary of Commerce may consider whether to establish the same or similar policies or impose the same or similar monitoring or other controls on virgin materials.

(Pub.L. 89–272, Title II, § 5005, as added Oct. 21, 1980, Pub.L. 96–482, § 21(c)(1), 94 Stat. 2346.)

§ 6956. Authorization of appropriations [SWDA § 5006]

There are authorized to be appropriated to the Secretary of Commerce $5,000,000 for each of fiscal years 1980, 1981, and 1982 and $1,500,000 for each of the fiscal years 1985 through 1988 to carry out the purposes of this subchapter.

(Pub.L. 89–272, Title II, § 5006, as added Oct. 21, 1980, Pub.L. 96–482, § 31(f)(1), 94 Stat. 2353, and amended Nov. 8, 1984, Pub.L. 98–616, § 2(h), 98 Stat. 3223.)

SUBCHAPTER VI—FEDERAL RESPONSIBILITIES

§ 6961. Application of Federal, State, and local law to Federal facilities [SWDA § 6001]

(a) In general

Each department, agency, and instrumentality of the executive, legislative, and judicial branches of the

Federal Government (1) having jurisdiction over any solid waste management facility or disposal site, or (2) engaged in any activity resulting, or which may result, in the disposal or management of solid waste or hazardous waste shall be subject to, and comply with, all Federal, State, interstate, and local requirements, both substantive and procedural (including any requirement for permits or reporting or any provisions for injunctive relief and such sanctions as may be imposed by a court to enforce such relief), respecting control and abatement of solid waste or hazardous waste disposal and management in the same manner, and to the same extent, as any person is subject to such requirements, including the payment of reasonable service charges. The Federal, State, interstate, and local substantive and procedural requirements referred to in this subsection include, but are not limited to, all administrative orders and all civil and administrative penalties and fines, regardless of whether such penalties or fines are punitive or coercive in nature or are imposed for isolated, intermittent, or continuing violations. The United States hereby expressly waives any immunity otherwise applicable to the United States with respect to any such substantive or procedural requirement (including, but not limited to, any injunctive relief, administrative order or civil or administrative penalty or fine referred to in the preceding sentence, or reasonable service charge). The reasonable service charges referred to in this subsection include, but are not limited to, fees or charges assessed in connection with the processing and issuance of permits, renewal of permits, amendments to permits, review of plans, studies, and other documents, and inspection and monitoring of facilities, as well as any other nondiscriminatory charges that are assessed in connection with a Federal, State, interstate, or local solid waste or hazardous waste regulatory program. Neither the United States, nor any agent, employee, or officer thereof, shall be immune or exempt from any process or sanction of any State or Federal Court with respect to the enforcement of any such injunctive relief. No agent, employee, or officer of the United States shall be personally liable for any civil penalty under any Federal, State, interstate, or local solid or hazardous waste law with respect to any act or omission within the scope of the official duties of the agent, employee, or officer. An agent, employee, or officer of the United States shall be subject to any criminal sanction (including, but not limited to, any fine or imprisonment) under any Federal or State solid or hazardous waste law, but no department, agency, or instrumentality of the executive, legislative, or judicial branch of the Federal Government shall be subject to any such sanction. The President may exempt any solid waste management facility of any department, agency, or instrumentality in the executive branch from compliance with such a requirement if he determines it to be in the paramount interest of the United States to do so. No such exemption shall be granted due to lack of appropriation unless the President shall have specifically requested such appropriation as a part of the budgetary process and the Congress shall have failed to make available such requested appropriation. Any exemption shall be for a period not in excess of one year, but additional exemptions may be granted for periods not to exceed one year upon the President's making a new determination. The President shall report each January to the Congress all exemptions from the requirements of this section granted during the preceding calendar year, together with his reason for granting each such exemption.

(b) Administrative enforcement actions

(1) The Administrator may commence an administrative enforcement action against any department, agency, or instrumentality of the executive, legislative, or judicial branch of the Federal Government pursuant to the enforcement authorities contained in this chapter. The Administrator shall initiate an administrative enforcement action against such a department, agency, or instrumentality in the same manner and under the same circumstances as an action would be initiated against another person. Any voluntary resolution or settlement of such an action shall be set forth in a consent order.

(2) No administrative order issued to such a department, agency, or instrumentality shall become final until such department, agency, or instrumentality has had the opportunity to confer with the Administrator.

(c) Limitation on State use of funds collected from Federal Government

Unless a State law in effect on October 6, 1992, or a State constitution requires the funds to be used in a different manner, all funds collected by a State from the Federal Government from penalties and fines imposed for violation of any substantive or procedural requirement referred to in subsection (a) of this section shall be used by the State only for projects designed to improve or protect the environment or to defray the costs of environmental protection or enforcement.

(Pub.L. 89–272, Title II, § 6001, as added Oct. 21, 1976, Pub.L. 94–580, § 2, 90 Stat. 2821, and amended Nov. 8, 1978, Pub.L. 95–609, § 7(m), 92 Stat. 3082; Oct. 6, 1992, Pub.L. 102–386, Title I, § 102(a), (b), 106 Stat. 1505, 1506.)

Effective Date of 1992 Amendments

Section 102(c) of Pub.L. 102–386 provided that:

"(1) **In general.**—Except as otherwise provided in paragraphs (2) and (3), the amendments made by subsection (a) [amending subsec. (a) of this section] shall take effect upon the date of the enactment of this Act [Oct. 6, 1992].

"(2) **Delayed effective date for certain mixed waste.**—Until the date that is 3 years after the date of the enactment of this Act [Oct. 6, 1992], the waiver of sovereign immunity contained in section 6001(a) of the Solid Waste Disposal Act with respect to civil, criminal, and administrative penalties and fines (as added by the amendments made by subsection (a) [subsec. (a) of this section]) shall not apply to departments, agencies, and instrumentalities of the executive branch of the Federal Government for violations of section 3004(j) of the Solid Waste Disposal Act [section 6924(j) of this title] involving storage of mixed waste that is not subject to an existing agreement, permit, or administrative or judicial order, so long as such waste is managed in compliance with all other applicable requirements.

"(3) **Effective date for certain mixed waste.**—(A) Except as provided in subparagraph (B), after the date that is 3 years after the date of the enactment of this Act [Oct. 6, 1992], the waiver of sovereign immunity contained in section 6001(a) of the Solid Waste Disposal Act with respect to civil, criminal, and administrative penalties and fines (as added by the amendments made by subsection (a) [subsec. (a) of this section]) shall apply to departments, agencies, and instrumentalities of the executive branch of the Federal Government for violations of section 3004(j) of the Solid Waste Disposal Act [section 6924(j) of this title] involving storage of mixed waste.

"(B) With respect to the Department of Energy, the waiver of sovereign immunity referred to in subparagraph (A) shall not apply after the date that is 3 years after the date of the enactment of this Act [Oct. 6, 1992] for violations of section 3004(j) of such Act [section 6924(j) of this title] involving storage of mixed waste, so long as the Department of Energy is in compliance with both—

"(i) a plan that has been submitted and approved pursuant to section 3021(b) of the Solid Waste Disposal Act [section 6939c(b) of this title] and which is in effect; and

"(ii) an order requiring compliance with such plan which has been issued pursuant to such section 3021(b) [section 6939c(b) of this title] and which is in effect.

"(4) **Application of waiver to agreements and orders.**—The waiver of sovereign immunity contained in section 6001(a) of the Solid Waste Disposal Act (as added by the amendments made by subsection (a) [subsec. (a) of this section]) shall take effect on the date of the enactment of this Act [Oct. 6, 1992] with respect to any agreement, permit, or administrative or judicial order existing on such date of enactment [Oct. 6, 1992] (and any subsequent modifications to such an agreement, permit, or order), including, without limitation, any provision of an agreement, permit, or order that addresses compliance with section 3004(j) of such Act [section 6924(j) of this title] with respect to mixed waste.

"(5) **Agreement or order.**—Except as provided in paragraph (4), nothing in this Act [see Short Title of 1992 Amendments note set out under section 6901 of this title] shall be construed to alter, modify, or change in any manner any agreement, permit, or administrative or judicial order, including, without limitation, any provision of an agreement, permit, or order—

"(i) that addresses compliance with section 3004(j) of the Solid Waste Disposal Act [section 6924(j) of this title] with respect to mixed waste;

"(ii) that is in effect on the date of enactment of this Act [Oct. 6, 1992]; and

"(iii) to which a department, agency, or instrumentality of the executive branch of the Federal Governmental is a party."

CODE OF FEDERAL REGULATIONS

Federal facilities and Native American Reservations, inclusion of, see 40 CFR 255.33 et seq.

LAW REVIEW COMMENTARIES

Hazardous Waste Law for the federal employee after the Federal Facility Compliance Act of 1992. Stephen J. Darmody, 40 Fed. B.News & J. 650 (Nov./Dec. 1993).

How well can states enforce their environmental laws when the polluter is the United States Government? 18 Rutgers L.J. 123 (1986).

West's Federal Practice Manual

Solid waste disposal, see § 4385.5.

United States Supreme Court

Section of Resource Conservation and Recovery Act (RCRA) which subjects government to all state requirements, including sanctions, and provides that United States is not immune from process or sanctions of any court with respect to enforcement of injunctive relief excludes punitive measures and does not waive government immunity as to punitive fines, see United States Department of Energy v. Ohio, 1992, 112 S.Ct. 1627, 118 L.Ed.2d 255.

§ 6962. Federal procurement [SWDA § 6002]

(a) Application of section

Except as provided in subsection (b) of this section, a procuring agency shall comply with the requirements set forth in this section and any regulations issued under this section, with respect to any purchase or acquisition of a procurement item where the purchase price of the item exceeds $10,000 or where the quantity of such items or of functionally equivalent items purchased or acquired in the course of the preceding fiscal year was $10,000 or more.

(b) Procurement subject to other law

Any procurement, by any procuring agency, which is subject to regulations of the Administrator under section 6964 of this title (as promulgated before October 21, 1976, under comparable provisions of prior law) shall not be subject to the requirements of this section to the extent that such requirements are inconsistent with such regulations.

(c) Requirements

(1) After the date specified in applicable guidelines prepared pursuant to subsection (e) of this section, each procuring agency which procures any items designated in such guidelines shall procure such items composed of the highest percentage of recovered materials practicable (and in the case of paper, the highest percentage of the postconsumer recovered materials referred to in subsection (h)(1) of this section practicable), consistent with maintaining a satisfactory level of competition, considering such guidelines. The decision not to procure such items shall be based on a determination that such procurement items—

(A) are not reasonably available within a reasonable period of time;

(B) fail to meet the performance standards set forth in the applicable specifications or fail to meet the reasonable performance standards of the procuring agencies; or

(C) are only available at an unreasonable price.
Any determination under subparagraph (B) shall be made on the basis of the guidelines of the National Institute of Standards and Technology in any case in which such material is covered by such guidelines.

(2) Agencies that generate heat, mechanical, or electrical energy from fossil fuel in systems that have the technical capability of using energy or fuels derived from solid waste as a primary or supplementary fuel shall use such capability to the maximum extent practicable.

(3)(A) After the date specified in any applicable guidelines prepared pursuant to subsection (e) of this section, contracting officers shall require that vendors:

(i) certify that the percentage of recovered materials to be used in the performance of the contract will be at least the amount required by applicable specifications or other contractual requirements, and

(ii) estimate the percentage of the total material utilized for the performance of the contract which is recovered materials.

(B) Clause (ii) of subparagraph (A) applies only to a contract in an amount greater than $100,000.

(d) Specifications

All Federal agencies that have the responsibility for drafting or reviewing specifications for procurement items procured by Federal agencies shall—

(1) as expeditiously as possible but in any event no later than eighteen months after November 8, 1984, eliminate from such specifications—

(A) any exclusion of recovered materials and

(B) any requirement that items be manufactured from virgin materials; and

(2) within one year after the date of publication of applicable guidelines under subsection (e) of this section, or as otherwise specified in such guidelines, assure that such specifications require the use of recovered materials to the maximum extent possible without jeopardizing the intended end use of the item.

(e) Guidelines

The Administrator, after consultation with the Administrator of General Services, the Secretary of Commerce (acting through the National Institute of Standards and Technology), and the Public Printer, shall prepare, and from time to time revise, guidelines for the use of procuring agencies in complying with the requirements of this section. Such guidelines shall—

(1) designate those items which are or can be produced with recovered materials and whose procurement by procuring agencies will carry out the objectives of this section, and in the case of paper, provide for maximizing the use of post consumer recovered materials referred to in subsection (h)(1) of this section;

(2) set forth recommended practices with respect to the procurement of recovered materials and items containing such materials and with respect to certification by vendors of the percentage of recovered materials used,

and shall provide information as to the availability, relative price, and performance of such materials and items and where appropriate shall recommend the level of recovered material to be contained in the procured product. The Administrator shall prepare final guidelines for paper within one hundred and eighty days after November 8, 1984, and for three additional product categories (including tires) by October 1, 1985. In making the designation under paragraph (1), the Administrator shall consider, but is not limited in his considerations, to—

(A) the availability of such items;

(B) the impact of the procurement of such items by procuring agencies on the volume of solid waste which must be treated, stored or disposed of;

(C) the economic and technological feasibility of producing and using such items; and

(D) other uses for such recovered materials.

(f) Procurement of services

A procuring agency shall, to the maximum extent practicable, manage or arrange for the procurement of solid waste management services in a manner which maximizes energy and resource recovery.

(g) Executive Office

The Office of Procurement Policy in the Executive Office of the President, in cooperation with the Administrator, shall implement the requirements of this section. It shall be the responsibility of the Office of Procurement Policy to coordinate this policy with other policies for Federal procurement, in such a way as to maximize the use of recovered resources, and to, every two years beginning in 1984, report to the Congress on actions taken by Federal agencies and the progress made in the implementation of this section, including agency compliance with subsection (d) of this section.

(h) Definitions

As used in this section, in the case of paper products, the term "recovered materials" includes—

(1) postconsumer materials such as—

(A) paper, paperboard, and fibrous wastes from retail stores, office buildings, homes, and so forth, after they have passed through their end-usage as a consumer item, including: used corrugated boxes; old newspapers; old magazines; mixed waste paper; tabulating cards; and used cordage; and

(B) all paper, paperboard, and fibrous wastes that enter and are collected from municipal solid waste, and

(2) manufacturing, forest residues, and other wastes such as—

(A) dry paper and paperboard waste generated after completion of the papermaking process (that is, those manufacturing operations up to and including the cutting and trimming of the paper machine reel into smaller rolls or rough sheets) including: envelope cuttings, bindery trimmings, and other paper and paperboard waste, resulting from printing, cutting, forming, and other converting operations; bag, box, and carton manufacturing wastes; and butt rolls, mill wrappers, and rejected unused stock; and

(B) finished paper and paperboard from obsolete inventories of paper and paperboard manufacturers, merchants, wholesalers, dealers, printers, converters, or others;

(C) fibrous byproducts of harvesting, manufacturing, extractive, or wood-cutting processes, flax, straw, linters, bagasse, slash, and other forest residues;

(D) wastes generated by the conversion of goods made from fibrous material (that is, waste rope from cordage manufacture, textile mill waste, and cuttings); and

(E) fibers recovered from waste water which otherwise would enter the waste stream.

(i) Procurement program

(1) Within one year after the date of publication of applicable guidelines under subsection (e) of this section, each procuring agency shall develop an affirmative procurement program which will assure that items composed of recovered materials will be purchased to the maximum extent practicable and which is consistent with applicable provisions of Federal procurement law.

(2) Each affirmative procurement program required under this subsection shall, at a minimum, contain—

(A) a recovered materials preference program;

(B) an agency promotion program to promote the preference program adopted under subparagraph (A);

(C) a program for requiring estimates of the total percentage of recovered material utilized in the performance of a contract; certification of minimum recovered material content actually utilized, where appropriate; and reasonable verification procedures for estimates and certifications; and

(D) annual review and monitoring of the effectiveness of an agency's affirmative procurement program.

In the case of paper, the recovered materials preference program required under subparagraph (A) shall provide for the maximum use of the post consumer recovered materials referred to in subsection (h)(1) of this section.

(3) In developing the preference program, the following options shall be considered for adoption:

(A) Case-by-Case Policy Development: Subject to the limitations of subsection (c)(1)(A) through (C) of this section, a policy of awarding contracts to the vendor offering an item composed of the highest percentage of recovered materials practicable (and in the case of paper, the highest percentage of the post consumer recovered materials referred to in subsection (h)(1) of this section). Subject to such limitations, agencies may make an award to a vendor offering items with less than the maximum recovered materials content.

(B) Minimum Content Standards: Minimum recovered materials content specifications which are set in such a way as to assure that the recovered materials content (and in the case of paper, the content of post consumer materials referred to in subsection (h)(1) of this section) required is the maximum available without jeopardizing the intended end use of the item, or violating the limitations of subsection (c)(1)(A) through (C) of this section.

Procuring agencies shall adopt one of the options set forth in subparagraphs (A) and (B) or a substantially equivalent alternative, for inclusion in the affirmative procurement program.

(j) Repealed. Pub.L. 103–355, Title I, § 1554(1), Oct. 13, 1994, 108 Stat. 3300

(Pub.L. 89–272, Title II, § 6002, as added Oct. 21, 1976, Pub.L. 94–580, § 2, 90 Stat. 2822, and amended Nov. 8, 1978, Pub.L. 95–609, § 7(n), 92 Stat. 3082; Oct. 21, 1980, Pub.L. 96–482, § 22, 94 Stat. 2346; Dec. 21, 1982, Pub.L. 97–375, Title I, § 102, 96 Stat. 1819; Nov. 8, 1984, Pub.L. 98–616, Title V, § 501(a)–(e), 98 Stat. 3274–3276; Pub.L. 100–418, Title V, § 5115(c), Aug. 23, 1988, 102 Stat. 1433; Oct. 6, 1992, Pub.L. 102–393, Title VI, § 630, 106 Stat. 1773; Pub.L. 103–355, Title I, § 1554(1), Title IV, § 4104(e), Oct. 13, 1994, 108 Stat. 3300, 3342.)

Effective Date of 1994 Amendments

Amendment by section 1554(1) of Pub.L. 103–355 effective Oct. 13, 1994, and applicable on and after such date; amendment by section

4104(e) of Pub.L. 103–355 effective Oct. 13, 1994, except as otherwise provided, see section 10001 of Pub.L. 103–355, set out as a note under section 251 of Title 41, Public Contracts.

Transfer of Functions

For transfer of certain enforcement functions of Administrator or other official of the Environmental Protection Agency under this chapter to Federal Inspector, Office of Federal Inspector for the Alaska Natural Gas Transportation System, see Transfer of Functions note set out under § 6903 of this title.

Procurement Preference for U.S. Made Remanufactured or Recycled Toner Cartridges

Pub.L. 103–123, Title IV, § 401, Oct. 28, 1993, 107 Stat. 1238, which provided in part that a Federal agency, when purchasing toner cartridges, give preference to remanufactured toner cartridges made in the U.S. by small businesses and to recycled toner cartridges, unless such cartridges do not exist, the cost is greater than new cartridges, or sufficient quantities are not available, but authorizing the purchase of one or more new cartridges as a part of an initial printer or copier acquisition, and providing that such purchasing preference directives shall not affect current law with respect to Organizations for the Blind or Other Severely Handicapped, was repealed by Pub.L. 103–355, Title I, § 1554(2), Title X, § 10001, Oct. 13, 1994, 108 Stat. 3300, 3404, effective Oct. 13, 1994, and applicable on and after such date.

Similar provisions were contained in the following prior appropriation Acts:

Pub.L. 102–393, Title VI, § 630, Oct. 6, 1992, 106 Stat. 1773.

CODE OF FEDERAL REGULATIONS

Cement and fly ash concrete, see 40 CFR 249.01 et seq.

§ 6963. Cooperation with Environmental Protection Agency [SWDA § 6003]

(a) General rule

All Federal agencies shall assist the Administrator in carrying out his functions under this chapter and shall promptly make available all requested information concerning past or present Agency waste management practices and past or present Agency owned, leased, or operated solid or hazardous waste facilities. This information shall be provided in such format as may be determined by the Administrator.

(b) Information relating to energy and materials conservation and recovery

The Administrator shall collect, maintain, and disseminate information concerning the market potential of energy and materials recovered from solid waste, including materials obtained through source separation, and information concerning the savings potential of conserving resources contributing to the waste stream. The Administrator shall identify the regions in which the increased substitution of such energy for energy derived from fossil fuels and other sources is most likely to be feasible, and provide information on the technical and economic aspects of developing integrated resource conservation or recovery systems which provide for the recovery of source-separated materials to be recycled or the conservation of resources. The Administrator shall utilize the authorities of subsection (a) of this section in carrying out this subsection.

(Pub.L. 89–272, Title II, § 6003, as added Oct. 21, 1976, Pub.L. 94–580, § 2, 90 Stat. 2823, and amended Oct. 21, 1980, Pub.L. 96–482, § 32(g), 94 Stat. 2355.)

§ 6964. Applicability of solid waste disposal guidelines to Executive agencies [SWDA § 6004]

(a) Compliance

(1) If—

(A) an Executive agency (as defined in section 105 of Title 5) or any unit of the legislative branch of the Federal Government has jurisdiction over any real property or facility the operation or administration of which involves such agency in solid waste management activities, or

(B) such an agency enters into a contract with any person for the operation by such person of any Federal property or facility, and the performance of such contract involves such person in solid waste management activities,

then such agency shall insure compliance with the guidelines recommended under section 6907 of this title and the purposes of this chapter in the operation or administration of such property or facility, or the performance of such contract, as the case may be.

(2) Each Executive agency or any unit of the legislative branch of the Federal Government which conducts any activity—

(A) which generates solid waste, and

(B) which, if conducted by a person other than such agency, would require a permit or license from such agency in order to dispose of such solid waste,

shall insure compliance with such guidelines and the purposes of this chapter in conducting such activity.

(3) Each Executive agency which permits the use of Federal property for purposes of disposal of solid waste shall insure compliance with such guidelines and the purposes of this chapter in the disposal of such waste.

(4) The President or the Committee on House Administration of the House of Representatives and the Committee on Rules and Administration of the Senate with regard to any unit of the legislative branch of the Federal Government shall prescribe regulations to carry out this subsection.

(b) Licenses and permits

Each Executive agency which issues any license or permit for disposal of solid waste shall, prior to the issuance of such license or permit, consult with the Administrator to insure compliance with guidelines recommended under section 6907 of this title and the purposes of this chapter.

(Pub.L. 89–272, Title II, § 6004, as added Oct. 21, 1976, Pub.L. 94–580, § 2, 90 Stat. 2823, and amended Nov. 8, 1978, Pub.L. 95–609, § 7(*o*), 92 Stat. 3083; Oct. 21, 1980, Pub.L. 96–482, § 23, 94 Stat. 2347.)

Change of Name

Any reference in any provision of law enacted before Jan. 4, 1995, to the Committee on House Administration of the House of Representatives treated as referring to the Committee on House Oversight of the House of Representatives, see section 1(a)(7) of Pub.L. 104–14, set out as a note preceding section 21 of Title 2, The Congress.

CODE OF FEDERAL REGULATIONS

Solid waste management guidelines and procedures, see 40 CFR 244.100 et seq., 245.100 et seq., 246.100 et seq.

§ 6965. Chief Financial Officer report

The Chief Financial Officer of each affected agency shall submit to Congress an annual report containing, to the extent practicable, a detailed description of the compliance activities undertaken by the agency for mixed waste streams, and an accounting of the fines and penalties imposed on the agency for violations involving mixed waste.

(Pub.L. 102–386, Title I, § 110, Oct. 6, 1992, 106 Stat. 1516.)

Codifications

Section was enacted as part of the Federal Facility Compliance Act of 1992 and not as part of the Solid Waste Disposal Act, which comprises this chapter.

SUBCHAPTER VII—MISCELLANEOUS PROVISIONS

§ 6971. Employee protection [SWDA § 7001]

(a) General

No person shall fire, or in any other way discriminate against, or cause to be fired or discriminated against, any employee or any authorized representative of employees by reason of the fact that such employee or representative has filed, instituted, or caused to be filed or instituted any proceeding under this chapter or under any applicable implementation plan, or has testified or is about to testify in any proceeding resulting from the administration or enforcement of the provisions of this chapter or of any applicable implementation plan.

(b) Remedy

Any employee or a representative of employees who believes that he has been fired or otherwise discriminated against by any person in violation of subsection (a) of this section may, within thirty days after such alleged violation occurs, apply to the Secretary of Labor for a review of such firing or alleged discrimination. A copy of the application shall be sent to such person who shall be the respondent. Upon receipt of such application, the Secretary of Labor shall cause such investigation to be made as he deems appropriate. Such investigation shall provide an opportunity for a public hearing at the request of any party to such review to enable the parties to present information relating to such alleged violation. The parties shall be given written notice of the time and place of the hearing at least five days prior to the hearing. Any such hearing shall be of record and shall be subject to section 554 of Title 5. Upon receiving the report of such investigation, the Secretary of Labor shall make findings of fact. If he finds that such violation did occur, he shall issue a decision, incorporating an order therein and his findings, requiring the party committing such violation to take such affirmative action to abate the violation as the Secretary of Labor deems appropriate, including, but not limited to, the rehiring or reinstatement of the employee or representative of employees to his former position with compensation. If he finds that there was no such violation, he shall issue an order denying the application. Such order issued by the Secretary of Labor under this subparagraph shall be subject to judicial review in the same manner as orders and decisions of the Administrator or subject to judicial review under this chapter.

(c) Costs

Whenever an order is issued under this section to abate such violation, at the request of the applicant, a sum equal to the aggregate amount of all costs and expenses (including the attorney's fees) as determined by the Secretary of Labor, to have been reasonably incurred by the applicant for, or in connection with, the institution and prosecution of such proceedings, shall be assessed against the person committing such violation.

(d) Exception

This section shall have no application to any employee who, acting without direction from his employer (or his agent) deliberately violates any requirement of this chapter.

(e) Employment shifts and loss

The Administrator shall conduct continuing evaluations of potential loss or shifts of employment which may result from the administration or enforcement of the provisions of this chapter and applicable implementation plans, including, where appropriate, investigating threatened plant closures or reductions in employment allegedly resulting from such administration or enforcement. Any employee who is discharged, or laid off, threatened with discharge or layoff, or otherwise discriminated against by any person because of the alleged results of such administration or enforcement, or any representative of such employee, may request the Administrator to conduct a full investigation of the matter. The Administrator shall thereupon investigate the matter and, at the request of any party, shall hold public hearings on not less than five days' notice, and shall at such hearings require the parties, including the employer involved, to present information relating to the actual or potential effect of such administration or enforcement on employment and on any alleged discharge, layoff, or other discrimination and the detailed reasons or justification therefor. Any such hearing shall be of record and shall be subject to section 554 of title 5. Upon receiving the report of such investigation, the Administrator shall make findings of fact as to the effect of such administration or enforcement on employment and on the alleged discharge, layoff, or discrimination and shall make such recommendations as he deems appropriate. Such report, findings, and recommendations shall be available to the public. Nothing in this subsection shall be construed to require or authorize the Administrator or any State to modify or withdraw any standard, limitation, or any other requirement of this chapter or any applicable implementation plan.

(f) Occupational safety and health

In order to assist the Secretary of Labor and the Director of the National Institute for Occupational Safety and Health in carrying out their duties under the Occupational Safety and Health Act of 1970 [29 U.S.C.A. § 651 et seq.], the Administrator shall—

(1) provide the following information, as such information becomes available, to the Secretary and the Director:

(A) the identity of any hazardous waste generation, treatment, storage, disposal facility or site where cleanup is planned or underway;

(B) information identifying the hazards to which persons working at a hazardous waste generation, treatment, storage, disposal facility or site or otherwise handling hazardous waste may be exposed, the nature and extent of the exposure, and methods to protect workers from such hazards; and

(C) incidents of worker injury or harm at a hazardous waste generation, treatment, storage or disposal facility or site; and

(2) notify the Secretary and the Director of the Administrator's receipt of notifications under section 6930 or reports under sections 6922, 6923, and 6924 of this title and make such notifications and reports available to the Secretary and the Director.

(Pub.L. 89–272, Title II, § 7001, as added Oct. 21, 1976, Pub.L. 94–580, § 2, 90 Stat. 2824, and amended Oct. 21, 1980, Pub.L. 96–482, § 24, 94 Stat. 2347.)

CODE OF FEDERAL REGULATIONS

Discrimination complaints, procedure, see 29 CFR 24.1 et seq.

§ 6972. Citizens' suits [SWDA § 7002]

(a) In general

Except as provided in subsection (b) or (c) of this section, any person may commence a civil action on his own behalf—

(1)(A) against any person (including (a) the United States, and (b) any other governmental instrumentality or agency, to the extent permitted by the eleventh amendment to the Constitution) who is alleged to be in violation of any permit, standard, regulation, condition, requirement, prohibition, or order which has become effective pursuant to this chapter; or

(B) against any person, including the United States, and any other governmental instrumentality or agency, to the extent permitted by the eleventh amendment to the Constitution, and including any past or present generator, past or present transporter, or past or present owner or operator of a treatment, storage, or disposal facility, who has contributed or who is contributing to the past or present handling, storage, treatment, transportation, or disposal of any solid or hazardous waste which may present an imminent and substantial endangerment to health or the environment; or

(2) against the Administrator where there is alleged a failure of the Administrator to perform any act or duty under this chapter which is not discretionary with the Administrator.

Any action under paragraph (a)(1) of this subsection shall be brought in the district court for the district in which the alleged violation occurred or the alleged endangerment may occur. Any action brought under paragraph (a)(2) of this subsection may be brought in the district court for the district in which the alleged violation occurred or in the District Court of the District of Columbia. The district court shall have jurisdiction, without regard to the amount in controversy or the citizenship of the parties, to enforce the permit, standard, regulation, condition, requirement, prohibition, or order, referred to in paragraph (1)(A), to restrain any person who has contributed or who is contributing to the past or present handling, storage, treatment, transportation, or disposal of any solid or hazardous waste referred to in paragraph (1)(B), to order such person to take such other action as may be necessary, or both, or to order the Administrator to perform the act or duty referred to in paragraph (2), as the case may be, and to apply any appropriate civil penalties under section 6928(a) and (g) of this title.

(b) Actions prohibited

(1) No action may be commenced under subsection (a)(1)(A) of this section—

(A) prior to 60 days after the plaintiff has given notice of the violation to—

(i) the Administrator;

(ii) the State in which the alleged violation occurs; and

(iii) to any alleged violator of such permit, standard, regulation, condition, requirement, prohibition, or order,

except that such action may be brought immediately after such notification in the case of an action under this section respecting a violation of subchapter III of this chapter; or

(B) if the Administrator or State has commenced and is diligently prosecuting a civil or criminal action in a court of the United States or a State to require compliance with such permit, standard, regulation, condition, requirement, prohibition, or order.

In any action under subsection (a)(1)(A) of this section in a court of the United States, any person may intervene as a matter of right.

(2)(A) No action may be commenced under subsection (a)(1)(B) of this section prior to ninety days after the plaintiff has given notice of the endangerment to—

(i) the Administrator;

(ii) the State in which the alleged endangerment may occur;

(iii) any person alleged to have contributed or to be contributing to the past or present handling, storage, treatment, transportation, or disposal of any solid or hazardous waste referred to in subsection (a)(1)(B) of this section,

except that such action may be brought immediately after such notification in the case of an action under this section respecting a violation of subchapter III of this chapter.

(B) No action may be commenced under subsection (a)(1)(B) of this section if the Administrator, in order to restrain or abate acts or conditions which may have contributed or are contributing to the activities which may present the alleged endangerment—

(i) has commenced and is diligently prosecuting an action under section 6973 of this title or under section 106 of the Comprehensive Environmental Response, Compensation and Liability Act of 1980 [42 U.S.C.A. § 9606];

(ii) is actually engaging in a removal action under section 104 of the Comprehensive Environmental Response, Compensation and Liability Act of 1980 [42 U.S.C.A. § 9604];

(iii) has incurred costs to initiate a Remedial Investigation and Feasibility Study under section 104 of the Comprehensive Environmental Response, Compensation and Liability Act of 1980 [42 U.S.C.A. § 9604] and is diligently proceeding with a remedial action under that Act [42 U.S.C.A. § 9601 et seq.]; or

(iv) has obtained a court order (including a consent decree) or issued an administrative order under section 106 of the Comprehensive Environmental Response, Compensation and Liability Act of 980[1] [42 U.S.C.A. § 9606] or section 6973 of this title pursuant to which a responsible party is diligently conducting a removal action, Remedial Investigation and Feasibility Study (RIFS), or proceeding with a remedial action.

In the case of an administrative order referred to in clause (iv), actions under subsection (a)(1)(B) of this section are prohibited only as to the scope and duration of the administrative order referred to in clause (iv).

(C) No action may be commenced under subsection (a)(1)(B) of this section if the State, in order to restrain or abate acts or conditions which may have contributed or are contributing to the activities which may present the alleged endangerment—

(i) has commenced and is diligently prosecuting an action under subsection (a)(1)(B) of this section;

(ii) is actually engaging in a removal action under section 104 of the Comprehensive Environmental Response, Compensation and Liability Act of 1980 [42 U.S.C.A. § 9604]; or

(iii) has incurred costs to initiate a Remedial Investigation and Feasibility Study under section 104 of the Comprehensive Environmental Response, Compensation and Liability Act of 1980 [42 U.S.C.A. § 9604] and is diligently proceeding with a remedial action under that Act [42 U.S.C.A. § 9601 et seq.].

(D) No action may be commenced under subsection (a)(1)(B) of this section by any person (other than a State or local government) with respect to the siting of a hazardous waste treatment, storage, or a disposal facility, nor to restrain or enjoin the issuance of a permit for such facility.

(E) In any action under subsection (a)(1)(B) of this section in a court of the United States, any person may intervene as a matter of right when the applicant claims an interest relating to the subject of the action and he is so situated that the disposition of the action may, as a practical matter, impair or impede his ability to protect that interest, unless the Administrator or the State shows that the applicant's interest is adequately represented by existing parties.

(F) Whenever any action is brought under subsection (a)(1)(B) of this section in a court of the United States, the plaintiff shall serve a copy of the complaint on the Attorney General of the United States and with the Administrator.

(c) Notice

No action may be commenced under paragraph (a)(2) of this section prior to sixty days after the plaintiff has given notice to the Administrator that he will commence such action, except that such action may be brought immediately after such notification in the case of an action under this section respecting a violation of subchapter III of this chapter. Notice under this subsection shall be given in such manner as the Administrator shall prescribe by regulation. Any action respecting a violation under this chapter may be brought under this section only in the judicial district in which such alleged violation occurs.

(d) Intervention

In any action under this section the Administrator, if not a party, may intervene as a matter of right.

(e) Costs

The court, in issuing any final order in any action brought pursuant to this section or section 6976 of this title, may award costs of litigation (including reasonable attorney and expert witness fees) to the prevailing or substantially prevailing party, whenever the court determines such an award is appropriate. The court may, if a temporary restraining order or preliminary injunction is sought, require the filing of a bond or equivalent security in accordance with the Federal Rules of Civil Procedure.

(f) Other rights preserved

Nothing in this section shall restrict any right which any person (or class of persons) may have under any statute or common law to seek enforcement of any standard or requirement relating to the management of solid waste or hazardous waste, or to seek any other relief (including relief against the Administrator or a State agency).

(g) Transporters

A transporter shall not be deemed to have contributed or to be contributing to the handling, storage, treatment, or disposal, referred to in subsection (a)(1)(B) of this section taking place after such solid waste or hazardous waste has left the possession or control of such transporter, if the transportation of such waste was under a sole contractual arrangement arising from a published tariff and acceptance for carriage by common carrier by rail and such transporter has exercised due care in the past or present handling, storage, treatment, transportation and disposal of such waste.

(Pub.L. 89–272, Title II, § 7002, as added Oct. 21, 1976, Pub.L. 94–580, § 2, 90 Stat. 2825, and amended Nov. 8, 1978, Pub.L. 95–609, § 7(p), 92 Stat. 3083; Nov. 8, 1984, Pub.L. 98–616, Title IV, § 401, 98 Stat. 3268.)

[1] So in original. Probably should be 1980.

CODE OF FEDERAL REGULATIONS

Citizen suits, prior notice of, see 40 CFR 254.1 et seq.

LAW REVIEW COMMENTARIES

Acid Rain: The Clean Air Act cannot handle the problem. Timothy Stein, 56 UMKC L.Rev. 139 (1987).

LIBRARY REFERENCES

Health and Environment ⚷25.15(4).
C.J.S. Health and Environment § 83 et seq.

United States Supreme Court

Inclusion in citizen suit sections of both Clean Water Act (CWA) and Resource Conservation and Recovery Act (RCRA) of United States as "person" went only to clauses subjecting government to suit, and broader waiver could not be inferred; authorization of district courts to impose punitive fines under Acts' civil penalties sections excluded United States from among "persons" who may be fined, see United States Department of Energy v. Ohio, 1992, 112 S.Ct. 1627, 118 L.Ed.2d 255.

§ 6973. Imminent hazard [SWDA § 7003]

(a) Authority of Administrator

Notwithstanding any other provision of this chapter, upon receipt of evidence that the past or present handling, storage, treatment, transportation or disposal of any solid waste or hazardous waste may present an imminent and substantial endangerment to health or the environment, the Administrator may bring suit on behalf of the United States in the appropriate district court against any person (including any past or present generator, past or present transporter, or past or present owner or operator of a treatment, storage, or disposal facility) who has contributed or who is contributing to such handling, storage, treatment, transportation or disposal to restrain such person from such handling, storage, treatment, transportation, or disposal, to order such person to take such other action as may be necessary, or both. A transporter shall not be deemed to have contributed or to be contributing to such handling, storage, treatment, or disposal taking place after such solid waste or hazardous waste has left the possession or control of such transporter if the transportation of such waste was under a sole contractural[1] arrangement arising from a published tariff and acceptance for carriage by common carrier by rail and such transporter has exercised due care in the past or present handling, storage, treatment, transportation and disposal of such waste. The Administrator shall provide notice to the affected State of any such suit. The Administrator may also, after notice to the affected State, take other action under this section including, but not limited to, issuing such orders as may be necessary to protect public health and the environment.

(b) Violations

Any person who willfully violates, or fails or refuses to comply with, any order of the Administrator under subsection (a) of this section may, in an action brought in the appropriate United States district court to enforce such order, be fined not more than $5,000 for each day in which such violation occurs or such failure to comply continues.

(c) Immediate notice

Upon receipt of information that there is hazardous waste at any site which has presented an imminent and substantial endangerment to human health or the environment, the Administrator shall provide immediate notice to the appropriate local government agencies. In addition, the Administrator shall require notice of such endangerment to be promptly posted at the site where the waste is located.

(d) Public participation in settlements

Whenever the United States or the Administrator proposes to covenant not to sue or to forbear from suit or to settle any claim arising under this section, notice, and opportunity for a public meeting in the affected area, and a reasonable opportunity to comment on the proposed settlement prior to its final entry shall be afforded to the public. The decision of the United States or the Administrator to enter into or not to enter into such Consent Decree, covenant or agreement shall not constitute a final agency action subject to judicial review under this chapter or subchapter II of chapter 5 of Title 5.

(Pub.L. 89–272, Title II, § 7003, as added Oct. 21, 1976, Pub.L. 94–580, § 2, 90 Stat. 2826, and amended Nov. 8, 1978, Pub.L. 95–609 § 7(q), 92 Stat. 3083; Oct. 21, 1980, Pub.L. 96–482, § 25, 94 Stat. 2348; Nov. 8, 1984, Pub.L. 98–616, Title IV, §§ 402, 403(a), 404, 98 Stat. 3271, 3273.)

[1] So in original. Probably should be contractual.

CROSS REFERENCES

Guidelines for using the imminent hazard, enforcement, and emergency response authorities to include powers authorized by this section, see section 9606 of this title.

LAW REVIEW COMMENTARIES

Abandoned hazardous waste sites and the RCRA imminent hazard provision: some suggestions for a sound judicial construction. Joel A. Mintz, 11 Harvard Environmental Law Review 247 (1987).

Interaction of the Bankruptcy Code and environmental laws: Grit, the grind, and the grease. Robert R. Graves, 29 Willamette L.Rev. 297 (1993).

Oil and gas exemptions under RCRA and CERCLA: Are they still "safe harbors" eleven years later? Michael M. Gibson and David P. Young, 32 S.Tex.L.Rev. 361 (1991).

Toxic tort litigation and the causation element: Is there any hope of reconciliation? Fred Harris, Jr., 40 Southwestern (Tex.) L.J. 909 (1986).

§ 6974. Petition for regulations; public participation [SWDA § 7004]

(a) Petition

Any person may petition the Administrator for the promulgation, amendment, or repeal of any regulation under this chapter. Within a reasonable time following receipt of such petition, the Administrator shall take action with respect to such petition and shall publish notice of such action in the Federal Register, together with the reasons therefor.

(b) Public participation

(1) Public participation in the development, revision, implementation, and enforcement of any regulation, guideline, information, or program under this chapter shall be provided for, encouraged, and assisted by the Administrator and the States. The Administrator, in cooperation with the States, shall develop and publish minimum guidelines for public participation in such processes.

(2) Before the issuing of a permit to any person with any respect to any facility for the treatment, storage, or disposal of hazardous wastes under section 6925 of this title, the Administrator shall—

(A) cause to be published in major local newspapers of general circulation and broadcast over local radio stations notice of the agency's intention to issue such permit, and

(B) transmit in writing notice of the agency's intention to issue such permit to each unit of local government having jurisdiction over the area in which such facility is proposed to be located and to each State agency having any authority under State law with respect to the construction or operation of such facility.

If within 45 days the Administrator receives written notice of opposition to the agency's intention to issue such permit and a request for a hearing, or if the Administrator determines on his own initiative, he shall hold an informal public hearing (including an opportunity for presentation of written and oral views) on whether he should issue a permit for the proposed facility. Whenever possible the Administrator shall schedule such hearing at a location convenient to the nearest population center to such proposed facility and give notice in the aforementioned manner of the date, time, and subject matter of such hearing. No State program which provides for the issuance of permits referred to in this paragraph may be authorized by the Administrator under section 6926 of this title unless such program provides for the notice and hearing required by the paragraph.

(Pub.L. 89–272, Title II, § 7004, as added Oct. 21, 1976, Pub.L. 94–580, § 2, 90 Stat. 2826, and amended Oct. 21, 1980, Pub.L. 96–482, § 26, 94 Stat. 2348.)

CODE OF FEDERAL REGULATIONS

Hazardous waste management, see 40 CFR 260.1 et seq.
Hazardous waste management generally, see 40 CFR 260.1 et seq. to 271.1 et seq.
National Pollutant Discharge Elimination System, see 40 CFR 122.1 et seq., 125.1 et seq.
Public participation, see 40 CFR 25.1 et seq.
State programs, see 40 CFR 123.1 et seq.
Underground Injection Control Program, see 40 CFR 146.1 et seq.

LAW REVIEW COMMENTARIES

Shelter from the storm? EPA's final lender liability rules. Meryl R. Lieberman and Michael J. Case, 65 N.Y.S.B.J. 32 (Dec. 1993).

§ 6975. Separability of provisions [SWDA § 7005]

If any provision of this chapter, or the application of any provision of this chapter to any person or circumstance, is held invalid, the application of such provision to other persons or circumstances, and the remainder of this chapter, shall not be affected thereby.

(Pub.L. 89–272, Title II, § 7005, as added Oct. 21, 1976, Pub.L. 94–580, § 2, 90 Stat. 2827.)

§ 6976. Judicial review [SWDA § 7006]

(a) Review of final regulations and certain petitions

Any judicial review of final regulations promulgated pursuant to this chapter and the Administrator's denial of any petition for the promulgation, amendment, or repeal of any regulation under this chapter shall be in accordance with sections 701 through 706 of Title 5, except that—

(1) a petition for review of action of the Administrator in promulgating any regulation, or requirement under this chapter or denying any petition for the promulgation, amendment or repeal of any regulation under this chapter may be filed only in the United States Court of Appeals for the District of Columbia, and such petition shall be filed within ninety days from the date of such promulgation or denial, or after such date if such petition for review is based solely on grounds arising after such ninetieth day; action of the Administrator with respect to which review could have been obtained under this subsection shall not be subject to judicial review in civil or criminal proceedings for enforcement; and

(2) in any judicial proceeding brought under this section in which review is sought of a determination under this chapter required to be made on the record after notice and opportunity for hearing, if a party seeking review under this chapter applies to the court for leave to adduce additional evidence, and shows to the satisfaction of the court that the information is material and that there were reasonable grounds for the failure to adduce such evidence in the proceeding before the Administrator, the court may order such additional evidence (and evidence in rebuttal thereof) to be taken before the Administrator, and to be adduced upon the hearing in such manner and upon such terms and conditions as the court may deem proper; the Administrator may modify his findings as to the facts, or make new findings, by reason of the additional evidence so taken, and he shall file with the court such modified or new findings and his recommendation, if any, for the modification or setting aside of his original order, with the return of such additional evidence.

(b) Review of certain actions under sections 6925 and 6926 of this title

Review of the Administrator's action (1) in issuing, denying, modifying, or revoking any permit under section 6925 of this title (or in modifying or revoking any permit which is deemed to have been issued under section 6935(d)(1) of this title), or (2) in granting, denying, or withdrawing authorization or interim authorization under section 6926 of this title, may be had by any interested person in the Circuit Court of Appeals of the United States for the Federal judicial district in which such person resides or transacts such business upon application by such person. Any such application shall be made within ninety days from the date of such issuance, denial, modification, revocation, grant, or withdrawal, or after such date only if such application is based solely on grounds which arose after such ninetieth day. Action of the Administrator with respect to which review could have been obtained under this subsection shall not be subject to judicial review in civil or criminal proceedings for enforcement. Such review shall be in accordance with sections 701 through 706 of Title 5.

(Pub.L. 89–272, Title II, § 7006, as added Oct. 21, 1976, Pub.L. 94–580, § 2, 90 Stat. 2827, and amended Oct. 21, 1980, Pub.L. 96–482, § 27, 94 Stat. 2349; Nov. 8, 1984, Pub.L. 98–616, Title II, § 241(b)(1), Title IV, § 403(d)(5), 98 Stat. 3259, 3273.)

ADMINISTRATIVE LAW

Enforcement and review, see Koch § 8.22.

United States Supreme Court

Supreme Court review, obtaining views of state supreme court on issue of preemption of state statute by this Chapter, see City of Philadelphia v. New Jersey 1977, 97 S.Ct. 987, 430 U.S. 141, 51 L.Ed.2d 224.

§ 6977. Grants or contracts for training projects [SWDA § 7007]

(a) General authority

The Administrator is authorized to make grants to, and contracts with any eligible organization. For purposes of this section the term "eligible organization" means a State or interstate agency, a municipality, educational institution, and any other organization which is capable of effectively carrying out a project which may be funded by grant under subsection (b) of this section.

(b) Purposes

(1) Subject to the provisions of paragraph (2), grants or contracts may be made to pay all or a part of the costs, as may be determined by the Administrator, of any project operated or to be operated by an eligible organization, which is designed—

(A) to develop, expand, or carry out a program (which may combine training, education, and employment) for training persons for occupations involving the management, supervision, design, operation, or maintenance of solid waste management and resource recovery equipment and facilities; or

(B) to train instructors and supervisory personnel to train or supervise persons in occupations involving the design, operation, and maintenance of solid waste management and resource recovery equipment and facilities.

(2) A grant or contract authorized by paragraph (1) of this subsection may be made only upon application to the Administrator at such time or times and containing such information as he may prescribe, except that no such application shall be approved unless it provides for the same procedures and reports (and access to such reports and to other records) as required by section 3254a(b)(4) and (5) of this title (as in effect before October 21, 1976) with respect to applications made under such section (as in effect before October 21, 1976).

(c) Study

The Administrator shall make a complete investigation and study to determine—

(1) the need for additional trained State and local personnel to carry out plans assisted under this chapter and other solid waste and resource recovery programs;

(2) means of using existing training programs to train such personnel; and

(3) the extent and nature of obstacles to employment and occupational advancement in the solid waste management and resource recovery field which may limit either available manpower or the advancement of personnel in such field.

He shall report the results of such investigation and study, including his recommendations to the President and the Congress.

(Pub.L. 89–272, Title II, § 7007, as added Oct. 21, 1976, Pub.L. 94–580, § 2, 90 Stat. 2827, and amended Nov. 8, 1978, Pub.L. 95–609, § 7(r), 92 Stat. 3083.)

CODE OF FEDERAL REGULATIONS

Grants and manpower forecasting, see 40 CFR 45.100 et seq.

LIBRARY REFERENCES

United States ⇐82(3).
C.J.S. United States § 122.

§ 6978. Payments [SWDA § 7008]

(a) General rule

Payments of grants under this chapter may be made (after necessary adjustment on account of previously made underpayments or overpayments) in advance or by way of reimbursement, and in such installments and on such conditions as the Administrator may determine.

(b) Prohibition

No grant may be made under this chapter to any private profitmaking organization.

(Pub.L. 89–272, Title II, § 7008, as added Oct. 21, 1976, Pub.L. 94–580, § 2, 90 Stat. 2828.)

§ 6979. Labor standards [SWDA § 7009]

No grant for a project of construction under this chapter shall be made unless the Administrator finds that the application contains or is supported by reasonable assurance that all laborers and mechanics employed by contractors or subcontractors on projects of the type covered by the Davis-Bacon Act, as amended (40 U.S.C. 276a—276a-5), will be paid wages at rates not less than those prevailing on similar work in the locality as determined by the Secretary of Labor in accordance with that Act; and the Secretary of Labor shall have with respect to the labor standards specified in this section the authority and functions set forth in Reorganization Plan Numbered 14 of 1950 (15 F.R. 3176) and section 276c of Title 40.

(Pub.L. 89–272, Title II, § 7009, as added Oct. 21, 1976, Pub.L. 94–580, § 2, 90 Stat. 2828, and amended Oct. 21, 1980, Pub.L. 96–482, § 28, 94 Stat. 2349.)

CODE OF FEDERAL REGULATIONS

Interpretation of fringe benefits provisions, see 29 CFR 5.20 et seq.
Wage rate predetermination, see 29 CFR 1.1 et seq.

LIBRARY REFERENCES

Labor Relations ⚷1129, 1132.
C.J.S. Labor Relations §§ 1039 et seq., 1042.

§ 6979a. Transferred

Codification

Section, Pub.L. 89–272, Title II, § 7010, as added Pub.L. 98–616, Title IV, § 405(a), Nov. 8, 1984, 98 Stat. 3273, was renumbered section 3020 of Pub.L. 89–272 by Pub.L. 99–339, Title II, § 201(c)(2), June 19, 1986, 100 Stat. 654, and transferred to section 6939b of this title.

§ 6979b. Law enforcement authority [SWDA § 7010]

The Attorney General of the United States shall, at the request of the Administrator and on the basis of a showing of need, deputize qualified employees of the Environmental Protection Agency to serve as special deputy United States marshals in criminal investigations with respect to violations of the criminal provisions of this chapter.

(Pub.L. 89–272, Title II, § 7010, formerly § 7012, as added Nov. 8, 1984, Pub.L. 98–616, Title IV, § 403(b)(1), 98 Stat. 3272, and renumbered June 19, 1986, Pub.L. 99–339, Title II, § 201(c)(1), 100 Stat. 654.)

LAW REVIEW COMMENTARIES

Interaction of the Bankruptcy Code and environmental laws: Grit, the grind, and the grease. Robert R. Graves, 29 Willamette L.Rev. 297 (1993).

SUBCHAPTER VIII—RESEARCH, DEVELOPMENT, DEMONSTRATION, AND INFORMATION

§ 6981. Research, demonstrations, training and other activities [SWDA § 8001]

(a) General authority

The Administrator, alone or after consultation with the Secretary of Energy, shall conduct, and encourage, cooperate with, and render financial and other assistance to appropriate public (whether Federal, State, interstate, or local) authorities, agencies, and institutions, private agencies and institutions, and individuals in the conduct of, and promote the coordination of, research, investigations, experiments, training, demonstrations, surveys, public education programs, and studies relating to—

(1) any adverse health and welfare effects of the release into the environment of material present in solid waste, and methods to eliminate such effects;

(2) the operation and financing of solid waste management programs;

(3) the planning, implementation, and operation of resource recovery and resource conservation systems and hazardous waste management systems, including the marketing of recovered resources;

(4) the production of usable forms of recovered resources, including fuel, from solid waste;

(5) the reduction of the amount of such waste and unsalvageable waste materials;

(6) the development and application of new and improved methods of collecting and disposing of solid waste and processing and recovering materials and energy from solid wastes;

(7) the identification of solid waste components and potential materials and energy recoverable from such waste components;

(8) small scale and low technology solid waste management systems, including but not limited to, resource recovery source separation systems;

(9) methods to improve the performance characteristics of resources recovered from solid waste and the relationship of such performance characteristics to available and potentially available markets for such resources;

(10) improvements in land disposal practices for solid waste (including sludge) which may reduce the adverse environmental effects of such disposal and other aspects of solid waste disposal on land, including means for reducing the harmful environmental effects of earlier and existing landfills, means for restoring areas damaged by such earlier or existing landfills, means for rendering landfills safe for purposes of construction and other uses, and techniques of recovering materials and energy from landfills;

(11) methods for the sound disposal of, or recovery of resources, including energy, from, sludge (including sludge from pollution control and treatment facilities, coal slurry pipelines, and other sources);

(12) methods of hazardous waste management, including methods of rendering such waste environmentally safe; and

(13) any adverse effects on air quality (particularly with regard to the emission of heavy metals) which result from solid waste which is burned (either alone or in conjunction with other substances) for purposes of treatment, disposal or energy recovery.

(b) Management program

(1)(A) In carrying out his functions pursuant to this chapter, and any other Federal legislation respecting solid waste or discarded material research, development, and demonstrations, the Administrator shall establish a management program or system to insure the coordination of all such activities and to facilitate and accelerate the process of development of sound new technology (or other discoveries) from the research phase, through development, and into the demonstration phase.

(B) The Administrator shall (i) assist, on the basis of any research projects which are developed with assistance under this chapter or without Federal assistance, the construction of pilot plant facilities for the purpose of investigating or testing the technological feasibility of any promising new fuel, energy, or resource recovery or resource conservation method or technology; and (ii) demonstrate each such method and technology that appears justified by an evaluation at such pilot plant stage or at a pilot plant stage developed without Federal assistance. Each such demonstration shall incorporate new or innovative technical advances or shall apply such advances to different circumstances and conditions, for the purpose of evaluating design concepts or to test the performance, efficiency, and economic feasibility of a particular method or technology under actual operating conditions. Each such demonstration shall be so planned and designed that, if successful, it can be expanded or utilized directly as a full-scale operational fuel, energy, or resource recovery or resource conservation facility.

(2) Any energy-related research, development, or demonstration project for the conversion including bioconversion, of solid waste carried out by the Environmental Protection Agency or by the Secretary of Energy pursuant to this chapter or any other Act shall be administered in accordance with the May 7, 1976, Interagency Agreement between the Environmental Protection Agency and the Secretary of Energy on the Development of Energy from Solid Wastes and specifically, that in accordance with this agreement, (A) for those energy-related projects of mutual interest, planning will be conducted jointly by the Environmental Protection Agency and the Secretary of Energy, following which project responsibility will be assigned to one agency; (B) energy-related portions of projects for recovery of synthetic fuels or other forms of energy from solid waste shall be the responsibility of the Secretary of Energy; (C) the Environmental Protection Agency shall retain responsibility for the environmental, economic, and institutional aspects of solid waste projects and for assurance that such projects are consistent with any applicable suggested guidelines published pursuant to section 6907 of this title, and any applicable State or regional solid waste management plan; and (D) any activities undertaken under provisions of sections 6982 and 6983 of this title as related to energy; as related to energy or synthetic fuels recovery from waste; or as related to energy conservation shall be accomplished through coordination and consultation with the Secretary of Energy.

(c) Authorities

(1) In carrying out subsection (a) of this section respecting solid waste research, studies, development, and demonstration, except as otherwise specifically provided in section 6984(d) of this title, the Administrator may make grants to or enter into contracts (including contracts for construction) with, public agencies and authorities or private persons.

(2) Contracts for research, development, or demonstrations or for both (including contracts for construction) shall be made in accordance with and subject to the limitations provided with respect to research contracts of the military departments in section 2353 of title 10, except that the determination, approval, and certification required thereby shall be made by the Administrator.

(3) Any invention made or conceived in the course of, or under, any contract under this chapter shall be subject to section 9 of the Federal Nonnuclear Energy Research and Development Act of 1974 [42 U.S.C. 5908] to the same extent and in the same manner as inventions made or conceived in the course of contracts under such Act [42 U.S.C.A. § 5901 et seq.], except that in applying such section, the Environmental Protection Agency shall be substituted for the Secretary of Energy and the words "solid waste" shall be substituted for the word "energy" where appropriate.

(4) For carrying out the purpose of this chapter the Administrator may detail personnel of the Environmental Protection Agency to agencies eligible for assistance under this section.

(Pub.L. 89–272, Title II, § 8001, as added Oct. 21, 1976, Pub.L. 94–580, § 2, 90 Stat. 2829, and amended Aug. 4, 1977, Pub.L. 95–91, Title III, § 301, Title VII, §§ 703, 707, 91 Stat. 577, 606, 607; Nov. 8, 1978, Pub.L. 95–609, § 7(s), 92 Stat. 3083.)

EPA Study of Methods to Reduce Plastic Pollution

Pub.L. 100–220, Title II, § 2202, Dec. 29, 1987, 101 Stat. 1465, authorized the Administrator of the Environmental Agency, in consultation with the Secretary of Commerce, to conduct a study of the adverse effects of the improper disposal of plastic articles on the environment and waste disposal, and various methods to reduce or eliminate such adverse effects, and directed the Administrator, within 18 months after Dec. 29, 1987, to report the results of this study to Congress.

Plastic Pollution Public Education Program

Pub.L. 100–220, Title II, § 2204, Dec. 29, 1987, 101 Stat. 1466, directed the Administrator of the National Oceanic and Atmospheric

Administration and the Administrator of the National Environmental Protection Agency, in consultation with the Secretary of Transportation, to jointly commence and conduct for a period of at least 3 years a public outreach program to educate the public, including recreational boaters, fishermen, and other users of the marine environment, regarding the harmful effects of plastic pollution and the need to reduce such pollution, recycle plastic materials, and reduce the quantity of plastic debris in the marine environment.

National Advisory Commission on Resource Conservation and Recovery

Pub.L. 96–482, § 33, Oct. 21, 1980, 94 Stat. 2356, provided for the establishment, membership, functions, etc., of a National Advisory Commission on Resource Conservation and Recovery, directed the Commission to submit an interim report for legislative and administrative actions relating to this chapter on Feb. 15, 1982, and upon the expiration of the two-year period beginning on the date when all initial members of the Commission have been appointed or the date initial funds become available, whichever is later, to transmit a final report to the President and Congress containing a detailed statement of the findings and conclusions of the Commission, and terminated the Commission 30 days after the submission of its final report.

Leachate Control Research Program in Delaware

Section 4 of Pub.L. 94–580 directed the Administrator of the Environmental Protection Agency, in order to demonstrate effective means of dealing with contamination of public water supplies by leachate from abandoned or other landfills, to provide technical and financial assistance for a research program, designed by the New Castle County areawide waste treatment management program, to control leachate from Llangollen Landfill in New Castle County, Delaware, and provided up to $200,000 in each of the fiscal years 1978 and 1979 for the operating costs of a counter-pumping program to contain the leachate from the Llangollen Landfill during the period of this study.

CROSS REFERENCES

Precedence of patent rights in inventions made with federal assistance over inventions within this section, see section 210 of Title 35, Patents.

CODE OF FEDERAL REGULATIONS.

Grants, see 40 CFR 40.100 et seq., 45.100 et seq.

§ 6982. Special studies; plans for research, development, and demonstrations [SWDA § 8002]

(a) Glass and plastic

The Administrator shall undertake a study and publish a report on resource recovery from glass and plastic waste, including a scientific, technological, and economic investigation of potential solutions to implement such recovery.

(b) Composition of waste stream

The Administrator shall undertake a systematic study of the composition of the solid waste stream and of anticipated future changes in the composition of such stream and shall publish a report containing the results of such study and quantitatively evaluating the potential utility of such components.

(c) Priorities study

For purposes of determining priorities for research on recovery of materials and energy from solid waste and developing materials and energy recovery research, development, and demonstration strategies, the Administrator shall review, and make a study of, the various existing and promising techniques of energy recovery from solid waste (including, but not limited to, waterwall furnace incinerators, dry shredded fuel systems, pyrolysis, densified refuse-derived fuel systems, anerobic digestion, and fuel and feedstock preparation systems). In carrying out such study the Administrator shall investigate with respect to each such technique—

(1) the degree of public need for the potential results of such research, development, or demonstration,

(2) the potential for research, development, and demonstration without Federal action, including the degree of restraint on such potential posed by the risks involved, and

(3) the magnitude of effort and period of time necessary to develop the technology to the point where Federal assistance can be ended.

(d) Small-scale and low technology study

The Administrator shall undertake a comprehensive study and analysis of, and publish a report on, systems of small-scale and low technology solid waste management, including household resource recovery and resource recovery systems which have special application to multiple dwelling units and high density housing and office complexes. Such study and analysis shall include an investigation of the degree to which such systems could contribute to energy conservation.

(e) Front-end source separation

The Administrator shall undertake research and studies concerning the compatibility of front-end source separation systems with high technology resource recovery systems and shall publish a report containing the results of such research and studies.

(f) Mining waste

The Administrator, in consultation with the Secretary of the Interior, shall conduct a detailed and comprehensive study on the adverse effects of solid wastes from active and abandoned surface and underground mines on the environment, including, but not limited to, the effects of such wastes on humans, water, air, health, welfare, and natural resources, and on the adequacy of means and measures currently employed by the mining industry, Government agencies, and others to dispose of and utilize such solid wastes and to prevent or substantially mitigate such adverse effects. Such study shall include an analysis of—

(1) the sources and volume of discarded material generated per year from mining;

(2) present disposal practices;

(3) potential dangers to human health and the environment from surface runoff of leachate and air pollution by dust;

(4) alternatives to current disposal methods;

(5) the cost of those alternatives in terms of the impact on mine product costs; and

(6) potential for use of discarded material as a secondary source of the mine product.

In furtherance of this study, the Administrator shall, as he deems appropriate, review studies and other actions of other Federal agencies concerning such wastes with a view toward avoiding duplication of effort and the need to expedite such study. Not later than thirty-six months after October 21, 1980, the Administrator shall publish a report of such study and shall include appropriate findings and recommendations for Federal and non-Federal actions concerning such effects. Such report shall be submitted to the Committee on Environment and Public Works of the United States Senate and the Committee on Energy and Commerce of the United States House of Representatives.

(g) Sludge

The Administrator shall undertake a comprehensive study and publish a report on sludge. Such study shall include an analysis of—

(1) what types of solid waste (including but not limited to sewage and pollution treatment residues and other residues from industrial operations such as extraction of oil from shale, liquefaction and gasification of coal and coal slurry pipeline operations) shall be classified as sludge;

(2) the effects of air and water pollution legislation on the creation of large volumes of sludge;

(3) the amounts of sludge originating in each State and in each industry producing sludge;

(4) methods of disposal of such sludge, including the cost, efficiency, and effectiveness of such methods;

(5) alternative methods for the use of sludge, including agricultural applications of sludge and energy recovery from sludge; and

(6) methods to reclaim areas which have been used for the disposal of sludge or which have been damaged by sludge.

(h) Tires

The Administrator shall undertake a study and publish a report respecting discarded motor vehicle tires which shall include an analysis of the problems involved in the collection, recovery of resources including energy, and use of such tires.

(i) Resource recovery facilities

The Administrator shall conduct research and report on the economics of, and impediments, to the effective functioning of resource recovery facilities.

(j) Resource Conservation Committee

(1) The Administrator shall serve as Chairman of a Committee composed of himself, the Secretary of Commerce, the Secretary of Labor, the Chairman of the Council on Environmental Quality, the Secretary of Treasury, the Secretary of the Interior, the Secretary of Energy, the Chairman of the Counsel of Economic Advisors, and a representative of the Office of Management and Budget, which shall conduct a full and complete investigation and study of all aspects of the economic, social, and environmental consequences of resource conservation with respect to—

(A) the appropriateness of recommended incentives and disincentives to foster resource conservation;

(B) the effect of existing public policies (including subsidies and economic incentives and disincentives, percentage depletion allowances, capital gains treatment and other tax incentives and disincentives) upon resource conservation, and the likely effect of the modification or elimination of such incentives and disincentives upon resource conservation;

(C) the appropriateness and feasibility of restricting the manufacture or use of categories of consumer products as a resource conservation strategy;

(D) the appropriateness and feasibility of employing as a resource conservation strategy the imposition of solid waste management charges on consumer products, which charges would reflect the costs of solid waste management services, litter pickup, the value of recoverable components of such product, final disposal, and any social value associated with the nonrecycling or uncontrolled disposal of such product; and

(E) the need for further research, development, and demonstration in the area of resource conservation.

(2) The study required in paragraph (1)(D) may include pilot scale projects, and shall consider and evaluate alternative strategies with respect to—

(A) the product categories on which such charges would be imposed;

(B) the appropriate state in the production of such consumer product at which to levy such charge;

(C) appropriate criteria for establishing such charges for each consumer product category;

(D) methods for the adjustment of such charges to reflect actions such as recycling which would reduce the overall quantities of solid waste requiring disposal; and

(E) procedures for amending, modifying, or revising such charges to reflect changing conditions.

(3) The design for the study required in paragraph (1) of this subsection shall include timetables for the completion of the study. A preliminary report putting forth the study design shall be sent to the President and the Congress within six months following October 21, 1976, and followup reports shall be sent six months thereafter. Each recommendation resulting from the study shall include at least two alternatives to the proposed recommendation.

(4) The results of such investigation and study, including recommendations, shall be reported to the President and the Congress not later than two years after October 21, 1976.

(5) There are authorized to be appropriated not to exceed $2,000,000 to carry out this subsection.

(k) Airport landfills

The Administrator shall undertake a comprehensive study and analysis of and publish a report on systems to alleviate the hazards to aviation from birds congregating and feeding on landfills in the vicinity of airports.

(*l*) Completion of research and studies

The Administrator shall complete the research and studies, and submit the reports, required under subsections (b), (c), (d), (e), (f), (g), and (k) of this section not later than October 1, 1978. The Administrator shall complete the research and studies, and submit the reports, required under subsections (a), (h), and (i) of this section not later than October 1, 1979. Upon completion, each study specified in subsections (a) through (k) of this section, the Administrator shall prepare a plan for research, development, and demonstration respecting the findings of the study and shall submit any legislative recommendations resulting from such study to appropriate committees of Congress.

(m) Drilling fluids, produced waters, and other wastes associated with the exploration, development, or production of crude oil or natural gas or geothermal energy

(1) The Administrator shall conduct a detailed and comprehensive study and submit a report on the adverse effects, if any, of drilling fluids, produced waters, and other wastes associated with the exploration, development, or production of crude oil or natural gas or geothermal energy on human health and the environment, including, but not limited to, the effects of such wastes on humans, water, air, health, welfare, and natural resources and on the adequacy of means and measures currently employed by the oil and gas and geothermal drilling and production industry, Government agencies, and others to dispose of and utilize such wastes and to prevent or substantially mitigate such adverse effects. Such study shall include an analysis of—

(A) the sources and volume of discarded material generated per year from such wastes;

(B) present disposal practices;

(C) potential danger to human health and the environment from the surface runoff or leachate;

(D) documented cases which prove or have caused danger to human health and the environment from surface runoff or leachate;

(E) alternatives to current disposal methods;

(F) the cost of such alternatives; and

(G) the impact of those alternatives on the exploration for, and development and production of, crude oil and natural gas or geothermal energy.

In furtherance of this study, the Administrator shall, as he deems appropriate, review studies and other actions of other Federal agencies concerning such wastes with a view toward avoiding duplication of effort and the need to expedite such study. The Administrator shall publish a report of such study and shall include appropriate findings and recommendations for Federal and non-Federal actions concerning such effects.

(2) The Administrator shall complete the research and study and submit the report required under paragraph (1) not later than twenty-four months from October 21, 1980. Upon completion of the study, the Administrator shall prepare a summary of the findings of the study, a plan for research, development, and demonstration respecting the findings of the study, and shall submit the findings and the study, along with any recommendations resulting from such study, to the Committee on Environment and Public Works of the United States Senate and the Committee on Energy and Commerce of the United States House of Representatives.

(3) There are authorized to be appropriated not to exceed $1,000,000 to carry out the provisions of this subsection.

(n) Materials generated from the combustion of coal and other fossil fuels

The Administrator shall conduct a detailed and comprehensive study and submit a report on the adverse effects on human health and the environment, if any, of the disposal and utilization of fly ash waste, bottom ash waste, slag waste, flue gas emission control waste, and other byproduct materials generated primarily from the combustion of coal or other fossil fuels. Such study shall include an analysis of—

(1) the source and volumes of such material generated per year;

(2) present disposal and utilization practices;

(3) potential danger, if any, to human health and the environment from the disposal and reuse of such materials;

(4) documented cases in which danger to human health or the environment from surface runoff or leachate has been proved;

(5) alternatives to current disposal methods;

(6) the costs of such alternatives;

(7) the impact of those alternatives on the use of coal and other natural resources; and

(8) the current and potential utilization of such materials.

In furtherance of this study, the Administrator shall, as he deems appropriate, review studies and other actions of other Federal and State agencies concerning such material and invite participation by other concerned parties, including industry and other Federal and State agencies, with a view toward avoiding duplication of effort. The Administrator shall publish a report on such study, which shall include appropriate findings, not later than twenty-four months after October 21, 1980. Such study and findings shall be submitted to the Committee on Environment and Public Works of the United States Senate and the Committee on Energy and Commerce of the United States House of Representatives.

(*o*) Cement kiln dust waste

The Administrator shall conduct a detailed and comprehensive study of the adverse effects on human health and the environment, if any, of the disposal of cement kiln dust waste. Such study shall include an analysis of—

(1) the source and volumes of such materials generated per year;

(2) present disposal practices;

(3) potential danger, if any, to human health and the environment from the disposal of such materials;

(4) documented cases in which danger to human health or the environment has been proved;

(5) alternatives to current disposal methods;

(6) the costs of such alternatives;

(7) the impact of those alternatives on the use of natural resources; and

(8) the current and potential utilization of such materials.

In furtherance of this study, the Administrator shall, as he deems appropriate, review studies and other actions of other Federal and State agencies concerning such waste or materials and invite participation by other concerned parties, including industry and other Federal and State agencies, with a view toward avoiding duplication of effort. The Administrator shall publish a report of such study, which shall include appropriate findings, not later than thirty-six months after October 21, 1980. Such report shall be submitted to the Committee on Environment and Public Works of the United States Senate and the Committee on Energy and Commerce of the United States House of Representatives.

(p) Materials generated from the extraction, beneficiation, and processing of ores and minerals, including phosphate rock and overburden from uranium mining

The Administrator shall conduct a detailed and comprehensive study on the adverse effects on human health and the environment, if any, of the disposal and utilization of solid waste from the extraction, beneficiation, and processing of ores and minerals, including phosphate rock and overburden from uranium mining. Such study shall be conducted in conjunction with the study of mining wastes required by subsection (f) of this section and shall include an analysis of—

(1) the source and volumes of such materials generated per year;

(2) present disposal and utilization practices;

(3) potential danger, if any, to human health and the environment from the disposal and reuse of such materials;

(4) documented cases in which danger to human health or the environment has been proved;

(5) alternatives to current disposal methods;

(6) the costs of such alternatives;

(7) the impact of those alternatives on the use of phosphate rock and uranium ore, and other natural resources; and

(8) the current and potential utilization of such materials.

In furtherance of this study, the Administrator shall, as he deems appropriate, review studies and other actions of other Federal and State agencies concerning such waste or materials and invite participation by other concerned parties, including industry and other Federal and State agencies, with a view toward avoiding duplication of effort. The Administrator shall publish a report of such study, which shall include appropriate findings, in conjunction with the publication of the report of the study of mining wastes required to be conducted under subsection (f) of this section. Such report and findings shall be submitted to the Committee on Environment and Public Works of the United States Senate and the Committee on Energy and Commerce of the United States House of Representatives.

(q) Authorization of appropriations

There are authorized to be appropriated not to exceed $8,000,000 for the fiscal years 1978 and 1979 to carry out this section other than subsection (j) of this section.

(r) Minimization of hazardous waste

The Administrator shall compile, and not later than October 1, 1986, submit to the Congress, a report on the feasibility and desirability of establishing standards of performance or of taking other additional actions under this chapter to require the generators of hazardous waste to reduce the volume or quantity and toxicity of the hazardous waste they generate, and of establishing with respect to hazardous wastes required management practices or other requirements to assure such wastes are managed in ways that minimize present and future risks to human health and the environment. Such report shall include any recommendations for legislative changes which the Administrator determines are feasible and desirable to implement the national policy established by section 6902 of this title.

(s) Extending the useful life of sanitary landfills

The Administrator shall conduct detailed, comprehensive studies of methods to extend the useful life of sanitary landfills and to better use sites in which filled or closed landfills are located. Such studies shall address—

(1) methods to reduce the volume of materials before placement in landfills;

(2) more efficient systems for depositing waste in landfills;

(3) methods to enhance the rate of decomposition of solid waste in landfills, in a safe and environmentally acceptable manner;

(4) methane production from closed landfill units;

(5) innovative uses of closed landfill sites, including use for energy production such as solar or wind energy and use for metals recovery;

(6) potential for use of sewage treatment sludge in reclaiming landfilled areas; and

(7) methods to coordinate use of a landfill owned by one municipality by nearby municipalities, and to establish equitable rates for such use, taking into account the need to provide future landfill capacity to replace that so used.

The Administrator is authorized to conduct demonstrations in the areas of study provided in this subsection. The Administrator shall periodically report on the results of such studies, with the first such report not later than October 1, 1986. In carrying out this subsection, the Administrator need not duplicate other studies which have been completed and may rely upon information which has previously been compiled.

(Pub.L. 89–272, Title II, § 8002, as added Oct. 21, 1976, Pub.L. 94–580, § 2, 90 Stat. 2831, and amended Nov. 8, 1978, Pub.L. 95–609, § 7(t), 92 Stat. 3083; H.Res. 549, Mar. 25, 1980; Oct. 21, 1980, Pub.L. 96–482, § 29, 94 Stat. 2349; Nov. 8, 1984, Pub.L. 98–616, Title II, § 224(c), Title VII, § 702, 98 Stat. 3253, 3289.)

Change of Name

Any reference in any provision of law enacted before Jan. 4, 1995, to the Committee on Energy and Commerce of the House of Representatives treated as referring to the Committee on Commerce of the House of Representatives, except that any reference in any provision of law enacted before Jan. 4, 1995, to the Committee on Energy and Commerce of the House of Representatives treated as referring to the Committee on Agriculture of the House of Representatives, in the case of a provision of law relating to inspection of seafood or seafood products, the Committee on Banking and Financial Services of the House of Representatives, in the case of a provision of law relating to bank capital markets activities generally or to depository institution securities activities generally, and the Committee on Transportation and Infrastructure of the House of Representatives, in the case of a provision of law relating to railroads, railway labor, or railroad retirement and unemployment (except revenue measures related thereto), see section 1(a)(4) and (c)(1) of Pub.L. 104–14, set out as a note preceding section 21 of Title 2, The Congress.

LAW REVIEW COMMENTARIES

Emerging federal law of mine waste: Administrative, judicial and legislative developments. John R. Jacus and Thomas E. Root, 26 Land and Water L.Rev. 461 (1991).

§ 6983. Coordination, collection, and dissemination of information [SWDA § 8003]

(a) Information

The Administrator shall develop, collect, evaluate, and coordinate information on—

(1) methods and costs of the collection of solid waste;

(2) solid waste management practices, including data on the different management methods and the cost, operation, and maintenance of such methods;

(3) the amounts and percentages of resources (including energy) that can be recovered from solid waste by use of various solid waste management practices and various technologies;

(4) methods available to reduce the amount of solid waste that is generated;

(5) existing and developing technologies for the recovery of energy or materials from solid waste and the costs, reliability, and risks associated with such technologies;

(6) hazardous solid waste, including incidents of damage resulting from the disposal of hazardous solid wastes; inherently and potentially hazardous solid wastes; methods of neutralizing or properly disposing of hazardous solid wastes; facilities that properly dispose of hazardous wastes;

(7) methods of financing resource recovery facilities or, sanitary landfills, or hazardous solid waste treatment facilities, whichever is appropriate for the entity developing such facility or landfill (taking into account the amount of solid waste reasonably expected to be available to such entity);

(8) the availability of markets for the purchase of resources, either materials or energy, recovered from solid waste; and

(9) research and development projects respecting solid waste management.

(b) Library

(1) The Administrator shall establish and maintain a central reference library for (A) the materials collected pursuant to subsection (a) of this section and (B) the actual performance and cost effectiveness records and other data and information with respect to—

(i) the various methods of energy and resource recovery from solid waste,

(ii) the various systems and means of resource conservation,

(iii) the various systems and technologies for collection, transport, storage, treatment, and final disposition of solid waste, and

(iv) other aspects of solid waste and hazardous solid waste management.

Such central reference library shall also contain, but not be limited to, the model codes and model accounting systems developed under this section, the information collected under subsection (d) of this section, and, subject to any applicable requirements of confidentiality, information respecting any aspect of solid waste provided by officers and employees of the Environmental Protection Agency which has been acquired by them in the conduct of their functions under this chapter and which may be of value to Federal, State, and local authorities and other persons.

(2) Information in the central reference library shall, to the extent practicable, be collated, analyzed, verified, and published and shall be made available to State and local governments and other persons at reasonable times and subject to such reasonable charges as may be necessary to defray expenses of making such information available.

(c) Model accounting system

In order to assist State and local governments in determining the cost and revenues associated with the collection and disposal of solid waste and with resource recovery operations, the Administrator shall develop and publish a recommended model cost and revenue accounting system applicable to the solid waste management functions of State and local governments. Such system shall be in accordance with generally accepted accounting principles. The Administrator shall periodically, but not less frequently than once every five years, review such accounting system and revise it as necessary.

(d) Model codes

The Administrator is authorized, in cooperation with appropriate State and local agencies, to recommend model codes, ordinances, and statutes, providing for sound solid waste management.

(e) Information programs

(1) The Administrator shall implement a program for the rapid dissemination of information on solid waste management, hazardous waste management, resource conservation, and methods of resource recovery from solid waste, including the results of any relevant research, investigations, experiments, surveys, studies, or other information which may be useful in the implementation of new or improved solid waste management practices and methods and information on any other technical, managerial, financial, or market aspect of resource conservation and recovery facilities.

(2) The Administrator shall develop and implement educational programs to promote citizen understanding of the need for environmentally sound solid waste management practices.

(f) Coordination

In collecting and disseminating information under this section, the Administrator shall coordinate his actions and cooperate to the maximum extent possible with State and local authorities.

(g) Special restriction

Upon request, the full range of alternative technologies, programs or processes deemed feasible to meet the resource recovery or resource conservation needs of a jurisdiction shall be described in such a manner as to provide a sufficient evaluative basis from which the jurisdiction can make its decisions, but no officer or employee of the Environmental Protection Agency shall, in an official capacity, lobby for or otherwise represent an agency position in favor of resource recovery or resource conservation, as a policy alternative for adoption into ordinances, codes, regulations, or law by any State or political subdivision thereof.

(Pub.L. 89–272, Title II, § 8003, as added Oct. 21, 1976, Pub.L. 94–580, § 2, 90 Stat. 2834, and amended Nov. 8, 1978, Pub.L. 95–609, § 7(u), 92 Stat. 3083.)

§ 6984. Full-scale demonstration facilities [SWDA § 8004]

(a) Authority

The Administrator may enter into contracts with public agencies or authorities or private persons for the construction and operation of a full-scale demonstration facility under this chapter, or provide financial assistance in the form of grants to a full-scale demonstration facility under this chapter only if the Administrator finds that—

(1) such facility or proposed facility will demonstrate at full scale a new or significantly improved technology or process, a practical and significant improvement in solid waste management practice, or the technological feasibility and cost effectiveness of an existing, but unproven technology, process, or practice, and will not duplicate any other Federal, State, local, or commercial facility which has been constructed or with respect to which construction has begun (determined as of the date action is taken by the Administrator under this chapter),

(2) such contract or assistance meets the requirements of section 6981 of this title and meets other applicable requirements of this chapter,

(3) such facility will be able to comply with the guidelines published under section 6907 of this title and with other laws and regulations for the protection of health and the environment,

(4) in the case of a contract for construction or operation, such facility is not likely to be constructed or operated by State, local, or private persons or in the case of an application for financial assistance, such facility is not likely to receive adequate financial assistance from other sources, and

(5) any Federal interest in, or assistance to, such facility will be disposed of or terminated, with appropriate compensation, within such period of time as may be necessary to carry out the basic objectives of this chapter.

(b) Time limitation

No obligation may be made by the Administrator for financial assistance under this subchapter for any full-scale demonstration facility after the date ten years after October 21, 1976. No expenditure of funds for any such full-scale demonstration facility under this subchapter may be made by the Administrator after the date fourteen years after October 21, 1976.

(c) Cost sharing

(1) Wherever practicable, in constructing, operating, or providing financial assistance under this subchapter to a full-scale demonstration facility, the Administrator shall endeavor to enter into agreements and make other arrangements for maximum practicable cost sharing with other Federal, State, and local agencies, private persons, or any combination thereof.

(2) The Administrator shall enter into arrangements, wherever practicable and desirable, to provide monitoring of full-scale solid waste facilities (whether or not constructed or operated under this chapter) for purposes of obtaining information concerning the performance, and other aspects, of such facilities. Where the Administrator provides only monitoring and evaluation instruments or personnel (or both) or funds for such instruments or personnel and provides no other financial assistance to a facility, notwithstanding section 6981(c)(3) of this title, title to any invention made or conceived of in the course of developing, constructing, or operating such facility shall not be required to vest in the United States and patents respecting such invention shall not be required to be issued to the United States.

(d) Prohibition

After October 21, 1976, the Administrator shall not construct or operate any full-scale facility (except by contract with public agencies or authorities or private persons).

(Pub.L. 89–272, Title II, § 8004, as added Oct. 21, 1976, Pub.L. 94–580, § 2, 90 Stat. 2836, and amended Nov. 8, 1978, Pub.L. 95–609, § 7(v), 92 Stat. 3084; Nov. 8, 1984, Pub.L. 98–616, Title V, § 502(f), 98 Stat. 3276.)

CROSS REFERENCES

Consultation with Environmental Protection Agency to insure compliance with this section relating to municipal waste reprocessing demonstration facilities, see section 5920 of this title.

CODE OF FEDERAL REGULATIONS

Grants, see 40 CFR 40.100 et seq.

§ 6985. Special study and demonstration projects on recovery of useful energy and materials [SWDA § 8005]

(a) Studies

The Administrator shall conduct studies and develop recommendations for administrative or legislative action on—

(1) means of recovering materials and energy from solid waste, recommended uses of such materials and energy for national or international welfare, including identification of potential markets for such recovered resources, the impact of distribution of such resources on existing markets, and potentials for energy conservation through resource conservation and resource recovery;

(2) actions to reduce waste generation which have been taken voluntarily or in response to governmental action, and those which practically could be taken in the future, and the economic, social, and environmental consequences of such actions;

(3) methods of collection, separation, and containerization which will encourage efficient utilization of facilities and contribute to more effective programs of reduction, reuse, or disposal of wastes;

(4) the use of Federal procurement to develop market demand for recovered resources;

(5) recommended incentives (including Federal grants, loans, and other assistance) and disincentives to accelerate the reclamation or recycling of materials from solid wastes, with special emphasis on motor vehicle hulks;

(6) the effect of existing public policies, including subsidies and economic incentives and disincentives, percentage depletion allowances, capital gains treatment and other tax incentives and disincentives, upon the recycling and reuse of materials, and the likely effect of the modification or elimination of such incentives and disincentives upon the reuse, recycling and conservation of such materials;

(7) the necessity and method of imposing disposal or other charges on packaging, containers, vehicles, and other manufactured goods, which charges would reflect the cost of final disposal, the value of recoverable components of the item, and any social costs associated with nonrecycling or uncontrolled disposal of such items;

(8) the legal constraints and institutional barriers to the acquisition of land needed for solid waste management, including land for facilities and disposal sites;

(9) in consultation with the Secretary of Agriculture, agricultural waste management problems and practices, the extent of reuse and recovery of resources in such wastes, the prospects for improvement, Federal, State, and local regulations governing such practices, and the economic, social, and environmental consequences of such practices; and

(10) in consultation with the Secretary of the Interior, mining waste management problems, and practices, including an assessment of existing authorities, technologies, and economics, and the environmental and public health consequences of such practices.

(b) Demonstration

The Administrator is also authorized to carry out demonstration projects to test and demonstrate methods and techniques developed pursuant to subsection (a) of this section.

(c) Application of other sections

Section 6981(b) and (c) of this title shall be applicable to investigations, studies, and projects carried out under this section.

(Pub.L. 89–272, Title II, § 8005, as added Oct. 21, 1976, Pub.L. 94–580, § 2, 90 Stat. 2837.)

CODE OF FEDERAL REGULATIONS

Grants, see 40 CFR 40.100 et seq.

§ 6986. Grants for resource recovery systems and improved solid waste disposal facilities [SWDA § 8006]

(a) Authority

The Administrator is authorized to make grants pursuant to this section to any State, municipal, or interstate or intermunicipal agency for the demonstration of resource recovery systems or for the construction of new or improved solid waste disposal facilities.

(b) Conditions

(1) Any grant under this section for the demonstration of a resource recovery system may be made only if it (A) is consistent with any plans which meet the requirements of subchapter IV of this chapter; (B) is consistent with the guidelines recommended pursuant to section 6907 of this title; (C) is designed to provide area-wide resource recovery systems consistent with the purposes of this chapter, as determined by the Administrator, pursuant to regulations promulgated under subsection (d) of this section; and (D) provides an equitable system for distributing the costs associated with construction, operation, and maintenance of any resource recovery system among the users of such system.

(2) The Federal share for any project to which paragraph (1) applies shall not be more than 75 percent.

(c) Limitations

(1) A grant under this section for the construction of a new or improved solid waste disposal facility may be made only if—

(A) a State or interstate plan for solid waste disposal has been adopted which applies to the area involved, and the facility to be constructed (i) is consistent with such plan, (ii) is included in a comprehensive plan for the area involved which is satisfactory to the Administrator for the purposes of this chapter, and (iii) is consistent with the guidelines recommended under section 6907 of this title, and

(B) the project advances the state of the art by applying new and improved techniques in reducing the environmental impact of solid waste disposal, in achieving recovery of energy or resources, or in recycling useful materials.

(2) The Federal share for any project to which paragraph (1) applies shall be not more than 50 percent in the case of a project serving an area which includes only one municipality, and not more than 75 percent in any other case.

(d) Regulations

(1) The Administrator shall promulgate regulations establishing a procedure for awarding grants under this section which—

(A) provides that projects will be carried out in communities of varying sizes, under such conditions as will assist in solving the community waste problems of urban-industrial centers, metropolitan regions, and rural areas, under representative geographic and environmental conditions; and

(B) provides deadlines for submission of, and action on, grant requests.

(2) In taking action on applications for grants under this section, consideration shall be given by the Administrator (A) to the public benefits to be derived by the construction and the propriety of Federal aid in making such grant; (B) to the extent applicable, to the economic and commercial viability of the project (including contractual arrangements with the private sector to market any resources recovered); (C) to the potential of such project for general application to community solid waste disposal problems; and (D) to the use by the applicant of comprehensive regional or metropolitan area planning.

(e) Additional limitations

A grant under this section—

(1) may be made only in the amount of the Federal share of (A) the estimated total design and construction costs, plus (B) in the case of a grant to which subsection (b)(1) of this section applies, the first-year operation and maintenance costs;

(2) may not be provided for land acquisition or (except as otherwise provided in paragraph (1)(B)) for operating or maintenance costs;

(3) may not be made until the applicant has made provision satisfactory to the Administrator for proper and efficient operation and maintenance of the project (subject to paragraph (1)(B)); and

(4) may be made subject to such conditions and requirements, in addition to those provided in this section, as the Administrator may require to properly carry out his functions pursuant to this chapter.

For purposes of paragraph (1), the non-Federal share may be in any form, including, but not limited to, lands or interests therein needed for the project or personal property or services, the value of which shall be determined by the Administrator.

(f) Single State

(1) Not more than 15 percent of the total of funds authorized to be appropriated for any fiscal year to carry out this section shall be granted under this section for projects in any one State.

(2) The Administrator shall prescribe by regulation the manner in which this subsection shall apply to a grant under this section for a project in an area which includes all or part of more than one State.

(Pub.L. 89–272, Title II, § 8006, as added Oct. 21, 1976, Pub.L. 94–580, § 2, 90 Stat. 2838.)

CODE OF FEDERAL REGULATIONS

Grants, see 40 CFR 40.100 et seq.

LIBRARY REFERENCES

United States ⟹82(3).
C.J.S. United States § 122.

§ 6987. Authorization of appropriations [SWDA § 8007]

There are authorized to be appropriated not to exceed $35,000,000 for the fiscal year 1978 to carry out the purposes of this subchapter (except for section 6982 of this title).

(Pub.L. 89–272, Title II, § 8007, as added Oct. 21, 1976, Pub.L. 94–580, § 2, 90 Stat. 2839.)

LIBRARY REFERENCES

United States ⟹82(3).
C.J.S. United States § 122.

SUBCHAPTER IX—REGULATION OF UNDERGROUND STORAGE TANKS

§ 6991. Definitions and exemptions [SWDA § 9001]

For the purposes of this subchapter—

(1) The term "underground storage tank" means any one or combination of tanks (including underground pipes connected thereto) which is used to contain an accumulation of regulated substances, and the volume of which (including the volume of the underground pipes connected thereto) is 10 per centum or more beneath the surface of the ground. Such term does not include any—

(A) farm or residential tank of 1,100 gallons or less capacity used for storing motor fuel for noncommercial purposes,

(B) tank used for storing heating oil for consumptive use on the premises where stored,

(C) septic tank,

(D) pipeline facility (including gathering lines)—

(i) which is regulated under chapter 601 of Title 49, or

(ii) which is an intrastate pipeline facility regulated under State laws as provided in chapter 601 of Title 49,

and which is determined by the Secretary to be connected to a pipeline or to be operated or intended to be capable of operating at pipeline pressure or as an integral part of a pipeline,

(E) surface impoundment, pit, pond, or lagoon,

(F) storm water or waste water collection system,

(G) flow-through process tank,

(H) liquid trap or associated gathering lines directly related to oil or gas production and gathering operations, or

(I) storage tank situated in an underground area (such as a basement, cellar, mineworking, drift, shaft, or tunnel) if the storage tank is situated upon or above the surface of the floor.

The term "underground storage tank" shall not include any pipes connected to any tank which is described in subparagraphs (A) through (I).

(2) The term "regulated substance" means—

(A) any substance defined in section 9601(14) of this title (but not including any substance regulated as a hazardous waste under subchapter III of this chapter), and

(B) petroleum.

(3) The term "owner" means—

(A) in the case of an underground storage tank in use on November 8, 1984, or brought into use after that date, any person who owns an underground storage tank used for the storage, use, or dispensing of regulated sustances,[1] and

(B) in the case of any underground storage tank in use before November 8, 1984, but no longer in use on November 8, 1984, any person who owned such tank immediately before the discontinuation of its use.

(4) The term "operator" means any person in control of, or having responsibility for, the daily operation of the underground storage tank.

(5) The term "release" means any spilling, leaking, emitting, discharging, escaping, leaching, or disposing from an underground storage tank into ground water, surface water or subsurface soils.

(6) The term "person" has the same meaning as provided in section 6903(15) of this title, except that such term includes a consortium, a joint venture, and a commercial entity, and the United States Government.

(7) The term "nonoperational storage tank" means any underground storage tank in which regulated substances will not be deposited or from which regulated substances will not be dispensed after November 8, 1984.

(8) The term "petroleum" means petroleum, including crude oil or any fraction thereof which is liquid at standard conditions of temperature and pressure (60 degrees Fahrenheit and 14.7 pounds per square inch absolute).

(Pub.L. 89–272, Title II, § 9001, as added Nov. 8, 1984, Pub.L. 98–616, Title VI, § 601(a), 98 Stat. 3277, and amended Oct. 17, 1986, Pub.L. 99–499, Title II, § 205(a), 100 Stat. 1696; Oct. 24, 1992, Pub.L. 102–508, Title III, § 302, 106 Stat. 3307; Pub.L. 103–429, § 7(d), Oct. 31, 1994, 108 Stat. 4389.)

1 So in original. Probably should be "substances".

LAW REVIEW COMMENTARIES

High penalties and citizen suits await small businesses unaware of EPCRA reporting requirements. Jeffrey T. Pender, 10 Corp. Counsel Rev. (Tex.) 81 (May 1991).

Interaction of the Bankruptcy Code and environmental laws: Grit, the grind, and the grease. Robert R. Graves, 29 Willamette L.Rev. 297 (1993).

Shelter from the storm? EPA's final lender liability rules. Meryl R. Lieberman and Michael J. Case, 65 N.Y.S.B.J. 32 (Dec. 1993).

Underground storage tanks: Rules of the game change yet again. Carey S. Rosemarin, 8 CBA Rec. 22 (Feb. 1994).

LIBRARY REFERENCES

Health and Environment ⇐25.5(3).
C.J.S. Health and Environment § 91 et seq.

§ 6991a. Notification [SWDA § 9002]

(a) Underground storage tanks

(1) Within 18 months after November 8, 1984, each owner of an underground storage tank shall notify the State or local agency or department designated pursuant to subsection (b)(1) of this section of the existence of such tank, specifying the age, size, type, location, and uses of such tank.

(2)(A) For each underground storage tank taken out of operation after January 1, 1974, the owner of such tank shall, within eighteen months after November 8, 1984, notify the State or local agency, or department designated pursuant to subsection (b)(1) of this section of the existence of such tanks (unless the owner knows the tank subsequently was removed from the ground). The owner of a tank taken out of operation on or before January 1, 1974, shall not be required to notify the State or local agency under this subsection.

(B) Notice under subparagraph (A) shall specify, to the extent known to the owner—

(i) the date the tank was taken out of operation,

(ii) the age of the tank on the date taken out of operation,

(iii) the size, type and location of the tank, and

(iv) the type and quantity of substances left stored in such tank on the date taken out of operation.

(3) Any owner which brings into use an underground storage tank after the initial notification period specified under paragraph (1), shall notify the designated State or local agency or department within thirty days of the existence of such tank, specifying the age, size, type, location and uses of such tank.

(4) Paragraphs (1) through (3) of this subsection shall not apply to tanks for which notice was given pursuant to section 9603(c) of this title.

(5) Beginning thirty days after the Administrator prescribes the form of notice pursuant to subsection (b)(2) of this section and for eighteen months thereafter, any person who deposits regulated substances in an underground storage tank shall reasonably notify the owner or operator of such tank of the owner's notification requirements pursuant to this subsection.

(6) Beginning thirty days after the Administrator issues new tank performance standards pursuant to section 6991b(c) of this title, any person who sells a tank intended to be used as an underground storage tank shall notify the purchaser of such tank of the owner's notification requirements pursuant to this subsection.

(b) Agency designation

(1) Within one hundred and eighty days after November 8, 1984, the Governors of each State shall designate the appropriate State agency or department or local agencies or departments to receive the notifications under subsection (a)(1), (2), or (3) of this section.

(2) Within twelve months after November 8, 1984, the Administrator, in consultation with State and local officials designated pursuant to subsection (b)(1) of this section, and after notice and opportunity for public comment, shall prescribe the form of the notice and the information to be included in the notifications under subsection (a)(1), (2), or (3) of this section. In prescribing the form of such notice, the Administrator shall take into account the effect on small businesses and other owners and operators.

(c) State inventories

Each State shall make 2 separate inventories of all underground storage tanks in such State containing regulated substances. One inventory shall be made with respect to petroleum and one with respect to other regulated substances. In making such inventories, the State shall utilize and aggregate the data in the notification forms submitted pursuant to subsections (a) and (b) of this section. Each State shall submit such aggregated data to the Administrator not later than 270 days after October 17, 1986.

(Pub.L. 89–272, Title II, § 9002, as added Nov. 8, 1984, Pub.L. 98–616, Title VI, § 601(a), 98 Stat. 3278, and amended Oct. 17, 1986, Pub.L. 99–499, Title II, § 205(b), 100 Stat. 1696.)

§ 6991b. Release, detection, prevention, and correction regulations [SWDA § 9003]

(a) Regulations

The Administrator, after notice and opportunity for public comment, and at least three months before the effective dates specified in subsection (f) of this section, shall promulgate release detection, prevention, and correction regulations applicable to all owners and operators of underground storage tanks, as may be necessary to protect human health and the environment.

(b) Distinctions in regulations

In promulgating regulations under this section, the Administrator may distinguish between types, classes, and ages of underground storage tanks. In making such distinctions, the Administrator may take into consideration factors, including, but not limited to: location of the tanks, soil and climate conditions, uses of the tanks, history of maintenance, age of the tanks, current industry recommended practices, national consensus codes, hydrogeology, water table, size of the tanks, quantity of regulated substances periodically deposited in or dispensed from the tank, the technical capability of the owners and operators, and the compatibility of the regulated substance and the materials of which the tank is fabricated.

(c) Requirements

The regulations promulgated pursuant to this section shall include, but need not be limited to, the following requirements respecting all underground storage tanks—

(1) requirements for maintaining a leak detection system, an inventory control system together with tank testing, or a comparable system or method designed to identify releases in a manner consistent with the protection of human health and the environment;

(2) requirements for maintaining records of any monitoring or leak detection system or inventory control system or tank testing or comparable system;

(3) requirements for reporting of releases and corrective action taken in response to a release from an underground storage tank;

(4) requirements for taking corrective action in response to a release from an underground storage tank;

(5) requirements for the closure of tanks to prevent future releases of regulated substances into the environment; and

(6) requirements for maintaining evidence of financial responsibility for taking corrective action and compensating third parties for bodily injury and property damage caused by sudden and nonsudden accidental releases arising from operating an underground storage tank.

(d) Financial responsibility

(1) Financial responsibility required by this subsection may be established in accordance with regulations promulgated by the Administrator by any one, or any combination, of the following: insurance, guarantee, surety bond, letter of credit, qualification as a self-insurer or any other method satisfactory to the Administrator. In promulgating requirements under this subsection, the Administrator is authorized to specify policy or other contractual terms, conditions, or defenses which are necessary or are unacceptable in establishing such evidence of financial responsibility in order to effectuate the purposes of this subchapter.

(2) In any case where the owner or operator is in bankruptcy, reorganization, or arrangement pursuant to the Federal Bankruptcy Code or where with reasonable diligence jurisdiction in any State court of the Federal Courts cannot be obtained over an owner or operator likely to be solvent at the time of judgment, any claim arising from conduct for which evidence of financial responsibility must be provided under this subsection may be asserted directly against the guarantor providing such evidence of financial responsibility. In the case of any action pursuant to this paragraph such guarantor shall be entitled to invoke all rights and defenses which would have been available to the owner or operator if any action had been brought against the owner or operator by the claimant and which would have been available to the guarantor if an action had been brought against the guarantor by the owner or operator.

(3) The total liability of any guarantor shall be limited to the aggregate amount which the guarantor has provided as evidence of financial responsibility to the owner or operator under this section. Nothing in this subsection shall be construed to limit any other State or Federal statutory, contractual or common law liability of a guarantor to its owner or operator including, but not limited to, the liability of such guarantor for bad faith either in negotiating or in failing to negotiate the settlement of any claim. Nothing in this subsection shall be construed to diminish the liability of any person under section 9607 or 9611 of this title or other applicable law.

(4) For the purpose of this subsection, the term "guarantor" means any person, other than the owner or operator, who provides evidence of financial responsibility for an owner or operator under this subsection.

(5)(A) The Administrator, in promulgating financial responsibility regulations under this section, may establish an amount of coverage for particular classes or categories of underground storage tanks containing petroleum which shall satisfy such regulations and which shall not be less than $1,000,000 for each occurrence with an appropriate aggregate requirement.

(B) The Administrator may set amounts lower than the amounts required by subparagraph (A) of this paragraph for underground storage tanks containing petroleum which are at facilities not engaged in petroleum production, refining, or marketing and which are not used to handle substantial quantities of petroleum.

(C) In establishing classes and categories for purposes of this paragraph, the Administrator may consider the following factors:

(i) The size, type, location, storage, and handling capacity of underground storage tanks in the class or category and the volume of petroleum handled by such tanks.

(ii) The likelihood of release and the potential extent of damage from any release from underground storage tanks in the class or category.

(iii) The economic impact of the limits on the owners and operators of each such class or category, particularly relating to the small business segment of the petroleum marketing industry.

(iv) The availability of methods of financial responsibility in amounts greater than the amount established by this paragraph.

(v) Such other factors as the Administrator deems pertinent.

(D) The Administrator may suspend enforcement of the financial responsibility requirements for a particular class or category of underground storage tanks or in a particular State, if the Administrator makes a determination that methods of financial responsibility satisfying the requirements of this subsection are not generally available for underground storage tanks in that class or category, and—

(i) steps are being taken to form a risk retention group for such class of tanks; or

(ii) such State is taking steps to establish a fund pursuant to section 6991c(c)(1) of this title to be submitted as evidence of financial responsibility.

A suspension by the Administrator pursuant to this paragraph shall extend for a period not to exceed 180 days. A determination to suspend may be made with respect to the same class or category or for the same State at the end of such period, but only if substantial progress has been made in establishing a risk retention group, or the owners or operators in the class or category demonstrate, and the Administrator finds, that the formation of such a group is not possible and that the State is unable or unwilling to establish such a fund pursuant to clause (ii).

(e) New tank performance standards

The Administrator shall, not later than three months prior to the effective date specified in subsection (f) of this section, issue performance standards for underground storage tanks brought into use on or after the effective date of such standards. The performance standards for new underground storage tanks shall include, but need not be limited to, design, construction, installation, release detection, and compatibility standards.

(f) Effective dates

(1) Regulations issued pursuant to subsection[1] (c) and (d) of this section, and standards issued pursuant to subsection (e) of this section, for underground storage tanks containing regulated substances defined in section 6991(2)(B) of this title (petroleum, including crude oil or any fraction thereof which is liquid at standard conditions of temperature and pressure) shall be effective not later than thirty months after November 8, 1984.

(2) Standards issued pursuant to subsection (e) of this section (entitled "New Tank Performance Standards") for underground storage tanks containing regulated substances defined in section 6991(2)(A) of this title shall be effective not later than thirty-six months after November 8, 1984.

(3) Regulations issued pursuant to subsection (c) of this section (entitled "Requirements") and standards issued pursuant to subsection (d) of this section (entitled "Financial Responsibility") for underground storage tanks containing regulated substances defined in section 6991(2)(A) of this title shall be effective not later than forty-eight months after November 8, 1984.

(g) Interim prohibition

(1) Until the effective date of the standards promulgated by the Administrator under subsection (e) of this section and after one hundred and eighty days after November 8, 1984, no person may install an underground storage tank for the purpose of storing regulated substances unless such tank (whether of single or double wall construction)—

(A) will prevent releases due to corrosion or structural failure for the operational life of the tank;

(B) is cathodically protected against corrosion, constructed of noncorrosive material, steel clad with a noncorrosive material, or designed in a manner to prevent the release or threatened release of any stored substance; and

(C) the material used in the construction or lining of the tank is compatible with the substance to be stored.

(2) Notwithstanding paragraph (1), if soil tests conducted in accordance with ASTM Standard G57–78, or another standard approved by the Administrator, show that soil resistivity in an installation location is 12,000 ohm/cm or more (unless a more stringent standard is prescribed by the Administrator by rule), a storage tank without corrosion protection may be installed in that location during the period referred to in paragraph (1).

(h) EPA Response Program for Petroleum

(1) Before regulations

Before the effective date of regulations under subsection (c) of this section, the Administrator (or a State pursuant to paragraph (7)) is authorized to—

(A) require the owner or operator of an underground storage tank to undertake corrective action with respect to any release of petroleum when the Administrator (or the State) determines that such corrective action will be done properly and promptly by the owner or operator of the underground storage tank from which the release occurs; or

(B) undertake corrective action with respect to any release of petroleum into the environment from an underground storage tank if such action is necessary, in the judgment of the Administrator (or the State), to protect human health and the environment.

The corrective action undertaken or required under this paragraph shall be such as may be necessary to protect human health and the environment. The Administrator shall use funds in the Leaking Underground Storage Tank Trust Fund for payment of costs incurred for corrective action under subparagraph (B), enforcement action under subparagraph (A), and cost recovery under paragraph (6) of this subsection. Subject to the priority requirements of paragraph (3), the Administrator (or the State) shall give priority in undertaking such actions under subparagraph (B) to cases where the Administrator (or the State) cannot identify a solvent owner or operator of the tank who will undertake action properly.

(2) After regulations

Following the effective date of regulations under subsection (c) of this section, all actions or orders of the Administrator (or a State pursuant to paragraph (7)) described in paragraph (1) of this subsection shall be in conformity with such regulations. Following such effective date, the Administrator (or the State) may undertake corrective action with respect to any release of petroleum into the environment from an underground storage tank only if such action is necessary, in the judgment of the Administrator (or the State), to protect human health and the environment and one or more of the following situations exists:

(A) No person can be found, within 90 days or such shorter period as may be necessary to protect human health and the environment, who is—

(i) an owner or operator of the tank concerned,

(ii) subject to such corrective action regulations, and

(iii) capable of carrying out such corrective action properly.

(B) A situation exists which requires prompt action by the Administrator (or the State) under this paragraph to protect human health and the environment.

(C) Corrective action costs at a facility exceed the amount of coverage required by the Administrator pursuant to the provisions of subsections (c) and (d)(5) of this section and, considering the class or category of underground storage tank from which the release occurred, expenditures from the Leaking Underground Storage Tank Trust Fund are necessary to assure an effective corrective action.

(D) The owner or operator of the tank has failed or refused to comply with an order of the Administrator under this subsection or section 6991e of this title or with the order of a State under this subsection to comply with the corrective action regulations.

(3) Priority of corrective actions

The Administrator (or a State pursuant to paragraph (7)) shall give priority in undertaking corrective actions under this subsection, and in issuing orders requiring owners or operators to undertake such actions, to releases of petroleum from underground storage tanks which pose the greatest threat to human health and the environment.

(4) Corrective action orders

The Administrator is authorized to issue orders to the owner or operator of an underground storage tank to carry out subparagraph (A) of paragraph (1) or to carry out regulations issued under subsection (c)(4) of this section. A State acting pursuant to paragraph (7) of this subsection is authorized to carry out subparagraph (A) of paragraph (1) only until the State's program is approved by the Administrator under section 6991c of this title. Such orders shall be issued and enforced in the same manner and subject to the same requirements as orders under section 6991e of this title.

(5) Allowable corrective actions

The corrective actions undertaken by the Administrator (or a State pursuant to paragraph (7)) under paragraph (1) or (2) may include temporary or permanent relocation of residents and alternative household water supplies. In connection with the performance of any corrective action under paragraph (1) or (2), the Administrator may undertake an exposure assessment as defined in paragraph (10) of this subsection or provide for such an assessment in a cooperative agreement with a State pursuant to paragraph (7) of this subsection. The costs of any such assessment may be treated as corrective action for purposes of paragraph (6), relating to cost recovery.

(6) Recovery of costs

(A) In general

Whenever costs have been incurred by the Administrator, or by a State pursuant to paragraph (7), for undertaking corrective action or enforcement action with respect to the release of petroleum from an underground storage tank, the owner or operator of such tank shall be liable to the Administrator or the State for such costs. The liability under this paragraph shall be construed to be the standard of liability which obtains under section 1321 of Title 33.

(B) Recovery

In determining the equities for seeking the recovery of costs under subparagraph (A), the Administrator (or a State pursuant to paragraph (7) of this subsection) may consider the amount of financial responsibility required to be maintained under subsections (c) and (d)(5) of this section and the factors considered in establishing such amount under subsection (d)(5) of this section.

(C) Effect on liability

(i) No transfers of liability

No indemnification, hold harmless, or similar agreement or conveyance shall be effective to transfer from the owner or operator of any underground storage tank or from any person who may be liable for a release or threat of release under this subsection, to any other person the liability imposed under this subsection. Nothing in this subsection shall bar any agreement to insure, hold harmless, or indemnify a party to such agreement for any liability under this section.

(ii) No bar to cause of action

Nothing in this subsection, including the provisions of clause (i) of this subparagraph, shall bar a cause of action that an owner or operator or any other person subject to liability under this section, or a guarantor, has or would have, by reason of subrogation or otherwise against any person.

(D) Facility

For purposes of this paragraph, the term "facility" means, with respect to any owner or operator, all underground storage tanks used for the storage of petroleum which are owned or operated by such owner or operator and located on a single parcel of property (or on any contiguous or adjacent property).

(7) State authorities

(A) General

A State may exercise the authorities in paragraphs (1) and (2) of this subsection, subject to the terms and conditions of paragraphs (3), (5), (9), (10), and (11), and including the authorities of paragraphs (4), (6), and (8) of this subsection if—

(i) the Administrator determines that the State has the capabilities to carry out effective corrective actions and enforcement activities; and

(ii) the Administrator enters into a cooperative agreement with the State setting out the actions to be undertaken by the State.

The Administrator may provide funds from the Leaking Underground Storage Tank Trust Fund for the reasonable costs of the State's actions under the cooperative agreement.

(B) Cost share

Following the effective date of the regulations under subsection (c) of this section, the State shall pay 10 per centum of the cost of corrective actions undertaken either by the Administrator or by the State under a cooperative agreement, except that the Administrator may take corrective action at a facility where immediate action is necessary to respond to an imminent and substantial endangerment to human health or the environment if the State fails to pay the cost share.

(8) Emergency procurement powers

Notwithstanding any other provision of law, the Administrator may authorize the use of such emergency procurement powers as he deems necessary.

(9) Definition of owner

As used in this subsection, the term "owner" does not include any person who, without participating in the management of an underground storage tank and otherwise not engaged in petroleum production, refining, and marketing, holds indicia of ownership primarily to protect the owner's security interest in the tank.

(10) Definition of exposure assessment

As used in this subsection, the term "exposure assessment" means an assessment to determine the extent of exposure of, or potential for exposure of, individuals to petroleum from a release from an underground storage tank based on such factors as the nature and extent of contamination and the existence of or potential for pathways of human exposure (including ground or surface water contamination, air emissions, and food chain contamination), the size of the community within the likely pathways of exposure, and the comparison of expected human exposure levels to the short-term and long-term health effects associated with identified contaminants and any available recommended exposure or tolerance limits for such contaminants. Such assessment shall not delay corrective action to abate immediate hazards or reduce exposure.

(11) **Facilities without financial responsibility**

At any facility where the owner or operator has failed to maintain evidence of financial responsibility in amounts at least equal to the amounts established by subsection (d)(5)(A) of this section (or a lesser amount if such amount is applicable to such facility as a result of subsection (d)(5)(B) of this section) for whatever reason the Administrator shall expend no monies from the Leaking Underground Storage Tank Trust Fund to clean up releases at such facility pursuant to the provisions of paragraph (1) or (2) of this subsection. At such facilities the Administrator shall use the authorities provided in subparagraph (A) of paragraph (1) and paragraph (4) of this subsection and section 6991e of this title to order corrective action to clean up such releases. States acting pursuant to paragraph (7) of this subsection shall use the authorities provided in subparagraph (A) of paragraph (1) and paragraph (4) of this subsection to order corrective action to clean up such releases. Notwithstanding the provisions of this paragraph, the Administrator may use monies from the fund to take the corrective actions authorized by paragraph (5) of this subsection to protect human health at such facilities and shall seek full recovery of the costs of all such actions pursuant to the provisions of paragraph (6)(A) of this subsection and without consideration of the factors in paragraph (6)(B) of this subsection. Nothing in this paragraph shall prevent the Administrator (or a State pursuant to paragraph (7) of this subsection) from taking corrective action at a facility where there is no solvent owner or operator or where immediate action is necessary to respond to an imminent and substantial endangerment of human health or the environment.

(Pub.L. 89–272, Title II, § 9003, as added Nov. 8, 1984, Pub.L. 98–616, Title VI, § 601(a), 98 Stat. 3279, and amended Oct. 17, 1986, Pub.L. 99–499, Title II, § 205(c), (d), 100 Stat. 1697, 1698.)

[1] So in original. Probably should be "subsections".

LAW REVIEW COMMENTARIES

Shelter from the storm? EPA's final lender liability rules. Meryl R. Lieberman and Michael J. Case, 65 N.Y.S.B.J. 32 (Dec. 1993).

§ 6991c. Approval of State programs [SWDA § 9004]

(a) **Elements of State program**

Beginning 30 months after November 8, 1984, any State may,[1] submit an underground storage tank release detection, prevention, and correction program for review and approval by the Administrator. The program may cover tanks used to store regulated substances referred to in[2] 6991(2)(A) or (B) or both of this title. A State program may be approved by the Administrator under this section only if the State demonstrates that the State program includes the following requirements and standards and provides for adequate enforcement of compliance with such requirements and standards—

(1) requirements for maintaining a leak detection system, an inventory control system together with tank testing, or a comparable system or method designed to identify releases in a manner consistent with the protection of human health and the environment;

(2) requirements for maintaining records of any monitoring or leak detection system or inventory control system or tank testing system;

(3) requirements for reporting of any releases and corrective action taken in response to a release from an underground storage tank;

(4) requirements for taking corrective action in response to a release from an underground storage tank;

(5) requirements for the closure of tanks to prevent future releases of regulated substances into the environment;

(6) requirements for maintaining evidence of financial responsibility for taking corrective action and compensating third parties for bodily injury and property damage caused by sudden and nonsudden accidental releases arising from operating an underground storage tank;

(7) standards of performance for new underground storage tanks; and

(8) requirements—

(A) for notifying the appropriate State agency or department (or local agency or department) designated according to section 6991a(b)(1) of this title of the existence of any operational or nonoperational underground storage tank; and

(B) for providing the information required on the form issued pursuant to section 6991a(b)(2) of this title.

(b) **Federal standards**

(1) A State program submitted under this section may be approved only if the requirements under paragraphs (1) through (7) of subsection (a) of this section are no less stringent than the corresponding requirements standards promulgated by the Administrator pursuant to section 6991b(a) of this title.

(2)(A) A State program may be approved without regard to whether or not the requirements referred to in paragraphs (1), (2), (3), and (5) of subsection (a) of this section are less stringent than the corresponding standards under section 6991b(a) of this title during the one-year period commencing on the date of promulgation of regulations under section 6991b(a) of this title if State regulatory action but no State legislative action is required in order to adopt a State program.

(B) If such State legislative action is required, the State program may be approved without regard to whether or not the requirements referred to in paragraphs (1), (2), (3), and (5) of subsection (a) of this section are less stringent than the corresponding standards under section 6991b(a) of this title during the two-year period commencing on the date of promulgation of regulations under section 6991b(a) of this title (and during an additional one-year period after such legislative action if regulations are required to be promulgated by the State pursuant to such legislative action).

(c) Financial responsibility

(1) Corrective action and compensation programs administered by State or local agencies or departments may be submitted for approval under subsection (a)(6) of this section as evidence of financial responsibility.

(2) Financial responsibility required by this subsection may be established in accordance with regulations promulgated by the Administrator by any one, or any combination, of the following: insurance, guarantee, surety bond, letter of credit, qualification as a self-insurer or any other method satisfactory to the Administrator. In promulgating requirements under this subsection, the Administrator is authorized to specify policy or other contractual terms including the amount of coverage required for various classes and categories of underground storage tanks pursuant to section 6991b(d)(5) of this title, conditions, or defenses which are necessary or are unacceptable in establishing such evidence of financial responsibility in order to effectuate the purposes of this subchapter.

(3) In any case where the owner or operator is in bankruptcy, reorganization, or arrangement pursuant to the Federal Bankruptcy Code or where with reasonable diligence jurisdiction in any State court of the Federal courts cannot be obtained over an owner or operator likely to be solvent at the time of judgment, any claim arising from conduct for which evidence of financial responsibility must be provided under this subsection may be asserted directly against the guarantor providing such evidence of financial responsibility. In the case of any action pursuant to this paragraph such guarantor shall be entitled to invoke all rights and defenses which would have been available to the owner or operator if any action had been brought against the owner or operator by the claimant and which would have been available to the guarantor if an action had been brought against the guarantor by the owner or operator.

(4) The total liability of any guarantor shall be limited to the aggregate amount which the guarantor has provided as evidence of financial responsibility to the owner or operator under this section. Nothing in this subsection shall be construed to limit any other State or Federal statutory, contractual or common law liability of a guarantor to its owner or operator including, but not limited to, the liability of such guarantor for bad faith either in negotiating or in failing to negotiate the settlement of any claim. Nothing in this subsection shall be construed to diminish the liability of any person under section 9607 or 9611 of this title or other applicable law.

(5) For the purpose of this subsection, the term "guarantor" means any person, other than the owner or operator, who provides evidence of financial responsibility for an owner or operator under this subsection.

(d) EPA determination

(1) Within one hundred and eighty days of the date of receipt of a proposed State program, the Administrator shall, after notice and opportunity for public comment, make a determination whether the State's program complies with the provisions of this section and provides for adequate enforcement of compliance with the requirements and standards adopted pursuant to this section.

(2) If the Administrator determines that a State program complies with the provisions of this section and provides for adequate enforcement of compliance with the requirements and standards adopted pursuant to this section, he shall approve the State program in lieu of the Federal program and the State shall have primary enforcement responsibility with respect to requirements of its program.

(e) Withdrawal of authorization

Whenever the Administrator determines after public hearing that a State is not administering and enforcing a program authorized under this subchapter in accordance with the provisions of this section, he shall so notify the State. If appropriate action is not taken within a reasonable time, not to exceed one hundred and twenty days after such notification, the Administrator shall withdraw approval of such program and reestablish the Federal program pursuant to this subchapter.

(Pub.L. 89–272, Title II, § 9004, as added Nov. 8, 1984, Pub.L. 98–616, Title VI, § 601(a), 98 Stat. 3282, and amended Oct. 17, 1986, Pub.L. 99–499, Title II, § 205(e), 100 Stat. 1702.)

[1] So in original.

[2] So in original. Probably should be followed by "section".

§ 6991d. Inspections, monitoring, testing, and corrective action [SWDA § 9005]

(a) Furnishing information

For the purposes of developing or assisting in the development of any regulation, conducting any study[1] taking any corrective action, or enforcing the provisions of this subchapter, any owner or operator of an underground storage tank (or any tank subject to study under section 6991h of this title that is used for storing regulated substances) shall, upon request of any officer, employee or representative of the Environmental Protection Agency, duly designated by the Administrator, or upon request of any duly designated officer, employee, or representative of a State acting pursuant to subsection (h)(7) of section 6991b of this title or with an approved program, furnish information relating to such tanks, their associated equipment, their contents, conduct monitoring or testing, permit such officer at all reasonable times to have access to, and to copy all records relating to such tanks and permit such officer to have access for corrective action. For the purposes of developing or assisting in the development of any regulation, conducting any study, taking corrective action, or enforcing the provisions of this subchapter, such officers, employees, or representatives are authorized—

(1) to enter at reasonable times any establishment or other place where an underground storage tank is located;

(2) to inspect and obtain samples from any person of any regulated substances contained in such tank;

(3) to conduct monitoring or testing of the tanks, associated equipment, contents, or surrounding soils, air, surface water or ground water; and

(4) to take corrective action.

Each such inspection shall be commenced and completed with reasonable promptness.

(b) Confidentiality

(1) Any records, reports, or information obtained from any persons under this section shall be available to the public, except that upon a showing satisfactory to the Administrator (or the State, as the case may be) by any person that records, reports, or information, or a particular part thereof, to which the Administrator (or the State, as the case may be) or any officer, employee, or representative thereof has access under this section if made public, would divulge information entitled to protection under section 1905 of Title 18, such information or particular portion thereof shall be considered confidential in accordance with the purposes of that section, except that such record, report, document, or information may be disclosed to other officers, employees, or authorized representatives of the United States concerned with carrying out this chapter, or when relevent[2] in any proceeding under this chapter.

(2) Any person not subject to the provisions of section 1905 of Title 18 who knowingly and willfully divulges or discloses any information entitled to protection under this subsection shall, upon conviction, be subject to a fine of not more than $5,000 or to imprisonment not to exceed one year, or both.

(3) In submitting data under this subchapter, a person required to provide such data may—

(A) designate the data which such person believes is entitled to protection under this subsection, and

(B) submit such designated data separately from other data submitted under this subchapter.

A designation under this paragraph shall be made in writing and in such manner as the Administrator may prescribe.

(4) Notwithstanding any limitation contained in this section or any other provision of law, all information reported to, or otherwise obtained, by the Administrator (or any representative of the Administrator) under this chapter shall be made available, upon written request of any duly authorized committee of the Congress, to such committee (including records, reports, or information obtained by representatives of the Environmental Protection Agency).

(Pub.L. 89–272, Title II, § 9005, as added Nov. 8, 1984, Pub.L. 98–616, Title VI, § 601(a), 98 Stat. 3284, and amended Oct. 17, 1986, Pub.L. 99–499, Title II, § 205(f), 100 Stat. 1702.)

[1] So in original. Probably should be followed by a comma.
[2] So in original. Probably should be "relevant".

§ 6991e. Federal enforcement [SWDA § 9006]

(a) Compliance orders

(1) Except as provided in paragraph (2), whenever on the basis of any information, the Administrator determines that any person is in violation of any requirement of this subchapter, the Administrator may issue an order requiring compliance within a reasonable specified time period or the Administrator may commence a civil action in the United States district court in which the violation occurred for appropriate relief, including a temporary or permanent injunction.

(2) In the case of a violation of any requirement of this subchapter where such violation occurs in a State with a program approved under section 6991c of this

title the Administrator shall give notice to the State in which such violation has occurred prior to issuing an order or commencing a civil action under this section.

(3) If a violator fails to comply with an order under this subsection within the time specified in the order, he shall be liable for a civil penalty of not more than $25,000 for each day of continued noncompliance.

(b) Procedure

Any order issued under this section shall become final unless, no later than thirty days after the order is served, the person or persons named therein request a public hearing. Upon such request the Administrator shall promptly conduct a public hearing. In connection with any proceeding under this section the Administrator may issue subpoenas for the attendance and testimony of witnesses and the production of relevant papers, books, and documents, and may promulgate rules for discovery procedures.

(c) Contents of order

Any order issued under this section shall state with reasonable specificity the nature of the violation, specify a reasonable time for compliance, and assess a penalty, if any, which the Administrator determines is reasonable taking into account the seriousness of the violation and any good faith efforts to comply with the applicable requirements.

(d) Civil penalties

(1) Any owner who knowingly fails to notify or submits false information pursuant to section 6991a(a) of this title shall be subject to a civil penalty not to exceed $10,000 for each tank for which notification is not given or false information is submitted.

(2) Any owner or operator of an underground storage tank who fails to comply with—

(A) any requirement or standard promulgated by the Administrator under section 6991b of this title;

(B) any requirement or standard of a State program approved pursuant to section 6991c of this title; or

(C) the provisions of section 6991b(g) of this title (entitled "Interim Prohibition")

shall be subject to a civil penalty not to exceed $10,000 for each tank for each day of violation.

(Pub.L. 89–272, Title II, § 9006, as added Nov. 8, 1984, Pub.L. 98–616, Title VI, § 601(a), 98 Stat. 3286.)

§ 6991f. Federal facilities [SWDA § 9007]

(a) Application of subchapter

Each department, agency, and instrumentality of the executive, legislative, and judicial branches of the Federal Government having jurisdiction over any underground storage tank shall be subject to and comply with all Federal, State, interstate, and local requirements, applicable to such tank, both substantive and procedural, in the same manner, and to the same extent, as any other person is subject to such requirements, including payment of reasonable service charges. Neither the United States, nor any agent, employee, or officer thereof, shall be immune or exempt from any process or sanction of any State or Federal court with respect to the enforcement of any such injunctive relief.

(b) Presidential exemption

The President may exempt any underground storage tanks of any department, agency, or instrumentality in the executive branch from compliance with such a requirement if he determines it to be in the paramount interest of the United States to do so. No such exemption shall be granted due to lack of appropriation unless the President shall have specifically requested such appropriation as a part of the budgetary process and the Congress shall have failed to make available such requested appropriations. Any exemption shall be for a period not in excess of one year, but additional exemptions may be granted for periods not to exceed one year upon the President's making a new determination. The President shall report each January to the Congress all exemptions from the requirements of this section granted during the preceding calendar year, together with his reason for granting each such exemption.

(Pub.L. 89–272, Title II, § 9007, as added Nov. 8, 1984, Pub.L. 98–616, Title VI, § 601(a), 98 Stat. 3286.)

§ 6991g. State authority [SWDA § 9008]

Nothing in this subchapter shall preclude or deny any right of any State or political subdivision thereof to adopt or enforce any regulation, requirement, or standard of performance respecting underground storage tanks that is more stringent than a regulation, requirement, or standard of performance in effect under this subchapter or to impose any additional liability with respect to the release of regulated substances within such State or political subdivision.

(Pub.L. 89–272, Title II, § 9008, as added Nov. 8, 1984, Pub.L. 98–616, Title VI, § 601(a), 98 Stat. 3286, and amended Oct. 17, 1986, Pub.L. 99–499, Title II, § 205(g), 100 Stat. 1702.)

§ 6991h. Study of underground storage tanks [SWDA § 9009]

(a) Petroleum tanks

Not later than twelve months after November 8, 1984, the Administrator shall complete a study of underground storage tanks used for the storage of regulated substances defined in section 6991(2)(B) of this title.

(b) Other tanks

Not later than thirty-six months after November 8, 1984, the Administrator shall complete a study of all other underground storage tanks.

(c) Elements of studies

The studies under subsections (a) and (b) of this section shall include an assessment of the ages, types (including methods of manufacture, coatings, protection systems, the compatibility of the construction materials and the installation methods) and locations (including the climate of the locations) of such tanks; soil conditions, water tables, and the hydrogeology of tank locations; the relationship between the foregoing factors and the likelihood of releases from underground storage tanks; the effectiveness and costs of inventory systems, tank testing, and leak detection systems; and such other factors as the Administrator deems appropriate.

(d) Farm and heating oil tanks

Not later than thirty-six months after November 8, 1984, the Administrator shall conduct a study regarding the tanks referred to in section 6991(1)(A) and (B) of this title. Such study shall include estimates of the number and location of such tanks and an analysis of the extent to which there may be releases or threatened releases from such tanks into the environment.

(e) Reports

Upon completion of the studies authorized by this section, the Administrator shall submit reports to the President and to the Congress containing the results of the studies and recommendations respecting whether or not such tanks should be subject to the preceding provisions of this subchapter.

(f) Reimbursement

(1) If any owner or operator (excepting an agency, department, or instrumentality of the United States Government, a State or a political subdivision thereof) shall incur costs, including the loss of business opportunity, due to the closure or interruption of operation of an underground storage tank solely for the purpose of conducting studies authorized by this section, the Administrator shall provide such person fair and equitable reimbursement for such costs.

(2) All claims for reimbursement shall be filed with the Administrator not later than ninety days after the closure or interruption which gives rise to the claim.

(3) Reimbursements made under this section shall be from funds appropriated by the Congress pursuant to the authorization contained in section 6916(g) of this title.

(4) For purposes of judicial review, a determination by the Administrator under this subsection shall be considered final agency action.

(Pub.L. 89–272, Title II, § 9009, as added Nov. 8, 1984, Pub.L. 98–616, Title VI, § 601(a), 98 Stat. 3287.)

§ 6991i. Authorization of appropriations [SWDA § 9010]

For authorization of appropriations to carry out this subchapter, see section 6916(g) of this title.

(Pub.L. 89–272, Title II, § 9010, as added Nov. 8, 1984, Pub.L. 98–616, Title VI, § 601(a), 98 Stat. 3287.)

SUBCHAPTER X—DEMONSTRATION MEDICAL WASTE TRACKING PROGRAM

§ 6992. Scope of demonstration program for medical waste [SWDA § 11001]

(a) Covered states

The States within the demonstration program established under this subchapter for tracking medical wastes shall be New York, New Jersey, Connecticut, the States contiguous to the Great Lakes and any State included in the program through the petition procedure described in subsection (c) of this section, except for any of such States in which the Governor notifies the Administrator under subsection (b) of this section that such State shall not be covered by the program.

(b) Opt out

(1) If the Governor of any State covered under subsection (a) of this section which is not contiguous to the Atlantic Ocean notifies the Administrator that such State elects not to participate in the demonstration program, the Administrator shall remove such State from the program.

(2) If the Governor of any other State covered under subsection (a) of this section notifies the Administrator that such State has implemented a medical waste tracking program that is no less stringent than the demonstration program under this subchapter and that such State elects not to participate in the demonstration program, the Administrator shall, if the Administrator determines that such State program is no less stringent than the demonstration program under this subchapter, remove such State from the demonstration program.

(3) Notifications under paragraphs (1) or (2) shall be submitted to the Administrator no later than 30 days after the promulgation of regulations implementing the demonstration program under this subchapter.

(c) Petition in

The Governor of any State may petition the Administrator to be included in the demonstration program and the Administrator may, in his discretion, include any such State. Such petition may not be made later than 30 days after promulgation of regulations establishing the demonstration program under this subchapter, and the Administrator shall determine whether to include the State within 30 days after receipt of the State's petition.

(d) Expiration of demonstration program

The demonstration program shall expire on the date 24 months after the effective date of the regulations under this subchapter.

(Pub.L. 89–272, Title II, § 11001, as added Nov. 1, 1988, Pub.L. 100–582, § 2(a), 102 Stat. 2950.)

§ 6992a. Listing of medical wastes [SWDA § 11002]

(a) List

Not later than 6 months after November 1, 1988, the Administrator shall promulgate regulations listing the types of medical waste to be tracked under the demonstration program. Except as provided in subsection (b) of this section, such list shall include, but need not be limited to, each of the following types of solid waste:

(1) Cultures and stocks of infectious agents and associated biologicals, including cultures from medical and pathological laboratories, cultures and stocks of infectious agents from research and industrial laboratories, wastes from the production of biologicals, discarded live and attenuated vaccines, and culture dishes and devices used to transfer, inoculate, and mix cultures.

(2) Pathological wastes, including tissues, organs, and body parts that are removed during surgery or autopsy.

(3) Waste human blood and products of blood, including serum, plasma, and other blood components.

(4) Sharps that have been used in patient care or in medical, research, or industrial laboratories, including hypodermic needles, syringes, pasteur pipettes, broken glass, and scalpel blades.

(5) Contaminated animal carcasses, body parts, and bedding of animals that were exposed to infectious agents during research, production of biologicals, or testing of pharmaceuticals.

(6) Wastes from surgery or autopsy that were in contact with infectious agents, including soiled dressings, sponges, drapes, lavage tubes, drainage sets, underpads, and surgical gloves.

(7) Laboratory wastes from medical, pathological, pharmaceutical, or other research, commercial, or industrial laboratories that were in contact with infectious agents, including slides and cover slips, disposable gloves, laboratory coats, and aprons.

(8) Dialysis wastes that were in contact with the blood of patients undergoing hemodialysis, including contaminated disposable equipment and supplies such as tubing, filters, disposable sheets, towels, gloves, aprons, and laboratory coats.

(9) Discarded medical equipment and parts that were in contact with infectious agents.

(10) Biological waste and discarded materials contaminated with blood, excretion, excudates or secretion from human beings or animals who are isolated to protect others from communicable diseases.

(11) Such other waste material that results from the administration of medical care to a patient by a health care provider and is found by the Administrator to pose a threat to human health or the environment.

(b) Exclusions from list

The Administrator may exclude from the list under this section any categories or items described in paragraphs (6) through (10) of subsection (a) of this section which he determines do not pose a substantial present or potential hazard to human health or the environment when improperly treated, stored, transported, disposed of, or otherwise managed.

(Pub.L. 89–272, Title II, § 11002, as added Nov. 1, 1988, Pub.L. 100–582, § 2(a), 102 Stat. 2951.)

§ 6992b. Tracking of medical waste [SWDA § 11003]

(a) Demonstration program

Not later than 6 months after November 1, 1988, the Administrator shall promulgate regulations establishing a program for the tracking of the medical waste listed in section 6992a of this title which is generated in a State subject to the demonstration program. The program shall (1) provide for tracking of the transportation of the waste from the generator to the disposal facility, except that waste that is incinerated need not be tracked after incineration, (2) include a system for providing the generator of the waste with assurance that the waste is received by the disposal facility, (3) use a uniform form for tracking in each of the demonstration States, and (4) include the following requirements:

(A) A requirement for segregation of the waste at the point of generation where practicable.

(B) A requirement for placement of the waste in containers that will protect waste handlers and the public from exposure.

(C) A requirement for appropriate labeling of containers of the waste.

(b) Small quantities

In the program under subsection (a) of this section, the Administrator may establish an exemption for generators of small quantities of medical waste listed under section 6992a of this title, except that the Administrator may not exempt from the program any person who, or facility that, generates 50 pounds or more of such waste in any calendar month.

(c) On-site incinerators

Concurrently with the promulgation of regulations under subsection (a) of this section, the Administrator shall promulgate a recordkeeping and reporting requirement for any generator in a demonstration State of medical waste listed in section 6992a of this title that (1) incinerates medical waste listed in section 6992a of this title on site and (2) does not track such waste under the regulations promulgated under subsection (a) of this section. Such requirement shall require the generator to report to the Administrator on the volume and types of medical waste listed in section 6992a of this title that the generator incinerated on site during the 6 months following the effective date of the requirements of this subsection.

(d) Type of medical waste and types of generators

For each of the requirements of this section, the regulations may vary for different types of medical waste and for different types of medical waste generators.

(Pub.L. 89–272, Title II, § 11003, as added Nov. 1, 1988, Pub.L. 100–582, § 2(a), 102 Stat. 2952.)

§ 6992c. Inspections [SWDA § 11004]

(a) Requirements for access

For purposes of developing or assisting in the development of any regulation or report under this subchapter or enforcing any provision of this subchapter, any person who generates, stores, treats, transports, disposes of, or otherwise handles or has handled medical waste shall, upon request of any officer, employee, or representative of the Environmental Protection Agency duly designated by the Administrator, furnish information relating to such waste, including any tracking forms required to be maintained under section 6992b of this title, conduct monitoring or testing, and permit such person at all reasonable times to have access to, and to copy, all records relating to such waste. For such purposes, such officers, employees, or representatives are authorized to—

(1) enter at reasonable times any establishment or other place where medical wastes are or have been generated, stored, treated, disposed of, or transported from;

(2) conduct monitoring or testing; and

(3) inspect and obtain samples from any person of any such wastes and samples of any containers or labeling for such wastes.

(b) Procedures

Each inspection under this section shall be commenced and completed with reasonable promptness. If the officer, employee, or representative obtains any samples, prior to leaving the premises he shall give to the owner, operator, or agent in charge a receipt describing the sample obtained and, if requested, a portion of each such sample equal in volume or weight to the portion retained if giving such an equal portion is feasible. If any analysis is made of such samples, a copy of the results of such analysis shall be furnished promptly to the owner, operator, or agent in charge of the premises concerned.

(c) Availability to public

The provisions of section 6927(b) of this title shall apply to records, reports, and information obtained under this section in the same manner and to the same extent as such provisions apply to records, reports, and information obtained under section 6927 of this title.

(Pub.L. 89–272, Title II, § 11004, as added Nov. 1, 1988, Pub.L. 100–582, § 2(a), 102 Stat. 2952.)

§ 6992d. Enforcement [SWDA § 11005]

(a) Compliance orders

(1) Violations

Whenever on the basis of any information the Administrator determines that any person has violated, or is in violation of, any requirement or prohibition in effect under this subchapter (including any requirement or prohibition in effect under regulations under this subchapter) (A) the Administrator may issue an order (i) assessing a civil penalty for any past or current violation, (ii) requiring compliance immediately or within a specified time period, or (iii) both, or (B) the Administrator may commence a civil action in the United States district court in the district in which the violation occurred for appropriate relief, including a temporary or permanent injunction. Any order issued pursuant to this subsection shall state with reasonable specificity the nature of the violation.

(2) Orders assessing penalties

Any penalty assessed in an order under this subsection shall not exceed $25,000 per day of noncompliance for each violation of a requirement or prohibition in effect under this subchapter. In assessing such a penalty, the Administrator shall take into account the seriousness of the violation and any good faith efforts to comply with applicable requirements.

(3) Public hearing

Any order issued under this subsection shall become final unless, not later than 30 days after issuance of the order, the persons named therein request a public hearing. Upon such request, the Administrator shall promptly conduct a public hearing. In connection with any proceeding under this section, the Administrator may issue subpoenas for the production of relevant papers, books and documents, and may promulgate rules for discovery procedures.

(4) Violation of compliance orders

In the case of an order under this subsection requiring compliance with any requirement of or regulation under this subchapter, if a violator fails to take corrective action within the time specified in an order, the Administrator may assess a civil penalty of not more than $25,000 for each day of continued noncompliance with the order.

(b) Criminal penalties

Any person who—

(1) knowingly violates the requirements of or regulations under this subchapter;

(2) knowingly omits material information or makes any false material statement or representation in any label, record, report, or other document filed, maintained, or used for purposes of compliance with this subchapter or regulations thereunder; or

(3) knowingly generates, stores, treats, transports, disposes of, or otherwise handles any medical waste (whether such activity took place before or takes place after November 1, 1988) and who knowingly destroys, alters, conceals, or fails to file any record, report, or other document required to be maintained or filed for purposes of compliance with this subchapter or regulations thereunder

shall, upon conviction, be subject to a fine of not more than $50,000 for each day of violation, or imprisonment not to exceed 2 years (5 years in the case of a violation of paragraph (1)). If the conviction is for a violation committed after a first conviction of such person under this paragraph, the maximum punishment under the respective paragraph shall be doubled with respect to both fine and imprisonment.

(c) Knowing endangerment

Any person who knowingly violates any provision of subsection (b) of this section who knows at that time that he thereby places another person in imminent danger of death or serious bodily injury, shall upon conviction be subject to a fine of not more than $250,000 or imprisonment for not more than 15 years, or both. A defendant that is an organization shall, upon conviction under this subsection, be subject to a fine of not more than $1,000,000. The terms of this paragraph shall be interpreted in accordance with the rules provided under section 6928(f) of this title.

(d) Civil penalties

Any person who violates any requirement of or regulation under this subchapter shall be liable to the United States for a civil penalty in an amount not to exceed $25,000 for each such violation. Each day of such violation shall, for purposes of this section, constitute a separate violation.

(e) Civil penalty policy

Civil penalties assessed by the United States or by the States under this subchapter shall be assessed in accordance with the Administrator's "RCRA Civil Penalty Policy", as such policy may be amended from time to time.

(Pub.L. 89–272, Title II, § 11005, as added Nov. 1, 1988, Pub.L. 100–582, § 2(a), 102 Stat. 2953.)

§ 6992e. Federal facilities [SWDA § 11006]

(a) In general

Each department, agency, and instrumentality of the executive, legislative, and judicial branches of the Federal Government in a demonstration State (1) having jurisdiction over any solid waste management facility or disposal site at which medical waste is disposed of or otherwise handled, or (2) engaged in any activity resulting, or which may result, in the disposal, management, or handling of medical waste shall be subject to, and comply with, all Federal, State, interstate, and local requirements, both substantive and procedural (including any requirement for permits or reporting or any provisions for injunctive relief and such sanctions as may be imposed by a court to enforce such relief), respecting control and abatement of medical waste disposal and management in the same manner, and to the same extent, as any person is subject to such requirements, including the payment of reasonable service charges. The Federal, State, interstate, and local substantive and procedural requirements referred to in this subsection include, but are not limited to, all administrative orders, civil, criminal, and administrative penalties, and other sanctions, including injunctive relief, fines, and imprisonment. Neither the United States, nor any agent, employee, or officer thereof, shall be immune or exempt from any process or sanction of any State or Federal court with respect to the enforcement of any such order, penalty, or other sanction. For purposes of enforcing any such substantive or procedural requirement (including, but not limited to, any injunctive relief, administrative order, or civil, criminal, administrative penalty, or other sanction), against any such department, agency, or instrumentality, the United States hereby expressly waives any immunity otherwise applicable to the United States. The President may exempt any department, agency, or instrumentality in the executive branch from compliance with such a requirement if he determines it to be in the paramount interest of the United States to do so. No such exemption shall be granted due to lack of appropriation unless the President shall have specifically requested such appropriation as a part of the budgetary process and the Congress shall have failed to make available such requested appropriation. Any exemption shall be for a period not in excess of one year, but additional exemptions may be granted for periods not to exceed one year upon the President's making a new determination. The President shall report each January to the Congress all exemptions from the requirements of this section granted during the preceding calendar year, together with his reason for granting each such exemption.

(b) Definition of person

For purposes of this chapter, the term "person" shall be treated as including each department, agency, and instrumentality of the United States.

(Pub.L. 89–272, Title II, § 11006, as added Nov. 1, 1988, Pub.L. 100–582, § 2(a), 102 Stat. 2954.)

§ 6992f. Relationship to state law [SWDA § 11007]

(a) State inspections and enforcement

A State may conduct inspections under 6992c of this title and take enforcement actions under section 6992d of this title against any person, including any person who has imported medical waste into a State in violation of the requirements of, or regulations under, this subchapter, to the same extent as the Administrator. At the time a State initiates an enforcement action under section 6992d of this title against any person, the State shall notify the Administrator in writing.

(b) Retention of State authority

Nothing in this subchapter shall—

(1) preempt any State or local law; or

(2) except as provided in subsection (c) of this section, otherwise affect any State or local law or the authority of any State or local government to adopt or enforce any State or local law.

(c) State forms

Any State or local law which requires submission of a tracking form from any person subject to this subchapter shall require that the form be identical in content and format to the form required under section 6992b of this title, except that a State may require the submission of other tracking information which is supplemental to the information required on the form required under section 6992b of this title through additional sheets or such other means as the State deems appropriate.

(Pub.L. 89–272, Title II, § 11007, as added Nov. 1, 1988, Pub.L. 100–582, § 2(a), 102 Stat. 2955.)

§ 6992g. Report to Congress [SWDA § 11008]

(a) Final report

Not later than 3 months after the expiration of the demonstration program, the Administrator shall report to Congress on the following topics:

(1) The types, number, and size of generators of medical waste (including small quantity generators) in the United States, the types and amounts of medical waste generated, and the on-site and off-site methods currently used to handle, store, transport, treat, and dispose of the medical waste, including the extent to which such waste is disposed of in sewer systems.

(2) The present or potential threat to human health and the environment posed by medical waste or the incineration thereof.

(3) The present and potential costs (A) to local economies, persons, and the environment from the improper handling, storage, transportation, treatment or disposal of medical waste and (B) to generators, transporters, and treatment, storage, and disposal facilities from regulations establishing requirements for tracking, handling, storage, transportation, treatment, and disposal of medical waste.

(4)(A) The success of the demonstration program established under this subchapter in tracking medical waste,

(B) changes in incineration and storage practices attributable to the demonstration program, and

(C) other available and potentially available methods for tracking medical waste and their advantages and disadvantages, including the advantages and disadvantages of extending tracking requirements to (i) rural areas and (ii) small quantity generators.

(5) Available and potentially available methods for handling, storing, transporting, and disposing of medical waste and their advantages and disadvantages.

(6) Available and potentially available methods for treating medical waste, including the methods of incineration, sterilization, chemical treatment, and grinding, and their advantages, including their ability to render medical waste noninfectious or less infectious, and unrecognizable and otherwise protect human health and the environment, and disadvantages.

(7) Factors affecting the effectiveness of the treatment methods identified in subsection (a)(5) of this section, including quality control and quality assurance procedures, maintenance procedures, and operator training.

(8) Existing State and local controls on the handling, storage, transportation, treatment, and disposal of medical waste, including the enforcement and regulatory supervision thereof.

(9) The appropriateness of using any existing State requirements or the requirements contained in subchapter III of this chapter as nationwide requirements to monitor and control medical waste.

(10) The appropriateness of the penalties provided in section 6992e of this title for insuring compliance with the requirements of this subchapter, including a review of the level of penalties imposed under this subchapter.

(11)(A) The effect of excluding households and small quantity generators from any regulations governing the handling, storage, transportation, treatment, and disposal of medical waste, and

(B) potential guidelines for the handling, storage, treatment, and disposal of medical waste by households and small quantity generators.

(12) Available and potentially available methods for the reuse or reduction of the volume of medical waste generated.

(b) Interim reports

The Administrator shall submit two interim reports to Congress on the topics listed in subsection (a) of this section. The interim reports shall contain the information on the topics available to the Administrator at the time of submission. One interim report shall be due 9 months after November 1, 1988, and one shall be due 12 months after the effective date of regulations under this subchapter.

(c) Consultation

In preparing the reports under this section, the Administrator shall consult with appropriate State and local agencies.

(Pub.L. 89–272, Title II, § 11008, as added Nov. 1, 1988, Pub.L. 100–582, § 2(a), 102 Stat. 2956.)

§ 6992h. Health impacts report [SWDA § 11009]

Within 24 months after November 1, 1988, the Administrator of the Agency for Toxic Substances and Disease Registry shall prepare for Congress a report on the health effects of medical waste, including each of the following—

(1) A description of the potential for infection or injury from the segregation, handling, storage, treatment, or disposal of medical wastes.

(2) An estimate of the number of people injured or infected annually by sharps, and the nature and seriousness of those injuries or infections.

(3) An estimate of the number of people infected annually by other means related to waste segregation, handling, storage, treatment, or disposal, and the nature and seriousness of those infections.

(4) For diseases possibly spread by medical waste, including Acquired Immune Deficiency Syndrome and hepatitis B, an estimate of what percentage of the total number of cases nationally may be traceable to medical wastes.

(Pub.L. 89–272, Title II, § 11009, as added Nov. 1, 1988, Pub.L. 100–582, § 2(a), 102 Stat. 2957.)

§ 6992i. General provisions [SWDA § 11010]

(a) Consultation

(1) In promulgating regulations under this subchapter, the Administrator shall consult with the affected States and may consult with other interested parties.

(2) The Administrator shall also consult with the International Joint Commission to determine how to monitor the disposal of medical waste emanating from Canada.

(b) Public comment

In the case of the regulations required by this subchapter to be promulgated within 9 months after November 1, 1988, the Administrator may promulgate such regulations in interim final form without prior opportunity for public comment, but the Administrator shall provide an opportunity for public comment on the interim final rule. The promulgation of such regulations shall not be subject to the Paperwork Reduction Act of 1980.

(c) **Relationship to subchapter III**

Nothing in this subchapter shall affect the authority of the Administrator to regulate medical waste, including medical waste listed under section 6992a of this title, under subchapter III of this chapter.

(Pub.L. 89–272, Title II, § 11010, as added Nov. 1, 1988, Pub.L. 100–582, § 2(a), 102 Stat. 2957.)

§ 6992j. Effective date [SWDA § 11011]

The regulations promulgated under this subchapter shall take effect within 90 days after promulgation, except that, at the time of promulgation, the Administrator may provide for a shorter period prior to the effective date if he finds the regulated community does not need 90 days to come into compliance.

(Pub.L. 89–272, Title II, § 11011, as added Nov. 1, 1988, Pub.L. 100–582, § 2(a), 102 Stat. 2958.)

§ 6992k. Authorization of appropriations [SWDA § 11012]

There are authorized to be appropriated to the Administrator such sums as may be necessary for each of the fiscal years 1989 through 1991 for purposes of carrying out activities under this subchapter.

(Pub.L. 89–272, Title II, § 11012, as added Nov. 1, 1988, Pub.L. 100–582, § 2(a), 102 Stat. 2958.)

AIR POLLUTION PREVENTION AND CONTROL

CLEAN AIR ACT [CAA § ___]

(42 U.S.C.A. §§ 7401 to 7671q)

CHAPTER 85—AIR POLLUTION PREVENTION AND CONTROL

SUBCHAPTER I—PROGRAMS AND ACTIVITIES

Part A—Air Quality and Emission Limitations

Sec.

7401. Congressional findings and declaration of purpose.
- (a) Congressional findings.
- (b) Declaration of purpose.
- (c) Pollution prevention.

7402. Cooperative activities.
- (a) Interstate cooperation; uniform State laws; State compacts.
- (b) Federal cooperation.
- (c) Consent of Congress to compacts.

7403. Research, investigation, training, and other activities.
- (a) Research and development program for prevention and control of air pollution.
- (b) Authorized activities of Administrator in establishing research and development program.
- (c) Air pollutant monitoring, analysis, modeling and inventory research.
- (d) Environmental health effects research.
- (e) Ecosystem research.
- (f) Liquefied gaseous fuels spill test facility.
- (g) Pollution prevention and emissions control.
- (h) NIEHS studies.
- (i) Coordination of research.
- (j) Continuation of the national acid precipitation assessment program.
- (k) Air pollution conferences.

7404. Research relating to fuels and vehicles.
- (a) Research programs; grants; contracts; pilot and demonstration plants; byproducts research.
- (b) Powers of Administrator in establishing research and development programs.
- (c) Clean alternative fuels.

7405. Grants for support of air pollution planning and control programs.
- (a) Amounts; limitations; assurances of plan development capability.
- (b) Terms and conditions; regulations; factors for consideration; State expenditure limitations.
- (c) Maintenance of effort.
- (d) Reduction of payments; availability of reduced amounts; reduced amount as deemed paid to agency for purpose of determining amount of grant.
- (e) Notice and opportunity for hearing when affected by adverse action.

Sec.

7406. Interstate air quality agencies; program cost limitations.

7407. Air quality control regions.
- (a) Responsibility of each State for air quality; submission of implementation plan.
- (b) Designated regions.
- (c) Authority of Administrator to designate regions; notification of Governors of affected States.
- (d) Designations.
- (e) Redesignation of air quality control regions.

7408. Air quality criteria and control techniques.
- (a) Air pollutant list; publication and revision by Administrator; issuance of air quality criteria for air pollutants.
- (b) Issuance by Administrator of information on air pollution control techniques; standing consulting committees for air pollutants; establishment; membership.
- (c) Review, modification, and reissuance of criteria or information.
- (d) Publication in Federal Register; availability of copies for general public.
- (e) Transportation planning and guidelines.
- (f) Information regarding processes, procedures, and methods to reduce or control pollutants in transportation; reduction of mobile source related pollutants; reduction of impact on public health.
- (g) Assessment of rises to ecosystems.
- (h) RACT/BACT/CAER clearing house.

7409. National primary and secondary ambient air quality standards.
- (a) Promulgation.
- (b) Protection of public health and welfare.
- (c) National primary ambient air quality standard for nitrogen dioxide.
- (d) Review and revision of criteria and standards; independent scientific review committee; appointment; advisory functions.

7410. State implementation plans for national primary and secondary ambient air quality standards.
- (a) Adoption of plan by State; submission to Administrator; content of plan; revision; new sources; indirect source review program; supplemental or intermittent control systems.
- (b) Extension of period for submission of plans.
- (c) Preparation and publication by Administrator of proposed regulations setting forth implementation plan; transportation regulations study and report; parking surcharge; suspension authority; plan implementation.
- (d) Repealed.
- (e) Repealed.
- (f) National or regional energy emergencies; determination by President.

Sec.
7410. State implementation plans for national primary and secondary ambient air quality standards.
(g) Governor's authority to issue temporary emergency suspensions.
(h) Annual publication of comprehensive document for each State setting forth requirements of applicable implementation plan.
(i) Modification of requirements prohibited.
(j) Technological systems of continuous emission reduction on new or modified stationary sources; compliance with performance standards.
(k) Environmental Protection Agency action on plan submissions.
(*l*) Plan revisions.
(m) Sanctions.
(n) Savings clauses.
(*o*) Indian tribes.
(p) Reports.
7411. Standards of performance for new stationary sources.
(a) Definitions.
(b) List of categories of stationary sources; standards of performance; information on pollution control techniques; sources owned or operated by United States; particular systems; revised standards.
(c) State implementation and enforcement of standards of performance.
(d) Standards of performance for existing sources; remaining useful life of source.
(e) Prohibited acts.
(f) New source standards of performance.
(g) Revision of regulations.
(h) Design, equipment, work practice, or operational standard; alternative emission limitation.
(i) Country elevators.
(j) Innovative technological systems of continuous emission reduction.
7412. Hazardous air pollutants.
(a) Definitions.
(b) List of pollutants.
(c) List of source categories.
(d) Emission standards.
(e) Schedule for standards and review.
(f) Standard to protect health and the environment.
(g) Modifications.
(h) Work practice standards and other requirements.
(i) Schedule for compliance.
(j) Equivalent emission limitation by permit.
(k) Area source program.
(*l*) State programs.
(m) Atmospheric deposition to Great Lakes and coastal waters.
(n) Other provisions.
(*o*) National Academy of Sciences study.
(p) Mickey Leland Urban Air Toxics Research Center.
(q) Savings provision.
(r) Prevention of accidental releases.
(s) Periodic report.
7413. Federal enforcement procedures.
(a) In general.
(b) Civil judicial enforcement.
(c) Criminal penalties.

Sec.
7413. Federal enforcement procedures.
(d) Administrative assessment of civil penalties.
(e) Penalty assessment criteria.
(f) Awards.
(g) Settlements; public participation.
(h) Operator.
7414. Recordkeeping, inspections, monitoring, and entry.
(a) Authority of Administrator or authorized representative.
(b) State enforcement.
(c) Availability of records, reports, and information to public; disclosure of trade secrets.
(d) Notice of proposed entry, inspection, or monitoring.
7415. International air pollution.
(a) Endangerment of public health or welfare in foreign countries from pollution emitted in United States.
(b) Prevention or elimination of endangerment.
(c) Reciprocity.
(d) Recommendations.
7416. Retention of State authority.
7417. Advisory committees.
(a) Establishment; membership.
(b) Compensation.
(c) Consultations by Administrator.
7418. Control of pollution from Federal facilities.
(a) General compliance.
(b) Exemption.
(c) Government vehicles.
(d) Vehicles operated on Federal installations.
7419. Primary nonferrous smelter orders.
(a) Issuance; hearing; enforcement orders; statement of grounds for application; findings.
(b) Prerequisites to issuance of orders.
(c) Second orders.
(d) Interim measures; continuous emission reduction technology.
(e) Termination of orders.
(f) Violation of requirements.
7420. Noncompliance penalty.
(a) Assessment and collection.
(b) Regulations.
(c) Contract to assist in determining amount of penalty assessment or payment schedule.
(d) Payment.
(e) Judicial review.
(f) Other orders, payments, sanctions, or requirements.
(g) More stringent emission limitations or other requirements.
7421. Consultation.
7422. Listing of certain unregulated pollutants.
(a) Radioactive pollutants, cadmium, arsenic, and polycyclic organic matter.
(b) Revision authority.
(c) Consultation with Nuclear Regulatory Commission; interagency agreement; notice and hearing.
7423. Stack heights.
(a) Heights in excess of good engineering practice; other dispersion techniques.
(b) Dispersion technique.
(c) Regulations; good engineering practice.

Sec.
7424. Assurance of adequacy of State plans.
(a) State review of implementation plans which relate to major fuel burning sources.
(b) Plan revision.
7425. Measures to prevent economic disruption or unemployment.
(a) Determination that action is necessary.
(b) Use of locally or regionally available coal or coal derivatives to comply with implementation plan requirements.
(c) Contracts; schedules.
(d) Existing or new major fuel burning stationary sources.
(e) Actions not to be deemed modifications of major fuel burning stationary sources.
(f) Treatment of prohibitions, rules, or orders as requirements or parts of plans under other provisions.
(g) Delegation of Presidential authority.
(h) Locally or regionally available coal or coal derivatives.
7426. Interstate pollution abatement.
(a) Written notice to all nearby States.
(b) Petition for finding that major sources emit or would emit prohibited air pollutants.
(c) Violations; allowable continued operation.
7427. Public notification.
(a) Warning signs; television, radio, or press notices or information.
(b) Grants.
7428. State boards.
7429. Solid waste combustion.
(a) New source performance standards.
(b) Existing units.
(c) Monitoring.
(d) Operator training.
(e) Permits.
(f) Effective date and enforcement.
(g) Definitions.
(h) Other authority.
7430. Emission factors.
7431. Land use authority.

PART B—OZONE PROTECTION [REPEALED]

7450 to 7459. Repealed.

PART C—PREVENTION OF SIGNIFICANT DETERIORATION OF AIR QUALITY

Subpart I—Clean Air

7470. Congressional declaration of purpose.
7471. Plan requirements.
7472. Initial classifications.
(a) Areas designated as class I.
(b) Areas designated as class II.
7473. Increments and ceilings.
(a) Sulfur oxide and particulate matter; requirement that maximum allowable increases and maximum allowable concentrations not be exceeded.
(b) Maximum allowable increases in concentrations over baseline concentrations.
(c) Orders or rules for determining compliance with maximum allowable increases in ambient concentrations of air pollutants.

Sec.
7474. Area redesignation.
(a) Authority of States to redesignate areas.
(b) Notice and hearing; notice to Federal land manager; written comments and recommendations; regulations; disapproval of redesignation.
(c) Indian reservations.
(d) Review of national monuments, primitive areas, and national preserves.
(e) Resolution of disputes between State and Indian Tribes.
7475. Preconstruction requirements.
(a) Major emitting facilities on which construction is commenced.
(b) Exception.
(c) Permit applications.
(d) Action taken on permit applications; notice; adverse impact on air quality related values; variance; emission limitations.
(e) Analysis; continuous air quality monitoring data; regulations; model adjustments.
7476. Other pollutants.
(a) Hydrocarbons, carbon monoxide, petrochemical oxidants, and nitrogen oxides.
(b) Effective date of regulations.
(c) Contents of regulations.
(d) Specific measures to fulfill goals and purposes.
(e) Area classification plan not required.
(f) PM–10 increments.
7477. Enforcement.
7478. Period before plan approval.
(a) Existing regulations to remain in effect.
(b) Regulations deemed amended; construction commenced after June 1, 1975.
7479. Definitions.

Subpart II—Visibility Protection

7491. Visibility protection for Federal class I areas.
(a) Impairment of visibility; list of areas; study and report.
(b) Regulations.
(c) Exemptions.
(d) Consultations with appropriate Federal land managers.
(e) Buffer zones.
(f) Nondiscretionary duty.
(g) Definitions.
7492. Visibility.
(a) Studies.
(b) Impacts of other provisions.
(c) Establishment of visibility transport regions and commissions.
(d) Duties of visibility transport commissions.
(e) Duties of the administrator.
(f) Grand Canyon visibility transport commission.

PART D—PLAN REQUIREMENTS FOR NONATTAINMENT AREAS

Subpart 1—Nonattainment Areas in General

7501. Definitions.
7502. Nonattainment plan provisions.
(a) Classifications and attainment dates.
(b) Schedule for plan submissions.
(c) Nonattainment plan provisions.

Sec.
7502. Nonattainment plan provisions.
(d) Plan revisions required in response to finding of plan inadequacy.
(e) Future modification of standard.
7503. Permit requirements.
(a) In general.
(b) Prohibition on use of old growth allowances.
(c) Offsets.
(d) Control technology information.
(e) Rocket engines or motors.
7504. Planning procedures.
(a) In general.
(b) Coordination.
(c) Joint planning.
7505. Environmental Protection Agency grants.
(a) Plan revision development costs.
(b) Uses of grant funds.
7505a. Maintenance plans.
(a) Plan revision.
(b) Subsequent plan revision.
(c) Nonattainment requirements applicable pending plan approval.
(d) Contingency provisions.
7506. Limitations on certain Federal assistance.
[(a), (b) Repealed.]
(c) Activities not conforming to approved or promulgated plans.
(d) Priority of achieving and maintaining national primary ambient air quality standards.
7506a. Interstate transport commissions.
(a) Authority to establish interstate transport regions.
(b) Transport commissions.
(c) Commission requests.
7507. New motor vehicle emission standards in nonattainment areas.
7508. Guidance documents.
7509. Sanctions and consequences of failure to attain.
(a) State failure.
(b) Sanctions.
(c) Notice of failure to attain.
(d) Consequences for failure to attain.
7509a. International border areas.
(a) Implementation plans and revisions.
(b) Attainment of ozone levels.
(c) Attainment of carbon monoxide levels.
(d) Attainment of PM–10 levels.

Subpart 2—Additional Provisions for Ozone Nonattainment Areas

7511. Classifications and attainment dates.
(a) Classification and attainment dates for 1989 nonattainment areas.
(b) New designations and reclassifications.
(c) References to terms.
7511a. Plan submissions and requirements.
(a) Marginal areas.
(b) Moderate areas.
(c) Serious areas.
(d) Severe areas.
(e) Extreme areas.
(f) No requirements.
(g) Milestones.
(h) Rural transport areas.
(i) Reclassified areas.

Sec.
7511a. Plan submissions and requirements.
(j) Multi–State ozone nonattainment areas.
7511b. Federal ozone measures.
(a) Control techniques guidelines for VOC sources.
(b) Existing and new CTGS.
(c) Alternative control techniques.
(d) Guidance for evaluating cost-effectiveness.
(e) Control of emissions from certain sources.
(f) Tank vessel standards.
(g) Ozone design value study.
7511c. Control of interstate ozone air pollution.
(a) Ozone transport regions.
(b) Plan provisions for states in ozone transport regions.
(c) Additional control measures.
(d) Best available air quality monitoring and modeling.
7511d. Enforcement for severe and extreme ozone nonattainment areas for failure to attain.
(a) General rule.
(b) Computation of fee.
(c) Exception.
(d) Fee collection by the Administrator.
(e) Exemptions for certain small areas.
7511e. Transitional areas.
7511f. NO_x and VOC study.

Subpart 3—Additional Provisions for Carbon Monoxide Nonattainment Areas

7512. Classification and attainment dates.
(a) Classification by operation of law and attainment dates for nonattainment areas.
(b) New designations and reclassifications.
(c) References to terms.
7512a. Plan submission and requirements.
(a) Moderate areas.
(b) Serious areas.
(c) Areas with significant stationary source emissions of CO.
(d) CO milestone.
(e) Multi-State CO nonattainment areas.
(f) Reclassified areas.
(g) Failure of serious area to attain standard.

Subpart 4—Additional Provisions for Particulate Matter Nonattainment Areas

7513. Classification and attainment dates.
(a) Initial classifications.
(b) Reclassification as serious.
(c) Attainment dates.
(d) Extension of attainment date for moderate areas.
(e) Extension of attainment date for serious areas.
(f) Waiver for certain areas.
7513a. Plan provisions and schedules for plan submissions.
(a) Moderate areas.
(b) Serious areas.
(c) Milestones.
(d) Failure to attain.
(e) PM–10 precursors.
7513b. Issuance of RACM and BACM guidance.

Sec.

Subpart 5—Additional Provisions for Areas Designated Nonattainment for Sulfur Oxides, Nitrogen Dioxide, or Lead

7514. Plan submission deadlines.
(a) Submission.
(b) States lacking fully approved State implementation plans.
7514a. Attainment dates.
(a) Plans under section 7514(a) of this title.
(b) Plans under section 7514(b) of this title.
(c) Inadequate plans.

Subpart 6—Savings Provisions

7515. General savings clause.

SUBCHAPTER II—EMISSION STANDARDS FOR MOVING SOURCES

PART A—MOTOR VEHICLE EMISSION AND FUEL STANDARDS

7521. Emission standards for new motor vehicles or new motor vehicle engines.
(a) Authority of Administrator to prescribe by regulation.
(b) Emissions of carbon monoxide, hydrocarbons, and oxides of nitrogen; annual report to Congress; waiver of emission standards; research objectives.
(c) Feasibility study and investigation by National Academy of Sciences; reports to Administrator and Congress; availability of information.
(d) Useful life of vehicles.
(e) New power sources or propulsion systems.
(f) Model years after 1990.
(g) Light-duty trucks up to 6,000 lbs. GVWR and light-duty vehicles; standards for model years after 1993.
(h) Light-duty trucks of more than 6,000 lbs. GVWR; standards for model years after 1995.
(i) Phase II study for certain light-duty vehicles and light-duty trucks.
(j) Cold CO standard.
(k) Control of evaporative emissions.
(*l*) Mobil source-related air toxics.
(m) Emissions control diagnostics.
7522. Prohibited acts.
(a) Enumerated prohibitions.
(b) Exemptions; refusal to admit vehicle or engine into United States; vehicles or engines intended for export.
[(c) Repealed.]
7523. Actions to restrain violations.
(a) Jurisdiction.
(b) Actions brought by or in name of United States; subpenas.
7524. Penalties.
(a) Violations.
(b) Civil actions.
(c) Administrative assessment of certain penalties.
7525. Motor vehicle and motor vehicle engine compliance testing and certification.
(a) Testing and issuance of certificate of conformity.

Sec.

7525. Motor vehicle and motor vehicle engine compliance testing and certification.
(b) Testing procedures; hearing; judicial review; additional evidence.
(c) Inspection.
(d) Rules and regulations.
(e) Publication of test results.
(f) High altitude regulations.
(g) Nonconformance penalty.
(h) Review and revision of regulations.
7541. Compliance by vehicles and engines in actual use.
(a) Warranty; certification; payment of replacement costs of parts, devices, or components designed for emission control.
(b) Testing methods and procedures.
(c) Nonconforming vehicles; plan for remedying nonconformity; instructions for maintenance and use; label or tag.
(d) Dealer costs borne by manufacturer.
(e) Cost statement.
(f) Inspection after sale to ultimate purchaser.
(g) Replacement and maintenance costs borne by owner.
(h) Dealer certification.
(i) Warranty period.
7542. Records and reports.
(a) Manufacturer's responsibility.
(b) Enforcement authority.
(c) Availability to the public; trade secrets.
7543. State standards.
(a) Prohibition.
(b) Waiver.
(c) Certification of vehicle parts or engine parts.
(d) Control, regulation, or restrictions on registered or licensed motor vehicles.
(e) Nonroad engines or vehicles.
7544. State grants.
7545. Regulation of fuels.
(a) Authority of Administrator to regulate.
(b) Registration requirement.
(c) Offending fuels and fuel additives; control; prohibition.
(d) Penalties and injunctions.
(e) Testing of fuels and fuel additives.
(f) New fuels and fuel additives.
(g) Misfueling.
(h) Reid Vapor Pressure requirements.
(i) Sulfur content requirements for diesel fuel.
(j) Lead substitute gasoline additives.
(k) Reformulated gasoline for conventional vehicles.
(*l*) Detergents.
(m) Oxygenated fuels.
(n) Prohibition on leaded gasoline for highway use.
(*o*) Fuel and fuel additive importers and importation.
7546. Repealed.
7547. Nonroad engines and vehicles.
(a) Emissions standards.
(b) Effective date.
(c) Safe controls.
(d) Enforcement.
7548. Study of particulate emissions from motor vehicles.
(a) Study and analysis.
(b) Report to Congress.
7549. High altitude performance adjustments.
(a) Instruction of manufacturer.

Sec.
7549. High altitude performance adjustments.
(b) Regulations.
(c) Manufacturer parts.
(d) State inspection and maintenance programs.
(e) High altitude testing.
7550. Definitions.
7551. Study and report on fuel consumption.
7552. Motor vehicle compliance program fees.
(a) Fee collection.
(b) Special Treasury fund.
(c) Limitation on fund use.
(d) Administrator's testing authority.
7553. Prohibition on production of engines requiring leaded gasoline.
7554. Urban bus standards.
(a) Standards for model years after 1993.
(b) PM standard.
(c) Low-polluting fuel requirement.
(d) Retrofit requirements.
(e) Procedures for Administration and enforcement.
(f) Definitions.

PART B—AIRCRAFT EMISSION STANDARDS

7571. Establishment of standards.
(a) Study; proposed standards; hearings; issuance of regulations.
(b) Effective date of regulations.
(c) Regulations which create hazards to aircraft safety.
7572. Enforcement of standards.
(a) Regulations to insure compliance with standards.
(b) Notice and appeal rights.
7573. State standards and controls.
7574. Definitions.

PART C—CLEAN FUEL VEHICLES

7581. Definitions.
7582. Requirements applicable to clean fuel vehicles.
(a) Promulgation of standards.
(b) Other requirements.
(c) In-use useful life and testing.
7583. Standards for light-duty clean fuel vehicles.
(a) Exhaust standards for light-duty vehicles and certain light-duty trucks.
(b) Exhaust standards for light-duty trucks of more than 3,750 lbs. LVW and up to 5,750 lbs. LVW and up to 6,000 lbs. GVWR.
(c) Exhaust standards for light-duty trucks greater than 6,000 lbs. GVWR.
(d) Flexible end dual-fuel vehicles.
(e) Replacement by CARB standards.
(f) Less stringent CARB standards.
(g) Not applicable to heavy-duty vehicles.
7584. Administration and enforcement as per California standards.
7585. Standards for heavy-duty clean-fuel vehicles (GVWR above 8,500 up to 26,000 lbs.)
(a) Model years after 1997; combined NOx and NMHC standard.
(b) Revised standards that are less stringent.
7586. Centrally fueled fleets.
(a) Fleet program required for certain nonattainment areas.

Sec.
7586. Centrally fueled fleets.
(b) Phase-in of requirements.
(c) Accelerated standard for light-duty trucks up to 6,000 lbs. GVWR and light-duty vehicles.
(d) Choice of vehicles and fuel.
(e) Availability of clean alternative fuel.
(f) Credits.
(g) Availability to the public.
(h) Transportation control measures.
7587. Vehicle conversions.
(a) Conversion of existing and new conventional vehicles to clean-fuel vehicles.
(b) Regulations.
(c) Enforcement.
(d) Tampering.
(e) Safety.
7588. Federal agency fleets.
(a) Additional provisions applicable.
(b) Cost of vehicles to Federal agency.
(c) Limitations on appropriations.
(d) Vehicle costs.
(e) Exemptions.
(f) Acquisition requirement.
(g) Authorization of appropriations.
7589. California pilot test program.
(a) Establishment.
(b) Applicability.
(c) Program requirements.
(d) Credits for motor vehicle manufacturers.
(e) Program evaluations.
(f) Voluntary opt-in for other States.
7590. General provisions.
(a) State refueling facilities.
(b) No production mandate.
(c) Tax and fuel system safety.
(d) Consultation with Department of Energy and Department of Transportation.

SUBCHAPTER III—GENERAL PROVISIONS

7601. Administration.
(a) Regulations; delegation of powers and duties; regional officers and employees.
(b) Detail of Environmental Protection Agency personnel to air pollution control agencies.
(c) Payments under grants; installments; advances or reimbursements.
(d) Tribal authority.
7602. Definitions.
7603. Emergency powers.
(a) Suits in United States district court; emergency orders; consultation.
(b) Willful violation or failure or refusal to comply with orders.
7604. Citizen suits.
(a) Authority to bring civil action; jurisdiction.
(b) Notice.
(c) Venue; intervention by administrator; service of complaint; consent judgment.
(d) Award of costs; security.
(e) Nonrestriction of other rights.
(f) Definition.
(g) Penalty fund.
7605. Representation in litigation.
(a) Attorney General; attorneys appointed by Administrator.

Sec.
7605. Representation in litigation.
(b) Memorandum of understanding regarding legal representation.
7606. Federal procurement.
(a) Contracts with violators prohibited.
(b) Notification procedures.
(c) Federal agency contracts.
(d) Exemptions; notification to Congress.
(e) Annual report to Congress.
7607. Administrative proceedings and judicial review.
(a) Administrative subpenas; confidentiality; witnesses.
(b) Judicial review.
(c) Additional evidence.
(d) Rulemaking.
(e) Other methods of judicial review not authorized.
(f) Costs.
(g) Stay, injunction, or similar relief in proceedings relating to noncompliance penalties.
(h) Public participation.
7608. Mandatory licensing.
7609. Policy review.
(a) Environmental impact.
(b) Unsatisfactory legislation, action, or regulation.
7610. Other authority.
(a) Authority and responsibilities under other laws not affected.
(b) Nonduplication of appropriations.
7611. Records and audit.
(a) Recipients of assistance to keep prescribed records.
(b) Audits.
7612. Economic impact analyses.
(a) Cost benefit analysis.
(b) Benefits.
(c) Costs.
(d) Initial report.
(e) Biennial updates; future projections.
(f) Appointment of advisory council on clean air compliance analysis.
(g) Duties of advisory council.
7613. Repealed.
7614. Labor standards.
7615. Separability of provisions.
7616. Sewage treatment grants.
(a) Construction.
(b) Withholding, conditioning, or restriction of construction grants.
(c) National Environmental Policy Act.
7617. Economic impact assessment.
(a) Notice of proposed rulemaking; substantial revisions.
(b) Preparation of assessment by Administrator.
(c) Analysis.
(d) Extensiveness of assessment.
(e) Limitations on construction of section.
(f) Citizen suits.
(g) Costs.
7618. Repealed.
7619. Air quality monitoring.
7620. Standardized air quality modeling.
(a) Conferences.
(b) Conferees.
(c) Comments; transcripts.

Sec.
7620. Standardized air quality modeling.
(d) Promulgation and revision of regulations relating to air quality modeling.
7621. Employment effects.
(a) Continuous evaluation of potential loss or shifts of employment.
(b) Request for investigation; hearings; record; report.
(c) Subpenas; confidential information; witnesses; penalty.
(d) Limitations on construction of section.
7622. Employee protection.
(a) Discharge or discrimination prohibited.
(b) Complaint charging unlawful discharge or discrimination; investigation; order.
(c) Review.
(d) Enforcement of order by Secretary.
(e) Enforcement of order by person on whose behalf order was issued.
(f) Mandamus.
(g) Deliberate violation by employee.
7623. Repealed.
7624. Cost of vapor recovery equipment.
(a) Costs to be borne by owner of retail outlet.
(b) Payment by lessee.
7625. Vapor recovery for small business marketers of petroleum products.
(a) Marketers of gasoline.
(b) State requirements.
(c) Refiners.
7625–1. Exemptions for certain territories.
7625a. Statutory construction.
7626. Authorization of appropriations.
(a) In general.
(b) Grants for planning.
7627. Air pollution from outer continental shelf activities.
(a) Applicable requirements for certain areas.
(b) Requirements for other offshore areas.
(c) Coastal waters.

SUBCHAPTER IV—NOISE POLLUTION

7641. Noise abatement.
(a) Office of Noise Abatement and Control.
(b) Investigation techniques; report and recommendations.
(c) Abatement of noise from Federal activities.
7642. Authorization of appropriations.

SUBCHAPTER IV–A—ACID DEPOSITION CONTROL

7651. Findings and purposes.
(a) Findings.
(b) Purposes.
7651a. Definitions.
7651b. Sulfur dioxide allowance program for existing and new units.
(a) Allocations of annual allowances for existing and new units.
(b) Allowance transfer system.
(c) Interpollutant trading.
(d) Allowance tracking system.
(e) New utility units.
(f) Nature of allowances.
(g) Prohibition.
(h) Competitive bidding for power supply.

Sec.
7651b. Sulfur dioxide allowance program for existing and new units.
(i) Applicability of the antitrust laws.
(j) Public Utility Holding Company Act.
7651c. Phase I sulfur dioxide requirements.
(a) Emission limitations.
(b) Substitutions.
(c) Administrator's action on substitution proposals.
(d) Eligible Phase I extension units.
(e) Allocation of allowances.
(f) Energy conservation and renewable energy.
(g) Conservation and renewable energy reserve.
(h) Alternative allowance allocation for units in certain utility systems with optional baseline.
7651d. Phase II sulfur dioxide requirements.
(a) Applicability.
(b) Units equal to, or above, 75 MWe and 1.20 lbs/mmBtu.
(c) Coal or oil-fired units below 75 MWe and above 1.20 lbs/mmBtu.
(d) Coal-fired units below 1.20 lbs/mmBtu.
(e) Oil and gas-fired units equal to or greater than 0.60 lbs/mmBtu and less than 1.20 lbs/mmBtu.
(f) Oil and gas-fired units less than 0.60 lbs/mmBtu.
(g) Units that commence operation between 1986 and December 31, 1995.
(h) Oil and gas-fired units less than 10 percent oil consumed.
(i) Units in high growth States.
(j) Certain municipally owned power plants.
7651e. Allowances for States with emissions rates at or below 0.80 lbs/mmBtu.
(a) Election of Governor.
(b) Notification of Administrator.
(c) Allowances after January 1, 2010.
7651f. Nitrogen oxides emission reduction program.
(a) Applicability.
(b) Emission limitations.
(c) Revised performance standards.
(d) Alternative emission limitations.
(e) Emissions averaging.
7651g. Permits and compliance plans.
(a) Permit program.
(b) Compliance plan.
(c) First phase permits.
(d) Second phase permits.
(e) New units.
(f) Units subject to certain other limits.
(g) Amendment of application and compliance plan.
(h) Prohibition.
(i) Multiple owners.
7651h. Repowered sources.
(a) Availability.
(b) Extension.
(c) Allowances.
(d) Control requirements.
(e) Expedited permitting.
(f) Prohibition.
7651i. Election for additional sources.
(a) Applicability.
(b) Establishment of baseline.

Sec.
7651i. Election for additional sources.
(c) Emission limitations.
(d) Process sources.
(e) Allowances and permits.
(f) Limitation.
(g) Implementation.
(h) Small diesel refineries.
7651j. Excess emissions penalty.
(a) Excess emissions penalty.
(b) Excess emissions offset.
(c) Penalty adjustment.
(d) Prohibition.
(e) Savings provision.
7651k. Monitoring, reporting, and recordkeeping requirements.
(a) Applicability.
(b) First phase requirements.
(c) Second phase requirements.
(d) Unavailability of emissions data.
(e) Prohibition.
7651*l*. General compliance with other provisions.
7651m. Enforcement.
7651n. Clean coal technology regulatory incentives.
(a) Definition.
(b) Revised regulations for clean coal technology demonstrations.
(c) Exemption for reactivation of very clean units.
7651*o*. Contingency guarantee; auctions, reserve.
(a) Definitions.
(b) Special reserve of allowances.
(c) Direct sale at $1,500 per ton.
(d) Auction sales.
(e) Changes in sales, auctions, and withholding.
(f) Termination of auctions.

SUBCHAPTER V—PERMITS

7661. Definitions.
7661a. Permit programs.
(a) Violations.
(b) Regulations.
(c) Single permit.
(d) Submission and approval.
(e) Suspension.
(f) Prohibition.
(g) Interim approval.
(h) Effective date.
(i) Administration and enforcement.
7661b. Permit applications.
(a) Applicable date.
(b) Compliance plan.
(c) Deadline.
(d) Timely and complete applications.
(e) Copies; availability.
7661c. Permit requirements and conditions.
(a) Conditions.
(b) Monitoring and analysis.
(c) Inspection, entry, monitoring certification and reporting.
(d) General permits.
(e) Temporary sources.
(f) Permit shield.
7611d. Notification to Administrator and contiguous States.
(a) Transmission and notice.
(b) Objection by EPA.
(c) Issuance or denial.

Sec.
7611d. Notification to Administrator and contiguous States.
(d) Waiver of notification requirements.
(e) Refusal of permitting authority to terminate, modify, or revoke and reissue.
7661e. Other authorities.
(a) In general.
(b) Permits implementing acid rain provisions.
7661f. Small business stationary source technical and environmental compliance assistance program.
(a) Plain revisions.
(b) Program.
(c) Eligibility.
(d) Monitoring.
(e) Compliance advisory panel.
(f) Fees.
(g) Continuous emission monitors.
(h) Control technique guidelines.

SUBCHAPTER VI—STRATOSPHERIC OZONE PROTECTION

7671. Definitions.
7671a. Listing of class I and class II substances.
(a) List of class I substances.
(b) List of class II substances.
(c) Additions to the lists.
(d) New listed substances.
(e) Ozone depletion and global warming potential.
7671b. Monitoring and reporting requirements.
(a) Regulations.
(b) Production, import, and export level reports.
(c) Baseline reports for class I substances.
(d) Monitoring and reports to Congress.
(e) Technology status report in 2015.
(f) Emergency report.
7671c. Phase-out of production and consumption of class I substances.
(a) Production phase-out.
(b) Termination of production of class I substances.
(c) Regulations regarding production and consumption of class I substances.
(d) Exceptions for essential uses of methyl chloroform, medical devices and aviation safety.
(e) Developing countries.
(f) National security.
(g) Fire suppression and explosion prevention.
7671d. Phase-out of production and consumption of class II substances.
(a) Restriction of use of class II substances.
(b) Production phase-out.
(c) Regulations regarding production and consumption of class II substances.
(d) Exemptions.
7671e. Accelerated schedule.
(a) In general.
(b) Petition.
7671f. Exchange authority.
(a) Transfers.
(b) Interpollutant transfers.
(c) Trades with other persons.
7671g. National recycling and emission reduction program.
(a) In general.
(b) Safe disposal.
(c) Prohibitions.

Sec.
7671h. Servicing of motor vehicle air conditioners.
(a) Regulations.
(b) Definitions.
(c) Servicing motor vehicle air conditioners.
(d) Certification.
(e) Small containers of class I or class II substances.
7671*i*. Nonessential products containing chlorofluorocarbons.
(a) Regulations.
(b) Nonessential products.
(c) Effective date.
(d) Other products.
(e) Medical devices.
7671j. Labeling.
(a) Regulations.
(b) Containers containing class I or class II substances and products containing class I substances.
(c) Products containing class II substances.
(d) Products manufactured with class I and class II substances.
(e) Petitions.
(f) Relationship to other law.
7671k. Safe alternatives policy.
(a) Policy.
(b) Reviews and reports.
(c) Alternatives for class I or II substances.
(d) Right to petition.
(e) Studies and notification.
7671*l*. Federal procurement.
7671m. Relationship to other laws.
(a) State laws.
(b) Montreal Protocol.
(c) Technology export and overseas investment.
7671n. Authority of administrator.
7671*o*. Transfers among parties to Montreal Protocol.
(a) In general.
(b) Effect of transfers on production limits.
(c) Regulations.
(d) Definition.
7671p. International cooperation.
(a) In general.
(b) Assistance to developing countries.
7671q. Miscellaneous provisions.

Former Sections

The Clean Air Act, which is set out in the following pages, was originally classified to CHAPTER 15B—AIR POLLUTION CONTROL, 42 U.S.C.A. § 1857 et seq. prior to the complete revision and expansion of its provisions by Pub.L. 95–95, Aug. 7, 1977, 91 Stat. 385. At that time its classification was changed to CHAPTER 85—AIR POLLUTION PREVENTION AND CONTROL, 42 U.S.C.A. § 7401 et seq. A researcher seeking to compare the original Code classifications with the present Code classifications of particular sections of the Act will find a transfer table set out in 42 U.S.C.A. §§ 1857 to 1858a.

CROSS REFERENCES

Action under this chapter not to be deemed major federal action within meaning of National Environmental Policy Act of 1969, see section 793 of Title 15, Commerce and Trade.

Applicable environmental requirements defined to include standard, limitation or requirement established by this chapter for purposes of Powerplant and Industrial Fuel Use Act of 1978, see section 8302 of this title.

Authority of Administrator under this chapter not affected by provisions of Atomic Energy Act of 1954 applicable to byproduct material, see section 2022 of this title.
Availability to Science Advisory Board of proposed environmental criteria document, standard, limitation or regulation under this chapter, see section 4365 of this title.
Certification of compliance with procedures for determination of environmental impact of proposed urban mass transportation projects, see section 1604 of Title 49, Transportation.
Coal leases to contain provisions requiring compliance with this chapter, see section 201 of Title 30, Mineral Lands and Mining.
Congressional finding under Solid Waste Disposal Act that greater amounts of solid waste have been created as result of this chapter, see section 6901 of this title.
Consideration of standards under this chapter in establishing noise emission standards for products distributed in commerce, see section 4905 of this title.
Construction of Coastal Zone Management Act of 1972 with existing requirements of water and air pollution programs, see section 1456 of Title 16, Conservation.
Construction of highways to be consistent with plans for implementation of ambient air quality standards, see section 109 of Title 23, Highways.
Construction of Surface Mining Control and Reclamation Act of 1977 as not superseding, amending, modifying or repealing this chapter, see section 1292 of Title 30, Mineral Lands and Mining.
Consumer Product Safety Commission to have no authority to regulate risk of injury if risk could be eliminated by actions taken under this chapter, see section 2080 of Title 15, Commerce and Trade.
Control of environmental impacts of surface coal mining, see section 1251 et seq. of Title 30, Mineral Lands and Mining.
Coordination of regulatory and inspection activities under Surface Mining Control and Reclamation Act of 1977 and this chapter, see section 1303 of Title 30.
Deepwater port to be considered new source for purposes of this chapter, see section 1502 of Title 33, Navigation and Navigable Waters.
Demonstrations of energy-related pollution control technologies to fulfill provisions of this chapter, see section 4363a of this title.
Federal Energy Administrator defined for purposes of this chapter, see section 798 of Title 15, Commerce and Trade.
Guarantee of loans for developing new underground coal mines, necessity of having contract for sale or resale of coal with person certified as able to burn such coal in compliance with this chapter, see section 6211 of this title.
Income tax deduction for amortization of pollution control facilities, see section 169 of Title 26, Internal Revenue Code.
Integration of Solid Waste Disposal Act with this chapter, see section 6905 of this title.
License for ownership, construction and operation of deepwater ports, conformance of port with this chapter as condition for issuance, see section 1503 of Title 33, Navigation and Navigable Waters.
Loans to assist powerplant acquisitions of air pollution control equipment, see section 8402 of this title.
Monitoring of emissions from new and existing electric powerplants required to use coal or other alternate fuels, see section 8455 of this title.
Permit for increased use of petroleum by existing powerplants, necessity of certification that powerplant cannot comply with requirements of this chapter, see section 8375 of this title.
Policy of Congress to promote substitution of methane-fueled vehicles in areas where substitution would facilitate plans under this chapter, see section 3801 of Title 15, Commerce and Trade.
Regulations for leasing of Outer Continental Shelf to include provisions for compliance with national ambient air quality standards, see section 1334 of Title 43, Public Lands.
Restriction on use of funds under Department of Energy Organization Act to pay penalties under this chapter, see section 7273 of this title.
Rural communities assistance for solid waste management facilities necessary to meet requirements under this chapter, see section 6949 of this title.
Solid waste management guidelines to describe levels of performance that provide for protection of ambient air quality, see section 6907 of this title.
State or local toxic substance requirements preempted by federal requirements unless requirement is adopted under this chapter, see section 2617 of Title 15, Commerce and Trade.
Testing of advanced automobile propulsion systems to determine whether vehicle complies with requirements of this chapter, see section 2706 of Title 15.

West's Federal Forms

Enforcement and review of administrative decisions and orders, see § 851 et seq.
Jurisdiction and venue of district courts, see § 1003 et seq.
Preliminary injunctions and temporary restraining orders, see § 5271 et seq.

West's Federal Practice Manual

Environmental Law, see § 4381 et seq.

CODE OF FEDERAL REGULATIONS

Air pollution from motor vehicles, control, see 40 CFR 85.401 et seq.
  New motor vehicles, certification and testing, see 40 CFR 86.078–3 et seq.
Air programs, generally, see 40 CFR 50.1 et seq.
Aircraft, control of air pollution, see 40 CFR 87.1 et seq.
Environmental Protection Agency—
  Ambient air quality surveillance, see 40 CFR 50.1 et seq.
  Emission standards for hazardous pollutants, see 40 CFR 61.01 et seq.
  State penalty programs, standards for approval, see 40 CFR 67.1 et seq.
Fuels, regulation of, see 40 CFR 80.1 et seq.
Hazardous pollutants, emission standards for, see 40 CFR 61.01 et seq.
Implementation plans, generally, see 40 CFR 51.40 et seq.
New stationary sources, standards, see 40 CFR 60.1 et seq.
Primary nonferrous smelter orders, see 40 CFR 57.101 et seq.
Public information, see 40 CFR 2.100 et seq.
State and local assistance, see 40 CFR 35.001 et seq.

United States Supreme Court

State plan for achieving federal ambient air quality standards, approval of variances, see Train v. Natural Resources Defense Council, Inc., 1975, 95 S.Ct. 1470, 421 U.S. 60, 43 L.Ed.2d 731.

WESTLAW ELECTRONIC RESEARCH

See WESTLAW guide following the Explanation pages of this pamphlet.

SUBCHAPTER I—PROGRAMS AND ACTIVITIES

PART A—AIR QUALITY AND EMISSION LIMITATIONS

§ 7401. Congressional findings and declaration of purpose [CAA § 101]

(a) Congressional findings

The Congress finds—

(1) that the predominant part of the Nation's population is located in its rapidly expanding metropolitan and other urban areas, which generally cross the boundary lines of local jurisdictions and often extend into two or more States;

(2) that the growth in the amount and complexity of air pollution brought about by urbanization, industrial development, and the increasing use of motor vehicles, has resulted in mounting dangers to the public health and welfare, including injury to agricultural crops and livestock, damage to and the deterioration of property, and hazards to air and ground transportation;

(3) that air pollution prevention (that is, the reduction or elimination, through any measures, of the amount of pollutants produced or created at the source) and air pollution control at its source is the primary responsibility of States and local governments; and

(4) that Federal financial assistance and leadership is essential for the development of cooperative Federal, State, regional, and local programs to prevent and control air pollution.

(b) Declaration of purpose

The purposes of this subchapter are—

(1) to protect and enhance the quality of the Nation's air resources so as to promote the public health and welfare and the productive capacity of its population;

(2) to initiate and accelerate a national research and development program to achieve the prevention and control of air pollution;

(3) to provide technical and financial assistance to State and local governments in connection with the development and execution of their air pollution prevention and control programs; and

(4) to encourage and assist the development and operation of regional air pollution prevention and control programs.

(c) Pollution prevention

A primary goal of this chapter is to encourage or otherwise promote reasonable Federal, State, and local governmental actions, consistent with the provisions of this chapter, for pollution prevention.

(July 14, 1955, ch. 360, title I, § 101, formerly § 1, as added Dec. 17, 1963, Pub.L. 88–206, § 1, 77 Stat. 392, and amended and renumbered Oct. 20, 1965, Pub.L. 89–272, title I, § 101(2), (3), 79 Stat. 992; Nov. 21, 1967, Pub.L. 90–148, § 2, 81 Stat. 485; Nov. 15, 1990, Pub.L. 101–549, title I, § 108(k), 104 Stat. 2468.)

Effective Date of 1990 Amendment

Pub.L. 101–549, Title VII, § 711(b), Nov. 15, 1990, 104 Stat. 2684, provided that:

"(1) Except as otherwise expressly provided, the amendments made by this Act [Pub.L. 101–549, Nov. 15, 1990, 104 Stat. 2399, for classifications of which see Tables] shall be effective on the date of enactment of this Act [Nov. 15, 1990].

"(2) The Administrator's authority to assess civil penalties under section 205(c) of the Clean Air Act, as amended by this Act [section 7524(c) of this title], shall apply to violations that occur or continue on or after the date of enactment of this Act [Nov. 15, 1990]. Civil penalties for violations that occur prior to such date and do not continue after such date shall be assessed in accordance with the provisions of the Clean Air Act [this chapter] in effect immediately prior to the date of enactment of this Act.

"(3) The civil penalties prescribed under sections 205(a) and 211(d)(1) of the Clean Air Act, as amended by this Act [sections 7524(a) and 7545(d)(1) of this title], shall apply to violations that occur on or after the date of enactment of this Act [Nov. 15, 1990]. Violations that occur prior to such date shall be subject to the civil penalty provisions prescribed in sections 205(a) and 211(d) of the Clean Air Act in effect immediately prior to the enactment of this Act. The injunctive authority prescribed under section 211(d)(2) of the Clean Air Act, as amended by this Act [section 7545(d)(2) of this title], shall apply to violations that occur or continue on or after the date of enactment of this Act [Nov. 15, 1990].

"(4) For purposes of paragraphs (2) and (3), where the date of a violation cannot be determined it will be assumed to be the date on which the violation is discovered."

Savings Provisions

Pub.L. 101–549, Title VII, § 711(a), Nov. 15, 1990, 104 Stat. 2684, provided that: "Except as otherwise expressly provided in this Act [Pub.L. 101–549, Nov. 15, 1990, 104 Stat. 2399, for classifications of which see Tables], no suit, action, or other proceeding lawfully commenced by the Administrator or any other officer or employee of the United States in his official capacity or in relation to the discharge of his official duties under the Clean Air Act [this chapter], as in effect immediately prior to the date of enactment of this Act [Nov. 15, 1990], shall abate by reason of the taking effect of the amendments made by this Act."

Short Title

Section 317, formerly section 14, of Act July 14, 1955, c. 360, as added by Pub.L. 88–206, § 1, Dec. 17, 1963, 77 Stat. 401, renumbered section 307 by Pub.L. 89–272, Title I, § 101(4), Oct. 20, 1965, 79 Stat. 992, renumbered section 310 by Pub.L. 90–148, § 2, Nov. 21, 1967, 81 Stat. 507, and renumbered section 317 by Pub.L. 91–604, § 12(a), Dec. 31, 1970, 84 Stat. 1705, provided that: "This Act [enacting this chapter] may be cited as the 'Clean Air Act'."

Impact on Small Counties

Pub.L. 101–549, Title VIII, § 810, Nov. 15, 1990, 104 Stat. 2690, provided that: "Before implementing a provision of this Act [Pub.L. 101–549, Nov. 15, 1990, 104 Stat. 2399, for classifications of which see Tables], the Administrator of the Environmental Protection Agency shall consult with the Small Communities Coordinator of the Environmental Protection Agency to determine the impact of such provision on small communities, including the estimated cost of compliance with such provision."

CROSS REFERENCES

Dioxins from resource recovery facilities. Solid Waste Disposal Act as not preempting or affecting authorities under this chapter to regulate emissions of polychlorinated dibenzo-p-dioxins, see section 6905 of this title.

West's Federal Practice Manual

Environmental law, see § 4381 et seq.

CODE OF FEDERAL REGULATIONS

Air planning, designation of areas for, see 40 CFR 81.1 et seq.
Air quality conformity, see 23 CFR 770.1 et seq.
Air quality legislation, see § 4384.5.
Hazardous pollutants, emission standards for, see 40 CFR 61.01 et seq.
Implementation plans, approval and promulgation of, see 40 CFR 52.01 et seq.
Implementation plans, generally, see 40 CFR 51.40 et seq.
New stationary sources, performance standards, see 40 CFR 60.1 et seq.
State plans, see 40 CFR 62.01 et seq.

ADMINISTRATIVE LAW

Cost/benefit analysis, see Koch § 4.35.

LAW REVIEW COMMENTARIES

Confidential business information versus the public's right to disclosure—Biotechnology renews the challenge. Stanley H. Abramson, 34 U.Kansas L.Rev. 681 (1986).

Criminal sanctions under federal and state environmental statutes. Richard H. Allan, 14 Ecology L.Q. 117 (1987).

Environmental claims in bankruptcy: Policy conflicts, procedural pitfalls and problematic precedent. Thomas G. Gruenert, 32 S.Tex. L.Rev. 399 (1991).

Federal consistency doctrine: Coastal zone management and "new federalism". Tim Eichenberg and Jack Archer, 14 Ecology L.Q. 9 (1987).

Groundwater pollution I: The problem and the law. Robert L. Glicksman and George Cameron Coggins, 35 U.Kan.L.Rev. 75 (1986).

Oil and gas exemptions under RCRA and CERCLA: Are they still "safe harbors" eleven years later? Michael M. Gibson and David P. Young, 32 S.Tex.L.Rev. 361 (1991).

Resolving conflicts between bankruptcy law and the state police power. Ellen E. Sward, 1987 Wis.L.Rev. 403 (1987).

Toxic tort litigation and the causation element: Is there any hope of reconciliation? Fred Harris, Jr., 40 Southwestern (Tex) L.J. 909 (1986).

LIBRARY REFERENCES

Health and Environment ⚷25.6(1) et seq., 28.
C.J.S. Health and Environment § 91 et seq.

§ 7402. Cooperative activities [CAA § 102]

(a) Interstate cooperation; uniform State laws; State compacts

The Administrator shall encourage cooperative activities by the States and local governments for the prevention and control of air pollution; encourage the enactment of improved and, so far as practicable in the light of varying conditions and needs, uniform State and local laws relating to the prevention and control of air pollution; and encourage the making of agreements and compacts between States for the prevention and control of air pollution.

(b) Federal cooperation

The Administrator shall cooperate with and encourage cooperative activities by all Federal departments and agencies having functions relating to the prevention and control of air pollution, so as to assure the utilization in the Federal air pollution control program of all appropriate and available facilities and resources within the Federal Government.

(c) Consent of Congress to compacts

The consent of the Congress is hereby given to two or more States to negotiate and enter into agreements or compacts, not in conflict with any law or treaty of the United States, for (1) cooperative effort and mutual assistance for the prevention and control of air pollution and the enforcement of their respective laws relating thereto, and (2) the establishment of such agencies, joint or otherwise, as they may deem desirable for making effective such agreements or compacts. No such agreement or compact shall be binding or obligatory upon any State a party thereto unless and until it has been approved by Congress. It is the intent of Congress that no agreement or compact entered into between States after November 21, 1967, which relates to the control and abatement of air pollution in an air quality control region, shall provide for participation by a State which is not included (in whole or in part) in such air quality control region.

(July 14, 1955, ch. 360, title I, § 102, formerly § 2, as added Dec. 17, 1963, Pub.L. 88–206, § 1, 77 Stat. 393, renumbered Oct. 20, 1965, Pub.L. 89–272, title I, § 101(3), 79 Stat. 992, and amended Nov. 21, 1967, Pub.L. 90–148, § 2, 81 Stat. 485; Dec. 31, 1970, Pub.L. 91–604, § 15(c)(2), 84 Stat. 1713.)

LIBRARY REFERENCES

States ⚷4.19, 6.
C.J.S. States §§ 28, 31 et seq.

§ 7403. Research, investigation, training, and other activities [CAA § 103]

(a) Research and development program for prevention and control of air pollution

The Administrator shall establish a national research and development program for the prevention and control of air pollution and as part of such program shall—

(1) conduct, and promote the coordination and acceleration of, research, investigations, experiments, demonstrations, surveys, and studies relating to the causes, effects (including health and welfare effects), extent, prevention, and control of air pollution;

(2) encourage, cooperate with, and render technical services and provide financial assistance to air pollution control agencies and other appropriate public or private agencies, institutions, and organizations, and individuals in the conduct of such activities;

(3) conduct investigations and research and make surveys concerning any specific problem of air pollution in cooperation with any air pollution control agency with a view to recommending a solution of such problem, if he is requested to do so by such agency or if, in his judgment, such problem may affect any community or communities in a State other than that in which the source of the matter causing or contributing to the pollution is located;

(4) establish technical advisory committees composed of recognized experts in various aspects of air pollution to assist in the examination and evaluation

of research progress and proposals and to avoid duplication of research, and

(5) conduct and promote coordination and acceleration of training for individuals relating to the causes, effects, extent, prevention, and control of air pollution.

(b) Authorized activities of Administrator in establishing research and development program

In carrying out the provisions of the preceding subsection the Administrator is authorized to—

(1) collect and make available, through publications and other appropriate means, the results of and other information, including appropriate recommendations by him in connection therewith, pertaining to such research and other activities;

(2) cooperate with other Federal departments and agencies, with air pollution control agencies, with other public and private agencies, institutions, and organizations, and with any industries involved, in the preparation and conduct of such research and other activities;

(3) make grants to air pollution control agencies, to other public or nonprofit private agencies, institutions, and organizations, and to individuals, for purposes stated in subsection (a)(1) of this section;

(4) contract with public or private agencies, institutions, and organizations, and with individuals, without regard to section 3324(a) and (b) of Title 31 and section 5 of Title 41;

(5) establish and maintain research fellowships, in the Environmental Protection Agency and at public or nonprofit private educational institutions or research organizations;

(6) collect and disseminate, in cooperation with other Federal departments and agencies, and with other public or private agencies, institutions, and organizations having related responsibilities, basic data on chemical, physical, and biological effects of varying air quality and other information pertaining to air pollution and the prevention and control thereof;

(7) develop effective and practical processes, methods, and prototype devices for the prevention or control of air pollution; and

(8) construct facilities, provide equipment, and employ staff as necessary to carry out this chapter.

In carrying out the provisions of subsection (a) of this section, the Administrator shall provide training for, and make training grants to, personnel of air pollution control agencies and other persons with suitable qualifications and make grants to such agencies, to other public or nonprofit private agencies, institutions, and organizations for the purposes stated in subsection (a)(5) of this section. Reasonable fees may be charged for such training provided to persons other than personnel of air pollution control agencies but such training shall be provided to such personnel of air pollution control agencies without charge.

(c) Air pollutant monitoring, analysis, modeling, and inventory research

In carrying out subsection (a) of this section, the Administrator shall conduct a program of research, testing, and development of methods for sampling, measurement, monitoring, analysis, and modeling of air pollutants. Such program shall include the following elements:

(1) Consideration of individual, as well as complex mixtures of, air pollutants and their chemical transformations in the atmosphere.

(2) Establishment of a national network to monitor, collect, and compile data with quantification of certainty in the status and trends of air emissions, deposition, air quality, surface water quality, forest condition, and visibility impairment, and to ensure the comparability of air quality data collected in different States and obtained from different nations.

(3) Development of improved methods and technologies for sampling, measurement, monitoring, analysis, and modeling to increase understanding of the sources of ozone percursors [1], ozone formation, ozone transport, regional influences on urban ozone, regional ozone trends, and interactions of ozone with other pollutants. Emphasis shall be placed on those techniques which—

(A) improve the ability to inventory emissions of volatile organic compounds and nitrogen oxides that contribute to urban air pollution, including anthropogenic and natural sources;

(B) improve the understanding of the mechanism through which anthropogenic and biogenic volatile organic compounds react to form ozone and other oxidants; and

(C) improve the ability to identify and evaluate region-specific prevention and control options for ozone pollution.

(4) Submission of periodic reports to the Congress, not less than once every 5 years, which evaluate and assess the effectiveness of air pollution control regulations and programs using monitoring and modeling data obtained pursuant to this subsection.

(d) Environmental health effects research

(1) The Administrator, in consultation with the Secretary of Health and Human Services, shall conduct a research program on the short-term and long-term effects of air pollutants, including wood smoke, on

human health. In conducting such research program the Administrator—

(A) shall conduct studies, including epidemiological, clinical, and laboratory and field studies, as necessary to identify and evaluate exposure to and effects of air pollutants on human health;

(B) may utilize, on a reimbursable basis, the facilities of existing Federal scientific laboratories and research centers; and

(C) shall consult with other Federal agencies to ensure that similar research being conducted in other agencies is coordinated to avoid duplication.

(2) In conducting the research program under this subsection, the Administrator shall develop methods and techniques necessary to identify and assess the risks to human health from both routine and accidental exposures to individual air pollutants and combinations thereof. Such research program shall include the following elements:

(A) The creation of an Interagency Task Force to coordinate such program. The Task Force shall include representatives of the National Institute for Environmental Health Sciences, the Environmental Protection Agency, the Agency for Toxic Substances and Disease Registry, the National Toxicology Program, the National Institute of Standards and Technology, the National Science Foundation, the Surgeon General, and the Department of Energy. This Interagency Task Force shall be chaired by a representative of the Environmental Protection Agency and shall convene its first meeting within 60 days after November 15, 1990.

(B) An evaluation, within 12 months after November 15, 1990, of each of the hazardous air pollutants listed under section 7412(b) of this chapter, to decide, on the basis of available information, their relative priority for preparation of environmental health assessments pursuant to subparagraph (C). The evaluation shall be based on reasonably anticipated toxicity to humans and exposure factors such as frequency of occurrence as an air pollutant and volume of emissions in populated areas. Such evaluation shall be reviewed by the Interagency Task Force established pursuant to subparagraph (A).

(C) Preparation of environmental health assessments for each of the hazardous air pollutants referred to in subparagraph (B), beginning 6 months after the first meeting of the Interagency Task Force and to be completed within 96 months thereafter. No fewer than 24 assessments shall be completed and published annually. The assessments shall be prepared in accordance with guidelines developed by the Administrator in consultation with the Interagency Task Force and the Science Advisory Board of the Environmental Protection Agency. Each such assessment shall include—

(i) an examination, summary, and evaluation of available toxicological and epidemiological information for the pollutant to ascertain the levels of human exposure which pose a significant threat to human health and the associated acute, subacute, and chronic adverse health effects;

(ii) a determination of gaps in available information related to human health effects and exposure levels; and

(iii) where appropriate, an identification of additional activities, including toxicological and inhalation testing, needed to identify the types or levels of exposure which may present significant risk of adverse health effects in humans.

(e) Ecosystem research

In carrying out subsection (a) of this section, the Administrator, in cooperation, where appropriate, with the Under Secretary of Commerce for Oceans and Atmosphere, the Director of the Fish and Wildlife Service, and the Secretary of Agriculture, shall conduct a research program to improve understanding of the short-term and long-term causes, effects, and trends of ecosystems damage from air pollutants on ecosystems. Such program shall include the following elements:

(1) Identification of regionally representative and critical ecosystems for research.

(2) Evaluation of risks to ecosystems exposed to air pollutants, including characterization of the causes and effects of chronic and episodic exposures to air pollutants and determination of the reversibility of those effects.

(3) Development of improved atmospheric dispersion models and monitoring systems and networks for evaluating and quantifying exposure to and effects of multiple environmental stresses associated with air pollution.

(4) Evaluation of the effects of air pollution on water quality, including assessments of the short-term and long-term ecological effects of acid deposition and other atmospherically derived pollutants on surface water (including wetlands and estuaries) and groundwater.

(5) Evaluation of the effects of air pollution on forests, materials, crops, biological diversity, soils, and other terrestrial and aquatic systems exposed to air pollutants.

(6) Estimation of the associated economic costs of ecological damage which have occurred as a result of exposure to air pollutants.

Consistent with the purpose of this program, the Administrator may use the estuarine research reserves established pursuant to section 1461 of Title 16 to carry out this research.

(f) Liquefied gaseous fuels spill test facility

(1) The Administrator, in consultation with the Secretary of Energy and the Federal Coordinating Council for Science, Engineering, and Technology, shall oversee an experimental and analytical research effort, with the experimental research to be carried out at the Liquefied Gaseous Fuels Spill Test Facility. In consultation with the Secretary of Energy, the Administrator shall develop a list of chemicals and a schedule for field testing at the Facility. Analysis of a minimum of 10 chemicals per year shall be carried out, with the selection of a minimum of 2 chemicals for field testing each year. Highest priority shall be given to those chemicals that would present the greatest potential risk to human health as a result of an accidental release—

(A) from a fixed site; or

(B) related to the transport of such chemicals.

(2) The purpose of such research shall be to—

(A) develop improved predictive models for atmospheric dispersion which at a minimum—

(i) describe dense gas releases in complex terrain including man-made structures or obstacles with variable winds;

(ii) improve understanding of the effects of turbulence on dispersion patterns; and

(iii) consider realistic behavior of aerosols by including physicochemical reactions with water vapor, ground deposition, and removal by water spray;

(B) evaluate existing and future atmospheric dispersion models by—

(i) the development of a rigorous, standardized methodology for dense gas models; and

(ii) the application of such methodology to current dense gas dispersion models using data generated from field experiments; and

(C) evaluate the effectiveness of hazard mitigation and emergency response technology for fixed site and transportation related accidental releases of toxic chemicals.

Models pertaining to accidental release shall be evaluated and improved periodically for their utility in planning and implementing evacuation procedures and other mitigative strategies designed to minimize human exposure to hazardous air pollutants released accidentally.

(3) The Secretary of Energy shall make available to interested persons (including other Federal agencies and businesses) the use of the Liquefied Gaseous Fuels Spill Test Facility to conduct research and other activities in connection with the activities described in this subsection.

(g) Pollution prevention and emissions control

In carrying out subsection (a) of this section, the Administrator shall conduct a basic engineering research and technology program to develop, evaluate, and demonstrate nonregulatory strategies and technologies for air pollution prevention. Such strategies and technologies shall be developed with priority on those pollutants which pose a significant risk to human health and the environment, and with opportunities for participation by industry, public interest groups, scientists, and other interested persons in the development of such strategies and technologies. Such program shall include the following elements:

(1) Improvements in nonregulatory strategies and technologies for preventing or reducing multiple air pollutants, including sulfur oxides, nitrogen oxides, heavy metals, PM–10 (particulate matter), carbon monoxide, and carbon dioxide, from stationary sources, including fossil fuel power plants. Such strategies and technologies shall include improvements in the relative cost effectiveness and long-range implications of various air pollutant reduction and nonregulatory control strategies such as energy conservation, including end-use efficiency, and fuel-switching to cleaner fuels. Such strategies and technologies shall be considered for existing and new facilities.

(2) Improvements in nonregulatory strategies and technologies for reducing air emissions from area sources.

(3) Improvements in nonregulatory strategies and technologies for preventing, detecting, and correcting accidental releases of hazardous air pollutants.

(4) Improvements in nonregulatory strategies and technologies that dispose of tires in ways that avoid adverse air quality impacts.

Nothing in this subsection shall be construed to authorize the imposition on any person of air pollution control requirements. The Administrator shall consult with other appropriate Federal agencies to ensure coordination and to avoid duplication of activities authorized under this subsection.

(h) NIEHS studies

(1) The Director of the National Institute of Environmental Health Sciences may conduct a program of basic research to identify, characterize, and quantify

risks to human health from air pollutants. Such research shall be conducted primarily through a combination of university and medical school-based grants, as well as through intramural studies and contracts.

(2) The Director of the National Institute of Environmental Health Sciences shall conduct a program for the education and training of physicians in environmental health.

(3) The Director shall assure that such programs shall not conflict with research undertaken by the Administrator.

(4) There are authorized to be appropriated to the National Institute of Environmental Health Sciences such sums as may be necessary to carry out the purposes of this subsection.

(i) Coordination of research

The Administrator shall develop and implement a plan for identifying areas in which activities authorized under this section can be carried out in conjunction with other Federal ecological and air pollution research efforts. The plan, which shall be submitted to Congress within 6 months after November 15, 1990, shall include—

(1) an assessment of ambient monitoring stations and networks to determine cost effective ways to expand monitoring capabilities in both urban and rural environments;

(2) a consideration of the extent of the feasibility and scientific value of conducting the research program under subsection (e) of this section to include consideration of the effects of atmospheric processes and air pollution effects; and

(3) a methodology for evaluating and ranking pollution prevention technologies, such as those developed under subsection (g) of this section, in terms of their ability to reduce cost effectively the emissions of air pollutants and other airborne chemicals of concern.

Not later than 2 years after November 15, 1990, and every 4 years thereafter, the Administrator shall report to Congress on the progress made in implementing the plan developed under this subsection, and shall include in such report any revisions of the plan.

(j) Continuation of the national acid precipitation assessment program

(1) The acid precipitation research program set forth in the Acid Precipitation Act of 1980 [42 U.S.C.A. § 8901 et seq.] shall be continued with modifications pursuant to this subsection.

(2) The Acid Precipitation Task Force shall consist of the Administrator of the Environmental Protection Agency, the Secretary of Energy, the Secretary of the Interior, the Secretary of Agriculture, the Administrator of the National Oceanic and Atmospheric Administration, the Administrator of the National Aeronautics and Space Administration, and such additional members as the President may select. The President shall appoint a chairman for the Task Force from among its members within 30 days after November 15, 1990.

(3) The responsibilities of the Task Force shall include the following:

(A) Review of the status of research activities conducted to date under the comprehensive research plan developed pursuant to the Acid Precipitation Act of 1980 [42 U.S.C.A. § 8901 et seq.], and development of a revised plan that identifies significant research gaps and establishes a coordinated program to address current and future research priorities. A draft of the revised plan shall be submitted by the Task Force to Congress within 6 months after November 15, 1990. The plan shall be available for public comment during the 60 day period after its submission, and a final plan shall be submitted by the President to the Congress within 45 days after the close of the comment period.

(B) Coordination with participating Federal agencies, augmenting the agencies' research and monitoring efforts and sponsoring additional research in the scientific community as necessary to ensure the availability and quality of data and methodologies needed to evaluate the status and effectiveness of the acid deposition control program. Such research and monitoring efforts shall include, but not be limited to—

(i) continuous monitoring of emissions of precursors of acid deposition;

(ii) maintenance, upgrading, and application of models, such as the Regional Acid Deposition Model, that describe the interactions of emissions with the atmosphere, and models that describe the response of ecosystems to acid deposition; and

(iii) analysis of the costs, benefits, and effectiveness of the acid deposition control program.

(C) Publication and maintenance of a National Acid Lakes Registry that tracks the condition and change over time of a statistically representative sample of lakes in regions that are known to be sensitive to surface water acidification.

(D) Submission every two years of a unified budget recommendation to the President for activities of the Federal Government in connection with the research program described in this subsection.

(E) Beginning in 1992 and biennially thereafter, submission of a report to Congress describing the results of its investigations and analyses. The reporting of technical information about acid deposition shall be provided in a format that facilitates communication with policymakers and the public. The report shall include—

(i) actual and projected emissions and acid deposition trends;

(ii) average ambient concentrations of acid deposition percursors [1] and their transformation products;

(iii) the status of ecosystems (including forests and surface waters), materials, and visibility affected by acid deposition;

(iv) the causes and effects of such deposition, including changes in surface water quality and forest and soil conditions;

(v) the occurrence and effects of episodic acidification, particularly with respect to high elevation watersheds; and

(vi) the confidence level associated with each conclusion to aid policymakers in use of the information.

(F) Beginning in 1996, and every 4 years thereafter, the report under subparagraph (E) shall include—

(i) the reduction in deposition rates that must be achieved in order to prevent adverse ecological effects; and

(ii) the costs and benefits of the acid deposition control program created by subchapter IV-A of this chapter.

(k) Air pollution conferences

If, in the judgment of the Administrator, an air pollution problem of substantial significance may result from discharge or discharges into the atmosphere, the Administrator may call a conference concerning this potential air pollution problem to be held in or near one or more of the places where such discharge or discharges are occurring or will occur. All interested persons shall be given an opportunity to be heard at such conference, either orally or in writing, and shall be permitted to appear in person or by representative in accordance with procedures prescribed by the Administrator. If the Administrator finds, on the basis of the evidence presented at such conference, that the discharge or discharges if permitted to take place or continue are likely to cause or contribute to air pollution subject to abatement under part A of subchapter I of this chapter, the Administrator shall send such findings, together with recommendations concerning the measures which the Administrator finds reasonable and suitable to prevent such pollution, to the person or persons whose actions will result in the discharge or discharges involved; to air pollution agencies of the State or States and of the municipality or municipalities where such discharge or discharges will originate; and to the interstate air pollution control agency, if any, in the jurisdictional area of which any such municipality is located. Such findings and recommendations shall be advisory only, but shall be admitted together with the record of the conference, as part of the proceedings under subsections (b), (c), (d), (e), and (f) of section 7408 of this title.

(July 14, 1955, ch. 360, title I, § 103, formerly § 3, as added Dec. 17, 1963, Pub.L. 88–206, § 1, 77 Stat. 394, and amended and renumbered Oct. 20, 1965, Pub.L. 89–272, title I, §§ 101(3), 103, 79 Stat. 992, 996; Nov. 21, 1967, Pub.L. 90–148, § 2, 81 Stat. 486; Dec. 31, 1970, Pub.L. 91–604, §§ 2(a), 4(2), 15(a)(2), (c)(2), 84 Stat. 1676, 1689, 1710, 1713; Aug. 7, 1977, Pub.L. 95–95, title I, § 101(a), (b), 91 Stat. 686, 687; Nov. 15, 1990, Pub.L. 101–549, title IX, § 901(a)–(c), 104 Stat. 2700–2703.)

[1] So in original. Probably should be "precursors".

References in Text

The Acid Precipitation Act of 1980, referred to in subsec. (j)(1) and (3)(A), is Title VII of Pub.L. 96–294, June 30, 1984, 94 Stat. 770, which is classified generally to chapter 97 (section 8901 et seq.) of this title. For complete classification of this Act to the Code, see Short Title note set out under section 8901 of this title and Tables.

Codification

In subsec. (b)(4), "section 3324(a) and (b) of Title 31" was substituted for reference to section 3648 of the Revised Statutes (31 U.S.C. 529) on authority of Pub.L. 97–258, § 4(b), Sept. 13, 1982, 96 Stat. 1067, the first section of which enacted Title 31, Money and Finance.

Effective Date of 1990 Amendment

Amendment by Pub.L. 101–549 effective Nov. 15, 1990, except as otherwise provided, see section 711(b) of Pub.L. 101–549, set out as a note under section 7401 of this title.

Savings Provisions

Suits, actions or proceedings commenced under this chapter as in effect prior to Nov. 15, 1990, not to abate by reason of the taking effect of amendments by Pub.L. 101–549, except as otherwise provided for, see section 711(a) of Pub.L. 101–549, set out as a note under section 7401 of this title.

National Acid Lakes Registry

Pub.L. 101–549, Title IV, § 405, Nov. 15, 1990, 104 Stat. 2632, provided that: "The Administrator of the Environmental Protection Agency shall create a National Acid Lakes Registry that shall list, to the extent practical, all lakes that are known to be acidified due to acid deposition, and shall publish such list within one year of the enactment of this Act [Nov. 15, 1990]. Lakes shall be added to the registry as they become acidic or as data becomes available to show they are acidic. Lakes shall be deleted from the registry as they become nonacidic."

Assessment of International Air Pollution Control Techniques

Section 901(e) of Pub.L. 101–549 provided that: "The Administrator of the Environmental Protection Agency shall conduct a study that compares international air pollution control technologies of selected industrialized countries to determine if there exist air pollution control technologies in countries outside the United States that may have beneficial applications to this Nation's air pollution control efforts. With respect to each country studied, the study shall include the topics of urban air quality, motor vehicle emissions, toxic air emissions, and acid deposition. The Administrator shall, within 2 years after the date of enactment of this Act [Nov. 15, 1990], submit to the Congress a report detailing the results of such study."

Western States Acid Deposition Research

Section 901(g) of Pub.L. 101–549 provided that:

"(1) The Administrator of the Environmental Protection Agency shall sponsor monitoring and research and submit to Congress annual and periodic assessment reports on—

"(A) the occurrence and effects of acid deposition on surface waters located in that part of the United States west of the Mississippi River;

"(B) the occurrence and effects of acid deposition on high elevation ecosystems (including forests, and surface waters); and

"(C) the occurrence and effects of episodic acidification, particularly with respect to high elevation watersheds.

"(2) The Administrator of the Environmental Protection Agency shall analyze data generated from the studies conducted under paragraph (1), data from the Western Lakes Survey, and other appropriate research and utilize predictive modeling techniques that take into account the unique geographic, climatological, and atmospheric conditions which exist in the western United States to determine the potential occurrence and effects of acid deposition due to any projected increases in the emission of sulfur dioxide and nitrogen oxides in that part of the United States located west of the Mississippi River. The Administrator shall include the results of the project conducted under this paragraph in the reports issued to Congress under paragraph (1)."

LIBRARY REFERENCES

Health and Environment ⟹25.6(1) et seq., 28.
C.J.S. Health and Environment § 91 et seq.

§ 7404. Research relating to fuels and vehicles [CAA § 104]

(a) Research programs; grants; contracts; pilot and demonstration plants; byproducts research

The Administrator shall give special emphasis to research and development into new and improved methods, having industry-wide application, for the prevention and control of air pollution resulting from the combustion of fuels. In furtherance of such research and development he shall—

(1) conduct and accelerate research programs directed toward development of improved, cost-effective techniques for—

(A) control of combustion byproducts of fuels,

(B) removal of potential air pollutants from fuels prior to combustion,

(C) control of emissions from the evaporation of fuels,

(D) improving the efficiency of fuels combustion so as to decrease atmospheric emissions, and

(E) producing synthetic or new fuels which, when used, result in decreased atmospheric emissions.

(2) provide for Federal grants to public or nonprofit agencies, institutions, and organizations and to individuals, and contracts with public or private agencies, institutions, or persons, for payment of (A) part of the cost of acquiring, constructing, or otherwise securing for research and development purposes, new or improved devices or methods having industrywide application of preventing or controlling discharges into the air of various types of pollutants; (B) part of the cost of programs to develop low emission alternatives to the present internal combustion engine; (C) the cost to purchase vehicles and vehicle engines, or portions thereof, for research, development, and testing purposes; and (D) carrying out the other provisions of this section, without regard to section 3324(a) and (b) of Title 31 and section 5 of Title 41: *Provided,* That research or demonstration contracts awarded pursuant to this subsection (including contracts for construction) may be made in accordance with, and subject to the limitations provided with respect to research contracts of the military departments in, section 2353 of Title 10, except that the determination, approval, and certification required thereby shall be made by the Secretary: *Provided further,* That no grant may be made under this paragraph in excess of $1,500,000;

(3) determine, by laboratory and pilot plant testing, the results of air pollution research and studies in order to develop new or improved processes and plant designs to the point where they can be demonstrated on a large and practical scale;

(4) construct, operate, and maintain, or assist in meeting the cost of the construction, operation, and maintenance of new or improved demonstration plants or processes which have promise of accomplishing the purposes of this chapter;

(5) study new or improved methods for the recovery and marketing of commercially valuable byproducts resulting from the removal of pollutants.

(b) Powers of Administrator in establishing research and development programs

In carrying out the provisions of this section, the Administrator may—

(1) conduct and accelerate research and development of cost-effective instrumentation techniques to facilitate determination of quantity and quality of air pollutant emissions, including, but not limited to, automotive emissions;

(2) utilize, on a reimbursable basis, the facilities of existing Federal scientific laboratories;

(3) establish and operate necessary facilities and test sites at which to carry on the research, testing, development, and programming necessary to effectuate the purposes of this section;

(4) acquire secret processes, technical data, inventions, patent applications, patents, licenses, and an interest in lands, plants, and facilities, and other property or rights by purchase, license, lease, or donation; and

(5) cause on-site inspections to be made of promising domestic and foreign projects, and cooperate and participate in their development in instances in which the purposes of the chapter will be served thereby.

(c) Clean alternative fuels

The Administrator shall conduct a research program to identify, characterize, and predict air emissions related to the production, distribution, storage, and use of clean alternative fuels to determine the risks and benefits to human health and the environment relative to those from using conventional gasoline and diesel fuels. The Administrator shall consult with other Federal agencies to ensure coordination and to avoid duplication of activities authorized under this subsection.

(July 14, 1955, ch. 360, title I, § 104, as added Nov. 21, 1967, Pub.L. 90–148, § 2, 81 Stat. 487, and amended Dec. 5, 1969, Pub.L. 91–137, 83 Stat. 283; Dec. 31, 1970, Pub.L. 91–604, §§ 2(b), (c), 13(a), 15(c)(2), 84 Stat. 1676, 1677, 1709, 1713; Apr. 9, 1973, Pub.L. 93–15, § 1(a), 87 Stat. 11; June 22, 1974, Pub.L. 93–319, § 13(a), 88 Stat. 265; Sept. 13, 1982, Pub.L. 97–258, § 4(b), 96 Stat. 1067; Nov. 15, 1990, Pub.L. 101–549, title IX, § 901(d), 104 Stat. 2706.)

Effective Date of 1990 Amendment

Amendment by Pub.L. 101–549 effective Nov. 15, 1990, except as otherwise provided, see section 711(b) of Pub.L. 101–549, set out as a note under section 7401 of this title.

Savings Provisions

Suits, actions or proceedings commenced under this chapter as in effect prior to Nov. 15, 1990, not to abate by reason of the taking effect of amendments by Pub.L. 101–549, except as otherwise provided for, see section 711(a) of Pub.L. 101–549, set out as a note under section 7401 of this title.

Combustion of Contaminated Used Oil in Ships

Pub.L. 101–549, Title VIII, § 813, Nov. 15, 1990, 104 Stat. 2693, provided that: "Within 2 years after the enactment of the Clean Air Act Amendments of 1990 [probably means the date of enactment of Pub.L. 101–549, which was approved Nov. 15, 1990], the Administrator of the Environmental Protection Agency shall complete a study and submit a report to Congress evaluating the health and environmental impacts of the combustion of contaminated used oil in ships, the reasons for using such oil for such purposes, the alternatives to such use, the costs of such alternatives, and other relevant factors and impacts. In preparing such study, the Administrator shall obtain the view and comments of all interested persons and shall consult with the Secretary of Transportation and the Secretary of the department in which the Coast Guard is operating."

LIBRARY REFERENCES

Health and Environment ⚖25.6(1) et seq., 28.
C.J.S. Health and Environment § 91 et seq.

§ 7405. Grants for support of air pollution planning and control programs [CAA § 105]

(a) Amounts; limitations; assurances of plan development capability

(1)(A) The Administrator may make grants to air pollution control agencies, within the meaning of paragraph (1), (2), (3), (4), or (5) of section 7602 of this title, in an amount up to three-fifths of the cost of implementing programs for the prevention and control of air pollution or implementation of national primary and secondary ambient air quality standards. For the purpose of this section, "implementing" means any activity related to the planning, developing, establishing, carrying-out, improving, or maintaining of such programs.

(B) Subject to subsections (b) and (c) of this section, an air pollution control agency which receives a grant under subparagraph (A) and which contributes less than the required two-fifths minimum shall have 3 years following November 15, 1990, in which to contribute such amount. If such an agency fails to meet and maintain this required level, the Administrator shall reduce the amount of the Federal contribution accordingly.

(C) With respect to any air quality control region or portion thereof for which there is an applicable implementation plan under section 7410 of this title, grants under subparagraph (A) may be made only to air pollution control agencies which have substantial responsibilities for carrying out such applicable implementation plan.

(2) Before approving any grant under this subsection to any air pollution control agency within the meaning of sections 7602(b)(2) and 7602(b)(4) of this title, the Administrator shall receive assurances that such agency provides for adequate representation of appropriate State, interstate, local, and (when appropriate) international, interests in the air quality control region.

(3) Before approving any planning grant under this subsection to any air pollution control agency within the meaning of sections 7602(b)(2) and 7602(b)(4) of this title, the Administrator shall receive assurances that such agency has the capability of developing a comprehensive air quality plan for the air quality control region, which plan shall include (when appropriate) a recommended system of alerts to avert and reduce the risk of situations in which there may be imminent and serious danger to the public health or welfare from air pollutants and the various aspects relevant to the establishment of air quality standards for such air quality control region, including the concentration of industries, other commercial establishments, population and naturally occurring factors which shall affect such standards.

(b) Terms and conditions; regulations; factors for consideration; State expenditure limitations

(1) From the sums available for the purposes of subsection (a) of this section for any fiscal year, the

Administrator shall from time to time make grants to air pollution control agencies upon such terms and conditions as the Administrator may find necessary to carry out the purpose of this section. In establishing regulations for the granting of such funds the Administrator shall, so far as practicable, give due consideration to (A) the population, (B) the extent of the actual or potential air pollution problem, and (C) the financial need of the respective agencies.

(2) Not more than 10 per centum of the total of funds appropriated or allocated for the purposes of subsection (a) of this section shall be granted for air pollution control programs in any one State. In the case of a grant for a program in an area crossing State boundaries, the Administrator shall determine the portion of such grant that is chargeable to the percentage limitation under this subsection for each State into which such area extends. Subject to the provisions of paragraph (1) of this subsection, no State shall have made available to it for application less than one-half of 1 per centum of the annual appropriation for grants under this section for grants to agencies within such State.

(c) Maintenance of effort

(1) No agency shall receive any grant under this section during any fiscal year when its expenditures of non-Federal funds for recurrent expenditures for air pollution control programs will be less than its expenditures were for such programs during the preceding fiscal year. In order for the Administrator to award grants under this section in a timely manner each fiscal year, the Administrator shall compare an agency's prospective expenditure level to that of its second preceding fiscal year. The Administrator shall revise the current regulations which define applicable nonrecurrent and recurrent expenditures, and in so doing, give due consideration to exempting an agency from the limitations of this paragraph and subsection (a) of this section due to periodic increases experienced by that agency from time to time in its annual expenditures for purposes acceptable to the Administrator for that fiscal year.

(2) The Administrator may still award a grant to an agency not meeting the requirements of paragraph (1) of this subsection if the Administrator, after notice and opportunity for public hearing, determines that a reduction in expenditures is attributable to a nonselective reduction in the expenditures in the programs of all Executive branch agencies of the applicable unit of Government. No agency shall receive any grant under this section with respect to the maintenance of a program for the prevention and control of air pollution unless the Administrator is satisfied that such a grant will be so used to supplement and, to the extent practicable, increase the level of State, local, or other non-Federal funds. No grants shall be made under this section until the Administrator has consulted with the appropriate official as designated by the Governor or Governors of the State or States affected.

(d) Reduction of payments; availability of reduced amounts; reduced amount as deemed paid to agency for purpose of determining amount of grant

The Administrator, with the concurrence of any recipient of a grant under this section, may reduce the payments to such recipient by the amount of the pay, allowances, traveling expenses, and any other costs in connection with the detail of any officer or employee to the recipient under section 7601 of this title, when such detail is for the convenience of, and at the request of, such recipient and for the purpose of carrying out the provisions of this chapter. The amount by which such payments have been reduced shall be available for payment of such costs by the Administrator, but shall, for the purpose of determining the amount of any grant to a recipient under subsection (a) of this section, be deemed to have been paid to such agency.

(e) Notice and opportunity for hearing when affected by adverse action

No application by a State for a grant under this section may be disapproved by the Administrator without prior notice and opportunity for a public hearing in the affected State, and no commitment or obligation of any funds under any such grant may be revoked or reduced without prior notice and opportunity for a public hearing in the affected State (or in one of the affected States if more than one State is affected).

(July 14, 1955, ch. 360, title I, § 105, formerly § 4, as added Dec. 17, 1963, Pub.L. 88–206, § 1, 77 Stat. 395, renumbered § 104 and amended Oct. 20, 1965, Pub.L. 89–272, title I, § 101(2)–(4), 79 Stat. 992; Oct. 15, 1966, Pub.L. 89–675, § 3, 80 Stat. 954, and renumbered § 105 and amended Nov. 21, 1967, Pub.L. 90–148, § 2, 81 Stat. 489; Dec. 31, 1970, Pub.L. 91–604, §§ 3(a), (b)(1), 15(c)(2), 84 Stat. 1677, 1713; Aug. 7, 1977, Pub.L. 95–95, title I, § 102, title III, § 305(b), 91 Stat. 687, 776; Nov. 15, 1990, Pub.L. 101–549, title VIII, § 802(a)–(e), 104 Stat. 2687, 2688.)

Effective Date of 1990 Amendment

Amendment by Pub.L. 101–549 effective Nov. 15, 1990, except as otherwise provided, see section 711(b) of Pub.L. 101–549, set out as a note under section 7401 of this title.

Savings Provisions

Suits, actions or proceedings commenced under this chapter as in effect prior to Nov. 15, 1990, not to abate by reason of the taking effect of amendments by Pub.L. 101–549, except as otherwise provided for, see section 711(a) of Pub.L. 101–549, set out as a note under section 7401 of this title.

CODE OF FEDERAL REGULATIONS

State and local assistance, see 40 CFR 35.001 et seq.

Library References

Health and Environment ⚖25.6(1) et seq., 28.
United States ⚖82(2).
C.J.S. Health and Environment § 91 et seq.
C.J.S. United States § 122.

§ 7406. Interstate air quality agencies; program cost limitations [CAA § 106]

For the purpose of developing implementation plans for any interstate air quality control region designated pursuant to section 7407 of this title or of implementing section 7506a of this title (relating to control of interstate air pollution) or section 7511c of this title (relating to control of interstate ozone pollution) the Administrator is authorized to pay, for two years, up to 100 per centum of the air quality planning program costs of any commission established under section 7506a of this title (relating to control of interstate air pollution) or section 7511c of this title (relating to control of interstate ozone pollution) or any agency designated by the Governors of the affected States, which agency shall be capable of recommending to the Governors plans for implementation of national primary and secondary ambient air quality standards and shall include representation from the States and appropriate political subdivisions within the air quality control region. After the initial two-year period the Administrator is authorized to make grants to such agency or such commission in an amount up to three-fifths of the air quality implementation program costs of such agency or commission.

(July 14, 1955, ch. 360, title I, § 106, as added Nov. 21, 1967, Pub.L. 90–148, § 2, 81 Stat. 490, and amended Dec. 31, 1970, Pub.L. 91–604, § 3(c), 84 Stat. 1677; Nov. 15, 1990, Pub.L. 101–549, title I, § 102(f)(2), title VIII, § 802(f), 104 Stat. 2420, 2688.)

Effective Date of 1990 Amendment

Amendment by Pub.L. 101–549 effective Nov. 15, 1990, except as otherwise provided, see section 711(b) of Pub.L. 101–549, set out as a note under section 7401 of this title.

Savings Provisions

Suits, actions or proceedings commenced under this chapter as in effect prior to Nov. 15, 1990, not to abate by reason of the taking effect of amendments by Pub.L. 101–549, except as otherwise provided for, see section 711(a) of Pub.L. 101–549, set out as a note under section 7401 of this title.

LIBRARY REFERENCES

Health and Environment ⚖25.6(1) et seq., 28.
C.J.S. Health and Environment § 91 et seq.

§ 7407. Air quality control regions [CAA § 107]

(a) Responsibility of each State for air quality; submission of implementation plan

Each State shall have the primary responsibility for assuring air quality within the entire geographic area comprising such State by submitting an implementation plan for such State which will specify the manner in which national primary and secondary ambient air quality standards will be achieved and maintained within each air quality control region in such State.

(b) Designated regions

For purposes of developing and carrying out implementation plans under section 7410 of this title—

(1) an air quality control region designated under this section before December 31, 1970, or a region designated after such date under subsection (c) of this section, shall be an air quality control region; and

(2) the portion of such State which is not part of any such designated region shall be an air quality control region, but such portion may be subdivided by the State into two or more air quality control regions with the approval of the Administrator.

(c) Authority of Administrator to designate regions; notification of Governors of affected States

The Administrator shall, within 90 days after December 31, 1970, after consultation with appropriate State and local authorities, designate as an air quality control region any interstate area or major intrastate area which he deems necessary or appropriate for the attainment and maintenance of ambient air quality standards. The Administrator shall immediately notify the Governors of the affected States of any designation made under this subsection.

(d) Designations

(1) Designations generally

(A) Submission by Governors of initial designations following promulgation of new or revised standards

By such date as the Administrator may reasonably require, but not later than 1 year after promulgation of a new or revised national ambient air quality standard for any pollutant under section 7409 of this title, the Governor of each State shall (and at any other time the Governor of a State deems appropriate the Governor may) submit to the Administrator a list of all areas (or portions thereof) in the State, designating as—

(i) nonattainment, any area that does not meet (or that contributes to ambient air quality in a nearby area that does not meet) the national primary or secondary ambient air quality standard for the pollutant,

(ii) attainment, any area (other than an area identified in clause (i)) that meets the national primary or secondary ambient air quality standard for the pollutant, or

(iii) unclassifiable, any area that cannot be classified on the basis of available information as meeting or not meeting the national primary or secondary ambient air quality standard for the pollutant.

The Administrator may not require the Governor to submit the required list sooner than 120 days after promulgating a new or revised national ambient air quality standard.

(B) Promulgation by EPA of designations

(i) Upon promulgation or revision of a national ambient air quality standard, the Administrator shall promulgate the designations of all areas (or portions thereof) submitted under subparagraph (A) as expeditiously as practicable, but in no case later than 2 years from the date of promulgation of the new or revised national ambient air quality standard. Such period may be extended for up to one year in the event the Administrator has insufficient information to promulgate the designations.

(ii) In making the promulgations required under clause (i), the Administrator may make such modifications as the Administrator deems necessary to the designations of the areas (or portions thereof) submitted under subparagraph (A) (including to the boundaries of such areas or portions thereof). Whenever the Administrator intends to make a modification, the Administrator shall notify the State and provide such State with an opportunity to demonstrate why any proposed modification is inappropriate. The Administrator shall give such notification no later than 120 days before the date the Administrator promulgates the designation, including any modification thereto. If the Governor fails to submit the list in whole or in part, as required under subparagraph (A), the Administrator shall promulgate the designation that the Administrator deems appropriate for any area (or portion thereof) not designated by the State.

(iii) If the Governor of any State, on the Governor's own motion, under subparagraph (A), submits a list of areas (or portions thereof) in the State designated as nonattainment, attainment, or unclassifiable, the Administrator shall act on such designations in accordance with the procedures under paragraph (3) (relating to redesignation).

(iv) A designation for an area (or portion thereof) made pursuant to this subsection shall remain in effect until the area (or portion thereof) is redesignated pursuant to paragraph (3) or (4).

(C) Designations by operation of law

(i) Any area designated with respect to any air pollutant under the provisions of paragraph (1)(A), (B), or (C) of this subsection (as in effect immediately before November 15, 1990) is designated, by operation of law, as a nonattainment area for such pollutant within the meaning of subparagraph (A)(i).

(ii) Any area designated with respect to any air pollutant under the provisions of paragraph (1)(E) (as in effect immediately before November 15, 1990) is designated by operation of law, as an attainment area for such pollutant within the meaning of subparagraph (A)(ii).

(iii) Any area designated with respect to any air pollutant under the provisions of paragraph (1)(D) (as in effect immediately before November 15, 1990) is designated, by operation of law, as an unclassifiable area for such pollutant within the meaning of subparagraph (A)(iii).

(2) Publication of designations and redesignations

(A) The Administrator shall publish a notice in the Federal Register promulgating any designation under paragraph (1) or (5), or announcing any designation under paragraph (4), or promulgating any redesignation under paragraph (3).

(B) Promulgation or announcement of a designation under paragraph (1), (4) or (5) shall not be subject to the provisions of sections 553 through 557 of Title 5 (relating to notice and comment), except nothing herein shall be construed as precluding such public notice and comment whenever possible.

(3) Redesignation

(A) Subject to the requirements of subparagraph (E), and on the basis of air quality data, planning and control considerations, or any other air quality-related considerations the Administrator deems appropriate, the Administrator may at any time notify the Governor of any State that available information indicates that the designation of any area or portion of an area within the State or interstate area should be revised. In issuing such notification, which shall be public, to the Governor, the Administrator shall provide such information as the Administrator may have available explaining the basis for the notice.

(B) No later than 120 days after receiving a notification under subparagraph (A), the Governor shall submit to the Administrator such redesignation, if any, of the appropriate area (or areas) or portion thereof within the State or interstate area, as the Governor considers appropriate.

(C) No later than 120 days after the date described in subparagraph (B) (or paragraph (1)(B)(iii)), the Administrator shall promulgate the redesignation, if any, of the area or portion thereof, submitted by the Governor in accordance with subparagraph (B), making such modifications as the Administrator may deem necessary, in the same manner and under the same procedure as is applicable under clause (ii) of paragraph (1)(B), except that the phrase "60 days" shall be substituted for the phrase "120 days" in that clause. If the Governor does not submit, in accordance with subparagraph (B), a redesignation for an area (or portion thereof) identified by the Administrator under subparagraph (A), the Administrator shall promulgate such redesignation, if any, that the Administrator deems appropriate.

(D) The Governor of any State may, on the Governor's own motion, submit to the Administrator a revised designation of any area or portion thereof within the State. Within 18 months of receipt of a complete State redesignation submittal, the Administrator shall approve or deny such redesignation. The submission of a redesignation by a Governor shall not affect the effectiveness or enforceability of the applicable implementation plan for the State.

(E) The Administrator may not promulgate a redesignation of a nonattainment area (or portion thereof) to attainment unless—

(i) the Administrator determines that the area has attained the national ambient air quality standard;

(ii) the Administrator has fully approved the applicable implementation plan for the area under section 7410(k) of this title;

(iii) the Administrator determines that the improvement in air quality is due to permanent and enforceable reductions in emissions resulting from implementation of the applicable implementation plan and applicable Federal air pollutant control regulations and other permanent and enforceable reductions;

(iv) the Administrator has fully approved a maintenance plan for the area as meeting the requirements of section 7505a of this title; and

(v) the State containing such area has met all requirements applicable to the area under section 7410 of this title and part D.

(F) The Administrator shall not promulgate any redesignation of any area (or portion thereof) from nonattainment to unclassifiable.

(4) Nonattainment designations for ozone, carbon monoxide and particulate matter (PM–10)

(A) Ozone and carbon monoxide

(i) Within 120 days after November 15, 1990, each Governor of each State shall submit to the Administrator a list that designates, affirms or reaffirms the designation of, or redesignates (as the case may be), all areas (or portions thereof) of the Governor's State as attainment, nonattainment, or unclassifiable with respect to the national ambient air quality standards for ozone and carbon monoxide.

(ii) No later than 120 days after the date the Governor is required to submit the list of areas (or portions thereof) required under clause (i) of this subparagraph, the Administrator shall promulgate such designations, making such modifications as the Administrator may deem necessary, in the same manner, and under the same procedure, as is applicable under clause (ii) of paragraph (1)(B), except that the phrase "60 days" shall be substituted for the phrase "120 days" in that clause. If the Governor does not submit, in accordance with clause (i) of this subparagraph, a designation for an area (or portion thereof), the Administrator shall promulgate the designation that the Administrator deems appropriate.

(iii) No nonattainment area may be redesignated as an attainment area under this subparagraph.

(iv) Notwithstanding paragraph (1)(C)(ii) of this subsection, if an ozone or carbon monoxide nonattainment area located within a metropolitan statistical area or consolidated metropolitan statistical area (as established by the Bureau of the Census) is classified under part D of this subchapter as a Serious, Severe, or Extreme Area, the boundaries of such area are hereby revised (on the date 45 days after such classification) by operation of law to include the entire metropolitan statistical area or consolidated metropolitan statistical area, as the case may be, unless within such 45–day period the Governor (in consultation with State and local air pollution control agencies) notifies the Administrator that additional time is necessary to evaluate the application of clause (v). Whenever a Governor has submitted such a notice to the Administrator, such boundary revision shall occur on the later of the date 8 months after such classification or 14 months after November 15, 1990, unless the Governor makes the finding referred to in clause (v), and the Administrator concurs in such finding, within such period. Except as otherwise provided in this paragraph, a boundary revision under this clause or clause (v) shall apply for purposes of any State implementation plan revision required to be submitted after November 15, 1990.

(v) Whenever the Governor of a State has submitted a notice under clause (iv), the Governor, in consultation with State and local air pollution control agencies, shall undertake a study to evaluate whether the entire metropolitan statistical area or consolidated metropolitan statistical area should be included within the nonattainment area. Whenever a Governor finds and demonstrates to the satisfaction of the Administrator, and the Administrator concurs in such finding, that with respect to a portion of a metropolitan statistical area or consolidated metropolitan statistical area, sources in the portion do not contribute significantly to violation of the national ambient air quality standard, the Administrator shall approve the Governor's request to exclude such portion from the nonattainment area. In making such finding, the Governor and the Administrator shall consider factors such as population density, traffic congestion, commercial development, industrial development, meteorological conditions, and pollution transport.

(B) PM–10 designations

By operation of law, until redesignation by the Administrator pursuant to paragraph (3)—

(i) each area identified in 52 Federal Register 29383 (Aug. 7, 1987) as a Group I area (except to the extent that such identification was modified by the Administrator before November 15, 1990) is designated nonattainment for PM–10;

(ii) any area containing a site for which air quality monitoring data show a violation of the national ambient air quality standard for PM–10 before January 1, 1989 (as determined under part 50, appendix K of title 40 of the Code of Federal Regulations) is hereby designated nonattainment for PM–10; and

(iii) each area not described in clause (i) or (ii) is hereby designated unclassifiable for PM–10.

Any designation for particulate matter (measured in terms of total suspended particulates) that the Administrator promulgated pursuant to this subsection (as in effect immediately before November 15, 1990) shall remain in effect for purposes of implementing the maximum allowable increases in concentrations of particulate matter (measured in terms of total suspended particulates) pursuant to section 7473(b) of this title until the Administrator determines that such designation is no longer necessary for that purpose.

(5) Designations for lead

The Administrator may, in the Administrator's discretion at any time the Administrator deems appropriate, require a State to designate areas (or portions thereof) with respect to the national ambient air quality standard for lead in effect as of November 15, 1990, in accordance with the procedures under subparagraphs (A) and (B) of paragraph (1), except that in applying subparagraph (B)(i) of paragraph (1) the phrase "2 years from the date of promulgation of the new or revised national ambient air quality standard" shall be replaced by the phrase "1 year from the date the Administrator notifies the State of the requirement to designate areas with respect to the standard for lead".

(e) Redesignation of air quality control regions

(1) Except as otherwise provided in paragraph (2), the Governor of each State is authorized, with the approval of the Administrator, to redesignate from time to time the air quality control regions within such State for purposes of efficient and effective air quality management. Upon such redesignation, the list under subsection (d) of this section shall be modified accordingly.

(2) In the case of an air quality control region in a State, or part of such region, which the Administrator finds may significantly affect air pollution concentrations in another State, the Governor of the State in which such region, or part of a region, is located may redesignate from time to time the boundaries of so much of such air quality control region as is located within such State only with the approval of the Administrator and with the consent of all Governors of all States which the Administrator determines may be significantly affected.

(3) No compliance date extension granted under section 7413(d)(5) of this title (relating to coal conversion) shall cease to be effective by reason of the regional limitation provided in section 7413(d)(5) of this title if the violation of such limitation is due solely to a redesignation of a region under this subsection.

(July 14, 1955, ch. 360, title I, § 107, as added Dec. 31, 1970, Pub.L. 91–604, § 4(a), 84 Stat. 1678, and amended Aug. 7, 1977, Pub.L. 95–95, title I, § 103, 91 Stat. 687; Nov. 15, 1990, Pub.L. 101–549, title I, § 101(a), 104 Stat. 2399.)

Effective Date of 1990 Amendment

Amendment by Pub.L. 101–549 effective Nov. 15, 1990, except as otherwise provided, see section 711(b) of Pub.L. 101–549, set out as a note under section 7401 of this title.

Savings Provisions

Suits, actions or proceedings commenced under this chapter as in effect prior to Nov. 15, 1990, not to abate by reason of the taking effect of amendments by Pub.L. 101–549, except as otherwise provided for, see section 711(a) of Pub.L. 101–549, set out as a note under section 7401 of this title.

West's Federal Practice Manual

Air quality legislation, see § 4384.5.

LIBRARY REFERENCES

Health and Environment ⚷25.6(1) et seq., 28.
C.J.S. Health and Environment § 91 et seq.

§ 7408. Air quality criteria and control techniques [CAA § 108]

(a) Air pollutant list; publication and revision by Administrator; issuance of air quality criteria for air pollutants

(1) For the purpose of establishing national primary and secondary ambient air quality standards, the Administrator shall within 30 days after December 31, 1970, publish, and shall from time to time thereafter revise, a list which includes each air pollutant—

(A) emissions of which, in his judgment, cause or contribute to air pollution which may reasonably be anticipated to endanger public health or welfare;

(B) the presence of which in the ambient air results from numerous or diverse mobile or stationary sources; and

(C) for which air quality criteria had not been issued before December 31, 1970 but for which he plans to issue air quality criteria under this section.

(2) The Administrator shall issue air quality criteria for an air pollutant within 12 months after he has included such pollutant in a list under paragraph (1). Air quality criteria for an air pollutant shall accurately reflect the latest scientific knowledge useful in indicating the kind and extent of all identifiable effects on public health or welfare which may be expected from the presence of such pollutant in the ambient air, in varying quantities. The criteria for an air pollutant, to the extent practicable, shall include information on—

(A) those variable factors (including atmospheric conditions) which of themselves or in combination with other factors may alter the effects on public health or welfare of such air pollutant;

(B) the types of air pollutants which, when present in the atmosphere, may interact with such pollutant to produce an adverse effect on public health or welfare; and

(C) any known or anticipated adverse effects on welfare.

(b) Issuance by Administrator of information on air pollution control techniques; standing consulting committees for air pollutants; establishment; membership

(1) Simultaneously with the issuance of criteria under subsection (a) of this section, the Administrator shall, after consultation with appropriate advisory committees and Federal departments and agencies, issue to the States and appropriate air pollution control agencies information on air pollution control techniques, which information shall include data relating to the cost of installation and operation, energy requirements, emission reduction benefits, and environmental impact of the emission control technology. Such information shall include such data as are available on available technology and alternative methods of prevention and control of air pollution. Such information shall also include data on alternative fuels, processes, and operating methods which will result in elimination or significant reduction of emissions.

(2) In order to assist in the development of information on pollution control techniques, the Administrator may establish a standing consulting committee for each air pollutant included in a list published pursuant to subsection (a)(1) of this section, which shall be comprised of technically qualified individuals representative of State and local governments, industry, and the academic community. Each such committee shall submit, as appropriate, to the Administrator information related to that required by paragraph (1).

(c) Review, modification, and reissuance of criteria or information

The Administrator shall from time to time review, and, as appropriate, modify, and reissue any criteria or information on control techniques issued pursuant to this section. Not later than six months after August 7, 1977, the Administrator shall revise and reissue criteria relating to concentrations of NO_2 over such period (not more than three hours) as he deems appropriate. Such criteria shall include a discussion of nitric and nitrous acids, nitrites, nitrates, nitrosamines, and other carcinogenic and potentially carcinogenic derivatives of oxides of nitrogen.

(d) Publication in Federal Register; availability of copies for general public

The issuance of air quality criteria and information on air pollution control techniques shall be announced in the Federal Register and copies shall be made available to the general public.

(e) Transportation planning and guidelines

The Administrator shall, after consultation with the Secretary of Transportation, and after providing public notice and opportunity for comment, and with State and local officials, within nine months after enactment of the Clean Air Act Amendments of 1989 and periodically thereafter as necessary to maintain a continuous transportation-air quality planning process, update the June 1978 Transportation-Air Quality Planning Guidelines and publish guidance on the development and implementation of transportation and other measures necessary to demonstrate and maintain attainment of national ambient air quality standards. Such guidelines shall include information on—

(1) methods to identify and evaluate alternative planning and control activities;

(2) methods of reviewing plans on a regular basis as conditions change or new information is presented;

(3) identification of funds and other resources necessary to implement the plan, including interagency agreements on providing such funds and resources;

(4) methods to assure participation by the public in all phases of the planning process; and

(5) such other methods as the Administrator determines necessary to carry out a continuous planning process.

(f) Information regarding processes, procedures, and methods to reduce or control pollutants in transportation; reduction of mobile source related pollutants; reduction of impact on public health

(1) The Administrator shall publish and make available to appropriate Federal, State, and local environmental and transportation agencies not later than one year after enactment of the Clean Air Act Amendments of 1990, and from time to time thereafter—

(A) information prepared, as appropriate, in consultation with the Secretary of Transportation, and after providing public notice and opportunity for comment, regarding the formulation and emission reduction potential of transportation control measures related to criteria pollutants and their precursors, including, but not limited to—

(i) programs for improved public transit;

(ii) restriction of certain roads or lanes to, or construction of such roads or lanes for use by, passenger buses or high occupancy vehicles;

(iii) employer-based transportation management plans, including incentives;

(iv) trip-reduction ordinances;

(v) traffic flow improvement programs that achieve emission reductions;

(vi) fringe and transportation corridor parking facilities serving multiple occupancy vehicle programs or transit service;

(vii) programs to limit or restrict vehicle use in downtown areas or other areas of emission concentration particularly during periods of peak use;

(viii) programs for the provision of all forms of high-occupancy, shared-ride services;

(ix) programs to limit portions of road surfaces or certain sections of the metropolitan area to the use of non-motorized vehicles or pedestrian use, both as to time and place;

(x) programs for secure bicycle storage facilities and other facilities, including bicycle lanes, for the convenience and protection of bicyclists, in both public and private areas;

(xi) programs to control extended idling of vehicles;

(xii) programs to reduce motor vehicle emissions, consistent with subchapter II of this chapter, which are caused by extreme cold start conditions;

(xiii) employer-sponsored programs to permit flexible work schedules;

(xiv) programs and ordinances to facilitate non-automobile travel, provision and utilization of mass transit, and to generally reduce the need for single-occupant vehicle travel, as part of transportation planning and development efforts of a locality, including programs and ordinances applicable to new shopping centers, special events, and other centers of vehicle activity;

(xv) programs for new construction and major reconstructions of paths, tracks or areas solely for the use by pedestrian or other non-motorized means of transportation when economically feasible and in the public interest. For purposes of this clause, the Administrator shall also consult with the Secretary of the Interior; and

(xvi) program to encourage the voluntary removal from use and the marketplace of pre-1980 model year light duty vehicles and pre-1980 model light duty trucks.

(B) information on additional methods or strategies that will contribute to the reduction of mobile source related pollutants during periods in which any primary ambient air quality standard will be exceeded and during episodes for which an air pollution alert, warning, or emergency has been declared;

(C) information on other measures which may be employed to reduce the impact on public health or protect the health of sensitive or susceptible individuals or groups; and

(D) information on the extent to which any process, procedure, or method to reduce or control such air pollutant may cause an increase in the emissions or formation of any other pollutant.

(2) In publishing such information the Administrator shall also include an assessment of—

(A) the relative effectiveness of such processes, procedures, and methods;

(B) the potential effect of such processes, procedures, and methods on transportation systems and the provision of transportation services; and

(C) the environmental, energy, and economic impact of such processes, procedures, and methods.

(3) The Secretary of Transportation and the Administrator shall submit to Congress by January 1, 1993, and every 3 years thereafter a report that—

(A) reviews and analyzes existing State and local air quality-related transportation programs, including specifically any analyses of whether adequate funding is available to complete transportation projects identified in State implementation plans in the time required by applicable State implementation plans and any Federal efforts to promote those programs;

(B) evaluates the extent to which the Department of Transportation's existing air quality-related transportation programs and such Department's proposed budget will achieve the goals of and compliance with this chapter; and

(C) recommends what, if any, changes to such existing programs and proposed budget as well as any statutory authority relating to air quality-related transportation programs that would improve the achievement of the goals of and compliance with this chapter.

(4) In each report to Congress after the first report required under paragraph (3), the Secretary of Transportation shall include a description of the actions taken to implement the changes recommended in the preceding report.

(g) Assessment of risks to ecosystems

The Administrator may assess the risks to ecosystems from exposure to criteria air pollutants (as identified by the Administrator in the Administrator's sole discretion).

(h) RACT/BACT/LAER clearinghouse

The Administrator shall make information regarding emission control technology available to the States and to the general public through a central database. Such information shall include all control technology information received pursuant to State plan provisions requiring permits for sources, including operating permits for existing sources.

(July 14, 1955, ch. 360, title I, § 108, as added Dec. 31, 1970, Pub.L. 91–604, § 4(a), 84 Stat. 1678, and amended Aug. 7, 1977, Pub.L. 95–95, title I, §§ 104, 105, title IV, § 401(a), 91 Stat. 689, 790; Nov. 15, 1990, Pub.L. 101–549, title I, §§ 108(a)–(c), (*o*), 111, 104 Stat. 2465, 2466, 2469, 2470.)

References in Text

The enactment of the Clean Air Act Amendments of 1989, referred to in subsecs. (e), (f)(1)(A), probably means the date of the enactment of Pub.L. 101–549, which was approved Nov. 15, 1990.

Effective Date of 1990 Amendment

Amendment by Pub.L. 101–549 effective Nov. 15, 1990, except as otherwise provided, see section 711(b) of Pub.L. 101–549, set out as a note under section 7401 of this title.

Savings Provisions

Suits, actions or proceedings commenced under this chapter as in effect prior to Nov. 15, 1990, not to abate by reason of the taking effect of amendments by Pub.L. 101–549, except as otherwise provided for, see section 711(a) of Pub.L. 101–549, set out as a note under section 7401 of this title.

WEST'S FEDERAL PRACTICE MANUAL

Air quality legislation, see § 4384 et seq.

LIBRARY REFERENCES

Health and Environment ⚷25.6(1) et seq., 28.
C.J.S. Health and Environment § 91 et seq.

§ 7409. National primary and secondary ambient air quality standards [CAA § 109]

(a) Promulgation

(1) The Administrator—

(A) within 30 days after December 31, 1970, shall publish proposed regulations prescribing a national primary ambient air quality standard and a national secondary ambient air quality standard for each air pollutant for which air quality criteria have been issued prior to such date; and

(B) after a reasonable time for interested persons to submit written comments thereon (but no later than 90 days after the initial publication of such proposed standards) shall by regulation promulgate such proposed national primary and secondary ambient air quality standards with such modifications as he deems appropriate.

(2) With respect to any air pollutant for which air quality criteria are issued after December 31, 1970, the Administrator shall publish, simultaneously with the issuance of such criteria and information, proposed national primary and secondary ambient air quality standards for any such pollutant. The procedure provided for in paragraph (1)(B) of this subsection shall apply to the promulgation of such standards.

(b) Protection of public health and welfare

(1) National primary ambient air quality standards, prescribed under subsection (a) of this section shall be ambient air quality standards the attainment and maintenance of which in the judgment of the Administrator, based on such criteria and allowing an adequate margin of safety, are requisite to protect the

public health. Such primary standards may be revised in the same manner as promulgated.

(2) Any national secondary ambient air quality standard prescribed under subsection (a) of this section shall specify a level of air quality the attainment and maintenance of which in the judgment of the Administrator, based on such criteria, is requisite to protect the public welfare from any known or anticipated adverse effects associated with the presence of such air pollutant in the ambient air. Such secondary standards may be revised in the same manner as promulgated.

(c) National primary ambient air quality standard for nitrogen dioxide

The Administrator shall, not later than one year after August 7, 1977, promulgate a national primary ambient air quality standard for NO_2 concentrations over a period of not more than 3 hours unless, based on the criteria issued under section 7408(c) of this title, he finds that there is no significant evidence that such a standard for such a period is requisite to protect public health.

(d) Review and revision of criteria and standards; independent scientific review committee; appointment; advisory functions

(1) Not later than December 31, 1980, and at five-year intervals thereafter, the Administrator shall complete a thorough review of the criteria published under section 7408 of this title and the national ambient air quality standards promulgated under this section and shall make such revisions in such criteria and standards and promulgate such new standards as may be appropriate in accordance with section 7408 of this title and subsection (b) of this section. The Administrator may review and revise criteria or promulgate new standards earlier or more frequently than required under this paragraph.

(2)(A) The Administrator shall appoint an independent scientific review committee composed of seven members including at least one member of the National Academy of Sciences, one physician, and one person representing State air pollution control agencies.

(B) Not later than January 1, 1980, and at five-year intervals thereafter, the committee referred to in subparagraph (A) shall complete a review of the criteria published under section 7408 of this title and the national primary and secondary ambient air quality standards promulgated under this section and shall recommend to the Administrator any new national ambient air quality standards and revisions of existing criteria and standards as may be appropriate under section 7408 of this title and subsection (b) of this section.

(C) Such committee shall also (i) advise the Administrator of areas in which additional knowledge is required to appraise the adequacy and basis of existing, new, or revised national ambient air quality standards, (ii) describe the research efforts necessary to provide the required information, (iii) advise the Administrator on the relative contribution to air pollution concentrations of natural as well as anthropogenic activity, and (iv) advise the Administrator of any adverse public health, welfare, social, economic, or energy effects which may result from various strategies for attainment and maintenance of such national ambient air quality standards.

(July 14, 1955, ch. 360, title I, § 109, as added Dec. 31, 1970, Pub.L. 91–604, § 4(a), 84 Stat. 1679, and amended Aug. 7, 1977, Pub.L. 95–95, title I, § 106, 91 Stat. 691.)

Role of Secondary Standards

Pub.L. 101–549, Title VIII, § 817, Nov. 15, 1990, 104 Stat. 2697, provided that:

"**(a) Report.**—The Administrator shall request the National Academy of Sciences to prepare a report to the Congress on the role of national secondary ambient air quality standards in protecting welfare and the environment. The report shall:

"(1) include information on the effects on welfare and the environment which are caused by ambient concentrations of pollutants listed pursuant to section 108 [section 7408 of this title] and other pollutants which may be listed;

"(2) estimate welfare and environmental costs incurred as a result of such effects;

"(3) examine the role of secondary standards and the State implementation planning process in preventing such effects;

"(4) determine ambient concentrations of each such pollutant which would be adequate to protect welfare and the environment from such effects;

"(5) estimate the costs and other impacts of meeting secondary standards; and

"(6) consider other means consistent with the goals and objectives of the Clean Air Act [this chapter] which may be more effective than secondary standards in preventing or mitigating such effects.

"**(b) Submission to Congress; comments; authorization.**—(1) The report shall be transmitted to the Congress not later than 3 years after the date of enactment of the Clean Air Act Amendments of 1990 [Nov. 15, 1990].

"(2) At least 90 days before issuing a report the Administrator shall provide an opportunity for public comment on the proposed report. The Administrator shall include in the final report a summary of the comments received on the proposed report.

"(3) There are authorized to be appropriated such sums as are necessary to carry out this section."

West's Federal Practice Manual

Air quality legislation, see § 4384.5.

CODE OF FEDERAL REGULATIONS

Air programs, generally, see 40 CFR 50.1 et seq.

LAW REVIEW COMMENTARIES

Toxic tort litigation and the causation element: Is there any hope of reconciliation? Fred Harris Jr., 40 Southwestern (Tex.) L.J. 909 (1986).

Library References

Health and Environment ⇨25.6(1) et seq., 28.
C.J.S. Health and Environment § 91 et seq.

§ 7410. State implementation plans for national primary and secondary ambient air quality standards [CAA § 110]

(a) Adoption of plan by State; submission to Administrator; content of plan; revision; indirect source review program; supplemental or intermittent control systems

(1) Each State shall, after reasonable notice and public hearings, adopt and submit to the Administrator, within 3 years (or such shorter period as the Administrator may prescribe) after the promulgation of a national primary ambient air quality standard (or any revision thereof) under section 7409 of this title for any air pollutant, a plan which provides for implementation, maintenance, and enforcement of such primary standard in each air quality control region (or portion thereof) within such State. In addition, such State shall adopt and submit to the Administrator (either as a part of a plan submitted under the preceding sentence or separately) within 3 years (or such shorter period as the Administrator may prescribe) after the promulgation of a national ambient air quality secondary standard (or revision thereof), a plan which provides for implementation, maintenance, and enforcement of such secondary standard in each air quality control region (or portion thereof) within such State. Unless a separate public hearing is provided, each State shall consider its plan implementing such secondary standard at the hearing required by the first sentence of this paragraph.

(2) Each implementation plan submitted by a State under this chapter shall be adopted by the State after reasonable notice and public hearing. Each such plan shall—

(A) include enforceable emission limitations and other control measures, means, or techniques (including economic incentives such as fees, marketable permits, and auctions of emissions rights), as well as schedules and timetables for compliance, as may be necessary or appropriate to meet the applicable requirements of this chapter;

(B) provide for establishment and operation of appropriate devices, methods, systems, and procedures necessary to—

(i) monitor, compile, and analyze data on ambient air quality, and

(ii) upon request, make such data available to the Administrator;

(C) include a program to provide for the enforcement of the measures described in subparagraph (A), and regulation of the modification and construction of any stationary source within the areas covered by the plan as necessary to assure that national ambient air quality standards are achieved, including a permit program as required in parts C and D;

(D) contain adequate provisions—

(i) prohibiting, consistent with the provisions of this subchapter, any source or other type of emissions activity within the State from emitting any air pollutant in amounts which will—

(I) contribute significantly to nonattainment in, or interfere with maintenance by, any other State with respect to any such national primary or secondary ambient air quality standard, or

(II) interfere with measures required to be included in the applicable implementation plan for any other State under part C to prevent significant deterioration of air quality or to protect visibility,

(ii) insuring compliance with the applicable requirements of sections 7426 and 7415 of this title (relating to interstate and international pollution abatement);

(E) provide (i) necessary assurances that the State (or, except where the Administrator deems inappropriate, the general purpose local government or governments, or a regional agency designated by the State or general purpose local governments for such purpose) will have adequate personnel, funding, and authority under State (and, as appropriate, local) law to carry out such implementation plan (and is not prohibited by any provision of Federal or State law from carrying out such implementation plan or portion thereof), (ii) requirements that the State comply with the requirements respecting State boards under section 7428 of this title, and (iii) necessary assurances that, where the State has relied on a local or regional government, agency, or instrumentality for the implementation of any plan provision, the State has responsibility for ensuring adequate implementation of such plan provision;

(F) require, as may be prescribed by the Administrator—

(i) the installation, maintenance, and replacement of equipment, and the implementation of other necessary steps, by owners or operators of stationary sources to monitor emissions from such sources,

(ii) periodic reports on the nature and amounts of emissions and emissions-related data from such sources, and

(iii) correlation of such reports by the State agency with any emission limitations or standards established pursuant to this chapter, which reports shall be available at reasonable times for public inspection;

(G) provide for authority comparable to that in section 7603 of this title and adequate contingency plans to implement such authority;

(H) provide for revision of such plan—

(i) from time to time as may be necessary to take account of revisions of such national primary or secondary ambient air quality standard or the availability of improved or more expeditious methods of attaining such standard, and

(ii) except as provided in paragraph (3)(C), whenever the Administrator finds on the basis of information available to the Administrator that the plan is substantially inadequate to attain the national ambient air quality standard which it implements or to otherwise comply with any additional requirements established under this chapter;

(I) in the case of a plan or plan revision for an area designated as a nonattainment area, meet the applicable requirements of part D (relating to nonattainment areas);

(J) meet the applicable requirements of section 7421 of this title (relating to consultation), section 7427 of this title (relating to public notification), and part C (relating to prevention of significant deterioration of air quality and visibility protection);

(K) provide for—

(i) the performance of such air quality modeling as the Administrator may prescribe for the purpose of predicting the effect on ambient air quality of any emissions of any air pollutant for which the Administrator has established a national ambient air quality standard, and

(ii) the submission, upon request, of data related to such air quality modeling to the Administrator;

(L) require the owner or operator of each major stationary source to pay to the permitting authority, as a condition of any permit required under this chapter, a fee sufficient to cover—

(i) the reasonable costs of reviewing and acting upon any application for such a permit, and

(ii) if the owner or operator receives a permit for such source, the reasonable costs of implementing and enforcing the terms and conditions of any such permit (not including any court costs or other costs associated with any enforcement action),

until such fee requirement is superseded with respect to such sources by the Administrator's approval of a fee program under subchapter V of this chapter; and

(M) provide for consultation and participation by local political subdivisions affected by the plan.

(3)(A) Repealed. Pub.L. 101–549, Title I, § 101(d)(1), Nov. 15, 1990, 104 Stat. 2409.

(B) As soon as practicable, the Administrator shall, consistent with the purposes of this chapter and the Energy Supply and Environmental Coordination Act of 1974 [15 U.S.C.A. § 791 et seq.], review each State's applicable implementation plans and report to the State on whether such plans can be revised in relation to fuel burning stationary sources (or persons supplying fuel to such sources) without interfering with the attainment and maintenance of any national ambient air quality standard within the period permitted in this section. If the Administrator determines that any such plan can be revised, he shall notify the State that a plan revision may be submitted by the State. Any plan revision which is submitted by the State shall, after public notice and opportunity for public hearing, be approved by the Administrator if the revision relates only to fuel burning stationary sources (or persons supplying fuel to such sources), and the plan as revised complies with paragraph (2) of this subsection. The Administrator shall approve or disapprove any revision no later than three months after its submission.

(C) Neither the State, in the case of a plan (or portion thereof) approved under this subsection, nor the Administrator, in the case of a plan (or portion thereof) promulgated under subsection (c) of this section, shall be required to revise an applicable implementation plan because one or more exemptions under section 7418 of this title (relating to Federal facilities), enforcement orders under section 7413(d) of this title, suspensions under subsection (f) or (g) of this section (relating to temporary energy or economic authority), orders under section 7419 of this title (relating to primary nonferrous smelters), or extensions of compliance in decrees entered under section 7413(e) of this title (relating to iron- and steel-producing operations) have been granted, if such plan would have met the requirements of this section if no such exemptions, orders, or extensions had been granted.

(D) Repealed. Pub.L. 101–549, Title I, § 101(d)(1), Nov. 15, 1990, 104 Stat. 2409.

(4) Repealed. Pub.L. 101–549, Title I, § 101(d)(2), Nov. 15, 1990, 104 Stat. 2409.

(5)(A)(i) Any State may include in a State implementation plan, but the Administrator may not require as a condition of approval of such plan under this section, any indirect source review program. The Administrator may approve and enforce, as part of an applicable implementation plan, an indirect source review program which the State chooses to adopt and submit as part of its plan.

(ii) Except as provided in subparagraph (B), no plan promulgated by the Administrator shall include any indirect source review program for any air quality control region, or portion thereof.

(iii) Any State may revise an applicable implementation plan approved under this subsection to suspend or revoke any such program included in such plan, provided that such plan meets the requirements of this section.

(B) The Administrator shall have the authority to promulgate, implement and enforce regulations under subsection (c) of this section respecting indirect source review programs which apply only to federally assisted highways, airports, and other major federally assisted indirect sources and federally owned or operated indirect sources.

(C) For purposes of this paragraph, the term "indirect source" means a facility, building, structure, installation, real property, road, or highway which attracts, or may attract, mobile sources of pollution. Such term includes parking lots, parking garages, and other facilities subject to any measure for management of parking supply (within the meaning of subsection (c)(2)(D)(ii) of this section), including regulation of existing off-street parking but such term does not include new or existing on-street parking. Direct emissions sources or facilities at, within, or associated with, any indirect source shall not be deemed indirect sources for the purpose of this paragraph.

(D) For purposes of this paragraph the term "indirect source review program" means the facility-by-facility review of indirect sources of air pollution, including such measures as are necessary to assure, or assist in assuring, that a new or modified indirect source will not attract mobile sources of air pollution, the emissions from which would cause or contribute to air pollution concentrations—

(i) exceeding any national primary ambient air quality standard for a mobile source-related air pollutant after the primary standard attainment date, or

(ii) preventing maintenance of any such standard after such date.

(E) For purposes of this paragraph and paragraph (2)(B), the term "transportation control measure" does not include any measure which is an "indirect source review program".

(6) No State plan shall be treated as meeting the requirements of this section unless such plan provides that in the case of any source which uses a supplemental, or intermittent control system for purposes of meeting the requirements of an order under section 7413(d) of this title or section 7419 of this title (relating to primary nonferrous smelter orders), the owner or operator of such source may not temporarily reduce the pay of any employee by reason of the use of such supplemental or intermittent or other dispersion dependent control system.

(b) Extension of period for submission of plans

The Administrator may, wherever he determines necessary, extend the period for submission of any plan or portion thereof which implements a national secondary ambient air quality standard for a period not to exceed 18 months from the date otherwise required for submission of such plan.

(c) Preparation and publication by Administrator of proposed regulations setting forth implementation plan; parking surcharge; plan implementation

(1) The Administrator shall promulgate a Federal implementation plan at any time within 2 years after the Administrator—

(A) finds that a State has failed to make a required submission or finds that the plan or plan revision submitted by the State does not satisfy the minimum criteria established under section 7410(k)(1)(A) of this title, or

(B) disapproves a State implementation plan submission in whole or in part,

unless the State corrects the deficiency, and the Administrator approves the plan or plan revision, before the Administrator promulgates such Federal implementation plan.

(2)(A) Repealed. Pub.L. 101–549, Title I, § 101(d)(3)(A), Nov. 15, 1990, 104 Stat. 2409.

(B) No parking surcharge regulation may be required by the Administrator under paragraph (1) of this subsection as a part of an applicable implementation plan. All parking surcharge regulations previously required by the Administrator shall be void upon June 22, 1974. This subparagraph shall not prevent the Administrator from approving parking surcharges if they are adopted and submitted by a State as part of an applicable implementation plan. The Administrator may not condition approval of any implementation plan submitted by a State on such plan's including a parking surcharge regulation.

(C) Repealed. Pub.L. 101–549, Title I, § 101(d)(3)(B), Nov. 15, 1990, 104 Stat. 2409.

(D) For purposes of this paragraph—

(i) The term "parking surcharge regulation" means a regulation imposing or requiring the imposition of any tax, surcharge, fee, or other charge on parking spaces, or any other area used for the temporary storage of motor vehicles.

(ii) The term "management of parking supply" shall include any requirement providing that any new facility containing a given number of parking spaces shall receive a permit or other prior approval, issuance of which is to be conditioned on air quality considerations.

(iii) The term "preferential bus/carpool lane" shall include any requirement for the setting aside of one or more lanes of a street or highway on a permanent or temporary basis for the exclusive use of buses or carpools, or both.

(E) No standard, plan, or requirement, relating to management of parking supply or preferential bus/carpool lanes shall be promulgated after June 22, 1974, by the Administrator pursuant to this section, unless such promulgation has been subjected to at least one public hearing which has been held in the area affected and for which reasonable notice has been given in such area. If substantial changes are made following public hearings, one or more additional hearings shall be held in such area after such notice.

(3) Upon application of the chief executive officer of any general purpose unit of local government, if the Administrator determines that such unit has adequate authority under State or local law, the Administrator may delegate to such unit the authority to implement and enforce within the jurisdiction of such unit any part of a plan promulgated under this subsection. Nothing in this paragraph shall prevent the Administrator from implementing or enforcing any applicable provision of a plan promulgated under this subsection.

(4) **Repealed.** Pub.L. 101–549, Title I, § 101(d)(3)(C), Nov. 15, 1990, 104 Stat. 2409.

(5)(A) Any measure in an applicable implementation plan which requires a toll or other charge for the use of a bridge located entirely within one city shall be eliminated from such plan by the Administrator upon application by the Governor of the State, which application shall include a certification by the Governor that he will revise such plan in accordance with subparagraph (B).

(B) In the case of any applicable implementation plan with respect to which a measure has been eliminated under subparagraph (A), such plan shall, not later than one year after August 7, 1977, be revised to include comprehensive measures to:

(i) establish, expand, or improve public transportation measures to meet basic transportation needs, as expeditiously as is practicable; and

(ii) implement transportation control measures necessary to attain and maintain national ambient air quality standards,

and such revised plan shall, for the purpose of implementing such comprehensive public transportation measures, include requirements to use (insofar as is necessary) Federal grants, State or local funds, or any combination of such grants and funds as may be consistent with the terms of the legislation providing such grants and funds. Such measures shall, as a substitute for the tolls or charges eliminated under subparagraph (A), provide for emissions reductions equivalent to the reductions which may reasonably be expected to be achieved through the use of the tolls or charges eliminated.

(C) Any revision of an implementation plan for purposes of meeting the requirements of subparagraph (B) shall be submitted in coordination with any plan revision required under part D of this subchapter.

(d), (e) Repealed. Pub.L. 101–549, Title I, § 101(d)(4), (5), Nov. 15, 1990, 104 Stat. 2409.

(f) National or regional energy emergencies; determination by President

(1) Upon application by the owner or operator of a fuel burning stationary source, and after notice and opportunity for public hearing, the Governor of the State in which such source is located may petition the President to determine that a national or regional energy emergency exists of such severity that—

(A) a temporary suspension of any part of the applicable implementation plan or of any requirement under section 7651j of this title (concerning excess emissions penalties or offsets) may be necessary, and

(B) other means of responding to the energy emergency may be inadequate.

Such determination shall not be delegable by the President to any other person. If the President determines that a national or regional energy emergency of such severity exists, a temporary emergency suspension of any part of an applicable implementation plan or of any requirement under section 7651j of this title (concerning excess emissions penalties or offsets) adopted by the State may be issued by the Governor of any State covered by the President's determination under the condition specified in paragraph (2) and may take effect immediately.

(2) A temporary emergency suspension under this subsection shall be issued to a source only if the Governor of such State finds that—

(A) there exists in the vicinity of such source a temporary energy emergency involving high levels of unemployment or loss of necessary energy supplies for residential dwellings; and

(B) such unemployment or loss can be totally or partially alleviated by such emergency suspension.

Not more than one such suspension may be issued for any source on the basis of the same set of circumstances or on the basis of the same emergency.

(3) A temporary emergency suspension issued by a Governor under this subsection shall remain in effect for a maximum of four months or such lesser period as may be specified in a disapproval order of the Administrator, if any. The Administrator may disapprove such suspension if he determines that it does not meet the requirements of paragraph (2).

(4) This subsection shall not apply in the case of a plan provision or requirement promulgated by the Administrator under subsection (c) of this section, but in any such case the President may grant a temporary emergency suspension for a four month period of any such provision or requirement if he makes the determinations and findings specified in paragraphs (1) and (2).

(5) The Governor may include in any temporary emergency suspension issued under this subsection a provision delaying for a period identical to the period of such suspension any compliance schedule (or increment of progress) to which such source is subject under section 1857c–10 of this title, as in effect before August 7, 1977, or section 7413(d) of this title, upon a finding that such source is unable to comply with such schedule (or increment) solely because of the conditions on the basis of which a suspension was issued under this subsection.

(g) Governor's authority to issue temporary emergency suspensions

(1) In the case of any State which has adopted and submitted to the Administrator a proposed plan revision which the State determines—

(A) meets the requirements of this section, and

(B) is necessary (i) to prevent the closing for one year or more of any source of air pollution, and (ii) to prevent substantial increases in unemployment which would result from such closing, and

which the Administrator has not approved or disapproved under this section within 12 months of submission of the proposed plan revision, the Governor may issue a temporary emergency suspension of the part of the applicable implementation plan for such State which is proposed to be revised with respect to such source. The determination under subparagraph (B) may not be made with respect to a source which would close without regard to whether or not the proposed plan revision is approved.

(2) A temporary emergency suspension issued by a Governor under this subsection shall remain in effect for a maximum of four months or such lesser period as may be specified in a disapproval order of the Administrator. The Administrator may disapprove such suspension if he determines that it does not meet the requirements of this subsection.

(3) The Governor may include in any temporary emergency suspension issued under this subsection a provision delaying for a period identical to the period of such suspension any compliance schedule (or increment of progress) to which such source is subject under section 1857c–10 of this title as in effect before August 7, 1977, or under section 7413(d) of this title upon a finding that such source is unable to comply with such schedule (or increment) solely because of the conditions on the basis of which a suspension was issued under this subsection.

(h) Publication of comprehensive document for each State setting forth requirements of applicable implementation plan

(1) Not later than 5 years after November 15, 1990, and every 3 years thereafter, the Administrator shall assemble and publish a comprehensive document for each State setting forth all requirements of the applicable implementation plan for such State and shall publish notice in the Federal Register of the availability of such documents.

(2) The Administrator may promulgate such regulations as may be reasonably necessary to carry out the purpose of this subsection.

(i) Modification of requirements prohibited

Except for a primary nonferrous smelter order under section 7419 of this title, a suspension under subsection (f) or (g) of this section (relating to emergency suspensions), an exemption under section 7418 of this title (relating to certain Federal facilities), an order under section 7413(d) of this title (relating to compliance orders), a plan promulgation under subsection (c) of this section, or a plan revision under subsection (a)(3) of this section; no order, suspension, plan revision, or other action modifying any requirement of an applicable implementation plan may be taken with respect to any stationary source by the State or by the Administrator.

(j) Technological systems of continuous emission reduction on new or modified stationary sources; compliance with performance standards

As a condition for issuance of any permit required under this subchapter, the owner or operator of each new or modified stationary source which is required to obtain such a permit must show to the satisfaction of the permitting authority that the technological system of continuous emission reduction which is to be used will enable such source to comply with the standards of performance which are to apply to such source and that the construction or modification and operation of such source will be in compliance with all other requirements of this chapter.

(k) Environmental Protection Agency action on plan submissions

(1) Completeness of plan submissions

(A) Completeness criteria

Within 9 months after November 15, 1990, the Administrator shall promulgate minimum criteria that any plan submission must meet before the Administrator is required to act on such submission under this subsection. The criteria shall be limited to the information necessary to enable the Administrator to determine whether the plan submission complies with the provisions of this chapter.

(B) Completeness finding

Within 60 days of the Administrator's receipt of a plan or plan revision, but no later than 6 months after the date, if any, by which a State is required to submit the plan or revision, the Administrator shall determine whether the minimum criteria established pursuant to subparagraph (A) have been met. Any plan or plan revision that a State submits to the Administrator, and that has not been determined by the Administrator (by the date 6 months after receipt of the submission) to have failed to meet the minimum criteria established pursuant to subparagraph (A), shall on that date be deemed by operation of law to meet such minimum criteria.

(C) Effect of finding of incompleteness

Where the Administrator determines that a plan submission (or part thereof) does not meet the minimum criteria established pursuant to subparagraph (A), the State shall be treated as not having made the submission (or, in the Administrator's discretion, part thereof).

(2) Deadline for action

Within 12 months of a determination by the Administrator (or a determination deemed by operation of law) under paragraph (1) that a State has submitted a plan or plan revision (or, in the Administrator's discretion, part thereof) that meets the minimum criteria established pursuant to paragraph (1), if applicable (or, if those criteria are not applicable, within 12 months of submission of the plan or revision), the Administrator shall act on the submission in accordance with paragraph (3).

(3) Full and partial approval and disapproval

In the case of any submittal on which the Administrator is required to act under paragraph (2), the Administrator shall approve such submittal as a whole if it meets all of the applicable requirements of this chapter. If a portion of the plan revision meets all the applicable requirements of this chapter, the Administrator may approve the plan revision in part and disapprove the plan revision in part. The plan revision shall not be treated as meeting the requirements of this chapter until the Administrator approves the entire plan revision as complying with the applicable requirements of this chapter.

(4) Conditional approval

The Administrator may approve a plan revision based on a commitment of the State to adopt specific enforceable measures by a date certain, but not later than 1 year after the date of approval of the plan revision. Any such conditional approval shall be treated as a disapproval if the State fails to comply with such commitment.

(5) Calls for plan revisions

Whenever the Administrator finds that the applicable implementation plan for any area is substantially inadequate to attain or maintain the relevant national ambient air quality standard, to mitigate adequately the interstate pollutant transport described in section 7506a or section 7511c of this title, or to otherwise comply with any requirement of this chapter, the Administrator shall require the State to revise the plan as necessary to correct such inadequacies. The Administrator shall notify the State of the inadequacies, and may establish reasonable deadlines (not to exceed 18 months after the date of such notice) for the submission of such plan revisions. Such findings and notice shall be public. Any finding under this paragraph shall, to the extent the Administrator deems appropriate, subject the State to the requirements of this chapter to which the State was subject when it developed and submitted the plan for which such finding was made, except that the Administrator may adjust any dates applicable under such requirements as appropriate (except that the Administrator may not adjust any attainment date prescribed under part D, unless such date has elapsed).

(6) Corrections

Whenever the Administrator determines that the Administrator's action approving, disapproving, or promulgating any plan or plan revision (or part thereof), area designation, redesignation, classification, or reclassification was in error, the Administrator may in the same manner as the approval, disapproval, or promulgation revise such action as appropriate without requiring any further submission from the State. Such determination and the basis thereof shall be provided to the State and public.

(*l*) Plan revisions

Each revision to an implementation plan submitted by a State under this chapter shall be adopted by such State after reasonable notice and public hearing. The Administrator shall not approve a revision of a plan if the revision would interfere with any applicable requirement concerning attainment and reasonable further progress (as defined in section 7501 of this title), or any other applicable requirement of this chapter.

(m) Sanctions

The Administrator may apply any of the sanctions listed in section 7509(b) of this title at any time (or at any time after) the Administrator makes a finding, disapproval, or determination under paragraphs (1) through (4), respectively, of section 7509(a) of this title in relation to any plan or plan item (as that term is defined by the Administrator) required under this chapter, with respect to any portion of the State the Administrator determines reasonable and appropriate, for the purpose of ensuring that the requirements of this chapter relating to such plan or plan item are met. The Administrator shall, by rule, establish criteria for exercising his authority under the previous sentence with respect to any deficiency referred to in section 7509(a) of this title to ensure that, during the 24-month period following the finding, disapproval, or determination referred to in section 7509(a) of this title, such sanctions are not applied on a statewide basis where one or more political subdivisions covered by the applicable implementation plan are principally responsible for such deficiency.

(n) Savings clauses

(1) Existing plan provisions

Any provision of any applicable implementation plan that was approved or promulgated by the Administrator pursuant to this section as in effect before November 15, 1990, shall remain in effect as part of such applicable implementation plan, except to the extent that a revision to such provision is approved or promulgated by the Administrator pursuant to this chapter.

(2) Attainment dates

For any area not designated non-attainment, any plan or plan revision submitted or required to be submitted by a State—

(A) in response to the promulgation or revision of a national primary ambient air quality standard in effect on November 15, 1990, or

(B) in response to a finding of substantial inadequacy under subsection (a)(2) of this section (as in effect immediately before November 15, 1990),

shall provide for attainment of the national primary ambient air quality standards within 3 years of November 15, 1990, or within 5 years of issuance of such finding of substantial inadequacy, whichever is later.

(3) Retention of construction moratorium in certain areas

In the case of an area to which, immediately before November 15, 1990, the prohibition on construction or modification of major stationary sources prescribed in subsection (a)(2)(I) of this section (as in effect immediately before November 15, 1990) applied by virtue of a finding of the Administrator that the State containing such area had not submitted an implementation plan meeting the requirements of section 7502(b)(6) (relating to establishment of a permit program) (as in effect immediately before November 15, 1990) or 7502(a)(1) of this title (to the extent such requirements relate to provision for attainment of the primary national ambient air quality standard for sulfur oxides by December 31, 1982) as in effect immediately before November 15, 1990, no major stationary source of the relevant air pollutant or pollutants shall be constructed or modified in such area until the Administrator finds that the plan for such area meets the applicable requirements of section 7502(c)(5) of this title (relating to permit programs) or subpart 5 of part D (relating to attainment of the primary national ambient air quality standard for sulfur dioxide), respectively.

(*o*) Indian tribes

If an Indian tribe submits an implementation plan to the Administrator pursuant to section 7601(d) of this title, the plan shall be reviewed in accordance with the provisions for review set forth in this section for State plans, except as otherwise provided by regulation promulgated pursuant to section 7601(d)(2) of this title. When such plan becomes effective in accordance with the regulations promulgated under section 7601(d) of this title, the plan shall become applicable to all areas (except as expressly provided otherwise in the plan) located within the exterior boundaries of the reservation, notwithstanding the issuance of any patent and including rights-of-way running through the reservation.

(p) Reports

Any State shall submit, according to such schedule as the Administrator may prescribe, such reports as the Administrator may require relating to emission reductions, vehicle miles traveled, congestion levels, and any other information the Administrator may deem necessary to assess the development effectiveness, need for revision, or implementation of any plan or plan revision required under this chapter.

(July 14, 1955, ch. 369, title I, § 110, as added Dec. 31, 1970, Pub.L. 91–604, § 4(a), 84 Stat. 1680, and amended June 22, 1974, Pub.L. 93–319, § 4, 88 Stat. 256; S.Res. 4, Feb. 4, 1977; Aug. 4, 1977, Pub.L. 95–91, title III, § 301(a), title VII, § 703, 91 Stat. 577, 606; Aug. 7, 1977, Pub.L. 95–95, title I, §§ 107, 108, 91 Stat. 691, 693; Nov. 16, 1977, Pub.L. 95–190, § 14(a)(1)–(6), 91 Stat. 1399; July 17, 1981, Pub.L. 97–23, § 3, 95 Stat. 142; Nov. 15, 1990, Pub.L. 101–549, title I, §§ 101(b)–(d), 102(h), 107(c), 108(d), title IV, § 412, 104 Stat. 2404–2408, 2422, 2464, 2466, 2634.)

References in Text

"Section 1857c–10 of this title, as in effect before August 7, 1977", referred to in subsecs. (f)(5) and (g)(3) was, in the original, "section 119, as in effect before the date of the enactment of this paragraph", meaning section 119 of Act July 14, 1955, c. 360, Title I, as added June 22, 1974, Pub.L. 93–319, § 3, 88 Stat. 248, (which was classified to section 1857c–10 of this title) as in effect prior to the enactment of subsecs. (f)(5) and (g)(3) of this section by Pub.L. 95–95, § 107, Aug. 7, 1977, 91 Stat. 691, effective Aug. 7, 1977. Section 112(b)(1) of Pub.L. 95–95 repealed section 119 of Act July 14, 1955, c. 360, Title I, as added by Pub.L. 93–319, and provided that all references to such section 119 in any subsequent enactment which supersedes Pub.L. 93–319 shall be construed to refer to section 113(d) of the Clean Air Act and to paragraph (5) thereof in particular which is classified to section 7413(d)(5) of this title. Section 117(b) of Pub.L. 95–95 added a new section 119 of Act July 14, 1955, which is classified to section 7419 of this title.

Effective Date of 1990 Amendment

Amendment by Pub.L. 101–549 effective Nov. 15, 1990, except as otherwise provided, see section 711(b) of Pub.L. 101–549, set out as a note under section 7401 of this title.

Savings Provisions

Suits, actions or proceedings commenced under this chapter as in effect prior to Nov. 15, 1990, not to abate by reason of the taking effect of amendments by Pub.L. 101–549, except as otherwise provided for, see section 711(a) of Pub.L. 101–549, set out as a note under section 7401 of this title.

CROSS REFERENCES

Documentation includable in petition to President to exercise authorities pursuant to section 7425 of this title with respect to major fuel burning stationary source to support finding of significant local or regional economic disruption or unemployment, see section 6215 of this title.

Federally permitted release defined to include emissions into air subject to permit or control regulation under state implementation plan submitted in accordance with this section for purposes of Comprehensive Environmental Response, Compensation, and Liability Act of 1980, see section 9601 of this title.

Permit authorizing increased uses of petroleum by existing powerplants, necessity of certification that powerplant cannot comply with requirements of implementation plan, see section 8375 of this title.

Suspension of emission limitations or other requirements of applicable implementation plans required by emergency prohibition on use of natural gas or petroleum to be issued in accordance with subsec. (f) of this section, see section 8374 of this title.

CODE OF FEDERAL REGULATIONS

Environmental Protection Agency,
- Ambient air quality surveillance, see 40 CFR 58.1 et seq.
- Emission standards for hazardous pollutants, see 40 CFR 61.01 et seq.

Implementation plans, generally, see 40 CFR 51.40 et seq.
- Implementation plans, requirements concerning, see 40 CFR 51.1 et seq.
- National primary and secondary ambient air quality standards, see 40 CFR 50.1 et seq.
- New stationary sources, performance standards for, see 40 CFR 60.1 et seq.
- Primary nonferrous smelter orders, see 40 CFR 57.101 et seq.

West's Federal Practice Manual

Air quality legislation, see § 4384.5.

LAW REVIEW COMMENTARIES

Resolving conflicts between bankruptcy law and the state police power. Ellen E. Sward, 1987 Wis.L.Rev. 403 (1987).

Toxic tort litigation and the causation element: Is there any hope of reconciliation? Or a Fred Harris, Jr., 40 Southwestern (Tex.) L.J. 909 (1986).

Library References

Health and Environment ⇐25.6(1) et seq., 28.
States ⇐4.19.
C.J.S. Health and Environment § 91 et seq.
C.J.S. States § 28.

United States Supreme Court

Approval of plan, economic and technological feasibility, see Union Elec. Co. v. Environmental Protection Agency, 1976, 96 S.Ct. 2518, 427 U.S. 246, 49 L.Ed.2d 474.

Extension of time for revision of plan, see Train v. Natural Resources Defense Council, Inc., 1975, 95 S.Ct. 1470, 421 U.S. 60, 43 L.Ed.2d 731.

§ 7411. Standards of performance for new stationary sources [CAA § 111]

(a) Definitions

For purposes of this section:

(1) The term "standard of performance" means a standard for emissions of air pollutants which reflects the degree of emission limitation achievable through the application of the best system of emission reduction which (taking into account the cost of achieving such reduction and any nonair quality health and environmental impact and energy requirements) the Administrator determines has been adequately demonstrated."

(2) The term "new source" means any stationary source, the construction or modification of which is commenced after the publication of regulations (or, if earlier, proposed regulations) prescribing a standard of performance under this section which will be applicable to such source.

(3) The term "stationary source" means any building, structure, facility, or installation which emits or may emit any air pollutant. Nothing in subchapter II of this chapter relating to nonroad

engines shall be construed to apply to stationary internal combustion engines.

(4) The term "modification" means any physical change in, or change in the method of operation of, a stationary source which increases the amount of any air pollutant emitted by such source or which results in the emission of any air pollutant not previously emitted.

(5) The term "owner or operator" means any person who owns, leases, operates, controls, or supervises a stationary source.

(6) The term "existing source" means any stationary source other than a new source.

(7) The term "technological system of continuous emission reduction" means—

(A) a technological process for production or operation by any source which is inherently low-polluting or nonpolluting, or

(B) a technological system for continuous reduction of the pollution generated by a source before such pollution is emitted into the ambient air, including precombustion cleaning or treatment of fuels.

(8) A conversion to coal (A) by reason of an order under section 2(a) of the Energy Supply and Environmental Coordination Act of 1974 [15 U.S.C.A. § 792(a)] or any amendment thereto, or any subsequent enactment which supersedes such Act [15 U.S.C.A. § 791 et seq.], or (B) which qualifies under section 7413(d)(5)(A)(ii) of this title, shall not be deemed to be a modification for purposes of paragraphs (2) and (4) of this subsection.

(b) List of categories of stationary sources; standards of performance; information on pollution control techniques; sources owned or operated by United States; particular systems; revised standards

(1)(A) The Administrator shall, within 90 days after December 31, 1970, publish (and from time to time thereafter shall revise) a list of categories of stationary sources. He shall include a category of sources in such list if in his judgment it causes, or contributes significantly to, air pollution which may reasonably be anticipated to endanger public health or welfare.

(B) Within one year after the inclusion of a category of stationary sources in a list under subparagraph (A), the Administrator shall publish proposed regulations, establishing Federal standards of performance for new sources within such category. The Administrator shall afford interested persons an opportunity for written comment on such proposed regulations. After considering such comments, he shall promulgate, within one year after such publication, such standards with such modifications as he deems appropriate. The Administrator shall, at least every 8 years, review and, if appropriate, revise such standards following the procedure required by this subsection for promulgation of such standards. Notwithstanding the requirements of the previous sentence, the Administrator need not review any such standard if the Administrator determines that such review is not appropriate in light of readily available information on the efficacy of such standard. Standards of performance or revisions thereof shall become effective upon promulgation. When implementation and enforcement of any requirement of this chapter indicate that emission limitations and percent reductions beyond those required by the standards promulgated under this section are achieved in practice, the Administrator shall, when revising standards promulgated under this section, consider the emission limitations and percent reductions achieved in practice.

(2) The Administrator may distinguish among classes, types, and sizes within categories of new sources for the purpose of establishing such standards.

(3) The Administrator shall, from time to time, issue information on pollution control techniques for categories of new sources and air pollutants subject to the provisions of this section.

(4) The provisions of this section shall apply to any new source owned or operated by the United States.

(5) Except as otherwise authorized under subsection (h) of this section, nothing in this section shall be construed to require, or to authorize the Administrator to require, any new or modified source to install and operate any particular technological system of continuous emission reduction to comply with any new source standard of performance.

(6) The revised standards of performance required by enactment of subsection (a)(1)(A)(i) and (ii) of this section shall be promulgated not later than one year after August 7, 1977. Any new or modified fossil fuel fired stationary source which commences construction prior to the date of publication of the proposed revised standards shall not be required to comply with such revised standards.

(c) State implementation and enforcement of standards of performance

(1) Each State may develop and submit to the Administrator a procedure for implementing and enforcing standards of performance for new sources located in such State. If the Administrator finds the State procedure is adequate, he shall delegate to such State any authority he has under this chapter to implement and enforce such standards.

(2) Nothing in this subsection shall prohibit the Administrator from enforcing any applicable standard of performance under this section.

(d) Standards of performance for existing sources; remaining useful life of source

(1) The Administrator shall prescribe regulations which shall establish a procedure similar to that provided by section 7410 of this title under which each State shall submit to the Administrator a plan which (A) establishes standards of performance for any existing source for any air pollutant (i) for which air quality criteria have not been issued or which is not included on a list published under section 7408(a) or emitted from a source category which is regulated under section 7412 of this title but (ii) to which a standard of performance under this section would apply if such existing source were a new source, and (B) provides for the implementation and enforcement of such standards of performance. Regulations of the Administrator under this paragraph shall permit the State in applying a standard of performance to any particular source under a plan submitted under this paragraph to take into consideration, among other factors, the remaining useful life of the existing source to which such standard applies.

(2) The Administrator shall have the same authority—

(A) to prescribe a plan for a State in cases where the State fails to submit a satisfactory plan as he would have under section 7410(c) of this title in the case of failure to submit an implementation plan, and

(B) to enforce the provisions of such plan in cases where the State fails to enforce them as he would have under sections 7413 and 7414 of this title with respect to an implementation plan.

In promulgating a standard of performance under a plan prescribed under this paragraph, the Administrator shall take into consideration, among other factors, remaining useful lives of the sources in the category of sources to which such standard applies.

(e) Prohibited acts

After the effective date of standards of performance promulgated under this section, it shall be unlawful for any owner or operator of any new source to operate such source in violation of any standard of performance applicable to such source.

(f) New source standards of performance

(1) For those categories of major stationary sources that the Administrator listed under subsection (b)(1)(A) of this section before November 15, 1990, and for which regulations had not been proposed by the Administrator by such date, the Administrator shall—

(A) propose regulations establishing standards of performance for at least 25 percent of such categories of sources within 2 years after November 15, 1990;

(B) propose regulations establishing standards of performance for at least 50 percent of such categories of sources within 4 years after November 15, 1990; and

(C) propose regulations for the remaining categories of sources within 6 years after November 15, 1990.

(2) In determining priorities for promulgating standards for categories of major stationary sources for the purpose of paragraph (1), the Administrator shall consider—

(A) the quantity of air pollutant emissions which each such category will emit, or will be designed to emit;

(B) the extent to which each such pollutant may reasonably be anticipated to endanger public health or welfare; and

(C) the mobility and competitive nature of each such category of sources and the consequent need for nationally applicable new source standards of performance.

(3) Before promulgating any regulations under this subsection or listing any category of major stationary sources as required under this subsection, the Administrator shall consult with appropriate representatives of the Governors and of State air pollution control agencies.

(g) Revision of regulations

(1) Upon application by the Governor of a State showing that the Administrator has failed to specify in regulations under subsection (f)(1) of this section any category of major stationary sources required to be specified under such regulations, the Administrator shall revise such regulations to specify any such category.

(2) Upon application of the Governor of a State, showing that any category of stationary sources which is not included in the list under subsection (b)(1)(A) of this section contributes significantly to air pollution which may reasonably be anticipated to endanger public health or welfare (notwithstanding that such category is not a category of major stationary sources), the Administrator shall revise such regulations to specify such category of stationary sources.

(3) Upon application of the Governor of a State showing that the Administrator has failed to apply

properly the criteria required to be considered under subsection (f)(2) of this section, the Administrator shall revise the list under subsection (b)(1)(A) of this section to apply properly such criteria.

(4) Upon application of the Governor of a State showing that—

(A) a new, innovative, or improved technology or process which achieves greater continuous emission reduction has been adequately demonstrated for any category of stationary sources, and

(B) as a result of such technology or process, the new source standard of performance in effect under this section for such category no longer reflects the greatest degree of emission limitation achievable through application of the best technological system of continuous emission reduction which (taking into consideration the cost of achieving such emission reduction, and any non-air quality health and environmental impact and energy requirements) has been adequately demonstrated,

the Administrator shall revise such standard of performance for such category accordingly.

(5) Unless later deadlines for action of the Administrator are otherwise prescribed under this section, the Administrator shall, not later than three months following the date of receipt of any application by a Governor of a State, either—

(A) find that such application does not contain the requisite showing and deny such application, or

(B) grant such application and take the action required under this subsection.

(6) Before taking any action required by subsection (f) of this section or by this subsection, the Administrator shall provide notice and opportunity for public hearing.

(h) Design, equipment, work practice, or operational standard; alternative emission limitation

(1) For purposes of this section, if in the judgment of the Administrator, it is not feasible to prescribe or enforce a standard of performance, he may instead promulgate a design, equipment, work practice, or operational standard, or combination thereof, which reflects the best technological system of continuous emission reduction which (taking into consideration the cost of achieving such emission reduction, and any non-air quality health and environmental impact and energy requirements) the Administrator determines has been adequately demonstrated. In the event the Administrator promulgates a design or equipment standard under this subsection, he shall include as part of such standard such requirements as will assure the proper operation and maintenance of any such element of design or equipment.

(2) For the purpose of this subsection, the phrase "not feasible to prescribe or enforce a standard of performance" means any situation in which the Administrator determines that (A) a pollutant or pollutants cannot be emitted through a conveyance designed and constructed to emit or capture such pollutant, or that any requirement for, or use of, such a conveyance would be inconsistent with any Federal, State, or local law, or (B) the application of measurement methodology to a particular class of sources is not practicable due to technological or economic limitations.

(3) If after notice and opportunity for public hearing, any person establishes to the satisfaction of the Administrator that an alternative means of emission limitation will achieve a reduction in emissions of any air pollutant at least equivalent to the reduction in emissions of such air pollutant achieved under the requirements of paragraph (1), the Administrator shall permit the use of such alternative by the source for purposes of compliance with this section with respect to such pollutant.

(4) Any standard promulgated under paragraph (1) shall be promulgated in terms of standard of performance whenever it becomes feasible to promulgate and enforce such standard in such terms.

(5) Any design, equipment, work practice, or operational standard, or any combination thereof, described in this subsection shall be treated as a standard of performance for purposes of the provisions of this chapter (other than the provisions of subsection (a) of this section and this subsection).

(i) Country elevators

Any regulations promulgated by the Administrator under this section applicable to grain elevators shall not apply to country elevators (as defined by the Administrator) which have a storage capacity of less than two million five hundred thousand bushels.

(j) Innovative technological systems of continuous emission reduction

(1)(A) Any person proposing to own or operate a new source may request the Administrator for one or more waivers from the requirements of this section for such source or any portion thereof with respect to any air pollutant to encourage the use of an innovative technological system or systems of continuous emission reduction. The Administrator may, with the consent of the Governor of the State in which the source is to be located, grant a waiver under this paragraph, if the Administrator determines after notice and opportunity for public hearing, that—

(i) the proposed system or systems have not been adequately demonstrated,

(ii) the proposed system or systems will operate effectively and there is a substantial likelihood that such system or systems will achieve greater continuous emission reduction than that required to be achieved under the standards of performance which would otherwise apply, or achieve at least an equivalent reduction at lower cost in terms of energy, economic, or nonair quality environmental impact,

(iii) the owner or operator of the proposed source has demonstrated to the satisfaction of the Administrator that the proposed system will not cause or contribute to an unreasonable risk to public health, welfare, or safety in its operation, function, or malfunction, and

(iv) the granting of such waiver is consistent with the requirements of subparagraph (C).

In making any determination under clause (ii), the Administrator shall take into account any previous failure of such system or systems to operate effectively or to meet any requirement of the new source performance standards. In determining whether an unreasonable risk exists under clause (iii), the Administrator shall consider, among other factors, whether and to what extent the use of the proposed technological system will cause, increase, reduce, or eliminate emissions of any unregulated pollutants; available methods for reducing or eliminating any risk to public health, welfare, or safety which may be associated with the use of such system; and the availability of other technological systems which may be used to conform to standards under this section without causing or contributing to such unreasonable risk. The Administrator may conduct such tests and may require the owner or operator of the proposed source to conduct such tests and provide such information as is necessary to carry out clause (iii) of this subparagraph. Such requirements shall include a requirement for prompt reporting of the emission of any unregulated pollutant from a system if such pollutant was not emitted, or was emitted in significantly lesser amounts without use of such system.

(B) A waiver under this paragraph shall be granted on such terms and conditions as the Administrator determines to be necessary to assure—

(i) emissions from the source will not prevent attainment and maintenance of any national ambient air quality standards, and

(ii) proper functioning of the technological system or systems authorized.

Any such term or condition shall be treated as a standard of performance for the purposes of subsection (e) of this section and section 7413 of this title.

(C) The number of waivers granted under this paragraph with respect to a proposed technological system of continuous emission reduction shall not exceed such number as the Administrator finds necessary to ascertain whether or not such system will achieve the conditions specified in clauses (ii) and (iii) of subparagraph (A).

(D) A waiver under this paragraph shall extend to the sooner of—

(i) the date determined by the Administrator, after consultation with the owner or operator of the source, taking into consideration the design, installation, and capital cost of the technological system or systems being used, or

(ii) the date on which the Administrator determines that such system has failed to—

(I) achieve at least an equivalent continuous emission reduction to that required to be achieved under the standards of performance which would otherwise apply, or

(II) comply with the condition specified in paragraph (1)(A)(iii),

and that such failure cannot be corrected.

(E) In carrying out subparagraph (D)(i), the Administrator shall not permit any waiver for a source or portion thereof to extend beyond the date—

(i) seven years after the date on which any waiver is granted to such source or portion thereof, or

(ii) four years after the date on which such source or portion thereof commences operation,

whichever is earlier.

(F) No waiver under this subsection shall apply to any portion of a source other than the portion on which the innovative technological system or systems of continuous emission reduction is used.

(2)(A) If a waiver under paragraph (1) is terminated under clause (ii) of paragraph (1)(D), the Administrator shall grant an extension of the requirements of this section for such source for such minimum period as may be necessary to comply with the applicable standard of performance under this section. Such period shall not extend beyond the date three years from the time such waiver is terminated.

(B) An extension granted under this paragraph shall set forth emission limits and a compliance schedule containing increments of progress which require compliance with the applicable standards of performance as expeditiously as practicable and include such measures as are necessary and practicable in the interim to minimize emissions. Such schedule shall be treated as a standard of performance for purposes of subsection (e) of this section and section 7413 of this title.

(July 14, 1955, ch. 360, title I, § 111, as added Dec. 31, 1970, Pub.L. 91–604, § 4(a), 84 Stat. 1683, and amended Nov. 18, 1971, Pub.L. 92–157, title III, § 302(f), 85 Stat. 464; Aug. 7, 1977, Pub.L. 95–95, title I, § 109(a)–(d)(1), (e), (f), title IV, § 401(b), 91 Stat. 697–703, 791; Nov. 16, 1977, Pub.L. 95–190, § 14(a)(7)–(9), 91 Stat. 1399; Nov. 9, 1978, Pub.L. 95–623, § 13(a), 92 Stat. 3457; Nov. 15, 1990, Pub.L. 101–549, title I, § 108(e)–(g), title III, § 302(a), (b), title IV, § 403(a), 104 Stat. 2467, 2574, 2631.)

Codification

Amendment of subsec. (d)(1) of this section by section 302(a) of Pub.L. 101–549, which directed that "112(b)" [7412(b)] be substituted for "112(b)(1)(A)" [7412(b)(1)(A)], could not be executed due to amendment by section 108(g) of Pub.L. 101–549, which directed substitution of "or emitted from a source category which is regulated under section 112 [7412]" for "or 112(b)(1)(A) [7412(b)(1)(A)]".

Effective Date

Section to take effect Nov. 15, 1990, except as otherwise provided, see section 711(b) of Pub.L. 101–549, set out as a note under section 7401 of this title.

Savings Provisions

Suits, actions or proceedings commenced under this chapter as in effect prior to Nov. 15, 1990, not to abate by reason of the taking effect of amendments by Pub.L. 101–549, except as otherwise provided for, see section 711(a) of Pub.L. 101–549, set out as a note under section 7401 of this title.

Revised Regulations; Applicability

Section 403(b), (c) of Pub.L. 101–549 provided that:

"**(b) Revised regulations.**—Not later than three years after the date of enactment of the Clean Air Act Amendments of 1990 [Nov. 15, 1990], the Administrator shall promulgate revised regulations for standards of performance for new fossil fuel fired electric utility units commencing construction after the date on which such regulations are proposed that, at a minimum, require any source subject to such revised standards to emit sulfur dioxide at a rate not greater than would have resulted from compliance by such source with the applicable standards of performance under this section prior to such revision.

"**(c) Applicability.**—The provisions of subsections (a) and (b) [amending subsec. (a)(1) of this section and enacting subsec. (b) of this note, respectively] apply only so long as the provisions of section 403(e) of the Clean Air Act [section 7651b(e) of this title] remain in effect."

CROSS REFERENCES

Federally permitted release defined to include emissions into air subject to permit or control regulation under this section for purposes of Comprehensive Environmental Response, Compensation, and Liability Act of 1980, see section 9601 of this title.

West's Federal Practice Manual

Air quality legislation, see § 4384.5.

Library References

Health and Environment ⚷25.6(1) et seq., 28.
C.J.S. Health and Environment § 91 et seq.

§ 7412. Hazardous air pollutants [CAA § 112]

(a) Definitions

For purposes of this section, except subsection (r) of this section—

(1) Major source

The term "major source" means any stationary source or group of stationary sources located within a contiguous area and under common control that emits or has the potential to emit considering controls, in the aggregate, 10 tons per year or more of any hazardous air pollutant or 25 tons per year or more of any combination of hazardous air pollutants. The Administrator may establish a lesser quantity, or in the case of radionuclides different criteria, for a major source than that specified in the previous sentence, on the basis of the potency of the air pollutant, persistence, potential for bioaccumulation, other characteristics of the air pollutant, or other relevant factors.

(2) Area source

The term "area source" means any stationary source of hazardous air pollutants that is not a major source. For purposes of this section, the term "area source" shall not include motor vehicles or nonroad vehicles subject to regulation under subchapter II of this chapter.

(3) Stationary source

The term "stationary source" shall have the same meaning as such term has under section 7411(a) of this title.

(4) New source

The term "new source" means a stationary source the construction or reconstruction of which is commenced after the Administrator first proposes regulations under this section establishing an emission standard applicable to such source.

(5) Modification

The term "modification" means any physical change in, or change in the method of operation of, a major source which increases the actual emissions of any hazardous air pollutant emitted by such source by more than a de minimis amount or which results in the emission of any hazardous air pollutant not previously emitted by more than a de minimis amount.

(6) Hazardous air pollutant

The term "hazardous air pollutant" means any air pollutant listed pursuant to subsection (b) of this section.

(7) Adverse environmental effect

The term "adverse environmental effect" means any significant and widespread adverse effect, which may reasonably be anticipated, to wildlife, aquatic life, or other natural resources, including adverse impacts on populations of endangered or threatened species or significant degradation of environmental quality over broad areas.

(8) Electric utility steam generating unit

The term "electric utility steam generating unit" means any fossil fuel fired combustion unit of more than 25 megawatts that serves a generator that produces electricity for sale. A unit that cogenerates steam and electricity and supplies more than one-third of its potential electric output capacity and more than 25 megawatts electrical output to any utility power distribution system for sale shall be considered an electric utility steam generating unit.

(9) Owner or operator

The term "owner or operator" means any person who owns, leases, operates, controls, or supervises a stationary source.

(10) Existing source

The term "existing source" means any stationary source other than a new source.

(11) Carcinogenic effect

Unless revised, the term "carcinogenic effect" shall have the meaning provided by the Administrator under Guidelines for Carcinogenic Risk Assessment as of the date of enactment. Any revisions in the existing Guidelines shall be subject to notice and opportunity for comment.

(b) List of pollutants

(1) Initial list

The Congress establishes for purposes of this section a list of hazardous air pollutants as follows:

CAS number	Chemical name
75070	Acetaldehyde
60355	Acetamide
75058	Acetonitrile
98862	Acetophenone
53963	2–Acetylaminofluorene
107028	Acrolein
79061	Acrylamide
79107	Acrylic acid
107131	Acrylonitrile
107051	Allyl chloride
92671	4–Aminobiphenyl
62533	Aniline
90040	o-Anisidine
1332214	Asbestos
71432	Benzene (including benzene from gasoline)
92875	Benzidine
98077	Benzotrichloride
100447	Benzyl chloride
92524	Biphenyl
117817	Bis(2–ethylhexyl)phthalate (DEHP)
542881	Bis(chloromethyl)ether
75252	Bromoform
106990	1,3–Butadiene
156627	Calcium cyanamide
105602	Caprolactam
133062	Captan
63252	Carbaryl
75150	Carbon disulfide
56235	Carbon tetrachloride
463581	Carbonyl sulfide
120809	Catechol
133904	Chloramben
57749	Chlordane
7782505	Chlorine
79118	Chloroacetic acid
532274	2–Chloroacetophenone
108907	Chlorobenzene
510156	Chlorobenzilate
67663	Chloroform
107302	Chloromethyl methyl ether
126998	Chloroprene
1319773	Cresols/Cresylic acid (isomers and mixture)
95487	o-Cresol
108394	m-Cresol
106445	p-Cresol
98828	Cumene
94757	2,4–D, salts and esters
3547044	DDE
334883	Diazomethane
132649	Dibenzofurans
96128	1,2–Dibromo–3–chloropropane
84742	Dibutylphthalate
106467	1,4–Dichlorobenzene(p)
91941	3,3–Dichlorobenzidene
111444	Dichloroethyl ether (Bis(2–chloroethyl)ether)
542756	1,3–Dichloropropene
62737	Dichlorvos
111422	Diethanolamine
121697	N,N–Diethyl aniline (N,N–Dimethylaniline)
64675	Diethyl sulfate
119904	3,3–Dimethoxybenzidine
60117	Dimethyl aminoazobenzene
119937	3,3′–Dimethyl benzidine
79447	Dimethyl carbamoyl chloride
68122	Dimethyl formamide
57147	1,1–Dimethyl hydrazine
131113	Dimethyl phthalate
77781	Dimethyl sulfate
534521	4,6–Dinitro–o–cresol, and salts
51285	2,4–Dinitrophenol
121142	2,4–Dinitrotoluene
123911	1,4–Dioxane (1,4–Diethyleneoxide)
122667	1,2–Diphenylhydrazine
106898	Epichlorohydrin (1–Chloro–2,3–epoxypropane)
106887	1,2–Expoxybutane
140885	Ethyl acrylate
100414	Ethyl benzene
51796	Ethyl carbamate (Urethane)
75003	Ethyl chloride (Chloroethane)
106934	Ethylene dibromide (Dibromoethane)
107062	Ethylene dichloride (1,2–Dichloroethane)
107211	Ethylene glycol
151564	Ethylene imine (Aziridine)
75218	Ethylene oxide
96457	Ethylene thiourea
75343	Ethylidene dichloride (1,1–Dichloroethane)
50000	Formaldehyde
76448	Heptachlor
118741	Hexachlorobenzene
87683	Hexachlorobutadiene
77474	Hexachlorocyclopentadiene

CAS number	Chemical name
67721	Hexachloroethane
822060	Hexamethylene–1,6–diisocyanate
680319	Hexamethylphosphoramide
110543	Hexane
302012	Hydrazine
7647010	Hydrochloric acid
7664393	Hydrogen fluoride (Hydrofluoric acid)
123319	Hydroquinone
78591	Isophorone
58899	Lindane (all isomers)
108316	Maleic anhydride
67561	Methanol
72435	Methoxychlor
74839	Methyl bromide (Bromomethane)
74873	Methyl chloride (Chloromethane)
71556	Methyl chloroform (1,1,1–Trichloroethane)
78933	Methyl ethyl ketone (2–Butanone)
60344	Methyl hydrazine
74884	Methyl iodide (Iodomethane)
108101	Methyl isobutyl ketone (Hexone)
624839	Methyl isocyanate
80626	Methyl methacrylate
1634044	Methyl tert butyl ether
101144	4,4–Methylene bis(2–chloroaniline)
75092	Methylene chloride (Dichloromethane)
101688	Methylene diphenyl diisocyanate (MDI)
101779	4,4′–Methylenedianiline
91203	Naphthalene
98953	Nitrobenzene
92933	4–Nitrobiphenyl
100027	4–Nitrophenol
79469	2–Nitropropane
684935	N–Nitroso-N-methylurea
62759	N–Nitrosodimethylamine
59892	N–Nitrosomorpholine
56382	Parathion
82688	Pentachloronitrobenzene (Quintobenzene)
87865	Pentachlorophenol
108952	Phenol
106503	p-Phenylenediamine
75445	Phosgene
7803512	Phosphine
7723140	Phosphorus
85449	Phthalic anhydride
1336363	Polychlorinated biphenyls (Aroclors)
1120714	1,3–Propane sultone
57578	beta-Propiolactone
123386	Propionaldehyde
114261	Propoxur (Baygon)
78875	Propylene dichloride (1,2–Dichloropropane)
75569	Propylene oxide
75558	1,2–Propylenimine (2–Methyl aziridine)
91225	Quinoline
106514	Quinone
100425	Styrene
96093	Styrene oxide
1746016	2,3,7,8–Tetrachlorodibenzo-p-dioxin
79345	1,1,2,2–Tetrachloroethane
127184	Tetrachloroethylene (Perchloroethylene)
7550450	Titanium tetrachloride
108883	Toluene
95807	2,4–Toluene diamine
584849	2,4–Toluene diisocyanate
95534	o-Toluidine
8001352	Toxaphene (chlorinated camphene)
120821	1,2,4–Trichlorobenzene
79005	1,1,2–Trichloroethane
79016	Trichloroethylene
95954	2,4,5–Trichlorophenol
88062	2,4,6–Trichlorophenol
121448	Triethylamine
1582098	Trifluralin
540841	2,2,4–Trimethylpentane
108054	Vinyl acetate
593602	Vinyl bromide
75014	Vinyl chloride
75354	Vinylidene chloride (1,1–Dichloroethylene)
1330207	Xylenes (isomers and mixture)
95476	o-Xylenes
108383	m-Xylenes
106423	p-Xylenes
0	Antimony Compounds
0	Arsenic Compounds (inorganic including arsine)
0	Beryllium Compounds
0	Cadmium Compounds
0	Chromium Compounds
0	Cobalt Compounds
0	Coke Oven Emissions
0	Cyanide Compounds [1]
0	Glycol ethers [2]
0	Lead Compounds
0	Manganese Compounds
0	Mercury Compounds
0	Fine mineral fibers [3]
0	Nickel Compounds
0	Polycylic Organic Matter [4]
0	Radionuclides (including radon) [5]
0	Selenium Compounds

NOTE: For all listings above which contain the word "compounds" and for glycol ethers, the following applies: Unless otherwise specified, these listings are defined as including any unique chemical substance that contains the named chemical (i.e., antimony, arsenic, etc.) as part of that chemical's infrastructure.

1 X′CN where X = H′ or any other group where a formal dissociation may occur. For example KCN or $Ca(CN)_2$

2 Includes mono- and di-ethers of ethylene glycol, diethylene glycol, and triethylene glycol $R\text{-}(OCH2CH2)_n\text{-}OR'$ where

n = 1, 2, or 3

R = alkyl or aryl groups

R′ = R, H, or groups which, when removed, yield glycol ethers with the structure: $R\text{-}(OCH2CH)_n\text{-}OH$. Polymers are excluded from the glycol category.

3 Includes mineral fiber emissions from facilities manufacturing or processing glass, rock, or slag fibers (or other mineral derived fibers) of average diameter 1 micrometer or less.

4 Includes organic compounds with more than one benzene ring, and which have a boiling point greater than or equal to 100°C.

5 A type of atom which spontaneously undergoes radioactive decay.

(2) Revision of the list

The Administrator shall periodically review the list established by this subsection and publish the results thereof and, where appropriate, revise such list by rule, adding pollutants which present, or may present, through inhalation or other routes of exposure, a threat of adverse human health effects (including, but not limited to, substances which are known to be, or may reasonably be anticipated to be, carcinogenic, mutagenic, teratogenic, neurotoxic, which cause reproductive dysfunction, or which are acutely or chronically toxic) or adverse environmental effects whether through ambient concentrations, bioaccumulation, deposition, or otherwise, but not including releases subject to regulation under subsection (r) of this section as a result of emissions to the air. No air pollutant which is listed under section 7408(a) of this title may be added to the list under this section, except that the prohibition of this sentence shall not apply to any pollutant which independently meets the listing criteria of this paragraph and is a precursor to a pollutant which is listed under section 7408(a) of this title or to any pollutant which is in a class of pollutants listed under such section. No substance, practice, process or activity regulated under subchapter VI of this chapter shall be subject to regulation under this section solely due to its adverse effects on the environment.

(3) Petitions to modify the list

(A) Beginning at any time after 6 months after November 15, 1990, any person may petition the Administrator to modify the list of hazardous air pollutants under this subsection by adding or deleting a substance or, in case of listed pollutants without CAS numbers (other than coke oven emissions, mineral fibers, or polycyclic organic matter) removing certain unique substances. Within 18 months after receipt of a petition, the Administrator shall either grant or deny the petition by publishing a written explanation of the reasons for the Administrator's decision. Any such petition shall include a showing by the petitioner that there is adequate data on the health or environmental defects of the pollutant or other evidence adequate to support the petition. The Administrator may not deny a petition solely on the basis of inadequate resources or time for review.

(B) The Administrator shall add a substance to the list upon a showing by the petitioner or on the Administrator's own determination that the substance is an air pollutant and that emissions, ambient concentrations, bioaccumulation or deposition of the substance are known to cause or may reasonably be anticipated to cause adverse effects to human health or adverse environmental effects.

(C) The Administrator shall delete a substance from the list upon a showing by the petitioner or on the Administrator's own determination that there is adequate data on the health and environmental effects of the substance to determine that emissions, ambient concentrations, bioaccumulation or deposition of the substance may not reasonably be anticipated to cause any adverse effects to the human health or adverse environmental effects.

(D) The Administrator shall delete one or more unique chemical substances that contain a listed hazardous air pollutant not having a CAS number (other than coke oven emissions, mineral fibers, or polycyclic organic matter) upon a showing by the petitioner or on the Administrator's own determination that such unique chemical substances that contain the named chemical of such listed hazardous air pollutant meet the deletion requirements of subparagraph (C). The Administrator must grant or deny a deletion petition prior to promulgating any emission standards pursuant to subsection (d) of this section applicable to any source category or subcategory of a listed hazardous air pollutant without a CAS number listed under subsection (b) for which a deletion petition has been filed within 12 months of November 15, 1990.

(4) Further information

If the Administrator determines that information on the health or environmental effects of a substance is not sufficient to make a determination required by this subsection, the Administrator may use any authority available to the Administrator to acquire such information.

(5) Test methods

The Administrator may establish, by rule, test measures and other analytic procedures for monitoring and measuring emissions, ambient concentrations, deposition, and bioaccumulation of hazardous air pollutants.

(6) Prevention of significant deterioration

The provisions of part C of this subchapter (prevention of significant deterioration) shall not apply to pollutants listed under this section.

(7) Lead

The Administrator may not list elemental lead as a hazardous air pollutant under this subsection.

(c) List of source categories

(1) In general

Not later than 12 months after November 15, 1990, the Administrator shall publish, and shall from time to time, but no less often than every 8 years, revise, if appropriate, in response to public comment or new information, a list of all categories and subcategories of major sources and area sources (listed under paragraph (3)) of the air pollutants listed pursuant to subsection (b) of this section. To the extent practicable, the categories and subcategories listed under this subsection shall be consistent with the list of source categories established pursuant to section 7411 of this title and part C of this subchapter. Nothing in the preceding sentence limits the Administrator's authority to establish subcategories under this section, as appropriate.

(2) Requirement for emissions standards

For the categories and subcategories the Administrator lists, the Administrator shall establish emissions standards under subsection (d) of this section, according to the schedule in this subsection and subsection (e) of this section.

(3) Area sources

The Administrator shall list under this subsection each category or subcategory of area sources which the Administrator finds presents a threat of adverse effects to human health or the environment (by such sources individually or in the aggregate) warranting regulation under this section. The Administrator shall, not later than 5 years after November 15, 1990, and pursuant to subsection (k)(3)(B) of this section, list, based on actual or estimated aggregate emissions of a listed pollutant or pollutants, sufficient categories or subcategories of area sources to ensure that area sources representing 90 percent of the area source emissions of the 30 hazardous air pollutants that present the greatest threat to public health in the largest number of urban areas are subject to regulation under this section. Such regulations shall be promulgated not later than 10 years after November 15, 1990.

(4) Previously regulated categories

The Administrator may, in the Administrator's discretion, list any category or subcategory of sources previously regulated under this section as in effect before November 15, 1990.

(5) Additional categories

In addition to those categories and subcategories of sources listed for regulation pursuant to paragraphs (1) and (3), the Administrator may at any time list additional categories and subcategories of sources of hazardous air pollutants according to the same criteria for listing applicable under such paragraphs. In the case of source categories and subcategories listed after publication of the initial list required under paragraph (1) or (3), emission standards under subsection (d) of this section for the category or subcategory shall be promulgated within 10 years after November 15, 1990, or within 2 years after the date on which such category or subcategory is listed, whichever is later.

(6) Specific pollutants

With respect to alkylated lead compounds, polycyclic organic matter, hexachlorobenzene, mercury, polychlorinated biphenyls, 2,3,7,8–tetrachlorodibenzofurans and 2,3,7,8–tetrachlorodibenzo-p-dioxin, the Administrator shall, not later than 5 years after November 15, 1990, list categories and subcategories of sources assuring that sources accounting for not less than 90 per centum of the aggregate emissions of each such pollutant are subject to standards under subsection (d)(2) or (d)(4) of this section. Such standards shall be promulgated not later than 10 years after November 15, 1990. This paragraph shall not be construed to require the Administrator to promulgate standards for such pollutants emitted by electric utility steam generating units.

(7) Research facilities

The Administrator shall establish a separate category covering research or laboratory facilities, as necessary to assure the equitable treatment of such facilities. For purposes of this section, "research or laboratory facility" means any stationary source whose primary purpose is to conduct research and development into new processes and products, where such source is operated under the close supervision of technically trained personnel and is not engaged in the manufacture of products for commercial sale in commerce, except in a de minimis manner.

(8) Boat manufacturing

When establishing emissions standards for styrene, the Administrator shall list boat manufacturing as a separate subcategory unless the Administrator finds that such listing would be inconsistent with the goals and requirements of this chapter.

(9) Deletions from the list

(A) Where the sole reason for the inclusion of a source category on the list required under this subsection is the emission of a unique chemical substance, the Administrator shall delete the source category from the list if it is appropriate because of action taken under either subparagraphs (C) or (D) of subsection (b)(3) of this section.

(B) The Administrator may delete any source category from the list under this subsection, on petition of any person or on the Administrator's own motion, whenever the Administrator makes the following determination or determinations, as applicable:

(i) In the case of hazardous air pollutants emitted by sources in the category that may result in cancer in humans, a determination that no source in the category (or group of sources in the case of area sources) emits such hazardous air pollutants in quantities which may cause a lifetime risk of cancer greater than one in one million to the individual in the population who is most exposed to emissions of such pollutants from the source (or group of sources in the case of area sources).

(ii) In the case of hazardous air pollutants that may result in adverse health effects in humans other than cancer or adverse environmental effects, a determination that emissions from no source in the category or subcategory concerned (or group of sources in the case of area sources) exceed a level which is adequate to protect public health with an ample margin of safety and no adverse environmental effect will result from emissions from any source (or from a group of sources in the case of area sources).

The Administrator shall grant or deny a petition under this paragraph within 1 year after the petition is filed.

(d) Emission standards

(1) In general

The Administrator shall promulgate regulations establishing emission standards for each category or subcategory of major sources and area sources of hazardous air pollutants listed for regulation pursuant to subsection (c) of this section in accordance with the schedules provided in subsections (c) and (e) of this section. The Administrator may distinguish among classes, types, and sizes of sources within a category or subcategory in establishing such standards except that, there shall be no delay in the compliance date for any standard applicable to any source under subsection (i) of this section as the result of the authority provided by this sentence.

(2) Standards and methods

Emissions standards promulgated under this subsection and applicable to new or existing sources of hazardous air pollutants shall require the maximum degree of reduction in emissions of the hazardous air pollutants subject to this section (including a prohibition on such emissions, where achievable) that the Administrator, taking into consideration the cost of achieving such emission reduction, and any non-air quality health and environmental impacts and energy requirements, determines is achievable for new or existing sources in the category or subcategory to which such emission standard applies, through application of measures, processes, methods, systems or techniques including, but not limited to, measures which—

(A) reduce the volume of, or eliminate emissions of, such pollutants through process changes, substitution of materials or other modifications,

(B) enclose systems or processes to eliminate emissions,

(C) collect, capture or treat such pollutants when released from a process, stack, storage or fugitive emissions point,

(D) are design, equipment, work practice, or operational standards (including requirements for operator training or certification) as provided in subsection (h) of this section, or

(E) are a combination of the above.

None of the measures described in subparagraphs (A) through (D) shall, consistent with the provisions of section 7414(c) of this title, in any way compromise any United States patent or United States trademark right, or any confidential business information, or any trade secret or any other intellectual property right.

(3) New and existing sources

The maximum degree of reduction in emissions that is deemed achievable for new sources in a category or subcategory shall not be less stringent than the emission control that is achieved in practice by the best controlled similar source, as determined by the Administrator. Emission standards promulgated under this subsection for existing sources in a category or subcategory may be less stringent than standards for new sources in the same category or subcategory but shall not be less stringent, and may be more stringent than—

(A) the average emission limitation achieved by the best performing 12 percent of the existing sources (for which the Administrator has emissions information), excluding those sources that have, within 18 months before the emission standard is proposed or within 30 months before such standard is promulgated, whichever is later, first achieved a level of emission rate or emission reduction which complies, or would comply if the source is not subject to such standard, with the lowest achievable emission rate (as defined by section 7501 of this title) applicable to the source category and prevailing at the time, in the category or subcategory for categories and subcategories with 30 or more sources, or

(B) the average emission limitation achieved by the best performing 5 sources (for which the Administrator has or could reasonably obtain emissions information) in the category or subcategory for categories or subcategories with fewer than 30 sources.

(4) Health threshold

With respect to pollutants for which a health threshold has been established, the Administrator may consider such threshold level, with an ample margin of safety, when establishing emission standards under this subsection.

(5) Alternative standard for area sources

With respect only to categories and subcategories of area sources listed pursuant to subsection (c) of this section, the Administrator may, in lieu of the authorities provided in paragraph (2) and subsection (f) of this section, elect to promulgate standards or requirements applicable to sources in such categories or subcategories which provide for the use of generally available control technologies or management practices by such sources to reduce emissions of hazardous air pollutants.

(6) Review and revision

The Administrator shall review, and revise as necessary (taking into account developments in practices, processes, and control technologies), emission standards promulgated under this section no less often than every 8 years.

(7) Other requirements preserved

No emission standard or other requirement promulgated under this section shall be interpreted, construed or applied to diminish or replace the requirements of a more stringent emission limitation or other applicable requirement established pursuant to section 7411 of this title, part C or D of this subchapter, or other authority of this chapter or a standard issued under State authority.

(8) Coke ovens

(A) Not later than December 31, 1992, the Administrator shall promulgate regulations establishing emission standards under paragraphs (2) and (3) of this subsection for coke oven batteries. In establishing such standards, the Administrator shall evaluate—

(i) the use of sodium silicate (or equivalent) luting compounds to prevent door leaks, and other operating practices and technologies for their effectiveness in reducing coke oven emissions, and their suitability for use on new and existing coke oven batteries, taking into account costs and reasonable commercial door warranties; and

(ii) as a basis for emission standards under this subsection for new coke oven batteries that begin construction after the date of proposal of such standards, the Jewell design Thompson non-recovery coke oven batteries and other non-recovery coke oven technologies, and other appropriate emission control and coke production technologies, as to their effectiveness in reducing coke oven emissions and their capability for production of steel quality coke.

Such regulations shall require at a minimum that coke oven batteries will not exceed 8 per centum leaking doors, 1 per centum leaking lids, 5 per centum leaking offtakes, and 16 seconds visible emissions per charge, with no exclusion for emissions during the period after the closing of self-sealing oven doors. Notwithstanding subsection (i) of this section, the compliance date for such emission standards for existing coke oven batteries shall be December 31, 1995.

(B) The Administrator shall promulgate work practice regulations under this subsection for coke oven batteries requiring, as appropriate—

(i) the use of sodium silicate (or equivalent) luting compounds, if the Administrator determines that use of sodium silicate is an effective means of emissions control and is achievable, taking into account costs and reasonable commercial warranties for doors and related equipment; and

(ii) door and jam cleaning practices.

Notwithstanding subsection (i) of this section, the compliance date for such work practice regulations for coke oven batteries shall be not later than the date 3 years after November 15, 1990.

(C) For coke oven batteries electing to qualify for an extension of the compliance date for standards promulgated under subsection (f) of this section in accordance with subsection (i)(8) of this section, the emission standards under this subsection for coke oven batteries shall require that coke oven batteries not exceed 8 per centum leaking doors, 1 per centum leaking lids, 5 per centum leaking offtakes, and 16 seconds visible emissions per charge, with no exclusion for emissions during the period after the closing of self-sealing doors. Notwithstanding subsection (i) of this section, the compliance date for such emission standards for existing coke oven batteries seeking an extension shall be not later than the date 3 years after November 15, 1990.

(9) Sources licensed by the Nuclear Regulatory Commission

No standard for radionuclide emissions from any category or subcategory of facilities licensed by the Nuclear Regulatory Commission (or an Agreement State) is required to be promulgated under this section if the Administrator determines, by rule, and after consultation with the Nuclear Regulatory Commission, that the regulatory program established by the Nuclear Regulatory Commission pursuant to the Atomic Energy Act [42 U.S.C.A. § 2011 et seq.] for such category or subcategory provides an ample margin of safety to protect the public health. Nothing in this subsection shall preclude or deny the right of any State or political subdivision thereof to adopt or enforce any standard or limitation respecting emissions of radionuclides which is more stringent than the standard or limitation in effect under section 7411 of this title or this section.

(10) Effective date

Emission standards or other regulations promulgated under this subsection shall be effective upon promulgation.

(e) Schedule for standards and review

(1) In general

The Administrator shall promulgate regulations establishing emission standards for categories and subcategories of sources initially listed for regulation pursuant to subsection (c)(1) of this section as expeditiously as practicable, assuring that—

(A) emission standards for not less than 40 categories and subcategories (not counting coke oven batteries) shall be promulgated not later than 2 years after November 15, 1990;

(B) emission standards for coke oven batteries shall be promulgated not later than December 31, 1992;

(C) emission standards for 25 per centum of the listed categories and subcategories shall be promulgated not later than 4 years after November 15, 1990;

(D) emission standards for an additional 25 per centum of the listed categories and subcategories shall be promulgated not later than 7 years after November 15, 1990; and

(E) emission standards for all categories and subcategories shall be promulgated not later than 10 years after November 15, 1990.

(2) In determining priorities for promulgating standards under subsection (d) of this section, the Administrator shall consider—

(A) the known or anticipated adverse effects of such pollutants on public health and the environment;

(B) the quantity and location of emissions or reasonably anticipated emissions of hazardous air pollutants that each category or subcategory will emit; and

(C) the efficiency of grouping categories or subcategories according to the pollutants emitted, or the processes or technologies used.

(3) Published schedule

Not later than 24 months after November 15, 1990, and after opportunity for comment, the Administrator shall publish a schedule establishing a date for the promulgation of emission standards for each category and subcategory of sources listed pursuant to subsection (c)(1) and (3) of this section which shall be consistent with the requirements of paragraphs (1) and (2). The determination of priorities for the promulgation of standards pursuant to this paragraph is not a rulemaking and shall not be subject to judicial review, except that, failure to promulgate any standard pursuant to the schedule established by this paragraph shall be subject to review under section 7604 of this title.

(4) Judicial review

Notwithstanding section 7607 of this title, no action of the Administrator adding a pollutant to the list under subsection (b) of this section or listing a source category or subcategory under subsection (c) of this section shall be a final agency action subject to judicial review, except that any such action may be reviewed under such section 7607 of this title when the Administrator issues emission standards for such pollutant or category.

(5) Publicly owned treatment works

The Administrator shall promulgate standards pursuant to subsection (d) of this section applicable to publicly owned treatment works (as defined in title II of the Federal Water Pollution Control Act [33 U.S.C.A. § 1281 et seq.]) not later than 5 years after November 15, 1990.

(f) Standard to protect health and the environment

(1) Report

Not later than 6 years after November 15, 1990, the Administrator shall investigate and report, after consultation with the Surgeon General and after opportunity for public comment, to Congress on—

(A) methods of calculating the risk to public health remaining, or likely to remain, from sources subject to regulation under this section after the application of standards under subsection (d) of this section;

(B) the public health significance of such estimated remaining risk and the technologically and commercially available methods and costs of reducing such risks;

(C) the actual health effects with respect to persons living in the vicinity of sources, any available epidemiological or other health studies, risks presented by background concentrations of hazardous air pollutants, any uncertainties in risk assessment methodology or other health assessment technique, and any negative health or environmental consequences to the community of efforts to reduce such risks; and

(D) recommendations as to legislation regarding such remaining risk.

(2) Emission standards

(A) If Congress does not act on any recommendation submitted under paragraph (1), the Administrator shall, within 8 years after promulgation of standards for each category or subcategory of sources pursuant to subsection (d) of this section, promulgate standards for such category or subcategory if promulgation of such standards is required in order to provide an ample margin of safety to protect public health in accordance with this section (as in effect before November 15, 1990) or to prevent, taking into consideration costs, energy, safety, and other relevant factors, an adverse environmental effect. Emission standards promulgated under this subsection shall provide an ample margin of safety to protect public health in accordance with this section (as in effect before November 15, 1990), unless the Administrator determines that a more stringent standard is necessary to prevent, taking into consideration costs, energy, safety, and other relevant factors, an adverse environmental effect. If standards promulgated pursuant to subsection (d) of this section and applicable to a category or subcategory of sources emitting a pollutant (or pollutants) classified as a known, probable or possible human carcinogen do not reduce lifetime excess cancer risks to the individual most exposed to emissions from a source in the category or subcategory to less than one in one million, the Administrator shall promulgate standards under this subsection for such source category.

(B) Nothing in subparagraph (A) or in any other provision of this section shall be construed as affecting, or applying to the Administrator's interpretation of this section, as in effect before November 15, 1990, and set forth in the Federal Register of September 14, 1989 (54 Federal Register 38044).

(C) The Administrator shall determine whether or not to promulgate such standards and, if the Administrator decides to promulgate such standards, shall promulgate the standards 8 years after promulgation of the standards under subsection (d) of this section for each source category or subcategory concerned. In the case of categories or subcategories for which standards under subsection (d) of this section are required to be promulgated within 2 years after November 15, 1990, the Administrator shall have 9 years after promulgation of the standards under subsection (d) of this section to make the determination under the preceding sentence and, if required, to promulgate the standards under this paragraph.

(3) Effective date

Any emission standard established pursuant to this subsection shall become effective upon promulgation.

(4) Prohibition

No air pollutant to which a standard under this subsection applies may be emitted from any stationary source in violation of such standard, except that in the case of an existing source—

(A) such standard shall not apply until 90 days after its effective date, and

(B) the Administrator may grant a waiver permitting such source a period of up to 2 years after the effective date of a standard to comply with the standard if the Administrator finds that such period is necessary for the installation of controls and that steps will be taken during the period of the waiver to assure that the health of persons will be protected from imminent endangerment.

(5) Area sources

The Administrator shall not be required to conduct any review under this subsection or promulgate emission limitations under this subsection for any category or subcategory of area sources that is listed pursuant to subsection (c)(3) of this section and for which an emission standard is promulgated pursuant to subsection (d)(5) of this section.

(6) Unique chemical substances

In establishing standards for the control of unique chemical substances of listed pollutants without CAS numbers under this subsection, the Administrator shall establish such standards with respect to the health and environmental effects of the substances actually emitted by sources and direct transformation byproducts of such emissions in the categories and subcategories.

(g) Modifications

(1) Offsets

(A) A physical change in, or change in the method of operation of, a major source which results in a greater than de minimis increase in actual emissions of a hazardous air pollutant shall not be considered a modification, if such increase in the quantity of actual emissions of any hazardous air pollutant from such source will be offset by an equal or greater decrease in the quantity of emissions of another hazardous air pollutant (or pollutants) from such source which is deemed more hazardous, pursuant to guidance issued by the Administrator under subparagraph (B). The owner or operator of such source shall submit a showing to the Administrator (or the State) that such increase has been offset under the preceding sentence.

(B) The Administrator shall, after notice and opportunity for comment and not later than 18 months after November 15, 1990, publish guidance with respect to implementation of this subsection. Such guidance shall include an identification, to the extent practicable, of the relative hazard to human health resulting from emissions to the ambient air of each of the pollutants listed under subsection (b) of this section sufficient to facilitate the offset showing authorized by subparagraph (A). Such guidance shall not authorize offsets between pollutants where the increased pollutant (or more than one pollutant in a stream of pollutants) causes adverse effects to human health for which no safety threshold for exposure can be determined unless there are corresponding decreases in such types of pollutant(s).

(2) Construction, reconstruction and modifications

(A) After the effective date of a permit program under subchapter V of this chapter in any State, no person may modify a major source of hazardous air pollutants in such State, unless the Administrator (or the State) determines that the maximum achievable control technology emission limitation under this section for existing sources will be met. Such determination shall be made on a case-by-case basis where no applicable emissions limitations have been established by the Administrator.

(B) After the effective date of a permit program under subchapter V of this chapter in any State, no person may construct or reconstruct any major source of hazardous air pollutants, unless the Administrator (or the State) determines that the maximum achievable control technology emission limitation under this section for new sources will be met. Such determination shall be made on a case-by-case basis where no applicable emission limitations have been established by the Administrator.

(3) Procedures for modifications

The Administrator (or the State) shall establish reasonable procedures for assuring that the requirements applying to modifications under this section are reflected in the permit.

(h) Work practice standards and other requirements

(1) In general

For purposes of this section, if it is not feasible in the judgment of the Administrator to prescribe or enforce an emission standard for control of a hazardous air pollutant or pollutants, the Administrator may, in lieu thereof, promulgate a design, equipment, work practice, or operational standard, or combination thereof, which in the Administrator's judgment is consistent with the provisions of subsection (d) or (f) of this section. In the event the Administrator promulgates a design or equipment standard under this subsection, the Administrator shall include as part of such standard such requirements as will assure the proper operation and maintenance of any such element of design or equipment.

(2) Definition

For the purpose of this subsection, the phrase "not feasible to prescribe or enforce an emission standard" means any situation in which the Administrator determines that—

(A) a hazardous air pollutant or pollutants cannot be emitted through a conveyance designed and constructed to emit or capture such pollutant, or that any requirement for, or use of, such a conveyance would be inconsistent with any Federal, State or local law, or

(B) the application of measurement methodology to a particular class of sources is not practicable due to technological and economic limitations.

(3) Alternative standard

If after notice and opportunity for comment, the owner or operator of any source establishes to the satisfaction of the Administrator that an alternative means of emission limitation will achieve a reduction in emissions of any air pollutant at least equivalent to the reduction in emissions of such pollutant achieved under the requirements of paragraph (1), the Administrator shall permit the use of such alternative by the source for purposes of compliance with this section with respect to such pollutant.

(4) Numerical standard required

Any standard promulgated under paragraph (1) shall be promulgated in terms of an emission standard whenever it is feasible to promulgate and enforce a standard in such terms.

(i) Schedule for compliance

(1) Preconstruction and operating requirements

After the effective date of any emission standard, limitation, or regulation under subsection (d), (f) or (h) of this section, no person may construct any new major source or reconstruct any existing major source subject to such emission standard, regulation or limitation unless the Administrator (or a State with a permit program approved under subchapter V of this chapter) determines that such source, if properly constructed, reconstructed and operated, will comply with the standard, regulation or limitation.

(2) Special rule

Notwithstanding the requirements of paragraph (1), a new source which commences construction or reconstruction after a standard, limitation or regulation applicable to such source is proposed and before such standard, limitation or regulation is promulgated shall not be required to comply with such promulgated standard until the date 3 years after the date of promulgation if—

(A) the promulgated standard, limitation or regulation is more stringent than the standard, limitation or regulation proposed; and

(B) the source complies with the standard, limitation, or regulation as proposed during the 3-year period immediately after promulgation.

(3) Compliance schedule for existing sources

(A) After the effective date of any emissions standard, limitation or regulation promulgated under this section and applicable to a source, no person may operate such source in violation of such standard, limitation or regulation except, in the case of an existing source, the Administrator shall establish a compliance date or dates for each category or subcategory of existing sources, which shall provide for compliance as expeditiously as practicable, but in no event later than 3 years after the effective date of such standard, except as provided in subparagraph (B) and paragraphs (4) through (8).

(B) The Administrator (or a State with a program approved under subchapter V of this chapter) may issue a permit that grants an extension permitting an existing source up to 1 additional year to comply with standards under subsection (d) of this section if such additional period is necessary for the installation of controls. An additional extension of up to 3 years may be added for mining waste operations, if the 4-year compliance time is insufficient to dry and cover mining waste in order to reduce emissions of any pollutant listed under subsection (b) of this section.

(4) Presidential exemption

The President may exempt any stationary source from compliance with any standard or limitation under this section for a period of not more than 2 years if the President determines that the technology to implement such standard is not available and that it is in the national security interests of the United States to do so. An exemption under this paragraph may be extended for 1 or more additional periods, each period not to exceed 2 years. The President shall report to Congress with respect to each exemption (or extension thereof) made under this paragraph.

(5) Early reduction

(A) The Administrator (or a State acting pursuant to a permit program approved under subchapter V of this chapter) shall issue a permit allowing an existing source, for which the owner or operator demonstrates that the source has achieved a reduction of 90 per centum or more in emissions of hazardous air pollutants (95 per centum in the case of hazardous air pollutants which are particulates) from the source, to meet an alternative emission limitation reflecting such reduction in lieu of an emission limitation promulgated under subsection (d) of this section for a period of 6 years from the compliance date for the otherwise applicable standard, provided that such reduction is achieved before the otherwise applicable standard under subsection (d) of this section is first proposed. Nothing in this paragraph shall preclude a State from requiring reductions in excess of those specified in this subparagraph as a condition of granting the extension authorized by the previous sentence.

(B) An existing source which achieves the reduction referred to in subparagraph (A) after the proposal of an applicable standard but before January 1, 1994, may qualify under subparagraph (A), if the source makes an enforceable commitment to achieve such reduction before the proposal of the standard. Such commitment shall be enforceable to the same extent as a regulation under this section.

(C) The reduction shall be determined with respect to verifiable and actual emissions in a base year not earlier than calendar year 1987, provided that, there is no evidence that emissions in the base year are artificially or substantially greater than emissions in other years prior to implementation of emissions reduction measures. The Administrator may allow a source to use a baseline year of 1985 or 1986 provided that the source can demonstrate to the satisfaction of the Administrator that emissions data for the source reflects verifiable data based on information for such source, received by the Administrator prior to the enactment of the Clean Air Act Amendments of 1990, pursuant to an information request issued under section 7411 of this title.

(D) For each source granted an alternative emission limitation under this paragraph there shall be established by a permit issued pursuant to subchapter V of this chapter an enforceable emission limitation for hazardous air pollutants reflecting the reduction which qualifies the source for an alternative emission limitation under this paragraph. An alternative emission limitation under this paragraph shall not be available with respect to standards or requirements promulgated pursuant to subsection

(f) of this section and the Administrator shall, for the purpose of determining whether a standard under subsection (f) of this section is necessary, review emissions from sources granted an alternative emission limitation under this paragraph at the same time that other sources in the category or subcategory are reviewed.

(E) With respect to pollutants for which high risks of adverse public health effects may be associated with exposure to small quantities including, but not limited to, chlorinated dioxins and furans, the Administrator shall by regulation limit the use of offsetting reductions in emissions of other hazardous air pollutants from the source as counting toward the 90 per centum reduction in such high-risk pollutants qualifying for an alternative emissions limitation under this paragraph.

(6) Other reductions

Notwithstanding the requirements of this section, no existing source that has installed—

(A) best available control technology (as defined in section 7479(3) of this title), or

(B) technology required to meet a lowest achievable emission rate (as defined in section 7501 of this title),

prior to the promulgation of a standard under this section applicable to such source and the same pollutant (or stream of pollutants) controlled pursuant to an action described in subparagraph (A) or (B) shall be required to comply with such standard under this section until the date 5 years after the date on which such installation or reduction has been achieved, as determined by the Administrator. The Administrator may issue such rules and guidance as are necessary to implement this paragraph.

(7) Extension for new sources

A source for which construction or reconstruction is commenced after the date an emission standard applicable to such source is proposed pursuant to subsection (d) of this section but before the date an emission standard applicable to such source is proposed pursuant to subsection (f) of this section shall not be required to comply with the emission standard under subsection (f) of this section until the date 10 years after the date construction or reconstruction is commenced.

(8) Coke ovens

(A) Any coke oven battery that complies with the emission limitations established under subsection (d)(8)(C) of this section, subparagraph (B), and subparagraph (C), and complies with the provisions of subparagraph (E), shall not be required to achieve emission limitations promulgated under subsection (f) of this section until January 1, 2020.

(B)(i) Not later than December 31, 1992, the Administrator shall promulgate emission limitations for coke oven emissions from coke oven batteries. Notwithstanding paragraph (3) of this subsection, the compliance date for such emission limitations for existing coke oven batteries shall be January 1, 1998. Such emission limitations shall reflect the lowest achievable emission rate as defined in section 7501 of this title for a coke oven battery that is rebuilt or a replacement at a coke oven plant for an existing battery. Such emission limitations shall be no less stringent than—

(I) 3 per centum leaking doors (5 per centum leaking doors for six meter batteries);

(II) 1 per centum leaking lids;

(III) 4 per centum leaking offtakes; and

(IV) 16 seconds visible emissions per charge,

with an exclusion for emissions during the period after the closing of self-sealing oven doors (or the total mass emissions equivalent). The rulemaking in which such emission limitations are promulgated shall also establish an appropriate measurement methodology for determining compliance with such emission limitations, and shall establish such emission limitations in terms of an equivalent level of mass emissions reduction from a coke oven battery, unless the Administrator finds that such a mass emissions standard would not be practicable or enforceable. Such measurement methodology, to the extent it measures leaking doors, shall take into consideration alternative test methods that reflect the best technology and practices actually applied in the affected industries, and shall assure that the final test methods are consistent with the performance of such best technology and practices.

(ii) If the Administrator fails to promulgate such emission limitations under this subparagraph prior to the effective date of such emission limitations, the emission limitations applicable to coke oven batteries under this subparagraph shall be—

(I) 3 per centum leaking doors (5 per centum leaking doors for six meter batteries);

(II) 1 per centum leaking lids;

(III) 4 per centum leaking offtakes; and

(IV) 16 seconds visible emissions per charge,

or the total mass emissions equivalent (if the total mass emissions equivalent is determined to be practicable and enforceable), with no exclusion for emissions during the period after the closing of self-sealing oven doors.

(C) Not later than January 1, 2007, the Administrator shall review the emission limitations promulgated under subparagraph (B) and revise, as necessary, such emission limitations to reflect the lowest achievable emission rate as defined in section 7501 of this title at the time for a coke oven battery that is rebuilt or a replacement at a coke oven plant for an existing battery. Such emission limitations shall be no less stringent than the emission limitation promulgated under subparagraph (B). Notwithstanding paragraph (2) of this subsection, the compliance date for such emission limitations for existing coke oven batteries shall be January 1, 2010.

(D) At any time prior to January 1, 1998, the owner or operator of any coke oven battery may elect to comply with emission limitations promulgated under subsection (f) of this section by the date such emission limitations would otherwise apply to such coke oven battery, in lieu of the emission limitations and the compliance dates provided under subparagraphs (B) and (C) of this paragraph. Any such owner or operator shall be legally bound to comply with such emission limitations promulgated under subsection (f) of this section with respect to such coke oven battery as of January 1, 2003. If no such emission limitations have been promulgated for such coke oven battery, the Administrator shall promulgate such emission limitations in accordance with subsection (f) of this section for such coke oven battery.

(E) Coke oven batteries qualifying for an extension under subparagraph (A) shall make available not later than January 1, 2000, to the surrounding communities the results of any risk assessment performed by the Administrator to determine the appropriate level of any emission standard established by the Administrator pursuant to subsection (f) of this section.

(F) Notwithstanding the provisions of this section, reconstruction of any source of coke oven emissions qualifying for an extension under this paragraph shall not subject such source to emission limitations under subsection (f) of this section more stringent than those established under subparagraphs (B) and (C) until January 1, 2020. For the purposes of this subparagraph, the term "reconstruction" includes the replacement of existing coke oven battery capacity with new coke oven batteries of comparable or lower capacity and lower potential emissions.

(j) Equivalent emission limitation by permit

(1) Effective date

The requirements of this subsection shall apply in each State beginning on the effective date of a permit program established pursuant to subchapter V of this chapter in such State, but not prior to the date 42 months after November 15, 1990.

(2) Failure to promulgate a standard

In the event that the Administrator fails to promulgate a standard for a category or subcategory of major sources by the date established pursuant to subsection (e)(1) and (3) of this section, and beginning 18 months after such date (but not prior to the effective date of a permit program under subchapter V of this chapter), the owner or operator of any major source in such category or subcategory shall submit a permit application under paragraph (3) and such owner or operator shall also comply with paragraphs (5) and (6).

(3) Applications

By the date established by paragraph (2), the owner or operator of a major source subject to this subsection shall file an application for a permit. If the owner or operator of a source has submitted a timely and complete application for a permit required by this subsection, any failure to have a permit shall not be a violation of paragraph (2), unless the delay in final action is due to the failure of the applicant to timely submit information required or requested to process the application. The Administrator shall not later than 18 months after November 15, 1990, and after notice and opportunity for comment, establish requirements for applications under this subsection including a standard application form and criteria for determining in a timely manner the completeness of applications.

(4) Review and approval

Permit applications submitted under this subsection shall be reviewed and approved or disapproved according to the provisions of section 7661d of this title. In the event that the Administrator (or the State) disapproves a permit application submitted under this subsection or determines that the application is incomplete, the applicant shall have up to 6 months to revise the application to meet the objections of the Administrator (or the State).

(5) Emission limitation

The permit shall be issued pursuant to subchapter V of this chapter and shall contain emission limitations for the hazardous air pollutants subject to regulation under this section and emitted by the source that the Administrator (or the State) determines, on a case-by-case basis, to be equivalent to the limitation that would apply to such source if an emission standard had been promulgated in a timely manner under subsection (d) of this section. In the alternative, if the applicable criteria are met, the permit may contain an emissions limitation established according to the provisions of subsection (i)(5) of this section. For purposes of the preceding sentence, the reduction required by subsection (i)(5)(A) of this section shall be achieved by the date on which the relevant standard should have been promulgated under subsection (d) of this section. No such pollutant may be emitted in amounts exceeding an emission limitation contained in a permit immediately for new sources and, as expeditiously as practicable, but not later than the date 3 years after the permit is issued for existing sources or such other compliance date as would apply under subsection (i) of this section.

(6) Applicability of subsequent standards

If the Administrator promulgates an emission standard that is applicable to the major source prior to the date on which a permit application is approved, the emission limitation in the permit shall reflect the promulgated standard rather than the emission limitation determined pursuant to paragraph (5), provided that the source shall have the compliance period provided under subsection (i) of this section. If the Administrator promulgates a standard under subsection (d) of this section that would be applicable to the source in lieu of the emission limitation established by permit under this subsection after the date on which the permit has been issued, the Administrator (or the State) shall revise such permit upon the next renewal to reflect the standard promulgated by the Administrator providing such source a reasonable time to comply, but no longer than 8 years after such standard is promulgated or 8 years after the date on which the source is first required to comply with the emissions limitation established by paragraph (5), whichever is earlier.

(k) Area source program

(1) Findings and purpose

The Congress finds that emissions of hazardous air pollutants from area sources may individually, or in the aggregate, present significant risks to public health in urban areas. Considering the large number of persons exposed and the risks of carcinogenic and other adverse health effects from hazardous air pollutants, ambient concentrations characteristic of large urban areas should be reduced to levels substantially below those currently experienced. It is the purpose of this subsection to achieve a substantial reduction in emissions of hazardous air pollutants from area sources and an equivalent reduction in the public health risks associated with such sources including a reduction of not less than 75 per centum in the incidence of cancer attributable to emissions from such sources.

(2) Research program

The Administrator shall, after consultation with State and local air pollution control officials, conduct a program of research with respect to sources of hazardous air pollutants in urban areas and shall include within such program—

(A) ambient monitoring for a broad range of hazardous air pollutants (including, but not limited to, volatile organic compounds, metals, pesticides and products of incomplete combustion) in a representative number of urban locations;

(B) analysis to characterize the sources of such pollution with a focus on area sources and the contribution that such sources make to public health risks from hazardous air pollutants; and

(C) consideration of atmospheric transformation and other factors which can elevate public health risks from such pollutants.

Health effects considered under this program shall include, but not be limited to, carcinogenicity, mutagenicity, teratogenicity, neurotoxicity, reproductive dysfunction and other acute and chronic effects including the role of such pollutants as precursors of ozone or acid aerosol formation. The Administrator shall report the preliminary results of such research not later than 3 years after November 15, 1990.

(3) National strategy

(A) Considering information collected pursuant to the monitoring program authorized by paragraph (2), the Administrator shall, not later than 5 years after November 15, 1990, and after notice and opportunity for public comment, prepare and transmit to the Congress a comprehensive strategy to control emissions of hazardous air pollutants from area sources in urban areas.

(B) The strategy shall—

(i) identify not less than 30 hazardous air pollutants which, as the result of emissions from area sources, present the greatest threat to public health in the largest number of urban areas and that are or will be listed pursuant to subsection (b) of this section, and

(ii) identify the source categories or subcategories emitting such pollutants that are or will be listed pursuant to subsection (c) of this section. When identifying categories and subcategories of sources under this subparagraph, the Administrator shall assure that sources accounting for 90 per centum or more of the aggregate emissions of each of the 30 identified hazardous air pollutants are subject to standards pursuant to subsection (d) of this section.

(C) The strategy shall include a schedule of specific actions to substantially reduce the public health risks posed by the release of hazardous air pollutants from area sources that will be implemented by the Administrator under the authority of this or other laws (including, but not limited to, the Toxic Substances Control Act [15 U.S.C.A. § 2601 et seq.], the Federal Insecticide, Fungicide and Rodenticide Act [7 U.S.C.A. § 136 et seq.] and the Resource Conservation and Recovery Act [42 U.S.C.A. § 6901 et seq.]) or by the States. The strategy shall achieve a reduction in the incidence of cancer attributable to exposure to hazardous air pollutants emitted by stationary sources of not less than 75 per centum, considering control of emissions of hazardous air pollutants from all stationary sources and resulting from measures implemented by the Administrator or by the States under this or other laws.

(D) The strategy may also identify research needs in monitoring, analytical methodology, modeling or pollution control techniques and recommendations for changes in law that would further the goals and objectives of this subsection.

(E) Nothing in this subsection shall be interpreted to preclude or delay implementation of actions with respect to area sources of hazardous air pollutants under consideration pursuant to this or any other law and that may be promulgated before the strategy is prepared.

(F) The Administrator shall implement the strategy as expeditiously as practicable assuring that all sources are in compliance with all requirements not later than 9 years after November 15, 1990.

(G) As part of such strategy the Administrator shall provide for ambient monitoring and emissions modeling in urban areas as appropriate to demonstrate that the goals and objectives of the strategy are being met.

(4) Areawide activities

In addition to the national urban air toxics strategy authorized by paragraph (3), the Administrator shall also encourage and support areawide strategies developed by State or local air pollution control agencies that are intended to reduce risks from emissions by area sources within a particular urban area. From the funds available for grants under this section, the Administrator shall set aside not less than 10 per centum to support areawide strategies addressing hazardous air pollutants emitted by area sources and shall award such funds on a demonstration basis to those States with innovative and effective strategies. At the request of State or local air pollution control officials, the Administrator shall prepare guidelines for control technologies or management practices which may be applicable to various categories or subcategories of area sources.

(5) Report

The Administrator shall report to the Congress at intervals not later than 8 and 12 years after November 15, 1990, on actions taken under this subsection and other parts of this chapter to reduce the risk to public health posed by the release of hazardous air pollutants from area sources. The reports shall also identify specific metropolitan areas that continue to experience high risks to public health as the result of emissions from area sources.

(*l*) State programs

(1) In general

Each State may develop and submit to the Administrator for approval a program for the implementation and enforcement (including a review of enforcement delegations previously granted) of emission standards and other requirements for air pollutants subject to this section or requirements for the prevention and mitigation of accidental releases pursuant to subsection (r) of this section. A program submitted by a State under this subsection may provide for partial or complete delegation of the Administrator's authorities and responsibilities to implement and enforce emissions standards and prevention requirements but shall not include authority to set standards less stringent than those promulgated by the Administrator under this chapter.

(2) Guidance

Not later than 12 months after November 15, 1990, the Administrator shall publish guidance that would be useful to the States in developing programs for submittal under this subsection. The guidance shall also provide for the registration of all facilities producing, processing, handling or storing any substance listed pursuant to subsection (r) of this section in amounts greater than the threshold quantity. The Administrator shall include as an element in such guidance an optional program begun in 1986 for the review of high-risk point sources of air pollutants including, but not limited to, hazardous air pollutants listed pursuant to subsection (b) of this section.

(3) Technical assistance

The Administrator shall establish and maintain an air toxics clearinghouse and center to provide technical information and assistance to State and local agencies and, on a cost recovery basis, to others on control technology, health and ecological risk assessment, risk analysis, ambient monitoring and modeling, and emissions measurement and monitoring. The Administrator shall use the authority of section 7403 of this title to examine methods for preventing, measuring, and controlling emissions and evaluating associated health and ecological risks. Where appropriate, such activity shall be conducted with not-for-profit organizations. The Administrator may conduct research on methods for preventing, measuring and controlling emissions and evaluating associated health and environment risks. All information collected under this paragraph shall be available to the public.

(4) Grants

Upon application of a State, the Administrator may make grants, subject to such terms and conditions as the Administrator deems appropriate, to such State for the purpose of assisting the State in developing and implementing a program for submittal and approval under this subsection. Programs assisted under this paragraph may include program elements addressing air pollutants or extremely hazardous substances other than those specifically subject to this section. Grants under this paragraph may include support for high-risk point source review as provided in paragraph (2) and support for the development and implementation of areawide area source programs pursuant to subsection (k) of this section.

(5) Approval or disapproval

Not later than 180 days after receiving a program submitted by a State, and after notice and opportunity for public comment, the Administrator shall either approve or disapprove such program. The Administrator shall disapprove any program submitted by a State, if the Administrator determines that—

(A) the authorities contained in the program are not adequate to assure compliance by all sources within the State with each applicable standard, regulation or requirement established by the Administrator under this section;

(B) adequate authority does not exist, or adequate resources are not available, to implement the program;

(C) the schedule for implementing the program and assuring compliance by affected sources is not sufficiently expeditious; or

(D) the program is otherwise not in compliance with the guidance issued by the Administrator under paragraph (2) or is not likely to satisfy, in whole or in part, the objectives of this chapter.

If the Administrator disapproves a State program, the Administrator shall notify the State of any revisions or modifications necessary to obtain approval. The State may revise and resubmit the proposed program for review and approval pursuant to the provisions of this subsection.

(6) Withdrawal

Whenever the Administrator determines, after public hearing, that a State is not administering and enforcing a program approved pursuant to this subsection in accordance with the guidance published pursuant to paragraph (2) or the requirements of paragraph (5), the Administrator shall so notify the State and, if action which will assure prompt compliance is not taken within 90 days, the Administrator shall withdraw approval of the program. The Administrator shall not withdraw approval of any program unless the State shall have been notified and the reasons for withdrawal shall have been stated in writing and made public.

(7) Authority to enforce

Nothing in this subsection shall prohibit the Administrator from enforcing any applicable emission standard or requirement under this section.

(8) Local program

The Administrator may, after notice and opportunity for public comment, approve a program developed and submitted by a local air pollution control agency (after consultation with the State) pursuant to this subsection and any such agency implementing an approved program may take any action authorized to be taken by a State under this section.

(9) Permit authority

Nothing in this subsection shall affect the authorities and obligations of the Administrator or the State under subchapter V of this chapter.

(m) Atmospheric deposition to Great Lakes and coastal waters

(1) Deposition assessment

The Administrator, in cooperation with the Under Secretary of Commerce for Oceans and Atmosphere, shall conduct a program to identify and assess the extent of atmospheric deposition of hazardous air pollutants (and in the discretion of the Administrator, other air pollutants) to the Great Lakes, the Chesapeake Bay, Lake Champlain and coastal waters. As part of such program, the Administrator shall—

(A) monitor the Great Lakes, the Chesapeake Bay, Lake Champlain and coastal waters, including monitoring of the Great Lakes through the monitoring network established pursuant to paragraph (2) of this subsection and designing and deploying an atmospheric monitoring network for coastal waters pursuant to paragraph (4);

(B) investigate the sources and deposition rates of atmospheric deposition of air pollutants (and their atmospheric transformation precursors);

(C) conduct research to develop and improve monitoring methods and to determine the relative contribution of atmospheric pollutants to total pollution loadings to the Great Lakes, the Chesapeake Bay, Lake Champlain, and coastal waters;

(D) evaluate any adverse effects to public health or the environment caused by such deposition (including effects resulting from indirect exposure pathways) and assess the contribution of such deposition to violations of water quality standards established pursuant to the Federal Water Pollution Control Act [33 U.S.C.A. § 1251 et seq.] and drinking water standards established pursuant to the Safe Drinking Water Act [42 U.S.C.A. § 300f et seq.]; and

(E) sample for such pollutants in biota, fish, and wildlife of the Great Lakes, the Chesapeake Bay, Lake Champlain and coastal waters and characterize the sources of such pollutants.

(2) Great Lakes monitoring network

The Administrator shall oversee, in accordance with Annex 15 of the Great Lakes Water Quality Agreement, the establishment and operation of a Great Lakes atmospheric deposition network to monitor atmospheric deposition of hazardous air pollutants (and in the Administrator's discretion, other air pollutants) to the Great Lakes.

(A) As part of the network provided for in this paragraph, and not later than December 31, 1991, the Administrator shall establish in each of the 5 Great Lakes at least 1 facility capable of monitoring the atmospheric deposition of hazardous air pollutants in both dry and wet conditions.

(B) The Administrator shall use the data provided by the network to identify and track the movement of hazardous air pollutants through the Great Lakes, to determine the portion of water pollution loadings attributable to atmospheric deposition of such pollutants, and to support development of remedial action plans and other management plans as required by the Great Lakes Water Quality Agreement.

(C) The Administrator shall assure that the data collected by the Great Lakes atmospheric deposition monitoring network is in a format compatible with data bases sponsored by the International Joint Commission, Canada, and the several States of the Great Lakes region.

(3) Monitoring for the Chesapeake Bay and Lake Champlain

The Administrator shall establish at the Chesapeake Bay and Lake Champlain atmospheric deposition stations to monitor deposition of hazardous air pollutants (and in the Administrator's discretion, other air pollutants) within the Chesapeake Bay and Lake Champlain watersheds. The Administrator shall determine the role of air deposition in the pollutant loadings of the Chesapeake Bay and Lake Champlain, investigate the sources of air pollutants deposited in the watersheds, evaluate the health and environmental effects of such pollutant loadings, and shall sample such pollutants in biota, fish and wildlife within the watersheds, as necessary to characterize such effects.

(4) Monitoring for coastal waters

The Administrator shall design and deploy atmospheric deposition monitoring networks for coastal waters and their watersheds and shall make any information collected through such networks available to the public. As part of this effort, the Administrator shall conduct research to develop and improve deposition monitoring methods, and to determine the relative contribution of atmospheric pollutants to pollutant loadings. For purposes of this subsection, "coastal waters" shall mean estuaries selected pursuant to section 320(a)(2)(A) of the Federal Water Pollution Control Act [33 U.S.C.A. § 1330(a)(2)(A)] . or listed pursuant to section 320(a)(2)(B) of such Act [33 U.S.C.A. § 1330(a)(2)(B)] or estuarine research reserves designated pursuant to section 1461 of Title 16.

(5) Report

Within 3 years of November 15, 1990, and biennially thereafter, the Administrator, in cooperation with the Under Secretary of Commerce for Oceans and Atmosphere, shall submit to the Congress a report on the results of any monitoring, studies, and investigations conducted pursuant to this subsection. Such report shall include, at a minimum, an assessment of—

(A) the contribution of atmospheric deposition to pollution loadings in the Great Lakes, the Chesapeake Bay, Lake Champlain and coastal waters;

(B) the environmental and public health effects of any pollution which is attributable to atmospheric deposition to the Great Lakes, the Chesapeake Bay, Lake Champlain and coastal waters;

(C) the source or sources of any pollution to the Great Lakes, the Chesapeake Bay, Lake Champlain and coastal waters which is attributable to atmospheric deposition;

(D) whether pollution loadings in the Great Lakes, the Chesapeake Bay, Lake Champlain or coastal waters cause or contribute to exceedances of drinking water standards pursuant to the Safe Drinking Water Act [42 U.S.C.A. § 300f et seq.] or water quality standards pursuant to the Federal Water Pollution Control Act [33 U.S.C.A. § 1251 et seq.] or, with respect to the Great Lakes, exceedances of the specific objectives of the Great Lakes Water Quality Agreement; and

(E) a description of any revisions of the requirements, standards, and limitations pursuant to this chapter and other applicable Federal laws as are necessary to assure protection of human health and the environment.

(6) Additional regulation

As part of the report to Congress, the Administrator shall determine whether the other provisions of this section are adequate to prevent serious adverse effects to public health and serious or widespread environmental effects, including such effects resulting from indirect exposure pathways, associated with atmospheric deposition to the Great Lakes, the Chesapeake Bay, Lake Champlain and coastal waters of hazardous air pollutants (and their atmospheric transformation products). The Administrator shall take into consideration the tendency of such pollutants to bioaccumulate. Within 5 years after November 15, 1990, the Administrator shall, based on such report and determination, promulgate, in accordance with this section, such further emission standards or control measures as may be necessary and appropriate to prevent such effects, including effects due to bioaccumulation and indirect exposure pathways. Any requirements promulgated pursuant to this paragraph with respect to coastal waters shall only apply to the coastal waters of the States which are subject to section 7627(a) of this title.

(n) Other provisions

(1) Electric utility steam generating units

(A) The Administrator shall perform a study of the hazards to public health reasonably anticipated to occur as a result of emissions by electric utility steam generating units of pollutants listed under subsection (b) of this section after imposition of the requirements of this chapter. The Administrator shall report the results of this study to the Congress within 3 years after November 15, 1990. The Administrator shall develop and describe in the Administrator's report to Congress alternative control strategies for emissions which may warrant regulation under this section. The Administrator shall regulate electric utility steam generating units under this section, if the Administrator finds such regulation is appropriate and necessary after considering the results of the study required by this subparagraph.

(B) The Administrator shall conduct, and transmit to the Congress not later than 4 years after November 15, 1990, a study of mercury emissions from electric utility steam generating units, municipal waste combustion units, and other sources, including area sources. Such study shall consider the rate and mass of such emissions, the health and environmental effects of such emissions, technologies which are available to control such emissions, and the costs of such technologies.

(C) The National Institute of Environmental Health Sciences shall conduct, and transmit to the Congress not later than 3 years after November 15, 1990, a study to determine the threshold level of mercury exposure below which adverse human health effects are not expected to occur. Such study shall include a threshold for mercury concentrations in the tissue of fish which may be consumed (including consumption by sensitive populations) without adverse effects to public health.

(2) Coke oven production technology study

(A) The Secretary of the Department of Energy and the Administrator shall jointly undertake a 6-year study to assess coke oven production emission control technologies and to assist in the development and commercialization of technically practicable and economically viable control technologies which have the potential to significantly reduce emissions of hazardous air pollutants from coke oven production facilities. In identifying control technologies, the Secretary and the Administrator shall consider the range of existing coke oven operations and battery design and the availability of sources of materials for such coke ovens as well as alternatives to existing coke oven production design.

(B) The Secretary and the Administrator are authorized to enter into agreements with persons who propose to develop, install and operate coke production emission control technologies which have the potential for significant emissions reductions of hazardous air pollutants provided that Federal funds shall not exceed 50 per centum of the cost of any project assisted pursuant to this paragraph.

(C) The Secretary shall prepare annual reports to Congress on the status of the research program and at the completion of the study shall make recommendations to the Administrator identifying practicable and economically viable control technologies for coke oven production facilities to reduce residual risks remaining after implementation of the standard under subsection (d) of this section.

(D) There are authorized to be appropriated $5,000,000 for each of the fiscal years 1992 through 1997 to carry out the program authorized by this paragraph.

(3) Publicly owned treatment works

The Administrator may conduct, in cooperation with the owners and operators of publicly owned treatment works, studies to characterize emissions of hazardous air pollutants emitted by such facilities, to identify industrial, commercial and residential discharges that contribute to such emissions and to demonstrate control measures for such emissions. When promulgating any standard under this section applicable to publicly owned treatment works, the Administrator may provide for control measures that include pretreatment of discharges causing emissions of hazardous air pollutants and process or product substitutions or limitations that may be effective in reducing such emissions. The Administrator may prescribe uniform sampling, modeling and risk assessment methods for use in implementing this subsection.

(4) Oil and gas wells; pipeline facilities

(A) Notwithstanding the provisions of subsection (a) of this section, emissions from any oil or gas exploration or production well (with its associated equipment) and emissions from any pipeline compressor or pump station shall not be aggregated with emissions from other similar units, whether or not such units are in a contiguous area or under common control, to determine whether such units or stations are major sources, and in the case of any oil or gas exploration or production well (with its associated equipment), such emissions shall not be aggregated for any purpose under this section.

(B) The Administrator shall not list oil and gas production wells (with its associated equipment) as an area source category under subsection (c) of this section, except that the Administrator may establish an area source category for oil and gas production wells located in any metropolitan statistical area or consolidated metropolitan statistical area with a population in excess of 1 million, if the Administrator determines that emissions of hazardous air pollutants from such wells present more than a negligible risk of adverse effects to public health.

(5) Hydrogen sulfide

The Administrator is directed to assess the hazards to public health and the environment resulting from the emission of hydrogen sulfide associated with the extraction of oil and natural gas resources. To the extent practicable, the assessment shall build upon and not duplicate work conducted for an assessment pursuant to section 8002(m) of the Solid Waste Disposal Act [42 U.S.C.A. § 6982(m)] and shall reflect consultation with the States. The assessment shall include a review of existing State and industry control standards, techniques and enforcement. The Administrator shall report to the Congress within 24 months after November 15, 1990, with the findings of such assessment, together with any recommendations, and shall, as appropriate, develop and implement a control strategy for emissions of hydrogen sulfide to protect human health and the environment, based on the findings of such assessment, using authorities under this chapter including sections [1] 7411 of this title and this section.

(6) Hydrofluoric acid

Not later than 2 years after November 15, 1990, the Administrator shall, for those regions of the country which do not have comprehensive health and safety regulations with respect to hydrofluoric acid, complete a study of the potential hazards of hydrofluoric acid and the uses of hydrofluoric acid in industrial and commercial applications to public health and the environment considering a range of events including worst-case accidental releases and shall make recommendations to the Congress for the reduction of such hazards, if appropriate.

(7) RCRA facilities

In the case of any category or subcategory of sources the air emissions of which are regulated under subtitle C of the Solid Waste Disposal Act [42 U.S.C.A. § 6921 et seq.], the Administrator shall take into account any regulations of such emissions which are promulgated under such subtitle and shall, to the maximum extent practicable and consistent with the provisions of this section, ensure that the requirements of such subtitle and this section are consistent.

(*o*) National Academy of Sciences Study

(1) Request of the Academy

Within 3 months of November 15, 1990, the Administrator shall enter into appropriate arrangements with the National Academy of Sciences to conduct a review of—

(A) risk assessment methodology used by the Environmental Protection Agency to determine the carcinogenic risk associated with exposure to hazardous air pollutants from source categories and subcategories subject to the requirements of this section; and

(B) improvements in such methodology.

(2) **Elements to be studied**

In conducting such review, the National Academy of Sciences should consider, but not be limited to, the following—

(A) the techniques used for estimating and describing the carcinogenic potency to humans of hazardous air pollutants; and

(B) the techniques used for estimating exposure to hazardous air pollutants (for hypothetical and actual maximally exposed individuals as well as other exposed individuals).

(3) **Other health effects of concern**

To the extent practicable, the Academy shall evaluate and report on the methodology for assessing the risk of adverse human health effects other than cancer for which safe thresholds of exposure may not exist, including, but not limited to, inheritable genetic mutations, birth defects, and reproductive dysfunctions.

(4) **Report**

A report on the results of such review shall be submitted to the Senate Committee on Environment and Public Works, the House Committee on Energy and Commerce, the Risk Assessment and Management Commission established by section 303 of the Clean Air Act Amendments of 1990 and the Administrator not later than 30 months after November 15, 1990.

(5) **Assistance**

The Administrator shall assist the Academy in gathering any information the Academy deems necessary to carry out this subsection. The Administrator may use any authority under this chapter to obtain information from any person, and to require any person to conduct tests, keep and produce records, and make reports respecting research or other activities conducted by such person as necessary to carry out this subsection.

(6) **Authorization**

Of the funds authorized to be appropriated to the Administrator by this chapter, such amounts as are required shall be available to carry out this subsection.

(7) **Guidelines for carcinogenic risk assessment**

The Administrator shall consider, but need not adopt, the recommendations contained in the report of the National Academy of Sciences prepared pursuant to this subsection and the views of the Science Advisory Board, with respect to such report. Prior to the promulgation of any standard under subsection (f) of this section, and after notice and opportunity for comment, the Administrator shall publish revised Guidelines for Carcinogenic Risk Assessment or a detailed explanation of the reasons that any recommendations contained in the report of the National Academy of Sciences will not be implemented. The publication of such revised Guidelines shall be a final Agency action for purposes of section 7607 of this title.

(p) **Mickey Leland Urban Air Toxics Research Center**

(1) **Establishment**

The Administrator shall oversee the establishment of a National Urban Air Toxics Research Center, to be located at a university, a hospital, or other facility capable of undertaking and maintaining similar research capabilities in the areas of epidemiology, oncology, toxicology, pulmonary medicine, pathology, and biostatistics. The center shall be known as the Mickey Leland National Urban Air Toxics Research Center. The geographic site of the National Urban Air Toxics Research Center should be further directed to Harris County, Texas, in order to take full advantage of the well developed scientific community presence on-site at the Texas Medical Center as well as the extensive data previously compiled for the comprehensive monitoring system currently in place.

(2) **Board of directors**

The National Urban Air Toxics Research Center shall be governed by a Board of Directors to be comprised of 9 members, the appointment of which shall be allocated pro rata among the Speaker of the House, the Majority Leader of the Senate and the President. The members of the Board of Directors shall be selected based on their respective academic and professional backgrounds and expertise in matters relating to public health, environmental pollution and industrial hygiene. The duties of the Board of Directors shall be to determine policy and research guidelines, submit views from center sponsors and the public and issue periodic reports of center findings and activities.

(3) **Scientific Advisory Panel**

The Board of Directors shall be advised by a Scientific Advisory Panel, the 13 members of which shall be appointed by the Board, and to include eminent members of the scientific and medical communities. The Panel membership may include scientists with relevant experience from the National Institute of Environmental Health Sciences, the

Center for Disease Control, the Environmental Protection Agency, the National Cancer Institute, and others, and the Panel shall conduct peer review and evaluate research results. The Panel shall assist the Board in developing the research agenda, reviewing proposals and applications, and advise on the awarding of research grants.

(4) Funding

The center shall be established and funded with both Federal and private source funds.

(q) Savings provision

(1) Standards previously promulgated

Any standard under this section in effect before November 15, 1990, shall remain in force and effect after such date unless modified as provided in this section before the date of enactment of such Amendments or under such Amendments. Except as provided in paragraph (4), any standard under this section which has been promulgated, but has not taken effect, before such date shall not be affected by such Amendments unless modified as provided in this section before such date or under such Amendments. Each such standard shall be reviewed and, if appropriate, revised, to comply with the requirements of subsection (d) of this section within 10 years after the date of enactment of the Clean Air Act Amendments of 1990. If a timely petition for review of any such standard under section 7607 of this title is pending on such date of enactment, the standard shall be upheld if it complies with this section as in effect before that date. If any such standard is remanded to the Administrator, the Administrator may in the Administrator's discretion apply either the requirements of this section, or those of this section as in effect before November 15, 1990.

(2) Special rule

Notwithstanding paragraph (1), no standard shall be established under this section, as amended by the Clean Air Act Amendments of 1990, for radionuclide emissions from (A) elemental phosphorous plants, (B) grate calcination elemental phosphorous plants, (C) phosphogypsum stacks, or (D) any subcategory of the foregoing. This section, as in effect prior to November 15, 1990, shall remain in effect for radionuclide emissions from such plants and stacks.

(3) Other categories

Notwithstanding paragraph (1), this section, as in effect prior to November 15, 1990, shall remain in effect for radionuclide emissions from non-Department of Energy Federal facilities that are not licensed by the Nuclear Regulatory Commission, coal-fired utility and industrial boilers, underground uranium mines, surface uranium mines, and disposal of uranium mill tailings piles, unless the Administrator, in the Administrator's discretion, applies the requirements of this section as modified by the Clean Air Act Amendments of 1990 to such sources of radionuclides.

(4) Medical facilities

Notwithstanding paragraph (1), no standard promulgated under this section prior to November 15, 1990, with respect to medical research or treatment facilities shall take effect for two years following November 15, 1990, unless the Administrator makes a determination pursuant to a rulemaking under section 7412(d)(9) of this title. If the Administrator determines that the regulatory program established by the Nuclear Regulatory Commission for such facilities does not provide an ample margin of safety to protect public health, the requirements of section 7412 of this title shall fully apply to such facilities. If the Administrator determines that such regulatory program does provide an ample margin of safety to protect the public health, the Administrator is not required to promulgate a standard under this section for such facilities, as provided in section 7412(d)(9) of this title.

(r) Prevention of accidental releases

(1) Purpose and general duty

It shall be the objective of the regulations and programs authorized under this subsection to prevent the accidental release and to minimize the consequences of any such release of any substance listed pursuant to paragraph (3) or any other extremely hazardous substance. The owners and operators of stationary sources producing, processing, handling or storing such substances have a general duty in the same manner and to the same extent as section 654 of Title 29 to identify hazards which may result from such releases using appropriate hazard assessment techniques, to design and maintain a safe facility taking such steps as are necessary to prevent releases, and to minimize the consequences of accidental releases which do occur. For purposes of this paragraph, the provisions of section 7604 of this title shall not be available to any person or otherwise be construed to be applicable to this paragraph. Nothing in this section shall be interpreted, construed, implied or applied to create any liability or basis for suit for compensation for bodily injury or any other injury or property damages to any person which may result from accidental releases of such substances.

(2) Definitions

(A) The term "accidental release" means an unanticipated emission of a regulated substance or other extremely hazardous substance into the ambient air from a stationary source.

(B) The term "regulated substance" means a substance listed under paragraph (3).

(C) The term "stationary source" means any buildings, structures, equipment, installations or substance emitting stationary activities (i) which belong to the same industrial group, (ii) which are located on one or more contiguous properties, (iii) which are under the control of the same person (or persons under common control), and (iv) from which an accidental release may occur.

(3) List of substances

The Administrator shall promulgate not later than 24 months after enactment of the Clean Air Act Amendments of 1990 an initial list of 100 substances which, in the case of an accidental release, are known to cause or may reasonably be anticipated to cause death, injury, or serious adverse effects to human health or the environment. For purposes of promulgating such list, the Administrator shall use, but is not limited to, the list of extremely hazardous substances published under the Emergency Planning and Community Right-to-Know Act of 1986 [42 U.S.C.A. § 11001 et seq.], with such modifications as the Administrator deems appropriate. The initial list shall include chlorine, anhydrous ammonia, methyl chloride, ethylene oxide, vinyl chloride, methyl isocyanate, hydrogen cyanide, ammonia, hydrogen sulfide, toluene diisocyanate, phosgene, bromine, anhydrous hydrogen chloride, hydrogen fluoride, anhydrous sulfur dioxide, and sulfur trioxide. The initial list shall include at least 100 substances which pose the greatest risk of causing death, injury, or serious adverse effects to human health or the environment from accidental releases. Regulations establishing the list shall include an explanation of the basis for establishing the list. The list may be revised from time to time by the Administrator on the Administrator's own motion or by petition and shall be reviewed at least every 5 years. No air pollutant for which a national primary ambient air quality standard has been established shall be included on any such list. No substance, practice, process, or activity regulated under subchapter VI of this chapter shall be subject to regulations under this subsection. The Administrator shall establish procedures for the addition and deletion of substances from the list established under this paragraph consistent with those applicable to the list in subsection (b) of this section.

(4) Factors to be considered

In listing substances under paragraph (3), the Administrator shall consider each of the following criteria—

(A) the severity of any acute adverse health effects associated with accidental releases of the substance;

(B) the likelihood of accidental releases of the substance; and

(C) the potential magnitude of human exposure to accidental releases of the substance.

(5) Threshold quantity

At the time any substance is listed pursuant to paragraph (3), the Administrator shall establish by rule, a threshold quantity for the substance, taking into account the toxicity, reactivity, volatility, dispersibility, combustibility, or flammability of the substance and the amount of the substance which, as a result of an accidental release, is known to cause or may reasonably be anticipated to cause death, injury or serious adverse effects to human health for which the substance was listed. The Administrator is authorized to establish a greater threshold quantity for, or to exempt entirely, any substance that is a nutrient used in agriculture when held by a farmer.

(6) Chemical safety board

(A) There is hereby established an independent safety board to be known as the Chemical Safety and Hazard Investigation Board.

(B) The Board shall consist of 5 members, including a Chairperson, who shall be appointed by the President, by and with the advice and consent of the Senate. Members of the Board shall be appointed on the basis of technical qualification, professional standing, and demonstrated knowledge in the fields of accident reconstruction, safety engineering, human factors, toxicology, or air pollution regulation. The terms of office of members of the Board shall be 5 years. Any member of the Board, including the Chairperson, may be removed for inefficiency, neglect of duty, or malfeasance in office. The Chairperson shall be the Chief Executive Officer of the Board and shall exercise the executive and administrative functions of the Board.

(C) The Board shall—

(i) investigate (or cause to be investigated), determine and report to the public in writing the facts, conditions, and circumstances and the cause or probable cause of any accidental release resulting in a fatality, serious injury or substantial property damages;

(ii) issue periodic reports to the Congress, Federal, State and local agencies, including the Environmental Protection Agency and the Occupational Safety and Health Administration, concerned with the safety of chemical production, processing, handling and storage, and other interested persons recommending measures to reduce the likelihood or the consequences of accidental releases and proposing corrective steps to make chemical production, processing, handling and storage as safe and free from risk of injury as is possible and may include in such reports proposed rules or orders which should be issued by the Administrator under the authority of this section or the Secretary of Labor under the Occupational Safety and Health Act [29 U.S.C.A. § 651 et seq.] to prevent or minimize the consequences of any release of substances that may cause death, injury or other serious adverse effects on human health or substantial property damage as the result of an accidental release; and

(iii) establish by regulation requirements binding on persons for reporting accidental releases into the ambient air subject to the Board's investigatory jurisdiction. Reporting releases to the National Response Center, in lieu of the Board directly, shall satisfy such regulations. The National Response Center shall promptly notify the Board of any releases which are within the Board's jurisdiction.

(D) The Board may utilize the expertise and experience of other agencies.

(E) The Board shall coordinate its activities with investigations and studies conducted by other agencies of the United States having a responsibility to protect public health and safety. The Board shall enter into a memorandum of understanding with the National Transportation Safety Board to assure coordination of functions and to limit duplication of activities which shall designate the National Transportation Safety Board as the lead agency for the investigation of releases which are transportation related. The Board shall not be authorized to investigate marine oil spills, which the National Transportation Safety Board is authorized to investigate. The Board shall enter into a memorandum of understanding with the Occupational Safety and Health Administration so as to limit duplication of activities. In no event shall the Board forego an investigation where an accidental release causes a fatality or serious injury among the general public, or had the potential to cause substantial property damage or a number of deaths or injuries among the general public.

(F) The Board is authorized to conduct research and studies with respect to the potential for accidental releases, whether or not an accidental release has occurred, where there is evidence which indicates the presence of a potential hazard or hazards. To the extent practicable, the Board shall conduct such studies in cooperation with other Federal agencies having emergency response authorities, State and local governmental agencies and associations and organizations from the industrial, commercial, and nonprofit sectors.

(G) No part of the conclusions, findings, or recommendations of the Board relating to any accidental release or the investigation thereof shall be admitted as evidence or used in any action or suit for damages arising out of any matter mentioned in such report.

(H) Not later than 18 months after November 15, 1990, the Board shall publish a report accompanied by recommendations to the Administrator on the use of hazard assessments in preventing the occurrence and minimizing the consequences of accidental releases of extremely hazardous substances. The recommendations shall include a list of extremely hazardous substances which are not regulated substances (including threshold quantities for such substances) and categories of stationary sources for which hazard assessments would be an appropriate measure to aid in the prevention of accidental releases and to minimize the consequences of those releases that do occur. The recommendations shall also include a description of the information and analysis which would be appropriate to include in any hazard assessment. The Board shall also make recommendations with respect to the role of risk management plans as required by paragraph (8)(B) in preventing accidental releases. The Board may from time to time review and revise its recommendations under this subparagraph.

(I) Whenever the Board submits a recommendation with respect to accidental releases to the Administrator, the Administrator shall respond to such recommendation formally and in writing not later than 180 days after receipt thereof. The response to the Board's recommendation by the Administrator shall indicate whether the Administrator will—

(i) initiate a rulemaking or issue such orders as are necessary to implement the recommendation in full or in part, pursuant to any timetable contained in the recommendation;

(ii) decline to initiate a rulemaking or issue orders as recommended.

Any determination by the Administrator not to implement a recommendation of the Board or to implement a recommendation only in part, including any variation from the schedule contained in the recommendation, shall be accompanied by a statement from the Administrator setting forth the reasons for such determination.

(J) The Board may make recommendations with respect to accidental releases to the Secretary of Labor. Whenever the Board submits such recommendation, the Secretary shall respond to such recommendation formally and in writing not later than 180 days after receipt thereof. The response to the Board's recommendation by the Administrator shall indicate whether the Secretary will—

(i) initiate a rulemaking or issue such orders as are necessary to implement the recommendation in full or in part, pursuant to any timetable contained in the recommendation;

(ii) decline to initiate a rulemaking or issue orders as recommended.

Any determination by the Secretary not to implement a recommendation or to implement a recommendation only in part, including any variation from the schedule contained in the recommendation, shall be accompanied by a statement from the Secretary setting forth the reasons for such determination.

(K) Within 2 years after enactment of the Clean Air Act Amendments of 1990, the Board shall issue a report to the Administrator of the Environmental Protection Agency and to the Administrator of the Occupational Safety and Health Administration recommending the adoption of regulations for the preparation of risk management plans and general requirements for the prevention of accidental releases of regulated substances into the ambient air (including recommendations for listing substances under paragraph (3)) and for the mitigation of the potential adverse effect on human health or the environment as a result of accidental releases which should be applicable to any stationary source handling any regulated substance in more than threshold amounts. The Board may include proposed rules or orders which should be issued by the Administrator under authority of this subsection or by the Secretary of Labor under the Occupational Safety and Health Act [29 U.S.C.A. § 651 et seq.]. Any such recommendations shall be specific and shall identify the regulated substance or class of regulated substances (or other substances) to which the recommendations apply. The Administrator shall consider such recommendations before promulgating regulations required by paragraph (7)(B).

(L) The Board, or upon authority of the Board, any member thereof, any administrative law judge employed by or assigned to the Board, or any officer or employee duly designated by the Board, may for the purpose of carrying out duties authorized by subparagraph (C)—

(i) hold such hearings, sit and act at such times and places, administer such oaths, and require by subpoena or otherwise attendance and testimony of such witnesses and the production of evidence and may require by order that any person engaged in the production, processing, handling, or storage of extremely hazardous substances submit written reports and responses to requests and questions within such time and in such form as the Board may require; and

(ii) upon presenting appropriate credentials and a written notice of inspection authority, enter any property where an accidental release causing a fatality, serious injury or substantial property damage has occurred and do all things therein necessary for a proper investigation pursuant to subparagraph (C) and inspect at reasonable times records, files, papers, processes, controls, and facilities and take such samples as are relevant to such investigation.

Whenever the Administrator or the Board conducts an inspection of a facility pursuant to this subsection, employees and their representatives shall have the same rights to participate in such inspections as provided in the Occupational Safety and Health Act [29 U.S.C.A. § 651 et seq.].

(M) In addition to that described in subparagraph (L), the Board may use any information gathering authority of the Administrator under this chapter, including the subpoena power provided in section 7607(a)(1) of this title.

(N) The Board is authorized to establish such procedural and administrative rules as are necessary to the exercise of its functions and duties. The Board is authorized without regard to section 5 of Title 41 to enter into contracts, leases, cooperative agreements or other transactions as may be necessary in the conduct of the duties and functions of the Board with any other agency, institution, or person.

(O) After the effective date of any reporting requirement promulgated pursuant to subparagraph (C)(iii) it shall be unlawful for any person to fail to report any release of any extremely hazardous substance as required by such subparagraph. The Administrator is authorized to enforce any regulation or requirements established by the Board pursuant to subparagraph (C)(iii) using the authorities of sections 7413 and 7414 of this title. Any request for information from the owner or operator of a stationary source made by the Board or by the Administrator under this section shall be treated, for purposes of sections 7413, 7414, 7416, 7420, 7603, 7604 and 7607 of this title and any other enforcement provisions of this chapter, as a request made by the Administrator under section 7414 of this title and may be enforced by the Chairperson of the Board or by the Administrator as provided in such section.

(P) The Administrator shall provide to the Board such support and facilities as may be necessary for operation of the Board.

(Q) Consistent with subsection (G)[2] and section 7414(c) of this title any records, reports or information obtained by the Board shall be available to the Administrator, the Secretary of Labor, the Congress and the public, except that upon a showing satisfactory to the Board by any person that records, reports, or information, or particular part thereof (other than release or emissions data) to which the Board has access, if made public, is likely to cause substantial harm to the person's competitive position, the Board shall consider such record, report, or information or particular portion thereof confidential in accordance with section 1905 of Title 18, except that such record, report, or information may be disclosed to other officers, employees, and authorized representatives of the United States concerned with carrying out this chapter or when relevant under any proceeding under this chapter. This subparagraph does not constitute authority to withhold records, reports, or information from the Congress.

(R) Whenever the Board submits or transmits any budget estimate, budget request, supplemental budget request, or other budget information, legislative recommendation, prepared testimony for congressional hearings, recommendation or study to the President, the Secretary of Labor, the Administrator, or the Director of the Office of Management and Budget, it shall concurrently transmit a copy thereof to the Congress. No report of the Board shall be subject to review by the Administrator or any Federal agency or to judicial review in any court. No officer or agency of the United States shall have authority to require the Board to submit its budget requests or estimates, legislative recommendations, prepared testimony, comments, recommendations or reports to any officer or agency of the United States for approval or review prior to the submission of such recommendations, testimony, comments or reports to the Congress. In the performance of their functions as established by this chapter, the members, officers and employees of the Board shall not be responsible to or subject to supervision or direction, in carrying out any duties under this subsection, of any officer or employee or agent of the Environmental Protection Agency, the Department of Labor or any other agency of the United States except that the President may remove any member, officer or employee of the Board for inefficiency, neglect of duty or malfeasance in office. Nothing in this section shall affect the application of Title 5 to officers or employees of the Board.

(S) The Board shall submit an annual report to the President and to the Congress which shall include, but not be limited to, information on accidental releases which have been investigated by or reported to the Board during the previous year, recommendations for legislative or administrative action which the Board has made, the actions which have been taken by the Administrator or the Secretary of Labor or the heads of other agencies to implement such recommendations, an identification of priorities for study and investigation in the succeeding year, progress in the development of risk-reduction technologies and the response to and implementation of significant research findings on chemical safety in the public and private sector.

(7) Accident prevention

(A) In order to prevent accidental releases of regulated substances, the Administrator is authorized to promulgate release prevention, detection, and correction requirements which may include monitoring, record-keeping, reporting, training, vapor recovery, secondary containment, and other design, equipment, work practice, and operational requirements. Regulations promulgated under this paragraph may make distinctions between various types, classes, and kinds of facilities, devices and systems taking into consideration factors including, but not limited to, the size, location, process, process controls, quantity of substances handled, potency of substances, and response capabilities present at any stationary source. Regulations promulgated pursuant to this subparagraph shall have an effective date, as determined by the Administrator, assuring compliance as expeditiously as practicable.

(B)(i) Within 3 years after November 15, 1990, the Administrator shall promulgate reasonable regulations and appropriate guidance to provide, to the greatest extent practicable, for the prevention and detection of accidental releases of regulated substances and for response to such releases by the owners or operators of the sources of such releases. The Administrator shall utilize the expertise of the Secretaries of Transportation and Labor in promulgating such regulations. As appropriate, such regulations shall cover the use, operation, repair, replacement, and maintenance of equipment to monitor, detect, inspect, and control such releases, including training of persons in the use and maintenance of such equipment and in the conduct of periodic inspections. The regulations shall include procedures and measures for emergency response after an accidental release of a regulated substance in order to protect human health and the environment. The regulations shall cover storage, as well as operations. The regulations shall, as appropriate, recognize differences in size, operations, processes, class and categories of sources and the voluntary actions of such sources to prevent such releases and respond to such releases. The regulations shall be applicable to a stationary source 3 years after the date of promulgation, or 3 years after the date on which a regulated substance present at the source in more than threshold amounts is first listed under paragraph (3), whichever is later.

(ii) The regulations under this subparagraph shall require the owner or operator of stationary sources at which a regulated substance is present in more than a threshold quantity to prepare and implement a risk management plan to detect and prevent or minimize accidental releases of such substances from the stationary source, and to provide a prompt emergency response to any such releases in order to protect human health and the environment. Such plan shall provide for compliance with the requirements of this subsection and shall also include each of the following:

(I) a hazard assessment to assess the potential effects of an accidental release of any regulated substance. This assessment shall include an estimate of potential release quantities and a determination of downwind effects, including potential exposures to affected populations. Such assessment shall include a previous release history of the past 5 years, including the size, concentration, and duration of releases, and shall include an evaluation of worst case accidental releases;

(II) a program for preventing accidental releases of regulated substances, including safety precautions and maintenance, monitoring and employee training measures to be used at the source; and

(III) a response program providing for specific actions to be taken in response to an accidental release of a regulated substance so as to protect human health and the environment, including procedures for informing the public and local agencies responsible for responding to accidental releases, emergency health care, and employee training measures.

At the time regulations are promulgated under this subparagraph, the Administrator shall promulgate guidelines to assist stationary sources in the preparation of risk management plans. The guidelines shall, to the extent practicable, include model risk management plans.

(iii) The owner or operator of each stationary source covered by clause (ii) shall register a risk management plan prepared under this subparagraph with the Administrator before the effective date of regulations under clause (i) in such form and manner as the Administrator shall, by rule, require. Plans prepared pursuant to this subparagraph shall also be submitted to the Chemical Safety and Hazard Investigation Board, to the State in which the stationary source is located, and to any local agency or entity having responsibility for planning for or responding to accidental releases which may occur at such source, and shall be available to the public under section 7414(c) of this title. The Administrator shall establish, by rule, an auditing system to regularly review and, if necessary, require revision in risk management plans to assure that the plans comply with this subparagraph. Each such plan shall be updated periodically as required by the Administrator, by rule.

(C) Any regulations promulgated pursuant to this subsection shall to the maximum extent practicable, consistent with this subsection, be consistent with the recommendations and standards established by the American Society of Mechanical Engineers (ASME), the American National Standards Institute (ANSI) or the American Society of Testing Materials (ASTM). The Administrator shall take into consideration the concerns of small business in promulgating regulations under this subsection.

(D) In carrying out the authority of this paragraph, the Administrator shall consult with the Secretary of Labor and the Secretary of Transportation and shall coordinate any requirements under this paragraph with any requirements established for comparable purposes by the Occupational Safety and Health Administration or the Department of Transportation. Nothing in this subsection shall be interpreted, construed or applied to impose requirements affecting, or to grant the Administrator, the Chemical Safety and Hazard Investigation Board, or any other agency any authority to regulate (including requirements for hazard assessment), the accidental release of radionuclides arising from the construction and operation of facilities licensed by the Nuclear Regulatory Commission.

(E) After the effective date of any regulation or requirement imposed under this subsection, it shall be unlawful for any person to operate any stationary source subject to such regulation or requirement in violation of such regulation or requirement. Each regulation or requirement under this subsection shall for purposes of sections 7413, 7414, 7416, 7420, 7604, and 7607 of this title and other enforcement provisions of this chapter, be treated as a standard in effect under subsection (d) of this section.

(F) Notwithstanding the provisions of subchapter V of this chapter or this section, no stationary source shall be required to apply for, or operate pursuant to, a permit issued under such subchapter solely because such source is subject to regulations or requirements under this subsection.

(G) In exercising any authority under this subsection, the Administrator shall not, for purposes of section 653(b)(1) of Title 29, be deemed to be exercising statutory authority to prescribe or enforce standards or regulations affecting occupational safety and health.

(8) Research on hazard assessments

The Administrator may collect and publish information on accident scenarios and consequences covering a range of possible events for substances listed under paragraph (3). The Administrator shall establish a program of long-term research to develop and disseminate information on methods and techniques for hazard assessment which may be useful in improving and validating the procedures employed in the preparation of hazard assessments under this subsection.

(9) Order authority

(A) In addition to any other action taken, when the Administrator determines that there may be an imminent and substantial endangerment to the human health or welfare or the environment because of an actual or threatened accidental release of a regulated substance, the Administrator may secure such relief as may be necessary to abate such danger or threat, and the district court of the United States in the district in which the threat occurs shall have jurisdiction to grant such relief as the public interest and the equities of the case may require. The Administrator may also, after notice to the State in which the stationary source is located, take other action under this paragraph including, but not limited to, issuing such orders as may be necessary to protect human health. The Administrator shall take action under section 7603 of this title rather than this paragraph whenever the authority of such section is adequate to protect human health and the environment.

(B) Orders issued pursuant to this paragraph may be enforced in an action brought in the appropriate United States district court as if the order were issued under section 7603 of this title.

(C) Within 180 days after enactment of the Clean Air Act Amendments of 1990, the Administrator shall publish guidance for using the order authorities established by this paragraph. Such guidance shall provide for the coordinated use of the authorities of this paragraph with other emergency powers authorized by section 9606 of this title, sections 311(c), 308, 309 and 504(a) of the Federal Water Pollution Control Act [15 U.S.C.A. §§ 1321(c), 1318, 1319 and 1364(a)], sections 3007, 3008, 3013, and 7003 of the Solid Waste Disposal Act [42 U.S.C.A. §§ 6927, 6928, 6934 and 6973], sections 1445 and 1431 of the Safe Drinking Water Act [42 U.S.C.A. §§ 300j–4 and 300], sections 5 and 7 of the Toxic Substances Control Act [15 U.S.C.A. §§ 2604, 2606], and sections 7413, 7414, and 7603 of this title.

(10) Presidential review

The President shall conduct a review of release prevention, mitigation and response authorities of the various Federal agencies and shall clarify and coordinate agency responsibilities to assure the most effective and efficient implementation of such authorities and to identify any deficiencies in authority or resources which may exist. The President may utilize the resources and solicit the recommendations of the Chemical Safety and Hazard Investigation Board in conducting such review. At the conclusion of such review, but not later than 24 months after November 15, 1990, the President shall transmit a message to the Congress on the release prevention, mitigation and response activities of the Federal Government making such recommendations for change in law as the President may deem appropriate. Nothing in this paragraph shall be interpreted, construed or applied to authorize the President to modify or reassign release prevention, mitigation or response authorities otherwise established by law.

(11) State authority

Nothing in this subsection shall preclude, deny or limit any right of a State or political subdivision thereof to adopt or enforce any regulation, requirement, limitation or standard (including any procedural requirement) that is more stringent than a regulation, requirement, limitation or standard in effect under this subsection or that applies to a substance not subject to this subsection.

(s) Periodic report

Not later than January 15, 1993 and every 3 years thereafter, the Administrator shall prepare and transmit to the Congress a comprehensive report on the measures taken by the Agency and by the States to implement the provisions of this section. The Administrator shall maintain a database on pollutants and sources subject to the provisions of this section and shall include aggregate information from the database in each annual report. The report shall include, but not be limited to—

(1) a status report on standard-setting under subsections (d) and (f) of this section;

(2) information with respect to compliance with such standards including the costs of compliance experienced by sources in various categories and subcategories;

(3) development and implementation of the national urban air toxics program; and

(4) recommendations of the Chemical Safety and Hazard Investigation Board with respect to the prevention and mitigation of accidental releases.

(July 14, 1955, ch. 360, title I, § 112, as added Dec. 31, 1970, Pub.L. 91–604, § 4(a), 84 Stat. 1685, and amended Aug. 7, 1977, Pub.L. 95–95, title I, §§ 109(d)(2), 110, title IV, § 401(c), 91 Stat. 701, 703, 791; Nov. 9, 1978, Pub.L. 95–623, § 13(b), 92 Stat. 3458; Nov. 15, 1990, Pub.L. 101–549, title III, § 301, 104 Stat. 2531; Dec. 4, 1991, Pub.L. 102–187, 105 Stat. 1285.)

1 So in original. Probably should be "section".

2 So in original. Probably should read "subparagraph (G)".

References in Text

The Atomic Energy Act of 1954, referred to in subsec. (d)(9), is Act Aug. 30, 1954, c. 1073, 68 Stat. 921, as amended, which is classified generally to chapter 23 (section 2011 et seq.) of this title. For complete classification of this Act to the Code, see Short Title note set out under section 2011 of this title and Tables.

The Federal Water Pollution Control Act, referred to in subsecs. (e)(4), (m)(1)(D), (m)(4), (m)(5)(D) and (r)(9)(C), is Act June 30, 1948, c. 758, as amended generally by Pub.L. 92–500, § 2, Oct. 18, 1972, 86 Stat. 816, which is classified generally to chapter 26 (section 1251 et seq.) of Title 33, Navigation and Navigable Waters. Title II of the Federal Water Pollution Control Act, referred to in subsec. (e)(4), is classified generally to subchapter II (section 1281 et seq.) of Title 33. Section 320 of such Act, referred to in subsec. (m)(4), is classified to section 1330 of Title 33. Sections 308, 309, 311(c) and 504(a) of such Act, referred to in subsec. (r)(9)(C), are classified to sections 1318, 1319, 1321(c) and 1364(a), respectively, of Title 33. For complete classification of this Act to the Code, see Short Title note set out under section 1251 of Title 33 and Tables.

The enactment of the Clean Air Act Amendments of 1990, referred to in subsecs. (i)(5)(C), (r)(3), (r)(6)(K) and (r)(9)(C), probably means the date of enactment of Pub.L. 101–549, Nov. 15, 1990, 104 Stat. 2399, which was approved Nov. 15, 1990.

The Toxic Substances Control Act, referred to in subsecs. (k)(3)(C) and (r)(9)(C), is Pub.L. 94–469, Oct. 11, 1976, 90 Stat. 2003, as amended, which is classified generally to chapter 53 (section 2601 et seq.) of Title 15, Commerce and Trade. Sections 5 and 7 of such Act, referred to in subsec. (r)(9)(C), are classified to section 2604 and 2606, respectively, of Title 15. For complete classification of this Act to the Code, see Short Title note set out under section 2601 of Title 15 and Tables.

The Federal Insecticide, Fungicide, and Rodenticide Act, referred to in subsec. (k)(3)(C), is Act June 25, 1947, c. 125, as amended, which is classified generally to subchapter II (section 136 et seq.) of chapter 6 of Title 7, Agriculture. For complete classification of this Act to the Code, see Short Title note set out under section 136 of Title 7 and Tables.

The Resource Conservation and Recovery Act of 1976, referred to in subsec. (k)(3)(C), is Pub.L. 94–580, Oct. 21, 1976, 90 Stat. 2796, as amended, which is classified generally to chapter 82 (section 6901 et seq.) of this title. For complete classification of this Act to the Code, see Short Title note set out under section 6901 of this title and Tables.

The Safe Drinking Water Act, referred to in subsecs. (m)(1)(D), (m)(5)(D) and (r)(9)(C), is Pub.L. 93–523, Dec. 16, 1974, 88 Stat. 1660, as amended, which is classified principally to subchapter XII (section 300f et seq.) of chapter 6A of this title. Sections 1431 and 1445 of such Act, referred to in subsec. (r)(9)(C), are classified to section 300i and 300j–4 of this title, respectively. For complete classification of this Act to the Code see Short Title note set out under section 201 of this title and Tables.

The Solid Waste Disposal Act, referred to in subsecs. (n)(5), (n)(7) and (r)(9)(C), is Title II of Pub.L. 89–272, Oct. 20, 1965, 79 Stat. 997, as amended generally by Pub.L. 94–580, § 2, Oct. 21, 1976, 90 Stat. 2795, which is classified generally to chapter 82 (section 6901 et seq.) of this title. Section 8002(m) of the Solid Waste Disposal Act, referred to in subsec. (n)(5), is classified to section 6982(m) of this title. Subtitle C of such Act, referred to in subsec. (n)(7), is classified generally to subchapter III (section 6921 et seq.) of chapter 82 of this title. Sections 3007, 3008, 3013 and 7003 of such Act, referred to in subsec. (r)(9)(C), are classified to sections 6927, 6928, 6934 and 6973, respectively, of this title. For complete classification of this Act to the Code, see Short Title note set out under section 6901 of this title and Tables.

The Clean Air Act Amendments of 1990, referred to in subsecs. (*o*)(4), (q)(1), (q)(2) and (q)(3), is Pub.L. 101–549, Nov. 15, 1990, 104 Stat. 2399. Section 303 of such Act, referred to in subsec. (*o*)(4), is set out as a note under this section. For complete classification of this Act to the Code, see Tables.

The Emergency Planning and Community Right-to-Know Act of 1986, referred to in subsec. (r)(3), is Title III of Pub.L. 99–499, Oct. 17, 1986, 100 Stat. 1728, which is classified generally to chapter 116 (section 11001 et seq.) of this title. For complete classification of this Act to the Code, see Short Title note set out under section 11001 of this title and Tables.

The Occupational Safety and Health Act of 1970, referred to in subsecs. (r)(6)(C)(ii), (r)(6)(K) and (r)(6)(L), is Pub.L. 91–596, Dec. 29, 1970, 84 Stat. 1590, as amended, which is classified principally to chapter 15 (section 651 et seq.) of Title 29, Labor. For complete classification of this Act to the Code, see Short Title note set out under section 651 of Title 29 and Tables.

Change of Name

Any reference in any provision of law enacted before Jan. 4, 1995, to the Committee on Energy and Commerce of the House of Representatives treated as referring to the Committee on Commerce of the House of Representatives, except that any reference in any provision of law enacted before Jan. 4, 1995, to the Committee on Energy and Commerce of the House of Representatives treated as referring to the Committee on Agriculture of the House of Representatives, in the case of a provision of law relating to inspection of seafood or seafood products, the Committee on Banking and Financial Services of the House of Representatives, in the case of a provision of law relating to bank capital markets activities generally or to depository institution securities activities generally, and the Committee on Transportation and Infrastructure of the House of Representatives, in the case of a provision of law relating to railroads, railway labor, or railroad retirement and unemployment (except revenue measures related thereto), see section 1(a)(4) and (c)(1) of Pub.L. 104–14, set out as a note preceding section 21 of Title 2, The Congress.

Effective Date of 1990 Amendment

Amendment by Pub.L. 101–549 effective Nov. 15, 1990, except as otherwise provided, see section 711(b) of Pub.L. 101–549, set out as a note under section 7401 of this title.

Savings Provisions

Suits, actions or proceedings commenced under this chapter as in effect prior to Nov. 15, 1990, not to abate by reason of the taking effect of amendments by Pub.L. 101–549, except as otherwise provided for, see section 711(a) of Pub.L. 101–549, set out as a note under section 7401 of this title.

Risk Assessment and Management Commission

Section 303 of Pub.L. 101–549 provided that:

"**(a) Establishment.**—There is hereby established a Risk Assessment and Management Commission (hereafter referred to in this section as the 'Commission'), which shall commence proceedings not later than 18 months after the date of enactment of the Clean Air Act Amendments of 1990 [Nov. 15, 1990] and which shall make a full investigation of the policy implications and appropriate uses of risk assessment and risk management in regulatory programs under various Federal laws to prevent cancer and other chronic human health effects which may result from exposure to hazardous substances.

"**(b) Charge.**—The Commission shall consider—

"(1) the report of the National Academy of Sciences authorized by section 112(*o*) of the Clean Air Act [subsec. (*o*) of this section] the use and limitations of risk assessment in establishing emission or effluent standards, ambient standards, exposure standards, acceptable concentration levels, tolerances or other environmental criteria for hazardous substances that present a risk of carcinogenic effects or other chronic health effects and the suitability of risk assessment for such purposes;

"(2) the most appropriate methods for measuring and describing cancer risks or risks of other chronic health effects from exposure to hazardous substances considering such alternative approaches as the lifetime risk of cancer or other effects to the individual or individuals most exposed to emissions from a source or sources on both an actual and worst case basis, the range of such risks, the total number of health effects avoided by exposure reductions, effluent standards, ambient standards, exposures standards, acceptable concentration levels, tolerances and other environmental criteria, reductions in the number of persons exposed at various levels of risk, the incidence of cancer, and other public health factors;

"(3) methods to reflect uncertainties in measurement and estimation techniques, the existence of synergistic or antagonistic effects among hazardous substances, the accuracy of extrapolating human health risks from animal exposure data, and the existence of unquantified direct or indirect effects on human health in risk assessment studies;

"(4) risk management policy issues including the use of lifetime cancer risks to individuals most exposed, incidence of cancer, the cost and technical feasibility of exposure reduction measures and the use of site-specific actual exposure information in setting emissions standards and other limitations applicable to sources of exposure to hazardous substances; and

"(5) and comment on the degree to which it is possible or desirable to develop a consistent risk assessment methodology, or a consistent standard of acceptable risk, among various Federal programs.

"**(c) Membership.**—Such Commission shall be composed of ten members who shall have knowledge or experience in fields of risk assessment or risk management, including three members to be appointed by the President, two members to be appointed by the Speaker of the House of Representatives, one member to be appointed by the Minority Leader of the House of Representatives, two members to be appointed by the Majority Leader of the Senate, one member to be appointed by the Minority Leader of the Senate, and one member to be appointed by the President of the National Academy of Sciences. Appointments shall be made not later than 18 months after the date of enactment of the Clean Air Act Amendments of 1990 [Nov. 15, 1990].

"**(d) Assistance from agencies.**—The Administrator of the Environmental Protection Agency and the heads of all other departments, agencies, and instrumentalities of the executive branch of the Federal Government shall, to the maximum extent practicable, assist the Commission in gathering such information as the Commission deems necessary to carry out this section subject to other provisions of law.

"**(e) Staff and contracts.**—

"(1) In the conduct of the study required by this section, the Commission is authorized to contract (in accordance with Federal contract law) with nongovernmental entities that are competent to perform research or investigations within the Commission's mandate, and to hold public hearings, forums, and workshops to enable full public participation.

"(2) The Commission may appoint and fix the pay of such staff as it deems necessary in accordance with the provisions of title 5, United States Code [Title 5, Government Organization and Employees]. The Commission may request the temporary assignment of personnel from the Environmental Protection Agency or other Federal agencies.

"(3) The members of the Commission who are not officers or employees of the United States, while attending conferences or meetings of the Commission or while otherwise serving at the request of the Chair, shall be entitled to receive compensation at a rate not in excess of the maximum rate of pay for Grade GS–18, as provided in the General Schedule under section 5332 of title 5 of the United States Code [section 5332 of Title 5], including travel time, and while away from their homes or regular places of business they may be allowed travel expenses, including per diem in lieu of subsistence as authorized by law for persons in the Government service employed intermittently.

"**(f) Report.**—A report containing the results of all Commission studies and investigations under this section, together with any appropriate legislative recommendations or administrative recommendations, shall be made available to the public for comment not later than 42 months after the date of enactment of the Clean Air Act Amendments of 1990 [Nov. 15, 1990] and shall be submitted to the President and to the Congress not later than 48 months after such date of enactment. In the report, the Commission shall make recommendations with respect to the appropriate use of risk assessment and risk management in Federal regulatory programs to prevent cancer or other chronic health effects which may result from exposure to hazardous substances. The Commission shall cease to exist upon the date determined by the Commission, but not later than 9 months after the submission of such report.

"**(g) Authorization.**—There are authorized to be appropriated such sums as are necessary to carry out the activities of the Commission established by this section."

CROSS REFERENCES

Federally permitted release defined to include emissions into air subject to permit or control regulation under this section for purposes of Comprehensive Environmental Response, Compensation, and Liability Act of 1980, see section 9601 of this title.

West's Federal Practice Manual

Air quality legislation, see § 4384.5.

CODE OF FEDERAL REGULATIONS

Emission standards for hazardous pollutants, see 40 CFR 61.01 et seq.

New stationary sources, standards of performance for, see 40 CFR 60.1 et seq.

LAW REVIEW COMMENTARIES

Encouraging safety through insurance-based incentives: financial responsibility for hazardous wastes. Jeffrey Kehne, 96 Yale L.J. 403 (1986).

The Clean Air Act: Economic and technological feasibility in setting standards under Section 112. John A. Coppede, 22 Land & Water L.Rev. 397 (1987).

Library References

Health and Environment ⚷25.6(1) et seq., 28.

C.J.S. Health and Environment § 91 et seq.

§ 7413. Federal enforcement [CAA § 113]

(a) In general

(1) Order to comply with SIP

Whenever, on the basis of any information available to the Administrator, the Administrator finds that any person has violated or is in violation of any requirement or prohibition of an applicable implementation plan or permit, the Administrator shall notify the person and the State in which the plan applies of such finding. At any time after the expiration of 30 days following the date on which such notice of a violation is issued, the Administrator may, without regard to the period of violation (subject to section 2462 of Title 28)—

(A) issue an order requiring such person to comply with the requirements or prohibitions of such plan or permit,

(B) issue an administrative penalty order in accordance with subsection (d) of this section, or

(C) bring a civil action in accordance with subsection (b) of this section.

(2) State failure to enforce SIP or permit program

Whenever, on the basis of information available to the Administrator, the Administrator finds that violations of an applicable implementation plan or an approved permit program under subchapter V of this chapter are so widespread that such violations appear to result from a failure of the State in which the plan or permit program applies to enforce the plan or permit program effectively, the Administrator shall so notify the State. In the case of a permit program, the notice shall be made in accordance with subchapter V of this chapter. If the Administrator finds such failure extends beyond the 30th day after such notice (90 days in the case of such permit program), the Administrator shall give public notice of such finding. During the period beginning with such public notice and ending when such State satisfies the Administrator that it will enforce such plan or permit program (hereafter referred to in this section as "period of federally assumed enforcement"), the Administrator may enforce any requirement or prohibition of such plan or permit program with respect to any person by—

(A) issuing an order requiring such person to comply with such requirement or prohibition,

(B) issuing an administrative penalty order in accordance with subsection (d) of this section, or

(C) bringing a civil action in accordance with subsection (b) of this section.

(3) EPA enforcement of other requirements

Except for a requirement or prohibition enforceable under the preceding provisions of this subsection, whenever, on the basis of any information available to the Administrator, the Administrator finds that any person has violated, or is in violation of, any other requirement or prohibition of this subchapter, section 7603 of this title, subchapter IV–A of this chapter, subchapter V of this chapter, or subchapter VI of this chapter, including, but not limited to, a requirement or prohibition of any rule, plan, order, waiver, or permit promulgated, issued, or approved under those provisions or titles, or for the payment of any fee owed to the United States under this chapter (other than subchapter II of this chapter), the Administrator may—

(A) issue an administrative penalty order in accordance with subsection (d) of this section,

(B) issue an order requiring such person to comply with such requirement or prohibition,

(C) bring a civil action in accordance with subsection (b) of this section or section 7605 of this title, or

(D) request the Attorney General to commence a criminal action in accordance with subsection (c) of this section.

(4) Requirements for orders

An order issued under this subsection (other than an order relating to a violation of section 7412 of this title) shall not take effect until the person to whom it is issued has had an opportunity to confer with the Administrator concerning the alleged violation. A copy of any order issued under this subsection shall be sent to the State air pollution control agency of any State in which the violation occurs. Any order issued under this subsection shall state with reasonable specificity the nature of the violation and specify a time for compliance which the Administrator determines is reasonable, taking into account the seriousness of the violation and any good faith efforts to comply with applicable requirements. In any case in which an order under this subsection (or notice to a violator under paragraph (1)) is issued to a corporation, a copy of such order (or notice) shall be issued to appropriate corporate officers. An order issued under this subsection shall require the person to whom it was issued to comply with the requirement as expeditiously as practicable, but in no event longer than one year after the date the order was issued, and shall be nonrenewable. No order issued under this subsection shall prevent the State or the Administrator from assessing any penalties nor otherwise affect or limit the State's or the United States authority to enforce under other provisions of this chapter, nor affect any person's obligations to comply with any section of this chapter or with a term or condition of any permit or applicable implementation plan promulgated or approved under this chapter.

(5) Failure to comply with new source requirements

Whenever, on the basis of any available information, the Administrator finds that a State is not acting in compliance with any requirement or prohibition of the chapter relating to the construction of new sources or the modification of existing sources, the Administrator may—

(A) issue an order prohibiting the construction or modification of any major stationary source in any area to which such requirement applies;

(B) issue an administrative penalty order in accordance with subsection (d) of this section, or

(C) bring a civil action under subsection (b) of this section.

Nothing in this subsection shall preclude the United States from commencing a criminal action under subsection (c) of this section at any time for any such violation.

(b) Civil judicial enforcement

The Administrator shall, as appropriate, in the case of any person that is the owner or operator of an affected source, a major emitting facility, or a major stationary source, and may, in the case of any other person, commence a civil action for a permanent or temporary injunction, or to assess and recover a civil penalty of not more than $25,000 per day for each violation, or both, in any of the following instances:

(1) Whenever such person has violated, or is in violation of, any requirement or prohibition of an applicable implementation plan or permit. Such an action shall be commenced (A) during any period of federally assumed enforcement, or (B) more than 30 days following the date of the Administrator's notification under subsection (a)(1) of this section that such person has violated, or is in violation of, such requirement or prohibition.

(2) Whenever such person has violated, or is in violation of, any other requirement or prohibition of this subchapter, section 7603 of this title, subchapter IV–A of this chapter, subchapter V of this chapter, or subchapter VI of this chapter, including, but not limited to, a requirement or prohibition of any rule, order, waiver or permit promulgated, issued, or approved under this chapter, or for the payment of any fee owed the United States under this chapter (other than subchapter II of this chapter).

(3) Whenever such person attempts to construct or modify a major stationary source in any area with respect to which a finding under subsection (a)(5) of this section has been made.

Any action under this subsection may be brought in the district court of the United States for the district in which the violation is alleged to have occurred, or is occurring, or in which the defendant resides, or where the defendant's principal place of business is located, and such court shall have jurisdiction to restrain such violation, to require compliance, to assess such civil penalty, to collect any fees owed the United States under this chapter (other than subchapter II of this chapter) and any noncompliance assessment and nonpayment penalty owed under section 7420 of this title, and to award any other appropriate relief. Notice of the commencement of such action shall be given to the appropriate State air pollution control agency. In the case of any action brought by the Administrator under this subsection, the court may award costs of litigation (including reasonable attorney and expert witness fees) to the party or parties against whom such action was brought if the court finds that such action was unreasonable.

(c) Criminal penalties

(1) Any person who knowingly violates any requirement or prohibition of an applicable implementation plan (during any period of federally assumed enforcement or more than 30 days after having been notified under subsection (a)(1) of this section by the Administrator that such person is violating such requirement or prohibition), any order under subsection (a) of this section, requirement or prohibition of section 7411(e) of this title (relating to new source performance standards), section 7412 of this title, section 7414 of this title (relating to inspections, etc.), section 7429 of this title (relating to solid waste combustion), section 7475(a) of this title (relating to preconstruction requirements), an order under section 7477 of this title (relating to preconstruction requirements), an order under section 7603 of this title (relating to emergency orders), section 7661a(a) or 7661b(c) of this title (relating to permits), or any requirement or prohibition of subchapter IV–A of this chapter (relating to acid deposition control), or subchapter VI of this chapter (relating to stratospheric ozone control), including a requirement of any rule, order, waiver, or permit promulgated or approved under such sections or titles, and including any requirement for the payment of any fee owed the United States under this chapter (other than subchapter II of this chapter) shall, upon conviction, be punished by a fine pursuant to Title 18, or by imprisonment for not to exceed 5 years, or both. If a conviction of any person under this paragraph is for a

violation committed after a first conviction of such person under this paragraph, the maximum punishment shall be doubled with respect to both the fine and imprisonment.

(2) Any person who knowingly—

(A) makes any false material statement, representation, or certification in, or omits material information from, or knowingly alters, conceals, or fails to file or maintain any notice, application, record, report, plan, or other document required pursuant to this chapter to be either filed or maintained (whether with respect to the requirements imposed by the Administrator or by a State);

(B) fails to notify or report as required under this chapter; or

(C) falsifies, tampers with, renders inaccurate, or fails to install any monitoring device or method required to be maintained or followed under this chapter

shall, upon conviction, be punished by a fine pursuant to Title 18, or by imprisonment for not more than 2 years, or both. If a conviction of any person under this paragraph is for a violation committed after a first conviction of such person under this paragraph, the maximum punishment shall be doubled with respect to both the fine and imprisonment.

(3) Any person who knowingly fails to pay any fee owed the United States under this subchapter, subchapter III of this chapter, subchapter IV–A of this chapter, subchapter V of this chapter, or subchapter VI of this chapter shall, upon conviction, be punished by a fine pursuant to Title 18, or by imprisonment for not more than 1 year, or both. If a conviction of any person under this paragraph is for a violation committed after a first conviction of such person under this paragraph, the maximum punishment shall be doubled with respect to both the fine and imprisonment.

(4) Any person who negligently releases into the ambient air any hazardous air pollutant listed pursuant to section 7412 of this title or any extremely hazardous substance listed pursuant to section 11002(a)(2) of this title that is not listed in section 7412 of this title, and who at the time negligently places another person in imminent danger of death or serious bodily injury shall, upon conviction, be punished by a fine under Title 18, or by imprisonment for not more than 1 year, or both. If a conviction of any person under this paragraph is for a violation committed after a first conviction of such person under this paragraph, the maximum punishment shall be doubled with respect to both the fine and imprisonment.

(5)**(A)** Any person who knowingly releases into the ambient air any hazardous air pollutant listed pursuant to section 7412 of this title or any extremely hazardous substance listed pursuant to section 11002(a)(2) of this title that is not listed in section 7412 of this title, and who knows at the time that he thereby places another person in imminent danger of death or serious bodily injury shall, upon conviction, be punished by a fine under Title 18, or by imprisonment of not more than 15 years, or both. Any person committing such violation which is an organization shall, upon conviction under this paragraph, be subject to a fine of not more than $1,000,000 for each violation. If a conviction of any person under this paragraph is for a violation committed after a first conviction of such person under this paragraph, the maximum punishment shall be doubled with respect to both the fine and imprisonment. For any air pollutant for which the Administrator has set an emissions standard or for any source for which a permit has been issued under subchapter V of this chapter, a release of such pollutant in accordance with that standard or permit shall not constitute a violation of this paragraph or paragraph (4).

(B) In determining whether a defendant who is an individual knew that the violation placed another person in imminent danger of death or serious bodily injury—

(i) the defendant is responsible only for actual awareness or actual belief possessed; and

(ii) knowledge possessed by a person other than the defendant, but not by the defendant, may not be attributed to the defendant;

except that in proving a defendant's possession of actual knowledge, circumstantial evidence may be used, including evidence that the defendant took affirmative steps to be shielded from relevant information.

(C) It is an affirmative defense to a prosecution that the conduct charged was freely consented to by the person endangered and that the danger and conduct charged were reasonably foreseeable hazards of—

(i) an occupation, a business, or a profession; or

(ii) medical treatment or medical or scientific experimentation conducted by professionally approved methods and such other person had been made aware of the risks involved prior to giving consent.

The defendant may establish an affirmative defense under this subparagraph by a preponderance of the evidence.

(D) All general defenses, affirmative defenses, and bars to prosecution that may apply with respect to other Federal criminal offenses may apply under subparagraph (A) of this paragraph and shall be determined by the courts of the United States according to the principles of common law as they may be interpreted in the light of reason and experience. Concepts of justification and excuse applicable under this section may be developed in the light of reason and experience.

(E) The term "organization" means a legal entity, other than a government, established or organized for any purpose, and such term includes a corporation, company, association, firm, partnership, joint stock company, foundation, institution, trust, society, union, or any other association of persons.

(F) The term "serious bodily injury" means bodily injury which involves a substantial risk of death, unconsciousness, extreme physical pain, protracted and obvious disfigurement or protracted loss or impairment of the function of a bodily member, organ, or mental faculty.

(6) For the purpose of this subsection, the term "person" includes, in addition to the entities referred to in section 7602(e) of this title, any responsible corporate officer.

(d) Administrative assessment of civil penalties

(1) The Administrator may issue an administrative order against any person assessing a civil administrative penalty of up to $25,000, per day of violation, whenever, on the basis of any available information, the Administrator finds that such person—

> **(A)** has violated or is violating any requirement or prohibition of an applicable implementation plan (such order shall be issued (i) during any period of federally assumed enforcement, or (ii) more than thirty days following the date of the Administrator's notification under subsection (a)(1) of this section of a finding that such person has violated or is violating such requirement or prohibition); or
>
> **(B)** has violated or is violating any other requirement or prohibition of subchapter I of this chapter, subchapter III of this chapter, subchapter IV–A of this chapter, subchapter V of this chapter, subchapter VI of this chapter, including, but not limited to, a requirement or prohibition of any rule, order, waiver, permit, or plan promulgated, issued, or approved under this chapter, or for the payment of any fee owed the United States under this chapter (other than subchapter II of this chapter); or
>
> **(C)** attempts to construct or modify a major stationary source in any area with respect to which a finding under subsection (a)(5) of this section has been made.

The Administrator's authority under this paragraph shall be limited to matters where the total penalty sought does not exceed $200,000 and the first alleged date of violation occurred no more than 12 months prior to the initiation of the administrative action, except where the Administrator and the Attorney General jointly determine that a matter involving a larger penalty amount or longer period of violation is appropriate for administrative penalty action. Any such determination by the Administrator and the Attorney General shall not be subject to judicial review.

(2)(A) An administrative penalty assessed under paragraph (1) shall be assessed by the Administrator by an order made after opportunity for a hearing on the record in accordance with sections 554 and 556 of Title 5. The Administrator shall issue reasonable rules for discovery and other procedures for hearings under this paragraph. Before issuing such an order, the Administrator shall give written notice to the person to be assessed an administrative penalty of the Administrator's proposal to issue such order and provide such person an opportunity to request such a hearing on the order, within 30 days of the date the notice is received by such person.

(B) The Administrator may compromise, modify, or remit, with or without conditions, any administrative penalty which may be imposed under this subsection.

(3) The Administrator may implement, after consultation with the Attorney General and the States, a field citation program through regulations establishing appropriate minor violations for which field citations assessing civil penalties not to exceed $5,000 per day of violation may be issued by officers or employees designated by the Administrator. Any person to whom a field citation is assessed may, within a reasonable time as prescribed by the Administrator through regulation, elect to pay the penalty assessment or to request a hearing on the field citation. If a request for a hearing is not made within the time specified in the regulation, the penalty assessment in the field citation shall be final. Such hearing shall not be subject to section 554 or 556 of Title 5, but shall provide a reasonable opportunity to be heard and to present evidence. Payment of a civil penalty required by a field citation shall not be a defense to further enforcement by the United States or a State to correct a violation, or to assess the statutory maximum penalty pursuant to other authorities in the chapter, if the violation continues.

(4) Any person against whom a civil penalty is assessed under paragraph (3) of this subsection or to whom an administrative penalty order is issued under paragraph (1) of this subsection may seek review of such assessment in the United States District Court for the District of Columbia or for the district in which the violation is alleged to have occurred, in which such person resides, or where such person's principal place of business is located, by filing in such court within 30 days following the date the administrative penalty order becomes final under paragraph (2), the assessment becomes final under paragraph (3), or a final decision following a hearing under paragraph (3) is rendered, and by simultaneously sending a copy of the filing by certified mail to the Administrator and the Attorney General. Within 30 days thereafter, the Administrator shall file in such court a certified copy, or certified index, as appropriate, of the record on which the administrative penalty order or assessment was issued. Such court shall not set aside or remand such order or assessment unless there is not substantial evidence in the record, taken as a whole, to support the finding of a violation or unless the order or penalty assessment constitutes an abuse of discretion. Such order or penalty assessment shall not be subject to review by any court except as provided in this paragraph. In any such proceedings, the United States may seek to recover civil penalties ordered or assessed under this section.

(5) If any person fails to pay an assessment of a civil penalty or fails to comply with an administrative penalty order—

(A) after the order or assessment has become final, or

(B) after a court in an action brought under paragraph (4) has entered a final judgment in favor of the Administrator, the Administrator shall request the Attorney General to bring a civil action in an appropriate district court to enforce the order or to recover the amount ordered or assessed (plus interest at rates established pursuant to section 6621(a)(2) of Title 26 from the date of the final order or decision or the date of the final judgment, as the case may be). In such an action, the validity, amount, and appropriateness of such order or assessment shall not be subject to review. Any person who fails to pay on a timely basis a civil penalty ordered or assessed under this section shall be required to pay, in addition to such penalty and interest, the United States enforcement expenses, including but not limited to attorneys fees and costs incurred by the United States for collection proceedings and a quarterly nonpayment penalty for each quarter during which such failure to pay persists. Such nonpayment penalty shall be 10 percent of the aggregate amount of such person's outstanding penalties and nonpayment penalties accrued as of the beginning of such quarter.

(e) Penalty assessment criteria

(1) In determining the amount of any penalty to be assessed under this section or section 7604(a) of this title, the Administrator or the court, as appropriate, shall take into consideration (in addition to such other factors as justice may require) the size of the business, the economic impact of the penalty on the business, the violator's full compliance history and good faith efforts to comply, the duration of the violation as established by any credible evidence (including evidence other than the applicable test method), payment by the violator of penalties previously assessed for the same violation, the economic benefit of noncompliance, and the seriousness of the violation. The court shall not assess penalties for noncompliance with administrative subpoenas under section 7607(a) of this title, or actions under section 7414 of this title, where the violator had sufficient cause to violate or fail or refuse to comply with such subpoena or action.

(2) A penalty may be assessed for each day of violation. For purposes of determining the number of days of violation for which a penalty may be assessed under subsection (b) or (d)(1) of this section, or section 7604(a) of this title, or an assessment may be made under section 7420 of this title, where the Administrator or an air pollution control agency has notified the source of the violation, and the plaintiff makes a prima facie showing that the conduct or events giving rise to the violation are likely to have continued or recurred past the date of notice, the days of violation shall be presumed to include the date of such notice and each and every day thereafter until the violator establishes that continuous compliance has been achieved, except to the extent that the violator can prove by a preponderance of the evidence that there were intervening days during which no violation occurred or that the violation was not continuing in nature.

(f) Awards

The Administrator may pay an award, not to exceed $10,000, to any person who furnishes information or services which lead to a criminal conviction or a judicial or administrative civil penalty for any violation of this subchapter or subchapter III, subchapter IV–A, subchapter V, or subchapter VI of this chapter enforced under this section. Such payment is subject to available appropriations for such purposes as provided in annual appropriation Acts. Any officer, or employee of the United States or any State or local government who furnishes information or renders service in the performance of an official duty is ineligible for payment under this subsection. The Administrator may, by regulation, prescribe additional criteria for eligibility for such an award.

(g) Settlements; public participation

At least 30 days before a consent order or settlement agreement of any kind under this chapter to which the United States is a party (other than enforcement actions under this section, section 7420 of this title, or subchapter II of this chapter, whether or not involving civil or criminal penalties, or judgments subject to Department of Justice policy on public participation) is final or filed with a court, the Administrator shall provide a reasonable opportunity by notice in the Federal Register to persons who are not named as parties or intervenors to the action or matter to comment in writing. The Administrator or the Attorney General, as appropriate, shall promptly consider any such written comments and may withdraw or withhold his consent to the proposed order or agreement if the comments disclose facts or considerations which indicate that such consent is inappropriate, improper, inadequate, or inconsistent with the requirements of this chapter. Nothing in this subsection shall apply to civil or criminal penalties under this chapter.

(h) Operator

For purposes of the provisions of this section and section 7420 of this title, the term "operator", as used in such provisions, shall include any person who is senior management personnel or a corporate officer. Except in the case of knowing and willful violations, such term shall not include any person who is a stationary engineer or technician responsible for the operation, maintenance, repair, or monitoring of equipment and facilities and who often has supervisory and training duties but who is not senior management personnel or a corporate officer. Except in the case of knowing and willful violations, for purposes of subsection (c)(4) of this section, the term "a person" shall not include an employee who is carrying out his normal activities and who is not a part of senior management personnel or a corporate officer. Except in the case of knowing and willful violations, for purposes of paragraphs (1), (2), (3), and (5) of subsection (c) of this section the term "a person" shall not include an employee who is carrying out his normal activities and who is acting under orders from the employer.

(July 14, 1955, ch. 360, title I, § 113, as added Dec. 31, 1970, Pub.L. 91–604, § 4(a), 84 Stat. 1686, and amended Nov. 18, 1971, Pub.L. 92–157, title III, § 302(b), (c), 85 Stat. 464; June 22, 1974, Pub.L. 93–319, § 6(a)(1)–(3), 88 Stat. 259; Aug. 7, 1977, Pub.L. 95–95, title I, §§ 111, 112(a), 91 Stat. 704, 705; Nov. 16, 1977, Pub.L. 95–190, § 14(a)(10)–(21), (b)(1), 91 Stat. 1400, 1404; July 17, 1981, Pub.L. 97–23, § 2, 95 Stat. 139; Nov. 15, 1990, Pub.L. 101–549, title VII, § 701, 104 Stat. 2672.)

Effective Date of 1990 Amendment

Amendment by Pub.L. 101–549 effective Nov. 15, 1990, except as otherwise provided, see section 711(b) of Pub.L. 101–549, set out as a note under section 7401 of this title.

Savings Provisions

Suits, actions or proceedings commenced under this chapter as in effect prior to Nov. 15, 1990, not to abate by reason of the taking effect of amendments by Pub.L. 101–549, except as otherwise provided for, see section 711(a) of Pub.L. 101–549, set out as a note under section 7401 of this title.

CROSS REFERENCES

Guidelines for using imminent hazard, enforcement, and emergency response authorities to include assignment of responsibility for coordinating response actions with imminent hazard and emergency powers authorized by this section, see section 9606 of this title.

Federal Practice and Procedure

Requirements for issuance of declaratory judgment in matters involving public law, see Wright, Miller & Kane: Civil 2d § 2763.

West's Federal Practice Manual

Air quality legislation, see § 4384.5.

CODE OF FEDERAL REGULATIONS

Delayed compliance orders, see 40 CFR 65.01 et seq.

LAW REVIEW COMMENTARIES

Bonfire of the executives: Criminal environmental enforcement unfolds. John E. Smith, II, 10 Corp. Counsel Rev. (Tex.) 67 (May 1991).

Erosion of mens rea in environmental criminal prosecution. Ruth Ann Weidel, John R. Mayo and F. Michael Zachara, 21 Seton Hall L.Rev. 1125 (1991).

Fair warning: The deterioration of scienter under environmental criminal statutes. M. Diane Barber, 26 Loy.L.A.L.Rev. 105 (1992).

Library References

Health and Environment ⟹25.6(1) et seq., 28, 37.
C.J.S. Health and Environment §§ 48 et seq., 91 et seq.

United States Supreme Court

Certiorari to supreme court, appeals concerning Administrator's authority to compel implement—and enforcement actions by states, see Environmental Protection Agency v. Brown, 1977, 97 S.Ct. 1635, 431 U.S. 99, 52 L.Ed.2d 166.

§ 7414. Recordkeeping, inspections, monitoring, and entry [CAA § 114]

(a) Authority of Administrator or authorized representative

For the purpose (i) of developing or assisting in the development of any implementation plan under section 7410 or section 7411(d) of this title, any standard of performance under section 7411 of this title, any emission standard under section 7412 of this title, or any regulation of solid waste combustion under section 7429 of this title, (ii) of determining whether any person is in violation of any such standard or any requirement of such a plan, or (iii) carrying out any provision of this chapter (except a provision of subchapter II of this chapter with respect to a manufacturer of new motor vehicles or new motor vehicle engines)—

(1) the Administrator may require any person who owns or operates any emission source, who manufactures emission control equipment or process equipment, who the Administrator believes may have information necessary for the purposes set forth in this subsection, or who is subject to any requirement of this chapter (other than a manufacturer subject to the provisions of section 7525(c) or 7542 of this title with respect to a provision of subchapter II of this chapter) on a one-time, periodic or continuous basis to—

(A) establish and maintain such records;

(B) make such reports;

(C) install, use, and maintain such monitoring equipment, and use such audit procedures, or methods;

(D) sample such emissions (in accordance with such procedures or methods, at such locations, at such intervals, during such periods and in such manner as the Administrator shall prescribe);

(E) keep records on control equipment parameters, production variables or other indirect data when direct monitoring of emissions is impractical;

(F) submit compliance certifications in accordance with section 7414(a)(3) of this title; and

(G) provide such other information as the Administrator may reasonably require; and

(2) the Administrator or his authorized representative, upon presentation of his credentials—

(A) shall have a right of entry to, upon, or through any premises of such person or in which any records required to be maintained under paragraph (1) of this section are located, and

(B) may at reasonable times have access to and copy any records, inspect any monitoring equipment or method required under paragraph (1), and sample any emissions which such person is required to sample under paragraph (1).

(3) The [1] Administrator shall in the case of any person which is the owner or operator of a major stationary source, and may, in the case of any other person, require enhanced monitoring and submission of compliance certifications. Compliance certifications shall include (A) identification of the applicable requirement that is the basis of the certification, (B) the method used for determining the compliance status of the source, (C) the compliance status, (D) whether compliance is continuous or intermittent, (E) such other facts as the Administrator may require. Compliance certifications and monitoring data shall be subject to subsection (c) of this section. Submission of a compliance certification shall in no way limit the Administrator's authorities to investigate or otherwise implement this chapter. The Administrator shall promulgate rules to provide guidance and to implement this paragraph within 2 years after the enactment of the Clean Air Act Amendments of 1990.

(b) State enforcement

(1) Each State may develop and submit to the Administrator a procedure for carrying out this section in such State. If the Administrator finds the State procedure is adequate, he may delegate to such State any authority he has to carry out this section.

(2) Nothing in this subsection shall prohibit the Administrator from carrying out this section in a State.

(c) Availability of records, reports, and information to public; disclosure of trade secrets

Any records, reports or information obtained under subsection (a) of this section shall be available to the public, except that upon a showing satisfactory to the Administrator by any person that records, reports, or information, or particular part thereof (other than emission data), to which the Administrator has access under this section if made public, would divulge methods or processes entitled to protection as trade secrets of such person, the Administrator shall consider such record, report, or information or particular portion thereof confidential in accordance with the purposes of section 1905 of title 18, except that such record, report, or information may be disclosed to other officers, employees, or authorized representatives of the United States concerned with carrying out this chapter or when relevant in any proceeding under this chapter.

(d) Notice of proposed entry, inspection, or monitoring

(1) In the case of any emission standard or limitation or other requirement which is adopted by a State, as part of an applicable implementation plan or as part of an order under section 7413(d) of this title, before carrying out an entry, inspection, or monitoring under paragraph (2) of subsection (a) of this section with respect to such standard, limitation, or other requirement, the Administrator (or his representatives) shall provide the State air pollution control agency with reasonable prior notice of such action, indicating the purpose of such action. No State agency which receives notice under this paragraph of an action proposed to be taken may use the information contained in the notice to inform the person whose property is proposed to be affected of the proposed action. If the Administrator has reasonable basis for

believing that a State agency is so using or will so use such information, notice to the agency under this paragraph is not required until such time as the Administrator determines the agency will no longer so use information contained in a notice under this paragraph. Nothing in this section shall be construed to require notification to any State agency of any action taken by the Administrator with respect to any standard, limitation, or other requirement which is not part of an applicable implementation plan or which was promulgated by the Administrator under section 7410(c) of this title.

(2) Nothing in paragraph (1) shall be construed to provide that any failure of the Administrator to comply with the requirements of such paragraph shall be a defense in any enforcement action brought by the Administrator or shall make inadmissible as evidence in any such action any information or material obtained notwithstanding such failure to comply with such requirements.

(July 14, 1955, ch. 360, title I, § 114, as added Dec. 31, 1970, Pub.L. 91–604, § 4(a), 84 Stat. 1687, and amended June 22, 1974, Pub.L. 93–319, § 6(a)(4), 88 Stat. 259; Aug. 7, 1977, Pub.L. 95–95, title I, §§ 109(d)(3), 113, title III, § 305(d), 91 Stat. 701, 709, 776; Nov. 16, 1977, Pub.L. 95–190, § 14(a)(22), (23), 91 Stat. 1400; Nov. 15, 1990, Pub.L. 101–549, title III, § 302(c), title VII, § 702(a), (b), 104 Stat. 2574, 2680, 2681.)

[1] So in original. Probably should be "the".

References in Text

The enactment of the Clean Air Act Amendments of 1990, referred to in subsec. (a)(3), probably means the date of enactment of Pub.L. 101–549, which was approved Nov. 15, 1990.

Codification

Amendment of subsec. (a) of this section by section 702(a)(1), (2) of Pub.L. 101–549 could not be executed due to prior amendment by section 302(c) of Pub.L. 101–549, which effected a similar change.

Effective Date of 1990 Amendment

Amendment by Pub.L. 101–549 effective Nov. 15, 1990, except as otherwise provided, see section 711(b) of Pub.L. 101–549, set out as a note under section 7401 of this title.

Savings Provisions

Suits, actions or proceedings commenced under this chapter as in effect prior to Nov. 15, 1990, not to abate by reason of the taking effect of amendments by Pub.L. 101–549, except as otherwise provided for, see section 711(a) of Pub.L. 101–549, set out as a note under section 7401 of this title.

CROSS REFERENCES

Guidelines for using imminent hazard, enforcement and emergency response authorities to include assignment of responsibility for coordinating response actions with imminent hazard and emergency powers authorized by this section, see section 9606 of this title.

Federal Practice and Procedure

Holding back of trade secrets, see Wright & Graham: Evidence § 5437.

CODE OF FEDERAL REGULATIONS

Emission standards for hazardous pollutants, see 40 CFR 61.01 et seq.
Implementation plans, generally, see 40 CFR 51.40 et seq.
New stationary sources, standards of performance for, see 40 CFR 60.1 et seq.
Primary nonferrous smelter orders, see 40 CFR 57.101 et seq.
Public information, see 40 CFR 2.100 et seq.

Library References

Health and Environment ⚡25.6(6).
Records ⚡30.
C.J.S. Health and Environment § 91 et seq.
C.J.S. Records §§ 4 et seq., 60 et seq.

United States Supreme Court

State trade secret law not protecting chemical company from federal aerial monitoring, see Dow Chemical Co. v. U.S., 1986, 106 S.Ct. 1819, 90 L.Ed.2d 226.

§ 7415. International air pollution [CAA § 115]

(a) Endangerment of public health or welfare in foreign countries from pollution emitted in United States

Whenever the Administrator, upon receipt of reports, surveys or studies from any duly constituted international agency has reason to believe that any air pollutant or pollutants emitted in the United States cause or contribute to air pollution which may reasonably be anticipated to endanger public health or welfare in a foreign country or whenever the Secretary of State requests him to do so with respect to such pollution which the Secretary of State alleges is of such a nature, the Administrator shall give formal notification thereof to the Governor of the State in which such emissions originate.

(b) Prevention or elimination of endangerment

The notice of the Administrator shall be deemed to be a finding under section 7410(a)(2)(H)(ii) of this title which requires a plan revision with respect to so much of the applicable implementation plan as is inadequate to prevent or eliminate the endangerment referred to in subsection (a) of this section. Any foreign country so affected by such emission of pollutant or pollutants shall be invited to appear at any public hearing associated with any revision of the appropriate portion of the applicable implementation plan.

(c) Reciprocity

This section shall apply only to a foreign country which the Administrator determines has given the United States essentially the same rights with respect to the prevention or control of air pollution occurring in that country as is given that country by this section.

(d) Recommendations

Recommendations issued following any abatement conference conducted prior to August 7, 1977, shall remain in effect with respect to any pollutant for which no national ambient air quality standard has been established under section 7409 of this title unless the Administrator, after consultation with all agencies which were party to the conference, rescinds any such recommendation on grounds of obsolescence.

(July 14, 1955, ch. 360, title I, § 115, formerly § 5, as added Dec. 17, 1963, Pub.L. 88–206, § 1, 77 Stat. 396, renumbered § 105 and amended Oct. 20, 1965, Pub.L. 89–272, title I, §§ 101(2), (3), 102, 79 Stat. 992, 995, renumbered § 108 and amended Nov. 21, 1967, Pub.L. 90–148, § 2, 81 Stat. 491, renumbered § 115 and amended Dec. 31, 1970, Pub.L. 91–604, §§ 4(a), (b)(2)–(10), 15(c)(2), 84 Stat. 1678, 1688, 1689, 1713; Aug. 7, 1977, Pub.L. 95–95, title I, § 114, 91 Stat. 710.)

Library References

Health and Environment ⇐25.6(1).
C.J.S. Health and Environment § 91 et seq.

§ 7416. Retention of State authority [CAA § 116]

Except as otherwise provided in sections 1857c–10(c), (e), and (f) (as in effect before August 7, 1977), 7543, 7545(c)(4), and 7573 of this title (preempting certain State regulation of moving sources) nothing in this chapter shall preclude or deny the right of any State or political subdivision thereof to adopt or enforce (1) any standard or limitation respecting emissions of air pollutants or (2) any requirement respecting control or abatement of air pollution; except that if an emission standard or limitation is in effect under an applicable implementation plan or under section 7411 or section 7412 of this title, such State or political subdivision may not adopt or enforce any emission standard or limitation which is less stringent than the standard or limitation under such plan or section.

(July 14, 1955, ch. 360, title I, § 116, formerly § 109, as added Nov. 21, 1967, Pub.L. 90–148, § 2, 81 Stat. 497, renumbered and amended Dec. 31, 1970, Pub.L. 91–604, § 4(a), (c), 84 Stat. 1678, 1689; June 22, 1974, Pub.L. 93–319, § 6(b), 88 Stat. 259; Nov. 16, 1977, Pub.L. 95–190, § 14(a)(24), 91 Stat. 1400.)

CODE OF FEDERAL REGULATIONS

Hazardous pollutants, emission standards for, see 40 CFR 61.01 et seq.
New stationary sources, performance standards, see 40 CFR 60.1 et seq.

Library References

States ⇐4.19.
C.J.S. States § 28.

§ 7417. Advisory committees [CAA § 117]

(a) Establishment; membership

In order to obtain assistance in the development and implementation of the purposes of this chapter including air quality criteria, recommended control techniques, standards, research and development, and to encourage the continued efforts on the part of industry to improve air quality and to develop economically feasible methods for the control and abatement of air pollution, the Administrator shall from time to time establish advisory committees. Committee members shall include, but not be limited to, persons who are knowledgeable concerning air quality from the standpoint of health, welfare, economics or technology.

(b) Compensation

The members of any other advisory committees appointed pursuant to this chapter who are not officers or employees of the United States while attending conferences or meetings or while otherwise serving at the request of the Administrator, shall be entitled to receive compensation at a rate to be fixed by the Administrator, but not exceeding $100 per diem, including traveltime, and while away from their homes or regular places of business they may be allowed travel expenses, including per diem in lieu of subsistence, as authorized by section 5703 of title 5 for persons in the Government service employed intermittently.

(c) Consultations by Administrator

Prior to—

(1) issuing criteria for an air pollutant under section 7408(a)(2) of this title,

(2) publishing any list under section 7411(b)(1)(A) or section 7412(b)(1)(A) of this title,

(3) publishing any standard under section 7411 or section 7412 of this title, or

(4) publishing any regulation under section 7521(a) of this title,

the Administrator shall, to the maximum extent practicable within the time provided, consult with appropriate advisory committees, independence experts, and Federal departments and agencies.

(July 14, 1955, ch. 360, title I, § 117, formerly § 6, as added Dec. 17, 1963, Pub.L. 88–206, § 1, 77 Stat. 399, renumbered § 106, Oct. 20, 1965, Pub.L. 89–272, title I, § 101(3), 79 Stat. 992, renumbered § 110 and amended Nov. 21, 1967, Pub.L. 90–148, § 2, 81 Stat. 498, renumbered § 117 and amended Dec. 31, 1970, Pub.L. 91–604, §§ 4(a), (d), 15(c)(2), 84 Stat. 1678, 1689, 1713; Aug. 7, 1977, Pub.L. 95–95, title I, § 115, 91 Stat. 711; Nov. 9, 1978, Pub.L. 95–623, § 13(c), 92 Stat. 3458.)

Library References

Health and Environment ⇐25.6(1) et seq., 28.
C.J.S. Health and Environment § 91 et seq.

§ 7418. Control of pollution from Federal facilities [CAA § 118]

(a) General compliance

Each department, agency, and instrumentality of the executive, legislative, and judicial branches of the Federal Government (1) having jurisdiction over any property or facility, or (2) engaged in any activity resulting, or which may result, in the discharge of air pollutants, and each officer, agent, or employee thereof, shall be subject to, and comply with, all Federal, State, interstate, and local requirements, administrative authority, and process and sanctions respecting the control and abatement of air pollution in the same manner, and to the same extent as any nongovernmental entity. The preceding sentence shall apply (A) to any requirement whether substantive or procedural (including any recordkeeping or reporting requirement, any requirement respecting permits and any other requirement whatsoever), (B) to any requirement to pay a fee or charge imposed by any State or local agency to defray the costs of its air pollution regulatory program, (C) to the exercise of any Federal, State, or local administrative authority, and (D) to any process and sanction, whether enforced in Federal, State, or local courts, or in any other manner. This subsection shall apply notwithstanding any immunity of such agencies, officers, agents, or employees under any law or rule of law. No officer, agent, or employee of the United States shall be personally liable for any civil penalty for which he is not otherwise liable.

(b) Exemption

The President may exempt any emission source of any department, agency, or instrumentality in the executive branch from compliance with such a requirement if he determines it to be in the paramount interest of the United States to do so, except that no exemption may be granted from section 7411 of this title, and an exemption from section 7412 of this title may be granted only in accordance with section 7412(i)(4) of this title. No such exemption shall be granted due to lack of appropriation unless the President shall have specifically requested such appropriation as a part of the budgetary process and the Congress shall have failed to make available such requested appropriation. Any exemption shall be for a period not in excess of one year, but additional exemptions may be granted for periods of not to exceed one year upon the President's making a new determination. In addition to any such exemption of a particular emission source, the President may, if he determines it to be in the paramount interest of the United States to do so, issue regulations exempting from compliance with the requirements of this section any weaponry, equipment, aircraft, vehicles, or other classes or categories of property which are owned or operated by the Armed Forces of the United States (including the Coast Guard) or by the National Guard of any State and which are uniquely military in nature. The President shall reconsider the need for such regulations at three-year intervals. The President shall report each January to the Congress all exemptions from the requirements of this section granted during the preceding calendar year, together with his reason for granting each such exemption.

(c) Government vehicles

Each department, agency, and instrumentality of executive, legislative, and judicial branches of the Federal Government shall comply with all applicable provisions of a valid inspection and maintenance program established under the provisions of subpart 2 of part D of this subchapter or subpart 3 of part D of this subchapter except for such vehicles that are considered military tactical vehicles.

(d) Vehicles operated on Federal installations

Each department, agency, and instrumentality of executive, legislative, and judicial branches of the Federal Government having jurisdiction over any property or facility shall require all employees which operate motor vehicles on the property or facility to furnish proof of compliance with the applicable requirements of any vehicle inspection and maintenance program established under the provisions of subpart 2 of part D of this subchapter or subpart 3 of part D of this subchapter for the State in which such property or facility is located (without regard to whether such vehicles are registered in the State). The installation shall use one of the following methods to establish proof of compliance—

(1) presentation by the vehicle owner of a valid certificate of compliance from the vehicle inspection and maintenance program;

(2) presentation by the vehicle owner of proof of vehicle registration within the geographic area covered by the vehicle inspection and maintenance program (except for any program whose enforcement mechanism is not through the denial of vehicle registration);

(3) another method approved by the vehicle inspection and maintenance program administrator.

(July 14, 1955, ch. 360, title I, § 118, formerly § 7, as added Dec. 17, 1963, Pub.L. 88–206, § 1, 77 Stat. 399, renumbered § 107, Oct. 20, 1965, Pub.L. 89–272, title I, § 101(3), 79 Stat. 992, renumbered § 111 and amended Nov. 21, 1967, Pub.L. 90–148, § 2, 81 Stat. 499, and renumbered § 118 and amended Dec. 31, 1970, Pub.L. 91–604, §§ 4(a), 5, 84 Stat. 1678, 1689; Aug. 7, 1977, Pub.L. 95–95, title I, § 116, 91 Stat. 711; Nov. 15, 1990, Pub.L. 101–549, title I, § 101(e), title II, § 235, title III, § 302(d), 104 Stat. 2409, 2530, 2574.)

Effective Date of 1990 Amendment

Amendment by Pub.L. 101-549 effective Nov. 15, 1990, except as otherwise provided, see section 711(b) of Pub.L. 101-549, set out as a note under section 7401 of this title.

Savings Provisions

Suits, actions or proceedings commenced under this chapter as in effect prior to Nov. 15, 1990, not to abate by reason of the taking effect of amendments by Pub.L. 101-549, except as otherwise provided for, see section 711(a) of Pub.L. 101-549, set out as a note under section 7401 of this title.

LAW REVIEW COMMENTARIES

How well can states enforce their environmental laws when the polluter is the United States Government? 18 Rutgers L.J. 123 (1986).

Library References

Health and Environment ⇐25.6(5).
C.J.S. Health and Environment § 91 et seq.

§ 7419. Primary nonferrous smelter orders [CAA § 119]

(a) Issuance; hearing; enforcement orders; statement of grounds for application; findings

(1) Upon application by the owner or operator of a primary nonferrous smelter, a primary nonferrous smelter order under subsection (b) of this section may be issued—

(A) by the Administrator, after thirty days' notice to the State, or

(B) by the State in which such source is located, but no such order issued by the State shall take effect until the Administrator determines that such order has been issued in accordance with the requirements of this chapter.

Not later than ninety days after submission by the State to the Administrator of notice of the issuance of a primary nonferrous smelter order under this section, the Administrator shall determine whether or not such order has been issued by the State in accordance with the requirements of this chapter. If the Administrator determines that such order has not been issued in accordance with such requirements, he shall conduct a hearing respecting the reasonably available control technology for primary nonferrous smelters.

(2)(A) An order issued under this section to a primary nonferrous smelter shall be referred to as a "primary nonferrous smelter order". No primary nonferrous smelter may receive both an enforcement order under section 7413(d) of this title and a primary nonferrous smelter order under this section.

(B) Before any hearing conducted under this section, in the case of an application made by the owner or operator of a primary nonferrous smelter for a second order under this section, the applicant shall furnish the Administrator (or the State as the case may be) with a statement of the grounds on which such application is based (including all supporting documents and information). The statement of the grounds for the proposed order shall be provided by the Administrator or the State in any case in which such State or Administrator is acting on its own initiative. Such statement (including such documents and information) shall be made available to the public for a thirty-day period before such hearing and shall be considered as part of such hearing. No primary nonferrous smelter order may be granted unless the applicant establishes that he meets the conditions required for the issuance of such order (or the Administrator or State establishes the meeting of such conditions when acting on their own initiative).

(C) Any decision with respect to the issuance of a primary nonferrous smelter order shall be accompanied by a concise statement of the findings and of the basis of such findings.

(3) For the purposes of sections 7410, 7604, and 7607 of this title, any order issued by the State and in effect pursuant to this subsection shall become part of the applicable implementation plan.

(b) Prerequisites to issuance of orders

A primary nonferrous smelter order under this section may be issued to a primary nonferrous smelter if—

(1) such smelter is in existence on August 7, 1977;

(2) the requirement of the applicable implementation plan with respect to which the order is issued is an emission limitation or standard for sulfur oxides which is necessary and intended to be itself sufficient to enable attainment and maintenance of national primary and secondary ambient air quality standards for sulfur oxides; and

(3) such smelter is unable to comply with such requirement by the applicable date for compliance because no means of emission limitation applicable to such smelter which will enable it to achieve compliance with such requirement has been adequately demonstrated to be reasonably available (as determined by the Administrator, taking into account the cost of compliance, non-air quality health and environmental impact, and energy consideration).

(c) Second orders

(1) A second order issued to a smelter under this section shall set forth compliance schedules containing increments of progress which require compliance with the requirement postponed as expeditiously as practicable. The increments of progress shall be limited to requiring compliance with subsection (d) of this section and, in the case of a second order, to procuring, installing, and operating the necessary means of emission limitation as expeditiously as practicable after the Administrator determines such means have been adequately demonstrated to be reasonably available within the meaning of subsection (b)(3) of this section.

(2) Not in excess of two primary nonferrous smelter orders may be issued under this section to any primary nonferrous smelter. The first such order issued to a smelter shall not result in the postponement of the requirement with respect to which such order is issued beyond January 1, 1983. The second such order shall not result in the postponement of such requirement beyond January 1, 1988.

(d) Interim measures; continuous emission reduction technology

(1)(A) Each primary nonferrous smelter to which an order is issued under this section shall be required to use such interim measures for the period during which such order is in effect as may be necessary in the judgment of the Administrator to assure attainment and maintenance of the national primary and secondary ambient air quality standards during such period, taking into account the aggregate effect on air quality of such order together with all variances, extensions, waivers, enforcement orders, delayed compliance orders and primary nonferrous smelter orders previously issued under this chapter.

(B) Such interim requirements shall include—

(i) a requirement that the source to which the order applies comply with such reporting requirements and conduct such monitoring as the Administrator determines may be necessary, and

(ii) such measures as the Administrator determines are necessary to avoid an imminent and substantial endangerment to health of persons.

(C) Such interim measures shall also, except as provided in paragraph (2), include continuous emission reduction technology. The Administrator shall condition the use of any such interim measures upon the agreement of the owner or operator of the smelter—

(i) to comply with such conditions as the Administrator determines are necessary to maximize the reliability and enforceability of such interim measures, as applied to the smelter, in attaining and maintaining the national ambient air quality standards to which the order relates, and

(ii) to commit reasonable resources to research and development of appropriate emission control technology.

(2) The requirement of paragraph (1) for the use of continuous emission reduction technology may be waived with respect to a particular smelter by the State or the Administrator, after notice and a hearing on the record, and upon a showing by the owner or operator of the smelter that such requirement would be so costly as to necessitate permanent or prolonged temporary cessation of operations of the smelter. Upon application for such waiver, the Administrator shall be notified and shall, within ninety days, hold a hearing on the record in accordance with section 554 of title 5. At such hearing the Administrator shall require the smelter involved to present information relating to any alleged cessation of operations and the detailed reasons or justifications therefor. On the basis of such hearing the Administrator shall make findings of fact as to the effect of such requirement and on the alleged cessation of operations and shall make such recommendations as he deems appropriate. Such report, findings, and recommendations shall be available to the public, and shall be taken into account by the State or the Administrator in making the decision whether or not to grant such waiver.

(3) In order to obtain information for purposes of a waiver under paragraph (2), the Administrator may, on his own motion, conduct an investigation and use the authority of section 7621 of this title.

(4) In the case of any smelter which on August 7, 1977, uses continuous emission reduction technology and supplemental controls and which receives an initial primary nonferrous smelter order under this section, no additional continuous emission reduction technology shall be required as a condition of such order unless the Administrator determines, at any time, after notice and public hearing, that such additional continuous emission reduction technology is adequately demonstrated to be reasonably available for the primary nonferrous smelter industry.

(e) Termination of orders

At any time during which an order under this section applies, the Administrator may enter upon a public hearing respecting the availability of technology. Any order under this section shall be terminated if the Administrator determines on the record, after notice and public hearing, that the conditions upon which the order was based no longer exist. If the owner or operator of the smelter to which the order is issued demonstrates that prompt termination of such order would result in undue hardship, the termination shall become effective at the earliest practicable date on which such undue hardship would not result, but in no event later than the date required under subsection (c) of this section.

(f) Violation of requirements

If the Administrator determines that a smelter to which an order is issued under this section is in violation of any requirement of subsection (c) or (d) of this section, he shall—

(1) enforce such requirement under section 7413 of this title,

(2) (after notice and opportunity for public hearing) revoke such order and enforce compliance with the requirement with respect to which such order was granted,

(3) give notice of noncompliance and commence action under section 7420 of this title, or

(4) take any appropriate combination of such actions.

(July 14, 1955, ch. 360, title I, § 119, as added Aug. 7, 1977, Pub.L. 95–95, title I, § 117(b), 91 Stat. 712, and amended Nov. 16, 1977, Pub.L. 95–190, § 14(a)(25)–(27), 91 Stat. 1401.)

Effective Date

Section 406(d) of Title IV of Pub.L. 95–95, Aug. 7, 1977, 91 Stat. 796, provided that, except as otherwise expressly provided, the amendments made by that Act [which enacted this section and sections 7420 to 7428 of this title] were effective on the date of enactment [Aug. 7, 1977].

CODE OF FEDERAL REGULATIONS

Primary nonferrous smelter orders, see 40 CFR 57.101 et seq.

Library References

Health and Environment ⚿25.6(5).
C.J.S. Health and Environment § 91 et seq.

§ 7420. Noncompliance penalty [CAA § 120]

(a) Assessment and collection

(1)(A) Not later than 6 months after August 7, 1977, and after notice and opportunity for a public hearing, the Administrator shall promulgate regulations requiring the assessment and collection of a noncompliance penalty against persons referred to in paragraph (2)(A).

(B)(i) Each State may develop and submit to the Administrator a plan for carrying out this section in such State. If the Administrator finds that the State plan meets the requirements of this section, he may delegate to such State any authority he has to carry out this section.

(ii) Notwithstanding a delegation to a State under clause (i), the Administrator may carry out this section in such State under the circumstances described in subsection (b)(2)(B) of this section.

(2)(A) Except as provided in subparagraph (B) or (C) of this paragraph, the State or the Administrator shall assess and collect a noncompliance penalty against every person who owns or operates—

(i) a major stationary source (other than a primary nonferrous smelter which has received a primary nonferrous smelter order under section 7419 of this title), which is not in compliance with any emission limitation, emission standard or compliance schedule under any applicable implementation plan (whether or not such source is subject to a Federal or State consent decree), or

(ii) a stationary source which is not in compliance with an emission limitation, emission standard, standard of performance, or other requirement established under section 7411, 7477, 7603, or 7412 of this title, or

(iii) a stationary source which is not in compliance with any requirement of subchapter IV–A, V, or VI of this chapter, or

(iv) any source referred to in clause (i), (ii), or (iii) (for which an extension, order, or suspension referred to in subparagraph (B), or Federal or State consent decree is in effect), or a primary nonferrous smelter which has received a primary nonferrous smelter order under section 7419 of this title which is not in compliance with any interim emission control requirement or schedule of compliance under such extension, order, suspension, or consent decree.

For purposes of subsection (d)(2) of this section, in the case of a penalty assessed with respect to a source referred to in clause (iii) of this subparagraph, the costs referred to in such subsection (d)(2) shall be the economic value of noncompliance with the interim emission control requirement or the remaining steps in the schedule of compliance referred to in such clause.

(B) Notwithstanding the requirements of subparagraph (A)(i) and (ii), the owner or operator of any source shall be exempted from the duty to pay a noncompliance penalty under such requirements with respect to that source if, in accordance with the procedures in subsection (b)(5) of this section, the owner or operator demonstrates that the failure of such source to comply with any such requirement is due solely to—

(i) a conversion by such source from the burning of petroleum products or natural gas, or both, as the permanent primary energy source to the burning of coal pursuant to an order under section 7413(d)(5) of this title or section 1857c–10 of this title (as in effect before August 7, 1977);

(ii) in the case of a coal-burning source granted an extension under the second sentence of section 1857c–10(c)(1) of this title (as in effect before August 7, 1977), a prohibition from using petroleum products or natural gas or both, by reason of an order under the provisions of section 792(a) and (b) of title 15 or under any legislation which amends or supersedes such provisions;

(iii) the use of innovative technology sanctioned by an enforcement order under section 7413(d)(4) of this title;

(iv) an inability to comply with any such requirement, for which inability the source has received an order under section 7413(d) of this title (or an order under section 7413 of this title issued before August 7, 1977) which has the effect of permitting a delay or violation of any requirement of this chapter (including a requirement of an applicable implementation plan) which inability results from reasons entirely beyond the control of the owner or operator of such source or of any entity controlling, controlled by, or under common control with the owner or operator of such source; or

(v) the conditions by reason of which a temporary emergency suspension is authorized under section 7410(f) or (g) of this title.

An exemption under this subparagraph shall cease to be effective if the source fails to comply with the interim emission control requirements or schedules of compliance (including increments of progress) under any such extension, order, or suspension.

(C) The Administrator may, after notice and opportunity for public hearing, exempt any source from the requirements of this section with respect to a particular instance of noncompliance if he finds that such instance of noncompliance is de minimis in nature and in duration.

(b) Regulations

Regulations under subsection (a) of this section shall—

(1) permit the assessment and collection of such penalty by the State if the State has a delegation of authority in effect under subsection (a)(1)(B)(i) of this section;

(2) provide for the assessment and collection of such penalty by the Administrator, if—

(A) the State does not have a delegation of authority in effect under subsection (a)(1)(B)(i) of this section, or

(B) the State has such a delegation in effect but fails with respect to any particular person or source to assess or collect the penalty in accordance with the requirements of this section;

(3) require the States, or in the event the States fail to do so, the Administrator, to give a brief but reasonably specific notice of noncompliance under this section to each person referred to in subsection (a)(2)(A) of this section with respect to each source owned or operated by such person which is not in compliance as provided in such subsection, not later than July 1, 1979, or thirty days after the discovery of such noncompliance, whichever is later;

(4) require each person to whom notice is given under paragraph (3) to—

(A) calculate the amount of the penalty owed (determined in accordance with subsection (d)(2) of this section) and the schedule of payments (determined in accordance with subsection (d)(3) of this section) for each such source and, within forty-five days after the issuance of such notice or after the denial of a petition under subparagraph (B), to submit that calculation and proposed schedule, together with the information necessary for an independent verification thereof, to the State and to the Administrator, or

(B) submit a petition, within forty-five days after the issuance of such notice, challenging such notice of noncompliance or alleging entitlement to an exemption under subsection (a)(2)(B) of this section with respect to a particular source;

(5) require the Administrator to provide a hearing on the record (within the meaning of subchapter II of chapter 5 of title 5) and to make a decision on such petition (including findings of fact and conclusions of law) not later than ninety days after the receipt of any petition under paragraph (4)(B), unless the State agrees to provide a hearing which is substantially similar to such a hearing on the record and to make a decision on such petition (including such findings and conclusions) within such ninety-day period;

(6)(A) authorize the Administrator on his own initiative to review the decision of the State under paragraph (5) and disapprove it if it is not in accordance with the requirements of this section, and (B) require the Administrator to do so not later than sixty days after receipt of a petition under this subparagraph, notice, and public hearing and a showing by such petitioner that the State decision under paragraph (5) is not in accordance with the requirements of this section;

(7) require payment, in accordance with subsection (d) of this section, of the penalty by each person to whom notice of noncompliance is given under paragraph (3) with respect to each noncomplying source for which such notice is given unless there has been a final determination granting a petition under paragraph (4)(B) with respect to such source;

(8) authorize the State or the Administrator to adjust (and from time to time to readjust) the amount of the penalty assessment calculated or the payment schedule proposed by such owner or operator under paragraph (4), if the Administrator finds after notice and opportunity for a hearing on the record that the penalty or schedule does not meet the requirements of this section; and

(9) require a final adjustment of the penalty within 180 days after such source comes into compliance in accordance with subsection (d)(4) of this section.

In any case in which the State establishes a noncompliance penalty under this section, the State shall provide notice thereof to the Administrator. A noncompliance penalty established by a State under this section shall apply unless the Administrator, within ninety days after the date of receipt of notice of the State penalty assessment under this section, objects in writing to the amount of the penalty as less than would be required to comply with guidelines established by the Administrator. If the Administrator objects, he shall immediately establish a substitute noncompliance penalty applicable to such source.

(c) Contract to assist in determining amount of penalty assessment or payment schedule

If the owner or operator of any stationary source to whom a notice is issued under subsection (b)(3) of this section—

(1) does not submit a timely petition under subsection (b)(4)(B) of this section, or

(2) submits a petition under subsection (b)(4)(B) of this section which is denied, and

fails to submit a calculation of the penalty assessment, a schedule for payment, and the information necessary for independent verification thereof, the State (or the Administrator, as the case may be) may enter into a contract with any person who has no financial interest in the owner or operator of the source (or in any person controlling, controlled by or under common control with such source) to assist in determining the amount of the penalty assessment or payment schedule with respect to such source. The cost of carrying out such contract may be added to the penalty to be assessed against the owner or operator of such source.

(d) Payment

(1) All penalties assessed by the Administrator under this section shall be paid to the United States Treasury. All penalties assessed by the State under this section shall be paid to such State.

(2) The amount of the penalty which shall be assessed and collected with respect to any source under this section shall be equal to—

(A) the amount determined in accordance with regulations promulgated by the Administrator under subsection (a) of this section, which is no less than the economic value which a delay in compliance beyond July 1, 1979, may have for the owner of such source, including the quarterly equivalent of the capital costs of compliance and debt service over a normal amortization period, not to exceed ten years, operation and maintenance costs foregone as a result of noncompliance, and any additional economic value which such a delay may have for the owner or operator of such source, minus

(B) the amount of any expenditure made by the owner or operator of that source during any such quarter for the purpose of bringing that source into, and maintaining compliance with, such requirement, to the extent that such expenditures have not been taken into account in the calculation of the penalty under subparagraph (A).

To the extent that any expenditure under subparagraph (B) made during any quarter is not subtracted for such quarter from the costs under subparagraph (A), such expenditure may be subtracted for any subsequent quarter from such costs. In no event shall the amount paid be less than the quarterly payment minus the amount attributed to actual cost of construction.

(3)(A) The assessed penalty required under this section shall be paid in quarterly installments for the period of covered noncompliance. All quarterly payments (determined without regard to any adjustment or any subtraction under paragraph (2)(B)) after the first payment shall be equal.

(B) The first payment shall be due on the date six months after the date of issuance of the notice of noncompliance under subsection (b)(3) of this section with respect to any source or on January 1, 1980, whichever is later. Such first payment shall be in the amount of the quarterly installment for the upcoming quarter, plus the amount owed for any preceding period within the period of covered noncompliance for such source.

(C) For the purpose of this section, the term "period of covered noncompliance" means the period which begins—

(i) two years after August 7, 1977, in the case of a source for which notice of noncompliance under subsection (b)(3) of this section is issued on or before the date two years after August 7, 1977, or

(ii) on the date of issuance of the notice of noncompliance under subsection (b)(3) of this section, in the case of a source for which such notice is issued after July 1, 1979, and ending on the date on which such source comes into (or for the purpose of establishing the schedule of payments, is estimated to come into) compliance with such requirement.

(4) Upon making a determination that a source with respect to which a penalty has been paid under this section is in compliance and is maintaining compliance with the applicable requirement, the State (or the Administrator as the case may be) shall review the actual expenditures made by the owner or operator of such source for the purpose of attaining and maintaining compliance, and shall within 180 days after such source comes into compliance—

(A) provide reimbursement with interest (to be paid by the State or Secretary of the Treasury, as the case may be) at appropriate prevailing rates (as determined by the Secretary of the Treasury) for any overpayment by such person, or

(B) assess and collect an additional payment with interest at appropriate prevailing rates (as determined by the Secretary of the Treasury) for any underpayment by such person.

(5) Any person who fails to pay the amount of any penalty with respect to any source under this section on a timely basis shall be required to pay in addition a quarterly nonpayment penalty for each quarter during which such failure to pay persists. Such nonpayment penalty shall be in an amount equal to 20 percent of the aggregate amount of such person's penalties and nonpayment penalties with respect to such source which are unpaid as of the beginning of such quarter.

(e) Judicial review

Any action pursuant to this section, including any objection of the Administrator under the last sentence of subsection (b) of this section, shall be considered a final action for purposes of judicial review of any penalty under section 7607 of this title.

(f) Other orders, payments, sanctions, or requirements

Any orders, payments, sanctions, or other requirements under this section shall be in addition to any other permits, orders, payments, sanctions, or other requirements established under this chapter, and shall in no way affect any civil or criminal enforcement proceedings brought under any provision of this chapter or State or local law.

(g) More stringent emission limitations or other requirements

In the case of any emission limitation or other requirement approved or promulgated by the Administrator under this chapter after August 7, 1977, which is more stringent than the emission limitation or requirement for the source in effect prior to such approval or promulgation, if any, or where there was no emission limitation or requirement approved or promulgated before August 7, 1977, the date for imposition of the non-compliance penalty under this section, shall be either July 1, 1979, or the date on which the source is required to be in full compliance with such emission limitation or requirement, whichever is later, but in no event later than three years after the approval or promulgation of such emission limitation or requirement.

(July 14, 1955, ch. 360, title I, § 120, as added Aug. 7, 1977, Pub.L. 95–95, title I, § 118, 91 Stat. 714, and amended Nov. 16, 1977, Pub.L. 95–190, § 14(a)(28)–(38), 91 Stat. 1401; Nov. 15, 1990, Pub.L. 101–549, title VII, § 710(a), 104 Stat. 2684.)

References in Text

Section 1857c–10 of this title (as in effect before August 7, 1977), referred to in subsec. (a)(2)(B)(i), was in the original "section 119 (as in effect before the date of the enactment of the Clean Air Act Amendments of 1977)", meaning section 119 of Act July 14, 1955, c. 360, Title I, as added June 22, 1974, Pub.L. 93–319, § 3, 88 Stat. 248, (which was classified to section 1857c–10 of this title) as in effect prior to the enactment of Pub.L. 95–95, Aug. 7, 1977, 91 Stat. 691, effective Aug. 7, 1977. Section 112(b)(1) of Pub.L. 95–95 repealed section 119 of Act July 14, 1955, c. 360, Title I, as added by Pub.L. 93–319, and provided that all references to such section 119 in any subsequent enactment which supersedes Pub.L. 93–319 shall be construed to refer to section 113(d) of the Clean Air Act and to paragraph (5) thereof in particular which is classified to subsec. (d)(5) of section 7413 of this title. Section 117(b) of Pub.L. 95–95 added a new section 119 of Act July 14, 1955, which is classified to section 7419 of this title.

Section 1857c–10(c)(1) of this title (as in effect before August 7, 1977), referred to in subsec. (a)(2)(B)(ii), was in the original "section 119(c)(1) (as in effect before the date of the enactment of the Clean Air Act Amendments of 1977)." See paragraph set out above for explanation of codification.

Effective Date of 1990 Amendment

Amendment by Pub.L. 101–549 effective Nov. 15, 1990, except as otherwise provided, see section 711(b) of Pub.L. 101–549, set out as a note under section 7401 of this title.

Savings Provisions

Suits, actions or proceedings commenced under this chapter as in effect prior to Nov. 15, 1990, not to abate by reason of the taking effect of amendments by Pub.L. 101–549, except as otherwise provided for, see section 711(a) of Pub.L. 101–549, set out as a note under section 7401 of this title.

West's Federal Practice Manual

Air quality legislation, see § 4384.5.

CODE OF FEDERAL REGULATIONS

Environmental Protection Agency,
- Non-compliance penalty, proceedings for assessment of, see 40 CFR 66.1 et seq.
- Standards for approval of state non-compliance penalty programs, see 40 CFR 67.1 et seq.

LAW REVIEW COMMENTARIES

Bonfire of the executives: Criminal environmental enforcement unfolds. John E. Smith, II, 10 Corp. Counsel Rev. (Tex.) 67 (May 1991).

Resolving conflicts between bankruptcy law and the state police power. Ellen E. Sward, 1987 Wis.L.Rev. 403 (1987).

Library References

Health and Environment ⇨25.6(9).

C.J.S. Health and Environment § 104 et seq.

§ 7421. Consultation [CAA § 121]

In carrying out the requirements of this chapter requiring applicable implementation plans to contain—

(1) any transportation controls, air quality maintenance plan requirements or preconstruction review of direct sources of air pollution, or

(2) any measure referred to—

(A) in part D (pertaining to nonattainment requirements), or

(B) in part C (pertaining to prevention of significant deterioration),

and in carrying out the requirements of section 7413(d) of this title (relating to certain enforcement orders), the State shall provide a satisfactory process of consultation with general purpose local governments, designated organizations of elected officials of local governments and any Federal land manager having authority over Federal land to which the State plan applies, effective with respect to any such requirement which is adopted more than one year after August 7, 1977, as part of such plan. Such process shall be in accordance with regulations promulgated by the Administrator to assure adequate consultation. The Administrator shall update as necessary the original regulations required and promulgated under this section (as in effect immediately before November 15, 1990) to ensure adequate consultation. Only a general purpose unit of local government, regional agency, or council of governments adversely affected by action of the Administrator approving any portion of a plan referred to in this subsection[1] may petition for judicial review of such action on the basis of a violation of the requirements of this section.

(July 14, 1955, ch. 360, title I, § 121, as added Aug. 7, 1977, Pub.L. 95–95, title I, § 119, 91 Stat. 719, and amended Nov. 15, 1990, Pub.L. 101–549, title I, § 108(h), 104 Stat. 2467.)

[1] So in original. Probably should be "section".

Effective Date of 1990 Amendment

Amendment by Pub.L. 101–549 to take effect Nov. 15, 1990, except as otherwise provided, see section 711(b) of Pub.L. 101–549, set out as a note under section 7401 of this title.

Savings Provisions

Suits, actions or proceedings commenced under this chapter as in effect prior to Nov. 15, 1990, not to abate by reason of the taking effect of amendments by Pub.L. 101–549, except as otherwise provided for, see section 711(a) of Pub.L. 101–549, set out as a note under section 7401 of this title.

CODE OF FEDERAL REGULATIONS

Implementation plans, generally, see 40 CFR 51.40 et seq.

§ 7422. Listing of certain unregulated pollutants [CAA § 122]

(a) Radioactive pollutants, cadmium, arsenic, and polycyclic organic matter

Not later than one year after August 7, 1977 (two years for radioactive pollutants) and after notice and opportunity for public hearing, the Administrator shall review all available relevant information and determine whether or not emissions of radioactive pollutants (including source material, special nuclear material, and byproduct material), cadmium, arsenic and polycyclic organic matter into the ambient air will cause, or contribute to, air pollution which may reasonably be anticipated to endanger public health. If the Administrator makes an affirmative determination with respect to any such substance, he shall simultaneously with such determination include such substance in the list published under section 7408(a)(1) or 7412(b)(1)(A) of this title (in the case of a substance which, in the judgment of the Administrator, causes, or contributes to, air pollution which may reasonably be anticipated to result in an increase in mortality or an increase in serious irreversible, or incapacitating reversible, illness), or shall include each category of stationary sources emitting such substance in significant amounts in the list published under section 7411(b)(1)(A) of this title, or take any combination of such actions.

(b) Revision authority

Nothing in subsection (a) of this section shall be construed to affect the authority of the Administrator to revise any list referred to in subsection (a) of this section with respect to any substance (whether or not enumerated in subsection (a) of this section).

(c) Consultation with Nuclear Regulatory Commission; interagency agreement; notice and hearing

(1) Before listing any source material, special nuclear, or byproduct material (or component or derivative thereof) as provided in subsection (a) of this section, the Administrator shall consult with the Nuclear Regulatory Commission.

(2) Not later than six months after listing any such material (or component or derivative thereof) the Administrator and the Nuclear Regulatory Commission shall enter into an interagency agreement with respect to those sources or facilities which are under the jurisdiction of the Commission. This agreement shall, to the maximum extent practicable consistent with this chapter, minimize duplication of effort and conserve administrative resources in the establishment, implementation, and enforcement of emission limitations, standards of performance, and other requirements and authorities (substantive and procedural) under this chapter respecting the emission of such material (or component or derivative thereof) from such sources or facilities.

(3) In case of any standard or emission limitation promulgated by the Administrator, under this chapter or by any State (or the Administrator) under any applicable implementation plan under this chapter, if the Nuclear Regulatory Commission determines, after notice and opportunity for public hearing that the application of such standard or limitation to a source or facility within the jurisdiction of the Commission would endanger public health or safety, such standard or limitation shall not apply to such facilities or sources unless the President determines otherwise within ninety days from the date of such finding.

(July 14, 1955, ch. 360, title I, § 122, as added Aug. 7, 1977, Pub.L. 95–95, title I, § 120(a), 91 Stat. 720.)

Library References

Health and Environment ⊂⊃25.6(5).
C.J.S. Health and Environment § 91 et seq.

§ 7423. Stack heights [CAA § 123]

(a) Heights in excess of good engineering practice; other dispersion techniques

The degree of emission limitation required for control of any air pollutant under an applicable implementation plan under this subchapter shall not be affected in any manner by—

(1) so much of the stack height of any source as exceeds good engineering practice (as determined under regulations promulgated by the Administrator), or

(2) any other dispersion technique.

The preceding sentence shall not apply with respect to stack heights in existence before December 31, 1970, or dispersion techniques implemented before such date. In establishing an emission limitation for coal-fired steam electric generating units which are subject to the provisions of section 7418 of this title and which commenced operation before July 1, 1957, the effect of the entire stack height of stacks for which a construction contract was awarded before February 8, 1974, may be taken into account.

(b) Dispersion technique

For the purpose of this section, the term "dispersion technique" includes any intermittent or supplemental control of air pollutants varying with atmospheric conditions.

(c) Regulations; good engineering practice

Not later than six months after August 7, 1977, the Administrator, shall after notice and opportunity for public hearing, promulgate regulations to carry out this section. For purposes of this section, good engineering practice means, with respect to stack heights, the height necessary to insure that emissions from the stack do not result in excessive concentrations of any air pollutant in the immediate vicinity of the source as a result of atmospheric downwash, eddies and wakes which may be created by the source itself, nearby structures or nearby terrain obstacles (as determined by the Administrator). For purposes of this section such height shall not exceed two and a half times the height of such source unless the owner or operator of the source demonstrates, after notice and opportunity for public hearing, to the satisfaction of the Administrator, that a greater height is necessary as provided under the preceding sentence. In no event may the Administrator prohibit any increase in any stack height or restrict in any manner the stack height of any source.

(July 14, 1955, ch. 360, title I, § 123, as added Aug. 7, 1977, Pub.L. 95–95, title I, § 121, 91 Stat. 721.)

CODE OF FEDERAL REGULATIONS

Implementation plans, generally, see 40 CFR 51.40 et seq.

Library References

Health and Environment ⊂⊃25.6(5).
C.J.S. Health and Environment § 91 et seq.

§ 7424. Assurance of adequacy of State plans [CAA § 124]

(a) State review of implementation plans which relate to major fuel burning sources

As expeditiously as practicable but not later than one year after August 7, 1977, each State shall review the provisions of its implementation plan which relate to major fuel burning sources and shall determine—

(1) the extent to which compliance with requirements of such plan is dependent upon the use by major fuel burning stationary sources of petroleum products or natural gas,

(2) the extent to which such plan may reasonably be anticipated to be inadequate to meet the requirements of this chapter in such State on a reliable and long-term basis by reason of its dependence upon the use of such fuels, and

(3) the extent to which compliance with the requirements of such plan is dependent upon use of coal or coal derivatives which is not locally or regionally available.

Each State shall submit the results of its review and its determination under this paragraph to the Administrator promptly upon completion thereof.

(b) Plan revision

(1) Not later than eighteen months after August 7, 1977, the Administrator shall review the submissions of the States under subsection (a) of this section and shall require each State to revise its plan if, in the judgment of the Administrator, such plan revision is necessary to assure that such plan will be adequate to assure compliance with the requirements of this chapter in such State on a reliable and long-term basis, taking into account the actual or potential prohibitions on use of petroleum products or natural gas, or both, under any other authority of law.

(2) Before requiring a plan revision under this subsection, with respect to any State the Administrator shall take into account the report of the review conducted by such State under paragraph (1) and shall consult with the Governor of the State respecting such required revision.

(July 14, 1955, ch. 360, title I, § 124, as added Aug. 7, 1977, Pub.L. 95–95, title I, § 122, 91 Stat. 722.)

Library References

Health and Environment ⟹25.6(2).
C.J.S. Health and Environment § 125 et seq.

§ 7425. Measures to prevent economic disruption or unemployment [CAA § 125]

(a) Determination that action is necessary

After notice and opportunity for a public hearing—

(1) the Governor of any State in which a major fuel burning stationary source referred to in this subsection (or class or category thereof) is located,

(2) the Administrator, or

(3) the President (or his designee),

may determine that action under subsection (b) of this section is necessary to prevent or minimize significant local or regional economic disruption or unemployment which would otherwise result from use by such source (or class or category) of—

(A) coal or coal derivatives other than locally or regionally available coal,

(B) petroleum products,

(C) natural gas, or

(D) any combination of fuels referred to in subparagraphs (A) through (C),

to comply with the requirements of a State implementation plan.

(b) Use of locally or regionally available coal or coal derivatives to comply with implementation plan requirements

Upon a determination under subsection (a) of this section—

(1) such Governor, with the written consent of the President or his designee,

(2) the President's designee with the written consent of such Governor, or

(3) the President

may by rule or order prohibit any such major fuel burning stationary source (or class or category thereof) from using fuels other than locally or regionally available coal or coal derivatives to comply with implementation plan requirements. In taking any action under this subsection, the Governor, the President, or the President's designee as the case may be, shall take into account, the final cost to the consumer of such an action.

(c) Contracts; schedules

The Governor, in the case of action under subsection (b)(1) of this section, or the Administrator, in the case of an action under subsection (b)(2) or (3) of this section shall, by rule or order, require each source to which such action applies to—

(1) enter into long-term contracts of at least ten years in duration (except as the President or his designee may otherwise permit or require by rule or order for good cause) for supplies of regionally available coal or coal derivatives,

(2) enter into contracts to acquire any additional means of emission limitation which the Administrator or the State determines may be necessary to comply with the requirements of this chapter while using such coal or coal derivatives as fuel, and

(3) comply with such schedules (including increments of progress), timetables and other requirements as may be necessary to assure compliance with the requirements of this chapter.

Requirements under this subsection shall be established simultaneously with, and as a condition of, any action under subsection (b) of this section.

(d) Existing or new major fuel burning stationary sources

This section applies only to existing or new major fuel burning stationary sources—

(1) which have the design capacity to produce 250,000,000 Btu's per hour (or its equivalent), as determined by the Administrator, and

(2) which are not in compliance with the requirements of an applicable implementation plan or which are prohibited from burning oil or natural gas, or both, under any other authority of law.

(e) Actions not to be deemed modifications of major fuel burning stationary sources

Except as may otherwise be provided by rule by the State or the Administrator for good cause, any action required to be taken by a major fuel burning stationary source under this section shall not be deemed to constitute a modification for purposes of section 7411(a)(2) and (4) of this title.

(f) Treatment of prohibitions, rules, or orders as requirements or parts of plans under other provisions

For purposes of sections 7413 and 7420 of this title a prohibition under subsection (b) of this section, and a corresponding rule or order under subsection (c) of this section, shall be treated as a requirement of section 7413 of this title. For purposes of any plan (or portion thereof) promulgated under section 7410(c) of this title, any rule or order under subsection (c) of this section corresponding to a prohibition under subsection (b) of this section, shall be treated as a part of such plan. For purposes of section 7413 of this title, a prohibition under subsection (b) of this section, applicable to any source, and a corresponding rule or order under subsection (c) of this section, shall be treated as part of the applicable implementation plan for the State in which subject source is located.

(g) Delegation of Presidential authority

The President may delegate his authority under this section to an officer or employee of the United States designated by him on a case-by-case basis or in any other manner he deems suitable.

(h) Locally or regionally available coal or coal derivatives

For the purpose of this section the term "locally or regionally available coal or coal derivatives" means coal or coal derivatives which is, or can in the judgment of the State or the Administrator feasibly be, mined or produced in the local or regional area (as determined by the Administrator) in which the major fuel burning stationary source is located.

(July 14, 1955, ch. 360, title I, § 125, as added Aug. 7, 1977, Pub.L. 95–95, title I, § 122, 91 Stat. 722.)

CROSS REFERENCES

Petition to President to exercise his authorities pursuant to this section with respect to major fuel burning stationary source, see section 6215 of this title.

Library References

Health and Environment ⚷25.6(2).
C.J.S. Health and Environment § 125 et seq.

§ 7426. Interstate pollution abatement [CAA § 126]

(a) Written notice to all nearby States

Each applicable implementation plan shall—

(1) require each major proposed new (or modified) source—

(A) subject to part C of this subchapter (relating to significant deterioration of air quality) or

(B) which may significantly contribute to levels of air pollution in excess of the national ambient air quality standards in any air quality control region outside the State in which such source intends to locate (or make such modification),

to provide written notice to all nearby States the air pollution levels of which may be affected by such source at least sixty days prior to the date on which commencement of construction is to be permitted by the State providing notice, and

(2) identify all major existing stationary sources which may have the impact described in paragraph (1) with respect to new or modified sources and provide notice to all nearby States of the identity of such sources not later than three months after August 7, 1977.

(b) Petition for finding that major sources emit or would emit prohibited air pollutants

Any State or political subdivision may petition the Administrator for a finding that any major source or group of stationary sources emits or would emit any air pollutant in violation of the prohibition of section 7410(a)(2)(D)(ii) of this title or this section. Within 60 days after receipt of any petition under this subsection and after public hearing, the Administrator shall make such a finding or deny the petition.

(c) Violations; allowable continued operation

Notwithstanding any permit which may have been granted by the State in which the source is located (or intends to locate), it shall be a violation of the this section and the applicable implementation plan in such State—

(1) for any major proposed new (or modified) source with respect to which a finding has been made under subsection (b) of this section to be constructed or to operate in violation of the prohibition of section 7410(a)(2)(D)(ii) of this title or this section, or

(2) for any major existing source to operate more than three months after such finding has been made with respect to it.

The Administrator may permit the continued operation of a source referred to in paragraph (2) beyond the expiration of such three-month period if such source complies with such emission limitations and compliance schedules (containing increments of progress) as may be provided by the Administrator to bring about compliance with the requirements contained in section 7410(a)(2)(D)(ii) of this title or this section as expeditiously as practicable, but in no case later than three years after the date of such finding. Nothing in the preceding sentence shall be construed to preclude any such source from being eligible for an enforcement order under section 7413(d) of this title after the expiration of such period during which the Administrator has permitted continuous operation.

(July 14, 1955, ch. 360, title I, § 126, as added Aug. 7, 1977, Pub.L. 95–95, title I, § 123, 91 Stat. 724, and amended Nov. 16, 1977, Pub.L. 95–190, § 14(a)(39), 91 Stat. 1401; Nov. 15, 1990, Pub.L. 101–549, title I, § 109(a), 104 Stat. 2469.)

Effective Date of 1990 Amendment

Amendment by Pub.L. 101–549 effective Nov. 15, 1990, except as otherwise provided, see section 711(b) of Pub.L. 101–549, set out as a note under section 7401 of this title.

Savings Provisions

Suits, actions or proceedings commenced under this chapter as in effect prior to Nov. 15, 1990, not to abate by reason of the taking effect of amendments by Pub.L. 101–549, except as otherwise provided for, see section 711(a) of Pub.L. 101–549, set out as a note under section 7401 of this title.

Library References

Health and Environment ⚷25.6(2).
C.J.S. Health and Environment § 125 et seq.

§ 7427. Public notification [CAA § 127]

(a) Warning signs; television, radio, or press notices or information

Each State plan shall contain measures which will be effective to notify the public during any calendar[1] on a regular basis of instances or areas in which any national primary ambient air quality standard is exceeded or was exceeded during any portion of the preceding calendar year to advise the public of the health hazards associated with such pollution, and to enhance public awareness of the measures which can be taken to prevent such standards from being exceeded and the ways in which the public can participate in regulatory and other efforts to improve air quality. Such measures may include the posting of warning signs on interstate highway access points to metropolitan areas or television, radio, or press notices or information.

(b) Grants

The Administrator is authorized to make grants to States to assist in carrying out the requirements of subsection (a) of this section.

(July 14, 1955, ch. 360, title I, § 127, as added Aug. 7, 1977, Pub.L. 95–95, title I, § 124, 91 Stat. 725.)

[1] So in original. Probably should read "calendar year".

Library References

Health and Environment ⚷25.6(2).
United States ⚷82(2).
C.J.S. Health and Environment § 125 et seq.
C.J.S. United States § 122.

§ 7428. State boards [CAA § 128]

(a)[1] Not later than the date one year after August 7, 1977, each applicable implementation plan shall contain requirements that—

(1) any board or body which approves permits or enforcement orders under this chapter shall have at least a majority of members who represent the public interest and do not derive any significant portion of their income from persons subject to permits or enforcement orders under this chapter, and

(2) any potential conflicts of interest by members of such board or body or the head of an executive agency with similar powers be adequately disclosed.

A State may adopt any requirements respecting conflicts of interest for such boards or bodies or heads of executive agencies, or any other entities which are more stringent than the requirements of paragraph (1) and (2), and the Administrator shall approve any such more stringent requirements submitted as part of an implementation plan.

(July 14, 1955, ch. 360, title I, § 128, as added Aug. 7, 1977, Pub.L. 95–95, title I, § 125, 91 Stat. 725.)

[1] So in original. Section enacted without subsec. (b).

§ 7429. Solid waste combustion [CAA § 129]

(a) New source performance standards

(1) In general

(A) The Administrator shall establish performance standards and other requirements pursuant to section 7411 of this title and this section for each category of solid waste incineration units. Such standards shall include emissions limitations and other requirements applicable to new units and guidelines (under section 7411(d) of this title and this section) and other requirements applicable to existing units.

(B) Standards under section 7411 of this title and this section applicable to solid waste incineration units with capacity greater than 250 tons per day combusting municipal waste shall be promulgated not later than 12 months after November 15, 1990. Nothing in this subparagraph shall alter any schedule for the promulgation of standards applicable to such units under section 7411 of this title pursuant to any settlement and consent decree entered by the Administrator before November 15, 1990: *Provided,* That, such standards are subsequently modified pursuant to the schedule established in this subparagraph to include each of the requirements of this section.

(C) Standards under section 7411 of this title and this section applicable to solid waste incineration units with capacity equal to or less than 250 tons per day combusting municipal waste and units combusting hospital waste, medical waste and infectious waste shall be promulgated not later than 24 months after November 15, 1990.

(D) Standards under section 7411 of this title and this section applicable to solid waste incineration units combusting commercial or industrial waste shall be proposed not later than 36 months after November 15, 1990, and promulgated not later than 48 months after November 15, 1990.

(E) Not later than 18 months after November 15, 1990, the Administrator shall publish a schedule for the promulgation of standards under section 111 and this section applicable to other categories of solid waste incineration units.

(2) Emissions standard

Standards applicable to solid waste incineration units promulgated under section 7411 of this title and this section shall reflect the maximum degree of reduction in emissions of air pollutants listed under section (a)(4)[1] that the Administrator, taking into consideration the cost of achieving such emission reduction, and any non-air quality health and environmental impacts and energy requirements, determines is achievable for new or existing units in each category. The Administrator may distinguish among classes, types (including mass-burn, refuse-derived fuel, modular and other types of units), and sizes of units within a category in establishing such standards. The degree of reduction in emissions that is deemed achievable for new units in a category shall not be less stringent than the emissions control that is achieved in practice by the best controlled similar unit, as determined by the Administrator. Emissions standards for existing units in a category may be less stringent than standards for new units in the same category but shall not be less stringent than the average emissions limitation achieved by the best performing 12 percent of units in the category (excluding units which first met lowest achievable emissions rates 18 months before the date such standards are proposed or 30 months before the date such standards are promulgated, whichever is later).

(3) Control methods and technologies

Standards under section 7411 of this title and this section applicable to solid waste incineration units shall be based on methods and technologies for removal or destruction of pollutants before, during, or after combustion, and shall incorporate for new units siting requirements that minimize, on a site specific basis, to the maximum extent practicable, potential risks to public health or the environment.

(4) Numerical emissions limitations

The performance standards promulgated under section 7411 of this title and this section and applicable to solid waste incineration units shall specify numerical emission limitations for the following substances or mixtures: particulate matter (total and fine), opacity (as appropriate), sulfur dioxide, hydrogen chloride, oxides of nitrogen, carbon monoxide, lead, cadmium, mercury, and dioxins and dibenzofurans. The Administrator may promulgate numerical emissions limitations or provide for the monitoring of postcombustion concentrations of surrogate substances, parameters or periods of residence time in excess of stated temperatures with respect to pollutants other than those listed in this paragraph.

(5) Review and revision

Not later than 5 years following the initial promulgation of any performance standards and other requirements under this section and section 7411 of this title applicable to a category of solid waste incineration units, and at 5 year intervals thereafter, the Administrator shall review, and in accordance with this section and section 7411 of this title, revise such standards and requirements.

(b) Existing units

(1) Guidelines

Performance standards under this section and section 7411 of this title for solid waste incineration units shall include guidelines promulgated pursuant to section 7411(d) of this title and this section applicable to existing units. Such guidelines shall include, as provided in this section, each of the elements required by subsection (a) of this section (emissions limitations, notwithstanding any restriction in section 7411(d) of this title regarding issuance of such limitations), subsection (c) of this section (monitoring), subsection (d) of this section (operator training), subsection (e) of this section (permits), and subsection (h)(4) of this section (residual risk).

(2) State plans

Not later than 1 year after the Administrator promulgates guidelines for a category of solid waste incineration units, each State in which units in the category are operating shall submit to the Administrator a plan to implement and enforce the guidelines with respect to such units. The State plan shall be at least as protective as the guidelines promulgated by the Administrator and shall provide that each unit subject to the guidelines shall be in compliance with all requirements of this section not later than 3 years after the State plan is approved by the Administrator but not later than 5 years after the guidelines were promulgated. The Administrator shall approve or disapprove any State plan within 180 days of the submission, and if a plan is disapproved, the Administrator shall state the reasons for disapproval in writing. Any State may modify and resubmit a plan which has been disapproved by the Administrator.

(3) Federal plan

The Administrator shall develop, implement and enforce a plan for existing solid waste incineration units within any category located in any State which has not submitted an approvable plan under this subsection with respect to units in such category within 2 years after the date on which the Administrator promulgated the relevant guidelines. Such plan shall assure that each unit subject to the plan is in compliance with all provisions of the guidelines not later than 5 years after the date the relevant guidelines are promulgated.

(c) Monitoring

The Administrator shall, as part of each performance standard promulgated pursuant to subsection (a) and section 111, promulgate regulations requiring the owner or operator of each solid waste incineration unit—

(1) to monitor emissions from the unit at the point at which such emissions are emitted into the ambient air (or within the stack, combustion chamber or pollution control equipment, as appropriate) and at such other points as necessary to protect public health and the environment;

(2) to monitor such other parameters relating to the operation of the unit and its pollution control technology as the Administrator determines are appropriate; and

(3) to report the results of such monitoring.

Such regulations shall contain provisions regarding the frequency of monitoring, test methods and procedures validated on solid waste incineration units, and the form and frequency of reports containing the results of monitoring and shall require that any monitoring reports or test results indicating an exceedance of any standard under this section shall be reported separately and in a manner that facilitates review for purposes of enforcement actions. Such regulations shall require that copies of the results of such monitoring be maintained on file at the facility concerned and that copies shall be made available for inspection and copying by interested members of the public during business hours.

(d) Operator training

Not later than 24 months after the enactment of the Clean Air Act Amendments of 1990, the Administrator shall develop and promote a model State program for the training and certification of solid waste incineration unit operators and high-capacity fossil fuel fired plant operators. The Administrator may authorize any State to implement a model program for the training of solid waste incineration unit operators and high-capacity fossil fuel fired plant operators, if the State has adopted a program which is at least as effective as the model program developed by the Administrator. Beginning on the date 36 months after the date on which performance standards and guidelines are promulgated under subsection (a) of this section and section 7411 of this title for any category of solid waste incineration units it shall be unlawful to operate any unit in the category unless each person with control over processes affecting emissions from such unit has satisfactorily completed a training program meeting the requirements established by the Administrator under this subsection.

(e) Permits

Beginning (1) 36 months after the promulgation of a performance standard under subsection (a) of this section and section 7411 of this title applicable to a category of solid waste incineration units, or (2) the effective date of a permit program under subchapter V of this chapter in the State in which the unit is located, whichever is later, each unit in the category shall operate pursuant to a permit issued under this subsection and subchapter V of this chapter. Permits required by this subsection may be renewed according to the provisions of subchapter V of this chapter. Notwithstanding any other provision of this chapter, each permit for a solid waste incineration unit combusting municipal waste issued under this chapter shall be issued for a period of up to 12 years and shall be reviewed every 5 years after date of issuance or reissuance. Each permit shall continue in effect after the date of issuance until the date of termination, unless the Administrator or State determines that the unit is not in compliance with all standards and conditions contained in the permit. Such determination shall be made at regular intervals during the term of the permit, such intervals not to exceed 5 years, and only after public comment and public hearing. No permit for a solid waste incineration unit may be issued under this chapter by an agency, instrumentality or person that is also responsible, in whole or part, for the design and construction or operation of the unit. Notwithstanding any other provision of this subsection, the Administrator or the State shall require the owner or operator of any unit to comply with emissions limitations or implement any other measures, if the Administrator or the State determines that emissions in the absence of such limitations or measures may reasonably be anticipated to endanger public health or the environment. The Administrator's determination under the preceding sentence is a discretionary decision.

(f) Effective date and enforcement

(1) New units

Performance standards and other requirements promulgated pursuant to this section and section 7411 of this title and applicable to new solid waste incineration units shall be effective as of the date 6 months after the date of promulgation.

(2) Existing units

Performance standards and other requirements promulgated pursuant to this section and section 7411 of this title and applicable to existing solid waste incineration units shall be effective as expeditiously as practicable after approval of a State plan under subsection (b)(2) of this section (or promulgation of a plan by the Administrator under subsection (b)(3) of this section) but in no event later than 3 years after the State plan is approved or 5 years after the date such standards or requirements are promulgated, whichever is earlier.

(3) Prohibition

After the effective date of any performance standard, emission limitation or other requirement promulgated pursuant to this section and section 7411 of this title, it shall be unlawful for any owner or operator of any solid waste incineration unit to which such standard, limitation or requirement applies to operate such unit in violation of such limitation, standard or requirement or for any other person to violate an applicable requirement of this section.

(4) Coordination with other authorities

For purposes of sections 7411(e), 7413, 7414, 7416, 7420, 7603, 7604, 7607 of this title and other provisions for the enforcement of this chapter, each performance standard, emission limitation or other requirement established pursuant to this section by the Administrator or a State or local government, shall be treated in the same manner as a standard of performance under section 7411 of this title which is an emission limitation.

(g) Definitions

For purposes of section 306 of the Clean Air Act Amendments of 1990 and this section only—

(1) Solid waste incineration unit

The term "solid waste incineration unit" means a distinct operating unit of any facility which combusts any solid waste material from commercial or industrial establishments or the general public (including single and multiple residences, hotels, and motels). Such term does not include incinerators or other units required to have a permit under section 3005 of the Solid Waste Disposal Act [42 U.S.C.A. § 6925]. The term "solid waste incineration unit" does not include (A) materials recovery facilities (including primary or secondary smelters) which combust waste for the primary purpose of recovering metals, (B) qualifying small power production facilities, as defined in section 769(17)(C) of Title 16, or qualifying cogeneration facilities, as defined in section 796(18)(B) of Title 16, which burn homogeneous waste (such as units which burn tires or used oil, but not including refuse-derived fuel) for the production of electric energy or in the case of qualifying cogeneration facilities which burn homogeneous waste for the production of electric energy and steam or forms of useful energy (such as heat) which are used for industrial, commercial, heating or cooling purposes, or (C) air curtain incinerators provided that such incinerators only burn wood wastes, yard wastes and clean lumber and that such air curtain incinerators comply with opacity limitations to be established by the Administrator by rule.

(2) New solid waste incineration unit

The term "new solid waste incineration unit" means a solid waste incineration unit the construction of which is commenced after the Administrator proposes requirements under this section establishing emissions standards or other requirements which would be applicable to such unit or a modified solid waste incineration unit.

(3) Modified solid waste incineration unit

The term "modified solid waste incineration unit" means a solid waste incineration unit at which modifications have occurred after the effective date of a standard under subsection (a) of this section if (A) the cumulative cost of the modifications, over the life of the unit, exceed 50 per centum of the original cost of construction and installation of the unit (not including the cost of any land purchased in connection with such construction or installation) updated to current costs, or (B) the modification is a physical change in or change in the method of operation of the unit which increases the amount of any air pollutant emitted by the unit for which standards have been established under this section or section 7411 of this title.

(4) Existing solid waste incineration unit

The term "existing solid waste incineration unit" means a solid waste unit which is not a new or modified solid waste incineration unit.

(5) Municipal waste

The term "municipal waste" means refuse (and refuse-derived fuel) collected from the general public and from residential, commercial, institutional, and industrial sources consisting of paper, wood, yard wastes, food wastes, plastics, leather, rubber, and other combustible materials and non-combustible materials such as metal, glass and rock, provided that: (A) the term does not include industrial process wastes or medical wastes that are segregated from such other wastes; and (B) an incineration unit shall not be considered to be combusting municipal waste for purposes of section 7411 of this title or this section if it combusts a fuel feed stream, 30 percent or less of the weight of which is comprised, in aggregate, of municipal waste.

(6) Other terms

The terms "solid waste" and "medical waste" shall have the meanings established by the Administrator pursuant to the Solid Waste Disposal Act [42 U.S.C.A. § 6901 et seq.].

(h) Other authority

(1) State authority

Nothing in this section shall preclude or deny the right of any State or political subdivision thereof to adopt or enforce any regulation, requirement, limitation or standard relating to solid waste incineration units that is more stringent than a regulation, requirement, limitation or standard in effect under this section or under any other provision of this chapter.

(2) Other authority under this chapter

Nothing in this section shall diminish the authority of the Administrator or a State to establish any other requirements applicable to solid waste incineration units under any other authority of law, including the authority to establish for any air pollutant a national ambient air quality standard, except that no solid waste incineration unit subject to performance standards under this section and section 7411 of this title shall be subject to standards under section 7412(d) of this title.

(3) Residual risk

The Administrator shall promulgate standards under section 7412(f) of this title for a category of solid waste incineration units, if promulgation of such standards is required under section 7412(f) of this title. For purposes of this preceding sentence only—

(A) the performance standards under subsection (a) of this section and section 7411 of this title applicable to a category of solid waste incineration units shall be deemed standards under section 7412(d)(2) of this title, and

(B) the Administrator shall consider and regulate, if required, the pollutants listed under subsection (a)(4) of this section and no others.

(4) Acid rain

A solid waste incineration unit shall not be a utility unit as defined in subchapter IV–A of this chapter: *Provided,* That, more than 80 per centum of its annual average fuel consumption measured on a Btu basis, during a period or periods to be determined by the Administrator, is from a fuel (including any waste burned as a fuel) other than a fossil fuel.

(5) Requirements of parts C and D of this subchapter

No requirement of an applicable implementation plan under section 7475 of this title (relating to construction of facilities in regions identified pursuant to section 7407(d)(1)(A)(ii) or (iii) of this title) or under section 7502(c)(5) of this title (relating to permits for construction and operation in nonattainment areas) may be used to weaken the standards in effect under this section.

(July 14, 1955, ch. 360, title I, § 129, as added Nov. 15, 1990, Pub.L. 101–549, title III, § 305(a), 104 Stat. 2578.)

1 So in original. Probably should read "subsection (a)(4) of this section".

References in Text

The enactment of the Clean Air Act Amendments of 1990, referred to in subsec. (d), probably means the date of enactment of Pub.L. 101–549, Nov. 15, 1990, 104 Stat. 2399, which was approved Nov. 15, 1990.

Section 306 of the Clean Air Act Amendments of 1990, referred to in subsec. (g), is set out as a note under section 6921 of this title.

The Solid Waste Disposal Act, referred to in subsecs. (g)(1) and (g)(6), is Title II of Pub.L. 89–272, Oct. 20, 1965, 79 Stat. 997, as amended generally by Pub.L. 94–580, § 2, Oct. 21, 1976, 90 Stat. 2795, which is classified generally to chapter 82 (section 6901 et seq.) of this title. Section 3005 of the Solid Waste Disposal Act, referred to in subsec. (g)(1), is classified to section 6925 of this title. For complete classification of this Act to the Code, see Short Title note set out under section 6901 of this title and Tables.

Effective Date

Section to take effect Nov. 15, 1990, except as otherwise provided, see section 711(b) of Pub.L. 101–549, set out as a note under section 7401 of this title.

Savings Provisions

Suits, actions or proceedings commenced under this chapter as in effect prior to Nov. 15, 1990, not to abate by reason of the taking effect of amendments by Pub.L. 101–549, except as otherwise provided for, see section 711(a) of Pub.L. 101–549, set out as a note under section 7401 of this title.

Review of Acid Gas Scrubbing Requirements

Section 305(c) of Pub.L. 101–549 provided that: "Prior to the promulgation of any performance standard for solid waste incineration units combusting municipal waste under section 111 [section 7411 of this title] or section 129 of the Clean Air Act [this section], the Administrator shall review the availability of acid gas scrubbers as a pollution control technology for small new units and for existing units (as defined in 54 Federal Register 52190 (December 20, 1989), taking into account the provisions of subsection (a)(2) of section 129 of the Clean Air Act [subsec. (a)(2) of this section]."

§ 7430. Emission factors [CAA § 130]

Within 6 months after enactment of the Clean Air Act Amendments of 1990, and at least every 3 years thereafter, the Administrator shall review and, if necessary, revise, the methods ("emission factors") used for purposes of this chapter to estimate the quantity of emissions of carbon monoxide, volatile organic compounds, and oxides of nitrogen from sources of such air pollutants (including area sources and mobile sources). In addition, the Administrator shall establish emission factors for sources for which no such methods have previously been established by the Administrator. The Administrator shall permit any person to demonstrate improved emissions estimating techniques, and following approval of such techniques, the Administrator shall authorize the use of such techniques. Any such technique may be approved only after appropriate public participation. Until the Administrator has completed the revision required by this section, nothing in this section shall be construed to affect the validity of emission factors established by the Administrator before November 15, 1990.

(July 14, 1955, ch. 360, title I, § 130, as added Nov. 15, 1990, Pub.L. 101–549, title VIII, § 804, 104 Stat. 2689.)

References in Text

The enactment of the Clean Air Act Amendments of 1990, referred to in text, probably means the date of enactment of Pub.L. 101–549, Nov. 15, 1990, 104 Stat. 2399, which was approved Nov. 15, 1990.

Effective Date

Section to take effect Nov. 15, 1990, except as otherwise provided, see section 711(b) of Pub.L. 101–549, set out as a note under section 7401 of this title.

Savings Provisions

Suits, actions or proceedings commenced under this chapter as in effect prior to Nov. 15, 1990, not to abate by reason of the taking effect of amendments by Pub.L. 101–549, except as otherwise provided for, see section 711(a) of Pub.L. 101–549, set out as a note under section 7401 of this title.

§ 7431. Land use authority [CAA § 131]

Nothing in this chapter constitutes an infringement on the existing authority of counties and cities to plan or control land use, and nothing in this chapter provides or transfers authority over such land use.

(July 14, 1955, ch. 360, title I, § 131, as added Nov. 15, 1990, Pub.L. 101–549, title VIII, § 805, 104 Stat. 2689.)

Effective Date

Section to take effect Nov. 15, 1990, except as otherwise provided, see section 711(b) of Pub.L. 101–549, set out as a note under section 7401 of this title.

Savings Provisions

Suits, actions or proceedings commenced under this chapter as in effect prior to Nov. 15, 1990, not to abate by reason of the taking effect of amendments by Pub.L. 101–549, except as otherwise provided for, see section 711(a) of Pub.L. 101–549, set out as a note under section 7401 of this title.

PART B—OZONE PROTECTION [REPEALED]

§§ 7450 to 7459. Repealed. Pub.L. 101–549, Title VI, § 601, Nov. 15, 1990, 104 Stat. 2648

Section 7450, July 14, 1955, c. 360, Title I, § 150, as added Aug. 7, 1977, Pub.L. 95–95, Title I, § 126, 91 Stat. 726, set forth the Congressional declaration of purpose.

Section 7451, July 14, 1955, c. 360, Title I, § 151, as added Aug. 7, 1977, Pub.L. 95–95, Title I, § 126, 91 Stat. 726, set forth Congressional findings.

Section 7452, July 14, 1955, c. 360, Title I, § 152, as added Aug. 7, 1977, Pub.L. 95–95, Title I, § 126, 91 Stat. 726, set forth definitions applicable to the part. See section 7671 of this title.

Section 7453, July 14, 1955, c. 360, Title I, § 153, as added Aug. 7, 1977, Pub.L. 95–95, Title I, § 126, 91 Stat. 726, related to studies by the Environmental Protection Agency.

Section 7454, July 14, 1955, c. 360, Title I, § 154, as added Aug. 7, 1977, Pub.L. 95–95, Title I, § 126, 91 Stat. 728, and amended Pub.L. 96–88, Title V, § 509(b), Oct. 17, 1979, 93 Stat. 695 related to research and monitoring activities by Federal agencies. See section 7671b of this title.

Section 7455, July 14, 1955, c. 360, Title I, § 155, as added Aug. 17, 1977, Pub.L. 95–95, Title I, § 126, 91 Stat. 726, related to reports on the progress of regulation. See section 7671b of this title.

Section 7456, July 14, 1955, c. 360, Title I, § 156, as added Aug. 7, 1977, Pub.L. 95–95, Title I, § 126, 91 Stat. 729, authorized the President to enter into international agreements to foster cooperative research. See section 7671p of this title.

Section 7457, July 14, 1955, c. 360, Title I, § 157, as added Aug. 7, 1977, Pub.L. 95–95, Title I, § 126, 91 Stat. 729, related to promulgation of regulations. See section 7671n of this title.

Section 7458, July 14, 1955, c. 360, Title I, § 158, as added Aug. 7, 1977, Pub.L. 95–95, Title I, § 126, 91 Stat. 730, set forth other provisions of law that would be unaffected by the provisions of this part. See section 7671m of this title.

Section 7459, July 14, 1955, c. 360, Title I, § 159, as added Aug. 7, 1977, Pub.L. 95–95, Title I, § 126, 91 Stat. 730, related to the authority of the State to protect the stratosphere. See section 7671m of this title.

Effective Date of Repeal

Repeal of sections 7450 to 7459 effective Nov. 15, 1990, except as otherwise provided, see section 711(b) of Pub.L. 101–549, set out as a note under section 7401 of this title.

Savings Provisions

Suits, actions or proceedings commenced under this chapter as in effect prior to Nov. 15, 1990, not to abate by reason of the taking effect of amendments by Pub.L. 101–549, except as otherwise provided for, see section 711(a) of Pub.L. 101–549, set out as a note under section 7401 of this title.

PART C—PREVENTION OF SIGNIFICANT DETERIORATION OF AIR QUALITY

CROSS REFERENCES

Class I or class II redesignation of New River Gorge National River for purposes of this part, see section 460m–24 of Title 16, Conservation.

Federally permitted release defined to include emissions into air subject to permit or control regulation under this part for purposes of Comprehensive Environmental Response, Compensation, and Liability Act of 1980, see section 9601 of this title.

Subpart I—Clean Air

§ 7470. Congressional declaration of purpose [CAA § 160]

The purposes of this part are as follows:

(1) to protect public health and welfare from any actual or potential adverse effect which in the Administrator's judgment may reasonably be anticipate[1] to occur from air pollution or from exposures to pollutants in other media, which pollutants originate as emissions to the ambient air)[2], notwithstanding attainment and maintenance of all national ambient air quality standards;

(2) to preserve, protect, and enhance the air quality in national parks, national wilderness areas, national monuments, national seashores, and other areas of special national or regional natural, recreational, scenic, or historic value;

(3) to insure that economic growth will occur in a manner consistent with the preservation of existing clean air resources;

(4) to assure that emissions from any source in any State will not interfere with any portion of the applicable implementation plan to prevent significant deterioration of air quality for any other State; and

(5) to assure that any decision to permit increased air pollution in any area to which this section applies is made only after careful evaluation of all the consequences of such a decision and after adequate procedural opportunities for informed public participation in the decisionmaking process.

(July 14, 1955, ch. 360, title I, § 160, as added Aug. 7, 1977, Pub.L. 95–95, title I, § 127(a), 91 Stat. 731.)

[1] So in original. Probably should read "anticipated".

[2] So in original. No opening parenthesis.

Effective Date

Section 406(d) of Title IV of Pub.L. 95–95, Aug. 7, 1977, 91 Stat. 796, provided that, except as otherwise expressly provided, the amendments made by that Act [which enacted this subpart] were effective on the date of enactment [Aug. 7, 1977].

CODE OF FEDERAL REGULATIONS

Emission standards for hazardous pollutants, see 40 CFR 61.01 et seq.

Implementation plans, generally, see 40 CFR 51.40 et seq.

New stationary sources, performance standards for, see 40 CFR 60.1 et seq.

Library References

Health and Environment ⟹25.6(1) et seq.

C.J.S. Health and Environment § 91 et seq.

§ 7471. Plan requirements [CAA § 161]

In accordance with the policy of section 7401(b)(1) of this title, each applicable implementation plan shall contain emission limitations and such other measures as may be necessary, as determined under regulations promulgated under this part, to prevent significant deterioration of air quality in each region (or portion thereof) designated pursuant to section 7407 of this title as attainment or unclassifiable.

(July 14, 1955, ch. 360, title I, § 161, as added Aug. 7, 1977, Pub.L. 95–95, title I, § 127(a), 91 Stat. 731, and amended Nov. 15, 1990, Pub.L. 101–549, title I, § 110(1), 104 Stat. 2470.)

Effective Date of 1990 Amendment

Amendment by Pub.L. 101–549 effective Nov. 15, 1990, except as otherwise provided, see section 711(b) of Pub.L. 101–549, set out as a note under section 7401 of this title.

Savings Provisions

Suits, actions or proceedings commenced under this chapter as in effect prior to Nov. 15, 1990, not to abate by reason of the taking effect of amendments by Pub.L. 101–549, except as otherwise provided for, see section 711(a) of Pub.L. 101–549, set out as a note under section 7401 of this title.

§ 7472. Initial classifications [CAA § 162]

(a) Areas designated as class I

Upon the enactment of this part, all—

(1) international parks,

(2) national wilderness areas which exceed 5,000 acres in size,

(3) national memorial parks which exceed 5,000 acres in size, and

(4) national parks which exceed six thousand acres in size,

and which are in existence on August 7, 1977, shall be class I areas and may not be redesignated. All areas which were redesignated as class I under regulations promulgated before August 7, 1977, shall be class I areas which may be redesignated as provided in this part. The extent of the areas designated as Class I under this section shall conform to any changes in the boundaries of such areas which have occurred subsequent to August 7, 1977, or which may occur subsequent to November 15, 1990.

(b) Areas designated as class II

All areas in such State designated pursuant to section 7407(d) of this title as attainment or unclassifiable which are not established as class I under subsection (a) of this section shall be class II areas unless redesignated under section 7474 of this title.

(July 14, 1955, ch. 360, title I, § 162, as added Aug. 7, 1977, Pub.L. 95–95, title I, § 127(a), 91 Stat. 731, and amended Nov. 16, 1977, Pub.L. 95–190, § 14(a)(40), 91 Stat. 1401; Nov. 15, 1990, Pub.L. 101–549, title I, §§ 108(m), 110(2), 104 Stat. 2469, 2470.)

Effective Date of 1990 Amendment

Amendment by Pub.L. 101–549 effective Nov. 15, 1990, except as otherwise provided, see section 711(b) of Pub.L. 101–549, set out as a note under section 7401 of this title.

Savings Provisions

Suits, actions or proceedings commenced under this chapter as in effect prior to Nov. 15, 1990, not to abate by reason of the taking effect of amendments by Pub.L. 101–549, except as otherwise provided for, see section 711(a) of Pub.L. 101–549, set out as a note under section 7401 of this title.

§ 7473. Increments and ceilings [CAA § 163]

(a) Sulfur oxide and particulate matter; requirement that maximum allowable increases and maximum allowable concentrations not be exceeded

In the case of sulfur oxide and particulate matter, each applicable implementation plan shall contain measures assuring that maximum allowable increases over baseline concentrations of, and maximum allowable concentrations of, such pollutant shall not be exceeded. In the case of any maximum allowable increase (except an allowable increase specified under section 7475(d)(2)(C)(iv) of this title) for a pollutant based on concentrations permitted under national ambient air quality standards for any period other than an annual period, such regulations shall permit such maximum allowable increase to be exceeded during one such period per year.

(b) Maximum allowable increases in concentrations over baseline concentrations

(1) For any class I area, the maximum allowable increase in concentrations of sulfur dioxide and particulate matter over the baseline concentration of such pollutants shall not exceed the following amounts:

Pollutant	Maximum allowable increase (in micrograms per cubic meter)
Particulate matter:	
Annual geometric mean	5
Twenty-four-hour maximum	10
Sulfur dioxide:	
Annual arithmetic mean	2
Twenty-four-hour maximum	5
Three-hour maximum	25

(2) For any class II area, the maximum allowable increase in concentrations of sulfur dioxide and particulate matter over the baseline concentration of such pollutants shall not exceed the following amounts:

Pollutant	Maximum allowable increase (in micrograms per cubic meter)
Particulate matter:	
Annual geometric mean	19
Twenty-four-hour maximum	37
Sulfur dioxide:	
Annual arithmetic mean	20
Twenty-four-hour maximum	91
Three-hour maximum	512

(3) For any class III area, the maximum allowable increase in concentrations of sulfur dioxide and particulate matter over the baseline concentration of such pollutants shall not exceed the following amounts:

Pollutant	Maximum allowable increase (in micrograms per cubic meter)
Particulate matter:	
Annual geometric mean	37
Twenty-four-hour maximum	75
Sulfur dioxide:	
Annual arithmetic mean	40
Twenty-four-hour maximum	182
Three-hour maximum	700

(4) The maximum allowable concentration of any air pollutant in any area to which this part applies shall not exceed a concentration for such pollutant for each period of exposure equal to—

(A) the concentration permitted under the national secondary ambient air quality standard, or

(B) the concentration permitted under the national primary ambient air quality standard,

whichever concentration is lowest for such pollutant for such period of exposure.

(c) Orders or rules for determining compliance with maximum allowable increases in ambient concentrations of air pollutants

(1) In the case of any State which has a plan approved by the Administrator for purposes of carry-

ing out this part, the Governor of such State may, after notice and opportunity for public hearing, issue orders or promulgate rules providing that for purposes of determining compliance with the maximum allowable increases in ambient concentrations of an air pollutant, the following concentrations of such pollutant shall not be taken into account:

(A) concentrations of such pollutant attributable to the increase in emissions from stationary sources which have converted from the use of petroleum products, or natural gas, or both, by reason of an order which is in effect under the provisions of sections 792(a) and (b) of title 15 (or any subsequent legislation which supersedes such provisions) over the emissions from such sources before the effective date of such order[1].

(B) the concentrations of such pollutant attributable to the increase in emissions from stationary sources which have converted from using natural gas by reason of a natural gas curtailment pursuant to a natural gas curtailment plan in effect pursuant to the Federal Power Act [16 U.S.C. 791a et seq.] over the emissions from such sources before the effective date of such plan,

(C) concentrations of particulate matter attributable to the increase in emissions from construction or other temporary emission-related activities, and

(D) the increase in concentrations attributable to new sources outside the United States over the concentrations attributable to existing sources which are included in the baseline concentration determined in accordance with section 7479(4) of this title.

(2) No action taken with respect to a source under paragraph (1)(A) or (1)(B) shall apply more than five years after the effective date of the order referred to in paragraph (1)(A) or the plan referred to in paragraph (1)(B), whichever is applicable. If both such order and plan are applicable, no such action shall apply more than five years after the later of such effective dates.

(3) No action under this subsection shall take effect unless the Governor submits the order or rule providing for such exclusion to the Administrator and the Administrator determines that such order or rule is in compliance with the provisions of this subsection.

(July 14, 1955, ch. 360, title I, § 163, as added Aug. 7, 1977, Pub.L. 95–95, title I, § 127(a), 91 Stat. 732, and amended Nov. 16, 1977, Pub.L. 95–190, § 14(a)(41), 91 Stat. 1401.)

[1] So in original. The period probably should be a comma.

Library References

Health and Environment ⇨25.6(4), 28.
C.J.S. Health and Environment §§ 91 et seq., 95 et seq.

§ 7474. Area redesignation [CAA § 164]

(a) Authority of States to redesignate areas

Except as otherwise provided under subsection (c) of this section, a State may redesignate such areas as it deems appropriate as class I areas. The following areas may be redesignated only as class I or II:

(1) an area which exceeds ten thousand acres in size and is a national monument, a national primitive area, a national preserve, a national recreation area, a national wild and scenic river, a national wildlife refuge, a national lakeshore or seashore, and

(2) a national park or national wilderness area established after August 7, 1977, which exceeds ten thousand acres in size.

The extent of the areas referred to in paragraph (1) and (2) shall conform to any changes in the boundaries of such areas which have occurred subsequent to August 7, 1977, or which may occur subsequent to November 15, 1990. Any area (other than an area referred to in paragraph (1) or (2) or an area established as class I under the first sentence of section 7472(a) of this title) may be redesignated by the State as class III if—

(A) such redesignation has been specifically approved by the Governor of the State, after consultation with the appropriate Committees of the legislature if it is in session or with the leadership of the legislature if it is not in session (unless State law provides that such redesignation must be specifically approved by State legislation) and if general purpose units of local government representing a majority of the residents of the area so redesignated enact legislation (including for such units of local government resolutions where appropriate) concurring in the State's redesignation;

(B) such redesignation will not cause, or contribute to, concentrations of any air pollutant which exceed any maximum allowable increase or maximum allowable concentration permitted under the classification of any other area; and

(C) such redesignation otherwise meets the requirements of this part.

Subparagraph (A) of this paragraph shall not apply to area redesignations by Indian tribes.

(b) Notice and hearing; notice to Federal land manager; written comments and recommendations; regulations; disapproval of redesignation

(1)(A) Prior to redesignation of any area under this part, notice shall be afforded and public hearings shall be conducted in areas proposed to be redesignated and in areas which may be affected by the proposed redesignation. Prior to any such public hearing a satisfactory description and analysis of the health, environmental, economic, social, and energy effects of the proposed redesignation shall be prepared and made available for public inspection and prior to any such redesignation, the description and analysis of such effects shall be reviewed and examined by the redesignating authorities.

(B) Prior to the issuance of notice under subparagraph (A) respecting the redesignation of any area under this subsection, if such area includes any Federal lands, the State shall provide written notice to the appropriate Federal land manager and afford adequate opportunity (but not in excess of 60 days) to confer with the State respecting the intended notice of redesignation and to submit written comments and recommendations with respect to such intended notice of redesignation. In redesignating any area under this section with respect to which any Federal land manager has submitted written comments and recommendations, the State shall publish a list of any inconsistency between such redesignation and such recommendations and an explanation of such inconsistency (together with the reasons for making such redesignation against the recommendation of the Federal land manager).

(C) The Administrator shall promulgate regulations not later than six months after August 7, 1977, to assure, insofar as practicable, that prior to any public hearing on redesignation of any area, there shall be available for public inspection any specific plans for any new or modified major emitting facility which may be permitted to be constructed and operated only if the area in question is designated or redesignated as class III.

(2) The Administrator may disapprove the redesignation of any area only if he finds, after notice and opportunity for public hearing, that such redesignation does not meet the procedural requirements of this section or is inconsistent with the requirements of section 7472(a) of this title or of subsection (a) of this section. If any such disapproval occurs, the classification of the area shall be that which was in effect prior to the redesignation which was disapproved.

(c) Indian reservations

Lands within the exterior boundaries of reservations of federally recognized Indian tribes may be redesignated only by the appropriate Indian governing body. Such Indian governing body shall be subject in all respect to the provisions of subsection (e) of this section.

(d) Review of national monuments, primitive areas, and national preserves

The Federal Land Manager shall review all national monuments, primitive areas, and national preserves, and shall recommend any appropriate areas for redesignation as class I where air quality related values are important attributes of the area. The Federal Land Manager shall report such recommendations, within[1] supporting analysis, to the Congress and the affected States within one year after August 7, 1977. The Federal Land Manager shall consult with the appropriate States before making such recommendations.

(e) Resolution of disputes between State and Indian Tribes

If any State affected by the redesignation of an area by an Indian tribe or any Indian tribe affected by the redesignation of an area by a State disagrees with such redesignation of any area, or if a permit is proposed to be issued for any new major emitting facility proposed for construction in any State which the Governor of an affected State or governing body of an affected Indian tribe determines will cause or contribute to a cumulative change in air quality in excess of that allowed in this part within the affected State or tribal reservation, the Governor or Indian ruling body may request the Administrator to enter into negotiations with the parties involved to resolve such dispute. If requested by any State or Indian tribe involved, the Administrator shall make a recommendation to resolve the dispute and protect the air quality related values of the lands involved. If the parties involved do not reach agreement, the Administrator shall resolve the dispute and his determination, or the results of agreements reached through other means, shall become part of the applicable plan and shall be enforceable as part of such plan. In resolving such disputes relating to area redesignation, the Administrator shall consider the extent to which the lands involved are of sufficient size to allow effective air quality management or have air quality related values of such an area.

(July 14, 1955, ch. 360, title I, § 164, as added Aug. 7, 1977, Pub.L. 95–95, title I, § 127(a), 91 Stat. 733, and amended Nov. 16, 1977, Pub.L. 95–190, § 14(a)(42), (43), 91 Stat. 1402; Nov. 15, 1990, Pub.L. 101–549, title I, § 108(n), 104 Stat. 2469.)

1 So in original. Probably should be "with".

Effective Date of 1990 Amendment

Amendment by Pub.L. 101–549 effective Nov. 15, 1990, except as otherwise provided, see section 711(b) of Pub.L. 101–549, set out as a note under section 7401 of this title.

Savings Provisions

Suits, actions or proceedings commenced under this chapter as in effect prior to Nov. 15, 1990, not to abate by reason of the taking effect of amendments by Pub.L. 101–549, except as otherwise provid-

ed for, see section 711(a) of Pub.L. 101–549, set out as a note under section 7401 of this title.

Library References

Health and Environment ⚖25.6(4).
C.J.S. Health and Environment § 95 et seq.

§ 7475. Preconstruction requirements [CAA § 165]

(a) Major emitting facilities on which construction is commenced

No major emitting facility on which construction is commenced after August 7, 1977, may be constructed in any area to which this part applies unless—

(1) a permit has been issued for such proposed facility in accordance with this part setting forth emission limitations for such facility which conform to the requirements of this part;

(2) the proposed permit has been subject to a review in accordance with this section, the required analysis has been conducted in accordance with regulations promulgated by the Administrator, and a public hearing has been held with opportunity for interested persons including representatives of the Administrator to appear and submit written or oral presentations on the air quality impact of such source, alternatives thereto, control technology requirements, and other appropriate considerations;

(3) the owner or operator of such facility demonstrates, as required pursuant to section 7410(j) of this title, that emissions from construction or operation of such facility will not cause, or contribute to, air pollution in excess of any (A) maximum allowable increase or maximum allowable concentration for any pollutant in any area to which this part applies more than one time per year, (B) national ambient air quality standard in any air quality control region, or (C) any other applicable emission standard or standard of performance under this chapter;

(4) the proposed facility is subject to the best available control technology for each pollutant subject to regulation under this chapter emitted from, or which results from, such facility;

(5) the provisions of subsection (d) of this section with respect to protection of class I areas have been complied with for such facility;

(6) there has been an analysis of any air quality impacts projected for the area as a result of growth associated with such facility;

(7) the person who owns or operates, or proposes to own or operate, a major emitting facility for which a permit is required under this part agrees to conduct such monitoring as may be necessary to determine the effect which emissions from any such facility may have, or is having, on air quality in any area which may be affected by emissions from such source; and

(8) in the case of a source which proposes to construct in a class III area, emissions from which would cause or contribute to exceeding the maximum allowable increments applicable in a class II area and where no standard under section 7411 of this title has been promulgated subsequent to August 7, 1977, for such source category, the Administrator has approved the determination of best available technology as set forth in the permit.

(b) Exception

The demonstration pertaining to maximum allowable increases required under subsection (a)(3) of this section shall not apply to maximum allowable increases for class II areas in the case of an expansion or modification of a major emitting facility which is in existence on August 7, 1977, whose allowable emissions of air pollutants, after compliance with subsection (a)(4) of this section, will be less than fifty tons per year and for which the owner or operator of such facility demonstrates that emissions of particulate matter and sulfur oxides will not cause or contribute to ambient air quality levels in excess of the national secondary ambient air quality standard for either of such pollutants.

(c) Permit applications

Any completed permit application under section 7410 of this title for a major emitting facility in any area to which this part applies shall be granted or denied not later than one year after the date of filing of such completed application.

(d) Action taken on permit applications; notice; adverse impact on air quality related values; variance; emission limitations

(1) Each State shall transmit to the Administrator a copy of each permit application relating to a major emitting facility received by such State and provide notice to the Administrator of every action related to the consideration of such permit.

(2)(A) The Administrator shall provide notice of the permit application to the Federal Land Manager and the Federal official charged with direct responsibility for management of any lands within a class I area which may be affected by emissions from the proposed facility.

(B) The Federal Land Manager and the Federal official charged with direct responsibility for management of such lands shall have an affirmative responsibility to protect the air quality related values (including visibility) of any such lands within a class I area and to consider, in consultation with the Administrator, whether a proposed major emitting facility will have an adverse impact on such values.

(C)(i) In any case where the Federal official charged with direct responsibility for management of any lands within a class I area or the Federal Land Manager of such lands, or the Administrator, or the Governor of an adjacent State containing such a class I area files a notice alleging that emissions from a proposed major emitting facility may cause or contribute to a change in the air quality in such area and identifying the potential adverse impact of such change, a permit shall not be issued unless the owner or operator of such facility demonstrates that emissions of particulate matter and sulfur dioxide will not cause or contribute to concentrations which exceed the maximum allowable increases for a class I area.

(ii) In any case where the Federal Land Manager demonstrates to the satisfaction of the State that the emissions from such facility will have an adverse impact on the air quality-related values (including visibility) of such lands, notwithstanding the fact that the change in air quality resulting from emissions from such facility will not cause or contribute to concentrations which exceed the maximum allowable increases for a class I area, a permit shall not be issued.

(iii) In any case where the owner or operator of such facility demonstrates to the satisfaction of the Federal Land Manager, and the Federal Land Manager so certifies, that the emissions from such facility will have no adverse impact on the air quality-related values of such lands (including visibility), notwithstanding the fact that the change in air quality resulting from emissions from such facility will cause or contribute to concentrations which exceed the maximum allowable increases for class I areas, the State may issue a permit.

(iv) In the case of a permit issued pursuant to clause (iii), such facility shall comply with such emission limitations under such permit as may be necessary to assure that emissions of sulfur oxides and particulates from such facility will not cause or contribute to concentrations of such pollutant which exceed the following maximum allowable increases over the baseline concentration for such pollutants:

Particulate matter:	Maximum allowable increase (in micrograms per cubic meter)
Annual geometric mean	19
Twenty-four-hour maximum	37
Sulfur dioxide:	
Annual arithmetic mean	20
Twenty-four-hour maximum	91
Three-hour maximum	325

(D)(i) In any case where the owner or operator of a proposed major emitting facility who has been denied a certification under subparagraph (C)(iii) demonstrates to the satisfaction of the Governor, after notice and public hearing, and the Governor finds, that the facility cannot be constructed by reason of any maximum allowable increase for sulfur dioxide for periods of twenty-four hours or less applicable to any class I area and, in the case of Federal mandatory class I areas, that a variance under this clause will not adversely affect the air quality related values of the area (including visibility), the Governor, after consideration of the Federal Land Manager's recommendation (if any) and subject to his concurrence, may grant a variance from such maximum allowable increase. If such variance is granted, a permit may be issued to such source pursuant to the requirements of this subparagraph.

(ii) In any case in which the Governor recommends a variance under this subparagraph in which the Federal Land Manager does not concur, the recommendations of the Governor and the Federal Land Manager shall be transmitted to the President. The President may approve the Governor's recommendation if he finds that such variance is in the national interest. No Presidential finding shall be reviewable in any court. The variance shall take effect if the President approves the Governor's recommendations. The President shall approve or disapprove such recommendation within ninety days after his receipt of the recommendations of the Governor and the Federal Land Manager.

(iii) In the case of a permit issued pursuant to this subparagraph, such facility shall comply with such emission limitations under such permit as may be necessary to assure that emissions of sulfur oxides from such facility will not (during any day on which the otherwise applicable maximum allowable increases are exceeded) cause or contribute to concentrations which exceed the following maximum allowable increases for such areas over the baseline concentration for such pollutant and to assure that such emissions will not cause or contribute to concentrations which exceed the otherwise applicable maximum allowable increases for periods of exposure of 24 hours or less on more than 18 days during any annual period:

MAXIMUM ALLOWABLE INCREASE

[In micrograms per cubic meter]

Period of exposure	Low terrain areas	High terrain areas
24-hr. maximum	36	62
3-hr. maximum	130	221

(iv) For purposes of clause (iii), the term "high terrain area" means with respect to any facility, any area having an elevation of 900 feet or more above the base of the stack of such facility, and the term "low terrain area" means any area other than a high terrain area.

(e) Analysis; continuous air quality monitoring data; regulations; model adjustments

(1) The review provided for in subsection (a) of this section shall be preceded by an analysis in accordance with regulations of the Administrator, promulgated under this subsection, which may be conducted by the State (or any general purpose unit of local government) or by the major emitting facility applying for such permit, of the ambient air quality at the proposed site and in areas which may be affected by emissions from such facility for each pollutant subject to regulation under this chapter which will be emitted from such facility.

(2) Effective one year after August 7, 1977, the analysis required by this subsection shall include continuous air quality monitoring data gathered for purposes of determining whether emissions from such facility will exceed the maximum allowable increases or the maximum allowable concentration permitted under this part. Such data shall be gathered over a period of one calendar year preceding the date of application for a permit under this part unless the State, in accordance with regulations promulgated by the Administrator, determines that a complete and adequate analysis for such purposes may be accomplished in a shorter period. The results of such analysis shall be available at the time of the public hearing on the application for such permit.

(3) The Administrator shall within six months after August 7, 1977, promulgate regulations respecting the analysis required under this subsection which regulations—

(A) shall not require the use of any automatic or uniform buffer zone or zones,

(B) shall require an analysis of the ambient air quality, climate and meteorology, terrain, soils and vegetation, and visibility at the site of the proposed major emitting facility and in the area potentially affected by the emissions from such facility for each pollutant regulated under this chapter which will be emitted from, or which results from the construction or operation of, such facility, the size and nature of the proposed facility, the degree of continuous emission reduction which could be achieved by such facility, and such other factors as may be relevant in determining the effect of emissions from a proposed facility on any air quality control region,

(C) shall require the results of such analysis shall be available at the time of the public hearing on the application for such permit, and

(D) shall specify with reasonable particularity each air quality model or models to be used under specified sets of conditions for purposes of this part.

Any model or models designated under such regulations may be adjusted upon a determination, after notice and opportunity for public hearing, by the Administrator that such adjustment is necessary to take into account unique terrain or meteorological characteristics of an area potentially affected by emissions from a source applying for a permit required under this part.

(July 14, 1955, ch. 360, title I, § 165, as added Aug. 7, 1977, Pub.L. 95–95, title I, § 127(a), 91 Stat. 735, and amended Nov. 16, 1977, Pub.L. 95–190, § 14(a)(44)–(51), 91 Stat. 1402.)

Library References

Health and Environment ⚷25.6(5).
C.J.S. Health and Environment § 91 et seq.

LAW REVIEW COMMENTARIES

Toxic tort litigation and the causation element: Is there any hope of reconciliation? Or a Fred Harris, Jr., 40 Southwestern (Tex.) L.J. 909 (1986).

§ 7476. Other pollutants [CAA § 166]

(a) Hydrocarbons, carbon monoxide, petrochemical oxidants, and nitrogen oxides

In the case of the pollutants hydrocarbons, carbon monoxide, photochemical oxidants, and nitrogen oxides, the Administrator shall conduct a study and not later than two years after August 7, 1977, promulgate regulations to prevent the significant deterioration of air quality which would result from the emissions of such pollutants. In the case of pollutants for which national ambient air quality standards are promulgated after August 7, 1977, he shall promulgate such regulations not more than 2 years after the date of promulgation of such standards.

(b) Effective date of regulations

Regulations referred to in subsection (a) of this section shall become effective one year after the date of promulgation. Within 21 months after such date of promulgation such plan revision shall be submitted to the Administrator who shall approve or disapprove the plan within 25 months after such date or promulgation in the same manner as required under section 7410 of this title.

(c) Contents of regulations

Such regulations shall provide specific numerical measures against which permit applications may be evaluated, a framework for stimulating improved control technology, protection of air quality values, and fulfill the goals and purposes set forth in section 7401 and section 7470 of this title.

(d) Specific measures to fulfill goals and purposes

The regulations of the Administrator under subsection (a) of this section shall provide specific measures at least as effective as the increments established in section 7473 of this title to fulfill such goals and purposes, and may contain air quality increments, emission density requirements, or other measures.

(e) Area classification plan not required

With respect to any air pollutant for which a national ambient air quality standard is established other than sulfur oxides or particulate matter, an area classification plan shall not be required under this section if the implementation plan adopted by the State and submitted for the Administrator's approval or promulgated by the Administrator under section 7410(c) of this title contains other provisions which when considered as a whole, the Administrator finds will carry out the purposes in section 7470 of this title at least as effectively as an area classification plan for such pollutant. Such other provisions referred to in the preceding sentence need not require the establishment of maximum allowable increases with respect to such pollutant for any area to which this section applies.

(f) PM–10 Increments

The Administrator is authorized to substitute, for the maximum allowable increases in particulate matter specified in section 7473(b) of this title and section 7475(d)(2)(C)(iv) of this title, maximum allowable increases in particulate matter with an aerodynamic diameter smaller than or equal to 10 micrometers. Such substituted maximum allowable increases shall be of equal stringency in effect as those specified in the provisions for which they are substituted. Until the Administrator promulgates regulations under the authority of this subsection, the current maximum allowable increases in concentrations of particulate matter shall remain in effect.

(July 14, 1955, ch. 360, title I, § 166, as added Aug. 7, 1977, Pub.L. 95–95, title I, § 127(a), 91 Stat. 739, and amended Nov. 15, 1990, Pub.L. 101–549, title I, § 105(b), 104 Stat. 2462.)

Effective Date of 1990 Amendment

Amendment by Pub.L. 101–549 effective Nov. 15, 1990, except as otherwise provided, see section 711(b) of Pub.L. 101–549, set out as a note under section 7401 of this title.

Savings Provisions

Suits, actions or proceedings commenced under this chapter as in effect prior to Nov. 15, 1990, not to abate by reason of the taking effect of amendments by Pub.L. 101–549, except as otherwise provided for, see section 711(a) of Pub.L. 101–549, set out as a note under section 7401 of this title.

Library References

Health and Environment ⚷25.6(3).
C.J.S. Health and Environment § 92.

§ 7477. Enforcement [CAA § 167]

The Administrator shall, and a State may, take such measures, including issuance of an order, or seeking injunctive relief, as necessary to prevent the construction or modification of a major emitting facility which does not conform to the requirements of this part, or which is proposed to be constructed in any area designated pursuant to section 7407(d) of this title as attainment or unclassifiable and which is not subject to an implementation plan which meets the requirements of this part.

(July 14, 1955, ch. 360, title I, § 167, as added Aug. 7, 1977, Pub.L. 95–95, title I, § 127(a), 91 Stat. 740, and amended Nov. 15, 1990, Pub.L. 101–549, title I, § 110(3), title VII, § 708, 104 Stat. 2470, 2684.)

Effective Date of 1990 Amendment

Amendment by Pub.L. 101–549 effective Nov. 15, 1990, except as otherwise provided, see section 711(b) of Pub.L. 101–549, set out as a note under section 7401 of this title.

Savings Provisions

Suits, actions or proceedings commenced under this chapter as in effect prior to Nov. 15, 1990, not to abate by reason of the taking effect of amendments by Pub.L. 101–549, except as otherwise provided for, see section 711(a) of Pub.L. 101–549, set out as a note under section 7401 of this title.

Library References

Health and Environment ⚷25.6(9).
C.J.S. Health and Environment § 104 et seq.

§ 7478. Period before plan approval [CAA § 168]

(a) Existing regulations to remain in effect

Until such time as an applicable implementation plan is in effect for any area, which plan meets the requirements of this part to prevent significant deterioration of air quality with respect to any air pollutant, applicable regulations under this chapter prior to August 7, 1977, shall remain in effect to prevent significant deterioration of air quality in any such area for any such pollutant except as otherwise provided in subsection (b) of this section.

(b) Regulations deemed amended; construction commenced after June 1, 1975

If any regulation in effect prior to August 7, 1977, to prevent significant deterioration of air quality would be inconsistent with the requirements of section 7472(a), section 7473(b) or section 7474(a) of this title, then such regulations shall be deemed amended so as to conform with such requirements. In the case of a facility on which construction was commenced (in accordance with the definition of "commenced" in section 7479(2) of this title) after June 1, 1975, and prior to August 7, 1977, the review and permitting of such facility shall be in accordance with the regulations for the prevention of significant deterioration in effect prior to August 7, 1977.

(July 14, 1955, ch. 360, title I, § 168, as added Aug. 7, 1977, Pub.L. 95–95, title I, § 127(a), 91 Stat. 740, and amended Nov. 16, 1977, Pub.L. 95–190, § 14(a)(52), 91 Stat. 1402.)

Library References

Health and Environment ⟹25.6(4).
C.J.S. Health and Environment § 95 et seq.

§ 7479. Definitions [CAA § 169]

For purposes of this part—

(1) The term "major emitting facility" means any of the following stationary sources of air pollutants which emit, or have the potential to emit, one hundred tons per year or more of any air pollutant from the following types of stationary sources: fossil-fuel fired steam electric plants of more than two hundred and fifty million British thermal units per hour heat input, coal cleaning plants (thermal dryers), kraft pulp mills, Portland Cement plants, primary zinc smelters, iron and steel mill plants, primary aluminum ore reduction plants, primary copper smelters, municipal incinerators capable of charging more than fifty tons of refuse per day, hydrofluoric, sulfuric, and nitric acid plants, petroleum refineries, lime plants, phosphate rock processing plants, coke oven batteries, sulfur recovery plants, carbon black plants (furnace process), primary lead smelters, fuel conversion plants, sintering plants, secondary metal production facilities, chemical process plants, fossil-fuel boilers of more than two hundred and fifty million British thermal units per hour heat input, petroleum storage and transfer facilities with a capacity exceeding three hundred thousand barrels, taconite ore processing facilities, glass fiber processing plants, charcoal production facilities. Such term also includes any other source with the potential to emit two hundred and fifty tons per year or more of any air pollutant. This term shall not include new or modified facilities which are nonprofit health or education institutions which have been exempted by the State.

(2)(A) The term "commenced" as applied to construction of a major emitting facility means that the owner or operator has obtained all necessary preconstruction approvals or permits required by Federal, State, or local air pollution emissions and air quality laws or regulations and either has (i) begun, or caused to begin, a continuous program of physical on-site construction of the facility or (ii) entered into binding agreements or contractual obligations, which cannot be canceled or modified without substantial loss to the owner or operator, to undertake a program of construction of the facility to be completed within a reasonable time.

(B) The term "necessary preconstruction approvals or permits" means those permits or approvals, required by the permitting authority as a precondition to undertaking any activity under clauses (i) or (ii) of subparagraph (A) of this paragraph.

(C) The term "construction" when used in connection with any source or facility, includes the modification (as defined in section 7411(a) of this title) of any source or facility.

(3) The term "best available control technology" means an emission limitation based on the maximum degree of reduction of each pollutant subject to regulation under this chapter emitted from or which results from any major emitting facility, which the permitting authority, on a case-by-case basis, taking into account energy, environmental, and economic impacts and other costs, determines is achievable for such facility through application of production processes and available methods, systems, and techniques, including fuel cleaning, clean fuels, or treatment or innovative fuel combustion techniques for control of each such pollutant. In no event shall application of "best available control technology" result in emissions of any pollutants which will exceed the emissions allowed by any applicable standard established pursuant to section 7411 or 7412 of this title. Emissions from any source utilizing clean fuels, or any other means, to comply with this paragraph shall not be allowed to increase above levels that would have been required under this paragraph as it existed prior to enactment of the Clean Air Act Amendments of 1990.

(4) The term "baseline concentration" means, with respect to a pollutant, the ambient concentration levels which exist at the time of the first application for a permit in an area subject to this part, based on air quality data available in the Environmental Protection Agency or a State air pollution control agency and on such monitoring data as the permit applicant is required to submit. Such ambient concentration levels shall take into account all projected emissions in, or which may affect, such area from any major emitting facility on which construction commenced prior to January 6, 1975, but which has not begun operation by the date of the baseline air quality concentration determination. Emissions of sulfur oxides and particulate matter from any major emitting facility on which construction commenced after January 6, 1975, shall not be included in the baseline and shall be counted against the maximum allowable increases in pollutant concentrations established under this part.

(July 14, 1955, ch. 360, title I, § 169, as added Aug. 7, 1977, Pub.L. 95–95, title I, § 127(a), 91 Stat. 740, and amended Nov. 16, 1977, Pub.L. 95–190, § 14(a)(54), 91 Stat. 1402; Nov. 15, 1990, Pub.L. 101–549, title III, § 305(b), title IV, § 403(d), 104 Stat. 2583, 2631.)

References in Text

Enactment of the Clean Air Act Amendments of 1990, referred to in par. (3), probably means the date of enactment of Pub.L. 101–549, Nov. 15, 1990, 104 Stat. 2399, which was approved Nov. 15, 1990.

Effective Date of 1990 Amendment

Amendment by Pub.L. 101–549 effective Nov. 15, 1990, except as otherwise provided, see section 711(b) of Pub.L. 101–549, set out as a note under section 7401 of this title.

Savings Provisions

Suits, actions or proceedings commenced under this chapter as in effect prior to Nov. 15, 1990, not to abate by reason of the taking effect of amendments by Pub.L. 101–549, except as otherwise provided for, see section 711(a) of Pub.L. 101–549, set out as a note under section 7401 of this title.

Library References

Health and Environment ⚡25.6(1) et seq.
C.J.S. Health and Environment § 91 et seq.

Subpart II—Visibility Protection

§ 7491. Visibility protection for Federal class I areas [CAA § 169A]

(a) Impairment of visibility; list of areas; study and report

(1) Congress hereby declares as a national goal the prevention of any future, and the remedying of any existing, impairment of visibility in mandatory class I Federal areas which impairment results from manmade air pollution.

(2) Not later than six months after August 7, 1977, the Secretary of the Interior in consultation with other Federal land managers shall review all mandatory class I Federal areas and identify those where visibility is an important value of the area. From time to time the Secretary of the Interior may revise such identifications. Not later than one year after August 7, 1977, the Administrator shall, after consultation with the Secretary of the Interior, promulgate a list of mandatory class I Federal areas in which he determines visibility is an important value.

(3) Not later than eighteen months after August 7, 1977, the Administrator shall complete a study and report to Congress on available methods for implementing the national goal set forth in paragraph (1). Such report shall include recommendations for—

(A) methods for identifying, characterizing, determining, quantifying, and measuring visibility impairment in Federal areas referred to in paragraph (1), and

(B) modeling techniques (or other methods) for determining the extent to which manmade air pollution may reasonably be anticipated to cause or contribute to such impairment, and

(C) methods for preventing and remedying such manmade air pollution and resulting visibility impairment.

Such report shall also identify the classes or categories of sources and the types of air pollutants which, alone or in conjunction with other sources or pollutants, may reasonably be anticipated to cause or contribute significantly to impairment of visibility.

(4) Not later than twenty-four months after August 7, 1977, and after notice and public hearing, the Administrator shall promulgate regulations to assure (A) reasonable progress toward meeting the national goal specified in paragraph (1), and (B) compliance with the requirements of this section.

(b) Regulations

Regulations under subsection (a)(4) of this section shall—

(1) provide guidelines to the States, taking into account the recommendations under subsection (a)(3) of this section on appropriate techniques and methods for implementing this section (as provided in subparagraphs (A) through (C) of such subsection (a)(3)), and

(2) require each applicable implementation plan for a State in which any area listed by the Administrator under subsection (a)(2) of this section is located (or for a State the emissions from which may reasonably be anticipated to cause or contribute to any impairment of visibility in any such area) to contain such emission limits, schedules of compliance and other measures as may be necessary to make reasonable progress toward meeting the national goal specified in subsection (a) of this section, including—

(A) except as otherwise provided pursuant to subsection (c) of this section, a requirement that each major stationary source which is in existence on August 7, 1977, but which has not been in operation for more than fifteen years as of such date, and which, as determined by the State (or the Administrator in the case of a plan promulgated under section 7410(c) of this title) emits any air pollutant which may reasonably be anticipated to cause or contribute to any impairment of visibility in any such area, shall procure, install, and operate, as expeditiously as practicable (and maintain thereafter) the best available retrofit technology, as determined by the State (or the Administrator in the case of a plan promulgated under section 7410(c) of this title) for controlling emissions from such source for the purpose of eliminating or reducing any such impairment, and

(B) a long-term (ten to fifteen years) strategy for making reasonable progress toward meeting the national goal specified in subsection (a) of this section.

In the case of a fossil-fuel fired generating powerplant having a total generating capacity in excess of 750 megawatts, the emission limitations required under this paragraph shall be determined pursuant to guidelines, promulgated by the Administrator under paragraph (1).

(c) Exemptions

(1) The Administrator may, by rule, after notice and opportunity for public hearing, exempt any major stationary source from the requirement of subsection (b)(2)(A) of this section, upon his determination that such source does not or will not, by itself or in combination with other sources, emit any air pollutant which may reasonably be anticipated to cause or contribute to a significant impairment of visibility in any mandatory class I Federal area.

(2) Paragraph (1) of this subsection shall not be applicable to any fossil-fuel fired powerplant with total design capacity of 750 megawatts or more, unless the owner or operator of any such plant demonstrates to the satisfaction of the Administrator that such powerplant is located at such distance from all areas listed by the Administrator under subsection (a)(2) of this section that such powerplant does not or will not, by itself or in combination with other sources, emit any air pollutant which may reasonably be anticipated to cause or contribute to significant impairment of visibility in any such area.

(3) An exemption under this subsection shall be effective only upon concurrence by the appropriate Federal land manager or managers with the Administrator's determination under this subsection.

(d) Consultations with appropriate Federal land managers

Before holding the public hearing on the proposed revision of an applicable implementation plan to meet the requirements of this section, the State (or the Administrator, in the case of a plan promulgated under section 7410(c) of this title) shall consult in person with the appropriate Federal land manager or managers and shall include a summary of the conclusions and recommendations of the Federal land managers in the notice to the public.

(e) Buffer zones

In promulgating regulations under this section, the Administrator shall not require the use of any automatic or uniform buffer zone or zones.

(f) Nondiscretionary duty

For purposes of section 7604(a)(2) of this title, the meeting of the national goal specified in subsection (a)(1) of this section by any specific date or dates shall not be considered a "nondiscretionary duty" of the Administrator.

(g) Definitions

For the purpose of this section—

(1) in determining reasonable progress there shall be taken into consideration the costs of compliance, the time necessary for compliance, and the energy and nonair quality environmental impacts of compliance, and the remaining useful life of any existing source subject to such requirements;

(2) in determining best available retrofit technology the State (or the Administrator in determining emission limitations which reflect such technology) shall take into consideration the costs of compliance, the energy and nonair quality environmental impacts of compliance, any existing pollution control technology in use at the source, the remaining useful life of the source, and the degree of improvement in visibility which may reasonably be anticipated to result from the use of such technology;

(3) the term "manmade air pollution" means air pollution which results directly or indirectly from human activities;

(4) the term "as expeditiously as practicable" means as expeditiously as practicable but in no event later than five years after the date of approval of a plan revision under this section (or the date of promulgation of such a plan revision in the case of action by the Administrator under section 7410(c) of this title for purposes of this section);

(5) the term "mandatory class I Federal areas" means Federal areas which may not be designated as other than class I under this part;

(6) the terms "visibility impairment" and "impairment of visibility" shall include reduction in visual range and atmospheric discoloration; and

(7) the term "major stationary source" means the following types of stationary sources with the potential to emit 250 tons or more of any pollutant: fossil-fuel fired steam electric plants of more than 250 million British thermal units per hour heat input, coal cleaning plants (thermal dryers), kraft pulp mills, Portland Cement plants, primary zinc smelters, iron and steel mill plants, primary aluminum ore reduction plants, primary copper smelters, municipal incenerators [1] capable of charging more than 250 tons of refuse per day, hydrofluoric, sulfuric, and nitric acid plants, petroleum refineries, lime plants, phosphate rock processing plants, coke oven batteries, sulfur recovery plants, carbon black plants (furnace process), primary lead smelters, fuel conversion plants, sintering plants, secondary metal production facilities, chemical process plants, fossil-fuel boilers of more than 250 million British thermal units per hour heat input, petroleum storage and transfer facilities with a capacity exceeding 300,000 barrels, taconite ore processing facilities, glass fiber processing plants, charcoal production facilities.

(July 14, 1955, ch. 360, title I, § 169A, as added Aug. 7, 1977, Pub.L. 95–95, title I, § 128, 91 Stat. 742.)

[1] So in original. Probably should be "incinerators".

Effective Date

Section 406(d) of Title IV of Pub.L. 95–95, Aug. 7, 1977, 91 Stat. 796, provided that, except as otherwise expressly provided, the amendments made by that Act [which enacted this subpart] were effective on the date of enactment [Aug. 7, 1977].

CODE OF FEDERAL REGULATIONS

Emission standards for hazardous pollutants, see 40 CFR 61.01 et seq.
New stationary sources, performance standards for, see 40 CFR 60.1 et seq.

Library References

Health and Environment ⚖25.6(3).
C.J.S. Health and Environment § 92.

§ 7492. Visibility [CAA § 169B]

(a) Studies

(1) The Administrator, in conjunction with the National Park Service and other appropriate Federal agencies, shall conduct research to identify and evaluate sources and source regions of both visibility impairment and regions that provide predominantly clean air in class I areas. A total of $8,000,000 per year for 5 years is authorized to be appropriated for the Environmental Protection Agency and the other Federal agencies to conduct this research. The research shall include—

(A) expansion of current visibility related monitoring in class I areas;

(B) assessment of current sources of visibility impairing pollution and clean air corridors;

(C) adaptation of regional air quality models for the assessment of visibility;

(D) studies of atmospheric chemistry and physics of visibility.

(2) Based on the findings available from the research required in subsection (a)(1) of this section as well as other available scientific and technical data, studies, and other available information pertaining to visibility source-receptor relationships, the Administrator shall conduct an assessment and evaluation that identifies, to the extent possible, sources and source regions of visibility impairment including natural sources as well as source regions of clear air for class I areas. The Administrator shall produce interim findings from this study within 3 years after enactment of the Clean Air Act Amendments of 1990.

(b) Impacts of other provisions

Within 24 months after enactment of the Clean Air Act Amendments of 1990, the Administrator shall conduct an assessment of the progress and improvements in visibility in class I areas that are likely to result from the implementation of the provisions of the Clean Air Act Amendments of 1990 other than the provisions of this section. Every 5 years thereafter the Administrator shall conduct an assessment of actual progress and improvement in visibility in class I areas. The Administrator shall prepare a written report on each assessment and transmit copies of these reports to the appropriate committees of Congress.

(c) Establishment of visibility transport regions and commissions

(1) Authority to establish visibility transport regions

Whenever, upon the Administrator's motion or by petition from the Governors of at least two affected States, the Administrator has reason to believe that the current or projected interstate transport of air pollutants from one or more States contributes significantly to visibility impairment in class I areas located in the affected States, the Administrator may establish a transport region for such pollutants that includes such States. The Administrator, upon the Administrator's own motion or upon petition from the Governor of any affected State, or upon the recommendations of a transport commission established under subsection (b) of this section may—

(A) add any State or portion of a State to a visibility transport region when the Administrator determines that the interstate transport of air pollutants from such State significantly contributes to visibility impairment in a class I area located within the transport region, or

(B) remove any State or portion of a State from the region whenever the Administrator has reason to believe that the control of emissions in that State or portion of the State pursuant to this section will not significantly contribute to the protection or enhancement of visibility in any class I area in the region.

(2) Visibility transport commissions

Whenever the Administrator establishes a transport region under subsection (c)(1) of this section, the Administrator shall establish a transport commission comprised of (as a minimum) each of the following members:

(A) the Governor of each State in the Visibility Transport Region, or the Governor's designee;

(B) The[1] Administrator or the Administrator's designee; and

(C) A [1] representative of each Federal agency charged with the direct management of each class I area or areas within the Visibility Transport Region.

(3) All representatives of the Federal Government shall be ex officio members.

(4) The visibility transport commissions shall be exempt from the requirements of the Federal Advisory Committee Act (5 U.S.C. Appendix 2, Section 1).

(d) Duties of visibility transport commissions

A Visibility Transport Commission—

(1) shall assess the scientific and technical data, studies, and other currently available information, including studies conducted pursuant to subsection (a)(1) of this section, pertaining to adverse impacts on visibility from potential or projected growth in emissions from sources located in the Visibility Transport Region; and

(2) shall, within 4 years of establishment, issue a report to the Administrator recommending what measures, if any, should be taken under this chapter to remedy such adverse impacts. The report required by this subsection shall address at least the following measures:

(A) the establishment of clean air corridors, in which additional restrictions on increases in emissions may be appropriate to protect visibility in affected class I areas;

(B) the imposition of the requirements of part D of this subchapter affecting the construction of new major stationary sources or major modifications to existing sources in such clean air corridors specifically including the alternative siting analysis provisions of section 7503(a)(5) of this title; and

(C) the promulgation of regulations under section 7491 of this title to address long range strategies for addressing regional haze which impairs visibility in affected class I areas.

(e) Duties of the administrator

(1) The Administrator shall, taking into account the studies pursuant to subsection (a)(1) of this section and the reports pursuant to subsection (d)(2) of this section and any other relevant information, within eighteen months of receipt of the report referred to in subsection (d)(2) of this section, carry out the Administrator's regulatory responsibilities under section 7491 of this title, including criteria for measuring "reasonable progress" toward the national goal.

(2) Any regulations promulgated under section 7491 of this title pursuant to this subsection shall require affected States to revise within 12 months their implementation plans under section 7410 of this title to contain such emission limits, schedules of compliance, and other measures as may be necessary to carry out regulations promulgated pursuant to this subsection.

(f) Grand Canyon visibility transport commission

The Administrator pursuant to subsection (c)(1) of this section shall, within 12 months, establish a visibility transport commission for the region affecting the visibility of the Grand Canyon National Park.

(July 14, 1955, ch. 360, title I, § 169B, as added Nov. 15, 1990, Pub.L. 101–549, title VIII, § 816, 104 Stat. 2695.)

[1] So in original. Probably should be lower case.

References in Text

The enactment of the Clean Air Act Amendments of 1990, referred to in subsecs. (a)(2) and (b), probably means the date of enactment of Pub.L. 101–549, Nov. 15, 1990, 104 Stat. 2399, which was approved Nov. 15, 1990.

The Clean Air Act Amendments of 1990, referred to in subsec. (b), is Pub.L. 101–549, Nov. 15, 1990, 104 Stat. 2399. For complete distribution of this Act to the Code, see Tables.

The Federal Advisory Committee Act, referred to in subsec. (c)(4), is Pub.L. 92–463, Oct. 6, 1972, 86 Stat. 770, as amended, which is set out in Appendix 2 to Title 5, Government Organization and Employees.

Effective Date

Section to take effect Nov. 15, 1990, except as otherwise provided, see section 711(b) of Pub.L. 101–549, set out as a note under section 7401 of this title.

Savings Provisions

Suits, actions or proceedings commenced under this chapter as in effect prior to Nov. 15, 1990, not to abate by reason of the taking effect of amendments by Pub.L. 101–549, except as otherwise provided for, see section 711(a) of Pub.L. 101–549, set out as a note under section 7401 of this title.

Part D—Plan Requirements for Nonattainment Areas

Cross References

Federally permitted release defined to include emissions into air subject to permit or control regulation under this part for purposes of Comprehensive Environmental Response, Compensation, and Liability Act of 1980, see section 9601 of this title.

Subpart 1—Nonattainment Areas in General

§ 7501. Definitions [CAA § 171]

For the purpose of this part—

(1) Reasonable further progress

The term "reasonable further progress" means such annual incremental reductions in emissions of the relevant air pollutant as are required by this part or may reasonably be required by the Administrator for the purpose of ensuring attainment of the applicable national ambient air quality standard by the applicable date.

(2) Nonattainment area

The term "nonattainment area" means, for any air pollutant, an area which is designated "nonattainment" with respect to that pollutant within the meaning of section 7407(d) of this title.

(3) The term "lowest achievable emission rate" means for any source, that rate of emissions which reflects—

(A) the most stringent emission limitation which is contained in the implementation plan of any State for such class or category of source, unless the owner or operator of the proposed source demonstrates that such limitations are not achievable, or

(B) the most stringent emission limitation which is achieved in practice by such class or category of source, whichever is more stringent.

In no event shall the application of this term permit a proposed new or modified source to emit any pollutant in excess of the amount allowable under applicable new source standards of performance.

(4) The terms "modifications" and "modified" mean the same as the term "modification" as used in section 7411(a)(4) of this title.

(July 14, 1955, ch. 360, title I, § 171, as added Aug. 7, 1977, Pub.L. 95–95, title I, § 129(b), 91 Stat. 746, and amended Nov. 15, 1990, Pub.L. 101–549, title I, § 102(a)(2), 104 Stat. 2412.)

Effective Date of 1990 Amendment

Amendment by Pub.L. 101–549 effective Nov. 15, 1990, except as otherwise provided, see section 711(b) of Pub.L. 101–549, set out as a note under section 7401 of this title.

Effective Date

Section 406(d) of Title IV of Pub.L. 95–95, Aug. 7, 1977, 91 Stat. 796, provided that, except as otherwise expressly provided, the amendments made by that Act [which enacted this part] were effective on the date of enactment [Aug. 7, 1977].

Savings Provisions

Suits, actions or proceedings commenced under this chapter as in effect prior to Nov. 15, 1990, not to abate by reason of the taking effect of amendments by Pub.L. 101–549, except as otherwise provided for, see section 711(a) of Pub.L. 101–549, set out as a note under section 7401 of this title.

CODE OF FEDERAL REGULATIONS

Air pollution from motor vehicles, control of, see 40 CFR 86.078–3 et seq.
Air programs, see 40 CFR 81.1 et seq.
Implementation plans, generally, see 40 CFR 51.40 et seq.

Library References

Health and Environment ⚷25.6(4).
C.J.S. Health and Environment § 95 et seq.

§ 7502. Nonattainment plan provisions in general [CAA § 172]

(a) Classifications and attainment dates

(1) Classifications

(A) On or after the date the Administrator promulgates the designation of an area as a nonattainment area pursuant to section 7407(d) of this title with respect to any national ambient air quality standard (or any revised standard, including a revision of any standard in effect on November 15, 1990), the Administrator may classify the area for the purpose of applying an attainment date pursuant to paragraph (2), and for other purposes. In determining the appropriate classification, if any, for a nonattainment area, the Administrator may consider such factors as the severity of nonattainment in such area and the availability and feasibility of the pollution control measures that the Administrator believes may be necessary to provide for attainment of such standard in such area.

(B) The Administrator shall publish a notice in the Federal Register announcing each classification under subparagraph (A), except the Administrator shall provide an opportunity for at least 30 days for written comment. Such classification shall not be subject to the provisions of sections 553 through 557 of Title 5 (concerning notice and comment) and shall not be subject to judicial review until the Administrator takes final action under subsection (k) or (*l*) of section 7410 of this title (concerning action on plan submissions) or section 7509 of this title (concerning sanctions) with respect to any plan submissions required by virtue of such classification.

(C) This paragraph shall not apply with respect to nonattainment areas for which classifications are specifically provided under other provisions of this part.

(2) Attainment dates for nonattainment areas

(A) The attainment date for an area designated nonattainment with respect to a national primary ambient air quality standard shall be the date by which attainment can be achieved as expeditiously as practicable, but no later than 5 years from the date such area was designated nonattainment under section 7407(d) of this title, except that the Administrator may extend the attainment date to the extent the Administrator determines appropriate, for a period no greater than 10 years from the date of designation as nonattainment, considering the severity of nonattainment and the availability and feasibility of pollution control measures.

(B) The attainment date for an area designated nonattainment with respect to a secondary national ambient air quality standard shall be the date by which attainment can be achieved as expeditiously as practicable after the date such area was designated nonattainment under section 7407(d) of this title.

(C) Upon application by any State, the Administrator may extend for 1 additional year (hereinafter referred to as the "Extension Year") the attainment date determined by the Administrator under subparagraph (A) or (B) if—

(i) the State has complied with all requirements and commitments pertaining to the area in the applicable implementation plan, and

(ii) in accordance with guidance published by the Administrator, no more than a minimal number of exceedances of the relevant national ambient air quality standard has occurred in the area in the year preceding the Extension Year.

No more than 2 one-year extensions may be issued under this subparagraph for a single nonattainment area.

(D) This paragraph shall not apply with respect to nonattainment areas for which attainment dates are specifically provided under other provisions of this part.

(b) Schedule for plan submissions

At the time the Administrator promulgates the designation of an area as nonattainment with respect to a national ambient air quality standard under section 7407(d) of this title, the Administrator shall establish a schedule according to which the State containing such area shall submit a plan or plan revision (including the plan items) meeting the applicable requirements of subsection (c) of this section and section 7410(a)(2) of this title. Such schedule shall at a minimum, include a date or dates, extending no later than 3 years from the date of the nonattainment designation, for the submission of a plan or plan revision (including the plan items) meeting the applicable requirements of subsection (c) of this section and section 7410(a)(2) of this title.

(c) Nonattainment plan provisions

The plan provisions (including plan items) required to be submitted under this part shall comply with each of the following:

(1) In general

Such plan provisions shall provide for the implementation of all reasonably available control measures as expeditiously as practicable (including such reductions in emissions from existing sources in the area as may be obtained through the adoption, at a minimum, of reasonably available control technology) and shall provide for attainment of the national primary ambient air quality standards.

(2) RFP

Such plan provisions shall require reasonable further progress.

(3) Inventory

Such plan provisions shall include a comprehensive, accurate, current inventory of actual emissions from all sources of the relevant pollutant or pollutants in such area, including such periodic revisions as the Administrator may determine necessary to assure that the requirements of this part are met.

(4) Identification and quantification

Such plan provisions shall expressly identify and quantify the emissions, if any, of any such pollutant or pollutants which will be allowed, in accordance with section 7503(a)(1)(B) of this title, from the construction and operation of major new or modified stationary sources in each such area. The plan shall demonstrate to the satisfaction of the Administrator that the emissions quantified for this purpose will be consistent with the achievement of reasonable further progress and will not interfere with attainment of the applicable national ambient air quality standard by the applicable attainment date.

(5) Permits for new and modified major stationary sources

Such plan provisions shall require permits for the construction and operation of new or modified major stationary sources anywhere in the nonattainment area, in accordance with section 7503 of this title.

(6) Other measures

Such plan provisions shall include enforceable emission limitations, and such other control measures, means or techniques (including economic incentives such as fees, marketable permits, and auctions of emission rights), as well as schedules and timetables for compliance, as may be necessary or appropriate to provide for attainment of such standard in such area by the applicable attainment date specified in this part.

(7) Compliance with section 7410(a)(2) of this title

Such plan provisions shall also meet the applicable provisions of section 7410(a)(2) of this title.

(8) Equivalent techniques

Upon application by any State, the Administrator may allow the use of equivalent modeling, emission inventory, and planning procedures, unless the Administrator determines that the proposed techniques are, in the aggregate, less effective than the methods specified by the Administrator.

(9) Contingency measures

Such plan shall provide for the implementation of specific measures to be undertaken if the area fails to make reasonable further progress, or to attain the national primary ambient air quality standard by the attainment date applicable under this part. Such measures shall be included in the plan revision as contingency measures to take effect in any such case without further action by the State or the Administrator.

(d) Plan revisions required in response to finding of plan inadequacy

Any plan revision for a nonattainment area which is required to be submitted in response to a finding by the Administrator pursuant to section 7410(k)(5) of this title (relating to calls for plan revisions) must correct the plan deficiency (or deficiencies) specified by the Administrator and meet all other applicable plan requirements of section 7410 of this title and this part. The Administrator may reasonably adjust the dates otherwise applicable under such requirements to such revision (except for attainment dates that have not yet elapsed), to the extent necessary to achieve a consistent application of such requirements. In order to facilitate submittal by the States of adequate and approvable plans consistent with the applicable requirements of this chapter, the Administrator shall, as appropriate and from time to time, issue written guidelines, interpretations, and information to the States which shall be available to the public, taking into consideration any such guidelines, interpretations, or information provided before November 15, 1990.

(e) Future modification of standard

If the Administrator relaxes a national primary ambient air quality standard after November 15, 1990, the Administrator shall, within 12 months after the relaxation, promulgate requirements applicable to all areas which have not attained that standard as of the date of such relaxation. Such requirements shall provide for controls which are not less stringent than the controls applicable to areas designated nonattainment before such relaxation.

(July 14, 1955, ch. 360, title I, § 172, as added Aug. 7, 1977, Pub.L. 95–95, title I, § 129(b), 91 Stat. 746, and amended Nov. 16, 1977, Pub.L. 95–190, § 14(a)(55), (56), 91 Stat. 1402; Nov. 15. 1990, Pub.L. 101–549, title I, § 102(b), 104 Stat. 2412.)

Effective Date of 1990 Amendment

Amendment by Pub.L. 101–549 effective Nov. 15, 1990, except as otherwise provided, see section 711(b) of Pub.L. 101–549, set out as a note under section 7401 of this title.

Savings Provisions

Suits, actions or proceedings commenced under this chapter as in effect prior to Nov. 15, 1990, not to abate by reason of the taking effect of amendments by Pub.L. 101–549, except as otherwise provided for, see section 711(a) of Pub.L. 101–549, set out as a note under section 7401 of this title.

CODE OF FEDERAL REGULATIONS

Emission regulations, see 40 CFR 86.078–3 et seq.
Implementation plans, generally, see 40 CFR 51.40 et seq.
New stationary sources, performance standards for, see 40 CFR 60.1 et seq.

Library References

Health and Environment ⚷25.6(4).
C.J.S. Health and Environment § 95 et seq.

§ 7503. Permit requirements [CAA § 173]

(a) In general

The permit program required by section 7502(b)(6) of this title shall provide that permits to construct and operate may be issued if—

(1) in accordance with regulations issued by the Administrator for the determination of baseline emissions in a manner consistent with the assumptions underlying the applicable implementation plan approved under section 7410 of this title and this part, the permitting agency determines that—

(A) by the time the source is to commence operation, sufficient offsetting emissions reductions have been obtained, such that total allowable emissions from existing sources in the region, from new or modified sources which are not major emitting facilities, and from the proposed source will be sufficiently less than total emissions from existing sources (as determined in accordance with the regulations under this paragraph) prior to the application for such permit to construct or modify so as to represent (when considered together with the plan provisions required under section 7502 of this title) reasonable further progress (as defined in section 7501 of this title); or

(B) in the case of a new or modified major stationary source which is located in a zone (within the nonattainment area) identified by the Administrator, in consultation with the Secretary of Housing and Urban Development, as a zone to which economic development should be targeted, that emissions of such pollutant resulting from the proposed new or modified major stationary source will not cause or contribute to emissions levels which exceed the allowance permitted for such pollutant for such area from new or modified major stationary sources under section 7502(c) of this title;

(2) the proposed source is required to comply with the lowest achievable emission rate;

(3) the owner or operator of the proposed new or modified source has demonstrated that all major stationary sources owned or operated by such person (or by any entity controlling, controlled by, or under common control with such person) in such State are subject to emission limitations and are in compliance, or on a schedule for compliance, with all applicable emission limitations and standards under this chapter; and

(4) the Administrator has not determined that the applicable implementation plan is not being adequately implemented for the nonattainment area in which the proposed source is to be constructed or modified in accordance with the requirements of this part; and

(5) an analysis of alternative sites, sizes, production processes, and environmental control techniques for such proposed source demonstrates that benefits of the proposed source significantly outweigh the environmental and social costs imposed as a result of its location, construction, or modification.

Any emission reductions required as a precondition of the issuance of a permit under paragraph (1) shall be federally enforceable before such permit may be issued.

(b) Prohibition on use of old growth allowances

Any growth allowance included in an applicable implementation plan to meet the requirements of section 7502(b)(5) of this title (as in effect immediately before November 15, 1990) shall not be valid for use in any area that received or receives a notice under section 7410(a)(2)(H)(ii) of this title (as in effect immediately before November 15, 1990) or under section 7410(k)(1) of this title that its applicable implementation plan containing such allowance is substantially inadequate.

(c) Offsets

(1) The owner or operator of a new or modified major stationary source may comply with any offset requirement in effect under this part for increased emissions of any air pollutant only by obtaining emission reductions of such air pollutant from the same source or other sources in the same nonattainment area, except that the State may allow the owner or operator of a source to obtain such emission reductions in another nonattainment area if (A) the other area has an equal or higher nonattainment classification than the area in which the source is located and (B) emissions from such other area contribute to a violation of the national ambient air quality standard in the nonattainment area in which the source is located. Such emission reductions shall be, by the time a new or modified source commences operation, in effect and enforceable and shall assure that the total tonnage of increased emissions of the air pollutant from the new or modified source shall be offset by an equal or greater reduction, as applicable, in the actual emissions of such air pollutant from the same or other sources in the area.

(2) Emission reductions otherwise required by this chapter shall not be creditable as emissions reductions for purposes of any such offset requirement. Incidental emission reductions which are not otherwise required by this chapter shall be creditable as emission reductions for such purposes if such emission reductions meet the requirements of paragraph (1).

(d) Control technology information

The State shall provide that control technology information from permits issued under this section will be promptly submitted to the Administrator for purposes of making such information available through the RACT/BACT/LAER clearinghouse to other States and to the general public.

(e) Rocket engines or motors

The permitting authority of a State shall allow a source to offset by alternative or innovative means emission increases from rocket engine and motor firing, and cleaning related to such firing, at an existing or modified major source that tests rocket engines or motors under the following conditions:

(1) Any modification proposed is solely for the purpose of expanding the testing of rocket engines or motors at an existing source that is permitted to test such engines on November 15, 1990.

(2) The source demonstrates to the satisfaction of the permitting authority of the State that it has used all reasonable means to obtain and utilize offsets, as determined on an annual basis, for the emissions increases beyond allowable levels, that all

available offsets are being used, and that sufficient offsets are not available to the source.

(3) The source has obtained a written finding from the Department of Defense, Department of Transportation, National Aeronautics and Space Administration or other appropriate Federal agency, that the testing of rocket motors or engines at the facility is required for a program essential to the national security.

(4) The source will comply with an alternative measure, imposed by the permitting authority, designed to offset any emission increases beyond permitted levels not directly offset by the source. In lieu of imposing any alternative offset measures, the permitting authority may impose an emissions fee to be paid to such authority of a State which shall be an amount no greater than 1.5 times the average cost of stationary source control measures adopted in that area during the previous 3 years. The permitting authority shall utilize the fees in a manner that maximizes the emissions reductions in that area.

(July 14, 1955, ch. 360, title I, § 173, as added Aug. 7, 1977, Pub.L. 95–95, title I, § 129(b), 91 Stat. 748, and amended Nov. 16, 1977, Pub.L. 95–190, § 14(a)(57), (58), 91 Stat. 1403; Nov. 15, 1990, Pub.L. 101–549, title I, § 102(c), 104 Stat. 2416.)

Effective Date of 1990 Amendment

Amendment by Pub.L. 101–549 effective Nov. 15, 1990, except as otherwise provided, see section 711(b) of Pub.L. 101–549, set out as a note under section 7401 of this title.

Savings Provisions

Suits, actions or proceedings commenced under this chapter as in effect prior to Nov. 15, 1990, not to abate by reason of the taking effect of amendments by Pub.L. 101–549, except as otherwise provided for, see section 711(a) of Pub.L. 101–549, set out as a note under section 7401 of this title.

CODE OF FEDERAL REGULATIONS

Implementation plans, generally, see 40 CFR 51.40 et seq.

§ 7504. Planning procedures [CAA § 174]

(a) In general

For any ozone, carbon monoxide, or PM–10 nonattainment area, the State containing such area and elected officials of affected local governments shall, before the date required for submittal of the inventory described under sections 7511a(a)(1) and 7512a(a)(1) of this title, jointly review and update as necessary the planning procedures adopted pursuant to this subsection as in effect immediately before November 15, 1990, or develop new planning procedures pursuant to this subsection, as appropriate. In preparing such procedures the State and local elected officials shall determine which elements of a revised implementation plan will be developed, adopted, and implemented (through means including enforcement) by the State and which by local governments or regional agencies, or any combination of local governments, regional agencies, or the State. The implementation plan required by this part shall be prepared by an organization certified by the State, in consultation with elected officials of local governments and in accordance with the determination under the second sentence of this subsection. Such organization shall include elected officials of local governments in the affected area, and representatives of the State air quality planning agency, the State transportation planning agency, the metropolitan planning organization designated to conduct the continuing, cooperative and comprehensive transportation planning process for the area under section 134 of Title 23, the organization responsible for the air quality maintenance planning process under regulations implementing this chapter, and any other organization with responsibilities for developing, submitting, or implementing the plan required by this part. Such organization may be one that carried out these functions before November 15, 1990.

(b) Coordination

The preparation of implementation plan provisions and subsequent plan revisions under the continuing transportation-air quality planning process described in section 7408(e) of this title shall be coordinated with the continuing, cooperative and comprehensive transportation planning process required under section 134 of Title 23, and such planning processes shall take into account the requirements of this part.

(c) Joint planning

In the case of a nonattainment area that is included within more than one State, the affected States may jointly, through interstate compact or otherwise, undertake and implement all or part of the planning procedures described in this section.

(July 14, 1955, ch. 360, title I, § 174, as added Aug. 7, 1977, Pub.L. 95–95, title I, § 129(b), 91 Stat. 748, and amended Nov. 15, 1990, Pub.L. 101–549, title I, § 102(d), 104 Stat. 2417.)

Effective Date of 1990 Amendment

Amendment by Pub.L. 101–549 effective Nov. 15, 1990, except as otherwise provided, see section 711(b) of Pub.L. 101–549, set out as a note under section 7401 of this title.

Savings Provisions

Suits, actions or proceedings commenced under this chapter as in effect prior to Nov. 15, 1990, not to abate by reason of the taking effect of amendments by Pub.L. 101–549, except as otherwise provided for, see section 711(a) of Pub.L. 101–549, set out as a note under section 7401 of this title.

CODE OF FEDERAL REGULATIONS

Implementation plans, generally, see 40 CFR 51.40 et seq.
Planning assistance and standards, see 23 CFR 450.100 et seq., 49 CFR 613.100 et seq.

§ 7505. Environmental Protection Agency grants [CAA § 175]

(a) Plan revision development costs

The Administrator shall make grants to any organization of local elected officials with transportation or air quality maintenance planning responsibilities recognized by the State under section 7504(a) of this title for payment of the reasonable costs of developing a plan revision under this part.

(b) Uses of grant funds

The amount granted to any organization under subsection (a) of this section shall be 100 percent of any additional costs of developing a plan revision under this part for the first two fiscal years following receipt of the grant under this paragraph, and shall supplement any funds available under Federal law to such organization for transportation or air quality maintenance planning. Grants under this section shall not be used for construction.

(July 14, 1955, ch. 360, title I, § 175, as added Aug. 7, 1977, Pub.L. 95–95, title I, § 129(b), 91 Stat. 749.)

CODE OF FEDERAL REGULATIONS

Implementation plans, generally, see 40 CFR 51.40 et seq.

Library References

Health and Environment ⚷25.6(1).
United States ⚷82(2).
C.J.S. Health and Environment § 91 et seq.
C.J.S. United States § 122.

§ 7505a. Maintenance plans [CAA § 175A]

(a) Plan revision

Each State which submits a request under section 7407(d) of this title for redesignation of a nonattainment area for any air pollutant as an area which has attained the national primary ambient air quality standard for that air pollutant shall also submit a revision of the applicable State implementation plan to provide for the maintenance of the national primary ambient air quality standard for such air pollutant in the area concerned for at least 10 years after the redesignation. The plan shall contain such additional measures, if any, as may be necessary to ensure such maintenance.

(b) Subsequent plan revisions

8 years after redesignation of any area as an attainment area under section 7407(d) of this title, the State shall submit to the Administrator an additional revision of the applicable State implementation plan for maintaining the national primary ambient air quality standard for 10 years after the expiration of the 10–year period referred to in subsection (a) of this section.

(c) Nonattainment requirements applicable pending plan approval

Until such plan revision is approved and an area is redesignated as attainment for any area designated as a nonattainment area, the requirements of this part shall continue in force and effect with respect to such area.

(d) Contingency provisions

Each plan revision submitted under this section shall contain such contingency provisions as the Administrator deems necessary to assure that the State will promptly correct any violation of the standard which occurs after the redesignation of the area as an attainment area. Such provisions shall include a requirement that the State will implement all measures with respect to the control of the air pollutant concerned which were contained in the State implementation plan for the area before redesignation of the area as an attainment area. The failure of any area redesignated as an attainment area to maintain the national ambient air quality standard concerned shall not result in a requirement that the State revise its State implementation plan unless the Administrator, in the Administrator's discretion, requires the State to submit a revised State implementation plan.

(July 14, 1955, ch. 360, title I, § 175A, as added Nov. 15, 1990, Pub.L. 101–549, title I, § 102(e), 104 Stat. 2418.)

Effective Date

Section to take effect Nov. 15, 1990, except as otherwise provided, see section 711(b) of Pub.L. 101–549, set out as a note under section 7401 of this title.

Savings Provisions

Suits, actions or proceedings commenced under this chapter as in effect prior to Nov. 15, 1990, not to abate by reason of the taking effect of amendments by Pub.L. 101–549, except as otherwise provided for, see section 711(a) of Pub.L. 101–549, set out as a note under section 7401 of this title.

§ 7506. Limitations on certain Federal assistance [CAA § 176]

(a), (b) Repealed. Pub.L. 101–549, Title I, § 110(4), Nov. 15, 1990, 104 Stat. 2470

(c) Activities not conforming to approved or promulgated plans

(1) No department, agency, or instrumentality of the Federal Government shall engage in, support in any way or provide financial assistance for, license or permit, or approve, any activity which does not conform to an implementation plan after it has been approved or promulgated under section 7410 of this title. No metropolitan planning organization designated under section 134 of Title 23, shall give its

approval to any project, program, or plan which does not conform to an implementation plan approved or promulgated under section 7410 of this title. The assurance of conformity to such an implementation plan shall be an affirmative responsibility of the head of such department, agency, or instrumentality. Conformity to an implementation plan means—

(A) conformity to an implementation plan's purpose of eliminating or reducing the severity and number of violations of the national ambient air quality standards and achieving expeditious attainment of such standards; and

(B) that such activities will not—

(i) cause or contribute to any new violation of any standard in any area;

(ii) increase the frequency or severity of any existing violation of any standard in any area; or

(iii) delay timely attainment of any standard or any required interim emission reductions or other milestones in any area.

The determination of conformity shall be based on the most recent estimates of emissions, and such estimates shall be determined from the most recent population, employment, travel and congestion estimates as determined by the metropolitan planning organization or other agency authorized to make such estimates.

(2) Any transportation plan or program developed pursuant to Title 23 or the Federal Transit Act [49 U.S.C.A. App. § 1601 et seq.] shall implement the transportation provisions of any applicable implementation plan approved under this chapter applicable to all or part of the area covered by such transportation plan or program. No Federal agency may approve, accept or fund any transportation plan, program or project unless such plan, program or project has been found to conform to any applicable implementation plan in effect under this chapter. In particular—

(A) no transportation plan or transportation improvement program may be adopted by a metropolitan planning organization designated under Title 23 or the Federal Transit Act [49 U.S.C.A.App. § 1601 et seq.], or be found to be in conformity by a metropolitan planning organization until a final determination has been made that emissions expected from implementation of such plans and programs are consistent with estimates of emissions from motor vehicles and necessary emissions reductions contained in the applicable implementation plan, and that the plan or program will conform to the requirements of paragraph (1)(B);

(B) no metropolitan planning organization or other recipient of funds under Title 23 or the Federal Transit Act [49 U.S.C.A.App. § 1601 et seq.] shall adopt or approve a transportation improvement program of projects until it determines that such program provides for timely implementation of transportation control measures consistent with schedules included in the applicable implementation plan;

(C) a transportation project may be adopted or approved by a metropolitan planning organization or any recipient of funds designated under Title 23 or the Federal Transit Act [49 U.S.C.A.App. § 1601 et seq.], or found in conformity by a metropolitan planning organization or approved, accepted, or funded by the Department of Transportation only if it meets either the requirements of subparagraph (D) or the following requirements—

(i) such a project comes from a conforming plan and program;

(ii) the design concept and scope of such project have not changed significantly since the conformity finding regarding the plan and program from which the project derived; and

(iii) the design concept and scope of such project at the time of the conformity determination for the program was adequate to determine emissions.

(D) Any project not referred to in subparagraph (C) shall be treated as conforming to the applicable implementation plan only if it is demonstrated that the projected emissions from such project, when considered together with emissions projected for the conforming transportation plans and programs within the nonattainment area, do not cause such plans and programs to exceed the emission reduction projections and schedules assigned to such plans and programs in the applicable implementation plan.

(3) Until such time as the implementation plan revision referred to in paragraph (4)(C) is approved, conformity of such plans, programs, and projects will be demonstrated if—

(A) the transportation plans and programs—

(i) are consistent with the most recent estimates of mobile source emissions;

(ii) provide for the expeditious implementation of transportation control measures in the applicable implementation plan; and

(iii) with respect to ozone and carbon monoxide nonattainment areas, contribute to annual emissions reductions consistent with sections 7511a(b)(1) and 7512a(a)(7) of this title; and

(B) the transportation projects—

(i) come from a conforming transportation plan and program as defined in subparagraph (A) or for 12 months after November 15, 1990, from a transportation program found to conform within 3 years prior to November 15, 1990; and

(ii) in carbon monoxide nonattainment areas, eliminate or reduce the severity and number of violations of the carbon monoxide standards in the area substantially affected by the project.

With regard to subparagraph (B)(ii), such determination may be made as part of either the conformity determination for the transportation program or for the individual project taken as a whole during the environmental review phase of project development.

(4)(A) No later than one year after November 15, 1990, the Administrator shall promulgate criteria and procedures for determining conformity (except in the case of transportation plans, programs, and projects) of, and for keeping the Administrator informed about, the activities referred to in paragraph (1). No later than one year after November 15, 1990, the Administrator, with the concurrence of the Secretary of Transportation, shall promulgate criteria and procedures for demonstrating and assuring conformity in the case of transportation plans, programs, and projects. A suit may be brought against the Administrator and the Secretary of Transportation under section 7604 of this title to compel promulgation of such criteria and procedures and the Federal district court shall have jurisdiction to order such promulgation.

(B) The procedures and criteria shall, at a minimum—

(i) address the consultation procedures to be undertaken by metropolitan planning organizations and the Secretary of Transportation with State and local air quality agencies and State departments of transportation before such organizations and the Secretary make conformity determinations;

(ii) address the appropriate frequency for making conformity determinations, but in no case shall such determinations for transportation plans and programs be less frequent than every three years; and

(iii) address how conformity determinations will be made with respect to maintenance plans.

(C) Such procedures shall also include a requirement that each State shall submit to the Administrator and the Secretary of Transportation within 24 months of November 15, 1990, a revision to its implementation plan that includes criteria and procedures for assessing the conformity of any plan, program, or project subject to the conformity requirements of this subsection.

(5) Applicability

This subsection shall apply only with respect to—

(A) a nonattainment area and each pollutant for which the area is designated as a nonattainment area; and

(B) an area that was designated as a nonattainment area but that was later redesignated by the Administrator as an attainment area and that is required to develop a maintenance plan under section 7505a of this title with respect to the specific pollutant for which the area was designated nonattainment.

(d) Priority of achieving and maintaining national primary ambient air quality standards

Each department, agency, or instrumentality of the Federal Government having authority to conduct or support any program with air- quality related transportation consequences shall give priority in the exercise of such authority, consistent with statutory requirements for allocation among States or other jurisdictions, to the implementation of those portions of plans prepared under this section to achieve and maintain the national primary ambient air quality standard. This paragraph extends to, but is not limited to, authority exercised under the Federal Transit Act [49 U.S.C.A.App. § 1601 et seq.], Title 23, and the Housing and Urban Development Act.

(July 14, 1955, ch. 360, title I, § 176, as added Aug. 7, 1977, Pub.L. 95–95, title I, § 129(b), 91 Stat. 749, and amended Nov. 16, 1977, Pub.L. 95–190, § 14(a)(59), 91 Stat. 1403; Nov. 15, 1990, Pub.L. 101–549, title I, §§ 101(f), 110(4), 104 Stat. 2409, 2470; Dec. 18, 1991, Pub.L. 102–240, Title III, § 3003(b) 105 Stat. 2088; Nov. 28, 1995, Pub.L. 104–59, Title III, § 305(b), 109 Stat. 580.)

References in Text.

Title 23, referred to in subsec. (c)(2), (2)(A)–(C), is Title 23, Highways.

The Federal Transit Act, originally the Urban Mass Transportation Act, referred to in text, probably meant the Urban Mass Transportation Act of 1964, Pub.L. 88–365, July 9, 1964, 78 Stat. 302, which was redesignated by Pub.L. 102–240, as the Federal Transit Act, is classified generally to chapter 21 (section 1601 et seq.) of Title 49, Transportation, Appendix. For complete classification of this Act to the Code, see Short Title note set out under section 1601 of Title 49, Appendix, and Tables.

Effective Date of 1990 Amendment

Amendment by Pub.L. 101–549 effective Nov. 15, 1990, except as otherwise provided, see section 711(b) of Pub.L. 101–549, set out as a note under section 7401 of this title.

Savings Provisions

Suits, actions or proceedings commenced under this chapter as in effect prior to Nov. 15, 1990, not to abate by reason of the taking effect of amendments by Pub.L. 101–549, except as otherwise provided for, see section 711(a) of Pub.L. 101–549, set out as a note under section 7401 of this title.

CODE OF FEDERAL REGULATIONS

Air quality conformity and priority procedures, see 23 CFR 770.1 et seq.

Implementation plans, generally, see 40 CFR 51.40 et seq.

Planning assistance and standards, see 23 CFR 450.100 et seq., 49 CFR 613.100 et seq.

§ 7506a. Interstate transport commissions [CAA § 176A]

(a) Authority to establish interstate transport regions

Whenever, on the Administrator's own motion or by petition from the Governor of any State, the Administrator has reason to believe that the interstate transport of air pollutants from one or more States contributes significantly to a violation of a national ambient air quality standard in one or more other States, the Administrator may establish, by rule, a transport region for such pollutant that includes such States. The Administrator, on the Administrator's own motion or upon petition from the Governor of any State, or upon the recommendation of a transport commission established under subsection (b) of this section, may—

(1) add any State or portion of a State to any region established under this subsection whenever the Administrator has reason to believe that the interstate transport of air pollutants from such State significantly contributes to a violation of the standard in the transport region, or

(2) remove any State or portion of a State from the region whenever the Administrator has reason to believe that the control of emissions in that State or portion of the State pursuant to this section will not significantly contribute to the attainment of the standard in any area in the region.

The Administrator shall approve or disapprove any such petition or recommendation within 18 months of its receipt. The Administrator shall establish appropriate proceedings for public participation regarding such petitions and motions, including notice and comment.

(b) Transport commissions

(1) Establishment

Whenever the Administrator establishes a transport region under subsection (a) of this section, the Administrator shall establish a transport commission comprised of (at a minimum) each of the following members:

(A) The Governor of each State in the region or the designee of each such Governor.

(B) The Administrator or the Administrator's designee.

(C) The Regional Administrator (or the Administrator's designee) for each Regional Office for each Environmental Protection Agency Region affected by the transport region concerned.

(D) An air pollution control official representing each State in the region, appointed by the Governor.

Decisions of, and recommendations and requests to, the Administrator by each transport commission may be made only by a majority vote of all members other than the Administrator and the Regional Administrators (or designees thereof).

(2) Recommendations

The transport commission shall assess the degree of interstate transport of the pollutant or precursors to the pollutant throughout the transport region, assess strategies for mitigating the interstate pollution, and recommend to the Administrator such measures as the Commission determines to be necessary to ensure that the plans for the relevant States meet the requirements of section 7410(a)(2)(D) of this title. Such commission shall not be subject to the provisions of the Federal Advisory Committee Act (5 U.S.C.App.).

(c) Commission requests

A transport commission established under subsection (b) of this section may request the Administrator to issue a finding under section 7410(k)(5) of this title that the implementation plan for one or more of the States in the transport region is substantially inadequate to meet the requirements of section 7410(a)(2)(D) of this title. The Administrator shall approve, disapprove, or partially approve and partially disapprove such a request within 18 months of its receipt and, to the extent the Administrator approves such request, issue the finding under section 7410(k)(5) of this title at the time of such approval. In acting on such request, the Administrator shall provide an opportunity for public participation and shall address each specific recommendation made by the commission. Approval or disapproval of such a request shall constitute final agency action within the meaning of section 7607(b) of this title.

(July 14, 1955, ch. 360, title I, § 176A, as added Nov. 15, 1990, Pub.L. 101–549, title I, § 102(f)(1), 104 Stat. 2419.)

References in Text

The Federal Advisory Committee Act, referred to in subsec. (b)(2), is Pub.L. 92–463, Oct. 6, 1972, 86 Stat. 770, as amended, which is set out in Appendix 2 to Title 5, Government Organization and Employees.

Effective Date

Section to take effect Nov. 15, 1990, except as otherwise provided, see section 711(b) of Pub.L. 101–549, set out as a note under section 7401 of this title.

Savings Provisions

Suits, actions or proceedings commenced under this chapter as in effect prior to Nov. 15, 1990, not to abate by reason of the taking effect of amendments by Pub.L. 101–549, except as otherwise provid-

ed for, see section 711(a) of Pub.L. 101–549, set out as a note under section 7401 of this title.

§ 7507. New motor vehicle emission standards in nonattainment areas [CAA § 177]

Notwithstanding section 7543(a) of this title, any State which has plan provisions approved under this part may adopt and enforce for any model year standards relating to control of emissions from new motor vehicles or new motor vehicle engines and take such other actions as are referred to in section 7543(a) of this title respecting such vehicles if—

(1) such standards are identical to the California standards for which a waiver has been granted for such model year, and

(2) California and such State adopt such standards at least two years before commencement of such model year (as determined by regulations of the Administrator).

Nothing in this section or in subchapter II of this chapter shall be construed as authorizing any such State to prohibit or limit, directly or indirectly, the manufacture or sale of a new motor vehicle or motor vehicle engine that is certified in California as meeting California standards, or to take any action of any kind to create, or have the effect of creating, a motor vehicle or motor vehicle engine different than a motor vehicle or engine certified in California under California standards (a "third vehicle") or otherwise create such a "third vehicle".

(July 14, 1955, ch. 360, title I, § 177, as added Aug. 7, 1977, Pub.L. 95–95, title I, § 129(b), 91 Stat. 750, and amended Nov. 15, 1990, Pub.L. 101–549, title II, § 232, 104 Stat. 2529.)

Effective Date of 1990 Amendment

Amendment by Pub.L. 101–549 effective Nov. 15, 1990, except as otherwise provided, see section 711(b) of Pub.L. 101–549, set out as a note under section 7401 of this title.

Savings Provisions

Suits, actions or proceedings commenced under this chapter as in effect prior to Nov. 15, 1990, not to abate by reason of the taking effect of amendments by Pub.L. 101–549, except as otherwise provided for, see section 711(a) of Pub.L. 101–549, set out as a note under section 7401 of this title.

CODE OF FEDERAL REGULATIONS

Implementation plans, generally, see 40 CFR 51.40 et seq.

§ 7508. Guidance documents [CAA § 178]

The Administrator shall issue guidance documents under section 7408 of this title for purposes of assisting States in implementing requirements of this part respecting the lowest achievable emission rate. Such a document shall be published not later than nine months after August 7, 1977, and shall be revised at least every two years thereafter.

(July 14, 1955, ch. 360, title I, § 178, as added Aug. 7, 1977, Pub.L. 95–95, title I, § 129(b), 91 Stat. 750.)

CODE OF FEDERAL REGULATIONS

Implementation plans, generally, see 40 CFR 51.40 et seq.

§ 7509. Sanctions and consequences of failure to attain [CAA § 179]

(a) State failure

For any implementation plan or plan revision required under this part (or required in response to a finding of substantial inadequacy as described in section 7410(k)(5) of this title), if the Administrator—

(1) finds that a State has failed, for an area designated nonattainment under section 7407(d) of this title, to submit a plan, or to submit 1 or more of the elements (as determined by the Administrator) required by the provisions of this chapter applicable to such an area, or has failed to make a submission for such an area that satisfies the minimum criteria established in relation to any such element under section 7410(k) of this title,

(2) disapproves a submission under section 7410(k) of this title, for an area designated nonattainment under section 7407 of this title, based on the submission's failure to meet one or more of the elements required by the provisions of this chapter applicable to such an area,

(3)(A) determines that a State has failed to make any submission as may be required under this chapter, other than one described under paragraph (1) or (2), including an adequate maintenance plan, or has failed to make any submission, as may be required under this chapter, other than one described under paragraph (1) or (2), that satisfies the minimum criteria established in relation to such submission under section 7410(k)(1)(A) of this title, or

(B) disapproves in whole or in part a submission described under subparagraph (A), or

(4) finds that any requirement of an approved plan (or approved part of a plan) is not being implemented,

unless such deficiency has been corrected within 18 months after the finding, disapproval, or determination referred to in paragraphs (1), (2), (3), and (4), one of the sanctions referred to in subsection (b) of this section shall apply, as selected by the Administrator, until the Administrator determines that the State has come into compliance, except that if the Administrator finds a lack of good faith, sanctions under both paragraph (1) and paragraph (2) of subsection (b) of this section shall apply until the Administrator determines that the State has come into compliance. If the Administrator has selected one of such sanctions and the deficiency has not been corrected within 6 months thereafter, sanctions under both paragraph (1) and paragraph (2) of subsection (b) of this section shall apply until the Administrator determines that the State has come into compliance. In addition to any other sanction applicable as provided in this section, the Administrator may withhold all or part of the grants for support of air pollution planning and control programs that the Administrator may award under section 7405 of this title.

(b) Sanctions

The sanctions available to the Administrator as provided in subsection (a) of this section are as follows:

(1) Highway sanctions

(A) The Administrator may impose a prohibition, applicable to a nonattainment area, on the approval by the Secretary of Transportation of any projects or the awarding by the Secretary of Transportation of any projects or the awarding by the Secretary of any grants, under Title 23, other than projects or grants for safety where the Secretary determines, based on accident or other appropriate data submitted by the State, that the principal purpose of the project is an improvement in safety to resolve a demonstrated safety problem and likely will result in a significant reduction in, or avoidance of, accidents. Such prohibition shall become effective upon the selection by the Administrator of this sanction.

(B) In addition to safety, projects or grants that may be approved by the Secretary, notwithstanding the prohibition in subparagraph (A), are the following—

(i) capital programs for public transit;

(ii) construction or restriction of certain roads or lanes solely for the use of passenger buses or high occupancy vehicles;

(iii) planning for requirements for employers to reduce employee work-trip-related vehicle emissions;

(iv) highway ramp metering, traffic signalization, and related programs that improve traffic flow and achieve a net emission reduction;

(v) fringe and transportation corridor parking facilities serving multiple occupancy vehicle programs or transit operations;

(vi) programs to limit or restrict vehicle use in downtown areas or other areas of emission concentration particularly during periods of peak use, through road use charges, tolls, parking surcharges, or other pricing mechanisms, vehicle restricted zones or periods, or vehicle registration programs;

(vii) programs for breakdown and accident scene management, nonrecurring congestion, and vehicle information systems, to reduce congestion and emissions; and

(viii) such other transportation-related programs as the Administrator, in consultation with the Secretary of Transportation, finds would improve air quality and would not encourage single occupancy vehicle capacity.

In considering such measures, the State should seek to ensure adequate access to downtown, other commercial, and residential areas, and avoid increasing or relocating emissions and congestion rather than reducing them.

(2) Offsets

In applying the emissions offset requirements of section 7503 of this title to new or modified sources or emissions units for which a permit is required under part D, the ratio of emission reductions to increased emissions shall be at least 2 to 1.

(c) Notice of failure to attain

(1) As expeditiously as practicable after the applicable attainment date for any nonattainment area, but not later than 6 months after such date, the Administrator shall determine, based on the area's air quality as of the attainment date, whether the area attained the standard by that date.

(2) Upon making the determination under paragraph (1), the Administrator shall publish a notice in the Federal Register containing such determination and identifying each area that the Administrator has determined to have failed to attain. The Administrator may revise or supplement such determination at any time based on more complete information or analysis concerning the area's air quality as of the attainment date.

(d) Consequences for failure to attain

(1) Within 1 year after the Administrator publishes the notice under subsection (c)(2) of this section (relating to notice of failure to attain), each State containing a nonattainment area shall submit a revision to the applicable implementation plan meeting the requirements of paragraph (2) of this subsection.

(2) The revision required under paragraph (1) shall meet the requirements of section 7410 and section 7502 of this title. In addition, the revision shall include such additional measures as the Administrator may reasonably prescribe, including all measures that can be feasibly implemented in the area in light of technological achievability, costs, and any nonair quality and other air quality-related health and environmental impacts.

(3) The attainment date applicable to the revision required under paragraph (1) shall be the same as provided in the provisions of section 7502(a)(2) of this title, except that in applying such provisions the phrase "from the date of the notice under section 7509(c)(2) of this title" shall be substituted for the phrase "from the date such area was designated nonattainment under section 7407(d) of this title" and for the phrase "from the date of designation as nonattainment".

(July 14, 1955, ch. 360, title I, § 179, as added Nov. 15, 1990, Pub.L. 101–549, title I, § 102(g), 104 Stat. 2420.)

References in Text

Title 23, referred to in subsec. (b)(1)(A), is Title 23, Highways.

Effective Date

Section to take effect Nov. 15, 1990, except as otherwise provided, see section 711(b) of Pub.L. 101–549, set out as a note under section 7401 of this title.

Savings Provisions

Suits, actions or proceedings commenced under this chapter as in effect prior to Nov. 15, 1990, not to abate by reason of the taking effect of amendments by Pub.L. 101–549, except as otherwise provided for, see section 711(a) of Pub.L. 101–549, set out as a note under section 7401 of this title.

§ 7509a. International border areas [CAA § 179B]

(a) Implementation plans and revisions

Notwithstanding any other provision of law, an implementation plan or plan revision required under this chapter shall be approved by the Administrator if—

(1) such plan or revision meets all the requirements applicable to it under the chapter other than a requirement that such plan or revision demonstrate attainment and maintenance of the relevant national ambient air quality standards by the attainment date specified under the applicable provision of this chapter, or in a regulation promulgated under such provision, and

(2) the submitting State establishes to the satisfaction of the Administrator that the implementation plan of such State would be adequate to attain and maintain the relevant national ambient air quality standards by the attainment date specified under the applicable provision of this chapter, or in a regulation promulgated under such provision, but for emissions emanating from outside of the United States.

(b) Attainment of ozone levels

Notwithstanding any other provision of law, any State that establishes to the satisfaction of the Administrator that, with respect to an ozone nonattainment area in such State, such State would have attained the national ambient air quality standard for ozone by the applicable attainment date, but for emissions emanating from outside of the United States, shall not be subject to the provisions of section 7511(a)(2) or (5) of this title or section 7511d of this title.

(c) Attainment of carbon monoxide levels

Notwithstanding any other provision of law, any State that establishes to the satisfaction of the Administrator, with respect to a carbon monoxide nonattainment area in such State, that such State has attained the national ambient air quality standard for carbon monoxide by the applicable attainment date, but for emissions emanating from outside of the United States, shall not be subject to the provisions of section 7512(b)(2) or (9) of this title [1].

(d) Attainment of PM–10 levels

Notwithstanding any other provision of law, any State that establishes to the satisfaction of the Administrator that, with respect to a PM–10 nonattainment area in such State, such State would have attained the national ambient air quality standard for carbon monoxide by the applicable attainment date, but for emissions emanating from outside the United States shall not be subject to the provisions of section 7513(b)(2) of this title.

(July 14, 1955, ch. 360, title I, § 179B, as added Nov. 15, 1990, Pub.L. 101–549, title VIII, § 818, 104 Stat. 2693.)

[1] So in original. There is no subsec. (b)(9) of section 7512 of this title.

Effective Date

Section to take effect Nov. 15, 1990, except as otherwise provided, see section 711(b) of Pub.L. 101–549, set out as a note under section 7401 of this title.

Savings Provisions

Suits, actions or proceedings commenced under this chapter as in effect prior to Nov. 15, 1990, not to abate by reason of the taking effect of amendments by Pub.L. 101–549, except as otherwise provided for, see section 711(a) of Pub.L. 101–549, set out as a note under section 7401 of this title.

Establishment of Program to Monitor and Improve Air Quality in Regions Along the Border Between the United States and Mexico

Section 815 of Pub.L. 101–549 provided that:

"(a) **In general.**—The Administrator of the Environmental Protection Agency (hereinafter referred to as the 'Administrator') is authorized, in cooperation with the Department of State and the affected States, to negotiate with representatives of Mexico to authorize a program to monitor and improve air quality in regions along the border between the United States and Mexico. The program established under this section shall not extend beyond July 1, 1995.

"(b) **Monitoring and remediation.**—

"(1) **Monitoring.**—The monitoring component of the program conducted under this section shall identify and determine sources of pollutants for which national ambient air quality standards (hereinafter referred to as "NAAQS") and other air quality goals have been established in regions along the border between the United

States and Mexico. Any such monitoring component of the program shall include, but not be limited to, the collection of meteorological data, the measurement of air quality, the compilation of an emissions inventory, and shall be sufficient to the extent necessary to successfully support the use of a state-of-the-art mathematical air modeling analysis. Any such monitoring component of the program shall collect and produce data projecting the level of emission reductions necessary in both Mexico and the United States to bring about attainment of both primary and secondary NAAQS, and other air quality goals, in regions along the border in the United States. Any such monitoring component of the program shall include to the extent possible, data from monitoring programs undertaken by other parties.

"(2) **Remediation.**—The Administrator is authorized to negotiate with appropriate representatives of Mexico to develop joint remediation measures to reduce the level of airborne pollutants to achieve and maintain primary and secondary NAAQS, and other air quality goals, in regions along the border between the United States and Mexico. Such joint remediation measures may include, but not be limited to measures included in the Environmental Protection Agency's Control Techniques and Control Technology documents. Any such remediation program shall also identify those control measures implementation of which in Mexico would be expedited by the use of material and financial assistance of the United States.

"(c) **Annual reports.**—The Administrator shall, each year the program authorized in this section is in operation, report to Congress on the progress of the program in bringing nonattainment areas along the border of the United States into attainment with primary and secondary NAAQS. The report issued by the Administrator under this paragraph shall include recommendations on funding mechanisms to assist in implementation of monitoring and remediation efforts.

"(d) **Funding and personnel.**—The Administrator may, where appropriate, make available, subject to the appropriations, such funds, personnel, and equipment as may be necessary to implement the provisions of this section. In those cases where direct financial assistance of the United States is provided to implement monitoring and remediation programs in Mexico, the Administrator shall develop grant agreements with appropriate representatives of Mexico to assure the accuracy and completeness of monitoring data and the performance of remediation measures which are financed by the United States. With respect to any control measures within Mexico funded by the United States, the Administrator shall, to the maximum extent practicable, utilize resources of Mexico where such utilization would reduce costs to the United States. Such funding agreements shall include authorization for the Administrator to—

"(1) review and agree to plans for monitoring and remediation;

"(2) inspect premises, equipment and records to insure compliance with the agreements established under and the purposes set forth in this section; and

"(3) where necessary, develop grant agreements with affected States to carry out the provisions of this section."

Subpart 2—Additional Provisions for Ozone Nonattainment Areas

§ 7511. Classifications and attainment dates [CAA § 181]

(a) Classification and attainment dates for 1989 nonattainment areas

(1) Each area designated nonattainment for ozone pursuant to section 7407(d) of this title shall be classified at the time of such designation, under table 1, by operation of law, as a Marginal Area, a Moderate Area, a Serious Area, a Severe Area, or an Extreme Area based on the design value for the area. The design value shall be calculated according to the interpretation methodology issued by the Administrator most recently before November 15, 1990. For each area classified under this subsection, the primary standard attainment date for ozone shall be as expeditiously as practicable but not later than the date provided in table 1.

TABLE 1

Area class	Design value *	Primary standard attainment date **
Marginal	0.121 up to 0.138	3 years after November 15, 1990
Moderate	0.138 up to 0.160	6 years after November 15, 1990
Serious	0.160 up to 0.180	9 years after November 15, 1990
Severe	0.180 up to 0.280	15 years after November 15, 1990
Extreme	0.280 and above	20 years after November 15, 1990

* The design value is measured in parts per million (ppm).

** The primary standard attainment date is measured from November 15, 1990.

(2) Notwithstanding table 1, in the case of a severe area with a 1988 ozone design value between 0.190 and 0.280 ppm, the attainment date shall be 17 years (in lieu of 15 years) after November 15, 1990.

(3) At the time of publication of the notice under section 7407(d)(4) of this title (relating to area designations) for each ozone nonattainment area, the Administrator shall publish a notice announcing the classification of such ozone nonattainment area. The provisions of section 7502(a)(1)(B) of this title (relating to lack of notice and comment and judicial review) shall apply to such classification.

(4) If an area classified under paragraph (1) (Table 1) would have been classified in another category if the design value in the area were 5 percent greater or 5 percent less than the level on which such classification was based, the Administrator may, in the Administrator's discretion, within 90 days after the initial classification, by the procedure required under paragraph (3), adjust the classification to place the area in such other category. In making such adjustment, the Administrator may consider the number of exceedances of the national primary ambient air quality standard for ozone in the area, the level of pollution transport between the area and other affected areas, including both intrastate and interstate transport, and the mix of sources and air pollutants in the area.

(5) Upon application by any State, the Administrator may extend for 1 additional year (hereinafter referred to as the "Extension Year") the date specified in table 1 of paragraph (1) of this subsection if—

(A) the State has complied with all requirements and commitments pertaining to the area in the applicable implementation plan, and

(B) no more than 1 exceedance of the national ambient air quality standard level for ozone has occurred in the area in the year preceding the Extension Year.

No more than 2 one-year extensions may be issued under this paragraph for a single nonattainment area.

(b) New designations and reclassifications

(1) New designations to nonattainment

Any area that is designated attainment or unclassifiable for ozone under section 7407(d)(4) of this title, and that is subsequently redesignated to nonattainment for ozone under section 7407(d)(3) of this title, shall, at the time of the redesignation, be classified by operation of law in accordance with table 1 under subsection (a) of this section. Upon its classification, the area shall be subject to the same requirements under section 7410 of this title, subpart 1 of this part, and this subpart that would have applied had the area been so classified at the time of the notice under subsection (a)(3) of this section, except that any absolute, fixed date applicable in connection with any such requirement is extended by operation of law by a period equal to the length of time between November 15, 1990, and the date the area is classified under this paragraph.

(2) Reclassification upon failure to attain

(A) Within 6 months following the applicable attainment date (including any extension thereof) for an ozone nonattainment area, the Administrator shall determine, based on the area's design value (as of the attainment date), whether the area attained the standard by that date. Except for any Severe or Extreme area, any area that the Administrator finds has not attained the standard by that date shall be reclassified by operation of law in accordance with table 1 of subsection (a) of this section to the higher of—

(i) the next higher classification for the area, or

(ii) the classification applicable to the area's design value as determined at the time of the notice required under subparagraph (B).

No area shall be reclassified as Extreme under clause (ii).

(B) The Administrator shall publish a notice in the Federal Register, no later than 6 months following the attainment date, identifying each area that the Administrator has determined under subparagraph (A) as having failed to attain and identifying the reclassification, if any, described under subparagraph (A).

(3) Voluntary reclassification

The Administrator shall grant the request of any State to reclassify a nonattainment area in that State in accordance with table 1 of subsection (a) to a higher classification. The Administrator shall publish a notice in the Federal Register of any such request and of action by the Administrator granting the request.

(4) Failure of severe areas to attain standard

(A) If any Severe Area fails to achieve the national primary ambient air quality standard for ozone by the applicable attainment date (including any extension thereof), the fee provisions under section 7511d of this title shall apply within the area, the percent reduction requirements of section 7511a(c)(2)(B) and (C) of this title (relating to reasonable further progress demonstration and NO_x control) shall continue to apply to the area, and the State shall demonstrate that such percent reduction has been achieved in each 3-year interval after such failure until the standard is attained. Any failure to make such a demonstration shall be subject to the sanctions provided under this part.

(B) In addition to the requirements of subparagraph (A), if the ozone design value for a Severe Area referred to in subparagraph (A) is above 0.140 ppm for the year of the applicable attainment date, or if the area has failed to achieve its most recent milestone under section 7511a(g) of this title, the new source review requirements applicable under this subpart in Extreme Areas shall apply in the area and the term "major source" and "major stationary source" shall have the same meaning as in Extreme Areas.

(C) In addition to the requirements of subparagraph (A) for those areas referred to in subparagraph (A) and not covered by subparagraph (B), the provisions referred to in subparagraph (B) shall apply after 3 years from the applicable attainment date unless the area has attained the standard by the end of such 3-year period.

(D) If, after November 15, 1990, the Administrator modifies the method of determining compliance with the national primary ambient air quality standard, a design value or other indicator comparable to 0.140 in terms of its relationship to the standard shall be used in lieu of 0.140 for purposes of applying the provisions of subparagraphs (B) and (C).

(c) References to terms

(1) Any reference in this subpart to a "Marginal Area", a "Moderate Area", a "Serious Area", a "Se-

vere Area", or an "Extreme Area" shall be considered a reference to a Marginal Area, a Moderate Area, a Serious Area, a Severe Area, or an Extreme Area as respectively classified under this section.

(2) Any reference in this subpart to "next higher classification" or comparable terms shall be considered a reference to the classification related to the next higher set of design values in table 1.

(July 14, 1955, ch. 360, title I, § 181, as added Nov. 15, 1990, Pub.L. 101–549, title I, § 103, 104 Stat. 2423.)

Effective Date

Section to take effect Nov. 15, 1990, except as otherwise provided, see section 711(b) of Pub.L. 101–549, set out as a note under section 7401 of this title.

Savings Provisions

Suits, actions or proceedings commenced under this chapter as in effect prior to Nov. 15, 1990, not to abate by reason of the taking effect of amendments by Pub.L. 101–549, except as otherwise provided for, see section 711(a) of Pub.L. 101–549, set out as a note under section 7401 of this title.

Exemptions for Stripper Wells

Section 819 of Pub.L. 101–549 provided that:

"Notwithstanding any other provision of law, the amendments to the Clean Air Act [this chapter] made by section 103 of the Clean Air Act Amendments of 1990 (relating to additional provisions for ozone nonattainment areas) [enacting sections 7511 to 7511f of this title], by section 104 of such amendments (relating to additional provisions for carbon monoxide nonattainment areas) [enacting sections 7512 and 7512a of this title], by section 105 of such amendments (relating to additional provisions for PM–10 nonattainment areas) [enacting sections 7513 to 7513b of this title and amending section 7476 of this title], and by section 106 of such amendments (relating to additional provisions for areas designated as nonattainment for sulfur oxides, nitrogen dioxide, and lead) [enacting sections 7514 and 7514a of this title] shall not apply with respect to the production of and equipment used in the exploration, production, development, storage or processing of—

"(1) oil from a stripper well property, within the meaning of the June 1979 energy regulations (within the meaning of section 4996(b)(7) of the Internal Revenue Code of 1986 [section 4996(b)(7) of Title 26, Internal Revenue Code], as in effect before the repeal of such section); and

"(2) stripper well natural gas, as defined in section 108(b) of the Natural Gas Policy Act of 1978 (15 U.S.C. 3318(b)) [section 3318(b) of Title 15, Commerce and Trade].

except to the extent that provisions of such amendments cover areas designated as Serious pursuant to part D of title I of the Clean Air Act [part D of subchapter I of this chapter] and having a population of 350,000 or more, or areas designated as Severe or Extreme pursuant to such part D."

§ 7511a. Plan submissions and requirements [CAA § 182]

(a) Marginal areas

Each State in which all or part of a Marginal Area is located shall, with respect to the Marginal Area (or portion thereof, to the extent specified in this subsection), submit to the Administrator the State implementation plan revisions (including the plan items) described under this subsection except to the extent the State has made such submissions as of November 15, 1990.

(1) Inventory

Within 2 years after November 15, 1990, the State shall submit a comprehensive, accurate, current inventory of actual emissions from all sources, as described in section 7502(c)(3) of this title, in accordance with guidance provided by the Administrator.

(2) Corrections to the State implementation plan

Within the periods prescribed in this paragraph, the State shall submit a revision to the State implementation plan that meets the following requirements—

(A) Reasonably available control technology corrections

For any Marginal Area (or, within the Administrator's discretion, portion thereof) the State shall submit, within 6 months of the date of classification under section 7511(a) of this title, a revision that includes such provisions to correct requirements in (or add requirements to) the plan concerning reasonably available control technology as were required under section 7502(b) of this title (as in effect immediately before November 15, 1990), as interpreted in guidance issued by the Administrator under section 7408 of this title before November 15, 1990.

(B) Savings clause for vehicle inspection and maintenance

(i) For any Marginal Area (or, within the Administrator's discretion, portion thereof), the plan for which already includes, or was required by section 7502(b)(11)(B) of this title (as in effect immediately before November 15, 1990) to have included, a specific schedule for implementation of a vehicle emission control inspection and maintenance program, the State shall submit, immediately after November 15, 1990, a revision that includes any provisions necessary to provide for a vehicle inspection and maintenance program of no less stringency than that of either the program defined in House Report Numbered 95–294, 95th Congress, 1st Session, 281–291 (1977) as interpreted in guidance of the Administrator issued pursuant to section 7502(b)(11)(B) of this title (as in effect immediately before November 15, 1990) or the program already included in the plan, whichever is more stringent.

(ii) Within 12 months after November 15, 1990, the Administrator shall review, revise, update, and republish in the Federal Register the guidance for the States for motor vehicle inspection and maintenance programs required by this chapter, taking into consideration the Administrator's investigations and audits of such program.

The guidance shall, at a minimum, cover the frequency of inspections, the types of vehicles to be inspected (which shall include leased vehicles that are registered in the nonattainment area), vehicle maintenance by owners and operators, audits by the State, the test method and measures, including whether centralized or decentralized, inspection methods and procedures, quality of inspection, components covered, assurance that a vehicle subject to a recall notice from a manufacturer has complied with that notice, and effective implementation and enforcement, including ensuring that any retesting of a vehicle after a failure shall include proof of corrective action and providing for denial of vehicle registration in the case of tampering or misfueling. The guidance which shall be incorporated in the applicable State implementation plans by the States shall provide the States with continued reasonable flexibility to fashion effective, reasonable, and fair programs for the affected consumer. No later than 2 years after the Administrator promulgates regulations under section 7521(m)(3) of this title (relating to emission control diagnostics), the State shall submit a revision to such program to meet any requirements that the Administrator may prescribe under that section.

(C) Permit programs

Within 2 years after November 15, 1990, the State shall submit a revision that includes each of the following:

(i) Provisions to require permits, in accordance with sections 7502(c)(5) and 7503 of this title, for the construction and operation of each new or modified major stationary source (with respect to ozone) to be located in the area.

(ii) Provisions to correct requirements in (or add requirements to) the plan concerning permit programs as were required under section 7502(b)(6) of this title (as in effect immediately before November 15, 1990), as interpreted in regulations of the Administrator promulgated as of November 15, 1990.

(3) Periodic inventory

(A) General requirement

No later than the end of each 3-year period after submission of the inventory under paragraph (1) until the area is redesignated to attainment, the State shall submit a revised inventory meeting the requirements of subsection (a)(1) of this section.

(B) Emissions statements

(i) Within 2 years after November 15, 1990, the State shall submit a revision to the State implementation plan to require that the owner or operator of each stationary source of oxides of nitrogen or volatile organic compounds provide the State with a statement, in such form as the Administrator may prescribe (or accept an equivalent alternative developed by the State), for classes or categories of sources, showing the actual emissions of oxides of nitrogen and volatile organic compounds from that source. The first such statement shall be submitted within 3 years after November 15, 1990. Subsequent statements shall be submitted at least every year thereafter. The statement shall contain a certification that the information contained in the statement is accurate to the best knowledge of the individual certifying the statement.

(ii) The State may waive the application of clause (i) to any class or category of stationary sources which emit less than 25 tons per year of volatile organic compounds or oxides of nitrogen if the State, in its submissions under subparagraphs (1) or (3)(A), provides an inventory of emissions from such class or category of sources, based on the use of the emission factors established by the Administrator or other methods acceptable to the Administrator.

(4) General offset requirement

For purposes of satisfying the emission offset requirements of this part, the ratio of total emission reductions of volatile organic compounds to total increased emissions of such air pollutant shall be at least 1.1 to 1.

The Administrator may, in the Administrator's discretion, require States to submit a schedule for submitting any of the revisions or other items required under this subsection. The requirements of this subsection shall apply in lieu of any requirement that the State submit a demonstration that the applicable implementation plan provides for attainment of the ozone standard by the applicable attainment date in any Marginal Area. Section 7502(c)(9) of this title (relating to contingency measures) shall not apply to Marginal Areas.

(b) Moderate areas

Each State in which all or part of a Moderate Area is located shall, with respect to the Moderate Area, make the submissions described under subsection (a) of this section (relating to Marginal Areas), and shall also submit the revisions to the applicable implementation plan described under this subsection.

(1) Plan provisions for reasonable further progress

(A) General rule

(i) By no later than 3 years after November 15, 1990, the State shall submit a revision to the applicable implementation plan to provide for volatile organic compound emission reductions, within 6 years after November 15, 1990, of at least 15 percent from baseline emissions, accounting for any growth in emissions after 1990. Such plan shall provide for such specific annual reductions in emissions of volatile organic compounds and oxides of nitrogen as necessary to attain the national primary ambient air quality standard for ozone by the attainment date applicable under this chapter. This subparagraph shall not apply in the case of oxides of nitrogen for those areas for which the Administrator determines (when the Administrator approves the plan or plan revision) that additional reductions of oxides of nitrogen would not contribute to attainment.

(ii) A percentage less than 15 percent may be used for purposes of clause (i) in the case of any State which demonstrates to the satisfaction of the Administrator that—

(I) new source review provisions are applicable in the nonattainment areas in the same manner and to the same extent as required under subsection (e) of this section in the case of Extreme Areas (with the exception that, in applying such provisions, the terms "major source" and "major stationary source" shall include (in addition to the sources described in section 7602 of this title) any stationary source or group of sources located within a contiguous area and under common control that emits, or has the potential to emit, at least 5 tons per year of volatile organic compounds);

(II) reasonably available control technology is required for all existing major sources (as defined in subclause (I)); and

(III) the plan reflecting a lesser percentage than 15 percent includes all measures that can feasibly be implemented in the area, in light of technological achievability.

To qualify for a lesser percentage under this clause, a State must demonstrate to the satisfaction of the Administrator that the plan for the area includes the measures that are achieved in practice by sources in the same source category in nonattainment areas of the next higher category.

(B) Baseline emissions

For purposes of subparagraph (A), the term "baseline emissions" means the total amount of actual VOC or NO_x emissions from all anthropogenic sources in the area during the calendar year of 1990, excluding emissions that would be eliminated under the regulations described in clauses (i) and (ii) of subparagraph (D).

(C) General rule for creditability of reductions

Except as provided under subparagraph (D), emissions reductions are creditable toward the 15 percent required under subparagraph (A) to the extent they have actually occurred, as of 6 years after November 15, 1990, from the implementation of measures required under the applicable implementation plan, rules promulgated by the Administrator, or a permit under subchapter V of this chapter.

(D) Limits on creditability of reductions

Emission reductions from the following measures are not creditable toward the 15 percent reductions required under subparagraph (A):

(i) Any measure relating to motor vehicle exhaust or evaporative emissions promulgated by the Administrator by January 1, 1990.

(ii) Regulations concerning Reid Vapor Pressure promulgated by the Administrator by November 15, 1990 or required to be promulgated under section 7545(h) of this title.

(iii) Measures required under subsection (a)(2)(A) of this section (concerning corrections to implementation plans prescribed under guidance by the Administrator).

(iv) Measures required under subsection (a)(2)(B) of this section to be submitted immediately after November 15, 1990 (concerning corrections to motor vehicle inspection and maintenance programs).

(2) Reasonably available control technology

The State shall submit a revision to the applicable implementation plan to include provisions to require the implementation of reasonably available control technology under section 7502(c)(1) of this title with respect to each of the following:

(A) Each category of VOC sources in the area covered by a CTG document issued by the Administrator between November 15, 1990 and the date of attainment.

(B) All VOC sources in the area covered by any CTG issued before November 15, 1990.

(C) All other major stationary sources of VOCs that are located in the area.

Each revision described in subparagraph (A) shall be submitted within the period set forth by the Administrator in issuing the relevant CTG document. The revisions with respect to sources described in subparagraphs (B) and (C) shall be submitted by 2 years after November 15, 1990, and shall provide for the implementation of the required measures as expeditiously as practicable but no later than May 31, 1995.

(3) Gasoline vapor recovery

(A) General rule

Not later than 2 years after November 15, 1990, the State shall submit a revision to the applicable implementation plan to require all owners or operators of gasoline dispensing systems to install and operate, by the date prescribed under subparagraph (B), a system for gasoline vapor recovery of emissions from the fueling of motor vehicles. The Administrator shall issue guidance as appropriate as to the effectiveness of such system. This subparagraph shall apply only to facilities which sell more than 10,000 gallons of gasoline per month (50,000 gallons per month in the case of an independent small business marketer of gasoline as defined in section 7625–1 of this title).

(B) Effective date

The date required under subparagraph (A) shall be—

(i) 6 months after the adoption date, in the case of gasoline dispensing facilities for which construction commenced after November 15, 1990;

(ii) one year after the adoption date, in the case of gasoline dispensing facilities which dispense at least 100,000 gallons of gasoline per month, based on average monthly sales for the 2–year period before the adoption date; or

(iii) 2 years after the adoption date, in the case of all other gasoline dispensing facilities.

Any gasoline dispensing facility described under both clause (i) and clause (ii) shall meet the requirements of clause (i).

(C) Reference to terms

For purposes of this paragraph, any reference to the term "adoption date" shall be considered a reference to the date of adoption by the State of requirements for the installation and operation of a system for gasoline vapor recovery of emissions from the fueling of motor vehicles.

(4) Motor vehicle inspection and maintenance

For all Moderate Areas, the State shall submit, immediately after November 15, 1990, a revision to the applicable implementation plan that includes provisions necessary to provide for a vehicle inspection and maintenance program as described in subsection (a)(2)(B) of this section (without regard to whether or not the area was required by section 7502(b)(11)(B) of this section (as in effect immediately before November 15, 1990) to have included a specific schedule for implementation of such a program).

(5) General offset requirement

For purposes of satisfying the emission offset requirements of this part, the ratio of total emission reductions of volatile organic compounds to total increase emissions of such air pollutant shall be at least 1.15 to 1.

(c) Serious areas

Except as otherwise specified in paragraph (4), each State in which all or part of a Serious Area is located shall, with respect to the Serious Area (or portion thereof, to the extent specified in this subsection), make the submissions described under subsection (b) of this section (relating to Moderate Areas), and shall also submit the revisions to the applicable implementation plan (including the plan items) described under this subsection. For any Serious Area, the terms "major source" and "major stationary source" include (in addition to the sources described in section 7602 of this title) any stationary source or group of sources located within a contiguous area and under common control that emits, or has the potential to emit, at least 50 tons per year of volatile organic compounds.

(1) Enhanced monitoring

In order to obtain more comprehensive and representative data on ozone air pollution, not later than 18 months after November 15, 1990 the Administrator shall promulgate rules, after notice and public comment, for enhanced monitoring of ozone, oxides of nitrogen, and volatile organic compounds. The rules shall, among other things, cover the location and maintenance of monitors. Immediately following the promulgation of rules by the Administrator relating to enhanced monitoring, the State shall commence such actions as may be necessary to adopt and implement a program based on such rules, to improve monitoring for ambient concentrations of ozone, oxides of nitrogen and volatile organic compounds and to improve monitoring of emissions of oxides of nitrogen and volatile organic compounds. Each State implementation plan for the area shall contain measures to improve the ambient monitoring of such air pollutants.

(2) Attainment and reasonable further progress demonstrations

Within 4 years after November 15, 1990, the State shall submit a revision to the applicable implementation plan that includes each of the following:

(A) Attainment demonstration

A demonstration that the plan, as revised, will provide for attainment of the ozone national ambient air quality standard by the applicable attainment date. This attainment demonstration must be based on photochemical grid modeling or any other analytical method determined by the Administrator, in the Administrator's discretion, to be at least as effective.

(B) Reasonable further progress demonstration

A demonstration that the plan, as revised, will result in VOC emissions reductions from the baseline emissions described in subsection (b)(1)(B) of this section equal to the following amount averaged over each consecutive 3–year period beginning 6 years after November 15, 1990, until the attainment date:

(i) at least 3 percent of baseline emissions each year; or

(ii) an amount less than 3 percent of such baseline emissions each year, if the State demonstrates to the satisfaction of the Administrator that the plan reflecting such lesser amount includes all measures that can feasibly be implemented in the area, in light of technological achievability.

To lessen the 3 percent requirement under clause (ii), a State must demonstrate to the satisfaction of the Administrator that the plan for the area includes the measures that are achieved in practice by sources in the same source category in nonattainment areas of the next higher classification. Any determination to lessen the 3 percent requirement shall be reviewed at each milestone under subsection (g) of this section and revised to reflect such new measures (if any) achieved in practice by sources in the same category in any State, allowing a reasonable time to implement such measures. The emission reductions described in this subparagraph shall be calculated in accordance with subsection (b)(1)(C) and (D) of this section (concerning creditability of reductions). The reductions creditable for the period beginning 6 years after November 15, 1990, shall include reductions that occurred before such period, computed in accordance with subsection (b)(1) of this section, that exceed the 15–percent amount of reductions required under subsection (b)(1)(A) of this section.

(C) NO_x control

The revision may contain, in lieu of the demonstration required under subparagraph (B), a demonstration to the satisfaction of the Administrator that the applicable implementation plan, as revised, provides for reductions of emissions of VOC's and oxides of nitrogen (calculated according to the creditability provisions of subsection (b)(1)(C) and (D) of this section), that would result in a reduction in ozone concentrations at least equivalent to that which would result from the amount of VOC emission reductions required under subparagraph (B). Within 1 year after November 15, 1990, the Administrator shall issue guidance concerning the conditions under which NO_x control may be substituted for VOC control or may be combined with VOC control in order to maximize the reduction in ozone air pollution. In accord with such guidance, a lesser percentage of VOCs may be accepted as an adequate demonstration for purposes of this subsection.

(3) Enhanced vehicle inspection and maintenance program

(A) Requirement for submission

Within 2 years after November 15, 1990, the State shall submit a revision to the applicable implementation plan to provide for an enhanced program to reduce hydrocarbon emissions and NO_x emissions from in-use motor vehicles registered in each urbanized area (in the nonattainment area), as defined by the Bureau of the Census, with a 1980 population of 200,000 or more.

(B) Effective date of State programs; guidance

The State program required under subparagraph (A) shall take effect no later than 2 years from November 15, 1990, and shall comply in all respects with guidance published in the Federal Register (and from time to time revised) by the Administrator for enhanced vehicle inspection and maintenance programs. Such guidance shall include—

(i) a performance standard achievable by a program combining emission testing, including on-road emission testing, with inspection to detect tampering with emission control devices and misfueling for all light-duty vehicles and all light-duty trucks subject to standards under section 7521 of this title; and

(ii) program administration features necessary to reasonably assure that adequate management resources, tools, and practices are in place to attain and maintain the performance standard.

Compliance with the performance standard under clause (i) shall be determined using a method to be established by the Administrator.

(C) State program

The State program required under subparagraph (A) shall include, at a minimum, each of the following elements—

(i) Computerized emission analyzers, including on-road testing devices.

(ii) No waivers for vehicles and parts covered by the emission control performance warranty as provided for in section 7541(b) of this title unless a warranty remedy has been denied in writing, or for tampering-related repairs.

(iii) In view of the air quality purpose of the program, if, for any vehicle, waivers are permitted for emissions-related repairs not covered by warranty, an expenditure to qualify for the waiver of an amount of $450 or more for such repairs (adjusted annually as determined by the Administrator on the basis of the Consumer Price Index in the same manner as provided in subchapter V of this chapter.

(iv) Enforcement through denial of vehicle registration (except for any program in operation before November 15, 1990 whose enforcement mechanism is demonstrated to the Administrator to be more effective than the applicable vehicle registration program in assuring that noncomplying vehicles are not operated on public roads).

(v) Annual emission testing and necessary adjustment, repair, and maintenance, unless the State demonstrates to the satisfaction of the Administrator that a biennial inspection, in combination with other features of the program which exceed the requirements of this chapter, will result in emission reductions which equal or exceed the reductions which can be obtained through such annual inspections.

(vi) Operation of the program on a centralized basis, unless the State demonstrates to the satisfaction of the Administrator that a decentralized program will be equally effective. An electronically connected testing system, a licensing system, or other measures (or any combination thereof) may be considered, in accordance with criteria established by the Administrator, as equally effective for such purposes.

(vii) Inspection of emission control diagnostic systems and the maintenance or repair of malfunctions or system deterioration identified by or affecting such diagnostics systems.

Each State shall biennially prepare a report to the Administrator which assesses the emission reductions achieved by the program required under this paragraph based on data collected during inspection and repair of vehicles. The methods used to assess the emission reductions shall be those established by the Administrator.

(4) Clean-fuel vehicle programs

(A) Except to the extent that substitute provisions have been approved by the Administrator under subparagraph (B), the State shall submit to the Administrator, within 42 months of November 15, 1990, a revision to the applicable implementation plan for each area described under part C of subchapter II of this chapter to include such measures as may be necessary to ensure the effectiveness of the applicable provisions of the clean-fuel vehicle program prescribed under part C of subchapter II of this chapter, including all measures necessary to make the use of clean alternative fuels in clean-fuel vehicles (as defined in part C of subchapter II of this chapter) economic from the standpoint of vehicle owners. Such a revision shall also be submitted for each area that opts into the clean fuel-vehicle program as provided in part C of subchapter II of this chapter.

(B) The Administrator shall approve, as a substitute for all or a portion of the clean-fuel vehicle program prescribed under part C of subchapter II of this chapter, any revision to the relevant applicable implementation plan that in the Administrator's judgment will achieve long-term reductions in ozone-producing and toxic air emissions equal to those achieved under part C of subchapter II of this chapter, or the percentage thereof attributable to the portion of the clean-fuel vehicle program for which the revision is to substitute. The Administrator may approve such revision only if it consists exclusively of provisions other than those required under this chapter for the area. Any State seeking approval of such revision must submit the revision to the Administrator within 24 months of November 15, 1990. The Administrator shall approve or disapprove any such revision within 30 months of November 15, 1990. The Administrator shall publish the revision submitted by a State in the Federal Register upon receipt. Such notice shall constitute a notice of proposed rulemaking on whether or not to approve such revision and shall be deemed to comply with the requirements concerning notices of proposed rulemaking contained in sections 553 through 557 of Title 5 (related to notice and comment). Where the Administrator approves such revision for any area, the State need not submit the revision required by subparagraph (A) for the area with respect to the portions of the Federal clean-fuel vehicle program for which the Administrator has approved the revision as a substitute.

(C) If the Administrator determines, under section 7509 of this title, that the State has failed to submit any portion of the program required under subparagraph (A), then, in addition to any sanctions available under section 7509 of this title, the State may not receive credit, in any demonstration of attainment or reasonable further progress for the area, for any emission reductions from implementation of the corresponding aspects of the Federal clean-fuel vehicle requirements established in part C of subchapter II of this chapter.

(5) Transportation control

(A) Beginning 6 years after November 15, 1990 and each third year thereafter, the State shall submit a demonstration as to whether current aggregate vehicle mileage, aggregate vehicle emissions, congestion levels, and other relevant parameters are consistent with those used for the area's demonstration of attainment. Where such parameters and emissions levels exceed the levels projected for purposes of the area's attainment demonstration, the State shall within 18 months develop and submit a revision of the applicable implementation plan that includes a transportation control measures program consisting of measures from, but not limited to, section 7408(f) of this title that will reduce emissions to levels that are consistent with emission levels projected in such demonstration. In considering such measures, the State should ensure adequate access to downtown, other commercial, and residential areas and should avoid measures that increase or relocate emissions and congestion rather than reduce them. Such revision shall be developed in accordance with guidance issued by the Administrator pursuant to section 7408(e) of this title and with the requirements of section 7504(b) of this title and shall include implementation and funding schedules that achieve expeditious emissions reductions in accordance with implementation plan projections.

(6) De minimis rule

The new source review provisions under this part shall ensure that increased emissions of volatile organic compounds resulting from any physical change in, or change in the method of operation of, a stationary source located in the area shall not be considered de minimis for purposes of determining the applicability of the permit requirements established by this chapter unless the increase in net emissions of such air pollutant from such source does not exceed 25 tons when aggregated with all other net increases in emissions from the source over any period of 5 consecutive calendar years which includes the calendar year in which such increase occurred.

(7) Special rule for modifications of sources emitting less than 100 tons

In the case of any major stationary source of volatile organic compounds located in the area (other than a source which emits or has the potential to emit 100 tons or more of volatile organic compounds per year), whenever any change (as described in section 7411(a)(4) of this title) at that source results in any increase (other than a de minimis increase) in emissions of volatile organic compounds from any discrete operation, unit, or other pollutant emitting activity at the source, such increase shall be considered a modification for purposes of section 7502(c)(5) of this title and section 7503(a) of this title, except that such increase shall not be considered a modification for such purposes if the owner or operator of the source elects to offset the increase by a greater reduction in emissions of volatile organic compounds concerned from other operations, units, or activities within the source at an internal offset ratio of at least 1.3 to 1. If the owner or operator does not make such election, such change shall be considered a modification for such purposes, but in applying section 7503(a)(2) of this title in the case of any such modification, the best available control technology (BACT), as defined in section 7479 of this title, shall be substituted for the lowest achievable emission rate (LAER). The Administrator shall establish and publish policies and procedures for implementing the provisions of this paragraph.

(8) Special rule for modifications of sources emitting 100 tons or more

In the case of any major stationary source of volatile organic compounds located in the area which emits or has the potential to emit 100 tons or more of volatile organic compounds per year, whenever any change (as described in section 7411(a)(4) of this title) at that source results in any increase (other than a de minimis increase) in emissions of volatile organic compounds from any discrete operation, unit, or other pollutant emitting activity at the source, such increase shall be considered a modification for purposes of section 7502(c)(5) of this title and section 7503(a) of this title, except that if the owner or operator of the source elects to offset the increase by a greater reduction in emissions of volatile organic compounds from other operations, units, or activities within the source at an internal offset ratio of at least 1.3 to 1, the requirements of section 7503(a)(2) of this title (concerning the lowest achievable emission rate (LAER)) shall not apply.

(9) Contingency provisions

In addition to the contingency provisions required under section 7502(c)(9) of this title, the plan revision shall provide for the implementation of specific measures to be undertaken if the area fails to meet any applicable milestone. Such measures shall be included in the plan revision as contingency measures to take effect without further action by the State or the Administrator upon a failure by the State to meet the applicable milestone.

(10) General offset requirement

For purposes of satisfying the emission offset requirements of this part, the ratio of total emission reductions of volatile organic compounds to total increase emissions of such air pollutant shall be at least 1.2 to 1.

Any reference to "attainment date" in subsection (b) of this section, which is incorporated by reference into this subsection, shall refer to the attainment date for serious areas.

(d) Severe areas

Each State in which all or part of a Severe Area is located shall, with respect to the Severe Area, make the submissions described under subsection (c) of this section (relating to Serious Areas), and shall also submit the revisions to the applicable implementation plan (including the plan items) described under this subsection. For any Severe Area, the terms "major source" and "major stationary source" include (in addition to the sources described in section 7602 of this title) any stationary source or group of sources located within a contiguous area and under common control that emits, or has the potential to emit, at least 25 tons per year of volatile organic compounds.

(1) Vehicle miles traveled

(A) Within 2 years after November 15, 1990, the State shall submit a revision that identifies and adopts specific enforceable transportation control strategies and transportation control measures to offset any growth in emissions from growth in vehicle miles traveled or numbers of vehicle trips in such area and to attain reduction in motor vehicle emissions as necessary, in combination with other emission reduction requirements of this subpart, to comply with the requirements of subsection [1] (b)(2)(B) and (c)(2)(B) of this section (pertaining to periodic emissions reduction requirements). The State shall consider measures specified in section 7408(f) of this title, and choose from among and implement such measures as necessary to demonstrate attainment with the national ambient air quality standards; in considering such measures, the State should ensure adequate access to downtown, other commercial, and residential areas and should avoid measures that increase or relocate emissions and congestion rather than reduce them.

(B) The State may also, in its discretion, submit a revision at any time requiring employers in such area to implement programs to reduce work-related vehicle trips and miles travelled by employees. Such revision shall be developed in accordance with guidance issued by the Administrator pursuant to section 7408(f) of this title and may require that employers in such area increase average passenger occupancy per vehicle in commuting trips between home and the workplace during peak travel periods. The guidance of the Administrator may specify average vehicle occupancy rates which vary for locations within a nonattainment area (suburban, center city, business district) or among nonattainment areas reflecting existing occupancy rates and the availability of high occupancy modes. Any State required to submit a revision under this subparagraph (as in effect before December 23, 1995) containing provisions requiring employers to reduce work-related vehicle trips and miles travelled by employees may, in accordance with State law, remove such provisions from the implementation plan, or withdraw its submission, if the State notifies the Administrator, in writing, that the State has undertaken, or will undertake, one or more alternative methods that will achieve emission reductions equivalent to those to be achieved by the removed or withdrawn provisions.

(2) Offset requirement

For purposes of satisfying the offset requirements pursuant to this part, the ratio of total emission reductions of VOCs to total increased emissions of such air pollutant shall be at least 1.3 to 1, except that if the State plan requires all existing major sources in the nonattainment area to use best available control technology (as defined in section 7479(3) of this title) for the control of volatile organic compounds, the ratio shall be at least 1.2 to 1.

(3) Enforcement under section 7511d of this title

By December 31, 2000, the State shall submit a plan revision which includes the provisions required under section 7511d of this title.

Any reference to the term "attainment date" in subsection (b) or (c) of this section, which is incorporated by reference into this subsection (d), shall refer to the attainment date for Severe Areas.

(e) Extreme areas

Each State in which all or part of an Extreme Area is located shall, with respect to the Extreme Area, make the submissions described under subsection (d) of this section (relating to Severe Areas), and shall also submit the revisions to the applicable implementation plan (including the plan items) described under this subsection. The provisions of clause (ii) of subsection (c)(2)(B) of this section (relating to reductions of less than 3 percent), the provisions of paragraphs (6), (7) and (8) of subsection (c) of this section (relating to de minimus rule and modification of sources), and the provisions of clause (ii) of subsection (b)(1)(A) of this section (relating to reductions of less than 15 percent) shall not apply in the case of an Extreme Area. For any Extreme Area, the terms "major source" and "major stationary source" includes (in addition to the sources described in section 7602 of this title) any stationary source or group of sources located within a contiguous area and under common control that emits, or has the potential to emit, at least 10 tons per year of volatile organic compounds.

(1) Offset requirement

For purposes of satisfying the offset requirements pursuant to this part, the ratio of total emission reductions of VOCs to total increased emissions of such air pollutant shall be at least 1.5 to 1, except that if the State plan requires all existing major sources in the nonattainment area to use best available control technology (as defined in section 7479(3) of this title) for the control of volatile organic compounds, the ratio shall be at least 1.2 to 1.

(2) Modifications

Any change (as described in section 7411(a)(4) of this title) at a major stationary source which results in any increase in emissions from any discrete operation, unit, or other pollutant emitting activity at the source shall be considered a modification for purposes of section 7502(c)(5) and section 7503(a) of this title, except that for purposes of complying with the offset requirement pursuant to section 7503(a)(1) of this title, any such increase shall not be considered a modification if the owner or operator of the source elects to offset the increase by a greater reduction in emissions of the air pollutant concerned from other discrete operations, units, or activities within the source at an internal offset ratio of at least 1.3 to 1. The offset requirements of this part shall not be applicable in Extreme Areas to a modification of an existing source if such modification consists of installation of equipment required to comply with the applicable implementation plan, permit, or this chapter.

(3) Use of clean fuels or advanced control technology

For Extreme Areas, a plan revision shall be submitted within 3 years after November 15, 1990 to require, effective 8 years after such date, that each new, modified, and existing electric utility and industrial and commercial boiler which emits more than 25 tons per year of oxides of nitrogen—

(A) burn as its primary fuel natural gas, methanol, or ethanol (or a comparably low polluting fuel), or

(B) use advanced control technology (such as catalytic control technology or other comparably effective control methods) for reduction of emissions of oxides of nitrogen.

For purposes of this subsection, the term "primary fuel" means the fuel which is used 90 percent or more of the operating time. This paragraph shall not apply during any natural gas supply emergency (as defined in title III of the Natural Gas Policy Act of 1978 [15 U.S.C.A. § 3361 et seq.]).

(4) Traffic control measures during heavy traffic hours

For Extreme Areas, each implementation plan revision under this subsection may contain provisions establishing traffic control measures applicable during heavy traffic hours to reduce the use of high polluting vehicles or heavy-duty vehicles, notwithstanding any other provision of law.

(5) New technologies

The Administrator may, in accordance with section 7410 of this title, approve provisions of an implementation plan for an Extreme Area which anticipate development of new control techniques or improvement of existing control technologies, and an attainment demonstration based on such provisions, if the State demonstrates to the satisfaction of the Administrator that—

(A) such provisions are not necessary to achieve the incremental emission reductions required during the first 10 years after November 15, 1990; and

(B) the State has submitted enforceable commitments to develop and adopt contingency measures to be implemented as set forth herein if the anticipated technologies do not achieve planned reductions.

Such contingency measures shall be submitted to the Administrator no later than 3 years before proposed implementation of the plan provisions and approved or disapproved by the Administrator in accordance with section 7410 of this title. The contingency measures shall be adequate to produce emission reductions sufficient, in conjunction with other approved plan provisions, to achieve the periodic emission reductions required by subsection (b)(1) or (c)(2) of this section and attainment by the applicable dates. If the Administrator determines that an Extreme Area has failed to achieve an emission reduction requirement set forth in subsection (b)(1) or (c)(2) of this section, and that such failure is due in whole or part to an inability to fully implement provisions approved pursuant to this subsection, the Administrator shall require the State to implement the contingency measures to the extent necessary to assure compliance with subsections (b)(1) and (c)(2) of this section.

Any reference to the term "attainment date" in subsection (b), (c), or (d) of this section which is incorporated by reference into this subsection, shall refer to the attainment date for Extreme Areas.

(f) NO_x Requirements

(1) The plan provisions required under this subpart for major stationary sources of volatile organic compounds shall also apply to major stationary sources (as defined in section 7602 of this title and subsections (c), (d), and (e) of this section) of oxides of nitrogen. This subsection shall not apply in the case of oxides of nitrogen for those sources for which the Administrator determines (when the Administrator approves a plan or plan revision) that net air quality benefits are greater in the absence of reductions of oxides of nitrogen from the sources concerned. This subsection shall also not apply in the case of oxides of nitrogen for—

(A) nonattainment areas not within an ozone transport region under section 7511c of this title if the Administrator determines (when the Administrator approves a plan or plan revision) that additional reductions of oxides of nitrogen would not contribute to attainment of the national ambient air quality standard for ozone in the area, or

(B) nonattainment areas within such an ozone transport region if the Administrator determines (when the Administrator approves a plan or plan revision) that additional reductions of oxides of nitrogen would not produce net ozone air quality benefits in such region.

The Administrator shall, in the Administrator's determinations, consider the study required under section 7511f of this title.

(2)(A) If the Administrator determines that excess reductions in emissions of NO_x would be achieved under paragraph (1), the Administrator may limit the application of paragraph (1) to the extent necessary to avoid achieving such excess reductions.

(B) For purposes of this paragraph, excess reductions in emissions of NO_x are emission reductions for which the Administrator determines that net air quality benefits are greater in the absence of such reductions. Alternatively, for purposes of this paragraph, excess reductions in emissions of NO_x are, for—

(i) nonattainment areas not within an ozone transport region under section 7511c of this title, emission reductions that the Administrator determines would not contribute to attainment of the national ambient air quality standard for ozone in the area, or

(ii) nonattainment areas within such ozone transport region, emission reductions that the Administrator determines would not produce net ozone air quality benefits in such region.

(3) At any time after the final report under section 7511f of this title is submitted to Congress, a person may petition the Administrator for a determination under paragraph (1) or (2) with respect to any nonattainment area or any ozone transport region under section 7511c of this title. The Administrator shall grant or deny such petition within 6 months after its filing with the Administrator.

(g) Milestones

(1) Reductions in emissions

6 years after November 15, 1990 and at intervals of every 3 years thereafter, the State shall determine whether each nonattainment area (other than an area classified as Marginal or Moderate) has achieved a reduction in emissions during the preceding intervals equivalent to the total emission reductions required to be achieved by the end of such interval pursuant to subsection (b)(1) of this section and the corresponding requirements of subsections (c)(2)(B) and (C), (d), and (e) of this section. Such reduction shall be referred to in this section as an applicable milestone.

(2) Compliance demonstration

For each nonattainment area referred to in paragraph (1), not later than 90 days after the date on which an applicable milestone occurs (not including an attainment date on which a milestone occurs in cases where the standard has been attained), each State in which all or part of such area is located shall submit to the Administrator a demonstration that the milestone has been met. A demonstration under this paragraph shall be submitted in such form and manner, and shall contain such information and analysis, as the Administrator shall require, by rule. The Administrator shall determine whether or not a State's demonstration is adequate within 90 days after the Administrator's receipt of a demonstration which contains the information and analysis required by the Administrator.

(3) Serious and severe areas; state election

If a State fails to submit a demonstration under paragraph (2) for any Serious or Severe Area within the required period or if the Administrator determines that the area has not met any applicable milestone, the State shall elect, within 90 days after such failure or determination—

(A) to have the area reclassified to the next higher classification,

(B) to implement specific additional measures adequate, as determined by the Administrator, to meet the next milestone as provided in the applicable contingency plan, or

(C) to adopt an economic incentive program as described in paragraph (4).

If the State makes an election under subparagraph (B), the Administrator shall, within 90 days after the election, review such plan and shall, if the Administrator finds the contingency plan inadequate, require further measures necessary to meet such milestone. Once the State makes an election, it shall be deemed accepted by the Administrator as meeting the election requirement. If the State fails to make an election required under this paragraph within the required 90–day period or within 6 months thereafter, the area shall be reclassified to the next higher classification by operation of law at the expiration of such 6–month period. Within 12 months after the date required for the State to make an election, the State shall submit a revision of the applicable implementation plan for the area that meets the requirements of this paragraph. The Administrator shall review such plan revision and approve or disapprove the revision within 9 months after the date of its submission.

(4) Economic incentive program

(A) An economic incentive program under this paragraph shall be consistent with rules published by the Administrator and sufficient, in combination with other elements of the State plan, to achieve the next milestone. The State program may include a nondiscriminatory system, consistent with applicable law regarding interstate commerce, of State established emissions fees or a system of marketable permits, or a system of State fees on sale or manufacture of products the use of which contributes to ozone formation, or any combination of the foregoing or other similar measures. The program may also include incentives and requirements to reduce vehicle emissions and vehicle miles traveled in the area, including any of the transportation control measures identified in section 7408(f) of this title.

(B) Within 2 years after November 15, 1990, the Administrator shall publish rules for the programs to be adopted pursuant to subparagraph (A). Such rules shall include model plan provisions which may be adopted for reducing emissions from permitted stationary sources, area sources, and mobile sources. The guidelines shall require that any revenues generated by the plan provisions adopted pursuant to subparagraph (A) shall be used by the State for any of the following:

(i) Providing incentives for achieving emission reductions.

(ii) Providing assistance for the development of innovative technologies for the control of ozone air pollution and for the development of lower-polluting solvents and surface coatings. Such assistance shall not provide for the payment of more than 75 percent of either the costs of any project to develop such a technology or the costs of development of a lower-polluting solvent or surface coating.

(iii) Funding the administrative costs of State programs under this chapter. Not more than 50 percent of such revenues may be used for purposes of this clause.

(5) Extreme areas

If a State fails to submit a demonstration under paragraph (2) for any Extreme Area within the required period, or if the Administrator determines that the area has not met any applicable milestone, the State shall, within 9 months after such failure or determination, submit a plan revision to implement an economic incentive program which meets the requirements of paragraph (4). The Administrator shall review such plan revision and approve or disapprove the revision within 9 months after the date of its submission.

(h) Rural transport areas

(1) Notwithstanding any other provision of section 7511 of this title or this section, a State containing an ozone nonattainment area that does not include, and is not adjacent to, any part of a Metropolitan Statistical Area or, where one exists, a Consolidated Metropolitan Statistical Area (as defined by the United States Bureau of the Census), which area is treated by the Administrator, in the Administrator's discretion, as a rural transport area within the meaning of paragraph (2), shall be treated by operation of law as satisfying the requirements of this section if it makes the submissions required under subsection (a) of this section (relating to marginal areas).

(2) The Administrator may treat an ozone nonattainment area as a rural transport area if the Administrator finds that sources of VOC (and, where the Administrator determines relevant, NO_x) emissions within the area do not make a significant contribution to the ozone concentrations measured in the area or in other areas.

(i) Reclassified areas

Each State containing an ozone nonattainment area reclassified under section 7511(b)(2) of this title shall meet such requirements of subsections (b) through (d) of this section as may be applicable to the area as reclassified, according to the schedules prescribed in connection with such requirements, except that the Administrator may adjust any applicable deadlines (other than attainment dates) to the extent such adjustment is necessary or appropriate to assure consistency among the required submissions.

(j) Multi-State ozone nonattainment areas

(1) Coordination among States

Each State in which there is located a portion of a single ozone nonattainment area which covers more than one State (hereinafter in this section referred to as a "multi-State ozone nonattainment area") shall—

(A) take all reasonable steps to coordinate, substantively and procedurally, the revisions and implementation of State implementation plans applicable to the nonattainment area concerned; and

(B) use photochemical grid modeling or any other analytical method determined by the Administrator, in his discretion, to be at least as effective.

The Administrator may not approve any revision of a State implementation plan submitted under this part for a State in which part of a multi-State ozone nonattainment area is located if the plan revision for that State fails to comply with the requirements of this subsection.

(2) Failure to demonstrate attainment

If any State in which there is located a portion of a multi-State ozone nonattainment area fails to provide a demonstration of attainment of the national ambient air quality standard for ozone in that portion within the required period, the State may petition the Administrator to make a finding that the State would have been able to make such demonstration but for the failure of one or more other States in which other portions of the area are located to commit to the implementation of all measures required under this section (relating to plan submissions and requirements for ozone nonattainment areas). If the Administrator makes such finding, the provisions of section 7509 of this title (relating to sanctions) shall not apply, by reason of the failure to make such demonstration, in the portion of the multi-State ozone nonattainment area within the State submitting such petition.

(July 14, 1955, ch. 360, title I, § 182, as added Nov. 15, 1990, Pub.L. 101–549, title I, § 103, 104 Stat. 2426, and amended Dec. 23, 1995, Pub.L. 104–70, § 1, 109 Stat. 773.)

[1] The term "subsection" in subsec. (d)(1)(A) of this section probably should read "subsections".

References in Text

The Natural Gas Policy Act of 1978, referred to in subsec. (e), the last sentence, is Pub.L. 95–621, Nov. 9, 1978, 92 Stat. 3350, as amended. Title III of the Natural Gas Policy Act of 1978 is classified to subchapter III (section 3361 et seq.) of chapter 60 of Title 15, Commerce and Trade. For complete classification of this Act to the Code, see Short Title note set out under section 3301 of Title 15 and Tables.

Effective Date

Section to take effect Nov. 15, 1990, except as otherwise provided, see section 711(b) of Pub.L. 101–549, set out as a note under section 7401 of this title.

Savings Provisions

Suits, actions or proceedings commenced under this chapter as in effect prior to Nov. 15, 1990, not to abate by reason of the taking effect of amendments by Pub.L. 101–549, except as otherwise provided for, see section 711(a) of Pub.L. 101–549, set out as a note under section 7401 of this title.

Moratorium on Certain Emissions Testing Requirements

Pub.L. 104–59, Title III, § 348, Nov. 28, 1995, 109 Stat. 617, provided that:

"**(a) In general.**—The Administrator of the Environmental Protection Agency (hereinafter in this section referred to as the 'Administrator') shall not require adoption or implementation by a State of a test-only I/M240 enhanced vehicle inspection and maintenance program as a means of compliance with section 182 or 187 of the Clean Air Act (42 U.S.C. 7511a; 7512a), but the Administrator may approve such a program if a State chooses to adopt the program as a means of compliance with such section.

"**(b) Limitation on plan disapproval.**—The Administrator shall not disapprove or apply an automatic discount to a State implementation plan revision under section 182 or 187 of the Clean Air Act (42 U.S.C. 7511a; 7512a) on the basis of a policy, regulation, or guidance providing for a discount of emissions credits because the inspection and maintenance program in such plan revision is decentralized or a test-and-repair program.

"**(c) Emissions reduction credits.**—

"**(1) State plan revision; approval.**—Within 120 days of the date of the enactment of this subsection [Nov. 28, 1995], a State may submit an implementation plan revision proposing an interim inspection and maintenance program under section 182 or 187 of the Clean Air Act (42 U.S.C. 7511a; 7512a). The Administrator shall approve the program based on the full amount of credits proposed by the State for each element of the program if the proposed credits reflect good faith estimates by the State and the revision is otherwise in compliance with such Act [this chapter]. If, within such 120-day period, the State submits to the Administrator proposed revisions to the implementation plan, has all of the statutory authority necessary to implement the revisions, and has proposed a regulation to make the revisions, the Administrator may approve the revisions without regard to whether or not such regulation has been issued as a final regulation by the State.

"(2) **Expiration of interim approval.**—The interim approval shall expire on the earlier of (A) the last day of the 18–month period beginning on the date of the interim approval, or (B) the date of final approval. The interim approval may not be extended.

"(3) **Final approval.**—The Administrator shall grant final approval of the revision based on the credits proposed by the State during or after the period of interim approval if data collected on the operation of the State program demonstrates that the credits are appropriate and the revision is otherwise in compliance with the Clean Air Act [this chapter].

"(4) **Basis of approval; no automatic discount.**—Any determination with respect to interim or full approval shall be based on the elements of the program and shall not apply any automatic discount because the program is decentralized or a test-and-repair program."

§ 7511b. Federal ozone measures [CAA § 183]

(a) Control techniques guidelines for VOC sources

Within 3 years after November 15, 1990, the Administrator shall issue control techniques guidelines, in accordance with section 7408 of this title, for 11 categories of stationary sources of VOC emissions for which such guidelines have not been issued as of November 15, 1990, not including the categories referred to in paragraphs (3) and (4) of subsection (b) of this section. The Administrator may issue such additional control techniques guidelines as the Administrator deems necessary.

(b) Existing and new CTGS

(1) Within 36 months after November 15, 1990, and periodically thereafter, the Administrator shall review and, if necessary, update control technique guidance issued under section 7408 of this title before November 15, 1990.

(2) In issuing the guidelines the Administrator shall give priority to those categories which the Administrator considers to make the most significant contribution to the formation of ozone air pollution in ozone nonattainment areas, including hazardous waste treatment, storage, and disposal facilities which are permitted under subtitle C of the Solid Waste Disposal Act [42 U.S.C.A. § 6921 et seq.]. Thereafter the Administrator shall periodically review and, if necessary, revise such guidelines.

(3) Within 3 years after November 15, 1990, the Administrator shall issue control techniques guidelines in accordance with section 7408 of this title to reduce the aggregate emissions of volatile organic compounds into the ambient air from aerospace coatings and solvents. Such control techniques guidelines shall, at a minimum, be adequate to reduce aggregate emissions of volatile organic compounds into the ambient air from the application of such coatings and solvents to such level as the Administrator determines may be achieved through the adoption of best available control measures. Such control technology guidance shall provide for such reductions in such increments and on such schedules as the Administrator determines to be reasonable, but in no event later than 10 years after the final issuance of such control technology guidance. In developing control technology guidance under this subsection, the Administrator shall consult with the Secretary of Defense, the Secretary of Transportation, and the Administrator of the National Aeronautics and Space Administration with regard to the establishment of specifications for such coatings. In evaluating VOC reduction strategies, the guidance shall take into account the applicable requirements of section 7412 of this title and the need to protect stratospheric ozone.

(4) Within 3 years after November 15, 1990, the Administrator shall issue control techniques guidelines in accordance with section 7408 of this title to reduce the aggregate emissions of volatile organic compounds and PM–10 into the ambient air from paints, coatings, and solvents used in shipbuilding operations and ship repair. Such control techniques guidelines shall, at a minimum, be adequate to reduce aggregate emissions of volatile organic compounds and PM–10 into the ambient air from the removal or application of such paints, coatings, and solvents to such level as the Administrator determines may be achieved through the adoption of the best available control measures. Such control techniques guidelines shall provide for such reductions in such increments and on such schedules as the Administrator determines to be reasonable, but in no event later than 10 years after the final issuance of such control technology guidance. In developing control techniques guidelines under this subsection, the Administrator shall consult with the appropriate Federal agencies.

(c) Alternative control techniques

Within 3 years after November 15, 1990, the Administrator shall issue technical documents which identify alternative controls for all categories of stationary sources of volatile organic compounds and oxides of nitrogen which emit, or have the potential to emit 25 tons per year or more of such air pollutant. The Administrator shall revise and update such documents as the Administrator determines necessary.

(d) Guidance for evaluating cost-effectiveness

Within 1 year after November 15, 1990, the Administrator shall provide guidance to the States to be used in evaluating the relative cost-effectiveness of various options for the control of emissions from existing stationary sources of air pollutants which contribute to nonattainment of the national ambient air quality standards for ozone.

(e) Control of emissions from certain sources

(1) Definitions

For purposes of this subsection—

(A) Best available controls

The term "best available controls" means the degree of emissions reduction that the Administrator determines, on the basis of technological and economic feasibility, health, environmental, and energy impacts, is achievable through the application of the most effective equipment, measures, processes, methods, systems or techniques, including chemical reformulation, product or feedstock substitution, repackaging, and directions for use, consumption, storage, or disposal.

(B) Consumer or commercial product

The term "consumer or commercial product" means any substance, product (including paints, coatings, and solvents), or article (including any container or packaging) held by any person, the use, consumption, storage, disposal, destruction, or decomposition of which may result in the release of volatile organic compounds. The term does not include fuels or fuel additives regulated under section 7545 of this title, or motor vehicles, non-road vehicles, and non-road engines as defined under section 7550 of this title.

(C) Regulated entities

The term "regulated entities" means—

(i) manufacturers, processors, wholesale distributors, or importers of consumer or commercial products for sale or distribution in interstate commerce in the United States; or

(ii) manufacturers, processors, wholesale distributors, or importers that supply the entities listed under clause (i) with such products for sale or distribution in interstate commerce in the United States.

(2) Study and report

(A) Study

The Administrator shall conduct a study of the emissions of volatile organic compounds into the ambient air from consumer and commercial products (or any combination thereof) in order to—

(i) determine their potential to contribute to ozone levels which violate the national ambient air quality standard for ozone; and

(ii) establish criteria for regulating consumer and commercial products or classes or categories thereof which shall be subject to control under this subsection.

The study shall be completed and a report submitted to Congress not later than 3 years after November 15, 1990.

(B) Consideration of certain factors

In establishing the criteria under subparagraph (A)(ii), the Administrator shall take into consideration each of the following:

(i) The uses, benefits, and commercial demand of consumer and commercial products.

(ii) The health or safety functions (if any) served by such consumer and commercial products.

(iii) Those consumer and commercial products which emit highly reactive volatile organic compounds into the ambient air.

(iv) Those consumer and commercial products which are subject to the most cost-effective controls.

(v) The availability of alternatives (if any) to such consumer and commercial products which are of comparable costs, considering health, safety, and environmental impacts.

(3) Regulations to require emission reductions

(A) In general

Upon submission of the final report under paragraph (2), the Administrator shall list those categories of consumer or commercial products that the Administrator determines, based on the study, account for at least 80 percent of the VOC emissions, on a reactivity-adjusted basis, from consumer or commercial products in areas that violate the NAAQS for ozone. Credit toward the 80 percent emissions calculation shall be given for emission reductions from consumer or commercial products made after November 15, 1990. At such time, the Administrator shall divide the list into 4 groups establishing priorities for regulation based on the criteria established in paragraph (2). Every 2 years after promulgating such list, the Administrator shall regulate one group of categories until all 4 groups are regulated. The regulations shall require best available controls as defined in this section. Such regulations may exempt health use products for which the Administrator determines there is no suitable substitute. In order to carry out this section, the Administrator may, by regulation, control or prohibit any activity, including the manufacture or introduction into commerce, offering for sale, or sale of any consumer or commercial product which results in emission of volatile organic compounds into the ambient air.

(B) Regulated entities

Regulations under this subsection may be imposed only with respect to regulated entities.

(C) Use of CTGS

For any consumer or commercial product the Administrator may issue control techniques guidelines under this chapter in lieu of regulations required under subparagraph (A) if the Administrator determines that such guidance will be substantially as effective as regulations in reducing emissions of volatile organic compounds which contribute to ozone levels in areas which violate the national ambient air quality standard for ozone.

(4) Systems of regulation

The regulations under this subsection may include any system or systems of regulation as the Administrator may deem appropriate, including requirements for registration and labeling, self-monitoring and reporting, prohibitions, limitations, or economic incentives (including marketable permits and auctions of emissions rights) concerning the manufacture, processing, distribution, use, consumption, or disposal of the product.

(5) Special fund

Any amounts collected by the Administrator under such regulations shall be deposited in a special fund in the United States Treasury for licensing and other services, which thereafter shall be available until expended, subject to annual appropriation Acts, solely to carry out the activities of the Administrator for which such fees, charges, or collections are established or made.

(6) Enforcement

Any regulation established under this subsection shall be treated, for purposes of enforcement of this chapter, as a standard under section 7411 of this title and any violation of such regulation shall be treated as a violation of a requirement of section 7411(e) of this title.

(7) State administration

Each State may develop and submit to the Administrator a procedure under State law for implementing and enforcing regulations promulgated under this subsection. If the Administrator finds the State procedure is adequate, the Administrator shall approve such procedure. Nothing in this paragraph shall prohibit the Administrator from enforcing any applicable regulations under this subsection.

(8) Size, etc.

No regulations regarding the size, shape, or labeling of a product may be promulgated, unless the Administrator determines such regulations to be useful in meeting any national ambient air quality standard.

(9) State consultation

Any State which proposes regulations other than those adopted under this subsection shall consult with the Administrator regarding whether any other State or local subdivision has promulgated or is promulgating regulations on any products covered under this part. The Administrator shall establish a clearinghouse of information, studies, and regulations proposed and promulgated regarding products covered under this subsection and disseminate such information collected as requested by State or local subdivisions.

(f) Tank vessel standards

(1) Schedule for standards

(A) Within 2 years after November 15, 1990, the Administrator, in consultation with the Secretary of the Department in which the Coast Guard is operating, shall promulgate standards applicable to the emission of VOCs and any other air pollutant from loading and unloading of tank vessels (as that term is defined in section 2101 of Title 46) which the Administrator finds causes, or contributes to, air pollution that may be reasonably anticipated to endanger public health or welfare. Such standards shall require the application of reasonably available control technology, considering costs, any nonair-quality benefits, environmental impacts, energy requirements and safety factors associated with alternative control techniques. To the extent practicable such standards shall apply to loading and unloading facilities and not to tank vessels.

(B) Any regulation prescribed under this subsection (and any revision thereof) shall take effect after such period as the Administrator finds (after consultation with the Secretary of the department in which the Coast Guard is operating) necessary to permit the development and application of the requisite technology, giving appropriate consideration to the cost of compliance within such period, except that the effective date shall not be more than 2 years after promulgation of such regulations.

(2) Regulations on equipment safety

Within 6 months after November 15, 1990, the Secretary of the Department in which the Coast Guard is operating shall issue regulations to ensure the safety of the equipment and operations which are to control emissions from the loading and unloading of tank vessels, under section 3703 of Title 46 and section 1225 of Title 33. The standards promulgated by the Administrator under paragraph (1) and the regulations issued by a State or political subdivision regarding emissions from the loading and unloading of tank vessels shall be consistent with the regulations regarding safety of the Department in which the Coast Guard is operating.

(3) Agency authority

(A) The Administrator shall ensure compliance with the tank vessel emission standards prescribed under paragraph (1)(A). The Secretary of the Department in which the Coast Guard is operating shall also ensure compliance with the tank vessel standards prescribed under paragraph (1)(A).

(B) The Secretary of the Department in which the Coast Guard is operating shall ensure compliance with the regulations issued under paragraph (2).

(4) State or local standards

After the Administrator promulgates standards under this section, no State or political subdivision thereof may adopt or attempt to enforce any standard respecting emissions from tank vessels subject to regulation under paragraph (1) unless such standard is no less stringent than the standards promulgated under paragraph (1).

(5) Enforcement

Any standard established under paragraph (1)(A) shall be treated, for purposes of enforcement of this chapter, as a standard under section 7411 of this title and any violation of such standard shall be treated as a violation of a requirement of section 7411(e) of this title.

(g) Ozone design value study

The Administrator shall conduct a study of whether the methodology in use by the Environmental Protection Agency as of November 15, 1990 for establishing a design value for ozone provides a reasonable indicator of the ozone air quality of ozone nonattainment areas. The Administrator shall obtain input from States, local subdivisions thereof, and others. The study shall be completed and a report submitted to Congress not later than 3 years after November 15, 1990. The results of the study shall be subject to peer and public review before submitting it to Congress.

(July 14, 1955, ch. 360, title I, § 183, as added Nov. 15, 1990, Pub.L. 101–549, title I, § 103, 104 Stat. 2443.)

References in Text

The Solid Waste Disposal Act, referred to in subsec. (b)(2), is Title II of Pub.L. 89–272, Oct. 20, 1965, 79 Stat. 997, as amended generally by Pub.L. 94–580, § 2, Oct. 21, 1976, 90 Stat. 2795. Subtitle C of the Solid Waste Disposal Act is classified generally to subchapter III (section 6921 et seq.) of chapter 82 of this title. For complete classification of this Act to the Code, see Short Title note set out under section 6901 of this title and Tables volume.

Effective Date

Section to take effect Nov. 15, 1990, except as otherwise provided, see section 711(b) of Pub.L. 101–549, set out as a note under section 7401 of this title.

Savings Provisions

Suits, actions or proceedings commenced under this chapter as in effect prior to Nov. 15, 1990, not to abate by reason of the taking effect of amendments by Pub.L. 101–549, except as otherwise provided for, see section 711(a) of Pub.L. 101–549, set out as a note under section 7401 of this title.

§ 7511c. Control of interstate ozone air pollution [CAA § 184]

(a) Ozone transport regions

A single transport region for ozone (within the meaning of section 7506a(a) of this title), comprised of the States of Connecticut, Delaware, Maine, Maryland, Massachusetts, New Hampshire, New Jersey, New York, Pennsylvania, Rhode Island, Vermont, and the Consolidated Metropolitan Statistical Area that includes the District of Columbia, is hereby established by operation of law. The provisions of section 7506a(a)(1) and (2) of this title shall apply with respect to the transport region established under this section and any other transport region established for ozone, except to the extent inconsistent with the provisions of this section. The Administrator shall convene the commission required (under section 7506a(b) of this title) as a result of the establishment of such region within 6 months of November 15, 1990.

(b) Plan provisions for States in ozone transport regions

(1) In accordance with section 7410 of this title, not later than 2 years after November 15, 1990 (or 9 months after the subsequent inclusion of a State in a transport region established for ozone), each State included within a transport region established for ozone shall submit a State implementation plan or revision thereof to the Administrator which requires the following—

(A) that each area in such State that is in an ozone transport region, and that is a metropolitan statistical area or part thereof with a population of 100,000 or more comply with the provisions of section 7511a(c)(2)(A) of this title (pertaining to enhanced vehicle inspection and maintenance programs); and

(B) implementation of reasonably available control technology with respect to all sources of volatile organic compounds in the State covered by a control techniques guideline issued before or after November 15, 1990.

(2) Within 3 years after November 15, 1990, the Administrator shall complete a study identifying control measures capable of achieving emission reductions comparable to those achievable through vehicle refueling controls contained in section 7511a(b)(3) of this title, and such measures or such vehicle refueling controls shall be implemented in accordance with the provisions of this section. Notwithstanding other deadlines in this section, the applicable implementation plan shall be revised to reflect such measures within 1 year of completion of the study. For purposes of this section any stationary source that emits or has the potential to emit at least 50 tons per year of volatile organic compounds shall be considered a major stationary source and subject to the requirements which would be applicable to major stationary sources if the area were classified as a Moderate nonattainment area.

(c) Additional control measures

(1) Recommendations

Upon petition of any State within a transport region established for ozone, and based on a majority vote of the Governors on the Commission (or their designees), the Commission may, after notice and opportunity for public comment, develop recommendations for additional control measures to be applied within all or a part of such transport region if the commission determines such measures are necessary to bring any area in such region into attainment by the dates provided by this subpart. The commission shall transmit such recommendations to the Administrator.

(2) Notice and review

Whenever the Administrator receives recommendations prepared by a commission pursuant to paragraph (1) (the date of receipt of which shall hereinafter in this section be referred to as the "receipt date"), the Administrator shall—

(A) immediately publish in the Federal Register a notice stating that the recommendations are available and provide an opportunity for public hearing within 90 days beginning on the receipt date; and

(B) commence a review of the recommendations to determine whether the control measures in the recommendations are necessary to bring any area in such region into attainment by the dates provided by this subpart and are otherwise consistent with this chapter.

(3) Consultation

In undertaking the review required under paragraph (2)(B), the Administrator shall consult with members of the commission of the affected States and shall take into account the data, views, and comments received pursuant to paragraph (2)(A).

(4) Approval and disapproval

Within 9 months after the receipt date, the Administrator shall (A) determine whether to approve, disapprove, or partially disapprove and partially approve the recommendations; (B) notify the commission in writing of such approval, disapproval, or partial disapproval; and (C) publish such determination in the Federal Register. If the Administrator disapproves or partially disapproves the recommendations, the Administrator shall specify—

(i) why any disapproved additional control measures are not necessary to bring any area in such region into attainment by the dates provided by this subpart or are otherwise not consistent with the chapter; and

(ii) recommendations concerning equal or more effective actions that could be taken by the commission to conform the disapproved portion of the recommendations to the requirements of this section.

(5) Finding

Upon approval or partial approval of recommendations submitted by a commission, the Administrator shall issue to each State which is included in the transport region and to which a requirement of the approved plan applies, a finding under section 7410(k)(5) of this title that the implementation plan for such State is inadequate to meet the requirements of section 7410(a)(2)(D) of this title. Such finding shall require each such State to revise its implementation plan to include the approved additional control measures within one year after the finding is issued.

(d) Best available air quality monitoring and modeling

For purposes of this section, not later than 6 months after November 15, 1990, the Administrator shall promulgate criteria for purposes of determining the contribution of sources in one area to concentrations of ozone in another area which is a nonattainment area for ozone. Such criteria shall require that the best available air quality monitoring and modeling techniques be used for purposes of making such determinations.

(July 14, 1955, ch. 360, title I, § 184, as added Nov. 15, 1990, Pub.L. 101–549, title I, § 103, 104 Stat. 2448.)

Effective Date

Section to take effect Nov. 15, 1990, except as otherwise provided, see section 711(b) of Pub.L. 101–549, set out as a note under section 7401 of this title.

Savings Provisions

Suits, actions or proceedings commenced under this chapter as in effect prior to Nov. 15, 1990, not to abate by reason of the taking effect of amendments by Pub.L. 101–549, except as otherwise provided for, see section 711(a) of Pub.L. 101–549, set out as a note under section 7401 of this title.

§ 7511d. Enforcement for severe and extreme ozone non-attainment areas for failure to attain [CAA § 185]

(a) General rule

Each implementation plan revision required under section 7511a(d) and (e) of this title (relating to the attainment plan for Severe and Extreme ozone nonattainment areas) shall provide that, if the area to which such plan revision applies has failed to attain the national primary ambient air quality standard for ozone by the applicable attainment date, each major stationary source of VOCs located in the area shall, except as otherwise provided under subsection (c) of this section, pay a fee to the State as a penalty for such failure, computed in accordance with subsection (b) of this section, for each calendar year beginning after the attainment date, until the area is redesignated as an attainment area for ozone. Each such plan revision should include procedures for assessment and collection of such fees.

(b) Computation of fee

(1) Fee amount

The fee shall equal $5,000, adjusted in accordance with paragraph (3), per ton of VOC emitted by the source during the calendar year in excess of 80 percent of the baseline amount, computed under paragraph (2).

(2) Baseline amount

For purposes of this section, the baseline amount shall be computed, in accordance with such guidance as the Administrator may provide, as the lower of the amount of actual VOC emissions ("actuals") or VOC emissions allowed under the permit applicable to the source (or, if no such permit has been issued for the attainment year, the amount of VOC emissions allowed under the applicable implementation plan ("allowables")) during the attainment year. Notwithstanding the preceding sentence, the Administrator may issue guidance authorizing the baseline amount to be determined in accordance with the lower of average actuals or average allowables, determined over a period of more than one calendar year. Such guidance may provide that such average calculation for a specific source may be used if that source's emissions are irregular, cyclical, or otherwise vary significantly from year to year.

(3) Annual adjustment

The fee amount under paragraph (1) shall be adjusted annually, beginning in the year beginning after 1990, in accordance with section 7661a(b)(3)(B)(v) of this title (relating to inflation adjustment).

(c) Exception

Notwithstanding any provision of this section, no source shall be required to pay any fee under subsection (a) of this title with respect to emissions during any year that is treated as an Extension Year under section 7511(a)(5) of this title.

(d) Fee collection by the Administrator

If the Administrator has found that the fee provisions of the implementation plan do not meet the requirements of this section, or if the Administrator makes a finding that the State is not administering and enforcing the fee required under this section, the Administrator shall, in addition to any other action authorized under this subchapter, collect, in accordance with procedures promulgated by the Administrator, the unpaid fees required under subsection (a) of this section. If the Administrator makes such a finding under section 7509(a)(4) of this title, the Administrator may collect fees for periods before the determination, plus interest computed in accordance with section 6621(a)(2) of Title 26 (relating to computation of interest on underpayment of Federal taxes), to the extent the Administrator finds such fees have not been paid to the State. The provisions of clauses (ii) through (iii) of section 7661a(b)(3)(C) of this title (relating to penalties and use of the funds, respectively) shall apply with respect to fees collected under this subsection.

(e) Exemptions for certain small areas

For areas with a total population under 200,000 which fail to attain the standard by the applicable attainment date, no sanction under this section or under any other provision of this chapter shall apply if the area can demonstrate, consistent with guidance issued by the Administrator, that attainment in the area is prevented because of ozone or ozone precursors transported from other areas. The prohibition applies only in cases in which the area has met all requirements and implemented all measures applicable to the area under this chapter.

(July 14, 1955, ch. 360, title I, § 185, as added Nov. 15, 1990, Pub.L. 101–549, title I, § 103, 104 Stat. 2450.)

Effective Date

Section to take effect Nov. 15, 1990, except as otherwise provided, see section 711(b) of Pub.L. 101–549, set out as a note under section 7401 of this title.

Savings Provisions

Suits, actions or proceedings commenced under this chapter as in effect prior to Nov. 15, 1990, not to abate by reason of the taking effect of amendments by Pub.L. 101–549, except as otherwise provided for, see section 711(a) of Pub.L. 101–549, set out as a note under section 7401 of this title.

§ 7511e. Transitional areas [CAA § 185A]

If an area designated as an ozone nonattainment area as of November 15, 1990 has not violated the national primary ambient air quality standard for ozone for the 36–month period commencing on January 1, 1987, and ending on December 31, 1989, the Administrator shall suspend the application of the requirements of this subpart to such area until December 31, 1991. By June 30, 1992, the Administrator shall determine by order, based on the area's design value as of the attainment date, whether the area attained such standard by December 31, 1991. If the Administrator determines that the area attained the standard, the Administrator shall require, as part of the order, the State to submit a maintenance plan for the area within 12 months of such determination. If the Administrator determines that the area failed to attain the standard, the Administrator shall, by June 30, 1992, designate the area as nonattainment under section 7407(d)(4) of this title.

(July 14, 1990, ch. 360, title I, § 185A, as added Nov. 15, 1990, Pub.L. 101–549, title I, § 103, 104 Stat. 2451.)

Effective Date

Section to take effect Nov. 15, 1990, except as otherwise provided, see section 711(b) of Pub.L. 101–549, set out as a note under section 7401 of this title.

Savings Provisions

Suits, actions or proceedings commenced under this chapter as in effect prior to Nov. 15, 1990, not to abate by reason of the taking effect of amendments by Pub.L. 101–549, except as otherwise provided for, see section 711(a) of Pub.L. 101–549, set out as a note under section 7401 of this title.

§ 7511f. NO_x and VOC study [CAA § 185B]

The Administrator, in conjunction with the National Academy of Sciences, shall conduct a study on the role of ozone precursors in tropospheric ozone formation and control. The study shall examine the roles of NO_x and VOC emission reductions, the extent to which NO_x reductions may contribute (or be counterproductive) to achievement of attainment in different nonattainment areas, the sensitivity of ozone to the control of NO_x, the availability and extent of controls for NO_x, the role of biogenic VOC emissions, and the basic information required for air quality models. The study shall be completed and a proposed report made public for 30 days comment within 1 year of November 15, 1990, and a final report shall be submitted to Congress within 15 months after November 15, 1990. The Administrator shall utilize all available information and studies, as well as develop additional information, in conducting the study required by this section.

(July 14, 1955, ch. 360, title I, § 185B, as added Nov. 15, 1990, Pub.L. 101–549, title I, § 103, 104 Stat. 2452.)

Effective Date

Section to take effect Nov. 15, 1990, except as otherwise provided, see section 711(b) of Pub.L. 101–549, set out as a note under section 7401 of this title.

Savings Provisions

Suits, actions or proceedings commenced under this chapter as in effect prior to Nov. 15, 1990, not to abate by reason of the taking effect of amendments by Pub.L. 101–549, except as otherwise provided for, see section 711(a) of Pub.L. 101–549, set out as a note under section 7401 of this title.

Subpart 3—Additional Provisions for Carbon Monoxide Nonattainment Areas

§ 7512. Classification and attainment dates [CAA § 186]

(a) Classification by operation of law and attainment dates for nonattainment areas

(1) Each area designated nonattainment for carbon monoxide pursuant to section 7407(d) of this title shall be classified at the time of such designation under table 1, by operation of law, as a Moderate Area or a Serious Area based on the design value for the area. The design value shall be calculated according to the interpretation methodology issued by the Administrator most recently before November 15, 1990. For each area classified under this subsection, the primary standard attainment date for carbon monoxide shall be as expeditiously as practicable but not later than the date provided in table 1:

TABLE 3

Area classification	Design value	Primary standard attainment date
Moderate	9.1–16.4 ppm	December 31, 1995
Serious	16.5 and above	December 31, 2000

(2) At the time of publication of the notice required under section 7407 of this title (designating carbon monoxide nonattainment areas), the Administrator shall publish a notice announcing the classification of each such carbon monoxide nonattainment area. The provisions of section 7502(a)(1)(B) of this title (relating to lack of notice-and-comment and judicial review) shall apply with respect to such classification.

(3) If an area classified under paragraph (1), table 1, would have been classified in another category if the design value in the area were 5 percent greater or 5 percent less than the level on which such classification was based, the Administrator may, in the Administrator's discretion, within 90 days after November 15, 1990 by the procedure required under paragraph (2), adjust the classification of the area. In making such adjustment, the Administrator may consider the number of exceedances of the national primary ambient air quality standard for carbon monoxide in the area, the level of pollution transport between the area and the other affected areas, and the mix of sources and air pollutants in the area. The Administrator may make the same adjustment for purposes of paragraphs (2), (3), (6), and (7) of section 7512a(a) of this title.

(4) Upon application by any State, the Administrator may extend for 1 additional year (hereinafter in this subpart referred to as the "Extension Year") the date specified in table 1 of subsection (a) of this section if—

(A) the State has complied with all requirements and commitments pertaining to the area in the applicable implementation plan, and

(B) no more than one exceedance of the national ambient air quality standard level for carbon monoxide has occurred in the area in the year preceding the Extension Year.

No more than 2 one-year extensions may be issued under this paragraph for a single nonattainment area.

(b) New designations and reclassifications

(1) New designations to nonattainment

Any area that is designated attainment or unclassifiable for carbon monoxide under section 7407(d)(4) of this title, and that is subsequently redesignated to nonattainment for carbon monoxide under section 7407(d)(3) of this title, shall, at the time of the redesignation, be classified by operation of law in accordance with table 1 under subsections (a)(1) and (a)(4) of this section. Upon its classification, the area shall be subject to the same requirements under section 7410 of this title, subpart 1 of this part, and this subpart that would have applied had the area been so classified at the time of the notice under subsection (a)(2) of this section, except that any absolute, fixed date applicable in connection with any such requirement is extended by operation of law by a period equal to the length of time between November 15, 1990 and the date the area is classified.

(2) Reclassification of moderate areas upon failure to attain

(A) General rule

Within 6 months following the applicable attainment date for a carbon monoxide nonattainment area, the Administrator shall determine, based on the area's design value as of the attainment date, whether the area has attained the standard by that date. Any Moderate Area that the Administrator finds has not attained the standard by that date shall be reclassified by operation of law in accordance with table 1 of subsection (a)(1) of this section as a Serious Area.

(B) Publication of notice

The Administrator shall publish a notice in the Federal Register, no later than 6 months following the attainment date, identifying each area that the Administrator has determined, under subparagraph (A), as having failed to attain and identifying the reclassification, if any, described under subparagraph (A).

(c) References to terms

Any reference in this subpart to a "Moderate Area" or a "Serious Area" shall be considered a reference to a Moderate Area or a Serious Area, respectively, as classified under this section.

(July 14, 1955, ch. 360, title I, § 186, as added Nov. 15, 1990, Pub.L. 101–549, title I, § 104, 104 Stat. 2452.)

Effective Date

Section to take effect Nov. 15, 1990, except as otherwise provided, see section 711(b) of Pub.L. 101–549, set out as a note under section 7401 of this title.

Savings Provisions

Suits, actions or proceedings commenced under this chapter as in effect prior to Nov. 15, 1990, not to abate by reason of the taking effect of amendments by Pub.L. 101–549, except as otherwise provided for, see section 711(a) of Pub.L. 101–549, set out as a note under section 7401 of this title.

§ 7512a. Plan submissions and requirements [CAA § 187]

(a) Moderate areas

Each State in which all or part of a Moderate Area is located shall, with respect to the Moderate Area (or portion thereof, to the extent specified in guidance of the Administrator issued before November 15, 1990, submit to the Administrator the State implementation plan revisions (including the plan items) described under this subsection, within such periods as are prescribed under this subsection, except to the extent the State has made such submissions as of November 15, 1990:

(1) Inventory

No later than 2 years from November 15, 1990, the State shall submit a comprehensive, accurate, current inventory of actual emissions from all sources, as described in section 7502(c)(3) of this title, in accordance with guidance provided by the Administrator.

(2)(A) Vehicle miles traveled

No later than 2 years after November 15, 1990, for areas with a design value above 12.7 ppm at the time of classification, the plan revision shall contain a forecast of vehicle miles traveled in the nonattainment area concerned for each year before the year in which the plan projects the national ambient air quality standard for carbon monoxide to be attained in the area. The forecast shall be based on guidance which shall be published by the Administrator, in consultation with the Secretary of Transportation, within 6 months after November 15, 1990. The plan revision shall provide for annual updates of the forecasts to be submitted to the Administrator together with annual reports regarding the extent to which such forecasts proved to be accurate. Such annual reports shall contain estimates of actual vehicle miles traveled in each year for which a forecast was required.

(B) Special rule for Denver

Within 2 years after November 15, 1990, in the case of Denver, the State shall submit a revision that includes the transportation control measures as required in section 7511a(d)(1)(A) of this title except that such revision shall be for the purpose of reducing CO emissions rather than volatile organic compound emissions. If the State fails to include any such measure, the implementation plan shall contain an explanation of why such measure was not adopted and what emissions reduction measure was adopted to provide a comparable reduction in emissions, or reasons why such reduction is not necessary to attain the national primary ambient air quality standard for carbon monoxide.

(3) Contingency provisions

No later than 2 years after November 15, 1990, for areas with a design value above 12.7 ppm at the time of classification, the plan revision shall provide for the implementation of specific measures to be undertaken if any estimate of vehicle miles traveled in the area which is submitted in an annual report under paragraph (2) exceeds the number predicted in the most recent prior forecast or if the area fails to attain the national primary ambient air quality standard for carbon monoxide by the primary standard attainment date. Such measures shall be included in the plan revision as contingency measures to take effect without further action by the State or the Administrator if the prior forecast has been exceeded by an updated forecast or if the national standard is not attained by such deadline.

(4) Savings clause for vehicle inspection and maintenance provisions of the State implementation plan

Immediately after November 15, 1990, for any Moderate Area (or, within the Administrator's discretion, portion thereof), the plan for which is of the type described in section 7511a(a)(2)(B) of this title any provisions necessary to ensure that the applicable implementation plan includes the vehicle inspection and maintenance program described in section 7511a(a)(2)(B) of this title.

(5) Periodic inventory

No later than September 30, 1995, and no later than the end of each 3 year period thereafter, until the area is redesignated to attainment, a revised inventory meeting the requirements of subsection (a)(1) of this section.

(6) Enhanced vehicle inspection and maintenance

No later than 2 years after November 15, 1990 in the case of Moderate Areas with a design value greater than 12.7 ppm at the time of classification, a revision that includes provisions for an enhanced vehicle inspection and maintenance program as required in section 7511a(c)(3) of this title (concerning serious ozone nonattainment areas), except that such program shall be for the purpose of reducing carbon monoxide rather than hydrocarbon emissions.

(7) Attainment demonstration and specific annual emission reductions

In the case of Moderate Areas with a design value greater than 12.7 ppm at the time of classification, no later than 2 years after November 15, 1990, a revision to provide, and a demonstration that the plan as revised will provide, for attainment of the carbon monoxide NAAQS by the applicable attainment date and provisions for such specific annual emission reductions as are necessary to attain the standard by that date.

The Administrator may, in the Administrator's discretion, require States to submit a schedule for submitting any of the revisions or other items required under this subsection. In the case of Moderate Areas with a design value of 12.7 ppm or lower at the time of classification, the requirements of this subsection shall apply in lieu of any requirement that the State submit a demonstration that the applicable implementation plan provides for attainment of the carbon monoxide standard by the applicable attainment date.

(b) Serious areas

(1) In general

Each State in which all or part of a Serious Area is located shall, with respect to the Serious Area, make the submissions (other than those required under subsection (a)(1)(B) of this section) applicable under subsection (a) of this section to Moderate Areas with a design value of 12.7 ppm or greater at the time of classification, and shall also submit the revision and other items described under this subsection.

(2) Vehicle miles traveled

Within 2 years after November 15, 1990 the State shall submit a revision that includes the transportation control measures as required in section 7511a(d)(1) of this title except that such revision shall be for the purpose of reducing CO emissions rather than volatile organic compound emissions. In the case of any such area (other than an area in New York State) which is a covered area (as defined in section 7586(a)(2)(B) of this title) for purposes of the Clean Fuel Fleet program under part C of subchapter II of this chapter, if the State fails to include any such measure, the implementation plan shall contain an explanation of why such measure was not adopted and what emissions reduction measure was adopted to provide a comparable reduction in emissions, or reasons why such reduction is not necessary to attain the national primary ambient air quality standard for carbon monoxide.

(3) Oxygenated gasoline

(A) Within 2 years after November 15, 1990, the State shall submit a revision to require that gasoline sold, supplied, offered for sale or supply, dispensed, transported or introduced into commerce in the larger of—

(i) the Consolidated Metropolitan Statistical Area (as defined by the United States Office of Management and Budget) (CMSA) in which the area is located, or

(ii) if the area is not located in a CMSA, the Metropolitan Statistical Area (as defined by the United States Office of Management and Budget) in which the area is located,

be blended, during the portion of the year in which the area is prone to high ambient concentrations of carbon monoxide (as determined by the Administrator), with fuels containing such level of oxygen as is necessary, in combination with other measures, to provide for attainment of the carbon monoxide national ambient air quality standard by the applicable attainment date and maintenance of the national ambient air quality standard thereafter in the area. The revision shall provide that such requirement shall take effect no later than October 1, 1993, and shall include a program for implementation and enforcement of the requirement consistent with guidance to be issued by the Administrator.

(B) Notwithstanding subparagraph (A), the revision described in this paragraph shall not be required for an area if the State demonstrates to the satisfaction of the Administrator that the revision is not necessary to provide for attainment of the carbon monoxide national ambient air quality standard by the applicable attainment date and maintenance of the national ambient air quality standard thereafter in the area.

(c) Areas with significant stationary source emissions of CO

(1) Serious areas

In the case of Serious Areas in which stationary sources contribute significantly to carbon monoxide levels (as determined under rules issued by the Administrator), the State shall submit a plan revision within 2 years after November 15, 1990, which provides that the term "major stationary source" includes (in addition to the sources described in section 7602 of this title) any stationary source which emits, or has the potential to emit, 50 tons per year or more of carbon monoxide.

(2) Waivers for certain areas

The Administrator may, on a case-by-case basis, waive any requirements that pertain to transportation controls, inspection and maintenance, or oxygenated fuels where the Administrator determines by rule that mobile sources of carbon monoxide do not contribute significantly to carbon monoxide levels in the area.

(3) Guidelines

Within 6 months after November 15, 1990, the Administrator shall issue guidelines for and rules determining whether stationary sources contribute significantly to carbon monoxide levels in an area.

(d) CO milestone

(1) Milestone demonstration

By March 31, 1996, each State in which all or part of a Serious Area is located shall submit to the Administrator a demonstration that the area has achieved a reduction in emissions of CO equivalent to the total of the specific annual emission reductions required by December 31, 1995. Such reductions shall be referred to in this subsection as the milestone.

(2) Adequacy of demonstration

A demonstration under this paragraph shall be submitted in such form and manner, and shall contain such information and analysis, as the Administrator shall require. The Administrator shall determine whether or not a State's demonstration is adequate within 90 days after the Administrator's receipt of a demonstration which contains the information and analysis required by the Administrator.

(3) Failure to meet emission reduction milestone

If a State fails to submit a demonstration under paragraph (1) within the required period, or if the Administrator notifies the State that the State has not met the milestone, the State shall, within 9 months after such a failure or notification, submit a plan revision to implement an economic incentive and transportation control program as described in section 7511a(g)(4) of this title. Such revision shall be sufficient to achieve the specific annual reductions in carbon monoxide emissions set forth in the plan by the attainment date.

(e) Multi–State CO nonattainment areas

(1) Coordination among states

Each State in which there is located a portion of a single nonattainment area for carbon monoxide which covers more than one State ("multi-State nonattainment area") shall take all reasonable steps to coordinate, substantively and procedurally, the revisions and implementation of State implementation plans applicable to the nonattainment area concerned. The Administrator may not approve any revision of a State implementation plan submitted under this part for a State in which part of a multi-State nonattainment area is located if the plan revision for that State fails to comply with the requirements of this subsection.

(2) Failure to demonstrate attainment

If any State in which there is located a portion of a multi-State nonattainment area fails to provide a demonstration of attainment of the national ambient air quality standard for carbon monoxide in that portion within the period required under this part the State may petition the Administrator to make a finding that the State would have been able to make such demonstration but for the failure of one or more other States in which other portions of the area are located to commit to the implementation of all measures required under section 7512a of this title (relating to plan submissions for carbon monoxide nonattainment areas). If the Administrator makes such finding, in the portion of the nonattainment area within the State submitting such petition, no sanction shall be imposed under section 7509 of this title or under any other provision of this chapter, by reason of the failure to make such demonstration.

(f) Reclassified areas

Each State containing a carbon monoxide nonattainment area reclassified under section 7512(b)(2) of this title shall meet the requirements of subsection (b) of this section, as may be applicable to the area as reclassified, according to the schedules prescribed in connection with such requirements, except that the Administrator may adjust any applicable deadlines (other than the attainment date) where such deadlines are shown to be infeasible.

(g) Failure of serious area to attain standard

If the Administrator determines under section 7512(b)(2) of this title that the national primary ambient air quality standard for carbon monoxide has not been attained in a Serious Area by the applicable attainment date, the State shall submit a plan revision for the area within 9 months after the date of such determination. The plan revision shall provide that a program of incentives and requirements as described in section 7511a(g)(4) of this title shall be applicable in the area, and such program, in combination with other elements of the revised plan, shall be adequate to reduce the total tonnage of emissions of carbon monoxide in the area by at least 5 percent per year in each year after approval of the plan revision and before attainment of the national primary ambient air quality standard for carbon monoxide.

(July 14, 1955, ch. 360, title I, § 187, as added Nov. 15, 1990, Pub.L. 101–549, title I, § 104, 104 Stat. 2454.)

Effective Date

Section to take effect Nov. 15, 1990, except as otherwise provided, see section 711(b) of Pub.L. 101–549, set out as a note under section 7401 of this title.

Savings Provisions

Suits, actions or proceedings commenced under this chapter as in effect prior to Nov. 15, 1990, not to abate by reason of the taking effect of amendments by Pub.L. 101–549, except as otherwise provided for, see section 711(a) of Pub.L. 101–549, set out as a note under section 7401 of this title.

Moratorium on Certain Emissions Testing Requirements

For provisions directing that the Administrator shall not require the adoption or implementation by a State of a test-only I/M240 enhanced vehicle inspection and maintenance program as a mean of compliance with this section, see section 348 of Pub.L. 104–59, set out as a note under section 7511a of this title.

Subpart 4—Additional Provisions for Particulate Matter Nonattainment Areas

§ 7513. Classifications and attainment dates [CAA § 188]

(a) Initial classifications

Every area designated nonattainment for PM–10 pursuant to section 7407(d) of this title shall be classified at the time of such designation, by operation of law, as a moderate PM–10 nonattainment area (also referred to in this subpart as a "Moderate Area") at the time of such designation. At the time of publication of the notice under section 7407(d)(4) of this title (relating to area designations) for each PM–10 nonattainment area, the Administrator shall publish a notice announcing the classification of such area. The provisions of section 7502(a)(1)(B) of this title (relating to lack of notice-and-comment and judicial review) shall apply with respect to such classification.

(b) Reclassification as serious

(1) Reclassification before attainment date

The Administrator may reclassify as a Serious PM–10 nonattainment area (identified in this subpart also as a "Serious Area") any area that the Administrator determines cannot practicably attain the national ambient air quality standard for PM–10 by the attainment date (as prescribed in subsection (c) of this section) for Moderate Areas. The Administrator shall reclassify appropriate areas as Serious by the following dates:

(A) For areas designated nonattainment for PM–10 under section 7407(d)(4) of this section, the Administrator shall propose to reclassify appropriate areas by June 30, 1991, and take final action by December 31, 1991.

(B) For areas subsequently designated nonattainment, the Administrator shall reclassify appropriate areas within 18 months after the required date for the State's submission of a SIP for the Moderate Area.

(2) Reclassification upon failure to attain

Within 6 months following the applicable attainment date for a PM–10 nonattainment area, the Administrator shall determine whether the area attained the standard by that date. If the Administrator finds that any Moderate Area is not in attainment after the applicable attainment date—

(A) the area shall be reclassified by operation of law as a Serious Area; and

(B) the Administrator shall publish a notice in the Federal Register no later than 6 months following the attainment date, identifying the area as having failed to attain and identifying the reclassification described under subparagraph (A).

(c) Attainment dates

Except as provided under subsection (d) of this section, the attainment dates for PM–10 nonattainment areas shall be as follows:

(1) Moderate areas

For a Moderate Area, the attainment date shall be as expeditiously as practicable but no later than the end of the sixth calendar year after the area's designation as nonattainment, except that, for areas designated nonattainment for PM–10 under section 7407(d)(4) of this title, the attainment date shall not extend beyond December 31, 1994.

(2) Serious areas

For a Serious Area, the attainment date shall be as expeditiously as practicable but no later than the end of the tenth calendar year beginning after the area's designation as nonattainment, except that, for areas designated nonattainment for PM–10 under section 7407(d)(4) of this title, the date shall not extend beyond December 31, 2001.

(d) Extension of attainment date for moderate areas

Upon application by any State, the Administrator may extend for 1 additional year (hereinafter referred to as the "Extension Year") the date specified in paragraph (c)(1) if—

(1) the State has complied with all requirements and commitments pertaining to the area in the applicable implementation plan; and

(2) no more than one exceedance of the 24-hour national ambient air quality standard level for PM–10 has occurred in the area in the year preceding the Extension Year, and the annual mean concentration of PM–10 in the area for such year is less than or equal to the standard level.

No more than 2 one-year extensions may be issued under the subsection for a single nonattainment area.

(e) Extension of attainment date for serious areas

Upon application by any State, the Administrator may extend the attainment date for a Serious Area beyond the date specified under subsection (c) of this section, if attainment by the date established under subsection (c) of this section would be impracticable, the State has complied with all requirements and commitments pertaining to that area in the implementation plan, and the State demonstrates to the satisfaction of the Administrator that the plan for that area includes the most stringent measures that are included in the implementation plan of any State or are achieved in practice in any State, and can feasibly be implemented in the area. At the time of such application, the State must submit a revision to the implementation plan that includes a demonstration of attainment by the most expeditious alternative date practicable. In determining whether to grant an extension, and the appropriate length of time for any such extension, the Administrator may consider the nature and extent of nonattainment, the types and numbers of sources or other emitting activities in the area (including the influence of uncontrollable natural sources and transboundary emissions from foreign countries), the population exposed to concentrations in excess of the standard, the presence and concentration of potentially toxic substances in the mix of particulate emissions in the area, and the technological and economic feasibility of various control measures. The Administrator may not approve an extension until the State submits an attainment demonstration for the area. The Administrator may grant at most one such extension for an area, of no more than 5 years.

(f) Waivers for certain areas

The Administrator may, on a case-by-case basis, waive any requirement applicable to any Serious Area under this subpart where the Administrator determines that anthropogenic sources of PM–10 do not contribute significantly to the violation of the PM–10 standard in the area. The Administrator may also waive a specific date for attainment of the standard where the Administrator determines that nonanthropogenic sources of PM–10 contribute significantly to the violation of the PM–10 standard in the area.

(July 14, 1955, ch. 360, title I, § 188, as added Nov. 15, 1990, Pub.L. 101–549, title I, § 105(a), 104 Stat. 2458.)

Effective Date

Section to take effect Nov. 15, 1990, except as otherwise provided, see section 711(b) of Pub.L. 101–549, set out as a note under section 7401 of this title.

Savings Provisions

Suits, actions or proceedings commenced under this chapter as in effect prior to Nov. 15, 1990, not to abate by reason of the taking effect of amendments by Pub.L. 101–549, except as otherwise provided for, see section 711(a) of Pub.L. 101–549, set out as a note under section 7401 of this title.

§ 7513a. Plan provisions and schedules for plan submissions [CAA § 189]

(a) Moderate areas

(1) Plan provisions

Each State in which all or part of a Moderate Area is located shall submit, according to the applicable schedule under paragraph (2), an implementation plan that includes each of the following:

(A) For the purpose of meeting the requirements of section 7502(c)(5) of this title, a permit program providing that permits meeting the requirements of section 7503 of this title are required for the construction and operation of new and modified major stationary sources of PM–10.

(B) Either (i) a demonstration (including air quality modeling) that the plan will provide for attainment by the applicable attainment date; or (ii) a demonstration that attainment by such date is impracticable.

(C) Provisions to assure that reasonably available control measures for the control of PM–10 shall be implemented no later than December 10, 1993, or 4 years after designation in the case of an area classified as moderate after November 15, 1990.

(2) Schedule for plan submissions

A State shall submit the plan required under subparagraph (1) no later than the following:

(A) Within 1 year of November 15, 1990, for areas designated nonattainment under section 7407(d)(4) of this title, except that the provision required under subparagraph (1)(A) shall be submitted no later than June 30, 1992.

(B) 18 months after the designation as nonattainment, for those areas designated nonattainment after the designations prescribed under section 7407(d)(4) of this title.

(b) Serious areas

(1) Plan provisions

In addition to the provisions submitted to meet the requirements of paragraph (a)(1) (relating to Moderate Areas), each State in which all or part of a Serious Area is located shall submit an implementation plan for such area that includes each of the following:

(A) A demonstration (including air quality modeling)—

(i) that the plan provides for attainment of the PM–10 national ambient air quality standard by the applicable attainment date, or

(ii) for any area for which the State is seeking, pursuant to section 7513(e) of this title, an extension of the attainment date beyond the date set forth in section 7513(c) of this title, that attainment by that date would be impracticable, and that the plan provides for attainment by the most expeditious alternative date practicable.

(B) Provisions to assure that the best available control measures for the control of PM–10 shall be implemented no later than 4 years after the date the area is classified (or reclassified) as a Serious Area.

(2) Schedule for plan submissions

A State shall submit the demonstration required for an area under paragraph (1)(A) no later than 4 years after reclassification of the area to Serious, except that for areas reclassified under section 7513(b)(2) of this title, the State shall submit the attainment demonstration within 18 months after reclassification to Serious. A State shall submit the provisions described under paragraph (1)(B) no later than 18 months after reclassification of the area as a Serious Area.

(3) Major sources

For any Serious Area, the terms "major source" and "major stationary source" include any stationary source or group of stationary sources located within a contiguous area and under common control that emits, or has the potential to emit, at least 70 tons per year of PM–10.

(c) Milestones

(1) Plan revisions demonstrating attainment submitted to the Administrator for approval under this subpart shall contain quantitative milestones which are to be achieved every 3 years until the area is redesignated attainment and which demonstrate reasonable further progress, as defined in section 7501(1) of this title, toward attainment by the applicable date.

(2) Not later than 90 days after the date on which a milestone applicable to the area occurs, each State in which all or part of such area is located shall submit to the Administrator a demonstration that all measures in the plan approved under this section have been implemented and that the milestone has been met. A demonstration under this subsection shall be submitted in such form and manner, and shall contain such information and analysis, as the Administrator shall require. The Administrator shall determine whether or not a State's demonstration under this subsection is adequate within 90 days after the Administrator's receipt of a demonstration which contains the information and analysis required by the Administrator.

(3) If a State fails to submit a demonstration under paragraph (2) with respect to a milestone within the required period or if the Administrator determines that the area has not met any applicable milestone, the Administrator shall require the State, within 9 months after such failure or determination to submit a plan revision that assures that the State will achieve the next milestone (or attain the national ambient air quality standard for PM–10, if there is no next milestone) by the applicable date.

(d) Failure to attain

In the case of a Serious PM–10 nonattainment area in which the PM–10 standard is not attained by the applicable attainment date, the State in which such area is located shall, after notice and opportunity for public comment, submit within 12 months after the applicable attainment date, plan revisions which provide for attainment of the PM–10 air quality standard and, from the date of such submission until attainment, for an annual reduction in PM–10 or PM–10 precursor emissions within the area of not less than 5 percent of the amount of such emissions as reported in the most recent inventory prepared for such area.

(e) PM–10 precursors

The control requirements applicable under plans in effect under this part for major stationary sources of PM–10 shall also apply to major stationary sources of PM–10 precursors, except where the Administrator determines that such sources do not contribute significantly to PM–10 levels which exceed the standard in the area. The Administrator shall issue guidelines regarding the application of the preceding sentence.

(July 14, 1955, ch. 360, title I, § 189, as added Nov. 15, 1990, Pub.L. 101–549, title I, § 105(a), 104 Stat. 2460.)

Effective Date

Section to take effect Nov. 15, 1990, except as otherwise provided, see section 711(b) of Pub.L. 101–549, set out as a note under section 7401 of this title.

Savings Provisions

Suits, actions or proceedings commenced under this chapter as in effect prior to Nov. 15, 1990, not to abate by reason of the taking effect of amendments by Pub.L. 101–549, except as otherwise provided for, see section 711(a) of Pub.L. 101–549, set out as a note under section 7401 of this title.

§ 7513b. Issuance of RACM and BACM guidance [CAA § 190]

The Administrator shall issue, in the same manner and according to the same procedure as guidance is issued under section 7408(c) of this title, technical guidance on reasonably available control measures and best available control measures for urban fugitive dust, and emissions from residential wood combustion (including curtailments and exemptions from such curtailments) and prescribed silvicultural and agricultural burning, no later than 18 months following November 15, 1990. The Administrator shall also examine other categories of sources contributing to nonattainment of the PM–10 standard, and determine whether additional guidance on reasonably available control measures and best available control measures is needed, and issue any such guidance no later than 3 years after November 15, 1990. In issuing guidelines and making determinations under this section, the Administrator (in consultation with the State) shall take into account emission reductions achieved, or expected to be achieved, under subchapter IV–A of this chapter and other provisions of this chapter.

(July 14, 1955, ch. 360, title I, § 190, as added Nov. 15, 1990, Pub.L. 101–549, title I, § 105(a), 104 Stat. 2462.)

Effective Date

Section to take effect Nov. 15, 1990, except as otherwise provided, see section 711(b) of Pub.L. 101–549, set out as a note under section 7401 of this title.

Savings Provisions

Suits, actions or proceedings commenced under this chapter as in effect prior to Nov. 15, 1990, not to abate by reason of the taking effect of amendments by Pub.L. 101–549, except as otherwise provided for, see section 711(a) of Pub.L. 101–549, set out as a note under section 7401 of this title.

Subpart 5—Additional Provisions for Areas Designated Nonattainment for Sulfur Oxides, Nitrogen Dioxide, or Lead

§ 7514. Plan submission deadlines [CAA § 191]

(a) Submission

Any State containing an area designated or redesignated under section 7407(d) of this title as nonattainment with respect to the national primary ambient air quality standards for sulfur oxides, nitrogen dioxide, or lead subsequent to November 15, 1990 shall submit to the Administrator, within 18 months of the designation, an applicable implementation plan meeting the requirements of this part.

(b) States lacking fully approved State implementation plans

Any State containing an area designated nonattainment with respect to national primary ambient air quality standards for sulfur oxides or nitrogen dioxide under section 7407(d)(1)(C)(i) of this title, but lacking a fully approved implementation plan complying with the requirements of this chapter (including part D) as in effect immediately before November 15, 1990, shall submit to the Administrator, within 18 months of November 15, 1990, an implementation plan meeting the requirements of subpart 1 (except as otherwise prescribed by section 7514a of this title).

(July 14, 1955, ch. 360, title I, § 191, as added Nov. 15, 1990, Pub.L. 101–549, Title I, § 106, 104 Stat. 2463.)

Effective Date

Section to take effect Nov. 15, 1990, except as otherwise provided, see section 711(b) of Pub.L. 101–549, set out as a note under section 7401 of this title.

Savings Provisions

Suits, actions or proceedings commenced under this chapter as in effect prior to Nov. 15, 1990, not to abate by reason of the taking effect of amendments by Pub.L. 101–549, except as otherwise provided for, see section 711(a) of Pub.L. 101–549, set out as a note under section 7401 of this title.

§ 7514a. Attainment dates [CAA § 192]

(a) Plans under section 7514(a) of this title

Implementation plans required under section 7514(b) of this title shall provide for attainment of the relevant primary standard as expeditiously as practicable but no later than 5 years from the date of the nonattainment designation.

(b) Plans under section 7514(b) of this title

Implementation plans required under section 7514(b) of this title shall provide for attainment of the relevant primary national ambient air quality standard within 5 years after November 15, 1990.

(c) Inadequate plans

Implementation plans for nonattainment areas for sulfur oxides or nitrogen dioxide with plans that were approved by the Administrator before November 15, 1990 but, subsequent to such approval, were found by the Administrator to be substantially inadequate, shall provide for attainment of the relevant primary standard within 5 years from the date of such finding.

(July 14, 1955, ch. 360, title I, § 192, as added Nov. 15, 1990, Pub.L. 101–549, Title I, § 106, 104 Stat. 2463.)

Effective Date

Section to take effect Nov. 15, 1990, except as otherwise provided, see section 711(b) of Pub.L. 101–549, set out as a note under section 7401 of this title.

Savings Provisions

Suits, actions or proceedings commenced under this chapter as in effect prior to Nov. 15, 1990, not to abate by reason of the taking effect of amendments by Pub.L. 101–549, except as otherwise provided for, see section 711(a) of Pub.L. 101–549, set out as a note under section 7401 of this title.

Subpart 6—Savings Provisions

§ 7515. General savings clause [CAA § 193]

Each regulation, standard, rule, notice, order and guidance promulgated or issued by the Administrator under this chapter, as in effect before November 15, 1990 shall remain in effect according to its terms, except to the extent otherwise provided under this chapter, inconsistent with any provision of this chapter, or revised by the Administrator. No control requirement in effect, or required to be adopted by an order, settlement agreement, or plan in effect before November 15, 1990 in any area which is a nonattainment area for any air pollutant may be modified after November 15, 1990 in any manner unless the modification insures equivalent or greater emission reductions of such air pollutant.

(July 14, 1955, ch. 360, title I, § 193, as added Nov. 15, 1990, Pub.L. 101–549, Title I, § 108(*l*), 104 Stat. 2469.)

Effective Date

Section to take effect Nov. 15, 1990, except as otherwise provided, see section 711(b) of Pub.L. 101–549, set out as a note under section 7401 of this title.

Savings Provisions

Suits, actions or proceedings commenced under this chapter as in effect prior to Nov. 15, 1990, not to abate by reason of the taking effect of amendments by Pub.L. 101–549, except as otherwise provided for, see section 711(a) of Pub.L. 101–549, set out as a note under section 7401 of this title.

SUBCHAPTER II—EMISSION STANDARDS FOR MOVING SOURCES

PART A—MOTOR VEHICLE EMISSION AND FUEL STANDARDS

§ 7521. Emission standards for new motor vehicles or new motor vehicle engines [CAA § 202]

(a) Authority of Administrator to prescribe by regulation

Except as otherwise provided in subsection (b) of this section—

(1) The Administrator shall by regulation prescribe (and from time to time revise) in accordance with the provisions of this section, standards applicable to the emission of any air pollutant from any class or classes of new motor vehicles or new motor vehicle engines, which in his judgment cause, or contribute to, air pollution which may reasonably be anticipated to endanger public health or welfare. Such standards shall be applicable to such vehicles and engines for their useful life (as determined under subsection (d) of this section, relating to useful life of vehicles for purposes of certification), whether such vehicles and engines are designed as complete systems or incorporate devices to prevent or control such pollution.

(2) Any regulation prescribed under paragraph (1) of this subsection (and any revision thereof) shall take effect after such period as the Administrator finds necessary to permit the development and application of the requisite technology, giving appropriate consideration to the cost of compliance within such period.

(3)(A) **In general.**—(i) Unless the standard is changed as provided in subparagraph (B), regulations under paragraph (1) of this subsection applicable to emissions of hydrocarbons, carbon monoxide, oxides of nitrogen, and particulate matter from classes or categories of heavy-duty vehicles or engines manufactured during or after model year 1983 shall contain standards which reflect the greatest degree of emission reduction achievable through the application of technology which the Administrator determines will be available for the model year to which such standards apply, giving appropriate consideration to cost, energy, and safety factors associated with the application of such technology.

(ii) In establishing classes or categories of vehicles or engines for purposes of regulations under this paragraph, the Administrator may base such classes or categories on gross vehicle weight, horsepower, type of fuel used, or other appropriate factors.

(B) **Revised standards for heavy duty trucks.**—(i) On the basis of information available to the Administrator concerning the effects of air pollutants emitted from heavy-duty vehicles or engines and from other sources of mobile source related pollutants on the public health and welfare, and taking costs into account, the Administrator may promulgate regulations under paragraph (1) of this subsection revising any standard promulgated under, or before November 15, 1990 (or previously revised under this subparagraph) and applicable to classes or categories of heavy-duty vehicles or engines.

(ii) Effective for the model year 1998 and thereafter, the regulations under paragraph (1) of this subsection applicable to emissions of oxides of nitrogen (NO_x) from gasoline and diesel-fueled heavy duty trucks shall contain standards which provide that such emissions may not exceed 4.0 grams per brake horsepower hour (gbh).

(C) **Lead time and stability.**—Any standard promulgated or revised under this paragraph and applicable to classes or categories of heavy-duty vehicles or engines shall apply for a period of no less than 3 model years beginning no earlier than the model year commencing 4 years after such revised standard is promulgated.

(D) **Rebuilding practices.**—The Administrator shall study the practice of rebuilding heavy-duty engines and the impact rebuilding has on engine emissions. On the basis of that study and other information available to the Administrator, the Administrator may prescribe requirements to control rebuilding practices, including standards applicable to emissions from any rebuilt heavy-duty engines (whether or not the engine is past its statutory useful life), which in the Administrator's judgment cause, or contribute to, air pollution which may reasonably be anticipated to endanger public health or welfare taking costs into account. Any regulation shall take effect after a period the Administrator finds necessary to permit the development and application of the requisite control measures, giving appropriate consideration to the cost of compliance within the period and energy and safety factors.

(E) **Motorcycles.**—For purposes of this paragraph, motorcycles and motorcycle engines shall be treated in the same manner as heavy-duty vehicles and engines (except as otherwise permitted under section 7525(f)(1) of this title) unless the Administrator promulgates a rule reclassifying motorcycles as light-duty vehicles within the meaning of this section or unless the Administrator promulgates regulations under subsection (a) of this section applying standards applicable to the emission of air pollutants from motorcycles as a separate class or category. In any case in which such standards are promulgated for such emissions from motorcycles as a separate class or category, the Administrator, in promulgating such standards, shall consider the need to achieve equivalency of emission reductions between motorcycles and other motor vehicles to the maximum extent practicable.

(4)(A) Effective with respect to vehicles and engines manufactured after model year 1978, no emission control device, system, or element of design shall be used in a new motor vehicle or new motor vehicle engine for purposes of complying with requirements prescribed under this subchapter if such device, system, or element of design will cause or contribute to an unreasonable risk to public health, welfare, or safety in its operation or function.

(B) In determining whether an unreasonable risk exists under subparagraph (A), the Administrator shall consider, among other factors, (i) whether and to what extent the use of any device, system, or element of design causes, increases, reduces, or eliminates emissions of any unregulated pollutants; (ii) available methods for reducing or eliminating any risk to public health, welfare, or safety which may be associated with the use of such device, system, or element of design, and (iii) the availability of other devices, systems, or elements of design which may be used to conform to requirements prescribed under this subchapter without causing or contributing to such unreasonable risk. The Administrator shall include in the consideration required by this paragraph all relevant information developed pursuant to section 7548 of this title.

(5)(A) If the Administrator promulgates final regulations which define the degree of control required and the test procedures by which compliance could be determined for gasoline vapor recovery of uncontrolled emissions from the fueling of motor vehicles, the Administrator shall, after consultation with the Secretary of Transportation with respect to motor vehicle safety, prescribe, by regulation, fill pipe standards for new motor vehicles in order to insure effective connection between such fill pipe and any vapor recovery system which the Administrator determines may be required to comply with such vapor recovery regulations. In promulgating such standards the Administrator shall take into consideration limits on fill pipe diameter, minimum design criteria for nozzle retainer lips, limits on the location of the unleaded fuel restrictors, a minimum access zone surrounding a fill pipe, a minimum pipe or nozzle insertion angle, and such other factors as he deems pertinent.

(B) Regulations prescribing standards under subparagraph (A) shall not become effective until the introduction of the model year for which it would be feasible to implement such standards, taking into consideration the restraints of an adequate leadtime for design and production.

(C) Nothing in subparagraph (A) shall (i) prevent the Administrator from specifying different nozzle and fill neck sizes for gasoline with additives and gasoline without additives or (ii) permit the Administrator to require a specific location, configuration, modeling, or styling of the motor vehicle body with respect to the fuel tank fill neck or fill nozzle clearance envelope.

(D) For the purpose of this paragraph, the term "fill pipe" shall include the fuel tank fill pipe, fill neck, fill inlet, and closure.

(6) Onboard vapor recovery.—Within 1 year after November 15, 1990, the Administrator shall, after consultation with the Secretary of Transportation regarding the safety of vehicle-based ('onboard') systems for the control of vehicle refueling emissions, promulgate standards under this section requiring that new light-duty vehicles manufactured beginning in the fourth model year after the model year in which the standards are promulgated and thereafter shall be equipped with such systems. The standards required under this paragraph shall apply to a percentage of each manufacturer's fleet of new light-duty vehicles beginning with the fourth model year after the model year in which the standards are promulgated. The percentage shall be as specified in the following table:

IMPLEMENTATION SCHEDULE FOR ONBOARD VAPOR RECOVERY REQUIREMENTS

Model year commencing after standards promulgated	Percentage*
Fourth	40
Fifth	80
After Fifth	100

*Percentages in the table refer to a percentage of the manufacturer's sales volume.

The standards shall require that such systems provide a minimum evaporative emission capture efficiency of 95 percent. The requirements of section 7511a(b)(3) of this title (relating to stage II gasoline vapor recovery) for areas classified under section 7511 of this title as moderate for ozone shall not apply after promulgation of such standards and the Administrator may, by rule, revise or waive the application of the requirements of such section 7511a(b)(3) of this title for areas classified under section 7511 of this title as Serious, Severe, or Extreme for ozone, as appropriate, after such time as the Administrator determines that onboard emissions control systems required under this paragraph are in widespread use throughout the motor vehicle fleet.

(b) Emissions of carbon monoxide, hydrocarbons, and oxides of nitrogen; waiver of emission standards; research objectives

(1)(A) The regulations under subsection (a) of this section applicable to emissions of carbon monoxide and hydrocarbons from light-duty vehicles and engines manufactured during model years 1977 through 1979 shall contain standards which provide that such emissions from such vehicles and engines may not exceed 1.5 grams per vehicle mile of hydrocarbons and 15.0 grams per vehicle mile of carbon monoxide. The regulations under subsection (a) of this section applicable to emissions of carbon monoxide from light-duty vehicles and engines manufactured during the model year 1980 shall contain standards which provide that such emissions may not exceed 7.0 grams per vehicle mile. The regulations under subsection (a) of this section applicable to emissions of hydrocarbons from light-duty vehicles and engines manufactured during or after model year 1980 shall contain standards which require a reduction of at least 90 percent from emissions of such pollutant allowable under the standards under this section applicable to light-duty vehicles and engines manufactured in model year 1970. Unless waived as provided in paragraph (5), regulations under subsection (a) of this section applicable to emissions of carbon monoxide from light-duty vehicles and engines manufactured during or after the model year 1981 shall contain standards which require a reduction of at least 90 percent from emissions of such pollutant allowable under the standards under this section applicable to light-duty vehicles and engines manufactured in model year 1970.

(B) The regulations under subsection (a) of this section applicable to emissions of oxides of nitrogen from light-duty vehicles and engines manufactured during model years 1977 through 1980 shall contain standards which provide that such emissions from such vehicles and engines may not exceed 2.0 grams per vehicle mile. The regulations under subsection (a) of this section applicable to emissions of oxides of nitrogen from light-duty vehicles and engines manufactured during the model year 1981 and thereafter shall contain standards which provide that such emissions from such vehicles and engines may not exceed 1.0 gram per vehicle mile. The Administrator shall prescribe standards in lieu of those required by the preceding sentence, which provide that emissions of oxides of nitrogen may not exceed 2.0 grams per vehicle mile for any light-duty vehicle manufactured during model years 1981 and 1982 by any manufacturer whose production, by corporate identity, for calendar year 1976 was less than three hundred thousand light-duty motor vehicles worldwide if the Administrator determines that—

(i) the ability of such manufacturer to meet emission standards in the 1975 and subsequent model years was, and is, primarily dependent upon technology developed by other manufacturers and purchased from such manufacturers; and

(ii) such manufacturer lacks the financial resources and technological ability to develop such technology.

(C) The Administrator may promulgate regulations under subsection (a)(1) of this section revising any standard prescribed or previously revised under this subsection, as needed to protect public health or welfare, taking costs, energy, and safety into account. Any revised standard shall require a reduction of emissions from the standard that was previously applicable. Any such revision under this subchapter may provide for a phase-in of the standard. It is the intent of Congress that the numerical emission standards specified in subsections (a)(3)(B)(ii), (g), (h), and (i) of this section shall not be modified by the Administrator after the enactment of the Clean Air Act Amendments of 1990 for any model year before the model year 2004.

(2) Emission standards under paragraph (1), and measurement techniques on which such standards are based (if not promulgated prior to November 15, 1990), shall be promulgated by regulation within 180 days after such date.

(3) For purposes of this part—

(A)(i) The term "model year" with reference to any specific calendar year means the manufacturer's annual production period (as determined by the Administrator) which includes January 1 of such calendar year. If the manufacturer has no annual production period, the term "model year" shall mean the calendar year.

(ii) For the purpose of assuring that vehicles and engines manufactured before the beginning of a model year were not manufactured for purposes of circumventing the effective date of a standard required to be prescribed by subsection (b) of this section, the Administrator may prescribe regulations defining "model year" otherwise than as provided in clause (i).

(B) Repealed. Pub.L. 101–549, title II, § 230(1), Nov. 15, 1990, 104 Stat. 2529.

(C) The term "heavy duty vehicle" means a truck, bus, or other vehicle manufactured primarily for use on the public streets, roads, and highways (not including any vehicle operated exclusively on a rail or rails) which has a gross vehicle weight (as determined under regulations promulgated by the Administrator) in excess of six thousand pounds. Such term includes any such vehicle which has special features enabling off-street or off-highway operation and use.

(3) [1] Upon the petition of any manufacturer, the Administrator, after notice and opportunity for public hearing, may waive the standard required under subparagraph (B) of paragraph (1) to not exceed 1.5 grams of oxides of nitrogen per vehicle mile for any class or category of light-duty vehicles or engines manufactured by such manufacturer during any period of up to four model years beginning after the model year 1980 if the manufacturer demonstrates that such waiver is necessary to permit the use of an innovative power train technology, or innovative emission control device or system, in such class or category of vehicles or engines and that such technology or system was not utilized by more than 1 percent of the light-duty vehicles sold in the United States in the 1975 model year. Such waiver may be granted only if the Administrator determines—

(A) that such waiver would not endanger public health,

(B) that there is a substantial likelihood that the vehicles or engines will be able to comply with the applicable standard under this section at the expiration of the waiver, and

(C) that the technology or system has a potential for long-term air quality benefit and has the potential to meet or exceed the average fuel economy standard applicable under the Energy Policy and Conservation Act [42 U.S.C. 6201 et seq.] upon the expiration of the waiver.

No waiver under this subparagraph granted to any manufacturer shall apply to more than 5 percent of such manufacturer's production or more than fifty thousand vehicles or engines, whichever is greater.

(c) Feasibility study and investigation by National Academy of Sciences; reports to Administrator and Congress; availability of information

(1) The Administrator shall undertake to enter into appropriate arrangements with the National Academy of Sciences to conduct a comprehensive study and investigation of the technological feasibility of meeting the emissions standards required to be prescribed by the Administrator by subsection (b) of this section.

(2) Of the funds authorized to be appropriated to the Administrator by this chapter, such amounts as are required shall be available to carry out the study and investigation authorized by paragraph (1) of this subsection.

(3) In entering into any arrangement with the National Academy of Sciences for conducting the study and investigation authorized by paragraph (1) of this subsection, the Administrator shall request the National Academy of Sciences to submit semiannual reports on the progress of its study and investigation to the Administrator and the Congress, beginning not later than July 1, 1971, and continuing until such study and investigation is completed.

(4) The Administrator shall furnish to such Academy at its request any information which the Academy deems necessary for the purpose of conducting the investigation and study authorized by paragraph (1) of this subsection. For the purpose of furnishing such information, the Administrator may use any authority he has under this chapter (A) to obtain information from any person, and (B) to require such person to conduct such tests, keep such records, and make such reports respecting research or other activities conducted by such person as may be reasonably necessary to carry out this subsection.

(d) Useful life of vehicles

The Administrator shall prescribe regulations under which the useful life of vehicles and engines shall be determined for purposes of subsection (a)(1) of this section and section 7541 of this title. Such regulations shall provide that except where a different useful life period is specified in this subchapter useful life shall—

(1) in the case of light duty vehicles and light duty vehicle engines and light-duty trucks up to 3,750 lbs. LVW and up to 6,000 lbs. GVWR, be a period of use of five years or of fifty thousand miles (or the equivalent), whichever first occurs, except that in the case of any requirement of this section which first becomes applicable after the enactment of the Clean Air Act Amendments of 1990 where the useful life period is not otherwise specified for such vehicles and engines, the period shall be 10 years or 100,000 miles (or the equivalent), whichever first occurs, with testing for purposes of in-use compliance under section 7541 of this title up to (but not beyond) 7 years or 75,000 miles (or the equivalent), whichever first occurs;

(2) in the case of any other motor vehicle or motor vehicle engine (other than motorcycles or motorcycle engines), be a period of use set forth in paragraph (1) unless the Administrator determines that a period of use of greater duration or mileage is appropriate; and

(3) in the case of any motorcycle or motorcycle engine, be a period of use the Administrator shall determine.

(e) New power sources or propulsion systems

In the event a new power source or propulsion system for new motor vehicles or new motor vehicle engines is submitted for certification pursuant to section 7525(a) of this title, the Administrator may postpone certification until he has prescribed standards for any air pollutants emitted by such vehicle or engine which in his judgment cause, or contribute to, air pollution which may reasonably be anticipated to endanger the public health or welfare but for which standards have not been prescribed under subsection (a) of this section.

(f)[2] High altitude regulations

(1) The high altitude regulation in effect with respect to model year 1977 motor vehicles shall not apply to the manufacture, distribution, or sale of 1978 and later model year motor vehicles. Any future regulation affecting the sale or distribution of motor vehicles or engines manufactured before the model year 1984 in high altitude areas of the country shall take effect no earlier than model year 1981.

(2) Any such future regulation applicable to high altitude vehicles or engines shall not require a percentage of reduction in the emissions of such vehicles which is greater than the required percentage of reduction in emissions from motor vehicles as set forth in subsection (b) of this section. This percentage reduction shall be determined by comparing any proposed high altitude emission standards to high altitude emissions from vehicles manufactured during model year 1970. In no event shall regulations applicable to high altitude vehicles manufactured before the model year 1984 establish a numerical standard which is more stringent than that applicable to vehicles certified under non-high altitude conditions.

(3) Section 7607(d) of this title shall apply to any high altitude regulation referred to in paragraph (2) and before promulgating any such regulation, the Administrator shall consider and make a finding with respect to—

(A) the economic impact upon consumers, individual high altitude dealers, and the automobile industry of any such regulation, including the economic impact which was experienced as a result of the regulation imposed during model year 1977 with respect to high altitude certification requirements;

(B) the present and future availability of emission control technology capable of meeting the applicable vehicle and engine emission requirements without reducing model availability; and

(C) the likelihood that the adoption of such a high altitude regulation will result in any significant improvement in air quality in any area to which it shall apply.

(g) Light-duty trucks up to 6,000 lbs. GVWR and light-duty vehicles; standards for model years after 1993

(1) NMHC, CO, and No_x

Effective with respect to the model year 1994 and thereafter, the regulations under subsection (a) of this section applicable to emissions of nonmethane hydrocarbons (NMHC), carbon monoxide (CO), and oxides of nitrogen (NO_x) from light-duty trucks (LDTs) of up to 6,000 lbs. gross vehicle weight rating (GVWR) and light-duty vehicles (LDVs) shall contain standards which provide that emissions from a percentage of each manufacturer's sales volume of such vehicles and trucks shall comply with the levels specified in table G. The percentage shall be as specified in the implementation schedule below:

TABLE G—EMISSION STANDARDS FOR NMHC, CO, AND NO_X FROM LIGHT-DUTY TRUCKS OF UP TO 6,000 LBS. GVWR AND LIGHT-DUTY VEHICLES

Vehicle type	Column A (5 yrs/50,000 mi)			Column B (10 yrs/100,000 mi)		
	NMHC	CO	NO_x	NMHC	CO	NO_x
LDTs (0–3,750 lbs. LVW) and light-duty vehicles	0.25	3.4	0.4*	0.31	4.2	0.6*
LDTs (3,751–5,750 lbs. LVW)	0.32	4.4	0.7**	0.40	5.5	0.97

Standards are expressed in grams per mile (gpm).

For standards under column A, for purposes of certification under section 7525 of this title, the applicable useful life shall be 5 years or 50,000 miles (or the equivalent), whichever first occurs.

For standards under column B, for purposes of certification under section 7525 of this title, the applicable useful life shall be 10 years or 100,000 miles (or the equivalent), whichever first occurs.

*In the case of diesel-fueled LDTs (0–3,750 lvw) and light-duty vehicles, before the model year 2004, in lieu of the 0.4 and 0.6 standards for NO_X the applicable standards for NO_X shall be 1.0 gpm for a useful life of 5 years or 50,000 miles (or the equivalent), whichever first occurs, and 1.25 gpm for a useful life of 10 years or 100,000 miles (or the equivalent) whichever first occurs.

**This standard does not apply to diesel-fueled LDTs (3,751–5,750 lbs. LVW).

IMPLEMENTATION SCHEDULE FOR TABLE G STANDARDS

Model year	Percentage*
1994	40
1995	80
after 1995	100

*Percentages in the table refer to a percentage of each manufacturer's sales volume.

(2) PM standard

Effective with respect to model year 1994 and thereafter in the case of light-duty vehicles and effective with respect to the model year 1995 and thereafter in the case of light-duty trucks (LDTs) of up to 6,000 lbs. gross vehicle weight rating (GVWR), the regulations under subsection (a) of this section applicable to emissions of particulate matter (PM) from such vehicles and trucks shall contain standards which provide that such emissions from a percentage of each manufacturer's sales volume of such vehicles and trucks shall not exceed the levels specified in the table below. The percentage shall be as specified in the Implementation Schedule below.

PM STANDARD FOR LDTs OF UP TO 6,000 LBS. GVWR

Useful life period	Standard
5/50,000	0.08 gpm
10/100,000	0.10 gpm

The applicable useful life, for purposes of certification under section 7525 of this title and for purposes of in-use compliance under section 7541 of this title, shall be 5 years or 50,000 miles (or the equivalent), whichever first occurs, in the case of the 5/50,000 standard.

The applicable useful life, for purposes of certification under section 7525 of this title and for purposes of in-use compliance under section 7541 of this title, shall be 10 years or 100,000 miles (or the equivalent), whichever first occurs in the case of the 10/100,000 standard.

IMPLEMENTATION SCHEDULE FOR PM STANDARDS

Model year	Light-duty vehicles	LDTs
1994	40% *	......
1995	80% *	40% *
1996	100% *	80% *
after 1996	100%*	100%*

* Percentages in the table refer to a percentage of each manufacturer's sales volume.

(h) Light-duty trucks of more than 6,000 lbs. GVWR; standards for model years after 1995

Effective with respect to the model year 1996 and thereafter, the regulations under subsection (a) of this section applicable to emissions of nonmethane hydrocarbons (NMHC), carbon monoxide (CO), oxides of nitrogen (NO_x), and particulate matter (PM) from light-duty trucks (LDTs) of more than 6,000 lbs. gross vehicle weight rating (GVWR) shall contain standards which provide that emissions from a specified percentage of each manufacturer's sales volume of such trucks shall comply with the levels specified in table H. The specified percentage shall be 50 percent in model year 1996 and 100 percent thereafter.

TABLE H—EMISSION STANDARDS FOR NMHC AND CO FROM GASOLINE AND DIESEL FUELED LIGHT-DUTY TRUCKS OF MORE THAN 6,000 LBS. GVWR

LDT Test weight	Column A (5 yrs/50,000 mi)			Column B (11 yrs/120,000 mi)			
	NMHC	CO	NO_x	NMHC	CO	NO_x	PM
3,751–5,750 lbs. TW	0.32	4.4	0.7*	0.46	6.4	0.98	0.10
Over 5,750 lbs. TW	0.39	5.0	1.1*	0.56	7.3	1.53	0.12

Standards are expressed in grams per mile (GPM).

For standards under column A, for purposes of certification under section 7525 of this title, the applicable useful life shall be 5 years or 50,000 miles (or the equivalent) whichever first occurs.

For standards under column B, for purposes of certification under section 7525 of this title, the applicable useful life shall be 11 years or 120,000 miles (or the equivalent), whichever first occurs.

* Not applicable to diesel-fueled LDTs.

(i) Phase II study for certain light-duty vehicles and light-duty trucks

(1) The Administrator, with the participation of the Office of Technology Assessment, shall study whether or not further reductions in emissions from light-duty vehicles and light-duty trucks should be required pursuant to this title. The study shall consider whether to establish with respect to model years commencing after January 1, 2003, the standards and useful life period for gasoline and diesel-fueled light-duty vehicles and light-duty trucks with a loaded vehicle weight (LVW) of 3,750 lbs. or less specified in the following table:

TABLE 3—PENDING EMISSION STANDARDS FOR GASOLINE AND DIESEL FUELED LIGHT-DUTY VEHICLES AND LIGHT-DUTY TRUCKS 3,750 LBS. LVW OR LESS

Pollutant	Emission level*
NMHC	0.125 GPM
NO_x	0.2 GPM
CO	1.7 GPM

*Emission levels are expressed in grams per mile (GPM). For vehicles and engines subject to this subsection for purposes of subsection (d) of this section and any reference thereto, the useful life of such vehicles and engines shall be a period of 10 years or 100,000 miles (or the equivalent), whichever first occurs.

Such study shall also consider other standards and useful life periods which are more stringent or less stringent than those set forth in table 3 (but more stringent than those referred to in subsections (g) and (h) of this section).

(2)(A) As part of the study under paragraph (1), the Administrator shall examine the need for further reductions in emissions in order to attain or maintain the national ambient air quality standards, taking into consideration the waiver provisions of section 7543(b) of this title. As part of such study, the Administrator shall also examine—

(i) the availability of technology (including the costs thereof), in the case of light-duty vehicles and light-duty trucks with a loaded vehicle weight (LVW) of 3,750 lbs. or less, for meeting more stringent emission standards than those provided in subsections (g) and (h) of this section for model years commencing not earlier than after January 1, 2003, and not later than model year 2006, including the lead time and safety and energy impacts of meeting more stringent emission standards; and

(ii) the need for, and cost effectiveness of, obtaining further reductions in emissions from such light-duty vehicles and light-duty trucks, taking into consideration alternative means of attaining or maintaining the national primary ambient air quality standards pursuant to State implementation plans and other requirements of this chapter, including their feasibility and cost effectiveness.

(B) The Administrator shall submit a report to Congress no later than June 1, 1997, containing the results of the study under this subsection, including the results of the examination conducted under subparagraph (A). Before submittal of such report the Administrator shall provide a reasonable opportunity for public comment and shall include a summary of such comments in the report to Congress.

(3)(A) Based on the study under paragraph (1) the Administrator shall determine, by rule, within 3 calendar years after the report is submitted to Congress, but not later than December 31, 1999, whether—

(i) there is a need for further reductions in emissions as provided in paragraph (2)(A);

(ii) the technology for meeting more stringent emission standards will be available, as provided in paragraph (2)(A)(i), in the case of light-duty vehicles and light-duty trucks with a loaded vehicle weight (LVW) of 3,750 lbs. or less, for model years commencing not earlier than January 1, 2003, and not later than model year 2006, considering the factors listed in paragraph (2)(A)(i); and

(iii) obtaining further reductions in emissions from such vehicles will be needed and cost effective, taking into consideration alternatives as provided in paragraph (2)(A)(ii).

The rulemaking under this paragraph shall commence within 3 months after submission of the report to Congress under paragraph (2)(B).

(B) If the Administrator determines under subparagraph (A) that—

(i) there is no need for further reductions in emissions as provided in paragraph (2)(A);

(ii) the technology for meeting more stringent emission standards will not be available as provided in paragraph (2)(A)(i), in the case of light-duty vehicles and light-duty trucks with a loaded vehicle weight (LVW) of 3,750 lbs. or less, for model years commencing not earlier than January 1, 2003, and not later than model year 2006, considering the factors listed in paragraph (2)(A)(i); or

(iii) obtaining further reductions in emissions from such vehicles will not be needed or cost effective, taking into consideration alternatives as provided in paragraph (2)(A)(ii),

the Administrator shall not promulgate more stringent standards than those in effect pursuant to subsections (g) and (h) of this section. Nothing in this paragraph shall prohibit the Administrator from exercising the Administrator's authority under subsection (a) of this section to promulgate more stringent standards for light-duty vehicles and light-duty trucks with a loaded vehicle weight (LVW) of 3,750 lbs. or less at any other time thereafter in accordance with subsection (a) of this section.

(C) If the Administrator determines under subparagraph (A) that—

(i) there is a need for further reductions in emissions as provided in paragraph (2)(A);

(ii) the technology for meeting more stringent emission standards will be available, as provided in paragraph (2)(A)(i), in the case of light-duty vehicles and light-duty trucks with a loaded vehicle weight (LVW) of 3,750 lbs. or less, for model years commencing not earlier than January 1, 2003, and not later than model year 2006, considering the factors listed in paragraph (2)(A)(i); and

(iii) obtaining further reductions in emissions from such vehicles will be needed and cost effective, taking into consideration alternatives as provided in paragraph (2)(A)(ii),

the Administrator shall either promulgate the standards (and useful life periods) set forth in Table 3 in paragraph (1) or promulgate alternative standards (and useful life periods) which are more stringent than those referred to in subsections (g) and (h) of this section. Any such standards (or useful life periods) promulgated by the Administrator shall take effect with respect to any such vehicles or engines no earlier than the model year 2003 but not later than model year 2006, as determined by the Administrator in the rule.

(D) Nothing in this paragraph shall be construed by the Administrator or by a court as a presumption that any standards (or useful life period) set forth in Table 3 shall be promulgated in the rulemaking required under this paragraph. The action required of the Administrator in accordance with this paragraph shall be treated as a nondiscretionary duty for purposes of section 7604(a)(2) of this title (relating to citizen suits).

(E) Unless the Administrator determines not to promulgate more stringent standards as provided in subparagraph (B) or to postpone the effective date of standards referred to in Table 3 in paragraph (1) or to establish alternative standards as provided in subparagraph (C), effective with respect to model years commencing after January 1, 2003, the regulations under subsection (a) of this section applicable to emissions of nonmethane hydrocarbons (NMHC), oxides of nitrogen (NO_x), and carbon monoxide (CO) from motor vehicles and motor vehicle engines in the classes specified in Table 3 in paragraph (1) above shall contain standards which provide that emissions may not exceed the pending emission levels specified in Table 3 in paragraph (1).

(j) Cold CO standard

(1) Phase I

Not later than 12 months after November 15, 1990, the Administrator shall promulgate regulations under subsection (a) of this section applicable to emissions of carbon monoxide from 1994 and later model year light-duty vehicles and light-duty trucks when operated at 20 degrees Fahrenheit. The regulations shall contain standards which provide that emissions of carbon monoxide from a manufacturer's vehicles when operated at 20 degrees Fahrenheit may not exceed, in the case of light-duty vehicles, 10.0 grams per mile, and in the case of light-duty trucks, a level comparable in stringency to the standard applicable to light-duty vehicles. The standards shall take effect after model year 1993 according to a phase-in schedule which requires a percentage of each manufacturer's sales volume of light-duty vehicles and light-duty trucks to comply with applicable standards after model year 1993. The percentage shall be as specified in the following table:

PHASE-IN SCHEDULE FOR COLD START STANDARDS

Model Year	Percentage
1994	40
1995	80
1996 and after	100

(2) Phase II

(A) Not later than June 1, 1997, the Administrator shall complete a study assessing the need for further reductions in emissions of carbon monoxide and the maximum reductions in such emissions achievable from model year 2001 and later model year light-duty vehicles and light-duty trucks when operated at 20 degrees Fahrenheit.

(B)(i) If as of June 1, 1997, 6 or more nonattainment areas have a carbon monoxide design value of 9.5 ppm or greater, the regulations under subsection (a)(1) of this section applicable to emissions of carbon monoxide from model year 2002 and later model year light-duty vehicles and light-duty trucks shall contain standards which provide that emissions of carbon monoxide from such vehicles and trucks when operated at 20 degrees Fahrenheit may not exceed 3.4 grams per mile (gpm) in the case of light-duty vehicles and 4.4 grams per mile (gpm) in the case of light-duty trucks up to 6,000 GVWR and a level comparable in stringency in the case of light-duty trucks 6,000 GVWR and above.

(ii) In determining for purposes of this subparagraph whether 6 or more nonattainment areas have a carbon monoxide design value of 9.5 ppm or greater, the Administrator shall exclude the areas of Steubenville, Ohio, and Oshkosh, Wisconsin.

(3) Useful-life for phase I and phase II standards

In the case of the standards referred to in paragraphs (1) and (2), for purposes of certification under section 7525 of this title and in-use compliance under section 7541 of this title, the applicable useful life period shall be 5 years or 50,000 miles, whichever first occurs, except that the Administrator may extend such useful life period (for purposes of section 7525 of this title, or section 7541 of this title, or both) if he determines that it is feasible for vehicles and engines subject to such standards to meet such standards for a longer useful life. If the Administrator extends such useful life period, the Administrator may make an appropriate adjustment of applicable standards for such extended useful life. No such extended useful life shall extend beyond the useful life period provided in regulations under subsection (d) of this section.

(4) Heavy-duty vehicles and engines

The Administrator may also promulgate regulations under subsection (a)(1) of this section applicable to emissions of carbon monoxide from heavy-duty vehicles and engines when operated at cold temperatures.

(k) Control of evaporative emissions

The Administrator shall promulgate (and from time to time revise) regulations applicable to evaporative emissions of hydrocarbons from all gasoline-fueled motor vehicles—

(1) during operation; and

(2) over 2 or more days of nonuse;

under ozone-prone summertime conditions (as determined by regulations of the Administrator). The regulations shall take effect as expeditiously as possible and shall require the greatest degree of emission reduction achievable by means reasonably expected to be available for production during any model year to which the regulations apply, giving appropriate consideration to fuel volatility, and to cost, energy, and safety factors associated with the application of the appropriate technology. The Administrator shall commence a rulemaking under this subsection within 12 months after November 15, 1990. If final regulations are not promulgated under this subsection within 18 months after November 15, 1990, the Administrator shall submit a statement to the Congress containing an explanation of the reasons for the delay and a date certain for promulgation of such final regulations in accordance with this chapter. Such date certain shall not be later than 15 months after the expiration of such 18 month deadline.

(*l*) Mobile source-related air toxics

(1) Study

Not later than 18 months after November 15, 1990, the Administrator shall complete a study of the need for, and feasibility of, controlling emissions of toxic air pollutants which are unregulated under this chapter and associated with motor vehicles and motor vehicle fuels, and the need for, and feasibility of, controlling such emissions and the means and measures for such controls. The study shall focus on those categories of emissions that pose the greatest risk to human health or about which significant uncertainties remain, including emissions of benzene, formaldehyde, and 1, 3 butadiene. The proposed report shall be available for public review and comment and shall include a summary of all comments.

(2) Standards

Within 54 months after November 15, 1990, the Administrator shall, based on the study under paragraph (1), promulgate (and from time to time revise) regulations under subsection (a)(1) of this section or section 7545(c)(1) of this title containing reasonable requirements to control hazardous air pollutants from motor vehicles and motor vehicle fuels. The regulations shall contain standards for such fuels or vehicles, or both, which the Administrator determines reflect the greatest degree of emission reduction achievable through the application of technology which will be available, taking into consideration the standards established under subsection (a) of this section, the availability and costs of the technology, and noise, energy, and safety factors, and lead time. Such regulations shall not be inconsistent with standards under subsection (a) of this section. The regulations shall, at a minimum, apply to emissions of benzene and formaldehyde.

(m) Emissions control diagnostics

(1) Regulations

Within 18 months after the enactment of the Clean Air Act Amendments of 1990, the Administrator shall promulgate regulations under subsection (a) of this section requiring manufacturers to install on all new light duty vehicles and light duty trucks diagnostics systems capable of—

(A) accurately identifying for the vehicle's useful life as established under this section, emission-related systems deterioration or malfunction, including, at a minimum, the catalytic converter and oxygen sensor, which could cause or result in failure of the vehicles to comply with emission standards established under this section,

(B) alerting the vehicle's owner or operator to the likely need for emission-related components or systems maintenance or repair,

(C) storing and retrieving fault codes specified by the Administrator, and

(D) providing access to stored information in a manner specified by the Administrator.

The Administrator may, in the Administrator's discretion, promulgate regulations requiring manufacturers to install such onboard diagnostic systems on heavy-duty vehicles and engines.

(2) Effective date

The regulations required under paragraph (1) of this subsection shall take effect in model year 1994, except that the Administrator may waive the application of such regulations for model year 1994 or 1995 (or both) with respect to any class or category of motor vehicles if the Administrator determines that it would be infeasible to apply the regulations to that class or category in such model year or years, consistent with corresponding regulations or policies adopted by the California Air Resources Board for such systems.

(3) State inspection

The Administrator shall by regulation require States that have implementation plans containing motor vehicle inspection and maintenance programs to amend their plans within 2 years after promulgation of such regulations to provide for inspection of onboard diagnostics systems (as prescribed by regulations under paragraph (1) of this subsection) and for the maintenance or repair of malfunctions or system deterioration identified by or affecting such diagnostics systems. Such regulations shall not be inconsistent with the provisions for warranties promulgated under section 7541(a) and (b) of this title.

(4) Specific requirements

In promulgating regulations under this subsection, the Administrator shall require—

(A) that any connectors through which the emission control diagnostics system is accessed for inspection, diagnosis, service, or repair shall be standard and uniform on all motor vehicles and motor vehicle engines;

(B) that access to the emission control diagnostics system through such connectors shall be unrestricted and shall not require any access code or any device which is only available from a vehicle manufacturer; and

(C) that the output of the data from the emission control diagnostics system through such connectors shall be usable without the need for any unique decoding information or device.

(5) Information availability

The Administrator, by regulation, shall require (subject to the provisions of section 7542(c) of this title regarding the protection of methods or processes entitled to protection as trade secrets) manufacturers to provide promptly to any person engaged in the repairing or servicing of motor vehicles or motor vehicle engines, and the Administrator for use by any such persons, with any and all information needed to make use of the emission control diagnostics system prescribed under this subsection and such other information including instructions for making emission related diagnosis and repairs. No such information may be withheld under section 7542(c) of this title if that information is provided (directly or indirectly) by the manufacturer to franchised dealers or other persons engaged in the repair, diagnosing, or servicing of motor vehicles or motor vehicle engines. Such information shall also be available to the Administrator, subject to section 7542(c) of this title, in carrying out the Administrator's responsibilities under this section.

(f)[3] Model years after 1990

For model years prior to model year 1994, the regulations under subsection (a) of this section applicable to buses other than those subject to standards under section 7554 of this title shall contain a standard which provides that emissions of particulate matter (PM) from such buses may not exceed the standards set forth in the following table:

PM STANDARD FOR BUSES

Model year	Standard*
1991	0.25
1992	0.25
1993 and thereafter	0.10

* Standards are expressed in grams per brake horsepower hour (g/bhp/hr).

(July 14, 1955, ch. 360, title II, § 202, as added Oct. 20, 1965, Pub.L. 89–272, title I, § 101(8), 79 Stat. 992, and amended Nov. 21, 1967, Pub.L. 90–148, § 2, 81 Stat. 499; Dec. 31, 1970, Pub.L. 91–604, § 6(a), 84 Stat. 1690; June 22, 1974, Pub.L. 93–319, § 5, 88 Stat. 258; Aug. 7, 1977, Pub.L. 95–95, title II, §§ 201, 202(b), 213(b), 214(a), 215–217, 224(a), (b), (g), title IV, § 401(d), 91 Stat. 751–753, 758–761, 765, 767, 769, 791; Nov. 16, 1977, Pub.L. 95–190, § 14(a)(60)–(65), (b)(5), 91 Stat. 1403, 1405; Nov. 15, 1990, Pub.L. 101–549, title II, §§ 201–207, 227[(b)], 230(1)–(5), 104 Stat. 2472–2481, 2507, 2529.)

1 Two pars. (3) have been enacted.

2 Another subsec. (f) is set out following subsec. (m).

3 So in original. Probably should be designated as subsec. (n). See Codification note set out under this section.

References in Text

The enactment of the Clean Air Act Amendments of 1990, referred to in subsecs. (b)(1)(C), (d)(1) and (m), probably means the date of enactment of the Clean Air Act Amendments of 1990, Pub.L. 101–549, which was approved November 15, 1990.

Codification

Amendment by Pub.L. 101–549, § 230(4)(C) to subsec. (b) resulted in there being two subsections (b)(3).

Pub.L. 101–549, § 203(b), directed that section 202(d) of the Clean Air Act (42 U.S.C. 7521(d)(1)) be amended. The amendment was executed to the opening paragraph of this subsec. as the probable intent of Congress.

Pub.L. 101–549, § 207(b), directed that subsec. (f), relating to PM standards for buses for model years after 1990, be set out at the end of this section.

Effective Date of 1990 Amendment

Amendment by Pub.L. 101–549 effective Nov. 15, 1990, except as otherwise provided, see section 711(b) of Pub.L. 101–549, set out as a note under section 7401 of this title.

Short Title

Section 201 of Act July 14, 1955, c. 360, Title II, as added Pub.L. 89–272, Title I, § 101(8), Oct. 20, 1965, 79 Stat. 992, and amended Pub.L. 90–148, § 2, Nov. 2, 1967, 81 Stat. 499, provided that Title II of Act July 14, 1955, c. 360 [this subchapter], may be cited as the "National Emission Standards Act".

Savings Provisions

Suits, actions or proceedings commenced under this chapter as in effect prior to Nov. 15, 1990, not to abate by reason of the taking effect of amendments by Pub.L. 101–549, except as otherwise provided for, see section 711(a) of Pub.L. 101–549, set out as a note under section 7401 of this title.

Cross References

Emissions standards under this section as category of federal standards for purposes of average fuel economy standards, see section 2002 of Title 15, Commerce and Trade.

Low-emission motor vehicle defined for purposes of exemption from safety standards, see section 1410 of Title 15.

West's Federal Practice Manual

Air quality legislation, see § 4384.5.

CODE OF FEDERAL REGULATIONS

Air pollution from motor vehicles, control of, see 40 CFR 85.401 et seq.

Control of air pollution from new motor vehicles, certification and test procedures, see 40 CFR 86.078–3 et seq.

Library References

Health and Environment ⚷25.6(6).
C.J.S. Health and Environment § 91 et seq.

§ 7522. Prohibited acts [CAA § 203]

(a) Enumerated prohibitions

The following acts and the causing thereof are prohibited—

(1) in the case of a manufacturer of new motor vehicles or new motor vehicle engines for distribution in commerce, the sale, or the offering for sale, or the introduction, or delivery for introduction, into commerce, or (in the case of any person, except as provided by regulation of the Administrator), the importation into the United States, of any new motor vehicle or new motor vehicle engine, manufactured after the effective date of regulations under this part which are applicable to such vehicle or engine unless such vehicle or engine is covered by a certificate of conformity issued (and in effect) under regulations prescribed under this part or part C of this subchapter in the case of clean-fuel vehicles (except as provided in subsection (b) of this section);

(2)(A) for any person to fail or refuse to permit access to or copying of records or to fail to make reports or provide information required under section 7542 of this title;

(B) for any person to fail or refuse to permit entry, testing or inspection authorized under section 7525(c) of this title or section 7542 of this title;

(C) for any person to fail or refuse to perform tests, or have tests performed as required under section 7542 of this title;

(D) for any manufacturer to fail to make information available as provided by regulation under section 7521(m)(5) of this title;

(3)(A) for any person to remove or render inoperative any device or element of design installed on or in a motor vehicle or motor vehicle engine in compliance with regulations under this subchapter prior to its sale and delivery to the ultimate purchaser, or for any person knowingly to remove or render inoperative any such device or element of design after such sale and delivery to the ultimate purchaser; or

(B) for any person to manufacture or sell, or offer to sell, or install, any part or component intended for use with, or as part of, any motor vehicle or motor vehicle engine, where a principal effect of the part or component is to bypass, defeat, or render inoperative any device or element of design installed on or in a motor vehicle or motor vehicle engine in compliance with regulations under this subchapter, and where the person knows or should know that such part or component is being offered for sale or installed for such use or put to such use; or

(4) for any manufacturer of a new motor vehicle or new motor vehicle engine subject to standards prescribed under section 7521 of this title or part C of this subchapter—

(A) to sell or lease any such vehicle or engine unless such manufacturer has complied with (i) the requirements of section 7541(a) and (b) of this title with respect to such vehicle or engine, and unless a label or tag is affixed to such vehicle or engine in accordance with section 7541(c)(3) of this title or (ii) the corresponding requirements of part C of this subchapter in the case of clean fuel vehicles unless the manufacturer has complied with the corresponding requirements of part C of this subchapter,

(B) to fail or refuse to comply with the requirements of section 7541(c) or (e) of this title or the corresponding requirements of part C of this subchapter in the case of clean fuel vehicles,

(C) except as provided in subsection (c)(3) of section 7541 of this title and the corresponding requirements of part C of this subchapter in the case of clean fuel vehicles, to provide directly or indirectly in any communication to the ultimate purchaser or any subsequent purchaser that the coverage of any warranty under this chapter is conditioned upon use of any part, component, or system manufactured by such manufacturer or any person acting for such manufacturer or under his control, or conditioned upon service performed by any such person, or

(D) to fail or refuse to comply with the terms and conditions of the warranty under section 7541(a) or (b) of this title or the corresponding requirements of part C of this subchapter in the case of clean fuel vehicles with respect to any vehicle.

No action with respect to any element of design referred to in paragraph (3) (including any adjustment or alteration of such element) shall be treated as a prohibited Act[1] under such paragraph (3) if such action is in accordance with section 7549 of this title. Nothing in paragraph (3) shall be construed to require the use of manufacturer parts in maintaining or repairing any motor vehicle or motor vehicle engine. For the purposes of the preceding sentence, the term "manufacturer parts" means, with respect to a motor vehicle engine, parts produced or sold by the manufacturer of the motor vehicle or motor vehicle engine. No action with respect to any device or element of design referred to in paragraph (3) shall be treated as a prohibited act under that paragraph if (i) the action is for the purpose of repair or replacement of the device or element, or is a necessary and temporary procedure to repair or replace any other item and the device or element is replaced upon completion of the procedure, and (ii) such action thereafter results in the proper functioning of the device or element referred to in paragraph (3). No action with respect to any device or element of design referred to in paragraph (3) shall be treated as a prohibited act under that paragraph if the action is for the purpose of a conversion of a motor vehicle for use of a clean alternative fuel (as defined in this subchapter) and if such vehicle complies with the applicable standard under section 7521 of this title when operating on such fuel, and if in the case of a clean alternative fuel vehicle (as defined by rule by the administrator), the device or element is replaced upon completion of the conversion procedure and such action results in proper functioning of the device or element when the motor vehicle operates on conventional fuel; or

(5) for any person to violate section 7553, 7554 of this title, or part C of this subchapter or any regulations under section 7553, 7554 of this title, or part C of this subchapter.

(b) Exemptions; refusal to admit vehicle or engine into United States; vehicles or engines intended for export

(1) The Administrator may exempt any new motor vehicle or new motor vehicle engine, from subsection (a) of this section, upon such terms and conditions as he may find necessary for the purpose of research, investigations, studies, demonstrations, or training, or for reasons of national security.

(2) A new motor vehicle or new motor vehicle engine offered for importation or imported by any person in violation of subsection (a) of this section shall be refused admission into the United States, but the Secretary of the Treasury and the Administrator may, by joint regulation, provide for deferring final determination as to admission and authorizing the delivery of such a motor vehicle or engine offered for import to the owner or consignee thereof upon such terms and conditions (including the furnishing of a bond) as may appear to them appropriate to insure that any such motor vehicle or engine will be brought into conformity with the standards, requirements, and limitations applicable to it under this part. The Secretary of the Treasury shall, if a motor vehicle or engine is finally refused admission under this paragraph, cause disposition thereof in accordance with the customs laws unless it is exported, under regulations prescribed by such Secretary, within ninety days of the date of notice of such refusal or such additional time as may be permitted pursuant to such regulations, except that disposition in accordance with the customs laws may not be made in such manner as may result, directly or indirectly, in the sale, to the ultimate consumer, of a new motor vehicle or new motor vehicle engine that fails to comply with applicable standards of the Administrator under this part.

(3) A new motor vehicle or new motor vehicle engine intended solely for export, and so labeled or tagged on the outside of the container and on the vehicle or engine itself, shall be subject to the provisions of subsection (a) of this section, except that if the country which is to receive such vehicle or engine has emission standards which differ from the standards prescribed under section 7521 of this title, then such vehicle or engine shall comply with the standards of such country which is to receive such vehicle or engine.

(c) Repealed. Pub.L. 101–549, title II, § 230(6), Nov. 15, 1990, 104 Stat. 2529

(July 14, 1955, ch. 360, title II, § 203, as added Oct. 20, 1965, Pub.L. 89–272, title I, § 101(8), 79 Stat. 993, and amended Nov. 21, 1967, Pub.L. 90–148, § 2, 81 Stat. 499; Dec. 31, 1970, Pub.L. 91–604, §§ 7(a), 11(a)(2)(A), 15(c)(2), 84 Stat. 1693, 1705, 1713; Aug. 7, 1977, Pub.L. 95–95, title II, §§ 206, 211(a), 218(a), (d), 219(a), (b), 91 Stat. 755, 757, 761, 762; Nov. 16, 1977, Pub.L. 95–190, § 14(a)(66)–(68), 91 Stat. 1403; Nov. 15, 1990, Pub.L. 101–549, title II, §§ 228(a), (b), (e), 230(6), 104 Stat. 2507, 2511, 2529.)

[1] So in original. Probably should be "act".

Effective Date of 1990 Amendment

Amendment by Pub.L. 101–549 effective Nov. 15, 1990, except as otherwise provided, see section 711(b) of Pub.L. 101–549, set out as a note under section 7401 of this title.

Savings Provisions

Suits, actions or proceedings commenced under this chapter as in effect prior to Nov. 15, 1990, not to abate by reason of the taking effect of amendments by Pub.L. 101–549, except as otherwise provided for, see section 711(a) of Pub.L. 101–549, set out as a note under section 7401 of this title.

CODE OF FEDERAL REGULATIONS

Air pollution from motor vehicles, control of, see 40 CFR 85.401 et seq.

Library References

Health and Environment ⟹25.6(6), 37, 38.
C.J.S. Health and Environment, §§ 48 et seq., 91 et seq.

§ 7523. Actions to restrain violations [CAA § 204]

(a) Jurisdiction

The district courts of the United States shall have jurisdiction to restrain violations of section 7522(a) of this title.

(b) Actions brought by or in name of United States; subpenas

Actions to restrain such violations shall be brought by and in the name of the United States. In any such action, subpenas for witnesses who are required to attend a district court in any district may run into any other district.

(July 14, 1955, ch. 360, title II, § 204, as added Oct. 20, 1965, Pub.L. 89–272, title I, § 101(8), 79 Stat. 994, and amended Nov. 21, 1967, Pub.L. 90–148, § 2, 81 Stat. 500; Dec. 31, 1970, Pub.L. 91–604, § 7(b), 84 Stat. 1694; Aug. 7, 1977, Pub.L. 95–95, title II, § 218(b), 91 Stat. 761.)

Library References

Federal Courts ⟹192.
C.J.S. Federal Courts § 30 et seq.

§ 7524. Civil penalties [CAA § 205]

(a) Violations

Any person who violates sections 7522(a)(1), 7522(a)(4), or 7522(a)(5) of this title or any manufacturer or dealer who violates section 7522(a)(3)(A) of this title shall be subject to a civil penalty of not more than $25,000. Any person other than a manufacturer or dealer who violates section 7522(a)(3)(A) of this title or any person who violates section 7522(a)(3)(B) of this title shall be subject to a civil penalty of not more than $2,500. Any such violation with respect to paragraph (1), (3)(A), or (4) of section 7522(a) of this title shall constitute a separate offense with respect to each motor vehicle or motor vehicle engine. Any such violation with respect to section 7522(a)(3)(B) of this title shall constitute a separate offense with respect to each part or component. Any person who violates section 7522(a)(2) of this title shall be subject to a civil penalty of not more than $25,000 per day of violation.

(b) Civil actions

The Administrator may commence a civil action to assess and recover any civil penalty under subsection (a) of this section, section 7545(d) of this title, or section 7547(d) of this title. Any action under this subsection may be brought in the district court of the United States for the district in which the violation is alleged to have occurred or in which the defendant resides or has the Administrator's principal place of business, and the court shall have jurisdiction to assess a civil penalty. In determining the amount of any civil penalty to be assessed under this subsection, the court shall take into account the gravity of the violation, the economic benefit or savings (if any) resulting from the violation, the size of the violator's business, the violator's history of compliance with this title, action taken to remedy the violation, the effect of the penalty on the violator's ability to continue in business, and such other matters as justice may require. In any such action, subpoenas for witnesses who are required to attend a district court in any district may run into any other district.

(c) Administrative assessment of certain penalties

(1) Administrative penalty authority

In lieu of commencing a civil action under subsection (b) of this section, the Administrator may assess any civil penalty prescribed in subsection (a) of this section, section 7545(d) of this title, or section 7547(d) of this title, except that the maximum amount of penalty sought against each violator in a penalty assessment proceeding shall not exceed $200,000, unless the Administrator and the Attorney General jointly determine that a matter involving a larger penalty amount is appropriate for administrative penalty assessment. Any such determination by the Administrator and the Attorney General shall not be subject to judicial review. Assessment of a civil penalty under this subsection shall be by an order made on the record after opportunity for a hearing in accordance with sections 554 and 556 of Title 5. The Administrator shall issue reasonable rules for discovery and other procedures for hearings under this paragraph. Before issuing such an order, the Administrator shall give written notice to the person to be assessed an administrative penalty of the Administrator's proposal to issue such order and provide such person an opportunity to request such a hearing on the order, within 30 days of the date the notice is received by such person. The Administrator may compromise, or remit, with or without conditions, any administrative penalty which may be imposed under this section.

(2) Determining amount

In determining the amount of any civil penalty assessed under this subsection, the Administrator shall take into account the gravity of the violation, the economic benefit or savings (if any) resulting from the violation, the size of the violator's business, the violator's history of compliance with this subchapter, action taken to remedy the violation, the effect of the penalty on the violator's ability to continue in business, and such other matters as justice may require.

(3) Effect of Administrator's action

(A) Action by the Administrator under this subsection shall not affect or limit the Administrator's authority to enforce any provision of this chapter, except that any violation,

(i) with respect to which the Administrator has commenced and is diligently prosecuting an action under this subsection, or

(ii) for which the Administrator has issued a final order not subject to further judicial review and the violator has paid a penalty assessment under this subsection,

shall not be the subject of civil penalty action under subsection (b) of this section.

(B) No action by the Administrator under this subsection shall affect any person's obligation to comply with any section of this chapter.

(4) Finality of order

An order issued under this subsection shall become final 30 days after its issuance unless a petition for judicial review is filed under paragraph (5).

(5) Judicial review

Any person against whom a civil penalty is assessed in accordance with this subsection may seek review of the assessment in the United States District Court for the District of Columbia, or for the district in which the violation is alleged to have occurred, in which such person resides, or where such person's principal place of business is located, within the 30–day period beginning on the date a civil penalty order is issued. Such person shall simultaneously send a copy of the filing by certified mail to the Administrator and the Attorney General. The Administrator shall file in the court a certified copy, or certified index, as appropriate, of the record on which the order was issued within 30 days. The court shall not set aside or remand any order issued in accordance with the requirements of this subsection unless there is not substantial evidence in the record, taken as a whole, to support the finding of a violation or unless the Administrator's assessment of the penalty constitutes an abuse of discretion, and the court shall not impose additional civil penalties unless the Administrator's assessment of the penalty constitutes an abuse of discretion. In any proceedings, the United States may seek to recover civil penalties assessed under this section.

(6) Collection

If any person fails to pay an assessment of a civil penalty imposed by the Administrator as provided in this subsection—

(A) after the order making the assessment has become final, or

(B) after a court in an action brought under paragraph (5) has entered a final judgment in favor of the Administrator,

the Administrator shall request the Attorney General to bring a civil action in an appropriate district court to recover the amount assessed (plus interest at rates established pursuant to section 6621(a)(2) of Title 26 from the date of the final order or the date of the final judgment, as the case may be). In such an action, the validity, amount, and appropriateness of the penalty shall not be subject to review. Any person who fails to pay on a timely basis the amount of an assessment of a civil penalty as described in the first sentence of this paragraph shall be required to pay, in addition to that amount and interest, the United States' enforcement expenses, including attorneys fees and costs for collection proceedings, and a quarterly nonpayment penalty for each quarter during which such failure to pay persists. The nonpayment penalty shall be in an amount equal to 10 percent of the aggregate amount of that person's penalties and nonpayment penalties which are unpaid as of the beginning of such quarter.

(July 14, 1955, ch. 360, title I, § 205, as added Oct. 20, 1965, Pub.L. 89–272, title I, § 101(8), 79 Stat. 994, and amended Nov. 21, 1967, Pub.L. 90–148, § 2, 81 Stat. 500; Dec. 31, 1970, Pub.L. 91–604, § 7(c), 84 Stat. 1694; Aug. 7, 1977, Pub.L. 95–95, title II, § 219(c), 91 Stat. 762; Nov. 15, 1990, Pub.L. 101–549, title II, § 228(c), 104 Stat. 2508.)

Effective Date of 1990 Amendment

Amendment by Pub.L. 101–549 effective Nov. 15, 1990, except as otherwise provided, see section 711(b) of Pub.L. 101–549, set out as a note under section 7401 of this title.

Savings Provisions

Suits, actions or proceedings commenced under this chapter as in effect prior to Nov. 15, 1990, not to abate by reason of the taking effect of amendments by Pub.L. 101–549, except as otherwise provid-

ed for, see section 711(a) of Pub.L. 101–549, set out as a note under section 7401 of this title.

CODE OF FEDERAL REGULATIONS

Control of air pollution from new motor vehicles, certification and test procedures, see 40 CFR 86.078–3 et seq.

Library References

Health and Environment ⚐38.
C.J.S. Health and Environment § 49 et seq.

§ 7525. Motor vehicle and motor vehicle engine compliance testing and certification [CAA § 206]

(a) Testing and issuance of certificate of conformity

(1) The Administrator shall test, or require to be tested in such manner as he deems appropriate, any new motor vehicle or new motor vehicle engine submitted by a manufacturer to determine whether such vehicle or engine conforms with the regulations prescribed under section 7521 of this title. If such vehicle or engine conforms to such regulations, the Administrator shall issue a certificate of conformity upon such terms, and for such period (not in excess of one year), as he may prescribe. In the case of any original equipment manufacturer (as defined by the Administrator in regulations promulgated before November 15, 1990) of vehicles or vehicle engines whose projected sales in the United States for any model year (as determined by the Administrator) will not exceed 300, the Administrator shall not require, for purposes of determining compliance with regulations under section 7521 of this title for the useful life of the vehicle or engine, operation of any vehicle or engine manufactured during such model year for more than 5,000 miles or 160 hours, respectively, unless the Administrator, by regulation, prescribes otherwise. The Administrator shall apply any adjustment factors that the Administrator deems appropriate to assure that each vehicle or engine will comply during its useful life (as determined under section 7521(d) of this title) with the regulations prescribed under section 7521 of this title.

(2) The Administrator shall test any emission control system incorporated in a motor vehicle or motor vehicle engine submitted to him by any person, in order to determine whether such system enables such vehicle or engine to conform to the standards required to be prescribed under section 7521(b) of this title. If the Administrator finds on the basis of such tests that such vehicle or engine conforms to such standards, the Administrator shall issue a verification of compliance with emission standards for such system when incorporated in vehicles of a class of which the tested vehicle is representative. He shall inform manufacturers and the National Academy of Sciences, and make available to the public, the results of such tests. Tests under this paragraph shall be conducted under such terms and conditions (including requirements for preliminary testing by qualified independent laboratories) as the Administrator may prescribe by regulations.

(3)(A) A certificate of conformity may be issued under this section only if the Administrator determines that the manufacturer (or in the case of a vehicle or engine for import, any person) has established to the satisfaction of the Administrator that any emission control device, system, or element of design installed on, or incorporated in, such vehicle or engine conforms to applicable requirements of section 7521(a)(4) of this title.

(B) The Administrator may conduct such tests and may require the manufacturer (or any such person) to conduct such tests and provide such information as is necessary to carry out subparagraph (A) of this paragraph. Such requirements shall include a requirement for prompt reporting of the emission of any unregulated pollutant from a system, device, or element of design if such pollutant was not emitted, or was emitted in significantly lesser amounts, from the vehicle or engine without use of the system, device, or element of design.

(4)(A) Not later than 12 months after November 15, 1990, the Administrator shall revise the regulations promulgated under this subsection to add test procedures capable of determining whether model year 1994 and later model year light-duty vehicles and light-duty trucks, when properly maintained and used, will pass the inspection methods and procedures established under section 7541(b) of this title for that model year, under conditions reasonably likely to be encountered in the conduct of inspection and maintenance programs, but which those programs cannot reasonably influence or control. The conditions shall include fuel characteristics, ambient temperature, and short (30 minutes or less) waiting periods before tests are conducted. The Administrator shall not grant a certificate of conformity under this subsection for any 1994 or later model year vehicle or engine that the Administrator concludes cannot pass the test procedures established under this paragraph.

(B) From time to time, the Administrator may revise the regulations promulgated under subparagraph (A), as the Administrator deems appropriate.

(b) Testing procedures; hearing; judicial review; additional evidence

(1) In order to determine whether new motor vehicles or new motor vehicle engines being manufactured by a manufacturer do in fact conform with the regulations with respect to which the certificate of conformity was issued, the Administrator is authorized to test such vehicles or engines. Such tests may be conducted by the Administrator directly or, in accordance with conditions specified by the Administrator, by the manufacturer.

(2)(A)(i) If, based on tests conducted under paragraph (1) on a sample of new vehicles or engines covered by a certificate of conformity, the Administrator determines that all or part of the vehicles or engines so covered do not conform with the regulations with respect to which the certificate of conformity was issued and with the requirements of section 7521(a)(4) of this title, he may suspend or revoke such certificate in whole or in part, and shall so notify the manufacturer. Such suspension or revocation shall apply in the case of any new motor vehicles or new motor vehicle engines manufactured after the date of such notification (or manufactured before such date if still in the hands of the manufacturer), and shall apply until such time as the Administrator finds that vehicles and engines manufactured by the manufacturer do conform to such regulations and requirements. If, during any period of suspension or revocation, the Administrator finds that a vehicle or engine actually conforms to such regulations and requirements, he shall issue a certificate of conformity applicable to such vehicle or engine.

(ii) If, based on tests conducted under paragraph (1) on any new vehicle or engine, the Administrator determines that such vehicle or engine does not conform with such regulations and requirements, he may suspend or revoke such certificate insofar as it applies to such vehicle or engine until such time as he finds such vehicle or engine actually so conforms with such regulations and requirements, and he shall so notify the manufacturer.

(B)(i) At the request of any manufacturer the Administrator shall grant such manufacturer a hearing as to whether the tests have been properly conducted or any sampling methods have been properly applied, and make a determination on the record with respect to any suspension or revocation under subparagraph (A); but suspension or revocation under subparagraph (A) shall not be stayed by reason of such hearing.

(ii) In any case of actual controversy as to the validity of any determination under clause (i), the manufacturer may at any time prior to the 60th day after such determination is made file a petition with the United States court of appeals for the circuit wherein such manufacturer resides or has his principal place of business for a judicial review of such determination. A copy of the petition shall be forthwith transmitted by the clerk of the court to the Administrator or other officer designated by him for that purpose. The Administrator thereupon shall file in the court the record of the proceedings on which the Administrator based his determination, as provided in section 2112 of Title 28.

(iii) If the petitioner applies to the court for leave to adduce additional evidence, and shows to the satisfaction of the court that such additional evidence is material and that there were reasonable grounds for the failure to adduce such evidence in the proceeding before the Administrator, the court may order such additional evidence (and evidence in rebuttal thereof) to be taken before the Administrator, in such manner and upon such terms and conditions as the court may deem proper. The Administrator may modify his findings as to the facts, or make new findings, by reason of the additional evidence so taken and he shall file such modified or new findings, and his recommendation, if any, for the modification or setting aside of his original determination, with the return of such additional evidence.

(iv) Upon the filing of the petition referred to in clause (ii), the court shall have jurisdiction to review the order in accordance with chapter 7 of Title 5 and to grant appropriate relief as provided in such chapter.

(c) Inspection

For purposes of enforcement of this section, officers or employees duly designated by the Administrator, upon presenting appropriate credentials to the manufacturer or person in charge, are authorized (1) to enter, at reasonable times, any plant or other establishment of such manufacturer, for the purpose of conducting tests of vehicles or engines in the hands of the manufacturer, or (2) to inspect, at reasonable times, records, files, papers, processes, controls, and facilities used by such manufacturer in conducting tests under regulations of the Administrator. Each such inspection shall be commenced and completed with reasonable promptness.

(d) Rules and regulations

The Administrator shall by regulation establish methods and procedures for making tests under this section.

(e) Publication of test results

The Administrator shall make available to the public the results of his tests of any motor vehicle or motor vehicle engine submitted by a manufacturer under subsection (a) of this section as promptly as possible after December 31, 1970, and at the beginning of each model year which begins thereafter. Such results shall be described in such nontechnical manner as will reasonably disclose to prospective ultimate purchasers of new motor vehicles and new motor vehicle engines the comparative performance of the vehicles and engines tested in meeting the standards prescribed under section 7521 of this title.

(f) High altitude regulations

All light duty vehicles and engines manufactured during or after model year 1984 and all light-duty trucks manufactured during or after model year 1995 shall comply with the requirements of section 7521 of this title regardless of the altitude at which they are sold.

(g) Nonconformance penalty

(1) In the case of any class or category of heavy-duty vehicles or engines to which a standard promulgated under section 7521(a) of this title applies, except as provided in paragraph (2), a certificate of conformity shall be issued under subsection (a) of this section and shall not be suspended or revoked under subsection (b) of this section for such vehicles or engines manufactured by a manufacturer notwithstanding the failure of such vehicles or engines to meet such standard if such manufacturer pays a nonconformance penalty as provided under regulations promulgated by the Administrator after notice and opportunity for public hearing. In the case of motorcycles to which such a standard applies, such a certificate may be issued notwithstanding such failure if the manufacturer pays such a penalty.

(2) No certificate of conformity may be issued under paragraph (1) with respect to any class or category of vehicle or engine if the degree by which the manufacturer fails to meet any standard promulgated under section 7521(a) of this title with respect to such class or category exceeds the percentage determined under regulations promulgated by the Administrator to be practicable. Such regulations shall require such testing of vehicles or engines being produced as may be necessary to determine the percentage of the classes or categories of vehicles or engines which are not in compliance with the regulations with respect to which a certificate of conformity was issued and shall be promulgated not later than one year after August 7, 1977.

(3) The regulations promulgated under paragraph (1) shall, not later than one year after August 7, 1977, provide for nonconformance penalties in amounts determined under a formula established by the Administrator. Such penalties under such formula—

(A) may vary from pollutant-to-pollutant;

(B) may vary by class or category or vehicle or engine;

(C) shall take into account the extent to which actual emissions of any air pollutant exceed allowable emissions under the standards promulgated under section 7521 of this title;

(D) shall be increased periodically in order to create incentives for the development of production vehicles or engines which achieve the required degree of emission reduction; and

(E) shall remove any competitive disadvantage to manufacturers whose engines or vehicles achieve the required degree of emission reduction (including any such disadvantage arising from the application of paragraph (4)).

(4) In any case in which a certificate of conformity has been issued under this subsection, any warranty required under section 7541(b)(2) of this title and any action under section 7541(c) of this title shall be required to be effective only for the emission levels which the Administrator determines that such certificate was issued and not for the emission levels required under the applicable standard.

(5) The authorities of section 7542(a) of this title shall apply, subject to the conditions of section 7542(b) of this title, for purposes of this subsection.

(h) Review and revision of regulations

Within 18 months after the enactment of the Clean Air Act Amendments of 1990, the Administrator shall review and revise as necessary the regulations under subsection (a) and (b) of this section regarding the testing of motor vehicles and motor vehicle engines to insure that vehicles are tested under circumstances which reflect the actual current driving conditions under which motor vehicles are used, including conditions relating to fuel, temperature, acceleration, and altitude.

(July 14, 1955, ch. 360, title II, § 206, as added Dec. 31, 1970, Pub.L. 91–604, § 8(a), 84 Stat. 1694, and amended Aug. 7, 1977, Pub.L. 95–95, title II, §§ 213(a), 214(b), (c), 220, 224(e), 91 Stat. 758–760, 762, 768; Nov. 16, 1977, Pub.L. 95–190, § 14(a)(69), 91 Stat. 1403; Nov. 15, 1990, Pub.L. 101–549, title II, §§ 208, 230(7), (8), 104 Stat. 2483, 2529.)

References in Text

The enactment of the Clean Air Act Amendments of 1990, referred to in subsec. (h), probably means the date of enactment of the Clean Air Act Amendments of 1990, Pub.L. 101–549, which was approved November 15, 1990.

Effective Date of 1990 Amendment

Amendment by Pub.L. 101–549 effective Nov. 15, 1990, except as otherwise provided, see section 711(b) of Pub.L. 101–549, set out as a note under section 7401 of this title.

Effective Date

Section 8(b) of Pub.L. 91–604, Dec. 31, 1970, 84 Stat. 1698, provided that: "The amendments made by this section [enacting sections 7525 and 7541 of this title] shall not apply to vehicles or engines imported into the United States before the sixtieth day after the date of enactment of this Act [Dec. 31, 1970]."

Savings Provisions

Suits, actions or proceedings commenced under this chapter as in effect prior to Nov. 15, 1990, not to abate by reason of the taking effect of amendments by Pub.L. 101–549, except as otherwise provided for, see section 711(a) of Pub.L. 101–549, set out as a note under section 7401 of this title.

Cross References

Determination of fuel economy for purposes of gas guzzler tax, see section 4064 of Title 26, Internal Revenue Code.

Fuel economy defined for purposes of Automobile Propulsion Research and Development Act of 1978, see section 2702 of Title 15, Commerce and Trade.

Testing and calculation procedures for measurement of average fuel economy, see section 2003 of Title 15.

CODE OF FEDERAL REGULATIONS

Control of air pollution from new motor vehicles, certification and test procedures, see 40 CFR 86.078–3 et seq.

Library References

Health and Environment ⚷25.6(6).
C.J.S. Health and Environment § 91 et seq.

§ 7541. Compliance by vehicles and engines in actual use [CAA § 207]

(a) Warranty; certification; payment of replacement costs of parts, devices, or components designed for emission control

(1) Effective with respect to vehicles and engines manufactured in model years beginning more than 60 days after December 31, 1970, the manufacturer of each new motor vehicle and new motor vehicle engine shall warrant to the ultimate purchaser and each subsequent purchaser that such vehicle or engine is (A) designed, built, and equipped so as to conform at the time of sale with applicable regulations under section 7521 of this title, and (B) free from defects in materials and workmanship which cause such vehicle or engine to fail to conform with applicable regulations for its useful life (as determined under section 7521(d) of this title). In the case of vehicles and engines manufactured in the model year 1995 and thereafter such warranty shall require that the vehicle or engine is free from any such defects for the warranty period provided under subsection (i) of this section.

(2) In the case of a motor vehicle part or motor vehicle engine part, the manufacturer or rebuilder of such part may certify that use of such part will not result in a failure of the vehicle or engine to comply with emission standards promulgated under section 7521 of this title. Such certification shall be made only under such regulations as may be promulgated by the Administrator to carry out the purposes of subsection (b) of this section. The Administrator shall promulgate such regulations no later than two years following August 7, 1977.

(3) The cost of any part, device, or component of any light-duty vehicle that is designed for emission control and which in the instructions issued pursuant to subsection (c)(3) of this section is scheduled for replacement during the useful life of the vehicle in order to maintain compliance with regulations under section 7521 of this title, the failure of which shall not interfere with the normal performance of the vehicle, and the expected retail price of which, including installation costs, is greater than 2 percent of the suggested retail price of such vehicle, shall be borne or reimbursed at the time of replacement by the vehicle manufacturer and such replacement shall be provided without cost to the ultimate purchaser, subsequent purchaser, or dealer. The term "designed for emission control" as used in the preceding sentence means a catalytic converter, thermal reactor, or other component installed on or in a vehicle for the sole or primary purpose of reducing vehicle emissions (not including those vehicle components which were in general use prior to model year 1968 and the primary function of which is not related to emission control).

(b) Testing methods and procedures

If the Administrator determines that (i) there are available testing methods and procedures to ascertain whether, when in actual use throughout its [1] the warranty period (as determined under subsection (i) of this section), each vehicle and engine to which regulations under section 7521 of this title apply complies with the emission standards of such regulations, (ii) such methods and procedures are in accordance with good engineering practices, and (iii) such methods and procedures are reasonably capable of being correlated with tests conducted under section 7525(a)(1) of this title, then—

(1) he shall establish such methods and procedures by regulation, and

(2) at such time as he determines that inspection facilities or equipment are available for purposes of carrying out testing methods and procedures established under paragraph (1), he shall prescribe regulations which shall require manufacturers to warrant the emission control device or system of each new motor vehicle or new motor vehicle engine to which a regulation under section 7521 of this title applies and which is manufactured in a model year beginning after the Administrator first prescribes warranty regulations under this paragraph (2). The warranty under such regulations shall run to the ultimate purchaser and each subsequent purchaser and shall provide that if—

(A) the vehicle or engine is maintained and operated in accordance with instructions under subsection (c)(3) of this section,

(B) it fails to conform at any time during its[1] the warranty period (as determined under subsection (i) of this section), to the regulations prescribed under section 7521 of this title, and

(C) such nonconformity results in the ultimate purchaser (or any subsequent purchaser) of such vehicle or engine having to bear any penalty or other sanction (including the denial of the right to use such vehicle or engine) under State or Federal law,

then such manufacturer shall remedy such nonconformity under such warranty with the cost thereof to be borne by the manufacturer. No such warranty shall be invalid on the basis of any part used in the maintenance or repair of a vehicle or engine if such part was certified as provided under subsection (a)(2) of this section.

(c) Nonconforming vehicles; plan for remedying nonconformity; instructions for maintenance and use; label or tag; in-use standards

Effective with respect to vehicles and engines manufactured during model years beginning more than 60 days after December 31, 1970—

(1) If the Administrator determines that a substantial number of any class or category of vehicles or engines, although properly maintained and used, do not conform to the regulations prescribed under section 7521 of this title, when in actual use throughout their useful life (as determined under section 7521(d) of this title), he shall immediately notify the manufacturer thereof of such nonconformity, and he shall require the manufacturer to submit a plan for remedying the nonconformity of the vehicles or engines with respect to which such notification is given. The plan shall provide that the nonconformity of any such vehicles or engines which are properly used and maintained will be remedied at the expense of the manufacturer. If the manufacturer disagrees with such determination of nonconformity and so advises the Administrator, the Administrator shall afford the manufacturer and other interested persons an opportunity to present their views and evidence in support thereof at a public hearing. Unless, as a result of such hearing the Administrator withdraws such determination of nonconformity, he shall, within 60 days after the completion of such hearing, order the manufacturer to provide prompt notification of such nonconformity in accordance with paragraph (2).

(2) Any notification required by paragraph (1) with respect to any class or category of vehicles or engines shall be given to dealers, ultimate purchasers, and subsequent purchasers (if known) in such manner and containing such information as the Administrator may by regulations require.

(3)(A) The manufacturer shall furnish with each new motor vehicle or motor vehicle engine written instructions for the proper maintenance and use of the vehicle or engine by the ultimate purchaser and such instructions shall correspond to regulations which the Administrator shall promulgate. The manufacturer shall provide in boldface type on the first page of the written maintenance instructions notice that maintenance, replacement, or repair of the emission control devices and systems may be performed by any automotive repair establishment or individual using any automotive part which has been certified as provided in subsection (a)(2) of this section.

(B) The instruction under subparagraph (A) of this paragraph shall not include any condition on the ultimate purchaser's using, in connection with such vehicle or engine, any component or service (other than a component or service provided without charge under the terms of the purchase agreement) which is identified by brand, trade, or corporate name; or directly or indirectly distinguishing between service performed by the franchised dealers of such manufacturer or any other service establishments with which such manufacturer has a commercial relationship, and service performed by independent automotive repair facilities with which such manufacturer has no commercial relationship; except that the prohibition of this subsection may be waived by the Administrator if—

(i) the manufacturer satisfies the Administrator that the vehicle or engine will function properly only if the component or service so identified is used in connection with such vehicle or engine, and

(ii) the Administrator finds that such a waiver is in the public interest.

(C) In addition, the manufacturer shall indicate by means of a label or tag permanently affixed to such vehicle or engine that such vehicle or engine is covered by a certificate of conformity issued for the purpose of assuring achievement of emissions standards prescribed under section 7521 of this title. Such label or tag shall contain such other information relating to control of motor vehicle emissions as the Administrator shall prescribe by regulation.

(4) Intermediate in-use standards.—

(A) Model years 1994 and 1995.—For light-duty trucks of up to 6,000 lbs. gross vehicle weight rating (GVWR) and light-duty vehicles which are subject to standards under table G of section 7521(g)(1) of this section in model years 1994 and 1995 (40 percent of the manufacturer's sales volume in model year 1994 and 80 percent in model year 1995), the standards applicable to NMHC, CO, and NO_x for purposes of this subsection shall be those set forth in table A below in lieu of the standards for such air pollutants otherwise applicable under this subchapter.

TABLE A—INTERMEDIATE IN-USE STANDARDS LDTs UP TO 6,000 LBS. GVWR AND LIGHT-DUTY VEHICLES

Vehicle type	NMHC	CO	NO_x
Light-duty vehicles	0.32	3.4	0.4 *
LDT's (0–3,750 LVW)	0.32	5.2	0.4 *
LDT's (3,751–5,750 LVW).....	0.41	6.7	0.7 *

* Not applicable to diesel-fueled vehicles.

(B) Model years 1996 and thereafter.—(i) In the model years 1996 and 1997, light-duty trucks (LDTs) up to 6,000 lbs. gross vehicle weight rating (GVWR) and light-duty vehicles which are not subject to final in-use standards under paragraph (5) (60 percent of the manufacturer's sales volume in model year 1996 and 20 percent in model year 1997) shall be subject to the standards set forth in table A of subparagraph (A) for NMHC, CO, and NO_x for purposes of this subsection in lieu of those set forth in paragraph (5).

(ii) For LDTs of more than 6,000 lbs. GVWR—

(I) in model year 1996 which are subject to the standards set forth in Table H of section 7521(h) of this title (50%);

(II) in model year 1997 (100%); and

(III) in model year 1998 which are not subject to final in-use standards under paragraph (5) (50%);

the standards for NMHC, CO, and NO_x for purposes of this subsection shall be those set forth in Table B below in lieu of the standards for such air pollutants otherwise applicable under this subchapter.

TABLE B—INTERMEDIATE IN-USE STANDARDS LDTs MORE THAN 6,000 LBS. GVWR

Vehicle type	NMHC	CO	No_x
LDTs (3,751–5,750 lbs. TW) ...	0.40	5.5	0.88 *
LDTs (over 5,750 lbs. TW)	0.49	6.2	1.38 *

* Not applicable to diesel-fueled vehicles.

(C) Useful life.—In the case of the in-use standards applicable under this paragraph, for purposes of applying this subsection, the applicable useful life shall be 5 years or 50,000 miles or the equivalent (whichever first occurs).

(5) Final in-use standards.—(A) After the model year 1995, for purposes of applying this subsection, in the case of the percentage specified in the implementation schedule below of each manufacturer's sales volume of light-duty trucks of up to 6,000 lbs. gross vehicle weight rating (GVWR) and light duty vehicles, the standards for NMHC, CO, and NO_x shall be as provided in Table G in section 7521(g) of this title, except that in applying the standards set forth in Table G for purposes of determining compliance with this subsection, the applicable useful life shall be (i) 5 years or 50,000 miles (or the equivalent) whichever first occurs in the case of standards applicable for purposes of certification at 50,000 miles; and (ii) 10 years or 100,000 miles (or the equivalent), whichever first occurs in the case of standards applicable for purposes of certification at 100,000 miles, except that no testing shall be done beyond 7 years or 75,000 miles, or the equivalent whichever first occurs.

LDTs UP TO 6,000 LBS. GVWR AND LIGHT-DUTY VEHICLE SCHEDULE FOR IMPLEMENTATION OF FINAL IN-USE STANDARDS

Model year	Percent
1996	40
1997	80
1998	100

(B) After the model year 1997, for purposes of applying this subsection, in the case of the percentage specified in the implementation schedule below of each manufacturer's sales volume of light-duty trucks of more than 6,000 lbs. gross vehicle weight rating (GVWR), the standards for NMHC, CO, and NO_x shall be as provided in Table H in section 7521(h) of this title, except that in applying the standards set forth in Table H for purposes of determining compliance with this subsection, the applicable useful life shall be (i) 5 years or 50,000 miles (or the equivalent) whichever first occurs in the case of standards applicable for purposes of certification at 50,000 miles; and (ii) 11 years or 120,000 miles (or the equivalent), whichever first occurs in the case of standards applicable for purposes of certification at 120,000 miles, except that no testing shall be done beyond 7 years or 90,000 miles (or the equivalent) whichever first occurs.

LDTs OF MORE THAN 6,000 LBS. GVWR IMPLEMENTATION SCHEDULE FOR IMPLEMENTATION OF FINAL IN-USE STANDARDS

Model year	Percent
1998	50
1999	100

(6) Diesel vehicles; in-use useful life and testing.—**(A)** In the case of diesel-fueled light-duty trucks up to 6,000 lbs. GVWR and light-duty vehicles, the useful life for purposes of determining in-use compliance with the standards under section 7521(g) of this title for NO_x shall be a period of 10 years or 100,000 miles (or the equivalent), whichever first occurs, in the case of standards applicable for purposes of certification at 100,000 miles, except that testing shall not be done for a period beyond 7 years or 75,000 miles (or the equivalent) whichever first occurs.

(B) In the case of diesel-fueled light-duty trucks of 6,000 lbs. GVWR or more, the useful life for purposes of determining in-use compliance with the standards under section 7521(h) of this title for NO_x shall be a period of 11 years or 120,000 miles (or the equivalent), whichever first occurs, in the case of standards applicable for purposes of certification at 120,000 miles, except that testing shall not be done for a period beyond 7 years or 90,000 miles (or the equivalent) whichever first occurs.

(d) Dealer costs borne by manufacturer

Any cost obligation of any dealer incurred as a result of any requirement imposed by subsection (a), (b), or (c) of this section shall be borne by the manufacturer. The transfer of any such cost obligation from a manufacturer to any dealer through franchise or other agreement is prohibited.

(e) Cost statement

If a manufacturer includes in any advertisement a statement respecting the cost or value of emission control devices or systems, such manufacturer shall set forth in such statement the cost or value attributed to such devices or systems by the Secretary of Labor (through the Bureau of Labor Statistics). The Secretary of Labor, and his representatives, shall have the same access for this purpose to the books, documents, papers, and records of a manufacturer as the Comptroller General has to those of a recipient of assistance for purposes of section 7611 of this title.

(f) Inspection after sale to ultimate purchaser

Any inspection of a motor vehicle or a motor vehicle engine for purposes of subsection (c)(1) of this section, after its sale to the ultimate purchaser, shall be made only if the owner of such vehicle or engine voluntarily permits such inspection to be made, except as may be provided by any State or local inspection program.

(g) Replacement and maintenance costs borne by owner

For the purposes of this section, the owner of any motor vehicle or motor vehicle engine warranted under this section is responsible in the proper maintenance of such vehicle or engine to replace and to maintain, at his expense at any service establishment or facility of his choosing, such items as spark plugs, points, condensers, and any other part, item, or device related to emission control (but not designed for emission control under the terms of the last sentence of subsection (a)(3) of this section), unless such part, item, or device is covered by any warranty not mandated by this chapter.

(h) Dealer certification

(1) Upon the sale of each new light-duty motor vehicle by a dealer, the dealer shall furnish to the purchaser a certificate that such motor vehicle conforms to the applicable regulations under section 7521 of this title, including notice of the purchaser's rights under paragraph (2).

(2) If at any time during the period for which the warranty applies under subsection (b) of this section, a motor vehicle fails to conform to the applicable regulations under section 7521 of this title as determined under subsection (b) of this section such nonconformity shall be remedied by the manufacturer at the cost of the manufacturer pursuant to such warranty as provided in subsection (b)(2) of this section (without regard to subparagraph (C) thereof).

(3) Nothing in section 7543(a) of this title shall be construed to prohibit a State from testing, or requiring testing of, a motor vehicle after the date of sale of such vehicle to the ultimate purchaser (except that no new motor vehicle manufacturer or dealer may be required to conduct testing under this paragraph).

(i) Warranty period.

(1) In general

For purposes of subsection (a)(1) of this section and subsection (b) of this section, the warranty period, effective with respect to new light-duty trucks and new light-duty vehicles and engines, manufactured in the model year 1995 and thereafter, shall be the first 2 years or 24,000 miles of use (whichever first occurs), except as provided in paragraph (2). For purposes of subsection (a)(1) and subsection (b) of this section, for other vehicles and engines the warranty period shall be the period established by the Administrator by regulation (promulgated prior to the enactment of the Clean Air Act Amendments of 1990) for such purposes unless the Administrator subsequently modifies such regulation.

(2) Specified major emission control components

In the case of a specified major emission control component, the warranty period for new light-duty trucks and new light-duty vehicles and engines manufactured in the model year 1995 and thereafter for purposes of subsection (a)(1) and subsection (b) of this section shall be 8 years or 80,000 miles of use (whichever first occurs). As used in this paragraph, the term 'specified major emission control component' means only a catalytic converter, an electronic emissions control unit, and an onboard emissions diagnostic device, except that the Administrator may designate any other pollution control device or component as a specified major emission control component if—

(A) the device or component was not in general use on vehicles and engines manufactured prior to the model year 1990; and

(B) the Administrator determines that the retail cost (exclusive of installation costs) of such device or component exceeds $200 (in 1989 dollars), adjusted for inflation or deflation as calculated by the Administrator at the time of such determination.

For purposes of this paragraph, the term 'onboard emissions diagnostic device' means any device installed for the purpose of storing or processing emissions related diagnostic information, but not including any parts or other systems which it monitors except specified major emissions control components. Nothing in this chapter shall be construed to provide that any part (other than a part referred to in the preceding sentence) shall be required to be warranted under this chapter for the period of 8 years or 80,000 miles referred to in this paragraph.

(3) Instructions

Subparagraph (A) of subsection (b)(2) of this section shall apply only where the Administrator has made a determination that the instructions concerned conform to the requirements of subsection (c)(3) of this section.

(July 14, 1955, ch. 360, title II, § 207, as added Dec. 31, 1970, Pub.L. 91–604, § 8(a), 84 Stat. 1696, and amended Aug. 7, 1977, Pub.L. 95–95, title II, §§ 205, 208–210, 212, 91 Stat. 754–756, 758; Nov. 16, 1977, Pub.L. 95–190, § 14(a)(70)–(72), 91 Stat. 1403; Nov. 15, 1990, Pub.L. 101–549, title II, §§ 209, 210, 230(9), 104 Stat. 2484, 2485, 2529.)

1 So in original.

References in Text

"Prior to the enactment of the Clean Air Act Amendments of 1990", referred to in subsec. (i)(1), probably means prior to the date of enactment of the Clean Air Act Amendments of 1990, Pub.L. 101–549, which was approved November 15, 1990.

Codification

Section was formerly classified to § 1857f–5a of this title.

Prior Provisions

A prior § 207 of Act July 14, 1955, was renumbered § 208 by Pub.L. 91–604 and is set out as § 7542 of this title.

Effective Date of 1990 Amendment

Amendment by Pub.L. 101–549 effective Nov. 15, 1990, except as otherwise provided, see section 711(b) of Pub.L. 101–549, set out as a note under section 7401 of this title.

Section 209 of Pub.L. 101–549, provided in part that the amendments made by such section [enacting subsec. (i) of this section and amending subsecs. (a) and (b) of this section] shall be effective with respect to new motor vehicles and engines manufactured in the model year 1995 and thereafter.

Effective Date

Section not applicable to vehicles or engines imported into the United States before the sixtieth day after Dec. 31, 1970, see section 8(b) of Pub.L. 91–604, set out as a note under section 7525 of this title.

Savings Provisions

Suits, actions or proceedings commenced under this chapter as in effect prior to Nov. 15, 1990, not to abate by reason of the taking effect of amendments by Pub.L. 101–549, except as otherwise provided for, see section 711(a) of Pub.L. 101–549, set out as a note under section 7401 of this title.

CODE OF FEDERAL REGULATIONS

Air pollution from motor vehicles, control of, see 40 CFR 85.401 et seq.
Control of air pollution from new motor vehicles, certification and test procedures, see 40 CFR 86.078–3 et seq.

Library References

Health and Environment ⚷25.6(6).
C.J.S. Health and Environment § 91 et seq.

§ 7542. Information collection [CAA § 208]

(a) Manufacturer's responsibility

Every manufacturer of new motor vehicles or new motor vehicle engines, and every manufacturer of new motor vehicle or engine parts or components, and other persons subject to the requirements of this part or part C of this subchapter, shall establish and maintain records, perform tests where such testing is not otherwise reasonably available under this part and part C of this subchapter (including fees for testing), make reports and provide information the Administrator may reasonably require to determine whether the manufacturer or other person has acted or is acting in compliance with this part and part C of this subchapter and regulations thereunder, or to otherwise carry out the provision of this part and part C of this subchapter, and shall, upon request of an officer or employee duly designated by the Administrator, permit such officer or employee at reasonable times to have access to and copy such records.

(b) Enforcement authority

For the purposes of enforcement of this section, officers or employees duly designated by the Administrator upon presenting appropriate credentials are authorized—

(1) to enter, at reasonable times, any establishment of the manufacturer, or of any person whom the manufacturer engages to perform any activity required by subsection (a) of this section, for the purposes of inspecting or observing any activity conducted pursuant to subsection (a) of this section, and

(2) to inspect records, files, papers, processes, controls, and facilities used in performing any activity required by subsection (a) of this section, by such manufacturer or by any person whom the manufacturer engages to perform any such activity.

(c) Availability to the public; trade secrets

Any records, reports, or information obtained under this part or part C of this subchapter shall be available to the public, except that upon a showing satisfactory to the Administrator by any person that records, reports, or information, or a particular portion thereof (other than emission data), to which the Administrator has access under this section, if made public, would divulge methods or processes entitled to protection as trade secrets of that person, the Administrator shall consider the record, report, or information or particular portion thereof confidential in accordance with the purposes of section 1905 of Title 18. Any authorized representative of the Administrator shall be considered an employee of the United States for purposes of section 1905 of Title 18. Nothing in this section shall prohibit the Administrator or authorized representative of the Administrator from disclosing records, reports or information to other officers, employees or authorized representatives of the United States concerned with carrying out this chapter or when relevant in any proceeding under this chapter. Nothing in this section shall authorize the withholding of information by the Administrator or any officer or employee under the Administrator's control from the duly authorized committees of the Congress.

(July 14, 1955, ch. 360, title II, § 208, formerly § 207, as added Oct. 20, 1965, Pub.L. 89–272, title I, § 101(8), 79 Stat. 994, and amended Nov. 21, 1967, Pub.L. 90–148, § 2, 81 Stat. 501, renumbered and amended Dec. 31, 1970, Pub.L. 91–604, §§ 8(a), 10(a), 11(a)(2)(A), 15(c)(2), 84 Stat. 1694, 1700, 1705, 1713; Nov. 15, 1990, Pub.L. 101–549, title II, § 211, 104 Stat. 2487.)

Effective Date of 1990 Amendment

Amendment by Pub.L. 101–549 effective Nov. 15, 1990, except as otherwise provided, see section 711(b) of Pub.L. 101–549, set out as a note under section 7401 of this title.

Savings Provisions

Suits, actions or proceedings commenced under this chapter as in effect prior to Nov. 15, 1990, not to abate by reason of the taking effect of amendments by Pub.L. 101–549, except as otherwise provided for, see section 711(a) of Pub.L. 101–549, set out as a note under section 7401 of this title.

CODE OF FEDERAL REGULATIONS

Air pollution from motor vehicles, control of, see 40 CFR 85.401 et seq.

Control of air pollution from new motor vehicles, certification and test procedures, see 40 CFR 86.078–3 et seq.

Public information, see 40 CFR 2.100 et seq.

Library References

Records ⚖30.

C.J.S. Records §§ 32, 33.

§ 7543. State standards [CAA § 209]

(a) Prohibition

No State or any political subdivision thereof shall adopt or attempt to enforce any standard relating to the control of emissions from new motor vehicles or new motor vehicle engines subject to this part. No State shall require certification, inspection, or any other approval relating to the control of emissions from any new motor vehicle or new motor vehicle engine as condition precedent to the initial retail sale, titling (if any), or registration of such motor vehicle, motor vehicle engine, or equipment.

(b) Waiver

(1) The Administrator shall, after notice and opportunity for public hearing, waive application of this section to any State which has adopted standards (other than crankcase emission standards) for the control of emissions from new motor vehicles or new motor vehicle engines prior to March 30, 1966, if the State determines that the State standards will be, in the aggregate, at least as protective of public health and welfare as applicable Federal standards. No such waiver shall be granted if the Administrator finds that—

(A) the determination of the State is arbitrary and capricious,

(B) such State does not need such State standards to meet compelling and extraordinary conditions, or

(C) such State standards and accompanying enforcement procedures are not consistent with section 7521(a) of this title.

(2) If each State standard is at least as stringent as the comparable applicable Federal standard, such State standard shall be deemed to be at least as protective of health and welfare as such Federal standards for purposes of paragraph (1).

(3) In the case of any new motor vehicle or new motor vehicle engine to which State standards apply pursuant to a waiver granted under paragraph (1), compliance with such State standards shall be treated as compliance with applicable Federal standards for purposes of this subchapter.

(c) Certification of vehicle parts or engine parts

Whenever a regulation with respect to any motor vehicle part or motor vehicle engine part is in effect under section 7541(a)(2) of this title, no State or political subdivision thereof shall adopt or attempt to enforce any standard or any requirement of certification, inspection, or approval which relates to motor vehicle emissions and is applicable to the same aspect of such part. The preceding sentence shall not apply in the case of a State with respect to which a waiver is in effect under subsection (b) of this section.

(d) Control, regulation, or restrictions on registered or licensed motor vehicles

Nothing in this part shall preclude or deny to any State or political subdivision thereof the right otherwise to control, regulate, or restrict the use, operation, or movement of registered or licensed motor vehicles.

(e) Nonroad engines or vehicles

(1) Prohibition on certain state standards

No State or any political subdivision thereof shall adopt or attempt to enforce any standard or other requirement relating to the control of emissions from either of the following new nonroad engines or nonroad vehicles subject to regulation under this chapter—

(A) New engines which are used in construction equipment or vehicles or used in farm equipment or vehicles and which are smaller than 175 horsepower.

(B) New locomotives or new engines used in locomotives.

Subsection (b) of this section shall not apply for purposes of this paragraph.

(2) Other nonroad engines or vehicles

(A) In the case of any nonroad vehicles or engines other than those referred to in subparagraph (A) or (B) of paragraph (1), the Administrator shall, after notice and opportunity for public hearing, authorize California to adopt and enforce standards and other requirements relating to the control of emissions from such vehicles or engines if California determines that California standards will be, in the aggregate, at least as protective of public health and welfare as applicable Federal standards. No such authorization shall be granted if the Administrator finds that—

(i) the determination of California is arbitrary and capricious,

(ii) California does not need such California standards to meet compelling and extraordinary conditions, or

(iii) California standards and accompanying enforcement procedures are not consistent with this section.

(B) Any State other than California which has plan provisions approved under part D of subchapter I of this chapter may adopt and enforce, after notice to the Administrator, for any period, standards relating to control of emissions from nonroad vehicles or engines (other than those referred to in subparagraph (A) or (B) of paragraph (1)) and take such other actions as are referred to in subparagraph (A) of this paragraph respecting such vehicles or engines if—

(i) such standards and implementation and enforcement are identical, for the period concerned, to the California standards authorized by the Administrator under subparagraph (A), and

(ii) California and such State adopt such standards at least 2 years before commencement of the period for which the standards take effect.

The Administrator shall issue regulations to implement this subsection.

(July 14, 1955, ch. 360, title II, § 209, formerly § 208, as added Nov. 21, 1967, Pub.L. 90–148, § 2, 81 Stat. 501, renumbered and amended Dec. 31, 1970, Pub.L. 91–604, §§ 8(a), 11(a)(2)(A), 15(c)(2), 84 Stat. 1694, 1705, 1713; Aug. 7, 1977, Pub.L. 95–95, title II, §§ 207, 221, 91 Stat. 755, 762; Nov. 15, 1990, Pub.L. 101–549, title II, § 222(b), 104 Stat. 2502.)

Effective Date of 1990 Amendment

Amendment by Pub.L. 101–549 effective Nov. 15, 1990, except as otherwise provided, see section 711(b) of Pub.L. 101–549, set out as a note under section 7401 of this title.

Savings Provisions

Suits, actions or proceedings commenced under this chapter as in effect prior to Nov. 15, 1990, not to abate by reason of the taking effect of amendments by Pub.L. 101–549, except as otherwise provided for, see section 711(a) of Pub.L. 101–549, set out as a note under section 7401 of this title.

Cross References

Emission standards applicable by reason of this section as category of federal standards for purposes of average fuel economy standards, see section 2002 of Title 15, Commerce and Trade.

LIBRARY REFERENCES

Health and Environment ⚷25.6(2).
C.J.S. Health and Environment § 125 et seq.

§ 7544. State grants [CAA § 210]

The Administrator is authorized to make grants to appropriate State agencies in an amount up to two-thirds of the cost of developing and maintaining effective vehicle emission devices and systems inspection and emission testing and control programs, except that—

(1) no such grant shall be made for any part of any State vehicle inspection program which does not directly relate to the cost of the air pollution control aspects of such a program;

(2) no such grant shall be made unless the Secretary of Transportation has certified to the Administrator that such program is consistent with any highway safety program developed pursuant to section 402 of Title 23; and

(3) no such grant shall be made unless the program includes provisions designed to insure that emission control devices and systems on vehicles in actual use have not been discontinued or rendered inoperative.

Grants may be made under this section by way of reimbursement in any case in which amounts have been expended by the State before the date on which any such grant was made.

(July 14, 1955, ch. 360, title II, § 210, formerly § 209, as added Nov. 21, 1967, Pub.L. 90–148, § 2, 81 Stat. 502, and renumbered and amended Dec. 31, 1970, Pub.L. 91–604, §§ 8(a), 10(b), 84 Stat. 1694, 1700; Aug. 7, 1977, Pub.L. 95–95, title II, § 204, 91 Stat. 754.)

LIBRARY REFERENCES

United States ⚷82(2).
C.J.S. United States § 122.

§ 7545. Regulation of fuels [CAA § 211]

(a) Authority of Administrator to regulate

The Administrator may by regulation designate any fuel or fuel additive (including any fuel or fuel additive used exclusively in nonroad engines or nonroad vehicles) and, after such date or dates as may be prescribed by him, no manufacturer or processor of any such fuel or additive may sell, offer for sale, or introduce into commerce such fuel or additive unless the Administrator has registered such fuel or additive in accordance with subsection (b) of this section.

(b) Registration requirement

(1) For the purpose of registration of fuels and fuel additives, the Administrator shall require—

(A) the manufacturer of any fuel to notify him as to the commercial identifying name and manufacturer of any additive contained in such fuel; the range of concentration of any additive in the fuel; and the purpose-in-use of any such additive; and

(B) the manufacturer of any additive to notify him as to the chemical composition of such additive.

(2) For the purpose of registration of fuels and fuel additives, the Administrator may also require the manufacturer of any fuel or fuel additive—

(A) to conduct tests to determine potential public health effects of such fuel or additive (including, but not limited to, carcinogenic, teratogenic, or mutagenic effects), and

(B) to furnish the description of any analytical technique that can be used to detect and measure any additive in such fuel, the recommended range of concentration of such additive, and the recommended purpose-in-use of such additive, and such other information as is reasonable and necessary to determine the emissions resulting from the use of the fuel or additive contained in such fuel, the effect of such fuel or additive on the emission control performance of any vehicle, vehicle engine, nonroad engine or nonroad vehicle, or the extent to which such emissions affect the public health or welfare.

Tests under subparagraph (A) shall be conducted in conformity with test procedures and protocols established by the Administrator. The result of such tests shall not be considered confidential.

(3) Upon compliance with the provision of this subsection, including assurances that the Administrator will receive changes in the information required, the Administrator shall register such fuel or fuel additive.

(c) Offending fuels and fuel additives; control; prohibition

(1) The Administrator may, from time to time on the basis of information obtained under subsection (b) of this section or other information available to him, by regulation, control or prohibit the manufacture, introduction into commerce, offering for sale, or sale of any fuel or fuel additive for use in a motor vehicle, motor vehicle engine, or nonroad engine or nonroad vehicle (A) if in the judgment of the Administrator any emission product of such fuel or fuel additive causes, or contributes, to air pollution which may reasonably be anticipated to endanger the public health or welfare, or (B) if emission products of such fuel or fuel additive will impair to a significant degree the performance of any emission control device or system which is in general use, or which the Administrator finds has been developed to a point where in a reasonable time it would be in general use were such regulation to be promulgated.

(2)(A) No fuel, class of fuels, or fuel additive may be controlled or prohibited by the Administrator pursuant to clause (A) of paragraph (1) except after consideration of all relevant medical and scientific evidence available to him, including consideration of other technologically or economically feasible means of achieving emission standards under section 7521 of this title.

(B) No fuel or fuel additive may be controlled or prohibited by the Administrator pursuant to clause (B) of paragraph (1) except after consideration of available scientific and economic data, including a cost benefit analysis comparing emission control devices or systems which are or will be in general use and require the proposed control or prohibition with emission control devices or systems which are or will be in general use and do not require the proposed control or prohibition. On request of a manufacturer of motor vehicles, motor vehicle engines, fuels, or fuel additives submitted within 10 days of notice of proposed rulemaking, the Administrator shall hold a public hearing and publish findings with respect to any matter he is required to consider under this subparagraph. Such findings shall be published at the time of promulgation of final regulations.

(C) No fuel or fuel additive may be prohibited by the Administrator under paragraph (1) unless he finds, and publishes such finding, that in his judgment such prohibition will not cause the use of any other fuel or fuel additive which will produce emissions which will endanger the public health or welfare to the same or greater degree than the use of the fuel or fuel additive proposed to be prohibited.

(3)(A) For the purpose of obtaining evidence and data to carry out paragraph (2), the Administrator may require the manufacturer of any motor vehicle or motor vehicle engine to furnish any information which has been developed concerning the emissions from motor vehicles resulting from the use of any fuel or fuel additive, or the effect of such use on the performance of any emission control device or system.

(B) In obtaining information under subparagraph (A), section 7607(a) of this title (relating to subpenas) shall be applicable.

(4)(A) Except as otherwise provided in subparagraph (B) or (C), no State (or political subdivision thereof) may prescribe or attempt to enforce, for purposes of motor vehicle emission control, any control or prohibition respecting any characteristic or component of a fuel or fuel additive in a motor vehicle or motor vehicle engine—

(i) if the Administrator has found that no control or prohibition of the characteristic or component of a fuel or fuel additive under paragraph (1) is necessary and has published his finding in the Federal Register, or

(ii) if the Administrator has prescribed under paragraph (1) a control or prohibition applicable to such characteristic or component of a fuel or fuel additive, unless State prohibition or control is identical to the prohibition or control prescribed by the Administrator.

(B) Any State for which application of section 7543(a) of this title has at any time been waived under section 7543(b) of this title may at any time prescribe and enforce, for the purpose of motor vehicle emission control, a control or prohibition respecting any fuel or fuel additive.

(C) A State may prescribe and enforce, for purposes of motor vehicle emission control, a control or prohibition respecting the use of a fuel or fuel additive in a motor vehicle or motor vehicle engine if an applicable implementation plan for such State under section 7410 of this title so provides. The Administrator may approve such provision in an implementation plan, or promulgate an implementation plan containing such a provision, only if he finds that the State control or prohibition is necessary to achieve the national primary or secondary ambient air quality standard which the plan implements. The Administrator may find that a State control or prohibition is necessary to achieve that standard if no other measures that would bring about timely attainment exist, or if other measures exist and are technically possible to implement, but are unreasonable or impracticable. The Administrator may make a finding of necessity under this subparagraph even if the plan for the area does not contain an approved demonstration of timely attainment.

(d) Penalties and injunctions

(1) Civil penalties

Any person who violates subsection (a), (f), (g), (k), (*l*), (m), or (n) of this section or the regulations prescribed under subsection (c), (h), (i), (k), (*l*), (m), or (n) of this section or who fails to furnish any information or conduct any tests required by the Administrator under subsection (b) of this section shall be liable to the United States for a civil penalty of not more than the sum of $25,000 for every day of such violation and the amount of economic benefit or savings resulting from the violation. Any violation with respect to a regulation prescribed under subsection (c), (k), (*l*), or (m) of this section which establishes a regulatory standard based upon a multiday averaging period shall constitute a separate day of violation for each and every day in the averaging period. Civil penalties shall be assessed in accordance with subsections (b) and (c) of section 7524 of this title.

(2) Injunctive authority

The district courts of the United States shall have jurisdiction to restrain violations of subsections (a), (f), (g), (k), (*l*), (m), and (n) of this section and of the regulations prescribed under subsections (c), (h), (i), (k), (*l*), (m), and (n) of this section, to award other appropriate relief, and to compel the furnishing of information and the conduct of tests required by the Administrator under subsection (b) of this section. Actions to restrain such violations and compel such actions shall be brought by and in the name of the United States. In any such action, subpoenas for witnesses who are required to attend a district court in any district may run into any other district.

(e) Testing of fuels and fuel additives

(1) Not later than one year after August 7, 1977, and after notice and opportunity for a public hearing, the Administrator shall promulgate regulations which implement the authority under subsection (b)(2)(A) and (B) of this section with respect to each fuel or fuel additive which is registered on the date of promulgation of such regulations and with respect to each fuel or fuel additive for which an application for registration is filed thereafter.

(2) Regulations under subsection (b) of this section to carry out this subsection shall require that the requisite information be provided to the Administrator by each such manufacturer—

(A) prior to registration, in the case of any fuel or fuel additive which is not registered on the date of promulgation of such regulations; or

(B) not later than three years after the date of promulgation of such regulations, in the case of any fuel or fuel additive which is registered on such date.

(3) In promulgating such regulations, the Administrator may—

(A) exempt any small business (as defined in such regulations) from or defer or modify the requirements of, such regulations with respect to any such small business;

(B) provide for cost-sharing with respect to the testing of any fuel or fuel additive which is manufactured or processed by two or more persons or otherwise provide for shared responsibility to meet the requirements of this section without duplication; or

(C) exempt any person from such regulations with respect to a particular fuel or fuel additive upon a finding that any additional testing of such fuel or fuel additive would be duplicative of adequate existing testing.

(f) New fuels and fuel additives

(1)(A) Effective upon March 31, 1977, it shall be unlawful for any manufacturer of any fuel or fuel additive to first introduce into commerce, or to increase the concentration in use of, any fuel or fuel additive for general use in light duty motor vehicles manufactured after model year 1974 which is not substantially similar to any fuel or fuel additive utilized in the certification of any model year 1975, or subsequent model year, vehicle or engine under section 7525 of this title.

(B) Effective upon November 15, 1990, it shall be unlawful for any manufacturer of any fuel or fuel additive to first introduce into commerce, or to increase the concentration in use of, any fuel or fuel additive for use by any person in motor vehicles manufactured after model year 1974 which is not substantially similar to any fuel or fuel additive utilized in the certification of any model year 1975, or subsequent model year, vehicle or engine under section 7525 of this title.

(2) Effective November 30, 1977, it shall be unlawful for any manufacturer of any fuel to introduce into commerce any gasoline which contains a concentration of manganese in excess of .0625 grams per gallon of fuel, except as otherwise provided pursuant to a waiver under paragraph (4).

(3) Any manufacturer of any fuel or fuel additive which prior to March 31, 1977, and after January 1, 1974, first introduced into commerce or increased the concentration in use of a fuel or fuel additive that would otherwise have been prohibited under paragraph (1)(A) if introduced on or after March 31, 1977 shall, not later than September 15, 1978, cease to distribute such fuel or fuel additive in commerce. During the period beginning 180 days after August 7, 1977, and before September 15, 1978, the Administrator shall prohibit, or restrict the concentration of any fuel additive which he determines will cause or contribute to the failure of an emission control device or system (over the useful life of any vehicle in which such device or system is used) to achieve compliance by the vehicle with the emission standards with respect to which it has been certified under section 7525 of this title.

(4) The Administrator, upon application of any manufacturer of any fuel or fuel additive, may waive the prohibitions established under paragraph (1) or (3) of this subsection or the limitation specified in paragraph (2) of this subsection, if he determines that the applicant has established that such fuel or fuel additive or a specified concentration thereof, and the emission products of such fuel or additive or specified concentration thereof, will not cause or contribute to a failure of any emission control device or system (over the useful life of any vehicle in which such device or system is used) to achieve compliance by the vehicle with the emission standards with respect to which it has been certified pursuant to section 7525 of this title. If the Administrator has not acted to grant or deny an application under this paragraph within one hundred and eighty days of receipt of such application, the waiver authorized by this paragraph shall be treated as granted.

(5) No action of the Administrator under this section may be stayed by any court pending judicial review of such action.

(g) Misfueling

(1) No person shall introduce, or cause or allow the introduction of, leaded gasoline into any motor vehicle which is labeled "unleaded gasoline only," which is equipped with a gasoline tank filler inlet designed for the introduction of unleaded gasoline, which is a 1990 or later model year motor vehicle, or which such person knows or should know is a vehicle designed solely for the use of unleaded gasoline.

(2) Beginning October 1, 1993, no person shall introduce or cause or allow the introduction into any motor vehicle of diesel fuel which such person knows or should know contains a concentration of sulfur in excess of 0.05 percent (by weight) or which fails to meet a cetane index minimum of 40 or such equivalent alternative aromatic level as prescribed by the Administrator under subsection (i)(2) of this section.

(h) Reid Vapor Pressure requirements

(1) Prohibition

Not later than 6 months after November 15, 1990, the Administrator shall promulgate regulations making it unlawful for any person during the high ozone season (as defined by the Administrator) to sell, offer for sale, dispense, supply, offer for supply, transport, or introduce into commerce gasoline with a Reid Vapor Pressure in excess of 9.0 pounds per square inch (psi). Such regulations shall also establish more stringent Reid Vapor Pressure standards in a nonattainment area as the Administrator finds necessary to generally achieve comparable evaporative emissions (on a per-vehicle basis) in nonattainment areas, taking into consideration the enforceability of such standards, the need of an area for emission control, and economic factors.

(2) Attainment areas

The regulations under this subsection shall not make it unlawful for any person to sell, offer for supply, transport, or introduce into commerce gasoline with a Reid Vapor Pressure of 9.0 pounds per square inch (psi) or lower in any area designated under section 7407 of this title as an attainment area. Notwithstanding the preceding sentence, the Administrator may impose a Reid vapor pressure requirement lower than 9.0 pounds per square inch (psi) in any area, formerly an ozone nonattainment area, which has been redesignated as an attainment area.

(3) Effective date; enforcement

The regulations under this subsection shall provide that the requirements of this subsection shall take effect not later than the high ozone season for 1992, and shall include such provisions as the Administrator determines are necessary to implement and enforce the requirements of this subsection.

(4) Ethanol waiver

For fuel blends containing gasoline and 10 percent denatured anhydrous ethanol, the Reid vapor pressure limitation under this subsection shall be one pound per square inch (psi) greater than the applicable Reid vapor pressure limitations established under paragraph (1); Provided, however, That a distributor, blender, marketer, reseller, carrier, retailer, or wholesale purchaser-consumer shall be deemed to be in full compliance with the provisions of this subsection and the regulations promulgated thereunder if it can demonstrate (by showing receipt of a certification or other evidence acceptable to the Administrator) that—

(A) the gasoline portion of the blend complies with the Reid vapor pressure limitations promulgated pursuant to this subsection;

(B) the ethanol portion of the blend does not exceed its waiver condition under subsection (f)(4) of this section; and

(C) no additional alcohol or other additive has been added to increase the Reid Vapor Pressure of the ethanol portion of the blend.

(5) Areas covered

The provisions of this subsection shall apply only to the 48 contiguous States and the District of Columbia.

(i) Sulfur content requirements for diesel fuel

(1) Effective October 1, 1993, no person shall manufacture, sell, supply, offer for sale or supply, dispense, transport, or introduce into commerce motor vehicle diesel fuel which contains a concentration of sulfur in excess of 0.05 percent (by weight) or which fails to meet a cetane index minimum of 40.

(2) Not later than 12 months after November 15, 1990, the Administrator shall promulgate regulations to implement and enforce the requirements of paragraph (1). The Administrator may require manufacturers and importers of diesel fuel not intended for use in motor vehicles to dye such fuel in a particular manner in order to segregate it from motor vehicle

diesel fuel. The Administrator may establish an equivalent alternative aromatic level to the cetane index specification in paragraph (1).

(3) The sulfur content of fuel required to be used in the certification of 1991 through 1993 model year heavy-duty diesel vehicles and engines shall be 0.10 percent (by weight). The sulfur content and cetane index minimum of fuel required to be used in the certification of 1994 and later model year heavy-duty diesel vehicles and engines shall comply with the regulations promulgated under paragraph (2).

(4) The States of Alaska and Hawaii may be exempted from the requirements of this subsection in the same manner as provided in section 7625 of this title. The Administrator shall take final action on any petition filed under section 7625 of this title or this paragraph for an exemption from the requirements of this subsection, within 12 months from the date of the petition.

(j) Lead substitute gasoline additives

(1) After November 15, 1990, any person proposing to register any gasoline additive under subsection (a) of this section or to use any previously registered additive as a lead substitute may also elect to register the additive as a lead substitute gasoline additive for reducing valve seat wear by providing the Administrator with such relevant information regarding product identity and composition as the Administrator deems necessary for carrying out the responsibilities of paragraph (2) of this subsection (in addition to other information which may be required under subsection (b) of this section).

(2) In addition to the other testing which may be required under subsection (b) of this section, in the case of the lead substitute gasoline additives referred to in paragraph (1), the Administrator shall develop and publish a test procedure to determine the additives' effectiveness in reducing valve seat wear and the additives' tendencies to produce engine deposits and other adverse side effects. The test procedures shall be developed in cooperation with the Secretary of Agriculture and with the input of additive manufacturers, engine and engine components manufacturers, and other interested persons. The Administrator shall enter into arrangements with an independent laboratory to conduct tests of each additive using the test procedures developed and published pursuant to this paragraph. The Administrator shall publish the results of the tests by company and additive name in the Federal Register along with, for comparison purposes, the results of applying the same test procedures to gasoline containing 0.1 gram of lead per gallon in lieu of the lead substitute gasoline additive. The Administrator shall not rank or otherwise rate the lead substitute additives. Test procedures shall be established within 1 year after November 15, 1990. Additives shall be tested within 18 months of November 15, 1990 or 6 months after the lead substitute additives are identified to the Administrator, whichever is later.

(3) The Administrator may impose a user fee to recover the costs of testing of any fuel additive referred to in this subsection. The fee shall be paid by the person proposing to register the fuel additive concerned. Such fee shall not exceed $20,000 for a single fuel additive.

(4) There are authorized to be appropriated to the Administrator not more than $1,000,000 for the second full fiscal year after November 15, 1990 to establish test procedures and conduct engine tests as provided in this subsection. Not more than $500,000 per year is authorized to be appropriated for each of the 5 subsequent fiscal years.

(5) Any fees collected under this subsection shall be deposited in a special fund in the United States Treasury for licensing and other services which thereafter shall be available for appropriation, to remain available until expended, to carry out the Agency's activities for which the fees were collected.

(k) Reformulated gasoline for conventional vehicles

(1) EPA regulations

Within 1 year after the enactment of the Clean Air Act Amendments of 1990, the Administrator shall promulgate regulations under this section establishing requirements for reformulated gasoline to be used in gasoline-fueled vehicles in specified nonattainment areas. Such regulations shall require the greatest reduction in emissions of ozone forming volatile organic compounds (during the high ozone season) and emissions of toxic air pollutants (during the entire year) achievable through the reformulation of conventional gasoline, taking into consideration the cost of achieving such emission reductions, any nonair-quality and other air-quality related health and environmental impacts and energy requirements.

(2) General requirements

The regulations referred to in paragraph (1) shall require that reformulated gasoline comply with paragraph (3) and with each of the following requirements (subject to paragraph (7)):

(A) NO_x emissions

The emissions of oxides of nitrogen (NO_x) from baseline vehicles when using the reformulated gasoline shall be no greater than the level of such emissions from such vehicles when using baseline gasoline. If the Administrator determines that compliance with the limitation on emissions of oxides of nitrogen under the preceding sentence is technically infeasible, considering the other requirements applicable under this subsection to such gasoline, the Administrator may, as appropriate to ensure compliance with this subparagraph, adjust (or waive entirely), any other requirements of this paragraph (including the oxygen content requirement contained in subparagraph (B)) or any requirements applicable under paragraph (3)(A).

(B) Oxygen content

The oxygen content of the gasoline shall equal or exceed 2.0 percent by weight (subject to a testing tolerance established by the Administrator) except as otherwise required by this chapter. The Administrator may waive, in whole or in part, the application of this subparagraph for any ozone nonattainment area upon a determination by the Administrator that compliance with such requirement would prevent or interfere with the attainment by the area of a national primary ambient air quality standard.

(C) Benzene content

The benzene content of the gasoline shall not exceed 1.0 percent by volume.

(D) Heavy metals

The gasoline shall have no heavy metals, including lead or manganese. The Administrator may waive the prohibition contained in this subparagraph for a heavy metal (other than lead) if the Administrator determines that addition of the heavy metal to the gasoline will not increase, on an aggregate mass or cancer-risk basis, toxic air pollutant emissions from motor vehicles.

(3) More stringent of formula or performance standards

The regulations referred to in paragraph (1) shall require compliance with the more stringent of either the requirements set forth in subparagraph (A) or the requirements of subparagraph (B) of this paragraph. For purposes of determining the more stringent provision, clause (i) and clause (ii) of subparagraph (B) shall be considered independently.

(A) Formula

(i) Benzene

The benzene content of the reformulated gasoline shall not exceed 1.0 percent by volume.

(ii) Aromatics

The aromatic hydrocarbon content of the reformulated gasoline shall not exceed 25 percent by volume.

(iii) Lead

The reformulated gasoline shall have no lead content.

(iv) Detergents

The reformulated gasoline shall contain additives to prevent the accumulation of deposits in engines or vehicle fuel supply systems.

(v) Oxygen content

The oxygen content of the reformulated gasoline shall equal or exceed 2.0 percent by weight (subject to a testing tolerance established by the Administrator) except as otherwise required by this chapter.

(B) Performance standard

(i) VOC emissions

During the high ozone season (as defined by the Administrator), the aggregate emissions of ozone forming volatile organic compounds from baseline vehicles when using the reformulated gasoline shall be 15 percent below the aggregate emissions of ozone forming volatile organic compounds from such vehicles when using baseline gasoline. Effective in calendar year 2000 and thereafter, 25 percent shall be substituted for 15 percent in applying this clause, except that the Administrator may adjust such 25 percent requirement to provide for a lesser or greater reduction based on technological feasibility, considering the cost of achieving such reductions in VOC emissions. No such adjustment shall provide for less than a 20 percent reduction below the aggregate emissions of such air pollutants from such vehicles when using baseline gasoline. The reductions required under this clause shall be on a mass basis.

(ii) Toxics

During the entire year, the aggregate emissions of toxic air pollutants from baseline vehicles when using the reformulated gasoline shall be 15 percent below the aggregate emissions of toxic air pollutants from such vehicles when using baseline gasoline. Effective in calendar year 2000 and thereafter, 25 percent shall be substituted for 15 percent in applying this clause, except that the Administrator may adjust such 25 percent requirement to provide for a lesser or greater reduction based on technological feasibility, considering the cost of achieving such reductions in toxic air pollutants. No such adjustment shall provide for less than a 20 percent reduction below the aggregate emissions of such air pollutants from such vehicles when using baseline gasoline. The reductions required under this clause shall be on a mass basis.

Any reduction greater than a specific percentage reduction required under this subparagraph shall be treated as satisfying such percentage reduction requirement.

(4) Certification procedures

(A) Regulations

The regulations under this subsection shall include procedures under which the Administrator shall certify reformulated gasoline as complying with the requirements established pursuant to this subsection. Under such regulations, the Administrator shall establish procedures for any person to petition the Administrator to certify a fuel formulation, or slate of fuel formulations. Such procedures shall further require that the Administrator shall approve or deny such petition within 180 days of receipt. If the Administrator fails to act within such 180-day period, the fuel shall be deemed certified until the Administrator completes action on the petition.

(B) Certification; equivalency

The Administrator shall certify a fuel formulation or slate of fuel formulations as complying with this subsection if such fuel or fuels—

(i) comply with the requirements of paragraph (2), and

(ii) achieve equivalent or greater reductions in emissions of ozone forming volatile organic compounds and emissions of toxic air pollutants than are achieved by a reformulated gasoline meeting the applicable requirements of paragraph (3).

(C) EPA determination of emissions level

Within 1 year after the enactment of the Clean Air Act Amendments of 1990, the Administrator shall determine the level of emissions of ozone forming volatile organic compounds and emissions of toxic air pollutants emitted by baseline vehicles when operating on baseline gasoline. For purposes of this subsection, within 1 year after the enactment of the Clean Air Act Amendments of 1990, the Administrator shall, by rule, determine appropriate measures of, and methodology for, ascertaining the emissions of air pollutants (including calculations, equipment, and testing tolerances).

(5) Prohibition

Effective beginning January 1, 1995, each of the following shall be a violation of this subsection:

(A) The sale or dispensing by any person of conventional gasoline to ultimate consumers in any covered area.

(B) The sale or dispensing by any refiner, blender, importer, or marketer of conventional gasoline for resale in any covered area, without (i) segregating such gasoline from reformulated gasoline, and (ii) clearly marking such conventional gasoline as "conventional gasoline, not for sale to ultimate consumer in a covered area".

Any refiner, blender, importer or marketer who purchases property segregated and marked conventional gasoline, and thereafter labels, represents, or wholesales such gasoline as reformulated gasoline shall also be in violation of this subsection. The Administrator may impose sampling, testing, and recordkeeping requirements upon any refiner, blender, importer, or marketer to prevent violations of this section.

(6) Opt-in areas

(A) Upon the application of the Governor of a State, the Administrator shall apply the prohibition set forth in paragraph (5) in any area in the State classified under subpart 2 of part D of subchapter I of this chapter as a Marginal, Moderate, Serious, or Severe Area (without regard to whether or not the 1980 population of the area exceeds 250,000). In any such case, the Administrator shall establish an effective date for such prohibition as he deems appropriate, not later than January 1, 1995, or 1 year after such application is received, whichever is later. The Administrator shall publish such application in the Federal Register upon receipt.

(B) If the Administrator determines, on the Administrator's own motion or on petition of any person, after consultation with the Secretary of Energy, that there is insufficient domestic capacity to produce gasoline certified under this subsection, the Administrator shall, by rule, extend the effective date of such prohibition in Marginal, Moderate, Serious, or Severe Areas referred to in subparagraph (A) for one additional year, and may, by rule, renew such extension for 2 additional one-year periods. The Administrator shall act on any petition submitted under this paragraph within 6 months after receipt of the petition. The Administrator shall issue such extensions for areas with a lower ozone classification before issuing any such extension for areas with a higher classification.

(7) Credits

(A) The regulations promulgated under this subsection shall provide for the granting of an appropriate amount of credits to a person who refines, blends, or imports and certifies a gasoline or slate of gasoline that—

(i) has an oxygen content (by weight) that exceeds the minimum oxygen content specified in paragraph (2);

(ii) has an aromatic hydrocarbon content (by volume) that is less than the maximum aromatic hydrocarbon content required to comply with paragraph (3); or

(iii) has a benzene content (by volume) that is less than the maximum benzene content specified in paragraph (2).

(B) The regulations described in subparagraph (A) shall also provide that a person who is granted credits may use such credits, or transfer all or a portion of such credits to another person for use within the same nonattainment area, for the purpose of complying with this subsection.

(C) The regulations promulgated under subparagraphs (A) and (B) shall ensure the enforcement of the requirements for the issuance, application, and transfer of the credits. Such regulations shall prohibit the granting or transfer of such credits for use with respect to any gasoline in a nonattainment area, to the extent the use of such credits would result in any of the following:

(i) An average gasoline aromatic hydrocarbon content (by volume) for the nonattainment (taking into account all gasoline sold for use in conventional gasoline-fueled vehicles in the nonattainment area) higher than the average fuel aromatic hydrocarbon content (by volume) that would occur in the absence of using any such credits.

(ii) An average gasoline oxygen content (by weight) for the nonattainment area (taking into account all gasoline sold for use in conventional gasoline-fueled vehicles in the nonattainment area) lower than the average gasoline oxygen content (by weight) that would occur in the absence of using any such credits.

(iii) An average benzene content (by volume) for the nonattainment area (taking into account all gasoline sold for use in conventional gasoline-fueled vehicles in the nonattainment area) higher than the average benzene content (by volume) that would occur in the absence of using any such credits.

(8) Anti-dumping rules

(A) In general

Within 1 year after the enactment of the Clean Air Act Amendments of 1990, the Administrator shall promulgate regulations applicable to each refiner, blender, or importer of gasoline ensuring that gasoline sold or introduced into commerce by such refiner, blender, or importer (other than reformulated gasoline subject to the requirements of paragraph (1)) does not result in average per gallon emissions (measured on a mass basis) of (i) volatile organic compounds, (ii) oxides of nitrogen, (iii) carbon monoxide, and (iv) toxic air pollutants in excess of such emissions of such pollutants attributable to gasoline sold or introduced into commerce in calendar year 1990 by that refiner, blender, or importer. Such regulations shall take effect beginning January 1, 1995.

(B) Adjustments

In evaluating compliance with the requirements of subparagraph (A), the Administrator shall make appropriate adjustments to insure that no credit is provided for improvement in motor vehicle emissions control in motor vehicles sold after the calendar year 1990.

(C) Compliance determined for each pollutant independently

In determining whether there is an increase in emissions in violation of the prohibition contained in subparagraph (A) the Administrator shall consider an increase in each air pollutant referred to in clauses (i) through (iv) as a separate violation of such prohibition, except that the Administrator shall promulgate regulations to provide that any increase in emissions of oxides of nitrogen resulting from adding oxygenates to gasoline may be offset by an equivalent or greater reduction (on a mass basis) in emissions of volatile organic compounds, carbon monoxide, or toxic air pollutants, or any combination of the foregoing.

(D) Compliance period

The Administrator shall promulgate an appropriate compliance period or appropriate compliance periods to be used for assessing compliance with the prohibition contained in subparagraph (A).

(E) Baseline for determining compliance

If the Administrator determines that no adequate and reliable data exists regarding the composition of gasoline sold or introduced into commerce by a refiner, blender, or importer in calendar year 1990, for such refiner, blender, or importer, baseline gasoline shall be substituted for such 1990 gasoline in determining compliance with subparagraph (A).

(9) Emissions from entire vehicle

In applying the requirements of this subsection, the Administrator shall take into account emissions from the entire motor vehicle, including evaporative, running, refueling, and exhaust emissions.

(10) Definitions

For purposes of this subsection—

(A) Baseline vehicles

The term "baseline vehicles" mean representative model year 1990 vehicles.

(B) Baseline gasoline

(i) Summertime

The term "baseline gasoline" means in the case of gasoline sold during the high ozone period (as defined by the Administrator) a gasoline which meets the following specifications:

BASELINE GASOLINE FUEL PROPERTIES

API Gravity	57.4
Sulfur, ppm	339
Benzene, %	1.53
RVP, psi	8.7
Octane, R + M/2	87.3
IBP, F	91
10%, F	128
50%, F	218
90%, F	330
End Point, F	415
Aromatics, %	32.0
Olefins, %	9.2
Saturates, %	58.8

(ii) Wintertime

The Administrator shall establish the specifications of "baseline gasoline" for gasoline sold at times other than the high ozone period (as defined by the Administrator). Such specifications shall be the specifications of 1990 industry average gasoline sold during such period.

(C) Toxic air pollutants

The term "toxic air pollutants" means the aggregate emissions of the following:

Benzene
1,3 Butadiene
Polycyclic organic matter (POM)
Acetaldehyde
Formaldehyde.

(D) Covered area

The 9 ozone nonattainment areas having a 1980 population in excess of 250,000 and having the highest ozone design value during the period 1987 through 1989 shall be "covered areas" for purposes of this subsection. Effective one year after the reclassification of any ozone nonattainment area as a Severe ozone nonattainment area under section 7511(b) of this title, such Severe area shall also be a "covered area" for purposes of this subsection.

(E) Reformulated gasoline

The term "reformulated gasoline" means any gasoline which is certified by the Administrator under this section as complying with this subsection.

(F) Conventional gasoline

The term "conventional gasoline" means any gasoline which does not meet specifications set by a certification under this subsection.

(*l*) Detergents

Effective beginning January 1, 1995, no person may sell or dispense to an ultimate consumer in the United States, and no refiner or marketer may directly or indirectly sell or dispense to persons who sell or dispense to ultimate consumers in the United States any gasoline which does not contain additives to prevent the accumulation of deposits in engines or fuel supply systems. Not later than 2 years after November 15, 1990, the Administrator shall promulgate a rule establishing specifications for such additives.

(m) Oxygenated fuels

(1) Plan revisions for CO nonattainment areas

(A) Each State in which there is located all or part of an area which is designated under subchapter I of this chapter as a nonattainment area for carbon monoxide and which has a carbon monoxide design value of 9.5 parts per million (ppm) or above based on data for the 2–year period of 1988 and 1989 and calculated according to the most recent interpretation methodology issued by the Administrator prior to the enactment of the Clean Air Act Amendments of 1990 shall submit to the Administrator a State implementation plan revision under section 7410 of this title and part D of subchapter I of this chapter for such area which shall contain the provisions specified under this subsection regarding oxygenated gasoline.

(B) A plan revision which contains such provisions shall also be submitted by each State in which there is located any area which, for any 2–year period after 1989 has a carbon monoxide design value of 9.5 ppm or above. The revision shall be submitted within 18 months after such 2–year period.

(2) Oxygenated gasoline in CO nonattainment areas

Each plan revision under this subsection shall contain provisions to require that any gasoline sold, or dispensed, to the ultimate consumer in the carbon monoxide nonattainment area or sold or dispensed directly or indirectly by fuel refiners or marketers to persons who sell or dispense to ultimate consumers, in the larger of—

(A) the Consolidated Metropolitan Statistical Area (CMSA) in which the area is located, or

(B) if the area is not located in a CMSA, the Metropolitan Statistical Area in which the area is located,

be blended, during the portion of the year in which the area is prone to high ambient concentrations of carbon monoxide to contain not less than 2.7 percent oxygen by weight (subject to a testing tolerance established by the Administrator). The portion of the year in which the area is prone to high ambient concentrations of carbon monoxide shall be as determined by the Administrator, but shall not be less than 4 months. At the request of a State with respect to any area designated as nonattainment for carbon monoxide, the Administrator may reduce the period specified in the preceding sentence if the State can demonstrate that because of meteorological conditions, a reduced period will assure that there will be no exceedances of the carbon monoxide standard outside of such reduced period. For areas with a carbon monoxide design value of 9.5 ppm or more of November 15, 1990,[1] the revision shall provide that such requirement shall take effect no later than November 1, 1992, (or at such other date during 1992 as the Administrator establishes under the preceding provisions of this paragraph). For other areas, the revision shall provide that such requirement shall take effect no later than November 1 of the third year after the last year of the applicable 2–year period referred to in paragraph (1) (or at such other date during such third year as the Administrator establishes under the preceding provisions of this paragraph) and shall include a program for implementation and enforcement of the requirement consistent with guidance to be issued by the Administrator.

(3) Waivers

(A) The Administrator shall waive, in whole or in part, the requirements of paragraph (2) upon a demonstration by the State to the satisfaction of the Administrator that the use of oxygenated gasoline would prevent or interfere with the attainment by the area of a national primary ambient air quality standard (or a State or local ambient air quality standard) for any air pollutant other than carbon monoxide.

(B) The Administrator shall, upon demonstration by the State satisfactory to the Administrator, waive the requirement of paragraph (2) where the Administrator determines that mobile sources of carbon monoxide do not contribute significantly to carbon monoxide levels in an area.

(C)(i) Any person may petition the Administrator to make a finding that there is, or is likely to be, for any area, an inadequate domestic supply of, or distribution capacity for, oxygenated gasoline meeting the requirements of paragraph (2) or fuel additives (oxygenates) necessary to meet such requirements. The Administrator shall act on such petition within 6 months after receipt of the petition.

(ii) If the Administrator determines, in response to a petition under clause (i), that there is an inadequate supply or capacity described in clause (i), the Administrator shall delay the effective date of paragraph (2) for 1 year. Upon petition, the Administrator may extend such effective date for one additional year. No partial delay or lesser waiver may be granted under this clause.

(iii) In granting waivers under this subparagraph the Administrator shall consider distribution capacity separately from the adequacy of domestic supply and shall grant such waivers in such manner as will assure that, if supplies of oxygenated gasoline are limited, areas having the highest design value for carbon monoxide will have a priority in obtaining oxygenated gasoline which meets the requirements of paragraph (2).

(iv) As used in this subparagraph, the term distribution capacity includes capacity for transportation, storage, and blending.

(4) Fuel dispensing systems

Any person selling oxygenated gasoline at retail pursuant to this subsection shall be required under regulations promulgated by the Administrator to label the fuel dispensing system with a notice that the gasoline is oxygenated and will reduce the carbon monoxide emissions from the motor vehicle.

(5) Guidelines for credit

The Administrator shall promulgate guidelines, within 9 months after November 15, 1990, allowing the use of marketable oxygen credits from gasolines during that portion of the year specified in paragraph (2) with higher oxygen content than required to offset the sale or use of gasoline with a lower oxygen content than required. No credits may be transferred between nonattainment areas.

(6) **Attainment areas**

Nothing in this subsection shall be interpreted as requiring an oxygenated gasoline program in an area which is in attainment for carbon monoxide, except that in a carbon monoxide nonattainment area which is redesignated as attainment for carbon monoxide, the requirements of this subsection shall remain in effect to the extent such program is necessary to maintain such standard thereafter in the area.

(7) **Failure to attain CO standard**

If the Administrator determines under section 7512(b)(2) of this title that the national primary ambient air quality standard for carbon monoxide has not been attained in a Serious Area by the applicable attainment date, the State shall submit a plan revision for the area within 9 months after the date of such determination. The plan revision shall provide that the minimum oxygen content of gasoline referred to in paragraph (2) shall be 3.1 percent by weight unless such requirement is waived in accordance with the provisions of this subsection.

(n) **Prohibition on leaded gasoline for highway use**

After December 31, 1995, it shall be unlawful for any person to sell, offer for sale, supply, offer for supply, dispense, transport, or introduce into commerce, for use as fuel in any motor vehicle (as defined in section 7554(2) of this title) any gasoline which contains lead or lead additives.

(*o*) **Fuel and fuel additive importers and importation**

For the purposes of this section, the term "manufacturer" includes an importer and the term "manufacture" includes importation.

(July 14, 1955, ch. 360, title II, § 211, formerly § 210, as added Nov. 21, 1967, Pub.L. 90–148, § 2, 81 Stat. 502, and renumbered and amended Dec. 31, 1970, Pub.L. 91–604, §§ 8(a), 9(a), 84 Stat. 1694, 1698; Nov. 18, 1971, Pub.L. 92–157, title III, § 302(d), (e), 85 Stat. 464; Aug. 7, 1977, Pub.L. 95–95, title II, §§ 222, 223, title IV, § 401(e), 91 Stat. 762, 764, 791; Nov. 16, 1977, Pub.L. 95–190, § 14(a)(73), (74), 91 Stat. 1403, 1404; Nov. 15, 1990, Pub.L. 101–549, title II, §§ 212–221, 228(d), 104 Stat. 2488–2500, 2510.)

[1] So in original.

References in Text

The enactment of the Clean Air Act Amendments of 1990, referred to in subsec. (k)(1), (4)(C), (8)(A) and (m), probably means the date of enactment of the Clean Air Act Amendments of 1990, Pub.L. 101–549, which was approved November 15, 1990.

Effective Date of 1990 Amendment

Amendment by Pub.L. 101–549 effective Nov. 15, 1990, except as otherwise provided, see section 711(b) of Pub.L. 101–549, set out as a note under section 7401 of this title.

Savings Provisions

Suits, actions or proceedings commenced under this chapter as in effect prior to Nov. 15, 1990, not to abate by reason of the taking effect of amendments by Pub.L. 101–549, except as otherwise provided for, see section 711(a) of Pub.L. 101–549, set out as a note under section 7401 of this title.

CODE OF FEDERAL REGULATIONS

Control of air pollution from motor vehicles, generally, see 40 CFR 85.401 et seq.
Fuels and fuel additives, registration and regulation of, see 40 CFR 79.1 et seq., 80.1 et seq.
Suspension and revocation of permits, rules governing, see 40 CFR 22.01 et seq.

LIBRARY REFERENCES

Health and Environment ⚷20, 25.6(1).
C.J.S. Health and Environment §§ 2 et seq., 91 et seq.

§ 7546. Repealed. Pub.L. 101–549, Title II, § 230(10), Nov. 15, 1990, 104 Stat. 2529

Section, July 14, 1955, c. 360, Title II, § 212, as added Dec. 31, 1970, Pub.L. 91–604, § 10(c), 84 Stat. 1700, and amended Dec. 31, 1970, Pub.L. 91–605, § 202(a), 84 Stat. 1739; Apr. 9, 1973, Pub.L. 93–15, § 1(b), 87 Stat. 11; June 22, 1974, Pub.L. 93–319, § 13(b), 88 Stat. 265, related to low-emission vehicles.

Effective Date of Repeal

Repeal of section effective Nov. 15, 1990, except as otherwise provided, see section 711(b) of Pub.L. 101–549, set out as a note under section 7401 of this title.

Savings Provisions

Suits, actions or proceedings commenced under this chapter as in effect prior to Nov. 15, 1990, not to abate by reason of the taking effect of amendments by Pub.L. 101–549, except as otherwise provided for, see section 711(a) of Pub.L. 101–549, set out as a note under section 7401 of this title.

§ 7547. Nonroad engines and vehicles [CAA § 213]

(a) **Emissions standards**

(1) The Administrator shall conduct a study of emissions from nonroad engines and nonroad vehicles (other than locomotives or engines used in locomotives) to determine if such emissions cause, or significantly contribute to, air pollution which may reasonably be anticipated to endanger public health or welfare. Such study shall be completed within 12 months of November 15, 1990.

(2) After notice and opportunity for public hearing, the Administrator shall determine within 12 months after completion of the study under paragraph (1), based upon the results of such study, whether emissions of carbon monoxide, oxides of nitrogen, and volatile organic compounds from new and existing nonroad engines or nonroad vehicles (other than locomotives or engines used in locomotives) are significant contributors to ozone or carbon monoxide concentrations in more than 1 area which has failed to attain the national ambient air quality standards for ozone or carbon monoxide. Such determination shall be included in the regulations under paragraph (3).

(3) If the Administrator makes an affirmative determination under paragraph (2) the Administrator shall, within 12 months after completion of the study under paragraph (1), promulgate (and from time to time revise) regulations containing standards applicable to emissions from those classes or categories of new nonroad engines and new nonroad vehicles (other than locomotives or engines used in locomotives) which in the Administrator's judgment cause, or contribute to, such air pollution. Such standards shall achieve the greatest degree of emission reduction achievable through the application of technology which the Administrator determines will be available for the engines or vehicles to which such standards apply, giving appropriate consideration to the cost of applying such technology within the period of time available to manufacturers and to noise, energy, and safety factors associated with the application of such technology. In determining what degree of reduction will be available, the Administrator shall first consider standards equivalent in stringency to standards for comparable motor vehicles or engines (if any) regulated under section 7521 of this title, taking into account the technological feasibility, costs, safety, noise, and energy factors associated with achieving, as appropriate, standards of such stringency and lead time. The regulations shall apply to the useful life of the engines or vehicles (as determined by the Administrator).

(4) If the Administrator determines that any emissions not referred to in paragraph (2) from new nonroad engines or vehicles significantly contribute to air pollution which may reasonably be anticipated to endanger public health or welfare, the Administrator may promulgate (and from time to time revise) such regulations as the Administrator deems appropriate containing standards applicable to emissions from those classes or categories of new nonroad engines and new nonroad vehicles (other than locomotives or engines used in locomotives) which in the Administrator's judgment cause, or contribute to, such air pollution, taking into account costs, noise, safety, and energy factors associated with the application of technology which the Administrator determines will be available for the engines and vehicles to which such standards apply. The regulations shall apply to the useful life of the engines or vehicles (as determined by the Administrator).

(5) Within 5 years after the enactment of the Clean Air Act Amendments of 1990, the Administrator shall promulgate regulations containing standards applicable to emissions from new locomotives and new engines used in locomotives. Such standards shall achieve the greatest degree of emission reduction achievable through the application of technology which the Administrator determines will be available for the locomotives or engines to which such standards apply, giving appropriate consideration to the cost of applying such technology within the period of time available to manufacturers and to noise, energy, and safety factors associated with the application of such technology.

(b) Effective date

Standards under this section shall take effect at the earliest possible date considering the lead time necessary to permit the development and application of the requisite technology, giving appropriate consideration to the cost of compliance within such period and energy and safety.

(c) Safe controls

Effective with respect to new engines or vehicles to which standards under this section apply, no emission control device, system, or element of design shall be used in such a new nonroad engine or new nonroad vehicle for purposes of complying with such standards if such device, system, or element of design will cause or contribute to an unreasonable risk to public health, welfare, or safety in its operation or function. In determining whether an unreasonable risk exists, the Administrator shall consider factors including those described in section 7521(a)(4)(B) of this title.

(d) Enforcement

The standards under this section shall be subject to sections 7525, 7541, 7542, and 7543 of this title, with such modifications of the applicable regulations implementing such sections as the Administrator deems appropriate, and shall be enforced in the same manner as standards prescribed under section 7521 of this title. The Administrator shall revise or promulgate regulations as may be necessary to determine compliance with, and enforce, standards in effect under this section.

(July 14, 1955, ch. 360, title II, § 213, as added June 22, 1974, Pub.L. 93–319, § 10, 88 Stat. 261, and amended Nov. 15, 1990, Pub.L. 101–549, title II, § 222(a), 104 Stat. 2500.)

References in Text

The enactment of the Clean Air Act Amendments of 1990, referred to in subsec. (a)(5), probably means the date of enactment of the Clean Air Act Amendments of 1990, Pub.L. 101–549, which was approved November 15, 1990.

Effective Date of 1990 Amendment

Amendment by Pub.L. 101–549 effective Nov. 15, 1990, except as otherwise provided, see section 711(b) of Pub.L. 101–549, set out as a note under section 7401 of this title.

Savings Provisions

Suits, actions or proceedings commenced under this chapter as in effect prior to Nov. 15, 1990, not to abate by reason of the taking effect of amendments by Pub.L. 101–549, except as otherwise provided for, see section 711(a) of Pub.L. 101–549, set out as a note under section 7401 of this title.

§ 7548. Study of particulate emissions from motor vehicles [CAA § 214]

(a) Study and analysis

(1) The Administrator shall conduct a study concerning the effects on health and welfare of particulate emissions from motor vehicles or motor vehicle engines to which section 7521 of this title applies. Such study shall characterize and quantify such emissions and analyze the relationship of such emissions to various fuels and fuel additives.

(2) The study shall also include an analysis of particulate emissions from mobile sources which are not related to engine emissions (including, but not limited to tire debris, and asbestos from brake lining).

(b) Report to Congress

The Administrator shall report to the Congress the findings and results of the study conducted under subsection (a) of this section not later than two years after August 7, 1977. Such report shall also include recommendations for standards or methods to regulate particulate emissions described in paragraph (2) of subsection (a) of this section.

(July 14, 1955, ch. 360, title II, § 214, as added Aug. 7, 1977, Pub.L. 95–95, title II, § 224(d), 91 Stat. 767.)

Effective Date

Section 406(d) of Title IV of Pub.L. 95–95, Aug. 7, 1977, 91 Stat. 796, provided that, except as otherwise expressly provided, the amendments made by that Act [which enacted this section] were effective on the date of enactment [Aug. 7, 1977].

§ 7549. High altitude performance adjustments [CAA § 215]

(a) Instruction of manufacturer

(1) Any action taken with respect to any element of design installed on or in a motor vehicle or motor vehicle engine in compliance with regulations under this subchapter (including any alteration or adjustment of such element), shall be treated as not in violation of section 7522(a) of this title if such action is performed in accordance with high altitude adjustment instructions provided by the manufacturer under subsection (b) of this section and approved by the Administrator.

(2) If the Administrator finds that adjustments or modifications made pursuant to instructions of the manufacturer under paragraph (1) will not insure emission control performance with respect to each standard under section 7521 of this title at least equivalent to that which would result if no such adjustments or modifications were made, he shall disapprove such instructions. Such finding shall be based upon minimum engineering evaluations consistent with good engineering practice.

(b) Regulations

(1) Instructions respecting each class or category of vehicles or engines to which this subchapter applies providing for such vehicle and engine adjustments and modifications as may be necessary to insure emission control performance at different altitudes shall be submitted by the manufacturer to the Administrator pursuant to regulations promulgated by the Administrator.

(2) Any knowing violation by a manufacturer of requirements of the Administrator under paragraph (1) shall be treated as a violation by such manufacturer of section 7522(a)(3) of this title for purposes of the penalties contained in section 7524 of this title.

(3) Such instructions shall provide, in addition to other adjustments, for adjustments for vehicles moving from high altitude areas to low altitude areas after the initial registration of such vehicles.

(c) Manufacturer parts

No instructions under this section respecting adjustments or modifications may require the use of any manufacturer parts (as defined in section 7522(a) of this title) unless the manufacturer demonstrates to the satisfaction of the Administrator that the use of such manufacturer parts is necessary to insure emission control performance.

(d) State inspection and maintenance programs

Before January 1, 1981 the authority provided by this section shall be available in any high altitude State (as determined under regulations of the Administrator under regulations promulgated before August 7, 1977) but after December 31, 1980, such authority shall be available only in any such State in which an inspection and maintenance program for the testing of motor vehicle emissions has been instituted for the portions of the State where any national ambient air quality standard for auto-related pollutants has not been attained.

(e) High altitude testing

(1) The Administrator shall promptly establish at least one testing center (in addition to the testing centers existing on November 15, 1990) located at a site that represents high altitude conditions, to ascertain in a reasonable manner whether, when in actual use throughout their useful life (as determined under

section 7521(d) of this title), each class or category of vehicle and engines to which regulations under section 7521(d) of this title apply conforms to the emissions standards established by such regulations. For purposes of this subsection, the term "high altitude conditions" refers to high altitude as defined in regulations of the Administrator in effect as of November 15, 1990.

(2) The Administrator, in cooperation with the Secretary of Energy and the Administrator of the Federal Transit Administration, and such other agencies as the Administrator deems appropriate, shall establish a research and technology assessment center to provide for the development and evaluation of less-polluting heavy-duty engines and fuels for use in buses, heavy-duty trucks, and non-road engines and vehicles, which shall be located at a high-altitude site that represents high-altitude conditions. In establishing and funding such a center, the Administrator shall give preference to proposals which provide for local cost-sharing of facilities and recovery of costs of operation through utilization of such facility for the purposes of this section.

(3) The Administrator shall designate at least one center at high-altitude conditions to provide research on after-market emission components, dual-fueled vehicles and conversion kits, the effects of tampering on emissions equipment, testing of alternate fuels and conversion kits, and the development of curricula, training courses, and materials to maximize the effectiveness of inspection and maintenance programs as they relate to promoting effective control of vehicle emissions at high-altitude elevations. Preference shall be given to existing vehicle emissions testing and research centers that have established reputations for vehicle emissions research and development and training, and that possess in-house Federal Test Procedure capacity.

(July 14, 1955, ch. 360, title II, § 215, as added Aug. 7, 1977, Pub.L. 95–95, title II, § 211(b), 91 Stat. 757, and amended Nov. 16, 1977, Pub.L. 95–190, § 14(a)(75), 91 Stat. 1404; Nov. 15, 1990, Pub.L. 101–549, title II, § 224, 104 Stat. 2503; Dec. 18, 1991, Pub.L. 102–240, Title III § 3004(b), 105 Stat. 2088.)

Effective Date of 1990 Amendment

Amendment by Pub.L. 101–549 effective Nov. 15, 1990, except as otherwise provided, see section 711(b) of Pub.L. 101–549, set out as a note under section 7401 of this title.

Effective Date

Section 406(d) of Title IV of Pub.L. 95–95, Aug. 7, 1977, 91 Stat. 796, provided that, except as otherwise expressly provided, the amendments made by that Act [which enacted this section] were effective on the date of enactment [Aug. 7, 1977].

Savings Provisions

Suits, actions or proceedings commenced under this chapter as in effect prior to Nov. 15, 1990, not to abate by reason of the taking effect of amendments by Pub.L. 101–549, except as otherwise provided for, see section 711(a) of Pub.L. 101–549, set out as a note under section 7401 of this title.

Change of Name

Any reference in a law, map, regulation, document, paper, or other record of the United States to the Urban Mass Transportation Administration deemed a reference to the Federal Transit Administration, see section 3004(b) of Pub.L. 102–240, set out as a note under section 107 of Title 49, Transportation.

§ 7550. Definitions [CAA § 216]

As used in this part—

(1) The term "manufacturer" as used in sections 7521, 7522, 7525, 7541, and 7542 of this title means any person engaged in the manufacturing or assembling of new motor vehicles, new motor vehicle engines, new nonroad vehicles or new nonroad engines, or importing such vehicles or engines for resale, or who acts for and is under the control of any such person in connection with the distribution of new motor vehicles, new motor vehicle engines, new nonroad vehicles or new nonroad engines, but shall not include any dealer with respect to new motor vehicles or new motor vehicle engines received by him in commerce.

(2) The term "motor vehicle" means any self-propelled vehicle designed for transporting persons or property on a street or highway.

(3) Except with respect to vehicles or engines imported or offered for importation, the term "new motor vehicle" means a motor vehicle the equitable or legal title to which has never been transferred to an ultimate purchaser; and the term "new motor vehicle engine" means an engine in a new motor vehicle or a motor vehicle engine the equitable or legal title to which has never been transferred to the ultimate purchaser; and with respect to imported vehicles or engines, such terms mean a motor vehicle and engine, respectively, manufactured after the effective date of a regulation issued under section 7521 of this title which is applicable to such vehicle or engine (or which would be applicable to such vehicle or engine had it been manufactured for importation into the United States).

(4) The term "dealer" means any person who is engaged in the sale or the distribution of new motor vehicles or new motor vehicle engines to the ultimate purchaser.

(5) The term "ultimate purchaser" means, with respect to any new motor vehicle or new motor vehicle engine, the first person who in good faith purchases such new motor vehicle or new engine for purposes other than resale.

(6) The term "commerce" means (A) commerce between any place in any State and any place

outside thereof; and (B) commerce wholly within the District of Columbia.

(7) Vehicle curb weight, gross vehicle weight rating, light-duty truck, light-duty vehicle, and loaded vehicle weight

The terms "vehicle curb weight", "gross vehicle weight rating" (GVWR), "light-duty truck" (LDT), "light-duty vehicle", and "loaded vehicle weight" (LVW) have the meaning provided in regulations promulgated by the Administrator and in effect as of the enactment of the Clean Air Act Amendments of 1990. The abbreviations in parentheses corresponding to any term referred to in this paragraph shall have the same meaning as the corresponding term.

(8) Test weight

The term "test weight" and the abbreviation "tw" mean the vehicle curb weight added to the gross vehicle weight rating (gvwr) and divided by 2.

(9) Motor vehicle or engine part manufacturer

The term "motor vehicle or engine part manufacturer" as used in sections 7541 and 7542 of this title means any person engaged in the manufacturing, assembling or rebuilding of any device, system, part, component or element of design which is installed in or on motor vehicles or motor vehicle engines.

(10) Nonroad engine

The term "nonroad engine" means an internal combustion engine (including the fuel system) that is not used in a motor vehicle or a vehicle used solely for competition, or that is not subject to standards promulgated under section 7411 or 7521 of this title.

(11) Nonroad vehicle

The term "nonroad vehicle" means a vehicle that is powered by a nonroad engine and that is not a motor vehicle or a vehicle used solely for competition.

(July 14, 1955, ch. 360, title II, § 216, formerly § 208, as added Oct. 20, 1965, Pub.L. 89–272, title I, § 101(8), 79 Stat. 994, renumbered § 212, and amended Nov. 21, 1967, Pub.L. 90–148, § 2, 81 Stat. 503, renumbered § 213, and amended Dec. 31, 1970, Pub.L. 91–604, §§ 8(a), 10(d), 11(a)(2)(A), 84 Stat. 1694, 1703, 1705, renumbered § 214, June 22, 1974, Pub.L. 93–319, § 10, 88 Stat. 261, renumbered § 216, Aug. 7, 1977, Pub.L. 95–95, title II, § 224(d), 91 Stat. 767; Nov. 15, 1990, Pub.L. 101–549, title II, § 223, 104 Stat. 2503.)

References in Text

The enactment of the Clean Air Act Amendments of 1990, referred to in par. (7), probably means the date of enactment of the Clean Air Act Amendments of 1990, Pub.L. 101–549, which was approved November 15, 1990.

CODE OF FEDERAL REGULATIONS

Control of air pollution from motor vehicles, generally, see 40 CFR 85.401 et seq.

Control of air pollution from new motor vehicles, certification and test procedures, see 40 CFR 86.078–3 et seq.

Suspension or revocation of permits, rules governing, see 40 CFR 22.01 et seq.

§ 7551. Study and report on fuel consumption

Following each motor vehicle model year, the Administrator of the Environmental Protection Agency shall report to the Congress respecting the motor vehicle fuel consumption associated with the standards applicable for the immediately preceding model year.

(Aug. 7, 1977, Pub.L. 95–95, title II, § 203, 91 Stat. 754; Dec. 21, 1982, Pub.L. 97–375, title I, § 106(a), 96 Stat. 1820.)

Codification

Section was enacted as part of Pub.L. 95–95, Aug. 7, 1977, 91 Stat. 685, known as the Clean Air Act Amendments of 1977, and not as part of Act July 14, 1955, c. 360, as amended generally by Pub.L. 88–206, Dec. 17, 1963, 77 Stat. 392, and later by Pub.L. 95–95, Aug. 7, 1977, 91 Stat. 685, known as the Clean Air Act, which comprises this chapter.

Effective Date of 1990 Amendment

Amendment by Pub.L. 101–549 effective Nov. 15, 1990, except as otherwise provided, see section 711(b) of Pub.L. 101–549, set out as a note under section 7401 of this title.

Effective Date

Section 406(d) of Title IV of Pub.L. 95–95, Aug. 7, 1977, 91 Stat. 796, provided that, except as otherwise expressly provided, the amendments made by that Act [which enacted this section] were effective on the date of enactment [Aug. 7, 1977].

Savings Provisions

Suits, actions or proceedings commenced under this chapter as in effect prior to Nov. 15, 1990, not to abate by reason of the taking effect of amendments by Pub.L. 101–549, except as otherwise provided for, see section 711(a) of Pub.L. 101–549, set out as a note under section 7401 of this title.

§ 7552. Motor vehicle compliance program fees [CAA § 217]

(a) Fee collection

Consistent with section 9701 of Title 31, the Administrator may promulgate (and from time to time revise) regulations establishing fees to recover all reasonable costs to the Administrator associated with—

(1) new vehicle or engine certification under section 7525(a) of this title or part C of this subchapter,

(2) new vehicle or engine compliance monitoring and testing under section 7525(b) of this title or part C of this subchapter, and

(3) in-use vehicle or engine compliance monitoring and testing under section 7541(c) of this title or part C of this subchapter.

The Administrator may establish for all foreign and domestic manufacturers a fee schedule based on such factors as the Administrator finds appropriate and equitable and nondiscriminatory, including the number of vehicles or engines produced under a certificate of conformity. In the case of heavy-duty engine and vehicle manufacturers, such fees shall not exceed a reasonable amount to recover an appropriate portion of such reasonable costs.

(b) Special treasury fund

Any fees collected under this section shall be deposited in a special fund in the United States Treasury for licensing and other services which thereafter shall be available for appropriation, to remain available until expended, to carry out the Agency's activities for which the fees were collected.

(c) Limitation on fund use

Moneys in the special fund referred to in subsection (b) of this section shall not be used until after the first fiscal year commencing after the first July 1 when fees are paid into the fund.

(d) Administrator's testing authority

Nothing in this subsection shall be construed to limit the Administrator's authority to require manufacturer or confirmatory testing as provided in this part.

(July 14, 1955, ch. 360, title II, § 217, as added Nov. 15, 1990, Pub.L. 101–549, title II, § 225, 104 Stat. 2504.)

Effective Date

Section to take effect Nov. 15, 1990, except as otherwise provided, see section 711(b) of Pub.L. 101–549, set out as a note under section 7401 of this title.

Savings Provisions

Suits, actions or proceedings commenced under this chapter as in effect prior to Nov. 15, 1990, not to abate by reason of the taking effect of amendments by Pub.L. 101–549, except as otherwise provided for, see section 711(a) of Pub.L. 101–549, set out as a note under section 7401 of this title.

§ 7553. Prohibition on production of engines requiring leaded gasoline [CAA § 218]

The Administrator shall promulgate regulations applicable to motor vehicle engines and nonroad engines manufactured after model year 1992 that prohibit the manufacture, sale, or introduction into commerce of any engine that requires leaded gasoline.

(July 14, 1955, ch. 360, title II, § 218, as added Nov. 15, 1990, Pub.L. 101–549, title II, § 226, 104 Stat. 2505.)

Effective Date

Section to take effect Nov. 15, 1990, except as otherwise provided, see section 711(b) of Pub.L. 101–549, set out as a note under section 7401 of this title.

Savings Provisions

Suits, actions or proceedings commenced under this chapter as in effect prior to Nov. 15, 1990, not to abate by reason of the taking effect of amendments by Pub.L. 101–549, except as otherwise provided for, see section 711(a) of Pub.L. 101–549, set out as a note under section 7401 of this title.

§ 7554. Urban bus standards [CAA § 219]

(a) Standards for model years after 1993

Not later than January 1, 1992, the Administrator shall promulgate regulations under section 7521(a) of this title applicable to urban buses for the model year 1994 and thereafter. Such standards shall be based on the best technology that can reasonably be anticipated to be available at the time such measures are to be implemented, taking costs, safety, energy, lead time, and other relevant factors into account. Such regulations shall require that such urban buses comply with the provisions of subsection (b) of this section (and subsection (c) of this subsection, if applicable) in addition to compliance with the standards applicable under section 7521(a) of this title for heavy-duty vehicles of the same type and model year.

(b) PM standard

(1) 50 percent reduction

The standards under section 7521(a) of this title applicable to urban buses shall require that, effective for the model year 1994 and thereafter, emissions of particulate matter (PM) from urban buses shall not exceed 50 percent of the emissions of particulate matter (PM) allowed under the emission standard applicable under section 7521(a) of this title as of November 15, 1990 for particulate matter (PM) in the case of heavy-duty diesel vehicles and engines manufactured in the model year 1994.

(2) Revised reduction

The Administrator shall increase the level of emissions of particulate matter allowed under the standard referred to in paragraph (1) if the Administrator determines that the 50 percent reduction referred to in paragraph (1) is not technologically achievable, taking into account durability, costs, lead time, safety, and other relevant factors. The Administrator may not increase such level of emissions above 70 percent of the emissions of particulate matter (PM) allowed under the emission standard applicable under section 7521(a) of this title as of November 15, 1990 for particulate matter (PM) in the case of heavy-duty diesel vehicles and engines manufactured in the model year 1994.

(3) Determination as part of rule

As part of the rulemaking under subsection (a) of this section, the Administrator shall make a determination as to whether the 50 percent reduction referred to in paragraph (1) is technologically achievable, taking into account durability, costs, lead time, safety, and other relevant factors.

(c) Low-polluting fuel requirement

(1) Annual testing

Beginning with model year 1994 buses, the Administrator shall conduct annual tests of a representative sample of operating urban buses subject to the particulate matter (PM) standard applicable pursuant to subsection (b) of this section to determine whether such buses comply with such standard in use over their full useful life.

(2) Promulgation of additional low-polluting fuel requirement

(A) If the Administrator determines, based on the testing under paragraph (1), that urban buses subject to the particulate matter (PM) standard applicable pursuant to subsection (b) of this section do not comply with such standard in use over their full useful life, he shall revise the standards applicable to such buses to require (in addition to compliance with the PM standard applicable pursuant to subsection (b) of this section) that all new urban buses purchased or placed into service by owners or operators of urban buses in all metropolitan statistical areas or consolidated metropolitan statistical areas with a 1980 population of 750,000 or more shall be capable of operating, and shall be exclusively operated, on low-polluting fuels. The Administrator shall establish the pass-fail rate for purposes of testing under this subparagraph.

(B) The Administrator shall promulgate a schedule phasing in any low-polluting fuel requirement established pursuant to this paragraph to an increasing percentage of new urban buses purchased or placed into service in each of the first 5 model years commencing 3 years after the determination under subparagraph (A). Under such schedule 100 percent of new urban buses placed into service in the fifth model year commencing 3 years after the determination under subparagraph (A) shall comply with the low-polluting fuel requirement established pursuant to this paragraph.

(C) The Administrator may extend the requirements of this paragraph to metropolitan statistical areas or consolidated metropolitan statistical areas with a 1980 population of less than 750,000, if the Administrator determines that a significant benefit to public health could be expected to result from such extension.

(d) Retrofit requirements

Not later than 12 months after the enactment of the Clean Air Act Amendments of 1990, the Administrator shall promulgate regulations under section 7521(a) of this title requiring that urban buses which—

(1) are operating in areas referred to in subparagraph (A) of subsection (c)(2) of this section (or subparagraph (C) of subsection (c)(2) of this section if the Administrator has taken action under that subparagraph);

(2) were not subject to standards in effect under the regulations under subsection (a) of this section; and

(3) have their engines replaced or rebuilt after January 1, 1995,

shall comply with an emissions standard or emissions control technology requirement established by the Administrator in such regulations. Such emissions standard or emissions control technology requirement shall reflect the best retrofit technology and maintenance practices reasonably achievable.

(e) Procedures for administration and enforcement

The Administrator shall establish, within 18 months after the enactment of the Clean Air Act Amendments to 1990, and in accordance with section 7525(h) of this title, procedures for the administration and enforcement of standards for buses subject to standards under this section, testing procedures, sampling protocols, in-use compliance requirements, and criteria governing evaluation of buses. Procedures for testing (including, but not limited to, certification testing) shall reflect actual operating conditions.

(f) Definitions

For purposes of this section—

(1) Urban bus

The term "urban bus" has the meaning provided under regulations of the Administrator promulgated under section 7521(a) of this title.

(2) Low-polluting fuel

The term "low-polluting fuel" means methanol, ethanol, propane, or natural gas, or any comparably low-polluting fuel. In determining whether a fuel is comparably low-polluting, the Administrator shall consider both the level of emissions of air pollutants from vehicles using the fuel and the contribution of such emissions to ambient levels of air pollutants. For purposes of this paragraph, the term "methanol" includes any fuel which contains at least 85 percent methanol unless the Administrator increases such percentage as he deems appropriate to protect public health and welfare.

(July 14, 1955, ch. 360, title II, § 219, as added Nov. 15, 1990, Pub.L. 101–549, title II, § 227, 104 Stat. 2505.)

References in Text

Enactment of the Clean Air Act Amendments of 1990, referred to in subsecs. (d), and (e), probably means the date of enactment of the Clean Air Act Amendments of 1990, Pub.L. 101–549, which was approved November 15, 1990.

Effective Date

Section to take effect Nov. 15, 1990, except as otherwise provided, see section 711(b) of Pub.L. 101–549, set out as a note under section 7401 of this title.

Savings Provisions

Suits, actions or proceedings commenced under this chapter as in effect prior to Nov. 15, 1990, not to abate by reason of the taking effect of amendments by Pub.L. 101–549, except as otherwise provided for, see section 711(a) of Pub.L. 101–549, set out as a note under section 7401 of this title.

PART B—AIRCRAFT EMISSION STANDARDS

§ 7571. Establishment of standards [CAA § 231]

(a) Study; proposed standards; hearings; issuance of regulations

(1) Within 90 days after December 31, 1970, the Administrator shall commence a study and investigation of emissions of air pollutants from aircraft in order to determine—

(A) the extent to which such emissions affect air quality in air quality control regions throughout the United States, and

(B) the technological feasibility of controlling such emissions.

(2) The Administrator shall, from time to time, issue proposed emission standards applicable to the emission of any air pollutant from any class or classes of aircraft engines which in his judgment causes, or contributes to, air pollution which may reasonably be anticipated to endanger public health or welfare.

(3) The Administrator shall hold public hearings with respect to such proposed standards. Such hearings shall, to the extent practicable, be held in air quality control regions which are most seriously affected by aircraft emissions. Within 90 days after the issuance of such proposed regulations, he shall issue such regulations with such modifications as he deems appropriate. Such regulations may be revised from time to time.

(b) Effective date of regulations

Any regulation prescribed under this section (and any revision thereof) shall take effect after such period as the Administrator finds necessary (after consultation with the Secretary of Transportation) to permit the development and application of the requisite technology, giving appropriate consideration to the cost of compliance within such period.

(c) Regulations which create hazards to aircraft safety

Any regulations in effect under this section on August 7, 1977, or proposed or promulgated thereafter, or amendments thereto, with respect to aircraft shall not apply if disapproved by the President, after notice and opportunity for public hearing, on the basis of a finding by the Secretary of Transportation that any such regulation would create a hazard to aircraft safety. Any such finding shall include a reasonably specific statement of the basis upon which the finding was made.

(July 14, 1955, ch. 360, title II, § 231, as added Dec. 31, 1970, Pub.L. 91–604, § 11(a)(1), 84 Stat. 1703, and amended Aug. 7, 1977, Pub.L. 95–95, title II, § 225, title IV, § 401(f), 91 Stat. 769, 791.)

Study And Investigation Of Uninstalled Aircraft Engines

Pub.L. 101–549, Title II, § 233, Nov. 15, 1990, 104 Stat. 2529, provided that:

"(a) **Study.**—The Administrator of the Environmental Protection Agency and the Secretary of Transportation, in consultation with the Secretary of Defense, shall commence a study and investigation of the testing of uninstalled aircraft engines in enclosed test cells that shall address at a minimum the following issues and such other issues as they shall deem appropriate—

"(1) whether technologies exist to control some or all emissions of oxides of nitrogen from test cells;

"(2) the effectiveness of such technologies;

"(3) the cost of implementing such technologies;

"(4) whether such technologies affect the safety, design, structure, operation, or performance of aircraft engines;

"(5) whether such technologies impair the effectiveness and accuracy of aircraft engine safety design, and performance tests conducted in test cells; and

"(6) the impact of not controlling such oxides of nitrogen in the applicable nonattainment areas and on other sources, stationary and mobile, on oxides of nitrogen in such areas.

"(b) **Report, authority to regulate.**—Not later than 24 months after enactment of the Clean Air Act Amendments of 1990 [probably means the date of enactment of Pub.L. 101–549, which was approved Nov. 15, 1990], the Administrator of the Environmental Protection Agency and the Secretary of Transportation shall submit to Congress a report of the study conducted under this section. Following the completion of such study, any of the States may adopt or enforce any standard for emissions of oxides of nitrogen from test cells only after issuing a public notice stating whether such standards are in accordance with the findings of the study."

CROSS REFERENCES

Aviation fuel standards, establishment, implementation and enforcement, see section 1421 of Title 49, Transportation.

West's Federal Practice Manual

Air quality legislation, see § 4384.5.

CODE OF FEDERAL REGULATIONS

Air pollution from aircrafts, control of, see 40 CFR 87.1 et seq.

LIBRARY REFERENCES

Health and Environment ⚷20, 25.6(6).
C.J.S. Health and Environment §§ 2 et seq., 91 et seq.

§ 7572. Enforcement of standards [CAA § 232]

(a) Regulations to insure compliance with standards

The Secretary of Transportation, after consultation with the Administrator, shall prescribe regulations to insure compliance with all standards prescribed under section 7571 of this title by the Administrator. The regulations of the Secretary of Transportation shall include provisions making such standards applicable in the issuance, amendment, modification, suspension, or revocation of any certificate authorized by the Federal Aviation Act [49 U.S.C.A. App. § 1301 et seq.] or the Department of Transportation Act [49 U.S.C.A. App. § 1651 et seq.]. Such Secretary shall insure that all necessary inspections are accomplished, and,[1] may execute any power or duty vested in him by any other provision of law in the execution of all powers and duties vested in him under this section.

(b) Notice and appeal rights

In any action to amend, modify, suspend, or revoke a certificate in which violation of an emission standard prescribed under section 7571 of this title or of a regulation prescribed under subsection (a) of this section is at issue, the certificate holder shall have the same notice and appeal rights as are prescribed for such holders in the Federal Aviation Act of 1958 [49 U.S.C.A. App. § 1301 et seq.] or the Department of Transportation Act [49 U.S.C.A. App. § 1651 et seq.], except that in any appeal to the National Transportation Safety Board, the Board may amend, modify, or revoke the order of the Secretary of Transportation only if it finds no violation of such standard or regulation and that such amendment, modification, or revocation is consistent with safety in air transportation.

(July 14, 1955, ch. 360, title II, § 232, as added Dec. 31, 1970, Pub.L. 91–604, § 11(a)(1), 84 Stat. 1704.)

[1] So in original. The comma probably should not have appeared.

LIBRARY REFERENCES

Health and Environment ⇔25.6(6).
C.J.S. Health and Environment § 91 et seq.

§ 7573. State standards and controls [CAA § 233]

No State or political subdivision thereof may adopt or attempt to enforce any standard respecting emissions of any air pollutant from any aircraft or engine thereof unless such standard is identical to a standard applicable to such aircraft under this part.

(July 14, 1955, ch. 360, title II, § 233, as added Dec. 31, 1970, Pub.L. 91–604, § 11(a)(1), 84 Stat. 1704.)

LIBRARY REFERENCES

States ⇔4.11.
C.J.S. States § 24.

§ 7574. Definitions [CAA § 234]

Terms used in this part (other than Administrator) shall have the same meaning as such terms have under section 1301 of Title 49 Appendix.

(July 14, 1955, ch. 360, title II, § 234, as added Dec. 31, 1970, Pub.L. 91–604, § 11(a)(1), 84 Stat. 1705.)

Part C—Clean Fuel Vehicles

§ 7581. Definitions [CAA § 241]

For purposes of this part—

(1) Terms defined in part A of this subchapter

The definitions applicable to part A of this subchapter under section 7550 of this title shall also apply for purposes of this part.

(2) Clean alternative fuel

The term "clean alternative fuel" means any fuel (including methanol, ethanol, or other alcohols (including any mixture thereof containing 85 percent or more by volume of such alcohol with gasoline or other fuels), reformulated gasoline, diesel, natural gas, liquefied petroleum gas, and hydrogen) or power source (including electricity) used in a clean-fuel vehicle that complies with the standards and requirements applicable to such vehicle under this subchapter when using such fuel or power source. In the case of any flexible fuel vehicle or dual fuel vehicle, the term "clean alternative fuel" means only a fuel with respect to which such vehicle was certified as a clean-fuel vehicle meeting the standards applicable to clean-fuel vehicles under section 7583(d)(2) of this title when operating on clean alternative fuel (or any CARB standards which replaces such standards pursuant to section 7583(e) of this title).

(3) NMOG

The term nonmethane organic gas ("NMOG") means the sum of nonoxygenated and oxygenated hydrocarbons contained in a gas sample, including, at a minimum, all oxygenated organic gases containing 5 or fewer carbon atoms (i.e., aldehydes, ketones, alcohols, ethers, etc.), and all known alkanes, alkenes, alkynes, and aromatics containing 12 or fewer carbon atoms. To demonstrate compliance with a NMOG standard, NMOG emissions shall be measured in accordance with the "California Non–Methane Organic Gas Test Procedures". In the case of vehicles using fuels other than base gasoline, the level of NMOG emissions shall be adjusted based on the reactivity of the emissions relative to vehicles using base gasoline.

(4) Base gasoline

The term "base gasoline" means gasoline which meets the following specifications:

Specifications of Base Gasoline Used as Basis for Reactivity Readjustment:

API gravity	57.8
Sulfur, ppm	317
Color	Purple

Benzene, vol. %	1.35
Reid vapor pressure	8.7
Drivability	1195
Antiknock index	87.3
Distillation, D–86 • F	
IBP	92
10%	126
50%	219
90%	327
EP	414
Hydrocarbon Type, Vol. % FIA:	
Aromatics	30.9
Olefins	8.2
Saturates	60.9

The Administrator shall modify the definitions of NMOG, base gasoline, and the methods for making reactivity adjustments, to conform to the definitions and method used in California under the Low–Emission Vehicle and Clean Fuel Regulations of the California Air Resources Board, so long as the California definitions are, in the aggregate, at least as protective of public health and welfare as the definitions in this section.

(5) Covered fleet

The term "covered fleet" means 10 or more motor vehicles which are owned or operated by a single person. In determining the number of vehicles owned or operated by a single person for purposes of this paragraph, all motor vehicles owned or operated, leased or otherwise controlled by such person, by any person who controls such person, by any person controlled by such person, and by any person under common control with such person shall be treated as owned by such person. The term "covered fleet" shall not include motor vehicles held for lease or rental to the general public, motor vehicles held for sale by motor vehicle dealers (including demonstration vehicles), motor vehicles used for motor vehicle manufacturer product evaluations or tests, law enforcement and other emergency vehicles, or nonroad vehicles (including farm and construction vehicles).

(6) Covered fleet vehicle

The term "covered fleet vehicle" means only a motor vehicle which is—

(i) in a vehicle class for which standards are applicable under this part; and

(ii) in a covered fleet which is centrally fueled (or capable of being centrally fueled).

No vehicle which under normal operations is garaged at a personal residence at night shall be considered to be a vehicle which is capable of being centrally fueled within the meaning of this paragraph.

(7) Clean-fuel vehicle

The term "clean-fuel vehicle" means a vehicle in a class or category of vehicles which has been certified to meet for any model year the clean-fuel vehicle standards applicable under this part for that model year to clean-fuel vehicles in that class or category.

(July 14, 1955, ch. 360, title II, § 241, as added Nov. 15, 1990, Pub.L. 101–549, title II, § 229(a), 104 Stat. 2511.)

Effective Date

Section to take effect Nov. 15, 1990, except as otherwise provided, see section 711(b) of Pub.L. 101–549, set out as a note under section 7401 of this title.

Savings Provisions

Suits, actions or proceedings commenced under this chapter as in effect prior to Nov. 15, 1990, not to abate by reason of the taking effect of amendments by Pub.L. 101–549, except as otherwise provided for, see section 711(a) of Pub.L. 101–549, set out as a note under section 7401 of this title.

§ 7582. Requirements applicable to clean fuel vehicles [CAA § 242]

(a) Promulgation of standards

Not later than 24 months after the enactment of the Clean Air Act Amendments of 1990, the Administrator shall promulgate regulations under this part containing clean-fuel vehicle standards for the clean-fuel vehicles specified in this part.

(b) Other requirements

Clean–fuel vehicles of up to 8,500 gvwr subject to standards set forth in this part shall comply with all motor vehicle requirements of this subchapter (such as requirements relating to on-board diagnostics, evaporative emissions, etc.) which are applicable to conventional gasoline-fueled vehicles of the same category and model year, except as provided in section 7584 of this title with respect to administration and enforcement, and except to the extent that any such requirement is in conflict with the provisions of this part. Clean-fuel vehicles of 8,500 gvwr or greater subject to standards set forth in this part shall comply with all requirements of this subchapter which are applicable in the case of conventional gasoline-fueled or diesel fueled vehicles of the same category and model year, except as provided in section 7584 of this title with respect to administration and enforcement, and except to the extent that any such requirement is in conflict with the provisions of this part.

(c) In-use useful life and testing

(1) In the case of light-duty vehicles and light-duty trucks up to 6,000 lbs gvwr, the useful life for purposes of determining in-use compliance with the standards under section 7583 of this title shall be—

(A) a period of 5 years or 50,000 miles (or the equivalent) whichever first occurs, in the case of standards applicable for purposes of certification at 50,000 miles; and

(B) a period of 10 years or 100,000 miles (or the equivalent) whichever first occurs, in the case of standards applicable for purposes of certification at 100,000 miles, except that in-use testing shall not be done for a period beyond 7 years or 75,000 miles (or the equivalent) whichever first occurs.

(2) In the case of light-duty trucks of more than 6,000 lbs gvwr, the useful life for purposes of determining in-use compliance with the standards under section 7583 of this title shall be—

(A) a period of 5 years or 50,000 miles (or the equivalent [1] whichever first occurs in the case of standards applicable for purposes of certification at 50,000 miles; and

(B) a period of 11 years or 120,000 miles (or the equivalent) whichever first occurs in the case of standards applicable for purposes of certification at 120,000 miles, except that in-use testing shall not be done for a period beyond 7 years or 90,000 miles (or the equivalent) whichever first occurs.

(July 14, 1955, ch. 360, title II, § 242, as added Nov. 15, 1990, Pub.L. 101–549, title II, § 229(a), 104 Stat. 2513.)

[1] So in original. Probably should be a closing parenthesis.

References in Text

The enactment of the Clean Air Act Amendments of 1990, referred to in subsec. (a), probably means the date of enactment of the Clean Air Act Amendments of 1990, Pub.L. 101–549, which was approved November 15, 1990.

Effective Date

Section to take effect Nov. 15, 1990, except as otherwise provided, see section 711(b) of Pub.L. 101–549, set out as a note under section 7401 of this title.

Savings Provisions

Suits, actions or proceedings commenced under this chapter as in effect prior to Nov. 15, 1990, not to abate by reason of the taking effect of amendments by Pub.L. 101–549, except as otherwise provided for, see section 711(a) of Pub.L. 101–549, set out as a note under section 7401 of this title.

§ 7583. Standards for light-duty clean fuel vehicles [CAA § 243]

(a) Exhaust standards for light-duty vehicles and certain light-duty trucks

The standards set forth in this subsection shall apply in the case of clean-fuel vehicles which are light-duty trucks of up to 6,000 lbs. gross vehicle weight rating (gvwr) (but not including light-duty trucks of more than 3,750 lbs. loaded vehicle weight (lvw)) or light-duty vehicles:

(1) Phase I

Beginning with model year 1996, for the air pollutants specified in the following table, the clean-fuel vehicle standards under this section shall provide that vehicle exhaust emissions shall not exceed the levels specified in the following table:

PHASE I CLEAN FUEL VEHICLE EMISSION STANDARDS FOR LIGHT-DUTY TRUCKS OF UP TO 3,750 LBS. LVW AND UP TO 6,000 LBS. GVWR AND LIGHT-DUTY VEHICLES

Pollutant	NMOG	CO	NO_x	PM	HCHO (formaldehyde)
50,000 mile standard	0.125	3.4	0.4	....	0.015
100,000 mile standard	0.156	4.2	0.6	0.08*	0.018

Standards are expressed in grams per mile (gpm).
*Standards for particulates (PM) shall apply only to diesel-fueled vehicles.
In the case of the 50,000 mile standards and the 100,000 mile standards, for purposes of certification, the applicable useful life shall be 50,000 miles or 100,000 miles, respectively.

(2) Phase II

Beginning with model year 2001, for air pollutants specified in the following table, the clean-fuel vehicle standards under this section shall provide that vehicle exhaust emissions shall not exceed the levels specified in the following table.

PHASE II CLEAN FUEL VEHICLE EMISSION STANDARDS FOR LIGHT-DUTY TRUCKS OF UP TO 3,750 LBS. LVW AND UP TO 6,000 LBS. GVWR AND LIGHT-DUTY VEHICLES

Pollutant	NMOG	CO	NO_x	PM*	HCHO (formaldehyde)
50,000 mile standard	0.075	3.4	0.2	....	0.015
100,000 mile standard	0.090	4.2	0.3	0.08	0.018

Standards are expressed in grams per mile (gpm).
*Standards for particulates (PM) shall apply only to diesel-fueled vehicles.
In the case of the 50,000 mile standards and the 100,000 mile standards, for purposes of certification, the applicable useful life shall be 50,000 miles or 100,000 miles, respectively.

(b) Exhaust standards for light-duty trucks of more than 3,750 lbs. LVW and up to 5,750 lbs. LVW and up to 6,000 lbs. GVWR

The standards set forth in this paragraph shall apply in the case of clean-fuel vehicles which are light-duty trucks of more than 3,750 lbs. loaded vehicle weight (lvw) but not more than 5,750 lbs. lvw and not more than 6,000 lbs. gross weight rating (GVWR):

(1) Phase I

Beginning with model year 1996, for the air pollutants specified in the following table, the clean-fuel vehicle standards under this section shall provide that vehicle exhaust emissions shall not exceed the levels specified in the following table.

PHASE I CLEAN FUEL VEHICLE EMISSION STANDARDS FOR LIGHT-DUTY TRUCKS OF MORE THAN 3,750 LBS. AND UP TO 5,750 LBS. LVW AND UP TO 6,000 LBS. GVWR

Pollutant	NMOG	CO	NO_x	PM*	HCHO (formaldehyde)
50,000 mile standard	0.160	4.4	0.7	....	0.018
100,000 mile standard	0.200	5.5	0.9	0.08	0.023

Standards are expressed in grams per mile (gpm).
*Standards for particulates (PM) shall apply only to diesel-fueled vehicles.
In the case of the 50,000 mile standards and the 100,000 mile standards, for purposes of certification, the applicable useful life shall be 50,000 miles or 100,000 miles, respectively.

(2) Phase II

Beginning with model year 2001, for the air pollutants specified in the following table, the clean-fuel vehicle standards under this section shall provide that vehicle exhaust emissions shall not exceed the levels specified in the following table.

PHASE II CLEAN FUEL VEHICLE EMISSION STANDARDS FOR LIGHT-DUTY TRUCKS OF MORE THAN 3,750 LBS. LVW AND UP TO 5,750 LBS. LVW AND UP TO 6,000 LBS. GVWR

Pollutant	NMOG	CO	NO_x	PM*	HCHO (formaldehyde)
50,000 mile standard	0.100	4.4	0.4	....	0.018
100,000 mile standard	0.130	5.5	0.5	0.08	0.023

Standards are expressed in grams per mile (gpm).
*Standards for particulates (PM) shall apply only to diesel-fueled vehicles.
In the case of the 50,000 mile standards and the 100,000 mile standards, for purposes of certification, the applicable useful life shall be 50,000 miles or 100,000 miles, respectively.

(c) Exhaust standards for light-duty trucks greater than 6,000 lbs. GVWR

The standards set forth in this subsection shall apply in the case of clean-fuel vehicles which are light-duty trucks of more than 6,000 lbs. gross weight rating (GVWR) and less than or equal to 8,500 lbs. GVWR, beginning with model year 1998. For the air pollutants specified in the following table, the clean-fuel vehicle standards under this section shall provide that vehicle exhaust emissions of vehicles within the test weight categories specified in the following table shall not exceed the levels specified in such table.

CLEAN FUEL VEHICLE EMISSION STANDARDS FOR LIGHT-DUTY TRUCKS GREATER THAN 6,000 LBS. GVWR

Test Weight Category: Up to 3,750 lbs. tw

Pollutant	NMOG	CO	NO_x	PM*	HCHO (formaldehyde)
50,000 mile standard	0.125	3.4	0.4**	....	0.015
120,000 mile standard	0.180	5.0	0.6	0.08	0.022

Test Weight Category: Above 3,750 but not above 5,750 lbs. tw

Pollutant	NMOG	CO	NO_x	PM*	HCHO (formaldehyde)
50,000 mile standard	0.160	4.4	0.7**	....	0.018
120,000 mile standard	0.230	6.4	1.0	0.10	0.027

Test Weight Category: Above 5,750 tw but not above 8,500 lbs. gvwr

Pollutant	NMOG	CO	NO_x	PM*	HCHO (formaldehyde)
50,000 mile standard	0.195	5.0	1.1**	....	0.022
120,000 mile standard	0.280	7.3	1.5	0.12	0.032

Standards are expressed in grams per mile (gpm).

*Standards for particulates (PM) shall apply only to diesel-fueled vehicles.

**Standard not applicable to diesel-fueled vehicles.

For the 50,000 mile standards and the 120,000 mile standards set forth in the table, the applicable useful life for purposes of certification shall be 50,000 miles or 120,000 miles, respectively.

(d) Flexible and dual-fuel vehicles

(1) In general

The Administrator shall establish standards and requirements under this section for the model year 1996 and thereafter for vehicles weighing not more than 8,500 lbs. gvwr which are capable of operating on more than one fuel. Such standards shall require that such vehicles meet the exhaust standards applicable under subsection (a), (b), and (c) of this section for CO, NO_x, and HCHO, and if appropriate, PM for single-fuel vehicles of the same vehicle category and model year.

(2) Exhaust NMOG standard for operation on clean alternative fuel

In addition to standards for the pollutants referred to in paragraph (1), the standards established under paragraph (1) shall require that vehicle exhaust emissions of NMOG not exceed the levels (expressed in grams per mile) specified in the tables below when the vehicle is operated on the clean alternative fuel for which such vehicle is certified:

NMOG STANDARDS FOR FLEXIBLE- AND DUAL-FUELED VEHICLES WHEN OPERATING ON CLEAN ALTERNATIVE FUEL

Light-duty Trucks up to 6,000 lbs. GVWR and Light-duty vehicles

Vehicle Type	Column A (50,000 mi.) Standard (gpm)	Column B (100,000 mi.) Standard (gpm)
Beginning MY 1996:		
LDT's (0–3,750 lbs. LVW) and light-duty vehicles	0.125	0.156
LDT's (3,751–3,750 lbs. LVW)	0.160	0.20
Beginning MY 2001:		
LDT's (0–3,750 lbs. LVW) and light-duty vehicles	0.075	0.090
LDT's (3,751–5,750 lbs. LVW)	0.100	0.130

For standards under column A, for purposes of certification under section 7525 of this title, the applicable useful life shall be 50,000 miles.

For standards under column B, for purposes of certification under section 7525 of this title, the applicable useful life shall be 100,000 miles.

Light-duty Trucks More than 6,000 lbs. GVWR

Vehicle Type	Column A (50,000 mi.) Standard	Column B (120,000 mi.) Standard
Beginning MY 1998:		
LDT's (0–3,750 lbs. TW)	0.125	0.180
LDT's (3,751–5,750 lbs. TW)	0.160	0.230
LDT's (above 5,750 lbs. TW)	0.195	0.280

For standards under column A, for purposes of certification under section 7525 of this title, the applicable useful life shall be 50,000 miles.

For standards under column B, for purposes of certification under section 7525 of this title, the applicable useful life shall be 120,000 miles.

(3) NMOG standard for operation on conventional fuel

In addition to the standards referred to in paragraph (1), the standards established under paragraph (1) shall require that vehicle exhaust emissions of NMOG not exceed the levels (expressed in grams per mile) specified in the tables below:

NMOG STANDARDS FOR FLEXIBLE- AND DUAL-FUELED VEHICLES WHEN OPERATING ON CONVENTIONAL FUEL

Light-duty Trucks of up to 6,000 lbs. GVWR and Light-duty vehicles

Vehicle Type	Column A (50,000 mi.) Standard (gpm)	Column B (100,000 mi.) Standard (gpm)
Beginning MY 1996:		
LDT's (0–3,750 lbs. LVW) and light-duty vehicles	0.25	0.31
LDT's (3,751–5,750 lbs. LVW)	0.32	0.40

Vehicle Type	Column A (50,000 mi.) Standard (gpm)	Column B (100,000 mi.) Standard (gpm)
Beginning MY 2001:		
LDT's (0–3,750 lbs. LVW) and light-duty vehicles	0.125	0.156
LDT's (3,750–5,750 lbs. LVW)	0.160	0.200

For standards under column A, for purposes of certification under section 7525 of this title, the applicable useful life shall be 50,000 miles.

For standards under column B, for purposes of certification under section 7525 of this title, the applicable useful life shall be 100,000 miles.

Light-duty Trucks of up to 6,000 lbs. GVWR

Vehicle Type	Column A (50,000 mi.) Standard	Column B (120,000 mi.) Standard
Beginning MY 1998:		
LDT's (0–3,750 lbs. TW)	0.25	0.36
LDT's (3,751–5,750 lbs. TW)	0.32	0.46
LDT's (above 5,750 lbs. TW)	0.39	0.56

For standards under column A, for purposes of certification under section 7525 of this title, the applicable useful life shall be 50,000 miles.

For standards under column B, for purposes of certification under section 7525 of this title, the applicable useful life shall be 120,000 miles.

(e) Replacement by CARB standards

(1) Single set of CARB standards

If the State of California promulgates regulations establishing and implementing a single set of standards applicable in California pursuant to a waiver approved under section 7543 of this title to any category of vehicles referred to in subsection (a), (b), (c), or (d) of this section and such set of standards is, in the aggregate, at least as protective of public health and welfare as the otherwise applicable standards set forth in section 7582 of this title and subsection (a), (b), (c), or (d) of this section, such set of California standards shall apply to clean-fuel vehicles in such category in lieu of the standards otherwise applicable under section 7582 of this title and subsection (a), (b), (c), or (d) of this section, as the case may be.

(2) Multiple sets of CARB standards

If the State of California promulgates regulations establishing and implementing several different sets of standards applicable in California pursuant to a waiver approved under section 7543 of this title to any category of vehicles referred to in subsection (a), (b), (c), or (d) of this section and each of such sets of California standards is, in the aggregate, at least as protective of public health and welfare as the otherwise applicable standards set forth in section 7582 of this title and subsection (a), (b), (c), or (d) of this section, such standards shall be treated as "qualifying California standards" for purposes of this paragraph. Where more than one set of qualifying standards are established and administered by the State of California, the least stringent set of qualifying California standards shall apply to the clean-fuel vehicles concerned in lieu of the standards otherwise applicable to such vehicles under section 7582 of this title and this section.

(f) Less stringent CARB standards

If the Low-Emission Vehicle and Clean Fuels Regulations of the California Air Resources Board applicable to any category of vehicles referred to in subsection (a), (b), (c), or (d) of this section are modified after the enactment of the Clean Air Act of 1990 to provide an emissions standard which is less stringent than the otherwise applicable standard set forth in subsection (a), (b), (c), or (d) of this section, or if any effective date contained in such regulations is delayed, such modified standards or such delay (or both, as the case may be) shall apply, for an interim period, in lieu of the standard or effective date otherwise applicable under subsection (a), (b), (c), or (d) of this section to any vehicles covered by such modified standard or delayed effective date. The interim period shall be a period of not more than 2 model years from the effective date otherwise applicable under subsection (a), (b), (c), or (d) of this section. After such interim period, the otherwise applicable standard set forth in subsection (a), (b), (c), or (d) of this section shall take effect with respect to such vehicles (unless subsequently replaced under subsection (e) of this section).

(g) Not applicable to heavy-duty vehicles

Notwithstanding any provision of the Low-Emission Vehicle and Clean Fuels Regulations of the California Air Resources Board nothing in this section shall apply to heavy-duty engines in vehicles of more than 8,500 lbs. GVWR.

(July 14, 1955, ch. 360, title II, § 243, as added Nov. 15, 1990, Pub.L. 101–549, title II, § 229(a), 104 Stat. 2514.)

References in Text

The enactment of the Clean Air Act of 1990, referred to in subsec. (f), probably means the date of enactment of the Clean Air Act Amendments of 1990, Pub.L. 101–549, which was approved November 15, 1990.

Effective Date

Section to take effect Nov. 15, 1990, except as otherwise provided, see section 711(b) of Pub.L. 101–549, set out as a note under section 7401 of this title.

Savings Provisions

Suits, actions or proceedings commenced under this chapter as in effect prior to Nov. 15, 1990, not to abate by reason of the taking effect of amendments by Pub.L. 101–549, except as otherwise provided for, see section 711(a) of Pub.L. 101–549, set out as a note under section 7401 of this title.

§ 7584. Administration and enforcement as per California standards [CAA § 244]

Where the numerical clean-fuel vehicle standards applicable under this part to vehicles of not more than 8,500 lbs. GVWR are the same as numerical emission standards applicable in California under the Low–Emission Vehicle and Clean Fuels Regulations of the California Air Resources Board ("CARB"), such standards shall be administered and enforced by the Administrator—

(1) in the same manner and with the same flexibility as the State of California administers and enforces corresponding standards applicable under the Low–Emission Vehicle and Clean Fuels Regulations of the California Air Resources Board ("CARB"); and

(2) subject to the same requirements, and utilizing the same interpretations and policy judgments, as are applicable in the case of such CARB standards, including, but not limited to, requirements regarding certification, production-line testing, and in-use compliance,

unless the Administrator determines (in promulgating the rules establishing the clean fuel vehicle program under this section) that any such administration and enforcement would not meet the criteria for a waiver under section 7543 of this title. Nothing in this section shall apply in the case of standards under section 7585 of this title for heavy-duty vehicles.

(July 14, 1955, ch. 360, title II, § 244, as added Nov. 15, 1990, Pub.L. 101–549, title II, § 229(a), 104 Stat. 2519.)

Effective Date

Section to take effect Nov. 15, 1990, except as otherwise provided, see section 711(b) of Pub.L. 101–549, set out as a note under section 7401 of this title.

Savings Provisions

Suits, actions or proceedings commenced under this chapter as in effect prior to Nov. 15, 1990, not to abate by reason of the taking effect of amendments by Pub.L. 101–549, except as otherwise provided for, see section 711(a) of Pub.L. 101–549, set out as a note under section 7401 of this title.

§ 7585. Standards for heavy-duty clean-fuel vehicles (GVWR above 8,500 up to 26,000 lbs.) [CAA § 245]

(a) Model years after 1997; combined NO_x and NMHC standard

For classes or categories of heavy-duty vehicles or engines manufactured for the model year 1998 or thereafter and having a GVWR greater than 8,500 lbs. and up to 26,000 lbs. GVWR, the standards under this part for clean-fuel vehicles shall require that combined emissions of oxides of nitrogen (NO_x) and nonmethane hydrocarbons (NMHC) shall not exceed 3.15 grams per brake horsepower hour (equivalent to 50 percent of the combined emission standards applicable under section 7521 of this title for such air pollutants in the case of a conventional model year 1994 heavy-duty diesel-fueled vehicle or engine). No standard shall be promulgated as provided in this section for any heavy-duty vehicle of more than 26,000 lbs. GVWR.

(b) Revised standards that are less stringent

(1) The Administrator may promulgate a revised less stringent standard for the vehicles or engines referred to in subsection (a) of this section if the Administrator determines that the 50 percent reduction required under subsection (a) of this section is not technologically feasible for clean diesel-fueled vehicles and engines, taking into account durability, costs, lead time, safety, and other relevant factors. To provide adequate lead time the Administrator shall make a determination with regard to the technological feasibility of such 50 percent reduction before December 31, 1993.

(2) Any person may at any time petition the Administrator to make a determination under paragraph (1). The Administrator shall act on such a petition within 6 months after the petition is filed.

(3) Any revised less stringent standards promulgated as provided in this subsection shall require at least a 30 percent reduction in lieu of the 50 percent reduction referred to in paragraph (1).

(July 14, 1955, ch. 360, title II, § 245, as added Nov. 15, 1990, Pub.L. 101–549, title II, § 229(a), 104 Stat. 2519.)

Effective Date

Section to take effect Nov. 15, 1990, except as otherwise provided, see section 711(b) of Pub.L. 101–549, set out as a note under section 7401 of this title.

Savings Provisions

Suits, actions or proceedings commenced under this chapter as in effect prior to Nov. 15, 1990, not to abate by reason of the taking effect of amendments by Pub.L. 101–549, except as otherwise provided for, see section 711(a) of Pub.L. 101–549, set out as a note under section 7401 of this title.

§ 7586. Centrally fueled fleets [CAA § 246]

(a) Fleet program required for certain nonattainment areas

(1) SIP revision

Each State in which there is located all or part of a covered area (as defined in paragraph (2)) shall submit, within 42 months after the enactment of the Clean Air Act Amendments of 1990, a State implementation plan revision under section 7410 of this title and part D of subchapter I of this chapter to establish a clean-fuel vehicle program for fleets under this section.

(2) Covered areas

For purposes of this subsection, each of the following shall be a "covered area":

(A) Ozone nonattainment areas

Any ozone nonattainment area with a 1980 population of 250,000 or more classified under subpart 2 of part D of subchapter I of this chapter as Serious, Severe, or Extreme based on data for the calendar years 1987, 1988, and 1989. In determining the ozone nonattainment areas to be treated as covered areas pursuant to this subparagraph, the Administrator shall use the most recent interpretation methodology issued by the Administrator prior to the enactment of the Clean Air Act Amendments of 1990.

(B) Carbon monoxide nonattainment areas

Any carbon monoxide nonattainment area with a 1980 population of 250,000 or more and a carbon monoxide design value at or above 16.0 parts per million based on data for calendar years 1988 and 1989 (as calculated according to the most recent interpretation methodology issued prior to enactment of the Clean Air Act Amendments of 1990 by the United States Environmental Protection Agency), excluding those carbon monoxide nonattainment areas in which mobile sources do not contribute significantly to carbon monoxide exceedances.

(3) Plan revisions for reclassified areas

In the case of ozone nonattainment areas reclassified as Serious, Severe, or Extreme under part D of subchapter I of this chapter with a 1980 population of 250,000 or more, the State shall submit a plan revision meeting the requirements of this subsection within 1 year after reclassification. Such plan revision shall implement the requirements applicable under this subsection at the time of reclassification and thereafter, except that the Administrator may adjust for a limited period the deadlines for compliance where compliance with such deadlines would be infeasible.

(4) Consultation; consideration of factors

Each State required to submit an implementation plan revision under this subsection shall develop such revision in consultation with fleet operators, vehicle manufacturers, fuel producers and distributors, motor vehicle fuel, and other interested parties, taking into consideration operational range, specialty uses, vehicle and fuel availability, costs, safety, resale values of vehicles and equipment and other relevant factors.

(b) Phase-in of requirements

The plan revision required under this section shall contain provisions requiring that at least a specified percentage of all new covered fleet vehicles in model year 1998 and thereafter purchased by each covered fleet operator in each covered area shall be clean-fuel vehicles and shall use clean alternative fuels when operating in the covered area. For the applicable model years (MY) specified in the following table and thereafter, the specified percentage shall be as provided in the table for the vehicle types set forth in the table:

CLEAN FUEL VEHICLE PHASE-IN REQUIREMENTS FOR FLEETS

Vehicle Type	MY1998	MY1999	MY2000
Light-duty trucks up to 6,000 lbs. GVWR and light-duty vehicles	30%	50%	70%
Heavy-duty trucks above 8,500 lbs. GVWR	50%	50%	50%

The term MY refers to model year.

(c) Accelerated standard for light-duty trucks up to 6,000 lbs. GVWR and light-duty vehicles

Notwithstanding the model years for which clean-fuel vehicle standards are applicable as provided in section 7583 of this title, for purposes of this section, light duty trucks of up to 6,000 lbs. GVWR and light-duty vehicles manufactured in model years 1998 through model year 2000 shall be treated as clean-fuel vehicles only if such vehicles comply with the standards applicable under section 7583 of this title for vehicles in the same class for the model year 2001. The requirements of subsection (b) of this section shall take effect on the earlier of the following:

(1) The first model year after model year 1997 in which new light-duty trucks up to 6,000 lbs. GVWR and light-duty vehicles which comply with the model year 2001 standards under section 7583 of this title are offered for sale in California.

(2) Model year 2001.

Whenever the effective date of subsection (b) of this section is delayed pursuant to paragraph (1) of this subsection, the phase-in schedule under subsection (b) of this section shall be modified to commence with the model year referred to in paragraph (1) in lieu of model year 1998.

(d) Choice of vehicles and fuel

The plan revision under this subsection shall provide that the choice of clean-fuel vehicles and clean alternative fuels shall be made by the covered fleet operator subject to the requirements of this subsection.

(e) Availability of clean alternative fuel

The plan revision shall require fuel providers to make clean alternative fuel available to covered fleet operators at locations at which covered fleet vehicles are centrally fueled.

(f) Credits

(1) Issuance of credits

The State plan revision required under this section shall provide for the issuance by the State of appropriate credits to a fleet operator for any of the following (or any combination thereof):

(A) The purchase of more clean-fuel vehicles than required under this section.

(B) The purchase of clean fuel vehicles which meet more stringent standards established by the Administrator pursuant to paragraph (4).

(C) The purchase of vehicles in categories which are not covered by this section but which meet standards established for such vehicles under paragraph (4).

(2) Use of credits; limitations based on weight classes

(A) Use of credits

Credits under this subsection may be used by the person holding such credits to demonstrate compliance with this section or may be traded or sold for use by any other person to demonstrate compliance with other requirements applicable under this section in the same nonattainment area. Credits obtained at any time may be held or banked for use at any later time, and when so used, such credits shall maintain the same value as if used at an earlier date.

(B) Limitations based on weight classes

Credits issued with respect to the purchase of vehicles of up to 8,500 lbs. GVWR may not be used to demonstrate compliance by any person with the requirements applicable under this subsection to vehicles of more than 8,500 lbs. GVWR. Credits issued with respect to the purchase of vehicles of more than 8,500 lbs. GVWR may not be used to demonstrate compliance by any person with the requirements applicable under this subsection to vehicles weighing up to 8,500 lbs. GVWR.

(C) Weighting

Credits issued for purchase of a clean fuel vehicle under this subsection shall be adjusted with appropriate weighting to reflect the level of emission reduction achieved by the vehicle.

(3) Regulations and administration

Within 12 months after the enactment of the Clean Air Act Amendments of 1990, the Administrator shall promulgate regulations for such credit program. The State shall administer the credit program established under this subsection.

(4) Standards for issuing credits for cleaner vehicles

Solely for purposes of issuing credits under paragraph (1)(B), the Administrator shall establish under this paragraph standards for Ultra–Low Emission Vehicles ("ULEV"s) and Zero Emissions Vehicles ("ZEV"s) which shall be more stringent than those otherwise applicable to clean-fuel vehicles under this part. The Administrator shall certify clean fuel vehicles as complying with such more stringent standards, and administer and enforce such more stringent standards, in the same manner as in the case of the otherwise applicable clean-fuel vehicle standards established under this section. The standards established by the Administrator under this paragraph for vehicles under 8,500 lbs. GVWR or greater shall conform as closely as possible to standards which are established by the State of California for ULEV and ZEV vehicles in the same class. For vehicles of 8,500 lbs. GVWR or more, the Administrator shall promulgate comparable standards for purposes of this subsection.

(5) Early fleet credits

The State plan revision shall provide credits under this subsection to fleet operators that purchase vehicles certified to meet clean-fuel vehicle standards under this part during any period after approval of the plan revision and prior to the effective date of the fleet program under this section.

(g) Availability to the public

At any facility owned or operated by a department, agency, or instrumentality of the United States where vehicles subject to this subsection are supplied with clean alternative fuel, such fuel shall be offered for sale to the public for use in other vehicles during reasonable business times and subject to national security concerns, unless such fuel is commercially available for vehicles in the vicinity of such Federal facilities.

(h) Transportation control measures

The Administrator shall by rule, within 1 year after the enactment of the Clean Air Act Amendments of 1990, ensure that certain transportation control measures including time-of-day or day-of-week restrictions, and other similar measures that restrict vehicle usage, do not apply to any clean-fuel vehicle that meets the requirements of this section. This subsection shall apply notwithstanding subchapter I of this chapter.

(July 14, 1955, ch. 360, title II, § 246, as added Nov. 15, 1990, Pub.L. 101–549, title II, § 229(a), 104 Stat. 2520.)

References in Text

Enactment of the Clean Air Act Amendments of 1990, referred to in subsec. (a)(1), (2), (f)(3) and (h) probably means the date of enactment of the Clean Air Act Amendments of 1990, Pub.L. 101–549, which was approved November 15, 1990.

Effective Date

Section to take effect Nov. 15, 1990, except as otherwise provided, see section 711(b) of Pub.L. 101–549, set out as a note under section 7401 of this title.

Savings Provisions

Suits, actions or proceeding commenced under this chapter as in effect prior to Nov. 15, 1990, not to abate by reason of the taking effect of amendments by Pub.L. 101–549, except as otherwise provided for, see section 711(a) of Pub.L. 101–549, set out as a note under section 7401 of this title.

§ 7587. Vehicle conversions [CAA § 247]

(a) Conversion of existing and new conventional vehicles to clean-fuel vehicles

The requirements of section 7586 of this title may be met through the conversion of existing or new gasoline or diesel-powered vehicles to clean-fuel vehicles which comply with the applicable requirements of that section. For purposes of such provisions the conversion of a vehicle to clean fuel vehicle shall be treated as the purchase of a clean fuel vehicle. Nothing in this part shall be construed to provide that any covered fleet operator subject to fleet vehicle purchase requirements under section 7586 of this title shall be required to convert existing or new gasoline or diesel-powered vehicles to clean-fuel vehicles or to purchase converted vehicles.

(b) Regulations

The Administrator shall, within 24 months after the enactment of the Clean Air Act Amendments of 1990, consistent with the requirements of this subchapter applicable to new vehicles, promulgate regulations governing conversions of conventional vehicles to clean-fuel vehicles. Such regulations shall establish criteria for such conversions which will ensure that a converted vehicle will comply with the standards applicable under this part to clean-fuel vehicles. Such regulations shall provide for the application to such conversions of the same provisions of this subchapter (including provisions relating to administration enforcement) as are applicable to standards under section 7582, 7583, 7584, and 7585 of this title, except that in the case of conversions the Administrator may modify the applicable regulations implementing such provisions as the Administrator deems necessary to implement this part.

(c) Enforcement

Any person who converts conventional vehicles to clean fuel vehicles pursuant to subsection (b) of this section, shall be considered a manufacturer for purposes of sections 7525 and 7541 of this title and related enforcement provisions. Nothing in the preceding sentence shall require a person who performs such conversions to warrant any part or operation of a vehicle other than as required under this part. Nothing in this paragraph shall limit the applicability of any other warranty to unrelated parts or operations.

(d) Tampering

The conversion from a vehicle capable of operating on gasoline or diesel fuel only to a clean-fuel vehicle shall not be considered a violation of section 7522(a)(3) of this title if such conversion complies with the regulations promulgated under subsection (b) of this section.

(e) Safety

The Secretary of Transportation shall, if necessary, promulgate rules under applicable motor vehicle laws regarding the safety of vehicles converted from existing and new vehicles to clean-fuel vehicles.

(July 14, 1955, ch. 360, title II, § 247, as added Nov. 15, 1990, Pub.L. 101–549, title II, § 229(a), 104 Stat. 2523.)

References in Text

The enactment of the Clean Air Act Amendments of 1990, referred to in subsec. (b), probably means the date of enactment of the Clean Air Act Amendments of 1990, Pub.L. 101–549, which was approved November 15, 1990.

Effective Date

Section to take effect Nov. 15, 1990, except as otherwise provided, see section 711(b) of Pub.L. 101–549, set out as a note under section 7401 of this title.

Savings Provisions

Suits, actions or proceedings commenced under this chapter as in effect prior to Nov. 15, 1990, not to abate by reason of the taking effect of amendments by Pub.L. 101–549, except as otherwise provided for, see section 711(a) of Pub.L. 101–549, set out as a note under section 7401 of this title.

§ 7588. Federal agency fleets [CAA § 248]

(a) Additional provisions applicable

The provisions of this section shall apply, in addition to the other provisions of this part, in the case of covered fleet vehicles owned or operated by an agency, department, or instrumentality of the United States, except as otherwise provided in subsection (e) of this section.

(b) Cost of vehicles to Federal agency

Notwithstanding the provisions of section 491 of Title 40, the Administrator of General Services shall not include the incremental costs of clean-fuel vehicles in the amount to be reimbursed by Federal agencies if the Administrator of General Services determines that appropriations provided pursuant to this paragraph are sufficient to provide for the incremental cost of such vehicles over the cost of comparable conventional vehicles.

(c) Limitations on appropriations

Funds appropriated pursuant to the authorization under this paragraph shall be applicable only—

(1) to the portion of the cost of acquisition, maintenance and operation of vehicles acquired under this subparagraph which exceeds the cost of acquisition, maintenance and operation of comparable conventional vehicles;

(2) to the portion of the costs of fuel storage and dispensing equipment attributable to such vehicles which exceeds the costs for such purposes required for conventional vehicles; and

(3) to the portion of the costs of acquisition of clean-fuel vehicles which represents a reduction in revenue from the disposal of such vehicles as compared to revenue resulting from the disposal of comparable conventional vehicles.

(d) Vehicle costs

The incremental cost of vehicles acquired under this part over the cost of comparable conventional vehicles shall not be applied to any calculation with respect to a limitation under law on the maximum cost of individual vehicles which may be required by the United States.

(e) Exemptions

The requirements of this part shall not apply to vehicles with respect to which the Secretary of Defense has certified to the Administrator that an exemption is needed based on national security consideration.

(f) Acquisition requirement

Federal agencies, to the extent practicable, shall obtain clean-fuel vehicles from original equipment manufacturers.

(g) Authorization of appropriations

There are authorized to be appropriated such sums as may be required to carry out the provisions of this section: *Provided,* That such sums as are appropriated for the Administrator of General Services pursuant to the authorization under this section shall be added to the General Supply Fund established in section 756 of Title 40.

(July 14, 1955, ch. 360, title II, § 248, as added Nov. 15, 1990, Pub.L. 101–549, title II, § 229(a), 104 Stat. 2524.)

Effective Date

Section to take effect Nov. 15, 1990, except as otherwise provided, see section 711(b) of Pub.L. 101–549, set out as a note under section 7401 of this title.

Savings Provisions

Suits, actions or proceedings commenced under this chapter as in effect prior to Nov. 15, 1990, not to abate by reason of the taking effect of amendments by Pub.L. 101–549, except as otherwise provided for, see section 711(a) of Pub.L. 101–549, set out as a note under section 7401 of this title.

§ 7589. California pilot test program [CAA § 249]

(a) Establishment

The Administrator shall establish a pilot program in the State of California to demonstrate the effectiveness of clean-fuel vehicles in controlling air pollution in ozone nonattainment areas.

(b) Applicability

The provisions of this section shall only apply to light-duty trucks and light-duty vehicles, and such provisions shall apply only in the State of California, except as provided in subsection (f) of this section.

(c) Program requirements

Not later than 24 months after the enactment of the Clean Air Act Amendments of 1990, the Administrator shall promulgate regulations establishing requirements under this section applicable in the State of California. The regulations shall provide the following:

(1) Clean-fuel vehicles

Clean-fuel vehicles shall be produced, sold, and distributed (in accordance with normal business practices and applicable franchise agreements) to ultimate purchasers in California (including owners of covered fleets referred to in section 7586 of this title) in numbers that meet or exceed the following schedule:

Model Years	Number of Clean–Fuel Vehicles
1996, 1997, 1998	150,000 vehicles
1999 and thereafter	300,000 vehicles

(2) Clean alternative fuels

(A) Within 2 years after the enactment of the Clean Air Act Amendments of 1990, the State of California shall submit a revision of the applicable implementation plan under part D of subchapter I of this chapter and section 7410 of this title containing a clean fuel plan that requires that clean alternative fuels on which the clean-fuel vehicles required under this paragraph can operate shall be produced and distributed by fuel suppliers and made available in California. At a minimum, sufficient clean alternative fuels shall be produced, distributed and made available to assure that all clean-fuel vehicles required under this section can operate, to the maximum extent practicable, exclusively on such fuels in California. The State shall require that clean alternative fuels be made available and offered for sale at an adequate number of locations with sufficient geographic distribution to ensure convenient refueling with clean alternative fuels, considering the number of, and type of, such vehicles sold and the geographic distribution of such vehicles within the State. The State shall determine the clean alternative fuels to be produced, distributed, and made available based on motor vehicle manufacturers' projections of future sales of such vehicles and consultations with the affected local governments and fuel suppliers.

(B) The State may by regulation grant persons subject to the requirements prescribed under this paragraph an appropriate amount of credits for exceeding such requirements, and any person granted credits may transfer some or all of the credits for use by one or more persons in demonstrating compliance with such requirements. The State may make the credits available for use after consideration of enforceability, environmental, and economic factors and upon such terms and conditions as the State finds appropriate.

(C) The State may also by regulation establish specifications for any clean alternative fuel produced and made available under this paragraph as the State finds necessary to reduce or eliminate an unreasonable risk to public health, welfare, or safety associated with its use or to ensure acceptable vehicle maintenance and performance characteristics.

(D) If a retail gasoline dispensing facility would have to remove or replace one or more motor vehicle fuel underground storage tanks and accompanying piping in order to comply with the provisions of this section, and it had removed and replaced such tank or tanks and accompanying piping in order to comply with subtitle I of the Solid Waste Disposal Act [42 U.S.C.A. § 6901 et seq.] prior to November 15, 1990, it shall not be required to comply with this subsection until a period of 7 years has passed from the date of the removal and replacement of such tank or tanks.

(E) Nothing in this section authorizes any State other than California to adopt provisions regarding clean alternative fuels.

(F) If the State of California fails to adopt a clean fuel program that meets the requirements of this paragraph, the Administrator shall, within 4 years after the enactment of the Clean Air Act Amendments of 1990, establish a clean fuel program for the State of California under this paragraph and section 7410(c) of this title that meets the requirements of this paragraph.

(d) Credits for motor vehicle manufacturers

(1) The Administrator may (by regulation) grant a motor vehicle manufacturer an appropriate amount of credits toward fulfillment of such manufacturer's share of the requirements of subsection (c)(1) of this section for any of the following (or any combination thereof):

(A) The sale of more clean-fuel vehicles than required under subsection (c)(1) of this section.

(B) The sale of clean fuel vehicles which meet standards established by the Administrator as provided in paragraph (3) which are more stringent than the clean-fuel vehicle standards otherwise applicable to such clean-fuel vehicle. A manufacturer granted credits under this paragraph may transfer some or all of the credits for use by one or more other manufacturers in demonstrating compliance with the requirements prescribed under this paragraph. The Administrator may make the credits available for use after consideration of enforceability, environmental, and economic factors and upon such terms and conditions as he finds appropriate. The Administrator shall grant credits in accordance with this paragraph, notwithstanding any requirements of State law or any credits granted with respect to the same vehicles under any State law, rule, or regulation.

(2) **Regulations and administration.**—The Administrator shall administer the credit program established under this subsection. Within 12 months after the enactment of the Clean Air Act Amendments of 1990, the Administrator shall promulgate regulations for such credit program.

(3) **Standards for issuing credits for cleaner vehicles.**—The more stringent standards and other requirements (including requirements relating to the weighting of credits) established by the Administrator for purposes of the credit program under section 7586(f) of this title (relating to credits for clean fuel

vehicles in the fleets program) shall also apply for purposes of the credit program under this paragraph.

(e) Program evaluation

(1) Not later than June 30, 1994 and again in connection with the report under paragraph (2), the Administrator shall provide a report to the Congress on the status of the California Air Resources Board Low–Emissions Vehicles and Clean Fuels Program. Such report shall examine the capability, from a technological standpoint, of motor vehicle manufacturers and motor vehicle fuel suppliers to comply with the requirements of such program and with the requirements of the California Pilot Program under this section.

(2) Not later than June 30, 1998, the Administrator shall complete and submit a report to Congress on the effectiveness of the California pilot program under this section. The report shall evaluate the level of emission reductions achieved under the program, the costs of the program, the advantages and disadvantages of extending the program to other nonattainment areas, and desirability of continuing or expanding the program in California.

(3) The program under this section cannot be extended or terminated by the Administrator except by Act of Congress enacted after the date of the Clean Air Act Amendments of 1990. Section 7507 of this title does not apply to the program under this section.

(f) Voluntary opt-in for other states

(1) EPA regulations

Not later than 2 years after the enactment of the Clean Air Act Amendments of 1990, the Administrator shall promulgate regulations establishing a voluntary opt-in program under this subsection pursuant to which—

(A) clean-fuel vehicles which are required to be produced, sold, and distributed in the State of California under this section, and

(B) clean alternative fuels required to be produced and distributed under this section by fuel suppliers and made available in California

may also be sold and used in other States which submit plan revisions under paragraph (2).

(2) Plan revisions

Any State in which there is located all or part of an ozone nonattainment area classified under subpart D of subchapter I of this chapter as Serious, Severe, or Extreme may submit a revision of the applicable implementation plan under part D of subchapter I of this chapter and section 7410 of this title to provide incentives for the sale or use in such an area or State of clean-fuel vehicles which are required to be produced, sold, and distributed in the State of California, and for the use in such an area or State of clean alternative fuels required to be produced and distributed by fuel suppliers and made available in California. Such plan provisions shall not take effect until 1 year after the State has provided notice of such provisions to motor vehicle manufacturers and to fuel suppliers.

(3) Incentives

The incentives referred to in paragraph (2) may include any or all of the following:

(A) A State registration fee on new motor vehicles registered in the State which are not clean-fuel vehicles in the amount of at least 1 percent of the cost of the vehicle. The proceeds of such fee shall be used to provide financial incentives to purchasers of clean-fuel vehicles and to vehicle dealers who sell high volumes or high percentages of clean-fuel vehicles and to defray the administrative costs of the incentive program.

(B) Provisions to exempt clean-fuel vehicles from high occupancy vehicle or trip reduction requirements.

(C) Provisions to provide preference in the use of existing parking spaces for clean-fuel vehicles.

The incentives under this paragraph shall not apply in the case of covered fleet vehicles.

(4) No sales or production mandate

The regulations and plan revisions under paragraphs (1) and (2) shall not include any production or sales mandate for clean-fuel vehicles or clean alternative fuels. Such regulations and plan revisions shall also provide that vehicle manufacturers and fuel suppliers may not be subject to penalties or sanctions for failing to produce or sell clean-fuel vehicles or clean alternative fuels.

(July 14, 1955, ch. 360, title II, § 249, as added Nov. 15, 1990, Pub.L. 101–549, title II, § 229(a), 104 Stat. 2525.)

References in Text

The enactment of the Clean Air Act Amendments of 1990, referred to in subsecs. (c), (c)(2)(A), (F), (d)(2) and (f)(1), probably means the date of enactment of the Clean Air Act Amendments of 1990, Pub.L. 101–549, which was approved November 15, 1990.

The Solid Waste Disposal Act, referred to in subsec. (c)(2)(D), is title II of Pub.L. 89–272, Oct. 20, 1965, 79 Stat. 997, as amended generally by Pub.L. 94–580, § 2, Oct. 21, 1976, 90 Stat. 2795, which is classified generally to chapter 82 (section 6901 et seq.) of this title. For complete classification of this Act to the Code, see Short Title note set out under section 6901 of this title and Tables.

The date of the Clean Air Act Amendments of 1990, referred to in subsec. (e)(3), probably means the date of enactment of the Clean Air Act Amendments of 1990, Pub.L. 101–549, which was approved November 15, 1990.

Codification

Section 7586(f) of this title, referred to in subsec. (d)(3) was substituted for section 245(e) as the probable intent of Congress.

Effective Date

Section to take effect Nov. 15, 1990, except as otherwise provided, see section 711(b) of Pub.L. 101–549, set out as a note under section 7401 of this title.

Savings Provisions

Suits, actions or proceedings commenced under this chapter as in effect prior to Nov. 15, 1990, not to abate by reason of the taking effect of amendments by Pub.L. 101–549, except as otherwise provided for, see section 711(a) of Pub.L. 101–549, set out as a note under section 7401 of this title.

§ 7590. General provisions [CAA § 250]

(a) State refueling facilities

If any State adopts enforceable provisions in an implementation plan applicable to a nonattainment area which provides that existing State refueling facilities will be made available to the public for the purchase of clean alternative fuels or that State-operated refueling facilities for such fuels will be constructed and operated by the State and made available to the public at reasonable times, taking into consideration safety, costs, and other relevant factors, in approving such plan under section 7410 of this title and part D of subchapter I of this chapter, the Administrator may credit a State with the emission reductions for purposes of part D of subchapter I of this chapter attributable to such actions.

(b) No production mandate

The Administrator shall have no authority under this part to mandate the production of clean-fuel vehicles except as provided in the California pilot test program or to specify as applicable the models, lines, or types of, or marketing or price practices, policies, or strategies for, vehicles subject to this part. Nothing in this part shall be construed to give the Administrator authority to mandate marketing or pricing practices, policies, or strategies for fuels.

(c) Tank and fuel system safety

The Secretary of Transportation shall, in accordance with the National Motor Vehicle Traffic Safety Act of 1966, promulgate applicable regulations regarding the safety and use of fuel storage cylinders and fuel systems, including appropriate testing and retesting, in conversions of motor vehicles.

(d) Consultation with Department of Energy and Department of Transportation

The Administrator shall coordinate with the Secretaries of the Department of Energy and the Department of Transportation in carrying out the Administrator's duties under this part.

(July 14, 1955, ch. 360, title II, § 250, as added Nov. 15, 1990, Pub.L. 101–549, title II, § 229(a), 104 Stat. 2528.)

References in Text

The National Motor Vehicle Traffic Safety Act of 1966, referred to in subsec. (c), probably means the National Traffic and Motor Vehicle Safety Act of 1966, Pub.L. 89–563, Sept. 9, 1966, 80 Stat. 718, as amended, which is classified generally to chapter 38 (section 1381 et seq.) of Title 15, Commerce and Trade. For complete classification of this Act to the Code, see Short Title note set out under section 1381 of Title 15 and Tables.

Codification

Reference to part D of subchapter I of this chapter, in subsec. (a), was substituted for part D, as the probable intent of Congress.

Effective Date

Section to take effect Nov. 15, 1990, except as otherwise provided, see section 711(b) of Pub.L. 101–549, set out as a note under section 7401 of this title.

Savings Provisions

Suits, actions or proceedings commenced under this chapter as in effect prior to Nov. 15, 1990, not to abate by reason of the taking effect of amendments by Pub.L. 101–549, except as otherwise provided for, see section 711(a) of Pub.L. 101–549, set out as a note under section 7401 of this title.

SUBCHAPTER III—GENERAL PROVISIONS

§ 7601. Administration [CAA § 301]

(a) Regulations; delegation of powers and duties; regional officers and employees

(1) The Administrator is authorized to prescribe such regulations as are necessary to carry out his functions under this chapter. The Administrator may delegate to any officer or employee of the Environmental Protection Agency such of his powers and duties under this chapter, except the making of regulations, subject to section 7607(d) of this title, as he may deem necessary or expedient.

(2) Not later than one year after August 7, 1977, the Administrator shall promulgate regulations establishing general applicable procedures and policies for regional officers and employees (including the Regional Administrator) to follow in carrying out a delegation under paragraph (1), if any. Such regulations shall be designed—

(A) to assure fairness and uniformity in the criteria, procedures, and policies applied by the various regions in implementing and enforcing the chapter;

(B) to assure at least an adequate quality audit of each State's performance and adherence to the requirements of this chapter in implementing and enforcing the chapter, particularly in the review of new sources and in enforcement of the chapter; and

(C) to provide a mechanism for identifying and standardizing inconsistent or varying criteria, procedures, and policies being employed by such officers and employees in implementing and enforcing the chapter.

(b) Detail of Environmental Protection Agency personnel to air pollution control agencies

Upon the request of an air pollution control agency, personnel of the Environmental Protection Agency may be detailed to such agency for the purpose of carrying out the provisions of this chapter.

(c) Payments under grants; installments; advances or reimbursements

Payments under grants made under this chapter may be made in installments, and in advance or by way of reimbursement, as may be determined by the Administrator.

(d) Tribal authority

(1) Subject to the provisions of paragraph (2), the Administrator—

(A) is authorized to treat Indian tribes as States under this chapter, except for purposes of the requirement that makes available for application by each State no less than one-half of 1 percent of annual appropriations under section 7405 of this title; and

(B) may provide any such Indian tribe grant and contract assistance to carry out functions provided by this chapter.

(2) The Administrator shall promulgate regulations within 18 months after November 15, 1990, specifying those provisions of this chapter for which it is appropriate to treat Indian tribes as States. Such treatment shall be authorized only if—

(A) the Indian tribe has a governing body carrying out substantial governmental duties and powers;

(B) the functions to be exercised by the Indian tribe pertain to the management and protection of air resources within the exterior boundaries of the reservation or other areas within the tribe's jurisdiction; and

(C) the Indian tribe is reasonably expected to be capable, in the judgment of the Administrator, of carrying out the functions to be exercised in a manner consistent with the terms and purposes of this chapter and all applicable regulations.

(3) The Administrator may promulgate regulations which establish the elements of tribal implementation plans and procedures for approval or disapproval of tribal implementation plans and portions thereof.

(4) In any case in which the Administrator determines that the treatment of Indian tribes as identical to States is inappropriate or administratively infeasible, the Administrator may provide, by regulation, other means by which the Administrator will directly administer such provisions so as to achieve the appropriate purpose.

(5) Until such time as the Administrator promulgates regulations pursuant to this subsection, the Administrator may continue to provide financial assistance to eligible Indian tribes under section 7405 of this title.

(July 14, 1955, ch. 360, title III, § 301, formerly § 8, as added Dec. 17, 1963, Pub.L. 88–206, § 1, 77 Stat. 400, renumbered Oct. 20, 1965, Pub.L. 89–272, title I, § 101(4), 79 Stat. 992, and amended Nov. 21, 1967, Pub.L. 90–148, § 2, 81 Stat. 504; Dec. 31, 1970, Pub.L. 91–604, §§ 3(b)(2), 15(c)(2), 84 Stat. 1677, 1713; Aug. 7, 1977, Pub.L. 95–95, title III, § 305(e), 91 Stat. 776; Nov. 15, 1990, Pub.L. 101–549, title I, §§ 107(d), 108(i), 104 Stat. 2464, 2467.)

Effective Date of 1990 Amendment

Amendment by Pub.L. 101–549 effective Nov. 15, 1990, except as otherwise provided, see section 711(b) of Pub.L. 101–549, set out as a note under section 7401 of this title.

Savings Provisions

Suits, actions or proceedings commenced under this chapter as in effect prior to Nov. 15, 1990, not to abate by reason of the taking effect of amendments by Pub.L. 101–549, except as otherwise provided for, see section 711(a) of Pub.L. 101–549, set out as a note under section 7401 of this title.

Disadvantaged Business Concerns

Title X of Pub.L. 101–549 provided that:

"Sec. 1001. Disadvantaged Business Concerns.

"(a) In general.—In providing for any research relating to the requirements of the amendments made by the Clean Air Act Amendments of 1990 [Pub.L. 101–549, Nov. 15, 1990, 104 Stat. 2399, for distribution to which see Tables] which uses funds of the Environmental Protection Agency, the Administrator of the Environmental Protection Agency shall, to the extent practicable, require that not less than 10 percent of total Federal funding for such research will be made available to disadvantaged business concerns.

"(b) Definition.—

"**(1)(A)** For purposes of subsection (a), the term 'disadvantaged business concern' means a concern—

"**(i)** which is at least 51 percent owned by one or more socially and economically disadvantaged individuals or, in the case of a publicly traded company, at least 51 percent of the stock of which is owned by one or more socially and economically disadvantaged individuals; and

"**(ii)** the management and daily business operations of which are controlled by such individuals.

"**(B)(i)** A for-profit business concern is presumed to be a disadvantaged business concern for purposes of subsection (a) if it is at least 51 percent owned by, or in the case of a concern which is a publicly traded company at least 51 percent of the stock of the company is owned by, one or more individuals who are members of the following groups:

"**(I)** Black Americans.

"**(II)** Hispanic Americans.

"**(III)** Native Americans.

"**(IV)** Asian Americans.

"**(V)** Women.

"**(VI)** Disabled Americans.

"**(ii)** The presumption established by clause (i) may be rebutted with respect to a particular business concern if it is reasonably established that the individual or individuals referred to in that clause with respect to that business concern are not experiencing impediments to establishing or developing such concern as a result of the individual's identification as a member of a group specified in that clause.

"**(C)** The following institutions are presumed to be disadvantaged business concerns for purposes of subsection (a):

"(i) Historically black colleges and universities, and colleges and universities having a student body in which 40 percent of the students are Hispanic.

"(ii) Minority institutions (as that term is defined by the Secretary of Education pursuant to the General Education Provision Act (20 U.S.C. 1221 et seq.).

"(iii) Private and voluntary organizations controlled by individuals who are socially and economically disadvantaged.

"(D) A joint venture may be considered to be a disadvantaged business concern under subsection (a), notwithstanding the size of such joint venture, if—

"(i) a party to the joint venture is a disadvantaged business concern; and

"(ii) that party owns at least 51 percent of the joint venture.

A person who is not an economically disadvantaged individual or a disadvantaged business concern, as a party to a joint venture, may not be a party to more than 2 awarded contracts in a fiscal year solely by reason of this subparagraph.

"(E) Nothing in this paragraph shall prohibit any member of a racial or ethnic group that is not listed in subparagraph (B)(i) from establishing that they have been impeded in establishing or developing a business concern as a result of racial or ethnic discrimination."

"Sec. 1002. **Use of quotas prohibited.**—Nothing in this title shall permit or require the use of quotas or a requirement that has the effect of a quota in determining eligibility under section 1001."

CODE OF FEDERAL REGULATIONS

Environmental Protection Agency,
- Aircraft, control of air pollution from, see 40 CFR 87.1 et seq.
- Air pollution from motor vehicles, control of, see 40 CFR 85.401 et seq.
- Air quality standards, see 40 CFR 50.1 et seq.
- Ambient air quality surveillance, see 40 CFR 58.1 et seq.
- Compliance orders, see 40 CFR 65.01 et seq.
- Fuels,
  - Registration of, see 40 CFR 79.1 et seq.
  - Regulation of, see 40 CFR 80.1 et seq.
- Hazardous air pollutants, emission standards, see 40 CFR 61.01 et seq.

Implementation plans, generally, see 40 CFR 51.40 et seq.
- Information, requests for, see 40 CFR 2.100 et seq.
- New stationary sources, performance standards, see 40 CFR 60.1 et seq.
- Nonferrous smelter orders, see 40 CFR 57.101 et seq.
- Regional consistency, see 40 CFR 56.1 et seq.

LIBRARY REFERENCES

Health and Environment ⇨20.
C.J.S. Health and Environment § 2 et seq.

§ 7602. Definitions [CAA § 302]

When used in this chapter—

(a) The term "Administrator" means the Administrator of the Environmental Protection Agency.

(b) The term "air pollution control agency" means any of the following:

(1) A single State agency designated by the Governor of that State as the official State air pollution control agency for purposes of this chapter.

(2) An agency established by two or more States and having substantial powers or duties pertaining to the prevention and control of air pollution.

(3) A city, county, or other local government health authority, or, in the case of any city, county, or other local government in which there is an agency other than the health authority charged with responsibility for enforcing ordinances or laws relating to the prevention and control of air pollution, such other agency.

(4) An agency of two or more municipalities located in the same State or in different States and having substantial powers or duties pertaining to the prevention and control of air pollution.

(5) An agency of an Indian tribe.

(c) The term "interstate air pollution control agency" means—

(1) an air pollution control agency established by two or more States, or

(2) an air pollution control agency of two or more municipalities located in different States.

(d) The term "State" means a State, the District of Columbia, the Commonwealth of Puerto Rico, the Virgin Islands, Guam, and American Samoa and includes the Commonwealth of the Northern Mariana Islands.

(e) The term "person" includes an individual, corporation, partnership, association, State, municipality, political subdivision of a State, and any agency, department, or instrumentality of the United States and any officer, agent, or employee thereof.

(f) The term "municipality" means a city, town, borough, county, parish, district, or other public body created by or pursuant to State law.

(g) The term "air pollutant" means any air pollution agent or combination of such agents, including any physical, chemical, biological, radioactive (including source material, special nuclear material, and byproduct material) substance or matter which is emitted into or otherwise enters the ambient air. Such term includes any precursors to the formation of any air pollutant, to the extent the Administrator has identified such precursor or precursors for the particular purpose for which the term "air pollutant" is used.

(h) All language referring to effects on welfare includes, but is not limited to, effects on soils, water, crops, vegetation, manmade materials, animals, wildlife, weather, visibility, and climate, damage to and deterioration of property, and hazards to transportation, as well as effects on economic values and on personal comfort and well-being, whether caused by transformation, conversion, or combination with other air pollutants.

(i) The term "Federal land manager" means, with respect to any lands in the United States, the

Secretary of the department with authority over such lands.

(j) Except as otherwise expressly provided, the terms "major stationary source" and "major emitting facility" mean any stationary facility or source of air pollutants which directly emits, or has the potential to emit, one hundred tons per year or more of any air pollutant (including any major emitting facility or source of fugitive emissions of any such pollutant, as determined by rule by the Administrator).

(k) The terms "emission limitation" and "emission standard" mean a requirement established by the State or the Administrator which limits the quantity, rate, or concentration of emissions of air pollutants on a continuous basis, including any requirement relating to the operation or maintenance of a source to assure continuous emission reduction, and any design, equipment, work practice or operational standard promulgated under this chapter.

(*l*) The term "standard of performance" means a requirement of continuous emission reduction, including any requirement relating to the operation or maintenance of a source to assure continuous emission reduction.

(m) The term "means of emission limitation" means a system of continuous emission reduction (including the use of specific technology or fuels with specified pollution characteristics).

(n) The term "primary standard attainment date" means the date specified in the applicable implementation plan for the attainment of a national primary ambient air quality standard for any air pollutant.

(*o*) The term "delayed compliance order" means an order issued by the State or by the Administrator to an existing stationary source, postponing the date required under an applicable implementation plan for compliance by such source with any requirement of such plan.

(p) The term "schedule and timetable of compliance" means a schedule of required measures including an enforceable sequence of actions or operations leading to compliance with an emission limitation, other limitation, prohibition, or standard.

(q) Applicable implementation plan defined. For purposes of this chapter, the term "applicable implementation plan" means the portion (or portions) of the implementation plan, or most recent revision thereof, which has been approved under section 7410 of this title, or promulgated under section 7410(c) of this title, or promulgated or approved pursuant to regulations promulgated under section 7601(d) of this title and which implements the relevant requirements of this chapter.

(r) Indian tribe.—The term "Indian tribe" means any Indian tribe, band, nation, or other organized group or community, including any Alaska Native village, which is Federally recognized as eligible for the special programs and services provided by the United States to Indians because of their status as Indians.

(s) VOC.—The term "VOC" means volatile organic compound, as defined by the Administrator.

(t) PM–10.—The term "PM–10" means particulate matter with an aerodynamic diameter less than or equal to a nominal ten micrometers, as measured by such method as the Administrator may determine.

(u) NAAQS AND CTG.—The term "NAAQS" means national ambient air quality standard. The term "CTG" means a Control Technique Guideline published by the Administrator under section 7408 of this title.

(v) NO_x.—The term "NO_x" means oxides of nitrogen.

(w) CO.—The term "CO" means carbon monoxide.

(x) Small source.—The term "small source" means a source that emits less than 100 tons of regulated pollutants per year, or any class of persons that the Administrator determines, through regulation, generally lack technical ability or knowledge regarding control of air pollution.

(y) Federal implementation plan.—The term "Federal implementation plan" means a plan (or portion thereof) promulgated by the Administrator to fill all or a portion of a gap or otherwise correct all or a portion of an inadequacy in a State implementation plan, and which includes enforceable emission limitations or other control measures, means or techniques (including economic incentives, such as marketable permits or auctions of emissions allowances), and provides for attainment of the relevant national ambient air quality standard.".

(z) Stationary source.—The term "stationary source" means generally any source of an air pollutant except those emissions resulting directly from an internal combustion engine for transportation purposes or from a nonroad engine or nonroad vehicle as defined in section 7550 of this title.

(July 14, 1955, ch. 360, title III, § 302, formerly § 9, as added Dec. 17, 1963, Pub.L. 88–206, § 1, 77 Stat. 400, renumbered Oct. 20, 1965, Pub.L. 89–272, title I, § 101(4), 79 Stat. 992, and amended Nov. 21, 1967, Pub.L. 90–148, § 2, 81 Stat. 504; Dec. 31, 1970, Pub.L. 91–604, § 15(a)(1), (c)(1), 84 Stat. 1710, 1713; Aug. 7, 1977, Pub.L. 95–95, title II, § 218(c), title III, § 301, 91 Stat. 761, 769; Nov. 16, 1977, Pub.L. 95–190, § 14(a)(76), 91 Stat. 1404; Nov. 15, 1990, Pub.L. 101–549, title I, §§ 101(d)(4), 107(a), (b), 108(j), 109(b), title III, § 302(e), title VII, § 709, 104 Stat. 2409, 2464, 2468, 2470, 2574, 2684.)

Effective Date of 1990 Amendment

Amendment by Pub.L. 101–549 effective Nov. 15, 1990, except as otherwise provided, see section 711(b) of Pub.L. 101–549, set out as a note under section 7401 of this title.

Savings Provisions

Suits, actions or proceedings commenced under this chapter as in effect prior to Nov. 15, 1990, not to abate by reason of the taking effect of amendments by Pub.L. 101–549, except as otherwise provided for, see section 711(a) of Pub.L. 101–549, set out as a note under section 7401 of this title.

CROSS REFERENCES

Air pollution control agency to have same meaning given such term by subsec. (b) of this section for purposes of Powerplant and Industrial Fuel Use Act of 1978, see section 8302 of this title.

State certifying authority to mean air pollution control agency as defined in subsec. (b) of this section for purposes of amortization of pollution control facilities, see section 169 of Title 26, Internal Revenue Code.

FEDERAL PRACTICE AND PROCEDURE

Review of administrative decisions in courts of appeals, see Wright, Miller, Cooper & Gressman: Jurisdiction § 3941.

CODE OF FEDERAL REGULATIONS

Fuels, regulation of, see 40 CFR 80.1 et seq.

§ 7603. Emergency powers [CAA § 303]

Notwithstanding any other provision of this chapter, the Administrator, upon receipt of evidence that a pollution source or combination of sources (including moving sources) is presenting an imminent and substantial endangerment to public health or welfare, or the environment, may bring suit on behalf of the United States in the appropriate United States district court to immediately restrain any person causing or contributing to the alleged pollution to stop the emission of air pollutants causing or contributing to such pollution or to take such other action as may be necessary. If it is not practicable to assure prompt protection of public health or welfare or the environment by commencement of such a civil action, the Administrator may issue such orders as may be necessary to protect public health or welfare or the environment. Prior to taking any action under this section, the Administrator shall consult with appropriate State and local authorities and attempt to confirm the accuracy of the information on which the action proposed to be taken is based. Any order issued by the Administrator under this section shall be effective upon issuance and shall remain in effect for a period of not more than 60 days, unless the Administrator brings an action pursuant to the first sentence of this section before the expiration of that period. Whenever the Administrator brings such an action within the 60-day period, such order shall remain in effect for an additional 14 days or for such longer period as may be authorized by the court in which such action is brought.

(July 14, 1955, ch. 360, title III, § 303, as added Dec. 31, 1970, Pub.L. 91–604, § 12(a), 84 Stat. 1705, and amended Aug. 7, 1977, Pub.L. 95–95, title III, § 302(a), 91 Stat. 770; Nov. 15, 1990, Pub.L. 101–549, title VII, § 704, 104 Stat. 2681.)

Effective Date of 1990 Amendment

Amendment by Pub.L. 101–549 effective Nov. 15, 1990, except as otherwise provided, see section 711(b) of Pub.L. 101–549, set out as a note under section 7401 of this title.

Savings Provisions

Suits, actions or proceedings commenced under this chapter as in effect prior to Nov. 15, 1990, not to abate by reason of the taking effect of amendments by Pub.L. 101–549, except as otherwise provided for, see section 711(a) of Pub.L. 101–549, set out as a note under section 7401 of this title.

CROSS REFERENCES

Guidelines for using imminent hazard, enforcement, and emergency response authorities to include assignment of responsibility for coordinating response actions with imminent hazard and emergency powers authorized by this section, see section 9606 of this title.

§ 7604. Citizen suits [CAA § 304]

(a) Authority to bring civil action; jurisdiction

Except as provided in subsection (b) of this section, any person may commence a civil action on his own behalf—

(1) against any person (including (i) the United States, and (ii) any other governmental instrumentality or agency to the extent permitted by the Eleventh Amendment to the Constitution) who is alleged to have violated (if there is evidence that the alleged violation has been repeated) or to be in violation of (A) an emission standard or limitation under this chapter or (B) an order issued by the Administrator or a State with respect to such a standard or limitation,

(2) against the Administrator where there is alleged a failure of the Administrator to perform any act or duty under this chapter which is not discretionary with the Administrator, or

(3) against any person who proposes to construct or constructs any new or modified major emitting facility without a permit required under part C of subchapter I of this chapter (relating to significant deterioration of air quality) or part D of subchapter I of this chapter (relating to nonattainment) or who is alleged to have violated (if there is evidence that the alleged violation has been repeated) or to be in violation of any condition of such permit.

The district courts shall have jurisdiction, without regard to the amount in controversy or the citizenship of the parties, to enforce such an emission standard or limitation, or such an order, or to order the Administrator to perform such act or duty, as the case may be, and to apply any appropriate civil penalties (except for actions under paragraph (2)). The district courts of the United States shall have jurisdiction to compel (consistent with paragraph (2) of this subsection) agency action unreasonably delayed, except that an action to compel agency action referred to in section 7607(b) of this title which is unreasonably delayed may only be filed in a United States District Court within the circuit in which such action would be reviewable under section 7607(b) of this title. In any such action for unreasonable delay, notice to the entities referred to in subsection (b)(1)(A) of this section shall be provided 180 days before commencing such action.

(b) Notice

No action may be commenced—

(1) under subsection (a)(1) of this section—

(A) prior to 60 days after the plaintiff has given notice of the violation (i) to the Administrator, (ii) to the State in which the violation occurs, and (iii) to any alleged violator of the standard, limitation, or order, or

(B) if the Administrator or State has commenced and is diligently prosecuting a civil action in a court of the United States or a State to require compliance with the standard, limitation, or order, but in any such action in a court of the United States any person may intervene as a matter of right.

(2) under subsection (a)(2) of this section prior to 60 days after the plaintiff has given notice of such action to the Administrator,

except that such action may be brought immediately after such notification in the case of an action under this section respecting a violation of section 7412(i)(3)(A) or (f)(4) of this title or an order issued by the Administrator pursuant to section 7413(a) of this title. Notice under this subsection shall be given in such manner as the Administrator shall prescribe by regulation.

(c) Venue; intervention by administrator; service of complaint; consent judgment

(1) Any action respecting a violation by a stationary source of an emission standard or limitation or an order respecting such standard or limitation may be brought only in the judicial district in which such source is located.

(2) In any action under this section, the Administrator, if not a party, may intervene as a matter of right at any time in the proceeding. A judgment in an action under this section to which the United States is not a party shall not, however, have any binding effect upon the United States.

(3) Whenever any action is brought under this section the plaintiff shall serve a copy of the complaint on the Attorney General of the United States and on the Administrator. No consent judgment shall be entered in an action brought under this section in which the United States is not a party prior to 45 days following the receipt of a copy of the proposed consent judgment by the Attorney General and the Administrator during which time the Government may submit its comments on the proposed consent judgment to the court and parties or may intervene as a matter of right.

(d) Award of costs; security

The court, in issuing any final order in any action brought pursuant to subsection (a) of this section, may award costs of litigation (including reasonable attorney and expert witness fees) to any party, whenever the court determines such award is appropriate. The court may, if a temporary restraining order or preliminary injunction is sought, require the filing of a bond or equivalent security in accordance with the Federal Rules of Civil Procedure.

(e) Nonrestriction of other rights

Nothing in this section shall restrict any right which any person (or class of persons) may have under any statute or common law to seek enforcement of any emission standard or limitation or to seek any other relief (including relief against the Administrator or a State agency). Nothing in this section or in any other law of the United States shall be construed to prohibit, exclude, or restrict any State, local, or interstate authority from—

(1) bringing any enforcement action or obtaining any judicial remedy or sanction in any State or local court, or

(2) bringing any administrative enforcement action or obtaining any administrative remedy or sanction in any State or local administrative agency, department or instrumentality,

against the United States, any department, agency, or instrumentality thereof, or any officer, agent, or employee thereof under State or local law respecting control and abatement of air pollution. For provisions requiring compliance by the United States, departments, agencies, instrumentalities, officers, agents, and employees in the same manner as nongovernmental entities, see section 7418 of this title.

(f) Definition

For purposes of this section, the term "emission standard or limitation under this chapter" means—

(1) a schedule or timetable of compliance, emission limitation, standard of performance or emission standard,

(2) a control or prohibition respecting a motor vehicle fuel or fuel additive, or

(3) any condition or requirement of a permit under part C of subchapter I of this chapter (relating to significant deterioration of air quality) or part D of subchapter I of this chapter (relating to nonattainment), section 7419 of this title (relating to primary nonferrous smelter orders), any condition or requirement under an applicable implementation plan relating to transportation control measures, air quality maintenance plans, vehicle inspection and maintenance programs or vapor recovery requirements, section 7545 (e) and (f) of this title (relating to fuels and fuel additives), section 7491 of this title (relating to visibility protection), any condition or requirement under subchapter VI of this chapter (relating to ozone protection), or any requirement under section 7411 or 7412 of this title (without regard to whether such requirement is expressed as an emission standard or otherwise); or

(4) any other standard, limitation, or schedule established under any permit issued pursuant to subchapter V of this chapter or under any applicable State implementation plan approved by the Administrator, any permit term or condition, and any requirement to obtain a permit as a condition of operations.

which is in effect under this chapter (including a requirement applicable by reason of section 7418 of this title) or under an applicable implementation plan.

(g) Penalty fund

(1) Penalties received under subsection (a) shall be deposited in a special fund in the United States Treasury for licensing and other services. Amounts in such fund are authorized to be appropriated and shall remain available until expended, for use by the Administrator to finance air compliance and enforcement activities. The Administrator shall annually report to the Congress about the sums deposited into the fund, the sources thereof, and the actual and proposed uses thereof.

(2) Notwithstanding paragraph (1) the court in any action under this subsection to apply civil penalties shall have discretion to order that such civil penalties, in lieu of being deposited in the fund referred to in paragraph (1), be used in beneficial mitigation projects which are consistent with this Act and enhance the public health or the environment. The court shall obtain the view of the Administrator in exercising such discretion and selecting any such projects. The amount of any such payment in any such action shall not exceed $100,000.

(July 14, 1955, ch. 360, title III, § 304, as added Dec. 31, 1970, Pub.L. 91–604, § 12(a), 84 Stat. 1706, and amended Aug. 7, 1977, Pub.L. 95–95, title III, § 303(a)–(c), 91 Stat. 771, 772; Nov. 16, 1977, Pub.L. 95–190, § 14(a)(77), (78), 91 Stat. 1404; Nov. 15, 1990, P.L. 101–549, title III, § 302(f), title VII, § 707(a)–(g), 104 Stat. 2574, 2682, 2683.)

Effective Date of 1990 Amendment

Amendment by section 302(f) of Pub.L. 101–549 effective Nov. 15, 1990, except as otherwise provided, see section 711(b) of Pub.L. 101–549, set out as a note under section 7401 of this title.

Section 707(g) of Pub.L. 101–549 provided, in part, that: "The amendment made by this subsection [amending subsec. (a)(1), (3) of this section] shall take effect with respect to actions brought after the date 2 years after the enactment of the Clean Air Act Amendments of 1990 [Nov. 15, 1990]."

Savings Provisions

Suits, actions or proceedings commenced under this chapter as in effect prior to Nov. 15, 1990, not to abate by reason of the taking effect of amendments by Pub.L. 101–549, except as otherwise provided for, see section 711(a) of Pub.L. 101–549, set out as a note under section 7401 of this title.

FEDERAL PRACTICE AND PROCEDURE

Allowability of suit by any person, see Wright, Miller & Cooper: Jurisdiction § 3531.
Attorney's fees, see Wright, Miller & Kane: Civil 2d § 2675.
Jurisdictional amount in controversy, see Wright, Miller & Cooper: Jurisdiction § 3701 et seq.
Venue in district courts, see Wright, Miller & Cooper: Jurisdiction § 3825.

LAW REVIEW COMMENTARIES

Note, effective assistance of counsel: *Strickland* and the Illinois Death Penalty Statute. U.Ill.L.Rev. 131 (1987).

Scope of attorney's fees under *Pennsylvania v. Delaware Valley Citizens' Council for Clean Air.* Ann Sprightley Ryan, 14 Ecology L.Q. 517 (1987).

LIBRARY REFERENCES

Health and Environment ⟹25.6(1), 28.
C.J.S. Health and Environment § 91 et seq.

United States Supreme Court

Attorney fees, superior quality of counsel's performance, see Pennsylvania v. Delaware Valley Citizens' Council for Clean Air, 1986, 106 S.Ct. 3088, 92 L.Ed.2d 439.

§ 7605. Representation in litigation [CAA § 305]

(a) Attorney General; attorneys appointed by Administrator

The Administrator shall request the Attorney General to appear and represent him in any civil action instituted under this chapter to which the Administrator is a party. Unless the Attorney General notifies the Administrator that he will appear in such action, within a reasonable time, attorneys appointed by the Administrator shall appear and represent him.

(b) Memorandum of understanding regarding legal representation

In the event the Attorney General agrees to appear and represent the Administrator in any such action, such representation shall be conducted in accordance with, and shall include participation by, attorneys appointed by the Administrator to the extent authorized by, the memorandum of understanding between the Department of Justice and the Environmental Protection Agency, dated June 13, 1977, respecting representation of the agency by the department in civil litigation.

(July 14, 1955, ch. 360, title III, § 305, as added Dec. 31, 1970, Pub.L. 91–604, § 12(a), 84 Stat. 1707, and amended Aug. 7, 1977, Pub.L. 95–95, title III, § 304(a), 91 Stat. 772.)

LIBRARY REFERENCES

Attorney General ⚷7.
C.J.S. Attorney General § 8 et seq.

§ 7606. Federal procurement [CAA § 306]

(a) Contracts with violators prohibited

No Federal agency may enter into any contract with any person who is convicted of any offense under section 7413 of this title for the procurement of goods, materials, and services to perform such contract at any facility at which the violation which gave rise to such conviction occurred if such facility is owned, leased, or supervised by such person. The prohibition in the preceding sentence shall continue until the Administrator certifies that the condition giving rise to such a conviction has been corrected. For convictions arising under section 7413(c)(2) of this title, the condition giving rise to the conviction also shall be considered to include any substantive violation of this chapter associated with the violation of 7413(c)(2) of this title. The Administrator may extend this prohibition to other facilities owned or operated by the convicted person.

(b) Notification procedures

The Administrator shall establish procedures to provide all Federal agencies with the notification necessary for the purposes of subsection (a) of this section.

(c) Federal agency contracts

In order to implement the purposes and policy of this chapter to protect and enhance the quality of the Nation's air, the President shall, not more than 180 days after December 31, 1970, cause to be issued an order (1) requiring each Federal agency authorized to enter into contracts and each Federal agency which is empowered to extend Federal assistance by way of grant, loan, or contract to effectuate the purpose and policy of this chapter in such contracting or assistance activities, and (2) setting forth procedures, sanctions, penalties, and such other provisions, as the President determines necessary to carry out such requirement.

(d) Exemptions; notification to Congress

The President may exempt any contract, loan, or grant from all or part of the provisions of this section where he determines such exemption is necessary in the paramount interest of the United States and he shall notify the Congress of such exemption.

(e) Annual report to Congress

The President shall annually report to the Congress on measures taken toward implementing the purpose and intent of this section, including but not limited to the progress and problems associated with implementation of this section.

(July 14, 1955, ch. 360, title III, § 306, as added Dec. 31, 1970, Pub.L. 91–604, § 12(a), 84 Stat. 1707, and amended Nov. 15, 1990, Pub.L. 101–549, title VII, § 705, 104 Stat. 2682.)

Effective Date of 1990 Amendment

Amendment by Pub.L. 101–549 effective Nov. 15, 1990, except as otherwise provided, see section 711(b) of Pub.L. 101–549, set out as a note under section 7401 of this title.

Savings Provisions

Suits, actions or proceedings commenced under this chapter as in effect prior to Nov. 15, 1990, not to abate by reason of the taking effect of amendments by Pub.L. 101–549, except as otherwise provided for, see section 711(a) of Pub.L. 101–549, set out as a note under section 7401 of this title.

Federal Acquisition Regulation: Contractor Certification or Contract Clause for Acquisition of Commercial Items

Pub.L. 103–355, Title VIII, § 8301(g), Oct. 13, 1994, 108 Stat. 3397, provided that: "The Federal Acquisition Regulation may not contain a requirement for a certification by a contractor under a contract for the acquisition of commercial items, or a requirement that such a contract include a contract clause, in order to implement a prohibition or requirement of section 306 of the Clean Air Act (42 U.S.C. 7606) [this section] or a prohibition or requirement issued in the implementation of that section [this section], since there is nothing in such section 306 [this section] that requires such a certification or contract clause."

LIBRARY REFERENCES

United States ⚷68.
C.J.S. United States § 90.

§ 7607. Administrative proceedings and judicial review [CAA § 307]

(a) Administrative subpenas; confidentiality; witnesses

In connection with any determination under section 7410(f), or for purposes of obtaining information under section 7521(b)(4) or 7545(c)(3) of this title, any investigation, monitoring, reporting requirement, entry, compliance inspection, or administrative enforcement proceeding under this chapter (including but not limited to section 7413, section 7414, section 7420, section

7424, section 7477, section 7524, section 7525, section 7542, section 7603, or section 7606 of this title), the Administrator may issue subpenas for the attendance and testimony of witnesses and the production of relevant papers, books, and documents, and he may administer oaths. Except for emission data, upon a showing satisfactory to the Administrator by such owner or operator that such papers, books, documents, or information or particular part thereof, if made public, would divulge trade secrets or secret processes of such owner or operator, the Administrator shall consider such record, report, or information or particular portion thereof confidential in accordance with the purposes of section 1905 of title 18, except that such paper, book, document, or information may be disclosed to other officers, employees, or authorized representatives of the United States concerned with carrying out this chapter, to persons carrying out the National Academy of Sciences' study and investigation provided for in section 7521(c) of this title, or when relevant in any proceeding under this chapter. Witnesses summoned shall be paid the same fees and mileage that are paid witnesses in the courts of the United States. In case of contumacy or refusal to obey a subpena served upon any person under this subparagraph, the district court of the United States for any district in which such person is found or resides or transacts business, upon application by the United States and after notice to such person, shall have jurisdiction to issue an order requiring such person to appear and give testimony before the Administrator to appear and produce papers, books, and documents before the Administrator, or both, and any failure to obey such order of the court may be punished by such court as a contempt thereof.

(b) Judicial review

(1) A petition for review of action of the Administrator in promulgating any national primary or secondary ambient air quality standard, any emission standard or requirement under section 7412 of this title, any standard of performance or requirement under section 7411 of this title, any standard under section 7521 of this title (other than a standard required to be prescribed under section 7521(b)(1) of this title), any determination under section 7521(b)(5) of this title, any control or prohibition under section 7545 of this title, any standard under section 7571 of this title, any rule issued under section 7413, 7419, or under section 7420 of this title, or any other nationally applicable regulations promulgated, or final action taken, by the Administrator under this chapter may be filed only in the United States Court of Appeals for the District of Columbia. A petition for review of the Administrator's action in approving or promulgating any implementation plan under section 7410 of this title or section 7411(d) of this title, any order under section 7411(j) of this title, under section 7412 of this title, under section 7419 of this title, or under section 7420 of this title, or his action under section 1857c–10(c)(2)(A), (B), or (C) of this title (as in effect before August 7, 1977) or under regulations thereunder, or revising regulations for enhanced monitoring and compliance certification programs under section 7414(a)(3) of this title, or any other final action of the Administrator under this chapter (including any denial or disapproval by the Administrator under subchapter I of this chapter) which is locally or regionally applicable may be filed only in the United States Court of Appeals for the appropriate circuit. Notwithstanding the preceding sentence a petition for review of any action referred to in such sentence may be filed only in the United States Court of Appeals for the District of Columbia if such action is based on a determination of nationwide scope or effect and if in taking such action the Administrator finds and publishes that such action is based on such a determination. Any petition for review under this subsection shall be filed within sixty days from the date notice of such promulgation, approval, or action appears in the Federal Register, except that if such petition is based solely on grounds arising after such sixtieth day, then any petition for review under this subsection shall be filed within sixty days after such grounds arise. The filing of a petition for reconsideration by the Administrator of any otherwise final rule or action shall not affect the finality of such rule or action for purposes of judicial review nor extend the time within which a petition for judicial review of such rule or action under this section may be filed, and shall not postpone the effectiveness of such rule or action.

(2) Action of the Administrator with respect to which review could have been obtained under paragraph (1) shall not be subject to judicial review in civil or criminal proceedings for enforcement. Where a final decision by the Administrator defers performance of any nondiscretionary statutory action to a later time, any person may challenge the deferral pursuant to paragraph (1).

(c) Additional evidence

In any judicial proceeding in which review is sought of a determination under this chapter required to be made on the record after notice and opportunity for hearing, if any party applies to the court for leave to adduce additional evidence, and shows to the satisfaction of the court that such additional evidence is material and that there were reasonable grounds for the failure to adduce such evidence in the proceeding before the Administrator, the court may order such additional evidence (and evidence in rebuttal thereof) to be taken before the Administrator, in such manner and upon such terms and conditions as to[1] the court may deem proper. The Administrator may modify his findings as to the facts, or make new findings, by reason of the additional evidence so taken and he shall file such modified or new findings, and his recommendation, if any, for the modification or setting aside of his original determination, with the return of such additional evidence.

(d) Rulemaking

(1) This subsection applies to—

(A) the promulgation or revision of any national ambient air quality standard under section 7409 of this title,

(B) the promulgation or revision of an implementation plan by the Administrator under section 7410(c) of this title,

(C) the promulgation or revision of any standard of performance under section 7411 of this title, or emission standard or limitation under section 7412(d) of this title, any standard under section 7412(f) of this title, or any regulation under section 7412(g)(1)(D) and (F) of this title, or any regulation under section 7412(m) or (n) of this title,

(D) the promulgation of any requirement for solid waste combustion under section 7429 of this title,

(E) the promulgation or revision of any regulation pertaining to any fuel or fuel additive under section 7545 of this title,

(F) the promulgation or revision of any regulation under subchapter IV–A of this chapter (relating to control of acid deposition),

(G) promulgation or revision of regulations pertaining to orders for coal conversion under section 7413(d)(5) of this title (but not including orders granting or denying any such orders),

(H) promulgation or revision of regulations pertaining to primary nonferrous smelter orders under section 7419 of this title (but not including the granting or denying of any such order),

(I) promulgation or revision of regulations under subchapter VI of this chapter (relating to stratosphere and ozone protection),

(J) promulgation or revision of regulations under part C of subchapter I of this chapter (relating to prevention of significant deterioration of air quality and protection of visibility),

(K) promulgation or revision of regulations under section 7521 of this title and test procedures for new motor vehicles or engines under section 7525 of this title and the revision of a standard under section 7521(a)(3) of this title,

(L) promulgation or revision of regulations for noncompliance penalties under section 7420 of this title,

(M) promulgation or revision of any regulations promulgated under section 7541 of this title (relating to warranties and compliance by vehicles in actual use),

(N) action of the Administrator under section 7426 of this title (relating to interstate pollution abatement),

(O) the promulgation or revision of any regulation pertaining to consumer and commercial products under section 7511b(e) of this title,

(P) the promulgation or revision of any regulation pertaining to field citations under section 7413(d)(3) of this title,

(Q) the promulgation or revision of any regulation pertaining to urban buses or the clean-fuel vehicle, clean-fuel fleet, and clean fuel programs under part C of subchapter II of this chapter,

(R) the promulgation or revision of any regulation pertaining to nonroad engines or nonroad vehicles under section 7547 of this title,

(S) the promulgation or revision of any regulation relating to motor vehicle compliance program fees under section 7552 of this title,

(T) the promulgation or revision of any regulation under subchapter IV–A of this chapter (relating to acid deposition),

(U) the promulgation or revision of any regulation under section 7511b(f) of this title pertaining to marine vessels, and

(V) such other actions as the Administrator may determine.

The provisions of section 553 through 557 and section 706 of Title 5 shall not, except as expressly provided in this subsection, apply to actions to which this subsection applies. This subsection shall not apply in the case of any rule or circumstance referred to in subparagraphs (A) or (B) of subsection 553(b) of Title 5.

(2) Not later than the date of proposal of any action to which this subsection applies, the Administrator shall establish a rulemaking docket for such action (hereinafter in this subsection referred to as a "rule"). Whenever a rule applies only within a particular State, a second (identical) docket shall be simultaneously established in the appropriate regional office of the Environmental Protection Agency.

(3) In the case of any rule to which this subsection applies, notice of proposed rulemaking shall be published in the Federal Register, as provided under section 553(b) of Title 5, shall be accompanied by a statement of its basis and purpose and shall specify the period available for public comment (hereinafter referred to as the "comment period"). The notice of proposed rulemaking shall also state the docket number, the location or locations of the docket, and the times it will be open to public inspection. The statement of basis and purpose shall include a summary of—

(A) the factual data on which the proposed rule is based;

(B) the methodology used in obtaining the data and in analyzing the data; and

(C) the major legal interpretations and policy considerations underlying the proposed rule.

The statement shall also set forth or summarize and provide a reference to any pertinent findings, recommendations, and comments by the Scientific Review Committee established under section 7409(d) of this title and the National Academy of Sciences, and, if the proposal differs in any important respect from any of these recommendations, an explanation of the reasons for such differences. All data, information, and documents referred to in this paragraph on which the proposed rule relies shall be included in the docket on the date of publication of the proposed rule.

(4)(A) The rulemaking docket required under paragraph (2) shall be open for inspection by the public at reasonable times specified in the notice of proposed rulemaking. Any person may copy documents contained in the docket. The Administrator shall provide copying facilities which may be used at the expense of the person seeking copies, but the Administrator may waive or reduce such expenses in such instances as the public interest requires. Any person may request copies by mail if the person pays the expenses, including personnel costs to do the copying.

(B)(i) Promptly upon receipt by the agency, all written comments and documentary information on the proposed rule received from any person for inclusion in the docket during the comment period shall be placed in the docket. The transcript of public hearings, if any, on the proposed rule shall also be included in the docket promptly upon receipt from the person who transcribed such hearings. All documents which become available after the proposed rule has been published and which the Administrator determines are of central relevance to the rulemaking shall be placed in the docket as soon as possible after their availability.

(ii) The drafts of proposed rules submitted by the Administrator to the Office of Management and Budget for any interagency review process prior to proposal of any such rule, all documents accompanying such drafts, and all written comments thereon by other agencies and all written responses to such written comments by the Administrator shall be placed in the docket no later than the date of proposal of the rule. The drafts of the final rule submitted for such review process prior to promulgation and all such written comments thereon, all documents accompanying such drafts, and written responses thereto shall be placed in the docket no later than the date of promulgation.

(5) In promulgating a rule to which this subsection applies (i) the Administrator shall allow any person to submit written comments, data, or documentary information; (ii) the Administrator shall give interested persons an opportunity for the oral presentation of data, views, or arguments, in addition to an opportunity to make written submissions; (iii) a transcript shall be kept of any oral presentation; and (iv) the Administrator shall keep the record of such proceeding open for thirty days after completion of the proceeding to provide an opportunity for submission of rebuttal and supplementary information.

(6)(A) The promulgated rule shall be accompanied by (i) a statement of basis and purpose like that referred to in paragraph (3) with respect to a proposed rule and (ii) an explanation of the reasons for any major changes in the promulgated rule from the proposed rule.

(B) The promulgated rule shall also be accompanied by a response to each of the significant comments, criticisms, and new data submitted in written or oral presentations during the comment period.

(C) The promulgated rule may not be based (in part or whole) on any information or data which has not been placed in the docket as of the date of such promulgation.

(7)(A) The record for judicial review shall consist exclusively of the material referred to in paragraph (3), clause (i) of paragraph (4)(B), and subparagraphs (A) and (B) of paragraph (6).

(B) Only an objection to a rule or procedure which was raised with reasonable specificity during the period for public comment (including any public hearing) may be raised during judicial review. If the person raising an objection can demonstrate to the Administrator that it was impracticable to raise such objection within such time or if the grounds for such objection arose after the period for public comment (but within the time specified for judicial review) and if such objection is of central relevance to the outcome of the rule, the Administrator shall convene a proceeding for reconsideration of the rule and provide the same procedural rights as would have been afforded had the information been available at the time the rule was proposed. If the Administrator refuses to convene such a proceeding, such person may seek review of such refusal in the United States court of appeals for the appropriate circuit (as provided in subsection (b) of this section). Such reconsideration shall not postpone the effectiveness of the rule. The effectiveness of the rule may be stayed during such reconsideration, however, by the Administrator or the court for a period not to exceed three months.

(8) The sole forum for challenging procedural determinations made by the Administrator under this subsection shall be in the United States court of appeals for the appropriate circuit (as provided in subsection (b) of this section) at the time of the substantive review of the rule. No interlocutory appeals shall be permitted with respect to such procedural determinations. In reviewing alleged procedural errors, the court may invalidate the rule only if the errors were so serious and related to matters of such central relevance to the rule that there is a substantial likelihood that the rule would have been significantly changed if such errors had not been made.

(9) In the case of review of any action of the Administrator to which this subsection applies, the court may reverse any such action found to be—

(A) arbitrary, capricious, an abuse of discretion, or otherwise not in accordance with law;

(B) contrary to constitutional right, power, privilege, or immunity;

(C) in excess of statutory jurisdiction, authority, or limitations, or short of statutory right; or

(D) without observance of procedure required by law, if (i) such failure to observe such procedure is arbitrary or capricious, (ii) the requirement of paragraph (7)(B) has been met, and (iii) the condition of the last sentence of paragraph (8) is met.

(10) Each statutory deadline for promulgation of rules to which this subsection applies which requires promulgation less than six months after date of proposal may be extended to not more than six months after date of proposal by the Administrator upon a determination that such extension is necessary to afford the public, and the agency, adequate opportunity to carry out the purposes of this subsection.

(11) The requirements of this subsection shall take effect with respect to any rule the proposal of which occurs after ninety days after August 7, 1977.

(e) Other methods of judicial review not authorized

Nothing in this chapter shall be construed to authorize judicial review of regulations or orders of the Administrator under this chapter, except as provided in this section.

(f) Costs

In any judicial proceeding under this section, the court may award costs of litigation (including reasonable attorney and expert witness fees) whenever it determines that such award is appropriate.

(g) Stay, injunction, or similar relief in proceedings relating to noncompliance penalties

In any action respecting the promulgation of regulations under section 7420 of this title or the administration or enforcement of section 7420 of this title no court shall grant any stay, injunctive, or similar relief before final judgment by such court in such action.

(h) Public participation

It is the intent of Congress that, consistent with the policy of the Administrative Procedures Act, the Administrator in promulgating any regulation under this chapter, including a regulation subject to a deadline, shall ensure a reasonable period for public participation of at least 30 days, except as otherwise expressly provided in section[2] 7407(d), 7502(a), 7511(a) and (b), and 7512(a) and (b) of this title.

(July 14, 1955, ch. 360, Title III, § 307, as added Dec. 31, 1970, Pub.L. 91–604, § 12(a), 84 Stat. 1707, and amended Nov. 18, 1971, Pub.L. 92–157, title III, § 302(a), 85 Stat. 464; June 22, 1974, Pub.L. 93–319, § 6(c), 88 Stat. 259; Aug. 7, 1977, Pub.L. 95–95, title III, §§ 303(d), 305(a), (c), (f)–(h), 91 Stat. 772, 776, 777; Nov. 16, 1977, Pub.L. 95–190, § 14(a)(79), (80), 91 Stat. 1404; Nov. 15, 1990, Pub.L. 101–549, title I, §§ 108(p), 110(5), title III, § 302(g), (h), title VII, §§ 702(c), 703, 706, 707(h), 710(b), 104 Stat. 2469, 2470, 2574, 2681–2684.)

1 So in original. The word "to" probably should not appear.

2 The word "section" probably should read "sections".

References in Text

Section 1857c–10(c)(2)(A), (B), or (C) of this title (as in effect before August 7, 1977), referred to in subsec. (b)(1), was in the original "section 119(c)(2)(A), (B), or (C) (as in effect before the date of enactment of the Clean Air Act Amendments of 1977)", meaning section 119 of Act July 14, 1955, c. 360, Title I, as added June 22, 1974, Pub.L. 93–319, § 3, 88 Stat. 248, (which was classified to section 1857c–10 of this title) as in effect prior to the enactment of Pub.L. 95–95, Aug. 7, 1977, 91 Stat. 691, effective Aug. 7, 1977. Section 112(b)(1) of Pub.L. 95–95 repealed section 119 of Act July 14, 1955, c. 360, Title I, as added by Pub.L. 93–319, and provided that all references to such section 119 in any subsequent enactment which supersedes Pub.L. 93–319 shall be construed to refer to section 113(d) of the Clean Air Act and to paragraph (5) thereof in particular which is classified to subsec. (d)(5) of section 7413 of this title. Section 117(b) of Pub.L. 95–95 added a new section 119 of Act July 14, 1955, which is classified to section 7419 of this title.

The Administrative Procedures Act, referred to in subsec. (h), is classified to subchapter II (section 551 et seq.) of chapter 5, and chapter 7 (section 701 et seq.) of Title 5, Government Organization and Employees.

Codification

Amendment by section 710(b) of Pub.L. 101–549 has been executed to subsec. (d)(1)(I) of this section as the probable intent of Congress.

Effective Date of 1990 Amendment

Amendment by Pub.L. 101–549 effective Nov. 15, 1990, except as otherwise provided, see section 711(b) of Pub.L. 101–549, set out as a note under section 7401 of this title.

Savings Provisions

Suits, actions or proceedings commenced under this chapter as in effect prior to Nov. 15, 1990, not to abate by reason of the taking effect of amendments by Pub.L. 101–549, except as otherwise provided for, see section 711(a) of Pub.L. 101–549, set out as a note under section 7401 of this title.

FEDERAL PRACTICE AND PROCEDURE

Holding back of trade secrets, see Wright & Graham: Evidence § 5437.

ADMINISTRATIVE LAW

Enforcement and review, see Koch § 8.22.

CODE OF FEDERAL REGULATIONS

Public information, see 40 CFR 2.100 et seq.

WEST'S FEDERAL FORMS

Administrative subpenas, enforcement of, see § 5901 et seq.

LAW REVIEW COMMENTARIES

Awarding attorney fees against adversaries: Introducing the problem. Dan B. Dobbs, Duke L.J. 435 (June 1986).

Coordinating judicial review in administrative law. Harold H. Bruff, 39 UCLA L.Rev. 1193 (1992).

The threat to investment in the hazardous waste industry: An analysis of individual and corporate shareholder liability under CERCLA. Utah L.Rev. 585 (1987).

LIBRARY REFERENCES

Health and Environment ⚷25.6(1), 28.
C.J.S. Health and Environment § 91 et seq.

United States Supreme Court

Attorney fees, appropriateness of award by federal court in absence of success on merits, see Ruckelshaus v. Sierra Club, 1983, 103 S.Ct. 3274, 462 U.S. 680, 77 L.Ed.2d 938.

§ 7608. Mandatory licensing [CAA § 308]

Whenever the Attorney General determines, upon application of the Administrator—

(1) that—

(A) in the implementation of the requirements of section 7411, 7412, or 7521 of this title, a right under any United States letters patent, which is being used or intended for public or commercial use and not otherwise reasonably available, is necessary to enable any person required to comply with such limitation to so comply, and

(B) there are no reasonable alternative methods to accomplish such purpose, and

(2) that the unavailability of such right may result in a substantial lessening of competition or tendency to create a monopoly in any line of commerce in any section of the country,

the Attorney General may so certify to a district court of the United States, which may issue an order requiring the person who owns such patent to license it on such reasonable terms and conditions as the court, after hearing, may determine. Such certification may be made to the district court for the district in which the person owning the patent resides, does business, or is found.

(July 14, 1955, ch. 360, title III, § 308, as added Dec. 31, 1970, Pub.L. 91–604, § 12(a), 84 Stat. 1708.)

LIBRARY REFERENCES

Health and Environment ⚷25.6(1).
C.J.S. Health and Environment § 91 et seq.

§ 7609. Policy review [CAA § 309]

(a) Environmental impact

The Administrator shall review and comment in writing on the environmental impact of any matter relating to duties and responsibilities granted pursuant to this chapter or other provisions of the authority of the Administrator, contained in any (1) legislation proposed by any Federal department or agency, (2) newly authorized Federal projects for construction and any major Federal agency action (other than a project for construction) to which section 4332(2)(C) of this title applies, and (3) proposed regulations published by any department or agency of the Federal Government. Such written comment shall be made public at the conclusion of any such review.

(b) Unsatisfactory legislation, action, or regulation

In the event the Administrator determines that any such legislation, action, or regulation is unsatisfactory from the standpoint of public health or welfare or environmental quality, he shall publish his determination and the matter shall be referred to the Council on Environmental Quality.

(July 14, 1955, ch. 360, title III, § 309, as added Dec. 31, 1970, Pub.L. 91–604, § 12(a), 84 Stat. 1709.)

CODE OF FEDERAL REGULATIONS

Council on Environmental Quality,
- Agency compliance, see 40 CFR 1507.1 et seq.
- Agency decisions, see 40 CFR 1505.1 et seq.
- Commenting, see 40 CFR 1503.1 et seq.
- Environmental quality, see 14 CFR 1216.100 et seq.
- Impact statements, see 40 CFR 1502.1 et seq.
- National Science Foundation, compliance with NEPA, see 45 CFR 640.1 et seq.
- NEPA,
  - Agency planning, see 40 CFR 1501.1 et seq.
  - Purpose, policy and mandate, see 40 CFR 1500.1 et seq.
- Other NEPA requirements, see 40 CFR 1506.1 et seq.
- Predecision referrals to Council, see 40 CFR 1504.1 et seq.
- Terminology, see 40 CFR 1508.1 et seq.

LIBRARY REFERENCES

Health and Environment ⚖25.6(1).
C.J.S. Health and Environment § 91 et seq.

§ 7610. Other authority [CAA § 310]

(a) Authority and responsibilities under other laws not affected

Except as provided in subsection (b) of this section, this chapter shall not be construed as superseding or limiting the authorities and responsibilities, under any other provision of law, of the Administrator or any other Federal officer, department, or agency.

(b) Nonduplication of appropriations

No appropriation shall be authorized or made under section 241, 243, or 246 of this title for any fiscal year after the fiscal year ending June 30, 1964, for any purpose for which appropriations may be made under authority of this chapter.

(July 14, 1955, ch. 360, title III, § 310, formerly § 10, as added Dec. 17, 1963, Pub.L. 88–206, § 1, 77 Stat. 401, renumbered § 303, Oct. 20, 1965, Pub.L. 89–272, title I, § 101(4), 79 Stat. 992, amended Nov. 21, 1967, Pub.L. 90–148, § 2, 81 Stat. 505, and renumbered § 310, and amended Dec. 31, 1970, Pub.L. 91–604, §§ 12(a), 15(c)(2), 84 Stat. 1705, 1713.)

LIBRARY REFERENCES

United States ⚖85.
C.J.S. United States § 123.

§ 7611. Records and audit [CAA § 311]

(a) Recipients of assistance to keep prescribed records

Each recipient of assistance under this chapter shall keep such records as the Administrator shall prescribe, including records which fully disclose the amount and disposition by such recipient of the proceeds of such assistance, the total cost of the project or undertaking in connection with which such assistance is given or used, and the amount of that portion of the cost of the project or undertaking supplied by other sources, and such other records as will facilitate an effective audit.

(b) Audits

The Administrator and the Comptroller General of the United States, or any of their duly authorized representatives, shall have access for the purpose of audit and examinations to any books, documents, papers, and records of the recipients that are pertinent to the grants received under this chapter.

(July 14, 1955, ch. 360, title III, § 311, formerly § 11, as added Dec. 17, 1963, Pub.L. 88–206, § 1, 77 Stat. 401, renumbered § 304, Oct. 20, 1965, Pub.L. 89–272, title I, § 101(4), 79 Stat. 992, and amended Nov. 21, 1967, Pub.L. 90–148, § 2, 81 Stat. 505, and renumbered § 311, and amended Dec. 31, 1970, Pub.L. 91–604, §§ 12(a), 15(c)(2), 84 Stat. 1705, 1713.)

LIBRARY REFERENCES

Health and Environment ⚖25.6(2).
C.J.S. Health and Environment § 125 et seq.

§ 7612. Economic impact analyses [CAA § 312]

(a) Cost-benefit analysis

The Administrator, in consultation with the Secretary of Commerce, the Secretary of Labor, and the Council on Clean Air Compliance Analysis (as established under subsection (f) of this section), shall conduct a comprehensive analysis of the impact of this chapter on the public health, economy, and environment of the United States. In performing such analysis, the Administrator should consider the costs, benefits and other effects associated with compliance with each standard issued for—

(1) a criteria air pollutant subject to a standard issued under section 7409 of this title;

(2) a hazardous air pollutant listed under section 7412 of this title, including any technology-based standard and any risk-based standard for such pollutant;

(3) emissions from mobile sources regulated under subchapter II of this chapter;

(4) a limitation under this chapter for emissions of sulfur dioxide or nitrogen oxides;

(5) a limitation under subchapter VI of this chapter on the production of any ozone-depleting substance; and

(6) any other section of this chapter.

(b) Benefits

In describing the benefits of a standard described in subsection (a) of this section, the Administrator shall consider all of the economic, public health, and environmental benefits of efforts to comply with such standard. In any case where numerical values are assigned to such benefits, a default assumption of zero value shall not be assigned to such benefits unless supported by specific data. The Administrator shall assess how benefits are measured in order to assure that damage to human health and the environment is more accurately measured and taken into account.

(c) Costs

In describing the costs of a standard described in subsection (a) of this section the Administrator shall consider the effects of such standard on employment, productivity, cost of living, economic growth, and the overall economy of the United States.

(d) Initial report

Not later than 12 months after November 15, 1990, the Administrator, in consultation with the Secretary of Commerce, the Secretary of Labor, and the Council on Clean Air Compliance Analysis, shall submit a report to the Congress that summarizes the results of the analysis described in subsection (a) of this section, which reports—

(1) all costs incurred previous to November 15, 1990 in the effort to comply with such standards; and

(2) all benefits that have accrued to the United States as a result of such costs.

(e) Biennial updates; future projections

Not later than 24 months after November 15, 1990, and every 24 months thereafter, the Administrator, in consultation with the Secretary of Commerce, the Secretary of Labor, and the Council on Clean Air Compliance Analysis, shall submit a report to the Congress that updates the report issued pursuant to subsection (d) of this section, and which, in addition, makes projections into the future regarding expected costs, benefits, and other effects of compliance with standards pursuant to this chapter as listed in subsection (a) of this section.

(f) Appointment of Advisory Council on Clean Air Compliance Analysis

Not later than 6 months after November 15, 1990, the Administrator, in consultation with the Secretary of Commerce and the Secretary of Labor, shall appoint an Advisory Council on Clean Air Compliance Analysis of not less than nine members (hereafter in this section referred to as the "Council"). In appointing such members, the Administrator shall appoint recognized experts in the fields of the health and environmental effects of air pollution, economic analysis, environmental sciences, and such other fields that the Administrator determines to be appropriate.

(g) Duties of advisory council

The Council shall—

(1) review the data to be used for any analysis required under this section and make recommendations to the Administrator on the use of such data;

(2) review the methodology used to analyze such data and make recommendations to the Administrator on the use of such methodology; and

(3) prior to the issuance of a report required under subsection (d) or (e) of this section, review the findings of such report, and make recommendations to the Administrator concerning the validity and utility of such findings.

(July 14, 1955, c. 360, Title III, § 312, formerly § 305, as added Nov. 21, 1967, Pub.L. 90–148, § 2, 81 Stat. 505, and renumbered and amended Dec. 31, 1970, Pub.L. 91–604, §§ 12(a), 15(c)(2), 84 Stat. 1705, 1713; Aug. 7, 1977, Pub.L. 95–95, title II, § 224(c), 91 Stat. 767; Nov. 15, 1990, Pub.L. 101–549, title VIII, § 812(a), 104 Stat. 2691.)

Effective Date of 1990 Amendment

Amendment by Pub.L. 101–549 effective Nov. 15, 1990, except as otherwise provided, see section 711(b) of Pub.L. 101–549, set out as a note under section 7401 of this title.

Savings Provisions

Suits, actions or proceedings commenced under this chapter as in effect prior to Nov. 15, 1990, not to abate by reason of the taking effect of amendments by Pub.L. 101–549, except as otherwise provided for, see section 711(a) of Pub.L. 101–549, set out as a note under section 7401 of this title.

Equivalent Air Quality Controls Among Trading Nations

Section 811 of Pub.L. 101–549 provided that:

"(a) **Findings.**—The Congress finds that—

"(1) all nations have the responsibility to adopt and enforce effective air quality standards and requirements and the United States, in enacting this Act [Pub.L. 101–549, Nov. 15, 1990, 104 Stat. 2399, for classifications to which see Tables], is carrying out its responsibility in this regard;

"(2) as a result of complying with this Act, businesses in the United States will make significant capital investments and incur incremental costs in implementing control technology standards;

"(3) such compliance may impair the competitiveness of certain United States jobs, production, processes, and products if foreign goods are produced under less costly environmental standards and requirements than are United States goods; and

"(4) mechanisms should be sought through which the United States and its trading partners can agree to eliminate or reduce competitive disadvantages.

"(b) **Action by the President.**—

"(1) **In general.**—Within 18 months after the date of the enactment of the Clean Air Act Amendments of 1990 [Nov. 15, 1990], the President shall submit to the Congress a report—

"(A) identifying and evaluating the economic effects of—

"(i) the significant air quality standards and controls required under this Act, and

"(ii) the differences between the significant standards and controls required under this Act and similar standards and controls adopted and enforced by the major trading partners of the United States,

on the international competitiveness of United States manufacturers; and

"(B) containing a strategy for addressing such economic effects through trade consultations and negotiations.

"(2) **Additional reporting requirements.—(A)** The evaluation required under paragraph (1)(A) shall examine the extent to which the significant air quality standards and controls required under this Act are comparable to existing internationally-agreed norms.

"(B) The strategy required to be developed under paragraph (1)(B) shall include recommended options (such as the harmonization of standards and trade adjustment measures) for reducing or eliminating competitive disadvantages caused by differences in standards and controls between the United States and each of its major trading partners.

"(3) **Public comment.**—Interested parties shall be given an opportunity to submit comments regarding the evaluations and strategy required in the report under paragraph (1). The President shall take any such comment into account in preparing the report.

"(4) **Interim report.**—Within 9 months after the date of the enactment of the Clean Air Act Amendments of 1990 [Nov. 15,

1990], the President shall submit to the Congress an interim report on the progress being made in complying with paragraph (1)."

GAO Reports on Costs and Benefits

Section 812(b) of Pub.L. 101–549 provided that: "Commencing on the second year after the date of the enactment of the Clean Air Act Amendments of 1990 [Nov. 15, 1990] and annually thereafter, the Comptroller General of the General Accounting Office, in consultation with other agencies, such as the Environmental Protection Agency, the Department of Labor, the Department of Commerce, the United States Trade Representative, the National Academy of Sciences, the Office of Technology Assessment, the National Academy of Engineering, the Council on Environmental Quality, and the Surgeon General, shall provide a report to the Congress on the incremental human health and environmental benefits, and incremental costs beyond current clean air requirements of the new control strategies and technologies required by this Act [Pub.L. 101–549, Nov. 15, 1990, 104 Stat. 2399, for classifications to which see Tables]. The report shall include, for such strategies and technologies, an analysis of the actual emissions reductions beyond existing practice, the effects on human life, human health and the environment (including both positive impacts and those that may be detrimental to jobs and communities resulting from loss of employers and employment, etc.), the energy security impacts, and the effect on United States products and industrial competitiveness in national and international markets."

§ 7613. Repealed. Pub.L. 101–549, Title VIII, § 803, 104 Stat. 2689

Section, July 14, 1955, c. 360, Title III, § 313, formerly § 306, as added Nov. 21, 1967, Pub.L. 90–148, § 2, 81 Stat. 506, and renumbered and amended Dec. 31, 1970, Pub.L. 91–604, §§ 12(a), 15(c)(2), 84 Stat. 1705, 1713; Aug. 7, 1977, Pub.L. 95–95, Title III, § 302(b), 91 Stat. 771, required annual report to Congress on progress of programs under this chapter.

Effective Date of Repeal

Repeal of section effective Nov. 15, 1990, except as otherwise provided, see section 711(b) of Pub.L. 101–549, set out as a note under section 7401 of this title.

Savings Provisions

Suits, actions or proceedings commenced under this chapter as in effect prior to Nov. 15, 1990, not to abate by reason of the taking effect of amendments by Pub.L. 101–549, except as otherwise provided for, see section 711(a) of Pub.L. 101–549, set out as a note under section 7401 of this title.

§ 7614. Labor standards [CAA § 314]

The Administrator shall take such action as may be necessary to insure that all laborers and mechanics employed by contractors or subcontractors on projects assisted under this chapter shall be paid wages at rates not less than those prevailing for the same type of work on similar construction in the locality as determined by the Secretary of Labor, in accordance with the Act of March 3, 1931, as amended, known as the Davis-Bacon Act (46 Stat. 1494; 40 U.S.C. 276a—276a–5). The Secretary of Labor shall have, with respect to the labor standards specified in this subsection, the authority and functions set forth in Reorganization Plan Numbered 14 of 1950 (15 F.R. 3176; 64 Stat. 1267) and section 276c of title 40.

(July 14, 1955, ch. 360, title III, § 314, formerly § 307, as added Nov. 21, 1967, Pub.L. 90–148, § 2, 81 Stat. 506, and renumbered and amended Dec. 31, 1970, Pub.L. 91–604, §§ 12(a), 15(c)(2), 84 Stat. 1705, 1713.)

LIBRARY REFERENCES

Labor Relations ⚷1129.
C.J.S. Labor Relations § 1039 et seq.

§ 7615. Separability of provisions [CAA § 315]

If any provision of this chapter, or the application of any provision of this chapter to any person or circumstance, is held invalid, the application of such provision to other persons or circumstances, and the remainder of this chapter shall not be affected thereby.

(July 14, 1955, ch. 360, title III, § 315, formerly § 12, as added Dec. 17, 1963, Pub.L. 88–206, § 1, 77 Stat. 401, renumbered § 305, Oct. 20, 1965, Pub.L. 89–272, title I, § 101(4), 79 Stat. 992, amended and renumbered § 308, Nov. 21, 1967, Pub.L. 90–148, § 2, 81 Stat. 506, and renumbered § 315, Dec. 31, 1970, Pub.L. 91–604, § 12(a), 84 Stat. 1705.)

LIBRARY REFERENCES

Statutes ⚷64(2).
C.J.S. Statutes § 96 et seq.

§ 7616. Sewage treatment grants [CAA § 316]

(a) Construction

No grant which the Administrator is authorized to make to any applicant for construction of sewage treatment works in any area in any State may be withheld, conditioned, or restricted by the Administrator on the basis of any requirement of this chapter except as provided in subsection (b) of this section.

(b) Withholding, conditioning, or restriction of construction grants

The Administrator may withhold, condition, or restrict the making of any grant for construction referred to in subsection (a) of this section only if he determines that—

(1) such treatment works will not comply with applicable standards under section 7411 or 7412 of this title,

(2) the State does not have in effect, or is not carrying out, a State implementation plan approved by the Administrator which expressly quantifies and provides for the increase in emissions of each air pollutant (from stationary and mobile sources in any area to which either part C or part D of subchapter I of this chapter applies for such pollutant) which increase may reasonably be anticipated to result directly or indirectly from the new sewage treatment capacity which would be created by such construction.

(3) the construction of such treatment works would create new sewage treatment capacity which—

(A) may reasonably be anticipated to cause or contribute to, directly or indirectly, an increase in emissions of any air pollutant in excess of the increase provided for under the provisions referred to in paragraph (2) for any such area, or

(B) would otherwise not be in conformity with the applicable implementation plan, or

(4) such increase in emissions would interfere with, or be inconsistent with, the applicable implementation plan for any other State.

In the case of construction of a treatment works which would result, directly or indirectly, in an increase in emissions of any air pollutant from stationary and mobile sources in an area to which part D of subchapter I of this chapter applies, the quantification of emissions referred to in paragraph (2) shall include the emissions of any such pollutant resulting directly or indirectly from areawide and nonmajor stationary source growth (mobile and stationary) for each such area.

(c) National Environmental Policy Act

Nothing in this section shall be construed to amend or alter any provision of the National Environmental Policy Act [42 U.S.C.A. § 4321 et seq.] or to affect any determination as to whether or not the requirements of such Act have been met in the case of the construction of any sewage treatment works.

(July 14, 1955, ch. 360, title III, § 316, as added Aug. 7, 1977, Pub.L. 95–95, title III, § 306, 91 Stat. 777.)

Effective Date

Section 406(d) of Title IV of Pub.L. 95–95, Aug. 7, 1977, 91 Stat. 796, provided that, except as otherwise expressly provided, the amendments made by that Act [which enacted this section and sections 7617 to 7625 of this title] were effective on the date of enactment [Aug. 7, 1977].

LIBRARY REFERENCES

Health and Environment ⚡25.7(7).
United States ⚡82(2).
C.J.S. Health and Environment § 108 et seq.
C.J.S. United States § 122.

§ 7617. Economic impact assessment [CAA § 317]

(a) Notice of proposed rulemaking; substantial revisions

This section applies to action of the Administrator in promulgating or revising—

(1) any new source standard of performance under section 7411 of this title,

(2) any regulation under section 7411(d) of this title,

(3) any regulation under part B of subchapter I of this chapter (relating to ozone and stratosphere protection),

(4) any regulation under part C of subchapter I of this chapter (relating to prevention of significant deterioration of air quality),

(5) any regulation establishing emission standards under section 7521 of this title and any other regulation promulgated under that section,

(6) any regulation controlling or prohibiting any fuel or fuel additive under section 7545(c) of this title, and

(7) any aircraft emission standard under section 7571 of this title.

Nothing in this section shall apply to any standard or regulation described in paragraphs (1) through (7) of this subsection unless the notice of proposed rulemaking in connection with such standard or regulation is published in the Federal Register after the date ninety days after August 7, 1977. In the case of revisions of such standards or regulations, this section shall apply only to revisions which the Administrator determines to be substantial revisions.

(b) Preparation of assessment by Administrator

Before publication of notice of proposed rulemaking with respect to any standard or regulation to which this section applies, the Administrator shall prepare an economic impact assessment respecting such standard or regulation. Such assessment shall be included in the docket required under section 7607(d)(2) of this title and shall be available to the public as provided in section 7607(d)(4) of this title. Notice of proposed rulemaking shall include notice of such availability together with an explanation of the extent and manner in which the Administrator has considered the analysis contained in such economic impact assessment in proposing the action. The Administrator shall also provide such an explanation in his notice of promulgation of any regulation or standard referred to in subsection (a) of this section. Each such explanation shall be part of the statements of basis and purpose required under sections 7607(d)(3) and 7607(d)(6) of this title.

(c) Analysis

Subject to subsection (d) of this section, the assessment required under this section with respect to any standard or regulation shall contain an analysis of—

(1) the costs of compliance with any such standard or regulation, including extent to which the costs of compliance will vary depending on (A) the effective date of the standard or regulation, and (B) the development of less expensive, more efficient

means or methods of compliance with the standard or regulation;

(2) the potential inflationary or recessionary effects of the standard or regulation;

(3) the effects on competition of the standard or regulation with respect to small business;

(4) the effects of the standard or regulation on consumer costs; and

(5) the effects of the standard or regulation on energy use.

Nothing in this section shall be construed to provide that the analysis of the factors specified in this subsection affects or alters the factors which the Administrator is required to consider in taking any action referred to in subsection (a) of this section.

(d) Extensiveness of assessment

The assessment required under this section shall be as extensive as practicable, in the judgment of the Administrator taking into account the time and resources available to the Environmental Protection Agency and other duties and authorities which the Administrator is required to carry out under this chapter.

(e) Limitations on construction of section

Nothing in this section shall be construed—

(1) to alter the basis on which a standard or regulation is promulgated under this chapter;

(2) to preclude the Administrator from carrying out his responsibility under this chapter to protect public health and welfare; or

(3) to authorize or require any judicial review of any such standard or regulation, or any stay or injunction of the proposal, promulgation, or effectiveness of such standard or regulation on the basis of failure to comply with this section.

(f) Citizen suits

The requirements imposed on the Administrator under this section shall be treated as nondiscretionary duties for purposes of section 7604(a)(2) of this title, relating to citizen suits. The sole method for enforcement of the Administrator's duty under this section shall be by bringing a citizen suit under such section 7604(a)(2) for a court order to compel the Administrator to perform such duty. Violation of any such order shall subject the Administrator to penalties for contempt of court.

(g) Costs

In the case of any provision of this chapter in which costs are expressly required to be taken into account, the adequacy or inadequacy of any assessment required under this section may be taken into consideration, but shall not be treated for purposes of judicial review of any such provision as conclusive with respect to compliance or noncompliance with the requirement of such provision to take cost into account.

(July 14, 1955, ch. 360, title III, § 317, as added Aug. 7, 1977, Pub.L. 95–95, title III, § 307, 91 Stat. 778, and amended Nov. 9, 1978, Pub.L. 95–623, § 13(d), 92 Stat. 3458.)

ADMINISTRATIVE LAW

Cost/benefit analysis, see Koch § 4.35.

§ 7618. Repealed. Pub.L. 101–549, title I, § 108(q), Nov. 15, 1990, 104 Stat. 2469

Section, July 14, 1955, ch. 360, title III, § 318, as added Aug. 7, 1977, Pub.L. 95–95, title III, § 308, 91 Stat. 780, related to financial disclosure and conflicts of interest.

Effective Date of Repeal

Repeal of section effective Nov. 15, 1990, except as otherwise provided, see section 711(b) of Pub.L. 101–549, set out as a note under section 7401 of this title.

Savings Provisions

Suits, actions or proceedings commenced under this chapter as in effect prior to Nov. 15, 1990, not to abate by reason of the taking effect of amendments by Pub.L. 101–549, except as otherwise provided for, see section 711(a) of Pub.L. 101–549, set out as a note under section 7401 of this title.

§ 7619. Air quality monitoring [CAA § 319]

Not later than one year after August 7, 1977, and after notice and opportunity for public hearing, the Administrator shall promulgate regulations establishing an air quality monitoring system throughout the United States which—

(1) utilizes uniform air quality monitoring criteria and methodology and measures such air quality according to a uniform air quality index,

(2) provides for air quality monitoring stations in major urban areas and other appropriate areas throughout the United States to provide monitoring such as will supplement (but not duplicate) air quality monitoring carried out by the States required under any applicable implementation plan,

(3) provides for daily analysis and reporting of air quality based upon such uniform air quality index, and

(4) provides for recordkeeping with respect to such monitoring data and for periodic analysis and reporting to the general public by the Administrator with respect to air quality based upon such data.

The operation of such air quality monitoring system may be carried out by the Administrator or by such other departments, agencies, or entities of the Federal Government (including the National Weather Service) as the President may deem appropriate. Any air quality monitoring system required under any applicable implementation plan under section 7410 of this title shall, as soon as practicable following promulgation of regulations under this section, utilize the standard criteria and methodology, and measure air quality according to the standard index, established under such regulations.

(July 14, 1955, ch. 360, title III, § 319, as added Aug. 7, 1977, Pub.L. 95–95, title III, § 309, 91 Stat. 781.)

CODE OF FEDERAL REGULATIONS

Air programs, generally, see 40 CFR 50.1 et seq.
Implementation plans, generally, see 40 CFR 51.40 et seq.
New stationary sources, performance standards, see 40 CFR 60.1 et seq.
Surveillance of ambient air quality, see 40 CFR 58.1 et seq.

LIBRARY REFERENCES

Health and Environment ⚷25.6(1).
C.J.S. Health and Environment § 91 et seq.

§ 7620. Standardized air quality modeling [CAA § 320]

(a) Conferences

Not later than six months after August 7, 1977, and at least every three years thereafter, the Administrator shall conduct a conference on air quality modeling. In conducting such conference, special attention shall be given to appropriate modeling necessary for carrying out part C of subchapter I of this chapter (relating to prevention of significant deterioration of air quality).

(b) Conferees

The conference conducted under this section shall provide for participation by the National Academy of Sciences, representatives of State and local air pollution control agencies, and appropriate Federal agencies, including the National Science Foundation; [1] the National Oceanic and Atmospheric Administration, and the National Institute of Standards and Technology.

(c) Comments; transcripts

Interested persons shall be permitted to submit written comments and a verbatim transcript of the conference proceedings shall be maintained.

(d) Promulgation and revision of regulations relating to air quality modeling

The comments submitted and the transcript maintained pursuant to subsection (c) of this section shall be included in the docket required to be established for purposes of promulgating or revising any regulation relating to air quality modeling under part C of subchapter I of this chapter.

(July 14, 1955, ch. 360, title III, § 320, as added Aug. 7, 1977, Pub.L. 95–95, title III, § 310, 91 Stat. 782, and amended Aug. 23, 1988, Pub.L. 100–418, Title V, § 5115(c), 102 Stat. 1433.)

[1] So in original. Probably should be a comma.

§ 7621. Employment effects [CAA § 321]

(a) Continuous evaluation of potential loss or shifts of employment

The Administrator shall conduct continuing evaluations of potential loss or shifts of employment which may result from the administration or enforcement of the provision of this chapter and applicable implementation plans, including where appropriate, investigating threatened plant closures or reductions in employment allegedly resulting from such administration or enforcement.

(b) Request for investigation; hearings; record; report

Any employee, or any representative of such employee, who is discharged or laid off, threatened with discharge or layoff, or whose employment is otherwise adversely affected or threatened to be adversely affected because of the alleged results of any requirement imposed or proposed to be imposed under this chapter, including any requirement applicable to Federal facilities and any requirement imposed by a State or political subdivision thereof, may request the Administrator to conduct a full investigation of the matter. Any such request shall be reduced to writing, shall set forth with reasonable particularity the grounds for the request, and shall be signed by the employee, or representative of such employee, making the request. The Administrator shall thereupon investigate the matter and, at the request of any party, shall hold public hearings on not less than five days' notice. At such hearings, the Administrator shall require the parties, including the employer involved, to present information relating to the actual or potential effect of such requirements on employment and the detailed reasons or justification therefor. If the Administrator determines that there are no reasonable grounds for conducting a public hearing he shall notify (in writing) the party requesting such hearing of such a determination and the reasons therefor. If the Administrator does convene such a hearing, the hearing shall be on the record. Upon receiving the report of such investigation, the Administrator shall make findings of fact as to the effect of such requirements on employment and on the alleged actual or potential discharge, layoff, or other adverse effect on employment, and shall make such recommendations as he deems appropriate. Such report, findings, and recommendations shall be available to the public.

(c) Subpenas; confidential information; witnesses; penalty

In connection with any investigation or public hearing conducted under subsection (b) of this section or as authorized in section 7419 of this title (relating to primary nonferrous smelter orders), the Administrator may issue subpenas for the attendance and testimony of witnesses and the production of relevant papers, books and documents, and he may administer oaths. Except for emission data, upon a showing satisfactory to the Administrator by such owner or operator that such papers, books, documents, or information or particular part thereof, if made public, would divulge trade secrets or secret processes of such owner, or operator, the Administrator shall consider such record, report, or information or particular portion thereof confidential in accordance with the purposes of section 1905 of title 18, except that such paper, book, document, or information may be disclosed to other officers, employees, or authorized representatives of the United States concerned with carrying out this chapter, or when relevant in any proceeding under this chapter. Witnesses summoned shall be paid the same fees and mileage that are paid witnesses in the courts of the United States. In cases of contumacy or refusal to obey a subpena served upon any person under this subparagraph, the district court of the United States for any district in which such person is found or resides or transacts business, upon application by the United States and after notice to such person, shall have jurisdiction to issue an order requiring such person to appear and give testimony before the Administrator, to appear and produce papers, books, and documents before the Administrator, or both, and any failure to obey such order of the court may be punished by such court as a contempt thereof.

(d) Limitations on construction of section

Nothing in this section shall be construed to require or authorize the Administrator, the States, or political subdivisions thereof, to modify or withdraw any requirement imposed or proposed to be imposed under this chapter.

(July 14, 1955, ch. 360, title III, § 321, as added Aug. 7, 1977, Pub.L. 95–95, title III, § 311, 91 Stat. 782.)

§ 7622. Employee protection [CAA § 322]

(a) Discharge or discrimination prohibited

No employer may discharge any employee or otherwise discriminate against any employee with respect to his compensation, terms, conditions, or privileges of employment because the employee (or any person acting pursuant to a request of the employee)—

(1) commenced, caused to be commenced, or is about to commence or cause to be commenced a proceeding under this chapter or a proceeding for the administration or enforcement of any requirement imposed under this chapter or under any applicable implementation plan,

(2) testified or is about to testify in any such proceeding, or

(3) assisted or participated or is about to assist or participate in any manner in such a proceeding or in any other action to carry out the purposes of this chapter.

(b) Complaint charging unlawful discharge or discrimination; investigation; order

(1) Any employee who believes that he has been discharged or otherwise discriminated against by any person in violation of subsection (a) of this section may, within thirty days after such violation occurs, file (or have any person file on his behalf) a complaint with the Secretary of Labor (hereinafter in this subsection referred to as the "Secretary") alleging such discharge or discrimination. Upon receipt of such a complaint, the Secretary shall notify the person named in the complaint of the filing of the complaint.

(2)(A) Upon receipt of a complaint filed under paragraph (1), the Secretary shall conduct an investigation of the violation alleged in the complaint. Within thirty days of the receipt of such complaint, the Secretary shall complete such investigation and shall notify in writing the complainant (and any person acting in his behalf) and the person alleged to have committed such violation of the results of the investigation conducted pursuant to this subparagraph. Within ninety days of the receipt of such complaint the Secretary shall, unless the proceeding on the complaint is terminated by the Secretary on the basis of a settlement entered into by the Secretary and the person alleged to have committed such violation, issue an order either providing the relief prescribed by subparagraph (B) or denying the complaint. An order of the Secretary shall be made on the record after notice and opportunity for public hearing. The Secretary may not enter into a settlement terminating a proceeding on a complaint without the participation and consent of the complainant.

(B) If, in response to a complaint filed under paragraph (1), the Secretary determines that a violation of subsection (a) of this section has occurred, the Secretary shall order the person who committed such violation to (i) take affirmative action to abate the violation, and (ii) reinstate the complainant to his former position together with the compensation (including back pay), terms, conditions, and privileges of his employment, and the Secretary may order such person to provide compensatory damages to the complainant. If an order is issued under this paragraph, the Secretary, at the request of the complainant, shall assess against the person against whom the order is issued a sum equal to the aggregate amount of all costs and expenses (including attorneys' and expert witness fees) reasonably incurred, as determined by the Secretary, by the complainant for, or in connection with, the bringing of the complaint upon which the order was issued.

(c) Review

(1) Any person adversely affected or aggrieved by an order issued under subsection (b) of this section may obtain review of the order in the United States court of appeals for the circuit in which the violation, with respect to which the order was issued, allegedly occurred. The petition for review must be filed within sixty days from the issuance of the Secretary's order. Review shall conform to chapter 7 of title 5. The commencement of proceedings under this subparagraph shall not, unless ordered by the court, operate as a stay of the Secretary's order.

(2) An order of the Secretary with respect to which review could have been obtained under paragraph (1) shall not be subject to judicial review in any criminal or other civil proceeding.

(d) Enforcement of order by Secretary

Whenever a person has failed to comply with an order issued under subsection (b)(2) of this section, the Secretary may file a civil action in the United States district court for the district in which the violation was found to occur to enforce such order. In actions brought under this subsection, the district courts shall have jurisdiction to grant all appropriate relief including, but not limited to, injunctive relief, compensatory, and exemplary damages.

(e) Enforcement of order by person on whose behalf order was issued

(1) Any person on whose behalf an order was issued under paragraph (2) of subsection (b) of this section may commence a civil action against the person to whom such order was issued to require compliance with such order. The appropriate United States district court shall have jurisdiction, without regard to the amount in controversy or the citizenship of the parties, to enforce such order.

(2) The court, in issuing any final order under this subsection, may award costs of litigation (including reasonable attorney and expert witness fees) to any party whenever the court determines such award is appropriate.

(f) Mandamus

Any nondiscretionary duty imposed by this section shall be enforceable in a mandamus proceeding brought under section 1361 of title 28.

(g) Deliberate violation by employee

Subsection (a) of this section shall not apply with respect to any employee who, acting without direction from his employer (or the employer's agent), deliberately causes a violation of any requirement of this chapter.

(July 14, 1955, ch. 360, title III, § 322, as added Aug. 7, 1977, Pub.L. 95–95, title III, § 312, 91 Stat. 783.)

CODE OF FEDERAL REGULATIONS

Discrimination complaints, procedures, see 29 CFR 24.1 et seq.

§ 7623. Repealed. Pub. L. 96–300, § 1(c), July 2, 1980, 94 Stat. 831

§ 7624. Cost of vapor recovery equipment [CAA § 323]

(a) Costs to be borne by owner of retail outlet

The regulations under this chapter applicable to vapor recovery with respect to mobile source fuels at retail outlets of such fuels shall provide that the cost of procurement and installation of such vapor recovery shall be borne by the owner of such outlet (as determined under such regulations). Except as provided in subsection (b) of this section, such regulations shall provide that no lease of a retail outlet by the owner thereof which is entered into or renewed after August 7, 1977, may provide for a payment by the lessee of the cost of procurement and installation of vapor recovery equipment. Such regulations shall also provide that the cost of procurement and installation of vapor recovery equipment may be recovered by the owner of such outlet by means of price increases in the cost of any product sold by such owner, notwithstanding any provision of law.

(b) Payment by lessee

The regulations of the Administrator referred to in subsection (a) of this section shall permit a lease of a retail outlet to provide for payment by the lessee of the cost of procurement and installation of vapor recovery equipment over a reasonable period (as determined in accordance with such regulations), if the owner of such outlet does not sell, trade in, or otherwise dispense any product at wholesale or retail at such outlet.

(July 14, 1955, ch. 360, title III, § 323 formerly § 324, as added Aug. 7, 1977, Pub.L. 95–95, title III, § 314(a), 91 Stat. 788, amended Nov. 16, 1977, Pub.L. 95–190, § 14(a)(82), 91 Stat. 1404, and renumbered and amended July 2, 1980, Pub.L. 96–300, § 1(b), (c), 94 Stat. 831.)

§ 7625. Vapor recovery for small business marketers of petroleum products [CAA § 324]

(a) Marketers of gasoline

The regulations under this chapter applicable to vapor recovery from fueling of motor vehicles at retail outlets of gasoline shall not apply to any outlet owned by an independent small business marketer of gasoline having monthly sales of less than 50,000 gallons. In the case of any other outlet owned by an independent small business marketer, such regulations shall provide, with respect to independent small business marketers of gasoline, for a three-year phase-in period for the installation of such vapor recovery equipment at such outlets under which such marketers shall have—

(1) 33 percent of such outlets in compliance at the end of the first year during which such regulations apply to such marketers,

(2) 66 percent at the end of such second year, and

(3) 100 percent at the end of the third year.

(b) State requirements

Nothing in subsection (a) of this section shall be construed to prohibit any State from adopting or enforcing, with respect to independent small business marketers of gasoline having monthly sales of less than 50,000 gallons, any vapor recovery requirements for mobile source fuels at retail outlets. Any vapor recovery requirement which is adopted by a State and submitted to the Administrator as part of its implementation plan may be approved and enforced by the Administrator as part of the applicable implementation plan for that State.

(c) Refiners

For purposes of this section, an independent small business marketer of gasoline is a person engaged in the marketing of gasoline who would be required to pay for procurement and installation of vapor recovery equipment under section 7624 of this title or under regulations of the Administrator, unless such person—

(1)(A) is a refiner, or

(B) controls, is controlled by, or is under common control with, a refiner,

(C) is otherwise directly or indirectly affiliated (as determined under the regulations of the Administrator) with a refiner or with a person who controls, is controlled by, or is under a common control with a refiner (unless the sole affiliation referred to herein is by means of a supply contract or an agreement or contract to use a trademark, trade name, service mark, or other identifying symbol or name owned by such refiner or any such person), or

(2) receives less than 50 percent of his annual income from refining or marketing of gasoline.

For the purpose of this section, the term "refiner" shall not include any refiner whose total refinery capacity (including the refinery capacity of any person who controls, is controlled by, or is under common control with, such refiner) does not exceed 65,000 barrels per day. For purposes of this section, "control" of a corporation means ownership of more than 50 percent of its stock.

(July 14, 1955, ch. 360, title III, § 324, formerly § 325, as added Aug. 7, 1977, Pub.L. 95–95, title III, § 314(b), 91 Stat. 789, and renumbered July 2, 1980, Pub.L. 96–300, § 1(c), 94 Stat. 831.)

§ 7625–1. Exemptions for certain territories [CAA § 325]

(a)(1) Upon petition by the governor of Guam, American Samoa, the Virgin Islands, or the Commonwealth of the Northern Mariana, Islands, the Administrator is authorized to exempt any person or source or class of persons or sources in such territory from any requirement under this chapter other than section 7412 of this title or any requirement under section 7410 of this title or part D of subchapter I of this chapter necessary to attain or maintain a national primary ambient air quality standard. Such exemption may be granted if the Administrator finds that compliance with such requirement is not feasible or is unreasonable due to unique geographical, meteorological, or economic factors of such territory, or such other local factors as the Administrator deems significant. Any such petition shall be considered in accordance with section 7607(d) of this title and any exemption under this subsection shall be considered final action by the Administrator for the purposes of section 7607(b) of this title.

(2) The Administrator shall promptly notify the Committees on Energy and Commerce and on Natural Resources of the House of Representatives and the Committees on Environment and Public Works and on Energy and Natural Resources of the Senate upon receipt of any petition under this subsection and of the approval or rejection of such petition and the basis for such action.

(b) Notwithstanding any other provision of this chapter, any fossil fuel fired steam electric power plant operating within Guam as of December 8, 1983 is hereby exempted from:

(1) any requirement of the new source performance standards relating to sulfur dioxide promulgated under section 7411 of this title as of December 8, 1983; and

(2) any regulation relating to sulfur dioxide standards or limitations contained in a State implementation plan approved under section 7410 of this title as of December 8, 1983: *Provided*, That such exemption shall expire eighteen months after December 8, 1983, unless the Administrator determines that such plant is making all emissions reductions practicable to prevent exceedances of the national ambient air quality standards for sulfur dioxide.

(July 14, 1955, ch. 360, title III, § 325, as added Dec. 8, 1983, Pub.L. 98–213, § 11, 97 Stat. 1461, and amended Nov. 5, 1990, Pub.L. 101–549, title VIII, § 806, 104 Stat. 2689; Nov. 2, 1994, Pub.L. 103–437, § 15(s), 108 Stat. 4594.)

Change of Name

Any reference in any provision of law enacted before Jan. 4, 1995, to the Committee on Energy and Commerce of the House of Representatives treated as referring to the Committee on Commerce of the House of Representatives, except that any reference in any provision of law enacted before Jan. 4, 1995, to the Committee on Energy and Commerce of the House of Representatives treated as referring to the Committee on Agriculture of the House of Representatives, in the case of a provision of law relating to inspection of seafood or seafood products, the Committee on Banking and Financial Services of the House of Representatives, in the case of a provision of law relating to bank capital markets activities generally or to depository institution securities activities generally, and the Committee on Transportation and Infrastructure of the House of Representatives, in the case of a provision of law relating to railroads, railway labor, or railroad retirement and unemployment (except revenue measures related thereto), see section 1(a)(4) and (c)(1) of Pub.L. 104–14, set out as a note preceding section 21 of Title 2, The Congress.

Any reference in any provision of law enacted before Jan. 4, 1995, to the Committee on Natural Resources of the House of Representatives treated as referring to the Committee on Resources of the House of Representatives, see section 1(a)(8) of Pub.L. 104–14, set out as a note preceding section 21 of Title 2, The Congress.

Effective Date of 1990 Amendment

Amendment by Pub.L. 101–549 effective Nov. 15, 1990, except as otherwise provided, see section 711(b) of Pub.L. 101–549, set out as a note under section 7401 of this title.

Savings Provisions

Suits, actions or proceedings commenced under this chapter as in effect prior to Nov. 15, 1990, not to abate by reason of the taking effect of amendments by Pub.L. 101–549, except as otherwise provided for, see section 711(a) of Pub.L. 101–549, set out as a note under section 7401 of this title.

§ 7625a. Statutory construction [CAA § 326]

The parenthetical cross references in any provision of this chapter to other provisions of the chapter, or other provisions of law, where the words "relating to" or "pertaining to" are used, are made only for convenience, and shall be given no legal effect.

(July 14, 1955, ch. 360, title III, § 326, as added Nov. 16, 1977, Pub.L. 95–190, § 14(a)(84), 91 Stat. 1404, and renumbered § 325, July 2, 1980, Pub.L. 96–300, § 1(c), 94 Stat. 831; renumbered § 326, Dec. 8, 1983, Pub.L. 98–213, § 11, 97 Stat. 1461.)

§ 7626. Authorization of appropriations [CAA § 327]

(a) In general

There are authorized to be appropriated to carry out this chapter such sums as may be necessary for the 7 fiscal years commencing after the enactment of the Clean Air Act Amendments of 1990.

(b) Grants for planning

There are authorized to be appropriated (1) not more than $50,000,000 to carry out section 7505 of this title beginning in fiscal year 1991, to be available until expended, to develop plan revisions required by subpart[1] 2, 3, or 4 of part D of subchapter I of this chapter, and (2) not more than $15,000,000 for each of the 7 fiscal years commencing after the enactment of the Clean Air Act Amendments of 1990 to make grants to the States to prepare implementation plans as required by subpart[1] 2, 3, or 4 of part D of subchapter I of this chapter.

(July 14, 1955, ch. 360, title III, § 327, formerly § 325, as added Aug. 7, 1977, Pub.L. 95–95, title III, § 315, 91 Stat. 790, renumbered § 327 and amended Nov. 16, 1977, Pub.L. 95–190, § 14(a)(83), 91 Stat. 1404; renumbered § 326, July 2, 1980, Pub.L. 96–300, § 1(c), 94 Stat. 831; renumbered § 327, Dec. 8, 1983, Pub.L. 98–213, § 11, 97 Stat. 1461; amended Nov. 15, 1990, Pub.L. 101–549, title VIII, § 822, 104 Stat. 2699.)

References in Text

The enactment of the Clean Air Act Amendments of 1990, referred to in text, probably means the date of enactment of Pub.L. 101–549, Nov. 15, 1990, 104 Stat. 2399, which was approved Nov. 15, 1990.

Effective Date of 1990 Amendment

Amendment by Pub.L. 101–549 effective Nov. 15, 1990, except as otherwise provided, see section 711(b) of Pub.L. 101–549, set out as a note under section 7401 of this title.

Effective Date

Section 406(d) of Title IV of Pub.L. 95–95, Aug. 7, 1977, 91 Stat. 796, provided that, except as otherwise expressly provided, the amendments made by that Act [which enacted this section] were effective on the date of enactment [Aug. 7, 1977].

Savings Provisions

Suits, actions or proceedings commenced under this chapter as in effect prior to Nov. 15, 1990, not to abate by reason of the taking effect of amendments by Pub.L. 101–549, except as otherwise provided for, see section 711(a) of Pub.L. 101–549, set out as a note under section 7401 of this title.

LIBRARY REFERENCES

United States ⚯85.

C.J.S. United States § 123.

§ 7627. Air pollution from outer continental shelf activities [CAA § 328]

(a)(1) Applicable requirements for certain areas.—Not later than 12 months after the enactment of the Clean Air Act Amendments of 1990, following consultation with the Secretary of the Interior and the Commandant of the United States Coast Guard, the Administrator, by rule, shall establish requirements to control air pollution from Outer Continental Shelf sources located offshore of the States along the Pacific, Arctic and Atlantic Coasts, and along the United States Gulf Coast off the State of Florida eastward of longitude 87 degrees and 30 minutes ("OCS sources") to attain and maintain Federal and State ambient air quality standards and to comply with the provisions of part C of title I. For such sources located within 25 miles of the seaward boundary of such States, such requirements shall be the same as would be applicable if the source were located in the corresponding onshore area, and shall include, but not be limited to, State and local requirements for emission controls, emission limitations, offsets, permitting, monitoring, testing, and reporting. New OCS sources shall comply with such requirements on the date of promulgation and existing OCS sources shall comply on the date 24 months thereafter. The Administrator shall update such requirements as necessary to maintain consistency with onshore regulations. The authority of this subsection shall supersede section 5(a)(8) of the Outer Continental Shelf Lands Act [43 U.S.C.A. § 1334(a)(8)] but shall not repeal or modify any other Federal, State, or local authorities with respect to air quality. Each requirement established under this section shall be treated, for purposes of sections 7413, 7414, 7416, 7420, and 7604 of this title, as a standard under section 7411 of this title and a violation of any such requirement shall be considered a violation of section 7411(e) of this title.

(2) Exemptions.—The Administrator may exempt an OCS source from a specific requirement in effect under regulations under this subsection if the Administrator finds that compliance with a pollution control technology requirement is technically infeasible or will cause an unreasonable threat to health and safety. The Administrator shall make written findings explaining the basis of any exemption issued pursuant to this subsection and shall impose another requirement equal to or as close in stringency to the original requirement as possible. The Administrator shall ensure that any increase in emissions due to the granting of an exemption is offset by reductions in actual emissions, not otherwise required by this chapter, from the same source or other sources in the area or in the corresponding onshore area. The Administrator shall establish procedures to provide for public notice and comment on exemptions proposed pursuant to this subsection.

(3) State procedures.—Each State adjacent to an OCS source included under this subsection may promulgate and submit to the Administrator regulations for implementing and enforcing the requirements of this subsection. If the Administrator finds that the State regulations are adequate, the Administrator shall delegate to that State any authority the Administrator has under this chapter to implement and enforce such requirements. Nothing in this subsection shall prohibit the Administrator from enforcing any requirement of this section.

(4) Definitions.—For purposes of subsections (a) and (b) of this section—

(A) Outer Continental Shelf.—The term "Outer Continental Shelf" has the meaning provided by section 2 of the Outer Continental Shelf Lands Act (43 U.S.C. 1331).

(B) Corresponding onshore area.—The term "corresponding onshore area" means, with respect to any OCS source, the onshore attainment or nonattainment area that is closest to the source, unless the Administrator determines that another area with more stringent requirements with respect to the control and abatement of air pollution may reasonably be expected to be affected by such emissions. Such determination shall be based on the potential for air pollutants from the OCS source to reach the other onshore area and the potential of such air pollutants to affect the efforts of the other onshore area to attain or maintain any Federal or State ambient air quality standard or to comply with the provisions of part C of subchapter I of this chapter.

(C) Outer Continental Shelf Source.—The terms "Outer Continental Shelf source" and "OCS source" include any equipment, activity, or facility which—

(i) emits or has the potential to emit any air pollutant,

(ii) is regulated or authorized under the Outer Continental Shelf Lands Act [43 U.S.C.A. § 1331 et seq.], and

(iii) is located on the Outer Continental Shelf or in or on waters above the Outer Continental Shelf.

Such activities include, but are not limited to, platform and drill ship exploration, construction, development, production, processing, and transportation.

For purposes of this subsection, emissions from any vessel servicing or associated with an OCS source, including emissions while at the OCS source or en route to or from the OCS source within 25 miles of the OCS source, shall be considered direct emissions from the OCS source.

(D) New and existing OCS sources.—The term "new OCS source" means an OCS source which is a new source within the meaning of section 7411(a) of this title. The term "existing OCS source" means any OCS source other than a new OCS source.

(b) Requirements for other offshore areas.—For portions of the United States Gulf Coast Outer Continental Shelf that are adjacent to the States not covered by subsection (a) of this section which are Texas, Louisiana, Mississippi, and Alabama, the Secretary shall consult with the Administrator to assure coordination of air pollution control regulation for Outer Continental Shelf emissions and emissions in adjacent onshore areas. Concurrently with this obligation, the Secretary shall complete within 3 years of enactment of this section a research study examining the impacts of emissions from Outer Continental Shelf activities in such areas that fail to meet the national ambient air quality standards for either ozone or nitrogen dioxide. Based on the results of this study, the Secretary shall consult with the Administrator and determine if any additional actions are necessary. There are authorized to be appropriated such sums as may be necessary to provide funding for the study required under this section.

(c)(1) Coastal waters.—The study report of section 7412(n) of this title shall apply to the coastal waters of the United States to the same extent and in the same manner as such requirements apply to the Great Lakes, the Chesapeake Bay, and their tributary waters.

(2) The regulatory requirements of section 7412(n) of this title shall apply to the coastal waters of the States which are subject to subsection (a) of this section, to the same extent and in the same manner as such requirements apply to the Great Lakes, the Chesapeake Bay, and their tributary waters.

(July 14, 1955, ch. 360, title III, § 328, as added Nov. 15, 1990, Pub.L. 101–549, title VIII, § 801, 104 Stat. 2685.)

References in Text

The enactment of the Clean Air Act Amendments of 1990, referred to in subsec. (a)(1), and the enactment of this section, referred to in subsec. (b), probably mean the date of enactment of Pub.L. 101–549, Nov. 15, 1990, 104 Stat. 2399, which was approved Nov. 15, 1990.

The Outer Continental Shelf Lands Act, referred to in subsecs. (a)(1), (a)(4)(A) and (a)(4)(C)(ii), is Act Aug. 7, 1953, c. 345, 67 Stat. 462, as amended, which is classified generally to subchapter III (section 1331 et seq.) of chapter 29 of Title 43, Public Lands. Section 5(a)(8) of such Act, referred to in subsec. (a)(1), is classified to section 1334(a)(8) of Title 43. Section 2 of such Act, referred to in subsec. (a)(4)(A), is classified to section 1331 of Title 43. For complete classification of this Act to the Code, see Short Title note set out under section 1331 of Title 43 and Tables.

Effective Date

Section to take effect Nov. 15, 1990, except as otherwise provided, see section 711(b) of Pub.L. 101–549, set out as a note under section 7401 of this title.

Savings Provisions

Suits, actions or proceedings commenced under this chapter as in effect prior to Nov. 15, 1990, not to abate by reason of the taking effect of amendments by Pub.L. 101–549, except as otherwise provided for, see section 711(a) of Pub.L. 101–549, set out as a note under section 7401 of this title.

SUBCHAPTER IV—NOISE POLLUTION

Codification

Another title IV was enacted by Pub.L. 101–549, Title IV, § 401, Nov. 15, 1990, 104 Stat. 2584, as added to Act July 14, 1955, c. 360, and is set out as subchapter IV–A (§§ 7651 to 7651*o*) of this chapter, post.

§ 7641. Noise abatement [CAA § 402]

(a) Office of Noise Abatement and Control

The Administrator shall establish within the Environmental Protection Agency an Office of Noise Abatement and Control, and shall carry out through such Office a full and complete investigation and study of noise and its effect on the public health and welfare in order to (1) identify and classify causes and sources of noise, and (2) determine—

(A) effects at various levels;

(B) projected growth of noise levels in urban areas through the year 2000;

(C) the psychological and physiological effect on humans;

(D) effects of sporadic extreme noise (such as jet noise near airports) as compared with constant noise;

(E) effect on wildlife and property (including values);

(F) effect of sonic booms on property (including values); and

(G) such other matters as may be of interest in the public welfare.

(b) Investigation techniques; report and recommendations

In conducting such investigation, the Administrator shall hold public hearings, conduct research, experiments, demonstrations, and studies. The Administrator shall report the results of such investigation and study, together with his recommendations for legislation or other action, to the President and the Congress not later than one year after December 31, 1970.

(c) Abatement of noise from Federal activities

In any case where any Federal department or agency is carrying out or sponsoring any activity resulting in noise which the Administrator determines amounts to a public nuisance or is otherwise objectionable, such department or agency shall consult with the Administrator to determine possible means of abating such noise.

(July 14, 1955, ch. 360, title IV, § 402, as added Dec. 31, 1970, Pub.L. 91–604, § 14, 84 Stat. 1709.)

Codification

There are two sections 401 and 402 of Act July 14, 1955, c. 360, Title IV, as amended. Section 401, as added Pub.L. 91–604, is classified in a Short Title note set out under this section. Section 401, as added Pub.L. 101–549, is classified as section 7651 of this title. Section 402, as added Pub.L. 91–604, is classified as this section. Section 402, as added Pub.L. 101–549, is classified as section 7651a of this title.

Short Title

Section 401 of Act July 14, 1955, c. 360, Title IV, as added Pub.L. 91–604, § 14, Dec. 31, 1970, 84 Stat. 1709, provided that Title IV of Act July 14, 1955, c. 360 [this subchapter], may be cited as the "Noise Pollution and Abatement Act of 1970".

WEST'S FEDERAL PRACTICE MANUAL

Noise pollution, see § 4389 et seq.

LIBRARY REFERENCES

Health and Environment ⚷25.8.
C.J.S. Health and Environment § 61 et seq.

§ 7642. Authorization of appropriations [CAA § 403]

There is authorized to be appropriated such amount, not to exceed $30,000,000, as may be necessary for the purposes of this subchapter.

(July 14, 1955, ch. 360, title IV, § 403, as added Dec. 31, 1970, Pub.L. 91–604, § 14, 84 Stat. 1710.)

Codification

There are two sections 403 of Act July 14, 1955, c. 360, Title IV, as amended. Section 403, as added Pub.L. 91–604, is classified as this section. Section 403, as added Pub.L. 101–549, is classified as section 7651b of this title.

SUBCHAPTER IV–A—ACID DEPOSITION CONTROL

Codification

Another title IV was enacted by Pub.L. 91–604, § 14, Dec. 31, 1970, 84 Stat. 1709, as added to Act July 14, 1955, c. 360, and is set out as subchapter IV (§§ 7641, 7642) of this chapter, ante.

§ 7651. Findings and purposes [CAA § 401]

(a) Findings

The Congress finds that—

(1) the presence of acidic compounds and their precursors in the atmosphere and in deposition from the atmosphere represents a threat to natural resources, ecosystems, materials, visibility, and public health;

(2) the principal sources of the acidic compounds and their precursors in the atmosphere are emissions of sulfur and nitrogen oxides from the combustion of fossil fuels;

(3) the problem of acid deposition is of national and international significance;

(4) strategies and technologies for the control of precursors to acid deposition exist now that are economically feasible, and improved methods are expected to become increasingly available over the next decade;

(5) current and future generations of Americans will be adversely affected by delaying measures to remedy the problem;

(6) reduction of total atmospheric loading of sulfur dioxide and nitrogen oxides will enhance protection of the public health and welfare and the environment; and

(7) control measures to reduce precursor emissions from steam-electric generating units should be initiated without delay.

(b) Purposes

The purpose of this subchapter is to reduce the adverse effects of acid deposition through reductions in annual emissions of sulfur dioxide of ten million tons from 1980 emission levels, and, in combination with other provisions of this chapter, of nitrogen oxides emissions of approximately two million tons from 1980 emission levels, in the forty-eight contiguous States and the District of Columbia. It is the intent of this subchapter to effectuate such reductions by requiring compliance by affected sources with prescribed emission limitations by specified deadlines, which limitations may be met through alternative methods of compliance provided by an emission allocation and transfer system. It is also the purpose of this subchapter to encourage energy conservation, use of renewable and clean alternative technologies, and pollution prevention as a long-range strategy, consistent with the provisions of this subchapter, for reducing air pollution and other adverse impacts of energy production and use.

(July 14, 1955, ch. 360, title IV, § 401, as added Nov. 15, 1990, Pub.L. 101–549, title IV, § 401, 104 Stat. 2584.)

Codification

There are two sections 401 of Act July 14, 1955, c. 360, Title IV, as amended. Section 401, as added Pub.L. 91–604, is classified as a Short Title of 1970 Amendment note set out under section 7641 of this title. Section 401, as added Pub.L. 101–549, is classified as this section.

Effective Date

Section to take effect Nov. 15, 1990, except as otherwise provided, see section 711(b) of Pub.L. 101–549, set out as a note under section 7401 of this title.

Savings Provisions

Suits, actions or proceedings commenced under this chapter as in effect prior to Nov. 15, 1990, not to abate by reason of the taking effect of amendments by Pub.L. 101–549, except as otherwise provided for, see section 711(a) of Pub.L. 101–549, set out as a note under section 7401 of this title.

Acid Deposition Standards

Section 404 of Pub.L. 101–549 provided that:

"Not later than 36 months after the date of enactment of this Act [Nov. 15, 1990], the Administrator of the Environmental Protection Agency shall transmit to the Committee on Environment and Public Works of the Senate and the Committee on Energy and Commerce of the House of Representatives a report on the feasibility and effectiveness of an acid deposition standard or standards to protect sensitive and critically sensitive aquatic and terrestrial resources. The study required by this section shall include, but not be limited to, consideration of the following matters:

"(1) identification of the sensitive and critically sensitive aquatic and terrestrial resources in the United States and Canada which may be affected by the deposition of acidic compounds;

"(2) description of the nature and numerical value of a deposition standard or standards that would be sufficient to protect such resources;

"(3) description of the use of such standard or standards in other Nations or by any of the several States in acid deposition control programs;

"(4) description of the measures that would need to be taken to integrate such standard or standards with the control program required by title IV of the Clean Air Act [this subchapter];

"(5) description of the state of knowledge with respect to source-receptor relationships necessary to develop a control program on such standard or standards and the additional research that is ongoing or would be needed to make such a control program feasible; and

"(6) description of the impediments to implementation of such control program and the cost-effectiveness of deposition standards compared to other control strategies including ambient air quality standards, new source performance standards and the requirements of title IV of the Clean Air Act [this subchapter]."

[Any reference in any provision of law enacted before Jan. 4, 1995, to the Committee on Energy and Commerce of the House of Representatives treated as referring to the Committee on Commerce of the House of Representatives, except that any reference in any provision of law enacted before Jan. 4, 1995, to the Committee on Energy and Commerce of the House of Representatives treated as referring to the Committee on Agriculture of the House of Representatives, in the case of a provision of law relating to inspection of seafood or seafood products, the Committee on Banking and Financial Services of the House of Representatives, in the case of a provision of law relating to bank capital markets activities generally or to depository institution securities activities generally, and the Committee on Transportation and Infrastructure of the House of Representatives, in the case of a provision of law relating to railroads, railway labor, or railroad retirement and unemployment (except revenue measures related thereto), see section 1(a)(4) and (c)(1) of Pub.L. 104–14, set out as a note preceding section 21 of Title 2, The Congress.]

Industrial SO_2 Emissions

Section 406 of Pub.L. 101–549 provided that:

"**(a) Report.**—Not later than January 1, 1995 and every 5 years thereafter, the Administrator of the Environmental Protection Agency shall transmit to the Congress a report containing an inventory of national annual sulfur dioxide emissions from industrial sources (as defined in title IV of the Act [this subchapter]), including units subject to section 405(g)(6) of the Clean Air Act [section 7651d(g)(6) of this title], for all years for which data are available, as well as the likely trend in such emissions over the following twenty-year period. The reports shall also contain estimates of the actual emission reduction in each year resulting from promulgation of the diesel fuel desulfurization regulations under section 214 [section 7548 of this title].

"**(b) 5.60 million ton cap.**—Whenever the inventory required by this section indicates that sulfur dioxide emissions from industrial sources, including units subject to section 405(g)(5) of the Clean Air Act [section 7651d(g)(5) of this title], may reasonably be expected to reach levels greater than 5.60 million tons per year, the Administrator of the Environmental Protection Agency shall take such actions under the Clean Air Act [this chapter] as may be appropriate to ensure that such emissions do not exceed 5.60 million tons per year. Such actions may include the promulgation of new and revised standards of performance for new sources, including units subject to section 405(g)(5) of the Clean Air Act [section 7651d(g)(5) of this title], under section 111(b) of the Clean Air Act [section 7411(b) of this title], as well as promulgation of standards of performance for existing sources, including units subject to section 405(g)(5) of the Clean Air Act [section 7651d(g)(5) of this title], under authority of this section. For an existing source regulated under this section, 'standard of performance' means a standard which the Administrator determines is applicable to that source and which reflects the degree of emission reduction achievable through the application of the best system of continuous emission reduction which (taking into consideration the cost of achieving such emission reduction, and any nonair quality health and environmental impact and energy requirements) the Administrator determines has been adequately demonstrated for that category of sources.

"**(c) Election.**—Regulations promulgated under section 405(b) of the Clean Air Act [section 7651d(b) of this title] shall not prohibit a source from electing to become an affected unit under section 410 of the Clean Air Act [section 7651i of this title]."

Sense of Congress on Emission Reductions Costs

Section 407 of Pub.L. 101–549 provided that: "It is the sense of the Congress that the Clean Air Act Amendments of 1990 [Pub.L. 101–549, Nov. 15, 1990, 104 Stat. 2399, for distribution of which see Tables], through the allowance program, allocates the costs of achieving the required reductions in emissions of sulfur dioxide and oxides of nitrogen among sources in the United States. Broad based taxes and emissions fees that would provide for payment of the costs of achieving required emissions reductions by any party or parties other than the sources required to achieve the reductions are undesirable."

Monitoring of Acid Rain Program in Canada

Section 408 of Pub.L. 101–549 provided that:

"**(a) Reports to Congress.**—The Administrator of the Environmental Protection Agency, in consultation with the Secretary of State, the Secretary of Energy, and other persons the Administrator deems appropriate, shall prepare and submit a report to Congress on January 1, 1994, January 1, 1999, and January 1, 2005.

"**(b) Contents.**—The report to Congress shall analyze the current emission levels of sulfur dioxide and nitrogen oxides in each of the provinces participating in Canada's acid rain control program, the amount of emission reductions of sulfur dioxide and oxides of nitrogen achieved by each province, the methods utilized by each province in making those reductions, the costs to each province and the employment impacts in each province of making and maintaining those reductions.

"**(c) Compliance.**—Beginning on January 1, 1999, the reports shall also assess the degree to which each province is complying with its stated emissions cap."

§ 7651a. Definitions [CAA § 402]

As used in this subchapter:

(1) The term "affected source" means a source that includes one or more affected units.

(2) The term "affected unit" means a unit that is subject to emission reduction requirements or limitations under this subchapter.

(3) The term "allowance" means an authorization, allocated to an affected unit by the Administrator under this subchapter, to emit, during or after a specified calendar year, one ton of sulfur dioxide.

(4) The term "baseline" means the annual quantity of fossil fuel consumed by an affected unit, measured in millions of British Thermal Units ("mmBtu's"), calculated as follows:

(A) For each utility unit that was in commercial operation prior to January 1, 1985, the baseline shall be the annual average quantity of mmBtu's consumed in fuel during calendar years 1985, 1986, and 1987, as recorded by the Department of Energy pursuant to Form 767. For any utility unit for which such form was not filed, the baseline shall be the level specified for such unit in the 1985 National Acid Precipitation Assessment Program (NAPAP) Emissions Inventory, Version 2, National Utility Reference File (NURF) or in a corrected data base as established by the Administrator pursuant to paragraph (3). For nonutility units, the baseline is the NAPAP Emissions Inventory, Version 2. The Administrator, in the Administrator's sole discretion, may exclude periods during which a unit is shutdown for a continuous period of four calendar months or longer, and make appropriate adjustments under this paragraph. Upon petition of the owner or operator of any unit, the Administrator may make appropriate baseline adjustments for accidents that caused prolonged outages.

(B) For any other nonutility unit that is not included in the NAPAP Emissions Inventory, Version 2, or a corrected data base as established by the Administrator pursuant to paragraph (3), the baseline shall be the annual average quantity, in mmBtu consumed in fuel by that unit, as calculated pursuant to a method which the administrator [1] shall prescribe by regulation to be promulgated not later than eighteen months after enactment of the Clean Air Act Amendments of 1990.

(C) The Administrator shall, upon application or on his own motion, by December 31, 1991, supplement data needed in support of this subchapter and correct any factual errors in data from which affected Phase II units' baselines or actual 1985 emission rates have been calculated. Corrected data shall be used for purposes of issuing allowances under the [2] subchapter. Such corrections shall not be subject to judicial review, nor shall the failure of the Administrator to correct an alleged factual error in such reports be subject to judicial review.

(5) The term "capacity factor" means the ratio between the actual electric output from a unit and the potential electric output from that unit.

(6) The term "compliance plan" means, for purposes of the requirements of this subchapter, either—

(A) a statement that the source will comply with all applicable requirements under this subchapter, or

(B) where applicable, a schedule and description of the method or methods for compliance and certification by the owner or operator that the source is in compliance with the requirements of this subchapter.

(7) The term "continuous emission monitoring system" (CEMS) means the equipment as required by section 7651k of this title, used to sample, analyze, measure, and provide on a continuous basis a permanent record of emissions and flow (expressed in pounds per million British thermal units (lbs/mmBtu), pounds per hour (lbs/hr) or such other form as the Administrator may prescribe by regulations under section 7651k of this title).

(8) The term "existing unit" means a unit (including units subject to section 7411 of this title) that commenced commercial operation before November 15, 1990. Any unit that commenced commercial operation before November 15, 1990 which is modified, reconstructed, or repowered after November 15, 1990 shall continue to be an existing unit for the purposes of this subchapter. For the purposes of this subchapter, existing units shall not include simple combustion turbines, or units which serve a generator with a nameplate capacity of 25MWe or less.

(9) The term "generator" means a device that produces electricity and which is reported as a generating unit pursuant to Department of Energy Form 860.

(10) The term "new unit" means a unit that commences commercial operation on or after November 15, 1990.

(11) The term "permitting authority" means the Administrator, or the State or local air pollution control agency, with an approved permitting program under part B of subchapter III of this chapter.

(12) The term "repowering" means replacement of an existing coal-fired boiler with one of the following clean coal technologies: atmospheric or pressurized fluidized bed combustion, integrated gasification combined cycle, magnetohydrodynamics, direct and indirect coal-fired turbines, integrated gasification fuel cells, or as determined by the

Administrator, in consultation with the Secretary of Energy, a derivative of one or more of these technologies, and any other technology capable of controlling multiple combustion emissions simultaneously with improved boiler or generation efficiency and with significantly greater waste reduction relative to the performance of technology in widespread commercial use as of November 15, 1990. Notwithstanding the provisions of section 7651h(a) of this title, for the purpose of this subchapter, the term "repowering" shall also include any oil and/or gas-fired unit which has been awarded clean coal technology demonstration funding as of January 1, 1991, by the Department of Energy.

(13) The term "reserve" means any bank of allowances established by the Administrator under this subchapter.

(14) The term "State" means one of the 48 contiguous States and the District of Columbia.

(15) The term "unit" means a fossil fuel-fired combustion device.

(16) The term "actual 1985 emission rate", for electric utility units means the annual sulfur dioxide or nitrogen oxides emission rate in pounds per million Btu as reported in the NAPAP Emissions Inventory, Version 2, National Utility Reference File. For nonutility units, the term "actual 1985 emission rate" means the annual sulfur dioxide or nitrogen oxides emission rate in pounds per million Btu as reported in the NAPAP Emission Inventory, Version 2.

(17)(A) The term "utility unit" means—

(i) a unit that serves a generator in any State that produces electricity for sale, or

(ii) a unit that, during 1985, served a generator in any State that produced electricity for sale.

(B) Notwithstanding subparagraph (A), a unit described in subparagraph (A) that—

(i) was in commercial operation during 1985, but

(ii) did not, during 1985, serve a generator in any State that produced electricity for sale shall not be a utility unit for purposes of this subchapter.

(C) A unit that cogenerates steam and electricity is not a "utility unit" for purposes of this subchapter unless the unit is constructed for the purpose of supplying, or commences construction after November 15, 1990, and supplies, more than one-third of its potential electric output capacity and more than 25 megawatts electrical output to any utility power distribution system for sale.

(18) The term "allowable 1985 emissions rate" means a federally enforceable emissions limitation for sulfur dioxide or oxides of nitrogen, applicable to the unit in 1985 or the limitation applicable in such other subsequent year as determined by the Administrator if such a limitation for 1985 does not exist. Where the emissions limitation for a unit is not expressed in pounds of emissions per million Btu, or the averaging period of that emissions limitation is not expressed on an annual basis, the Administrator shall calculate the annual equivalent of that emissions limitation in pounds per million Btu to establish the allowable 1985 emissions rate.

(19) The term "qualifying phase I technology" means a technological system of continuous emission reduction which achieves a 90 percent reduction in emissions of sulfur dioxide from the emissions that would have resulted from the use of fuels which were not subject to treatment prior to combustion.

(20) The term "alternative method of compliance" means a method of compliance in accordance with one or more of the following authorities:

(A) a substitution plan submitted and approved in accordance with subsections (b) and (c) of section 7651c of this title;

(B) a Phase I extension plan approved by the Administrator under section 7651c(d) of this title, using qualifying phase I technology as determined by the Administrator in accordance with that section; or

(C) repowering with a qualifying clean coal technology under section 7651h of this title.

(21) The term "commenced" as applied to construction of any new electric utility unit means that an owner or operator has undertaken a continuous program of construction or that an owner or operator has entered into a contractual obligation to undertake and complete, within a reasonable time, a continuous program of construction.

(22) The term "commenced commercial operation" means to have begun to generate electricity for sale.

(23) The term "construction" means fabrication, erection, or installation of an affected unit.

(24) The term "industrial source" means a unit that does not serve a generator that produces electricity, a 'nonutility unit' as defined in this section, or a process source as defined in section 7651i(e) of this title.

(25) The term "nonutility unit" means a unit other than a utility unit.

(26) The term "designated representative" means a responsible person or official authorized by the owner or operator of a unit to represent the owner or operator in matters pertaining to the holding, transfer, or disposition of allowances allocated to a unit, and the submission of and compliance with permits, permit applications, and compliance plans for the unit.

(27) The term "life-of-the-unit, firm power contractual arrangement" means a unit participation power sales agreement under which a utility or industrial customer reserves, or is entitled to receive, a specified amount or percentage of capacity and associated energy generated by a specified generating unit (or units) and pays its proportional amount of such unit's total costs, pursuant to a contract either—

(A) for the life of the unit;

(B) for a cumulative term of no less than 30 years, including contracts that permit an election for early termination; or

(C) for a period equal to or greater than 25 years or 70 percent of the economic useful life of the unit determined as of the time the unit was built, with option rights to purchase or re-lease some portion of the capacity and associated energy generated by the unit (or units) at the end of the period.

(28) The term "basic Phase II allowance allocations" means:

(A) For calendar years 2000 through 2009 inclusive, allocations of allowances made by the Administrator pursuant to section 7651b of this title and subsections (b)(1), (3), and (4); (c)(1), (2), (3), and (5); (d)(1), (2), (4), and (5); (e); (f); (g)(1), (2), (3), (4), and (5); (h)(1); (i) and (j) of section 7651d of this title.

(B) For each calendar year beginning in 2010, allocations of allowances made by the Administrator pursuant to section 7651b of this title and subsections (b)(1), (3), and (4); (c)(1), (2), (3), and (5); (d)(1), (2), (4) and (5); (e); (f); (g)(1), (2), (3), (4), and (5); (h)(1) and (3); (i) and (j) of section 7651d of this title.

(29) The term "Phase II bonus allowance allocations" means, for calendar year 2000 through 2009, inclusive, and only for such years, allocations made by the Administrator pursuant to section 7651b of this title, subsections (a)(2), (b)(2), (c)(4), (d)(3) (except as otherwise provided therein), and (h)(2) of section 7651d of this title, and section 7651e of this title.

(July 14, 1955, ch. 360, title IV, § 402, as added Nov. 15, 1990, Pub.L. 101–549, title IV, § 401, 104 Stat. 2585.)

1 So in original. Probably should be capitalized.

2 So in original. Probably should be "this".

Codification

There are two sections 402 of Act July 14, 1955, c. 360, Title IV, as amended. Section 402, as added Pub.L. 91–604, is classified as section 7641 of this title. Section 402, as added Pub.L. 101–549, is classified as this section.

References in Text

Enactment of the Clean Air Act Amendments of 1990, referred to in par. (4)(B), probably means the date of enactment of Pub.L. 101–549, Nov. 15, 1990, 104 Stat. 2399, which was approved Nov. 15, 1990.

An approved permitting program under part B of title III of the Act, referred to in par. (11), probably means an approved permitting program under subchapter V of this chapter. A literal interpretation of part B of title III of this Act would mean part B of title III (section 301 et seq.) of Act July 14, 1955, c. 360, as added Dec. 17, 1963, Pub.L. 88–206, 77 Stat. 400, as amended, which is classified to subchapter III of this chapter, however, such title and such chapter have no part B. Likewise, subchapter V of this chapter contains no part B, however, subchapter V of this chapter specifically addresses permit programs.

Sections 7651c(b) and 7651c(c) of this title, referred to in par. (20)(A), was in the original subsections 404(b) and (c). The translation was made to sections 7651c(b) and 7651c(c) of this title as the probable intent of Congress.

Effective Date

Section to take effect Nov. 15, 1990, except as otherwise provided, see section 711(b) of Pub.L. 101–549, set out as a note under section 7401 of this title.

Savings Provisions

Suits, actions or proceedings commenced under this chapter as in effect prior to Nov. 15, 1990, not to abate by reason of the taking effect of amendments by Pub.L. 101–549, except as otherwise provided for, see section 711(a) of Pub.L. 101–549, set out as a note under section 7401 of this title.

§ 7651b. Sulfur dioxide allowance program for existing and new units [CAA § 403]

(a) Allocations of annual allowances for existing and new units

(1) For the emission limitation programs under this subchapter, the Administrator shall allocate annual allowances for the unit, to be held or distributed by the designated representative of the owner or operator of each affected unit at an affected source in accordance with this subchapter, in an amount equal to the annual tonnage emission limitation calculated under section[1] 7651c, 7651d, 7651e, 7651h, or 7651i of this title except as otherwise specifically provided elsewhere in this title. Except as provided in sections 7651d(a)(2), 7651d(a)(3), 7651h and 7651i of this title beginning January 1, 2000, the Administrator shall not allocate annual allowances to emit sulfur dioxide pursuant to section 7651d of this title in such an amount as would result in total annual emissions of sulfur dioxide from utility units in excess of 8.90 million tons except that the Administrator shall not take into account unused allowances carried forward by owners and operators of affected units or by other persons holding such allowances, following the year for which they were allocated. If necessary to meeting the restrictions imposed in the preceding sentence, the Administrator shall reduce, pro rata, the basic Phase II allowance allocations for each unit subject to the requirements of section 7651d of this title. Subject to the provisions of section 7651*o* of this title, the Administrator shall allocate allowances for each affected unit at an affected source annually, as provided in paragraphs (2) and (3) and section 7651g of this title. Except as provided in sections 7651h and 7651i of this title, the removal of an existing affected unit or source from commercial operation at any time after November 15, 1990 (whether before or after January 1, 1995, or January 1, 2000) shall not terminate or otherwise affect the allocation of allowances pursuant to section 7651c or 7651d of this title to which the unit is entitled. Allowances shall be allocated by the Administrator without cost to the recipient, except for allowances sold by the Administrator pursuant to section 7651*o* of this title. Not later than December 31, 1991, the Administrator shall publish a proposed list of the basic Phase II allowance allocations, the Phase II bonus allowance allocations and, if applicable, allocations pursuant to section 7651d(a)(3) of this title for each unit subject to the emissions limitation requirements of section 7651d of this title for the year 2000 and the year 2010. After notice and opportunity for public comment, but not later than December 31, 1992, the Administrator shall publish a final list of such allocations, subject to the provisions of section 7651d(a)(2) of this title. Any owner or operator of an existing unit subject to the requirements of section 7651d(b) or (c) of this title who is considering applying for an extension of the emission limitation requirement compliance deadline for that unit from January 1, 2000, until not later than December 31, 2000, pursuant to section 7651h of this title, shall notify the Administrator no later than March 31, 1991. Such notification shall be used as the basis for estimating the basic Phase II allowances under this subsection. Prior to June 1, 1998, the Administrator shall publish a revised final statement of allowance allocations, subject to the provisions of section 7651d(a)(2) of this title and taking into account the effect of any compliance date extensions granted pursuant to section 7651h of this title on such allocations. Any person who may make an election concerning the amount of allowances to be allocated to a unit or units shall make such election and so inform the Administrator not later than March 31, 1991, in the case of an election under section 7651d of this title (or June 30, 1991, in the case of an election under section 7651e of this title). If such person fails to make such election, the Administrator shall set forth for each unit owned or operated by such person, the amount of allowances reflecting the election that would, in the judgment of the Administrator, provide the greatest benefit for the owner or operator of the unit. If such person is a Governor who may make an election under section 7651e of this title and the Governor fails to make an election, the Administrator shall set forth for each unit in the State the amount of allowances reflecting the election that would, in the judgment of the Administrator, provide the greatest benefit for units in the State.

(b) Allowance transfer system

Allowances allocated under this subchapter may be transferred among designated representatives of the owners or operators of affected sources under this subchapter and any other person who holds such allowances, as provided by the allowance system regulations to be promulgated by the Administrator not later than eighteen months after November 15, 1990. Such regulations shall establish the allowance system prescribed under this section, including, but not limited to, requirements for the allocation, transfer, and use of allowances under this subchapter. Such regulations shall prohibit the use of any allowance prior to the calendar year for which the allowance was allocated, and shall provide, consistent with the purposes of this subchapter, for the identification of unused allowances, and for such unused allowances to be carried forward and added to allowances allocated in subsequent years, including allowances allocated to units subject to Phase I requirements (as described in section 7651c of this title) which are applied to emissions limitations requirements in Phase II (as described in section 7651d of this title). Transfers of allowances shall not be effective until written certification of the transfer, signed by a responsible official of each party to the transfer, is received and recorded by the Administrator. Such regulations shall permit the transfer of allowances prior to the issuance of such allowances. Recorded pre-allocation transfers shall be deducted by the Administrator from the number of allowances which would otherwise be allocated to the transferor, and added to those allowances allocated to the transferee. Pre-allocation transfers shall not affect the prohibition contained in this subsection against the use of allowances prior to the year for which they are allocated.

(c) Interpollutant trading

Not later than January 1, 1994, the Administrator shall furnish to the Congress a study evaluating the environmental and economic consequences of amending this subchapter to permit trading sulfur dioxide allowances for nitrogen oxides allowances.

(d) Allowance tracking system

(1) The Administrator shall promulgate, not later than 18 months after November 15, 1990, a system for issuing, recording, and tracking allowances, which shall specify all necessary procedures and requirements for an orderly and competitive functioning of the allowance system. All allowance allocations and transfers shall, upon recordation by the Administrator, be deemed a part of each unit's permit requirements pursuant to section 7651g of this title, without any further permit review and revision.

(2) In order to insure electric reliability, such regulations shall not prohibit or affect temporary increases and decreases in emissions within utility systems, power pools, or utilities entering into allowance pool agreements, that result from their operations, including emergencies and central dispatch, and such temporary emissions increases and decreases shall not require transfer of allowances among units nor shall it require recordation. The owners or operators of such units shall act through a designated representative. Notwithstanding the preceding sentence, the total tonnage of emissions in any calendar year (calculated at the end thereof) from all units in such a utility system, power pool, or allowance pool agreements shall not exceed the total allowances for such units for the calendar year concerned.

(e) New utility units

After January 1, 2000, it shall be unlawful for a new utility unit to emit an annual tonnage of sulfur dioxide in excess of the number of allowances to emit held for the unit by the unit's owner or operator. Such new utility units shall not be eligible for an allocation of sulfur dioxide allowances under subsection (a)(1) of this section, unless the unit is subject to the provisions of subsection (g)(2) or (3) of section 7651d of this title. New utility units may obtain allowances from any person, in accordance with this subchapter. The owner or operator of any new utility unit in violation of this subsection shall be liable for fulfilling the obligations specified in section 7651j of this title.

(f) Nature of allowances

An allowance allocated under this subchapter is a limited authorization to emit sulfur dioxide in accordance with the provisions of this subchapter. Such allowance does not constitute a property right. Nothing in this subchapter or in any other provision of law shall be construed to limit the authority of the United States to terminate or limit such authorization. Nothing in this section relating to allowances shall be construed as affecting the application of, or compliance with, any other provision of this chapter to an affected unit or source, including the provisions related to applicable National Ambient Air Quality Standards and State implementation plans. Nothing in this section shall be construed as requiring a change of any kind in any State law regulating electric utility rates and charges or affecting any State law regarding such State regulation or as limiting State regulation (including any prudency review) under such a State law. Nothing in this section shall be construed as modifying the Federal Power Act [16 U.S.C.A. § 791a et seq.] or as affecting the authority of the Federal Energy Regulatory Commission under that Act. Nothing in this subchapter shall be construed to interfere with or impair any program for competitive bidding for power supply in a State in which such program is established. Allowances, once allocated to a person by the Administrator, may be received, held, and temporarily or permanently transferred in accordance with this subchapter and the regulations of the Administrator without regard to whether or not a permit is in effect under subchapter V of this chapter or section 7651g of this title with respect to the unit for which such allowance was originally allocated and recorded. Each permit under this subchapter and each permit issued under subchapter V of this chapter for any affected unit shall provide that the affected unit may not emit an annual tonnage of sulfur dioxide in excess of the allowances held for that unit.

(g) Prohibition

It shall be unlawful for any person to hold, use, or transfer any allowance allocated under this subchapter, except in accordance with regulations promulgated by the Administrator. It shall be unlawful for any affected unit to emit sulfur dioxide in excess of the number of allowances held for that unit for that year by the owner or operator of the unit. Upon the allocation of allowances under this subchapter, the prohibition contained in the preceding sentence shall supersede any other emission limitation applicable under this subchapter to the units for which such allowances are allocated. Allowances may not be used prior to the calendar year for which they are allocated. Nothing in this section or in the allowance system regulations shall relieve the Administrator of the Administrator's permitting, monitoring and enforcement obligations under this chapter, nor relieve affected sources of their requirements and liabilities under this chapter.

(h) Competitive bidding for power supply

Nothing in this subchapter shall be construed to interfere with or impair any program for competitive bidding for power supply in a State in which such program is established.

(i) Applicability of the antitrust laws

(1) Nothing in this section affects—

(A) the applicability of the antitrust laws to the transfer, use, or sale of allowances, or

(B) the authority of the Federal Energy Regulatory Commission under any provision of law respecting unfair methods of competition or anticompetitive acts or practices.

(2) As used in this section, "antitrust laws" means those Acts set forth in section 12 of Title 15.

(j) Public Utility Holding Company Act

The acquisition or disposition of allowances pursuant to this subchapter including the issuance of securities or the undertaking of any other financing transaction in connection with such allowances shall not be subject to the provisions of the Public Utility Holding Company Act of 1935 [15 U.S.C.A. § 79 et seq.].

(July 14, 1955, ch. 360, title IV, § 403, as added Nov. 15, 1990, Pub.L. 101–549, title IV, § 401, 104 Stat. 2589.)

1 So in original. Probably should be "sections".

Codification

There are two sections 403 of Act July 14, 1955, c. 360, Title IV, as amended. Section 403, as added Pub.L. 91–604, is classified as section 7642 of this title. Section 403, as added Pub.L. 101–549, is classified as this section.

References in Text

The Federal Power Act, referred to in subsec. (f), is Act June 10, 1920, c. 285, 41 Stat. 1063, as amended, which is classified generally to chapter 12 (section 791a et seq.) of Title 16, Conservation.

That Act, referred to in subsec. (f), is a reference to this same Act. For complete classification of this Act to the Code, see section 791a of Title 16 and Tables.

The antitrust laws, referred to in subsec. (i), are classified generally to Title 15, Commerce and Trade.

The Public Utility Holding Company Act of 1935, referred to in subsec. (j), is the Public Utility Holding Company Act of 1935, Act Aug. 26, 1935, c. 687, Title I, 49 Stat. 838, as amended, which is classified generally to chapter 2C (section 79 et seq.) of Title 15, Commerce and Trade. For complete classification of this Act to the Code, see section 79 of Title 15 and Tables.

Effective Date

Section to take effect Nov. 15, 1990, except as otherwise provided, see section 711(b) of Pub.L. 101–549, set out as a note under section 7401 of this title.

Savings Provisions

Suits, actions or proceedings commenced under this chapter as in effect prior to Nov. 15, 1990, not to abate by reason of the taking effect of amendments by Pub.L. 101–549, except as otherwise provided for, see section 711(a) of Pub.L. 101–549, set out as a note under section 7401 of this title.

Fossil Fuel Use

Section 402 of Pub.L. 101–549 provided that:

"**(a) Contracts for hydroelectric energy.**—Any person who, after the date of the enactment of the Clean Air Act Amendments of 1990 [Nov. 15, 1990], enters into a contract under which such person receives hydroelectric energy in return for the provision of electric energy by such person shall use allowances held by such person as necessary to satisfy such person's obligations under such contract.

"**(b) Federal Power Marketing Administration.**—A Federal Power Marketing Administration shall not be subject to the provisions and requirements of this title [this subchapter] with respect to electric energy generated by hydroelectric facilities and marketed by such Power Marketing Administration. Any person who sells or provides electric energy to a Federal Power Marketing Administration shall comply with the provisions and requirements of this title [this subchapter]."

§ 7651c. Phase I sulfur dioxide requirements [CAA § 404]

(a) Emission limitations

(1) After January 1, 1995, each source that includes one or more affected units listed in table A is an affected source under this section. After January 1, 1995, it shall be unlawful for any affected unit (other than an eligible phase I unit under subsection (d)(2) of this section) to emit sulfur dioxide in excess of the tonnage limitation stated as a total number of allowances in table A for phase I, unless (A) the emissions reduction requirements applicable to such unit have been achieved pursuant to subsection (b) or (d) of this section, or (B) the owner or operator of such unit holds allowances to emit not less than the unit's total annual emissions, except that, after January 1, 2000, the emissions limitations established in this section shall be superseded by those established in section 7651d of this title. The owner or operator of any unit in violation of this section shall be fully liable for such violation including, but not limited to, liability for fulfilling the obligations specified in section 7651j of this title.

(2) Not later than December 31, 1991, the Administrator shall determine the total tonnage of reductions in the emissions of sulfur dioxide from all utility units in calendar year 1995 that will occur as a result of compliance with the emissions limitation requirements of this section, and shall establish a reserve of allowances equal in amount to the number of tons determined thereby not to exceed a total of 3.50 million tons. In making such a determination, the Administrator shall compute for each unit subject to the emissions limitation requirements of this section the difference between:

(A) the product of its baseline multiplied by the lesser of each unit's allowable 1985 emissions rate and its actual 1985 emissions rate, divided by 2,000, and

(B) the product of each unit's baseline multiplied by 2.50 lbs/mmBtu divided by 2,000,

and sum the computations. The Administrator shall adjust the foregoing calculation to reflect projected calendar year 1995 utilization of the units subject to the emissions limitations of this subchapter that the Administrator finds would have occurred in the absence of the imposition of such requirements. Pursuant to subsection (d) of this section, the Administrator shall allocate allowances from the reserve established hereinunder until the earlier of such time as all such allowances in the reserve are allocated or December 31, 1999.

(3) In addition to allowances allocated pursuant to paragraph (1), in each calendar year beginning in 1995 and ending in 1999, inclusive, the Administrator shall allocate for each unit on Table A that is located in the States of Illinois, Indiana, or Ohio (other than units at Kyger Creek, Clifty Creek and Joppa Steam [1]), allowances in an amount equal to 200,000 multiplied by the unit's pro rata share of the total number of allowances allocated for all units on Table A in the 3 States (other than units at Kyger Creek, Clifty Creek, and Joppa Steam [1]) pursuant to paragraph (1). Such allowances shall be excluded from the calculation of the reserve under paragraph (2).

(b) Substitutions

The owner or operator of an affected unit under subsection (a) of this section may include in its section 7651g of this title permit application and proposed compliance plan a proposal to reassign, in whole or in part, the affected unit's sulfur dioxide reduction requirements to any other unit(s) under the control of such owner or operator. Such proposal shall specify—

(1) the designation of the substitute unit or units to which any part of the reduction obligations of subsection (a) of this section shall be required, in addition to, or in lieu of, any original affected units designated under such subsection;

(2) the original affected unit's baseline, the actual and allowable 1985 emissions rate for sulfur dioxide, and the authorized annual allowance allocation stated in table A;

(3) calculation of the annual average tonnage for calendar years 1985, 1986, and 1987, emitted by the substitute unit or units, based on the baseline for each unit, as defined in section 7651a(d) of this title, multiplied by the lesser of the unit's actual or allowable 1985 emissions rate;

(4) the emissions rates and tonnage limitations that would be applicable to the original and substitute affected units under the substitution proposal;

(5) documentation, to the satisfaction of the Administrator, that the reassigned tonnage limits will, in total, achieve the same or greater emissions reduction than would have been achieved by the original affected unit and the substitute unit or units without such substitution; and

(6) such other information as the Administrator may require.

(c) Administrator's action on substitution proposals

(1) The Administrator shall take final action on such substitution proposal in accordance with section 7651g(c) of this title if the substitution proposal fulfills the requirements of this subsection. The Administrator may approve a substitution proposal in whole or in part and with such modifications or conditions as may be consistent with the orderly functioning of the allowance system and which will ensure the emissions reductions contemplated by this subchapter. If a proposal does not meet the requirements of subsection (b) of this section, the Administrator shall disapprove it. The owner or operator of a unit listed in table A shall not substitute another unit or units without the prior approval of the Administrator.

(2) Upon approval of a substitution proposal, each substitute unit, and each source with such unit, shall be deemed affected under this subchapter, and the Administrator shall issue a permit to the original and substitute affected source and unit in accordance with the approved substitution plan and section 7651g of this title. The Administrator shall allocate allowances for the original and substitute affected units in accordance with the approved substitution proposal pursuant to section 7651b of this title. It shall be unlawful for any source or unit that is allocated allowances pursuant to this section to emit sulfur dioxide in excess of the emissions limitation provided for in the approved substitution permit and plan unless the owner or operator of each unit governed by the permit and approved substitution plan holds allowances to emit not less than the units total annual emissions. The owner or operator of any original or substitute affected unit operated in violation of this subsection shall be fully liable for such violation, including liability for fulfilling the obligations specified in section 7651j of this title. If a substitution proposal is disapproved, the Administrator shall allocate allowances to the original affected unit or units in accordance with subsection (a) of this section.

(d) Eligible Phase I extension units

(1) The owner or operator of any affected unit subject to an emissions limitation requirement under this section may petition the Administrator in its permit application under section 7651g of this title for an extension of 2 years of the deadline for meeting such requirement, provided that the owner or operator of any such unit holds allowances to emit not less than the unit's total annual emissions for each of the 2 years of the period of extension. To qualify for such an extension, the affected unit must either employ a qualifying phase I technology, or transfer its phase I emissions reduction obligation to a unit employing a qualifying phase I technology. Such transfer shall be accomplished in accordance with a compliance plan, submitted and approved under section 7651g of this title, that shall govern operations at all units included in the transfer, and that specifies the emissions reduc-

tion requirements imposed pursuant to this subchapter.

(2) Such extension proposal shall—

(A) specify the unit or units proposed for designation as an eligible phase I extension unit;

(B) provide a copy of an executed contract, which may be contingent upon the Administrator approving the proposal, for the design engineering, and construction of the qualifying phase I technology for the extension unit, or for the unit or units to which the extension unit's emission reduction obligation is to be transferred;

(C) specify the unit's or units' baseline, actual 1985 emissions rate, allowable 1985 emissions rate, and projected utilization for calendar years 1995 through 1999;

(D) require CEMS on both the eligible phase I extension unit or units and the transfer unit or units beginning no later than January 1, 1995; and

(E) specify the emission limitation and number of allowances expected to be necessary for annual operation after the qualifying phase I technology has been installed.

(3) The Administrator shall review and take final action on each extension proposal in order of receipt, consistent with section 7651g of this title, and for an approved proposal shall designate the unit or units as an eligible phase I extension unit. The Administrator may approve an extension proposal in whole or in part, and with such modifications or conditions as may be necessary, consistent with the orderly functioning of the allowance system, and to ensure the emissions reductions contemplated by the subchapter.

(4) In order to determine the number of proposals eligible for allocations from the reserve under subsection (a)(2) and the number of allowances remaining available after each proposal is acted upon, the Administrator shall reduce the total number of allowances remaining available in the reserve by the number of allowances calculated according to subparagraphs (A), (B) and (C) until either no allowances remain available in the reserve for further allocation or all approved proposals have been acted upon. If no allowances remain available in the reserve for further allocation before all proposals have been acted upon by the Administrator, any pending proposals shall be disapproved. The Administrator shall calculate allowances equal to—

(A) the difference between the lesser of the average annual emissions in calendar years 1988 and 1989 or the projected emissions tonnage for calendar year 1995 of each eligible phase I extension unit, as designated under paragraph (3), and the product of the unit's baseline multiplied by an emission rate of 2.50 lbs/mmBtu, divided by 2,000;

(B) the difference between the lesser of the average annual emissions in calendar years 1988 and 1989 or the projected emissions tonnage for calendar year 1996 of each eligible phase I extension unit, as designated under paragraph (3), and the product of the unit's baseline multiplied by an emission rate of 2.50 lbs/mmBtu, divided by 2,000; and

(C) the amount by which (i) the product of each unit's baseline multiplied by an emission rate of 1.20 lbs/mmBtu, divided by 2,000, exceeds (ii) the tonnage level specified under subparagraph (E) of paragraph (2) of this subsection multiplied by a factor of 3.

(5) Each eligible Phase I extension unit shall receive allowances determined under subsection (a)(1) or (c) of this section. In addition, for calendar year 1995, the Administrator shall allocate to each eligible Phase I extension unit, from the allowance reserve created pursuant to subsection (a)(2) of this section, allowances equal to the difference between the lesser of the average annual emissions in calendar years 1988 and 1989 or its projected emissions tonnage for calendar year 1995 and the product of the unit's baseline multiplied by an emission rate of 2.50 lbs/mmBtu, divided by 2,000. In calendar year 1996, the Administrator shall allocate for each eligible unit, from the allowance reserve created pursuant to subsection (a)(2) of this section, allowances equal to the difference between the lesser of the average annual emissions in calendar years 1988 and 1989 or its projected emissions tonnage for calendar year 1996 and the product of the unit's baseline multiplied by an emission rate of 2.50 lbs/mmBtu, divided by 2,000. It shall be unlawful for any source or unit subject to an approved extension plan under this subsection to emit sulfur dioxide in excess of the emissions limitations provided for in the permit and approved extension plan, unless the owner or operator of each unit governed by the permit and approved plan holds allowances to emit not less than the unit's total annual emissions.

(6) In addition to allowances specified in paragraph (5), the Administrator shall allocate for each eligible Phase I extension unit employing qualifying Phase I technology, for calendar years 1997, 1998, and 1999, additional allowances, from any remaining allowances in the reserve created pursuant to subsection (a)(2) of this section, following the reduction in the reserve provided for in paragraph (4), not to exceed the amount by which (A) the product of each eligible unit's baseline times an emission rate of 1.20 lbs/mmBtu, divided by 2,000, exceeds (B) the tonnage level speci-

fied under subparagraph (E) of paragraph (2) of this subsection.

(7) After January 1, 1997, in addition to any liability under this chapter, including under section 7651j of this title, if any eligible phase I extension unit employing qualifying phase I technology or any transfer unit under this subsection emits sulfur dioxide in excess of the annual tonnage limitation specified in the extension plan, as approved in paragraph (3) of this subsection, the Administrator shall, in the calendar year following such excess, deduct allowances equal to the amount of such excess from such unit's annual allowance allocation.

(e) Allocation of allowances

(1) In the case of a unit that receives authorization from the Governor of the State in which such unit is located to make reductions in the emissions of sulfur dioxide prior to calendar year 1995 and that is part of a utility system that meets the following requirements: (A) the total coal-fired generation within the utility system as a percentage of total system generation decreased by more than 20 percent between January 1, 1980, and December 31, 1985; and (B) the weighted capacity factor of all coal-fired units within the utility system averaged over the period from January 1, 1985, through December 31, 1987, was below 50 percent, the Administrator shall allocate allowances under this paragraph for the unit pursuant to this subsection. The Administrator shall allocate allowances for a unit that is an affected unit pursuant to section 7651d of this title (but is not also an affected unit under this section) and part of a utility system that includes 1 or more affected units under section 7651d of this title for reductions in the emissions of sulfur dioxide made during the period 1995–1999 if the unit meets the requirements of this subsection and the requirements of the preceding sentence, except that for the purposes of applying this subsection to any such unit, the prior year concerned as specified below, shall be any year after January 1, 1995 but prior to January 1, 2000.

(2) In the case of an affected unit under this section described in subparagraph (A), the allowances allocated under this subsection for early reductions in any prior year may not exceed the amount which (A) the product of the unit's baseline multiplied by the unit's 1985 actual sulfur dioxide emission rate (in lbs. per mmBtu), divided by 2,000, exceeds (B) the allowances specified for such unit in Table A. In the case of an affected unit under section 7651d of this title described in subparagraph (A), the allowances awarded under this subsection for early reductions in any prior year may not exceed the amount by which (i) the product of the quantity of fossil fuel consumed by the unit (in mmBtu) in the prior year multiplied by the lesser of 2.50 or the most stringent emission rate (in lbs. per mmBtu) applicable to the unit under the applicable implementation plan, divided by 2,000, exceeds (ii) the unit's actual tonnage of sulfur dioxide emission for the prior year concerned. Allowances allocated under this subsection for units referred to in subparagraph (A) may be allocated only for emission reductions achieved as a result of physical changes or changes in the method of operation made after November 15, 1990, including changes in the type or quality of fossil fuel consumed.

(3) In no event shall the provisions of this paragraph be interpreted as an event of force majeur or a commercial impractibility[2] or in any other way as a basis for excused nonperformance by a utility system under a coal sales contract in effect before November 15, 1990.

TABLE A.—AFFECTED SOURCES AND UNITS IN PHASE I AND THEIR SULFUR DIOXIDE ALLOWANCES (TONS)

State	Plant Name	Generator	Phase I Allowances
Alabama	Colbert	1	13,570
		2	15,310
		3	15,400
		4	15,410
		5	37,180
	E.C. Gaston	1	18,100
		2	18,540
		3	18,310
		4	19,280
		5	59,840
Florida	Big Bend	1	28,410
		2	27,100
		3	26,740
	Crist	6	19,200
		7	31,680
Georgia	Bowen	1	56,320
		2	54,770
		3	71,750
		4	71,740
	Hammond	1	8,780
		2	9,220
		3	8,910
		4	37,640
	J. McDonough	1	19,910
		2	20,600
	Wansley	1	70,770
		2	65,430
	Yates	1	7,210
		2	7,040
		3	6,950
		4	8,910
		5	9,410
		6	24,760
		7	21,480
Illinois	Baldwin	1	42,010
		2	44,420
		3	42,550
	Coffeen	1	11,790
		2	35,670
	Grand Tower	4	5,910
	Hennepin	2	18,410
	Joppa Steam 1	1	12,590

State	Plant Name	Generator	Phase I Allowances
		2	10,770
		3	12,270
		4	11,360
		5	11,420
		6	10,620
	Kincaid	1	31,530
		2	33,810
	Meredosia	3	13,890
	Vermilion	2	8,880
Indiana	Bailly	7	11,180
		8	15,630
	Breed	1	18,500
	Cayuga	1	33,370
		2	34,130
	Clifty Creek	1	20,150
		2	19,810
		3	20,410
		4	20,080
		5	19,360
		6	20,380
	E.W. Stout	5	3,880
		6	4,770
		7	23,610
	F.B. Culley	2	4,290
		3	16,970
	F.E. Ratts	1	8,330
		2	8,480
	Gibson	1	40,400
		2	41,010
		3	41,080
		4	40,320
	H.T. Pritchard	6	5,770
	Michigan City	12	23,310
	Petersburg	1	16,430
		2	32,380
	R. Gallagher	1	6,490
		2	7,280
		3	6,530
		4	7,650
	Tanners Creek	4	24,820
	Wabash River	1	4,000
		2	2,860
		3	3,750
		5	3,670
		6	12,280
	Warrick	4	26,980
Iowa	Burlington	1	10,710
	Des Moines	7	2,320
	George Neal	1	1,290
	M.L. Kapp	2	13,800
	Prairie Creek	4	8,180
	Riverside	5	3,990
Kansas	Quindaro	2	4,220
Kentucky	Coleman	1	11,250
		2	12,840
		3	12,340
	Cooper	1	7,450
		2	15,320
	E.W. Brown	1	7,110
		2	10,910
		3	26,100
	Elmer Smith	1	6,520
		2	14,410
	Ghent	1	28,410
	Green River	4	7,820
	H.L. Spurlock	1	22,780
	Henderson II	1	13,340
		2	12,310
	Paradise	3	59,170
	Shawnee	10	10,170
Maryland	Chalk Point	1	21,910
		2	24,330

State	Plant Name	Generator	Phase I Allowances
	C.P. Crane	1	10,330
		2	9,230
	Morgantown	1	35,260
		2	38,480
Michigan	J.H. Campbell	1	19,280
		2	23,060
Minnesota	High Bridge	6	4,270
Mississippi	Jack Watson	4	17,910
		5	36,700
Missouri	Asbury	1	16,190
	James River	5	4,850
	Labadie	1	40,110
		2	37,710
		3	40,310
		4	35,940
	Montrose	1	7,390
		2	8,200
		3	10,090
	New Madrid	1	28,240
		2	32,480
	Sibley	3	15,580
	Sioux	1	22,570
		2	23,690
	Thomas Hill	1	10,250
		2	19,390
New Hampshire	Merrimack	1	10,190
		2	22,000
New Jersey	B.L. England	1	9,060
		2	11,720
New York	Dunkirk	3	12,600
		4	14,060
	Greenidge	4	7,540
	Milliken	1	11,170
		2	12,410
	Northport	1	19,810
		2	24,110
		3	26,480
	Port Jefferson	3	10,470
		4	12,330
Ohio	Ashtabula	5	16,740
	Avon Lake	8	11,650
		9	30,480
	Cardinal	1	34,270
		2	38,320
	Conesville	1	4,210
		2	4,890
		3	5,500
		4	48,770
	Eastlake	1	7,800
		2	8,640
		3	10,020
		4	14,510
		5	34,070
	Edgewater	4	5,050
	Gen. J.M. Gavin	1	79,080
		2	80,560
	Kyger Creek	1	19,280
		2	18,560
		3	17,910
		4	18,710
		5	18,740
	Miami Fort	5	760
		6	11,380
		7	38,510
	Muskingum River	1	14,880
		2	14,170
		3	13,950
		4	11,780
		5	40,470
	Niles	1	6,940
		2	9,100
	Picway	5	4,930

State	Plant Name	Generator	Phase I Allowances
	R.E. Burger	3	6,150
		4	10,780
		5	12,430
	W.H. Sammis	5	24,170
		6	39,930
		7	43,220
	W.C. Beckjord	5	8,950
		6	23,020
Pennsylvania	Armstrong	1	14,410
		2	15,430
	Brunner Island	1	27,760
		2	31,100
		3	53,820
	Cheswick	1	39,170
	Conemaugh	1	59,790
		2	66,450
	Hatfield's Ferry	1	37,830
		2	37,320
		3	40,270
	Martins Creek	1	12,660
		2	12,820
	Portland	1	5,940
		2	10,230
	Shawville	1	10,320
		2	10,320
		3	14,220
		4	14,070
	Sunbury	3	8,760
		4	11,450
Tennessee	Allen	1	15,320
		2	16,770
		3	15,670
	Cumberland	1	86,700
		2	94,840
	Gallatin	1	17,870
		2	17,310
		3	20,020
		4	21,260
	Johnsonville	1	7,790
		2	8,040
		3	8,410
		4	7,990
		5	8,240
		6	7,890
		7	8,980
		8	8,700
		9	7,080
		10	7,550
West Virginia	Albright	3	12,000
	Fort Martin	1	41,590
		2	41,200
	Harrison	1	48,620
		2	46,150
		3	41,500
	Kammer	1	18,740
		2	19,460
		3	17,390
	Mitchell	1	43,980
		2	45,510
	Mount Storm	1	43,720
		2	35,580
		3	42,430
Wisconsin	Edgewater	4	24,750
	La Crosse/Genoa	3	22,700
	Nelson Dewey	1	6,010
		2	6,680
	N. Oak Creek	1	5,220
		2	5,140
		3	5,370
		4	6,320
	Pulliam	8	7,510
	S. Oak Creek	5	9,670
		6	12,040
		7	16,180
		8	15,790

(f) Energy conservation and renewable energy

(1) Definitions

As used in this subsection:

(A) Qualified energy conservation measure

The term "qualified energy conservation measure" means a cost effective measure, as identified by the Administrator in consultation with the Secretary of Energy, that increases the efficiency of the use of electricity provided by an electric utility to its customers.

(B) Qualified renewable energy

The term "qualified renewable energy" means energy derived from biomass, solar, geothermal, or wind as identified by the Administrator in consultation with the Secretary of Energy.

(C) Electric utility

The term "electric utility" means any person, State agency, or Federal agency, which sells electric energy.

(2) Allowances for emissions avoided through energy conservation and renewable energy

(A) In general

The regulations under paragraph (4) of this subsection shall provide that for each ton of sulfur dioxide emissions avoided by an electric utility, during the applicable period, through the use of qualified energy conservation measures or qualified renewable energy, the Administrator shall allocate a single allowance to such electric utility, on a first-come-first-served basis from the Conservation and Renewable Energy Reserve established under subsection (g) of this section, up to a total of 300,000 allowances for allocation from such Reserve.

(B) Requirements for issuance

The Administrator shall allocate allowances to an electric utility under this subsection only if all of the following requirements are met:

(i) Such electric utility is paying for the qualified energy conservation measures or qualified renewable energy directly or through purchase from another person.

(ii) The emissions of sulfur dioxide avoided through the use of qualified energy conservation measures or qualified renewable energy are quantified in accordance with regulations promulgated by the Administrator under this subsection.

(iii)(I) Such electric utility has adopted and is implementing a least cost energy conservation and electric power plan which evaluates a range of resources, including new power supplies, energy conservation, and renewable energy resources, in order to meet expected future demand at the lowest system cost.

(II) The qualified energy conservation measures or qualified renewable energy, or both, are consistent with that plan.

(III) Electric utilities subject to the jurisdiction of a State regulatory authority must have such plan approved by such authority. For electric utilities not subject to the jurisdiction of a State regulatory authority such plan shall be approved by the entity with ratemaking authority for such utility.

(iv) In the case of qualified energy conservation measures undertaken by a State regulated electric utility, the Secretary of Energy certifies that the State regulatory authority with jurisdiction over the electric rates of such electric utility has established rates and charges which ensure that the net income of such electric utility after implementation of specific cost effective energy conservation measures is at least as high as such net income would have been if the energy conservation measures had not been implemented. Upon the date of any such certification by the Secretary of Energy, all allowances which, but for this paragraph, would have been allocated under subparagraph (A) before such date, shall be allocated to the electric utility. This clause is not a requirement for qualified renewable energy.

(v) Such utility or any subsidiary of the utility's holding company owns or operates at least one affected unit.

(C) Period of applicability

Allowances under this subsection shall be allocated only with respect to kilowatt hours of electric energy saved by qualified energy conservation measures or generated by qualified renewable energy after January 1, 1992 and before the earlier of (i) December 31, 2000, or (ii) the date on which any electric utility steam generating unit owned or operated by the electric utility to which the allowances are allocated becomes subject to this subchapter (including those sources that elect to become affected by this title, pursuant to section 7651i of this title).

(D) Determination of avoided emissions

(i) Application

In order to receive allowances under this subsection, an electric utility shall make an application which—

(I) designates the qualified energy conservation measures implemented and the qualified renewable energy sources used for purposes of avoiding emissions,

(II) calculates, in accordance with subparagraphs (F) and (G), the number of tons of emissions avoided by reason of the implementation of such measures or the use of such renewable energy sources; and

(III) demonstrates that the requirements of subparagraph (B) have been met.

Such application for allowances by a State-regulated electric utility shall require approval by the State regulatory authority with jurisdiction over such electric utility. The authority shall review the application for accuracy and compliance with this subsection and the rules under this subsection. Electric utilities whose retail rates are not subject to the jurisdiction of a State regulatory authority shall apply directly to the Administrator for such approval.

(E) Avoided emissions from qualified energy conservation measures

For the purposes of this subsection, the emission tonnage deemed avoided by reason of the implementation of qualified energy conservation measures for any calendar year shall be a tonnage equal to the product of multiplying—

(i) the kilowatt hours that would otherwise have been supplied by the utility during such year in the absence of such qualified energy conservation measures, by

(ii) 0.004,

and dividing by 2,000.

(F) Avoided emissions from the use of qualified renewable energy

The emissions tonnage deemed avoided by reason of the use of qualified renewable energy by an electric utility for any calendar year shall be a tonnage equal to the product of multiplying—

(i) the actual kilowatt hours generated by, or purchased from, qualified renewable energy, by

(ii) 0.004,

and dividing by 2,000.

(G) Prohibitions

(i) No allowances shall be allocated under this subsection for the implementation of programs that are exclusively informational or educational in nature.

(ii) No allowances shall be allocated for energy conservation measures or renewable energy that were operational before January 1, 1992.

(3) Savings provision

Nothing in this subsection precludes a State or State regulatory authority from providing additional incentives to utilities to encourage investment in demand-side resources.

(4) Regulations

Not later than 18 months after November 15, 1990 and in conjunction with the regulations required to be promulgated under subsections (b) and (c) of this section, the Administrator shall, in consultation with the Secretary of Energy, promulgate regulations under this subsection. Such regulations shall list energy conservation measures and renewable energy sources which may be treated as qualified energy conservation measures and qualified renewable energy for purposes of this subsection. Allowances shall only be allocated if all requirements of this subsection and the rules promulgated to implement this subsection are complied with. The Administrator shall review the determinations of each State regulatory authority under this subsection to encourage consistency from electric utility to electric utility and from State to State in accordance with the Administrator's rules. The Administrator shall publish the findings of this review no less than annually.

(g) Conservation and Renewable Energy Reserve

The Administrator shall establish a Conservation and Renewable Energy Reserve under this subsection. Beginning on January 1, 1995, the Administrator may allocate from the Conservation and Renewable Energy Reserve an amount equal to a total of 300,000 allowances for emissions of sulfur dioxide pursuant to section 7651b of this title. In order to provide 300,000 allowances for such reserve, in each year beginning in calendar year 2000 and until calendar year 2009, inclusive, the Administrator shall reduce each unit's basic Phase II allowance allocation on the basis of its pro rata share of 30,000 allowances. If allowances remain in the reserve after January 2, 2010, the Administrator shall allocate such allowances for affected units under section 7651d of this title on a pro rata basis. For purposes of this subsection, for any unit subject to the emissions limitation requirements of section 7651d of this title, the term "pro rata basis" refers to the ratio which the reductions made in such unit's allowances in order to establish the reserve under this subsection bears to the total of such reductions for all such units.

(h) Alternative allowance allocation for units in certain utility systems with optional baseline

(1) Optional baseline for units in certain systems

In the case of a unit subject to the emissions limitation requirements of this section which (as of November 15, 1990)—

(A) has an emission rate below 1.0 lbs/mmBtu,

(B) has decreased its sulfur dioxide emissions rate by 60 percent or greater since 1980, and

(C) is part of a utility system which has a weighted average sulfur dioxide emissions rate for all fossil fueled-fired units below 1.0 lbs/mmBtu,

at the election of the owner or operator of such unit, the unit's baseline may be calculated (i) as provided under section 7651a(d) of this title, or (ii) by utilizing the unit's average annual fuel consumption at a 60 percent capacity factor. Such election shall be made no later than March 1, 1991.

(2) Allowance allocation

Whenever a unit referred to in paragraph (1) elects to calculate its baseline as provided in clause (ii) of paragraph (1), the Administrator shall allocate allowances for the unit pursuant to section 7651b(a)(1) of this title, this section, and section 7651d of this title (as basic Phase II allowance allocations) in an amount equal to the baseline selected multiplied by the lower of the average annual emission rate for such unit in 1989, or 1.0 lbs./mmBtu. Such allowance allocation shall be in lieu of any allocation of allowances under this section and section 7651d of this title.

(July 14, 1955, ch. 360, title IV, § 404, as added Nov. 15, 1990, Pub.L. 101–549, title IV, § 401, 104 Stat. 2592.)

1 So in original. Probably should be "Stream".

2 So in original. Probably should be "impracticability".

Effective Date

Section to take effect Nov. 15, 1990, except as otherwise provided, see section 711(b) of Pub.L. 101–549, set out as a note under section 7401 of this title.

Savings Provisions

Suits, actions or proceedings commenced under this chapter as in effect prior to Nov. 15, 1990, not to abate by reason of the taking effect of amendments by Pub.L. 101–549, except as otherwise provided for, see section 711(a) of Pub.L. 101–549, set out as a note under section 7401 of this title.

§ 7651d. Phase II sulfur dioxide requirements [CAA § 405]

(a) Applicability

(1) After January 1, 2000, each existing utility unit as provided below is subject to the limitations or requirements of this section. Each utility unit subject to an annual sulfur dioxide tonnage emission limitation under this section is an affected unit under this subchapter. Each source that includes one or more affected units is an affected source. In the case of an existing unit that was not in operation during calendar year 1985, the emission rate for a calendar year after 1985, as determined by the Administrator, shall be used in lieu of the 1985 rate. The owner or operator of any unit operated in violation of this section shall be fully liable under this chapter for fulfilling the obligations specified in section 7651j of this title.

(2) In addition to basic Phase II allowance allocations, in each year beginning in calendar year 2000 and ending in calendar year 2009, inclusive, the Administrator shall allocate up to 530,000 Phase II bonus allowances pursuant to subsections (b)(2), (c)(4), (d)(3)(A) and (B), and (h)(2) of this section and section 7651e of this title. Not later than June 1, 1998, the Administrator shall calculate, for each unit granted an extension pursuant to section 7651h of this title the difference between (A) the number of allowances allocated for the unit in calendar year 2000, and (B) the product of the unit's baseline multiplied by 1.20 lbs/mmBtu, divided by 2000, and sum the computations. In each year, beginning in calendar year 2000 and ending in calendar year 2009, inclusive, the Administrator shall deduct from each unit's basic Phase II allowance allocation its pro rata share of 10 percent of the sum calculated pursuant to the preceding sentence.

(3) In addition to basic Phase II allowance allocations and Phase II bonus allowance allocations, beginning January 1, 2000, the Administrator shall allocate for each unit listed on Table A in section 7651c of this title (other than units at Kyger Creek, Clifty Creek, and Joppa Steam) and located in the States of Illinois, Indiana, Ohio, Georgia, Alabama, Missouri, Pennsylvania, West Virginia, Kentucky, or Tennessee allowances in an amount equal to 50,000 multiplied by the unit's pro rata share of the total number of basic allowances allocated for all units listed on Table A (other than units at Kyger Creek, Clifty Creek, and Joppa Steam). Allowances allocated pursuant to this paragraph shall not be subject to the 8,900,000 ton limitation in section 403(a).

(b) Units equal to, or above, 75 MWe and 1.20 lbs/mmBtu

(1) Except as otherwise provided in paragraph (3), after January 1, 2000, it shall be unlawful for any existing utility unit that serves a generator with nameplate capacity equal to, or greater, than 75 MWe and an actual 1985 emission rate equal to or greater than 1.20 lbs/mmBtu to exceed an annual sulfur dioxide tonnage emission limitation equal to the product of the unit's baseline multiplied by an emission rate equal to 1.20 lbs/mmBtu, divided by 2,000, unless the owner or operator of such unit holds allowances to emit not less than the unit's total annual emissions.

(2) In addition to allowances allocated pursuant to paragraph (1) and section 7651b(a)(1) of this title as basic Phase II allowance allocations, beginning January 1, 2000, and for each calendar year thereafter until and including 2009, the Administrator shall allocate annually for each unit subject to the emissions limitation requirements of paragraph (1) with an actual 1985 emissions rate greater than 1.20 lbs/mmBtu and less than 2.50 lbs/mmBtu and a baseline capacity factor of less than 60 percent, allowances from the reserve created pursuant to subsection (a)(2) of this section in an amount equal to 1.20 lbs/mmBtu multiplied by 50 percent of the difference, on a Btu basis, between the unit's baseline and the unit's fuel consumption at a 60 percent capacity factor.

(3) After January 1, 2000, it shall be unlawful for any existing utility unit with an actual 1985 emissions rate equal to or greater than 1.20 lbs/mmBtu whose annual average fuel consumption during 1985, 1986, and 1987 on a Btu basis exceeded 90 percent in the form of lignite coal which is located in a State in which, as of July 1, 1989, no county or portion of a county was designated nonattainment under section 7407 of this title for any pollutant subject to the requirements of section 7409 of this title to exceed an annual sulfur dioxide tonnage limitation equal to the product of the unit's baseline multiplied by the lesser of the unit's actual 1985 emissions rate or its allowable 1985 emissions rate, divided by 2,000, unless the owner or operator of such unit holds allowances to emit not less than the unit's total annual emissions.

(4) After January 1, 2000, the Administrator shall allocate annually for each unit, subject to the emissions limitation requirements of paragraph (1), which is located in a State with an installed electrical generating capacity of more than 30,000,000 kw in 1988 and for which was issued a prohibition order or a proposed prohibition order (from burning oil), which unit subsequently converted to coal between January 1, 1980 and December 31, 1985, allowances equal to the difference between (A) the product of the unit's annual fuel

consumption, on a Btu basis, at a 65 percent capacity factor multiplied by the lesser of its actual or allowable emissions rate during the first full calendar year after conversion, divided by 2,000, and (B) the number of allowances allocated for the unit pursuant to paragraph (1): *Provided,* That the number of allowances allocated pursuant to this paragraph shall not exceed an annual total of five thousand. If necessary to meeting the restriction imposed in the preceding sentence the Administrator shall reduce, pro rata, the annual allowances allocated for each unit under this paragraph.

(c) Coal or oil-fired units below 75 MWe and above 1.20 lbs/mmBtu

(1) Except as otherwise provided in paragraph (3), after January 1, 2000, it shall be unlawful for a coal or oil-fired existing utility unit that serves a generator with nameplate capacity of less than 75 MWe and an actual 1985 emission rate equal to, or greater than, 1.20 lbs/mmBtu and which is a unit owned by a utility operating company whose aggregate nameplate fossil fuel steam-electric capacity is, as of December 31, 1989, equal to, or greater than, 250 MWe to exceed an annual sulfur dioxide emissions limitation equal to the product of the unit's baseline multiplied by an emission rate equal to 1.20 lbs/mmBtu, divided by 2,000, unless the owner or operator of such unit holds allowances to emit not less than the unit's total annual emissions.

(2) After January 1, 2000, it shall be unlawful for a coal or oil-fired existing utility unit that serves a generator with nameplate capacity of less than 75 MWe and an actual 1985 emission rate equal to, or greater than, 1.20 lbs/mmBtu (excluding units subject to section 7411 of this title or to a federally enforceable emissions limitation for sulfur dioxide equivalent to an annual rate of less than 1.20 lbs/mmBtu) and which is a unit owned by a utility operating company whose aggregate nameplate fossil fuel steam-electric capacity is, as of December 31, 1989, less than 250 MWe, to exceed an annual sulfur dioxide tonnage emissions limitation equal to the product of the unit's baseline multiplied by the lesser of its actual 1985 emissions rate or its allowable 1985 emissions rate, divided by 2,000, unless the owner or operator of such unit holds allowances to emit not less than the unit's total annual emissions.

(3) After January 1, 2000, it shall be unlawful for any existing utility unit with a nameplate capacity below 75 MWe and an actual 1985 emissions rate equal to, or greater than, 1.20 lbs/mmBtu which became operational on or before December 31, 1965, which is owned by a utility operating company with, as of December 31, 1989, a total fossil fuel steam-electric generating capacity greater than 250 MWe, and less than 450 MWe which serves fewer than 78,000 electrical customers as of November 15, 1990 to exceed an annual sulfur dioxide emissions tonnage limitation equal to the product of its baseline multiplied by the lesser of its actual or allowable 1985 emission rate, divided by 2,000, unless the owner or operator holds allowances to emit not less than the units total annual emissions. After January 1, 2010, it shall be unlawful for each unit subject to the emissions limitation requirements of this paragraph to exceed an annual emissions tonnage limitation equal to the product of its baseline multiplied by an emissions rate of 1.20 lbs/mmBtu, divided by 2,000, unless the owner or operator holds allowances to emit not less than the unit's total annual emissions.

(4) In addition to allowances allocated pursuant to paragraph (1) and section 7651b(a)(1) of this title as basic Phase II allowance allocations, beginning January 1, 2000, and for each calendar year thereafter until and including 2009, inclusive, the Administrator shall allocate annually for each unit subject to the emissions limitation requirements of paragraph (1) with an actual 1985 emissions rate equal to, or greater than, 1.20 lbs/mmBtu and less than 2.50 lbs/mmBtu and a baseline capacity factor of less than 60 percent, allowances from the reserve created pursuant to subsection (a)(2) of this section in an amount equal to 1.20 lbs/mmBtu multiplied by 50 percent of the difference, on a Btu basis, between the unit's baseline and the unit's fuel consumption at a 60 percent capacity factor.

(5) After January 1, 2000, it shall be unlawful for any existing utility unit with a nameplate capacity below 75 MWe and an actual 1985 emissions rate equal to, or greater than, 1.20 lbs/mmBtu which is part of an electric utility system which, as of November 15, 1990, (A) has at least 20 percent of its fossil-fuel capacity controlled by flue gas desulfurization devices, (B) has more than 10 percent of its fossil-fuel capacity consisting of coal-fired units of less than 75 MWe, and (C) has large units (greater than 400 MWe) all of which have difficult or very difficult FGD Retrofit Cost Factors (according to the Emissions and the FGD Retrofit Feasibility at the 200 Top Emitting Generating Stations, prepared for the United States Environmental Protection Agency on January 10, 1986) to exceed an annual sulfur dioxide emissions tonnage limitation equal to the product of its baseline multiplied by an emissions rate of 2.5 lbs/mmBtu, divided by 2,000, unless the owner or operator holds allowances to emit not less than the unit's total annual emissions. After January 1, 2010, it shall be unlawful for each unit subject to the emissions limitation requirements of this paragraph to exceed an annual

emissions tonnage limitation equal to the product of its baseline multiplied by an emissions rate of 1.20 lbs/mmBtu, divided by 2,000, unless the owner or operator holds for use allowances to emit not less than the unit's total annual emissions.

(d) Coal-fired units below 1.20 lbs/mmBtu

(1) After January 1, 2000, it shall be unlawful for any existing coal-fired utility unit the lesser of whose actual or allowable 1985 sulfur dioxide emissions rate is less than 0.60 lbs/mmBtu to exceed an annual sulfur dioxide tonnage emission limitation equal to the product of the unit's baseline multiplied by (A) the lesser of 0.60 lbs/mmBtu or the unit's allowable 1985 emissions rate, and (B) a numerical factor of 120 percent, divided by 2,000, unless the owner or operator of such unit holds allowances to emit not less than the unit's total annual emissions.

(2) After January 1, 2000, it shall be unlawful for any existing coal-fired utility unit the lesser of whose actual or allowable 1985 sulfur dioxide emissions rate is equal to, or greater than, 0.60 lbs/mmBtu and less than 1.20 lbs/mmBtu to exceed an annual sulfur dioxide tonnage emissions limitation equal to the product of the unit's baseline multiplied by (A) the lesser of its actual 1985 emissions rate or its allowable 1985 emissions rate, and (B) a numerical factor of 120 percent, divided by 2,000, unless the owner or operator of such unit holds allowances to emit not less than the unit's total annual emissions.

(3)(A) In addition to allowances allocated pursuant to paragraph (1) and section 7651b(a)(1) of this title as basic Phase II allowance allocations, at the election of the designated representative of the operating company, beginning January 1, 2000, and for each calendar year thereafter until and including 2009, the Administrator shall allocate annually for each unit subject to the emissions limitation requirements of paragraph (1) allowances from the reserve created pursuant to subsection (a)(2) of this section in an amount equal to the amount by which (i) the product of the lesser of 0.60 lbs/mmBtu or the unit's allowable 1985 emissions rate multiplied by the unit's baseline adjusted to reflect operation at a 60 percent capacity factor, divided by 2,000, exceeds (ii) the number of allowances allocated for the unit pursuant to paragraph (1) and section 7651b(a)(1) of this title as basic Phase II allowance allocations.

(B) In addition to allowances allocated pursuant to paragraph (2) and section 7651b(a)(1) of this title as basic Phase II allowance allocations, at the election of the designated representative of the operating company, beginning January 1, 2000, and for each calendar year thereafter until and including 2009, the Administrator shall allocate annually for each unit subject to the emissions limitation requirements of paragraph (2) allowances from the reserve created pursuant to subsection (a)(2) of this section in an amount equal to the amount by which (i) the product of the lesser of the unit's actual 1985 emissions rate or its allowable 1985 emissions rate multiplied by the unit's baseline adjusted to reflect operation at a 60 percent capacity factor, divided by 2,000, exceeds (ii) the number of allowances allocated for the unit pursuant to paragraph (2) and section 7651b(a)(1) of this title as basic Phase II allowance allocations.

(C) An operating company with units subject to the emissions limitation requirements of this subsection may elect the allocation of allowances as provided under subparagraphs (A) and (B). Such election shall apply to the annual allowance allocation for each and every unit in the operating company subject to the emissions limitation requirements of this subsection. The Administrator shall allocate allowances pursuant to subparagraphs (A) and (B) only in accordance with this subparagraph.

(4) Notwithstanding any other provision of this section, at the election of the owner or operator, after January 1, 2000, the Administrator shall allocate in lieu of allocation, pursuant to paragraph (1), (2), (3), (5), or (6), allowances for a unit subject to the emissions limitation requirements of this subsection which commenced commercial operation on or after January 1, 1981 and before December 31, 1985, which was subject to, and in compliance with, section 7411 of this title in an amount equal to the unit's annual fuel consumption, on a Btu basis, at a 65 percent capacity factor multiplied by the unit's allowable 1985 emissions rate, divided by 2,000.

(5) For the purposes of this section, in the case of an oil- and gas-fired unit which has been awarded a clean coal technology demonstration grant as of January 1, 1991, by the United States Department of Energy, beginning January 1, 2000, the Administrator shall allocate for the unit allowances in an amount equal to the unit's baseline multiplied by 1.20 lbs/mmBtu, divided by 2,000.

(e) Oil and gas-fired units equal to or greater than 0.60 lbs/mmBtu and less than 1.20 lbs/mmBtu

After January 1, 2000, it shall be unlawful for any existing oil and gas-fired utility unit the lesser of whose actual or allowable 1985 sulfur dioxide emission rate is equal to, or greater than, 0.60 lbs/mmBtu, but less than 1.20 lbs/mmBtu to exceed an annual sulfur dioxide tonnage limitation equal to the product of the unit's baseline multiplied by (A) the lesser of the unit's allowable 1985 emissions rate or its actual 1985 emissions rate and (B) a numerical factor of 120 percent divided by 2,000, unless the owner or operator of such unit holds allowances to emit not less than the unit's total annual emissions.

(f) Oil and gas-fired units less than 0.60 lbs/mmBtu

(1) After January 1, 2000, it shall be unlawful for any oil and gas-fired existing utility unit the lesser of whose actual or allowable 1985 emission rate is less than 0.60 lbs/mmBtu and whose average annual fuel consumption during the period 1980 through 1989 on a Btu basis was 90 percent or less in the form of natural gas to exceed an annual sulfur dioxide tonnage emissions limitation equal to the product of the unit's baseline multiplied by (A) the lesser of 0.60 lbs/mmBtu or the unit's allowable 1985 emissions, and (B) a numerical factor of 120 percent, divided by 2,000, unless the owner or operator of such unit holds allowances to emit not less than the unit's total annual emissions.

(2) In addition to allowances allocated pursuant to paragraph (1) as basic Phase II allowance allocations and section 7651b(a)(1) of this title, beginning January 1, 2000, the Administrator shall, in the case of any unit operated by a utility that furnishes electricity, electric energy, steam, and natural gas within an area consisting of a city and 1 contiguous county, and in the case of any unit owned by a State authority, the output of which unit is furnished within that same area consisting of a city and 1 contiguous county, the Administrator shall allocate for each unit in the utility its pro rata share of 7,000 allowances and for each unit in the State authority its pro rata share of 2,000 allowances.

(g) Units that commence operation between 1986 and December 31, 1995

(1) After January 1, 2000, it shall be unlawful for any utility unit that has commenced commercial operation on or after January 1, 1986, but not later than September 30, 1990 to exceed an annual tonnage emission limitation equal to the product of the unit's annual fuel consumption, on a Btu basis, at a 65 percent capacity factor multiplied by the unit's allowable 1985 sulfur dioxide emission rate (converted, if necessary, to pounds per mmBtu), divided by 2,000 unless the owner or operator of such unit holds allowances to emit not less than the unit's total annual emissions.

(2) After January 1, 2000, the Administrator shall allocate allowances pursuant to section 7651b of this title to each unit which is listed in Table B of this paragraph in an annual amount equal to the amount specified in Table B.

TABLE B

Unit	Allowances
Brandon Shores	8,907
Miller 4	9,197
TNP One 2	4,000
Zimmer 1	18,458
Spruce 1	7,647
Clover 1	2,796
Clover 2	2,796
Twin Oak 2	1,760
Twin Oak 1	9,158
Cross 1	6,401
Malakoff 1	1,759

Notwithstanding any other paragraph of this subsection, for units subject to this paragraph, the Administrator shall not allocate allowances pursuant to any other paragraph of this subsection, Provided that the owner or operator of a unit listed on Table B may elect an allocation of allowances under another paragraph of this subsection in lieu of an allocation under this paragraph.

(3) Beginning January 1, 2000, the Administrator shall allocate to the owner or operator of any utility unit that commences commercial operation, or has commenced commercial operation, on or after October 1, 1990, but not later than December 31, 1992 allowances in an amount equal to the product of the unit's annual fuel consumption, on a Btu basis, at a 65 percent capacity factor multiplied by the lesser of 0.30 lbs/mmBtu or the unit's allowable sulfur dioxide emission rate (converted, if necessary, to pounds per mmBtu), divided by 2,000.

(4) Beginning January 1, 2000, the Administrator shall allocate to the owner or operator of any utility unit that has commenced construction before December 31, 1990 and that commences commercial operation between January 1, 1993 and December 31, 1995, allowances in an amount equal to the product of the unit's annual fuel consumption, on a Btu basis, at a 65 percent capacity factor multiplied by the lesser of 0.30 lbs/mmBtu or the unit's allowable sulfur dioxide emission rate (converted, if necessary, to pounds per mmBtu), divided by 2,000.

(5) After January 1, 2000, it shall be unlawful for any existing utility unit that has completed conversion from predominantly gas fired existing operation to coal fired operation between January 1, 1985 and December 31, 1987, for which there has been allocated a proposed or final prohibition order pursuant to section 301(b) of the Powerplant and Industrial Fuel Use Act of 1978 (42 U.S.C. 8301 et seq., repealed 1987) to exceed an annual sulfur dioxide tonnage emissions limitation equal to the product of the unit's annual fuel consumption, on a Btu basis, at a 65 percent capacity factor multiplied by the lesser of 1.20

lbs/mmBtu or the unit's allowable 1987 sulfur dioxide emissions rate, divided by 2,000, unless the owner or operator of such unit has obtained allowances equal to its actual emissions.

(6)(A) [1] Unless the Administrator has approved a designation of such facility under section 7651i of this title, the provisions of this subchapter shall not apply to a "qualifying small power production facility" or "qualifying cogeneration facility" (within the meaning of section 796(17)(C) or 796(18)(B) of Title 16) or to a "new independent power production facility" as defined in section 7651*o* of this title except that clause (iii) of such definition in section 416 shall not apply for purposes of this paragraph if, as of November 15, 1990,

(i) an applicable power sales agreement has been executed;

(ii) the facility is the subject of a State regulatory authority order requiring an electric utility to enter into a power sales agreement with, purchase capacity from, or (for purposes of establishing terms and conditions of the electric utility's purchase of power) enter into arbitration concerning, the facility;

(iii) an electric utility has issued a letter of intent or similar instrument committing to purchase power from the facility at a previously offered or lower price and a power sales agreement is executed within a reasonable period of time; or

(iv) the facility has been selected as a winning bidder in a utility competitive bid solicitation.

(h) Oil and gas-fired units less than 10 percent oil consumed

(1) After January 1, 2000, it shall be unlawful for any oil- and gas-fired utility unit whose average annual fuel consumption during the period 1980 through 1989 on a Btu basis exceeded 90 percent in the form of natural gas to exceed an annual sulfur dioxide tonnage limitation equal to the product of the unit's baseline multiplied by the unit's actual 1985 emissions rate divided by 2,000 unless the owner or operator of such unit holds allowances to emit not less than the unit's total annual emissions.

(2) In addition to allowances allocated pursuant to paragraph (1) and section 7651b(a)(1) of this title as basic Phase II allowance allocations, beginning January 1, 2000, and for each calendar year thereafter until and including 2009, the Administrator shall allocate annually for each unit subject to the emissions limitation requirements of paragraph (1) allowances from the reserve created pursuant to subsection (a)(2) of this section in an amount equal to the unit's baseline multiplied by 0.050 lbs/mmBtu, divided by 2,000.

(3) In addition to allowances allocated pursuant to paragraph (1) and section 7651b(a)(1) of this title, beginning January 1, 2010, the Administrator shall allocate annually for each unit subject to the emissions limitation requirements of paragraph (1) allowances in an amount equal to the unit's baseline multiplied by 0.050 lbs/mmBtu, divided by 2,000.

(i) Units in high growth States

(1) In addition to allowances allocated pursuant to this section and section 7651b(a)(1) of this title as basic Phase II allowance allocations, beginning January 1, 2000, the Administrator shall allocate annually allowances for each unit, subject to an emissions limitation requirement under this section, and located in a State that—

(A) has experienced a growth in population in excess of 25 percent between 1980 and 1988 according to State Population and Household Estimates, With Age, Sex, and Components of Change: 1981–1988 allocated by the United States Department of Commerce, and

(B) had an installed electrical generating capacity of more than 30,000,000 kw in 1988,

in an amount equal to the difference between (A) the number of allowances that would be allocated for the unit pursuant to the emissions limitation requirements of this section applicable to the unit adjusted to reflect the unit's annual average fuel consumption on a Btu basis of any three consecutive calendar years between 1980 and 1989 (inclusive) as elected by the owner or operator and (B) the number of allowances allocated for the unit pursuant to the emissions limitation requirements of this section: *Provided*, That the number of allowances allocated pursuant to this subsection shall not exceed an annual total of 40,000. If necessary to meeting the 40,000 allowance restriction imposed under this subsection the Administrator shall reduce, pro rata, the additional annual allowances allocated to each unit under this subsection.

(2) Beginning January 1, 2000, in addition to allowances allocated pursuant to this section and section 7651b(a)(1) of this title as basic Phase II allowance allocations, the Administrator shall allocate annually for each unit subject to the emissions limitation requirements of subsection (b)(1) of this section, (A) the lesser of whose actual or allowable 1980 emissions rate has declined by 50 percent or more as of November 15, 1990, (B) whose actual emissions rate is less than 1.2 lbs/mmBtu as of January 1, 2000, (C) which commenced operation after January 1, 1970, (D) which is owned by a utility company whose combined commercial and industrial kilowatt-hour sales have increased by more than 20 percent between calendar year 1980 and November 15, 1990, and (E) whose company-wide fossil-fuel sulfur dioxide emissions rate has declined 40 per centum or more from 1980 to 1988, allowances in an amount equal to the difference between (i) the number of allowances that would be allocated for the unit pursuant to the emissions limitation requirements of subsection (b)(1) of this section adjusted to reflect the unit's annual average fuel consumption on a Btu basis for any three consecutive years between 1980 and 1989 (inclusive) as elected by the owner or operator and (ii) the number of allowances allocated for the unit pursuant to the emissions limitation requirements of subsection (b)(1) of this section: *Provided,* That the number of allowances allocated pursuant to this paragraph shall not exceed an annual total of 5,000. If necessary to meeting the 5,000–allowance restriction imposed in the last clause of the preceding sentence the Administrator shall reduce, pro rata, the additional allowances allocated to each unit pursuant to this paragraph.

(j) Certain municipally owned power plants

Beginning January 1, 2000, in addition to allowances allocated pursuant to this section and section 7651b(a)(1) of this title as basic Phase II allowance allocations, the Administrator shall allocate annually for each existing municipally owned oil and gas-fired utility unit with nameplate capacity equal to, or less than, 40 MWe, the lesser of whose actual or allowable 1985 sulfur dioxide emission rate is less than 1.20 lbs/mmBtu, allowances in an amount equal to the product of the unit's annual fuel consumption on a Btu basis at a 60 percent capacity factor multiplied by the lesser of its allowable 1985 emission rate or its actual 1985 emission rate, divided by 2,000.

(July 14, 1955, ch. 360, title IV, § 405, as added Nov. 15, 1990, Pub.L. 101–549, title IV, § 401, 104 Stat. 2605.)

1 No par. (B) has been enacted.

References in Text

Section 301(b) of the Powerplant and Industrial Fuel Use Act of 1978, referred to in subsec. (g)(5), is a reference to section 301(b) of Pub.L. 95–620, Title III, Nov. 9, 1978, 92 Stat. 3305, which was formerly classified to section 8341(b) of this title. Such section was repealed by Pub.L. 97–35, Title X, § 1021(a), Aug. 13, 1981, 95 Stat. 614. Such section related to the authority of the Secretary to prohibit the use of petroleum or natural gas, or both, as a primary energy source in existing electric powerplants where coal or alternate fuel capability exists and its use feasible. For complete text of prior section 8341(b) of this title see 92 Stat. 3305.

Effective Date

Section to take effect Nov. 15, 1990, except as otherwise provided, see section 711(b) of Pub.L. 101–549, set out as a note under section 7401 of this title.

Savings Provisions

Suits, actions or proceedings commenced under this chapter as in effect prior to Nov. 15, 1990, not to abate by reason of the taking effect of amendments by Pub.L. 101–549, except as otherwise provided for, see section 711(a) of Pub.L. 101–549, set out as a note under section 7401 of this title.

§ 7651e. Allowances for States with emissions rates at or below 0.80 lbs/mmBtu [CAA § 406]

(a) Election of Governor

In addition to basic Phase II allowance allocations, upon the election of the Governor of any State, with a 1985 state-wide annual sulfur dioxide emissions rate equal to or less than, 0.80 lbs/mmBtu, averaged over all fossil fuel-fired utility steam generating units, beginning January 1, 2000, and for each calendar year thereafter until and including 2009, the Administrator shall allocate, in lieu of other Phase II bonus allowance allocations, allowances from the reserve created pursuant to section 7651d(a)(2) of this title to all such units in the State in an amount equal to 125,000 multiplied by the unit's pro rata share of electricity generated in calendar year 1985 at fossil fuel-fired utility steam units in all States eligible for the election.

(b) Notification of Administrator

Pursuant to section 7651b(a)(1) of this title, each Governor of a State eligible to make an election under paragraph (a) shall notify the Administrator of such election. In the event that the Governor of any such State fails to notify the Administrator of the Governor's elections, the Administrator shall allocate allowances pursuant to section 7651d of this title.

(c) Allowances after January 1, 2010

After January 1, 2010, the Administrator shall allocate allowances to units subject to the provisions of this section pursuant to section 7651d of this title.

(July 14, 1955, ch. 360, title IV, § 406, as added Nov. 15, 1990, Pub.L. 101–549, title IV, § 401, 104 Stat. 2613.)

Effective Date

Section to take effect Nov. 15, 1990, except as otherwise provided, see section 711(b) of Pub.L. 101–549, set out as a note under section 7401 of this title.

Savings Provisions

Suits, actions or proceedings commenced under this chapter as in effect prior to Nov. 15, 1990, not to abate by reason of the taking effect of amendments by Pub.L. 101–549, except as otherwise provided for, see section 711(a) of Pub.L. 101–549, set out as a note under section 7401 of this title.

§ 7651f. Nitrogen oxides emission reduction program [CAA § 407]

(a) Applicability

On the date that a coal-fired utility unit becomes an affected unit pursuant to sections 7651c, 7651d, 7651h of this title, or on the date a unit subject to the provisions of section 7651c(d) or 7651h(b) of this title, must meet the SO_2 reduction requirements, each such unit shall become an affected unit for purposes of this section and shall be subject to the emission limitations for nitrogen oxides set forth herein.

(b) Emission limitations

(1) Not later than eighteen months after enactment of the Clean Air Act Amendments of 1990, the Administrator shall by regulation establish annual allowable emission limitations for nitrogen oxides for the types of utility boilers listed below, which limitations shall not exceed the rates listed below: *Provided,* That the Administrator may set a rate higher than that listed for any type of utility boiler if the Administrator finds that the maximum listed rate for that boiler type cannot be achieved using low NO_x burner technology. The maximum allowable emission rates are as follows:

(A) for tangentially fired boilers, 0.45 lb/mmBtu;

(B) for dry bottom wall-fired boilers (other than units applying cell burner technology), 0.50 lb/mmBtu.

After January 1, 1995, it shall be unlawful for any unit that is an affected unit on that date and is of the type listed in this paragraph to emit nitrogen oxides in excess of the emission rates set by the Administrator pursuant to this paragraph.

(2) Not later than January 1, 1997, the Administrator shall, by regulation, establish allowable emission limitations on a lb/mmBtu, annual average basis, for nitrogen oxides for the following types of utility boilers:

(A) wet bottom wall-fired boilers;

(B) cyclones;

(C) units applying cell burner technology;

(D) all other types of utility boilers.

The Administrator shall base such rates on the degree of reduction achievable through the retrofit application of the best system of continuous emission reduction, taking into account available technology, costs and energy and environmental impacts; and which is comparable to the costs of nitrogen oxides controls set pursuant to subsection (b)(1) of this section. Not later than January 1, 1997, the Administrator may revise the applicable emission limitations for tangentially fired and dry bottom, wall-fired boilers (other than cell burners) to be more stringent if the Administrator determines that more effective low NO_x burner technology is available: *Provided,* That, no unit that is an affected unit pursuant to section 7651c of this title and that is subject to the requirements of subsection (b)(1) of this section, shall be subject to the revised emission limitations, if any.

(c) Revised performance standards

(1) [1] Not later than January 1, 1993, the Administrator shall propose revised standards of performance to section 7411 of this title for nitrogen oxides emissions from fossil-fuel fired steam generating units, including both electric utility and nonutility units. Not later than January 1, 1994, the Administrator shall promulgate such revised standards of performance. Such revised standards of performance shall reflect improvements in methods for the reduction of emissions of oxides of nitrogen.

(d) Alternative emission limitations

The permitting authority shall, upon request of an owner or operator of a unit subject to this section, authorize an emission limitation less stringent than the applicable limitation established under subsection (b)(1) or (b)(2) of this section upon a determination that—

(1) a unit subject to subsection (b)(1) of this section cannot meet the applicable limitation using low NO_x burner technology; or

(2) a unit subject to subsection (b)(2) of this section cannot meet the applicable rate using the technology on which the Administrator based the applicable emission limitation.

The permitting authority shall base such determination upon a showing satisfactory to the permitting authority, in accordance with regulations established by the Administrator not later than eighteen months after enactment of the Clean Air Act Amendments of 1990, that the owner or operator—

(1) has properly installed appropriate control equipment designed to meet the applicable emission rate;

(2) has properly operated such equipment for a period of fifteen months (or such other period of time as the Administrator determines through the regulations), and provides operating and monitoring data for such period demonstrating that the unit cannot meet the applicable emission rate; and

(3) has specified an emission rate that such unit can meet on an annual average basis.

The permitting authority shall issue an operating permit for the unit in question, in accordance with section 7651g of this title and part B of title III—

(i) that permits the unit during the demonstration period referred to in subparagraph (2) above, to emit at a rate in excess of the applicable emission rate;

(ii) at the conclusion of the demonstration period to revise the operating permit to reflect the alternative emission rate demonstrated in paragraphs (2) and (3) above.

Units subject to subsection (b)(1) of this section for which an alternative emission limitation is established shall not be required to install any additional control technology beyond low NO_x burners. Nothing in this section shall preclude an owner or operator from installing and operating an alternative NO_x control technology capable of achieving the applicable emission limitation. If the owner or operator of a unit subject to the emissions limitation requirements of subsection (b)(1) of this section demonstrates to the satisfaction of the Administrator that the technology necessary to meet such requirements is not in adequate supply to enable its installation and operation at the unit, consistent with system reliability, by January 1, 1995, then the Administrator shall extend the deadline for compliance for the unit by a period of 15 months. Any owner or operator may petition the Administrator to make a determination under the previous sentence. The Administrator shall grant or deny such petition within 3 months of submittal.

(e) Emissions averaging

In lieu of complying with the applicable emission limitations under subsection (b)(1), (2), or (d) of this section, the owner or operator of two or more units subject to one or more of the applicable emission limitations set pursuant to these sections, may petition the permitting authority for alternative contemporaneous annual emission limitations for such units that ensure that (1) the actual annual emission rate in pounds of nitrogen oxides per million Btu averaged over the units in question is a rate that is less than or equal to (2) the Btu-weighted average annual emission rate for the same units if they had been operated, during the same period of time, in compliance with limitations set in accordance with the applicable emission rates set pursuant to subsections (b)(1) and (2) of this section.

If the permitting authority determines, in accordance with regulations issued by the Administrator not later than eighteen months after enactment of the Clean Air Act Amendments of 1990; that the conditions in the paragraph above can be met, the permitting authority shall issue operating permits for such units, in accordance with section 7651g of this title and part B of title III, that allow alternative contemporaneous annual emission limitations. Such emission limitations shall only remain in effect while both units continue operation under the conditions specified in their respective operating permits.

(July 14, 1955, ch. 360, title IV, § 407, as added Nov. 15, 1990, Pub.L. 101–549, title IV, § 401, 104 Stat. 2613.)

[1] No par. (2) has been enacted.

References in Text

Enactment of the Clean Air Act Amendments of 1990, referred to in subsecs. (b)(1), (d) and (e), probably means the date of enactment of Pub.L. 101–549, Nov. 15, 1990, 104 Stat. 2399, which was approved Nov. 15, 1990.

An approved permitting program under part B of title III of the Act, referred to in subsecs. (d) and (e), probably means an approved permitting program under subchapter V of this chapter. A literal interpretation of part B of title III of this Act would mean part B of title III (section 301 et seq.) of Act July 14, 1955, c. 360, as added Dec. 17, 1963, Pub.L. 88–206, 77 Stat. 400, as amended, which is classified to subchapter III of this chapter, however, such title and such chapter have no part B. Likewise, subchapter V of this chapter contains no part B, however, subchapter V of this chapter specifically addresses permit programs.

Effective Date

Section to take effect Nov. 15, 1990, except as otherwise provided, see section 711(b) of Pub.L. 101–549, set out as a note under section 7401 of this title.

Savings Provisions

Suits, actions or proceedings commenced under this chapter as in effect prior to Nov. 15, 1990, not to abate by reason of the taking effect of amendments by Pub.L. 101–549, except as otherwise provided for, see section 711(a) of Pub.L. 101–549, set out as a note under section 7401 of this title.

§ 7651g. Permits and compliance plans [CAA § 408]

(a) Permit program

The provisions of this subchapter shall be implemented, subject to section 7651b of this title, by permits issued to units subject to this subchapter (and enforced) in accordance with the provisions of subchapter V of this chapter, as modified by this subchapter. Any such permit issued by the Administrator, or by a State with an approved permit program, shall prohibit—

(1) annual emissions of sulfur dioxide in excess of the number of allowances to emit sulfur dioxide the owner or operator, or the designated representative of the owners or operators, of the unit hold for the unit,

(2) exceedances of applicable emissions rates,

(3) the use of any allowance prior to the year for which it was allocated, and

(4) contravention of any other provision of the permit.

Permits issued to implement this subchapter shall be issued for a period of 5 years, notwithstanding subchapter V of this chapter. No permit shall be issued that is inconsistent with the requirements of this subchapter, and subchapter V of this chapter as applicable.

(b) Compliance plan

Each initial permit application shall be accompanied by a compliance plan for the source to comply with its requirements under this subchapter. Where an affected source consists of more than one affected unit, such plan shall cover all such units, and for purposes of section 7661a(c) of this title, such source shall be considered a "facility". Nothing in this section regarding compliance plans or in subchapter V of this chapter shall be construed as affecting allowances. Except as provided under subsection (c)(1)(B) of this section, submission of a statement by the owner or operator, or the designated representative of the owners and operators, of a unit subject to the emissions limitation requirements of sections 7651c, 7651d, and 7651f of this title, that the unit will meet the applicable emissions limitation requirements of such sections in a timely manner or that, in the case of the emissions limitation requirements of sections 7651c and 7651d of this title, the owners and operators will hold allowances to emit not less than the total annual emissions of the unit, shall be deemed to meet the proposed and approved compliance planning requirements of this section and subchapter V of this chapter, except that, for any unit that will meet the requirements of this subchapter by means of an alternative method of compliance authorized under section 7651c(b), (c), (d), or (f) of this title[1] section 7651f(d) or (e) of this title, section 7651h of this title and section 7651i of this title, the proposed and approved compliance plan, permit application and permit shall include, pursuant to regulations promulgated by the Administrator, for each alternative method of compliance a comprehensive description of the schedule and means by which the unit will rely on one or more alternative methods of compliance in the manner and time authorized under this subchapter. Recordation by the Administrator of transfers of allowances shall amend automatically all applicable proposed or approved permit applications, compliance plans and permits. The Administrator may also require—

(1) for a source, a demonstration of attainment of national ambient air quality standards, and

(2) from the owner or operator of two or more affected sources, an integrated compliance plan providing an overall plan for achieving compliance at the affected sources.

(c) First phase permits

The Administrator shall issue permits to affected sources under sections 7651c and 7651f of this title.

(1) Permit application and compliance plan

(A) Not later than 27 months after November 15, 1990, the designated representative of the owners or operators, or the owner and operator, of each affected source under sections 7651c and 7651f of this title shall submit a permit application and compliance plan for that source in accordance with regulations issued by the Administrator under paragraph (3). The permit application and the compliance plan shall be binding on the owner or operator or the designated representative of owners and operators for purposes of this subchapter and section 7651a(a) of this title, and shall be enforceable in lieu of a permit until a permit is issued by the Administrator for the source.

(B) In the case of a compliance plan for an affected source under sections 7651c and 7651f of this title for which the owner or operator proposes to meet the requirements of that section by reducing utilization of the unit as compared with its baseline or by shutting down the unit, the owner or operator shall include in the proposed compliance plan a specification of the unit or units that will provide electrical generation to compensate for the reduced output at the affected source, or a demonstration that such reduced utilization will be accomplished through energy conservation or improved unit efficiency. The unit to be used for such compensating generation, which is not otherwise an affected unit under sections 7651c and 7651f of this title, shall be deemed an affected unit under section 7651c of this title, subject to all of the requirements for such units under this subchapter, except that allowances shall be allocated to such compensating unit in the amount of an annual limitation equal to the product of the unit's baseline multiplied by the lesser of the unit's actual 1985 emissions rate or its allowable 1985 emissions rate, divided by 2,000.

(2) EPA action on compliance plans

The Administrator shall review each proposed compliance plan to determine whether it satisfies the requirements of this subchapter, and shall approve or disapprove such plan within 6 months after receipt of a complete submission. If a plan is disapproved, it may be resubmitted for approval with such changes as the Administrator shall require consistent with the requirements of this subchapter and within such period as the Administrator prescribes as part of such disapproval.

(3) Regulations; issuance of permits

Not later than 18 months after November 15, 1990, the Administrator shall promulgate regulations, in accordance with subchapter V of this chapter, to implement a Federal permit program to issue permits for affected sources under this subchapter. Following promulgation, the Administrator shall issue a permit to implement the requirements of section 7651c of this title and the allowances provided under section 7651b of this title to the owner or operator of each affected source under section 7651c of this title. Such a permit shall supersede any permit application and compliance plan submitted under paragraph (1).

(4) Fees

During the years 1995 through 1999 inclusive, no fee shall be required to be paid under section 7661a(b)(3) of this title or under section 7410(a)(2)(L) of this title with respect to emissions from any unit which is an affected unit under section 7651c of this title.

(d) Second phase permits

(1) To provide for permits for (A) new electric utility steam generating units required under section 7651b(e) of this title to have allowances, (B) affected units or sources under section 7651d of this title, and (C) existing units subject to nitrogen oxide emission reductions under section 7651f of this title, each State in which one or more such units or sources are located shall submit in accordance with subchapter V of this chapter, a permit program for approval as provided by that subchapter. Upon approval of such program, for the units or sources subject to such approved program the Administrator shall suspend the issuance of permits as provided in subchapter V of this chapter.

(2) The owner or operator or the designated representative of each affected source under section 7651d of this title shall submit a permit application and compliance plan for that source to the permitting authority, not later than January 1, 1996.

(3) Not later than December 31, 1997, each State with an approved permit program shall issue permits to the owner or operator, or the designated representative of the owners and operators, of affected sources under section 7651d of this title that satisfy the requirements of subchapter V of this chapter and this subchapter and that submitted to such State a permit application and compliance plan pursuant to paragraph (2). In the case of a State without an approved permit program by July 1, 1996, the Administrator shall, not later than January 1, 1998, issue a permit to the owner or operator or the designated representative of each such affected source. In the case of affected sources for which applications and plans are timely received under paragraph (2), the permit application and the compliance plan, including amendments thereto, shall be binding on the owner or operator or the designated representative of the owners or operators and shall be enforceable as a permit for purposes of this subchapter and subchapter V of this chapter until a permit is issued by the permitting authority for the affected source. The provisions of section 558(c) of Title 5 (relating to renewals) shall apply to permits issued by a permitting authority under this subchapter and subchapter V of this chapter.

(4) The permit issued in accordance with this subsection for an affected source shall provide that the affected units at the affected source may not emit an annual tonnage of sulfur dioxide in excess of the number of allowances to emit sulfur dioxide the owner or operator or designated representative hold for the unit.

(e) New units

The owner or operator of each source that includes a new electric utility steam generating unit shall submit a permit application and compliance plan to the permitting authority not later than 24 months before the later of (1) January 1, 2000, or (2) the date on which the unit commences operation. The permitting authority shall issue a permit to the owner or operator, or the designated representative thereof, of the unit that satisfies the requirements of subchapter V of this chapter and this subchapter.

(f) Units subject to certain other limits

The owner or operator, or designated representative thereof, of any unit subject to an emission rate requirement under section 7651f of this title shall submit a permit application and compliance plan for such unit to the permitting authority, not later than January 1, 1998. The permitting authority shall issue a permit to the owner or operator that satisfies the requirements of subchapter V of this chapter and this subchapter, including any appropriate monitoring and reporting requirements.

(g) Amendment of application and compliance plan

At any time after the submission of an application and compliance plan under this section, the applicant may submit a revised application and compliance plan, in accordance with the requirements of this section. In considering any permit application and compliance plan under this subchapter, the permitting authority shall ensure coordination with the applicable electric ratemaking authority, in the case of regulated utilities, and with unregulated public utilities.

(h) Prohibition

(1) It shall be unlawful for an owner or operator, or designated representative, required to submit a permit application or compliance plan under this subchapter to fail to submit such application or plan in accordance with the deadlines specified in this section or to otherwise fail to comply with regulations implementing this section.

(2) It shall be unlawful for any person to operate any source subject to this subchapter except in compliance with the terms and requirements of a permit application and compliance plan (including amendments thereto) or permit issued by the Administrator

or a State with an approved permit program. For purposes of this subsection, compliance, as provided in section 7661c(f) of this title, with a permit issued under subchapter V of this chapter which complies with this subchapter for sources subject to this subchapter shall be deemed compliance with this subsection as well as section 7661a(a) of this title.

(3) In order to ensure reliability of electric power, nothing in this subchapter or subchapter V of this chapter shall be construed as requiring termination of operations of an electric utility steam generating unit for failure to have an approved permit or compliance plan, except that any such unit may be subject to the applicable enforcement provisions of section 7413 of this title.

(i) Multiple owners

No permit shall be issued under this section to an affected unit until the designated representative of the owners or operators has filed a certificate of representation with regard to matters under this subchapter, including the holding and distribution of allowances and the proceeds of transactions involving allowances. Where there are multiple holders of a legal or equitable title to, or a leasehold interest in, such a unit, or where a utility or industrial customer purchases power from an affected unit (or units) under life-of-the-unit, firm power contractual arrangements, the certificate shall state (1) that allowances and the proceeds of transactions involving allowances will be deemed to be held or distributed in proportion to each holder's legal, equitable, leasehold, or contractual reservation or entitlement, or (2) if such multiple holders have expressly provided for a different distribution of allowances by contract, that allowances and the proceeds of transactions involving allowances will be deemed to be held or distributed in accordance with the contract. A passive lessor, or a person who has an equitable interest through such lessor, whose rental payments are not based, either directly or indirectly, upon the revenues or income from the affected unit shall not be deemed to be a holder of a legal, equitable, leasehold, or contractual interest for the purpose of holding or distributing allowances as provided in this subsection, during either the term of such leasehold or thereafter, unless expressly provided for in the leasehold agreement. Except as otherwise provided in this subsection, where all legal or equitable title to or interest in an affected unit is held by a single person, the certification shall state that all allowances received by the unit are deemed to be held for that person.

(July 14, 1955, ch. 360, title IV, § 408, as added Nov. 15, 1990, Pub.L. 101–549, title IV, § 401, 104 Stat. 2616.)

[1] So in original. Probably should be a comma.

References in Text

Section 558(c) of Title 5, referred to in subsec. (d)(3), was in the original section 558(c) of title V of the United States Code. Editorial translation was made to section 558(c) of Title 5, as the probable intent of Congress.

Effective Date

Section to take effect Nov. 15, 1990, except as otherwise provided, see section 711(b) of Pub.L. 101–549, set out as a note under section 7401 of this title.

Savings Provisions

Suits, actions or proceedings commenced under this chapter as in effect prior to Nov. 15, 1990, not to abate by reason of the taking effect of amendments by Pub.L. 101–549, except as otherwise provided for, see section 711(a) of Pub.L. 101–549, set out as a note under section 7401 of this title.

§ 7651h. Repowered sources [CAA § 409]

(a) Availability

Not later than December 31, 1997, the owner or operator of an existing unit subject to the emissions limitation requirements of section 7651d(b) and (c) of this title may demonstrate to the permitting authority that one or more units will be repowered with a qualifying clean coal technology to comply with the requirements under section 7651d of this title. The owner or operator shall, as part of any such demonstration, provide, not later than January 1, 2000, satisfactory documentation of a preliminary design and engineering effort for such repowering and an executed and binding contract for the majority of the equipment to repower such unit and such other information as the Administrator may require by regulation. The replacement of an existing utility unit with a new utility unit using a repowering technology referred to in section 7651a(2) of this title which is located at a different site, shall be treated as repowering of the existing unit for purposes of this subchapter, if—

(1) the replacement unit is designated by the owner or operator to replace such existing unit, and

(2) the existing unit is retired from service on or before the date on which the designated replacement unit enters commercial operation.

(b) Extension

(1) An owner or operator satisfying the requirements of subsection (a) of this section shall be granted an extension of the emission limitation requirement compliance date for that unit from January 1, 2000, to December 31, 2003. The extension shall be specified in the permit issued to the source under section 7651g of this title, together with any compliance schedule and other requirements necessary to meet second phase requirements by the extended date. Any unit that is granted an extension under this section shall not be eligible for a waiver under section 7411(j) of this title, and shall continue to be subject to require-

ments under this subchapter as if it were a unit subject to section 7651d of this title.

(2) If (A) the owner or operator of an existing unit has been granted an extension under paragraph (1) in order to repower such unit with a clean coal unit, and (B) such owner or operator demonstrates to the satisfaction of the Administrator that the repowering technology to be utilized by such unit has been properly constructed and tested on such unit, but nevertheless has been unable to achieve the emission reduction limitations and is economically or technologically infeasible, such existing unit may be retrofitted or repowered with equipment or facilities utilizing another clean coal technology or other available control technology.

(c) Allowances

(1) For the period of the extension under this section, the Administrator shall allocate to the owner or operator of the affected unit, annual allowances for sulfur dioxide equal to the affected unit's baseline multiplied by the lesser of the unit's federally approved State Implementation Plan emissions limitation or its actual emission rate for 1995 in lieu of any other allocation. Such allowances may not be transferred or used by any other source to meet emission requirements under this subchapter. The source owner or operator shall notify the Administrator sixty days in advance of the date on which the affected unit for which the extension has been granted is to be removed from operation to install the repowering technology.

(2) Effective on that date, the unit shall be subject to the requirements of section 7651d of this title. Allowances for the year in which the unit is removed from operation to install the repowering technology shall be calculated as the product of the unit's baseline multiplied by 1.20 lbs/mmBtu, divided by 2,000, and prorated accordingly, and are transferable.

(3) Allowances for such existing utility units for calendar years after the year the repowering is complete shall be calculated as the product of the existing unit's baseline multiplied by 1.20 lbs/mmBtu, divided by 2,000.

(4) Notwithstanding the provisions of section 7651b(a) and (e) of this title, allowances shall be allocated under this section for a designated replacement unit which replaces an existing unit (as provided in the last sentence of subsection (a) of this section) in lieu of any further allocations of allowances for the existing unit.

(5) For the purpose of meeting the aggregate emissions limitation requirement set forth in section 7651b(a)(1) of this title, the units with an extension under this subsection shall be treated in each calendar year during the extension period as holding allowances allocated under paragraph (3).

(d) Control requirements

Any unit qualifying for an extension under this section that does not increase actual hourly emissions for any pollutant regulated under this chapter shall not be subject to any standard of performance under section 7411 of this title. Notwithstanding the provisions of this subsection, no new unit (1) designated as a replacement for an existing unit, (2) qualifying for the extension under subsection (b) of this section, and (3) located at a different site than the existing unit shall receive an exemption from the requirements imposed under section 7411 of this title.

(e) Expedited permitting

State permitting authorities and, where applicable, the Administrator, are encouraged to give expedited consideration to permit applications under parts C and D of subchapter I of this chapter for any source qualifying for an extension under this section.

(f) Prohibition

It shall be unlawful for the owner or operator of a repowered source to fail to comply with the requirement of this section, or any regulations of permit requirements to implement this section, including the prohibition against emitting sulfur dioxide in excess of allowances held.

(July 14, 1955, ch. 360, title IV, § 409, as added Nov. 15, 1990, Pub.L. 101–549, title IV, § 401, 104 Stat. 2619.)

Effective Date

Section to take effect Nov. 15, 1990, except as otherwise provided, see section 711(b) of Pub.L. 101–549, set out as a note under section 7401 of this title.

Savings Provisions

Suits, actions or proceedings commenced under this chapter as in effect prior to Nov. 15, 1990, not to abate by reason of the taking effect of amendments by Pub.L. 101–549, except as otherwise provided for, see section 711(a) of Pub.L. 101–549, set out as a note under section 7401 of this title.

§ 7651i. Election for additional sources [CAA § 410]

(a) Applicability

The owner or operator of any unit that is not, nor will become, an affected unit under section 7651b(e), 7651c, or 7651d of this title, or that is a process source under subsection (d) of this section, that emits sulfur dioxide, may elect to designate that unit or source to become an affected unit and to receive allowances under this subchapter. An election shall be submitted to the Administrator for approval, along with a permit application and proposed compliance plan in accordance with section 7651g of this title. The Administrator shall approve a designation that meets the requirements of this section, and such designated unit, or source, shall be allocated allowances, and be an affected unit for purposes of this subchapter.

(b) Establishment of baseline

The baseline for a unit designated under this section shall be established by the Administrator by regulation, based on fuel consumption and operating data for the unit for calendar years 1985, 1986, and 1987, or if such data is not available, the Administrator may prescribe a baseline based on alternative representative data.

(c) Emission limitations

Annual emissions limitations for sulfur dioxide shall be equal to the product of the baseline multiplied by the lesser of the unit's 1985 actual or allowable emission rate in lbs/mmBtu, or, if the unit did not operate in 1985, by the lesser of the unit's actual or allowable emission rate for a calendar year after 1985 (as determined by the Administrator), divided by 2,000.

(d) Process sources

Not later than 18 months after enactment of the Clean Air Act Amendments of 1990, the Administrator shall establish a program under which the owner or operator of a process source that emits sulfur dioxide may elect to designate that source as an affected unit for the purpose of receiving allowances under this subchapter. The Administrator shall, by regulation, define the sources that may be designated; specify the emissions limitation; specify the operating, emission baseline, and other data requirements; prescribe CEMS or other monitoring requirements; and promulgate permit, reporting, and any other requirements necessary to implement such a program.

(e) Allowances and permits

The Administrator shall issue allowances to an affected unit under this section in an amount equal to the emissions limitation calculated under subsection (c) or (d) of this section, in accordance with section 7651b of this title. Such allowance may be used in accordance with, and shall be subject to, the provisions of section 7651b of this title. Affected sources under this section shall be subject to the requirements of sections 7651b, 7651g, 7651j, 7651k, 7651l, and 7651m of this title.

(f) Limitation

Any unit designated under this section shall not transfer or bank allowances produced as a result of reduced utilization or shutdown, except that, such allowances may be transferred or carried forward for use in subsequent years to the extent that the reduced utilization or shutdown results from the replacement of thermal energy from the unit designated under this section, with thermal energy generated by any other unit or units subject to the requirements of this subchapter, and the designated unit's allowances are transferred or carried forward for use at such other replacement unit or units. In no case may the Administrator allocate to a source designated under this section allowances in an amount greater than the emissions resulting from operation of the source in full compliance with the requirements of this chapter. No such allowances shall authorize operation of a unit in violation of any other requirements of this chapter.

(g) Implementation

The Administrator shall issue regulations to implement this section not later than eighteen months after enactment of the Clean Air Act Amendments of 1990.

(h) Small diesel refineries

The Administrator shall issue allowances to owners or operators of small diesel refineries who produce diesel fuel after October 1, 1993, meeting the requirements of section 7545(i) of this title.

(1) Allowance period

Allowances may be allocated under this subsection only for the period from October 1, 1993, through December 31, 1999.

(2) Allowance determination

The number of allowances allocated pursuant to this paragraph shall equal the annual number of pounds of sulfur dioxide reduction attributable to desulfurization by a small refinery divided by 2,000. For the purposes of this calculation, the concentration of sulfur removed from diesel fuel shall be the difference between 0.274 percent (by weight) and 0.050 percent (by weight).

(3) Refinery eligibility

As used in this subsection, the term "small refinery" shall mean a refinery or portion of a refinery—

(A) which, as of November 15, 1990, has bona fide crude oil through-put of less than 18,250,000 barrels per year, as reported to the Department of Energy, and

(B) which, as of November 15, 1990, is owned or controlled by a refiner with a total combined bona fide crude oil through-put of less than 50,187,500 barrels per year, as reported to the Department of Energy.

(4) Limitation per refinery

The maximum number of allowances that can be annually allocated to a small refinery pursuant to this subsection is one thousand and five hundred.

(5) Limitation on total

In any given year, the total number of allowances allocated pursuant to this subsection shall not exceed thirty-five thousand.

(6) Required certification

The Administrator shall not allocate any allowances pursuant to this subsection unless the owner or operator of a small diesel refinery shall have certified, at a time and in a manner prescribed by the Administrator, that all motor diesel fuel produced by the refinery for which allowances are claimed, including motor diesel fuel for off-highway use, shall have met the requirements of section 7545(i) of this title.

(July 14, 1955, ch. 360, title IV, § 410, as added Nov. 15, 1990, Pub.L. 101–549, title IV, § 401, 104 Stat. 2621.)

References in Text

Enactment of the Clean Air Act Amendments of 1990, referred to in subsecs. (d) and (g), probably means the date of enactment of Pub.L. 101–549, Nov. 15, 1990, 104 Stat. 2399, which was approved Nov. 15, 1990.

Section 7545(i) of this title, referred to in subsecs. (h) and (h)(6), was in the original subsection 211(i) of this Act. The translation was made to section 7545(i) of this title as the probable intent of Congress.

Effective Date

Section to take effect Nov. 15, 1990, except as otherwise provided, see section 711(b) of Pub.L. 101–549, set out as a note under section 7401 of this title.

Savings Provisions

Suits, actions or proceedings commenced under this chapter as in effect prior to Nov. 15, 1990, not to abate by reason of the taking effect of amendments by Pub.L. 101–549, except as otherwise provided for, see section 711(a) of Pub.L. 101–549, set out as a note under section 7401 of this title.

§ 7651j. Excess emissions penalty [CAA § 411]

(a) Excess emissions penalty

The owner or operator of any unit or process source subject to the requirements of sections 7651b, 7651c, 7651d, 7651e, 7651f or 7651h of this title, or designated under section 7651i of this title, that emits sulfur dioxide or nitrogen oxides for any calendar year in excess of the unit's emissions limitation requirement or, in the case of sulfur dioxide, of the allowances the owner or operator holds for use for the unit for that calendar year shall be liable for the payment of an excess emissions penalty, except where such emissions were authorized pursuant to section 7410(f) of this title. That penalty shall be calculated on the basis of the number of tons emitted in excess of the unit's emissions limitation requirement or, in the case of sulfur dioxide, of the allowances the operator holds for use for the unit for that year, multiplied by $2,000. Any such penalty shall be due and payable without demand to the Administrator as provided in regulations to be issued by the Administrator by no later than eighteen months after November 15, 1990. Any such payment shall be deposited in the United States Treasury pursuant to the Miscellaneous Receipts Act. Any penalty due and payable under this section shall not diminish the liability of the unit's owner or operator for any fine, penalty or assessment against the unit for the same violation under any other section of this chapter.

(b) Excess emissions offset

The owner or operator of any affected source that emits sulfur dioxide during any calendar year in excess of the unit's emissions limitation requirement or of the allowances held for the unit for the calendar year, shall be liable to offset the excess emissions by an equal tonnage amount in the following calendar year, or such longer period as the Administrator may prescribe. The owner or operator of the source shall, within sixty days after the end of the year in which the excess emissions occured [1], submit to the Administrator, and to the State in which the source is located, a proposed plan to achieve the required offsets. Upon approval of the proposed plan by the Administrator, as submitted, modified or conditioned, the plan shall be deemed at a condition of the operating permit for the unit without further review or revision of the permit. The Administrator shall also deduct allowances equal to the excess tonnage from those allocated for the source for the calendar year, or succeeding years during which offsets are required, following the year in which the excess emissions occurred.

(c) Penalty adjustment

The Administrator shall, by regulation, adjust the penalty specified in subsection (a) of this section for inflation, based on the Consumer Price Index, on November 15, 1990, and annually thereafter.

(d) Prohibition

It shall be unlawful for the owner or operator of any source liable for a penalty and offset under this section to fail (1) to pay the penalty under subsection (a) of this section, (2) to provide, and thereafter comply with, a compliance plan as required by subsection (b) of this section, or (3) to offset excess emissions as required by subsection (b) of this section.

(e) Savings provision

Nothing in this subchapter shall limit or otherwise affect the application of section 7413, 7414, 7420, or

7604 of this title except as otherwise explicitly provided in this subchapter.

(July 14, 1955, ch. 360, title IV, § 411, as added Nov. 15, 1990, Pub.L. 101–549, title IV, § 401, 104 Stat. 2623.)

1 So in original. Probably should be "occurred".

References in Text

Pursuant to the "Miscellaneous Receipts Act", referred to in subsec. (a), probably means "as miscellaneous receipts". No Miscellaneous Receipts Act was enacted by Congress at time of publication.

Effective Date

Section to take effect Nov. 15, 1990, except as otherwise provided, see section 711(b) of Pub.L. 101–549, set out as a note under section 7401 of this title.

Savings Provisions

Suits, actions or proceedings commenced under this chapter as in effect prior to Nov. 15, 1990, not to abate by reason of the taking effect of amendments by Pub.L. 101–549, except as otherwise provided for, see section 711(a) of Pub.L. 101–549, set out as a note under section 7401 of this title.

§ 7651k. Monitoring, reporting, and recordkeeping requirements [CAA § 412]

(a) Applicability

The owner and operator of any source subject to this subchapter shall be required to install and operate CEMS on each affected unit at the source, and to quality assure the data for sulfur dioxide, nitrogen oxides, opacity and volumetric flow at each such unit. The Administrator shall, by regulations issued not later than eighteen months after enactment of the Clean Air Act Amendments of 1990, specify the requirements for CEMS, for any alternative monitoring system that is demonstrated as providing information with the same precision, reliability, accessibility, and timeliness as that provided by CEMS, and for recordkeeping and reporting of information from such systems. Such regulations may include limitations or the use of alternative compliance methods by units equipped with an alternative monitoring system as may be necessary to preserve the orderly functioning of the allowance system, and which will ensure the emissions reductions contemplated by this subchapter. Where 2 or more units utilize a single stack, a separate CEMS shall not be required for each unit, and for such units the regulations shall require that the owner or operator collect sufficient information to permit reliable compliance determinations for each such unit.

(b) First phase requirements

Not later than thirty-six months after enactment of the Clean Air Act Amendments of 1990, the owner or operator of each affected unit under section 7651c of this title, including, but not limited to, units that become affected units pursuant to subsections (b) and (c) of this section and eligible units under subsection (d) of this section, shall install and operate CEMS, quality assure the data, and keep records and reports in accordance with the regulations issued under subsection (a) of this section.

(c) Second phase requirements

Not later than January 1, 1995, the owner or operator of each affected unit that has not previously met the requirements of subsections (a) and (b) of this section shall install and operate CEMS, quality assure the data, and keep records and reports in accordance with the regulations issued under subsection (a) of this section. Upon commencement of commercial operation of each new utility unit, the unit shall comply with the requirements of subsection (a) of this section.

(d) Unavailability of emissions data

If CEMS data or data from an alternative monitoring system approved by the Administrator under subsection (a) of this section is not available for any affected unit during any period of a calendar year in which such data is required under this subchapter, and the owner or operator cannot provide information, satisfactory to the Administrator, on emissions during that period, the Administrator shall deem the unit to be operating in an uncontrolled manner during the entire period for which the data was not available and shall, by regulation which shall be issued not later than eighteen months after enactment of the Clean Air Act Amendments of 1990, prescribe means to calculate emissions for that period. The owner or operator shall be liable for excess emissions fees and offsets under section 7651j of this title in accordance with such regulations. Any fee due and payable under this subsection shall not diminish the liability of the unit's owner or operator for any fine, penalty, fee or assessment against the unit for the same violation under any other section of this chapter.

(e) Prohibition

It shall be unlawful for the owner or operator of any source subject to this subchapter to operate a source without complying with the requirements of this section, and any regulations implementing this section.

(July 14, 1955, ch. 360, title IV, § 412, as added Nov. 15, 1990, Pub.L. 101–549, title IV, § 401, 104 Stat. 2624.)

References in Text

Enactment of the Clean Air Act Amendments of 1990, referred to in subsecs. (a), (b) and (d), probably means the date of enactment of Pub.L. 101–549, Nov. 15, 1990, 104 Stat. 2399, which was approved Nov. 15, 1990.

Effective Date

Section to take effect Nov. 15, 1990, except as otherwise provided, see section 711(b) of Pub.L. 101–549, set out as a note under section 7401 of this title.

Savings Provisions

Suits, actions or proceedings commenced under this chapter as in effect prior to Nov. 15, 1990, not to abate by reason of the taking effect of amendments by Pub.L. 101–549, except as otherwise provided for, see section 711(a) of Pub.L. 101–549, set out as a note under section 7401 of this title.

Information Gathering on Greenhouse Gases Contributing to Global Climate Change

Section 821 of Pub.L. 101–549 provided that:

"(a) **Monitoring.**—The Administrator of the Environmental Protection Agency shall promulgate regulations within 18 months after the enactment of the Clean Air Act Amendments of 1990 [probably means the date of enactment of Pub.L. 101–549, Nov. 15, 1990, 104 Stat. 2399, which was approved Nov. 15, 1990] to require that all affected sources subject to title V of the Clean Air Act [subchapter V of this chapter] shall also monitor carbon dioxide emissions according to the same timetable as in section 511(b) and (c). The regulations shall require that such data be reported to the Administrator. The provisions of section 511(e) of title V of the Clean Air Act shall apply for purposes of this section in the same manner and to the same extent as such provision applies to the monitoring and data referred to in section 511.

"(b) **Public availability of carbon dioxide information.**—For each unit required to monitor and provide carbon dioxide data under subsection (a), the Administrator shall compute the unit's aggregate annual total carbon dioxide emissions, incorporate such data into a computer data base, and make such aggregate annual data available to the public."

§ 7651*l*. General compliance with other provisions [CAA § 413]

Except as expressly provided, compliance with the requirements of this subchapter shall not exempt or exclude the owner or operator of any source subject to this subchapter from compliance with any other applicable requirements of this chapter.

(July 14, 1955, ch. 360, title IV, § 413, as added Nov. 15, 1990, Pub.L. 101–549, title IV, § 401, 104 Stat. 2625.)

Effective Date of 1990 Amendment

Amendment by Pub.L. 101–549 effective Nov. 15, 1990, except as otherwise provided, see section 711(b) of Pub.L. 101–549, set out as a note under section 7401 of this title.

Savings Provisions

Suits, actions or proceedings commenced under this chapter as in effect prior to Nov. 15, 1990, not to abate by reason of the taking effect of amendments by Pub.L. 101–549, except as otherwise provided for, see section 711(a) of Pub.L. 101–549, set out as a note under section 7401 of this title.

§ 7651m. Enforcement [CAA § 414]

It shall be unlawful for any person subject to this subchapter to violate any prohibition of, requirement of, or regulation promulgated pursuant to this subchapter shall be a violation of this chapter. In addition to the other requirements and prohibitions provided for in this subchapter, the operation of any affected unit to emit sulfur dioxide in excess of allowances held for such unit shall be deemed a violation, with each ton emitted in excess of allowances held constituting a separate violation.

(July 14, 1955, ch. 360, title IV, § 414, as added Nov. 15, 1990, Pub.L. 101–549, title IV, § 401, 104 Stat. 2625.)

Effective Date

Section to take effect Nov. 15, 1990, except as otherwise provided, see section 711(b) of Pub.L. 101–549, set out as a note under section 7401 of this title.

Savings Provisions

Suits, actions or proceedings commenced under this chapter as in effect prior to Nov. 15, 1990, not to abate by reason of the taking effect of amendments by Pub.L. 101–549, except as otherwise provided for, see section 711(a) of Pub.L. 101–549, set out as a note under section 7401 of this title.

§ 7651n. Clean coal technology regulatory incentives [CAA § 415]

(a) Definition

For purposes of this section, "clean coal technology" means any technology, including technologies applied at the precombustion, combustion, or post combustion stage, at a new or existing facility which will achieve significant reductions in air emissions of sulfur dioxide or oxides of nitrogen associated with the utilization of coal in the generation of electricity, process steam, or industrial products, which is not in widespread use as of November 15, 1990.

(b) Revised regulations for clean coal technology demonstrations

(1) Applicability

This subsection applies to physical or operational changes to existing facilities for the sole purpose of installation, operation, cessation, or removal of a temporary or permanent clean coal technology demonstration project. For the purposes of this section, a clean coal technology demonstration project shall mean a project using funds appropriated under the heading "Department of Energy—Clean Coal Technology", up to a total amount of $2,500,000,000 for commercial demonstration of clean coal technology, or similar projects funded through appropriations for the Environmental Protection Agency. The Federal contribution for a qualifying project shall be at least 20 percent of the total cost of the demonstration project.

(2) Temporary projects

Installation, operation, cessation, or removal of a temporary clean coal technology demonstration project that is operated for a period of five years or less, and which complies with the State implementation plans for the State in which the project is located and other requirements necessary to attain and maintain the national ambient air quality standards during and after the project is terminated, shall not subject such facility to the requirements of section 7411 of this title or part C or D of subchapter I of this chapter.

(3) Permanent projects

For permanent clean coal technology demonstration projects that constitute repowering as defined in section 7651a(1) of this title, any qualifying project shall not be subject to standards of performance under section 7411 of this title or to the review and permitting requirements of part C of subchapter I of this chapter for any pollutant the potential emissions of which will not increase as a result of the demonstration project.

(4) EPA regulations

Not later than 12 months after November 15, 1990, the Administrator shall promulgate regulations or interpretive rulings to revise requirements under section 7411 of this title and parts C and D of subchapter I of this chapter, as appropriate, to facilitate projects consistent in this subsection. With respect to parts C and D of subchapter I of this chapter, such regulations or rulings shall apply to all areas in which EPA is the permitting authority. In those instances in which the State is the permitting authority under part C or D of subchapter I of this chapter, any State may adopt and submit to the Administrator for approval revisions to its implementation plan to apply the regulations or rulings promulgated under this subsection.

(c) Exemption for reactivation of very clean units

Physical changes or changes in the method of operation associated with the commencement of commercial operations by a coal-fired utility unit after a period of discontinued operation shall not subject the unit to the requirements of section 7411 of this title or part C of subchapter I of this chapter where the unit (1) has not been in operation for the two-year period prior to the enactment of the Clean Air Act Amendments of 1990, and the emissions from such unit continue to be carried in the permitting authority's emissions inventory at the time of enactment, (2) was equipped prior to shut-down with a continuous system of emissions control that achieves a removal efficiency for sulfur dioxide of no less than 85 percent and a removal efficiency for particulates of no less than 98 percent, (3) is equipped with low-NO_x burners prior to the time of commencement, and (4) is otherwise in compliance with the requirements of this chapter.

(July 14, 1955, ch. 360, title IV, § 415, as added Nov. 15, 1990, Pub.L. 101–549, title IV, § 401, 104 Stat. 2625.)

References in Text

Enactment of the Clean Air Act Amendments of 1990, referred to in subsec. (c), probably means the date of enactment of Pub.L. 101–549, Nov. 15, 1990, 104 Stat. 2399, which was approved Nov. 15, 1990.

Effective Date

Section to take effect Nov. 15, 1990, except as otherwise provided, see section 711(b) of Pub.L. 101–549, set out as a note under section 7401 of this title.

Savings Provisions

Suits, actions or proceedings commenced under this chapter as in effect prior to Nov. 15, 1990, not to abate by reason of the taking effect of amendments by Pub.L. 101–549, except as otherwise provided for, see section 711(a) of Pub.L. 101–549, set out as a note under section 7401 of this title.

§ 7651*o*. Contingency guarantee; auctions, reserve [CAA § 416]

(a) Definitions

For purposes of this section—

(1) The term "independent power producer" means any person who owns or operates, in whole or in part, one or more new independent power production facilities.

(2) The term "new independent power production facility" means a facility that—

(A) is used for the generation of electric energy, 80 percent or more of which is sold at wholesale;

(B) is nonrecourse project-financed (as such term is defined by the Secretary of Energy within 3 months of November 15, 1990);

(C) does not generate electric energy sold to any affiliate (as defined in section 79b(a)(11) of Title 15) of the facility's owner or operator unless the owner or operator of the facility demonstrates that it cannot obtain allowances from the affiliate; and

(D) is a new unit required to hold allowances under this subchapter.

(3) The term "required allowances" means the allowances required to operate such unit for so much of the unit's useful life as occurs after January 1, 2000.

(b) Special reserve of allowances

Within 36 months after November 15, 1990, the Administrator shall promulgate regulations establishing a Special Allowance Reserve containing allowances to be sold under this section. For purposes of establishing the Special Allowance Reserve, the Administrator shall withhold—

(1) 2.8 percent of the allocation of allowances for each year from 1995 through 1999 inclusive; and

(2) 2.8 percent of the basic Phase II allowance allocation of allowances for each year beginning in the year 2000

which would (but for this subsection) be issued for each affected unit at an affected source. The Administrator shall record such withholding for purposes of transferring the proceeds of the allowance sales under this subsection. The allowances so withheld shall be deposited in the Reserve under this section.

(c) Direct sale at $1,500 per ton

(1) Subaccount for direct sales

In accordance with regulations under this section, the Administrator shall establish a Direct Sale Subaccount in the Special Allowance Reserve established under this section. The Direct Sale Subaccount shall contain allowances in the amount of 50,000 tons per year for each year beginning in the year 2000.

(2) Sales

Allowances in the subaccount shall be offered for direct sale to any person at the times and in the amounts specified in table 1 at a price of $1,500 per allowance, adjusted by the Consumer Price Index in the same manner as provided in paragraph (3). Requests to purchase allowances from the Direct Sale Subaccount established under paragraph (1) shall be approved in the order of receipt until no allowances remain in such subaccount, except that an opportunity to purchase such allowances shall be provided to the independent power producers referred to in this subsection before such allowances are offered to any other person. Each applicant shall be required to pay 50 percent of the total purchase price of the allowances within 6 months after the approval of the request to purchase. The remainder shall be paid on or before the transfer of the allowances.

TABLE 1—NUMBER OF ALLOWANCES AVAILABLE FOR SALE AT $1,500 PER TON

Year of Sale	Spot Sale (same year)	Advance Sale
1993–1999		25,000
2000 and after	25,000	25,000

Allowances sold in the spot sale in any year are allowances which may only be used in that year (unless banked for use in a later year). Allowances sold in the advance sale in any year are allowances which may only be used in the 7th year after the year in which they are first offered for sale (unless banked for use in a later year).

(3) Entitlement to written guarantee

Any independent power producer that submits an application to the Administrator establishing that such independent power producer—

(A) proposes to construct a new independent power production facility for which allowances are required under this subchapter;

(B) will apply for financing to construct such facility after January 1, 1990, and before the date of the first auction under this section;

(C) has submitted to each owner or operator of an affected unit listed in table A (in section 7651c of this title) a written offer to purchase the required allowances for $750 per ton; and

(D) has not received (within 180 days after submitting offers to purchase under subparagraph (C)) an acceptance of the offer to purchase the required allowances,

shall, within 30 days after submission of such application, be entitled to receive the Administrator's written guarantee (subject to the eligibility requirements set forth in paragraph (4)) that such required allowances will be made available for purchase from the Direct Sale Subaccount established under this subsection and at a guaranteed price. The guaranteed price at which such allowances shall be made available for purchase shall be $1,500 per ton, adjusted by the percentage, if any, by which the Consumer Price Index (as determined under section 7661a(b)(3)(B)(v) of this title) for the year in which the allowance is purchased exceeds the Consumer Price Index for the calendar year 1990.

(4) Eligibility requirements

The guarantee issued by the Administrator under paragraph (3) shall be subject to a demonstration by the independent power producer, satisfactory to the Administrator, that—

(A) the independent power producer has—

(i) made good faith efforts to purchase the required allowances from the owners or operators of affected units to which allowances will be allocated, including efforts to purchase at annual auctions under this section, and from industrial sources that have elected to become affected units pursuant to section 7651i of this title; and

(ii) such bids and efforts were unsuccessful in obtaining the required allowances; and

(B) the independent power producer will continue to make good faith efforts to purchase the required allowances from the owners or operators of affected units and from industrial sources.

(5) Issuance of guaranteed allowances from direct sale subaccount under this section

From the allowances available in the Direct Sale Subaccount established under this subsection, upon payment of the guaranteed price, the Administrator shall issue to any person exercising the right to purchase allowances pursuant to a guarantee under this subsection the allowances covered by such guarantee. Persons to which guarantees under this subsection have been issued shall have the opportunity to purchase allowances pursuant to such guarantee from such subaccount before the allowances in such reserve are offered for sale to any other person.

(6) Proceeds

Notwithstanding section 3302 of Title 31 or any other provision of law, the Administrator shall require that the proceeds of any sale under this subsection be transferred, within 90 days after the sale, without charge, on a pro rata basis to the owners or operators of the affected units from whom the allowances were withheld under subsection (b) of this section and that any unsold allowances be transferred to the Subaccount for Auction Sales established under subsection (d) of this section. No proceeds of any sale under this subsection shall be held by any officer or employee of the United States or treated for any purpose as revenue to the United States or to the Administrator.

(7) Termination of subaccount

If the Administrator determines that, during any period of 2 consecutive calendar years, less than 20 percent of the allowances available in the subaccount for direct sales established under this subsection have been purchased under this paragraph, the Administrator shall terminate the subaccount and transfer such allowances to the Auction Subaccount under subsection (d) of this section.

(d) Auction sales

(1) Subaccount for auctions

The Administrator shall establish an Auction Subaccount in the Special Reserve established under this section. The Auction Subaccount shall contain allowances to be sold at auction under this section in the amount of 150,000 tons per year for each year from 1995 through 1999, inclusive and 250,000 tons per year for each year beginning in the calendar year 2000.

(2) Annual auctions

Commencing in 1993 and in each year thereafter, the Administrator shall conduct auctions at which the allowances referred to in paragraph (1) shall be offered for sale in accordance with regulations promulgated by the Administrator, in consultation with the Secretary of the Treasury, within 12 months of enactment of the Clean Air Act Amendments of 1990. The allowances referred to in paragraph (1) shall be offered for sale at auction in the amounts specified in table 2. The auction shall be open to any person. A person wishing to bid for such allowances shall submit (by a date set by the Administrator) to the Administrator (on a sealed bid schedule provided by the Administrator) offers to purchase specified numbers of allowances at specified prices. Such regulations shall specify that the auctioned allowances shall be allocated and sold on the basis of bid price, starting with the highest-priced bid and continuing until all allowances for sale at such auction have been allocated. The regulations shall not permit that a minimum price be set for the purchase of withheld allowances. Allowances purchased at the auction may be used for any purpose and at any time after the auction, subject to the provisions of this subchapter.

TABLE 2—NUMBER OF ALLOWANCES AVAILABLE FOR AUCTION

Year of Sale	Spot Auction (same year)	Advance Auction
1993	50,000*	100,000
1994	50,000*	100,000
1995	50,000*	100,000
1996	150,000	100,000
1997	150,000	100,000
1998	150,000	100,000
1999	150,000	100,000
2000 and after	100,000	100,000

Allowances sold in the spot sale in any year are allowances which may only be used in that year (unless banked for use in a later year), except as otherwise noted. Allowances sold in the advance auction in any year are allowances which may only be used in the 7th year after the year in which they are first offered for sale (unless banked for use in a later year).

* Available for use only in 1995 (unless banked for use in a later year).

(3) Proceeds

(A) Notwithstanding section 3302 of Title 31 or any other provision of law, within 90 days of receipt, the Administrator shall transfer the proceeds from the auction under this section, on a pro rata basis, to the owners or operators of the affected units at an affected source from whom allowances were withheld under subsection (b) of this section. No funds transferred from a purchaser to a seller of allowances under this paragraph shall be held by any officer or employee of the United States or treated for any purpose as revenue to the United States or the Administrator

(B) At the end of each year, any allowances offered for sale but not sold at the auction shall be returned without charge, on a pro rata basis, to the owner or operator of the affected units from whose allocation the allowances were withheld.

(4) Additional auction participants

Any person holding allowances or to whom allowances are allocated by the Administrator may submit those allowances to the Administrator to be offered for sale at auction under this subsection. The proceeds of any such sale shall be transferred at the time of sale by the purchaser to the person submitting such allowances for sale. The holder of allowances offered for sale under this paragraph may specify a minimum sale price. Any person may purchase allowances offered for auction under this paragraph. Such allowances shall be allocated and sold to purchasers on the basis of bid price after the auction under paragraph (2) is complete. No funds transferred from a purchaser to a seller of allowances under this paragraph shall be held by any officer or employee of the United States or treated for any purpose as revenue to the United States or the Administrator.

(5) Recording by EPA

The Administrator shall record and publicly report the nature, prices and results of each auction under this subsection, including the prices of successful bids, and shall record the transfers of allowances as a result of each auction in accordance with the requirements of this section. The transfer of allowances at such auction shall be recorded in accordance with the regulations promulgated by the Administrator under this subchapter.

(e) Changes in sales, auctions, and withholding

Pursuant to rulemaking after public notice and comment the Administrator may at any time after the year 1998 (in the case of advance sales or advance auctions) and 2005 (in the case of spot sales or spot auctions) decrease the number of allowances withheld and sold under this section.

(f) Termination of auctions

The Administrator may terminate the withholding of allowances and the auction sales under this section if the Administrator determines that, during any period of 3 consecutive calendar years after 2002, less than 20 percent of the allowances available in the auction subaccount have been purchased. Pursuant to regulations under this section, the Administrator may by delegation or contract provide for the conduct of sales or auctions under the Administrator's supervision by other departments or agencies of the United States Government or by nongovernmental agencies, groups, or organizations.

(July 14, 1955, ch. 360, title IV, § 416, as added Nov. 15, 1990, Pub.L. 101–549, title IV, § 401, 104 Stat. 2626.)

References in Text

Enactment of the Clean Air Act Amendments of 1990, referred to in subsec. (d)(2), probably means the date of enactment of Pub.L. 101–549, Nov. 15, 1990, 104 Stat. 2399, which was approved Nov. 15, 1990.

Effective Date

Section to take effect Nov. 15, 1990, except as otherwise provided, see section 711(b) of Pub.L. 101–549, set out as a note under section 7401 of this title.

Savings Provisions

Suits, actions or proceedings commenced under this chapter as in effect prior to Nov. 15, 1990, not to abate by reason of the taking effect of amendments by Pub.L. 101–549, except as otherwise provided for, see section 711(a) of Pub.L. 101–549, set out as a note under section 7401 of this title.

SUBCHAPTER V—PERMITS

§ 7661. Definitions [CAA § 501]

As used in this subchapter—

(1) Affected source

The term "affected source" shall have the meaning given such term in subchapter IV–A of this chapter.

(2) Major source

The term "major source" means any stationary source (or any group of stationary sources located within a contiguous area and under common control) that is either of the following:

(A) A major source as defined in section 7412 of this title.

(B) A major stationary source as defined in section 7602 of this title or part D of subchapter I of this chapter.

(3) Schedule of compliance

The term "schedule of compliance" means a schedule of remedial measures, including an enforceable sequence of actions or operations, leading to compliance with an applicable implementation plan, emission standard, emission limitation, or emission prohibition.

(4) Permitting authority

The term "permitting authority" means the Administrator or the air pollution control agency authorized by the Administrator to carry out a permit program under this subchapter.

(July 14, 1955, ch. 360, title V, § 501, as added Nov. 15, 1990, Pub.L. 101–549, title V, § 501, 104 Stat. 2635.)

Effective Date

Section to take effect Nov. 15, 1990, except as otherwise provided, see section 711(b) of Pub.L. 101–549, set out as a note under section 7401 of this title.

Savings Provisions

Suits, actions or proceedings commenced under this chapter as in effect prior to Nov. 15, 1990, not to abate by reason of the taking effect of amendments by Pub.L. 101–549, except as otherwise provided for, see section 711(a) of Pub.L. 101–549, set out as a note under section 7401 of this title.

§ 7661a. Permit programs [CAA § 502]

(a) Violations

After the effective date of any permit program approved or promulgated under this subchapter, it shall be unlawful for any person to violate any requirement of a permit issued under this subchapter, or to operate an affected source (as provided in subchapter IV–A of this chapter), a major source, any other source (including an area source) subject to standards or regulations under section 7411 or 7412 of this title, any other source required to have a permit under parts C or D of subchapter I of this chapter, or any other stationary source in a category designated (in whole or in part) by regulations promulgated by the Administrator (after notice and public comment) which shall include a finding setting forth the basis for such designation, except in compliance with a permit issued by a permitting authority under this subchapter. (Nothing in this subsection shall be construed to alter the applicable requirements of this chapter that a permit be obtained before construction or modification.) The Administrator may, in the Administrator's discretion and consistent with the applicable provisions of this chapter, promulgate regulations to exempt one or more source categories (in whole or in part) from the requirements of this subsection if the Administrator finds that compliance with such requirements is impracticable, infeasible, or unnecessarily burdensome on such categories, except that the Administrator may not exempt any major source from such requirements.

(b) Regulations

The Administrator shall promulgate within 12 months after November 15, 1990 regulations establishing the minimum elements of a permit program to be administered by any air pollution control agency. These elements shall include each of the following:

(1) Requirements for permit applications, including a standard application form and criteria for determining in a timely fashion the completeness of applications.

(2) Monitoring and reporting requirements.

(3)(A) A requirement under State or local law or interstate compact that the owner or operator of all sources subject to the requirement to obtain a permit under this subchapter pay an annual fee, or the equivalent over some other period, sufficient to cover all reasonable (direct and indirect) costs required to develop and administer the permit program requirements of this subchapter, including section 7661f of this title, including the reasonable costs of—

(i) reviewing and acting upon any application for such a permit,

(ii) if the owner or operator receives a permit for such source, whether before or after November 15, 1990, implementing and enforcing the terms and conditions of any such permit (not including any court costs or other costs associated with any enforcement action),

(iii) emissions and ambient monitoring,

(iv) preparing generally applicable regulations, or guidance,

(v) modeling, analyses, and demonstrations, and

(vi) preparing inventories and tracking emissions.

(B) The total amount of fees collected by the permitting authority shall conform to the following requirements:

(i) The Administrator shall not approve a program as meeting the requirements of this paragraph unless the State demonstrates that, except as otherwise provided in subparagraphs (ii) through (v) of this subparagraph, the program will result in the collection, in the aggregate, from all sources subject to subparagraph (A), of an amount not less than $25 per ton of each regulated pollutant, or such other amount as the Administrator may determine adequately reflects the reasonable costs of the permit program.

(ii) As used in this subparagraph, the term "regulated pollutant" shall mean (I) a volatile organic compound; (II) each pollutant regulated under section 7411 or 7412 of this title; and (III) each pollutant for which a national primary ambient air quality standard has been promulgated (except that carbon monoxide shall be excluded from this reference).

(iii) In determining the amount under clause (i), the permitting authority is not required to include any amount of regulated pollutant emitted by any source in excess of 4,000 tons per year of that regulated pollutant.

(iv) The requirements of clause (i) shall not apply if the permitting authority demonstrates that collecting an amount less than the amount specified under clause (i) will meet the requirements of subparagraph (A).

(v) The fee calculated under clause (i) shall be increased (consistent with the need to cover the reasonable costs authorized by subparagraph (A)) in each year beginning after 1990 by the percentage, if any, by which the Consumer Price Index for the most recent calendar year ending before the beginning of such year exceeds the Consumer Price Index for the calendar year 1989. For purposes of this clause—

(I) the Consumer Price Index for any calendar year is the average of the Consumer Price Index for all-urban consumers published by the Department of Labor, as of the close of the 12–month period ending on August 31 of each calendar year, and

(II) the revision of the Consumer Price Index which is most consistent with the Consumer Price Index for calendar year 1989 shall be used.

(C)(i) If the Administrator determines, under subsection (d) of this section, that the fee provisions of the operating permit program do not meet the requirements of this paragraph, or if the Administrator makes a determination, under subsection (i) of this section, that the permitting authority is not adequately administering or enforcing an approved fee program, the Administrator may, in addition to taking any other action authorized under this subchapter, collect reasonable fees from the sources identified under subparagraph (A). Such fees shall be designed solely to cover the Administrator's costs of administering the provisions of the permit program promulgated by the Administrator.

(ii) Any source that fails to pay fees lawfully imposed by the Administrator under this subparagraph shall pay a penalty of 50 percent of the fee amount, plus interest on the fee amount computed in accordance with section 6621(a)(2) of Title 26 (relating to computation of interest on underpayment of Federal taxes).

(iii) Any fees, penalties, and interest collected under this subparagraph shall be deposited in a special fund in the United States Treasury for licensing and other services, which thereafter shall be available for appropriation, to remain available until expended, subject to appropriation, to carry out the Agency's activities for which the fees were collected. Any fee required to be collected by a State, local, or interstate agency under this subsection shall be utilized solely to cover all reasonable (direct and indirect) costs required to support the permit program as set forth in subparagraph (A).

(4) Requirements for adequate personnel and funding to administer the program.

(5) A requirement that the permitting authority have adequate authority to:

(A) issue permits and assure compliance by all sources required to have a permit under this title with each applicable standard, regulation or requirement under this Act;

(B) issue permits for a fixed term, not to exceed 5 years;

(C) assure that upon issuance or renewal permits incorporate emission limitations and other requirements in an applicable implementation plan;

(D) terminate, modify, or revoke and reissue permits for cause;

(E) enforce permits, permit fee requirements, and the requirement to obtain a permit, including authority to recover civil penalties in a maximum amount of not less than $10,000 per day for each violation, and provide appropriate criminal penalties; and

(F) assure that no permit will be issued if the Administrator objects to its issuance in a timely manner under this subchapter.

(6) Adequate, streamlined, and reasonable procedures for expeditiously determining when applications are complete, for processing such applications, for public notice, including offering an opportunity for public comment and a hearing, and for expeditious review of permit actions, including applications, renewals, or revisions, and including an opportunity for judicial review in State court of the final permit action by the applicant, any person who participated in the public comment process, and any other person who could obtain judicial review of that action under applicable law.

(7) To ensure against unreasonable delay by the permitting authority, adequate authority and procedures to provide that a failure of such permitting authority to act on a permit application or permit renewal application (in accordance with the time periods specified in section 7661b of this title or, as appropriate, subchapter IV–A of this chapter) shall be treated as a final permit action solely for purposes of obtaining judicial review in State court of an action brought by any person referred to in paragraph (6) to require that action be taken by the permitting authority on such application without additional delay.

(8) Authority, and reasonable procedures consistent with the need for expeditious action by the permitting authority on permit applications and related matters, to make available to the public any permit application, compliance plan, permit, and monitoring or compliance report under section 7661b(e) of this title, subject to the provisions of section 7414(c) of this title.

(9) A requirement that the permitting authority, in the case of permits with a term of 3 or more years for major sources, shall require revisions to the permit to incorporate applicable standards and regulations promulgated under this chapter after the issuance of such permit. Such revisions shall occur as expeditiously as practicable and consistent with the procedures established under paragraph (6) but not later than 18 months after the promulgation of such standards and regulations. No such revision shall be required if the effective date of the standards or regulations is a date after the expiration of the permit term. Such permit revision shall be treated as a permit renewal if it complies with the requirements of this subchapter regarding renewals.

(10) Provisions to allow changes within a permitted facility (or one operating pursuant to section 7661b(d) of this title) without requiring a permit revision, if the changes are not modifications under any provision of subchapter I of this chapter and the changes do not exceed the emissions allowable under the permit (whether expressed therein as a rate of emissions or in terms of total emissions: *Provided,* That the facility provides the Administrator and the permitting authority with written notification in advance of the proposed changes which shall be a minimum of 7 days, unless the permitting authority provides in its regulations a different timeframe for emergencies.

(c) Single permit

A single permit may be issued for a facility with multiple sources.

(d) Submission and approval

(1) Not later than 3 years after November 15, 1990, the Governor of each State shall develop and submit to the Administrator a permit program under State or local law or under an interstate compact meeting the requirements of this subchapter. In addition, the Governor shall submit a legal opinion from the attorney general (or the attorney for those State air pollution control agencies that have independent legal counsel), or from the chief legal officer of an interstate agency, that the laws of the State, locality, or the interstate compact provide adequate authority to carry out the program. Not later than 1 year after receiving a program, and after notice and opportunity for public comment, the Administrator shall approve or disapprove such program, in whole or in part. The Administrator may approve a program to the extent that the program meets the requirements of this chapter, including the regulations issued under subsection (b) of this section. If the program is disapproved, in whole or in part, the Administrator shall notify the Governor of any revisions or modifications necessary to obtain approval. The Governor shall revise and resubmit the program for review under this section within 180 days after receiving notification.

(2)(A) If the Governor does not submit a program as required under paragraph (1) or if the Administrator disapproves a program submitted by the Governor under paragraph (1), in whole or in part, the Administrator may, prior to the expiration of the 18–month period referred to in subparagraph (B), in the Administrator's discretion, apply any of the sanctions specified in section 7509(b) of this title.

(B) If the Governor does not submit a program as required under paragraph (1), or if the Administrator disapproves any such program submitted by the Governor under paragraph (1), in whole or in part, 18 months after the date required for such submittal or the date of such disapproval, as the case may be, the Administrator shall apply sanctions under section 7509(b) of this title in the same manner and subject to the same deadlines and other conditions as are applicable in the case of a determination, disapproval, or finding under section 7509(a) of this title.

(C) The sanctions under section 7509(b)(2) of this title shall not apply pursuant to this paragraph in any area unless the failure to submit or the disapproval referred to in subparagraph (A) or (B) relates to an air pollutant for which such area has been designated a nonattainment area (as defined in part D of subchapter I of this chapter).

(3) If a program meeting the requirements of this subchapter has not been approved in whole for any State, the Administrator shall, 2 years after the date required for submission of such a program under paragraph (1), promulgate, administer, and enforce a program under this subchapter for that State.

(e) Suspension

The Administrator shall suspend the issuance of permits promptly upon publication of notice of approval of a permit program under this section, but may, in such notice, retain jurisdiction over permits that have been federally issued, but for which the administrative or judicial review process is not complete. The Administrator shall continue to administer and enforce federally issued permits under this subchapter until they are replaced by a permit issued by a permitting program. Nothing in this subsection should be construed to limit the Administrator's ability to enforce permits issued by a State.

(f) Prohibition

No partial permit program shall be approved unless, at a minimum, it applies, and ensures compliance with, this subchapter and each of the following:

(1) All requirements established under subchapter IV–A of this chapter applicable to "affected sources".

(2) All requirements established under section 7412 of this title applicable to "major sources", "area sources", and "new sources".

(3) All requirements of subchapter I of this chapter (other than section 7412 of this title) applicable to sources required to have a permit under this subchapter. Approval of a partial program shall not relieve the State of its obligation to submit a complete program, nor from the application of any sanctions under this chapter for failure to submit an approvable permit program.

Approval of a partial program shall not relieve the State of its obligation to submit a complete program, nor from the application of any sanctions under this chapter for failure to submit an approvable permit program.

(g) Interim approval

If a program (including a partial permit program) submitted under this subchapter substantially meets the requirements of this subchapter, but is not fully approvable, the Administrator may by rule grant the program interim approval. In the notice of final rulemaking, the Administrator shall specify the changes that must be made before the program can receive full approval. An interim approval under this subsection shall expire on a date set by the Administrator not later than 2 years after such approval, and may not be renewed. For the period of any such interim approval, the provisions of subsection (d)(2) of this section, and the obligation of the Administrator to promulgate a program under this subchapter for the State pursuant to subsection (d)(3) of this section, shall be suspended. Such provisions and such obligation of the Administrator shall apply after the expiration of such interim approval.

(h) Effective date

The effective date of a permit program, or partial or interim program, approved under this subchapter, shall be the effective date of approval by the Administrator. The effective date of a permit program, or partial permit program, promulgated by the Administrator shall be the date of promulgation.

(i) Administration and enforcement

(1) Whenever the Administrator makes a determination that a permitting authority is not adequately administering and enforcing a program, or portion thereof, in accordance with the requirements of this subchapter, the Administrator shall provide notice to the State and may, prior to the expiration of the 18–month period referred to in paragraph (2), in the Administrator's discretion, apply any of the sanctions specified in section 7509(b) of this title.

(2) Whenever the Administrator makes a determination that a permitting authority is not adequately administering and enforcing a program, or portion thereof, in accordance with the requirements of this subchapter, 18 months after the date of the notice under paragraph (1), the Administrator shall apply the sanctions under section 7509(b) of this title in the same manner and subject to the same deadlines and other conditions as are applicable in the case of a determination, disapproval, or finding under section 7509(a) of this title.

(3) The sanctions under section 7509(b)(2) of this title shall not apply pursuant to this subsection in any area unless the failure to adequately enforce and administer the program relates to an air pollutant for which such area has been designated a nonattainment area.

(4) Whenever the Administrator has made a finding under paragraph (1) with respect to any State, unless the State has corrected such deficiency within 18 months after the date of such finding, the Administrator shall, 2 years after the date of such finding, promulgate, administer, and enforce a program under this subchapter for that State. Nothing in this paragraph shall be construed to affect the validity of a program which has been approved under this subchapter or the authority of any permitting authority acting under such program until such time as such program is promulgated by the Administrator under this paragraph.

(July 14, 1955, ch. 360, title V, § 502, as added Nov. 15, 1990, Pub.L. 101–549, title V, § 501, 104 Stat. 2635.)

Effective Date

Section to take effect Nov. 15, 1990, except as otherwise provided, see section 711(b) of Pub.L. 101–549, set out as a note under section 7401 of this title.

Savings Provisions

Suits, actions or proceedings commenced under this chapter as in effect prior to Nov. 15, 1990, not to abate by reason of the taking effect of amendments by Pub.L. 101–549, except as otherwise provided for, see section 711(a) of Pub.L. 101–549, set out as a note under section 7401 of this title.

§ 7661b. Permit applications [CAA § 503]

(a) Applicable date

Any source specified in section 7661a(a) of this title shall become subject to a permit program, and required to have a permit, on the later of the following dates—

(1) the effective date of a permit program or partial or interim permit program applicable to the source; or

(2) the date such source becomes subject to section 7661a(a) of this title.

(b) Compliance plan

(1) The regulations required by section 7661a(b) of this title shall include a requirement that the applicant submit with the permit application a compliance plan describing how the source will comply with all applicable requirements under this chapter. The compliance plan shall include a schedule of compliance, and a schedule under which the permittee will submit progress reports to the permitting authority no less frequently than every 6 months.

(2) The regulations shall further require the permittee to periodically (but no less frequently than annually) certify that the facility is in compliance with any applicable requirements of the permit, and to promptly report any deviations from permit requirements to the permitting authority.

(c) Deadline

Any person required to have a permit shall, not later than 12 months after the date on which the source becomes subject to a permit program approved or promulgated under this subchapter, or such earlier date as the permitting authority may establish, submit to the permitting authority a compliance plan and an application for a permit signed by a responsible official, who shall certify the accuracy of the information submitted. The permitting authority shall approve or disapprove a completed application (consistent with the procedures established under this subchapter for consideration of such applications), and shall issue or deny the permit, within 18 months after the date of receipt thereof, except that the permitting authority shall establish a phased schedule for acting on permit applications submitted within the first full year after the effective date of a permit program (or a partial or interim program). Any such schedule shall assure that at least one-third of such permits will be acted on by such authority annually over a period of not to exceed 3 years after such effective date. Such authority shall establish reasonable procedures to prioritize such approval or disapproval actions in the case of applications for construction or modification under the applicable requirements of this chapter.

(d) Timely and complete applications

Except for sources required to have a permit before construction or modification under the applicable requirements of this chapter, if an applicant has submitted a timely and complete application for a permit required by this subchapter (including renewals), but final action has not been taken on such application, the source's failure to have a permit shall not be a violation of this chapter, unless the delay in final action was due to the failure of the applicant timely to submit information required or requested to process the application. No source required to have a permit under this subchapter shall be in violation of section 7661a(a) of this title before the date on which the source is required to submit an application under subsection (c) of this section.

(e) Copies; availability

A copy of each permit application, compliance plan (including the schedule of compliance), emissions or compliance monitoring report, certification, and each permit issued under this subchapter, shall be available to the public. If an applicant or permittee is required to submit information entitled to protection from disclosure under section 7414(c) of this title, the applicant or permittee may submit such information separately. The requirements of section 7414(c) of this title shall apply to such information. The contents of a permit shall not be entitled to protection under section 7414(c) of this title.

(July 14, 1955, ch. 360, title V, § 503, as added Nov. 15, 1990, Pub.L. 101–549, title V, § 501, 104 Stat. 2641.)

Effective Date

Section to take effect Nov. 15, 1990, except as otherwise provided, see section 711(b) of Pub.L. 101–549, set out as a note under section 7401 of this title.

Savings Provisions

Suits, actions or proceedings commenced under this chapter as in effect prior to Nov. 15, 1990, not to abate by reason of the taking effect of amendments by Pub.L. 101–549, except as otherwise provided for, see section 711(a) of Pub.L. 101–549, set out as a note under section 7401 of this title.

§ 7661c. Permit requirements and conditions [CAA § 504]

(a) Conditions

Each permit issued under this subchapter shall include enforceable emission limitations and standards, a schedule of compliance, a requirement that the permittee submit to the permitting authority, no less often than every 6 months, the results of any required monitoring, and such other conditions as are necessary to assure compliance with applicable requirements of this chapter, including the requirements of the applicable implementation plan.

(b) Monitoring and analysis

The Administrator may by rule prescribe procedures and methods for determining compliance and for monitoring and analysis of pollutants regulated under this Act, but continuous emissions monitoring need not be required if alternative methods are available that provide sufficiently reliable and timely information for determining compliance. Nothing in this subsection shall be construed to affect any continuous emissions monitoring requirement of subchapter IV–A of this chapter, or where required elsewhere in this chapter.

(c) Inspection, entry, monitoring, certification, and reporting

Each permit issued under this subchapter shall set forth inspection, entry, monitoring, compliance certification, and reporting requirements to assure compliance with the permit terms and conditions. Such monitoring and reporting requirements shall conform to any applicable regulation under subsection (b) of this section. Any report required to be submitted by a permit issued to a corporation under this subchapter shall be signed by a responsible corporate official, who shall certify its accuracy.

(d) General permits

The permitting authority may, after notice and opportunity for public hearing, issue a general permit covering numerous similar sources. Any general permit shall comply with all requirements applicable to permits under this subchapter. No source covered by a general permit shall thereby be relieved from the obligation to file an application under section 7661b of this title.

(e) Temporary sources

The permitting authority may issue a single permit authorizing emissions from similar operations at multiple temporary locations. No such permit shall be issued unless it includes conditions that will assure compliance with all the requirements of this chapter at all authorized locations, including, but not limited to, ambient standards and compliance with any applicable increment or visibility requirements under part C of subchapter I of this chapter. Any such permit shall in addition require the owner or operator to notify the permitting authority in advance of each change in location. The permitting authority may require a separate permit fee for operations at each location.

(f) Permit shield

Compliance with a permit issued in accordance with this subchapter shall be deemed compliance with section 7661a of this title. Except as otherwise provided by the Administrator by rule, the permit may also provide that compliance with the permit shall be deemed compliance with other applicable provisions of this chapter that relate to the permittee if—

(1) the permit includes the applicable requirements of such provisions, or

(2) the permitting authority in acting on the permit application makes a determination relating to the permittee that such other provisions (which shall be referred to in such determination) are not applicable and the permit includes the determination or a concise summary thereof.

Nothing in the preceding sentence shall alter or affect the provisions of section 7603 of this title, including the authority of the Administrator under that section.

(July 14, 1955, ch. 360, title V, § 504, as added Nov. 15, 1990, Pub.L. 101–549, title V, § 501, 104 Stat. 2642.)

Effective Date

Section to take effect Nov. 15, 1990, except as otherwise provided, see section 711(b) of Pub.L. 101–549, set out as a note under section 7401 of this title.

Savings Provisions

Suits, actions or proceedings commenced under this chapter as in effect prior to Nov. 15, 1990, not to abate by reason of the taking effect of amendments by Pub.L. 101–549, except as otherwise provided for, see section 711(a) of Pub.L. 101–549, set out as a note under section 7401 of this title.

§ 7661d. Notification to administrator and contiguous States [CAA § 505]

(a) Transmission and notice

(1) Each permitting authority—

(A) shall transmit to the Administrator a copy of each permit application (and any application for a permit modification or renewal) or such portion thereof, including any compliance plan, as the Administrator may require to effectively review the application and otherwise to carry out the Administrator's responsibilities under this chapter, and

(B) shall provide to the Administrator a copy of each permit proposed to be issued and issued as a final permit.

(2) The permitting authority shall notify all States—

(A) whose air quality may be affected and that are contiguous to the State in which the emission originates, or

(B) that are within 50 miles of the source,

of each permit application or proposed permit forwarded to the Administrator under this section, and shall provide an opportunity for such States to submit written recommendations respecting the issuance of the permit and its terms and conditions. If any part of those recommendations are not accepted by the permitting authority, such authority shall notify the State submitting the recommendations and the Administrator in writing of its failure to accept those recommendations and the reasons therefor.

(b) Objection by EPA

(1) If any permit contains provisions that are determined by the Administrator as not in compliance with the applicable requirements of this chapter, including the requirements of an applicable implementation plan, the Administrator shall, in accordance with this subsection, object to its issuance. The permitting authority shall respond in writing if the Administrator (A) within 45 days after receiving a copy of the proposed permit under subsection (a)(1), or (B) of this section within 45 days after receiving notification under subsection (a)(2) of this section, objects in writing to its issuance as not in compliance with such requirements. With the objection, the Administrator shall provide a statement of the reasons for the objection. A copy of the objection and statement shall be provided to the applicant.

(2) If the Administrator does not object in writing to the issuance of a permit pursuant to paragraph (1), any person may petition the Administrator within 60 days after the expiration of the 45–day review period specified in paragraph (1) to take such action. A copy of such petition shall be provided to the permitting authority and the applicant by the petitioner. The petition shall be based only on objections to the permit that were raised with reasonable specificity during the public comment period provided by the permitting agency (unless the petitioner demonstrates in the petition to the Administrator that it was impracticable to raise such objections within such period or unless the grounds for such objection arose after such period). The petition shall identify all such objections. If the permit has been issued by the permitting agency, such petition shall not postpone the effectiveness of the permit. The Administrator shall grant or deny such petition within 60 days after the petition is filed. The Administrator shall issue an objection within such period if the petitioner demonstrates to the Administrator that the permit is not in compliance with the requirements of this chapter, including the requirements of the applicable implementation plan. Any denial of such petition shall be subject to judicial review under section 7607 of this title. The Administrator shall include in regulations under this subchapter provisions to implement this paragraph. The Administrator may not delegate the requirements of this paragraph.

(3) Upon receipt of an objection by the Administrator under this subsection, the permitting authority may not issue the permit unless it is revised and issued in accordance with subsection (c) of this section. If the permitting authority has issued a permit prior to receipt of an objection by the Administrator under paragraph (2) of this subsection, the Administrator shall modify, terminate, or revoke such permit and the permitting authority may thereafter only issue a revised permit in accordance with subsection (c) of this section.

(c) Issuance or denial

If the permitting authority fails, within 90 days after the date of an objection under subsection (b) of this section, to submit a permit revised to meet the objection, the Administrator shall issue or deny the permit in accordance with the requirements of this subchapter. No objection shall be subject to judicial review until the Administrator takes final action to issue or deny a permit under this subsection.

(d) Waiver of notification requirements

(1) The Administrator may waive the requirements of subsections (a) and (b) of this section at the time of approval of a permit program under this subchapter for any category (including any class, type, or size within such category) of sources covered by the program other than major sources.

(2) The Administrator may, by regulation, establish categories of sources (including any class, type, or size within such category) to which the requirements of subsections (a) and (b) of this section shall not apply. The preceding sentence shall not apply to major sources.

(3) The Administrator may exclude from any waiver under this subsection notification under subsection (a)(2) of this section. Any waiver granted under this subsection may be revoked or modified by the Administrator by rule.

(e) Refusal of permitting authority to terminate, modify, or revoke and reissue

If the Administrator finds that cause exists to terminate, modify, or revoke and reissue a permit under this subchapter, the Administrator shall notify the permitting authority and the source of the Administrator's finding. The permitting authority shall, within 90 days after receipt of such notification, forward to the Administrator under this section a proposed determination of termination, modification, or revocation and reissuance, as appropriate. The Administrator may extend such 90 day period for an additional 90 days if the Administrator finds that a new or revised permit application is necessary, or that the permitting authority must require the permittee to submit additional information. The Administrator may review such proposed determination under the provisions of subsections (a) and (b) of this section. If the permitting authority fails to submit the required proposed determination, or if the Administrator objects and the permitting authority fails to resolve the objection within 90 days, the Administrator may, after notice and in accordance with fair and reasonable procedures, terminate, modify, or revoke and reissue the permit.

(July 14, 1955, ch. 360, title V, § 505, as added Nov. 15, 1990, Pub.L. 101–549, title V, § 501, 104 Stat. 2643.)

Effective Date

Section to take effect Nov. 15, 1990, except as otherwise provided, see section 711(b) of Pub.L. 101–549, set out as a note under section 7401 of this title.

Savings Provisions

Suits, actions or proceeding commenced under this chapter as in effect prior to Nov. 15, 1990, not to abate by reason of the taking effect of amendments by Pub.L. 101–549, except as otherwise provided for, see section 711(a) of Pub.L. 101–549, set out as a note under section 7401 of this title.

§ 7661e. Other authorities [CAA § 506]

(a) In general

Nothing in this subchapter shall prevent a State, or interstate permitting authority, from establishing additional permitting requirements not inconsistent with this chapter.

(b) Permits implementing acid rain provisions

The provisions of this subchapter, including provisions regarding schedules for submission and approval or disapproval of permit applications, shall apply to permits implementing the requirements of subchapter IV–A of this chapter except as modified by that subchapter.

(July 14, 1955, ch. 360, title V, § 506, as added Nov. 15, 1990, Pub.L. 101–549, title V, § 501, 104 Stat. 2645.)

Effective Date

Section to take effect Nov. 15, 1990, except as otherwise provided, see section 711(b) of Pub.L. 101–549, set out as a note under section 7401 of this title.

Savings Provisions

Suits, actions or proceedings commenced under this chapter as in effect prior to Nov. 15, 1990, not to abate by reason of the taking effect of amendments by Pub.L. 101–549, except as otherwise provided for, see section 711(a) of Pub.L. 101–549, set out as a note under section 7401 of this title.

§ 7661f. Small business stationary source technical and environmental compliance assistance program [CAA § 507]

(a) Plan revisions

Consistent with sections 7410 and 7412 of this title, each State shall, after reasonable notice and public hearings, adopt and submit to the Administrator as part of the State implementation plan for such State or as a revision to such State implementation plan under section 7410 of this title, plans for establishing a small business stationary source technical and environmental compliance assistance program. Such submission shall be made within 24 months after November 15, 1990. The Administrator shall approve such program if it includes each of the following:

(1) Adequate mechanisms for developing, collecting, and coordinating information concerning compliance methods and technologies for small business stationary sources, and programs to encourage lawful cooperation among such sources and other persons to further compliance with this chapter.

(2) Adequate mechanisms for assisting small business stationary sources with pollution prevention and accidental release detection and prevention, including providing information concerning alternative technologies, process changes, products, and methods of operation that help reduce air pollution.

(3) A designated State office within the relevant State agency to serve as ombudsman for small business stationary sources in connection with the implementation of this chapter.

(4) A compliance assistance program for small business stationary sources which assists small business stationary sources in determining applicable requirements and in receiving permits under this chapter in a timely and efficient manner.

(5) Adequate mechanisms to assure that small business stationary sources receive notice of their rights under this Act in such manner and form as to assure reasonably adequate time for such sources to evaluate compliance methods and any relevant or applicable proposed or final regulation or standard issued under this chapter.

(6) Adequate mechanisms for informing small business stationary sources of their obligations under this chapter, including mechanisms for referring such sources to qualified auditors or, at the option of the State, for providing audits of the operations of such sources to determine compliance with this chapter.

(7) Procedures for consideration of requests from a small business stationary source for modification of—

(A) any work practice or technological method of compliance, or

(B) the schedule of milestones for implementing such work practice or method of compliance preceding any applicable compliance date,

based on the technological and financial capability of any such small business stationary source. No such modification may be granted unless it is in compliance with the applicable requirements of this chapter, including the requirements of the applicable implementation plan. Where such applicable requirements are set forth in Federal regulations, only modifications authorized in such regulations may be allowed.

(b) Program

The Administrator shall establish within 9 months after November 15, 1990 a small business stationary source technical and environmental compliance assistance program. Such program shall—

(1) assist the States in the development of the program required under subsection (a) of this section (relating to assistance for small business stationary sources);

(2) issue guidance for the use of the States in the implementation of these programs that includes alternative control technologies and pollution prevention methods applicable to small business stationary sources; and

(3) provide for implementation of the program provisions required under subsection (a)(4) of this section in any State that fails to submit such a program under that subsection.

(c) Eligibility

(1) Except as provided in paragraphs (2) and (3), for purposes of this section, the term "small business stationary source" means a stationary source that—

(A) is owned or operated by a person that employs 100 or fewer individuals,

(B) is a small business concern as defined in the Small Business Act [42 U.S.C.A. § 631 et seq.];

(C) is not a major stationary source;

(D) does not emit 50 tons or more per year of any regulated pollutant; and

(E) emits less than 75 tons per year of all regulated pollutants.

(2) Upon petition by a source, the State may, after notice and opportunity for public comment, include as a small business stationary source for purposes of this section any stationary source which does not meet the criteria of subparagraphs (C), (D), or (E) of paragraph (1) but which does not emit more than 100 tons per year of all regulated pollutants.

(3)(A) The Administrator, in consultation with the Administrator of the Small Business Administration and after providing notice and opportunity for public comment, may exclude from the small business stationary source definition under this section any category or subcategory of sources that the Administrator determines to have sufficient technical and financial capabilities to meet the requirements of this chapter without the application of this subsection.

(B) The State, in consultation with the Administrator and the Administrator of the Small Business Administration and after providing notice and opportunity for public hearing, may exclude from the small business stationary source definition under this section any category or subcategory of sources that the State determines to have sufficient technical and financial capabilities to meet the requirements of this chapter without the application of this subsection.

(d) Monitoring

The Administrator shall direct the Agency's Office of Small and Disadvantaged Business Utilization through the Small Business Ombudsman (hereinafter in this section referred to as the "Ombudsman") to monitor the small business stationary source technical and environmental compliance assistance program under this section. In carrying out such monitoring activities, the Ombudsman shall—

(1) render advisory opinions on the overall effectiveness of the Small Business Stationary Source Technical and Environmental Compliance Assistance Program, difficulties encountered, and degree and severity of enforcement;

(2) make periodic reports to the Congress on the compliance of the Small Business Stationary Source Technical and Environmental Compliance Assistance Program with the requirements of the Paperwork Reduction Act [44 U.S.C.A. § 3501 et seq.], the Regulatory Flexibility Act [5 U.S.C.A. § 601 et seq.], and the Equal Access to Justice Act;

(3) review information to be issued by the Small Business Stationary Source Technical and Environmental Compliance Assistance Program for small business stationary sources to ensure that the information is understandable by the layperson; and

(4) have the Small Business Stationary Source Technical and Environmental Compliance Assistance Program serve as the secretariat for the development and dissemination of such reports and advisory opinions.

(e) Compliance advisory panel

(1) There shall be created a Compliance Advisory Panel (hereinafter referred to as the "Panel") on the State level of not less than 7 individuals. This Panel shall—

(A) render advisory opinions concerning the effectiveness of the small business stationary source technical and environmental compliance assistance program, difficulties encountered, and degree and severity of enforcement;

(B) make periodic reports to the Administrator concerning the compliance of the State Small Business Stationary Source Technical and Environmental Compliance Assistance Program with the requirements of the Paperwork Reduction Act [44

U.S.C.A. § 3501 et seq.], the Regulatory Flexibility Act [5 U.S.C.A. § 601 et seq.], and the Equal Access to Justice Act;

(C) review information for small business stationary sources to assure such information is understandable by the layperson; and

(D) have the Small Business Stationary Source Technical and Environmental Compliance Assistance Program serve as the secretariat for the development and dissemination of such reports and advisory opinions.

(2) The Panel shall consist of—

(A) 2 members, who are not owners, or representatives of owners, of small business stationary sources, selected by the Governor to represent the general public;

(B) 2 members selected by the State legislature who are owners, or who represent owners, of small business stationary sources (1 member each by the majority and minority leadership of the lower house, or in the case of a unicameral State legislature, 2 members each shall be selected by the majority leadership and the minority leadership, respectively, of such legislature, and subparagraph (C) shall not apply);

(C) 2 members selected by the State legislature who are owners, or who represent owners, of small business stationary sources (1 member each by the majority and minority leadership of the upper house, or the equivalent State entity); and

(D) 1 member selected by the head of the department or agency of the State responsible for air pollution permit programs to represent that agency.

(f) Fees

The State (or the Administrator) may reduce any fee required under this chapter to take into account the financial resources of small business stationary sources.

(g) Continuous emission monitors

In developing regulations and CTGs under this chapter that contain continuous emission monitoring requirements, the Administrator, consistent with the requirements of this chapter, before applying such requirements to small business stationary sources, shall consider the necessity and appropriateness of such requirements for such sources. Nothing in this subsection shall affect the applicability of subchapter IV–A of this chapter provisions relating to continuous emissions monitoring.

(h) Control technique guidelines

The Administrator shall consider, consistent with the requirements of this chapter, the size, type, and technical capabilities of small business stationary sources (and sources which are eligible under subsection (c)(2) of this section to be treated as small business stationary sources) in developing CTGs applicable to such sources under this chapter.

(July 14, 1955, ch. 360, title V, § 507, as added Nov. 15, 1990, Pub.L. 101–549, title V, § 501, 104 Stat. 2645.)

References in Text

The Small Business Act, referred to in subsec. (c)(1)(B), is Pub.L. 85–536, July 18, 1958, 72 Stat. 384, as amended, which is classified generally to chapter 14A (section 631 et seq.) of Title 15, Commerce and Trade. For complete classification of this Act to the Code, see Short Title note set out under section 631 of Title 15 and Tables.

The Paperwork Reduction Act, referred to in subsecs. (d)(2) and (e)(1)(B), probably means the Paperwork Reduction Act of 1980, Pub.L. 96–511, Dec. 11, 1980, 94 Stat. 2812, as amended, which is classified principally to chapter 35 (section 3501 et seq.) of Title 44, Public Printing and Documents. For complete classification of this Act to the Code, see Short Title of 1980 Amendment note set out under section 101 of Title 44 and Tables.

The Regulatory Flexibility Act, referred to in subsecs. (d)(2) and (e)(1)(B), is Pub.L. 96–354, Sept. 19, 1980, 94 Stat. 1164, which is classified generally to chapter 6 (section 601 et seq.) of Title 5, Government Organization and Employees. For complete classification of this Act to the Code, see Short Title note set out under section 601 of Title 5 and Tables.

The Equal Access to Justice Act, referred to in subsecs. (d)(2) and (e)(1)(B), is Title II of Pub.L. 96–481, Oct. 21, 1980, 94 Stat. 2325. For complete classification of this Act to the Code, see Short Title note set out under section 504 of Title 5, Government Organization and Employees and Tables.

Effective Date

Section to take effect Nov. 15, 1990, except as otherwise provided, see section 711(b) of Pub.L. 101–549, set out as a note under section 7401 of this title.

Savings Provisions

Suits, actions or proceedings commenced under this chapter as in effect prior to Nov. 15, 1990, not to abate by reason of the taking effect of amendments by Pub.L. 101–549, except as otherwise provided for, see section 711(a) of Pub.L. 101–549, set out as a note under section 7401 of this title.

SUBCHAPTER VI—STRATOSPHERIC OZONE PROTECTION

§ 7671. Definitions [CAA § 601]

As used in this subchapter—

(1) Appliance

The term "appliance" means any device which contains and uses a class I or class II substance as a refrigerant and which is used for household or commercial purposes, including any air conditioner, refrigerator, chiller, or freezer.

(2) Baseline year

The term "baseline year" means—

(A) the calendar year 1986, in the case of any class I substance listed in Group I or II under section 7671a(a) of this title,

(B) the calendar year 1989, in the case of any class I substance listed in Group III, IV, or V under section 7671a(a) of this title, and

(C) a representative calendar year selected by the Administrator, in the case of—

(i) any substance added to the list of class I substances after the publication of the initial list under section 7671a(a) of this title, and

(ii) any class II substance.

(3) Class I substance

The term "class I substance" means each of the substances listed as provided in section 7671a(a) of this title.

(4) Class II substance

The term "class II substance" means each of the substances listed as provided in section 7671a(b) of this title.

(5) Commissioner

The term "Commissioner" means the Commissioner of the Food and Drug Administration.

(6) Consumption

The term "consumption" means, with respect to any substance, the amount of that substance produced in the United States, plus the amount imported, minus the amount exported to Parties to the Montreal Protocol. Such term shall be construed in a manner consistent with the Montreal Protocol.

(7) Import

The term "import" means to land on, bring into, or introduce into, or attempt to land on, bring into, or introduce into, any place subject to the jurisdiction of the United States, whether or not such landing, bringing, or introduction constitutes an importation within the meaning of the customs laws of the United States.

(8) Medical device

The term "medical device" means any device (as defined in the Federal Food, Drug, and Cosmetic Act (21 U.S.C. 321)), diagnostic product, drug (as defined in the Federal Food, Drug, and Cosmetic Act [21 U.S.C.A. § 301 et seq.]), and drug delivery system—

(A) if such device, product, drug, or drug delivery system utilizes a class I or class II substance for which no safe and effective alternative has been developed, and where necessary, approved by the Commissioner; and

(B) if such device, product, drug, or drug delivery system, has, after notice and opportunity for public comment, been approved and determined to be essential by the Commissioner in consultation with the Administrator.

(9) Montreal protocol

The terms "Montreal Protocol" and "the Protocol" mean the Montreal Protocol on Substances that Deplete the Ozone Layer, a protocol to the Vienna Convention for the Protection of the Ozone Layer, including adjustments adopted by Parties thereto and amendments that have entered into force.

(10) Ozone-depletion potential

The term "ozone-depletion potential" means a factor established by the Administrator to reflect the ozone-depletion potential of a substance, on a mass per kilogram basis, as compared to chlorofluorocarbon–11 (CFC–11). Such factor shall be based upon the substance's atmospheric lifetime, the molecular weight of bromine and chlorine, and the substance's ability to be photolytically disassociated, and upon other factors determined to be an accurate measure of relative ozone-depletion potential.

(11) Produce, produced, and production

The terms "produce", "produced", and "production", refer to the manufacture of a substance from any raw material or feedstock chemical, but such terms do not include—

(A) the manufacture of a substance that is used and entirely consumed (except for trace quantities) in the manufacture of other chemicals, or

(B) the reuse or recycling of a substance.

(July 14, 1955, ch. 360, title VI, § 601, as added Nov. 15, 1990, Pub.L. 101–549, title VI, § 602(a), 104 Stat. 2649.)

References in Text

The Federal Food, Drug, and Cosmetic Act, referred to in (par. 8), is Act June 25, 1938, c. 675, 52 Stat. 1040, as amended, which is classified generally to chapter 9 (section 301 et seq.) of Title 21, Food and Drugs. For complete classification of this Act to the Code, see section 301 of Title 21 and Tables.

Effective Date

Section to take effect Nov. 15, 1990, except as otherwise provided, see section 711(b) of Pub.L. 101–549, set out as a note under section 7401 of this title.

Savings Provisions

Suits, actions or proceedings commenced under this chapter as in effect prior to Nov. 15, 1990, not to abate by reason of the taking effect of amendments by Pub.L. 101–549, except as otherwise provided for, see section 711(a) of Pub.L. 101–549, set out as a note under section 7401 of this title.

§ 7671a. Listing of class I and class II substances [CAA § 602]

(a) List of class I substances

Within 60 days after enactment of the Clean Air Act Amendments of 1990, the Administrator shall publish an initial list of class I substances, which list shall contain the following substances:

Group I
chlorofluorocarbon–11 (CFC–11)
chlorofluorocarbon–12 (CFC–12)
chlorofluorocarbon–113 (CFC–113)
chlorofluorocarbon–114 (CFC–114)
chlorofluorocarbon–115 (CFC–115)

Group II
halon–1211
halon–1301
halon–2402

Group III
chlorofluorocarbon–13 (CFC–13)
chlorofluorocarbon–111 (CFC–111)
chlorofluorocarbon–112 (CFC–112)
chlorofluorocarbon–211 (CFC–211)
chlorofluorocarbon–212 (CFC–212)
chlorofluorocarbon–213 (CFC–213)
chlorofluorocarbon–214 (CFC–214)
chlorofluorocarbon–215 (CFC–215)
chlorofluorocarbon–216 (CFC–216)
chlorofluorocarbon–217 (CFC–217)

Group IV
carbon tetrachloride

Group V
methyl chloroform

The initial list under this subsection shall also include the isomers of the substances listed above, other than 1,1,2–trichloroethane (an isomer of methyl chloroform). Pursuant to subsection (c) of this section, the Administrator shall add to the list of class I substances any other substance that the Administrator finds causes or contributes significantly to harmful effects on the stratospheric ozone layer. The Administrator shall, pursuant to subsection (c) of this section, add to such list all substances that the Administrator determines have an ozone depletion potential of 0.2 or greater.

(b) List of class II substances

Simultaneously with publication of the initial list of class I substances, the Administrator shall publish an initial list of class II substances, which shall contain the following substances:

hydrochlorofluorocarbon–21 (HCFC–21)
hydrochlorofluorocarbon–22 (HCFC–22)
hydrochlorofluorocarbon–31 (HCFC–31)
hydrochlorofluorocarbon–121 (HCFC–121)
hydrochlorofluorocarbon–122 (HCFC–122)
hydrochlorofluorocarbon–123 (HCFC–123)
hydrochlorofluorocarbon–124 (HCFC–124)
hydrochlorofluorocarbon–131 (HCFC–131)
hydrochlorofluorocarbon–132 (HCFC–132)
hydrochlorofluorocarbon–133 (HCFC–133)
hydrochlorofluorocarbon–141 (HCFC–141)
hydrochlorofluorocarbon–142 (HCFC–142)
hydrochlorofluorocarbon–221 (HCFC–221)
hydrochlorofluorocarbon–222 (HCFC–222)
hydrochlorofluorocarbon–223 (HCFC–223)
hydrochlorofluorocarbon–224 (HCFC–224)
hydrochlorofluorocarbon–225 (HCFC–225)
hydrochlorofluorocarbon–226 (HCFC–226)
hydrochlorofluorocarbon–231 (HCFC–231)
hydrochlorofluorocarbon–232 (HCFC–232)
hydrochlorofluorocarbon–233 (HCFC–233)
hydrochlorofluorocarbon–234 (HCFC–234)
hydrochlorofluorocarbon–235 (HCFC–235)
hydrochlorofluorocarbon–241 (HCFC–241)
hydrochlorofluorocarbon–242 (HCFC–242)
hydrochlorofluorocarbon–243 (HCFC–243)
hydrochlorofluorocarbon–244 (HCFC–244)
hydrochlorofluorocarbon–251 (HCFC–251)
hydrochlorofluorocarbon–252 (HCFC–252)
hydrochlorofluorocarbon–253 (HCFC–253)
hydrochlorofluorocarbon–261 (HCFC–261)
hydrochlorofluorocarbon–262 (HCFC–262)
hydrochlorofluorocarbon–271 (HCFC–271)

The initial list under this subsection shall also include the isomers of the substances listed above. Pursuant to subsection (c) of this section, the Administrator shall add to the list of class II substances any other substance that the Administrator finds is known or may reasonably be anticipated to cause or contribute to harmful effects on the stratospheric ozone layer.

(c) Additions to the lists

(1) The Administrator may add, by rule, in accordance with the criteria set forth in subsection (a) or (b) of this section, as the case may be, any substance to the list of class I or class II substances under subsection (a) or (b) of this section. For purposes of exchanges under section 7671f of this title, whenever a substance is added to the list of class I substances the Administrator shall, to the extent consistent with the Montreal Protocol, assign such substance to existing Group I, II, III, IV, or V or place such substance in a new Group.

(2) Periodically, but not less frequently than every 3 years after the enactment of the Clean Air Act Amendments of 1990, the Administrator shall list, by rule, as additional class I or class II substances those substances which the Administrator finds meet the criteria of subsection (a) or (b) of this section, as the case may be.

(3) At any time, any person may petition the Administrator to add a substance to the list of class I or class II substances. Pursuant to the criteria set forth in subsection (a) or (b) of this section as the case may be, within 180 days after receiving such a petition, the Administrator shall either propose to add the substance to such list or publish an explanation of the petition denial. In any case where the Administrator proposes to add a substance to such list, the Administrator shall add, by rule, (or make a final determination not to add) such substance to such list within 1 year after receiving such petition. Any petition under this paragraph shall include a showing by the petitioner that there are data on the substance adequate to support the petition. If the Administrator determines that information on the substance is not sufficient to make a determination under this paragraph, the Administrator shall use any authority available to the Administrator, under any law administered by the Administrator, to acquire such information.

(4) Only a class II substance which is added to the list of class I substances may be removed from the list of class II substances. No substance referred to in subsection (a) of this section, including methyl chloroform, may be removed from the list of class I substances.

(d) New listed substances

In the case of any substance added to the list of class I or class II substances after publication of the initial list of such substances under this section, the Administrator may extend any schedule or compliance deadline contained in section 7671c or 7671d of this title to a later date than specified in such sections if such schedule or deadline is unattainable, considering when such substance is added to the list. No extension under this subsection may extend the date for termination of production of any class I substance to a date more than 7 years after January 1 of the year after the year in which the substance is added to the list of class I substances. No extension under this subsection may extend the date for termination of production of any class II substance to a date more than 10 years after January 1 of the year after the year in which the substance is added to the list of class II substances.

(e) Ozone-depletion and global warming potential

Simultaneously with publication of the lists under this section and simultaneously with any addition to either of such lists, the Administrator shall assign to each listed substance a numerical value representing the substance's ozone-depletion potential. In addition, the Administrator shall publish the chlorine and bromine loading potential and the atmospheric lifetime of each listed substance. One year after enactment of the Clean Air Act Amendments of 1990 (one year after the addition of a substance to either of such lists in the case of a substance added after the publication of the initial lists of such substances), and after notice and opportunity for public comment, the Administrator shall publish the global warming potential of each listed substance. The preceding sentence shall not be construed to be the basis of any additional regulation under this chapter. In the case of the substances referred to in table 1, the ozone-depletion potential shall be as specified in table 1, unless the Administrator adjusts the substance's ozone-depletion potential based on criteria referred to in section 7671(10) of this title:

TABLE 1

Substance	Ozone-depletion potential
chlorofluorocarbon–11 (CFC–11)	1.0
chlorofluorocarbon–12 (CFC–12)	1.0
chlorofluorocarbon–13 (CFC–13)	1.0
chlorofluorocarbon–111 (CFC–111)	1.0
chlorofluorocarbon–112 (CFC–112)	1.0
chlorofluorocarbon–113 (CFC–113)	0.8
chlorofluorocarbon–114 (CFC–114)	1.0
chlorofluorocarbon–115 (CFC–115)	0.6
chlorofluorocarbon–211 (CFC–211)	1.0
chlorofluorocarbon–212 (CFC–212)	1.0
chlorofluorocarbon–213 (CFC–213)	1.0
chlorofluorocarbon–214 (CFC–214)	1.0
chlorofluorocarbon–215 (CFC–215)	1.0
chlorofluorocarbon–216 (CFC–216)	1.0
chlorofluorocarbon–217 (CFC–217)	1.0
halon–1211	3.0
halon–1301	10.0
halon–2402	6.0
carbon tetrachloride	1.1
methyl chloroform	0.1
hydrochlorofluorocarbon–22 (HCFC–22)	0.05
hydrochlorofluorocarbon–123 (HCFC–123)	0.02
hydrochlorofluorocarbon–124 (HCFC–124)	0.02
hydrochlorofluorocarbon–141(b) (HCFC–141(b))	0.1
hydrochlorofluorocarbon–142(b) (HCFC–142(b))	0.06

Where the ozone-depletion potential of a substance is specified in the Montreal Protocol, the ozone-depletion potential specified for that substance under this section shall be consistent with the Montreal Protocol.

(July 14, 1955, ch. 360, title VI, § 602, as added Nov. 15, 1990, Pub.L. 101–549, title VI, § 602(a), 104 Stat. 2650.)

References in Text

Enactment of the Clean Air Act Amendments of 1990, referred to in subsecs. (a), (c)(2) and (e), probably means the date of enactment of the Clean Air Act Amendments of 1990, Pub.L. 101–549, which was approved November 15, 1990.

Codification

Section 7671f of this title, referred to in subsec. (c), was substituted for section 507 as the probable intent of Congress.

Effective Date

Section to take effect Nov. 15, 1990, except as otherwise provided, see section 711(b) of Pub.L. 101–549, set out as a note under section 7401 of this title.

Savings Provisions

Suits, actions or proceedings commenced under this chapter as in effect prior to Nov. 15, 1990, not to abate by reason of the taking effect of amendments by Pub.L. 101–549, except as otherwise provided for, see section 711(a) of Pub.L. 101–549, set out as a note under section 7401 of this title.

§ 7671b. Monitoring and reporting requirements [CAA § 603]

(a) Regulations

Within 270 days after the enactment of the Clean Air Act Amendments of 1990, the Administrator shall amend the regulations of the Administrator in effect on such date regarding monitoring and reporting of class I and class II substances. Such amendments shall conform to the requirements of this section. The amended regulations shall include requirements with respect to the time and manner of monitoring and reporting as required under this section.

(b) Production, import, and export level reports

On a quarterly basis, or such other basis (not less than annually) as determined by the Administrator, each person who produced, imported, or exported a class I or class II substance shall file a report with the Administrator setting forth the amount of the substance that such person produced, imported, and exported during the preceding reporting period. Each such report shall be signed and attested by a responsible officer. No such report shall be required from a person after April 1 of the calendar year after such person permanently ceases production, importation, and exportation of the substance and so notifies the Administrator in writing.

(c) Baseline reports for class I substances

Unless such information has previously been reported to the Administrator, on the date on which the first report under subsection (b) of this section is required to be filed, each person who produced, imported, or exported a class I substance (other than a substance added to the list of class I substances after the publication of the initial list of such substances under this section) shall file a report with the Administrator setting forth the amount of such substance that such person produced, imported, and exported during the baseline year. In the case of a substance added to the list of class I substances after publication of the initial list of such substances under this section, the regulations shall require that each person who produced, imported, or exported such substance shall file a report with the Administrator within 180 days after the date on which such substance is added to the list, setting forth the amount of the substance that such person produced, imported, and exported in the baseline year.

(d) Monitoring and reports to Congress

(1) The Administrator shall monitor and, not less often than every 3 years following enactment of the Clean Air Act Amendments of 1990, submit a report to Congress on the production, use and consumption of class I and class II substances. Such report shall include data on domestic production, use and consumption, and an estimate of worldwide production, use and consumption of such substances. Not less frequently than every 6 years the Administrator shall report to Congress on the environmental and economic effects of any stratospheric ozone depletion.

(2) The Administrators of the National Aeronautics and Space Administration and the National Oceanic and Atmospheric Administration shall monitor, and not less often than every 3 years following enactment of the Clean Air Act Amendments of 1990, submit a report to Congress on the current average tropospheric concentration of chlorine and bromine and on the level of stratospheric ozone depletion. Such reports shall include updated projections of—

(A) peak chlorine loading;

(B) the rate at which the atmospheric abundance of chlorine is projected to decrease after the year 2000; and

(C) the date by which the atmospheric abundance of chlorine is projected to return to a level of two parts per billion.

Such updated projections shall be made on the basis of current international and domestic controls on substances covered by this title as well as on the basis of such controls supplemented by a year 2000 global phase out of all halocarbon emissions (the base case). It is the purpose of the Congress through the provisions of this section to monitor closely the production and consumption of class II substances to assure that the production and consumption of such substances will not:

(i) increase significantly the peak chlorine loading that is projected to occur under the base case established for purposes of this section;

(ii) reduce significantly the rate at which the atmospheric abundance of chlorine is projected to decrease under the base case; or

(iii) delay the date by which the average atmospheric concentration of chlorine is projected under the base case to return to a level of two parts per billion.

(e) Technology status report in 2015

The Administrator shall review, on a periodic basis, the progress being made in the development of alternative systems or products necessary to manufacture and operate appliances without class II substances. If the Administrator finds, after notice and opportunity for public comment, that as a result of technological development problems, the development of such alternative systems or products will not occur within the time necessary to provide for the manufacture of such equipment without such substances prior to the applicable deadlines under section 7671d of this title, the Administrator shall, not later than January 1, 2015, so inform the Congress.

(f) Emergency report

If, in consultation with the Administrators of the National Aeronautics and Space Administration and the National Oceanic and Atmospheric Administration, and after notice and opportunity for public comment, the Administrator determines that the global production, consumption, and use of class II substances are projected to contribute to an atmospheric chlorine loading in excess of the base case projections by more than 4/10ths parts per billion, the Administrator shall so inform the Congress immediately. The determination referred to in the preceding sentence shall be based on the monitoring under subsection (d) of this title and updated not less often than every 3 years.

(July 14, 1955, ch. 360, title VI, § 603, as added Nov. 15, 1990, Pub.L. 101–549, title VI, § 602(a), 104 Stat. 2653.)

References in Text

Enactment of the Clean Air Act Amendments of 1990, referred to in subsecs. (a) and (d), probably means the date of enactment of the Clean Air Act Amendments of 1990, Pub.L. 101–549, which was approved November 15, 1990.

Effective Date

Section to take effect Nov. 15, 1990, except as otherwise provided, see section 711(b) of Pub.L. 101–549, set out as a note under section 7401 of this title.

Savings Provisions

Suits, actions or proceedings commenced under this chapter as in effect prior to Nov. 15, 1990, not to abate by reason of the taking effect of amendments by Pub.L. 101–549, except as otherwise provided for, see section 711(a) of Pub.L. 101–549, set out as a note under section 7401 of this title.

Methane Studies

Section 603 of Pub.L. 101–549 provided that:

"**(a) Economically justified actions.**—Not later than 2 years after enactment of this Act [probably means date of enactment of Pub.L. 101–549, which was approved Nov. 15, 1990], the Administrator shall prepare and submit a report to the Congress that identifies activities, substances, processes, or combinations thereof that could reduce methane emissions and that are economically and technologically justified with and without consideration of environmental benefit.

"**(b) Domestic methane source inventory and control.**—Not later than 2 years after the enactment of this Act, the Administrator, in consultation and coordination with the Secretary of Energy and the Secretary of Agriculture, shall prepare and submit to the Congress reports on each of the following:

"(1) Methane emissions associated with natural gas extraction, transportation, distribution, storage, and use. Such report shall include an inventory of methane emissions associated with such activities within the United States. Such emissions include, but are not limited to, accidental and intentional releases from natural gas and oil wells, pipelines, processing facilities, and gas burners. The report shall also include an inventory of methane generation with such activities.

"(2) Methane emissions associated with coal extraction, transportation, distribution, storage, and use. Such report shall include an inventory of methane emissions associated with such activities within the United States. Such emissions include, but are not limited to, accidental and intentional releases from mining shafts, degasification wells, gas recovery wells and equipment, and from the processing and use of coal. The report shall also include an inventory of methane generation with such activities.

"(3) Methane emissions associated with management of solid waste. Such report shall include an inventory of methane emissions associated with all forms of waste management in the United States, including storage, treatment, and disposal.

"(4) Methane emissions associated with agriculture. Such report shall include an inventory of methane emissions associated with rice and livestock production in the United States.

"(5) Methane emissions associated with biomass burning. Such report shall include an inventory of methane emissions associated with the intentional burning of agricultural wastes, wood, grasslands, and forests.

"(6) Other methane emissions associated with human activities. Such report shall identify and inventory other domestic sources of methane emissions that are deemed by the Administrator and other such agencies to be significant.

"**(c) International studies.**—

"**(1) Methane emissions.**—Not later than 2 years after the enactment of this Act, the Administrator shall prepare and submit to the Congress a report on methane emissions from countries other than the United States. Such report shall include inventories of methane emissions associated with the activities listed in subsection (b).

"**(2) Preventing increases in methane concentrations.**—Not later than 2 years after the enactment of this Act, the Administrator shall prepare and submit to the Congress a report that analyzes the potential for preventing an increase in atmospheric concentrations of methane from activities and sources in other countries. Such report shall identify and evaluate the technical options for reducing methane emission from each of the activities listed in subsection (b), as well as other activities or sources that are deemed by the Administrator in consultation with other relevant Federal agencies and departments to be significant and shall include an evaluation of costs. The report shall identify the emissions reductions that would need to be achieved to prevent increasing atmospheric concentrations of methane. The report shall also identify technology transfer programs that could promote methane emissions reductions in lesser developed countries.

"**(d) Natural sources.**—Not later than 2 years after the enactment of this Act, the Administrator shall prepare and submit to the Congress a report on—

"(1) methane emissions from biogenic sources such as (A) tropical, temperate, and subarctic forests, (B) tundra, and (C) freshwater and saltwater wetlands; and

"(2) the changes in methane emissions from biogenic sources that may occur as a result of potential increases in temperatures and atmospheric concentrations of carbon dioxide.

"**(e) Study of measures to limit growth in methane concentrations.**—Not later than 2 years after the completion of the studies in subsections (b), (c), and (d), the Administrator shall prepare and submit to the Congress a report that presents options outlining measures that could be implemented to stop or reduce the growth in atmospheric concentrations of methane from sources within the United States referred to in paragraphs (1) through (6) of subsection (b). This study shall identify and evaluate the technical options for reducing methane emissions from each of the activities listed in subsection (b), as well as other activities or sources deemed by such agencies to be significant, and shall include an evaluation of costs, technology, safety, energy, and other factors. The study shall be based on the other studies under this section. The study shall also identify programs of the United States and international lending agencies that could be used to induce lesser developed countries to undertake measures that will reduce methane emissions and the resource needs of such programs.

"(f) **Information gathering.**—In carrying out the studies under this section, the provisions and requirements of section 114 of the Clean Air Act [section 7414 of this title] shall be available for purposes of obtaining information to carry out such studies.

"(g) **Consultation and coordination.**—In preparing the studies under this section the Administrator shall consult and coordinate with the Secretary of Energy, the Administrators of the National Aeronautics and Space Administration and the National Oceanic and Atmospheric Administration, and the heads of other relevant Federal agencies and departments. In the case of the studies under subsections (a), (b), and (e), such consultation and coordination shall include the Secretary of Agriculture."

§ 7671c. Phase-out of production and consumption of class I substances [CAA § 604]

(a) Production phase-out

Effective on January 1 of each year specified in Table 2, it shall be unlawful for any person to produce any class I substance in an annual quantity greater than the relevant percentage specified in Table 2. The percentages in Table 2 refer to a maximum allowable production as a percentage of the quantity of the substance produced by the person concerned in the baseline year.

TABLE 2

Date	Carbon tetrachloride	Methyl chloroform	Other class I substances
1991	100%	100%	85%
1992	90%	100%	80%
1993	80%	90%	75%
1994	70%	85%	65%
1995	15%	70%	50%
1996	15%	50%	40%
1997	15%	50%	15%
1998	15%	50%	15%
1999	15%	50%	15%
2000		20%	
2001		20%	

(b) Termination of production of class I substances

Effective January 1, 2000 (January 1, 2002 in the case of methyl chloroform), it shall be unlawful for any person to produce any amount of a class I substance.

(c) Regulations regarding production and consumption of class I substances

The Administrator shall promulgate regulations within 10 months after the enactment of the Clean Air Act Amendments of 1990 phasing out the production of class I substances in accordance with this section and other applicable provisions of this subchapter. The Administrator shall also promulgate regulations to insure that the consumption of class I substances in the United States is phased out and terminated in accordance with the same schedule (subject to the same exceptions and other provisions) as is applicable to the phase-out and termination of production of class I substances under this subchapter.

(d) Exceptions for essential uses of methyl chloroform, medical devices, and aviation safety

(1) Essential uses of methyl chloroform

Notwithstanding the termination of production required by subsection (b) of this section, during the period beginning on January 1, 2002, and ending on January 1, 2005, the Administrator, after notice and opportunity for public comment, may, to the extent such action is consistent with the Montreal Protocol, authorize the production of limited quantities of methyl chloroform solely for use in essential applications (such as nondestructive testing for metal fatigue and corrosion of existing airplane engines and airplane parts susceptible to metal fatigue) for which no safe and effective substitute is available. Notwithstanding this paragraph, the authority to produce methyl chloroform for use in medical devices shall be provided in accordance with paragraph (2).

(2) Medical devices

Notwithstanding the termination of production required by subsection (b) of this section, the Administrator, after notice and opportunity for public comment, shall, to the extent such action is consistent with the Montreal Protocol, authorize the production of limited quantities of class I substances solely for use in medical devices if such authorization is determined by the Commissioner, in consultation with the Administrator, to be necessary for use in medical devices.

(3) Aviation safety

(A) Notwithstanding the termination of production required by subsection (b) of this section, the Administrator, after notice and opportunity for public comment, may, to the extent such action is consistent with the Montreal Protocol, authorize the production of limited quantities of halon–1211 (bromochlorodifluoromethane), halon–1301 (bromotrifluoromethane), and halon–2402 (dibromotetrafluoroethane) solely for purposes of aviation safety if the Administrator of the Federal Aviation Administration, in consultation with the Administrator, determines that no safe and effective substitute has been developed and that such authorization is necessary for aviation safety purposes.

(B) The Administrator of the Federal Aviation Administration shall, in consultation with the Administrator, examine whether safe and effective substitutes for methyl chloroform or alternative techniques will be available for nondestructive testing for metal fatigue and corrosion of existing airplane engines and airplane parts susceptible to metal fatigue and whether an exception for such uses of methyl chloroform under this paragraph will be necessary for purposes of airline safety after January 1, 2005 and provide a report to Congress in 1998.

(4) Cap on certain exceptions

Under no circumstances may the authority set forth in paragraphs (1), (2), and (3) of subsection (d) of this section be applied to authorize any person to produce a class I substance in annual quantities greater than 10 percent of that produced by such person during the baseline year.

(e) Developing countries

(1) Exception

Notwithstanding the phase-out and termination of production required under subsections (a) and (b) of this section, the Administrator, after notice and opportunity for public comment, may, consistent with the Montreal Protocol, authorize the production of limited quantities of a class I substance in excess of the amounts otherwise allowable under subsection (a) or (b) of this section, or both, solely for export to, and use in, developing countries that are Parties to the Montreal Protocol and are operating under article 5 of such Protocol. Any production authorized under this paragraph shall be solely for purposes of satisfying the basic domestic needs of such countries.

(2) Cap on exception

(A) Under no circumstances may the authority set forth in paragraph (1) be applied to authorize any person to produce a class I substance in any year for which a production percentage is specified in Table 2 of subsection (a) of this section in an annual quantity greater than the specified percentage, plus an amount equal to 10 percent of the amount produced by such person in the baseline year.

(B) Under no circumstances may the authority set forth in paragraph (1) be applied to authorize any person to produce a class I substance in the applicable termination year referred to in subsection (b) of this section, or in any year thereafter, in an annual quantity greater than 15 percent of the baseline quantity of such substance produced by such person.

(C) An exception authorized under this subsection shall terminate no later than January 1, 2010 (2012 in the case of methyl chloroform).

(f) National security

The President may, to the extent such action is consistent with the Montreal Protocol, issue such orders regarding production and use of CFC–114 (chlorofluorocarbon–114), halon–1211, halon–1301, and halon–2402, at any specified site or facility or on any vessel as may be necessary to protect the national security interests of the United States if the President finds that adequate substitutes are not available and that the production and use of such substance are necessary to protect such national security interest. Such orders may include, where necessary to protect such interests, an exemption from any prohibition or requirement contained in this subchapter. The President shall notify the Congress within 30 days of the issuance of an order under this paragraph providing for any such exemption. Such notification shall include a statement of the reasons for the granting of the exemption. An exemption under this paragraph shall be for a specified period which may not exceed one year. Additional exemptions may be granted, each upon the President's issuance of a new order under this paragraph. Each such additional exemption shall be for a specified period which may not exceed one year. No exemption shall be granted under this paragraph due to lack of appropriation unless the President shall have specifically requested such appropriation as a part of the budgetary process and the Congress shall have failed to make available such requested appropriation.

(g) Fire suppression and explosion prevention

(1) Notwithstanding the production phase-out set forth in subsection (a) of this section, the Administrator, after notice and opportunity for public comment, may, to the extent such action is consistent with the Montreal Protocol, authorize the production of limited quantities of halon–1211, halon–1301, and halon–2402 in excess of the amount otherwise permitted pursuant to the schedule under subsection (a) of this section solely for purposes of fire suppression or explosion prevention if the Administrator, in consultation with the Administrator of the United States Fire Administration, determines that no safe and effective substitute has been developed and that such authorization is necessary for fire suppression or explosion prevention purposes. The Administrator shall not authorize production under this paragraph for purposes of fire safety or explosion prevention training or testing of fire suppression or explosion prevention equipment. In no event shall the Administrator grant an exception under this paragraph that permits production after December 31, 1999.

(2) The Administrator shall periodically monitor and assess the status of efforts to obtain substitutes for the substances referred to in paragraph (1) for purposes of fire suppression or explosion prevention and the probability of such substitutes being available by December 31, 1999. The Administrator, as part of such assessment, shall consider any relevant assessments under the Montreal Protocol and the actions of the Parties pursuant to Article 2B of the Montreal Protocol in identifying essential uses and in permitting a level of production or consumption that is necessary to satisfy such uses for which no adequate alternatives are available after December 31, 1999. The Administrator shall report to Congress the results of such assessment in 1994 and again in 1998.

(3) Notwithstanding the termination of production set forth in subsection (b) of this section, the Administrator, after notice and opportunity for public comment, may, to the extent consistent with the Montreal Protocol, authorize the production of limited quantities of halon–1211, halon–1301, and halon–2402 in the period after December 31, 1999, and before December 31, 2004, solely for purposes of fire suppression or explosion prevention in association with domestic production of crude oil and natural gas energy supplies on the North Slope of Alaska, if the Administrator, in consultation with the Administrator of the United States Fire Administration, determines that no safe and effective substitute has been developed and that such authorization is necessary for fire suppression and explosion prevention purposes. The Administrator shall not authorize production under the paragraph for purposes of fire safety or explosion prevention training or testing of fire suppression or explosion prevention equipment. In no event shall the Administrator authorize under this paragraph any person to produce any such halon in an amount greater than 3 percent of that produced by such person during the baseline year.

(July 14, 1955, ch. 360, title VI, § 604, as added Nov. 15, 1990, Pub.L. 101–549, title VI, § 602(a), 104 Stat. 2655.)

References in Text

The enactment of the Clean Air Act Amendments of 1990, referred to in subsec. (c), probably means the date of enactment of the Clean Air Act Amendments of 1990, Pub.L. 101–549, which was approved November 15, 1990.

Effective Date

Section to take effect Nov. 15, 1990, except as otherwise provided, see section 711(b) of Pub.L. 101–549, set out as a note under section 7401 of this title.

Savings Provisions

Suits, actions or proceedings commenced under this chapter as in effect prior to Nov. 15, 1990, not to abate by reason of the taking effect of amendments by Pub.L. 101–549, except as otherwise provided for, see section 711(a) of Pub.L. 101–549, set out as a note under section 7401 of this title.

§ 7671d. Phase-out of production and consumption of class II substances [CAA § 605]

(a) Restriction of use of class II substances

Effective January 1, 2015, it shall be unlawful for any person to introduce into interstate commerce or use any class II substance unless such substance—

(1) has been used, recovered, and recycled;

(2) is used and entirely consumed (except for trace quantities) in the production of other chemicals; or

(3) is used as a refrigerant in appliances manufactured prior to January 1, 2020.

As used in this subsection, the term "refrigerant" means any class II substance used for heat transfer in a refrigerating system.

(b) Production phase-out

(1) Effective January 1, 2015, it shall be unlawful for any person to produce any class II substance in an annual quantity greater than the quantity of such substance produced by such person during the baseline year.

(2) Effective January 1, 2030, it shall be unlawful for any person to produce any class II substance.

(c) Regulations regarding production and consumption of class II substances

By December 31, 1999, the Administrator shall promulgate regulations phasing out the production, and restricting the use, of class II substances in accordance with this section, subject to any acceleration of the phase-out of production under section 7671 of this title. The Administrator shall also promulgate regulations to insure that the consumption of class II substances in the United States is phased out and terminated in accordance with the same schedule (subject to the same exceptions and other provisions) as is applicable to the phase-out and termination of production of class II substances under this subchapter.

(d) Exceptions

(1) Medical devices

(A) In general

Notwithstanding the termination of production required under subsection (b)(2) of this section and the restriction on use referred to in subsection (a) of this section, the Administrator, after notice and opportunity for public comment, shall, to the extent such action is consistent with the Montreal Protocol, authorize the production and use of limited quantities of class II substances solely for purposes of use in medical devices if such authorization is determined by the Commissioner, in consultation with the Administrator, to be necessary for use in medical devices.

(B) Cap on exception

Under no circumstances may the authority set forth in subparagraph (A) be applied to authorize any person to produce a class II substance in annual quantities greater than 10 percent of that produced by such person during the baseline year.

(2) **Developing countries**

(A) **In general**

Notwithstanding the provisions of subsection (a) or (b) of this section, the Administrator, after notice and opportunity for public comment, may authorize the production of limited quantities of a class II substance in excess of the quantities otherwise permitted under such provisions solely for export to and use in developing countries that are Parties to the Montreal Protocol, as determined by the Administrator. Any production authorized under this subsection shall be solely for purposes of satisfying the basic domestic needs of such countries.

(B) **Cap on exception**

(i) Under no circumstances may the authority set forth in subparagraph (A) be applied to authorize any person to produce a class II substance in any year following the effective date of subsection (b)(1) of this section and before the year 2030 in annual quantities greater than 110 percent of the quantity of such substance produced by such person during the baseline year.

(ii) Under no circumstances may the authority set forth in subparagraph (A) be applied to authorize any person to produce a class II substance in the year 2030, or any year thereafter, in an annual quantity greater than 15 percent of the quantity of such substance produced by such person during the baseline year.

(iii) Each exception authorized under this paragraph shall terminate no later than January 1, 2040.

(July 14, 1955, ch. 360, title VI, § 605, as added Nov. 15, 1990, Pub.L. 101–549, title VI, § 602(a), 104 Stat. 2658.)

Effective Date

Section to take effect Nov. 15, 1990, except as otherwise provided, see section 711(b) of Pub.L. 101–549, set out as a note under section 7401 of this title.

Savings Provisions

Suits, actions or proceedings commenced under this chapter as in effect prior to Nov. 15, 1990, not to abate by reason of the taking effect of amendments by Pub.L. 101–549, except as otherwise provided for, see section 711(a) of Pub.L. 101–549, set out as a note under section 7401 of this title.

§ 7671e. Accelerated schedule [CAA § 606]

(a) **In general**

The Administrator shall promulgate regulations, after notice and opportunity for public comment, which establish a schedule for phasing out the production and consumption of class I and class II substances (or use of class II substances) that is more stringent than set forth in section 7671c or 7671d of this title, or both, if—

(1) based on an assessment of credible current scientific information (including any assessment under the Montreal Protocol) regarding harmful effects on the stratospheric ozone layer associated with a class I or class II substance, the Administrator determines that such more stringent schedule may be necessary to protect human health and the environment against such effects,

(2) based on the availability of substitutes for listed substances, the Administrator determines that such more stringent schedule is practicable, taking into account technological achievability, safety, and other relevant factors, or

(3) the Montreal Protocol is modified to include a schedule to control or reduce production, consumption, or use of any substance more rapidly than the applicable schedule under this subchapter.

In making any determination under paragraphs (1) and (2), the Administrator shall consider the status of the period remaining under the applicable schedule under this subchapter.

(b) **Petition**

Any person may petition the Administrator to promulgate regulations under this section. The Administrator shall grant or deny the petition within 180 days after receipt of any such petition. If the Administrator denies the petition, the Administrator shall publish an explanation of why the petition was denied. If the Administrator grants such petition, such final regulations shall be promulgated within 1 year. Any petition under this subsection shall include a showing by the petitioner that there are data adequate to support the petition. If the Administrator determines that information is not sufficient to make a determination under this subsection, the Administrator shall use any authority available to the Administrator, under any law administered by the Administrator, to acquire such information.

(July 14, 1955, ch. 360, title VI, § 606, as added Nov. 15, 1990, Pub.L. 101–549, title VI, § 602(a), 104 Stat. 2660.)

Effective Date

Section to take effect Nov. 15, 1990, except as otherwise provided, see section 711(b) of Pub.L. 101–549, set out as a note under section 7401 of this title.

Savings Provisions

Suits, actions or proceedings commenced under this chapter as in effect prior to Nov. 15, 1990, not to abate by reason of the taking effect of amendments by Pub.L. 101–549, except as otherwise provided for, see section 711(a) of Pub.L. 101–549, set out as a note under section 7401 of this title.

§ 7671f. Exchange authority [CAA § 607]

(a) Transfers

The Administrator shall, within 10 months after the enactment of the Clean Air Act Amendments of 1990, promulgate rules under this subchapter providing for the issuance of allowances for the production of class I and II substances in accordance with the requirements of this subchapter and governing the transfer of such allowances. Such rules shall insure that the transactions under the authority of this section will result in greater total reductions in the production in each year of class I and class II substances than would occur in that year in the absence of such transactions.

(b) Interpollutant transfers

(1) The rules under this section shall permit a production allowance for a substance for any year to be transferred for a production allowance for another substance for the same year on an ozone depletion weighted basis.

(2) Allowances for substances in each group of class I substances (as listed pursuant to section 7671a of this title) may only be transferred for allowances for other substances in the same Group.

(3) The Administrator shall, as appropriate, establish groups of class II substances for trading purposes and assign class II substances to such groups. In the case of class II substances, allowances may only be transferred for allowances for other class II substances that are in the same Group.

(c) Trades with other persons

The rules under this section shall permit 2 or more persons to transfer production allowances (including interpollutant transfers which meet the requirements of subsections (a) and (b) of this section) if the transferor of such allowances will be subject, under such rules, to an enforceable and quantifiable reduction in annual production which—

(1) exceeds the reduction otherwise applicable to the transferor under this subchapter,

(2) exceeds the production allowances transferred to the transferee, and

(3) would not have occurred in the absence of such transaction.

(d) Consumption

The rules under this section shall also provide for the issuance of consumption allowances in accordance with the requirements of this subchapter and for the trading of such allowances in the same manner as is applicable under this section to the trading of production allowances under this section.

(July 14, 1955, ch. 360, title VI, § 607, as added Nov. 15, 1990, Pub.L. 101–549, title VI, § 602(a), 104 Stat. 2660.)

References in Text

Enactment of the Clean Air Act Amendments of 1990, referred to in subsec. (a), probably means the date of enactment of the Clean Air Act Amendments of 1990, Pub.L. 101–549, which was approved November 15, 1990.

Effective Date

Section to take effect Nov. 15, 1990, except as otherwise provided, see section 711(b) of Pub.L. 101–549, set out as a note under section 7401 of this title.

Savings Provisions

Suits, actions or proceedings commenced under this chapter as in effect prior to Nov. 15, 1990, not to abate by reason of the taking effect of amendments by Pub.L. 101–549, except as otherwise provided for, see section 711(a) of Pub.L. 101–549, set out as a note under section 7401 of this title.

§ 7671g. National recycling and emission reduction program [CAA § 608]

(a) In general

(1) The Administrator shall, by not later than January 1, 1992, promulgate regulations establishing standards and requirements regarding the use and disposal of class I substances during the service, repair, or disposal of appliances and industrial process refrigeration. Such standards and requirements shall become effective not later than July 1, 1992.

(2) The Administrator shall, within 4 years after the enactment of the Clean Air Act Amendments of 1990, promulgate regulations establishing standards and requirements regarding use and disposal of class I and II substances not covered by paragraph (1), including the use and disposal of class II substances during service, repair, or disposal of appliances and industrial process refrigeration. Such standards and requirements shall become effective not later than 12 months after promulgation of the regulations.

(3) The regulations under this subsection shall include requirements that—

(A) reduce the use and emission of such substances to the lowest achievable level, and

(B) maximize the recapture and recycling of such substances.

Such regulations may include requirements to use alternative substances (including substances which are not class I or class II substances) or to minimize use of class I or class II substances, or to promote the use of safe alternatives pursuant to section 7671k of this title or any combination of the foregoing.

(b) Safe disposal

The regulations under subsection (a) of this section shall establish standards and requirements for the safe disposal of class I and II substances. Such regulations shall include each of the following—

(1) Requirements that class I or class II substances contained in bulk in appliances, machines or other goods shall be removed from each such appliance, machine or other good prior to the disposal of such items or their delivery for recycling.

(2) Requirements that any appliance, machine or other good containing a class I or class II substance in bulk shall not be manufactured, sold, or distributed in interstate commerce or offered for sale or distribution in interstate commerce unless it is equipped with a servicing aperture or an equally effective design feature which will facilitate the recapture of such substance during service and repair or disposal of such item.

(3) Requirements that any product in which a class I or class II substance is incorporated so as to constitute an inherent element of such product shall be disposed of in a manner that reduces, to the maximum extent practicable, the release of such substance into the environment. If the Administrator determines that the application of this paragraph to any product would result in producing only insignificant environmental benefits, the Administrator shall include in such regulations an exception for such product.

(c) Prohibitions

(1) Effective July 1, 1992, it shall be unlawful for any person, in the course of maintaining, servicing, repairing, or disposing of an appliance or industrial process refrigeration, to knowingly vent or otherwise knowingly release or dispose of any class I or class II substance used as a refrigerant in such appliance (or industrial process refrigeration) in a manner which permits such substance to enter the environment. De minimis releases associated with good faith attempts to recapture and recycle or safely dispose of any such substance shall not be subject to the prohibition set forth in the preceding sentence.

(2) Effective 5 years after the enactment of the Clean Air Act Amendments of 1990, paragraph (1) shall also apply to the venting, release, or disposal of any substitute substance for a class I or class II substance by any person maintaining, servicing, repairing, or disposing of an appliance or industrial process refrigeration which contains and uses as a refrigerant any such substance, unless the Administrator determines that venting, releasing, or disposing of such substance does not pose a threat to the environment. For purposes of this paragraph, the term 'appliance' includes any device which contains and uses as a refrigerant a substitute substance and which is used for household or commercial purposes, including any air conditioner, refrigerator, chiller, or freezer.

(July 14, 1955, ch. 360, title VI, § 608, as added Nov. 15, 1990, Pub.L. 101–549, title VI, § 602(a), 104 Stat. 2661.)

References in Text

Enactment of the Clean Air Act Amendments of 1990, referred to in subsecs. (a)(2) and (c)(2), probably means the date of enactment of the Clean Air Act Amendments of 1990, Pub.L. 101–549, which was approved November 15, 1990.

Effective Date

Section to take effect Nov. 15, 1990, except as otherwise provided, see section 711(b) of Pub.L. 101–549, set out as a note under section 7401 of this title.

Savings Provisions

Suits, actions or proceedings commenced under this chapter as in effect prior to Nov. 15, 1990, not to abate by reason of the taking effect of amendments by Pub.L. 101–549, except as otherwise provided for, see section 711(a) of Pub.L. 101–549, set out as a note under section 7401 of this title.

§ 7671h. Servicing of motor vehicle air conditioners [CAA § 609]

(a) Regulations

Within 1 year after the enactment of the Clean Air Act Amendments of 1990, the Administrator shall promulgate regulations in accordance with this section establishing standards and requirements regarding the servicing of motor vehicle air conditioners.

(b) Definitions

As used in this section—

(1) The term "refrigerant" means any class I or class II substance used in a motor vehicle air conditioner. Effective 5 years after the enactment of the Clean Air Act Amendments of 1990, the term "refrigerant" shall also include any substitute substance.

(2)(A) The term "approved refrigerant recycling equipment" means equipment certified by the Administrator (or an independent standards testing organization approved by the Administrator) to meet the standards established by the Administrator and applicable to equipment for the extraction and reclamation of refrigerant from motor vehicle air conditioners. Such standards shall, at a minimum, be at least as stringent as the standards of the Society of Automotive Engineers in effect as of November 15, 1990 and applicable to such equipment (SAE standard J–1990).

(B) Equipment purchased before the proposal of regulations under this section shall be considered certified if it is substantially identical to equipment certified as provided in subparagraph (A).

(3) The term "properly using" means, with respect to approved refrigerant recycling equipment, using such equipment in conformity with standards established by the Administrator and applicable to the use of such equipment. Such standards shall, at a minimum, be at least as stringent as the standards of the Society of Automotive Engineers in effect as of November 15, 1990 and applicable to the use of such equipment (SAE standard J–1989).

(4) The term "properly trained and certified" means training and certification in the proper use of approved refrigerant recycling equipment for motor vehicle air conditioners in conformity with standards established by the Administrator and applicable to the performance of service on motor vehicle air conditioners. Such standards shall, at a minimum, be at least as stringent as specified, as of November 15, 1990, in SAE standard J–1989 under the certification program of the National Institute for Automotive Service Excellence (ASE) or under a similar program such as the training and certification program of the Mobile Air Conditioning Society (MACS).

(c) Servicing motor vehicle air conditioners

Effective January 1, 1992, no person repairing or servicing motor vehicles for consideration may perform any service on a motor vehicle air conditioner involving the refrigerant for such air conditioner without properly using approved refrigerant recycling equipment and no such person may perform such service unless such person has been properly trained and certified. The requirements of the previous sentence shall not apply until January 1, 1993 in the case of a person repairing or servicing motor vehicles for consideration at an entity which performed service on fewer than 100 motor vehicle air conditioners during calendar year 1990 and if such person so certifies, pursuant to subsection (d)(2) of this section, to the Administrator by January 1, 1992.

(d) Certification

(1) Effective 2 years after the enactment of the Clean Air Act Amendments of 1990, each person performing service on motor vehicle air conditioners for consideration shall certify to the Administrator either—

(A) that such person has acquired, and is properly using, approved refrigerant recycling equipment in service on motor vehicle air conditioners involving refrigerant and that each individual authorized by such person to perform such service is properly trained and certified; or

(B) that such person is performing such service at an entity which serviced fewer than 100 motor vehicle air conditioners in 1991.

(2) Effective January 1, 1993, each person who certified under paragraph (1)(B) shall submit a certification under paragraph (1)(A).

(3) Each certification under this subsection shall contain the name and address of the person certifying under this subsection and the serial number of each unit of approved recycling equipment acquired by such person and shall be signed and attested by the owner or another responsible officer. Certifications under paragraph (1)(A) may be made by submitting the required information to the Administrator on a standard form provided by the manufacturer of certified refrigerant recycling equipment.

(e) Small containers of class I or class II substances

Effective 2 years after November 15, 1990, it shall be unlawful for any person to sell or distribute, or offer for sale or distribution, in interstate commerce to any person (other than a person performing service for consideration on motor vehicle air-conditioning systems in compliance with this section) any class I or class II substance that is suitable for use as a refrigerant in a motor vehicle air-conditioning system and that is in a container which contains less than 20 pounds of such refrigerant.

(July 14, 1955, ch. 360, title VI, § 609, as added Nov. 15, 1990, Pub.L. 101–549, title VI, § 602(a), 104 Stat. 2662.)

References in Text

Enactment of the Clean Air Act Amendments of 1990, referred to in subsecs. (a), (b)(1) and (d)(1), probably means the date of enactment of the Clean Air Act Amendments of 1990, Pub.L. 101–549, which was approved November 15, 1990.

Effective Date

Section to take effect Nov. 15, 1990, except as otherwise provided, see section 711(b) of Pub.L. 101–549, set out as a note under section 7401 of this title.

Savings Provisions

Suits, actions or proceedings commenced under this chapter as in effect prior to Nov. 15, 1990, not to abate by reason of the taking effect of amendments by Pub.L. 101–549, except as otherwise provided for, see section 711(a) of Pub.L. 101–549, set out as a note under section 7401 of this title.

§ 7671i. Nonessential products containing chlorofluorocarbons [CAA § 610]

(a) Regulations

The Administrator shall promulgate regulations to carry out the requirements of this section within 1 year after the enactment of the Clean Air Act Amendments of 1990.

(b) Nonessential products

The regulations under this section shall identify nonessential products that release class I substances into the environment (including any release occurring during manufacture, use, storage, or disposal) and prohibit any person from selling or distributing any such product, or offering any such product for sale or distribution, in interstate commerce. At a minimum, such prohibition shall apply to—

(1) chlorofluorocarbon-propelled plastic party streamers and noise horns,

(2) chlorofluorocarbon-containing cleaning fluids for noncommercial electronic and photographic equipment, and

(3) other consumer products that are determined by the Administrator—

(A) to release class I substances into the environment (including any release occurring during manufacture, use, storage, or disposal), and

(B) to be nonessential.

In determining whether a product is nonessential, the Administrator shall consider the purpose or intended use of the product, the technological availability of substitutes for such product and for such class I substance, safety, health, and other relevant factors.

(c) Effective date

Effective 24 months after the enactment of the Clean Air Act Amendments of 1990, it shall be unlawful for any person to sell or distribute, or offer for sale or distribution, in interstate commerce any nonessential product to which regulations under subsection (a) of this section implementing subsection (b) of this section are applicable.

(d) Other products

(1) Effective January 1, 1994, it shall be unlawful for any person to sell or distribute, or offer for sale or distribution, in interstate commerce—

(A) any aerosol product or other pressurized dispenser which contains a class II substance; or

(B) any plastic foam product which contains, or is manufactured with, a class II substance.

(2) The Administrator is authorized to grant exceptions from the prohibition under subparagraph (A) of paragraph (1) where—

(A) the use of the aerosol product or pressurized dispenser is determined by the Administrator to be essential as a result of flammability or worker safety concerns, and

(B) the only available alternative to use of a class II substance is use of a class I substance which legally could be substituted for such class II substance.

(3) Subparagraph (B) of paragraph (1) shall not apply to—

(A) a foam insulation product, or

(B) an integral skin, rigid, or semi-rigid foam utilized to provide for motor vehicle safety in accordance with Federal Motor Vehicle Safety Standards where no adequate substitute substance (other than a class I or class II substance) is practicable for effectively meeting such Standards.

(e) Medical devices

Nothing in this section shall apply to any medical device as defined in section 7671(8) of this title.

(July 14, 1955, ch. 360, title VI, § 610, as added Nov. 15, 1990, Pub.L. 101–549, title VI, § 602(a), 104 Stat. 2664.)

References in Text

Enactment of the Clean Air Act Amendments of 1990, referred to in subsecs. (a) and (c), probably means the date of enactment of the Clean Air Act Amendments of 1990, Pub.L. 101–549, which was approved November 15, 1990.

Effective Date

Section to take effect Nov. 15, 1990, except as otherwise provided, see section 711(b) of Pub.L. 101–549, set out as a note under section 7401 of this title.

Savings Provisions

Suits, actions or proceedings commenced under this chapter as in effect prior to Nov. 15, 1990, not to abate by reason of the taking effect of amendments by Pub.L. 101–549, except as otherwise provided for, see section 711(a) of Pub.L. 101–549, set out as a note under section 7401 of this title.

§ 7671j. Labeling [CAA § 611]

(a) Regulations

The Administrator shall promulgate regulations to implement the labeling requirements of this section within 18 months after enactment of the Clean Air Act Amendments of 1990, after notice and opportunity for public comment.

(b) Containers containing class I or class II substances and products containing class I substances

Effective 30 months after the enactment of the Clean Air Act Amendments of 1990, no container in which a class I or class II substance is stored or transported, and no product containing a class I substance, shall be introduced into interstate commerce unless it bears a clearly legible and conspicuous label stating:

"Warning: Contains [insert name of substance], a substance which harms public health and environment by destroying ozone in the upper atmosphere".

(c) Products containing class II substances

(1) After 30 months after the enactment of the Clean Air Act Amendments of 1990, and before Janu-

ary 1, 2015, no product containing a class II substance shall be introduced into interstate commerce unless it bears the label referred to in subsection (b) of this section if the Administrator determines, after notice and opportunity for public comment, that there are substitute products or manufacturing processes (A) that do not rely on the use of such class II substance, (B) that reduce the overall risk to human health and the environment, and (C) that are currently or potentially available.

(2) Effective January 1, 2015, the requirements of subsection (b) of this section shall apply to all products containing a class II substance.

(d) Products manufactured with class I and class II substances

(1) In the case of a class II substance, after 30 months after the enactment of the Clean Air Act Amendments of 1990, and before January 1, 2015, if the Administrator, after notice and opportunity for public comment, makes the determination referred to in subsection (c) of this section with respect to a product manufactured with a process that uses such class II substance, no such product shall be introduced into interstate commerce unless it bears a clearly legible and conspicuous label stating:

"Warning: Manufactured with [insert name of substance], a substance which harms public health and environment by destroying ozone in the upper atmosphere" [1]

(2) In the case of a class I substance, effective 30 months after the enactment of the Clean Air Act Amendments of 1990, and before January 1, 2015, the labeling requirements of this subsection shall apply to all products manufactured with a process that uses such class I substance unless the Administrator determines that there are no substitute products or manufacturing processes that (A) do not rely on the use of such class I substance, (B) reduce the overall risk to human health and the environment, and (C) are currently or potentially available.

(e) Petitions

(1) Any person may, at any time after 18 months after the enactment of the Clean Air Act Amendments of 1990, petition the Administrator to apply the requirements of this section to a product containing a class II substance or a product manufactured with a class I or II substance which is not otherwise subject to such requirements. Within 180 days after receiving such petition, the Administrator shall, pursuant to the criteria set forth in subsection (c) of this section, either propose to apply the requirements of this section to such product or publish an explanation of the petition denial. If the Administrator proposes to apply such requirements to such product, the Administrator shall, by rule, render a final determination pursuant to such criteria within 1 year after receiving such petition.

(2) Any petition under this paragraph shall include a showing by the petitioner that there are data on the product adequate to support the petition.

(3) If the Administrator determines that information on the product is not sufficient to make the required determination the Administrator shall use any authority available to the Administrator under any law administered by the Administrator to acquire such information.

(4) In the case of a product determined by the Administrator, upon petition or on the Administrator's own motion, to be subject to the requirements of this section, the Administrator shall establish an effective date for such requirements. The effective date shall be 1 year after such determination or 30 months after the enactment of the Clean Air Act Amendments of 1990, whichever is later.

(5) Effective January 1, 2015, the labeling requirements of this subsection shall apply to all products manufactured with a process that uses a class I or class II substance.

(f) Relationship to other law

(1) The labeling requirements of this section shall not constitute, in whole or part, a defense to liability or a cause for reduction in damages in any suit, whether civil or criminal, brought under any law, whether Federal or State, other than a suit for failure to comply with the labeling requirements of this section.

(2) No other approval of such label by the Administrator under any other law administered by the Administrator shall be required with respect to the labeling requirements of this section.

(July 14, 1955, ch. 360, title VI, § 611, as added Nov. 15, 1990, Pub.L. 101–549, title VI, § 602(a), 104 Stat. 2665.)

[1] So in original. Probably should be a closing period.

References in Text

Enactment of the Clean Air Act Amendments of 1990, referred to in subsecs. (a), (b), (c)(1), (d), (e)(1) and (4), probably means the date of enactment of the Clean Air Act Amendments of 1990, Pub.L. 101–549, which was approved November 15, 1990.

Effective Date

Section to take effect Nov. 15, 1990, except as otherwise provided, see section 711(b) of Pub.L. 101–549, set out as a note under section 7401 of this title.

Savings Provisions

Suits, actions or proceedings commenced under this chapter as in effect prior to Nov. 15, 1990, not to abate by reason of the taking effect of amendments by Pub.L. 101–549, except as otherwise provid-

ed for, see section 711(a) of Pub.L. 101–549, set out as a note under section 7401 of this title.

§ 7671k. Safe alternatives policy [CAA § 612]

(a) Policy

To the maximum extent practicable, class I and class II substances shall be replaced by chemicals, product substitutes, or alternative manufacturing processes that reduce overall risks to human health and the environment.

(b) Reviews and reports

The Administrator shall—

(1) in consultation and coordination with interested members of the public and the heads of relevant Federal agencies and departments, recommend Federal research programs and other activities to assist in identifying alternatives to the use of class I and class II substances as refrigerants, solvents, fire retardants, foam blowing agents, and other commercial applications and in achieving a transition to such alternatives, and, where appropriate, seek to maximize the use of Federal research facilities and resources to assist users of class I and class II substances in identifying and developing alternatives to the use of such substances as refrigerants, solvents, fire retardants, foam blowing agents, and other commercial applications;

(2) examine in consultation and coordination with the Secretary of Defense and the heads of other relevant Federal agencies and departments, including the General Services Administration, Federal procurement practices with respect to class I and class II substances and recommend measures to promote the transition by the Federal Government, as expeditiously as possible, to the use of safe substitutes;

(3) specify initiatives, including appropriate intergovernmental, international, and commercial information and technology transfers, to promote the development and use of safe substitutes for class I and class II substances, including alternative chemicals, product substitutes, and alternative manufacturing processes; and

(4) maintain a public clearinghouse of alternative chemicals, product substitutes, and alternative manufacturing processes that are available for products and manufacturing processes which use class I and class II substances.

(c) Alternatives for class I or II substances

Within 2 years after enactment of the Clean Air Act Amendments of 1990, the Administrator shall promulgate rules under this section providing that it shall be unlawful to replace any class I or class II substance with any substitute substance which the Administrator determines may present adverse effects to human health or the environment, where the Administrator has identified an alternative to such replacement that—

(1) reduces the overall risk to human health and the environment; and

(2) is currently or potentially available.

The Administrator shall publish a list of (A) the substitutes prohibited under this subsection for specific uses and (B) the safe alternatives identified under this subsection for specific uses.

(d) Right to petition

Any person may petition the Administrator to add a substance to the lists under subsection (c) of this section or to remove a substance from either of such lists. The Administrator shall grant or deny the petition within 90 days after receipt of any such petition. If the Administrator denies the petition, the Administrator shall publish an explanation of why the petition was denied. If the Administrator grants such petition the Administrator shall publish such revised list within 6 months thereafter. Any petition under this subsection shall include a showing by the petitioner that there are data on the substance adequate to support the petition. If the Administrator determines that information on the substance is not sufficient to make a determination under this subsection, the Administrator shall use any authority available to the Administrator, under any law administered by the Administrator, to acquire such information.

(e) Studies and notification

The Administrator shall require any person who produces a chemical substitute for a class I substance to provide the Administrator with such person's unpublished health and safety studies on such substitute and require producers to notify the Administrator not less than 90 days before new or existing chemicals are introduced into interstate commerce for significant new uses as substitutes for a class I substance. This subsection shall be subject to section 7414(c) of this title.

(July 14, 1955, ch. 360, title VI, § 612, as added Nov. 15, 1990, Pub.L. 101–549, title VI, § 602(a), 104 Stat. 2667.)

References in Text

Enactment of the Clean Air Act Amendments of 1990, referred to in subsec. (c), probably means the date of enactment of Pub.L. 101–549, Nov. 15, 1990, 104 Stat. 2399, which was approved Nov. 15, 1990.

Effective Date

Section to take effect Nov. 15, 1990, except as otherwise provided, see section 711(b) of Pub.L. 101–549, set out as a note under section 7401 of this title.

Savings Provisions

Suits, actions or proceedings commenced under this chapter as in effect prior to Nov. 15, 1990, not to abate by reason of the taking effect of amendments by Pub.L. 101–549, except as otherwise provided for, see section 711(a) of Pub.L. 101–549, set out as a note under section 7401 of this title.

§ 7671*l*. Federal procurement [CAA § 613]

Not later than 18 months after the enactment of the Clean Air Act Amendments of 1990, the Administrator, in consultation with the Administrator of the General Services Administration and the Secretary of Defense, shall promulgate regulations requiring each department, agency, and instrumentality of the United States to conform its procurement regulations to the policies and requirements of this subchapter and to maximize the substitution of safe alternatives identified under section 7671k of this title for class I and class II substances. Not later than 30 months after the enactment of the Clean Air Act Amendments of 1990, each department, agency, and instrumentality of the United States shall so conform its procurement regulations and certify to the President that its regulations have been modified in accordance with this section.

(July 14, 1955, ch. 360, title VI, § 613, as added Nov. 15, 1990, Pub.L. 101–549, title VI, § 602(a), 104 Stat. 2668.)

References in Text

Enactment of the Clean Air Act Amendments of 1990, referred to in text, probably means the date of enactment of Pub.L. 101–549, Nov. 15, 1990, 104 Stat. 2399, which was approved Nov. 15, 1990.

Effective Date

Section to take effect Nov. 15, 1990, except as otherwise provided, see section 711(b) of Pub.L. 101–549, set out as a note under section 7401 of this title.

Savings Provisions

Suits, actions or proceedings commenced under this chapter as in effect prior to Nov. 15, 1990, not to abate by reason of the taking effect of amendments by Pub.L. 101–549, except as otherwise provided for, see section 711(a) of Pub.L. 101–549, set out as a note under section 7401 of this title.

§ 7671m. Relationship to other laws [CAA § 614]

(a) State laws

Notwithstanding section 7416 of this title, during the 2–year period beginning on the enactment of the Clean Air Act Amendments of 1990, no State or local government may enforce any requirement concerning the design of any new or recalled appliance for the purpose of protecting the stratospheric ozone layer.

(b) Montreal Protocol

This subchapter as added by the Clean Air Act Amendments of 1990 shall be construed, interpreted, and applied as a supplement to the terms and conditions of the Montreal Protocol, as provided in Article 2, paragraph 11 thereof, and shall not be construed, interpreted, or applied to abrogate the responsibilities or obligations of the United States to implement fully the provisions of the Montreal Protocol. In the case of conflict between any provision of this subchapter and any provision of the Montreal Protocol, the more stringent provision shall govern. Nothing in this subchapter shall be construed, interpreted, or applied to affect the authority or responsibility of the Administrator to implement Article 4 of the Montreal Protocol with other appropriate agencies.

(c) Technology export and overseas investment

Upon enactment of this subchapter, the President shall—

(1) prohibit the export of technologies used to produce a class I substance;

(2) prohibit direct or indirect investments by any person in facilities designed to produce a class I or class II substance in nations that are not parties to the Montreal Protocol; and

(3) direct that no agency of the government provide bilateral or multilateral subsidies, aids, credits, guarantees, or insurance programs, for the purpose of producing any class I substance.

(July 14, 1955, ch. 360, title VI, § 614, as added Nov. 15, 1990, Pub.L. 101–549, title VI, § 602(a), 104 Stat. 2668.)

References in Text

The Clean Air Act Amendments of 1990, referred to in subsec. (b), is Pub.L. 101–549, Nov. 15, 1990, 104 Stat. 2399, which is classified generally to this chapter. For complete classification of this Act to the Code, see Tables.

Effective Date

Section to take effect Nov. 15, 1990, except as otherwise provided, see section 711(b) of Pub.L. 101–549, set out as a note under section 7401 of this title.

Savings Provisions

Suits, actions or proceedings commenced under this chapter as in effect prior to Nov. 15, 1990, not to abate by reason of the taking effect of amendments by Pub.L. 101–549, except as otherwise provided for, see section 711(a) of Pub.L. 101–549, set out as a note under section 7401 of this title.

§ 7671n. Authority of Administrator [CAA § 615]

If, in the Administrator's judgment, any substance, practice, process, or activity may reasonably be anticipated to affect the stratosphere, especially ozone in the stratosphere, and such effect may reasonably be anticipated to endanger public health or welfare, the Administrator shall promptly promulgate regulations respecting the control of such substance, practice, process, or activity, and shall submit notice of the proposal and promulgation of such regulation to the Congress.

(July 14, 1955, ch. 360, title VI, § 615, as added Nov. 15, 1990, Pub.L. 101–549, title VI, § 602(a), 104 Stat. 2669.)

Effective Date

Section to take effect Nov. 15, 1990, except as otherwise provided, see section 711(b) of Pub.L. 101–549, set out as a note under section 7401 of this title.

Savings Provisions

Suits, actions or proceedings commenced under this chapter as in effect prior to Nov. 15, 1990, not to abate by reason of the taking effect of amendments by Pub.L. 101–549, except as otherwise provided for, see section 711(a) of Pub.L. 101–549, set out as a note under section 7401 of this title.

§ 7671*o*. Transfers among parties to Montreal Protocol [CAA § 616]

(a) In general

Consistent with the Montreal Protocol, the United States may engage in transfers with other Parties to the Protocol under the following conditions:

(1) The United States may transfer production allowances to another Party if, at the time of such transfer, the Administrator establishes revised production limits for the United States such that the aggregate national United States production permitted under the revised production limits equals the lesser of (A) the maximum production level permitted for the substance or substances concerned in the transfer year under the Protocol minus the production allowances transferred, (B) the maximum production level permitted for the substance or substances concerned in the transfer year under applicable domestic law minus the production allowances transferred, or (C) the average of the actual national production level of the substance or substances concerned for the 3 years prior to the transfer minus the production allowances transferred.

(2) The United States may acquire production allowances from another Party if, at the time of such transfer, the Administrator finds that the other Party has revised its domestic production limits in the same manner as provided with respect to transfers by the United States in subsection (a) of this section.

(b) Effect of transfers on production limits

The Administrator is authorized to reduce the production limits established under this chapter as required as a prerequisite to transfers under paragraph (1) of subsection (a) of this section or to increase production limits established under this chapter to reflect production allowances acquired under a transfer under paragraph (2) of subsection (a) of this section.

(c) Regulations

The Administrator shall promulgate, within 2 years after November 15, 1990, regulations to implement this section.

(d) Definition

In the case of the United States, the term "applicable domestic law" means this chapter.

(July 14, 1955, ch. 360, title VI, § 616, as added Nov. 15, 1990, Pub.L. 101–549, title VI, § 602(a), 104 Stat. 2669.)

Effective Date

Section to take effect Nov. 15, 1990, except as otherwise provided, see section 711(b) of Pub.L. 101–549, set out as a note under section 7401 of this title.

Savings Provisions

Suits, actions or proceedings commenced under this chapter as in effect prior to Nov. 15, 1990, not to abate by reason of the taking effect of amendments by Pub.L. 101–549, except as otherwise provided for, see section 711(a) of Pub.L. 101–549, set out as a note under section 7401 of this title.

§ 7671p. International cooperation [CAA § 617]

(a) In general

The President shall undertake to enter into international agreements to foster cooperative research which complements studies and research authorized by this title, and to develop standards and regulations which protect the stratosphere consistent with regulations applicable within the United States. For these purposes the President through the Secretary of State and the Assistant Secretary of State for Oceans and International Environmental and Scientific Affairs, shall negotiate multilateral treaties, conventions, resolutions, or other agreements, and formulate, present, or support proposals at the United Nations and other appropriate international forums and shall report to the Congress periodically on efforts to arrive at such agreements.

(b) Assistance to developing countries

The Administrator, in consultation with the Secretary of State, shall support global participation in the Montreal Protocol by providing technical and financial assistance to developing countries that are Parties to the Montreal Protocol and operating under article 5 of the Protocol. There are authorized to be appropriated not more than $30,000,000 to carry out this section in fiscal years 1991, 1992 and 1993 and such sums as may be necessary in fiscal years 1994 and 1995. If China and India become Parties to the Montreal Protocol, there are authorized to be appropriated not more than an additional $30,000,000 to carry out this section in fiscal years 1991, 1992, and 1993.

(July 14, 1955, ch. 360, title VI, § 617, as added Nov. 15, 1990, Pub.L. 101–549, title VI, § 602(a), 104 Stat. 2669.)

Effective Date

Section to take effect Nov. 15, 1990, except as otherwise provided, see section 711(b) of Pub.L. 101–549, set out as a note under section 7401 of this title.

Savings Provisions

Suits, actions or proceedings commenced under this chapter as in effect prior to Nov. 15, 1990, not to abate by reason of the taking effect of amendments by Pub.L. 101–549, except as otherwise provided for, see section 711(a) of Pub.L. 101–549, set out as a note under section 7401 of this title.

§ 7671q. Miscellaneous provisions [CAA § 618]

For purposes of section 7416 of this title, requirements concerning the areas addressed by this subchapter for the protection of the stratosphere against ozone layer depletion shall be treated as requirements for the control and abatement of air pollution. For purposes of section 7418 of this title, the requirements of this subchapter and corresponding State, interstate, and local requirements, administrative authority, and process, and sanctions respecting the protection of the stratospheric ozone layer shall be treated as requirements for the control and abatement of air pollution within the meaning of section 7418 of this title.

(July 14, 1955, ch. 360, title VI, § 618, as added Nov. 15, 1990, Pub.L. 101–549, title VI, § 602(a), 104 Stat. 2670.)

Effective Date

Section to take effect Nov. 15, 1990, except as otherwise provided, see section 711(b) of Pub.L. 101–549, set out as a note under section 7401 of this title.

Savings Provisions

Suits, actions or proceedings commenced under this chapter as in effect prior to Nov. 15, 1990, not to abate by reason of the taking effect of amendments by Pub.L. 101–549, except as otherwise provided for, see section 711(a) of Pub.L. 101–549, set out as a note under section 7401 of this title.

COMPREHENSIVE ENVIRONMENTAL RESPONSE, COMPENSATION AND LIABILITY

COMPREHENSIVE ENVIRONMENTAL RESPONSE, COMPENSATION, AND LIABILITY ACT OF 1980 [CERCLA § ___]

(42 U.S.C.A. §§ 9601 to 9675)

CHAPTER 103—COMPREHENSIVE ENVIRONMENTAL RESPONSE, COMPENSATION, AND LIABILITY

SUBCHAPTER I—HAZARDOUS SUBSTANCES RELEASES, LIABILITY, COMPENSATION

Sec.

9601. Definitions.
9602. Designation of additional hazardous substances and establishment of reportable released quantities; regulations.
9603. Notification requirements respecting released substances.
- (a) Notice to National Response Center upon release from vessel or offshore or onshore facility by person in charge; conveyance of notice by Center.
- (b) Penalties for failure to notify; use of notice or information pursuant to notice in criminal case.
- (c) Notice to Administrator of EPA of existence of storage, etc., facility by owner or operator; exceptions; time, manner, and form of notice; penalties for failure to notify; use of notice or information pursuant to notice in criminal case.
- (d) Recordkeeping requirements; promulgation of rules and regulations by Administrator of EPA; penalties for violations; waiver of retention requirements.
- (e) Applicability to registered pesticide product.
- (f) Exemptions from notice and penalty provisions for substances reported under other Federal law or is in continuous release, etc.

9604. Response authorities.
- (a) Removal and other remedial action by President; applicability of national contingency plan; response by potentially responsible parties; public health threats; limitations on response; exception.
- (b) Investigations, monitoring, etc., by President.
- (c) Criteria for continuance of obligations from Fund over specified amount for response actions; consultation by President with affected States; contracts or cooperative agreements by States with President prior to remedial actions; cost-sharing agreements; selection

Sec.

9604. Response authorities.
by President of remedial actions; State credits: granting of credit, expenses before listing or agreement, response actions between 1978 and 1980, State expenses after December 11, 1980, in excess of 10 percent of costs, item-by-item approval, use of credits; operation and maintenance; limitation on source of funds for O & M; recontracting; siting.
- (d) Contracts or cooperative agreements by President with States or political subdivisions or Indian tribes; State applications, terms and conditions; reimbursements; cost-sharing provisions; enforcement requirements and procedures.
- (e) Information gathering and access.
- (f) Contracts for response action; compliance with Federal health and safety standards.
- (g) Rates for wages and labor standards applicable to covered work.
- (h) Emergency procurement powers; exercise by President.
- (i) Agency for Toxic Substances and Disease Registry; establishment, functions, etc.
- (j) Acquisition of property.

9605. National contingency plan; preparation, contents, etc.
- (a) Revision and republication.
- (b) Revision of plan.
- (c) Hazard ranking system.
  - (1) Revision.
  - (2) Health assessment of water contamination risks.
  - (3) Reevaluation not required.
  - (4) New information.
- (d) Petition for assessment of release.
- (e) Releases from earlier sites.
- (f) Minority contractors.
- (g) Special study wastes.
  - (1) Application.
  - (2) Considerations in adding facilities to NPL.
  - (3) Savings provisions.
  - (4) Information gathering and analysis.

9606. Abatement actions.
- (a) Maintenance, jurisdiction, etc.
- (b) Fines; reimbursement.
- (c) Guidelines for using imminent hazard, enforcement, and emergency response authorities;

Sec.
9606. Abatement actions.
promulgation by Administrator of EPA, scope, etc.
9607. Liability.
(a) Covered persons; scope; recoverable costs and damages; interest rate; "comparable maturity" date.
(b) Defenses.
(c) Determination of amounts.
(d) Rendering care or advice.
(1) In general.
(2) State and local governments.
(3) Savings provision.
(e) Indemnification, hold harmless, etc., agreements or conveyances; subrogation rights.
(f) Actions involving natural resources; maintenance, scope, etc.
(1) Natural resources liability.
(2) Designation of Federal and State officials.
(A) Federal.
(B) State.
(C) Rebuttable presumption.
(g) Federal agencies.
(h) Owner or operator of vessel.
(i) Application of a registered pesticide product.
(j) Obligations or liability pursuant to federally permitted release.
(k) Transfer to, and assumption by Post-Closure Liability Fund of liability of owner or operator of hazardous waste disposal facility in receipt of permit under applicable solid waste disposal law; time, criteria applicable, procedures, etc.; monitoring costs; reports.
(5) Suspension of liability transfer.
(6) Study of options for post-closure program.
(A) Study.
(B) Program elements.
(C) Assessments.
(D) Procedures.
(E) Consideration of options.
(F) Recommendations.
(*l*) Federal lien.
(1) In general.
(2) Duration.
(3) Notice and validity.
(4) Action in rem.
(m) Maritime lien.
9608. Financial responsibility.
(a) Establishment and maintenance by owner or operator of vessel; amount; failure to obtain certification of compliance.
(b) Establishment and maintenance by owner or operator of production, etc., facilities; amount; adjustment; consolidated form of responsibility; coverage of motor carriers.
(c) Direct action.
(1) Releases from vessels.
(2) Releases from facilities.
(d) Limitation of guarantor liability.
(1) Total liability.
(2) Other liability.
9609. Civil penalties and awards.
(a) Class 1 administrative penalty.
(1) Violations.
(2) Notice and hearings.
(3) Determining amount.

Sec.
9609. Civil penalties and awards.
(4) Review.
(5) Subpoenas.
(b) Class II administrative penalty.
(c) Judicial assessment.
(d) Awards.
(e) Procurement procedures.
(f) Savings clause.
9610. Employee protection.
(a) Activities of employee subject to protection.
(b) Administrative grievance procedure in cases of alleged violations.
(c) Assessment of costs and expenses against violator subsequent to issuance of order of abatement.
(d) Defenses.
(e) Presidential evaluations of potential loss of shifts of employment resulting from administration or enforcement of provisions; investigations; procedures applicable, etc.
9611. Use of Fund.
(a) In general.
(b) Additional authorized purposes.
(c) Peripheral matters and limitations.
(d) Additional limitations.
(e) Funding requirements respecting moneys in Fund; limitation on certain claims; Fund use outside Federal property boundaries.
(f) Obligation of moneys by Federal officials; obligation of moneys or settlement of claims by State officials or Indian tribe.
(g) Notice to potential injured parties by owner and operator of vessel or facility causing release of substance; rules and regulations.
(h) Repealed.
(i) Restoration, etc., of natural resources.
(j) Use of Post-closure Liability Fund.
(k) Inspector General.
(*l*) Foreign claimants.
(m) Agency for Toxic Substances and Disease Registry.
(n) Limitations on research, development, and demonstration program.
(1) Section 9660(b).
(2) Section 9660(a).
(3) Section 9660(d).
(*o*) Notification procedures for limitations on certain payments.
(p) General revenue share of Superfund.
(1) In general.
(2) Computation.
9612. Claims procedure.
(a) Claims against Fund for response costs.
(b) Forms and procedures applicable.
(1) Prescribing forms and procedures.
(2) Payment or request for hearing.
(3) Burden of proof.
(4) Decisions.
(5) Finality and appeal.
(6) Payment.
(c) Subrogation rights; actions maintainable.
(d) Statute of limitations.
(1) Claims for recovery of costs.
(2) Claims for recovery of damages.
(3) Minors and incompetents.

Sec.
9612. Claims procedure.
(e) Other statutory or common law claims not waived, etc.
(f) Double recovery prohibited.
9613. Civil proceedings.
(a) Review of regulations in Circuit Court of Appeals of the United States for the District of Columbia.
(b) Jurisdiction; venue.
(c) Controversies or other matters resulting from tax collection or tax regulation review.
(d) Litigation commenced prior to December 11, 1980.
(e) Nationwide service of process.
(f) Contribution.
(1) Contribution.
(2) Settlement.
(3) Persons not party to settlement.
(g) Period in which action may be brought.
(1) Actions for natural resource damages.
(2) Actions for recovery of costs.
(3) Contribution.
(4) Subrogation.
(5) Actions to recover indemnification payments.
(6) Minors and incompetents.
(h) Timing of review.
(i) Intervention.
(j) Judicial review.
(1) Limitation.
(2) Standard.
(3) Remedy.
(4) Procedural errors.
(k) Administrative record and participation procedures.
(1) Administrative record.
(2) Participation procedures.
(A) Removal action.
(B) Remedial action.
(C) Interim record.
(D) Potentially responsible parties.
(*l*) Notice of actions.
9614. Relationship to other law.
(a) Additional State liability or requirements with respect to release of substances within State.
(b) Recovery under other State or Federal law of compensation for removal costs or damages, or payment of claims.
(c) Recycled oil.
(1) Service station dealers, etc.
(2) Presumption.
(3) Definition.
(4) Effective date.
(d) Financial responsibility of owner or operator of vessel or facility under State or local law, rule or regulation.
9615. Presidential delegation and assignment of duties or powers and promulgation of regulations.
9616. Schedules.
(a) Assessment and listing of facilities.
(b) Evaluation.
(c) Explanations.
(d) Commencement of RI/FS.
(e) Commencement of remedial action.
9617. Public participation.
(a) Proposed plan.

Sec.
9617. Public participation.
(b) Final plan.
(c) Explanation of differences.
(d) Publication.
(e) Grants for technical assistance.
(1) Authority.
(2) Amount.
9618. High priority for drinking water supplies.
9619. Response action contractors.
(a) Liability of response action contractors.
(1) Response action contractors.
(2) Negligence, etc.
(3) Effect on warranties; employer liability.
(4) Governmental employees.
(b) Savings provisions.
(1) Liability of other persons.
(2) Burden of plaintiff.
(c) Indemnification.
(1) In general.
(2) Applicability.
(3) Source of funding.
(4) Requirements.
(5) Limitations.
(A) Liability covered.
(B) Deductibles and limits.
(C) Contracts with potentially responsible parties.
(i) Decision to indemnify.
(ii) Conditions.
(D) RCRA facilities.
(E) Persons retained or hired.
(6) Cost recovery.
(7) Regulations.
(8) Study.
(d) Exception.
(e) Definitions.
(1) Response action contract.
(2) Response action contractor.
(3) Insurance.
(f) Competition.
(g) Surety bonds.
9620. Federal facilities.
(a) Application of chapter to Federal Government.
(1) In general.
(2) Application or requirements to Federal facilities.
(3) Exceptions.
(4) State laws.
(b) Notice.
(c) Federal Agency Hazardous Waste Compliance Docket.
(d) Assessment and evaluation.
(e) Required action by department.
(1) RI/FS.
(2) Commencement of remedial action; interagency agreement.
(3) Completion of remedial actions.
(4) Contents of agreement.
(5) Annual report.
(6) Settlements with other parties.
(f) State and local participation.
(g) Transfer of authorities.
(h) Property transferred by Federal agencies.
(1) Notice.
(2) Form of notice; regulations.
(3) Contents of certain deeds.

Sec.
9620. Federal facilities.
(i) Obligations under Solid Waste Disposal Act.
(j) National security.
(1) Site specific Presidential orders.
(2) Classified information.
9621. Cleanup standards.
(a) Selection of remedial action.
(b) General rules.
(c) Review.
(d) Degree of cleanup.
(e) Permits and enforcement.
(f) State involvement.
9622. Settlements.
(a) Authority to enter into agreements.
(b) Agreements with potentially responsible parties.
(1) Mixed funding.
(2) Reviewability.
(3) Retention of funds.
(4) Future obligation of fund.
(c) Effect of agreement.
(1) Liability.
(2) Actions against other persons.
(d) Enforcement.
(1) Cleanup agreements.
(A) Consent decree.
(B) Effect.
(C) Structure.
(2) Public participation.
(A) Filing of proposed judgment.
(B) Opportunity for comment.
(3) 9604(b) agreements.
(e) Special notice procedures.
(1) Notice.
(2) Negotiation.
(A) Moratorium.
(B) Proposals.
(C) Additional parties.
(3) Preliminary allocation of responsibility.
(A) In general.
(B) Collection of information.
(C) Effect.
(D) Costs.
(E) Decision to reject offer.
(4) Failure to propose.
(5) Significant threats.
(6) Inconsistent response action.
(f) Covenant not to sue.
(1) Discretionary covenants.
(2) Special covenants not to sue.
(3) Requirement that remedial action be completed.
(4) Factors.
(5) Satisfactory performance.
(6) Additional condition for future liability.
(g) De minimis settlements.
(1) Expedited final settlement.
(2) Covenant not to sue.
(3) Expedited agreement.
(4) Consent decree or administrative order.
(5) Effect of agreement.
(6) Settlements with other potentially responsible parties.
(h) Cost recovery settlement authority.
(1) Authority to settle.
(2) Use of arbitration.
(3) Recovery of claims.

Sec.
9622. Settlements.
(4) Claims for contribution.
(i) Settlement procedures.
(1) Publication in Federal Register.
(2) Comment period.
(3) Consideration of comments.
(j) Natural resources.
(1) Notification of trustees.
(2) Covenant not to sue.
(k) Section not applicable to vessels.
(*l*) Civil penalties.
(m) Applicability of general principles of law.
9623. Reimbursement to local governments.
(a) Application.
(b) Reimbursement.
(1) Temporary emergency measures.
(2) Local funds not supplanted.
(c) Amount.
(d) Procedure.
9624. Methane recovery.
(a) In general.
(b) Exceptions.
9625. Section 6921(b)(3)(A)(i) waste.
(a) Revision of hazard ranking system.
(b) Inclusion prohibited.
9626. Indian tribes.
(a) Treatment generally.
(b) Community relocation.
(c) Study.
(d) Limitation.

SUBCHAPTER II—HAZARDOUS SUBSTANCE RESPONSE REVENUE

PART A—HAZARDOUS SUBSTANCE RESPONSE TRUST FUND

9631 to 9633. Repealed.

PART B—POST-CLOSURE LIABILITY TRUST FUND

9641. Repealed.

SUBCHAPTER III—MISCELLANEOUS PROVISIONS

9651. Reports and studies.
(a) Implementation experiences; identification and disposal of waste.
(b) Private insurance protection.
(c) Regulations respecting assessment of damages to natural resources.
(d) Issues, alternatives, and policy considerations involving selection of locations for waste treatment, storage, and disposal facilities.
(e) Adequacy of existing common law and statutory remedies.
(f) Modification of national contingency plan.
(g) Insurability study.
(1) Study by Comptroller General.
(2) Consultation.
(3) Items evaluated.
(4) Submission.
(h) Report and oversight requirements.
(1) Annual report by EPA.
(2) Review by Inspector General.
(3) Congressional oversight.
9652. Effective dates; savings provisions.
9653. Repealed.

Sec.
9654. Applicability of Federal water pollution control funding, etc., provisions.
9655. Legislative veto of rule or regulation.
(a) Transmission to Congress upon promulgation or repromulgation of rule or regulation; disapproval procedures.
(b) Approval; effective dates.
(c) Sessions of Congress as applicable.
(d) Congressional inaction on, or rejection of, resolution of disapproval.
9656. Transportation of hazardous substances; listing as hazardous material; liability for release.
9657. Separability of provisions; contribution.
9658. Actions under State law for damages from exposure to hazardous substances.
(a) State statutes of limitations for hazardous substance cases.
(1) Exception to state statutes.
(2) State law generally applicable.
(3) Actions under section 9607.
(b) Definitions.
(1) Subchapter I terms.
(2) Applicable limitations period.
(3) Commencement date.
(4) Federally required commencement date.
(A) In general.
(B) Special rules.
9659. Citizens suits.
(a) Authority to bring civil actions.
(b) Venue.
(1) Actions under subsection (a)(1).
(2) Actions under subsection (a)(2).
(c) Relief.
(d) Rules applicable to subsection (a)(1) actions.
(1) Notice.
(2) Diligent prosecution.
(e) Rules applicable to subsection (a)(2) actions.
(f) Costs.
(g) Intervention.
(h) Other rights.
(i) Definitions.
9660. Research, development, and demonstrator.
(a) Hazardous substance research and training.
(1) Authorities of secretary.
(2) Director of NIEHS.
(3) Recipients of grants, etc.
(4) Procedures.
(5) Advisory council.
(6) Planning.
(b) Alternative or innovative treatment technology research and demonstration program.
(1) Establishment.
(2) Administration.
(3) Contracts and grants.
(4) Use of sites.
(5) Demonstration assistance.
(A) Program components.
(B) Solicitation.
(C) Applications.
(D) Project selection.
(E) Site selection.
(F) Demonstration plan.
(G) Supervision and testing.
(H) Project completion.
(I) Extensions.
(J) Funding restrictions.

Sec.
9660. Research, development, and demonstrator.
(6) Field demonstrations.
(7) Criteria.
(8) Technology transfer.
(9) Training.
(10) Definition.
(c) Hazardous substance research.
(d) University hazardous substance research centers.
(1) Grant program.
(2) Responsibilities of centers.
(3) Applications.
(4) Selection criteria.
(5) Maintenance of effort.
(6) Federal share.
(7) Limitation on use of funds.
(8) Administration through the Office of the Administrator.
(9) Equitable distribution of funds.
(10) Technology transfer activities.
(e) Report to Congress.
(f) Saving provision.
(g) Small business participation.
9660a. Grant program.
(1) Grant purposes.
(2) Administration.
(3) Grant recipients.
9661. Love Canal property acquisition.
(a) Acquisition of property in Emergency Declaration Area.
(b) Procedures for acquisition.
(c) State ownership.
(d) Maintenance of property.
(e) Habitability and land use study.
(f) Funding.
(g) Response.
(h) Definitions.
(1) Emergency Declaration Area.
(2) Private property.
9662. Limitation on contract and borrowing authority.

SUBCHAPTER IV—POLLUTION INSURANCE

9671. Definitions.
(1) Insurance.
(2) Pollution liability.
(3) Risk retention group.
(4) Purchasing group.
(5) State.
9672. State laws; scope of subchapter.
(a) State laws.
(b) Scope of title.
9673. Risk retention groups.
(a) Exemption.
(b) Exceptions.
(1) State laws generally applicable.
(2) State regulations not subject to exemption.
(c) Application of exemptions.
(d) Agents or brokers.
9674. Purchasing groups.
(a) Exemption.
(b) Application of exemptions.
(c) Agents or brokers.
9675. Applicability of securities laws.
(a) Ownership interests.
(b) Investment Company Act.

Sec.
9675. Applicability of securities laws.
(c) Blue sky law.

WEST'S FEDERAL FORMS

Administrative agency decisions and orders, enforcement and review, see § 851 et seq.
Depositions and discovery, see §§ 3271 et seq., 3681 et seq.
Intervention, motion for leave, see § 3111 et seq.
Jurisdiction and venue in district courts, see § 1003 et seq.
Production of documents, motions and orders pertaining to, see § 3551 et seq.
Sentence and fine, see § 7531 et seq.
Subpoenas, see § 3981 et seq.

CODE OF FEDERAL REGULATIONS

Assistance agreements, procurement under, see 40 CFR 33.001 et seq.
Superfund cost share eligibility criteria for permanent and temporary relocation, see 44 CFR 222.1 et seq.

LAW REVIEW COMMENTARIES

Groundwater pollution I: The problem and the law. Robert L. Glicksman and George Cameron Coggins, 35 U.Kan.L.Rev. 75 (1986).

Confidential business information versus the public's right to disclosure—Biotechnology renews the challenge. Stanley H. Abramson, 34 U.Kansas L.Rev. 681 (1986).

Corporate officer liability for hazardous waste disposal: What are the consequences? 38 Mercer L.Rev. 677 (1987).

Criminal sanctions under federal and state environmental statutes. Richard H. Allan, 14 Ecology L.Q. 117 (1987).

Direct liability for hazardous substance cleanups under CERCLA: A comprehensive approach. Michael P. Healy, 42 Case W.Res.L.Rev. 65 (1992).

Emerging theories of lender liability in Texas. John O. Tyler, Jr., 24 Houston L.Rev. 411 (1987).

Environmental liability of creditors under superfund (with forms). Joel R. Burcat, 33 Prac.Law. 13 (1987).

Expansive reach of CERCLA liability: Potential liability of executors of wills and inter vivos and testamentary trustees. Denise Rodosevich, 55 Alb.L.Rev. 97 (1991).

Federal preemption, federal conscription under the New Superfund Act. Alfred R. Light, 38 Mercer L.Rev. 643 (1987).

Hazardous waste issues in real estate transactions. Elliott H. Levitas and John Vance Hughes, 38 Mercer L.Rev. 581 (1987).

Patterns of judicial interpretation of insurance coverage for hazardous waste site liability. Robert D. Chesler, Michael L. Rodburg and Cornelius C. Smith, Jr., 18 Rutgers L.J. 9 (1986).

Significant developments affecting ECRA. David B. Farer, 119 N.J.L.J. 681 (1987).

Successor landowner suits for recovery of hazardous waste cleanup costs: CERCLA Section 107(a)(4). 33 UCLA Law R. 1737 (1986).

The impact of bankruptcy on environmental obligations. Robert P. Dresdner, Nat.Env.L.J. (May 1993) p. 3.

The impact of the 1986 Superfund Amendments and Reauthorization Act on the commercial lending industry: A critical assessment. 41 U.Miami L.Rev. 879 (1987).

Toxic tort litigation and the causation element: Is there any hope of reconciliation? Or a Fred Harris, Jr., 40 Southwestern (Tex.) L.J. 909 (1986).

WESTLAW ELECTRONIC RESEARCH

See WESTLAW guide following the Explanation pages of this pamphlet.

SUBCHAPTER I—HAZARDOUS SUBSTANCES RELEASES, LIABILITY, COMPENSATION

LAW REVIEW COMMENTARIES

Case for a Bankruptcy Code priority for environmental cleanup claims. Gary E. Claar, 18 Wm.Mitchell L.Rev. 29 (1992).

Discharging CERCLA liability in bankruptcy: When does a claim arise? 76 Minn.L.Rev. 327 (1991).

Renouncing the rule of limited liability: Shareholder liability under CERCLA. J. Patrick Berry and Eric T. Furey, 9 Corp.Counsel Rev. (Tex.) 71 (Nov.1990).

§ 9601. Definitions [CERCLA § 101]

For purpose of this subchapter—

(1) The term "act of God" means an unanticipated grave natural disaster or other natural phenomenon of an exceptional, inevitable, and irresistible character, the effects of which could not have been prevented or avoided by the exercise of due care or foresight.

(2) The term "Administrator" means the Administrator of the United States Environmental Protection Agency.

(3) The term "barrel" means forty-two United States gallons at sixty degrees Fahrenheit.

(4) The term "claim" means a demand in writing for a sum certain.

(5) The term "claimant" means any person who presents a claim for compensation under this chapter.

(6) The term "damages" means damages for injury or loss of natural resources as set forth in section 9607(a) or 9611(b) of this title.

(7) The term "drinking water supply" means any raw or finished water source that is or may be used by a public water system (as defined in the Safe Drinking Water Act [42 U.S.C.A. § 300f et seq.]) or as drinking water by one or more individuals.

(8) The term "environment" means (A) the navigable waters, the waters of the contiguous zone, and the ocean waters for which the natural resources are under the exclusive management authority of the United States under the Magnuson Fishery Conservation and Management Act [16 U.S.C.A. § 1801 et seq.], and (B) any other surface water, ground water, drinking water supply, land surface or subsurface strata, or ambient air within the United States or under the jurisdiction of the United States.

(9) The term "facility" means (A) any building, structure, installation, equipment, pipe or pipeline (including any pipe into a sewer or publicly owned treatment works), well, pit, pond, lagoon, impoundment, ditch, landfill, storage container, motor vehicle, rolling stock, or aircraft, or (B) any site or area where a hazardous substance has been deposited, stored, disposed of, or placed, or otherwise come to be located; but does not include any consumer product in consumer use or any vessel.

(10) The term "federally permitted release" means (A) discharges in compliance with a permit under section 1342 of Title 33, (B) discharges resulting from circumstances identified and reviewed and made part of the public record with respect to a permit issued or modified under section 1342 of Title 33 and subject to a condition of such permit, (C) continuous or anticipated intermittent discharges from a point source, identified in a permit or permit application under section 1342 of Title 33, which are caused by events occurring within the scope of relevant operating or treatment systems, (D) discharges in compliance with a legally enforceable permit under section 1344 of Title 33, (E) releases in compliance with a legally enforceable final permit issued pursuant to section 3005(a) through (d) of the Solid Waste Disposal Act [42 U.S.C.A. § 6925(a) to (d)] from a hazardous waste treatment, storage, or disposal facility when such permit specifically identifies the hazardous substances and makes such substances subject to a standard of practice, control procedure or bioassay limitation or condition, or other control on the hazardous substances in such releases, (F) any release in compliance with a legally enforceable permit issued under section 1412 of Title 33 of[1] section 1413 of Title 33, (G) any injection of fluids authorized under Federal underground injection control programs or State programs submitted for Federal approval (and not disapproved by the Administrator of the Environmental Protection Agency) pursuant to part C of the Safe Drinking Water Act [42 U.S.C.A. § 300h et seq.], (H) any emission into the air subject to a permit or control regulation under section 111 [42 U.S.C.A. § 7411], section 112 [42 U.S.C.A. § 7412], Title I part C [42 U.S.C.A. § 7470 et seq.], Title I part D [42 U.S.C.A. § 7501 et seq.], or State implementation plans submitted in accordance with section 110 of the Clean Air Act [42 U.S.C.A. § 7410] (and not disapproved by the Administrator of the Environmental Protection Agency), including any schedule or waiver granted, promulgated, or approved under these sections, (I) any injection of fluids or other materials authorized under applicable State law (i) for the purpose of stimulating or treating wells for the production of crude oil, natural gas, or water, (ii) for the purpose of secondary, tertiary, or other enhanced recovery of crude oil or natural gas, or (iii) which are brought to the surface in conjunction with the production of crude oil or natural gas and which are reinjected, (J) the introduction of any pollutant into a publicly owned treatment works when such pollutant is specified in and in compliance with applicable pretreatment standards of section 1317(b) or (c) of Title 33 and enforceable requirements in a pretreatment program submitted by a State or municipality for Federal approval under section 1342 of Title 33, and (K) any release of source, special nuclear, or byproduct material, as those terms are defined in the Atomic Energy Act of 1954 [42 U.S.C.A. § 2011 et seq.], in compliance with a legally enforceable license, permit, regulation, or order issued pursuant to the Atomic Energy Act of 1954.

(11) The term "Fund" or "Trust Fund" means the Hazardous Substance Superfund established by section 9507 of Title 26.

(12) The term "ground water" means water in a saturated zone or stratum beneath the surface of land or water.

(13) The term "guarantor" means any person, other than the owner or operator, who provides evidence of financial responsibility for an owner or operator under this chapter.

(14) The term "hazardous substance" means (A) any substance designated pursuant to section 1321(b)(2)(A) of Title 33, (B) any element, compound, mixture, solution, or substance designated pursuant to section 9602 of this title, (C) any hazardous waste having the characteristics identified under or listed pursuant to section 3001 of the Solid Waste Disposal Act [42 U.S.C.A. § 6921] (but not including any waste the regulation of which under the Solid Waste Disposal Act [42 U.S.C.A. § 6901 et seq.] has been suspended by Act of Congress), (D) any toxic pollutant listed under section 1317(a) of Title 33, (E) any hazardous air pollutant listed under section 112 of the Clean Air Act [42 U.S.C.A. § 7412], and (F) any imminently hazardous chemical substance or mixture with respect to which the Administrator has taken action pursuant to section 2606 of Title 15. The term does not include petroleum, including crude oil or any fraction thereof which is not otherwise specifically listed or designated as a hazardous substance under subparagraphs (A) through (F) of this paragraph, and the term does not include natural gas, natural gas liquids, liquefied natural gas, or synthetic gas usable for fuel (or mixtures of natural gas and such synthetic gas).

(15) The term "navigable waters" or "navigable waters of the United States" means the waters of the United States, including the territorial seas.

(16) The term "natural resources" means land, fish, wildlife, biota, air, water, ground water, drinking water supplies, and other such resources belonging to, managed by, held in trust by, appertaining to, or otherwise controlled by the United States (including the resources of the fishery conservation zone established by the Magnuson Fishery Conservation and Management Act [16 U.S.C.A. § 1801 et seq.]), any State or local government, any foreign government, any Indian tribe, or, if such resources are subject to a trust restriction on alienation, any member of an Indian tribe.

(17) The term "offshore facility" means any facility of any kind located in, on, or under, any of the navigable waters of the United States, and any facility of any kind which is subject to the jurisdiction of the United States and is located in, on, or under any other waters, other than a vessel or a public vessel.

(18) The term "onshore facility" means any facility (including, but not limited to, motor vehicles and rolling stock) of any kind located in, on, or under, any land or nonnavigable waters within the United States.

(19) The term "otherwise subject to the jurisdiction of the United States" means subject to the jurisdiction of the United States by virtue of United States citizenship, United States vessel documentation or numbering, or as provided by international agreement to which the United States is a party.

(20)(A) The term "owner or operator" means (i) in the case of a vessel, any person owning, operating, or chartering by demise, such vessel, (ii) in the case of an onshore facility or an offshore facility, any person owning or operating such facility, and (iii) in the case of any facility, title or control of which was conveyed due to bankruptcy, foreclosure, tax delinquency, abandonment, or similar means to a unit of State or local government, any person who owned, operated, or otherwise controlled activities at such facility immediately beforehand. Such term does not include a person, who, without participating in the management of a vessel or facility, holds indicia of ownership primarily to protect his security interest in the vessel or facility.

(B) In the case of a hazardous substance which has been accepted for transportation by a common or contract carrier and except as provided in section 9607(a)(3) or (4) of this title, (i) the term "owner or operator" shall mean such common carrier or other bona fide for hire carrier acting as an independent contractor during such transportation, (ii) the shipper of such hazardous substance shall not be considered to have caused or contributed to any release during such transportation which resulted solely from circumstances or conditions beyond his control.

(C) In the case of a hazardous substance which has been delivered by a common or contract carrier to a disposal or treatment facility and except as provided in section 9607(a)(3) or (4) of this title, (i) the term "owner or operator" shall not include such common or contract carrier, and (ii) such common or contract carrier shall not be considered to have caused or contributed to any release at such disposal or treatment facility resulting from circumstances or conditions beyond its control.

(D) The term "owner or operator" does not include a unit of State or local government which acquired ownership or control involuntarily through bankruptcy, tax delinquency, abandonment, or other circumstances in which the government involuntarily acquires title by virtue of its function as sovereign. The exclusion provided under this paragraph shall not apply to any State or local government which has caused or contributed to the release or threatened release of a hazardous substance from the facility, and such a State or local government shall be subject to the provisions of this chapter in the same manner and to the same extent, both procedurally and substantively, as any nongovernmental entity, including liability under section 9607 of this title.

(21) The term "person" means an individual, firm, corporation, association, partnership, consortium, joint venture, commercial entity, United States Government, State, municipality, commission, political subdivision of a State, or any interstate body.

(22) The term "release" means any spilling, leaking, pumping, pouring, emitting, emptying, discharging, injecting, escaping, leaching, dumping, or disposing into the environment (including the abandonment or discarding of barrels, containers, and other closed receptacles containing any hazardous substance or pollutant or contaminant), but excludes (A) any release which results in exposure to persons solely within a workplace, with respect to a claim which such persons may assert against the employer of such persons, (B) emissions from the engine exhaust of a motor vehicle, rolling stock, aircraft, vessel, or pipeline pumping station engine, (C) release of source, byproduct, or special nuclear material from a nuclear incident, as those terms are defined in the Atomic Energy Act of 1954 [42 U.S.C.A. § 2011 et seq.], if such release is subject to requirements with respect to financial protection established by the Nuclear Regulatory Commission under section 170 of such Act [42 U.S.C.A. § 2210], or, for the purposes of section 9604 of this title or any other response action, any release of source byproduct, or special nuclear material from any processing site designated under section 7912(a)(1) or 7942(a) of this title, and (D) the normal application of fertilizer.

(23) The terms "remove" or "removal" means[2] the cleanup or removal of released hazardous substances from the environment, such actions as may be necessary[3] taken in the event of the threat of release of hazardous substances into the environment, such actions as may be necessary to monitor, assess, and evaluate the release or threat of release of hazardous substances, the disposal of removed material, or the taking of such other actions as may be necessary to prevent, minimize, or mitigate damage to the public health or welfare or to the environment, which may otherwise result from a release or threat of release. The term includes, in addition, without being limited to, security fencing or other measures to limit access, provision of alternative water supplies, temporary evacuation and housing of threatened individuals not otherwise provided for, action taken under section 9604(b) of this title, and any emergency assistance which may be provided under the Disaster Relief and Emergency Assistance Act [42 U.S.C.A. § 5121 et seq.].

(24) The terms "remedy" or "remedial action" means[2] those actions consistent with permanent remedy taken instead of or in addition to removal actions in the event of a release or threatened release of a hazardous substance into the environment, to prevent or minimize the release of hazardous substances so that they do not migrate to cause substantial danger to present or future public health or welfare or the environment. The term includes, but is not limited to, such actions at the location of the release as storage, confinement, perimeter protection using dikes, trenches, or ditches, clay cover, neutralization, cleanup of released hazardous substances and associated contaminated materials, recycling or reuse, diversion, destruction, segregation of reactive wastes, dredging or excavations, repair or replacement of leaking containers, collection of leachate and runoff, onsite treatment or incineration, provision of alternative water supplies, and any monitoring reasonably required to assure that such actions protect the public health and welfare and the environment. The term includes the costs of permanent relocation of residents and businesses and community facilities where the President determines that, alone or in combination with other measures, such relocation is more cost-effective than and environmentally preferable to the transportation, storage, treatment, destruction, or secure disposition offsite of hazardous substances, or may otherwise be necessary to protect the public health or welfare; the term includes offsite transport and offsite storage, treatment, destruction, or secure disposition of hazardous substances and associated contaminated materials.

(25) The terms "respond" or "response" means[2] remove, removal, remedy, and remedial action;,[4] all such terms (including the terms "removal" and "remedial action") include enforcement activities related thereto.

(26) The terms "transport" or "transportation" means[2] the movement of a hazardous substance by any mode, including a hazardous liquid pipeline facility (as defined in the Pipeline Safety Act), and in the case of a hazardous substance which has been accepted for transportation by a common or contract carrier, the term "transport" or "transportation" shall include any stoppage in transit which is temporary, incidental to the transportation movement, and at the ordinary operating convenience of a common or contract carrier, and any such stoppage shall be considered as a continuity of movement and not as the storage of a hazardous substance.

(27) The terms "United States" and "State" include the several States of the United States, the District of Columbia, the Commonwealth of Puerto Rico, Guam, American Samoa, the United States Virgin Islands, the Commonwealth of the Northern Marianas, and any other territory or possession over which the United States has jurisdiction.

(28) The term "vessel" means every description of watercraft or other artificial contrivance used, or capable of being used, as a means of transportation on water.

(29) The terms "disposal", "hazardous waste", and "treatment" shall have the meaning provided in section 1004 of the Solid Waste Disposal Act [42 U.S.C.A. § 6903].

(30) The terms "territorial sea" and "contiguous zone" shall have the meaning provided in section 1362 of Title 33.

(31) The term "national contingency plan" means the national contingency plan published under section 1321(c) of Title 33 or revised pursuant to section 9605 of this title.

(32) The term "liable" or "liability" under this subchapter shall be construed to be the standard of liability which obtains under section 1321 of Title 33.

(33) The term "pollutant or contaminant" shall include, but not be limited to, any element, substance, compound, or mixture, including disease-causing agents, which after release into the environment and upon exposure, ingestion, inhalation, or assimilation into any organism, either directly from the environment or indirectly by ingestion through food chains, will or may reasonably be anticipated to cause death, disease, behavioral abnormalities, cancer, genetic mutation, physiological malfunctions (including malfunctions in reproduction) or physical deformations, in such organisms or their offspring; except that the term "pollutant or contaminant" shall not include petroleum, including crude oil or any fraction thereof which is not otherwise specifically listed or designated as a hazardous substance under subparagraphs (A) through (F) of paragraph (14) and shall not include natural gas, liquefied natural gas, or synthetic gas of pipeline quality (or mixtures of natural gas and such synthetic gas).

(34) The term "alternative water supplies" includes, but is not limited to, drinking water and household water supplies.

(35)(A) The term "contractual relationship", for the purpose of section 9607(b)(3) of this title, includes, but is not limited to, land contracts, deeds or other instruments transferring title or possession, unless the real property on which the facility concerned is located was acquired by the defendant after the disposal or placement of the hazardous substance on, in, or at the facility, and one or more of the circumstances described in clause (i), (ii), or (iii) is also established by the defendant by a preponderance of the evidence:

(i) At the time the defendant acquired the facility the defendant did not know and had no reason to know that any hazardous substance which is the subject of the release or threatened release was disposed of on, in, or at the facility.

(ii) The defendant is a government entity which acquired the facility by escheat, or through any other involuntary transfer or acquisition, or through the exercise of eminent domain authority by purchase or condemnation.

(iii) The defendant acquired the facility by inheritance or bequest.

In addition to establishing the foregoing, the defendant must establish that he has satisfied the requirements of section 9607(b)(3)(a) and (b) of this title.

(B) To establish that the defendant had no reason to know, as provided in clause (i) of subparagraph (A) of this paragraph, the defendant must have undertaken, at the time of acquisition, all appropriate inquiry into the previous ownership and uses of the property consistent with good commercial or customary practice in an effort to minimize liability. For purposes of the preceding sentence the court shall take into account any specialized knowledge or experience on the part of the defendant, the relationship of the purchase price to the value of the property if uncontaminated, commonly known or reasonably ascertainable information about the property, the obviousness of the presence or likely presence of contamination at the property, and the ability to detect such contamination by appropriate inspection.

(C) Nothing in this paragraph or in section 9607(b)(3) of this title shall diminish the liability of any previous owner or operator of such facility who would otherwise be liable under this chapter. Notwithstanding this paragraph, if the defendant obtained actual knowledge of the release or threatened release of a hazardous substance at such facility when the defendant owned the real property and then subsequently transferred ownership of the property to another person without disclosing such knowledge, such defendant shall be treated as liable under section 9607(a)(1) of this title and no defense under section 9607(b)(3) of this title shall be available to such defendant.

(D) Nothing in this paragraph shall affect the liability under this chapter of a defendant who, by any act or omission, caused or contributed to the release or threatened release of a hazardous substance which is the subject of the action relating to the facility.

(36) The term "Indian tribe" means any Indian tribe, band, nation, or other organized group or community, including any Alaska Native village but not including any Alaska Native regional or village corporation, which is recognized as eligible for the special programs and services provided by the United States to Indians because of their status as Indians.

(37)(A) The term "service station dealer" means any person—

(i) who owns or operates a motor vehicle service station, filling station, garage, or similar retail establishment engaged in the business of selling, repairing, or servicing motor vehicles, where a significant percentage of the gross revenue of the establishment is derived from the fueling, repairing, or servicing of motor vehicles, and

(ii) who accepts for collection, accumulation, and delivery to an oil recycling facility, recycled oil that (I) has been removed from the engine of a light duty motor vehicle or household appliances by the owner of such vehicle or appliances, and (II) is presented, by such owner, to such person for collection, accumulation, and delivery to an oil recycling facility.

(B) For purposes of section 9614(c) of this title the term "service station dealer" shall, notwithstanding the provisions of subparagraph (A), include any government agency that establishes a facility solely for the purpose of accepting recycled oil that satisfies the criteria set forth in subclauses (I) and (II) of subparagraph (A)(ii), and, with respect to recycled oil that satisfies the criteria set forth in subclauses (I) and (II), owners or operators of refuse collection services who are compelled by State law to collect, accumulate, and deliver such oil to an oil recycling facility.

(C) The President shall promulgate regulations regarding the determination of what constitutes a significant percentage of the gross revenues of an establishment for purposes of this paragraph.

(38) The term "incineration vessel" means any vessel which carries hazardous substances for the purpose of incineration of such substances, so long as such substances or residues of such substances are on board.

(Dec. 11, 1980, Pub.L. 96–510, Title I, § 101, 94 Stat. 2767; Dec. 22, 1980, Pub.L. 96–561, Title II, § 238(b), 94 Stat. 3300; Oct. 17, 1986, Pub.L. 99–499, Title I, §§ 101, 114(b), 127(a), Title V, § 517(c)(2), 100 Stat. 1615, 1652, 1692, 1774; Nov. 23, 1988, Pub.L. 100–707, Title I, § 109(v), 102 Stat. 4710; Oct. 31, 1994, Pub.L. 103–429, § 7(e)(1), 108 Stat. 4390.)

[1] So in original. Probably should be "or".

[2] So in original. Probably should be "mean".

[3] So in original. Probably should be "necessarily".

[4] So in original.

Short Title of 1992 Amendments

Pub.L. 102–426, § 1, Oct. 19, 1992, 106 Stat. 2174, provided that: "This Act [amending section 9620 of this title and enacting provisions set out as a note under section 9620 of this title] may be cited as the 'Community Environmental Response Facilitation Act'."

Short Title

Section 1 of Pub.L. 96–510, Dec. 11, 1980, 94 Stat. 2767, provided: "That this Act [enacting this chapter, section 6911a of this title, and sections 4611, 4612, 4661, 4662, 4681, and 4682 of Title 26, Internal Revenue Code, amending section 6911 of this title, section 1364 of Title 33, Navigation and Navigable Waters, and section 11901 of Title 49, Transportation, and enacting provisions set out as notes under section 6911 of this title and sections 1 and 4611 of Title 26] may be cited as the 'Comprehensive Environmental Response, Compensation, and Liability Act of 1980'."

CROSS REFERENCES

Storage and disposal of nondefense materials on Department of Defense installations, definition of materials to include materials referred to in par. (14) of this section, see section 2692 of Title 10, Armed Forces.

CODE OF FEDERAL REGULATIONS

Grants and other federal assistance, see 40 CFR 30.100 et seq.

LAW REVIEW COMMENTARIES

Ability of CERCLA defendants to challenge cost-effectiveness of government cleanups. Daniel W. Coffey, 65 N.Y.S.B.J. 42 (Mar./Apr. 1993).

Allocation of liability under CERCLA: A "carrot and stick" formula. Thomas C.L. Roberts, 14 Ecology L.Q. 601 (1987).

Breaking new ground: Recovery of transaction costs in private CERCLA cost-recovery actions. Christopher D. Knopf, 28 Willamette L.Rev. 495 (1992).

Cleaning up after federal and state pollution programs: Local government hazardous waste regulation. William L. Earl and George F. Gramling, 17 Stetson L.Rev. (Fla.) 639 (1988).

Cost recovery by private parties under CERCLA: Planning a response action for maximum recovery. Arnold W. Reitze, Jr., Andrew J. Harrison, Jr., and Monica J. Palko, 27 Tulsa L.J. 365 (1992).

Crying wolf or is a wolf at the door?: Lender liability for environmental cleanup. Jeanmarie B. Tade, 32 S.Tex.L.Rev. 555 (1991).

Enforcing environmental indemnification against a settling party under CERCLA. Daniel R. Avery, 23 Seton Hall L.Rev. 872 (1993).

EPA inspections of hazardous waste sites: A valid exception to the warrant requirement for administrative searches? Note, 65 U.Det.L.Rev. 333 (1988).

Environmental claims in bankruptcy: Policy conflicts, procedural pitfalls and problematic precedent. Thomas G. Gruenert, 32 S.Tex. L.Rev. 399 (1991).

Environmental liability of creditors: open season on banks, creditors, and other deep pockets. Joel R. Burcat, 103 Banking L.J. 509 (1986).

Environmental obligations in bankruptcy: A fundamental framework. Kathryn R. Heidt, 44 Fla.L.Rev. 153 (1992).

Erosion of mens rea in environmental criminal prosecution. Ruth Ann Weidel, John R. Mayo and F. Michael Zachara, 21 Seton Hall L.Rev. 1125 (1991).

High penalties and citizen suits await small businesses unaware of EPCRA reporting requirements. Jeffrey T. Pender, 10 Corp. Counsel Rev. (Tex.) 81 (May 1991).

Impact of the new EPA regulation on lender liability. Cathy Stricklin Krendl and Thomas J. Gibson, 21 Colo.Law. 2339 (1992).

Insurance industry's 1970 pollution exclusion: An exercise in ambiguity. John S. Vishneski, III, Todd G. Zimmerman, Robert A. Creamer, and Judith N. Levi, 23 Loy.U.Chi.L.J. 25 (1991).

Interaction of the Bankruptcy Code and environmental laws: Grit, the grind, and the grease. Robert R. Graves, 29 Willamette L.Rev. 297 (1993).

Lender liability dilemma: Fleet Factors history and aftermath. Brent Nicholson and Todd Zuiderhoek, 38 S.D.L.Rev. 22 (1993).

Lessor and lessee liability under the Comprehensive Environmental Response, Compensation, and Liability Act (CERCLA): The catch–22 of lease agreements. William P. Jensen, 32 S.Tex.L.Rev. 447 (1991).

Liability of officers, directors and stockholders under CERCLA: The case for adopting state law. Richard G. Dennis, 36 Vill.L.Rev. 1367 (1991).

New federalism, old due process, retroactive revival: Constitutional problems with CERCLA's Amendment of state law. Alfred R. Light, 40 U.Kan.L.Rev. 365 (1992).

Note, In search of effective hazardous waste legislation: Corporate officer criminal liability. Brett L. Warning, 22 Val.U.L.Rev. 385 (1988).

Oil and gas exemptions under RCRA and CERCLA: Are they still "safe harbors" eleven years later? Michael M. Gibson and David P. Young, 32 S.Tex.L.Rev. 361 (1991).

Property owner liability for environmental contamination in California. Michael B. Hingerty, 22 U.S.F.L.Rev. 31 (1987).

Resolving conflicts between bankruptcy law and the state police power. Ellen E. Sward, 1987 Wis.L.Rev. 403 (1987).

Shockwave: Lender liability under CERCLA after United States v. Fleet Factors Corporation. 18 Pepperdine L.Rev. 513 (1991).

Surveying the superfund settlement dilemma. Lynnette Boomgaarden and Charles Breer, 27 Land & Water L.Rev. 83 (1992).

The removal/remedial action conundrum for recovery of private-party response costs under CERCLA. Colburn T. Cherney, Roscoe

Trimmer, Jr. and Paul R. Noe, 24 Chem. Waste Litig. Rep. 724 (1993).

Unsuspecting fiduciary and beneficiary as "owner or operator" of a hazardous waste facility under CERCLA. H. Lewis McReynolds, 44 Baylor L.Rev. 71 (1992).

LIBRARY REFERENCES

Health and Environment ⚬25.5(5.5).
C.J.S. Health and Environment §§ 61 et seq., 91 et seq., 106 to 133 et seq.

§ 9602. Designation of additional hazardous substances and establishment of reportable released quantities; regulations [CERCLA § 102]

(a) The Administrator shall promulgate and revise as may be appropriate, regulations designating as hazardous substances, in addition to those referred to in section 9601(14) of this title, such elements, compounds, mixtures, solutions, and substances which, when released into the environment may present substantial danger to the public health or welfare or the environment, and shall promulgate regulations establishing that quantity of any hazardous substance the release of which shall be reported pursuant to section 9603 of this title. The Administrator may determine that one single quantity shall be the reportable quantity for any hazardous substance, regardless of the medium into which the hazardous substance is released. For all hazardous substances for which proposed regulations establishing reportable quantities were published in the Federal Register under this subsection on or before March 1, 1986, the Administrator shall promulgate under this subsection final regulations establishing reportable quantities not later than December 31, 1986. For all hazardous substances for which proposed regulations establishing reportable quantities were not published in the Federal Register under this subsection on or before March 1, 1986, the Administrator shall publish under this subsection proposed regulations establishing reportable quantities not later than December 31, 1986, and promulgate final regulations under this subsection establishing reportable quantities not later than April 30, 1988.

(b) Unless and until superseded by regulations establishing a reportable quantity under subsection (a) of this section for any hazardous substance as defined in section 9601(14) of this title, (1) a quantity of one pound, or (2) for those hazardous substances for which reportable quantities have been established pursuant to section 1321(b)(4) of Title 33, such reportable quantity, shall be deemed that quantity, the release of which requires notification pursuant to section 9603(a) or (b) of this title.

(Dec. 11, 1980, Pub.L. 96–510, Title I, § 102, 94 Stat. 2772; Oct. 17, 1986, Pub.L. 99–499, Title I, § 102, 100 Stat. 1617.)

CROSS REFERENCES

Storage and disposal of nondefense materials on Department of Defense installations, definition of materials to include materials designated under this section, see § 2692 of Title 10, Armed Forces.

WEST'S FEDERAL PRACTICE MANUAL

Environmental common law background, see § 4382 et seq.
Environmental litigation problems, see § 4390 et seq.

CODE OF FEDERAL REGULATIONS

Designation, reportable quantities, see 40 CFR 302.1 et seq.

LAW REVIEW COMMENTARIES

Erosion of mens rea in environmental criminal prosecution. Ruth Ann Weidel, John R. Mayo and F. Michael Zachara, 21 Seton Hall L.Rev. 1125 (1991).

LIBRARY REFERENCES

Health and Environment ⚬25.5(1), 25.6, 25.7.
C.J.S. Health and Environment §§ 61 et seq., 91 et seq., 106 et seq.

§ 9603. Notification requirements respecting released substances [CERCLA § 103]

(a) Notice to National Response Center upon release from vessel or offshore or onshore facility by person in charge; conveyance of notice by Center

Any person in charge of a vessel or an offshore or an onshore facility shall, as soon as he has knowledge of any release (other than a federally permitted release) of a hazardous substance from such vessel or facility in quantities equal to or greater than those determined pursuant to section 9602 of this title, immediately notify the National Response Center established under the Clean Water Act [33 U.S.C.A. § 1251 et seq.] of such release. The National Response Center shall convey the notification expeditiously to all appropriate Government agencies, including the Governor of any affected State.

(b) Penalties for failure to notify; use of notice or information pursuant to notice in criminal case

Any person—

(1) in charge of a vessel from which a hazardous substance is released, other than a federally permitted release, into or upon the navigable waters of the United States, adjoining shorelines, or into or upon the waters of the contiguous zone, or

(2) in charge of a vessel from which a hazardous substance is released, other than a federally permitted release, which may affect natural resources belonging to, appertaining to, or under the exclusive management authority of the United States (including resources under the Magnuson Fishery Conservation and Management Act [16 U.S.C.A. § 1801 et seq.]), and who is otherwise subject to the jurisdiction of the United States at the time of the release, or

(3) in charge of a facility from which a hazardous substance is released, other than a federally permitted release,

in a quantity equal to or greater than that determined pursuant to section 9602 of this title who fails to notify immediately the appropriate agency of the United States Government as soon as he has knowledge of such release or who submits in such a notification any information which he knows to be false or misleading shall, upon conviction, be fined in accordance with the applicable provisions of Title 18 or imprisoned for not more than 3 years (or not more than 5 years in the case of a second or subsequent conviction), or both. Notification received pursuant to this subsection or information obtained by the exploitation of such notification shall not be used against any such person in any criminal case, except a prosecution for perjury or for giving a false statement.

(c) Notice to Administrator of EPA of existence of storage, etc., facility by owner or operator; exceptions; time, manner, and form of notice; penalties for failure to notify; use of notice or information pursuant to notice in criminal case

Within one hundred and eighty days after December 11, 1980, any person who owns or operates or who at the time of disposal owned or operated, or who accepted hazardous substances for transport and selected, a facility at which hazardous substances (as defined in section 9601(14)(C) of this title) are or have been stored, treated, or disposed of shall, unless such facility has a permit issued under, or has been accorded interim status under, subtitle C of the Solid Waste Disposal Act [42 U.S.C.A. § 6921 et seq.], notify the Administrator of the Environmental Protection Agency of the existence of such facility, specifying the amount and type of any hazardous substance to be found there, and any known, suspected, or likely releases of such substances from such facility. The Administrator may prescribe in greater detail the manner and form of the notice and the information included. The Administrator shall notify the affected State agency, or any department designated by the Governor to receive such notice, of the existence of such facility. Any person who knowingly fails to notify the Administrator of the existence of any such facility shall, upon conviction, be fined not more than $10,000, or imprisoned for not more than one year, or both. In addition, any such person who knowingly fails to provide the notice required by this subsection shall not be entitled to any limitation of liability or to any defenses to liability set out in section 9607 of this title: *Provided however*, That notification under this subsection is not required for any facility which would be reportable hereunder solely as a result of any stoppage in transit which is temporary, incidental to the transportation movement, or at the ordinary operating convenience of a common or contract carrier, and such stoppage shall be considered as a continuity of movement and not as the storage of a hazardous substance. Notification received pursuant to this subsection or information obtained by the exploitation of such notification shall not be used against any such person in any criminal case, except a prosecution for perjury or for giving a false statement.

(d) Recordkeeping requirements; promulgation of rules and regulations by Administrator of EPA; penalties for violations; waiver of retention requirements

(1) The Administrator of the Environmental Protection Agency is authorized to promulgate rules and regulations specifying, with respect to—

(A) the location, title, or condition of a facility, and

(B) the identity, characteristics, quantity, origin, or condition (including containerization and previous treatment) of any hazardous substances contained or deposited in a facility;

the records which shall be retained by any person required to provide the notification of a facility set out in subsection (c) of this section. Such specification shall be in accordance with the provisions of this subsection.

(2) Beginning with December 11, 1980, for fifty years thereafter or for fifty years after the date of establishment of a record (whichever is later), or at any such earlier time as a waiver if obtained under paragraph (3) of this subsection, it shall be unlawful for any such person knowingly to destroy, mutilate, erase, dispose of, conceal, or otherwise render unavailable or unreadable or falsify any records identified in paragraph (1) of this subsection. Any person who violates this paragraph shall, upon conviction, be fined in accordance with the applicable provisions of Title 18 or imprisoned for not more than 3 years (or not more than 5 years in the case of a second or subsequent conviction), or both.

(3) At any time prior to the date which occurs fifty years after December 11, 1980, any person identified under paragraph (1) of this subsection may apply to the Administrator of the Environmental Protection Agency for a waiver of the provisions of the first sentence of paragraph (2) of this subsection. The Administrator is authorized to grant such waiver if, in

his discretion, such waiver would not unreasonably interfere with the attainment of the purposes and provisions of this chapter. The Administrator shall promulgate rules and regulations regarding such a waiver so as to inform parties of the proper application procedure and conditions for approval of such a waiver.

(4) Notwithstanding the provisions of this subsection, the Administrator of the Environmental Protection Agency may in his discretion require any such person to retain any record identified pursuant to paragraph (1) of this subsection for such a time period in excess of the period specified in paragraph (2) of this subsection as the Administrator determines to be necessary to protect the public health or welfare.

(e) Applicability to registered pesticide product

This section shall not apply to the application of a pesticide product registered under the Federal Insecticide, Fungicide, and Rodenticide Act [7 U.S.C.A. § 136 et seq.] or to the handling and storage of such a pesticide product by an agricultural producer.

(f) Exemptions from notice and penalty provisions for substances reported under other Federal law or is in continuous release, etc.

No notification shall be required under subsection (a) or (b) of this section for any release of a hazardous substance—

(1) which is required to be reported (or specifically exempted from a requirement for reporting) under subtitle C of the Solid Waste Disposal Act [42 U.S.C.A. § 6921 et seq.] or regulations thereunder and which has been reported to the National Response Center, or

(2) which is a continuous release, stable in quantity and rate, and is—

(A) from a facility for which notification has been given under subsection (c) of this section, or

(B) a release of which notification has been given under subsections (a) and (b) of this section for a period sufficient to establish the continuity, quantity, and regularity of such release:

Provided, That notification in accordance with subsections (a) and (b) of this paragraph shall be given for releases subject to this paragraph annually, or at such time as there is any statistically significant increase in the quantity of any hazardous substance or constituent thereof released, above that previously reported or occurring.

(Dec. 11, 1980, Pub.L. 96–510, Title I, § 103, 94 Stat. 2772; Dec. 22, 1980, Pub.L. 96–561, Title II, § 238(b), 94 Stat. 3300; Oct. 17, 1986, Pub.L. 99–499, Title I, §§ 103, 109(a)(1), (2), 100 Stat. 1617, 1632, 1633.)

WEST'S FEDERAL PRACTICE MANUAL

Environmental litigation problems, see § 4390 et seq.
Environmental regulatory framework, see § 4381.5 et seq.

CODE OF FEDERAL REGULATIONS

Grants and other federal assistance, see 40 CFR 30.100 et seq.

LAW REVIEW COMMENTARIES

Erosion of mens rea in environmental criminal prosecution. Ruth Ann Weidel, John R. Mayo and F. Michael Zachara, 21 Seton Hall L.Rev. 1125 (1991).

Insurance coverage for superfund liability: A plain meaning approach to the pollution exclusion clause. Note, 27 Washburn L.J. 161 (1987).

LIBRARY REFERENCES

Health and Environment ⚷25.5(10), 25.6(3), (9), 25.7(3), (24).
C.J.S. Health and Environment §§ 92, 103 et seq., 106, 113 et seq.

§ 9604. Response authorities [CERCLA § 104]

(a) Removal and other remedial action by President; applicability of national contingency plan; response by potentially responsible parties; public health threats; limitations on response; exception

(1) Whenever (A) any hazardous substance is released or there is a substantial threat of such a release into the environment, or (B) there is a release or substantial threat of release into the environment of any pollutant or contaminant which may present an imminent and substantial danger to the public health or welfare, the President is authorized to act, consistent with the national contingency plan, to remove or arrange for the removal of, and provide for remedial action relating to such hazardous substance, pollutant, or contaminant at any time (including its removal from any contaminated natural resource), or take any other response measure consistent with the national contingency plan which the President deems necessary to protect the public health or welfare or the environment. When the President determines that such action will be done properly and promptly by the owner or operator of the facility or vessel or by any other responsible party, the President may allow such person to carry out the action, conduct the remedial investigation, or conduct the feasibility study in accordance with section 9622 of this title. No remedial investigation or feasibility study (RI/FS) shall be authorized except on a determination by the President that the party is qualified to conduct the RI/FS and only if the President contracts with or arranges for a qualified person to assist the President in overseeing and reviewing the conduct of such RI/FS and if the responsible party agrees to reimburse the Fund for any cost incurred by the President under, or in connection with, the oversight contract or arrangement. In no event shall a potentially responsible party be subject to a lesser standard of liability, receive preferential treatment, or in any other way, whether direct or indirect, benefit from any such arrangements as a response action contractor, or as a person hired or retained by such a response action contractor, with respect to the release or facility in question. The President shall give primary attention to those releases which the President deems may present a public health threat.

(2) Removal action

Any removal action undertaken by the President under this subsection (or by any other person referred to in section 9622 of this title) should, to the extent the President deems practicable, contribute to the efficient performance of any long term remedial action with respect to the release or threatened release concerned.

(3) Limitations on response

The President shall not provide for a removal or remedial action under this section in response to a release or threat of release—

(A) of a naturally occurring substance in its unaltered form, or altered solely through naturally occurring processes or phenomena, from a location where it is naturally found;

(B) from products which are part of the structure of, and result in exposure within, residential buildings or business or community structures; or

(C) into public or private drinking water supplies due to deterioration of the system through ordinary use.

(4) Exception to limitations

Notwithstanding paragraph (3) of this subsection, to the extent authorized by this section, the President may respond to any release or threat of release if in the President's discretion, it constitutes a public health or environmental emergency and no other person with the authority and capability to respond to the emergency will do so in a timely manner.

(b) Investigations, monitoring, etc., by President

(1) Information; studies and investigations

Whenever the President is authorized to act pursuant to subsection (a) of this section, or whenever the President has reason to believe that a release has occurred or is about to occur, or that illness, disease, or complaints thereof may be attributable to exposure to a hazardous substance, pollutant, or contaminant and that a release may have occurred or be occurring, he may undertake such investigations, monitoring, surveys, testing, and other information gathering as he may deem necessary or appropriate to identify the existence and extent of the release or threat thereof, the source and nature of the hazardous substances, pollutants or contaminants involved, and the extent of danger to the public health or welfare or to the environment. In addition, the President may undertake such planning, legal, fiscal, economic, engineering, architectural, and other studies or investigations as he may deem necessary or appropriate to plan and direct response actions, to recover the costs thereof, and to enforce the provisions of this chapter.

(2) Coordination of investigations

The President shall promptly notify the appropriate Federal and State natural resource trustees of potential damages to natural resources resulting from releases under investigation pursuant to this section and shall seek to coordinate the assessments, investigations, and planning under this section with such Federal and State trustees.

(c) Criteria for continuance of obligations from Fund over specified amount for response actions; consultation by President with affected States; contracts or cooperative agreements by States with President prior to remedial actions; cost-sharing agreements; selection by President of remedial actions; State credits: granting of credit, expenses before listing or agreement, response actions between 1978 and 1980, State expenses after December 11, 1980, in excess of 10 percent of costs, item-by-item approval, use of credits; operation and maintenance; limitation on source of funds for O&M; recontracting; siting

(1) Unless (A) the President finds that (i) continued response actions are immediately required to prevent, limit, or mitigate an emergency, (ii) there is an immediate risk to public health or welfare or the environment, and (iii) such assistance will not otherwise be provided on a timely basis, or (B) the President has determined the appropriate remedial actions pursuant to paragraph (2) of this subsection and the State or States in which the source of the release is located have complied with the requirements of paragraph (3) of this subsection, or (C) continued response action is otherwise appropriate and consistent with the remedial action to be taken [1] obligations from the Fund, other than those authorized by subsection (b) of this section, shall not continue after $2,000,000 has been obligated for response actions or 12 months has elapsed from the date of initial response to a release or threatened release of hazardous substances.

(2) The President shall consult with the affected State or States before determining any appropriate remedial action to be taken pursuant to the authority granted under subsection (a) of this section.

(3) The President shall not provide any remedial actions pursuant to this section unless the State in which the release occurs first enters into a contract or cooperative agreement with the President providing assurances deemed adequate by the President that (A) the State will assure all future maintenance of the removal and remedial actions provided for the expected life of such actions as determined by the President; (B) the State will assure the availability of a hazardous waste disposal facility acceptable to the President and in compliance with the requirements of subtitle C of the Solid Waste Disposal Act [42 U.S.C.A. § 6921 et seq.] for any necessary offsite storage, destruction, treatment, or secure disposition of the hazardous substances; and (C) the State will pay or assure payment of (i) 10 per centum of the costs of the remedial action, including all future maintenance, or (ii) 50 percent (or such greater amount as the President may determine appropriate, taking into account the degree of responsibility of the State or political subdivision for the release) of any sums expended in response to a release at a facility, that was operated by the State or a political subdivision thereof, either directly or through a contractual relationship or otherwise, at the time of any disposal of hazardous substances therein. For the purpose of clause (ii) of this subparagraph, the term "facility" does not include navigable waters or the beds underlying those waters. In the case of remedial action to be taken on land or water held by an Indian tribe, held by the United States in trust for Indians, held by a member of an Indian tribe (if such land or water is subject to a trust restriction on alienation), or otherwise within the borders of an Indian reservation, the requirements of this paragraph for assurances regarding future maintenance and cost-sharing shall not apply, and the President shall provide the assurance required by this paragraph regarding the availability of a hazardous waste disposal facility.

(4) Selection of remedial action

The President shall select remedial actions to carry out this section in accordance with section 9621 of this title (relating to cleanup standards).

(5) State credits

(A) Granting of credit

The President shall grant a State a credit against the share of the costs, for which it is responsible under paragraph (3) with respect to a facility listed on the National Priorities List under the National Contingency Plan, for amounts expended by a State for remedial action at such facility pursuant to a contract or cooperative agreement with the President. The credit under this paragraph shall be limited to those State expenses which the President determines to be reasonable, documented, direct out-of-pocket expenditures of non-Federal funds.

(B) Expenses before listing or agreement

The credit under this paragraph shall include expenses for remedial action at a facility incurred before the listing of the facility on the National Priorities List or before a contract or cooperative agreement is entered into under subsection (d) of this section for the facility if—

(i) after such expenses are incurred the facility is listed on such list and a contract or cooperative agreement is entered into for the facility, and

(ii) the President determines that such expenses would have been credited to the State under subparagraph (A) had the expenditures been made after listing of the facility on such list and after the date on which such contract or cooperative agreement is entered into.

(C) Response actions between 1978 and 1980

The credit under this paragraph shall include funds expended or obligated by the State or a political subdivision thereof after January 1, 1978, and before December 11, 1980, for cost-eligible response actions and claims for damages compensable under section 9611 of this title.

(D) State expenses after December 11, 1980, in excess of 10 percent of costs

The credit under this paragraph shall include 90 percent of State expenses incurred at a facility owned, but not operated, by such State or by a political subdivision thereof. Such credit applies only to expenses incurred pursuant to a contract or cooperative agreement under subsection (d) of this section and only to expenses incurred after December 11, 1980, but before October 17, 1986.

(E) Item-by-item approval

In the case of expenditures made after October 17, 1986, the President may require prior approval of each item of expenditure as a condition of granting a credit under this paragraph.

(F) Use of credits

Credits granted under this paragraph for funds expended with respect to a facility may be used by the State to reduce all or part of the share of costs otherwise required to be paid by the State under paragraph (3) in connection with remedial actions at such facility. If the amount of funds for which credit is allowed under this paragraph exceeds such share of costs for such facility, the State may use the amount of such excess to reduce all or part of the share of such costs at other facilities in that

State. A credit shall not entitle the State to any direct payment.

(6) Operation and maintenance

For the purposes of paragraph (3) of this subsection, in the case of ground or surface water contamination, completed remedial action includes the completion of treatment or other measures, whether taken onsite or offsite, necessary to restore ground and surface water quality to a level that assures protection of human health and the environment. With respect to such measures, the operation of such measures for a period of up to 10 years after the construction or installation and commencement of operation shall be considered remedial action. Activities required to maintain the effectiveness of such measures following such period or the completion of remedial action, whichever is earlier, shall be considered operation or maintenance.

(7) Limitation on source of funds for O&M

During any period after the availability of funds received by the Hazardous Substance Superfund established under subchapter A of chapter 98 of Title 26 from tax revenues or appropriations from general revenues, the Federal share of the payment of the cost of operation or maintenance pursuant to paragraph (3)(C)(i) or paragraph (6) of this subsection (relating to operation and maintenance) shall be from funds received by the Hazardous Substance Superfund from amounts recovered on behalf of such fund under this chapter.

(8) Recontracting

The President is authorized to undertake or continue whatever interim remedial actions the President determines to be appropriate to reduce risks to public health or the environment where the performance of a complete remedial action requires recontracting because of the discovery of sources, types, or quantities of hazardous substances not known at the time of entry into the original contract. The total cost of interim actions undertaken at a facility pursuant to this paragraph shall not exceed $2,000,000.

(9) Siting

Effective 3 years after October 17, 1986, the President shall not provide any remedial actions pursuant to this section unless the State in which the release occurs first enters into a contract or cooperative agreement with the President providing assurances deemed adequate by the President that the State will assure the availability of hazardous waste treatment or disposal facilities which—

(A) have adequate capacity for the destruction, treatment, or secure disposition of all hazardous wastes that are reasonably expected to be generated within the State during the 20-year period following the date of such contract or cooperative agreement and to be disposed of, treated, or destroyed,

(B) are within the State or outside the State in accordance with an interstate agreement or regional agreement or authority,

(C) are acceptable to the President, and

(D) are in compliance with the requirements of subtitle C of the Solid Waste Disposal Act [42 U.S.C.A. § 6921 et seq.]

(d) Contracts or cooperative agreements by President with States or political subdivisions or Indian tribes; State applications, terms and conditions; reimbursements; cost-sharing provisions; enforcement requirements and procedures

(1) Cooperative agreements

(A) State applications

A State or political subdivision thereof or Indian tribe may apply to the President to carry out actions authorized in this section. If the President determines that the State or political subdivision or Indian tribe has the capability to carry out any or all of such actions in accordance with the criteria and priorities established pursuant to section 9605(a)(8) of this title and to carry out related enforcement actions, the President may enter into a contract or cooperative agreement with the State or political subdivision or Indian tribe to carry out such actions. The President shall make a determination regarding such an application within 90 days after the President receives the application.

(B) Terms and conditions

A contract or cooperative agreement under this paragraph shall be subject to such terms and conditions as the President may prescribe. The contract or cooperative agreement may cover a specific facility or specific facilities.

(C) Reimbursements

Any State which expended funds during the period beginning September 30, 1985, and ending on October 17, 1986, for response actions at any site included on the National Priorities List and subject to a cooperative agreement under this chapter shall be reimbursed for the share of costs of such actions for which the Federal Government is responsible under this chapter.

(2) If the President enters into a cost-sharing agreement pursuant to subsection (c) of this section or a contract or cooperative agreement pursuant to this subsection, and the State or political subdivision thereof fails to comply with any requirements of the contract, the President may, after providing sixty days notice, seek in the appropriate Federal district court to enforce the contract or to recover any funds advanced or any costs incurred because of the breach of the contract by the State or political subdivision.

(3) Where a State or a political subdivision thereof is acting in behalf of the President, the President is authorized to provide technical and legal assistance in the administration and enforcement of any contract or subcontract in connection with response actions assisted under this subchapter, and to intervene in any civil action involving the enforcement of such contract or subcontract.

(4) Where two or more noncontiguous facilities are reasonably related on the basis of geography, or on the basis of the threat, or potential threat to the public health or welfare or the environment, the President may, in his discretion, treat these related facilities as one for purposes of this section.

(e) Information gathering and access

(1) Action authorized

Any officer, employee, or representative of the President, duly designated by the President, is authorized to take action under paragraph (2), (3), or (4) (or any combination thereof) at a vessel, facility, establishment, place, property, or location or, in the case of paragraph (3) or (4), at any vessel, facility, establishment, place, property, or location which is adjacent to the vessel, facility, establishment, place, property, or location referred to in such paragraph (3) or (4). Any duly designated officer, employee, or representative of a State or political subdivision under a contract or cooperative agreement under subsection (d)(1) of this section is also authorized to take such action. The authority of paragraphs (3) and (4) may be exercised only if there is a reasonable basis to believe there may be a release or threat of release of a hazardous substance or pollutant or contaminant. The authority of this subsection may be exercised only for the purposes of determining the need for response, or choosing or taking any response action under this subchapter, or otherwise enforcing the provisions of this subchapter.

(2) Access to information

Any officer, employee, or representative described in paragraph (1) may require any person who has or may have information relevant to any of the following to furnish, upon reasonable notice, information or documents relating to such matter:

(A) The identification, nature, and quantity of materials which have been or are generated, treated, stored, or disposed of at a vessel or facility or transported to a vessel or facility.

(B) The nature or extent of a release or threatened release of a hazardous substance or pollutant or contaminant at or from a vessel or facility.

(C) Information relating to the ability of a person to pay for or to perform a cleanup.

In addition, upon reasonable notice, such person either (i) shall grant any such officer, employee, or representative access at all reasonable times to any vessel, facility, establishment, place, property, or location to inspect and copy all documents or records relating to such matters or (ii) shall copy and furnish to the officer, employee, or representative all such documents or records, at the option and expense of such person.

(3) Entry

Any officer, employee, or representative described in paragraph (1) is authorized to enter at reasonable times any of the following:

(A) Any vessel, facility, establishment, or other place or property where any hazardous substance or pollutant or contaminant may be or has been generated, stored, treated, disposed of, or transported from.

(B) Any vessel, facility, establishment, or other place or property from which or to which a hazardous substance or pollutant or contaminant has been or may have been released.

(C) Any vessel, facility, establishment, or other place or property where such release is or may be threatened.

(D) Any vessel, facility, establishment, or other place or property where entry is needed to determine the need for response or the appropriate response or to effectuate a response action under this subchapter.

(4) Inspection and samples

(A) Authority

Any officer, employee or representative described in paragraph (1) is authorized to inspect and obtain samples from any vessel, facility, establishment, or other place or property referred to in paragraph (3) or from any location of any suspected hazardous substance or pollutant or contaminant. Any such officer, employee, or representative is authorized to inspect and obtain samples of any containers or labeling for suspected hazardous substances or pollutants or contaminants. Each such inspection shall be completed with reasonable promptness.

(B) Samples

If the officer, employee, or representative obtains any samples, before leaving the premises he shall give to the owner, operator, tenant, or other person in charge of the place from which the samples were obtained a receipt describing the sample obtained and, if requested, a portion of each such sample. A copy of the results of any analysis made of such samples shall be furnished promptly to the owner, operator, tenant, or other person in charge, if such person can be located.

(5) Compliance orders

(A) Issuance

If consent is not granted regarding any request made by an officer, employee, or representative under paragraph (2), (3), or (4), the President may issue an order directing compliance with the request. The order may be issued after such notice and opportunity for consultation as is reasonably appropriate under the circumstances.

(B) Compliance

The President may ask the Attorney General to commence a civil action to compel compliance with a request or order referred to in subparagraph (A). Where there is a reasonable basis to believe there may be a release or threat of a release of a hazardous substance or pollutant or contaminant, the court shall take the following actions:

(i) In the case of interference with entry or inspection, the court shall enjoin such interference or direct compliance with orders to prohibit interference with entry or inspection unless under the circumstances of the case the demand for entry or inspection is arbitrary and capricious, an abuse of discretion, or otherwise not in accordance with law.

(ii) In the case of information or document requests or orders, the court shall enjoin interference with such information or document requests or orders or direct compliance with the requests or orders to provide such information or documents unless under the circumstances of the case the demand for information or documents is arbitrary and capricious, an abuse of discretion, or otherwise not in accordance with law.

The court may assess a civil penalty not to exceed $25,000 for each day of noncompliance against any person who unreasonably fails to comply with the provisions of paragraph (2), (3), or (4) or an order issued pursuant to subparagraph (A) of this paragraph.

(6) Other authority

Nothing in this subsection shall preclude the President from securing access or obtaining information in any other lawful manner.

(7) Confidentiality of information

(A) Any records, reports, or information obtained from any person under this section (including records, reports, or information obtained by representatives of the President) shall be available to the public, except that upon a showing satisfactory to the President (or the State, as the case may be) by any person that records, reports, or information, or particular part thereof (other than health or safety effects data), to which the President (or the State, as the case may be) or any officer, employee, or representative has access under this section if made public would divulge information entitled to protection under section 1905 of Title 18, such information or particular portion thereof shall be considered confidential in accordance with the purposes of that section, except that such record, report, document or information may be disclosed to other officers, employees, or authorized representatives of the United States concerned with carrying out this chapter, or when relevant in any proceeding under this chapter.

(B) Any person not subject to the provisions of section 1905 of Title 18 who knowingly and willfully divulges or discloses any information entitled to protection under this subsection shall, upon conviction, be subject to a fine of not more than $5,000 or to imprisonment not to exceed one year, or both.

(C) In submitting data under this chapter, a person required to provide such data may (i) designate the data which such person believes is entitled to protection under this subsection and (ii) submit such designated data separately from other data submitted under this chapter. A designation under this paragraph shall be made in writing and in such manner as the President may prescribe by regulation.

(D) Notwithstanding any limitation contained in this section or any other provision of law, all information reported to or otherwise obtained by the President (or any representative of the President) under this chapter shall be made available, upon written request of any duly authorized committee of the Congress, to such committee.

(E) No person required to provide information under this chapter may claim that the information is entitled to protection under this paragraph unless such person shows each of the following:

(i) Such person has not disclosed the information to any other person, other than a member of a local emergency planning committee established under title III of the Amendments and Reauthorization Act of 1986 [42 U.S.C.A. § 11001 et seq.], an officer or employee of the United States or a State or local government, an employee of such person, or a person who is bound by a confidentiality agreement, and such person has taken reasonable measures to protect the confidentiality of such information and intends to continue to take such measures.

(ii) The information is not required to be disclosed, or otherwise made available, to the public under any other Federal or State law.

(iii) Disclosure of the information is likely to cause substantial harm to the competitive position of such person.

(iv) The specific chemical identity, if sought to be protected, is not readily discoverable through reverse engineering.

(F) The following information with respect to any hazardous substance at the facility or vessel shall not be entitled to protection under this paragraph:

(i) The trade name, common name, or generic class or category of the hazardous substance.

(ii) The physical properties of the substance, including its boiling point, melting point, flash point, specific gravity, vapor density, solubility in water, and vapor pressure at 20 degrees Celsius.

(iii) The hazards to health and the environment posed by the substance, including physical hazards (such as explosion) and potential acute and chronic health hazards.

(iv) The potential routes of human exposure to the substance at the facility, establishment, place, or property being investigated, entered, or inspected under this subsection.

(v) The location of disposal of any waste stream.

(vi) Any monitoring data or analysis of monitoring data pertaining to disposal activities.

(vii) Any hydrogeologic or geologic data.

(viii) Any groundwater monitoring data.

(f) Contracts for response action; compliance with Federal health and safety standards

In awarding contracts to any person engaged in response actions, the President or the State, in any case where it is awarding contracts pursuant to a contract entered into under subsection (d) of this section, shall require compliance with Federal health and safety standards established under section 9651(f) of this title by contractors and subcontractors as a condition of such contracts.

(g) Rates for wages and labor standards applicable to covered work

(1) All laborers and mechanics employed by contractors or subcontractors in the performance of construction, repair, or alteration work funded in whole or in part under this section shall be paid wages at rates not less than those prevailing on projects of a character similar in the locality as determined by the Secretary of Labor in accordance with the Davis-Bacon Act [40 U.S.C.A. § 276a et seq.]. The President shall not approve any such funding without first obtaining adequate assurance that required labor standards will be maintained upon the construction work.

(2) The Secretary of Labor shall have, with respect to the labor standards specified in paragraph (1), the authority and functions set forth in Reorganization Plan Numbered 14 of 1950 (15 F.R. 3176; 64 Stat. 1267) and section 276c of Title 40.

(h) Emergency procurement powers; exercise by President

Notwithstanding any other provision of law, subject to the provisions of section 9611 of this title, the President may authorize the use of such emergency procurement powers as he deems necessary to effect the purpose of this chapter. Upon determination that such procedures are necessary, the President shall promulgate regulations prescribing the circumstances under which such authority shall be used and the procedures governing the use of such authority.

(i) Agency for Toxic Substances and Disease Registry; establishment, functions, etc.

(1) There is hereby established within the Public Health Service an agency, to be known as the Agency for Toxic Substances and Disease Registry, which shall report directly to the Surgeon General of the United States. The Administrator of said Agency shall, with the cooperation of the Administrator of the Environmental Protection Agency, the Commissioner of the Food and Drug Administration, the Directors of the National Institute of Medicine, National Institute of Environmental Health Sciences, National Institute of Occupational Safety and Health, Centers for Disease Control and Prevention, the Administrator of the Occupational Safety and Health Administration, the Administrator of the Social Security Administration, the Secretary of Transportation, and appropriate State and local health officials, effectuate and implement the health related authorities of this chapter. In addition, said Administrator shall—

(A) in cooperation with the States, establish and maintain a national registry of serious diseases and illnesses and a national registry of persons exposed to toxic substances;

(B) establish and maintain inventory of literature, research, and studies on the health effects of toxic substances;

(C) in cooperation with the States, and other agencies of the Federal Government, establish and maintain a complete listing of areas closed to the public or otherwise restricted in use because of toxic substance contamination;

(D) in cases of public health emergencies caused or believed to be caused by exposure to toxic substances, provide medical care and testing to exposed individuals, including but not limited to tissue sampling, chromosomal testing where appropriate, epidemiological studies, or any other assistance appropriate under the circumstances; and

(E) either independently or as part of other health status survey, conduct periodic survey and screening programs to determine relationships between exposure to toxic substances and illness. In cases of public health emergencies, exposed persons shall be eligible for admission to hospitals and other facilities and services operated or provided by the Public Health Service.

(2)(A) Within 6 months after October 17, 1986, the Administrator of the Agency for Toxic Substances and Disease Registry (ATSDR) and the Administrator of the Environmental Protection Agency (EPA) shall prepare a list, in order of priority, of at least 100 hazardous substances which are most commonly found at facilities on the National Priorities List and which, in their sole discretion, they determine are posing the most significant potential threat to human health due to their known or suspected toxicity to humans and the potential for human exposure to such substances at facilities on the National Priorities List or at facilities to which a response to a release or a threatened release under this section is under consideration.

(B) Within 24 months after October 17, 1986, the Administrator of ATSDR and the Administrator of EPA shall revise the list prepared under subparagraph (A). Such revision shall include, in order of priority, the addition of 100 or more such hazardous substances. In each of the 3 consecutive 12-month periods that follow, the Administrator of ATSDR and the Administrator of EPA shall revise, in the same manner as provided in the 2 preceding sentences, such list to include not fewer than 25 additional hazardous substances per revision. The Administrator of ATSDR and the Administrator of EPA shall not less often than once every year thereafter revise such list to include additional hazardous substances in accordance with the criteria in subparagraph (A).

(3) Based on all available information, including information maintained under paragraph (1)(B) and data developed and collected on the health effects of hazardous substances under this paragraph, the Administrator of ATSDR shall prepare toxicological profiles of each of the substances listed pursuant to paragraph (2). The toxicological profiles shall be prepared in accordance with guidelines developed by the Administrator of ATSDR and the Administrator of EPA. Such profiles shall include, but not be limited to each of the following:

(A) An examination, summary, and interpretation of available toxicological information and epidemiologic evaluations on a hazardous substance in order to ascertain the levels of significant human exposure for the substance and the associated acute, subacute, and chronic health effects.

(B) A determination of whether adequate information on the health effects of each substance is available or in the process of development to determine levels of exposure which present a significant risk to human health of acute, subacute, and chronic health effects.

(C) Where appropriate, an identification of toxicological testing needed to identify the types or levels of exposure that may present significant risk of adverse health effects in humans.

Any toxicological profile or revision thereof shall reflect the Administrator of ATSDR's assessment of all relevant toxicological testing which has been peer reviewed. The profiles required to be prepared under this paragraph for those hazardous substances listed under subparagraph (A) of paragraph (2) shall be completed, at a rate of no fewer than 25 per year, within 4 years after October 17, 1986. A profile required on a substance listed pursuant to subparagraph (B) of paragraph (2) shall be completed within 3 years after addition to the list. The profiles prepared under this paragraph shall be of those substances highest on the list of priorities under paragraph (2) for which profiles have not previously been prepared. Profiles required under this paragraph shall be revised and republished as necessary, but no less often than once every 3 years. Such profiles shall be provided to the States and made available to other interested parties.

(4) The Administrator of the ATSDR shall provide consultations upon request on health issues relating to exposure to hazardous or toxic substances, on the basis of available information, to the Administrator of EPA, State officials, and local officials. Such consultations to individuals may be provided by States under cooperative agreements established under this chapter.

(5)(A) For each hazardous substance listed pursuant to paragraph (2), the Administrator of ATSDR (in consultation with the Administrator of EPA and other agencies and programs of the Public Health Service) shall assess whether adequate information on the health effects of such substance is available. For any such substance for which adequate information is not available (or under development), the Administrator of ATSDR, in cooperation with the Director of the National Toxicology Program, shall assure the initiation of a program of research designed to determine the health effects (and techniques for development of methods to determine such health effects) of such substance. Where feasible, such program shall seek to develop methods to determine the health effects of such substance in combination with other substances with which it is commonly found. Before assuring the initiation of such program, the Administrator of ATSDR shall consider recommendations of the Interagency Testing Committee established under section 4(e) of the Toxic Substances Control Act [15 U.S.C.A. § 2603(e)] on the types of research that should be done. Such program shall include, to the extent necessary to supplement existing information, but shall not be limited to—

(i) laboratory and other studies to determine short, intermediate, and long-term health effects;

(ii) laboratory and other studies to determine organ-specific, site-specific, and system-specific acute and chronic toxicity;

(iii) laboratory and other studies to determine the manner in which such substances are metabolized or to otherwise develop an understanding of the biokinetics of such substances; and

(iv) where there is a possibility of obtaining human data, the collection of such information.

(B) In assessing the need to perform laboratory and other studies, as required by subparagraph (A), the Administrator of ATSDR shall consider—

(i) the availability and quality of existing test data concerning the substance on the suspected health effect in question;

(ii) the extent to which testing already in progress will, in a timely fashion, provide data that will be adequate to support the preparation of toxicological profiles as required by paragraph (3); and

(iii) such other scientific and technical factors as the Administrator of ATSDR may determine are necessary for the effective implementation of this subsection.

(C) In the development and implementation of any research program under this paragraph, the Administrator of ATSDR and the Administrator of EPA shall coordinate such research program implemented under this paragraph with the National Toxicology Program and with programs of toxicological testing established under the Toxic Substances Control Act [15 U.S.C.A. § 2601 et seq.] and the Federal Insecticide, Fungicide and Rodenticide Act [7 U.S.C.A. § 136 et seq.]. The purpose of such coordination shall be to avoid duplication of effort and to assure that the hazardous substances listed pursuant to this subsection are tested thoroughly at the earliest practicable date. Where appropriate, consistent with such purpose, a research program under this paragraph may be carried out using such programs of toxicological testing.

(D) It is the sense of the Congress that the costs of research programs under this paragraph be borne by the manufacturers and processors of the hazardous substance in question, as required in programs of toxicological testing under the Toxic Substances Control Act [15 U.S.C.A. § 2601 et seq.]. Within 1 year after October 17, 1986, the Administrator of EPA shall promulgate regulations which provide, where appropriate, for payment of such costs by manufacturers and processors under the Toxic Substances Control Act, and registrants under the Federal Insecticide, Fungicide, and Rodenticide Act [7 U.S.C.A. § 136 et seq.], and recovery of such costs from responsible parties under this chapter.

(6)(A) The Administrator of ATSDR shall perform a health assessment for each facility on the National Priorities List established under section 9605 of this title. Such health assessment shall be completed not later than December 10, 1988, for each facility proposed for inclusion on such list prior to October 17, 1986, or not later than one year after the date of proposal for inclusion on such list for each facility proposed for inclusion on such list after October 17, 1986.

(B) The Administrator of ATSDR may perform health assessments for releases or facilities where individual persons or licensed physicians provide information that individuals have been exposed to a hazardous substance, for which the probable source of such exposure is a release. In addition to other methods (formal or informal) of providing such information, such individual persons or licensed physicians may submit a petition to the Administrator of ATSDR providing such information and requesting a health assessment. If such a petition is submitted and the Administrator of ATSDR does not initiate a health assessment, the Administrator of ATSDR shall provide a written explanation of why a health assessment is not appropriate.

(C) In determining the priority in which to conduct health assessments under this subsection, the Administrator of ATSDR, in consultation with the Administrator of EPA, shall give priority to those facilities at which there is documented evidence of the release of hazardous substances, at which the potential risk to human health appears highest, and for which in the judgment of the Administrator of ATSDR existing health assessment data are inadequate to assess the potential risk to human health as provided in subparagraph (F). In determining the priorities for conducting health assessments under this subsection, the Administrator of ATSDR shall consider the National Priorities List schedules and the needs of the Environmental Protection Agency and other Federal agencies pursuant to schedules for remedial investigation and feasibility studies.

(D) Where a health assessment is done at a site on the National Priorities List, the Administrator of ATSDR shall complete such assessment promptly and, to the maximum extent practicable, before the completion of the remedial investigation and feasibility study at the facility concerned.

(E) Any State or political subdivision carrying out a health assessment for a facility shall report the results of the assessment to the Administrator of ATSDR and the Administrator of EPA and shall include recommendations with respect to further activities which need to be carried out under this section. The Administrator of ATSDR shall state such recommendation in any report on the results of any assessment carried out directly by the Administrator of ATSDR for such facility and shall issue periodic reports which include the results of all the assessments carried out under this subsection.

(F) For the purposes of this subsection and section 9611(c)(4) of this title, the term "health assessments" shall include preliminary assessments of the potential risk to human health posed by individual sites and facilities, based on such factors as the nature and extent of contamination, the existence of potential pathways of human exposure (including ground or surface water contamination, air emissions, and food chain contamination), the size and potential susceptibility of the community within the likely pathways of exposure, the comparison of expected human exposure levels to the short-term and long-term health effects associated with identified hazardous substances and any available recommended exposure or tolerance limits for such hazardous substances, and the comparison of existing morbidity and mortality data on diseases that may be associated with the observed levels of exposure. The Administrator of ATSDR shall use appropriate data, risk assessments, risk evaluations and studies available from the Administrator of EPA.

(G) The purpose of health assessments under this subsection shall be to assist in determining whether actions under paragraph (11) of this subsection should be taken to reduce human exposure to hazardous substances from a facility and whether additional information on human exposure and associated health risks is needed and should be acquired by conducting epidemiological studies under paragraph (7), establishing a registry under paragraph (8), establishing a health surveillance program under paragraph (9), or through other means. In using the results of health assessments for determining additional actions to be taken under this section, the Administrator of ATSDR may consider additional information on the risks to the potentially affected population from all sources of such hazardous substances including known point or nonpoint sources other than those from the facility in question.

(H) At the completion of each health assessment, the Administrator of ATSDR shall provide the Administrator of EPA and each affected State with the results of such assessment, together with any recommendations for further actions under this subsection or otherwise under this chapter. In addition, if the health assessment indicates that the release or threatened release concerned may pose a serious threat to human health or the environment, the Administrator of ATSDR shall so notify the Administrator of EPA who shall promptly evaluate such release or threatened release in accordance with the hazard ranking system referred to in section 9605(a)(8)(A) of this title to determine whether the site shall be placed on the National Priorities List or, if the site is already on the list, the Administrator of ATSDR may recommend to the Administrator of EPA that the site be accorded a higher priority.

(7)(A) Whenever in the judgment of the Administrator of ATSDR it is appropriate on the basis of the results of a health assessment, the Administrator of ATSDR shall conduct a pilot study of health effects for selected groups of exposed individuals in order to determine the desirability of conducting full scale epidemiological or other health studies of the entire exposed population.

(B) Whenever in the judgment of the Administrator of ATSDR it is appropriate on the basis of the results of such pilot study or other study or health assessment, the Administrator of ATSDR shall conduct such full scale epidemiological or other health studies as may be necessary to determine the health effects on the population exposed to hazardous substances from a release or threatened release. If a significant excess of disease in a population is identified, the letter of transmittal of such study shall include an assessment of other risk factors, other than a release, that may, in the judgment of the peer review group, be associated with such disease, if such risk factors were not taken into account in the design or conduct of the study.

(8) In any case in which the results of a health assessment indicate a potential significant risk to human health, the Administrator of ATSDR shall consider whether the establishment of a registry of exposed persons would contribute to accomplishing the purposes of this subsection, taking into account circumstances bearing on the usefulness of such a registry, including the seriousness or unique character of identified diseases or the likelihood of population migration from the affected area.

(9) Where the Administrator of ATSDR has determined that there is a significant increased risk of adverse health effects in humans from exposure to hazardous substances based on the results of a health assessment conducted under paragraph (6), an epidemiologic study conducted under paragraph (7), or an exposure registry that has been established under paragraph (8), and the Administrator of ATSDR has determined that such exposure is the result of a release from a facility, the Administrator of ATSDR shall initiate a health surveillance program for such population. This program shall include but not be limited to—

(A) periodic medical testing where appropriate of population subgroups to screen for diseases for which the population or subgroup is at significant increased risk; and

(B) a mechanism to refer for treatment those individuals within such population who are screened positive for such diseases.

(10) Two years after October 17, 1986, and every 2 years thereafter, the Administrator of ATSDR shall prepare and submit to the Administrator of EPA and to the Congress a report on the results of the activities of ATSDR regarding—

(A) health assessments and pilot health effects studies conducted;

(B) epidemiologic studies conducted;

(C) hazardous substances which have been listed under paragraph (2), toxicological profiles which have been developed, and toxicologic testing which has been conducted or which is being conducted under this subsection;

(D) registries established under paragraph (8); and

(E) an overall assessment, based on the results of activities conducted by the Administrator of ATSDR, of the linkage between human exposure to individual or combinations of hazardous substances due to releases from facilities covered by this chapter or the Solid Waste Disposal Act [42 U.S.C.A. § 6901 et seq.] and any increased incidence or prevalence of adverse health effects in humans.

(11) If a health assessment or other study carried out under this subsection contains a finding that the exposure concerned presents a significant risk to human health, the President shall take such steps as may be necessary to reduce such exposure and eliminate or substantially mitigate the significant risk to human health. Such steps may include the use of any authority under this chapter, including, but not limited to—

(A) provision of alternative water supplies, and

(B) permanent or temporary relocation of individuals.

In any case in which information is insufficient, in the judgment of the Administrator of ATSDR or the President to determine a significant human exposure level with respect to a hazardous substance, the President may take such steps as may be necessary to reduce the exposure of any person to such hazardous substance to such level as the President deems necessary to protect human health.

(12) In any case which is the subject of a petition, a health assessment or study, or a research program under this subsection, nothing in this subsection shall be construed to delay or otherwise affect or impair the authority of the President, the Administrator of ATSDR, or the Administrator of EPA to exercise any authority vested in the President, the Administrator of ATSDR or the Administrator of EPA under any other provision of law (including, but not limited to, the imminent hazard authority of section 7003 of the Solid Waste Disposal Act [42 U.S.C.A. § 6973]) or the response and abatement authorities of this chapter.

(13) All studies and results of research conducted under this subsection (other than health assessments) shall be reported or adopted only after appropriate peer review. Such peer review shall be completed, to the maximum extent practicable, within a period of 60 days. In the case of research conducted under the National Toxicology Program, such peer review may be conducted by the Board of Scientific Counselors. In the case of other research, such peer review shall be conducted by panels consisting of no less than three nor more than seven members, who shall be disinterested scientific experts selected for such purpose by the Administrator of ATSDR or the Administrator of EPA, as appropriate, on the basis of their reputation for scientific objectivity and the lack of institutional ties with any person involved in the conduct of the study or research under review. Support services for such panels shall be provided by the Agency for Toxic Substances and Disease Registry, or by the Environmental Protection Agency, as appropriate.

(14) In the implementation of this subsection and other health-related authorities of this chapter, the Administrator of ATSDR shall assemble, develop as necessary, and distribute to the States, and upon request to medical colleges, physicians, and other health professionals, appropriate educational materials (including short courses) on the medical surveillance, screening, and methods of diagnosis and treatment of injury or disease related to exposure to hazardous substances (giving priority to those listed in paragraph (2)), through such means as the Administrator of ATSDR deems appropriate.

(15) The activities of the Administrator of ATSDR described in this subsection and section 9611(c)(4) of this title shall be carried out by the Administrator of ATSDR, either directly or through cooperative agreements with States (or political subdivisions thereof) which the Administrator of ATSDR determines are capable of carrying out such activities. Such activities shall include provision of consultations on health information, the conduct of health assessments, including those required under section 3019(b) of the Solid Waste Disposal Act [42 U.S.C.A. 6939a(b)], health studies, registries, and health surveillance.

(16) The President shall provide adequate personnel for ATSDR, which shall not be fewer than 100 employees. For purposes of determining the number of employees under this subsection, an employee employed by ATSDR on a part-time career employment basis shall be counted as a fraction which is determined by dividing 40 hours into the average number of hours of such employee's regularly scheduled workweek.

(17) In accordance with section 9620 of this title (relating to Federal facilities), the Administrator of ATSDR shall have the same authorities under this section with respect to facilities owned or operated by a department, agency, or instrumentality of the United States as the Administrator of ATSDR has with respect to any nongovernmental entity.

(18) If the Administrator of ATSDR determines that it is appropriate for purposes of this section to treat a pollutant or contaminant as a hazardous substance, such pollutant or contaminant shall be treated as a hazardous substance for such purpose.

(j) Acquisition of property

(1) Authority

The President is authorized to acquire, by purchase, lease, condemnation, donation, or otherwise, any real property or any interest in real property that the President in his discretion determines is needed to conduct a remedial action under this chapter. There shall be no cause of action to compel the President to acquire any interest in real property under this chapter.

(2) State assurance

The President may use the authority of paragraph (1) for a remedial action only if, before an interest in real estate is acquired under this subsection, the State in which the interest to be acquired is located assures the President, through a contract or cooperative agreement or otherwise, that the State will accept transfer of the interest following completion of the remedial action.

(3) Exemption

No Federal, State, or local government agency shall be liable under this chapter solely as a result of acquiring an interest in real estate under this subsection.

(Dec. 11, 1980, Pub.L. 96–510, Title I, § 104, 94 Stat. 2774; Oct. 17, 1986, Pub.L. 99–499, Title I, §§ 104, 110, Title II, § 207(b), 100 Stat. 1617, 1642, 1705; Oct. 22, 1986, Pub.L. 99–514, § 2, 100 Stat. 2095; Oct. 27, 1992, Pub.L. 102–531, Title III, § 312(h), 106 Stat. 3506.)

[1] So in original. Probably should be followed by a comma.

CROSS REFERENCES

Solid Waste Disposal Act, action prohibited under if State is engaging in a removal action or is proceeding with a remedial action under this section, see section 6972(b) of this title.

WEST'S FEDERAL PRACTICE MANUAL

Environmental common law background, see § 4382 et seq.

LAW REVIEW COMMENTARIES

Bankruptcy versus environmental protection: Discharging future CERCLA liability in Chapter 11. Note, 14 Cardozo L.Rev. 1999 (1993).

Insurance coverage for superfund liability: A plain meaning approach to the pollution exclusion clause. Note, 27 Washburn L.J. 161 (1987).

Interstate waste: A key issue in resolving the national hazardous waste capacity crisis. B.J. Wynne, III and Terri Hamby, 32 S.Tex. L.Rev. 601 (1991).

Lender liability dilemma: Fleet Factors history and aftermath. Brent Nicholson and Todd Zuiderhoek, 38 S.D.L.Rev. 22 (1993).

New federalism, old due process, retroactive revival: Constitutional problems with CERCLA's Amendment of state law. Alfred R. Light, 40 U.Kan.L.Rev. 365 (1992).

Property owner liability for environmental contamination in California. Michael B. Hingerty, 22 U.S.F.L.Rev. 31 (1987).

LIBRARY REFERENCES

Health and Environment ⟹25.6, 25.7.

C.J.S. Health and Environment §§ 91 et seq., 106 et seq.

§ 9605. National contingency plan; preparation, contents, etc. [CERCLA § 105]

(a) Revision and republication

Within one hundred and eighty days after December 11, 1980, the President shall, after notice and opportunity for public comments, revise and republish the national contingency plan for the removal of oil and hazardous substances, originally prepared and published pursuant to section 1321 of Title 33, to reflect and effectuate the responsibilities and powers created by this chapter, in addition to those matters specified in section 1321(c)(2) of Title 33. Such revision shall include a section of the plan to be known as the national hazardous substance response plan which shall establish procedures and standards for responding to releases of hazardous substances, pollutants, and contaminants, which shall include at a minimum:

(1) methods for discovering and investigating facilities at which hazardous substances have been disposed of or otherwise come to be located;

(2) methods for evaluating, including analyses of relative cost, and remedying any releases or threats of releases from facilities which pose substantial danger to the public health or the environment;

(3) methods and criteria for determining the appropriate extent of removal, remedy, and other measures authorized by this chapter;

(4) appropriate roles and responsibilities for the Federal, State, and local governments and for interstate and nongovernmental entities in effectuating the plan;

(5) provision for identification, procurement, maintenance, and storage of response equipment and supplies;

(6) a method for and assignment of responsibility for reporting the existence of such facilities which may be located on federally owned or controlled properties and any releases of hazardous substances from such facilities;

(7) means of assuring that remedial action measures are cost-effective over the period of potential exposure to the hazardous substances or contaminated materials;

(8)(A) criteria for determining priorities among releases or threatened releases throughout the United States for the purpose of taking remedial action and, to the extent practicable taking into account the potential urgency of such action, for the purpose of taking removal action. Criteria and priorities under this paragraph shall be based upon relative risk or danger to public health or welfare or the environment, in the judgment of the President, taking into account to the extent possible the population at risk, the hazard potential of the hazardous substances at such facilities, the potential for contamination of drinking water supplies, the potential for direct human contact, the potential for destruction of sensitive ecosystems, the damage to natural resources which may affect the human food chain and which is associated with any release or threatened release, the contamination or potential contamination of the ambient air which is associated with the release or threatened release, State preparedness to assume State costs and responsibilities, and other appropriate factors;

(B) based upon the criteria set forth in subparagraph (A) of this paragraph, the President shall list as part of the plan national priorities among the known releases or threatened releases throughout the United States and shall revise the list no less often than annually. Within one year after December 11, 1980, and annually thereafter, each State shall establish and submit for consideration by the President priorities for remedial action among known releases and potential releases in that State based upon the criteria set forth in subparagraph (A) of this paragraph. In assembling or revising the national list, the President shall consider any priorities established by the States. To the extent practicable, the highest priority facilities shall be designated individually and shall be referred to as the "top priority among known response targets", and, to the extent practicable, shall include among the one hundred highest priority facilities one such facility from each State which shall be the facility designated by the State as presenting the greatest danger to public health or welfare or the environment among the known facilities in such State. A State shall be allowed to designate its highest priority facility only once. Other priority facilities or incidents may be listed singly or grouped for response priority purposes;

(9) specified roles for private organizations and entities in preparation for response and in responding to releases of hazardous substances, including identification of appropriate qualifications and capacity therefor and including consideration of minority firms in accordance with subsection (f) of this section; and

(10) standards and testing procedures by which alternative or innovative treatment technologies can be determined to be appropriate for utilization in response actions authorized by this chapter.

The plan shall specify procedures, techniques, materials, equipment, and methods to be employed in identifying, removing, or remedying releases of hazardous substances comparable to those required under section 1321(c)(2)(F) and (G) and (j)(1) of Title 33. Following publication of the revised national contingency plan, the response to and actions to minimize damage from hazardous substances releases shall, to the greatest extent possible, be in accordance with the provisions of the plan. The President may, from time to time, revise and republish the national contingency plan.

(b) Revision of plan

Not later than 18 months after the enactment of the Superfund Amendments and Reauthorization Act of 1986 [October 17, 1986], the President shall revise the National Contingency Plan to reflect the requirements of such amendments. The portion of such Plan known as "the National Hazardous Substance Response Plan" shall be revised to provide procedures and standards for remedial actions undertaken pursuant to this chapter which are consistent with amendments made by the Superfund Amendments and Reauthorization Act of 1986 relating to the selection of remedial action.

(c) Hazard ranking system

(1) Revision

Not later than 18 months after October 17, 1986, and after publication of notice and opportunity for submission of comments in accordance with section 553 of Title 5, the President shall by rule promulgate amendments to the hazard ranking system in effect on September 1, 1984. Such amendments shall assure, to the maximum extent feasible, that the hazard ranking system accurately assesses the relative degree of risk to human health and the environment posed by sites and facilities subject to review. The President shall establish an effective date for the amended hazard ranking system which is not later than 24 months after October 17, 1986. Such amended hazard ranking system shall be applied to any site or facility to be newly listed on the National Priorities List after the effective date established by the President. Until such effective date of the regulations, the hazard ranking system in effect on September 1, 1984, shall continue in full force and effect.

(2) Health assessment of water contamination risks

In carrying out this subsection, the President shall ensure that the human health risks associated with the contamination or potential contamination (either directly or as a result of the runoff of any hazardous substance or pollutant or contaminant from sites or facilities) of surface water are appropriately assessed where such surface water is, or can be, used for recreation or potable water consumption. In making the assessment required pursuant to the preceding sentence, the President shall take into account the potential migration of any hazardous substance or pollutant or contaminant through such surface water to downstream sources of drinking water.

(3) Reevaluation not required

The President shall not be required to reevaluate, after October 17, 1986, the hazard ranking of any facility which was evaluated in accordance with the criteria under this section before the effective date of the amendments to the hazard ranking system under this subsection and which was assigned a national priority under the National Contingency Plan.

(4) New information

Nothing in paragraph (3) shall preclude the President from taking new information into account in undertaking response actions under this chapter.

(d) Petition for assessment of release

Any person who is, or may be, affected by a release or threatened release of a hazardous substance or pollutant or contaminant, may petition the President to conduct a preliminary assessment of the hazards to public health and the environment which are associated with such release or threatened release. If the President has not previously conducted a preliminary assessment of such release, the President shall, within 12 months after the receipt of any such petition, complete such assessment or provide an explanation of why the assessment is not appropriate. If the preliminary assessment indicates that the release or threatened release concerned may pose a threat to human health or the environment, the President shall promptly evaluate such release or threatened release in accordance with the hazard ranking system referred to in paragraph (8)(A) of subsection (a) of this section to determine the national priority of such release or threatened release.

(e) Releases from earlier sites

Whenever there has been, after January 1, 1985, a significant release of hazardous substances or pollutants or contaminants from a site which is listed by the President as a "Site Cleaned Up To Date" on the National Priorities List (revised edition, December 1984) the site shall be restored to the National Priorities List, without application of the hazard ranking system.

(f) Minority contractors

In awarding contracts under this chapter, the President shall consider the availability of qualified minority firms. The President shall describe, as part of any annual report submitted to the Congress under this chapter, the participation of minority firms in contracts carried out under this chapter. Such report shall contain a brief description of the contracts which have been awarded to minority firms under this chapter and of the efforts made by the President to encourage the participation of such firms in programs carried out under this chapter.

(g) Special study wastes

(1) Application

This subsection applies to facilities—

(A) which as of October 17, 1986, were not included on, or proposed for inclusion on, the National Priorities List; and

(B) at which special study wastes described in paragraph (2), (3)(A)(ii) or (3)(A)(iii) of section 6921(b) of this title are present in significant quantities, including any such facility from which there has been a release of a special study waste.

(2) Considerations in adding facilities to NPL

Pending revision of the hazard ranking system under subsection (c) of this section, the President shall consider each of the following factors in adding facilities covered by this section to the National Priorities List:

(A) The extent to which hazard ranking system score for the facility is affected by the presence of any special study waste at, or any release from, such facility.

(B) Available information as to the quantity, toxicity, and concentration of hazardous substances that are constituents of any special study waste at, or released from such facility, the extent of or potential for release of such hazardous constituents, the exposure or potential exposure to human population and the environment, and the degree of hazard to human health or the environment posed by the release of such hazardous constituents at such facility. This subparagraph refers only to available information on actual concentrations of hazardous substances and not on the total quantity of special study waste at such facility.

(3) Savings provisions

Nothing in this subsection shall be construed to limit the authority of the President to remove any facility which as of October 17, 1986, is included on the National Priorities List from such List, or not to list any facility which as of such date is proposed for inclusion on such list.

(4) Information gathering and analysis

Nothing in this chapter shall be construed to preclude the expenditure of monies from the Fund for gathering and analysis of information which will enable the President to consider the specific factors required by paragraph (2).

(Dec. 11, 1980, Pub.L. 96–510, Title I, § 105, 94 Stat. 2779; Oct. 17, 1986, Pub.L. 99–499, Title I, § 105, 100 Stat. 1625.)

WEST'S FEDERAL PRACTICE MANUAL

Environmental regulatory framework, see § 4381.5 et seq.

CODE OF FEDERAL REGULATIONS

Oil and hazardous substances pollution contingency plan, see 40 CFR 300.1 et seq.

LAW REVIEW COMMENTARIES

Ability of CERCLA defendants to challenge cost-effectiveness of government cleanups. Daniel W. Coffey, 65 N.Y.S.B.J. 42 (Mar./Apr. 1993).

Bankruptcy versus environmental protection: Discharging future CERCLA liability in Chapter 11. Note, 14 Cardozo L.Rev. 1999 (1993).

Environmental liability and the limits of insurance. Kenneth S. Abraham, 88 Columbia L.Rev. 942 (1988).

Lender liability dilemma: Fleet Factors history and aftermath. Brent Nicholson and Todd Zuiderhoek, 38 S.D.L.Rev. 22 (1993).

Property owner liability for environmental contamination in California. Michael B. Hingerty, 22 U.S.F.L.Rev. 31 (1987).

LIBRARY REFERENCES

Health and Environment ⚿25.6, 25.7.
C.J.S. Health and Environment §§ 91 et seq., 106 et seq.

§ 9606. Abatement actions [CERCLA § 106]

(a) Maintenance, jurisdiction, etc.

In addition to any other action taken by a State or local government, when the President determines that there may be an imminent and substantial endangerment to the public health or welfare or the environment because of an actual or threatened release of a hazardous substance from a facility, he may require the Attorney General of the United States to secure such relief as may be necessary to abate such danger or threat, and the district court of the United States in the district in which the threat occurs shall have jurisdiction to grant such relief as the public interest and the equities of the case may require. The President may also, after notice to the affected State, take other action under this section including, but not limited to, issuing such orders as may be necessary to protect public health and welfare and the environment.

(b) Fines; reimbursement

(1) Any person who, without sufficient cause, willfully violates, or fails or refuses to comply with, any order of the President under subsection (a) of this section may, in an action brought in the appropriate United States district court to enforce such order, be fined not more than $25,000 for each day in which such violation occurs or such failure to comply continues.

(2)(A) Any person who receives and complies with the terms of any order issued under subsection (a) of this section may, within 60 days after completion of the required action, petition the President for reimbursement from the Fund for the reasonable costs of such action, plus interest. Any interest payable under this paragraph shall accrue on the amounts expended from the date of expenditure at the same rate as specified for interest on investments of the Hazardous Substance Superfund established under subchapter A of chapter 98 of Title 26.

(B) If the President refuses to grant all or part of a petition made under this paragraph, the petitioner may within 30 days of receipt of such refusal file an action against the President in the appropriate United States district court seeking reimbursement from the Fund.

(C) Except as provided in subparagraph (D), to obtain reimbursement, the petitioner shall establish by a preponderance of the evidence that it is not liable for response costs under section 9607(a) of this title and that costs for which it seeks reimbursement are reasonable in light of the action required by the relevant order.

(D) A petitioner who is liable for response costs under section 9607(a) of this title may also recover its reasonable costs of response to the extent that it can demonstrate, on the administrative record, that the President's decision in selecting the response action ordered was arbitrary and capricious or was otherwise not in accordance with law. Reimbursement awarded under this subparagraph shall include all reasonable response costs incurred by the petitioner pursuant to the portions of the order found to be arbitrary and capricious or otherwise not in accordance with law.

(E) Reimbursement awarded by a court under subparagraph (C) or (D) may include appropriate costs, fees, and other expenses in accordance with subsections (a) and (d) of section 2412 of Title 28.

(c) Guidelines for using imminent hazard, enforcement, and emergency response authorities; promulgation by Administrator of EPA, scope, etc.

Within one hundred and eighty days after December 11, 1980, the Administrator of the Environmental Protection Agency shall, after consultation with the Attorney General, establish and publish guidelines for using the imminent hazard, enforcement, and emergency response authorities of this section and other existing statutes administered by the Administrator of the Environmental Protection Agency to effectuate the responsibilities and powers created by this chapter. Such guidelines shall to the extent practicable be consistent with the national hazardous substance response plan, and shall include, at a minimum, the assignment of responsibility for coordinating response actions with the issuance of administrative orders, enforcement of standards and permits, the gathering of information, and other imminent hazard and emergency powers authorized by (1) sections 1321(c)(2), 1318, 1319, and 1364(a) of Title 33, (2) sections 6927, 6928, 6934, and 6973 of this title, (3) sections 300j–4 and 300i of this title, (4) sections 7413, 7414, and 7603 of this title, and (5) section 2606 of Title 15.

(Dec. 11, 1980, Pub.L. 96–510, Title I, § 106, 94 Stat. 2780; Oct. 17, 1986, Pub.L. 99–499, Title I, §§ 106, 109(b), 100 Stat. 1628, 1633.)

CROSS REFERENCES

Solid Waste Disposal Act, actions prohibited under if Administrator of EPA is diligently prosecuting an action under this section, see section 6972(b) of this title.

CODE OF FEDERAL REGULATIONS

Grants and other federal assistance, see 40 CFR 30.100 et seq.

LAW REVIEW COMMENTARIES

Environmental liability and the limits of insurance. Kenneth S. Abraham, 88 Columbia L.Rev. 942 (1988).

Lender liability dilemma: Fleet Factors history and aftermath. Brent Nicholson and Todd Zuiderhoek, 38 S.D.L.Rev. 22 (1993).

LIBRARY REFERENCES

Health and Environment ⟹25.5(10), 25.6(3), (9), 25.7(3), (24).
C.J.S. Health and Environment §§ 92, 103 et seq., 106, 113 et seq.

§ 9607. Liability [CERCLA § 107]

(a) Covered persons; scope; recoverable costs and damages; interest rate; "comparable maturity" date

Notwithstanding any other provision or rule of law, and subject only to the defenses set forth in subsection (b) of this section—

(1) the owner and operator of a vessel or a facility,

(2) any person who at the time of disposal of any hazardous substance owned or operated any facility at which such hazardous substances were disposed of,

(3) any person who by contract, agreement, or otherwise arranged for disposal or treatment, or arranged with a transporter for transport for disposal or treatment, of hazardous substances owned or possessed by such person, by any other party or entity, at any facility or incineration vessel owned or operated by another party or entity and containing such hazardous substances, and

(4) any person who accepts or accepted any hazardous substances for transport to disposal or treatment facilities, incineration vessels or sites selected by such person, from which there is a release, or a threatened release which causes the incurrence of response costs, of a hazardous substance, shall be liable for—

(A) all costs of removal or remedial action incurred by the United States Government or a State or an Indian tribe not inconsistent with the national contingency plan;

(B) any other necessary costs of response incurred by any other person consistent with the national contingency plan;

(C) damages for injury to, destruction of, or loss of natural resources, including the reasonable costs of assessing such injury, destruction, or loss resulting from such a release; and

(D) the costs of any health assessment or health effects study carried out under section 9604(i) of this title.

The amounts recoverable in an action under this section shall include interest on the amounts recoverable under subparagraphs (A) through (D). Such interest shall accrue from the later of (i) the date payment of a specified amount is demanded in writing, or (ii) the date of the expenditure concerned. The rate of interest on the outstanding unpaid balance of the amounts recoverable under this section shall be the same rate as is specified for interest on investments of the Hazardous Substance Superfund established under subchapter A of chapter 98 of Title 26. For purposes of applying such amendments to interest under this subsection, the term "comparable maturity" shall be determined with reference to the date on which interest accruing under this subsection commences.

(b) Defenses

There shall be no liability under subsection (a) of this section for a person otherwise liable who can establish by a preponderance of the evidence that the release or threat of release of a hazardous substance and the damages resulting therefrom were caused solely by—

(1) an act of God;

(2) an act of war;

(3) an act or omission of a third party other than an employee or agent of the defendant, or than one whose act or omission occurs in connection with a contractual relationship, existing directly or indirectly, with the defendant (except where the sole contractual arrangement arises from a published tariff and acceptance for carriage by a common carrier by rail), if the defendant establishes by a preponderance of the evidence that (a) he exercised due care with respect to the hazardous substance concerned, taking into consideration the characteristics of such hazardous substance, in light of all relevant facts and circumstances, and (b) he took precautions against foreseeable acts or omissions of any such third party and the consequences that could foreseeably result from such acts or omissions; or

(4) any combination of the foregoing paragraphs.

(c) Determination of amounts

(1) Except as provided in paragraph (2) of this subsection, the liability under this section of an owner or operator or other responsible person for each release of a hazardous substance or incident involving release of a hazardous substance shall not exceed—

(A) for any vessel, other than an incineration vessel, which carries any hazardous substance as cargo or residue, $300 per gross ton, or $5,000,000, whichever is greater;

(B) for any other vessel, other than an incineration vessel, $300 per gross ton, or $500,000, whichever is greater;

(C) for any motor vehicle, aircraft, hazardous liquid pipeline facility (as defined in the Hazardous Liquid Pipeline Safety Act of 1979 [49 U.S.C.A. 2001 et seq.]), or rolling stock, $50,000,000 or such lesser amount as the President shall establish by regulation, but in no event less than $5,000,000 (or, for releases of hazardous substances as defined in section 9601(14)(A) of this title into the navigable waters, $8,000,000). Such regulations shall take into account the size, type, location, storage, and handling capacity and other matters relating to the likelihood of release in each such class and to the economic impact of such limits on each such class; or

(D) for any incineration vessel or any facility other than those specified in subparagraph (C) of this paragraph, the total of all costs of response plus $50,000,000 for any damages under this subchapter.

(2) Notwithstanding the limitations in paragraph (1) of this subsection, the liability of an owner or operator or other responsible person under this section shall be the full and total costs of response and damages, if (A)(i) the release or threat of release of a hazardous substance was the result of willful misconduct or willful negligence within the privity or knowledge of such person, or (ii) the primary cause of the release was a violation (within the privity or knowledge of such person) of applicable safety, construction, or operating standards or regulations; or (B) such person fails or refuses to provide all reasonable cooperation and assistance requested by a responsible public official in connection with response activities under the national contingency plan with respect to regulated carriers subject to the provisions of Title 49 or vessels subject to the provisions of Title 33, 46, or 46 Appendix, subparagraph (A)(ii) of this paragraph shall be deemed to refer to Federal standards or regulations.

(3) If any person who is liable for a release or threat of release of a hazardous substance fails without sufficient cause to properly provide removal or remedial action upon order of the President pursuant to section 9604 or 9606 of this title, such person may be liable to the United States for punitive damages in an amount at least equal to, and not more than three times, the amount of any costs incurred by the Fund as a result of such failure to take proper action. The President is authorized to commence a civil action against any such person to recover the punitive damages, which shall be in addition to any costs recovered from such person pursuant to section 9612(c) of this title. Any moneys received by the United States pursuant to this subsection shall be deposited in the Fund.

(d) Rendering care or advice

(1) In general

Except as provided in paragraph (2), no person shall be liable under this subchapter for costs or damages as a result of actions taken or omitted in the course of rendering care, assistance, or advice in accordance with the National Contingency Plan ("NCP") or at the direction of an onscene coordinator appointed under such plan, with respect to an incident creating a danger to public health or welfare or the environment as a result of any releases of a hazardous substance or the threat thereof. This paragraph shall not preclude liability for costs or damages as the result of negligence on the part of such person.

(2) State and local governments

No State or local government shall be liable under this subchapter for costs or damages as a result of actions taken in response to an emergency created by the release or threatened release of a hazardous substance generated by or from a facility owned by another person. This paragraph shall not preclude liability for costs or damages as a result of gross negligence or intentional misconduct by the State or local government. For the purpose of the preceding sentence, reckless, willful, or wanton misconduct shall constitute gross negligence.

(3) Savings provision

This subsection shall not alter the liability of any person covered by the provisions of paragraph (1), (2), (3), or (4) of subsection (a) of this section with respect to the release or threatened release concerned.

(e) Indemnification, hold harmless, etc., agreements or conveyances; subrogation rights

(1) No indemnification, hold harmless, or similar agreement or conveyance shall be effective to transfer from the owner or operator of any vessel or facility or from any person who may be liable for a release or threat of release under this section, to any other person the liability imposed under this section. Nothing in this subsection shall bar any agreement to insure, hold harmless, or indemnify a party to such agreement for any liability under this section.

(2) Nothing in this subchapter, including the provisions of paragraph (1) of this subsection, shall bar a cause of action that an owner or operator or any other person subject to liability under this section, or a guarantor, has or would have, by reason of subrogation or otherwise against any person.

(f) Actions involving natural resources; maintenance, scope, etc.

(1) Natural resources liability

In the case of an injury to, destruction of, or loss of natural resources under subparagraph (C) of subsection (a) of this section liability shall be to the United States Government and to any State for natural resources within the State or belonging to, managed by, controlled by, or appertaining to such State and to any Indian tribe for natural resources belonging to, managed by, controlled by, or appertaining to such tribe, or held in trust for the benefit of such tribe, or belonging to a member of such tribe if such resources are subject to a trust restriction on alienation: *Provided, however,* That no liability to the United States or State or Indian tribe shall be imposed under subparagraph (C) of subsection (a) of this section, where the party sought to be charged has demonstrated that the damages to natural resources complained of were specifically identified as an irreversible and irretrievable commitment of natural resources in an environmental impact statement, or other comparable environment analysis, and the decision to grant a permit or license authorizes such commitment of natural resources, and the facility or project was otherwise operating within the terms of its permit or license, so long as, in the case of damages to an Indian tribe occurring pursuant to a Federal permit or license, the issuance of that permit or license was not inconsistent with the fiduciary duty of the United States with respect to such Indian tribe. The President, or the authorized representative of any State, shall act on behalf of the public as trustee of such natural resources to recover for such damages. Sums recovered by the United States Government as trustee under this subsection shall be retained by the trustee, without further appropriation, for use only to restore, replace, or acquire the equivalent of such natural resources. Sums recovered by a State as trustee under this subsection shall be available for use only to restore, replace, or acquire the equivalent of such natural resources by the State. The measure of damages in any action under subparagraph (C) of subsection (a) of this section shall not be limited by the sums which can be used to restore or replace such resources. There shall be no double recovery under this chapter for natural resource damages, including the costs of damage assessment or restoration, rehabilitation, or acquisition for the same release and natural resource. There shall be no recovery under the authority of subparagraph (C) of subsection (a) of this section where such damages and the release of a hazardous substance from which such damages resulted have occurred wholly before December 11, 1980.

(2) Designation of Federal and State officials

(A) Federal

The President shall designate in the National Contingency Plan published under section 9605 of this title the Federal officials who shall act on behalf of the public as trustees for natural resources under this chapter and section 1321 of Title 33. Such officials shall assess damages for injury to, destruction of, or loss of natural resources for purposes of this chapter and such section 1321 of Title 33 for those resources under their trusteeship and may, upon request of and reimbursement from a State and at the Federal officials' discretion, assess damages for those natural resources under the State's trusteeship.

(B) State

The Governor of each State shall designate State officials who may act on behalf of the public as trustees for natural resources under this chapter and section 1321 of Title 33 and shall notify the President of such designations. Such State officials shall assess damages to natural resources for the purposes of this chapter and such section 1321 of Title 33 for those natural resources under their trusteeship.

(C) Rebuttable presumption

Any determination or assessment of damages to natural resources for the purposes of this chapter and section 1321 of Title 33 made by a Federal or State trustee in accordance with the regulations promulgated under section 9651(c) of this title shall have the force and effect of a rebuttable presumption on behalf of the trustee in any administrative or judicial proceeding under this chapter or section 1321 of Title 33.

(g) Federal agencies

For provisions relating to Federal agencies, see section 9620 of this title.

(h) Owner or operator of vessel

The owner or operator of a vessel shall be liable in accordance with this section, under maritime tort law, and as provided under section 9614 of this title notwithstanding any provision of the Act of March 3, 1851 (46 U.S.C. 183ff) [46 App.U.S.C.A. 182, 183, 184–188] or the absence of any physical damage to the proprietary interest of the claimant.

(i) Application of a registered pesticide product

No person (including the United States or any State or Indian tribe) may recover under the authority of this section for any response costs or damages resulting from the application of a pesticide product registered under the Federal Insecticide, Fungicide, and Rodenticide Act [7 U.S.C.A. § 136 et seq.]. Nothing in this paragraph shall affect or modify in any way the obligations or liability of any person under any other provision of State or Federal law, including common law, for damages, injury, or loss resulting from a release of any hazardous substance or for removal or remedial action or the costs of removal or remedial action of such hazardous substance.

(j) Obligations or liability pursuant to federally permitted release

Recovery by any person (including the United States or any State or Indian tribe) for response costs or damages resulting from a federally permitted release shall be pursuant to existing law in lieu of this section. Nothing in this paragraph shall affect or modify in any way the obligations or liability of any person under any other provision of State or Federal law, including common law, for damages, injury, or loss resulting from a release of any hazardous substance or for removal or remedial action or the costs of removal or remedial action of such hazardous substance. In addition, costs of response incurred by the Federal Government in connection with a discharge specified in section 9601(10)(B) or (C) of this title shall be recoverable in an action brought under section 1319(b) of Title 33.

(k) Transfer to, and assumption by, Post-Closure Liability Fund of liability of owner or operator of hazardous waste disposal facility in receipt of permit under applicable solid waste disposal law; time, criteria applicable, procedures, etc.; monitoring costs; reports

(1) The liability established by this section or any other law for the owner or operator of a hazardous waste disposal facility which has received a permit under subtitle C of the Solid Waste Disposal Act [42 U.S.C.A. § 6921 et seq.], shall be transferred to and assumed by the Post-closure Liability Fund established by section 9641 of this title when—

(A) such facility and the owner and operator thereof has complied with the requirements of subtitle C of the Solid Waste Disposal Act [42 U.S.C.A. § 6921 et seq.] and regulations issued thereunder, which may affect the performance of such facility after closure; and

(B) such facility has been closed in accordance with such regulations and the conditions of such permit, and such facility and the surrounding area have been monitored as required by such regulations and permit conditions for a period not to exceed five years after closure to demonstrate that there is no substantial likelihood that any migration offsite or release from confinement of any hazardous substance or other risk to public health or welfare will occur.

(2) Such transfer of liability shall be effective ninety days after the owner or operator of such facility notifies the Administrator of the Environmental Protection Agency (and the State where it has an authorized program under section 3006(b) of the Solid Waste Disposal Act [42 U.S.C.A. § 6926(b)]) that the conditions imposed by this subsection have been satisfied. If within such ninety-day period the Administrator of the Environmental Protection Agency or such State determines that any such facility has not complied with all the conditions imposed by this subsection or that insufficient information has been provided to demonstrate such compliance, the Administrator or such State shall so notify the owner and operator of such facility and the administrator of the Fund established by section 9641 of this title, and the owner and operator of such facility shall continue to be liable with respect to such facility under this section and other law until such time as the Administrator and such State determines that such facility has complied with all conditions imposed by this subsection. A determination by the Administrator or such State that a facility has not complied with all conditions imposed by this subsection or that insufficient information has been supplied to demonstrate compliance, shall be a final administrative action for purposes of judicial review. A request for additional information shall state in specific terms the data required.

(3) In addition to the assumption of liability of owners and operators under paragraph (1) of this subsection, the Post-closure Liability Fund established by section 9641 of this title may be used to pay costs of monitoring and care and maintenance of a site incurred by other persons after the period of monitoring required by regulations under subtitle C of the Solid Waste Disposal Act [42 U.S.C.A. § 6921 et seq.] for hazardous waste disposal facilities meeting the conditions of paragraph (1) of this subsection.

(4)(A) Not later than one year after December 11, 1980, the Secretary of the Treasury shall conduct a study and shall submit a report thereon to the Congress on the feasibility of establishing or qualifying an optional system of private insurance for postclosure financial responsibility for hazardous waste disposal facilities to which this subsection applies. Such study shall include a specification of adequate and realistic minimum standards to assure that any such privately placed insurance will carry out the purposes of this subsection in a reliable, enforceable, and practical manner. Such a study shall include an examination of the public and private incentives, programs, and actions necessary to make privately placed insurance a practical and effective option to the financing system for the Post-closure Liability Fund provided in subchapter II of this chapter.

(B) Not later than eighteen months after December 11, 1980, and after a public hearing, the President shall by rule determine whether or not it is feasible to establish or qualify an optional system of private insurance for postclosure financial responsibility for hazardous waste disposal facilities to which this subsection applies. If the President determines the establishment or qualification of such a system would be infeasible, he shall promptly publish an explanation of the reasons for such a determination. If the President determines the establishment or qualification of such a system would be feasible, he shall promptly publish notice of such determination. Not later than six months after an affirmative determination under the preceding sentence and after a public hearing, the President shall by rule promulgate adequate and realistic minimum standards which must be met by any such privately placed insurance, taking into account the purposes of this chapter and this subsection. Such rules shall also specify reasonably expeditious procedures by which privately placed insurance plans can qualify as meeting such minimum standards.

(C) In the event any privately placed insurance plan qualifies under subparagraph (B), any person enrolled in, and complying with the terms of, such plan shall be excluded from the provisions of paragraphs (1), (2), and (3) of this subsection and exempt from the requirements to pay any tax or fee to the Post-closure Liability Fund under subchapter II of this chapter.

(D) The President may issue such rules and take such other actions as are necessary to effectuate the purposes of this paragraph.

(5) Suspension of liability transfer

Notwithstanding paragraphs (1), (2), (3), and (4) of this subsection and subsection (j) of section 9611 of this title, no liability shall be transferred to or assumed by the Post-Closure Liability Trust Fund established by section 9641 of this title prior to completion of the study required under paragraph (6) of this subsection, transmission of a report of such study to both Houses of Congress, and authorization of such a transfer or assumption by Act of Congress following receipt of such study and report.

(6) Study of options for post-closure program

(A) Study

The Comptroller General shall conduct a study of options for a program for the management of the liabilities associated with hazardous waste treatment, storage, and disposal sites after their closure which complements the policies set forth in the Hazardous and Solid Waste Amendments of 1984 and assures the protection of human health and the environment.

(B) Program elements

The program referred to in subparagraph (A) shall be designed to assure each of the following:

(i) Incentives are created and maintained for the safe management and disposal of hazardous wastes so as to assure protection of human health and the environment.

(ii) Members of the public will have reasonable confidence that hazardous wastes will be managed and disposed of safely and that resources will be available to address any problems that may arise and to cover costs of long-term monitoring, care, and maintenance of such sites.

(iii) Persons who are or seek to become owners and operators of hazardous waste disposal facilities will be able to manage their potential future liabilities and to attract the investment capital necessary to build, operate, and close such facilities in a manner which assures protection of human health and the environment.

(C) Assessments

The study under this paragraph shall include assessments of treatment, storage, and disposal facilities which have been or are likely to be issued a permit under section 3005 of the Solid Waste Disposal Act [42 U.S.C.A. § 6925] and the likelihood of future insolvency on the part of owners and operators of such facilities. Separate assessments shall be made for different classes of facilities and for different classes of land disposal facilities and shall include but not be limited to—

(i) the current and future financial capabilities of facility owners and operators;

(ii) the current and future costs associated with facilities, including the costs of routine monitoring and maintenance, compliance monitoring, corrective action, natural resource damages, and liability for damages to third parties; and

(iii) the availability of mechanisms by which owners and operators of such facilities can assure that current and future costs, including post-closure costs, will be financed.

(D) Procedures

In carrying out the responsibilities of this paragraph, the Comptroller General shall consult with the Administrator, the Secretary of Commerce, the Secretary of the Treasury, and the heads of other appropriate Federal agencies.

(E) Consideration of options

In conducting the study under this paragraph, the Comptroller General shall consider various mechanisms and combinations of mechanisms to complement the policies set forth in the Hazardous and Solid Waste Amendments of 1984 to serve the purposes set forth in subparagraph (B) and to assure that the current and future costs associated with hazardous waste facilities, including post-closure costs, will be adequately financed and, to the greatest extent possible, borne by the owners and operators of such facilities. Mechanisms to be considered include, but are not limited to—

(i) revisions to closure, post-closure, and financial responsibility requirements under subtitles C and I of the Solid Waste Disposal Act [42 U.S.C.A. § 6921 et seq. and § 6991 et seq.];

(ii) voluntary risk pooling by owners and operators;

(iii) legislation to require risk pooling by owners and operators;

(iv) modification of the Post-Closure Liability Trust Fund previously established by section 9641 of this title, and the conditions for transfer of liability under this subsection, including limiting the transfer of some or all liability under this subsection only in the case of insolvency of owners and operators;

(v) private insurance;

(vi) insurance provided by the Federal Government;

(vii) coinsurance, reinsurance, or pooled-risk insurance, whether provided by the private sector or provided or assisted by the Federal Government; and

(viii) creation of a new program to be administered by a new or existing Federal agency or by a federally chartered corporation.

(F) Recommendations

The Comptroller General shall consider options for funding any program under this section and shall, to the extent necessary, make recommendations to the appropriate committees of Congress for additional authority to implement such program.

(*l*) Federal lien

(1) In general

All costs and damages for which a person is liable to the United States under subsection (a) of this section (other than the owner or operator of a vessel under paragraph (1) of subsection (a) of this section) shall constitute a lien in favor of the United States upon all real property and rights to such property which—

(A) belong to such person; and

(B) are subject to or affected by a removal or remedial action.

(2) Duration

The lien imposed by this subsection shall arise at the later of the following:

(A) The time costs are first incurred by the United States with respect to a response action under this chapter.

(B) The time that the person referred to in paragraph (1) is provided (by certified or registered mail) written notice of potential liability.

Such lien shall continue until the liability for the costs (or a judgment against the person arising out of such liability) is satisfied or becomes unenforceable through operation of the statute of limitations provided in section 9613 of this title.

(3) Notice and validity

The lien imposed by this subsection shall be subject to the rights of any purchaser, holder of a security interest, or judgment lien creditor whose interest is perfected under applicable State law before notice of the lien has been filed in the appropriate office within the State (or county or other governmental subdivision), as designated by State law, in which the real property subject to the lien is located. Any such purchaser, holder of a security interest, or judgment lien creditor shall be afforded the same protections against the lien imposed by this subsection as are afforded under State law against a judgment lien which arises out of an unsecured obligation and which arises as of the time of the filing of the notice of the lien imposed by this subsection. If the State has not by law designated one office for the receipt of such notices of liens, the notice shall be filed in the office of the clerk of the United States district court for the district in which the real property is located. For purposes of this subsection, the terms "purchaser" and "security interest" shall have the definitions provided under section 6323(h) of Title 26.

(4) Action in rem

The costs constituting the lien may be recovered in an action in rem in the United States district court for the district in which the removal or remedial action is occurring or has occurred. Nothing in this subsection shall affect the right of the United States to bring an action against any person to recover all costs and damages for which such person is liable under subsection (a) of this section.

(m) Maritime lien

All costs and damages for which the owner or operator of a vessel is liable under subsection (a)(1) of this section with respect to a release or threatened release from such vessel shall constitute a maritime lien in favor of the United States on such vessel. Such costs may be recovered in an action in rem in the district court of the United States for the district in which the vessel may be found. Nothing in this subsection shall affect the right of the United States to bring an action against the owner or operator of such vessel in any court of competent jurisdiction to recover such costs.

(Dec. 11, 1980, Pub.L. 96–510, Title I, § 107, 94 Stat. 2781; Oct. 17, 1986, Pub.L. 99–499, Title I, §§ 107(a)–(d)(2), (e), (f), 127(b), (e), Title II, §§ 201, 207(c), 100 Stat. 1628–1630, 1692, 1693, 1705, 1706; Oct. 22, 1986, Pub.L. 99–514, § 2, 100 Stat. 2095; Oct. 31, 1994, Pub.L. 103–429, § 7(e)(2), 108 Stat. 4390.)

CROSS REFERENCES

Solid Waste Disposal Act, financial responsibility provisions under as not diminishing liabilities of persons under this section, see sections 6924(t)(3), 6991b(d)(3), and 6991c(c)(4) of this title.

CODE OF FEDERAL REGULATIONS

Grants and other federal assistance, see 40 CFR 30.100 et seq.

LAW REVIEW COMMENTARIES

Ability of CERCLA defendants to challenge cost-effectiveness of government cleanups. Daniel W. Coffey, 65 N.Y.S.B.J. 42 (Mar./Apr. 1993).

Bankruptcy versus environmental protection: Discharging future CERCLA liability in Chapter 11. Note, 14 Cardozo L.Rev. 1999 (1993).

Cost recovery by private parties under CERCLA: Planning a response action for maximum recovery. Arnold W. Reitze, Jr., Andrew J. Harrison, Jr., and Monica J. Palko, 27 Tulsa L.J. 365 (1992).

Crying wolf or is a wolf at the door?: Lender liability for environmental cleanup. Jeanmarie B. Tade, 32 S.Tex.L.Rev. 555 (1991).

Enforcing environmental indemnification against a settling party under CERCLA. Daniel R. Avery, 23 Seton Hall L.Rev. 872 (1993).

Environmental liability and the limits of insurance. Kenneth S. Abraham, 88 Columbia L.Rev. 942 (1988).

Groundwater contamination claims in Connecticut. Dean M. Cordiano and Lynn Anne Glover, 60 Conn.B.J. 167 (1986).

Hazardous Waste: A threat to the lender's environment. Marcy Sharon Cohen, 19 UCC L.J. 99 (1986).

Impact of the new EPA regulation on lender liability. Cathy Stricklin Krendl and Thomas J. Gibson, 21 Colo.Law. 2339 (1992).

Insurance industry's 1970 pollution exclusion: An exercise in ambiguity. John S. Vishneski, III, Todd G. Zimmerman, Robert A. Creamer, and Judith N. Levi, 23 Loy.U.Chi.L.J. 25 (1991).

Lessor and lessee liability under the Comprehensive Environmental Response, Compensation, and Liability Act (CERCLA): The catch–22 of lease agreements. William P. Jensen, 32 S.Tex.L.Rev. 447 (1991).

Liability of officers, directors and stockholders under CERCLA: The case for adopting state law. Richard G. Dennis, 36 Vill.L.Rev. 1367 (1991).

Municipal liability for household hazardous wastes: An analysis of the superfund statute and its policy implications. Molly A. Meegan, 79 Geo.L.J. 1783 (1991).

New federalism, old due process, retroactive revival: Constitutional problems with CERCLA's Amendment of state law. Alfred R. Light, 40 U.Kan.L.Rev. 365 (1992).

Property owner liability for environmental contamination in California. Michael B. Hingerty, 22 U.S.F.L.Rev. 31 (1987).

Resolving conflicts between bankruptcy law and the state police power. Ellen E. Sward, 1987 Wis.L.Rev. 403 (1987).

The impact of the 1986 Superfund Amendments and Reauthorization Act on the commercial lending industry: A critical assessment. 41 U.Miami L.Rev. 879 (1987).

Third-party defense to hazardous waste liability: Narrowing the contractual relationship exception. J.B. Ruhl, 29 South Texas L.Rev. 291 (1988).

Toxic tort litigation and the causation element: Is there any hope of reconciliation? Or a Fred Harris, Jr., 40 Southwestern (Tex.) L.J. 909 (1986).

Toxics and title insurance. Oscar H. Beasley and Maureen M. Muranaka, 10 L.A.Law. 19 (January 1988).

United States v. Maryland Bank & Trust Co.: Lender liability under CERCLA. Carolyn Rashby, 14 Ecology L.Q. 569 (1987).

When a security becomes a liability: Claims against lenders in hazardous waste cleanup. 38 Hast.L.J. 1261 (1987).

United States Supreme Court

Private litigant's activities in identifying other potentially responsible parties were "necessary costs of response" recoverable under the Comprehensive Environmental Response, Compensation and Liability Act but fees incurred by private litigant for legal services performed in connection with negotiations with Environmental Protection Agency resulting in consent decree were not "necessary costs of response" and not recoverable under such Act, see Key Tronic Corp. v. U.S., 1994, 114 S.Ct. 1960, 128 L.Ed.2d 797.

LIBRARY REFERENCES

Health and Environment ⚷25.7(23).
C.J.S. Health and Environment § 113 et seq.

§ 9608. Financial responsibility [CERCLA § 108]

(a) Establishment and maintenance by owner or operator of vessel; amount; failure to obtain certification of compliance

(1) The owner or operator of each vessel (except a nonself-propelled barge that does not carry hazardous substances as cargo) over three hundred gross tons that uses any port or place in the United States or the navigable waters or any offshore facility, shall establish and maintain, in accordance with regulations promulgated by the President, evidence of financial responsibility of $300 per gross ton (or for a vessel carrying hazardous substances as cargo, or $5,000,000, whichever is greater) to cover the liability prescribed under paragraph (1) of section 9607(a) of this title. Financial responsibility may be established by any one, or any combination, of the following: insurance, guarantee, surety bond, or qualification as a self-insurer. Any bond filed shall be issued by a bonding company authorized to do business in the United States. In cases where an owner or operator owns, operates, or charters more than one vessel subject to this subsection, evidence of financial responsibility need be established only to meet the maximum liability applicable to the largest of such vessels.

(2) The Secretary of the Treasury shall withhold or revoke the clearance required by section 91 of Title 46, Appendix, of any vessel subject to this subsection that does not have certification furnished by the President that the financial responsibility provisions of paragraph (1) of this subsection have been complied with.

(3) The Secretary of Transportation, in accordance with regulations issued by him, shall (A) deny entry to any port or place in the United States or navigable waters to, and (B) detain at the port or place in the United States from which it is about to depart for any other port or place in the United States, any vessel subject to this subsection that, upon request, does not produce certification furnished by the President that the financial responsibility provisions of paragraph (1) of this subsection have been complied with.

(4) In addition to the financial responsibility provisions of paragraph (1) of this subsection, the President shall require additional evidence of financial responsibility for incineration vessels in such amounts, and to cover such liabilities recognized by law, as the President deems appropriate, taking into account the potential risks posed by incineration and transport for incineration, and any other factors deemed relevant.

(b) Establishment and maintenance by owner or operator of production, etc., facilities; amount; adjustment; consolidated form of responsibility; coverage of motor carriers

(1) Beginning not earlier than five years after December 11, 1980, the President shall promulgate requirements (for facilities in addition to those under subtitle C of the Solid Waste Disposal Act [42 U.S.C.A. § 6921 et seq.] and other Federal law) that classes of facilities establish and maintain evidence of financial responsibility consistent with the degree and duration of risk associated with the production, transportation, treatment, storage, or disposal of hazardous substances. Not later than three years after December 11, 1980, the President shall identify those classes for which requirements will be first developed and publish notice of such identification in the Federal Register. Priority in the development of such requirements shall be accorded to those classes of facilities, owners, and operators which the President determines present the highest level of risk of injury.

(2) The level of financial responsibility shall be initially established, and, when necessary, adjusted to protect against the level of risk which the President in his discretion believes is appropriate based on the payment experience of the Fund, commercial insurers, courts settlements and judgments, and voluntary claims satisfaction. To the maximum extent practicable, the President shall cooperate with and seek the advice of the commercial insurance industry in developing financial responsibility requirements. Financial responsibility may be established by any one, or any combination, of the following: insurance, guarantee, surety bond, letter of credit, or qualification as a self-insurer. In promulgating requirements under this section, the President is authorized to specify policy or other contractual terms, conditions, or defenses which are necessary, or which are unacceptable, in establishing such evidence of financial responsibility in order to effectuate the purposes of this chapter.

(3) Regulations promulgated under this subsection shall incrementally impose financial responsibility requirements as quickly as can reasonably be achieved but in no event more than 4 years after the date of promulgation. Where possible, the level of financial responsibility which the President believes appropriate as a final requirement shall be achieved through incremental, annual increases in the requirements.

(4) Where a facility is owned or operated by more than one person, evidence of financial responsibility covering the facility may be established and maintained by one of the owners or operators, or, in consolidated form, by or on behalf of two or more owners or operators. When evidence of financial responsibility is established in a consolidated form, the proportional share of each participant shall be shown. The evidence shall be accompanied by a statement authorizing the applicant to act for and in behalf of each participant in submitting and maintaining the evidence of financial responsibility.

(5) The requirements for evidence of financial responsibility for motor carriers covered by this chapter shall be determined under section 30 of the Motor Carrier Act of 1980, Public Law 96–296.

(c) Direct action

(1) Releases from vessels

In the case of a release or threatened release from a vessel, any claim authorized by section 9607 or 9611 of this title may be asserted directly against any guarantor providing evidence of financial responsibility for such vessel under subsection (a) of this section. In defending such a claim, the guarantor may invoke all rights and defenses which would be available to the owner or operator under this subchapter. The guarantor may also invoke the defense that the incident was caused by the willful misconduct of the owner or operator, but the guarantor may not invoke any other defense that the guarantor might have been entitled to invoke in a proceeding brought by the owner or operator against him.

(2) Releases from facilities

In the case of a release or threatened release from a facility, any claim authorized by section 9607 or 9611 of this title may be asserted directly against any guarantor providing evidence of financial responsibility for such facility under subsection (b) of this section, if the person liable under section 9607 of this title is in bankruptcy, reorganization, or arrangement pursuant to the Federal Bankruptcy Code, or if, with reasonable diligence, jurisdiction in the Federal courts cannot be obtained over a person liable under section 9607 of this title who is likely to be solvent at the time of judgment. In the case of any action pursuant to this paragraph, the guarantor shall be entitled to invoke all rights and defenses which would have been available to the person liable under section 9607 of this title if any action had been brought against such person by the claimant and all rights and defenses which would have been available to the guarantor if an action had been brought against the guarantor by such person.

(d) Limitation of guarantor liability

(1) Total liability

The total liability of any guarantor in a direct action suit brought under this section shall be limited to the aggregate amount of the monetary limits of the policy of insurance, guarantee, surety bond, letter of credit, or similar instrument obtained from the guarantor by the person subject to liability under section 9607 of this title for the purpose of satisfying the requirement for evidence of financial responsibility.

(2) Other liability

Nothing in this subsection shall be construed to limit any other State or Federal statutory, contractual, or common law liability of a guarantor, including, but not limited to, the liability of such guarantor for bad faith either in negotiating or in failing to negotiate the settlement of any claim. Nothing in this subsection shall be construed, interpreted, or applied to diminish the liability of any person under section 9607 of this title or other applicable law.

(Dec. 11, 1980, Pub.L. 96–510, Title I, § 108, 94 Stat. 2785; Oct. 17, 1986, Pub.L. 99–499, Title I, §§ 108, 127(c), 100 Stat. 1631, 1692.)

CODE OF FEDERAL REGULATIONS

Grants and other federal assistance, see 40 CFR 30.100 et seq.

LIBRARY REFERENCES

Health and Environment ⚷25.7(3).
C.J.S. Health and Environment § 106.

§ 9609. Civil penalties and awards [CERCLA § 109]

(a) Class I administrative penalty

(1) Violations

A civil penalty of not more than $25,000 per violation may be assessed by the President in the case of any of the following—

(A) A violation of the requirements of section 9603(a) or (b) of this title (relating to notice).

(B) A violation of the requirements of section 9603(d)(2) of this title (relating to destruction of records, etc.).

(C) A violation of the requirements of section 9608 of this title (relating to financial responsibility, etc.), the regulations issued under section 9608 of this title, or with any denial or detention order under section 9608 of this title.

(D) A violation of an order under section 9622(d)(3) of this title (relating to settlement agreements for action under section 9604(b) of this title).

(E) Any failure or refusal referred to in section 9622(*l*) of this title (relating to violations of administrative orders, consent decrees, or agreements under section 9620 of this title).

(2) Notice and hearings

No civil penalty may be assessed under this subsection unless the person accused of the violation is given notice and opportunity for a hearing with respect to the violation.

(3) Determining amount

In determining the amount of any penalty assessed pursuant to this subsection, the President shall take into account the nature, circumstances, extent and gravity of the violation or violations and, with respect to the violator, ability to pay, any prior history of such violations, the degree of culpability, economic benefit or savings (if any) resulting from the violation, and such other matters as justice may require.

(4) Review

Any person against whom a civil penalty is assessed under this subsection may obtain review thereof in the appropriate district court of the United States by filing a notice of appeal in such court within 30 days from the date of such order and by simultaneously sending a copy of such notice by certified mail to the President. The President shall promptly file in such court a certified copy of the record upon which such violation was found or such penalty imposed. If any person fails to pay an assessment of a civil penalty after it has become a final and unappealable order or after the appropriate court has entered final judgment in favor of the United States, the President may request the Attorney General of the United States to institute a civil action in an appropriate district court of the United States to collect the penalty, and such court shall have jurisdiction to hear and decide any such action. In hearing such action, the court shall have authority to review the violation and the assessment of the civil penalty on the record.

(5) Subpoenas

The President may issue subpoenas for the attendance and testimony of witnesses and the production of relevant papers, books, or documents in connection with hearings under this subsection. In case of contumacy or refusal to obey a subpoena issued pursuant to this paragraph and served upon any person, the district court of the United States for any district in which such person is found, resides, or transacts business, upon application by the United States and after notice to such person, shall have jurisdiction to issue an order requiring such person to appear and give testimony before the administrative law judge or to appear and produce documents before the administrative law judge, or both, and any failure to obey such order of the court may be punished by such court as a contempt thereof.

(b) Class II administrative penalty

A civil penalty of not more than $25,000 per day for each day during which the violation continues may be assessed by the President in the case of any of the following—

(1) A violation of the notice requirements of section 9603(a) or (b) of this title.

(2) A violation of section 9603(d)(2) of this title (relating to destruction of records, etc.).

(3) A violation of the requirements of section 9608 of this title (relating to financial responsibility, etc.), the regulations issued under section 9608 of this title, or with any denial or detention order under section 9608 of this title.

(4) A violation of an order under section 9622(d)(3) of this title (relating to settlement agreements for action under section 9604(b) of this title).

(5) Any failure or refusal referred to in section 9622(*l*) of this title (relating to violations of administrative orders, consent decrees, or agreements under section 9620 of this title).

In the case of a second or subsequent violation the amount of such penalty may be not more than $75,000 for each day during which the violation continues. Any civil penalty under this subsection shall be assessed and collected in the same manner, and subject to the same provisions, as in the case of civil penalties assessed and collected after notice and opportunity for hearing on the record in accordance with section 554 of Title 5. In any proceeding for the assessment of a civil penalty under this subsection the President may issue subpoenas for the attendance and testimony of witnesses and the production of relevant papers, books, and documents and may promulgate rules for discovery procedures. Any person who requested a hearing with respect to a civil penalty under this subsection and who is aggrieved by an order assessing the civil penalty may file a petition for judicial review of such order with the United States Court of Appeals for the District of Columbia Circuit or for any other circuit in which such person resides or transacts business. Such a petition may only be filed within the 30-day period beginning on the date the order making such assessment was issued.

(c) Judicial assessment

The President may bring an action in the United States district court for the appropriate district to assess and collect a penalty of not more than $25,000 per day for each day during which the violation (or failure or refusal) continues in the case of any of the following—

(1) A violation of the notice requirements of section 9603(a) or (b) of this title.

(2) A violation of section 9603(d)(2) of this title (relating to destruction of records, etc.).

(3) A violation of the requirements of section 9608 of this title (relating to financial responsibility, etc.), the regulations issued under section 9608 of this title, or with any denial or detention order under section 9608 of this title.

(4) A violation of an order under section 9622(d)(3) of this title (relating to settlement agreements for action under section 9604(b) of this title).

(5) Any failure or refusal referred to in section 9622(*l*) of this title (relating to violations of administrative orders, consent decrees, or agreements under section 9620 of this title).

In the case of a second or subsequent violation (or failure or refusal), the amount of such penalty may be not more than $75,000 for each day during which the violation (or failure or refusal) continues. For additional provisions providing for judicial assessment of civil penalties for failure to comply with a request or order under section 9604(e) of this title (relating to information gathering and access authorities), see section 9604(e) of this title.

(d) Awards

The President may pay an award of up to $10,000 to any individual who provides information leading to the arrest and conviction of any person for a violation subject to a criminal penalty under this chapter, including any violation of section 9603 of this title and any other violation referred to in this section. The President shall, by regulation, prescribe criteria for such an award and may pay any award under this subsection from the Fund, as provided in section 9611 of this title.

(e) Procurement procedures

Notwithstanding any other provision of law, any executive agency may use competitive procedures or procedures other than competitive procedures to procure the services of experts for use in preparing or prosecuting a civil or criminal action under this chapter, whether or not the expert is expected to testify at trial. The executive agency need not provide any written justification for the use of procedures other than competitive procedures when procuring such expert services under this chapter and need not furnish for publication in the Commerce Business Daily or otherwise any notice of solicitation or synopsis with respect to such procurement.

(f) Savings clause

Action taken by the President pursuant to this section shall not affect or limit the President's authority to enforce any provisions of this chapter.

(Dec. 11, 1980, Pub.L. 96–510, Title I, § 109, 94 Stat. 2787; Oct. 17, 1986, Pub.L. 99–499, Title I, § 109(c), 100 Stat. 1633.)

LAW REVIEW COMMENTARIES

Insurance coverage for superfund liability: A plain meaning approach to the pollution exclusion clause. Note, 27 Washburn L.J. 161 (1987).

LIBRARY REFERENCES

Health and Environment ⟹25.7(24).
C.J.S. Health and Environment § 113 et seq.

§ 9610. Employee protection [CERCLA § 110]

(a) Activities of employee subject to protection

No person shall fire or in any other way discriminate against, or cause to be fired or discriminated against, any employee or any authorized representative of employees by reason of the fact that such employee or representative has provided information to a State or to the Federal Government, filed, instituted, or caused to be filed or instituted any proceeding under this chapter, or has testified or is about to testify in any proceeding resulting from the administration or enforcement of the provisions of this chapter.

(b) Administrative grievance procedure in cases of alleged violations

Any employee or a representative of employees who believes that he has been fired or otherwise discriminated against by any person in violation of subsection (a) of this section may, within thirty days after such alleged violation occurs, apply to the Secretary of Labor for a review of such firing or alleged discrimination. A copy of the application shall be sent to such person, who shall be the respondent. Upon receipt of such application, the Secretary of Labor shall cause such investigation to be made as he deems appropriate. Such investigation shall provide an opportunity for a public hearing at the request of any party to such review to enable the parties to present information relating to such alleged violation. The parties shall be given written notice of the time and place of the hearing at least five days prior to the hearing. Any such hearing shall be of record and shall be subject to section 554 of Title 5. Upon receiving the report of such investigation, the Secretary of Labor shall make findings of fact. If he finds that such violation did occur, he shall issue a decision, incorporating an order therein and his findings, requiring the party committing such violation to take such affirmative action to abate the violation as the Secretary of Labor deems appropriate, including, but not limited to, the rehiring or reinstatement of the employee or representative of employees to his former position with compensation. If he finds that there was no such violation, he shall issue an order denying the application. Such order issued by the Secretary of Labor under this subparagraph shall be subject to judicial review in the same manner as orders and decisions are subject to judicial review under this chapter.

(c) Assessment of costs and expenses against violator subsequent to issuance of order of abatement

Whenever an order is issued under this section to abate such violation, at the request of the applicant a sum equal to the aggregate amount of all costs and expenses (including the attorney's fees) determined by the Secretary of Labor to have been reasonably incurred by the applicant for, or in connection with, the institution and prosecution of such proceedings, shall be assessed against the person committing such violation.

(d) Defenses

This section shall have no application to any employee who acting without discretion from his employer (or his agent) deliberately violates any requirement of this chapter.

(e) Presidential evaluations of potential loss of shifts of employment resulting from administration or enforcement of provisions; investigations; procedures applicable, etc.

The President shall conduct continuing evaluations of potential loss of shifts of employment which may result from the administration or enforcement of the provisions of this chapter, including, where appropriate, investigating threatened plant closures or reductions in employment allegedly resulting from such administration or enforcement. Any employee who is discharged, or laid off, threatened with discharge or layoff, or otherwise discriminated against by any person because of the alleged results of such administration or enforcement, or any representative of such employee, may request the President to conduct a full investigation of the matter and, at the request of any party, shall hold public hearings, require the parties, including the employer involved, to present information relating to the actual or potential effect of such administration or enforcement on employment and any alleged discharge, layoff, or other discrimination, and the detailed reasons or justification therefore.

Any such hearing shall be of record and shall be subject to section 554 of Title 5. Upon receiving the report of such investigation, the President shall make findings of fact as to the effect of such administration or enforcement on employment and on the alleged discharge, layoff, or discrimination and shall make such recommendations as he deems appropriate. Such report, findings, and recommendations shall be available to the public. Nothing in this subsection shall be construed to require or authorize the President or any State to modify or withdraw any action, standard, limitation, or any other requirement of this chapter.

(Dec. 11, 1980, Pub.L. 96–510, Title I, § 110, 94 Stat. 2787.)

CODE OF FEDERAL REGULATIONS

Grants and other federal assistance, see 40 CFR 30.100 et seq.

LIBRARY REFERENCES

Health and Environment ⚷25.6(3), 25.7(3).
C.J.S. Health and Environment §§ 92, 106.

§ 9611. Use of Fund [CERCLA § 111]

(a) In general

For the purposes specified in this section there is authorized to be appropriated from the Hazardous Substance Superfund established under subchapter A of chapter 98 of Title 26 not more than $8,500,000,000 for the 5-year period beginning on October 17, 1986, and not more than $5,100,000,000 for the period commencing October 1, 1991, and ending September 30, 1994, and such sums shall remain available until expended. The preceding sentence constitutes a specific authorization for the funds appropriated under title II of Public Law 99–160 (relating to payment to the Hazardous Substances Trust Fund). The President shall use the money in the Fund for the following purposes:

(1) Payment of governmental response costs incurred pursuant to section 9604 of this title, including costs incurred pursuant to the Intervention on the High Seas Act [33 U.S.C.A. § 1471 et seq.].

(2) Payment of any claim for necessary response costs incurred by any other person as a result of carrying out the national contingency plan established under section 1321(c) of Title 33 and amended by section 9605 of this title: *Provided, however,* That such costs must be approved under said plan and certified by the responsible Federal official.

(3) Payment of any claim authorized by subsection (b) of this section and finally decided pursuant to section 9612 of this title, including those costs set out in subsection 9612(c)(3) of this title.

(4) Payment of costs specified under subsection (c) of this section.

(5) Grants for technical assistance

The cost of grants under section 9617(e) of this title (relating to public participation grants for technical assistance).

(6) Lead contaminated soil

Payment of not to exceed $15,000,000 for the costs of a pilot program for removal, decontamination, or other action with respect to lead-contaminated soil in one to three different metropolitan areas.

The President shall not pay for any administrative costs or expenses out of the Fund unless such costs and expenses are reasonably necessary for and incidental to the implementation of this subchapter.

(b) Additional authorized purposes

(1) In general

Claims asserted and compensable but unsatisfied under provisions of section 1321 of Title 33, which are modified by section 304 of this Act may be asserted against the Fund under this subchapter; and other claims resulting from a release or threat of release of a hazardous substance from a vessel or a facility may be asserted against the Fund under this subchapter for injury to, or destruction or loss of, natural resources, including cost for damage assessment: *Provided, however,* That any such claim may be asserted only by the President, as trustee, for natural resources over which the United States has sovereign rights, or natural resources within the territory or the fishery conservation zone of the United States to the extent they are managed or protected by the United States, or by any State for natural resources within the boundary of that State belonging to, managed by, controlled by, or appertaining to the State, or by any Indian tribe or by the United States acting on behalf of any Indian tribe for natural resources belonging to, managed by, controlled by, or appertaining to such tribe, or held in trust for the benefit of such tribe, or belonging to a member of such tribe if such resources are subject to a trust restriction on alienation.

(2) Limitation on payment of natural resource claims

(A) General requirements

No natural resource claim may be paid from the Fund unless the President determines that the claimant has exhausted all administrative and judicial remedies to recover the amount of such claim from persons who may be liable under section 9607 of this title.

(B) Definition

As used in this paragraph, the term "natural resource claim" means any claim for injury to, or destruction or loss of, natural resources. The term does not include any claim for the costs of natural resource damage assessment.

(c) Peripheral matters and limitations

Uses of the Fund under subsection (a) of this section include—

(1) The costs of assessing both short-term and long-term injury to, destruction of, or loss of any natural resources resulting from a release of a hazardous substance.

(2) The costs of Federal or State or Indian tribe efforts in the restoration, rehabilitation, or replacement or acquiring the equivalent of any natural resources injured, destroyed, or lost as a result of a release of a hazardous substance.

(3) Subject to such amounts as are provided in appropriation Acts, the costs of a program to identify, investigate, and take enforcement and abatement action against releases of hazardous substances.

(4) Any costs incurred in accordance with subsection (m) of this section (relating to ATSDR) and section 9604(i) of this title, including the costs of epidemiologic and laboratory studies, health assessments, preparation of toxicologic profiles, development and maintenance of a registry of persons exposed to hazardous substances to allow long-term health effect studies, and diagnostic services not otherwise available to determine whether persons in populations exposed to hazardous substances in connection with a release or a suspected release are suffering from long-latency diseases.

(5) Subject to such amounts as are provided in appropriation Acts, the costs of providing equipment and similar overhead, related to the purposes of this chapter and section 1321 of Title 33, and needed to supplement equipment and services available through contractors or other non-Federal entities, and of establishing and maintaining damage assessment capability, for any Federal agency involved in strike forces, emergency task forces, or other response teams under the national contingency plan.

(6) Subject to such amounts as are provided in appropriation Acts, the costs of a program to protect the health and safety of employees involved in response to hazardous substance releases. Such program shall be developed jointly by the Environmental Protection Agency, the Occupational Safety and Health Administration, and the National Institute for Occupational Safety and Health and shall include, but not be limited to, measures for identifying and assessing hazards to which persons engaged in removal, remedy, or other response to hazardous substances may be exposed, methods to protect workers from such hazards, and necessary regulatory and enforcement measures to assure adequate protection of such employees.

(7) Evaluation costs under petition provisions of section 9605(d)

Costs incurred by the President in evaluating facilities pursuant to petitions under section 9605(d) of this title (relating to petitions for assessment of release).

(8) Contract costs under section 9604(a)(1)

The costs of contracts or arrangements entered into under section 9604(a)(1) of this title to oversee and review the conduct of remedial investigations and feasibility studies undertaken by persons other than the President and the costs of appropriate Federal and State oversight of remedial activities at National Priorities List sites resulting from consent orders or settlement agreements.

(9) Acquisition costs under section 9604(j)

The costs incurred by the President in acquiring real estate or interests in real estate under section 9604(j) of this title (relating to acquisition of property).

(10) Research, development, and demonstration costs under section 9660

The cost of carrying out section 9660a of this title (relating to research, development, and demonstration), except that the amounts available for such purposes shall not exceed the amounts specified in subsection (n) of this section.

(11) Local government reimbursement

Reimbursements to local governments under section 9623 of this title, except that during the 8-fiscal year period beginning October 1, 1986, not more than 0.1 percent of the total amount appropriated from the Fund may be used for such reimbursements.

(12) Worker training and education grants

The costs of grants under section 9660a of this title for training and education of workers to the extent that such costs do not exceed $20,000,000 for each of the fiscal years 1987, 1988, 1989, 1990, 1991, 1992, 1993, and 1994.

(13) Awards under section 9609

The costs of any awards granted under section 9609(d) of this title.

(14) Lead poisoning study

The cost of carrying out the study under subsection (f) of section 118 of the Superfund Amendments and Reauthorization Act of 1986 [42 U.S.C.A. § 6981 note] (relating to lead poisoning in children).

(d) Additional limitations

(1) No money in the Fund may be used under subsection (c)(1) and (2) of this section, nor for the payment of any claim under subsection (b) of this section, where the injury, destruction, or loss of natural resources and the release of a hazardous substance from which such damages resulted have occurred wholly before December 11, 1980.

(2) No money in the Fund may be used for the payment of any claim under subsection (b) of this section where such expenses are associated with injury or loss resulting from long-term exposure to ambient concentrations of air pollutants from multiple or diffuse sources.

(e) Funding requirements respecting moneys in Fund; limitation on certain claims; Fund use outside Federal property boundaries

(1) Claims against or presented to the Fund shall not be valid or paid in excess of the total money in the Fund at any one time. Such claims become valid only when additional money is collected, appropriated, or otherwise added to the Fund. Should the total claims outstanding at any time exceed the current balance of the Fund, the President shall pay such claims, to the extent authorized under this section, in full in the order in which they were finally determined.

(2) In any fiscal year, 85 percent of the money credited to the Fund under subchapter II of this chapter shall be available only for the purposes specified in paragraphs (1), (2), and (4) of subsection (a) of this section. No money in the Fund may be used for the payment of any claim under subsection (a)(3) or subsection (b) of this section in any fiscal year for which the President determines that all of the Fund is needed for response to threats to public health from releases or threatened releases of hazardous substances.

(3) No money in the Fund shall be available for remedial action, other than actions specified in subsection (c) of this section, with respect to federally owned facilities; except that money in the Fund shall be available for the provision of alternative water supplies (including the reimbursement of costs incurred by a municipality) in any case involving groundwater contamination outside the boundaries of a federally owned facility in which the federally owned facility is not the only potentially responsible party.

(4) Paragraphs (1) and (4) of subsection (a) of this section shall in the aggregate be subject to such amounts as are provided in appropriation Acts.

(f) Obligation of moneys by Federal officials; obligation of moneys or settlement of claims by State officials or Indian tribe

The President is authorized to promulgate regulations designating one or more Federal officials who may obligate money in the Fund in accordance with this section or portions thereof. The President is also authorized to delegate authority to obligate money in the Fund or to settle claims to officials of a State or Indian tribe operating under a contract or cooperative agreement with the Federal Government pursuant to section 9604(d) of this title.

(g) Notice to potential injured parties by owner and operator of vessel or facility causing release of substance; rules and regulations

The President shall provide for the promulgation of rules and regulations with respect to the notice to be provided to potential injured parties by an owner and operator of any vessel, or facility from which a hazardous substance has been released. Such rules and regulations shall consider the scope and form of the notice which would be appropriate to carry out the purposes of this subchapter. Upon promulgation of such rules and regulations, the owner and operator of any vessel or facility from which a hazardous substance has been released shall provide notice in accordance with such rules and regulations. With respect to releases from public vessels, the President shall provide such notification as is appropriate to potential injured parties. Until the promulgation of such rules and regulations, the owner and operator of any vessel or facility from which a hazardous substance has been released shall provide reasonable notice to potential injured parties by publication in local newspapers serving the affected area.

(h) Repealed. Pub.L. 99–499, Title I, § 111(c)(2), Oct. 17, 1986, 100 Stat. 1643

(i) Restoration, etc., of natural resources

Except in a situation requiring action to avoid an irreversible loss of natural resources or to prevent or reduce any continuing danger to natural resources or similar need for emergency action, funds may not be used under this chapter for the restoration, rehabilitation, or replacement or acquisition of the equivalent of any natural resources until a plan for the use of such funds for such purposes has been developed and adopted by affected Federal agencies and the Governor or Governors of any State having sustained damage to natural resources within its borders, belonging to, managed by or appertaining to such State, and by the governing body of any Indian tribe having sustained damage to natural resources belonging to, managed by, controlled by, or appertaining to such tribe, or held in trust for the benefit of such tribe, or belonging to a member of such tribe if such resources are subject to a trust restriction on alienation, after adequate public notice and opportunity for hearing and consideration of all public comment.

(j) Use of Post-closure Liability Fund

The President shall use the money in the Post-closure Liability Fund for any of the purposes specified in subsection (a) of this section with respect to a hazardous waste disposal facility for which liability has transferred to such fund under section 9607(k) of this title, and, in addition, for payment of any claim or appropriate request for costs of response, damages, or other compensation for injury or loss under section 9607 of this title or any other State or Federal law, resulting from a release of a hazardous substance from such a facility.

(k) Inspector General

In each fiscal year, the Inspector General of each department, agency, or instrumentality of the United States which is carrying out any authority of this chapter shall conduct an annual audit of all payments, obligations, reimbursements, or other uses of the Fund in the prior fiscal year, to assure that the Fund is being properly administered and that claims are being appropriately and expeditiously considered. The audit shall include an examination of a sample of agreements with States (in accordance with the provisions of the Single Audit Act [31 U.S.C.A. 7501 et seq.]) carrying out response actions under this subchapter and an examination of remedial investigations and feasibility studies prepared for remedial actions. The Inspector General shall submit to the Congress an annual report regarding the audit report required under this subsection. The report shall contain such recommendations as the Inspector General deems appropriate. Each department, agency, or instrumentality of the United States shall cooperate with its inspector general in carrying out this subsection.

(*l*) Foreign claimants

To the extent that the provisions of this chapter permit, a foreign claimant may assert a claim to the same extent that a United States claimant may assert a claim if—

(1) the release of a hazardous substance occurred (A) in the navigable waters or (B) in or on the territorial sea or adjacent shoreline of a foreign country of which the claimant is a resident;

(2) the claimant is not otherwise compensated for his loss;

(3) the hazardous substance was released from a facility or from a vessel located adjacent to or within the navigable waters or was discharged in connection with activities conducted under the Outer Continental Shelf Lands Act, as amended (43 U.S.C. 1331 et seq.) or the Deepwater Port Act of 1974, as amended (33 U.S.C. 1501 et seq.); and

(4) recovery is authorized by a treaty or an executive agreement between the United States and foreign country involved, or if the Secretary of State, in consultation with the Attorney General and other appropriate officials, certifies that such country provides a comparable remedy for United States claimants.

(m) Agency for Toxic Substances and Disease Registry

There shall be directly available to the Agency for Toxic Substances and Disease Registry to be used for the purpose of carrying out activities described in subsection (c)(4) of this section and section 9604(i) of this title not less than $50,000,000 per fiscal year for each of fiscal years 1987 and 1988, not less than $55,000,000 for fiscal year 1989, and not less than $60,000,000 per fiscal year for each of fiscal years 1990, 1991, 1992, 1993, and 1994. Any funds so made available which are not obligated by the end of the fiscal year in which made available shall be returned to the Fund.

(n) Limitations on research, development, and demonstration program

(1) Section 9660(b)

For each of the fiscal years 1987, 1988, 1989, 1990, 1991, 1992, 1993, and 1994, not more than $20,000,000 of the amounts available in the Fund may be used for the purposes of carrying out the applied research, development, and demonstration program for alternative or innovative technologies and training program authorized under section 9660(b) of this title (relating to research, development, and demonstration) other than basic research. Such amounts shall remain available until expended.

(2) Section 9660(a)

From the amounts available in the Fund, not more than the following amounts may be used for the purposes of section 9660(a) of this title (relating to hazardous substance research, demonstration, and training activities):

(A) For the fiscal year 1987, $3,000,000.

(B) For the fiscal year 1988, $10,000,000.

(C) For the fiscal year 1989, $20,000,000.

(D) For the fiscal year 1990, $30,000,000.

(E) For each of the fiscal years 1991, 1992, 1993, and 1994, $35,000,000.

No more than 10 percent of such amounts shall be used for training under section 9660(a) of this title in any fiscal year.

(3) Section 9660(d)

For each of the fiscal years 1987, 1988, 1989, 1990, 1991, 1992, 1993, and 1994, not more than $5,000,000 of the amounts available in the Fund may be used for the purposes of section 9660(d) of this title (relating to university hazardous substance research centers).

(*o*) Notification procedures for limitations on certain payments

Not later than 90 days after October 17, 1986, the President shall develop and implement procedures to adequately notify, as soon as practicable after a site is included on the National Priorities List, concerned local and State officials and other concerned persons of the limitations, set forth in subsection (a)(2) of this section, on the payment of claims for necessary response costs incurred with respect to such site.

(p) General revenue share of Superfund

(1) In general

The following sums are authorized to be appropriated, out of any money in the Treasury not otherwise appropriated, to the Hazardous Substance Superfund:

(A) For fiscal year 1987, $212,500,000.
(B) For fiscal year 1988, $212,500,000.
(C) For fiscal year 1989, $212,500,000.
(D) For fiscal year 1990, $212,500,000.
(E) For fiscal year 1991, $212,500,000.
(F) For fiscal year 1992, $212,500,000.
(G) For fiscal year 1993, $212,500,000.
(H) For fiscal year 1994, $212,500,000.

In addition there is authorized to be appropriated to the Hazardous Substance Superfund for each fiscal year an amount equal to so much of the aggregate amount authorized to be appropriated under this subsection (and paragraph (2) of section 9631(b) of this title) as has not been appropriated before the beginning of the fiscal year involved.

(2) Computation

The amounts authorized to be appropriated under paragraph (1) of this subsection in a given fiscal year shall be available only to the extent that such amount exceeds the amount determined by the Secretary under section 9507(b)(2) of Title 26 for the prior fiscal year.

(Dec. 11, 1980, Pub.L. 96–510, Title I, § 111, 94 Stat. 2788; Oct. 17, 1986, Pub.L. 99–499, Title I, § 111, Title II, § 207(d), 100 Stat. 1642, 1706; Pub.L. 101–144, Title III, Nov. 9, 1989, 103 Stat. 857; Nov. 5, 1990, Pub.L. 101–508, Title VI, § 6301, 104 Stat. 1388–319.)

CROSS REFERENCES

Solid Waste Disposal Act, financial responsibility provisions under as not diminishing liabilities of persons under this section, see sections 6924(t)(3), 6991b(d)(3), and 6991c(c)(4) of this title.

CODE OF FEDERAL REGULATIONS

Grants and other federal assistance, see 40 CFR 30.100 et seq.

LAW REVIEW COMMENTARIES

Cost recovery by private parties under CERCLA: Planning a response action for maximum recovery. Arnold W. Reitze, Jr., Andrew J. Harrison, Jr., and Monica J. Palko, 27 Tulsa L.J. 365 (1992).

Direct liability for hazardous substance cleanups under CERCLA: A comprehensive approach. Michael P. Healy, 42 Case W.Res.L.Rev. 65 (1992).

Hazardous wastes in New Jersey: An overview. Anne F. Morris, 38 Rutgers L.Rev. 623 (1986).

Interaction of the Bankruptcy Code and environmental laws: Grit, the grind, and the grease. Robert R. Graves, 29 Willamette L.Rev. 297 (1993).

Property owner liability for environmental contamination in California. Michael B. Hingerty, 22 U.S.F.L.Rev. 31 (1987).

Toxic tort litigation and the causation element: Is there any hope of reconciliation? Ora Fred Harris, Jr., 40 Southwestern (Tex.) L.J. 909 (1986).

Toxic waste: Who pays the piper? A private party's federal and Texas rights to recovery of voluntary cleanup costs of toxic waste. Barbara Hanson Nellermoe, 20 St. Mary's L.J. 339 (1989).

LIBRARY REFERENCES

Health and Environment ⚷25.6(3), 25.7(3).
C.J.S. Health and Environment §§ 92, 106.

§ 9612. Claims procedure [CERCLA § 112]

(a) Claims against the Fund for response costs

No claim may be asserted against the Fund pursuant to section 9611(a) of this title unless such claim is presented in the first instance to the owner, operator, or guarantor of the vessel or facility from which a hazardous substance has been released, if known to the claimant, and to any other person known to the claimant who may be liable under section 9607 of this title. In any case where the claim has not been satisfied within 60 days of presentation in accordance with this subsection, the claimant may present the claim to the Fund for payment. No claim against the Fund may be approved or certified during the pendency of an action by the claimant in court to recover costs which are the subject of the claim.

(b) Forms and procedures applicable

(1) Prescribing forms and procedures

The President shall prescribe appropriate forms and procedures for claims filed hereunder, which shall include a provision requiring the claimant to make a sworn verification of the claim to the best of his knowledge. Any person who knowingly gives or causes to be given any false information as a part of any such claim shall, upon conviction, be fined in accordance with the applicable provisions of Title 18 or imprisoned for not more than 3 years (or not more than 5 years in the case of a second or subsequent conviction), or both.

(2) Payment or request for hearing

The President may, if satisfied that the information developed during the processing of the claim warrants it, make and pay an award of the claim, except that no claim may be awarded to the extent that a judicial judgment has been made on the costs that are the subject of the claim. If the President declines to pay all or part of the claim, the claimant may, within 30 days after receiving notice of the President's decision, request an administrative hearing.

(3) Burden of proof

In any proceeding under this subsection, the claimant shall bear the burden of proving his claim.

(4) Decisions

All administrative decisions made hereunder shall be in writing, with notification to all appropriate parties, and shall be rendered within 90 days of submission of a claim to an administrative law judge, unless all the parties to the claim agree in writing to an extension or unless the President, in his discretion, extends the time limit for a period not to exceed sixty days.

(5) Finality and appeal

All administrative decisions hereunder shall be final, and any party to the proceeding may appeal a decision within 30 days of notification of the award or decision. Any such appeal shall be made to the Federal district court for the district where the release or threat of release took place. In any such appeal, the decision shall be considered binding and conclusive, and shall not be overturned except for arbitrary or capricious abuse of discretion.

(6) Payment

Within 20 days after the expiration of the appeal period for any administrative decision concerning an award, or within 20 days after the final judicial determination of any appeal taken pursuant to this subsection, the President shall pay any such award from the Fund. The President shall determine the method, terms, and time of payment.

(c) Subrogation rights; actions maintainable

(1) Payment of any claim by the Fund under this section shall be subject to the United States Government acquiring by subrogation the rights of the claimant to recover those costs of removal or damages for which it has compensated the claimant from the person responsible or liable for such release.

(2) Any person, including the Fund, who pays compensation pursuant to this chapter to any claimant for damages or costs resulting from a release of a hazardous substance shall be subrogated to all rights, claims, and causes of action for such damages and costs of removal that the claimant has under this chapter or any other law.

(3) Upon request of the President, the Attorney General shall commence an action on behalf of the Fund to recover any compensation paid by the Fund to any claimant pursuant to this subchapter, and, without regard to any limitation of liability, all interest, administrative and adjudicative costs, and attorney's fees incurred by the Fund by reason of the claim. Such an action may be commenced against any owner, operator, or guarantor, or against any other person who is liable, pursuant to any law, to the compensated claimant or to the Fund, for the damages or costs for which compensation was paid.

(d) Statute of limitations

(1) Claims for recovery of costs

No claim may be presented under this section for recovery of the costs referred to in section 9607(a) of this title after the date 6 years after the date of completion of all response action.

(2) Claims for recovery of damages

No claim may be presented under this section for recovery of the damages referred to in section 9607(a) of this title unless the claim is presented within 3 years after the later of the following:

(A) The date of the discovery of the loss and its connection with the release in question.

(B) The date on which final regulations are promulgated under section 9651(c) of this title.

(3) Minors and incompetents

The time limitations contained herein shall not begin to run—

(A) against a minor until the earlier of the date when such minor reaches 18 years of age or the date on which a legal representative is duly appointed for the minor, or

(B) against an incompetent person until the earlier of the date on which such person's incompetency ends or the date on which a legal representative is duly appointed for such incompetent person.

(e) Other statutory or common law claims not waived, etc.

Regardless of any State statutory or common law to the contrary, no person who asserts a claim against the Fund pursuant to this subchapter shall be deemed or held to have waived any other claim not covered or assertable against the Fund under this subchapter arising from the same incident, transaction, or set of circumstances, nor to have split a cause of action. Further, no person asserting a claim against the Fund pursuant to this subchapter shall as a result of any determination of a question of fact or law made in connection with that claim be deemed or held to be collaterally estopped from raising such question in connection with any other claim not covered or assertable against the Fund under this subchapter arising from the same incident, transaction, or set of circumstances.

(f) Double recovery prohibited

Where the President has paid out of the Fund for any response costs or any costs specified under section 9611(c)(1) or (2) of this title, no other claim may be paid out of the Fund for the same costs.

(Dec. 11, 1980, Pub.L. 96–510, Title I, § 112, 94 Stat. 2792; Oct. 17, 1986, Pub.L. 99–499, Title I, §§ 109(a)(3), 112, 100 Stat. 1633, 1646.)

WEST'S FEDERAL FORMS

Administrative subpenas, enforcement of, see § 5901 et seq.

LIBRARY REFERENCES

Health and Environment ⚷25.6(3), 25.7(3).
C.J.S. Health and Environment §§ 92, 106.

§ 9613. Civil proceedings [CERCLA § 113]

(a) Review of regulations in Circuit Court of Appeals of the United States for the District of Columbia

Review of any regulation promulgated under this chapter may be had upon application by any interested person only in the Circuit Court of Appeals of the United States for the District of Columbia. Any such application shall be made within ninety days from the date of promulgation of such regulations. Any matter with respect to which review could have been obtained under this subsection shall not be subject to judicial review in any civil or criminal proceeding for enforcement or to obtain damages or recovery of response costs.

(b) Jurisdiction; venue

Except as provided in subsections (a) and (h) of this section, the United States district courts shall have exclusive original jurisdiction over all controversies arising under this chapter, without regard to the citizenship of the parties or the amount in controversy. Venue shall lie in any district in which the release or damages occurred, or in which the defendant resides, may be found, or has his principal office. For the purposes of this section, the Fund shall reside in the District of Columbia.

(c) Controversies or other matters resulting from tax collection or tax regulation review

The provisions of subsections (a) and (b) of this section shall not apply to any controversy or other matter resulting from the assessment of collection of any tax, as provided by subchapter II of this chapter, or to the review of any regulation promulgated under Title 26.

(d) Litigation commenced prior to December 11, 1980

No provision of this chapter shall be deemed or held to moot any litigation concerning any release of any hazardous substance, or any damages associated therewith, commenced prior to December 11, 1980.

(e) Nationwide service of process

In any action by the United States under this chapter, process may be served in any district where the defendant is found, resides, transacts business, or has appointed an agent for the service of process.

(f) Contribution

(1) Contribution

Any person may seek contribution from any other person who is liable or potentially liable under section 9607(a) of this title, during or following any civil action under section 9606 of this title or under section 9607(a) of this title. Such claims shall be brought in accordance with this section and the Federal Rules of Civil Procedure, and shall be governed by Federal law. In resolving contribution claims, the court may allocate response costs among liable parties using such equitable factors as the court determines are appropriate. Nothing in this subsection shall diminish the right of any person to bring an action for contribution in the absence of a civil action under section 9606 of this title or section 9607 of this title.

(2) Settlement

A person who has resolved its liability to the United States or a State in an administrative or judicially approved settlement shall not be liable for claims for contribution regarding matters addressed in the settlement. Such settlement does not discharge any of the other potentially liable persons unless its terms so provide, but it reduces the potential liability of the others by the amount of the settlement.

(3) Persons not party to settlement

(A) If the United States or a State has obtained less than complete relief from a person who has resolved its liability to the United States or the State in an administrative or judicially approved settlement, the United States or the State may bring an action against any person who has not so resolved its liability.

(B) A person who has resolved its liability to the United States or a State for some or all of a response action or for some or all of the costs of such action in an administrative or judicially approved settlement may seek contribution from any person who is not party to a settlement referred to in paragraph (2).

(C) In any action under this paragraph, the rights of any person who has resolved its liability to the United States or a State shall be subordinate to the rights of the United States or the State. Any contribution action brought under this paragraph shall be governed by Federal law.

(g) Period in which action may be brought

(1) Actions for natural resource damages

Except as provided in paragraphs (3) and (4), no action may be commenced for damages (as defined in section 9601(6) of this title) under this chapter, unless that action is commenced within 3 years after the later of the following:

(A) The date of the discovery of the loss and its connection with the release in question.

(B) The date on which regulations are promulgated under section 9651(c) of this title.

With respect to any facility listed on the National Priorities List (NPL), any Federal facility identified under section 9620 of this title (relating to Federal facilities), or any vessel or facility at which a remedial action under this chapter is otherwise scheduled, an action for damages under this chapter must be commenced within 3 years after the completion of the remedial action (excluding operation and maintenance activities) in lieu of the dates referred to in subparagraph (A) or (B). In no event may an action for damages under this chapter with respect to such a vessel or facility be commenced (i) prior to 60 days after the Federal or State natural resource trustee provides to the President and the potentially responsible party a notice of intent to file suit, or (ii) before selection of the remedial action if the President is diligently proceeding with a remedial investigation and feasibility study under section 9604(b) of this title or section 9620 of this title (relating to Federal facilities). The limitation in the preceding sentence on commencing an action before giving notice or before selection of the remedial action does not apply to actions filed on or before October 17, 1986.

(2) Actions for recovery of costs

An initial action for recovery of the costs referred to in section 9607 of this title must be commenced—

(A) for a removal action, within 3 years after completion of the removal action, except that such cost recovery action must be brought within 6 years after a determination to grant a waiver under section 9604(c)(1)(C) of this title for continued response action; and

(B) for a remedial action, within 6 years after initiation of physical on-site construction of the remedial action, except that, if the remedial action is initiated within 3 years after the completion of the removal action, costs incurred in the removal action may be recovered in the cost recovery action brought under this subparagraph.

In any such action described in this subsection, the court shall enter a declaratory judgment on liability for response costs or damages that will be binding on any subsequent action or actions to recover further response costs or damages. A subsequent action or actions under section 9607 of this title for further response costs at the vessel or facility may be maintained at any time during the response action, but must be commenced no later than 3 years after the date of completion of all response action. Except as otherwise provided in this paragraph, an action may be commenced under section 9607 of this title for recovery of costs at any time after such costs have been incurred.

(3) Contribution

No action for contribution for any response costs or damages may be commenced more than 3 years after—

(A) the date of judgment in any action under this chapter for recovery of such costs or damages, or

(B) the date of an administrative order under section 9622(g) of this title (relating to de minimis settlements) or 9622(h) of this title (relating to cost recovery settlements) or entry of a judicially approved settlement with respect to such costs or damages.

(4) Subrogation

No action based on rights subrogated pursuant to this section by reason of payment of a claim may be commenced under this subchapter more than 3 years after the date of payment of such claim.

(5) Actions to recover indemnification payments

Notwithstanding any other provision of this subsection, where a payment pursuant to an indemnification agreement with a response action contractor is made under section 9619 of this title, an action under section 9607 of this title for recovery of such indemnification payment from a potentially responsible party may be brought at any time before the expiration of 3 years from the date on which such payment is made.

(6) Minors and incompetents

The time limitations contained herein shall not begin to run—

(A) against a minor until the earlier of the date when such minor reaches 18 years of age or the date on which a legal representative is duly appointed for such minor, or

(B) against an incompetent person until the earlier of the date on which such incompetent's incompetency ends or the date on which a legal representative is duly appointed for such incompetent.

(h) Timing of review

No Federal court shall have jurisdiction under Federal law other than under section 1332 of Title 28 (relating to diversity of citizenship jurisdiction) or under State law which is applicable or relevant and appropriate under section 9621 of this title (relating to cleanup standards) to review any challenges to removal or remedial action selected under section 9604 of this title, or to review any order issued under section 9606(a) of this title, in any action except one of the following:

(1) An action under section 9607 of this title to recover response costs or damages or for contribution.

(2) An action to enforce an order issued under section 9606(a) of this title or to recover a penalty for violation of such order.

(3) An action for reimbursement under section 9606(b)(2) of this title.

(4) An action under section 9659 of this title (relating to citizens suits) alleging that the removal or remedial action taken under section 9604 of this title or secured under section 9606 of this title was in violation of any requirement of this chapter. Such an action may not be brought with regard to a removal where a remedial action is to be undertaken at the site.

(5) An action under section 9606 of this title in which the United States has moved to compel a remedial action.

(i) Intervention

In any action commenced under this chapter or under the Solid Waste Disposal Act [42 U.S.C.A. § 6901 et seq.] in a court of the United States, any person may intervene as a matter of right when such person claims an interest relating to the subject of the action and is so situated that the disposition of the action may, as a practical matter, impair or impede the person's ability to protect that interest, unless the President or the State shows that the person's interest is adequately represented by existing parties.

(j) Judicial review

(1) Limitation

In any judicial action under this chapter, judicial review of any issues concerning the adequacy of any response action taken or ordered by the President shall be limited to the administrative record. Otherwise applicable principles of administrative law shall govern whether any supplemental materials may be considered by the court.

(2) Standard

In considering objections raised in any judicial action under this chapter, the court shall uphold the President's decision in selecting the response action unless the objecting party can demonstrate, on the administrative record, that the decision was arbitrary and capricious or otherwise not in accordance with law.

(3) Remedy

If the court finds that the selection of the response action was arbitrary and capricious or otherwise not in accordance with law, the court shall award (A) only the response costs or damages that are not inconsistent with the National Contingency Plan, and (B) such other relief as is consistent with the National Contingency Plan.

(4) Procedural errors

In reviewing alleged procedural errors, the court may disallow costs or damages only if the errors were so serious and related to matters of such central relevance to the action that the action would have been significantly changed had such errors not been made.

(k) Administrative record and participation procedures

(1) Administrative record

The President shall establish an administrative record upon which the President shall base the selection of a response action. The administrative record shall be available to the public at or near the facility at issue. The President also may place duplicates of the administrative record at any other location.

(2) Participation procedures

(A) Removal action

The President shall promulgate regulations in accordance with chapter 5 of Title 5 establishing procedures for the appropriate participation of interested persons in the development of the administrative record on which the President will base the selection of removal actions and on which judicial review of removal actions will be based.

(B) Remedial action

The President shall provide for the participation of interested persons, including potentially responsible parties, in the development of the administrative record on which the President will base the selection of remedial actions and on which judicial review of remedial actions will be based. The procedures developed under this subparagraph shall include, at a minimum, each of the following:

(i) Notice to potentially affected persons and the public, which shall be accompanied by a brief analysis of the plan and alternative plans that were considered.

(ii) A reasonable opportunity to comment and provide information regarding the plan.

(iii) An opportunity for a public meeting in the affected area, in accordance with section 9617(a)(2) of this title (relating to public participation).

(iv) A response to each of the significant comments, criticisms, and new data submitted in written or oral presentations.

(v) A statement of the basis and purpose of the selected action.

For purposes of this subparagraph, the administrative record shall include all items developed and received under this subparagraph and all items described in the second sentence of section 9617(d) of this title. The President shall promulgate regulations in accordance with chapter 5 of Title 5 to carry out the requirements of this subparagraph.

(C) Interim record

Until such regulations under subparagraphs (A) and (B) are promulgated, the administrative record shall consist of all items developed and received pursuant to current procedures for selection of the response action, including procedures for the participation of interested parties and the public. The development of an administrative record and the selection of response action under this chapter shall not include an adjudicatory hearing.

(D) Potentially responsible parties

The President shall make reasonable efforts to identify and notify potentially responsible parties as early as possible before selection of a response action. Nothing in this paragraph shall be construed to be a defense to liability.

(*l*) Notice of actions

Whenever any action is brought under this chapter in a court of the United States by a plaintiff other than the United States, the plaintiff shall provide a copy of the complaint to the Attorney General of the United States and to the Administrator of the Environmental Protection Agency.

(Dec. 11, 1980, Pub.L. 96–510, Title I, § 113, 94 Stat. 2795; Oct. 17, 1986, Pub.L. 99–499, Title I, § 113, 100 Stat. 1647.)

CODE OF FEDERAL REGULATIONS

Grants and other federal assistance, see 40 CFR 30.100 et seq.

LAW REVIEW COMMENTARIES

Ability of CERCLA defendants to challenge cost-effectiveness of government cleanups. Daniel W. Coffey, 65 N.Y.S.B.J. 42 (Mar./Apr. 1993).

Bankruptcy versus environmental protection: Discharging future CERCLA liability in Chapter 11. Note, 14 Cardozo L.Rev. 1999 (1993).

Enforcing environmental indemnification against a settling party under CERCLA. Daniel R. Avery, 23 Seton Hall L.Rev. 872 (1993).

Environmental liability and the limits of insurance. Kenneth S. Abraham, 88 Columbia L.Rev. 942 (1988).

Insurance coverage for superfund liability: A plain meaning approach to the pollution exclusion clause. Note, 27 Washburn L.J. 161 (1987).

Insurance industry's 1970 pollution exclusion: An exercise in ambiguity. John S. Vishneski, III, Todd G. Zimmerman, Robert A. Creamer, and Judith N. Levi, 23 Loy.U.Chi.L.J. 25 (1991).

Lender liability dilemma: Fleet Factors history and aftermath. Brent Nicholson and Todd Zuiderhoek, 38 S.D.L.Rev. 22 (1993).

Property owner liability for environmental contamination in California. Michael B. Hingerty, 22 U.S.F.L.Rev. 31 (1987).

LIBRARY REFERENCES

Health and Environment ⚷25.6(3), 25.7(3).
C.J.S. Health and Environment §§ 92, 106.

§ 9614. Relationship to other law [CERCLA § 114]

(a) Additional State liability or requirements with respect to release of substances within State

Nothing in this chapter shall be construed or interpreted as preempting any State from imposing any additional liability or requirements with respect to the release of hazardous substances within such State.

(b) Recovery under other State or Federal law of compensation for removal costs or damages, or payment of claims

Any person who receives compensation for removal costs or damages or claims pursuant to this chapter shall be precluded from recovering compensation for the same removal costs or damages or claims pursuant to any other State or Federal law. Any person who receives compensation for removal costs or damages or claims pursuant to any other Federal or State law shall be precluded from receiving compensation for the same removal costs or damages or claims as provided in this chapter.

(c) Recycled oil

(1) Service station dealers, etc.

No person (including the United States or any State) may recover, under the authority of subsection (a)(3) or (a)(4) of section 9607 of this title, from a service station dealer for any response costs or damages resulting from a release or threatened release of recycled oil, or use the authority of section 9606 of this title against a service station dealer other than a person described in subsection (a)(1) or (a)(2) of section 9607 of this title, if such recycled oil—

(A) is not mixed with any other hazardous substance, and

(B) is stored, treated, transported, or otherwise managed in compliance with regulations or standards promulgated pursuant to section 3014 of the Solid Waste Disposal Act [42 U.S.C.A. § 6935] and other applicable authorities.

Nothing in this paragraph shall affect or modify in any way the obligations or liability of any person under any other provision of State or Federal law, including common law, for damages, injury, or loss resulting from a release or threatened release of any hazardous substance or for removal or remedial action or the costs of removal or remedial action.

(2) Presumption

Solely for the purposes of this subsection, a service station dealer may presume that a small quantity of used oil is not mixed with other hazardous substances if it—

(A) has been removed from the engine of a light duty motor vehicle or household appliances by the owner of such vehicle or appliances, and

(B) is presented, by such owner, to the dealer for collection, accumulation, and delivery to an oil recycling facility.

(3) Definition

For purposes of this subsection, the terms "used oil" and "recycled oil" have the same meanings as set forth in sections 1004(36) and 1004(37) of the Solid Waste Disposal Act [42 U.S.C.A. § 6903(36), (37)] and regulations promulgated pursuant to that Act [42 U.S.C.A. § 6901 et seq.].

(4) Effective date

The effective date of paragraphs (1) and (2) of this subsection shall be the effective date of regulations or standards promulgated under section 3014 of the Solid Waste Disposal Act [42 U.S.C.A. § 6935] that include, among other provisions, a requirement to conduct corrective action to respond to any releases of recycled oil under subtitle C or subtitle I of such Act [42 U.S.C.A. § 6921 et seq. or § 6991 et seq.].

(d) Financial responsibility of owner or operator of vessel or facility under State or local law, rule, or regulation

Except as provided in this subchapter, no owner or operator of a vessel or facility who establishes and maintains evidence of financial responsibility in accordance with this subchapter shall be required under any State or local law, rule, or regulation to establish or maintain any other evidence of financial responsibility in connection with liability for the release of a hazardous substance from such vessel or facility. Evidence of compliance with the financial responsibility requirements of this subchapter shall be accepted by a State in lieu of any other requirement of financial responsibility imposed by such State in connection with liability for the release of a hazardous substance from such vessel or facility.

(Dec. 11, 1980, Pub.L. 96–510, Title I, § 114, 94 Stat. 2795; Oct. 17, 1986, Pub.L. 99–499, Title I, § 114(a), 100 Stat. 1652.)

LAW REVIEW COMMENTARIES

Oil Pollution Act of 1990: Opening a new era in federal and Texas regulation of oil spill prevention, containment and cleanup, and liability. J.B. Ruhl and Michael J. Jewell, 32 S.Tex.L.Rev. 475 (1991).

LIBRARY REFERENCES

Health and Environment ⇐25.6(3), 25.7(3).
C.J.S. Health and Environment §§ 92, 106.

United States Supreme Court

Intention of Congress to prohibit state funds that cover Superfund-eligible expenses, see Exxon Corp. v. Hunt, 1986, 106 S.Ct. 1103, 89 L.Ed.2d 364.

§ 9615. Presidential delegation and assignment of duties or powers and promulgation of regulations [CERCLA § 115]

The President is authorized to delegate and assign any duties or powers imposed upon or assigned to him and to promulgate any regulations necessary to carry out the provisions of this subchapter.

(Dec. 11, 1980, Pub.L. 96–510, Title I, § 115, 94 Stat. 2796.)

LIBRARY REFERENCES

Health and Environment ⇐25.6(3), 25.7(3).
C.J.S. Health and Environment §§ 92, 106.

§ 9616. Schedules [CERCLA § 116]

(a) Assessment and listing of facilities

It shall be a goal of this chapter that, to the maximum extent practicable—

(1) not later than January 1, 1988, the President shall complete preliminary assessments of all facilities that are contained (as of October 17, 1986) on the Comprehensive Environmental Response, Compensation, and Liability Information System (CERCLIS) including in each assessment a statement as to whether a site inspection is necessary and by whom it should be carried out; and

(2) not later than January 1, 1989, the President shall assure the completion of site inspections at all facilities for which the President has stated a site inspection is necessary pursuant to paragraph (1).

(b) Evaluation

Within 4 years after October 17, 1986, each facility listed (as of October 17, 1986) in the CERCLIS shall be evaluated if the President determines that such evaluation is warranted on the basis of a site inspection or preliminary assessment. The evaluation shall be in accordance with the criteria established in section 9605 of this title under the National Contingency Plan for determining priorities among release for inclusion on the National Priorities List. In the case of a facility listed in the CERCLIS after October 17, 1986, the facility shall be evaluated within 4 years after the date of such listing if the President determines that such evaluation is warranted on the basis of a site inspection or preliminary assessment.

(c) Explanations

If any of the goals established by subsection (a) or (b) of this section are not achieved, the President shall publish an explanation of why such action could not be completed by the specified date.

(d) Commencement of RI/FS

The President shall assure that remedial investigations and feasibility studies (RI/FS) are commenced for facilities listed on the National Priorities List, in addition to those commenced prior to October 17, 1986, in accordance with the following schedule:

(1) not fewer than 275 by the date 36 months after October 17, 1986, and

(2) if the requirement of paragraph (1) is not met, not fewer than an additional 175 by the date 4 years after October 17, 1986, an additional 200 by the date 5 years after October 17, 1986, and a total of 650 by the date 5 years after October 17, 1986.

(e) Commencement of remedial action

The President shall assure that substantial and continuous physical on-site remedial action commences at facilities on the National Priorities List, in addition to those facilities on which remedial action has commenced prior to October 17, 1986, at a rate not fewer than:

(1) 175 facilities during the first 36-month period after October 17, 1986; and

(2) 200 additional facilities during the following 24 months after such 36-month period.

(Pub.L. 96–510, Title I, § 116, as added Oct. 17, 1986, Pub.L. 99–499, Title I, § 116, 100 Stat. 1653.)

Effective Date

Section 4 of Pub.L. 99–499, Oct. 17, 1986, 100 Stat. 1614, provided that title I of Pub.L. 99–499 [which enacted this section and sections 9617 to 9620 of this title] is effective Oct. 17, 1986.

LAW REVIEW COMMENTARIES

Interstate waste: A key issue in resolving the national hazardous waste capacity crisis. B.J. Wynne, III and Terri Hamby, 32 S.Tex. L.Rev. 601 (1991).

§ 9617. Public participation [CERCLA § 117]

(a) Proposed plan

Before adoption of any plan for remedial action to be undertaken by the President, by a State, or by any other person, under section 9604, 9606, 9620, or 9622 of this title, the President or State, as appropriate, shall take both of the following actions:

(1) Publish a notice and brief analysis of the proposed plan and make such plan available to the public.

(2) Provide a reasonable opportunity for submission of written and oral comments and an opportunity for a public meeting at or near the facility at issue regarding the proposed plan and regarding any proposed findings under section 9621(d)(4) of this title (relating to cleanup standards). The President or the State shall keep a transcript of the meeting and make such transcript available to the public.

The notice and analysis published under paragraph (1) shall include sufficient information as may be necessary to provide a reasonable explanation of the proposed plan and alternative proposals considered.

(b) Final plan

Notice of the final remedial action plan adopted shall be published and the plan shall be made available to the public before commencement of any remedial action. Such final plan shall be accompanied by a discussion of any significant changes (and the reasons for such changes) in the proposed plan and a response to each of the significant comments, criticisms, and new data submitted in written or oral presentations under subsection (a) of this section.

(c) Explanation of differences

After adoption of a final remedial action plan—

(1) if any remedial action is taken,

(2) if any enforcement action under section 9606 of this title is taken, or

(3) if any settlement or consent decree under section 9606 of this title or section 9622 of this title is entered into,

and if such action, settlement, or decree differs in any significant respects from the final plan, the President or the State shall publish an explanation of the significant differences and the reasons such changes were made.

(d) Publication

For the purposes of this section, publication shall include, at a minimum, publication in a major local newspaper of general circulation. In addition, each item developed, received, published, or made available to the public under this section shall be available for public inspection and copying at or near the facility at issue.

(e) Grants for technical assistance

(1) Authority

Subject to such amounts as are provided in appropriations Acts and in accordance with rules promulgated by the President, the President may make grants available to any group of individuals which may be affected by a release or threatened release at any facility which is listed on the National Priorities List under the National Contingency Plan. Such grants may be used to obtain technical assistance in interpreting information with regard to the nature of the hazard, remedial investigation and feasibility study, record of decision, remedial design, selection and construction of remedial action, operation and maintenance, or removal action at such facility.

(2) Amount

The amount of any grant under this subsection may not exceed $50,000 for a single grant recipient. The President may waive the $50,000 limitation in any case where such waiver is necessary to carry out the purposes of this subsection. Each grant recipient shall be required, as a condition of the grant, to contribute at least 20 percent of the total of costs of the technical assistance for which such grant is made. The President may waive the 20 percent contribution requirement if the grant recipient demonstrates financial need and such waiver is necessary to facilitate public participation in the selection of remedial action at the facility. Not more than one grant may be made under this subsection with respect to a single facility, but the grant may be renewed to facilitate public participation at all stages of remedial action.

(Pub.L. 96–510, Title I, § 117, as added Oct. 17, 1986, Pub.L. 99–499, Title I, § 117, 100 Stat. 1654.)

CODE OF FEDERAL REGULATIONS

State and local assistance, see 40 CFR 35.001 et seq.

§ 9618. High priority for drinking water supplies [CERCLA § 118]

For purposes of taking action under section 9604 or 9606 of this title and listing facilities on the National Priorities List, the President shall give a high priority to facilities where the release of hazardous substances or pollutants or contaminants has resulted in the closing of drinking water wells or has contaminated a principal drinking water supply.

(Pub.L. 96–510, Title I, § 118, as added Oct. 17, 1986, Pub.L. 99–499, Title I, § 118, 100 Stat. 1655.)

LIBRARY REFERENCES

Health and Environment ⚷25.7(3).
Waters and Water Courses ⚷196.
C.J.S. Health and Environment § 106.
C.J.S. Waters §§ 232 et seq.

§ 9619. Response action contractors [CERCLA § 119]

(a) Liability of response action contractors

(1) Response action contractors

A person who is a response action contractor with respect to any release or threatened release of a hazardous substance or pollutant or contaminant from a vessel or facility shall not be liable under this subchapter or under any other Federal law to any person for injuries, costs, damages, expenses, or other liability (including but not limited to claims for indemnification or contribution and claims by third parties for death, personal injury, illness or loss of or damage to property or economic loss) which results from such release or threatened release.

(2) Negligence, etc.

Paragraph (1) shall not apply in the case of a release that is caused by conduct of the response action contractor which is negligent, grossly negligent, or which constitutes intentional misconduct.

(3) **Effect on warranties; employer liability**

Nothing in this subsection shall affect the liability of any person under any warranty under Federal, State, or common law. Nothing in this subsection shall affect the liability of an employer who is a response action contractor to any employee of such employer under any provision of law, including any provision of any law relating to worker's compensation.

(4) **Governmental employees**

A state employee or an employee of a political subdivision who provides services relating to response action while acting within the scope of his authority as a governmental employee shall have the same exemption from liability (subject to the other provisions of this section) as is provided to the response action contractor under this section.

(b) **Savings provisions**

(1) **Liability of other persons**

The defense provided by section 9607(b)(3) of this title shall not be available to any potentially responsible party with respect to any costs or damages caused by any act or omission of a response action contractor. Except as provided in subsection (a)(4) of this section and the preceding sentence, nothing in this section shall affect the liability under this chapter or under any other Federal or State law of any person, other than a response action contractor.

(2) **Burden of plaintiff**

Nothing in this section shall affect the plaintiff's burden of establishing liability under this subchapter.

(c) **Indemnification**

(1) **In general**

The President may agree to hold harmless and indemnify any response action contractor meeting the requirements of this subsection against any liability (including the expenses of litigation or settlement) for negligence arising out of the contractor's performance in carrying out response action activities under this subchapter, unless such liability was caused by conduct of the contractor which was grossly negligent or which constituted intentional misconduct.

(2) **Applicability**

This subsection shall apply only with respect to a response action carried out under written agreement with—

(A) the President;

(B) any Federal agency;

(C) a State or political subdivision which has entered into a contract or cooperative agreement in accordance with section 9604(d)(1) of this title; or

(D) any potentially responsible party carrying out any agreement under section 9622 of this title (relating to settlements) or section 9606 of this title (relating to abatement).

(3) **Source of funding**

This subsection shall not be subject to section 1301 or 1341 of Title 31 or section 11 of Title 41 or to section 9662 of this title. For purposes of section 9611 of this title, amounts expended pursuant to this subsection for indemnification of any response action contractor (except with respect to federally owned or operated facilities) shall be considered governmental response costs incurred pursuant to section 9604 of this title. If sufficient funds are unavailable in the Hazardous Substance Superfund established under subchapter A of chapter 98 of Title 26 to make payments pursuant to such indemnification or if the Fund is repealed, there are authorized to be appropriated such amounts as may be necessary to make such payments.

(4) **Requirements**

An indemnification agreement may be provided under this subsection only if the President determines that each of the following requirements are met:

(A) The liability covered by the indemnification agreement exceeds or is not covered by insurance available, at a fair and reasonable price, to the contractor at the time the contractor enters into the contract to provide response action, and adequate insurance to cover such liability is not generally available at the time the response action contract is entered into.

(B) The response action contractor has made diligent efforts to obtain insurance coverage from non-Federal sources to cover such liability.

(C) In the case of a response action contract covering more than one facility, the response action contractor agrees to continue to make such diligent efforts each time the contractor begins work under the contract at a new facility.

(5) **Limitations**

(A) **Liability covered**

Indemnification under this subsection shall apply only to response action contractor liability which results from a release of any hazardous substance or pollutant or contaminant if such release arises out of response action activities.

(B) Deductibles and limits

An indemnification agreement under this subsection shall include deductibles and shall place limits on the amount of indemnification to be made available.

(C) Contracts with potentially responsible parties

(i) Decision to indemnify

In deciding whether to enter into an indemnification agreement with a response action contractor carrying out a written contract or agreement with any potentially responsible party, the President shall determine an amount which the potentially responsible party is able to indemnify the contractor. The President may enter into such an indemnification agreement only if the President determines that such amount of indemnification is inadequate to cover any reasonable potential liability of the contractor arising out of the contractor's negligence in performing the contract or agreement with such party. The President shall make the determinations in the preceding sentences (with respect to the amount and the adequacy of the amount) taking into account the total net assets and resources of potentially responsible parties with respect to the facility at the time of such determinations.

(ii) Conditions

The President may pay a claim under an indemnification agreement referred to in clause (i) for the amount determined under clause (i) only if the contractor has exhausted all administrative, judicial, and common law claims for indemnification against all potentially responsible parties participating in the clean-up of the facility with respect to the liability of the contractor arising out of the contractor's negligence in performing the contract or agreement with such party. Such indemnification agreement shall require such contractor to pay any deductible established under subparagraph (B) before the contractor may recover any amount from the potentially responsible party or under the indemnification agreement.

(D) RCRA facilities

No owner or operator of a facility regulated under the Solid Waste Disposal Act [42 U.S.C.A. § 6901 et seq.] may be indemnified under this subsection with respect to such facility.

(E) Persons retained or hired

A person retained or hired by a person described in subsection (e)(2)(B) of this section shall be eligible for indemnification under this subsection only if the President specifically approves of the retaining or hiring of such person.

(6) Cost recovery

For purposes of section 9607 of this title, amounts expended pursuant to this subsection for indemnification of any person who is a response action contractor with respect to any release or threatened release shall be considered a cost of response incurred by the United States Government with respect to such release.

(7) Regulations

The President shall promulgate regulations for carrying out the provisions of this subsection. Before promulgation of the regulations, the President shall develop guidelines to carry out this section. Development of such guidelines shall include reasonable opportunity for public comment.

(8) Study

The Comptroller General shall conduct a study in the fiscal year ending September 30, 1989, on the application of this subsection, including whether indemnification agreements under this subsection are being used, the number of claims that have been filed under such agreements, and the need for this subsection. The Comptroller General shall report the findings of the study to Congress no later than September 30, 1989.

(d) Exception

The exemption provided under subsection (a) of this section and the authority of the President to offer indemnification under subsection (c) of this section shall not apply to any person covered by the provisions of paragraph (1), (2), (3), or (4) of section 9607(a) of this title with respect to the release or threatened release concerned if such person would be covered by such provisions even if such person had not carried out any actions referred to in subsection (e) of this section.

(e) Definitions

For purposes of this section—

(1) Response action contract

The term "response action contract" means any written contract or agreement entered into by a response action contractor (as defined in paragraph (2)(A) of this subsection) with—

(A) the President;

(B) any Federal agency;

(C) a State or political subdivision which has entered into a contract or cooperative agreement in accordance with section 9604(d)(1) of this title; or

(D) any potentially responsible party carrying out an agreement under section 9606 or 9622 of this title;

to provide any remedial action under this chapter at a facility listed on the National Priorities List, or any removal under this chapter, with respect to any release or threatened release of a hazardous substance or pollutant or contaminant from the facility or to provide any evaluation, planning, engineering, surveying and mapping, design, construction, equipment, or any ancillary services thereto for such facility.

(2) Response action contractor

The term "response action contractor" means—

(A) any—

(i) person who enters into a response action contract with respect to any release or threatened release of a hazardous substance or pollutant or contaminant from a facility and is carrying out such contract; and

(ii) person, public or nonprofit private entity, conducting a field demonstration pursuant to section 9660(b) of this title; and

(iii) Recipients of grants (including subgrantees) under section 9660a of this title for the training and education of workers who are or may be engaged in activities related to hazardous waste removal, containment, or emergency response under this chapter; and

(B) any person who is retained or hired by a person described in subparagraph (A) to provide any services relating to a response action; and

(C) any surety who after October 16, 1990, and before January 1, 1996, provides a bid, performance or payment bond to a response action contractor, and begins activities to meet its obligations under such bond, but only in connection with such activities or obligations.

(3) Insurance

The term "insurance" means liability insurance which is fair and reasonably priced, as determined by the President, and which is made available at the time the contractor enters into the response action contract to provide response action.

(f) Competition

Response action contractors and subcontractors for program management, construction management, architectural and engineering, surveying and mapping, and related services shall be selected in accordance with title IX of the Federal Property and Administrative Services Act of 1949 [40 U.S.C.A. § 541 et seq.]. The Federal selection procedures shall apply to appropriate contracts negotiated by all Federal governmental agencies involved in carrying out this chapter. Such procedures shall be followed by response action contractors and subcontractors.

(g) Surety bonds

(1) If under the Act of August 24, 1935 (40 U.S.C. 270a–270d), commonly referred to as the "Miller Act", surety bonds are required for any direct Federal procurement of any response action contract and are not waived pursuant to the Act of April 29, 1941 (40 U.S.C. 270e–270f), they shall be issued in accordance with such Act of August 24, 1935.

(2) If under applicable Federal law surety bonds are required for any direct Federal procurement of any response action contract, no right of action shall accrue on the performance bond issued on such response action contract to or for the use of any person other than the obligee named in the bond.

(3) If under applicable Federal law surety bonds are required for any direct Federal procurement of any response action contract, unless otherwise provided for by the procuring agency in the bond, in the event of a default, the surety's liability on a performance bond shall be only for the cost of completion of the contract work in accordance with the plans and specifications less the balance of funds remaining to be paid under the contract, up to the penal sum of the bond. The surety shall in no event be liable on bonds to indemnify or compensate the obligee for loss or liability arising from personal injury or property damage whether or not caused by a breach of the bonded contract.

(4) Nothing in this subsection shall be construed as preempting, limiting, superseding, affecting, applying to, or modifying any State laws, regulations, requirements, rules, practices or procedures. Nothing in this subsection shall be construed as affecting, applying to, modifying, limiting, superseding, or preempting any rights, authorities, liabilities, demands, actions, causes of action, losses, judgments, claims, statutes of limitation, or obligations under Federal or State law, which do not arise on or under the bond.

(5) This subsection shall not apply to bonds executed before October 17, 1990, or after December 31, 1995.

(Pub.L. 96–510, Title I, § 119, as added Oct. 17, 1986, Pub.L. 99–499, Title I, § 119, 100 Stat. 1662, and amended Pub.L. 99–514, § 2, Oct. 22, 1986, 100 Stat. 2095; Pub.L. 100–202, § 101(f) [Title II], Dec. 22, 1987, 101 Stat. 1329–198; Pub.L. 101–584, § 1, Nov. 15, 1990, 104 Stat. 2872; Pub.L. 102–484, Div. A, Title III, § 331(a), Oct. 23, 1992, 106 Stat. 2373.)

[1] So in original. Probably should be "1993,".

References in Text

Act of August 24, 1935, referred to in subsec. (g)(1), is Act Aug. 24, 1935, c. 642, 49 Stat. 793, as amended, popularly known as the Miller Act, which is classified generally to section 270a et seq. of Title 40, Public Buildings, Property, and Works. For complete classification of this Act to the Code, see Short Title note set out under section 270a of Title 40 and Tables.

Act of April 29, 1941, referred to in subsec. (g)(1), is Act Apr. 29, 1941, c. 81, § 1, 55 Stat. 147 and § 2 as added Oct. 21, 1970, Pub.L. 91–469, § 39, 84 Stat. 1036, which enacted section 270e and 270f of Title 40, Public Buildings, Property, and Works.

CODE OF FEDERAL REGULATIONS

Grants and other federal assistance, see 40 CFR 30.100 et seq.

LIBRARY REFERENCES

Health and Environment ⚷18, 25.7(23).
C.J.S. Health and Environment §§ 54 et seq., 113 et seq.

§ 9620. Federal facilities [CERCLA § 120]

(a) Application of chapter to Federal Government

(1) In general

Each department, agency, and instrumentality of the United States (including the executive, legislative, and judicial branches of government) shall be subject to, and comply with, this chapter in the same manner and to the same extent, both procedurally and substantively, as any nongovernmental entity, including liability under section 9607 of this title. Nothing in this section shall be construed to affect the liability of any person or entity under sections 9606 and 9607 of this title.

(2) Application or requirements to Federal facilities

All guidelines, rules, regulations, and criteria which are applicable to preliminary assessments carried out under this chapter for facilities at which hazardous substances are located, applicable to evaluations of such facilities under the National Contingency Plan, applicable to inclusion on the National Priorities List, or applicable to remedial actions at such facilities shall also be applicable to facilities which are owned or operated by a department, agency, or instrumentality of the United States in the same manner and to the extent as such guidelines, rules, regulations, and criteria are applicable to other facilities. No department, agency, or instrumentality of the United States may adopt or utilize any such guidelines, rules, regulations, or criteria which are inconsistent with the guidelines, rules, regulations, and criteria established by the Administrator under this chapter.

(3) Exceptions

This subsection shall not apply to the extent otherwise provided in this section with respect to applicable time periods. This subsection shall also not apply to any requirements relating to bonding, insurance, or financial responsibility. Nothing in this chapter shall be construed to require a State to comply with section 9604(c)(3) of this title in the case of a facility which is owned or operated by any department, agency, or instrumentality of the United States.

(4) State laws

State laws concerning removal and remedial action, including State laws regarding enforcement, shall apply to removal and remedial action at facilities owned or operated by a department, agency, or instrumentality of the United States when such facilities are not included on the National Priorities List. The preceding sentence shall not apply to the extent a State law would apply any standard or requirement to such facilities which is more stringent than the standards and requirements applicable to facilities which are not owned or operated by any such department, agency, or instrumentality.

(b) Notice

Each department, agency, and instrumentality of the United States shall add to the inventory of Federal agency hazardous waste facilities required to be submitted under section 3016 of the Solid Waste Disposal Act [42 U.S.C.A. § 6937] (in addition to the information required under section 3016(a)(3) of such Act [42 U.S.C.A. § 6937(a)(3)]) information on contamination from each facility owned or operated by the department, agency, or instrumentality if such contamination affects contiguous or adjacent property owned by the department, agency, or instrumentality or by any other person, including a description of the monitoring data obtained.

(c) Federal Agency Hazardous Waste Compliance Docket

The Administrator shall establish a special Federal Agency Hazardous Waste Compliance Docket (hereinafter in this section referred to as the "docket") which shall contain each of the following:

(1) All information submitted under section 3016 of the Solid Waste Disposal Act [42 U.S.C.A. § 6937] and subsection (b) of this section regarding any Federal facility and notice of each subsequent action taken under this chapter with respect to the facility.

(2) Information submitted by each department, agency, or instrumentality of the United States under section 3005 or 3010 of such Act [42 U.S.C.A. § 6925 or 6930].

(3) Information submitted by the department, agency, or instrumentality under section 9603 of this title.

The docket shall be available for public inspection at reasonable times. Six months after establishment of the docket and every 6 months thereafter, the Administrator shall publish in the Federal Register a list of the Federal facilities which have been included in the docket during the immediately preceding 6-month period. Such publication shall also indicate where in the appropriate regional office of the Environmental Protection Agency additional information may be obtained with respect to any facility on the docket. The Administrator shall establish a program to provide information to the public with respect to facilities which are included in the docket under this subsection.

(d) Assessment and evaluation

Not later than 18 months after October 17, 1986, the Administrator shall take steps to assure that a preliminary assessment is conducted for each facility on the docket. Following such preliminary assessment, the Administrator shall, where appropriate—

(1) evaluate such facilities in accordance with the criteria established in accordance with section 9605 of this title under the National Contingency Plan for determining priorities among releases; and

(2) include such facilities on the National Priorities List maintained under such plan if the facility meets such criteria.

Such criteria shall be applied in the same manner as the criteria are applied to facilities which are owned or operated by other persons. Evaluation and listing under this subsection shall be completed not later than 30 months after October 17, 1986. Upon the receipt of a petition from the Governor of any State, the Administrator shall make such an evaluation of any facility included in the docket.

(e) Required action by department

(1) RI/FS

Not later than 6 months after the inclusion of any facility on the National Priorities List, the department, agency, or instrumentality which owns or operates such facility shall, in consultation with the Administrator and appropriate State authorities, commence a remedial investigation and feasibility study for such facility. In the case of any facility which is listed on such list before October 17, 1986, the department, agency, or instrumentality which owns or operates such facility shall, in consultation with the Administrator and appropriate State authorities, commence such an investigation and study for such facility within one year after October 17, 1986. The Administrator and appropriate State authorities shall publish a timetable and deadlines for expeditious completion of such investigation and study.

(2) Commencement of remedial action; interagency agreement

The Administrator shall review the results of each investigation and study conducted as provided in paragraph (1). Within 180 days thereafter, the head of the department, agency, or instrumentality concerned shall enter into an interagency agreement with the Administrator for the expeditious completion by such department, agency, or instrumentality of all necessary remedial action at such facility. Substantial continuous physical onsite remedial action shall be commenced at each facility not later than 15 months after completion of the investigation and study. All such interagency agreements, including review of alternative remedial action plans and selection of remedial action, shall comply with the public participation requirements of section 9617 of this title.

(3) Completion of remedial actions

Remedial actions at facilities subject to interagency agreements under this section shall be completed as expeditiously as practicable. Each agency shall include in its annual budget submissions to the Congress a review of alternative agency funding which could be used to provide for the costs of remedial action. The budget submission shall also include a statement of the hazard posed by the facility to human health, welfare, and the environment and identify the specific consequences of failure to begin and complete remedial action.

(4) Contents of agreement

Each interagency agreement under this subsection shall include, but shall not be limited to, each of the following:

(A) A review of alternative remedial actions and selection of a remedial action by the head of the relevant department, agency, or instrumentality and the Administrator or, if unable to reach agreement on selection of a remedial action, selection by the Administrator.

(B) A schedule for the completion of each such remedial action.

(C) Arrangements for long-term operation and maintenance of the facility.

(5) Annual report

Each department; agency, or instrumentality responsible for compliance with this section shall furnish an annual report to the Congress concerning its progress in implementing the requirements of this section. Such reports shall include, but shall not be limited to, each of the following items:

(A) A report on the progress in reaching interagency agreements under this section.

(B) The specific cost estimates and budgetary proposals involved in each interagency agreement.

(C) A brief summary of the public comments regarding each proposed interagency agreement.

(D) A description of the instances in which no agreement was reached.

(E) A report on progress in conducting investigations and studies under paragraph (1).

(F) A report on progress in conducting remedial actions.

(G) A report on progress in conducting remedial action at facilities which are not listed on the National Priorities List.

With respect to instances in which no agreement was reached within the required time period, the department, agency, or instrumentality filing the report under this paragraph shall include in such report an explanation of the reasons why no agreement was reached. The annual report required by this paragraph shall also contain a detailed description on a State-by-State basis of the status of each facility subject to this section, including a description of the hazard presented by each facility, plans and schedules for initiating and completing response action, enforcement status (where appropriate), and an explanation of any postponements or failure to complete response action. Such reports shall also be submitted to the affected States.

(6) Settlements with other parties

If the Administrator, in consultation with the head of the relevant department, agency, or instrumentality of the United States, determines that remedial investigations and feasibility studies or remedial action will be done properly at the Federal facility by another potentially responsible party within the deadlines provided in paragraphs (1), (2), and (3) of this subsection, the Administrator may enter into an agreement with such party under section 9622 of this title (relating to settlements). Following approval by the Attorney General of any such agreement relating to a remedial action, the agreement shall be entered in the appropriate United States district court as a consent decree under section 9606 of this title.

(f) State and local participation

The Administrator and each department, agency, or instrumentality responsible for compliance with this section shall afford to relevant State and local officials the opportunity to participate in the planning and selection of the remedial action, including but not limited to the review of all applicable data as it becomes available and the development of studies, reports, and action plans. In the case of State officials, the opportunity to participate shall be provided in accordance with section 9621 of this title.

(g) Transfer of authorities

Except for authorities which are delegated by the Administrator to an officer or employee of the Environmental Protection Agency, no authority vested in the Administrator under this section may be transferred, by executive order of the President or otherwise, to any other officer or employee of the United States or to any other person.

(h) Property transferred by Federal agencies

(1) Notice

After the last day of the 6-month period beginning on the effective date of regulations under paragraph (2) of this subsection, whenever any department, agency, or instrumentality of the United States enters into any contract for the sale or other transfer of real property which is owned by the United States and on which any hazardous substance was stored for one year or more, known to have been released, or disposed of, the head of such department, agency, or instrumentality shall include in such contract notice of the type and quantity of such hazardous substance and notice of the time at which such storage, release, or disposal took place, to the extent such information is available on the basis of a complete search of agency files.

(2) Form of notice; regulations

Notice under this subsection shall be provided in such form and manner as may be provided in regulations promulgated by the Administrator. As promptly as practicable after October 17, 1986, but not later than 18 months after October 17, 1986, and after consultation with the Administrator of the General Services Administration, the Administrator shall promulgate regulations regarding the notice required to be provided under this subsection.

(3) Contents of certain deeds

After the last day of the 6-month period beginning on the effective date of regulations under paragraph (2) of this subsection, in the case of any real property owned by the United States on which any hazardous substance was stored for one year or more, known to have been released, or disposed of, each deed entered into for the transfer of such property by the United States to any other person or entity shall contain—

(A) to the extent such information is available on the basis of a complete search of agency files—

(i) a notice of the type and quantity of such hazardous substances,

(ii) notice of the time at which such storage, release, or disposal took place, and

(iii) a description of the remedial action taken, if any, and

(B) a covenant warranting that—

(i) all remedial action necessary to protect human health and the environment with respect to any such substance remaining on the property has been taken before the date of such transfer, and

(ii) any additional remedial action found to be necessary after the date of such transfer shall be conducted by the United States; and

(C) a clause granting the United States access to the property in any case in which remedial action or corrective action is found to be necessary after the date of such transfer.

For purposes of subparagraph (B)(i), all remedial action described in such subparagraph has been taken if the construction and installation of an approved remedial design has been completed, and the remedy has been demonstrated to the Administrator to be operating properly and successfully. The carrying out of long-term pumping and treating, or operation and maintenance, after the remedy has been demonstrated to the Administrator to be operating properly and successfully does not preclude the transfer of the property.

The requirements of subparagraph (B) shall not apply in any case in which the person or entity to whom the real property is transferred is a potentially responsible party with respect to such property. The requirements of subparagraph (B) shall not apply in any case in which the transfer of the property occurs or has occurred by means of a lease, without regard to whether the lessee has agreed to purchase the property or whether the duration of the lease is longer than 55 years. In the case of a lease entered into after September 30, 1995, with respect to real property located at an installation approved for closure or realignment under a base closure law, the agency leasing the property, in consultation with the Administrator, shall determine before leasing the property that the property is suitable for lease, that the uses contemplated for the lease are consistent with protection of human health and the environment, and that there are adequate assurances that the United States will take all remedial action referred to in subparagraph (B) that has not been taken on the date of the lease.

(4) Identification of uncontaminated property

(A) In the case of real property to which this paragraph applies (as set forth in subparagraph (E)), the head of the department, agency, or instrumentality of the United States with jurisdiction over the property shall identify the real property on which no hazardous substances and no petroleum products or their derivatives were stored for one year or more, known to have been released, or disposed of. Such identification shall be based on an investigation of the real property to determine or discover the obviousness of the presence or likely presence of a release or threatened release of any hazardous substance or any petroleum product or its derivatives, including aviation fuel and motor oil, on the real property. The identification shall consist, at a minimum, of a review of each of the following sources of information concerning the current and previous uses of the real property:

(i) A detailed search of Federal Government records pertaining to the property.

(ii) Recorded chain of title documents regarding the real property.

(iii) Aerial photographs that may reflect prior uses of the real property and that are reasonably obtainable through State or local government agencies.

(iv) A visual inspection of the real property and any buildings, structures, equipment, pipe, pipeline, or other improvements on the real property, and a visual inspection of properties immediately adjacent to the real property.

(v) A physical inspection of property adjacent to the real property, to the extent permitted by owners or operators of such property.

(vi) Reasonably obtainable Federal, State, and local government records of each adjacent facility where there has been a release of any hazardous substance or any petroleum product or its derivatives, including aviation fuel and motor oil, and which is likely to cause or contribute to a release or threatened release of any hazardous substance or any petroleum product or its derivatives, including aviation fuel and motor oil, on the real property.

(vii) Interviews with current or former employees involved in operations on the real property.

Such identification shall also be based on sampling, if appropriate under the circumstances. The results of the identification shall be provided immediately to the Administrator and State and local government officials and made available to the public.

(B) The identification required under subparagraph (A) is not complete until concurrence in the results of the identification is obtained, in the case of real property that is part of a facility on the National Priorities List, from the Administrator, or, in the case of real property that is not part of a facility on the National Priorities List, from the appropriate State official. In the case of a concurrence which is required from a State official, the concurrence is deemed to be obtained if, within 90 days after receiving a request for the concurrence, the State official has not acted (by either concurring or declining to concur) on the request for concurrence.

(C)(i) Except as provided in clauses (ii), (iii), and (iv), the identification and concurrence required under subparagraphs (A) and (B), respectively, shall be made at least 6 months before the termination of operations on the real property.

(ii) In the case of real property described in subparagraph (E)(i)(II) on which operations have been closed or realigned or scheduled for closure or realignment pursuant to a base closure law described in subparagraph (E)(ii)(I) or (E)(ii)(II) by October 19, 1992, the identification and concurrence required under subparagraphs (A) and (B), respectively, shall be made not later than 18 months after October 19, 1992.

(iii) In the case of real property described in subparagraph (E)(i)(II) on which operations are closed or realigned or become scheduled for closure or realignment pursuant to the base closure law described in subparagraph (E)(ii)(II) after October 19, 1992, the identification and concurrence required under subparagraphs (A) and (B), respectively, shall be made not later than 18 months after the date by which a joint resolution disapproving the closure or realignment of the real property under section 2904(b) of such base closure law must be enacted, and such a joint resolution has not been enacted.

(iv) In the case of real property described in subparagraphs (E)(i)(II) on which operations are closed or realigned pursuant to a base closure law described in subparagraph (E)(ii)(III) or (E)(ii)(IV), the identification and concurrence required under subparagraphs (A) and (B), respectively, shall be made not later than 18 months after the date on which the real property is selected for closure or realignment pursuant to such a base closure law.

(D) In the case of the sale or other transfer of any parcel of real property identified under subparagraph (A), the deed entered into for the sale or transfer of such property by the United States to any other person or entity shall contain—

(i) a covenant warranting that any response action or corrective action found to be necessary after the date of such sale or transfer shall be conducted by the United States; and

(ii) a clause granting the United States access to the property in any case in which a response action or corrective action is found to be necessary after such date at such property, or such access is necessary to carry out a response action or corrective action on adjoining property.

(E)(i) This paragraph applies to—

(I) real property owned by the United States and on which the United States plans to terminate Federal Government operations, other than real property described in subclause (II); and

(II) real property that is or has been used as a military installation and on which the United States plans to close or realign military operations pursuant to base closure law.

(ii) For purposes of this paragraph, the term "base closure law" includes the following:

(I) Title II of the Defense Authorization Amendments and Base Closure and Realignment Act (Public Law 100–526; 10 U.S.C. 2687 note).

(II) The Defense Base Closure and Realignment Act of 1990 (part A of title XXIX of Public Law 101–510; 10 U.S.C. 2687 note).

(III) Section 2687 of Title 10.

(IV) Any provision of law authorizing the closure or realignment of a military installation enacted on or after October 19, 1992.

(F) Nothing in this paragraph shall affect, preclude, or otherwise impair the termination of Federal Government operations on real property owned by the United States.

(5) Notification of States regarding certain leases

In the case of real property owned by the United States, on which any hazardous substance or any petroleum product or its derivatives (including aviation fuel and motor oil) was stored for one year or more, known to have been released, or disposed of, and on which the United States plans to terminate Federal Government operations, the head of the department, agency, or instrumentality of the United States with jurisdiction over the property shall notify the State in which the property is located of any lease entered into by the United States that will encumber the property beyond the date of termination of operations on the property. Such notification shall be made before entering into the lease and shall include the length of the lease, the name of person[1] to whom the property is leased, and a description of the uses that will be allowed under the lease of the property and buildings and other structures on the property.

(i) Obligations under Solid Waste Disposal Act

Nothing in this section shall affect or impair the obligation of any department, agency, or instrumentality of the United States to comply with any requirement of the Solid Waste Disposal Act [42 U.S.C.A. § 6901 et seq.] (including corrective action requirements).

(j) National security

(1) Site specific Presidential orders

The President may issue such orders regarding response actions at any specified site or facility of the Department of Energy or the Department of Defense as may be necessary to protect the national security interests of the United States at that site or facility. Such orders may include, where necessary to protect such interests, an exemption from any requirement contained in this subchapter or under title III of the Superfund Amendments and Reauthorization Act of 1986 [42 U.S.C.A. § 11001 et seq.] with respect to the site or facility concerned. The President shall notify the Congress within 30 days of the issuance of an order under this paragraph providing for any such exemption. Such notification shall include a statement of the reasons for the granting of the exemption. An exemption under this paragraph shall be for a specified period which may not exceed one year. Additional exemptions may be granted, each upon the President's issuance of a new order under this paragraph for the site or facility concerned. Each such additional exemption shall be for a specified period which may not exceed one year. It is the intention of the Congress that whenever an exemption is issued under this paragraph the response action shall proceed as expeditiously as practicable. The Congress shall be notified periodically of the progress of any response action with respect to which an exemption has been issued under this paragraph. No exemption shall be granted under this paragraph due to lack of appropriation unless the President shall have specifically requested such appropriation as a part of the budgetary process and the Congress shall have failed to make available such requested appropriation.

(2) Classified information

Notwithstanding any other provision of law, all requirements of the Atomic Energy Act [42 U.S.C.A. § 2011 et seq.] and all Executive orders concerning the handling of restricted data and national security information, including "need to know" requirements, shall be applicable to any grant of access to classified information under the provisions of this chapter or under title III of the Superfund Amendments and Reauthorization Act of 1986 [42 U.S.C.A. § 11001 et seq.]

(Pub.L. 96–510, Title I, § 120, as added Oct. 17, 1986, Pub.L. 99–499, Title I, § 120(a), 100 Stat. 1666, and amended Pub.L. 102–426, §§ 3–5, Oct. 19, 1992, 106 Stat. 2175–2177; Pub.L. 104–106, Title XXVIII, § 2834, Feb. 10, 1996, 110 Stat. 559.)

1 So in original. Probably should be "the person".

References in Text

This chapter, referred to in subsecs. (a) catchline and pars. (1), (2), (3), (c)(1), and (j)(2), was in the original, "this Act", meaning Pub.L. 96–510, Dec. 11, 1980, 94 Stat. 2767, known as the Comprehensive Environmental Response, Compensation, and Liability Act of 1980. For complete classification of this Act to the Code, see Short Title note set out under section 9601 of this title and Tables.

Section 2904(b) of such base closure law, referred to in subsec. (h)(4)(C)(iii), is Pub.L. 101–510, Div. B, Title XXIX, § 2904(b), Nov. 5, 1990, 104 Stat. 1812, as amended, which is set out as a note under section 2687 of Title 10, Armed Forces.

Title II of the Defense Authorization Amendments and Base Closure and Realignment Act, referred to in subsec. (h)(4)(E)(ii)(I), is Pub.L. 100–526, Title II, Oct. 24, 1988, 102 Stat. 2627, as amended, which is set out as a note under section 2687 of Title 10, Armed Forces.

The Defense Base Closure and Realignment Act of 1990, referred to in subsec. (h)(4)(E)(ii)(II), is Pub.L. 101–510, Div. B, Title XXIX, §§ 2901–2910, Nov. 5, 1990, 104 Stat. 1808, as amended, which is set out as a note under section 2687 of Title 10, Armed Forces.

The Solid Waste Disposal Act, referred to in subsec. (i), is Title II of Pub.L. 89–272, Oct. 20, 1965, 79 Stat. 997, as amended generally by Pub.L. 94–580, § 2, Oct. 21, 1976, 90 Stat. 2795, which is classified generally to chapter 82 (section 6901 et seq.) of this title. For complete classification of this Act to the Code, see Short Title note set out under section 6901 of this title and Tables.

Title III of the Superfund Amendments and Reauthorization Act of 1986, referred to in subsec. (j), is Title III (section 300 et seq.) of Pub.L. 99–499, Oct. 17, 1986, 100 Stat. 1728, known as the Emergency Planning and Community Right–To–Know Act of 1986, which is classified principally to chapter 116 (section 11001 et seq.) of this title. For complete classification of the Emergency Planning and Community Right–To–Know Act of 1986 to the Code, see Short Title note set out under section 11001 of this title and Tables.

The Atomic Energy Act, referred to in subsec. (j)(2), probably means the Atomic Energy Act of 1954, Act Aug. 30, 1954, c. 1073, § 1, 68 Stat. 921, as amended, which is classified principally to chapter 23 (section 2011 et seq.) of this title. For complete classification of this Act to the Code, see Short Title note set out under section 2011 of this title and Tables.

Identification of Uncontaminated Property at Installations to Be Closed

Pub.L. 103–160, Div. B, Title XXIX, § 2910, Nov. 30, 1993, 107 Stat. 1924, provided that: "The identification by the Secretary of Defense required under section 120(h)(4)(A) of the Comprehensive Environmental Response, Compensation, and Liability Act of 1980 (42 U.S.C. 9620(h)(4)(A)) [subsec. (h)(4)(A) of this section], and the concurrence required under section 120(h)(4)(B) of such Act [subsec. (h)(4)(B) of this section], shall be made not later than the earlier of—

"(1) the date that is 9 months after the date of the submittal, if any, to the transition coordinator for the installation concerned of a specific use proposed for all or a portion of the real property of the installation; or

"(2) the date specified in section 120(h)(4)(C)(iii) of such Act [subsec. (h)(4)(C)(iii) of this section]."

Congressional Findings

Section 2 of Pub.L. 102–426 provided that:

"The Congress finds the following:

"(1) The closure of certain Federal facilities is having adverse effects on the economies of local communities by eliminating jobs associated with such facilities, and delay in remediation of environmental contamination of real property at such facilities is preventing transfer and private development of such property.

"(2) Each department, agency, or instrumentality of the United States, in cooperation with local communities, should expeditiously identify real property that offers the greatest opportunity for reuse and redevelopment on each facility under the jurisdiction of the department, agency, or instrumentality where operations are terminating.

"(3) Remedial actions, including remedial investigations and feasibility studies, and corrective actions at such Federal facilities should be expedited in a manner to facilitate environmental protection and the sale or transfer of such excess real property for the purpose of mitigating adverse economic effects on the surrounding community.

"(4) Each department, agency, or instrumentality of the United States, in accordance with applicable law, should make available without delay such excess real property.

"(5) In the case of any real property owned by the United States and transferred to another person, the United States Government should remain responsible for conducting any remedial action or corrective action necessary to protect human health and the environment with respect to any hazardous substance or petroleum product or its derivatives, including aviation fuel and motor oil, that was present on such real property at the time of transfer."

Limited Grandfather Application

Section 120(b) of Pub.L. 99–499 Title I, Oct. 17, 1986, 100 Stat. 1671, provided that: "Section 120 of CERCLA [this section] shall not apply to any response action or remedial action for which a plan is under development by the Department of Energy on the date of enactment of this Act [October 17, 1986] with respect to facilities—

"(1) owned or operated by the United States and subject to the jurisdiction of such Department;

"(2) located in St. Charles and St. Louis counties, Missouri, or the city of St. Louis, Missouri, and

"(3) published in the National Priorities List.

"In preparing such plans, the Secretary of Energy shall consult with the Administrator of the Environmental Protection Agency."

LAW REVIEW COMMENTARIES

Determining cleanup standards for hazardous waste sites. William D. Turkula, 135 Mil.L.Rev. 167 (1992).

LIBRARY REFERENCES

Health and Environment ⚷25.5(5.5).
C.J.S. Health and Environment § 91 et seq.

§ 9621. Cleanup standards [CERCLA § 121]

(a) Selection of remedial action

The President shall select appropriate remedial actions determined to be necessary to be carried out under section 9604 of this title or secured under section 9606 of this title which are in accordance with this section and, to the extent practicable, the national contingency plan, and which provide for cost-effective response. In evaluating the cost effectiveness of proposed alternative remedial actions, the President shall take into account the total short- and long-term costs of such actions, including the costs of operation and maintenance for the entire period during which such activities will be required.

(b) General rules

(1) Remedial actions in which treatment which permanently and significantly reduces the volume, toxicity or mobility of the hazardous substances, pollutants, and contaminants is a principal element, are to be preferred over remedial actions not involving such treatment. The offsite transport and disposal of hazardous substances or contaminated materials without such treatment should be the least favored alternative remedial action where practicable treatment technologies are available. The President shall conduct an assessment of permanent solutions and alternative treatment technologies or resource recovery technologies that, in whole or in part, will result in a permanent and significant decrease in the toxicity, mobility, or volume of the hazardous substance, pollutant, or contaminant. In making such assessment, the President shall specifically address the long-term effectiveness of various alternatives. In assessing alternative remedial actions, the President shall, at a minimum, take into account:

(A) the long-term uncertainties associated with land disposal;

(B) the goals, objectives, and requirements of the Solid Waste Disposal Act [42 U.S.C.A. § 6901 et seq.];

(C) the persistence, toxicity, mobility, and propensity to bioaccumulate of such hazardous substances and their constituents;

(D) short- and long-term potential for adverse health effects from human exposure;

(E) long-term maintenance costs;

(F) the potential for future remedial action costs if the alternative remedial action in question were to fail; and

(G) the potential threat to human health and the environment associated with excavation, transportation, and redisposal, or containment.

The President shall select a remedial action that is protective of human health and the environment, that is cost effective, and that utilizes permanent solutions and alternative treatment technologies or resource recovery technologies to the maximum extent practicable. If the President selects a remedial action not appropriate for a preference under this subsection, the President shall publish an explanation as to why a remedial action involving such reductions was not selected.

(2) The President may select an alternative remedial action meeting the objectives of this subsection whether or not such action has been achieved in practice at any other facility or site that has similar characteristics. In making such a selection, the President may take into account the degree of support for such remedial action by parties interested in such site.

(c) Review

If the President selects a remedial action that results in any hazardous substances, pollutants, or contaminants remaining at the site, the President shall review such remedial action no less often than each 5 years after the initiation of such remedial action to assure that human health and the environment are being protected by the remedial action being implemented. In addition, if upon such review it is the judgment of the President that action is appropriate at such site in accordance with section 9604 or 9606 of this title, the President shall take or require such action. The President shall report to the Congress a list of facilities for which such review is required, the results of all such reviews, and any actions taken as a result of such reviews.

(d) Degree of cleanup

(1) Remedial actions selected under this section or otherwise required or agreed to by the President under this chapter shall attain a degree of cleanup of hazardous substances, pollutants, and contaminants released into the environment and of control of further release at a minimum which assures protection of human health and the environment. Such remedial actions shall be relevant and appropriate under the circumstances presented by the release or threatened release of such substance, pollutant, or contaminant.

(2)(A) With respect to any hazardous substance, pollutant or contaminant that will remain onsite, if—

(i) any standard, requirement, criteria, or limitation under any Federal environmental law, including, but not limited to, the Toxic Substances Control Act [15 U.S.C.A. § 2601 et seq.], the Safe Drinking Water Act [42 U.S.C.A. § 300f et seq.], the Clear Air Act [42 U.S.C.A. § 7401 et seq.], the Clean Water Act [33 U.S.C.A. § 1251 et seq.], the Marine Protection, Research and Sanctuaries Act [33 U.S.C.A. § 1401 et seq.], or the Solid Waste Disposal Act [42 U.S.C.A. § 6901 et seq.]; or

(ii) any promulgated standard, requirement, criteria, or limitation under a State environmental or facility siting law that is more stringent than any Federal standard, requirement, criteria, or limitation, including each such State standard, requirement, criteria, or limitation contained in a program approved, authorized or delegated by the Administrator under a statute cited in subparagraph (A), and that has been identified to the President by the State in a timely manner,

is legally applicable to the hazardous substance or pollutant or contaminant concerned or is relevant and appropriate under the circumstances of the release or threatened release of such hazardous substance or pollutant or contaminant, the remedial action selected under section 9604 of this title or secured under section 9606 of this title shall require, at the completion of the remedial action, a level or standard of control for such hazardous substance or pollutant or contaminant which at least attains such legally applicable or relevant and appropriate standard, requirement, criteria, or limitation. Such remedial action shall require a level or standard of control which at least attains Maximum Contaminant Level Goals established under the Safe Drinking Water Act [42 U.S.C.A. § 300f et seq.] and water quality criteria established under section 304 or 303 of the Clean Water Act [33 U.S.C.A. § 1314 or 1313], where such goals or criteria are relevant and appropriate under the circumstances of the release or threatened release.

(B)(i) In determining whether or not any water quality criteria under the Clean Water Act [33 U.S.C.A. § 1251 et seq.] is relevant and appropriate under the circumstances of the release or threatened release, the President shall consider the designated or potential use of the surface or groundwater, the environmental media affected, the purposes for which such criteria were developed, and the latest information available.

(ii) For the purposes of this section, a process for establishing alternate concentration limits to those otherwise applicable for hazardous constituents in groundwater under subparagraph (A) may not be used to establish applicable standards under this paragraph if the process assumes a point of human exposure beyond the boundary of the facility, as defined at the conclusion of the remedial investigation and feasibility study, except where—

(I) there are known and projected points of entry of such groundwater into surface water; and

(II) on the basis of measurements or projections, there is or will be no statistically significant increase of such constituents from such groundwater in such surface water at the point of entry or at any point where there is reason to believe accumulation of constituents may occur downstream; and

(III) the remedial action includes enforceable measures that will preclude human exposure to the contaminated groundwater at any point between the facility boundary and all known and projected points of entry of such groundwater into surface water,

then the assumed point of human exposure may be at such known and projected points of entry.

(C)(i) Clause (ii) of this subparagraph shall be applicable only in cases where, due to the President's selection, in compliance with subsection (b)(1) of this section, of a proposed remedial action which does not permanently and significantly reduce the volume, toxicity, or mobility of hazardous substances, pollutants, or contaminants, the proposed disposition of waste generated by or associated with the remedial action selected by the President is land disposal in a State referred to in clause (ii).

(ii) Except as provided in clauses (iii) and (iv), a State standard, requirement, criteria, or limitation (including any State siting standard or requirement) which could effectively result in the statewide prohibition of land disposal of hazardous substances, pollutants, or contaminants shall not apply.

(iii) Any State standard, requirement, criteria, or limitation referred to in clause (ii) shall apply where each of the following conditions is met:

(I) The State standard, requirement, criteria, or limitation is of general applicability and was adopted by formal means.

(II) The State standard, requirement, criteria, or limitation was adopted on the basis of hydrologic, geologic, or other relevant considerations and was not adopted for the purpose of precluding onsite remedial actions or other land disposal for reasons unrelated to protection of human health and the environment.

(III) The State arranges for, and assures payment of the incremental costs of utilizing, a facility for disposition of the hazardous substances, pollutants, or contaminants concerned.

(iv) Where the remedial action selected by the President does not conform to a State standard and the State has initiated a law suit against the Environmental Protection Agency prior to May 1, 1986, to seek to have the remedial action conform to such standard, the President shall conform the remedial action to the State standard. The State shall assure the availability of an offsite facility for such remedial action.

(3) In the case of any removal or remedial action involving the transfer of any hazardous substance or pollutant or contaminant offsite, such hazardous substance or pollutant or contaminant shall only be transferred to a facility which is operating in compliance with section 3004 and 3005 of the Solid Waste Disposal Act [42 U.S.C.A. §§ 6924 and 6925] (or, where applicable, in compliance with the Toxic Substances Control Act [15 U.S.C.A. § 2601 et seq.] or other applicable Federal law) and all applicable State requirements. Such substance or pollutant or contaminant may be transferred to a land disposal facility only if the President determines that both of the following requirements are met:

(A) The unit to which the hazardous substance or pollutant or contaminant is transferred is not releasing any hazardous waste, or constituent thereof, into the groundwater or surface water or soil.

(B) All such releases from other units at the facility are being controlled by a corrective action program approved by the Administrator under subtitle C of the Solid Waste Disposal Act [42 U.S.C.A. § 6921 et seq.].

The President shall notify the owner or operator of such facility of determinations under this paragraph.

(4) The President may select a remedial action meeting the requirements of paragraph (1) that does not attain a level or standard of control at least equivalent to a legally applicable or relevant and appropriate standard, requirement, criteria, or limitation as required by paragraph (2) (including subparagraph (B) thereof), if the President finds that—

(A) the remedial action selected is only part of a total remedial action that will attain such level or standard of control when completed;

(B) compliance with such requirement at that facility will result in greater risk to human health and the environment than alternative options;

(C) compliance with such requirements is technically impracticable from an engineering perspective;

(D) the remedial action selected will attain a standard of performance that is equivalent to that required under the otherwise applicable standard, requirement, criteria, or limitation, through use of another method or approach;

(E) with respect to a State standard, requirement, criteria, or limitation, the State has not consistently applied (or demonstrated the intention to consistently apply) the standard, requirement, criteria, or limitation in similar circumstances at other remedial actions within the State; or

(F) in the case of a remedial action to be undertaken solely under section 9604 of this title using the Fund, selection of a remedial action that attains such level or standard of control will not provide a balance between the need for protection of public health and welfare and the environment at the facility under consideration, and the availability of amounts from the Fund to respond to other sites which present or may present a threat to public health or welfare or the environment, taking into consideration the relative immediacy of such threats.

The President shall publish such findings, together with an explanation and appropriate documentation.

(e) Permits and enforcement

(1) No Federal, State, or local permit shall be required for the portion of any removal or remedial action conducted entirely onsite, where such remedial action is selected and carried out in compliance with this section.

(2) A State may enforce any Federal or State standard, requirement, criteria, or limitation to which the remedial action is required to conform under this chapter in the United States district court for the district in which the facility is located. Any consent decree shall require the parties to attempt expeditiously to resolve disagreements concerning implementation of the remedial action informally with the appropriate Federal and State agencies. Where the parties agree, the consent decree may provide for administrative enforcement. Each consent decree shall also contain stipulated penalties for violations of the decree in an amount not to exceed $25,000 per day, which may be enforced by either the President or the State. Such stipulated penalties shall not be construed to impair or affect the authority of the court to order compliance with the specific terms of any such decree.

(f) State involvement

(1) The President shall promulgate regulations providing for substantial and meaningful involvement by each State in initiation, development, and selection of remedial actions to be undertaken in that State. The regulations, at a minimum, shall include each of the following:

(A) State involvement in decisions whether to perform a preliminary assessment and site inspection.

(B) Allocation of responsibility for hazard ranking system scoring.

(C) State concurrence in deleting sites from the National Priorities List.

(D) State participation in the long-term planning process for all remedial sites within the State.

(E) A reasonable opportunity for States to review and comment on each of the following:

(i) The remedial investigation and feasibility study and all data and technical documents leading to its issuance.

(ii) The planned remedial action identified in the remedial investigation and feasibility study.

(iii) The engineering design following selection of the final remedial action.

(iv) Other technical data and reports relating to implementation of the remedy.

(v) Any proposed finding or decision by the President to exercise the authority of subsection (d)(4) of this section.

(F) Notice to the State of negotiations with potentially responsible parties regarding the scope of any response action at a facility in the State and an opportunity to participate in such negotiations and, subject to paragraph (2), be a party to any settlement.

(G) Notice to the State and an opportunity to comment on the President's proposed plan for remedial action as well as on alternative plans under consideration. The President's proposed decision regarding the selection of remedial action shall be accompanied by a response to the comments submitted by the State, including an explanation regarding any decision under subsection (d)(4) of this section on compliance with promulgated State standards. A copy of such response shall also be provided to the State.

(H) Prompt notice and explanation of each proposed action to the State in which the facility is located.

Prior to the promulgation of such regulations, the President shall provide notice to the State of negotiations with potentially responsible parties regarding the scope of any response action at a facility in the State, and such State may participate in such negotiations and, subject to paragraph (2), any settlements.

(2)(A) This paragraph shall apply to remedial actions secured under section 9606 of this title. At least 30 days prior to the entering of any consent decree, if the President proposes to select a remedial action that does not attain a legally applicable or relevant and appropriate standard, requirement, criteria, or limitation, under the authority of subsection (d)(4) of this section, the President shall provide an opportunity for the State to concur or not concur in such selection. If the State concurs, the State may become a signatory to the consent decree.

(B) If the State does not concur in such selection, and the State desires to have the remedial action conform to such standard, requirement, criteria, or limitation, the State shall intervene in the action under section 9606 of this title before entry of the consent decree, to seek to have the remedial action so conform. Such intervention shall be a matter of right. The remedial action shall conform to such standard, requirement, criteria, or limitation if the State establishes, on the administrative record, that the finding of the President was not supported by substantial evidence. If the court determines that the remedial action shall conform to such standard, requirement, criteria, or limitation, the remedial action shall be so modified and the State may become a signatory to the decree. If the court determines that the remedial action need not conform to such standard, requirement, criteria, or limitation, and the State pays or assures the payment of the additional costs attributable to meeting such standard, requirement, criteria, or limitation, the remedial action shall be so modified and the State shall become a signatory to the decree.

(C) The President may conclude settlement negotiations with potentially responsible parties without State concurrence.

(3)(A) This paragraph shall apply to remedial actions at facilities owned or operated by a department, agency, or instrumentality of the United States. At least 30 days prior to the publication of the President's final remedial action plan, if the President proposes to select a remedial action that does not attain a legally applicable or relevant and appropriate standard, requirement, criteria, or limitation, under the authority of subsection (d)(4) of this section, the President shall provide an opportunity for the State to concur or not concur in such selection. If the State concurs, or does not act within 30 days, the remedial action may proceed.

(B) If the State does not concur in such selection as provided in subparagraph (A), and desires to have the remedial action conform to such standard, requirement, criteria, or limitation, the State may maintain an action as follows:

(i) If the President has notified the State of selection of such a remedial action, the State may bring an action within 30 days of such notification for the sole purpose of determining whether the finding of the President is supported by substantial evidence. Such action shall be brought in the United States district court for the district in which the facility is located.

(ii) If the State establishes, on the administrative record, that the President's finding is not supported by substantial evidence, the remedial action shall be modified to conform to such standard, requirement, criteria, or limitation.

(iii) If the State fails to establish that the President's finding was not supported by substantial evidence and if the State pays, within 60 days of judgment, the additional costs attributable to meeting such standard, requirement, criteria, or limitation, the remedial action shall be selected to meet such standard, requirement, criteria, or limitation. If the State fails to pay within 60 days, the remedial action selected by the President shall proceed through completion.

(C) Nothing in this section precludes, and the court shall not enjoin, the Federal agency from taking any remedial action unrelated to or not inconsistent with such standard, requirement, criteria, or limitation.

(Pub.L. 96–510, Title I, § 121, as added Oct. 17, 1986, Pub.L. 99–499, Title I, § 121(a), Oct. 17, 1986, 100 Stat. 1672.)

Effective Date

Section 121(b) of Pub.L. 99–499, Title I, Oct. 17, 1986, 100 Stat. 1678, provided that: "With respect to section 121 of CERCLA [this section] as added by this section—

"(1) The requirements of section 121 of CERCLA [this section] shall not apply to any remedial action for which the Record of Decision (hereinafter in this section referred to as the 'ROD') was signed, or the consent decree was lodged, before date of enactment [Oct. 17, 1986].

"(2) If the ROD was signed, or the consent decree lodged, within the 30-day period immediately following enactment of the Act [Oct. 17, 1986], the Administrator shall certify in writing that the portion of the remedial action covered by the ROD or consent decree complies to the maximum extent practicable with section 121 of CERCLA [this section].

"Any ROD signed before enactment of this Act [Oct. 17, 1986] and reopened after enactment of this Act [Oct. 17, 1986] to modify or supplement the selection of remedy shall be subject to the requirements of section 121 of CERCLA [this section]".

CODE OF FEDERAL REGULATIONS

Grants and other federal assistance, see 40 CFR 30.100 et seq.

LAW REVIEW COMMENTARIES

Environmental liability and the limits of insurance. Kenneth S. Abraham, 88 Columbia L.Rev. 942 (1988).

LIBRARY REFERENCES

Health and Environment ⚷25.5(5.5), 25.7(23).
C.J.S. Health and Environment §§ 91 et seq., 113 et seq.

§ 9622. Settlements [CERCLA § 122]

(a) Authority to enter into agreements

The President, in his discretion, may enter into an agreement with any person (including the owner or operator of the facility from which a release or substantial threat of release emanates, or any other potentially responsible person), to perform any response action (including any action described in section 9604(b) of this title) if the President determines that such action will be done properly by such person. Whenever practicable and in the public interest, as determined by the President, the President shall act to facilitate agreements under this section that are in the public interest and consistent with the National Contingency Plan in order to expedite effective remedial actions and minimize litigation. If the President decides not to use the procedures in this section, the President shall notify in writing potentially responsible parties at the facility of such decision and the reasons why use of the procedures is inappropriate.

A decision of the President to use or not to use the procedures in this section is not subject to judicial review.

(b) Agreements with potentially responsible parties

(1) Mixed funding

An agreement under this section may provide that the President will reimburse the parties to the agreement from the Fund, with interest, for certain costs of actions under the agreement that the parties have agreed to perform but which the President has agreed to finance. In any case in which the President provides such reimbursement, the President shall make all reasonable efforts to recover the amount of such reimbursement under section 9607 of this title or under other relevant authorities.

(2) Reviewability

The President's decisions regarding the availability of fund financing under this subsection shall not be subject to judicial review under subsection (d) of this section.

(3) Retention of funds

If, as part of any agreement, the President will be carrying out any action and the parties will be paying amounts to the President, the President may, notwithstanding any other provision of law, retain and use such amounts for purposes of carrying out the agreement.

(4) Future obligation of Fund

In the case of a completed remedial action pursuant to an agreement described in paragraph (1), the Fund shall be subject to an obligation for subsequent remedial actions at the same facility but only to the extent that such subsequent actions are necessary by reason of the failure of the original remedial action. Such obligation shall be in a proportion equal to, but not exceeding, the proportion contributed by the Fund for the original remedial action. The Fund's obligation for such future remedial action may be met through Fund expenditures or through payment, following settlement or enforcement action, by parties who were not signatories to the original agreement.

(c) Effect of agreement

(1) Liability

Whenever the President has entered into an agreement under this section, the liability to the United States under this chapter of each party to the agreement, including any future liability to the United States, arising from the release or threatened release that is the subject of the agreement shall be limited as provided in the agreement pursuant to a covenant not to sue in accordance with subsection (f) of this section. A covenant not to sue may provide that future liability to the United States of a settling potentially responsible party under the agreement may be limited to the same proportion as that established in the original settlement agreement. Nothing in this section shall limit or otherwise affect the authority of any court to review in the consent decree process under subsection (d) of this section any covenant not to sue contained in an agreement under this section. In determining the extent to which the liability of parties to an agreement shall be limited pursuant to a covenant not to sue, the President shall be guided by the principle that a more complete covenant not to sue shall be provided for a more permanent remedy undertaken by such parties.

(2) Actions against other persons

If an agreement has been entered into under this section, the President may take any action under section 9606 of this title against any person who is not a party to the agreement, once the period for submitting a proposal under subsection (e)(2)(B) of this section has expired. Nothing in this section shall be construed to affect either of the following:

(A) The liability of any person under section 9606 or 9607 of this title with respect to any costs or damages which are not included in the agreement.

(B) The authority of the President to maintain an action under this chapter against any person who is not a party to the agreement.

(d) Enforcement

(1) Cleanup agreements

(A) Consent decree

Whenever the President enters into an agreement under this section with any potentially responsible party with respect to remedial action under section 9606 of this title, following approval of the agreement by the Attorney General, except as otherwise provided in the case of certain administrative settlements referred to in subsection (g) of this section, the agreement shall be entered in the appropriate United States district court as a consent decree. The President need not make any finding regarding an imminent and substantial endangerment to the public health or the environment in connection with any such agreement or consent decree.

(B) Effect

The entry of any consent decree under this subsection shall not be construed to be an acknowledgment by the parties that the release or threatened release concerned constitutes an imminent and substantial endangerment to the public health or welfare or the environment. Except as otherwise provided in the Federal Rules of Evidence, the participation by any party in the process under this section shall not be considered an admission of liability for any purpose, and the fact of such participation shall not be admissible in any judicial or administrative proceeding, including a subsequent proceeding under this section.

(C) Structure

The President may fashion a consent decree so that the entering of such decree and compliance with such decree or with any determination or agreement made pursuant to this section shall not be considered an admission of liability for any purpose.

(2) Public participation

(A) Filing of proposed judgment

At least 30 days before a final judgment is entered under paragraph (1), the proposed judgment shall be filed with the court.

(B) Opportunity for comment

The Attorney General shall provide an opportunity to persons who are not named as parties to the action to comment on the proposed judgment before its entry by the court as a final judgment. The Attorney General shall consider, and file with the court, any written comments, views, or allegations relating to the proposed judgment. The Attorney General may withdraw or withhold its consent to the proposed judgment if the comments, views, and allegations concerning the judgment disclose facts or considerations which indicate that the proposed judgment is inappropriate, improper, or inadequate.

(3) 9604(b) agreements

Whenever the President enters into an agreement under this section with any potentially responsible party with respect to action under section 9604(b) of this title, the President shall issue an order or enter into a decree setting forth the obligations of such party. The United States district court for the district in which the release or threatened release occurs may enforce such order or decree.

(e) Special notice procedures

(1) Notice

Whenever the President determines that a period of negotiation under this subsection would facilitate an agreement with potentially responsible parties for taking response action (including any action described in section 9604(b) of this title) and would expedite remedial action, the President shall so notify all such parties and shall provide them with information concerning each of the following:

(A) The names and addresses of potentially responsible parties (including owners and operators and other persons referred to in section 9607(a) of this title), to the extent such information is available.

(B) To the extent such information is available, the volume and nature of substances contributed by each potentially responsible party identified at the facility.

(C) A ranking by volume of the substances at the facility, to the extent such information is available.

The President shall make the information referred to in this paragraph available in advance of notice under this paragraph upon the request of a potentially responsible party in accordance with procedures provided by the President. The provisions of subsection (e) of section 9604 of this title regarding protection of confidential information apply to information provided under this paragraph. Disclosure of information generated by the President under this section to persons other than the Congress, or any duly authorized Committee thereof, is subject to other privileges or protections provided by law, including (but not limited to) those applicable to attorney work product. Nothing contained in this paragraph or in other provisions of this chapter shall be construed, interpreted, or applied to diminish the required disclosure of information under other provisions of this or other Federal or State laws.

(2) Negotiation

(A) Moratorium

Except as provided in this subsection, the President may not commence action under section 9604(a) of this title or take any action under section 9606 of this title for 120 days after providing notice and information under this subsection with respect to such action. Except as provided in this subsection, the President may not commence a remedial investigation and feasibility study under section 9604(b) of this title for 90 days after providing notice and information under this subsection with respect to such action. The President may commence any additional studies or investigations authorized under section 9604(b) of this title, including remedial design, during the negotiation period.

(B) Proposals

Persons receiving notice and information under paragraph (1) of this subsection with respect to action under section 9606 of this title shall have 60 days from the date of receipt of such notice to make a proposal to the President for undertaking or financing the action under section 9606 of this title. Persons receiving notice and information under paragraph (1) of this subsection with respect to action under section 9604(b) of this title shall have 60 days from the date of receipt of such notice to make a proposal to the President for undertaking or financing the action under section 9604(b) of this title.

(C) Additional parties

If an additional potentially responsible party is identified during the negotiation period or after an agreement has been entered into under this subsection concerning a release or threatened release, the President may bring the additional party into the negotiation or enter into a separate agreement with such party.

(3) Preliminary allocation of responsibility

(A) In general

The President shall develop guidelines for preparing nonbinding preliminary allocations of responsibility. In developing these guidelines the President may include such factors as the President considers relevant, such as: volume, toxicity, mobility, strength of evidence, ability to pay, litigative risks, public interest considerations, precedential value, and inequities and aggravating factors. When it would expedite settlements under this section and remedial action, the President may, after completion of the remedial investigation and feasibility study, provide a nonbinding preliminary allocation of responsibility which allocates percentages of the total cost of response among potentially responsible parties at the facility.

(B) Collection of information

To collect information necessary or appropriate for performing the allocation under subparagraph (A) or for otherwise implementing this section, the President may by subpoena require the attendance and testimony of witnesses and the production of reports, papers, documents, answers to questions, and other information that the President deems necessary. Witnesses shall be paid the same fees and mileage that are paid witnesses in the courts of the United States. In the event of contumacy or failure or refusal of any person to obey any such subpoena, any district court of the United States in which venue is proper shall have jurisdiction to order any such person to comply with such subpoena. Any failure to obey such an order of the court is punishable by the court as a contempt thereof.

(C) Effect

The nonbinding preliminary allocation of responsibility shall not be admissible as evidence in any proceeding, and no court shall have jurisdiction to review the nonbinding preliminary allocation of responsibility. The nonbinding preliminary allocation of responsibility shall not constitute an apportionment or other statement on the divisibility of harm or causation.

(D) Costs

The costs incurred by the President in producing the nonbinding preliminary allocation of responsibility shall be reimbursed by the potentially responsible parties whose offer is accepted by the President. Where an offer under this section is not accepted, such costs shall be considered costs of response.

(E) Decision to reject offer

Where the President, in his discretion, has provided a nonbinding preliminary allocation of responsibility and the potentially responsible parties have made a substantial offer providing for response to the President which he rejects, the reasons for the rejection shall be provided in a written explanation. The President's decision to reject such an offer shall not be subject to judicial review.

(4) Failure to propose

If the President determines that a good faith proposal for undertaking or financing action under section 9606 of this title has not been submitted within 60 days of the provision of notice pursuant to this subsection, the President may thereafter commence action under section 9604(a) of this title or take an action against any person under section 9606 of this title. If the President determines that a good faith proposal for undertaking or financing action under section 9604(b) of this title has not been submitted within 60 days after the provision of notice pursuant to this subsection, the President may thereafter commence action under section 9604(b) of this title.

(5) Significant threats

Nothing in this subsection shall limit the President's authority to undertake response or enforcement action regarding a significant threat to public health or the environment within the negotiation period established by this subsection.

(6) **Inconsistent response action**

When either the President, or a potentially responsible party pursuant to an administrative order or consent decree under this chapter, has initiated a remedial investigation and feasibility study for a particular facility under this chapter, no potentially responsible party may undertake any remedial action at the facility unless such remedial action has been authorized by the President.

(f) **Covenant not to sue**

(1) **Discretionary covenants**

The President may, in his discretion, provide any person with a covenant not to sue concerning any liability to the United States under this chapter, including future liability, resulting from a release or threatened release of a hazardous substance addressed by a remedial action, whether that action is onsite or offsite, if each of the following conditions is met:

(A) The covenant not to sue is in the public interest.

(B) The covenant not to sue would expedite response action consistent with the National Contingency Plan under section 9605 of this title.

(C) The person is in full compliance with a consent decree under section 9606 of this title (including a consent decree entered into in accordance with this section) for response to the release or threatened release concerned.

(D) The response action has been approved by the President.

(2) **Special covenants not to sue**

In the case of any person to whom the President is authorized under paragraph (1) of this subsection to provide a covenant not to sue, for the portion of remedial action—

(A) which involves the transport and secure disposition offsite of hazardous substances in a facility meeting the requirements of sections 6924(c), (d), (e), (f), (g), (m), (*o*), (p), (u), and (v) of 6925(c) of this title, where the President has rejected a proposed remedial action that is consistent with the National Contingency Plan that does not include such offsite disposition and has thereafter required offsite disposition; or

(B) which involves the treatment of hazardous substances so as to destroy, eliminate, or permanently immobilize the hazardous constituents of such substances, such that, in the judgment of the President, the substances no longer present any current or currently foreseeable future significant risk to public health, welfare or the environment, no byproduct of the treatment or destruction process presents any significant hazard to public health, welfare or the environment, and all byproducts are themselves treated, destroyed, or contained in a manner which assures that such byproducts do not present any current or currently foreseeable future significant risk to public health, welfare or the environment,

the president shall provide such person with a covenant not to sue with respect to future liability to the United States under this chapter for a future release or threatened release of hazardous substances from such facility, and a person provided such covenant not to sue shall not be liable to the United States under section 9606 or 9607 of this title with respect to such release or threatened release at a future time.

(3) **Requirement that remedial action be completed**

A covenant not to sue concerning future liability to the United States shall not take effect until the President certifies that remedial action has been completed in accordance with the requirements of this chapter at the facility that is the subject of such covenant.

(4) **Factors**

In assessing the appropriateness of a covenant not to sue under paragraph (1) and any condition to be included in a covenant not to sue under paragraph (1) or (2), the President shall consider whether the covenant or condition is in the public interest on the basis of such factors as the following:

(A) The effectiveness and reliability of the remedy, in light of the other alternative remedies considered for the facility concerned.

(B) The nature of the risks remaining at the facility.

(C) The extent to which performance standards are included in the order or decree.

(D) The extent to which the response action provides a complete remedy for the facility, including a reduction in the hazardous nature of the substances at the facility.

(E) The extent to which the technology used in the response action is demonstrated to be effective.

(F) Whether the Fund or other sources of funding would be available for any additional remedial actions that might eventually be necessary at the facility.

(G) Whether the remedial action will be carried out, in whole or in significant part, by the responsible parties themselves.

(5) Satisfactory performance

Any covenant not to sue under this subsection shall be subject to the satisfactory performance by such party of its obligations under the agreement concerned.

(6) Additional condition for future liability

(A) Except for the portion of the remedial action which is subject to a covenant not to sue under paragraph (2) or under subsection (g) of this section (relating to de minimis settlements), a covenant not to sue a person concerning future liability to the United States shall include an exception to the covenant that allows the President to sue such person concerning future liability resulting from the release or threatened release that is the subject of the covenant where such liability arises out of conditions which are unknown at the time the President certifies under paragraph (3) that remedial action has been completed at the facility concerned.

(B) In extraordinary circumstances, the President may determine, after assessment of relevant factors such as those referred to in paragraph (4) and volume, toxicity, mobility, strength of evidence, ability to pay, litigative risks, public interest considerations, precedential value, and inequities and aggravating factors, not to include the exception referred to in subparagraph (A) if other terms, conditions, or requirements of the agreement containing the covenant not to sue are sufficient to provide all reasonable assurances that public health and the environment will be protected from any future releases at or from the facility.

(C) The President is authorized to include any provisions allowing future enforcement action under section 9606 or 9607 of this title that in the discretion of the President are necessary and appropriate to assure protection of public health, welfare, and the environment.

(g) De minimis settlements

(1) Expedited final settlement

Whenever practicable and in the public interest, as determined by the President, the President shall as promptly as possible reach a final settlement with a potentially responsible party in an administrative or civil action under section 9606 or 9607 of this title if such settlement involves only a minor portion of the response costs at the facility concerned and, in the judgment of the President, the conditions in either of the following subparagraph (A) or (B) are met:

(A) Both of the following are minimal in comparison to other hazardous substances at the facility:

(i) The amount of the hazardous substances contributed by that party to the facility.

(ii) The toxic or other hazardous effects of the substances contributed by that party to the facility.

(B) The potentially responsible party—

(i) is the owner of the real property on or in which the facility is located;

(ii) did not conduct or permit the generation, transportation, storage, treatment, or disposal of any hazardous substance at the facility; and

(iii) did not contribute to the release or threat of release of a hazardous substance at the facility through any action or omission.

This subparagraph (B) does not apply if the potentially responsible party purchased the real property with actual or constructive knowledge that the property was used for the generation, transportation, storage, treatment, or disposal of any hazardous substance.

(2) Covenant not to sue

The President may provide a covenant not to sue with respect to the facility concerned to any party who has entered into a settlement under this subsection unless such a covenant would be inconsistent with the public interest as determined under subsection (f) of this section.

(3) Expedited agreement

The President shall reach any such settlement or grant any such covenant not to sue as soon as possible after the President has available the information necessary to reach such a settlement or grant such a covenant.

(4) Consent decree or administrative order

A settlement under this subsection shall be entered as a consent decree or embodied in an administrative order setting forth the terms of the settlement. In the case of any facility where the total response costs exceed $500,000 (excluding interest), if the settlement is embodied as an administrative order, the order may be issued only with the prior written approval of the Attorney General. If the Attorney General or his designee has not approved or disapproved the order within 30 days of this referral, the order shall be deemed to be approved unless the Attorney General and the Administrator have agreed to extend the time. The district court for the district in which the release or threatened release occurs may enforce any such administrative order.

(5) **Effect of agreement**

A party who has resolved its liability to the United States under this subsection shall not be liable for claims for contribution regarding matters addressed in the settlement. Such settlement does not discharge any of the other potentially responsible parties unless its terms so provide, but it reduces the potential liability of the others by the amount of the settlement.

(6) **Settlements with other potentially responsible parties**

Nothing in this subsection shall be construed to affect the authority of the President to reach settlements with other potentially responsible parties under this chapter.

(h) **Cost recovery settlement authority**

(1) **Authority to settle**

The head of any department or agency with authority to undertake a response action under this chapter pursuant to the national contingency plan may consider, compromise, and settle a claim under section 9607 of this title for costs incurred by the United States Government if the claim has not been referred to the Department of Justice for further action. In the case of any facility where the total response costs exceed $500,000 (excluding interest), any claim referred to in the preceding sentence may be compromised and settled only with the prior written approval of the Attorney General.

(2) **Use of arbitration**

Arbitration in accordance with regulations promulgated under this subsection may be used as a method of settling claims of the United States where the total response costs for the facility concerned do not exceed $500,000 (excluding interest). After consultation with the Attorney General, the department or agency head may establish and publish regulations for the use of arbitration or settlement under this subsection.

(3) **Recovery of claims**

If any person fails to pay a claim that has been settled under this subsection, the department or agency head shall request the Attorney General to bring a civil action in an appropriate district court to recover the amount of such claim, plus costs, attorneys' fees, and interest from the date of the settlement. In such an action, the terms of the settlement shall not be subject to review.

(4) **Claims for contribution**

A person who has resolved its liability to the United States under this subsection shall not be liable for claims for contribution regarding matters addressed in the settlement. Such settlement shall not discharge any of the other potentially liable persons unless its terms so provide, but it reduces the potential liability of the others by the amount of the settlement.

(i) **Settlement procedures**

(1) **Publication in Federal Register**

At least 30 days before any settlement (including any settlement arrived at through arbitration) may become final under subsection (h) of this section, or under subsection (g) of this section in the case of a settlement embodied in an administrative order, the head of the department or agency which has jurisdiction over the proposed settlement shall publish in the Federal Register notice of the proposed settlement. The notice shall identify the facility concerned and the parties to the proposed settlement.

(2) **Comment period**

For a 30-day period beginning on the date of publication of notice under paragraph (1) of a proposed settlement, the head of the department or agency which has jurisdiction over the proposed settlement shall provide an opportunity for persons who are not parties to the proposed settlement to file written comments relating to the proposed settlement.

(3) **Consideration of comments**

The head of the department or agency shall consider any comments filed under paragraph (2) in determining whether or not to consent to the proposed settlement and may withdraw or withhold consent to the proposed settlement if such comments disclose facts or considerations which indicate the proposed settlement is inappropriate, improper, or inadequate.

(j) **Natural resources**

(1) **Notification of trustee**

Where a release or threatened release of any hazardous substance that is the subject of negotiations under this section may have resulted in damages to natural resources under the trusteeship of the United States, the President shall notify the Federal natural resource trustee of the negotiations and shall encourage the participation of such trustee in the negotiations.

(2) **Covenant not to sue**

An agreement under this section may contain a covenant not to sue under section 9607(a)(4)(C) of this title for damages to natural resources under the trusteeship of the United States resulting from the release or threatened release of hazardous substances that is the subject of the agreement, but only if the Federal natural resource trustee has agreed in writing to such covenant. The Federal natural resource trustee may agree to such covenant if the potentially responsible party agrees to undertake appropriate actions necessary to protect and restore the natural resources damaged by such release or threatened release of hazardous substances.

(k) Section not applicable to vessels

The provisions of this section shall not apply to releases from a vessel.

(*l*) Civil penalties

A potentially responsible party which is a party to an administrative order or consent decree entered pursuant to an agreement under this section or section 9620 of this title (relating to Federal facilities) or which is a party to an agreement under section 9620 of this title and which fails or refuses to comply with any term or condition of the order, decree or agreement shall be subject to a civil penalty in accordance with section 9609 of this title.

(m) Applicability of general principles of law

In the case of consent decrees and other settlements under this section (including covenants not to sue), no provision of this chapter shall be construed to preclude or otherwise affect the applicability of general principles of law regarding the setting aside or modification of consent decrees or other settlements.

(Pub.L. 96–510, Title I, § 122, as added Oct. 17, 1986, Pub.L. 99–499, Title I, § 122(a), 100 Stat. 1678.)

Effective Date

Section 4 of Pub.L. 99–499, Oct. 17, 1986, 100 Stat. 1614, provided that title I of Pub.L. 99–499 [which enacted this section and sections 9623 to 9625 of this title] is effective Oct. 17, 1986.

CODE OF FEDERAL REGULATIONS

Grants and other federal assistance, see 40 CFR 30.100 et seq.

LAW REVIEW COMMENTARIES

Bankruptcy versus environmental protection: Discharging future CERCLA liability in Chapter 11. Note, 14 Cardozo L.Rev. 1999 (1993).

Environmental liability and the limits of insurance. Kenneth S. Abraham, 88 Columbia L.Rev. 942 (1988).

Property owner liability for environmental contamination in California. Michael B. Hingerty, 22 U.S.F.L.Rev. 31 (1987).

Surveying the superfund settlement dilemma. Lynnette Boomgaarden and Charles Breer, 27 Land & Water L.Rev. 83 (1992).

LIBRARY REFERENCES

Health and Environment ⇨25.5(5.5), 25.7(23).
C.J.S. Health and Environment §§ 91 et seq., 113 et seq.

§ 9623. Reimbursement to local governments [CERCLA § 123]

(a) Application

Any general purpose unit of local government for a political subdivision which is affected by a release or threatened release at any facility may apply to the President for reimbursement under this section.

(b) Reimbursement

(1) Temporary emergency measures

The President is authorized to reimburse local community authorities for expenses incurred (before or after October 17, 1986) in carrying out temporary emergency measures necessary to prevent or mitigate injury to human health or the environment associated with the release or threatened release of any hazardous substance or pollutant or contaminant. Such measures may include, where appropriate, security fencing to limit access, response to fires and explosions, and other measures which require immediate response at the local level.

(2) Local funds not supplanted

Reimbursement under this section shall not supplant local funds normally provided for response.

(c) Amount

The amount of any reimbursement to any local authority under subsection (b)(1) of this section may not exceed $25,000 for a single response. The reimbursement under this section with respect to a single facility shall be limited to the units of local government having jurisdiction over the political subdivision in which the facility is located.

(d) Procedure

Reimbursements authorized pursuant to this section shall be in accordance with rules promulgated by the Administrator within one year after October 17, 1986.

(Pub.L. 96–510, Title I, § 123, as added Oct. 17, 1986, Pub.L. 99–499, Title I, § 123(a), 100 Stat. 1688.)

CODE OF FEDERAL REGULATIONS

Grants and other federal assistance, see 40 CFR 30.100 et seq.

§ 9624. Methane recovery [CERCLA § 124]

(a) In general

In the case of a facility at which equipment for the recovery or processing (including recirculation of condensate) of methane has been installed, for purposes of this chapter:

(1) The owner or operator of such equipment shall not be considered an "owner or operator", as

defined in section 9601(20) of this title, with respect to such facility.

(2) The owner or operator of such equipment shall not be considered to have arranged for disposal or treatment of any hazardous substance at such facility pursuant to section 9607 of this title.

(3) The owner or operator of such equipment shall not be subject to any action under section 9606 of this title with respect to such facility.

(b) Exceptions

Subsection (a) of this section does not apply with respect to a release or threatened release of a hazardous substance from a facility described in subsection (a) of this section if either of the following circumstances exist:

(1) The release or threatened release was primarily caused by activities of the owner or operator of the equipment described in subsection (a) of this section.

(2) The owner or operator of such equipment would be covered by paragraph (1), (2), (3), or (4) of subsection (a) of section 9607 of this title with respect to such release or threatened release if he were not the owner or operator of such equipment.

In the case of any release or threatened release referred to in paragraph (1), the owner or operator of the equipment described in subsection (a) shall be liable under this chapter only for costs or damages primarily caused by the activities of such owner or operator.

(Pub.L. 96–510, Title I, § 124, as added Oct. 17, 1986, Pub.L. 99–499, Title I, § 124(a), 100 Stat. 1688.)

LAW REVIEW COMMENTARIES

Environmental liability and the limits of insurance. Kenneth S. Abraham, 88 Columbia L.Rev. 942 (1988).

§ 9625. Section 6921(b)(3)(A)(i) waste [CERCLA § 125]

(a) Revision of hazard ranking system

This section shall apply only to facilities which are not included or proposed for inclusion on the National Priorities List and which contain substantial volumes of waste described in section 6921(b)(3)(A)(i) of this title. As expeditiously as practicable, the President shall revise the hazard ranking system in effect under the National Contingency Plan with respect to such facilities in a manner which assures appropriate consideration of each of the following site-specific characteristics of such facilities:

(1) The quantity, toxicity, and concentrations of hazardous constituents which are present in such waste and a comparison thereof with other wastes.

(2) The extent of, and potential for, release of such hazardous constituents into the environment.

(3) The degree of risk to human health and the environment posed by such constituents.

(b) Inclusion prohibited

Until the hazard ranking system is revised as required by this section, the President may not include on the National Priorities List any facility which contains substantial volumes of waste described in section 6921(b)(3)(A)(i) of this title on the basis of an evaluation made principally on the volume of such waste and not on the concentrations of the hazardous constituents of such waste. Nothing in this section shall be construed to affect the President's authority to include any such facility on the National Priorities List based on the presence of other substances at such facility or to exercise any other authority of this chapter with respect to such other substances.

(Pub.L. 96–510, Title I, § 125, as added Oct. 17, 1986, Pub.L. 99–499, Title I, § 125, 100 Stat. 1689.)

CODE OF FEDERAL REGULATIONS

Grants and other federal assistance, see 40 CFR 30.100 et seq.

§ 9626. Indian tribes [CERCLA § 126]

(a) Treatment generally

The governing body of an Indian tribe shall be afforded substantially the same treatment as a State with respect to the provisions of section 9603(a) of this title (regarding notification of releases), section 9604(c)(2) of this title (regarding consultation on remedial actions), section 9604(e) of this title (regarding access to information), section 9604(i) of this title (regarding health authorities) and section 9605 of this title (regarding roles and responsibilities under the national contingency plan and submittal of priorities for remedial action, but not including the provision regarding the inclusion of at least one facility per State on the National Priorities List).

(b) Community relocation

Should the President determine that proper remedial action is the permanent relocation of tribal members away from a contaminated site because it is cost effective and necessary to protect their health and welfare, such finding must be concurred in by the affected tribal government before relocation shall occur. The President, in cooperation with the Secretary of the Interior, shall also assure that all benefits of the relocation program are provided to the affected tribe and that alternative land of equivalent value is available and satisfactory to the tribe. Any lands acquired for relocation of tribal members shall be held in trust by the United States for the benefit of the tribe.

(c) Study

The President shall conduct a survey, in consultation with the Indian tribes, to determine the extent of hazardous waste sites on Indian lands. Such survey shall be included within a report which shall make recommendations on the program needs of tribes under this chapter, with particular emphasis on how tribal participation in the administration of such programs can be maximized. Such report shall be submitted to Congress along with the President's budget request for fiscal year 1988.

(d) Limitation

Notwithstanding any other provision of this chapter, no action under this chapter by an Indian tribe shall be barred until the later of the following:

(1) The applicable period of limitations has expired.

(2) 2 years after the United States, in its capacity as trustee for the tribe, gives written notice to the governing body of the tribe that it will not present a claim or commence an action on behalf of the tribe or fails to present a claim or commence an action within the time limitations specified in this chapter.

(Pub.L. 96–510, Title I, § 126, as added Oct. 17, 1986, Pub.L. 99–499, Title II, § 207(e), 100 Stat. 1706.)

Effective Date

Section 4 of Pub.L. 99–499, Oct. 17, 1986, 100 Stat. 1614, provided that title II of Pub.L. 99–499, [which enacted this section] is effective Oct. 17, 1986.

CODE OF FEDERAL REGULATIONS

Grants and other federal assistance, see 40 CFR 30.100 et seq.

SUBCHAPTER II—HAZARDOUS SUBSTANCE RESPONSE REVENUE

PART A—HAZARDOUS SUBSTANCE RESPONSE TRUST FUND

§§ 9631 to 9633. Repealed. Pub.L. 99–499, Title V, § 517(c)(1), Oct. 17, 1986, 100 Stat. 1774

PART B—POST-CLOSURE LIABILITY TRUST FUND

§ 9641. Repealed. Pub.L. 99–499, Title V, § 514(b), Oct. 17, 1986, 100 Stat. 1767

SUBCHAPTER III—MISCELLANEOUS PROVISIONS

§ 9651. Reports and studies [CERCLA § 301]

(a) Implementation experiences; identification and disposal of waste

(1) The President shall submit to the Congress, within four years after December 11, 1980, a comprehensive report on experience with the implementation of this chapter including, but not limited to—

(A) the extent to which the chapter and Fund are effective in enabling Government to respond to and mitigate the effects of releases of hazardous substances;

(B) a summary of past receipts and disbursements from the Fund;

(C) a projection of any future funding needs remaining after the expiration of authority to collect taxes, and of the threat to public health, welfare, and the environment posed by the projected releases which create any such needs;

(D) the record and experience of the Fund in recovering Fund disbursements from liable parties;

(E) the record of State participation in the system of response, liability, and compensation established by this chapter;

(F) the impact of the taxes imposed by subchapter II of this chapter on the Nation's balance of trade with other countries;

(G) an assessment of the feasibility and desirability of a schedule of taxes which would take into account one or more of the following: the likelihood of a release of a hazardous substance, the degree of hazard and risk of harm to public health, welfare, and the environment resulting from any such release, incentives to proper handling, recycling, incineration, and neutralization of hazardous wastes, and disincentives to improper or illegal handling or disposal of hazardous materials, administrative and reporting burdens on Government and industry, and the extent to which the tax burden falls on the substances and parties which create the problems addressed by this chapter. In preparing the report, the President shall consult with appropriate Federal, State, and local agencies, affected industries and claimants, and such other interested parties as he may find useful. Based upon the analyses and consultation required by this subsection, the President shall also include in the report any recommendations for legislative changes he may deem necessary for the better effectuation of the purposes of this chapter, including but not limited to recommendations concerning authorization levels, taxes, State participation, liability and liability limits, and financial responsibility provisions for the Response Trust Fund and the Post-closure Liability Trust Fund;

(H) an exemption from or an increase in the substances or the amount of taxes imposed by section 4661 of Title 26 for copper, lead, and zinc oxide, and for feedstocks when used in the manufacture and production of fertilizers, based upon the expenditure experience of the Response Trust Fund;

(I) the economic impact of taxing coal-derived substances and recycled metals.

(2) The Administrator of the Environmental Protection Agency (in consultation with the Secretary of the Treasury) shall submit to the Congress (i) within four years after December 11, 1980, a report identifying additional wastes designated by rule as hazardous after the effective date of this chapter and pursuant to section 3001 of the Solid Waste Disposal Act [42 U.S.C.A. § 6921] and recommendations on appropriate tax rates for such wastes for the Post-closure Liability Trust Fund. The report shall, in addition, recommend a tax rate, considering the quantity and potential danger to human health and the environment posed by the disposal of any wastes which the Administrator, pursuant to subsection 3001(b)(2)(B) and subsection 3001(b)(3)(A) of the Solid Waste Disposal Act of 1980 [42 U.S.C.A. §§ 6921(b)(2)(B) and 6921(b)(3)(A)], has determined should be subject to regulation under subtitle C of such Act [42 U.S.C.A. § 6921 et seq.], (ii) within three years after December 11, 1980, a report on the necessity for and the adequacy of the revenue raised, in relation to estimated future requirements, of the Post-closure Liability Trust Fund.

(b) Private insurance protection

The President shall conduct a study to determine (1) whether adequate private insurance protection is available on reasonable terms and conditions to the owners and operators of vessels and facilities subject to liability under section 9607 of this title, and (2) whether the market for such insurance is sufficiently competitive to assure purchasers of features such as a reasonable range of deductibles, coinsurance provisions, and exclusions. The President shall submit the results of his study, together with his recommendations, within two years of December 11, 1980, and shall submit an interim report on his study within one year of December 11, 1980.

(c) Regulations respecting assessment of damages to natural resources

(1) The President, acting through Federal officials designated by the National Contingency Plan published under section 9605 of this title, shall study and, not later than two years after December 11, 1980, shall promulgate regulations for the assessment of damages for injury to, destruction of, or loss of natural resources resulting from a release of oil or a hazardous substance for the purposes of this chapter and section 1321(f)(4) and (5) of Title 33. Notwithstanding the failure of the President to promulgate the regulations required under this subsection on the required date, the President shall promulgate such regulations not later than 6 months after October 17, 1986.

(2) Such regulations shall specify (A) standard procedures for simplified assessments requiring minimal field observation, including establishing measures of damages based on units of discharge or release or units of affected area, and (B) alternative protocols for conducting assessments in individual cases to determine the type and extent of short- and long-term injury, destruction, or loss. Such regulations shall identify the best available procedures to determine such damages, including both direct and indirect injury, destruction, or loss and shall take into consideration factors including, but not limited to, replacement value, use value, and ability of the ecosystem or resource to recover.

(3) Such regulations shall be reviewed and revised as appropriate every two years.

(d) Issues, alternatives, and policy considerations involving selection of locations for waste treatment, storage, and disposal facilities

The Administrator of the Environmental Protection Agency shall, in consultation with other Federal agencies and appropriate representatives of State and local governments and nongovernmental agencies, conduct a study and report to the Congress within two years of December 11, 1980, on the issues, alternatives, and policy considerations involved in the selection of locations for hazardous waste treatment, storage, and disposal facilities. This study shall include—

(A) an assessment of current and projected treatment, storage, and disposal capacity needs and shortfalls for hazardous waste by management category on a State-by-State basis;

(B) an evaluation of the appropriateness of a regional approach to siting and designing hazardous waste management facilities and the identification of hazardous waste management regions, interstate or intrastate, or both, with similar hazardous waste management needs;

(C) solicitation and analysis of proposals for the construction and operation of hazardous waste management facilities by nongovernmental entities, except that no proposal solicited under terms of this subsection shall be analyzed if it involves cost to the United States Government or fails to comply with the requirements of subtitle C of the Solid Waste Disposal Act [42 U.S.C.A. § 6921 et seq.] and other applicable provisions of law;

(D) recommendations on the appropriate balance between public and private sector involvement in the siting, design, and operation of new hazardous waste management facilities;

(E) documentation of the major reasons for public opposition to new hazardous waste management facilities; and

(F) an evaluation of the various options for overcoming obstacles to siting new facilities, including needed legislation for implementing the most suitable option or options.

(e) Adequacy of existing common law and statutory remedies

(1) In order to determine the adequacy of existing common law and statutory remedies in providing legal redress for harm to man and the environment caused by the release of hazardous substances into the environment, there shall be submitted to the Congress a study within twelve months of December 11, 1980.

(2) This study shall be conducted with the assistance of the American Bar Association, the American Law Institute, the Association of American Trial Lawyers, and the National Association of State Attorneys General with the President of each entity selecting three members from each organization to conduct the study. The study chairman and one reporter shall be elected from among the twelve members of the study group.

(3) As part of their review of the adequacy of existing common law and statutory remedies, the study group shall evaluate the following:

(A) the nature, adequacy, and availability of existing remedies under present law in compensating for harm to man from the release of hazardous substances;

(B) the nature of barriers to recovery (particularly with respect to burdens of going forward and of proof and relevancy) and the role such barriers play in the legal system;

(C) the scope of the evidentiary burdens placed on the plaintiff in proving harm from the release of hazardous substances, particularly in light of the scientific uncertainty over causation with respect to—

(i) carcinogens, mutagens, and teratogens, and

(ii) the human health effects of exposure to low doses of hazardous substances over long periods of time;

(D) the nature and adequacy of existing remedies under present law in providing compensation for damages to natural resources from the release of hazardous substances;

(E) the scope of liability under existing law and the consequences, particularly with respect to obtaining insurance, of any changes in such liability;

(F) barriers to recovery posed by existing statutes of limitations.

(4) The report shall be submitted to the Congress with appropriate recommendations. Such recommendations shall explicitly address—

(A) the need for revisions in existing statutory or common law, and

(B) whether such revisions should take the form of Federal statutes or the development of a model code which is recommended for adoption by the States.

(5) The Fund shall pay administrative expenses incurred for the study. No expenses shall be available to pay compensation, except expenses on a per diem basis for the one reporter, but in no case shall the total expenses of the study exceed $300,000.

(f) Modification of national contingency plan

The President, acting through the Administrator of the Environmental Protection Agency, the Secretary of Transportation, the Administrator of the Occupational Safety and Health Administration, and the Director of the National Institute for Occupational Safety and Health shall study and, not later than two years after December 11, 1980, shall modify the national contingency plan to provide for the protection of the health and safety of employees involved in response actions.

(g) Insurability study

(1) Study by Comptroller General

The Comptroller General of the United States, in consultation with the persons described in paragraph (2), shall undertake a study to determine the insurability, and effects on the standard of care, of the liability of each of the following:

(A) Persons who generate hazardous substances: liability for costs and damages under this chapter.

(B) Persons who own or operate facilities: liability for costs and damages under this chapter.

(C) Persons liable for injury to persons or property caused by the release of hazardous substances into the environment.

(2) Consultation

In conducting the study under this subsection, the Comptroller General shall consult with the following:

(A) Representatives of the Administrator.

(B) Representatives of persons described in subparagraphs (A) through (C) of the preceding paragraph.

(C) Representatives (i) of groups or organizations comprised generally of persons adversely affected by releases or threatened releases of hazardous substances and (ii) of groups organized for protecting the interests of consumers.

(D) Representatives of property and casualty insurers.

(E) Representatives of reinsurers.

(F) Persons responsible for the regulation of insurance at the State level.

(3) Items evaluated

The study under this section shall include, among other matters, an evaluation of the following:

(A) Current economic conditions in, and the future outlook for, the commercial market for insurance and reinsurance.

(B) Current trends in statutory and common law remedies.

(C) The impact of possible changes in traditional standards of liability, proof, evidence, and damages on existing statutory and common law remedies.

(D) The effect of the standard of liability and extent of the persons upon whom it is imposed under this chapter on the protection of human health and the environment and on the availability, underwriting, and pricing of insurance coverage.

(E) Current trends, if any, in the judicial interpretation and construction of applicable insurance contracts, together with the degree to which amendments in the language of such contracts and the description of the risks assumed, could affect such trends.

(F) The frequency and severity of a representative sample of claims closed during the calendar year immediately preceding Oct. 17, 1986.

(G) Impediments to the acquisition of insurance or other means of obtaining liability coverage other than those referred to in the preceding subparagraphs.

(H) The effects of the standards of liability and financial responsibility requirements imposed pursuant to this chapter on the cost of, and incentives for, developing and demonstrating alternative and innovative treatment technologies, as well as waste generation minimization.

(4) Submission

The Comptroller General shall submit a report on the results of the study to Congress with appropriate recommendations within 12 months after October 17, 1986.

(h) Report and oversight requirements

(1) Annual report by EPA

On January 1 of each year the Administrator of the Environmental Protection Agency shall submit an annual report to Congress of such Agency on the progress achieved in implementing this chapter during the preceding fiscal year. In addition such report shall specifically include each of the following:

(A) A detailed description of each feasibility study carried out at a facility under subchapter I of this chapter.

(B) The status and estimated date of completion of each such study.

(C) Notice of each such study which will not meet a previously published schedule for completion and the new estimated date for completion.

(D) An evaluation of newly developed feasible and achievable permanent treatment technologies.

(E) Progress made in reducing the number of facilities subject to review under section 9621(c) of this title.

(F) A report on the status of all remedial and enforcement actions undertaken during the prior fiscal year, including a comparison to remedial and enforcement actions undertaken in prior fiscal years.

(G) An estimate of the amount of resources, including the number of work years or personnel, which would be necessary for each department, agency, or instrumentality which is carrying out any activities of this chapter to complete the implementation of all duties vested in the department, agency, or instrumentality under this chapter.

(2) Review by Inspector General

Consistent with the authorities of the Inspector General Act of 1978 [5 U.S.C.A. App. 3, § 1 et seq.] the Inspector General of the Environmental Protection Agency shall review any report submitted under paragraph (1) related to EPA's activities for reasonableness and accuracy and submit to Congress, as a part of such report a report on the results of such review.

(3) Congressional oversight

After receiving the reports under paragraphs (1) and (2) of this subsection in any calendar year, the appropriate authorizing committees of Congress shall conduct oversight hearings to ensure that this chapter is being implemented according to the purposes of this chapter and congressional intent in enacting this chapter.

(Dec. 11, 1980, Pub.L. 96–510, Title III, § 301, 94 Stat. 2805; Oct. 17, 1986, Pub.L. 99–499, Title I, § 107(d)(3), Title II, §§ 208, 212, 100 Stat. 1630, 1707, 1726.)

LAW REVIEW COMMENTARIES

New federalism, old due process, retroactive revival: Constitutional problems with CERCLA's Amendment of state law. Alfred R. Light, 40 U.Kan.L.Rev. 365 (1992).

LIBRARY REFERENCES

Health and Environment ⚖25.5.
C.J.S. Health and Environment § 61 et seq.

§ 9652. Effective dates; savings provisions [CERCLA § 302]

(a) Unless otherwise provided, all provisions of this chapter shall be effective on December 11, 1980.

(b) Any regulation issued pursuant to any provisions of section 1321 of Title 33 which is repealed or superseded by this chapter and which is in effect on the date immediately preceding the effective date of this chapter shall be deemed to be a regulation issued pursuant to the authority of this chapter and shall remain in full force and effect unless or until superseded by new regulations issued thereunder.

(c) Any regulation—

(1) respecting financial responsibility,

(2) issued pursuant to any provision of law repealed or superseded by this chapter, and

(3) in effect on the date immediately preceding the effective date of this chapter shall be deemed to be a regulation issued pursuant to the authority of this chapter and shall remain in full force and effect unless or until superseded by new regulations issued thereunder.

(d) Nothing in this chapter shall affect or modify in any way the obligations or liabilities of any person under other Federal or State law, including common law, with respect to releases of hazardous substances or other pollutants or contaminants. The provisions of this chapter shall not be considered, interpreted, or construed in any way as reflecting a determination, in part or whole, of policy regarding the inapplicability of strict liability, or strict liability doctrines, to activities relating to hazardous substances, pollutants, or contaminants or other such activities.

(Dec. 11, 1980, Pub.L. 96–510, Title III, § 302, 94 Stat. 2808.)

§ 9653. Repealed. Pub.L. 99–499, Title V, § 511(b), Oct. 17, 1986, 100 Stat. 1761

§ 9654. Applicability of Federal water pollution control funding, etc., provisions [CERCLA § 304]

(a) Omitted.

(b) One-half of the unobligated balance remaining before December 11, 1980, under subsection (k) of section 1321 of Title 33 and all sums appropriated under section 1364(b) of Title 33 shall be transferred to the Fund established under subchapter II of this chapter.

(c) In any case in which any provision of section 1321 of Title 33 is determined to be in conflict with any provisions of this chapter, the provisions of this chapter shall apply.

(Dec. 11, 1980, Pub.L. 96–510, Title III, § 304, 94 Stat. 2809.)

CODE OF FEDERAL REGULATIONS

Grants and other federal assistance, see 40 CFR 30.100 et seq.

§ 9655. Legislative veto of rule or regulation [CERCLA § 305]

(a) Transmission to Congress upon promulgation or repromulgation of rule or regulation; disapproval procedures

Notwithstanding any other provision of law, simultaneously with promulgation or repromulgation of any rule or regulation under authority of subchapter I of this chapter, the head of the department, agency, or instrumentality promulgating such rule or regulation shall transmit a copy thereof to the Secretary of the Senate and the Clerk of the House of Representatives. Except as provided in subsection (b) of this section, the rule or regulation shall not become effective, if—

(1) within ninety calendar days of continuous session of Congress after the date of promulgation, both Houses of Congress adopt a concurrent resolution, the matter after the resolving clause of which is as follows: "That Congress disapproves the rule or regulation promulgated by the ______ dealing with the matter of ______, which rule or regulation was transmitted to Congress on ______.", the blank spaces therein being appropriately filled; or

(2) within sixty calendar days of continuous session of Congress after the date of promulgation, one House of Congress adopts such a concurrent resolution and transmits such resolution to the other House, and such resolution is not disapproved by such other House within thirty calendar days of continuous session of Congress after such transmittal.

(b) Approval; effective dates

If, at the end of sixty calendar days of continuous session of Congress after the date of promulgation of a rule or regulation, no committee of either House of Congress has reported or been discharged from further consideration of a concurrent resolution disapproving the rule or regulation and neither House has adopted such a resolution, the rule or regulation may go into effect immediately. If, within such sixty calendar days, such a committee has reported or been discharged from further consideration of such a resolution, or either House has adopted such a resolution, the rule or regulation may go into effect not sooner than ninety calendar days of continuous session of Congress after such rule is prescribed unless disapproved as provided in subsection (a) of this section.

(c) Sessions of Congress as applicable

For purposes of subsections (a) and (b) of this section—

(1) continuity of session is broken only by an adjournment of Congress sine die; and

(2) the days on which either House is not in session because of an adjournment of more than three days to a day certain are excluded in the computation of thirty, sixty, and ninety calendar days of continuous session of Congress.

(d) Congressional inaction on, or rejection of, resolution of disapproval

Congressional inaction on, or rejection of, a resolution of disapproval shall not be deemed an expression of approval of such rule or regulation.

(Dec. 11, 1980, Pub.L. 96–510, Title III, § 305, 94 Stat. 2809.)

LIBRARY REFERENCES

Health and Environment ⇔25.5(1).
C.J.S. Health and Environment § 61 et seq.

§ 9656. Transportation of hazardous substances; listing as hazardous material; liability for release [CERCLA § 306]

(a) Each hazardous substance which is listed or designated as provided in section 9601(14) of this title shall, within 30 days after October 17, 1986, or at the time of such listing or designation, whichever is later, be listed and regulated as a hazardous material under the Hazardous Materials Transportation Act [49 App. U.S.C.A. § 1801 et seq.].

(b) A common or contract carrier shall be liable under other law in lieu of section 9607 of this title for damages or remedial action resulting from the release of a hazardous substance during the course of transportation which commenced prior to the effective date of the listing and regulation of such substance as a hazardous material under the Hazardous Materials Transportation Act [49 App.U.S.C.A. § 1801 et seq.], or for substances listed pursuant to subsection (a) of this section, prior to the effective date of such listing: *Provided, however,* That this subsection shall not apply where such a carrier can demonstrate that he did not have actual knowledge of the identity or nature of the substance released.

(Dec. 11, 1980, Pub.L. 96–510, Title III, § 306(a), (b), 94 Stat. 2810; Oct. 17, 1986, Pub.L. 99–499, Title II, § 202, 100 Stat. 1695.)

CODE OF FEDERAL REGULATIONS

Grants and other federal assistance, see 40 CFR 30.100 et seq.

§ 9657. Separability of provisions; contribution [CERCLA § 308]

If any provision of this chapter, or the application of any provision of this chapter to any person or circumstance, is held invalid, the application of such provision to other persons or circumstances and the remainder of this chapter shall not be affected thereby. If an administrative settlement under section 9622 of this title has the effect of limiting any person's right to obtain contribution from any party to such settlement, and if the effect of such limitation would constitute a taking without just compensation in violation of the fifth amendment of the Constitution of the United States, such person shall not be entitled, under other laws of the United States, to recover compensation from the United States for such taking, but in any such case, such limitation on the right to obtain contribution shall be treated as having no force and effect.

(Dec. 11, 1980, Pub.L. 96–510, Title III, § 308, 94 Stat. 2811; Oct. 7, 1986, Pub.L. 99–499, Title I, § 122(b), 100 Stat. 1688.)

LIBRARY REFERENCES

Statutes ⇔64.
C.J.S. Statutes § 92.

§ 9658. Actions under State law for damages from exposure to hazardous substances [CERCLA § 309]

(a) State statutes of limitations for hazardous substance cases

(1) Exception to State statutes

In the case of any action brought under State law for personal injury, or property damages, which are caused or contributed to by exposure to any hazardous substance, or pollutant or contaminant, released into the environment from a facility, if the applicable limitations period for such action (as specified in the State statute of limitations or under common law) provides a commencement date which is earlier than the federally required commencement date, such period shall commence at the federally required commencement date in lieu of the date specified in such State statute.

(2) State law generally applicable

Except as provided in paragraph (1), the statute of limitations established under State law shall apply in all actions brought under State law for personal injury, or property damages, which are caused or contributed to by exposure to any hazardous substance, or pollutant or contaminant, released into the environment from a facility.

(3) Actions under section 9607

Nothing in this section shall apply with respect to any cause of action brought under section 9607 of this title.

(b) Definitions

As used in this section—

(1) Subchapter I terms

The terms used in this section shall have the same meaning as when used in subchapter I of this chapter.

(2) Applicable limitations period

The term "applicable limitations period" means the period specified in a statute of limitations during which a civil action referred to in subsection (a)(1) of this section may be brought.

(3) Commencement date

The term "commencement date" means the date specified in a statute of limitations as the beginning of the applicable limitations period.

(4) Federally required commencement date

(A) In general

Except as provided in subparagraph (B), the term "federally required commencement date" means the date the plaintiff knew (or reasonably should have known) that the personal injury or property damages referred to in subsection (a)(1) of this section were caused or contributed to by the hazardous substance or pollutant or contaminant concerned.

(B) Special rules

In the case of a minor or incompetent plaintiff, the term "federally required commencement date" means the later of the date referred to in subparagraph (A) or the following:

(i) In the case of a minor, the date on which the minor reaches the age of majority, as determined by State law, or has a legal representative appointed.

(ii) In the case of an incompetent individual, the date on which such individual becomes competent or has had a legal representative appointed.

(Pub.L. 96–510, Title III, § 309, as added Oct. 17, 1986, Pub.L. 99–499, Title II, § 203(a), 100 Stat. 1695.)

Effective Date

Section 203(b) of Pub.L. 99–499 Title II, Oct. 17, 1986, 100 Stat. 1696, provided that: "The amendment made by subsection (a) of this section [enacting this section] shall take effect with respect to actions brought after December 11, 1980."

LAW REVIEW COMMENTARIES

Choosing law: The limitations debates. Louise Weinberg, 1991 U.Ill.L.Rev. 365 (1992).

New federalism, old due process, retroactive revival: Constitutional problems with CERCLA's Amendment of state law. Alfred R. Light, 40 U.Kan.L.Rev. 365 (1992).

Superfund amended: A new emphasis on the public health. James M. Strock, 16 Colo.Law. 1845 (1987).

LIBRARY REFERENCES

Health and Environment ⇐25.5(5.5), 38.
C.J.S. Health and Environment §§ 49 et seq., 91 et seq.

§ 9659. Citizens suits [CERCLA § 310]

(a) Authority to bring civil actions

Except as provided in subsections (d) and (e) of this section and in section 9613(h) of this title (relating to timing of judicial review), any person may commence a civil action on his own behalf—

(1) against any person (including the United States and any other governmental instrumentality or agency, to the extent permitted by the eleventh amendment to the Constitution) who is alleged to be in violation of any standard, regulation, condition, requirement, or order which has become effective pursuant to this chapter (including any provision of an agreement under section 9620 of this title, relating to Federal facilities); or

(2) against the President or any other officer of the United States (including the Administrator of the Environmental Protection Agency and the Administrator of the ATSDR) where there is alleged a failure of the President or of such other officer to perform any act or duty under this chapter, including an act or duty under section 9620 of this title (relating to Federal facilities), which is not discretionary with the President or such other officer.

Paragraph (2) shall not apply to any act or duty under the provisions of section 9660 of this title (relating to research, development, and demonstration).

(b) Venue

(1) Actions under subsection (a)(1)

Any action under subsection (a)(1) of this section shall be brought in the district court for the district in which the alleged violation occurred.

(2) Actions under subsection (a)(2)

Any action brought under subsection (a)(2) of this section may be brought in the United States District Court for the District of Columbia.

(c) Relief

The district court shall have jurisdiction in actions brought under subsection (a)(1) of this section to enforce the standard, regulation, condition, requirement, or order concerned (including any provision of an agreement under section 9620 of this title), to order such action as may be necessary to correct the violation, and to impose any civil penalty provided for the violation. The district court shall have jurisdiction in actions brought under subsection (a)(2) of this section to order the President or other officer to perform the act or duty concerned.

(d) Rules applicable to subsection (a)(1) actions

(1) Notice

No action may be commenced under subsection (a)(1) of this section before 60 days after the plaintiff has given notice of the violation to each of the following:

(A) The President.

(B) The State in which the alleged violation occurs.

(C) Any alleged violator of the standard, regulation, condition, requirement, or order concerned (including any provision of an agreement under section 9620 of this title).

Notice under this paragraph shall be given in such manner as the President shall prescribe by regulation.

(2) Diligent prosecution

No action may be commenced under paragraph (1) of subsection (a) of this section if the President has commenced and is diligently prosecuting an action under this chapter, or under the Solid Waste Disposal Act [42 U.S.C.A. § 6901 et seq.] to require compliance with the standard, regulation, condition, requirement, or order concerned (including any provision of an agreement under section 9620 of this title).

(e) Rules applicable to subsection (a)(2) actions

No action may be commenced under paragraph (2) of subsection (a) of this section before the 60th day following the date on which the plaintiff gives notice to the Administrator or other department, agency, or instrumentality that the plaintiff will commence such action. Notice under this subsection shall be given in such manner as the President shall prescribe by regulation.

(f) Costs

The court, in issuing any final order in any action brought pursuant to this section, may award costs of litigation (including reasonable attorney and expert witness fees) to the prevailing or the substantially prevailing party whenever the court determines such an award is appropriate. The court may, if a temporary restraining order or preliminary injunction is sought, require the filing of a bond or equivalent security in accordance with the Federal Rules of Civil Procedure.

(g) Intervention

In any action under this section, the United States or the State, or both, if not a party may intervene as a matter of right. For other provisions regarding intervention, see section 9613 of this title.

(h) Other rights

This chapter does not affect or otherwise impair the rights of any person under Federal, State, or common law, except with respect to the timing of review as provided in section 9613(h) of this title or as otherwise provided in section 9658 of this title (relating to actions under State law).

(i) Definitions

The terms used in this section shall have the same meanings as when used in subchapter I of this chapter.

(Pub.L. 96–510, Title III, § 310, as added Oct. 17, 1986, Pub.L. 99–499, Title II, § 206, 100 Stat. 1703.)

Effective Date

Section 4 of Pub.L. 99–499, Oct. 17, 1986, 100 Stat. 1614, provided that title II of Pub.L. 99–499 [which enacted this section and sections 9660 and 9661 of this title] is effective Oct. 17, 1986.

CODE OF FEDERAL REGULATIONS

Grants and other federal assistance, see 40 CFR 30.100 et seq.

LAW REVIEW COMMENTARIES

Insurance coverage for superfund liability: A plain meaning approach to the pollution exclusion clause. Note, 27 Washburn L.J. 161 (1987).

LIBRARY REFERENCES

Health and Environment ⟹38.
C.J.S. Health and Environment § 49 et seq.

§ 9660. Research, development, and demonstration [CERCLA § 311]

(a) Hazardous substance research and training

(1) Authorities of secretary

The Secretary of Health and Human Services (hereinafter in this subsection referred to as the Secretary), in consultation with the Administrator, shall establish and support a basic research and training program (through grants, cooperative agreements, and contracts) consisting of the following:

(A) Basic research (including epidemiologic and ecologic studies) which may include each of the following:

(i) Advanced techniques for the detection, assessment, and evaluation of the effects on human health of hazardous substances.

(ii) Methods to assess the risks to human health presented by hazardous substances.

(iii) Methods and technologies to detect hazardous substances in the environment and basic biological, chemical, and physical methods to reduce the amount and toxicity of hazardous substances.

(B) Training, which may include each of the following:

(i) Short courses and continuing education for State and local health and environment agency personnel and other personnel engaged in the handling of hazardous substances, in the management of facilities at which hazardous substances are located, and in the evaluation of the hazards to human health presented by such facilities.

(ii) Graduate or advanced training in environmental and occupational health and safety and in the public health and engineering aspects of hazardous waste control.

(iii) Graduate training in the geosciences, including hydrogeology, geological engineering, geophysics, geochemistry, and related fields necessary to meet professional personnel needs in the public and private sectors and to effectuate the purposes of this chapter.

(2) Director of NIEHS

The Director of the National Institute for Environmental Health Sciences shall cooperate fully with the relevant Federal agencies referred to in subparagraph (A) of paragraph (5) in carrying out the purposes of this section.

(3) Recipients of grants, etc.

A grant, cooperative agreement, or contract may be made or entered into under paragraph (1) with an accredited institution of higher education. The institution may carry out the research or training under the grant, cooperative agreement, or contract through contracts, including contracts with any of the following:

(A) Generators of hazardous wastes.

(B) Persons involved in the detection, assessment, evaluation, and treatment of hazardous substances.

(C) Owners and operators of facilities at which hazardous substances are located.

(D) State and local governments.

(4) Procedures

In making grants and entering into cooperative agreements and contracts under this subsection, the Secretary shall act through the Director of the National Institute for Environmental Health Sciences. In considering the allocation of funds for training purposes, the Director shall ensure that at least one grant, cooperative agreement, or contract shall be awarded for training described in each of clauses (i), (ii), and (iii) of paragraph (1)(B). Where applicable, the Director may choose to operate training activities in cooperation with the Director of the National Institute for Occupational Safety and Health. The procedures applicable to grants and contracts under title IV of the Public Health Service Act [42 U.S.C.A. § 281 et seq.] shall be followed under this subsection.

(5) Advisory council

To assist in the implementation of this subsection and to aid in the coordination of research and demonstration and training activities funded from the Fund under this section, the Secretary shall appoint an advisory council (hereinafter in this subsection referred to as the "Advisory Council") which shall consist of representatives of the following:

(A) The relevant Federal agencies.

(B) The chemical industry.

(C) The toxic waste management industry.

(D) Institutions of higher education.

(E) State and local health and environmental agencies.

(F) The general public.

(6) Planning

Within nine months after October 17, 1986, the Secretary, acting through the Director of the National Institute for Environmental Health Sciences, shall issue a plan for the implementation of paragraph (1). The plan shall include priorities for actions under paragraph (1) and include research and training relevant to scientific and technological issues resulting from site specific hazardous substance response experience. The Secretary shall, to the maximum extent practicable, take appropriate steps to coordinate program activities under this plan with the activities of other Federal agencies in order to avoid duplication of effort. The plan shall be consistent with the need for the development of new technologies for meeting the goals of response actions in accordance with the provisions of this chapter. The Advisory Council shall be provided an opportunity to review and comment on the plan and priorities and assist appropriate coordination among the relevant Federal agencies referred to in subparagraph (A) of paragraph (5).

(b) Alternative or innovative treatment technology research and demonstration program

(1) Establishment

The Administrator is authorized and directed to carry out a program of research, evaluation, testing, development, and demonstration of alternative or innovative treatment technologies (hereinafter in this subsection referred to as the "program") which may be utilized in response actions to achieve more permanent protection of human health and welfare and the environment.

(2) Administration

The program shall be administered by the Administrator, acting through an office of technology demonstration and shall be coordinated with programs carried out by the Office of Solid Waste and Emergency Response and the Office of Research and Development.

(3) Contracts and grants

In carrying out the program, the Administrator is authorized to enter into contracts and cooperative agreements with, and make grants to, persons, public entities, and nonprofit private entities which are exempt from tax under section 501(c)(3) of Title 26. The Administrator shall, to the maximum extent possible, enter into appropriate cost sharing arrangements under this subsection.

(4) Use of sites

In carrying out the program, the Administrator may arrange for the use of sites at which a response may be undertaken under section 9604 of this title for the purposes of carrying out research, testing, evaluation, development, and demonstration projects. Each such project shall be carried out under such terms and conditions as the Administrator shall require to assure the protection of human health and the environment and to assure adequate control by the Administrator of the research, testing, evaluation, development, and demonstration activities at the site.

(5) Demonstration assistance

(A) Program components

The demonstration assistance program shall include the following:

(i) The publication of a solicitation and the evaluation of applications for demonstration projects utilizing alternative or innovative technologies.

(ii) The selection of sites which are suitable for the testing and evaluation of innovative technologies.

(iii) The development of detailed plans for innovative technology demonstration projects.

(iv) The supervision of such demonstration projects and the providing of quality assurance for data obtained.

(v) The evaluation of the results of alternative innovative technology demonstration projects and the determination of whether or not the technologies used are effective and feasible.

(B) Solicitation

Within 90 days after October 17, 1986, and no less often than once every 12 months thereafter, the Administrator shall publish a solicitation for innovative or alternative technologies at a stage of development suitable for full-scale demonstrations at sites at which a response action may be undertaken under section 9604 of this title. The purpose of any such project shall be to demonstrate the use of an alternative or innovative treatment technology with respect to hazardous substances or pollutants or contaminants which are located at the site or which are to be removed from the site. The solicitation notice shall prescribe information to be included in the application, including technical and economic data derived from the applicant's own research and development efforts, and other information sufficient to permit the Administrator to assess the technology's potential and the types of remedial action to which it may be applicable.

(C) Applications

Any person and any public or private nonprofit entity may submit an application to the Administrator in response to the solicitation. The application shall contain a proposed demonstration plan setting forth how and when the project is to be carried out and such other information as the Administrator may require.

(D) Project selection

In selecting technologies to be demonstrated, the Administrator shall fully review the applications submitted and shall consider at least the criteria specified in paragraph (7). The Administrator shall select or refuse to select a project for demonstration under this subsection within 90 days of receiving the completed application for such project. In the case of a refusal to select the project, the Administrator shall notify the applicant within such 90-day period of the reasons for his refusal.

(E) Site selection

The Administrator shall propose 10 sites at which a response may be undertaken under section 9604 of this title to be the location of any demonstration project under this subsection within 60 days after the close of the public comment period. After an opportunity for notice and public comment, the Administrator shall select such sites and projects. In selecting any such site, the Administrator shall take into account the applicant's technical data and preferences either for onsite operation or for utilizing the site as a source of hazardous substances or pollutants or contaminants to be treated offsite.

(F) Demonstration plan

Within 60 days after the selection of the site under this paragraph to be the location of a demonstration project, the Administrator shall establish a final demonstration plan for the project, based upon the demonstration plan contained in the application for the project. Such plan shall clearly set forth how and when the demonstration project will be carried out.

(G) Supervision and testing

Each demonstration project under this subsection shall be performed by the applicant, or by a person satisfactory to the applicant, under the supervision of the Administrator. The Administrator shall enter into a written agreement with each applicant granting the Administrator the responsibility and authority for testing procedures, quality control, monitoring, and other measurements necessary to determine and evaluate the results of the demonstration project. The Administrator may pay the costs of testing, monitoring, quality control, and other measurements required by the Administrator to determine and evaluate the results of the demonstration project, and the limitations established by subparagraph (J) shall not apply to such costs.

(H) Project completion

Each demonstration project under this subsection shall be completed within such time as is established in the demonstration plan.

(I) Extensions

The Administrator may extend any deadline established under this paragraph by mutual agreement with the applicant concerned.

(J) Funding restrictions

The Administrator shall not provide any Federal assistance for any part of a full-scale field demonstration project under this subsection to any applicant unless such applicant can demonstrate that it cannot obtain appropriate private financing on reasonable terms and conditions sufficient to carry out such demonstration project without such Federal assistance. The total Federal funds for any full-scale field demonstration project under this subsection shall not exceed 50 percent of the total cost of such project estimated at the time of the award of such assistance. The Administrator shall not expend more than $10,000,000 for assistance under the program in any fiscal year and shall not expend more than $3,000,000 for any single project.

(6) Field demonstrations

In carrying out the program, the Administrator shall initiate or cause to be initiated at least 10 field demonstration projects of alternative or innovative treatment technologies at sites at which a response may be undertaken under section 9604 of this title, in fiscal year 1987 and each of the succeeding three fiscal years. If the Administrator determines that 10 field demonstration projects under this subsection cannot be initiated consistent with the criteria set forth in paragraph (7) in any of such fiscal years, the Administrator shall transmit to the appropriate committees of Congress a report explaining the reasons for his inability to conduct such demonstration projects.

(7) Criteria

In selecting technologies to be demonstrated under this subsection, the Administrator shall, consistent with the protection of human health and the environment, consider each of the following criteria:

(A) The potential for contributing to solutions to those waste problems which pose the greatest threat to human health, which cannot be adequately controlled under present technologies, or which otherwise pose significant management difficulties.

(B) The availability of technologies which have been sufficiently developed for field demonstration and which are likely to be cost-effective and reliable.

(C) The availability and suitability of sites for demonstrating such technologies, taking into account the physical, biological, chemical, and geological characteristics of the sites, the extent and type of contamination found at the site, and the capability to conduct demonstration projects in such a manner as to assure the protection of human health and the environment.

(D) The likelihood that the data to be generated from the demonstration project at the site will be applicable to other sites.

(8) Technology transfer

In carrying out the program, the Administrator shall conduct a technology transfer program including the development, collection, evaluation, coordination, and dissemination of information relating to the utilization of alternative or innovative treatment technologies for response actions. The Administrator shall establish and maintain a central reference library for such information. The information maintained by the Administrator shall be made available to the public, subject to the provisions of section 552 of Title 5 and section 1905 of Title 18, and to other Government agencies in a manner that will facilitate its dissemination; except, that upon a showing satisfactory to the Administrator by any person that any information or portion thereof obtained under this subsection by the Administrator directly or indirectly from such person, would, if made public, divulge—

(A) trade secrets; or

(B) other proprietary information of such person,

the Administrator shall not disclose such information and disclosure thereof shall be punishable under section 1905 of Title 18. This subsection is not authority to withhold information from Congress or any committee of Congress upon the request of the chairman of such committee.

(9) Training

The Administrator is authorized and directed to carry out, through the Office of Technology Demonstration, a program of training and an evaluation of training needs for each of the following:

(A) Training in the procedures for the handling and removal of hazardous substances for employees who handle hazardous substances.

(B) Training in the management of facilities at which hazardous substances are located and in the evaluation of the hazards to human health presented by such facilities for State and local health and environment agency personnel.

(10) Definition

For purposes of this subsection, the term "alternative or innovative treatment technologies" means those technologies, including proprietary or patented methods, which permanently alter the composition of hazardous waste through chemical, biological, or physical means so as to significantly reduce the toxicity, mobility, or volume (or any combination thereof) of the hazardous waste or contaminated materials being treated. The term also includes technologies that characterize or assess the extent of contamination, the chemical and physical character of the contaminants, and the stresses imposed by the contaminants on complex ecosystems at sites.

(c) Hazardous substance research

The Administrator may conduct and support, through grants, cooperative agreements, and contracts, research with respect to the detection, assessment, and evaluation of the effects on and risks to human health of hazardous substances and detection of hazardous substances in the environment. The Administrator shall coordinate such research with the Secretary of Health and Human Services, acting through the advisory council established under this section, in order to avoid duplication of effort.

(d) University hazardous substance research centers

(1) Grant program

The Administrator shall make grants to institutions of higher learning to establish and operate not fewer than 5 hazardous substance research centers in the United States. In carrying out the program under this subsection, the Administrator should seek to have established and operated 10 hazardous substance research centers in the United States.

(2) Responsibilities of centers

The responsibilities of each hazardous substance research center established under this subsection shall include, but not be limited to, the conduct of research and training relating to the manufacture, use, transportation, disposal, and management of hazardous substances and publication and dissemination of the results of such research.

(3) Applications

Any institution of higher learning interested in receiving a grant under this subsection shall submit to the Administrator an application in such form and containing such information as the Administrator may require by regulation.

(4) Selection criteria

The Administrator shall select recipients of grants under this subsection on the basis of the following criteria:

(A) The hazardous substance research center shall be located in a State which is representative of the needs of the region in which such State is located for improved hazardous waste management.

(B) The grant recipient shall be located in an area which has experienced problems with hazardous substance management.

(C) There is available to the grant recipient for carrying out this subsection demonstrated research resources.

(D) The capability of the grant recipient to provide leadership in making national and regional contributions to the solution of both long-range and immediate hazardous substance management problems.

(E) The grant recipient shall make a commitment to support ongoing hazardous substance research programs with budgeted institutional funds of at least $100,000 per year.

(F) The grant recipient shall have a interdisciplinary staff with demonstrated expertise in hazardous substance management and research.

(G) The grant recipient shall have a demonstrated ability to disseminate results of hazardous substance research and educational programs through an interdisciplinary continuing education program.

(H) The projects which the grant recipient proposes to carry out under the grant are necessary and appropriate.

(5) Maintenance of effort

No grant may be made under this subsection in any fiscal year unless the recipient of such grant enters into such agreements with the Administrator as the Administrator may require to ensure that such recipient will maintain its aggregate expenditures from all other sources for establishing and operating a regional hazardous substance research center and related research activities at or above the average level of such expenditures in its 2 fiscal years preceding October 17, 1986.

(6) Federal share

The Federal share of a grant under this subsection shall not exceed 80 percent of the costs of establishing and operating the regional hazardous substance research center and related research activities carried out by the grant recipient.

(7) Limitation on use of funds

No funds made available to carry out this subsection shall be used for acquisition of real property (including buildings) or construction of any building.

(8) Administration through the Office of the Administrator

Administrative responsibility for carrying out this subsection shall be in the Office of the Administrator.

(9) Equitable distribution of funds

The Administrator shall allocate funds made available to carry out this subsection equitably among the regions of the United States.

(10) Technology transfer activities

Not less than five percent of the funds made available to carry out this subsection for any fiscal year shall be available to carry out technology transfer activities.

(e) Report to Congress

At the time of the submission of the annual budget request to Congress, the Administrator shall submit to the appropriate committees of the House of Representatives and the Senate and to the advisory council established under subsection (a) of this section, a report on the progress of the research, development, and demonstration program authorized by subsection (b) of this section, including an evaluation of each demonstration project completed in the preceding fiscal year, findings with respect to the efficacy of such demonstrated technologies in achieving permanent and significant reductions in risk from hazardous wastes, the costs of such demonstration projects, and the potential applicability of, and projected costs for, such technologies at other hazardous substance sites.

(f) Saving provision

Nothing in this section shall be construed to affect the provisions of the Solid Waste Disposal Act [42 U.S.C. 6901 et seq.].

(g) Small business participation

The Administrator shall ensure, to the maximum extent practicable, an adequate opportunity for small business participation in the program established by subsection (b) of this section.

(Pub.L. 96–510, Title III, § 311, as added Oct. 17, 1986, Pub.L. 99–499, Title II, § 209(b), 100 Stat. 1708.)

LIBRARY REFERENCES

Health and Environment ⚷25.5(5.5).
C.J.S. Health and Environment § 91 et seq.

§ 9660a. Grant program

(1) Grant purposes

Grants for the training and education of workers who are or may be engaged in activities related to hazardous waste removal or containment or emergency response may be made under this section.

(2) Administration

Grants under this section shall be administered by the National Institute of Environmental Health Sciences.

(3) Grant recipients

Grants shall be awarded to nonprofit organizations which demonstrate experience in implementing and operating worker health and safety training and education programs and demonstrate the ability to reach and involve in training programs target populations of workers who are or will be engaged in hazardous waste removal or containment or emergency response operations.

(Oct. 17, 1986, Pub.L. 99–499, Title I, § 126(g), 100 Stat. 1692.)

Codification

Section was enacted as a part of the Superfund Amendments and Reauthorization Act of 1986, and not as a part of the Comprehensive Environmental Response, Compensation and Liability Act of 1980, which is classified to this chapter.

CODE OF FEDERAL REGULATIONS

Grants and other federal assistance, see 40 CFR 30.100 et seq.

§ 9661. Love Canal property acquisition [CERCLA § 312]

(a) Acquisition of property in Emergency Declaration Area

The Administrator of the Environmental Protection Agency (hereinafter referred to as the "Administrator") may make grants not to exceed $2,500,000 to the State of New York (or to any duly constituted public agency or authority thereof) for purposes of acquisition of private property in the Love Canal Emergency Declaration Area. Such acquisition shall include (but shall not be limited to) all private property within the Emergency Declaration Area, including non-owner occupied residential properties, commercial, industrial, public, religious, non-profit, and vacant properties.

(b) Procedures for acquisition

No property shall be acquired pursuant to this section unless the property owner voluntarily agrees to such acquisition. Compensation for any property acquired pursuant to this section shall be based upon the fair market value of the property as it existed prior to the emergency declaration. Valuation procedures for property acquired with funds provided under this section shall be in accordance with those set forth in the agreement entered into between the New York State Disaster Preparedness Commission and the Love Canal Revitalization Agency on October 9, 1980.

(c) State ownership

The Administrator shall not provide any funds under this section for the acquisition of any properties pursuant to this section unless a public agency or authority of the State of New York first enters into a cooperative agreement with the Administrator providing assurances deemed adequate by the Administrator that the State or an agency created under the laws of the State shall take title to the properties to be so acquired.

(d) Maintenance of property

The Administrator shall enter into a cooperative agreement with an appropriate public agency or authority of the State of New York under which the Administrator shall maintain or arrange for the maintenance of all properties within the Emergency Declaration Area that have been acquired by any public agency or authority of the State. Ninety (90) percent of the costs of such maintenance shall be paid by the Administrator. The remaining portion of such costs shall be paid by the State (unless a credit is available under section 9604(c) of this title). The Administrator is authorized, in his discretion, to provide technical assistance to any public agency or authority of the State of New York in order to implement the recommendations of the habitability and land-use study in order to put the land within the Emergency Declaration Area to its best use.

(e) Habitability and land use study

The Administrator shall conduct or cause to be conducted a habitability and land-use study. The study shall—

(1) assess the risks associated with inhabiting of the Love Canal Emergency Declaration Area;

(2) compare the level of hazardous waste contamination in that Area to that present in other comparable communities; and

(3) assess the potential uses of the land within the Emergency Declaration Area, including but not limited to residential, industrial, commercial and recreational, and the risks associated with such potential uses.

The Administrator shall publish the findings of such study and shall work with the State of New York to develop recommendations based upon the results of such study.

(f) Funding

For purposes of section 9611 of this title [and 9631(c) of this title], the expenditures authorized by this section shall be treated as a cost specified in section 9611(c) of this title.

(g) Response

The provisions of this section shall not affect the implementation of other response actions within the Emergency Declaration Area that the Administrator has determined (before October 17, 1986) to be necessary to protect the public health or welfare or the environment.

(h) Definitions

For purposes of this section:

(1) Emergency Declaration Area

The terms "Emergency Declaration Area" and "Love Canal Emergency Declaration Area" mean the Emergency Declaration Area as defined in section 950, paragraph (2) of the General Municipal Law of the State of New York, Chapter 259, Laws of 1980 [McKinney N.Y. General Municipal Law § 950, par. 2] as in effect on October 17, 1986.

(2) Private property

As used in subsection (a) of this section, the term "private property" means all property which is not owned by a department, agency, or instrumentality of—

(A) the United States, or

(B) the State of New York (or any public agency or authority thereof).

(Pub.L. 96–510, Title III, § 312, as added Oct. 17, 1986, Pub.L. 99–499, Title II, § 213(b), 100 Stat. 1727.)

LIBRARY REFERENCES

United States ⇔59, 60.
C.J.S. United States §§ 81 et seq., 83 et seq.

§ 9662. Limitation on contract and borrowing authority

Any authority provided by this Act, including any amendment made by this Act, to enter into contracts to obligate the United States or to incur indebtedness for the repayment of which the United States is liable shall be effective only to such extent or in such amounts as are provided in appropriation Acts.

(Oct. 17, 1986, Pub.L. 99–499, § 3, 100 Stat. 1614.)

References in Text

This Act, referred to in text, is Pub.L. 99–499, Oct. 17, 1986, 100 Stat. 1613, as amended, known as the Superfund Amendments and Reauthorization Act of 1986. For complete classification of this Act to the Code, see Tables.

Codification

Section was enacted as a part of the Superfund Amendments and Reauthorization Act of 1986, and not as a part of the Comprehensive Environmental Response, Compensation, and Liability Act of 1980, which is classified to this chapter.

LIBRARY REFERENCES

Health and Environment ⇔25.7(23).
C.J.S. Health and Environment § 113 et seq.

SUBCHAPTER IV—POLLUTION INSURANCE

§ 9671. Definitions [CERCLA § 401]

As used in this subchapter—

(1) Insurance

The term "insurance" means primary insurance, excess insurance, reinsurance, surplus lines insurance, and any other arrangement for shifting and distributing risk which is determined to be insurance under applicable State or Federal law.

(2) Pollution liability

The term "pollution liability" means liability for injuries arising from the release of hazardous substances or pollutants or contaminants.

(3) Risk retention group

The term "risk retention group" means any corporation or other limited liability association taxable as a corporation, or as an insurance company, formed under the laws of any State—

(A) whose primary activity consists of assuming and spreading all, or any portion, of the pollution liability of its group members;

(B) which is organized for the primary purpose or conducting the activity described under subparagraph (A);

(C) which is chartered or licensed as an insurance company and authorized to engage in the business of insurance under the laws of any State; and

(D) which does not exclude any person from membership in the group solely to provide for members of such a group a competitive advantage over such a person.

(4) Purchasing group

The term "purchasing group" means any group of persons which has as one of its purposes the purchase of pollution liability insurance on a group basis.

(5) State

The term "State" means any State of the United States, the District of Columbia, the Commonwealth of Puerto Rico, Guam, American Samoa, the Virgin Islands, the Commonwealth of the Northern Marianas, and any other territory or possession over which the United States has jurisdiction.

(Pub.L. 96–510, Title IV, § 401, as added Oct. 17, 1986, Pub.L. 99–499, Title II, § 210(a), formerly § 210, 100 Stat. 1716, as renumbered Oct. 27, 1986, Pub.L. 99–563, § 11(c)(1), 100 Stat. 3177.)

Effective Date

Section 4 of Pub.L. 99–499, Oct. 17, 1986, 100 Stat. 1614, provided that title II of Pub.L. 99–499 [which enacted this subchapter] is effective Oct. 17, 1986.

LIBRARY REFERENCES

Health and Environment ⚷25.6(1), 25.7(1).
Insurance ⚷124.1.
C.J.S. Health and Environment §§ 91 et seq., 106 et seq.
C.J.S. Insurance §§ 3 et seq., 59, 60.

§ 9672. State laws; scope of subchapter [CERCLA § 402]

(a) State laws

Nothing in this subchapter shall be construed to affect either the tort law or the law governing the interpretation of insurance contracts of any State. The definitions of pollution liability and pollution liability insurance under any State law shall not be applied for the purposes of this subchapter, including recognition or qualification of risk retention groups or purchasing groups.

(b) Scope of subchapter

The authority to offer or to provide insurance under this subchapter shall be limited to coverage of pollution liability risks and this subchapter does not authorize a risk retention group or purchasing group to provide coverage of any other line of insurance.

(Pub.L. 96–510, Title IV, § 402, as added Oct. 17, 1986, Pub.L. 99–499, Title II, § 210(a), formerly § 210, 100 Stat. 1716, as renumbered Oct. 27, 1986, Pub.L. 99–563, § 11(c)(1), 100 Stat. 3177.)

LIBRARY REFERENCES

Health and Environment ⚷25.6(1), 25.7(1).
Insurance ⚷124.1.
C.J.S. Health and Environment §§ 91 et seq., 106 et seq.
C.J.S. Insurance §§ 3 et seq., 59, 60.

§ 9673. Risk retention groups [CERCLA § 403]

(a) Exemption

Except as provided in this section, a risk retention group shall be exempt from the following:

(1) A State law, rule, or order which makes unlawful, or regulates, directly or indirectly, the operation of a risk retention group.

(2) A State law, rule, or order which requires or permits a risk retention group to participate in any insurance insolvency guaranty association to which an insurer licensed in the State is required to belong.

(3) A State law, rule, or order which requires any insurance policy issued to a risk retention group or any member of the group to be countersigned by an insurance agent or broker residing in the State.

(4) A State law, rule, or order which otherwise discriminates against a risk retention group or any of its members.

(b) Exceptions

(1) State laws generally applicable

Nothing in subsection (a) of this section shall be construed to affect the applicability of State laws generally applicable to persons or corporations. The State in which a risk retention group is chartered may regulate the formation and operation of the group.

(2) State regulations not subject to exemption

Subsection (a) of this section shall not apply to any State law which requires a risk retention group to do any of the following:

(A) Comply with the unfair claim settlement practices law of the State.

(B) Pay, on a nondiscriminatory basis, applicable premium and other taxes which are levied on admitted insurers and surplus line insurers, brokers, or policyholders under the laws of the State.

(C) Participate, on a nondiscriminatory basis, in any mechanism established or authorized under the law of the State for the equitable apportionment among insurers of pollution liability insurance losses and expenses incurred on policies written through such mechanism.

(D) Submit to the appropriate authority reports and other information required of licensed insurers under the laws of a State relating solely to pollution liability insurance losses and expenses.

(E) Register with and designate the State insurance commissioner as its agent solely for the purpose of receiving service of legal documents or process.

(F) Furnish, upon request, such commissioner a copy of any financial report submitted by the risk retention group to the commissioner of the chartering or licensing jurisdiction.

(G) Submit to an examination by the State insurance commissioner in any State in which the group is doing business to determine the group's financial condition, if—

(i) the commissioner has reason to believe the risk retention group is in a financially impaired condition; and

(ii) the commissioner of the jurisdiction in which the group is chartered has not begun or has refused to initiate an examination of the group.

(H) Comply with a lawful order issued in a delinquency proceeding commenced by the State insurance commissioner if the commissioner of the jurisdiction in which the group is chartered has failed to initiate such a proceeding after notice of a finding of financial impairment under subparagraph (G).

(c) Application of exemptions

The exemptions specified in subsection (a) of this section apply to—

(1) pollution liability insurance coverage provided by a risk retention group for—

(A) such group; or

(B) any person who is a member of such group;

(2) the sale of pollution liability insurance coverage for a risk retention group; and

(3) the provision of insurance related services or management services for a risk retention group or any member of such a group.

(d) Agents or brokers

A State may require that a person acting, or offering to act, as an agent or broker for a risk retention group obtain a license from that State, except that a State may not impose any qualification or requirement which discriminates against a nonresident agent or broker.

(Pub.L. 96–510, Title IV, § 403, as added Oct. 17, 1986, Pub.L. 99–499, Title II, § 210(a), formerly § 210, 100 Stat. 1717, as renumbered Oct. 27, 1986, Pub.L. 99–563, § 11(c)(1), 100 Stat. 3177.)

WEST'S FEDERAL PRACTICE MANUAL

Environmental common law background, see § 4382 et seq.
Environmental litigation problems, see § 4390 et seq.

LIBRARY REFERENCES

Health and Environment ⚷25.6(1), 25.7(1).
Insurance ⚷124.1.
C.J.S. Health and Environment §§ 91 et seq., 106 et seq.
C.J.S. Insurance §§ 3 et seq., 59, 60.

§ 9674. Purchasing groups [CERCLA § 404]

(a) Exemption

Except as provided in this section, a purchasing group is exempt from the following:

(1) A State law, rule, or order which prohibits the establishment of a purchasing group.

(2) A State law, rule, or order which makes it unlawful for an insurer to provide or offer to provide insurance on a basis providing, to a purchasing group or its member, advantages, based on their loss and expense experience, not afforded to other persons with respect to rates, policy forms, coverages, or other matters.

(3) A State law, rule, or order which prohibits a purchasing group or its members from purchasing insurance on the group basis described in paragraph (2) of this subsection.

(4) A State law, rule, or order which prohibits a purchasing group from obtaining insurance on a group basis because the group has not been in existence for a minimum period of time or because any member has not belonged to the group for a minimum period of time.

(5) A State law, rule, or order which requires that a purchasing group must have a minimum number of members, common ownership or affiliation, or a certain legal form.

(6) A State law, rule, or order which requires that a certain percentage of a purchasing group must obtain insurance on a group basis.

(7) A State law, rule, or order which requires that any insurance policy issued to a purchasing group or any members of the group be countersigned by an insurance agent or broker residing in that State.

(8) A State law, rule, or order which otherwise discriminate [1] against a purchasing group or any of its members.

(b) Application of exemptions

The exemptions specified in subsection (a) of this section apply to the following:

(1) Pollution liability insurance, and comprehensive general liability insurance which includes this coverage, provided to—

(A) a purchasing group; or

(B) any person who is a member of a purchasing group.

(2) The sale of any one of the following to a purchasing group or a member of the group:

(A) Pollution liability insurance and comprehensive general liability coverage.

(B) Insurance related services.

(C) Management services.

(c) Agents or brokers

A State may require that a person acting, or offering to act, as an agent or broker for a purchasing group obtain a license from that State, except that a State may not impose any qualification or requirement which discriminates against a nonresident agent or broker.

(Pub.L. 96–510, Title IV, § 404, as added Oct. 17, 1986, Pub.L. 99–499, Title II, § 210(a), formerly § 210, 100 Stat. 1718, as renumbered Oct. 27, 1986, Pub.L. 99–563, § 11(c)(1), 100 Stat. 3177.)

[1] So in original. Probably should be "discriminates".

LIBRARY REFERENCES

Health and Environment ⇨25.6(1), 25.7(1).
Insurance ⇨124.1.
C.J.S. Health and Environment §§ 91 et seq., 106 et seq.
C.J.S. Insurance §§ 3 et seq., 59, 60.

§ 9675. Applicability of securities laws [CERCLA § 405]

(a) Ownership interests

The ownership interests of members of a risk retention group shall be considered to be—

(1) exempted securities for purposes of section 77e of Title 15 and for purposes of section 78*l* of Title 15; and

(2) securities for purposes of the provisions of section 77q of Title 15 and the provisions of section 78j of Title 15.

(b) Investment Company Act

A risk retention group shall not be considered to be an investment company for purposes of the Investment Company Act of 1940 (15 U.S.C. 80a–1 et seq.).

(c) Blue sky law

The ownership interests of members in a risk retention group shall not be considered securities for purposes of any State blue sky law.

(Pub.L. 96–510, Title IV, § 405, as added Oct. 17, 1986, Pub.L. 99–499, Title II, § 210(a), formerly § 210, 100 Stat. 1719, as renumbered Oct. 27, 1986, Pub.L. 99–563, § 11(c)(1), 100 Stat. 3177.)

EMERGENCY PLANNING AND COMMUNITY RIGHT-TO-KNOW

EMERGENCY PLANNING AND COMMUNITY RIGHT-TO-KNOW ACT OF 1986 [EPCRTKA § ___]

(42 U.S.C.A. §§ 11001 to 11050)

CHAPTER 116—EMERGENCY PLANNING AND COMMUNITY RIGHT-TO-KNOW

SUBCHAPTER I—EMERGENCY PLANNING AND NOTIFICATION

Sec.

11001. Establishment of State commissions, planning districts, and local committees.
(a) Establishment of State emergency response commissions.
(b) Establishment of emergency planning districts.
(c) Establishment of local emergency planning committees.
(d) Revisions.

11002. Substances and facilities covered and notification.
(a) Substances covered.
(b) Facilities covered.
(c) Emergency planning notification.
(d) Notification of Administrator.

11003. Comprehensive emergency response plans.
(a) Plan required.
(b) Resources.
(c) Plan provisions.
(d) Providing of information.
(e) Review by the State emergency response commission.
(f) Guidance documents.
(g) Review of plans by regional response teams.

11004. Emergency notification.
(a) Types of releases.
(b) Notification.
(c) Followup emergency notice.
(d) Transportation exemption not applicable.

11005. Emergency training and review of emergency systems.
(a) Emergency training.
(b) Review of emergency systems.

SUBCHAPTER II—REPORTING REQUIREMENTS

11021. Material safety data sheets.
(a) Basic requirement.
(b) Thresholds.
(c) Availability of MSDS on request.
(d) Initial submission and updating.
(e) Hazardous chemical defined.

11022. Emergency and hazardous chemical inventory forms.
(a) Basic requirement.
(b) Thresholds.
(c) Hazardous chemicals covered.

Sec.

11022. Emergency and hazardous chemical inventory forms.
(d) Contents of form.
(e) Availability of tier II information.
(f) Fire department access.
(g) Format of forms.

11023. Toxic chemical release forms.
(a) Basic requirement.
(b) Covered owners and operators of facilities.
(c) Toxic chemicals covered.
(d) Revisions by Administrator.
(e) Petitions.
(f) Threshold for reporting.
(g) Form.
(h) Use of release form.
(i) Modifications in reporting frequency.
(j) EPA management of data.
(k) Report.
(*l*) Mass balance study.

SUBCHAPTER III—GENERAL PROVISIONS

11041. Relationship to other law.
(a) In general.
(b) Effect on MSDS requirements.

11042. Trade secrets.
(a) Authority to withhold information.
(b) Trade secret factors.
(c) Trade secret regulations.
(d) Petition for review.
(e) Exception for information provided to health professionals.
(f) Providing information to the Administrator; availability to public.
(g) Information provided to State.
(h) Information on adverse effects.
(i) Information provided to Congress.

11043. Provision of information to health professionals, doctors, and nurses.
(a) Diagnosis or treatment by health professional.
(b) Medical emergency.
(c) Preventive measures by local health professionals.
(d) Confidentiality agreement.
(e) Regulations.

11044. Public availability of plans, data sheets, forms, and followup notices.
(a) Availability to public.
(b) Notice of public availability.

Sec.
11045. Enforcement.
(a) Civil penalties for emergency planning.
(b) Civil, administrative, and criminal penalties for emergency notification.
(c) Civil and administrative penalties for reporting requirements.
(d) Civil, administrative, and criminal penalties with respect to trade secrets.
(e) Special enforcement provisions for section 11043.
(f) Procedures for administrative penalties.
11046. Civil actions.
(a) Authority to bring civil actions.
(b) Venue.
(c) Relief.
(d) Notice.
(e) Limitation.
(f) Costs.
(g) Other rights.
(h) Intervention.
11047. Exemption.
11048. Regulations.
11049. Definitions.
11050. Authorization of appropriations.

WESTLAW ELECTRONIC RESEARCH

See WESTLAW guide following the Explanation pages of this pamphlet.

SUBCHAPTER I—EMERGENCY PLANNING AND NOTIFICATION

§ 11001. Establishment of State commissions, planning districts, and local committees [EPCRTKA § 301]

(a) Establishment of State emergency response commissions

Not later than six months after October 17, 1986, the Governor of each State shall appoint a State emergency response commission. The Governor may designate as the State emergency response commission one or more existing emergency response organizations that are State-sponsored or appointed. The Governor shall, to the extent practicable, appoint persons to the State emergency response commission who have technical expertise in the emergency response field. The State emergency response commission shall appoint local emergency planning committees under subsection (c) of this section and shall supervise and coordinate the activities of such committees. The State emergency response commission shall establish procedures for receiving and processing requests from the public for information under section 11044 of this title, including tier II information under section 11022 of this title. Such procedures shall include the designation of an official to serve as coordinator for information. If the Governor of any State does not designate a State emergency response commission within such period, the Governor shall operate as the State emergency response commission until the Governor makes such designation.

(b) Establishment of emergency planning districts

Not later than nine months after October 17, 1986, the State emergency response commission shall designate emergency planning districts in order to facilitate preparation and implementation of emergency plans. Where appropriate, the State emergency response commission may designate existing political subdivisions or multijurisdictional planning organizations as such districts. In emergency planning areas that involve more than one State, the State emergency response commissions of all potentially affected States may designate emergency planning districts and local emergency planning committees by agreement. In making such designation, the State emergency response commission shall indicate which facilities subject to the requirements of this subchapter are within such emergency planning district.

(c) Establishment of local emergency planning committees

Not later than 30 days after designation of emergency planning districts or 10 months after October 17, 1986, whichever is earlier, the State emergency response commission shall appoint members of a local emergency planning committee for each emergency planning district. Each committee shall include, at a minimum, representatives from each of the following groups or organizations: elected State and local officials; law enforcement, civil defense, firefighting, first aid, health, local environmental, hospital, and transportation personnel; broadcast and print media; community groups; and owners and operators of facilities subject to the requirements of this subchapter. Such committee shall appoint a chairperson and shall establish rules by which the committee shall function. Such rules shall include provisions for public notification of committee activities, public meetings to discuss the emergency plan, public comments, response to such comments by the committee, and distribution of the emergency plan. The local emergency planning committee shall establish procedures for receiving and processing requests from the public for information under section 11044 of this title, including tier II information under section 11022 of this title. Such procedures shall include the designation of an official to serve as coordinator for information.

(d) Revisions

A State emergency response commission may revise its designations and appointments under subsections (b) and (c) of this section as it deems appropriate.

Interested persons may petition the State emergency response commission to modify the membership of a local emergency planning committee.

(Pub.L. 99-499, Title III, § 301, Oct. 17, 1986, 100 Stat. 1729.)

Effective Date

Section 4 of Pub.L. 99-499, Oct. 17, 1986, 100 Stat. 1614, provided that title III of Pub.L. 99-499 [this chapter] is effective Oct. 17, 1986.

CERCLA and Administrator

Section 2 of Pub.L. 99-499, Oct. 17, 1986, 100 Stat. 1613, provided that, as used in this chapter—

(1) CERCLA.—The term "CERCLA" means the Comprehensive Environmental Response, Compensation, and Liability Act of 1980 [42 U.S.C.A. § 9601 et seq.].

(2) Administrator.—The term "Administrator" means the Administrator of the Environmental Protection Agency.

Short Title

Section 300(a) of Pub.L. 99-499, Title III, Oct. 17, 1986, 100 Stat. 1729, provided that: "This title [enacting this chapter] may be cited as the 'Emergency Planning and Community Right-To-Know Act of 1986'."

LAW REVIEW COMMENTARIES

Bonfire of the executives: Criminal environmental enforcement unfolds. John E. Smith, II, 10 Corp. Counsel Rev. (Tex.) 67 (May 1991).

High penalties and citizen suits await small businesses unaware of EPCRA reporting requirements. Jeffrey T. Pender, 10 Corp. Counsel Rev. (Tex.) 81 (May 1991).

LIBRARY REFERENCES

Health and Environment ⚖25.5(9).
C.J.S. Health and Environment §§ 65, 66, 103, 107, 140 et seq.

§ 11002. Substances and facilities covered and notification [EPCRTKA § 302]

(a) Substances covered

(1) In general

A substance is subject to the requirements of this subchapter if the substance is on the list published under paragraph (2).

(2) List of extremely hazardous substances

Within 30 days after October 17, 1986, the Administrator shall publish a list of extremely hazardous substances. The list shall be the same as the list of substances published in November 1985 by the Administrator in Appendix A of the "Chemical Emergency Preparedness Program Interim Guidance".

(3) Thresholds

(A) At the time the list referred to in paragraph (2) is published the Administrator shall—

(i) publish an interim final regulation establishing a threshold planning quantity for each substance on the list, taking into account the criteria described in paragraph (4), and

(ii) initiate a rulemaking in order to publish final regulations establishing a threshold planning quantity for each substance on the list.

(B) The threshold planning quantities may, at the Administrator's discretion, be based on classes of chemicals or categories of facilities.

(C) If the Administrator fails to publish an interim final regulation establishing a threshold planning quantity for a substance within 30 days after October 17, 1986, the threshold planning quantity for the substance shall be 2 pounds until such time as the Administrator publishes regulations establishing a threshold for the substance.

(4) Revisions

The Administrator may revise the list and thresholds under paragraphs (2) and (3) from time to time. Any revisions to the list shall take into account the toxicity, reactivity, volatility, dispersability, combustability, or flammability of a substance. For purposes of the preceding sentence, the term "toxicity" shall include any short- or long-term health effect which may result from a short-term exposure to the substance.

(b) Facilities covered

(1) Except as provided in section 11004 of this title, a facility is subject to the requirements of this subchapter if a substance on the list referred to in subsection (a) of this section is present at the facility in an amount in excess of the threshold planning quantity established for such substance.

(2) For purposes of emergency planning, a Governor or a State emergency response commission may designate additional facilities which shall be subject to the requirements of this subchapter, if such designation is made after public notice and opportunity for comment. The Governor or State emergency response commission shall notify the facility concerned of any facility designation under this paragraph.

(c) Emergency planning notification

Not later than seven months after October 17, 1986, the owner or operator of each facility subject to the requirements of this subchapter by reason of subsection (b)(1) of this section shall notify the State emergency response commission for the State in which such facility is located that such facility is subject to the requirements of this subchapter. Thereafter, if a substance on the list of extremely hazardous substances referred to in subsection (a) of this section first becomes present at such facility in excess of the threshold planning quantity established for such substance, or if there is a revision of such list and the facility has present a substance on the revised list in excess of the threshold planning quantity established for such substance, the owner or operator of the facility shall notify the State emergency response commission and the local emergency planning committee within 60 days after such acquisition or revision that such facility is subject to the requirements of this subchapter.

(d) Notification of Administrator

The State emergency response commission shall notify the Administrator of facilities subject to the requirements of this subchapter by notifying the Administrator of—

(1) each notification received from a facility under subsection (c) of this section, and

(2) each facility designated by the Governor or State emergency response commission under subsection (b)(2) of this section.

(Pub.L. 99–499, Title III, § 302, Oct. 17, 1986, 100 Stat. 1730.)

LIBRARY REFERENCES

Health and Environment ⟹25.5(5.5).
C.J.S. Health and Environment §§ 91, 92, 106, 109, 129 to 131.

§ 11003. Comprehensive emergency response plans [EPCRTKA § 303]

(a) Plan required

Each local emergency planning committee shall complete preparation of an emergency plan in accordance with this section not later than two years after October 17, 1986. The committee shall review such plan once a year, or more frequently as changed circumstances in the community or at any facility may require.

(b) Resources

Each local emergency planning committee shall evaluate the need for resources necessary to develop, implement, and exercise the emergency plan, and shall make recommendations with respect to additional resources that may be required and the means for providing such additional resources.

(c) Plan provisions

Each emergency plan shall include (but is not limited to) each of the following:

(1) Identification of facilities subject to the requirements of this subchapter that are within the emergency planning district, identification of routes likely to be used for the transportation of substances on the list of extremely hazardous substances referred to in section 11002(a) of this title, and identification of additional facilities contributing or subjected to additional risk due to their proximity to facilities subject to the requirements of this subchapter, such as hospitals or natural gas facilities.

(2) Methods and procedures to be followed by facility owners and operators and local emergency and medical personnel to respond to any release of such substances.

(3) Designation of a community emergency coordinator and facility emergency coordinators, who shall make determinations necessary to implement the plan.

(4) Procedures providing reliable, effective, and timely notification by the facility emergency coordinators and the community emergency coordinator to persons designated in the emergency plan, and to the public, that a release has occurred (consistent with the emergency notification requirements of section 11004 of this title).

(5) Methods for determining the occurrence of a release, and the area or population likely to be affected by such release.

(6) A description of emergency equipment and facilities in the community and at each facility in the community subject to the requirements of this subchapter, and an identification of the persons responsible for such equipment and facilities.

(7) Evacuation plans, including provisions for a precautionary evacuation and alternative traffic routes.

(8) Training programs, including schedules for training of local emergency response and medical personnel.

(9) Methods and schedules for exercising the emergency plan.

(d) Providing of information

For each facility subject to the requirements of this subchapter:

(1) Within 30 days after establishment of a local emergency planning committee for the emergency planning district in which such facility is located, or within 11 months after October 17, 1986, whichever is earlier, the owner or operator of the facility shall notify the emergency planning committee (or the Governor if there is no committee) of a facility representative who will participate in the emergency planning process as a facility emergency coordinator.

(2) The owner or operator of the facility shall promptly inform the emergency planning committee of any relevant changes occurring at such facility as such changes occur or are expected to occur.

(3) Upon request from the emergency planning committee, the owner or operator of the facility shall promptly provide information to such commit-

tee necessary for developing and implementing the emergency plan.

(e) Review by the State emergency response commission

After completion of an emergency plan under subsection (a) of this section for an emergency planning district, the local emergency planning committee shall submit a copy of the plan to the State emergency response commission of each State in which such district is located. The commission shall review the plan and make recommendations to the committee on revisions of the plan that may be necessary to ensure coordination of such plan with emergency response plans of other emergency planning districts. To the maximum extent practicable, such review shall not delay implementation of such plan.

(f) Guidance documents

The national response team, as established pursuant to the National Contingency Plan as established under section 9605 of this title, shall publish guidance documents for preparation and implementation of emergency plans. Such documents shall be published not later than five months after October 17, 1986.

(g) Review of plans by regional response teams

The regional response teams, as established pursuant to the National Contingency Plan as established under section 9605 of this title, may review and comment upon an emergency plan or other issues related to preparation, implementation, or exercise of such a plan upon request of a local emergency planning committee. Such review shall not delay implementation of the plan.

(Pub.L. 99-499, Title III, § 303, Oct. 17, 1986, 100 Stat. 1731.)

LIBRARY REFERENCES

Health and Environment ⚷25.5(9).
C.J.S. Health and Environment §§ 65, 66, 103, 107, 140 et seq.

§ 11004. Emergency notification [EPCRTKA § 304]

(a) Types of releases

(1) 11002(a) substance which requires CERCLA notice

If a release of an extremely hazardous substance referred to in section 11002(a) of this title occurs from a facility at which a hazardous chemical is produced, used, or stored, and such release requires a notification under section 103(a) of the Comprehensive Environmental Response, Compensation, and Liability Act of 1980 [42 U.S.C.A. § 9603(a)] (hereafter in this section referred to as "CERCLA") (42 U.S.C. 9601 et seq.), the owner or operator of the facility shall immediately provide notice as described in subsection (b) of this section.

(2) Other section 11002(a) substance

If a release of an extremely hazardous substance referred to in section 11002(a) of this title occurs from a facility at which a hazardous chemical is produced, used, or stored, and such release is not subject to the notification requirements under section 103(a) of CERCLA [42 U.S.C.A. § 9603(a)] the owner or operator of the facility shall immediately provide notice as described in subsection (b) of this section, but only if the release—

(A) is not a federally permitted release as defined in section 101(10) of CERCLA [42 U.S.C.A. § 9601(10)],

(B) is in an amount in excess of a quantity which the Administrator has determined (by regulation) requires notice, and

(C) occurs in a manner which would require notification under section 103(a) of CERCLA [42 U.S.C.A. § 9603(a)].

Unless and until superseded by regulations establishing a quantity for an extremely hazardous substance described in this paragraph, a quantity of 1 pound shall be deemed that quantity the release of which requires notice as described in subsection (b) of this section.

(3) Non-11002(a) substance which requires CERCLA notice

If a release of a substance which is not on the list referred to in section 11002(a) of this title occurs at a facility at which a hazardous chemical is produced, used, or stored, and such release requires notification under section 103(a) of CERCLA [42 U.S.C.A. § 9603(a)], the owner or operator shall provide notice as follows:

(A) If the substance is one for which a reportable quantity has been established under section 102(a) of CERCLA [42 U.S.C.A. 9602(a)], the owner or operator shall provide notice as described in subsection (b) of this section.

(B) If the substance is one for which a reportable quantity has not been established under section 102(a) of CERCLA [42 U.S.C.A. § 9602(a)]—

(i) Until April 30, 1988, the owner or operator shall provide, for releases of one pound or more of the substance, the same notice to the community emergency coordinator for the local emergency planning committee, at the same time and in the same form, as notice is provided to the National Response Center under section 103(a) of CERCLA [42 U.S.C.A. § 9603(a)].

(ii) On and after April 30, 1988, the owner or operator shall provide, for releases of one pound or more of the substance, the notice as described in subsection (b) of this section.

(4) Exempted releases

This section does not apply to any release which results in exposure to persons solely within the site or sites on which a facility is located.

(b) Notification

(1) Recipients of notice

Notice required under subsection (a) of this section shall be given immediately after the release by the owner or operator of a facility (by such means as telephone, radio, or in person) to the community emergency coordinator for the local emergency planning committees, if established pursuant to section 11001(c) of this title, for any area likely to be affected by the release and to the State emergency planning commission of any State likely to be affected by the release. With respect to transportation of a substance subject to the requirements of this section, or storage incident to such transportation, the notice requirements of this section with respect to a release shall be satisfied by dialing 911 or, in the absence of a 911 emergency telephone number, calling the operator.

(2) Contents

Notice required under subsection (a) of this section shall include each of the following (to the extent known at the time of the notice and so long as no delay in responding to the emergency results):

(A) The chemical name or identity of any substance involved in the release.

(B) An indication of whether the substance is on the list referred to in section 11002(a) of this title.

(C) An estimate of the quantity of any such substance that was released into the environment.

(D) The time and duration of the release.

(E) The medium or media into which the release occurred.

(F) Any known or anticipated acute or chronic health risks associated with the emergency and, where appropriate, advice regarding medical attention necessary for exposed individuals.

(G) Proper precautions to take as a result of the release, including evacuation (unless such information is readily available to the community emergency coordinator pursuant to the emergency plan).

(H) The name and telephone number of the person or persons to be contacted for further information.

(c) Followup emergency notice

As soon as practicable after a release which requires notice under subsection (a) of this section, such owner or operator shall provide a written followup emergency notice (or notices, as more information becomes available) setting forth and updating the information required under subsection (b) of this section, and including additional information with respect to—

(1) actions taken to respond to and contain the release,

(2) any known or anticipated acute or chronic health risks associated with the release, and

(3) where appropriate, advice regarding medical attention necessary for exposed individuals.

(d) Transportation exemption not applicable

The exemption provided in section 11047 of this title (relating to transportation) does not apply to this section.

(Pub.L. 99–499, Title III, § 304, Oct. 17, 1986, 100 Stat. 1733.)

LIBRARY REFERENCES

Health and Environment ⚡25.5(5.5).
C.J.S. Health and Environment §§ 91, 92, 106, 109, 129 to 131.

CODE OF FEDERAL REGULATIONS

Emergency planning and notification, see 40 CFR 355.10 et seq.

§ 11005. Emergency training and review of emergency systems [EPCRTKA § 305]

(a) Emergency training

(1) Programs

Officials of the United States Government carrying out existing Federal programs for emergency training are authorized to specifically provide training and education programs for Federal, State, and local personnel in hazard mitigation, emergency preparedness, fire prevention and control, disaster response, long-term disaster recovery, national security, technological and natural hazards, and emergency processes. Such programs shall provide special emphasis for such training and education with respect to hazardous chemicals.

(2) State and local program support

There is authorized to be appropriated to the Federal Emergency Management Agency for each of the fiscal years 1987, 1988, 1989, and 1990, $5,000,000 for making grants to support programs of State and local governments, and to support university-sponsored programs, which are designed to improve emergency planning, preparedness, mitigation, response, and recovery capabilities. Such programs shall provide special emphasis with respect to emergencies associated with hazardous chemicals. Such grants may not exceed 80 percent of the cost of any such program. The remaining 20 percent of such costs shall be funded from non-Federal sources.

(3) Other programs

Nothing in this section shall affect the availability of appropriations to the Federal Emergency Management Agency for any programs carried out by such agency other than the programs referred to in paragraph (2).

(b) Review of emergency systems

(1) Review

The Administrator shall initiate, not later than 30 days after October 17, 1986, a review of emergency systems for monitoring, detecting, and preventing releases of extremely hazardous substances at representative domestic facilities that produce, use, or store extremely hazardous substances. The Administrator may select representative extremely hazardous substances from the substances on the list referred to in section 11002(a) of this title, for the purposes of this review. The Administrator shall report interim findings to the Congress not later than seven months after October 17, 1986, and issue a final report of findings and recommendations to the Congress not later than 18 months after October 17, 1986. Such report shall be prepared in consultation with the States and appropriate Federal agencies.

(2) Report

The report required by this subsection shall include the Administrator's findings regarding each of the following:

(A) The status of current technological capabilities to (i) monitor, detect, and prevent, in a timely manner, significant releases of extremely hazardous substances, (ii) determine the magnitude and direction of the hazard posed by each release, (iii) identify specific substances, (iv) provide data on the specific chemical composition of such releases, and (v) determine the relative concentrations of the constituent substances.

(B) The status of public emergency alert devices or systems for providing timely and effective public warning of an accidental release of extremely hazardous substances into the environment, including releases into the atmosphere, surface water, or groundwater from facilities that produce, store, or use significant quantities of such extremely hazardous substances.

(C) The technical and economic feasibility of establishing, maintaining, and operating perimeter alert systems for detecting releases of such extremely hazardous substances into the atmosphere, surface water, or groundwater, at facilities that manufacture, use, or store significant quantities of such substances.

(3) Recommendations

The report required by this subsection shall also include the Administrator's recommendations for—

(A) initiatives to support the development of new or improved technologies or systems that would facilitate the timely monitoring, detection, and prevention of releases of extremely hazardous substances, and

(B) improving devices or systems for effectively alerting the public in a timely manner, in the event of an accidental release of such extremely hazardous substances.

(Pub.L. 99–499, Title III, § 305, Oct. 17, 1986, 100 Stat. 1735.)

LIBRARY REFERENCES

Health and Environment ⚷25.5(9), (10).
C.J.S. Health and Environment §§ 65, 66, 103 to 113, 139 to 150 et seq.

SUBCHAPTER II—REPORTING REQUIREMENTS

LIBRARY REFERENCES

Health and Environment ⚷25.5(5.5).
C.J.S. Health and Environment §§ 91, 92, 106 to 109, 129 to 131.

§ 11021. Material safety data sheets [EPCRTKA § 311]

(a) Basic requirement

(1) Submission of MSDS or list

The owner or operator of any facility which is required to prepare or have available a material safety data sheet for a hazardous chemical under the Occupational Safety and Health Act of 1970 and regulations promulgated under that Act [29 U.S.C.A. § 651 et seq.] shall submit a material safety data sheet for each such chemical, or a list of such chemicals as described in paragraph (2), to each of the following:

(A) The appropriate local emergency planning committee.

(B) The State emergency response commission.

(C) The fire department with jurisdiction over the facility.

(2) **Contents of list**

(A) The list of chemicals referred to in paragraph (1) shall include each of the following:

(i) A list of the hazardous chemicals for which a material safety data sheet is required under the Occupational Safety and Health Act of 1970 [29 U.S.C.A. § 651 et seq.] and regulations promulgated under that Act, grouped in categories of health and physical hazards as set forth under such Act and regulations promulgated under such Act, or in such other categories as the Administrator may prescribe under subparagraph (B).

(ii) The chemical name or the common name of each such chemical as provided on the material safety data sheet.

(iii) Any hazardous component of each such chemical as provided on the material safety data sheet.

(B) For purposes of the list under this paragraph, the Administrator may modify the categories of health and physical hazards as set forth under the Occupational Safety and Health Act of 1970 [29 U.S.C.A. § 651 et seq.] and regulations promulgated under that Act by requiring information to be reported in terms of groups of hazardous chemicals which present similar hazards in an emergency.

(3) **Treatment of mixtures**

An owner or operator may meet the requirements of this section with respect to a hazardous chemical which is a mixture by doing one of the following:

(A) Submitting a material safety data sheet for, or identifying on a list, each element or compound in the mixture which is a hazardous chemical. If more than one mixture has the same element or compound, only one material safety data sheet, or one listing, of the element or compound is necessary.

(B) Submitting a material safety data sheet for, or identifying on a list, the mixture itself.

(b) Thresholds

The Administrator may establish threshold quantities for hazardous chemicals below which no facility shall be subject to the provisions of this section. The threshold quantities may, in the Administrator's discretion, be based on classes of chemicals or categories of facilities.

(c) Availability of MSDS on request

(1) **To local emergency planning committee**

If an owner or operator of a facility submits a list of chemicals under subsection (a)(1) of this section, the owner or operator, upon request by the local emergency planning committee, shall submit the material safety data sheet for any chemical on the list to such committee.

(2) **To public**

A local emergency planning committee, upon request by any person, shall make available a material safety data sheet to the person in accordance with section 11044 of this title. If the local emergency planning committee does not have the requested material safety data sheet, the committee shall request the sheet from the facility owner or operator and then make the sheet available to the person in accordance with section 11044 of this title.

(d) Initial submission and updating

(1) The initial material safety data sheet or list required under this section with respect to a hazardous chemical shall be provided before the later of—

(A) 12 months after October 17, 1986, or

(B) 3 months after the owner or operator of a facility is required to prepare or have available a material safety data sheet for the chemical under the Occupational Safety and Health Act of 1970 [29 U.S.C.A. § 651 et seq.] and regulations promulgated under that Act.

(2) Within 3 months following discovery by an owner or operator of significant new information concerning an aspect of a hazardous chemical for which a material safety data sheet was previously submitted to the local emergency planning committee under subsection (a) of this section, a revised sheet shall be provided to such person.

(e) "Hazardous chemical" defined

For purposes of this section, the term "hazardous chemical" has the meaning given such term by section 1910.1200(c) of title 29 of the Code of Federal Regulations, except that such term does not include the following:

(1) Any food, food additive, color additive, drug, or cosmetic regulated by the Food and Drug Administration.

(2) Any substance present as a solid in any manufactured item to the extent exposure to the substance does not occur under normal conditions of use.

(3) Any substance to the extent it is used for personal, family, or household purposes, or is present in the same form and concentration as a product packaged for distribution and use by the general public.

(4) Any substance to the extent it is used in a research laboratory or a hospital or other medical facility under the direct supervision of a technically qualified individual.

(5) Any substance to the extent it is used in routine agricultural operations or is a fertilizer held for sale by a retailer to the ultimate customer.

(Pub.L. 99-499, Title III, § 311, Oct. 17, 1986, 100 Stat. 1736.)

LAW REVIEW COMMENTARIES

Bonfire of the executives: Criminal environmental enforcement unfolds. John E. Smith, II, 10 Corp. Counsel Rev. (Tex.) 67 (May 1991).

High penalties and citizen suits await small businesses unaware of EPCRA reporting requirements. Jeffrey T. Pender, 10 Corp. Counsel Rev. (Tex.) 81 (May 1991).

§ 11022. Emergency and hazardous chemical inventory forms [EPCRTKA § 312]

(a) Basic requirement

(1) The owner or operator of any facility which is required to prepare or have available a material safety data sheet for a hazardous chemical under the Occupational Safety and Health Act of 1970 [29 U.S.C.A. § 651 et seq.] and regulations promulgated under that Act shall prepare and submit an emergency and hazardous chemical inventory form (hereafter in this chapter referred to as an "inventory form") to each of the following:

(A) The appropriate local emergency planning committee.

(B) The State emergency response commission.

(C) The fire department with jurisdiction over the facility.

(2) The inventory form containing tier I information (as described in subsection (d)(1) of this section) shall be submitted on or before March 1, 1988, and annually thereafter on March 1, and shall contain data with respect to the preceding calendar year. The preceding sentence does not apply if an owner or operator provides, by the same deadline and with respect to the same calendar year, tier II information (as described in subsection (d)(2) of this section) to the recipients described in paragraph (1).

(3) An owner or operator may meet the requirements of this section with respect to a hazardous chemical which is a mixture by doing one of the following:

(A) Providing information on the inventory form on each element or compound in the mixture which is a hazardous chemical. If more than one mixture has the same element or compound, only one listing on the inventory form for the element or compound at the facility is necessary.

(B) Providing information on the inventory form on the mixture itself.

(b) Thresholds

The Administrator may establish threshold quantities for hazardous chemicals covered by this section below which no facility shall be subject to the provisions of this section. The threshold quantities may, in the Administrator's discretion, be based on classes of chemicals or categories of facilities.

(c) Hazardous chemicals covered

A hazardous chemical subject to the requirements of this section is any hazardous chemical for which a material safety data sheet or a listing is required under section 11021 of this title.

(d) Contents of form

(1) Tier I information

(A) Aggregate information by category

An inventory form shall provide the information described in subparagraph (B) in aggregate terms for hazardous chemicals in categories of health and physical hazards as set forth under the Occupational Safety and Health Act of 1970 [29 U.S.C.A. § 651 et seq.] and regulations promulgated under that Act.

(B) Required information

The information referred to in subparagraph (A) is the following:

(i) An estimate (in ranges) of the maximum amount of hazardous chemicals in each category present at the facility at any time during the preceding calendar year.

(ii) An estimate (in ranges) of the average daily amount of hazardous chemicals in each category present at the facility during the preceding calendar year.

(iii) The general location of hazardous chemicals in each category.

(C) Modifications

For purposes of reporting information under this paragraph, the Administrator may—

(i) modify the categories of health and physical hazards as set forth under the Occupational Safety and Health Act of 1970 [29 U.S.C.A. § 651 et seq.] and regulations promulgated under that Act by requiring information to be reported in terms of groups of hazardous chemicals which present similar hazards in an emergency, or

(ii) require reporting on individual hazardous chemicals of special concern to emergency response personnel.

(2) Tier II information

An inventory form shall provide the following additional information for each hazardous chemical present at the facility, but only upon request and in accordance with subsection (e) of this section:

(A) The chemical name or the common name of the chemical as provided on the material safety data sheet.

(B) An estimate (in ranges) of the maximum amount of the hazardous chemical present at the facility at any time during the preceding calendar year.

(C) An estimate (in ranges) of the average daily amount of the hazardous chemical present at the facility during the preceding calendar year.

(D) A brief description of the manner of storage of the hazardous chemical.

(E) The location at the facility of the hazardous chemical.

(F) An indication of whether the owner elects to withhold location information of a specific hazardous chemical from disclosure to the public under section 11044 of this title.

(e) Availability of tier II information

(1) Availability to State commissions, local committees, and fire departments

Upon request by a State emergency planning commission, a local emergency planning committee, or a fire department with jurisdiction over the facility, the owner or operator of a facility shall provide tier II information, as described in subsection (d) of this section, to the person making the request. Any such request shall be with respect to a specific facility.

(2) Availability to other State and local officials

A State or local official acting in his or her official capacity may have access to tier II information by submitting a request to the State emergency response commission or the local emergency planning committee. Upon receipt of a request for tier II information, the State commission or local committee shall, pursuant to paragraph (1), request the facility owner or operator for the tier II information and make available such information to the official.

(3) Availability to public

(A) In general

Any person may request a State emergency response commission or local emergency planning committee for tier II information relating to the preceding calendar year with respect to a facility. Any such request shall be in writing and shall be with respect to a specific facility.

(B) Automatic provision of information to public

Any tier II information which a State emergency response commission or local emergency planning committee has in its possession shall be made available to a person making a request under this paragraph in accordance with section 11044 of this title. If the State emergency response commission or local emergency planning committee does not have the tier II information in its possession, upon a request for tier II information the State emergency response commission or local emergency planning committee shall, pursuant to paragraph (1), request the facility owner or operator for tier II information with respect to a hazardous chemical which a facility has stored in an amount in excess of 10,000 pounds present at the facility at any time during the preceding calendar year and make such information available in accordance with section 11044 of this title to the person making the request.

(C) Discretionary provision of information to public

In the case of tier II information which is not in the possession of a State emergency response commission or local emergency planning committee and which is with respect to a hazardous chemical which a facility has stored in an amount less than 10,000 pounds present at the facility at any time during the preceding calendar year, a request from a person must include the general need for the information. The State emergency response commission or local emergency planning committee may, pursuant to paragraph (1), request the facility owner or operator for the tier II information on behalf of the person making the request. Upon receipt of any information requested on behalf of such person, the State emergency response commission or local emergency planning committee shall make the information available in accordance with section 11044 of this title to the person.

(D) Response in 45 days

A State emergency response commission or local emergency planning committee shall respond to a request for tier II information under this paragraph no later than 45 days after the date of receipt of the request.

(f) Fire department access

Upon request to an owner or operator of a facility which files an inventory form under this section by the fire department with jurisdiction over the facility, the owner or operator of the facility shall allow the fire department to conduct an on-site inspection of the facility and shall provide to the fire department specific location information on hazardous chemicals at the facility.

(g) Format of forms

The Administrator shall publish a uniform format for inventory forms within three months after October 17, 1986. If the Administrator does not publish such forms, owners and operators of facilities subject to the requirements of this section shall provide the information required under this section by letter.

(Pub.L. 99–499, Title III, § 312, Oct. 17, 1986, 100 Stat. 1738.)

CODE OF FEDERAL REGULATIONS

Hazardous chemical reporting, community right to know, see 40 CFR 370.1 et seq.

LAW REVIEW COMMENTARIES

High penalties and citizen suits await small businesses unaware of EPCRA reporting requirements. Jeffrey T. Pender, 10 Corp. Counsel Rev. (Tex.) 81 (May 1991).

§ 11023. Toxic chemical release forms [EPCRTKA § 313]

(a) Basic requirement

The owner or operator of a facility subject to the requirements of this section shall complete a toxic chemical release form as published under subsection (g) of this section for each toxic chemical listed under subsection (c) of this section that was manufactured, processed, or otherwise used in quantities exceeding the toxic chemical threshold quantity established by subsection (f) of this section during the preceding calendar year at such facility. Such form shall be submitted to the Administrator and to an official or officials of the State designated by the Governor on or before July 1, 1988, and annually thereafter on July 1 and shall contain data reflecting releases during the preceding calendar year.

(b) Covered owners and operators of facilities

(1) In general

(A) The requirements of this section shall apply to owners and operators of facilities that have 10 or more full-time employees and that are in Standard Industrial Classification Codes 20 through 39 (as in effect on July 1, 1985) and that manufactured, processed, or otherwise used a toxic chemical listed under subsection (c) of this section in excess of the quantity of that toxic chemical established under subsection (f) of this section during the calendar year for which a release form is required under this section.

(B) The Administrator may add or delete Standard Industrial Classification Codes for purposes of subparagraph (A), but only to the extent necessary to provide that each Standard Industrial Code to which this section applies is relevant to the purposes of this section.

(C) For purposes of this section—

(i) The term "manufacture" means to produce, prepare, import, or compound a toxic chemical.

(ii) The term "process" means the preparation of a toxic chemical, after its manufacture, for distribution in commerce—

(I) in the same form or physical state as, or in a different form or physical state from, that in which it was received by the person so preparing such chemical, or

(II) as part of an article containing the toxic chemical.

(2) Discretionary application to additional facilities

The Administrator, on his own motion or at the request of a Governor of a State (with regard to facilities located in that State), may apply the requirements of this section to the owners and operators of any particular facility that manufactures, processes, or otherwise uses a toxic chemical listed under subsection (c) of this section if the Administrator determines that such action is warranted on the basis of toxicity of the toxic chemical, proximity to other facilities that release the toxic chemical or to population centers, the history of releases of such chemical at such facility, or such other factors as the Administrator deems appropriate.

(c) Toxic chemicals covered

The toxic chemicals subject to the requirements of this section are those chemicals on the list in Committee Print Number 99–169 of the Senate Committee on Environment and Public Works, titled "Toxic Chemicals Subject to Section 313 of the Emergency Planning and Community Right-To-Know Act of 1986" [42 U.S.C.A. § 11023] (including any revised version of the list as may be made pursuant to subsection (d) or (e) of this section).

(d) Revisions by Administrator

(1) In general

The Administrator may by rule add or delete a chemical from the list described in subsection (c) of this section at any time.

(2) Additions

A chemical may be added if the Administrator determines, in his judgment, that there is sufficient evidence to establish any one of the following:

(A) The chemical is known to cause or can reasonably be anticipated to cause significant adverse acute human health effects at concentration levels that are reasonably likely to exist beyond facility site boundaries as a result of continuous, or frequently recurring, releases.

(B) The chemical is known to cause or can reasonably be anticipated to cause in humans—

(i) cancer or teratogenic effects, or

(ii) serious or irreversible—

(I) reproductive dysfunctions,

(II) neurological disorders,

(III) heritable genetic mutations, or

(IV) other chronic health effects.

(C) The chemical is known to cause or can reasonably be anticipated to cause, because of—

(i) its toxicity,

(ii) its toxicity and persistence in the environment, or

(iii) its toxicity and tendency to bioaccumulate in the environment,

a significant adverse effect on the environment of sufficient seriousness, in the judgment of the Administrator, to warrant reporting under this section. The number of chemicals included on the list described in subsection (c) of this section on the basis of the preceding sentence may constitute in the aggregate no more than 25 percent of the total number of chemicals on the list. A determination under this paragraph shall be based on generally accepted scientific principles or laboratory tests, or appropriately designed and conducted epidemiological or other population studies, available to the Administrator.

(3) Deletions

A chemical may be deleted if the Administrator determines there is not sufficient evidence to establish any of the criteria described in paragraph (2).

(4) Effective date

Any revision made on or after January 1 and before December 1 of any calendar year shall take effect beginning with the next calendar year. Any revision made on or after December 1 of any calendar year and before January 1 of the next calendar year shall take effect beginning with the calendar year following such next calendar year.

(e) Petitions

(1) In general

Any person may petition the Administrator to add or delete a chemical from the list described in subsection (c) of this section on the basis of the criteria in subparagraph (A) or (B) of subsection (d)(2) of this section. Within 180 days after receipt of a petition, the Administrator shall take one of the following actions:

(A) Initiate a rulemaking to add or delete the chemical to the list, in accordance with subsection (d)(2) or (d)(3) of this section.

(B) Publish an explanation of why the petition is denied.

(2) Governor petitions

A State Governor may petition the Administrator to add or delete a chemical from the list described in subsection (c) of this section on the basis of the criteria in subparagraph (A), (B), or (C) of subsection (d)(2) of this section. In the case of such a petition from a State Governor to delete a chemical, the petition shall be treated in the same manner as a petition received under paragraph (1) to delete a chemical. In the case of such a petition from a State Governor to add a chemical, the chemical will be added to the list within 180 days after receipt of the petition, unless the Administrator—

(A) initiates a rulemaking to add the chemical to the list, in accordance with subsection (d)(2) of this section, or

(B) publishes an explanation of why the Administrator believes the petition does not meet the requirements of subsection (d)(2) of this section for adding a chemical to the list.

(f) Threshold for reporting

(1) Toxic chemical threshold amount

The threshold amounts for purposes of reporting toxic chemicals under this section are as follows:

(A) With respect to a toxic chemical used at a facility, 10,000 pounds of the toxic chemical per year.

(B) With respect to a toxic chemical manufactured or processed at a facility—

(i) For the toxic chemical release form required to be submitted under this section on or before July 1, 1988, 75,000 pounds of the toxic chemical per year.

(ii) For the form required to be submitted on or before July 1, 1989, 50,000 pounds of the toxic chemical per year.

(iii) For the form required to be submitted on or before July 1, 1990, and for each form thereafter, 25,000 pounds of the toxic chemical per year.

(2) Revisions

The Administrator may establish a threshold amount for a toxic chemical different from the amount established by paragraph (1). Such revised threshold shall obtain reporting on a substantial majority of total releases of the chemical at all facilities subject to the requirements of this section. The amounts established under this paragraph may, at the Administrator's discretion, be based on classes of chemicals or categories of facilities.

(g) Form

(1) Information required

Not later than June 1, 1987, the Administrator shall publish a uniform toxic chemical release form for facilities covered by this section. If the Administrator does not publish such a form, owners and operators of facilities subject to the requirements of this section shall provide the information required under this subsection by letter postmarked on or before the date on which the form is due. Such form shall—

(A) provide for the name and location of, and principal business activities at, the facility;

(B) include an appropriate certification, signed by a senior official with management responsibility for the person or persons completing the report, regarding the accuracy and completeness of the report; and

(C) provide for submission of each of the following items of information for each listed toxic chemical known to be present at the facility:

(i) Whether the toxic chemical at the facility is manufactured, processed, or otherwise used, and the general category or categories of use of the chemical.

(ii) An estimate of the maximum amounts (in ranges) of the toxic chemical present at the facility at any time during the preceding calendar year.

(iii) For each wastestream, the waste treatment or disposal methods employed, and an estimate of the treatment efficiency typically achieved by such methods for that wastestream.

(iv) The annual quantity of the toxic chemical entering each environmental medium.

(2) Use of available data

In order to provide the information required under this section, the owner or operator of a facility may use readily available data (including monitoring data) collected pursuant to other provisions of law, or, where such data are not readily available, reasonable estimates of the amounts involved. Nothing in this section requires the monitoring or measurement of the quantities, concentration, or frequency of any toxic chemical released into the environment beyond that monitoring and measurement required under other provisions of law or regulation. In order to assure consistency, the Administrator shall require that data be expressed in common units.

(h) Use of release form

The release forms required under this section are intended to provide information to the Federal, State, and local governments and the public, including citizens of communities surrounding covered facilities. The release form shall be available, consistent with section 11044(a) of this title, to inform persons about releases of toxic chemicals to the environment; to assist governmental agencies, researchers, and other persons in the conduct of research and data gathering; to aid in the development of appropriate regulations, guidelines, and standards; and for other similar purposes.

(i) Modifications in reporting frequency

(1) In general

The Administrator may modify the frequency of submitting a report under this section, but the Administrator may not modify the frequency to be any more often than annually. A modification may apply, either nationally or in a specific geographic area, to the following:

(A) All toxic chemical release forms required under this section.

(B) A class of toxic chemicals or a category of facilities.

(C) A specific toxic chemical.

(D) A specific facility.

(2) Requirements

A modification may be made under paragraph (1) only if the Administrator—

(A) makes a finding that the modification is consistent with the provisions of subsection (h) of this section, based on—

(i) experience from previously submitted toxic chemical release forms, and

(ii) determinations made under paragraph (3), and

(B) the finding is made by a rulemaking in accordance with section 553 of Title 5.

(3) Determinations

The Administrator shall make the following determinations with respect to a proposed modification before making a modification under paragraph (1):

(A) The extent to which information relating to the proposed modification provided on the toxic chemical release forms has been used by the Administrator or other agencies of the Federal Government, States, local governments, health professionals, and the public.

(B) The extent to which the information is (i) readily available to potential users from other sources, such as State reporting programs, and (ii) provided to the Administrator under another Federal law or through a State program.

(C) The extent to which the modification would impose additional and unreasonable burdens on facilities subject to the reporting requirements under this section.

(4) 5-year review

Any modification made under this subsection shall be reviewed at least once every 5 years. Such review shall examine the modification and ensure that the requirements of paragraphs (2) and (3) still justify continuation of the modification. Any change to a modification reviewed under this paragraph shall be made in accordance with this subsection.

(5) Notification to Congress

The Administrator shall notify Congress of an intention to initiate a rulemaking for a modification under this subsection. After such notification, the Administrator shall delay initiation of the rulemaking for at least 12 months, but no more than 24 months, after the date of such notification.

(6) Judicial review

In any judicial review of a rulemaking which establishes a modification under this subsection, a court may hold unlawful and set aside agency action, findings, and conclusions found to be unsupported by substantial evidence.

(7) Applicability

A modification under this subsection may apply to a calendar year or other reporting period beginning no earlier than January 1, 1993.

(8) Effective date

Any modification made on or after January 1 and before December 1 of any calendar year shall take effect beginning with the next calendar year. Any modification made on or after December 1 of any calendar year and before January 1 of the next calendar year shall take effect beginning with the calendar year following such next calendar year.

(j) EPA management of data

The Administrator shall establish and maintain in a computer data base a national toxic chemical inventory based on data submitted to the Administrator under this section. The Administrator shall make these data accessible by computer telecommunication and other means to any person on a cost reimbursable basis.

(k) Report

Not later than June 30, 1991, the Comptroller General, in consultation with the Administrator and appropriate officials in the States, shall submit to the Congress a report including each of the following:

(1) A description of the steps taken by the Administrator and the States to implement the requirements of this section, including steps taken to make information collected under this section available to and accessible by the public.

(2) A description of the extent to which the information collected under this section has been used by the Environmental Protection Agency, other Federal agencies, the States, and the public, and the purposes for which the information has been used.

(3) An identification and evaluation of options for modifications to the requirements of this section for the purpose of making information collected under this section more useful.

(*l*) Mass balance study

(1) In general

The Administrator shall arrange for a mass balance study to be carried out by the National Academy of Sciences using mass balance information collected by the Administrator under paragraph (3). The Administrator shall submit to Congress a report on such study no later than 5 years after October 17, 1986.

(2) Purposes

The purposes of the study are as follows:

(A) To assess the value of mass balance analysis in determining the accuracy of information on toxic chemical releases.

(B) To assess the value of obtaining mass balance information, or portions thereof, to determine the waste reduction efficiency of different facilities, or categories of facilities, including the effectiveness of toxic chemical regulations promulgated under laws other than this chapter.

(C) To assess the utility of such information for evaluating toxic chemical management practices at facilities, or categories of facilities, covered by this section.

(D) To determine the implications of mass balance information collection on a national scale similar to the mass balance information collection carried out by the Administrator under paragraph (3), including implications of the use of such collection as part of a national annual quantity toxic chemical release program.

(3) **Information collection**

(A) The Administrator shall acquire available mass balance information from States which currently conduct (or during the 5 years after October 17, 1986, initiate) a mass balance-oriented annual quantity toxic chemical release program. If information from such States provides an inadequate representation of industry classes and categories to carry out the purposes of the study, the Administrator also may acquire mass balance information necessary for the study from a representative number of facilities in other States.

(B) Any information acquired under this section shall be available to the public, except that upon a showing satisfactory to the Administrator by any person that the information (or a particular part thereof) to which the Administrator or any officer, employee, or representative has access under this section if made public would divulge information entitled to protection under section 1905 of Title 18, such information or part shall be considered confidential in accordance with the purposes of that section, except that such information or part may be disclosed to other officers, employees, or authorized representatives of the United States concerned with carrying out this section.

(C) The Administrator may promulgate regulations prescribing procedures for collecting mass balance information under this paragraph.

(D) For purposes of collecting mass balance information under subparagraph (A), the Administrator may require the submission of information by a State or facility.

(4) **Mass balance definition**

For purposes of this subsection, the term "mass balance" means an accumulation of the annual quantities of chemicals transported to a facility, produced at a facility, consumed at a facility, used at a facility, accumulated at a facility, released from a facility, and transported from a facility as a waste or as a commercial product or byproduct or component of a commercial product or byproduct.

(Pub.L. 99–499, Title III, § 313, Oct. 17, 1986, 100 Stat. 1741.)

LAW REVIEW COMMENTARIES

High penalties and citizen suits await small businesses unaware of EPCRA reporting requirements. Jeffrey T. Pender, 10 Corp. Counsel Rev. (Tex.) 81 (May 1991).

SUBCHAPTER III—GENERAL PROVISIONS

§ 11041. Relationship to other law [EPCRTKA § 321]

(a) **In general**

Nothing in this chapter shall—

(1) preempt any State or local law,

(2) except as provided in subsection (b) of this section, otherwise affect any State or local law or the authority of any State or local government to adopt or enforce any State or local law, or

(3) affect or modify in any way the obligations or liabilities of any person under other Federal law.

(b) **Effect on MSDS requirements**

Any State or local law enacted after August 1, 1985, which requires the submission of a material safety data sheet from facility owners or operators shall require that the data sheet be identical in content and format to the data sheet required under subsection (a) of section 11021 of this title. In addition, a State or locality may require the submission of information which is supplemental to the information required on the data sheet (including information on the location and quantity of hazardous chemicals present at the facility), through additional sheets attached to the data sheet or such other means as the State or locality considers appropriate.

(Pub.L. 99–499, Title III, § 321, Oct. 17, 1986, 100 Stat. 1747.)

LAW REVIEW COMMENTARIES

Bonfire of the executives: Criminal environmental enforcement unfolds. John E. Smith, II, 10 Corp. Counsel Rev. (Tex.) 67 (May 1991).

LIBRARY REFERENCES

Health and Environment ⇐25.5(5.5).
C.J.S. Health and Environment §§ 91, 92, 106, 109, 129 to 131.

§ 11042. Trade secrets [EPCRTKA § 322]

(a) **Authority to withhold information**

(1) **General authority**

(A) With regard to a hazardous chemical, an extremely hazardous substance, or a toxic chemical, any person required under section 11003(d)(2), 11003(d)(3), 11021, 11022, or 11023 of this title to submit information to any other person may withhold from such submittal the specific chemical identity (including the chemical name and other specific identification), as defined in regulations prescribed by the Administrator under subsection (c) of this section, if the person complies with paragraph (2).

(B) Any person withholding the specific chemical identity shall, in the place on the submittal where the chemical identity would normally be included, include the generic class or category of the hazardous chemical, extremely hazardous substance, or toxic chemical (as the case may be).

(2) Requirements

(A) A person is entitled to withhold information under paragraph (1) if such person—

(i) claims that such information is a trade secret, on the basis of the factors enumerated in subsection (b) of this section,

(ii) includes in the submittal referred to in paragraph (1) an explanation of the reasons why such information is claimed to be a trade secret, based on the factors enumerated in subsection (b) of this section, including a specific description of why such factors apply, and

(iii) submits to the Administrator a copy of such submittal, and the information withheld from such submittal.

(B) In submitting to the Administrator the information required by subparagraph (A)(iii), a person withholding information under this subsection may—

(i) designate, in writing and in such manner as the Administrator may prescribe by regulation, the information which such person believes is entitled to be withheld under paragraph (1), and

(ii) submit such designated information separately from other information submitted under this subsection.

(3) Limitation

The authority under this subsection to withhold information shall not apply to information which the Administrator has determined, in accordance with subsection (c) of this section, is not a trade secret.

(b) Trade secret factors

No person required to provide information under this chapter may claim that the information is entitled to protection as a trade secret under subsection (a) of this section unless such person shows each of the following:

(1) Such person has not disclosed the information to any other person, other than a member of a local emergency planning committee, an officer or employee of the United States or a State or local government, an employee of such person, or a person who is bound by a confidentiality agreement, and such person has taken reasonable measures to protect the confidentiality of such information and intends to continue to take such measures.

(2) The information is not required to be disclosed, or otherwise made available, to the public under any other Federal or State law.

(3) Disclosure of the information is likely to cause substantial harm to the competitive position of such person.

(4) The chemical identity is not readily discoverable through reverse engineering.

(c) Trade secret regulations

As soon as practicable after October 17, 1986, the Administrator shall prescribe regulations to implement this section. With respect to subsection (b)(4) of this section, such regulations shall be equivalent to comparable provisions in the Occupational Safety and Health Administration Hazard Communication Standard (29 C.F.R. 1910.1200) and any revisions of such standard prescribed by the Secretary of Labor in accordance with the final ruling of the courts of the United States in United Steelworkers of America, AFL-CIO-CLC v. Thorne G. Auchter.

(d) Petition for review

(1) In general

Any person may petition the Administrator for the disclosure of the specific chemical identity of a hazardous chemical, an extremely hazardous substance, or a toxic chemical which is claimed as a trade secret under this section. The Administrator may, in the absence of a petition under this paragraph, initiate a determination, to be carried out in accordance with this subsection, as to whether information withheld constitutes a trade secret.

(2) Initial review

Within 30 days after the date of receipt of a petition under paragraph (1) (or upon the Administrator's initiative), the Administrator shall review the explanation filed by a trade secret claimant under subsection (a)(2) of this section and determine whether the explanation presents assertions which, if true, are sufficient to support a finding that the specific chemical identity is a trade secret.

(3) Finding of sufficient assertions

(A) If the Administrator determines pursuant to paragraph (2) that the explanation presents sufficient assertions to support a finding that the specific chemical identity is a trade secret, the Administrator shall notify the trade secret claimant that he has 30 days to supplement the explanation with detailed information to support the assertions.

(B) If the Administrator determines, after receipt of any supplemental supporting detailed information under subparagraph (A), that the assertions in the explanation are true and that the specific chemical identity is a trade secret, the Administrator shall so notify the petitioner and the petitioner may seek judicial review of the determination.

(C) If the Administrator determines, after receipt of any supplemental supporting detailed information under subparagraph (A), that the assertions in the explanation are not true and that the specific chemical identity is not a trade secret, the Administrator shall notify the trade secret claimant that the Administrator intends to release the specific chemical identity. The trade secret claimant has 30 days in which he may appeal the Administrator's determination under this subparagraph to the Administrator. If the Administrator does not reverse his determination under this subparagraph in such an appeal by the trade secret claimant, the trade secret claimant may seek judicial review of the determination.

(4) Finding of insufficient assertions

(A) If the Administrator determines pursuant to paragraph (2) that the explanation presents insufficient assertions to support a finding that the specific chemical identity is a trade secret, the Administrator shall notify the trade secret claimant that he has 30 days to appeal the determination to the Administrator, or, upon a showing of good cause, amend the original explanation by providing supplementary assertions to support the trade secret claim.

(B) If the Administrator does not reverse his determination under subparagraph (A) after an appeal or an examination of any supplementary assertions under subparagraph (A), the Administrator shall so notify the trade secret claimant and the trade secret claimant may seek judicial review of the determination.

(C) If the Administrator reverses his determination under subparagraph (A) after an appeal or an examination of any supplementary assertions under subparagraph (A), the procedures under paragraph (3) of this subsection apply.

(e) Exception for information provided to health professionals

Nothing in this section, or regulations adopted pursuant to this section, shall authorize any person to withhold information which is required to be provided to a health professional, a doctor, or a nurse in accordance with section 11043 of this title.

(f) Providing information to the Administrator; availability to public

Any information submitted to the Administrator under subsection (a)(2) of this section or subsection (d)(3) of this section (except a specific chemical identity) shall be available to the public, except that upon a showing satisfactory to the Administrator by any person that the information (or a particular part thereof) to which the Administrator has access under this section if made public would divulge information entitled to protection under section 1905 of Title 18, such information or part shall be considered confidential in accordance with the purposes of that section, except that such information or part may be disclosed to other officers, employees, or authorized representatives of the United States concerned with carrying out this chapter.

(g) Information provided to State

Upon request by a State, acting through the Governor of the State, the Administrator shall provide to the State any information obtained under subsection (a)(2) of this section and subsection (d)(3) of this section.

(h) Information on adverse effects

(1) In any case in which the identity of a hazardous chemical or an extremely hazardous substance is claimed as a trade secret, the Governor or State emergency response commission established under section 11001 of this title shall identify the adverse health effects associated with the hazardous chemical or extremely hazardous substance and shall assure that such information is provided to any person requesting information about such hazardous chemical or extremely hazardous substance.

(2) In any case in which the identity of a toxic chemical is claimed as a trade secret, the Administrator shall identify the adverse health and environmental effects associated with the toxic chemical and shall assure that such information is included in the computer database required by section 11023(j) of this title and is provided to any person requesting information about such toxic chemical.

(i) Information provided to Congress

Notwithstanding any limitatio [1] contained in this section or any other provision of law, all information reported to or otherwise obtained by the Administrator (or any representative of the Administrator) under this chapter shall be made available to a duly authorized committee of the Congress upon written request by such a committee.

(Pub.L. 99–499, Title III, § 322, Oct. 17, 1986, 100 Stat. 1747.)

[1] So in original. Probably should be "limitation".

CODE OF FEDERAL REGULATIONS

Trade secrecy claims for emergency planning, etc., see 40 CFR 350.1 et seq.

LIBRARY REFERENCES

Health and Environment ⟹25.5(5.5), (9).
C.J.S. Health and Environment §§ 65, 66, 91, 92, 103 to 109, 129 to 140 et seq.

§ 11043. Provision of information to health professionals, doctors, and nurses [EPCRTKA § 323]

(a) Diagnosis or treatment by health professional

An owner or operator of a facility which is subject to the requirements of section 11021, 11022, or 11023 of this title shall provide the specific chemical identity, if known, of a hazardous chemical, extremely hazardous substance, or a toxic chemical to any health professional who requests such information in writing if the health professional provides a written statement of need under this subsection and a written confidentiality agreement under subsection (d) of this section. The written statement of need shall be a statement that the health professional has a reasonable basis to suspect that—

(1) the information is needed for purposes of diagnosis or treatment of an individual,

(2) the individual or individuals being diagnosed or treated have been exposed to the chemical concerned, and

(3) knowledge of the specific chemical identity of such chemical will assist in diagnosis or treatment.

Following such a written request, the owner or operator to whom such request is made shall promptly provide the requested information to the health professional. The authority to withhold the specific chemical identity of a chemical under section 11042 of this title when such information is a trade secret shall not apply to information required to be provided under this subsection, subject to the provisions of subsection (d) of this section.

(b) Medical emergency

An owner or operator of a facility which is subject to the requirements of section 11021, 11022, or 11023 of this title shall provide a copy of a material safety data sheet, an inventory form, or a toxic chemical release form, including the specific chemical identity, if known, of a hazardous chemical, extremely hazardous substance, or a toxic chemical, to any treating physician or nurse who requests such information if such physician or nurse determines that—

(1) a medical emergency exists,

(2) the specific chemical identity of the chemical concerned is necessary for or will assist in emergency or first-aid diagnosis or treatment, and

(3) the individual or individuals being diagnosed or treated have been exposed to the chemical concerned.

Immediately following such a request, the owner or operator to whom such request is made shall provide the requested information to the physician or nurse. The authority to withhold the specific chemical identity of a chemical from a material safety data sheet, an inventory form, or a toxic chemical release form under section 11042 of this title when such information is a trade secret shall not apply to information required to be provided to a treating physician or nurse under this subsection. No written confidentiality agreement or statement of need shall be required as a precondition of such disclosure, but the owner or operator disclosing such information may require a written confidentiality agreement in accordance with subsection (d) of this section and a statement setting forth the items listed in paragraphs (1) through (3) as soon as circumstances permit.

(c) Preventive measures by local health professionals

(1) Provision of information

An owner or operator of a facility subject to the requirements of section 11021, 11022, or 11023 of this title shall provide the specific chemical identity, if known, of a hazardous chemical, an extremely hazardous substance, or a toxic chemical to any health professional (such as a physician, toxicologist, or epidemiologist)—

(A) who is a local government employee or a person under contract with the local government, and

(B) who requests such information in writing and provides a written statement of need under paragraph (2) and a written confidentiality agreement under subsection (d) of this section.

Following such a written request, the owner or operator to whom such request is made shall promptly provide the requested information to the local health professional. The authority to withhold the specific chemical identity of a chemical under section 11042 of this title when such information is a trade secret shall not apply to information required to be provided under this subsection, subject to the provisions of subsection (d) of this section.

(2) Written statement of need

The written statement of need shall be a statement that describes with reasonable detail one or more of the following health needs for the information:

(A) To assess exposure of persons living in a local community to the hazards of the chemical concerned.

(B) To conduct or assess sampling to determine exposure levels of various population groups.

(C) To conduct periodic medical surveillance of exposed population groups.

(D) To provide medical treatment to exposed individuals or population groups.

(E) To conduct studies to determine the health effects of exposure.

(F) To conduct studies to aid in the identification of a chemical that may reasonably be anticipated to cause an observed health effect.

(d) Confidentiality agreement

Any person obtaining information under subsection (a) or (c) of this section shall, in accordance with such subsection (a) or (c) of this section, be required to agree in a written confidentiality agreement that he will not use the information for any purpose other than the health needs asserted in the statement of need, except as may otherwise be authorized by the terms of the agreement or by the person providing such information. Nothing in this subsection shall preclude the parties to a confidentiality agreement from pursuing any remedies to the extent permitted by law.

(e) Regulations

As soon as practicable after October 17, 1986, the Administrator shall promulgate regulations describing criteria and parameters for the statement of need under subsection[1] (a) and (c) of this section and the confidentiality agreement under subsection (d) of this section.

(Pub.L. 99–499, Title III, § 323, Oct. 17, 1986, 100 Stat. 1750.)

[1] So in original. Probably should be "subsections".

CODE OF FEDERAL REGULATIONS

Trade secret disclosures to health professionals, etc., see 40 CFR 350.1 et seq.

§ 11044. Public availability of plans, data sheets, forms, and followup notices [EPCRTKA § 324]

(a) Availability to public

Each emergency response plan, material safety data sheet, list described in section 11021(a)(2) of this title, inventory form, toxic chemical release form, and followup emergency notice shall be made available to the general public, consistent with section 11042 of this title, during normal working hours at the location or locations designated by the Administrator, Governor, State emergency response commission, or local emergency planning committee, as appropriate. Upon request by an owner or operator of a facility subject to the requirements of section 11022 of this title, the State emergency response commission and the appropriate local emergency planning committee shall withhold from disclosure under this section the location of any specific chemical required by section 11022(d)(2) of this title to be contained in an inventory form as tier II information.

(b) Notice of public availability

Each local emergency planning committee shall annually publish a notice in local newspapers that the emergency response plan, material safety data sheets, and inventory forms have been submitted under this section. The notice shall state that followup emergency notices may subsequently be issued. Such notice shall announce that members of the public who wish to review any such plan, sheet, form, or followup notice may do so at the location designated under subsection (a) of this section.

(Pub.L. 99–499, Title III, § 324, Oct. 17, 1986, 100 Stat. 1752.)

LAW REVIEW COMMENTARIES

Environmental liability and the limits of insurance. Kenneth S. Abraham, 88 Columbia L.Rev. 942 (1988).

LIBRARY REFERENCES

Health and Environment ⟹25.5(5.5).
C.J.S. Health and Environment §§ 91, 92, 106, 109, 129 to 131.

§ 11045. Enforcement [EPCRTKA § 325]

(a) Civil penalties for emergency planning

The Administrator may order a facility owner or operator (except an owner or operator of a facility designated under section 11002(b)(2) of this title) to comply with section 11002(c) of this title and section 11003(d) of this title. The United States district court for the district in which the facility is located shall have jurisdiction to enforce the order, and any person who violates or fails to obey such an order shall be liable to the United States for a civil penalty of not more than $25,000 for each day in which such violation occurs or such failure to comply continues.

(b) Civil, administrative, and criminal penalties for emergency notification

(1) Class I administrative penalty

(A) A civil penalty of not more than $25,000 per violation may be assessed by the Administrator in the case of a violation of the requirements of section 11004 of this title.

(B) No civil penalty may be assessed under this subsection unless the person accused of the violation is given notice and opportunity for a hearing with respect to the violation.

(C) In determining the amount of any penalty assessed pursuant to this subsection, the Administrator shall take into account the nature, circumstances, extent and gravity of the violation or violations and, with respect to the violator, ability to pay, any prior history of such violations, the degree of culpability, economic benefit or savings (if any) resulting from the violation, and such other matters as justice may require.

(2) Class II administrative penalty

A civil penalty of not more than $25,000 per day for each day during which the violation continues may be assessed by the Administrator in the case of a violation of the requirements of section 11004 of this title. In the case of a second or subsequent violation the amount of such penalty may be not more than $75,000 for each day during which the violation continues. Any civil penalty under this subsection shall be assessed and collected in the same manner, and subject to the same provisions, as in the case of civil penalties assessed and collected under section 2615 of Title 15. In any proceeding for the assessment of a civil penalty under this subsection the Administrator may issue subpoenas for the attendance and testimony of witnesses and the production of relevant papers, books, and documents and may promulgate rules for discovery procedures.

(3) Judicial assessment

The Administrator may bring an action in the United States District court for the appropriate district to assess and collect a penalty of not more than $25,000 per day for each day during which the violation continues in the case of a violation of the requirements of section 11004 of this title. In the case of a second or subsequent violation, the amount of such penalty may be not more than $75,000 for each day during which the violation continues.

(4) Criminal penalties

Any person who knowingly and willfully fails to provide notice in accordance with section 11004 of this title shall, upon conviction, be fined not more than $25,000 or imprisoned for not more than two years, or both (or in the case of a second or subsequent conviction, shall be fined not more than $50,000 or imprisoned for not more than five years, or both).

(c) Civil and administrative penalties for reporting requirements

(1) Any person (other than a governmental entity) who violates any requirement of section 11022 or 11023 of this title shall be liable to the United States for a civil penalty in an amount not to exceed $25,000 for each such violation.

(2) Any person (other than a governmental entity) who violates any requirement of section 11021 or 11043(b) of this title, and any person who fails to furnish to the Administrator information required under section 11042(a)(2) of this title shall be liable to the United States for a civil penalty in an amount not to exceed $10,000 for each such violation.

(3) Each day a violation described in paragraph (1) or (2) continues shall, for purposes of this subsection, constitute a separate violation.

(4) The Administrator may assess any civil penalty for which a person is liable under this subsection by administrative order or may bring an action to assess and collect the penalty in the United States district court for the district in which the person from whom the penalty is sought resides or in which such person's principal place of business is located.

(d) Civil, administrative, and criminal penalties with respect to trade secrets

(1) Civil and administrative penalty for frivolous claims

If the Administrator determines—

(A)(i) under section 11042(d)(4) of this title that an explanation submitted by a trade secret claimant presents insufficient assertions to support a finding that a specific chemical identity is a trade secret, or (ii) after receiving supplemental supporting detailed information under section 11042(d)(3)(A) of this title, that the specific chemical identity is not a trade secret; and

(B) that the trade secret claim is frivolous,

the trade secret claimant is liable for a penalty of $25,000 per claim. The Administrator may assess the penalty by administrative order or may bring an action in the appropriate district court of the United States to assess and collect the penalty.

(2) Criminal penalty for disclosure of trade secret information

Any person who knowingly and willfully divulges or discloses any information entitled to protection under section 11042 of this title shall, upon conviction, be subject to a fine of not more than $20,000 or to imprisonment not to exceed one year, or both.

(e) Special enforcement provisions for section 11043

Whenever any facility owner or operator required to provide information under section 11043 of this title to a health professional who has requested such information fails or refuses to provide such information in accordance with such section, such health professional may bring an action in the appropriate United States district court to require such facility owner or operator to provide the information. Such court shall have jurisdiction to issue such orders and take such other action as may be necessary to enforce the requirements of section 11043 of this title.

(f) Procedures for administrative penalties

(1) Any person against whom a civil penalty is assessed under this section may obtain review thereof in the appropriate district court of the United States by filing a notice of appeal in such court within 30 days after the date of such order and by simultaneously sending a copy of such notice by certified mail to the Administrator. The Administrator shall promptly file in such court a certified copy of the record upon which such violation was found or such penalty imposed. If any person fails to pay an assessment of a civil penalty after it has become a final and unappealable order or after the appropriate court has entered final judgment in favor of the United States, the Administrator may request the Attorney General of the United States to institute a civil action in an appropriate district court of the United States to collect the penalty, and such court shall have jurisdiction to hear and decide any such action. In hearing such action, the court shall have authority to review the violation and the assessment of the civil penalty on the record.

(2) The Administrator may issue subpoenas for the attendance and testimony of witnesses and the production of relevant papers, books, or documents in connection with hearings under this section. In case of contumacy or refusal to obey a subpoena issued pursuant to this paragraph and served upon any person, the district court of the United States for any district in which such person is found, resides, or transacts business, upon application by the United States and after notice to such person, shall have jurisdiction to issue an order requiring such person to appear and give testimony before the administrative law judge or to appear and produce documents before the administrative law judge, or both, and any failure to obey such order of the court may be punished by such court as a contempt thereof.

(Pub.L. 99-499, Title III, § 325, Oct. 17, 1986, 100 Stat. 1753.)

WEST'S FEDERAL FORMS

Complaint for enforcement, see § 1714.15.

LAW REVIEW COMMENTARIES

High penalties and citizen suits await small businesses unaware of EPCRA reporting requirements. Jeffrey T. Pender, 10 Corp. Counsel Rev. (Tex.) 81 (May 1991).

LIBRARY REFERENCES

Health and Environment ⚷25.5(10), 38.
C.J.S. Health and Environment §§ 49, 50, 103 et seq., 113, 134 to 156.

§ 11046. Civil actions [EPCRTKA § 326]

(a) Authority to bring civil actions

(1) Citizen suits

Except as provided in subsection (e) of this section, any person may commence a civil action on his own behalf against the following:

(A) An owner or operator of a facility for failure to do any of the following:

(i) Submit a followup emergency notice under section 11004(c) of this title.

(ii) Submit a material safety data sheet or a list under section 11021(a) of this title.

(iii) Complete and submit an inventory form under section 11022(a) of this title containing tier I information as described in section 11022(d)(1) of this title unless such requirement does not apply by reason of the second sentence of section 11022(a)(2) of this title.

(iv) Complete and submit a toxic chemical release form under section 11023(a) of this title.

(B) The Administrator for failure to do any of the following:

(i) Publish inventory forms under section 11022(g) of this title.

(ii) Respond to a petition to add or delete a chemical under section 11023(e)(1) of this title within 180 days after receipt of the petition.

(iii) Publish a toxic chemical release form under[1] 11023(g) of this title.

(iv) Establish a computer database in accordance with section 11023(j) of this title.

(v) Promulgate trade secret regulations under section 11042(c) of this title.

(vi) Render a decision in response to a petition under section 11042(d) of this title within 9 months after receipt of the petition.

(C) The Administrator, a State Governor, or a State emergency response commission, for failure to provide a mechanism for public availability of information in accordance with section 11044(a) of this title.

(D) A State Governor or a State emergency response commission for failure to respond to a request for tier II information under section 11022(e)(3) of this title within 120 days after the date of receipt of the request.

(2) State or local suits

(A) Any State or local government may commence a civil action against an owner or operator of a facility for failure to do any of the following:

(i) Provide notification to the emergency response commission in the State under section 11002(c) of this title.

(ii) Submit a material safety data sheet or a list under section 11021(a) of this title.

(iii) Make available information requested under section 11021(c) of this title.

(iv) Complete and submit an inventory form under section 11022(a) of this title containing tier I information unless such requirement does not apply by reason of the second sentence of section 11022(a)(2) of this title.

(B) Any State emergency response commission or local emergency planning committee may commence a civil action against an owner or operator of a facility for failure to provide information under section 11003(d) of this title or for failure to submit tier II information under section 11022(e)(1) of this title.

(C) Any State may commence a civil action against the Administrator for failure to provide information to the State under section 11042(g) of this title.

(b) Venue

(1) Any action under subsection (a) of this section against an owner or operator of a facility shall be brought in the district court for the district in which the alleged violation occurred.

(2) Any action under subsection (a) of this section against the Administrator may be brought in the United States District Court for the District of Columbia.

(c) Relief

The district court shall have jurisdiction in actions brought under subsection (a) of this section against an owner or operator of a facility to enforce the requirement concerned and to impose any civil penalty provided for violation of that requirement. The district court shall have jurisdiction in actions brought under subsection (a) of this section against the Administrator to order the Administrator to perform the act or duty concerned.

(d) Notice

(1) No action may be commenced under subsection (a)(1)(A) of this section prior to 60 days after the plaintiff has given notice of the alleged violation to the Administrator, the State in which the alleged violation occurs, and the alleged violator. Notice under this paragraph shall be given in such manner as the Administrator shall prescribe by regulation.

(2) No action may be commenced under subsection (a)(1)(B) or (a)(1)(C) of this section prior to 60 days after the date on which the plaintiff gives notice to the Administrator, State Governor, or State emergency response commission (as the case may be) that the plaintiff will commence the action. Notice under this paragraph shall be given in such manner as the Administrator shall prescribe by regulation.

(e) Limitation

No action may be commenced under subsection (a) of this section against an owner or operator of a facility if the Administrator has commenced and is diligently pursuing an administrative order or civil action to enforce the requirement concerned or to impose a civil penalty under this chapter with respect to the violation of the requirement.

(f) Costs

The court, in issuing any final order in any action brought pursuant to this section, may award costs of litigation (including reasonable attorney and expert witness fees) to the prevailing or the substantially prevailing party whenever the court determines such an award is appropriate. The court may, if a temporary restraining order or preliminary injunction is sought, require the filing of a bond or equivalent security in accordance with the Federal Rules of Civil Procedure.

(g) Other rights

Nothing in this section shall restrict or expand any right which any person (or class of persons) may have under any Federal or State statute or common law to seek enforcement of any requirement or to seek any other relief (including relief against the Administrator or a State agency).

(h) Intervention

(1) By the United States

In any action under this section the United States or the State, or both, if not a party, may intervene as a matter of right.

(2) By persons

In any action under this section, any person may intervene as a matter of right when such person has a direct interest which is or may be adversely affected by the action and the disposition of the action may, as a practical matter, impair or impede the person's ability to protect that interest unless the Administrator or the State shows that the person's interest is adequately represented by existing parties in the action.

(Pub.L. 99–499, Title III, § 326, Oct. 17, 1986, 100 Stat. 1755.)

[1] So in original. Probably should be preceded by "section".

WEST'S FEDERAL FORMS

Complaint for enforcement, see § 1714.15.

LAW REVIEW COMMENTARIES

Environmental liability and the limits of insurance. Kenneth S. Abraham, 88 Columbia L.Rev. 942 (1988).

High penalties and citizen suits await small businesses unaware of EPCRA reporting requirements. Jeffrey T. Pender, 10 Corp. Counsel Rev. (Tex.) 81 (May 1991).

§ 11047. Exemption [EPCRTKA § 327]

Except as provided in section 11004 of this title, this chapter does not apply to the transportation, including the storage incident to such transportation, of any substance or chemical subject to the requirements of this chapter, including the transportation and distribution of natural gas.

(Pub.L. 99–499, Title III, § 327, Oct. 17, 1986, 100 Stat. 1757.)

LIBRARY REFERENCES

Health and Environment ⇐25.5(5.5).
C.J.S. Health and Environment §§ 91, 92, 106, 109, 129 to 131.

§ 11048. Regulations [EPCRTKA § 328]

The Administrator may prescribe such regulations as may be necessary to carry out this chapter.

(Pub.L. 99–499, Title III, § 328, Oct. 17, 1986, 100 Stat. 1757.)

LIBRARY REFERENCES

Health and Environment ⇐25.5(1).
C.J.S. Health and Environment §§ 61 et seq., 91 et seq., 106 to 133 et seq.

§ 11049. Definitions [EPCRTKA § 329]

For purposes of this chapter—

(1) Administrator

The term "Administrator" means the Administrator of the Environmental Protection Agency.

(2) Environment

The term "environment" includes water, air, and land and the interrelationship which exists among and between water, air, and land and all living things.

(3) Extremely hazardous substance

The term "extremely hazardous substance" means a substance on the list described in section 11002(a)(2) of this title.

(4) Facility

The term "facility" means all buildings, equipment, structures, and other stationary items which are located on a single site or on contiguous or adjacent sites and which are owned or operated by the same person (or by any person which controls, is controlled by, or under common control with, such person). For purposes of section 11004 of this title, the term includes motor vehicles, rolling stock, and aircraft.

(5) Hazardous chemical

The term "hazardous chemical" has the meaning given such term by section 11021(e) of this title.

(6) Material safety data sheet

The term "material safety data sheet" means the sheet required to be developed under section 1910.1200(g) of title 29 of the Code of Federal Regulations, as that section may be amended from time to time.

(7) Person

The term "person" means any individual, trust, firm, joint stock company, corporation (including a government corporation), partnership, association, State, municipality, commission, political subdivision of a State, or interstate body.

(8) Release

The term "release" means any spilling, leaking, pumping, pouring, emitting, emptying, discharging, injecting, escaping, leaching, dumping, or disposing into the environment (including the abandonment or discarding of barrels, containers, and other closed receptacles) of any hazardous chemical, extremely hazardous substance, or toxic chemical.

(9) State

The term "State" means any State of the United States, the District of Columbia, the Commonwealth of Puerto Rico, Guam, American Samoa, the United States Virgin Islands, the Northern Mariana Islands, and any other territory or possession over which the United States has jurisdiction.

(10) Toxic chemical

The term "toxic chemical" means a substance on the list described in section 11023(c) of this title.

(Pub.L. 99–499, Title III, § 329, Oct. 17, 1986, 100 Stat. 1757.)

LAW REVIEW COMMENTARIES

Erosion of mens rea in environmental criminal prosecution. Ruth Ann Weidel, John R. Mayo and F. Michael Zachara, 21 Seton Hall L.Rev. 1125 (1991).

High penalties and citizen suits await small businesses unaware of EPCRA reporting requirements. Jeffrey T. Pender, 10 Corp. Counsel Rev. (Tex.) 81 (May 1991).

LIBRARY REFERENCES

Health and Environment ⚷25.5(5.5).
C.J.S. Health and Environment §§ 91, 92, 106, 109, 129 to 131.

§ 11050. Authorization of appropriations [EPCRTKA § 330]

There are authorized to be appropriated for fiscal years beginning after September 30, 1986, such sums as may be necessary to carry out this chapter.

(Pub.L. 99–499, Title III, § 330, Oct. 17, 1986, 100 Stat. 1758.)

LIBRARY REFERENCES

United States ⚷85.
C.J.S. United States § 123.

POLLUTION PREVENTION

POLLUTION PREVENTION ACT OF 1990 [PPA § ___]

(42 U.S.C.A. §§ 13101 to 13109)

CHAPTER 133—POLLUTION PREVENTION

Sec.
13101. Findings and policy.
(a) Findings.
(b) Policy.
13102. Definitions.
13103. EPA activities.
(a) Authorities.
(b) Functions.
13104. Grants to states for state technical assistance programs.
(a) General authority.
(b) Criteria.
(c) Matching funds.
(d) Effectiveness.
(e) Information.
13105. Source reduction clearinghouse.
(a) Authority.
(b) Public availability.
13106. Source reduction and recycling data collection.
(a) Reporting requirements.
(b) Items included in report.
(c) SARA provisions.
(d) Additional optional information.
(e) Availability of data.
13107. EPA report.
(a) Biennial reports.
(b) Subsequent reports.
13108. Savings provisions.
13109. Authorization of appropriations.

§ 13101. Findings and policy [PPA § 6602]

(a) Findings

The Congress finds that:

(1) The United States of America annually produces millions of tons of pollution and spends tens of billions of dollars per year controlling this pollution.

(2) There are significant opportunities for industry to reduce or prevent pollution at the source through cost-effective changes in production, operation, and raw materials use. Such changes offer industry substantial savings in reduced raw material, pollution control, and liability costs as well as help protect the environment and reduce risks to worker health and safety.

(3) The opportunities for source reduction are often not realized because existing regulations, and the industrial resources they require for compliance, focus upon treatment and disposal, rather than source reduction; existing regulations do not emphasize multi-media management of pollution; and businesses need information and technical assistance to overcome institutional barriers to the adoption of source reduction practices.

(4) Source reduction is fundamentally different and more desirable than waste management and pollution control. The Environmental Protection Agency needs to address the historical lack of attention to source reduction.

(5) As a first step in preventing pollution through source reduction, the Environmental Protection Agency must establish a source reduction program which collects and disseminates information, provides financial assistance to States, and implements the other activities provided for in this chapter.

(b) Policy

The Congress hereby declares it to be the national policy of the United States that pollution should be prevented or reduced at the source whenever feasible; pollution that cannot be prevented should be recycled in an environmentally safe manner, whenever feasible; pollution that cannot be prevented or recycled should be treated in an environmentally safe manner whenever feasible; and disposal or other release into the environment should be employed only as a last resort and should be conducted in an environmentally safe manner.

(Pub.L. 101–508, Title VI, § 6602, Nov. 5, 1990, 104 Stat. 1388–321.)

Short Title

Section 6601 of Pub.L. 101–508 provided that: "This subtitle [enacting this chapter] may be cited as the 'Pollution Prevention Act of 1990'."

LAW REVIEW COMMENTARIES

From elephants to mice: The development of EBMUD's program to control small source wastewater discharges. Raoul Stewardson, 20 Ecology L.Q. 441 (1993).

§ 13102. Definitions [PPA § 6603]

For purposes of this chapter—

(1) The term "Administrator" means the Administrator of the Environmental Protection Agency.

(2) The term "Agency" means the Environmental Protection Agency.

(3) The term "toxic chemical" means any substance on the list described in section 11023(c) of this title.

(4) The term "release" has the same meaning as provided by section 11049(8) of this title.

(5)(A) The term "source reduction" means any practice which—

(i) reduces the amount of any hazardous substance, pollutant, or contaminant entering any waste stream or otherwise released into the environment (including fugitive emissions) prior to recycling, treatment, or disposal; and

(ii) reduces the hazards to public health and the environment associated with the release of such substances, pollutants, or contaminants.

The term includes equipment or technology modifications, process or procedure modifications, reformulation or redesign of products, substitution of raw materials, and improvements in housekeeping, maintenance, training, or inventory control.

(B) The term "source reduction" does not include any practice which alters the physical, chemical, or biological characteristics or the volume of a hazardous substance, pollutant, or contaminant through a process or activity which itself is not integral to and necessary for the production of a product or the providing of a service.

(6) The term "multi-media" means water, air, and land.

(7) The term "SIC codes" refers to the 2-digit code numbers used for classification of economic activity in the Standard Industrial Classification Manual.

(Pub.L. 101–508, Title VI, § 6603, Nov. 5, 1990, 104 Stat. 1388–321.)

LAW REVIEW COMMENTARIES

From elephants to mice: The development of EBMUD's program to control small source wastewater discharges. Raoul Stewardson, 20 Ecology L.Q. 441 (1993).

§ 13103. EPA activities [PPA § 6604]

(a) Authorities

The Administrator shall establish in the Agency an office to carry out the functions of the Administrator under this chapter. The office shall be independent of the Agency's single-medium program offices but shall have the authority to review and advise such offices on their activities to promote a multi-media approach to source reduction. The office shall be under the direction of such officer of the Agency as the Administrator shall designate.

(b) Functions

The Administrator shall develop and implement a strategy to promote source reduction. As part of the strategy, the Administrator shall—

(1) establish standard methods of measurement of source reduction;

(2) ensure that the Agency considers the effect of its existing and proposed programs on source reduction efforts and shall review regulations of the Agency prior and subsequent to their proposal to determine their effect on source reduction;

(3) coordinate source reduction activities in each Agency Office and coordinate with appropriate offices to promote source reduction practices in other Federal agencies, and generic research and development on techniques and processes which have broad applicability;

(4) develop improved methods of coordinating, streamlining and assuring public access to data collected under Federal environmental statutes;

(5) facilitate the adoption of source reduction techniques by businesses. This strategy shall include the use of the Source Reduction Clearinghouse and State matching grants provided in this chapter to foster the exchange of information regarding source reduction techniques, the dissemination of such information to businesses, and the provision of technical assistance to businesses. The strategy shall also consider the capabilities of various businesses to make use of source reduction techniques;

(6) identify, where appropriate, measurable goals which reflect the policy of this chapter, the tasks necessary to achieve the goals, dates at which the principal tasks are to be accomplished, required resources, organizational responsibilities, and the means by which progress in meeting the goals will be measured;

(8)[1] establish an advisory panel of technical experts comprised of representatives from industry, the States, and public interest groups, to advise the Administrator on ways to improve collection and dissemination of data;

(9) establish a training program on source reduction opportunities, including workshops and guidance documents, for State and Federal permit issuance, enforcement, and inspection officials working within all agency program offices.

(10) identify and make recommendations to Congress to eliminate barriers to source reduction including the use of incentives and disincentives;

(11) identify opportunities to use Federal procurement to encourage source reduction;

(12) develop, test and disseminate model source reduction auditing procedures designed to highlight source reduction opportunities; and

(13) establish an annual award program to recognize a company or companies which operate outstanding or innovative source reduction programs.

(Pub.L. 101–508, Title VI, § 6604, Nov. 5, 1990, 104 Stat. 1388–322.)

1 No par. (7) has been enacted.

§ 13104. Grants to states for state technical assistance programs [PPA § 6605]

(a) General authority

The Administrator shall make matching grants to States for programs to promote the use of source reduction techniques by businesses.

(b) Criteria

When evaluating the requests for grants under this section, the Administrator shall consider, among other things, whether the proposed State program would accomplish the following:

(1) Make specific technical assistance available to businesses seeking information about source reduction opportunities, including funding for experts to provide onsite technical advice to business seeking assistance and to assist in the development of source reduction plans.

(2) Target assistance to businesses for whom lack of information is an impediment to source reduction.

(3) Provide training in source reduction techniques. Such training may be provided through local engineering schools or any other appropriate means.

(c) Matching funds

Federal funds used in any State program under this section shall provide no more than 50 per centum of the funds made available to a State in each year of that State's participation in the program.

(d) Effectiveness

The Administrator shall establish appropriate means for measuring the effectiveness of the State grants made under this section in promoting the use of source reduction techniques by businesses.

(e) Information

States receiving grants under this section shall make information generated under the grants available to the Administrator.

(Pub.L. 101–508, Title VI, § 6605, Nov. 5, 1990, 104 Stat. 1388–323.)

§ 13105. Source reduction clearinghouse [PPA § 6606]

(a) Authority

The Administrator shall establish a Source Reduction Clearinghouse to compile information including a computer data base which contains information on management, technical, and operational approaches to source reduction. The Administrator shall use the clearinghouse to—

(1) serve as a center for source reduction technology transfer;

(2) mount active outreach and education programs by the States to further the adoption of source reduction technologies; and

(3) collect and compile information reported by States receiving grants under section 13104 of this title on the operation and success of State source reduction programs.

(b) Public availability

The Administrator shall make available to the public such information on source reduction as is gathered pursuant to this chapter and such other pertinent information and analysis regarding source reduction as may be available to the Administrator. The data base shall permit entry and retrieval of information to any person.

(Pub.L. 101–508, Title VI, § 6606, Nov. 5, 1990, 104 Stat. 1388–324.)

§ 13106. Source reduction and recycling data collection [PPA § 6607]

(a) Reporting requirements

Each owner or operator of a facility required to file an annual toxic chemical release form under section 11023 of this title for any toxic chemical shall include with each such annual filing a toxic chemical source reduction and recycling report for the preceding calendar year. The toxic chemical source reduction and recycling report shall cover each toxic chemical required to be reported in the annual toxic chemical release form filed by the owner or operator under section 11023(c) of this title. This section shall take effect with the annual report filed under section 11023 of this title for the first full calendar year beginning after the enactment of this chapter.

(b) Items included in report

The toxic chemical source reduction and recycling report required under subsection (a) of this section shall set forth each of the following on a facility-by-facility basis for each toxic chemical:

(1) The quantity of the chemical entering any waste stream (or otherwise released into the environment) prior to recycling, treatment, or disposal during the calendar year for which the report is filed and the percentage change from the previous year. The quantity reported shall not include any amount reported under paragraph (7). When actual measurements of the quantity of a toxic chemical entering the waste streams are not readily available, reasonable estimates should be made based on best engineering judgment.

(2) The amount of the chemical from the facility which is recycled (at the facility or elsewhere) during such calendar year, the percentage change from the previous year, and the process of recycling used.

(3) The source reduction practices used with respect to that chemical during such year at the facility. Such practices shall be reported in accordance with the following categories unless the Administrator finds other categories to be more appropriate:

(A) Equipment, technology, process, or procedure modifications.

(B) Reformulation or redesign of products.

(C) Substitution of raw materials.

(D) Improvement in management, training, inventory control, materials handling, or other general operational phases of industrial facilities.

(4) The amount expected to be reported under paragraph (1) and (2) for the two calendar years immediately following the calendar year for which the report is filed. Such amount shall be expressed as a percentage change from the amount reported in paragraphs (1) and (2).

(5) A ratio of production in the reporting year to production in the previous year. The ratio should be calculated to most closely reflect all activities involving the toxic chemical. In specific industrial classifications subject to this section, where a feedstock or some variable other than production is the primary influence on waste characteristics or volumes, the report may provide an index based on that primary variable for each toxic chemical. The Administrator is encouraged to develop production indexes to accommodate individual industries for use on a voluntary basis.

(6) The techniques which were used to identify source reduction opportunities. Techniques listed should include, but are not limited to, employee recommendations, external and internal audits, participative team management, and material balance audits. Each type of source reduction listed under paragraph (3) should be associated with the techniques or multiples of techniques used to identify the source reduction technique.

(7) The amount of any toxic chemical released into the environment which resulted from a catastrophic event, remedial action, or other one-time event, and is not associated with production processes during the reporting year.

(8) The amount of the chemical from the facility which is treated (at the facility or elsewhere) during such calendar year and the percentage change from the previous year. For the first year of reporting under this subsection, comparison with the previous year is required only to the extent such information is available.

For the first year of reporting under this subsection, comparison with the previous year is required only to the extent such information is available.

(c) SARA provisions

The provisions of sections 11042, 11045(c), and 11046 of this title shall apply to the reporting requirements of this section in the same manner as to the reports required under section 11023 of this title. The Administrator may modify the form required for purposes of reporting information under section 11023 of this title to the extent he deems necessary to include the additional information required under this section.

(d) Additional optional information

Any person filing a report under this section for any year may include with the report additional information regarding source reduction, recycling, and other pollution control techniques in earlier years.

(e) Availability of data

Subject to section 11042 of this title, the Administrator shall make data collected under this section publicly available in the same manner as the data collected under section 11023 of this title.

(Pub.L. 101–508, Title VI, § 6607, Nov. 5, 1990, 104 Stat. 1388–324.)

§ 13107. EPA report [PPA § 6608]

(a) Biennial reports

The Administrator shall provide Congress with a report within eighteen months after enactment of this chapter and biennially thereafter, containing a detailed description of the actions taken to implement the strategy to promote source reduction developed under section 13103(b) of this title and of the results of such actions. The report shall include an assessment of the effectiveness of the clearinghouse and grant program established under this chapter in promoting the goals of the strategy, and shall evaluate data gaps and data duplication with respect to data collected under Federal environmental statutes.

(b) Subsequent reports

Each biennial report submitted under subsection (a) of this section after the first report shall contain each of the following:

(1) An analysis of the data collected under section 13106 of this title on an industry-by-industry basis for not less than five SIC codes or other categories as the Administrator deems appropriate. The analysis shall begin with those SIC codes or other categories of facilities which generate the largest quantities of toxic chemical waste. The analysis shall include an evaluation of trends in source reduction by industry, firm size, production, or other useful means. Each such subsequent report shall cover five SIC codes or other categories which were not covered in a prior report until all SIC codes or other categories have been covered.

(2) An analysis of the usefulness and validity of the data collected under section 13106 of this title for measuring trends in source reduction and the adoption of source reduction by business.

(3) Identification of regulatory and nonregulatory barriers to source reduction, and of opportunities for using existing regulatory programs, and incentives and disincentives to promote and assist source reduction.

(4) Identification of industries and pollutants that require priority assistance in multi-media source reduction.

(5) Recommendations as to incentives needed to encourage investment and research and development in source reduction.

(6) Identification of opportunities and development of priorities for research and development in source reduction methods and techniques.

(7) An evaluation of the cost and technical feasibility, by industry and processes, of source reduction opportunities and current activities and an identification of any industries for which there are significant barriers to source reduction with an analysis of the basis of this identification.

(8) An evaluation of methods of coordinating, streamlining, and improving public access to data collected under Federal environmental statutes.

(9) An evaluation of data gaps and data duplication with respect to data collected under environmental statutes.

In the report following the first biennial report provided for under this subsection, paragraphs (3) through (9) may be included at the discretion of the Administrator.

(Pub.L. 101–508, Title VI, § 6608, Nov. 5, 1990, 104 Stat. 1388–326.)

§ 13108. Savings provisions [PPA § 6609]

(a) Nothing in this chapter shall be construed to modify or interfere with the implementation of title III of the Superfund Amendments and Reauthorization Act of 1986 [42 U.S.C.A. § 11001 et seq.].

(b) Nothing contained in this chapter shall be construed, interpreted or applied to supplant, displace, preempt or otherwise diminish the responsibilities and liabilities under other State or Federal law, whether statutory or common.

(Pub.L. 101–508, Title VI, § 6609, Nov. 5, 1990, 104 Stat. 1388–327.)

§ 13109. Authorization of appropriations [PPA § 6610]

There is authorized to be appropriated to the Administrator $8,000,000 for each of the fiscal years 1991, 1992 and 1993 for functions carried out under this chapter (other than state grants), and $8,000,000 for each of the fiscal years 1991, 1992 and 1993, for grant programs to States issued pursuant to section 13104 of this title.

(Pub.L. 101–508, Title VI, § 6610, Nov. 5, 1990, 104 Stat. 1388–327.)

*

TITLE 43—PUBLIC LANDS

FEDERAL LAND POLICY AND MANAGEMENT

FEDERAL LAND POLICY AND MANAGEMENT ACT OF 1976 [FLPMA § ___]

(43 U.S.C.A. §§ 1701 to 1784)

CHAPTER 35—FEDERAL LAND POLICY AND MANAGEMENT

SUBCHAPTER I—GENERAL PROVISIONS

Sec.

1701. Congressional declaration of policy.
1702. Definitions.

SUBCHAPTER II—LAND USE PLANNING AND LAND ACQUISITION AND DISPOSITION

1711. Continuing inventory and identification of public lands; preparation and maintenance.
1712. Land use plans.
 (a) Development, maintenance and revision by Secretary.
 (b) Coordination of plans for National Forest System lands with Indian land use planning and management programs for purposes of development and revision.
 (c) Criteria for development and revision.
 (d) Review and inclusion of classified public lands; review of existing land use plans; modification and termination of classifications.
 (e) Management decisions for implementation of developed or revised plans.
 (f) Procedures applicable to formulation of plans and programs for public land management.
1713. Sales of public land tracts.
 (a) Criteria for disposal; excepted lands.
 (b) Conveyance of land of agricultural value and desert in character.
 (c) Congressional approval procedures applicable to tracts in excess of two thousand five hundred acres.
 (d) Sale price.
 (e) Maximum size of tracts.
 (f) Competitive bidding requirements.
 (g) Acceptance or rejection of offers to purchase.
1714. Withdrawals of lands.
 (a) Authorization and limitation; delegation of authority.
 (b) Application and procedures applicable subsequent to submission of application.
 (c) Congressional approval procedures applicable to withdrawals aggregating five thousand acres or more.

Sec.

1714. Withdrawals of lands.
 (d) Withdrawals aggregating less than five thousand acres; procedure applicable.
 (e) Emergency withdrawals; procedure applicable; duration.
 (f) Review of existing withdrawals and extensions; procedure applicable to extensions; duration.
 (g) Processing and adjudication of existing applications.
 (h) Public hearing required for new withdrawals.
 (i) Consent for withdrawal of lands under administration of department or agency other than Department of the Interior.
 (j) Applicability of other Federal laws withdrawing lands as limiting authority.
 (k) Authorization of appropriations for processing applications.
 (*l*) Review of existing withdrawals in certain States; procedure applicable for determination of future status of lands; authorization of appropriations.
1715. Acquisitions of public lands and access over non-Federal lands to National Forest System units.
 (a) Authorization and limitations on authority of Secretary of the Interior and Secretary of Agriculture.
 (b) Conformity to departmental policies and land-use plan of acquisitions.
 (c) Status of lands and interests in lands upon acquisition by Secretary of the Interior; transfers to Secretary of Agriculture of lands and interests in lands acquired within National Forest System boundaries.
 (d) Status of lands and interests in lands upon acquisition by Secretary of Agriculture.
 (e) Status and administration of lands acquired in exchange for lands revested in or reconveyed to United States.
1716. Exchanges of public lands or interests therein within the National Forest System.
 (a) Authorization and limitations on authority of Secretary of the Interior and Secretary of Agriculture.
 (b) Implementation requirements; cash equalization waiver.
 (c) Status of lands acquired upon exchange by Secretary of the Interior.

Sec.
1716. Exchanges of public lands or interests therein within the National Forest System.
(d) Appraisal of land; submission to arbitrator; determination to proceed or withdraw from exchange; use of other valuation process; suspension of deadlines.
(e) Simultaneous issue of patents or titles.
(f) New rules and regulations; appraisal rules and regulations; "costs and other responsibilities or requirements" defined.
(g) Exchanges to proceed under existing laws and regulations pending new rules and regulations.
(h) Exchanges of lands or interests of approximately equal value; conditions; "approximate equal value" defined.
(i) Segregation from appropriation under mining and public land laws.
1717. Qualifications of conveyees.
1718. Documents of conveyance; terms, covenants, etc.
1719. Mineral interests; reservation and conveyance requirements and procedures.
1720. Coordination by Secretary of the Interior with State and local governments.
1721. Conveyances of public lands to States, local governments, etc.
(a) Unsurveyed islands; authorization and limitations on authority.
(b) Omitted lands, authorization and limitations on authority.
(c) Conformity with land use plans and programs and coordination with State and local governments of conveyances.
(d) Applicability of other statutory requirements for authorized use of conveyed lands.
(e) Limitations on uses of conveyed lands.
(f) Applicability to lands within National Forest System, National Park System, National Wildlife Refuge System, and National Wild and Scenic Rivers System.
(g) Applicability to other statutory provisions authorizing sale of specific omitted lands.
1722. Sale of public lands subject to unintentional trespass.
(a) Preference right of contiguous landowners; offering price.
(b) Procedures applicable.
(c) Time for processing of applications and sales.
1723. Temporary revocation authority.
(a) Exchange involved.
(b) Requirements.
(c) Limitations.
(d) Termination.

SUBCHAPTER III—ADMINISTRATION

1731. Bureau of Land Management.
(a) Director; appointment, qualifications, functions, and duties.
(b) Statutory transfer of functions, powers and duties relating to administration of laws.
(c) Associate Director, Assistant Directors, and other employees; appointment and compensation.
(d) Existing regulations relating to administration of laws.

Sec.
1732. Management of use, occupancy, and development of public lands.
(a) Multiple use and sustained yield requirements applicable; exception.
(b) Easements, permits, etc., for utilization through habitation, cultivation, and development of small trade or manufacturing concerns; applicable statutory requirements.
(c) Revocation or suspension provision in instrument authorizing use, occupancy or development; violation of provision; procedure applicable.
(d) Temporary use of Alaska public lands for military purposes.
1733. Enforcement authority.
(a) Regulations for implementation of management, use, and protection requirements, violations; criminal penalties.
(b) Civil actions by Attorney General for violations of regulations; nature of relief; jurisdiction.
(c) Contracts for enforcement of Federal laws and regulations by local law enforcement officials; procedure applicable; contract requirements and implementation.
(d) Cooperation with regulatory and law enforcement officials of any State or political subdivision in enforcement of laws or ordinances.
(e) Uniformed desert ranger force in California Desert Conservation Area; establishment; enforcement of Federal laws and regulations.
(f) Applicability of other Federal enforcement provisions.
(g) Unlawful activities.
1734. Fees, charges, and commissions.
(a) Authority to establish and modify.
(b) Deposits for payments to reimburse reasonable costs of United States.
(c) Refunds.
1735. Forfeiture and deposits.
(a) Credit to separate account in Treasury; appropriation and availability.
(b) Expenditure of moneys collected administering Oregon and California Railroad and Coos Bay Wagon Road Grant lands.
(c) Refunds.
1736. Working capital fund.
(a) Establishment; availability of fund.
(b) Initial funding; subsequent transfers.
(c) Payments credited to fund; amount; advancement or reimbursement.
(d) Authorization of appropriations.
1736a. Revolving fund derived from disposal of salvage timber.
1737. Implementation provisions.
(a) Investigations, studies, and experiments.
(b) Contracts and cooperative agreements.
(c) Contributions and donations of money, services, and property.
(d) Recruitment of volunteers.
(e) Restrictions on activities of volunteers.
(f) Federal employment status of volunteers.
(g) Authorization of appropriations.
1738. Contracts for surveys and resource protection; renewals; funding requirements.
1739. Advisory councils.
(a) Establishment; membership; operation.

Sec.
1739. Advisory councils.
(b) Meetings.
(c) Travel and per diem payments.
(d) Functions.
(e) Public participation; procedures applicable.
1740. Rules and regulations.
1741. Annual reports.
(a) Purpose; time for submission.
(b) Format.
(c) Contents.
1742. Search, rescue, and protection forces; emergency situations authorizing hiring.
1743. Disclosure of financial interests by officers or employees.
(a) Annual written statement; availability to public.
(b) Implementation of requirements.
(c) Exempted personnel.
(d) Violations; criminal penalties.
1744. Recordation of mining claims.
(a) Filing requirements.
(b) Additional filing requirements.
(c) Failure to file as constituting abandonment; defective or untimely filing.
(d) Validity of claims, waiver of assessment, etc., as unaffected.
1745. Disclaimer of interest in lands.
(a) Issuance of recordable document; criteria.
(b) Procedures applicable.
(c) Construction and quit-claim deed from United States.
1746. Correction of conveyance documents.
1747. Loans to States and political subdivisions; purposes; amounts; allocation; terms and conditions; interest rate; security; limitations; forbearance for benefit of borrowers; recordkeeping requirements; discrimination prohibited; deposit of receipts.
1748. Funding requirements.
(a) Authorization of appropriations.
(b) Procedure applicable for authorization of appropriations.
(c) Distribution of receipts from Bureau from disposal of lands, etc.
(d) Purchase of certain public lands from Land and Water Conservation Fund.

SUBCHAPTER IV—RANGE MANAGEMENT

1751. Grazing fees; feasibility study; contents; submission of report; annual distribution and use of range betterment funds; nature of distributions.
1752. Grazing leases and permits.
(a) Terms and conditions.
(b) Terms of lesser duration.
(c) First priority for renewal of expiring permit or lease.
(d) Allotment management plan requirements.
(e) Omission of allotment management plan requirements and incorporation of appropriate terms and conditions; reexamination of range conditions.
(f) Allotment management plan applicability to non-Federal lands; appeal rights.
(g) Cancellation of permit or lease; determination of reasonable compensation; notice.

Sec.
1752. Grazing leases and permits.
(h) Applicability of provisions to rights, etc., in or to public lands or lands in National Forests.
1753. Grazing advisory boards.
(a) Establishment; maintenance.
(b) Functions.
(c) Appointment and terms of members.
(d) Meetings.
(e) Federal Advisory Committee Act applicability.
(f) Expiration date.

SUBCHAPTER V—RIGHTS-OF-WAY

1761. Grant, issue, or renewal of rights-of-way.
(a) Authorized purposes.
(b) Procedures applicable; administration.
(c) Permanent easement for water systems; issuance, preconditions, etc.
(d) Rights-of-way on certain Federal lands.
1762. Roads.
(a) Authority to acquire, construct, and maintain; financing arrangements.
(b) Recordation of copies of affected instruments.
(c) Maintenance or reconstruction of facilities by users.
(d) Fund for user fees for delayed payment to grantor.
1763. Right-of-way corridors; criteria and procedures applicable for designation.
1764. General requirements.
(a) Boundary specifications; criteria; temporary use of additional lands.
(b) Terms and conditions of right-of-way or permit.
(c) Applicability of regulations or stipulations.
(d) Submission of plan of construction, operation, and rehabilitation by new project applicants; plan requirements.
(e) Regulatory requirements for terms and conditions; revision and applicability of regulations.
(f) Removal or use of mineral and vegetative materials.
(g) Rental payments; amount, waiver, etc.
(h) Liability for damage or injury incurred by United States for use and occupancy of rights-of-way; indemnifications of United States; no-fault liability; amount of damages.
(i) Bond or security requirements.
(j) Criteria for grant, issue, or renewal of right-of-way.
1765. Terms and conditions.
1766. Suspension or termination; grounds; procedures applicable.
1767. Rights-of-way for Federal departments and agencies.
1768. Conveyance of lands covered by right-of-way; terms and conditions.
1769. Existing right-of-way or right-of-use unaffected; exceptions; rights-of-way for railroad and appurtenant communication facilities; applicability of existing terms and conditions.
1770. Applicability of provisions to other Federal laws.
(a) Right-of-way.
(b) Highway use.
(c) Application of antitrust laws.
1771. Coordination of applications.

Sec.

SUBCHAPTER VI. DESIGNATED MANAGEMENT AREAS

1781. California Desert Conservation Area.
(a) Congressional findings.
(b) Statement of purpose.
(c) Description of Area.
(d) Preparation and implementation of comprehensive long-range plan for management, use, etc.
(e) Interim program for management, use, etc.
(f) Applicability of mining laws.
(g) Advisory Committee; establishment; functions.
(h) Management of lands under jurisdiction of Secretary of Agriculture and Secretary of Defense.
(i) Annual report; contents.
(j) Authorization of appropriations.
1782. Bureau of Land Management Wilderness Study.
(a) Lands subject to review and designation as wilderness.

Sec.
1782. Bureau of Land Management Wilderness Study.
(b) Presidential recommendation for designation as wilderness.
(c) Status of lands during period of review and determination.
1783. Yaquina Head Outstanding Natural Area.
(a) Establishment.
(b) Administration by Secretary of the Interior; management plan; quarrying permits.
(c) Revocation of 1866 reservation of lands for lighthouse purposes; restoration to public lands status.
(d) Acquisition of lands not already in Federal ownership.
(e) Wind energy research.
(f) Reclamation and restoration of lands affected by quarrying operations.
(g) Authorization of appropriations.
1784. Lands in Alaska; designation as wilderness; management by Bureau of Land Management pending Congressional action.

Related Provisions

See, also, Coastal Zone Management, 16 U.S.C.A. § 1451 et seq., ante; Rural Environmental Conservation Program, 16 U.S.C.A. § 1501 et seq., ante; and Soil and Water Resources, 16 U.S.C.A. § 2001 et seq., ante.

CROSS REFERENCES

Acquisition of land not already in Federal ownership for Yaquina Head Outstanding Natural Area, see section 1783 of this title.

Alaska national interest lands conservation—

Access to nonfederally-owned land surrounded by lands managed under this chapter, see section 3210 of Title 16, Conservation.

Management under this chapter of Federal lands outside boundaries established by Alaska National Interest Lands Conservation Act, see section 3209 of Title 16.

Chaco Culture National Historic Park, Federal lands excluded therefrom managed in accordance with this chapter, see section 410ii–3 of Title 16.

Designations pursuant to this chapter, effect on State selections and conveyances in implementation of Alaska native claims settlement and Alaska statehood, see section 1635 of this title.

Establishment of Indian tribal reservations from lands administered under this chapter, see section 713f of Title 25, Indians.

Management of public rangelands in accordance with this chapter, see section 1903 of this title.

Redwood National Park, management of lands in accordance with this chapter, see section 79b of Title 16, Conservation.

Steese National Conservation Area, administration pursuant to this chapter, see section 460mm–1 of Title 16.

White Mountains National Recreation Area, administration in accordance with this chapter, see section 460mm–2 of Title 16.

WEST'S FEDERAL FORMS

Eminent domain proceedings, see § 5711 et seq.

Jurisdiction and venue in district courts, see § 1003 et seq.

Preliminary injunctions and temporary restraining order, see § 5271 et seq.

Sentence and fine, see § 7531 et seq.

WEST'S FEDERAL PRACTICE MANUAL

Bureau of Land Management, see §§ 14, 5226.

CODE OF FEDERAL REGULATIONS

Coal management, see 43 CFR 3400.0–3 et seq.

Color-of-title and omitted lands, see 43 CFR 2540.0–3 et seq.

Criminal law enforcement, see 43 CFR 9260.0–1 et seq.

Environment, see 43 CFR 3461.0–3 et seq.

Exchanges, acquisition of lands by, see 43 CFR 2200.0–1 et seq.

Forest management decisions, administration of, see 43 CFR 5003.1 et seq.

Land ownership adjustments, see 36 CFR 254.1 et seq.

Land uses, see 36 CFR 251.9 et seq.

Land withdrawals, see 43 CFR 2300.0–1 et seq.

Leases, generally, see 43 CFR 3420.0–1 et seq., 3430.0–1 et seq., 3451.1 et seq.

Local governments, financial assistance, see 43 CFR 1881.0–1 et seq.

Mineral interest reservation and conveyance procedure, see 43 CFR 2720.0–1 et seq.

Minerals management, see 43 CFR Chap. II, Subchap. C.

Mining claims under general laws, see 43 CFR 3802.0–1 et seq.

Oil and gas leases, see 43 CFR 3130.0–1 et seq.

Planning, programming, and budgeting, see 43 CFR 1601.0–1 et seq.

Public entry and use of lands, see 50 CFR 26.11 et seq.

Range management, see 43 CFR Chap. II, Subchap. D.

Recreation and public purposes, see 43 CFR 2742.1 et seq.

Recreation programs, see 43 CFR Chap. II, Subchap. H.

Wildfire prevention, see 43 CFR 9212.0–1 et seq.

WESTLAW ELECTRONIC RESEARCH

See WESTLAW guide following the Explanation pages of this pamphlet.

SUBCHAPTER I—GENERAL PROVISIONS

§ 1701. Congressional declaration of policy [FLPMA § 102]

(a) The Congress declares that it is the policy of the United States that—

(1) the public lands be retained in Federal ownership, unless as a result of the land use planning procedure provided for in this Act, it is determined that disposal of a particular parcel will serve the national interest;

(2) the national interest will be best realized if the public lands and their resources are periodically and systematically inventoried and their present and future use is projected through a land use planning process coordinated with other Federal and State planning efforts;

(3) public lands not previously designated for any specific use and all existing classifications of public lands that were effected by executive action or statute before October 21, 1976, be reviewed in accordance with the provisions of this Act;

(4) the Congress exercise its constitutional authority to withdraw or otherwise designate or dedicate Federal lands for specified purposes and that Congress delineate the extent to which the Executive may withdraw lands without legislative action;

(5) in administering public land statutes and exercising discretionary authority granted by them, the Secretary be required to establish comprehensive rules and regulations after considering the views of the general public; and to structure adjudication procedures to assure adequate third party participation, objective administrative review of initial decisions, and expeditious decisionmaking;

(6) judicial review of public land adjudication decisions be provided by law;

(7) goals and objectives be established by law as guidelines for public land use planning, and that management be on the basis of multiple use and sustained yield unless otherwise specified by law;

(8) the public lands be managed in a manner that will protect the quality of scientific, scenic, historical, ecological, environmental, air and atmospheric, water resource, and archeological values; that, where appropriate, will preserve and protect certain public lands in their natural condition; that will provide food and habitat for fish and wildlife and domestic animals; and that will provide for outdoor recreation and human occupancy and use;

(9) the United States receive fair market value of the use of the public lands and their resources unless otherwise provided for by statute;

(10) uniform procedures for any disposal of public land, acquisition of non-Federal land for public purposes, and the exchange of such lands be established by statute, requiring each disposal, acquisition, and exchange to be consistent with the prescribed mission of the department or agency involved, and reserving to the Congress review of disposals in excess of a specified acreage;

(11) regulations and plans for the protection of public land areas of critical environmental concern be promptly developed;

(12) the public lands be managed in a manner which recognizes the Nation's need for domestic sources of minerals, food, timber, and fiber from the public lands including implementation of the Mining and Minerals Policy Act of 1970 (84 Stat. 1876, 30 U.S.C. 21a) as it pertains to the public lands; and

(13) the Federal Government should, on a basis equitable to both the Federal and local taxpayer, provide for payments to compensate States and local governments for burdens created as a result of the immunity of Federal lands from State and local taxation.

(b) The policies of this Act shall become effective only as specific statutory authority for their implementation is enacted by this Act or by subsequent legislation and shall then be construed as supplemental to and not in derogation of the purposes for which public lands are administered under other provisions of law.

(Oct. 21, 1976, Pub.L. 94–579, Title I, § 102, 90 Stat. 2744.)

Short Title

Section 101 of Pub.L. 94–579, Title I, Oct. 21, 1976, 90 Stat. 2744, provided that: "This Act [enacting this chapter and amending and repealing numerous other laws, which for complete distribution, see Tables Volume] may be cited as the 'Federal Land Policy and Management Act of 1976'."

Section 1 of Pub.L. 100–409, Aug. 20, 1988, 102 Stat. 1086, provided that: "This Act [enacting section 1723 of this title, amending section 1716 of this title and sections 505a, 505b, and 521b of Title 16, Conservation, and enacting provisions set out as notes under sections 751 and 1716 of this title] may be cited as the 'Federal Land Exchange Facilitation Act of 1988'."

Severability of Provisions

Section 707 of Pub.L. 94–579, Title VII, Oct. 21, 1976, 90 Stat. 2794, provided that: "If any provision of this Act [see Short Title note set out under this section] or the application thereof is held invalid, the remainder of the Act and the application thereof shall not be affected thereby."

Existing Right-of-Way

Section 706(b) of Pub.L. 94–579, Title VII, Oct. 21, 1976, 90 Stat. 2794, provided that: "Nothing in section 706(a), except as it pertains to rights-of-way, may be construed as affecting the authority of the Secretary of Agriculture under the Act of June 4, 1897 (30 Stat. 35, as amended, 16 U.S.C. 551) [section 551 of Title 16]; the Act of July 22, 1937 (50 Stat. 525, as amended, 7 U.S.C. 1010–1212) [sections 1010 to 1012 of Title 7]; or the Act of September 3, 1954 (68 Stat. 1146, 43 U.S.C. 931c) [section 931c of this title]."

Savings Provisions

Section 701 of Pub.L. 94–579, Title VII, Oct. 21, 1976, 90 Stat. 2786, provided that:

"(a) Nothing in this Act [see Short Title note set out under this section], or in any amendment made by this Act, shall be construed as terminating any valid lease, permit, patent, right-of-way, or other land use right or authorization existing on the date of approval of this Act [Oct. 21, 1976].

"(b) Notwithstanding any provision of this Act, in the event of conflict with or inconsistency between this Act and the Acts of August 28, 1937 (50 Stat. 874; 43 U.S.C. 1181a–1181j) [sections 1181a to 1181j of this title], and May 24, 1939 (53 Stat. 753), insofar as they relate to management of timber resources, and disposition of revenues from lands and resources, the latter Acts shall prevail.

"(c) All withdrawals, reservations, classifications, and designations in effect as of the date of approval of this Act [Oct. 21, 1976] shall remain in full force and effect until modified under the provisions of this Act or other applicable law.

"(d) Nothing in this Act, or in any amendments made by this Act, shall be construed as permitting any person to place, or allow to be placed, spent oil shale, overburden, or byproducts from the recovery of other minerals found with oil shale, on any Federal land other than Federal land which has been leased for the recovery of shale oil under the Act of February 25, 1920 (41 Stat. 437, as amended; 30 U.S.C. 181 et seq.) [section 181 et seq. of Title 30].

"(e) Nothing in this Act shall be construed as modifying, revoking, or changing any provision of the Alaska Native Claims Settlement Act (85 Stat. 688, as amended; 43 U.S.C. 1601 et seq.) [section 1601 et seq. of this title].

"(f) Nothing in this Act shall be deemed to repeal any existing law by implication.

"(g) Nothing in this Act shall be construed as limiting or restricting the power and authority of the United States or—

"(1) as affecting in any way any law governing appropriation or use of, or Federal right to, water on public lands;

"(2) as expanding or diminishing Federal or State jurisdiction, responsibility, interests, or rights in water resources development or control;

"(3) as displacing, superseding, limiting, or modifying any interstate compact or the jurisdiction or responsibility of any legally established joint or common agency of two or more States or of two or more States and the Federal Government;

"(4) as superseding, modifying, or repealing, except as specifically set forth in this Act, existing laws applicable to the various Federal agencies which are authorized to develop or participate in the development of water resources or to exercise licensing or regulatory functions in relation thereto;

"(5) as modifying the terms of any interstate compact;

"(6) as a limitation upon any State criminal statute or upon the police power of the respective States, or as derogating the authority of a local police officer in the performance of his duties, or as depriving any State or political subdivision thereof of any right it may have to exercise civil and criminal jurisdiction on the national resource lands; or as amending, limiting, or infringing the existing laws providing grants of lands to the States.

"(h) All actions by the Secretary concerned under this Act shall be subject to valid existing rights.

"(i) The adequacy of reports required by this Act to be submitted to the Congress or its committees shall not be subject to judicial review.

"(j) Nothing in this Act shall be construed as affecting the distribution of livestock grazing revenues to local governments under the Granger-Thye Act (64 Stat. 85, 16 U.S.C. 580h) [section 580h of Title 16], under the Act of May 23, 1908 (35 Stat. 260, as amended; 16 U.S.C. 500) [section 500 of Title 16], under the Act of March 4, 1913 (37 Stat. 843, as amended; 16 U.S.C. 501) [section 501 of Title 16], and under the Act of June 20, 1910 (36 Stat. 557)."

CODE OF FEDERAL REGULATIONS

Administration of forest management decisions, see 43 CFR 5003.1 et seq.
Cooperative relations, see 43 CFR 1784.0–1 et seq.
Minerals management, see 43 CFR Chap. II, Subchap. C.

LAW REVIEW COMMENTARIES

Grazing management on the public lands: Opening the process to public participation. Joseph M. Feller, 26 Land and Water L.Rev. 571 (1991).

Mountain bicycles on federal lands. 7 J.Energy L. & Pol'y 123 (1986).

Natural environments and natural resources: An economic analysis and new interpretation of general mining law. Michael Braunstein (1985) 32 U.C.L.A.Law Rev. 1133.

Protecting national park system buffer zones: Existing, proposed, and suggested authority. John W. Hiscock. 7 J.Energy L. & Pol'y 35 (1986).

LIBRARY REFERENCES

Public Lands ⚷96.
C.J.S. Public Lands § 168.

§ 1702. Definitions [FLPMA § 103]

Without altering in any way the meaning of the following terms as used in any other statute, whether or not such statute is referred to in, or amended by, this Act, as used in this Act—

(a) The term "areas of critical environmental concern" means areas within the public lands where special management attention is required (when such areas are developed or used or where no development is required) to protect and prevent irreparable damage to important historic, cultural, or scenic values, fish and wildlife resources or other natural systems or processes, or to protect life and safety from natural hazards.

(b) The term "holder" means any State or local governmental entity, individual, partnership, corporation, association, or other business entity receiving or using a right-of-way under subchapter V of this chapter.

(c) The term "multiple use" means the management of the public lands and their various resource values so that they are utilized in the combination that will best meet the present and future needs of the American people; making the most judicious use of the land for some or all of these resources or related services over areas large enough to provide sufficient latitude for periodic adjustments in use to conform to changing needs and conditions; the use of some land for less than all of the resources; a combination of balanced and diverse resource uses that takes into account the long-term needs of future generations for renewable and nonrenewable resources, including, but not limited to, recreation, range, timber, minerals, watershed, wildlife and fish, and natural scenic, scientific and historical values; and harmonious and coordinated management of the various resources without permanent impairment of the productivity of the land and the quality of the environment with consideration being given to the relative values of the resources and not necessarily to the combination of uses that will give the greatest economic return or the greatest unit output.

(d) The term "public involvement" means the opportunity for participation by affected citizens in rulemaking, decisionmaking, and planning with respect to the public lands, including public meetings or hearings held at locations near the affected lands, or advisory mechanisms, or such other procedures as may be necessary to provide public comment in a particular instance.

(e) The term "public lands" means any land and interest in land owned by the United States within the several States and administered by the Secretary of the Interior through the Bureau of Land Management, without regard to how the United States acquired ownership, except—

(1) lands located on the Outer Continental Shelf; and

(2) lands held for the benefit of Indians, Aleuts, and Eskimos.

(f) The term "right-of-way" includes an easement, lease, permit, or license to occupy, use, or traverse public lands granted for the purpose listed in subchapter V of this chapter.

(g) The term "Secretary", unless specifically designated otherwise, means the Secretary of the Interior.

(h) The term "sustained yield" means the achievement and maintenance in perpetuity of a high-level annual or regular periodic output of the various renewable resources of the public lands consistent with multiple use.

(i) The term "wilderness" as used in section 1782 of this title shall have the same meaning as it does in section 1131(c) of Title 16.

(j) The term "withdrawal" means withholding an area of Federal land from settlement, sale, location, or entry, under some or all of the general land laws, for the purpose of limiting activities under those laws in order to maintain other public values in the area or reserving the area for a particular public purpose or program; or transferring jurisdiction over an area of Federal land, other than "property" governed by the Federal Property and Administrative Services Act, as amended (40 U.S.C. 472) from one department, bureau or agency to another department, bureau or agency.

(k) An "allotment management plan" means a document prepared in consultation with the lessees or permittees involved, which applies to livestock operations on the public lands or on lands within National Forests in the eleven contiguous Western States and which:

(1) prescribes the manner in, and extent to, which livestock operations will be conducted in order to meet the multiple-use, sustained-yield, economic and other needs and objectives as determined for the lands by the Secretary concerned; and

(2) describes the type, location, ownership, and general specifications for the range improvements to be installed and maintained on the lands to meet the livestock grazing and other objectives of land management; and

(3) contains such other provisions relating to livestock grazing and other objectives found by the Secretary concerned to be consistent with the provisions of this Act and other applicable law.

(*l*) The term "principal or major uses" includes, and is limited to, domestic livestock grazing, fish and wildlife development and utilization, mineral exploration and production, rights-of-way, outdoor recreation, and timber production.

(m) The term "department" means a unit of the executive branch of the Federal Government which is headed by a member of the President's Cabinet and the term "agency" means a unit of the executive branch of the Federal Government which is not under the jurisdiction of a head of a department.

(n) The term "Bureau[1] means the Bureau of Land Management.

(*o*) The term "eleven contiguous Western States" means the States of Arizona, California, Colorado, Idaho, Montana, Nevada, New Mexico, Oregon, Utah, Washington, and Wyoming.

(p) The term "grazing permit and lease" means any document authorizing use of public lands or lands in National Forests in the eleven contiguous western States for the purpose of grazing domestic livestock.

(Oct. 21, 1976, Pub.L. 94–579, Title I, § 103, 90 Stat. 2745.)

1 So in original. Probably should have a close quote.

CROSS REFERENCES

Allotment management plan defined for public rangelands improvement, see section 1902 of this title.

Chaco Canyon National Monument; Federal lands exchanged for non-Federal property, see section 410ii–3 of Title 16, Conservation.

Chaco Culture Archeological Protection Sites; protection, preservation, and maintenance of cultural resources, see section 410ii–5 of Title 16.

Minerals in outer Continental Shelf lands as including minerals authorized to be produced from public lands defined in this section, see section 1331 of this title.

Yaquina Head Outstanding Natural Area; restoration to public lands status, see section 1783 of this title.

WEST'S FEDERAL PRACTICE MANUAL

Bureau of Land Management, see §§ 14, 5226.

LAW REVIEW COMMENTARIES

Public access to landlocked public lands. Note, 39 Stan.L.Rev. 1373 (1987).

SUBCHAPTER II—LAND USE PLANNING AND LAND ACQUISITION AND DISPOSITION

§ 1711. Continuing inventory and identification of public lands; preparation and maintenance [FLPMA § 201]

(a) The Secretary shall prepare and maintain on a continuing basis an inventory of all public lands and their resource and other values (including, but not limited to, outdoor recreation and scenic values), giving priority to areas of critical environmental concern. This inventory shall be kept current so as to reflect changes in conditions and to identify new and emerging resource and other values. The preparation and maintenance of such inventory or the identification of such areas shall not, of itself, change or prevent change of the management or use of public lands.

(b) As funds and manpower are made available, the Secretary shall ascertain the boundaries of the public lands; provide means of public identification thereof including, where appropriate, signs and maps; and provide State and local governments with data from the inventory for the purpose of planning and regulating the uses of non-Federal lands in proximity of such public lands.

(Oct. 21, 1976, Pub.L. 94–579, Title II, § 201, 90 Stat. 2747.)

CROSS REFERENCES

Lands in Alaska, designation as wilderness, see section 1784 of this title.
Lands subject to review and designation as wilderness, see section 1782 of this title.
Public rangelands, inventory and identification of, see section 1901 of this title.
Rangelands inventory, duties of Secretary of the Interior and Secretary of Agriculture, see section 1903 of this title.

CODE OF FEDERAL REGULATIONS

Planning, programming, and budgeting, see 43 CFR 1601.0–1 et seq.

LIBRARY REFERENCES

Public Lands ⚷4, 5, 51, 96.
C.J.S. Public Lands §§ 2 et seq., 76 et seq., 168.

§ 1712. Land use plans [FLPMA § 202]

(a) Development, maintenance, and revision by Secretary

The Secretary shall, with public involvement and consistent with the terms and conditions of this Act, develop, maintain, and, when appropriate, revise land use plans which provide by tracts or areas for the use of the public lands. Land use plans shall be developed for the public lands regardless of whether such lands previously have been classified, withdrawn, set aside, or otherwise designated for one or more uses.

(b) Coordination of plans for National Forest System lands with Indian land use planning and management programs for purposes of development and revision

In the development and revision of land use plans, the Secretary of Agriculture shall coordinate land use plans for lands in the National Forest System with the land use planning and management programs of and for Indian tribes by, among other things, considering the policies of approved tribal land resource management programs.

(c) Criteria for development and revision

In the development and revision of land use plans, the Secretary shall—

(1) use and observe the principles of multiple use and sustained yield set forth in this and other applicable law;

(2) use a systematic interdisciplinary approach to achieve integrated consideration of physical, biological, economic, and other sciences;

(3) give priority to the designation and protection of areas of critical environmental concern;

(4) rely, to the extent it is available, on the inventory of the public lands, their resources, and other values;

(5) consider present and potential uses of the public lands;

(6) consider the relative scarcity of the values involved and the availability of alternative means (including recycling) and sites for realization of those values;

(7) weigh long-term benefits to the public against short-term benefits;

(8) provide for compliance with applicable pollution control laws, including State and Federal air, water, noise, or other pollution standards or implementation plans; and

(9) to the extent consistent with the laws governing the administration of the public lands, coordinate the land use inventory, planning, and management activities of or for such lands with the land use planning and management programs of other Federal departments and agencies and of the States and local governments within which the lands are located, including, but not limited to, the statewide outdoor recreation plans developed under the Act of September 3, 1964 (78 Stat. 897), as amended [16 U.S.C.A. § 460*l*–4 et seq.], and of or for Indian tribes by, among other things, considering the policies of approved State and tribal land resource management programs. In implementing this directive, the Secretary shall, to the extent he finds practical, keep apprised of State, local, and tribal land use plans; assure that consideration is given to those State, local, and tribal plans that are germane in the development of land use plans for public lands; assist in resolving, to the extent practical, inconsistencies between Federal and non-Federal Government plans, and shall provide for meaningful public involvement of State and local government officials, both elected and appointed, in the development of land use programs, land use regulations, and land use decisions for public lands, including early public notice of proposed decisions which may have a significant impact on non-Federal lands. Such officials in each State are authorized to furnish advice to the Secretary with respect to the development and revision of land use plans, land use guidelines, land use rules, and land use regulations for the public lands within such State and with respect to such other land use matters as may be referred to them by him. Land use plans of the Secretary under this section shall be consistent with State and local plans to the maximum extent he finds consistent with Federal law and the purposes of this Act.

(d) Review and inclusion of classified public lands; review of existing land use plans; modification and termination of classifications

Any classification of public lands or any land use plan in effect on October 21, 1976, is subject to review in the land use planning process conducted under this section, and all public lands, regardless of classification, are subject to inclusion in any land use plan developed pursuant to this section. The Secretary may modify or terminate any such classification consistent with such land use plans.

(e) Management decisions for implementation of developed or revised plans

The Secretary may issue management decisions to implement land use plans developed or revised under this section in accordance with the following:

(1) Such decisions, including but not limited to exclusions (that is, total elimination) of one or more of the principal or major uses made by a management decision shall remain subject to reconsideration, modification, and termination through revision by the Secretary or his delegate, under the provisions of this section, of the land use plan involved.

(2) Any management decision or action pursuant to a management decision that excludes (that is, totally eliminates) one or more of the principal or major uses for two or more years with respect to a tract of land of one hundred thousand acres or more shall be reported by the Secretary to the House of Representatives and the Senate. If within ninety days from the giving of such notice (exclusive of days on which either House has adjourned for more than three consecutive days), the Congress adopts a concurrent resolution of nonapproval of the management decision or action, then the management decision or action shall be promptly terminated by the Secretary. If the committee to which a resolution has been referred during the said ninety day period, has not reported it at the end of thirty calendar days after its referral, it shall be in order to either discharge the committee from further consideration of such resolution or to discharge the committee from consideration of any other resolution with respect to the management decision or action. A motion to discharge may be made only by an individual favoring the resolution, shall be highly privileged (except that it may not be made after the committee has reported such a resolution), and debate thereon shall be limited to not more than one hour, to be divided equally between those favoring and those opposing the resolution. An amendment to the motion shall not be in order, and it shall not be in order to move to reconsider the vote by which the motion was agreed to or disagreed to. If the motion to discharge is agreed to or disagreed to, the motion may not be made with respect to any other resolution with respect to the same management decision or action. When the committee has reprinted, or has been discharged from further consideration of a resolution, it shall at any time thereafter be in order (even though a previous motion to the same effect has been disagreed to) to move to proceed to the consideration of the resolution. The motion shall be highly privileged and shall not be debatable. An amendment to the motion shall not be in order, and it shall not be in order to move to reconsider the vote by which the motion was agreed to or disagreed to.

(3) Withdrawals made pursuant to section 1714 of this title may be used in carrying out management decisions, but public lands shall be removed from or restored to the operation of the Mining Law of 1872, as amended (R.S. 2318–2352; 30 U.S.C.A. § 21 et seq.) or transferred to another department, bureau, or agency only by withdrawal action pursuant to section 1714 of this title or other action pursuant to applicable law: *Provided*, That nothing in this section shall prevent a wholly owned Government corporation from acquiring and holding rights as a citizen under the Mining Law of 1872.

(f) Procedures applicable to formulation of plans and programs for public land management

The Secretary shall allow an opportunity for public involvement and by regulation shall establish procedures, including public hearings where appropriate, to give Federal, State, and local governments and the public, adequate notice and opportunity to comment upon and participate in the formulation of plans and programs relating to the management of the public lands.

(Oct. 21, 1976, Pub.L. 94–579, Title II, § 202, 90 Stat. 2747.)

CROSS REFERENCES

California Desert Conservation Area; preparation and implementation of comprehensive long-range plan for management, see section 1781 of this title.

Grazing leases and permits; first priority for renewal, see section 1752 of this title.

Lands in Alaska; designation as wilderness, see section 1784 of this title.

Management of public lands; multiple use and sustained yield requirements, see section 1732 of this title.

National Petroleum Reserve in Alaska; competitive leasing of oil and gas, see section 6508 of Title 42, The Public Health and Welfare.

Public rangelands management; Congressional declaration of policy, see section 1901 of this title.

Range improvement funding; fund limitations for prescribed uses, see section 1904 of this title.

Rangelands management, see section 1903 of this title.

Sales of public land tracts; criteria for disposal, see section 1713 of this title.

Snake River Birds of Prey National Conservation Area, Congressional findings of compliance with section, see 16 USCA § 460iii.

Wild horses and burros; inventory, see section 1333 of Title 16, Conservation.

Yaquina Head Outstanding Natural Area; development of management plan, see section 1783 of this title.

CODE OF FEDERAL REGULATIONS

Environment, see 43 CFR 3461.0–3 et seq.
Planning, programming, and budgeting, see 43 CFR 1601.0–1 et seq.
Recreation programs, see 43 CFR Chap. II, Subchap. H.

LAW REVIEW COMMENTARIES

Federal lands and local communities. Eric T. Freyfogle, 27 Ariz. L.Rev. 653 (1985).

Grazing management on the public lands: Opening the process to public participation. Joseph M. Feller, 26 Land and Water L.Rev. 571 (1991).

§ 1713. Sales of public land tracts [FLPMA § 203]

(a) Criteria for disposal; excepted lands

A tract of the public lands (except land in units of the National Wilderness Preservation System, National Wild and Scenic Rivers Systems, and National System of Trails) may be sold under this Act where, as a result of land use planning required under section 1712 of this title, the Secretary determines that the sale of such tract meets the following disposal criteria:

(1) such tract because of its location or other characteristics is difficult and uneconomic to manage as part of the public lands, and is not suitable for management by another Federal department or agency; or

(2) such tract was acquired for a specific purpose and the tract is no longer required for that or any other Federal purpose; or

(3) disposal of such tract will serve important public objectives, including but not limited to, expansion of communities and economic development, which cannot be achieved prudently or feasibly on land other than public land and which outweigh other public objectives and values, including, but not limited to, recreation and scenic values, which would be served by maintaining such tract in Federal ownership.

(b) Conveyance of land of agricultural value and desert in character

Where the Secretary determines that land to be conveyed under clause (3) of subsection (a) of this section is of agricultural value and is desert in character, such land shall be conveyed either under the sale authority of this section or in accordance with other existing law.

(c) Congressional approval procedures applicable to tracts in excess of two thousand five hundred acres

Where a tract of the public lands in excess of two thousand five hundred acres has been designated for sale, such sale may be made only after the end of the ninety days (not counting days on which the House of Representatives or the Senate has adjourned for more than three consecutive days) beginning on the day the Secretary has submitted notice of such designation to the Senate and the House of Representatives, and then only if the Congress has not adopted a concurrent resolution stating that such House does not approve of such designation. If the committee to which a resolution has been referred during the said ninety day period, has not reported it at the end of thirty calendar days after its referral, it shall be in order to either discharge the committee from further consideration of such resolution or to discharge the committee from consideration of any other resolution with respect to the designation. A motion to discharge may be made only by an individual favoring the resolution, shall be highly privileged (except that it may not be made after the committee has reported such a resolution), and debate thereon shall be limited to not more than one hour, to be divided equally between those favoring and those opposing the resolution. An amendment to the motion shall not be in order, and it shall not be in order to move to reconsider the vote by which the motion was agreed to or disagreed to. If the motion to discharge is agreed to or disagreed to, the motion may not be made with respect to any other resolution with respect to the same designation. When the committee has reprinted, or has been discharged from further consideration of a resolution, it shall at any time thereafter be in order (even though a previous motion to the same effect has been disagreed to) to move to proceed to the consideration of the resolution. The motion shall be highly privileged and shall not be debatable. An amendment to the motion shall not be in order, and it shall not be in order to move to reconsider the vote by which the motion was agreed to or disagreed to.

(d) Sale price

Sales of public lands shall be made at a price not less than their fair market value as determined by the Secretary.

(e) Maximum size of tracts

The Secretary shall determine and establish the size of tracts of public lands to be sold on the basis of the land use capabilities and development requirements of the lands; and, where any such tract which is judged by the Secretary to be chiefly valuable for agriculture is sold, its size shall be no larger than necessary to support a family-sized farm.

(f) Competitive bidding requirements

Sales of public lands under this section shall be conducted under competitive bidding procedures to be established by the Secretary. However, where the Secretary determines it necessary and proper in order (1) to assure equitable distribution among purchasers of lands, or (2) to recognize equitable considerations or public policies, including but not limited to, a preference to users, he may sell those lands with modified competitive bidding or without competitive bidding. In recognizing public policies, the Secretary shall give consideration to the following potential purchasers:

(1) the State in which the land is located;

(2) the local government entities in such State which are in the vicinity of the land;

(3) adjoining landowners;

(4) individuals; and

(5) any other person.

(g) Acceptance or rejection of offers to purchase

The Secretary shall accept or reject, in writing, any offer to purchase made through competitive bidding at his invitation no later than thirty days after the receipt of such offer or, in the case of a tract in excess of two thousand five hundred acres, at the end of thirty days after the end of the ninety-day period provided in subsection (c) of this section, whichever is later, unless the offeror waives his right to a decision within such thirty-day period. Prior to the expiration of such periods the Secretary may refuse to accept any offer or may withdraw any land or interest in land from sale under this section when he determines that consummation of the sale would not be consistent with this Act or other applicable law.

(Oct. 21, 1976, Pub.L. 94–579, Title II, § 203, 90 Stat. 2750.)

CODE OF FEDERAL REGULATIONS

Sales, see 43 CFR 2710.0–1 et seq.

LIBRARY REFERENCES

Public Lands ⇐33.
C.J.S. Public Lands § 42.

§ 1714. Withdrawals of lands [FLPMA § 204]

(a) Authorization and limitation; delegation of authority

On and after the effective date of this Act the Secretary is authorized to make, modify, extend, or revoke withdrawals but only in accordance with the provisions and limitations of this section. The Secretary may delegate this withdrawal authority only to individuals in the Office of the Secretary who have been appointed by the President, by and with the advice and consent of the Senate.

(b) Application and procedures applicable subsequent to submission of application

(1) Within thirty days of receipt of an application for withdrawal, and whenever he proposes a withdrawal on his own motion, the Secretary shall publish a notice in the Federal Register stating that the application has been submitted for filing or the proposal has been made and the extent to which the land is to be segregated while the application is being considered by the Secretary. Upon publication of such notice the land shall be segregated from the operation of the public land laws to the extent specified in the notice. The segregative effect of the application shall terminate upon (a) rejection of the application by the Secretary, (b) withdrawal of lands by the Secretary, or (c) the expiration of two years from the date of the notice.

(2) The publication provisions of this subsection are not applicable to withdrawals under subsection (e) hereof.

(c) Congressional approval procedures applicable to withdrawals aggregating five thousand acres or more

(1) On and after October 21, 1976, a withdrawal aggregating five thousand acres or more may be made (or such a withdrawal or any other withdrawal involving in the aggregate five thousand acres or more which terminates after such date of approval may be extended) only for a period of not more than twenty years by the Secretary on his own motion or upon request by a department or agency head. The Secretary shall notify both Houses of Congress of such a

withdrawal no later than its effective date and the withdrawal shall terminate and become ineffective at the end of ninety days (not counting days on which the Senate or the House of Representatives has adjourned for more than three consecutive days) beginning on the day notice of such withdrawal has been submitted to the Senate and the House of Representatives, if the Congress has adopted a concurrent resolution stating that such House does not approve the withdrawal. If the committee to which a resolution has been referred during the said ninety day period, has not reported it at the end of thirty calendar days after its referral, it shall be in order to either discharge the committee from further consideration of such resolution or to discharge the committee from consideration of any other resolution with respect to the Presidential recommendation. A motion to discharge may be made only by an individual favoring the resolution, shall be highly privileged (except that it may not be made after the committee has reported such a resolution), and debate thereon shall be limited to not more than one hour, to be divided equally between those favoring and those opposing the resolution. An amendment to the motion shall not be in order, and it shall not be in order to move to reconsider the vote by which the motion was agreed to or disagreed to. If the motion to discharge is agreed to or disagreed to, the motion may not be made with respect to any other resolution with respect to the same Presidential recommendation. When the committee has reprinted, or has been discharged from further consideration of a resolution, it shall at any time thereafter be in order (even though a previous motion to the same effect has been disagreed to) to move to proceed to the consideration of the resolution. The motion shall be highly privileged and shall not be debatable. An amendment to the motion shall not be in order, and it shall not be in order to move to reconsider the vote by which the motion was agreed to or disagreed to.

(2) With the notices required by subsection (c)(1) of this section and within three months after filing the notice under subsection (e) of this section, the Secretary shall furnish to the committees—

(1) a clear explanation of the proposed use of the land involved which led to the withdrawal;

(2) an inventory and evaluation of the current natural resource uses and values of the site and adjacent public and nonpublic land and how it appears they will be affected by the proposed use, including particularly aspects of use that might cause degradation of the environment, and also the economic impact of the change in use on individuals, local communities, and the Nation;

(3) an identification of present users of the land involved, and how they will be affected by the proposed use;

(4) an analysis of the manner in which existing and potential resource uses are incompatible with or in conflict with the proposed use, together with a statement of the provisions to be made for continuation or termination of existing uses, including an economic analysis of such continuation or termination;

(5) an analysis of the manner in which such lands will be used in relation to the specific requirements for the proposed use;

(6) a statement as to whether any suitable alternative sites are available (including cost estimates) for the proposed use or for uses such a withdrawal would displace;

(7) a statement of the consultation which has been or will be had with other Federal departments and agencies, with regional, State, and local government bodies, and with other appropriate individuals and groups;

(8) a statement indicating the effect of the proposed uses, if any, on State and local government interests and the regional economy;

(9) a statement of the expected length of time needed for the withdrawal;

(10) the time and place of hearings and of other public involvement concerning such withdrawal;

(11) the place where the records on the withdrawal can be examined by interested parties; and

(12) a report prepared by a qualified mining engineer, engineering geologist, or geologist which shall include but not be limited to information on: general geology, known mineral deposits, past and present mineral production, mining claims, mineral leases, evaluation of future mineral potential, present and potential market demands.

(d) Withdrawals aggregating less than five thousand acres; procedure applicable

A withdrawal aggregating less than five thousand acres may be made under this subsection by the Secretary on his own motion or upon request by a department or an agency head—

(1) for such period of time as he deems desirable for a resource use; or

(2) for a period of not more than twenty years for any other use, including but not limited to use for administrative sites, location of facilities, and other proprietary purposes; or

(3) for a period of not more than five years to preserve such tract for a specific use then under consideration by the Congress.

(e) Emergency withdrawals; procedure applicable; duration

When the Secretary determines, or when the Committee on Natural Resources of the House of Representatives or the Committee on Energy and Natural Resources of the Senate notifies the Secretary, that an emergency situation exists and that extraordinary measures must be taken to preserve values that would otherwise be lost, the Secretary notwithstanding the provisions of subsections (c)(1) and (d) of this section, shall immediately make a withdrawal and file notice of such emergency withdrawal with both of those Committees. Such emergency withdrawal shall be effective when made but shall last only for a period not to exceed three years and may not be extended except under the provisions of subsection (c)(1) or (d), whichever is applicable, and (b)(1) of this section. The information required in subsection (c)(2) of this subsection shall be furnished the committees within three months after filing such notice.

(f) Review of existing withdrawals and extensions; procedure applicable to extensions; duration

All withdrawals and extensions thereof, whether made prior to or after October 21, 1976, having a specific period shall be reviewed by the Secretary toward the end of the withdrawal period and may be extended or further extended only upon compliance with the provisions of subsection (c)(1) or (d) of this section, whichever is applicable, and only if the Secretary determines that the purpose for which the withdrawal was first made requires the extension, and then only for a period no longer than the length of the original withdrawal period. The Secretary shall report on such review and extensions to the Committee on Natural Resources of the House of Representatives and the Committee on Energy and Natural Resources of the Senate.

(g) Processing and adjudication of existing applications

All applications for withdrawal pending on October 21, 1976 shall be processed and adjudicated to conclusion within fifteen years of October 21, 1976, in accordance with the provisions of this section. The segregative effect of any application not so processed shall terminate on that date.

(h) Public hearing required for new withdrawals

All new withdrawals made by the Secretary under this section (except an emergency withdrawal made under subsection (e) of this section) shall be promulgated after an opportunity for a public hearing.

(i) Consent for withdrawal of lands under administration of department or agency other than Department of the Interior

In the case of lands under the administration of any department or agency other than the Department of the Interior, the Secretary shall make, modify, and revoke withdrawals only with the consent of the head of the department or agency concerned, except when the provisions of subsection (e) of this section apply.

(j) Applicability of other Federal laws withdrawing lands as limiting authority

The Secretary shall not make, modify, or revoke any withdrawal created by Act of Congress; make a withdrawal which can be made only by Act of Congress; modify or revoke any withdrawal creating national monuments under the Act of June 8, 1906 (34 Stat. 225; 16 U.S.C. 431–433); or modify, or revoke any withdrawal which added lands to the National Wildlife Refuge System prior to October 21, 1976, or which thereafter adds lands to that System under the terms of this Act. Nothing in this Act is intended to modify or change any provision of the Act of February 27, 1976 (90 Stat. 199; 16 U.S.C. 668dd(a)).

(k) Authorization of appropriations for processing applications

There is hereby authorized to be appropriated the sum of $10,000,000 for the purpose of processing withdrawal applications pending on the effective date of this Act, to be available until expended.

(*l*) Review of existing withdrawals in certain States; procedure applicable for determination of future status of lands; authorization of appropriations

(1) The Secretary shall, within fifteen years of October 21, 1976, review withdrawals existing on October 21, 1976, in the States of Arizona, California, Colorado, Idaho, Montana, Nevada, New Mexico, Oregon, Utah, Washington, and Wyoming of (1) all Federal lands other than withdrawals of the public lands administered by the Bureau of Land Management and of lands which, on October 21, 1976, were part of Indian reservations and other Indian holdings, the National Forest System, the National Park System, the National Wildlife Refuge System, other lands administered by the Fish and Wildlife Service or the Secretary through the Fish and Wildlife Service, the National Wild and Scenic Rivers System, and the National System of Trails; and (2) all public lands administered by the Bureau of Land Management and of lands in the National Forest System (except those in wilderness areas, and those areas formally identified as primitive or natural areas or designated as national recreation areas) which closed the lands to appropriation under the Mining Law of 1872 (17 Stat. 91, as amended; 30 U.S.C. 22 et seq.) or to leasing under the

Mineral Leasing Act of 1920 (41 Stat. 437, as amended; 30 U.S.C. 181 et seq.).

(2) In the review required by paragraph (1) of this subsection, the Secretary shall determine whether, and for how long, the continuation of the existing withdrawal of the lands would be, in his judgment, consistent with the statutory objectives of the programs for which the lands were dedicated and of the other relevant programs. The Secretary shall report his recommendations to the President, together with statements of concurrence or nonconcurrence submitted by the heads of the departments or agencies which administer the lands. The President shall transmit this report to the President of the Senate and the Speaker of the House of Representatives, together with his recommendations for action by the Secretary, or for legislation. The Secretary may act to terminate withdrawals other than those made by Act of the Congress in accordance with the recommendations of the President unless before the end of ninety days (not counting days on which the Senate and the House of Representatives has adjourned for more than three consecutive days) beginning on the day the report of the President has been submitted to the Senate and the House of Representatives the Congress has adopted a concurrent resolution indicating otherwise. If the committee to which a resolution has been referred during the said ninety day period, has not reported it at the end of thirty calendar days after its referral, it shall be in order to either discharge the committee from further consideration of such resolution or to discharge the committee from consideration of any other resolution with respect to the Presidential recommendation. A motion to discharge may be made only by an individual favoring the resolution, shall be highly privileged (except that it may not be made after the committee has reported such a resolution), and debate thereon shall be limited to not more than one hour, to be divided equally between those favoring and those opposing the resolution. An amendment to the motion shall not be in order, and it shall not be in order to move to reconsider the vote by which the motion was agreed to or disagreed to. If the motion to discharge is agreed to or disagreed to, the motion may not be made with respect to any other resolution with respect to the same Presidential recommendation. When the committee has reprinted, or has been discharged from further consideration of a resolution, it shall at any time thereafter be in order (even though a previous motion to the same effect has been disagreed to) to move to proceed to the consideration of the resolution. The motion shall be highly privileged and shall not be debatable. An amendment to the motion shall not be in order, and it shall not be in order to move to reconsider the vote by which the motion was agreed to or disagreed to.

(3) There are hereby authorized to be appropriated not more than $10,000,000 for the purpose of paragraph (1) of this subsection to be available until expended to the Secretary and to the heads of other departments and agencies which will be involved.

(Oct. 21, 1976, Pub.L. 94–579, Title II, § 204, 90 Stat. 2751; Nov. 2, 1994, Pub.L. 103–437, § 16(d)(1), 108 Stat. 4594.)

Change of Name

Any reference in any provision of law enacted before Jan. 4, 1995, to the Committee on Natural Resources of the House of Representatives treated as referring to the Committee on Resources of the House of Representatives, see section 1(a)(8) of Pub.L. 104–14, set out as a note preceding section 21 of Title 2, The Congress.

CROSS REFERENCES

Withdrawals of public land for—
  Carrying out management decisions for implementation of land use plans, see section 1712 of this title.
  Management of use, occupancy and development, see section 1732 of this title.
Withdrawals of public land under consideration for wilderness status, see section 1782 of this title.

CODE OF FEDERAL REGULATIONS

Land withdrawals, see 43 CFR 2300.0–1 et seq.
Public entry and use, see 50 CFR 26.11 et seq.

LIBRARY REFERENCES

Public Lands ⇨29.
C.J.S. Public Lands § 36 et seq.

§ 1715. Acquisitions of public lands and access over non-Federal lands to National Forest System units [FLPMA § 205]

(a) Authorization and limitations on authority of Secretary of the Interior and Secretary of Agriculture

Notwithstanding any other provisions of law, the Secretary, with respect to the public lands and the Secretary of Agriculture, with respect to the acquisition of access over non-Federal lands to units of the National Forest System, are authorized to acquire pursuant to this Act by purchase, exchange, donation, or eminent domain, lands or interests therein: *Provided*, That with respect to the public lands, the Secretary may exercise the power of eminent domain only if necessary to secure access to public lands, and then only if the lands so acquired are confined to as narrow a corridor as is necessary to serve such purpose. Nothing in this subsection shall be construed as expanding or limiting the authority of the Secretary of Agriculture to acquire land by eminent domain within the boundaries of units of the National Forest System.

(b) Conformity to departmental policies and land-use plan of acquisitions

Acquisitions pursuant to this section shall be consistent with the mission of the department involved and with applicable departmental land-use plans.

(c) Status of lands and interests in lands upon acquisition by Secretary of the Interior; transfers to Secretary of Agriculture of lands and interests in lands acquired within National Forest System boundaries

Except as provided in subsection (e) of this section lands and interests in lands acquired by the Secretary pursuant to this section or section 1716 of this title shall, upon acceptance of title, become public lands and, for the administration of public land laws not repealed by this Act, shall remain public lands. If such acquired lands or interests in lands are located within the exterior boundaries of a grazing district established pursuant to section 315 of this title, they shall become a part of that district. Lands and interests in lands acquired pursuant to this section which are within boundaries of the National Forest System may be transferred to the Secretary of Agriculture and shall then become National Forest System lands and subject to all the laws, rules, and regulations applicable thereto.

(d) Status of lands and interests in lands upon acquisition by Secretary of Agriculture

Lands and interests in lands acquired by the Secretary of Agriculture pursuant to this section shall, upon acceptance of title, become National Forest System lands subject to all the laws, rules, and regulations applicable thereto.

(e) Status and administration of lands acquired in exchange for lands revested in or reconveyed to United States

Lands acquired by the Secretary pursuant to this section or section 1716 of this title in exchange for lands which were revested in the United States pursuant to the provisions of the Act of June 9, 1916 (39 Stat. 218) or reconveyed to the United States pursuant to the provisions of the Act of February 26, 1919 (40 Stat. 1179), shall be considered for all purposes to have the same status as, and shall be administered in accordance with the same provisions of law applicable to, the revested or reconveyed lands exchanged for the lands acquired by the Secretary.

(Oct. 21, 1976, Pub.L. 94–579, Title II, § 205, 90 Stat. 2755; Nov. 7, 1986, Pub.L. 99–632, § 5, 100 Stat. 3521.)

CROSS REFERENCES

Exchanges of public lands or interests therein within the National Forest System; implementation requirements, see section 1716 of this title.

Purchase pursuant to this section of certain public lands from Land and Water Conservation Fund, see section 1748 of this title.

CODE OF FEDERAL REGULATIONS

Landownership adjustments, see 36 CFR 254.1 et seq.

LIBRARY REFERENCES

Public Lands ⟹6.
C.J.S. Public Lands § 3.

§ 1716. Exchanges of public lands or interests therein within the National Forest System [FLPMA § 206]

(a) Authorization and limitations on authority of Secretary of the Interior and Secretary of Agriculture

A tract of public land or interests therein may be disposed of by exchange by the Secretary under this Act and a tract of land or interests therein within the National Forest System may be disposed of by exchange by the Secretary of Agriculture under applicable law where the Secretary concerned determines that the public interest will be well served by making that exchange: *Provided*, That when considering public interest the Secretary concerned shall give full consideration to better Federal land management and the needs of State and local people, including needs for lands for the economy, community expansion, recreation areas, food, fiber, minerals, and fish and wildlife and the Secretary concerned finds that the values and the objectives which Federal lands or interests to be conveyed may serve if retained in Federal ownership are not more than the values of the non-Federal lands or interests and the public objectives they could serve if acquired.

(b) Implementation requirements; cash equalization waiver

In exercising the exchange authority granted by subsection (a) of this section or by section 1715(a) of this title, the Secretary concerned may accept title to any non-Federal land or interests therein in exchange for such land, or interests therein which he finds proper for transfer out of Federal ownership and which are located in the same State as the non-Federal land or interest to be acquired. For the purposes of this subsection, unsurveyed school sections which, upon survey by the Secretary, would become State lands, shall be considered as "non-Federal lands". The values of the lands exchanged by the Secretary under this Act and by the Secretary of Agriculture under applicable law relating to lands within the National Forest System either shall be equal, or if they are not equal, the values shall be equalized by the payment of money to the grantor or to the Secretary concerned as the circumstances require so long as payment does not exceed 25 per centum of the total value of the lands or interests transferred out of Federal ownership. The Secretary concerned and the other party or parties involved in the exchange may mutually agree to waive the requirement for the payment of money to equalize values where the Secretary concerned determines that the exchange will be expedited thereby and that the public interest will be better served by such a waiver of cash equalization payments and where the amount to be waived is no more than 3 per centum of the value of the lands being transferred out of Federal ownership or $15,000, whichever is less, except that the Secretary of Agriculture shall not agree to waive any such requirement for payment of money to the United States. The Secretary concerned shall try to reduce the amount of the payment of money to as small an amount as possible.

(c) Status of lands acquired upon exchange by Secretary of the Interior

Lands acquired by the Secretary by exchange under this section which are within the boundaries of any unit of the National Forest System, National Park System, National Wildlife Refuge System, National Wild and Scenic Rivers System, National Trails System, National Wilderness Preservation System, or any other system established by Act of Congress, or the boundaries of the California Desert Conservation Area, or the boundaries of any national conservation area or national recreation area established by Act of Congress, upon acceptance of title by the United States shall immediately be reserved for and become a part of the unit or area within which they are located, without further action by the Secretary, and shall thereafter be managed in accordance with all laws, rules, and regulations applicable to such unit or area.

(d) Appraisal of land; submission to arbitrator; determination to proceed or withdraw from exchange; use of other valuation process; suspension of deadlines

(1) No later than ninety days after entering into an agreement to initiate an exchange of land or interests therein pursuant to this Act or other applicable law, the Secretary concerned and other party or parties involved in the exchange shall arrange for appraisal (to be completed within a time frame and under such terms as are negotiated by the parties) of the lands or interests therein involved in the exchange in accordance with subsection (f) of this section.

(2) If within one hundred and eighty days after the submission of an appraisal or appraisals for review and approval by the Secretary concerned, the Secretary concerned and the other party or parties involved cannot agree to accept the findings of an appraisal or appraisals, the appraisal or appraisals shall be submitted to an arbitrator appointed by the Secretary from a list of arbitrators submitted to him by the American Arbitration Association for arbitration to be conducted in accordance with the real estate valuation arbitration rules of the American Arbitration Association. Such arbitration shall be binding for a period of not to exceed two years on the Secretary concerned and the other party or parties involved in the exchange insofar as concerns the value of the lands which were the subject of the appraisal or appraisals.

(3) Within thirty days after the completion of the arbitration, the Secretary concerned and the other party or parties involved in the exchange shall determine whether to proceed with the exchange, modify the exchange to reflect the findings of the arbitration or any other factors, or to withdraw from the exchange. A decision to withdraw from the exchange may be made by either the Secretary concerned or the other party or parties involved.

(4) Instead of submitting the appraisal to an arbitrator, as provided in paragraph (2) of this section, the Secretary concerned and the other party or parties involved in an exchange may mutually agree to employ a process of bargaining or some other process to determine the values of the properties involved in the exchange.

(5) The Secretary concerned and the other party or parties involved in an exchange may mutually agree to suspend or modify any of the deadlines contained in this subsection.

(e) Simultaneous issue of patents or titles

Unless mutually agreed otherwise by the Secretary concerned and the other party or parties involved in an exchange pursuant to this Act or other applicable law, all patents or titles to be issued for land or interests therein to be acquired by the Federal Government and lands or interest therein to be transferred out of Federal ownership shall be issued simultaneously after the Secretary concerned has taken any necessary steps to assure that the United States will receive acceptable title.

(f) New rules and regulations; appraisal rules and regulations; "costs and other responsibilities or requirements" defined

(1) Within one year after August 20, 1988, the Secretaries of the Interior and Agriculture shall promulgate new and comprehensive rules and regulations governing exchanges of land and interests therein pursuant to this Act and other applicable law. Such rules and regulations shall fully reflect the changes in law made by subsections (d) through (i) of this section and shall include provisions pertaining to appraisals of lands and interests therein involved in such exchanges.

(2) The provisions of the rules and regulations issued pursuant to paragraph (1) of this subsection governing appraisals shall reflect nationally recognized appraisal standards, including, to the extent appropriate, the Uniform Appraisal Standards for Federal Land Acquisitions: *Provided, however,* That the provisions of such rules and regulations shall—

(A) ensure that the same nationally approved appraisal standards are used in appraising lands or interest therein being acquired by the Federal Government and appraising lands or interests therein being transferred out of Federal ownership; and

(B) with respect to costs or other responsibilities or requirements associated with land exchanges—

(i) recognize that the parties involved in an exchange may mutually agree that one party (or parties) will assume, without compensation, all or part of certain costs or other responsibilities or requirements ordinarily borne by the other party or parties; and

(ii) also permit the Secretary concerned, where such Secretary determines it is in the public interest and it is in the best interest of consummating an exchange pursuant to this Act or other applicable law, and upon mutual agreement of the parties, to make adjustments to the relative values involved in an exchange transaction in order to compensate a party or parties to the exchange for assuming costs or other responsibilities or requirements which would ordinarily be borne by the other party or parties.

As used in this subparagraph, the term "costs or other responsibilities or requirements" shall include, but not be limited to, costs or other requirements associated with land surveys and appraisals, mineral examinations, title searches, archeological surveys and salvage, removal of encumbrances, arbitration pursuant to subsection (d) of this section, curing deficiencies preventing highest and best use, and other costs to comply with laws, regulations and policies applicable to exchange transactions, or which are necessary to bring the Federal or non-Federal lands or interests involved in the exchange to their highest and best use for the appraisal and exchange purposes. Prior to making any adjustments pursuant to this subparagraph, the Secretary concerned shall be satisfied that the amount of such adjustment is reasonable and accurately reflects the approximate value of any costs or services provided or any responsibilities or requirements assumed.

(g) Exchanges to proceed under existing laws and regulations pending new rules and regulations

Until such time as new and comprehensive rules and regulations governing exchange of land and interests therein are promulgated pursuant to subsection (f) of this section, land exchanges may proceed in accordance with existing laws and regulations, and nothing in the Act shall be construed to require any delay in, or otherwise hinder, the processing and consummation of land exchanges pending the promulgation of such new and comprehensive rules and regulations. Where the Secretary concerned and the party or parties involved in an exchange have agreed to initiate an exchange of land or interests therein prior to August 20, 1988, subsections (d) through (i) of this section shall not apply to such exchanges unless the Secretary concerned and the party or parties involved in the exchange mutually agree otherwise.

(h) Exchange of lands or interests of approximately equal value; conditions; "approximately equal value" defined

(1) Notwithstanding the provisions of this Act and other applicable laws which require that exchanges of land or interests therein be for equal value, where the Secretary concerned determines it is in the public interest and that the consummation of a particular exchange will be expedited thereby, the Secretary concerned may exchange lands or interests therein which are of approximately equal value in cases where—

(A) the combined value of the lands or interests therein to be transferred from Federal ownership by the Secretary concerned in such exchange is not more than $150,000; and

(B) the Secretary concerned finds in accordance with the regulations to be promulgated pursuant to subsection (f) of this section that a determination of approximately equal value can be made without formal appraisals, as based on a statement of value made by a qualified appraiser and approved by an authorized officer; and

(C) the definition of and procedure for determining "approximately equal value" has been set forth in regulations by the Secretary concerned and the Secretary concerned documents how such determination was made in the case of the particular exchange involved.

(2) As used in this subsection, the term "approximately equal value" shall have the same meaning with respect to lands managed by the Secretary of Agriculture as it does in the Act of January 22, 1983 (commonly known as the "Small Tracts Act").

(i) Segregation from appropriation under mining and public land laws

(1) Upon receipt of an offer to exchange lands or interests in lands pursuant to this Act or other applicable laws, at the request of the head of the depart-

ment or agency having jurisdiction over the lands involved, the Secretary of the Interior may temporarily segregate the Federal lands under consideration for exchange from appropriation under the mining laws. Such temporary segregation may only be made for a period of not to exceed five years. Upon a decision not to proceed with the exchange or upon deletion of any particular parcel from the exchange offer, the Federal lands involved or deleted shall be promptly restored to their former status under the mining laws. Any segregation pursuant to this paragraph shall be subject to valid existing rights as of the date of such segregation.

(2) All non-Federal lands which are acquired by the United States through exchange pursuant to this Act or pursuant to other law applicable to lands managed by the Secretary of Agriculture shall be automatically segregated from appropriation under the public land law, including the mining laws, for ninety days after acceptance of title by the United States. Such segregation shall be subject to valid existing rights as of the date of such acceptance of title. At the end of such ninety day period, such segregation shall end and such lands shall be open to operation of the public land laws and to entry, location, and patent under the mining laws except to the extent otherwise provided by this Act or other applicable law, or appropriate actions pursuant thereto.

(Oct. 21, 1976, Pub.L. 94–579, Title II, § 206, 90 Stat. 2756; Aug. 20, 1988, Pub.L. 100–409, §§ 3, 9, 102 Stat. 1087, 1092.)

References in Text

This Act, referred to in subsecs. (a), (b), (d)(1), (e), (f)(1), (2)(B)(ii), (g), (h)(1), and (i), is Pub.L. 94–579, Oct. 21, 1976, 90 Stat. 2743, as amended, known as the Federal Land Policy and Management Act of 1976.

Act of January 22, 1983 (commonly known as the "Small Tracts Act)", referred to in subsec. (h)(1), is Pub.L. 97–465, Jan. 12, 1983, 96 Stat. 2535, which enacted sections 521c to 521i of Title 16, Conservation, and amended section 484a of Title 16. For complete classification of this Act to the Code, see Tables volume.

The mining laws, referred to in subsec. (i), are classified generally to Title 30, Mineral Lands and Mining.

The public land laws, referred to in subsec. (i)(1), are classified generally to this title.

Congressional Statement of Findings and Purposes

Section 2 of Pub.L. 100–409 provided that:

"(a) **Findings.**—The Congress finds and declares that—

"(1) land exchanges are a very important tool for Federal and State land managers and private landowners to consolidate Federal, State, and private holdings of land or interests in land for purposes of more efficient management and to secure important objectives including the protection of fish and wildlife habitat and aesthetic values; the enhancement of recreation opportunities; the consolidation of mineral and timber holdings for more logical and efficient development; the expansion of communities; the promotion of multiple-use values; and fulfillment of public needs;

"(2) needs for land ownership adjustments and consolidation consistently outpace available funding for land purchases by the Federal Government and thereby make land exchanges an increasingly important method of land acquisition and consolidation for both Federal and State land managers and private landowners;

"(3) the Federal Land Policy and Management Act of 1976 [Pub.L. 94–579, see Short Title note set out under section 1701 of this title] and other laws provide a basic framework and authority for land exchanges involving lands under the jurisdiction of the Secretary of the Interior and the Secretary of Agriculture; and

"(4) such existing laws are in need of certain revisions to streamline and facilitate land exchange procedures and expedite exchanges.

"(b) **Purposes.**—The purposes of this Act [see Short Title of 1988 Amendment note set out under section 1701 of this title] are:

"(1) to facilitate and expedite land exchanges pursuant to the Federal Land Policy and Management Act of 1976 and other laws applicable to exchanges involving lands managed by the Departments of the Interior and Agriculture by—

"(A) providing more uniform rules and regulations pertaining to land appraisals which reflect nationally recognized appraisal standards; and

"(B) establishing procedures and guidelines for the resolution of appraisal disputes.

"(2) to provide sufficient resources to the Secretaries of the Interior and Agriculture to ensure that land exchange activities can proceed consistent with the public interest; and

"(3) to require a study and report concerning improvements in the handling of certain information related to Federal and other lands."

Land Exchange Funding Authorization

Section 4 of Pub.L. 100–409 provided that: "In order to ensure that there are increased funds and personnel available to the Secretaries of the Interior and Agriculture to consider, process, and consummate land exchanges pursuant to the Federal Land Policy and Management Act of 1976 [Pub.L. 94–579, see Short Title note set out under section 1701 of this title] and other applicable law, there are hereby authorized to be appropriated for fiscal years 1989 through 1998 an annual amount not to exceed $4,000,000 which shall be used jointly or divided among the Secretaries as they determine appropriate for the consideration, processing, and consummation of land exchanges pursuant to the Federal Land Policy and Management Act of 1976, as amended, and other applicable law. Such moneys are expressly intended by Congress to be in addition to, and not offset against, moneys otherwise annually requested by the Secretaries, and appropriated by Congress for land exchange purposes."

Savings Provisions; Severability of Provisions

Section 5 of Pub.L. 100–409 provided that: "Nothing in this Act [see Short Title of 1988 Amendment note set out section 1701 of this title] shall be construed as amending the Alaska Native Claims Settlement Act (Public Law 92–203, as amended) [section 1601 et seq. of this title] or the Alaska National Interest Lands Conservation Act (Public Law 96–487, as amended) [Pub.L. 96–487, Dec. 2, 1980, 94 Stat. 2371, see Short Title note set out under section 3101 of Title 16, Conservation] or as enlarging or diminishing the authority with regard to exchanges conferred upon either the Secretary of the Interior or the Secretary of Agriculture by either such Acts. If any provision of this Act or the application thereof is held invalid, the remainder of the Act and the application thereof shall not be affected thereby. Nothing in this Act shall be construed to change the discretionary nature of land exchanges or to prohibit the Secretary concerned or any other party or parties involved in a land exchange from withdrawing from the exchange at any time, unless the Secretary concerned and the other party or parties specifically commit otherwise by written agreement."

CROSS REFERENCES

Administration of Steese National Conservation Area, transfer of lands, see section 460mm–1 of Title 16, Conservation.

Disposition of deposits of coal, etc., as provided by this section, see section 193 of Title 30, Mineral Lands and Mining.

Documents of conveyance; terms, covenants, etc., see section 1718 of this title.

Exchange of lands within national forests by Secretary of Agriculture, see section 516 of Title 16, Conservation.

Mineral interests; reservation, see section 1719 of this title.

Report of Secretary of Agriculture prior to purchase or exchange of lands relating to National Forest System, see section 521b of Title 16, Conservation.
Sale, exchange or interchange of National Forest System lands, see section 521d of Title 16.
Status of lands and interests in lands upon acquisition by Secretary of Interior pursuant to this section, see section 1715 of this title.
Surface mining control and reclamation; requirements for permit approval or denial, see section 1260 of Title 30, Mineral Lands and Mining.

CODE OF FEDERAL REGULATIONS

Exchanges, see 43 CFR 2200.0–1 et seq.
Landownership adjustments, see 36 CFR 254.1 et seq.

LIBRARY REFERENCES

United States ⚖58(3).
C.J.S. United States § 75 et seq.

§ 1717. Qualifications of conveyees [FLPMA § 207]

No tract of land may be disposed of under this Act, whether by sale, exchange, or donation, to any person who is not a citizen of the United States, or in the case of a corporation, is not subject to the laws of any State or of the United States.

(Oct. 21, 1976, Pub.L. 94–579, Title II, § 207, 90 Stat. 2757.)

LIBRARY REFERENCES

Public Lands ⚖30.
C.J.S. Public Lands § 39.

§ 1718. Documents of conveyance; terms, covenants, etc. [FLPMA § 208]

The Secretary shall issue all patents or other documents of conveyance after any disposal authorized by this Act. The Secretary shall insert in any such patent or other document of conveyance he issues, except in the case of land exchanges, for which the provisions of subsection[1] 1716(b) of this title shall apply, such terms, covenants, conditions, and reservations as he deems necessary to insure proper land use and protection of the public interest: *Provided*, That a conveyance of lands by the Secretary, subject to such terms, covenants, conditions, and reservations, shall not exempt the grantee from compliance with applicable Federal or State law or State land use plans: *Provided further*, That the Secretary shall not make conveyances of public lands containing terms and conditions which would, at the time of the conveyance, constitute a violation of any law or regulation pursuant to State and local land use plans, or programs.

(Oct. 21, 1976, Pub.L. 94–579, Title II, § 208, 90 Stat. 2757.)

[1] So in original. Probably should be "section".

CROSS REFERENCES

Correction of conveyance documents, see section 1746 of this title.

CODE OF FEDERAL REGULATIONS

Color-of-title and omitted lands, see 43 CFR 2540.0–3 et seq.

LIBRARY REFERENCES

Public Lands ⚖30.
C.J.S. Public Lands § 39.

§ 1719. Mineral interests; reservation and conveyance requirements and procedures [FLPMA § 209]

(a) All conveyances of title issued by the Secretary, except those involving land exchanges provided for in section 1716 of this title, shall reserve to the United States all minerals in the lands, together with the right to prospect for, mine, and remove the minerals under applicable law and such regulations as the Secretary may prescribe, except that if the Secretary makes the findings specified in subsection (b) of this section, the minerals may then be conveyed together with the surface to the prospective surface owner as provided in subsection (b) of this section.

(b)(1) The Secretary, after consultation with the appropriate department or agency head, may convey mineral interests owned by the United States where the surface is or will be in non-Federal ownership, regardless of which Federal entity may have administered the surface, if he finds (1) that there are no known mineral values in the land, or (2) that the reservation of the mineral rights in the United States is interfering with or precluding appropriate nonmineral development of the land and that such development is a more beneficial use of the land than mineral development.

(2) Conveyance of mineral interests pursuant to this section shall be made only to the existing or proposed record owner of the surface, upon payment of administrative costs and the fair market value of the interests being conveyed.

(3) Before considering an application for conveyance of mineral interests pursuant to this section—

(i) the Secretary shall require the deposit by the applicant of a sum of money which he deems sufficient to cover administrative costs including, but not limited to, costs of conducting an exploratory program to determine the character of the mineral deposits in the land, evaluating the data obtained under the exploratory program to determine the fair market value of the mineral interests to be conveyed, and preparing and issuing the documents of conveyance: *Provided*, That, if the administrative costs exceed the deposit, the applicant shall pay the outstanding amount; and, if the deposit exceeds the administrative costs, the applicant shall be given a credit for or refund of the excess; or

(ii) the applicant, with the consent of the Secretary, shall have conducted, and submitted to the Secretary the results of, such an exploratory program, in accordance with standards promulgated by the Secretary.

(4) Moneys paid to the Secretary for administrative costs pursuant to this subsection shall be paid to the agency which rendered the service and deposited to the appropriation then current.

(Oct. 21, 1976, Pub.L. 94–579, Title II, § 209, 90 Stat. 2757.)

CROSS REFERENCES

Disposition of deposits of coal, etc., as provided by this section, see section 193 of Title 30, Mineral Lands and Mining.

Stock-raising homesteads, reservations of coal and mineral rights, see section 299 of this title.

CODE OF FEDERAL REGULATIONS

Color-of-title and omitted lands, see 43 CFR 2540.0–3 et seq.

Procedure, see 43 CFR 2720.0–1 et seq.

LIBRARY REFERENCES

Mines and Minerals ⚬=2.
Public Lands ⚬=113.
C.J.S. Mines and Minerals § 4 et seq.
C.J.S. Public Lands § 137.

§ 1720. Coordination by Secretary of the Interior with State and local governments [FLPMA § 210]

At least sixty days prior to offering for sale or otherwise conveying public lands under this Act, the Secretary shall notify the Governor of the State within which such lands are located and the head of the governing body of any political subdivision of the State having zoning or other land use regulatory jurisdiction in the geographical area within which such lands are located, in order to afford the appropriate body the opportunity to zone or otherwise regulate, or change or amend existing zoning or other regulations concerning the use of such lands prior to such conveyance. The Secretary shall also promptly notify such public officials of the issuance of the patent or other document of conveyance for such lands.

(Oct. 21, 1976, Pub.L. 94–579, Title II, § 210, 90 Stat. 2758.)

CROSS REFERENCES

Conveyances of public lands to States, local governments, etc., see section 1721 of this title.

§ 1721. Conveyances of public lands to States, local governments, etc. [FLPMA § 211]

(a) Unsurveyed islands; authorization and limitations on authority

The Secretary is hereby authorized to convey to States or their political subdivisions under the Recreation and Public Purposes Act (44 Stat. 741 as amended; 43 U.S.C. 869 et seq.), as amended, but without regard to the acreage limitations contained therein, unsurveyed islands determined by the Secretary to be public lands of the United States. The conveyance of any such island may be made without survey: *Provided, however*, That such island may be surveyed at the request of the applicant State or its political subdivision if such State or subdivision donates money or services to the Secretary for such survey, the Secretary accepts such money or services, and such services are conducted pursuant to criteria established by the Director of the Bureau of Land Management. Any such island so surveyed shall not be conveyed without approval of such survey by the Secretary prior to the conveyance.

(b) Omitted lands; authorization and limitations on authority

(1) The Secretary is authorized to convey to States and their political subdivisions under the Recreation and Public Purposes Act [43 U.S.C.A. §§ 869 to 869–4], but without regard to the acreage limitations contained therein, lands other than islands determined by him after survey to be public lands of the United States erroneously or fraudulently omitted from the original surveys (hereinafter referred to as "omitted lands"). Any such conveyance shall not be made without a survey: *Provided*, That the prospective recipient may donate money or services to the Secretary for the surveying necessary prior to conveyance if the Secretary accepts such money or services, such services are conducted pursuant to criteria established by the Director of the Bureau of Land Management, and such survey is approved by the Secretary prior to the conveyance.

(2) The Secretary is authorized to convey to the occupant of any omitted lands which, after survey, are found to have been occupied and developed for a five-year period prior to January 1, 1975, if the Secretary determines that such conveyance is in the public interest and will serve objectives which outweigh all public objectives and values which would be served by retaining such lands in Federal ownership. Conveyance under this subparagraph shall be made at not less than the fair market value of the land, as determined by the Secretary, and upon payment in addition of administrative costs, including the cost of making the survey, the cost of appraisal, and the cost of making the conveyance.

(c) Conformity with land use plans and programs and coordination with State and local governments of conveyances

(1) No conveyance shall be made pursuant to this section until the relevant State government, local gov-

ernment, and areawide planning agency designated pursuant to section 204 of the Demonstration Cities and Metropolitan Development Act of 1966 (80 Stat. 1255, 1262) [42 U.S.C.A. § 3334] and/or section 6506 of Title 31 have notified the Secretary as to the consistency of such conveyance with applicable State and local government land use plans and programs.

(2) The provisions of section 1720 of this title shall be applicable to all conveyances under this section.

(d) Applicability of other statutory requirements for authorized use of conveyed lands

The final sentence of section 1(c) of the Recreation and Public Purposes Act [43 U.S.C.A. § 869(c)] shall not be applicable to conveyances under this section.

(e) Limitations on uses of conveyed lands

No conveyance pursuant to this section shall be used as the basis for determining the baseline between Federal and State ownership, the boundary of any State for purposes of determining the extent of a State's submerged lands or the line of demarcation of Federal jurisdiction, or any similar or related purpose.

(f) Applicability to lands within National Forest System, National Park System, National Wildlife Refuge System, and National Wild and Scenic Rivers System

The provisions of this section shall not apply to any lands within the National Forest System, defined in the Act of August 17, 1974 (88 Stat. 476; 16 U.S.C. 1601), the National Park System, the National Wildlife Refuge System, and the National Wild and Scenic Rivers System.

(g) Applicability to other statutory provisions authorizing sale of specific omitted lands

Nothing in this section shall supersede the provisions of the Act of December 22, 1928 (45 Stat. 1069; 43 U.S.C. 1068), as amended, and the Act of May 31, 1962 (76 Stat. 89), or any other Act authorizing the sale of specific omitted lands.

(Oct. 21, 1976, Pub.L. 94–579, Title II, § 211, 90 Stat. 2758.)

CODE OF FEDERAL REGULATIONS

Cadastral survey, see 43 CFR 9180.0–2 et seq.
Color-of-title and omitted lands, see 43 CFR 2540.0–3 et seq.
Recreation and public purposes, omitted lands and unsurveyed islands, see 43 CFR 2742.1 et seq.

§ 1722. Sale of public lands subject to unintentional trespass [FLPMA § 212]

(a) Preference right of contiguous landowners; offering price

Notwithstanding the provisions of the Act of September 26, 1968 (82 Stat. 870; 43 U.S.C. 1431–1435), hereinafter called the "1968 Act", with respect to applications under the 1968 Act which were pending before the Secretary as of the effective date of this subsection and which he approves for sale under the criteria prescribed by the 1968 Act, he shall give the right of first refusal to those having a preference right under section 2 of the 1968 Act [43 U.S.C.A. § 1432]. The Secretary shall offer such lands to such preference right holders at their fair market value (exclusive of any values added to the land by such holders and their predecessors in interest) as determined by the Secretary as of September 26, 1973.

(b) Procedures applicable

Within three years after October 21, 1976, the Secretary shall notify the filers of applications subject to paragraph (a) of this section whether he will offer them the lands applied for and at what price; that is, their fair market value as of September 26, 1973, excluding any value added to the lands by the applicants or their predecessors in interest. He will also notify the President of the Senate and the Speaker of the House of Representatives of the lands which he has determined not to sell pursuant to paragraph (a) of this section and the reasons therefor. With respect to such lands which the Secretary determined not to sell, he shall take no other action to convey those lands or interests in them before the end of ninety days (not counting days on which the House of Representatives or the Senate has adjourned for more than three consecutive days) beginning on the date the Secretary has submitted such notice to the Senate and House of Representatives. If, during that ninety-day period, the Congress adopts a concurrent resolution stating the length of time such suspension of action should continue, he shall continue such suspension for the specified time period. If the committee to which a resolution has been referred during the said ninety-day period, has not reported it at the end of thirty calendar days after its referral, it shall be in order to either discharge the committee from further consideration of such resolution or to discharge the committee from consideration of any other resolution with respect to the suspension of action. A motion to discharge may be made only by an individual favoring the resolution, shall be highly privileged (except that it may not be made after the committee has reported such a resolution), and debate thereon shall be limited to not more than one hour, to be divided equally between those favoring and those opposing the resolution. An amendment to the motion shall not be in order, and it shall not be in order to move to reconsider the vote by which the motion was agreed to or disagreed to. If the motion to discharge is agreed to or disagreed to, the motion may not be made with respect to any other resolution with respect to the same suspension of action. When the committee has reprinted, or has been discharged from further consideration of a resolution, it shall at any time thereafter be in order (even though a previous motion to the same effect has been disagreed to) to move to proceed to the consideration of the resolution. The motion shall be highly privileged and shall not be debatable. An amendment to the motion shall not be in order, and it shall not be in order to move to reconsider the vote by which the motion was agreed to or disagreed to.

(c) Time for processing of applications and sales

Within five years after October 21, 1976, the Secretary shall complete the processing of all applications filed under the 1968 Act and hold sales covering all lands which he has determined to sell thereunder. (Oct. 21, 1976, Pub.L. 94–579, Title II, § 214, 90 Stat. 2760.)

LIBRARY REFERENCES

Public Lands ⟹8, 33.
C.J.S. Public Lands §§ 6, 42.

§ 1723. Temporary revocation authority [FLPMA § 215]

(a) Exchange involved

When the sole impediment to consummation of an exchange of lands or interests therein (hereinafter referred to as an exchange) determined to be in the public interest, is the inability of the Secretary of the Interior to revoke, modify, or terminate part or all of a withdrawal or classification because of the order (or subsequent modification or continuance thereof) of the United States District Court for the District of Columbia dated February 10, 1986, in Civil Action No. 85–2238 (National Wildlife Federation v. Robert E. Burford, et al.), the Secretary of the Interior is hereby authorized, notwithstanding such order (or subsequent modification or continuance thereof), to use the authority contained herein, in lieu of other authority provided in this Act including section 1714 of this title, to revoke, modify, or terminate in whole or in part, withdrawals or classifications to the extent deemed necessary by the Secretary to enable the United States to transfer land or interests therein out of Federal ownership pursuant to an exchange.

(b) Requirements

The authority specified in subsection (a) of this section may be exercised only in cases where—

(1) a particular exchange is proposed to be carried out pursuant to this Act, as amended, or other applicable law authorizing such an exchange;

(2) the proposed exchange has been prepared in compliance with all laws applicable to such exchange;

(3) the head of each Federal agency managing the lands proposed for such transfer has submitted to the Secretary of the Interior a statement of concurrence with the proposed revocation, modification, or termination;

(4) at least sixty days have elapsed since the Secretary of the Interior has published in the Federal Register a notice of the proposed revocation, modification, or termination; and

(5) at least sixty days have elapsed since the Secretary of the Interior has transmitted to the Committee on Natural Resources of the House of Representatives and the Committee on Energy and Natural Resources of the United States Senate a report which includes—

(A) a justification for the necessity of exercising such authority in order to complete an exchange;

(B) an explanation of the reasons why the continuation of the withdrawal or a classification or portion thereof proposed for revocation, modification, or termination is no longer necessary for the purposes of the statutory or other program or programs for which the withdrawal or classification was made or other relevant programs;

(C) assurances that all relevant documents concerning the proposed exchange or purchase for which such authority is proposed to be exercised (including documents related to compliance with the National Environmental Policy Act of 1969 [42 U.S.C.A. § 4321 et seq.] and all other applicable provisions of law) are available for public inspection in the office of the Secretary concerned located nearest to the lands proposed for transfer out of Federal ownership in furtherance of such exchange and that the relevant portions of such documents are also available in the offices of the Secretary concerned in Washington, District of Columbia; and

(D) an explanation of the effect of the revocation, modification, or termination of a withdrawal or classification or portion thereof and the transfer of lands out of Federal ownership pursuant to the particular proposed exchange, on the objectives of the land management plan which is applicable at the time of such transfer to the land to be transferred out of Federal ownership.

(c) Limitations

(1) Nothing in this section shall be construed as affirming or denying any of the allegations made by any party in the civil action specified in subsection (a)

of this section, or as constituting an expression of congressional opinion with respect to the merits of any allegation, contention, or argument made or issue raised by any party in such action, or as expanding or diminishing the jurisdiction of the United States District Court for the District of Columbia.

(2) Except as specifically provided in this section, nothing in this section shall be construed as modifying, terminating, revoking, or otherwise affecting any provision of law applicable to land exchanges, withdrawals, or classifications.

(3) The availability or exercise of the authority granted in subsection (a) of this section may not be considered by the Secretary of the Interior in making a determination pursuant to this Act or other applicable law as to whether or not any proposed exchange is in the public interest.

(d) Termination

The authority specified in subsection (a) of this section shall expire either (1) on December 31, 1990, or (2) when the Court order (or subsequent modification or continuation thereof) specified in subsection (a) of this section is no longer in effect, whichever occurs first.

(Pub.L. 94–579, Title II, § 215, as added Pub.L. 100–409, § 10, Aug. 20, 1988, 102 Stat. 1092, and amended Pub.L. 103–437, § 16(d)(2), Nov. 2, 1994, 108 Stat. 4595.)

References in Text

This Act, referred to in subsecs. (a), (b)(1), and (c)(3), is Pub.L. 94–579, Oct. 21, 1976, 90 Stat. 2743, as amended, known as the Federal Land Policy and Management Act of 1976. For complete classification of this Act to the Code, see Tables volume.

The National Environmental Policy Act of 1969, referred to in subsec. (b)(5)(C), is Pub.L. 91–190, Jan. 1, 1970, 83 Stat. 852, as amended, which is classified generally to chapter 55 (section 4321 et seq.) of Title 42, The Public Health and Welfare. For complete classification of this Act to the Code, see Short Title note set out under section 4321 of Title 42 and Tables volume.

Change of Name

Any reference in any provision of law enacted before Jan. 4, 1995, to the Committee on Natural Resources of the House of Representatives treated as referring to the Committee on Resources of the House of Representatives, see section 1(a)(8) of Pub.L. 104–14, set out as a note preceding section 21 of Title 2, The Congress.

Savings Provisions; Severability of Provisions

Nothing in Pub.L. 100–409 construed as amending the Alaska Native Claims Settlement Act, Pub.L. 92–203, or the Alaska National Interest Lands Conservation Act, Pub.L. 96–487, as enlarging or diminishing the authority with regard to exchanges conferred upon either the Secretary of the Interior or the Secretary of Agriculture by either such Acts, or as changing the discretionary nature of land exchanges or prohibiting the Secretary concerned or any other party or parties involved in a land exchange from withdrawing from the exchange at any time, unless the Secretary concerned and the other party or parties specifically commit otherwise by written agreement, with any provision of Pub.L. 100–409 or the application thereof being held invalid not affecting the remainder of Pub.L. 100–409 and the application thereof, see section 5 of Pub.L. 100–409, set out as a note under section 1716 of this title.

SUBCHAPTER III—ADMINISTRATION

§ 1731. Bureau of Land Management [FLPMA § 301]

(a) Director; appointment, qualifications, functions, and duties

The Bureau of Land Management established by Reorganization Plan Numbered 3, of 1946 shall have as its head a Director. Appointments to the position of Director shall hereafter be made by the President, by and with the advice and consent of the Senate. The Director of the Bureau shall have a broad background and substantial experience in public land and natural resource management. He shall carry out such functions and shall perform such duties as the Secretary may prescribe with respect to the management of lands and resources under his jurisdiction according to the applicable provisions of this Act and any other applicable law.

(b) Statutory transfer of functions, powers and duties relating to administration of laws

Subject to the discretion granted to him by Reorganization Plan Numbered 3 of 1950, the Secretary shall carry out through the Bureau all functions, powers, and duties vested in him and relating to the administration of laws which, on October 21, 1976, were carried out by him through the Bureau of Land Management established by section 403 of Reorganization Plan Numbered 3 of 1946. The Bureau shall administer such laws according to the provisions thereof existing as of October 21, 1976, as modified by the provisions of this Act or by subsequent law.

(c) Associate Director, Assistant Directors, and other employees; appointment and compensation

In addition to the Director, there shall be an Associate Director of the Bureau and so many Assistant Directors, and other employees, as may be necessary, who shall be appointed by the Secretary subject to the provisions of Title 5 governing appointments in the competitive service, and shall be paid in accordance with the provisions of chapter 51 and subchapter 3[1] of chapter 53 of such title relating to classification and General Schedule pay rates.

(d) Existing regulations relating to administration of laws

Nothing in this section shall affect any regulation of the Secretary with respect to the administration of laws administered by him through the Bureau on October 21, 1976.

(Oct. 21, 1976 Pub.L. 94–579, Title III, § 301, 90 Stat. 2762.)

[1] So in original. Probably should be "III".

Use of Appropriated Funds For Protection of Lands and Surveys of Federal Lands in Alaska

Pub.L. 102–381, Title I, Oct. 5, 1992, 106 Stat. 1378, provided in part: "That appropriations herein made, in fiscal year 1993 and thereafter, may be expended for surveys of Federal lands and on a reimbursable basis for surveys of Federal lands and for protection of lands for the State of Alaska[.]".

§ 1732. Management of use, occupancy, and development of public lands [FLPMA § 302]

(a) Multiple use and sustained yield requirements applicable; exception

The Secretary shall manage the public lands under principles of multiple use and sustained yield, in accordance with the land use plans developed by him under section 1712 of this title when they are available, except that where a tract of such public land has been dedicated to specific uses according to any other provisions of law it shall be managed in accordance with such law.

(b) Easements, permits, etc., for utilization through habitation, cultivation, and development of small trade or manufacturing concerns; applicable statutory requirements

In managing the public lands, the Secretary shall, subject to this Act and other applicable law and under such terms and conditions as are consistent with such law, regulate, through easements, permits, leases, licenses, published rules, or other instruments as the Secretary deems appropriate, the use, occupancy, and development of the public lands, including, but not limited to, long-term leases to permit individuals to utilize public lands for habitation, cultivation, and the development of small trade or manufacturing concerns: *Provided*, That unless otherwise provided for by law, the Secretary may permit Federal departments and agencies to use, occupy, and develop public lands only through rights-of-way under section 1767 of this title, withdrawals under section 1714 of this title, and, where the proposed use and development are similar or closely related to the programs of the Secretary for the public lands involved, cooperative agreements under section 1737(b) of this title: *Provided further*, That nothing in this Act shall be construed as authorizing the Secretary concerned to require Federal permits to hunt and fish on public lands or on lands in the National Forest System and adjacent waters or as enlarging or diminishing the responsibility and authority of the States for management of fish and resident wildlife. However, the Secretary concerned may designate areas of public land and of lands in the National Forest System where, and establish periods when, no hunting or fishing will be permitted for reasons of public safety, administration, or compliance with provisions of applicable law. Except in emergencies, any regulations of the Secretary concerned relating to hunting and fishing pursuant to this section shall be put into effect only after consultation with the appropriate State fish and game department. Nothing in this Act shall modify or change any provision of Federal law relating to migratory birds or to endangered or threatened species. Except as provided in section 1744, section 1782, and subsection (f) of section 1781 of this title and in the last sentence of this paragraph, no provision of this section or any other section of this Act shall in any way amend the Mining Law of 1872 or impair the rights of any locators or claims under that Act, including, but not limited to, rights of ingress and egress. In managing the public lands the Secretary shall, by regulation or otherwise, take any action necessary to prevent unnecessary or undue degradation of the lands.

(c) Revocation or suspension provision in instrument authorizing use, occupancy or development; violation of provision; procedure applicable

The Secretary shall insert in any instrument providing for the use, occupancy, or development of the public lands a provision authorizing revocation or suspension, after notice and hearing, of such instrument upon a final administrative finding of a violation of any term or condition of the instrument, including, but not limited to, terms and conditions requiring compliance with regulations under Acts applicable to the public lands and compliance with applicable State or Federal air or water quality standard or implementation plan: *Provided*, That such violation occurred on public lands covered by such instrument and occurred in connection with the exercise of rights and privileges granted by it: *Provided further*, That the Secretary shall terminate any such suspension no later than the date upon which he determines the cause of said violation has been rectified: *Provided further*, That the Secretary may order an immediate temporary suspension prior to a hearing or final administrative finding if he determines that such a suspension is necessary to protect health or safety or the environment: *Provided further*, That, where other applicable law contains specific provisions for suspension, revocation, or cancellation of a permit, license, or other authorization to use, occupy, or develop the public lands, the specific provisions of such law shall prevail.

(d) Temporary use of Alaska public lands for military purposes

(1) The Secretary of the Interior, after consultation with the Governor of Alaska, may issue to the Secretary of Defense or to the Secretary of a military department within the Department of Defense or to the Commandant of the Coast Guard a nonrenewable general authorization to utilize public lands in Alaska

(other than within a conservation system unit or the Steese National Conservation Area or the White Mountains National Recreation Area) for purposes of military maneuvering, military training, or equipment testing not involving artillery firing, aerial or other gunnery, or other use of live ammunition or ordnance.

(2) Use of public lands pursuant to a general authorization under this subsection shall be limited to areas where such use would not be inconsistent with the plans prepared pursuant to section 1712 of this title. Each such use shall be subject to a requirement that the using department shall be responsible for any necessary cleanup and decontamination of the lands used, and to such other terms and conditions (including but not limited to restrictions on use of off-road or all-terrain vehicles) as the Secretary of the Interior may require to—

(A) minimize adverse impacts on the natural, environmental, scientific, cultural, and other resources and values (including fish and wildlife habitat) of the public lands involved; and

(B) minimize the period and method of such use and the interference with or restrictions on other uses of the public lands involved.

(3)(A) A general authorization issued pursuant to this subsection shall not be for a term of more than three years and shall be revoked in whole or in part, as the Secretary of the Interior finds necessary, prior to the end of such term upon a determination by the Secretary of the Interior that there has been a failure to comply with its terms and conditions or that activities pursuant to such an authorization have had or might have a significant adverse impact on the resources or values of the affected lands.

(B) Each specific use of a particular area of public lands pursuant to a general authorization under this subsection shall be subject to specific authorization by the Secretary and to appropriate terms and conditions, including such as are described in paragraph (2) of this subsection.

(4) Issuance of a general authorization pursuant to this subsection shall be subject to the provisions of section 1712(f) of this title, section 3120 of Title 16, and all other applicable provisions of law. The Secretary of a military department (or the commandant of the Coast Guard) requesting such authorization shall reimburse the Secretary of the Interior for the costs of implementing this paragraph. An authorization pursuant to this subsection shall not authorize the construction of permanent structures or facilities on the public lands.

(5) To the extent that public safety may require closure to public use of any portion of the public lands covered by an authorization issued pursuant to this subsection, the Secretary of the military department concerned or the Commandant of the Coast Guard shall take appropriate steps to notify the public concerning such closure and to provide appropriate warnings of risks to public safety.

(6) For purposes of this subsection, the term "conservation system unit" has the same meaning as specified in section 3102 of Title 16.

(Oct. 21, 1976, Pub.L. 94–579, Title III, § 302, 90 Stat. 2762; Nov. 3, 1988, Pub.L. 100–586, 102 Stat. 2980.)

CROSS REFERENCES

Snake River Birds of Prey National Conservation Area, Congressional findings of compliance with section, see 16 USCA § 460iii.

CODE OF FEDERAL REGULATIONS

Coal management, see 43 CFR 3400.0–3 et seq.
Exchanges, see 43 CFR 2200.0–1 et seq.
Land withdrawals, see 43 CFR 2300.0–1 et seq.
Leases, permits and easements, see 43 CFR 2920.0–1 et seq.
Leases generally, see 43 CFR 3420.0–1 et seq., 3430.0–1 et seq., 3451.1 et seq.
Mining claims under general mining laws, see 43 CFR 3802.0–1 et seq.
Oil and gas leasing, see 43 CFR 3130.0–1 et seq.

LAW REVIEW COMMENTARIES

Grazing management on the public lands: Opening the process to public participation. Joseph M. Feller, 26 Land and Water L.Rev. 571 (1991).

LIBRARY REFERENCES

Game ⚷3½.
C.J.S. Game § 7.
C.J.S. States § 24.

§ 1733. Enforcement authority [FLPMA § 303]

(a) Regulations for implementation of management, use, and protection requirements; violations; criminal penalties

The Secretary shall issue regulations necessary to implement the provisions of this Act with respect to the management, use, and protection of the public lands, including the property located thereon. Any person who knowingly and willfully violates any such regulation which is lawfully issued pursuant to this Act shall be fined no more than $1,000 or imprisoned no more than twelve months, or both. Any person charged with a violation of such regulation may be tried and sentenced by any United States magistrate judge designated for that purpose by the court by which he was appointed, in the same manner and subject to the same conditions and limitations as provided for in section 3401 of Title 18.

(b) Civil actions by Attorney General for violations of regulations; nature of relief; jurisdiction

At the request of the Secretary, the Attorney General may institute a civil action in any United States district court for an injunction or other appropriate order to prevent any person from utilizing public lands in violation of regulations issued by the Secretary under this Act.

(c) Contracts for enforcement of Federal laws and regulations by local law enforcement officials; procedure applicable; contract requirements and implementation

(1) When the Secretary determines that assistance is necessary in enforcing Federal laws and regulations relating to the public lands or their resources he shall offer a contract to appropriate local officials having law enforcement authority within their respective jurisdictions with the view of achieving maximum feasible reliance upon local law enforcement officials in enforcing such laws and regulations. The Secretary shall negotiate on reasonable terms with such officials who have authority to enter into such contracts to enforce such Federal laws and regulations. In the performance of their duties under such contracts such officials and their agents are authorized to carry firearms; execute and serve any warrant or other process issued by a court or officer of competent jurisdiction; make arrests without warrant or process for a misdemeanor he has reasonable grounds to believe is being committed in his presence or view, or for a felony if he has reasonable grounds to believe that the person to be arrested has committed or is committing such felony; search without warrant or process any person, place, or conveyance according to any Federal law or rule of law; and seize without warrant or process any evidentiary item as provided by Federal law. The Secretary shall provide such law enforcement training as he deems necessary in order to carry out the contracted for responsibilities. While exercising the powers and authorities provided by such contract pursuant to this section, such law enforcement officials and their agents shall have all the immunities of Federal law enforcement officials.

(2) The Secretary may authorize Federal personnel or appropriate local officials to carry out his law enforcement responsibilities with respect to the public lands and their resources. Such designated personnel shall receive the training and have the responsibilities and authority provided for in paragraph (1) of this subsection.

(d) Cooperation with regulatory and law enforcement officials of any State or political subdivision in enforcement of laws or ordinances

In connection with the administration and regulation of the use and occupancy of the public lands, the Secretary is authorized to cooperate with the regulatory and law enforcement officials of any State or political subdivision thereof in the enforcement of the laws or ordinances of such State or subdivision. Such cooperation may include reimbursement to a State or its subdivision for expenditures incurred by it in connection with activities which assist in the administration and regulation of use and occupancy of the public lands.

(e) Uniformed desert ranger force in California Desert Conservation Area; establishment; enforcement of Federal laws and regulations

Nothing in this section shall prevent the Secretary from promptly establishing a uniformed desert ranger force in the California Desert Conservation Area established pursuant to section 1781 of this title for the purpose of enforcing Federal laws and regulations relating to the public lands and resources managed by him in such area. The officers and members of such ranger force shall have the same responsibilities and authority as provided for in paragraph (1) of subsection (c) of this section.

(f) Applicability of other Federal enforcement provisions

Nothing in this Act shall be construed as reducing or limiting the enforcement authority vested in the Secretary by any other statute.

(g) Unlawful activities

The use, occupancy, or development of any portion of the public lands contrary to any regulation of the Secretary or other responsible authority, or contrary to any order issued pursuant to any such regulation, is unlawful and prohibited.

(Oct. 21, 1976, Pub.L. 94–579, Title III, § 303, 90 Stat. 2763; Dec. 1, 1991, Pub.L. 101–650, Title III, § 321, 104 Stat. 5117.)

Change of Name

United States magistrate appointed under section 631 of Title 28, Judiciary and Judicial Procedure, to be known as United States magistrate judge after Dec. 1, 1990, with any reference to United States magistrate or magistrate in Title 28, in any other Federal statute, etc., deemed a reference to United States magistrate judge appointed under section 631 of Title 28, see section 321 of Pub.L. 101–650, set out as a note under section 631 of Title 28.

CODE OF FEDERAL REGULATIONS

Criminal law enforcement, see 43 CFR 9260.0–1 et seq.
Wildfire prevention, see 43 CFR 9212.0–1 et seq.

§ 1734. Fees, charges, and commissions [FLPMA § 304]

(a) Authority to establish and modify

Notwithstanding any other provision of law, the Secretary may establish reasonable filing and service fees and reasonable charges, and commissions with respect to applications and other documents relating to the public lands and may change and abolish such fees, charges, and commissions.

(b) Deposits for payments to reimburse reasonable costs of United States

The Secretary is authorized to require a deposit of any payments intended to reimburse the United States for reasonable costs with respect to applications and other documents relating to such lands. The moneys received for reasonable costs under this subsection shall be deposited with the Treasury in a special account and are hereby authorized to be appropriated and made available until expended. As used in this section "reasonable costs" include, but are not limited to, the costs of special studies; environmental impact statements; monitoring construction, operation, maintenance, and termination of any authorized facility; or other special activities. In determining whether costs are reasonable under this section, the Secretary may take into consideration actual costs (exclusive of management overhead), the monetary value of the rights or privileges sought by the applicant, the efficiency to the government processing involved, that portion of the cost incurred for the benefit of the general public interest rather than for the exclusive benefit of the applicant, the public service provided, and other factors relevant to determining the reasonableness of the costs.

(c) Refunds

In any case where it shall appear to the satisfaction of the Secretary that any person has made a payment under any statute relating to the sale, lease, use, or other disposition of public lands which is not required or is in excess of the amount required by applicable law and the regulations issued by the Secretary, the Secretary, upon application or otherwise, may cause a refund to be made from applicable funds.

(Oct. 21, 1976, Pub.L. 94–579, Title III, § 304, 90 Stat. 2765.)

CROSS REFERENCES

Crude oil transportation systems; additional information required for review of applications, see section 2005 of this title.

Transportation and utility systems in and across, and access to, Alaskan conservation system units; environmental impact statement, see section 3164 of Title 16, Conservation.

LIBRARY REFERENCES

Mines and Minerals ⟹5.1(5).

C.J.S. Mines and Minerals § 128.

§ 1735. Forfeitures and deposits [FLPMA § 305]

(a) Credit to separate account in Treasury; appropriation and availability

Any moneys received by the United States as a result of the forfeiture of a bond or other security by a resource developer or purchaser or permittee who does not fulfill the requirements of his contract or permit or does not comply with the regulations of the Secretary; or as a result of a compromise or settlement of any claim whether sounding in tort or in contract involving present or potential damage to the public lands shall be credited to a separate account in the Treasury and are hereby authorized to be appropriated and made available, until expended as the Secretary may direct, to cover the cost to the United States of any improvement, protection, or rehabilitation work on those public lands which has been rendered necessary by the action which has led to the forfeiture, compromise, or settlement.

(b) Expenditure of moneys collected administering Oregon and California Railroad and Coos Bay Wagon Road Grant lands

Any moneys collected under this Act in connection with lands administered under the Act of August 28, 1937 (50 Stat. 874; 43 U.S.C. 1181a–1181j), shall be expended for the benefit of such land only.

(c) Refunds

If any portion of a deposit or amount forfeited under this Act is found by the Secretary to be in excess of the cost of doing the work authorized under this Act, the Secretary, upon application or otherwise, may cause a refund of the amount in excess to be made from applicable funds.

(Oct. 21, 1976, Pub.L. 94–579, Title III, § 305, 90 Stat. 2765.)

Availability of Moneys for Improvement, Protection, or Rehabilitation of Public Lands Damaged by Unauthorized Persons

Pub.L. 103–332, Title I, Sept. 30, 1994, 108 Stat. 2501, provided in part: "That notwithstanding any provision to the contrary of section 305(a) of the Act of October 21, 1976 (43 U.S.C. 1735(a)) [subsec. (a) of this section], any moneys that have been or will be received pursuant to that section, whether as a result of forfeiture, compromise, or settlement, if not appropriate for refund pursuant to section 305(c) of that Act (43 U.S.C. 1735(c)) [subsec. (c) of this section], shall be available and may be expended under the authority of this or subsequent appropriations Acts by the Secretary to improve, protect, or rehabilitate any public lands administered through the Bureau of Land Management which have been damaged by the action of a resource developer, purchaser, permittee, or any unauthorized person, without regard to whether all moneys collected from each such forfeiture, compromise, or settlement are used on the exact lands damage to which led to the forfeiture, compromise, or settlement: *Provided further*, That such moneys are in excess of amounts needed to repair damage to the exact land for which collected."

Similar provisions were contained in the following prior Appropriations Acts:

Pub.L. 103–138, Title I, Nov. 11, 1993, 107 Stat. 1381.

Pub.L. 102–381, Title I, Oct. 5, 1992, 106 Stat. 1377.

Pub.L. 102–154, Title I, Nov. 13, 1991, 105 Stat. 992.

Pub.L. 101–512, Title I, Nov. 5, 1990, 104 Stat. 1917.

Pub.L. 101–121, Title I, Oct. 23, 1989, 103 Stat. 703.

Pub.L. 100–446, Title I, Sept. 27, 1988, 102 Stat. 1776.

Pub.L. 100–202, § 101(g) [Title I], Dec. 22, 1987, 101 Stat. 1329–215.

§ 1736. Working capital fund [FLPMA § 306]

(a) Establishment; availability of fund

There is hereby established a working capital fund for the management of the public lands. This fund shall be available without fiscal year limitation for expenses necessary for furnishing, in accordance with the Federal Property and Administrative Services Act of 1949 (63 Stat. 377, as amended), and regulations promulgated thereunder, supplies and equipment services in support of Bureau programs, including but not limited to, the purchase or construction of storage facilities, equipment yards, and related improvements and the purchase, lease, or rent of motor vehicles, aircraft, heavy equipment, and fire control and other resource management equipment within the limitations set forth in appropriations made to the Secretary for the Bureau.

(b) Initial funding; subsequent transfers

The initial capital of the fund shall consist of appropriations made for that purpose together with the fair and reasonable value at the fund's inception of the inventories, equipment, receivables, and other assets, less the liabilities, transferred to the fund. The Secretary is authorized to make such subsequent transfers to the fund as he deems appropriate in connection with the functions to be carried on through the fund.

(c) Payments credited to fund; amount; advancement or reimbursement

The fund shall be credited with payments from appropriations, and funds of the Bureau, other agencies of the Department of the Interior, other Federal agencies, and other sources, as authorized by law, at rates approximately equal to the cost of furnishing the facilities, supplies, equipment, and services (including depreciation and accrued annual leave). Such payments may be made in advance in connection with firm orders, or by way of reimbursement.

(d) Authorization of appropriations

There is hereby authorized to be appropriated a sum not to exceed $3,000,000 as initial capital of the working capital fund.

(Oct. 21, 1976, Pub.L. 94–579, Title III, § 306, 90 Stat. 2766.)

§ 1736a. Revolving fund derived from disposal of salvage timber

There is hereby established in the Treasury of the United States a special fund to be derived hereafter from the Federal share of moneys received from the disposal of salvage timber prepared for sale from the lands under the jurisdiction of the Bureau of Land Management, Department of the Interior. The money in this fund shall be immediately available to the Bureau of Land Management without further appropriation, for the purposes of planning and preparing salvage timber for disposal, the administration of salvage timber sales, and subsequent site preparation and reforestation.

(Pub.L. 102–381, Title I, Oct. 5, 1992, 106 Stat. 1376.)

References in Text

Reference in text to funds "derived hereafter" probably means funds derived after Oct. 5, 1992, the date of approval of Pub.L. 102–381.

Codification

Section was enacted as part of the Department of the Interior and Related Agencies Appropriations Act, 1993, and not as part of the Federal Land Policy and Management Act of 1976, which comprises this chapter.

Distribution of Receipts

Title I of Pub.L. 102–381 provided in part that: "Nothing in this provision [this section] shall alter the formulas currently in existence by law for the distribution of receipts for the applicable lands and timber resources."

§ 1737. Implementation provisions [FLPMA § 307]

(a) Investigations, studies, and experiments

The Secretary may conduct investigations, studies, and experiments, on his own initiative or in cooperation with others, involving the management, protection, development, acquisition, and conveying of the public lands.

(b) Contracts and cooperative agreements

Subject to the provisions of applicable law, the Secretary may enter into contracts and cooperative agreements involving the management, protection, development, and sale of public lands.

(c) Contributions and donations of money, services, and property

The Secretary may accept contributions or donations of money, services, and property, real, personal, or mixed, for the management, protection, development, acquisition, and conveying of the public lands, including the acquisition of rights-of-way for such purposes. He may accept contributions for cadastral surveying performed on federally controlled or intermingled lands. Moneys received hereunder shall be credited to a separate account in the Treasury and are hereby authorized to be appropriated and made available until expended, as the Secretary may direct, for payment of expenses incident to the function toward the administration of which the contributions were made and for refunds to depositors of amounts contributed by them in specific instances where contributions are in excess of their share of the cost.

(d) Recruitment of volunteers

The Secretary may recruit, without regard to the civil service classification laws, rules, or regulations, the services of individuals contributed without compensation as volunteers for aiding in or facilitating the activities administered by the Secretary through the Bureau of Land Management.

(e) Restrictions on activities of volunteers

In accepting such services of individuals as volunteers, the Secretary—

(1) shall not permit the use of volunteers in hazardous duty or law enforcement work, or in policymaking processes or to displace any employee; and

(2) may provide for services or costs incidental to the utilization of volunteers, including transportation, supplies, lodging, subsistence, recruiting, training, and supervision.

(f) Federal employment status of volunteers

Volunteers shall not be deemed employees of the United States except for the purposes of—

(1) the tort claims provisions of Title 28;

(2) subchapter 1 of chapter 81 of Title 5; and

(3) claims relating to damage to, or loss of, personal property of a volunteer incident to volunteer service, in which case the provisions of section 3721 of Title 31 shall apply.

(g) Authorization of appropriations

Effective with fiscal years beginning after September 30, 1984, there are authorized to be appropriated such sums as may be necessary to carry out the provisions of subsection (d) of this section, but not more than $250,000 may be appropriated for any one fiscal year.

(Oct. 21, 1976, Pub.L. 94–579, Title III, § 307, 90 Stat. 2766; Oct. 24, 1984, Pub.L. 98–540, § 2, 98 Stat. 2718; May 9, 1990, Pub.L. 101–286, Title II, § 204(c), 104 Stat. 175.)

CROSS REFERENCES

Cooperative agreements with Federal departments and agencies to use, occupy, and develop public lands, see section 1732 of this title.
Surveys, see section 52 et seq. of this title.

§ 1738. Contracts for surveys and resource protection; renewals; funding requirements [FLPMA § 308]

(a) The Secretary is authorized to enter into contracts for the use of aircraft, and for supplies and services, prior to the passage of an appropriation therefor, for airborne cadastral survey and resource protection operations of the Bureau. He may renew such contracts annually, not more than twice, without additional competition. Such contracts shall obligate funds for the fiscal years in which the costs are incurred.

(b) Each such contract shall provide that the obligation of the United States for the ensuing fiscal years is contingent upon the passage of an applicable appropriation, and that no payment shall be made under the contract for the ensuing fiscal years until such appropriation becomes available for expenditure.

(Oct. 21, 1976, Pub.L. 94–579, Title III, § 308, 90 Stat. 2767.)

CROSS REFERENCES

Surveys, see section 52 et seq. of this title.

§ 1739. Advisory councils [FLPMA § 309]

(a) Establishment; membership; operation

The Secretary shall establish advisory councils of not less than ten and not more than fifteen members appointed by him from among persons who are representative of the various major citizens' interests concerning the problems relating to land use planning or the management of the public lands located within the area for which an advisory council is established. At least one member of each council shall be an elected official of general purpose government serving the people of such area. To the extent practicable there shall be no overlap or duplication of such councils. Appointments shall be made in accordance with rules prescribed by the Secretary. The establishment and operation of an advisory council established under this section shall conform to the requirements of the Federal Advisory Committee Act (86 Stat. 770).

(b) Meetings

Notwithstanding the provisions of subsection (a) of this section, each advisory council established by the Secretary under this section shall meet at least once a year with such meetings being called by the Secretary.

(c) Travel and per diem payments

Members of advisory councils shall serve without pay, except travel and per diem will be paid each member for meetings called by the Secretary.

(d) Functions

An advisory council may furnish advice to the Secretary with respect to the land use planning, classification, retention, management, and disposal of the public lands within the area for which the advisory council is established and such other matters as may be referred to it by the Secretary.

(e) Public participation; procedures applicable

In exercising his authorities under this Act, the Secretary, by regulation, shall establish procedures, including public hearings where appropriate, to give the Federal, State, and local governments and the public adequate notice and an opportunity to comment upon the formulation of standards and criteria for, and to participate in, the preparation and execution of plans and programs for, and the management of, the public lands.

(Oct. 21, 1976, Pub.L. 94–579, Title III, § 309, 90 Stat. 2767; Oct. 25, 1978, Pub.L. 95–514, § 13, 92 Stat. 1808.)

CROSS REFERENCES

California Desert Conservation Area; establishment of advisory committee, see section 1781 of this title.
Distribution of range improvement funds; consultation with advisory councils, see section 1904 of this title.
Land use plans, see section 1712 of this title.
Management of use, occupancy and development of public lands, see section 1732 of this title.

LAW REVIEW COMMENTARIES

Grazing management on the public lands: Opening the process to public participation. Joseph M. Feller, 26 Land and Water L.Rev. 571 (1991).

§ 1740. Rules and regulations [FLPMA § 310]

The Secretary, with respect to the public lands, shall promulgate rules and regulations to carry out the purposes of this Act and of other laws applicable to the public lands, and the Secretary of Agriculture, with respect to lands within the National Forest System, shall promulgate rules and regulations to carry out the purposes of this Act. The promulgation of such rules and regulations shall be governed by the provisions of chapter 5 of Title 5, without regard to section 553(a)(2). Prior to the promulgation of such rules and regulations, such lands shall be administered under existing rules and regulations concerning such lands to the extent practical.

(Oct. 21, 1976, Pub.L. 94–579, Title III, § 310, 90 Stat. 2767.)

CODE OF FEDERAL REGULATIONS

Administrative regulations of Department of Agriculture implementing Freedom of Information Act, see 7 CFR 1.1 et seq.
Color-of-title and omitted lands, see 43 CFR 2540.0–3 et seq.
Exchanges, see 43 CFR 2200.0–1 et seq.
Land sales, see 43 CFR 2710.0–1 et seq.
Land withdrawals, see 43 CFR 2300.0–1 et seq.
Recreation and public purposes, see 43 CFR 2742.1 et seq.

LIBRARY REFERENCES

Public Lands ⇐97.
C.J.S. Public Lands § 170 et seq.

§ 1741. Annual reports [FLPMA § 311]

(a) Purpose; time for submission

For the purpose of providing information that will aid Congress in carrying out its oversight responsibilities for public lands programs and for other purposes, the Secretary shall prepare a report in accordance with subsections (b) and (c) of this section and submit it to the Congress no later than one hundred and twenty days after the end of each fiscal year beginning with the report for fiscal year 1979.

(b) Format

A list of programs and specific information to be included in the report as well as the format of the report shall be developed by the Secretary after consulting with the Committee on Natural Resources of the House of Representatives and the Committee on Energy and Natural Resources of the Senate and shall be provided to the committees prior to the end of the second quarter of each fiscal year.

(c) Contents

The report shall include, but not be limited to, program identification information, program evaluation information, and program budgetary information for the preceding current and succeeding fiscal years.

(Oct. 21, 1976, Pub.L. 94–579, Title III, § 311, 90 Stat. 2768; Nov. 2, 1994, Pub.L. 103–437, § 16(d)(3), 108 Stat. 4595.)

Change of Name

Any reference in any provision of law enacted before Jan. 4, 1995, to the Committee on Natural Resources of the House of Representatives treated as referring to the Committee on Resources of the House of Representatives, see section 1(a)(8) of Pub.L. 104–14, set out as a note preceding section 21 of Title 2, The Congress.

§ 1742. Search, rescue, and protection forces; emergency situations authorizing hiring [FLPMA § 312]

Where in his judgment sufficient search, rescue, and protection forces are not otherwise available, the Secretary is authorized in cases of emergency to incur such expenses as may be necessary (a) in searching for and rescuing, or in cooperating in the search for and rescue of, persons lost on the public lands, (b) in protecting or rescuing, or in cooperating in the protection and rescue of, persons or animals endangered by an act of God, and (c) in transporting deceased persons or persons seriously ill or injured to the nearest place where interested parties or local authorities are located.

(Oct. 21, 1976, Pub.L. 94–579, Title III, § 312, 90 Stat. 2768.)

§ 1743. Disclosure of financial interests by officers or employees [FLPMA § 313]

(a) Annual written statement; availability to public

Each officer or employee of the Secretary and the Bureau who—

(1) performs any function or duty under this Act; and

(2) has any known financial interest in any person who (A) applies for or receives any permit, lease, or right-of-way under, or (B) applies for or acquires any land or interests therein under, or (C) is otherwise subject to the provisions of, this Act,

shall, beginning on February 1, 1977, annually file with the Secretary a written statement concerning all such interests held by such officer or employee during the preceding calendar year. Such statement shall be available to the public.

(b) Implementation of requirements

The Secretary shall—

(1) act within ninety days after October 21, 1976—

(A) to define the term "known financial interests" for the purposes of subsection (a) of this section; and

(B) to establish the methods by which the requirement to file written statements specified in subsection (a) of this section will be monitored and enforced, including appropriate provisions for the filing by such officers and employees of such statements and the review by the Secretary of such statements; and

(2) report to the Congress on June 1 of each calendar year with respect to such disclosures and the actions taken in regard thereto during the preceding calendar year.

(c) Exempted personnel

In the rules prescribed in subsection (b) of this section, the Secretary may identify specific positions within the Department of the Interior which are of a nonregulatory or nonpolicymaking nature and provide that officers or employees occupying such positions shall be exempt from the requirements of this section.

(d) Violations; criminal penalties

Any officer or employee who is subject to, and knowingly violates, this section, shall be fined not more than $2,500 or imprisoned not more than one year, or both.

(Oct. 21, 1976, Pub.L. 94–579, Title III, § 313, 90 Stat. 2768.)

§ 1744. Recordation of mining claims [FLPMA § 314]

(a) Filing requirements

The owner of an unpatented lode or placer mining claim located prior to October 21, 1976, shall, within the three-year period following October 21, 1976, and prior to December 31 of each year thereafter, file the instruments required by paragraphs (1) and (2) of this subsection. The owner of an unpatented lode or placer mining claim located after October 21, 1976 shall, prior to December 31 of each year following the calendar year in which the said claim was located, file the instruments required by paragraphs (1) and (2) of this subsection:

(1) File for record in the office where the location notice or certificate is recorded either a notice of intention to hold the mining claim (including but not limited to such notices as are provided by law to be filed when there has been a suspension or deferment of annual assessment work), an affidavit of assessment work performed thereon, on a detailed report provided by section 28–1 of Title 30, relating thereto.

(2) File in the office of the Bureau designated by the Secretary a copy of the official record of the instrument filed or recorded pursuant to paragraph (1) of this subsection, including a description of the location of the mining claim sufficient to locate the claimed lands on the ground.

(b) Additional filing requirements

The owner of an unpatented lode or placer mining claim or mill or tunnel site located prior to October 21, 1976 shall, within the three-year period following October 21, 1976, file in the office of the Bureau designated by the Secretary a copy of the official record of the notice of location or certificate of location, including a description of the location of the mining claim or mill or tunnel site sufficient to locate the claimed lands on the ground. The owner of an unpatented lode or placer mining claim or mill or tunnel site located after October 21, 1976, shall, within ninety days after the date of location of such claim, file in the office of the Bureau designated by the Secretary a copy of the official record of the notice of location or certificate of location, including a description of the location of the mining claim or mill or tunnel site sufficient to locate the claimed lands on the ground.

(c) Failure to file as constituting abandonment; defective or untimely filing

The failure to file such instruments as required by subsections (a) and (b) of this section shall be deemed conclusively to constitute an abandonment of the mining claim or mill or tunnel site by the owner; but it shall not be considered a failure to file if the instrument is defective or not timely filed for record under other Federal laws permitting filing or recording thereof, or if the instrument is filed for record by or on behalf of some but not all of the owners of the mining claim or mill or tunnel site.

(d) Validity of claims, waiver of assessment, etc., as unaffected

Such recordation or application by itself shall not render valid any claim which would not be otherwise valid under applicable law. Nothing in this section shall be construed as a waiver of the assessment and other requirements of such law.

(Oct. 21, 1976, Pub.L. 94–579, Title III, § 314, 90 Stat. 2769.)

CROSS REFERENCES

Locators or claimants under Mining Law of 1872, impairment of claims of, see section 1732 of this title.

Unpatented oil placer mining claims, abandonment of, see section 188 of Title 30, Mineral Lands and Mining.

United States Supreme Court

Miner failing to timely file annual proof of labor, presumption of abandonment, extinguishment of claims, see United States v. Locke, 1985, 105 S.Ct. 1785, 85 L.Ed.2d 64.

§ 1745. Disclaimer of interest in lands [FLPMA § 315]

(a) Issuance of recordable document; criteria

After consulting with any affected Federal agency, the Secretary is authorized to issue a document of disclaimer of interest or interests in any lands in any form suitable for recordation, where the disclaimer will help remove a cloud on the title of such lands and where he determines (1) a record interest of the United States in lands has terminated by operation of law or is otherwise invalid; or (2) the lands lying between the meander line shown on a plat of survey approved by the Bureau or its predecessors and the actual shoreline of a body of water are not lands of the United States; or (3) accreted, relicted, or avulsed lands are not lands of the United States.

(b) Procedures applicable

No document or disclaimer shall be issued pursuant to this section unless the applicant therefor has filed with the Secretary an application in writing and notice of such application setting forth the grounds supporting such application has been published in the Federal Register at least ninety days preceding the issuance of such disclaimer and until the applicant therefor has paid to the Secretary the administrative costs of issuing the disclaimer as determined by the Secretary. All receipts shall be deposited to the then-current appropriation from which expended.

(c) Construction as quit-claim deed from United States

Issuance of a document of disclaimer by the Secretary pursuant to the provisions of this section and regulations promulgated hereunder shall have the same effect as a quit-claim deed from the United States.

(Oct. 21, 1976, Pub.L. 94–579, Title III, § 315, 90 Stat. 2770.)

CODE OF FEDERAL REGULATIONS

Conveyances, disclaimers, and correction documents, see 43 CFR 1862.0–3 et seq.

LIBRARY REFERENCES

Public Lands ⚷7.
C.J.S. Public Lands § 3 et seq.

§ 1746. Correction of conveyance documents [FLPMA § 316]

The Secretary may correct patents or documents of conveyance issued pursuant to section 1718 of this title or to other Acts relating to the disposal of public lands where necessary in order to eliminate errors. In addition, the Secretary may make corrections of errors in any documents of conveyance which have heretofore been issued by the Federal Government to dispose of public lands.

(Oct. 21, 1976, Pub.L. 94–579, Title III, § 316, 90 Stat. 2770.)

CODE OF FEDERAL REGULATIONS

Conveyances, disclaimers, and correction documents, see 43 CFR 1862.0–3 et seq.

§ 1747. Loans to States and political subdivisions; purposes; amounts; allocation; terms and conditions; interest rate; security; limitations; forbearance for benefit of borrowers; recordkeeping requirements; discrimination prohibited; deposit of receipts [FLPMA § 317]

(1) The Secretary is authorized to make loans to States and their political subdivisions in order to relieve social or economic impacts occasioned by the development of minerals leased in such States pursuant to the Act of February 25, 1920, as amended [30 U.S.C.A. § 181 et seq.]. Such loans shall be confined to the uses specified for the 50 per centum of mineral leasing revenues to be received by such States and subdivisions pursuant to section 35 of such Act [30 U.S.C.A. § 191].

(2) The total amount of loans outstanding pursuant to this section for any State and political subdivisions thereof in any year shall be not more than the antici-

pated mineral leasing revenues to be received by that State pursuant to section 35 of the Act of February 25, 1920, as amended [30 U.S.C.A. § 191], for the ten years following.

(3) The Secretary, after consultation with the Governors of the affected States, shall allocate such loans among the States and their political subdivisions in a fair and equitable manner, giving priority to those States and subdivisions suffering the most severe impacts.

(4) Loans made pursuant to this section shall be subject to such terms and conditions as the Secretary determines necessary to assure the achievement of the purpose of this section. The Secretary shall promulgate such regulations as may be necessary to carry out the provisions of this section no later than three months after August 20, 1978.

(5) Loans made pursuant to this section shall bear interest equivalent to the lowest interest rate paid on an issue of at least $1,000,000 of tax exempt bonds of such State or any agency thereof within the preceding calendar year.

(6) Any loan made pursuant to this section shall be secured only by a pledge of the revenues received by the State or the political subdivision thereof pursuant to section 35 of the Act of February 25, 1920, as amended [30 U.S.C.A. § 191], and shall not constitute an obligation upon the general property or taxing authority of such unit of government.

(7) Notwithstanding any other provision of law, loans made pursuant to this section may be used for the non-Federal share of the aggregate cost of any project or program otherwise funded by the Federal Government which requires a non-Federal share for such project or program and which provides planning or public facilities otherwise eligible for assistance under this section.

(8) Nothing in this section shall be construed to preclude any forebearance [1] for the benefit of the borrower including loan restructuring, which may be determined by the Secretary as justified by the failure of anticipated mineral development or related revenues to materialize as expected when the loan was made pursuant to this section.

(9) Recipients of loans made pursuant to this section shall keep such records as the Secretary shall prescribe by regulation, including records which fully disclose the disposition of the proceeds of such assistance and such other records as the Secretary may require to facilitate an effective audit. The Secretary and the Comptroller General of the United States or their duly authorized representatives shall have access, for the purpose of audit, to such records.

(10) No person in the United States shall, on the grounds of race, color, religion, national origin, or sex be excluded from participation in, be denied the benefits of, or be subjected to discrimination under, any program or activity funded in whole or part with funds made available under this section.

(11) All amounts collected in connection with loans made pursuant to this section, including interest payments or repayments of principal on loans, fees, and other moneys, derived in connection with this section, shall be deposited in the Treasury as miscellaneous receipts.

(Oct. 21, 1976, Pub.L. 94–579, Title III, § 317(c), 90 Stat. 2771; Aug. 20, 1978, Pub.L. 95–352, § 1(f), 92 Stat. 515.)

[1] So in original.

CODE OF FEDERAL REGULATIONS

Financial assistance, local governments, see 43 CFR 1881.0–1 et seq.

§ 1748. Funding requirements [FLPMA § 318]

(a) Authorization of appropriations

There are hereby authorized to be appropriated such sums as are necessary to carry out the purposes and provisions of this Act, but no amounts shall be appropriated to carry out after October 1, 1978, any program, function, or activity of the Bureau under this or any other Act unless such sums are specifically authorized to be appropriated as of October 21, 1976 or are authorized to be appropriated in accordance with the provisions of subsection (b) of this section.

(b) Procedure applicable for authorization of appropriations

Consistent with section 1110 of Title 31, beginning May 15, 1977, and not later than May 15 of each second even numbered year thereafter, the Secretary shall submit to the Speaker of the House of Representatives and the President of the Senate a request for the authorization of appropriations for all programs, functions, and activities of the Bureau to be carried out during the four-fiscal-year period beginning on October 1 of the calendar year following the calendar year in which such request is submitted. The Secretary shall include in his request, in addition to the information contained in his budget request and justification statement to the Office of Management and Budget, the funding levels which he determines can be efficiently and effectively utilized in the execution of his responsibilities for each such program, function, or activity, notwithstanding any budget guidelines or limitations imposed by any official or agency of the executive branch.

(c) Distribution of receipts from Bureau from disposal of lands, etc.

Nothing in this section shall apply to the distribution of receipts of the Bureau from the disposal of lands, natural resources, and interests in lands in accordance with applicable law, nor to the use of contributed funds, private deposits for public survey work, and townsite trusteeships, nor to fund allocations from other Federal agencies, reimbursements from both Federal and non-Federal sources, and funds expended for emergency firefighting and rehabilitation.

(d) Purchase of certain public lands from Land and Water Conservation Fund

In exercising the authority to acquire by purchase granted by section 1715(a) of this title, the Secretary may use the Land and Water Conservation Fund to purchase lands which are necessary for proper management of public lands which are primarily of value for outdoor recreation purposes.

(Oct. 21, 1976, Pub.L. 94–579, Title III, § 318, 90 Stat. 2771.)

CROSS REFERENCES

Conservation programs on public lands; functions and responsibilities of Secretary of the Interior, see section 670*o* of Title 16, Conservation.

Range improvement funding; authorization of additional appropriations, see section 1904 of this title.

Snake River Birds of Prey National Conservation Area, land acquisition, appropriation authorization, see 16 USCA § 460iii–4.

SUBCHAPTER IV—RANGE MANAGEMENT

CROSS REFERENCES

Grazing lands, see section 315 et seq. of this title.

LIBRARY REFERENCES

Public Lands ⇐17.
C.J.S. Public Lands § 19 et seq.

§ 1751. Grazing fees; feasibility study; contents; submission of report; annual distribution and use of range betterment funds; nature of distributions [FLPMA § 401]

(a) The Secretary of Agriculture and the Secretary of the Interior shall jointly cause to be conducted a study to determine the value of grazing on the lands under their jurisdiction in the eleven Western States with a view to establishing a fee to be charged for domestic livestock grazing on such lands which is equitable to the United States and to the holders of grazing permits and leases on such lands. In making such study, the Secretaries shall take into consideration the costs of production normally associated with domestic livestock grazing in the eleven Western States, differences in forage values, and such other factors as may relate to the reasonableness of such fees. The Secretaries shall report the result of such study to the Congress not later than one year from and after October 21, 1976, together with recommendations to implement a reasonable grazing fee schedule based upon such study. If the report required herein has not been submitted to the Congress within one year after October 21, 1976, the grazing fee charge then in effect shall not be altered and shall remain the same until such report has been submitted to the Congress. Neither Secretary shall increase the grazing fee in the 1977 grazing year.

(b)(1) Congress finds that a substantial amount of the Federal range lands is deteriorating in quality, and that installation of additional range improvements could arrest much of the continuing deterioration and could lead to substantial betterment of forage conditions with resulting benefits to wildlife, watershed protection, and livestock production. Congress therefore directs that 50 per centum or $10,000,000 per annum, whichever is greater of all moneys received by the United States as fees for grazing domestic livestock on public lands (other than from ceded Indian lands) under the Taylor Grazing Act (48 Stat. 1269; 43 U.S.C. 315 et seq.) and the Act of August 28, 1937 (50 Stat. 874; 43 U.S.C. 1181d), and on lands in National Forests in the sixteen contiguous Western States under the provisions of this section shall be credited to a separate account in the Treasury, one-half of which is authorized to be appropriated and made available for use in the district, region, or national forest from which such moneys were derived, as the respective Secretary may direct after consultation with district, regional, or national forest user representatives, for the purpose of on-the-ground range rehabilitation, protection, and improvements on such lands, and the remaining one-half shall be used for on-the-ground range rehabilitation, protection, and improvements as the Secretary concerned directs. Any funds so appropriated shall be in addition to any other appropriations made to the respective Secretary for planning and administration of the range betterment program and for other range management. Such rehabilitation, protection, and improvements shall include all forms of range land betterment including, but not limited to, seeding and reseeding, fence construction, weed control, water development, and fish and wildlife habitat enhancement as the respective Secretary may direct after consultation with user representatives. The annual distribution and use of range betterment funds authorized by this paragraph shall not be considered a major Federal action requiring a detailed statement pursuant to section 4332(c) of Title 42.

(2) All distributions of moneys made under subsection (b)(1) of this section shall be in addition to distributions made under section 10 of the Taylor Grazing Act [43 U.S.C.A. § 315i] and shall not apply to distribution of moneys made under section 11 of that Act [43 U.S.C.A. § 315j]. The remaining moneys received by the United States as fees for grazing domestic livestock on the public lands shall be deposited in the Treasury as miscellaneous receipts.

(Oct. 21, 1976, Pub.L. 94–579, Title IV, § 401(a), (b)(1), (2), 90 Stat. 2772; Oct. 25, 1978, Pub.L. 95–514, § 6(b), 92 Stat. 1806.)

CROSS REFERENCES

Grazing fees—
Generally, see section 315b of this title.
Alaska, see section 316g of this title.
Range improvement funding; authorization of additional appropriations, see section 1904 of this title.

CODE OF FEDERAL REGULATIONS

Range management, see 36 CFR 222.1 et seq., 43 CFR 4100.0–1 et seq.

§ 1752. Grazing leases and permits [FLPMA § 402]

(a) Terms and conditions

Except as provided in subsection (b) of this section, permits and leases for domestic livestock grazing on public lands issued by the Secretary under the Act of June 28, 1934 (48 Stat. 1269, as amended; 43 U.S.C. 315 et seq.) or the Act of August 28, 1937 (50 Stat. 874, as amended; 43 U.S.C. 1181a–1181j), or by the Secretary of Agriculture, with respect to lands within National Forests in the sixteen contiguous Western States, shall be for a term of ten years subject to such terms and conditions the Secretary concerned deems appropriate and consistent with the governing law, including, but not limited to, the authority of the Secretary concerned to cancel, suspend, or modify a grazing permit or lease, in whole or in part, pursuant to the terms and conditions thereof, or to cancel or suspend a grazing permit or lease for any violation of a grazing regulation or of any term or condition of such grazing permit or lease.

(b) Terms of lesser duration

Permits or leases may be issued by the Secretary concerned for a period shorter than ten years where the Secretary concerned determines that—

(1) the land is pending disposal; or

(2) the land will be devoted to a public purpose prior to the end of ten years; or

(3) it will be in the best interest of sound land management to specify a shorter term: *Provided*, That the absence from an allotment management plan of details the Secretary concerned would like to include but which are undeveloped shall not be the basis for establishing a term shorter than ten years: *Provided further*, That the absence of completed land use plans or court ordered environmental statements shall not be the sole basis for establishing a term shorter than ten years unless the Secretary determines on a case-by-case basis that the information to be contained in such land use plan or court ordered environmental impact statement is necessary to determine whether a shorter term should be established for any of the reasons set forth in items (1) through (3) of this subsection.

(c) First priority for renewal of expiring permit or lease

So long as (1) the lands for which the permit or lease is issued remain available for domestic livestock grazing in accordance with land use plans prepared pursuant to section 1712 of this title or section 1604 of Title 16, (2) the permittee or lessee is in compliance with the rules and regulations issued and the terms and conditions in the permit or lease specified by the Secretary concerned, and (3) the permittee or lessee accepts the terms and conditions to be included by the Secretary concerned in the new permit or lease, the holder of the expiring permit or lease shall be given first priority for receipt of the new permit or lease.

(d) Allotment management plan requirements

All permits and leases for domestic livestock grazing issued pursuant to this section may incorporate an allotment management plan developed by the Secretary concerned. However, nothing in this subsection shall be construed to supersede any requirement for completion of court ordered environmental impact statements prior to development and incorporation of allotment management plans. If the Secretary concerned elects to develop an allotment management plan for a given area, he shall do so in careful and considered consultation, cooperation and coordination with the lessees, permittees, and landowners involved, the district grazing advisory boards established pursuant to section 1753 of this title, and any State or States having lands within the area to be covered by such allotment management plan. Allotment management plans shall be tailored to the specific range condition of the area to be covered by such plan, and shall be reviewed on a periodic basis to determine whether they have been effective in improving the range condition of the lands involved or whether such lands can be better managed under the provisions of subsection (e) of this section. The Secretary concerned may revise or terminate such plans or develop new plans from time to time after such review and careful and considered consultation, cooperation and coordination with the parties involved. As used in this subsection, the terms "court ordered environmental impact statement" and "range condition" shall be defined as in the "Public Rangelands Improvement Act of 1978 [43 U.S.C.A. § 1901 et seq.]".

(e) Omission of allotment management plan requirements and incorporation of appropriate terms and conditions; reexamination of range conditions

In all cases where the Secretary concerned has not completed an allotment management plan or determines that an allotment management plan is not necessary for management of livestock operations and will not be prepared, the Secretary concerned shall incorporate in grazing permits and leases such terms and conditions as he deems appropriate for management of the permitted or leased lands pursuant to applicable law. The Secretary concerned shall also specify therein the numbers of animals to be grazed and the seasons of use and that he may reexamine the condition of the range at any time and, if he finds on reexamination that the condition of the range requires adjustment in the amount or other aspect of grazing use, that the permittee or lessee shall adjust his use to the extent the Secretary concerned deems necessary. Such readjustment shall be put into full force and effect on the date specified by the Secretary concerned.

(f) Allotment management plan applicability to non-Federal lands; appeal rights

Allotment management plans shall not refer to livestock operations or range improvements on non-Federal lands except where the non-Federal lands are intermingled with, or, with the consent of the permittee or lessee involved, associated with, the Federal lands subject to the plan. The Secretary concerned under appropriate regulations shall grant to lessees and permittees the right of appeal from decisions which specify the terms and conditions of allotment management plans. The preceding sentence of this subsection shall not be construed as limiting any other right of appeal from decisions of such officials.

(g) Cancellation of permit or lease; determination of reasonable compensation; notice

Whenever a permit or lease for grazing domestic livestock is canceled in whole or in part, in order to devote the lands covered by the permit or lease to another public purpose, including disposal, the permittee or lessee shall receive from the United States a reasonable compensation for the adjusted value, to be determined by the Secretary concerned, of his interest in authorized permanent improvements placed or constructed by the permittee or lessee on lands covered by such permit or lease, but not to exceed the fair market value of the terminated portion of the permittee's or lessee's interest therein. Except in cases of emergency, no permit or lease shall be canceled under this subsection without two years' prior notification.

(h) Applicability of provisions to rights, etc., in or to public lands or lands in National Forests

Nothing in this Act shall be construed as modifying in any way law existing on October 21, 1976, with respect to the creation of right, title, interest or estate in or to public lands or lands in National Forests by issuance of grazing permits and leases.

(Oct. 21, 1976, Pub.L. 94–579, Title IV, § 402, 90 Stat. 2773; Oct. 25, 1978, Pub.L. 95–514, §§ 7, 8, 92 Stat. 1807.)

Reductions in Grazing Allotments on Public Rangelands

Pub.L. 102–381, Title I, Oct. 5, 1992, 106 Stat. 1378, provided in part: "That an appeal of any reductions in grazing allotments on public rangelands must be taken within thirty days after receipt of a final grazing allotment decision. Reductions of up to 10 per centum in grazing allotments shall become effective when so designated by the Secretary of the Interior. Upon appeal any proposed reduction in excess of 10 per centum shall be suspended pending final action on the appeal, which shall be completed within two years after the appeal is filed[.]".

Similar provisions were contained in the following prior appropriations acts:

Pub.L. 102–154, Title I, Nov. 13, 1991, 105 Stat. 993.

Pub.L. 101–512, Title I, Nov. 5, 1990, 104 Stat. 1917.

Pub.L. 101–121, Title I, Oct. 23, 1989, 103 Stat. 704.

Pub.L. 100–446, Title I, Sept. 27, 1988, 102 Stat. 1776.

Pub.L. 100–202, § 101(g) [Title I], Dec. 22, 1987, 101 Stat. 1329–216.

Pub.L. 99–591, Title I, § 101(h) [Title I, § 100], Oct. 30, 1986, 100 Stat. 3341–245.

Pub.L. 99–500, Title I, § 101(h) [Title I, § 100], Oct. 18, 1986, 100 Stat. 1783.

Pub.L. 99–190, § 101(d) [Title I, § 100], Dec. 19, 1985, 99 Stat. 1226.

CROSS REFERENCES

Grazing permits, see section 315b of this title.

Navajo and Hopi Tribes; settlement of rights and interests; cancellation of grazing leases and permits, see section 640d–26 of Title 25, Indians.

Snake River Birds of Prey National Conservation Area, livestock grazing, see 16 USCA § 460iii–3.

Terms and conditions of Alaska grazing leases, see section 316f of this title.

CODE OF FEDERAL REGULATIONS

Range management, see 43 CFR Chap. II, Subchap. D.

LAW REVIEW COMMENTARIES

Federal lands and local communities. Eric T. Freyfogle, 27 Ariz. L.Rev. 653 (1985).

Grazing management on the public lands: Opening the process to public participation. Joseph M. Feller, 26 Land and Water L.Rev. 571 (1991).

§ 1753. Grazing advisory boards [FLPMA § 403]

(a) Establishment; maintenance

For each Bureau district office and National Forest headquarters office in the sixteen contiguous Western States having jurisdiction over more than five hundred thousand acres of lands subject to commercial livestock grazing (hereinafter in this section referred to as "office"), the Secretary and the Secretary of Agriculture, upon the petition of a simple majority of the livestock lessees and permittees under the jurisdiction of such office, shall establish and maintain at least one grazing advisory board of not more than fifteen advisers.

(b) Functions

The function of grazing advisory boards established pursuant to this section shall be to offer advice and make recommendations to the head of the office involved concerning the development of allotment management plans and the utilization of range-betterment funds.

(c) Appointment and terms of members

The number of advisers on each board and the number of years an adviser may serve shall be determined by the Secretary concerned in his discretion. Each board shall consist of livestock representatives who shall be lessees or permittees in the area administered by the office concerned and shall be chosen by the lessees and permittees in the area through an election prescribed by the Secretary concerned.

(d) Meetings

Each grazing advisory board shall meet at least once annually.

(e) Federal Advisory Committee Act applicability

Except as may be otherwise provided by this section, the provisions of the Federal Advisory Committee Act (86 Stat. 770) shall apply to grazing advisory boards.

(f) Expiration date

The provisions of this section shall expire December 31, 1985.

(Oct. 21, 1976, Pub.L. 94–579, Title IV, § 403, 90 Stat. 2775; Oct. 25, 1978, Pub.L. 95–514, § 10, 92 Stat. 1808.)

CROSS REFERENCES

Allotment management plans, consultation with grazing advisory boards, see section 1752 of this title.

Range improvement funding; distribution, consultation and coordination, see section 1904 of this title.

SUBCHAPTER V—RIGHTS–OF–WAY

CROSS REFERENCES

Negotiated sales of coal on exercise of right-of-way permits, see section 201 of Title 30, Mineral Lands and Mining.

Right-of-way defined, see section 1702 of this title.

Rights-of-way and other easements in public lands, see section 931 et seq. of this title.

Transportation and utility systems in and across, and access into, conservation system units in Alaska; Congressional approval, see section 3166 of Title 16, Conservation.

LIBRARY REFERENCES

United States ⚖57.

C.J.S. United States § 74.

§ 1761. Grant, issue, or renewal of rights-of-way [FLPMA § 501]

(a) Authorized purposes

The Secretary, with respect to the public lands (including public lands, as defined in section 1702(e) of this title, which are reserved from entry pursuant to section 24 of the Federal Power Act [16 U.S.C.A. § 818]) and, the Secretary of Agriculture, with respect to lands within the National Forest System (except in each case land designated as wilderness), are authorized to grant, issue, or renew rights-of-way over, upon, under, or through such lands for—

(1) reservoirs, canals, ditches, flumes, laterals, pipes, pipelines, tunnels, and other facilities and systems for the impoundment, storage, transportation, or distribution of water;

(2) pipelines and other systems for the transportation or distribution of liquids and gases, other than water and other than oil, natural gas, synthetic liquid or gaseous fuels, or any refined product produced therefrom, and for storage and terminal facilities in connection therewith;

(3) pipelines, slurry and emulsion systems, and conveyor belts for transportation and distribution of solid materials, and facilities for the storage of such materials in connection therewith;

(4) systems for generation, transmission, and distribution of electric energy, except that the applicant shall also comply with all applicable requirements of the Federal Energy Regulatory Commission under the Federal Power Act [16 U.S.C.A. §§ 791a–825r], including part 1 thereof [16 U.S.C.A. §§ 792–823b] (41 Stat. 1063, 16 U.S.C. 791a–825r).[1];

(5) systems for transmission or reception of radio, television, telephone, telegraph, and other electronic signals, and other means of communication;

(6) roads, trails, highways, railroads, canals, tunnels, tramways, airways, livestock driveways, or other means of transportation except where such facilities are constructed and maintained in connection with commercial recreation facilities on lands in the National Forest System; or

(7) such other necessary transportation or other systems or facilities which are in the public interest and which require rights-of-way over, upon, under, or through such lands.

(b) Procedures applicable; administration

(1) The Secretary concerned shall require, prior to granting, issuing, or renewing a right-of-way, that the applicant submit and disclose those plans, contracts, agreements, or other information reasonably related to the use, or intended use, of the right-of-way, including its effect on competition, which he deems necessary to a determination, in accordance with the provisions of this Act, as to whether a right-of-way shall be granted, issued, or renewed and the terms and conditions which should be included in the right-of-way.

(2) If the applicant is a partnership, corporation, association, or other business entity, the Secretary concerned, prior to granting a right-to-way[1] pursuant to this subchapter, shall require the applicant to disclose the identity of the participants in the entity, when he deems it necessary to a determination, in accordance with the provisions of this subchapter, as to whether a right-of-way shall be granted, issued, or renewed and the terms and conditions which should be included in the right-of-way. Such disclosures shall include, where applicable: (A) the name and address of each partner; (B) the name and address of each shareholder owning 3 per centum or more of the shares, together with the number and percentage of any class of voting shares of the entity which such shareholder is authorized to vote; and (C) the name and address of each affiliate of the entity together with, in the case of an affiliate controlled by the entity, the number of shares and the percentage of any class of voting stock of that affiliate owned, directly or indirectly, by that entity, and, in the case of an affiliate which controls that entity, the number of shares and the percentage of any class of voting stock of that entity owned, directly or indirectly, by the affiliate.

(3) The Secretary of Agriculture shall have the authority to administer all rights-of-way granted or issued under authority of previous Acts with respect to lands under the jurisdiction of the Secretary of Agriculture, including rights-of-way granted or issued pursuant to authority given to the Secretary of the Interior by such previous Acts.

(c) Permanent easement for water systems; issuance, preconditions, etc.

(1) Upon receipt of a written application pursuant to paragraph (2) of this subsection from an applicant meeting the requirements of this subsection, the Secretary of Agriculture shall issue a permanent easement, without a requirement for reimbursement, for a water system as described in subsection (a)(1) of this section, traversing Federal lands within the National Forest System ("National Forest Lands"), constructed and in operation or placed into operation prior to October 21, 1976, if—

(A) the traversed National Forest lands are in a State where the appropriation doctrine governs the ownership of water rights;

(B) at the time of submission of the application the water system is used solely for agricultural irrigation or livestock watering purposes;

(C) the use served by the water system is not located solely on Federal lands;

(D) the originally constructed facilities comprising such system have been in substantially continuous operation without abandonment;

(E) the applicant has a valid existing right, established under applicable State law, for water to be conveyed by the water system;

(F) a recordable survey and other information concerning the location and characteristics of the system as necessary for proper management of National Forest lands is provided to the Secretary of Agriculture by the applicant for the easement; and

(G) the applicant submits such application on or before December 31, 1996.

(2)(A) Nothing in this subsection shall be construed as affecting any grants made by any previous Act. To the extent any such previous grant of right-of-way is a valid existing right, it shall remain in full force and effect unless an owner thereof notifies the Secretary of Agriculture that such owner elects to have a water system on such right-of-way governed by the provisions of this subsection and submits a written application for issuance of an easement pursuant to this subsection, in which case upon the issuance of an easement pursuant to this subsection such previous grant shall be deemed to have been relinquished and shall terminate.

(B) Easements issued under the authority of this subsection shall be fully transferable with all existing conditions and without the imposition of fees or new conditions or stipulations at the time of transfer. The holder shall notify the Secretary of Agriculture within sixty days of any address change of the holder or change in ownership of the facilities.

(C) Easements issued under the authority of this subsection shall include all changes or modifications to the original facilities in existence as of October 21, 1976, the date of enactment of this Act.

(D) Any future extension or enlargement of facilities after October 21, 1976, shall require the issuance of a separate authorization, not authorized under this subsection.

(3)(A) Except as otherwise provided in this subsection, the Secretary of Agriculture may terminate or suspend an easement issued pursuant to this subsection in accordance with the procedural and other provisions of section 1766 of this title. An easement issued pursuant to this subsection shall terminate if the water system for which such easement was issued is used for any purpose other than agricultural irrigation or livestock watering use. For purposes of subparagraph (D) of paragraph (1) of this subsection, non-use of a water system for agricultural irrigation or livestock watering purposes for any continuous five-year period shall constitute a rebuttable presumption of abandonment of the facilities comprising such system.

(B) Nothing in this subsection shall be deemed to be an assertion by the United States of any right or claim with regard to the reservation, acquisition, or use of water. Nothing in this subsection shall be deemed to confer on the Secretary of Agriculture any power or authority to regulate or control in any manner the appropriation, diversion, or use of water for any purpose (nor to diminish any such power or authority of such Secretary under applicable law) or to require the conveyance or transfer to the United States of any right or claim to the appropriation, diversion, or use of water.

(C) Except as otherwise provided in this subsection, all rights-of-way issued pursuant to this subsection are subject to all conditions and requirements of this Act.

(D) In the event a right-of-way issued pursuant to this subsection is allowed to deteriorate to the point of threatening persons or property and the holder of the right-of-way, after consultation with the Secretary of Agriculture, refuses to perform the repair and maintenance necessary to remove the threat to persons or property, the Secretary shall have the right to undertake such repair and maintenance on the right-of-way and to assess the holder for the costs of such repair and maintenance, regardless of whether the Secretary had required the holder to furnish a bond or other security pursuant to subsection (i) of this section.

(d) Rights-of-way on certain Federal lands

With respect to any project or portion thereof that was licensed pursuant to, or granted an exemption from, part I of the Federal Power Act [16 U.S.C.A. §§ 792–823b] which is located on lands subject to a reservation under section 24 of the Federal Power Act [16 U.S.C.A. § 818] and which did not receive a permit, right-of-way, or other approval under this section prior to October 24, 1992, no such permit, right-of-way, or other approval shall be required for continued operation, including continued operation pursuant to section 15 of the Federal Power Act [16 U.S.C.A. § 808], of such project unless the Commission determines that such project involves the use of any additional public lands or National Forest lands not subject to such reservation.

(Oct. 21, 1976, Pub.L. 94–579, Title V, § 501, 90 Stat. 2776; Oct. 27, 1986, Pub.L. 99–545, § 1(b), (c), 100 Stat. 3047, 3048; Oct. 24, 1992, Pub.L. 102–486, Title XXIV, § 2401, 106 Stat. 3096.)

1 So in original.

References in Text

The Federal Power Act, referred to in text, is Act June 10, 1920, c. 285, 41 Stat. 1063, as amended. Part I of the Federal Power Act is classified generally to subchapter I (section 791a et seq.) of chapter 12 of Title 16, Conservation. For complete classification of this Act to the Code, see section 791a of Title 16 and Tables.

This Act, referred to in subsec. (b)(1), is Pub.L. 94–579, Oct. 21, 1976, 90 Stat. 2743, as amended, known as the Federal Land Policy and Management Act of 1976. For complete classification of this Act to the Code, see Tables.

CROSS REFERENCES

Applicability of right-of-way provisions to other Federal laws, see section 1770 of this title.

CODE OF FEDERAL REGULATIONS

Land uses, see 36 CFR 251.9 et seq.
Principles and procedures, see 43 CFR 2800.0–1 et seq.

§ 1762. Roads [FLPMA § 502]

(a) Authority to acquire, construct, and maintain; financing arrangements

The Secretary, with respect to the public lands, is authorized to provide for the acquisition, construction, and maintenance of roads within and near the public lands in locations and according to specifications which will permit maximum economy in harvesting timber from such lands tributary to such roads and at the same time meet the requirements for protection, development, and management of such lands for utilization of the other resources thereof. Financing of such roads may be accomplished (1) by the Secretary utilizing appropriated funds, (2) by requirements on purchasers of timber and other products from the public lands, including provisions for amortization of road costs in contracts, (3) by cooperative financing with other public agencies and with private agencies or persons, or (4) by a combination of these methods: *Provided*, That, where roads of a higher standard than that needed in the harvesting and removal of the timber and other products covered by the particular sale are to be constructed, the purchaser of timber and other products from public lands shall not, except when the provisions of the second proviso of this subsection apply, be required to bear that part of the costs necessary to meet such higher standard, and the Secretary is authorized to make such arrangements to this end as may be appropriate: *Provided further*, That when timber is offered with the condition that the purchaser thereof will build a road or roads in accordance with standards specified in the offer, the purchaser of the timber will be responsible for paying the full costs of construction of such roads.

(b) Recordation of copies of affected instruments

Copies of all instruments affecting permanent interests in land executed pursuant to this section shall be recorded in each county where the lands are located.

(c) Maintenance or reconstruction of facilities by users

The Secretary may require the user or users of a road, trail, land, or other facility administered by him through the Bureau, including purchasers of Government timber and other products, to maintain such facilities in a satisfactory condition commensurate with the particular use requirements of each. Such maintenance to be borne by each user shall be proportionate to total use. The Secretary may also require the user or users of such a facility to reconstruct the same when such reconstruction is determined to be necessary to accommodate such use. If such maintenance or reconstruction cannot be so provided or if the Secretary determines that maintenance or reconstruction by a user would not be practical, then the Secretary may require that sufficient funds be deposited by the user to provide his portion of such total maintenance or reconstruction. Deposits made to cover the maintenance or reconstruction of roads are hereby made available until expended to cover the cost to the United States of accomplishing the purposes for which deposited: *Provided*, That deposits received for work on adjacent and overlapping areas may be combined when it is the most practicable and efficient manner of performing the work, and cost thereof may be determined by estimates: *And provided further*, That unexpended balances upon accomplishment of the purpose for which deposited shall be transferred to miscellaneous receipts or refunded.

(d) Fund for user fees for delayed payment to grantor

Whenever the agreement under which the United States has obtained for the use of, or in connection with, the public lands a right-of-way or easement for a road or an existing road or the right to use an existing road provides for delayed payments to the Government's grantor, any fees or other collections received by the Secretary for the use of the road may be placed in a fund to be available for making payments to the grantor.

(Oct. 21, 1976, Pub.L. 94–579, Title V, § 502, 90 Stat. 2777.)

§ 1763. Right-of-way corridors; criteria and procedures applicable for designation [FLPMA § 503]

In order to minimize adverse environmental impacts and the proliferation of separate rights-of-way, the utilization of rights-of-way in common shall be required to the extent practical, and each right-of-way or permit shall reserve to the Secretary concerned the right to grant additional rights-of-way or permits for compatible uses on or adjacent to rights-of-way granted pursuant to this Act. In designating right-of-way corridors and in determining whether to require that rights-of-way be confined to them, the Secretary concerned shall take into consideration national and State land use policies, environmental quality, economic efficiency, national security, safety, and good engineering and technological practices. The Secretary concerned shall issue regulations containing the criteria and procedures he will use in designating such corridors. Any existing transportation and utility corridors may be designated as transportation and utility corridors pursuant to this subsection without further review.

(Oct. 21, 1976, Pub.L. 94–579, Title V, § 503, 90 Stat. 2778.)

§ 1764. General requirements [FLPMA § 504]

(a) Boundary specifications; criteria; temporary use of additional lands

The Secretary concerned shall specify the boundaries of each right-of-way as precisely as is practical. Each right-of-way shall be limited to the ground which the Secretary concerned determines (1) will be occupied by facilities which constitute the project for which the right-of-way is granted, issued, or renewed, (2) to be necessary for the operation or maintenance of the project, (3) to be necessary to protect the public safety, and (4) will do no unnecessary damage to the environment. The Secretary concerned may authorize the temporary use of such additional lands as he determines to be reasonably necessary for the construction, operation, maintenance, or termination of the project or a portion thereof, or for access thereto.

(b) Terms and conditions of right-of-way or permit

Each right-of-way or permit granted, issued, or renewed pursuant to this section shall be limited to a reasonable term in light of all circumstances concerning the project. In determining the duration of a right-of-way the Secretary concerned shall, among other things, take into consideration the cost of the facility, its useful life, and any public purpose it serves. The right-of-way shall specify whether it is or is not renewable and the terms and conditions applicable to the renewal.

(c) Applicability of regulations or stipulations

Rights-of-way shall be granted, issued, or renewed pursuant to this subchapter under such regulations or stipulations, consistent with the provisions of this subchapter or any other applicable law, and shall also be subject to such terms and conditions as the Secretary concerned may prescribe regarding extent, duration, survey, location, construction, maintenance, transfer or assignment, and termination.

(d) Submission of plan of construction, operation, and rehabilitation by new project applicants; plan requirements

The Secretary concerned prior to granting or issuing a right-of-way pursuant to this subchapter for a new project which may have a significant impact on the environment, shall require the applicant to submit a plan of construction, operation, and rehabilitation for such right-of-way which shall comply with stipulations or with regulations issued by that Secretary, including the terms and conditions required under section 1765 of this title.

(e) Regulatory requirements for terms and conditions; revision and applicability of regulations

The Secretary concerned shall issue regulations with respect to the terms and conditions that will be included in rights-of-way pursuant to section 1765 of this title. Such regulations shall be regularly revised as needed. Such regulations shall be applicable to every right-of-way granted or issued pursuant to this subchapter and to any subsequent renewal thereof, and may be applicable to rights-of-way not granted or issued, but renewed pursuant to this subchapter.

(f) Removal or use of mineral and vegetative materials

Mineral and vegetative materials, including timber, within or without a right-of-way, may be used or disposed of in connection with construction or other purposes only if authorization to remove or use such materials has been obtained pursuant to applicable laws or for emergency repair work necessary for those rights-of-way authorized under section 1761(c) of this title.

(g) Rental payments; amount, waiver, etc.

The holder of a right-of-way shall pay in advance the fair market value thereof, as determined by the Secretary granting, issuing, or renewing such right-of-way. The Secretary concerned may require either annual payment or a payment covering more than one year at a time except that private individuals may make at their option either annual payments or payments covering more than one year if the annual fee is greater than one hundred dollars. The Secretary concerned may waive rentals where a right-of-way is granted, issued or renewed in consideration of a right-of-way conveyed to the United States in connection with a cooperative cost share program between the United States and the holder. The Secretary concerned may, by regulation or prior to promulgation of such regulations, as a condition of a right-of-way, require an applicant for or holder of a right-of-way to reimburse the United States for all reasonable administrative and other costs incurred in processing an application for such right-of-way and in inspection and monitoring of construction, operation, and termination of the facility pursuant to such right-of-way: *Provided, however,* That the Secretary concerned need not secure reimbursement in any situation where there is in existence a cooperative cost share right-of-way program between the United States and the holder of a right-of-way. Rights-of-way may be granted, issued, or renewed to a Federal, State, or local government or any agency or instrumentality thereof, to nonprofit associations or nonprofit corporations which are not themselves controlled or owned by profitmaking corporations or business enterprises, or to a holder where he provides without or at reduced charges a valuable benefit to the public or to the programs of the Secretary concerned, or to a holder in connection with the authorized use or occupancy of Federal land for which the United States is already receiving compensation for such lesser charge, including free use as the Secretary concerned finds equitable and in the public interest. Such rights-of-way issued at less than fair market value are not assignable except with the approval of the Secretary issuing the right-of-way. The moneys received for reimbursement of reasonable costs shall be deposited with the Treasury in a special account and are hereby authorized to be appropriated and made available until expended. Rights-of-way shall be granted, issued, or renewed, without rental fees, for electric or telephone facilities financed pursuant to the Rural Electrification Act of 1936, as amended [7 U.S.C.A. § 901 et seq.], or any extensions from such facilities: *Provided,* That nothing in this sentence shall be construed to affect the authority of the Secretary granting, issuing, or renewing the right-of-way to require reimbursement of reasonable administrative and other costs pursuant to the second sentence of this subsection.

(h) Liability for damage or injury incurred by United States for use and occupancy of rights-of-way; indemnification of United States; no-fault liability; amount of damages

(1) The Secretary concerned shall promulgate regulations specifying the extent to which holders of rights-of-way under this subchapter shall be liable to the United States for damage or injury incurred by the United States caused by the use and occupancy of the rights-of-way. The regulations shall also specify

the extent to which such holders shall indemnify or hold harmless the United States for liabilities, damages, or claims caused by their use and occupancy of the rights-of-way.

(2) Any regulation or stipulation imposing liability without fault shall include a maximum limitation on damages commensurate with the foreseeable risks or hazards presented. Any liability for damage or injury in excess of this amount shall be determined by ordinary rules of negligence.

(i) Bond or security requirements

Where he deems it appropriate, the Secretary concerned may require a holder of a right-of-way to furnish a bond, or other security, satisfactory to him to secure all or any of the obligations imposed by the terms and conditions of the right-of-way or by any rule or regulation of the Secretary concerned.

(j) Criteria for grant, issue, or renewal of right-of-way

The Secretary concerned shall grant, issue, or renew a right-of-way under this subchapter only when he is satisfied that the applicant has the technical and financial capability to construct the project for which the right-of-way is requested, and in accord with the requirements of this subchapter.

(Oct. 21, 1976, Pub.L. 94–579, Title V, § 504, 90 Stat. 2778; May 25, 1984, Pub.L. 98–300, 98 Stat. 215; Oct. 27, 1986, Pub.L. 99–545, § 2, 100 Stat. 3048.)

§ 1765. Terms and conditions [FLPMA § 505]

Each right-of-way shall contain—

(a) terms and conditions which will (i) carry out the purposes of this Act and rules and regulations issued thereunder; (ii) minimize damage to scenic and esthetic values and fish and wildlife habitat and otherwise protect the environment; (iii) require compliance with applicable air and water quality standards established by or pursuant to applicable Federal or State law; and (iv) require compliance with State standards for public health and safety, environmental protection, and siting, construction, operation, and maintenance of or for rights-of-way for similar purposes if those standards are more stringent than applicable Federal standards; and

(b) such terms and conditions as the Secretary concerned deems necessary to (i) protect Federal property and economic interests; (ii) manage efficiently the lands which are subject to the right-of-way or adjacent thereto and protect the other lawful users of the lands adjacent to or traversed by such right-of-way; (iii) protect lives and property; (iv) protect the interests of individuals living in the general area traversed by the right-of-way who rely on the fish, wildlife, and other biotic resources of the area for subsistence purposes; (v) require location of the right-of-way along a route that will cause least damage to the environment, taking into consideration feasibility and other relevant factors; and (vi) otherwise protect the public interest in the lands traversed by the right-of-way or adjacent thereto.

(Oct. 21, 1976, Pub.L. 94–579, Title V, § 505, 90 Stat. 2780.)

CROSS REFERENCES

Regulatory requirements for terms and conditions, see section 1764 of this title.

§ 1766. Suspension or termination; grounds; procedures applicable [FLPMA § 506]

Abandonment of a right-of-way or noncompliance with any provision of this subchapter, condition of the right-of-way, or applicable rule or regulation of the Secretary concerned may be grounds for suspension or termination of the right-of-way if, after due notice to the holder of the right-of-way and, and[1] with respect to easements, an appropriate administrative proceeding pursuant to section 554 of Title 5, the Secretary concerned determines that any such ground exists and that suspension or termination is justified. No administrative proceeding shall be required where the right-of-way by its terms provides that it terminates on the occurrence of a fixed or agreed-upon condition, event, or time. If the Secretary concerned determines that an immediate temporary suspension of activities within a right-of-way for violation of its terms and conditions is necessary to protect public health or safety or the environment, he may abate such activities prior to an administrative proceeding. Prior to commencing any proceeding to suspend or terminate a right-of-way the Secretary concerned shall give written notice to the holder of the grounds for such action and shall give the holder a reasonable time to resume use of the right-of-way or to comply with this subchapter, condition, rule, or regulation as the case may be. Failure of the holder of the right-of-way to use the right-of-way for the purpose for which it was granted, issued, or renewed, for any continuous five-year period, shall constitute a rebuttable presumption of abandonment of the right-of-way, except that where the failure of the holder to use the right-of-way for the purpose for which it was granted, issued, or renewed for any continuous five-year period is due to circumstances not within the holder's control, the Secretary concerned is not required to commence proceedings to suspend or terminate the right-of-way.

(Oct. 21, 1976, Pub.L. 94–579, Title V, § 506, 90 Stat. 2780.)

[1] So in original.

§ 1767. Rights-of-way for Federal departments and agencies [FLPMA § 507]

(a) The Secretary concerned may provide under applicable provisions of this subchapter for the use of any department or agency of the United States a right-of-way over, upon, under or through the land administered by him, subject to such terms and conditions as he may impose.

(b) Where a right-of-way has been reserved for the use of any department or agency of the United States, the Secretary shall take no action to terminate, or otherwise limit, that use without the consent of the head of such department or agency.

(Oct. 21, 1976, Pub.L. 94–579, Title V, § 507, 90 Stat. 2781.)

CROSS REFERENCES

Federal departments and agencies to use, occupy, and develop public lands only through rights-of-way, see section 1732 of this title.

§ 1768. Conveyance of lands covered by right-of-way; terms and conditions [FLPMA § 508]

If under applicable law the Secretary concerned decides to transfer out of Federal ownership any lands covered in whole or in part by a right-of-way, including a right-of-way granted under the Act of November 16, 1973 (87 Stat. 576; 30 U.S.C. 185), the lands may be conveyed subject to the right-of-way; however, if the Secretary concerned determines that retention of Federal control over the right-of-way is necessary to assure that the purposes of this subchapter will be carried out, the terms and conditions of the right-of-way complied with, or the lands protected, he shall (a) reserve to the United States that portion of the lands which lies within the boundaries of the right-of-way, or (b) convey the lands, including that portion within the boundaries of the right-of-way, subject to the right-of-way and reserving to the United States the right to enforce all or any of the terms and conditions of the right-of-way, including the right to renew it or extend it upon its termination and to collect rents.

(Oct. 21, 1976, Pub.L. 94–579, Title V, § 508, 90 Stat. 2781.)

§ 1769. Existing right-of-way or right-of-use unaffected; exceptions; rights-of-way for railroad and appurtenant communication facilities; applicability of existing terms and conditions [FLPMA § 509]

(a) Nothing in this subchapter shall have the effect of terminating any right-of-way or right-of-use heretofore issued, granted, or permitted. However, with the consent of the holder thereof, the Secretary concerned may cancel such a right-of-way or right-of-use and in its stead issue a right-of-way pursuant to the provisions of this subchapter.

(b) When the Secretary concerned issues a right-of-way under this subchapter for a railroad and appurtenant communication facilities in connection with a realinement[1] of a railroad on lands under his jurisdiction by virtue of a right-of-way granted by the United States, he may, when he considers it to be in the public interest and the lands involved are not within an incorporated community and are of approximately equal value, notwithstanding the provisions of this subchapter, provide in the new right-of-way the same terms and conditions as applied to the portion of the existing right-of-way relinquished to the United States with respect to the payment of annual rental, duration of the right-of-way, and the nature of the interest in lands granted. The Secretary concerned or his delegate shall take final action upon all applications for the grant, issue, or renewal of rights-of-way under subsection (b) of this section no later than six months after receipt from the applicant of all information required from the applicant by this subchapter.

(Oct. 21, 1976, Pub.L. 94–579, Title V, § 509, 90 Stat. 2781.)

[1] So in original. Probably should be "realignment".

§ 1770. Applicability of provisions to other Federal laws [FLPMA § 510]

(a) Right-of-way

Effective on and after October 21, 1976, no right-of-way for the purposes listed in this subchapter shall be granted, issued, or renewed over, upon, under, or through such lands except under and subject to the provisions, limitations, and conditions of this subchapter: *Provided,* That nothing in this subchapter shall be construed as affecting or modifying the provisions of sections 532 to 538 of Title 16 and in the event of conflict with, or inconsistency between, this subchapter and sections 532 to 538 of Title 16, the latter shall prevail: *Provided further,* That nothing in this Act should be construed as making it mandatory that, with respect to forest roads, the Secretary of Agriculture limit rights-of-way grants or their term of years or require disclosure pursuant to section 1761(b) of this title or impose any other condition contemplated by this Act that is contrary to present practices of that Secretary under sections 532 to 538 of Title 16. Any pending application for a right-of-way under any other law on the effective date of this section shall be considered as an application under this subchapter. The Secretary concerned may require the applicant to submit any additional information he deems necessary to comply with the requirements of this subchapter.

(b) Highway use

Nothing in this subchapter shall be construed to preclude the use of lands covered by this subchapter for highway purposes pursuant to sections 107 and 317 of Title 23.

(c) Application of antitrust laws

(1) Nothing in this subchapter shall be construed as exempting any holder of a right-of-way issued under this subchapter from any provision of the antitrust laws of the United States.

(2) For the purposes of this subsection, the term "antitrust laws" includes the Act of July 2, 1890 (26 Stat. 15 U.S.C. 1 et seq.); the Act of October 15, 1914 (38 Stat. 730, 15 U.S.C. 12 et seq.); the Federal Trade Commission Act (38 Stat. 717; 15 U.S.C. 41 et seq.); and sections 73 and 74 of the Act of August 27, 1894 [15 U.S.C.A. §§ 8, 9].

(Oct. 21, 1976, Pub.L. 94–579, Title V, § 510, 90 Stat. 2782.)

§ 1771. Coordination of applications [FLPMA § 511]

Applicants before Federal departments and agencies other than the Department of the Interior or Agriculture seeking a license, certificate, or other authority for a project which involve a right-of-way over, upon, under, or through public land or National Forest System lands must simultaneously apply to the Secretary concerned for the appropriate authority to use public lands or National Forest System lands and submit to the Secretary concerned all information furnished to the other Federal department or agency.

(Oct. 21, 1976, Pub.L. 94–579, Title V, § 511, 90 Stat. 2782.)

SUBCHAPTER VI—DESIGNATED MANAGEMENT AREAS

§ 1781. California Desert Conservation Area [FLPMA § 601]

(a) Congressional findings

The Congress finds that—

(1) the California desert contains historical, scenic, archeological, environmental, biological, cultural, scientific, educational, recreational, and economic resources that are uniquely located adjacent to an area of large population;

(2) the California desert environment is a total ecosystem that is extremely fragile, easily scarred, and slowly healed;

(3) the California desert environment and its resources, including certain rare and endangered species of wildlife, plants, and fishes, and numerous archeological and historic sites, are seriously threatened by air pollution, inadequate Federal management authority, and pressures of increased use, particularly recreational use, which are certain to intensify because of the rapidly growing population of southern California;

(4) the use of all California desert resources can and should be provided for in a multiple use and sustained yield management plant[1] to conserve these resources for future generations, and to provide present and future use and enjoyment, particularly outdoor recreation uses, including the use, where appropriate, of off-road recreational vehicles;

(5) the Secretary has initiated a comprehensive planning process and established an interim management program for the public lands in the California desert; and

(6) to insure further study of the relationship of man and the California desert environment, preserve the unique and irreplaceable resources, including archeological values, and conserve the use of the economic resources of the California desert, the public must be provided more opportunity to participate in such planning and management, and additional management authority must be provided to the Secretary to facilitate effective implementation of such planning and management.

(b) Statement of purpose

It is the purpose of this section to provide for the immediate and future protection and administration of the public lands in the California desert within the framework of a program of multiple use and sustained yield, and the maintenance of environmental quality.

(c) Description of Area

(1) For the purpose of this section, the term "California desert" means the area generally depicted on a map entitled "California Desert Conservation Area—Proposed" dated April 1974, and described as provided in subsection (c)(2) of this section.

(2) As soon as practicable after October 21, 1976, the Secretary shall file a revised map and a legal description of the California Desert Conservation Area with the Committees on Interior and Insular Affairs of the United States Senate and the House of Representatives, and such map and description shall have the same force and effect as if included in this Act. Correction of clerical and typographical errors in such legal description and a map may be made by the Secretary. To the extent practicable, the Secretary shall make such legal description and map available to the public promptly upon request.

(d) Preparation and implementation of comprehensive long-range plan for management, use, etc.

The Secretary, in accordance with section 1712 of this title, shall prepare and implement a comprehensive, long-range plan for the management, use, development, and protection of the public lands within the California Desert Conservation Area. Such plan shall take into account the principles of multiple use and sustained yield in providing for resource use and development, including, but not limited to, maintenance of environmental quality, rights-of-way, and mineral development. Such plan shall be completed and implementation thereof initiated on or before September 30, 1980.

(e) Interim program for management, use, etc.

During the period beginning on October 21, 1976, and ending on the effective date of implementation of the comprehensive, long-range plan, the Secretary shall execute an interim program to manage, use, and protect the public lands, and their resources now in danger of destruction, in the California Desert Conservation Area, to provide for the public use of such lands in an orderly and reasonable manner such as through the development of campgrounds and visitor centers, and to provide for a uniformed desert ranger force.

(f) Applicability of mining laws

Subject to valid existing rights, nothing in this Act shall affect the applicability of the United States mining laws on the public lands within the California Desert Conservation Area, except that all mining claims located on public lands within the California Desert Conservation Area shall be subject to such reasonable regulations as the Secretary may prescribe to effectuate the purposes of this section. Any patent issued on any such mining claim shall recite this limitation and continue to be subject to such regulations. Such regulations shall provide for such measures as may be reasonable to protect the scenic, scientific, and environmental values of the public lands of the California Desert Conservation Area against undue impairment, and to assure against pollution of the streams and waters within the California Desert Conservation Area.

(g) Advisory Committee; establishment; functions

(1) The Secretary, within sixty days after October 21, 1976, shall establish a California Desert Conservation Area Advisory Committee (hereinafter referred to as "advisory committee") in accordance with the provisions of section 1739 of this title.

(2) It shall be the function of the advisory committee to advise the Secretary with respect to the preparation and implementation of the comprehensive, long-range plan required under subsection (d) of this section.

(h) Management of lands under jurisdiction of Secretary of Agriculture and Secretary of Defense

The Secretary of Agriculture and the Secretary of Defense shall manage lands within their respective jurisdictions located in or adjacent to the California Desert Conservation Area, in accordance with the laws relating to such lands and wherever practicable, in a manner consonant with the purpose of this section. The Secretary, the Secretary of Agriculture, and the Secretary of Defense are authorized and directed to consult among themselves and take cooperative actions to carry out the provisions of this subsection, including a program of law enforcement in accordance with applicable authorities to protect the archeological and other values of the California Desert Conservation Area and adjacent lands.

(i) Annual report; contents

The Secretary shall report to the Congress no later than two years after October 21, 1976, and annually thereafter, on the progress in, and any problems concerning, the implementation of this section, together with any recommendations, which he may deem necessary, to remedy such problems.

(j) Authorization of appropriations

There are authorized to be appropriated for fiscal years 1977 through 1981 not to exceed $40,000,000 for the purpose of this section, such amount to remain available until expended.

(Oct. 21, 1976, Pub.L. 94–579, Title VI, § 601, 90 Stat. 2782.)

[1] So in original. Probably should be "plan".

Change of Name

Any reference in any provision of law enacted before Jan. 4, 1995, to the Committee on Natural Resources of the House of Representatives treated as referring to the Committee on Resources of the House of Representatives, see section 1(a)(8) of Pub.L. 104–14, set out as a note preceding section 21 of Title 2, The Congress.

Committee on Interior and Insular Affairs of the House of Representatives changed to Committee on Natural Resources of the House of Representatives on Jan. 5, 1993, by House Resolution No. 5, One Hundred Third Congress.

Desert Lily Sanctuary

Pub.L. 103–433, Title I, § 107, Oct. 31, 1994, 108 Stat. 4483, provided that:

"**(a) Designation.**—There is hereby established the Desert Lily Sanctuary within the California Desert Conservation Area, California, of the Bureau of Land Management, comprising approximately two thousand forty acres, as generally depicted on a map entitled 'Desert Lily Sanctuary', dated February 1986. The Secretary shall administer the area to provide maximum protection to the desert lily.

"**(b) Withdrawal.**—Subject to valid existing rights, all Federal lands within the Desert Lily Sanctuary are hereby withdrawn from all forms of entry, appropriation, or disposal under the public land laws; from location, entry, and patent under the United States mining laws;

and from disposition under all laws pertaining to mineral and geothermal leasing, and mineral materials, and all amendments thereto."

Dinosaur Trackway Area of Critical Environmental Concern

Pub.L. 103–433, Title I, § 108, Oct. 31, 1994, 108 Stat. 4483, provided that:

"**(a) Designation.**—There is hereby established the Dinosaur Trackway Area of Critical Environmental Concern within the California Desert Conservation Area, of the Bureau of Land Management, comprising approximately five hundred and ninety acres as generally depicted on a map entitled 'Dinosaur Trackway Area of Critical Environmental Concern', dated July 1993. The Secretary shall administer the area to preserve the paleontological resources within the area.

"**(b) Withdrawal.**—Subject to valid existing rights, the Federal lands within and adjacent to the Dinosaur Trackway Area of Critical Environmental Concern, as generally depicted on a map entitled 'Dinosaur Trackway Mineral Withdrawal Area', dated July 1993, are hereby withdrawn from all forms of entry, appropriation, or disposal under the public land laws; from location, entry, and patent under the United States mining laws; and from disposition under all laws pertaining to mineral and geothermal leasing, and mineral materials, and all amendments thereto."

CROSS REFERENCES

Locators or claimants under Mining Law of 1872, impairment of claims of, see section 1732 of this title.

Uniformed desert ranger force in California Desert Conservation Area; establishment; enforcement of Federal laws and regulations, see section 1733 of this title.

§ 1782. Bureau of Land Management Wilderness Study [FLPMA § 603]

(a) Lands subject to review and designation as wilderness

Within fifteen years after October 21, 1976, the Secretary shall review those roadless areas of five thousand acres or more and roadless islands of the public lands, identified during the inventory required by section 1711(a) of this title as having wilderness characteristics described in the Wilderness Act of September 3, 1964 (78 Stat. 890; 16 U.S.C. 1131 et seq.) and shall from time to time report to the President his recommendation as to the suitability or nonsuitability of each such area or island for preservation as wilderness: *Provided*, That prior to any recommendations for the designation of an area as wilderness the Secretary shall cause mineral surveys to be conducted by the United States Geological Survey and the United States Bureau of Mines to determine the mineral values, if any, that may be present in such areas: *Provided further*, That the Secretary shall report to the President by July 1, 1980, his recommendations on those areas which the Secretary has prior to November 1, 1975, formally identified as natural or primitive areas. The review required by this subsection shall be conducted in accordance with the procedure specified in section 3(d) of the Wilderness Act [16 U.S.C.A. § 1132(d)].

(b) Presidential recommendation for designation as wilderness

The President shall advise the President of the Senate and the Speaker of the House of Representatives of his recommendations with respect to designation as wilderness of each such area, together with a map thereof and a definition of its boundaries. Such advice by the President shall be given within two years of the receipt of each report from the Secretary. A recommendation of the President for designation as wilderness shall become effective only if so provided by an Act of Congress.

(c) Status of lands during period of review and determination

During the period of review of such areas and until Congress has determined otherwise, the Secretary shall continue to manage such lands according to his authority under this Act and other applicable law in a manner so as not to impair the suitability of such areas for preservation as wilderness, subject, however, to the continuation of existing mining and grazing uses and mineral leasing in the manner and degree in which the same was being conducted on October 21, 1976: *Provided*, That, in managing the public lands the Secretary shall by regulation or otherwise take any action required to prevent unnecessary or undue degradation of the lands and their resources or to afford environmental protection. Unless previously withdrawn from appropriation under the mining laws, such lands shall continue to be subject to such appropriation during the period of review unless withdrawn by the Secretary under the procedures of section 1714 of this title for reasons other than preservation of their wilderness character. Once an area has been designated for preservation as wilderness, the provisions of the Wilderness Act [16 U.S.C.A. § 1131 et seq.] which apply to national forest wilderness areas shall apply with respect to the administration and use of such designated area, including mineral surveys required by section 4(d)(2) of the Wilderness Act [16 U.S.C.A. § 1133(d)(2)], and mineral development, access, exchange of lands, and ingress and egress for mining claimants and occupants.

(Oct. 21, 1976, Pub.L. 94–579, Title VI, § 603, 90 Stat. 2785; Pub.L. 102–154, Title I, Nov. 13, 1991, 105 Stat. 1000; Pub.L. 102–285, § 10, May 18, 1992, 106 Stat. 171.)

Change of Name

Pub.L. 102–285, § 10(a), May 18, 1992, 106 Stat. 171, redesignated the Geological Survey and provided that on and after May 18, 1992, it shall be known as the United States Geological Survey. An earlier statute [Pub.L. 102–154, Title I, Nov. 13, 1991, 105 Stat. 1000] had provided for the identical change of name effective on and after Nov. 13, 1991. See note under section 31 of Title 43, Public Lands.

Pub.L. 102–285, §10(b), May 18, 1992, 106 Stat. 172, provided that, on and after May 18, 1992, the Bureau of Mines is redesignated and shall thereafter be known as the United States Bureau of Mines. See note under section 1 of Title 30, Mineral Lands and Mining.

CROSS REFERENCES

Lands in Alaska; designation as wilderness, see section 1784 of this title.
Locators or claimants under Mining Law of 1872, impairment of claims of, see section 1732 of this title.
National Petroleum Reserve in Alaska, competitive leasing of oil and gas, application of this section, see section 6508 of Title 42, The Public Health and Welfare.
Navajo and Hopi tribes, settlement of rights and interests, application of this section, see section 640d–26 of Title 25, Indians.
Snake River Birds of Prey National Conservation Area, release from wilderness designation and management, see 16 USCA § 460iii–5.
Wilderness defined, see section 1702 of this title.

CODE OF FEDERAL REGULATIONS

Mining claims, see 43 CFR 3802.0–1 et seq.

LIBRARY REFERENCES

Public Lands ⚷96.
C.J.S. Public Lands § 168.

§ 1783. Yaquina Head Outstanding Natural Area

(a) Establishment

In order to protect the unique scenic, scientific, educational, and recreational values of certain lands in and around Yaquina Head, in Lincoln County, Oregon, there is hereby established, subject to valid existing rights, the Yaquina Head Outstanding Natural Area (hereinafter referred to as the "area"). The boundaries of the area are those shown on the map entitled "Yaquina Head Area", dated July 1979, which shall be on file and available for public inspection in the Office of the Director, Bureau of Land Management, United States Department of the Interior, and the State Office of the Bureau of Land Management in the State of Oregon.

(b) Administration by Secretary of the Interior; management plan; quarrying permits

(1) The Secretary of the Interior (hereinafter referred to as the "Secretary") shall administer the Yaquina Head Outstanding Natural Area in accordance with the laws and regulations applicable to the public lands as defined in section 103(e) of the Federal Land Policy and Management Act of 1976, as amended (43 U.S.C. 1702) [43 U.S.C.A. § 1702(e)], in such a manner as will best provide for—

(A) the conservation and development of the scenic, natural, and historic values of the area;

(B) the continued use of the area for purposes of education, scientific study, and public recreation which do not substantially impair the purposes for which the area is established; and

(C) protection of the wildlife habitat of the area.

(2) The Secretary shall develop a management plan for the area which accomplishes the purposes and is consistent with the provisions of this section. This plan shall be developed in accordance with the provisions of section 202 of the Federal Land Policy and Management Act of 1976, as amended (43 U.S.C. 1712).

(3) Notwithstanding any other provision of this section, the Secretary is authorized to issue permits or to contract for the quarrying of materials from the area in accordance with the management plan for the area on condition that the lands be reclaimed and restored to the satisfaction of the Secretary. Such authorization to quarry shall require payment of fair market value for the materials to be quarried, as established by the Secretary, and shall also include any terms and conditions which the Secretary determines necessary to protect the values of such quarry lands for purposes of this section.

(c) Revocation of 1866 reservation of lands for lighthouse purposes; restoration to public lands status

The reservation of lands for lighthouse purposes made by Executive order of June 8, 1866, of certain lands totaling approximately 18.1 acres, as depicted on the map referred to in subsection (a) of this section, is hereby revoked. The lands referred to in subsection (a) of this section are hereby restored to the status of public lands as defined in section 103(e) of the Federal Land Policy and Management Act of 1976, as amended (43 U.S.C. 1702) [43 U.S.C.A. § 1702(e)], and shall be administered in accordance with the management plan for the area developed pursuant to subsection (b) of this section, except that such lands are hereby withdrawn from settlement, sale, location, or entry, under the public land laws, including the mining laws (30 U.S.C., ch. 2), leasing under the mineral leasing laws (30 U.S.C. 181 et seq.), and disposals under the Materials Act of July 31, 1947, as amended (30 U.S.C. 601, 602) [43 U.S.C.A. § 601 et seq.].

(d) Acquisition of lands not already in Federal ownership

The Secretary shall, as soon as possible but in no event later than twenty-four months following March 5, 1980, acquire by purchase, exchange, donation, or condemnation all or any part of the lands and waters and interests in lands and waters within the area referred to in subsection (a) of this section which are not in Federal ownership except that State land shall not be acquired by purchase or condemnation. Any lands or interests acquired by the Secretary pursuant to this section shall become public lands as defined in the Federal Land Policy and Management Act of 1976, as amended [43 U.S.C.A. § 1701 et seq.]. Upon acquisition by the United States, such lands are automatically withdrawn under the provisions of subsection (c) of this section except that lands affected by quarrying operations in the area shall be subject to disposals under the Materials Act of July 31, 1947, as amended (30 U.S.C. 601, 602) [30 U.S.C.A. § 601 et seq.]. Any lands acquired pursuant to this subsection shall be administered in accordance with the management plan for the area developed pursuant to subsection (b) of this section.

(e) Wind energy research

The Secretary is authorized to conduct a study relating to the use of lands in the area for purposes of wind energy research. If the Secretary determines after such study that the conduct of wind energy research activity will not substantially impair the values of the lands in the area for purposes of this section, the Secretary is further authorized to issue permits for the use of such lands as a site for installation and field testing of an experimental wind turbine generating system. Any permit issued pursuant to this subsection shall contain such terms and conditions as the Secretary determines necessary to protect the values of such lands for purposes of this section.

(f) Reclamation and restoration of lands affected by quarrying operations

The Secretary shall develop and administer, in addition to any requirements imposed pursuant to subsection (b)(3) of this section, a program for the reclamation and restoration of all lands affected by quarrying operations in the area acquired pursuant to subsection (d) of this section. All revenues received by the United States in connection with quarrying operations authorized by subsection (b)(3) of this section shall be deposited in a separate fund account which shall be established by the Secretary of the Treasury. Such revenues are hereby authorized to be appropriated to the Secretary as needed for reclamation and restoration of any lands acquired pursuant to subsection (d) of this section. After completion of such reclamation and restoration to the satisfaction of the Secretary, any unexpended revenues in such fund shall be returned to the general fund of the United States Treasury.

(g) Authorization of appropriations

There are hereby authorized to be appropriated in addition to that authorized by subsection (f) of this section, such sums as may be necessary to carry out the provisions of this section.

(Mar. 5, 1980, Pub.L. 96–199, Title I, § 119, 94 Stat. 71.)

Codification

Section was not enacted as part of the Federal Land Policy and Management Act of 1976 which enacted this chapter.

§ 1784. Lands in Alaska; designation as wilderness; management by Bureau of Land Management pending Congressional action

Notwithstanding any other provision of law, section 1782 of this title shall not apply to any lands in Alaska. However, in carrying out his duties under sections 1711 and 1712 of this title and other applicable laws, the Secretary may identify areas in Alaska which he determines are suitable as wilderness and may, from time to time, make recommendations to the Congress for inclusion of any such areas in the National Wilderness Preservation System, pursuant to the provisions of the Wilderness Act [16 U.S.C.A. § 1131 et seq.]. In the absence of congressional action relating to any such recommendation of the Secretary, the Bureau of Land Management shall manage all such areas which are within its jurisdiction in accordance with the applicable land use plans and applicable provisions of law.

(Dec. 2, 1980, Pub.L. 96–487, Title XIII, § 1320, 94 Stat. 2487.)

Codification

Section was enacted as part of the Alaska National Interest Lands Conservation Act and not as part of the Federal Land Policy and Management Act of 1976, which comprises this chapter.

LIBRARY REFERENCES

Public Lands ⟹49.
C.J.S. Public Lands § 58 et seq.

APPENDIX A

OCCUPATIONAL SAFETY AND HEALTH ACT

(Selections From 29 U.S.C.A. § 651 et seq.)

CHAPTER 15

OCCUPATIONAL SAFETY AND HEALTH

Table of Contents

Sec.
651. Congressional statement of findings and declaration of purpose and policy.
652. Definitions.
* * *
654. Duties of employers and employees.
655. Standards.
(a) Promulgation by Secretary of national consensus standards and established Federal standards; time for promulgation; conflicting standards.
(b) Procedure for promulgation, modification, or revocation of standards.
(c) Emergency temporary standards.
(d) Variances from standards; procedure.
(e) Statement of reasons for Secretary's determinations; publication in Federal Register.
(f) Judicial review.
(g) Priority for establishment of standards.
* * *
657. Inspections, investigations, and recordkeeping.
(a) Authority of Secretary to enter, inspect, and investigate places of employment; time and manner.
(b) Attendance and testimony of witnesses and production of evidence; enforcement of subpoena.
(c) Maintenance, preservation, and availability of records; issuance of regulations; scope of records; periodic inspections by employer; posting of notices by employer; notification of employee of corrective action.
(d) Obtaining of information.
(e) Employer and authorized employee representatives to accompany Secretary or his authorized representative on inspection of workplace; consultation with employees where no authorized employee representative is present.
(f) Request for inspection by employees or representative of employees; grounds; procedure; determination of request; notification of Secretary or representative prior to or during any inspection of violations; procedure for review of refusal by representative of Secretary to issue citation for alleged violations.
(g) Compilation, analysis, and publication of reports and information; rules and regulations.

Sec.

658. Citations.
  (a) Authority to issue; grounds; contents; notice in lieu of citation for de minimis violations.
  (b) Posting.
  (c) Time for issuance.
659. Enforcement procedures.
  (a) Notification of employer of proposed assessment of penalty subsequent to issuance of citation; time for notification of Secretary by employer of contest by employer of citation or proposed assessment; citation and proposed assessment as final order upon failure of employer to notify of contest and failure of employees to file notice.
  (b) Notification of employer of failure to correct in allotted time period violation for which citation was issued and proposed assessment of penalty for failure to correct; time for notification of Secretary by employer of contest by employer of notification of failure to correct or proposed assessment; notification or proposed assessment as final order upon failure of employer to notify of contest.
  (c) Advisement of Commission by Secretary of notification of contest by employer of citation or notification or of filing of notice by any employee or representative of employees; hearing by Commission; orders of Commission and Secretary; rules of procedure.
660. Judicial review.
  (a) Filing of petition by persons adversely affected or aggrieved; orders subject to review; jurisdiction; venue; procedure; conclusiveness of record and findings of Commission; appropriate relief; finality of judgment.
  (b) Filing of petition by Secretary; orders subject to review; jurisdiction; venue; procedure; conclusiveness of record and findings of Commission; enforcement of orders; contempt proceedings.
  (c) Discharge or discrimination against employee for exercise of rights under this chapter; prohibition; procedure for relief.
661. Occupational Safety and Health Review Commission.
  (a) Establishment; membership; appointment; Chairman.
  (b) Terms of office; removal by President.
  (c) Omitted.
  (d) Principal office; hearings or other proceedings at other places.
  (e) Functions and duties of Chairman; appointment and compensation of administrative law judges and other employees.
  (f) Quorum; official action.
  (g) Hearings and records open to public; promulgation of rules; applicability of Federal Rules of Civil Procedure.
  (h) Depositions and production of documentary evidence; fees.
  (i) Investigatory powers.
  (j) Administrative law judges; determination; report as final order of Commission.
  (k) Appointment and compensation of administrative law judges.
662. Injunction proceedings.
  (a) Petition by Secretary to restrain imminent dangers; scope of order.
  (b) Appropriate injunctive relief or temporary restraining order pending outcome of enforcement proceeding; applicability of Rule 65 of Federal Rules of Civil Procedure.
  (c) Notification of affected employees and employers by inspector of danger and of recommendation to Secretary to seek relief.
  (d) Failure of Secretary to seek relief; writ of mandamus.
663. Representation in civil litigation.
664. Disclosure of trade secrets; protective orders.

Sec.
665. Variations, tolerances, and exemptions from required provisions; procedure; duration.
666. Civil and criminal penalties.
(a) Willful or repeated violation.
(b) Citation for serious violation.
(c) Citation for violation determined not serious.
(d) Failure to correct violation.
(e) Willful violation causing death to employee.
(f) Giving advance notice of inspection.
(g) False statements, representations or certification.
(h) Omitted.
(i) Violation of posting requirements.
(j) Authority of Commission to assess civil penalties.
(k) Determination of serious violation.
(*l*) Procedure for payment of civil penalties.
667. State jurisdiction and plans.
(a) Assertion of State standards in absence of applicable Federal standards.
(b) Submission of State plan for development and enforcement of State standards to preempt applicable Federal standards.
(c) Conditions for approval of plan.
(d) Rejection of plan; notice and opportunity for hearing.
(e) Discretion of Secretary to exercise authority over comparable standards subsequent to approval of State plan; duration; retention of jurisdiction by Secretary upon determination of enforcement of plan by State.
(f) Continuing evaluation by Secretary of State enforcement of approved plan; withdrawal of approval of plan by Secretary; grounds; procedure; conditions for retention of jurisdiction by State.
(g) Judicial review of Secretary's withdrawal of approval or rejection of plan; jurisdiction; venue; procedure; appropriate relief; finality of judgment.
(h) Temporary enforcement of State standards.
* * *

---

§ 651. Congressional statement of findings and declaration of purpose and policy

(a)[1] The Congress finds that personal injuries and illnesses arising out of work situations impose a substantial burden upon, and are a hindrance to, interstate commerce in terms of lost production, wage loss, medical expenses, and disability compensation payments.

(b) The Congress declares it to be its purpose and policy, through the exercise of its powers to regulate commerce among the several States and with foreign nations and to provide for the general welfare, to assure so far as possible every working man and woman in the Nation safe and healthful working conditions and to preserve our human resources—

(1) by encouraging employers and employees in their efforts to reduce the number of occupational safety and health hazards at their

1. Section was enacted without subsec. (a) designation, which has been supplied editorially.

places of employment, and to stimulate employers and employees to institute new and to perfect existing programs for providing safe and healthful working conditions;

(2) by providing that employers and employees have separate but dependent responsibilities and rights with respect to achieving safe and healthful working conditions;

(3) by authorizing the Secretary of Labor to set mandatory occupational safety and health standards applicable to businesses affecting interstate commerce, and by creating an Occupational Safety and Health Review Commission for carrying out adjudicatory functions under this chapter;

(4) by building upon advances already made through employer and employee initiative for providing safe and healthful working conditions;

(5) by providing for research in the field of occupational safety and health, including the psychological factors involved, and by developing innovative methods, techniques, and approaches for dealing with occupational safety and health problems;

(6) by exploring ways to discover latent diseases, establishing causal connections between diseases and work in environmental conditions, and conducting other research relating to health problems, in recognition of the fact that occupational health standards present problems often different from those involved in occupational safety;

(7) by providing medical criteria which will assure insofar as practicable that no employee will suffer diminished health, functional capacity, or life expectancy as a result of his work experience;

(8) by providing for training programs to increase the number and competence of personnel engaged in the field of occupational safety and health;

(9) by providing for the development and promulgation of occupational safety and health standards;

(10) by providing an effective enforcement program which shall include a prohibition against giving advance notice of any inspection and sanctions for any individual violating this prohibition;

(11) by encouraging the States to assume the fullest responsibility for the administration and enforcement of their occupational safety and health laws by providing grants to the States to assist in identifying their needs and responsibilities in the area of occupational safety and health, to develop plans in accordance with the provisions of this chapter, to improve the administration and enforcement of State occupational safety and health laws, and to conduct experimental and demonstration projects in connection therewith;

(12) by providing for appropriate reporting procedures with respect to occupational safety and health which procedures will help achieve the objectives of this chapter and accurately describe the nature of the occupational safety and health problems;

(13) by encouraging joint labor-management efforts to reduce injuries and disease arising out of employment.

Pub.L. 91–596, § 2, Dec. 29, 1970, 84 Stat. 1590.

§ 652. Definitions

For the purposes of this chapter—

(1) The term "Secretary" mean [1] the Secretary of Labor.

(2) The term "Commission" means the Occupational Safety and Health Review Commission established under this chapter.

(3) The term "commerce" means trade, traffic, commerce, transportation, or communication among the several States, or between a State and any place outside thereof, or within the District of Columbia, or a possession of the United States (other than the Trust Territory of the Pacific Islands), or between points in the same State but through a point outside thereof.

(4) The term "person" means one or more individuals, partnerships, associations, corporations, business trusts, legal representatives, or any organized group of persons.

(5) The term "employer" means a person engaged in a business affecting commerce who has employees, but does not include the United States or any State or political subdivision of a State.

(6) The term "employee" means an employee of an employer who is employed in a business of his employer which affects commerce.

(7) The term "State" includes a State of the United States, the District of Columbia, Puerto Rico, the Virgin Islands, American Samoa, Guam, and the Trust Territory of the Pacific Islands.

(8) The term "occupational safety and health standard" means a standard which requires conditions, or the adoption or use of one or more practices, means, methods, operations, or processes, reasonably necessary or appropriate to provide safe or healthful employment and places of employment.

(9) The term "national consensus standard" means any occupational safety and health standard or modification thereof which (1) has been adopted and promulgated by a nationally recognized standards-producing organization under procedures whereby it can be determined by the Secretary that persons interested and affected by the scope or provisions of the standard have reached substantial agreement on its adoption, (2) was formulated in a manner which afforded an opportunity for diverse views to be considered and (3) has been designated as such a standard by the Secretary, after consultation with other appropriate Federal agencies.

(10) The term "established Federal standard" means any operative occupational safety and health standard established by any agency of

1. So in original. Probably should be "means".

the United States and presently in effect, or contained in any Act of Congress in force on December 29, 1970.

(11) The term "Committee" means the National Advisory Committee on Occupational Safety and Health established under this chapter.

(12) The term "Director" means the Director of the National Institute for Occupational Safety and Health.

(13) The term "Institute" means the National Institute for Occupational Safety and Health established under this chapter.

(14) The term "Workmen's Compensation Commission" means the National Commission on State Workmen's Compensation Laws established under this chapter.

Pub.L. 91–596, § 3, Dec. 29, 1970, 84 Stat. 1591.

* * *

§ 654. Duties of employers and employees

(a) Each employer—

(1) shall furnish to each of his employees employment and a place of employment which are free from recognized hazards that are causing or are likely to cause death or serious physical harm to his employees;

(2) shall comply with occupational safety and health standards promulgated under this chapter.

(b) Each employee shall comply with occupational safety and health standards and all rules, regulations, and orders issued pursuant to this chapter which are applicable to his own actions and conduct.

Pub.L. 91–596, § 5, Dec. 29, 1970, 84 Stat. 1593.

§ 655. Standards

(a) Promulgation by Secretary of National Consensus Standards and Established Federal Standards; Time for Promulgation; Conflicting Standards. Without regard to chapter 5 of Title 5 or to the other subsections of this section, the Secretary shall, as soon as practicable during the period beginning with the effective date of this chapter and ending two years after such date, by rule promulgate as an occupational safety or health standard any national consensus standard, and any established Federal standard, unless he determines that the promulgation of such a standard would not result in improved safety or health for specifically designated employees. In the event of conflict among any such standards, the Secretary shall promulgate the standard which assures the greatest protection of the safety or health of the affected employees.

(b) Procedure for Promulgation, Modification, or Revocation of Standards. The Secretary may by rule promulgate, modify, or revoke any occupational safety or health standard in the following manner:

(1) Whenever the Secretary, upon the basis of information submitted to him in writing by an interested person, a representative of any organization of employers or employees, a nationally recognized stan-

dards-producing organization, the Secretary of Health and Human Services, the National Institute for Occupational Safety and Health, or a State or political subdivision, or on the basis of information developed by the Secretary or otherwise available to him, determines that a rule should be promulgated in order to serve the objectives of this chapter, the Secretary may request the recommendations of an advisory committee appointed under section 656 of this title. The Secretary shall provide such an advisory committee with any proposals of his own or of the Secretary of Health and Human Services, together with all pertinent factual information developed by the Secretary or the Secretary of Health and Human Services, or otherwise available, including the results of research, demonstrations, and experiments. An advisory committee shall submit to the Secretary its recommendations regarding the rule to be promulgated within ninety days from the date of its appointment or within such longer or shorter period as may be prescribed by the Secretary, but in no event for a period which is longer than two hundred and seventy days.

(2) The Secretary shall publish a proposed rule promulgating, modifying, or revoking an occupational safety or health standard in the Federal Register and shall afford interested persons a period of thirty days after publication to submit written data or comments. Where an advisory committee is appointed and the Secretary determines that a rule should be issued, he shall publish the proposed rule within sixty days after the submission of the advisory committee's recommendations or the expiration of the period prescribed by the Secretary for such submission.

(3) On or before the last day of the period provided for the submission of written data or comments under paragraph (2), any interested person may file with the Secretary written objections to the proposed rule, stating the grounds therefor and requesting a public hearing on such objections. Within thirty days after the last day for filing such objections, the Secretary shall publish in the Federal Register a notice specifying the occupational safety or health standard to which objections have been filed and a hearing requested, and specifying a time and place for such hearing.

(4) Within sixty days after the expiration of the period provided for the submission of written data or comments under paragraph (2), or within sixty days after the completion of any hearing held under paragraph (3), the Secretary shall issue a rule promulgating, modifying, or revoking an occupational safety or health standard or make a determination that a rule should not be issued. Such a rule may contain a provision delaying its effective date for such period (not in excess of ninety days) as the Secretary determines may be necessary to insure that affected employers and employees will be informed of the existence of the standard and of its terms and that employers affected are given an opportunity to familiarize themselves and their employees with the existence of the requirements of the standard.

(5) The Secretary, in promulgating standards dealing with toxic materials or harmful physical agents under this subsection, shall set the standard which most adequately assures, to the extent feasible, on the basis of the best available evidence, that no employee will suffer material impairment of health or functional capacity even if such employee has regular exposure to the hazard dealt with by such standard for the period of his working life. Development of standards under this subsection shall be based upon research, demonstrations, experiments, and such other information as may be appropriate. In addition to the attainment of the highest degree of health and safety protection for the employee, other considerations shall be the latest available scientific data in the field, the feasibility of the standards, and experience gained under this and other health and safety laws. Whenever practicable, the standard promulgated shall be expressed in terms of objective criteria and of the performance desired.

(6)(A) Any employer may apply to the Secretary for a temporary order granting a variance from a standard or any provision thereof promulgated under this section. Such temporary order shall be granted only if the employer files an application which meets the requirements of clause (B) and establishes that (i) he is unable to comply with a standard by its effective date because of unavailability of professional or technical personnel or of materials and equipment needed to come into compliance with the standard or because necessary construction or alteration of facilities cannot be completed by the effective date, (ii) he is taking all available steps to safeguard his employees against the hazards covered by the standard, and (iii) he has an effective program for coming into compliance with the standard as quickly as practicable. Any temporary order issued under this paragraph shall prescribe the practices, means, methods, operations, and processes which the employer must adopt and use while the order is in effect and state in detail his program for coming into compliance with the standard. Such a temporary order may be granted only after notice to employees and an opportunity for a hearing: *Provided,* That the Secretary may issue one interim order to be effective until a decision is made on the basis of the hearing. No temporary order may be in effect for longer than the period needed by the employer to achieve compliance with the standard or one year, whichever is shorter, except that such an order may be renewed not more than twice (I) so long as the requirements of this paragraph are met and (II) if an application for renewal is filed at least 90 days prior to the expiration date of the order. No interim renewal of an order may remain in effect for longer than 180 days.

(B) An application for a temporary order under this paragraph (6) shall contain:

(i) a specification of the standard or portion thereof from which the employer seeks a variance,

(ii) a representation by the employer, supported by representations from qualified persons having firsthand knowledge of the facts represented, that he is unable to comply with the standard or portion thereof and a detailed statement of the reasons therefor,

(iii) a statement of the steps he has taken and will take (with specific dates) to protect employees against the hazard covered by the standard,

(iv) a statement of when he expects to be able to comply with the standard and what steps he has taken and what steps he will take (with dates specified) to come into compliance with the standard, and

(v) a certification that he has informed his employees of the application by giving a copy thereof to their authorized representative, posting a statement giving a summary of the application and specifying where a copy may be examined at the place or places where notices to employees are normally posted, and by other appropriate means.

A description of how employees have been informed shall be contained in the certification. The information to employees shall also inform them of their right to petition the Secretary for a hearing.

(C) The Secretary is authorized to grant a variance from any standard or portion thereof whenever he determines, or the Secretary of Health and Human Services certifies, that such variance is necessary to permit an employer to participate in an experiment approved by him or the Secretary of Health and Human Services designed to demonstrate or validate new and improved techniques to safeguard the health or safety of workers.

(7) Any standard promulgated under this subsection shall prescribe the use of labels or other appropriate forms of warning as are necessary to insure that employees are apprised of all hazards to which they are exposed, relevant symptoms and appropriate emergency treatment, and proper conditions and precautions of safe use or exposure. Where appropriate, such standard shall also prescribe suitable protective equipment and control or technological procedures to be used in connection with such hazards and shall provide for monitoring or measuring employee exposure at such locations and intervals, and in such manner as may be necessary for the protection of employees. In addition, where appropriate, any such standard shall prescribe the type and frequency of medical examinations or other tests which shall be made available, by the employer or at his cost, to employees exposed to such hazards in order to most effectively determine whether the health of such employees is adversely affected by such exposure. In the event such medical examinations are in the nature of research, as determined by the Secretary of Health and Human Services, such examinations may be furnished at the expense of the Secretary of Health and Human Services. The results of such examinations or tests shall be furnished only to the Secretary or the Secretary of Health and Human Services, and, at the request of the employee, to his physician. The Secretary, in consultation with the Secretary of Health and Human Services, may by rule promulgated pursuant to section 553 of Title 5, make appropriate

modifications in the foregoing requirements relating to the use of labels or other forms of warning, monitoring or measuring, and medical examinations, as may be warranted by experience, information, or medical or technological developments acquired subsequent to the promulgation of the relevant standard.

(8) Whenever a rule promulgated by the Secretary differs substantially from an existing national consensus standard, the Secretary shall, at the same time, publish in the Federal Register a statement of the reasons why the rule as adopted will better effectuate the purposes of this chapter than the national consensus standard.

(c)(1) Emergency Temporary Standards. The Secretary shall provide, without regard to the requirements of chapter 5 of Title 5, for an emergency temporary standard to take immediate effect upon publication in the Federal Register if he determines (A) that employees are exposed to grave danger from exposure to substances or agents determined to be toxic or physically harmful or from new hazards, and (B) that such emergency standard is necessary to protect employees from such danger.

(2) Such standard shall be effective until superseded by a standard promulgated in accordance with the procedures prescribed in paragraph (3) of this subsection.

(3) Upon publication of such standard in the Federal Register the Secretary shall commence a proceeding in accordance with subsection (b) of this section, and the standard as published shall also serve as a proposed rule for the proceeding. The Secretary shall promulgate a standard under this paragraph no later than six months after publication of the emergency standard as provided in paragraph (2) of this subsection.

(d) Variances from Standards; Procedure. Any affected employer may apply to the Secretary for a rule or order for a variance from a standard promulgated under this section. Affected employees shall be given notice of each such application and an opportunity to participate in a hearing. The Secretary shall issue such rule or order if he determines on the record, after opportunity for an inspection where appropriate and a hearing, that the proponent of the variance has demonstrated by a preponderance of the evidence that the conditions, practices, means, methods, operations, or processes used or proposed to be used by an employer will provide employment and places of employment to his employees which are as safe and healthful as those which would prevail if he complies with the standard. The rule or order so issued shall prescribe the conditions the employer must maintain, and the practices, means, methods, operations, and processes which he must adopt and utilize to the extent they differ from the standard in question. Such a rule or order may be modified or revoked upon application by an employer, employees, or by the Secretary on his own motion, in the manner prescribed for its issuance under this subsection at any time after six months from its issuance.

(e) Statement of Reasons for Secretary's Determinations; Publication in Federal Register. Whenever the Secretary promulgates any standard, makes any rule, order, or decision, grants any exemption or extension of time, or compromises, mitigates, or settles any penalty assessed under this chapter, he shall include a statement of the reasons for such action, which shall be published in the Federal Register.

(f) Judicial Review. Any person who may be adversely affected by a standard issued under this section may at any time prior to the sixtieth day after such standard is promulgated file a petition challenging the validity of such standard with the United States court of appeals for the circuit wherein such person resides or has his principal place of business, for a judicial review of such standard. A copy of the petition shall be forthwith transmitted by the clerk of the court to the Secretary. The filing of such petition shall not, unless otherwise ordered by the court, operate as a stay of the standard. The determinations of the Secretary shall be conclusive if supported by substantial evidence in the record considered as a whole.

(g) Priority for Establishment of Standards. In determining the priority for establishing standards under this section, the Secretary shall give due regard to the urgency of the need for mandatory safety and health standards for particular industries, trades, crafts, occupations, businesses, workplaces or work environments. The Secretary shall also give due regard to the recommendations of the Secretary of Health and Human Services regarding the need for mandatory standards in determining the priority for establishing such standards.

(Pub.L. 91–596, § 6, Dec. 29, 1970, 84 Stat. 1593; Pub.L. 96–88, Title V, § 509(b), Oct. 17, 1979, 93 Stat. 695.)

Editorial Notes

Hazardous Waste Operations. Pub.L. 99–499, Title I, § 126(a)–(f), Oct. 17, 1986, 100 Stat. 1690, as amended Pub.L. 100–202, § 101(f) [Title II], Dec. 22, 1987, 101 Stat. 1329–198, provided that:

"(a) Promulgation.—Within one year after the date of the enactment of this section [Oct. 17, 1986], the Secretary of Labor shall, pursuant to section 6 of the Occupational Safety and Health Act of 1970 [this section] promulgate standards for the health and safety protection of employees engaged in hazardous waste operations.

"(b) Proposed standards.—The Secretary of Labor shall issue proposed regulations on such standards which shall include, but need not be limited to, the following worker protection provisions:

"(1) Site analysis.—Requirements for a formal hazard analysis of the site and development of a site specific plan for worker protection.

"(2) Training.—Requirements for contractors to provide initial and routine training of workers before such workers are permitted to engage in hazardous waste operations which would expose them to toxic substances.

"(3) Medical surveillance.—A program of regular medical examination, monitoring, and surveillance of workers engaged in hazardous waste operations which would expose them to toxic substances.

"(4) Protective equipment.—Requirements for appropriate personal protective equipment, clothing, and respirators for work in hazardous waste operations.

"(5) Engineering controls.—Requirements for engineering controls concerning the use of equipment and exposure of workers engaged in hazardous waste operations.

"(6) Maximum exposure limits.—Requirements for maximum exposure limitations for workers engaged in hazardous waste operations, including necessary monitoring and assessment procedures.

"(7) Informational program.—A program to inform workers engaged in hazardous waste operations of the nature and degree of toxic exposure likely as a result of such hazardous waste operations.

"(8) Handling.—Requirements for the handling, transporting, labeling, and disposing of hazardous wastes.

"(9) New technology program.—A program for the introduction of new equipment or technologies that will maintain worker protections.

"(10) Decontamination procedures.—Procedures for decontamination.

"(11) Emergency response.—Requirements for emergency response and protection of workers engaged in hazardous waste operations.

"(c) Final regulations.—Final regulations under subsection (a) shall take effect one year after the date they are promulgated. In promulgating final regulations on standards under subsection (a), the Secretary of Labor shall include each of the provisions listed in paragraphs (1) through (11) of subsection (b) unless the Secretary determines that the evidence in the public record considered as a whole does not support inclusion of any such provision.

"(d) Specific training standards.—

"(1) Offsite instruction; field experience.—Standards promulgated under subsection (a) shall include training standards requiring that general site workers (such as equipment operators, general laborers, and other supervised personnel) engaged in hazardous substance removal or other activities which expose or potentially expose such workers to hazardous substances receive a minimum of 40 hours of initial instruction off the site, and a minimum of three days of actual field experience under the direct supervision of a trained, experienced supervisor, at the time of assignment. The requirements of the preceding sentence shall not apply to any general site worker who has received the equivalent of such training. Workers who may be exposed to unique or special hazards shall be provided additional training.

"(2) Training of supervisors.—Standards promulgated under subsection (a) shall include training standards requiring that onsite managers and supervisors directly responsible for the hazardous waste operations (such as foremen) receive the same training as general site workers set forth in paragraph (1) of this subsection and at least eight additional hours of specialized training on managing hazardous waste operations. The requirements of the preceding sentence shall not apply to any person who has received the equivalent of such training.

"(3) Certification; enforcement.—Such training standards shall contain provisions for certifying that general site workers, onsite managers, and supervisors have received the specified training and shall prohibit any individual who has not received the specified training from engaging in hazardous waste operations covered by the standard. The certification procedures shall be no less comprehensive than those adopted by the Environmental Protection Agency in its Model Accreditation Plan for

Asbestos Abatement Training as required under the Asbestos Hazard Emergency Response Act of 1986 [Pub.L. 99–519].

"(4) Training of emergency response personnel.—Such training standards shall set forth requirements for the training of workers who are responsible for responding to hazardous emergency situations who may be exposed to toxic substances in carrying out their responsibilities.

"(e) Interim regulations.—The Secretary of Labor shall issue interim final regulations under this section within 60 days after the enactment of this section which shall provide no less protection under this section for workers employed by contractors and emergency response workers than the protections contained in the Environmental Protection Agency Manual (1981) 'Health and Safety Requirements for Employees Engaged in Field Activities' and existing standards under the Occupational Safety and Health Act of 1970 found in subpart C of part 1926 of title 29 of the Code of Federal Regulations. Such interim final regulations shall take effect upon issuance and shall apply until final regulations become effective under subsection (c).

"(f) Coverage of certain State and local employees.—Not later than 90 days after the promulgation of final regulations under subsection (a), the Administrator shall promulgate standards identical to those promulgated by the Secretary of Labor under subsection (a). Standards promulgated under this subsection shall apply to employees of State and local governments in each State which does not have in effect an approved State plan under section 18 of the Occupational Safety and Health Act of 1970 [section 667 of this title] providing for standards for the health and safety protection of employees engaged in hazardous waste operations."

§ 657. Inspections, investigations, and recordkeeping

(a) Authority of Secretary to Enter, Inspect, and Investigate Places of Employment; Time and Manner. In order to carry out the purposes of this chapter, the Secretary, upon presenting appropriate credentials to the owner, operator, or agent in charge, is authorized—

(1) to enter without delay and at reasonable times any factory, plant, establishment, construction site, or other area, workplace or environment where work is performed by an employee of an employer; and

(2) to inspect and investigate during regular working hours and at other reasonable times, and within reasonable limits and in a reasonable manner, any such place of employment and all pertinent conditions, structures, machines, apparatus, devices, equipment, and materials therein, and to question privately any such employer, owner, operator, agent or employee.

(b) Attendance and Testimony of Witnesses and Production of Evidence; Enforcement of Subpoena. In making his inspections and investigations under this chapter the Secretary may require the attendance and testimony of witnesses and the production of evidence under oath. Witnesses shall be paid the same fees and mileage that are paid witnesses in the courts of the United States. In case of a contumacy, failure, or refusal of any person to obey such an order, any district court of the United States or the United States courts of any territory or possession, within the jurisdiction of which such person is found, or resides or transacts business, upon the application by the Secretary, shall have jurisdiction to issue to such person an order requiring such person to appear to produce evidence if, as, and when so ordered, and to give testimony relating to the matter under investigation or in question, and any failure to obey such order of the court may be punished by said court as a contempt thereof.

(c)(1) Maintenance, Preservation, and Availability of Records; Issuance of Regulations; Scope of Records; Periodic Inspections by Employer; Posting of Notices by Employer; Notification of Employee of Corrective Action. Each employer shall make, keep and preserve, and make available to the Secretary or the Secretary of Health and Human Services, such records regarding his activities relating to this chapter as the Secretary, in cooperation with the Secretary of Health and Human Services, may prescribe by regulation as necessary or appropriate for the enforcement of this chapter or for developing information regarding the causes and prevention of occupational accidents and illnesses. In order to carry out the provisions of this paragraph such regulations may include provisions requiring employers to conduct periodic inspections. The Secretary shall also issue regulations requiring that employers, through posting of notices or other appropriate means, keep their employees informed of their protections and obligations under this chapter, including the provisions of applicable standards.

(2) The Secretary, in cooperation with the Secretary of Health and Human Services, shall prescribe regulations requiring employers to maintain accurate records of, and to make periodic reports on, work-related deaths, injuries and illnesses other than minor injuries requiring only first aid treatment and which do not involve medical treatment, loss of consciousness, restriction of work or motion, or transfer to another job.

(3) The Secretary, in cooperation with the Secretary of Health and Human Services, shall issue regulations requiring employers to maintain accurate records of employee exposures to potentially toxic materials or harmful physical agents which are required to be monitored or measured under section 655 of this title. Such regulations shall provide employees or their representatives with an opportunity to observe such monitoring or measuring, and to have access to the records thereof. Such regulations shall also make appropriate provision for each employee or former employee to have access to such records as will indicate his own exposure to toxic materials or harmful physical agents. Each employer shall promptly notify any employee who has been or is being exposed to toxic materials or harmful physical agents in concentrations or at levels which exceed those prescribed by an applicable occupational safety and health standard promulgated under section 655 of this title, and shall inform any employee who is being thus exposed of the corrective action being taken.

(d) Obtaining of Information. Any information obtained by the Secretary, the Secretary of Health and Human Services, or a State agency under this chapter shall be obtained with a minimum burden upon employers, especially those operating small businesses. Unnecessary duplication of efforts in obtaining information shall be reduced to the maximum extent feasible.

(e) Employer and Authorized Employee Representatives to Accompany Secretary or his Authorized Representative on Inspection of Workplace; Consultation with Employees Where no Authorized Employee Representative is Present. Subject to regulations issued by the Secretary, a representative of the employer and a representative authorized by his employees shall be given an opportunity to accompany the Secretary or his authorized representative during the physical inspection of any workplace under subsection (a) of this section for the purpose of aiding such inspection. Where there is no authorized employee representative, the Secretary or his authorized representative shall consult with a reasonable number of employees concerning matters of health and safety in the workplace.

(f)(1) Request for Inspection by Employees or Representative of Employees; Grounds; Procedure; Determination of Request; Notification of Secretary or Representative Prior to or During any Inspection of Violations; Procedure for Review of Refusal by Representative of Secretary to Issue Citation for Alleged Violations. Any employees or representative of employees who believe that a violation of a safety or health standard exists that threatens physical harm, or that an imminent danger exists, may request an inspection by giving notice to the Secretary or his authorized representative of such violation or danger. Any such notice shall be reduced to writing, shall set forth with reasonable particularity the grounds for the notice, and shall be signed by the employees or representative of employees, and a copy shall be provided the employer or his agent no later than at the time of inspection, except that, upon the request of the person giving such notice, his name and the names of individual employees referred to therein shall not appear in such copy or on any record published, released, or made available pursuant to subsection (g) of this section. If upon receipt of such notification the Secretary determines there are reasonable grounds to believe that such violation or danger exists, he shall make a special inspection in accordance with the provisions of this section as soon as practicable, to determine if such violation or danger exists. If the Secretary determines there are no reasonable grounds to believe that a violation or danger exists he shall notify the employees or representative of the employees in writing of such determination.

(2) Prior to or during any inspection of a workplace, any employees or representative of employees employed in such workplace may notify the Secretary or any representative of the Secretary responsible for conducting the inspection, in writing, of any violation of this chapter which they have reason to believe exists in such workplace. The Secretary shall, by regulation, establish procedures for informal review of any refusal by a representative of the Secretary to issue a citation with respect to any such alleged violation and shall furnish the employees or representative of employees requesting such review a written statement of the reasons for the Secretary's final disposition of the case.

(g)(1) Compilation, Analysis, and Publication of Reports and Information; Rules and Regulations. The Secretary and Secretary of Health and Human Services are authorized to compile, analyze, and publish, either in summary or detailed form, all reports or information obtained under this section.

(2) The Secretary and the Secretary of Health and Human Services shall each prescribe such rules and regulations as he may deem necessary to carry out their responsibilities under this chapter, including rules and regulations dealing with the inspection of an employer's establishment.

(Pub.L. 91–596, § 8, Dec. 29, 1970, 84 Stat. 1598; Pub.L. 96–88, Title V, § 509(b), Oct. 17, 1979, 93 Stat. 695.)

§ 658. Citations

(a) Authority to Issue; Grounds; Contents; Notice in Lieu of Citation for De Minimis Violations. If, upon inspection or investigation, the Secretary or his authorized representative believes that an employer has violated a requirement of section 654 of this title, of any standard, rule or order promulgated pursuant to section 655 of this title, or of any regulations prescribed pursuant to this chapter, he shall with reasonable promptness issue a citation to the employer. Each citation shall be in writing and shall describe with particularity the nature of the violation, including a reference to the provision of the chapter, standard, rule, regulation, or order alleged to have been violated. In addition, the citation shall fix a reasonable time for the abatement of the violation. The Secretary may prescribe procedures for the issuance of a notice in lieu of a citation with respect to de minimis violations which have no direct or immediate relationship to safety or health.

(b) Posting. Each citation issued under this section, or a copy or copies thereof, shall be prominently posted, as prescribed in regulations issued by the Secretary, at or near each place a violation referred to in the citation occurred.

(c) Time for Issuance. No citation may be issued under this section after the expiration of six months following the occurrence of any violation.

(Pub.L. 91–596, § 9, Dec. 29, 1970, 84 Stat. 1601.)

§ 659. Enforcement procedures

(a) Notification of Employer of Proposed Assessment of Penalty Subsequent to Issuance of Citation; Time for Notification of Secretary by Employer of Contest by Employer of Citation or Proposed Assessment; Citation and Proposed Assessment as Final Order Upon Failure of Employer to Notify of Contest and Failure of Employees to File Notice. If, after an inspection or investigation, the Secretary issues a citation under section 658(a) of this title, he shall, within a reasonable time after the termination of such inspection or investigation, notify the employer by certified mail of the penalty, if any, proposed to be assessed under section 666 of this title and that the employer has fifteen working days within which to notify the Secretary that he wishes to contest the citation or proposed assessment of penalty. If, within fifteen working days from the receipt of the notice issued by the Secretary the employer fails to notify the Secretary that he intends to contest the citation or proposed assessment of penalty, and no notice is filed by any employee or representative of employees under subsection (c) of this section within such time, the citation and the assessment, as proposed, shall be deemed a final order of the Commission and not subject to review by any court or agency.

(b) Notification of Employer of Failure to Correct in Allotted Time Period Violation for Which Citation was Issued and Proposed Assessment of Penalty for Failure to Correct; Time for Notification of Secretary by Employer of Contest by Employer of Notification of Failure to Correct or Proposed Assessment; Notification or Proposed Assessment as Final Order Upon Failure of Employer to Notify of Contest. If the Secretary has reason to believe that an employer has failed to correct a violation for which a citation has been issued within the period permitted for its correction (which period shall not begin to run until the entry of a final order by the Commission in the case of any review proceedings under this section initiated by the employer in good faith and not solely for delay or avoidance of penalties), the Secretary shall notify the employer by certified mail of such failure and of the penalty proposed to be assessed under section 666 of this title by reason of such failure, and that the employer has fifteen working days within which to notify the Secretary that he wishes to contest the Secretary's notification or the proposed assessment of penalty. If, within fifteen working days from the receipt of notification issued by the Secretary, the employer fails to notify the Secretary that he intends to contest the notification or proposed assessment of penalty, the notification and assessment, as proposed, shall be deemed a final order of the Commission and not subject to review by any court or agency.

(c) Advisement of Commission by Secretary of Notification of Contest by Employer of Citation or Notification or of Filing of Notice by any Employee or Representative of Employees; Hearing by Commission; Orders of Commission and Secretary; Rules of Procedure. If an employer notifies the Secretary that he intends to contest a citation issued under section 658(a) of this title or notification issued under subsection (a) or (b) of this section, or if, within fifteen working days of the issuance of a citation under section 658(a) of this title, any employee or representative of employees files a notice with the Secretary alleging that the period of time fixed in the citation for the abatement of the violation is unreasonable, the Secretary shall immediately advise the Commission of such notification, and the Commission shall afford an opportunity for a hearing (in accordance with section 554 of Title 5 but without regard to subsection (a)(3) of such section). The Commission shall thereafter issue an order, based on findings of fact, affirming, modifying, or vacating the Secretary's citation or proposed penalty, or directing other appropriate relief, and such order shall become final thirty days after its issuance. Upon a showing by an employer of a good faith effort to comply with the abatement requirements of a citation, and that abatement has not been completed because of factors beyond his reasonable control, the Secretary, after an opportunity for a hearing as provided in this subsection, shall issue an order affirming or modifying the abatement requirements in such citation. The rules of procedure prescribed by the Commission shall provide affected employees or representatives of affected employees an opportunity to participate as parties to hearings under this subsection.

(Pub.L. 91–596, § 10, Dec. 29, 1970, 84 Stat. 1601.)

§ 660. Judicial review

(a) Filing of Petition by Persons Adversely Affected or Aggrieved; Orders Subject to Review; Jurisdiction; Venue; Procedure; Conclusiveness of Record and Findings of Commission; Appropriate Relief; Finality of Judgment. Any person adversely affected or aggrieved on an order of the Commission issued under subsection (c) of section 659 of this title may obtain a review of such order in any United States court of appeals for the circuit in which the violation is alleged to have occurred or where the employer has its principal office, or in the Court of Appeals for the District of Columbia Circuit, by filing in such court within sixty days following the issuance of such order a written petition praying that the order be modified or set aside. A copy of such petition shall be forthwith transmitted by the clerk of the court to the Commission and to the other parties, and thereupon the Commission shall file in the court the record in the proceeding as provided in section 2112 of Title 28. Upon such filing, the court shall have jurisdiction of the proceeding and of the question determined therein, and shall have power to grant such temporary relief or restraining order as it deems just and proper, and to make and enter upon the pleadings, testimony, and proceedings set forth in such record a decree affirming, modifying, or setting aside in whole or in part, the order of the Commission and enforcing the same to the extent that such order is affirmed or modified. The commencement of proceedings under this subsection shall not, unless ordered by the court, operate as a stay of the order of the Commission. No objection that has not been urged before the Commission shall be considered by the court, unless the failure or neglect to urge such objection shall be excused because of extraordinary circumstances. The findings of the Commission with respect to questions of fact, if supported by substantial evidence on the record considered as a whole, shall be conclusive. If any party shall apply to the court for leave to adduce additional evidence and shall show to the satisfaction of the court that such additional evidence is material and that there were reasonable grounds for the failure to adduce such evidence in the hearing before the Commission, the court may order such additional evidence to be taken before the Commission and to be made a part of the record. The Commission may modify its findings as to the facts, or make new findings, by reason of additional evidence so taken and filed, and it shall file such modified or new findings, which findings with respect to questions of fact, if supported by substantial evidence on the record considered as a whole, shall be conclusive, and its recommendations, if any, for the modification or setting aside of its original order. Upon the filing of the record with it, the jurisdiction of the court shall be exclusive and its judgment and decree shall be final, except that the same shall be subject to review by the Supreme Court of the United States, as provided in section 1254 of Title 28.

(b) Filing of Petition by Secretary; Orders Subject to Review; Jurisdiction; Venue; Procedure; Conclusiveness of Record and Findings of Commission; Enforcement of Orders; Contempt Proceedings. The Secretary may also obtain review or enforcement of any final order of the Commission by filing a petition for such relief in the United States court of appeals for the circuit in which the alleged violation occurred or in which the employer has its principal office, and the provisions of subsection (a) of this section shall govern such proceedings to the extent applicable. If no petition for review, as provided in subsection (a) of this section is filed within sixty days after service of the Commission's order, the Commission's findings of fact and order shall be conclusive in connection with any petition for enforcement which is filed by the Secretary after the expiration of such sixty-day period. In any such case, as well as in the case of a noncontested citation or notification by the Secretary which has become a final order of the Commission under subsection (a) or (b) of section 659 of this title, the clerk of the court, unless otherwise ordered by the court, shall forthwith enter a decree enforcing the order and shall transmit a copy of such decree to the Secretary and the employer named in the petition. In any contempt proceeding brought to enforce a decree of a court of appeals entered pursuant to this subsection or subsection (a) of this section, the court of appeals may assess the penalties provided in section 666 of this title, in addition to invoking any other available remedies.

(c)(1) Discharge or Discrimination Against Employee for Exercise of Rights Under this Chapter; Prohibition; Procedure for Relief. No person shall discharge or in any manner discriminate against any employee because such employee has filed any complaint or instituted or caused to be instituted any proceeding under or related to this chapter or has testified or is about to testify in any such proceeding or because of the exercise by such employee on behalf of himself or others of any right afforded by this chapter.

(2) Any employee who believes that he has been discharged or otherwise discriminated against by any person in violation of this subsection may, within thirty days after such violation occurs, file a complaint with the Secretary alleging such discrimination. Upon receipt of such complaint, the Secretary shall cause such investigation to be made as he deems appropriate. If upon such investigation, the Secretary determines that the provisions of this subsection have been violated, he shall bring an action in any appropriate United States district court against such person. In any such action the United States district courts shall have jurisdiction, for cause shown to restrain violations of paragraph (1) of this subsection and order all appropriate relief including rehiring or reinstatement of the employee to his former position with back pay.

(3) Within 90 days of the receipt of a complaint filed under this subsection the Secretary shall notify the complainant of his determination under paragraph (2) of this subsection.

(Pub.L. 91–596, § 11, Dec. 29, 1970, 84 Stat. 1602; Pub.L. 98–620, Title IV, § 402(32), Nov. 8, 1984, 98 Stat. 3360.)

§ 661. Occupational Safety and Health Review Commission

(a) Establishment; Membership; Appointment; Chairman. The Occupational Safety and Health Review Commission is hereby established. The Commission shall be composed of three members who shall be appointed by the President, by and with the advice and consent of the Senate, from among persons who by reason of training, education, or experience are qualified to carry out the functions of the Commission under this chapter. The President shall designate one of the members of the Commission to serve as Chairman.

(b) Terms of Office; Removal by President. The terms of members of the Commission shall be six years except that (1) the members of the Commission first taking office shall serve, as designated by the President at the time of appointment, one for a term of two years, one for a term of four years, and one for a term of six years, and (2) a vacancy caused by the death, resignation, or removal of a member prior to the expiration of the term for which he was appointed shall be filled only for the remainder of such unexpired term. A member of the Commission may be removed by the President for inefficiency, neglect of duty, or malfeasance in office.

(c) Omitted

(d) Principal Office; Hearings or Other Proceedings at Other Places. The principal office of the Commission shall be in the District of Columbia. Whenever the Commission deems that the convenience of the public or of the parties may be promoted, or delay or expense may be minimized, it may hold hearings or conduct other proceedings at any other place.

(e) Functions and Duties of Chairman; Appointment and Compensation of Administrative Law Judges and Other Employees. The Chairman shall be responsible on behalf of the Commission for the administrative operations of the Commission and shall appoint such administrative law judges and other employees as he deems necessary to assist in the performance of the Commission's functions and to fix their compensation in accordance with the provisions of chapter 51 and subchapter III of chapter 53 of Title 5 relating to classification and General Schedule pay rates: *Provided,* That assignment, removal and compensation of administrative law judges shall be in accordance with sections 3105, 3344, 5372, and 7521 of Title 5.

(f) Quorum; Official Action. For the purpose of carrying out its functions under this chapter, two members of the Commission shall constitute a quorum and official action can be taken only on the affirmative vote of at least two members.

(g) Hearings and Records Open to Public; Promulgation of Rules; Applicability of Federal Rules of Civil Procedure. Every official act of the Commission shall be entered of record, and its hearings and records shall be open to the public. The Commission is authorized to make such rules as are necessary for the orderly transaction of its proceedings. Unless the Commission has adopted a different rule, its proceedings shall be in accordance with the Federal Rules of Civil Procedure.

(h) Depositions and Production of Documentary Evidence; Fees. The Commission may order testimony to be taken by deposition in any proceedings pending before it at any state of such proceeding. Any person may be compelled to appear and depose, and to produce books, papers, or documents, in the same manner as witnesses may be compelled to appear and testify and produce like documentary evidence before the Commission. Witnesses whose depositions are taken under this subsection, and the persons taking such depositions, shall be entitled to the same fees as are paid for like services in the courts of the United States.

(i) Investigatory Powers. For the purpose of any proceeding before the Commission, the provisions of section 161 of this title are hereby made applicable to the jurisdiction and powers of the Commission.

(j) Administrative Law Judges; Determinations; Report as Final Order of Commission. A[1] administrative law judge appointed by the Commission shall hear, and make a determination upon, any proceeding instituted before the Commission and any motion in connection therewith, assigned to such administrative law judge by the Chairman of the Commission, and shall make a report of any such determination which constitutes his final disposition of the proceedings. The report of the administrative law judge shall become the final order of the Commission within thirty days after such report by the administrative law judge, unless within such period any Commission member has directed that such report shall be reviewed by the Commission.

(k) Appointment and Compensation of Administrative Law Judges. Except as otherwise provided in this chapter, the administrative law judges shall be subject to the laws governing employees in the classified civil service, except that appointments shall be made without regard to section 5108 of Title 5. Each administrative law judge shall receive compensation at a rate not less than that prescribed for GS–16 under section 5332 of Title 5.

(Pub.L. 91–596, § 12, Dec. 29, 1970, 84 Stat. 1603; amended Pub.L. 95–251, § 2(a)(7), Mar. 27, 1978, 92 Stat. 183.)

§ 662. Injunction proceedings

(a) Petition by Secretary to Restrain Imminent Dangers; Scope of Order. The United States district courts shall have jurisdiction, upon petition of the Secretary, to restrain any conditions or practices in any place of employment which are such that a danger exists which could reasonably be expected to cause death or serious physical harm immediately or before the imminence of such danger can be eliminated through the enforcement procedures otherwise provided by this chapter. Any order issued under this section may require such steps to be taken as may be necessary to avoid, correct, or remove such imminent danger and prohibit the employ-

1. So in original. Probably should be "An".

ment or presence of any individual in locations or under conditions where such imminent danger exists, except individuals whose presence is necessary to avoid, correct, or remove such imminent danger or to maintain the capacity of a continuous process operation to resume normal operations without a complete cessation of operations, or where a cessation of operations is necessary, to permit such to be accomplished in a safe and orderly manner.

(b) Appropriate Injunctive Relief or Temporary Restraining Order Pending Outcome of Enforcement Proceeding; Applicability of Rule 65 of Federal Rules of Civil Procedure. Upon the filing of any such petition the district court shall have jurisdiction to grant such injunctive relief or temporary restraining order pending the outcome of an enforcement proceeding pursuant to this chapter. The proceeding shall be as provided by Rule 65 of the Federal Rules, Civil Procedure, except that no temporary restraining order issued without notice shall be effective for a period longer than five days.

(c) Notification of Affected Employees and Employers by Inspector of Danger and of Recommendation to Secretary to Seek Relief. Whenever and as soon as an inspector concludes that conditions or practices described in subsection (a) of this section exist in any place of employment, he shall inform the affected employees and employers of the danger and that he is recommending to the Secretary that relief be sought.

(d) Failure of Secretary to Seek Relief; Writ of Mandamus. If the Secretary arbitrarily or capriciously fails to seek relief under this section, any employee who may be injured by reason of such failure, or the representative of such employees, might bring an action against the Secretary in the United States district court for the district in which the imminent danger is alleged to exist or the employer has its principal office, or for the District of Columbia, for a writ of mandamus to compel the Secretary to seek such an order and for such further relief as may be appropriate.

(Pub.L. 91–596, § 13, Dec. 29, 1970, 84 Stat. 1605.)

§ 663. Representation in civil litigation

Except as provided in section 518(a) of Title 28 relating to litigation before the Supreme Court, the Solicitor of Labor may appear for and represent the Secretary in any civil litigation brought under this chapter but all such litigation shall be subject to the direction and control of the Attorney General.

(Pub.L. 91–596, § 14, Dec. 29, 1970, 84 Stat. 1606.)

§ 664. Disclosure of trade secrets; protective orders

All information reported to or otherwise obtained by the Secretary or his representative in connection with any inspection or proceeding under this chapter which contains or which might reveal a trade secret referred to in section 1905 of Title 18 shall be considered confidential for the purpose of that section, except that such information may be disclosed to other officers or employees concerned with carrying out this chapter or when relevant in any proceeding under this chapter. In any such proceeding the Secretary, the Commission, or the court shall issue such orders as may be appropriate to protect the confidentiality of trade secrets.

(Pub.L. 91–596, § 15, Dec. 29, 1970, 84 Stat. 1606.)

§ 665. Variations, tolerances, and exemptions from required provisions; procedure; duration

The Secretary, on the record, after notice and opportunity for a hearing may provide such reasonable limitations and may make such rules and regulations allowing reasonable variations, tolerances, and exemptions to and from any or all provisions of this chapter as he may find necessary and proper to avoid serious impairment of the national defense. Such action shall not be in effect for more than six months without notification to affected employees and an opportunity being afforded for a hearing.

(Pub.L. 91–596, § 16, Dec. 29, 1970, 84 Stat. 1606.)

§ 666. Civil and criminal penalties

(a) Willful or Repeated Violation. Any employer who willfully or repeatedly violates the requirements of section 654 of this title, any standard, rule, or order promulgated pursuant to section 655 of this title, or regulations prescribed pursuant to this chapter, may be assessed a civil penalty of not more than $70,000 for each violation, but not less than $5,000 for each willful violation.

(b) Citation for Serious Violation. Any employer who has received a citation for a serious violation of the requirements of section 654 of this title, of any standard, rule, or order promulgated pursuant to section 655 of this title, or of any regulations prescribed pursuant to this chapter, shall be assessed a civil penalty of up to $7,000 for each such violation.

(c) Citation for Violation Determined Not Serious. Any employer who has received a citation for a violation of the requirements of section 654 of this title, of any standard, rule, or order promulgated pursuant to section 655 of this title, or of regulations prescribed pursuant to this chapter, and such violation is specifically determined not to be of a serious nature, may be assessed a civil penalty of up to $7,000 for each such violation.

(d) Failure to Correct Violation. Any employer who fails to correct a violation for which a citation has been issued under section 658(a) of this title within the period permitted for its correction (which period shall not begin to run until the date of the final order of the Commission in the case of any review proceeding under section 659 of this title initiated by the employer in good faith and not solely for delay or avoidance of penalties), may be assessed a civil penalty of not more than $7,000 for each day during which such failure or violation continues.

(e) Willful Violation Causing Death to Employee. Any employer who willfully violates any standard, rule, or order promulgated pursuant to section 655 of this title, or of any regulations prescribed pursuant to this chapter, and that violation caused death to any employee, shall, upon conviction, be punished by a fine of not more than $10,000 or by imprisonment for not more than six months, or by both; except that if the conviction is for a violation committed after a first conviction of such person, punishment shall be by a fine of not more than $20,000 or by imprisonment for not more than one year, or by both.

(f) Giving Advance Notice of Inspection. Any person who gives advance notice of any inspection to be conducted under this chapter, without authority from the Secretary or his designees, shall, upon conviction, be punished by a fine of not more than $1,000 or by imprisonment for not more than six months, or by both.

(g) False Statements, Representations or Certification. Whoever knowingly makes any false statement, representation, or certification in any application, record, report, plan, or other document filed or required to be maintained pursuant to this chapter shall, upon conviction, be punished by a fine of not more than $10,000, or by imprisonment for not more than six months, or by both.

(h) Omitted

(i) Violation of Posting Requirements. Any employer who violates any of the posting requirements, as prescribed under the provisions of this chapter, shall be assessed a civil penalty of up to $7,000 for each violation.

(j) Authority of Commission to Assess Civil Penalties. The Commission shall have authority to assess all civil penalties provided in this section, giving due consideration to the appropriateness of the penalty with respect to the size of the business of the employer being charged, the gravity of the violation, the good faith of the employer, and the history of previous violations.

(k) Determination of Serious Violation. For purposes of this section, a serious violation shall be deemed to exist in a place of employment if there is a substantial probability that death or serious physical harm could result from a condition which exists, or from one or more practices, means, methods, operations, or processes which have been adopted or are in use, in such place of employment unless the employer did not, and could not with the exercise of reasonable diligence, know of the presence of the violation.

(*l*) Procedure for Payment of Civil Penalties. Civil penalties owed under this chapter shall be paid to the Secretary for deposit into the Treasury of the United States and shall accrue to the United States and may be recovered in a civil action in the name of the United States brought in the United States district court for the district where the violation is alleged to have occurred or where the employer has its principal office.

(Pub.L. 91–596, § 17, Dec. 29, 1970, 84 Stat. 1606; amended Pub.L. 101–508, Title III, § 3101, Nov. 5, 1990, 104 Stat. 1388–29.)

§ 667. State jurisdiction and plans

(a) Assertion of State Standards in Absence of Applicable Federal Standards. Nothing in this chapter shall prevent any State agency or court from asserting jurisdiction under State law over any occupational safety or health issue with respect to which no standard is in effect under section 655 of this title.

(b) Submission of State Plan for Development and Enforcement of State Standards to Preempt Applicable Federal Standards. Any State which, at any time, desires to assume responsibility for development and enforcement therein of occupational safety and health standards relating to any occupational safety or health issue with respect to which a Federal standard has been promulgated under section 655 of this title shall submit a State plan for the development of such standards and their enforcement.

(c) Conditions for Approval of Plan. The Secretary shall approve the plan submitted by a State under subsection (b) of this section, or any modification thereof, if such plan in his judgment—

(1) designates a State agency or agencies as the agency or agencies responsible for administering the plan throughout the State,

(2) provides for the development and enforcement of safety and health standards relating to one or more safety or health issues, which standards (and the enforcement of which standards) are or will be at least as effective in providing safe and healthful employment and places of employment as the standards promulgated under section 655 of this title which relate to the same issues, and which standards, when applicable to products which are distributed or used in interstate commerce, are required by compelling local conditions and do not unduly burden interstate commerce,

(3) provides for a right of entry and inspection of all workplaces subject to this chapter which is at least as effective as that provided in section 657 of this title, and includes a prohibition on advance notice of inspections,

(4) contains satisfactory assurances that such agency or agencies have or will have the legal authority and qualified personnel necessary for the enforcement of such standards,

(5) gives satisfactory assurances that such State will devote adequate funds to the administration and enforcement of such standards,

(6) contains satisfactory assurances that such State will, to the extent permitted by its law, establish and maintain an effective and comprehensive occupational safety and health program applicable to all employees of public agencies of the State and its political subdivisions, which program is as effective as the standards contained in an approved plan,

(7) requires employers in the State to make reports to the Secretary in the same manner and to the same extent as if the plan were not in effect, and

(8) provides that the State agency will make such reports to the Secretary in such form and containing such information, as the Secretary shall from time to time require.

(d) Rejection of Plan; Notice and Opportunity for Hearing. If the Secretary rejects a plan submitted under subsection (b) of this section, he shall afford the State submitting the plan due notice and opportunity for a hearing before so doing.

(e) Discretion of Secretary to Exercise Authority Over Comparable Standards Subsequent to Approval of State Plan; Duration; Retention of Jurisdiction by Secretary Upon Determination of Enforcement of Plan by State. After the Secretary approves a State plan submitted under subsection (b) of this section, he may, but shall not be required to, exercise his authority under sections 657, 658, 659, 662, and 666 of this title with respect to comparable standards promulgated under section 655 of this title, for the period specified in the next sentence. The Secretary may exercise the authority referred to above until he determines, on the basis of actual operations under the State plan, that the criteria set forth in subsection (c) of this section are being applied, but he shall not make such determination for at least three years after the plan's approval under subsection (c) of this section. Upon making the determination referred to in the preceding sentence, the provisions of sections 654(a)(2), 657 (except for the purpose of carrying out subsection (f) of this section), 658, 659, 662, and 666 of this title, and standards promulgated under section 655 of this title, shall not apply with respect to any occupational safety or health issues covered under the plan, but the Secretary may retain jurisdiction under the above provisions in any proceeding commenced under section 658 or 659 of this title before the date of determination.

(f) Continuing Evaluation by Secretary of State Enforcement of Approved Plan; Withdrawal of Approval of Plan by Secretary; Grounds; Procedure; Conditions for Retention of Jurisdiction by State. The Secretary shall, on the basis of reports submitted by the State agency and his own inspections make a continuing evaluation of the manner in which each State having a plan approved under this section is carrying out such plan. Whenever the Secretary finds, after affording due notice and opportunity for a hearing, that in the administration of the State plan there is a failure to comply substantially with any provision of the State plan (or any assurance contained therein), he shall notify the State agency of his withdrawal of approval of such plan and upon receipt of such notice such plan shall cease to be in effect, but the State may retain jurisdiction in any case commenced before the withdrawal of the plan in order to enforce standards under the plan whenever the issues involved do not relate to the reasons for the withdrawal of the plan.

(g) Judicial Review of Secretary's Withdrawal of Approval or Rejection of Plan; Jurisdiction; Venue; Procedure; Appropriate Relief; Finality of Judgment. The State may obtain a review of a decision of the Secretary withdrawing approval of or rejecting its plan by the United States court of appeals for the circuit in which the State is located by filing in such court within thirty days following receipt of notice of such decision a petition to modify or set aside in whole or in part the action of the Secretary. A copy of such petition shall forthwith be served upon the Secretary, and thereupon the Secretary shall certify and file in the court the record upon which the decision complained of was issued as provided in section 2112 of Title 28. Unless the court finds that the Secretary's decision in rejecting a proposed State plan or withdrawing his approval of such a plan is not supported by substantial evidence the court shall affirm the Secretary's decision. The judgment of the court shall be subject to review by the Supreme Court of the United States upon certiorari or certification as provided in section 1254 of Title 28.

(h) Temporary Enforcement of State Standards. The Secretary may enter into an agreement with a State under which the State will be permitted to continue to enforce one or more occupational health and safety standards in effect in such State until final action is taken by the Secretary with respect to a plan submitted by a State under subsection (b) of this section, or two years from December 29, 1970, whichever is earlier.

(Pub.L. 91–596, § 18, Dec. 29, 1970, 84 Stat. 1608.)

*

APPENDIX B

CODE OF FEDERAL REGULATIONS

TITLE 40—PROTECTION OF ENVIRONMENT

CHAPTER V

COUNCIL ON ENVIRONMENTAL QUALITY

Table of Contents

Part

1500. Purpose, policy, and mandate.
1501. NEPA and Agency planning.
1502. Environmental impact statement.
1503. Commenting.
1504. Predecision referrals to the Council of proposed Federal actions determined to be environmentally unsatisfactory.
1505. NEPA and Agency decisionmaking.
1506. Other requirements of NEPA.
1507. Agency compliance.
1508. Terminology and index.
1515. Freedom of Information Act procedures.
1516. Privacy Act implementation.
1517. Public meeting procedures of the Council on Environmental Quality.

Part 1500

Purpose, Policy, and Mandate

Sec.

1500.1 Purpose.
1500.2 Policy.
1500.3 Mandate.
1500.4 Reducing paperwork.
1500.5 Reducing delay.
1500.6 Agency authority.

AUTHORITY: NEPA, the Environmental Quality Improvement Act of 1970, as amended (42 U.S.C. 4371 *et seq.*), sec. 309 of the Clean Air Act, as amended (42 U.S.C. 7609) and E.O. 11514 (Mar. 5, 1970, as amended by E.O. 11991, May 24, 1977).

SOURCE: 43 FR 55990, Nov. 28, 1978, unless otherwise noted.

§ 1500.1 Purpose

(a) The National Environmental Policy Act (NEPA) is our basic national charter for protection of the environment. It establishes policy, sets goals (section 101), and provides means (section 102) for carrying out the policy. Section 102(2) contains "action-forcing" provisions to make sure that federal agencies act according to the letter and spirit of the Act. The regulations that follow implement section 102(2). Their purpose is to tell federal agencies what they must do to comply with the procedures and achieve the goals of the Act. The President, the federal agencies, and the courts share responsibility for enforcing the Act so as to achieve the substantive requirements of section 101.

(b) NEPA procedures must insure that environmental information is available to public officials and citizens before decisions are made and before actions are taken. The information must be of high quality. Accurate scientific analysis, expert agency comments, and public scrutiny are essential to implementing NEPA. Most important, NEPA documents must concentrate on the issues that are truly significant to the action in question, rather than amassing needless detail.

(c) Ultimately, of course, it is not better documents but better decisions that count. NEPA's purpose is not to generate paperwork—even excellent paperwork—but to foster excellent action. The NEPA process is intended to help public officials make decisions that are based on understanding of environmental consequences, and take actions that protect, restore, and enhance the environment. These regulations provide the direction to achieve this purpose.

§ 1500.2 Policy

Federal agencies shall to the fullest extent possible:

(a) Interpret and administer the policies, regulations, and public laws of the United States in accordance with the policies set forth in the Act and in these regulations.

(b) Implement procedures to make the NEPA process more useful to decisionmakers and the public; to reduce paperwork and the accumulation of extraneous background data; and to emphasize real environmental issues and alternatives. Environmental impact statements shall be concise, clear, and to the point, and shall be supported by evidence that agencies have made the necessary environmental analyses.

(c) Integrate the requirements of NEPA with other planning and environmental review procedures required by law or by agency practice so that all such procedures run concurrently rather than consecutively.

(d) Encourage and facilitate public involvement in decisions which affect the quality of the human environment.

(e) Use the NEPA process to identify and assess the reasonable alternatives to proposed actions that will avoid or minimize adverse effects of these actions upon the quality of the human environment.

(f) Use all practicable means, consistent with the requirements of the Act and other essential considerations of national policy, to restore and enhance the quality of the human environment and avoid or minimize any possible adverse effects of their actions upon the quality of the human environment.

§ 1500.3 Mandate

Parts 1500 through 1508 of this title provide regulations applicable to and binding on all Federal agencies for implementing the procedural provisions of the National Environmental Policy Act of 1969, as amended (Pub.L. 91–190, 42 U.S.C. 4321 et seq.) (NEPA or the Act) except where compliance would be inconsistent with other statutory requirements. These regulations are issued pursuant to NEPA, the Environmental Quality Improvement Act of 1970, as amended (42 U.S.C. 4371 et seq.) section 309 of the Clean Air Act, as amended (42 U.S.C. 7609) and Executive Order 11514, Protection and Enhancement of Environmental Quality (March 5, 1970, as amended by Executive Order 11991, May 24, 1977). These regulations unlike the predecessor guidelines, are not confined to sec. 102(2)(C) (environmental impact statements). The regulations apply to the whole of section 102(2). The provisions of the Act and of these regulations must be read together as a whole in order to comply with the spirit and letter of the law. It is the Council's intention that judicial review of agency compliance with these regulations not occur before an agency has filed the final environmental impact statement, or has made a final finding of no significant impact (when such a finding will result in action affecting the environment), or takes action that will result in irreparable injury. Furthermore, it is the Council's intention that any trivial violation of these regulations not give rise to any independent cause of action.

§ 1500.4 Reducing paperwork

Agencies shall reduce excessive paperwork by:

(a) Reducing the length of environmental impact statements (§ 1502.2(c)), by means such as setting appropriate page limits (§§ 1501.7(b)(1) and 1502.7).

(b) Preparing analytic rather than encyclopedic environmental impact statements (§ 1502.2(a)).

(c) Discussing only briefly issues other than significant ones (§ 1502.2(b)).

(d) Writing environmental impact statements in plain language (§ 1502.8).

(e) Following a clear format for environmental impact statements (§ 1502.10).

(f) Emphasizing the portions of the environmental impact statement that are useful to decisionmakers and the public (§§ 1502.14 and 1502.15) and reducing emphasis on background material (§ 1502.16).

(g) Using the scoping process, not only to identify significant environmental issues deserving of study, but also to deemphasize insignificant issues, narrowing the scope of the environmental impact statement process accordingly (§ 1501.7).

(h) Summarizing the environmental impact statement (§ 1502.12) and circulating the summary instead of the entire environmental impact statement if the latter is unusually long (§ 1502.19).

(i) Using program, policy, or plan environmental impact statements and tiering from statements of broad scope to those of narrower scope, to eliminate repetitive discussions of the same issues (§§ 1502.4 and 1502.20).

(j) Incorporating by reference (§ 1502.21).

(k) Integrating NEPA requirements with other environmental review and consultation requirements (§ 1502.25).

(*l*) Requiring comments to be as specific as possible (§ 1503.3).

(m) Attaching and circulating only changes to the draft environmental impact statement, rather than rewriting and circulating the entire statement when changes are minor (§ 1503.4(c)).

(n) Eliminating duplication with State and local procedures, by providing for joint preparation (§ 1506.2), and with other Federal procedures, by providing that an agency may adopt appropriate environmental documents prepared by another agency (§ 1506.3).

(*o*) Combining environmental documents with other documents (§ 1506.4).

(p) Using categorical exclusions to define categories of actions which do not individually or cumulatively have a significant effect on the human environment and which are therefore exempt from requirements to prepare an environmental impact statement (§ 1508.4).

(q) Using a finding of no significant impact when an action not otherwise excluded will not have a significant effect on the human environment and is therefore exempt from requirements to prepare an environmental impact statement (§ 1508.13).

[43 FR 55990, Nov. 29, 1978; 44 FR 873, Jan. 3, 1979]

§ 1500.5 Reducing delay

Agencies shall reduce delay by:

(a) Integrating the NEPA process into early planning (§ 1501.2).

(b) Emphasizing interagency cooperation before the environmental impact statement is prepared, rather then submission of adversary comments on a completed document (§ 1501.6).

(c) Insuring the swift and fair resolution of lead agency disputes (§ 1501.5).

(d) Using the scoping process for an early identification of what are and what are not the real issues (§ 1501.7).

(e) Establishing appropriate time limits for the environmental impact statement process (§§ 1501.7(b)(2) and 1501.8).

(f) Preparing environmental impact statements early in the process (§ 1502.5).

(g) Integrating NEPA requirements with other environmental review and consultation requirements (§ 1502.25).

(h) Eliminating duplication with State and local procedures by providing for joint preparation (§ 1506.2) and with other Federal procedures by providing that an agency may adopt appropriate environmental documents prepared by another agency (§ 1506.3).

(i) Combining environmental documents with other documents (§ 1506.4).

(j) Using accelerated procedures for proposals for legislation (§ 1506.8).

(k) Using categorical exclusions to define categories of actions which do not individually or cumulatively have a significant effect on the human environment (§ 1508.4) and which are therefore exempt from requirements to prepare an environmental impact statement.

(*l*) Using a finding of no significant impact when an action not otherwise excluded will not have a significant effect on the human environment (§ 1508.13) and is therefore exempt from requirements to prepare an environmental impact statement.

§ 1500.6 Agency authority

Each agency shall interpret the provisions of the Act as a supplement to its existing authority and as a mandate to view traditional policies and missions in the light of the Act's national environmental objectives. Agencies shall review their policies, procedures, and regulations accordingly and revise them as necessary to insure full compliance with the purposes and provisions of the Act. The phrase "to the fullest extent possible" in section 102 means that each agency of the Federal Government shall comply with that section unless existing law applicable to the agency's operations expressly prohibits or makes compliance impossible.

Part 1501

NEPA and Agency Planning

Sec.

1501.1 Purpose.
1501.2 Apply NEPA early in the process.
1501.3 When to prepare an environmental assessment.
1501.4 Whether to prepare an environmental impact statement.
1501.5 Lead agencies.
1501.6 Cooperating agencies.
1501.7 Scoping.
1501.8 Time limits.

Authority: NEPA, the Environmental Quality Improvement Act of 1970, as amended (42 U.S.C. 4371 *et seq.*), sec. 309 of the Clean Air Act, as amended (42 U.S.C. 7609), and E.O. 11514 (Mar. 5, 1970, as amended by E.O. 11991, May 24, 1977).

Source: 43 FR 55992, Nov. 29, 1978, unless otherwise noted.

§ 1501.1 Purpose

The purposes of this part include:

(a) Integrating the NEPA process into early planning to insure appropriate consideration of NEPA's policies and to eliminate delay.

(b) Emphasizing cooperative consultation among agencies before the environmental impact statement is prepared rather than submission of adversary comments on a completed document.

(c) Providing for the swift and fair resolution of lead agency disputes.

(d) Identifying at an early stage the significant environmental issues deserving of study and deemphasizing insignificant issues, narrowing the scope of the environmental impact statement accordingly.

(e) Providing a mechanism for putting appropriate time limits on the environmental impact statement process.

§ 1501.2 Apply NEPA early in the process

Agencies shall integrate the NEPA process with other planning at the earliest possible time to insure that planning and decisions reflect environmental values, to avoid delays later in the process, and to head off potential conflicts. Each agency shall:

(a) Comply with the mandate of section 102(2)(A) to "utilize a systematic, interdisciplinary approach which will insure the integrated use of the natural and social sciences and the environmental design arts in planning and in decisionmaking which may have an impact on man's environment," as specified by § 1507.2.

(b) Identify environmental effects and values in adequate detail so they can be compared to economic and technical analyses. Environmental documents and appropriate analyses shall be circulated and reviewed at the same time as other planning documents.

(c) Study, develop, and describe appropriate alternatives to recommended courses of action in any proposal which involves unresolved conflicts concerning alternative uses of available resources as provided by section 102(2)(E) of the Act.

(d) Provide for cases where actions are planned by private applicants or other non-Federal entities before Federal involvement so that:

(1) Policies or designated staff are available to advise potential applicants of studies or other information foreseeably required for later Federal action.

(2) The Federal agency consults early with appropriate State and local agencies and Indian tribes and with interested private persons and organizations when its own involvement is reasonably foreseeable.

(3) The Federal agency commences its NEPA process at the earliest possible time.

§ 1501.3 When to prepare an environmental assessment

(a) Agencies shall prepare an environmental assessment (§ 1508.9) when necessary under the procedures adopted by individual agencies to supplement these regulations as described in § 1507.3. An assessment is not necessary if the agency has decided to prepare an environmental impact statement.

(b) Agencies may prepare an environmental assessment on any action at any time in order to assist agency planning and decisionmaking.

§ 1501.4 Whether to prepare an environmental impact statement

In determining whether to prepare an environmental impact statement the Federal agency shall:

(a) Determine under its procedures supplementing these regulations (described in § 1507.3) whether the proposal is one which:

(1) Normally requires an environmental impact statement, or

(2) Normally does not require either an environmental impact statement or an environmental assessment (categorical exclusion).

(b) If the proposed action is not covered by paragraph (a) of this section, prepare an environmental assessment (§ 1508.9). The agency shall involve environmental agencies, applicants, and the public, to the extent practicable, in preparing assessments required by § 1508.9(a)(1).

(c) Based on the environmental assessment make its determination whether to prepare an environmental impact statement.

(d) Commence the scoping process (§ 1507.7), if the agency will prepare an environmental impact statement.

(e) Prepare a finding of no significant impact (§ 1508.13), if the agency determines on the basis of the environmental assessment not to prepare a statement.

(1) The agency shall make the finding of no significant impact available to the affected public as specified in § 1506.6.

(2) In certain limited circumstances, which the agency may cover in its procedures under § 1507.3, the agency shall make the finding of no significant impact available for public review (including State and areawide clearinghouses) for 30 days before the agency makes its final determination whether to prepare an environmental impact statement and before the action may begin. The circumstances are:

(i) The proposed action is, or is closely similar to, one which normally requires the preparation of an environmental impact statement under the procedures adopted by the agency pursuant to § 1507.3, or

(ii) The nature of the proposed action is one without precedent.

§ 1501.5 Lead agencies

(a) A lead agency shall supervise the preparation of an environmental impact statement if more than one Federal agency either:

(1) Proposes or is involved in the same action; or

(2) Is involved in a group of actions directly related to each other because of their functional interdependence or geographical proximity.

(b) Federal, State, or local agencies, including at least one Federal agency, may act as joint lead agencies to prepare an environmental impact statement (§ 1506.2).

(c) If an action falls within the provisions of paragraph (a) of this section the potential lead agencies shall determine by letter or memorandum which agency shall be the lead agency and which shall be cooperating agencies. The agencies shall resolve the lead agency question so as not to cause delay. If there is disagreement among the agencies, the following factors (which are listed in order of descending importance) shall determine lead agency designation:

(1) Magnitude of agency's involvement.

(2) Project approval/disapproval authority.

(3) Expertise concerning the action's environmental effects.

(4) Duration of agency's involvement.

(5) Sequence of agency's involvement.

(d) Any Federal agency, or any State or local agency or private person substantially affected by the absence of lead agency designation, may make a written request to the potential lead agencies that a lead agency be designated.

(e) If Federal agencies are unable to agree on which agency will be the lead agency or if the procedure described in paragraph (c) of this section has not resulted within 45 days in a lead agency designation, any of the agencies or persons concerned may file a request with the Council asking it to determine which Federal agency shall be the lead agency.

A copy of the request shall be transmitted to each potential lead agency. The request shall consist of:

(1) A precise description of the nature and extent of the proposed action.

(2) A detailed statement of why each potential lead agency should or should not be the lead agency under the criteria specified in paragraph (c) of this section.

(f) A response may be filed by any potential lead agency concerned within 20 days after a request is filed with the Council. The Council shall determine as soon as possible but not later than 20 days after receiving the request and all responses to it which Federal agency shall be the lead agency and which other Federal agencies shall be cooperating agencies.

[43 FR 55992, Nov. 29, 1978; 44 FR 873, Jan. 3, 1979]

§ 1501.6 Cooperating agencies

The purpose of this section is to emphasize agency cooperation early in the NEPA process. Upon request of the lead agency, any other Federal agency which has jurisdiction by law shall be a cooperating agency. In addition any other Federal agency which has special expertise with respect to any environmental issue, which should be addressed in the statement may be a cooperating agency upon request of the lead agency. An agency may request the lead agency to designate it a cooperating agency.

(a) The lead agency shall:

(1) Request the participation of each cooperating agency in the NEPA process at the earliest possible time.

(2) Use the environmental analysis and proposals of cooperating agencies with jurisdiction by law or special expertise, to the maximum extent possible consistent with its responsibility as lead agency.

(3) Meet with a cooperating agency at the latter's request.

(b) Each cooperating agency shall:

(1) Participate in the NEPA process at the earliest possible time.

(2) Participate in the scoping process (described below in § 1501.7).

(3) Assume on request of the lead agency responsibility for developing information and preparing environmental analyses including portions of the environmental impact statement concerning which the cooperating agency has special expertise.

(4) Make available staff support at the lead agency's request to enhance the latter's interdisciplinary capability.

(5) Normally use its own funds. The lead agency shall, to the extent available funds permit, fund those major activities or analyses it requests from cooperating agencies. Potential lead agencies shall include such funding requirements in their budget requests.

(c) A cooperating agency may in response to a lead agency's request for assistance in preparing the environmental impact statement (described in paragraph (b)(3), (4) or (5) of this section) reply that other program commitments preclude any involvement or the degree of involvement requested in the action that is the subject of the environmental impact statement. A copy of this reply shall be submitted to the Council.

§ 1501.7 Scoping

There shall be an early and open process for determining the scope of issues to be addressed and for identifying the significant issues related to a proposed action. This process shall be termed scoping. As soon as practicable after its decision to prepare an environmental impact statement and before the scoping process the lead agency shall publish a notice of intent (§ 1508.22) in the Federal Register except as provided in § 1507.3(e).

(a) As part of the scoping process the lead agency shall:

(1) Invite the participation of affected Federal, State, and local agencies, any affected Indian tribe, the proponent of the action, and other interested persons (including those who might not be in accord with the action on environmental grounds), unless there is a limited exception under § 1507.3(c). An agency may give notice in accordance with § 1506.6.

(2) Determine the scope (§ 1508.25) and the significant issues to be analyzed in depth in the environmental impact statement.

(3) Identify and eliminate from detailed study the issues which are not significant or which have been covered by prior environmental review (§ 1506.3), narrowing the discussion of these issues in the statement to a brief presentation of why they will not have a significant effect on the human environment or providing a reference to their coverage elsewhere.

(4) Allocate assignments for preparation of the environmental impact statement among the lead and cooperating agencies, with the lead agency retaining responsibility for the statement.

(5) Indicate any public environmental assessments and other environmental impact statements which are being or will be prepared that are related to but are not part of the scope of the impact statement under consideration.

(6) Identify other environmental review and consultation requirements so the lead and cooperating agencies may prepare other required analyses and studies concurrently with, and integrated with, the environmental impact statement as provided in § 1502.25.

(7) Indicate the relationship between the timing of the preparation of environmental analyses and the agency's tentative planning and decisionmaking schedule.

(b) As part of the scoping process the lead agency may:

(1) Set page limits on environmental documents (§ 1502.7).

(2) Set time limits (§ 1501.8).

(3) Adopt procedures under § 1507.3 to combine its environmental assessment process with its scoping process.

(4) Hold an early scoping meeting or meetings which may be integrated with any other early planning meeting the agency has. Such a scoping meeting will often be appropriate when the impacts of a particular action are confined to specific sites.

(c) An agency shall revise the determinations made under paragraphs (a) and (b) of this section if substantial changes are made later in the proposed action, or if significant new circumstances or information arise which bear on the proposal or its impacts.

§ 1501.8 Time limits

Although the Council has decided that prescribed universal time limits for the entire NEPA process are too inflexible, Federal agencies are encouraged to set time limits appropriate to individual actions (consistent with the time intervals required by § 1506.10). When multiple agencies are involved the reference to agency below means lead agency.

(a) The agency shall set time limits if an applicant for the proposed action requests them: *Provided,* That the limits are consistent with the purposes of NEPA and other essential considerations of national policy.

(b) The agency may:

(1) Consider the following factors in determining time limits:

(i) Potential for environmental harm.

(ii) Size of the proposed action.

(iii) State of the art of analytic techniques.

(iv) Degree of public need for the proposed action, including the consequences of delay.

(v) Number of persons and agencies affected.

(vi) Degree to which relevant information is known and if not known the time required for obtaining it.

(vii) Degree to which the action is controversial.

(viii) Other time limits imposed on the agency by law, regulations, or executive order.

(2) Set overall time limits or limits for each constituent part of the NEPA process, which may include:

(i) Decision on whether to prepare an environmental impact statement (if not already decided).

(ii) Determination of the scope of the environmental impact statement.

(iii) Preparation of the draft environmental impact statement.

(iv) Review of any comments on the draft environmental impact statement from the public and agencies.

(v) Preparation of the final environmental impact statement.

(vi) Review of any comments on the final environmental impact statement.

(vii) Decision on the action based in part on the environmental impact statement.

(3) Designate a person (such as the project manager or a person in the agency's office with NEPA responsibilities) to expedite the NEPA process.

(c) State or local agencies or members of the public may request a Federal Agency to set time limits.

Part 1502

Environmental Impact Statement

Sec.
1502.1 Purpose.
1502.2 Implementation.
1502.3 Statutory requirements for statements.
1502.4 Major Federal actions requiring the preparation of environmental impact statements.
1502.5 Timing.
1502.6 Interdisciplinary preparation.
1502.7 Page limits.
1502.8 Writing.
1502.9 Draft, final, and supplemental statements.
1502.10 Recommended format.
1502.11 Cover sheet.
1502.12 Summary.
1502.13 Purpose and need.
1502.14 Alternatives including the proposed action.
1502.15 Affected environment.
1502.16 Environmental consequences.
1502.17 List of preparers.
1502.18 Appendix.
1502.19 Circulation of the environmental impact statement.
1502.20 Tiering.
1502.21 Incorporation by reference.
1502.22 Incomplete or unavailable information.
1502.23 Cost-benefit analysis.
1502.24 Methodology and scientific accuracy.
1502.25 Environmental review and consultation requirements.

AUTHORITY: NEPA, the Environmental Quality Improvement Act of 1970, as amended (42 U.S.C. 4371 *et seq.*), sec. 309 of the Clean Air Act, as amended (42 U.S.C. 7609), and E.O. 11514 (Mar. 5, 1970, as amended by E.O. 11991, May 24, 1977).

SOURCE: 43 FR 55994, Nov. 29, 1978, unless otherwise noted.

§ 1502.1 Purpose

The primary purpose of an environmental impact statement is to serve as an action-forcing device to insure that the policies and goals defined in the Act are infused into the ongoing programs and actions of the Federal Government. It shall provide full and fair discussion of significant environmental impacts and shall inform decisionmakers and the public of the reasonable alternatives which would avoid or minimize adverse impacts or enhance the quality of the human environment. Agencies shall focus on significant environmental issues and alternatives and shall reduce paperwork and the accumulation of extraneous background data. Statements shall be concise, clear, and to the point, and shall be supported by evidence that the agency has made the necessary environmental analyses. An environmental impact statement is more than a disclosure document. It shall be used by Federal officials in conjunction with other relevant material to plan actions and make decisions.

§ 1502.2 Implementation

To achieve the purposes set forth in § 1502.1 agencies shall prepare environmental impact statements in the following manner:

(a) Environmental impact statements shall be analytic rather than encyclopedic.

(b) Impacts shall be discussed in proportion to their significance. There shall be only brief discussion of other than significant issues. As in a finding of no significant impact, there should be only enough discussion to show why more study is not warranted.

(c) Environmental impact statements shall be kept concise and shall be no longer than absolutely necessary to comply with NEPA and with these regulations. Length should vary first with potential environmental problems and then with project size.

(d) Environmental impact statements shall state how alternatives considered in it and decisions based on it will or will not achieve the requirements of sections 101 and 102(1) of the Act and other environmental laws and policies.

(e) The range of alternatives discussed in environmental impact statements shall encompass those to be considered by the ultimate agency decisionmaker.

(f) Agencies shall not commit resources prejudicing selection of alternatives before making a final decision (§ 1506.1).

(g) Environmental impact statements shall serve as the means of assessing the environmental impact of proposed agency actions, rather than justifying decisions already made.

§ 1502.3 Statutory requirements for statements

As required by sec. 102(2)(C) of NEPA environmental impact statements (§ 1508.11) are to be included in every recommendation or report.

On proposals (§ 1508.23).

For legislation and (§ 1508.17).

Other major Federal actions (§ 1508.18).

Significantly (§ 1508.27).

Affecting (§§ 1508.3, 1508.8).

The quality of the human environment (§ 1508.14).

§ 1502.4 Major Federal actions requiring the preparation of environmental impact statements

(a) Agencies shall make sure the proposal which is the subject of an environmental impact statement is properly defined. Agencies shall use the criteria for scope (§ 1508.25) to determine which proposal(s) shall be the subject of a particular statement. Proposals or parts of proposals which are related to each other closely enough to be, in effect, a single course of action shall be evaluated in a single impact statement.

(b) Environmental impact statements may be prepared, and are sometimes required, for broad Federal actions such as the adoption of new agency programs or regulations (§ 1508.18). Agencies shall prepare statements on broad actions so that they are relevant to policy and are timed to coincide with meaningful points in agency planning and decisionmaking.

(c) When preparing statements on broad actions (including proposals by more than one agency), agencies may find it useful to evaluate the proposal(s) in one of the following ways:

(1) Geographically, including actions occurring in the same general location, such as body of water, region, or metropolitan area.

(2) Generically, including actions which have relevant similarities, such as common timing, impacts, alternatives, methods of implementation, media, or subject matter.

(3) By stage of technological development including federal or federally assisted research, development or demonstration programs for new technologies which, if applied, could significantly affect the quality of the human environment. Statements shall be prepared on such programs and shall be available before the program has reached a stage of investment or commitment to implementation likely to determine subsequent development or restrict later alternatives.

(d) Agencies shall as appropriate employ scoping (§ 1501.7), tiering (§ 1502.20), and other methods listed in §§ 1500.4 and 1500.5 to relate broad and narrow actions and to avoid duplication and delay.

§ 1502.5 Timing

An agency shall commence preparation of an environmental impact statement as close as possible to the time the agency is developing or is presented with a proposal (§ 1508.23) so that preparation can be completed in time for the final statement to be included in any recommendation or report on the proposal. The statement shall be prepared early enough so that it can serve practically as an important contribution to the decisionmaking process and will not be used to rationalize or justify decisions already made (§§ 1500.2(c), 1501.2, and 1502.2). For instance:

(a) For projects directly undertaken by Federal agencies the environmental impact statement shall be prepared at the feasibility analysis (go-no go) stage and may be supplemented at a later stage if necessary.

(b) For applications to the agency appropriate environmental assessments or statements shall be commenced no later than immediately after the application is received. Federal agencies are encouraged to begin preparation of such assessments or statements earlier, preferably jointly with applicable State or local agencies.

(c) For adjudication, the final environmental impact statement shall normally precede the final staff recommendation and that portion of the public hearing related to the impact study. In appropriate circumstances the statement may follow preliminary hearings designed to gather information for use in the statements.

(d) For informal rulemaking the draft environmental impact statement shall normally accompany the proposed rule.

§ 1502.6 Interdisciplinary preparation

Environmental impact statements shall be prepared using an interdisciplinary approach which will insure the integrated use of the natural and social sciences and the environmental design arts (section 102(2)(A) of the Act). The disciplines of the preparers shall be appropriate to the scope and issues identified in the scoping process (§ 1501.7).

§ 1502.7 Page limits

The text of final environmental impact statements (e.g., paragraphs (d) through (g) of § 1502.10) shall normally be less than 150 pages and for proposals of unusual scope or complexity shall normally be less than 300 pages.

§ 1502.8 Writing

Environmental impact statements shall be written in plain language and may use appropriate graphics so that decisionmakers and the public can readily understand them. Agencies should employ writers of clear prose or editors to write, review, or edit statements, which will be based upon the analysis and supporting data from the natural and social sciences and the environmental design arts.

§ 1502.9 Draft, final, and supplemental statements

Except for proposals for legislation as provided in § 1506.8 environmental impact statements shall be prepared in two stages and may be supplemented.

(a) Draft environmental impact statements shall be prepared in accordance with the scope decided upon in the scoping process. The lead agency shall work with the cooperating agencies and shall obtain comments as required in Part 1503 of this chapter. The draft statement must fulfill and satisfy to the fullest extent possible the requirements established for final statements in section 102(2)(C) of the Act. If a draft statement is so inadequate as to preclude meaningful analysis, the agency shall prepare and circulate a revised draft of the appropriate portion. The agency shall make every effort to disclose and discuss at appropriate points in the draft statement all major points of view on the environmental impacts of the alternatives including the proposed action.

(b) Final environmental impact statements shall respond to comments as required in Part 1503 of this chapter. The agency shall discuss at appropriate points in the final statement any responsible opposing view which was not adequately discussed in the draft statement and shall indicate the agency's response to the issues raised.

(c) Agencies:

(1) Shall prepare supplements to either draft or final environmental impact statements if:

(i) The agency makes substantial changes in the proposed action that are relevant to environmental concerns; or

(ii) There are significant new circumstances or information relevant to environmental concerns and bearing on the proposed action or its impacts.

(2) May also prepare supplements when the agency determines that the purposes of the Act will be furthered by doing so.

(3) Shall adopt procedures for introducing a supplement into its formal administrative record, if such a record exists.

(4) Shall prepare, circulate, and file a supplement to a statement in the same fashion (exclusive of scoping) as a draft and final statement unless alternative procedures are approved by the Council.

§ 1502.10 Recommended format

Agencies shall use a format for environmental impact statements which will encourage good analysis and clear presentation of the alternatives including the proposed action. The following standard format for environmental impact statements should be followed unless the agency determines that there is a compelling reason to do otherwise:

(a) Cover sheet.

(b) Summary.

(c) Table of contents.

(d) Purpose of and need for action.

(e) Alternatives including proposed action (sections 102(2)(C)(iii) and 102(2)(E) of the Act).

(f) Affected environment.

(g) Environmental consequences (especially sections 102(2)(C)(i), (ii), (iv), and (v) of the Act).

(h) List of preparers.

(i) List of Agencies, Organizations, and persons to whom copies of the statement are sent.

(j) Index.

(k) Appendices (if any).

If a different format is used, it shall include paragraphs (a), (b), (c), (h), (i), and (j), of this section and shall include the substance of paragraphs (d), (e), (f), (g), and (k) of this section, as further described in §§ 1502.11 through 1502.18, in any appropriate format.

§ 1502.11 Cover sheet

The cover sheet shall not exceed one page. It shall include:

(a) A list of the responsible agencies including the lead agency and any cooperating agencies.

(b) The title of the proposed action that is the subject of the statement (and if appropriate the titles of related cooperating agency actions), together with the State(s) and county(ies) (or other jurisdiction if applicable) where the action is located.

(c) The name, address, and telephone number of the person at the agency who can supply further information.

(d) A designation of the statement as a draft, final, or draft or final supplement.

(e) A one paragraph abstract of the statement.

(f) The date by which comments must be received (computed in cooperation with EPA under § 1506.10).

The information required by this section may be entered on Standard Form 424 (in items 4, 6, 7, 10, and 18).

§ 1502.12 Summary

Each environmental impact statement shall contain a summary which adequately and accurately summarizes the statement. The summary shall stress the major conclusions, areas of controversy (including issues raised by agencies and the public), and the issues to be resolved (including the choice among alternatives). The summary will normally not exceed 15 pages.

§ 1502.13 Purpose and need

The statement shall briefly specify the underlying purpose and need to which the agency is responding in proposing the alternatives including the proposed action.

§ 1502.14 Alternatives including the proposed action

This section is the heart of the environmental impact statement. Based on the information and analysis presented in the sections on the Affected Environment (§ 1502.15) and the Environmental Consequences (§ 1502.16), it should present the environmental impacts of the proposal and the alternatives in comparative form, thus sharply defining the issues and providing a clear basis for choice among options by the decisionmaker and the public. In this section agencies shall:

(a) Rigorously explore and objectively evaluate all reasonable alternatives, and for alternatives which were eliminated from detailed study, briefly discuss the reasons for their having been eliminated.

(b) Devote substantial treatment to each alternative considered in detail including the proposed action so that reviewers may evaluate their comparative merits.

(c) Include reasonable alternatives not within the jurisdiction of the lead agency.

(d) Include the alternative of no action.

(e) Identify the agency's preferred alternative or alternatives, if one or more exists, in the draft statement and identify such alternative in the final statement unless another law prohibits the expression of such a preference.

(f) Include appropriate mitigation measures not already included in the proposed action or alternatives.

§ 1502.15 Affected environment

The environmental impact statement shall succinctly describe the environment of the area(s) to be affected or created by the alternatives under consideration. The descriptions shall be no longer than is necessary to understand the effects of the alternatives. Data and analyses in a statement shall be commensurate with the importance of the impact, with less important material summarized, consolidated, or simply referenced. Agencies shall avoid useless bulk in statements and shall concentrate effort and attention on important issues. Verbose descriptions of the affected environment are themselves no measure of the adequacy of an environmental impact statement.

§ 1502.16 Environmental consequences

This section forms the scientific and analytic basis for the comparisons under § 1502.14. It shall consolidate the discussions of those elements required by sections 102(2)(C)(i), (ii), (iv), and (v) of NEPA which are within the scope of the statement and as much of section 102(2)(C)(iii) as is necessary to support the comparisons. The discussion will include the environmental impacts of the alternatives including the proposed action, any adverse environmental effects which cannot be avoided should the proposal be implemented, the relationship between short-term uses of man's environment and the maintenance and enhancement of long-term productivity, and any irreversible or irretrievable commitments of resources which would be involved in the proposal should it be implemented. This section should not duplicate discussions in § 1502.14. It shall include discussions of:

(a) Direct effects and their significance (§ 1508.8).

(b) Indirect effects and their significance (§ 1508.8).

(c) Possible conflicts between the proposed action and the objectives of Federal, regional, State, and local (and in the case of a reservation, Indian tribe) land use plans, policies and controls for the area concerned. (See § 1506.2(d).)

(d) The environmental effects of alternatives including the proposed action. The comparisons under § 1502.14 will be based on this discussion.

(e) Energy requirements and conservation potential of various alternatives and mitigation measures.

(f) Natural or depletable resource requirements and conservation potential of various alternatives and mitigation measures.

(g) Urban quality, historic and cultural resources, and the design of the built environment, including the reuse and conservation potential of various alternatives and mitigation measures.

(h) Means to mitigate adverse environmental impacts (if not fully covered under § 1502.14(f)).

[43 FR 55994, Nov. 29, 1978; 44 FR 873, Jan. 3, 1979]

§ 1502.17 List of preparers

The environmental impact statement shall list the names, together with their qualifications (expertise, experience, professional disciplines), of the persons who were primarily responsible for preparing the environmental impact statement or significant background papers, including basic components of the statement (§§ 1502.6 and 1502.8). Where possible the persons who are responsible for a particular analysis, including analyses in background papers, shall be identified. Normally the list will not exceed two pages.

§ 1502.18 Appendix

If an agency prepares an appendix to an environmental impact statement the appendix shall:

(a) Consist of material prepared in connection with an environmental impact statement (as distinct from material which is not so prepared and which is incorporated by reference (§ 1502.21)).

(b) Normally consist of material which substantiates any analysis fundamental to the impact statement.

(c) Normally be analytic and relevant to the decision to be made.

(d) Be circulated with the environmental impact statement or be readily available on request.

§ 1502.19 Circulation of the environmental impact statement

Agencies shall circulate the entire draft and final environmental impact statements except for certain appendices as provided in § 1502.18(d) and unchanged statements as provided in § 1503.4(c). However, if the statement is unusually long, the agency may circulate the summary instead, except that the entire statement shall be furnished to:

(a) Any Federal agency which has jurisdiction by law or special expertise with respect to any environmental impact involved and any appropriate Federal, State or local agency authorized to develop and enforce environmental standards.

(b) The applicant, if any.

(c) Any person, organization, or agency requesting the entire environmental impact statement.

(d) In the case of a final environmental impact statement any person, organization, or agency which submitted substantive comments on the draft.

If the agency circulates the summary and thereafter receives a timely request for the entire statement and for additional time to comment, the time for that requestor only shall be extended by at least 15 days beyond the minimum period.

§ 1502.20 Tiering

Agencies are encouraged to tier their environmental impact statements to eliminate repetitive discussions of the same issues and to focus on the actual issues ripe for decision at each level of environmental review (§ 1508.28). Whenever a broad environmental impact statement has been prepared (such as a program or policy statement) and a subsequent statement or environmental assessment is then prepared on an action included within the entire program or policy (such as a site specific action) the subsequent statement or environmental assessment need only summarize the issues discussed in the broader statement and incorporate discussions from the broader statement by reference and shall concentrate on the issues specific to the subsequent action. The subsequent document shall state where the earlier document is available. Tiering may also be appropriate for different stages of actions. (Section 1508.28).

§ 1502.21 Incorporation by reference

Agencies shall incorporate material into an environmental impact statement by reference when the effect will be to cut down on bulk without impeding agency and public review of the action. The incorporated material shall be cited in the statement and its content briefly described. No material may be incorporated by reference unless it is reasonably available for inspection by potentially interested persons within the time allowed for comment. Material based on proprietary data which is itself not available for review and comment shall not be incorporated by reference.

§ 1502.22 Incomplete or unavailable information

When an agency is evaluating reasonably foreseeable significant adverse effects on the human environment in an environmental impact statement and there is incomplete or unavailable information, the agency shall always make clear that such information is lacking.

(a) If the incomplete information relevant to reasonably foreseeable significant adverse impacts is essential to a reasoned choice among alternatives and the overall costs of obtaining it are not exorbitant, the agency shall include the information in the environmental impact statement.

(b) If the information relevant to reasonably foreseeable significant adverse impacts cannot be obtained because the overall costs of obtaining it are exorbitant or the means to obtain it are not known, the agency shall include within the environmental impact statement: (1) A statement that such information is incomplete or unavailable; (2) a statement of the relevance of the incomplete or unavailable information to evaluating reasonably foreseeable significant adverse impacts on the human environment; (3) a summary of existing credible scientific evidence which is relevant to evaluating the reasonably foreseeable significant adverse impacts on the human environment, and (4) the agency's evaluation of such impacts based upon theoretical approaches or research methods generally accepted in the scientific community. For the purposes of this section, "reasonably foreseeable" includes impacts which have catastrophic consequences, even if their probability of occurrence is low, provided that the analysis of the impacts is supported by credible scientific evidence, is not based on pure conjecture, and is within the rule of reason.

(c) The amended regulation will be applicable to all environmental impact statements for which a Notice of Intent (40 CFR 1508.22) is published in the Federal Register on or after May 27, 1986. For environmental impact statements in progress, agencies may choose to comply with the requirements of either the original or amended regulation.

[51 FR 15625, Apr. 25, 1986]

§ 1502.23 Cost-benefit analysis

If a cost-benefit analysis relevant to the choice among environmentally different alternatives is being considered for the proposed action, it shall be incorporated by reference or appended to the statement as an aid in evaluating the environmental consequences. To assess the adequacy of compliance with section 102(2)(B) of the Act the statement shall, when a cost-benefit analysis is prepared, discuss the relationship between the analysis and any analyses of unquantified environmental impacts, values, and amenities. For purposes of complying with the Act, the weighing of the merits and drawbacks of the various alternatives need not be displayed in a monetary cost-benefit analysis and should not be when there are important qualitative considerations. In any event, an environmental impact statement should at least indicate those considerations, including factors not related to environmental quality, which are likely to be relevant and important to a decision.

§ 1502.24 Methodology and scientific accuracy

Agencies shall insure the professional integrity, including scientific integrity, of the discussions and analyses in environmental impact statements. They shall identify any methodologies used and shall make explicit reference by footnote to the scientific and other sources relied upon for conclusions in the statement. An agency may place discussion of methodology in an appendix.

§ 1502.25 Environmental review and consultation requirements

(a) To the fullest extent possible, agencies shall prepare draft environmental impact statements concurrently with and integrated with environmental impact analyses and related surveys and studies required by the Fish and Wildlife Coordination Act (16 U.S.C. 661 et seq.), the National Historic Preservation Act of 1966 (16 U.S.C. 470 et seq.), the Endangered

Species Act of 1973 (16 U.S.C. 1531 et seq.), and other environmental review laws and executive orders.

(b) The draft environmental impact statement shall list all Federal permits, licenses, and other entitlements which must be obtained in implementing the proposal. If it is uncertain whether a Federal permit, license, or other entitlement is necessary, the draft environmental impact statement shall so indicate.

Part 1503

Commenting

Sec.
1503.1 Inviting comments.
1503.2 Duty to comment.
1503.3 Specificity of comments.
1503.4 Response to comments.

AUTHORITY: NEPA, the Environmental Quality Improvement Act of 1970, as amended (42 U.S.C. 4371 *et seq.*), sec. 309 of the Clean Air Act, as amended (42 U.S.C. 7609), and E.O. 11514 (Mar. 5, 1970, as amended by E.O. 11991, May 24, 1977).

SOURCE: 43 FR 55997, Nov. 29, 1978, unless otherwise noted.

§ 1503.1 Inviting comments

(a) After preparing a draft environmental impact statement and before preparing a final environmental impact statement the agency shall:

(1) Obtain the comments of any Federal agency which has jurisdiction by law or special expertise with respect to any environmental impact involved or which is authorized to develop and enforce environmental standards.

(2) Request the comments of:

(i) Appropriate State and local agencies which are authorized to develop and enforce environmental standards;

(ii) Indian tribes, when the effects may be on a reservation; and

(iii) Any agency which has requested that it receive statements on actions of the kind proposed.

Office of Management and Budget Circular A–95 (Revised), through its system of clearinghouses, provides a means of securing the views of State and local environmental agencies. The clearinghouses may be used, by mutual agreement of the lead agency and the clearinghouse, for securing State and local reviews of the draft environmental impact statements.

(3) Request comments from the applicant, if any.

(4) Request comments from the public, affirmatively soliciting comments from those persons or organizations who may be interested or affected.

(b) An agency may request comments on a final environmental impact statement before the decision is finally made. In any case other agencies or persons may make comments before the final decision unless a different time is provided under § 1506.10.

§ 1503.2 Duty to comment

Federal agencies with jurisdiction by law or special expertise with respect to any environmental impact involved and agencies which are authorized to develop and enforce environmental standards shall comment on statements within their jurisdiction, expertise, or authority. Agencies shall comment within the time period specified for comment in § 1506.10. A Federal agency may reply that it has no comment. If a cooperating agency is satisfied that its views are adequately reflected in the environmental impact statement, it should reply that it has no comment.

§ 1503.3 Specificity of comments

(a) Comments on an environmental impact statement or on a proposed action shall be as specific as possible and may address either the adequacy of the statement or the merits of the alternatives discussed or both.

(b) When a commenting agency criticizes a lead agency's predictive methodology, the commenting agency should describe the alternative methodology which it prefers and why.

(c) A cooperating agency shall specify in its comments whether it needs additional information to fulfill other applicable environmental reviews or consultation requirements and what information it needs. In particular, it shall specify any additional information it needs to comment adequately on the draft statement's analysis of significant site-specific effects associated with the granting or approving by that cooperating agency of necessary Federal permits, licenses, or entitlements.

(d) When a cooperating agency with jurisdiction by law objects to or expresses reservations about the proposal on grounds of environmental impacts, the agency expressing the objection or reservation shall specify the mitigation measures it considers necessary to allow the agency to grant or approve applicable permit, license, or related requirements or concurrences.

§ 1503.4 Response to comments

(a) An agency preparing a final environmental impact statement shall assess and consider comments both individually and collectively, and shall respond by one or more of the means listed below, stating its response in the final statement. Possible responses are to:

(1) Modify alternatives including the proposed action.

(2) Develop and evaluate alternatives not previously given serious consideration by the agency.

(3) Supplement, improve, or modify its analyses.

(4) Make factual corrections.

(5) Explain why the comments do not warrant further agency response, citing the sources, authorities, or reasons which support the agency's position and, if appropriate, indicate those circumstances which would trigger agency reappraisal or further response.

(b) All substantive comments received on the draft statement (or summaries thereof where the response has been exceptionally voluminous), should be attached to the final statement whether or not the comment is thought to merit individual discussion by the agency in the text of the statement.

(c) If changes in response to comments are minor and are confined to the responses described in paragraphs (a)(4) and (5) of this section, agencies may write them on errata sheets and attach them to the statement instead of rewriting the draft statement. In such cases only the comments, the responses, and the changes and not the final statement need be circulated (§ 1502.19). The entire document with a new cover sheet shall be filed as the final statement (§ 1506.9).

Part 1504

Predecision Referrals to the Council of Proposed Federal Actions Determined to be Environmentally Unsatisfactory

Sec.

1504.1 Purpose.
1504.2 Criteria for referral.
1504.3 Procedure for referrals and response.

AUTHORITY: NEPA, the Environmental Quality Improvement Act of 1970, as amended (42 U.S.C. 4371 *et seq.*), sec. 309 of the Clean Air Act, as amended (42 U.S.C. 7609), and E.O. 11514 (Mar. 5, 1970, as amended by E.O. 11991, May 24, 1977).

SOURCE: 43 FR 55998, Nov. 29, 1978, unless otherwise noted.

§ 1504.1 Purpose

(a) This part establishes procedures for referring to the Council Federal interagency disagreements concerning proposed major Federal actions that might cause unsatisfactory environmental effects. It provides means for early resolution of such disagreements.

(b) Under section 309 of the Clean Air Act (42 U.S.C. 7609), the Administrator of the Environmental Protection Agency is directed to review and comment publicly on the environmental impacts of Federal activities, including actions for which environmental impact statements are prepared. If after this review the Administrator determines that the matter is "unsatisfactory from the standpoint of public health or welfare or environmental quality," section 309 directs that the matter be referred to the Council (hereafter "environmental referrals").

(c) Under section 102(2)(C) of the Act other Federal agencies may make similar reviews of environmental impact statements, including judgments on the acceptability of anticipated environmental impacts. These reviews must be made available to the President, the Council and the public.

§ 1504.2 Criteria for referral

Environmental referrals should be made to the Council only after concerted, timely (as early as possible in the process), but unsuccessful attempts to resolve differences with the lead agency. In determining what environmental objections to the matter are appropriate to refer to the Council, an agency should weigh potential adverse environmental impacts, considering:

(a) Possible violation of national environmental standards or policies.

(b) Severity.

(c) Geographical scope.

(d) Duration.

(e) Importance as precedents.

(f) Availability of environmentally preferable alternatives.

§ 1504.3 Procedure for referrals and response

(a) A Federal agency making the referral to the Council shall:

(1) Advise the lead agency at the earliest possible time that it intends to refer a matter to the Council unless a satisfactory agreement is reached.

(2) Include such advice in the referring agency's comments on the draft environmental impact statement, except when the statement does not contain adequate information to permit an assessment of the matter's environmental acceptability.

(3) Identify any essential information that is lacking and request that it be made available at the earliest possible time.

(4) Send copies of such advice to the Council.

(b) The referring agency shall deliver its referral to the Council not later than twenty-five (25) days after the final environmental impact statement has been made available to the Environmental Protection Agency, commenting agencies, and the public. Except when an extension of this period has been granted by the lead agency, the Council will not accept a referral after that date.

(c) The referral shall consist of:

(1) A copy of the letter signed by the head of the referring agency and delivered to the lead agency informing the lead agency of the referral and the reasons for it, and requesting that no action be taken to implement the matter until the Council acts upon the referral. The letter shall include a copy of the statement referred to in (c)(2) of this section.

(2) A statement supported by factual evidence leading to the conclusion that the matter is unsatisfactory from the standpoint of public health or welfare or environmental quality. The statement shall:

(i) Identify any material facts in controversy and incorporate (by reference if appropriate) agreed upon facts.

(ii) Identify any existing environmental requirements or policies which would be violated by the matter,

(iii) Present the reasons why the referring agency believes the matter is environmentally unsatisfactory,

(iv) Contain a finding by the agency whether the issue raised is of national importance because of the threat to national environmental resources or policies or for some other reason,

(v) Review the steps taken by the referring agency to bring its concerns to the attention of the lead agency at the earliest possible time, and

(vi) Give the referring agency's recommendations as to what mitigation alternative, further study, or other course of action (including abandonment of the matter) are necessary to remedy the situation.

(d) Not later than twenty-five (25) days after the referral to the Council the lead agency may deliver a response to the Council, and the referring agency. If the lead agency requests more time and gives assurance that the matter will not go forward in the interim, the Council may grant an extension. The response shall:

(1) Address fully the issues raised in the referral.

(2) Be supported by evidence.

(3) Give the lead agency's response to the referring agency's recommendations.

(e) Interested persons (including the applicant) may deliver their views in writing to the Council. Views in support of the referral should be delivered not later than the referral. Views in support of the response shall be delivered not later than the response.

(f) Not later than twenty-five (25) days after receipt of both the referral and any response or upon being informed that there will be no response (unless the lead agency agrees to a longer time), the Council may take one or more of the following actions:

(1) Conclude that the process of referral and response has successfully resolved the problem.

(2) Initiate discussions with the agencies with the objective of mediation with referring and lead agencies.

(3) Hold public meetings or hearings to obtain additional views and information.

(4) Determine that the issue is not one of national importance and request the referring and lead agencies to pursue their decision process.

(5) Determine that the issue should be further negotiated by the referring and lead agencies and is not appropriate for Council consideration until one or more heads of agencies report to the Council that the agencies' disagreements are irreconcilable.

(6) Publish its findings and recommendations (including where appropriate a finding that the submitted evidence does not support the position of an agency).

(7) When appropriate, submit the referral and the response together with the Council's recommendation to the President for action.

(g) The Council shall take no longer than 60 days to complete the actions specified in paragraph (f)(2), (3), or (5) of this section.

(h) When the referral involves an action required by statute to be determined on the record after opportunity for agency hearing, the referral shall be conducted in a manner consistent with 5 U.S.C. 557(d) (Administrative Procedure Act).

[43 FR 55998, Nov. 29, 1978; 44 FR 873, Jan. 3, 1979]

Part 1505

NEPA and Agency Decisionmaking

Sec.

1505.1 Agency decisionmaking procedures.
1505.2 Record of decision in cases requiring environmental impact statements.
1505.3 Implementing the decision.

AUTHORITY: NEPA, the Environmental Quality Improvement Act of 1970, as amended (42 U.S.C. 4371 *et seq.*), sec. 309 of the Clean Air Act, as amended (42 U.S.C. 7609), and E.O. 11514 (Mar. 5, 1970, as amended by E.O. 11991, May 24, 1977).

SOURCE: 43 FR 55999, Nov. 29, 1978, unless otherwise noted.

§ 1505.1 Agency decisionmaking procedures

Agencies shall adopt procedures (§ 1507.3) to ensure that decisions are made in accordance with the policies and purposes of the Act. Such procedures shall include but not be limited to:

(a) Implementing procedures under section 102(2) to achieve the requirements of sections 101 and 102(1).

(b) Designating the major decision points for the agency's principal programs likely to have a significant effect on the human environment and assuring that the NEPA process corresponds with them.

(c) Requiring that relevant environmental documents, comments, and responses be part of the record in formal rulemaking or adjudicatory proceedings.

(d) Requiring that relevant environmental documents, comments, and responses accompany the proposal through existing agency review processes so that agency officials use the statement in making decisions.

(e) Requiring that the alternatives considered by the decisionmaker are encompassed by the range of alternatives discussed in the relevant environmental documents and that the decisionmaker consider the alternatives described in the environmental impact statement. If another decision document accompanies the relevant environmental documents to the decisionmaker, agencies are encouraged to make available to the public before the decision is made any part of that document that relates to the comparison of alternatives.

§ 1505.2 Record of decision in cases requiring environmental impact statements

At the time of its decision (§ 1506.10) or, if appropriate, its recommendation to Congress, each agency shall prepare a concise public record of decision. The record, which may be integrated into any other record prepared by the agency, including that required by OMB Circular A–95 (Revised), part I, sections 6(c) and (d), and part II, section 5(b)(4), shall:

(a) State what the decision was.

(b) Identify all alternatives considered by the agency in reaching its decision, specifying the alternative or alternatives which were considered to be environmentally preferable. An agency may discuss preferences among alternatives based on relevant factors including economic and technical considerations and agency statutory missions. An agency shall identify and discuss all such factors including any essential considerations of national policy which were balanced by the agency in making its decision and state how those considerations entered into its decision.

(c) State whether all practicable means to avoid or minimize environmental harm from the alternative selected have been adopted, and if not, why they were not. A monitoring and enforcement program shall be adopted and summarized where applicable for any mitigation.

§ 1505.3 Implementing the decision

Agencies may provide for monitoring to assure that their decisions are carried out and should do so in important cases. Mitigation (§ 1505.2(c)) and other conditions established in the environmental impact statement or during its review and committed as part of the decision shall be implemented by the lead agency or other appropriate consenting agency. The lead agency shall:

(a) Include appropriate conditions in grants, permits or other approvals.

(b) Condition funding of actions on mitigation.

(c) Upon request, inform cooperating or commenting agencies on progress in carrying out mitigation measures which they have proposed and which were adopted by the agency making the decision.

(d) Upon request, make available to the public the results of relevant monitoring.

Part 1506

Other Requirements of NEPA

Sec.
1506.1 Limitations on actions during NEPA process.
1506.2 Elimination of duplication with State and local procedures.
1506.3 Adoption.
1506.4 Combining documents.
1506.5 Agency responsibility.
1506.6 Public involvement.
1506.7 Further guidance.
1506.8 Proposals for legislation.
1506.9 Filing requirements.
1506.10 Timing of agency action.
1506.11 Emergencies.
1506.12 Effective date.

AUTHORITY: NEPA, the Environmental Quality Improvement Act of 1970, as amended (42 U.S.C. 4371 *et seq.*), sec. 309 of the Clean Air Act, as amended (42 U.S.C. 7609), and E.O. 11514 (Mar. 5, 1970, as amended by E.O. 11991, May 24, 1977).

SOURCE: 43 FR 56000, Nov. 29, 1978, unless otherwise noted.

§ 1506.1 Limitations on actions during NEPA process

(a) Until an agency issues a record of decision as provided in § 1505.2 (except as provided in paragraph (c) of this section), no action concerning the proposal shall be taken which would:

(1) Have an adverse environmental impact; or

(2) Limit the choice of reasonable alternatives.

(b) If any agency is considering an application from a non-Federal entity, and is aware that the applicant is about to take an action within the agency's jurisdiction that would meet either of the criteria in paragraph (a) of this section, then the agency shall promptly notify the applicant that the agency will take appropriate action to insure that the objectives and procedures of NEPA are achieved.

(c) While work on a required program environmental impact statement is in progress and the action is not covered by an existing program statement, agencies shall not undertake in the interim any major Federal action covered by the program which may significantly affect the quality of the human environment unless such action:

(1) Is justified independently of the program;

(2) Is itself accompanied by an adequate environmental impact statement; and

(3) Will not prejudice the ultimate decision on the program. Interim action prejudices the ultimate decision on the program when it tends to determine subsequent development or limit alternatives.

(d) This section does not preclude development by applicants of plans or designs or performance of other work necessary to support an application for Federal, State or local permits or assistance. Nothing in this section shall preclude Rural Electrification Administration approval of minimal expenditures not affecting the environment (*e.g.* long leadtime equipment and purchase options) made by non-governmental entities seeking loan guarantees from the Administration.

§ 1506.2 Elimination of duplication with State and local procedures

(a) Agencies authorized by law to cooperate with State agencies of statewide jurisdiction pursuant to section 102(2)(D) of the Act may do so.

(b) Agencies shall cooperate with State and local agencies to the fullest extent possible to reduce duplication between NEPA and State and local requirements, unless the agencies are specifically barred from doing so by some other law. Except for cases covered by paragraph (a) of this section, such cooperation shall to the fullest extent possible include:

(1) Joint planning processes.

(2) Joint environmental research and studies.

(3) Joint public hearings (except where otherwise provided by statute.

(4) Joint environmental assessments.

(c) Agencies shall cooperate with State and local agencies to the fullest extent possible to reduce duplication between NEPA and comparable State and local requirements, unless the agencies are specifically barred from doing so by some other law. Except for cases covered by paragraph (a) of this section, such cooperation shall to the fullest extent possible include joint environmental impact statements. In such cases one or more Federal agencies and one or more State or local agencies shall be joint lead agencies. Where State laws or local ordinances have environmental impact statement requirements in addition to but not in conflict with those in NEPA, Federal agencies shall cooperate in fulfilling these requirements as well as those of Federal laws so that one document will comply with all applicable laws.

(d) To better integrate environmental impact statements into State or local planning processes, statements shall discuss any inconsistency of a proposed action with any approved State or local plan and laws (whether or not federally sanctioned). Where an inconsistency exists, the statement should describe the extent to which the agency would reconcile its proposed action with the plan or law.

§ 1506.3 Adoption

(a) An agency may adopt a Federal draft or final environmental impact statement or portion thereof provided that the statement or portion thereof meets the standards for an adequate statement under these regulations.

(b) If the actions covered by the original environmental impact statement and the proposed action are substantially the same, the agency adopting another agency's statement is not required to recirculate it except as a final statement. Otherwise the adopting agency shall treat the statement as a draft and recirculate it (except as provided in paragraph (c) of this section).

(c) A cooperating agency may adopt without recirculating the environmental impact statement of a lead agency when, after an independent review of the statement, the cooperating agency concludes that its comments and suggestions have been satisfied.

(d) When an agency adopts a statement which is not final within the agency that prepared it, or when the action it assesses is the subject of a referral under Part 1504, or when the statement's adequacy is the subject of a judicial action which is not final, the agency shall so specify.

§ 1506.4 Combining documents

Any environmental document in compliance with NEPA may be combined with any other agency document to reduce duplication and paperwork.

§ 1506.5 Agency responsibility

(a) *Information.* If an agency requires an applicant to submit environmental information for possible use by the agency in preparing an environmental impact statement, then the agency should assist the applicant by outlining the types of information required. The agency shall independently evaluate the information submitted and shall be responsible for its accuracy. If the agency chooses to use the information submitted by the applicant in the environmental impact statement, either directly or by reference, then the names of the persons responsible for the independent evaluation shall be included in the list of preparers (§ 1502.17). It is the intent of this paragraph that acceptable work not be redone, but that it be verified by the agency.

(b) *Environmental assessments.* If an agency permits an applicant to prepare an environmental assessment, the agency, besides fulfilling the requirements of paragraph (a) of this section, shall make its own evaluation of the environmental issues and take responsibility for the scope and content of the environmental assessment.

(c) *Environmental impact statements.* Except as provided in §§ 1506.2 and 1506.3 any environmental impact statement prepared pursuant to the requirements of NEPA shall be prepared directly by or by a contractor selected by the lead agency or where appropriate under § 1501.6(b), a cooperating agency. It is the intent of these regulations that the contractor be chosen solely by the lead agency, or by the lead agency in cooperation with cooperating agencies, or where appropriate by a cooperating agency to avoid any conflict of interest. Contractors shall execute a disclosure statement prepared by the lead agency, or where appropriate the cooperating agency, specifying that they have no financial or other interest in the outcome of the project. If the document is prepared by contract, the responsible Federal official shall furnish guidance and participate in the preparation and shall independently evaluate the statement prior to its approval and take responsibility for its scope and contents. Nothing in this section is intended to prohibit any agency from requesting any person to submit information to it or prohibit any person from submitting information to any agency.

§ 1506.6 Public involvement

Agencies shall:

(a) Make diligent efforts to involve the public in preparing and implementing their NEPA procedures.

(b) Provide public notice of NEPA-related hearings, public meetings, and the availability of environmental documents so as to inform those persons and agencies who may be interested or affected.

(1) In all cases the agency shall mail notice to those who have requested it on an individual action.

(2) In the case of an action with effects of national concern notice shall include publication in the FEDERAL REGISTER and notice by mail to national organizations reasonably expected to be interested in the matter and may include listing in the *102 Monitor.* An agency engaged in rulemaking may provide notice by mail to national organizations who have requested that notice regularly be provided. Agencies shall maintain a list of such organizations.

(3) In the case of an action with effects primarily of local concern the notice may include:

(i) Notice to State and areawide clearinghouses pursuant to OMB Circular A–95 (Revised).

(ii) Notice to Indian tribes when effects may occur on reservations.

(iii) Following the affected State's public notice procedures for comparable actions.

(iv) Publication in local newspapers (in papers of general circulation rather than legal papers).

(v) Notice through other local media.

(vi) Notice to potentially interested community organizations including small business associations.

(vii) Publication in newsletters that may be expected to reach potentially interested persons.

(viii) Direct mailing to owners and occupants of nearby or affected property.

(ix) Posting of notice on and off site in the area where the action is to be located.

(c) Hold or sponsor public hearings or public meetings whenever appropriate or in accordance with statutory requirements applicable to the agency. Criteria shall include whether there is:

(1) Substantial environmental controversy concerning the proposed action or substantial interest in holding the hearing.

(2) A request for a hearing by another agency with jurisdiction over the action supported by reasons why a hearing will be helpful. If a draft environmental impact statement is to be considered at a public hearing, the agency should make the statement available to the public at least 15 days in advance (unless the purpose of the hearing is to provide information for the draft environmental impact statement).

(d) Solicit appropriate information from the public.

(e) Explain in its procedures where interested persons can get information or status reports on environmental impact statements and other elements of the NEPA process.

(f) Make environmental impact statements, the comments received, and any underlying documents available to the public pursuant to the provisions of the Freedom of Information Act (5 U.S.C. 552), without regard to the exclusion for interagency memoranda where such memoranda transmit comments of Federal agencies on the environmental impact of the proposed action. Materials to be made available to the public shall be provided to the public without charge to the extent practicable, or at a fee which is not more than the actual costs of reproducing copies required to be sent to other Federal agencies, including the Council.

§ 1506.7 Further guidance

The Council may provide further guidance concerning NEPA and its procedures including:

(a) A handbook which the Council may supplement from time to time, which shall in plain language provide guidance and instructions concerning the application of NEPA and these regulations.

(b) Publication of the Council's Memoranda to Heads of Agencies.

(c) In conjunction with the Environmental Protection Agency and the publication of the 102 Monitor, notice of:

(1) Research activities;

(2) Meetings and conferences related to NEPA; and

(3) Successful and innovative procedures used by agencies to implement NEPA.

§ 1506.8 Proposals for legislation

(a) The NEPA process for proposals for legislation (§ 1508.17) significantly affecting the quality of the human environment shall be integrated with the legislative process of the Congress. A legislative environmental impact statement is the detailed statement required by law to be included in a recommendation or report on a legislative proposal to Congress. A legislative environmental impact statement shall be considered part of the formal transmittal of a legislative proposal to Congress; however, it may be transmitted to Congress up to 30 days later in order to allow time for completion of an accurate statement which can serve as the basis for public and Congressional debate. The statement must be available in time for Congressional hearings and deliberations.

(b) Preparation of a legislative environmental impact statement shall conform to the requirements of these regulations except as follows:

(1) There need not be a scoping process.

(2) The legislative statement shall be prepared in the same manner as a draft statement, but shall be considered the "detailed statement" required by statute; *Provided*, That when any of the following conditions exist both the draft and final environmental impact statement on the legislative proposal shall be prepared and circulated as provided by §§ 1503.1 and 1506.10.

(i) A Congressional Committee with jurisdiction over the proposal has a rule requiring both draft and final environmental impact statements.

(ii) The proposal results from a study process required by statute (such as those required by the Wild and Scenic Rivers Act (16 U.S.C. 1271 et seq.) and the Wilderness Act (16 U.S.C. 1131 et seq.)).

(iii) Legislative approval is sought for Federal or federally assisted construction or other projects which the agency recommends be located at specific geographic locations. For proposals requiring an environmental impact statement for the acquisition of space by the General Services Administration, a draft statement shall accompany the Prospectus or the 11(b) Report of Building Project Surveys to the Congress, and a final statement shall be completed before site acquisition.

(iv) The agency decides to prepare draft and final statements.

(c) Comments on the legislative statement shall be given to the lead agency which shall forward them along with its own responses to the Congressional committees with jurisdiction.

§ 1506.9 Filing requirements

Environmental impact statements together with comments and responses shall be filed with the Environmental Protection Agency, attention Office of Federal Activities (A–104), 401 M Street SW., Washington, D.C. 20460. Statements shall be filed with EPA no earlier than they are also transmitted to commenting agencies and made available to the public. EPA shall deliver one copy of each statement to the Council, which shall satisfy the requirement of availability to the President. EPA may issue guidelines to agencies to implement its responsibilities under this section and § 1506.10.

§ 1506.10 Timing of agency action

(a) The Environmental Protection Agency shall publish a notice in the FEDERAL REGISTER each week of the environmental impact statements filed during the preceding week. The minimum time periods set forth in this section shall be calculated from the date of publication of this notice.

(b) No decision on the proposed action shall be made or recorded under § 1505.2 by a Federal agency until the later of the following dates:

(1) Ninety (90) days after publication of the notice described above in paragraph (a) of this section for a draft environmental impact statement.

(2) Thirty (30) days after publication of the notice described above in paragraph (a) of this section for a final environmental impact statement.

An exception to the rules on timing may be made in the case of an agency decision which is subject to a formal internal appeal. Some agencies have a formally established appeal process which allows other agencies or the public to take appeals on a decision and make their views known, after publication of the final environmental impact statement. In such cases, where a real opportunity exists to alter the decision, the decision may be made and recorded at the same time the environmental impact statement is published. This means that the period for appeal of the decision and the 30–day period prescribed in paragraph (b)(2) of this section may run concurrently. In such cases the environmental impact statement shall explain the timing and the public's right of appeal. An agency engaged in rulemaking under the Administrative Procedure Act or other statute for the purpose of protecting the public health or safety, may waive the time period in paragraph (b)(2) of this section and publish a decision on the final rule simultaneously with publication of the notice of the availability of the final environmental impact statement as described in paragraph (a) of this section.

(c) If the final environmental impact statement is filed within ninety (90) days after a draft environmental impact statement is filed with the Environmental Protection Agency, the minimum thirty (30) day period and the minimum ninety (90) day period may run concurrently. However, subject to paragraph (d) of this section agencies shall allow not less than 45 days for comments on draft statements.

(d) The lead agency may extend prescribed periods. The Environmental Protection Agency may upon a showing by the lead agency of compelling reasons of national policy reduce the prescribed periods and may upon a showing by any other Federal agency of compelling reasons of national policy also extend prescribed periods, but only after consultation with the lead agency. (Also see § 1507.3(d).) Failure to file timely comments shall not be a sufficient reason for extending a period. If the lead agency does not concur with the extension of time, EPA may not extend it for more than 30 days. When the Environmental Protection Agency reduces or extends any period of time it shall notify the Council.

[43 FR 56000, Nov. 29, 1978; 44 FR 874, Jan. 3, 1979]

§ 1506.11 Emergencies

Where emergency circumstances make it necessary to take an action with significant environmental impact without observing the provisions of these regulations, the Federal agency taking the action should consult with the Council about alternative arrangements. Agencies and the Council will limit such arrangements to actions necessary to control the immediate impacts of the emergency. Other actions remain subject to NEPA review.

§ 1506.12 Effective date

The effective date of these regulations is July 30, 1979, except that for agencies that administer programs that qualify under section 102(2)(D) of the Act or under sec. 104(h) of the Housing and Community Development Act of 1974 an additional four months shall be allowed for the State or local agencies to adopt their implementing procedures.

(a) These regulations shall apply to the fullest extent practicable to ongoing activities and environmental documents begun before the effective date. These regulations do not apply to an environmental impact statement or supplement if the draft statement was filed before the effective date of these regulations. No completed environmental documents need be redone by reasons of these regulations. Until these regulations are applicable, the Council's guidelines published in the FEDERAL REGISTER of August 1, 1973, shall continue to be applicable. In cases where these regulations are applicable the guidelines are superseded. However, nothing shall prevent an agency from proceeding under these regulations at an earlier time.

(b) NEPA shall continue to be applicable to actions begun before January 1, 1970, to the fullest extent possible.

Part 1507

Agency Compliance

Sec.

1507.1 Compliance.
1507.2 Agency capability to comply.
1507.3 Agency procedures.

AUTHORITY: NEPA, the Environmental Quality Improvement Act of 1970, as amended (42 U.S.C. 4371 *et seq.*), sec. 309 of the Clean Air Act, as amended (42 U.S.C. 7609), and E.O. 11514 (Mar. 5, 1970, as amended by E.O. 11991, May 24, 1977).

SOURCE: 43 FR 56002, Nov. 29, 1978, unless otherwise noted.

§ 1507.1 Compliance

All agencies of the Federal Government shall comply with these regulations. It is the intent of these regulations to allow each agency flexibility in adapting its implementing procedures authorized by § 1507.3 to the requirements of other applicable laws.

§ 1507.2 Agency capability to comply

Each agency shall be capable (in terms of personnel and other resources) of complying with the requirements enumerated below. Such compliance may include use of other's resources, but the using agency shall itself have sufficient capability to evaluate what others do for it. Agencies shall:

(a) Fulfill the requirements of section 102(2)(A) of the Act to utilize a systematic, interdisciplinary approach which will insure the integrated use of the natural and social sciences and the environmental design arts in planning and in decisionmaking which may have an impact on the human environment. Agencies shall designate a person to be responsible for overall review of agency NEPA compliance.

(b) Identify methods and procedures required by section 102(2)(B) to insure that presently unquantified environmental amenities and value may be given appropriate consideration.

(c) Prepare adequate environmental impact statements pursuant to section 102(2)(C) and comment on statements in the areas where the agency has jurisdiction by law or special expertise or is authorized to develop and enforce environmental standards.

(d) Study, develop, and describe alternatives to recommended courses of action in any proposal which involves unresolved conflicts concerning alternative uses of available resources. This requirement of section 102(2)(E) extends to all such proposals, not just the more limited scope of section 102(2)(C)(iii) where the discussion of alternatives is confined to impact statements.

(e) Comply with the requirements of section 102(2)(H) that the agency initiate and utilize ecological information in the planning and development of resource-oriented projects.

(f) Fulfill the requirements of sections 102(2)(F), 102(2)(G), and 102(2)(I), of the Act and of Executive Order 11514, Protection and Enhancement of Environmental Quality, Sec. 2.

§ 1507.3 Agency procedures

(a) Not later than eight months after publication of these regulations as finally adopted in the Federal Register, or five months after the establishment of an agency, whichever shall come later, each agency shall as necessary adopt procedures to supplement these regulations. When the agency is a department, major subunits are encouraged (with the consent of the department) to adopt their own procedures. Such procedures shall not paraphrase these regulations. They shall confine themselves to implementing procedures. Each agency shall consult with the Council while developing its procedures and before publishing them in the Federal Register for comment. Agencies with similar programs should consult with each other and the Council to coordinate their procedures, especially for programs requesting similar information from applicants. The procedures shall be adopted only after an opportunity for public review and after review by the Council for conformity with the Act and these regulations. The Council shall complete its review within 30 days. Once in effect they shall be filed with the Council and made readily available to the public. Agencies are encouraged to publish explanatory guidance for these regulations and their own procedures. Agencies shall continue to review their policies and procedures and in consultation with the Council to revise them as necessary to ensure full compliance with the purposes and provisions of the Act.

(b) Agency procedures shall comply with these regulations except where compliance would be inconsistent with statutory requirements and shall include:

(1) Those procedures required by §§ 1501.2(d), 1502.9(c)(3), 1505.1, 1506.6(e), and 1508.4.

(2) Specific criteria for and identification of those typical classes of action:

(i) Which normally do require environmental impact statements.

(ii) Which normally do not require either an environmental impact statement or an environmental assessment (categorical exclusions (§ 1508.4)).

(iii) Which normally require environmental assessments but not necessarily environmental impact statements.

(c) Agency procedures may include specific criteria for providing limited exceptions to the provisions of these regulations for classified proposals. They are proposed actions which are specifically authorized under criteria established by an Executive Order or statute to be kept secret in the interest of national defense or foreign policy and are in fact properly classified pursuant to such Executive Order or statute. Environmental assessments and environmental impact statements which address classified proposals may be safeguarded and restricted from public dissemination in accordance with agencies' own regulations applicable to classified information. These documents may be organized so that classified portions can be included as annexes, in order that the unclassified portions can be made available to the public.

(d) Agency procedures may provide for periods of time other than those presented in § 1506.10 when necessary to comply with other specific statutory requirements.

(e) Agency procedures may provide that where there is a lengthy period between the agency's decision to prepare an environmental impact statement and the time of actual preparation, the notice of intent required by § 1501.7 may be published at a reasonable time in advance of preparation of the draft statement.

Part 1508

Terminology and Index

Sec.

1508.1 Terminology.
1508.2 Act.
1508.3 Affecting.

Sec.
1508.4 Categorical exclusion.
1508.5 Cooperating agency.
1508.6 Council.
1508.7 Cumulative impact.
1508.8 Effects.
1508.9 Environmental assessment.
1508.10 Environmental document.
1508.11 Environmental impact statement.
1508.12 Federal agency.
1508.13 Finding of no significant impact.
1508.14 Human environment.
1508.15 Jurisdiction by law.
1508.16 Lead agency.
1508.17 Legislation.
1508.18 Major Federal action.
1508.19 Matter.
1508.20 Mitigation.
1508.21 NEPA process.
1508.22 Notice of intent.
1508.23 Proposal.
1508.24 Referring agency.
1508.25 Scope.
1508.26 Special expertise.
1508.27 Significantly.
1508.28 Tiering.

AUTHORITY: NEPA, the Environmental Quality Improvement Act of 1970, as amended (42 U.S.C. 4371 *et seq.*), sec. 309 of the Clear Air Act, as amended (42 U.S.C. 7609), and E.O. 11514 (Mar. 5, 1970, as amended by E.O. 11991, May 24, 1977).

SOURCE: 43 FR 56003, Nov. 29, 1978, unless otherwise noted.

§ 1508.1 Terminology

The terminology of this part shall be uniform throughout the Federal Government.

§ 1508.2 Act

"Act" means the National Environmental Policy Act, as amended (42 U.S.C. 4321, et seq.) which is also referred to as "NEPA."

§ 1508.3 Affecting

"Affecting" means will or may have an effect on.

§ 1508.4 Categorical exclusion

"Categorical exclusion" means a category of actions which do not individually or cumulatively have a significant effect on the human environment and which have been found to have no such effect in procedures adopted by a Federal agency in implementation of these regulations

(§ 1507.3) and for which, therefore, neither an environmental assessment nor an environmental impact statement is required. An agency may decide in its procedures or otherwise, to prepare environmental assessments for the reasons stated in § 1508.9 even though it is not required to do so. Any procedures under this section shall provide for extraordinary circumstances in which a normally excluded action may have a significant environmental effect.

§ 1508.5 Cooperating agency

"Cooperating agency" means any Federal agency other than a lead agency which has jurisdiction by law or special expertise with respect to any environmental impact involved in a proposal (or a reasonable alternative) for legislation or other major Federal action significantly affecting the quality of the human environment. The selection and responsibilities of a cooperating agency are described in § 1501.6. A State or local agency of similar qualifications or, when the effects are on a reservation, an Indian Tribe, may by agreement with the lead agency become a cooperating agency.

§ 1508.6 Council

"Council" means the Council on Environmental Quality established by Title II of the Act.

§ 1508.7 Cumulative impact

"Cumulative impact" is the impact on the environment which results from the incremental impact of the action when added to other past, present, and reasonably foreseeable future actions regardless of what agency (Federal or non–Federal) or person undertakes such other actions. Cumulative impacts can result from individually minor but collectively significant actions taking place over a period of time.

§ 1508.8 Effects

"Effects" include:

(a) Direct effects, which are caused by the action and occur at the same time and place.

(b) Indirect effects, which are caused by the action and are later in time or farther removed in distance, but are still reasonably foreseeable. Indirect effects may include growth inducing effects and other effects related to induced changes in the pattern of land use, population density or growth rate, and related effects on air and water and other natural systems, including ecosystems.

Effects and impacts as used in these regulations are synonymous. Effects includes ecological (such as the effects on natural resources and on the components, structures, and functioning of affected ecosystems), aesthetic, historic, cultural, economic, social, or health, whether direct, indirect, or cumulative. Effects may also include those resulting from actions which may have both beneficial and detrimental effects, even if on balance the agency believes that the effect will be beneficial.

§ 1508.9 Environmental assessment

"Environmental assessment":

(a) Means a concise public document for which a Federal agency is responsible that serves to:

(1) Briefly provide sufficient evidence and analysis for determining whether to prepare an environmental impact statement or a finding of no significant impact.

(2) Aid an agency's compliance with the Act when no environmental impact statement is necessary.

(3) Facilitate preparation of a statement when one is necessary.

(b) Shall include brief discussions of the need for the proposal, of alternatives as required by section 102(2)(E), of the environmental impacts of the proposed action and alternatives, and a listing of agencies and persons consulted.

§ 1508.10 Environmental document

"Environmental document" includes the documents specified in § 1508.9 (environmental assessment), § 1508.11 (environmental impact statement), § 1508.13 (finding of no significant impact), and § 1508.22 (notice of intent).

§ 1508.11 Environmental impact statement

"Environmental impact statement" means a detailed written statement as required by section 102(2)(C) of the Act.

§ 1508.12 Federal agency

"Federal agency" means all agencies of the Federal Government. It does not mean the Congress, the Judiciary, or the President, including the performance of staff functions for the President in his Executive Office. It also includes for purposes of these regulations States and units of general local government and Indian tribes assuming NEPA responsibilities under section 104(h) of the Housing and Community Development Act of 1974.

§ 1508.13 Finding of no significant impact

"Finding of no significant impact" means a document by a Federal agency briefly presenting the reasons why an action, not otherwise excluded (§ 1508.4), will not have a significant effect on the human environment and for which an environmental impact statement therefore will not be prepared. It shall include the environmental assessment or a summary of it and shall note any other environmental documents related to it (§ 1501.7(a)(5)). If the assessment is included, the finding need not repeat any of the discussion in the assessment but may incorporate it by reference.

§ 1508.14 Human environment

"Human environment" shall be interpreted comprehensively to include the natural and physical environment and the relationship of people with that environment. (See the definition of "effects" (§ 1508.8).) This means that economic or social effects are not intended by themselves to require preparation of an environmental impact statement. When an environmental impact statement is prepared and economic or social and natural or physical environmental effects are interrelated, then the environmental impact statement will discuss all of these effects on the human environment.

§ 1508.15 Jurisdiction by law

"Jurisdiction by law" means agency authority to approve, veto, or finance all or part of the proposal.

§ 1508.16 Lead agency

"Lead agency" means the agency or agencies preparing or having taken primary responsibility for preparing the environmental impact statement.

§ 1508.17 Legislation

"Legislation" includes a bill or legislative proposal to Congress developed by or with the significant cooperation and support of a Federal agency, but does not include requests for appropriations. The test for significant cooperation is whether the proposal is in fact predominantly that of the agency rather than another source. Drafting does not by itself constitute significant cooperation. Proposals for legislation include requests for ratification of treaties. Only the agency which has primary responsibility for the subject matter involved will prepare a legislative environmental impact statement.

§ 1508.18 Major Federal action

"Major Federal action" includes actions with effects that may be major and which are potentially subject to Federal control and responsibility. Major reinforces but does not have a meaning independent of significantly (§ 1508.27). Actions include the circumstance where the responsible officials fail to act and that failure to act is reviewable by courts or administrative tribunals under the Administrative Procedure Act or other applicable law as agency action.

(a) Actions include new and continuing activities, including projects and programs entirely or partly financed, assisted, conducted, regulated, or approved by federal agencies; new or revised agency rules, regulations, plans, policies, or procedures; and legislative proposals (§§ 1506.8, 1508.17). Actions do not include funding assistance solely in the form of general revenue sharing funds, distributed under the State and Local Fiscal Assistance Act of 1972, 31 U.S.C. 1221 et seq., with no Federal agency control over the subsequent use of such funds. Actions do not include bringing judicial or administrative civil or criminal enforcement actions.

(b) Federal actions tend to fall within one of the following categories:

(1) Adoption of official policy, such as rules, regulations, and interpretations adopted pursuant to the Administrative Procedure Act,

5 U.S.C. 551 et seq.; treaties and international conventions or agreements; formal documents establishing an agency's policies which will result in or substantially alter agency programs.

(2) Adoption of formal plans, such as official documents prepared or approved by federal agencies which guide or prescribe alternative uses of federal resources, upon which future agency actions will be based.

(3) Adoption of programs, such as a group of concerted actions to implement a specific policy or plan; systematic and connected agency decisions allocating agency resources to implement a specific statutory program or executive directive.

(4) Approval of specific projects, such as construction or management activities located in a defined geographic area. Projects include actions approved by permit or other regulatory decision as well as federal and federally assisted activities.

§ 1508.19 Matter

"Matter" includes for purposes of Part 1504:

(a) With respect to the Environmental Protection Agency, any proposed legislation, project, action or regulation as those terms are used in section 309(a) of the Clean Air Act (42 U.S.C. 7609).

(b) With respect to all other agencies, any proposed major federal action to which section 102(2)(C) of NEPA applies.

§ 1508.20 Mitigation

"Mitigation" includes:

(a) Avoiding the impact altogether by not taking a certain action or parts of an action.

(b) Minimizing impacts by limiting the degree or magnitude of the action and its implementation.

(c) Rectifying the impact by repairing, rehabilitating, or restoring the affected environment.

(d) Reducing or eliminating the impact over time by preservation and maintenance operations during the life of the action.

(e) Compensating for the impact by replacing or providing substitute resources or environments.

§ 1508.21 NEPA process

"NEPA process" means all measures necessary for compliance with the requirements of section 2 and Title I of NEPA.

§ 1508.22 Notice of intent

"Notice of intent" means a notice that an environmental impact statement will be prepared and considered. The notice shall briefly:

(a) Describe the proposed action and possible alternatives.

(b) Describe the agency's proposed scoping process including whether, when, and where any scoping meeting will be held.

(c) State the name and address of a person within the agency who can answer questions about the proposed action and the environmental impact statement.

§ 1508.23 Proposal

"Proposal" exists at that stage in the development of an action when an agency subject to the Act has a goal and is actively preparing to make a decision on one or more alternative means of accomplishing that goal and the effects can be meaningfully evaluated. Preparation of an environmental impact statement on a proposal should be timed (§ 1502.5) so that the final statement may be completed in time for the statement to be included in any recommendation or report on the proposal. A proposal may exist in fact as well as by agency declaration that one exists.

§ 1508.24 Referring agency

"Referring agency" means the federal agency which has referred any matter to the Council after a determination that the matter is unsatisfactory from the standpoint of public health or welfare or environmental quality.

§ 1508.25 Scope

Scope consists of the range of actions, alternatives, and impacts to be considered in an environmental impact statement. The scope of an individual statement may depend on its relationships to other statements (§§ 1502.20 and 1508.28). To determine the scope of environmental impact statements, agencies shall consider 3 types of actions, 3 types of alternatives, and 3 types of impacts. They include:

(a) Actions (other than unconnected single actions) which may be:

(1) Connected actions, which means that they are closely related and therefore should be discussed in the same impact statement. Actions are connected if they:

(i) Automatically trigger other actions which may require environmental impact statements.

(ii) Cannot or will not proceed unless other actions are taken previously or simultaneously.

(iii) Are interdependent parts of a larger action and depend on the larger action for their justification.

(2) Cumulative actions, which when viewed with other proposed actions have cumulatively significant impacts and should therefore be discussed in the same impact statement.

(3) Similar actions, which when viewed with other reasonably foreseeable or proposed agency actions, have similarities that provide a basis for evaluating their environmental consequences together, such as common timing or geography. An agency may wish to analyze these actions in the same impact statement. It

should do so when the best way to assess adequately the combined impacts of similar actions or reasonable alternatives to such actions is to treat them in a single impact statement.

(b) Alternatives, which include: (1) No action alternative.

(2) Other reasonable courses of actions.

(3) Mitigation measures (not in the proposed action).

(c) Impacts, which may be: (1) Direct; (2) indirect; (3) cumulative.

§ 1508.26 Special expertise

"Special expertise" means statutory responsibility, agency mission, or related program experience.

§ 1508.27 Significantly

"Significantly" as used in NEPA requires considerations of both context and intensity:

(a) *Context.* This means that the significance of an action must be analyzed in several contexts such as society as a whole (human, national), the affected region, the affected interests, and the locality. Significance varies with the setting of the proposed action. For instance, in the case of a site-specific action, significance would usually depend upon the effects in the locale rather than in the world as a whole. Both short- and long-term effects are relevant.

(b) *Intensity.* This refers to the severity of impact. Responsible officials must bear in mind that more than one agency may make decisions about partial aspects of a major action. The following should be considered in evaluating intensity:

(1) Impacts that may be both beneficial and adverse. A significant effect may exist even if the Federal agency believes that on balance the effect will be beneficial.

(2) The degree to which the proposed action affects public health or safety.

(3) Unique characteristics of the geographic area such as proximity to historic or cultural resources, park lands, prime farmlands, wetlands, wild and scenic rivers, or ecologically critical areas.

(4) The degree to which the effects on the quality of the human environment are likely to be highly controversial.

(5) The degree to which the possible effects on the human environment are highly uncertain or involve unique or unknown risks.

(6) The degree to which the action may establish a precedent for future actions with significant effects or represents a decision in principle about a future consideration.

(7) Whether the action is related to other actions with individually insignificant but cumulatively significant impacts. Signifi-

cance exists if it is reasonable to anticipate a cumulatively significant impact on the environment. Significance cannot be avoided by terming an action temporary or by breaking it down into small component parts.

(8) The degree to which the action may adversely affect districts, sites, highways, structures, or objects listed in or eligible for listing in the National Register of Historic Places or may cause loss or destruction of significant scientific, cultural, or historical resources.

(9) The degree to which the action may adversely affect an endangered or threatened species or its habitat that has been determined to be critical under the Endangered Species Act of 1973.

(10) Whether the action threatens a violation of Federal, State, or local law or requirements imposed for the protection of the environment.

[43 FR 56003, Nov. 29, 1978; 44 FR 874, Jan. 3, 1979]

§ 1508.28 Tiering

"Tiering" refers to the coverage of general matters in broader environmental impact statements (such as national program or policy statements) with subsequent narrower statements or environmental analyses (such as regional or basinwide program statements or ultimately site-specific statements) incorporating by reference the general discussions and concentrating solely on the issues specific to the statement subsequently prepared. Tiering is appropriate when the sequence of statements or analyses is:

(a) From a program, plan, or policy environmental impact statement to a program, plan, or policy statement or analysis of lesser scope or to a site-specific statement or analysis.

(b) From an environmental impact statement on a specific action at an early stage (such as need and site selection) to a supplement (which is preferred) or a subsequent statement or analysis at a later stage (such as environmental mitigation). Tiering in such cases is appropriate when it helps the lead agency to focus on the issues which are ripe for decision and exclude from consideration issues already decided or not yet ripe.

Part 1515

Freedom of Information Act Procedures

Purposes

Sec.
1515.1 What are these procedures?

Organization of CEQ

1515.2 What is the Council on Environmental Quality (CEQ)?
1515.3 How is CEQ organized?

Sec.

PROCEDURES FOR REQUESTING RECORDS

1515.5 How to make a Freedom of Information Act request.

AVAILABILITY OF INFORMATION

1515.10 What information is available, and how can it be obtained?

COSTS

1515.15 What fees may be charged, and how should they be paid?

AUTHORITY: 5 U.S.C. 552, as amended by Pub.L. 93–502.

SOURCE: 42 FR 65158, Dec. 30, 1977, unless otherwise noted.

PURPOSES

§ 1515.1 What are these procedures?

The Freedom of Information Act (5 U.S.C. 552, commonly known as FOIA) is a law which creates a procedure for any person to request official documents and other records from United States Government agencies. The law requires every Federal agency to make available to the public the material requested, unless the material falls under one of the limited exceptions stated in section 552(b)(5) of the Act, and the agency has good reason to refuse the request. These procedures explain how the Council on Environmental Quality—one of several offices in the Executive Office of the President—will carry out the Freedom of Information Act. They are written from the standpoint of a member of the public requesting material from the Council.

ORGANIZATION OF CEQ

§ 1515.2 What is the Council on Environmental Quality (CEQ)?

(a) The Council on Environmental Quality ("CEQ" or "the Council") was created by the National Environmental Policy Act of 1969, as amended (42 U.S.C. 4321–4347). The Council's authority is derived from that Act, the Environmental Quality Improvement Act of 1970, as amended (42 U.S.C. 4371–4374), Reorganization Plan No. 1 of 1977 (July 15, 1977), and Executive Order 11514, Protection and Enhancement of Environmental Quality, March 5, 1970, as amended by Executive Order 11991, May 24, 1977.

(b) The Council's primary responsibilities include the following:

(1) To review and evaluate the programs and activities of the Federal Government to determine how they are contributing to the attainment of the national environmental policy;

(2) To assist Federal agencies and departments in appraising the effectiveness of their existing and proposed facilities, programs, policies, and activities affecting environmental quality;

(3) To develop and recommend to the President policies to improve environmental quality to meet the conservation, social, economic, health, and other requirements and goals of the Nation;

(4) To advise and assist the President in achieving international cooperation for dealing with environmental problems;

(5) To assist in coordinating among Federal agencies and departments those programs which affect, protect, and improve environmental quality, including Federal compliance with the environmental impact statement process, and to seek resolution of significant environmental issues;

(6) To foster research relating to environmental quality and the impacts of new or changing technologies; and

(7) To analyze long and short term environmental problems and trends and assist in preparing an annual Environmental Quality Report to the President and the Congress.

(c) The Council maintains a "Quarterly Index" which lists its current policies and procedures, as required by section 552(a)(2) of the Freedom of Information Act. This index is updated and published in the FEDERAL REGISTER quarterly, starting in 1976. The Quarterly Index—and the specific items listed in the index—are available on request from the Freedom of Information Officer. You may also inspect or copy any of these materials at the Council's office during the hours stated below in § 1515.3(f).

§ 1515.3 How is CEQ organized?

(a) The Council is made up of three members appointed by the President and subject to approval by the Senate. One member is designated as chairman by the President. All three serve in a full-time capacity.

(b) The National Environmental Policy Act and the Environmental Quality Improvement Act give the Council the authority to hire any officers and staff that may be necessary to carry out responsibilities and functions specified in these two Acts. Also, the use of consultants and experts is permitted.

(c) In addition to the three members, the Council has program and legal staff.

(d) The Council has no field or regional offices.

(e) The Council has a public affairs office which is responsible for providing information to the general public, the Congress, and the press. If you are interested in general information about the Council or have questions about the Council's recent activities or policy positions, you should call this office at (202) 633–7005 or write to the "Public Affairs Office" of the Council at the address given in the next paragraph.

NOTE: The CEQ public affairs office can respond fully and promptly to most questions you may have; the Council suggests that the Freedom of Information Act procedures be used when you are seeking a specific document and have had difficulty obtaining it.

(f) The Council is located at 722 Jackson Place NW., Washington, D.C. 20006. Office hours are 9–5:30, Monday through Friday, except legal holidays. If you wish to meet with any of the staff, please write or phone ahead for an appointment. The main number is 202–633–7027.

PROCEDURES FOR REQUESTING RECORDS

§ 1515.5 How to make a Freedom of Information Act request

(a) The Chairman has appointed a Freedom of Information Officer who will be responsible for overseeing the Council's administration of the Freedom of Information Act and for receiving, routing, and overseeing the processing of all Freedom of Information requests. The Chairman has also appointed an Appeals Officer who is responsible for processing any appeals.

(b) *Requesting information from the Council.* (1) When you make a Freedom of Information Act request to the Council, the Freedom of Information Officer shall decide how to respond to—or "make an initial determination on"—your request within 10 working days from the date the Officer receives the request. The Freedom of Information Officer will then provide you with written notification of the determination.

(2) You can make a Freedom of Information Act request by writing a letter which states that you are making a Freedom of Information Act request. Address your letter to:

Freedom of Information Officer, Council on Environmental Quality, Executive Office of the President, 722 Jackson Place NW., Washington, D.C. 20006.

(3) In your request you should identify the desired record or reasonably describe it. The request should be as specific as possible so that the item can be readily found. You should not make blanket requests, such as requests for "the entire file of" or "all materials relating to" a specified subject.

(4) The Council will make a reasonable effort to assist you in defining the request to eliminate extraneous and unwanted materials and to keep search and copying fees to a minimum. If you have budgetary constraints and anticipate that your request might be costly you may wish to indicate the maximum fee you are prepared to pay for acquiring the information. (See § 1515.15(c) also.)

(5) The 10 day period for making a determination on a request will begin when the records requested are specified or reasonably identifiable.

(6) Despite its name, the Freedom of Information Act does not require a government agency to create or research information that you would like or that you may think the agency should have. The Act only requires that existing records be made available to the public.

(c) *Council's response to a request.* (1) Upon receipt of any request under the Act, the Freedom of Information Officer shall direct the request to the appropriate staff member at the Council, who will review the request and advise the Freedom of Information Officer as soon as possible.

(2) If it is appropriate to grant the request, the staff member will immediately collect the requested materials in order to accompany, wherever possible, the Freedom of Information Officer's letter notifying you of the decision.

(3) If your request is denied, in part or in full, the letter notifying you of the decision will be signed by the Freedom of Information Officer, and will include the names of any other individuals who participated in the decision. The letter will include the reasons for any denial and the procedure for filing an appeal.

(d) *Appeals.* (1) If you are not satisfied with the response you have received from the Freedom of Information Officer, you may ask the Council to reconsider the decision. You should explain what material you still wish to receive, and why you believe the Council should disclose this to you. This is called an "appeal." You must make your appeal within 45 days of the date on the letter which denied your request.

(2) You can make an appeal by writing a letter to:

> FOIA Appeals Officer, Council on Environmental Quality, Executive Office of the President, 722 Jackson Place NW., Washington, D.C. 20006.

(3) Your letter should specify the records being requested and ask the Appeals Officer to review the determination made by the Freedom of Information Officer. The letter should explain the basis for the appeal.

(4) The Appeals Officer shall decide the appeal—or "make a final determination"—within 20 working days from the date the Officer receives the appeal. The Appeals Officer (or designee) will send you a letter informing you of the decision as soon as it is made. If the Appeals Officer denies your request, in part or in whole, the letter will also notify you of the provisions for judicial review and the names of any persons who participated in the final determination of the appeal.

(e) *Extending the Council's time to respond.* In unusual circumstances, the time limits for response to your request (paragraphs (b) and (d) of this section) may be extended by the Council for not more than 10 working days. Extensions may be granted by the Freedom of Information Officer in the case of initial requests and by the Appeals Officer in the case of any appeals. The extension period may be split between the initial request and the appeal but may not exceed 10 working days overall. Any extension will be made or confirmed to you in writing and will set forth the reasons for the extension and the date that the final determination is expected. The term "unusual circumstances" means:

> (i) The need to search for and collect the requested records from * * * establishments that are separate from the office processing the request;
>
> (ii) The need to search for, collect, and appropriately examine a voluminous amount of separate and distinct records which are demanded in a single request; or
>
> (iii) The need for consultation, which shall be conducted with all practicable speed, with another agency having a substantial interest in the determination of the request or among two or more components of the agency having substantial subject-matter interest therein.

(5 U.S.C. 552(a)(6)(B))

AVAILABILITY OF INFORMATION

§ 1515.10 What information is available, and how can it be obtained?

(a) When a request for information has been approved, in whole or in part, you may make an appointment to inspect or copy the materials requested during regular business hours by writing or telephoning the Freedom of Information Officer at the address or phone number given in § 1515.3(f). You may be charged reasonable fees for copying materials, as explained by § 1515.15. The Council on Environmental Quality will permit copying of any available material but will reserve the right to limit the number of copies made with the Council's copying facilities.

(b) In general, all records of the Council are available to the public, as required by the Freedom of Information Act. The Council claims the right, where it is applicable, to withhold material under the provisions specified in the Freedom of Information Act as amended (5 U.S.C. 552(b)).

(c) The legislative history of the establishment of the Council states that the Congress intended the Council to be a confidential advisor to the President on matters of environmental policy. Therefore, members of the public should presume that communications between the Council and the President (and their staffs) are confidential and ordinarily will not be released; they will usually fall, at a minimum, within Exemption 5 of the Act. The Freedom of Information Officer shall review each request, however, to determine whether the record is exclusively factual or may have factual portions which may be reasonably segregated and made available to the requester. Furthermore, on the recommendation of the FOIA Officer or Appeals Officer, the Council will consider the release of an entire record, even if it comes within an exemption or contains policy advice, if its disclosure would not impair Executive policy-making processes or the Council's participation in decisionmaking.

COSTS

§ 1515.15 What fees may be charged, and how should they be paid?

(a) Following is the schedule of fees you may be charged for the search and reproduction of information available under the Freedom of Information Act, 5 U.S.C. 552, as amended.

(1) *Search for records.* Five dollars per hour when the search is conducted by a clerical employee. Eight dollars per hour when the search is conducted by a professional employee. There will be no charge for searches of less than one hour.

(2) *Duplication of records.* Records will be duplicated at a rate of $0.10 per page for copying of 10 pages or more. There will be no charge for duplicating 9 pages or less.

(3) *Other.* When no specific fee has been established for a service, or the request for a service does not fall under categories (1) and (2), the Administrative Officer is authorized to establish an appropriate fee based on "direct costs" as provided in the Freedom of Information Act. Examples of

services covered by this provision include searches involving computer time or special travel, transportation, or communication costs.

(b) If the Council anticipates that the fees chargeable under this section will amount to more than $25, or the maximum amount specified in your request, you shall be promptly notified of the amount of the anticipated fee or the closest estimate of the amount. In such instances you will be advised of your option to consult with Council personnel in order to reformulate the request in a manner which will reduce the fees, yet still meet your needs. A reformulated request shall be considered a new request, thus beginning a new 10 working day period for processing.

(c) Fees must be paid in full prior to issuance of the requested copies. In the event you owe money for previous request, copies of records will not be provided for any subsequent request until the debt has been paid in full.

(d) Search costs are due and payable even if the record which was requested cannot be located after all reasonable efforts have been made, or if the FOI Officer determines that a record which has been requested is exempt under the Freedom of Information Act as amended and is to be withheld.

(e) Payment shall be in the form either of a personal check or bank draft drawn on a bank in the United States, or a postal money order. Checks shall be made payable to General Services Administration. You should mail or deliver any payment for services to the Administrative Office, Council on Environmental Quality, 722 Jackson Place NW., Washington, D.C. 20006.

(f) A receipt for fees paid will be given upon request. Refunds of fees paid for services actually rendered will not be made.

(g) The Council may waive all or part of any fee provided for in this section when the Freedom of Information Officer (or designee) deems it to be in either the Council's interest or in the general public's interest.

Part 1516

Privacy Act Implementation

Sec.

1516.1 Purpose and scope.
1516.2 Definitions.
1516.3 Procedures for requests pertaining to individual records in a record system.
1516.4 Times, places, and requirements for the identification of the individual making a request.
1516.5 Disclosure of requested information to the individual.
1516.6 Request for correction or amendment to the record.
1516.7 Agency review of request for correction or amendment of the record.
1516.8 Appeal of an initial adverse agency determination on correction or amendment of the record.
1516.9 Disclosure of a record to a person other than the individual to whom the record pertains.
1516.10 Fees.

AUTHORITY: 5 U.S.C. 552a; Pub.L. 93–579.

SOURCE: 42 FR 32537, June 27, 1977, unless otherwise noted.

§ 1516.1 Purpose and scope

The purposes of these regulations are to:

(a) Establish a procedure by which an individual can determine if the Council on Environmental Quality (hereafter known as the Council) maintains a system of records which includes a record pertaining to the individual; and

(b) Establish a procedure by which an individual can gain access to a record pertaining to him or her for the purpose of review, amendment and/or correction.

§ 1516.2 Definitions

For the purpose of these regulations:

(a) The term "individual" means a citizen of the United States or an alien lawfully admitted for permanent residence;

(b) The term "maintain" means maintain, collect, use or disseminate;

(c) The term "record" means any item or collection or grouping of information about an individual that is maintained by the Council (including, but not limited to, his or her employment history, payroll information, and financial transactions), and that contains his or her name, or an identifying number, symbol, or other identifying particular assigned to the individual such as a social security number;

(d) The term "system of records" means a group of any records under the control of the Council from which information is retrieved by the name of the individual or by some identifying number, symbol, or other identifying particular assigned to the individual; and

(e) The term "routine use" means with respect to the disclosure of a record, the use of such record for a purpose which is compatible with the purpose for which it was collected.

§ 1516.3 Procedures for requests pertaining to individual records in a record system

An individual shall submit a written request to the Administrative Officer of the Council to determine if a system of records named by the individual contains a record pertaining to the individual. The individual shall submit a written request to the Administrative Officer of the Council which states the individual's desire to review his or her record. The Administrative Officer of the Council is available to answer questions regarding these regulations and to provide assistance in locating records in the Council's system of records.

[42 FR 32537, June 27, 1977; 42 FR 35960, July 13, 1977]

§ 1516.4 Times, places, and requirements for the identification of the individual making a request

An individual making a request to the Administrative Officer of the Council pursuant to § 1516.3 shall present the request at the Council's office, 722 Jackson Place, N.W., Washington, D.C. 20006, on any business day between the hours of 9 a.m. and 5 p.m. and should be prepared to identify himself by signature. Requests will also be accepted in writing if mailed to the Council's offices and signed by the requester.

§ 1516.5 Disclosure of requested information to the individual

Upon verification of identity, the Council shall disclose to the individual the information contained in the record which pertains to that individual.

(a) The individual may be accompanied for this purpose by a person of his choosing.

(b) Upon request of the individual to whom the record pertains, all information in the accounting of disclosures will be made available.

[42 FR 35960, July 13, 1977]

§ 1516.6 Request for correction or amendment to the record

The individual may submit a request to the Administrative Officer of the Council which states the individual's desire to correct or to amend his or her record. This request must be made in accordance with the procedures of § 1516.4 and shall describe in detail the change which is requested.

[42 FR 32537, June 27, 1977. Redesignated at 42 FR 35960, July 13, 1977]

§ 1516.7 Agency review of request for correction or amendment of the record

Within ten working days of the receipt of a request to correct or to amend a record, the Administrative Officer of the Council will acknowledge in writing such receipt and promptly either:

(a) Make any correction or amendment of any portion thereof which the individual believes is not accurate, relevant, timely, or complete; or

(b) Inform the individual of his or her refusal to correct or amend the record in accordance with the request, the reason for the refusal, and the procedure established by the Council for the individual to request a review of that refusal.

§ 1516.8 Appeal of an initial adverse agency determination on correction or amendment of the record

An individual may appeal refusal by the Administrative Officer of the Council to correct or to amend his or her record by submitting a request for a review of such refusal to the General Counsel, Council on Environmental Quality, 722 Jackson Place, N.W., Washington, D.C. 20006. The General Counsel shall, not later than thirty working days from the date on which the individual requests such a review, complete such review and make a final determination unless, for good cause shown, the General Counsel extends such thirty day period. If, after his or her review, the General Counsel also refuses to correct or to amend the record in accordance with the request, the individual may file with the Council a concise statement setting forth the reasons for his or her disagreement with the General Counsel's decision and may seek judicial relief under 5 U.S.C. 552a(g)(1)(A).

§ 1516.9 Disclosure of a record to a person other than the individual to whom the record pertains

The Council will not disclose a record to any individual other than to the individual to whom the record pertains without receiving the prior written consent of the individual to whom the record pertains, unless the disclosure either has been listed as a "routine use" in the Council's notices of its systems of records or falls within the special conditions of disclosure set forth in section 3 of the Privacy Act of 1974.

§ 1516.10 Fees

If an individual requests copies of his or her record, he or she shall be charged ten cents per page, excluding the cost of any search for the record, in advance of receipt of the pages.

Part 1517

Public Meeting Procedures of the Council on Environmental Quality

Sec.

1517.1 Policy and scope.
1517.2 Definitions.
1517.3 Open meeting requirement.
1517.4 Exceptions.
1517.5 Procedure for closing meetings.
1517.6 Notice of meetings.
1517.7 Records of closed meetings.

AUTHORITY: 5 U.S.C. 552b(g); Pub.L. 94–409.

SOURCE: 42 FR 20818, Apr. 22, 1977, unless otherwise noted.

§ 1517.1 Policy and scope

Consistent with the policy that the public is entitled to the fullest information regarding the decisionmaking processes of the Federal Government, it is the purpose of this part to open the meetings of the Council on Environmental Quality to public observation while protecting the rights of individuals and the ability of the Council to carry out its primary responsibility of providing advice to the President. Actions taken by the Chairman acting as Director of the Office of Environmental Quality and Council actions involving advice to the President when such advice is not formulated collegially during a meeting are outside the scope of this part. In addition to conducting the meetings required by this part, it is the Council's policy to conduct, open to public observation, periodic meetings involving Council discussions of Council business, including where appropriate, matters outside the scope of this part. This part does not affect the procedures set forth in Part 1515 pursuant to which records of the Council are made available to the public for inspection and copying, except that the exemptions set forth in § 1517.4(a) shall govern in the case of any request made to copy or inspect the transcripts, recording or minutes described in § 1517.7.

[47 FR 6277, Feb. 11, 1982]

§ 1517.2 Definitions

For the purpose of this part:

(a) The term "Council" shall mean the Council on Environmental Quality established under Title II of the National Environmental Policy Act of 1969 (42 U.S.C. 4321–4347).

(b) The term "meeting" means the deliberations of at least two Council members where such deliberations determine or result in the joint conduct or disposition of official collegial Council business, but does not include deliberations to take actions to open or close a meeting under §§ 1517.4 and 1517.5 or to release or withhold information under §§ 1517.4 and 1517.7. "Meeting" shall not be construed to prevent Council members from considering individually Council business that is circulated to them sequentially in writing.

(c) "Director" means the Chairman of the Council on Environmental Quality acting as the head of the Office of Environmental Quality pursuant to the Environmental Quality Improvement Act of 1970, Pub.L. 91–224, 42 U.S.C. 4371–4374.

[44 FR 34946, June 18, 1979, as amended at 47 FR 6277, Feb. 11, 1982]

§ 1517.3 Open meeting requirement

(a) Every portion of every meeting of the Council is open to public observation subject to the exemptions provided in § 1517.4. Members of the Council may not jointly conduct or dispose of the business of the Council other than in accordance with this part.

(b) The Council will conduct open to public observation periodic meetings involving Council discussions of Council business including where appropriate matters outside the scope of this part. Such meetings will be noticed pursuant to § 1517.6.

(c) Members of the public may attend open meetings of the Council for the sole purpose of observation and may not participate in or photograph any meeting without prior permission of the Council. Members of the public who desire to participate in or photograph an open meeting of the Council may request permission to do so from the General Counsel of the Council before such meeting. Members of the public may record open meetings of the Council by means of any mechanical or electronic device unless the Council determines such recording would disrupt the orderly conduct of such meeting.

[44 FR 34946, June 18, 1979, as amended at 47 FR 6277, Feb. 11, 1982]

§ 1517.4 Exceptions

(a) A meeting or portion thereof may be closed to public observation, and information pertaining to such meeting or portion thereof may be withheld from the public, if the Council determines that such meeting or portion thereof or disclosure of such information is likely to:

(1) Disclose matters that are (i) specifically authorized under criteria established by an Executive order to be kept secret in the interest of national defense or foreign policy and (ii) in fact properly classified pursuant to that Executive order;

(2) Relate solely to the internal personnel rules and practices of the Council;

(3) Disclose matters specifically exempted from disclosure by statute (other than the Freedom of Information Act, 5 U.S.C. 552), provided that the statute: (i) Requires that the matters be withheld from the public in such a manner as to leave no discretion on the issue, or (ii) establishes particular criteria for withholding or refers to particular types of matters to be withheld;

(4) Disclose the trade secrets and commercial or financial information obtained from a person and privileged or confidential;

(5) Involve accusing any person of a crime, or formally censuring any person;

(6) Disclose information of a personal nature if disclosure would constitute a clearly unwarranted invasion of personal privacy;

(7) Disclose investigatory records compiled for law enforcement purposes, or information which if written would be contained in such records, but only to the extent that the production of those records or information would:

(i) Interfere with enforcement proceedings,

(ii) Deprive a person of a right to a fair trial or an impartial adjudication,

(iii) Constitute an unwarranted invasion of personal privacy,

(iv) Disclose the identity of a confidential source and, in the case of a record compiled by a criminal law enforcement authority in the course of a criminal investigation, or by an agency conducting a lawful national security intelligence investigation, confidential information furnished only by the confidential source,

(v) Disclose investigative techniques and procedures, or,

(vi) Endanger the life or physical safety of law enforcement personnel;

(8) Disclose information contained in or related to examination, operating, or condition reports prepared by, on behalf of, or for the use of an agency responsible for the regulation or supervision of financial institutions;

(9) Disclose information the premature disclosure of which would be likely to significantly frustrate implementation of a proposed action of the Council. This exception shall not apply in any instance where the Council has already disclosed to the public the content or nature of the proposed action, or where the Council is required by law to make such disclosure on its own initiative prior to taking final action on the proposal; or

(10) Specifically concern the issuance of a subpoena by the Council, or the participation of the Council in a civil action or proceeding, an action in a foreign court or international tribunal, or an arbitration, or the initiation, conduct, or disposition by the Council of a particular case of formal adjudication pursuant to the procedures in 5 U.S.C. 554 or otherwise involving a determination on the record after opportunity for a hearing.

(b) Before a meeting is closed to public observation the Council shall determine whether or not the public interest requires that the meeting be open. The Council may open a meeting to public observation which could be closed under paragraph (a) of this section, if the Council finds it to be in the public interest to do so.

§ 1517.5 Procedure for closing meetings

(a) A majority of the entire membership of the Council may vote to close to public observation a meeting or a portion or portions thereof, or to withhold information pertaining to such meeting. A separate vote of the members of the Council shall be taken with respect to each meeting of the Council, a portion or portions of which are proposed to be closed to the observation of the public or with respect to any information concerning such meetings or portion thereof. A single vote may be taken with respect to a series of meetings, a portion or portions of which are proposed to be closed to the public, or with respect to information concerning such series of meetings, so long as each meeting in such series involves the same particular matters and is scheduled to be held no more than thirty days after the initial meeting in such series. The vote of each member of the Council participating in a vote shall be recorded and no proxies shall be allowed.

(b) Whenever any person whose interest may be directly affected by a portion of a meeting requests that the Council close that portion to public observation for any of the reasons referred to in § 1517.4(a) the Council, upon request of any of the members of the Council, shall decide by recorded vote whether to close that portion of the meeting.

(c) For every meeting or portion thereof closed under this part, the General Counsel of the Council before such meeting is closed shall publicly certify that, in his or her opinion, the meeting may properly be closed to the public stating each relevant exemptive provision. The Council shall retain a copy of the General Counsel's certification, together with a statement from the presiding officer of the meeting setting forth the time and place of the meeting and listing the persons present.

(d) Within one day of any vote taken on a proposal to close a meeting, the Council shall make publicly available a record reflecting the vote of each member on the question. In addition, within one day of any vote which closes a portion or portions of a meeting to the public, the Council shall make publicly available a full written explanation of its closure action together with a list naming all persons expected to attend and identifying their affiliation, unless such disclosure would reveal the information that the meeting itself was closed to protect.

(e) Following any announcement that the Council intends to close a meeting or portion thereof, any person may make a request that the meeting or portion thereof be opened. Such request shall be made of the Chairman of the Council who shall ensure that the request is circulated to all members of the Council on the same business day on which it is received. The request shall set forth the reasons why the requestor believes the meeting should be open. The Council upon the request of any member or its General Counsel, shall vote on the request.

§ 1517.6 Notice of meetings

(a) Except as otherwise provided in this section, the Council shall make a public announcement at least one week before a meeting, to include the following:

(1) Time, place, and subject matter of the meeting;

(2) Whether the meeting is to be open or closed; and

(3) Name and telephone number of the official who will respond to requests for information about the meeting.

(b) A majority of the members of the Council may determine by recorded vote that the business of the Council requires a meeting to be called with less than one week's notice. At the earliest practicable time, the Council shall publicly announce the time, place and subject matter of the meeting, and whether or not it is to be open or closed to the public.

(c) If announcement of the subject matter of a closed meeting would reveal the information that the meeting itself was closed to protect, the subject matter shall not be announced.

(d) Following the public announcement required by paragraphs (a) or (b) of this section:

(1) A majority of the members of the Council may change the time or place of a meeting. At the earliest practicable time, the Council shall publicly announce the change.

(2) A majority of the entire membership of the Council may change the subject matter of a meeting, or the determination to open or close a meeting to the public, if it determines by a recorded vote that the change is required by the business of the Council and that no earlier announcement of the change was possible. At the earliest practicable time, the Council shall publicly announce the change, and the vote of each member upon the change.

(e) Individuals or organizations having a special interest in activities of the Council may request the Council to place them on a mailing list for receipt of information available under this section.

(f) Following public announcement of a meeting, the time or place of a meeting may be changed only if the change is announced publicly at the earliest practicable time. The subject matter of a meeting or the determination to open or close a meeting may be changed following public announcement of a meeting only if both of the following conditions are met:

(1) There must be a recorded vote of a majority of the Council that the business of the Council requires the change and that no earlier announcement of such change was possible; and

(2) There must be a public announcement of the change and of the individual Council members' votes at the earliest practicable time.

(g) Immediately following each public announcement required by this this section, the following information, as applicable, shall be submitted for publication in the FEDERAL REGISTER.

(1) Notice of the time, place, and subject matter of a meeting;

(2) Whether the meeting is open or closed;

(3) Any change in one of the preceding; and

(4) The name and telephone number of the official who will respond to requests for information about the meeting.

§ 1517.7 Records of closed meetings

(a) A record of each meeting or portion thereof which is closed to the public shall be made and retained for two years or for one year after the conclusion of any Council proceeding involved in the meeting whichever occurs later. The record of any portion of a meeting closed to the public shall be a verbatim transcript or electronic recording. In lieu of a transcript or recording, a comprehensive set of minutes may be produced if the closure decision was made pursuant to § 1517.4(a)(8) or (10).

(b) If minutes are produced, such minutes shall fully and clearly describe all matters discussed, provide a full and accurate summary of any actions taken and the reasons expressed therefor, and include a description of each of the views expressed on any item. The minutes shall also reflect the vote of each member of the Council on any roll call vote taken during the proceedings and identify all documents produced at the meeting.

(c) The following documents shall be retained by the Council as part of the transcript, recording, or minutes of the meeting:

(1) Certification by the General Counsel that the meeting may properly be closed; and

(2) Statement from the presiding officer of the meeting setting forth the date, time, and place of the meeting and listing the persons present.

(d) The Council shall make promptly available to the public at its offices at 722 Jackson Place, N.W., Washington, D.C. the transcript, electronic recording, or minutes maintained as a record of a closed meeting, except for such information as may be withheld under one of the provisions of § 1517.5. Copies of such transcript, minutes, or transcription of an electronic recording, disclosing the identity of each speaker, shall be furnished to any person at the actual cost of duplication or transcription.

(e) [Reserved]

(f) Requests to review or obtain copies of records other than transcripts, electronic recordings or minutes of a meeting will be processed under the Freedom of Information Act (5 U.S.C. 552) or, where applicable, the Privacy Act of 1974. (5 U.S.C. 552a). Nothing in these regulations authorizes the Council to withhold from any individual any record, including the transcripts or electronic recordings described in § 1517.8, to which the individual may have access under the Privacy Act of 1974 (5 U.S.C. 552a).

*

APPENDIX C

ADMINISTRATIVE PROCEDURE ACT

Administrative Procedure Act

A. Internal Procedures

B. Judicial Review

A. INTERNAL PROCEDURES

5 U.S.C.A., Chapter 5

Table of Contents

Sec.

551. Definitions.
552. Public information; agency rules, opinions, orders, records, and proceedings.

* * *

552b. Open meetings.
553. Rule making.
554. Adjudications.
555. Ancillary matters.
556. Hearings; presiding employees; powers and duties; burden of proof; evidence; record as basis of decision.
557. Initial decisions; conclusiveness; review by agency; submissions by parties; contents of decisions; record.
558. Imposition of sanctions; determination of applications for licenses; suspension, revocation, and expiration of licenses.
559. Effect on other laws; effect of subsequent statute.

---

§ 551. Definitions

For the purpose of this subchapter—

(1) "agency" means each authority of the Government of the United States, whether or not it is within or subject to review by another agency, but does not include—

(A) the Congress;

(B) the courts of the United States;

(C) the governments of the territories or possessions of the United States;

(D) the government of the District of Columbia, or except as to the requirements of section 552 of this title—

(E) agencies composed of representatives of the parties or of representatives of organizations of the parties to the disputes determined by them;

(F) courts martial and military commissions;

(G) military authority exercised in the field in time of war or in occupied territory; or

(H) functions conferred by sections 1738, 1739, 1743, and 1744 of title 12; chapter 2 of title 41; subchapter II of chapter 471 of title 49; or sections 1884, 1891–1902, and former section 1641(b)(2), of title 50, appendix;

(2) "person" includes an individual, partnership, corporation, association, or public or private organization other than an agency;

(3) "party" includes a person or agency named or admitted as a party, or properly seeking and entitled as of right to be admitted as a party, in an agency proceeding, and a person or agency admitted by an agency as a party for limited purposes;

(4) "rule" means the whole or a part of an agency statement of general or particular applicability and future effect designed to implement, interpret, or prescribe law or policy or describing the organization, procedure, or practice requirements of an agency and includes the approval or prescription for the future of rates, wages, corporate or financial structures or reorganization thereof, prices, facilities, appliances, services or allowances therefor or of valuations, costs, or accounting, or practices bearing on any of the foregoing;

(5) "rule making" means agency process for formulating, amending, or repealing a rule;

(6) "order" means the whole or a part of a final disposition, whether affirmative, negative, injunctive, or declaratory in form, of an agency in a matter other than rule making but including licensing;

(7) "adjudication" means agency process for the formulation of an order;

(8) "license" includes the whole or a part of an agency permit, certificate, approval, registration, charter, membership, statutory exemption or other form of permission;

(9) "licensing" includes agency process respecting the grant, renewal, denial, revocation, suspension, annulment, withdrawal, limitation, amendment, modification, or conditioning of a license;

(10) "sanction" includes the whole or a part of an agency—

(A) prohibition, requirement, limitation, or other condition affecting the freedom of a person;

(B) withholding of relief;

(C) imposition of penalty or fine;

(D) destruction, taking, seizure, or withholding of property;

(E) assessment of damages, reimbursement, restitution, compensation, costs, charges, or fees;

(F) requirement, revocation, or suspension of a license; or

(G) taking other compulsory or restrictive action;

(11) "relief" includes the whole or a part of an agency—

(A) grant of money, assistance, license, authority, exemption, exception, privilege, or remedy;

(B) recognition of a claim, right, immunity, privilege, exemption, or exception; or

(C) taking of other action on the application or petition of, and beneficial to, a person;

(12) "agency proceeding" means an agency process as defined by paragraphs (5), (7), and (9) of this section;

(13) "agency action" includes the whole or a part of an agency rule, order, license, sanction, relief, or the equivalent or denial thereof, or failure to act; and

(14) "ex parte communication" means an oral or written communication not on the public record with respect to which reasonable prior notice to all parties is not given, but it shall not include requests for status reports on any matter or proceeding covered by this subchapter.

§ 552. Public Information; Agency Rules, Opinions, Orders, Records, and Proceedings [Freedom of Information Act]

(a) Each agency shall make available to the public information as follows:

(1) Each agency shall separately state and currently publish in the Federal Register for the guidance of the public—

(A) descriptions of its central and field organization and the established places at which, the employees (and in the case of a uniformed service, the members) from whom, and the methods whereby, the public may obtain information, make submittals or requests, or obtain decisions;

(B) statements of the general course and method by which its functions are channeled and determined, including the nature and requirements of all formal and informal procedures available;

(C) rules of procedure, descriptions of forms available or the places at which forms may be obtained, and instructions as to the scope and contents of all papers, reports, or examinations;

(D) substantive rules of general applicability adopted as authorized by law, and statements of general policy or interpretations of general applicability formulated and adopted by the agency; and

(E) each amendment, revision, or repeal of the foregoing.

Except to the extent that a person has actual and timely notice of the terms thereof, a person may not in any manner be required to resort to, or be adversely affected by, a matter required to be published in the Federal Register and not so published. For the purpose of this paragraph, matter reasonably available to the class of persons affected thereby is deemed published in the Federal Register when incorporated by reference therein with the approval of the Director of the Federal Register.

(2) Each agency, in accordance with published rules, shall make available for public inspection and copying—

(A) final opinions, including concurring and dissenting opinions, as well as orders, made in the adjudication of cases;

(B) those statements of policy and interpretations which have been adopted by the agency and are not published in the Federal Register; and

(C) administrative staff manuals and instructions to staff that affect a member of the public;

unless the materials are promptly published and copies offered for sale. To the extent required to prevent a clearly unwarranted invasion of personal privacy, an agency may delete identifying details when it makes available or publishes an opinion, statement of policy, interpretation, or staff manual or instruction. However, in each case the justification for the deletion shall be explained fully in writing. Each agency shall also maintain and make available for public inspection and copying current indexes providing identifying information to the public as to any matter issued, adopted, or promulgated after July 4, 1967, and required by this paragraph to be made available or published. Each agency shall promptly publish, quarterly or more frequently, and distribute (by sale or otherwise) copies of each index or supplements thereto unless it determines by order published in the Federal Register that the publication would be unnecessary and impracticable, in which case the agency shall nonetheless provide copies of such index on request at a cost not to exceed the direct cost of duplication. A final order, opinion, statement of policy, interpretation, or staff manual or instruction that affects a member of the public may be relied on, used, or cited as precedent by an agency against a party other than an agency only if—

(i) it has been indexed and either made available or published as provided by this paragraph; or

(ii) the party has actual and timely notice of the terms thereof.

(3) Except with respect to the records made available under paragraphs (1) and (2) of this subsection, each agency, upon any request for records which (A) reasonably describes such records and (B) is made in accordance with published rules stating the time, place, fees (if any), and procedures to be followed, shall make the records promptly available to any person.

(4)(A)(i) In order to carry out the provisions of this section, each agency shall promulgate regulations, pursuant to notice and receipt of public comment, specifying the schedule of fees applicable to the processing of requests under this section and establishing procedures and guidelines for determining when such fees should be waived or reduced. Such schedule shall conform to the guidelines which shall be promulgated, pursuant to notice and receipt of public comment, by the Director of the Office of Management and Budget and which shall provide for a uniform schedule of fees for all agencies.

(ii) Such agency regulations shall provide that—

(I) fees shall be limited to reasonable standard charges for document search, duplication, and review, when records are requested for commercial use;

(II) fees shall be limited to reasonable standard charges for document duplication when records are not sought for commercial use and the request is made by an educational or noncommercial scientific institution, whose purpose is scholarly or scientific research; or a representative of the news media; and

(III) for any request not described in (I) or (II), fees shall be limited to reasonable standard charges for document search and duplication.

(iii) Documents shall be furnished without any charge or at a charge reduced below the fees established under clause (ii) if disclosure of the information is in the public interest because it is likely to contribute significantly to public understanding of the operations or activities of the government and is not primarily in the commercial interest of the requester.

(iv) Fee schedules shall provide for the recovery of only the direct costs of search, duplication, or review. Review costs shall include only the direct costs incurred during the initial examination of a document for the purposes of determining whether the documents must be disclosed under this section and for the purposes of withholding any portions exempt from disclosure under this section. Review costs may not include any costs incurred in resolving issues of law or policy that may be raised in the course of processing a request under this section. No fee may be charged by any agency under this section—

(I) if the costs of routine collection and processing of the fee are likely to equal or exceed the amount of the fee; or

(II) for any request described in clause (ii)(II) or (III) of this subparagraph for the first two hours of search time or for the first one hundred pages of duplication.

(v) No agency may require advance payment of any fee unless the requester has previously failed to pay fees in a timely fashion, or the agency has determined that the fee will exceed $250.

(vi) Nothing in this subparagraph shall supersede fees chargeable under a statute specifically providing for setting the level of fees for particular types of records.

(vii) In any action by a requester regarding the waiver of fees under this section, the court shall determine the matter de novo: *Provided,* That the court's review of the matter shall be limited to the record before the agency.

(B) On complaint, the district court of the United States in the district in which the complainant resides, or has his principal place of business, or in which the agency records are situated, or in the District of Columbia, has jurisdiction to enjoin the agency from withholding agency records and to order the production of any agency records improperly withheld from the complainant. In such a case the court shall determine the matter de novo, and may examine the contents of such agency records in camera to determine whether such records or any part thereof shall be withheld under any of the exemptions set forth in subsection (b) of this section, and the burden is on the agency to sustain its action.

(C) Notwithstanding any other provision of law, the defendant shall serve an answer or otherwise plead to any complaint made under this subsection within thirty days after service upon the defendant of the pleading in which such complaint is made, unless the court otherwise directs for good cause shown.

[(D) Repealed. Pub.L. 98–620, Title IV, § 402(2), Nov. 8, 1984, 98 Stat. 3357].

(E) The court may assess against the United States reasonable attorney fees and other litigation costs reasonably incurred in any case under this section in which the complainant has substantially prevailed.

(F) Whenever the court orders the production of any agency records improperly withheld from the complainant and assesses against the United States reasonable attorney fees and other litigation costs, and the court additionally issues a written finding that the circumstances surrounding the withholding raise questions whether agency personnel acted arbitrarily or capriciously with respect to the withholding, the Special Counsel shall promptly initiate a proceeding to determine whether disciplinary action is warranted against the officer or employee who was primarily responsible for the withholding. The Special Counsel, after investigation and consideration of the evidence submitted, shall submit his findings and recommendations to the administrative authority of the agency concerned and shall send copies of the findings and recommendations to the officer or employee or his representative. The administrative authority shall take the corrective action that the Special Counsel recommends.

(G) In the event of noncompliance with the order of the court, the district court may punish for contempt the responsible employee, and in the case of a uniformed service, the responsible member.

(5) Each agency having more than one member shall maintain and make available for public inspection a record of the final votes of each member in every agency proceeding.

(6)(A) Each agency, upon any request for records made under paragraph (1), (2), or (3) of this subsection, shall—

(i) determine within ten days (excepting Saturdays, Sundays and legal public holidays) after the receipt of any such request whether to comply with such request and shall immediately notify the person making such request of such determination and the reasons therefor, and of the right of such person to appeal to the head of the agency any adverse determination; and

(ii) make a determination with respect to any appeal within twenty days (excepting Saturdays, Sundays, and legal public holidays) after the receipt of such appeal. If on appeal the denial of the request for records is in whole or in part upheld, the agency shall notify the person making such request of the provisions for judicial review of that determination under paragraph (4) of this subsection.

(B) In unusual circumstances as specified in this subparagraph, the time limits prescribed in either clause (i) or clause (ii) of subparagraph (A) may be extended by written notice to the person making such request setting forth the reasons for such extension and the date on which a determination is expected to be dispatched. No such notice shall specify a date that would result in an extension for more than ten working days. As used in this subparagraph, "unusual circumstances" means, but only to the extent reasonably necessary to the proper processing of the particular request—

(i) the need to search for and collect the requested records from field facilities or other establishments that are separate from the office processing the request;

(ii) the need to search for, collect, and appropriately examine a voluminous amount of separate and distinct records which are demanded in a single request; or

(iii) the need for consultation, which shall be conducted with all practicable speed, with another agency having a substantial interest in the determination of the request or among two or more components of the agency having substantial subject-matter interest therein.

(C) Any person making a request to any agency for records under paragraph (1), (2), or (3) of this subsection shall be deemed to have exhausted his administrative remedies with respect to such request if the agency fails to comply with the applicable time limit provisions of this paragraph. If the Government can show exceptional circumstances exist and that the agency is exercising due diligence in responding to the request, the court may retain jurisdiction and allow the agency additional time to complete its review of the records. Upon any determination by an agency to comply with a request for records, the records shall be made promptly available to such person making such request. Any notification of denial of any request for records under this subsection shall set forth the names and titles or positions of each person responsible for the denial of such request.

(b) This section does not apply to matters that are—

(1)(A) specifically authorized under criteria established by an Executive order to be kept secret in the interest of national defense or foreign policy and (B) are in fact properly classified pursuant to such Executive order;

(2) related solely to the internal personnel rules and practices of an agency;

(3) specifically exempted from disclosure by statute (other than section 552b of this title), provided that such statute (A) requires that the matters be withheld from the public in such a manner as to leave no discretion on the issue, or (B) establishes particular criteria for withholding or refers to particular types of matters to be withheld;

(4) trade secrets and commercial or financial information obtained from a person and privileged or confidential;

(5) inter-agency or intra-agency memorandums or letters which would not be available by law to a party other than an agency in litigation with the agency;

(6) personnel and medical files and similar files the disclosure of which would constitute a clearly unwarranted invasion of personal privacy;

(7) records or information compiled for law enforcement purposes, but only to the extent that the production of such law enforcement records or information (A) could reasonably be expected to interfere with enforcement proceedings, (B) would deprive a person of a right to a fair trial or an impartial adjudication, (C) could reasonably be expected to constitute an unwarranted invasion of personal privacy, (D) could reasonably be expected to disclose the identity of a confidential source, including a State, local, or foreign agency or authority or any private institution which furnished information on a confidential basis, and, in the case of a record or information compiled by criminal law enforcement authority in the course of a criminal investigation or by an agency conducting a lawful national security intelligence investigation, information furnished by a confidential source, (E) would disclose techniques and procedures for law enforcement investigations or prosecutions, or would disclose guidelines for law enforcement investigations or prosecutions if such disclosure could reasonably be expected to risk circumvention of the law, or (F) could reasonably be expected to endanger the life or physical safety of any individual;

(8) contained in or related to examination, operating, or condition reports prepared by, on behalf of, or for the use of an agency responsible for the regulation or supervision of financial institutions; or

(9) geological and geophysical information and data, including maps, concerning wells.

Any reasonable segregable portion of a record shall be provided to any person requesting such record after deletion of the portions which are exempt under this subsection.

(c)(1) Whenever a request is made which involves access to records described in subsection (b)(7)(A) and—

(A) the investigation or proceeding involves a possible violation of criminal law; and

(B) there is reason to believe that (i) the subject of the investigation or proceeding is not aware of its pendency, and (ii) disclosure of the existence of the records could reasonably be expected to interfere with enforcement proceedings,

the agency may, during only such time as that circumstance continues, treat the records as not subject to the requirements of this section.

(2) Whenever informant records maintained by a criminal law enforcement agency under an informant's name or personal identifier are requested by a third party according to the informant's name or personal identifier, the agency may treat the records as not subject to the requirements of this section unless the informant's status as an informant has been officially confirmed.

(3) Whenever a request is made which involves access to records maintained by the Federal Bureau of Investigation pertaining to foreign intelligence or counterintelligence, or international terrorism, and the existence of the records is classified information as provided in subsection (b)(1), the Bureau may, as long as the existence of the records remains classified information, treat the records as not subject to the requirements of this section.

(d) This section does not authorize withholding of information or limit the availability of records to the public, except as specifically stated in this section. This section is not authority to withhold information from Congress.

(e) On or before March 1 of each calendar year, each agency shall submit a report covering the preceding calendar year to the Speaker of the House of Representatives and President of the Senate for referral to the appropriate committees of the Congress. The report shall include—

(1) the number of determinations made by such agency not to comply with requests for records made to such agency under subsection (a) and the reasons for each such determination;

(2) the number of appeals made by persons under subsection (a)(6), the result of such appeals, and the reason for the action upon each appeal that results in a denial of information;

(3) the names and titles or positions of each person responsible for the denial of records requested under this section, and the number of instances of participation for each;

(4) the results of each proceeding conducted pursuant to subsection (a)(4)(F), including a report of the disciplinary action taken against the officer or employee who was primarily responsible for improperly withholding records or an explanation of why disciplinary action was not taken;

(5) a copy of every rule made by such agency regarding this section;

(6) a copy of the fee schedule and the total amount of fees collected by the agency for making records available under this section; and

(7) such other information as indicates efforts to administer fully this section.

The Attorney General shall submit an annual report on or before March 1 of each calendar year which shall include for the prior calendar year a listing of the number of cases arising under this section, the exemption involved in each case, the disposition of such case, and the cost, fees, and penalties assessed under subsections (a)(4)(E), (F), and (G). Such report shall also include a description of the efforts undertaken by the Department of Justice to encourage agency compliance with this section.

(f) For purposes of this section, the term "agency" as defined in section 551(1) of this title includes any executive department, military department, Government corporation, Government controlled corporation, or other establishment in the executive branch of the Government (including the Executive Office of the President), or any independent regulatory agency.

(As amended Pub.L. 95–454, Title IX, § 906(a)(10), Oct. 13, 1978, 92 Stat. 1225; Pub.L. 98–620, Title IV, § 402(2), Nov. 8, 1984, 98 Stat. 3357; Pub.L. 99–570, Title I, §§ 1802, 1803, Oct. 27, 1986, 100 Stat. 3207–48, 3207–49.)

[5 U.S.C.A. § 552a, The Privacy Protection Act, is omitted.—Ed.]

§ 552b. Open Meetings [Government in the Sunshine Act]

(a) For purposes of this section—

(1) the term "agency" means any agency, as defined in section 552(e) of this title, headed by a collegial body composed of two or more individual members, a majority of whom are appointed to such position by the President with the advice and consent of the Senate, and any subdivision thereof authorized to act on behalf of the agency;

(2) the term "meeting" means the deliberations of at least the number of individual agency members required to take action on behalf of the agency where such deliberations determine or result in the joint conduct or disposition of official agency business, but does not include deliberations required or permitted by subsection (d) or (e); and

(3) the term "member" means an individual who belongs to a collegial body heading an agency.

(b) Members shall not jointly conduct or dispose of agency business other than in accordance with this section. Except as provided in subsection (c), every portion of every meeting of an agency shall be open to public observation.

(c) Except in a case where the agency finds that the public interest requires otherwise, the second sentence of subsection (b) shall not apply to any portion of an agency meeting, and the requirements of subsections (d) and (e) shall not apply to any information pertaining to such meeting otherwise required by this section to be disclosed to the public, where the agency properly determines that such portion or portions of its meeting or the disclosure of such information is likely to—

(1) disclose matters that are (A) specifically authorized under criteria established by an Executive order to be kept secret in the interests of national defense or foreign policy and (B) in fact properly classified pursuant to such Executive order;

(2) relate solely to the internal personnel rules and practices of an agency;

(3) disclose matters specifically exempted from disclosure by statute (other than section 552 of this title), provided that such statute (A) requires that the matters be withheld from the public in such a manner as to leave no discretion on the issue, or (B) establishes particular criteria for withholding or refers to particular types of matters to be withheld;

(4) disclose trade secrets and commercial or financial information obtained from a person and privileged or confidential;

(5) involve accusing any person of a crime, or formally censuring any person;

(6) disclose information of a personal nature where disclosure would constitute a clearly unwarranted invasion of personal privacy;

(7) disclose investigatory records compiled for law enforcement purposes, or information which if written would be contained in such records, but only to the extent that the production of such records or information would (A) interfere with enforcement proceedings, (B) deprive a person of a right to a fair trial or an impartial adjudication, (C) constitute an unwarranted invasion of personal privacy, (D) disclose the identity of a confidential source and, in the case of a record compiled by a criminal law enforcement authority in the course of a criminal investigation, or by an agency conducting a lawful national security intelligence investigation, confidential information furnished only by the confidential source, (E) disclose investigative techniques and procedures, or (F) endanger the life or physical safety of law enforcement personnel;

(8) disclose information contained in or related to examination, operating, or condition reports prepared by, on behalf of, or for the use of an agency responsible for the regulation or supervision of financial institutions;

(9) disclose information the premature disclosure of which would—

(A) in the case of an agency which regulates currencies, securities, commodities, or financial institutions, be likely to (i) lead to significant financial speculation in currencies, securities, or commodities, or (ii) significantly endanger the stability of any financial institution; or

(B) in the case of any agency, be likely to significantly frustrate implementation of a proposed agency action,

except that subparagraph (B) shall not apply in any instance where the agency has already disclosed to the public the content or nature of its proposed action, or where the agency is required by law to make such disclosure on its own initiative prior to taking final agency action on such proposal; or

(10) specifically concern the agency's issuance of a subpoena, or the agency's participation in a civil action or proceeding, an action in a foreign court or international tribunal, or an arbitration, or the initiation, conduct, or disposition by the agency of a particular case of formal agency adjudication pursuant to the procedures in section 554 of this title or otherwise involving a determination on the record after opportunity for a hearing.

(d)(1) Action under subsection (c) shall be taken only when a majority of the entire membership of the agency (as defined in subsection (a)(1)) votes to take such action. A separate vote of the agency members shall be taken with respect to each agency meeting a portion or portions of which are proposed to be closed to the public pursuant to subsection (c), or with respect to any information which is proposed to be withheld under subsection (c). A single vote may be taken with respect to a series of meetings, a portion or portions of which are proposed to be closed to the public, or with respect to any information concerning such series of meetings, so long as each meeting in such series involves the same particular matters and is scheduled to be held no more than thirty days after the initial meeting in such series. The vote of each agency member participating in such vote shall be recorded and no proxies shall be allowed.

(2) Whenever any person whose interests may be directly affected by a portion of a meeting requests that the agency close such portion to the public for any of the reasons referred to in paragraph (5), (6), or (7) of subsection (c), the agency, upon request of any one of its members, shall vote by recorded vote whether to close such meeting.

(3) Within one day of any vote taken pursuant to paragraph (1) or (2), the agency shall make publicly available a written copy of such vote reflecting the vote of each member on the question. If a portion of a meeting is to be closed to the public, the agency shall, within one day of the vote taken pursuant to paragraph (1) or (2) of this subsection, make publicly available a full written explanation of its action closing the portion together with a list of all persons expected to attend the meeting and their affiliation.

(4) Any agency, a majority of whose meetings may properly be closed to the public pursuant to paragraph (4), (8), (9)(A), or (10) of subsection (c), or any combination thereof, may provide by regulation for the closing of such meetings or portions thereof in the event that a majority of the members of the agency votes by recorded vote at the beginning of such meeting, or portion thereof, to close the exempt portion or portions of the meeting, and a copy of such vote, reflecting the vote of each member on the question, is made available to the public. The provisions of paragraphs (1), (2), and (3) of this subsection and subsection (e) shall not apply to any portion of a meeting to which such regulations apply: *Provided,* That the agency shall, except to the extent that such information is exempt from disclosure under the provisions of subsection (c), provide the public with public announcement of the time, place, and subject matter of the meeting and of each portion thereof at the earliest practicable time.

(e)(1) In the case of each meeting, the agency shall make public announcement, at least one week before the meeting, of the time, place, and subject matter of the meeting, whether it is to be open or closed to the public, and the name and phone number of the official designated by the agency to respond to requests for information about the meeting. Such announcement shall be made unless a majority of the members of the agency determines by a recorded vote that agency business requires that such meeting be called at an earlier date, in which case the agency shall make public announcement of the time, place, and subject matter of such meeting, and whether open or closed to the public, at the earliest practicable time.

(2) The time or place of a meeting may be changed following the public announcement required by paragraph (1) only if the agency publicly announces such change at the earliest practicable time. The subject matter of a meeting, or the determination of the agency to open or close a meeting, or portion of a meeting, to the public, may be changed following the public announcement required by this subsection only if (A) a majority of the entire membership of the agency determines by a recorded vote that agency business so requires and that no earlier announcement of the change was possible, and (B) the agency publicly announces such change and the vote of each member upon such change at the earliest practicable time.

(3) Immediately following each public announcement required by this subsection, notice of the time, place, and subject matter of a meeting, whether the meeting is open or closed, any change in one of the preceding, and the name and phone number of the official designated by the agency to respond to requests for information about the meeting, shall also be submitted for publication in the Federal Register.

(f)(1) For every meeting closed pursuant to paragraphs (1) through (10) of subsection (c), the General Counsel or chief legal officer of the agency shall publicly certify that, in his or her opinion, the meeting may be closed to the public and shall state each relevant exemptive provision. A copy of such certification, together with a statement from the presiding officer of the meeting setting forth the time and place of the meeting, and the persons present, shall be retained by the agency. The agency shall maintain a complete transcript or electronic recording adequate to record fully the proceedings of each meeting, or portion of a meeting, closed to the public, except that in the case of a meeting, or portion of a meeting, closed to the public pursuant to paragraph (8), (9)(A), or (10) of subsection (c), the agency shall maintain either such a transcript or recording, or a set of minutes. Such minutes shall fully and clearly describe all matters discussed and shall provide a full and accurate summary of any actions taken, and the reasons therefor, including a description of each of the views expressed on any item and the record of any rollcall vote (reflecting the vote of each member on the question). All documents considered in connection with any action shall be identified in such minutes.

(2) The agency shall make promptly available to the public, in a place easily accessible to the public, the transcript, electronic recording, or minutes (as required by paragraph (1)) of the discussion of any item on the agenda, or of any item of the testimony of any witness received at the meeting, except for such item or items of such discussion or testimony as the agency determines to contain information which may be withheld under subsection (c). Copies of such transcript, or minutes, or a transcription of such recording disclosing the identity of each speaker, shall be furnished to any person at the actual cost of duplication or transcription. The agency shall maintain a complete verbatim copy of the transcript, a complete copy of the minutes, or a complete electronic recording of each meeting, or portion of a meeting, closed to the public, for a period of at least two years after such meeting, or until one year after the conclusion of any agency proceeding with respect to which the meeting or portion was held, whichever occurs later.

(g) Each agency subject to the requirements of this section shall, within 180 days after the date of enactment of this section, following consultation with the Office of the Chairman of the Administrative Conference of the United States and published notice in the Federal Register of at least thirty days and opportunity for written comment by any person, promulgate regulations to implement the requirements of subsections (b) through (f) of this section. Any person may bring a proceeding in the United States District Court for the District of Columbia to require an agency to promulgate such regulations if such agency has not promulgated such regulations within the time period specified herein. Subject to any limitations of time provided by law, any person may bring a proceeding in the United States Court of Appeals for the District of Columbia to set aside agency regulations issued pursuant to this subsection that are not in accord with the requirements of subsections (b) through (f) of this section and to require the promulgation of regulations that are in accord with such subsections.

(h)(1) The district courts of the United States shall have jurisdiction to enforce the requirements of subsections (b) through (f) of this section by declaratory judgment, injunctive relief, or other relief as may be appropriate. Such actions may be brought by any person against an agency prior to, or within sixty days after, the meeting out of which the violation of this section arises, except that if public announcement of such meeting is not initially provided by the agency in accordance with the requirements of this section, such action may be instituted pursuant to this section at any time prior to sixty days after any public announcement of such meeting. Such actions may be brought in the district court of the United States for the district in which the agency meeting is held or in which the agency in question has its headquarters, or in the District Court for the District of Columbia. In such actions a defendant shall serve his answer within thirty days after the service of the complaint. The burden is on the defendant to sustain his action. In deciding such cases the court may examine in camera any portion of the transcript, electronic recording, or minutes of a meeting closed to the public, and may take such additional evidence as it deems necessary. The court, having due regard for orderly administration and the public interest, as well as the interests of the parties, may grant such equitable relief as it deems appropriate, including granting an injunction against future violations of this section or ordering the agency to make available to the public such portion of the transcript, recording, or minutes of a meeting as is not authorized to be withheld under subsection (c) of this section.

(2) Any Federal court otherwise authorized by law to review agency action may, at the application of any person properly participating in the proceeding pursuant to other applicable law, inquire into violations by the agency of the requirements of this section and afford such relief as it deems appropriate. Nothing in this section authorizes any Federal court having jurisdiction solely on the basis of paragraph (1) to set aside, enjoin, or invalidate any agency action (other than an action to close a meeting or to withhold information under this section) taken or discussed at any agency meeting out of which the violation of this section arose.

(i) The court may assess against any party reasonable attorney fees and other litigation costs reasonably incurred by any other party who substantially prevails in any action brought in accordance with the provisions of subsection (g) or (h) of this section, except that costs may be assessed against the plaintiff only where the court finds that the suit was initiated by the plaintiff primarily for frivolous or dilatory purposes. In the case of assessment of costs against an agency, the costs may be assessed by the court against the United States.

(j) Each agency subject to the requirements of this section shall annually report to the Congress regarding the following:

(1) The changes in the policies and procedures of the agency under this section that have occurred during the preceding 1-year period.

(2) A tabulation of the number of meetings held, the exemptions applied to close meetings, and the days of public notice provided to close meetings.

(3) A brief description of litigation or formal complaints concerning the implementation of this section by the agency.

(4) A brief explanation of any changes in law that have affected the responsibilities of the agency under this section.

(k) Nothing herein expands or limits the present rights of any person under section 552 of this title, except that the exemptions set forth in subsection (c) of this section shall govern in the case of any request made pursuant to section 552 to copy or inspect the transcripts, recordings, or minutes described in subsection (f) of this section. The requirements of chapter 33 of title 44, United States Code, shall not apply to the transcripts, recordings, and minutes described in subsection (f) of this section.

(*l*) This section does not constitute authority to withhold any information from Congress, and does not authorize the closing of any agency meeting or portion thereof required by any other provision of law to be open.

(m) Nothing in this section authorizes any agency to withhold from any individual any record, including transcripts, recording, or minutes required by this section, which is otherwise accessible to such individual under section 552a of this title.

§ 553. Rule Making

(a) This section applies, accordingly to the provisions thereof, except to the extent that there is involved—

(1) a military or foreign affairs function of the United States; or

(2) a matter relating to agency management or personnel or to public property, loans, grants, benefits, or contracts.

(b) General notice of proposed rule making shall be published in the Federal Register, unless persons subject thereto are named and either personally served or otherwise have actual notice thereof in accordance with law. The notice shall include—

(1) a statement of the time, place, and nature of public rule making proceedings;

(2) reference to the legal authority under which the rule is proposed; and

(3) either the terms or substance of the proposed rule or a description of the subjects and issues involved.

Except when notice or hearing is required by statute, this subsection does not apply—

(A) to interpretative rules, general statements of policy, or rules of agency organization, procedure, or practice; or

(B) when the agency for good cause finds (and incorporates the finding and a brief statement of reasons therefor in the rules issued) that notice and public procedure thereon are impracticable, unnecessary, or contrary to the public interest.

(c) After notice required by this section, the agency shall give interested persons an opportunity to participate in the rule making through submission of written data, views, or arguments with or without opportunity for oral presentation. After consideration of the relevant matter presented, the agency shall incorporate in the rules adopted a concise general statement of their basis and purpose. When rules are required by statute to be made on the record after opportunity for an agency hearing, sections 556 and 557 of this title apply instead of this subsection.

(d) The required publication or service of a substantive rule shall be made not less than 30 days before its effective date, except—

(1) a substantive rule which grants or recognizes an exemption or relieves a restriction;

(2) interpretative rules and statements of policy; or

(3) as otherwise provided by the agency for good cause found and published with the rule.

(e) Each agency shall give an interested person the right to petition for the issuance, amendment, or repeal of a rule.

§ 554. Adjudications

(a) This section applies, according to the provisions thereof, in every case of adjudication required by statute to be determined on the record after opportunity for an agency hearing, except to the extent that there is involved—

(1) a matter subject to a subsequent trial of the law and the facts de novo in a court;

(2) the selection or tenure of an employee, except an administrative law judge appointed under section 3105 of this title;

(3) proceedings in which decisions rest solely on inspections, tests, or elections;

(4) the conduct of military or foreign affairs functions;

(5) cases in which an agency is acting as an agent for a court; or

(6) the certification of worker representatives.

(b) Persons entitled to notice of an agency hearing shall be timely informed of—

(1) the time, place, and nature of the hearing;

(2) the legal authority and jurisdiction under which the hearing is to be held; and

(3) the matters of fact and law asserted.

When private persons are the moving parties, other parties to the proceeding shall give prompt notice of issues controverted in fact or law; and in other instances agencies may by rule require responsive pleading. In fixing the time and place for hearings, due regard shall be had for the convenience and necessity of the parties or their representatives.

(c) The agency shall give all interested parties opportunity for—

(1) the submission and consideration of facts, arguments, offers of settlement, or proposals of adjustment when time, the nature of the proceeding, and the public interest permit; and

(2) to the extent that the parties are unable so to determine a controversy by consent, hearing and decision on notice and in accordance with sections 556 and 557 of this title.

(d) The employee who presides at the reception of evidence pursuant to section 556 of this title shall make the recommended decision or initial decision required by section 557 of this title, unless he becomes unavailable to the agency. Except to the extent required for the disposition of ex parte matters as authorized by law, such an employee may not—

(1) consult a person or party on a fact in issue, unless on notice and opportunity for all parties to participate; or

(2) be responsible to or subject to the supervision or direction of an employee or agent engaged in the performance of investigative or prosecuting functions for an agency.

An employee or agent engaged in the performance of investigative or prosecuting functions for an agency in a case may not, in that or a factually related case, participate or advise in the decision, recommended decision, or agency review pursuant to section 557 of this title, except as witness or counsel in public proceedings. This subsection does not apply—

(A) in determining applications for initial licenses;

(B) to proceedings involving the validity or application of rates, facilities, or practices of public utilities or carriers; or

(C) to the agency or a member or members of the body comprising the agency.

(e) The agency, with like effect as in the case of other orders, and in its sound discretion, may issue a declaratory order to terminate a controversy or remove uncertainty.

(As amended Pub.L. 95–251, § 2(a)(1), Mar. 27, 1978, 92 Stat. 183.)

§ 555. Ancillary Matters

(a) This section applies, according to the provisions thereof, except as otherwise provided by this subchapter.

(b) A person compelled to appear in person before an agency or representative thereof is entitled to be accompanied, represented, and advised by counsel or, if permitted by the agency, by other qualified representative. A party is entitled to appear in person or by or with counsel or other duly qualified representative in an agency proceeding. So far as the orderly conduct of public business permits, an interested person may appear before an agency or its responsible employees for the presentation, adjustment, or determination of an issue, request, or controversy in a proceeding, whether interlocutory, summary, or otherwise, or in connection with an agency function. With due regard for the convenience and necessity of the parties or their representatives and within a reasonable time, each agency shall proceed to conclude a matter presented to it. This subsection does not grant or deny a person who is not a lawyer the right to appear for or represent others before an agency or in an agency proceeding.

(c) Process, requirement of a report, inspection, or other investigative act or demand may not be issued, made, or enforced except as authorized by law. A person compelled to submit data or evidence is entitled to retain or, on payment of lawfully prescribed costs, procure a copy or transcript thereof, except that in a non-public investigatory proceeding the witness may for good cause be limited to inspection of the official transcript of his testimony.

(d) Agency subpoenas authorized by law shall be issued to a party on request and, when required by rules of procedure, on a statement or showing of general relevance and reasonable scope of the evidence sought. On contest, the court shall sustain the subpoena or similar process or demand to the extent that it is found to be in accordance with law. In a proceeding for enforcement, the court shall issue an order requiring the appearance of the witness or the production of the evidence or data within a reasonable time under penalty of punishment for contempt in cases of contumacious failure to comply.

(e) Prompt notice shall be given of the denial in whole or in part of a written application, petition, or other request of an interested person made in connection with any agency proceeding. Except in affirming a prior denial or when the denial is self-explanatory, the notice shall be accompanied by a brief statement of the grounds for denial.

§ 556. Hearings; Presiding Employees; Powers and Duties; Burden of Proof; Evidence; Record as Basis of Decision

(a) This section applies, according to the provisions thereof, to hearings required by section 553 or 554 of this title to be conducted in accordance with this section.

(b) There shall preside at the taking of evidence—

(1) the agency;

(2) one or more members of the body which comprises the agency; or

(3) one or more administrative law judges appointed under section 3105 of this title.

This subchapter does not supersede the conduct of specified classes of proceedings, in whole or in part, by or before boards or other employees specially provided for by or designated under statute. The functions of presiding employees and of employees participating in decisions in accordance with section 557 of this title shall be conducted in an impartial manner. A presiding or participating employee may at any time disqualify himself. On the filing in good faith of a timely and sufficient affidavit of personal bias or other disqualification of a presiding or participating employee, the agency shall determine the matters as a part of the record and decision in the case.

(c) Subject to published rules of the agency and within its powers, employees presiding at hearings may—

(1) administer oaths and affirmations;

(2) issue subpoenas authorized by law;

(3) rule on offers of proof and receive relevant evidence;

(4) take depositions or have depositions taken when the ends of justice would be served;

(5) regulate the course of the hearing;

(6) hold conferences for the settlement or simplification of the issues by consent of the parties or by the use of alternative means of dispute resolution as provided in subchapter IV of this chapter;

(7) inform the parties as to the availability of one or more alternative means of dispute resolution, and encourage use of such methods;

(8) require the attendance at any conference held pursuant to paragraph (6) of at least one representative of each party who has authority to negotiate concerning resolution of issues in controversy;

(9) dispose of procedural requests or similar matters;

(10) make or recommend decisions in accordance with section 557 of this title; and

(11) take other action authorized by agency rule consistent with this subchapter.

(d) Except as otherwise provided by statute, the proponent of a rule or order has the burden of proof. Any oral or documentary evidence may be received, but the agency as a matter of policy shall provide for the exclusion of irrelevant, immaterial, or unduly repetitious evidence. A sanction may not be imposed or rule or order issued except on consideration of the whole record or those parts thereof cited by a party and supported by and in accordance with the reliable, probative, and substantial evidence. The agency may, to the extent consistent with the interests of justice and the policy of the underlying statutes administered by the agency, consider a violation of section 557(d) of this title sufficient grounds for a decision adverse to a party who has knowingly committed such violation or knowingly caused such violation to occur. A party is entitled to present his case or defense by oral or documentary evidence, to submit rebuttal evidence, and to conduct such cross-examination as may be required for a full and true disclosure of the facts. In rule making or determining claims for money or benefits or applications for initial licenses an agency may, when a party will not be prejudiced thereby, adopt procedures for the submission of all or part of the evidence in written form.

(e) The transcript of testimony and exhibits, together with all papers and requests filed in the proceeding, constitutes the exclusive record for decision in accordance with section 557 of this title and, on payment of lawfully prescribed costs, shall be made available to the parties. When an agency decision rests on official notice of a material fact not appearing in the evidence in the record, a party is entitled, on timely request, to an opportunity to show the contrary.

(As amended Pub.L. 95–251, § 2(a)(1), Mar. 27, 1978, 92 Stat. 183; Pub.L. 101–552, § 4(a), Nov. 15, 1990, 104 Stat. 2737.)

STATUTORY NOTE

Sunset Provisions

For termination of amendments by Pub.L. 101–552 and authority to use dispute resolution proceedings on Oct. 1, 1995, except with respect to certain pending proceedings, see section 11 of Pub.L. 101–552, set out as a note under section 581 of this title.

§ 557. Initial Decisions; Conclusiveness; Review by Agency; Submissions by Parties; Contents of Decisions; Record

(a) This section applies, according to the provisions thereof, when a hearing is required to be conducted in accordance with section 556 of this title.

(b) When the agency did not preside at the reception of the evidence, the presiding employee or, in cases not subject to section 554(d) of this title, an employee qualified to preside at hearings pursuant to section 556 of this title, shall initially decide the case unless the agency requires, either in specific cases or by general rule, the entire record to be certified to it for decision. When the presiding employee makes an initial decision, that decision then becomes the decision of the agency without further proceedings unless there is an appeal to, or review on motion of, the agency within time provided by rule. On appeal from or review of the initial decision, the agency has all the powers which it would have in making the initial decision except as it may limit the issues on notice or by rule. When the agency makes the decision without having presided at the reception of the evidence, the presiding employee or an employee qualified to preside at hearings pursuant to section 556 of this title shall first recommend a decision, except that in rule making or determining application for initial licenses—

(1) instead thereof the agency may issue a tentative decision or one of its responsible employees may recommend a decision; or

(2) this procedure may be omitted in a case in which the agency finds on the record that due and timely execution of its functions imperatively and unavoidably so requires.

(c) Before a recommended, initial, or tentative decision, or a decision on agency review of the decision of subordinate employees, the parties are entitled to a reasonable opportunity to submit for the consideration of the employees participating in the decisions—

(1) proposed finding and conclusions; or

(2) exceptions to the decisions or recommended decisions of subordinate employees or to tentative agency decisions; and

(3) supporting reasons for the exceptions or proposed findings or conclusions.

The record shall show the ruling on each finding, conclusion, or exception presented. All decisions, including initial, recommended, and tentative decisions, are a part of the record and shall include a statement of—

(A) findings and conclusions, and the reasons or basis therefor, on all the material issues of fact, law, or discretion presented on the record; and

(B) the appropriate rule, order, sanction, relief, or denial thereof.

(d)(1) In any agency proceeding which is subject to subsection (a) of this section, except to the extent required for the disposition of ex parte matters as authorized by law—

(A) no interested person outside the agency shall make or knowingly cause to be made to any member of the body comprising the agency, administrative law judge, or other employee who is or may reasonably be expected to be involved in the decisional process of the proceeding, an ex parte communication relevant to the merits of the proceeding;

(B) no member of the body comprising the agency, administrative law judge, or other employee who is or may reasonably be expected to be involved in the decisional process of the proceeding, shall make or knowingly cause to be made to any interested person outside the agency an ex parte communication relevant to the merits of the proceeding;

(C) a member of the body comprising the agency, administrative law judge, or other employee who is or may reasonably be expected to be involved in the decisional process of such proceeding who receives, or who makes or knowingly causes to be made, a communication prohibited by this subsection shall place on the public record of the proceeding:

(i) all such written communications;

(ii) memoranda stating the substance of all such oral communications; and

(iii) all written responses, and memoranda stating the substance of all oral responses, to the materials described in clauses (i) and (ii) of this subparagraph;

(D) upon receipt of a communication knowingly made or knowingly caused to be made by a party in violation of this subsection, the agency, administrative law judge, or other employee presiding at the hearing may, to the extent consistent with the interests of justice and the policy of the underlying statutes, require the party to show cause why his claim or interest in the proceeding should not be dismissed, denied, disregarded, or otherwise adversely affected on account of such violation; and

(E) the prohibitions of this subsection shall apply beginning at such time as the agency may designate, but in no case shall they begin to apply later than the time at which a proceeding is noticed for hearing unless the person responsible for the communication has knowledge that it will be noticed, in which case the prohibitions shall apply beginning at the time of his acquisition of such knowledge.

(2) This subsection does not constitute authority to withhold information from Congress.

§ 558. Imposition of Sanctions; Determination of Applications for Licenses; Suspension, Revocation, and Expiration of Licenses

(a) This section applies, according to the provisions thereof, to the exercise of a power or authority.

(b) A sanction may not be imposed or a substantive rule or order issued except with jurisdiction delegated to the agency and as authorized by law.

(c) When application is made for a license, required by law, the agency, with due regard for the rights and privileges of all the interested parties or adversely affected persons and within a reasonable time, shall set and complete proceedings required to be conducted in accordance with sections 556 and 557 of this title or other proceedings required by law and shall make its decision. Except in cases of willfulness or those in which public health, interest, or safety requires otherwise, the withdrawal, suspension, revocation, or annulment of a license is lawful only if, before the institution of agency proceedings therefor, the licensee has been given—

(1) notice by the agency in writing of the facts or conduct which may warrant the action; and

(2) opportunity to demonstrate or achieve compliance with all lawful requirements.

When the licensee has made timely and sufficient application for a renewal or a new license in accordance with agency rules, a license with reference to an activity of a continuing nature does not expire until the application has been finally determined by the agency.

§ 559. Effect on Other Laws; Effect of Subsequent Statute

This subchapter, chapter 7, and sections 1305, 3105, 3344, 4301(2)(E), 5372 and 7521 of this title, and the provisions of section 5335(a)(B) of this title that relate to administrative law judges, do not limit or repeal additional requirements imposed by statute or otherwise recognized by law. Except as otherwise required by law, requirements or privileges relating to evidence or procedure apply equally to agencies and persons. Each agency is granted the authority necessary to comply with the requirements of this subchapter through the issuance of rules or otherwise. Subsequent statute may not be held to supersede or modify this subchapter, chapter 7, sections 1305, 3105, 3344, 4301(2)(E), 5372 or 7521 of this title, or the provisions of section 5335(a)(B) of this title that relate to administrative law judges, except to the extent that it does so expressly.

(As amended Pub.L. 95–251, § 2(a)(1), Mar. 27, 1978, 92 Stat. 183; Pub.L. 95–454, Title VIII, § 801(a)(3)(B)(iii), Oct. 13, 1978, 92 Stat. 1221.)

B. JUDICIAL REVIEW

5 U.S.C.A., Chapter 7

Table of Contents

Sec.
701. Application; definitions.
702. Right of review.
703. Form and venue of proceeding.
704. Actions reviewable.
705. Relief pending review.
706. Scope of review.

§ 701. Application; Definitions

(a) This chapter applies, according to the provisions thereof, except to the extent that—

(1) statutes preclude judicial review; or

(2) agency action is committed to agency discretion by law.

(b) For the purpose of this chapter—

(1) "agency" means each authority of the Government of the United States, whether or not it is within or subject to review by another agency, but does not include—

(A) the Congress;

(B) the courts of the United States;

(C) the governments of the territories or possessions of the United States;

(D) the government of the District of Columbia;

(E) agencies composed of representatives of the parties or of representatives of organizations of the parties to the disputes determined by them;

(F) courts martial and military commissions;

(G) military authority exercised in the field in time of war or in occupied territory; or

(H) functions conferred by sections 1738, 1739, 1743, and 1744 of title 12; chapter 2 of title 41; or sections 1622, 1884, 1891–1902, and former section 1641(b)(2), of title 50, appendix; and

(2) "person", "rule", "order", "license", "sanction", "relief", and "agency action" have the meanings given them by section 551 of this title.

§ 702. Right of Review

A person suffering legal wrong because of agency action, or adversely affected or aggrieved by agency action within the meaning of a relevant statute, is entitled to judicial review thereof. An action in a court of the United States seeking relief other than money damages and stating a claim that an agency or an officer or employee thereof acted or failed to act in an official capacity or under color of legal authority shall not be dismissed nor relief therein be denied on the ground that it is against the United States or that the United States is an indispensable party. The United States may be named as a defendant in any such action, and a judgment or decree may be entered against the United States: *Provided*, That any mandatory or injunctive decree shall specify the Federal officer or officers (by name or by title), and their successors in office, personally responsible for compliance. Nothing herein (1) affects other limitations on judicial review or the power or duty of the court to dismiss any action or deny relief on any other appropriate legal or equitable ground; or (2) confers authority to grant relief if any other statute that grants consent to suit expressly or impliedly forbids the relief which is sought.

§ 703. Form and Venue of Proceeding

The form of proceeding for judicial review is the special statutory review proceeding relevant to the subject matter in a court specified by statute or, in the absence or inadequacy thereof, any applicable form of legal action, including actions for declaratory judgments or writs of prohibitory or mandatory injunction or habeas corpus, in a court of competent jurisdiction. If no special statutory review proceeding is applicable, the action for judicial review may be brought against the United States, the agency by its official title, or the appropriate officer. Except to the extent that prior, adequate, and exclusive opportunity for judicial review is provided by law, agency action is subject to judicial review in civil or criminal proceedings for judicial enforcement.

§ 704. Actions Reviewable

Agency action made reviewable by statute and final agency action for which there is no adequate remedy in a court are subject to judicial review. A preliminary, procedural, or intermediate agency action or ruling not directly reviewable is subject to review on the review of the final agency action. Except as otherwise expressly required by statute, agency action otherwise final is final for the purposes of this section whether or not there has been presented or determined an application for a declaratory order, for any form of reconsideration, or, unless the agency otherwise requires by rule and provides that the action meanwhile is inoperative, for an appeal to superior agency authority.

§ 705. Relief Pending Review

When an agency finds that justice so requires, it may postpone the effective date of action taken by it, pending judicial review. On such conditions as may be required and to the extent necessary to prevent irreparable injury, the reviewing court, including the court to which a case may be taken on appeal from or on application for certiorari or other writ to a reviewing court, may issue all necessary and appropriate process to postpone the effective date of an agency action or to preserve status or rights pending conclusion of the review proceedings.

§ 706. Scope of Review

To the extent necessary to decision and when presented, the reviewing court shall decide all relevant questions of law, interpret constitutional and statutory provisions, and determine the meaning or applicability of the terms of an agency action. The reviewing court shall—

(1) compel agency action unlawfully withheld or unreasonably delayed; and

(2) hold unlawful and set aside agency action, findings, and conclusions found to be—

(A) arbitrary, capricious, an abuse of discretion, or otherwise not in accordance with law;

(B) contrary to constitutional right, power, privilege, or immunity;

(C) in excess of statutory jurisdiction, authority, or limitations, or short of statutory right;

(D) without observance of procedure required by law;

(E) unsupported by substantial evidence in a case subject to section 556 and 557 of this title or otherwise reviewed on the record of an agency hearing provided by statute; or

(F) unwarranted by the facts to the extent that the facts are subject to trial de novo by the reviewing court.

In making the foregoing determinations, the court shall review the whole record or those parts of it cited by a party, and due account shall be taken of the rule of prejudicial error.

APPENDIX D
EQUAL ACCESS TO JUSTICE ACT
28 U.S.C.A. § 2412

EDITORIAL NOTE: *In a citizen suit, attorney fees may be recovered under provisions of the Equal Access to Justice Act, codified in Section 2412 of Title 28, United States Code. That statute is set out below. Attorney fees may similarly be awarded by agencies in adjudicatory proceedings under like administrative procedure provisions of the Equal Access to Justice Act, codified at 5 U.S.C.A. § 504. The costs and fee provisions relating to actions in federal court and those relating to adversary adjudications are synonymous; the latter are not duplicated here.*

---

§ 2412. Costs and fees

(a)(1) Except as otherwise specifically provided by statute, a judgment for costs, as enumerated in section 1920 of this title, but not including the fees and expenses of attorneys, may be awarded to the prevailing party in any civil action brought by or against the United States or any agency or any official of the United States acting in his or her official capacity in any court having jurisdiction of such action. A judgment for costs when taxed against the United States shall, in an amount established by statute, court rule, or order, be limited to reimbursing in whole or in part the prevailing party for the costs incurred by such party in the litigation.

(2) A judgment for costs, when awarded in favor of the United States in an action brought by the United States, may include an amount equal to the filing fee prescribed under section 1914(a) of this title. The preceding sentence shall not be construed as requiring the United States to pay any filing fee.

(b) Unless expressly prohibited by statute, a court may award reasonable fees and expenses of attorneys, in addition to the costs which may be awarded pursuant to subsection (a), to the prevailing party in any civil action brought by or against the United States or any agency or any official of the United States acting in his or her official capacity in any court having jurisdiction of such action. The United States shall be liable for such fees and expenses to the same extent that any other party would be liable under the common law or under the terms of any statute which specifically provides for such an award.

(c)(1) Any judgment against the United States or any agency and any official of the United States acting in his or her official capacity for costs pursuant to subsection (a) shall be paid as provided in sections 2414 and 2517 of this title and shall be in addition to any relief provided in the judgment.

(2) Any judgment against the United States or any agency and any official of the United States acting in his or her official capacity for fees and expenses of attorneys pursuant to subsection (b) shall be paid as provided in sections 2414 and 2517 of this title, except that if the basis for the award is a finding that the United States acted in bad faith, then the award shall be paid by any agency found to have acted in bad faith and shall be in addition to any relief provided in the judgment.

(d)(1)(A) Except as otherwise specifically provided by statute, a court shall award to a prevailing party other than the United States fees and other expenses, in addition to any costs awarded pursuant to subsection (a), incurred by that party in any civil action (other than cases sounding in tort), including proceedings for judicial review of agency action, brought by or against the United States in any court having jurisdiction of that action, unless the court finds that the position of the United States was substantially justified or that special circumstances make an award unjust.

(B) A party seeking an award of fees and other expenses shall, within thirty days of final judgment in the action, submit to the court an application for fees and other expenses which shows that the party is a prevailing party and is eligible to receive an award under this subsection, and the amount sought, including an itemized statement from any attorney or expert witness representing or appearing in behalf of the party stating the actual time expended and the rate at which fees and other expenses are computed. The party shall also allege that the position of the United States was not substantially justified. Whether or not the position of the United States was substantially justified shall be determined on the basis of the record (including the record with respect to the action or failure to act by the agency upon which the civil action is based) which is made in the civil action for which fees and other expenses are sought.

(C) The court, in its discretion, may reduce the amount to be awarded, pursuant to this subsection, or deny an award, to the extent that the prevailing party during the course of the proceedings engaged in conduct which unduly and unreasonably protracted the final resolution of the matter in controversy.

(D) If, in a civil action brought by the United States or a proceeding for judicial review of an adversary adjudication described in section 504(a)(4) of title 5, the demand by the United States is substantially in excess of the judgment finally obtained by the United States and is unreasonable when compared with such judgment, under the facts and circumstances of the case, the court shall award to the party the fees and other expenses related to defending against the excessive demand, unless the party has committed a willful violation of law or otherwise acted in bad faith, or special circumstances making an award unjust. Fees and expenses awarded under this subparagraph shall be paid only as a consequence of appropriations provided in advance.

(2) For the purposes of this subsection—

(A) "fees and other expenses" includes the reasonable expenses of expert witnesses, the reasonable cost of any study, analysis, engineering report, test, or project which is found by the court to be necessary for the preparation of the party's case, and reasonable attorney fees (The amount of fees awarded under this subsection shall be based upon prevailing market rates for the kind and quality of the services furnished, except that (i) no expert witness shall be compensated at a rate in excess of the highest rate of compensation for expert witnesses paid by the United States; and (ii) attorney fees shall not be awarded in excess of $125 per hour unless the court determines that an increase in the cost of living or a special factor, such as the limited availability of qualified attorneys for the proceedings involved, justifies a higher fee.);

(B) "party" means (i) an individual whose net worth did not exceed $2,000,000 at the time the civil action was filed, or (ii) any owner of an unincorporated business, or any partnership, corporation, association, unit of local government, or organization, the net worth of which did not exceed $7,000,000 at the time the civil action was filed, and which had not more than 500 employees at the time the civil action was filed; except that an organization described in section 501(c)(3) of the Internal Revenue Code of 1954 (26 U.S.C. 501(c)(3)) exempt from taxation under section 501(a) of such Code, or a cooperative association as defined in section 15(a) of the Agricultural Marketing Act (12 U.S.C. 1141j(a)), may be a party regardless of the net worth of such organization or cooperative association or for purposes of subsection (d)(1)(D), a small entity as defined in section 601 of title 5;

(C) "United States" includes any agency and any official of the United States acting in his or her official capacity;

(D) "position of the United States" means, in addition to the position taken by the United States in the civil action, the action or failure to act by the agency upon which the civil action is based; except that fees and expenses may not be awarded to a party for any portion of the litigation in which the party has unreasonably protracted the proceedings;

(E) "civil action brought by or against the United States" includes an appeal by a party, other than the United States, from a decision of a contracting officer rendered pursuant to a disputes clause in a contract with the Government or pursuant to the Contract Disputes Act of 1978;

(F) "court" includes the United States Claims Court and the United States Court of Veterans Appeals;

(G) "final judgment" means a judgment that is final and not appealable, and includes an order of settlement;

(H) "prevailing party", in the case of eminent domain proceedings, means a party who obtains a final judgment (other than by settlement), exclusive of interest, the amount of which is at least as close to the highest valuation of the property involved that is attested to at trial on behalf of the property owner as it is to the highest valuation of the property involved that is attested to at trial on behalf of the Government; and

(I) "demand" means the express demand of the United States which led to the adversary adjudication, but shall not include a recitation of the maximum statutory penalty (i) in the complaint, or (ii) elsewhere when accompanied by an express demand for a lesser amount.

(3) In awarding fees and other expenses under this subsection to a prevailing party in any action for judicial review of an adversary adjudication, as defined in subsection (b)(1)(C) of section 504 of title 5, United States Code, or an adversary adjudication subject to the Contract Disputes Act of 1978, the court shall include in that award fees and other expenses to the same extent authorized in subsection (a) of such section, unless the court finds that during such adversary adjudication the position of the United States was substantially justified, or that special circumstances make an award unjust.

(4) Fees and other expenses awarded under this subsection to a party shall be paid by any agency over which the party prevails from any funds made available to the agency by appropriation or otherwise.

[(5) Repealed. Pub.L. 104–66, Title I, § 1091(b), Dec. 21, 1995, 109 Stat. 722]

(e) The provisions of this section shall not apply to any costs, fees, and other expenses in connection with any proceeding to which section 7430 of the Internal Revenue Code of 1954 applies (determined without regard to subsections (b) and (f) of such section). Nothing in the preceding sentence shall prevent the awarding under subsection (a) of section 2412 of title 28, United States Code, of costs enumerated in section 1920 of such title (as in effect on October 1, 1981).

(f) If the United States appeals an award of costs or fees and other expenses made against the United States under this section and the award is affirmed in whole or in part, interest shall be paid on the amount of the award as affirmed. Such interest shall be computed at the rate determined under section 1961(a) of this title, and shall run from the date of the award through the day before the date of the mandate of affirmance.

(As amended Oct. 21, 1980, Pub.L. 96–481, Title II, § 204(a), (c), 94 Stat. 2327, 2329; Sept. 3, 1982, Pub.L. 97–248, Title II, § 292(c), 96 Stat. 574; Aug. 5, 1985, Pub.L. 99–80, §§ 2, 6, 99 Stat. 184, 186; Oct. 29, 1992, Pub.L. 102–572, Title III, § 301(a), Title V, §§ 502(b), 506(a), 106 Stat. 4511, 4512, 4513.)

†